Peterson's

Graduate Schools in the U.S. 2011

About Peterson's
To succeed on your lifelong educational journey, you will need accurate, dependable, and practical tools and resources. That is why Peterson's is everywhere education happens. Because whenever and however you need education content delivered, you can rely on Peterson's to provide the information, know-how, and guidance to help you reach your goals. Tools to match the right students with the right school. It's here. Personalized resources and expert guidance. It's here. Comprehensive and dependable education content—delivered whenever and however you need it. It's all here.

For more information, contact Peterson's, 2000 Lenox Drive, Lawrenceville, NJ 08648; 800-338-3282; or find us on the World Wide Web at www.petersons.com/about.

Stephen Clemente, Managing Director, Publishing and Institutional Research; Bernadette Webster, Director of Publishing; Jill C. Schwartz, Editor; Ken Britschge, Research Project Manager; Amy Weber, Research Associate; Phyllis Johnson, Programmer; Ray Golaszewski, Manufacturing Manager; Linda M. Williams, Composition Manager

ISSN 1528-5901
ISBN 13: 978-0-7689-2861-7
ISBN 10: 0-7689-2861-3

Printed in the United States of America

10 9 8 7 6 5 4 3 2 1 12 11 10

Eleventh Edition

By producing this book on recycled paper (40% post-consumer waste) 132 trees were saved.

Contents

A Note from the Peterson's Editors

If you are a student seeking to continue your education beyond college, *Peterson's Graduate Schools in the U.S.* is just what you need to discover an array of possibilities in a wide variety of academic disciplines available at more than 950 graduate schools across the United States.

Inside you'll find advice on graduate education, including topics such as admission tests, financial aid, and accreditation. **The Graduate Adviser** includes two essays and information about accreditation. The first essay, "The Admissions Process," discusses general admission requirements, admission tests, factors to consider when selecting a graduate school or program, when and how to apply, and how admission decisions are made. Special information for international students and tips for minority students are also included. The second essay, "Financial Support," is an overview of the broad range of support available at the graduate level. Fellowships, scholarships, and grants; assistantships and internships; federal and private loan programs, as well as Federal Work-Study; and the GI bill are detailed. This essay concludes with advice on applying for need-based financial aid. "Accreditation and Accrediting Agencies" gives information on accreditation and its purpose and lists first institutional accrediting agencies and then specialized accrediting agencies relevant to specific fields of study.

If you know the field of study that interests you, turn to the **Directory of Graduate and Professional Programs by Field.** You will find, at a glance, all institutions that offer that field of study.

For geographical or financial reasons, you may already have a specific institution in mind. Turn to the **Profiles of Institutions Offering Graduate and Professional Work,** which contain information on more than 950 graduate schools. **Profiles** detail information from student enrollment and the number of full-time faculty members to tuition and application contacts and are followed by a list of graduate units and the specific programs of study they offer.

Peterson's Web site provides a wealth of information and services involving all aspects of the grad school search and graduate admissions process. To access these resources, go to www.petersons.com/gradchannel.

Peterson's publishes a full line of resources to help guide you through the graduate admissions process. Peterson's publications can be found in college libraries and career centers and at your local bookstore or library. *Peterson's Graduate Schools in the U.S.* is also available to purchase as an e-book. Continue to check www.petersons.com for more information about our e-book program.

We welcome any comments or suggestions you may have about this publication and invite you to complete our online survey at www.petersons.com/booksurvey. Or you can fill out the survey at the back of this book, tear it out, and mail it to us at:

Publishing Department
Peterson's, a Nelnet company
2000 Lenox Drive
Lawrenceville, NJ 08648

Your feedback will help us make your educational dreams possible.

Colleges and universities will be pleased to know that Peterson's helped you in your selection. Admissions staff members are more than happy to answer questions, address specific problems, and help in any way they can. The editors at Peterson's wish you great success in your graduate school search!

The Graduate Adviser

The Admissions Process

Generalizations about graduate admissions practices are not always helpful because each institution has its own set of guidelines and procedures. Nevertheless, some broad statements can be made about the admissions process that may help you plan your strategy.

Factors Involved in Selecting a Graduate School or Program

Selecting a graduate school and a specific program of study is a complex matter. Quality of the faculty; program and course offerings; the nature, size, and location of the institution; admission requirements; cost; and the availability of financial assistance are among the many factors that affect one's choice of institution. Other considerations are job placement and achievements of the program's graduates and the institution's resources, such as libraries, laboratories, and computer facilities. If you are to make the best possible choice, you need to learn as much as you can about the schools and programs you are considering before you apply.

The following steps may help you narrow your choices.

- Talk to alumni of the programs or institutions you are considering to get their impressions of how well they were prepared for work in their fields of study.
- Remember that graduate school requirements change, so be sure to get the most up-to-date information possible.
- Talk to department faculty members and the graduate adviser at your undergraduate institution. They often have information about programs of study at other institutions.
- Visit the Web sites of the graduate schools in which you are interested to request a graduate catalog. Contact the department chair in your chosen field of study for additional information about the department and the field.
- Visit as many campuses as possible. Call ahead for an appointment with the graduate adviser in your field of interest and be sure to check out the facilities and talk to students.

General Requirements

Graduate schools and departments have requirements that applicants for admission must meet. Typically, these requirements include undergraduate transcripts (which provide information about undergraduate grade point average and course work applied toward a major), admission test scores, and letters of recommendation. Most graduate programs also ask for an essay or personal statement that describes your personal reasons for seeking graduate study. In some fields, such as art and music, portfolios or auditions may be required in addition to other evidence of talent. Some institutions require that the applicant have an undergraduate degree in the same subject as the intended graduate major.

Most institutions evaluate each applicant on the basis of the applicant's total record, and the weight accorded any given factor varies widely from institution to institution and from program to program.

The Application Process

You should begin the application process at least one year before you expect to begin your graduate study. Find out the application deadline for each institution (many are provided in the **Profile** section of this guide). Go to the institution's Web site and find out if you can apply online. If not, request a paper application form. Fill out this form thoroughly and neatly. Assume that the school needs all the information it is requesting and that the admissions officer will be sensitive to the neatness and overall quality of what you submit. Do not supply more information than the school requires.

The institution may ask at least one question that will require a three- or four-paragraph answer. Compose your response on the assumption that the admissions officer is interested in both what you think and how you express yourself. Keep your statement brief and to the point, but, at the same time, include all pertinent information about your past experiences and your educational goals. Individual statements vary greatly in style and content, which helps admissions officers differentiate among applicants. Many graduate departments give considerable weight to the statement in making their admissions decisions, so be sure to take the time to prepare a thoughtful and concise statement.

If recommendations are a part of the admissions requirements, carefully choose the individuals you ask to write them. It is generally best to ask current or former professors to write the recommendations, provided they are able to attest to your intellectual ability and motivation for doing the work required of a graduate student. It is advisable to provide stamped, preaddressed envelopes to people being asked to submit recommendations on your behalf.

Completed applications, including references, transcripts, and admission test scores, should be received at the institution by the specified date.

Be advised that institutions do not usually make admissions decisions until all materials have been received. Enclose a self-addressed postcard with your application, requesting confirmation of receipt. Allow at least 10 days for the return of the postcard before making further inquiries.

If you plan to apply for financial support, it is imperative that you file your application early.

Admission Tests

The major testing program used in graduate admissions is the Graduate Record Examinations (GRE) testing program, sponsored by the GRE Board and administered by Educational Testing Service, Princeton, New Jersey.

The Graduate Record Examinations testing program consists of a General Test and eight Subject Tests. The General Test measures critical thinking, verbal reasoning, quantitative reasoning, and analytical writing skills. It is offered as an Internet-based test (iBT) in the United States, Canada, and many other countries.

The typical computer-based General Test consists of one 30-minute verbal reasoning section, one 45-minute quantitative reasoning section, one 45-minute issue analysis (writing) section, and one 30-minute argument analysis (writing) section. In addition, an unidentified verbal or quantitative section that doesn't count toward a score may be included, and an identified research section that is not scored may also be included.

The Subject Tests measure achievement and assume undergraduate majors or extensive background in the following eight disciplines:

- Biochemistry, Cell and Molecular Biology
- Biology
- Chemistry
- Computer Science
- Literature in English
- Mathematics
- Physics
- Psychology

The Subject Tests are available three times per year as paper-based administrations around the world. Testing time is approximately 2 hours 50 minutes. You can obtain more information about the GRE by visiting the ETS Web site at www.ets.org or consulting the *GRE Information and Registration Bulletin*. The *Bulletin* can be obtained at many undergraduate colleges. You can also download it from the ETS Web site or obtain it by contacting Graduate Record Examinations,

Educational Testing Service, P.O. Box 6000, Princeton, NJ 08541-6000; Phone: 609-771-7670 or 866-473-4373 (toll-free in the U.S., U.S. territories, and Canada), Monday–Friday 8 a.m.–7:45 p.m. Eastern Time.

If you expect to apply for admission to a program that requires any of the GRE tests, you should select a test date well in advance of the application deadline. Scores on the computer-based General Test are reported within ten to fifteen days; scores on the paper-based Subject Tests are reported within six weeks.

Another testing program, the Miller Analogies Test (MAT), is administered at more than 500 Controlled Testing Centers, licensed by Pearson Education, Inc., in the United States, Canada, and other countries. The MAT computer-based test is now available. Testing time is 60 minutes. The test consists of 120 partial analogies. You can obtain the *Candidate Information Booklet*, which contains a list of test centers and instructions for taking the test, from the Web site at www.MillerAnalogies.com or by calling 800-622-3231 (toll-free).

Check the specific requirements of the programs to which you are applying.

How Admission Decisions Are Made

The program you apply to is directly involved in the admissions process. Although the final decision is usually made by the graduate dean (or an associate) or the faculty admissions committee, recommendations from faculty members in your intended field are important. At some institutions, an interview is incorporated into the decision process.

A Special Note for International Students

In addition to the steps already described, there are some special considerations for international students who intend to apply for graduate study in the United States. All graduate schools require an indication of competence in English. The purpose of the Test of English as a Foreign Language (TOEFL) is to evaluate the English proficiency of people who are nonnative speakers of English and want to study at colleges and universities where English is the language of instruction. The TOEFL is administered by Educational Testing Service (ETS) under the general direction of a policy board established by the College Board and the Graduate Record Examinations Board.

The TOEFL iBT assesses the four basic language skills: listening, reading, writing, and speaking. It was administered for the first time in September 2005, and ETS continues to introduce the TOEFL iBT in selected cities. The Internet-based test is administered at secure, official test centers. The testing time is approximately 4 hours. Because the TOEFL iBT includes a speaking section, the Test of Spoken English (TSE) is no longer needed.

The TOEFL is also offered in the paper-based format in areas of the world where Internet-based testing is not available. The TOEFL paper-based Test (PBT) consists of three sections—listening comprehension, structure and written expression, and reading comprehension—plus a 30-minute writing test, the Test of Written English® (TWE), which measures the examinee's ability to compose in English. The total testing time is approximately 3 hours. Examinees receive separate TOEFL and TWE scores. The *Information Bulletin* contains information on local fees and registration procedures.

Additional information and registration materials are available from TOEFL Services, Educational Testing Service, P.O. Box 6151, Princeton, New Jersey 08541-6151. Phone: 609-771-7100. Web site: www.toefl.org.

International students should apply especially early because of the number of steps required to complete the admissions process. Furthermore, many United States graduate schools have a limited number of spaces for international students, and many more students apply than the schools can accommodate.

International students may find financial assistance from institutions very limited. The U.S. government requires international applicants to submit a certification of support, which is a statement attesting to the applicant's financial resources. In addition, international students *must* have health insurance coverage.

Tips for Minority Students

Indicators of a university's values in terms of diversity are found both in its recruitment programs and its resources directed to student success. Important questions: Does the institution vigorously recruit minorities for its graduate programs? Is there funding available to help with the costs associated with visiting the school? Are minorities represented in the institution's brochures or Web site or on their faculty rolls? What campus-based resources or services (including assistance in locating housing or career counseling and placement) are available? Is funding available to members of underrepresented groups?

At the program level, it is particularly important for minority students to investigate the "climate" of a program under consideration. How many minority students are enrolled and how many have graduated? What opportunities are there to work with diverse faculty and mentors whose research interests match yours? How are conflicts resolved or concerns addressed? How interested are faculty members in building strong and supportive relations with students? "Climate" concerns should be addressed by posing questions to various individuals, including faculty members, current students, and alumni.

Information is also available through various organizations, such as the Hispanic Association of Colleges & Universities (HACU), and publications such as *Diverse Issues in Higher Education* and *Hispanic Outlook* magazine. There are also books devoted to this topic, such as *The Multicultural Student's Guide to Colleges* by Robert Mitchell.

Financial Support

The range of financial support at the graduate level is very broad. The following descriptions will give you a general idea of what you might expect and what will be expected of you as a financial support recipient.

Fellowships, Scholarships, and Grants

These are usually outright awards of a few hundred to many thousands of dollars with no service to the institution required in return. Fellowships and scholarships are usually awarded on the basis of merit and are highly competitive. Grants are made on the basis of financial need or special talent in a field of study. Many fellowships, scholarships, and grants not only cover tuition, fees, and supplies but also include stipends for living expenses with allowances for dependents. However, the terms of each should be examined because some do not permit recipients to supplement their income with outside work. Fellowships, scholarships, and grants may vary in the number of years for which they are awarded.

In addition to the availability of these funds at the university or program level, many excellent fellowship programs are available at the national level and may be applied for before and during enrollment in a graduate program. A listing of many of these programs can be found at the Council of Graduate Schools' Web site: http://www.cgsnet.org. There is a wealth of information in the "Programs" and "Awards" sections.

Assistantships and Internships

Many graduate students receive financial support through assistantships, particularly involving teaching or research duties. It is important to recognize that such appointments should not be viewed simply as employment relationships but rather should constitute an integral and important part of a student's graduate education. As such, the appointments should be accompanied by strong faculty mentoring and increasingly responsible apprenticeship experiences. The specific nature of these appointments in a given program should be considered in selecting that graduate program.

Teaching Assistantships

These usually provide a salary and full or partial tuition remission and may also provide health benefits. Unlike fellowships, scholarships, and grants, which require no service to the institution, teaching assistantships require recipients to provide the institution with a specific amount of undergraduate teaching, ideally related to the student's field of study. Some teaching assistants are limited to grading papers, compiling bibliographies, taking notes, or monitoring laboratories. At some graduate schools, teaching assistants must carry lighter course loads than regular full-time students.

Research Assistantships

These are very similar to teaching assistantships in the manner in which financial assistance is provided. The difference is that recipients are given basic research assignments in their disciplines rather than teaching responsibilities. The work required is normally related to the student's field of study; in most instances, the assistantship supports the student's thesis or dissertation research.

Administrative Internships

These are similar to assistantships in application of financial assistance funds, but the student is given an assignment on a part-time basis, usually as a special assistant with one of the university's administrative offices. The assignment may not necessarily be directly related to the recipient's discipline.

Residence Hall and Counseling Assistantships

These assistantships are frequently assigned to graduate students in psychology, counseling, and social work, but they may be offered to students in other disciplines, especially if the student has worked in this capacity during his or her undergraduate years. Duties can vary from being available in a dean's office for a specific number of hours for consultation with undergraduates to living in campus residences and being responsible for both counseling and administrative tasks or advising student activity groups. Residence hall assistantships often include a room and board allowance and, in some cases, tuition assistance and stipends. Contact the Housing and Student Life Office for more information.

Health Insurance

The availability and affordability of health insurance is an important issue and one that should be considered in an applicant's choice of institution and program. While often included with assistantships and fellowships, this is not always the case and, even if provided, the benefits may be limited. It is important to note that the U.S. government requires international students to have health insurance.

The GI Bill

This provides financial assistance for students who are veterans of the United States armed forces. If you are a veteran, contact your local Veterans Administration office to determine your eligibility and to get full details about benefits. There are a number of programs that offer educational benefits to current military enlistees. Some states have tuition assistance programs for members of the National Guard. Contact the VA office at the college for more information.

Federal Work-Study Program (FWS)

Employment is another way some students finance their graduate studies. The federally funded Federal Work-Study Program provides eligible students with employment opportunities, usually in public and private nonprofit organizations. Federal funds pay up to 75 percent of the wages, with the remainder paid by the employing agency. FWS is available to graduate students who demonstrate financial need. Not all schools have these funds, and some only award them to undergraduates. Each school sets its application deadline and work-study earnings limits. Wages vary and are related to the type of work done. You must file the Free Application for Federal Student Aid (FAFSA) to be eligible for this program.

Loans

Many graduate students borrow to finance their graduate programs when other sources of assistance (which do not have to be repaid) prove insufficient. You should always read and understand the terms of any loan program before submitting your application.

Federal Loans

Federal Stafford Loans. The Federal Stafford Loan Program offers government-sponsored, low-interest loans to students through a private lender such as a bank, credit union, or savings and loan association.

There are two components of the Federal Stafford Loan program. Under the *subsidized* component of the program, the federal government pays the interest on the loan while you are enrolled in graduate school on at least a half-time basis during the six-month grace period after you drop below half-time enrollment, as well as during any period of deferment. Under the *unsubsidized* component of the program, you pay the interest on the loan from the day proceeds are issued. Eligibility for the federal subsidy is based on demonstrated financial need as determined by the financial aid office from the information you provide on the FAFSA. A cosigner is not required, since the loan is not based on creditworthiness.

Although *unsubsidized* Federal Stafford Loans may not be as desirable as *subsidized* Federal Stafford Loans from the student's perspective, they are a useful source of support for those who may not qualify for the subsidized loans or who need additional financial assistance.

Graduate students may borrow up to $20,500 per year through the Stafford Loan Program, up to a cumulative maximum of $138,500, including undergraduate borrowing. This may include up to $8500 in *subsidized* Stafford Loans annually, depending on eligibility, up to a cumulative maximum of $65,500, including undergraduate borrowing. The amount of the loan borrowed through the *unsubsidized* Stafford Program equals the total amount of the loan (as much as $20,500) minus your eligibility for a *subsidized* Stafford Loan (as much as $8500). You may borrow up to the cost of attendance at the school in which you are enrolled or will attend, minus estimated financial assistance from other federal, state, and private sources, up to a maximum of $20,500.

Stafford Loans made on or after July 1, 2006, carry a fixed interest rate of 6.8% both for in-school and in-repayment borrowers.

Two fees may be deducted from the loan proceeds upon disbursement: a Federal Default Fee of 1 percent, which is deposited in an insurance pool to ensure repayment to the lender if the borrower defaults, and a federally mandated 0.5 percent origination fee, for loans made after July 1, 2009, which is used to offset the administrative cost of the Federal Stafford Loan Program. The origination fees are scheduled to be eliminated by July 1, 2010.

Under the *subsidized* Federal Stafford Loan Program, repayment begins six months after your last date of enrollment on at least a half-time basis. Under the *unsubsidized* program, repayment of interest begins within thirty days from disbursement of the loan proceeds, and repayment of the principal begins six months after your last enrollment on at least a half-time basis. Some borrowers may choose to defer interest payments while they are in school. The accrued interest is added to the loan balance when the borrower begins repayment. There are several repayment options.

Federal Direct Loans. Some schools participate in the Department of Education's William D. Ford Direct Loan Program instead of the Federal Stafford Loan Program. The two programs are essentially the same except that with the Direct Loans, schools themselves provide the loans with funds from the federal government. Terms and interest rates are virtually the same except that there are a few additional repayment options with Federal Direct Loans.

Federal Perkins Loans. The Federal Perkins Loan is available to students demonstrating financial need and is administered directly by the school. Not all schools have these funds, and some may award them to undergraduates only. Eligibility is determined from the information you provide on the FAFSA. The school will notify you of your eligibility.

Eligible graduate students may borrow up to $6000 per year, up to a maximum of $40,000, including undergraduate borrowing (even if your previous Perkins Loans have been repaid). The interest rate for Federal Perkins Loans is 5 percent, and no interest accrues while you remain in school at least half-time. There are no guarantee, loan, or disbursement fees. Repayment begins nine months after your last date of enrollment on at least a half-time basis and may extend over a maximum of ten years with no prepayment penalty.

Federal Graduate PLUS Loans. Effective July 1, 2006, graduate and professional students are eligible for Graduate PLUS loans. This program allows students to borrow up to the cost of attendance, less any other aid received. These loans have a fixed interest rate of 8.5% (7.9% for the Federal Direct PLUS), and interest begins to accrue at the time of disbursement. The PLUS loans do involve a credit check; a PLUS borrower may obtain a loan with a cosigner if his or her credit is not good enough. Grad PLUS loans may be deferred while a student in school and for the six months following a drop below half-time enrollment. For more information, contact your FFELP lender or your college financial aid office.

Deferring Your Federal Loan Repayments. If you borrowed under the Federal Stafford Loan Program, Federal Direct Loan Program, or the Federal Perkins Loan Program for previous undergraduate or graduate study, your repayments may be deferred when you return to graduate school, depending on when you borrowed and under which program.

There are other deferment options available if you are temporarily unable to repay your loan. Information about these deferments is provided at your entrance and exit interviews. If you believe you are eligible for a deferment of your loan repayments, you must contact your lender to request a deferment form. The deferment must be filed prior to the time your repayment is due, and it must be refiled when it expires if you remain eligible for deferment at that time.

Supplemental (Private) Loans

Many lending institutions offer supplemental loan programs and other financing plans, such as the ones described here, to students seeking additional assistance in meeting their education expenses. Some loan programs target all types of graduate students; others are designed specifically for business, law, or medical students. In addition, you can use private loans not specifically designed for education to help finance your graduate degree.

If you are considering borrowing through a supplemental or private loan program, you should carefully consider the terms and be sure to "read the fine print." Check with the program sponsor for the most current terms that will be applicable to the amounts you intend to borrow for graduate study. Most supplemental loan programs for graduate study offer unsubsidized, credit-based loans. In general, a credit-ready borrower is one who has a satisfactory credit history or no credit history at all. A creditworthy borrower generally must pass a credit test to be eligible to borrow or act as a cosigner for the loan funds.

Many supplemental loan programs have minimum and maximum annual loan limits. Some offer amounts equal to the cost of attendance minus any other aid you will receive for graduate study. If you are planning to borrow for several years of graduate study, consider whether there is a cumulative or aggregate limit on the amount you may borrow. Often this cumulative or aggregate limit will include any amounts you borrowed and have not repaid for undergraduate or previous graduate study.

The combination of the annual interest rate, loan fees, and the repayment terms you choose will determine how much you will repay over time. Compare these features in combination before you decide which loan program to use. Some loans offer interest rates that are adjusted monthly, some quarterly, some annually. Some offer interest rates that are lower during the in-school, grace, and deferment periods and then increase when you begin repayment. Some programs include a loan "origination" fee, which is usually deducted from the principal amount you receive when the loan is disbursed and must be repaid along with the interest and other principal when you graduate, withdraw from school, or drop below half-time study. Sometimes the loan fees are reduced if you borrow with a qualified cosigner. Some programs allow you to defer interest and/or principal payments while you are enrolled in graduate school. Many programs allow you to capitalize your interest payments; the interest due on your loan is added to the outstanding balance of your loan, so you don't have to repay immediately, but this increases the amount you owe. Other programs allow you to pay the interest as you go, which reduces the amount you later have to repay.

Some examples of supplemental programs follow. The private loan market is very competitive, and your financial aid office can help you evaluate these and other programs.

CitiAssist® Graduate Loans. Offered by Citibank, these loans help graduate students fill the gap between the financial aid they receive and the money they need for school. Graduate students can borrow up to $150,000. A one-time minimum loan amount of $1,000 may apply. Visit www.studentloan.com for more loan information from Citibank.

Chase Select[SM] Private Student Loans. Offered by Chase, these loans are subject to credit approval, receipt of a completed and signed Application/Promissory Note, verification of application information including enrollment at a participating school, and verification that the requested loan amount does not exceed the student's actual cost of attendance. For more information, visit www.chasestudentloans.com.

Graduate Access Loans. Sponsored by the Access Group, this is for graduate students enrolled at least half-time. The Web site is www.accessgroup.com.

Smart Option Student Loans. Sponsored by Sallie Mae, this loan program is for graduate students who are enrolled at least half-time. Visit www.salliemae.com for more information.

Applying for Need-Based Financial Aid

Schools that award federal and institutional financial assistance based on need will require you to complete the FAFSA and, in some cases, an institutional financial aid application.

If you are applying for federal student assistance, you **must** complete the FAFSA. A service of the U.S. Department of Education, the FAFSA is free to all applicants. Most applicants apply online at www.fafsa.ed.gov. Paper applications are available at the financial aid office of your local college.

After your FAFSA information has been processed, you will receive a Student Aid Report (SAR). If you provided an e-mail address on the FAFSA, this will be sent to you electronically; otherwise, it will be mailed to your home address.

Follow the instructions on the SAR if you need to correct information reported on your original application. If your situation changes after you file your FAFSA, contact your financial aid officer to discuss amending your information. You can also appeal your financial aid award if you have extenuating circumstances.

If you would like more information on federal student financial aid, visit the FAFSA Web site or download the most recent version of *Funding Education Beyond High School: The Guide to Federal Student Aid* at http://studentaid.ed.gov/students/publications/student_guide/index.html. This guide is also available in Spanish.

The U.S. Department of Education also has a toll-free number for questions concerning federal student aid programs. The number is 1-800-4-FED AID (1-800-433-3243). If you are hearing impaired, call toll-free, 1-800-730-8913.

Summary

Remember that these are generalized statements about financial assistance at the graduate level. Because each institution allots its aid differently, you should communicate directly with the school and the specific department of interest to you. It is not unusual, for example, to find that an endowment vested within a specific department supports one or more fellowships. You may fit its requirements and specifications precisely.

Accreditation and Accrediting Agencies

Colleges and universities in the United States, and their individual academic and professional programs, are accredited by nongovernmental agencies concerned with monitoring the quality of education in this country. Agencies with both regional and national jurisdictions grant accreditation to institutions as a whole, while specialized bodies acting on a nationwide basis—often national professional associations—grant accreditation to departments and programs in specific fields.

Institutional and specialized accrediting agencies share the same basic concerns: the purpose an academic unit—whether university or program—has set for itself and how well it fulfills that purpose, the adequacy of its financial and other resources, the quality of its academic offerings, and the level of services it provides. Agencies that grant institutional accreditation take a broader view, of course, and examine university-wide or college-wide services with which a specialized agency may not concern itself.

Both types of agencies follow the same general procedures when considering an application for accreditation. The academic unit prepares a self-evaluation, focusing on the concerns mentioned above and usually including an assessment of both its strengths and weaknesses; a team of representatives of the accrediting body reviews this evaluation, visits the campus, and makes its own report; and finally, the accrediting body makes a decision on the application. Often, even when accreditation is granted, the agency makes a recommendation regarding how the institution or program can improve. All institutions and programs are also reviewed every few years to determine whether they continue to meet established standards; if they do not, they may lose their accreditation.

Accrediting agencies themselves are reviewed and evaluated periodically by the U.S. Department of Education and the Council for Higher Education Accreditation (CHEA). Recognized agencies adhere to certain standards and practices, and their authority in matters of accreditation is widely accepted in the educational community.

This does not mean, however, that accreditation is a simple matter, either for schools wishing to become accredited or for students deciding where to apply. Indeed, in certain fields the very meaning and methods of accreditation are the subject of a good deal of debate. For their part, those applying to graduate school should be aware of the safeguards provided by regional accreditation, especially in terms of degree acceptance and institutional longevity. Beyond this, applicants should understand the role that specialized accreditation plays in their field, as this varies considerably from one discipline to another. In certain professional fields, it is necessary to have graduated from a program that is accredited in order to be eligible for a license to practice, and in some fields the federal government also makes this a hiring requirement. In other disciplines, however, accreditation is not as essential, and there can be excellent programs that are not accredited. In fact, some programs choose not to seek accreditation, although most do.

Institutions and programs that present themselves for accreditation are sometimes granted the status of candidate for accreditation, or what is known as "preaccreditation." This may happen, for example, when an academic unit is too new to have met all the requirements for accreditation. Such status signifies initial recognition and indicates that the school or program in question is working to fulfill all requirements; it does not, however, guarantee that accreditation will be granted.

Institutional Accrediting Agencies—Regional

MIDDLE STATES ASSOCIATION OF COLLEGES AND SCHOOLS

Accredits institutions in Delaware, District of Columbia, Maryland, New Jersey, New York, Pennsylvania, Puerto Rico, and the Virgin Islands.
Jean Avnet Morse, President
Middle States Commission on Higher Education
3624 Market Street, Second Floor Annex
Philadelphia, Pennsylvania 19104
Phone: 267-284-5000
Fax: 215-662-5501
E-mail: info@msche.org
Web: www.msche.org

NEW ENGLAND ASSOCIATION OF SCHOOLS AND COLLEGES

Accredits institutions in Connecticut, Maine, Massachusetts, New Hampshire, Rhode Island, and Vermont.
Barbara E. Brittingham, Director
Commission on Institutions of Higher Education
209 Burlington Road, Suite 201
Bedford, Massachusetts 01730-1433
Phone: 781-271-0022
Fax: 781-271-0950
E-mail: CIHE@neasc.org
Web: www.neasc.org

NORTH CENTRAL ASSOCIATION OF COLLEGES AND SCHOOLS

Accredits institutions in Arizona, Arkansas, Colorado, Illinois, Indiana, Iowa, Kansas, Michigan, Minnesota, Missouri, Nebraska, New Mexico, North Dakota, Ohio, Oklahoma, South Dakota, West Virginia, Wisconsin, and Wyoming.
Sylvia Manning, President
The Higher Learning Commission
30 North LaSalle Street, Suite 2400
Chicago, Illinois 60602
Phone: 312-263-0456
Fax: 312-263-7462
E-mail: smanning@hlcommission.org
Web: www.ncahigherlearningcommission.org

NORTHWEST COMMISSION ON COLLEGES AND UNIVERSITIES

Accredits institutions in Alaska, Idaho, Montana, Nevada, Oregon, Utah, and Washington.
Sandra E. Elman, President
8060 165th Avenue, NE, Suite 100
Redmond, Washington 98052
Phone: 425-558-4224
Fax: 425-376-0596
E-mail: selman@nwccu.org
Web: www.nwccu.org

SOUTHERN ASSOCIATION OF COLLEGES AND SCHOOLS

Accredits institutions in Alabama, Florida, Georgia, Kentucky, Louisiana, Mississippi, North Carolina, South Carolina, Tennessee, Texas, and Virginia.
Belle S. Wheelan, President
Commission on Colleges
1866 Southern Lane
Decatur, Georgia 30033-4097
Phone: 404-679-4512
Fax: 404-679-4528
E-mail: bwheelan@sacscoc.org
Web: www.sacsoc.org

WESTERN ASSOCIATION OF SCHOOLS AND COLLEGES

Accredits institutions in California, Guam, and Hawaii.
Ralph A. Wolff, President and Executive Director
Accrediting Commission for Senior Colleges and Universities
985 Atlantic Avenue, Suite 100
Alameda, California 94501
Phone: 510-748-9001
Fax: 510-748-9797
E-mail: wascsr@wascsenior.org
Web: www.wascweb.org

Institutional Accrediting Agencies—Other

ACCREDITING COUNCIL FOR INDEPENDENT COLLEGES AND SCHOOLS

Albert C. Gray, Ph.D., Executive Director and CEO
750 First Street, NE, Suite 980
Washington, DC 20002-4242
Phone: 202-336-6780
Fax: 202-842-2593
E-mail: info@acics.org
Web: www.acics.org

DISTANCE EDUCATION AND TRAINING COUNCIL (DETC)

Accrediting Commission
Michael P. Lambert, Executive Director
1601 18th Street, NW, Suite 2
Washington, DC 20009
Phone: 202-234-5100
Fax: 202-332-1386
E-mail: detc@detc.org
Web: www.detc.org

Specialized Accrediting Agencies

ACUPUNCTURE AND ORIENTAL MEDICINE

Dort S. Bigg, J.D., Executive Director
Accreditation Commission for Acupuncture and Oriental Medicine
Maryland Trade Center #3
7501 Greenway Center Drive, Suite 760
Greenbelt, Maryland 20770
Phone: 301-313-0855
Fax: 301-313-0912
E-mail: coordinator@acaom.org
Web: www.acaom.org

ART AND DESIGN

Samuel Hope, Executive Director
Karen P. Moynahan, Associate Director
National Association of Schools of Art and Design (NASAD)
Commission on Accreditation
11250 Roger Bacon Drive, Suite 21
Reston, Virginia 20190-5243
Phone: 703-437-0700
Fax: 703-437-6312
E-mail: info@arts-accredit.org
Web: www.arts-accredit.org

BUSINESS

Jerry Trapnell, Executive Vice President/Chief Accreditation Officer
AACSB International--The Association to Advance Collegiate Schools of Business
777 South Harbour Island Boulevard, Suite 700
Tampa, Florida 33602
Phone: 813-769-6500
Fax: 813-769-6559
E-mail: jerryt@aacsb.edu
Web: www.aacsb.edu

CHIROPRACTIC

G. Lansing Bradshaw, Interim Executive Director
Council on Chiropractic Education (CCE)
8049 North 85th Way
Scottsdale, Arizona 85258-4321
Phone: 480-443-8877
Fax: 480-483-7333
E-mail: cce@cce-usa.org
Web: www.cce-usa.org

CLINICAL LABORATORY SCIENCES

Dianne M. Cearlock, Ph.D., Chief Executive Officer
National Accrediting Agency for Clinical Laboratory Sciences
5600 N. River Road, Suite 720
Rosemont, Illinois 60018-5119
Phone: 773-714-8880
Fax: 773-714-8886
E-mail: infonaacls.org
Web: www.naacls.org

CLINICAL PASTORAL EDUCATION

Teresa E. Snorton, Executive Director
Accreditation Commission
Association for Clinical Pastoral Education, Inc.
1549 Claremont Road, Suite 103
Decatur, Georgia 30033-4611
Phone: 404-320-1472
Fax: 404-320-0849
E-mail: acpe@acpe.edu
Web: www.acpe.edu

DANCE

Samuel Hope, Executive Director
Karen P. Moynahan, Associate Director
National Association of Schools of Dance (NASD)
Commission on Accreditation
11250 Roger Bacon Drive, Suite 21
Reston, Virginia 20190-5248
Phone: 703-437-0700
Fax: 703-437-6312
E-mail: info@arts-accredit.org
Web: www.arts-accredit.org

DENTISTRY

Anthony Ziebert, Director
Commission on Dental Accreditation
American Dental Association
211 East Chicago Avenue, Suite 1900
Chicago, Illinois 60611
Phone: 312-440-4643
E-mail: accreditation@ada.org
Web: www.ada.org

DIETETICS

Ulric K. Chung, Ph.D., Senior Director
American Dietetic Association
Commission on Accreditation for Dietetics Education (CADE-ADA)
120 South Riverside Plaza, Suite 2000
Chicago, Illinois 60606-6995
Phone: 800-877-1600
Fax: 312-899-4817
E-mail: cade@eatright.org
Web: www.eatright.org/cade

ENGINEERING

Michael Milligan, Ph.D., PE, Executive Director
Accreditation Board for Engineering and Technology, Inc. (ABET)
111 Market Place, Suite 1050
Baltimore, Maryland 21202
Phone: 410-347-7700
Fax: 410-625-2238
E-mail: info@abet.org
Web: www.abet.org

FORESTRY

Terrance Clark
Associate Director of Science and Education
Society of American Foresters (SAF)
5400 Grosvenor Lane
Bethesda, Maryland 20814-2198
Phone: 301-897-8720 Ext. 123
Fax: 301-897-3690
E-mail: clarkt@safnet.org
Web: www.safnet.org

HEALTH SERVICES ADMINISTRATION

Commission on Accreditation of Healthcare Management Education (CAHME)
John S. Lloyd, President and CEO
2000 14th Street North, Suite 780
Arlington, Virginia 22201
Phone: 703-894-0960
Fax: 703-894-0941
E-mail: info@cahme.org
Web: www.cahme.org

INTERIOR DESIGN

Holly Mattson, Executive Director
Council for Interior Design Accreditation
206 Grandview Avenue, Suite 350
Grand Rapids, Michigan 49503
Phone: 616-458-0400
Fax: 616-458-0460
E-mail: info@accredit-id.org
Web: www.accredit-id.org

JOURNALISM AND MASS COMMUNICATIONS

Susanne Shaw, Executive Director
Accrediting Council on Education in Journalism and Mass Communications (ACEJMC)
School of Journalism
Stauffer-Flint Hall
University of Kansas
1435 Jayhawk Boulevard
Lawrence, Kansas 66045-7575
Phone: 785-864-3986
Fax: 785-864-5225
E-mail: sshaw@ku.edu
Web: www2.ku.edu/~acejmc

LANDSCAPE ARCHITECTURE

Ronald C. Leighton, Executive Director
Landscape Architectural Accreditation Board
American Society of Landscape Architects
636 Eye Street, NW
Washington, DC 20001-3736
Phone: 202-898-2444
Fax: 202-898-1185
E-mail: info@asla.org
Web: www.asla.org

LAW

Hulett H. Askew, Consultant on Legal Education
American Bar Association
321 North Clark Street, 21st Floor
Chicago, Illinois 60654
Phone: 312-988-6738
Fax: 312-988-5681
E-mail: askewh@staff.abanet.org
Web: www.abanet.org/legaled/

LIBRARY

Karen O'Brien, Director
Office for Accreditation
American Library Association
50 East Huron Street
Chicago, Illinois 60611
Phone: 800-545-2433 Ext. 2432
Fax: 312-280-2433
E-mail: accred@ala.org
Web: www.ala.org/accreditation/

MARRIAGE AND FAMILY THERAPY

Jeff S. Harmon, Director of Accreditation Services
Commission on Accreditation for Marriage and Family Therapy Education
American Association for Marriage and Family Therapy
112 South Alfred Street
Alexandria, Virginia 22314-3061
Phone: 703-838-9808
Fax: 703-838-9805
E-mail: coamfle@aamft.org
Web: www.aamft.org

MEDICAL ILLUSTRATION

Commission on Accreditation of Allied Health Education
Programs (CAAHEP)
Kathleen Megivern, Executive Director
1361 Park Street
Clearwater, Florida 33756
Phone: 727-210-2350
Fax: 727-210-2354
E-mail: mail@caahep.org
Web: www.caahep.org

MEDICINE

Liaison Committee on Medical Education (LCME)
In odd-numbered years beginning each July 1, contact:
Barbara Barzansky, Ph.D., LCME Secretary
American Medical Association
Council on Medical Education
515 North State Street
Chicago, Illinois 60654
Phone: 312-464-4933
Fax: 312-464-5830
E-mail: cme@aamc.org
Web: www.ama-assn.org
In even-numbered years beginning each July 1, contact:
Dan Hunt, M.D., LCME Secretary
Association of American Medical Colleges
2450 N Street, NW
Washington, DC 20037
Phone: 202-828-0596
Fax: 202-828-1125
E-mail: dhunt@aamc.org
Web: www.lcme.org

MUSIC

Samuel Hope, Executive Director
Karen P. Moynahan, Associate Director
National Association of Schools of Music (NASM)
Commission on Accreditation
11250 Roger Bacon Drive, Suite 21
Reston, Virginia 20190-5248
Phone: 703-437-0700
Fax: 703-437-6312
E-mail: info@arts-accredit.org
Web: www.arts-accredit.org

NATUROPATHIC MEDICINE

Daniel Seitz, J.D., Ed.D., Executive Director
Council on Naturopathic Medical Education
P.O. Box 178
Great Barrington, Massachusetts 01230
Phone: 413-528-8877
Fax: 413-528-8880
E-mail: staff@cnme.org
Web: www.cnme.org

NURSE ANESTHESIA

Francis R. Gerbasi, Executive Director
Council on Accreditation of Nurse Anesthesia Educational Programs
American Association of Nurse Anesthetists
222 South Prospect Avenue, Suite 304
Park Ridge, Illinois 60068
Phone: 847-692-7050 Ext. 1154
Fax: 847-692-6968
E-mail: fgerbasi@aana.com
Web: www.aana.com

NURSE EDUCATION

Jennifer L. Butlin, Director
Commission on Collegiate Nursing Education (CCNE)
One Dupont Circle, NW, Suite 530
Washington, DC 20036-1120
Phone: 202-887-6791
Fax: 202-887-8476
E-mail: jbutlin@aacn.nche.edu
Web: www.aacn.nche.edu/accreditation

NURSE MIDWIFERY

Mary Brucker, Chair
Accreditation Commission for Midwifery Education
American College of Nurse-Midwives
Nurse-Midwifery Program
8403 Colesville Road, Suite 1550
Silver Spring, Maryland 20910
Phone: 240-485-1800
Fax: 240-485-1818
E-mail: mary_brucker@baylor.edu
Web: www.midwife.org/acme.cfm

Jo Anne Myers-Ciecko, Executive Director
Midwifery Education Accreditation Council
P.O. Box 984
La Conner, Washington 98257
Phone: 360-466-2080
Fax: 480-907-2936
E-mail: executivedirector@meacschools.org
Web: www.meacschools.org

NURSE PRACTITIONER
Susan Wysocki, President
National Association of Nurse Practitioners in Women's Health
Council on Accreditation
505 C Street, NE
Washington, DC 20002
Phone: 202-543-9693
Fax: 202-543-9858
E-mail: info@npwh.org
Web: www.npwh.org

NURSING
Sharon J. Tanner, Ed.D., RN, Executive Director
National League for Nursing Accrediting Commission (NLNAC)
3343 Peachtree Road, NE, Suite 500
Atlanta, Georgia 30326
Phone: 404-975-5000
Fax: 404-975-5020
E-mail: sjtanner@nlnac.org
Web: www.nlnac.org

OCCUPATIONAL THERAPY
Neil Harvison, Ph.D., OTR/L
Director of Accreditation and Academic Affairs
The American Occupational Therapy Association
4720 Montgomery Lane
P.O. Box 31220
Bethesda, Maryland 20824-1220
Phone: 301-652-2682 Ext. 2914
Fax: 301-652-7711
E-mail: accred@aota.org
Web: www.aota.org

OPTOMETRY
Joyce L. Urbeck, Administrative Director
Accreditation Council on Optometric Education
American Optometric Association (AOA)
243 North Lindbergh Boulevard
St. Louis, Missouri 63141
Phone: 800-365-2219
Fax: 314-991-4101
E-mail: ACOE@aoa.org
Web: www.theacoe.org

OSTEOPATHIC MEDICINE
Konrad C. Miskowicz-Retz, Ph.D., CAE
Director, Department of Accreditation
Commission on Osteopathic College Accreditation
American Osteopathic Association
142 East Ontario Street
Chicago, Illinois 60611
Phone: 312-202-8048
Fax: 312-202-8202
E-mail: kretz@osteopathic.org
Web: www.osteopathic.org

PHARMACY
Peter H. Vlasses, Executive Director
Accreditation Council for Pharmacy Education
20 North Clark Street, Suite 2500
Chicago, Illinois 60602-5109
Phone: 312-664-3575
Fax: 312-664-4652
E-mail: info@acpe-accredit.org
Web: www.acpe-accredit.org

PHYSICAL THERAPY
Mary Jane Harris, Director
Commission on Accreditation in Physical Therapy Education (CAPTE)
American Physical Therapy Association (APTA)
1111 North Fairfax Street
Alexandria, Virginia 22314
Phone: 703-706-3245
Fax: 703-706-3387
E-mail: accreditation@apta.org
Web: www.capteonline.org

PHYSICIAN ASSISTANT STUDIES
John E. McCarty, Executive Director
Accreditation Review Commission on Education for the
Physician Assistant, Inc. (ARC-PA)
12000 Findley Road, Suite 240
Duluth, Georgia 30097
Phone: 770-476-1224
Fax: 770-476-1738
E-mail: arc-pa@arc-pa.org
Web: www.arc-pa.org

PLANNING
Shonagh Merits, Executive Director
American Institute of Certified Planners/Association of Collegiate Schools of Planning/American Planning Association
Planning Accreditation Board (PAB)
122 South Michigan Avenue, Suite 1600
Chicago, Illinois 60603
Phone: 312-334-1271
Fax: 312-334-1273
E-mail: pab@planning.org
Web: www.planningaccreditationboard.org

PODIATRIC MEDICINE
Alan R. Tinkleman, Director
Council on Podiatric Medical Education (CPME)
American Podiatric Medical Association
9312 Old Georgetown Road
Bethesda, Maryland 20814-1621
Phone: 301-571-9200
Fax: 301-571-4903
E-mail: artinkleman@apma.org
Web: www.cpme.org

PSYCHOLOGY AND COUNSELING
Susan Zlotlow, Executive Director
Office of Program Consultation and Accreditation
American Psychological Association
750 First Street, NE
Washington, DC 20002-4242
Phone: 202-336-5979
Fax: 202-336-5978
E-mail: apaaccred@apa.org
Web: www.apa.org/ed/accreditation

Carol L. Bobby, Executive Director
Council for Accreditation of Counseling and Related Educational Programs (CACREP)
1001 North Fairfax Street, Suite 510
Alexandria, Virginia 22314
Phone: 703-535-5990
Fax: 703-739-6209
E-mail: cacrep@cacrep.org
Web: www.cacrep.org

PUBLIC AFFAIRS AND ADMINISTRATION
Crystal Calarusse, Executive Director
Commission on Peer Review and Accreditation
National Association of Schools of Public Affairs and Administration
1120 G Street, NW, Suite 730
Washington, DC 20005
Phone: 202-628-8965
Fax: 202-626-4978
E-mail: calarusse@naspaa.org
Web: www.naspaa.org

PUBLIC HEALTH
Laura Rasar King, M.P.H., CHES, Executive Director
Council on Education for Public Health
800 Eye Street, NW, Suite 202
Washington, DC 20001-3710
Phone: 202-789-1050
Fax: 202-789-1895
E-mail: Lking@ceph.org
Web: www.ceph.org

REHABILITATION EDUCATION
Marvin D. Kuehn, Executive Director
Council on Rehabilitation Education (CORE)
Commission on Standards and Accreditation
300 North Martingale Road, Suite 460
Schaumburg, Illinois 60173
Phone: 847-944-1345
Fax: 847-944-1324
E-mail: mkuehn@emporia.edu
Web: www.core-rehab.org

SOCIAL WORK
Judith Bremner, Interim Director of Accreditation
Commission on Accreditation
Council on Social Work Education
1725 Duke Street, Suite 500
Alexandria, Virginia 22314
Phone: 703-519-2044
Fax: 703-683-8099
E-mail: jbermner@cswe.org
Web: www.cswe.org

SPEECH-LANGUAGE PATHOLOGY AND AUDIOLOGY
Patrima L. Tice, Director of Accreditation
American Speech-Language-Hearing Association
2200 Research Boulevard
Rockville, Maryland 20850-3289
Phone: 301-897-5700
Fax: 301-296-8750
E-mail: ptice@asha.org
Web: www.asha.org/about/credentialing/accreditation

TEACHER EDUCATION
James G. Cibulka, President
National Council for Accreditation of Teacher Education
2010 Massachusetts Avenue, NW, Suite 500
Washington, DC 20036-1023
Phone: 202-466-7496
Fax: 202-296-6620
E-mail: ncate@ncate.org
Web: www.ncate.org

Frank B. Murray, President
Teacher Education Accreditation Council (TEAC)
Accreditation Committee
One Dupont Circle, Suite 320
Washington, DC 20036-0110
Phone: 202-831-0400
Fax: 202-831-3013
E-mail: teac@teac.org
Web: www.teac.org

TECHNOLOGY

Elise Scanlon, Executive Director
Accrediting Commission of Career Schools and Colleges of Technology
2101 Wilson Boulevard, Suite 302
Arlington, Virginia 22201
Phone: 703-247-4212
Fax: 703-247-4533
E-mail: escanlon@accsct.org
Web: www.accsct.org

THEATER

Samuel Hope, Executive Director
Karen P. Moynahan, Associate Director
National Association of Schools of Theatre
Commission on Accreditation
11250 Roger Bacon Drive, Suite 21
Reston, Virginia 20190
Phone: 703-437-0700
Fax: 703-437-6312
E-mail: info@arts-accredit.org
Web: www.arts-accredit.org

THEOLOGY

Bernard Fryshman, Executive Vice President
Association of Advanced Rabbinical and Talmudic Schools (AARTS)
Accreditation Commission
11 Broadway, Suite 405
New York, New York 10004
Phone: 212-363-1991
Fax: 212-533-5335

Daniel O. Aleshire, Executive Director
Association of Theological Schools in the United States and Canada (ATS)
Commission on Accrediting
10 Summit Park Drive
Pittsburgh, Pennsylvania 15275-1103
Phone: 412-788-6505
Fax: 412-788-6510
E-mail: ats@ats.edu
Web: www.ats.edu

Russell Guy Fitzgerald, Executive Director
Transnational Association of Christian Colleges and Schools (TRACS)
Accreditation Commission
P.O. Box 328
Forest, Virginia 24551
Phone: 434-525-9539
Fax: 434-525-9538
E-mail: info@tracs.org
Web: www.tracs.org

VETERINARY MEDICINE

Dr. David Granstrom, Director
Education and Research Division
American Veterinary Medical Association (AVMA)
Council on Education
1931 North Meacham Road, Suite 100
Schaumburg, Illinois 60173
Phone: 847-925-8070
Fax: 847-925-1329
E-mail: avmainfo@avma.org
Web: www.avma.org

How to Use This Guide

The graduate and professional programs in *Peterson's Graduate Schools in the U.S.* are offered by colleges and universities in the United States and U.S. territories that are accredited by U.S. accrediting bodies recognized by the Department of Education or the Council for Higher Education Accreditation. Each institution qualifies as a Doctorate-granting University or Master's College and University according to the most recent available *Carnegie Classification of Institutions of Higher Education*–Basic Classification, and most are regionally accredited.

Profiles of Institutions Offering Graduate and Professional Work

Information in this guide is presented in **Profile** form. Each **Profile** provides basic information about an institution. The format of the **Profiles** is consistent throughout the guide, making it easier to compare institutions. Any item that does not apply to or was not provided by a graduate unit is omitted. Information about the overall institution comes first. Information about autonomous graduate units follows with lists of the specific graduate degree programs offered. For complex institutions that combine their graduate studies under a unified administrative structure, degrees may be listed under divisional subheadings.

Institution Information

The institution's name, city, and Web address make up the heading. The following paragraph begins with information about the institution's control, gender makeup of the student body, and category of institutional structure. The total figure for graduate, professional, and undergraduate student enrollment precedes specific figures for full-time and part-time graduate students, including number of women. Next comes the number of full-time and part-time graduate faculty members. Information about the institution's computer and library facilities follows. Graduate tuition and fee information for full-time and part-time students follows. (Please be aware that tuition can be different, and frequently higher, in specific graduate programs. You should always check with the particular program if a tuition difference will be a factor in your selection.) A general graduate program application contact and telephone number ends this first paragraph.

Graduate Units

The name of the unit is followed by the name and title of the head of the unit. Institutions have varying levels of discreteness in defining administrative units, and these are presented according to the information that the institution has provided to Peterson's. Each degree-program field of study offered by the unit is listed with abbreviations for all postbaccalaureate degrees awarded.

Data Collection Procedures

The information published in this book was collected through *Peterson's Annual Survey of Graduate and Professional Institutions*. Each spring and summer, this survey is sent to accredited institutions in the United States and U.S. territories that offer postbaccalaureate degree programs. Deans and other administrators provide information on specific programs as well as overall institutional information.

While every effort is made to ensure the accuracy and completeness of the data, information is sometimes unavailable or changes occur after publication deadlines. The omission of any particular item from a **Profile** signifies either that the item is not applicable to the institution or program or that information was not available.

Directory of Graduate and Professional Programs by Field

Directory of Graduate and Professional Programs by Field

■ ACCOUNTING

Abilene Christian University M
Adelphi University M
Alabama State University M
American InterContinental University Buckhead Campus M
American InterContinental University South Florida M
American International College M
American University M
Anderson University (IN) M,D
Andrews University M
Angelo State University M
Appalachian State University M
Argosy University, Orange County M,D,O
Argosy University, Sarasota M,D,O
Argosy University, Tampa M,D
Argosy University, Twin Cities M,D
Arizona State University M,D
Arkansas State University M
Assumption College M,O
Auburn University M
Avila University M
Baldwin-Wallace College M
Ball State University M
Barry University M
Bayamón Central University M
Baylor University M
Benedictine University M
Bentley University M,D
Bernard M. Baruch College of the City University of New York M,D
Bob Jones University P,M,D,O
Boise State University M
Boston College M
Boston University M,D,O
Bowling Green State University M
Bradley University M
Brenau University M
Bridgewater State College M
Brigham Young University M
Brooklyn College of the City University of New York M
Bryant University M
Caldwell College M
California State University, East Bay M
California State University, Fresno M
California State University, Fullerton M
California State University, Los Angeles M
California State University, Sacramento M
Canisius College M
Capella University M,D,O
Carnegie Mellon University D
Case Western Reserve University M,D
Centenary College M
Central Michigan University M
Central Washington University M
Charleston Southern University M
Chatham University M
City University of Seattle M,O
Clark Atlanta University M
Clark University M
Clemson University M
Cleveland State University M
The College at Brockport, State University of New York M
College of Charleston M
The College of Saint Rose M
The College of William and Mary M
Colorado State University M
Colorado Technical University Colorado Springs M,D
Colorado Technical University Denver M
Columbia University M,D
Cornell University D
Dallas Baptist University M
Davenport University M
Delta State University M
DePaul University M
DeSales University M
Dominican University M
Drexel University M,D,O
Duquesne University M
East Carolina University M
Eastern Illinois University M,O
Eastern Michigan University M
East Tennessee State University M
Edgewood College M
Elmhurst College M
Emory University M,D
Fairfield University M,O
Fairleigh Dickinson University, College at Florham M
Fairleigh Dickinson University, Metropolitan Campus M,O
Fitchburg State College M
Florida Agricultural and Mechanical University M
Florida Atlantic University M,D
Florida Gulf Coast University M
Florida Institute of Technology M
Florida International University M
Florida State University M,D
Fontbonne University M
Fordham University M
Freed-Hardeman University M
Gannon University O
George Mason University M
The George Washington University M,D
Georgia College & State University M
Georgia Institute of Technology M,D,O
Georgian Court University M,O
Georgia Southern University M
Georgia State University M,D,O
Golden Gate University M,D,O
Gonzaga University M
Governors State University M
Graduate School and University Center of the City University of New York D
Grand Canyon University M
Grand Valley State University M
Harding University M
Harvard University D
Hawai'i Pacific University M
Hofstra University M
Hood College M
Houston Baptist University M
Howard University M
Hunter College of the City University of New York M
Illinois State University M
Indiana University Northwest M,O
Indiana University–Purdue University Indianapolis M
Indiana University South Bend M
Indiana Wesleyan University M
Inter American University of Puerto Rico, Metropolitan Campus M
Inter American University of Puerto Rico, San Germán Campus M,D
Iowa State University of Science and Technology M
Ithaca College M
Jackson State University M
James Madison University M
John Carroll University M
Johnson & Wales University M
Jones International University M

Kansas State University M
Kean University M
Kennesaw State University M
Kent State University M,D
Lakeland College M
Lamar University M
La Sierra University M,O
Lehigh University M
Lehman College of the City University of New York M
Lewis University M
Lincoln University (MO) M
Lindenwood University M
Lipscomb University M
Long Island University, Brooklyn Campus M
Long Island University, C.W. Post Campus M,O
Louisiana State University and Agricultural and Mechanical College M,D
Louisiana Tech University M,D
Loyola University Chicago M
Loyola University Maryland M
Maharishi University of Management M,D
Marquette University M
Maryville University of Saint Louis M,O
McNeese State University M
Mercy College M
Miami University M
Michigan State University M,D
Middle Tennessee State University M
Minnesota State University Mankato M
Mississippi College M,O
Mississippi State University M,D
Missouri State University M
Molloy College M
Monmouth University M,O
Montana State University M
Montclair State University M,O
Murray State University M
National University M
New Jersey City University M
New Mexico State University M
New York Institute of Technology M,O
New York University M,D
North Carolina State University M
Northeastern Illinois University M
Northeastern State University M
Northeastern University M,O
Northern Illinois University M
Northern Kentucky University M,O
Northwestern University D
Northwest Missouri State University M
Nova Southeastern University M,D
Nyack College M
Oakland University M,O
The Ohio State University M
Oklahoma City University M
Oklahoma State University M,D
Old Dominion University M
Oral Roberts University M
Our Lady of the Lake University of San Antonio M
Pace University M
Pittsburg State University M
Pontifical Catholic University of Puerto Rico M
Prairie View A&M University M
Providence College M
Purdue University Calumet M
Queens College of the City University of New York M
Quinnipiac University M
Regis University M,O
Rhode Island College M,O
Rider University M
Rochester Institute of Technology M
Roosevelt University M
Rutgers, The State University of New Jersey, Newark M,D,O
St. Ambrose University M
St. Bonaventure University M
St. Edward's University M,O
St. John's University (NY) M,O
St. Joseph's College, Long Island Campus M
Saint Joseph's University M
Saint Leo University M
Saint Louis University M
St. Mary's University (United States) M
Saint Peter's College M
St. Thomas University M,O
Salisbury University M
Sam Houston State University M
San Diego State University M
San Jose State University M
Seattle University M
Seton Hall University M
Southeast Missouri State University M
Southern Illinois University Carbondale M,D
Southern Illinois University Edwardsville M
Southern Methodist University M
Southern New Hampshire University M,D,O
Southern Polytechnic State University M,O
Southern Utah University M
State University of New York at Binghamton M,D
State University of New York at Fredonia M
State University of New York at New Paltz M
State University of New York College at Geneseo M
State University of New York Institute of Technology M
Stephen F. Austin State University M
Stetson University M
Strayer University M
Suffolk University M,O
Syracuse University M,D
Tarleton State University M
Temple University M,D
Texas A&M International University M
Texas A&M University M,D
Texas A&M University–Corpus Christi M
Texas A&M University–Texarkana M
Texas Christian University M
Texas State University–San Marcos M
Texas Tech University M,D
Towson University M
Trinity University M
Truman State University M
Universidad del Turabo M
Universidad Metropolitana M,O
University at Albany, State University of New York M
University at Buffalo, the State University of New York M,D,O
The University of Akron M
The University of Alabama M,D
The University of Alabama at Birmingham M
The University of Alabama in Huntsville M,O
The University of Arizona M
University of Arkansas M
University of Arkansas at Little Rock M,O
University of Baltimore M,O
University of California, Berkeley D,O
University of Central Arkansas M
University of Central Florida M
University of Central Missouri M
University of Cincinnati M,D
University of Colorado at Boulder M,D
University of Colorado at Colorado Springs M
University of Colorado Denver M
University of Connecticut M,D
University of Dallas M
University of Dayton M
University of Delaware M
University of Denver M
University of Florida M,D
University of Georgia M
University of Hartford M,O
University of Hawaii at Manoa M,D
University of Houston M,D
University of Houston–Clear Lake M

M—master's degree; P—first professional degree; D—doctorate; O—other advanced degree

University of Houston–Victoria	M
University of Idaho	M
University of Illinois at Chicago	M
University of Illinois at Springfield	M
University of Illinois at Urbana–Champaign	M,D
The University of Iowa	M,D
The University of Kansas	M
University of Kentucky	M
University of La Verne	M
University of Louisville	M
University of Maine	M
University of Mary Hardin-Baylor	M
University of Maryland University College	M,O
University of Massachusetts Amherst	M
University of Massachusetts Dartmouth	M,O
University of Memphis	M,D
University of Miami	M
University of Michigan–Dearborn	M
University of Minnesota, Twin Cities Campus	M,D
University of Mississippi	M,D
University of Missouri–Columbia	M,D
University of Missouri–Kansas City	M,D
University of Missouri–St. Louis	M,O
The University of Montana	M
University of Nebraska at Omaha	M
University of Nebraska–Lincoln	M,D
University of Nevada, Las Vegas	M
University of Nevada, Reno	M
University of New Hampshire	M
University of New Haven	M
University of New Orleans	M
The University of North Carolina at Chapel Hill	M,D
The University of North Carolina at Charlotte	M
The University of North Carolina at Greensboro	M,O
The University of North Carolina Wilmington	M
University of North Dakota	M
University of Northern Iowa	M
University of North Florida	M
University of North Texas	M,D
University of Notre Dame	M
University of Oklahoma	M
University of Oregon	M,D
University of Pennsylvania	M,D
University of Phoenix	M
University of Phoenix–Central Florida Campus	M
University of Phoenix–Denver Campus	M
University of Phoenix–Hawaii Campus	M
University of Phoenix–Las Vegas Campus	M
University of Phoenix–Louisiana Campus	M
University of Phoenix–New Mexico Campus	M
University of Phoenix–North Florida Campus	M
University of Phoenix–Oregon Campus	M
University of Phoenix–Philadelphia Campus	M
University of Phoenix–Phoenix Campus	M
University of Phoenix–Sacramento Valley Campus	M
University of Phoenix–San Diego Campus	M
University of Phoenix–Southern Arizona Campus	M
University of Phoenix–Southern California Campus	M
University of Phoenix–Southern Colorado Campus	M
University of Phoenix–South Florida Campus	M
University of Phoenix–Utah Campus	M
University of Phoenix–West Florida Campus	M
University of Phoenix–West Michigan Campus	M
University of Pittsburgh	M,D
University of Puerto Rico, Río Piedras	M,D
University of Rhode Island	M
University of St. Thomas (MN)	M
University of San Diego	M,O
The University of Scranton	M
University of South Alabama	M
University of South Carolina	M
The University of South Dakota	M
University of Southern California	M
University of Southern Indiana	M
University of Southern Maine	M
University of Southern Mississippi	M
University of South Florida	M
The University of Tampa	M
The University of Tennessee	M,D
The University of Tennessee at Chattanooga	M
The University of Texas at Arlington	M,D
The University of Texas at Austin	M,D
The University of Texas at Dallas	M,D
The University of Texas at El Paso	M
The University of Texas at San Antonio	M,D
The University of Texas of the Permian Basin	M
The University of Texas–Pan American	M
University of the Incarnate Word	M
The University of Toledo	M
University of Tulsa	M
University of Utah	M,D
University of Vermont	M
University of Virginia	M
University of Washington	M,D
University of Washington, Tacoma	M
University of West Florida	M
University of West Georgia	M
University of Wisconsin–Madison	D
University of Wisconsin–Whitewater	M
University of Wyoming	M
Upper Iowa University	M
Utah State University	M
Utica College	M
Villanova University	M
Virginia Commonwealth University	M,D
Virginia Polytechnic Institute and State University	M,D
Wagner College	M
Wake Forest University	M
Walden University	M,D
Washington State University	M,D
Washington University in St. Louis	M
Wayne State University	M,D
Weber State University	M
Western Carolina University	M
Western Connecticut State University	M
Western Illinois University	M
Western Michigan University	M
Western New England College	M
West Texas A&M University	M
West Virginia University	M
Wheeling Jesuit University	M
Wichita State University	M
Widener University	M
Wilkes University	M
Worcester State College	M
Wright State University	M
Yale University	D
Yeshiva University	M
Youngstown State University	M

■ ACOUSTICS

Penn State University Park	M,D
University of Massachusetts Dartmouth	M,D,O

■ ACTUARIAL SCIENCE

Ball State University	M
Boston University	M
Central Connecticut State University	M,O
Columbia University	M
Georgia State University	M

Maryville University of Saint Louis M
Roosevelt University M
St. John's University (NY) M
Temple University M
University of Central Florida M,O
University of Connecticut M,D
University of Illinois at Urbana–Champaign M,D
The University of Iowa M,D
University of Nebraska–Lincoln M
The University of Texas at Austin M,D
University of Wisconsin–Madison M

■ ACUPUNCTURE AND ORIENTAL MEDICINE

Touro College M,D
University of Bridgeport M

■ ACUTE CARE/CRITICAL CARE NURSING

Barry University M,O
Case Western Reserve University M,D
The College of New Rochelle M,O
Columbia University M,O
Duke University M,D,O
Duquesne University O
Georgetown University M
Indiana University–Purdue University Indianapolis M,D
The Johns Hopkins University M,O
Loyola University Chicago M,O
New York University M,O
Northeastern University M,O
Seton Hall University M
Texas Woman's University M,D
University at Buffalo, the State University of New York M,D,O
The University of Alabama in Huntsville M,D,O
University of Cincinnati M,D
University of Illinois at Chicago M
University of Miami M,D
University of Michigan M
University of Pennsylvania M
University of Pittsburgh M,D
University of Rochester M,D,O
University of South Carolina M,O
University of Virginia M,D
Vanderbilt University M,D
Virginia Polytechnic Institute and State University M,D
Wayne State University M
Wright State University M

■ ADDICTIONS/SUBSTANCE ABUSE COUNSELING

Cambridge College M,O
Capella University M,D,O
Cleveland State University M,O
The College of New Jersey M,O
College of St. Joseph M
The College of William and Mary M,D
Coppin State University M
East Carolina University M
Eastern Michigan University M,O
Governors State University M
Grand Canyon University M
Indiana University–Purdue University Indianapolis M,D
Indiana Wesleyan University M
The Johns Hopkins University M,D
Kean University M
Lewis & Clark College M
Maryville University of Saint Louis M
Marywood University M
McNeese State University M
Mercy College M,O
Monmouth University M,O
Montclair State University M,D,O
National-Louis University M,O
Pace University M
Palm Beach Atlantic University M
St. Mary's University (United States) M,D,O
Shippensburg University of Pennsylvania M,O
Southern New Hampshire University M,O
Springfield College M
Stony Brook University, State University of New York M
University of California, Berkeley O
University of Central Florida M,O
University of Central Oklahoma M
University of Detroit Mercy M,O
University of Illinois at Springfield M
University of Louisiana at Monroe M
University of Louisville M,D,O
University of Mary M
University of Nevada, Las Vegas M,O
University of New England M,O
Wayne State University O

■ ADULT EDUCATION

Alverno College M
Armstrong Atlantic State University M
Auburn University M,D,O
Ball State University M,D
Buffalo State College, State University of New York M,O
Capella University M,D,O
Central Michigan University M
Cheyney University of Pennsylvania M
Cleveland State University M,O
Colorado State University M,D
Coppin State University M
Cornell University M,D
Delaware State University M
DePaul University M
Drake University M
East Carolina University M,O
Eastern Washington University M
Florida Agricultural and Mechanical University M,D
Florida Atlantic University M,D,O
Florida International University M,D
Fordham University M,D,O
Grand Valley State University M,O
Indiana University of Pennsylvania M,D
Indiana University–Purdue University Indianapolis M
The Johns Hopkins University M,O
Jones International University M
Kansas State University M,D
Kean University M
Marshall University M
Michigan State University M,D,O
Montana State University M,D,O
Morehead State University M,O
National-Louis University M,D,O
North Carolina Agricultural and Technical State University M,D
North Carolina State University M,D
North Dakota State University M,D,O
Northern Illinois University M,D
Northwestern State University of Louisiana M
Nova Southeastern University D
Oregon State University M
Penn State University Park M,D
Plymouth State University D
Portland State University M,D
Regis University M,O
Saint Joseph's University M,O
San Francisco State University M,O
Seattle University M,O
Suffolk University M,O
Syracuse University O
Texas A&M University–Kingsville M
Texas A&M University–Texarkana M
Troy University M
Tusculum College M
University of Alaska Anchorage M
University of Arkansas at Little Rock M
University of California, Berkeley O
University of Central Oklahoma M
University of Cincinnati M,D,O
University of Connecticut M,D
University of Denver M,D,O
University of Georgia M,D,O
University of Idaho M,D,O
University of Memphis M,D
University of Minnesota, Twin Cities Campus M,D,O
University of Missouri–Columbia M,D,O
University of Missouri–St. Louis M,D,O

M—master's degree; P—first professional degree; D—doctorate; O—other advanced degree

University of Nebraska–Lincoln	M,D,O
The University of North Carolina at Charlotte	D
The University of North Carolina at Greensboro	M,D,O
University of Oklahoma	M,D
University of Phoenix	M
University of Phoenix–Phoenix Campus	M
University of Phoenix–Sacramento Valley Campus	M,O
University of Phoenix–Southern Arizona Campus	M,O
University of Phoenix–Southern California Campus	M
University of Rhode Island	M
University of Southern Maine	M,O
University of Southern Mississippi	M,D,O
University of South Florida	M,D,O
The University of Tennessee	M,D
University of the Incarnate Word	M,D,O
The University of West Alabama	M
University of Wisconsin–Milwaukee	D
University of Wisconsin–Platteville	M
University of Wyoming	M,D,O
Virginia Commonwealth University	M
Virginia Polytechnic Institute and State University	M,D
Walden University	M,D,O
Wayne State University	M,D,O
Western Washington University	M
Widener University	M,D
Wright State University	O

■ ADULT NURSING

Angelo State University	M
Bloomsburg University of Pennsylvania	M
Boston College	M,D
California State University, Long Beach	M
Case Western Reserve University	M,D
The Catholic University of America	M,D,O
College of Mount Saint Vincent	M,O
College of Staten Island of the City University of New York	M,O
Columbia University	M,O
Daemen College	M,O
DeSales University	M
Duke University	M,D,O
Eastern Michigan University	M,O
Emory University	M
The George Washington University	M,D,O
Georgia College & State University	M
Georgia State University	M,D,O
Grand Canyon University	M
Gwynedd-Mercy College	M
Hampton University	M
Hunter College of the City University of New York	M
Indiana University–Purdue University Fort Wayne	M,O
Indiana University–Purdue University Indianapolis	M,D
The Johns Hopkins University	M,O
Kent State University	M,D
Lehman College of the City University of New York	M
Lewis University	M
Long Island University, Brooklyn Campus	M,O
Loyola University Chicago	M,O
Loyola University New Orleans	M,D
Madonna University	M
Marian University (WI)	M
Marquette University	M,D,O
Maryville University of Saint Louis	M
Molloy College	M,O
Mount Saint Mary College	M
New Mexico State University	M
New York University	M,O
North Park University	M
Oakland University	M
Otterbein College	M,O
Quinnipiac University	M,O
Radford University	M
Rutgers, The State University of New Jersey, Newark	M
Saint Peter's College	M
Saint Xavier University	M,O
Seattle Pacific University	M,O
Seton Hall University	M
Spalding University	M
State University of New York Institute of Technology	M,O
Stony Brook University, State University of New York	M,O
Texas Christian University	M,D
Texas Woman's University	M,D
Universidad del Turabo	M
University at Buffalo, the State University of New York	M,D,O
University of Central Florida	M,D,O
University of Cincinnati	M,D
University of Colorado at Colorado Springs	M,D
University of Delaware	M,O
University of Hawaii at Manoa	M,D,O
University of Illinois at Chicago	M
University of Louisville	M,D
University of Massachusetts Dartmouth	M,D,O
University of Miami	M,D
University of Michigan	M,O
University of Minnesota, Twin Cities Campus	M
University of Missouri–Kansas City	M,D
The University of North Carolina at Chapel Hill	M,D,O
The University of North Carolina at Charlotte	M
The University of North Carolina at Greensboro	M,D,O
University of Pennsylvania	M
University of Pittsburgh	M,D
University of Rochester	M,D,O
University of St. Francis (IL)	M,D
University of San Diego	M,D
The University of Scranton	M,O
University of South Alabama	M,D
University of South Carolina	M
University of Southern Maine	M,O
University of Southern Mississippi	M,D
The University of Tampa	M
The University of Tennessee at Chattanooga	M,O
The University of Texas–Pan American	M
The University of Toledo	M,O
University of Wisconsin–Oshkosh	M
Vanderbilt University	M,D
Villanova University	M,D,O
Virginia Commonwealth University	M,D,O
Wayne State University	M
Western Connecticut State University	M
Wilmington University	M
Winona State University	M,D,O
Wright State University	M

■ ADVERTISING AND PUBLIC RELATIONS

Ball State University	M
Boston University	M
California State University, Fullerton	M
Central Connecticut State University	M,O
Colorado State University	M,D
DePaul University	M
Emerson College	M
Georgetown University	M,D
Golden Gate University	M,D,O
Immaculata University	M
Iona College	M
La Sierra University	M
Marquette University	M
Michigan State University	M,D
Mississippi College	M
Monmouth University	M,O
Montana State University–Billings	M
Montclair State University	M
New York University	M
Northwestern University	M

Quinnipiac University	M
Rowan University	M
San Diego State University	M
Seton Hall University	M
Suffolk University	M
Syracuse University	M
Texas Christian University	M
Towson University	O
The University of Alabama	M
University of Denver	M
University of Florida	M
University of Houston	M
University of Illinois at Urbana–Champaign	M
University of Maryland, College Park	M,D
University of Miami	M,D
University of Nebraska–Lincoln	M,D
University of New Haven	M
University of Oklahoma	M
University of Southern California	M
University of Southern Mississippi	M,D
The University of Tennessee	M,D
The University of Texas at Austin	M,D
University of Wisconsin–Stevens Point	M
Virginia Commonwealth University	M
Wayne State University	M,D
Webster University	M

■ AEROSPACE/AERONAUTICAL ENGINEERING

Arizona State University	M,D
Auburn University	M,D
California Institute of Technology	M,D,O
California Polytechnic State University, San Luis Obispo	M
California State University, Long Beach	M
Case Western Reserve University	M,D
Cornell University	M,D
Embry-Riddle Aeronautical University (FL)	M
Embry-Riddle Aeronautical University Worldwide	M
Florida Institute of Technology	M,D
The George Washington University	M,D,O
Georgia Institute of Technology	M,D
Illinois Institute of Technology	M,D
Iowa State University of Science and Technology	M,D
Massachusetts Institute of Technology	M,D,O
Middle Tennessee State University	M
Mississippi State University	M,D
Missouri University of Science and Technology	M,D
North Carolina State University	M,D
The Ohio State University	M,D
Old Dominion University	M,D
Penn State University Park	M,D
Princeton University	M,D
Purdue University	M,D
Rensselaer Polytechnic Institute	M,D
Rutgers, The State University of New Jersey, New Brunswick	M,D
San Diego State University	M,D
San Jose State University	M
Stanford University	M,D,O
Stevens Institute of Technology	M,O
Syracuse University	M,D
Texas A&M University	M,D
University at Buffalo, the State University of New York	M,D
The University of Alabama	M,D
The University of Alabama in Huntsville	M,D
The University of Arizona	M,D
University of California, Davis	M,D,O
University of California, Irvine	M,D
University of California, Los Angeles	M,D
University of California, San Diego	M,D
University of Central Florida	M
University of Cincinnati	M,D
University of Colorado at Boulder	M,D
University of Colorado at Colorado Springs	M
University of Dayton	M,D
University of Florida	M,D,O
University of Houston	M,D
University of Illinois at Urbana–Champaign	M,D
The University of Kansas	M,D
University of Maryland, College Park	M,D,O
University of Miami	M,D
University of Michigan	M,D
University of Minnesota, Twin Cities Campus	M,D
University of Missouri–Columbia	M,D
University of Nevada, Las Vegas	M,D
University of Notre Dame	M,D
University of Oklahoma	M,D
University of Southern California	M,D,O
The University of Tennessee	M,D
The University of Texas at Arlington	M,D
The University of Texas at Austin	M,D
University of Virginia	M,D
University of Washington	M,D
Utah State University	M,D
Virginia Polytechnic Institute and State University	M,D
Washington University in St. Louis	M,D
Webster University	M,D
West Virginia University	M,D
Wichita State University	M,D

■ AFRICAN-AMERICAN STUDIES

Boston University	M
Carnegie Mellon University	M,D
Clark Atlanta University	M,D
Columbia University	M
Cornell University	M,D
Eastern Michigan University	O
Florida Agricultural and Mechanical University	M
Harvard University	D
Indiana University Bloomington	M
Michigan State University	M,D
Morgan State University	M,D
North Carolina Agricultural and Technical State University	M
The Ohio State University	M
Rutgers, The State University of New Jersey, New Brunswick	D
Syracuse University	M
Temple University	M,D
University at Albany, State University of New York	M
University of California, Berkeley	D
University of California, Los Angeles	M
The University of Iowa	M
The University of Kansas	M,O
University of Louisville	M
University of Massachusetts Amherst	M,D
University of Wisconsin–Madison	M
West Virginia University	M,D
Yale University	D

■ AFRICAN STUDIES

Boston University	M,O
California State University, Long Beach	M
Carnegie Mellon University	M,D
Claremont Graduate University	M,D,O
Columbia University	O
Cornell University	M,D
Florida International University	M
Harvard University	D
Howard University	M,D
Indiana University Bloomington	M
Michigan State University	M,D
New York University	M,D,O
Northwestern University	O
The Ohio State University	M
Ohio University	M
Rutgers, The State University of New Jersey, New Brunswick	D
St. John's University (NY)	M,O
Stony Brook University, State University of New York	M
Syracuse University	M
University at Albany, State University of New York	M

M—master's degree; P—first professional degree; D—doctorate; O—other advanced degree

University of California, Los Angeles M
University of Connecticut M
University of Florida O
University of Illinois at Urbana–Champaign M
The University of Kansas M,O
University of Louisville M
University of Pittsburgh O
University of South Florida M
The University of Texas at Austin M,D
University of Wisconsin–Madison M,D
University of Wisconsin–Milwaukee D
West Virginia University M,D
Yale University M

■ AGRICULTURAL ECONOMICS AND AGRIBUSINESS

Alabama Agricultural and Mechanical University M
Alcorn State University M
Arizona State University M,D
Auburn University M,D
California Polytechnic State University, San Luis Obispo M
Colorado State University M,D
Cornell University M,D
Florida Agricultural and Mechanical University M
Illinois State University M
Iowa State University of Science and Technology M,D
Kansas State University M,D
Louisiana State University and Agricultural and Mechanical College M,D
Michigan State University M,D
Mississippi State University M
New Mexico State University M,D
North Carolina Agricultural and Technical State University M
North Carolina State University M
North Dakota State University M
Northwest Missouri State University M
The Ohio State University M,D
Oklahoma State University M,D
Oregon State University M,D
Penn State University Park M,D
Prairie View A&M University M
Purdue University M,D
Rutgers, The State University of New Jersey, New Brunswick M
South Carolina State University M
Southern Illinois University Carbondale M
Texas A&M University M,D
Texas A&M University–Kingsville M
Texas Tech University M,D
The University of Arizona M
University of Arkansas M
University of California, Berkeley D
University of California, Davis M,D
University of California, Santa Barbara M,D
University of Connecticut M,D
University of Delaware M
University of Florida M,D
University of Georgia M,D
University of Idaho M
University of Illinois at Urbana–Champaign M,D
University of Kentucky M,D
University of Maine M
University of Maryland, College Park M,D
University of Massachusetts Amherst M,D
University of Missouri–Columbia M,D
University of Nevada, Reno M,D
University of Puerto Rico, Mayagüez Campus M
University of Vermont M
University of Wisconsin–Madison M,D
University of Wyoming M
Virginia Polytechnic Institute and State University M,D
Washington State University M,D,O
West Texas A&M University M
West Virginia University M
William Woods University M,O

■ AGRICULTURAL EDUCATION

Alcorn State University M,O
Arkansas State University M,D,O
Clemson University M
Cornell University M,D
Eastern Kentucky University M
Iowa State University of Science and Technology M,D
Louisiana State University and Agricultural and Mechanical College M,D
Mississippi State University M,D,O
Missouri State University M
Montana State University M
Murray State University M
New Mexico State University M
North Carolina Agricultural and Technical State University M
North Carolina State University M,O
North Dakota State University M
Northwest Missouri State University M
The Ohio State University M,D
Oklahoma State University M,D
Oregon State University M
Penn State University Park M,D
Purdue University M,D,O
State University of New York at Oswego M
Stephen F. Austin State University M
Tarleton State University M
Texas A&M University M,D
Texas A&M University–Commerce M
Texas A&M University–Kingsville M
Texas State University–San Marcos M
Texas Tech University M,D
The University of Arizona M
University of Arkansas M
University of Connecticut M,D,O
University of Delaware M
University of Florida M,D
University of Georgia M
University of Idaho M
University of Illinois at Urbana–Champaign M,D
University of Minnesota, Twin Cities Campus M,D,O
University of Missouri–Columbia M,D,O
University of Nebraska–Lincoln M
University of Puerto Rico, Mayagüez Campus M
The University of Tennessee M
University of Wisconsin–River Falls M
Utah State University M
Virginia Polytechnic Institute and State University M,D
West Virginia University M,D

■ AGRICULTURAL ENGINEERING

Cornell University M,D
Illinois Institute of Technology M,D
Iowa State University of Science and Technology M,D
Kansas State University M,D
Louisiana State University and Agricultural and Mechanical College M,D
New York University M,D
North Carolina State University M,D,O
North Dakota State University M,D
The Ohio State University M,D
Oklahoma State University M,D
Penn State Great Valley M
Penn State University Park M,D
Purdue University M,D
South Dakota State University M,D
Texas A&M University M,D
The University of Arizona M,D
University of Arkansas M,D
University of Dayton M
University of Florida M,D,O
University of Georgia M,D
University of Idaho M,D
University of Illinois at Urbana–Champaign M,D
University of Kentucky M,D
University of Missouri–Columbia M,D
University of Nebraska–Lincoln M,D
The University of Tennessee M
University of Wisconsin–Madison M,D

Utah State University M,D
Virginia Polytechnic Institute and State University M,D
Washington State University M,D

■ AGRICULTURAL SCIENCES—GENERAL

Alabama Agricultural and Mechanical University M,D
Alcorn State University M
Angelo State University M
Arkansas State University M,D,O
Auburn University M,D
Brigham Young University M,D
California Polytechnic State University, San Luis Obispo M
California State Polytechnic University, Pomona M
Clemson University M,D
Colorado State University M,D
Florida Agricultural and Mechanical University M
Illinois State University M
Iowa State University of Science and Technology M,D
Kansas State University M,D
Louisiana State University and Agricultural and Mechanical College M,D
McNeese State University M
Michigan State University M,D
Mississippi State University M,D,O
Missouri State University M
Montana State University M,D
Murray State University M
New Mexico State University M
North Carolina Agricultural and Technical State University M
North Carolina State University M,D,O
North Dakota State University M,D
Northwest Missouri State University M
The Ohio State University M,D
Oklahoma State University M,D
Oregon State University M,D
Penn State University Park M,D
Prairie View A&M University M
Purdue University M,D
Sam Houston State University M
South Dakota State University M,D
Southern Illinois University Carbondale M
Southern University and Agricultural and Mechanical College M
Tarleton State University M
Tennessee State University M
Texas A&M University M,D
Texas A&M University–Commerce M
Texas A&M University–Kingsville M,D
Texas Tech University M,D
The University of Arizona M,D
University of Arkansas M,D
University of California, Davis M
University of Connecticut M,D
University of Delaware M,D
University of Florida M,D
University of Georgia M,D
University of Hawaii at Manoa M,D
University of Illinois at Urbana–Champaign M,D
University of Kentucky M,D
University of Maine M,D
University of Maryland, College Park P,M,D
University of Maryland Eastern Shore M,D
University of Minnesota, Twin Cities Campus M,D
University of Missouri–Columbia M,D
University of Nebraska–Lincoln M,D
University of Nevada, Reno M,D
University of Puerto Rico, Mayagüez Campus M
The University of Tennessee M,D
The University of Tennessee at Martin M
University of Vermont M,D
University of Wisconsin–Madison M,D
University of Wisconsin–River Falls M
University of Wyoming M,D
Utah State University M,D
Virginia Polytechnic Institute and State University M,D
Virginia State University M
Washington State University M
Western Kentucky University M
West Texas A&M University M,D
West Virginia University M,D

■ AGRONOMY AND SOIL SCIENCES

Alabama Agricultural and Mechanical University M,D
Alcorn State University M
Auburn University M,D
Colorado State University M,D
Cornell University M,D
Iowa State University of Science and Technology M,D
Kansas State University M,D
Louisiana State University and Agricultural and Mechanical College M,D
Michigan State University M,D
Mississippi State University M,D
North Carolina Agricultural and Technical State University M
North Carolina State University M,D
North Dakota State University M,D
The Ohio State University M,D
Oklahoma State University M,D
Oregon State University M,D
Penn State University Park M,D
Prairie View A&M University M
Purdue University M,D
South Dakota State University M,D
Southern Illinois University Carbondale M
Texas A&M University M,D
Texas A&M University–Kingsville M,D
Texas Tech University M,D
The University of Arizona M,D
University of Arkansas M,D
University of California, Davis M,D
University of California, Riverside M,D
University of Connecticut M,D
University of Delaware M,D
University of Florida M,D
University of Georgia M,D
University of Idaho M,D
University of Illinois at Urbana–Champaign M,D
University of Kentucky M,D
University of Maine M,D
University of Maryland, College Park M,D
University of Massachusetts Amherst M,D
University of Minnesota, Twin Cities Campus M,D
University of Missouri–Columbia M,D
University of Nebraska–Lincoln M,D
University of New Hampshire M
University of Puerto Rico, Mayagüez Campus M
University of Vermont M,D
University of Wisconsin–Madison M,D
University of Wyoming M,D
Utah State University M,D
Virginia Polytechnic Institute and State University M,D
Washington State University M,D
West Virginia University D

■ ALLIED HEALTH—GENERAL

Alabama State University D
Andrews University M
Baylor University M,D
Belmont University P,M,D
Bennington College O
Boston University M,D,O
Chatham University M
Cleveland State University M
Creighton University P,M,D
Dominican College M,D
Drexel University M,D,O
Duquesne University M,D
East Carolina University M,D
Eastern Kentucky University M
East Tennessee State University M,D,O

M—master's degree; P—first professional degree; D—doctorate; O—other advanced degree

Emory University M,D
Ferris State University M
Florida Agricultural and Mechanical University M
Florida Gulf Coast University M,D
Georgia Southern University M,D,O
Georgia State University M,D,O
Grand Valley State University M,D
Idaho State University M,D,O
Ithaca College M,D
Long Island University, C.W. Post Campus M,O
Marymount University M,D,O
Maryville University of Saint Louis M,D
Mercy College M,D,O
Minnesota State University Mankato M,D,O
Misericordia University M,D
Mountain State University M
New Jersey City University M
Northeastern University P,M,D,O
Northern Arizona University M,D
Nova Southeastern University M,D
Oakland University M,D,O
The Ohio State University M
Old Dominion University M,D
Quinnipiac University M,D,O
Regis University P,M,D,O
Saint Louis University M,D,O
Seton Hall University M,D
Shenandoah University M,D,O
South Carolina State University M
Southwestern Oklahoma State University M
Temple University M,D
Tennessee State University M,D
Texas Christian University M,D
Texas State University–San Marcos M,D
Texas Woman's University M,D
Towson University M
University at Buffalo, the State University of New York M,D,O
The University of Alabama at Birmingham M,D,O
University of Arkansas at Little Rock M
University of Connecticut M
University of Detroit Mercy M,O
University of Florida M,D
University of Illinois at Chicago M,D
The University of Kansas M,D,O
University of Kentucky M,D
University of Massachusetts Lowell M,D,O
University of Nevada, Las Vegas M,D
The University of North Carolina at Chapel Hill M,D
University of North Florida M,O
University of Phoenix–Las Vegas Campus M
University of St. Francis (IL) M,D
University of Saint Francis (IN) M
University of South Alabama M,D
The University of South Dakota M,D
The University of Texas at El Paso D
University of Vermont M,D
University of Wisconsin–Milwaukee M,D,O
Virginia Commonwealth University D
Washington University in St. Louis M,D,O
Wichita State University M

■ ALLOPATHIC MEDICINE

Boston University P
Brown University P
Case Western Reserve University P
Columbia University P
Creighton University P
Dartmouth College P
Drexel University P
Duke University P
East Carolina University P
East Tennessee State University P
Emory University P
Georgetown University P
The George Washington University P
Harvard University P,D
Howard University P,D
Indiana University–Purdue University Indianapolis P,M,D
The Johns Hopkins University P
Loyola University Chicago P
Marshall University P
Mercer University P,M
Michigan State University P
New York University P
Northwestern University
The Ohio State University P
Saint Louis University P
Stanford University P
Stony Brook University, State University of New York P
Temple University P
Tufts University P
Tulane University P
University at Buffalo, the State University of New York P
The University of Alabama at Birmingham P,M,D
The University of Arizona P
University of California, Berkeley
University of California, Davis P
University of California, Irvine P
University of California, Los Angeles P
University of California, San Diego P
University of Chicago P
University of Cincinnati P,M
University of Colorado Denver P
University of Florida P
University of Hawaii at Manoa P
University of Illinois at Chicago P
University of Illinois at Urbana–Champaign
The University of Iowa P
The University of Kansas P,M,D
University of Kentucky P
University of Louisville P
University of Miami P
University of Michigan P
University of Minnesota, Duluth P
University of Minnesota, Twin Cities Campus P
University of Missouri–Columbia P
University of Missouri–Kansas City P
University of New Mexico P
The University of North Carolina at Chapel Hill P
University of North Dakota P
University of Pennsylvania P
University of Pittsburgh P
University of Rochester P
University of South Alabama P
University of South Carolina P
The University of South Dakota P
University of Southern California P
University of Utah P
University of Vermont P
University of Virginia P,M,D
University of Washington P
University of Wisconsin–Madison P
Vanderbilt University M,D
Virginia Commonwealth University P
Wake Forest University P
Washington University in St. Louis P
Wayne State University P
West Virginia University P
Wright State University P
Yale University P

■ AMERICAN INDIAN/NATIVE AMERICAN STUDIES

Central Michigan University M
Montana State University M
The University of Arizona M,D
University of California, Davis M,D
University of California, Los Angeles M
The University of Kansas M
University of Oklahoma M

■ AMERICAN STUDIES

American University M,D,O
Appalachian State University M
Baylor University M
Boston University D
Bowling Green State University M,D

Brown University M,D
California State University, Fullerton M
California State University, Long Beach M
The Catholic University of America M,D
Central Michigan University M,D,O
Claremont Graduate University M,D,O
Clark University D
The College at Brockport, State University of New York M
The College of William and Mary M,D
Columbia University M
Cornell University M,D
Drake University M
East Carolina University M
Eastern Michigan University M,O
Fairfield University M
Florida State University M,O
Georgetown University M,D
The George Washington University M,D
Harvard University D
Lehigh University M
Lindenwood University M
Michigan State University M,D
Mississippi State University M,D
New Mexico Highlands University M
New York University M,D
Northeastern State University M
Penn State Harrisburg M,D
Pepperdine University M
Providence College M
Purdue University M,D
Rutgers, The State University of New Jersey, Newark M,D
Saint Louis University M,D
State University of New York College at Cortland O
University at Buffalo, the State University of New York M,D
The University of Alabama M
University of Central Oklahoma M
University of Dallas M
University of Delaware M
University of Hawaii at Manoa M,D,O
The University of Iowa M,D
The University of Kansas M,D
University of Louisiana at Lafayette D
University of Maryland, College Park M,D
University of Massachusetts Boston M
University of Michigan M,D
University of Michigan–Flint M
University of Minnesota, Twin Cities Campus D
University of Mississippi M
University of New Mexico M,D
University of Southern California D
University of Southern Maine M
University of South Florida M
The University of Texas at Austin M,D
University of Utah M,D
University of Wisconsin–Madison M,D
University of Wyoming M
Utah State University M
Washington State University M,D
West Virginia University M,D
Wheaton College M
Yale University D

■ ANALYTICAL CHEMISTRY

Auburn University M,D
Brigham Young University M,D
California State University, Los Angeles M
Clarkson University M,D
Cleveland State University M,D
Cornell University D
Florida State University M,D
Georgetown University D
The George Washington University M,D
Governors State University M
Howard University M,D
Illinois Institute of Technology M,D
Indiana University Bloomington M,D
Kansas State University M,D
Kent State University M,D
Marquette University M,D
Miami University M,D
Northeastern University M,D
Old Dominion University M,D
Oregon State University M,D
Purdue University M,D
Rensselaer Polytechnic Institute M,D
Rutgers, The State University of New Jersey, Newark M,D
Seton Hall University M,D
Southern University and Agricultural and Mechanical College M
State University of New York at Binghamton M,D
Stevens Institute of Technology M,D,O
Tufts University M,D
University of Cincinnati M,D
University of Georgia M,D
University of Louisville M,D
University of Maryland, College Park M,D
University of Massachusetts Lowell M,D
University of Michigan D
University of Missouri–Columbia M,D
University of Missouri–Kansas City M,D
The University of Montana M,D
University of Nebraska–Lincoln M,D
University of Southern Mississippi M,D
University of South Florida M,D
The University of Tennessee M,D
The University of Texas at Austin M,D
The University of Toledo M,D
Vanderbilt University M,D
Virginia Commonwealth University M,D
Wake Forest University M,D
West Virginia University M,D
Youngstown State University M

■ ANATOMY

Auburn University M,D
Barry University M
Boston University M,D
Case Western Reserve University M
Columbia University M,D
Cornell University M,D
Creighton University M
Duke University D
East Carolina University D
East Tennessee State University M,D
Howard University M,D
Indiana University–Purdue University Indianapolis M,D
The Johns Hopkins University D
Kansas State University M,D
Loyola University Chicago M,D
The Ohio State University M,D
Purdue University M,D
Saint Louis University M,D
Stony Brook University, State University of New York D
Temple University M,D
Texas A&M University M,D
University at Buffalo, the State University of New York M,D
The University of Arizona D
University of California, Irvine M,D
University of California, Los Angeles D
University of Chicago D
University of Georgia M
University of Illinois at Chicago D
The University of Iowa D
The University of Kansas M,D
University of Kentucky D
University of Louisville M,D
University of Missouri–Columbia M
University of North Dakota M,D
University of Rochester M,D
University of South Florida M,D
The University of Tennessee M,D
University of Utah D
Virginia Commonwealth University D,O
Wake Forest University D
Wayne State University M,D

M—master's degree; P—first professional degree; D—doctorate; O—other advanced degree

Wright State University M
Youngstown State University M

■ ANESTHESIOLOGIST ASSISTANT STUDIES

Case Western Reserve University M
Emory University M

■ ANIMAL BEHAVIOR

Bucknell University M
Cornell University D
Emory University D
Illinois State University M,D
University of California, Davis D
University of Colorado at Boulder M,D
University of Minnesota, Twin Cities Campus M,D
University of Missouri–St. Louis M,D,O
The University of Montana M,D,O
The University of Tennessee M,D
The University of Texas at Austin M,D
University of Washington D

■ ANIMAL SCIENCES

Alabama Agricultural and Mechanical University M,D
Alcorn State University M
Angelo State University M
Auburn University M,D
Boise State University M
Brigham Young University M,D
California State University, Fresno M
Clemson University M,D
Colorado State University M,D
Cornell University M,D
Florida Agricultural and Mechanical University M
Fort Valley State University M
Iowa State University of Science and Technology M,D
Kansas State University M,D
Louisiana State University and Agricultural and Mechanical College M,D
Michigan State University M,D
Mississippi State University M,D
Montana State University M,D
New Mexico State University M,D
North Carolina Agricultural and Technical State University M
North Carolina State University M,D
North Dakota State University M,D
The Ohio State University M,D
Oklahoma State University M,D
Oregon State University M,D
Penn State University Park M,D
Prairie View A&M University M
Purdue University M,D
Rutgers, The State University of New Jersey, New Brunswick M,D
South Dakota State University M,D
Southern Illinois University Carbondale M
Sul Ross State University M
Texas A&M University M,D
Texas A&M University–Kingsville M
Texas Tech University M,D
The University of Arizona M,D
University of Arkansas M,D
University of California, Davis M,D
University of Connecticut M,D
University of Delaware M,D
University of Florida M,D
University of Georgia M,D
University of Hawaii at Manoa M
University of Idaho M,D
University of Illinois at Urbana–Champaign M,D
University of Kentucky M,D
University of Maine M
University of Maryland, College Park M,D
University of Massachusetts Amherst M,D
University of Minnesota, Twin Cities Campus M,D
University of Missouri–Columbia M,D
University of Nebraska–Lincoln M,D
University of Nevada, Reno M
University of New Hampshire M,D
University of Puerto Rico, Mayagüez Campus M
University of Rhode Island M,D
The University of Tennessee M,D
University of Vermont M,D
University of Wisconsin–Madison M,D
University of Wyoming M,D
Utah State University M,D
Virginia Polytechnic Institute and State University M,D
Washington State University M,D
West Texas A&M University M
West Virginia University M,D

■ ANTHROPOLOGY

American University M,D,O
Arizona State University M,D
Ball State University M
Boston University M,D
Brandeis University M,D
Brigham Young University M
Brown University M,D
California Institute of Integral Studies M,D
California State University, Bakersfield M
California State University, Chico M
California State University, East Bay M
California State University, Fullerton M
California State University, Long Beach M
California State University, Los Angeles M
California State University, Northridge M
California State University, Sacramento M
Case Western Reserve University M,D
The Catholic University of America M
The College of William and Mary M,D
Colorado State University M
Columbia University M,D
Cornell University D
Duke University D
East Carolina University M
Eastern New Mexico University M
Emory University D
Florida Atlantic University M
Florida State University M,D
George Mason University M,D
The George Washington University M,D
Georgia State University M
Graduate School and University Center of the City University of New York D
Harvard University M,D
Hunter College of the City University of New York M
Idaho State University M
Indiana University Bloomington M,D
Iowa State University of Science and Technology M
The Johns Hopkins University D
Kent State University M
Louisiana State University and Agricultural and Mechanical College M,D
Michigan State University M,D
Minnesota State University Mankato M
Mississippi State University M
New Mexico Highlands University M
New Mexico State University M
The New School: A University M,D
New York University M,D
North Carolina State University M
Northern Arizona University M
Northern Illinois University M
Northwestern University D
The Ohio State University M,D
Oregon State University M
Penn State University Park M,D
Portland State University M,D,O
Princeton University D
Purdue University M,D
Rice University M,D
Roosevelt University M
Rutgers, The State University of New Jersey, New Brunswick M,D
San Diego State University M
San Francisco State University M
San Jose State University M

Sonoma State University	M
Southern Illinois University Carbondale	M,D
Southern Methodist University	M,D
Stanford University	M,D
State University of New York at Binghamton	M,D
Stony Brook University, State University of New York	M,D
Syracuse University	M,D
Temple University	D
Texas A&M University	M,D
Texas State University–San Marcos	M
Texas Tech University	M
Tulane University	M,D
University at Albany, State University of New York	M,D
University at Buffalo, the State University of New York	M,D
The University of Alabama	M,D
The University of Alabama at Birmingham	M
University of Alaska Anchorage	M
University of Alaska Fairbanks	M,D
The University of Arizona	M,D
University of Arkansas	M,D
University of California, Berkeley	D
University of California, Davis	M,D
University of California, Irvine	M,D
University of California, Los Angeles	M,D
University of California, Riverside	M,D
University of California, San Diego	D
University of California, Santa Barbara	M,D
University of California, Santa Cruz	D
University of Central Florida	M
University of Chicago	M,D
University of Cincinnati	M
University of Colorado at Boulder	M,D
University of Colorado Denver	M
University of Connecticut	M,D
University of Denver	M
University of Florida	M,D
University of Georgia	M,D
University of Hawaii at Manoa	M,D
University of Houston	M
University of Idaho	M
University of Illinois at Chicago	M,D
University of Illinois at Urbana–Champaign	M,D
The University of Iowa	M,D
The University of Kansas	M,D
University of Kentucky	M,D
University of Maryland, College Park	M
University of Massachusetts Amherst	M,D
University of Memphis	M
University of Michigan	D
University of Minnesota, Duluth	M
University of Minnesota, Twin Cities Campus	M,D
University of Mississippi	M
University of Missouri–Columbia	M,D
The University of Montana	M,D
University of Nebraska–Lincoln	M
University of Nevada, Las Vegas	M,D
University of Nevada, Reno	M,D
University of New Mexico	M,D
The University of North Carolina at Chapel Hill	M,D
University of North Texas	M
University of Oklahoma	M,D
University of Oregon	M,D
University of Pennsylvania	M,D
University of Pittsburgh	M,D
University of South Carolina	M,D
University of Southern Mississippi	M
University of South Florida	M,D
The University of Tennessee	M,D
The University of Texas at Arlington	M
The University of Texas at Austin	M,D
The University of Texas at San Antonio	M,D
University of Tulsa	M
University of Utah	M,D
University of Virginia	M,D
University of Washington	M,D
University of West Florida	M
University of Wisconsin–Madison	D
University of Wisconsin–Milwaukee	M,D,O
University of Wyoming	M,D
Vanderbilt University	M,D
Washington State University	M,D
Washington University in St. Louis	D
Wayne State University	M,D
West Chester University of Pennsylvania	M,O
Western Kentucky University	M
Western Michigan University	M
Western Washington University	M
Wichita State University	M
Yale University	M,D

■ APPLIED ARTS AND DESIGN—GENERAL

Alfred University	M
Arizona State University	M
Bowling Green State University	M
Bradley University	M
California State University, Fresno	M
California State University, Fullerton	M
California State University, Los Angeles	M
Cardinal Stritch University	M
Carnegie Mellon University	D
Drexel University	M
Ferris State University	M
Florida Atlantic University	M
Howard University	M
Illinois Institute of Technology	M,D
Indiana University–Purdue University Indianapolis	M
Iowa State University of Science and Technology	M
Lamar University	M
Louisiana State University and Agricultural and Mechanical College	M
Louisiana Tech University	M
New Mexico State University	M
The New School: A University	M
New York University	M
North Carolina State University	M,D
Oklahoma State University	M,D
Purdue University	M
Rutgers, The State University of New Jersey, New Brunswick	M
San Diego State University	M
San Jose State University	M
Southern Illinois University Carbondale	M
Stephen F. Austin State University	M
Suffolk University	M
Sul Ross State University	M
Syracuse University	M
University of Baltimore	M
University of California, Berkeley	M,O
University of California, Los Angeles	M
University of Central Oklahoma	M
University of Cincinnati	M
University of Delaware	M
University of Idaho	M
University of Illinois at Urbana–Champaign	M,D
The University of Kansas	M
University of Kentucky	M
University of Massachusetts Dartmouth	M
University of Michigan	M
University of Minnesota, Twin Cities Campus	M,D,O
University of North Texas	M
University of Notre Dame	M
University of Oklahoma	M
The University of Texas at Austin	M
University of Washington	M
University of Wisconsin–Madison	M,D
Virginia Commonwealth University	M
Virginia Polytechnic Institute and State University	M,D
Wayne State University	M
Western Carolina University	M

M—master's degree; P—first professional degree; D—doctorate; O—other advanced degree

Western Michigan University M
Yale University M

■ APPLIED ECONOMICS

American University M,D,O
Auburn University M,D
Buffalo State College, State University of New York M
Clemson University M,D
Cornell University D
Eastern Michigan University M
Georgia Southern University M
The Johns Hopkins University M
Mississippi State University M,D
New York University M,D,O
North Carolina Agricultural and Technical State University M
Northeastern University M,D
Ohio University M
Old Dominion University M
Portland State University M,D
Roosevelt University M
St. Cloud State University M
San Jose State University M
Southern Methodist University M,D
Texas Tech University M,D
University of California, Santa Cruz M
University of Georgia M,D
University of Idaho M
University of Michigan M
University of Minnesota, Twin Cities Campus M,D
University of Nevada, Reno M,D
The University of North Carolina at Greensboro M
University of North Dakota M
University of North Texas M
University of Pennsylvania D
University of Vermont M
University of Wisconsin–Madison M,D
University of Wyoming M
Utah State University M
Virginia Polytechnic Institute and State University M,D
Washington State University M,D,O
Western Michigan University M,D
Wright State University M

■ APPLIED MATHEMATICS

Arizona State University M,D
Auburn University M,D
Bowie State University M
Brown University M,D
California Institute of Technology M,D
California State Polytechnic University, Pomona M
California State University, Fullerton M
California State University, Long Beach M,D
California State University, Los Angeles M
California State University, Northridge M
Carnegie Mellon University M,D
Case Western Reserve University M,D
Claremont Graduate University M,D
Clemson University M,D
Columbia University M,D,O
Cornell University M,D
Delaware State University M,D
DePaul University M,O
East Carolina University M
Florida Atlantic University M,D
Florida Institute of Technology M,D
Florida State University M,D
The George Washington University M,D
Georgia Institute of Technology M,D
Hampton University M
Harvard University M,D
Hofstra University M
Howard University M,D
Hunter College of the City University of New York M
Illinois Institute of Technology M,D
Indiana University Bloomington M,D
Indiana University of Pennsylvania M
Indiana University–Purdue University Fort Wayne M,O
Indiana University–Purdue University Indianapolis M,D
Indiana University South Bend M
Inter American University of Puerto Rico, San Germán Campus M
Iowa State University of Science and Technology M,D
The Johns Hopkins University M,D,O
Kent State University M,D
Lehigh University M,D
Long Island University, C.W. Post Campus M
Michigan State University M,D
Missouri University of Science and Technology M,D
Montclair State University M,D,O
New Jersey Institute of Technology M
New Mexico Institute of Mining and Technology M,D
North Carolina Central University M
North Carolina State University M,D
North Dakota State University M,D
Northeastern University M,D
Northwestern University M,D
Oakland University M,D
Oklahoma State University M,D
Penn State University Park M,D
Princeton University D
Rensselaer Polytechnic Institute M
Rice University M,D
Rochester Institute of Technology M
Rutgers, The State University of New Jersey, New Brunswick M,D
St. John's University (NY) M
San Diego State University M
San Jose State University M
Santa Clara University M
Southern Methodist University M,D
Stevens Institute of Technology M
Stony Brook University, State University of New York M,D
Temple University M,D
Texas A&M University–Corpus Christi M
Texas State University–San Marcos M
Towson University M
Tulane University M,D
The University of Akron M,D
The University of Alabama M,D
The University of Alabama at Birmingham M,D
The University of Alabama in Huntsville M,D
The University of Arizona M,D
University of Arkansas at Little Rock M,O
University of California, Berkeley D
University of California, Davis M,D
University of California, San Diego M,D
University of California, Santa Barbara M,D
University of California, Santa Cruz M,D
University of Central Arkansas M
University of Central Florida M,D,O
University of Central Missouri M
University of Central Oklahoma M
University of Chicago M,D
University of Cincinnati M,D
University of Colorado at Boulder M,D
University of Colorado at Colorado Springs M
University of Colorado Denver M,D
University of Connecticut M
University of Dayton M
University of Delaware M,D
University of Denver M,D
University of Georgia M,D
University of Illinois at Chicago M,D
University of Illinois at Urbana–Champaign M,D
The University of Iowa D
University of Kentucky M,D
University of Louisville M,D
University of Maryland, Baltimore County M,D
University of Maryland, College Park M,D
University of Massachusetts Amherst M

University of Massachusetts Lowell M,D
University of Memphis M,D
University of Michigan–Dearborn M
University of Minnesota, Duluth M
University of Missouri–Columbia M
University of Missouri–St. Louis M,D
University of New Hampshire M,D,O
The University of North Carolina at Charlotte M,D
University of Notre Dame M,D
University of Pennsylvania D
University of Pittsburgh M,D
University of Puerto Rico, Mayagüez Campus M
University of Rhode Island M,D,O
University of Southern California M,D
The University of Tennessee M,D
The University of Texas at Austin M,D
The University of Texas at Dallas M,D
The University of Texas at El Paso M
The University of Texas at San Antonio M
The University of Toledo M,D
University of Washington M,D
University of West Georgia M
Utah State University M,D
Virginia Commonwealth University M,O
Virginia Polytechnic Institute and State University M,D
Washington State University M,D
Wayne State University M,D
Western Illinois University M,O
Western Michigan University M
West Virginia University M,D
Wichita State University M,D
Worcester Polytechnic Institute M,D,O
Wright State University M
Yale University M,D
Youngstown State University M

■ APPLIED PHYSICS

Alabama Agricultural and Mechanical University M,D
Brooklyn College of the City University of New York M,D
California Institute of Technology M,D
California State University, Long Beach M
Carnegie Mellon University M,D
Colorado School of Mines M,D
Columbia University M,D,O
Cornell University M,D
DePaul University M
George Mason University M
Harvard University M,D
Idaho State University M,D
Iowa State University of Science and Technology M,D
The Johns Hopkins University M,O
Mississippi State University M,D
New Jersey Institute of Technology M,D
Northern Arizona University M
Oregon State University M,D
Pittsburg State University M
Princeton University M,D
Rensselaer Polytechnic Institute M,D
Rice University M,D
Rutgers, The State University of New Jersey, Newark M,D
Southern Illinois University Carbondale M,D
Stanford University M,D
State University of New York at Binghamton M
Texas A&M University M,D
Texas Tech University M,D
The University of Arizona M
University of Arkansas M
University of California, San Diego M,D
University of Denver M,D
University of Maryland, Baltimore County M,D
University of Massachusetts Boston M
University of Massachusetts Lowell M,D
University of Michigan D
University of Missouri–St. Louis M,D
The University of North Carolina at Charlotte M,D
University of South Florida M,D
The University of Texas at Austin M,D
University of Washington M,D
Virginia Commonwealth University M
Virginia Polytechnic Institute and State University M,D
West Virginia University M,D
Yale University M,D

■ APPLIED SCIENCE AND TECHNOLOGY

American University M
The College of William and Mary M,D
Harvard University M,O
James Madison University M
Louisiana State University and Agricultural and Mechanical College M
Missouri State University M
Oklahoma State University M,D
Rensselaer Polytechnic Institute M
Southeastern Louisiana University M
Southern Methodist University M,D
University of Arkansas at Little Rock M,D
University of California, Berkeley D
University of California, Davis M,D
University of Colorado Denver M
University of Mississippi M,D

■ APPLIED SOCIAL RESEARCH

American University M,O
California State University, Dominguez Hills M,O
Hofstra University M
Hunter College of the City University of New York M
The New School: A University M,D
Portland State University M,D
University of California, Los Angeles M,D
Virginia Commonwealth University M,O
West Virginia University M

■ APPLIED STATISTICS

American University M,O
Bowling Green State University M,D
Brigham Young University M
California State University, East Bay M
California State University, Long Beach M
Cornell University M,D
DePaul University M,O
Eastern Michigan University M
Florida State University M,D
Indiana University–Purdue University Fort Wayne M,O
Indiana University–Purdue University Indianapolis M
Kennesaw State University M
Louisiana State University and Agricultural and Mechanical College M
Loyola University Chicago M
Michigan State University M,D
Montclair State University M,O
New Jersey Institute of Technology M
North Dakota State University M,D,O
Oakland University M
Penn State University Park M,D
Rochester Institute of Technology M,O
Rutgers, The State University of New Jersey, New Brunswick M,D
St. Cloud State University M
Stevens Institute of Technology O
Syracuse University M
The University of Alabama M,D
University of Arkansas at Little Rock M,O
University of California, Riverside M,D
University of California, Santa Barbara M,D
University of Illinois at Urbana–Champaign M,D
University of Memphis M,D

M—master's degree; P—first professional degree; D—doctorate; O—other advanced degree

University of Michigan	M,D
University of Northern Colorado	M,D
University of Pittsburgh	M,D
University of South Carolina	M,D,O
The University of Texas at San Antonio	M,D
Villanova University	M
Washington State University	M
West Chester University of Pennsylvania	M,O
Western Michigan University	M
Worcester Polytechnic Institute	M,D,O
Wright State University	M

■ AQUACULTURE

Auburn University	M,D
Clemson University	M,D
Purdue University	M,D
Texas A&M University–Corpus Christi	M
University of Florida	M,D
University of Rhode Island	M,D

■ ARCHAEOLOGY

Boston University	M,D
Brown University	M,D
California State University, Northridge	M
Columbia University	M,D
Cornell University	M,D
Florida State University	M,D
Graduate School and University Center of the City University of New York	D
Harvard University	M,D
Illinois State University	M
Massachusetts Institute of Technology	M,D,O
Michigan Technological University	M,D
New York University	M,D
Northern Arizona University	M
Northwestern State University of Louisiana	M
Princeton University	D
St. Cloud State University	M
Trinity International University	P,M,D,O
Tufts University	M
University of California, Berkeley	M,D
University of California, Los Angeles	M,D
University of California, Santa Barbara	M,D
University of California, Santa Cruz	D
University of Chicago	M,D
University of Georgia	M,D
University of Massachusetts Boston	M
University of Memphis	M,O
University of Michigan	D
University of Minnesota, Twin Cities Campus	M,D
University of Missouri–Columbia	M,D
University of Nebraska–Lincoln	M,D
The University of North Carolina at Chapel Hill	M,D
University of Pennsylvania	M,D
The University of Tennessee	M,D
The University of Texas at Austin	M,D
University of Virginia	M,D
University of West Florida	M
University of Wisconsin–Madison	D
Washington State University	M,D
Washington University in St. Louis	M,D
Wheaton College	M
Yale University	M,D

■ ARCHITECTURAL ENGINEERING

Carnegie Mellon University	M,D
Drexel University	M,D
Illinois Institute of Technology	M,D
Kansas State University	M
Penn State University Park	M,D
University of Colorado at Boulder	M,D
University of Detroit Mercy	M
The University of Kansas	M
University of Louisiana at Lafayette	M
University of Miami	M,D
University of Nebraska–Lincoln	M,D
The University of Texas at Austin	M

■ ARCHITECTURAL HISTORY

Arizona State University	D
Cornell University	M,D
Graduate School and University Center of the City University of New York	D
Harvard University	D
Massachusetts Institute of Technology	M,D
University of California, Berkeley	M,D
University of Pittsburgh	M,D
The University of Texas at Austin	M,D
University of Virginia	M,D
Virginia Commonwealth University	M,D

■ ARCHITECTURE

Andrews University	M
Arizona State University	M
Auburn University	M
Ball State University	M
California Polytechnic State University, San Luis Obispo	M
California State Polytechnic University, Pomona	M
Carnegie Mellon University	M,D
The Catholic University of America	M
City College of the City University of New York	M
Clemson University	M
Columbia College Chicago	M
Columbia University	M,D
Cornell University	M,D
Drury University	M
Florida Agricultural and Mechanical University	M
Florida International University	M
Georgia Institute of Technology	M,D
Harvard University	M,D
Illinois Institute of Technology	M,D
Iowa State University of Science and Technology	M
Kansas State University	M
Kent State University	M,O
Lawrence Technological University	M
Louisiana State University and Agricultural and Mechanical College	M
Marywood University	M
Massachusetts Institute of Technology	M,D
Miami University	M
Mississippi State University	M
Montana State University	M
Morgan State University	M
New Jersey Institute of Technology	M
The New School: A University	M
New York Institute of Technology	M
North Carolina State University	M
Northeastern University	M
The Ohio State University	M
Penn State University Park	M
Philadelphia University	M
Prairie View A&M University	M
Princeton University	M,D
Rensselaer Polytechnic Institute	M,D
Rice University	M,D
Roger Williams University	M
Southern Illinois University Carbondale	M
Syracuse University	M
Texas A&M University	M,D
Texas Tech University	M
Tulane University	M
University at Buffalo, the State University of New York	M
The University of Arizona	M
University of California, Berkeley	M,D
University of California, Los Angeles	M,D
University of Cincinnati	M
University of Colorado Denver	M
University of Florida	M,D
University of Hartford	M
University of Hawaii at Manoa	D
University of Houston	M
University of Idaho	M
University of Illinois at Chicago	M

University of Illinois at Urbana–Champaign M,D
The University of Kansas M,D,O
University of Kentucky M
University of Maryland, College Park M
University of Massachusetts Amherst M
University of Memphis M
University of Miami M
University of Michigan M,D
University of Minnesota, Twin Cities Campus M
University of Missouri–Columbia M
University of Nebraska–Lincoln M,D
University of Nevada, Las Vegas M
University of New Mexico M
The University of North Carolina at Charlotte M
The University of North Carolina at Greensboro M,O
University of Notre Dame M
University of Oklahoma M
University of Oregon M
University of Pennsylvania M,D,O
University of Puerto Rico, Río Piedras M
University of Southern California M,D
University of South Florida M
The University of Tennessee M
The University of Texas at Arlington M
The University of Texas at Austin M,D
The University of Texas at San Antonio M,O
University of Utah M
University of Virginia M
University of Washington M,D,O
University of Wisconsin–Milwaukee M,D,O
Virginia Polytechnic Institute and State University M,D
Washington State University M
Washington University in St. Louis M
Woodbury University M
Yale University M

■ ART/FINE ARTS

Adams State College M
Adelphi University M
Alfred University M,D
American University M
Anna Maria College M,O
Antioch University McGregor M
Arizona State University M,D
Arkansas State University M
Arkansas Tech University M
Azusa Pacific University M
Ball State University M
Barry University M
Bob Jones University P,M,D,O
Boise State University M
Boston University M
Bowling Green State University M
Bradley University M
Brandeis University O
Brigham Young University M
Brooklyn College of the City University of New York M,D
California State University, Chico M
California State University, Fresno M
California State University, Fullerton M
California State University, Long Beach M
California State University, Los Angeles M
California State University, Northridge M
California State University, Sacramento M
California State University, San Bernardino M
California State University, Stanislaus O
Carnegie Mellon University M
Central Washington University M
City College of the City University of New York M
Claremont Graduate University M
Clemson University M
Cleveland State University M
The College at Brockport, State University of New York M
The College of New Rochelle M
Colorado State University M
Columbia University M
Cornell University M
Drake University M
Drury University M
Duke University D
East Carolina University M
Eastern Illinois University M
Eastern Michigan University M
East Tennessee State University M
Edinboro University of Pennsylvania M
Fairleigh Dickinson University, Metropolitan Campus M
Ferris State University M
Florida Atlantic University M
Florida International University M
Florida State University M
Fontbonne University M
Fort Hays State University M
Framingham State College M
The George Washington University M
Georgia Southern University M
Georgia State University M
Governors State University M
Hofstra University M
Hollins University M,O
Hood College M,O
Howard University M
Hunter College of the City University of New York M
Idaho State University M
Illinois State University M
Indiana State University M
Indiana University Bloomington M,D
Indiana University of Pennsylvania M
Indiana University–Purdue University Indianapolis M
Inter American University of Puerto Rico, San Germán Campus M
James Madison University M
John F. Kennedy University M
Johnson State College M
Kansas State University M
Kean University M
Kent State University M
Lamar University M
Lehman College of the City University of New York M
Lesley University M
Lindenwood University M
Long Island University, C.W. Post Campus M
Louisiana State University and Agricultural and Mechanical College M
Louisiana Tech University M
Marshall University M
Marywood University M
Miami University M
Michigan State University M
Mills College M
Minnesota State University Mankato M
Mississippi College M
Missouri State University M
Montana State University M
Montclair State University M,O
Morehead State University M
National University M
New Jersey City University M
New Mexico State University M
The New School: A University M
New York University M,D
Norfolk State University M
Northeastern University M
Northern Illinois University M
Northwestern State University of Louisiana M
Northwestern University M
The Ohio State University M
Ohio University M
Oklahoma City University M
Penn State University Park M,D
Pittsburg State University M

M—master's degree; P—first professional degree; D—doctorate; O—other advanced degree

Portland State University M
Purchase College, State University of New York M
Purdue University M
Queens College of the City University of New York M
Radford University M
Regis University M,O
Rensselaer Polytechnic Institute M,D
Rhode Island College M
Rochester Institute of Technology M
Rutgers, The State University of New Jersey, New Brunswick M
San Diego State University M
San Francisco State University M
San Jose State University M
Seton Hall University M
Southern Illinois University Carbondale M
Southern Illinois University Edwardsville M
Southern Methodist University M
Stanford University M,D
State University of New York at New Paltz M
State University of New York at Oswego M
Stephen F. Austin State University M
Stony Brook University, State University of New York M
Sul Ross State University M
Syracuse University M
Temple University M
Texas A&M University–Commerce M
Texas A&M University–Corpus Christi M
Texas A&M University–Kingsville M
Texas Christian University M
Texas Southern University M
Texas Tech University M,D
Texas Woman's University M
Towson University M
Troy University M
Tufts University M
Tulane University M
Universidad del Turabo M
University at Albany, State University of New York M
University at Buffalo, the State University of New York M,O
The University of Alabama M
University of Alaska Fairbanks M
The University of Arizona M
University of Arkansas M
University of Arkansas at Little Rock M
University of California, Berkeley M,O
University of California, Davis M
University of California, Irvine M
University of California, Los Angeles M
University of California, Riverside M
University of California, San Diego M,D
University of California, Santa Barbara M,D
University of California, Santa Cruz M
University of Central Florida M
University of Chicago M
University of Cincinnati M
University of Colorado at Boulder M
University of Connecticut M
University of Dallas M
University of Delaware M
University of Denver M
University of Florida M,D
University of Georgia M
University of Guam M
University of Hartford M
University of Hawaii at Manoa M
University of Houston M
University of Idaho M
University of Illinois at Chicago M
University of Illinois at Urbana–Champaign M
University of Indianapolis M
The University of Iowa M
The University of Kansas M
University of Kentucky M
University of Louisville M
University of Maryland, Baltimore County M
University of Maryland, College Park M
University of Massachusetts Amherst M
University of Massachusetts Dartmouth M,O
University of Memphis M,O
University of Miami M
University of Michigan M
University of Minnesota, Duluth M
University of Minnesota, Twin Cities Campus M
University of Mississippi M
University of Missouri–Columbia M
University of Missouri–Kansas City M,D
The University of Montana M
University of Nebraska–Lincoln M
University of Nevada, Las Vegas M
University of Nevada, Reno M
University of New Hampshire M
University of New Mexico M
University of New Orleans M
The University of North Carolina at Chapel Hill M
The University of North Carolina at Greensboro M
University of North Dakota M
University of Northern Colorado M
University of Northern Iowa M
University of North Texas M
University of Notre Dame M
University of Oklahoma M
University of Oregon M
University of Pennsylvania M
University of Rochester M,D
University of Saint Francis (IN) M
University of South Carolina M
The University of South Dakota M
University of Southern California M,D,O
University of South Florida M
The University of Tennessee M
The University of Texas at Arlington M
The University of Texas at Austin M
The University of Texas at El Paso M
The University of Texas at San Antonio M
The University of Texas at Tyler M
The University of Texas–Pan American M
University of Tulsa M
University of Utah M
University of Washington M
University of Wisconsin–Madison M
University of Wisconsin–Milwaukee M
University of Wisconsin–River Falls M
University of Wisconsin–Superior M
Utah State University M
Virginia Commonwealth University M,D
Washington State University M
Washington University in St. Louis M
Wayne State University M
Webster University M
Western Carolina University M
Western Connecticut State University M
West Texas A&M University M
West Virginia University M
Wichita State University M
William Paterson University of New Jersey M
Winthrop University M
Yale University M

■ ART EDUCATION

Adelphi University M
Anna Maria College M
Arcadia University M,D,O
Ball State University M
Bennington College M
Boise State University M
Boston University M
Bowling Green State University M
Bridgewater State College M
Brigham Young University M

Institution	Degrees
Brooklyn College of the City University of New York	M,O
Buffalo State College, State University of New York	M
California State University, Long Beach	M
California State University, Los Angeles	M
California State University, Northridge	M
Cambridge College	M,D,O
Carlow University	M
Case Western Reserve University	M
Central Connecticut State University	M,O
Chatham University	M
Cleveland State University	M
College of Mount St. Joseph	M
The College of New Rochelle	M
The College of Saint Rose	M,O
Columbus State University	M
Concordia University Wisconsin	M
Converse College	M,O
Delaware State University	M
Eastern Illinois University	M
Eastern Kentucky University	M
Eastern Michigan University	M
East Tennessee State University	M
Endicott College	M
Fitchburg State College	M,O
Florida Atlantic University	M
Florida International University	M,D
Florida State University	M,D,O
George Mason University	M
Georgia Southern University	M
Georgia State University	M,D,O
Harding University	M,O
Harvard University	M
Hofstra University	M
Indiana University Bloomington	M,D,O
Indiana University–Purdue University Indianapolis	M
Indiana University South Bend	M
James Madison University	M
Kean University	M
Kent State University	M
Kutztown University of Pennsylvania	M,O
Lesley University	M,D,O
Long Island University, C.W. Post Campus	M
Manhattanville College	M
Mansfield University of Pennsylvania	M
Maryville University of Saint Louis	M,D
Marywood University	M
Miami University	M
Millersville University of Pennsylvania	M
Mills College	M,D
Minnesota State University Mankato	M
Mississippi College	M,D,O
Missouri State University	M
Montclair State University	M,O
Morehead State University	M
Nazareth College of Rochester	M
New Jersey City University	M
New York University	M,D
North Carolina Agricultural and Technical State University	M
North Georgia College & State University	M,O
Nova Southeastern University	M,O
The Ohio State University	M,D
Penn State University Park	M,D
Pittsburg State University	M
Purdue University	M,D,O
Queens College of the City University of New York	M,O
Rhode Island College	M
Rochester Institute of Technology	M
Saint Michael's College	M,O
Salem State College	M
San Jose State University	M
Southern Connecticut State University	M
Southern Illinois University Edwardsville	M
Southwestern Oklahoma State University	M
Stanford University	M,D
State University of New York at New Paltz	M
State University of New York at Oswego	M
Sul Ross State University	M
Syracuse University	M,O
Temple University	M
Texas Tech University	M,D
Towson University	M,O
The University of Alabama at Birmingham	M
The University of Arizona	M
University of Arkansas at Little Rock	M
University of Central Florida	M
University of Cincinnati	M
University of Dayton	M
University of Florida	M,D
University of Georgia	M,D,O
University of Houston	M,D
University of Idaho	M
University of Illinois at Urbana–Champaign	M,D
University of Indianapolis	M
The University of Iowa	M,D
The University of Kansas	M
University of Kentucky	M
University of Louisville	M
University of Massachusetts Dartmouth	M
University of Minnesota, Twin Cities Campus	M,D,O
University of Mississippi	M
University of Missouri–Columbia	M,D,O
University of Nebraska at Kearney	M
University of New Mexico	M
The University of North Carolina at Charlotte	M
The University of North Carolina at Pembroke	M
University of Northern Iowa	M
University of North Texas	M,D,O
University of Rio Grande	M
University of South Carolina	M,D
University of Southern Mississippi	M
The University of Tennessee	M,D,O
The University of Texas at Austin	M
The University of Texas at El Paso	M
The University of Toledo	M
University of Utah	M
University of West Georgia	M
University of Wisconsin–Madison	M,D
University of Wisconsin–Milwaukee	M
University of Wisconsin–Superior	M
Ursuline College	M
Virginia Commonwealth University	M
Wayne State University	M,D,O
Western Kentucky University	M
Western Michigan University	M
West Virginia University	M
Wichita State University	M
William Carey University	M,O
Winthrop University	M

■ ART HISTORY

Institution	Degrees
American University	M
Boston University	M,D,O
Bowling Green State University	M
Brigham Young University	M
Brooklyn College of the City University of New York	M,D
Brown University	M,D
California State University, Chico	M
California State University, Fullerton	M
California State University, Long Beach	M
California State University, Los Angeles	M
California State University, Northridge	M
Case Western Reserve University	M,D
City College of the City University of New York	M
Cleveland State University	M

M—master's degree; P—first professional degree; D—doctorate; O—other advanced degree

Columbia University M,D
Cornell University D
Duke University D
East Tennessee State University M
Emory University D
Florida State University M,D,O
George Mason University M
The George Washington University M
Georgia State University M
Graduate School and University Center of the City University of New York D
Harvard University D
Howard University M
Hunter College of the City University of New York M
Illinois State University M
Indiana University Bloomington M,D
James Madison University M
The Johns Hopkins University M,D
Kent State University M
Lamar University M
Louisiana State University and Agricultural and Mechanical College M
Massachusetts Institute of Technology M,D
Montclair State University M,O
New Mexico State University M
New York University M,D
Northwestern University D
The Ohio State University M,D
Ohio University M
Penn State University Park M,D
Purchase College, State University of New York M
Queens College of the City University of New York M
Rutgers, The State University of New Jersey, New Brunswick M,D,O
San Diego State University M
San Francisco State University M
San Jose State University M
Southern Methodist University M
State University of New York at Binghamton M,D
Stony Brook University, State University of New York M,D
Sul Ross State University M
Syracuse University M
Temple University M,D
Texas A&M University–Commerce M
Texas Christian University M
Tufts University M
Tulane University M
University at Buffalo, the State University of New York M,O
The University of Alabama M
The University of Alabama at Birmingham M
The University of Arizona M,D
University of Arkansas at Little Rock M
University of California, Berkeley D
University of California, Davis M
University of California, Irvine M,D
University of California, Los Angeles M,D
University of California, Riverside M
University of California, Santa Barbara D
University of Chicago M,D
University of Cincinnati M
University of Colorado at Boulder M
University of Connecticut M
University of Delaware M,D
University of Denver M
University of Florida M,D
University of Georgia M
University of Hawaii at Manoa M
University of Illinois at Chicago M,D
University of Illinois at Urbana–Champaign M,D
The University of Iowa M,D
The University of Kansas M,D
University of Kentucky M
University of Louisville M,D
University of Maryland, College Park M,D
University of Massachusetts Amherst M
University of Memphis M,O
University of Miami M
University of Michigan D
University of Minnesota, Twin Cities Campus M,D
University of Mississippi M
University of Missouri–Columbia M,D
University of Missouri–Kansas City M,D
University of Nebraska–Lincoln M
University of New Mexico M,D
The University of North Carolina at Chapel Hill M,D
University of North Texas M,D,O
University of Notre Dame M
University of Oklahoma M
University of Oregon M,D
University of Pennsylvania M,D
University of Pittsburgh M,D
University of Rochester M,D
University of St. Thomas (MN) M
University of South Carolina M
University of Southern California M,D,O
University of South Florida M
The University of Texas at Austin M,D
The University of Texas at San Antonio M
The University of Texas at Tyler M
University of Utah M
University of Virginia M,D
University of Washington M,D
University of Wisconsin–Madison M,D
University of Wisconsin–Milwaukee M,O
University of Wisconsin–Superior M
Virginia Commonwealth University M,D
Washington University in St. Louis M,D
Wayne State University M
West Virginia University M
Yale University D

■ ARTIFICIAL INTELLIGENCE/ ROBOTICS

California State University, Northridge M
Carnegie Mellon University M,D
Cornell University M,D
Eastern Michigan University M,O
Indiana University–Purdue University Indianapolis M,D
Portland State University M,D,O
University of California, Irvine M
University of California, Riverside M,D
University of California, San Diego M,D
University of Georgia M
University of Pittsburgh D
University of Southern California M,D
The University of Tennessee M,D
Villanova University M,O
Worcester Polytechnic Institute M,D,O

■ ARTS ADMINISTRATION

American University M,O
Boston University M,O
Carnegie Mellon University M
Claremont Graduate University M
The College at Brockport, State University of New York M,O
College of Charleston M,O
Columbia College Chicago M
Drexel University M
Eastern Michigan University M
Florida State University M,D
George Mason University M
Montclair State University M
New York University M
The Ohio State University M
Regis University M,O
Rhode Island College M
Saint Mary's University of Minnesota M
St. Thomas University M
Shenandoah University M,D,O
Southern Methodist University
Southern Utah University M
Temple University M,D
Universidad del Turabo M
The University of Akron M
University of Cincinnati M,D
University of Florida M

University of New Orleans M
University of Oregon M
University of Southern California M
University of Wisconsin–Madison M
University of Wisconsin–Superior M
Webster University M
Winthrop University M

■ ARTS JOURNALISM

Syracuse University M

■ ART THERAPY

Caldwell College M
California Institute of Integral Studies M,D
California State University, Los Angeles M
The College of New Rochelle M
Drexel University M,O
Emporia State University M
The George Washington University M
Hofstra University M
Lesley University M,D,O
Long Island University, C.W. Post Campus M
Marylhurst University M,O
Marywood University M,O
Mount Mary College M
Naropa University M
Nazareth College of Rochester M
New York University M
Notre Dame de Namur University M
Prescott College M
Salve Regina University M,O
Seton Hill University M,O
Southern Illinois University Edwardsville M
Springfield College M,O
University of Maryland, College Park M,D,O
University of Wisconsin–Superior M
Ursuline College M

■ ASIAN-AMERICAN STUDIES

California State University, Long Beach M,O
San Francisco State University M
University of California, Los Angeles M

■ ASIAN LANGUAGES

Columbia University M,D
Cornell University M,D
Harvard University M,D
Indiana University Bloomington M,D
Naropa University M
The Ohio State University M,D
St. John's College (NM) M
Seton Hall University M
University of California, Berkeley M,D
University of California, Irvine M,D
University of California, Los Angeles M,D
University of California, Santa Barbara M,D
University of Chicago M,D
University of Hawaii at Manoa M,D
University of Illinois at Urbana–Champaign M,D
The University of Kansas M
University of Michigan M,D
University of Minnesota, Twin Cities Campus D
University of Oregon M,D
University of Southern California M,D
The University of Texas at Austin M,D
University of Washington M,D
University of Wisconsin–Madison M,D
Washington University in St. Louis M,D
Yale University D

■ ASIAN STUDIES

California Institute of Integral Studies M,D
California State University, Long Beach M,O
Columbia University M,D,O
Cornell University M,D
Duke University M,O
Florida International University M
Florida State University M
The George Washington University M
Harvard University M,D
Indiana University Bloomington M,D
The Johns Hopkins University M,D,O
Maharishi University of Management M,D
New York University M,D
Ohio University M
Princeton University D
Rutgers, The State University of New Jersey, New Brunswick D
St. John's College (NM) M
St. John's University (NY) M,O
San Diego State University M
Seton Hall University M
Stanford University M
The University of Arizona M,D
University of California, Berkeley M,D
University of California, Los Angeles M,D
University of California, Riverside M
University of California, Santa Barbara M,D
University of Chicago M,D
University of Colorado at Boulder M,D
University of Hawaii at Manoa O
University of Illinois at Urbana–Champaign M,D
The University of Iowa M
The University of Kansas M
University of Michigan M,D,O
University of Minnesota, Twin Cities Campus D
University of Oregon M
University of Pennsylvania M,D
University of Pittsburgh M,O
University of San Francisco M
University of Southern California M,D
The University of Texas at Austin M,D
University of Utah M
University of Virginia M
University of Washington M,D
University of Wisconsin–Madison M,D
Valparaiso University M
Washington State University M,D
Washington University in St. Louis M
West Virginia University M,D
Yale University M

■ ASTRONOMY

Boston University M,D
Brigham Young University M,D
California Institute of Technology D
Case Western Reserve University M,D
Clemson University M,D
Columbia University M,D
Cornell University D
Dartmouth College M,D
Georgia State University D
Harvard University D
Indiana University Bloomington M,D
Iowa State University of Science and Technology M,D
The Johns Hopkins University D
Louisiana State University and Agricultural and Mechanical College M,D
Michigan State University M,D
Minnesota State University Mankato M
New Mexico State University M,D
Northwestern University M,D
The Ohio State University M,D
Ohio University M,D
Penn State University Park M,D
Princeton University D
Rice University M,D
Rutgers, The State University of New Jersey, New Brunswick M,D
San Diego State University M
Stony Brook University, State University of New York D
The University of Arizona M,D
University of California, Los Angeles M,D
University of California, Santa Cruz D
University of Chicago M,D

M—master's degree; P—first professional degree; D—doctorate; O—other advanced degree

University of Delaware M,D
University of Denver M,D
University of Florida M,D
University of Georgia M,D
University of Hawaii at Manoa M,D
University of Illinois at Urbana–Champaign M,D
The University of Iowa M
The University of Kansas M,D
University of Kentucky M,D
University of Maryland, College Park M,D
University of Massachusetts Amherst M,D
University of Michigan D
University of Minnesota, Twin Cities Campus M,D
University of Missouri–Columbia M,D
University of Nebraska–Lincoln M,D
University of Nevada, Las Vegas M,D
The University of North Carolina at Chapel Hill M,D
University of Rochester M,D
University of South Carolina M,D
The University of Texas at Austin M,D
University of Virginia M,D
University of Washington M,D
University of Wisconsin–Madison D
Vanderbilt University M,D
West Chester University of Pennsylvania M,O
Yale University M,D

■ ASTROPHYSICS

Arizona State University M,D
Clemson University M,D
Cornell University D
Harvard University D
Indiana University Bloomington M,D
Iowa State University of Science and Technology M,D
Louisiana State University and Agricultural and Mechanical College M,D
Michigan State University M,D
New Mexico Institute of Mining and Technology M,D
Northwestern University M,D
Penn State University Park M,D
Princeton University D
Rensselaer Polytechnic Institute M,D
Rochester Institute of Technology M,D
Texas Christian University M,D
University of Alaska Fairbanks M,D
University of California, Berkeley D
University of California, Los Angeles M,D
University of California, Santa Cruz D
University of Chicago M,D
University of Colorado at Boulder M,D
University of Maryland, Baltimore County M,D
University of Michigan D
University of Minnesota, Twin Cities Campus M,D
University of Missouri–St. Louis M,D
The University of North Carolina at Chapel Hill M,D
University of Oklahoma M,D
University of Pennsylvania M,D
Yale University M,D

■ ATHLETIC TRAINING AND SPORTS MEDICINE

Armstrong Atlantic State University M
Barry University M
Bloomsburg University of Pennsylvania M
Boston University D
Brigham Young University M,D
California Baptist University M
California State University, Long Beach M
California University of Pennsylvania M
Eastern Michigan University M,O
Florida International University M
Georgia State University M
Humboldt State University M
Indiana State University M
Indiana University Bloomington M,D
Inter American University of Puerto Rico, Metropolitan Campus M
Kent State University M
Long Island University, Brooklyn Campus M
Montana State University–Billings M
Ohio University M
Old Dominion University M
Plymouth State University M
Saint Louis University M,D
Seton Hall University M
Shenandoah University M
Springfield College M,D
Stephen F. Austin State University M
Texas State University–San Marcos M
Universidad del Turabo M
The University of Findlay M
University of Florida M,D
University of Miami M
The University of North Carolina at Chapel Hill M
University of Pittsburgh M
The University of Tennessee M,D
The University of West Alabama M
University of Wisconsin–La Crosse M
Virginia Commonwealth University M
Weber State University M
Western Michigan University M
West Virginia University M,D

■ ATMOSPHERIC SCIENCES

City College of the City University of New York M,D
Clemson University M,D
Colorado State University M,D
Columbia University M,D
Cornell University M,D
Creighton University M
George Mason University D
Georgia Institute of Technology M,D
Hampton University M,D
Howard University M,D
Massachusetts Institute of Technology M,D
Michigan Technological University D
New Mexico Institute of Mining and Technology M,D
North Carolina State University M,D
The Ohio State University M,D
Oregon State University M,D
Princeton University D
Purdue University M,D
Rutgers, The State University of New Jersey, New Brunswick M,D
Stony Brook University, State University of New York M,D
Texas Tech University M,D
University at Albany, State University of New York M,D
The University of Alabama in Huntsville M,D
University of Alaska Fairbanks M,D
The University of Arizona M,D
University of California, Davis M,D
University of California, Los Angeles M,D
University of Chicago M,D
University of Colorado at Boulder M,D
University of Delaware M,D
University of Illinois at Urbana–Champaign M,D
University of Maryland, Baltimore County M,D
University of Massachusetts Lowell M,D
University of Michigan M,D
University of Missouri–Columbia M,D
University of Nevada, Reno M,D
The University of North Carolina at Chapel Hill M,D
University of North Dakota M,D
University of Utah M,D
University of Washington M,D
University of Wisconsin–Madison M,D
University of Wyoming M,D
Yale University D

■ AUTOMOTIVE ENGINEERING

Central Michigan University M,O

Clemson University M,D
Lawrence Technological University M,D
Minnesota State University Mankato M
Old Dominion University M
University of Michigan M
University of Michigan–Dearborn M,D

■ AVIATION

Lewis University M
Southeastern Oklahoma State University M
University of Central Missouri M
University of Illinois at Urbana–Champaign M
University of North Dakota M
The University of Tennessee M

■ AVIATION MANAGEMENT

Delta State University M
Dowling College M,O
Embry-Riddle Aeronautical University (FL) M
Embry-Riddle Aeronautical University Worldwide M,O
Lynn University M,D
Middle Tennessee State University M
Southeastern Oklahoma State University M

■ BACTERIOLOGY

Illinois State University M,D
The University of Iowa M,D
University of Washington D
University of Wisconsin–Madison M

■ BIOCHEMICAL ENGINEERING

Cornell University M,D
Dartmouth College M,D
Drexel University M
Rutgers, The State University of New Jersey, New Brunswick M,D
University of California, Irvine M,D
The University of Iowa M,D
University of Maryland, Baltimore County M,D,O

■ BIOCHEMISTRY

Arizona State University M,D
Auburn University M,D
Boston College D
Boston University M,D
Brandeis University M,D
Brigham Young University M,D
Brown University M,D
California Institute of Technology M,D
California Polytechnic State University, San Luis Obispo M
California State University, East Bay M
California State University, Long Beach M
California State University, Los Angeles M
California State University, Northridge M
Carnegie Mellon University M,D
Case Western Reserve University M,D
Central Connecticut State University M
City College of the City University of New York M,D
Clemson University M,D
Colorado State University M,D
Columbia University M,D
Cornell University D
Dartmouth College D
DePaul University M
Drexel University M,D
Duke University D,O
Duquesne University M,D
East Carolina University D
East Tennessee State University M,D
Emory University D
Florida State University M,D
Georgetown University M,D
The George Washington University M,D
Georgia Institute of Technology M,D
Georgia State University M,D
Graduate School and University Center of the City University of New York D
Harvard University D
Howard University M,D
Hunter College of the City University of New York M,D
Illinois State University M,D
Indiana University Bloomington M,D
Indiana University–Purdue University Indianapolis D
Iowa State University of Science and Technology M,D
The Johns Hopkins University M,D
Kansas State University M,D
Kent State University M,D
Lehigh University M,D
Louisiana State University and Agricultural and Mechanical College M,D
Loyola University Chicago M,D
Massachusetts Institute of Technology D
Mayo Graduate School D
Miami University M,D
Michigan State University M,D
Mississippi College M
Mississippi State University M,D
Montana State University M,D
Montclair State University M
New Mexico Institute of Mining and Technology M,D
New Mexico State University M,D
North Carolina State University D
North Dakota State University M,D
Northeastern University M,D
Northern Arizona University M
Northwestern University D
The Ohio State University D
Ohio University M,D
Oklahoma State University M,D
Old Dominion University M,D
Oregon State University M,D
Penn State University Park M,D
Purdue University M,D
Queens College of the City University of New York M
Rensselaer Polytechnic Institute M,D
Rice University M,D
Rutgers, The State University of New Jersey, Newark M,D
Rutgers, The State University of New Jersey, New Brunswick M,D
Saint Joseph College M
Saint Louis University D
San Francisco State University M
Seton Hall University M,D
Southern Illinois University Carbondale M,D
Southern University and Agricultural and Mechanical College M
Stanford University D
State University of New York College of Environmental Science and Forestry M,D
Stevens Institute of Technology M,D,O
Stony Brook University, State University of New York D
Syracuse University D
Temple University M,D
Texas A&M University M,D
Texas State University–San Marcos M
Tufts University D
Tulane University M,D
University at Albany, State University of New York M,D
University at Buffalo, the State University of New York M,D
The University of Alabama at Birmingham M,D
University of Alaska Fairbanks M,D
The University of Arizona M,D
University of California, Berkeley D
University of California, Davis M,D
University of California, Irvine M,D
University of California, Los Angeles M,D
University of California, Riverside M,D
University of California, San Diego M,D
University of California, Santa Barbara M,D

M—master's degree; P—first professional degree; D—doctorate; O—other advanced degree

University of California, Santa Cruz M,D
University of Chicago D
University of Cincinnati M,D
University of Colorado at Boulder M,D
University of Colorado Denver D
University of Connecticut M,D
University of Delaware M,D
University of Detroit Mercy M
University of Florida M,D
University of Georgia M,D
University of Houston M,D
University of Idaho M,D
University of Illinois at Chicago D
University of Illinois at Urbana–Champaign M,D
The University of Iowa M,D
The University of Kansas M,D
University of Kentucky D
University of Louisville M,D
University of Maine M,D
University of Maryland, Baltimore County M,D
University of Maryland, College Park M,D
University of Massachusetts Amherst M,D
University of Massachusetts Lowell M,D
University of Miami D
University of Michigan D
University of Minnesota, Duluth M,D
University of Minnesota, Twin Cities Campus D
University of Missouri–Columbia M,D
University of Missouri–Kansas City D
University of Missouri–St. Louis M,D,O
The University of Montana M,D
University of Nebraska–Lincoln M,D
University of Nevada, Las Vegas M,D
University of Nevada, Reno M,D
University of New Hampshire M,D
University of New Mexico M,D
The University of North Carolina at Chapel Hill M,D
The University of North Carolina at Greensboro M
University of North Dakota M,D
University of North Texas M,D
University of Notre Dame M,D
University of Oklahoma M,D
University of Oregon M,D
University of Pennsylvania D
University of Pittsburgh M,D
University of Rhode Island M,D
University of Rochester M,D
The University of Scranton M
University of South Alabama D
University of South Carolina M,D
University of Southern California M,D
University of Southern Mississippi M,D
University of South Florida M,D
The University of Tennessee M,D
The University of Texas at Austin M,D
The University of Toledo M,D
University of Tulsa M
University of Utah M,D
University of Vermont M,D
University of Virginia D
University of Washington D
University of West Florida M
University of Wisconsin–Madison M,D
University of Wisconsin–Milwaukee M,D
Utah State University M,D
Vanderbilt University M,D
Virginia Commonwealth University M,D,O
Virginia Polytechnic Institute and State University M,D
Wake Forest University D
Washington State University M,D
Washington University in St. Louis D
Wayne State University M,D
West Virginia University M,D
Worcester Polytechnic Institute M,D
Wright State University M
Yale University D
Youngstown State University M

■ BIOENGINEERING

Alfred University M,D
Arizona State University M,D
California Institute of Technology M,D
Carnegie Mellon University M,D
Clemson University M,D
Cornell University M,D
Georgia Institute of Technology M,D
Illinois Institute of Technology M,D
Iowa State University of Science and Technology M,D
The Johns Hopkins University M,D
Kansas State University M,D
Lehigh University M,D
Louisiana State University and Agricultural and Mechanical College M,D
Massachusetts Institute of Technology M,D
Mississippi State University M,D
North Carolina State University M,D,O
The Ohio State University M,D
Oklahoma State University M,D
Oregon State University M,D
Penn State University Park M,D
Rensselaer Polytechnic Institute M,D
Rice University M,D
Stanford University M,D
Syracuse University M,D
Texas A&M University M,D
Tufts University M,D,O
University at Buffalo, the State University of New York M,D
University of Arkansas M
University of California, Berkeley D
University of California, Davis M,D
University of California, Riverside M,D
University of California, San Diego M,D
University of Denver M,D
University of Florida M,D,O
University of Georgia M,D
University of Hawaii at Manoa M
University of Idaho M,D
University of Illinois at Chicago M,D
University of Illinois at Urbana–Champaign M,D
The University of Kansas M,D
University of Maine M
University of Maryland, College Park M,D
University of Missouri–Columbia M,D
University of Nebraska–Lincoln M,D
University of Notre Dame M,D
University of Oklahoma M,D
University of Pennsylvania M,D
University of Pittsburgh M,D
The University of Texas at Arlington M,D
The University of Toledo M,D
University of Utah M,D
University of Washington M,D
University of Wisconsin–Madison M,D
Virginia Commonwealth University M,D
Virginia Polytechnic Institute and State University M,D
Washington State University M,D

■ BIOETHICS

Boston University M
Case Western Reserve University M
Cleveland State University M,O
Columbia University M
Drew University M,D,O
Duquesne University M,D,O
Indiana University–Purdue University Indianapolis M,O
The Johns Hopkins University M,D
Loyola Marymount University M
Michigan State University M
New York University M
Saint Louis University D,O
Trinity International University M
University of Pittsburgh M
The University of Tennessee M,D
University of Virginia M
University of Washington M

■ BIOINFORMATICS

Arizona State University M,D
Boston University M,D
Brandeis University M,O

California State University, Dominguez Hills M
The Catholic University of America M,D
Duke University D
Eastern Michigan University M,O
George Mason University M,D,O
Georgetown University M
The George Washington University M
Georgia Institute of Technology M,D
Grand Valley State University M
Indiana University Bloomington M,D
Iowa State University of Science and Technology D
The Johns Hopkins University M,D,O
Marquette University M,D
Mississippi Valley State University M
Morgan State University M
New Jersey Institute of Technology M,D
North Carolina State University M,D
North Dakota State University M,D
Northeastern University M
Northwestern University M
Polytechnic Institute of NYU M
Rochester Institute of Technology M
Stevens Institute of Technology M,D,O
Texas Tech University M,D
University of Arkansas at Little Rock M,D
University of California, Riverside D
University of California, San Diego D
University of California, Santa Cruz M,D
University of Cincinnati D
University of Colorado Denver D
University of Idaho M,D
University of Illinois at Urbana–Champaign M,D,O
University of Michigan M,D
University of Missouri–Columbia D
University of Missouri–Kansas City M,D
University of Nebraska–Lincoln M,D
University of Pittsburgh M,D,O
University of Southern California M,D
University of South Florida M,D
The University of Texas at El Paso M
The University of Toledo M,O
University of Utah M,D,O
University of Washington M,D
Vanderbilt University M,D
Virginia Commonwealth University M
Virginia Polytechnic Institute and State University D
Yale University D

■ BIOLOGICAL AND BIOMEDICAL SCIENCES—GENERAL

Adelphi University M
Alabama Agricultural and Mechanical University M
Alabama State University M
Alcorn State University M
American University M
Andrews University M
Angelo State University M
Appalachian State University M
Arizona State University M,D
Arkansas State University M,O
Auburn University M,D
Austin Peay State University M
Ball State University M,D
Barry University M
Baylor University M,D
Bemidji State University M
Bloomsburg University of Pennsylvania M
Boise State University M
Boston College D
Boston University M,D
Bowling Green State University M,D
Bradley University M
Brandeis University O
Brigham Young University M,D
Brooklyn College of the City University of New York M,D
Brown University M,D
Bucknell University M
Buffalo State College, State University of New York M
California Institute of Technology M,D
California Polytechnic State University, San Luis Obispo M
California State Polytechnic University, Pomona M
California State University, Bakersfield M
California State University, Chico M
California State University, Dominguez Hills M
California State University, East Bay M
California State University, Fresno M
California State University, Fullerton M
California State University, Long Beach M
California State University, Los Angeles M
California State University, Northridge M
California State University, Sacramento M
California State University, San Bernardino M
California State University, San Marcos M
California State University, Stanislaus M
Carnegie Mellon University M,D
Case Western Reserve University M,D
The Catholic University of America M,D
Central Connecticut State University M,O
Central Michigan University M
Central Washington University M
Chatham University M
Chicago State University M
The Citadel, The Military College of South Carolina M
City College of the City University of New York M,D
Clarion University of Pennsylvania M
Clark Atlanta University M,D
Clark University M,D
Clemson University M,D
Cleveland State University M,D
The College at Brockport, State University of New York M
College of Staten Island of the City University of New York M
The College of William and Mary M
Colorado State University M,D
Columbia University P,M,D,O
Cornell University M,D
Creighton University M,D
Dartmouth College D
Delaware State University M
Delta State University M
DePaul University M
Dominican University of California M
Drexel University M,D,O
Duke University D,O
Duquesne University M,D
East Carolina University M,D
Eastern Illinois University M
Eastern Kentucky University M
Eastern Michigan University M
Eastern New Mexico University M
Eastern Washington University M
East Stroudsburg University of Pennsylvania M
East Tennessee State University M,D
Edinboro University of Pennsylvania M
Emory University D
Emporia State University M
Fairleigh Dickinson University, College at Florham M
Fairleigh Dickinson University, Metropolitan Campus M
Fayetteville State University M
Fitchburg State College M
Florida Agricultural and Mechanical University M

M—master's degree; P—first professional degree; D—doctorate; O—other advanced degree

Florida Atlantic University M,D
Florida Institute of Technology M,D
Florida International University M,D
Florida State University P,M,D
Fordham University M,D
Fort Hays State University M
Frostburg State University M
George Mason University M,D,O
Georgetown University M,D
The George Washington University M,D
Georgia College & State University M
Georgia Institute of Technology M,D
Georgian Court University M,O
Georgia Southern University M
Georgia State University M,D
Graduate School and University Center of the City University of New York D
Grand Valley State University M
Hampton University M
Harvard University M,D,O
Heritage University M
Hofstra University M
Hood College M,O
Howard University M,D
Humboldt State University M
Hunter College of the City University of New York M,D
Idaho State University M,D
Illinois Institute of Technology M,D
Illinois State University M,D
Indiana State University M,D
Indiana University Bloomington M,D
Indiana University of Pennsylvania M
Indiana University–Purdue University Fort Wayne M
Indiana University–Purdue University Indianapolis M,D
Iowa State University of Science and Technology M,D
Jackson State University M,D
Jacksonville State University M
James Madison University M
John Carroll University M
The Johns Hopkins University M,D
Kansas State University M,D
Kent State University M,D
Lamar University M
Lehigh University M,D
Lehman College of the City University of New York M
Long Island University, Brooklyn Campus M
Long Island University, C.W. Post Campus M
Louisiana State University and Agricultural and Mechanical College M,D
Louisiana Tech University M
Loyola University Chicago M
Marquette University M,D
Marshall University M,D
Massachusetts Institute of Technology P,M,D
Mayo Graduate School D
McNeese State University M
Michigan State University M,D
Michigan Technological University M,D
Middle Tennessee State University M
Midwestern State University M
Millersville University of Pennsylvania M
Mills College O
Minnesota State University Mankato M
Mississippi College M
Mississippi State University M,D
Missouri State University M
Missouri University of Science and Technology M
Montana State University M,D
Montclair State University M,O
Morehead State University M
Morgan State University M,D
Murray State University M,D
New Jersey Institute of Technology M,D
New Mexico Institute of Mining and Technology M
New Mexico State University M,D
New York University M,D
North Carolina Agricultural and Technical State University M
North Carolina Central University M
North Carolina State University M,D,O
North Dakota State University M,D
Northeastern Illinois University M
Northeastern University M,D
Northern Arizona University M,D
Northern Illinois University M,D
Northern Michigan University M
Northwestern University D
Northwest Missouri State University M
Notre Dame de Namur University O
Nova Southeastern University M
Oakland University M,D
The Ohio State University M,D
Ohio University M,D
Old Dominion University M,D
Penn State University Park M,D
Pittsburg State University M
Point Loma Nazarene University M
Pontifical Catholic University of Puerto Rico M
Portland State University M,D
Prairie View A&M University M
Purdue University M,D
Purdue University Calumet M
Queens College of the City University of New York M
Quinnipiac University M
Rensselaer Polytechnic Institute M,D
Rhode Island College M
Rochester Institute of Technology M
Rutgers, The State University of New Jersey, Camden M
Rutgers, The State University of New Jersey, Newark M,D
Rutgers, The State University of New Jersey, New Brunswick D
St. Cloud State University M
Saint Francis University M
St. John's University (NY) M,D
Saint Joseph College M
Saint Joseph's University M
Saint Louis University M,D
Sam Houston State University M
San Diego State University M,D
San Francisco State University M
San Jose State University M
Seton Hall University M,D
Shippensburg University of Pennsylvania M
Sonoma State University M
South Dakota State University M,D
Southeastern Louisiana University M
Southeast Missouri State University M
Southern Connecticut State University M
Southern Illinois University Carbondale M,D
Southern Illinois University Edwardsville M
Southern Methodist University M,D
Southern University and Agricultural and Mechanical College M
Stanford University M,D
State University of New York at Binghamton M,D
State University of New York at Fredonia M
State University of New York at New Paltz M
State University of New York College at Oneonta M
Stephen F. Austin State University M
Stony Brook University, State University of New York D
Sul Ross State University M
Syracuse University M,D
Tarleton State University M
Temple University M,D
Tennessee State University M,D
Tennessee Technological University M
Texas A&M International University M
Texas A&M University M,D

Institution	Degree
Texas A&M University–Commerce	M
Texas A&M University–Corpus Christi	M
Texas A&M University–Kingsville	M
Texas Christian University	M
Texas Southern University	M
Texas State University–San Marcos	M
Texas Tech University	M,D
Texas Woman's University	M,D
Towson University	M
Truman State University	M
Tufts University	M,D
Tulane University	M,D
University at Albany, State University of New York	M,D
University at Buffalo, the State University of New York	M,D
The University of Akron	M,D
The University of Alabama	M,D
The University of Alabama at Birmingham	M,D
The University of Alabama in Huntsville	M
University of Alaska Anchorage	M
University of Alaska Fairbanks	M,D
The University of Arizona	M,D
University of Arkansas	M,D
University of Arkansas at Little Rock	M
University of California, Berkeley	D
University of California, Irvine	M,D
University of California, Los Angeles	M,D
University of California, Riverside	M,D
University of California, San Diego	M,D
University of Central Arkansas	M
University of Central Florida	M,D,O
University of Central Missouri	M
University of Central Oklahoma	M
University of Chicago	D
University of Cincinnati	M,D
University of Colorado at Colorado Springs	M
University of Colorado Denver	M,D
University of Connecticut	M,D
University of Dayton	M,D
University of Delaware	M,D
University of Denver	M,D
University of Florida	D
University of Georgia	D
University of Guam	M
University of Hartford	M
University of Hawaii at Manoa	M,D
University of Houston	M,D
University of Houston–Clear Lake	M
University of Idaho	M,D
University of Illinois at Chicago	M,D
University of Illinois at Springfield	M
University of Illinois at Urbana–Champaign	M,D
University of Indianapolis	M
The University of Iowa	M,D
The University of Kansas	M,D
University of Kentucky	M,D
University of Louisiana at Lafayette	M,D
University of Louisiana at Monroe	M
University of Louisville	M
University of Maine	D
University of Maryland, Baltimore County	M,D
University of Maryland, College Park	M,D
University of Massachusetts Amherst	M,D
University of Massachusetts Boston	M
University of Massachusetts Dartmouth	M
University of Massachusetts Lowell	M,D
University of Memphis	M,D
University of Miami	M,D
University of Michigan	M,D
University of Michigan–Flint	M
University of Minnesota, Duluth	M,D
University of Minnesota, Twin Cities Campus	M,D
University of Mississippi	M,D
University of Missouri–Columbia	M,D
University of Missouri–Kansas City	M,D
University of Missouri–St. Louis	M,D,O
The University of Montana	M,D
University of Nebraska at Kearney	M
University of Nebraska at Omaha	M
University of Nebraska–Lincoln	M,D
University of Nevada, Las Vegas	M,D
University of Nevada, Reno	M
University of New England	M
University of New Hampshire	M,D
University of New Mexico	M,D
University of New Orleans	M,D
The University of North Carolina at Chapel Hill	M,D
The University of North Carolina at Charlotte	M,D
The University of North Carolina at Greensboro	M
The University of North Carolina Wilmington	M,D
University of North Dakota	M,D
University of Northern Colorado	M
University of Northern Iowa	M
University of North Florida	M
University of North Texas	M,D
University of Notre Dame	M,D
University of Oregon	M,D
University of Pennsylvania	M,D
University of Pittsburgh	D
University of Puerto Rico, Mayagüez Campus	M
University of Puerto Rico, Río Piedras	M,D
University of Rhode Island	M,D
University of Rochester	M,D
University of San Francisco	M
University of South Alabama	M,D
University of South Carolina	M,D,O
The University of South Dakota	M,D
University of Southern California	M,D
University of Southern Maine	M
University of Southern Mississippi	M,D
University of South Florida	M,D
The University of Tennessee	M,D
The University of Texas at Arlington	M,D
The University of Texas at Austin	M,D
The University of Texas at Brownsville	M
The University of Texas at Dallas	M,D
The University of Texas at El Paso	M,D
The University of Texas at San Antonio	M,D
The University of Texas at Tyler	M
The University of Texas of the Permian Basin	M
The University of Texas–Pan American	M
University of the Incarnate Word	M
University of the Pacific	M
The University of Toledo	M,D,O
University of Tulsa	M,D
University of Utah	M,D,O
University of Vermont	M,D
University of Virginia	M,D
University of Washington	M,D
University of West Florida	M
University of West Georgia	M
University of Wisconsin–La Crosse	M
University of Wisconsin–Madison	M,D
University of Wisconsin–Milwaukee	M,D
University of Wisconsin–Oshkosh	M
Utah State University	M,D
Vanderbilt University	M,D
Villanova University	M
Virginia Commonwealth University	M,D,O
Virginia Polytechnic Institute and State University	M,D
Virginia State University	M
Wagner College	M
Wake Forest University	M,D
Walla Walla University	M

M—master's degree; P—first professional degree; D—doctorate; O—other advanced degree

Washington State University M
Washington University in St. Louis D
Wayne State University M,D
West Chester University of Pennsylvania M,O
Western Carolina University M
Western Connecticut State University M
Western Illinois University M,O
Western Kentucky University M
Western Michigan University M,D
Western Washington University M
West Texas A&M University M
West Virginia University M,D
Wichita State University M
William Paterson University of New Jersey M
Winthrop University M
Worcester Polytechnic Institute M,D
Wright State University M,D
Yale University D
Youngstown State University M

■ BIOLOGICAL ANTHROPOLOGY

Duke University D
Kent State University D
Mercyhurst College M

■ BIOMATHEMATICS

North Carolina State University M,D
University of California, Los Angeles M,D

■ BIOMEDICAL ENGINEERING

Baylor University M
Boston University M,D
Brown University M,D
Carnegie Mellon University M,D
Case Western Reserve University M,D
The Catholic University of America M,D
City College of the City University of New York M,D
Cleveland State University D
Colorado State University M,D
Columbia University M,D
Cornell University M,D
Drexel University M,D
Duke University M,D
Emory University D
Florida Agricultural and Mechanical University M,D
Florida International University M,D
Florida State University M,D
Georgia Institute of Technology D
Graduate School and University Center of the City University of New York D
Harvard University M,D
Illinois Institute of Technology D
Indiana University–Purdue University Indianapolis M,D,O
The Johns Hopkins University M,D,O
Louisiana Tech University M,D
Marquette University M,D
Massachusetts Institute of Technology M,D
Mayo Graduate School D
Mercer University M
Michigan Technological University D
Mississippi State University M,D
New Jersey Institute of Technology M,D
North Carolina State University M,D
Northwestern University M,D
The Ohio State University M,D
Ohio University M
Penn State University Park M,D
Polytechnic Institute of NYU M,D
Purdue University M,D
Rensselaer Polytechnic Institute M,D
Rice University M,D
Rutgers, The State University of New Jersey, New Brunswick M,D
St. Cloud State University M
Saint Louis University M,D
Southern Illinois University Carbondale M
Stanford University M
Stevens Institute of Technology M,O
Stony Brook University, State University of New York M,D,O
Texas A&M University M,D
Tufts University M,D
Tulane University M,D
The University of Akron M,D
The University of Alabama at Birmingham M,D
The University of Arizona M,D
University of Arkansas M
University of California, Davis M,D
University of California, Irvine M,D
University of California, Los Angeles M,D
University of Cincinnati D
University of Connecticut M,D
University of Florida M,D,O
University of Houston M,D
The University of Iowa M,D
University of Kentucky M,D
University of Massachusetts Dartmouth D
University of Memphis M,D
University of Miami M,D
University of Michigan M,D
University of Minnesota, Twin Cities Campus M,D
University of Nevada, Las Vegas M,D
University of Nevada, Reno M,D
The University of North Carolina at Chapel Hill M,D
University of Rhode Island M,D
University of Rochester M,D
University of Southern California M,D
University of South Florida M,D
The University of Tennessee M,D
The University of Texas at Austin M,D
The University of Texas at San Antonio M,D
The University of Toledo D
University of Vermont M
University of Virginia M,D
University of Wisconsin–Madison M,D
Vanderbilt University M,D
Virginia Commonwealth University M,D
Virginia Polytechnic Institute and State University M,D
Wake Forest University M,D
Washington University in St. Louis M,D
Wayne State University M,D
Worcester Polytechnic Institute M,D,O
Wright State University M
Yale University M,D

■ BIOMETRY

Cornell University M,D
San Diego State University M
University of California, Los Angeles M,D
University of Southern California M
University of Wisconsin–Madison M

■ BIOPHYSICS

Boston University D
Brandeis University M,D
California Institute of Technology D
Carnegie Mellon University M,D
Case Western Reserve University M,D
Clemson University M,D
Columbia University M,D
Cornell University D
East Carolina University M,D
East Tennessee State University M,D
Emory University D
Georgetown University M,D
Harvard University D
Howard University D
Illinois State University M,D
Iowa State University of Science and Technology M,D
The Johns Hopkins University D
Northwestern University D
The Ohio State University M,D
Oregon State University M,D
Purdue University M,D
Rensselaer Polytechnic Institute M,D
Stanford University D
Stony Brook University, State University of New York D
Syracuse University D
Texas A&M University M,D
University at Buffalo, the State University of New York M,D

The University of Alabama at Birmingham	D
University of California, Berkeley	D
University of California, Davis	M,D
University of California, Irvine	D
University of California, San Diego	M,D
University of Chicago	D
University of Cincinnati	D
University of Colorado Denver	M,D
University of Connecticut	M,D
University of Illinois at Chicago	M,D
University of Illinois at Urbana–Champaign	M,D
The University of Iowa	D
The University of Kansas	M,D
University of Louisville	M,D
University of Miami	D
University of Michigan	D
University of Minnesota, Duluth	M,D
University of Minnesota, Twin Cities Campus	M,D
University of Missouri–Kansas City	D
University of New Mexico	M,D
The University of North Carolina at Chapel Hill	M,D
University of Rochester	M,D
University of Southern California	M,D
University of South Florida	M,D
University of Vermont	M,D
University of Virginia	M,D
University of Washington	D
University of Wisconsin–Madison	D
Vanderbilt University	M,D
Washington State University	M,D
Wright State University	M
Yale University	D

■ BIOPSYCHOLOGY

American University	M
Argosy University, Twin Cities	M,D,O
Brown University	D
Carnegie Mellon University	D
Columbia University	M,D
Cornell University	D
Drexel University	M,D
Duke University	D
George Mason University	M,D
Graduate School and University Center of the City University of New York	D
Harvard University	D
Howard University	M,D
Hunter College of the City University of New York	M
Indiana University–Purdue University Indianapolis	M,D
Louisiana State University and Agricultural and Mechanical College	M,D
Northwestern University	D
Penn State University Park	M,D
Rutgers, The State University of New Jersey, Newark	D
Rutgers, The State University of New Jersey, New Brunswick	D
State University of New York at Binghamton	M,D
Stony Brook University, State University of New York	D
Texas A&M University	M,D
University at Albany, State University of New York	M,D,O
University of Connecticut	M,D,O
University of Michigan	D
University of Minnesota, Twin Cities Campus	D
University of Nebraska at Omaha	M,D,O
University of Nebraska–Lincoln	M,D
University of Oregon	M,D
The University of Texas at Austin	D
The University of Toledo	M,D
University of Wisconsin–Madison	D
Wayne State University	M

■ BIOSTATISTICS

Boston University	M,D
Brown University	M,D
California State University, East Bay	M
Case Western Reserve University	M,D
Columbia University	M,D
Drexel University	M,D,O
Emory University	M,D
Florida International University	M,D
Florida State University	M,D
George Mason University	M,D,O
Georgetown University	M
The George Washington University	M,D
Georgia Southern University	M,D
Grand Valley State University	M
Harvard University	M,D
Hunter College of the City University of New York	M
Iowa State University of Science and Technology	D
The Johns Hopkins University	M,D
Middle Tennessee State University	M
New Jersey Institute of Technology	M
The Ohio State University	D
Rice University	M,D
Rutgers, The State University of New Jersey, New Brunswick	M,D
San Diego State University	M,D
Tufts University	M,D
Tulane University	M,D
University at Albany, State University of New York	M,D
University at Buffalo, the State University of New York	M,D
The University of Alabama at Birmingham	M,D
The University of Arizona	M,D
University of California, Berkeley	M,D
University of California, Davis	M,D
University of California, Los Angeles	M,D
University of Cincinnati	M,D
University of Colorado Denver	M,D
University of Florida	M
University of Illinois at Chicago	M,D
The University of Iowa	M,D
University of Louisville	M,D
University of Maryland, Baltimore County	M,D
University of Maryland, College Park	M,D
University of Michigan	M,D
University of Minnesota, Twin Cities Campus	M,D
The University of North Carolina at Chapel Hill	M,D
University of Pennsylvania	M,D
University of Pittsburgh	M,D
University of Rochester	M,D
University of South Carolina	M,D
University of Southern California	M,D
University of Southern Mississippi	M
University of South Florida	M,D
The University of Toledo	M,O
University of Utah	M,D
University of Vermont	M
University of Washington	M,D
Virginia Commonwealth University	M,D
Yale University	M,D

■ BIOSYSTEMS ENGINEERING

Clemson University	M,D
Iowa State University of Science and Technology	M,D
Michigan State University	M,D
North Dakota State University	M,D
South Dakota State University	M,D
The University of Arizona	M,D
University of Minnesota, Twin Cities Campus	M,D
The University of Tennessee	M,D

■ BIOTECHNOLOGY

Arizona State University	P,M
Brigham Young University	M,D
Brown University	M,D
Cabrini College	M,O
Carnegie Mellon University	M,D
Dartmouth College	M,D
Duquesne University	M
East Carolina University	M
Florida Institute of Technology	M,D

M—master's degree; P—first professional degree; D—doctorate; O—other advanced degree

The George Washington University M
Harvard University M,O
Hood College M,O
Howard University M,D
Illinois State University M
Indiana University Bloomington M,D
The Johns Hopkins University M
Kean University M
Marywood University M
Middle Tennessee State University M
North Carolina State University M
Northeastern University M,D
Northwestern University D
Oklahoma State University M,D
Penn State University Park M,D
Polytechnic Institute of NYU M
Purdue University Calumet M
Regis College (MA) M
Roosevelt University M
St. John's University (NY) M
Southern Illinois University Edwardsville M
Stephen F. Austin State University M
Texas Tech University M
Tufts University O
University at Buffalo, the State University of New York M
The University of Alabama in Huntsville D
University of California, Berkeley O
University of California, Irvine M
University of Central Florida M
University of Connecticut M
University of Delaware M,D
University of Houston–Clear Lake M
University of Illinois at Chicago D
The University of Kansas M
University of Maryland, Baltimore County O
University of Maryland University College M,O
University of Massachusetts Amherst M,D
University of Massachusetts Boston M
University of Massachusetts Dartmouth D
University of Massachusetts Lowell M,D
University of Minnesota, Twin Cities Campus M
University of Missouri–St. Louis M,D,O
University of Nevada, Reno M
University of Pennsylvania M
University of Rhode Island M
The University of Texas at Dallas M,D
The University of Texas at San Antonio M,D
University of Utah M
University of Washington D
University of West Florida M
University of Wyoming D
Western Michigan University M,D
William Paterson University of New Jersey M
Worcester Polytechnic Institute M,D
Worcester State College M

■ BOTANY

Auburn University M,D
California State University, Chico M
Claremont Graduate University M,D
Colorado State University M,D
Emporia State University M
Illinois State University M,D
Miami University M,D
North Carolina State University M,D
North Dakota State University M,D
Oklahoma State University M,D
Oregon State University M,D
Purdue University M,D
Texas A&M University M,D
University of Alaska Fairbanks M,D
University of California, Riverside M,D
University of Connecticut M,D
University of Florida M,D
University of Hawaii at Manoa M,D
The University of Kansas M,D
University of Maine M
University of Missouri–St. Louis M,D,O
The University of North Carolina at Chapel Hill M,D
University of North Dakota M,D
University of Oklahoma M,D
University of Wisconsin–Madison M,D
University of Wisconsin–Oshkosh M
University of Wyoming M,D
Virginia Polytechnic Institute and State University M,D
Washington State University M,D

■ BROADCAST JOURNALISM

American University M
Boston University M
Emerson College M
Northwestern University M
Syracuse University M
University of Maryland, College Park M,D
University of Miami M,D
University of Southern California M

■ BUILDING SCIENCE

Arizona State University M
Auburn University M
Carnegie Mellon University M,D
Cornell University M,D
Georgia Institute of Technology M,D
University of California, Berkeley M,D
University of Florida M,D

■ BUSINESS ADMINISTRATION AND MANAGEMENT—GENERAL

Adelphi University M
Alabama Agricultural and Mechanical University M
Alabama State University M
Alaska Pacific University M
Albany State University M
Alcorn State University M
Alfred University M
Alliant International University–San Diego M,D
Alvernia University M
Alverno College M
Amberton University M
American InterContinental University Buckhead Campus M
American InterContinental University South Florida M
American International College M
American University M,D,O
Anderson University (IN) M,D
Andrews University M
Angelo State University M
Anna Maria College M,O
Antioch University Los Angeles M
Antioch University McGregor M
Antioch University New England M
Antioch University Seattle M
Appalachian State University M
Aquinas College M
Arcadia University M
Argosy University, Orange County M,D,O
Argosy University, Sarasota M,D,O
Argosy University, Tampa M,D
Argosy University, Twin Cities M,D
Arizona State University M,D
Arkansas State University M,O
Ashland University M
Assumption College M,O
Auburn University M,D
Auburn University Montgomery M
Augsburg College M
Augusta State University M
Aurora University M
Austin Peay State University M
Avila University M
Azusa Pacific University M
Baldwin-Wallace College M
Ball State University M
Barry University M,O
Bayamón Central University M
Baylor University M
Belhaven College (MS) M
Bellarmine University M
Bellevue University M,D
Belmont University M
Benedictine College M
Benedictine University M
Bentley University M,D,O
Bernard M. Baruch College of the City University of New York M,D,O
Bethel University M
Biola University M

Institution	Degrees
Bloomsburg University of Pennsylvania	M
Bob Jones University	P,M,D,O
Boise State University	M
Boston College	M
Boston University	M,D,O
Bowie State University	M
Bowling Green State University	M
Bradley University	M
Brandeis University	M
Brenau University	M
Bridgewater State College	M
Brigham Young University	M
Bryant University	M
Butler University	M
Caldwell College	M
California Baptist University	M
California Lutheran University	M,O
California Polytechnic State University, San Luis Obispo	M
California State Polytechnic University, Pomona	M
California State University, Bakersfield	M
California State University, Chico	M
California State University, Dominguez Hills	M
California State University, East Bay	M
California State University, Fresno	M
California State University, Fullerton	M
California State University, Long Beach	M
California State University, Los Angeles	M
California State University, Northridge	M
California State University, Sacramento	M
California State University, San Bernardino	M
California State University, San Marcos	M
California State University, Stanislaus	M
California University of Pennsylvania	M
Cambridge College	M
Cameron University	M
Campbell University	M
Canisius College	M
Capella University	M,D,O
Capital University	M
Cardinal Stritch University	M
Carlow University	M
Carnegie Mellon University	M,D
Case Western Reserve University	M,D
The Catholic University of America	M
Centenary College	M
Central Connecticut State University	M,O
Central Michigan University	M,O
Chaminade University of Honolulu	M
Chapman University	M
Charleston Southern University	M
Chatham University	M
Christian Brothers University	M,O
The Citadel, The Military College of South Carolina	M
City University of Seattle	M,O
Claremont Graduate University	M,D,O
Clarion University of Pennsylvania	M
Clark Atlanta University	M
Clarkson University	M
Clark University	M
Clemson University	M
Cleveland State University	M,D
College of Charleston	M
College of Notre Dame of Maryland	M
College of Saint Elizabeth	M
College of St. Joseph	M
The College of Saint Rose	M
The College of St. Scholastica	M,O
College of Santa Fe	M
College of Staten Island of the City University of New York	M
The College of William and Mary	M
Colorado Christian University	M
Colorado State University	M
Colorado Technical University Colorado Springs	M,D
Colorado Technical University Denver	M
Colorado Technical University Sioux Falls	M
Columbia College (MO)	M
Columbia University	M,D
Columbus State University	M
Concordia University (CA)	M
Concordia University (OR)	M
Concordia University Chicago	M
Concordia University, St. Paul	M
Concordia University Wisconsin	M
Cornell University	M,D
Cornerstone University	M,O
Creighton University	M
Cumberland University	M
Daemen College	M
Dallas Baptist University	M
Dartmouth College	M
Davenport University	M
Delaware State University	M
Delta State University	M
DePaul University	M
DeSales University	M
DeVry University (AZ)	M,O
DeVry University (CA)	M,O
DeVry University (FL)	M,O
DeVry University (GA)	M,O
DeVry University (IL)	M,O
DeVry University (OH)	M,O
DeVry University (TX)	M,O
DeVry University (VA)	M,O
Doane College	M
Dominican College	M
Dominican University	M
Dominican University of California	M
Dowling College	M,O
Drake University	M
Drexel University	M,D,O
Drury University	M
Duke University	M,D
Duquesne University	M
D'Youville College	M
East Carolina University	M,D,O
Eastern Illinois University	M,O
Eastern Kentucky University	M
Eastern Mennonite University	M
Eastern Michigan University	M,O
Eastern New Mexico University	M
Eastern University	M
Eastern Washington University	M
East Tennessee State University	M,O
Edgewood College	M
Elmhurst College	M
Elon University	M
Embry-Riddle Aeronautical University (FL)	M
Emmanuel College	M,O
Emory University	M,D
Emporia State University	M
Endicott College	M
Everest University	M
Fairfield University	M,O
Fairleigh Dickinson University, College at Florham	M,O
Fairleigh Dickinson University, Metropolitan Campus	M,O
Fayetteville State University	M
Ferris State University	M
Fitchburg State College	M
Florida Agricultural and Mechanical University	M
Florida Atlantic University	M,D,O
Florida Gulf Coast University	M
Florida Institute of Technology	M
Florida International University	M,D
Florida State University	M,D
Fontbonne University	M
Fordham University	M
Fort Hays State University	M
Framingham State College	M
Franciscan University of Steubenville	M
Francis Marion University	M
Freed-Hardeman University	M
Fresno Pacific University	M

M—master's degree; P—first professional degree; D—doctorate; O—other advanced degree

Institution	Degrees
Friends University	M
Frostburg State University	M
Gannon University	M,O
Gardner-Webb University	M
Geneva College	M
George Fox University	M,D
George Mason University	M
Georgetown University	M
The George Washington University	M,D,O
Georgia College & State University	M
Georgia Institute of Technology	M,D,O
Georgian Court University	M,O
Georgia Southern University	M
Georgia Southwestern State University	M
Georgia State University	M,D
Goddard College	M
Golden Gate University	M,D,O
Gonzaga University	M
Governors State University	M
Graduate School and University Center of the City University of New York	D
Grand Canyon University	M
Grand Valley State University	M
Gwynedd-Mercy College	M
Hamline University	M,D
Hampton University	M
Harding University	M
Hardin-Simmons University	M
Harvard University	M,D,O
Hawai'i Pacific University	M
Heidelberg University	M
Henderson State University	M
High Point University	M
Hodges University	M
Hofstra University	M
Holy Family University	M
Holy Names University	M
Hood College	M
Hope International University	M
Houston Baptist University	M
Howard University	M
Humboldt State University	M
Husson University	M
Idaho State University	M,O
Illinois Institute of Technology	M,D
Illinois State University	M
Indiana State University	M
Indiana University Bloomington	M,D
Indiana University Northwest	M,O
Indiana University of Pennsylvania	M
Indiana University–Purdue University Fort Wayne	M
Indiana University–Purdue University Indianapolis	M
Indiana University South Bend	M
Indiana University Southeast	M
Indiana Wesleyan University	M
Inter American University of Puerto Rico, Metropolitan Campus	M
Inter American University of Puerto Rico, San Germán Campus	M,D
Iona College	M,O
Iowa State University of Science and Technology	M
Ithaca College	M
Jackson State University	M,D
Jacksonville State University	M
Jacksonville University	M
James Madison University	M
John Brown University	M
John Carroll University	M
John F. Kennedy University	M,O
The Johns Hopkins University	M,O
Jones International University	M
Kansas State University	M
Kean University	M
Kennesaw State University	M
Kent State University	M
King's College	M
Kutztown University of Pennsylvania	M
Lakeland College	M
Lamar University	M
La Salle University	M,O
La Sierra University	M,O
Lawrence Technological University	M,D
Lehigh University	M,D,O
Le Moyne College	M
LeTourneau University	M
Lewis University	M
Liberty University	M
Lincoln Memorial University	M
Lincoln University (MO)	M
Lincoln University (PA)	M
Lindenwood University	M,O
Lipscomb University	M
Long Island University, Brooklyn Campus	M
Long Island University, C.W. Post Campus	M,O
Longwood University	M
Louisiana State University and Agricultural and Mechanical College	M,D
Louisiana State University in Shreveport	M
Louisiana Tech University	M,D
Loyola Marymount University	M
Loyola University Chicago	M
Loyola University Maryland	M
Loyola University New Orleans	M
Lynchburg College	M
Lynn University	M,D
Madonna University	M
Maharishi University of Management	M,D
Malone University	M
Marian University (WI)	M
Marist College	M,O
Marquette University	M
Marshall University	M,D,O
Marylhurst University	M
Marymount University	M,O
Maryville University of Saint Louis	M,O
Marywood University	M
Massachusetts Institute of Technology	M,D
McNeese State University	M
Medaille College	M
Mercer University	M
Mercy College	M
Metropolitan College of New York	M
Metropolitan State University	M,O
Miami University	M
Michigan State University	M,D
Michigan Technological University	M
MidAmerica Nazarene University	M
Middle Tennessee State University	M
Midwestern State University	M
Mills College	M
Minnesota State University Mankato	M
Minot State University	M
Misericordia University	M
Mississippi College	M,O
Mississippi State University	M,D
Missouri Baptist University	M,O
Missouri State University	M
Molloy College	M
Monmouth University	M,O
Montclair State University	M,O
Monterey Institute of International Studies	M
Morehead State University	M
Morgan State University	D
Mount Marty College	M
Mount Mary College	M
Mount Saint Mary College	M
Mount St. Mary's College	M
Mount St. Mary's University	M
Murray State University	M
National-Louis University	M
National University	M
Nazareth College of Rochester	M
New Jersey City University	M
New Jersey Institute of Technology	M
Newman University	M
New Mexico Highlands University	M
New Mexico State University	M,D
New York Institute of Technology	M,O
New York University	P,M,D,O
Niagara University	M
Nicholls State University	M

North Carolina Agricultural and Technical State University	M,D
North Carolina Central University	M
North Carolina State University	M
North Central College	M
Northcentral University	M,D,O
North Dakota State University	M
Northeastern Illinois University	M
Northeastern State University	M
Northeastern University	M,O
Northern Arizona University	M
Northern Illinois University	M
Northern Kentucky University	M,O
North Park University	M
Northwestern University	M
Northwest Missouri State University	M
Northwest Nazarene University	M
Norwich University	M
Notre Dame de Namur University	M
Nova Southeastern University	M,D
Nyack College	M
Oakland City University	M
Oakland University	M,O
Ohio Dominican University	M
The Ohio State University	M,D
Ohio University	M
Oklahoma City University	M
Oklahoma State University	M,D
Old Dominion University	M,D
Olivet Nazarene University	M
Oral Roberts University	M
Oregon State University	M,O
Otterbein College	M
Our Lady of the Lake University of San Antonio	M
Pace University	M,D,O
Pacific Lutheran University	M
Palm Beach Atlantic University	M
Park University	M
Penn State Great Valley	M
Penn State Harrisburg	M
Penn State University Park	M,D
Pepperdine University	M
Pfeiffer University	M
Philadelphia University	M
Piedmont College	M
Pittsburg State University	M
Plymouth State University	M
Point Loma Nazarene University	M
Point Park University	M
Polytechnic Institute of NYU	M,D
Polytechnic Institute of NYU, Westchester Graduate Center	M
Pontifical Catholic University of Puerto Rico	M,D
Portland State University	M,D,O
Prairie View A&M University	M
Providence College	M
Purdue University	M,D
Purdue University Calumet	M
Queens University of Charlotte	M
Quinnipiac University	M
Radford University	M
Regent University	M,D,O
Regis College (MA)	M
Regis University	M,O
Rensselaer Polytechnic Institute	M,D
Rice University	M
The Richard Stockton College of New Jersey	M
Rider University	M
Rivier College	M
Robert Morris University	M
Roberts Wesleyan College	M,O
Rochester Institute of Technology	M
Rockford College	M
Rockhurst University	M
Rollins College	M
Roosevelt University	M
Rosemont College	M
Rowan University	M
Rutgers, The State University of New Jersey, Camden	M
Rutgers, The State University of New Jersey, Newark	M,D,O
Sacred Heart University	M
Saginaw Valley State University	M
St. Ambrose University	M,D
St. Bonaventure University	M
St. Cloud State University	M
St. Edward's University	M,O
Saint Francis University	M
St. John Fisher College	M
St. John's University (NY)	M,O
Saint Joseph College	M
St. Joseph's College, Long Island Campus	M,O
Saint Joseph's College of Maine	M
Saint Joseph's University	M,O
Saint Leo University	M
Saint Louis University	M
Saint Martin's University	M
Saint Mary's College of California	M
St. Mary's University (United States)	M
Saint Mary's University of Minnesota	M
Saint Michael's College	M,O
Saint Peter's College	M
St. Thomas Aquinas College	M
St. Thomas University	M,O
Saint Xavier University	M,O
Salem State College	M
Salisbury University	M
Salve Regina University	M,O
Samford University	M
Sam Houston State University	M
San Diego State University	M
San Francisco State University	M
San Jose State University	M
Santa Clara University	M
Savannah State University	M
Schiller International University (United States)	M
Seattle Pacific University	M
Seattle University	M,O
Seton Hall University	M,O
Seton Hill University	M
Shenandoah University	M,O
Shippensburg University of Pennsylvania	M,O
Silver Lake College	M
Simmons College	M,O
SIT Graduate Institute	M
Sonoma State University	M
Southeastern Louisiana University	M
Southeastern Oklahoma State University	M
Southeast Missouri State University	M
Southern Connecticut State University	M
Southern Illinois University Carbondale	M,D
Southern Illinois University Edwardsville	M
Southern Methodist University	M
Southern Nazarene University	M
Southern New Hampshire University	M,D,O
Southern Oregon University	M
Southern Polytechnic State University	M,O
Southern University and Agricultural and Mechanical College	M
Southern Utah University	M
Southern Wesleyan University	M
Southwest Baptist University	M
Southwestern College (KS)	M
Southwestern Oklahoma State University	M
Southwest Minnesota State University	M
Spalding University	M
Spring Arbor University	M
Spring Hill College	M
Stanford University	M,D
State University of New York at Binghamton	M,D
State University of New York at Fredonia	M
State University of New York at New Paltz	M
State University of New York at Oswego	M
State University of New York College at Geneseo	M
State University of New York Empire State College	M

M—master's degree; P—first professional degree; D—doctorate; O—other advanced degree

State University of New York Institute of Technology M
Stephen F. Austin State University M
Stetson University M
Stevens Institute of Technology M
Stony Brook University, State University of New York M,O
Strayer University M
Suffolk University M,O
Sullivan University P,M
Sul Ross State University M
Syracuse University M,D
Tarleton State University M
Temple University M,D
Tennessee State University M
Tennessee Technological University M
Texas A&M International University M
Texas A&M University M,D
Texas A&M University–Commerce M
Texas A&M University–Corpus Christi M
Texas A&M University–Kingsville M
Texas A&M University–Texarkana M
Texas Christian University M,D
Texas Southern University M
Texas State University–San Marcos M
Texas Tech University M,D
Texas Wesleyan University M
Texas Woman's University M
Thomas More College M
Tiffin University M
Towson University M
Trevecca Nazarene University M
Trinity International University P,M,D,O
Trinity University M
Trinity (Washington) University M
Troy University M
Tulane University M,D
Union University M
Universidad del Turabo M
Universidad Metropolitana M,O
University at Albany, State University of New York M
University at Buffalo, the State University of New York M,D,O
The University of Akron M
The University of Alabama M,D
The University of Alabama at Birmingham M,D
The University of Alabama in Huntsville M,O
University of Alaska Anchorage M
University of Alaska Fairbanks M
University of Alaska Southeast M
The University of Arizona M,D
University of Arkansas M,D
University of Arkansas at Little Rock M,O
University of Baltimore M,O
University of Bridgeport M
University of California, Berkeley M,D,O
University of California, Davis M
University of California, Irvine M,D
University of California, Los Angeles M,D
University of California, Riverside M
University of California, San Diego M
University of Central Arkansas M
University of Central Florida M,D,O
University of Central Missouri M
University of Central Oklahoma M
University of Chicago M,D
University of Cincinnati M,D
University of Colorado at Boulder M
University of Colorado at Colorado Springs M
University of Colorado Denver M
University of Connecticut M,D
University of Dallas M
University of Dayton M
University of Delaware M,D
University of Denver M,O
University of Detroit Mercy M,O
University of Dubuque M
University of Evansville M
The University of Findlay M
University of Florida M,D,O
University of Georgia M,D
University of Guam M
University of Hartford M
University of Hawaii at Manoa M
University of Houston M,D
University of Houston–Clear Lake M
University of Houston–Victoria M
University of Idaho M
University of Illinois at Chicago M,D
University of Illinois at Springfield M
University of Illinois at Urbana–Champaign M,D
University of Indianapolis M,O
The University of Iowa M,D
The University of Kansas M,D
University of Kentucky M,D
University of La Verne M,O
University of Louisiana at Lafayette M
University of Louisiana at Monroe M
University of Louisville M
University of Maine M
University of Mary M
University of Mary Hardin-Baylor M
University of Maryland, College Park M,D
University of Maryland University College M,D,O
University of Mary Washington M
University of Massachusetts Amherst M,D
University of Massachusetts Boston M
University of Massachusetts Dartmouth M,O
University of Massachusetts Lowell M,O
University of Memphis M,D
University of Miami M
University of Michigan D
University of Michigan–Dearborn M
University of Michigan–Flint M
University of Minnesota, Duluth M
University of Minnesota, Twin Cities Campus M,D
University of Mississippi M,D
University of Missouri–Columbia M,D
University of Missouri–Kansas City M,D
University of Missouri–St. Louis M,O
University of Mobile M
The University of Montana M
University of Nebraska at Kearney M
University of Nebraska at Omaha M
University of Nebraska–Lincoln M,D
University of Nevada, Las Vegas M
University of Nevada, Reno M
University of New Hampshire M,O
University of New Haven M
University of New Mexico M
University of New Orleans M
University of North Alabama M
The University of North Carolina at Chapel Hill M,D
The University of North Carolina at Charlotte M,D
The University of North Carolina at Greensboro M,O
The University of North Carolina at Pembroke M
The University of North Carolina Wilmington M
University of North Dakota M
University of Northern Iowa M
University of North Florida M
University of North Texas M,D
University of Notre Dame M
University of Oklahoma M,D
University of Oregon M,D
University of Pennsylvania M,D
University of Phoenix M,D
University of Phoenix–Central Florida Campus M
University of Phoenix–Denver Campus M
University of Phoenix–Hawaii Campus M
University of Phoenix–Las Vegas Campus M

University of Phoenix–Louisiana Campus M
University of Phoenix–New Mexico Campus M
University of Phoenix–North Florida Campus M
University of Phoenix–Oregon Campus M
University of Phoenix–Philadelphia Campus M
University of Phoenix–Phoenix Campus M
University of Phoenix–Sacramento Valley Campus M
University of Phoenix–San Diego Campus M
University of Phoenix–Southern Arizona Campus M
University of Phoenix–Southern California Campus M
University of Phoenix–Southern Colorado Campus M
University of Phoenix–South Florida Campus M
University of Phoenix–Utah Campus M
University of Phoenix–West Florida Campus M
University of Phoenix–West Michigan Campus M
University of Pittsburgh M,D
University of Portland M
University of Puerto Rico, Mayagüez Campus M
University of Puerto Rico, Río Piedras M,D
University of Redlands M
University of Rhode Island M,D
University of Richmond M
University of Rochester M,D
University of St. Francis (IL) M
University of Saint Francis (IN) M
University of Saint Mary M
University of St. Thomas (MN) M
University of St. Thomas (TX) M
University of San Diego M,O
University of San Francisco M
The University of Scranton M
University of Sioux Falls M
University of South Alabama M
University of South Carolina M,D
The University of South Dakota M
University of Southern California M,D
University of Southern Indiana M
University of Southern Maine M
University of Southern Mississippi M
University of South Florida M,D
The University of Tampa M
The University of Tennessee M,D
The University of Tennessee at Chattanooga M
The University of Tennessee at Martin M
The University of Texas at Arlington M,D
The University of Texas at Austin M,D
The University of Texas at Brownsville M
The University of Texas at Dallas M,D
The University of Texas at El Paso M
The University of Texas at San Antonio M,D
The University of Texas at Tyler M
The University of Texas of the Permian Basin M
The University of Texas–Pan American M,D
University of the District of Columbia M
University of the Incarnate Word M,O
University of the Pacific M
University of the Southwest M
The University of Toledo M,D
University of Tulsa M
University of Utah M,D
University of Vermont M
University of Virginia M,D
University of Washington M,D
University of Washington, Bothell M
University of West Florida M
University of West Georgia M
University of Wisconsin–Eau Claire M
University of Wisconsin–La Crosse M
University of Wisconsin–Madison M
University of Wisconsin–Milwaukee M,D,O
University of Wisconsin–Oshkosh M
University of Wisconsin–River Falls M
University of Wisconsin–Stevens Point M
University of Wisconsin–Whitewater M
University of Wyoming M
Upper Iowa University M
Ursuline College M
Utah State University M
Valdosta State University M
Valparaiso University M,O
Vanderbilt University M,D
Vanguard University of Southern California M
Villanova University M
Virginia Commonwealth University M,O
Virginia Polytechnic Institute and State University M,D
Viterbo University M
Wagner College M
Wake Forest University M
Walden University M,D
Walsh University M
Washburn University M
Washington State University M,D
Washington University in St. Louis M,D
Wayland Baptist University M
Waynesburg University M,D
Wayne State College M
Wayne State University M,D
Weber State University M
Webster University M,D
Wesley College M
West Chester University of Pennsylvania M,O
Western Carolina University M
Western Connecticut State University M
Western Illinois University M
Western International University M
Western Kentucky University M
Western Michigan University M
Western New England College M
Western New Mexico University M
Western Washington University M
Westminster College (UT) M,O
West Texas A&M University M
West Virginia University M
Wheeling Jesuit University M
Whitworth University M
Wichita State University M
Widener University M
Wilkes University M
Willamette University M
William Carey University M
William Paterson University of New Jersey M
Wilmington University M
Winthrop University M
Woodbury University M
Worcester Polytechnic Institute M,O
Worcester State College M
Wright State University M
Xavier University M
Yale University M,D
Youngstown State University M,O

■ BUSINESS EDUCATION

Arkansas State University M,O
Armstrong Atlantic State University M
Auburn University M,D,O
Ball State University M
Bloomsburg University of Pennsylvania M
Bowling Green State University M
Buffalo State College, State University of New York M
Central Connecticut State University M,O

M—master's degree; P—first professional degree; D—doctorate; O—other advanced degree

The College of Saint Rose M,O
Drake University M
Eastern Kentucky University M
Emporia State University M
Florida Agricultural and Mechanical University M
Georgia Southern University M
Hofstra University M
Inter American University of Puerto Rico, San Germán Campus M
Lehman College of the City University of New York M
Louisiana State University and Agricultural and Mechanical College M,D
Louisiana Tech University M,D
Maryville University of Saint Louis M,O
Middle Tennessee State University M
Mississippi College M,D,O
Nazareth College of Rochester M
New York University M,O
North Carolina State University M
Northwestern State University of Louisiana M
Old Dominion University M,D
Penn State Harrisburg M,D
Pontifical Catholic University of Puerto Rico M,D
Rider University O
Robert Morris University M,D,O
South Carolina State University M
Southern New Hampshire University M,O
State University of New York at Oswego M
University of Delaware M,D
University of Minnesota, Twin Cities Campus M,D,O
University of Missouri–Columbia M,D,O
University of South Carolina M,D
The University of Toledo M
University of Washington M,D
University of West Georgia M,O
University of Wisconsin–Whitewater M
Utah State University M,D
Wayne State College M
Wayne State University M,D,O
Western Kentucky University M,O
Wright State University M

■ CANCER BIOLOGY/ONCOLOGY

Brown University M,D
Case Western Reserve University D
Dartmouth College D
Duke University D
Mayo Graduate School D
New York University P,M,D
Northwestern University D
Stanford University D
University at Buffalo, the State University of New York D
The University of Arizona D
University of California, San Diego D
University of Chicago D
University of Cincinnati D
University of Colorado Denver D
University of Delaware M,D
University of Miami D
University of Minnesota, Twin Cities Campus D
University of Pennsylvania D
University of South Florida D
The University of Toledo M,D
University of Utah M,D
University of Wisconsin–Madison D
Vanderbilt University M,D
Wake Forest University D
Wayne State University M,D
West Virginia University M,D
Yale University D

■ CARDIOVASCULAR SCIENCES

Dartmouth College D
Long Island University, C.W. Post Campus M
Loyola University Chicago M,O
The Ohio State University M
Quinnipiac University M
University of California, San Diego D
The University of South Dakota M,D
The University of Toledo M,D

■ CELL BIOLOGY

Appalachian State University M
Arizona State University M,D
Auburn University M,D
Boston University M,D
Brandeis University M,D
Brown University M,D
California Institute of Technology D
Carnegie Mellon University M,D
Case Western Reserve University M,D
The Catholic University of America M,D
Colorado State University M,D
Columbia University M,D
Cornell University M,D
Dartmouth College D
Drexel University M,D
Duke University D,O
East Carolina University D
Eastern Michigan University M
Emory University D
Emporia State University M
Florida Institute of Technology M,D
Florida State University M,D
George Mason University M,D,O
Georgetown University D
Georgia State University M,D
Grand Valley State University M
Harvard University D
Illinois State University M,D
Indiana University Bloomington M,D
Indiana University–Purdue University Indianapolis M,D
Iowa State University of Science and Technology M,D
The Johns Hopkins University D
Kent State University M,D
Loyola University Chicago M,D
Marquette University M,D
Massachusetts Institute of Technology D
Mayo Graduate School D
Michigan State University M,D
Missouri State University M
New York University P,M,D
North Carolina State University M,D
North Dakota State University M,D
Northwestern University D
The Ohio State University M,D
Ohio University M,D
Oregon State University M,D
Penn State University Park M,D
Purdue University M,D
Quinnipiac University M
Rensselaer Polytechnic Institute M,D
Rice University M,D
Rutgers, The State University of New Jersey, New Brunswick M,D
San Diego State University M,D
San Francisco State University M
Stony Brook University, State University of New York M,D
Temple University M,D
Texas A&M University M,D
Tufts University D
Tulane University M,D
University at Albany, State University of New York M,D
University at Buffalo, the State University of New York D
The University of Alabama at Birmingham D
The University of Arizona M,D
University of Arkansas M,D
University of California, Berkeley D
University of California, Davis M,D
University of California, Irvine M,D
University of California, Los Angeles D
University of California, Riverside M,D
University of California, San Diego D
University of California, Santa Barbara M,D
University of California, Santa Cruz M,D
University of Chicago D
University of Cincinnati D
University of Colorado at Boulder M,D

University of Colorado Denver	D
University of Connecticut	M,D
University of Delaware	M,D
University of Florida	M,D
University of Georgia	M,D
University of Illinois at Chicago	D
University of Illinois at Urbana–Champaign	D
The University of Iowa	M,D
The University of Kansas	M,D
University of Maryland, Baltimore County	D
University of Maryland, College Park	M,D
University of Massachusetts Amherst	D
University of Massachusetts Boston	D
University of Miami	D
University of Michigan	M,D
University of Minnesota, Twin Cities Campus	M,D
University of Missouri–Columbia	M,D
University of Missouri–Kansas City	D
University of Missouri–St. Louis	M,D,O
University of Nevada, Reno	M,D
University of New Haven	M
University of New Mexico	M,D
The University of North Carolina at Chapel Hill	D
University of Notre Dame	M,D
University of Pennsylvania	D
University of Pittsburgh	M,D
University of Rhode Island	M,D
University of South Alabama	D
University of South Carolina	M,D
The University of South Dakota	M,D
University of Southern California	M,D
University of South Florida	M,D
The University of Texas at Austin	D
The University of Texas at Dallas	M,D
The University of Texas at San Antonio	M,D
University of Vermont	M,D
University of Virginia	D
University of Washington	D
University of Wisconsin–La Crosse	M
University of Wisconsin–Madison	D
University of Wyoming	D
Vanderbilt University	M,D
Washington State University	M,D
Washington University in St. Louis	D
West Virginia University	M,D
Yale University	D

■ CELTIC LANGUAGES

Harvard University	D

■ CERAMIC SCIENCES AND ENGINEERING

Alfred University	M,D
Case Western Reserve University	M,D
Missouri University of Science and Technology	M,D
Rensselaer Polytechnic Institute	M,D
University of Cincinnati	M,D

■ CHEMICAL ENGINEERING

Arizona State University	M,D
Auburn University	M,D
Brigham Young University	M,D
Brown University	M,D
Bucknell University	M
California Institute of Technology	M,D
Carnegie Mellon University	M,D
Case Western Reserve University	M,D
City College of the City University of New York	M,D
Clarkson University	M,D
Clemson University	M,D
Cleveland State University	M,D
Colorado School of Mines	M,D
Colorado State University	M,D
Columbia University	M,D
Cornell University	M,D
Drexel University	M,D
Fairleigh Dickinson University, College at Florham	M,O
Florida Agricultural and Mechanical University	M,D
Florida Institute of Technology	M,D
Florida State University	M,D
Georgia Institute of Technology	M,D
Graduate School and University Center of the City University of New York	D
Howard University	M
Illinois Institute of Technology	M,D
Iowa State University of Science and Technology	M,D
The Johns Hopkins University	M,D
Kansas State University	M,D
Lamar University	M,D
Lehigh University	M,D
Louisiana State University and Agricultural and Mechanical College	M,D
Louisiana Tech University	M,D
Manhattan College	M
Massachusetts Institute of Technology	M,D
McNeese State University	M
Michigan State University	M,D
Michigan Technological University	M,D
Mississippi State University	M,D
Missouri University of Science and Technology	M,D
Montana State University	M,D
New Jersey Institute of Technology	M,D
New Mexico State University	M,D
North Carolina Agricultural and Technical State University	M,D
North Carolina State University	M,D
Northeastern University	M,D
Northwestern University	M,D
The Ohio State University	M,D
Ohio University	M,D
Oklahoma State University	M,D
Oregon State University	M,D
Penn State University Park	M,D
Polytechnic Institute of NYU	M,D
Polytechnic Institute of NYU, Westchester Graduate Center	M
Princeton University	M,D
Purdue University	M,D
Rensselaer Polytechnic Institute	M,D
Rice University	M,D
Rutgers, The State University of New Jersey, New Brunswick	M,D
San Jose State University	M
Stanford University	M,D,O
Stevens Institute of Technology	M,D,O
Syracuse University	M,D
Tennessee Technological University	M,D
Texas A&M University	M,D
Texas A&M University–Kingsville	M
Texas Tech University	M,D
Tufts University	M,D
Tulane University	D
University at Buffalo, the State University of New York	M,D
The University of Akron	M,D
The University of Alabama	M,D
The University of Alabama in Huntsville	M
The University of Arizona	M,D
University of Arkansas	M,D
University of California, Berkeley	M,D
University of California, Davis	M,D
University of California, Irvine	M,D
University of California, Los Angeles	M,D
University of California, Riverside	M,D
University of California, San Diego	M,D
University of California, Santa Barbara	M,D
University of Cincinnati	M,D
University of Colorado at Boulder	M,D
University of Connecticut	M,D
University of Dayton	M
University of Delaware	M,D
University of Florida	M,D
University of Houston	M,D
University of Idaho	M,D
University of Illinois at Chicago	M,D

M—master's degree; P—first professional degree; D—doctorate; O—other advanced degree

University of Illinois at Urbana–Champaign	M,D
The University of Iowa	M,D
The University of Kansas	M,D
University of Kentucky	M,D
University of Louisiana at Lafayette	M
University of Louisville	M,D
University of Maine	M,D
University of Maryland, Baltimore County	M,D,O
University of Maryland, College Park	M,D,O
University of Massachusetts Amherst	M,D
University of Massachusetts Lowell	M,D
University of Michigan	M,D,O
University of Minnesota, Twin Cities Campus	M,D
University of Missouri–Columbia	M,D
University of Nebraska–Lincoln	M,D
University of Nevada, Reno	M,D
University of New Hampshire	M,D
University of New Mexico	M,D
University of North Dakota	M
University of Notre Dame	M,D
University of Oklahoma	M,D
University of Pennsylvania	M,D
University of Pittsburgh	M,D
University of Puerto Rico, Mayagüez Campus	M,D
University of Rhode Island	M,D
University of Rochester	M,D
University of South Alabama	M
University of South Carolina	M,D
University of Southern California	M,D,O
University of South Florida	M,D
The University of Tennessee	M,D
The University of Tennessee at Chattanooga	M
The University of Texas at Austin	M,D
The University of Toledo	M,D
University of Tulsa	M,D
University of Utah	M,D
University of Virginia	M,D
University of Washington	M,D
University of Wisconsin–Madison	M,D
University of Wyoming	M,D
Vanderbilt University	M,D
Villanova University	M
Virginia Commonwealth University	M,D
Virginia Polytechnic Institute and State University	M,D
Washington State University	M,D
Washington University in St. Louis	M,D
Wayne State University	M,D
Western Michigan University	M,D
West Virginia University	M,D
Widener University	M
Worcester Polytechnic Institute	M,D
Yale University	M,D

■ CHEMICAL PHYSICS

Columbia University	M,D
Cornell University	D
Harvard University	D
Kent State University	M,D
Marquette University	M,D
Michigan State University	M,D
The Ohio State University	M,D
University of Colorado at Boulder	M,D
University of Illinois at Urbana–Champaign	M,D
University of Louisville	M,D
University of Maryland, College Park	M,D
University of Nevada, Reno	D
University of Southern California	D
The University of Tennessee	M,D
University of Utah	M,D
Virginia Commonwealth University	M,D
West Virginia University	M,D

■ CHEMISTRY

American University	M
Arizona State University	M,D
Arkansas State University	M,O
Auburn University	M,D
Ball State University	M
Baylor University	M,D
Boston College	M,D
Boston University	M,D
Bowling Green State University	M,D
Bradley University	M
Brandeis University	M,D
Brigham Young University	M,D
Brooklyn College of the City University of New York	M,D
Brown University	M,D
Bucknell University	M
Buffalo State College, State University of New York	M
California Institute of Technology	M,D
California Polytechnic State University, San Luis Obispo	M
California State Polytechnic University, Pomona	M
California State University, East Bay	M
California State University, Fresno	M
California State University, Fullerton	M
California State University, Long Beach	M
California State University, Los Angeles	M
California State University, Northridge	M
California State University, Sacramento	M
California State University, San Bernardino	M
Carnegie Mellon University	M,D
Case Western Reserve University	M,D
The Catholic University of America	M
Central Connecticut State University	M
Central Michigan University	M
Central Washington University	M
City College of the City University of New York	M,D
Clark Atlanta University	M,D
Clarkson University	M,D
Clark University	M,D
Clemson University	M,D
Cleveland State University	M,D
The College of William and Mary	M
Colorado School of Mines	M,D
Colorado State University	M,D
Columbia University	M,D
Cornell University	D
Dartmouth College	D
Delaware State University	M
DePaul University	M
Drexel University	M,D
Duke University	D
Duquesne University	M,D
East Carolina University	M
Eastern Illinois University	M
Eastern Kentucky University	M
Eastern Michigan University	M
Eastern New Mexico University	M
East Tennessee State University	M
Emory University	D
Fairleigh Dickinson University, College at Florham	M
Fairleigh Dickinson University, Metropolitan Campus	M
Florida Agricultural and Mechanical University	M
Florida Atlantic University	M,D
Florida Institute of Technology	M,D
Florida International University	M,D
Florida State University	M,D
Furman University	M
George Mason University	M
Georgetown University	D
The George Washington University	M,D
Georgia Institute of Technology	M,D
Georgia State University	M,D
Graduate School and University Center of the City University of New York	D
Hampton University	M
Harvard University	D
Howard University	M,D
Hunter College of the City University of New York	M,D
Idaho State University	M
Illinois Institute of Technology	M,D

Institution	Degrees
Illinois State University	M
Indiana University Bloomington	M,D
Indiana University of Pennsylvania	M
Indiana University–Purdue University Indianapolis	M,D
Iowa State University of Science and Technology	M,D
Jackson State University	M,D
The Johns Hopkins University	D
Kansas State University	M,D
Kent State University	M,D
Lamar University	M
Lehigh University	M,D
Long Island University, Brooklyn Campus	M
Louisiana State University and Agricultural and Mechanical College	M,D
Louisiana Tech University	M
Loyola University Chicago	M,D
Marquette University	M,D
Marshall University	M
Massachusetts Institute of Technology	D
McNeese State University	M
Miami University	M,D
Michigan State University	M,D
Michigan Technological University	M,D
Middle Tennessee State University	M,D
Mississippi College	M
Mississippi State University	M,D
Missouri State University	M
Missouri University of Science and Technology	M,D
Montana State University	M,D
Montclair State University	M
Morgan State University	M
Murray State University	M
New Jersey Institute of Technology	M,D
New Mexico Highlands University	M
New Mexico Institute of Mining and Technology	M,D
New Mexico State University	M,D
New York University	M,D
North Carolina Agricultural and Technical State University	M
North Carolina Central University	M
North Carolina State University	M,D
North Dakota State University	M,D
Northeastern Illinois University	M
Northeastern University	M,D
Northern Arizona University	M
Northern Illinois University	M,D
Northwestern University	D
Oakland University	M,D
The Ohio State University	M,D
Oklahoma State University	M,D
Old Dominion University	M,D
Oregon State University	M,D
Penn State University Park	M,D
Pittsburg State University	M
Polytechnic Institute of NYU	M,D
Polytechnic Institute of NYU, Westchester Graduate Center	M
Pontifical Catholic University of Puerto Rico	M
Portland State University	M,D
Prairie View A&M University	M
Princeton University	M,D
Purdue University	M,D
Queens College of the City University of New York	M
Rensselaer Polytechnic Institute	M,D
Rice University	M,D
Rochester Institute of Technology	M
Roosevelt University	M
Rutgers, The State University of New Jersey, Camden	M
Rutgers, The State University of New Jersey, Newark	M,D
Rutgers, The State University of New Jersey, New Brunswick	M,D
Sacred Heart University	M
St. John's University (NY)	M
Saint Joseph College	M
Saint Louis University	M,D
Sam Houston State University	M
San Diego State University	M,D
San Francisco State University	M
San Jose State University	M
Seton Hall University	M,D
South Dakota State University	M,D
Southeast Missouri State University	M
Southern Connecticut State University	M
Southern Illinois University Carbondale	M,D
Southern Illinois University Edwardsville	M
Southern Methodist University	M,D
Southern University and Agricultural and Mechanical College	M
Stanford University	D
State University of New York at Binghamton	M,D
State University of New York at Fredonia	M
State University of New York at Oswego	M
State University of New York College of Environmental Science and Forestry	M,D
Stephen F. Austin State University	M
Stevens Institute of Technology	M,D,O
Stony Brook University, State University of New York	M,D
Syracuse University	M,D
Temple University	M,D
Tennessee State University	M
Tennessee Technological University	M
Texas A&M University	M,D
Texas A&M University–Commerce	M
Texas A&M University–Kingsville	M
Texas Christian University	M,D
Texas Southern University	M
Texas State University–San Marcos	M
Texas Tech University	M,D
Texas Woman's University	M
Tufts University	M,D
Tulane University	M,D
University at Albany, State University of New York	M,D
University at Buffalo, the State University of New York	M,D
The University of Akron	M,D
The University of Alabama	M,D
The University of Alabama at Birmingham	M,D
The University of Alabama in Huntsville	M
University of Alaska Fairbanks	M,D
The University of Arizona	M,D
University of Arkansas	M,D
University of Arkansas at Little Rock	M
University of California, Berkeley	D
University of California, Davis	M,D
University of California, Irvine	M,D
University of California, Los Angeles	M,D
University of California, Riverside	M,D
University of California, San Diego	M,D
University of California, Santa Barbara	M,D
University of California, Santa Cruz	M,D
University of Central Florida	M,D,O
University of Central Oklahoma	M
University of Chicago	D
University of Cincinnati	M,D
University of Colorado at Boulder	M,D
University of Colorado at Colorado Springs	M
University of Colorado Denver	M
University of Connecticut	M,D
University of Dayton	M
University of Delaware	M,D
University of Denver	M,D
University of Detroit Mercy	M
University of Florida	M,D
University of Georgia	M,D
University of Hawaii at Manoa	M,D
University of Houston	M,D

M—master's degree; P—first professional degree; D—doctorate; O—other advanced degree

University of Houston–Clear Lake M
University of Idaho M,D
University of Illinois at Chicago M,D
University of Illinois at Urbana–Champaign M,D
The University of Iowa M,D
The University of Kansas M,D
University of Kentucky M,D
University of Louisville M,D
University of Maine M,D
University of Maryland, Baltimore County M,D
University of Maryland, College Park M,D
University of Massachusetts Amherst M,D
University of Massachusetts Boston M
University of Massachusetts Dartmouth M,D
University of Massachusetts Lowell M,D
University of Memphis M,D
University of Miami M,D
University of Michigan D
University of Minnesota, Duluth M
University of Minnesota, Twin Cities Campus M,D
University of Mississippi M,D
University of Missouri–Columbia M,D
University of Missouri–Kansas City M,D
University of Missouri–St. Louis M,D
The University of Montana M,D
University of Nebraska–Lincoln M,D
University of Nevada, Las Vegas M,D
University of Nevada, Reno M,D
University of New Hampshire M,D
University of New Mexico M,D
University of New Orleans M,D
The University of North Carolina at Chapel Hill M,D
The University of North Carolina at Charlotte M
The University of North Carolina at Greensboro M
The University of North Carolina Wilmington M
University of North Dakota M,D
University of Northern Colorado M,D
University of Northern Iowa M
University of North Texas M,D
University of Notre Dame M,D
University of Oklahoma M,D
University of Oregon M,D
University of Pennsylvania M,D
University of Pittsburgh M,D
University of Puerto Rico, Mayagüez Campus M,D
University of Puerto Rico, Río Piedras M,D
University of Rhode Island M,D
University of Rochester M,D
University of San Francisco M
The University of Scranton M
University of South Carolina M,D
The University of South Dakota M,D
University of Southern California M,D
University of Southern Mississippi M,D
University of South Florida M,D
The University of Tennessee M,D
The University of Texas at Arlington M,D
The University of Texas at Austin M,D
The University of Texas at Dallas M,D
The University of Texas at El Paso M,D
The University of Texas at San Antonio M,D
The University of Texas–Pan American M
The University of Toledo M,D
University of Tulsa M,D
University of Utah M,D
University of Vermont M,D
University of Virginia M,D
University of Washington M,D
University of Wisconsin–Madison M,D
University of Wisconsin–Milwaukee M,D
University of Wyoming M,D
Utah State University M,D
Vanderbilt University M,D
Villanova University M
Virginia Commonwealth University M,D
Virginia Polytechnic Institute and State University M,D
Wake Forest University M,D
Washington State University M,D
Washington University in St. Louis D
Wayne State University M,D
West Chester University of Pennsylvania M
Western Carolina University M
Western Illinois University M
Western Kentucky University M
Western Michigan University M,D
Western Washington University M
West Texas A&M University M
West Virginia University M,D
Wichita State University M,D
Worcester Polytechnic Institute M,D
Wright State University M
Yale University D
Youngstown State University M

■ CHILD AND FAMILY STUDIES

Arizona State University M,D
Assumption College M,O
Auburn University M,D
Bowling Green State University M
Brandeis University M,D
Brigham Young University M,D
California State University, Los Angeles M
Capella University M,D,O
Central Michigan University M,O
Central Washington University M
Colorado State University M,D
Concordia University, St. Paul M,O
Concordia University Wisconsin M
Cornell University D
East Carolina University M
Eastern Michigan University M,O
Florida State University M,D
Indiana University Bloomington M,D
Indiana University–Purdue University Indianapolis M
Iowa State University of Science and Technology M,D
Kansas State University M,D
Miami University M
Michigan State University M,D
Middle Tennessee State University M
Missouri State University M
North Dakota State University M,D
Northern Illinois University M
Nova Southeastern University M,D
The Ohio State University M,D
Ohio University M
Oklahoma State University M,D
Oregon State University M,D
Penn State University Park M,D
Purdue University M,D
Roberts Wesleyan College M
St. Cloud State University M
Saint Joseph College M
San Diego State University M
San Jose State University M
South Carolina State University M
Spring Arbor University M
Stanford University D
State University of New York at Oswego M
Syracuse University M,D
Texas State University–San Marcos M
Texas Tech University M,D
Texas Woman's University M,D
Towson University O
Tufts University M,D,O
The University of Akron M
The University of Alabama M
The University of Arizona M,D
University of California, Santa Barbara M,D
University of Central Florida M,O
University of Connecticut M,D,O
University of Delaware M,D
University of Denver M,D,O
University of Georgia M,D,O
University of Illinois at Springfield M
University of Kentucky M,D

University of La Verne M
University of Maryland, College Park M,D
University of Massachusetts Amherst M,D,O
University of Minnesota, Twin Cities Campus M,D
University of Missouri–Columbia M,D
University of Nevada, Reno M
University of New Hampshire M
University of New Mexico M,D
The University of North Carolina at Greensboro M,D
University of North Texas M,O
University of Rhode Island M
University of Southern California M,D
University of Southern Mississippi M
The University of Tennessee M,D
The University of Tennessee at Martin M
The University of Texas at Austin M,D
The University of Texas at Dallas M,D
University of Utah M
University of Wisconsin–Madison M,D
University of Wisconsin–Stout M
Utah State University M,D
Vanderbilt University M
Virginia Polytechnic Institute and State University M,D
Walden University M,D
Wayne State University O
West Virginia University M
Wheelock College M

■ CHILD DEVELOPMENT

Appalachian State University M
Arcadia University M,D,O
California State University, Los Angeles M
California State University, San Bernardino M
California State University, Stanislaus M,O
East Carolina University M
Michigan State University M,D
Middle Tennessee State University M
North Dakota State University M,D
Ohio University M
Purdue University M,D
Rutgers, The State University of New Jersey, Camden M,D
San Diego State University M
Sarah Lawrence College M
Southern New Hampshire University M,O
Texas Woman's University M,D
Tufts University M,D,O
The University of Akron M
University of California, Davis M
University of La Verne M
University of Minnesota, Twin Cities Campus M,D
University of Nebraska–Lincoln M,D
The University of North Carolina at Charlotte M,D
The University of Tennessee at Martin M
The University of Texas at Austin M,D
University of Wyoming M
Virginia Polytechnic Institute and State University M,D

■ CHINESE

Arizona State University M
Cornell University M,D
Harvard University D
Indiana University Bloomington M,D
The Ohio State University M,D
San Francisco State University M
Seton Hall University M
Stanford University M,D
University of California, Berkeley D
University of California, Irvine M,D
University of Colorado at Boulder M,D
University of Hawaii at Manoa M,D,O
University of Massachusetts Amherst M
University of Oregon M,D
University of Washington M,D
University of Wisconsin–Madison M,D
Washington University in St. Louis M,D

■ CHIROPRACTIC

D'Youville College P
University of Bridgeport P

■ CIVIL ENGINEERING

Arizona State University M,D
Auburn University M,D
Boise State University M
Bradley University M
Brigham Young University M,D
Bucknell University M
California Institute of Technology M,D,O
California Polytechnic State University, San Luis Obispo M
California State Polytechnic University, Pomona M
California State University, Fresno M
California State University, Fullerton M
California State University, Long Beach M
California State University, Los Angeles M
California State University, Northridge M
California State University, Sacramento M
Case Western Reserve University M,D
The Catholic University of America M,D,O
City College of the City University of New York M,D
Clarkson University M,D
Clemson University M,D
Cleveland State University M,D
Colorado State University M,D
Columbia University M,D,O
Cornell University M,D
Drexel University M,D
Duke University M,D
Florida Agricultural and Mechanical University M,D
Florida Atlantic University M
Florida Institute of Technology M,D
Florida International University M,D
Florida State University M,D
George Mason University M,D,O
The George Washington University M,D,O
Georgia Institute of Technology M,D
Graduate School and University Center of the City University of New York D
Howard University M
Idaho State University M
Illinois Institute of Technology M,D
Iowa State University of Science and Technology M,D
The Johns Hopkins University M,D
Kansas State University M,D
Lamar University M,D
Lawrence Technological University M,D
Lehigh University M,D
Louisiana State University and Agricultural and Mechanical College M,D
Louisiana Tech University M,D
Loyola Marymount University M
Manhattan College M
Marquette University M,D
Massachusetts Institute of Technology M,D,O
McNeese State University M
Michigan State University M,D
Michigan Technological University M,D
Mississippi State University M,D
Missouri University of Science and Technology M,D
Montana State University M,D
Morgan State University M,D
New Jersey Institute of Technology M,D
New Mexico State University M,D
North Carolina Agricultural and Technical State University M
North Carolina State University M,D
North Dakota State University M,D

M—master's degree; P—first professional degree; D—doctorate; O—other advanced degree

Northeastern University	M,D
Northern Arizona University	M
Northwestern University	M,D
Norwich University	M
The Ohio State University	M,D
Ohio University	M,D
Oklahoma State University	M,D
Old Dominion University	M,D
Oregon State University	M,D
Penn State University Park	M,D
Polytechnic Institute of NYU	M,D
Portland State University	M,D,O
Princeton University	M,D
Purdue University	M,D
Rensselaer Polytechnic Institute	M,D
Rice University	M,D
Rutgers, The State University of New Jersey, New Brunswick	M,D
Saint Martin's University	M
San Diego State University	M
San Jose State University	M
Santa Clara University	M
South Carolina State University	M
South Dakota State University	M
Southern Illinois University Carbondale	M
Southern Illinois University Edwardsville	M
Southern Methodist University	M,D
Stanford University	M,D,O
Stevens Institute of Technology	M,D,O
Syracuse University	M,D
Temple University	M
Tennessee Technological University	M,D
Texas A&M University	M,D
Texas A&M University–Kingsville	M
Texas Tech University	M,D
Tufts University	M,D
University at Buffalo, the State University of New York	M,D
The University of Akron	M,D
The University of Alabama	M,D
The University of Alabama at Birmingham	M,D
The University of Alabama in Huntsville	M,D
University of Alaska Anchorage	M,O
University of Alaska Fairbanks	M,D
The University of Arizona	M,D
University of Arkansas	M,D
University of California, Berkeley	M,D
University of California, Davis	M,D,O
University of California, Irvine	M,D
University of California, Los Angeles	M,D
University of Central Florida	M,D,O
University of Cincinnati	M,D
University of Colorado at Boulder	M,D
University of Colorado Denver	M,D
University of Connecticut	M,D
University of Dayton	M
University of Delaware	M,D
University of Detroit Mercy	M,D
University of Florida	M,D,O
University of Hawaii at Manoa	M,D
University of Houston	M,D
University of Idaho	M,D
University of Illinois at Chicago	M,D
University of Illinois at Urbana–Champaign	M,D
The University of Iowa	M,D
The University of Kansas	M,D
University of Kentucky	M,D
University of Louisiana at Lafayette	M
University of Louisville	M,D
University of Maine	M,D
University of Maryland, Baltimore County	M,D
University of Maryland, College Park	M,D,O
University of Massachusetts Amherst	M,D
University of Massachusetts Dartmouth	M
University of Massachusetts Lowell	M,D,O
University of Memphis	M,D
University of Miami	M,D
University of Michigan	M,D,O
University of Minnesota, Twin Cities Campus	M,D
University of Missouri–Columbia	M,D
University of Missouri–Kansas City	M,D
University of Nebraska–Lincoln	M,D
University of Nevada, Las Vegas	M,D
University of Nevada, Reno	M,D
University of New Hampshire	M,D
University of New Mexico	M,D
The University of North Carolina at Charlotte	M,D
University of North Dakota	M
University of Notre Dame	M,D
University of Oklahoma	M,D
University of Pittsburgh	M,D
University of Puerto Rico, Mayagüez Campus	M,D
University of Rhode Island	M,D
University of South Alabama	M
University of South Carolina	M,D
University of Southern California	M,D,O
University of South Florida	M,D
The University of Tennessee	M,D
The University of Tennessee at Chattanooga	M
The University of Texas at Arlington	M,D
The University of Texas at Austin	M,D
The University of Texas at El Paso	M,D
The University of Texas at San Antonio	M,D
The University of Texas at Tyler	M
The University of Toledo	M,D
University of Utah	M,D
University of Vermont	M,D
University of Virginia	M,D
University of Washington	M,D
University of Wisconsin–Madison	M,D
University of Wisconsin–Milwaukee	M,D,O
University of Wyoming	M,D
Utah State University	M,D,O
Vanderbilt University	M,D
Villanova University	M
Virginia Polytechnic Institute and State University	M,D
Washington State University	M,D
Wayne State University	M,D
Western Michigan University	M
West Virginia University	M,D
Widener University	M
Worcester Polytechnic Institute	M,D,O
Youngstown State University	M

■ CLASSICS

Boston College	M
Boston University	M,D
Brandeis University	M,O
Brown University	M,D
The Catholic University of America	M,D
Columbia University	M,D
Cornell University	D
Duke University	D
Florida State University	M,D
Fordham University	M,D
Graduate School and University Center of the City University of New York	M,D
Harvard University	D
Hunter College of the City University of New York	M
Indiana University Bloomington	M,D
The Johns Hopkins University	D
Kent State University	M,D
Marshall University	M
New York University	M,D,O
The Ohio State University	M,D
Princeton University	D
Rutgers, The State University of New Jersey, New Brunswick	M,D
San Francisco State University	M
Stanford University	M,D
Texas Tech University	M
Tufts University	M
Tulane University	M
University at Buffalo, the State University of New York	M,D
The University of Arizona	M
University of California, Berkeley	M,D
University of California, Irvine	M,D

University of California, Los Angeles	M,D
University of California, Riverside	D
University of California, Santa Barbara	M,D
University of Chicago	M,D
University of Cincinnati	M,D
University of Colorado at Boulder	M,D
University of Florida	M,D
University of Georgia	M
University of Illinois at Urbana–Champaign	M,D
The University of Iowa	M,D
The University of Kansas	M
University of Kentucky	M
University of Maryland, College Park	M
University of Massachusetts Amherst	M
University of Michigan	M,D,O
University of Minnesota, Twin Cities Campus	M,D
University of Mississippi	M
University of Missouri–Columbia	M,D
University of Nebraska–Lincoln	M
The University of North Carolina at Chapel Hill	M,D
The University of North Carolina at Greensboro	M
University of Oregon	M
University of Pennsylvania	M,D
University of Pittsburgh	M,D
University of Southern California	M,D
University of South Florida	M
The University of Texas at Austin	M,D
University of Vermont	M
University of Virginia	M,D
University of Washington	M,D
University of Wisconsin–Madison	M,D
University of Wisconsin–Milwaukee	M,O
Vanderbilt University	M
Washington University in St. Louis	M
Wayne State University	M
West Chester University of Pennsylvania	M,O
Yale University	M,D

■ CLINICAL LABORATORY SCIENCES/MEDICAL TECHNOLOGY

Austin Peay State University	M
The Catholic University of America	M,D
Duke University	M
Emory University	M,D
Fairleigh Dickinson University, Metropolitan Campus	M
Inter American University of Puerto Rico, Metropolitan Campus	M
Long Island University, C.W. Post Campus	M
Michigan State University	M
Pontifical Catholic University of Puerto Rico	O
Quinnipiac University	M
Rochester Institute of Technology	M
San Francisco State University	M
University at Buffalo, the State University of New York	M
University of Colorado Denver	M,D
University of Kentucky	M,D
University of Massachusetts Lowell	M,O
University of New Mexico	M
University of North Dakota	M
University of Pittsburgh	M,D,O
University of Rhode Island	M
University of Southern Mississippi	M
University of Utah	M
University of Vermont	M,D
University of Washington	M
University of Wisconsin–Milwaukee	M
Virginia Commonwealth University	M,D
Wayne State University	M,O

■ CLINICAL PSYCHOLOGY

Abilene Christian University	M
Adelphi University	D
Alabama Agricultural and Mechanical University	M,O
Alliant International University–San Diego	M,D
American International College	M
American University	D
Antioch University Los Angeles	M
Antioch University New England	M,D
Antioch University Santa Barbara	D
Appalachian State University	M,O
Argosy University, Orange County	M,D
Argosy University, Tampa	M,D
Argosy University, Twin Cities	M,D,O
Arizona State University	D
Azusa Pacific University	M,D
Ball State University	M
Barry University	M,O
Baylor University	M,D
Benedictine University	M
Bowling Green State University	M,D
Brigham Young University	M,D
California Institute of Integral Studies	M,D
California Lutheran University	M,D
California State University, Dominguez Hills	M
California State University, Fullerton	M
California State University, Northridge	M
California State University, San Bernardino	M
Capella University	M,D,O
Cardinal Stritch University	M
Carlos Albizu University	M,D
Case Western Reserve University	D
The Catholic University of America	M,D
Central Michigan University	M,D
Chestnut Hill College	M,D,O
City College of the City University of New York	M,D
Clark University	D
Cleveland State University	M,D,O
College of St. Joseph	M
The College of William and Mary	M,D
DePaul University	M,D
Drexel University	D
Duke University	D
Duquesne University	D
East Carolina University	M
Eastern Illinois University	M,O
Eastern Kentucky University	M,O
Eastern Michigan University	M,D
Eastern Washington University	M
East Tennessee State University	M
Edinboro University of Pennsylvania	M
Emory University	D
Emporia State University	M
Fairleigh Dickinson University, Metropolitan Campus	M,D
Florida Institute of Technology	M,D
Florida State University	D
Fordham University	D
Francis Marion University	M
Gallaudet University	D
George Fox University	M,D
George Mason University	M,D
The George Washington University	D
Graduate School and University Center of the City University of New York	D
Hofstra University	M,D
Howard University	M,D
Idaho State University	D
Illinois Institute of Technology	M,D
Illinois State University	M,D,O
Immaculata University	M,D,O
Indiana State University	M,D
Indiana University of Pennsylvania	D
Indiana University–Purdue University Indianapolis	M,D
Jackson State University	D
James Madison University	D
The Johns Hopkins University	M,D
Kean University	D
Kent State University	M,D
Lamar University	M
La Salle University	M,D

M—master's degree; P—first professional degree; D—doctorate; O—other advanced degree

Lesley University M,D,O
Long Island University, Brooklyn Campus D
Long Island University, C.W. Post Campus D
Louisiana State University and Agricultural and Mechanical College M,D
Loyola University Chicago M,D
Loyola University Maryland M,D,O
Madonna University M
Marquette University M,D
Marshall University M,D
Marywood University M,D
Miami University D
Middle Tennessee State University M,O
Millersville University of Pennsylvania M
Minnesota State University Mankato M,D
Mississippi State University M,D
Missouri State University M
Montclair State University M,O
Morehead State University M
Murray State University M
Naropa University M
New Mexico Highlands University M
The New School: A University M,D
Norfolk State University M
North Dakota State University M,D
Northern Arizona University M
Northwestern State University of Louisiana M
Northwestern University D
Notre Dame de Namur University M
Nova Southeastern University D,O
The Ohio State University M,D
Ohio University D
Oklahoma State University M,D
Old Dominion University D
Pacifica Graduate Institute M,D
Penn State Harrisburg M,D
Penn State University Park M,D
Pepperdine University M
Pontifical Catholic University of Puerto Rico M,D
Prairie View A&M University M,D
Queens College of the City University of New York M
Radford University M,D,O
Regent University M,D,O
Roosevelt University M,D
Rutgers, The State University of New Jersey, New Brunswick M,D
St. John's University (NY) D
Saint Louis University M,D
St. Mary's University (United States) M
Saint Michael's College M
Sam Houston State University M,D
San Diego State University M,D
San Jose State University M
Seattle Pacific University D
Southern Illinois University Carbondale M,D
Southern Illinois University Edwardsville M
Southern Methodist University D
Southern New Hampshire University M,O
Spalding University M,D
State University of New York at Binghamton M,D
Stony Brook University, State University of New York D
Suffolk University D
Syracuse University D
Temple University D
Texas A&M University M,D
Texas Tech University M,D
Towson University M
Troy University M
Union College (KY) M
Union Institute & University D
University at Albany, State University of New York M,D,O
University at Buffalo, the State University of New York M,D
The University of Alabama D
University of Alaska Anchorage M,D
University of Alaska Fairbanks D
University of California, San Diego D
University of California, Santa Barbara M,D
University of Central Florida M,D
University of Cincinnati D
University of Colorado Denver D
University of Connecticut M,D,O
University of Dayton M
University of Delaware D
University of Denver M,D
University of Detroit Mercy M,D
University of Florida D
University of Hartford M,D
University of Hawaii at Manoa M,D,O
University of Houston M,D
University of Houston–Clear Lake M
University of Indianapolis M,D
The University of Kansas M,D
University of Kentucky M,D
University of La Verne D
University of Louisville M,D
University of Maine M,D
University of Maryland, College Park M,D
University of Massachusetts Amherst M,D
University of Massachusetts Boston D
University of Massachusetts Dartmouth M,O
University of Memphis M,D
University of Miami M,D
University of Michigan D
University of Michigan–Dearborn M
University of Minnesota, Twin Cities Campus D
University of Mississippi M,D
University of Missouri–Kansas City M,D
University of Missouri–St. Louis M,D,O
The University of Montana M,D,O
University of Nebraska–Lincoln M,D
University of Nevada, Reno M,D
University of New Mexico M,D
The University of North Carolina at Chapel Hill D
The University of North Carolina at Charlotte M
The University of North Carolina at Greensboro M,D
University of North Dakota M,D
University of North Texas M,D
University of Oregon D
University of Puerto Rico, Río Piedras M,D
University of Rhode Island M,D
University of Rochester M,D
University of South Carolina M,D
The University of South Dakota M,D
University of Southern California M,D
University of Southern Mississippi M,D
University of South Florida M,D
The University of Tennessee M,D
The University of Texas at El Paso M,D
The University of Texas at Tyler M
The University of Texas of the Permian Basin M
The University of Texas–Pan American M
University of the District of Columbia M
The University of Toledo M,D
University of Tulsa M,D
University of Utah D
University of Vermont D
University of Virginia M,D,O
University of Washington D
University of Wisconsin–Madison D
University of Wisconsin–Milwaukee M,D
Utah State University M,D
Valdosta State University M,O
Valparaiso University M,O
Vanguard University of Southern California M
Virginia Commonwealth University D
Virginia Polytechnic Institute and State University M,D
Virginia State University M,D
Walden University M,D,O

Washburn University M
Washington State University M,D
Washington University in St. Louis D
Wayne State University M,D,O
West Chester University of Pennsylvania M,O
Western Illinois University M,O
Western Michigan University M,D
West Virginia University M,D
Wheaton College M,D
Wichita State University M,D
Widener University D
William Paterson University of New Jersey M
Wright State University D
Xavier University M,D
Yale University D
Yeshiva University D

■ CLINICAL RESEARCH

Case Western Reserve University M
Duke University M
Eastern Michigan University M,O
Emory University M
The Johns Hopkins University M,D
New York University P,M,D
Northwestern University M,O
Tufts University M,D
University of California, Berkeley O
University of California, Davis M
University of California, Los Angeles M
University of California, San Diego M
University of Connecticut M
University of Florida M
The University of Iowa M,D
University of Louisville M,O
University of Michigan M
University of Minnesota, Twin Cities Campus M
University of Pittsburgh M,D,O
University of Southern California M,D,O
University of South Florida M,D
University of Virginia M
University of Washington M,D
University of Wisconsin–Madison M,D
Vanderbilt University M
Walden University M,D
Washington University in St. Louis M

■ CLOTHING AND TEXTILES

Auburn University M
Central Michigan University M,O
Cornell University M,D
Eastern Michigan University M
Iowa State University of Science and Technology M,D
Kansas State University M,D
North Carolina State University D
The Ohio State University M,D
Oklahoma State University M,D
Oregon State University M,D
Philadelphia University M
Purdue University M,D
South Dakota State University M
The University of Akron M
The University of Alabama M
University of California, Davis M
University of Georgia M,D
University of Kentucky M
University of Minnesota, Twin Cities Campus M,D,O
University of Missouri–Columbia M
University of North Texas M
University of Rhode Island M
The University of Tennessee M,D
Virginia Polytechnic Institute and State University M,D
Washington State University M,D

■ COGNITIVE SCIENCES

Arizona State University D
Ball State University M
Boston University M,D
Brandeis University M,D
Brown University M,D
Carnegie Mellon University D
Case Western Reserve University M
Claremont Graduate University M,D,O
Cornell University D
Dartmouth College D
Duke University D
Emory University D
Florida State University D
The George Washington University D
Graduate School and University Center of the City University of New York D
Harvard University M,D
Hunter College of the City University of New York M
Indiana University Bloomington M,D
Iowa State University of Science and Technology D
The Johns Hopkins University D
Louisiana State University and Agricultural and Mechanical College M,D
Loyola University Chicago M
Massachusetts Institute of Technology D
Mississippi State University M,D
New York University M,D,O
North Dakota State University M,D
Northwestern University D
The Ohio State University M,D
Penn State University Park M,D
Rensselaer Polytechnic Institute D
Rice University M,D
Rutgers, The State University of New Jersey, Newark D
Rutgers, The State University of New Jersey, New Brunswick D
State University of New York at Binghamton M,D
Temple University D
Texas A&M University M,D
Texas A&M University–Commerce M,D
University at Buffalo, the State University of New York M,D
The University of Akron M,D
University of California, San Diego D
University of California, Santa Barbara M,D
University of Connecticut M,D,O
University of Delaware D
University of Florida M,D
The University of Kansas M,D
University of Louisiana at Lafayette D
University of Maryland, Baltimore County D
University of Maryland, College Park D
University of Massachusetts Amherst M,D
University of Minnesota, Twin Cities Campus D
University of Nebraska–Lincoln M,D,O
University of Nevada, Reno M,D
The University of North Carolina at Chapel Hill D
The University of North Carolina at Greensboro M,D
University of Notre Dame D
University of Oregon M,D
University of Pittsburgh D
University of Rochester M,D
University of Southern California M,D
University of South Florida M,D
The University of Texas at Austin M,D
The University of Texas at Dallas M,D
The University of Toledo M,D
University of Washington D
University of Wisconsin–Madison D
Wayne State University M,D
Yale University D

■ COMMUNICATION—GENERAL

Abilene Christian University M
American University M
Andrews University M
Angelo State University M
Arizona State University M,D
Arkansas State University M,O
Arkansas Tech University M
Auburn University M

M—master's degree; P—first professional degree; D—doctorate; O—other advanced degree

Institution	Degrees
Austin Peay State University	M
Ball State University	M
Barry University	M,O
Baylor University	M
Bellarmine University	M
Bethel University	M,O
Boise State University	M
Boston University	M
Bowling Green State University	M,D
Brandeis University	M,O
Brigham Young University	M
California State University, Chico	M
California State University, East Bay	M
California State University, Fresno	M
California State University, Fullerton	M
California State University, Long Beach	M
California State University, Los Angeles	M
California State University, Northridge	M
California State University, Sacramento	M
California State University, San Bernardino	M
Carnegie Mellon University	M,D
Central Connecticut State University	M,O
Central Michigan University	M
Clarion University of Pennsylvania	M
Clark University	M
Clemson University	M,D
Cleveland State University	M,O
The College at Brockport, State University of New York	M
College of Charleston	M
The College of New Rochelle	M,O
College of Notre Dame of Maryland	M
Columbia University	M,D
Cornell University	M,D
DePaul University	M
Drake University	M
Drexel University	M
Drury University	M
Duquesne University	M,D
Eastern Michigan University	M
Eastern New Mexico University	M
Eastern Washington University	M
East Tennessee State University	M
Edinboro University of Pennsylvania	M
Emerson College	M
Fairfield University	M
Fairleigh Dickinson University, Metropolitan Campus	M
Fitchburg State College	M,O
Florida Atlantic University	M,O
Florida Institute of Technology	M
Florida State University	M,D
Fordham University	M
Fort Hays State University	M
George Mason University	M,D
Georgetown University	M
The George Washington University	M
Georgia State University	M,D
Gonzaga University	M
Governors State University	M
Grand Valley State University	M
Harvard University	M,O
Hawai'i Pacific University	M
Hofstra University	M
Howard University	M,D
Illinois Institute of Technology	M,D
Illinois State University	M
Immaculata University	M
Indiana State University	M
Indiana University Bloomington	M,D
Indiana University of Pennsylvania	M,D
Indiana University–Purdue University Fort Wayne	M
Ithaca College	M
The Johns Hopkins University	M
Kansas State University	M
Kean University	M
Kent State University	M,D
La Sierra University	M
Liberty University	M
Lindenwood University	M,O
Louisiana State University and Agricultural and Mechanical College	M,D
Marquette University	M
Marshall University	M
Marywood University	M,O
Miami University	M
Michigan State University	M,D
Mississippi College	M
Missouri State University	M
Monmouth University	M,O
Montana State University–Billings	M
Montclair State University	M
Morehead State University	M
National University	M
New Mexico State University	M
The New School: A University	M
New York Institute of Technology	M
New York University	M,D
Norfolk State University	M
North Carolina State University	M
North Dakota State University	M,D
Northeastern State University	M
Northern Arizona University	M
Northern Illinois University	M
Northern Kentucky University	M
Northwestern University	M,D
The Ohio State University	M,D
Ohio University	M,D
Our Lady of the Lake University of San Antonio	M
Penn State University Park	M,D
Pepperdine University	M
Pittsburg State University	M
Point Park University	M
Polytechnic Institute of NYU	O
Purdue University	M,D
Purdue University Calumet	M
Quinnipiac University	M
Regent University	M,D
Regis University	M,O
Rensselaer Polytechnic Institute	M,D
Rochester Institute of Technology	M
Roosevelt University	M
Rutgers, The State University of New Jersey, New Brunswick	D
Saginaw Valley State University	M
St. John's University (NY)	M,D,O
Saint Louis University	M
St. Mary's University (United States)	M
St. Thomas University	M,D,O
San Diego State University	M
San Jose State University	M
Seton Hall University	M
Shippensburg University of Pennsylvania	M
South Dakota State University	M
Southeastern Louisiana University	M
Southern Illinois University Carbondale	M,D
Southern Methodist University	M
Southern Polytechnic State University	M,O
Southern Utah University	M
Spalding University	M
Spring Arbor University	M
Stanford University	M,D
State University of New York College at Potsdam	M
State University of New York College of Environmental Science and Forestry	M,D
Stephen F. Austin State University	M
Stevens Institute of Technology	M,D,O
Suffolk University	M
Syracuse University	M,D
Temple University	M,D
Texas A&M University	M,D
Texas Southern University	M
Texas State University–San Marcos	M
Texas Tech University	M
Towson University	M,O
Trinity International University	M
Trinity (Washington) University	M
Troy University	M
University at Albany, State University of New York	M,D
University at Buffalo, the State University of New York	M,D
The University of Akron	M
The University of Alabama	M,D

The University of Alabama at Birmingham M
University of Alaska Fairbanks M
The University of Arizona M,D
University of Arkansas M
University of California, Davis M
University of California, San Diego M,D
University of California, Santa Barbara D
University of California, Santa Cruz O
University of Central Florida M
University of Central Missouri M
University of Cincinnati M
University of Colorado at Boulder M,D
University of Colorado at Colorado Springs M
University of Colorado Denver M
University of Connecticut M,D
University of Dayton M
University of Delaware M
University of Denver M,D,O
University of Dubuque M
University of Florida M,D
University of Georgia M,D
University of Hartford M
University of Hawaii at Manoa M,O
University of Houston M
University of Illinois at Chicago M,D
University of Illinois at Springfield M
University of Illinois at Urbana–Champaign M,D
The University of Iowa M,D
The University of Kansas M,D
University of Kentucky M,D
University of Louisiana at Lafayette M
University of Louisiana at Monroe M
University of Maine M
University of Maryland, Baltimore County M
University of Maryland, College Park M,D
University of Massachusetts Amherst M,D
University of Memphis M,D
University of Miami M,D
University of Michigan D
University of Minnesota, Twin Cities Campus M,D,O
University of Missouri–Columbia M,D
University of Missouri–St. Louis M
The University of Montana M
University of Nebraska at Omaha M
University of Nebraska–Lincoln M,D
University of Nevada, Las Vegas M
University of New Mexico M,D
The University of North Carolina at Chapel Hill M,D
The University of North Carolina at Charlotte M
The University of North Carolina at Greensboro M
University of North Dakota M,D
University of Northern Colorado M
University of Northern Iowa M
University of North Texas M
University of Oklahoma M,D
University of Oregon M,D
University of Pennsylvania D
University of Pittsburgh M,D
University of Portland M
University of Rhode Island M
University of South Alabama M
The University of South Dakota M
University of Southern California M,D
University of South Florida M,D
The University of Tennessee M,D
The University of Texas at Arlington M
The University of Texas at Austin M,D
The University of Texas at Dallas M,D
The University of Texas at El Paso M
The University of Texas at San Antonio M
The University of Texas at Tyler M
The University of Texas–Pan American M
University of the Incarnate Word M,O
University of the Pacific M
The University of Toledo O
University of Utah M,D
University of Vermont M
University of Washington M,D
University of West Florida M
University of Wisconsin–Madison M,D
University of Wisconsin–Milwaukee M,D,O
University of Wisconsin–Stevens Point M
University of Wisconsin–Superior M
University of Wisconsin–Whitewater M
University of Wyoming M
Utah State University M
Villanova University M
Virginia Commonwealth University D
Virginia Polytechnic Institute and State University M
Wake Forest University M
Washington State University M,D
Wayne State College M
Wayne State University M,D
Webster University M
West Chester University of Pennsylvania M
Western Illinois University M
Western Kentucky University M
Western Michigan University M
Westminster College (UT) M
West Texas A&M University M
West Virginia University M,D
Wichita State University M
William Paterson University of New Jersey M

■ COMMUNICATION DISORDERS

Abilene Christian University M
Adelphi University M,D
Alabama Agricultural and Mechanical University M
Appalachian State University M
Arizona State University M,D
Arkansas State University M
Armstrong Atlantic State University M
Auburn University M,D
Ball State University M,D
Barry University M
Baylor University M
Bloomsburg University of Pennsylvania M,D
Boston University M,D,O
Bowling Green State University M,D
Brigham Young University M
Brooklyn College of the City University of New York M,D
Buffalo State College, State University of New York M
California State University, Chico M
California State University, East Bay M
California State University, Fresno M
California State University, Fullerton M
California State University, Long Beach M
California State University, Los Angeles M
California State University, Northridge M
California State University, Sacramento M
California University of Pennsylvania M
Canisius College M
Carlos Albizu University M,D
Case Western Reserve University M,D
Central Michigan University M,D
Chapman University M
Clarion University of Pennsylvania M
Cleveland State University M
The College of Saint Rose M
Duquesne University M,D
East Carolina University M,D
Eastern Illinois University M
Eastern Kentucky University M
Eastern Michigan University M

M—master's degree; P—first professional degree; D—doctorate; O—other advanced degree

Eastern New Mexico University M
Eastern Washington University M
East Stroudsburg University of Pennsylvania M
East Tennessee State University M,D
Edinboro University of Pennsylvania M
Emerson College M
Florida Atlantic University M
Florida International University M
Florida State University M,D
Fontbonne University M
Fort Hays State University M
Gallaudet University M,D,O
The George Washington University M
Georgia State University M
Governors State University M
Graduate School and University Center of the City University of New York D
Hampton University M
Harding University M
Harvard University D
Hofstra University M,D
Howard University M,D
Hunter College of the City University of New York M
Idaho State University M,D,O
Illinois State University M
Indiana University Bloomington M,D
Indiana University of Pennsylvania M
Indiana University–Purdue University Fort Wayne M
Ithaca College M
Jackson State University M
James Madison University M,D
Kean University M
Kent State University M,D
Lamar University M,D
La Salle University M
Lehman College of the City University of New York M
Lewis & Clark College M
Long Island University, Brooklyn Campus M
Long Island University, C.W. Post Campus M
Longwood University M
Louisiana State University and Agricultural and Mechanical College M,D
Louisiana Tech University M
Loyola University Maryland M,O
Marquette University M
Marshall University M
Marywood University M
Massachusetts Institute of Technology D
Mercy College M
Miami University M
Michigan State University M,D
Minnesota State University Mankato M
Minnesota State University Moorhead M
Minot State University M
Misericordia University M
Mississippi University for Women M,O
Missouri State University M,D
Montclair State University M,D
Murray State University M
National University M
Nazareth College of Rochester M
New Mexico State University M,D
New York University M,D
North Carolina Central University M
Northeastern State University M
Northeastern University M,D
Northern Arizona University M
Northern Illinois University M,D
Northwestern University M,D
Nova Southeastern University M,D
The Ohio State University M,D
Ohio University M,D
Oklahoma State University M
Old Dominion University M
Our Lady of the Lake University of San Antonio M
Penn State University Park M,D
Portland State University M
Purdue University M,D
Queens College of the City University of New York M
Radford University M
Rockhurst University M
St. Cloud State University M
Saint Louis University M
Saint Xavier University M
San Diego State University M,D
San Francisco State University M
San Jose State University M
Seton Hall University M
South Carolina State University M
Southeastern Louisiana University M
Southeast Missouri State University M
Southern Connecticut State University M
Southern Illinois University Carbondale M
Southern Illinois University Edwardsville M
State University of New York at Fredonia M
State University of New York at New Paltz M
State University of New York at Plattsburgh M
State University of New York College at Geneseo M
Stephen F. Austin State University M
Syracuse University M,D
Temple University M
Tennessee State University M
Texas A&M University–Kingsville M
Texas Christian University M
Texas State University–San Marcos M
Texas Woman's University M
Touro College M,D
Towson University M,D
Truman State University M
Universidad del Turabo M
University at Buffalo, the State University of New York M,D
The University of Akron M,D
The University of Alabama M
The University of Arizona M,D
University of Arkansas M
University of California, San Diego D
University of Central Arkansas M,D
University of Central Florida M,D,O
University of Central Missouri M
University of Central Oklahoma M
University of Cincinnati M,D,O
University of Colorado at Boulder M,D
University of Connecticut M,D
University of Florida M,D
University of Georgia M,D,O
University of Hawaii at Manoa M
University of Houston M
University of Illinois at Urbana–Champaign M,D
The University of Iowa M,D
The University of Kansas M,D
University of Kentucky M
University of Louisiana at Lafayette M,D
University of Louisiana at Monroe M
University of Louisville M,D
University of Maine M
University of Maryland, College Park M,D
University of Massachusetts Amherst M,D
University of Memphis M,D
University of Minnesota, Duluth M
University of Minnesota, Twin Cities Campus M,D
University of Mississippi M
University of Missouri–Columbia M
University of Montevallo M
University of Nebraska at Kearney M
University of Nebraska at Omaha M
University of Nebraska–Lincoln M,D
University of Nevada, Reno M,D
University of New Hampshire M,O
University of New Mexico M
The University of North Carolina at Chapel Hill M,D
The University of North Carolina at Greensboro M,D
University of North Dakota M,D

University of Northern Colorado M,D
University of Northern Iowa M
University of North Florida M
University of North Texas M,D
University of Pittsburgh M,D
University of Redlands M
University of Rhode Island M,D
University of South Alabama M,D
University of South Carolina M,D
The University of South Dakota M,D
University of Southern Mississippi M,D
University of South Florida M,D
The University of Tennessee M,D,O
The University of Texas at Austin M,D
The University of Texas at Dallas M,D
The University of Texas at El Paso M
The University of Texas–Pan American M
University of the District of Columbia M
University of the Pacific M
The University of Toledo M
University of Tulsa M
University of Utah M,D
University of Virginia M
University of Washington M,D
University of West Georgia M,O
University of Wisconsin–Eau Claire M
University of Wisconsin–Madison M,D
University of Wisconsin–Milwaukee M,O
University of Wisconsin–River Falls M
University of Wisconsin–Stevens Point M,D
University of Wisconsin–Whitewater M
University of Wyoming M
Utah State University M,D,O
Vanderbilt University M,D
Washington University in St. Louis M,D
Wayne State University M,D
West Chester University of Pennsylvania M,O
Western Carolina University M
Western Illinois University M
Western Kentucky University M
Western Michigan University M,D
Western Washington University M
West Texas A&M University M
West Virginia University M,D
Wichita State University M,D
William Paterson University of New Jersey M
Worcester State College M

■ COMMUNITY COLLEGE EDUCATION

Argosy University, Orange County M,D
Argosy University, Tampa M,D,O
Arkansas State University M,D,O
California State University, Stanislaus M,D
Central Michigan University M
Colorado State University M,D
George Mason University M,D,O
Mississippi State University M,D,O
Morgan State University D
North Carolina State University M,D
Northern Arizona University M,D
Old Dominion University M,D
Pittsburg State University O
University of Central Florida M,D,O
University of South Florida M,D,O
Walden University M,D,O
Western Carolina University M

■ COMMUNITY HEALTH

Adelphi University M,O
Arcadia University M
Arizona State University M,D,O
Austin Peay State University M
Bloomsburg University of Pennsylvania M
Brooklyn College of the City University of New York M
Brown University M,D
The Catholic University of America M,D,O
The College at Brockport, State University of New York M
Columbia University M,D
Duquesne University M
Eastern Kentucky University M
East Stroudsburg University of Pennsylvania M
East Tennessee State University M,O
George Mason University M,O
The George Washington University M
Georgia Southern University M,D
Hofstra University M
Hunter College of the City University of New York M
Idaho State University O
Indiana State University M
The Johns Hopkins University M,D
Kean University
Long Island University, Brooklyn Campus M
Minnesota State University Mankato M
New Jersey City University M
New Mexico State University M
Old Dominion University M
Saint Louis University M
Southern Illinois University Carbondale M
Southern New Hampshire University M,O
Stony Brook University, State University of New York M,D
Temple University M
Texas Woman's University M,D
University at Buffalo, the State University of New York M,D
The University of Alabama M
University of California, Los Angeles M,D
University of Illinois at Chicago M,D
University of Illinois at Urbana–Champaign M,D
The University of Iowa M,D
University of Minnesota, Twin Cities Campus M
University of Nevada, Las Vegas M,O
The University of North Carolina at Greensboro M,D
University of Northern Iowa M,D
University of North Florida M,O
University of North Texas M,D
University of Phoenix M
University of Phoenix–Hawaii Campus M
University of Pittsburgh M,D,O
University of South Florida M,D
The University of Tennessee M,D
University of Virginia M,D
University of Washington M,D
University of Wisconsin–La Crosse M
University of Wyoming M,D
Virginia Commonwealth University D
Virginia State University M,D
Walden University M,D
Wayne State University M,O
West Virginia University M

■ COMMUNITY HEALTH NURSING

Arizona State University M,D,O
Augsburg College M
Boston College M,D
Case Western Reserve University M
The Catholic University of America M,D,O
Cleveland State University M
D'Youville College M,O
Georgia Southern University M,D,O
Hampton University M
Hawai'i Pacific University M
Holy Family University M
Holy Names University M,O
Hunter College of the City University of New York M
Husson University M,O

M—master's degree; P—first professional degree; D—doctorate; O—other advanced degree

Indiana University–Purdue University Indianapolis M,D
Indiana Wesleyan University M,O
The Johns Hopkins University M
Kean University M
New Mexico State University M
Rutgers, The State University of New Jersey, Newark M
Saint Xavier University M,O
Seattle University M
University of Cincinnati M,D
University of Colorado at Colorado Springs M,D
University of Hartford M
University of Hawaii at Manoa M,D,O
University of Illinois at Chicago M
The University of Kansas M,D,O
University of Massachusetts Dartmouth M,D,O
University of Michigan M,O
University of Minnesota, Twin Cities Campus M
The University of North Carolina at Chapel Hill M
University of South Alabama M,D
University of South Carolina M
University of Southern Mississippi M,D
The University of Texas at Brownsville M
Wayne State University M
Worcester State College M
Wright State University M

■ COMPARATIVE AND INTERDISCIPLINARY ARTS

Bradley University M
Brigham Young University M
Columbia College Chicago M
Florida Atlantic University D
Goddard College M
John F. Kennedy University M
Ohio University D

■ COMPARATIVE LITERATURE

American University M
Antioch University McGregor M
Arizona State University M,D
Brigham Young University M
Brown University D
California State University, Fullerton M
California State University, Northridge M
Carnegie Mellon University M,D
Case Western Reserve University M
The Catholic University of America M
Claremont Graduate University M,D
Columbia University M,D
Cornell University D
Dartmouth College M
Duke University D
Emory University D,O
Fairleigh Dickinson University, Metropolitan Campus M
Florida Atlantic University M
Georgetown University M,D
Graduate School and University Center of the City University of New York M,D
Harvard University D
Hofstra University M
Indiana State University M
Indiana University Bloomington M,D
The Johns Hopkins University D
Kent State University M,D
Long Island University, Brooklyn Campus M
Louisiana State University and Agricultural and Mechanical College M,D
New York University M,D
Northwestern University M,D,O
Oklahoma City University M
Penn State University Park M,D
Princeton University D
Purdue University M,D
Rutgers, The State University of New Jersey, New Brunswick M,D
San Francisco State University M
San Jose State University M,O
Stanford University D
State University of New York at Binghamton M,D
Stony Brook University, State University of New York M,D
University at Buffalo, the State University of New York M,D
University of Arkansas M,D
University of California, Berkeley D
University of California, Davis D
University of California, Irvine M,D
University of California, Los Angeles M,D
University of California, Riverside M,D
University of California, San Diego M,D
University of California, Santa Barbara D
University of California, Santa Cruz M,D
University of Chicago M,D
University of Colorado at Boulder M,D
University of Connecticut M,D
University of Dallas D
University of Georgia M,D
University of Illinois at Urbana–Champaign M,D
The University of Iowa M,D
University of Maryland, College Park M,D
University of Massachusetts Amherst M,D
University of Michigan D
University of Minnesota, Twin Cities Campus D
University of Missouri–Columbia M,D
University of Nebraska–Lincoln M,D
University of New Hampshire M,D
University of New Mexico M,D
The University of North Carolina at Chapel Hill M,D
University of Notre Dame D
University of Oregon M,D
University of Pennsylvania M,D
University of Puerto Rico, Río Piedras M
University of South Carolina M,D
University of Southern California M,D
The University of Texas at Austin M,D
The University of Texas at Dallas M,D
University of Utah M,D
University of Washington M,D
University of Wisconsin–Madison M,D
University of Wisconsin–Milwaukee M,D,O
Washington University in St. Louis M,D
Wayne State University M
Western Kentucky University M
Yale University D

■ COMPUTATIONAL BIOLOGY

Arizona State University M
Carnegie Mellon University M,D
Claremont Graduate University M,D
Cornell University D
Florida State University D
George Mason University M,D,O
Iowa State University of Science and Technology D
Massachusetts Institute of Technology D
New Jersey Institute of Technology M
New York University D
Northwestern University M
Princeton University D
Rutgers, The State University of New Jersey, Newark M
Rutgers, The State University of New Jersey, New Brunswick D
University of Idaho M,D
University of Illinois at Urbana–Champaign M,D
The University of Iowa M,D,O
University of Pennsylvania D
University of Pittsburgh D
University of Rochester M,D
University of Southern California M,D
University of Wyoming D
Virginia Polytechnic Institute and State University D
Washington University in St. Louis D
Yale University D

■ COMPUTATIONAL SCIENCES

California Institute of Technology	M,D
Carnegie Mellon University	M,D
Claremont Graduate University	M,D
Clemson University	M,D
The College at Brockport, State University of New York	M
The College of William and Mary	M
Cornell University	M,D
George Mason University	M,D,O
Hampton University	M
Kean University	M
Lehigh University	M,D
Louisiana Tech University	M,D
Marquette University	M,D
Massachusetts Institute of Technology	M
Michigan Technological University	D
Northwestern University	M
Princeton University	D
Rice University	M,D
Sam Houston State University	M
San Diego State University	M,D
South Dakota State University	M,D
Southern Methodist University	M,D
Stanford University	M,D
Temple University	M,D
University of Alaska Fairbanks	M,D
University of California, Santa Barbara	M,D
University of Central Florida	M,D
The University of Iowa	D
The University of Kansas	M,D
University of Massachusetts Lowell	M,D
University of Michigan–Dearborn	M
University of Minnesota, Duluth	M
University of Minnesota, Twin Cities Campus	M,D
University of Mississippi	M,D
University of New Mexico	O
University of Pennsylvania	D
University of Puerto Rico, Mayagüez Campus	M
The University of South Dakota	M,D
University of Southern Mississippi	M,D
University of South Florida	M,D
The University of Tennessee at Chattanooga	M,D
The University of Texas at Austin	M,D
University of Utah	M
University of Washington	M,D
Western Michigan University	M

■ COMPUTER AND INFORMATION SYSTEMS SECURITY

American InterContinental University South Florida	M
Benedictine University	M
Brandeis University	M,O
Capella University	M,D,O
Carnegie Mellon University	M
The Catholic University of America	M,D
City University of Seattle	M,O
Colorado Technical University Colorado Springs	M,D
Colorado Technical University Denver	M
Colorado Technical University Sioux Falls	M
Davenport University	M
DePaul University	M,D
Eastern Illinois University	M,O
Eastern Michigan University	M,O
Florida State University	M,D
George Mason University	M,D,O
Georgia Institute of Technology	M,D
The Johns Hopkins University	M,O
Jones International University	M
Lewis University	M
Marymount University	M,O
Mercy College	M
Northern Kentucky University	M,O
Nova Southeastern University	M,D
Our Lady of the Lake University of San Antonio	M
Polytechnic Institute of NYU	O
Purdue University	M
Regis University	M,O
Robert Morris University	M,D
Rochester Institute of Technology	M,O
Sacred Heart University	M,O
St. Cloud State University	M
Saint Leo University	M
Southern Polytechnic State University	M,O
Stevens Institute of Technology	M,D,O
Strayer University	M
Syracuse University	O
Towson University	D,O
University of Minnesota, Twin Cities Campus	M
University of St. Thomas (MN)	M,O
University of Southern California	M,D
The University of Texas at Dallas	M
University of Wisconsin–Madison	M
West Chester University of Pennsylvania	M,O
Wilmington University	M
Worcester Polytechnic Institute	M,O

■ COMPUTER ART AND DESIGN

Alfred University	M
Arizona State University	M
Bowling Green State University	M
Carnegie Mellon University	M,D
The Catholic University of America	M
Chatham University	M
Claremont Graduate University	M
Clemson University	M
Cornell University	M,D
DePaul University	M,D
Drexel University	M
East Tennessee State University	M
Florida Atlantic University	M
Georgia Institute of Technology	M,D
Indiana University Bloomington	M,D
Long Island University, Brooklyn Campus	M
Long Island University, C.W. Post Campus	M
Michigan State University	M
Mississippi State University	M
National University	M
The New School: A University	M
New York University	M
North Carolina State University	D
Philadelphia University	M
Regent University	M,D
Rensselaer Polytechnic Institute	M,D
Rochester Institute of Technology	M
St. Edward's University	M
San Jose State University	M
Stevens Institute of Technology	M,D,O
Syracuse University	M
Texas State University–San Marcos	M
University of Alaska Fairbanks	M
University of Baltimore	M,D
University of California, Santa Cruz	M
University of Central Arkansas	M
University of Central Florida	M
University of Denver	M
University of Florida	M,D
The University of Kansas	M
University of Massachusetts Dartmouth	M
University of Missouri–Columbia	M
University of Pennsylvania	M
University of Southern California	M
Washington State University	M

■ COMPUTER EDUCATION

Arcadia University	M,D,O
California State University, Dominguez Hills	M,O
Cardinal Stritch University	M
DeSales University	M
Eastern Washington University	M
Florida Institute of Technology	M,D,O
Fontbonne University	M
Indiana University–Purdue University Indianapolis	M,O
Jacksonville University	M
Kean University	M
Lesley University	M,D,O
Long Island University, C.W. Post Campus	M
Mississippi College	M,D,O

M—master's degree; P—first professional degree; D—doctorate; O—other advanced degree

Nova Southeastern University M,D,O
Ohio University M,D
Southern New Hampshire University M,O
Stanford University M,D
State University of New York College at Potsdam M
Stony Brook University, State University of New York M
University of Bridgeport M,O
University of Central Oklahoma M
University of Detroit Mercy M
University of Michigan M,D
University of North Texas M,D
University of Phoenix M
University of Phoenix–Central Florida Campus M
University of Phoenix–North Florida Campus M
University of Phoenix–Phoenix Campus M
University of Phoenix–San Diego Campus M
University of Phoenix–South Florida Campus M
University of Phoenix–West Florida Campus M
Wilkes University M,D
Wright State University M

■ COMPUTER ENGINEERING

Arizona State University M
Auburn University M,D
Baylor University M
Boise State University M,D
Boston University M,D
Brown University M,D
California State University, Chico M
California State University, East Bay M
California State University, Long Beach M
Carnegie Mellon University M,D
Case Western Reserve University M,D
Clarkson University M,D
Clemson University M,D
Colorado Technical University Colorado Springs M
Colorado Technical University Denver M
Columbia University M,D,O
Cornell University M,D
Dartmouth College M,D
Drexel University M
Duke University M,D
Fairfield University M
Fairleigh Dickinson University, Metropolitan Campus M
Florida Atlantic University M,D
Florida Institute of Technology M,D
Florida International University M
George Mason University M,D,O
The George Washington University M,D
Georgia Institute of Technology M,D
Grand Valley State University M
Illinois Institute of Technology M,D
Indiana State University M
Indiana University–Purdue University Fort Wayne M
Indiana University–Purdue University Indianapolis M,D
Iowa State University of Science and Technology M,D
The Johns Hopkins University M,D,O
Kansas State University M,D
Lawrence Technological University M,D
Lehigh University M,D
Louisiana State University and Agricultural and Mechanical College M,D
Manhattan College M
Marquette University M,D
Mercer University M
Michigan Technological University D
Mississippi State University M,D
Missouri University of Science and Technology M,D
Montana State University M,D
New Jersey Institute of Technology M,D
New Mexico State University M,D
New York Institute of Technology M
Norfolk State University M
North Carolina Agricultural and Technical State University M,D
North Carolina State University M,D
North Dakota State University M,D
Northeastern University M,D
Northwestern University M,D,O
Oakland University M
The Ohio State University M,D
Oklahoma State University M,D
Old Dominion University M,D
Oregon State University M,D
Penn State University Park M,D
Polytechnic Institute of NYU M,O
Polytechnic Institute of NYU, Westchester Graduate Center M
Portland State University M,D
Purdue University M,D
Purdue University Calumet M
Rensselaer Polytechnic Institute M,D
Rice University M,D
Rochester Institute of Technology M
Rutgers, The State University of New Jersey, New Brunswick M,D
St. Mary's University (United States) M
San Jose State University M
Santa Clara University M,D,O
Southern Illinois University Carbondale M,D
Southern Methodist University M,D
Southern Polytechnic State University M
State University of New York at New Paltz M
Stevens Institute of Technology M,D,O
Stony Brook University, State University of New York M,D,O
Syracuse University M,D,O
Temple University M
Texas A&M University M,D
The University of Akron M,D
The University of Alabama M,D
The University of Alabama at Birmingham D
The University of Alabama in Huntsville M,D
University of Alaska Fairbanks M,D
The University of Arizona M,D
University of Arkansas M,D
University of Bridgeport M,D
University of California, Davis M,D
University of California, Riverside M,D
University of California, San Diego M,D
University of California, Santa Barbara M,D
University of California, Santa Cruz M,D
University of Central Florida M,D
University of Cincinnati M,D
University of Colorado at Boulder M,D
University of Colorado Denver M,D
University of Dayton M,D
University of Delaware M,D
University of Denver M
University of Detroit Mercy M,D
University of Florida M,D,O
University of Houston M,D
University of Houston–Clear Lake M
University of Idaho M
University of Illinois at Chicago M,D
University of Illinois at Urbana–Champaign M,D
The University of Iowa M,D
The University of Kansas M
University of Louisiana at Lafayette M,D
University of Louisville M,D
University of Maine M,D
University of Maryland, Baltimore County M,D
University of Maryland, College Park M,D
University of Massachusetts Amherst M,D
University of Massachusetts Dartmouth M,D,O
University of Massachusetts Lowell M

University of Memphis	M,D
University of Miami	M,D
University of Michigan	M,D
University of Michigan–Dearborn	M
University of Minnesota, Duluth	M
University of Minnesota, Twin Cities Campus	M,D
University of Missouri–Kansas City	M,D
University of Nebraska–Lincoln	M,D
University of Nevada, Las Vegas	M,D
University of Nevada, Reno	M,D
University of New Mexico	M,D
The University of North Carolina at Charlotte	M,D
University of North Texas	M,D
University of Notre Dame	M,D
University of Oklahoma	M,D
University of Puerto Rico, Mayagüez Campus	M
University of Rhode Island	M,D
University of Rochester	M,D
University of South Carolina	M,D
University of Southern California	M,D,O
University of South Florida	M,D
The University of Tennessee	M,D
The University of Texas at Arlington	M,D
The University of Texas at Austin	M,D
The University of Texas at Dallas	M,D
The University of Texas at El Paso	M,D
The University of Texas at San Antonio	M,D
University of Virginia	M,D
University of Washington, Tacoma	M
University of Wisconsin–Milwaukee	M,D,O
Villanova University	M,O
Virginia Polytechnic Institute and State University	M,D
Washington State University	M,D
Washington University in St. Louis	M,D
Wayne State University	M,D
Western Michigan University	M,D
West Virginia University	D
Widener University	M
Worcester Polytechnic Institute	M,D,O
Wright State University	M,D
Youngstown State University	M

■ COMPUTER SCIENCE

Alabama Agricultural and Mechanical University	M
Alcorn State University	M
American University	M,O
Appalachian State University	M
Arizona State University	M,D
Arkansas State University	M
Armstrong Atlantic State University	M
Auburn University	M,D
Ball State University	M
Baylor University	M
Boise State University	M
Boston University	M,D
Bowie State University	M,D
Bowling Green State University	M
Bradley University	M
Brandeis University	M,D,O
Bridgewater State College	M
Brigham Young University	M,D
Brooklyn College of the City University of New York	M,D,O
Brown University	M,D
California Institute of Technology	M,D
California Polytechnic State University, San Luis Obispo	M
California State Polytechnic University, Pomona	M
California State University, Chico	M
California State University, Dominguez Hills	M
California State University, East Bay	M
California State University, Fresno	M
California State University, Fullerton	M
California State University, Long Beach	M
California State University, Los Angeles	M
California State University, Northridge	M
California State University, Sacramento	M
California State University, San Bernardino	M
California State University, San Marcos	M
Carnegie Mellon University	M,D
Case Western Reserve University	M,D
The Catholic University of America	M,D
Central Connecticut State University	M
Central Michigan University	M
Chicago State University	M
The Citadel, The Military College of South Carolina	M
City College of the City University of New York	M,D
Clark Atlanta University	M
Clarkson University	M
Clemson University	M,D
Cleveland State University	M,D
College of Charleston	M
The College of Saint Rose	M
College of Staten Island of the City University of New York	M
The College of William and Mary	M,D
Colorado School of Mines	M,D
Colorado State University	M,D
Colorado Technical University Colorado Springs	M,D
Colorado Technical University Denver	M
Colorado Technical University Sioux Falls	M
Columbia University	M,D,O
Columbus State University	M
Cornell University	M,D
Dartmouth College	M,D
DePaul University	M,D
Drexel University	M,D
Duke University	M,D
East Carolina University	M,D,O
Eastern Illinois University	M,O
Eastern Michigan University	M,O
Eastern Washington University	M
East Stroudsburg University of Pennsylvania	M
East Tennessee State University	M
Elmhurst College	M
Emory University	M,D
Fairleigh Dickinson University, Metropolitan Campus	M
Ferris State University	M
Fitchburg State College	M
Florida Atlantic University	M,D
Florida Gulf Coast University	M
Florida Institute of Technology	M,D
Florida International University	M,D
Florida State University	M,D
Fordham University	M
Frostburg State University	M
Gannon University	M
George Mason University	M,D,O
Georgetown University	M
The George Washington University	M,D
Georgia Institute of Technology	M,D
Georgia Southwestern State University	M
Georgia State University	M,D
Governors State University	M
Graduate School and University Center of the City University of New York	D
Grand Valley State University	M
Hampton University	M
Harvard University	M,D
Hofstra University	M
Hood College	M
Howard University	M
Illinois Institute of Technology	M,D
Indiana State University	M
Indiana University Bloomington	M,D
Indiana University–Purdue University Fort Wayne	M

M—master's degree; P—first professional degree; D—doctorate; O—other advanced degree

Institution	Degrees
Indiana University–Purdue University Indianapolis	M,D
Indiana University South Bend	M
Inter American University of Puerto Rico, Metropolitan Campus	M
Iona College	M
Iowa State University of Science and Technology	M,D
Jackson State University	M
Jacksonville State University	M
James Madison University	M
The Johns Hopkins University	M,D,O
Kansas State University	M,D
Kennesaw State University	M
Kent State University	M,D
Kutztown University of Pennsylvania	M
Lamar University	M
La Salle University	M
Lawrence Technological University	M
Lehigh University	M,D
Lehman College of the City University of New York	M
Long Island University, Brooklyn Campus	M
Long Island University, C.W. Post Campus	M
Louisiana State University and Agricultural and Mechanical College	M,D
Louisiana State University in Shreveport	M
Louisiana Tech University	M
Loyola Marymount University	M
Loyola University Chicago	M
Loyola University Maryland	M
Maharishi University of Management	M
Marist College	M,O
Marquette University	M,D
Massachusetts Institute of Technology	M,D,O
McNeese State University	M
Metropolitan State University	M
Michigan State University	M,D
Michigan Technological University	M,D
Middle Tennessee State University	M
Midwestern State University	M
Mills College	M,O
Minnesota State University Mankato	M,O
Mississippi College	M
Mississippi State University	M,D
Missouri State University	M
Missouri University of Science and Technology	M,D
Monmouth University	M
Montana State University	M,D
Montclair State University	M,D,O
National University	M
New Jersey Institute of Technology	M,D
New Mexico Highlands University	M
New Mexico Institute of Mining and Technology	M,D
New Mexico State University	M,D
New York Institute of Technology	M
New York University	M,D
Nicholls State University	M
Norfolk State University	M
North Carolina Agricultural and Technical State University	M
North Carolina State University	M,D
North Central College	M
North Dakota State University	M,D,O
Northeastern Illinois University	M
Northeastern University	M,D
Northern Arizona University	M
Northern Illinois University	M
Northern Kentucky University	M,O
Northwestern University	M,D,O
Northwest Missouri State University	M,O
Nova Southeastern University	M,D
Oakland University	M
The Ohio State University	M,D
Ohio University	M,D
Oklahoma City University	M
Oklahoma State University	M,D
Old Dominion University	M,D
Oregon State University	M,D
Pace University	M,D,O
Penn State Harrisburg	M
Penn State University Park	M,D
Polytechnic Institute of NYU	M,D
Polytechnic Institute of NYU, Westchester Graduate Center	M,D
Portland State University	M,D
Prairie View A&M University	M,D
Princeton University	M,D
Purdue University	M,D
Queens College of the City University of New York	M
Regis University	M,O
Rensselaer Polytechnic Institute	M,D
Rice University	M,D
Rivier College	M
Rochester Institute of Technology	M,D,O
Roosevelt University	M
Rutgers, The State University of New Jersey, Camden	M
Rutgers, The State University of New Jersey, New Brunswick	M,D
Sacred Heart University	M,O
St. Cloud State University	M
St. John's University (NY)	M
Saint Joseph's University	M,O
St. Mary's University (United States)	M
Saint Xavier University	M
Sam Houston State University	M
San Diego State University	M
San Francisco State University	M
San Jose State University	M
Santa Clara University	M,D,O
Shippensburg University of Pennsylvania	M
Southern Connecticut State University	M
Southern Illinois University Carbondale	M,D
Southern Illinois University Edwardsville	M
Southern Methodist University	M,D
Southern Oregon University	M
Southern Polytechnic State University	M,O
Southern University and Agricultural and Mechanical College	M
Stanford University	M,D
State University of New York at Binghamton	M,D
State University of New York at New Paltz	M
State University of New York Institute of Technology	M
Stephen F. Austin State University	M
Stevens Institute of Technology	M,D,O
Stony Brook University, State University of New York	M,D,O
Suffolk University	M
Syracuse University	M
Temple University	M,D
Tennessee Technological University	M
Texas A&M University	M,D
Texas A&M University–Commerce	M
Texas A&M University–Corpus Christi	M
Texas A&M University–Kingsville	M
Texas Southern University	M
Texas State University–San Marcos	M
Texas Tech University	M,D
Towson University	M
Troy University	M
Tufts University	M,D,O
University at Albany, State University of New York	M,D
University at Buffalo, the State University of New York	M,D
The University of Akron	M
The University of Alabama	M,D
The University of Alabama at Birmingham	M,D
The University of Alabama in Huntsville	M,D,O
University of Alaska Fairbanks	M
The University of Arizona	M,D

University of Arkansas M,D
University of Arkansas at Little Rock M
University of Bridgeport M,D
University of California, Berkeley M,D
University of California, Davis M,D
University of California, Irvine M,D
University of California, Los Angeles M,D
University of California, Riverside M,D
University of California, San Diego M,D
University of California, Santa Barbara M,D
University of California, Santa Cruz M,D
University of Central Arkansas M
University of Central Florida M,D
University of Central Oklahoma M
University of Chicago M
University of Cincinnati M,D
University of Colorado at Boulder M,D
University of Colorado at Colorado Springs M,D
University of Colorado Denver M,D
University of Connecticut M,D
University of Dayton M
University of Delaware M,D
University of Denver M,D,O
University of Detroit Mercy M
University of Evansville M
University of Florida M,D
University of Georgia M,D
University of Hawaii at Manoa M,D,O
University of Houston M,D
University of Houston–Clear Lake M
University of Houston–Victoria M
University of Idaho M,D
University of Illinois at Chicago M,D
University of Illinois at Springfield M
University of Illinois at Urbana–Champaign M,D
The University of Iowa M,D
The University of Kansas M,D
University of Kentucky M,D
University of Louisiana at Lafayette M,D
University of Louisville M,D
University of Maine M,D
University of Maryland, Baltimore County M,D
University of Maryland, College Park M,D
University of Maryland Eastern Shore M
University of Massachusetts Amherst M,D
University of Massachusetts Boston M,D
University of Massachusetts Dartmouth M,O
University of Massachusetts Lowell M,D
University of Memphis M,D
University of Miami M,D
University of Michigan M,D
University of Michigan–Dearborn M
University of Michigan–Flint M
University of Minnesota, Duluth M
University of Minnesota, Twin Cities Campus M,D
University of Missouri–Columbia M,D
University of Missouri–Kansas City M,D
University of Missouri–St. Louis M,D
The University of Montana M
University of Nebraska at Omaha M
University of Nebraska–Lincoln M,D
University of Nevada, Las Vegas M,D
University of Nevada, Reno M,D
University of New Hampshire M,D
University of New Haven M
University of New Mexico M,D
University of New Orleans M
The University of North Carolina at Chapel Hill M,D
The University of North Carolina at Charlotte M
The University of North Carolina at Greensboro M
The University of North Carolina Wilmington M
University of North Dakota M
University of Northern Iowa M
University of North Florida M
University of North Texas M,D
University of Notre Dame M,D
University of Oklahoma M,D
University of Oregon M,D
University of Pennsylvania M,D
University of Pittsburgh M,D
University of Rhode Island M,D,O
University of Rochester M,D
University of San Francisco M
University of South Alabama M
University of South Carolina M,D
The University of South Dakota M,D
University of Southern California M,D
University of Southern Maine M
University of Southern Mississippi M,D
University of South Florida M,D
The University of Tennessee M,D
The University of Tennessee at Chattanooga M,O
The University of Texas at Arlington M,D
The University of Texas at Austin M,D
The University of Texas at Dallas M,D
The University of Texas at El Paso M,D
The University of Texas at San Antonio M,D
The University of Texas at Tyler M
The University of Texas of the Permian Basin M
The University of Texas–Pan American M
The University of Toledo M,D
University of Tulsa M,D
University of Utah M,D
University of Vermont M,D
University of Virginia M,D
University of Washington M,D
University of West Florida M
University of West Georgia M,O
University of Wisconsin–Madison M,D
University of Wisconsin–Milwaukee M,D
University of Wisconsin–Platteville M
University of Wyoming M,D
Utah State University M,D
Vanderbilt University M,D
Villanova University M,O
Virginia Commonwealth University M,D,O
Virginia Polytechnic Institute and State University M,D
Virginia State University M
Wake Forest University M
Washington State University M,D
Washington University in St. Louis M,D
Wayne State University M,D,O
Webster University M,O
West Chester University of Pennsylvania M,O
Western Carolina University M
Western Illinois University M
Western Kentucky University M
Western Michigan University M,D
Western Washington University M
West Virginia University M,D
Wichita State University M
Worcester Polytechnic Institute M,D,O
Wright State University M,D
Yale University M,D
Youngstown State University M

■ CONDENSED MATTER PHYSICS

Cleveland State University M
Emory University D
Iowa State University of Science and Technology M,D
Rutgers, The State University of New Jersey, New Brunswick M,D
West Virginia University M,D

■ CONFLICT RESOLUTION AND MEDIATION/PEACE STUDIES

Abilene Christian University M,O
American University M,D,O

M—master's degree; P—first professional degree; D—doctorate; O—other advanced degree

Antioch University McGregor M
Arcadia University M
Brandeis University M
California State University, Dominguez Hills M
Cambridge College M
Chaminade University of Honolulu M
Colorado Technical University Colorado Springs M,D
Colorado Technical University Denver M
Columbia College (SC) M,O
Columbia University M
Cornell University M,D
Creighton University M,O
Dallas Baptist University M
Duquesne University M,O
Eastern Mennonite University M,O
Florida International University O
Fresno Pacific University M
George Mason University M,D
Georgetown University M
Jones International University M
Kennesaw State University M
Lipscomb University M,O
Montclair State University M,O
National University M
Norwich University M
Nova Southeastern University M,D
Old Dominion University M,D
Pepperdine University M
Portland State University M
Regis University M,O
St. Edward's University M,O
SIT Graduate Institute M
Southern Methodist University M,O
Sullivan University P,M
Syracuse University O
Tufts University M,D
University of Arkansas at Little Rock O
University of Baltimore M
University of Bridgeport M
University of Denver M
University of Hawaii at Manoa O
University of Massachusetts Amherst M,D
University of Massachusetts Boston M,O
University of Missouri–Columbia M
University of Missouri–St. Louis M
The University of North Carolina at Greensboro M,O
University of Notre Dame M,D
University of Pittsburgh M
University of San Diego M
University of Wisconsin–Milwaukee M,O
Walden University M,D,O
Wayne State University M,O

■ CONSERVATION BIOLOGY

Antioch University New England M
Central Michigan University M
Colorado State University M,D
Columbia University M,D,O
Frostburg State University M
Illinois State University M,D
North Dakota State University M,D
San Francisco State University M
State University of New York College of Environmental Science and Forestry M,D
Texas State University–San Marcos M
University at Albany, State University of New York M
University of Central Florida M,D,O
University of Hawaii at Manoa M,D
University of Illinois at Urbana–Champaign M,D
University of Maryland, College Park M
University of Michigan M,D
University of Minnesota, Twin Cities Campus M,D
University of Missouri–St. Louis M,D,O
University of Nevada, Reno D
University of South Florida M,D
University of Wisconsin–Madison M

■ CONSTRUCTION ENGINEERING

Arizona State University M
Auburn University M,D
Bradley University M
Columbia University M,D,O
Illinois Institute of Technology M,D
Iowa State University of Science and Technology M,D
Lawrence Technological University M,D
Massachusetts Institute of Technology M,D,O
Missouri University of Science and Technology M,D
Montana State University M,D
Ohio University M,D
Oregon State University M,D
Stevens Institute of Technology M,O
Texas A&M University M,D
The University of Alabama M,D
University of Central Florida M,D,O
University of Colorado at Boulder M,D
University of Florida M,D
University of Michigan M,D,O
University of Southern Mississippi M
University of Washington M,D
Virginia Polytechnic Institute and State University M
Western Michigan University M

■ CONSTRUCTION MANAGEMENT

Arizona State University M
Auburn University M
Bowling Green State University M
Brigham Young University M
Carnegie Mellon University M,D
The Catholic University of America M,D,O
Central Connecticut State University M,O
Clemson University M
Colorado State University M
Columbia University M,D,O
Drexel University M
Eastern Michigan University M
Florida International University M
Marquette University M,D
Michigan State University M,D
Missouri State University M
New York University M,O
North Carolina Agricultural and Technical State University M
North Dakota State University M
Philadelphia University M
Polytechnic Institute of NYU M
Roger Williams University M
Southern Polytechnic State University M
State University of New York College of Environmental Science and Forestry M,D
Stevens Institute of Technology M,O
Texas A&M University M,D
University of Arkansas at Little Rock M,O
University of California, Berkeley O
University of Denver M
University of Houston M
The University of Kansas M
University of Nevada, Las Vegas M
University of New Mexico M
University of Southern California M,D,O
University of Southern Mississippi M
University of Washington M
Western Carolina University M
Western Michigan University M
Worcester Polytechnic Institute M,D,O

■ CONSUMER ECONOMICS

California State University, Long Beach M
Colorado State University M
Cornell University M,D
Eastern Illinois University M
Indiana State University M
Iowa State University of Science and Technology M,D
Montana State University M
North Dakota State University M,D
The Ohio State University M,D
Oklahoma State University M,D
Purdue University M,D
State University of New York at Oswego M
Texas Tech University M,D

The University of Alabama	M
The University of Arizona	M,D
University of Georgia	M,D
University of Idaho	M
University of Illinois at Urbana–Champaign	M,D
University of Missouri–Columbia	M
University of South Carolina	M
The University of Tennessee	M,D
University of Utah	M
University of Wisconsin–Madison	M,D
University of Wyoming	M
Utah State University	M
Virginia Polytechnic Institute and State University	M,D

■ CORPORATE AND ORGANIZATIONAL COMMUNICATION

American International College	M
Antioch University Seattle	M
Barry University	M,O
Bernard M. Baruch College of the City University of New York	M
Bowie State University	M,O
California State University, San Bernardino	M
Canisius College	M
Carnegie Mellon University	M
Central Connecticut State University	M,O
Central Michigan University	M,O
College of Charleston	O
Columbia University	M
Concordia University Wisconsin	M
Dallas Baptist University	M
DePaul University	M
Drexel University	M
Emerson College	M
Fairleigh Dickinson University, College at Florham	M
Florida State University	M,D
Fordham University	M
Howard University	M,D
Illinois Institute of Technology	M
Iowa State University of Science and Technology	M,D
John Carroll University	M
Jones International University	M
La Salle University	M
Loyola University Chicago	M
Marist College	M
Marywood University	M,O
Metropolitan College of New York	M
Mississippi College	M
Monmouth University	M,O
Montclair State University	M
Murray State University	M
National University	M
New Mexico State University	M,D
New York University	M
Northwestern University	M
Oklahoma City University	M
Queens University of Charlotte	M
Radford University	M
Regis College (MA)	M
Roosevelt University	M
Seton Hall University	M
Simmons College	M
Southern Illinois University Edwardsville	O
Southern Polytechnic State University	M,O
Spalding University	M
Stevens Institute of Technology	O
Suffolk University	M
Temple University	M,D
Towson University	M
University of Alaska Fairbanks	M
University of California, Berkeley	O
University of Central Florida	M
University of Connecticut	M,D
University of Nebraska–Lincoln	M,D
University of Portland	M
University of St. Thomas (MN)	M
University of Southern California	M,D
University of Wisconsin–Stevens Point	M
University of Wisconsin–Whitewater	M
Washington State University	M,D
Wayne State University	M,D
Webster University	M
Western Michigan University	M
West Virginia University	M,D

■ COUNSELING PSYCHOLOGY

Abilene Christian University	M
Adelphi University	M
Alabama Agricultural and Mechanical University	M,O
Alaska Pacific University	M
Amberton University	M
Andrews University	D
Angelo State University	M
Anna Maria College	M
Antioch University McGregor	M
Antioch University New England	M
Argosy University, Orange County	M,D
Argosy University, Sarasota	M,D,O
Argosy University, Tampa	M,D
Arizona State University	D
Assumption College	M,O
Auburn University	M,D,O
Avila University	M
Ball State University	M,D
Bemidji State University	M
Bethel University	M,O
Boston College	M,D
Boston University	D
Bowie State University	M
Bowling Green State University	M
Brigham Young University	M,D,O
Brooklyn College of the City University of New York	M,D,O
Caldwell College	M
California Baptist University	M
California Institute of Integral Studies	M,D
California State University, Bakersfield	M
California State University, Sacramento	M
California State University, San Bernardino	M
Cambridge College	M,O
Capella University	M,D,O
Carlow University	M
Centenary College	M
Central Michigan University	M,D,O
Central Washington University	M
Chaminade University of Honolulu	M
Chatham University	M,D
Chestnut Hill College	M,O
City College of the City University of New York	M
City University of Seattle	M
Cleveland State University	M,D,O
The College at Brockport, State University of New York	M,O
The College of New Rochelle	M,O
College of Saint Elizabeth	M,O
College of St. Joseph	M
College of Staten Island of the City University of New York	M
Colorado Christian University	M
Columbus State University	M,D,O
Concordia University Chicago	M
Concordia University Wisconsin	M
Dallas Baptist University	M
Dominican University of California	M
Eastern Nazarene College	M
Eastern University	M,O
Eastern Washington University	M
Emporia State University	M
Fairleigh Dickinson University, College at Florham	M
Fitchburg State College	M,O
Florida Atlantic University	M,D,O
Florida International University	M
Florida State University	M,D,O
Fordham University	M,D,O
Fort Valley State University	M
Franciscan University of Steubenville	M
Frostburg State University	M
Gallaudet University	M
Gannon University	D
Gardner-Webb University	M
Geneva College	M

M—master's degree; P—first professional degree; D—doctorate; O—other advanced degree

George Fox University	M,O
Georgian Court University	M,O
Georgia State University	M,D,O
Goddard College	M
Gonzaga University	M
Governors State University	M
Harding University	M
Heidelberg University	M
Hofstra University	M,O
Holy Family University	M
Holy Names University	M,O
Houston Baptist University	M
Howard University	M,D,O
Humboldt State University	M
Husson University	M
Idaho State University	M,D,O
Illinois State University	M,D,O
Immaculata University	M,D,O
Indiana State University	M,D,O
Indiana University Bloomington	M,D,O
Indiana Wesleyan University	M
Inter American University of Puerto Rico, San Germán Campus	M,D
Iona College	M
Iowa State University of Science and Technology	D
James Madison University	M,O
John Carroll University	M,O
John F. Kennedy University	M
Kean University	M
Kent State University	M
Kutztown University of Pennsylvania	M
La Salle University	M
Lee University	M
Lehigh University	M,D,O
Lesley University	M
Lewis & Clark College	M,O
Lewis University	M
Liberty University	M,D
Lindenwood University	M,D,O
Lipscomb University	M,O
Long Island University, Brentwood Campus	M
Louisiana State University in Shreveport	M
Louisiana Tech University	M,D
Loyola University Chicago	D
Loyola University Maryland	M,O
Marist College	M,O
Marylhurst University	M,O
Marymount University	M,O
Marywood University	M
McNeese State University	M
Medaille College	M
Mercy College	M,O
MidAmerica Nazarene University	M,O
Middle Tennessee State University	M,O
Mississippi College	M,O
Monmouth University	M,O
Montclair State University	M,D,O
Morehead State University	M
Mount St. Mary's College	M
Naropa University	M
National University	M
New Jersey City University	M
New Mexico State University	M,D,O
New York Institute of Technology	M
New York University	M,D,O
Nicholls State University	M,O
Northeastern State University	M
Northeastern University	M,D,O
Northern Arizona University	D
Northwestern University	M
Nova Southeastern University	M
Oakland University	M,D,O
Our Lady of the Lake University of San Antonio	M,D
Pace University	M
Pacifica Graduate Institute	M,D
Palm Beach Atlantic University	M
Penn State University Park	M,D
Prescott College	M
Purdue University Calumet	M
Radford University	M,D,O
Regent University	M,D,O
Regis University	M,O
Rivier College	M,D,O
Rosemont College	M
Rowan University	M
Rutgers, The State University of New Jersey, New Brunswick	M
St. Bonaventure University	M,O
St. Edward's University	M,O
St. John Fisher College	M
Saint Joseph College	M
Saint Martin's University	M
St. Mary's University (United States)	M
Saint Mary's University of Minnesota	M,D
St. Thomas University	M
Saint Xavier University	M,O
Salem State College	M
Salve Regina University	M,O
San Francisco State University	M
Santa Clara University	M
Seton Hall University	M,D
Shippensburg University of Pennsylvania	M,O
Sonoma State University	M
Southeast Missouri State University	M,O
Southern Illinois University Carbondale	M,D
Southern Nazarene University	M
Spring Arbor University	M
Springfield College	M,O
Stanford University	D
State University of New York at New Paltz	M
State University of New York at Oswego	M,O
Suffolk University	M,O
Tarleton State University	M,O
Temple University	M,D
Tennessee State University	M,D
Texas A&M International University	M
Texas A&M University	M,D
Texas A&M University–Commerce	M,D
Texas A&M University–Texarkana	M
Texas Tech University	M,D
Texas Wesleyan University	M
Texas Woman's University	M,D,O
Towson University	O
Trevecca Nazarene University	M
Trinity International University	P,M,D,O
Union College (KY)	M
Union Institute & University	M
Universidad del Turabo	M,D
University at Albany, State University of New York	M,D,O
University at Buffalo, the State University of New York	M,D,O
The University of Akron	M,D
University of Baltimore	M
University of California, Berkeley	O
University of California, Santa Barbara	M,D
University of Central Arkansas	M
University of Central Oklahoma	M
University of Colorado Denver	M
University of Connecticut	M,D,O
University of Denver	M,D,O
University of Florida	M,D
University of Great Falls	M
University of Houston	M,D
University of Houston–Victoria	M
University of Indianapolis	M,D
The University of Iowa	M,D,O
The University of Kansas	M,D
University of Kentucky	M,D,O
University of La Verne	M
University of Mary Hardin-Baylor	M
University of Maryland, College Park	M,D,O
University of Massachusetts Boston	M,O
University of Memphis	M,D
University of Miami	D
University of Minnesota, Twin Cities Campus	D
University of Missouri–Columbia	M,D,O
University of Missouri–Kansas City	M,D,O
The University of Montana	M,D,O
University of Nebraska–Lincoln	M,D,O
The University of North Carolina at Greensboro	M,D,O
University of North Dakota	M
University of Northern Colorado	D

University of North Florida M
University of North Texas M,D
University of Notre Dame D
University of Oklahoma D
University of Pennsylvania M,D
University of Phoenix–Las Vegas Campus M
University of Phoenix–Sacramento Valley Campus M
University of Phoenix–Utah Campus M
University of Puget Sound M
University of Rhode Island M
University of Saint Francis (IN) M
University of St. Thomas (MN) M,D,O
University of San Diego M
University of San Francisco M,D
The University of Scranton M,O
University of Southern Mississippi M,D
The University of Tennessee M,D
The University of Texas at Austin M,D
The University of Texas at Tyler M
University of the District of Columbia M
University of Utah M,D
University of Vermont M
University of West Florida M
University of Wisconsin–Madison D
University of Wisconsin–Milwaukee M,D
University of Wisconsin–Stout M
Utah State University M,D
Valdosta State University M,O
Valparaiso University M,O
Virginia Commonwealth University M,D,O
Walden University M,D,O
Walla Walla University M
Walsh University M
Washington State University M,D,O
Wayland Baptist University M
Waynesburg University M,D
Webster University M
Western Michigan University M,D
Western Washington University M
Westfield State College M
Westminster College (UT) M
West Virginia University D
William Carey University M
William Paterson University of New Jersey M
Yeshiva University M
Youngstown State University M

■ COUNSELOR EDUCATION

Adams State College M
Alabama Agricultural and Mechanical University M,O
Alabama State University M,O
Albany State University M
Alcorn State University M,O
Alfred University M,D,O
American International College M,D,O
Angelo State University M
Appalachian State University M
Argosy University, Sarasota M,D,O
Argosy University, Tampa M,D
Arizona State University M
Arkansas State University M,O
Auburn University M,D,O
Auburn University Montgomery M,O
Augusta State University M
Austin Peay State University M,O
Azusa Pacific University M
Barry University M,D,O
Bayamón Central University M
Bellevue University M,D
Bloomsburg University of Pennsylvania M
Bob Jones University P,M,D,O
Boise State University M
Boston University M,O
Bowie State University M
Bowling Green State University M
Bradley University M
Bridgewater State College M,O
Brooklyn College of the City University of New York M,O
Bucknell University M
Butler University M
Caldwell College M
California Baptist University M
California Lutheran University M
California State University, Bakersfield M
California State University, Dominguez Hills M
California State University, East Bay M
California State University, Fresno M
California State University, Fullerton M
California State University, Long Beach M
California State University, Los Angeles M,D
California State University, Northridge M
California State University, Sacramento M
California State University, San Bernardino M
California State University, Stanislaus M,D,O
California University of Pennsylvania M
Cambridge College M,D,O
Campbell University M
Canisius College M
Carlow University M
Carson-Newman College M
Central Connecticut State University M,O
Central Michigan University M
Central Washington University M
Chapman University M
Chicago State University M
The Citadel, The Military College of South Carolina M
Clark Atlanta University M
Clemson University M
Cleveland State University M,D,O
The College at Brockport, State University of New York M,O
The College of New Jersey M
College of St. Joseph M
The College of Saint Rose M
College of Santa Fe M
The College of William and Mary M,D
Colorado State University M,D
Columbus State University M,D,O
Concordia University Chicago M,O
Concordia University Wisconsin M
Creighton University M
Dallas Baptist University M
Delta State University M,D
DePaul University M,D
Doane College M
Drake University M
Duquesne University M,D
East Carolina University M,O
East Central University M
Eastern Illinois University M
Eastern Kentucky University M
Eastern Michigan University M,O
Eastern New Mexico University M
Eastern University M,O
Eastern Washington University M
East Tennessee State University M
Edinboro University of Pennsylvania M,O
Emporia State University M
Fairfield University M,O
Fitchburg State College M,O
Florida Agricultural and Mechanical University M,D
Florida Atlantic University M,D,O
Florida Gulf Coast University M
Florida International University M
Florida State University M,D,O
Fordham University M,D,O
Fort Hays State University M
Fort Valley State University M,O
Freed-Hardeman University M,O
Fresno Pacific University M
Frostburg State University M
Gallaudet University M
Gannon University M,O
Geneva College M
George Fox University M,O
George Mason University M

M—master's degree; P—first professional degree; D—doctorate; O—other advanced degree

Institution	Degrees
The George Washington University	M,D,O
Georgia Southern University	M,O
Georgia State University	M,D,O
Grambling State University	M,D
Grand Canyon University	M
Gwynedd-Mercy College	M
Hampton University	M
Harding University	M,O
Hardin-Simmons University	M
Henderson State University	M
Heritage University	M
Hofstra University	M,O
Houston Baptist University	M
Howard University	M,O
Hunter College of the City University of New York	M
Husson University	M
Idaho State University	M,D,O
Immaculata University	M,D,O
Indiana State University	M,D,O
Indiana University Bloomington	M,D,O
Indiana University of Pennsylvania	M
Indiana University–Purdue University Fort Wayne	M
Indiana University–Purdue University Indianapolis	M,O
Indiana University South Bend	M
Indiana University Southeast	M
Indiana Wesleyan University	M
Inter American University of Puerto Rico, San Germán Campus	M,D
Iowa State University of Science and Technology	M,D
Jackson State University	M,O
Jacksonville State University	M
John Brown University	M
John Carroll University	M,O
The Johns Hopkins University	M,O
Johnson State College	M
Kansas State University	M,D
Kean University	M
Kent State University	M,D,O
Kutztown University of Pennsylvania	M
Lakeland College	M
Lamar University	M,D,O
La Sierra University	M,O
Lee University	M
Lehigh University	M,D,O
Lehman College of the City University of New York	M
Lewis University	M
Liberty University	M,D,O
Lincoln Memorial University	M,O
Lincoln University (MO)	M,O
Long Island University, Brentwood Campus	M
Long Island University, Brooklyn Campus	M,O
Long Island University, C.W. Post Campus	M
Longwood University	M
Louisiana State University and Agricultural and Mechanical College	M,D,O
Louisiana Tech University	M,D
Loyola Marymount University	M
Loyola University Chicago	M,O
Loyola University Maryland	M,O
Loyola University New Orleans	M
Lynchburg College	M
Malone University	M
Manhattan College	M,O
Marshall University	M,O
Marymount University	M
Marywood University	M,O
McDaniel College	M
McNeese State University	M
Mercy College	M,O
Michigan State University	M,D,O
Middle Tennessee State University	M,O
Midwestern State University	M
Minnesota State University Mankato	M,D,O
Minnesota State University Moorhead	M
Mississippi College	M,O
Mississippi State University	M,D,O
Missouri Baptist University	M,O
Missouri State University	M
Montana State University	M
Montana State University–Billings	M
Montclair State University	M,D,O
Morehead State University	M,O
Mount Mary College	M
Murray State University	M,O
Naropa University	M
National-Louis University	M,O
National University	M
New Mexico Highlands University	M
New Mexico State University	M,D,O
New York Institute of Technology	M
New York University	M,D,O
Niagara University	M,O
Nicholls State University	M
North Carolina Agricultural and Technical State University	M,D
North Carolina Central University	M
North Carolina State University	M,D
North Dakota State University	M,D
Northeastern Illinois University	M
Northeastern State University	M
Northeastern University	M
Northern Arizona University	M
Northern Illinois University	M,D
Northern Kentucky University	M,O
Northern Michigan University	M
Northwestern State University of Louisiana	M,O
Northwest Missouri State University	M
Northwest Nazarene University	M
Nova Southeastern University	M
Ohio University	M,D
Old Dominion University	M,D,O
Oregon State University	M,D
Our Lady of the Lake University of San Antonio	M
Palm Beach Atlantic University	M
Penn State University Park	M,D
Pittsburg State University	M
Plymouth State University	M
Pontifical Catholic University of Puerto Rico	M
Portland State University	M,D
Prairie View A&M University	M,D
Prescott College	M,D
Providence College	M
Purdue University	M,D,O
Purdue University Calumet	M
Queens College of the City University of New York	M
Radford University	M
Regent University	M,D,O
Rhode Island College	M,O
Rider University	M,O
Rivier College	M,D,O
Roberts Wesleyan College	M
Rollins College	M
Roosevelt University	M
Rosemont College	M
Rowan University	M
St. Bonaventure University	M,O
St. Cloud State University	M
St. John's University (NY)	M,O
Saint Joseph College	M
Saint Louis University	M,D,O
Saint Martin's University	M
Saint Mary's College of California	M
St. Mary's University (United States)	D
St. Thomas University	M,O
Saint Xavier University	M
Salem State College	M
Sam Houston State University	M,D
San Diego State University	M
San Jose State University	M
Santa Clara University	M
Seattle Pacific University	M,D,O
Seattle University	M,O
Shippensburg University of Pennsylvania	M,O
Simmons College	M,D,O
Slippery Rock University of Pennsylvania	M
Sonoma State University	M
South Carolina State University	M
South Dakota State University	M
Southeastern Louisiana University	M
Southeastern Oklahoma State University	M

Southeast Missouri State University M,O
Southern Connecticut State University M,O
Southern Illinois University Carbondale M,D
Southern Methodist University M,O
Southern Oregon University M
Southern University and Agricultural and Mechanical College M
Southwestern Oklahoma State University M
Spalding University M
Springfield College M,O
State University of New York at New Paltz M
State University of New York at Plattsburgh M,O
State University of New York College at Oneonta M,O
Stephen F. Austin State University M
Stetson University M
Suffolk University M,O
Sul Ross State University M
Syracuse University M,D
Tarleton State University M,O
Tennessee State University M,D
Texas A&M International University M
Texas A&M University M,D
Texas A&M University–Commerce M,D
Texas A&M University–Corpus Christi M,D
Texas A&M University–Kingsville M
Texas Christian University M,O
Texas Southern University M,D
Texas State University–San Marcos M
Texas Tech University M,D
Texas Wesleyan University M
Texas Woman's University M,D
Trevecca Nazarene University M,D
Trinity (Washington) University M
Troy University M,O
Universidad del Turabo M
University at Albany, State University of New York M,D,O
University at Buffalo, the State University of New York M,D,O
The University of Akron M,D
The University of Alabama M,D,O
The University of Alabama at Birmingham M
University of Alaska Anchorage M
University of Alaska Fairbanks M
University of Arkansas M,D,O
University of Arkansas at Little Rock M
University of Central Arkansas M
University of Central Florida M,D,O
University of Central Missouri M,O
University of Central Oklahoma M
University of Cincinnati M,D,O
University of Colorado at Colorado Springs M,D
University of Colorado Denver M
University of Connecticut M,D,O
University of Dayton M,O
University of Detroit Mercy M
University of Florida M,D,O
University of Georgia M,D,O
University of Guam M
University of Hartford M,O
University of Houston–Clear Lake M
University of Houston–Victoria M
University of Idaho M,D,O
University of Illinois at Urbana–Champaign M,D,O
The University of Iowa M,D
University of La Verne M,O
University of Louisiana at Lafayette M
University of Louisiana at Monroe M
University of Louisville M,D
University of Maine M,D,O
University of Mary Hardin-Baylor M
University of Maryland, College Park M,D,O
University of Maryland Eastern Shore M
University of Massachusetts Amherst M,D,O
University of Massachusetts Boston M,O
University of Memphis M,D
University of Miami M,O
University of Minnesota, Twin Cities Campus M,D,O
University of Mississippi M,D,O
University of Missouri–St. Louis M,D
The University of Montana M,D,O
University of Montevallo M
University of Nebraska at Kearney M,O
University of Nebraska at Omaha M
University of Nevada, Las Vegas M,O
University of Nevada, Reno M,D,O
University of New Hampshire M,O
University of New Mexico M,D
University of New Orleans M,D,O
University of North Alabama M
The University of North Carolina at Chapel Hill M
The University of North Carolina at Charlotte M,D
The University of North Carolina at Greensboro M,D,O
The University of North Carolina at Pembroke M
University of Northern Colorado M,D
University of Northern Iowa M,D
University of North Florida M
University of North Texas M,D,O
University of Oklahoma M
University of Phoenix–New Mexico Campus M
University of Phoenix–Southern Arizona Campus M,O
University of Puerto Rico, Río Piedras M,D
University of Puget Sound M
University of Saint Francis (IN) M
University of San Diego M
University of San Francisco M,D
The University of Scranton M
University of South Alabama M,D
University of South Carolina D,O
The University of South Dakota M,D,O
University of Southern California M
University of Southern Maine M,O
University of South Florida M,D,O
The University of Tennessee M,D,O
The University of Tennessee at Chattanooga M,O
The University of Tennessee at Martin M
The University of Texas at Austin M,D
The University of Texas at Brownsville M
The University of Texas at El Paso M
The University of Texas at San Antonio M,D
The University of Texas of the Permian Basin M
The University of Texas–Pan American M
University of the District of Columbia M
University of the Southwest M
The University of Toledo M,D,O
University of Utah M,D
University of Vermont M
University of Virginia M,D,O
The University of West Alabama M
University of West Florida M
University of West Georgia M,O
University of Wisconsin–Madison M
University of Wisconsin–Milwaukee M,D
University of Wisconsin–Oshkosh M
University of Wisconsin–Platteville M
University of Wisconsin–River Falls M,O
University of Wisconsin–Stevens Point M
University of Wisconsin–Superior M
University of Wisconsin–Whitewater M
University of Wyoming M,D
Utah State University M,D

M—master's degree; P—first professional degree; D—doctorate; O—other advanced degree

Valdosta State University M,O
Vanderbilt University M
Villanova University M
Virginia Commonwealth University M
Virginia Polytechnic Institute and State University M,D,O
Wake Forest University M
Walsh University M
Wayne State College M
Wayne State University M,D,O
West Chester University of Pennsylvania M,O
Western Carolina University M
Western Connecticut State University M
Western Illinois University M
Western Kentucky University M,O
Western Michigan University M,D
Western New Mexico University M
Western Washington University M
Westfield State College M
West Texas A&M University M
West Virginia University M
Whitworth University M
Wichita State University M,D,O
Widener University M,D
William Paterson University of New Jersey M
Wilmington University M
Winona State University M
Winthrop University M
Wright State University M
Xavier University M
Xavier University of Louisiana M
Youngstown State University M

■ CRIMINAL JUSTICE AND CRIMINOLOGY

Albany State University M
American University M,D
Anna Maria College M
Appalachian State University M
Arizona State University M,D
Arkansas State University M,O
Armstrong Atlantic State University M
Auburn University Montgomery M
Bayamón Central University M
Bellevue University M,D
Boise State University M
Boston University M
Bowling Green State University M
Bridgewater State College M
Buffalo State College, State University of New York M
California State University, Fresno M
California State University, Long Beach M
California State University, Los Angeles M
California State University, Sacramento M
California State University, San Bernardino M
California State University, Stanislaus M
California University of Pennsylvania M
Calumet College of Saint Joseph M
Capella University M,D,O
Carnegie Mellon University M
Central Connecticut State University M
Chaminade University of Honolulu M,O
Charleston Southern University M
Chicago State University M
Clark Atlanta University M
Colorado Technical University Colorado Springs M
Colorado Technical University Denver M
Colorado Technical University Sioux Falls M
Columbia College (MO) M
Columbus State University M
Concordia University, St. Paul M
Coppin State University M
Dallas Baptist University M
Delta State University M
DeSales University M
Drury University M
East Carolina University M
East Central University M
Eastern Kentucky University M
Eastern Michigan University M,O
East Tennessee State University M
Fayetteville State University M
Ferris State University M
Fitchburg State College M
Florida Agricultural and Mechanical University M
Florida Atlantic University M
Florida Gulf Coast University M
Florida International University M
Florida State University M,D
George Mason University M,D
The George Washington University M
Georgia College & State University M
Georgia State University M,D,O
Graduate School and University Center of the City University of New York D
Grambling State University M
Grand Valley State University M
Hodges University M
Holy Family University M
Husson University M
Illinois State University M
Indiana State University M
Indiana University Bloomington M,D
Indiana University Northwest M,O
Indiana University of Pennsylvania M,D
Indiana University–Purdue University Indianapolis M
Inter American University of Puerto Rico, Metropolitan Campus M
Iona College M
Jackson State University M
Jacksonville State University M
John Jay College of Criminal Justice of the City University of New York M,D
The Johns Hopkins University M
Kean University M
Kent State University M
Lamar University M
Lewis University M
Lincoln University (MO) M
Lindenwood University M,O
Long Island University, Brentwood Campus M
Long Island University, C.W. Post Campus M
Longwood University M
Loyola University Chicago M
Loyola University New Orleans M
Lynn University M,O
Madonna University M
Marshall University M
Marywood University M
Mercyhurst College M,O
Michigan State University M,D
Middle Tennessee State University M
Midwestern State University M
Minot State University M
Mississippi College M,O
Mississippi Valley State University M
Missouri State University M
Molloy College M
Monmouth University M,O
Morehead State University M
Mountain State University M
National University M
New Jersey City University M
New Mexico State University M
Niagara University M
Norfolk State University M
North Carolina Central University M
North Dakota State University M,D
Northeastern State University M
Northeastern University M,D
Northern Arizona University M,O
Northern Michigan University M
Norwich University M
Nova Southeastern University M
Oklahoma City University M
Old Dominion University D
Penn State Harrisburg M,D
Penn State University Park M,D
Point Park University M
Polytechnic Institute of NYU M,D,O

Pontifical Catholic University of Puerto Rico M
Portland State University M,D
Radford University M
Regis University M,O
The Richard Stockton College of New Jersey M
Rochester Institute of Technology M
Roger Williams University M
Rowan University M
Rutgers, The State University of New Jersey, Camden M
Rutgers, The State University of New Jersey, Newark D
Sacred Heart University M
St. Ambrose University M
St. Cloud State University M
St. John's University (NY) M
Saint Joseph's University M,O
Saint Leo University M
St. Thomas University M,O
Salem State College M
Salve Regina University M
Sam Houston State University M,D
San Diego State University M
San Jose State University M
Seattle University M
Shippensburg University of Pennsylvania M
Southeast Missouri State University M
Southern Illinois University Carbondale M
Southern University and Agricultural and Mechanical College M
Southwestern College (KS) M
Suffolk University M
Sul Ross State University M
Tarleton State University M
Temple University M,D
Tennessee State University M
Texas A&M International University M
Texas Southern University M,D
Texas State University–San Marcos M,D
Tiffin University M
Troy University M
Universidad del Turabo M
University at Albany, State University of New York M,D
The University of Alabama M
The University of Alabama at Birmingham M
The University of Alabama in Huntsville O
University of Alaska Fairbanks M
University of Arkansas at Little Rock M,D
University of Baltimore M
University of California, Irvine M,D
University of Central Florida M,O
University of Central Missouri M,O
University of Central Oklahoma M
University of Cincinnati M,D
University of Colorado at Colorado Springs M
University of Colorado Denver M
University of Delaware M,D
University of Denver M,O
University of Detroit Mercy M
University of Florida M,D
University of Great Falls M
University of Houston–Clear Lake M
University of Illinois at Chicago M,D
University of Louisiana at Monroe M
University of Louisville M
University of Maryland, College Park M,D
University of Maryland Eastern Shore M
University of Massachusetts Lowell M
University of Memphis M
University of Minnesota, Duluth M
University of Missouri–Kansas City M
University of Missouri–St. Louis M,D
The University of Montana M
University of Nebraska at Omaha M,D
University of Nevada, Las Vegas M
University of Nevada, Reno M
University of New Haven M
University of North Alabama M
The University of North Carolina at Charlotte M
The University of North Carolina at Greensboro M
The University of North Carolina Wilmington M
University of North Dakota D
University of Northern Iowa M
University of North Florida M
University of North Texas M
University of Pennsylvania M,D
University of Phoenix M
University of Phoenix–Denver Campus M
University of Phoenix–Hawaii Campus M
University of Phoenix–Las Vegas Campus M
University of Phoenix–Louisiana Campus M
University of Phoenix–New Mexico Campus M
University of Phoenix–Oregon Campus M
University of Phoenix–Philadelphia Campus M
University of Phoenix–Sacramento Valley Campus M
University of Phoenix–San Diego Campus M
University of Phoenix–Southern Arizona Campus M,O
University of Phoenix–Southern California Campus M,O
University of Phoenix–Southern Colorado Campus M
University of Pittsburgh M,D
University of South Carolina M,D
University of Southern Mississippi M,D
University of South Florida M,D
The University of Tennessee M,D
The University of Tennessee at Chattanooga M
The University of Texas at Arlington M
The University of Texas at Dallas M,D
The University of Texas at San Antonio M
The University of Texas at Tyler M
The University of Texas of the Permian Basin M
The University of Texas–Pan American M
University of the Pacific P,M,D
The University of Toledo M,O
University of West Florida M
University of West Georgia M
University of Wisconsin–Milwaukee M
University of Wisconsin–Platteville M
Upper Iowa University M
Utica College M
Valdosta State University M
Villanova University M
Virginia Commonwealth University M,O
Walden University M,D,O
Washburn University M
Washington State University M,D
Wayland Baptist University M
Wayne State University M
Webster University M,D
West Chester University of Pennsylvania M
Western Connecticut State University M
Western Illinois University M,O
Western Oregon University M
Westfield State College M
West Texas A&M University M
Wichita State University M
Widener University M
Wilmington University M
Wright State University M
Xavier University M
Youngstown State University M

M—master's degree; P—first professional degree; D—doctorate; O—other advanced degree

■ CULTURAL STUDIES

American University M,D,O
Appalachian State University M
Arizona State University M
Biola University M,D,O
Brandeis University M
Carnegie Mellon University M,D
The Catholic University of America M
Central Michigan University M
Chapman University D
Claremont Graduate University M,D,O
Cornell University M,D
Eastern Michigan University M
George Mason University D
Lewis & Clark College M,O
New York University M,D,O
San Francisco State University M
Simmons College M
Southern Illinois University Carbondale M
State University of New York at Binghamton M,D
Stony Brook University, State University of New York M,D
Union Institute & University M
Union University M
University of Alaska Fairbanks M
University of California, Davis M,D
University of Houston–Clear Lake M
University of Minnesota, Twin Cities Campus D
University of Pittsburgh M,D
The University of Texas at San Antonio M,D
Washington State University M,D
Wheaton College M,O

■ CURRICULUM AND INSTRUCTION

Abilene Christian University M
American University M,O
Andrews University M,D,O
Angelo State University M
Appalachian State University M
Arizona State University M,D
Arkansas State University M,D,O
Arkansas Tech University M,O
Armstrong Atlantic State University M
Ashland University M
Auburn University M,D,O
Augusta State University M
Aurora University M,D
Austin Peay State University M,O
Azusa Pacific University M
Ball State University M,O
Barry University D,O
Baylor University M,D,O
Benedictine University M
Bloomsburg University of Pennsylvania M
Bob Jones University P,M,D,O
Boise State University D
Boston College M,D,O
Boston University M,D,O
Bowling Green State University M
Bradley University M,O
Bucknell University M
Caldwell College M
California Baptist University M
California State University, Bakersfield M
California State University, Chico M
California State University, Dominguez Hills M
California State University, East Bay M
California State University, Fresno M
California State University, Northridge M
California State University, Sacramento M
California State University, San Bernardino M
California State University, Stanislaus M,O
Cambridge College M,D,O
Capella University M,D,O
Carson-Newman College M
Castleton State College M
The Catholic University of America M,D,O
Central Michigan University M,D,O
Chapman University M,D
Christian Brothers University M
City University of Seattle M,O
Clarion University of Pennsylvania M
Clark Atlanta University M
Clemson University D
The College at Brockport, State University of New York M
The College of Saint Rose M,O
College of Santa Fe M
The College of William and Mary M,D
Colorado Christian University M
Columbus State University M,D,O
Concordia University (CA) M
Concordia University (OR) M
Concordia University Chicago M
Concordia University, St. Paul M,O
Concordia University Wisconsin M
Converse College O
Coppin State University M
Cornell University M,D
Dallas Baptist University M
Delaware State University M
DePaul University D
Doane College M
Dominican University M
Drexel University M
Duquesne University M,D,O
East Carolina University M
Eastern Kentucky University M
Eastern Michigan University M
Eastern Washington University M
East Tennessee State University M
Emporia State University M
Fairleigh Dickinson University, Metropolitan Campus M
Ferris State University M
Fitchburg State College M
Florida Atlantic University M,D,O
Florida Gulf Coast University M
Florida International University M,D,O
Fordham University M,D,O
Framingham State College M
Franciscan University of Steubenville M
Freed-Hardeman University M,O
Fresno Pacific University M
Frostburg State University M
Furman University M
Gannon University M
Gardner-Webb University D
George Fox University M,D,O
The George Washington University M,D,O
Georgia College & State University M,O
Georgia Southern University D
Grambling State University M,D
Grand Canyon University M,D
Harvard University M
Henderson State University M
Hood College M
Houston Baptist University M
Idaho State University M,O
Illinois State University M,D
Indiana State University M,D
Indiana University Bloomington M,D,O
Indiana University of Pennsylvania M,D
Indiana University–Purdue University Indianapolis M,O
Indiana Wesleyan University M
Inter American University of Puerto Rico, Metropolitan Campus M,D
Inter American University of Puerto Rico, San Germán Campus D
Iowa State University of Science and Technology M,D
The Johns Hopkins University M,O
Johnson State College M
Jones International University M
Kansas State University M,D
Kean University M
Keene State College M,O
Kent State University M,D,O
Kutztown University of Pennsylvania M,O
La Sierra University M,D,O
Lesley University M,D,O
LeTourneau University M
Lewis University M

Liberty University M,D,O
Lincoln Memorial University M,O
Lipscomb University M
Louisiana State University in Shreveport M
Louisiana Tech University M,D
Loyola University Chicago M,D
Loyola University Maryland M,O
Lynchburg College M
Malone University M
McDaniel College M
McNeese State University M
Medaille College M
Mercer University M,D,O
Miami University M
Michigan State University M,D,O
Middle Tennessee State University M,O
Midwestern State University M
Mills College M,D
Minnesota State University Mankato M,O
Minnesota State University Moorhead M
Misericordia University M
Mississippi College M,D,O
Mississippi State University M,D,O
Mississippi University for Women M
Missouri State University M
Montana State University M,D,O
Montana State University–Billings M
Montclair State University M,D,O
Morehead State University M,O
National-Louis University M,D,O
Newman University M
New Mexico Highlands University M
New Mexico State University M,D,O
Nicholls State University M
North Carolina Central University M
North Carolina State University M,D
North Central College M
Northern Arizona University D
Northern Illinois University M,D
Northwestern State University of Louisiana M
Northwest Nazarene University M
Nova Southeastern University M,O
Ohio University M,D
Oklahoma State University M,D
Old Dominion University M,D
Olivet Nazarene University M
Oral Roberts University M,D
Our Lady of the Lake University of San Antonio M
Pace University M,O
Pacific Lutheran University M
Penn State Great Valley M
Penn State Harrisburg M,D
Penn State University Park M,D
Philadelphia Biblical University M
Piedmont College M,O
Point Park University M
Pontifical Catholic University of Puerto Rico M,D
Portland State University M,D
Prairie View A&M University M
Purdue University M,D,O
Regis University M,O
Rider University M,O
Rivier College M,D,O
Rosemont College M
Rowan University M
St. Bonaventure University M,O
St. Cloud State University M
Saint Leo University M
Saint Louis University M,D
Saint Mary's College of California M
Saint Mary's University of Minnesota M,O
Saint Michael's College M,O
Saint Peter's College M,O
Saint Xavier University M,O
Sam Houston State University M
San Diego State University M
Seattle Pacific University M
Seattle University M,O
Shippensburg University of Pennsylvania M
Sonoma State University M
South Dakota State University M
Southeastern Louisiana University M
Southern Illinois University Carbondale M,D
Southern Illinois University Edwardsville M
Southern Nazarene University M
Southern New Hampshire University M,O
Southwestern College (KS) M
Stanford University M,D
State University of New York at Plattsburgh M
State University of New York College at Potsdam M
Syracuse University M,D,O
Tarleton State University M
Tennessee State University M,D
Tennessee Technological University M,O
Texas A&M International University M,D
Texas A&M University M,D
Texas A&M University–Commerce M,D
Texas A&M University–Corpus Christi M,D
Texas A&M University–Texarkana M
Texas Christian University M
Texas Southern University M,D
Texas Tech University M,D
Texas Woman's University M,D
Trevecca Nazarene University M
Trinity (Washington) University M
Universidad del Turabo M,D
Universidad Metropolitana M
University at Albany, State University of New York M,D,O
University of Alaska Fairbanks M,D,O
University of Arkansas D
University of California, Davis M,D
University of California, Riverside M,D
University of Central Florida M,D,O
University of Central Missouri M,O
University of Cincinnati M,D
University of Colorado at Boulder M,D
University of Colorado at Colorado Springs M,D
University of Colorado Denver M
University of Delaware M,D,O
University of Denver M,D,O
University of Detroit Mercy M
University of Florida M,D,O
University of Hawaii at Manoa M,D
University of Houston M,D
University of Houston–Clear Lake M
University of Houston–Victoria M
University of Idaho M,D
University of Illinois at Chicago M,D
University of Illinois at Urbana–Champaign M,D,O
University of Indianapolis M
The University of Iowa M,D
The University of Kansas M,D
University of Kentucky M,D
University of Louisiana at Lafayette M
University of Louisiana at Monroe M,D
University of Louisville D
University of Maine M
University of Mary M
University of Maryland, Baltimore County M,O
University of Maryland, College Park M,D,O
University of Massachusetts Boston M
University of Massachusetts Lowell M,D,O
University of Memphis M,D
University of Michigan M,D
University of Minnesota, Twin Cities Campus M,D,O
University of Mississippi M,D,O
University of Missouri–Columbia M,D,O
University of Missouri–Kansas City M,D,O
University of Missouri–St. Louis M,O
The University of Montana M,D
University of Nebraska at Kearney M
University of Nebraska–Lincoln M,D,O
University of Nevada, Las Vegas M,D

M—master's degree; P—first professional degree; D—doctorate; O—other advanced degree

University of Nevada, Reno D
University of New Orleans M,D,O
The University of North Carolina at Chapel Hill M,D
The University of North Carolina at Charlotte M,D,O
The University of North Carolina at Greensboro M,D,O
The University of North Carolina Wilmington M
University of Northern Iowa M,D
University of North Texas M,D
University of Oklahoma M,D,O
University of Phoenix M
University of Phoenix–Central Florida Campus M
University of Phoenix–Denver Campus M
University of Phoenix–Hawaii Campus M
University of Phoenix–Las Vegas Campus M
University of Phoenix–Louisiana Campus M
University of Phoenix–New Mexico Campus M
University of Phoenix–North Florida Campus M
University of Phoenix–Oregon Campus M
University of Phoenix–Phoenix Campus M
University of Phoenix–Sacramento Valley Campus M,O
University of Phoenix–San Diego Campus M
University of Phoenix–Southern Arizona Campus M,O
University of Phoenix–Southern California Campus M
University of Phoenix–Southern Colorado Campus M,O
University of Phoenix–South Florida Campus M
University of Phoenix–Utah Campus M
University of Phoenix–West Florida Campus M
University of Phoenix–West Michigan Campus M
University of Puerto Rico, Río Piedras M,D
University of St. Francis (IL) M
University of Saint Mary M
University of St. Thomas (MN) M,D,O
University of San Diego M
University of San Francisco M,D
The University of Scranton M
University of South Carolina D
The University of South Dakota M,D,O
University of Southern Mississippi M,D,O
University of South Florida M,D,O
The University of Tampa M
The University of Tennessee M,D,O
The University of Texas at Arlington M,D
The University of Texas at Austin M,D
The University of Texas at Brownsville M
The University of Texas at El Paso M,D
The University of Texas at San Antonio M
University of the Pacific M,D
University of the Southwest M
The University of Toledo M,D,O
University of Vermont M
University of Virginia M,D,O
University of Washington M,D
University of West Florida D,O
University of Wisconsin–Madison M,D
University of Wisconsin–Milwaukee M,D
University of Wisconsin–Oshkosh M
University of Wisconsin–Superior M
University of Wisconsin–Whitewater M
University of Wyoming M,D
Utah State University D
Virginia Commonwealth University M,O
Virginia Polytechnic Institute and State University M,D,O
Walden University M,D,O
Walla Walla University M
Washburn University M
Washington State University M,D
Wayne State College M
Wayne State University M,D,O
Weber State University M
Western Connecticut State University M
West Texas A&M University M
West Virginia University M,D
Wichita State University M
William Woods University M,O
Wright State University M,O
Xavier University of Louisiana M
Youngstown State University M

■ DANCE

Arizona State University M
Bennington College M
California State University, Fullerton M
California State University, Long Beach M
California State University, Sacramento M
Case Western Reserve University M
The College at Brockport, State University of New York M
Florida State University M
George Mason University M
Hollins University M
Mills College M
New York University M,D
Northern Illinois University M
The Ohio State University D
Oklahoma City University M
Purchase College, State University of New York M
Sam Houston State University M
Sarah Lawrence College M
Southern Methodist University M
Temple University M,D
Texas Tech University M,D
Texas Woman's University M,D
Tufts University M,D
Tulane University M
University of California, Irvine M
University of California, Los Angeles M,D
University of California, Riverside M,D
University of Colorado at Boulder M,D
University of Hawaii at Manoa M,D
University of Illinois at Urbana–Champaign M
The University of Iowa M
University of Maryland, College Park M
University of Michigan M
University of Minnesota, Twin Cities Campus M,D
University of New Mexico M
The University of North Carolina at Charlotte M
The University of North Carolina at Greensboro M
University of Oklahoma M
University of Oregon M
The University of Texas at Austin M,D
University of Utah M
University of Washington M
University of Wisconsin–Milwaukee M

■ DATABASE SYSTEMS

Colorado Technical University Colorado Springs M,D
Colorado Technical University Denver M
Ferris State University M
George Mason University M,D,O
Minnesota State University Mankato M,O
National University M
New York University M,O
Regis University M,O
Rochester Institute of Technology M,O
Sacred Heart University M,O
Stevens Institute of Technology M,D,O
Towson University D,O
University of California, Berkeley O

■ DECORATIVE ARTS

The New School: A University M

■ DEMOGRAPHY AND POPULATION STUDIES

Bowling Green State University M,D
Cornell University M,D
Emory University M
Florida State University M,O
Harvard University M,D
The Johns Hopkins University M,D
Penn State University Park M,D
Princeton University D,O
University at Albany, State University of New York M,D,O
University of California, Berkeley M,D
University of California, Irvine M
University of Hawaii at Manoa O
University of Pennsylvania M,D
The University of Texas at San Antonio D
University of Washington M,D
Washington State University M,D

■ DENTAL HYGIENE

Boston University P,M,D,O
Eastern Washington University M
Idaho State University M
Old Dominion University M
University of Bridgeport M
University of Michigan M
University of Missouri–Kansas City P,M,D,O
University of New Mexico M
The University of North Carolina at Chapel Hill M,D

■ DENTISTRY

Boston University P,M,D,O
Case Western Reserve University P
Columbia University P
Creighton University P
Harvard University P,M,D,O
Howard University P,O
Idaho State University O
Indiana University–Purdue University Indianapolis P,M,D,O
Marquette University P
New York University P
Nova Southeastern University P,M
The Ohio State University P,M
Saint Louis University M
Southern Illinois University Edwardsville P
Stony Brook University, State University of New York P,O
Temple University P
Tufts University P
University at Buffalo, the State University of New York P,M,D,O
The University of Alabama at Birmingham P
University of California, Los Angeles P,O
University of Colorado Denver P
University of Detroit Mercy P
University of Florida P,O
University of Illinois at Chicago P
The University of Iowa P,M,D,O
University of Kentucky P
University of Louisville P
University of Michigan P
University of Minnesota, Twin Cities Campus P
University of Missouri–Kansas City P,M,D,O
The University of North Carolina at Chapel Hill P
University of Pennsylvania P
University of Pittsburgh P,M,O
University of Southern California P
University of the Pacific P,M,O
University of Washington P
Virginia Commonwealth University P,M
West Virginia University P

■ DEVELOPMENTAL BIOLOGY

Brigham Young University M,D
Brown University M,D
California Institute of Technology D
Carnegie Mellon University M,D
Columbia University M,D
Cornell University M,D
Duke University D,O
Emory University D
Illinois State University M,D
Iowa State University of Science and Technology M,D
The Johns Hopkins University D
Marquette University M,D
Massachusetts Institute of Technology D
New York University M,D
Northwestern University D
The Ohio State University M,D
Penn State University Park M,D
Purdue University M,D
Rensselaer Polytechnic Institute M,D
Rutgers, The State University of New Jersey, New Brunswick M,D
Stanford University D
Stony Brook University, State University of New York M,D
Tufts University D
University at Albany, State University of New York M,D
University of California, Davis M,D
University of California, Irvine M,D
University of California, Los Angeles D
University of California, Riverside M,D
University of California, San Diego D
University of California, Santa Barbara M,D
University of California, Santa Cruz M,D
University of Chicago D
University of Cincinnati D
University of Colorado at Boulder M,D
University of Colorado Denver D
University of Connecticut M,D
University of Delaware M,D
University of Hawaii at Manoa M,D
University of Illinois at Urbana–Champaign D
The University of Kansas M,D
University of Massachusetts Amherst D
University of Miami D
University of Michigan M,D
University of Minnesota, Twin Cities Campus M,D
University of Missouri–St. Louis M,D,O
The University of North Carolina at Chapel Hill M,D
University of Pennsylvania D
University of Pittsburgh D
University of South Carolina M,D
Virginia Polytechnic Institute and State University M,D
Washington University in St. Louis D
West Virginia University M,D
Yale University D

■ DEVELOPMENTAL EDUCATION

Eastern Michigan University M,O
Edinboro University of Pennsylvania M,O
Ferris State University M
Grambling State University M,D
National-Louis University M,O
North Carolina State University M,D,O
Rutgers, The State University of New Jersey, New Brunswick M
Texas State University–San Marcos M,D
University of California, Berkeley
The University of Iowa M,D

■ DEVELOPMENTAL PSYCHOLOGY

Andrews University M,D
Arizona State University D
Boston College M,D
Bowling Green State University M,D
Brandeis University M,D
Brown University D
Capella University M,D,O
Carnegie Mellon University D
Chatham University M,D
Claremont Graduate University M,D,O

M—master's degree; P—first professional degree; D—doctorate; O—other advanced degree

Clark University D
Cornell University D
Duke University D
Emory University D
Florida State University D
Fordham University D
Gallaudet University M,O
George Mason University M,D
Graduate School and University Center of the City University of New York D
Harvard University D
Howard University M,D
Illinois State University M,D,O
Indiana University Bloomington M,D
Louisiana State University and Agricultural and Mechanical College M,D
Loyola University Chicago M,D
New York University M,D
North Carolina State University D
The Ohio State University M,D
Penn State University Park M,D
Stanford University D
Temple University D
Texas A&M University M,D
University of California, Santa Barbara M,D
University of Connecticut M,D,O
University of Florida M,D
The University of Kansas M,D
University of Maine M,D
University of Maryland, Baltimore County D
University of Maryland, College Park M,D
University of Massachusetts Amherst M,D
University of Miami M,D
University of Michigan D
The University of Montana M,D,O
University of Nebraska at Omaha M,D,O
University of Nebraska–Lincoln M,D,O
The University of North Carolina at Chapel Hill D
The University of North Carolina at Greensboro M,D
University of Notre Dame D
University of Oregon M,D
University of Pittsburgh M,D
University of Rochester M,D
University of Southern California M,D
University of Washington D
University of Wisconsin–Madison D
University of Wisconsin–Milwaukee M,D
Virginia Polytechnic Institute and State University M,D
Walden University M,D,O
Wayne State University M,D
West Virginia University M,D
Yale University D

■ DISABILITY STUDIES

Brandeis University D
Chapman University D
Syracuse University O
University of Hawaii at Manoa O
University of Illinois at Chicago M,D
University of Pittsburgh O
Utah State University M,D,O

■ DISTANCE EDUCATION DEVELOPMENT

Barry University O
Endicott College M
Florida State University M,D,O
Jones International University M
New York Institute of Technology M,O
Nova Southeastern University M,D
Saginaw Valley State University M
University of Maryland, Baltimore County M,O
University of Maryland University College M,O
University of Nebraska–Lincoln M
University of Wyoming M,D,O
Western Illinois University M,O
Wilkes University M,D

■ EARLY CHILDHOOD EDUCATION

Adelphi University M,O
Alabama Agricultural and Mechanical University M,O
Alabama State University M,O
Albany State University M
American International College M,D,O
American University M,O
Anna Maria College M,O
Antioch University New England M
Arcadia University M,D,O
Arkansas State University M,O
Armstrong Atlantic State University M
Auburn University M,D,O
Auburn University Montgomery M,O
Austin Peay State University M,O
Barry University M,D,O
Bayamón Central University M
Bellarmine University M
Belmont University M
Bennington College M
Bloomsburg University of Pennsylvania M
Boise State University M
Boston College M
Boston University M,D,O
Bowling Green State University M
Brenau University M,O
Bridgewater State College M
Brooklyn College of the City University of New York M
Buffalo State College, State University of New York M
California State University, Bakersfield M
California State University, Fresno M
California State University, Northridge M
California State University, Sacramento M
Cambridge College M,D,O
Canisius College M
Carlow University M
Central Connecticut State University M
Central Michigan University M,O
Chatham University M
Chestnut Hill College M
Cheyney University of Pennsylvania O
Chicago State University M
City College of the City University of New York M
Clarion University of Pennsylvania M
Cleveland State University M
College of Charleston M
College of Mount St. Joseph M
The College of New Jersey M
The College of New Rochelle M
The College of Saint Rose M,O
Columbus State University M,O
Concordia University Chicago M,D
Concordia University, Nebraska M
Concordia University, St. Paul M,O
Concordia University Wisconsin M
Converse College M,O
Daemen College M
Dominican University M
Duquesne University M
Eastern Connecticut State University M
Eastern Illinois University M
Eastern Michigan University M
Eastern Nazarene College M,O
Eastern Washington University M
East Tennessee State University M
Edinboro University of Pennsylvania M,O
Emporia State University M
Endicott College M
Fitchburg State College M
Florida Agricultural and Mechanical University M
Florida Atlantic University M,D,O
Florida Gulf Coast University M
Florida International University M,D
Florida State University M,D,O
Fordham University M,D,O
Framingham State College M
Francis Marion University M
Furman University M
Gallaudet University M,D,O
Gannon University M
George Mason University M,O

The George Washington University M
Georgia College & State University M,O
Georgia Southern University M
Georgia Southwestern State University M,O
Georgia State University M,D,O
Governors State University M
Grand Valley State University M,O
Hampton University M
Harding University M,O
Henderson State University M
Hofstra University M,O
Hood College M
Howard University M,O
Hunter College of the City University of New York M,O
Indiana State University M
Indiana University–Purdue University Indianapolis M,O
Jackson State University M,D,O
Jacksonville State University M
Jacksonville University M,O
James Madison University M
John Carroll University M
The Johns Hopkins University M,D,O
Kean University M
Kennesaw State University M
Kent State University M
Kutztown University of Pennsylvania M,O
Lehman College of the City University of New York M
Le Moyne College M,O
Lesley University M,D,O
Lewis & Clark College M
Liberty University M,D,O
Lincoln University (PA) M
Long Island University, Brentwood Campus M
Long Island University, C.W. Post Campus M
Loyola Marymount University M
Loyola University Maryland M,O
Manhattan College M
Manhattanville College M
Marshall University M
Maryville University of Saint Louis M,D
Marywood University M
McNeese State University M
Mercer University M,D,O
Mercy College M
Miami University M
Middle Tennessee State University M,O
Millersville University of Pennsylvania M
Mills College M,D
Minnesota State University Mankato M
Minot State University M
Missouri State University M
Montana State University–Billings M
Montclair State University M,O
Mount Saint Mary College M
Murray State University M
National-Louis University M,O
Nazareth College of Rochester M
New Jersey City University M
New York University M,D,O
Niagara University M,O
Norfolk State University M
Northeastern State University M
Northern Arizona University M
Northern Illinois University M,D
North Georgia College & State University M,O
Northwestern State University of Louisiana M
Northwest Missouri State University M
Nova Southeastern University M,O
Oakland University M,D,O
Ohio University M
Oklahoma City University M
Old Dominion University M,D
Our Lady of the Lake University of San Antonio M
Pacific University M
Penn State University Park M,D
Piedmont College M,O
Pittsburg State University M
Portland State University M,D
Prescott College M,D
Queens College of the City University of New York M,O
Regis University M,O
Rhode Island College M
Rivier College M,D,O
Roberts Wesleyan College M,O
Roosevelt University M
Rutgers, The State University of New Jersey, New Brunswick M,D
Saginaw Valley State University M
St. John's University (NY) M
St. Joseph's College, Long Island Campus M
Saint Mary's College of California M
Saint Xavier University M,O
Salem State College M
Samford University M,D,O
San Francisco State University M
Shippensburg University of Pennsylvania M
Siena Heights University M
South Carolina State University M
Southern Oregon University M
Southwestern Oklahoma State University M
Springfield College M
Spring Hill College M
State University of New York at Binghamton M
State University of New York at New Paltz M
State University of New York College at Cortland M
State University of New York College at Geneseo M
State University of New York College at Potsdam M
Stephen F. Austin State University M
Syracuse University M
Temple University M,D
Tennessee Technological University M,O
Texas A&M International University M,D
Texas A&M University–Commerce M,D
Texas A&M University–Corpus Christi M,D
Texas A&M University–Kingsville M
Texas State University–San Marcos M
Texas Woman's University M,D
Towson University M,O
Trinity (Washington) University M
Troy University M,O
Tufts University M,D,O
Universidad del Turabo M
Universidad Metropolitana M
University at Buffalo, the State University of New York M,D,O
The University of Alabama at Birmingham M,D
University of Alaska Anchorage M,O
University of Alaska Southeast M
University of Arkansas M
University of Arkansas at Little Rock M
University of Bridgeport M,O
University of Central Arkansas M
University of Central Florida M
University of Central Oklahoma M
University of Cincinnati M
University of Dayton M
The University of Findlay M
University of Florida M,D,O
University of Georgia M,D,O
University of Hartford M
University of Hawaii at Manoa M
University of Houston M,D
University of Houston–Clear Lake M
The University of Iowa M,D
University of Kentucky M,D
University of Louisville M
University of Mary M
University of Maryland, Baltimore County M
University of Maryland, College Park M,D

M—master's degree; P—first professional degree; D—doctorate; O—other advanced degree

University of Massachusetts Amherst M,D,O
University of Memphis M,D
University of Miami M,O
University of Michigan M,D
University of Michigan–Flint M
University of Minnesota, Twin Cities Campus M,D,O
University of Missouri–Columbia M,D,O
University of Missouri–St. Louis M,O
University of Nebraska–Lincoln M,D
University of Nevada, Las Vegas M,D,O
University of New Hampshire M
The University of North Carolina at Chapel Hill M,D
The University of North Carolina at Greensboro M,D,O
University of North Dakota M
University of Northern Colorado M,D
University of Northern Iowa M
University of North Texas M,D,O
University of Oklahoma M,D,O
University of Phoenix M
University of Phoenix–Central Florida Campus M
University of Phoenix–Louisiana Campus M
University of Phoenix–North Florida Campus M
University of Phoenix–Oregon Campus M
University of Phoenix–Phoenix Campus M
University of Phoenix–South Florida Campus M
University of Phoenix–West Florida Campus M
University of Pittsburgh M
University of Puerto Rico, Río Piedras M
The University of Scranton M
University of South Alabama M,O
University of South Carolina M,D
University of Southern Mississippi M,D,O
University of South Florida M,D,O
The University of Tennessee M,D,O
The University of Texas at Brownsville M
The University of Texas at San Antonio M
The University of Texas at Tyler M
The University of Texas of the Permian Basin M
The University of Texas–Pan American M
University of the District of Columbia M
University of the Incarnate Word M,D
University of the Southwest M
The University of Toledo M,O
University of Utah M,D
University of Virginia M,D
The University of West Alabama M
University of West Florida M
University of West Georgia M,O
University of Wisconsin–Milwaukee M
University of Wisconsin–Oshkosh M
Ursuline College M
Valdosta State University M,O
Virginia Commonwealth University M,O
Wagner College M
Walden University M,D,O
Wayne State College M
Wayne State University M,D,O
Webster University M
West Chester University of Pennsylvania M,O
Western Kentucky University M
Western Oregon University M
Westfield State College M
West Virginia University M,D
Wheelock College M
Widener University M,D
Worcester State College M
Wright State University M
Xavier University M
Youngstown State University M

■ EAST EUROPEAN AND RUSSIAN STUDIES

Boston College M
Brown University M,D
Columbia University M,O
Cornell University M,D
Florida State University M
Georgetown University M
The George Washington University M
Harvard University M
Indiana University Bloomington M,O
La Salle University M
The Ohio State University M
Stanford University M
University of Illinois at Urbana–Champaign M
The University of Kansas M
University of Michigan M,O
The University of North Carolina at Chapel Hill M
University of Pittsburgh O
The University of Texas at Austin M
University of Washington M
Yale University M,D

■ ECOLOGY

Brown University D
California State University, Stanislaus M
Clemson University M,D
Colorado State University M,D
Columbia University D,O
Cornell University M,D
Dartmouth College D
Duke University M,D,O
Eastern Kentucky University M
Eastern Michigan University M
Emory University D
Florida Institute of Technology M
Florida State University M,D
Frostburg State University M
Illinois State University M,D
Indiana State University M,D
Indiana University Bloomington M,D
Iowa State University of Science and Technology M,D
Kent State University M,D
Lesley University M,D,O
Marquette University M,D
Michigan State University D
Michigan Technological University M
Montana State University M,D
North Dakota State University M,D
The Ohio State University M,D
Ohio University M,D
Old Dominion University D
Penn State University Park M,D
Princeton University D
Purdue University M,D
Rice University M,D
Rutgers, The State University of New Jersey, New Brunswick M,D
San Diego State University M,D
San Francisco State University M
San Jose State University M
State University of New York College of Environmental Science and Forestry M,D
Stony Brook University, State University of New York M,D
Texas Christian University M
Tulane University M,D
University at Albany, State University of New York M,D
University at Buffalo, the State University of New York M,D,O
The University of Arizona M,D
University of California, Davis M,D
University of California, Irvine M,D
University of California, Los Angeles M,D
University of California, San Diego D
University of California, Santa Barbara M,D
University of California, Santa Cruz M,D
University of Chicago D
University of Colorado at Boulder M,D
University of Connecticut M,D,O
University of Delaware M,D
University of Florida M,D

University of Georgia M,D
University of Hawaii at Manoa M,D
University of Illinois at Urbana–Champaign M,D
The University of Kansas M,D
University of Maine M,D
University of Maryland, College Park M,D
University of Michigan M,D
University of Minnesota, Twin Cities Campus M,D
University of Missouri–Columbia M,D
University of Missouri–St. Louis M,D,O
The University of Montana M,D
University of Nevada, Reno D
The University of North Carolina at Chapel Hill M,D
University of North Dakota M,D
University of Notre Dame M,D
University of Oklahoma D
University of Oregon M,D
University of Pittsburgh D
University of South Carolina M,D
The University of Tennessee M,D
The University of Texas at Austin M,D
The University of Toledo M,D
University of Washington M,D
University of Wisconsin–Madison M
University of Wyoming M,D
Utah State University M,D
Virginia Polytechnic Institute and State University M,D
Washington University in St. Louis D
William Paterson University of New Jersey M
Yale University D

■ ECONOMIC DEVELOPMENT

Albany State University M
Boston University M
Chicago State University M
Claremont Graduate University M,D,O
Cleveland State University M,D,O
Cornell University M,D
Eastern Michigan University M
Eastern University M
East Tennessee State University M
Florida Atlantic University M,O
Fordham University M,O
Georgetown University D
Georgia Institute of Technology M,D
Georgia State University M,D,O
New Mexico State University M,D
Southern New Hampshire University M,D
University of Central Arkansas M
University of Houston–Victoria M
University of Massachusetts Lowell M,O
University of Miami M,D
University of Minnesota, Twin Cities Campus M
The University of North Carolina at Greensboro M,D,O
University of Southern California M,D
University of Southern Mississippi M,D
Vanderbilt University M,D
Virginia Polytechnic Institute and State University M,D
Wayne State University O
West Virginia University M,D
Yale University M

■ ECONOMICS

Albany State University M
American University M,D,O
Andrews University M
Arizona State University D
Assumption College M,O
Auburn University M
Baylor University M
Bernard M. Baruch College of the City University of New York M
Boston College D
Boston University M,D
Bowling Green State University M
Brandeis University M,D
Brooklyn College of the City University of New York M
Brown University D
Buffalo State College, State University of New York M
California State Polytechnic University, Pomona M
California State University, East Bay M
California State University, Fullerton M
California State University, Long Beach M
California State University, Los Angeles M
Carnegie Mellon University D
Case Western Reserve University M
The Catholic University of America M
Central Michigan University M
Chapman University P,M
City College of the City University of New York M
Claremont Graduate University M,D,O
Clark Atlanta University M
Clark University D
Clemson University M,D
Cleveland State University M,D,O
Colorado State University M,D
Columbia University M,D
Cornell University M,D
DePaul University M
Drexel University M,D,O
Duke University M,D
East Carolina University M
Eastern Illinois University M
Eastern Michigan University M
East Tennessee State University M
Emory University D
Florida Agricultural and Mechanical University M
Florida Atlantic University M
Florida International University M,D
Florida State University M,D
Fordham University M,D,O
Georgetown University D
The George Washington University M,D
Georgia Institute of Technology M
Georgia State University M,D
Graduate School and University Center of the City University of New York D
Harvard University D
Hawai'i Pacific University M
Howard University M,D
Hunter College of the City University of New York M
Illinois State University M
Indiana University Bloomington M,D
Indiana University–Purdue University Indianapolis M
Iowa State University of Science and Technology M,D
The Johns Hopkins University D
Kansas State University M,D
Kent State University M
Lehigh University M,D
Long Island University, Brooklyn Campus M
Louisiana State University and Agricultural and Mechanical College M,D
Louisiana Tech University M,D
Marquette University M
Massachusetts Institute of Technology M,D
Miami University M
Michigan State University M,D
Middle Tennessee State University M,D
Mississippi State University M,D
Montclair State University M
Morgan State University M
Murray State University M
National University M
New Mexico State University M,D
The New School: A University M,D
New York University M,D,O
North Carolina State University M,D
Northeastern University M,D
Northern Illinois University M,D
Northwestern University M,D
Oakland University O
The Ohio State University M,D

M—master's degree; P—first professional degree; D—doctorate; O—other advanced degree

Ohio University M
Oklahoma State University M,D
Old Dominion University M
Oregon State University M,D
Pace University M
Penn State University Park M,D
Pepperdine University M
Portland State University M,D,O
Princeton University D,O
Providence College M
Purdue University D
Regent University M
Rensselaer Polytechnic Institute M
Rice University M,D
Roosevelt University M
Rutgers, The State University of New Jersey, Newark M
Rutgers, The State University of New Jersey, New Brunswick M,D
St. Cloud State University M
San Diego State University M
San Francisco State University M
San Jose State University M
South Dakota State University M
Southern Illinois University Carbondale M,D
Southern Illinois University Edwardsville M
Southern Methodist University M,D
Stanford University D
State University of New York at Binghamton M,D
Stony Brook University, State University of New York M,D
Suffolk University M,D
Syracuse University M,D
Tarleton State University M
Texas A&M University M,D
Texas A&M University–Commerce M
Texas Tech University M,D
Tufts University M
Tulane University M,D
University at Albany, State University of New York M,D,O
University at Buffalo, the State University of New York M,D,O
The University of Akron M
The University of Alabama M,D
University of Alaska Fairbanks M
The University of Arizona M,D
University of Arkansas M,D
University of California, Berkeley D
University of California, Davis M,D
University of California, Irvine M,D
University of California, Los Angeles M,D
University of California, Riverside M,D
University of California, San Diego M,D
University of California, Santa Barbara M,D
University of California, Santa Cruz D
University of Central Arkansas M
University of Central Florida M,D
University of Chicago D
University of Cincinnati M
University of Colorado at Boulder M,D
University of Colorado Denver M
University of Connecticut M,D
University of Delaware M,D
University of Denver M
University of Florida M,D
University of Georgia M,D
University of Hawaii at Manoa M,D
University of Houston M,D
University of Illinois at Chicago M,D
University of Illinois at Urbana–Champaign M,D
The University of Iowa D
The University of Kansas M,D
University of Kentucky M,D
University of Maine M
University of Maryland, Baltimore County M
University of Maryland, College Park M,D
University of Massachusetts Amherst M,D
University of Massachusetts Lowell M,O
University of Memphis M,D
University of Miami M,D
University of Michigan M,D
University of Minnesota, Twin Cities Campus D
University of Mississippi M,D
University of Missouri–Columbia M,D
University of Missouri–Kansas City M,D
University of Missouri–St. Louis M,O
The University of Montana M
University of Nebraska at Omaha M
University of Nebraska–Lincoln M,D
University of Nevada, Las Vegas M
University of Nevada, Reno M
University of New Hampshire M,D
University of New Mexico M,D
University of New Orleans D
The University of North Carolina at Chapel Hill M,D
The University of North Carolina at Charlotte M
The University of North Carolina at Greensboro D
University of North Texas M
University of Notre Dame M,D
University of Oklahoma M,D
University of Oregon M,D
University of Pennsylvania M,D
University of Pittsburgh M,D
University of Puerto Rico, Río Piedras M
University of Rhode Island M,D
University of Rochester M,D
University of San Francisco M
University of South Carolina M,D
University of Southern California M,D
University of Southern Mississippi M,D
University of South Florida M,D
The University of Tampa M
The University of Tennessee M,D
The University of Texas at Arlington M
The University of Texas at Austin M,D
The University of Texas at Dallas M,D
The University of Texas at El Paso M
The University of Texas at San Antonio M
The University of Texas–Pan American D
The University of Toledo M
University of Utah M,D
University of Virginia M,D
University of Washington M,D
University of Wisconsin–Madison D
University of Wisconsin–Milwaukee M,D
University of Wyoming M,D
Utah State University M,D
Vanderbilt University P,M,D
Virginia Commonwealth University M
Virginia Polytechnic Institute and State University M,D
Virginia State University M
Washington State University M,D,O
Washington University in St. Louis D
Wayne State University M,D,O
West Chester University of Pennsylvania M
Western Illinois University M,O
Western Michigan University M,D
West Texas A&M University M
West Virginia University M,D
Wichita State University M
Wright State University M
Yale University M,D
Youngstown State University M

■ EDUCATION—GENERAL

Abilene Christian University M
Adams State College M
Adelphi University M,D,O
Alabama Agricultural and Mechanical University M,O
Alabama State University M,D,O
Alaska Pacific University M
Albany State University M,O
Alcorn State University M,O
Alfred University M

Institution	Degrees
Alliant International University–San Diego	M,O
Alvernia University	M
Alverno College	M
American International College	M,D,O
American University	M,O
Anderson University (IN)	M
Andrews University	M,D,O
Angelo State University	M
Anna Maria College	M,O
Antioch University Los Angeles	M
Antioch University McGregor	M
Antioch University New England	M
Antioch University Santa Barbara	M
Antioch University Seattle	M
Aquinas College	M
Arcadia University	M,D,O
Argosy University, Orange County	M,D
Argosy University, Sarasota	M,D,O
Argosy University, Tampa	M,D,O
Argosy University, Twin Cities	M,D,O
Arizona State University	M,D,O
Arkansas State University	M,D,O
Arkansas Tech University	M,O
Armstrong Atlantic State University	M
Ashland University	M,D
Auburn University	M,D,O
Auburn University Montgomery	M,O
Augsburg College	M
Augusta State University	M,O
Aurora University	M,D
Austin Peay State University	M,O
Avila University	M,O
Azusa Pacific University	M,D
Baldwin-Wallace College	M
Ball State University	M,D,O
Barry University	M,D,O
Bayamón Central University	M
Baylor University	M,D,O
Belhaven College (MS)	M
Bellarmine University	M
Belmont University	M
Bemidji State University	M
Benedictine University	M
Bennington College	M
Bethel University (TN)	M
Bethel University	M,D,O
Biola University	M
Bloomsburg University of Pennsylvania	M
Boise State University	M,D
Boston College	M,D,O
Boston University	M,D,O
Bowie State University	M
Bradley University	M,D,O
Brenau University	M,O
Bridgewater State College	M,O
Brigham Young University	M,D,O
Brooklyn College of the City University of New York	M,O
Brown University	M
Bucknell University	M
Butler University	M
Cabrini College	M,O
California Baptist University	M
California Lutheran University	M,D
California Polytechnic State University, San Luis Obispo	M
California State Polytechnic University, Pomona	M
California State University, Bakersfield	M,O
California State University, Chico	M
California State University, Dominguez Hills	M,O
California State University, East Bay	M
California State University, Fresno	M,D
California State University, Fullerton	M
California State University, Long Beach	M,D
California State University, Los Angeles	M,D
California State University, Northridge	M,D
California State University, Sacramento	M
California State University, San Bernardino	M,D
California State University, San Marcos	M
California State University, Stanislaus	M,D,O
California University of Pennsylvania	M
Cambridge College	M,D,O
Cameron University	M
Campbell University	M
Canisius College	M
Capella University	M,D,O
Cardinal Stritch University	M,D
Carlow University	M
Carnegie Mellon University	M,D
Carroll University	M
Carson-Newman College	M
Castleton State College	M,O
The Catholic University of America	M,D,O
Centenary College	M
Central Connecticut State University	M,D,O
Central Michigan University	M,D,O
Central Washington University	M
Chaminade University of Honolulu	M
Chapman University	M,D,O
Charleston Southern University	M
Chatham University	M
Chestnut Hill College	M
Cheyney University of Pennsylvania	M,O
Chicago State University	M,D
Christian Brothers University	M
The Citadel, The Military College of South Carolina	M,O
City College of the City University of New York	M,O
City University of Seattle	M,O
Claremont Graduate University	M,D,O
Clarion University of Pennsylvania	M,O
Clark Atlanta University	M,D,O
Clark University	M
Clemson University	M,D,O
Cleveland State University	M,D,O
The College at Brockport, State University of New York	M,O
College of Charleston	M,O
College of Mount St. Joseph	M
College of Mount Saint Vincent	M,O
The College of New Jersey	M,O
The College of New Rochelle	M,O
College of Notre Dame of Maryland	M
College of Saint Elizabeth	M,D,O
College of St. Joseph	M
The College of Saint Rose	M,O
The College of St. Scholastica	M,O
College of Santa Fe	M
College of Staten Island of the City University of New York	M,O
The College of William and Mary	M,D,O
Colorado Christian University	M
Colorado State University	M,D
Columbia College (MO)	M
Columbia College (SC)	M
Columbia College Chicago	M
Columbus State University	M,D,O
Concordia University (CA)	M
Concordia University (OR)	M
Concordia University Chicago	M
Concordia University, Nebraska	M
Concordia University, St. Paul	M,O
Concordia University Wisconsin	M
Converse College	M,O
Coppin State University	M
Cornell University	M,D
Cornerstone University	M,O
Creighton University	M
Cumberland University	M
Daemen College	M
Dallas Baptist University	M
Delaware State University	M,D
Delta State University	M,D,O
DePaul University	M,D
DeSales University	M
Doane College	M
Dominican College	M
Dominican University	M

M—master's degree; P—first professional degree; D—doctorate; O—other advanced degree

Dominican University of California M,O
Dowling College M,D,O
Drake University M,D,O
Drexel University M,D,O
Drury University M
Duke University M
Duquesne University M,D,O
D'Youville College M,O
East Carolina University M,D,O
East Central University M
Eastern Connecticut State University M
Eastern Illinois University M,O
Eastern Kentucky University M
Eastern Mennonite University M
Eastern Michigan University M,D,O
Eastern Nazarene College M,O
Eastern New Mexico University M
Eastern Oregon University M
Eastern University M,O
Eastern Washington University M
East Stroudsburg University of Pennsylvania M
East Tennessee State University M,D,O
Edgewood College M,D,O
Edinboro University of Pennsylvania M,O
Elon University M
Embry-Riddle Aeronautical University Worldwide M,O
Emmanuel College M,O
Emory University M,D,O
Emporia State University M,O
The Evergreen State College M
Fairfield University M,O
Fairleigh Dickinson University, College at Florham M,O
Fairleigh Dickinson University, Metropolitan Campus M,O
Ferris State University M
Florida Agricultural and Mechanical University M,D
Florida Atlantic University M,D,O
Florida Gulf Coast University M
Florida International University M,D,O
Florida State University M,D,O
Fontbonne University M
Fordham University M,D,O
Fort Hays State University M,O
Franciscan University of Steubenville M
Francis Marion University M
Freed-Hardeman University M,O
Fresno Pacific University M
Friends University M
Frostburg State University M
Furman University M
Gannon University M,D,O
Gardner-Webb University M,D
Geneva College M
George Fox University M,D,O
George Mason University M,D,O
Georgetown College M
The George Washington University M,D,O
Georgia College & State University M,O
Georgian Court University M
Georgia Southern University M,D,O
Georgia Southwestern State University M,O
Georgia State University M,D,O
Goddard College M
Gonzaga University M
Governors State University M
Graceland University (IA) M
Grambling State University M,D
Grand Canyon University M,D
Grand Valley State University M,O
Gratz College M
Gwynedd-Mercy College M
Hamline University M,D
Hampton University M
Harding University M,O
Hardin-Simmons University M
Harvard University M,D
Heidelberg University M
Henderson State University M,O
Heritage University M
Hodges University M
Hofstra University M,D,O
Hollins University M
Holy Family University M
Holy Names University M,O
Hood College M
Hope International University M
Houston Baptist University M
Howard University M,D,O
Humboldt State University M
Hunter College of the City University of New York M,O
Idaho State University M,D,O
Illinois State University M,D
Indiana State University M,D,O
Indiana University Bloomington M,D,O
Indiana University Northwest M
Indiana University of Pennsylvania M,D,O
Indiana University–Purdue University Fort Wayne M,O
Indiana University–Purdue University Indianapolis M,O
Indiana University South Bend M
Indiana University Southeast M
Indiana Wesleyan University M
Inter American University of Puerto Rico, Metropolitan Campus M,D
Iona College M
Jackson State University M,D,O
Jacksonville State University M,O
Jacksonville University M,O
John Carroll University M
John F. Kennedy University M
The Johns Hopkins University M,D,O
Johnson & Wales University M
Johnson State College M,O
Jones International University M
Kansas State University M,D
Kean University M
Keene State College M,O
Kennesaw State University M,D,O
Kent State University M,D,O
Kutztown University of Pennsylvania M,O
Lakeland College M
Lamar University M,D,O
La Salle University M
La Sierra University M,D,O
Lee University M,O
Lehigh University M,D,O
Lehman College of the City University of New York M
Le Moyne College M,O
Lesley University M,D,O
LeTourneau University M
Lewis & Clark College M
Lewis University M,D,O
Liberty University M,D,O
Lincoln Memorial University M,O
Lincoln University (MO) M,O
Lindenwood University M,D,O
Lipscomb University M
Lock Haven University of Pennsylvania M
Long Island University, Brentwood Campus M
Long Island University, Brooklyn Campus M,O
Long Island University, C.W. Post Campus M,D,O
Longwood University M
Louisiana State University and Agricultural and Mechanical College M,D,O
Louisiana State University in Shreveport M
Louisiana Tech University M,D
Loyola Marymount University M,D
Loyola University Chicago M,D,O
Loyola University Maryland M,O
Lynchburg College M
Madonna University M
Maharishi University of Management M
Malone University M
Manhattan College M,O
Manhattanville College M
Mansfield University of Pennsylvania M
Marian University (WI) M,D
Marist College M,O
Marquette University M,D,O
Marshall University M,D,O
Mary Baldwin College M

Marygrove College M
Marylhurst University M
Marymount University M
Maryville University of Saint Louis M,D
Marywood University M
McNeese State University M
Medaille College M
Mercer University M,D,O
Mercy College M,O
Miami University M,D,O
Michigan State University M,D,O
MidAmerica Nazarene University M
Middle Tennessee State University M,D,O
Midwestern State University M
Millersville University of Pennsylvania M
Mills College M,D
Minnesota State University Mankato M,D,O
Minnesota State University Moorhead M,O
Misericordia University M
Mississippi College M,D,O
Mississippi State University M,D,O
Mississippi University for Women M
Mississippi Valley State University M
Missouri Baptist University M,O
Monmouth University M,O
Montana State University M,D,O
Montana State University–Billings M,O
Montclair State University M,D,O
Morehead State University M,O
Morgan State University M,D
Morningside College M
Mount Mary College M
Mount Saint Mary College M
Mount St. Mary's College M
Mount St. Mary's University M
Murray State University M,D,O
Muskingum University M
Naropa University M
National-Louis University M,D,O
National University M
Nazareth College of Rochester M
Neumann University M,D
Newman University M
New Mexico Highlands University M
New Mexico State University M,D,O
New York Institute of Technology M,O
New York University M,D,O
Niagara University M,O
Nicholls State University M
Norfolk State University M
North Carolina Agricultural and Technical State University M
North Carolina Central University M
North Carolina State University M,D,O
North Central College M
Northcentral University M,D,O
North Dakota State University M,D,O
Northeastern Illinois University M
Northeastern State University M
Northern Arizona University M,D,O
Northern Illinois University M,D,O
Northern Kentucky University M,D,O
Northern Michigan University M,O
North Georgia College & State University M,O
North Park University M
Northwestern State University of Louisiana M,O
Northwestern University M,D
Northwest Missouri State University M,O
Northwest Nazarene University M
Notre Dame de Namur University M,O
Nova Southeastern University M,D,O
Nyack College M
Oakland City University M,D
Oakland University M,D,O
Ohio Dominican University M
The Ohio State University M,D
Ohio University M,D
Oklahoma City University M
Oklahoma State University M,D,O
Old Dominion University M,D,O
Olivet Nazarene University M
Oral Roberts University M,D
Oregon State University M,D
Otterbein College M
Our Lady of the Lake University of San Antonio M,D
Pace University M,O
Pacific Lutheran University M
Pacific University M
Palm Beach Atlantic University M
Park University M
Penn State Great Valley M
Penn State Harrisburg M,D
Penn State University Park M,D
Pfeiffer University M
Philadelphia Biblical University M
Piedmont College M,O
Pittsburg State University M,O
Plymouth State University O
Point Loma Nazarene University M,O
Point Park University M
Pontifical Catholic University of Puerto Rico M,D
Portland State University M,D
Prairie View A&M University M,D
Prescott College M,D
Providence College M
Purdue University M,D,O
Purdue University Calumet M
Queens College of the City University of New York M,O
Queens University of Charlotte M
Quinnipiac University M
Radford University M
Regent University M,D,O
Regis College (MA) M
Regis University M,O
Rhode Island College D
Rice University M
The Richard Stockton College of New Jersey M
Rider University M,O
Rivier College M,D,O
Robert Morris University M,D,O
Roberts Wesleyan College M,O
Rockford College M
Rockhurst University M
Roger Williams University M
Rollins College M
Roosevelt University M,D
Rowan University M,D,O
Rutgers, The State University of New Jersey, New Brunswick M,D
Sacred Heart University M,O
Saginaw Valley State University M,O
St. Ambrose University M
St. Bonaventure University M,O
St. Catherine University M
St. Cloud State University M,D,O
St. Edward's University M,O
Saint Francis University M
St. John Fisher College M,D,O
St. John's University (NY) M,D,O
Saint Joseph College M
Saint Joseph's College of Maine M
Saint Joseph's University M,D
Saint Leo University M
Saint Louis University M,D
Saint Martin's University M
Saint Mary's College of California M,D
St. Mary's University (United States) M,O
Saint Mary's University of Minnesota M,O
Saint Michael's College M,O
Saint Peter's College M,O
St. Thomas Aquinas College M,O
St. Thomas University M,D,O
Saint Xavier University M,O
Salem State College M
Salisbury University M
Samford University M,D,O
Sam Houston State University M,D
San Diego State University M,D
San Francisco State University M,D,O
San Jose State University M,O
Santa Clara University M,O
Sarah Lawrence College M
Seattle University M,D,O
Seton Hall University M,D,O
Seton Hill University M
Shenandoah University M,D,O

M—master's degree; P—first professional degree; D—doctorate; O—other advanced degree

Institution	Degrees
Shippensburg University of Pennsylvania	M,O
Siena Heights University	M
Silver Lake College	M
Simmons College	M,D,O
SIT Graduate Institute	M
Slippery Rock University of Pennsylvania	M
Sonoma State University	M
South Carolina State University	M
South Dakota State University	M,D
Southeastern Louisiana University	M,D
Southeastern Oklahoma State University	M
Southern Connecticut State University	M,D,O
Southern Illinois University Carbondale	M,D
Southern Illinois University Edwardsville	M,O
Southern Methodist University	M,D,O
Southern Nazarene University	M
Southern New Hampshire University	M,O
Southern Oregon University	M
Southern University and Agricultural and Mechanical College	M,D
Southern Utah University	M
Southern Wesleyan University	M
Southwest Baptist University	M,O
Southwestern College (KS)	M
Southwestern Oklahoma State University	M
Southwest Minnesota State University	M
Spalding University	M,D
Spring Arbor University	M
Springfield College	M
Spring Hill College	M
Stanford University	M,D
State University of New York at Binghamton	M,D
State University of New York at Fredonia	M,O
State University of New York at New Paltz	M,O
State University of New York at Oswego	M,O
State University of New York College at Cortland	M,O
State University of New York College at Geneseo	M
State University of New York College at Oneonta	M,O
State University of New York Empire State College	M
Stephen F. Austin State University	M,D
Stetson University	M
Strayer University	M
Suffolk University	M,O
Sul Ross State University	M
Syracuse University	M,D,O
Tarleton State University	M,D,O
Temple University	M,D
Tennessee State University	M,D,O
Tennessee Technological University	M,D,O
Texas A&M International University	M,D
Texas A&M University	M,D
Texas A&M University–Commerce	M,D
Texas A&M University–Corpus Christi	M,D
Texas A&M University–Kingsville	M,D
Texas A&M University–Texarkana	M
Texas Christian University	M,D,O
Texas Southern University	M,D
Texas State University–San Marcos	M,D
Texas Tech University	M,D
Texas Wesleyan University	M
Texas Woman's University	M,D
Thomas More College	M
Towson University	M
Trevecca Nazarene University	M,D
Trinity International University	M
Trinity University	M
Trinity (Washington) University	M
Troy University	M,O
Truman State University	M
Tufts University	M,D,O
Tusculum College	M
Union College (KY)	M
Union Institute & University	M,D,O
Union University	M,D,O
Universidad del Turabo	M,D
Universidad Metropolitana	M
University at Albany, State University of New York	M,D,O
University at Buffalo, the State University of New York	M,D,O
The University of Akron	M,D
The University of Alabama at Birmingham	M,D,O
University of Alaska Anchorage	M,O
University of Alaska Fairbanks	M,D,O
University of Alaska Southeast	M
The University of Arizona	M,D,O
University of Arkansas	M,D,O
University of Arkansas at Little Rock	M,D,O
University of Arkansas at Monticello	M
University of Bridgeport	M,D,O
University of California, Berkeley	M,D,O
University of California, Davis	M,D
University of California, Irvine	M,D
University of California, Los Angeles	M,D
University of California, Riverside	M,D
University of California, San Diego	M,D
University of California, Santa Barbara	M,D
University of California, Santa Cruz	M,D
University of Central Arkansas	M,O
University of Central Florida	M,D,O
University of Central Missouri	M,D,O
University of Central Oklahoma	M
University of Cincinnati	M,D,O
University of Colorado at Boulder	M,D
University of Colorado at Colorado Springs	M,D
University of Colorado Denver	M,D,O
University of Connecticut	M,D,O
University of Dayton	M,D,O
University of Delaware	M,D,O
University of Denver	M,D,O
University of Detroit Mercy	M
University of Evansville	M,D
The University of Findlay	M
University of Florida	M,D,O
University of Georgia	M,D,O
University of Great Falls	M
University of Guam	M
University of Hartford	M,D,O
University of Hawaii at Manoa	M,D,O
University of Houston	M,D
University of Houston–Clear Lake	M,D
University of Houston–Victoria	M
University of Idaho	M,D,O
University of Illinois at Chicago	M,D
University of Illinois at Springfield	M
University of Illinois at Urbana–Champaign	M,D,O
University of Indianapolis	M
The University of Iowa	M,D,O
The University of Kansas	M,D,O
University of Kentucky	M,D,O
University of La Verne	M,O
University of Louisiana at Lafayette	M,D
University of Louisiana at Monroe	M,D,O
University of Louisville	M,D,O
University of Maine	M,D,O
University of Mary	M
University of Mary Hardin-Baylor	M,D
University of Maryland, Baltimore County	M,O
University of Maryland, College Park	M,D,O
University of Maryland Eastern Shore	M
University of Maryland University College	M
University of Mary Washington	M
University of Massachusetts Amherst	M,D,O
University of Massachusetts Boston	M,D,O

University of Massachusetts Dartmouth	M,O
University of Massachusetts Lowell	M,D,O
University of Memphis	M,D,O
University of Miami	M,D,O
University of Michigan	M,D
University of Michigan–Dearborn	M
University of Michigan–Flint	M
University of Minnesota, Duluth	D
University of Minnesota, Twin Cities Campus	M,D,O
University of Mississippi	M,D,O
University of Missouri–Columbia	M,D,O
University of Missouri–Kansas City	M,D,O
University of Missouri–St. Louis	M,D,O
University of Mobile	M
The University of Montana	M,D,O
University of Montevallo	M,O
University of Nebraska at Kearney	M,O
University of Nebraska at Omaha	M,D,O
University of Nevada, Las Vegas	M,D,O
University of Nevada, Reno	M,D,O
University of New England	M
University of New Hampshire	M,D,O
University of New Haven	M
University of New Mexico	M,O
University of New Orleans	M,D,O
University of North Alabama	M,O
The University of North Carolina at Chapel Hill	M,D
The University of North Carolina at Charlotte	M
The University of North Carolina at Greensboro	M,D,O
The University of North Carolina at Pembroke	M
The University of North Carolina Wilmington	M,D
University of North Dakota	M,D,O
University of Northern Colorado	M,D,O
University of Northern Iowa	M,D,O
University of North Florida	M,D
University of North Texas	M,D,O
University of Notre Dame	M
University of Oklahoma	M,D,O
University of Oregon	M,D
University of Pennsylvania	M,D
University of Phoenix	M,D
University of Phoenix–Central Florida Campus	M
University of Phoenix–Denver Campus	M
University of Phoenix–Hawaii Campus	M
University of Phoenix–Las Vegas Campus	M
University of Phoenix–Louisiana Campus	M
University of Phoenix–New Mexico Campus	M
University of Phoenix–North Florida Campus	M
University of Phoenix–Oregon Campus	M
University of Phoenix–Phoenix Campus	M
University of Phoenix–Sacramento Valley Campus	M,O
University of Phoenix–San Diego Campus	M
University of Phoenix–Southern Arizona Campus	M,O
University of Phoenix–Southern California Campus	M
University of Phoenix–Southern Colorado Campus	M,O
University of Phoenix–South Florida Campus	M
University of Phoenix–Utah Campus	M
University of Phoenix–West Florida Campus	M
University of Phoenix–West Michigan Campus	M
University of Pittsburgh	M,D
University of Portland	M
University of Puerto Rico, Río Piedras	M,D
University of Puget Sound	M
University of Redlands	M,D,O
University of Rhode Island	M,D
University of Rio Grande	M
University of Rochester	M,D
University of St. Francis (IL)	M
University of Saint Francis (IN)	M
University of Saint Mary	M
University of St. Thomas (MN)	M,O
University of St. Thomas (TX)	M
University of San Diego	M,D,O
University of San Francisco	M,D
The University of Scranton	M
University of Sioux Falls	M,O
University of South Alabama	M,D,O
University of South Carolina	M,D,O
The University of South Dakota	M,D,O
University of Southern Indiana	M
University of Southern Maine	M,D,O
University of Southern Mississippi	M,D,O
University of South Florida	M,D,O
The University of Tampa	M
The University of Tennessee	M,D,O
The University of Tennessee at Chattanooga	M,D,O
The University of Tennessee at Martin	M
The University of Texas at Arlington	M,D
The University of Texas at Austin	M,D
The University of Texas at Brownsville	M
The University of Texas at El Paso	M,D
The University of Texas at San Antonio	M
The University of Texas of the Permian Basin	M
The University of Texas–Pan American	M,D
University of the District of Columbia	M
University of the Incarnate Word	M,D
University of the Pacific	M,D,O
University of the Southwest	M
The University of Toledo	M,D,O
University of Tulsa	M
University of Utah	M,D
University of Vermont	M,D
University of Virginia	M,D,O
University of Washington	M,D,O
University of Washington, Bothell	M
University of Washington, Tacoma	M
The University of West Alabama	M
University of West Georgia	M,D,O
University of Wisconsin–Eau Claire	M
University of Wisconsin–La Crosse	M
University of Wisconsin–Madison	M,D,O
University of Wisconsin–Milwaukee	M,D,O
University of Wisconsin–Oshkosh	M
University of Wisconsin–Platteville	M
University of Wisconsin–River Falls	M
University of Wisconsin–Stevens Point	M
University of Wisconsin–Stout	M,O
University of Wisconsin–Superior	M
University of Wisconsin–Whitewater	M
Ursuline College	M
Utah State University	M,D,O
Utica College	M,O
Valparaiso University	M
Vanderbilt University	M,D
Vanguard University of Southern California	M
Villanova University	M
Virginia Commonwealth University	M,D,O
Virginia State University	M,O
Viterbo University	M
Wagner College	M,O

M—master's degree; P—first professional degree; D—doctorate; O—other advanced degree

Wake Forest University M
Walden University M,D,O
Walla Walla University M
Walsh University M
Washburn University M
Washington State University M,D,O
Washington University in St. Louis M,D
Wayland Baptist University M
Waynesburg University M,D
Wayne State College M,O
Wayne State University M,D,O
Weber State University M
Webster University M,O
Wesley College M
West Chester University of Pennsylvania M,O
Western Carolina University M,D,O
Western Connecticut State University M,D
Western Illinois University M,D,O
Western Michigan University M,D,O
Western New Mexico University M
Western Oregon University M
Western Washington University M
Westfield State College M,O
Westminster College (UT) M
West Texas A&M University M
West Virginia University M,D
Wheaton College M
Wheelock College M
Whitworth University M
Wichita State University M,D,O
Widener University M,D
Wilkes University M,D
Willamette University M
William Carey University M,O
William Paterson University of New Jersey M
Wilmington University M
Winona State University M
Winthrop University M
Worcester State College M,O
Wright State University M,O
Xavier University M
Xavier University of Louisiana M
Youngstown State University M,D

■ EDUCATIONAL LEADERSHIP AND ADMINISTRATION

Abilene Christian University M
Adelphi University M,O
Alabama Agricultural and Mechanical University M,O
Alabama State University M,D,O
Albany State University M,O
Alliant International University–San Diego M,D,O
Alverno College M
American International College M,D,O
Andrews University M,D,O
Angelo State University M
Antioch University McGregor M
Antioch University New England M
Appalachian State University M,D,O
Arcadia University M,D,O
Argosy University, Orange County M,D
Argosy University, Sarasota M,D,O
Argosy University, Tampa M,D,O
Argosy University, Twin Cities M,D,O
Arizona State University M,D,O
Arkansas State University M,D,O
Arkansas Tech University M,O
Ashland University M,D
Auburn University M,D,O
Auburn University Montgomery M,O
Augusta State University M,O
Aurora University M,D
Austin Peay State University M,O
Azusa Pacific University M,D
Baldwin-Wallace College M
Ball State University M,D,O
Barry University M,D,O
Bayamón Central University M
Baylor University M,O
Bellarmine University M
Benedictine College M
Benedictine University M,D
Bernard M. Baruch College of the City University of New York M,O
Bethel University (TN) M
Bethel University M,D,O
Bob Jones University P,M,D,O
Boise State University M,D
Boston College M,D,O
Boston University M,O
Bowie State University M,D
Bowling Green State University M,D,O
Bradley University M
Bridgewater State College M,O
Brigham Young University M,D
Brooklyn College of the City University of New York M
Bucknell University M
Buffalo State College, State University of New York O
Butler University M
Caldwell College M
California Baptist University M
California Lutheran University M,D
California State University, Bakersfield M
California State University, Dominguez Hills M
California State University, East Bay M
California State University, Fresno M,D
California State University, Fullerton M,D
California State University, Northridge M,D
California State University, Sacramento M
California State University, San Bernardino M,D
California State University, Stanislaus M,D
California University of Pennsylvania M
Calumet College of Saint Joseph M
Cambridge College M,D,O
Cameron University M
Campbell University M
Canisius College M
Capella University M,D,O
Cardinal Stritch University M,D
Carlow University M
Carson-Newman College M
Castleton State College M,O
The Catholic University of America P,M,D,O
Centenary College M
Central Connecticut State University M,D,O
Central Michigan University M,D,O
Chapman University M
Charleston Southern University M
Chestnut Hill College M
Cheyney University of Pennsylvania M,O
Chicago State University M,D
Christian Brothers University M
The Citadel, The Military College of South Carolina M,O
City College of the City University of New York M,O
City University of Seattle M,O
Claremont Graduate University M,D,O
Clark Atlanta University M,D,O
Clemson University M,D,O
Cleveland State University M,D,O
The College at Brockport, State University of New York O
College of Mount St. Joseph M
The College of New Jersey M,O
The College of New Rochelle M,O
College of Notre Dame of Maryland M,D
College of Saint Elizabeth M,D,O
The College of Saint Rose M,O
College of Santa Fe M
College of Staten Island of the City University of New York O
The College of William and Mary M,D
Colorado State University M,D
Columbus State University M,D,O
Concordia University (CA) M
Concordia University (OR) M
Concordia University Chicago M,D,O
Concordia University, Nebraska M
Concordia University, St. Paul M,O
Concordia University Wisconsin M
Converse College M,O
Creighton University M
Dallas Baptist University M
Delaware State University M,D
Delta State University M,D,O

Institution	Degrees
DePaul University	D
Doane College	M
Dominican University	M
Dowling College	M,D,O
Drake University	M,D,O
Drexel University	M,D
Duquesne University	M,D,O
D'Youville College	D
East Carolina University	M,D,O
Eastern Illinois University	M,O
Eastern Kentucky University	M
Eastern Michigan University	M,D,O
Eastern Nazarene College	M,O
Eastern Washington University	M
East Tennessee State University	M,D,O
Edgewood College	M,D,O
Edinboro University of Pennsylvania	M,O
Elmhurst College	M
Emmanuel College	M,O
Emporia State University	M
Fairleigh Dickinson University, College at Florham	M
Fairleigh Dickinson University, Metropolitan Campus	M
Fayetteville State University	M,D
Ferris State University	M
Fitchburg State College	M,O
Florida Agricultural and Mechanical University	M,D
Florida Atlantic University	M,D,O
Florida Gulf Coast University	M
Florida International University	M,D,O
Florida State University	M,D,O
Fordham University	M,D,O
Fort Hays State University	M,O
Framingham State College	M
Franciscan University of Steubenville	M
Freed-Hardeman University	M,O
Fresno Pacific University	M
Frostburg State University	M
Furman University	M
Gallaudet University	M,D,O
Gannon University	M,D,O
Gardner-Webb University	M,D
Geneva College	M
George Fox University	M,D,O
George Mason University	M,O
The George Washington University	M,D,O
Georgia College & State University	M,O
Georgian Court University	M,O
Georgia Southern University	M,D,O
Georgia State University	M,D,O
Gonzaga University	M,D
Governors State University	M
Graceland University (IA)	M
Grambling State University	M,D
Grand Canyon University	M,D
Grand Valley State University	M,O
Gwynedd-Mercy College	M
Harding University	M,O
Harvard University	M,D
Henderson State University	M,O
Heritage University	M
High Point University	M
Hofstra University	M,D,O
Holy Family University	M
Hood College	M
Hope International University	M
Houston Baptist University	M
Howard University	M,D,O
Hunter College of the City University of New York	O
Idaho State University	M,D,O
Illinois State University	M,D
Immaculata University	M,D,O
Indiana State University	M,D,O
Indiana University Bloomington	M,D,O
Indiana University of Pennsylvania	M,D,O
Indiana University–Purdue University Fort Wayne	M
Indiana University–Purdue University Indianapolis	M,O
Inter American University of Puerto Rico, Metropolitan Campus	M,D
Inter American University of Puerto Rico, San Germán Campus	M,D
Iona College	M
Iowa State University of Science and Technology	M,D
Jackson State University	M,D,O
Jacksonville State University	M,O
James Madison University	M
John Carroll University	M
The Johns Hopkins University	M,D,O
Johnson & Wales University	D
Jones International University	M
Kansas State University	M,D
Kean University	M,D
Keene State College	M,O
Kennesaw State University	M,D,O
Kent State University	M,D,O
Kutztown University of Pennsylvania	M
Lamar University	M,D,O
La Sierra University	M,D,O
Lee University	M,O
Lehigh University	M,D,O
Le Moyne College	M,O
LeTourneau University	M
Lewis & Clark College	M,D
Lewis University	M,D,O
Liberty University	M,D,O
Lincoln Memorial University	M,O
Lincoln University (MO)	M,O
Lindenwood University	M,D,O
Lipscomb University	M
Long Island University, Brooklyn Campus	M
Long Island University, C.W. Post Campus	M,D,O
Longwood University	M
Louisiana State University and Agricultural and Mechanical College	M,D,O
Louisiana State University in Shreveport	M
Louisiana Tech University	M,D
Loyola Marymount University	M,D
Loyola University Chicago	M,D,O
Loyola University Maryland	M,O
Lynchburg College	M
Lynn University	M,D
Madonna University	M
Manhattan College	M,O
Manhattanville College	M
Marian University (WI)	M,D
Marshall University	M,D,O
Marygrove College	M
Marymount University	M,O
Maryville University of Saint Louis	M,D
Marywood University	M,D
McDaniel College	M
McNeese State University	M,O
Mercer University	M,D,O
Mercy College	M,O
Mercyhurst College	M,O
Miami University	M,D
Michigan State University	M,D,O
Middle Tennessee State University	M,O
Midwestern State University	M
Mills College	M,D
Minnesota State University Mankato	M,O
Minnesota State University Moorhead	M,O
Mississippi College	M,D,O
Mississippi State University	M,D,O
Missouri Baptist University	M,O
Missouri State University	M,O
Monmouth University	M,O
Montana State University	M,D,O
Montclair State University	M,D,O
Morehead State University	M,O
Morgan State University	M,D
Mount St. Mary's College	M
Murray State University	M,O
National-Louis University	M,D,O
National University	M
New Jersey City University	M
Newman University	M
New Mexico Highlands University	M
New Mexico State University	M,D
New York Institute of Technology	O
New York University	M,D,O

M—master's degree; P—first professional degree; D—doctorate; O—other advanced degree

Niagara University M,O
Nicholls State University M
Norfolk State University M
North Carolina Agricultural and Technical State University M,D
North Carolina Central University M
North Carolina State University M,D
North Central College M
North Dakota State University M,O
Northeastern Illinois University M
Northeastern State University M
Northern Arizona University M,D
Northern Illinois University M,D,O
Northern Kentucky University M,D,O
Northern Michigan University M,O
North Georgia College & State University M,O
Northwestern State University of Louisiana M,O
Northwest Missouri State University M,O
Northwest Nazarene University M
Notre Dame de Namur University M,O
Nova Southeastern University M,D,O
Oakland City University M,D
Oakland University M,D,O
The Ohio State University M,D
Ohio University M,D
Oklahoma State University M,D
Old Dominion University M,D,O
Olivet Nazarene University M
Oral Roberts University M,D
Oregon State University M
Our Lady of the Lake University of San Antonio M
Pace University M,O
Pacific Lutheran University M
Park University M
Penn State Great Valley M
Penn State University Park M,D
Philadelphia Biblical University M
Pittsburg State University M,O
Plymouth State University M
Point Park University M
Pontifical Catholic University of Puerto Rico D
Portland State University M,D
Prairie View A&M University M,D
Prescott College M,D
Providence College M
Purdue University M,D,O
Purdue University Calumet M
Queens College of the City University of New York O
Queens University of Charlotte M
Radford University M
Regent University M,D,O
Regis University M,O
Rhode Island College M,O
Rider University M,O
Rivier College M,D,O
Robert Morris University M,D,O
Roosevelt University M
Rowan University M,D
Rutgers, The State University of New Jersey, Camden M
Rutgers, The State University of New Jersey, New Brunswick M,D
Sacred Heart University M,O
Saginaw Valley State University M,O
St. Ambrose University M
St. Bonaventure University M,O
St. Cloud State University M,D
St. Edward's University M,O
Saint Francis University M
St. John Fisher College M,D
St. John's University (NY) M,D,O
Saint Joseph's University M,D
Saint Leo University M
Saint Louis University M,D,O
Saint Martin's University M
Saint Mary's College of California M,D
St. Mary's University (United States) M,O
Saint Mary's University of Minnesota M,D,O
Saint Michael's College M,O
Saint Peter's College M,O
St. Thomas Aquinas College M,O
St. Thomas University M,D,O
Saint Xavier University M,O
Salem State College M
Salisbury University M
Samford University M,D,O
Sam Houston State University M,D
San Diego State University M
San Francisco State University M,O
San Jose State University M,O
Santa Clara University M
Seattle Pacific University M,D,O
Seattle University M,D,O
Seton Hall University D,O
Shenandoah University M,D,O
Shippensburg University of Pennsylvania M
Siena Heights University M
Silver Lake College M
Simmons College M,O
Slippery Rock University of Pennsylvania M
Sonoma State University M
South Carolina State University D,O
South Dakota State University M
Southeastern Louisiana University M,D
Southeastern Oklahoma State University M
Southeast Missouri State University M,O
Southern Connecticut State University M,D,O
Southern Illinois University Carbondale M,D
Southern Illinois University Edwardsville M,O
Southern Nazarene University M
Southern New Hampshire University M,O
Southern Oregon University M
Southern University and Agricultural and Mechanical College M
Southwest Baptist University M,O
Southwestern Oklahoma State University M
Spalding University M,D
Springfield College M
Stanford University M,D
State University of New York at Fredonia O
State University of New York at New Paltz M,O
State University of New York at Oswego O
State University of New York at Plattsburgh O
State University of New York College at Cortland O
Stephen F. Austin State University M,D
Stetson University M
Stony Brook University, State University of New York M,O
Suffolk University M,O
Sul Ross State University M
Syracuse University M,D,O
Tarleton State University M,D,O
Temple University M,D
Tennessee State University M,D,O
Tennessee Technological University M,O
Texas A&M International University M
Texas A&M University M,D
Texas A&M University–Commerce M,D
Texas A&M University–Corpus Christi M,D
Texas A&M University–Kingsville M,D
Texas A&M University–Texarkana M
Texas Christian University M
Texas Southern University M,D
Texas State University–San Marcos M
Texas Tech University M,D
Texas Woman's University M,D
Trevecca Nazarene University M,D
Trinity International University M
Trinity University M
Trinity (Washington) University M
Troy University M,O
Union College (KY) M
Union Institute & University D
Union University M,D,O
Universidad del Turabo M,D
Universidad Metropolitana M

University at Albany, State University of New York	M,D,O
University at Buffalo, the State University of New York	M,D,O
The University of Akron	M,D
The University of Alabama	M,D,O
The University of Alabama at Birmingham	M,D,O
University of Alaska Anchorage	M,O
The University of Arizona	M,D,O
University of Arkansas	M,D,O
University of Arkansas at Little Rock	M,D,O
University of Arkansas at Monticello	M
University of Bridgeport	D,O
University of California, Berkeley	M,D
University of California, Irvine	M,D
University of California, Los Angeles	D
University of California, Riverside	M,D
University of California, Santa Barbara	M,D
University of Central Arkansas	M,O
University of Central Florida	M,D,O
University of Central Missouri	M,O
University of Central Oklahoma	M
University of Cincinnati	M,D,O
University of Colorado at Colorado Springs	M,D
University of Colorado Denver	M,D,O
University of Connecticut	D,O
University of Dayton	M,D,O
University of Delaware	M,D,O
University of Denver	M,D,O
University of Detroit Mercy	M
The University of Findlay	M
University of Florida	M,D,O
University of Georgia	M,D,O
University of Guam	M
University of Hartford	D,O
University of Hawaii at Manoa	M,D
University of Houston	M,D
University of Houston–Clear Lake	M,D
University of Houston–Victoria	M
University of Idaho	M,D,O
University of Illinois at Chicago	M,D
University of Illinois at Springfield	M
University of Illinois at Urbana–Champaign	M,D,O
University of Indianapolis	M
The University of Iowa	M,D,O
The University of Kansas	M,D
University of Kentucky	M,D,O
University of La Verne	M,D,O
University of Louisiana at Lafayette	M,D
University of Louisiana at Monroe	M,D
University of Louisville	M,D,O
University of Maine	M,D,O
University of Mary	M
University of Mary Hardin-Baylor	M,D
University of Maryland, College Park	M,D,O
University of Maryland Eastern Shore	D
University of Massachusetts Amherst	M,D,O
University of Massachusetts Boston	M,D,O
University of Massachusetts Lowell	M,D,O
University of Memphis	M,D
University of Miami	M,D,O
University of Michigan	M,D
University of Minnesota, Twin Cities Campus	M,D
University of Mississippi	M,D,O
University of Missouri–Columbia	M,D,O
University of Missouri–Kansas City	M,D,O
University of Missouri–St. Louis	M,D,O
The University of Montana	M,D,O
University of Montevallo	M,O
University of Nebraska at Kearney	M,O
University of Nebraska at Omaha	M,D,O
University of Nebraska–Lincoln	M,D,O
University of Nevada, Las Vegas	M,D
University of Nevada, Reno	M,D,O
University of New England	O
University of New Hampshire	M,O
University of New Mexico	M,D,O
University of New Orleans	M,D,O
University of North Alabama	O
The University of North Carolina at Chapel Hill	M,D
The University of North Carolina at Charlotte	M,D,O
The University of North Carolina at Greensboro	M,D,O
The University of North Carolina at Pembroke	M
The University of North Carolina Wilmington	M,D
University of North Dakota	M,D,O
University of Northern Colorado	M,D,O
University of Northern Iowa	M,D
University of North Florida	M,D
University of North Texas	M,D
University of Oklahoma	M,D
University of Pennsylvania	M,D
University of Phoenix	M
University of Phoenix–Central Florida Campus	M
University of Phoenix–Denver Campus	M
University of Phoenix–Hawaii Campus	M
University of Phoenix–Las Vegas Campus	M
University of Phoenix–New Mexico Campus	M
University of Phoenix–North Florida Campus	M
University of Phoenix–Phoenix Campus	M
University of Phoenix–Southern Arizona Campus	M,O
University of Phoenix–Southern Colorado Campus	M,O
University of Phoenix–South Florida Campus	M
University of Phoenix–Utah Campus	M
University of Phoenix–West Florida Campus	M
University of Phoenix–West Michigan Campus	M
University of Pittsburgh	M,D
University of Puerto Rico, Río Piedras	M,D
University of St. Francis (IL)	M
University of St. Thomas (MN)	M,D,O
University of San Diego	M,D,O
University of San Francisco	M,D
The University of Scranton	M
University of Sioux Falls	M,O
University of South Alabama	M,O
University of South Carolina	M,D,O
The University of South Dakota	M,D,O
University of Southern California	D
University of Southern Maine	M,O
University of Southern Mississippi	M,D,O
University of South Florida	M,D,O
The University of Tennessee	M,D,O
The University of Tennessee at Chattanooga	M,D,O
The University of Tennessee at Martin	M
The University of Texas at Arlington	M,D
The University of Texas at Austin	M,D
The University of Texas at Brownsville	M
The University of Texas at El Paso	M,D
The University of Texas at San Antonio	M,D
The University of Texas at Tyler	M
The University of Texas of the Permian Basin	M
The University of Texas–Pan American	M,D
University of the Incarnate Word	M,D
University of the Pacific	M,D
University of the Southwest	M
The University of Toledo	M,D,O
University of Utah	M,D

M—master's degree; P—first professional degree; D—doctorate; O—other advanced degree

University of Vermont M,D
University of Virginia M,D,O
University of Washington M,D
University of Washington, Tacoma M
The University of West Alabama M
University of West Florida M,O
University of West Georgia M,O
University of Wisconsin–Madison M,D,O
University of Wisconsin–Milwaukee M,D,O
University of Wisconsin–Oshkosh M
University of Wisconsin–Stevens Point M
University of Wisconsin–Superior M,O
University of Wisconsin–Whitewater M
University of Wyoming M,D,O
Ursuline College M
Valdosta State University M,D,O
Vanderbilt University M,D
Villanova University M
Virginia Commonwealth University D
Virginia Polytechnic Institute and State University D,O
Virginia State University M
Wagner College O
Walden University M,D,O
Walla Walla University M
Washburn University M
Washington State University M,D
Wayne State College M,O
Wayne State University M,D,O
Webster University M,O
Western Carolina University M,D,O
Western Connecticut State University D
Western Illinois University M,D,O
Western Kentucky University M,O
Western Michigan University M,D,O
Western New Mexico University M
Western Washington University M
Westfield State College M,O
West Texas A&M University M
West Virginia University M,D
Wheelock College M
Whitworth University M
Wichita State University M,D,O
Widener University M,D
Wilkes University M,D
William Paterson University of New Jersey M
William Woods University M,O
Wilmington University M,D
Winona State University M,O
Winthrop University M
Worcester State College M,O
Wright State University M,O
Xavier University M
Xavier University of Louisiana M
Yeshiva University M,D,O
Youngstown State University M,D

■ EDUCATIONAL MEASUREMENT AND EVALUATION

Angelo State University M
Arkansas State University M,O
Boston College M,D
Bucknell University M
Cambridge College M,D,O
Claremont Graduate University M,D,O
Eastern Michigan University M,O
Florida State University M,D,O
Gallaudet University M,O
George Mason University M
Georgia State University M,D
Harvard University D
Houston Baptist University M
Indiana University Bloomington M,D,O
Iowa State University of Science and Technology M,D
Kent State University M,D
Louisiana State University and Agricultural and Mechanical College M,D,O
Loyola University Chicago M,D
Michigan State University M,D,O
North Carolina State University D
Ohio University M,D
Rutgers, The State University of New Jersey, New Brunswick M
Seton Hall University M,D,O
Southern Connecticut State University M
Southern Illinois University Carbondale M,D
Southwestern Oklahoma State University M
Stanford University M,D
Sul Ross State University M
Syracuse University M,D,O
Texas A&M University M,D
University at Albany, State University of New York M,D,O
University of Arkansas M,D
University of California, Berkeley M,D
University of California, Santa Barbara M,D
University of Colorado at Boulder D
University of Connecticut M,D,O
University of Denver M,D,O
University of Florida M,D,O
The University of Iowa M,D,O
The University of Kansas M,D
University of Kentucky M,D
University of Louisiana at Monroe M,D
University of Maryland, College Park M,D
University of Massachusetts Amherst M,D,O
University of Memphis M,D
University of Miami M,D
University of Michigan M,D
University of Michigan–Dearborn M,O
University of Minnesota, Twin Cities Campus M,D
University of Missouri–St. Louis M,D,O
University of Nebraska–Lincoln M,D,O
University of New England M
The University of North Carolina at Chapel Hill M,D
The University of North Carolina at Greensboro D
University of North Dakota D
University of Northern Colorado M,D
University of North Texas D
University of Pennsylvania M,D
University of Pittsburgh M,D
University of Puerto Rico, Río Piedras M
University of South Carolina M,D
University of South Florida M,D,O
The University of Tennessee M,D,O
The University of Texas at El Paso M
The University of Texas–Pan American M
University of the Southwest M
The University of Toledo M,D
University of Virginia M,D,O
University of Washington M,D
University of West Georgia D
University of Wisconsin–Milwaukee M,D
Utah State University M,D
Vanderbilt University M,D
Virginia Commonwealth University D
Virginia Polytechnic Institute and State University D
Washington University in St. Louis D
Wayne State University M,D,O
West Chester University of Pennsylvania M,O
Western Michigan University M,D,O
West Texas A&M University M
Wilkes University M,D

■ EDUCATIONAL MEDIA/ INSTRUCTIONAL TECHNOLOGY

Adelphi University M,O
Alabama State University M,O
Alverno College M
American InterContinental University South Florida M
Appalachian State University M,O
Arcadia University M,D,O
Argosy University, Orange County M,D
Argosy University, Sarasota M,D,O
Arizona State University M,D
Auburn University M,D,O
Azusa Pacific University M
Baldwin-Wallace College M
Barry University M,D,O
Bellevue University M,D

Bloomsburg University of Pennsylvania M
Boise State University M
Boston University M,D,O
Bowling Green State University M
Bridgewater State College M
Brigham Young University M,D
Buffalo State College, State University of New York M
Cabrini College M,O
California Baptist University M
California State University, Bakersfield M
California State University, East Bay M
California State University, Fullerton M
California State University, Northridge M
California State University, San Bernardino M
California State University, Stanislaus M,D
Cambridge College M,D,O
Capella University M,D,O
Cardinal Stritch University M
Carlow University M
Central Connecticut State University M
Central Michigan University M,D,O
Chestnut Hill College M,O
Chicago State University M
City University of Seattle M,O
College of Mount Saint Vincent M,O
The College of New Jersey M
College of Saint Elizabeth M,D,O
The College of Saint Rose M,O
The College of St. Scholastica M
The College of William and Mary M,D
Concordia University Chicago M
Dowling College M,D,O
Drexel University M,D
Drury University M
Duquesne University M,D
East Carolina University M,O
Eastern Connecticut State University M
Eastern Michigan University M,O
Eastern Washington University M
East Stroudsburg University of Pennsylvania M
East Tennessee State University M
Emporia State University M
Fairfield University M,O
Fairleigh Dickinson University, College at Florham M,O
Fairleigh Dickinson University, Metropolitan Campus M,O
Ferris State University M
Fitchburg State College M,O
Florida Gulf Coast University M
Florida International University M,D,O
Florida State University M,D,O
Fort Hays State University M
Framingham State College M
Fresno Pacific University M
Frostburg State University M
Gannon University M,O
George Fox University M,D,O
George Mason University M,O
The George Washington University M
Georgia College & State University M,O
Georgia Southern University M
Georgia State University M,D,O
Governors State University M
Graceland University (IA) M
Grambling State University M,D
Grand Valley State University M,O
Harvard University M,O
Hofstra University M,O
Idaho State University M,D,O
Indiana State University M,D
Indiana University Bloomington M,D,O
Indiana University of Pennsylvania M,D
Inter American University of Puerto Rico, Metropolitan Campus M
Iona College M,O
Iowa State University of Science and Technology M,D
Jackson State University M,D,O
Jacksonville State University M
Jacksonville University M
The Johns Hopkins University M,D,O
Jones International University M
Kennesaw State University M
Kent State University M
Kutztown University of Pennsylvania M,O
Lamar University M,D,O
La Salle University M
Lawrence Technological University M
Lehigh University M,D,O
Lewis University M
Lindenwood University M,D,O
Long Island University, Brooklyn Campus M
Long Island University, C.W. Post Campus M
Longwood University M
Louisiana State University and Agricultural and Mechanical College M,D,O
Loyola University Chicago M
Loyola University Maryland M
Malone University M
McDaniel College M
McNeese State University M,O
Michigan State University M,D,O
MidAmerica Nazarene University M
Middle Tennessee State University M,O
Midwestern State University M
Minnesota State University Mankato M,O
Mississippi State University M,D,O
Missouri State University M
Montana State University–Billings M
Montclair State University M,O
National-Louis University M,O
National University M
Nazareth College of Rochester M
New Jersey City University M
New York Institute of Technology M,O
New York University M,D,O
North Carolina Agricultural and Technical State University M
North Carolina Central University M
North Carolina State University M,D
Northeastern State University M
Northern Arizona University M,O
Northern Illinois University M,D
Northwestern State University of Louisiana M,O
Northwestern University M,D
Northwest Missouri State University M
Nova Southeastern University M,D,O
Oakland University O
Ohio University M,D
Old Dominion University M,D
Our Lady of the Lake University of San Antonio M
Penn State Great Valley M
Penn State University Park M,D
Pittsburg State University M
Portland State University M,D
Purdue University M,D,O
Purdue University Calumet M
Ramapo College of New Jersey M
Regis University M,O
The Richard Stockton College of New Jersey M
Sacred Heart University M,O
Saginaw Valley State University M
St. Cloud State University M
St. Edward's University M,O
Saint Joseph's University M,D
Saint Leo University M
Saint Michael's College M,O
St. Thomas University M,D,O
Salem State College M
Sam Houston State University M
San Diego State University M,D
San Francisco State University M,O
San Jose State University M,O
Seton Hall University M
Simmons College M,D,O
Southeastern Louisiana University M,D

M—master's degree; P—first professional degree; D—doctorate; O—other advanced degree

Southern Illinois University Edwardsville M,O
Southern Polytechnic State University M,O
Southern University and Agricultural and Mechanical College M
State University of New York College at Potsdam M
Stony Brook University, State University of New York M,O
Strayer University M
Syracuse University M,O
Texas A&M University M,D
Texas A&M University–Commerce M,D
Texas A&M University–Corpus Christi M,D
Texas A&M University–Texarkana M
Texas Tech University M,D
Towson University M,D
University at Albany, State University of New York M,D,O
University of Alaska Southeast M
University of Arkansas M
University of Arkansas at Little Rock M
University of Central Arkansas M
University of Central Florida M,D,O
University of Central Missouri M,O
University of Central Oklahoma M
University of Colorado Denver M
University of Connecticut M,D,O
University of Dayton M
The University of Findlay M
University of Georgia M,D,O
University of Hartford M
University of Hawaii at Manoa M,D
University of Houston–Clear Lake M
University of Kentucky M,D
University of Louisville M
University of Maine M
University of Maryland, Baltimore County M,O
University of Maryland, College Park M,D,O
University of Massachusetts Amherst M,D,O
University of Memphis M,D
University of Michigan M,D
University of Michigan–Flint M
University of Minnesota, Twin Cities Campus M,D,O
University of Missouri–Columbia M,D,O
University of Nebraska at Kearney M
University of Nebraska at Omaha M,O
University of Nevada, Las Vegas M,D,O
University of New Mexico M,D,O
The University of North Carolina at Charlotte M,D,O
The University of North Carolina at Greensboro M,D,O
The University of North Carolina Wilmington M
University of North Dakota M
University of Northern Colorado M,D
University of Northern Iowa M
University of North Texas D
University of Pennsylvania M
University of Phoenix M
University of Phoenix–West Florida Campus M
University of St. Thomas (MN) M,D,O
University of San Francisco M,D
University of Sioux Falls M,O
University of South Alabama M,D
University of South Carolina M
The University of South Dakota M,O
University of Southern California M
University of South Florida M,D,O
The University of Tennessee M,D,O
The University of Tennessee at Chattanooga O
The University of Texas at Brownsville M
The University of Texas at San Antonio M
University of the Incarnate Word M,D,O
The University of Toledo M,D,O
University of Virginia M,D,O
University of Washington M,D
The University of West Alabama M
University of West Florida M
University of West Georgia M,O
University of Wisconsin–Milwaukee D
University of Wyoming M,D,O
Utah State University M,D,O
Virginia Polytechnic Institute and State University M,D,O
Walden University M,D,O
Waynesburg University M,D
Wayne State University M,D,O
Webster University M,O
West Chester University of Pennsylvania M,O
Western Connecticut State University M
Western Illinois University M,O
Western Kentucky University M
Western Michigan University M,D,O
Western Oregon University M
Westfield State College M
West Texas A&M University M
West Virginia University M,D
Widener University M,D
Wilkes University M,D
Wilmington University M
Youngstown State University M

■ EDUCATIONAL POLICY

Alabama State University M,D,O
The College of William and Mary M,D
Florida State University M,D,O
The George Washington University M,D
Georgia State University M,D,O
Harvard University M
Illinois State University M,D
Indiana University Bloomington M,D,O
Loyola University Chicago M,D
Michigan State University D
New York University M,D
The Ohio State University M,D
Portland State University M,D
Rutgers, The State University of New Jersey, Camden M
Rutgers, The State University of New Jersey, New Brunswick D
University of Arkansas D
University of California, Riverside M,D
University of California, Santa Cruz M,D
University of Georgia M,D,O
University of Hawaii at Manoa D
University of Illinois at Chicago M,D
University of Illinois at Urbana–Champaign M,D
The University of Iowa M,D,O
The University of Kansas D
University of Kentucky M,D
University of Maryland, College Park M,D
University of Massachusetts Amherst M,D,O
University of Minnesota, Twin Cities Campus M,D,O
University of St. Thomas (MN) M,D,O
University of Southern California D
University of Washington M,D
University of Wisconsin–Madison M,D,O
Vanderbilt University M,D
Virginia Commonwealth University D
Wayne State University M,D,O

■ EDUCATIONAL PSYCHOLOGY

Alliant International University–San Diego M,D,O
American International College M,D
Andrews University M,D
Arcadia University M,D,O
Arizona State University M,D
Auburn University M,D,O
Ball State University M,D,O
Baylor University M,D,O
Boston College M,D
Brigham Young University M,D
California State University, Northridge M
Capella University M,D,O

The Catholic University of America M,D,O
Chapman University M,O
Clark Atlanta University M
The College of Saint Rose M,O
Eastern Michigan University M,O
Edinboro University of Pennsylvania M,O
Florida State University M,D,O
Fordham University M,D,O
George Mason University M
Georgian Court University M,O
Georgia State University M,D
Graduate School and University Center of the City University of New York D
Harvard University M
Holy Names University M,O
Howard University M,D,O
Illinois State University M,D,O
Indiana University Bloomington M,D,O
Indiana University of Pennsylvania M,O
John Carroll University M
The Johns Hopkins University M,O
Johnson State College M
Kean University M
Kent State University M,D
La Sierra University M,O
Loyola University Chicago M
Marist College M,O
Maryville University of Saint Louis M,D
Miami University M,O
Michigan State University M,D,O
Mississippi State University M,D,O
Montclair State University M,O
National-Louis University M,D,O
New Jersey City University M,O
New York University M,D
Northeastern University M
Northern Arizona University D
Northern Illinois University M,D,O
Oklahoma City University M
Oklahoma State University M,D,O
Penn State University Park M,D
Pontifical Catholic University of Puerto Rico M
Purdue University M,D,O
Rutgers, The State University of New Jersey, New Brunswick M,D
Southern Illinois University Carbondale M,D
Stanford University D
State University of New York College at Oneonta M,O
Temple University M,D
Tennessee Technological University M,O
Texas A&M University M,D
Texas Christian University M,O
Texas Tech University M,D
University at Albany, State University of New York M,D,O
University at Buffalo, the State University of New York M,D,O
The University of Arizona M,D,O
University of California, Davis M,D
University of California, Riverside M,D
University of Colorado at Boulder M,D
University of Connecticut M,D,O
University of Denver M,D,O
University of Florida M,D,O
University of Georgia M,D,O
University of Hawaii at Manoa M,D
University of Houston M,D
University of Illinois at Chicago D
University of Illinois at Urbana–Champaign M,D,O
The University of Iowa M,D,O
The University of Kansas M,D
University of Kentucky M,D,O
University of Louisville M,D
University of Mary Hardin-Baylor M,D
University of Maryland, College Park M,D
University of Memphis M,D
University of Minnesota, Twin Cities Campus M,D,O
University of Missouri–Columbia M,D,O
University of Missouri–St. Louis D,O
University of Nebraska at Omaha M,D,O
University of Nebraska–Lincoln M,D,O
University of Nevada, Las Vegas M,D,O
University of Nevada, Reno M,D,O
University of New Mexico M,D
The University of North Carolina at Chapel Hill M,D
University of Northern Colorado M,D
University of Northern Iowa M,O
University of North Texas M
University of Oklahoma M,D
University of Pennsylvania M,D
University of Phoenix–Southern Arizona Campus M,O
University of South Carolina M,D
The University of South Dakota M,D,O
University of Southern California M,D
University of Southern Maine M,O
The University of Tennessee M,D,O
The University of Texas at Austin M,D
The University of Texas at El Paso M
The University of Texas–Pan American M
University of the Pacific M,D,O
The University of Toledo M,D
University of Utah M,D
University of Virginia M,D,O
University of Washington M,D
University of Wisconsin–Madison M,D
University of Wisconsin–Milwaukee M,D
Virginia Commonwealth University D
Virginia Polytechnic Institute and State University M,D,O
Washington State University M,D,O
Wayne State University M,D,O
Western Kentucky University M,O
West Virginia University M
Wichita State University M,D,O
Widener University M,D

■ EDUCATION OF STUDENTS WITH SEVERE/MULTIPLE DISABILITIES

Cleveland State University M
Fresno Pacific University M
Gallaudet University M,D,O
Georgia State University M
Hunter College of the City University of New York M
Minot State University M
Montclair State University M,O
Norfolk State University M
Syracuse University M
University of Illinois at Urbana–Champaign M,D,O
West Virginia University M,D

■ EDUCATION OF THE GIFTED

Arkansas State University M,D,O
Arkansas Tech University M,O
Ashland University M
Barry University M,D,O
Bowling Green State University M
The College of New Rochelle M,O
The College of William and Mary M
Converse College M
Drury University M
Elon University M
Emporia State University M
George Mason University M,O
Hardin-Simmons University M
Hofstra University M,O
The Johns Hopkins University M,D,O
Johnson State College M
Kent State University M
Liberty University M,D,O
Lynn University M,D
Maryville University of Saint Louis M,D
Millersville University of Pennsylvania M
Minnesota State University Mankato M,O
Mississippi University for Women M
Northeastern Illinois University M
Nova Southeastern University M,O
Purdue University M,D,O
Saint Leo University M
Saint Mary's University of Minnesota M,O

M—master's degree; P—first professional degree; D—doctorate; O—other advanced degree

St. Thomas University M,D,O
Samford University M,D,O
Southern Methodist University M,D,O
Tennessee Technological University D
Texas A&M University M,D
University at Buffalo, the State University of New York M,D,O
The University of Alabama M,D,O
The University of Arizona M,D,O
University of Arkansas at Little Rock M
University of Central Florida M,D,O
University of Connecticut M,D,O
University of Houston M,D
University of Louisiana at Lafayette M
University of Louisiana at Monroe M,D
University of Minnesota, Twin Cities Campus M,D,O
University of Missouri–Columbia M,D
The University of North Carolina at Charlotte M,D
University of St. Thomas (MN) M,D,O
University of Southern Mississippi M,D,O
University of South Florida M,D
The University of Texas–Pan American M
The University of Toledo D,O
University of Virginia M,D,O
Western Washington University M
West Virginia University M,D
Whitworth University M
William Carey University M,O
Wilmington University M
Wright State University M
Youngstown State University M

■ ELECTRICAL ENGINEERING

Alfred University M,D
Arizona State University M,D
Auburn University M,D
Baylor University M
Boise State University M,D
Boston University M,D
Bradley University M
Brigham Young University M,D
Brown University M,D
Bucknell University M
California Institute of Technology M,D,O
California Polytechnic State University, San Luis Obispo M
California State Polytechnic University, Pomona M
California State University, Chico M
California State University, Fresno M
California State University, Fullerton M
California State University, Long Beach M
California State University, Los Angeles M
California State University, Northridge M
California State University, Sacramento M
Carnegie Mellon University M,D
Case Western Reserve University M,D
The Catholic University of America M,D
City College of the City University of New York M,D
Clarkson University M,D
Clemson University M,D
Cleveland State University M,D
Colorado State University M,D
Colorado Technical University Colorado Springs M
Colorado Technical University Denver M
Columbia University M,D,O
Cornell University M,D
Dartmouth College M,D
Drexel University M
Duke University M,D
Fairfield University M
Fairleigh Dickinson University, Metropolitan Campus M
Florida Agricultural and Mechanical University M,D
Florida Atlantic University M,D
Florida Institute of Technology M,D
Florida International University M,D
Florida State University M,D
Gannon University M
George Mason University M,D,O
The George Washington University M,D
Georgia Institute of Technology M,D
Georgia Southern University M
Graduate School and University Center of the City University of New York D
Grand Valley State University M
Howard University M,D
Illinois Institute of Technology M,D
Indiana University–Purdue University Fort Wayne M
Indiana University–Purdue University Indianapolis M,D
Iowa State University of Science and Technology M,D
The Johns Hopkins University M,D,O
Kansas State University M,D
Lamar University M,D
Lawrence Technological University M,D
Lehigh University M,D
Louisiana State University and Agricultural and Mechanical College M,D
Louisiana Tech University M,D
Loyola Marymount University M
Manhattan College M
Marquette University M,D
Massachusetts Institute of Technology M,D,O
McNeese State University M
Mercer University M
Michigan State University M,D
Michigan Technological University M,D
Minnesota State University Mankato M
Mississippi State University M,D
Missouri University of Science and Technology M,D
Montana State University M,D
Morgan State University M,D
New Jersey Institute of Technology M,D
New Mexico Institute of Mining and Technology M
New Mexico State University M,D
New York Institute of Technology M
Norfolk State University M
North Carolina Agricultural and Technical State University M,D
North Carolina State University M,D
North Dakota State University M,D
Northeastern University M,D
Northern Arizona University M
Northern Illinois University M
Northwestern University M,D,O
Oakland University M
The Ohio State University M,D
Ohio University M,D
Oklahoma State University M,D
Old Dominion University M,D
Oregon State University M,D
Penn State Harrisburg M
Penn State University Park M,D
Polytechnic Institute of NYU M,D
Polytechnic Institute of NYU, Westchester Graduate Center M,D
Portland State University M,D
Prairie View A&M University M,D
Princeton University M,D
Purdue University M,D
Purdue University Calumet M
Rensselaer Polytechnic Institute M,D
Rice University M,D
Rochester Institute of Technology M
Rutgers, The State University of New Jersey, New Brunswick M,D
St. Cloud State University M
St. Mary's University (United States) M
San Diego State University M
San Jose State University M
Santa Clara University M,D,O
South Dakota State University M,D
Southern Illinois University Carbondale M,D

Southern Illinois University Edwardsville M
Southern Methodist University M,D
Southern Polytechnic State University M
Stanford University M,D,O
State University of New York at Binghamton M,D
State University of New York at New Paltz M
Stevens Institute of Technology M,D,O
Stony Brook University, State University of New York M,D
Syracuse University M,D,O
Temple University M
Tennessee Technological University M,D
Texas A&M University M,D
Texas A&M University–Kingsville M
Texas Tech University M,D
Tufts University M,D,O
University at Buffalo, the State University of New York M,D
The University of Akron M,D
The University of Alabama M,D
The University of Alabama at Birmingham M
The University of Alabama in Huntsville M,D
University of Alaska Fairbanks M,D
The University of Arizona M,D
University of Arkansas M,D
University of Bridgeport M
University of California, Berkeley M,D,O
University of California, Davis M,D
University of California, Irvine M,D
University of California, Los Angeles M,D
University of California, Riverside M,D
University of California, San Diego M,D
University of California, Santa Barbara M,D
University of California, Santa Cruz M,D
University of Central Florida M,D,O
University of Cincinnati M,D
University of Colorado at Boulder M,D
University of Colorado at Colorado Springs M,D
University of Colorado Denver M
University of Connecticut M,D
University of Dayton M,D
University of Delaware M,D
University of Denver M
University of Detroit Mercy M,D
University of Evansville M
University of Florida M,D,O
University of Hawaii at Manoa M,D
University of Houston M,D
University of Idaho M,D
University of Illinois at Chicago M,D
University of Illinois at Urbana–Champaign M,D
The University of Iowa M,D
The University of Kansas M,D
University of Kentucky M,D
University of Louisville M,D
University of Maine M,D
University of Maryland, Baltimore County M,D
University of Maryland, College Park M,D,O
University of Massachusetts Amherst M,D
University of Massachusetts Dartmouth M,D,O
University of Massachusetts Lowell M,D
University of Memphis M,D
University of Miami M,D
University of Michigan M,D
University of Michigan–Dearborn M
University of Minnesota, Duluth M
University of Minnesota, Twin Cities Campus M,D
University of Missouri–Columbia M,D
University of Missouri–Kansas City M,D
University of Nebraska–Lincoln M,D
University of Nevada, Las Vegas M,D
University of Nevada, Reno M,D
University of New Hampshire M,D
University of New Haven M
University of New Mexico M,D
The University of North Carolina at Charlotte M,D
University of North Dakota M
University of North Texas M
University of Notre Dame M,D
University of Oklahoma M,D
University of Pennsylvania M,D
University of Pittsburgh M,D
University of Puerto Rico, Mayagüez Campus M
University of Rhode Island M,D
University of Rochester M,D
University of South Alabama M
University of South Carolina M,D
University of Southern California M,D,O
University of South Florida M,D
The University of Tennessee M,D
The University of Tennessee at Chattanooga M
The University of Texas at Arlington M,D
The University of Texas at Austin M,D
The University of Texas at Dallas M,D
The University of Texas at El Paso M,D
The University of Texas at San Antonio M,D
The University of Texas at Tyler M
The University of Texas–Pan American M
The University of Toledo M,D
University of Tulsa M
University of Utah M,D,O
University of Vermont M,D
University of Virginia M,D
University of Washington M,D
University of Wisconsin–Madison M,D
University of Wisconsin–Milwaukee M,D,O
University of Wyoming M,D
Utah State University M,D
Vanderbilt University M,D
Villanova University M,O
Virginia Commonwealth University M,D
Virginia Polytechnic Institute and State University M,D
Washington State University M,D
Washington University in St. Louis M,D
Wayne State University M,D
Western Michigan University M,D
Western New England College M
West Virginia University M,D
Wichita State University M,D
Wilkes University M
Worcester Polytechnic Institute M,D,O
Wright State University M
Yale University M,D
Youngstown State University M

■ ELECTRONIC COMMERCE

Adelphi University M
Arkansas State University M
Boston University M
California State University, East Bay M
California State University, Fullerton M
Carnegie Mellon University M
Claremont Graduate University M,D,O
Dallas Baptist University M
DePaul University M,D
Eastern Michigan University M,O
Fairleigh Dickinson University, Metropolitan Campus M
Ferris State University M
Florida Institute of Technology M
George Mason University M,D,O
Georgia Institute of Technology M,O
Hawai'i Pacific University M
Lewis University M
Maryville University of Saint Louis M,O
Marywood University M,O
Mercy College M

M—master's degree; P—first professional degree; D—doctorate; O—other advanced degree

National University	M
Northwestern University	M
Regis University	M,O
Saint Xavier University	M,O
Stevens Institute of Technology	M,O
University at Buffalo, the State University of New York	M,D,O
The University of Akron	M
University of Dayton	M
University of Denver	M
University of Florida	M
University of Massachusetts Dartmouth	M,O
University of Phoenix	M
University of Phoenix–Denver Campus	M
University of Phoenix–New Mexico Campus	M
University of Phoenix–West Michigan Campus	M
University of San Francisco	M
The University of Texas at Dallas	M
Xavier University	M

■ ELECTRONIC MATERIALS

Colorado School of Mines	M,D
Massachusetts Institute of Technology	M,D,O
Northwestern University	M,D,O
Princeton University	D
University of Arkansas	M,D

■ ELEMENTARY EDUCATION

Adelphi University	M
Alabama Agricultural and Mechanical University	M,O
Alabama State University	M,O
Alaska Pacific University	M
Alcorn State University	M,O
American International College	M,D,O
American University	M,O
Andrews University	M,D,O
Anna Maria College	M,O
Antioch University New England	M
Appalachian State University	M
Arcadia University	M,D,O
Argosy University, Orange County	M,D
Argosy University, Sarasota	M,D,O
Argosy University, Tampa	M,D,O
Argosy University, Twin Cities	M,D,O
Arizona State University	M,D,O
Arkansas State University	M,D,O
Armstrong Atlantic State University	M
Auburn University	M,D,O
Auburn University Montgomery	M,O
Austin Peay State University	M,O
Ball State University	M,D
Barry University	M,D,O
Bayamón Central University	M
Belhaven College (MS)	M
Belmont University	M
Benedictine University	M
Bennington College	M
Bethel University (TN)	M
Bloomsburg University of Pennsylvania	M
Bob Jones University	P,M,D,O
Boston College	M
Boston University	M
Bowie State University	M
Brandeis University	M
Bridgewater State College	M
Brooklyn College of the City University of New York	M
Brown University	M
Buffalo State College, State University of New York	M
Butler University	M
California Lutheran University	M,D
California State University, Fullerton	M
California State University, Los Angeles	M
California State University, Northridge	M
California State University, San Bernardino	M
California State University, Stanislaus	M,O
California University of Pennsylvania	M
Cambridge College	M,D,O
Campbell University	M
Canisius College	M
Capella University	M,D,O
Carlow University	M
Carson-Newman College	M
Central Connecticut State University	M,O
Central Michigan University	M,O
Chapman University	M
Charleston Southern University	M
Chatham University	M
Chestnut Hill College	M
Cheyney University of Pennsylvania	M
Chicago State University	M
The Citadel, The Military College of South Carolina	M
City University of Seattle	M,O
Clarion University of Pennsylvania	M
Clemson University	M
College of Charleston	M
The College of New Jersey	M
The College of New Rochelle	M
College of St. Joseph	M
The College of Saint Rose	M,O
College of Staten Island of the City University of New York	M
The College of William and Mary	M
Columbia College (SC)	M
Columbia College Chicago	M
Concordia University (OR)	M
Concordia University Chicago	M
Concordia University, Nebraska	M
Converse College	M
Creighton University	M
Dallas Baptist University	M
Delta State University	M,D,O
DePaul University	M,D
DeSales University	M
Dominican College	M
Dominican University	M
Drake University	M
Drury University	M
Duquesne University	M
D'Youville College	M,O
East Carolina University	M
Eastern Connecticut State University	M
Eastern Illinois University	M
Eastern Kentucky University	M
Eastern Michigan University	M
Eastern Nazarene College	M,O
Eastern Oregon University	M
Eastern Washington University	M
East Stroudsburg University of Pennsylvania	M
East Tennessee State University	M
Edinboro University of Pennsylvania	M,O
Elon University	M
Emmanuel College	M,O
Emporia State University	M
Endicott College	M
Fairfield University	M,O
Fayetteville State University	M
Ferris State University	M
Fitchburg State College	M
Florida Agricultural and Mechanical University	M
Florida Atlantic University	M
Florida Gulf Coast University	M
Florida Institute of Technology	M,D,O
Florida International University	M,D
Florida State University	M,D,O
Fordham University	M,D,O
Framingham State College	M
Francis Marion University	M
Fresno Pacific University	M
Friends University	M
Frostburg State University	M
Gallaudet University	M,D,O
Gardner-Webb University	M
The George Washington University	M
Georgia Southern University	M
Grand Canyon University	M,D
Grand Valley State University	M,O
Hampton University	M
Harding University	M,O
High Point University	M
Hofstra University	M,O
Holy Family University	M
Hood College	M

Howard University M
Hunter College of the City University of New York M
Idaho State University M,O
Immaculata University M,D,O
Indiana State University M
Indiana University Bloomington M,D,O
Indiana University Northwest M
Indiana University of Pennsylvania M
Indiana University–Purdue University Fort Wayne M,O
Indiana University South Bend M
Indiana University Southeast M
Inter American University of Puerto Rico, Metropolitan Campus M
Inter American University of Puerto Rico, San Germán Campus M
Iowa State University of Science and Technology M,D
Ithaca College M
Jackson State University M,D,O
Jacksonville State University M
Jacksonville University M
James Madison University M
The Johns Hopkins University M,O
Johnson & Wales University D
Jones International University M
Kennesaw State University M
Kent State University M,D,O
Kutztown University of Pennsylvania M,O
Lee University M,O
Lehigh University M,D,O
Lehman College of the City University of New York M
Le Moyne College M,O
Lesley University M,D,O
Lewis & Clark College M
Lewis University M
Liberty University M,D,O
Lincoln University (MO) M,O
Lincoln University (PA) M
Lock Haven University of Pennsylvania M
Long Island University, Brooklyn Campus M
Long Island University, C.W. Post Campus M
Longwood University M
Louisiana State University and Agricultural and Mechanical College M,D,O
Loyola Marymount University M
Loyola University Chicago M
Maharishi University of Management M
Manhattanville College M
Mansfield University of Pennsylvania M
Marshall University M
Mary Baldwin College M
Marygrove College M
Marymount University M
Maryville University of Saint Louis M,D
Marywood University M
McDaniel College M
McNeese State University M
Medaille College M
Mercy College M
Metropolitan College of New York M
Miami University M
Middle Tennessee State University M,O
Millersville University of Pennsylvania M
Mills College M,D
Minnesota State University Mankato M
Minot State University M
Mississippi College M,D,O
Mississippi State University M,D,O
Mississippi Valley State University M
Missouri State University M,O
Monmouth University M,O
Montclair State University M,O
Morehead State University M,O
Morgan State University M
Mount Saint Mary College M
Mount St. Mary's College M
Murray State University M,O
National-Louis University M
Nazareth College of Rochester M
New Jersey City University M
New York Institute of Technology M,O
New York University M,D,O
Niagara University M,O
North Carolina Agricultural and Technical State University M
North Carolina Central University M
North Carolina State University M
Northern Arizona University M
Northern Illinois University M,D
Northern Michigan University M
Northwestern State University of Louisiana M,O
Northwestern University M
Northwest Missouri State University M,O
Nova Southeastern University M,O
Nyack College M
Oklahoma City University M
Old Dominion University M
Olivet Nazarene University M
Oregon State University M
Our Lady of the Lake University of San Antonio M
Pacific University M
Penn State University Park M,D
Pfeiffer University M
Pittsburg State University M
Plymouth State University M
Portland State University M,D
Prescott College M,D
Providence College M
Purdue University M,D,O
Queens College of the City University of New York M,O
Queens University of Charlotte M
Quinnipiac University M
Regent University M,D,O
Regis College (MA) M
Regis University M,O
Rhode Island College M
Rider University O
Rivier College M,D,O
Rockford College M
Roger Williams University M
Rollins College M
Roosevelt University M
Rosemont College M
Rowan University M
Rutgers, The State University of New Jersey, New Brunswick M,D
Sacred Heart University M,O
Saginaw Valley State University M
St. John Fisher College M
St. John's University (NY) M
Saint Joseph's University M,D
Saint Mary's University of Minnesota M,O
Saint Peter's College M,O
St. Thomas Aquinas College M,O
St. Thomas University M,D,O
Saint Xavier University M,O
Salem State College M
Samford University M,D,O
San Diego State University M
San Francisco State University M
San Jose State University M,O
Seton Hill University M,O
Shenandoah University M,D,O
Shippensburg University of Pennsylvania M
Siena Heights University M
Simmons College M,O
Slippery Rock University of Pennsylvania M
Sonoma State University M
South Carolina State University M
Southeastern Louisiana University M
Southeastern Oklahoma State University M
Southeast Missouri State University M
Southern Connecticut State University M,O
Southern New Hampshire University M,O
Southern Oregon University M

M—master's degree; P—first professional degree; D—doctorate; O—other advanced degree

Southern University and Agricultural and Mechanical College M
Southwestern Oklahoma State University M
Spalding University M
Springfield College M
Spring Hill College M
State University of New York at Fredonia M
State University of New York at New Paltz M
State University of New York at Oswego M
State University of New York at Plattsburgh M
State University of New York College at Geneseo M
State University of New York College at Oneonta M
State University of New York College at Potsdam M
Stephen F. Austin State University M
Sul Ross State University M
Temple University M,D
Tennessee State University M,D
Tennessee Technological University M,O
Texas A&M University–Commerce M,D
Texas A&M University–Corpus Christi M
Texas A&M University–Kingsville M
Texas Christian University M,O
Texas State University–San Marcos M
Texas Tech University M,D
Texas Woman's University M,D
Towson University M
Trevecca Nazarene University M
Trinity (Washington) University M
Troy University M,O
Union College (KY) M
University at Buffalo, the State University of New York M,D,O
The University of Akron M,D
The University of Alabama M,D,O
The University of Alabama at Birmingham M
University of Alaska Fairbanks M,D,O
University of Alaska Southeast M
The University of Arizona M,D
University of Arkansas M,O
University of Bridgeport M,O
University of California, Irvine M,D
University of Central Florida M,D
University of Central Missouri M,O
University of Central Oklahoma M
University of Cincinnati M
University of Connecticut M,D,O
The University of Findlay M
University of Florida M,D,O
University of Georgia M,D,O
University of Hartford M
University of Houston M,D
University of Illinois at Chicago M,D
University of Indianapolis M
The University of Iowa M,D
University of Louisiana at Monroe M,D
University of Louisville M
University of Maine M,O
University of Maryland, Baltimore County M
University of Massachusetts Amherst M,D,O
University of Massachusetts Boston M,D,O
University of Massachusetts Dartmouth M,O
University of Memphis M,D
University of Miami M
University of Michigan–Flint M
University of Minnesota, Twin Cities Campus M,D,O
University of Missouri–Columbia M,D,O
University of Missouri–St. Louis M,O
University of Montevallo M
University of Nebraska at Omaha M
University of Nevada, Reno M
University of New Hampshire M
University of New Mexico M,O
University of North Alabama M,O
The University of North Carolina at Charlotte M
The University of North Carolina at Greensboro D
The University of North Carolina at Pembroke M
The University of North Carolina Wilmington M
University of North Dakota M,D
University of Northern Iowa M
University of North Florida M
University of Oklahoma M,D,O
University of Pennsylvania M
University of Phoenix M
University of Phoenix–Central Florida Campus M
University of Phoenix–Denver Campus M
University of Phoenix–Hawaii Campus M
University of Phoenix–Las Vegas Campus M
University of Phoenix–New Mexico Campus M
University of Phoenix–North Florida Campus M
University of Phoenix–Oregon Campus M
University of Phoenix–Phoenix Campus M
University of Phoenix–Sacramento Valley Campus M,O
University of Phoenix–San Diego Campus M
University of Phoenix–Southern Arizona Campus M,O
University of Phoenix–Southern California Campus M
University of Phoenix–Southern Colorado Campus M,O
University of Phoenix–South Florida Campus M
University of Phoenix–Utah Campus M
University of Phoenix–West Florida Campus M
University of Pittsburgh M
University of Puget Sound M
University of Rhode Island M
University of St. Francis (IL) M
University of St. Thomas (MN) M,O
The University of Scranton M
University of South Alabama M,O
University of South Carolina M,D
The University of South Dakota M
University of Southern Indiana M
University of Southern Mississippi M,D,O
University of South Florida M,D,O
The University of Tennessee M,D,O
The University of Tennessee at Chattanooga M,O
The University of Tennessee at Martin M
The University of Texas–Pan American M
University of the Incarnate Word M
The University of Toledo D,O
University of Utah M,D
University of Virginia M,D,O
The University of West Alabama M
University of West Florida M
University of Wisconsin–Eau Claire M
University of Wisconsin–La Crosse M
University of Wisconsin–Milwaukee M
University of Wisconsin–Platteville M
University of Wisconsin–River Falls M
University of Wisconsin–Stevens Point M
Utah State University M
Vanderbilt University M
Villanova University M
Wagner College M
Walden University M,D,O
Washington State University M,D
Washington University in St. Louis M

Wayne State College M
Wayne State University M,D,O
West Chester University of Pennsylvania M,O
Western Illinois University M
Western Kentucky University M,O
Western New England College M
Western New Mexico University M
Western Washington University M
Westfield State College M
West Virginia University M
Wheaton College M
Wheelock College M
Whitworth University M
Widener University M,D
Wilkes University M,D
William Carey University M,O
William Paterson University of New Jersey M
William Woods University M,O
Wilmington University M
Worcester State College M
Wright State University M
Xavier University M

■ EMERGENCY MANAGEMENT

Adelphi University O
Anna Maria College M,O
Arkansas Tech University M
Benedictine University M
California State University, Long Beach M
Capella University M,D
Drexel University M
The George Washington University M,D,O
Georgia State University M,D,O
Indiana University of Pennsylvania M
Jacksonville State University M
The Johns Hopkins University M,O
Lynn University M,O
Millersville University of Pennsylvania M
New Jersey Institute of Technology M,D
North Dakota State University M,D
Oklahoma State University M,D
Park University M
Philadelphia University M
San Diego State University M,D
University of Central Florida M,O
University of Hawaii at Manoa O
University of Nevada, Las Vegas M,D,O
University of Pittsburgh M,D,O
University of Rochester M,D,O
Virginia Commonwealth University M,O
West Chester University of Pennsylvania M,O

■ EMERGENCY MEDICAL SERVICES

Baylor University D
Drexel University M
San Diego State University M,D

■ ENERGY AND POWER ENGINEERING

New Jersey Institute of Technology M
New York Institute of Technology M,O
North Carolina Agricultural and Technical State University M,D
Northeastern University M
Rensselaer Polytechnic Institute M,D
Southern Illinois University Carbondale D
University of Massachusetts Lowell M,D
University of Memphis M,D
University of Wisconsin–Madison M,D
Worcester Polytechnic Institute M,D

■ ENERGY MANAGEMENT AND POLICY

Holy Names University M
New York Institute of Technology M,O
University of California, Berkeley M,D
University of Delaware M,D
University of Tulsa M
University of Washington M,D

■ ENGINEERING AND APPLIED SCIENCES—GENERAL

Alabama Agricultural and Mechanical University M
Alfred University M,D
Andrews University M
Arizona State University M,D
Arkansas State University M
Arkansas Tech University M
Auburn University M,D
Baylor University M
Boise State University M,D
Boston University M,D
Bradley University M
Brigham Young University M,D
Brown University M,D
Bucknell University M
California Institute of Technology M,D,O
California Polytechnic State University, San Luis Obispo M
California State Polytechnic University, Pomona M
California State University, Chico M
California State University, Fresno M
California State University, Fullerton M
California State University, Los Angeles M
California State University, Northridge M
California State University, Sacramento M
Case Western Reserve University M,D
The Catholic University of America M,D,O
Central Connecticut State University M
Central Michigan University M
Central Washington University M
Christian Brothers University M
City College of the City University of New York M,D
Clarkson University M,D
Clemson University M,D
Cleveland State University M,D
Colorado School of Mines M,D,O
Colorado State University M,D
Columbia University M,D,O
Cornell University M,D
Dartmouth College M,D
Drexel University M,D,O
Duke University M,D
Eastern Illinois University M,O
Eastern Michigan University M
Fairfield University M
Fairleigh Dickinson University, Metropolitan Campus M
Florida Agricultural and Mechanical University M,D
Florida Atlantic University M,D
Florida Institute of Technology M,D
Florida International University M,D
Florida State University M,D
George Mason University M,D,O
The George Washington University M,D,O
Georgia Institute of Technology M,D
Graduate School and University Center of the City University of New York D
Grand Valley State University M
Harvard University M,D
Howard University M,D
Idaho State University M,D,O
Illinois Institute of Technology M,D
Indiana State University M
Indiana University–Purdue University Fort Wayne M
Iowa State University of Science and Technology M,D
The Johns Hopkins University M,D,O
Kansas State University M,D
Kent State University M
Lamar University M,D
Lawrence Technological University M,D
Lehigh University M,D

M—master's degree; P—first professional degree; D—doctorate; O—other advanced degree

Louisiana State University and Agricultural and Mechanical College	M,D
Louisiana Tech University	M,D
Manhattan College	M
Marquette University	M,D
Marshall University	M
Massachusetts Institute of Technology	M,D,O
McNeese State University	M
Mercer University	M
Miami University	M,O
Michigan State University	M,D
Michigan Technological University	M,D
Mississippi State University	M,D
Missouri University of Science and Technology	M,D
Montana State University	M,D
Morgan State University	M,D
National University	M
New Jersey Institute of Technology	M,D,O
New Mexico State University	M,D
New York Institute of Technology	M,O
North Carolina Agricultural and Technical State University	M,D
North Carolina State University	M,D
North Dakota State University	M,D
Northeastern University	M,D,O
Northern Arizona University	M,D
Northern Illinois University	M
Northwestern University	M,D,O
Oakland University	M,D
The Ohio State University	M,D
Ohio University	M,D
Oklahoma State University	M,D
Old Dominion University	M,D
Oregon State University	M,D
Penn State Harrisburg	M
Penn State University Park	M,D
Pittsburg State University	M
Portland State University	M,D,O
Prairie View A&M University	M,D
Purdue University	M,D,O
Purdue University Calumet	M
Rensselaer Polytechnic Institute	M,D
Rice University	M,D
Robert Morris University	M
Rochester Institute of Technology	M,D,O
Rowan University	M
St. Cloud State University	M
St. Mary's University (United States)	M
San Diego State University	M,D
San Francisco State University	M
San Jose State University	M
Santa Clara University	M,D,O
Seattle University	M
South Dakota State University	M,D
Southern Illinois University Carbondale	M,D
Southern Illinois University Edwardsville	M
Southern Methodist University	M,D
Southern Polytechnic State University	M,O
Southern University and Agricultural and Mechanical College	M
Stanford University	M,D,O
State University of New York at Binghamton	M,D
State University of New York Institute of Technology	M
Stevens Institute of Technology	M,D,O
Stony Brook University, State University of New York	M,D,O
Syracuse University	M,D,O
Temple University	M,D
Tennessee State University	M,D
Tennessee Technological University	M,D
Texas A&M University	M,D
Texas A&M University–Kingsville	M,D
Texas Tech University	M,D
Tufts University	M,D
University at Buffalo, the State University of New York	M,D
The University of Akron	M,D
The University of Alabama	M,D
The University of Alabama at Birmingham	M,D
The University of Alabama in Huntsville	M,D
University of Alaska Anchorage	M,O
University of Alaska Fairbanks	M,D
The University of Arizona	M,D,O
University of Arkansas	M,D
University of Bridgeport	M,D
University of California, Berkeley	M,D,O
University of California, Davis	M,D,O
University of California, Irvine	M,D
University of California, Los Angeles	M,D
University of California, Santa Barbara	M,D
University of California, Santa Cruz	M,D
University of Central Florida	M,D,O
University of Central Oklahoma	M
University of Cincinnati	M,D
University of Colorado at Boulder	M,D
University of Colorado at Colorado Springs	M,D
University of Connecticut	M,D
University of Dayton	M,D
University of Delaware	M,D
University of Detroit Mercy	M,D
University of Evansville	M
University of Florida	M,D,O
University of Hartford	M
University of Hawaii at Manoa	M,D
University of Houston	M,D
University of Idaho	M,D
University of Illinois at Chicago	M,D
University of Illinois at Urbana–Champaign	M,D
The University of Iowa	M,D
The University of Kansas	M,D
University of Kentucky	M,D
University of Louisville	M,D
University of Maine	M,D
University of Maryland, Baltimore County	M,D,O
University of Maryland, College Park	M
University of Massachusetts Amherst	M,D
University of Massachusetts Dartmouth	M,D,O
University of Massachusetts Lowell	M,D,O
University of Memphis	M,D
University of Miami	M,D
University of Michigan	M,D,O
University of Michigan–Dearborn	M,D
University of Minnesota, Twin Cities Campus	M,D
University of Mississippi	M,D
University of Missouri–Columbia	M,D
University of Missouri–Kansas City	M,D
University of Nebraska–Lincoln	M,D
University of Nevada, Las Vegas	M,D
University of Nevada, Reno	M,D
University of New Haven	M,O
University of New Mexico	M,D
University of New Orleans	M,D,O
The University of North Carolina at Charlotte	M,D
University of North Dakota	D
University of North Texas	M
University of Notre Dame	M,D
University of Oklahoma	M,D
University of Pennsylvania	M,D,O
University of Pittsburgh	M,D
University of Portland	M
University of Puerto Rico, Mayagüez Campus	M,D
University of Rhode Island	M,D
University of Rochester	M,D
University of St. Thomas (MN)	M,O
University of South Alabama	M
University of South Carolina	M,D
University of Southern California	M,D,O
University of Southern Indiana	M
University of Southern Mississippi	M,D
University of South Florida	M,D
The University of Tennessee	M,D
The University of Tennessee at Chattanooga	M,D,O

The University of Texas at Arlington M,D
The University of Texas at Austin M,D
The University of Texas at Dallas M,D
The University of Texas at El Paso M,D
The University of Texas at San Antonio M,D
The University of Toledo M
University of Tulsa M,D
University of Utah M,D,O
University of Vermont M,D
University of Virginia M,D
University of Wisconsin–Madison M,D,O
University of Wisconsin–Milwaukee M,D,O
University of Wisconsin–Platteville M
University of Wyoming M,D
Utah State University M,D,O
Vanderbilt University M,D
Villanova University M,D,O
Virginia Commonwealth University M,D,O
Virginia Polytechnic Institute and State University M,D
Walden University M,O
Washington State University M,D
Washington University in St. Louis M,D
Wayne State University M,D,O
Western Michigan University M,D
Western New England College M
West Texas A&M University M
West Virginia University M,D
Wichita State University M,D
Widener University M
Wilkes University M
Worcester Polytechnic Institute M,D,O
Wright State University M,D
Yale University M,D
Youngstown State University M

■ ENGINEERING DESIGN

Northwestern University M
Rochester Institute of Technology M
San Diego State University M,D
Santa Clara University M,D,O
Stanford University M
Stevens Institute of Technology M
University of Central Florida M,D,O
University of New Haven M,O
Worcester Polytechnic Institute M,O

■ ENGINEERING MANAGEMENT

California State Polytechnic University, Pomona M
California State University, East Bay M
California State University, Long Beach M,D
California State University, Northridge M
Case Western Reserve University M
The Catholic University of America M,O
Clarkson University M
Colorado School of Mines M,D
Columbia University M,D,O
Cornell University M,D
Dallas Baptist University M
Dartmouth College M
Drexel University M,O
Duke University M
Eastern Michigan University M
Florida Institute of Technology M
Gannon University M
The George Washington University M,D,O
Kansas State University M,D
Lamar University M,D
Lawrence Technological University M,D
Long Island University, C.W. Post Campus M
Loyola Marymount University M
Marquette University M,D
Marshall University M
Massachusetts Institute of Technology M,D
McNeese State University M
Mercer University M
Missouri University of Science and Technology M,D
National University M
New Jersey Institute of Technology M
New Mexico Institute of Mining and Technology M
Northeastern University M,D
Northwestern University M
Oakland University M
Old Dominion University M,D
Penn State Great Valley M
Penn State Harrisburg M
Point Park University M
Portland State University M,D,O
Rensselaer Polytechnic Institute M,D
Robert Morris University M
Rochester Institute of Technology M
Rowan University M
St. Cloud State University M
Saint Martin's University M
St. Mary's University (United States) M
Santa Clara University M
Southern Methodist University M,D
Stanford University M,D
Stevens Institute of Technology M,D
Syracuse University M
Texas Tech University M,D
Tufts University M
The University of Akron M
The University of Alabama in Huntsville M,D
University of Alaska Anchorage M
University of Alaska Fairbanks M,D
University of California, Berkeley M,D
University of Central Florida M,D,O
University of Colorado at Boulder M
University of Colorado at Colorado Springs M
University of Dayton M
University of Detroit Mercy M
University of Idaho M
The University of Kansas M
University of Louisiana at Lafayette M
University of Louisville M
University of Maryland, Baltimore County M,O
University of Massachusetts Amherst
University of Michigan–Dearborn M,D
University of Minnesota, Duluth M
University of Nebraska–Lincoln M,D
University of New Haven M
University of New Orleans M,O
The University of North Carolina at Charlotte M
University of St. Thomas (MN) M,O
University of Southern California M,D,O
University of South Florida M,D
The University of Tennessee M,D
The University of Tennessee at Chattanooga M,O
University of Wisconsin–Madison M
University of Wisconsin–Milwaukee M,D,O
Valparaiso University M,O
Virginia Polytechnic Institute and State University M,D
Walden University M,D,O
Wayne State University M
Webster University M
Western Michigan University M
Widener University M

■ ENGINEERING PHYSICS

Appalachian State University M
Cornell University M,D
Dartmouth College M,D
Embry-Riddle Aeronautical University (FL) M
George Mason University M
Michigan Technological University D
The Ohio State University M,D
Polytechnic Institute of NYU M
Rensselaer Polytechnic Institute M,D
Stevens Institute of Technology M,D,O

M—master's degree; P—first professional degree; D—doctorate; O—other advanced degree

University of California, San Diego M,D
University of Maine M
University of Oklahoma M,D
University of Tulsa M
University of Virginia M,D
University of Wisconsin–Madison M,D
Yale University M,D

■ ENGLISH

Abilene Christian University M
Andrews University M
Angelo State University M
Appalachian State University M
Arcadia University M
Arizona State University M,D
Arkansas State University M,O
Arkansas Tech University M
Auburn University M,D
Austin Peay State University M
Ball State University M,D
Baylor University M,D
Belmont University M
Bemidji State University M
Bennington College M
Bob Jones University P,M,D,O
Boise State University M
Boston College M,D
Boston University M,D
Bowie State University M
Bowling Green State University M,D
Bradley University M
Brandeis University M,D
Bridgewater State College M
Brigham Young University M
Brooklyn College of the City University of New York M,D
Brown University M,D
Bucknell University M
Buffalo State College, State University of New York M
Butler University M
California Baptist University M
California Polytechnic State University, San Luis Obispo M
California State Polytechnic University, Pomona M
California State University, Bakersfield M
California State University, Chico M
California State University, Dominguez Hills M,O
California State University, East Bay M
California State University, Fresno M
California State University, Fullerton M
California State University, Long Beach M
California State University, Los Angeles M
California State University, Northridge M
California State University, Sacramento M
California State University, San Bernardino M
California State University, San Marcos M
California State University, Stanislaus M,O
Carnegie Mellon University M,D
Case Western Reserve University M,D
The Catholic University of America M,D
Central Connecticut State University M,O
Central Michigan University M
Central Washington University M
Chapman University M
Chicago State University M
The Citadel, The Military College of South Carolina M
City College of the City University of New York M
Claremont Graduate University M,D
Clarion University of Pennsylvania M
Clark Atlanta University M,D
Clark University M
Clemson University M,D
Cleveland State University M
The College at Brockport, State University of New York M
College of Charleston M
The College of New Jersey M
The College of Saint Rose M
College of Staten Island of the City University of New York M
Columbia University M,D
Converse College M
Cornell University M,D
Creighton University M
DePaul University M
Drew University M,D
Duke University D
Duquesne University M,D
East Carolina University M
Eastern Illinois University M
Eastern Kentucky University M
Eastern Michigan University M,O
Eastern New Mexico University M
Eastern Washington University M
East Tennessee State University M
Elmhurst College M
Emory University D,O
Emporia State University M
Fairleigh Dickinson University, Metropolitan Campus M
Fayetteville State University M
Fitchburg State College M,O
Florida Atlantic University M
Florida Gulf Coast University M
Florida International University M
Florida State University M,D
Fordham University M,D
Fort Hays State University M
Gannon University M
Gardner-Webb University M
Georgetown University M
The George Washington University M,D
Georgia College & State University M
Georgia Southern University M
Georgia State University M,D
Governors State University M
Graduate School and University Center of the City University of New York D
Grambling State University M,D
Grand Valley State University M
Hardin-Simmons University M
Harvard University M,D,O
Heritage University M
Hofstra University M
Hollins University M
Howard University M,D
Humboldt State University M
Hunter College of the City University of New York M
Idaho State University M,D,O
Illinois State University M,D
Indiana State University M
Indiana University Bloomington M,D
Indiana University of Pennsylvania M,D
Indiana University–Purdue University Fort Wayne M,O
Indiana University–Purdue University Indianapolis M
Indiana University South Bend M
Inter American University of Puerto Rico, Metropolitan Campus M
Iona College M
Iowa State University of Science and Technology M,D
Jackson State University M
Jacksonville State University M
James Madison University M
John Carroll University M
The Johns Hopkins University D
Kansas State University M
Kent State University M,D
Kutztown University of Pennsylvania M
Lamar University M
La Sierra University M
Lehigh University M,D
Lehman College of the City University of New York M
Long Island University, Brooklyn Campus M
Long Island University, C.W. Post Campus M

Longwood University M
Louisiana State University and Agricultural and Mechanical College M,D
Louisiana Tech University M
Loyola Marymount University M
Loyola University Chicago M,D
Lynchburg College M
Marquette University M,D
Marshall University M
Mary Baldwin College M
Marygrove College M
Marymount University M
McNeese State University M
Mercy College M
Miami University M,D
Michigan State University M,D
Middle Tennessee State University M,D
Midwestern State University M
Millersville University of Pennsylvania M
Mills College M
Minnesota State University Mankato M,O
Mississippi College M
Mississippi State University M
Missouri State University M
Monmouth University M
Montana State University M
Montclair State University M,O
Morehead State University M
Morgan State University M,D
Mount Mary College M
Murray State University M
National University M
New Mexico Highlands University M
New Mexico State University M,D
New York University M,D
North Carolina Agricultural and Technical State University M
North Carolina Central University M
North Carolina State University M
North Dakota State University M
Northeastern Illinois University M
Northeastern State University M
Northeastern University M,D,O
Northern Arizona University M
Northern Illinois University M,D
Northern Kentucky University M,O
Northern Michigan University M
Northwestern State University of Louisiana M
Northwestern University M,D
Northwest Missouri State University M
Notre Dame de Namur University M,O
Oakland University M
The Ohio State University M,D
Ohio University M,D
Oklahoma State University M,D
Old Dominion University M,D
Oregon State University M
Our Lady of the Lake University of San Antonio M
Penn State University Park M,D
Pittsburg State University M
Portland State University M
Prairie View A&M University M
Princeton University D
Purdue University M,D
Purdue University Calumet M
Queens College of the City University of New York M
Radford University M
Rhode Island College M
Rice University M,D
Rivier College M
Roosevelt University M
Rosemont College M
Rutgers, The State University of New Jersey, Camden M
Rutgers, The State University of New Jersey, Newark M
Rutgers, The State University of New Jersey, New Brunswick D
St. Bonaventure University M
St. Cloud State University M
St. John's University (NY) M,D
Saint Louis University M,D
St. Mary's University (United States) M
Saint Xavier University M,O
Salem State College M
Salisbury University M
Sam Houston State University M
San Diego State University M
San Francisco State University M,O
San Jose State University M,O
Seton Hall University M
Simmons College M
Slippery Rock University of Pennsylvania M
Sonoma State University M
South Dakota State University M
Southeastern Louisiana University M
Southeast Missouri State University M
Southern Connecticut State University M
Southern Illinois University Carbondale M,D
Southern Illinois University Edwardsville M,O
Southern Methodist University M,D
Stanford University M,D
State University of New York at Binghamton M,D
State University of New York at Fredonia M
State University of New York at New Paltz M
State University of New York at Oswego M
State University of New York College at Cortland M
State University of New York College at Potsdam M
Stephen F. Austin State University M
Stetson University M
Stony Brook University, State University of New York M,D,O
Sul Ross State University M
Syracuse University M,D
Tarleton State University M
Temple University M,D
Tennessee State University M
Tennessee Technological University M
Texas A&M International University M,D
Texas A&M University M,D
Texas A&M University–Commerce M,D
Texas A&M University–Corpus Christi M
Texas A&M University–Kingsville M
Texas A&M University–Texarkana M
Texas Christian University M,D
Texas Southern University M
Texas State University–San Marcos M
Texas Tech University M,D
Texas Woman's University M,D
Truman State University M
Tufts University M,D
Tulane University M,D
University at Albany, State University of New York M,D
University at Buffalo, the State University of New York M,D
The University of Akron M
The University of Alabama M,D
The University of Alabama at Birmingham M
The University of Alabama in Huntsville M,O
University of Alaska Anchorage M
University of Alaska Fairbanks M
The University of Arizona M,D
University of Arkansas M,D
University of California, Berkeley D
University of California, Davis M,D
University of California, Irvine M,D
University of California, Los Angeles M,D
University of California, Riverside M,D
University of California, San Diego M
University of California, Santa Barbara D

M—master's degree; P—first professional degree; D—doctorate; O—other advanced degree

University of California, Santa Cruz	M,D
University of Central Arkansas	M
University of Central Florida	M
University of Central Missouri	M
University of Central Oklahoma	M
University of Chicago	M,D
University of Cincinnati	M,D
University of Colorado at Boulder	M,D
University of Colorado Denver	M,O
University of Connecticut	M,D
University of Dallas	M
University of Dayton	M
University of Delaware	M,D
University of Denver	M,D
University of Florida	M,D
University of Georgia	M,D
University of Guam	M
University of Hawaii at Manoa	M,D
University of Houston	M,D
University of Houston–Clear Lake	M
University of Idaho	M
University of Illinois at Chicago	M,D
University of Illinois at Springfield	M
University of Illinois at Urbana–Champaign	M,D
University of Indianapolis	M
The University of Iowa	M,D
The University of Kansas	M,D
University of Kentucky	M,D
University of Louisiana at Lafayette	M,D
University of Louisiana at Monroe	M
University of Louisville	M,D
University of Maine	M
University of Maryland, College Park	M,D
University of Massachusetts Amherst	M,D
University of Massachusetts Boston	M
University of Memphis	M,D,O
University of Miami	M,D
University of Michigan	M,D,O
University of Michigan–Flint	M
University of Minnesota, Duluth	M
University of Minnesota, Twin Cities Campus	M,D
University of Mississippi	M,D
University of Missouri–Columbia	M,D
University of Missouri–Kansas City	M,D
University of Missouri–St. Louis	M,O
The University of Montana	M
University of Montevallo	M
University of Nebraska at Kearney	M
University of Nebraska at Omaha	M,O
University of Nebraska–Lincoln	M,D
University of Nevada, Las Vegas	M,D
University of Nevada, Reno	M,D
University of New Hampshire	M,D
University of New Mexico	M,D
University of New Orleans	M
University of North Alabama	M
The University of North Carolina at Chapel Hill	M,D
The University of North Carolina at Charlotte	M
The University of North Carolina at Greensboro	M,D
The University of North Carolina Wilmington	M
University of North Dakota	M,D
University of Northern Colorado	M
University of Northern Iowa	M
University of North Florida	M
University of North Texas	M,D
University of Notre Dame	M,D
University of Oklahoma	M,D
University of Oregon	M,D
University of Pennsylvania	M,D
University of Pittsburgh	M,D
University of Puerto Rico, Mayagüez Campus	M
University of Puerto Rico, Río Piedras	M,D
University of Rhode Island	M,D
University of Rochester	M,D
University of St. Thomas (MN)	M
University of South Alabama	M
University of South Carolina	M,D
The University of South Dakota	M,D
University of Southern California	M,D
University of Southern Mississippi	M,D
University of South Florida	M,D
The University of Tennessee	M,D
The University of Tennessee at Chattanooga	M
The University of Texas at Arlington	M,D
The University of Texas at Austin	M,D
The University of Texas at Brownsville	M
The University of Texas at El Paso	M,D
The University of Texas at San Antonio	M,D,O
The University of Texas at Tyler	M
The University of Texas of the Permian Basin	M
The University of Texas–Pan American	M
University of the District of Columbia	M
The University of Toledo	M,O
University of Tulsa	M,D
University of Utah	M,D
University of Vermont	M
University of Virginia	M,D,O
University of Washington	M,D
University of West Florida	M
University of West Georgia	M
University of Wisconsin–Eau Claire	M
University of Wisconsin–Madison	M,D
University of Wisconsin–Milwaukee	M,D,O
University of Wisconsin–Oshkosh	M
University of Wisconsin–Stevens Point	M
University of Wyoming	M
Utah State University	M
Valdosta State University	M
Valparaiso University	M,O
Vanderbilt University	M,D
Villanova University	M
Virginia Commonwealth University	M
Virginia Polytechnic Institute and State University	M,D
Virginia State University	M
Wake Forest University	M
Washington State University	M,D
Washington University in St. Louis	M,D
Wayne State University	M,D
Weber State University	M
West Chester University of Pennsylvania	M,O
Western Carolina University	M
Western Connecticut State University	M
Western Illinois University	M,O
Western Kentucky University	M
Western Michigan University	M,D
Western Washington University	M
Westfield State College	M
West Texas A&M University	M
West Virginia University	M,D
Wichita State University	M
William Paterson University of New Jersey	M
Winona State University	M
Winthrop University	M
Wright State University	M
Xavier University	M
Yale University	M,D
Youngstown State University	M

■ ENGLISH AS A SECOND LANGUAGE

Adelphi University	M,O
Alliant International University–San Diego	M,D,O
American University	M,O
Andrews University	M,D,O
Arizona State University	M,D
Arkansas Tech University	M
Avila University	M,O
Azusa Pacific University	M
Ball State University	M,D
Barry University	M,D,O
Biola University	M,D,O
Boston University	M,O
Brigham Young University	M,O

California Baptist University	M
California State University, Dominguez Hills	M,O
California State University, Fresno	M
California State University, Fullerton	M
California State University, Long Beach	M
California State University, Sacramento	M
California State University, San Bernardino	M,D
California State University, Stanislaus	M,O
Cambridge College	M,D,O
Cardinal Stritch University	M
Carson-Newman College	M
Central Connecticut State University	M,O
Central Michigan University	M
Central Washington University	M
Cleveland State University	M
College of Charleston	O
The College of New Jersey	M,O
The College of New Rochelle	M,O
College of Notre Dame of Maryland	M
Cornerstone University	M,O
Dallas Baptist University	M
DeSales University	M
Dominican University	M
Drexel University	M,D,O
Duquesne University	M,D
Eastern Michigan University	M,O
Eastern Nazarene College	M,O
Eastern Washington University	M
Emporia State University	M
The Evergreen State College	M
Fairfield University	M,O
Florida Atlantic University	M,D,O
Florida International University	M,D,O
Fordham University	M,D,O
Framingham State College	M
Fresno Pacific University	M
Furman University	M
Gannon University	O
George Fox University	M,D,O
George Mason University	M,O
Georgetown University	M,D,O
Georgia State University	M,D,O
Gonzaga University	M
Grand Valley State University	M,O
Harding University	M,O
Hawai'i Pacific University	M
Heritage University	M
Hofstra University	M,O
Holy Names University	M,O
Houston Baptist University	M
Hunter College of the City University of New York	M
Indiana State University	M,O
Indiana University Bloomington	M,D
Indiana University of Pennsylvania	M,D
Indiana University–Purdue University Fort Wayne	M,O
Indiana University–Purdue University Indianapolis	M,O
Inter American University of Puerto Rico, Metropolitan Campus	M
Inter American University of Puerto Rico, San Germán Campus	M
The Johns Hopkins University	M,O
Kean University	M
Kennesaw State University	M
Kent State University	M,D
Lehigh University	M,O
Lehman College of the City University of New York	M
Lewis University	M
Lipscomb University	M
Long Island University, Brooklyn Campus	M
Long Island University, C.W. Post Campus	M
Loyola Marymount University	M
Madonna University	M
Manhattanville College	M
Marymount University	M
Mercy College	M
Michigan State University	M,D
MidAmerica Nazarene University	M
Middle Tennessee State University	M,O
Millersville University of Pennsylvania	M
Minnesota State University Mankato	M,O
Mississippi College	M
Montclair State University	M,O
Monterey Institute of International Studies	M
Murray State University	M
Nazareth College of Rochester	M
New Jersey City University	M
Newman University	M
The New School: A University	M
New York University	M,D,O
Northern Arizona University	M,D,O
Northwest Missouri State University	M,O
Notre Dame de Namur University	M,O
Nova Southeastern University	M,O
Oakland University	M,O
Ohio Dominican University	M
Ohio University	M
Oklahoma City University	M
Oral Roberts University	M,D
Our Lady of the Lake University of San Antonio	M
Pontifical Catholic University of Puerto Rico	M
Portland State University	M
Prescott College	M,D
Queens College of the City University of New York	M
Regent University	M,D,O
Regis University	M,O
Rhode Island College	M
Rider University	O
Rutgers, The State University of New Jersey, New Brunswick	M,D
St. Cloud State University	M
St. John's University (NY)	M
Saint Martin's University	M
Saint Michael's College	M,O
St. Thomas University	M,D,O
Salem State College	M
Salisbury University	M
San Diego State University	M,O
San Francisco State University	M
San Jose State University	M,O
Seattle Pacific University	M
Seattle University	M,O
Shenandoah University	M,D,O
Simmons College	M,O
SIT Graduate Institute	M
Southeast Missouri State University	M
Southern Connecticut State University	M
Southern Illinois University Carbondale	M
Southern Illinois University Edwardsville	M,O
Southern New Hampshire University	M,O
State University of New York at Fredonia	M
State University of New York at New Paltz	M
State University of New York College at Cortland	M
Stony Brook University, State University of New York	M
Syracuse University	M
Temple University	M,D
Texas A&M University–Commerce	M,D
Texas A&M University–Kingsville	M
Trevecca Nazarene University	M
Trinity (Washington) University	M
Universidad del Turabo	M
University at Buffalo, the State University of New York	M,D,O
The University of Alabama	M,D
The University of Alabama in Huntsville	M,O
The University of Arizona	D
University of Arkansas at Little Rock	M

M—master's degree; P—first professional degree; D—doctorate; O—other advanced degree

University of California, Berkeley O
University of California, Los Angeles M,D,O
University of Central Florida M,O
University of Central Missouri M
University of Central Oklahoma M
University of Cincinnati M,D,O
University of Colorado Denver M,O
University of Delaware M,D,O
The University of Findlay M
University of Florida M,D,O
University of Guam M
University of Hawaii at Manoa M,D,O
University of Houston M,D
University of Idaho M
University of Illinois at Chicago M
University of Illinois at Urbana–Champaign M,D
University of Maryland, Baltimore County M,O
University of Maryland, College Park M,D,O
University of Massachusetts Amherst M,D,O
University of Massachusetts Boston M
University of Miami M
University of Michigan M,D
University of Minnesota, Twin Cities Campus M
University of Missouri–St. Louis M,O
University of Nebraska at Omaha M,O
University of Nevada, Reno M
The University of North Carolina at Charlotte M
The University of North Carolina at Greensboro M,D,O
University of Northern Iowa M
University of Pennsylvania M,D
University of Phoenix M
University of Phoenix–Phoenix Campus M
University of Phoenix–San Diego Campus M
University of Pittsburgh O
University of Puerto Rico, Río Piedras M
University of San Francisco M,D
The University of Scranton M
University of South Carolina M,D,O
University of Southern California M
University of Southern Maine M,O
University of South Florida M,D,O
The University of Tennessee M,D,O
The University of Texas at Arlington M
The University of Texas at Brownsville M
The University of Texas at San Antonio M,D
The University of Texas of the Permian Basin M
The University of Texas–Pan American M
The University of Toledo M,O
University of Washington M,D
University of West Florida M
University of Wisconsin–River Falls M
Valparaiso University M,O
Wayne State College M
Webster University M
West Chester University of Pennsylvania M,O
Western Carolina University M
Western Connecticut State University M
Western Kentucky University M
Western New Mexico University M
West Virginia University M
Wheaton College M,O
Wright State University M

■ ENGLISH EDUCATION

Alabama State University M,O
Albany State University M
Andrews University M,D,O
Anna Maria College M,O
Appalachian State University M
Arcadia University M,D,O
Arkansas State University M,O
Arkansas Tech University M,O
Armstrong Atlantic State University M
Auburn University M,D,O
Belmont University M
Bennington College M
Bethel University (TN) M
Bob Jones University P,M,D,O
Boston College M
Boston University M,O
Brooklyn College of the City University of New York M,O
Brown University M
Buffalo State College, State University of New York M
California Baptist University M
California State University, Northridge M
California State University, San Bernardino M,D
Campbell University M
Chatham University M
The Citadel, The Military College of South Carolina M
City College of the City University of New York M,O
Clarion University of Pennsylvania M
Clemson University M
The College at Brockport, State University of New York M
College of St. Joseph M
The College of William and Mary M
Columbia College Chicago M
Columbus State University M,O
Converse College M
Delta State University M
Drake University M
Duquesne University M
East Carolina University M
Eastern Kentucky University M
Eastern Michigan University M,O
Fitchburg State College M,O
Florida Agricultural and Mechanical University M
Florida Atlantic University M
Florida Gulf Coast University M
Florida International University M,D
Florida State University M,D,O
Framingham State College M
Gardner-Webb University M
Georgia Southern University M
Georgia State University M,D,O
Grand Valley State University M
Harding University M,O
Hofstra University M
Humboldt State University M
Hunter College of the City University of New York M
Indiana State University M
Indiana University of Pennsylvania M,D
Indiana University–Purdue University Fort Wayne M,O
Indiana University–Purdue University Indianapolis M
Iona College M
Ithaca College M
Jackson State University M
The Johns Hopkins University M,O
Kennesaw State University M
Kent State University M,D
Kutztown University of Pennsylvania M,O
Lehman College of the City University of New York M
Lincoln Memorial University M,O
Long Island University, Brooklyn Campus M
Long Island University, C.W. Post Campus M
Longwood University M
Louisiana Tech University M,D
Lynchburg College M
Manhattanville College M
Maryville University of Saint Louis M,D
Miami University M,D
Millersville University of Pennsylvania M
Mills College M,D
Minnesota State University Mankato M,O
Mississippi College M,D,O
Montclair State University M,O
National-Louis University M,O

New York University M,D,O
North Carolina Agricultural and Technical State University M
North Carolina State University M
Northeastern Illinois University M
Northern Arizona University M
North Georgia College & State University M,O
Northwestern State University of Louisiana M
Northwest Missouri State University M
Nova Southeastern University M,O
Our Lady of the Lake University of San Antonio M
Penn State University Park M,D
Plymouth State University M
Purdue University M,D,O
Queens College of the City University of New York M,O
Quinnipiac University M
Rhode Island College M
Rider University O
Rollins College M
Rutgers, The State University of New Jersey, New Brunswick M
St. John Fisher College M
Salem State College M
San Francisco State University M,O
San Jose State University M,O
Shippensburg University of Pennsylvania M
South Carolina State University M
Southern Illinois University Edwardsville M,O
Southwestern Oklahoma State University M
Stanford University M,D
State University of New York at Binghamton M
State University of New York at New Paltz M
State University of New York at Plattsburgh M
State University of New York College at Cortland M
Stony Brook University, State University of New York M,D,O
Syracuse University M,D
Temple University M,D
Texas A&M University M,D
Texas A&M University–Commerce M,D
Texas Tech University M,D
Trinity (Washington) University M
University at Buffalo, the State University of New York M,D,O
University of Alaska Fairbanks M,D,O
The University of Arizona D
University of California, Berkeley O
University of Central Florida M
University of Colorado Denver M,O
University of Connecticut M,D,O
University of Florida M,D,O
University of Georgia M,D,O
University of Illinois at Chicago M,D
University of Indianapolis M
The University of Iowa M,D
University of Michigan M,D
University of Minnesota, Twin Cities Campus M
University of Missouri–Columbia M,D,O
The University of Montana M
University of New Hampshire M,D
University of New Orleans M
The University of North Carolina at Chapel Hill M
The University of North Carolina at Charlotte M
The University of North Carolina at Greensboro M,D
The University of North Carolina at Pembroke M
University of Oklahoma M,D,O
University of Phoenix M
University of Phoenix–Phoenix Campus M
University of Pittsburgh M,D
University of Puerto Rico, Mayagüez Campus M
University of Puerto Rico, Río Piedras M,D
University of St. Francis (IL) M
University of South Carolina M,D
University of South Florida M,D,O
The University of Tennessee M,D,O
The University of Texas at El Paso M,D
The University of Toledo M
University of Virginia M,D
University of Washington M,D
The University of West Alabama M
University of West Georgia M,O
University of Wisconsin–Eau Claire M
Vanderbilt University M
Virginia Polytechnic Institute and State University M,D,O
Washington State University M,D
Wayne State College M
Wayne State University M,D,O
Western Carolina University M
Western Connecticut State University M
Western Kentucky University M
Western Michigan University M,D
Western New England College M
Widener University M,D
Wilkes University M,D
William Carey University M,O
Worcester State College M

■ ENTERTAINMENT MANAGEMENT

Carnegie Mellon University M
Columbia College Chicago M
Hofstra University M
University of Dallas M
University of South Carolina M

■ ENTOMOLOGY

Auburn University M,D
Clemson University M,D
Colorado State University M,D
Cornell University M,D
Florida Agricultural and Mechanical University M
Illinois State University M,D
Iowa State University of Science and Technology M,D
Kansas State University M,D
Louisiana State University and Agricultural and Mechanical College M,D
Michigan State University M,D
Mississippi State University M,D
New Mexico State University M
North Carolina State University M,D
North Dakota State University M,D
The Ohio State University M,D
Oklahoma State University M,D
Penn State University Park M,D
Purdue University M,D
Rutgers, The State University of New Jersey, New Brunswick M,D
State University of New York College of Environmental Science and Forestry M,D
Texas A&M University M,D
Texas Tech University M,D
The University of Arizona M,D
University of Arkansas M,D
University of California, Davis M,D
University of California, Riverside M,D
University of Connecticut M,D
University of Delaware M,D
University of Florida M,D
University of Georgia M,D
University of Hawaii at Manoa M,D
University of Idaho M,D
University of Illinois at Urbana–Champaign M,D
The University of Kansas M,D
University of Kentucky M,D
University of Maine M
University of Maryland, College Park M,D
University of Massachusetts Amherst M,D
University of Minnesota, Twin Cities Campus M,D
University of Missouri–Columbia M,D
University of Nebraska–Lincoln M,D
University of North Dakota M,D

M—master's degree; P—first professional degree; D—doctorate; O—other advanced degree

University of Rhode Island M,D
The University of Tennessee M,D
University of Wisconsin–Madison M,D
University of Wyoming M,D
Virginia Polytechnic Institute and State University M,D
Washington State University M,D
West Virginia University M,D

■ ENTREPRENEURSHIP

American University M
Baldwin-Wallace College M
Benedictine University M
Bernard M. Baruch College of the City University of New York M,D
Boston University M,O
California Lutheran University M,O
California State University, East Bay M
California State University, Fullerton M
Cambridge College M
Cameron University M
Carnegie Mellon University D
Clarkson University M
Columbia University M
Dallas Baptist University M
DePaul University M
Eastern Michigan University M,O
Fairleigh Dickinson University, College at Florham M,O
Fairleigh Dickinson University, Metropolitan Campus M,O
Florida Atlantic University M,D
Georgia Institute of Technology M,O
Georgia State University M,D
Inter American University of Puerto Rico, San Germán Campus D
Jones International University M
Lamar University M
Lincoln University (MO) M
Lindenwood University M
Marquette University O
North Carolina State University M
Northeastern University M
Northern Kentucky University M,O
Nova Southeastern University M
Oakland University M,O
Oral Roberts University M
Park University M
Penn State Great Valley M
Polytechnic Institute of NYU M
Providence College M
Regent University M,D,O
Rensselaer Polytechnic Institute M,D
St. Edward's University M,O
San Diego State University M
Simmons College M,O
SIT Graduate Institute M
South Carolina State University M
Southeast Missouri State University M
Southern Methodist University M
Stevens Institute of Technology M,O
Suffolk University M,O
Syracuse University M
Temple University D
Texas Tech University M
The University of Akron M
University of Central Florida M,O
University of Colorado at Boulder M,D
University of Dallas M
University of Dayton M
University of Delaware M,D
University of Florida M,D,O
University of Hawaii at Manoa M
University of Houston D
University of Houston–Victoria M
The University of Iowa M
University of Louisville M,D
University of Massachusetts Lowell M,O
University of Minnesota, Twin Cities Campus M
University of Missouri–Kansas City M,D
University of San Francisco M
University of South Florida M,O
The University of Tampa M
The University of Texas at Austin M
The University of Texas at Dallas M
University of the Incarnate Word M,D
University of Wisconsin–Madison M
Wake Forest University M
Walden University M,D
West Chester University of Pennsylvania M,O
Western Carolina University M
Wilkes University M

■ ENVIRONMENTAL AND OCCUPATIONAL HEALTH

Anna Maria College M
Boston University M,D
California State University, Northridge M
Capella University M,D
Colorado State University M,D
Columbia University M,D
Duke University M,D,O
East Carolina University M
Eastern Kentucky University M
East Tennessee State University M
Emory University M
Florida International University M,D
Fort Valley State University M
Gannon University O
The George Washington University M,D
Georgia Southern University M,D
Harvard University M,D
Hunter College of the City University of New York M
Illinois Institute of Technology M
Indiana State University M
Indiana University of Pennsylvania M
The Johns Hopkins University M,D
Lewis University M
Loyola University Chicago M,O
Mississippi Valley State University M
Montclair State University M,D,O
Murray State University M
New York University M,D
North Carolina Agricultural and Technical State University M
Oakland University M
Old Dominion University M
Oregon State University M
Saint Joseph's University M,O
Saint Mary's University of Minnesota M
San Diego State University M,D
Stony Brook University, State University of New York M,O
Temple University M
Towson University D
Tufts University M,D
Tulane University M,D
University at Albany, State University of New York M,D
The University of Alabama at Birmingham D
University of California, Berkeley M,D
University of California, Los Angeles M,D
University of Central Missouri M,O
University of Cincinnati M,D
University of Connecticut M
University of Florida M
University of Georgia M,D
University of Illinois at Chicago M,D
The University of Iowa M,D,O
University of Louisville M,D
University of Maryland, College Park M,D
University of Miami M
University of Michigan M,D
University of Minnesota, Twin Cities Campus M,D,O
University of Nevada, Las Vegas M
University of Nevada, Reno M,D
University of New Haven M
The University of North Carolina at Chapel Hill M,D
University of Oklahoma M,D
University of Pittsburgh M
University of South Alabama M
University of South Carolina M,D
University of Southern Mississippi M
University of South Florida M,D
The University of Toledo M,O
University of Washington M,D
University of Wisconsin–Whitewater M

Virginia Commonwealth University M
Wayne State University M,O
West Virginia University D
Yale University M,D

■ ENVIRONMENTAL BIOLOGY

Baylor University M,D
Chatham University M
Emporia State University M
Georgia State University M,D
Governors State University M
Hampton University M
Hood College M
Inter American University of Puerto Rico, San Germán Campus M
Massachusetts Institute of Technology M,D,O
Missouri University of Science and Technology M
Morgan State University D
Nicholls State University M
Ohio University M,D
Rutgers, The State University of New Jersey, New Brunswick M,D
Sonoma State University M
State University of New York College of Environmental Science and Forestry M,D
Tennessee Technological University M
University of California, Santa Cruz M,D
University of Louisiana at Lafayette M,D
University of Louisville D
University of Massachusetts Amherst M,D
University of Massachusetts Boston D
University of North Dakota M,D
University of Southern Mississippi M,D
University of West Florida M
University of Wisconsin–Madison M,D
Washington University in St. Louis D
West Virginia University M,D
Youngstown State University M

■ ENVIRONMENTAL DESIGN

Arizona State University D
Clemson University D
Columbia University M
Cornell University M
Florida Atlantic University M,O
Michigan State University M,D
San Diego State University M
Texas Tech University M,D
University of California, Berkeley M
University of Georgia M
University of Missouri–Columbia M
Virginia Polytechnic Institute and State University D
Yale University M

■ ENVIRONMENTAL EDUCATION

Alaska Pacific University M
Antioch University New England M
Arcadia University M,D,O
Brooklyn College of the City University of New York M
California State University, San Bernardino M
Chatham University M
Concordia University Wisconsin M
Florida Atlantic University M
Florida Institute of Technology M,D,O
Gannon University M
Lesley University M,D,O
Maryville University of Saint Louis M,D
New York University M
Nova Southeastern University M,O
Prescott College M,D
Slippery Rock University of Pennsylvania M
Southern Connecticut State University M,O
Southern Oregon University M
Universidad Metropolitana M
University of Minnesota, Twin Cities Campus M,D,O
University of New Hampshire M
The University of North Carolina Wilmington M
Western Washington University M
West Virginia University M,D

■ ENVIRONMENTAL ENGINEERING

Arizona State University M,D
Auburn University M,D
California Institute of Technology M,D
California Polytechnic State University, San Luis Obispo M
Carnegie Mellon University M,D
The Catholic University of America M,D,O
Clarkson University M,D
Clemson University M,D
Cleveland State University M,D
Colorado School of Mines M,D
Columbia University M,D,O
Cornell University M,D
Drexel University M,D
Duke University M,D
Florida Agricultural and Mechanical University M,D
Florida International University M
Florida State University M,D
Gannon University M
The George Washington University M,D,O
Georgia Institute of Technology M,D
Idaho State University M
Illinois Institute of Technology M,D
Iowa State University of Science and Technology M,D
The Johns Hopkins University M,D,O
Lamar University M,D
Lehigh University M,D
Louisiana State University and Agricultural and Mechanical College M,D
Loyola Marymount University M
Manhattan College M
Marquette University M,D
Marshall University M
Massachusetts Institute of Technology M,D,O
Mercer University M
Michigan State University M,D
Michigan Technological University M,D
Missouri University of Science and Technology M,D
Montana State University M,D
National University M
New Jersey Institute of Technology M,D
New Mexico Institute of Mining and Technology M
New Mexico State University M,D
New York Institute of Technology M
North Dakota State University M,D
Northeastern University M,D
Northern Arizona University M
Northwestern University M,D
Ohio University M,D
Oklahoma State University M,D
Old Dominion University M,D
Oregon State University M,D
Penn State Harrisburg M
Penn State University Park M,D
Polytechnic Institute of NYU M
Portland State University M,D
Princeton University M,D
Rensselaer Polytechnic Institute M,D
Rice University M,D
Rutgers, The State University of New Jersey, New Brunswick M,D
Southern Methodist University M,D
Stanford University M,D,O
State University of New York College of Environmental Science and Forestry M,D
Stevens Institute of Technology M,D,O
Syracuse University M,D
Texas A&M University M,D
Texas A&M University–Kingsville M,D
Texas Tech University M,D
Tufts University M,D
University at Buffalo, the State University of New York M,D

M—master's degree; P—first professional degree; D—doctorate; O—other advanced degree

The University of Alabama M,D
The University of Alabama at Birmingham D
The University of Alabama in Huntsville M,D
University of Alaska Anchorage M
University of Alaska Fairbanks M,D
The University of Arizona M,D
University of Arkansas M
University of California, Berkeley M,D
University of California, Davis M,D,O
University of California, Irvine M,D
University of California, Los Angeles M,D
University of California, Riverside M,D
University of Central Florida M,D
University of Cincinnati M,D
University of Colorado at Boulder M,D
University of Connecticut M,D
University of Dayton M
University of Delaware M,D
University of Detroit Mercy M,D
University of Florida M,D,O
University of Hawaii at Manoa M,D
University of Houston M,D
University of Idaho M
University of Illinois at Urbana–Champaign M,D
The University of Iowa M,D
The University of Kansas M,D
University of Louisville M,D
University of Maine M,D
University of Maryland, Baltimore County M,D
University of Maryland, College Park M,D
University of Massachusetts Amherst M
University of Massachusetts Dartmouth M
University of Massachusetts Lowell M,D,O
University of Memphis M,D
University of Michigan M,D,O
University of Missouri–Columbia M,D
University of Nebraska–Lincoln M,D
University of New Haven M,O
The University of North Carolina at Chapel Hill M,D
The University of North Carolina at Charlotte D
University of North Dakota M
University of Notre Dame M,D
University of Oklahoma M,D
University of Pittsburgh M,D
University of Rhode Island M
University of Southern California M,D,O
University of South Florida M,D
The University of Tennessee M
The University of Texas at Austin M,D
The University of Texas at El Paso M,D
The University of Texas at San Antonio M,D
University of Utah M,D
University of Vermont M,D
University of Washington M,D
University of Wisconsin–Madison M,D
University of Wyoming M
Utah State University M,D,O
Vanderbilt University M,D
Villanova University M
Virginia Polytechnic Institute and State University M,D
Washington State University M
Washington University in St. Louis M,D
West Virginia University M,D
Worcester Polytechnic Institute M,D,O
Yale University M,D
Youngstown State University M

■ ENVIRONMENTAL LAW

Chapman University P,M
Golden Gate University P,M,D
Lewis & Clark College P,M
Pace University P,M,D
University of Florida P,M,D
University of Pittsburgh M,O
University of Tulsa P,M,O

■ ENVIRONMENTAL MANAGEMENT AND POLICY

Adelphi University M
American University M,D,O
Antioch University New England M,D
Antioch University Seattle M
Arizona State University M
Baylor University M
Bemidji State University M
Boise State University M
Boston University M,D,O
Brown University M
California State University, Fullerton M
The Catholic University of America M,D,O
Clarkson University M
Clark University M
Clemson University M,D
Cleveland State University M,O
Columbia University M
Cornell University M,D
Drexel University M
Duke University M,D
Duquesne University M,O
The Evergreen State College M
Florida Atlantic University M,O
Florida Gulf Coast University M
Florida Institute of Technology M,D
Florida International University M
The George Washington University M,D
Georgia Institute of Technology M,D
Goddard College M
Hardin-Simmons University M
Harvard University M,O
Humboldt State University M
Illinois Institute of Technology M
Indiana University–Purdue University Indianapolis M
Inter American University of Puerto Rico, Metropolitan Campus M
The Johns Hopkins University M,O
Kean University M
Lamar University M,D
Lehigh University M
Long Island University, C.W. Post Campus M
Louisiana State University and Agricultural and Mechanical College M
Michigan Technological University M
Missouri State University M
Montclair State University M,D
Monterey Institute of International Studies M
Morehead State University M
Naropa University M
New Jersey Institute of Technology M
New York Institute of Technology M,O
New York University M
Northeastern Illinois University M
Northern Arizona University M
Ohio University M
Penn State University Park M
Plymouth State University M
Point Park University M
Portland State University M,D
Prescott College M
Princeton University M,D
Purdue University M,D
Rensselaer Polytechnic Institute M,D
Rice University M
Rochester Institute of Technology M
St. Cloud State University M
Samford University M
San Francisco State University M
San Jose State University M
Shippensburg University of Pennsylvania M
Slippery Rock University of Pennsylvania M
Southeast Missouri State University M
Southern Illinois University Edwardsville M
Stanford University M
State University of New York College of Environmental Science and Forestry M,D

Stony Brook University, State University of New York M,O
Texas State University–San Marcos M
Texas Tech University D
Towson University M
Troy University M
Tufts University M,D,O
Universidad del Turabo M
Universidad Metropolitana M
University at Albany, State University of New York M
University of Alaska Fairbanks M,D
University of California, Berkeley M,D,O
University of California, Santa Barbara M,D
University of California, Santa Cruz D
University of Chicago M,D
University of Colorado at Boulder M,D
University of Dayton M,D
University of Delaware M,D
University of Denver M,O
The University of Findlay M
University of Hawaii at Manoa M,D,O
University of Houston–Clear Lake M
University of Illinois at Springfield M
University of Maryland, Baltimore County M,D
University of Maryland University College M,O
University of Massachusetts Dartmouth M,O
University of Massachusetts Lowell M,D,O
University of Miami M,D
University of Michigan M,D
University of Minnesota, Twin Cities Campus M
University of Missouri–St. Louis M,D,O
The University of Montana M
University of Nevada, Reno M
University of New Hampshire M
The University of North Carolina at Chapel Hill M,D
The University of North Carolina Wilmington M
University of Oregon M,D
University of Pennsylvania M
University of Pittsburgh M,O
University of Rhode Island M,D
University of South Carolina M
University of South Florida M
The University of Tennessee M,D
University of Washington M,D
Utah State University M,D
Vanderbilt University M,D
Virginia Commonwealth University M
Virginia Polytechnic Institute and State University M,D
Webster University M,D
Wesley College M
West Virginia University M,D
Yale University M,D
Youngstown State University M,O

■ ENVIRONMENTAL SCIENCES

Alabama Agricultural and Mechanical University M,D
Alaska Pacific University M
American University M
Antioch University New England M,D
Arizona State University M,D
Arkansas State University M,D
Brigham Young University M,D
California State Polytechnic University, Pomona M
California State University, Chico M
California State University, East Bay M
California State University, Fullerton M
California State University, Northridge M
California State University, San Bernardino M
City College of the City University of New York M,D
Clarkson University M,D
Clemson University M,D
Cleveland State University M,D
The College at Brockport, State University of New York M
College of Charleston M
College of Staten Island of the City University of New York M
Colorado School of Mines M,D
Columbia University M
Columbus State University M
Cornell University M,D
Drexel University M,D
Duke University M,D
Duquesne University M,O
Florida Agricultural and Mechanical University M,D
Florida Atlantic University M
Florida Gulf Coast University M
Florida Institute of Technology M,D
Florida International University M
Gannon University M,O
George Mason University M,D
Georgia Institute of Technology M,D
Graduate School and University Center of the City University of New York D
Harvard University M
Howard University M,D
Humboldt State University M
Hunter College of the City University of New York M,O
Idaho State University M
Indiana University Bloomington M,D
Indiana University Northwest M,O
Inter American University of Puerto Rico, San Germán Campus M
Iowa State University of Science and Technology M,D
Jackson State University M,D
The Johns Hopkins University M
Lehigh University M,D
Louisiana State University and Agricultural and Mechanical College M,D
Loyola Marymount University M
Marshall University M
Massachusetts Institute of Technology M,D,O
McNeese State University M
Mercer University M
Miami University M
Michigan State University M,D
Minnesota State University Mankato M
Montana State University M,D
Montclair State University M,D,O
Murray State University M
New Jersey Institute of Technology M,D
New Mexico Institute of Mining and Technology M,D
New Mexico State University M,D
North Carolina Agricultural and Technical State University M
North Dakota State University M,D
Northern Arizona University M
Nova Southeastern University M
Oakland University M,D
The Ohio State University M,D
Oklahoma State University M,D
Oregon State University M,D
Pace University M
Penn State Harrisburg M
Penn State University Park M
Polytechnic Institute of NYU M
Pontifical Catholic University of Puerto Rico M
Portland State University M,D
Queens College of the City University of New York M
Rensselaer Polytechnic Institute M,D
Rice University M,D
Rochester Institute of Technology M
Rutgers, The State University of New Jersey, Newark M,D
Rutgers, The State University of New Jersey, New Brunswick M,D
Southern Illinois University Carbondale D

M—master's degree; P—first professional degree; D—doctorate; O—other advanced degree

Southern Illinois University Edwardsville M
Southern Methodist University M,D
Southern University and Agricultural and Mechanical College M
Stanford University M,D,O
State University of New York College of Environmental Science and Forestry M,D
Stephen F. Austin State University M
Tarleton State University M
Tennessee Technological University D
Texas A&M University–Corpus Christi M
Texas Christian University M
Texas Tech University M,D
Towson University M,O
Tufts University M,D
Tulane University M,D
Universidad del Turabo M,D
University at Albany, State University of New York M
The University of Alabama in Huntsville M,D
University of Alaska Anchorage M
University of Alaska Fairbanks M,D
The University of Arizona M,D
University of California, Berkeley M,D
University of California, Davis M,D
University of California, Los Angeles M,D
University of California, Riverside M,D
University of California, Santa Barbara M,D
University of Chicago M,D
University of Cincinnati M,D
University of Colorado at Colorado Springs M
University of Colorado Denver M
University of Guam M
University of Houston–Clear Lake M
University of Idaho M,D
University of Illinois at Springfield M
University of Illinois at Urbana–Champaign M,D
The University of Kansas M,D
University of Maine M,D
University of Maryland, Baltimore County M,D
University of Maryland, College Park M,D
University of Maryland Eastern Shore M,D
University of Massachusetts Boston D
University of Massachusetts Lowell M,D,O
University of Michigan M,D
University of Michigan–Dearborn M
The University of Montana M
University of Nevada, Las Vegas M,D
University of Nevada, Reno M,D
University of New Haven M
University of New Orleans M
The University of North Carolina at Chapel Hill M,D
University of Northern Iowa M
University of North Texas M,D
University of Oklahoma M,D
University of Pennsylvania M,D
University of Rhode Island M,D
University of South Florida M,D
The University of Tennessee at Chattanooga M
The University of Texas at Arlington M,D
The University of Texas at El Paso D
The University of Texas at San Antonio M,D
The University of Toledo M,D
University of Utah M
University of Virginia M,D
University of West Florida M
University of Wisconsin–Madison M,D
Vanderbilt University M
Virginia Commonwealth University M
Virginia Polytechnic Institute and State University M,D
Washington State University M,D
Western Connecticut State University M
Western Washington University M
West Texas A&M University M
Wichita State University M
Wright State University M,D
Yale University M,D

■ EPIDEMIOLOGY

Boston University M,D
Brown University M,D
Case Western Reserve University M,D
Columbia University M,D
Cornell University M,D
Drexel University M,D,O
East Tennessee State University M,O
Emory University M,D
Florida International University M,D
George Mason University M,D,O
Georgetown University M
The George Washington University M,D
Georgia Southern University M,D
Harvard University M,D
Hunter College of the City University of New York M
Indiana University–Purdue University Indianapolis M
The Johns Hopkins University M,D
Michigan State University M,D
New York University M,D
North Carolina State University M,D
Purdue University M,D
San Diego State University M,D
Stanford University M,D
Temple University M
Texas A&M University M,D
Tufts University M,D,O
Tulane University M,D
University at Albany, State University of New York M,D
University at Buffalo, the State University of New York M,D
The University of Alabama at Birmingham D
The University of Arizona M,D
University of California, Berkeley M,D
University of California, Davis M,D
University of California, Irvine M,D
University of California, Los Angeles M,D
University of California, San Diego D
University of Cincinnati M,D
University of Colorado Denver D
University of Florida M
University of Hawaii at Manoa M,D,O
University of Illinois at Chicago M,D
The University of Iowa M,D
University of Louisville M,D
University of Maryland, Baltimore County M,O
University of Maryland, College Park M,D
University of Massachusetts Lowell M,D,O
University of Miami D
University of Michigan M,D
University of Minnesota, Twin Cities Campus M,D
The University of North Carolina at Chapel Hill M,D
University of Pennsylvania M,D
University of Pittsburgh M,D
University of Rochester M,D
University of South Carolina M,D
University of Southern California M,D
University of Southern Mississippi M
University of South Florida M,D
The University of Toledo M,O
University of Washington M,D
University of Wisconsin–Madison M,D
Virginia Commonwealth University D
Walden University M,D
Yale University M,D

■ ERGONOMICS AND HUMAN FACTORS

Bentley University M
California State University, Long Beach M

California State University, Northridge	M
The Catholic University of America	M,D
Clemson University	D
Cornell University	M
Embry-Riddle Aeronautical University (FL)	M
Florida Institute of Technology	M
Georgia Institute of Technology	M,D
Indiana University Bloomington	M,D
New York University	M,D
North Carolina State University	D
Old Dominion University	D
San Jose State University	M
Tufts University	M,D
The University of Alabama	M
University of Central Florida	M,D,O
University of Cincinnati	M,D
University of Illinois at Urbana–Champaign	M
The University of Iowa	M,D
University of Massachusetts Lowell	M,D,O
University of Miami	M
The University of Tennessee	M,D
University of Wisconsin–Milwaukee	M,O
Wright State University	M,D

■ ETHICS

American University	M,D,O
Azusa Pacific University	M
Biola University	P,M,D
Claremont Graduate University	M,D
Drew University	M,D
Duquesne University	M
Emory University	P,M,D
Fordham University	M,O
Freed-Hardeman University	M
Georgetown University	M,D
Marquette University	M,D
Oregon State University	M
St. Edward's University	M
Suffolk University	M
University of Baltimore	M
University of Nevada, Las Vegas	M
University of North Florida	M,O
University of Pennsylvania	M,D
Valparaiso University	M,O
West Chester University of Pennsylvania	M,O

■ ETHNIC STUDIES

Cornell University	M,D
Minnesota State University Mankato	M
San Francisco State University	M
University of California, Berkeley	D
University of California, Riverside	D
University of California, San Diego	M,D
Washington State University	M,D

■ EVOLUTIONARY BIOLOGY

Brown University	D
Clemson University	M,D
Columbia University	D,O
Cornell University	D
Dartmouth College	D
Emory University	D
Florida State University	M,D
George Mason University	M,D,O
Harvard University	D
Illinois State University	M,D
Indiana University Bloomington	M,D
Iowa State University of Science and Technology	M,D
The Johns Hopkins University	D
Marquette University	M,D
Michigan State University	D
Northwestern University	D
The Ohio State University	M,D
Ohio University	M,D
Penn State University Park	M,D
Princeton University	D
Purdue University	M,D
Rice University	M,D
Rutgers, The State University of New Jersey, New Brunswick	M,D
Stony Brook University, State University of New York	M,D
Tulane University	M,D
University at Albany, State University of New York	M,D
University at Buffalo, the State University of New York	M,D,O
The University of Arizona	M,D
University of California, Davis	D
University of California, Irvine	M,D
University of California, Los Angeles	M,D
University of California, Riverside	M,D
University of California, San Diego	D
University of California, Santa Barbara	M,D
University of California, Santa Cruz	M,D
University of Chicago	D
University of Colorado at Boulder	M,D
University of Delaware	M,D
University of Hawaii at Manoa	M,D
University of Illinois at Urbana–Champaign	M,D
The University of Iowa	M,D
The University of Kansas	M,D
University of Louisiana at Lafayette	M,D
University of Maryland, College Park	M,D
University of Massachusetts Amherst	M,D
University of Miami	M,D
University of Michigan	M,D
University of Minnesota, Twin Cities Campus	M,D
University of Missouri–Columbia	M,D
University of Missouri–St. Louis	M,D,O
University of Nevada, Reno	D
The University of North Carolina at Chapel Hill	M,D
University of Notre Dame	M,D
University of Oklahoma	D
University of Oregon	M,D
University of Pittsburgh	D
University of South Carolina	M,D
University of Southern California	M,D
The University of Tennessee	M,D
The University of Texas at Austin	M,D
Virginia Polytechnic Institute and State University	M,D
Washington University in St. Louis	D
West Virginia University	M,D
Yale University	D

■ EXERCISE AND SPORTS SCIENCE

American University	M
Appalachian State University	M
Arizona State University	M,D
Arkansas State University	M,O
Armstrong Atlantic State University	M
Ashland University	M
Auburn University	M,D,O
Austin Peay State University	M
Ball State University	D
Barry University	M
Baylor University	M,D
Bemidji State University	M
Benedictine University	M
Bloomsburg University of Pennsylvania	M
Boise State University	M
Brigham Young University	M,D
Brooklyn College of the City University of New York	M
California State University, Fresno	M
California State University, Long Beach	M
California University of Pennsylvania	M
Central Connecticut State University	M,O
Central Michigan University	M
Cleveland State University	M
The College of St. Scholastica	M
Colorado State University	M,D
Concordia University Chicago	M
Delaware State University	M
East Carolina University	M,D

M—master's degree; P—first professional degree; D—doctorate; O—other advanced degree

Eastern Michigan University M
Eastern Washington University M
East Stroudsburg University of Pennsylvania M
East Tennessee State University M
Florida Atlantic University M
Florida International University M
Florida State University M,D
Gardner-Webb University M
George Mason University M
The George Washington University M
Georgia State University M
High Point University M
Howard University M
Humboldt State University M
Indiana State University M
Indiana University Bloomington M,D
Indiana University of Pennsylvania M
Inter American University of Puerto Rico, Metropolitan Campus M
Ithaca College M
Kean University M
Kennesaw State University M
Kent State University M,D
Long Island University, Brooklyn Campus M
Louisiana Tech University M
Manhattanville College M
Marshall University M
Marywood University M
McNeese State University M
Miami University M
Middle Tennessee State University M,D
Mississippi State University M
Montana State University M
Montclair State University M,O
Morehead State University M
Murray State University M
New Mexico Highlands University M
North Dakota State University M
Northeastern University M
Northern Michigan University M
Oakland University M,O
Ohio University M,D
Old Dominion University M
Oregon State University M,D
Purdue University M,D
Queens College of the City University of New York M
Sacred Heart University M,D
St. Cloud State University M
San Diego State University M
Southeast Missouri State University M
Southern Connecticut State University M
Southern Utah University M
Springfield College M,D
State University of New York College at Cortland M
Syracuse University M
Tennessee State University M
Texas A&M University–Commerce M,D
Texas Tech University M
Texas Woman's University M
University at Buffalo, the State University of New York M,D
The University of Akron M
The University of Alabama M,D
University of California, Davis M
University of Central Florida M
University of Central Missouri M
University of Connecticut M,D
University of Dayton M,D
University of Delaware M
University of Florida M,D
University of Houston M,D
University of Houston–Clear Lake M
The University of Iowa M,D
University of Kentucky M,D
University of Louisiana at Monroe M
University of Louisville M
University of Mary Hardin-Baylor M,D
University of Memphis M
University of Miami M,D
University of Minnesota, Twin Cities Campus M,D,O
University of Mississippi M,D
University of Missouri–Columbia M,D
The University of Montana M
University of Nebraska at Kearney M
University of Nebraska–Lincoln M,D
University of Nevada, Las Vegas M
University of New Mexico D
The University of North Carolina at Chapel Hill M
The University of North Carolina at Charlotte M
The University of North Carolina at Greensboro M,D
University of Northern Colorado M,D
University of Oklahoma M,D
University of Pittsburgh M,D
University of Puerto Rico, Río Piedras M
University of Rhode Island M,D
University of South Alabama M
University of South Carolina M,D
University of Southern Mississippi M,D
University of South Florida M
The University of Tennessee M,D,O
The University of Texas at Arlington M,D
University of the Pacific M
The University of Toledo M,D
University of Utah M,D
University of West Florida M
University of Wisconsin–La Crosse M
University of Wyoming M
Virginia Commonwealth University M
Wake Forest University M
Washington State University M,D
Wayne State College M
West Chester University of Pennsylvania M,O
Western Michigan University M
Western Washington University M
West Texas A&M University M
West Virginia University M,D
Wichita State University M

■ EXPERIMENTAL PSYCHOLOGY

American University M
Appalachian State University M,O
Auburn University M,D
Bowling Green State University M,D
Brooklyn College of the City University of New York M,D
California State University, Northridge M
California State University, San Bernardino M
Case Western Reserve University D
The Catholic University of America M,D
Central Michigan University M,D
Central Washington University M
City College of the City University of New York M,D
Cleveland State University M,D,O
The College of William and Mary M,D
Columbia University M,D
Cornell University D
Dallas Baptist University M
DePaul University M,D
Duke University D
Eastern Washington University M
Fairleigh Dickinson University, Metropolitan Campus M,O
Georgia Institute of Technology M,D
Graduate School and University Center of the City University of New York D
Harvard University D
Howard University M,D
Illinois State University M,D,O
Iona College M
Kent State University M,D
McNeese State University M
Miami University D
Mississippi State University M,D
Missouri State University M
Morehead State University M
North Carolina State University D
Northeastern University M,D
Ohio University D
Old Dominion University D

Radford University M,D,O
St. John's University (NY) M
Saint Louis University M,D
San Jose State University M
Seton Hall University M
Southern Illinois University Carbondale M,D
Stony Brook University, State University of New York D
Syracuse University D
Texas Tech University M,D
University at Albany, State University of New York M,D,O
The University of Alabama D
University of Central Florida M,D
University of Cincinnati D
University of Connecticut M,D,O
University of Hartford M
University of Kentucky M,D
University of Louisiana at Monroe M
University of Louisville D
University of Maine M,D
University of Maryland, College Park M,D
University of Memphis M,D
University of Michigan D
University of Mississippi M,D
The University of Montana M,D,O
The University of North Carolina at Chapel Hill D
University of North Dakota M,D
University of North Texas M,D
University of South Carolina M,D
University of Southern Mississippi M,D
The University of Tennessee M,D
The University of Tennessee at Chattanooga M
The University of Texas at Arlington M,D
The University of Texas at El Paso M,D
The University of Texas of the Permian Basin M
The University of Texas–Pan American M
The University of Toledo M,D
University of Wisconsin–Oshkosh M
Washington State University M,D
Washington University in St. Louis D
Western Michigan University M,D
Western Washington University M
Xavier University M,D

■ FACILITIES MANAGEMENT

Cornell University M
Indiana University of Pennsylvania M
Southern Methodist University M,D
University of California, Berkeley O
The University of Kansas M,D,O

■ FAMILY AND CONSUMER SCIENCES-GENERAL

Alabama Agricultural and Mechanical University M,D
Appalachian State University M
Ball State University M
Bowling Green State University M
California State University, Fresno M
California State University, Long Beach M
California State University, Northridge M
Central Michigan University M,O
Central Washington University M
Cornell University M,D
Eastern Illinois University M
Florida State University M,D
Fontbonne University M
Illinois State University M
Indiana State University M
Iowa State University of Science and Technology M
Kansas State University M,D
Kent State University M
Lamar University M,O
Louisiana State University and Agricultural and Mechanical College M,D
Louisiana Tech University M
Marshall University M
Missouri State University M
New Mexico State University M
North Carolina Central University M
North Dakota State University M
The Ohio State University M
Ohio University M
Oklahoma State University M,D
Oregon State University M
Prairie View A&M University M
Purdue University M,D
Queens College of the City University of New York M
Sam Houston State University M
San Francisco State University M
South Carolina State University M
South Dakota State University M
State University of New York College at Oneonta M
Stephen F. Austin State University M
Tennessee State University M
Texas A&M University–Kingsville M
Texas Southern University M
Texas Tech University M,D
Tufts University M,D,O
The University of Akron M
The University of Alabama M,D
The University of Arizona M,D
University of Arkansas M
University of Central Arkansas M
University of Central Oklahoma M
University of Florida M
University of Georgia M,D
University of Houston M
University of Maryland, College Park M,D
University of Memphis M
University of Mississippi M
University of Missouri–Columbia M,D
University of Nebraska–Lincoln M,D
The University of North Carolina at Greensboro M,D,O
University of Puerto Rico, Río Piedras M
The University of Tennessee D
The University of Tennessee at Martin M
The University of Texas at Austin M,D
University of Wisconsin–Madison M,D
University of Wisconsin–Stevens Point M
Utah State University M,D
Western Michigan University M

■ FAMILY NURSE PRACTITIONER STUDIES

Abilene Christian University M,O
Austin Peay State University M
Barry University M,O
Baylor University M
Bellarmine University M,D
Bloomsburg University of Pennsylvania M
Bowie State University M
Brenau University M
Brigham Young University M
California State University, Fresno M
Carlow University M,D
Carson-Newman College M
Case Western Reserve University M,D
The Catholic University of America M,D,O
College of Mount Saint Vincent M,O
The College of New Rochelle M,O
Columbia University M,O
Concordia University Wisconsin M
Coppin State University M,O
Delta State University M
DeSales University M
Dominican College M
Duke University M,D,O
Duquesne University M,O
D'Youville College M,O
Eastern Kentucky University M
Edinboro University of Pennsylvania M
Emory University M
Fairfield University M,O
Florida State University M,O
Gannon University M,O
George Mason University M,D,O
Georgetown University M

M—master's degree; P—first professional degree; D—doctorate; O—other advanced degree

The George Washington University M,D,O
Georgia College & State University M
Georgia Southern University M,O
Georgia State University M,D,O
Graceland University (IA) M,O
Grambling State University M,O
Grand Canyon University M
Gwynedd-Mercy College M
Hardin-Simmons University M
Hawai'i Pacific University M
Holy Names University M,O
Howard University M,O
Husson University M,O
Illinois State University M,D,O
Indiana University–Purdue University Indianapolis M,D
The Johns Hopkins University M,O
Kent State University M,D
Lincoln Memorial University M
Long Island University, C.W. Post Campus M,O
Loyola University Chicago M,O
Loyola University New Orleans M,D
Malone University M
Marymount University M,O
Maryville University of Saint Louis M
McNeese State University M
Middle Tennessee State University M,O
Midwestern State University M
Minnesota State University Mankato M,D
Missouri State University M
Molloy College M,O
Montana State University M,O
Mountain State University M,O
Murray State University M
Northern Arizona University M
Northern Kentucky University M,O
North Georgia College & State University M
Oakland University M,O
Old Dominion University M
Otterbein College M,O
Pace University M,D,O
Pacific Lutheran University M
Prairie View A&M University M
Quinnipiac University M,O
Radford University M
Regis College (MA) M,O
Regis University P,M,D,O
Rivier College M
Rutgers, The State University of New Jersey, Newark M
Sacred Heart University M,D
Saginaw Valley State University M
St. John Fisher College M,O
Saint Joseph College M,O
Saint Xavier University M,O
Samford University M,D
San Francisco State University M
Seattle Pacific University M,O
Shenandoah University M,O
Sonoma State University M
Southern Illinois University Edwardsville M,O
Southern University and Agricultural and Mechanical College M,D,O
Spalding University M
State University of New York Institute of Technology M,O
Stony Brook University, State University of New York M,O
Tennessee State University M
Texas A&M University–Corpus Christi M
Texas Woman's University M,D
Union University M,D,O
Universidad del Turabo M,O
University at Buffalo, the State University of New York M,D,O
The University of Alabama in Huntsville M,D,O
University of Alaska Anchorage M,O
The University of Arizona M,D,O
University of Central Arkansas M
University of Central Florida M,D,O
University of Colorado at Colorado Springs M,D
University of Delaware M,O
University of Detroit Mercy M,O
University of Hawaii at Manoa M,D,O
University of Illinois at Chicago M
The University of Kansas M,D,O
University of Louisville M,D
University of Mary M
University of Massachusetts Lowell M
University of Miami M,D
University of Michigan M,O
University of Minnesota, Twin Cities Campus M
University of Missouri–Kansas City M,D
University of Missouri–St. Louis M,D,O
University of Nevada, Las Vegas M,D,O
The University of North Carolina at Chapel Hill M,D,O
The University of North Carolina Wilmington M
University of Northern Colorado M,D
University of Pennsylvania M,O
University of Phoenix M
University of Phoenix–Hawaii Campus M
University of Phoenix–Phoenix Campus M,O
University of Phoenix–Sacramento Valley Campus M
University of Phoenix–Southern Arizona Campus M,O
University of Phoenix–Southern California Campus M,O
University of Pittsburgh M,D
University of Rhode Island M,D
University of Rochester M,D,O
University of St. Francis (IL) M,D
University of San Diego M,D
University of San Francisco D
The University of Scranton M,O
University of South Carolina M
University of Southern Maine M,O
University of Southern Mississippi M,D
The University of Tampa M
The University of Tennessee at Chattanooga M,O
The University of Texas at Arlington M,D
The University of Texas at El Paso M,O
The University of Texas at Tyler M,D
The University of Texas–Pan American M
The University of Toledo M,O
University of Wisconsin–Milwaukee M,D,O
University of Wisconsin–Oshkosh M
Vanderbilt University M,D
Virginia Commonwealth University M,O
Wagner College O
Westminster College (UT) M
Wichita State University M
Wilmington University M
Winona State University M,D,O
Wright State University M

■ FILM, TELEVISION, AND VIDEO PRODUCTION

American University M
Antioch University McGregor M
Arizona State University M
Bob Jones University P,M,D,O
Boston University M
Bowling Green State University M,D
Brigham Young University M
Brooklyn College of the City University of New York M
California State University, Fullerton M
California State University, Los Angeles M
California State University, Northridge M
Carnegie Mellon University M
Central Michigan University M
Chapman University M
Chatham University M
Columbia College Chicago M
Columbia University M
Drexel University M
Florida Atlantic University M,O
Florida State University M

George Mason University	M
Georgia State University	M,D
Hofstra University	M
Hollins University	M
Howard University	M
Humboldt State University	M
Loyola Marymount University	M
Marywood University	M,O
Montana State University	M
New York University	M
Northwestern University	M,D
Ohio University	M
Polytechnic Institute of NYU	O
Regent University	M,D
Rochester Institute of Technology	M
St. Thomas University	M
San Diego State University	M
San Francisco State University	M
San Jose State University	M
Southern Methodist University	M
Syracuse University	M
Temple University	M
The University of Alabama	M
University of California, Los Angeles	M,D,O
University of California, Santa Barbara	D
University of Central Arkansas	M
University of Central Florida	M
University of Denver	M
The University of Iowa	M
University of Memphis	M,D
University of Miami	M,D
University of Nevada, Las Vegas	M
University of New Orleans	M
The University of North Carolina at Greensboro	M
University of North Texas	M
University of Oklahoma	M
University of Southern California	M,O
The University of Texas at Austin	M,D
University of Utah	M
University of Wisconsin–Milwaukee	M

■ FILM, TELEVISION, AND VIDEO THEORY AND CRITICISM

Boston University	M
Central Michigan University	M
Claremont Graduate University	M,D
College of Staten Island of the City University of New York	M
Emory University	M,D,O
Florida Atlantic University	M,O
Hollins University	M
Indiana University Bloomington	M,D
New York University	M,D
The Ohio State University	M
Ohio University	M
San Francisco State University	M
Syracuse University	M
University of Chicago	M,D
The University of Iowa	M,D
The University of Kansas	M,D
University of Miami	M,D
University of Michigan	D,O
University of Southern California	M,D
University of Wisconsin–Madison	M,D
Yale University	D

■ FINANCE AND BANKING

Adelphi University	M
Alliant International University–San Diego	M,D
American InterContinental University Buckhead Campus	M
American InterContinental University South Florida	M
American International College	M
American University	M,D,O
Andrews University	M
Argosy University, Orange County	M,D,O
Argosy University, Sarasota	M,D,O
Argosy University, Tampa	M,D
Argosy University, Twin Cities	M,D
Arizona State University	M,D
Assumption College	M,O
Auburn University	M
Avila University	M
Barry University	O
Bayamón Central University	M
Benedictine University	M
Bentley University	M
Bernard M. Baruch College of the City University of New York	M,D
Boston College	M,D
Boston University	P,M,D,O
Brandeis University	M,D
Bridgewater State College	M
California Lutheran University	M,O
California State University, East Bay	M
California State University, Fullerton	M
California State University, Los Angeles	M
California State University, Stanislaus	M
Capella University	M,D,O
Carnegie Mellon University	D
Case Western Reserve University	M,D
Central Michigan University	M
Charleston Southern University	M
Christian Brothers University	M,O
City University of Seattle	M,O
Clark University	M
Cleveland State University	M,D,O
College of Santa Fe	M
Colorado State University	M
Colorado Technical University Colorado Springs	M,D
Colorado Technical University Denver	M
Columbia University	M,D
Concordia University Wisconsin	M
Cornell University	D
Dallas Baptist University	M
Davenport University	M
DePaul University	M,O
DeSales University	M
Dowling College	M,O
Drexel University	M,D,O
Eastern Michigan University	M,O
East Tennessee State University	M
Emory University	M,D
Fairfield University	M,O
Fairleigh Dickinson University, College at Florham	M,O
Fairleigh Dickinson University, Metropolitan Campus	M,O
Florida Agricultural and Mechanical University	M
Florida Atlantic University	M,D
Florida Institute of Technology	M
Florida International University	M
Florida State University	M,D
Fordham University	M
Gannon University	O
Georgetown University	D
The George Washington University	M,D
Georgia Institute of Technology	M,D,O
Georgia State University	M,D,O
Golden Gate University	M,D,O
Graduate School and University Center of the City University of New York	D
Grand Canyon University	M
Hawai'i Pacific University	M
Hofstra University	M
Holy Family University	M
Holy Names University	M
Hood College	M
Howard University	M
Illinois Institute of Technology	P,M
Indiana University Southeast	M
Inter American University of Puerto Rico, Metropolitan Campus	M
Inter American University of Puerto Rico, San Germán Campus	M,D
Iona College	M,O
The Johns Hopkins University	M,O
Johnson & Wales University	M,O
Jones International University	M
Kent State University	D
Lakeland College	M
Lamar University	M
La Sierra University	M,O
Lehigh University	M
Lewis University	M

M—master's degree; P—first professional degree; D—doctorate; O—other advanced degree

Lincoln University (PA) M
Lindenwood University M
Lipscomb University M
Long Island University, C.W. Post Campus M,O
Louisiana State University and Agricultural and Mechanical College M,D
Louisiana Tech University M,D
Loyola University Chicago M
Loyola University Maryland M
Manhattanville College M
Marylhurst University M
Marywood University M
Miami University M
Michigan State University M,D
MidAmerica Nazarene University M
Minnesota State University Mankato M
Mississippi College M,O
Mississippi State University M,D
Molloy College M
Montclair State University M,O
Mount Saint Mary College M
National University M
New Jersey City University M
The New School: A University M
New York Institute of Technology M,O
New York University M,D,O
Northeastern Illinois University M
Northeastern State University M
Northeastern University M
Northern Kentucky University M,O
Northwestern University D
Notre Dame de Namur University M
Nova Southeastern University M,D
Oakland University M,O
The Ohio State University M,D
Ohio University M
Oklahoma City University M
Oklahoma State University M,D
Old Dominion University M,D
Oral Roberts University M
Our Lady of the Lake University of San Antonio M
Pace University M
Philadelphia University M
Polytechnic Institute of NYU M,O
Polytechnic Institute of NYU, Westchester Graduate Center M,O
Pontifical Catholic University of Puerto Rico M
Portland State University M
Princeton University M
Providence College M
Purdue University M
Quinnipiac University M
Regis University M,O
Rhode Island College M,O
Rochester Institute of Technology M
Rutgers, The State University of New Jersey, Newark M,D,O
St. Bonaventure University M
St. Cloud State University M
St. Edward's University M,O
St. John's University (NY) M,O
Saint Joseph's University M
Saint Louis University M
St. Mary's University (United States) M
Saint Peter's College M
St. Thomas Aquinas College M
Saint Xavier University M,O
Sam Houston State University M
San Diego State University M
Schiller International University (United States) M
Seattle University M,O
Seton Hall University M
Southeast Missouri State University M
Southern Illinois University Edwardsville M
Southern Methodist University M
Southern New Hampshire University M,D,O
State University of New York at Binghamton M,D
Stevens Institute of Technology M
Stony Brook University, State University of New York M,O
Strayer University M
Suffolk University M,O
Syracuse University M,D
Tarleton State University M
Temple University M,D
Texas A&M International University M
Texas A&M University M,D
Texas Tech University M,D
Universidad Metropolitana M
University at Albany, State University of New York M
University at Buffalo, the State University of New York M,D,O
The University of Akron M
The University of Alabama M,D
The University of Alabama in Huntsville M,O
University of Alaska Fairbanks M
The University of Arizona M,D
University of Baltimore M
University of California, Berkeley D,O
University of California, Santa Cruz M
University of Central Florida D
University of Cincinnati D
University of Colorado at Boulder M,D
University of Colorado at Colorado Springs M
University of Colorado Denver M
University of Connecticut M,D,O
University of Dallas M
University of Dayton M
University of Delaware M
University of Denver M
The University of Findlay M
University of Florida M,D,O
University of Hawaii at Manoa M,D
University of Houston M
University of Houston–Clear Lake M
University of Houston–Victoria M
University of Illinois at Urbana–Champaign M,D
The University of Iowa M,D
University of La Verne M
University of Maryland University College M,O
University of Massachusetts Dartmouth M,O
University of Memphis M,D
University of Miami M
University of Michigan–Dearborn M
University of Minnesota, Twin Cities Campus M,D
University of Missouri–St. Louis M,O
University of Nebraska–Lincoln M,D
University of Nevada, Reno M
University of New Haven M
University of New Orleans M,D
The University of North Carolina at Chapel Hill D
The University of North Carolina at Greensboro M,O
University of North Texas M,D
University of Oregon D
University of Pennsylvania M,D
University of Pittsburgh M,D
University of Puerto Rico, Mayagüez Campus M
University of Puerto Rico, Río Piedras M,D
University of Rhode Island D
University of San Francisco M
The University of Scranton M
University of South Florida M
The University of Tampa M
The University of Tennessee M,D
The University of Texas at Arlington M,D
The University of Texas at Austin D
The University of Texas at Dallas M,D
The University of Texas at San Antonio M,D
The University of Texas–Pan American D
The University of Toledo M
University of Tulsa M
University of Utah M,D
University of Virginia M
University of Washington M,D
University of Washington, Tacoma M
University of Wisconsin–Madison M,D

University of Wisconsin–Whitewater M
University of Wyoming M
Upper Iowa University M
Valparaiso University M
Vanderbilt University M,D
Villanova University M
Virginia Commonwealth University M
Virginia Polytechnic Institute and State University M,D
Wagner College M
Wake Forest University M
Walden University M,D
Washington State University M,D
Washington University in St. Louis M
Webster University M
Western International University M
Western Michigan University M
West Texas A&M University M
Wilkes University M
Wilmington University M
Wright State University M
Xavier University M
Yale University D
Youngstown State University M

■ FINANCIAL ENGINEERING

Claremont Graduate University M
Columbia University M,D,O
Kent State University M
North Carolina State University M
Polytechnic Institute of NYU M,O
Polytechnic Institute of NYU, Westchester Graduate Center M,O
Princeton University M,D
Rensselaer Polytechnic Institute M,D
Stevens Institute of Technology M
Temple University M
University of California, Berkeley M
University of Hawaii at Manoa M
University of Michigan M
University of Tulsa M

■ FIRE PROTECTION ENGINEERING

Anna Maria College M
Oklahoma State University M,D
University of Central Missouri M,O
University of Maryland, College Park M,O
University of New Haven M
Worcester Polytechnic Institute M,D,O

■ FISH, GAME, AND WILDLIFE MANAGEMENT

Arkansas Tech University M
Auburn University M,D
Brigham Young University M,D
Clemson University M,D
Colorado State University M,D
Cornell University M,D
Frostburg State University M
Humboldt State University M
Iowa State University of Science and Technology M,D
Louisiana State University and Agricultural and Mechanical College M,D
Michigan State University M,D
Mississippi State University M,D
Montana State University M,D
New Mexico Highlands University M
New Mexico State University M
North Carolina State University M,D
Oregon State University M,D
Penn State University Park M,D
Purdue University M,D
South Dakota State University M,D
State University of New York College of Environmental Science and Forestry M,D
Sul Ross State University M
Tennessee Technological University M
Texas A&M University M,D
Texas A&M University–Kingsville M,D
Texas State University–San Marcos M
Texas Tech University M,D
University of Alaska Fairbanks M,D
The University of Arizona M,D
University of Delaware M,D
University of Florida M,D
University of Idaho M
University of Maine M,D
University of Massachusetts Amherst M,D
University of Miami M,D
University of Missouri–Columbia M,D
The University of Montana M,D
University of New Hampshire M
University of North Dakota M,D
University of Rhode Island M,D
The University of Tennessee M
University of Washington M,D
University of Wisconsin–Madison M,D
Utah State University M,D
Virginia Polytechnic Institute and State University M,D
West Virginia University M

■ FOLKLORE

George Mason University M
The George Washington University M,D
Indiana University Bloomington M,D
University of California, Berkeley M
University of Louisiana at Lafayette M,D
The University of North Carolina at Chapel Hill M
University of Oregon M
The University of Texas at Austin M,D
University of Wisconsin–Madison M,D
Utah State University M

■ FOOD SCIENCE AND TECHNOLOGY

Alabama Agricultural and Mechanical University M,D
Auburn University M,D
Boston University M
Brigham Young University M
California State University, Fresno M
California State University, Long Beach M
Chapman University M
Clemson University M,D
Colorado State University M,D
Cornell University M,D
Drexel University M
Florida Agricultural and Mechanical University M
Florida State University M,D
Framingham State College M
Illinois Institute of Technology M
Iowa State University of Science and Technology M,D
Kansas State University M,D
Louisiana State University and Agricultural and Mechanical College M,D
Michigan State University M,D
Middle Tennessee State University M
Mississippi State University M,D
Montclair State University M,O
New York University M,D
North Carolina State University M,D
North Dakota State University M,D
The Ohio State University M,D
Oklahoma State University M,D
Oregon State University M,D
Penn State University Park M,D
Purdue University M,D
Rutgers, The State University of New Jersey, New Brunswick M,D
South Dakota State University M,D
Texas A&M University M,D
Texas Tech University M,D
Texas Woman's University M,D
University of Arkansas M,D
University of California, Davis M,D
University of Delaware M,D
University of Florida M,D
University of Georgia M,D
University of Hawaii at Manoa M
University of Idaho M,D
University of Illinois at Urbana–Champaign M,D
University of Maine M,D
University of Maryland, College Park M,D

M—master's degree; P—first professional degree; D—doctorate; O—other advanced degree

University of Maryland Eastern Shore M,D
University of Massachusetts Amherst M,D
University of Minnesota, Twin Cities Campus M,D
University of Missouri–Columbia M,D
University of Nebraska–Lincoln M,D
University of Puerto Rico, Mayagüez Campus M
University of Rhode Island M,D
University of Southern California M,D,O
University of Southern Mississippi M,D
The University of Tennessee M,D
The University of Tennessee at Martin M
University of Vermont D
University of Wisconsin–Madison M,D
University of Wisconsin–Stout M
University of Wyoming M
Utah State University M,D
Virginia Polytechnic Institute and State University M,D
Washington State University M,D
Wayne State University M,D
West Virginia University M,D

■ FOREIGN LANGUAGES EDUCATION

Andrews University M,D,O
Appalachian State University M
Auburn University M,D,O
Bennington College M
Boston College M
Boston University M
Bowling Green State University M
Brigham Young University M
Brooklyn College of the City University of New York M,O
California State University, Chico M
California State University, Sacramento M
Central Connecticut State University M,O
Cleveland State University M
The College at Brockport, State University of New York M,O
College of Charleston M
The College of William and Mary M
Colorado State University M
Cornell University M,D
Delaware State University M
Duquesne University M
Eastern Washington University M
Florida International University M,D,O
Framingham State College M
George Mason University M
Georgia Southern University M
Harding University M,O
Hofstra University M
Hunter College of the City University of New York M
Indiana University Bloomington M,D
Indiana University–Purdue University Indianapolis M,O
Iona College M
Ithaca College M
The Johns Hopkins University M,O
Kean University M
Kent State University M,D
Long Island University, C.W. Post Campus M
Louisiana Tech University M,D
Manhattanville College M
Marquette University M
Michigan State University D
Middle Tennessee State University M
Mills College M,D
Mississippi State University M
Missouri State University M
Monterey Institute of International Studies M
New York University M,D,O
Northern Arizona University M
Oregon State University M
Portland State University M
Purdue University M,D,O
Queens College of the City University of New York M,O
Quinnipiac University M
Rhode Island College M
Rider University O
Rivier College M
Rutgers, The State University of New Jersey, New Brunswick M,D
St. John Fisher College M
Shippensburg University of Pennsylvania M
SIT Graduate Institute M
Southern Illinois University Edwardsville M
Stanford University M
State University of New York at Binghamton M
State University of New York at Plattsburgh M
State University of New York College at Cortland M
Stony Brook University, State University of New York M,O
Temple University M,D
Texas A&M International University M,D
Texas A&M University–Kingsville M
University at Buffalo, the State University of New York M,D,O
University of Arkansas at Little Rock M
University of California, Irvine M,D
University of Central Arkansas M
University of Connecticut M,D,O
University of Delaware M
University of Georgia M,D,O
University of Hawaii at Manoa M,D,O
University of Illinois at Urbana–Champaign M,D
University of Indianapolis M
The University of Iowa M,D
University of Kentucky M
University of Maine M
University of Maryland, College Park M,D
University of Massachusetts Amherst M
University of Massachusetts Boston M
University of Michigan M,D
University of Minnesota, Twin Cities Campus M
University of Missouri–Columbia M,D,O
University of Nebraska at Kearney M
University of Nebraska at Omaha M
University of Nevada, Reno M
The University of North Carolina at Chapel Hill M
The University of North Carolina at Charlotte M
The University of North Carolina at Greensboro M,D,O
University of Northern Colorado M
University of Pittsburgh M,D
University of Puerto Rico, Río Piedras M,D
University of San Diego M
University of South Carolina M,D
University of Southern Mississippi M
University of South Florida M,D,O
The University of Tennessee M,D,O
The University of Texas at Austin M,D
The University of Toledo M
University of Utah M,D
University of Vermont M
University of Virginia M,D,O
University of West Georgia M,O
University of Wisconsin–Madison M,D
Vanderbilt University M,D
Virginia Polytechnic Institute and State University M
Washington State University M
Wayne State University M,D,O
West Chester University of Pennsylvania M,O
Worcester State College M

■ FORENSIC NURSING

Boston College M,D
Cleveland State University M
Duquesne University M,O
Fitchburg State College M,O
University of Colorado at Colorado Springs M,D
Vanderbilt University M,D

■ FORENSIC PSYCHOLOGY

American International College M
Argosy University, Orange County M
Argosy University, Sarasota M,D,O
Argosy University, Twin Cities M,D,O
California Baptist University M
Cambridge College M,O
Castleton State College M
College of Saint Elizabeth M,O
Drexel University D
Fairleigh Dickinson University, Metropolitan Campus M
Holy Names University M,O
John Jay College of Criminal Justice of the City University of New York M,D
Marymount University M
Prairie View A&M University M,D
Roger Williams University M
Tiffin University M
University of Massachusetts Boston M,O
University of North Dakota M,D
Walden University M,D,O

■ FORENSIC SCIENCES

Arcadia University M
Chaminade University of Honolulu M
Duquesne University M
Florida Gulf Coast University M
Florida International University M
George Mason University M,D,O
The George Washington University M
John Jay College of Criminal Justice of the City University of New York M,D
Mercyhurst College M
Michigan State University M,D
National University M
Pace University M
Sam Houston State University M,D
Southeast Missouri State University M
Southern Utah University M
Syracuse University M
Towson University M
Universidad del Turabo M
University at Albany, State University of New York M,D
The University of Alabama at Birmingham M
University of California, Davis M
University of Central Florida M,D,O
University of Florida M,O
University of Illinois at Chicago M
University of Nevada, Las Vegas M,O
University of New Haven M
University of Rhode Island M,D,O
Virginia Commonwealth University M
West Virginia University M,D

■ FORESTRY

Auburn University M,D
California Polytechnic State University, San Luis Obispo M
Clemson University M,D
Colorado State University M,D
Cornell University M,D
Duke University M
Harvard University M
Humboldt State University M
Iowa State University of Science and Technology M,D
Louisiana State University and Agricultural and Mechanical College M,D
Michigan State University M,D
Michigan Technological University M,D
Mississippi State University M,D
North Carolina State University M,D
Northern Arizona University M,D
Oklahoma State University M,D
Oregon State University M,D
Penn State University Park M,D
Purdue University M,D
Southern Illinois University Carbondale M
Southern University and Agricultural and Mechanical College M
State University of New York College of Environmental Science and Forestry M,D
Stephen F. Austin State University M,D
Texas A&M University M,D
The University of Arizona M,D
University of Arkansas at Monticello M
University of California, Berkeley M,D
University of Florida M,D
University of Georgia M,D
University of Idaho M
University of Kentucky M
University of Maine M,D
University of Massachusetts Amherst M,D
University of Michigan M,D,O
University of Missouri–Columbia M,D
The University of Montana M,D
University of New Hampshire M
The University of Tennessee M
University of Vermont M,D
University of Washington M,D
University of Wisconsin–Madison M,D
Utah State University M,D
Virginia Polytechnic Institute and State University M,D
West Virginia University M,D
Yale University M,D

■ FOUNDATIONS AND PHILOSOPHY OF EDUCATION

Antioch University New England M
Arizona State University M
Arkansas State University M,D,O
Ashland University M
Ball State University D
Brigham Young University M,D
Central Connecticut State University M
Chicago State University M
Duquesne University M
Eastern Michigan University M
Eastern Washington University M
Fairfield University M,O
Fairleigh Dickinson University, Metropolitan Campus M
Florida Atlantic University M
Florida State University M,D,O
George Fox University M,D,O
Georgia State University M,D
Harvard University M,O
Hofstra University M,O
Indiana University Bloomington M,D,O
Iowa State University of Science and Technology M,D
Kent State University M,D
Millersville University of Pennsylvania M
Montclair State University M,D,O
New York University M,D
Niagara University M
Northeastern State University M
Northern Arizona University M,D
Northern Illinois University M,D,O
Oakland University M
Penn State University Park M,D
Purdue University M,D,O
Regis University M,O
Rutgers, The State University of New Jersey, New Brunswick M,D
Saint Louis University M,D
Southeast Missouri State University M
Southern Connecticut State University O
Southern Illinois University Edwardsville M
Stanford University M,D
State University of New York at Binghamton D
Suffolk University M,O
Syracuse University M,D
Texas A&M University M,D
University of California, Berkeley M,D
University of Cincinnati M,D
University of Connecticut D
University of Florida M,D,O

M—master's degree; P—first professional degree; D—doctorate; O—other advanced degree

University of Georgia M,D,O
University of Hawaii at Manoa M,D
University of Houston M,D
University of Houston–Clear Lake M
The University of Iowa M,D,O
The University of Kansas D
University of Maryland, College Park M,D,O
University of Michigan M,D
University of Minnesota, Twin Cities Campus M,D,O
University of New Mexico M,D
University of Oklahoma M,D
University of Pittsburgh M,D
University of South Carolina D
The University of Tennessee M,D,O
The University of Texas of the Permian Basin M
The University of Toledo M,D
University of Utah M,D
University of Virginia M,D
University of Washington M,D
The University of West Alabama M
University of Wisconsin–Milwaukee M,D
Wayne State University M,D,O
Western Illinois University M
Widener University M,D
Youngstown State University M,D

■ FRENCH

American University O
Arizona State University M
Bennington College M
Boston College M,D
Boston University M,D
Bowling Green State University M
Brigham Young University M
Brooklyn College of the City University of New York M,D
Brown University D
California State University, Fullerton M
California State University, Long Beach M
California State University, Los Angeles M
California State University, Sacramento M
Case Western Reserve University M
Central Connecticut State University M,O
Cleveland State University M
Columbia University M,D
Cornell University D
Duke University D
Eastern Michigan University M,O
Emory University D,O
Florida Atlantic University M
Florida State University M,D
Georgia State University M,O
Graduate School and University Center of the City University of New York D
Harvard University M,D
Hofstra University M
Howard University M
Hunter College of the City University of New York M
Illinois State University M
Indiana University Bloomington M,D
The Johns Hopkins University D
Kansas State University M
Kent State University M,D
Louisiana State University and Agricultural and Mechanical College M,D
Miami University M
Michigan State University M,D
Millersville University of Pennsylvania M
Minnesota State University Mankato M
Mississippi State University M
Missouri State University M
Montclair State University M,O
New York University M,D,O
North Carolina State University M
Northern Illinois University M
Northwestern University D,O
The Ohio State University M,D
Ohio University M
Penn State University Park M,D
Portland State University M
Princeton University D
Purdue University M,D
Queens College of the City University of New York M
Rice University M,D
Rider University O
Rutgers, The State University of New Jersey, New Brunswick M,D
Saint Louis University M
San Francisco State University M
San Jose State University M
Stanford University M,D
State University of New York at Binghamton M
Stony Brook University, State University of New York M
Syracuse University M
Texas Tech University M
Tufts University M
Tulane University M,D
University at Albany, State University of New York M,D
University at Buffalo, the State University of New York M,D
The University of Alabama M,D
The University of Arizona M
University of Arkansas M
University of California, Berkeley D
University of California, Davis D
University of California, Irvine M,D
University of California, Los Angeles M,D
University of California, San Diego M
University of California, Santa Barbara M,D
University of Chicago M,D
University of Cincinnati M,D
University of Colorado at Boulder M,D
University of Connecticut M,D
University of Delaware M
University of Florida M,D
University of Georgia M
University of Hawaii at Manoa M
University of Houston M,D
University of Illinois at Chicago M
University of Illinois at Urbana–Champaign M,D
The University of Iowa M,D
The University of Kansas M,D
University of Kentucky M
University of Louisiana at Lafayette M,D
University of Louisville M
University of Maine M
University of Maryland, College Park M,D
University of Massachusetts Amherst M
University of Memphis M
University of Miami D
University of Michigan D
University of Minnesota, Twin Cities Campus M,D
University of Mississippi M
University of Missouri–Columbia M,D
The University of Montana M
University of Nebraska–Lincoln M,D
University of Nevada, Reno M
University of New Mexico M,D
The University of North Carolina at Chapel Hill M,D
The University of North Carolina at Greensboro M
University of Northern Iowa M
University of North Texas M
University of Notre Dame M
University of Oklahoma M,D
University of Oregon M
University of Pennsylvania M,D
University of Pittsburgh M,D
University of South Carolina M,D
University of South Florida M
The University of Tennessee M,D
The University of Texas at Arlington M
The University of Texas at Austin M,D
The University of Toledo M
University of Utah M,D
University of Vermont M
University of Virginia M,D

University of Washington M,D
University of Wisconsin–Madison M,D,O
University of Wisconsin–Milwaukee M,O
University of Wyoming M
Vanderbilt University M,D
Washington University in St. Louis M,D
Wayne State University M
West Chester University of Pennsylvania M,O
West Virginia University M
Yale University M,D

■ GAME DESIGN AND DEVELOPMENT

DePaul University M,D
George Mason University M,D,O
Michigan State University M
National University M
Rochester Institute of Technology M
University of Pennsylvania M
University of Southern California M,D

■ GENDER STUDIES

Arizona State University D
Brandeis University M
Carnegie Mellon University M,D
Central Michigan University M
Cornell University M,D
Eastern Michigan University M
George Mason University M
Indiana University Bloomington D
Indiana University–Purdue University Indianapolis M
Northwestern University
Roosevelt University M,O
Rutgers, The State University of New Jersey, New Brunswick M,D
Simmons College M
University of Florida M,O
The University of North Carolina at Greensboro M,O
University of Northern Iowa M
Virginia Commonwealth University O

■ GENETIC COUNSELING

Arcadia University M
Brandeis University M
California State University, Stanislaus M
Case Western Reserve University M
The Johns Hopkins University M,D
Northwestern University M
Sarah Lawrence College M
University of California, Irvine M
University of Cincinnati M
University of Colorado Denver M
University of Michigan M,D
University of Minnesota, Twin Cities Campus M,D
The University of North Carolina at Greensboro M
University of Pittsburgh M
University of South Carolina M
University of Wisconsin–Madison M

■ GENETICS

Brandeis University M,D
California Institute of Technology D
Carnegie Mellon University M,D
Case Western Reserve University D
Clemson University M,D
Columbia University M,D
Cornell University D
Dartmouth College D
Drexel University M,D
Duke University D
Emory University D
Florida State University M,D
The George Washington University D
Harvard University D
Illinois State University M,D
Indiana University Bloomington M,D
Iowa State University of Science and Technology M,D
The Johns Hopkins University M,D
Kansas State University M,D
Marquette University M,D
Massachusetts Institute of Technology D
Mayo Graduate School D
Michigan State University M,D
Mississippi State University M,D
New York University M,D
North Carolina State University M,D
Northwestern University D
The Ohio State University M,D
Oregon State University M,D
Penn State University Park M,D
Purdue University M,D
Rutgers, The State University of New Jersey, New Brunswick M,D
Stanford University D
Stony Brook University, State University of New York D
Temple University D
Texas A&M University M,D
Tufts University D
University at Albany, State University of New York M,D
The University of Alabama at Birmingham D
The University of Arizona M,D
University of California, Davis M,D
University of California, Irvine D
University of California, Riverside D
University of California, San Diego D
University of Chicago D
University of Colorado at Boulder M,D
University of Colorado Denver M,D
University of Connecticut M,D
University of Delaware M,D
University of Florida D
University of Georgia M,D
University of Hawaii at Manoa M,D
University of Illinois at Chicago D
The University of Iowa M,D
University of Miami M,D
University of Minnesota, Twin Cities Campus M,D
University of Missouri–Columbia M,D
University of Missouri–St. Louis M,D,O
University of New Hampshire M,D
University of New Mexico M,D
The University of North Carolina at Chapel Hill M,D
University of North Dakota M,D
University of Notre Dame M,D
University of Oregon M,D
University of Pennsylvania D
University of Rochester M,D
University of Southern California M,D
The University of Tennessee M,D
University of Washington M,D
University of Wisconsin–Madison M,D
University of Wyoming D
Virginia Commonwealth University M,D
Virginia Polytechnic Institute and State University M,D
Washington State University M,D
Washington University in St. Louis M,D,O
Wayne State University M,D
West Virginia University M,D
Yale University D

■ GENOMIC SCIENCES

Case Western Reserve University D
The George Washington University M
Harvard University D
North Carolina State University M,D
North Dakota State University M,D
Texas Tech University M
University of California, Riverside D
University of Chicago D
University of Cincinnati M,D
University of Connecticut M
University of Florida D
University of Pennsylvania D
The University of Tennessee M,D
The University of Toledo M,O
University of Washington D
Wake Forest University D
West Virginia University M,D
Yale University D

M—master's degree; P—first professional degree; D—doctorate; O—other advanced degree

■ GEOCHEMISTRY

California Institute of Technology M,D
California State University, Fullerton M
Colorado School of Mines M,D
Columbia University M,D
Cornell University M,D
Georgia Institute of Technology M,D
Indiana University Bloomington M,D
Massachusetts Institute of Technology M,D
Missouri University of Science and Technology M,D
New Mexico Institute of Mining and Technology M,D
Ohio University M
Penn State University Park M,D
Rensselaer Polytechnic Institute M,D
University of California, Los Angeles M,D
University of Hawaii at Manoa M,D
University of Michigan M,D
University of Nevada, Reno M,D
University of New Hampshire M
The University of Texas at Dallas M,D
University of Wisconsin–Milwaukee M,D
Yale University D

■ GEODETIC SCIENCES

Columbia University M,D
George Mason University M,D,O
The Ohio State University M,D

■ GEOGRAPHIC INFORMATION SYSTEMS

Appalachian State University M
Arizona State University M,D
Boston University M,D
Clark University M
Cleveland State University M,D,O
Eastern Michigan University M,O
Florida State University M,D
George Mason University M,D,O
Georgia Institute of Technology M,D
Georgia State University O
Hunter College of the City University of New York M,O
Idaho State University M,O
Indiana University–Purdue University Indianapolis M,O
Montclair State University M,D,O
North Carolina State University M,D
Northern Arizona University M,O
Northwest Missouri State University M,O
Saint Louis University M,D,O
Saint Mary's University of Minnesota M,O
Salisbury University M
San Jose State University M,O
Texas State University–San Marcos M,D
University at Albany, State University of New York M,O
University at Buffalo, the State University of New York M,D,O
The University of Akron M
University of Central Arkansas M,O
University of Colorado Denver M,D
University of Connecticut M,D,O
University of Denver M,O
University of Maryland, Baltimore County M,O
University of Minnesota, Twin Cities Campus M
The University of Montana M
The University of North Carolina at Greensboro M,D,O
University of Pittsburgh M,D
University of Redlands M
University of Southern California M,O
The University of Texas at Dallas M,D
The University of Toledo M,O
University of West Georgia O
University of Wisconsin–Madison M,D,O
University of Wisconsin–Milwaukee M,O
Virginia Commonwealth University O
West Chester University of Pennsylvania M,O
Western Illinois University M,O
West Virginia University M,D

■ GEOGRAPHY

Appalachian State University M
Arizona State University M,D
Auburn University M
Boston University M,D
Brigham Young University M
California State University, Chico M
California State University, East Bay M
California State University, Fullerton M
California State University, Long Beach M
California State University, Los Angeles M
California State University, Northridge M
Central Connecticut State University M
Chicago State University M
Clark University M,D
East Carolina University M
Eastern Michigan University M,O
Florida Atlantic University M
Florida State University M,D
Fort Hays State University M
George Mason University M
The George Washington University M
Georgia State University M
Hunter College of the City University of New York M,O
Indiana State University M,D
Indiana University Bloomington M,D
Indiana University of Pennsylvania M
The Johns Hopkins University M,D
Kansas State University M,D
Kent State University M,D
Louisiana State University and Agricultural and Mechanical College M,D
Marshall University M
Miami University M
Michigan State University M,D
Minnesota State University Mankato M
Missouri State University M
New Mexico State University M
Northeastern Illinois University M
Northern Arizona University M,O
Northern Illinois University M
Northwest Missouri State University M,O
The Ohio State University M,D
Ohio University M
Oklahoma State University M,D
Oregon State University M,D
Portland State University M,D
Rutgers, The State University of New Jersey, New Brunswick M,D
St. Cloud State University M
Salem State College M
San Diego State University M,D
San Francisco State University M
San Jose State University M,O
Shippensburg University of Pennsylvania M
South Dakota State University M
Southern Illinois University Carbondale M,D
Southern Illinois University Edwardsville M
State University of New York at Binghamton M
Syracuse University M,D
Temple University M
Texas A&M University M,D
Texas State University–San Marcos M,D
Towson University M
University at Albany, State University of New York M,O
University at Buffalo, the State University of New York M,D,O
The University of Akron M
The University of Alabama M
The University of Arizona M,D
University of Arkansas M
University of California, Berkeley D
University of California, Davis M,D

University of California, Los Angeles M,D
University of California, Santa Barbara M,D
University of Central Arkansas M,O
University of Cincinnati M,D
University of Colorado at Boulder M,D
University of Colorado at Colorado Springs M
University of Connecticut M,D,O
University of Delaware M,D
University of Denver M,D
University of Florida M,D
University of Georgia M,D
University of Hawaii at Manoa M,D,O
University of Idaho M,D
University of Illinois at Chicago M
University of Illinois at Urbana–Champaign M,D
The University of Iowa M,D
The University of Kansas M,D
University of Kentucky M,D
University of Maryland, Baltimore County M,D
University of Maryland, College Park M,D
University of Massachusetts Amherst M
University of Miami M
University of Minnesota, Twin Cities Campus M,D
University of Missouri–Columbia M
The University of Montana M
University of Nebraska at Omaha M,O
University of Nebraska–Lincoln M,D
University of Nevada, Reno M,D
University of New Mexico M
University of New Orleans M
The University of North Carolina at Chapel Hill M,D
The University of North Carolina at Charlotte M,D
The University of North Carolina at Greensboro M,D,O
University of North Dakota M
University of Northern Iowa M
University of North Texas M
University of Oklahoma M,D
University of Oregon M,D
University of South Carolina M,D
University of Southern California M,O
University of Southern Mississippi M,D
University of South Florida M,D
The University of Tennessee M,D
The University of Texas at Austin M,D
The University of Toledo M,O
University of Utah M,D
University of Washington M,D
University of Wisconsin–Madison M,D,O
University of Wisconsin–Milwaukee M,D
University of Wyoming M
Utah State University M,D
Virginia Polytechnic Institute and State University M,D
Wayne State University M
West Chester University of Pennsylvania M,O
Western Illinois University M,O
Western Kentucky University M
Western Michigan University M
Western Washington University M
West Virginia University M,D

■ GEOLOGICAL ENGINEERING

Arizona State University M,D
Colorado School of Mines M,D
Michigan Technological University M,D
Missouri University of Science and Technology M,D
University of Alaska Anchorage M
University of Alaska Fairbanks M,D
The University of Arizona M,D,O
University of Hawaii at Manoa M,D
University of Idaho M
University of Minnesota, Twin Cities Campus M,D
University of Nevada, Reno M,D
University of North Dakota M
University of Oklahoma M,D
University of Utah M,D
University of Wisconsin–Madison M,D

■ GEOLOGY

Arizona State University M,D
Auburn University M
Ball State University M
Baylor University M,D
Boise State University M,D
Boston College M
Bowling Green State University M
Brigham Young University M
Brooklyn College of the City University of New York M,D
California Institute of Technology M,D
California State University, Bakersfield M
California State University, Chico M
California State University, East Bay M
California State University, Fresno M
California State University, Fullerton M
California State University, Long Beach M
California State University, Los Angeles M
California State University, Northridge M
Case Western Reserve University M,D
Central Washington University M
Colorado School of Mines M,D
Cornell University M,D
Duke University M,D
East Carolina University M
Eastern Kentucky University M,D
Florida Atlantic University M
Florida State University M,D
Fort Hays State University M
Georgia State University M
Humboldt State University M
Idaho State University M,O
Indiana University Bloomington M,D
Indiana University–Purdue University Indianapolis M
Iowa State University of Science and Technology M,D
Kansas State University M
Kent State University M,D
Lehigh University M,D
Louisiana State University and Agricultural and Mechanical College M,D
Massachusetts Institute of Technology M,D
Miami University M,D
Michigan Technological University M,D
Missouri State University M
Missouri University of Science and Technology M,D
New Mexico Institute of Mining and Technology M,D
New Mexico State University M
Northern Arizona University M
Northern Illinois University M,D
Northwestern University M,D
The Ohio State University M,D
Ohio University M
Oklahoma State University M,D
Oregon State University M,D
Portland State University M,D
Queens College of the City University of New York M
Rensselaer Polytechnic Institute M,D
Rutgers, The State University of New Jersey, Newark M
Rutgers, The State University of New Jersey, New Brunswick M,D
San Diego State University M
San Jose State University M
Southern Illinois University Carbondale M,D
Southern Methodist University M,D
State University of New York at Binghamton M,D
Stephen F. Austin State University M
Sul Ross State University M
Syracuse University M,D
Temple University M
Texas A&M University M,D

M—master's degree; P—first professional degree; D—doctorate; O—other advanced degree

Texas A&M University–Kingsville M
Texas Christian University M
Tulane University M,D
University at Albany, State University of New York M,D
University at Buffalo, the State University of New York M,D
The University of Akron M
The University of Alabama M,D
University of Alaska Fairbanks M,D
University of Arkansas M
University of California, Berkeley M,D
University of California, Davis M,D
University of California, Los Angeles M,D
University of California, Riverside M,D
University of California, Santa Barbara M,D
University of Cincinnati M,D
University of Colorado at Boulder M,D
University of Connecticut M,D
University of Florida M,D
University of Georgia M,D
University of Hawaii at Manoa M,D
University of Houston M,D
University of Idaho M,D
University of Illinois at Chicago M,D
University of Illinois at Urbana–Champaign M,D
The University of Kansas M,D
University of Kentucky M,D
University of Louisiana at Lafayette M
University of Maine M,D
University of Maryland, College Park M,D
University of Memphis M,D,O
University of Michigan M,D
University of Minnesota, Duluth M,D
University of Minnesota, Twin Cities Campus M,D
University of Missouri–Columbia M,D
University of Missouri–Kansas City M,D
The University of Montana M,D
University of Nevada, Reno M,D
University of New Hampshire M
The University of North Carolina at Chapel Hill M,D
The University of North Carolina Wilmington M
University of North Dakota M,D
University of Oklahoma M,D
University of Oregon M,D
University of Pittsburgh M,D
University of Puerto Rico, Mayagüez Campus M
University of Rochester M,D
University of South Carolina M,D
University of Southern Mississippi M,D
University of South Florida M,D
The University of Tennessee M,D
The University of Texas at Arlington M,D
The University of Texas at Austin M,D
The University of Texas at El Paso M,D
The University of Texas at San Antonio M
The University of Texas of the Permian Basin M
The University of Toledo M,D
University of Utah M,D
University of Vermont M
University of Washington M,D
University of Wisconsin–Madison M,D
University of Wisconsin–Milwaukee M,D
University of Wyoming M,D
Utah State University M
Virginia Polytechnic Institute and State University M,D
Washington State University M,D
Wayne State University M
West Chester University of Pennsylvania M,O
Western Kentucky University M
Western Washington University M
West Virginia University M,D
Wichita State University M
Wright State University M
Yale University D

■ GEOPHYSICS

Boise State University M,D
Boston College M
Bowling Green State University M
California Institute of Technology M,D
California State University, Long Beach M
Colorado School of Mines M,D
Columbia University M,D
Cornell University M,D
Florida State University D
Georgia Institute of Technology M,D
Idaho State University M,O
Indiana University Bloomington M,D
Louisiana State University and Agricultural and Mechanical College M,D
Massachusetts Institute of Technology M,D
Michigan Technological University M
Missouri University of Science and Technology M,D
New Mexico Institute of Mining and Technology M,D
Ohio University M
Oregon State University M,D
Rensselaer Polytechnic Institute M,D
Rice University M
Saint Louis University M,D
Southern Methodist University M,D
Stanford University M,D
Texas A&M University M,D
The University of Akron M
University of Alaska Fairbanks M,D
University of California, Berkeley M,D
University of California, Los Angeles M,D
University of California, Santa Barbara M,D
University of Chicago M,D
University of Colorado at Boulder M,D
University of Hawaii at Manoa M,D
University of Houston M,D
University of Miami M,D
University of Minnesota, Twin Cities Campus M,D
University of Nevada, Reno M,D
University of Oklahoma M
The University of Texas at Dallas M,D
The University of Texas at El Paso M,D
University of Utah M,D
University of Washington M,D
University of Wisconsin–Madison M,D
University of Wyoming M,D
Virginia Polytechnic Institute and State University M,D
West Virginia University M,D
Wright State University M
Yale University D

■ GEOSCIENCES

Arizona State University M,D
Ball State University M
Baylor University M,D
Boise State University M
Boston University M,D
Brooklyn College of the City University of New York M
Brown University M,D
California State University, Chico M
Case Western Reserve University M,D
Central Connecticut State University M,O
City College of the City University of New York M,D
Colorado State University M,D
Columbia University M,D
Cornell University M,D
Dartmouth College M,D
Eastern Michigan University M
Emporia State University M,O
Florida International University M,D
Fort Hays State University M
Georgia Institute of Technology M,D
Georgia State University M,O
Graduate School and University Center of the City University of New York D
Harvard University M,D

Hunter College of the City University of New York M,O
Idaho State University M,O
Indiana University Bloomington M,D
Iowa State University of Science and Technology M,D
The Johns Hopkins University M,D
Lehigh University M,D
Long Island University, C.W. Post Campus M
Massachusetts Institute of Technology M,D
Michigan State University M,D
Middle Tennessee State University O
Mississippi State University M
Missouri State University M
Montana State University M,D
Montclair State University M,D,O
Murray State University M
New Mexico Institute of Mining and Technology M,D
North Carolina Central University M
North Carolina State University M,D
Northeastern Illinois University M
Northern Arizona University M
Northwestern University M,D
Oregon State University M,D
Penn State University Park M,D
Princeton University D
Purdue University M,D
Rensselaer Polytechnic Institute M,D
Rice University M,D
Saint Louis University M,D
St. Thomas University M,D,O
San Francisco State University M
South Dakota State University M,D
Stanford University M,D,O
State University of New York College at Oneonta M
Stony Brook University, State University of New York M,D
Texas A&M University–Commerce M
Texas Christian University M
Texas Tech University M,D
Tulane University M,D
University at Albany, State University of New York M,D
The University of Akron M
The University of Arizona M,D
University of Arkansas at Little Rock O
University of California, Irvine M,D
University of California, Los Angeles M,D
University of California, San Diego M,D
University of California, Santa Barbara M,D
University of California, Santa Cruz M,D
University of Chicago M,D
University of Florida M,D
University of Illinois at Chicago M,D
University of Illinois at Urbana–Champaign M,D
The University of Iowa M,D
University of Maine M,D
University of Massachusetts Amherst M,D
University of Missouri–Kansas City M,D
The University of Montana M,D
University of Nebraska–Lincoln M,D
University of Nevada, Las Vegas M,D
University of New Hampshire M
University of New Mexico M,D
University of New Orleans M
The University of North Carolina at Charlotte M
The University of North Carolina Wilmington M
University of North Dakota M,D
University of Northern Colorado M
University of Notre Dame M,D
University of Pennsylvania M,D
University of Rhode Island M,D
University of Rochester M,D
University of South Carolina M,D
University of Southern California M,D
The University of Texas at Austin M,D
The University of Texas at Dallas M,D
The University of Toledo M,D
University of Tulsa M,D
Virginia Polytechnic Institute and State University M,D
Washington State University M,D
Washington University in St. Louis M,D
Western Connecticut State University M
Western Michigan University M,D
Yale University D

■ GEOTECHNICAL ENGINEERING

Auburn University M,D
The Catholic University of America M,D,O
Cornell University M,D
Drexel University M,D
Illinois Institute of Technology M,D
Iowa State University of Science and Technology M,D
Louisiana State University and Agricultural and Mechanical College M,D
Marquette University M,D
Massachusetts Institute of Technology M,D,O
Missouri University of Science and Technology M,D
Northwestern University M,D
Ohio University M,D
Oregon State University M,D
Rensselaer Polytechnic Institute M,D
Texas A&M University M,D
Tufts University M,D
The University of Alabama in Huntsville M,D
University of California, Berkeley M,D
University of Colorado at Boulder M,D
University of Delaware M,D
University of Maine M,D
University of Missouri–Columbia M,D
University of Oklahoma M,D
University of Rhode Island M,D
The University of Texas at Austin M,D
University of Washington M,D

■ GERMAN

Arizona State University M
Bowling Green State University M
Brigham Young University M
Brown University D
California State University, Fullerton M
California State University, Long Beach M
California State University, Sacramento M
Columbia University M,D
Cornell University M,D
Duke University D
Eastern Michigan University M,O
Florida State University M
Georgetown University M,D
Georgia State University M,O
Graduate School and University Center of the City University of New York M,D
Harvard University D
Hofstra University M
Illinois State University M
Indiana University Bloomington M,D
The Johns Hopkins University D
Kansas State University M
Kent State University M,D
Michigan State University M,D
Millersville University of Pennsylvania M
Mississippi State University M
Missouri State University M
New York University M,D
Northwestern University D
The Ohio State University M,D
Penn State University Park M,D
Portland State University M
Princeton University D
Purdue University M,D
Rider University O

M—master's degree; P—first professional degree; D—doctorate; O—other advanced degree

Rutgers, The State University of New Jersey, New Brunswick M,D
San Francisco State University M
Stanford University M,D
Texas Tech University M
Tufts University M
The University of Alabama M,D
The University of Arizona M
University of Arkansas M
University of California, Berkeley D
University of California, Davis M,D
University of California, Irvine M,D
University of California, Los Angeles M,D
University of California, San Diego M
University of California, Santa Barbara M,D
University of Chicago M,D
University of Cincinnati M,D
University of Colorado at Boulder M
University of Connecticut M,D
University of Delaware M
University of Florida M,D
University of Georgia M
University of Illinois at Chicago M,D
University of Illinois at Urbana–Champaign M,D
The University of Iowa M,D
The University of Kansas M,D
University of Kentucky M
University of Maryland, College Park M,D
University of Massachusetts Amherst M,D
University of Michigan M,D
University of Minnesota, Twin Cities Campus M,D
University of Mississippi M
University of Missouri–Columbia M
The University of Montana M
University of Nebraska–Lincoln M,D
University of Nevada, Reno M
University of New Mexico M,D
The University of North Carolina at Chapel Hill M,D
University of Northern Iowa M
University of Oklahoma M
University of Oregon M,D
University of Pennsylvania M,D
University of Pittsburgh M,D
University of South Carolina M,D
The University of Tennessee M,D
The University of Texas at Austin M,D
The University of Toledo M
University of Utah M,D
University of Vermont M
University of Virginia M,D
University of Washington M,D
University of Wisconsin–Madison M,D
University of Wisconsin–Milwaukee M,O
University of Wyoming M
Vanderbilt University M,D
Washington University in St. Louis M,D
Wayne State University M,D
West Chester University of Pennsylvania M,O
Yale University D

■ GERONTOLOGICAL NURSING

Boston College M,D
Case Western Reserve University M,D
The Catholic University of America M,D,O
College of Mount Saint Vincent M,O
College of Staten Island of the City University of New York M,O
Columbia University M,O
Concordia University Wisconsin M
Duke University M,D,O
Emory University M
Gwynedd-Mercy College M
Hampton University M
Hunter College of the City University of New York M
Kent State University M,D
Lehman College of the City University of New York M
Marquette University M,D,O
Nazareth College of Rochester M
New York University M,O
Oakland University M,O
Rutgers, The State University of New Jersey, Newark M
San Jose State University M,O
Seattle Pacific University M,O
Seton Hall University M
Southern University and Agricultural and Mechanical College M,D,O
State University of New York Institute of Technology M,O
University at Buffalo, the State University of New York M,D,O
University of Colorado at Colorado Springs M,D
University of Delaware M,O
University of Illinois at Chicago M
University of Massachusetts Lowell M,O
University of Michigan M
University of Minnesota, Twin Cities Campus M
The University of North Carolina at Greensboro M,D,O
University of Rhode Island M,D
University of Utah M,O
Vanderbilt University M,D
Villanova University M,D,O

■ GERONTOLOGY

Abilene Christian University M,O
Adelphi University M,O
Appalachian State University M
Arizona State University M,O
Arkansas State University M,D,O
Ball State University M
Bethel University M
California State University, Fullerton M
California State University, Long Beach M
California State University, Stanislaus O
Capella University M,D
Chestnut Hill College M,O
Cleveland State University M,D,O
The College of New Rochelle M,O
Concordia University Chicago M
Dominican University of California M
Eastern Illinois University M
Eastern Michigan University M,O
East Tennessee State University M,O
Emory University M
Gannon University O
Georgia State University M
Hofstra University M,O
Kent State University M
Lindenwood University M,O
Long Island University, C.W. Post Campus M,O
Marywood University M,O
Miami University M
Middle Tennessee State University O
Minnesota State University Mankato M,O
Morehead State University M
National-Louis University M,O
North Dakota State University M,D
Northeastern Illinois University M
Notre Dame de Namur University M,O
Oregon State University M
Portland State University O
Rochester Institute of Technology M,O
Sacred Heart University M
St. Cloud State University M
Saint Joseph College M,O
Saint Joseph's University M,O
San Diego State University M
San Francisco State University M
San Jose State University M,O
Shippensburg University of Pennsylvania M,O
Texas A&M University–Kingsville M
Texas Tech University M,D
Towson University M,O
University of Arkansas at Little Rock O
University of Central Florida M,O
University of Central Missouri M
University of Central Oklahoma M
University of Georgia O

University of Illinois at Springfield M
University of Indianapolis M,O
The University of Kansas M,D,O
University of Kentucky D
University of La Verne M,O
University of Louisiana at Monroe M,O
University of Louisville M,D,O
University of Maryland, Baltimore County D
University of Massachusetts Boston M,D,O
University of Missouri–St. Louis M,O
University of Nebraska at Omaha M,O
University of Nebraska–Lincoln M,D
University of New England M,O
The University of North Carolina at Charlotte M
The University of North Carolina at Greensboro M,O
The University of North Carolina Wilmington M
University of Northern Colorado M
University of North Florida M,O
University of North Texas M,D,O
University of Phoenix M
University of Phoenix–Hawaii Campus M
University of Phoenix–Phoenix Campus M,O
University of Phoenix–Southern Colorado Campus M
University of Pittsburgh M,D,O
University of Rhode Island M,D
University of South Alabama O
University of South Carolina O
University of Southern California M,D,O
University of South Florida M,D
The University of Tennessee M
The University of Toledo O
University of Utah M,O
University of Wisconsin–Milwaukee M,D,O
Valparaiso University M,O
Virginia Commonwealth University M,D,O
Virginia Polytechnic Institute and State University M,D
Wayne State University O
Webster University M
West Chester University of Pennsylvania M,O
Wichita State University M
Wilmington University M

■ GRAPHIC DESIGN

Bob Jones University P,M,D,O
Boston University M
Bowling Green State University M
California State University, Los Angeles M
Cardinal Stritch University M
City College of the City University of New York M
The College of New Rochelle M
Florida Atlantic University M
George Mason University M
Illinois State University M
Indiana State University M
Iowa State University of Science and Technology M
Kean University M
Kent State University M
Louisiana State University and Agricultural and Mechanical College M
Louisiana Tech University M
Marywood University M
New York University M
North Carolina State University M
Ohio University M
Pittsburg State University M,O
Rochester Institute of Technology M
San Diego State University M
Southern Polytechnic State University M,O
Suffolk University M
Temple University M
Texas State University–San Marcos M
University of Baltimore M,D
University of California, Berkeley O
University of Cincinnati M
University of Florida M,D
University of Guam M
University of Illinois at Chicago M
University of Illinois at Urbana–Champaign M
University of Massachusetts Dartmouth M
University of Memphis M,O
University of Miami M
University of Minnesota, Duluth M
University of Notre Dame M
The University of Tennessee M
University of Utah M
Western Illinois University M,O
Western Michigan University M
West Virginia University M
Yale University M

■ HAZARDOUS MATERIALS MANAGEMENT

Humboldt State University M
Idaho State University M
New Mexico Institute of Mining and Technology M
Rutgers, The State University of New Jersey, New Brunswick M,D
Southern Methodist University M,D
Stony Brook University, State University of New York M,O
Tufts University M,D
University of Oklahoma M,D
University of South Carolina M,D
Wayne State University M,O

■ HEALTH COMMUNICATION

Boston University M
Chapman University M
Cleveland State University M,O
East Carolina University M
Emerson College M
The George Washington University M
The Johns Hopkins University M,D
Marquette University M
Marywood University M,O
Michigan State University M
Tufts University M
Tulane University M
University of Florida M,D,O
University of Southern California M
Washington State University M,D

■ HEALTH EDUCATION

Adelphi University M,O
Alabama State University M
Albany State University M
Alcorn State University M,O
American University M,O
Arcadia University M
Auburn University M,D,O
Augusta State University M
Austin Peay State University M
Ball State University M
Baylor University M,D
Benedictine University M
Boston University M,O
Brandeis University D
Brigham Young University M
Brooklyn College of the City University of New York M,O
California State University, Dominguez Hills M
California State University, Long Beach M
California State University, Los Angeles M
California State University, San Bernardino M
Cambridge College M,D,O
Central Washington University M
The Citadel, The Military College of South Carolina M
Cleveland State University M
The College at Brockport, State University of New York M
The College of New Jersey M
D'Youville College D
East Carolina University M
Eastern Kentucky University M
Eastern Michigan University M
Eastern University M

M—master's degree; P—first professional degree; D—doctorate; O—other advanced degree

East Stroudsburg University of Pennsylvania M
Emory University M
Florida Agricultural and Mechanical University M
Florida State University M,D
Fort Hays State University M
Framingham State College M
Georgia College & State University M
Georgia Southern University M,D
Georgia Southwestern State University M,O
Georgia State University M
Harding University M,O
Hofstra University M
Howard University M
Idaho State University M
Illinois State University M
Indiana State University M
Indiana University Bloomington M,D
Indiana University of Pennsylvania M
Indiana University–Purdue University Indianapolis M,D
Inter American University of Puerto Rico, Metropolitan Campus M
Ithaca College M
Jackson State University M
Jacksonville State University M
James Madison University M
John F. Kennedy University M
The Johns Hopkins University M,D
Kent State University M,D
Lehman College of the City University of New York M
Long Island University, Brooklyn Campus M
Louisiana Tech University M,D
Marshall University M
Marywood University D
Middle Tennessee State University M
Mills College M,D
Minnesota State University Mankato M
Mississippi University for Women M
Montana State University M
Montclair State University M,O
Morehead State University M
Mount Mary College M
New Jersey City University M
New Mexico Highlands University M
New Mexico State University M
New York University M,D
North Carolina Agricultural and Technical State University M
Northeastern State University M
Northwestern State University of Louisiana M
Northwest Missouri State University M
Nova Southeastern University M,D
Oklahoma State University M,D,O
Penn State Harrisburg M,D
Plymouth State University M
Portland State University M,O
Prairie View A&M University M
Regis University P,M,D,O
Rhode Island College M,O
Saint Francis University M
Saint Joseph's University M,O
San Francisco State University M
San Jose State University M,O
Simmons College M,D,O
South Dakota State University M
Southeastern Louisiana University M
Southern Connecticut State University M
Southern Illinois University Carbondale M,D
Southern Illinois University Edwardsville M,O
Springfield College M,D,O
State University of New York College at Cortland M
Suffolk University M
Temple University M
Tennessee Technological University M
Texas A&M University M,D
Texas A&M University–Commerce M,D
Texas A&M University–Kingsville M
Texas Southern University M
Texas State University–San Marcos M
Texas Woman's University M,D
Tulane University M
Union College (KY) M
The University of Alabama M,D
The University of Alabama at Birmingham M,D
University of Arkansas M,D
University of California, Berkeley M,O
University of Central Arkansas M
University of Central Oklahoma M
University of Cincinnati M,D
University of Colorado Denver D
University of Florida M,D,O
University of Georgia M,D
University of Houston M,D
University of Illinois at Chicago M
The University of Kansas M,D,O
University of Louisville M,D
University of Maryland, Baltimore County M,O
University of Maryland, College Park M,D
University of Michigan–Flint M
University of Missouri–Columbia M,D,O
The University of Montana M
University of Nebraska at Omaha M
University of Nebraska–Lincoln M
University of New Mexico M
The University of North Carolina at Chapel Hill M,D
University of Northern Colorado M
University of Northern Iowa M,D
University of Phoenix–Phoenix Campus M,O
University of Phoenix–Southern Colorado Campus M
University of Pittsburgh M,D,O
University of Rhode Island M,D
University of Rochester M,D,O
University of South Alabama M
University of South Carolina M,D,O
The University of South Dakota M
University of Southern Mississippi M
The University of Tennessee M
The University of Texas at Austin M,D
The University of Texas at El Paso M
The University of Texas at San Antonio M
The University of Texas at Tyler M
The University of Toledo M,D
University of Utah M,D
University of Virginia M,D
University of West Florida M
University of Wisconsin–La Crosse M
University of Wisconsin–Milwaukee M,D,O
University of Wyoming M
Utah State University M
Virginia Polytechnic Institute and State University M,D,O
Virginia State University M,D
Wayne State University M,D,O
West Chester University of Pennsylvania M,O
Western Illinois University M,O
Western Oregon University M
West Virginia University M,D
Widener University M,D
Worcester State College M
Wright State University M

■ HEALTH INFORMATICS

Barry University O
Benedictine University M
Claremont Graduate University M,D,O
The College of St. Scholastica M,O
Emory University M,D
Indiana University Bloomington M,D
The Johns Hopkins University M
Northeastern University M,D
Northern Kentucky University M,O
Saint Joseph's University M,O
Stevens Institute of Technology M,D,O
The University of Alabama at Birmingham M

University of Illinois at Chicago M
University of Illinois at Urbana–Champaign M,D,O
The University of Iowa M,D,O
University of La Verne M
University of Maryland University College M,O
University of Massachusetts Lowell M,O
University of Minnesota, Twin Cities Campus M,D
University of Missouri–Columbia M
The University of North Carolina at Charlotte M,O
University of Phoenix M
University of Phoenix–Phoenix Campus M,O
University of Pittsburgh M
University of Virginia M
University of Washington M,D
University of Wisconsin–Milwaukee M,O

■ HEALTH LAW

Boston University M
DePaul University P,M,O
Georgetown University P,M,D
Loyola University Chicago P,M,D
Nova Southeastern University M
Quinnipiac University P,M
Southern Illinois University Carbondale M
Suffolk University P,M
University of California, San Diego M
University of Pittsburgh M,O
University of Tulsa P,M,O
Widener University P,M,D
Xavier University M

■ HEALTH PHYSICS/ RADIOLOGICAL HEALTH

Bloomsburg University of Pennsylvania M
Emory University D
Georgetown University M
Georgia Institute of Technology M,D
Idaho State University M,D
Illinois Institute of Technology M,D
Midwestern State University M
Oregon State University M,D
Quinnipiac University M
San Diego State University M
Texas A&M University M,D
University of Cincinnati M
University of Kentucky M
University of Massachusetts Lowell M
University of Michigan M,D,O
University of Missouri–Columbia M,D
University of Nevada, Las Vegas M
The University of Toledo M
Virginia Commonwealth University D
Wayne State University M,D

■ HEALTH PROMOTION

Auburn University M,D,O
Ball State University M
Benedictine University M
Boston University M,D
Bridgewater State College M
Brigham Young University M,D
California State University, Fresno M
Canisius College M
Chatham University M
Eastern Kentucky University M
Eastern Michigan University M,O
Emory University M
Florida Atlantic University M
Florida International University M,D
George Mason University M
Georgetown University M,D
The George Washington University M
Georgia College & State University M
Georgia State University M,D,O
Goddard College M
Harvard University M,D
Indiana State University M
Indiana University Bloomington M,D
Lehman College of the City University of New York M
Marymount University M
McNeese State University M
Mississippi State University M,D
Missouri State University M
Montana State University M
New York University M,D,O
Oakland University O
Old Dominion University M
Oregon State University M,D
Portland State University M,O
Purdue University M,D
San Diego State University M,D
Simmons College M,O
Springfield College M,D
Texas A&M University–Commerce M,D
Union Institute & University M
Universidad del Turabo M
The University of Alabama M,D
The University of Alabama at Birmingham D
University of Chicago M,D
University of Delaware M
University of Georgia M,D
University of Kentucky M,D
University of Louisville M,D
University of Massachusetts Lowell D
University of Memphis M
University of Michigan M,D
The University of Montana M
University of Nebraska–Lincoln M,D
University of Nevada, Las Vegas M
The University of North Carolina at Chapel Hill M
University of Pittsburgh M,D,O
University of Rochester M,D,O
University of South Carolina M,D,O
University of Southern California M
The University of Tennessee M
The University of Texas at El Paso M
The University of Texas at San Antonio M
University of the Incarnate Word M
University of Utah M,D
University of Wisconsin–Stevens Point M
University of Wyoming M
Virginia Polytechnic Institute and State University M,D,O
Walden University M,D
West Virginia University M,D
Wright State University M

■ HEALTH PSYCHOLOGY

Appalachian State University M,O
Argosy University, Twin Cities M,D,O
California Institute of Integral Studies M,D
Central Connecticut State University M
Chatham University M,D
Claremont Graduate University M,D,O
Drexel University D
Duke University D
East Carolina University D
The George Washington University D
John F. Kennedy University M
Lesley University M
National-Louis University M,O
North Dakota State University M,D
Northern Arizona University M
Northern Kentucky University M,O
Prescott College M
Rutgers, The State University of New Jersey, New Brunswick D
San Diego State University M,D
Stony Brook University, State University of New York D
Texas State University–San Marcos M
University of Colorado Denver D
University of Connecticut M,D,O
University of Florida D
University of Michigan–Dearborn M
The University of North Carolina at Charlotte D
University of North Texas M,D

M—master's degree; P—first professional degree; D—doctorate; O—other advanced degree

The University of Texas at Arlington	M,D
Virginia State University	M,D
Walden University	M,D,O
West Chester University of Pennsylvania	M,O
Yeshiva University	D

■ HEALTH SERVICES MANAGEMENT AND HOSPITAL ADMINISTRATION

Alaska Pacific University	M
Albany State University	M
Argosy University, Orange County	M,D,O
Argosy University, Sarasota	M,D,O
Argosy University, Tampa	M,D,O
Argosy University, Twin Cities	M,D
Arizona State University	M,D
Armstrong Atlantic State University	M
Avila University	M
Baldwin-Wallace College	M
Barry University	M,O
Baylor University	M
Bellevue University	M
Benedictine University	M
Bernard M. Baruch College of the City University of New York	M
Boston University	M,D,O
Brandeis University	M
Brenau University	M
Brooklyn College of the City University of New York	M
California State University, Bakersfield	M
California State University, Chico	M
California State University, East Bay	M
California State University, Fresno	M
California State University, Long Beach	M,O
California State University, Los Angeles	M
California State University, Northridge	M
California State University, San Bernardino	M
Cambridge College	M
Capella University	M,D,O
Carnegie Mellon University	M
Central Michigan University	M,D,O
Charleston Southern University	M
Clark University	M
Cleveland State University	M
The College at Brockport, State University of New York	M,O
College of Saint Elizabeth	M
Colorado Technical University Sioux Falls	M
Columbia University	M
Columbus State University	M
Concordia University Wisconsin	M
Cornell University	M,D
Dallas Baptist University	M
Dartmouth College	M,D
Davenport University	M
Delta State University	M
DePaul University	M,O
DeSales University	M
Duke University	O
Duquesne University	M,D
D'Youville College	M,D,O
Eastern Kentucky University	M
Eastern Michigan University	M,O
Eastern University	M
East Tennessee State University	M,D,O
Emory University	M,D
Fairfield University	M,O
Fairleigh Dickinson University, College at Florham	M
Fairleigh Dickinson University, Metropolitan Campus	M
Florida Institute of Technology	M
Florida International University	M,D
Framingham State College	M
Francis Marion University	M
Friends University	M
The George Washington University	M,D,O
Georgia Institute of Technology	M
Georgia Southern University	M,D
Georgia State University	M
Governors State University	M
Grambling State University	M
Grand Canyon University	M
Grand Valley State University	M,D
Harding University	M
Harvard University	M,D
Hofstra University	M
Holy Family University	M
Houston Baptist University	M
Hunter College of the City University of New York	M
Husson University	M
Indiana University Northwest	M,O
Indiana University–Purdue University Indianapolis	M
Indiana University South Bend	M,O
Iona College	M,O
The Johns Hopkins University	M,D,O
Jones International University	M
Kean University	M
Kennesaw State University	M
King's College	M
Lakeland College	M
Lamar University	M
Lewis University	M
Lindenwood University	M,O
Lipscomb University	M
Long Island University, Brooklyn Campus	M
Long Island University, C.W. Post Campus	M,O
Louisiana State University in Shreveport	M
Loyola University Chicago	M,O
Loyola University New Orleans	M,D
Madonna University	M
Marshall University	M,D
Marylhurst University	M
Marymount University	M,O
Marywood University	M
Mercy College	M
Middle Tennessee State University	O
Midwestern State University	M
Mississippi College	M
Missouri State University	M
Monmouth University	M,O
Montana State University–Billings	M
National University	M
New Jersey City University	M
The New School: A University	M,O
New York University	M,O
Northeastern University	M,O
Northwest Missouri State University	M
The Ohio State University	M,D
Ohio University	M
Oklahoma City University	M
Old Dominion University	M
Oregon State University	M,D
Our Lady of the Lake University of San Antonio	M
Pace University	M
Pacific University	M
Park University	M
Penn State Great Valley	M
Penn State Harrisburg	M,D
Penn State University Park	M,D
Pfeiffer University	M
Philadelphia University	M
Portland State University	M
Quinnipiac University	M
Regent University	M
Regis University	P,M,D,O
Roberts Wesleyan College	M
Rochester Institute of Technology	M,O
Rutgers, The State University of New Jersey, Newark	M,D
Sacred Heart University	M,D
Saginaw Valley State University	M
St. Ambrose University	M,D
St. Joseph's College, Long Island Campus	M,O
Saint Joseph's College of Maine	M
Saint Joseph's University	M,O
Saint Leo University	M
Saint Louis University	M,D
Saint Mary's University of Minnesota	M
Saint Peter's College	M
St. Thomas University	M,O
Saint Xavier University	M,O
Salve Regina University	M,O
San Diego State University	M,D

Seton Hall University M,O
Shenandoah University M,O
Simmons College M,O
Southeast Missouri State University M
Southern Illinois University Carbondale M
Southwest Baptist University M
Springfield College M
State University of New York at Binghamton M,D
State University of New York Institute of Technology M
Stony Brook University, State University of New York M,D,O
Strayer University M
Suffolk University M,O
Syracuse University O
Temple University M
Texas A&M University–Corpus Christi M
Texas State University–San Marcos M
Texas Tech University M
Texas Wesleyan University M
Texas Woman's University M,D
Towson University O
Trinity University M
Troy University M
Tulane University M,D
University at Albany, State University of New York M
The University of Akron M
The University of Alabama at Birmingham M,D
The University of Alabama in Huntsville M,D,O
University of Baltimore M
University of California, Berkeley M,D
University of California, Los Angeles M,D
University of California, San Diego M
University of Central Florida M,O
University of Colorado at Colorado Springs M
University of Colorado Denver M
University of Connecticut M,D
University of Dallas M
University of Detroit Mercy M
University of Evansville M
University of Florida M,D
University of Houston–Clear Lake M
University of Illinois at Chicago M,D
The University of Iowa M,D
The University of Kansas M
University of Kentucky M
University of La Verne M,O
University of Louisville M,D
University of Mary M
University of Maryland, Baltimore County M,O
University of Maryland, College Park M,D
University of Maryland University College M,O
University of Massachusetts Boston M,D,O
University of Massachusetts Lowell M,O
University of Memphis M
University of Michigan M,D
University of Minnesota, Twin Cities Campus M,D
University of Missouri–Columbia M
University of Missouri–St. Louis M,O
University of Nevada, Las Vegas M
University of New Haven M
University of New Orleans M
The University of North Carolina at Chapel Hill M,D
The University of North Carolina at Charlotte M
University of North Florida M,O
University of Oklahoma M
University of Pennsylvania M,D
University of Phoenix M,D
University of Phoenix–Central Florida Campus M
University of Phoenix–Denver Campus M
University of Phoenix–Hawaii Campus M
University of Phoenix–Las Vegas Campus M
University of Phoenix–Louisiana Campus M
University of Phoenix–New Mexico Campus M
University of Phoenix–North Florida Campus M
University of Phoenix–Oregon Campus M
University of Phoenix–Philadelphia Campus M
University of Phoenix–Phoenix Campus M,O
University of Phoenix–Sacramento Valley Campus M
University of Phoenix–San Diego Campus M
University of Phoenix–Southern Arizona Campus M,O
University of Phoenix–Southern California Campus M,O
University of Phoenix–Southern Colorado Campus M
University of Phoenix–South Florida Campus M
University of Phoenix–Utah Campus M
University of Phoenix–West Florida Campus M
University of Phoenix–West Michigan Campus M
University of Pittsburgh M,D,O
University of St. Francis (IL) M
University of St. Thomas (MN) M
University of San Francisco M
The University of Scranton M
University of South Carolina M,D
University of Southern California M
University of Southern Indiana M
University of Southern Maine M,O
University of Southern Mississippi M
University of South Florida M,D
The University of Tennessee M
The University of Texas at Arlington M
The University of Texas at Dallas M
The University of Texas at El Paso M,O
The University of Texas at Tyler M
University of the Incarnate Word M,O
The University of Toledo M,O
University of Virginia M
University of Washington M
University of Wisconsin–Oshkosh M
Utica College M
Villanova University M,D,O
Virginia Commonwealth University M,D
Wagner College M
Wake Forest University M
Walden University M,D,O
Washington State University M
Wayland Baptist University M
Weber State University M
Webster University M,D
West Chester University of Pennsylvania M,O
Western Carolina University M
Western Connecticut State University M
Western Illinois University M,O
Western Kentucky University M
Western Michigan University M,D,O
Widener University M
William Woods University M,O
Wilmington University M
Worcester State College M
Wright State University M
Xavier University M
Yale University M,D
Youngstown State University M

■ HEALTH SERVICES RESEARCH

Brown University M,D
Case Western Reserve University M,D
Dartmouth College M,D
Emory University M,D

M—master's degree; P—first professional degree; D—doctorate; O—other advanced degree

The George Washington University M,D,O
The Johns Hopkins University M,D
Old Dominion University D
Stanford University M
Texas State University–San Marcos M
University of Colorado Denver D
University of Florida M,D
University of Illinois at Chicago M,D
University of La Verne M
University of Minnesota, Twin Cities Campus M,D
The University of North Carolina at Charlotte D
University of North Florida M,O
University of Rochester M,D,O
University of Southern California D
University of Virginia M
University of Washington M,D
University of Wisconsin–Madison M,D
Virginia Commonwealth University D
Wake Forest University M

■ HIGHER EDUCATION

Abilene Christian University M
Alliant International University–San Diego M,D,O
Angelo State University M
Appalachian State University M,O
Argosy University, Orange County M,D
Argosy University, Sarasota M,D,O
Argosy University, Tampa M,D,O
Argosy University, Twin Cities M,D,O
Arizona State University M
Auburn University M,D,O
Azusa Pacific University M,D
Ball State University M,D
Barry University M,D
Benedictine University D
Bernard M. Baruch College of the City University of New York M
Bethel University M,O
Boston College M,D
Bowling Green State University D
California Lutheran University M,D
California State University, Long Beach M,D
Capella University M,D,O
Central Michigan University M,D,O
Chicago State University M,D
Claremont Graduate University M,D,O
College of Saint Elizabeth M,O
Dallas Baptist University M
Delta State University D
Drexel University M
Eastern Kentucky University M
Fitchburg State College M,O
Florida Atlantic University M,D,O
Florida International University D
Florida State University M,D,O
Geneva College M
George Fox University M,D,O
George Mason University M,D,O
The George Washington University M,D,O
Georgia Southern University M
Grambling State University M,D
Grand Valley State University M,O
Harvard University D
Illinois State University M,D
Indiana State University M,D,O
Indiana University Bloomington M,D,O
Indiana University of Pennsylvania M
Indiana University–Purdue University Indianapolis M,O
Inter American University of Puerto Rico, Metropolitan Campus M
Iowa State University of Science and Technology M,D
John Brown University M
Johnson & Wales University D
Jones International University M
Kent State University M
Louisiana State University and Agricultural and Mechanical College M,D,O
Loyola University Chicago M,D
Marywood University M,D
Michigan State University M,D,O
Minnesota State University Mankato M,D,O
Mississippi College M,D,O
Montana State University M,D,O
Morehead State University M,O
Morgan State University D
New York University M,D
North Carolina State University M,D
Northeastern State University M
Northern Arizona University M,D
Northern Illinois University M,D
Northwestern University M
Northwest Missouri State University M,O
Nova Southeastern University D
Oakland University M,D,O
The Ohio State University M
Ohio University M,D
Oklahoma State University M,D
Old Dominion University M,D,O
Oral Roberts University M,D
Penn State University Park M,D
Pittsburg State University M,O
Portland State University M,D
Purdue University M,D,O
Rowan University M
St. Cloud State University M,D
Saint Louis University M,D,O
Salem State College M
San Diego State University M
San Jose State University M,O
Seton Hall University D
Shippensburg University of Pennsylvania M
Southeast Missouri State University M,O
Southern Illinois University Carbondale M
Stanford University M,D
Syracuse University M,D
Texas A&M University–Commerce M,D
Texas A&M University–Kingsville D
Texas Southern University M,D
Texas Tech University M,D
Union Institute & University D
Union University M,D,O
University at Buffalo, the State University of New York M,D,O
The University of Akron M
The University of Alabama M,D
The University of Arizona M,D
University of Arkansas M,D,O
University of Arkansas at Little Rock D
University of California, Riverside M,D
University of Central Florida M,D,O
University of Central Oklahoma M
University of Connecticut M
University of Delaware M,D,O
University of Denver M,D,O
University of Florida M,D,O
University of Georgia D
University of Houston M,D
University of Illinois at Urbana–Champaign M,D,O
The University of Iowa M,D,O
The University of Kansas M,D
University of Kentucky M,D
University of Louisville M
University of Maine M,D,O
University of Mary M
University of Maryland, College Park M,D
University of Massachusetts Amherst M,D,O
University of Massachusetts Boston M,D,O
University of Memphis M,D
University of Miami M,D,O
University of Michigan M,D
University of Minnesota, Twin Cities Campus M,D
University of Mississippi M,D,O
University of Missouri–Columbia M,D,O
University of Missouri–St. Louis M,D,O
University of New Hampshire M
The University of North Carolina at Greensboro D
University of Northern Colorado D
University of Northern Iowa M
University of North Texas M,D,O
University of Oklahoma M,D

University of Pittsburgh M,D
University of San Diego M,D,O
University of South Carolina M
University of Southern California D
University of Southern Mississippi M,D,O
University of South Florida M,D,O
University of the Incarnate Word M,D
The University of Toledo M,D
University of Virginia M,D,O
University of Washington M,D
University of Wisconsin–Whitewater M
Vanderbilt University M,D
Villanova University M
Virginia Polytechnic Institute and State University M,D,O
Walden University M,D,O
Washington State University M,D,O
Wayne State University M,D,O
Western Carolina University M
Western Washington University M
West Virginia University M,D
Wilkes University M,D
Wright State University M,O

■ HISPANIC STUDIES

Brown University M,D
California State University, Los Angeles M
California State University, Northridge M
Eastern Michigan University M,O
La Salle University M
Louisiana State University and Agricultural and Mechanical College M
Michigan State University M,D
New York University M,D
Oregon State University M
Pontifical Catholic University of Puerto Rico M,O
St. Thomas University M,O
San Jose State University M
Stony Brook University, State University of New York M,D
Texas A&M International University M,D
University of California, Berkeley D
University of California, Los Angeles D
University of California, Riverside M,D
University of California, Santa Barbara M,D
University of Illinois at Chicago M,D
University of Kentucky M,D
University of Nevada, Las Vegas M,O
The University of North Carolina at Greensboro M,O
The University of North Carolina Wilmington M,O
University of Pittsburgh M,D
University of Puerto Rico, Mayagüez Campus M
University of Puerto Rico, Río Piedras M,D
The University of Texas at Austin M
University of Washington M
Villanova University M

■ HISTORIC PRESERVATION

Arkansas State University M,D
Ball State University M
Boston University M
Buffalo State College, State University of New York M,O
Clemson University M
College of Charleston M
Columbia University M,O
Cornell University M,D
Delaware State University M
Eastern Michigan University M,O
The George Washington University M
Georgia State University M,O
Kent State University M,O
Michigan Technological University D
New York University
Northwestern State University of Louisiana M
Rutgers, The State University of New Jersey, New Brunswick M,D,O
St. Cloud State University M
Texas Tech University M
University of California, Riverside M,D
University of Delaware M,D
University of Georgia M
University of Hawaii at Manoa O
University of Kentucky M
University of Maryland, College Park M,O
University of Massachusetts Amherst M
University of New Mexico O
The University of North Carolina at Greensboro M,O
University of Oregon M
University of Pennsylvania M,O
University of South Carolina M,O
The University of Texas at Austin M,D
The University of Texas at San Antonio M,O
University of Vermont M
University of Washington O
University of West Florida M
University of Wisconsin–Milwaukee M,D,O
Ursuline College M
Virginia Commonwealth University O

■ HISTORY

Adams State College M
American University M,D
Andrews University M
Angelo State University M
Appalachian State University M
Arizona State University M,D
Arkansas State University M,O
Arkansas Tech University M
Armstrong Atlantic State University M
Ashland University M
Auburn University M,D
Ball State University M
Baylor University M
Bob Jones University P,M,D,O
Boise State University M
Boston College M,D
Boston University M,D
Bowling Green State University M,D
Brandeis University M,D
Brooklyn College of the City University of New York M,D
Brown University M,D
Buffalo State College, State University of New York M
Butler University M
California Polytechnic State University, San Luis Obispo M
California State Polytechnic University, Pomona M
California State University, Bakersfield M
California State University, Chico M
California State University, East Bay M
California State University, Fresno M
California State University, Fullerton M
California State University, Long Beach M
California State University, Los Angeles M
California State University, Northridge M
California State University, Stanislaus M
Cardinal Stritch University M
Carnegie Mellon University M,D
Case Western Reserve University M,D
The Catholic University of America M,D
Central Connecticut State University M,O
Central Michigan University M,D,O
Central Washington University M
Chicago State University M
The Citadel, The Military College of South Carolina M
City College of the City University of New York M

M—master's degree; P—first professional degree; D—doctorate; O—other advanced degree

Claremont Graduate University M,D,O
Clark Atlanta University M,D
Clark University M,D,O
Clemson University M
Cleveland State University M
The College at Brockport, State University of New York M
College of Charleston M
The College of Saint Rose M
College of Staten Island of the City University of New York M
The College of William and Mary M,D
Colorado State University M
Columbia University M,D
Converse College M
Cornell University M,D
DePaul University M
Drake University M
Drew University M,D
Duke University M,D
Duquesne University M
East Carolina University M
Eastern Illinois University M
Eastern Kentucky University M
Eastern Michigan University M,O
Eastern Washington University M
East Stroudsburg University of Pennsylvania M
East Tennessee State University M
Emory University D
Emporia State University M
Fairleigh Dickinson University, Metropolitan Campus M
Fayetteville State University M
Fitchburg State College M,O
Florida Agricultural and Mechanical University M
Florida Atlantic University M,O
Florida Gulf Coast University M
Florida International University M,D
Florida State University M,D
Fordham University M,D
Fort Hays State University M
George Mason University M,D,O
Georgetown University M,D
The George Washington University M,D
Georgia College & State University M
Georgia Southern University M
Georgia State University M,D
Graduate School and University Center of the City University of New York D
Hardin-Simmons University M
Harvard University D
High Point University M
Howard University M,D
Hunter College of the City University of New York M
Idaho State University M
Illinois State University M
Indiana State University M
Indiana University Bloomington M,D
Indiana University of Pennsylvania M
Indiana University–Purdue University Indianapolis M
Inter American University of Puerto Rico, Metropolitan Campus M,D
Iona College M
Iowa State University of Science and Technology M,D
Jackson State University M
Jacksonville State University M
James Madison University M
John Carroll University M
The Johns Hopkins University D
Kansas State University M,D
Kent State University M,D
Lamar University M
La Salle University M
Lehigh University M,D
Lehman College of the City University of New York M
Lincoln University (MO) M
Long Island University, Brooklyn Campus M,O
Long Island University, C.W. Post Campus M
Louisiana State University and Agricultural and Mechanical College M,D
Louisiana Tech University M
Loyola University Chicago M,D
Lynchburg College M
Marquette University M,D
Marshall University M
Miami University M,D
Michigan State University M,D
Middle Tennessee State University M
Midwestern State University M
Millersville University of Pennsylvania M
Minnesota State University Mankato M
Mississippi College M,O
Mississippi State University M,D
Missouri State University M
Monmouth University M
Montana State University M,D
Montclair State University M,O
Morgan State University M,D
Murray State University M
National University M
New Jersey Institute of Technology M
New Mexico State University M
The New School: A University M,D
New York University M,D,O
North Carolina Central University M
North Carolina State University M
North Dakota State University M,D
Northeastern Illinois University M
Northeastern University M,D
Northern Arizona University M,D
Northern Illinois University M,D
Northwestern University D
Northwest Missouri State University M
Oakland University M
The Ohio State University M,D
Ohio University M,D
Oklahoma State University M,D
Old Dominion University M
Oregon State University M,D
Penn State University Park M,D
Pepperdine University M
Pittsburg State University M
Pontifical Catholic University of Puerto Rico M
Portland State University M
Princeton University D
Providence College M
Purdue University M,D
Purdue University Calumet M
Queens College of the City University of New York M
Rhode Island College M
Rice University M,D
Roosevelt University M
Rutgers, The State University of New Jersey, Camden M
Rutgers, The State University of New Jersey, Newark M
Rutgers, The State University of New Jersey, New Brunswick D
St. Cloud State University M
St. John's University (NY) M,D
Saint Louis University M,D
Salem State College M
Salisbury University M
Sam Houston State University M
San Diego State University M
San Francisco State University M
San Jose State University M
Sarah Lawrence College M
Seton Hall University M
Shippensburg University of Pennsylvania M,O
Slippery Rock University of Pennsylvania M
Sonoma State University M
Southeastern Louisiana University M
Southeast Missouri State University M
Southern Connecticut State University M
Southern Illinois University Carbondale M,D
Southern Illinois University Edwardsville M
Southern Methodist University M,D

Southern University and Agricultural and Mechanical College M
Stanford University M,D
State University of New York at Binghamton M,D
State University of New York at Oswego M
State University of New York College at Cortland M
Stephen F. Austin State University M
Stony Brook University, State University of New York M,D
Sul Ross State University M
Syracuse University M,D
Tarleton State University M
Temple University M,D
Texas A&M International University M
Texas A&M University M,D
Texas A&M University–Commerce M
Texas A&M University–Corpus Christi M
Texas A&M University–Kingsville M
Texas Christian University M,D
Texas Southern University M
Texas State University–San Marcos M
Texas Tech University M,D
Texas Woman's University M
Tufts University M,D
Tulane University M,D
Union Institute & University M
University at Albany, State University of New York M,D,O
University at Buffalo, the State University of New York M,D
The University of Akron M,D
The University of Alabama M,D
The University of Alabama at Birmingham M
The University of Alabama in Huntsville M
University of Alaska Fairbanks M
The University of Arizona M,D
University of Arkansas M,D
University of California, Berkeley M,D
University of California, Davis M,D
University of California, Irvine M,D
University of California, Los Angeles M,D
University of California, Riverside M,D
University of California, San Diego M,D
University of California, Santa Barbara D
University of California, Santa Cruz M,D
University of Central Arkansas M
University of Central Florida M
University of Central Missouri M
University of Central Oklahoma M
University of Chicago D
University of Cincinnati M,D
University of Colorado at Boulder M,D
University of Colorado at Colorado Springs M
University of Colorado Denver M
University of Connecticut M,D
University of Delaware M,D
University of Florida M,D
University of Georgia M,D
University of Hawaii at Manoa M,D
University of Houston M,D
University of Houston–Clear Lake M
University of Idaho M,D
University of Illinois at Chicago M,D
University of Illinois at Springfield M
University of Illinois at Urbana–Champaign M,D
University of Indianapolis M
The University of Iowa M,D
The University of Kansas M,D
University of Kentucky M,D
University of Louisiana at Lafayette M
University of Louisiana at Monroe M
University of Louisville M
University of Maine M,D
University of Maryland, Baltimore County M
University of Maryland, College Park M,D
University of Massachusetts Amherst M,D
University of Massachusetts Boston M
University of Memphis M,D
University of Miami M,D
University of Michigan D,O
University of Minnesota, Twin Cities Campus M,D
University of Mississippi M,D
University of Missouri–Columbia M,D
University of Missouri–Kansas City M,D
The University of Montana M,D
University of Nebraska at Kearney M
University of Nebraska at Omaha M
University of Nebraska–Lincoln M,D
University of Nevada, Las Vegas M,D
University of Nevada, Reno M,D
University of New Hampshire M,D
University of New Mexico M,D
University of New Orleans M
University of North Alabama M
The University of North Carolina at Chapel Hill M,D
The University of North Carolina at Charlotte M
The University of North Carolina at Greensboro M,D,O
The University of North Carolina Wilmington M
University of North Dakota M,D
University of Northern Colorado M
University of Northern Iowa M
University of North Florida M
University of North Texas M,D
University of Notre Dame M,D
University of Oklahoma M,D
University of Oregon M,D
University of Pennsylvania M,D
University of Pittsburgh M,D
University of Puerto Rico, Río Piedras M,D
University of Rhode Island M
University of Rochester M,D
University of San Diego M
The University of Scranton M
University of South Alabama M
University of South Carolina M,D,O
The University of South Dakota M
University of Southern California D
University of Southern Mississippi M,D
University of South Florida M,D
The University of Tennessee M,D
The University of Texas at Arlington M,D
The University of Texas at Austin M,D
The University of Texas at Brownsville M
The University of Texas at El Paso M,D
The University of Texas at San Antonio M
The University of Texas at Tyler M
The University of Texas of the Permian Basin M
The University of Texas–Pan American M
The University of Toledo M,D
University of Tulsa M
University of Utah M,D
University of Vermont M
University of Virginia M,D
University of Washington M,D
University of West Florida M
University of West Georgia M
University of Wisconsin–Eau Claire M
University of Wisconsin–Madison M,D
University of Wisconsin–Milwaukee M,D
University of Wisconsin–Stevens Point M
University of Wyoming M
Utah State University M
Valdosta State University M
Valparaiso University M,O

M—master's degree; P—first professional degree; D—doctorate; O—other advanced degree

Vanderbilt University M,D
Villanova University M
Virginia Commonwealth University M,D
Virginia Polytechnic Institute and State University M
Virginia State University M
Washington State University M,D
Washington University in St. Louis M,D
Wayne State University M,D
West Chester University of Pennsylvania M,O
Western Carolina University M
Western Connecticut State University M
Western Illinois University M
Western Kentucky University M
Western Michigan University M,D
Western Washington University M
Westfield State College M
West Texas A&M University M
West Virginia University M,D
Wichita State University M
William Paterson University of New Jersey M
Winthrop University M
Worcester State College M
Wright State University M
Yale University M,D
Youngstown State University M

■ HISTORY OF MEDICINE

Rutgers, The State University of New Jersey, New Brunswick D
University of Minnesota, Twin Cities Campus M,D
Yale University M,D

■ HISTORY OF SCIENCE AND TECHNOLOGY

Carnegie Mellon University M,D
Cornell University M,D
Drexel University M
Georgia Institute of Technology M,D
Harvard University M,D
Indiana University Bloomington M,D
Iowa State University of Science and Technology M,D
The Johns Hopkins University M,D
Massachusetts Institute of Technology D
Oregon State University M,D
Polytechnic Institute of NYU M
Princeton University D
Rensselaer Polytechnic Institute M,D
Rutgers, The State University of New Jersey, New Brunswick D
University of California, Berkeley D
University of California, San Diego M,D
University of Delaware M,D
University of Massachusetts Amherst M,D
University of Minnesota, Twin Cities Campus M,D
University of Notre Dame M,D
University of Oklahoma M,D
University of Pennsylvania M,D
University of Pittsburgh M,D
University of Wisconsin–Madison M,D
Virginia Polytechnic Institute and State University M,D
West Virginia University M,D
Yale University M,D

■ HIV/AIDS NURSING

Duke University M,D,O
University of Delaware M,O

■ HOLOCAUST AND GENOCIDE STUDIES

Clark University D
Drew University M,D,O
Gratz College M,O
Kean University M
The Richard Stockton College of New Jersey M
Seton Hall University M
Seton Hill University O
West Chester University of Pennsylvania M,O

■ HOME ECONOMICS EDUCATION

Appalachian State University M
Cambridge College M,D,O
Central Washington University M
Eastern Kentucky University M
Harding University M,O
Indiana State University M
Iowa State University of Science and Technology M,D
Louisiana State University and Agricultural and Mechanical College M,D
Montana State University M
Montclair State University M,O
Northwestern State University of Louisiana M
The Ohio State University M
Purdue University M,D,O
Queens College of the City University of New York M
South Carolina State University M
State University of New York College at Oneonta M
Texas Tech University M,D
University of Central Oklahoma M
University of Nebraska–Lincoln M,D
Utah State University M
Wayne State College M

■ HOMELAND SECURITY

Arkansas Tech University M
Chaminade University of Honolulu M,O
Drexel University M
Fairleigh Dickinson University, Metropolitan Campus M
George Mason University M,D
The Johns Hopkins University M,O
Monterey Institute of International Studies M
National University M
Regent University M
Saint Joseph's University M,O
Salve Regina University M,O
Texas A&M University M,O
Tiffin University M
Towson University M,O
University of Central Florida M,O
University of Connecticut M
The University of Toledo M,O
Upper Iowa University M
Virginia Commonwealth University M,O
Walden University M,D,O
Wayland Baptist University M
Wilmington University M

■ HORTICULTURE

Auburn University M,D
Colorado State University M,D
Cornell University M,D
Iowa State University of Science and Technology M,D
Kansas State University M,D
Louisiana State University and Agricultural and Mechanical College M,D
Michigan State University M,D
Mississippi State University M,D
New Mexico State University M,D
North Carolina State University M,D,O
The Ohio State University M,D
Oklahoma State University M,D
Oregon State University M,D
Penn State University Park M,D
Purdue University M,D
Rutgers, The State University of New Jersey, New Brunswick M,D
Southern Illinois University Carbondale M
Texas A&M University M,D
Texas Tech University M,D
University of Arkansas M
University of California, Davis M
University of Delaware M
University of Florida M,D
University of Georgia M,D
University of Hawaii at Manoa M,D
University of Maine M
University of Maryland, College Park D
University of Missouri–Columbia M,D
University of Nebraska–Lincoln M,D
University of Puerto Rico, Mayagüez Campus M

University of Vermont M,D
University of Washington M,D
University of Wisconsin–Madison M,D
Virginia Polytechnic Institute and State University M,D
Washington State University M,D
West Virginia University M,D

■ HOSPICE NURSING

Madonna University M

■ HOSPITALITY MANAGEMENT

American International College M
California State University, Northridge M
Central Michigan University M
Cornell University M,D
Drexel University M
Eastern Michigan University M,O
East Stroudsburg University of Pennsylvania M
Endicott College M
Fairleigh Dickinson University, College at Florham M
Fairleigh Dickinson University, Metropolitan Campus M
Florida International University M
The George Washington University M,O
Iowa State University of Science and Technology M,D
Johnson & Wales University M,O
Kansas State University M,D
Lynn University M,D
Michigan State University M
New York University M,D,O
The Ohio State University M,D
Oklahoma State University M,D
Penn State University Park M,D
Purdue University M,D
Rochester Institute of Technology M
Roosevelt University M
Schiller International University (United States) M
South Dakota State University M,D
Southern New Hampshire University M,D,O
Strayer University M
Temple University M,D
Texas Tech University M,D
The University of Alabama M
University of Central Florida M
University of Delaware M
University of Houston M
University of Kentucky M
University of Massachusetts Amherst M
University of Missouri–Columbia M,D
University of Nevada, Las Vegas M,D,O
University of New Orleans M
University of North Texas M
University of South Carolina M
The University of Tennessee M
Virginia Polytechnic Institute and State University M,D

■ HUMAN-COMPUTER INTERACTION

Carnegie Mellon University M,D
Cornell University D
DePaul University M,D
Georgia Institute of Technology M
Indiana University Bloomington M,D
Iowa State University of Science and Technology M,D
Old Dominion University M,D
Rensselaer Polytechnic Institute M
Rochester Institute of Technology M
State University of New York at Oswego M
Tufts University O
University of Baltimore M,D
University of Illinois at Urbana–Champaign M,D,O
University of Michigan M,D

■ HUMAN DEVELOPMENT

Arizona State University M,D
Auburn University M,D
Boston University M,D,O
Bowling Green State University M
Bradley University M
Brigham Young University M,D
California State University, San Bernardino M
Central Michigan University M,O
Claremont Graduate University M,D,O
Clemson University M
Colorado State University M,D
Cornell University D
DePaul University M,D
Dowling College M,D,O
Duke University D
East Tennessee State University M
The George Washington University M
Harvard University M,D
Hofstra University M,D,O
Hood College M,O
Howard University M
Indiana University Bloomington M,D
Iowa State University of Science and Technology M,D
Kansas State University D
Kent State University M,D
Lehigh University M,D
Marywood University D
Montana State University M
National-Louis University M,D,O
New York Institute of Technology M
New York University M,D,O
North Dakota State University D
Northwestern University D
The Ohio State University M,D
Oklahoma State University M,D
Oregon State University M,D
Our Lady of the Lake University of San Antonio M
Penn State University Park M,D
Purdue University M,D
Saint Joseph College M,O
Saint Louis University M,D,O
Saint Mary's University of Minnesota M
South Dakota State University M
Southern Illinois University Carbondale M,D
Texas A&M University M,D
Texas Tech University M,D
The University of Alabama M
The University of Arizona M,D
University of California, Berkeley M,D
University of California, Davis D
University of California, Santa Barbara D
University of Central Oklahoma M
University of Chicago D
University of Connecticut M,D,O
University of Dayton M,O
University of Delaware M,D
University of Houston M
University of Illinois at Chicago M,D
University of Illinois at Springfield M
University of Illinois at Urbana–Champaign M,D
University of Maine M
University of Maryland, College Park M,D
University of Missouri–Columbia M,D
University of Nebraska–Lincoln M,D,O
University of Nevada, Reno M
The University of North Carolina at Greensboro M,D
University of North Texas M,O
University of Pennsylvania M,D
University of St. Thomas (MN) M,D,O
The University of Texas at Austin M,D
University of Utah M
University of Washington M,D
University of Wisconsin–Madison M,D
University of Wisconsin–Stevens Point M
University of Wisconsin–Stout M
Utah State University M,D
Vanderbilt University M
Virginia Polytechnic Institute and State University M,D
Washington State University M
Wayne State University M
West Virginia University M,D
Wheelock College M

■ HUMAN GENETICS

Case Western Reserve University D

M—master's degree; P—first professional degree; D—doctorate; O—other advanced degree

The Johns Hopkins University D
Sarah Lawrence College M
Tulane University M,D
University of California, Los Angeles M,D
University of Chicago D
University of Michigan M,D
University of Pittsburgh M,D,O
University of Utah M,D
Vanderbilt University D
Virginia Commonwealth University M,D,O
Wake Forest University D
West Virginia University M,D

■ HUMANITIES

Arcadia University M
Brigham Young University M
California Institute of Integral Studies M,D
California State University, Dominguez Hills M
Carlow University M
Central Michigan University M
Claremont Graduate University M,D,O
Dominican University of California M
Drew University M,D,O
Duke University M
Florida State University M,D,O
Georgetown University M,D
Hofstra University M
Hollins University M,O
Hood College M
John Carroll University M
Marshall University M
Marymount University M
Massachusetts Institute of Technology M
Michigan State University M
Mount St. Mary's College M
National University M
New York University M,O
Nova Southeastern University M,O
Old Dominion University M
Penn State Harrisburg M,D
Pepperdine University M
Polytechnic Institute of NYU M,O
Prescott College M
St. Edward's University M,O
Salve Regina University M,D,O
Sam Houston State University M,D
San Francisco State University M
Stanford University M
Texas Tech University M,D
Tiffin University M
Towson University M
University of California, Santa Cruz D
University of Chicago M
University of Colorado Denver M
University of Dallas M
University of Houston–Clear Lake M
University of Louisville M,D
The University of Texas at Arlington M
The University of Texas at Dallas M,D
University of Utah M
University of West Florida M
Villanova University M
Virginia Commonwealth University M,D,O
Wright State University M

■ HUMAN RESOURCES DEVELOPMENT

Abilene Christian University M
Amberton University M
American International College M
Antioch University Los Angeles M
Azusa Pacific University M
Barry University M,D
Bowie State University M
California State University, Sacramento M
Claremont Graduate University M,D,O
Clemson University M
The College of New Rochelle M
Florida International University M,D
Florida State University M,D,O
Friends University M
The George Washington University M,D,O
Illinois Institute of Technology M,D
Indiana State University M
Indiana University of Pennsylvania M
Inter American University of Puerto Rico, Metropolitan Campus M
Inter American University of Puerto Rico, San Germán Campus M,D
Iowa State University of Science and Technology M,D
John F. Kennedy University M,O
The Johns Hopkins University M,O
Johnson & Wales University O
Louisiana State University and Agricultural and Mechanical College M,D
Manhattanville College M
Marquette University M
McDaniel College M
Midwestern State University M
Mississippi State University M,D,O
National-Louis University M
The New School: A University M,O
New York University M,O
North Carolina Agricultural and Technical State University M,D
North Carolina State University M
Northeastern Illinois University M
Oakland University M
Penn State University Park M,O
Pittsburg State University M
Rochester Institute of Technology M
Rollins College M
Roosevelt University M
St. John Fisher College M
Salve Regina University M,O
Southern New Hampshire University M,O
Suffolk University M,O
Syracuse University D
Texas A&M University M,D
Towson University M
University of Bridgeport M
University of Connecticut M
University of Illinois at Urbana–Champaign M,D,O
University of Louisville M
University of Minnesota, Twin Cities Campus M,D,O
University of Missouri–St. Louis M,O
The University of Scranton M
The University of Tennessee M
The University of Texas at Tyler M,D
University of Wisconsin–Milwaukee M,O
University of Wisconsin–Stout M
Vanderbilt University M,D
Villanova University M
Virginia Commonwealth University M
Virginia Polytechnic Institute and State University M,D
Webster University M,D
Western Carolina University M
Western Michigan University M,D,O
William Woods University M,O
Xavier University M

■ HUMAN RESOURCES MANAGEMENT

Adelphi University M,O
Alabama Agricultural and Mechanical University M,O
Albany State University M
Amberton University M
American InterContinental University South Florida M
Assumption College M,O
Auburn University M,D
Baldwin-Wallace College M
Barry University O
Benedictine University M
Bernard M. Baruch College of the City University of New York M,D
Boston University M,O
Buffalo State College, State University of New York M,O
California State University, East Bay M
California State University, Sacramento M
Capella University M,D,O
Case Western Reserve University M

The Catholic University of America M
Central Michigan University M,O
Claremont Graduate University M
Cleveland State University M
College of Santa Fe M
Colorado Technical University Colorado Springs M,D
Colorado Technical University Denver M
Colorado Technical University Sioux Falls M
Columbia University M
Concordia University, St. Paul M
Concordia University Wisconsin M
Cornell University M,D
Cumberland University M
Dallas Baptist University M
Davenport University M
DePaul University M
East Central University M
Eastern Michigan University M,O
Emmanuel College M,O
Fairfield University M,O
Fairleigh Dickinson University, College at Florham M
Fairleigh Dickinson University, Metropolitan Campus M,O
Fitchburg State College M
Florida Institute of Technology M
Florida International University M
Fordham University M,D,O
Framingham State College M
Gannon University O
George Mason University M
Georgetown University M,D
The George Washington University M,D
Georgia State University M,D
Golden Gate University M,D,O
Grambling State University M
Hawai'i Pacific University M
Hofstra University M
Holy Family University M
Hood College M
Houston Baptist University M
Howard University M
Indiana Wesleyan University M
Inter American University of Puerto Rico, Metropolitan Campus M
Inter American University of Puerto Rico, San Germán Campus M,D
Iona College M,O
La Roche College M,O
La Sierra University M,O
Lewis University M
Lincoln University (PA) M
Lindenwood University M,O
Long Island University, Brooklyn Campus M
Loyola University Chicago M
Marquette University M
Marshall University M
Marygrove College M
Marymount University M,O
Mercy College M,O
Michigan State University M,D
National-Louis University M
National University M
Nazareth College of Rochester M
New Mexico Highlands University M
New York Institute of Technology M,O
New York University M,D,O
Notre Dame de Namur University M
Nova Southeastern University M,D
Oakland University M,O
The Ohio State University M,D
Penn State University Park M,O
Pontifical Catholic University of Puerto Rico M
Portland State University M
Purdue University M,D
Regis University M,O
Robert Morris University M
Rollins College M
Roosevelt University M
Rutgers, The State University of New Jersey, Newark M,D
Rutgers, The State University of New Jersey, New Brunswick M,D
St. Ambrose University M,D
St. Edward's University M,O
Saint Francis University M
St. Joseph's College, Long Island Campus M,O
Saint Joseph's University M
Saint Leo University M
Saint Mary's University of Minnesota M
St. Thomas University M,O
Salve Regina University M,O
San Diego State University M
Southern New Hampshire University M,D,O
Stevens Institute of Technology M
Stony Brook University, State University of New York M,O
Strayer University M
Tarleton State University M
Temple University M,D
Texas A&M University M,D
Trinity (Washington) University M
Troy University M
Universidad del Turabo M
Universidad Metropolitana M
University at Albany, State University of New York M
University at Buffalo, the State University of New York M,D,O
The University of Akron M
The University of Alabama in Huntsville M,O
University of California, Berkeley O
University of Central Florida M,O
University of Connecticut M
University of Dallas M
University of Denver M,O
The University of Findlay M
University of Florida M
University of Georgia M,D,O
University of Hawaii at Manoa M
University of Houston–Clear Lake M
University of Illinois at Urbana–Champaign M,D
University of Louisville M
University of Mary M
University of Minnesota, Twin Cities Campus M,D
University of Missouri–St. Louis M,O
University of New Haven M
University of New Mexico M
University of Phoenix M
University of Phoenix–Central Florida Campus M
University of Phoenix–Denver Campus M
University of Phoenix–Hawaii Campus M
University of Phoenix–Las Vegas Campus M
University of Phoenix–Louisiana Campus M
University of Phoenix–New Mexico Campus M
University of Phoenix–North Florida Campus M
University of Phoenix–Oregon Campus M
University of Phoenix–Philadelphia Campus M
University of Phoenix–Phoenix Campus M
University of Phoenix–Sacramento Valley Campus M
University of Phoenix–San Diego Campus M
University of Phoenix–Southern Arizona Campus M
University of Phoenix–Southern California Campus M
University of Phoenix–Southern Colorado Campus M
University of Phoenix–South Florida Campus M
University of Phoenix–Utah Campus M
University of Phoenix–West Florida Campus M

M—master's degree; P—first professional degree; D—doctorate; O—other advanced degree

University of Phoenix–West Michigan Campus M
University of Pittsburgh M,D
University of Puerto Rico, Mayagüez Campus M
University of Puerto Rico, Río Piedras M,D
University of Rhode Island M
University of St. Thomas (MN) M,D,O
The University of Scranton M
University of South Carolina M
The University of Texas at Arlington M
The University of Toledo M
University of Wisconsin–Madison M,D
University of Wisconsin–Whitewater M
Upper Iowa University M
Utah State University M
Walden University M,D
Wayland Baptist University M
Webster University M,D
West Chester University of Pennsylvania M,O
Widener University M
Wilkes University M
Wilmington University M

■ HUMAN SERVICES

Abilene Christian University M,O
Andrews University M
Bellevue University M
Brandeis University M
California State University, Sacramento M
Capella University M,D,O
Chestnut Hill College M,O
Concordia University Chicago M
Concordia University Wisconsin M,D
Coppin State University M
DePaul University M,D
Drury University M
Eastern Michigan University M,O
Eastern New Mexico University M
Fairfield University M,O
Ferris State University M
Georgia State University M
Indiana University Northwest M,O
Kansas State University M
Kent State University M,D,O
Lehigh University M,D,O
Lincoln University (PA) M
Louisiana State University in Shreveport M
McDaniel College M
Minnesota State University Mankato M
Minnesota State University Moorhead M,O
Montana State University–Billings M
Murray State University M
National-Louis University M,O
National University M
Nova Southeastern University M,D
Pontifical Catholic University of Puerto Rico M,D
Purdue University Calumet M
Roberts Wesleyan College M
Rosemont College M
St. Edward's University M,O
Saint Joseph's University M,O
St. Mary's University (United States) M,D,O
South Carolina State University M
Southern Oregon University M
Springfield College M
State University of New York at Oswego M
Texas Southern University M
Universidad del Turabo M
University of Baltimore M
University of Bridgeport M
University of Central Missouri M,O
University of Colorado at Colorado Springs M,D
University of Great Falls M
University of Illinois at Springfield M
University of Maryland, Baltimore County M,D
University of Massachusetts Boston M
University of Oklahoma M
Upper Iowa University M
Walden University M,D
Wayne State University O
West Virginia University M
Wichita State University M
Wilmington University M
Youngstown State University M

■ HYDRAULICS

Auburn University M,D
Drexel University M,D
Missouri University of Science and Technology M,D

■ HYDROGEOLOGY

California State University, Chico M
Clemson University M
Georgia State University M,O
Illinois State University M
Indiana University Bloomington M,D
Ohio University M
Rensselaer Polytechnic Institute M,D
University of Hawaii at Manoa M,D
University of Nevada, Reno M,D
The University of Texas at Dallas M,D
West Virginia University M,D

■ HYDROLOGY

Auburn University M,D
California State University, Bakersfield M
California State University, Chico M
Colorado State University M,D
Cornell University M,D
Drexel University M,D
Idaho State University M,O
Illinois State University M
Massachusetts Institute of Technology M,D,O
Missouri University of Science and Technology M,D
Murray State University M
New Mexico Institute of Mining and Technology M,D
State University of New York College of Environmental Science and Forestry M,D
Stevens Institute of Technology M,D,O
The University of Arizona M,D
University of California, Davis M,D
University of Idaho M
University of Nevada, Reno M,D
University of New Hampshire M
University of Southern Mississippi M,D
University of Washington M,D

■ ILLUSTRATION

Bob Jones University P,M,D,O
Bradley University M
Kent State University M
Marywood University M
Mills College M
Syracuse University M
University of California, Santa Cruz O
University of Massachusetts Dartmouth M
Western Connecticut State University M

■ IMMUNOLOGY

Boston University D
Brown University M,D
California Institute of Technology D
Case Western Reserve University M,D
Colorado State University M,D
Cornell University M,D
Creighton University M,D
Dartmouth College D
Drexel University M,D
Duke University D
East Carolina University D
Emory University D
Georgetown University M,D
The George Washington University D
Harvard University D
Hood College M,O
Illinois State University M,D
Indiana University–Purdue University Indianapolis M,D
Iowa State University of Science and Technology M,D
The Johns Hopkins University M,D

Long Island University, C.W. Post Campus M
Loyola University Chicago M,D
Massachusetts Institute of Technology D
Mayo Graduate School D
New York University P,M,D
North Carolina State University M,D
Northwestern University D
The Ohio State University M,D
Penn State University Park M,D
Purdue University M,D
Rutgers, The State University of New Jersey, New Brunswick M,D
Saint Louis University D
Stanford University D
Stony Brook University, State University of New York M,D
Temple University M,D
Tufts University D
Tulane University M,D
University at Albany, State University of New York M,D
University at Buffalo, the State University of New York M,D
The University of Arizona M,D
University of California, Berkeley D
University of California, Davis M,D
University of California, Los Angeles M,D
University of California, San Diego D
University of Chicago D
University of Cincinnati M,D
University of Colorado Denver D
University of Florida D
University of Illinois at Chicago D
The University of Iowa M,D
The University of Kansas D
University of Louisville M,D
University of Miami D
University of Michigan D
University of Minnesota, Duluth M,D
University of Minnesota, Twin Cities Campus D
University of Missouri–Columbia M,D
The University of North Carolina at Chapel Hill M,D
University of North Dakota M,D
University of Pennsylvania D
University of Pittsburgh M,D
University of Rochester M,D
University of South Alabama D
The University of South Dakota M,D
University of Southern California M,D
University of Southern Maine M
University of South Florida M,D
The University of Toledo M,D
University of Virginia D
University of Washington M,D
Vanderbilt University M,D
Virginia Commonwealth University M,D
Wake Forest University D
Washington University in St. Louis D
Wayne State University M,D
West Virginia University M,D
Wright State University M
Yale University D

■ INDUSTRIAL/MANAGEMENT ENGINEERING

Arizona State University M,D
Auburn University M,D
Bradley University M
Buffalo State College, State University of New York M
California Polytechnic State University, San Luis Obispo M
California State University, Fresno M
California State University, Northridge M
Central Washington University M
Clemson University M,D
Cleveland State University M,D
Columbia University M,D,O
Cornell University M,D
East Carolina University M,D,O
Eastern Kentucky University M
Florida Agricultural and Mechanical University M,D
Florida State University M,D
Georgia Institute of Technology M,D
Illinois State University M
Indiana State University M
Indiana University–Purdue University Fort Wayne M
Iowa State University of Science and Technology M,D
Kansas State University M,D
Lamar University M,D
Lehigh University M,D
Louisiana State University and Agricultural and Mechanical College M,D
Louisiana Tech University M
Mississippi State University M,D
Montana State University M,D
Morehead State University M
Morgan State University M,D
New Jersey Institute of Technology M,D
New Mexico State University M,D
North Carolina Agricultural and Technical State University M,D
North Carolina State University M,D
North Dakota State University M,D
Northeastern University M,D
Northern Illinois University M
Northwestern University M,D
The Ohio State University M,D
Ohio University M,D
Oklahoma State University M,D
Oregon State University M,D
Penn State University Park M,D
Polytechnic Institute of NYU M
Purdue University M,D
Rensselaer Polytechnic Institute M,D
Rochester Institute of Technology M
Rutgers, The State University of New Jersey, New Brunswick M,D
St. Mary's University (United States) M
Sam Houston State University M
San Jose State University M
South Dakota State University M
Southern Illinois University Edwardsville M
Southern Polytechnic State University M,O
Stanford University M,D
State University of New York at Binghamton M,D
Texas A&M University M,D
Texas A&M University–Commerce M
Texas A&M University–Kingsville M
Texas Southern University M
Texas State University–San Marcos M
Texas Tech University M,D
University at Buffalo, the State University of New York M,D
The University of Alabama M
The University of Alabama in Huntsville M,D
The University of Arizona M,D
University of Arkansas M,D
University of California, Berkeley M,D
University of Central Florida M,D,O
University of Central Missouri M
University of Cincinnati M,D
University of Florida M,D,O
University of Houston M,D
University of Illinois at Chicago M,D
University of Illinois at Urbana–Champaign M,D
The University of Iowa M,D
University of Louisville M,D
University of Massachusetts Amherst M,D
University of Massachusetts Lowell M,D,O
University of Memphis M,D
University of Miami M,D
University of Michigan M,D
University of Michigan–Dearborn M,D
University of Minnesota, Twin Cities Campus M,D
University of Missouri–Columbia M,D
University of Nebraska–Lincoln M,D
University of New Haven M,O

M—master's degree; P—first professional degree; D—doctorate; O—other advanced degree

University of Oklahoma M,D
University of Pittsburgh M,D
University of Puerto Rico, Mayagüez Campus M
University of Rhode Island D
University of Southern California M,D,O
University of South Florida M,D
The University of Tennessee M,D
The University of Tennessee at Chattanooga M
The University of Texas at Arlington M
The University of Texas at Austin M,D
The University of Texas at El Paso M
The University of Toledo M,D
University of Washington M,D
University of Wisconsin–Madison M,D
University of Wisconsin–Milwaukee M,D,O
University of Wisconsin–Stout M
Virginia Polytechnic Institute and State University M,D
Wayne State University M,D
Western Carolina University M
Western Michigan University M
Western New England College M
West Virginia University M,D
Wichita State University M,D
Youngstown State University M

■ INDUSTRIAL AND LABOR RELATIONS

Bernard M. Baruch College of the City University of New York M
Carnegie Mellon University M,D
Case Western Reserve University M
Cleveland State University P,M
Cornell University M,D
Georgetown University D
Indiana University of Pennsylvania M
Inter American University of Puerto Rico, Metropolitan Campus M,D
Inter American University of Puerto Rico, San Germán Campus M,D
Loyola University Chicago M
Michigan State University M,D
New York Institute of Technology M,O
The Ohio State University M,D
Penn State University Park M,O
Rutgers, The State University of New Jersey, New Brunswick M,D
State University of New York Empire State College M
University of California, Berkeley D
University of Cincinnati M
University of Illinois at Urbana–Champaign M,D
University of Massachusetts Amherst M
University of Minnesota, Twin Cities Campus M,D
University of New Haven M
University of North Texas M
University of Rhode Island M
University of Wisconsin–Milwaukee M,O
Wayne State University M
West Virginia University M

■ INDUSTRIAL AND MANUFACTURING MANAGEMENT

Boston University D
California Polytechnic State University, San Luis Obispo M
California State University, East Bay M
Carnegie Mellon University M,D
Case Western Reserve University M,D
Central Michigan University M
Cleveland State University D
Colorado Technical University Colorado Springs M,D
Colorado Technical University Denver M
DePaul University M
Florida Institute of Technology M
Friends University M
Georgetown University D
Harvard University D
Illinois Institute of Technology M
Inter American University of Puerto Rico, Metropolitan Campus M
Lawrence Technological University M,D
Marist College M,O
Northeastern State University M
Northern Illinois University M
Nova Southeastern University D
Oakland University M,O
Penn State University Park M
Portland State University M,D
Purdue University M
Regis University M,O
Rochester Institute of Technology M
San Diego State University M
San Jose State University M
Southeastern Oklahoma State University M
Southeast Missouri State University M
Stevens Institute of Technology M
Syracuse University D
Texas A&M University M,D
Texas Tech University M,D
University of Arkansas M
University of Central Missouri M
University of Cincinnati D
University of Dayton M
The University of Iowa M
University of Minnesota, Twin Cities Campus M,D
University of Missouri–St. Louis M,O
University of Puerto Rico, Mayagüez Campus M
University of Puerto Rico, Río Piedras M,D
University of Rhode Island M,D
University of St. Thomas (MN) M,O
University of Southern Indiana M
The University of Tennessee M,D
The University of Texas at Austin D
The University of Texas at Tyler M,D
The University of Toledo M,D
Wake Forest University M
Washington State University M,D

■ INDUSTRIAL AND ORGANIZATIONAL PSYCHOLOGY

Alliant International University–San Diego M,D
Angelo State University M
Antioch University Seattle M
Appalachian State University M,O
Auburn University M,D
Bernard M. Baruch College of the City University of New York M,D,O
Bowling Green State University M,D
Brooklyn College of the City University of New York M
California State University, San Bernardino M
Capella University M,D,O
Carlos Albizu University M,D
Central Michigan University M,D
Chatham University M,D
Claremont Graduate University M,D,O
Clemson University D
Cleveland State University M,D,O
DePaul University M,D
Eastern Kentucky University M,O
Elmhurst College M
Emporia State University M
Fairfield University M,O
Fairleigh Dickinson University, College at Florham M
Florida Institute of Technology M,D
George Mason University M,D
The George Washington University M,D
Georgia Institute of Technology M,D
Goddard College M
Graduate School and University Center of the City University of New York D
Hofstra University M,D
Illinois Institute of Technology M,D
Illinois State University M,D,O
Indiana University–Purdue University Indianapolis M
Inter American University of Puerto Rico, Metropolitan Campus M,D
Iona College M
John F. Kennedy University M,O

Kean University M
Lamar University M
Louisiana State University and Agricultural and Mechanical College M,D
Louisiana Tech University M,D
Marshall University M,D
Middle Tennessee State University M,O
Minnesota State University Mankato M,D
Missouri State University M
Montclair State University M,O
National-Louis University M,O
New York University M,D,O
North Carolina State University D
Northern Kentucky University M,O
Ohio University D
Old Dominion University D
Penn State University Park M,D
Pontifical Catholic University of Puerto Rico M,D
Radford University M,D,O
Rice University M,D
Roosevelt University M
Rutgers, The State University of New Jersey, New Brunswick M,D
St. Cloud State University M
Saint Joseph's University M,O
Saint Louis University M,D
St. Mary's University (United States) M
San Diego State University M,D
San Jose State University M
Seattle Pacific University M,D
Southern Illinois University Edwardsville M
Springfield College M,O
Temple University M
Texas A&M University M,D
University at Albany, State University of New York M,D,O
The University of Akron M,D
University of Baltimore M
University of Central Florida M,D
University of Connecticut M,D,O
University of Detroit Mercy M
University of Houston M,D
University of Maryland, College Park M,D
University of Minnesota, Twin Cities Campus D
University of Missouri–St. Louis M,D,O
University of Nebraska at Omaha M,D,O
University of New Haven M,O
The University of North Carolina at Charlotte M,D
University of Puerto Rico, Río Piedras M,D
University of South Florida M,D
The University of Tennessee D
The University of Tennessee at Chattanooga M
The University of Texas at Arlington M,D
University of Tulsa M,D
University of West Florida M
University of Wisconsin–Oshkosh M
Valdosta State University M,O
Virginia Polytechnic Institute and State University M,D
Walden University M,D,O
Wayne State University M,D
West Chester University of Pennsylvania M,O
Western Michigan University M,D
Wright State University M,D
Xavier University M,D

■ INDUSTRIAL DESIGN

Arizona State University M
Auburn University M
Brigham Young University M
North Carolina State University M
The Ohio State University M
Rochester Institute of Technology M
San Francisco State University M
University of Cincinnati M
University of Illinois at Chicago M
University of Illinois at Urbana–Champaign M
University of Notre Dame M
University of Washington M

■ INDUSTRIAL HYGIENE

California State University, Northridge M
Murray State University M
University of Central Missouri M,O
University of Cincinnati M,D
University of Massachusetts Lowell M,D,O
University of Michigan M,D
University of Minnesota, Twin Cities Campus M,D
University of New Haven M
The University of North Carolina at Chapel Hill M,D
University of South Carolina M,D
University of Wisconsin–Stout M
West Virginia University M

■ INFECTIOUS DISEASES

Cornell University M,D
Georgetown University M,D
The George Washington University M
Harvard University D
The Johns Hopkins University M,D
Loyola University Chicago M,O
North Carolina State University M,D
Tulane University M,D,O
University of California, Berkeley M,D
University of Georgia M,D
University of Minnesota, Twin Cities Campus M,D
The University of Montana D
University of Pittsburgh M,D,O
University of South Florida M,D
Yale University D

■ INFORMATION SCIENCE

Alcorn State University M
American InterContinental University Dunwoody Campus M
American InterContinental University South Florida M
Arizona State University M
Arkansas Tech University M
Ball State University M
Barry University M
Bellevue University M
Bentley University M
Bradley University M
Brigham Young University M
Brooklyn College of the City University of New York M,D,O
California State University, Fullerton M
Carnegie Mellon University M,D
Case Western Reserve University M,D
The Citadel, The Military College of South Carolina M
Claremont Graduate University M,D,O
Clark Atlanta University M
Clarkson University M
Clark University M
Cleveland State University M,D
The College of Saint Rose M
Cornell University D
DePaul University M,D
DeSales University M
Drexel University M,D
East Carolina University M
East Tennessee State University M
Florida Gulf Coast University M
Florida Institute of Technology M
Florida International University M,D
Gannon University M
George Mason University M,D,O
Georgia Southwestern State University M
Georgia State University M
Grand Valley State University M
Harvard University M,D,O
Hood College M
Indiana University Bloomington M,D,O
Indiana University–Purdue University Fort Wayne M
Indiana University–Purdue University Indianapolis M,D
Iowa State University of Science and Technology M
The Johns Hopkins University M

M—master's degree; P—first professional degree; D—doctorate; O—other advanced degree

Kansas State University	M,D
Kennesaw State University	M
Kent State University	M
Lamar University	M
Lehigh University	M
Long Island University, C.W. Post Campus	M
Loyola University Chicago	M
Marshall University	M
Marywood University	M
Massachusetts Institute of Technology	M,D,O
Missouri University of Science and Technology	M
Montclair State University	M,O
National University	M
New Jersey Institute of Technology	M,D
Northeastern University	M,D,O
Northern Kentucky University	M,O
Northwestern University	M
Nova Southeastern University	M,D
The Ohio State University	M,D
Oklahoma State University	M,D
Old Dominion University	D
Pace University	M,D,O
Penn State Great Valley	M
Polytechnic Institute of NYU, Westchester Graduate Center	M
Regis University	M,O
Rensselaer Polytechnic Institute	M
Robert Morris University	M,D
Rochester Institute of Technology	M,D
Sacred Heart University	M,O
St. Mary's University (United States)	M
Saint Xavier University	M
Sam Houston State University	M
Southern Methodist University	M,D
Southern Polytechnic State University	M,O
State University of New York Institute of Technology	M
Stevens Institute of Technology	M,O
Strayer University	M
Syracuse University	D
Temple University	M,D
Towson University	M,D,O
Trevecca Nazarene University	M
University at Albany, State University of New York	M,D,O
The University of Alabama at Birmingham	M,D
University of Arkansas at Little Rock	M
University of Baltimore	M,D
University of California, Irvine	M,D
University of Colorado at Colorado Springs	M
University of Colorado Denver	D
University of Delaware	M,D
University of Detroit Mercy	M
University of Florida	M,D
University of Hawaii at Manoa	M,D
University of Houston	M,D
University of Houston–Clear Lake	M
University of Illinois at Urbana–Champaign	M,D,O
The University of Iowa	M,D,O
University of Maryland, Baltimore County	M,D
University of Maryland University College	M,O
University of Michigan	M,D
University of Michigan–Dearborn	M,D
University of Michigan–Flint	M
University of Minnesota, Twin Cities Campus	M,D
University of Nebraska at Omaha	M,D,O
University of Nebraska–Lincoln	M,D
University of Nevada, Las Vegas	M,D
University of New Haven	M
The University of North Carolina at Charlotte	M,D
University of North Florida	M
University of Oregon	M,D
University of Pennsylvania	M,D
University of Phoenix–Phoenix Campus	M
University of Pittsburgh	M,D,O
University of Puerto Rico, Mayagüez Campus	D
University of South Alabama	M
The University of Tennessee	M,D
The University of Texas at El Paso	M,D
The University of Texas at San Antonio	M,D
University of Washington	M,D
University of Wisconsin–Stout	M
Virginia Polytechnic Institute and State University	M
Youngstown State University	M

■ INFORMATION STUDIES

The Catholic University of America	M
Central Connecticut State University	M
Claremont Graduate University	M,D,O
Columbia University	M
Cornell University	D
Dominican University	M,D,O
Drexel University	M
Emporia State University	M,D,O
Florida State University	M,D,O
Indiana University Bloomington	M,D,O
Long Island University, C.W. Post Campus	M,D,O
Louisiana State University and Agricultural and Mechanical College	M,O
Mansfield University of Pennsylvania	M
Metropolitan State University	M,O
North Carolina Central University	M
Queens College of the City University of New York	M,O
Rutgers, The State University of New Jersey, New Brunswick	M,D
St. Catherine University	M
St. John's University (NY)	M,O
San Jose State University	M,D
Simmons College	M,D,O
Southern Connecticut State University	M,O
Syracuse University	M,D
Universidad del Turabo	M
University at Albany, State University of New York	M,O
University at Buffalo, the State University of New York	M,O
The University of Alabama	M,D
The University of Arizona	M,D
University of California, Berkeley	M,D
University of California, Los Angeles	M,D,O
University of Central Missouri	M,O
University of Denver	M,O
University of Hawaii at Manoa	M,O
University of Illinois at Urbana–Champaign	M,D,O
The University of Iowa	M
University of Maryland, College Park	M,D
University of Michigan	M,D
University of Missouri–Columbia	M,D,O
The University of North Carolina at Chapel Hill	M,D,O
The University of North Carolina at Greensboro	M
University of North Texas	M,D
University of Oklahoma	M,O
University of Pittsburgh	M,D,O
University of Puerto Rico, Río Piedras	M,O
University of Rhode Island	M
University of South Carolina	M,D,O
University of South Florida	M
The University of Texas at Austin	M,D
University of Wisconsin–Madison	M,D
University of Wisconsin–Milwaukee	M,D,O
Valdosta State University	M
Wayne State University	M,O

■ INORGANIC CHEMISTRY

Auburn University	M,D
Boston College	M,D
Brandeis University	M,D
California State University, Los Angeles	M

Carnegie Mellon University	M,D
Clarkson University	M,D
Cleveland State University	M,D
Columbia University	M,D
Cornell University	D
Florida State University	M,D
Georgetown University	D
The George Washington University	M,D
Harvard University	D
Howard University	M,D
Indiana University Bloomington	M,D
Kansas State University	M,D
Kent State University	M,D
Marquette University	M,D
Massachusetts Institute of Technology	D
Miami University	M,D
Northeastern University	M,D
Oregon State University	M,D
Purdue University	M,D
Rensselaer Polytechnic Institute	M,D
Rice University	M,D
Rutgers, The State University of New Jersey, Newark	M,D
Rutgers, The State University of New Jersey, New Brunswick	M,D
Seton Hall University	M,D
Southern University and Agricultural and Mechanical College	M
State University of New York at Binghamton	M,D
Tufts University	M,D
University of Cincinnati	M,D
University of Georgia	M,D
University of Louisville	M,D
University of Maryland, College Park	M,D
University of Massachusetts Lowell	M,D
University of Miami	M,D
University of Michigan	D
University of Missouri–Columbia	M,D
University of Missouri–Kansas City	M,D
University of Missouri–St. Louis	M,D
The University of Montana	M,D
University of Nebraska–Lincoln	M,D
University of Notre Dame	M,D
University of Southern Mississippi	M,D
University of South Florida	M,D
The University of Tennessee	M,D
The University of Texas at Austin	M,D
The University of Toledo	M,D
Vanderbilt University	M,D
Virginia Commonwealth University	M,D
Wake Forest University	M,D
West Virginia University	M,D
Yale University	D
Youngstown State University	M

■ INSURANCE

Florida State University	M,D
Georgia State University	M,D,O
St. John's University (NY)	M
Temple University	D
University of Florida	M,D,O
University of Pennsylvania	M,D
University of Wisconsin–Madison	M,D
Virginia Commonwealth University	M
Washington State University	D

■ INTERDISCIPLINARY STUDIES

Alaska Pacific University	M
Amberton University	M
American University	M
Angelo State University	M
Antioch University New England	M
Arizona State University	M
Baylor University	M,D
Boise State University	M
Boston University	M
Bowling Green State University	M,D
Buffalo State College, State University of New York	M
California State University, Bakersfield	M
California State University, Chico	M
California State University, East Bay	M,O
California State University, Long Beach	M
California State University, Northridge	M
California State University, San Bernardino	M
California State University, Stanislaus	M
Cambridge College	M,D,O
Campbell University	M
Central Washington University	M
Columbia University	M
Dallas Baptist University	M
DePaul University	M
Drew University	M,D,O
Eastern Washington University	M
Emory University	D
Fitchburg State College	O
Florida Gulf Coast University	M
Fresno Pacific University	M
Frostburg State University	M
Georgetown University	M,D
Goddard College	M
Graduate School and University Center of the City University of New York	M,D
Hodges University	M
Hofstra University	M
Hollins University	M,O
Idaho State University	M
Iowa State University of Science and Technology	M
John F. Kennedy University	M
Lesley University	M
Long Island University, C.W. Post Campus	M
Marquette University	M,D
Marylhurst University	M
Marywood University	M,O
Mills College	M,O
Minnesota State University Mankato	M
Montana State University–Billings	M
Mountain State University	M
New Mexico State University	M,D
New York University	M
Niagara University	M
Nova Southeastern University	M,O
The Ohio State University	M,D
Oregon State University	M
Regis University	M,O
Rensselaer Polytechnic Institute	M,D
Rochester Institute of Technology	M
Rutgers, The State University of New Jersey, New Brunswick	D
San Diego State University	M
San Jose State University	M
Sarah Lawrence College	M
Sonoma State University	M
Stanford University	M,D
State University of New York at Fredonia	M
State University of New York at New Paltz	M
Stephen F. Austin State University	M
Texas A&M University–Texarkana	M
Texas State University–San Marcos	M
Texas Tech University	M
Tulane University	D
Union Institute & University	M,D
The University of Alabama in Huntsville	M,D,O
University of Alaska Anchorage	M
University of Alaska Fairbanks	M,D
The University of Arizona	M,D
University of Arkansas	M,D
University of Central Florida	M
University of Chicago	D
University of Cincinnati	D
University of Houston–Victoria	M
University of Idaho	M
University of Illinois at Springfield	M
The University of Kansas	M,D
University of Louisville	M
University of Maine	D
University of Minnesota, Twin Cities Campus	D

M—master's degree; P—first professional degree; D—doctorate; O—other advanced degree

University of Missouri–Kansas City D
The University of Montana M,D
University of North Texas M
University of Oklahoma M,D
University of Oregon M
University of Pittsburgh D
The University of South Dakota M
The University of Texas at Arlington M
The University of Texas at Brownsville M
The University of Texas at Dallas M
The University of Texas at El Paso M
The University of Texas at San Antonio M
The University of Texas at Tyler M
The University of Texas–Pan American M
University of the Incarnate Word M
University of Virginia M,D
University of Washington, Tacoma M
University of Wisconsin–Milwaukee D
Virginia Commonwealth University M
Virginia Polytechnic Institute and State University M,D,O
Virginia State University M
Washington State University D
Wayland Baptist University M
Western Kentucky University M
Western New Mexico University M
West Texas A&M University M
Worcester Polytechnic Institute M,D,O
Wright State University M

■ INTERIOR DESIGN

Arizona State University M
Brenau University M
Chatham University M
Columbia College Chicago M
Cornell University M
Drexel University M
Eastern Michigan University M
Florida International University M
Florida State University M
The George Washington University M
Iowa State University of Science and Technology M
Lawrence Technological University M
Louisiana Tech University M
Marymount University M
Marywood University M
Michigan State University M,D
Missouri State University M
The New School: A University M
The Ohio State University M
San Diego State University M
South Dakota State University M
Suffolk University M
Texas Tech University M,D
The University of Alabama M
University of California, Berkeley O
University of Central Oklahoma M
University of Cincinnati M
University of Florida M,D
University of Georgia M,D
University of Houston M
University of Kentucky M
University of Massachusetts Amherst M
University of Memphis M,O
University of Minnesota, Twin Cities Campus M,D,O
University of Nebraska–Lincoln M,D
The University of North Carolina at Greensboro M,O
University of Oregon M
Utah State University M
Virginia Commonwealth University M
Virginia Polytechnic Institute and State University M,D
Washington State University M,D

■ INTERNATIONAL AFFAIRS

Alliant International University–San Diego M
American University M,D,O
Appalachian State University M
Arcadia University M
Baylor University M,D
Boston University M,D,O
Brandeis University M,D
Brooklyn College of the City University of New York M,D
California State University, Fresno M
California State University, Sacramento M
California State University, Stanislaus M
The Catholic University of America M,D
Central Connecticut State University M
Central Michigan University M,O
Chapman University M
City College of the City University of New York M
Claremont Graduate University M,D
Colorado School of Mines M,O
Columbia University M
Concordia University (CA) M
Cornell University D
Creighton University M
East Carolina University M
Fairleigh Dickinson University, Metropolitan Campus M
Florida Agricultural and Mechanical University M
Florida International University M,D
Florida State University M
Fordham University M,O
George Mason University M
Georgetown University P,M,D
The George Washington University M
Georgia Institute of Technology M,D
Harvard University P,D
The Johns Hopkins University M,D,O
Kansas State University M
Lesley University M,O
Long Island University, Brooklyn Campus M,O
Long Island University, C.W. Post Campus M
Marquette University M
Michigan State University M
Missouri State University M
Monterey Institute of International Studies M
Morgan State University M
The New School: A University M
New York University M,D,O
North Carolina State University M
Northeastern University M,D,O
Northwestern University P,M,O
Norwich University M
Ohio University M
Old Dominion University M,D
Pepperdine University M
Princeton University M,D
Rutgers, The State University of New Jersey, Camden M
Rutgers, The State University of New Jersey, Newark M,D
Rutgers, The State University of New Jersey, New Brunswick D
St. John Fisher College M
St. Mary's University (United States) M
Salve Regina University M,O
San Francisco State University M
Seton Hall University M
SIT Graduate Institute M
Stanford University M
Syracuse University
Texas A&M University M,O
Texas State University–San Marcos M
Troy University M
Tufts University M,D
University of Bridgeport M
University of California, Berkeley M
University of California, San Diego M,D
University of California, Santa Barbara M,D
University of California, Santa Cruz D

University of Central Florida M
University of Central Oklahoma M
University of Chicago M
University of Colorado at Boulder M,D
University of Connecticut M
University of Delaware M,D
University of Denver M,D
University of Florida M
University of Indianapolis M
The University of Kansas M
University of Kentucky M
University of Miami M,D
University of Oklahoma M
University of Oregon M
University of Pennsylvania M
University of Pittsburgh M,D,O
University of Rhode Island M,O
University of San Diego M
University of San Francisco M
University of South Carolina M,D
University of Southern California M,D
University of Southern Mississippi M,D
University of South Florida M,D
University of the Pacific P,M,D
University of Utah M
University of Virginia M,D
University of Washington M
University of Wyoming M
Virginia Polytechnic Institute and State University M,D
Walden University M,D,O
Washington State University M,D
Webster University M
West Virginia University M,D
Yale University M,O

■ INTERNATIONAL AND COMPARATIVE EDUCATION

American University M
Boston University M
Bowling Green State University M
California State University, Dominguez Hills M
The College of New Jersey M,O
Drexel University M
Florida International University M,D
Florida State University M,D,O
Gallaudet University M,O
The George Washington University M
Harvard University M
Indiana University Bloomington M,D,O
Lehigh University M,O
Louisiana State University and Agricultural and Mechanical College M,D
Lynn University M,D
Morehead State University M,O
New York University M,D,O
SIT Graduate Institute M
Stanford University M,D
Tufts University M,D
University of Bridgeport M,O
University of California, Santa Barbara M,D
University of Central Florida M,D,O
University of Maryland, College Park M,D
University of Massachusetts Amherst M,D,O
University of Minnesota, Twin Cities Campus M,D
University of North Texas M,D
University of Pennsylvania M,D
University of Pittsburgh M,D
University of San Francisco M,D
Vanderbilt University M,D
Wright State University M

■ INTERNATIONAL BUSINESS

Alliant International University–San Diego M,D
American InterContinental University Dunwoody Campus M
American InterContinental University South Florida M
American International College M
American University M,O
Argosy University, Orange County M,D,O
Argosy University, Sarasota M,D,O
Argosy University, Tampa M,D
Argosy University, Twin Cities M,D
Assumption College M,O
Avila University M
Azusa Pacific University M
Baldwin-Wallace College M
Barry University O
Baylor University M
Benedictine University M
Bernard M. Baruch College of the City University of New York M
Boston University M,O
Brandeis University M,D
California Lutheran University M,O
California State University, East Bay M
California State University, Fullerton M
California State University, Los Angeles M
California State University, Stanislaus M
Canisius College M
Central Michigan University M,O
City University of Seattle M,O
Clarkson University M
Clark University M
Cleveland State University M,D,O
Columbia University M
Concordia University Wisconsin M
Daemen College M
Dallas Baptist University M
DePaul University M
Dominican University of California M
D'Youville College M
Eastern Michigan University M,O
Emerson College M
Fairfield University M,O
Fairleigh Dickinson University, College at Florham M,O
Fairleigh Dickinson University, Metropolitan Campus M
Florida Atlantic University M,D
Florida International University M
Georgetown University P,M,D
The George Washington University M,D
Georgia Institute of Technology M,O
Georgia State University M
Golden Gate University M,D,O
Harding University M
Hawai'i Pacific University M
Hofstra University M
Hope International University M
Howard University M
Inter American University of Puerto Rico, Metropolitan Campus M
Inter American University of Puerto Rico, San Germán Campus M,D
Iona College M,O
John Brown University M
Johnson & Wales University M
Kean University M
Lewis University M
Lindenwood University M
Long Island University, C.W. Post Campus M,O
Loyola University Maryland M
Lynn University M,D
Madonna University M
Manhattanville College M
MidAmerica Nazarene University M
Minnesota State University Mankato M
Montclair State University M,O
Monterey Institute of International Studies M
National University M
Newman University M
New Mexico Highlands University M
The New School: A University M
New York Institute of Technology M,O
New York University M,D
Northern Kentucky University M,O
Norwich University M
Nova Southeastern University M,D
Oakland University M,O

M—master's degree; P—first professional degree; D—doctorate; O—other advanced degree

Oklahoma City University M
Old Dominion University M
Oral Roberts University M
Pace University M
Park University M
Pepperdine University M
Philadelphia University M
Pontifical Catholic University of Puerto Rico M
Portland State University M
Providence College M
Purdue University M
Quinnipiac University M
Regis University M,O
Rochester Institute of Technology M
Roosevelt University M
Rutgers, The State University of New Jersey, Newark M,D
St. Bonaventure University M
St. Edward's University M,O
St. John's University (NY) M,O
Saint Joseph's University M
Saint Louis University M,D
St. Mary's University (United States) M
Saint Mary's University of Minnesota M
Saint Peter's College M
St. Thomas University M,O
San Diego State University M
Schiller International University (United States) M
Seton Hall University M,O
SIT Graduate Institute M
Southeast Missouri State University M
Southern New Hampshire University M,D,O
Stevens Institute of Technology M
Suffolk University M,D,O
Temple University M,D
Texas A&M International University M
Texas A&M University–Corpus Christi M
Texas Christian University M
Texas Tech University M
Tufts University M,D
Universidad Metropolitana M
The University of Akron M
University of California, Berkeley O
University of Chicago M
University of Colorado at Colorado Springs M
University of Colorado Denver M
University of Dallas M
University of Dayton M
University of Denver M
The University of Findlay M
University of Florida P,M,D
University of Hawaii at Manoa M,D
University of Houston–Victoria M
University of Kentucky M
University of La Verne M
University of Maryland University College M,O
University of Memphis M,D
University of Miami M
University of Minnesota, Twin Cities Campus M
University of New Haven M
University of New Mexico M
University of Oklahoma M
University of Pennsylvania M
University of Phoenix–Central Florida Campus M
University of Phoenix–Denver Campus M
University of Phoenix–Hawaii Campus M
University of Phoenix–Las Vegas Campus M
University of Phoenix–Louisiana Campus M
University of Phoenix–New Mexico Campus M
University of Phoenix–North Florida Campus M
University of Phoenix–Oregon Campus M
University of Phoenix–Philadelphia Campus M
University of Phoenix–Phoenix Campus M
University of Phoenix–Sacramento Valley Campus M
University of Phoenix–San Diego Campus M
University of Phoenix–Southern Arizona Campus M
University of Phoenix–Southern California Campus M
University of Phoenix–Southern Colorado Campus M
University of Phoenix–South Florida Campus M
University of Phoenix–Utah Campus M
University of Phoenix–West Florida Campus M
University of Phoenix–West Michigan Campus M
University of Pittsburgh M
University of Puerto Rico, Río Piedras M,D
University of Rhode Island M,D
University of San Francisco M
The University of Scranton M
University of South Carolina M
The University of Tampa M
The University of Texas at Dallas M,D
The University of Texas at San Antonio M,D
The University of Texas–Pan American D
University of the Incarnate Word M,O
The University of Toledo M
University of Tulsa M
University of Washington M,D,O
University of Wisconsin–Milwaukee M,O
University of Wisconsin–Oshkosh M
University of Wisconsin–Whitewater M
Upper Iowa University M
Valparaiso University M
Villanova University M
Wagner College M
Walden University M,D
Washington State University M,D,O
Wayland Baptist University M
Webster University M
Western International University M
Whitworth University M
Wilkes University M
Wright State University M
Xavier University M

■ INTERNATIONAL DEVELOPMENT

American University M,D,O
Andrews University M
Brandeis University M
Clark University M
Cornell University M
Duke University M,O
Eastern University M
Fordham University M,O
The George Washington University M
Harvard University M
Hope International University M
The Johns Hopkins University M,D,O
The New School: A University M
Ohio University M
Rutgers, The State University of New Jersey, Camden M
Texas A&M University M,O
Tufts University M,D
Tulane University M,D
University of Florida M,D,O
University of Pittsburgh M,O
University of San Francisco M
University of Southern Mississippi M,D
Virginia Polytechnic Institute and State University M,D

■ INTERNATIONAL ECONOMICS

Claremont Graduate University M,D,O
Eastern Michigan University M
Fordham University M,O
The Johns Hopkins University M,D,O
Regent University M
University of Miami M,D
Valparaiso University M

Virginia Polytechnic Institute and State University M,D
West Virginia University M,D
Yale University M

■ INTERNATIONAL HEALTH

Boston University M,D,O
Brandeis University M
The Catholic University of America M,D,O
Duke University M
Emory University M
George Mason University M,O
Georgetown University P,M,D
The George Washington University M,D
Harvard University M,D
The Johns Hopkins University M,D
New York University M,D
San Diego State University M,D
Tufts University M,D
Tulane University M,D
University of Michigan M,D
University of Minnesota, Twin Cities Campus M,D
University of Southern California M
University of South Florida M,D
The University of Toledo M,O
University of Washington M,D
Yale University M

■ INTERNATIONAL TRADE POLICY

The George Washington University M
Monterey Institute of International Studies M

■ INTERNET AND INTERACTIVE MULTIMEDIA

Alfred University M
Brooklyn College of the City University of New York M,O
California State University, East Bay M
DePaul University M,D
Duquesne University M,O
Elon University M
George Mason University M,D,O
Georgetown University M
Georgia Institute of Technology M,D
Indiana University–Purdue University Indianapolis M,D
Long Island University, C.W. Post Campus M
National University M
New Mexico Highlands University M
New York University M
Polytechnic Institute of NYU M,O
Quinnipiac University M
Robert Morris University M,D
Rochester Institute of Technology M,O
Sacred Heart University M,O
San Diego State University M
Southern Polytechnic State University M,O
Stevens Institute of Technology M,D,O
Towson University D,O
University of Central Florida M
University of Florida M,D
University of Georgia M
University of Miami M
University of San Francisco M
University of Southern California M,D,O
Virginia Commonwealth University M
Western Illinois University M,O
Wilmington University M

■ INTERNET ENGINEERING

New Jersey Institute of Technology M
University of Georgia M
University of San Francisco M
Wilmington University M

■ INVESTMENT MANAGEMENT

Alaska Pacific University M,O
Boston University M
Gannon University O
The George Washington University M,D
The Johns Hopkins University M,O
Lynn University M,D
Marywood University M
Pace University M
Quinnipiac University M
The University of Iowa M
University of San Francisco M
University of Tulsa M
University of Wisconsin–Madison D

■ ITALIAN

Boston College M,D
Brown University D
Central Connecticut State University M,O
Columbia University M,D
Cornell University D
Florida State University M
Graduate School and University Center of the City University of New York M,D
Harvard University M,D
Hunter College of the City University of New York M
Indiana University Bloomington M,D
Iona College M
The Johns Hopkins University D
Montclair State University M,O
New York University M,D
Northwestern University D,O
The Ohio State University M,D
Queens College of the City University of New York M
Rutgers, The State University of New Jersey, New Brunswick M,D
San Francisco State University M
Stanford University M,D
State University of New York at Binghamton M
Stony Brook University, State University of New York M
University at Albany, State University of New York M
University of California, Berkeley D
University of California, Los Angeles M,D
University of Chicago M,D
University of Connecticut M,D
University of Illinois at Urbana–Champaign M,D
University of Massachusetts Amherst M
The University of North Carolina at Chapel Hill M,D
University of Notre Dame M
University of Oregon M
University of Pennsylvania M,D
University of Pittsburgh M
The University of Tennessee D
The University of Texas at Austin M,D
University of Virginia M
University of Washington M,D
University of Wisconsin–Madison M,D
University of Wisconsin–Milwaukee M,O
Wayne State University M
Yale University D

■ JAPANESE

Arizona State University M
Cornell University M,D
Eastern Michigan University M,O
Harvard University D
Indiana University Bloomington M,D
Kent State University M,D
The Ohio State University M,D
Portland State University M
San Francisco State University M
Stanford University M,D
University at Buffalo, the State University of New York M,D,O
University of California, Berkeley D
University of California, Irvine M,D
University of Colorado at Boulder M,D
University of Hawaii at Manoa M,D,O
University of Maryland, College Park M,D
University of Massachusetts Amherst M
University of Oregon M,D
University of Washington M,D
University of Wisconsin–Madison M,D

M—master's degree; P—first professional degree; D—doctorate; O—other advanced degree

Washington University in St. Louis M,D

■ JEWISH STUDIES

Brandeis University M,D
Brooklyn College of the City University of New York M
Brown University D
Columbia University M,D
Cornell University M,D
Emory University M
Gratz College M,O
Harvard University M,D
New York University M,D,O
Seton Hall University M
Touro College M
Towson University M
University of California, Berkeley D
University of California, San Diego M,D
University of Connecticut M
University of Maryland, College Park M
University of Michigan M,D,O
The University of Montana M
University of Wisconsin–Madison M,D
University of Wisconsin–Milwaukee M,O
Yeshiva University M,D

■ JOURNALISM

American University M
Angelo State University M
Arizona State University M
Arkansas State University M
Arkansas Tech University M
Ball State University M
Baylor University M
Bob Jones University P,M,D,O
Boston University M
California State University, Fresno M
California State University, Fullerton M
California State University, Northridge M
Columbia College Chicago M
Columbia University M,D
DePaul University M
Drake University M
Drexel University M
Emerson College M
Florida Agricultural and Mechanical University M
Florida Atlantic University M,O
Georgetown University M,D
Harvard University M,O
Hofstra University M
Indiana University Bloomington M,D
Iona College M
Iowa State University of Science and Technology M
Kent State University M
Marquette University M
Marshall University M
Michigan State University M
New York University M,D,O
Northeastern University M
Northwestern University M
The Ohio State University M
Ohio University M,D
Point Park University M
Polytechnic Institute of NYU M
Quinnipiac University M
Regent University M,D
Roosevelt University M
South Dakota State University M
Southern Illinois University Carbondale D
Stanford University M,D
Syracuse University M
Temple University M
Texas Christian University M
The University of Alabama M
University of Arkansas M
University of Arkansas at Little Rock M
University of California, Berkeley M
University of Colorado at Boulder M,D
University of Florida M
University of Georgia M,D
University of Illinois at Springfield M
University of Illinois at Urbana–Champaign M
The University of Iowa M
The University of Kansas M
University of Maryland, College Park M,D
University of Memphis M
University of Miami M,D
University of Mississippi M
University of Missouri–Columbia M,D
The University of Montana M
University of Nebraska–Lincoln M
University of Nevada, Las Vegas M
University of Nevada, Reno M
University of North Texas M,O
University of Oklahoma M
University of Oregon M,D
University of South Carolina M,D
University of Southern California M
The University of Tennessee M,D
The University of Texas at Austin M,D
University of Wisconsin–Madison M,D
Virginia Commonwealth University M
West Virginia University M

■ KINESIOLOGY AND MOVEMENT STUDIES

Angelo State University M
Arizona State University D
Auburn University M,D,O
Barry University M
Bowling Green State University M
California Baptist University M
California Polytechnic State University, San Luis Obispo M
California State Polytechnic University, Pomona M
California State University, Chico M
California State University, Fresno M
California State University, Long Beach M
California State University, Los Angeles M
California State University, Northridge M
California State University, San Bernardino M
Columbia University M,D
Dallas Baptist University M
Eastern Michigan University M
Fresno Pacific University M
Georgia Southern University M
Georgia State University D
Hardin-Simmons University M
Humboldt State University M
Indiana University Bloomington M,D
Inter American University of Puerto Rico, San Germán Campus M
Iowa State University of Science and Technology M,D
James Madison University M
Kansas State University M
Lamar University M
Louisiana State University and Agricultural and Mechanical College M,D
Michigan State University M,D
Midwestern State University M
Mississippi College M
Mississippi State University M
New York University M,D,O
Northwestern University D
Old Dominion University D
Oregon State University M
Penn State University Park M,D
Saint Mary's College of California M
Sam Houston State University M
San Diego State University M
San Francisco State University M
San Jose State University M
Sonoma State University M
Southeastern Louisiana University M
Southern Illinois University Edwardsville M,O
Southwestern Oklahoma State University M
Stephen F. Austin State University M
Temple University M,D
Tennessee Technological University M
Texas A&M University M,D
Texas A&M University–Commerce M,D

Texas A&M University–Corpus Christi	M,D
Texas A&M University–Kingsville	M
Texas Christian University	M
Texas Woman's University	M,D
Towson University	M
The University of Alabama	M,D
University of Arkansas	M,D
University of Central Arkansas	M
University of Colorado at Boulder	M,D
University of Delaware	M,D
University of Florida	M,D
University of Georgia	M,D
University of Hawaii at Manoa	M,D
University of Houston	M,D
University of Illinois at Chicago	M,D
University of Illinois at Urbana–Champaign	M,D
University of Kentucky	M,D
University of Maine	M
University of Maryland, College Park	M,D
University of Massachusetts Amherst	M,D
University of Michigan	M,D
University of Minnesota, Twin Cities Campus	M,D
University of Nevada, Las Vegas	M
University of New Hampshire	M
The University of North Carolina at Chapel Hill	M,D
The University of North Carolina at Charlotte	M
University of North Dakota	M
University of North Texas	M
University of Southern California	M,D
The University of Tennessee	M,D
The University of Texas at Austin	M,D
The University of Texas at El Paso	M
The University of Texas at San Antonio	M
The University of Texas at Tyler	M
The University of Texas of the Permian Basin	M
The University of Texas–Pan American	M
University of the Incarnate Word	M,D
University of Virginia	M,D
University of Wisconsin–Madison	M,D
University of Wisconsin–Milwaukee	M
University of Wyoming	M
Washington University in St. Louis	D
Wayne State University	M
West Chester University of Pennsylvania	M,O
Western Illinois University	M

■ LANDSCAPE ARCHITECTURE

Arizona State University	M
Auburn University	M
Ball State University	M
California State Polytechnic University, Pomona	M
Chatham University	M
City College of the City University of New York	M,O
Clemson University	M
Columbia University	M
Cornell University	M
Florida Agricultural and Mechanical University	M
Florida International University	M
Harvard University	M,D
Illinois Institute of Technology	M,D
Iowa State University of Science and Technology	M
Kansas State University	M
Louisiana State University and Agricultural and Mechanical College	M
Mississippi State University	M
Morgan State University	M
North Carolina State University	M
The Ohio State University	M
Oklahoma State University	M,D
Penn State University Park	M
State University of New York College of Environmental Science and Forestry	M
Texas A&M University	M,D
Texas Tech University	M
The University of Arizona	M
University of California, Berkeley	M,O
University of Colorado Denver	M
University of Florida	M,D
University of Georgia	M
University of Idaho	M
University of Illinois at Urbana–Champaign	M,D
University of Massachusetts Amherst	M
University of Michigan	M,D
University of Minnesota, Twin Cities Campus	M
University of New Mexico	M
University of Oklahoma	M
University of Oregon	M
University of Pennsylvania	M,O
The University of Tennessee	M
The University of Texas at Arlington	M
The University of Texas at Austin	M,D
University of Virginia	M
University of Washington	M
University of Wisconsin–Madison	M
Utah State University	M
Virginia Polytechnic Institute and State University	M,D
Washington State University	M,D

■ LATIN AMERICAN STUDIES

American University	M,O
Arizona State University	M,D
Brown University	M,D
California State University, Long Beach	M
California State University, Los Angeles	M
Cleveland State University	M
Columbia University	M,O
Cornell University	M,D
Duke University	M,D,O
Florida International University	M
Fordham University	M,O
Georgetown University	M
The George Washington University	M
Georgia State University	M,D,O
Indiana University Bloomington	M
La Salle University	M
Michigan State University	D
New York University	M,D,O
Ohio University	M
San Diego State University	M
Tulane University	M,D
University at Albany, State University of New York	M,O
The University of Arizona	M
University of California, Berkeley	M
University of California, Los Angeles	M
University of California, San Diego	M
University of California, Santa Barbara	M,D
University of Central Florida	M,D,O
University of Chicago	M
University of Connecticut	M
University of Florida	M,O
University of Illinois at Urbana–Champaign	M
The University of Kansas	M,O
University of Massachusetts Dartmouth	M,D
University of Miami	M
University of New Mexico	M,D
The University of North Carolina at Chapel Hill	M,D,O
The University of North Carolina at Charlotte	M
University of Notre Dame	M
University of Pittsburgh	O
University of South Florida	M,D,O
The University of Texas at Austin	M,D
University of Wisconsin–Madison	M,D
Vanderbilt University	M
West Virginia University	M,D
Yale University	D

M—master's degree; P—first professional degree; D—doctorate; O—other advanced degree

■ LAW

American University P,M,O
Arizona State University P,M
Barry University P
Baylor University P
Boston College P
Boston University P,M
Brigham Young University P,M
Campbell University P
Capital University P,M
Case Western Reserve University P,M
The Catholic University of America P
Chapman University P,M
Cleveland State University P,M
The College of William and Mary P,M
Columbia University P,M,D
Cornell University P,M,D
Creighton University P,M,O
DePaul University P,M
Drake University P
Duke University P,M,D
Duquesne University P,M
Elon University P
Emory University P,M,O
Florida Agricultural and Mechanical University P
Florida International University P
Florida State University P,M
Fordham University P,M
Friends University M
George Mason University P,M
Georgetown University P,M,D
The George Washington University P,M,D
Georgia State University P
Golden Gate University P,M,D
Gonzaga University P
Hamline University P,M
Harvard University P,M,D
Hodges University M
Hofstra University P,M
Howard University P,M
Illinois Institute of Technology P,M
Indiana University Bloomington P,M,D,O
Indiana University–Purdue University Indianapolis P,M,D
John F. Kennedy University P
Lewis & Clark College P,M
Liberty University P
Louisiana State University and Agricultural and Mechanical College M
Loyola Marymount University P,M
Loyola University Chicago P,M,D
Loyola University New Orleans P,M
Marquette University P
Mercer University P
Mississippi College P,O
New York University P,M,D,O
North Carolina Central University P
Northeastern University P
Northern Illinois University P
Northern Kentucky University P
Northwestern University P,M,O
Nova Southeastern University P,M,O
The Ohio State University P,M
Oklahoma City University P
Pace University P,M,D
Park University M
Pepperdine University P
Pontifical Catholic University of Puerto Rico P
Quinnipiac University P,M
Regent University P,M
Roger Williams University P
Rutgers, The State University of New Jersey, Camden P
Rutgers, The State University of New Jersey, Newark P
St. John's University (NY) P
Saint Joseph's University M,O
Saint Louis University P,M
St. Mary's University (United States) P
St. Thomas University P,M
Samford University P,M
Santa Clara University P,M,O
Seattle University P,O
Seton Hall University P,M
Southern Illinois University Carbondale P,M
Southern Methodist University P,M,D
Southern University and Agricultural and Mechanical College P
Stanford University P,M,D
Stetson University P,M
Suffolk University P,M
Syracuse University P
Temple University P,M,D
Texas Southern University P
Texas Tech University P
Texas Wesleyan University P
Touro College P,M
Trinity International University P
Tulane University P,M,D
University at Buffalo, the State University of New York P,M
The University of Akron P
The University of Alabama P,M
The University of Arizona P,M
University of Arkansas P,M
University of Arkansas at Little Rock P
University of Baltimore M
University of California, Berkeley P,M,D
University of California, Davis P,M
University of California, Los Angeles P,M,D
University of California, San Diego M
University of Chicago P,M,D
University of Cincinnati P
University of Colorado at Boulder P
University of Connecticut P
University of Dayton P,M
University of Denver P,M
University of Detroit Mercy P
University of Florida P,M,D
University of Georgia P,M
University of Hawaii at Manoa P,M,O
University of Houston P,M
University of Idaho P
University of Illinois at Urbana–Champaign P,M,D
The University of Iowa P,M
The University of Kansas P
University of Kentucky P
University of La Verne P
University of Louisville P
University of Maryland, College Park
University of Memphis P
University of Miami P,M
University of Michigan P,M,D
University of Minnesota, Twin Cities Campus P,M
University of Mississippi P
University of Missouri–Columbia P,M
University of Missouri–Kansas City P,M
The University of Montana P
University of Nebraska–Lincoln P,M
University of Nevada, Las Vegas P
University of New Mexico P
The University of North Carolina at Chapel Hill P
University of North Dakota P
University of Notre Dame P,M,D
University of Oklahoma P
University of Oregon P,M
University of Pennsylvania P,M,D
University of Pittsburgh P,M,O
University of Puerto Rico, Río Piedras P,M
University of Richmond P
University of St. Thomas (MN) P
University of San Diego P,M,O
University of San Francisco P,M
University of South Carolina P
The University of South Dakota P
University of Southern Maine P
The University of Tennessee P
The University of Texas at Austin P,M
University of the District of Columbia P
University of the Pacific P,M,D
The University of Toledo P
University of Tulsa P,M,O
University of Utah P,M
University of Virginia P,M,D,O

University of Washington P,M,D
University of Wisconsin–Madison P,M,D
University of Wyoming P
Valparaiso University P,M
Vanderbilt University P,M,D
Villanova University P
Wake Forest University P,M,D
Walden University M,D,O
Washburn University P
Washington University in St. Louis P,M,D
Wayne State University P,M,D
Western New England College P,M
West Virginia University P
Widener University P,M,D
Willamette University P,M
Yale University P,M,D
Yeshiva University P,M

■ LEGAL AND JUSTICE STUDIES

American University M,D,O
Arizona State University P,M,D
Boston University M
California University of Pennsylvania M
Capital University M
Case Western Reserve University P,M
The Catholic University of America D,O
College of Charleston M,O
Eastern Michigan University O
Georgetown University P,M,D
The George Washington University M,O
Golden Gate University P,M,D
Governors State University M
Harvard University P
Hofstra University P,M
Hollins University M,O
John Jay College of Criminal Justice of the City University of New York M,D
Marygrove College M
Marymount University M,O
Mississippi College M,O
Montclair State University M,O
New York University M,D
Northeastern University M,D
Nova Southeastern University M,O
Pace University P,M,D
Prairie View A&M University M,D
Regent University P,M
Regis University M,O
The Richard Stockton College of New Jersey O
Rutgers, The State University of New Jersey, New Brunswick D
St. John's University (NY) M
Salve Regina University M
San Francisco State University M,O
Southern Illinois University Carbondale M
State University of New York at Binghamton M,D
Temple University P,M,D
Texas State University–San Marcos M
University of Baltimore M
University of California, Berkeley D,O
University of California, San Diego M
University of Denver M,O
University of Illinois at Springfield M
University of Mississippi M
University of Nebraska–Lincoln M
University of Nevada, Reno M,D
University of New Hampshire M
University of Pennsylvania M,D
University of Pittsburgh M,O
University of San Diego P,M,O
University of the Pacific P,M,D
University of Washington P,M,D
University of Wisconsin–Madison M,D
Weber State University M
Webster University M
West Virginia University M

■ LEISURE STUDIES

Aurora University M
Bowling Green State University M
California State University, Long Beach M
Central Michigan University M
The College at Brockport, State University of New York M
East Carolina University M
Florida International University M
Gallaudet University M
Howard University M
Indiana University Bloomington M,D,O
Kent State University M
Murray State University M
Penn State University Park M,D
Prescott College M
San Francisco State University M
Southeast Missouri State University M
Southern Connecticut State University M
Temple University M
Texas State University–San Marcos M
Universidad Metropolitana M
University of Connecticut M,D
University of Georgia M,D,O
University of Illinois at Urbana–Champaign M,D
The University of Iowa M
University of Memphis M
University of Minnesota, Twin Cities Campus M,D
University of Mississippi M,D
University of Nevada, Las Vegas M
The University of North Carolina at Chapel Hill M
University of Northern Iowa M,D
University of North Texas M,O
University of South Alabama M
University of Southern Mississippi M,D
The University of Tennessee M,D
The University of Toledo M
University of Utah M,D
University of West Florida M

■ LIBERAL STUDIES

Abilene Christian University M
Alaska Pacific University M
Alvernia University M
Antioch University McGregor M
Armstrong Atlantic State University M
Auburn University Montgomery M
Barry University M
Boston University M
Bradley University M
Brooklyn College of the City University of New York M
California State University, Sacramento M
Cardinal Stritch University M
Clark University M
The College at Brockport, State University of New York M
College of Notre Dame of Maryland M
College of Staten Island of the City University of New York M
Columbia University M
Concordia University Chicago M
Converse College M
Creighton University M
Dallas Baptist University M
Dartmouth College M
Dowling College M
Duke University M
Duquesne University M
East Tennessee State University M
Florida Atlantic University M
Florida International University M
Fordham University M
Fort Hays State University M
Georgetown University M,D
Graduate School and University Center of the City University of New York M
Hamline University M,O
Harvard University M,O
Henderson State University M
Hollins University M,O

M—master's degree; P—first professional degree; D—doctorate; O—other advanced degree

Houston Baptist University	M
Indiana University–Purdue University Fort Wayne	M
Indiana University–Purdue University Indianapolis	M,D,O
Indiana University South Bend	M
Indiana University Southeast	M
Jacksonville State University	M
The Johns Hopkins University	M,O
Kean University	M
Kent State University	M
Lock Haven University of Pennsylvania	M
Louisiana State University and Agricultural and Mechanical College	M
Louisiana State University in Shreveport	M
Loyola University Maryland	M
Madonna University	M
Manhattanville College	M
McDaniel College	M
Metropolitan State University	M
Minnesota State University Moorhead	M
Mississippi College	M
Monmouth University	M
Nazareth College of Rochester	M
The New School: A University	M
North Carolina State University	M
North Central College	M
Northern Arizona University	M
Northern Kentucky University	M,O
Northwestern University	M
Oakland University	M
Ohio Dominican University	M
Oklahoma City University	M
Queens College of the City University of New York	M
Ramapo College of New Jersey	M
Rollins College	M
Rutgers, The State University of New Jersey, Camden	M
Rutgers, The State University of New Jersey, Newark	M
St. Edward's University	M,O
St. John's College (MD)	M
St. John's College (NM)	M
St. John's University (NY)	M
Saint Mary's College of California	M
San Diego State University	M
Spring Hill College	M
State University of New York at Plattsburgh	M
State University of New York Empire State College	M
Stony Brook University, State University of New York	M,O
Tarleton State University	M
Temple University	M
Texas Christian University	M
Towson University	M
Tulane University	M
University at Albany, State University of New York	M
University of Arkansas at Little Rock	M
University of Delaware	M
University of Denver	M,O
University of Detroit Mercy	M
The University of Findlay	M
University of Maine	M
University of Memphis	M
University of Miami	M
University of Michigan–Dearborn	M
University of Minnesota, Duluth	M
University of New Hampshire	M
The University of North Carolina at Charlotte	M
The University of North Carolina at Greensboro	M
The University of North Carolina Wilmington	M
University of Oklahoma	M
University of Pennsylvania	M
University of St. Thomas (TX)	M
University of Southern Indiana	M
University of South Florida	M
The University of Toledo	M
University of Wisconsin–Milwaukee	M
Ursuline College	M
Utica College	M
Valparaiso University	M,O
Vanderbilt University	M
Villanova University	M
Wake Forest University	M
Washburn University	M
Western Illinois University	M
West Virginia University	M
Wichita State University	M
Widener University	M
Winthrop University	M

■ LIBRARY SCIENCE

Appalachian State University	M,O
Azusa Pacific University	M
The Catholic University of America	M
Chicago State University	M
Clarion University of Pennsylvania	M,O
Dominican University	M,D,O
Drexel University	M,D,O
East Carolina University	M,O
Eastern Kentucky University	M
Emporia State University	M,D,O
Florida State University	M,D,O
George Mason University	M,O
Indiana University Bloomington	M,D,O
Indiana University–Purdue University Indianapolis	M
Inter American University of Puerto Rico, San Germán Campus	M
Kent State University	M
Kutztown University of Pennsylvania	M,O
Long Island University, C.W. Post Campus	M,D,O
Louisiana State University and Agricultural and Mechanical College	M,O
Mansfield University of Pennsylvania	M
Marywood University	M,O
McDaniel College	M
North Carolina Central University	M
Old Dominion University	M
Olivet Nazarene University	M
Queens College of the City University of New York	M,O
Rowan University	M
Rutgers, The State University of New Jersey, New Brunswick	M,D
St. Catherine University	M
St. John's University (NY)	M,O
Sam Houston State University	M
San Jose State University	M,D
Simmons College	M,D,O
Southern Connecticut State University	M,O
Syracuse University	M,O
Tennessee Technological University	M,O
Texas Woman's University	M,D
Trevecca Nazarene University	M
Universidad del Turabo	M
University at Buffalo, the State University of New York	M,O
The University of Alabama	M,D
The University of Arizona	M,D
University of California, Los Angeles	M,D,O
University of Central Arkansas	M
University of Central Missouri	M,O
University of Denver	M,D,O
University of Hawaii at Manoa	M,O
University of Houston–Clear Lake	M
University of Illinois at Urbana–Champaign	M,D,O
The University of Iowa	M
University of Kentucky	M
University of Maryland, College Park	
University of Michigan	M,D
University of Missouri–Columbia	M,D,O
The University of North Carolina at Chapel Hill	M,D,O
The University of North Carolina at Greensboro	M
University of Northern Colorado	M
University of North Texas	M,D

University of Oklahoma M,O
University of Pittsburgh M,D,O
University of Puerto Rico, Río Piedras M,O
University of Rhode Island M
University of South Carolina M,D,O
University of Southern Mississippi M,O
University of South Florida M
University of Washington M,D
University of Wisconsin–Madison M,D
University of Wisconsin–Milwaukee M,D,O
Valdosta State University M
Wayne State University M,O
Wright State University M

■ LIGHTING DESIGN

The New School: A University M
Rensselaer Polytechnic Institute M
University of Washington M,D,O

■ LIMNOLOGY

Baylor University M,D
Cornell University D
University of Alaska Fairbanks M,D
University of Florida M,D
University of Wisconsin–Madison M,D
William Paterson University of New Jersey M

■ LINGUISTICS

Arizona State University M,D
Ball State University D
Biola University M,D,O
Boston College M
Boston University M,D
Brandeis University M
Brigham Young University M,O
Brown University M,D
California State University, Fresno M
California State University, Fullerton M
California State University, Long Beach M
California State University, Northridge M
Carnegie Mellon University D
Case Western Reserve University M
Cleveland State University M
Cornell University M,D
Eastern Michigan University M
Florida Atlantic University M
Florida International University M
Gallaudet University M,D
George Mason University M,O
Georgetown University M,D,O
Georgia State University M,D
Graduate School and University Center of the City University of New York M,D
Harvard University D
Hofstra University M,D,O
Indiana State University M,O
Indiana University Bloomington M,D
Indiana University of Pennsylvania M,D
Louisiana State University and Agricultural and Mechanical College M,D
Massachusetts Institute of Technology D
Michigan State University M,D
Montclair State University M,O
New York University M,D
Northeastern Illinois University M
Northern Arizona University M,D,O
Northwestern University M,D
Oakland University M,O
The Ohio State University M,D
Ohio University M
Old Dominion University M
Purdue University M,D
Queens College of the City University of New York M
Rice University M,D
Rutgers, The State University of New Jersey, New Brunswick D
San Diego State University M,O
San Francisco State University M
San Jose State University M,O
Southern Illinois University Carbondale M
Stanford University M,D
Stony Brook University, State University of New York M,D
Syracuse University M
Temple University M
Texas Tech University M
University at Buffalo, the State University of New York M,D
University of Alaska Fairbanks M
The University of Arizona M,D
University of California, Berkeley D
University of California, Davis M,D
University of California, Los Angeles M,D
University of California, San Diego D
University of California, Santa Barbara M,D
University of California, Santa Cruz M,D
University of Chicago M,D
University of Colorado at Boulder M,D
University of Colorado Denver M,O
University of Connecticut M,D
University of Delaware M,D
University of Florida M,D,O
University of Georgia M,D
University of Hawaii at Manoa M,D
University of Houston M,D
University of Illinois at Chicago M
University of Illinois at Urbana–Champaign M,D
The University of Iowa M,D
The University of Kansas M,D
University of Maryland, Baltimore County M
University of Maryland, College Park M,D
University of Massachusetts Amherst M,D
University of Massachusetts Boston M
University of Michigan D
University of Minnesota, Twin Cities Campus M,D
University of Missouri–St. Louis M,O
The University of Montana M,D
University of New Hampshire M,D
University of New Mexico M,D
The University of North Carolina at Chapel Hill M,D
University of North Dakota M
University of Oregon M,D
University of Pennsylvania M,D
University of Pittsburgh M,D
University of Puerto Rico, Río Piedras M
University of South Carolina M,D,O
University of Southern California M,D
University of South Florida M
The University of Tennessee D
The University of Texas at Arlington M,D
The University of Texas at Austin M,D
The University of Texas at El Paso M
University of Utah M,D
University of Virginia M
University of Washington M,D
University of Wisconsin–Madison M,D
University of Wisconsin–Milwaukee M,D,O
Wayne State University M
West Virginia University M
Yale University D

■ LOGISTICS

Benedictine University M
Case Western Reserve University M,D
Colorado Technical University Colorado Springs M,D
East Carolina University M,D,O
Florida Institute of Technology M
George Mason University M
Georgia College & State University M
Massachusetts Institute of Technology M,D
North Dakota State University M,D
The Ohio State University M
Stevens Institute of Technology M,D,O

M—master's degree; P—first professional degree; D—doctorate; O—other advanced degree

Universidad del Turabo M
University at Buffalo, the State University of New York M,D,O
The University of Alabama in Huntsville M,O
University of Alaska Anchorage M,O
University of Dallas M
University of Houston M
University of Minnesota, Twin Cities Campus M,D
University of Missouri–St. Louis M,D,O
University of New Hampshire M,D
University of New Haven M,O
The University of Tennessee M,D
The University of Texas at Arlington M
University of Washington O
Virginia Polytechnic Institute and State University M,D
Wilmington University M
Wright State University M

■ MANAGEMENT INFORMATION SYSTEMS

Adelphi University M
Alliant International University–San Diego M,D
American InterContinental University Dunwoody Campus M
American International College M
American University M,O
Argosy University, Orange County M,D,O
Argosy University, Sarasota M,D,O
Argosy University, Tampa M,D
Argosy University, Twin Cities M,D
Arizona State University M,D
Arkansas State University M
Auburn University M,D
Avila University M
Barry University O
Baylor University M
Bellarmine University M
Bellevue University M
Benedictine University M
Bernard M. Baruch College of the City University of New York M,D
Boise State University M
Boston University D
Bowie State University M,O
Brandeis University M,O
Brigham Young University M
California Lutheran University M,O
California State University, Fullerton M
California State University, Los Angeles M
California State University, Sacramento M
Capella University M,D,O
Carnegie Mellon University M,D
Case Western Reserve University M,D
Central Michigan University M,O
Charleston Southern University M
City University of Seattle M,O
Claremont Graduate University M,D,O
Clark University M
Cleveland State University M,D
College of Charleston M
The College of St. Scholastica M,O
Colorado State University M
Colorado Technical University Sioux Falls M
Concordia University Wisconsin M
Creighton University M
Dallas Baptist University M
DePaul University M,D
DeSales University M
Dominican University M
Duquesne University M
East Carolina University M,D,O
Eastern Michigan University M,O
Emory University M,D
Endicott College M
Fairfield University M,O
Fairleigh Dickinson University, Metropolitan Campus M,O
Ferris State University M
Florida Agricultural and Mechanical University M
Florida Atlantic University M
Florida Institute of Technology M
Florida International University M
Florida State University M,D
Fordham University M
Friends University M
George Mason University M,D,O
The George Washington University M,D
Georgia College & State University M
Georgia Institute of Technology M,D,O
Georgia State University M,D
Golden Gate University M,D,O
Governors State University M
Graduate School and University Center of the City University of New York D
Grand Canyon University M
Grand Valley State University M
Harding University M
Hawai'i Pacific University M
Hodges University M
Hofstra University M
Holy Family University M
Hood College M
Howard University M
Idaho State University M,O
Illinois Institute of Technology M,D
Illinois State University M
Indiana University South Bend M
Inter American University of Puerto Rico, Metropolitan Campus M
Inter American University of Puerto Rico, San Germán Campus M,D
Iowa State University of Science and Technology M
The Johns Hopkins University M,O
Kean University M
Kent State University D
Lawrence Technological University M,D
Lewis University M
Lindenwood University M,O
Long Island University, C.W. Post Campus M,O
Louisiana State University and Agricultural and Mechanical College M,D
Loyola University Chicago M
Loyola University Maryland M
Marist College M,O
Marymount University M,O
Marywood University M
Metropolitan State University M,O
Miami University M
Michigan State University M,D
Middle Tennessee State University M
Minnesota State University Mankato M,O
Minot State University M
Mississippi State University M,D
Missouri State University M
Montclair State University M,O
Morehead State University M
National University M
New Jersey Institute of Technology M,D
Newman University M
New Mexico Highlands University M
New York Institute of Technology M,O
New York University M,D,O
North Central College M
Northeastern University M,D
Northern Illinois University M
Northwestern University M
Northwest Missouri State University M
Norwich University M
Nova Southeastern University M,D
Oakland University M,O
The Ohio State University M,D
Oklahoma City University M
Oklahoma State University M,D
Old Dominion University M
Our Lady of the Lake University of San Antonio M
Pace University M
Park University M
Penn State Great Valley M
Penn State Harrisburg M
Polytechnic Institute of NYU, Westchester Graduate Center M,O

Pontifical Catholic University of Puerto Rico M
Prairie View A&M University M,D
Quinnipiac University M
Regis University M,O
Rivier College M
Robert Morris University M,D
Rochester Institute of Technology M
Roosevelt University M
Rutgers, The State University of New Jersey, Newark M,D
Sacred Heart University M,O
St. Edward's University M,O
St. John's University (NY) M,O
Saint Peter's College M
San Diego State University M
San Jose State University M
Santa Clara University M
Schiller International University (United States) M
Seattle Pacific University M
Seton Hall University M
Shenandoah University M,O
Southern Illinois University Edwardsville M
Southern Methodist University M
Southern New Hampshire University M,D,O
State University of New York College at Potsdam M
Stevens Institute of Technology M,D,O
Stony Brook University, State University of New York M,D,O
Strayer University M
Sullivan University P,M
Syracuse University M,D,O
Tarleton State University M
Temple University M,D
Texas A&M International University M
Texas A&M University M,D
Texas Southern University M
Texas State University–San Marcos M
Texas Tech University M,D
Towson University D,O
Troy University M
Universidad del Turabo M,D
University at Buffalo, the State University of New York M,D,O
The University of Akron M
The University of Alabama at Birmingham M
The University of Alabama in Huntsville M,O
The University of Arizona M
University of Arkansas M
University of Arkansas at Little Rock M,O
University of Baltimore M,O
University of California, Berkeley O
University of Central Florida M
University of Central Missouri M
University of Cincinnati M,D
University of Colorado at Boulder M,D
University of Colorado at Colorado Springs M
University of Colorado Denver M,D
University of Dallas M
University of Dayton M
University of Delaware M
University of Denver M
University of Detroit Mercy M
University of Florida M,D
University of Hawaii at Manoa M,D,O
University of Houston–Clear Lake M
University of Illinois at Chicago M,D
University of Illinois at Springfield M
The University of Iowa M
The University of Kansas M
University of La Verne M
University of Maine M
University of Mary Hardin-Baylor M
University of Maryland University College M,O
University of Mary Washington M
University of Memphis M,D
University of Miami M
University of Minnesota, Twin Cities Campus M,D
University of Mississippi M,D
University of Missouri–St. Louis M,D
University of Nebraska at Omaha M,D,O
University of Nebraska–Lincoln M
University of Nevada, Las Vegas M
University of Nevada, Reno M
University of New Haven M
University of New Mexico M
The University of North Carolina at Chapel Hill D
The University of North Carolina at Greensboro M,D,O
University of North Texas M,D
University of Oklahoma M
University of Oregon M
University of Pennsylvania M,D
University of Phoenix M
University of Phoenix–Central Florida Campus M
University of Phoenix–Denver Campus M
University of Phoenix–Hawaii Campus M
University of Phoenix–Las Vegas Campus M
University of Phoenix–Louisiana Campus M
University of Phoenix–New Mexico Campus M
University of Phoenix–North Florida Campus M
University of Phoenix–Oregon Campus M
University of Phoenix–Philadelphia Campus M
University of Phoenix–Sacramento Valley Campus M
University of Phoenix–San Diego Campus M
University of Phoenix–Southern Arizona Campus M
University of Phoenix–Southern California Campus M
University of Phoenix–Southern Colorado Campus M
University of Phoenix–South Florida Campus M
University of Phoenix–Utah Campus M
University of Phoenix–West Florida Campus M
University of Phoenix–West Michigan Campus M
University of Pittsburgh M
University of Redlands M
University of Rhode Island D
University of St. Thomas (MN) M,O
University of San Francisco M
The University of Scranton M
University of South Alabama M
University of Southern Mississippi M
University of South Florida M
The University of Tampa M
The University of Texas at Arlington M,D
The University of Texas at Austin D
The University of Texas at Dallas M,D
The University of Texas at San Antonio M,D
The University of Texas–Pan American D
The University of Toledo M
University of Tulsa M
University of Virginia M
University of Wisconsin–Madison D
Utah State University M,D
Valparaiso University M
Villanova University M
Virginia Commonwealth University M,D
Virginia Polytechnic Institute and State University M,D
Walden University M,D
Washington State University M,D
Wayland Baptist University M
Webster University M,D,O
West Chester University of Pennsylvania M,O
Western International University M

M—master's degree; P—first professional degree; D—doctorate; O—other advanced degree

Wilmington University M
Worcester Polytechnic Institute M,D,O
Wright State University M
Xavier University M

■ MANAGEMENT OF TECHNOLOGY

Alliant International University–San Diego M,D
Boston University M
California Lutheran University M,O
California State University, Los Angeles M
Cambridge College M
Capella University M,D,O
Carnegie Mellon University M,D
Central Connecticut State University M,O
City University of Seattle M,O
Colorado School of Mines M,D
Colorado Technical University Colorado Springs M,D
Colorado Technical University Denver M
Colorado Technical University Sioux Falls M
Columbia University M
Dallas Baptist University M
DePaul University M,D
East Carolina University M,D,O
Eastern Michigan University M,D
Embry-Riddle Aeronautical University Worldwide M,O
Fairfield University M
Fairleigh Dickinson University, College at Florham M,O
George Mason University M,D
The George Washington University M,D
Georgia Institute of Technology M,O
Golden Gate University M,D,O
Harvard University D
Hodges University M
Idaho State University M
Illinois State University M
Indiana State University D
Iona College M,O
The Johns Hopkins University M,O
Jones International University M
La Salle University M
Lawrence Technological University M,D
Lewis University M
Marist College M,O
Marquette University M,D
Marshall University M
Mercer University M
Murray State University M
National University M
New Jersey Institute of Technology M
North Carolina Agricultural and Technical State University M,D
North Carolina State University D
Notre Dame de Namur University M
Old Dominion University M
Pacific Lutheran University M
Polytechnic Institute of NYU M,D
Polytechnic Institute of NYU, Westchester Graduate Center M
Portland State University M,D
Regis University M,O
St. Ambrose University M
Southeast Missouri State University M
State University of New York Institute of Technology M
Stevens Institute of Technology M,D,O
Stony Brook University, State University of New York M
Sullivan University P,M
Texas A&M University–Commerce M
Texas State University–San Marcos M
University at Albany, State University of New York M
The University of Akron M
University of Arkansas at Little Rock M,O
University of Bridgeport M
University of Colorado at Colorado Springs M
University of Dallas M
University of Delaware M
University of Denver M,O
University of Illinois at Urbana–Champaign M,D
University of Maryland University College M,O
University of Miami M,D
University of Minnesota, Twin Cities Campus M
University of New Hampshire M,O
University of New Haven M
University of New Mexico M
University of Pennsylvania M
University of Phoenix M
University of Phoenix–Central Florida Campus M
University of Phoenix–Denver Campus M
University of Phoenix–Hawaii Campus M
University of Phoenix–Las Vegas Campus M
University of Phoenix–Louisiana Campus M
University of Phoenix–New Mexico Campus M
University of Phoenix–Oregon Campus M
University of Phoenix–Philadelphia Campus M
University of Phoenix–Phoenix Campus M
University of Phoenix–Sacramento Valley Campus M
University of Phoenix–San Diego Campus M
University of Phoenix–Southern Arizona Campus M
University of Phoenix–Southern California Campus M
University of Phoenix–Southern Colorado Campus M
University of Phoenix–Utah Campus M
University of Phoenix–West Florida Campus M
University of Phoenix–West Michigan Campus M
University of St. Thomas (MN) M,O
University of Washington M,D
University of Wisconsin–Madison M
University of Wisconsin–Stout M
University of Wisconsin–Whitewater M
Walden University M,D,O
West Chester University of Pennsylvania M
Westminster College (UT) M,O

■ MANAGEMENT STRATEGY AND POLICY

Alliant International University–San Diego M,D
Azusa Pacific University M
Bernard M. Baruch College of the City University of New York M,D
Boston University M,O
California State University, East Bay M
Case Western Reserve University M
Claremont Graduate University M,D,O
Davenport University M
DePaul University M
Dominican University of California M
Drexel University M,D,O
Duquesne University M
Freed-Hardeman University M
The George Washington University M,D
Georgia Institute of Technology M,D,O
Georgia State University M,D
Harvard University D
Lamar University M
Manhattanville College M
Middle Tennessee State University M
Mountain State University M
Neumann University M
New York University M,D,O
Northwestern University D
Pace University M
Regent University M,D,O
Roberts Wesleyan College M,O

Rutgers, The State University of New Jersey, Newark M
Saint Joseph's University M
Southern Methodist University M
Stevens Institute of Technology M
Suffolk University M,O
Syracuse University D
Temple University D
Tennessee Technological University M
Towson University O
Tufts University O
The University of Arizona D
University of California, Berkeley O
University of Dallas M
University of Dayton M
University of Denver M,O
University of Florida M
The University of Iowa M
University of Mary M
University of Minnesota, Twin Cities Campus M,D
University of New Haven M
University of New Mexico M
The University of North Carolina at Chapel Hill D
University of Oklahoma M
University of Pittsburgh M
The University of Texas at Dallas M
University of Wisconsin–Madison M
Western International University M

■ MANUFACTURING ENGINEERING

Arizona State University M,D
Bowling Green State University M
Bradley University M
California State University, Northridge M
Clemson University M
Cornell University M,D
Dartmouth College M,D
East Carolina University M,D,O
Eastern Kentucky University M
East Tennessee State University M
Florida State University M,D
Grand Valley State University M
Illinois Institute of Technology M,D
Kansas State University M,D
Lawrence Technological University M,D
Lehigh University M
Marquette University M,D
Massachusetts Institute of Technology M,D,O
Michigan State University M,D
Minnesota State University Mankato M
Missouri University of Science and Technology M,D
New Jersey Institute of Technology M
North Carolina State University M
North Dakota State University M,D
Northeastern University M,D
Northwestern University M
Ohio University M,D
Old Dominion University M,D
Oregon State University M,D
Penn State University Park M,D
Polytechnic Institute of NYU M
Portland State University M
Rochester Institute of Technology M
Southern Illinois University Carbondale M
Southern Methodist University M,D
Stevens Institute of Technology M
Texas A&M University M
Texas Tech University M,D
Tufts University O
University of California, Los Angeles M
University of Central Florida M,D,O
University of Colorado at Colorado Springs M
The University of Iowa M,D
University of Kentucky M
University of Maryland, College Park M,D
University of Memphis M
University of Michigan M,D
University of Michigan–Dearborn M,D
University of Missouri–Columbia M,D
University of Nebraska–Lincoln M,D
University of New Mexico M
University of Rhode Island M
University of St. Thomas (MN) M,O
University of Southern California M,D,O
University of Southern Maine M
The University of Tennessee M,D
The University of Texas at El Paso M
The University of Texas–Pan American M
University of Wisconsin–Madison M
University of Wisconsin–Milwaukee M,D,O
University of Wisconsin–Stout M
Villanova University M,O
Wayne State University M
Western Illinois University M
Western Michigan University M
Western New England College M
Wichita State University M,D
Worcester Polytechnic Institute M,D,O

■ MARINE AFFAIRS

Duke University M
East Carolina University D
Florida Institute of Technology M,D
Louisiana State University and Agricultural and Mechanical College M,D
Nova Southeastern University M
Old Dominion University M
Oregon State University M
Stevens Institute of Technology M
University of Delaware M,D
University of Maine M
University of Miami M
University of Rhode Island M,D
University of San Diego M
University of Washington M,O
University of West Florida M

■ MARINE BIOLOGY

College of Charleston M
Florida Institute of Technology M
Nicholls State University M
Northeastern University M,D
Nova Southeastern University M,D
Princeton University D
Rutgers, The State University of New Jersey, New Brunswick M,D
San Francisco State University M
Texas State University–San Marcos M,D
University of Alaska Fairbanks M,D
University of California, San Diego M,D
University of California, Santa Barbara M,D
University of Colorado at Boulder M,D
University of Guam M
University of Hawaii at Manoa M,D
University of Maine M,D
University of Massachusetts Dartmouth M
University of Miami M,D
The University of North Carolina Wilmington M,D
University of Oregon M,D
University of Southern California M,D
University of Southern Mississippi M,D
University of South Florida M,D
Western Illinois University M,O

■ MARINE GEOLOGY

Cornell University M,D
Massachusetts Institute of Technology M,D
University of Delaware M,D
University of Hawaii at Manoa M,D
University of Miami M,D
University of Michigan M,D
University of Washington M,D

■ MARINE SCIENCES

American University M
California State University, East Bay M
California State University, Fresno M
California State University, Sacramento M

M—master's degree; P—first professional degree; D—doctorate; O—other advanced degree

California State University, Stanislaus	M
The College of William and Mary	M,D
Cornell University	M,D
Duke University	M
Florida Institute of Technology	M,D
Georgia Institute of Technology	M,D
Hawai'i Pacific University	M
North Carolina State University	M,D
Nova Southeastern University	M
Oregon State University	M
San Francisco State University	M
San Jose State University	M
Savannah State University	M
Stony Brook University, State University of New York	M,D
Texas A&M University–Corpus Christi	D
University of Alaska Fairbanks	M,D
University of California, San Diego	M
University of California, Santa Barbara	M,D
University of California, Santa Cruz	M,D
University of Connecticut	M,D
University of Delaware	M,D
University of Florida	M,D
University of Georgia	M,D
University of Hawaii at Manoa	O
University of Maine	M,D
University of Maryland, Baltimore County	M,D
University of Maryland, College Park	M,D
University of Maryland Eastern Shore	M,D
University of Massachusetts Amherst	M
University of Massachusetts Boston	D
University of Massachusetts Dartmouth	M,D
University of Miami	M,D
University of Michigan	M,D
University of New England	M
The University of North Carolina at Chapel Hill	M,D
The University of North Carolina Wilmington	M,D
University of Puerto Rico, Mayagüez Campus	M,D
University of Rhode Island	M,D
University of San Diego	M
University of South Alabama	M,D
University of South Carolina	M,D
University of Southern California	M,D
University of Southern Mississippi	M,D
University of South Florida	M,D
The University of Texas at Austin	M,D
University of Wisconsin–La Crosse	M
University of Wisconsin–Madison	M,D
Western Washington University	M

■ MARKETING

Adelphi University	M
Alabama Agricultural and Mechanical University	M
Alliant International University–San Diego	M,D
American InterContinental University Buckhead Campus	M
American InterContinental University South Florida	M
American International College	M
American University	M
Andrews University	M
Argosy University, Orange County	M,D,O
Argosy University, Sarasota	M,D,O
Argosy University, Tampa	M,D
Argosy University, Twin Cities	M,D
Arizona State University	M,D
Assumption College	M,O
Avila University	M
Barry University	O
Bayamón Central University	M
Benedictine University	M
Bentley University	M
Bernard M. Baruch College of the City University of New York	M,D
Boston University	M,D,O
California Lutheran University	M,O
California State University, East Bay	M
California State University, Fullerton	M
California State University, Los Angeles	M
Canisius College	M
Capella University	M,D,O
Carnegie Mellon University	D
Case Western Reserve University	M,D
Central Michigan University	M
City University of Seattle	M,O
Clark University	M
Clemson University	M
Cleveland State University	M,D,O
Colorado Technical University Colorado Springs	M,D
Colorado Technical University Denver	M
Columbia University	M,D
Concordia University Wisconsin	M
Cornell University	D
Dallas Baptist University	M
Delta State University	M
DePaul University	M
DeSales University	M
Drexel University	M,D,O
Eastern Michigan University	M
Emerson College	M
Emory University	M,D
Fairfield University	M,O
Fairleigh Dickinson University, College at Florham	M,O
Fairleigh Dickinson University, Metropolitan Campus	M,O
Florida Agricultural and Mechanical University	M
Florida Institute of Technology	M
Florida State University	M,D
Fordham University	M
Gannon University	O
The George Washington University	M,D
Georgia Institute of Technology	M,D,O
Georgia State University	M,D
Golden Gate University	M,D,O
Grand Canyon University	M
Harvard University	D
Hawai'i Pacific University	M
Hofstra University	M
Holy Names University	M
Hood College	M
Howard University	M
Illinois Institute of Technology	M
Inter American University of Puerto Rico, Metropolitan Campus	M
Inter American University of Puerto Rico, San Germán Campus	M,D
Iona College	M,O
The Johns Hopkins University	M
Johnson & Wales University	M
Kent State University	D
La Sierra University	M,O
Lewis University	M
Lindenwood University	M,O
Long Island University, C.W. Post Campus	M,O
Louisiana State University and Agricultural and Mechanical College	D
Louisiana Tech University	M,D
Loyola University Chicago	M
Loyola University Maryland	M
Lynn University	M,D
Manhattanville College	M
Marylhurst University	M
Maryville University of Saint Louis	M,O
Miami University	M
Michigan State University	M,D
Middle Tennessee State University	M
Minnesota State University Mankato	M
Mississippi State University	D
Montclair State University	M,O
National University	M
New Mexico State University	D
New York Institute of Technology	M,O

New York University M,D,O
Northeastern Illinois University M
Northern Kentucky University M,O
Northwestern University M,D
Notre Dame de Namur University M
Oakland University M,O
Oklahoma City University M
Oklahoma State University M,D
Old Dominion University D
Oral Roberts University M
Pace University M
Philadelphia University M
Pontifical Catholic University of Puerto Rico M
Providence College M
Quinnipiac University M
Regis University M,O
Roberts Wesleyan College M,O
Rutgers, The State University of New Jersey, Newark M,D
St. Bonaventure University M
St. Cloud State University M
St. Edward's University M,O
St. John's University (NY) M,O
Saint Joseph's University M,O
Saint Peter's College M
St. Thomas Aquinas College M
Saint Xavier University M,O
San Diego State University M
Seton Hall University M
Southern Methodist University M
Southern New Hampshire University M,D,O
Stephen F. Austin State University M
Stony Brook University, State University of New York M,O
Strayer University M
Suffolk University M,O
Syracuse University M,D
Temple University M,D
Texas A&M University M,D
Texas Tech University M,D
Universidad del Turabo M
Universidad Metropolitana M
University at Albany, State University of New York M
The University of Akron M
The University of Alabama M,D
The University of Alabama in Huntsville M,O
The University of Arizona M,D
University of Baltimore M
University of California, Berkeley D,O
University of Central Florida D
University of Cincinnati M,D
University of Colorado at Boulder M,D
University of Colorado at Colorado Springs M
University of Colorado Denver M
University of Connecticut M,D
University of Dallas M
University of Dayton M
University of Denver M
The University of Findlay M
University of Florida M,D
University of Hawaii at Manoa M,D
University of Houston D
University of Houston–Victoria M
The University of Iowa M,D
University of La Verne M
University of Massachusetts Dartmouth M,O
University of Memphis M,D
University of Miami M
University of Minnesota, Twin Cities Campus M,D
University of Missouri–St. Louis M,O
University of Nebraska–Lincoln M,D
University of New Haven M
The University of North Carolina at Chapel Hill D
The University of North Carolina at Charlotte M
The University of North Carolina at Greensboro M,D
University of North Texas D
University of Oregon D
University of Pennsylvania M,D
University of Phoenix M
University of Phoenix–Central Florida Campus M
University of Phoenix–Denver Campus M
University of Phoenix–Hawaii Campus M
University of Phoenix–Las Vegas Campus M
University of Phoenix–Louisiana Campus M
University of Phoenix–New Mexico Campus M
University of Phoenix–North Florida Campus M
University of Phoenix–Oregon Campus M
University of Phoenix–Philadelphia Campus M
University of Phoenix–Phoenix Campus M
University of Phoenix–Sacramento Valley Campus M
University of Phoenix–San Diego Campus M
University of Phoenix–Southern Arizona Campus M
University of Phoenix–Southern California Campus M
University of Phoenix–Southern Colorado Campus M
University of Phoenix–South Florida Campus M
University of Phoenix–Utah Campus M
University of Phoenix–West Florida Campus M
University of Pittsburgh M,D
University of Puerto Rico, Río Piedras M,D
University of Rhode Island D
University of San Francisco M
The University of Scranton M
The University of Tampa M
The University of Tennessee M,D
The University of Texas at Arlington M,D
The University of Texas at Austin D
The University of Texas at Dallas D
The University of Texas at San Antonio M,D
The University of Texas–Pan American D
The University of Toledo M
University of Virginia M
University of Wisconsin–Madison D
University of Wisconsin–Whitewater M
Vanderbilt University D
Villanova University M
Virginia Commonwealth University O
Virginia Polytechnic Institute and State University M,D
Wagner College M
Wake Forest University M
Walden University M,D
Washington State University M,D
Webster University M,D
West Chester University of Pennsylvania M
Western International University M
West Virginia University M
Wilkes University M
Worcester Polytechnic Institute M,O
Wright State University M
Xavier University M
Yale University D
Youngstown State University M

■ MARKETING RESEARCH

American University M
Hofstra University M
Pace University M
Southern Illinois University Edwardsville M
University of Georgia M
The University of Texas at Arlington M
University of Wisconsin–Madison M

■ MARRIAGE AND FAMILY THERAPY

Abilene Christian University M

M—master's degree; P—first professional degree; D—doctorate; O—other advanced degree

Alliant International University–San Diego	M,D
Antioch University New England	M,D
Appalachian State University	M
Argosy University, Orange County	M,D
Argosy University, Sarasota	M,D,O
Argosy University, Tampa	M,D
Argosy University, Twin Cities	M,D,O
Arizona State University	M,D
Azusa Pacific University	M,D
Barry University	M,O
Brigham Young University	M,D
California Lutheran University	M,D
California State University, Chico	M
California State University, Dominguez Hills	M
California State University, Fresno	M
California State University, Long Beach	M
California State University, Northridge	M
Cambridge College	M,O
Capella University	M,D,O
Central Connecticut State University	M,O
Chapman University	M
Chatham University	M,D
The College of New Jersey	O
The College of William and Mary	M,D
Converse College	O
Dominican University of California	M
Drexel University	M,D
East Carolina University	M
Eastern Nazarene College	M
Eastern University	D
East Tennessee State University	M
Edgewood College	M
Fairfield University	M
Fitchburg State College	M,O
Florida Atlantic University	M,D,O
Florida State University	M,D
Friends University	M
Geneva College	M
George Fox University	M,O
Harding University	M
Hardin-Simmons University	M
Hofstra University	M
Hope International University	M
Idaho State University	M,D,O
Indiana Wesleyan University	M
Iona College	M,O
John Brown University	M
Kansas State University	D
Kean University	O
Kutztown University of Pennsylvania	M
La Salle University	D
Lewis & Clark College	M
Loyola Marymount University	M
Maryville University of Saint Louis	M
Mercy College	M
Michigan State University	M,D
Minnesota State University Mankato	M,D,O
Mississippi College	M,O
Montclair State University	M,O
North Dakota State University	M,D
Northwestern University	M
Northwest Nazarene University	M
Notre Dame de Namur University	M
Nova Southeastern University	M,D,O
Oral Roberts University	P,M,D
Our Lady of the Lake University of San Antonio	M,D
Pacific Lutheran University	M
Palm Beach Atlantic University	M
Purdue University	M,D
Purdue University Calumet	M
Regis University	M,O
St. Cloud State University	M
Saint Joseph College	M
Saint Louis University	M,D,O
Saint Mary's College of California	M
St. Mary's University (United States)	M,D
Saint Mary's University of Minnesota	M,O
St. Thomas University	M,O
San Francisco State University	M
Seattle Pacific University	M,O
Seton Hall University	M,D,O
Seton Hill University	M
Shippensburg University of Pennsylvania	M,O
Sonoma State University	M
Southern Connecticut State University	M
Southern Nazarene University	M
Springfield College	M,O
Stetson University	M
Syracuse University	M
Texas Tech University	M,D
Texas Woman's University	M,D
Trevecca Nazarene University	M
The University of Akron	M
University of Arkansas at Little Rock	O
University of Central Florida	M,O
University of Florida	M,D,O
University of Houston–Clear Lake	M
University of La Verne	M
University of Louisiana at Monroe	M,D
University of Louisville	M,D,O
University of Mary Hardin-Baylor	M
University of Maryland, College Park	M,D
University of Massachusetts Boston	M,O
University of Miami	M,O
University of Minnesota, Twin Cities Campus	M,D
University of Mobile	M
University of Montevallo	M
University of Nebraska–Lincoln	M,D
University of Nevada, Las Vegas	M,O
University of New Hampshire	M
The University of North Carolina at Greensboro	M,D,O
University of Phoenix	M
University of Phoenix–Denver Campus	M
University of Phoenix–Hawaii Campus	M
University of Phoenix–Las Vegas Campus	M
University of Phoenix–New Mexico Campus	M
University of Phoenix–Phoenix Campus	M,O
University of Phoenix–Sacramento Valley Campus	M
University of Phoenix–San Diego Campus	M
University of Phoenix–Southern Arizona Campus	M,O
University of Phoenix–Southern California Campus	M,O
University of Phoenix–Southern Colorado Campus	M
University of Rochester	M
University of St. Thomas (MN)	M,D,O
University of San Diego	M
University of San Francisco	M,D
University of Southern California	M
University of Southern Mississippi	M
The University of Texas at Tyler	M
University of Wisconsin–Milwaukee	M,D,O
University of Wisconsin–Stout	M
Utah State University	M,D
Valdosta State University	M
Virginia Polytechnic Institute and State University	M,D
Western Michigan University	M,D

■ MASS COMMUNICATION

American University	M,D,O
Arizona State University	M
Auburn University	M
Boston University	M
Brigham Young University	M
California State University, Fresno	M
California State University, Northridge	M
Central Michigan University	M
The College of Saint Rose	M
Colorado State University	M,D
Drexel University	M
Florida International University	M
Florida State University	M,D

Fordham University	M
The George Washington University	M
Georgia State University	M,D
Grambling State University	M
Howard University	M,D
Indiana University Bloomington	M,D
Iona College	M
Iowa State University of Science and Technology	M
Jackson State University	M
Kansas State University	M
Kent State University	M
Louisiana State University and Agricultural and Mechanical College	M,D
Lynn University	M,D
Marquette University	M
Marshall University	M
Miami University	M
Middle Tennessee State University	M
Murray State University	M
The New School: A University	M
North Dakota State University	M,D
Oklahoma City University	M
Oklahoma State University	M
Point Park University	M
St. Cloud State University	M
San Jose State University	M
Southern Illinois University Carbondale	M
Southern Illinois University Edwardsville	M
Southern University and Agricultural and Mechanical College	M
Stephen F. Austin State University	M
Syracuse University	M,D
Temple University	D
Texas State University–San Marcos	M
Texas Tech University	M,D
The University of Alabama	D
University of Arkansas at Little Rock	M
University of Central Florida	M
University of Central Missouri	M
University of Colorado at Boulder	M,D
University of Denver	M
University of Florida	M,D
University of Georgia	M,D
University of Houston	M
The University of Iowa	M,D
University of Louisiana at Lafayette	M
University of Michigan	D
University of Minnesota, Twin Cities Campus	M,D
University of Nebraska–Lincoln	M
The University of North Carolina at Chapel Hill	M,D
University of Oklahoma	M
University of Puerto Rico, Río Piedras	M
University of Southern California	M,D
University of Southern Mississippi	M,D
University of South Florida	M
University of Wisconsin–Madison	M,D
University of Wisconsin–Stevens Point	M
University of Wisconsin–Superior	M
University of Wisconsin–Whitewater	M
Virginia Commonwealth University	M

■ MATERIALS ENGINEERING

Arizona State University	M,D
Auburn University	M,D
Boise State University	M
Boston University	M,D
California State University, Northridge	M
Carnegie Mellon University	M,D
Case Western Reserve University	M,D
Clemson University	M,D
Colorado School of Mines	M,D
Columbia University	M,D,O
Cornell University	M,D
Dartmouth College	M,D
Drexel University	M,D
Florida International University	M,D
Georgia Institute of Technology	M,D
Illinois Institute of Technology	M,D
Iowa State University of Science and Technology	M,D
The Johns Hopkins University	M,D
Lehigh University	M,D
Massachusetts Institute of Technology	M,D,O
Michigan State University	M,D
Michigan Technological University	M,D
New Jersey Institute of Technology	M,D
New Mexico Institute of Mining and Technology	M,D
North Carolina State University	M,D
Northwestern University	M,D,O
The Ohio State University	M,D
Penn State University Park	M,D
Purdue University	M,D
Rensselaer Polytechnic Institute	M,D
Rochester Institute of Technology	M
Rutgers, The State University of New Jersey, New Brunswick	M,D
San Jose State University	M
Santa Clara University	M,D,O
Stanford University	M,D,O
State University of New York at Binghamton	M,D
Stevens Institute of Technology	M,D
Stony Brook University, State University of New York	M,D
Texas A&M University	M,D
The University of Alabama	M,D
The University of Alabama at Birmingham	M,D
The University of Arizona	M,D
University of California, Berkeley	M,D
University of California, Davis	M,D
University of California, Irvine	M,D
University of California, Los Angeles	M,D
University of California, Riverside	M,D
University of California, Santa Barbara	M,D
University of Central Florida	M,D
University of Cincinnati	M,D
University of Connecticut	M,D
University of Dayton	M,D
University of Delaware	M,D
University of Denver	M,D
University of Florida	M,D,O
University of Houston	M,D
University of Idaho	M,D
University of Illinois at Chicago	M,D
University of Illinois at Urbana–Champaign	M,D
University of Maryland, College Park	M,D,O
University of Massachusetts Lowell	M,D,O
University of Michigan	M,D
University of Minnesota, Twin Cities Campus	M,D
University of Nebraska–Lincoln	M,D
University of Nevada, Las Vegas	M,D
University of Pennsylvania	M,D
University of Southern California	M,D,O
The University of Tennessee	M,D
The University of Texas at Arlington	M,D
The University of Texas at Austin	M,D
The University of Texas at Dallas	M,D
The University of Texas at El Paso	D
University of Utah	M,D
University of Washington	M,D
University of Wisconsin–Madison	M,D
University of Wisconsin–Milwaukee	M,D,O
Virginia Polytechnic Institute and State University	M,D
Washington State University	M
Wayne State University	M,D,O
Worcester Polytechnic Institute	M,D,O
Wright State University	M

■ MATERIALS SCIENCES

Alabama Agricultural and Mechanical University	M,D

M—master's degree; P—first professional degree; D—doctorate; O—other advanced degree

Alfred University	M,D
Arizona State University	M,D
Boston University	M,D
Brown University	M,D
California Institute of Technology	M,D
Carnegie Mellon University	M,D
Case Western Reserve University	M,D
Central Michigan University	D
Clemson University	M,D
Colorado School of Mines	M,D
Columbia University	M,D,O
Cornell University	M,D
Dartmouth College	M,D
Duke University	M,D
Florida State University	M
Georgetown University	D
The George Washington University	M,D
Illinois Institute of Technology	M,D
Iowa State University of Science and Technology	M,D
Jackson State University	M
The Johns Hopkins University	M,D
Lehigh University	M,D
Massachusetts Institute of Technology	M,D,O
Michigan State University	M,D
Missouri State University	M
New Jersey Institute of Technology	M,D
Norfolk State University	M
North Carolina State University	M,D
North Dakota State University	D
Northwestern University	M,D,O
The Ohio State University	M,D
Oregon State University	M,D
Penn State University Park	M,D
Polytechnic Institute of NYU	M
Polytechnic Institute of NYU, Westchester Graduate Center	D
Princeton University	D
Rensselaer Polytechnic Institute	M,D
Rice University	M,D
Rochester Institute of Technology	M
Rutgers, The State University of New Jersey, New Brunswick	M,D
Stanford University	M,D,O
State University of New York at Binghamton	M,D
Stony Brook University, State University of New York	M,D
University at Buffalo, the State University of New York	M
The University of Alabama	D
The University of Alabama at Birmingham	D
The University of Alabama in Huntsville	M,D
The University of Arizona	M,D
University of California, Berkeley	M,D
University of California, Davis	M,D
University of California, Irvine	M,D
University of California, Los Angeles	M,D
University of California, Riverside	M,D
University of California, San Diego	M,D
University of California, Santa Barbara	M,D
University of Central Florida	M,D
University of Cincinnati	M,D
University of Connecticut	M,D
University of Delaware	M,D
University of Florida	M,D,O
University of Idaho	M,D
University of Illinois at Urbana–Champaign	M,D
University of Kentucky	M,D
University of Maryland, College Park	M,D,O
University of Michigan	M,D
University of Minnesota, Twin Cities Campus	M,D
University of Nebraska–Lincoln	M,D
University of New Hampshire	M,D
The University of North Carolina at Chapel Hill	M,D
University of North Texas	M,D
University of Pennsylvania	M,D
University of Pittsburgh	M,D
University of Rochester	M,D
University of Southern California	M,D,O
University of South Florida	M
The University of Tennessee	M,D
The University of Texas at Arlington	M,D
The University of Texas at Austin	M,D
The University of Texas at Dallas	M,D
The University of Texas at El Paso	D
University of Utah	M,D
University of Vermont	M,D
University of Virginia	M,D
University of Washington	M,D
University of Wisconsin–Madison	M,D
Vanderbilt University	M,D
Virginia Polytechnic Institute and State University	M,D
Washington State University	M,D
Wayne State University	M,D,O
Worcester Polytechnic Institute	M,D,O
Wright State University	M

■ MATERNAL AND CHILD/ NEONATAL NURSING

Baylor University	M
Boston College	M,D
Case Western Reserve University	M,D
Columbia University	M,O
Duke University	M,D,O
Hardin-Simmons University	M
Indiana University–Purdue University Indianapolis	M,D
Lehman College of the City University of New York	M
Marquette University	M,D,O
Northeastern University	M,O
Regis University	P,M,D,O
Rutgers, The State University of New Jersey, Newark	M
Stony Brook University, State University of New York	M,O
University at Buffalo, the State University of New York	M,D,O
University of Cincinnati	M,D
University of Colorado at Colorado Springs	M,D
University of Delaware	M,O
University of Illinois at Chicago	M
University of Louisville	M,D
University of Missouri–Kansas City	M,D
University of Pennsylvania	M,O
University of Rochester	M,D,O
University of South Alabama	M,D
University of Southern Mississippi	M,D
Vanderbilt University	M,D
Wayne State University	M,O

■ MATERNAL AND CHILD HEALTH

Boston University	M,D
Columbia University	M
The George Washington University	M
Oakland University	M,D,O
Tulane University	M,D
University of California, Berkeley	M
University of California, Davis	M
University of Maryland, College Park	M,D
University of Minnesota, Twin Cities Campus	M
The University of North Carolina at Chapel Hill	M,D
University of Washington	M,D

■ MATHEMATICAL AND COMPUTATIONAL FINANCE

Bernard M. Baruch College of the City University of New York	M
Boston University	M,D
Carnegie Mellon University	M,D
DePaul University	M,D
Florida State University	M,D
Georgia Institute of Technology	M,D
Illinois Institute of Technology	M
The Johns Hopkins University	M,D
New York University	M,D
North Carolina State University	M
Polytechnic Institute of NYU	M,O
Polytechnic Institute of NYU, Westchester Graduate Center	M,O
Rice University	M,D
Stanford University	M,D
University of California, Santa Barbara	M,D
University of Chicago	M

University of Connecticut	M
University of Dayton	M
University of Illinois at Chicago	M,D
The University of North Carolina at Charlotte	M
University of Pittsburgh	M,D

■ MATHEMATICAL PHYSICS

New Mexico Institute of Mining and Technology	M,D
University of Colorado at Boulder	M,D
Virginia Polytechnic Institute and State University	M,D

■ MATHEMATICS

Alabama State University	M,O
American University	M
Andrews University	M
Appalachian State University	M
Arizona State University	M,D
Arkansas State University	M
Auburn University	M,D
Aurora University	M
Ball State University	M
Baylor University	M,D
Boston College	M
Boston University	M,D
Bowling Green State University	M,D
Brandeis University	M,D,O
Brigham Young University	M,D
Brooklyn College of the City University of New York	M,D
Brown University	M,D
Bucknell University	M
California Institute of Technology	D
California Polytechnic State University, San Luis Obispo	M
California State Polytechnic University, Pomona	M
California State University, East Bay	M
California State University, Fresno	M
California State University, Fullerton	M
California State University, Long Beach	M
California State University, Los Angeles	M
California State University, Northridge	M
California State University, Sacramento	M
California State University, San Bernardino	M
California State University, San Marcos	M
Carnegie Mellon University	M,D
Case Western Reserve University	M,D
Central Connecticut State University	M,O
Central Michigan University	M,D
Central Washington University	M
Chicago State University	M
City College of the City University of New York	M
Claremont Graduate University	M,D
Clark Atlanta University	M
Clarkson University	M,D
Clemson University	M,D
Cleveland State University	M
The College at Brockport, State University of New York	M
College of Charleston	M,O
Colorado School of Mines	M,D
Colorado State University	M,D
Columbia University	M,D
Cornell University	D
Dartmouth College	D
Delaware State University	M
DePaul University	M,O
Dowling College	M
Drexel University	M,D
Duke University	D
Duquesne University	M
East Carolina University	M
Eastern Illinois University	M
Eastern Kentucky University	M
Eastern Michigan University	M
Eastern New Mexico University	M
Eastern Washington University	M
East Tennessee State University	M
Emory University	M,D
Emporia State University	M
Fairfield University	M
Fairleigh Dickinson University, Metropolitan Campus	M
Fayetteville State University	M
Florida Atlantic University	M,D
Florida International University	M
Florida State University	M,D
George Mason University	M,D
Georgetown University	M
The George Washington University	M,D
Georgia Institute of Technology	M,D
Georgian Court University	M,O
Georgia Southern University	M
Georgia State University	M,D
Graduate School and University Center of the City University of New York	D
Hardin-Simmons University	M,D
Harvard University	D
Hofstra University	M
Howard University	M,D
Hunter College of the City University of New York	M
Idaho State University	M,D
Illinois State University	M
Indiana State University	M
Indiana University Bloomington	M,D
Indiana University of Pennsylvania	M
Indiana University–Purdue University Fort Wayne	M,O
Indiana University–Purdue University Indianapolis	M,D
Iowa State University of Science and Technology	M,D
Jackson State University	M
Jacksonville State University	M
James Madison University	M
John Carroll University	M
The Johns Hopkins University	D
Kansas State University	M,D
Kean University	M
Kent State University	M,D
Lamar University	M
Lehigh University	M,D
Lehman College of the City University of New York	M
Long Island University, C.W. Post Campus	M
Louisiana State University and Agricultural and Mechanical College	M,D
Louisiana Tech University	M
Loyola University Chicago	M
Marquette University	M,D
Marshall University	M
Massachusetts Institute of Technology	D
McNeese State University	M
Miami University	M
Michigan State University	M,D
Michigan Technological University	M,D
Middle Tennessee State University	M
Minnesota State University Mankato	M
Mississippi College	M
Mississippi State University	M,D
Missouri State University	M
Missouri University of Science and Technology	M,D
Montana State University	M,D
Montclair State University	M,D,O
Morgan State University	M
Murray State University	M
New Jersey Institute of Technology	D
New Mexico Institute of Mining and Technology	M,D
New Mexico State University	M,D
New York University	M,D
Nicholls State University	M
North Carolina Central University	M
North Carolina State University	M,D
North Dakota State University	M,D
Northeastern Illinois University	M
Northeastern University	M,D
Northern Arizona University	M
Northern Illinois University	M,D

M—master's degree; P—first professional degree; D—doctorate; O—other advanced degree

Northwestern University D
Oakland University M
The Ohio State University M,D
Ohio University M,D
Oklahoma State University M,D
Old Dominion University M,D
Oregon State University M,D
Penn State University Park M,D
Pittsburg State University M
Polytechnic Institute of NYU M,D
Portland State University M,D,O
Prairie View A&M University M
Princeton University D
Purdue University M,D
Purdue University Calumet M
Queens College of the City University of New York M
Rensselaer Polytechnic Institute M,D
Rhode Island College M
Rice University M,D
Rivier College M
Roosevelt University M
Rowan University M
Rutgers, The State University of New Jersey, Camden M
Rutgers, The State University of New Jersey, Newark D
Rutgers, The State University of New Jersey, New Brunswick M,D
St. Cloud State University M
St. John's University (NY) M
Saint Joseph's University M,O
Saint Louis University M,D
Saint Xavier University M
Salem State College M
Sam Houston State University M
San Diego State University M,D
San Francisco State University M
San Jose State University M
South Dakota State University M,D
Southeast Missouri State University M
Southern Connecticut State University M
Southern Illinois University Carbondale M,D
Southern Illinois University Edwardsville M
Southern Methodist University M,D
Southern Oregon University M
Southern University and Agricultural and Mechanical College M
Stanford University M,D
State University of New York at Binghamton M,D
State University of New York at Fredonia M
State University of New York College at Cortland M
State University of New York College at Potsdam M
Stephen F. Austin State University M
Stevens Institute of Technology M,D
Stony Brook University, State University of New York M,D
Syracuse University M,D
Tarleton State University M
Temple University M,D
Tennessee State University M
Tennessee Technological University M
Texas A&M International University M
Texas A&M University M,D
Texas A&M University–Commerce M
Texas A&M University–Corpus Christi M
Texas A&M University–Kingsville M
Texas Christian University M
Texas Southern University M
Texas State University–San Marcos M,D
Texas Tech University M,D
Texas Woman's University M
Tufts University M,D
Tulane University M,D
University at Albany, State University of New York M,D
University at Buffalo, the State University of New York M,D
The University of Akron M
The University of Alabama M,D
The University of Alabama at Birmingham M,D
The University of Alabama in Huntsville M,D
University of Alaska Fairbanks M,D
The University of Arizona M,D
University of Arkansas M,D
University of Arkansas at Little Rock M,O
University of California, Berkeley M,D
University of California, Davis M,D
University of California, Irvine M,D
University of California, Los Angeles M,D
University of California, Riverside M,D
University of California, San Diego M,D
University of California, Santa Barbara M,D
University of California, Santa Cruz M,D
University of Central Arkansas M
University of Central Florida M,D,O
University of Central Missouri M
University of Central Oklahoma M
University of Chicago M,D
University of Cincinnati M,D
University of Colorado at Boulder M,D
University of Colorado at Colorado Springs M
University of Colorado Denver M
University of Connecticut M,D
University of Delaware M,D
University of Denver M,D
University of Florida M,D
University of Georgia M,D
University of Hawaii at Manoa M,D
University of Houston M,D
University of Houston–Clear Lake M
University of Idaho M,D
University of Illinois at Chicago M,D
University of Illinois at Urbana–Champaign M,D
The University of Iowa M,D
The University of Kansas M,D
University of Kentucky M,D
University of Louisiana at Lafayette M,D
University of Louisville M,D
University of Maine M
University of Maryland, College Park M,D
University of Massachusetts Amherst M,D
University of Massachusetts Lowell M,D
University of Memphis M,D
University of Miami M,D
University of Michigan M,D
University of Minnesota, Twin Cities Campus M,D
University of Mississippi M,D
University of Missouri–Columbia M,D
University of Missouri–Kansas City M,D
University of Missouri–St. Louis M,D
The University of Montana M,D
University of Nebraska at Omaha M
University of Nebraska–Lincoln M,D
University of Nevada, Las Vegas M,D
University of Nevada, Reno M
University of New Hampshire M,D,O
University of New Mexico M,D
University of New Orleans M
The University of North Carolina at Chapel Hill M,D
The University of North Carolina at Charlotte M,D
The University of North Carolina at Greensboro M,D
The University of North Carolina Wilmington M
University of North Dakota M
University of Northern Colorado M,D
University of Northern Iowa M
University of North Florida M
University of North Texas M,D
University of Notre Dame M,D
University of Oklahoma M,D
University of Oregon M,D
University of Pennsylvania M,D

University of Pittsburgh M,D
University of Puerto Rico, Mayagüez Campus M
University of Puerto Rico, Río Piedras M,D
University of Rhode Island M,D
University of Rochester M,D
University of South Alabama M
University of South Carolina M,D
The University of South Dakota M
University of Southern California M,D
University of Southern Mississippi M,D
University of South Florida M,D,O
The University of Tennessee M,D
The University of Texas at Arlington M,D
The University of Texas at Austin M,D
The University of Texas at Brownsville M
The University of Texas at Dallas M,D
The University of Texas at El Paso M
The University of Texas at San Antonio M
The University of Texas at Tyler M
The University of Texas–Pan American M
University of the Incarnate Word M
The University of Toledo M,D
University of Tulsa M
University of Utah M,D
University of Vermont M,D
University of Virginia M,D
University of Washington M,D
University of West Florida M
University of West Georgia M
University of Wisconsin–Madison D
University of Wisconsin–Milwaukee M,D
University of Wyoming M,D
Utah State University M,D
Vanderbilt University M,D
Villanova University M
Virginia Commonwealth University M,O
Virginia Polytechnic Institute and State University M,D
Virginia State University M
Wake Forest University M
Washington State University M,D
Washington University in St. Louis M,D
Wayne State University M,D
West Chester University of Pennsylvania M,O
Western Carolina University M
Western Connecticut State University M
Western Illinois University M,O
Western Kentucky University M
Western Michigan University M,D
Western Washington University M
West Texas A&M University M
West Virginia University M,D
Wichita State University M,D
Wilkes University M
Worcester Polytechnic Institute M,D,O
Wright State University M
Yale University M,D
Youngstown State University M

■ MATHEMATICS EDUCATION

Alabama State University M,O
Albany State University M
Alfred University M
Appalachian State University M
Arcadia University M,D,O
Arkansas State University M
Arkansas Tech University M
Armstrong Atlantic State University M
Auburn University M,D,O
Ball State University M
Belmont University M
Bemidji State University M
Bennington College M
Bob Jones University P,M,D,O
Boston College M
Boston University M,D,O
Bowling Green State University M,D
Bridgewater State College M
Brigham Young University M
Brooklyn College of the City University of New York M,O
Buffalo State College, State University of New York M
California State University, Bakersfield M
California State University, Chico M
California State University, Dominguez Hills M
California State University, Fresno M
California State University, Fullerton M
California State University, Long Beach M
California State University, Northridge M
California State University, San Bernardino M
Cambridge College M,D,O
Campbell University M
Central Michigan University M,D
Chatham University M
The Citadel, The Military College of South Carolina M
City College of the City University of New York M,O
Clemson University M
Cleveland State University M
The College at Brockport, State University of New York M
College of Charleston M
The College of William and Mary M
Columbus State University M,O
Converse College M
Cornell University M,D
Delaware State University M
Delta State University M
DePaul University M,O
DeSales University M
Drake University M
Drury University M
Duquesne University M
East Carolina University M
Eastern Illinois University M
Eastern Kentucky University M
Eastern Michigan University M
Eastern Washington University M
The Evergreen State College M
Florida Agricultural and Mechanical University M
Florida Institute of Technology M,D,O
Florida International University M,D
Florida State University M,D,O
Framingham State College M
Fresno Pacific University M
George Mason University M,O
Georgia Southern University M
Georgia State University M,D,O
Grambling State University M,D
Harding University M,O
Harvard University M,O
Hofstra University M
Hood College M,O
Hunter College of the City University of New York M
Idaho State University M,D
Illinois Institute of Technology M,D
Illinois State University D
Indiana State University M
Indiana University Bloomington M,D,O
Indiana University of Pennsylvania M
Indiana University–Purdue University Indianapolis M
Inter American University of Puerto Rico, Metropolitan Campus M
Iona College M
Iowa State University of Science and Technology M,D
Ithaca College M
Jackson State University M
Jacksonville University M
The Johns Hopkins University M,O
Kean University M
Kennesaw State University M
Kutztown University of Pennsylvania M,O
Lehman College of the City University of New York M

M—master's degree; P—first professional degree; D—doctorate; O—other advanced degree

Lewis University M
Long Island University, Brooklyn Campus M
Long Island University, C.W. Post Campus M
Louisiana Tech University M,D
Loyola Marymount University M
Manhattanville College M
Marquette University M,D
Miami University M
Michigan State University M,D
Middle Tennessee State University M
Millersville University of Pennsylvania M
Mills College M,D
Minnesota State University Mankato M
Minot State University M
Mississippi College M,D,O
Missouri University of Science and Technology M,D
Montana State University M,D
Montclair State University M,D,O
Morgan State University M,D
National-Louis University M,O
New Jersey City University M
New York University M
Nicholls State University M
North Carolina Agricultural and Technical State University M
North Carolina Central University M
North Carolina State University M,D
North Dakota State University M,D,O
Northeastern Illinois University M
Northeastern State University M
Northern Arizona University M
North Georgia College & State University M,O
Northwestern State University of Louisiana M
Northwest Missouri State University M
Nova Southeastern University M,O
Oakland University M,D,O
Ohio University M,D
Oklahoma State University M,D
Oregon State University M,D
Our Lady of the Lake University of San Antonio M
Penn State University Park M,D
Plymouth State University M
Portland State University M,D
Providence College M
Purdue University M,D,O
Purdue University Calumet M
Queens College of the City University of New York M,O
Quinnipiac University M
Regent University M,D,O
Rhode Island College M
Rider University O
Rollins College M
Rutgers, The State University of New Jersey, New Brunswick M,D
St. John Fisher College M
Salem State College M
Salisbury University M
San Diego State University M,D
San Francisco State University M
San Jose State University M
Shippensburg University of Pennsylvania M
Siena Heights University M
Slippery Rock University of Pennsylvania M
South Carolina State University M
Southeastern Oklahoma State University M
Southern Illinois University Edwardsville M
Southern University and Agricultural and Mechanical College D
Southwestern Oklahoma State University M
Stanford University M,D
State University of New York at Binghamton M
State University of New York at Plattsburgh M
State University of New York College at Cortland M
State University of New York College at Potsdam M
Stephen F. Austin State University M
Stony Brook University, State University of New York M,O
Syracuse University M,D
Temple University M,D
Texas A&M University M,D
Texas A&M University–Corpus Christi M
Texas State University–San Marcos M,D
Texas Woman's University M
Towson University M
University at Albany, State University of New York M,D
University at Buffalo, the State University of New York M,D,O
University of Arkansas M
University of California, Berkeley M,D
University of California, San Diego D
University of California, Santa Cruz M,D
University of Central Arkansas M
University of Central Florida M,D,O
University of Central Oklahoma M
University of Cincinnati M,D
University of Connecticut M,D,O
University of Detroit Mercy M
University of Florida M,D,O
University of Georgia M,D,O
University of Houston M,D
University of Illinois at Chicago M
University of Illinois at Urbana–Champaign M,D
University of Indianapolis M
The University of Iowa M,D
University of Maryland, Baltimore County M,O
University of Massachusetts Lowell M,D,O
University of Miami D
University of Michigan M,D
University of Minnesota, Twin Cities Campus M
University of Missouri–Columbia M,D,O
The University of Montana M,D
University of Nevada, Reno M
University of New Hampshire M,D,O
The University of North Carolina at Chapel Hill M
The University of North Carolina at Charlotte M
The University of North Carolina at Greensboro M,D,O
The University of North Carolina at Pembroke M
University of Northern Colorado M,D
University of Northern Iowa M
University of Oklahoma M,D,O
University of Phoenix M
University of Phoenix–Central Florida Campus M
University of Phoenix–North Florida Campus M
University of Phoenix–Phoenix Campus M
University of Phoenix–South Florida Campus M
University of Phoenix–West Florida Campus M
University of Pittsburgh M,D
University of Puerto Rico, Río Piedras M,D
University of Rio Grande M
University of St. Francis (IL) M
University of San Diego M
University of South Carolina M,D
University of Southern Mississippi M,D
University of South Florida M,D,O
The University of Tampa M
The University of Tennessee M,D,O
The University of Texas at Austin M,D
The University of Texas at Dallas M
The University of Texas–Pan American M
University of the District of Columbia M
University of the Incarnate Word M,D
The University of Toledo M

University of Tulsa M
University of Vermont M,D
University of Virginia M,D,O
University of Washington M,D
The University of West Alabama M
University of West Georgia M,O
University of Wisconsin–Eau Claire M
University of Wisconsin–Madison M,D
University of Wisconsin–Oshkosh M
University of Wisconsin–River Falls M
University of Wyoming M,D
Ursuline College M
Virginia Polytechnic Institute and State University M,D,O
Virginia State University M
Walden University M,D,O
Washington State University M,D
Wayne State College M
Wayne State University M,D,O
Webster University M,O
Western Carolina University M
Western Connecticut State University M
Western Michigan University M,D
Western New England College M
Western Oregon University M
West Virginia University M,D
Widener University M,D
Wilkes University M
Wright State University M
Youngstown State University M

■ MECHANICAL ENGINEERING

Alfred University M,D
Arizona State University M,D
Auburn University M,D
Baylor University M
Boise State University M
Boston University M,D
Bradley University M
Brigham Young University M,D
Brown University M,D
Bucknell University M
California Institute of Technology M,D,O
California Polytechnic State University, San Luis Obispo M
California State Polytechnic University, Pomona M
California State University, Fresno M
California State University, Fullerton M
California State University, Long Beach M,D
California State University, Los Angeles M
California State University, Northridge M
California State University, Sacramento M
Carnegie Mellon University M,D
Case Western Reserve University M,D
The Catholic University of America M,D
City College of the City University of New York M,D
Clarkson University M,D
Clemson University M,D
Cleveland State University M,D
Colorado State University M,D
Columbia University M,D,O
Cornell University M,D
Dartmouth College M,D
Drexel University M,D
Duke University M,D
Embry-Riddle Aeronautical University (FL) M
Fairfield University M
Florida Agricultural and Mechanical University M,D
Florida Atlantic University M,D
Florida Institute of Technology M,D
Florida International University M,D
Florida State University M,D
Gannon University M
The George Washington University M,D,O
Georgia Institute of Technology M,D
Georgia Southern University M
Graduate School and University Center of the City University of New York D
Grand Valley State University M
Howard University M,D
Idaho State University M
Illinois Institute of Technology M,D
Indiana University–Purdue University Fort Wayne M
Indiana University–Purdue University Indianapolis M,D,O
Iowa State University of Science and Technology M,D
The Johns Hopkins University M,D
Kansas State University M,D
Lamar University M,D
Lawrence Technological University M,D
Lehigh University M,D
Louisiana State University and Agricultural and Mechanical College M,D
Louisiana Tech University M,D
Loyola Marymount University M
Manhattan College M
Marquette University M,D
Massachusetts Institute of Technology M,D,O
McNeese State University M
Mercer University M
Michigan State University M,D
Michigan Technological University M,D
Mississippi State University M,D
Missouri University of Science and Technology M,D
Montana State University M,D
New Jersey Institute of Technology M,D,O
New Mexico State University M,D
North Carolina Agricultural and Technical State University M,D
North Carolina State University M,D
North Dakota State University M,D
Northeastern University M,D
Northern Arizona University M
Northern Illinois University M
Northwestern University M,D
Oakland University M,D
The Ohio State University M,D
Ohio University M,D
Oklahoma State University M,D
Old Dominion University M,D
Oregon State University M,D
Penn State University Park M,D
Polytechnic Institute of NYU M,D
Portland State University M,D,O
Princeton University M,D
Purdue University M,D,O
Purdue University Calumet M
Rensselaer Polytechnic Institute M,D
Rice University M,D
Rochester Institute of Technology M
Rutgers, The State University of New Jersey, New Brunswick M,D
St. Cloud State University M
San Diego State University M,D
San Jose State University M
Santa Clara University M,D,O
South Carolina State University M
South Dakota State University M
Southern Illinois University Carbondale M
Southern Illinois University Edwardsville M
Southern Methodist University M,D
Stanford University M,D,O
State University of New York at Binghamton M,D
Stevens Institute of Technology M,D,O
Stony Brook University, State University of New York M,D
Syracuse University M,D
Temple University M
Tennessee Technological University M,D
Texas A&M University M,D
Texas A&M University–Kingsville M
Texas Tech University M,D
Tufts University M,D

M—master's degree; P—first professional degree; D—doctorate; O—other advanced degree

University at Buffalo, the State University of New York M,D
The University of Akron M,D
The University of Alabama M,D
The University of Alabama at Birmingham M,D
The University of Alabama in Huntsville M,D
University of Alaska Fairbanks M,D
The University of Arizona M,D
University of Arkansas M,D
University of Bridgeport M
University of California, Berkeley M,D
University of California, Davis M,D,O
University of California, Irvine M,D
University of California, Los Angeles M,D
University of California, Riverside M,D
University of California, San Diego M,D
University of California, Santa Barbara M,D
University of Central Florida M,D,O
University of Cincinnati M,D
University of Colorado at Boulder M,D
University of Colorado at Colorado Springs M
University of Colorado Denver M
University of Connecticut M,D
University of Dayton M,D
University of Delaware M,D
University of Denver M,D
University of Detroit Mercy M,D
University of Florida M,D,O
University of Hawaii at Manoa M,D
University of Houston M,D
University of Idaho M,D
University of Illinois at Chicago M,D
University of Illinois at Urbana–Champaign M,D
The University of Iowa M,D
The University of Kansas M,D
University of Kentucky M,D
University of Louisiana at Lafayette M
University of Louisville M
University of Maine M,D
University of Maryland, College Park M,D,O
University of Massachusetts Amherst M,D
University of Massachusetts Dartmouth M
University of Massachusetts Lowell M,D
University of Memphis M,D
University of Miami M,D
University of Michigan M,D
University of Michigan–Dearborn M
University of Minnesota, Twin Cities Campus M,D
University of Missouri–Columbia M,D
University of Missouri–Kansas City M,D
University of Nebraska–Lincoln M,D
University of Nevada, Las Vegas M,D
University of Nevada, Reno M,D
University of New Hampshire M,D
University of New Haven M
University of New Mexico M,D
University of New Orleans M
The University of North Carolina at Charlotte M,D
University of North Dakota M
University of Notre Dame M,D
University of Oklahoma M,D
University of Pennsylvania M,D
University of Pittsburgh M,D
University of Puerto Rico, Mayagüez Campus M
University of Rhode Island M,D
University of Rochester M,D
University of South Alabama M
University of South Carolina M,D
University of Southern California M,D,O
University of South Florida M,D
The University of Tennessee M,D
The University of Tennessee at Chattanooga M
The University of Texas at Arlington M,D
The University of Texas at Austin M,D
The University of Texas at Dallas M
The University of Texas at El Paso M
The University of Texas at San Antonio M
The University of Texas at Tyler M
The University of Texas–Pan American M
The University of Toledo M,D
University of Tulsa M,D
University of Utah M,D
University of Vermont M,D
University of Virginia M,D
University of Washington M,D
University of Wisconsin–Madison M,D
University of Wisconsin–Milwaukee M,D,O
University of Wyoming M,D
Utah State University M,D
Vanderbilt University M,D
Villanova University M,O
Virginia Commonwealth University M,D
Virginia Polytechnic Institute and State University M,D
Washington State University M,D
Washington University in St. Louis M,D
Wayne State University M,D
Western Michigan University M,D
Western New England College M
West Virginia University M,D
Wichita State University M,D
Widener University M
Worcester Polytechnic Institute M,D,O
Wright State University M
Yale University M,D
Youngstown State University M

■ MECHANICS

Brown University M,D
California Institute of Technology M,D
California State University, Fullerton M
Case Western Reserve University M,D
The Catholic University of America M,D,O
Columbia University M,D,O
Cornell University M,D
Drexel University M,D
Georgia Institute of Technology M,D
Iowa State University of Science and Technology M,D
The Johns Hopkins University M
Lehigh University M,D
Louisiana State University and Agricultural and Mechanical College M,D
Michigan State University M,D
Michigan Technological University M
Missouri University of Science and Technology M,D
Montana State University M,D
New Mexico Institute of Mining and Technology M
North Dakota State University M,D
Northwestern University M,D
The Ohio State University M,D
Penn State University Park M,D
Rutgers, The State University of New Jersey, New Brunswick M,D
San Diego State University M,D
Southern Illinois University Carbondale M,D
The University of Alabama M,D
The University of Arizona M,D
University of California, Berkeley M,D
University of California, San Diego M,D
University of Cincinnati M,D
University of Dayton M
University of Illinois at Urbana–Champaign M,D
University of Maryland, College Park M,D
University of Massachusetts Lowell M,D
University of Minnesota, Twin Cities Campus M,D
University of Nebraska–Lincoln M,D
University of Pennsylvania M,D
University of Rhode Island M,D
University of Southern California M,D,O

The University of Tennessee M,D
The University of Texas at Austin M,D
University of Wisconsin–Madison M,D
University of Wisconsin–Milwaukee M,D,O
Virginia Polytechnic Institute and State University M,D
Worcester Polytechnic Institute M,D,O

■ MEDIA STUDIES

American University M
Arizona State University M
Arkansas State University M
Bob Jones University P,M,D,O
Boston University M
California State University, Fullerton M
Carnegie Mellon University M
Central Michigan University M
City College of the City University of New York M
Claremont Graduate University M,D,O
College of Staten Island of the City University of New York M
Columbia College Chicago M
DePaul University M
Drexel University M
Edinboro University of Pennsylvania M
Emerson College M
Fairleigh Dickinson University, Metropolitan Campus M
Florida State University M,D
Fordham University M
Georgetown University M,D
Governors State University M
Howard University M,D
Hunter College of the City University of New York M
Indiana State University M
Indiana University Bloomington M,D
Indiana University of Pennsylvania M,D
Kutztown University of Pennsylvania M
Louisiana State University and Agricultural and Mechanical College M,D
Lynn University M,D
Marquette University M
Marywood University M,O
Massachusetts Institute of Technology M,D
Metropolitan College of New York M
Michigan State University M,D
Monmouth University M,O
National University M
New Mexico Highlands University M
The New School: A University M
New York University M,D
Norfolk State University M
Northwestern University M,D
Ohio University M,D
Rochester Institute of Technology M
Saginaw Valley State University M
San Diego State University M
San Francisco State University M
Southern Illinois University Carbondale M
Southern Illinois University Edwardsville O
Syracuse University M
Temple University M,D
University at Buffalo, the State University of New York M,O
The University of Alabama M
The University of Arizona M
University of California, Santa Barbara M,D
University of Chicago M,D
University of Colorado at Boulder D
University of Denver M
University of Florida M
University of Illinois at Urbana–Champaign D
The University of Iowa M,D
University of Maryland, College Park M,D
University of Michigan M
University of Nevada, Las Vegas M
The University of North Carolina at Greensboro M
University of Oregon M
University of South Carolina M
University of Southern California M,D
The University of Tennessee M,D
The University of Texas at Austin M,D
University of Wisconsin–Madison M,D
University of Wisconsin–Milwaukee M,O
Virginia Commonwealth University D
Washington State University M,D
Wayne State University M,D
Webster University M
William Paterson University of New Jersey M

■ MEDICAL/SURGICAL NURSING

Angelo State University M
Boston College M,D
Case Western Reserve University M,D
Columbia University M,O
Daemen College M,O
Emory University M
Gannon University M,O
New Mexico State University M
Pontifical Catholic University of Puerto Rico M
University of Massachusetts Lowell M,D,O
University of Michigan M
University of South Carolina M
University of Southern Maine M,O
Ursuline College M
Vanderbilt University M,D

■ MEDICAL ILLUSTRATION

The Johns Hopkins University M
Rochester Institute of Technology M
University of Illinois at Chicago M

■ MEDICAL IMAGING

The Catholic University of America M,D
Cleveland State University M
Illinois Institute of Technology M,D
University of Cincinnati D
University of Florida M,D
University of Southern California M,D

■ MEDICAL INFORMATICS

Arizona State University M,D
Cambridge College M
Columbia University M,D,O
Drexel University M,D,O
Grand Valley State University M
Harvard University M
Marymount University M,O
Massachusetts Institute of Technology M
Middle Tennessee State University M
Stanford University M,D
The University of Arizona M,D,O
University of California, Davis M
University of Illinois at Urbana–Champaign M,D,O
The University of Kansas M,D,O
University of Washington M,D
University of Wisconsin–Milwaukee D

■ MEDICAL MICROBIOLOGY

Creighton University M,D
Idaho State University M,D
Rutgers, The State University of New Jersey, New Brunswick M,D
University of Hawaii at Manoa M,D
University of Minnesota, Duluth M,D
University of South Florida M,D
University of Wisconsin–La Crosse M
University of Wisconsin–Madison D

■ MEDICAL PHYSICS

Cleveland State University M
Columbia University M,D,O
East Carolina University M,D
Georgia Institute of Technology M,D
Hampton University M,D
Harvard University D
Louisiana State University and Agricultural and Mechanical College M,D

M—master's degree; P—first professional degree; D—doctorate; O—other advanced degree

Massachusetts Institute of Technology D
Oakland University M,D
Stony Brook University, State University of New York M,D
University of California, Los Angeles M,D
University of Central Arkansas M
University of Chicago D
University of Cincinnati M
University of Colorado at Boulder M,D
University of Kentucky M
University of Minnesota, Twin Cities Campus M,D
University of Missouri–Columbia M,D
University of Pennsylvania M,D
The University of Toledo M
University of Utah D
University of Wisconsin–Madison M,D
Vanderbilt University M
Virginia Commonwealth University M,D
Wayne State University M,D
Wright State University M

■ MEDICINAL AND PHARMACEUTICAL CHEMISTRY

Duquesne University M,D
Florida Agricultural and Mechanical University M,D
Idaho State University M,D
Long Island University, C.W. Post Campus M
The Ohio State University M,D
Purdue University M,D
Rutgers, The State University of New Jersey, New Brunswick M,D
Temple University M,D
University at Buffalo, the State University of New York M,D
University of Connecticut M,D
University of Florida P,M,D
The University of Kansas M,D
University of Michigan D
University of Minnesota, Twin Cities Campus M,D
University of Mississippi M,D
University of Rhode Island M,D
The University of Toledo M,D
University of Utah M,D
University of Washington D
Wayne State University P,M,D
West Virginia University M,D

■ MEDIEVAL AND RENAISSANCE STUDIES

California State University, Long Beach M
The Catholic University of America M,D,O
Columbia University M
Cornell University M,D
Duke University O
Fordham University M,O
Georgetown University M,D
Graduate School and University Center of the City University of New York M,D
Harvard University D
Indiana University Bloomington M,D
Marquette University M,D
Rutgers, The State University of New Jersey, New Brunswick D
Southern Methodist University M
University of California, Santa Barbara M,D
University of Colorado at Boulder M,D
University of Connecticut M,D
University of Michigan O
University of Minnesota, Twin Cities Campus M,D
University of Notre Dame M,D
Western Michigan University M
Yale University M,D

■ METALLURGICAL ENGINEERING AND METALLURGY

Colorado School of Mines M,D
Columbia University M,D,O
Massachusetts Institute of Technology M,D,O
Michigan Technological University M,D
Missouri University of Science and Technology M,D
The Ohio State University M,D
Rensselaer Polytechnic Institute M,D
The University of Alabama M,D
University of Cincinnati M,D
University of Connecticut M,D
University of Idaho M,D
University of Nebraska–Lincoln M,D
The University of Texas at El Paso M
University of Utah M,D
Wayne State University M,D,O

■ METEOROLOGY

Columbia University M
Florida Institute of Technology M,D
Florida State University M,D
Georgia Institute of Technology M,D
Iowa State University of Science and Technology M,D
North Carolina State University M,D
Penn State University Park M,D
Plymouth State University M
Saint Louis University M,D
San Jose State University M
Texas A&M University M,D
University of Hawaii at Manoa M,D
University of Maryland, College Park M,D
University of Miami M,D
University of Oklahoma M,D
Utah State University M,D
Yale University D

■ MICROBIOLOGY

Arizona State University M,D
Auburn University M,D
Boston University M,D
Brandeis University M,D
Brigham Young University M,D
Brown University M,D
California State University, Long Beach M
Case Western Reserve University D
The Catholic University of America M,D
Clemson University M,D
Colorado State University M,D
Columbia University M,D
Cornell University D
Dartmouth College D
Drexel University M,D
Duke University D
East Carolina University D
East Tennessee State University M,D
Emory University D
Emporia State University M
George Mason University M,D,O
Georgetown University M,D
The George Washington University M,D,O
Georgia State University M,D
Harvard University D
Hood College M,O
Howard University D
Idaho State University M,D
Illinois State University M,D
Indiana State University M,D
Indiana University Bloomington M,D
Indiana University–Purdue University Indianapolis M,D
Inter American University of Puerto Rico, Metropolitan Campus M
Iowa State University of Science and Technology M,D
The Johns Hopkins University M,D
Kansas State University D
Long Island University, C.W. Post Campus M
Loyola University Chicago M,D
Marquette University M,D
Massachusetts Institute of Technology D
Miami University M,D
Michigan State University M,D
Montana State University M,D
New York University P,M,D
North Carolina State University M,D
North Dakota State University M,D
Northwestern University D
The Ohio State University M,D
Ohio University M,D
Oklahoma State University M,D

Oregon State University M,D
Penn State University Park M,D
Purdue University M,D
Quinnipiac University M
Rensselaer Polytechnic Institute M,D
Rutgers, The State University of New Jersey, New Brunswick M,D
Saint Louis University D
San Diego State University M
San Francisco State University M
San Jose State University M
Seton Hall University M,D
South Dakota State University M,D
Southern Illinois University Carbondale M,D
Southwestern Oklahoma State University M
Stanford University D
Stony Brook University, State University of New York D
Temple University M,D
Texas A&M University M,D
Texas Tech University M,D
Tufts University D
Tulane University M,D
University at Buffalo, the State University of New York M,D
The University of Alabama at Birmingham D
The University of Arizona M,D
University of California, Berkeley D
University of California, Davis M,D
University of California, Irvine M,D
University of California, Los Angeles M,D
University of California, Riverside M,D
University of California, San Diego D
University of Central Florida M
University of Chicago D
University of Cincinnati M,D
University of Colorado at Boulder M,D
University of Colorado Denver D
University of Connecticut M,D
University of Delaware M,D
University of Florida M,D
University of Georgia M,D
University of Hawaii at Manoa M,D
University of Idaho M,D
University of Illinois at Chicago D
University of Illinois at Urbana–Champaign M,D
The University of Iowa M,D
The University of Kansas M,D
University of Kentucky D
University of Louisville M,D
University of Maine M,D
University of Massachusetts Amherst M,D
University of Miami D
University of Michigan D
University of Minnesota, Twin Cities Campus D
University of Missouri–Columbia M,D
The University of Montana M,D
University of New Hampshire M,D
University of New Mexico M,D
The University of North Carolina at Chapel Hill M,D
University of North Dakota M,D
University of Oklahoma M,D
University of Pennsylvania D
University of Pittsburgh M,D,O
University of Rhode Island M,D
University of Rochester M,D
University of South Alabama D
The University of South Dakota M,D
University of Southern California M,D
University of Southern Mississippi M,D
The University of Tennessee M,D
The University of Texas at Austin D
University of Vermont M,D
University of Virginia D
University of Washington D
University of Wisconsin–La Crosse M
University of Wisconsin–Madison D
University of Wisconsin–Oshkosh M
University of Wyoming D
Utah State University M,D
Vanderbilt University M,D
Virginia Commonwealth University M,D,O
Virginia Polytechnic Institute and State University M,D
Wagner College M
Wake Forest University D
Washington State University M,D
Washington University in St. Louis D
Wayne State University M,D
Western Michigan University M,D
West Virginia University M,D
Wright State University M
Yale University D
Youngstown State University M

■ MIDDLE SCHOOL EDUCATION

Alaska Pacific University M
Albany State University M
American International College M,D,O
Appalachian State University M
Arkansas State University M,O
Armstrong Atlantic State University M
Bellarmine University M
Belmont University M
Brenau University M,O
Brooklyn College of the City University of New York M
California Lutheran University M,D
California State University, Bakersfield M
California State University, Fullerton M
California State University, Stanislaus M,O
Cambridge College M,D,O
Campbell University M
Canisius College M
Capella University M,D,O
Central Michigan University M
Chicago State University M
City College of the City University of New York M,O
Clemson University M
Cleveland State University M
The College at Brockport, State University of New York M
College of Mount St. Joseph M
College of Mount Saint Vincent M,O
Columbus State University M,O
Daemen College M
Drury University M
East Carolina University M
Eastern Illinois University M
Eastern Michigan University M
Eastern Nazarene College M,O
Emory University M,D,O
Fayetteville State University M
Fitchburg State College M
Fresno Pacific University M
Gardner-Webb University M
Georgia College & State University M,O
Georgia Southern University M
Georgia Southwestern State University M,O
Georgia State University M,O
Grand Valley State University M,O
Hampton University M
Henderson State University M
Hofstra University O
Hood College M,O
James Madison University M
John Carroll University M
Kennesaw State University M
Kent State University M
Le Moyne College M,O
Lesley University M,D,O
Lewis & Clark College M
Long Island University, C.W. Post Campus M
Manhattanville College M
Mary Baldwin College M
Maryville University of Saint Louis M,D
Mercer University M,D,O
Mercy College M
Middle Tennessee State University M,O
Montclair State University M,D,O
Morehead State University M,O

M—master's degree; P—first professional degree; D—doctorate; O—other advanced degree

Morgan State University M
Mount Saint Mary College M
Murray State University M,O
Nazareth College of Rochester M
Niagara University M,O
North Carolina Central University M
North Carolina State University M
North Georgia College & State University M,O
Northwestern State University of Louisiana M
Northwest Missouri State University M
Ohio University M,D
Old Dominion University M
Our Lady of the Lake University of San Antonio M
Pacific University M
Park University M
Plymouth State University M
Quinnipiac University M
Roberts Wesleyan College M,O
Saginaw Valley State University M
St. John Fisher College M
St. Thomas Aquinas College M,O
Salem State College M
Shenandoah University M,D,O
Shippensburg University of Pennsylvania M
Siena Heights University M
Simmons College M,O
Southeast Missouri State University M
Spalding University M
State University of New York College at Oneonta M
State University of New York College at Potsdam M
Suffolk University M,O
Texas Christian University M
Tufts University M,D
Union College (KY) M
University at Buffalo, the State University of New York M,D,O
University of Arkansas M,D,O
University of Arkansas at Little Rock M
University of Central Florida M
University of Dayton M
University of Georgia M,D,O
University of Kentucky M,D
University of Louisiana at Monroe M
University of Louisville M
University of Massachusetts Dartmouth M,O
University of Memphis M,D
University of Missouri–St. Louis M,O
The University of North Carolina at Charlotte M
The University of North Carolina at Greensboro M,D,O
The University of North Carolina at Pembroke M
The University of North Carolina Wilmington M
University of Northern Iowa M
University of Phoenix–Oregon Campus M
University of Southern Maine M,O
The University of Toledo M
University of West Florida M
University of West Georgia M,O
University of Wisconsin–Milwaukee M
University of Wisconsin–Platteville M
Ursuline College M
Valdosta State University M,O
Virginia Commonwealth University M,O
Wagner College M
Walden University M,D,O
Western Kentucky University M,O
Widener University M,D
Winthrop University M
Worcester State College M
Wright State University M
Youngstown State University M

■ MILITARY AND DEFENSE STUDIES

Austin Peay State University M
The George Washington University M
Hawai'i Pacific University M
The Johns Hopkins University M
Missouri State University M
Norwich University M
University of Detroit Mercy M
University of Pittsburgh M
The University of Texas at El Paso M

■ MINERAL/MINING ENGINEERING

Colorado School of Mines M,D
Columbia University M,D,O
Michigan Technological University M,D
Missouri University of Science and Technology M,D
New Mexico Institute of Mining and Technology M
Southern Illinois University Carbondale M
University of Alaska Fairbanks M
The University of Arizona M,O
University of Idaho M,D
University of Kentucky M,D
University of Nevada, Reno M
University of North Dakota M
The University of Texas at Austin M
University of Utah M,D
Virginia Polytechnic Institute and State University M,D
West Virginia University M,D

■ MINERAL ECONOMICS

Colorado School of Mines M,D
Michigan Technological University M
The University of Texas at Austin M

■ MINERALOGY

Cornell University M,D
Indiana University Bloomington M,D

■ MISSIONS AND MISSIOLOGY

Abilene Christian University M
Anderson University (IN) P,M,D
Biola University M,D,O
Dallas Baptist University M
Eastern University D
Gardner-Webb University P,D
George Fox University P,M,D,O
Hope International University M
Northwest Nazarene University P,M
Oral Roberts University P,M,D
Regent University P,M,D
Trinity International University P,M,D,O
Wheaton College M,O

■ MOLECULAR BIOLOGY

Appalachian State University M
Arizona State University M,D
Arkansas State University D
Auburn University M,D
Boston University M,D
Brandeis University M,D
Brigham Young University M,D
Brown University M,D
California Institute of Technology D
Carnegie Mellon University M,D
Case Western Reserve University D
Central Connecticut State University M
Clemson University M,D
Colorado State University M,D
Columbia University M,D
Cornell University D
Dartmouth College D
Drexel University M,D
Duke University D,O
East Carolina University M,D
Eastern Michigan University M
Emory University D
Florida Institute of Technology M,D
Florida State University M,D
George Mason University M,D,O
Georgetown University M,D
The George Washington University M,D
Georgia State University M,D
Grand Valley State University M
Harvard University D
Hood College M,O
Howard University M,D
Illinois Institute of Technology M,D

Illinois State University	M,D
Indiana University Bloomington	M,D
Indiana University–Purdue University Indianapolis	D
Inter American University of Puerto Rico, Metropolitan Campus	M
Iowa State University of Science and Technology	M,D
The Johns Hopkins University	M,D
Kent State University	M,D
Lehigh University	M,D
Loyola University Chicago	D
Marquette University	M,D
Massachusetts Institute of Technology	D
Mayo Graduate School	D
Michigan State University	M,D
Mississippi State University	M,D
Missouri State University	M
Montana State University	M,D
Montclair State University	M,O
New Mexico State University	M,D
New York University	P,M,D
North Dakota State University	M,D
Northwestern University	D
The Ohio State University	M,D
Ohio University	M,D
Oklahoma State University	M,D
Oregon State University	M,D
Penn State University Park	M,D
Princeton University	D
Purdue University	M,D
Quinnipiac University	M
Rensselaer Polytechnic Institute	M,D
Rutgers, The State University of New Jersey, New Brunswick	M,D
Saint Louis University	D
San Diego State University	M,D
San Francisco State University	M
San Jose State University	M
Seton Hall University	M,D
Southern Illinois University Carbondale	M,D
Stony Brook University, State University of New York	M,D
Temple University	D
Texas Woman's University	M,D
Tufts University	D
Tulane University	M,D
University at Albany, State University of New York	M,D
University at Buffalo, the State University of New York	D
The University of Alabama at Birmingham	D
The University of Arizona	M,D
University of Arkansas	M,D
University of California, Berkeley	D
University of California, Davis	M,D
University of California, Irvine	M,D
University of California, Los Angeles	M,D
University of California, Riverside	M,D
University of California, San Diego	D
University of California, Santa Barbara	M,D
University of California, Santa Cruz	M,D
University of Central Florida	M
University of Chicago	D
University of Cincinnati	M,D
University of Colorado at Boulder	M,D
University of Colorado Denver	D
University of Connecticut	M
University of Delaware	M,D
University of Florida	M,D
University of Georgia	M,D
University of Hawaii at Manoa	M,D
University of Idaho	M,D
University of Illinois at Chicago	D
The University of Iowa	D
The University of Kansas	M,D
University of Louisville	M,D
University of Maine	M,D
University of Maryland, Baltimore County	M,D
University of Maryland, College Park	D
University of Massachusetts Boston	D
University of Miami	D
University of Michigan	M,D
University of Minnesota, Duluth	M,D
University of Minnesota, Twin Cities Campus	M,D
University of Missouri–Kansas City	D
University of Missouri–St. Louis	M,D,O
University of Nevada, Reno	M,D
University of New Haven	M
University of New Mexico	M,D
The University of North Carolina at Chapel Hill	M,D
University of North Texas	M,D
University of Notre Dame	M,D
University of Oregon	M,D
University of Pennsylvania	D
University of Pittsburgh	D
University of Rhode Island	M,D
University of South Alabama	D
University of South Carolina	M,D
The University of South Dakota	M,D
University of Southern California	M,D
University of Southern Maine	M
University of Southern Mississippi	M,D
University of South Florida	M,D
The University of Texas at Austin	D
The University of Texas at Dallas	M,D
The University of Texas at San Antonio	M,D
The University of Toledo	M
University of Utah	D
University of Vermont	M,D
University of Washington	D
University of Wisconsin–La Crosse	M
University of Wisconsin–Madison	D
University of Wyoming	M,D
Utah State University	M,D
Vanderbilt University	M,D
Virginia Commonwealth University	M,D
Wake Forest University	D
Washington State University	M,D
Washington University in St. Louis	D
Wayne State University	M,D
West Virginia University	M,D
William Paterson University of New Jersey	M
Wright State University	M
Yale University	D
Youngstown State University	M

■ MOLECULAR BIOPHYSICS

California Institute of Technology	M,D
Carnegie Mellon University	D
Duke University	O
Florida State University	D
Illinois Institute of Technology	M,D
The Johns Hopkins University	M,D
Rutgers, The State University of New Jersey, New Brunswick	D
University of Massachusetts Amherst	D
University of Pennsylvania	D
University of Pittsburgh	D
Washington University in St. Louis	D
Yale University	D

■ MOLECULAR GENETICS

Duke University	D
Emory University	D
The George Washington University	D
Georgia State University	M,D
Harvard University	D
Illinois State University	M,D
Indiana University–Purdue University Indianapolis	M,D
Michigan State University	M,D
New York University	M,D
The Ohio State University	M,D
Oklahoma State University	M,D
Rutgers, The State University of New Jersey, New Brunswick	M,D
Stony Brook University, State University of New York	D

M—master's degree; P—first professional degree; D—doctorate; O—other advanced degree

The University of Alabama at Birmingham D
University of California, Irvine M,D
University of California, Los Angeles M,D
University of California, Riverside D
University of Cincinnati M,D
University of Colorado Denver D
University of Florida M,D
University of Illinois at Chicago D
The University of Kansas D
University of Maryland, College Park M,D
University of Pittsburgh M,D
University of Rhode Island M,D
University of Vermont M,D
University of Virginia D
Wake Forest University D
Washington University in St. Louis D

■ MOLECULAR MEDICINE

Boston University D
Case Western Reserve University D
Cleveland State University M,D
Cornell University M,D
Dartmouth College D
The George Washington University D
The Johns Hopkins University D
Penn State University Park M,D
University of Cincinnati D
University of South Florida M,D
University of Washington D
Wake Forest University M,D
Yale University D

■ MOLECULAR PATHOGENESIS

Dartmouth College D
Emory University D
Massachusetts Institute of Technology M,D
North Dakota State University M,D
University at Albany, State University of New York M,D
Washington University in St. Louis D

■ MOLECULAR PATHOLOGY

University of California, San Diego D
University of Michigan D
University of Pittsburgh M,D
Yale University D

■ MOLECULAR PHARMACOLOGY

Brown University M,D
Dartmouth College D
Harvard University D
Massachusetts Institute of Technology M,D
Mayo Graduate School D
New York University D
Purdue University M,D
Rutgers, The State University of New Jersey, New Brunswick D
Stanford University D
University at Buffalo, the State University of New York D
University of Nevada, Reno D
University of Pittsburgh D
University of Southern California M,D
University of South Florida M,D

■ MOLECULAR PHYSIOLOGY

Case Western Reserve University M,D
Loyola University Chicago M,D
Stony Brook University, State University of New York D
Tufts University D
The University of Alabama at Birmingham M,D
University of Chicago D
University of Illinois at Urbana–Champaign M,D
The University of North Carolina at Chapel Hill D
University of Pittsburgh M,D
University of Vermont M,D
University of Virginia M,D
Vanderbilt University M,D
Yale University D

■ MOLECULAR TOXICOLOGY

Massachusetts Institute of Technology M,D
New York University M,D
North Carolina State University M,D
Oregon State University M,D
University of California, Berkeley D
University of California, Los Angeles D
University of Cincinnati M,D

■ MULTILINGUAL AND MULTICULTURAL EDUCATION

Azusa Pacific University M
Belhaven College (MS) M
Bennington College M
Boston University M,O
Brooklyn College of the City University of New York M
Brown University M,D
Buffalo State College, State University of New York M
California Baptist University M
California State University, Bakersfield M
California State University, Chico M
California State University, Dominguez Hills M
California State University, Fullerton M
California State University, Northridge M
California State University, Sacramento M
California State University, San Bernardino M
California State University, Stanislaus M,O
Capella University M,D,O
Chicago State University M
City College of the City University of New York M
The College at Brockport, State University of New York M,O
College of Mount St. Joseph M
College of Mount Saint Vincent M,O
The College of New Rochelle M,O
The College of Saint Rose M,O
College of Santa Fe M
Columbia College Chicago M
DePaul University M,D
Eastern Michigan University M,D,O
Eastern University M
Fairfield University M,O
Fairleigh Dickinson University, Metropolitan Campus M
Florida Atlantic University M,D,O
Fordham University M,D,O
Fresno Pacific University M
George Fox University M,D,O
Georgetown University M,D,O
Harvard University D
Heritage University M
Hofstra University M,O
Howard University M,D
Hunter College of the City University of New York M
Immaculata University M
Indiana State University M,O
Indiana University Bloomington M,D
Kean University M
Lehman College of the City University of New York M
Long Island University, Brooklyn Campus M
Long Island University, C.W. Post Campus M
Loyola Marymount University M
Mercy College M,O
Mercyhurst College M,O
Minnesota State University Mankato M
National University M
New Jersey City University M
New York University M,D,O
Northeastern Illinois University M
Northern Arizona University M
Nova Southeastern University M,O
Ohio University M,D
Our Lady of the Lake University of San Antonio M
Park University M
Penn State University Park M,D
Prescott College M,D
Queens College of the City University of New York M,O

Rutgers, The State University of New Jersey, New Brunswick M,D
St. John's University (NY) M,O
Salem State College M
San Diego State University M,D
Seton Hall University O
Southern Connecticut State University M
Southern Methodist University M,D,O
State University of New York at New Paltz M
State University of New York College at Geneseo M
Sul Ross State University M
Texas A&M International University M,D
Texas A&M University M,D
Texas A&M University–Commerce M,D
Texas A&M University–Kingsville M,D
Texas Southern University M,D
Texas State University–San Marcos M
Texas Tech University M,D
Universidad del Turabo M
University at Buffalo, the State University of New York M,D,O
University of Alaska Fairbanks M,D,O
The University of Arizona M,D,O
University of California, Berkeley M,D
University of Colorado at Boulder M,D
University of Connecticut M,D,O
University of Delaware M,D,O
The University of Findlay M
University of Florida M,D,O
University of Houston M,D
University of Houston–Clear Lake M
University of Illinois at Chicago M,D
University of La Verne O
University of Maryland, Baltimore County M,D
University of Massachusetts Amherst M,D,O
University of Massachusetts Boston M
University of Miami D
University of Michigan M,D
University of Minnesota, Twin Cities Campus M
University of New Mexico D,O
The University of North Carolina at Greensboro M,D,O
University of Oklahoma M,D,O
University of Pennsylvania M,D
University of St. Thomas (MN) M,O
University of San Francisco M,D
University of Southern California D
The University of Tennessee M,D,O
The University of Texas at Brownsville M
The University of Texas at San Antonio M,D
The University of Texas–Pan American M
University of the Incarnate Word M,D
University of Washington M,D
University of Wisconsin–Milwaukee D
Utah State University M
Vanderbilt University M,D
Washington State University M,D
Wayne State University M,D,O
Western New Mexico University M
Western Oregon University M
Xavier University M

■ MUSEUM EDUCATION

The George Washington University M
Seton Hall University M

■ MUSEUM STUDIES

Arizona State University M,D
Baylor University M
Boston University M,D,O
Brown University M,D
California State University, Chico M
Case Western Reserve University M,D
City College of the City University of New York M
Claremont Graduate University M,D,O
Cleveland State University M,D
Duquesne University M
Florida State University M,D,O
The George Washington University M,O
Harvard University M,O
Indiana University–Purdue University Indianapolis M,O
John F. Kennedy University M,O
The Johns Hopkins University M
New York University M,D,O
San Francisco State University M
Seton Hall University M
Southern Illinois University Edwardsville O
State University of New York College at Oneonta M
Syracuse University M
Texas Tech University M
Tufts University O
University at Buffalo, the State University of New York M,O
University of California, Riverside M,D
University of Central Oklahoma M
University of Colorado at Boulder M
University of Denver M
University of Florida M,D
University of Hawaii at Manoa O
The University of Kansas M,O
University of Louisville M,D
University of Missouri–St. Louis M,O
University of New Hampshire M,D
The University of North Carolina at Greensboro M,D,O
University of North Texas M,D,O
University of Oklahoma M
University of South Carolina M,O
University of Washington M
University of West Georgia O
University of Wisconsin–Milwaukee M,D,O
Virginia Commonwealth University M,D
Western Illinois University M

■ MUSIC

Alabama Agricultural and Mechanical University M
Alabama State University M
Andrews University M
Appalachian State University M
Arizona State University M,D
Arkansas State University M,O
Austin Peay State University M
Azusa Pacific University M
Baylor University M
Belmont University M
Bennington College M
Bob Jones University P,M,D,O
Boise State University M
Boston University M,D,O
Bowling Green State University M,D
Brandeis University M,D
Brigham Young University M
Brooklyn College of the City University of New York M,D,O
Brown University D
Butler University M
California Baptist University M
California State University, Chico M
California State University, East Bay M
California State University, Fresno M
California State University, Fullerton M
California State University, Long Beach M
California State University, Los Angeles M
California State University, Northridge M
California State University, Sacramento M
Capital University M
Cardinal Stritch University M
Carnegie Mellon University M
Case Western Reserve University M,D
The Catholic University of America M,D,O
Central Michigan University M
Central Washington University M

M—master's degree; P—first professional degree; D—doctorate; O—other advanced degree

City College of the City University of New York M
Claremont Graduate University M,D
Cleveland State University M
The College of Saint Rose M
Colorado State University M
Columbia University M,D
Concordia University Chicago M
Concordia University Wisconsin M
Converse College M
Cornell University M,D
Dartmouth College M
DePaul University M,O
Duke University M,D
Duquesne University M,O
East Carolina University M
Eastern Illinois University M
Eastern Kentucky University M
Eastern Michigan University M
Eastern Washington University M
Emory University M
Emporia State University M
Florida Atlantic University M
Florida International University M
Florida State University M,D
George Mason University M,O
Georgia Southern University M
Georgia State University M
Graduate School and University Center of the City University of New York D
Gratz College M,O
Hardin-Simmons University M
Harvard University M,D
Hofstra University M
Hollins University M,O
Holy Names University M,O
Hope International University M
Howard University M
Hunter College of the City University of New York M
Illinois State University M
Indiana State University M
Indiana University Bloomington M,D,O
Indiana University of Pennsylvania M
Indiana University–Purdue University Indianapolis M
Indiana University South Bend M
Ithaca College M
Jacksonville State University M
James Madison University D
The Johns Hopkins University M,D,O
Kansas State University M
Kent State University M,D
Lamar University M
Lee University M
Long Island University, C.W. Post Campus M
Louisiana State University and Agricultural and Mechanical College M,D
Loyola University New Orleans M
Lynchburg College M
Lynn University M,O
Mansfield University of Pennsylvania M
Marshall University M
Mercer University M
Miami University M
Michigan State University M,D
Middle Tennessee State University M
Mills College M
Minnesota State University Mankato M
Mississippi College M
Missouri State University M
Montclair State University M,O
Morehead State University M
Morgan State University M
Murray State University M
New Jersey City University M
New Mexico State University M
The New School: A University M,O
New York University M,D,O
Norfolk State University M
North Carolina Central University M
North Dakota State University M,D
Northeastern Illinois University M
Northern Arizona University M
Northern Illinois University M,O
Northwestern State University of Louisiana M
Northwestern University M,D,O
Notre Dame de Namur University M
Oakland University M,D
The Ohio State University M,D
Ohio University M,O
Oklahoma City University M
Oklahoma State University M
Penn State University Park M,D
Pittsburg State University M
Point Park University M
Portland State University M
Princeton University D
Purchase College, State University of New York M
Queens College of the City University of New York M
Radford University M
Regis University M,O
Rice University M,D
Roosevelt University M,O
Rowan University M
Rutgers, The State University of New Jersey, Newark M
Rutgers, The State University of New Jersey, New Brunswick M,D,O
St. Cloud State University M
Samford University M
Sam Houston State University M
San Diego State University M
San Francisco State University M
San Jose State University M
Santa Clara University M
Shenandoah University M,D,O
Southeastern Louisiana University M
Southern Illinois University Carbondale M
Southern Illinois University Edwardsville M
Southern Methodist University M,O
Southern Oregon University M
Southwestern Oklahoma State University M
Stanford University M,D
State University of New York at Binghamton M
State University of New York at Fredonia M
State University of New York at New Paltz M
State University of New York College at Potsdam M
Stephen F. Austin State University M
Stony Brook University, State University of New York M,D
Syracuse University M
Temple University M,D
Texas A&M University–Commerce M
Texas Christian University M,O
Texas Southern University M
Texas State University–San Marcos M
Texas Tech University M,D
Texas Woman's University M
Towson University M
Truman State University M
Tufts University M
Tulane University M
University at Buffalo, the State University of New York M,D
The University of Akron M
The University of Alabama M,D
University of Alaska Fairbanks M
The University of Arizona M,D
University of Arkansas M
University of California, Berkeley D
University of California, Davis M,D
University of California, Irvine M
University of California, Los Angeles M,D
University of California, Riverside M,D
University of California, San Diego M,D
University of California, Santa Barbara M,D
University of California, Santa Cruz M,D
University of Central Arkansas M
University of Central Florida M
University of Central Missouri M
University of Central Oklahoma M
University of Chicago M,D

University of Cincinnati M,D,O
University of Colorado at Boulder M,D
University of Colorado Denver M
University of Connecticut M,D,O
University of Delaware M
University of Denver M,O
University of Florida M,D
University of Georgia M,D
University of Hartford M,D,O
University of Hawaii at Manoa M,D
University of Houston M,D
University of Idaho M
University of Illinois at Urbana–Champaign M,D,O
The University of Iowa M,D
The University of Kansas M,D
University of Kentucky M,D
University of Louisiana at Lafayette M
University of Louisiana at Monroe M
University of Louisville M,D
University of Maine M
University of Maryland, Baltimore County O
University of Maryland, College Park M,D
University of Massachusetts Amherst M,D
University of Massachusetts Lowell M
University of Memphis M,D
University of Miami M,D,O
University of Michigan M,D,O
University of Minnesota, Duluth M
University of Minnesota, Twin Cities Campus M,D
University of Mississippi M,D
University of Missouri–Columbia M
University of Missouri–Kansas City M,D
The University of Montana M
University of Nebraska at Omaha M
University of Nebraska–Lincoln M,D
University of Nevada, Las Vegas M,D
University of Nevada, Reno M
University of New Hampshire M
University of New Mexico M
University of New Orleans M
The University of North Carolina at Chapel Hill M,D
The University of North Carolina at Greensboro M,D
University of North Dakota M,D
University of Northern Colorado M,D
University of Northern Iowa M
University of North Texas M,D
University of Oklahoma M,D
University of Oregon M,D
University of Pennsylvania M,D
University of Pittsburgh M,D
University of Portland M
University of Redlands M
University of Rhode Island M
University of Rochester M,D
University of South Carolina M,D,O
The University of South Dakota M
University of Southern California M,D
University of Southern Maine M
University of Southern Mississippi M,D
University of South Florida M,D
The University of Tennessee M
The University of Tennessee at Chattanooga M
The University of Texas at Arlington M
The University of Texas at Austin M,D
The University of Texas at El Paso M
The University of Texas at San Antonio M,O
The University of Texas–Pan American M
University of the Pacific M
The University of Toledo M
University of Utah M,D
University of Virginia M,D
University of Washington M,D
University of West Georgia M
University of Wisconsin–Madison M,D
University of Wisconsin–Milwaukee M,O
University of Wyoming M
Virginia Commonwealth University M
Washington State University M
Washington University in St. Louis M,D
Wayne State University M,O
Webster University M
West Chester University of Pennsylvania M,O
Western Carolina University M
Western Illinois University M
Western Michigan University M
Western Oregon University M
Western Washington University M
West Texas A&M University M
West Virginia University M,D
Wichita State University M
William Paterson University of New Jersey M
Winthrop University M
Wright State University M
Yale University M,D,O
Youngstown State University M

■ MUSIC EDUCATION

Alabama Agricultural and Mechanical University M
Albany State University M
Appalachian State University M
Arcadia University M,D,O
Arizona State University M,D
Arkansas State University M,O
Auburn University M,D,O
Austin Peay State University M
Azusa Pacific University M
Ball State University M,D
Belmont University M
Bennington College M
Bob Jones University P,M,D,O
Boise State University M
Boston University M,D
Bowling Green State University M,D
Brigham Young University M
Brooklyn College of the City University of New York M,D,O
Butler University M
California Baptist University M
California State University, Fresno M
California State University, Fullerton M
California State University, Los Angeles M
California State University, Northridge M
Capital University M
Carnegie Mellon University M
Case Western Reserve University M,D
The Catholic University of America M,D,O
Central Connecticut State University M,O
Central Michigan University M
Cleveland State University M
College of Charleston M
College of Mount St. Joseph M
The College of Saint Rose M,O
Columbus State University M
Converse College M
DePaul University M,O
Duquesne University M,O
East Carolina University M
Eastern Kentucky University M
Eastern Michigan University M
Eastern Washington University M
Emporia State University M
Florida International University M
Florida State University M,D
George Mason University M,O
Georgia College & State University M
Georgia State University M,D,O
Hampton University M
Hardin-Simmons University M
Hofstra University M
Holy Names University M,O
Howard University M
Hunter College of the City University of New York M
Indiana University of Pennsylvania M

M—master's degree; P—first professional degree; D—doctorate; O—other advanced degree

Inter American University of Puerto Rico, Metropolitan Campus M
Inter American University of Puerto Rico, San Germán Campus M
Ithaca College M
Jackson State University M
Jacksonville University M
James Madison University M,D
Kansas State University M
Kent State University M,D
Kutztown University of Pennsylvania O
Lamar University M
Lee University M
Lehman College of the City University of New York M
Long Island University, C.W. Post Campus M
Louisiana State University and Agricultural and Mechanical College M,D
Manhattanville College M
Marywood University M
McNeese State University M
Miami University M
Michigan State University M,D
Minot State University M
Mississippi College M
Missouri State University M
Montclair State University M,O
Morehead State University M
Murray State University M
Nazareth College of Rochester M
New Jersey City University M
New Mexico State University M
New York University M,D,O
Norfolk State University M
North Dakota State University M,D,O
Northern Arizona University M
Northwestern University M,D
Northwest Missouri State University M
Notre Dame de Namur University M
Oakland University M,D
Ohio University M,O
Oklahoma State University M
Old Dominion University M
Oregon State University M
Penn State University Park M,D
Pittsburg State University M
Portland State University M
Queens College of the City University of New York M,O
Radford University M
Rhode Island College M
Rollins College M
Roosevelt University M,O
Rutgers, The State University of New Jersey, New Brunswick M,D,O
St. Cloud State University M
Samford University M
Sam Houston State University M
San Diego State University M
San Francisco State University M
Shenandoah University M,D,O
Silver Lake College M
Southeast Missouri State University M
Southern Illinois University Carbondale M
Southern Illinois University Edwardsville M,O
Southern Methodist University M,O
Southwestern Oklahoma State University M
State University of New York at Fredonia M
State University of New York College at Potsdam M
Syracuse University M
Tarleton State University M
Temple University M,D
Tennessee State University M
Texas A&M University–Commerce M
Texas A&M University–Kingsville M
Texas Christian University M,O
Texas State University–San Marcos M
Texas Tech University M,D
Towson University M,O
Union College (KY) M
University at Buffalo, the State University of New York M,D,O
The University of Akron M
The University of Alabama M,D,O
University of Alaska Fairbanks M
The University of Arizona M,D
University of Central Arkansas M
University of Central Oklahoma M
University of Cincinnati M
University of Colorado at Boulder M,D
University of Connecticut M,D,O
University of Dayton M
University of Delaware M
University of Denver M,O
University of Florida M,D
University of Georgia M,D,O
University of Hartford M,D,O
University of Houston M,D
University of Illinois at Urbana–Champaign M,D,O
The University of Kansas M,D
University of Kentucky M,D
University of Louisiana at Lafayette M
University of Louisville M
University of Maryland, College Park M,D
University of Massachusetts Lowell M
University of Memphis M,D
University of Miami M,D,O
University of Michigan M,D,O
University of Minnesota, Duluth M
University of Missouri–Columbia M,D,O
University of Missouri–Kansas City M,D
University of Missouri–St. Louis M
The University of Montana M
University of Nebraska at Kearney M
University of Nebraska–Lincoln M,D
University of New Hampshire M
The University of North Carolina at Chapel Hill M
The University of North Carolina at Charlotte M
The University of North Carolina at Greensboro M,D
The University of North Carolina at Pembroke M
University of North Dakota M,D
University of Northern Colorado M,D
University of Northern Iowa M
University of North Texas M,D
University of Oklahoma M,D
University of Oregon M,D
University of Rhode Island M,D
University of Rochester M,D
University of St. Thomas (MN) M
University of South Carolina M,D,O
University of Southern California M,D
University of Southern Mississippi M,D
University of South Florida M,D
The University of Tennessee M
The University of Texas at Arlington M
The University of Texas at El Paso M
The University of Texas–Pan American M
University of the Pacific M
The University of Toledo M
University of Washington M,D
University of West Georgia M
University of Wisconsin–Madison M,D
University of Wisconsin–Milwaukee M,O
University of Wisconsin–Stevens Point M
University of Wyoming M
Virginia Commonwealth University M
Washington State University M
Wayne State College M
Wayne State University M,O
Webster University M
West Chester University of Pennsylvania M,O
Western Connecticut State University M

Western Kentucky University	M
Western Michigan University	M
West Virginia University	M,D
Wichita State University	M
Winthrop University	M
Wright State University	M
Youngstown State University	M

■ NANOTECHNOLOGY

Arizona State University	M,D
George Mason University	M,D,O
The Johns Hopkins University	M
North Dakota State University	D
Oregon State University	M,D
University at Albany, State University of New York	M,D
University of California, Riverside	M,D
University of New Mexico	M,D
University of Washington	M,D
Virginia Commonwealth University	D
Western Michigan University	M,D

■ NATIONAL SECURITY

California State University, San Bernardino	M
Kansas State University	M,D
New York University	M
Texas A&M University	M,O
Trinity (Washington) University	M
Troy University	M
University of New Haven	M
University of Pittsburgh	M
The University of Texas at El Paso	M

■ NATURAL RESOURCES

American University	M,D,O
Auburn University	M,D
Ball State University	M
California Polytechnic State University, San Luis Obispo	M
Central Washington University	M
Colorado State University	M,D
Cornell University	M,D
Delaware State University	M
Duke University	M,D
East Carolina University	D
Georgia Institute of Technology	M,D
Humboldt State University	M
Iowa State University of Science and Technology	M,D
Louisiana State University and Agricultural and Mechanical College	M,D
Michigan State University	M,D
Missouri State University	M
Montana State University	M
North Carolina State University	M,D
North Dakota State University	M,D
The Ohio State University	M,D
Oklahoma State University	M,D
Penn State University Park	M,D
Purdue University	M,D
San Francisco State University	M
State University of New York College of Environmental Science and Forestry	M,D
Texas A&M University	M,D
Texas Tech University	M,D
Universidad Metropolitana	M
University of Alaska Fairbanks	M
University of Arkansas at Monticello	M
University of California, Berkeley	M,D
University of Connecticut	M,D
University of Florida	M,D
University of Georgia	M,D
University of Hawaii at Manoa	M,D
University of Idaho	M,D
University of Illinois at Urbana–Champaign	M,D
University of Maine	M,D
University of Maryland, College Park	M,D
University of Michigan	M,D
University of Minnesota, Twin Cities Campus	M,D
University of Missouri–Columbia	M
The University of Montana	M,D
University of Nebraska–Lincoln	M,D
University of New Hampshire	M,D
University of Oklahoma	M,D
University of Rhode Island	M,D
University of San Francisco	M
The University of Texas at Austin	M
University of Vermont	M,D
University of Washington	M,D
University of Wisconsin–Madison	M,D
University of Wisconsin–Stevens Point	M
University of Wyoming	M,D
Utah State University	M
Virginia Polytechnic Institute and State University	M
Washington State University	M,D
West Virginia University	M,D

■ NATUROPATHIC MEDICINE

University of Bridgeport	D

■ NEAR AND MIDDLE EASTERN LANGUAGES

Brandeis University	M,D
The Catholic University of America	M,D
Columbia University	M,D
Georgetown University	M,D
Harvard University	M,D
Indiana University Bloomington	M,D
The Ohio State University	M,D
Oral Roberts University	P,M,D
University of California, Los Angeles	M,D
University of Chicago	M,D
University of Maryland, College Park	M,O
University of Michigan	M,D
The University of Texas at Austin	M,D
University of Utah	M,D
University of Wisconsin–Madison	M,D
Yale University	M,D

■ NEAR AND MIDDLE EASTERN STUDIES

Brandeis University	M,D
California State University, Long Beach	M
The Catholic University of America	M,D
Columbia University	M,D,O
Cornell University	M,D
Drew University	M,D
Emory University	D,O
Georgetown University	M,D,O
The George Washington University	M
Harvard University	M,D
The Johns Hopkins University	D
New York University	M,D,O
Princeton University	M,D
Regent University	M
SIT Graduate Institute	M
The University of Arizona	M,D
University of California, Berkeley	M,D
University of California, Los Angeles	M,D
University of Chicago	M,D
The University of Kansas	M
University of Michigan	M,D
University of Pennsylvania	M,D
The University of Texas at Austin	M,D
University of Utah	M,D
University of Washington	M,D
University of Wisconsin–Madison	M,D
Wayne State University	M
Yale University	M,D

■ NEUROBIOLOGY

Brandeis University	M,D
California Institute of Technology	D
Carnegie Mellon University	M,D
Case Western Reserve University	D
Columbia University	D
Cornell University	D
Duke University	D
Georgia State University	M,D
Harvard University	D
Illinois State University	M,D
Loyola University Chicago	M,D
Marquette University	M,D
Massachusetts Institute of Technology	D
New York University	M,D
Northwestern University	M,D
Purdue University	M,D

M—master's degree; P—first professional degree; D—doctorate; O—other advanced degree

University at Albany, State University of New York M,D
The University of Alabama at Birmingham D
University of California, Irvine M,D
University of California, Los Angeles D
University of California, San Diego D
University of Chicago D
University of Colorado at Boulder M,D
University of Connecticut M,D
University of Illinois at Chicago D
The University of Iowa M,D
University of Kentucky D
University of Louisville M,D
University of Minnesota, Twin Cities Campus M,D
University of Missouri–Columbia M,D
The University of North Carolina at Chapel Hill D
University of Oklahoma D
University of Pittsburgh D
University of Rochester M,D
University of Southern California M,D
The University of Texas at Austin D
The University of Texas at San Antonio M,D
University of Utah D
University of Washington D
University of Wisconsin–Madison D
Virginia Commonwealth University D
Wake Forest University D
Wayne State University D
West Virginia University M,D
Yale University D

■ NEUROSCIENCE

American University D
Argosy University, Tampa M,D
Arizona State University M,D
Baylor University M,D
Boston University M,D
Brandeis University M,D
Brigham Young University M,D
Brown University D
California Institute of Technology M,D
Carnegie Mellon University D
Case Western Reserve University D
Central Michigan University M,D
College of Staten Island of the City University of New York M
Colorado State University D
Dartmouth College D
Delaware State University M,D
Drexel University M,D
Duke University D,O
Emory University D
Florida Atlantic University D
Florida State University D
George Mason University M,D,O
Georgetown University D
Graduate School and University Center of the City University of New York D
Harvard University D
Illinois State University M,D
Indiana University Bloomington D
Iowa State University of Science and Technology M,D
The Johns Hopkins University D
Kent State University M,D
Lehigh University M,D
Loyola University Chicago M,D
Massachusetts Institute of Technology D
Mayo Graduate School D
Michigan State University M,D
Montana State University M,D
New York University P,M,D
Northwestern University D
The Ohio State University M,D
Ohio University M,D
Penn State University Park M,D
Princeton University D
Rutgers, The State University of New Jersey, Newark D
Rutgers, The State University of New Jersey, New Brunswick D
Seton Hall University M,D
Stanford University D
Stony Brook University, State University of New York D
Temple University M,D
Texas A&M University M,D
Tufts University D
Tulane University M,D
University at Albany, State University of New York M,D
University at Buffalo, the State University of New York M,D
The University of Alabama at Birmingham D
The University of Arizona D
University of California, Berkeley D
University of California, Davis D
University of California, Los Angeles D
University of California, Riverside D
University of California, San Diego D
University of Chicago D
University of Cincinnati D
University of Colorado Denver D
University of Connecticut M,D,O
University of Delaware D
University of Florida M,D
University of Georgia D
University of Hartford M
University of Idaho M,D
University of Illinois at Chicago D
University of Illinois at Urbana–Champaign D
The University of Iowa D
The University of Kansas M,D
University of Maryland, Baltimore County D
University of Maryland, College Park M,D
University of Massachusetts Amherst M,D
University of Miami M,D
University of Michigan D
University of Minnesota, Twin Cities Campus M,D
University of Missouri–Columbia M,D
University of Missouri–St. Louis M,D,O
The University of Montana M,D
University of New Mexico M,D
University of Oregon M,D
University of Pennsylvania D
University of Pittsburgh D
University of Rochester M,D
University of South Alabama D
The University of South Dakota M,D
University of Southern California M,D
University of South Florida M,D
The University of Texas at Austin D
The University of Texas at Dallas M,D
The University of Toledo M,D
University of Utah D
University of Vermont D
University of Virginia D
University of Wisconsin–Madison D
Vanderbilt University D
Virginia Commonwealth University M,D
Wake Forest University D
Washington State University M,D
Washington University in St. Louis D
West Virginia University D
Yale University D

■ NONPROFIT MANAGEMENT

American International College M
American University M,D,O
Arizona State University M,D
Assumption College M,O
Azusa Pacific University M
Bernard M. Baruch College of the City University of New York M
Boston University M,O
Brandeis University M
Cambridge College M
Capella University M,D,O
Carlow University M
Case Western Reserve University M,O
Cleveland State University M,D,O
The College at Brockport, State University of New York M,O
College of Notre Dame of Maryland M
The College of Saint Rose O
Columbia University M

Dallas Baptist University M
DePaul University M,O
Eastern Michigan University M,O
Eastern University M
Fairleigh Dickinson University, Metropolitan Campus M,O
Florida Atlantic University M
The George Washington University M
Georgia State University M,D,O
Hamline University M,D
High Point University M
Hope International University M
Husson University M
Illinois Institute of Technology M
Indiana University Bloomington M,D,O
Indiana University Northwest M,O
Indiana University–Purdue University Indianapolis M
Indiana University South Bend M,O
John Carroll University M
Kean University M
Lipscomb University M
Long Island University, C.W. Post Campus M,O
Marylhurst University M
Metropolitan State University M,O
MidAmerica Nazarene University M
New Mexico Highlands University M
The New School: A University M
New York University M,D,O
North Carolina State University M,D,O
North Central College M
Northern Kentucky University M,O
Oral Roberts University M
Our Lady of the Lake University of San Antonio M
Pace University M
Park University M
Providence College M
Regis College (MA) M,O
Regis University M,O
Robert Morris University M
Roberts Wesleyan College M,O
St. Cloud State University M
Saint Xavier University M,O
San Francisco State University M
Seattle University M
Seton Hall University M,O
Southern New Hampshire University M,D,O
Suffolk University M,O
Texas A&M University M,O
Trinity (Washington) University M
Troy University M
Tufts University O
University of Arkansas at Little Rock O
University of Central Florida M,O
University of Connecticut M,O
University of Dallas M
University of Delaware M,D
University of Georgia M,O
The University of Iowa M
University of La Verne M,O
University of Louisville M
University of Maryland, Baltimore County M,O
University of Memphis M
University of Michigan–Dearborn M,O
University of Missouri–St. Louis M,O
University of Nevada, Las Vegas M,D,O
The University of North Carolina at Greensboro M,O
University of Northern Iowa M
University of Notre Dame M
University of Pittsburgh M
University of San Diego M,D,O
University of San Francisco M
University of Southern Maine M,O
The University of Tampa M
University of Wisconsin–Milwaukee M,D,O
Virginia Commonwealth University O
Walden University M,D,O
West Chester University of Pennsylvania M,O
Western Illinois University M,O
Western Michigan University M,D,O
Worcester State College M

■ NORTHERN STUDIES

University of Alaska Fairbanks M

■ NUCLEAR ENGINEERING

Colorado School of Mines M,D
Cornell University M,D
Georgia Institute of Technology M,D
Idaho State University M,D,O
Kansas State University M,D
Massachusetts Institute of Technology M,D,O
Missouri University of Science and Technology M,D
North Carolina State University M,D
The Ohio State University M,D
Oregon State University M,D
Penn State University Park M,D
Purdue University M,D
Rensselaer Polytechnic Institute M,D
Texas A&M University M,D
University of California, Berkeley M,D
University of Cincinnati M,D
University of Florida M,D,O
University of Idaho M,D
University of Illinois at Urbana–Champaign M,D
University of Maryland, College Park M,D
University of Massachusetts Lowell M,D
University of Michigan M,D,O
University of Missouri–Columbia M,D
University of Nevada, Las Vegas M,D
University of New Mexico M,D
University of South Carolina M,D
The University of Tennessee M,D
University of Utah M,D
University of Wisconsin–Madison M,D
Virginia Commonwealth University M

■ NURSE ANESTHESIA

Arkansas State University M
Barry University M
Boston College M,D
Bradley University M
Case Western Reserve University M
Central Connecticut State University M,O
Columbia University M,O
DePaul University M
Drexel University M
Duke University M,D,O
Emory University M,D
Fairfield University M,O
Gannon University M,O
Georgetown University M
Gonzaga University M
La Roche College M
Lincoln Memorial University M
Missouri State University M
Mountain State University M,O
Mount Marty College M
Murray State University M
Newman University M
Northeastern University M,O
Oakland University M,O
Old Dominion University M
Saint Joseph's University M,O
Saint Mary's University of Minnesota M
Samford University M,D
Southern Illinois University Edwardsville M,O
Texas Christian University M
Texas Wesleyan University M,D
Union University M,D,O
University at Buffalo, the State University of New York M,D,O
The University of Alabama at Birmingham M
University of Cincinnati M,D
University of Detroit Mercy M
The University of Kansas M
University of Miami M,D
University of Michigan–Flint M
University of Minnesota, Twin Cities Campus M
University of New England M
The University of North Carolina at Charlotte M

M—master's degree; P—first professional degree; D—doctorate; O—other advanced degree

The University of North Carolina at Greensboro	M,D,O
University of Pennsylvania	M
University of Pittsburgh	M
The University of Scranton	M,O
University of South Carolina	M
The University of Tennessee at Chattanooga	M,O
University of Wisconsin–La Crosse	M
Villanova University	M,D,O
Virginia Commonwealth University	M,D
Wayne State University	M,O
Webster University	M
Westminster College (UT)	M

■ NURSE MIDWIFERY

Case Western Reserve University	M,D
Columbia University	M
DeSales University	M
Emory University	M
Georgetown University	M
Marquette University	M,D,O
New York University	M,O
Old Dominion University	M
Philadelphia University	M,O
Shenandoah University	M,O
Stony Brook University, State University of New York	M,O
University of Cincinnati	M,D
University of Illinois at Chicago	M
University of Indianapolis	M
The University of Kansas	M,D,O
University of Miami	M,D
University of Michigan	M,O
University of Minnesota, Twin Cities Campus	M
University of Pennsylvania	M
Vanderbilt University	M,D
Wichita State University	M

■ NURSING—GENERAL

Abilene Christian University	M,O
Adelphi University	M,D,O
Albany State University	M
Alcorn State University	M
Alverno College	M
American International College	M
Andrews University	M
Arizona State University	M,D,O
Arkansas State University	M
Arkansas Tech University	M
Armstrong Atlantic State University	M
Augsburg College	M
Austin Peay State University	M
Azusa Pacific University	M,D
Ball State University	M
Barry University	M,D,O
Baylor University	M
Bellarmine University	M,D
Belmont University	M
Bethel University	M,O
Bloomsburg University of Pennsylvania	M
Boston College	M,D
Bowie State University	M
Bradley University	M
Brigham Young University	M
California Baptist University	M
California State University, Bakersfield	M
California State University, Chico	M
California State University, Dominguez Hills	M
California State University, Fresno	M
California State University, Fullerton	M
California State University, Long Beach	M
California State University, Los Angeles	M
California State University, Sacramento	M
California State University, San Bernardino	M
Capital University	M
Cardinal Stritch University	M
Carlow University	M,D
Carson-Newman College	M
Case Western Reserve University	M,D
The Catholic University of America	M,D,O
Chatham University	M,D
Clarion University of Pennsylvania	M
Clemson University	M
Cleveland State University	M
College of Mount St. Joseph	M
College of Mount Saint Vincent	M,O
The College of New Jersey	M,O
The College of New Rochelle	M,O
College of Saint Elizabeth	M
The College of St. Scholastica	M,O
College of Staten Island of the City University of New York	M,O
Columbia University	M,D,O
Concordia University Wisconsin	M
Coppin State University	M,O
Creighton University	M,D
Daemen College	M,O
Delaware State University	M
Delta State University	M
DePaul University	M
DeSales University	M
Dominican College	M
Dominican University of California	M
Drexel University	M
Duke University	D
Duquesne University	M,D,O
D'Youville College	M,O
East Carolina University	M,D
Eastern Kentucky University	M
Eastern Washington University	M
East Tennessee State University	M,D,O
Edgewood College	M
Edinboro University of Pennsylvania	M
Elmhurst College	M
Emory University	M,D
Fairfield University	M,O
Fairleigh Dickinson University, Metropolitan Campus	M,D,O
Ferris State University	M
Florida Agricultural and Mechanical University	M
Florida Atlantic University	M,D,O
Florida Gulf Coast University	M
Florida International University	M,D
Florida State University	M,O
Fort Hays State University	M
Framingham State College	M
Franciscan University of Steubenville	M
Gannon University	M,O
Gardner-Webb University	M,O
George Mason University	M,D,O
Georgetown University	M
The George Washington University	M,D,O
Georgia College & State University	M
Georgia Southern University	M,D,O
Georgia State University	M,D,O
Gonzaga University	M
Governors State University	M
Graceland University (IA)	M,O
Graduate School and University Center of the City University of New York	D
Grambling State University	M,O
Grand Canyon University	M
Grand Valley State University	M,D
Gwynedd-Mercy College	M
Hampton University	M
Hardin-Simmons University	M
Hawai'i Pacific University	M
Holy Family University	M
Holy Names University	M,O
Howard University	M,O
Hunter College of the City University of New York	M,O
Husson University	M,O
Idaho State University	M,O
Illinois State University	M,D,O
Immaculata University	M
Indiana State University	M
Indiana University of Pennsylvania	M
Indiana University–Purdue University Fort Wayne	M,O
Indiana University–Purdue University Indianapolis	M,D
Indiana Wesleyan University	M,O
Jacksonville State University	M
Jacksonville University	M

James Madison University M
The Johns Hopkins University M,D,O
Kean University M
Kennesaw State University M
Kent State University M,D
Lamar University M
La Roche College M
La Salle University M,O
Lehman College of the City University of New York M
Le Moyne College M,O
Lewis University M
Liberty University M,D
Lincoln Memorial University M
Long Island University, Brooklyn Campus M,O
Long Island University, C.W. Post Campus M,O
Loyola University Chicago M,D
Lynchburg College M,D
Madonna University M
Malone University M
Mansfield University of Pennsylvania M
Marian University (WI) M
Marquette University M,D,O
Marshall University M
Marymount University M,O
Maryville University of Saint Louis M
McNeese State University M
Mercer University M,D,O
Mercy College M
Metropolitan State University M,D
Michigan State University M,D
Middle Tennessee State University M,O
Midwestern State University M
Millersville University of Pennsylvania M
Minnesota State University Mankato M,D
Minnesota State University Moorhead M,O
Misericordia University M
Mississippi University for Women M,O
Missouri State University M
Molloy College M,O
Monmouth University M,O
Montana State University M,O
Morgan State University M,D
Mountain State University M,O
Mount Saint Mary College M
Mount St. Mary's College M
Murray State University M
Nazareth College of Rochester M
Neumann University M
New Mexico State University M
New York University M,O
North Dakota State University M,D
Northeastern University M,O
Northern Arizona University M
Northern Illinois University M
Northern Kentucky University M,O
Northern Michigan University M
North Park University M
Northwestern State University of Louisiana M
Nova Southeastern University M,D
Oakland University M,D,O
The Ohio State University M,D
Oklahoma City University M
Old Dominion University M,D
Otterbein College M,O
Pace University M,D,O
Pacific Lutheran University M
Penn State University Park M,D
Pittsburg State University M
Point Loma Nazarene University M
Pontifical Catholic University of Puerto Rico M
Prairie View A&M University M
Purdue University Calumet M
Queens University of Charlotte M
Quinnipiac University M,O
Radford University M
Ramapo College of New Jersey M
Regis College (MA) M,O
Regis University P,M,D,O
Rhode Island College M
The Richard Stockton College of New Jersey M
Rivier College M
Robert Morris University M,D
Roberts Wesleyan College M
Rutgers, The State University of New Jersey, Newark M
Sacred Heart University M,D
Saginaw Valley State University M
St. Ambrose University M
St. Catherine University M,D
St. John Fisher College M,D,O
Saint Joseph College M,O
St. Joseph's College, Long Island Campus M
Saint Joseph's College of Maine M,O
Saint Louis University M,D,O
Saint Peter's College M
Saint Xavier University M,O
Salem State College M
Salisbury University M
Samford University M,D
San Diego State University M
San Francisco State University M
San Jose State University M,O
Seattle Pacific University M
Seattle University M
Seton Hall University M,D
Shenandoah University M,O
Simmons College M,D,O
South Dakota State University M,D
Southeastern Louisiana University M
Southeast Missouri State University M
Southern Connecticut State University M
Southern Illinois University Edwardsville M,O
Southern Nazarene University M
Southern University and Agricultural and Mechanical College M,D,O
Spalding University M
Spring Arbor University M
Spring Hill College M
State University of New York at Binghamton M,D,O
State University of New York Institute of Technology M,O
Stony Brook University, State University of New York M,D,O
Temple University M
Tennessee State University M
Tennessee Technological University M
Texas A&M International University M
Texas A&M University–Corpus Christi M
Texas Christian University M,D
Texas Woman's University M,D
Towson University M,O
Troy University M
Union University M,D,O
Universidad del Turabo M
University at Buffalo, the State University of New York M,D,O
The University of Akron M,D
The University of Alabama M,D
The University of Alabama at Birmingham M,D
The University of Alabama in Huntsville M,D,O
University of Alaska Anchorage M,O
The University of Arizona M,D,O
University of Arkansas M
University of California, Los Angeles M,D
University of Central Arkansas M
University of Central Florida M,D,O
University of Central Missouri M
University of Cincinnati M,D
University of Colorado at Colorado Springs M,D
University of Colorado Denver D
University of Connecticut M,D,O
University of Delaware M,O
University of Evansville M
University of Florida M,D
University of Hartford M
University of Hawaii at Manoa M,D,O
University of Houston–Victoria M
University of Illinois at Chicago M,D

M—master's degree; P—first professional degree; D—doctorate; O—other advanced degree

University of Indianapolis M
The University of Iowa M,D
The University of Kansas M,D,O
University of Kentucky M,D
University of Louisiana at Lafayette M
University of Louisville M,D
University of Maine M,O
University of Mary M
University of Mary Hardin-Baylor M
University of Massachusetts Amherst M,D
University of Massachusetts Boston M,D
University of Massachusetts Dartmouth M,D,O
University of Massachusetts Lowell M,D,O
University of Memphis M,O
University of Miami M,D
University of Michigan M,D,O
University of Michigan–Flint D
University of Minnesota, Twin Cities Campus M,D
University of Missouri–Columbia M,D
University of Missouri–Kansas City M,D
University of Missouri–St. Louis M,D,O
University of Mobile M
University of Nevada, Las Vegas M,D,O
University of Nevada, Reno M
University of New Hampshire M,O
University of New Mexico M,D
University of North Alabama M
The University of North Carolina at Chapel Hill M,D,O
The University of North Carolina at Charlotte M
The University of North Carolina at Greensboro M,D,O
The University of North Carolina Wilmington M
University of North Dakota M,D
University of Northern Colorado M,D
University of North Florida M,O
University of Pennsylvania M,D,O
University of Phoenix M
University of Phoenix–Central Florida Campus M
University of Phoenix–Denver Campus M
University of Phoenix–Hawaii Campus M
University of Phoenix–Las Vegas Campus M
University of Phoenix–Louisiana Campus M
University of Phoenix–New Mexico Campus M
University of Phoenix–North Florida Campus M
University of Phoenix–Philadelphia Campus M
University of Phoenix–Phoenix Campus M,O
University of Phoenix–Sacramento Valley Campus M
University of Phoenix–San Diego Campus M
University of Phoenix–Southern California Campus M,O
University of Phoenix–Southern Colorado Campus M
University of Phoenix–South Florida Campus M
University of Phoenix–Utah Campus M
University of Phoenix–West Florida Campus M
University of Phoenix–West Michigan Campus M
University of Pittsburgh M
University of Portland M,D
University of Rhode Island M,D
University of Rochester M,D,O
University of St. Francis (IL) M,D
University of Saint Francis (IN) M
University of San Diego M,D
University of San Francisco M,D
The University of Scranton M,O
University of South Alabama M,D
University of South Carolina M,O
University of Southern Indiana M,D
University of Southern Maine M,O
University of Southern Mississippi M,D
University of South Florida M,D
The University of Tampa M
The University of Tennessee M,D
The University of Tennessee at Chattanooga M,O
The University of Texas at Arlington M,D
The University of Texas at Austin M,D
The University of Texas at El Paso M,O
The University of Texas at Tyler M,D
The University of Texas–Pan American M
University of the Incarnate Word M
The University of Toledo M,O
University of Utah M,D
University of Vermont M
University of Virginia M,D
University of Washington M,D,O
University of Washington, Bothell M
University of Washington, Tacoma M
University of West Georgia M
University of Wisconsin–Eau Claire M
University of Wisconsin–Madison D
University of Wisconsin–Milwaukee M,D,O
University of Wisconsin–Oshkosh M
University of Wyoming M
Ursuline College M
Valparaiso University M,O
Vanderbilt University M,D
Villanova University M,D,O
Virginia Commonwealth University M,D,O
Viterbo University M
Wagner College M
Walden University M,O
Waynesburg University M,D
Wayne State University D
Webster University M
Wesley College M
West Chester University of Pennsylvania M,O
Western Carolina University M
Western Connecticut State University M
Western Kentucky University M
Westminster College (UT) M
West Texas A&M University M
West Virginia University M,D,O
Wheeling Jesuit University M
Wichita State University M
Widener University M,D,O
Wilkes University M
William Carey University M
William Paterson University of New Jersey M
Wilmington University M
Winona State University M,D,O
Wright State University M
Xavier University M
Yale University M,D,O
Youngstown State University M

■ NURSING AND HEALTHCARE ADMINISTRATION

Abilene Christian University M,O
American International College M
Austin Peay State University M
Barry University M,D,O
Baylor University M
Bellarmine University M,D
Bloomsburg University of Pennsylvania M
Bowie State University M
Bradley University M
Brenau University M
California State University, Long Beach M,O
Capital University M
Carlow University M,D
Chatham University M,D
College of Mount Saint Vincent M,O
The College of New Rochelle M,O
Daemen College M,O
Duke University M,D,O

D'Youville College	M,O
Eastern Michigan University	M,O
Emory University	M
Fairfield University	M,O
Ferris State University	M
Florida Agricultural and Mechanical University	M
Framingham State College	M
Gannon University	M,O
George Mason University	M,D,O
The George Washington University	M,D,O
Georgia College & State University	M
Graceland University (IA)	M,O
Grand Canyon University	M
Grand Valley State University	M,D
Holy Family University	M
Holy Names University	M,O
Indiana University–Purdue University Fort Wayne	M,O
Indiana Wesleyan University	M,O
The Johns Hopkins University	M
Kean University	M
Kent State University	M,D
Lamar University	M
La Roche College	M
Le Moyne College	M,O
Lewis University	M
Long Island University, Brooklyn Campus	M
Loyola University Chicago	M,O
Lynchburg College	M,D
Madonna University	M
Marywood University	M
McNeese State University	M
Mercy College	M
Minnesota State University Mankato	M,D
Molloy College	M,O
Mountain State University	M,O
Mount Saint Mary College	M
New Mexico State University	M
Northeastern University	M
North Park University	M
Norwich University	M
Otterbein College	M,O
Pacific Lutheran University	M
Prairie View A&M University	M
Queens University of Charlotte	M
Regis University	P,M,D,O
Roberts Wesleyan College	M
Sacred Heart University	M,D
Saginaw Valley State University	M
Saint Joseph's College of Maine	M,O
Saint Peter's College	M
Saint Xavier University	M,O
Samford University	M,D
San Francisco State University	M
San Jose State University	M,O
Seattle Pacific University	M
Seattle University	M
Seton Hall University	M
Southern Connecticut State University	M
Southern Illinois University Edwardsville	M,O
Southern Nazarene University	M
Southern University and Agricultural and Mechanical College	M,D,O
Spalding University	M
State University of New York Institute of Technology	M,O
Texas A&M University–Corpus Christi	M
Union University	M,D,O
University of Central Florida	M,D,O
University of Cincinnati	M,D
University of Colorado at Colorado Springs	M,D
University of Delaware	M,O
University of Hawaii at Manoa	M,D,O
University of Illinois at Chicago	M
University of Indianapolis	M
University of Mary	M
University of Massachusetts Lowell	D
University of Michigan	M
University of Minnesota, Twin Cities Campus	M
University of Missouri–Kansas City	M,D
The University of North Carolina at Chapel Hill	M,D,O
The University of North Carolina at Greensboro	M,D,O
University of Pennsylvania	M,D
University of Pittsburgh	M
University of Rhode Island	M,D
University of Rochester	M,D,O
University of San Diego	M,D
University of San Francisco	D
University of South Carolina	M
University of Southern Mississippi	M,D
The University of Tennessee at Chattanooga	M,O
The University of Texas at Arlington	M,D
The University of Texas at Dallas	M
The University of Texas at El Paso	M,O
The University of Texas at Tyler	M,D
University of Virginia	M,D
University of West Florida	M
Ursuline College	M
Vanderbilt University	M,D
Villanova University	M,D,O
Virginia Commonwealth University	M,D,O
Walden University	M,O
Wichita State University	M
Winona State University	M,D,O
Wright State University	M
Xavier University	M

■ NURSING EDUCATION

Abilene Christian University	M,O
American International College	M
Angelo State University	M
Arizona State University	M,D,O
Austin Peay State University	M
Azusa Pacific University	M,D
Barry University	M,O
Bellarmine University	M,D
Bethel University	M,O
Bowie State University	M
Brenau University	M
California State University, Fresno	M
Capella University	M,D
Carson-Newman College	M
The Catholic University of America	M,D,O
Chatham University	M,D
Cleveland State University	M
College of Mount Saint Vincent	M,O
The College of New Rochelle	M,O
College of Staten Island of the City University of New York	O
Concordia University Wisconsin	M
Daemen College	M,O
Delta State University	M
DeSales University	M
Dominican University of California	M
Duke University	M,D,O
Duquesne University	M
D'Youville College	M,O
Eastern Michigan University	M,O
Eastern Washington University	M
Ferris State University	M
Florida State University	M,O
Framingham State College	M
George Mason University	M,D,O
Georgetown University	M
Graceland University (IA)	M,O
Grambling State University	M,O
Grand Canyon University	M
Grand Valley State University	M,D
Holy Family University	M
Holy Names University	M,O
Indiana University–Purdue University Fort Wayne	M,O
Indiana Wesleyan University	M,O
Lamar University	M
La Roche College	M
Le Moyne College	M,O
Lewis University	M
Lynchburg College	M,D
Marian University (WI)	M
Marymount University	M,O

M—master's degree; P—first professional degree; D—doctorate; O—other advanced degree

Maryville University of Saint Louis M
McNeese State University M
Mercy College M
Midwestern State University M
Minnesota State University Mankato M,D
Minnesota State University Moorhead M
Missouri State University M
Molloy College M,O
Montana State University M,O
Mountain State University M,O
Mount Saint Mary College M
New York University M,O
Northern Arizona University M
North Georgia College & State University M
Oakland University M,O
Old Dominion University M
Pace University M,D,O
Prairie View A&M University M
Ramapo College of New Jersey M
Regis College (MA) M,O
Rivier College M
Roberts Wesleyan College M
St. John Fisher College M,O
Saint Joseph's College of Maine M,O
Samford University M,D
San Francisco State University M
San Jose State University M,O
Seattle Pacific University M
Seton Hall University M
Southern Connecticut State University M
Southern Illinois University Edwardsville M,O
Southern Nazarene University M
Southern University and Agricultural and Mechanical College M,D,O
State University of New York Institute of Technology M,O
Texas Woman's University M,D
Towson University M,O
Union University M,D,O
The University of Alabama in Huntsville M,D,O
University of Alaska Anchorage M,O
University of Central Florida M,D,O
University of Hartford M
University of Indianapolis M
University of Mary M
University of Massachusetts Lowell M,D,O
University of Missouri–Kansas City M,D
University of Nevada, Las Vegas M,D,O
The University of North Carolina at Greensboro M,D,O
The University of North Carolina Wilmington M
University of Northern Colorado M,D
University of Phoenix M
University of Phoenix–Central Florida Campus M
University of Phoenix–Hawaii Campus M
University of Phoenix–Las Vegas Campus M
University of Phoenix–New Mexico Campus M
University of Phoenix–North Florida Campus M
University of Phoenix–Philadelphia Campus M
University of Phoenix–Phoenix Campus M,O
University of Phoenix–Sacramento Valley Campus M
University of Phoenix–San Diego Campus M
University of Phoenix–Southern California Campus M,O
University of Phoenix–South Florida Campus M
University of Phoenix–Utah Campus M
University of Phoenix–West Florida Campus M
University of Pittsburgh M
University of Rhode Island M,D
The University of Tennessee at Chattanooga M,O
The University of Texas at Arlington M,D
The University of Texas at El Paso M,O
The University of Texas at Tyler M,D
The University of Toledo M,O
Ursuline College M
Valparaiso University M,O
Villanova University M,D,O
Walden University M,O
Wayne State University M,O
West Chester University of Pennsylvania M,O
Westminster College (UT) M
Winona State University M,D,O

■ NURSING INFORMATICS

Austin Peay State University M
Case Western Reserve University M
Duke University M,D,O
Ferris State University M
Loyola University Chicago M,O
Molloy College M,O
New York University M,O
Seattle Pacific University M
Tennessee State University M
Vanderbilt University M,D
Walden University M,O

■ NUTRITION

Andrews University M
Appalachian State University M
Arizona State University M
Auburn University M,D
Baylor University M,D
Benedictine University M
Boston University M
Bowling Green State University M
Brigham Young University M
Brooklyn College of the City University of New York M
California State University, Chico M
California State University, Long Beach M
California State University, Los Angeles M
Case Western Reserve University M,D
Central Michigan University M,O
Central Washington University M
Chapman University M
Clemson University M
College of Saint Elizabeth M,O
Colorado State University M,D
Columbia University M,D
Cornell University M,D
Drexel University M
D'Youville College M
East Carolina University M
Eastern Illinois University M
Eastern Kentucky University M
Eastern Michigan University M
East Tennessee State University M
Emory University M,D
Florida International University M,D
Florida State University M,D
Framingham State College M
George Mason University M,O
Georgia State University M
Harvard University D
Howard University M,D
Hunter College of the City University of New York M
Idaho State University M,O
Immaculata University M
Indiana State University M
Indiana University Bloomington M,D
Indiana University of Pennsylvania M
Indiana University–Purdue University Indianapolis M,D
Iowa State University of Science and Technology M,D
The Johns Hopkins University M,D
Kansas State University M,D
Kent State University M
Lehman College of the City University of New York M
Long Island University, C.W. Post Campus M,O
Louisiana Tech University M
Marshall University M
Marywood University M,O

McNeese State University M
Michigan State University M,D
Middle Tennessee State University M
Mississippi State University M,D
Montana State University M
Montclair State University M,O
Mount Mary College M
New York Institute of Technology M
New York University M,D
North Carolina Agricultural and Technical State University M
North Carolina State University M,D
North Dakota State University M
Northern Illinois University M
The Ohio State University M,D
Ohio University M
Oklahoma State University M,D
Oregon State University M,D
Penn State University Park M,D
Purdue University M,D
Rutgers, The State University of New Jersey, New Brunswick M,D
Sacred Heart University M,D
Saint Joseph College M
Saint Louis University M
Sam Houston State University M
San Diego State University M
San Jose State University M
Simmons College M,O
South Carolina State University M
South Dakota State University M,D
Southeast Missouri State University M
Southern Illinois University Carbondale M
State University of New York College at Oneonta M
Syracuse University M
Texas State University–San Marcos M
Texas Tech University M,D
Texas Woman's University M,D
Tufts University M,D
Tulane University M
University at Buffalo, the State University of New York M,D
The University of Akron M
The University of Alabama M
The University of Alabama at Birmingham M,D,O
University of Alaska Fairbanks M,D
The University of Arizona M,D
University of Bridgeport M
University of California, Berkeley M,D
University of California, Davis M,D
University of Central Oklahoma M
University of Chicago D
University of Cincinnati M
University of Connecticut M,D
University of Delaware M
University of Florida M,D
University of Georgia M,D
University of Hawaii at Manoa M,D
University of Houston M,D
University of Illinois at Chicago M,D
University of Illinois at Urbana–Champaign M,D
The University of Kansas M,O
University of Kentucky M,D
University of Maine M,D
University of Maryland, College Park M,D
University of Massachusetts Amherst M,D
University of Massachusetts Lowell M,O
University of Memphis M
University of Michigan M,D
University of Minnesota, Twin Cities Campus M,D
University of Missouri–Columbia M,D
University of Nebraska–Lincoln M,D
University of Nevada, Reno M
University of New Hampshire M,D
University of New Haven M
University of New Mexico M
The University of North Carolina at Chapel Hill M,D
The University of North Carolina at Greensboro M,D
University of North Florida M,O
University of Pittsburgh M
University of Puerto Rico, Río Piedras M
University of Rhode Island M,D
University of Southern Mississippi M,D
The University of Tennessee M
The University of Tennessee at Martin M
The University of Texas at Austin M,D
University of the Incarnate Word M,O
University of Utah M
University of Vermont M,D
University of Washington M,D
University of Wisconsin–Madison M,D
University of Wisconsin–Stevens Point M
University of Wisconsin–Stout M
University of Wyoming M
Utah State University M,D
Vanderbilt University M,D
Virginia Polytechnic Institute and State University M,D
Washington State University M,D
Wayne State University M,D
West Virginia University M
Winthrop University M

■ OCCUPATIONAL HEALTH NURSING

University of Cincinnati M,D
University of Illinois at Chicago M
University of Michigan M,O
University of Minnesota, Twin Cities Campus M,D
The University of North Carolina at Chapel Hill M
University of Pennsylvania M

■ OCCUPATIONAL THERAPY

Alvernia University M
American International College M
Barry University M
Belmont University M,D
Boston University M,D
Brenau University M
California State University, Dominguez Hills M
Chatham University M,D
Cleveland State University M
The College of St. Scholastica M
Colorado State University M
Columbia University M,D
Concordia University Wisconsin M
Creighton University D
Dominican College M
Dominican University of California M
Duquesne University M,D
D'Youville College M
East Carolina University M
Eastern Kentucky University M
Eastern Michigan University M
Eastern Washington University M
Florida Gulf Coast University M
Florida International University M
Gannon University M
Governors State University M
Grand Valley State University M
Husson University M
Idaho State University M
Indiana University–Purdue University Indianapolis M,D
Ithaca College M
James Madison University M
Kean University M
Maryville University of Saint Louis M
Mercy College M
Misericordia University M,D
Mount Mary College M
New York Institute of Technology M
New York University M,D
Nova Southeastern University M,D
The Ohio State University M
Pacific University M
Philadelphia University M
Quinnipiac University M
The Richard Stockton College of New Jersey M
Rockhurst University M
Sacred Heart University M

M—master's degree; P—first professional degree; D—doctorate; O—other advanced degree

Saginaw Valley State University M
St. Ambrose University M
St. Catherine University M
Saint Francis University M
Saint Louis University M
Salem State College M
San Jose State University M
Seton Hall University M
Shenandoah University M
Spalding University M
Springfield College M,O
Stony Brook University, State University of New York M,D,O
Temple University M
Texas Woman's University M,D
Touro College M
Towson University M
Tufts University M,D,O
University at Buffalo, the State University of New York M
The University of Alabama at Birmingham M
University of Central Arkansas M
The University of Findlay M
University of Florida M
University of Illinois at Chicago M,D
University of Indianapolis M,D
The University of Kansas M,D
University of Mary M
University of Missouri–Columbia M
University of New England M
University of New Hampshire M,O
University of New Mexico M
The University of North Carolina at Chapel Hill M,D
University of North Dakota M
University of Pittsburgh M
University of Puget Sound M
The University of Scranton M
University of South Alabama M
The University of South Dakota M
University of Southern California M,D
University of Southern Indiana M
University of Southern Maine M
The University of Texas at El Paso M
The University of Texas–Pan American M
The University of Toledo D
University of Utah M
University of Washington M,D
University of Wisconsin–La Crosse M
University of Wisconsin–Madison M,D
University of Wisconsin–Milwaukee M,O
Utica College M
Virginia Commonwealth University M,D
Washington University in St. Louis M,D
Wayne State University M
Western Michigan University M
Western New Mexico University M
West Virginia University M
Worcester State College M
Xavier University M

■ OCEAN ENGINEERING

Florida Atlantic University M,D
Florida Institute of Technology M,D
Massachusetts Institute of Technology M,D,O
Oregon State University M,D
Princeton University D
Stevens Institute of Technology M,D
Texas A&M University M,D
University of Alaska Anchorage M,O
University of California, San Diego M,D
University of Delaware M,D
University of Florida M,D,O
University of Hawaii at Manoa M,D
University of Michigan M,D,O
University of New Hampshire M,D,O
University of Rhode Island M,D
Virginia Polytechnic Institute and State University M,D

■ OCEANOGRAPHY

Columbia University M,D
Cornell University D
Florida Institute of Technology M,D
Florida State University M,D
Georgia Institute of Technology M,D
Louisiana State University and Agricultural and Mechanical College M,D
Massachusetts Institute of Technology M,D,O
North Carolina State University M,D
Nova Southeastern University M,D
Old Dominion University M,D
Oregon State University M,D
Princeton University D
Rutgers, The State University of New Jersey, New Brunswick M,D
Texas A&M University M,D
University of Alaska Fairbanks M,D
University of California, San Diego M,D
University of Colorado at Boulder M,D
University of Connecticut M,D
University of Delaware M,D
University of Georgia M,D
University of Hawaii at Manoa M,D
University of Maine M,D
University of Maryland, College Park M,D
University of Miami M,D
University of Michigan M,D
University of New Hampshire M,D,O
University of Rhode Island M,D
University of South Florida M,D
University of Washington M,D
University of Wisconsin–Madison M,D
Yale University D

■ ONCOLOGY NURSING

Columbia University M,O
Duke University M,D,O
Emory University M
Gwynedd-Mercy College M
Loyola University Chicago M,O
University of Delaware M,O
University of Pennsylvania M

■ OPERATIONS RESEARCH

Bowling Green State University M
California State University, East Bay M
Carnegie Mellon University D
Case Western Reserve University M
Claremont Graduate University M,D
Clemson University M,D
The College of William and Mary M
Columbia University M,D,O
Cornell University M,D
Florida Institute of Technology M,D
George Mason University M,D,O
Georgia Institute of Technology M,D
Georgia State University M,D
Idaho State University M
Indiana University–Purdue University Fort Wayne M,O
Iowa State University of Science and Technology M,D
The Johns Hopkins University M,D
Kansas State University M,D
Massachusetts Institute of Technology M,D
Miami University M
New Mexico Institute of Mining and Technology M,D
North Carolina State University M,D
North Dakota State University M,D,O
Northeastern University M,D
Northwestern University M,D
Oregon State University M,D
Penn State University Park M,D
Princeton University M,D
Rutgers, The State University of New Jersey, New Brunswick D
St. Mary's University (United States) M
Southern Methodist University M,D
The University of Alabama in Huntsville M
University of Arkansas M
University of California, Berkeley M,D
University of Central Florida M,D,O
University of Colorado at Boulder M
University of Delaware M,D
University of Illinois at Chicago D
The University of Iowa M,D
University of Massachusetts Amherst M,D
University of Michigan M,D

The University of North Carolina at Chapel Hill M,D
University of Southern California M,D,O
The University of Texas at Austin M,D
Virginia Commonwealth University M,O
Virginia Polytechnic Institute and State University M,D

■ OPTICAL SCIENCES

Alabama Agricultural and Mechanical University M,D
The Catholic University of America M,D
Cleveland State University M
Delaware State University M,D
Norfolk State University M
North Carolina Agricultural and Technical State University M,D
The Ohio State University M,D
Rochester Institute of Technology M,D
The University of Alabama in Huntsville M,D
The University of Arizona M,D
University of Central Florida M,D
University of Colorado at Boulder M,D
University of Dayton M,D
University of Maryland, Baltimore County M,D
University of Massachusetts Lowell M,D
University of New Mexico M,D
The University of North Carolina at Charlotte M,D
University of Rochester M,D

■ OPTOMETRY

Ferris State University P
Indiana University Bloomington P,M,D
Northeastern State University P
Nova Southeastern University P,M
The Ohio State University P
The University of Alabama at Birmingham P
University of California, Berkeley P,O
University of Houston P
University of Missouri–St. Louis P
University of the Incarnate Word P

■ ORAL AND DENTAL SCIENCES

Boston University P,M,D,O
Case Western Reserve University M,O
Columbia University M,D,O
Harvard University M,D,O
Howard University P,O
Idaho State University O
Jacksonville University O
Marquette University M
New York University M,D,O
The Ohio State University D
Saint Louis University M
Stony Brook University, State University of New York P,M,D,O
Temple University M,O
Tufts University M,O
University at Buffalo, the State University of New York M,D,O
The University of Alabama at Birmingham M
University of California, Los Angeles M,D
University of Connecticut M
University of Detroit Mercy M,O
University of Florida M,D,O
University of Illinois at Chicago M,D
The University of Iowa M,D,O
University of Kentucky M
University of Louisville M
University of Michigan M,D
University of Minnesota, Twin Cities Campus M,D,O
University of Missouri–Kansas City P,M,D,O
The University of North Carolina at Chapel Hill M,D
University of Pittsburgh M,O
University of Rochester M
University of Southern California M,D,O
University of the Pacific M,O
The University of Toledo M
University of Washington P,M,O
West Virginia University M

■ ORGANIC CHEMISTRY

Auburn University M,D
Boston College M,D
Brandeis University M,D
California State University, Los Angeles M
Carnegie Mellon University M,D
Clarkson University M,D
Cleveland State University M,D
Columbia University M,D
Cornell University D
Florida State University M,D
Georgetown University D
The George Washington University M,D
Harvard University D
Howard University M,D
Kansas State University M,D
Kent State University M,D
Marquette University M,D
Massachusetts Institute of Technology M,D,O
Miami University M,D
Northeastern University M,D
Old Dominion University M,D
Oregon State University M,D
Purdue University M,D
Rensselaer Polytechnic Institute M,D
Rice University M,D
Rutgers, The State University of New Jersey, Newark M,D
Rutgers, The State University of New Jersey, New Brunswick M,D
Seton Hall University M,D
Southern University and Agricultural and Mechanical College M
State University of New York at Binghamton M,D
State University of New York College of Environmental Science and Forestry M,D
Stevens Institute of Technology M,D,O
Tufts University M,D
University of Cincinnati M,D
University of Georgia M,D
University of Louisville M,D
University of Maryland, College Park M,D
University of Massachusetts Lowell M,D
University of Miami M,D
University of Michigan D
University of Missouri–Columbia M,D
University of Missouri–Kansas City M,D
University of Missouri–St. Louis M,D
The University of Montana M,D
University of Nebraska–Lincoln M,D
University of Notre Dame M,D
University of Southern Mississippi M,D
University of South Florida M,D
The University of Tennessee M,D
The University of Texas at Austin M,D
The University of Toledo M,D
Vanderbilt University M,D
Virginia Commonwealth University M,D
Wake Forest University M,D
West Virginia University M,D
Yale University D
Youngstown State University M

■ ORGANIZATIONAL BEHAVIOR

Benedictine University M
Bernard M. Baruch College of the City University of New York M,D
Boston College D
Boston University D
California Lutheran University M,O
Carnegie Mellon University D
Case Western Reserve University M
Columbia College (SC) M,O
Cornell University M,D
Drexel University M,D,O
Fairleigh Dickinson University, College at Florham M,O
Georgia Institute of Technology M,D,O

M—master's degree; P—first professional degree; D—doctorate; O—other advanced degree

Graduate School and University Center of the City University of New York D
Harvard University D
John Jay College of Criminal Justice of the City University of New York M,D
Marylhurst University M
New York University M,D
Northwestern University M,D
Oral Roberts University M
Polytechnic Institute of NYU M
Purdue University D
Silver Lake College M
Suffolk University M,O
Syracuse University D
Towson University O
University of California, Berkeley D
University of Hartford M
University of Hawaii at Manoa M
The University of North Carolina at Chapel Hill D
University of Oklahoma M
University of Pennsylvania M
University of Pittsburgh M,D

■ ORGANIZATIONAL MANAGEMENT

Alvernia University D
American International College M
American University M
Antioch University Los Angeles M
Antioch University New England M,O
Antioch University Santa Barbara M
Antioch University Seattle M
Argosy University, Orange County D
Argosy University, Sarasota M,D,O
Argosy University, Tampa M,D
Argosy University, Twin Cities M,D,O
Augsburg College M
Avila University M,O
Azusa Pacific University M
Benedictine University M,D
Bernard M. Baruch College of the City University of New York M,D
Bethel University M
Biola University M
Boston College D
Bowling Green State University M
Brenau University M
Cabrini College M,O
Cambridge College M
Capella University M,D,O
Carlow University M
Charleston Southern University M
City University of Seattle M,O
College of Mount St. Joseph M
Colorado State University M
Colorado Technical University Sioux Falls M
Concordia University, St. Paul M
Cumberland University M
Dominican University M
Duquesne University M
Eastern Connecticut State University M
Eastern Michigan University M
Eastern University M,D
Emory University M,D
Endicott College M
Fairleigh Dickinson University, College at Florham M,O
Gannon University D
Geneva College M
George Mason University M
The George Washington University M,D
Georgia State University M,D
Gonzaga University M
Grand Canyon University M,D
Harding University M
Hawai'i Pacific University M
Immaculata University M
Indiana University–Purdue University Fort Wayne M
Indiana Wesleyan University D
John F. Kennedy University M,O
Johnson & Wales University M
Jones International University M
Lewis University M
Manhattanville College M
Marian University (WI) M
Marymount University M,O
Medaille College M
Mercy College M
Mercyhurst College M,O
MidAmerica Nazarene University M
Misericordia University M
National University M
Newman University M
The New School: A University M
New York University M,D
North Carolina Agricultural and Technical State University M,D
Northern Kentucky University M
Northwestern University M,D
Norwich University M
Nova Southeastern University D
Nyack College M
Olivet Nazarene University M
Our Lady of the Lake University of San Antonio M,D
Palm Beach Atlantic University M
Pfeiffer University M
Philadelphia Biblical University M
Point Park University M
Regent University M,D,O
Regis College (MA) M
Regis University M,O
Rider University M
Rivier College M
Robert Morris University M,D
Roosevelt University M,D
Rutgers, The State University of New Jersey, Newark D
St. Ambrose University M
St. Catherine University M
St. Edward's University M
St. Joseph's College, Long Island Campus M,O
Saint Joseph's University M,D,O
Saint Louis University M,D,O
Saint Mary's University of Minnesota M
Seattle University M,O
Shippensburg University of Pennsylvania M
SIT Graduate Institute M
Southern New Hampshire University M,D,O
Southwestern College (KS) M
Spring Arbor University M
Springfield College M
State University of New York College at Potsdam M
Suffolk University M,O
Trevecca Nazarene University M
Trinity (Washington) University M
Tusculum College M
University of Cincinnati M
University of Colorado at Boulder M,D
University of Dallas M
University of Denver M,O
University of Hawaii at Manoa M,D
The University of Kansas M,D,O
University of La Verne M,D,O
University of Maryland Eastern Shore D
University of Massachusetts Dartmouth M,O
University of New Mexico M
University of Pennsylvania M
University of Phoenix D
University of St. Thomas (MN) M,D,O
University of San Francisco M
The University of Scranton M
University of Southern California M
The University of Texas at San Antonio M,D
University of the Incarnate Word M,D,O
Upper Iowa University M
Vanderbilt University M,D
Walden University M,D,O
Wayland Baptist University M
Wayne State College M
Webster University M
Western International University M
Wheeling Jesuit University M
Wilmington University M
Woodbury University M
Worcester Polytechnic Institute M,O
Worcester State College M

■ OSTEOPATHIC MEDICINE

Lincoln Memorial University P
Michigan State University P
New York Institute of Technology P
Nova Southeastern University P,M
Ohio University P
University of New England P

■ PACIFIC AREA/PACIFIC RIM STUDIES

University of California, San Diego M,D
University of Guam M
University of Hawaii at Manoa M,O
University of San Francisco M

■ PALEONTOLOGY

Cornell University M,D
Duke University D
University of Chicago M,D
The University of Texas at Dallas M,D
West Virginia University M,D
Yale University D

■ PAPER AND PULP ENGINEERING

Miami University M
North Carolina State University M,D
Oregon State University M,D
State University of New York College of Environmental Science and Forestry M,D
Western Michigan University M,D

■ PARASITOLOGY

Illinois State University M,D
New York University P,M,D
Texas A&M University M,D
Tulane University M,D,O
University of Notre Dame M,D
University of Pennsylvania D
University of Washington D
Yale University D

■ PASTORAL MINISTRY AND COUNSELING

Abilene Christian University M,D
Andrews University P,M,D,O
Anna Maria College M
Argosy University, Sarasota M,D,O
Azusa Pacific University P,M
Barry University M,D
Bob Jones University P,M,D,O
Boston College P,M,D,O
Caldwell College M
California Baptist University M
Cardinal Stritch University M
The Catholic University of America P,M,D,O
Chaminade University of Honolulu M
College of Mount St. Joseph M
Concordia University, Nebraska M
Concordia University, St. Paul M,O
Dallas Baptist University M
Eastern Mennonite University P,M,O
Eastern University D
Fordham University M,D,O
Freed-Hardeman University M
Gannon University M,O
Gardner-Webb University P,D
George Fox University P,M,D,O
Georgian Court University M,O
Gonzaga University M
Graceland University (IA) M
Hampton University M
Harding University M
Hardin-Simmons University M
Holy Names University M,O
Houston Baptist University M
Indiana Wesleyan University M
Inter American University of Puerto Rico, Metropolitan Campus D
Iona College M,O
John Brown University M
La Salle University M
La Sierra University P,M
Liberty University M,D
Loyola Marymount University M
Loyola University Chicago M,O
Loyola University Maryland M,D,O
Madonna University M
Malone University M
Marymount University M,O
Missouri Baptist University M,O
Mount Marty College M
Neumann University M,O
Northwest Nazarene University P,M
Oklahoma Christian University P,M
Oral Roberts University P,M,D
Philadelphia Biblical University M
Regent University P,M,D
Roberts Wesleyan College M
St. Ambrose University M
St. John's University (NY) P,M,O
Saint Leo University M
St. Mary's University (United States) M
Saint Mary's University of Minnesota M,O
St. Thomas University M,D,O
Santa Clara University M
Seattle University M
Seton Hall University P,M
Southern Wesleyan University M
Southwestern College (KS) M
Spring Arbor University M
Trinity International University P,M,D,O
Union University M,D
University of Dallas M
University of Dayton M,D
University of Portland M
University of Puget Sound M
University of Saint Francis (IN) M
University of St. Thomas (MN) M
Wayland Baptist University M
Wheaton College M,D
Xavier University of Louisiana M

■ PATHOBIOLOGY

Auburn University M,D
Brown University M,D
Columbia University M,D
Drexel University M,D
The Johns Hopkins University D
Kansas State University M,D
Michigan State University M,D
New York University P,M,D
The Ohio State University M,D
Penn State University Park D
Purdue University M,D
Texas A&M University M,D
The University of Arizona M,D
University of Cincinnati D
University of Connecticut M,D
University of Illinois at Urbana–Champaign M,D
University of Missouri–Columbia M,D
University of Southern California M,D
University of Washington D
University of Wyoming M
Wake Forest University M,D
Yale University D

■ PATHOLOGY

Brown University M,D
Case Western Reserve University M,D
Colorado State University M,D
Columbia University M,D
Duke University M,D
East Carolina University D
Georgetown University M,D
Harvard University D
Indiana University–Purdue University Indianapolis M,D
Iowa State University of Science and Technology M,D
The Johns Hopkins University D
Michigan State University M,D
North Carolina State University M,D
North Dakota State University M,D
The Ohio State University M
Purdue University M,D
Quinnipiac University M
Saint Louis University D
Stony Brook University, State University of New York M,D
Temple University D
Texas A&M University M,D
University at Buffalo, the State University of New York M,D
The University of Alabama at Birmingham D
University of California, Davis M,D

M—master's degree; P—first professional degree; D—doctorate; O—other advanced degree

University of California, Los Angeles M,D
University of Chicago D
University of Cincinnati D
University of Colorado Denver D
University of Florida D
University of Georgia M,D
The University of Iowa M
The University of Kansas M,D
University of Massachusetts Lowell M,O
University of Michigan D
University of Missouri–Columbia M
University of New Mexico M,D
The University of North Carolina at Chapel Hill D
University of Pittsburgh M,D
University of Rochester M,D
University of Southern California M,D
University of South Florida M,D
The University of Toledo O
University of Utah M,D
University of Vermont M
University of Virginia D
University of Washington D
University of Wisconsin–Madison D
Vanderbilt University D
Virginia Commonwealth University M,D
Wayne State University M,D
Yale University M,D

■ PEDIATRIC NURSING

Case Western Reserve University M,D
The Catholic University of America M,D,O
Columbia University M,O
Duke University M,D,O
Emory University M
Georgia State University M,D,O
Gwynedd-Mercy College M
Hampton University M
Indiana University–Purdue University Indianapolis M,D
The Johns Hopkins University M,O
Kent State University M,D
Lehman College of the City University of New York M
Marquette University M,D,O
Molloy College M,O
New York University M,O
Seton Hall University M
Spalding University M
Stony Brook University, State University of New York M,O
Texas Woman's University M,D
University at Buffalo, the State University of New York M,D,O
University of Central Florida M,D,O
University of Cincinnati M,D
University of Colorado Denver M
University of Delaware M,O
University of Illinois at Chicago M
University of Michigan M,O
University of Minnesota, Twin Cities Campus M
University of Missouri–Kansas City M,D
The University of North Carolina at Chapel Hill M,D,O
University of Pennsylvania M
University of Pittsburgh M,D
University of Rochester M,D,O
University of San Diego M,D
University of South Carolina M
The University of Texas–Pan American M
The University of Toledo M,O
Vanderbilt University M,D
Villanova University M,D,O
Virginia Commonwealth University M,D,O
Wayne State University M,O
Wright State University M

■ PERFUSION

Long Island University, C.W. Post Campus M
Quinnipiac University M
The University of Arizona M,D

■ PETROLEUM ENGINEERING

Colorado School of Mines M,D
Louisiana State University and Agricultural and Mechanical College M,D
Missouri University of Science and Technology M,D
New Mexico Institute of Mining and Technology M,D
Stanford University M,D,O
Texas A&M University M,D
Texas A&M University–Kingsville M
Texas Tech University M,D
University of Alaska Fairbanks M,D
University of Houston M,D
The University of Kansas M,D
University of Louisiana at Lafayette M
University of Oklahoma M,D
University of Pittsburgh M,D
University of Southern California M,D,O
The University of Texas at Austin M,D
University of Tulsa M,D
University of Wyoming M,D
West Virginia University M,D

■ PHARMACEUTICAL ADMINISTRATION

Duquesne University M
Fairleigh Dickinson University, Metropolitan Campus M,O
Florida Agricultural and Mechanical University M,D
Idaho State University P,M,D
Long Island University, Brooklyn Campus M
The Ohio State University M,D
Purdue University M,D,O
St. John's University (NY) M
San Diego State University M
Seton Hall University M
Temple University M
University of Florida M,D
University of Houston P,M,D
University of Illinois at Chicago M,D
University of Michigan D
University of Minnesota, Twin Cities Campus M,D
University of Mississippi M,D
The University of Toledo M
University of West Florida M
University of Wisconsin–Madison M,D
Wayne State University P,M,D,O
West Virginia University M,D

■ PHARMACEUTICAL ENGINEERING

New Jersey Institute of Technology M
University of Michigan M

■ PHARMACEUTICAL SCIENCES

Auburn University M,D
Boston University M,D
Butler University P,M
Campbell University P,M
Creighton University M,D
Dartmouth College D
Drake University P
Duquesne University M,D
Florida Agricultural and Mechanical University M,D
Idaho State University M,D
The Johns Hopkins University M
Long Island University, Brooklyn Campus M,D
Mercer University P,M,D
North Dakota State University M,D
Northeastern University P,M,D
The Ohio State University M,D
Oregon State University P,M,D
Purdue University M,D
Rutgers, The State University of New Jersey, New Brunswick M,D
St. John's University (NY) M,D
South Dakota State University M,D
Stevens Institute of Technology M,O
Temple University M,D
University at Buffalo, the State University of New York M,D
The University of Arizona M,D
University of California, Berkeley O
University of Cincinnati M,D
University of Colorado Denver P
University of Connecticut M,D
University of Florida D
University of Georgia M,D,O

University of Houston P,M,D
University of Illinois at Chicago M,D
The University of Kansas M
University of Kentucky M,D
University of Louisiana at Monroe M
University of Michigan D
University of Minnesota, Twin Cities Campus M,D
University of Mississippi M,D
University of Missouri–Kansas City P,M,D
The University of Montana M,D
University of New Mexico M,D
The University of North Carolina at Chapel Hill M,D
University of Pittsburgh M,D
University of Rhode Island M,D
University of South Carolina M,D
University of Southern California M,D
The University of Texas at Austin M,D
University of the Pacific M,D
The University of Toledo M
University of Utah M
University of Washington M,D
University of Wisconsin–Madison M,D
Virginia Commonwealth University P,M,D
Wayne State University P,M,D,O
West Virginia University M,D

■ PHARMACOLOGY

Auburn University M,D
Boston University M,D
Case Western Reserve University D
Columbia University M,D
Cornell University M,D
Creighton University M,D
Dartmouth College D
Drexel University M,D
Duke University D
Duquesne University M,D
East Carolina University D
East Tennessee State University M,D
Emory University D
Fairleigh Dickinson University, College at Florham M,O
Florida Agricultural and Mechanical University M,D
Georgetown University M,D
Howard University M,D
Idaho State University M,D
Indiana University–Purdue University Indianapolis M,D
The Johns Hopkins University D
Kent State University M,D
Long Island University, Brooklyn Campus M,D
Loyola University Chicago M,D
Michigan State University M,D
New York University P,M,D
North Carolina State University M,D
Northeastern University M,D
Northwestern University D
Nova Southeastern University M
The Ohio State University M,D
Purdue University M,D
Saint Louis University D
Southern Illinois University Carbondale M,D
Stony Brook University, State University of New York D
Temple University M,D
Tufts University D
Tulane University M,D
University at Buffalo, the State University of New York M,D
The University of Alabama at Birmingham D
The University of Arizona M,D
University of California, Davis M,D
University of California, Irvine M,D
University of California, Los Angeles D
University of California, San Diego D
University of Chicago D
University of Cincinnati D
University of Colorado Denver D
University of Connecticut M,D
University of Florida M,D
University of Georgia M,D
University of Houston P,M,D
University of Illinois at Chicago D
The University of Iowa M,D
The University of Kansas M,D
University of Kentucky D
University of Louisville M,D
University of Miami D
University of Michigan D
University of Minnesota, Duluth M,D
University of Minnesota, Twin Cities Campus M,D
University of Mississippi M,D
University of Missouri–Columbia M,D
The University of North Carolina at Chapel Hill D
University of North Dakota M,D
University of Pennsylvania D
University of Rhode Island M,D
University of Rochester M,D
University of South Alabama D
The University of South Dakota M,D
University of South Florida M,D
The University of Toledo M
University of Utah D
University of Vermont M,D
University of Virginia D
University of Washington D
University of Wisconsin–Madison D
Vanderbilt University D
Virginia Commonwealth University M,D,O
Wake Forest University D
Washington State University M,D
Wayne State University P,M,D
West Virginia University M,D
Wright State University M
Yale University D

■ PHARMACY

Auburn University P
Belmont University P
Butler University P,M
Campbell University P,M
Creighton University P
Drake University P
Duquesne University P
Ferris State University P
Florida Agricultural and Mechanical University P,D
Harding University P
Howard University P
Idaho State University P,M,D
Lipscomb University P
Mercer University P,M,D
Nova Southeastern University P
The Ohio State University P
Oregon State University P,M,D
Pacific University P
Palm Beach Atlantic University P
Purdue University P
Regis University P,M,D,O
Rutgers, The State University of New Jersey, New Brunswick P,M,D
St. John Fisher College P
St. John's University (NY) P
Samford University P
Shenandoah University P
South Dakota State University P
Southern Illinois University Edwardsville P
Southwestern Oklahoma State University P
Temple University P
Texas Southern University P,M,D
University at Buffalo, the State University of New York P
The University of Arizona P
University of California, San Diego P
University of Cincinnati P
University of Colorado Denver P,D
University of Connecticut P
The University of Findlay P
University of Florida P
University of Georgia P
University of Houston P,M,D
University of Illinois at Chicago P,D
The University of Iowa M,D
University of Kentucky P
University of Louisiana at Monroe P,D
University of Michigan P

M—master's degree; P—first professional degree; D—doctorate; O—other advanced degree

University of Minnesota, Twin Cities Campus P,M,D
University of Mississippi P
University of Missouri–Kansas City P,M,D
The University of Montana P,M,D
University of New Mexico P
University of Pittsburgh P
University of Rhode Island M,D
University of South Carolina P
University of Southern California P
The University of Texas at Austin P
University of the Incarnate Word P
University of the Pacific P
University of Utah P
University of Washington P,M,D
University of Wisconsin–Madison P
University of Wyoming P
Virginia Commonwealth University P
Washington State University P
Wayne State University P,M,D,O
West Virginia University P,M,D
Wilkes University P
Xavier University of Louisiana P

■ PHILANTHROPIC STUDIES

Indiana University–Purdue University Indianapolis M,D
Saint Mary's University of Minnesota M

■ PHILOSOPHY

American University M
Arizona State University M,D
Baylor University M,D
Boston College M,D
Boston University M,D
Bowling Green State University M,D
Brandeis University M
Brown University M,D
California Institute of Integral Studies M,D
California State University, Long Beach M
California State University, Los Angeles M
Carnegie Mellon University M,D
The Catholic University of America M,D,O
Claremont Graduate University M,D
Cleveland State University M,O
Colorado State University M
Columbia University M,D
Cornell University D
DePaul University M,D
Duke University M,D
Duquesne University M,D
Emory University D,O
Florida State University M,D
Fordham University M,D
Franciscan University of Steubenville M
George Mason University M
Georgetown University M,D
The George Washington University M,D
Georgia State University M
Gonzaga University M
Graduate School and University Center of the City University of New York M,D
Harvard University M,D
Howard University M
Indiana University Bloomington M,D
Indiana University–Purdue University Indianapolis M,O
The Johns Hopkins University M,D
Kent State University M
Louisiana State University and Agricultural and Mechanical College M
Loyola Marymount University M
Loyola University Chicago M,D
Marquette University M,D
Massachusetts Institute of Technology D
Miami University M
Michigan State University M,D
Montclair State University M,D,O
The New School: A University M,D
New York University M,D
Northern Illinois University M
Northwestern University D
The Ohio State University M,D
Ohio University M
Oklahoma City University M
Oklahoma State University M
Oregon State University M
Penn State University Park M,D
Princeton University D
Purdue University M,D
Rice University M,D
Rutgers, The State University of New Jersey, New Brunswick D
St. John's University (NY) M
Saint Louis University M,D
San Diego State University M
San Francisco State University M,O
San Jose State University M,O
Southern Illinois University Carbondale M,D
Stanford University M,D
State University of New York at Binghamton M,D
Stony Brook University, State University of New York M,D
Syracuse University M,D
Temple University M,D
Texas A&M University M,D
Texas Tech University M
Tufts University M
Tulane University M,D
University at Albany, State University of New York M,D
University at Buffalo, the State University of New York M,D
The University of Arizona M,D
University of Arkansas M,D
University of California, Berkeley D
University of California, Davis M,D
University of California, Irvine M,D
University of California, Los Angeles M,D
University of California, Riverside M,D
University of California, San Diego D
University of California, Santa Barbara D
University of California, Santa Cruz M,D
University of Chicago M,D
University of Cincinnati M,D
University of Colorado at Boulder M,D
University of Connecticut M,D
University of Dallas M,D
University of Florida M,D
University of Georgia M,D
University of Hawaii at Manoa M,D
University of Houston M
University of Illinois at Chicago M,D
University of Illinois at Urbana–Champaign M,D
The University of Iowa M,D
The University of Kansas M,D
University of Kentucky M,D
University of Louisville M
University of Maryland, College Park M,D
University of Massachusetts Amherst M,D
University of Memphis M,D
University of Miami M,D
University of Michigan M,D
University of Minnesota, Twin Cities Campus M,D
University of Mississippi M
University of Missouri–Columbia M,D
University of Missouri–St. Louis M
The University of Montana M
University of Nebraska–Lincoln M,D
University of Nevada, Reno M
University of New Mexico M,D
The University of North Carolina at Chapel Hill M,D
University of North Florida M,O
University of North Texas M,D
University of Notre Dame D
University of Oklahoma M,D
University of Oregon M,D
University of Pennsylvania M,D
University of Pittsburgh M,D
University of Puerto Rico, Río Piedras M
University of Rochester M,D
University of St. Thomas (TX) M,D
University of South Carolina M,D

University of Southern California M,D
University of Southern Mississippi M
University of South Florida M,D
The University of Tennessee M,D
The University of Texas at Austin D
The University of Toledo M
University of Utah M,D
University of Virginia M,D
University of Washington M,D
University of Wisconsin–Madison M,D
University of Wisconsin–Milwaukee M
University of Wyoming M
Vanderbilt University M,D
Villanova University D
Virginia Polytechnic Institute and State University M
Washington State University M
Washington University in St. Louis M,D
Wayne State University M,D
West Chester University of Pennsylvania M,O
Western Michigan University M
Yale University D

■ PHOTOGRAPHY

Barry University M
Bradley University M
Brooklyn College of the City University of New York M,D
California State University, Fullerton M
California State University, Los Angeles M
Claremont Graduate University M
Columbia College Chicago M
Columbia University M
Cornell University M
The George Washington University M
Georgia State University M,D
Howard University M
Illinois State University M
Indiana State University M
Inter American University of Puerto Rico, San Germán Campus M
James Madison University M
Lamar University M
Louisiana State University and Agricultural and Mechanical College M
Louisiana Tech University M
Marywood University M
Mills College M
New Mexico State University M
The New School: A University M
The Ohio State University M
Ohio University M
Penn State University Park M,D
Rochester Institute of Technology M
San Jose State University M
Southern Methodist University M
Syracuse University M
Temple University M
The University of Alabama M
University of Alaska Fairbanks M
University of Colorado at Boulder M
University of Florida M,D
University of Houston M
University of Illinois at Chicago M
University of Illinois at Urbana–Champaign M
University of Massachusetts Dartmouth M
University of Memphis M,O
University of Miami M
University of Notre Dame M
University of Oklahoma M
The University of Tennessee M
University of Utah M
University of Washington M
Virginia Commonwealth University M
Washington State University M
Yale University M

■ PHOTONICS

Boston University M,D
Lehigh University M,D
Oklahoma State University M,D
Princeton University D
Stevens Institute of Technology M,D,O
The University of Alabama in Huntsville M,D
University of Arkansas M,D
University of California, San Diego M,D
University of Central Florida M,D

■ PHYSICAL CHEMISTRY

Auburn University M,D
Boston College M,D
Brandeis University M,D
California State University, Los Angeles M
Clarkson University M,D
Cleveland State University M,D
Cornell University D
Florida State University M,D
Georgetown University D
The George Washington University M,D
Harvard University D
Howard University M,D
Indiana University Bloomington M,D
Kansas State University M,D
Kent State University M,D
Marquette University M,D
Massachusetts Institute of Technology D
Miami University M,D
Northeastern University M,D
Old Dominion University M,D
Oregon State University M,D
Purdue University M,D
Rensselaer Polytechnic Institute M,D
Rice University M,D
Rutgers, The State University of New Jersey, Newark M,D
Rutgers, The State University of New Jersey, New Brunswick M,D
Seton Hall University M,D
Southern University and Agricultural and Mechanical College M
State University of New York at Binghamton M,D
Stevens Institute of Technology M,D,O
Tufts University M,D
University of Cincinnati M,D
University of Georgia M,D
University of Louisville M,D
University of Maryland, College Park M,D
University of Miami M,D
University of Michigan D
University of Missouri–Columbia M,D
University of Missouri–Kansas City M,D
University of Missouri–St. Louis M,D
The University of Montana M,D
University of Nebraska–Lincoln M,D
University of Notre Dame M,D
University of Puerto Rico, Río Piedras M,D
University of Southern Mississippi M,D
University of South Florida M,D
The University of Tennessee M,D
The University of Texas at Austin M,D
The University of Toledo M,D
Vanderbilt University M,D
Virginia Commonwealth University M,D
Wake Forest University M,D
West Virginia University M,D
Yale University D
Youngstown State University M

■ PHYSICAL EDUCATION

Adams State College M
Adelphi University M,O
Alabama Agricultural and Mechanical University M
Alabama State University M
Albany State University M
Alcorn State University M,O
Arizona State University M,D,O
Arkansas State University M,O
Ashland University M
Auburn University M,D,O

M—master's degree; P—first professional degree; D—doctorate; O—other advanced degree

Auburn University Montgomery M,O
Augusta State University M
Azusa Pacific University M
Ball State University M,D
Bayamón Central University M
Baylor University M,D
Bethel University (TN) M
Boston University M,D,O
Bridgewater State College M
Brooklyn College of the City University of New York M,O
California Baptist University M
California State University, Dominguez Hills M
California State University, East Bay M
California State University, Fullerton M
California State University, Long Beach M
California State University, Los Angeles M
California State University, Sacramento M
California State University, Stanislaus M
Campbell University M
Canisius College M
Central Connecticut State University M,O
Central Michigan University M
Central Washington University M
Chicago State University M
The Citadel, The Military College of South Carolina M
Cleveland State University M
The College at Brockport, State University of New York M
The College of New Jersey M
Columbus State University M,O
Concordia University (CA) M
Delta State University M
DePaul University M,D
Eastern Illinois University M
Eastern Kentucky University M
Eastern Michigan University M
Eastern New Mexico University M
Eastern Washington University M
East Stroudsburg University of Pennsylvania M
East Tennessee State University M
Emporia State University M
Florida Agricultural and Mechanical University M
Florida International University M,D,O
Florida State University M,D,O
Fort Hays State University M
Gardner-Webb University M
George Mason University M,O
Georgia College & State University M
Georgia Southern University M
Georgia Southwestern State University M,O
Georgia State University M
Henderson State University M
Hofstra University M,D,O
Howard University M
Humboldt State University M
Idaho State University M
Illinois State University M
Indiana State University M
Indiana University Bloomington M,D
Indiana University of Pennsylvania M
Indiana University–Purdue University Indianapolis M
Inter American University of Puerto Rico, Metropolitan Campus M
Inter American University of Puerto Rico, San Germán Campus M
Ithaca College M
Jackson State University M
Jacksonville State University M
Kent State University M,D
Long Island University, Brooklyn Campus M
Louisiana Tech University M,D
McDaniel College M
Middle Tennessee State University M
Minnesota State University Mankato M,O
Mississippi State University M
Missouri State University M
Montana State University–Billings M
Montclair State University M,O
Morehead State University M
Murray State University M,O
North Carolina Agricultural and Technical State University M
North Carolina Central University M
North Dakota State University M
Northern Illinois University M
North Georgia College & State University M,O
Northwest Missouri State University M
The Ohio State University M,D
Ohio University M
Old Dominion University M
Oregon State University M
Pittsburg State University M
Prairie View A&M University M
Purdue University M,D
Rhode Island College M,O
Saginaw Valley State University M
St. Cloud State University M
Salem State College M
San Diego State University M
Slippery Rock University of Pennsylvania M
South Dakota State University M
Southern Connecticut State University M
Southern Illinois University Carbondale M
Springfield College M,D,O
State University of New York College at Cortland M
Stony Brook University, State University of New York M,O
Sul Ross State University M
Tarleton State University M
Temple University M,D
Tennessee State University M
Tennessee Technological University M
Texas A&M University M,D
Texas A&M University–Commerce M,D
Texas Southern University M
Texas State University–San Marcos M
Union College (KY) M
Universidad del Turabo M
Universidad Metropolitana M
The University of Akron M
The University of Alabama M,D
The University of Alabama at Birmingham M
University of Arkansas M
University of California, Berkeley M,D
University of Central Florida M
University of Central Missouri M
University of Dayton M,D
University of Florida M,D
University of Georgia M,D
University of Houston M,D
University of Idaho M,D
University of Indianapolis M
The University of Iowa M,D
The University of Kansas M,D
University of Louisville M
University of Maine M
University of Memphis M
University of Minnesota, Twin Cities Campus M,D,O
The University of Montana M
University of Nebraska at Kearney M
University of Nebraska at Omaha M
University of Nevada, Las Vegas M,D
University of New Mexico M,D,O
The University of North Carolina at Chapel Hill M
The University of North Carolina at Pembroke M
University of Northern Colorado M,D
University of Northern Iowa M
University of Rhode Island M,D
University of South Alabama M
University of South Carolina M,D
The University of South Dakota M

University of Southern Mississippi	M,D
University of South Florida	M
The University of Tennessee at Chattanooga	M
The University of Texas at Arlington	M,D
University of the Incarnate Word	M,O
The University of Toledo	M
University of Virginia	M,D
University of Washington	M,D
The University of West Alabama	M
University of West Florida	M
University of West Georgia	M
University of Wisconsin–La Crosse	M
University of Wyoming	M
Utah State University	M
Virginia Commonwealth University	M,D
Virginia Polytechnic Institute and State University	M,D,O
Wayne State College	M
Wayne State University	M
West Chester University of Pennsylvania	M,O
Western Carolina University	M
Western Kentucky University	M
Western Michigan University	M
Western Washington University	M
Westfield State College	M
West Virginia University	M,D
Wichita State University	M
William Woods University	M,O
Winthrop University	M
Wright State University	M

■ PHYSICAL THERAPY

Alabama State University	D
American International College	D
Andrews University	D
Angelo State University	D
Arcadia University	D
Arkansas State University	M,D,O
Armstrong Atlantic State University	D
Azusa Pacific University	D
Baylor University	M,D
Bellarmine University	M,D
Belmont University	D
Boston University	D
Bradley University	D
California State University, Fresno	M,D
California State University, Long Beach	M
California State University, Northridge	M
Carroll University	M,D
Central Michigan University	M,D
Chapman University	D
Chatham University	D
Clarkson University	D
Cleveland State University	D
College of Mount St. Joseph	M,D
The College of St. Scholastica	D
Columbia University	D
Concordia University Wisconsin	M,D
Creighton University	D
Daemen College	D,O
Dominican College	M,D
Drexel University	M,D,O
Duke University	D
Duquesne University	M,D
D'Youville College	M,D,O
East Carolina University	M,D
Eastern Washington University	D
East Tennessee State University	D
Elon University	D
Emory University	D
Florida Agricultural and Mechanical University	M
Florida Gulf Coast University	M,D
Florida International University	D
Gannon University	D
The George Washington University	D
Georgia State University	D
Governors State University	M,D
Graduate School and University Center of the City University of New York	D
Grand Valley State University	D
Hampton University	D
Hardin-Simmons University	D
Humboldt State University	M
Husson University	D
Idaho State University	D
Indiana University–Purdue University Indianapolis	M,D
Ithaca College	M,D
Long Island University, Brooklyn Campus	D
Lynchburg College	M,D
Marquette University	D
Marymount University	D
Maryville University of Saint Louis	D
Mercy College	M,D
Misericordia University	M,D
Missouri State University	D
Mount St. Mary's College	D
Nazareth College of Rochester	M,D
Neumann University	D
New York Institute of Technology	M,D
New York University	M,D,O
Northern Arizona University	D
Northern Illinois University	M
North Georgia College & State University	D
Northwestern University	D
Nova Southeastern University	D
Oakland University	M,D,O
The Ohio State University	M
Ohio University	D
Old Dominion University	D
Pacific University	D
Quinnipiac University	M,D
Regis University	P,M,D,O
The Richard Stockton College of New Jersey	D
Rockhurst University	D
Rutgers, The State University of New Jersey, Camden	D
Sacred Heart University	M,D
St. Ambrose University	D
St. Catherine University	D
Saint Francis University	D
Saint Louis University	M,D
San Francisco State University	M,D
Seton Hall University	D
Shenandoah University	D
Simmons College	D
Slippery Rock University of Pennsylvania	D
Southwest Baptist University	D
Springfield College	D
Stony Brook University, State University of New York	M,D,O
Temple University	D
Tennessee State University	M,D
Texas State University–San Marcos	D
Texas Woman's University	M,D
Touro College	M,D
University at Buffalo, the State University of New York	D
The University of Alabama at Birmingham	D
University of Central Arkansas	D
University of Central Florida	D
University of Colorado Denver	D
University of Connecticut	D
University of Dayton	M,D
University of Delaware	D
University of Evansville	D
The University of Findlay	M
University of Florida	D
University of Hartford	M,D
University of Illinois at Chicago	M,D
University of Indianapolis	M,D
The University of Iowa	D
The University of Kansas	D
University of Kentucky	M
University of Mary	D
University of Maryland Eastern Shore	D
University of Massachusetts Lowell	D
University of Miami	D
University of Michigan–Flint	D
University of Minnesota, Twin Cities Campus	D
University of Missouri–Columbia	M

M—master's degree; P—first professional degree; D—doctorate; O—other advanced degree

The University of Montana	D
University of Nevada, Las Vegas	D
University of New England	D
University of New Mexico	M
The University of North Carolina at Chapel Hill	M,D
University of North Dakota	M,D
University of North Florida	M
University of Pittsburgh	M,D
University of Puget Sound	D
University of Rhode Island	D
The University of Scranton	M,D
University of South Alabama	D
The University of South Dakota	D
University of Southern California	D
University of South Florida	M,D
The University of Tennessee at Chattanooga	D
The University of Texas at El Paso	M
University of the Pacific	M,D
The University of Toledo	M,D
University of Utah	D,O
University of Vermont	D
University of Washington	M,D
University of Wisconsin–La Crosse	M,D
University of Wisconsin–Milwaukee	D
Utica College	D
Virginia Commonwealth University	M,D
Walsh University	D
Washington University in St. Louis	D,O
Wayne State University	M
Western Carolina University	M
West Virginia University	D
Wheeling Jesuit University	D
Wichita State University	M
Widener University	M,D
Youngstown State University	D

■ PHYSICIAN ASSISTANT STUDIES

Augsburg College	M
Barry University	M
Butler University	P,M
California State University, Dominguez Hills	M
Central Michigan University	M,D
Chatham University	M
Cleveland State University	M,D
Daemen College	M
DeSales University	M
Drexel University	M
Duke University	M
Duquesne University	M,D
D'Youville College	M
East Carolina University	M
Emory University	M
Gannon University	M
The George Washington University	M
Grand Valley State University	M
Harding University	M
Idaho State University	M
James Madison University	M
King's College	M
Le Moyne College	M
Lock Haven University of Pennsylvania	M
Marquette University	M
Marywood University	M
Mercy College	M
Missouri State University	M
Mountain State University	M
New York Institute of Technology	M
Northeastern University	M
Nova Southeastern University	M
Pace University	M
Pacific University	M
Philadelphia University	M
Quinnipiac University	M
Regis University	P,M,D,O
Saint Francis University	M
Saint Louis University	M
Seton Hall University	M
Seton Hill University	M
Shenandoah University	M
Southern Illinois University Carbondale	M
Springfield College	M
Stony Brook University, State University of New York	M,D,O
Towson University	M
Trevecca Nazarene University	M
The University of Alabama at Birmingham	M
University of Detroit Mercy	M
University of Florida	M
The University of Iowa	M
University of Kentucky	M
University of New England	M
University of North Dakota	M
University of St. Francis (IL)	M,D
University of Saint Francis (IN)	M
University of South Alabama	M
The University of South Dakota	M
University of Southern California	M
The University of Toledo	M
University of Utah	M
University of Wisconsin–La Crosse	M
Wagner College	M
Wayne State University	M
Western Michigan University	M
Yale University	M,O

■ PHYSICS

Adelphi University	M
Alabama Agricultural and Mechanical University	M,D
Arizona State University	M,D
Auburn University	M,D
Ball State University	M
Baylor University	M,D
Boston College	M,D
Boston University	M,D
Bowling Green State University	M
Brandeis University	M,D
Brigham Young University	M,D
Brooklyn College of the City University of New York	M,D
Brown University	M,D
California Institute of Technology	D
California State University, Fresno	M
California State University, Fullerton	M
California State University, Long Beach	M
California State University, Los Angeles	M
California State University, Northridge	M
Carnegie Mellon University	M,D
Case Western Reserve University	M,D
The Catholic University of America	M,D
Central Connecticut State University	M,O
Central Michigan University	M,D
City College of the City University of New York	M,D
Clark Atlanta University	M
Clarkson University	M,D
Clark University	M,D
Clemson University	M,D
Cleveland State University	M
The College of William and Mary	M,D
Colorado School of Mines	M,D
Colorado State University	M,D
Columbia University	M,D
Cornell University	M,D
Creighton University	M
Dartmouth College	M,D
Delaware State University	M,D
DePaul University	M
Drexel University	M,D
Duke University	M,D
East Carolina University	M,D
Eastern Michigan University	M
Emory University	D
Florida Agricultural and Mechanical University	M,D
Florida Atlantic University	M,D
Florida Institute of Technology	M,D
Florida International University	M,D
Florida State University	M,D
George Mason University	M
The George Washington University	M,D
Georgia Institute of Technology	M,D
Georgia State University	M,D

Graduate School and University Center of the City University of New York D
Hampton University M,D
Harvard University D
Howard University M,D
Hunter College of the City University of New York M,D
Idaho State University M,D
Illinois Institute of Technology M,D
Indiana University Bloomington M,D
Indiana University of Pennsylvania M
Indiana University–Purdue University Indianapolis M,D
Iowa State University of Science and Technology M,D
The Johns Hopkins University D
Kent State University M,D
Lehigh University M,D
Louisiana State University and Agricultural and Mechanical College M,D
Louisiana Tech University M,D
Marshall University M
Massachusetts Institute of Technology M,D
Miami University M
Michigan State University M,D
Michigan Technological University M,D
Minnesota State University Mankato M
Mississippi State University M,D
Missouri University of Science and Technology M,D
Montana State University M,D
New Mexico Institute of Mining and Technology M,D
New Mexico State University M,D
New York University M,D
North Carolina Central University M
North Carolina State University M,D
North Dakota State University M,D
Northeastern University M,D
Northern Arizona University M
Northern Illinois University M,D
Northwestern University M,D
Oakland University M,D
The Ohio State University M,D
Ohio University M,D
Oklahoma State University M,D
Old Dominion University M,D
Oregon State University M,D
Penn State University Park M,D
Pittsburg State University M
Polytechnic Institute of NYU M,D
Portland State University M,D
Princeton University D
Purdue University M,D
Queens College of the City University of New York M,D
Rensselaer Polytechnic Institute M,D
Rice University M,D
Rutgers, The State University of New Jersey, New Brunswick M,D
San Diego State University M
San Francisco State University M
San Jose State University M
South Dakota State University M
Southern Illinois University Carbondale M,D
Southern Illinois University Edwardsville M
Southern Methodist University M,D
Southern University and Agricultural and Mechanical College M
Stanford University D
State University of New York at Binghamton M
Stephen F. Austin State University M
Stevens Institute of Technology M,D,O
Stony Brook University, State University of New York M,D
Syracuse University M,D
Temple University M,D
Texas A&M International University M
Texas A&M University M,D
Texas A&M University–Commerce M
Texas Christian University M,D
Texas State University–San Marcos M
Texas Tech University M,D
Tufts University M,D
Tulane University D
University at Albany, State University of New York M,D
University at Buffalo, the State University of New York M,D
The University of Akron M
The University of Alabama M,D
The University of Alabama at Birmingham M,D
The University of Alabama in Huntsville M,D
University of Alaska Fairbanks M,D
The University of Arizona M,D
University of Arkansas M,D
University of California, Berkeley D
University of California, Davis M,D
University of California, Irvine M,D
University of California, Los Angeles M,D
University of California, Riverside M,D
University of California, San Diego M,D
University of California, Santa Barbara D
University of California, Santa Cruz M,D
University of Central Florida M,D
University of Central Oklahoma M
University of Chicago M,D
University of Cincinnati M,D
University of Colorado at Boulder M,D
University of Colorado at Colorado Springs M
University of Connecticut M,D
University of Delaware M,D
University of Denver M,D
University of Florida M,D
University of Georgia M,D
University of Hawaii at Manoa M,D
University of Houston M,D
University of Houston–Clear Lake M
University of Idaho M,D
University of Illinois at Chicago M,D
University of Illinois at Urbana–Champaign M,D
The University of Iowa M,D
The University of Kansas M,D
University of Kentucky M,D
University of Louisiana at Lafayette M
University of Louisville M,D
University of Maine M,D
University of Maryland, Baltimore County M,D
University of Maryland, College Park M,D
University of Massachusetts Amherst M,D
University of Massachusetts Dartmouth M
University of Massachusetts Lowell M,D
University of Memphis M
University of Miami M,D
University of Michigan M,D
University of Minnesota, Duluth M
University of Minnesota, Twin Cities Campus M,D
University of Mississippi M,D
University of Missouri–Columbia M,D
University of Missouri–Kansas City M,D
University of Missouri–St. Louis M,D
University of Nebraska–Lincoln M,D
University of Nevada, Las Vegas M,D
University of Nevada, Reno M,D
University of New Hampshire M,D
University of New Mexico M,D
University of New Orleans M,D
The University of North Carolina at Chapel Hill M,D
University of North Dakota M,D
University of Northern Iowa M
University of North Texas M,D
University of Notre Dame M,D

M—master's degree; P—first professional degree; D—doctorate; O—other advanced degree

University of Oklahoma M,D
University of Oregon M,D
University of Pennsylvania M,D
University of Pittsburgh M,D
University of Puerto Rico, Mayagüez Campus M
University of Puerto Rico, Río Piedras M,D
University of Rhode Island M,D
University of Rochester M,D
University of South Carolina M,D
The University of South Dakota M,D
University of Southern California M,D
University of Southern Mississippi M,D
University of South Florida M,D
The University of Tennessee M,D
The University of Texas at Arlington M,D
The University of Texas at Austin M,D
The University of Texas at Brownsville M
The University of Texas at Dallas M,D
The University of Texas at El Paso M
The University of Texas at San Antonio M,D
The University of Toledo M,D
University of Tulsa M
University of Utah M,D
University of Vermont M
University of Virginia M,D
University of Washington M,D
University of Wisconsin–Madison M,D
University of Wisconsin–Milwaukee M,D
Utah State University M,D
Vanderbilt University M,D
Virginia Commonwealth University M
Virginia Polytechnic Institute and State University M,D
Virginia State University M
Wake Forest University M,D
Washington State University M,D
Washington University in St. Louis D
Wayne State University M,D
Western Illinois University M
Western Michigan University M,D
West Virginia University M,D
Wichita State University M
Worcester Polytechnic Institute M,D
Wright State University M
Yale University D

■ PHYSIOLOGY

Ball State University M
Boston University M,D
Brigham Young University M,D
Brown University M,D
Case Western Reserve University M,D
Columbia University M,D
Cornell University M,D
Dartmouth College D
East Carolina University D
Eastern Michigan University M
East Tennessee State University M,D
Georgetown University M,D
Georgia Institute of Technology M
Georgia State University M,D
Harvard University M,D
Howard University D
Illinois State University M,D
Indiana State University M,D
The Johns Hopkins University M,D
Kansas State University M,D
Kent State University M,D
Marquette University M,D
Michigan State University M,D
New York University P,M,D
North Carolina State University M,D
Northwestern University M
The Ohio State University M,D
Ohio University M,D
Penn State University Park M,D
Purdue University M,D
Saint Louis University D
Salisbury University M
San Francisco State University M
San Jose State University M
Southern Illinois University Carbondale M,D
Stanford University D
Stony Brook University, State University of New York D
Temple University D
Texas A&M University M,D
Tufts University D
Tulane University M,D
University at Buffalo, the State University of New York M,D
The University of Alabama at Birmingham D
The University of Arizona M,D
University of California, Berkeley M,D
University of California, Davis M,D
University of California, Irvine D
University of California, Los Angeles M,D
University of California, San Diego D
University of Chicago D
University of Cincinnati D
University of Colorado at Boulder M,D
University of Colorado Denver D
University of Connecticut M,D
University of Delaware M,D
University of Florida M,D
University of Georgia M,D
University of Hawaii at Manoa M,D
University of Illinois at Chicago M,D
University of Illinois at Urbana–Champaign M,D
The University of Iowa D
The University of Kansas M,D
University of Kentucky M,D
University of Louisville M,D
University of Miami D
University of Michigan D
University of Minnesota, Duluth M,D
University of Minnesota, Twin Cities Campus D
University of Missouri–Columbia M,D
University of Missouri–St. Louis M,D,O
University of Nevada, Reno D
University of New Mexico M,D
University of North Dakota M,D
University of Notre Dame M,D
University of Oregon M,D
University of Pennsylvania D
University of Rochester M,D
University of South Alabama D
The University of South Dakota M,D
University of Southern California M,D
University of South Florida M,D
The University of Tennessee M,D
University of Utah D
University of Virginia D
University of Washington D
University of Wisconsin–La Crosse M
University of Wisconsin–Madison M,D
University of Wyoming M,D
Virginia Commonwealth University M,D,O
Wake Forest University D
Wayne State University M,D
Western Michigan University M
West Virginia University M,D
William Paterson University of New Jersey M
Wright State University M
Yale University D
Youngstown State University M

■ PLANETARY AND SPACE SCIENCES

California Institute of Technology M,D
Columbia University M,D
Cornell University D
Embry-Riddle Aeronautical University (FL) M
Florida Institute of Technology M,D
Georgia Institute of Technology M,D
Harvard University M,D
Massachusetts Institute of Technology M,D
St. Thomas University M,D,O
The University of Arizona M,D
University of Arkansas M,D
University of California, Los Angeles M,D
University of California, Santa Cruz M,D
University of Chicago M,D

University of Hawaii at Manoa	M,D
University of Houston	M,D
University of Michigan	M,D
University of New Mexico	M,D
University of North Dakota	M
University of Pittsburgh	M,D
Washington University in St. Louis	M,D
West Chester University of Pennsylvania	M,O
Western Connecticut State University	M
Yale University	M,D

■ PLANT BIOLOGY

Arizona State University	M,D
Clemson University	M,D
Cornell University	M,D
Illinois State University	M,D
Indiana University Bloomington	M,D
Iowa State University of Science and Technology	M,D
Miami University	M,D
Michigan State University	M,D
New York University	M,D
North Carolina State University	M,D
The Ohio State University	M,D
Ohio University	M,D
Rutgers, The State University of New Jersey, New Brunswick	M,D
Southern Illinois University Carbondale	M,D
Texas A&M University	M,D
University of California, Berkeley	D
University of California, Davis	M,D
University of California, Riverside	M,D
University of California, San Diego	D
University of Connecticut	M,D
University of Florida	M,D
University of Georgia	M,D
University of Illinois at Urbana–Champaign	M,D
The University of Iowa	M,D
University of Maine	M,D
University of Maryland, College Park	M,D
University of Massachusetts Amherst	M,D
University of Minnesota, Twin Cities Campus	M,D
University of Missouri–Columbia	M,D
University of New Hampshire	M,D
The University of Texas at Austin	M,D
University of Vermont	M,D
Washington University in St. Louis	D
Yale University	D

■ PLANT MOLECULAR BIOLOGY

Cornell University	M,D
Illinois State University	M,D
Michigan Technological University	M,D
Rutgers, The State University of New Jersey, New Brunswick	M,D
University of California, San Diego	D
University of Connecticut	M,D
University of Florida	M,D
University of Massachusetts Amherst	M,D
Washington State University	M,D

■ PLANT PATHOLOGY

Auburn University	M,D
Colorado State University	M,D
Cornell University	M,D
Iowa State University of Science and Technology	M,D
Kansas State University	M,D
Louisiana State University and Agricultural and Mechanical College	M,D
Michigan State University	M,D
Mississippi State University	M,D
Montana State University	M,D
New Mexico State University	M
North Carolina State University	M,D
North Dakota State University	M,D
The Ohio State University	M,D
Oklahoma State University	M,D
Oregon State University	M,D
Penn State University Park	M,D
Purdue University	M,D
Rutgers, The State University of New Jersey, New Brunswick	M,D
State University of New York College of Environmental Science and Forestry	M,D
Texas A&M University	M,D
The University of Arizona	M,D
University of Arkansas	M
University of California, Davis	M,D
University of California, Riverside	M,D
University of Florida	M,D
University of Georgia	M,D
University of Hawaii at Manoa	M,D
University of Kentucky	M,D
University of Maine	M
University of Minnesota, Twin Cities Campus	M,D
University of Missouri–Columbia	M,D
The University of Tennessee	M,D
University of Wisconsin–Madison	M,D
Virginia Polytechnic Institute and State University	M,D
Washington State University	M,D
West Virginia University	M,D

■ PLANT PHYSIOLOGY

Cornell University	M,D
Oregon State University	M,D
Penn State University Park	M,D
Purdue University	M,D
University of Kentucky	D
University of Massachusetts Amherst	M,D
The University of Tennessee	M,D
Virginia Polytechnic Institute and State University	M,D

■ PLANT SCIENCES

Alabama Agricultural and Mechanical University	M,D
Brigham Young University	M,D
California State University, Fresno	M
Clemson University	M,D
Colorado State University	M,D
Cornell University	M,D
Delaware State University	M
Florida Agricultural and Mechanical University	M
Illinois State University	M,D
Lehman College of the City University of New York	D
Miami University	M,D
Michigan State University	M,D
Mississippi State University	M,D
Missouri State University	M
Montana State University	M,D
New Mexico State University	M,D
North Carolina Agricultural and Technical State University	M
North Dakota State University	M,D
Oklahoma State University	M,D
South Dakota State University	M,D
Southern Illinois University Carbondale	M
State University of New York College of Environmental Science and Forestry	M,D
Texas A&M University	M,D
Texas A&M University–Kingsville	M,D
Texas Tech University	M,D
The University of Arizona	M,D
University of Arkansas	D
University of California, Riverside	M,D
University of Connecticut	M,D
University of Delaware	M,D
University of Florida	D
University of Hawaii at Manoa	M,D
University of Idaho	M,D
University of Kentucky	M
University of Maine	M,D
University of Massachusetts Amherst	M,D
University of Minnesota, Twin Cities Campus	M,D
University of Missouri–Columbia	M,D
University of Rhode Island	M,D
The University of Tennessee	M
University of Vermont	M,D
University of Wisconsin–Madison	M,D
Utah State University	M,D

M—master's degree; P—first professional degree; D—doctorate; O—other advanced degree

Virginia State University M
West Texas A&M University M
West Virginia University D

■ PLASMA PHYSICS

Princeton University D
University of Colorado at Boulder M,D
West Virginia University M,D

■ PODIATRIC MEDICINE

Barry University P
Temple University P

■ POLITICAL SCIENCE

American University M,D,O
Appalachian State University M
Arizona State University M,D
Arkansas State University M,O
Ashland University M
Auburn University M,D
Auburn University Montgomery M,D
Augusta State University M
Ball State University M
Baylor University M,D
Boston College M,D
Boston University M,D
Bowling Green State University
Brandeis University M,D
Brigham Young University M
Brooklyn College of the City University of New York M,D
Brown University D
California Polytechnic State University, San Luis Obispo M
California State University, Chico M
California State University, Fullerton M
California State University, Long Beach M
California State University, Los Angeles M
California State University, Northridge M
California State University, Sacramento M
Case Western Reserve University M,D
The Catholic University of America M,D
Central Michigan University M,O
Claremont Graduate University M,D
Clark Atlanta University M,D
The College of Saint Rose M
Colorado State University M,D
Columbia University M,D
Converse College M
Cornell University D
Duke University M,D
East Carolina University M
Eastern Illinois University M
Eastern Kentucky University M
Eastern Michigan University M
East Stroudsburg University of Pennsylvania M
Emory University D
Fairleigh Dickinson University, Metropolitan Campus M
Fayetteville State University M
Florida Agricultural and Mechanical University M
Florida Atlantic University M
Florida International University M,D
Florida State University M,D
Fordham University M
George Mason University M,D
Georgetown University M,D
The George Washington University M,D
Georgia State University M,D
Governors State University M
Graduate School and University Center of the City University of New York M,D
Grambling State University M
Harvard University M,D
Howard University M,D
Idaho State University M,D
Illinois State University M
Indiana State University M
Indiana University Bloomington M,D
Indiana University of Pennsylvania M
Indiana University–Purdue University Indianapolis M,O
Iowa State University of Science and Technology M
Jackson State University M
Jacksonville State University M
James Madison University M
The Johns Hopkins University M,D,O
Kansas State University M
Kean University M
Kent State University M,D
Lamar University M
Lehigh University M
Lincoln University (MO) M
Long Island University, Brooklyn Campus M
Long Island University, C.W. Post Campus M
Louisiana State University and Agricultural and Mechanical College M,D
Loyola University Chicago M,D
Marquette University M
Marshall University M
Massachusetts Institute of Technology M,D
Miami University M,D
Michigan State University M,D
Midwestern State University M
Mississippi College M,O
Mississippi State University M,D
Missouri State University M
New Mexico State University M
The New School: A University M,D
New York University M,D
Northeastern Illinois University M
Northeastern University M,D,O
Northern Arizona University M,D,O
Northern Illinois University M,D
Northwestern University M,D
The Ohio State University M,D
Ohio University M
Oklahoma State University M,D
Penn State University Park M,D
Pepperdine University M
Portland State University M,D
Princeton University D
Purdue University M,D
Regent University M
Rice University M,D
Roosevelt University M
Rutgers, The State University of New Jersey, Newark M
Rutgers, The State University of New Jersey, New Brunswick D
St. John's University (NY) M,O
Saint Louis University M
St. Mary's University (United States) M
Sam Houston State University M
San Diego State University M
San Francisco State University M
Sonoma State University M
Southern Connecticut State University M
Southern Illinois University Carbondale M,D
Southern University and Agricultural and Mechanical College M
Stanford University M,D
State University of New York at Binghamton M,D
Stony Brook University, State University of New York M,D
Suffolk University M,O
Sul Ross State University M
Syracuse University M,D
Tarleton State University M
Temple University M,D
Texas A&M International University M
Texas A&M University M,D
Texas A&M University–Kingsville M
Texas State University–San Marcos M
Texas Tech University M,D
Texas Woman's University M
Tulane University M,D
University at Albany, State University of New York M,D
University at Buffalo, the State University of New York M,D
The University of Akron M
The University of Alabama M,D
The University of Arizona M,D
University of Arkansas M

University of California, Berkeley D
University of California, Davis M,D
University of California, Irvine D
University of California, Los Angeles M,D
University of California, Riverside M,D
University of California, San Diego M,D
University of California, Santa Barbara M,D
University of California, Santa Cruz D
University of Central Florida M
University of Central Oklahoma M
University of Chicago D
University of Cincinnati M,D
University of Colorado at Boulder M,D
University of Colorado Denver M
University of Connecticut M,D
University of Dallas M,D
University of Delaware M,D
University of Florida M,D,O
University of Georgia M,D
University of Hawaii at Manoa M,D
University of Houston M,D
University of Idaho M,D
University of Illinois at Chicago M,D
University of Illinois at Springfield M
University of Illinois at Urbana–Champaign M,D
The University of Iowa M,D
The University of Kansas M,D
University of Kentucky M,D
University of Louisville M
University of Maryland, College Park D
University of Massachusetts Amherst M,D
University of Massachusetts Boston M,D,O
University of Memphis M
University of Miami M
University of Michigan M,D
University of Minnesota, Twin Cities Campus D
University of Mississippi M,D
University of Missouri–Columbia M,D
University of Missouri–Kansas City M,D
University of Missouri–St. Louis M,D
The University of Montana M
University of Nebraska at Omaha M
University of Nevada, Las Vegas M,D
University of Nevada, Reno M,D
University of New Hampshire M
University of New Mexico M,D
University of New Orleans M,D
The University of North Carolina at Chapel Hill M,D
The University of North Carolina at Greensboro M,O
University of Northern Iowa M
University of North Texas M,D
University of Notre Dame D
University of Oklahoma M,D
University of Oregon M,D
University of Pennsylvania M,D
University of Pittsburgh M,D
University of Rhode Island M,O
University of Rochester M,D
University of South Carolina M,D
The University of South Dakota M,D
University of Southern California M,D
University of Southern Mississippi M,D
University of South Florida M,D
The University of Tennessee M,D
The University of Texas at Arlington M
The University of Texas at Austin D
The University of Texas at Brownsville M
The University of Texas at Dallas M,D
The University of Texas at El Paso M
The University of Texas at San Antonio M
The University of Texas at Tyler M
The University of Texas of the Permian Basin M
The University of Toledo M
University of Utah M,D
University of Virginia M,D
University of Washington M,D
University of West Florida M
University of Wisconsin–Madison D
University of Wisconsin–Milwaukee M,D
University of Wyoming M
Utah State University M
Vanderbilt University M,D
Villanova University M
Virginia Commonwealth University M,D,O
Virginia Polytechnic Institute and State University M
Washington State University M,D
Washington University in St. Louis M,D
Wayne State University M,D
West Chester University of Pennsylvania M,O
Western Illinois University M,O
Western Kentucky University M
Western Michigan University M,D
Western Washington University M
West Texas A&M University M
West Virginia University M,D
Wichita State University M
Yale University D

■ POLYMER SCIENCE AND ENGINEERING

California Polytechnic State University, San Luis Obispo M
Carnegie Mellon University M,D
Case Western Reserve University M,D
Clemson University M,D
Cornell University M,D
DePaul University M
Eastern Michigan University M
Florida State University M
Georgia Institute of Technology M,D
Lehigh University M,D
Massachusetts Institute of Technology M,D,O
North Carolina State University D
North Dakota State University M,D
Polytechnic Institute of NYU M
Rensselaer Polytechnic Institute M,D
Stevens Institute of Technology M,D,O
The University of Akron M,D
University of Cincinnati M,D
University of Connecticut M,D
University of Massachusetts Amherst M,D
University of Massachusetts Lowell M,D,O
University of Missouri–Kansas City M,D
University of Southern Mississippi M,D
University of South Florida M,D
The University of Tennessee M,D
University of Wisconsin–Madison M,D
Wayne State University M,D,O

■ PORTUGUESE

Brigham Young University M
Emory University D,O
Harvard University M,D
Indiana University Bloomington M,D
Michigan State University M,D
New York University M,D
The Ohio State University M,D
Princeton University D
Tulane University M,D
University of California, Los Angeles M
University of California, Santa Barbara M,D
University of Illinois at Urbana–Champaign M,D
University of Maryland, College Park M,D
University of Massachusetts Amherst M,D
University of Massachusetts Dartmouth M,D
University of Minnesota, Twin Cities Campus M,D
University of New Mexico M,D

M—master's degree; P—first professional degree; D—doctorate; O—other advanced degree

The University of North Carolina at Chapel Hill M,D
The University of Tennessee D
The University of Texas at Austin M,D
University of Washington M
University of Wisconsin–Madison M,D
Vanderbilt University M,D
Yale University D

■ PROJECT MANAGEMENT

Avila University M,O
Boston University M
Brandeis University M,O
Brenau University M
Capella University M,D,O
Christian Brothers University M,O
City University of Seattle M,O
Colorado Technical University Colorado Springs M,D
Colorado Technical University Denver M
Colorado Technical University Sioux Falls M
Dallas Baptist University M
DePaul University M,D
DeSales University M
Drexel University M
Embry-Riddle Aeronautical University Worldwide M
The George Washington University M,D
Jones International University M
Lakeland College M
Lehigh University M,D,O
Lewis University M
Marymount University M,O
Metropolitan State University M,O
Mississippi State University M,D
Missouri State University M
Northern Kentucky University M,O
Northwestern University M
Notre Dame de Namur University M
Regis University M,O
Robert Morris University M,D
St. Edward's University M
Saint Mary's University of Minnesota M,O
Southern Illinois University Edwardsville M
Southern New Hampshire University M,D,O
Stevens Institute of Technology M,O
Universidad del Turabo M
The University of Alabama in Huntsville M,O
University of Alaska Anchorage M
University of California, Berkeley O
University of Dallas M
University of Denver M,O
University of Mary M
University of San Francisco M
The University of Texas at Dallas M
University of the Incarnate Word M,O
University of Wisconsin–Platteville M
Walden University M,D,O
Western Carolina University M
Winthrop University M,O
Wright State University M

■ PSYCHIATRIC NURSING

Arizona State University M,D,O
Boston College M,D
Case Western Reserve University M,D
The Catholic University of America M,D,O
Columbia University M,O
Fairfield University M,O
Georgia State University M,D,O
Hampton University M
Hunter College of the City University of New York M,O
Husson University M,O
Indiana University–Purdue University Indianapolis M,D
Kent State University M,D
Molloy College M,O
New Mexico State University M
New York University M,O
Northeastern University M,O
Pontifical Catholic University of Puerto Rico M
Rutgers, The State University of New Jersey, Newark M
Saint Xavier University M,O
Seattle University M
Shenandoah University M,O
Stony Brook University, State University of New York M,O
University at Buffalo, the State University of New York M,D,O
University of Alaska Anchorage M,O
University of Cincinnati M,D
University of Delaware M,O
University of Illinois at Chicago M
The University of Kansas M,D,O
University of Louisville M,D
University of Massachusetts Lowell M,O
University of Michigan M
University of Minnesota, Twin Cities Campus M
The University of North Carolina at Chapel Hill M,D,O
University of Pennsylvania M
University of Pittsburgh M,D
University of Rhode Island M,D
University of Rochester M,D,O
University of South Carolina M,O
University of Southern Maine M,O
University of Southern Mississippi M,D
University of Virginia M,D
Vanderbilt University M,D
Virginia Commonwealth University M,D,O
Wayne State University M,O

■ PSYCHOANALYSIS AND PSYCHOTHERAPY

Naropa University M
New York University M,D,O
Prescott College M

■ PSYCHOLOGY—GENERAL

Abilene Christian University M
Adelphi University M,D
Alabama Agricultural and Mechanical University M,O
Alliant International University–San Diego M,D
American International College M,D
American University D
Andrews University M,D,O
Angelo State University M
Antioch University Los Angeles M
Antioch University McGregor M
Antioch University New England M,D,O
Antioch University Santa Barbara M
Antioch University Seattle M,D
Appalachian State University M,O
Arcadia University M,D,O
Argosy University, Orange County M,D,O
Argosy University, Sarasota M,D,O
Argosy University, Tampa M,D
Argosy University, Twin Cities M,D,O
Arizona State University M,D
Assumption College M,O
Auburn University M,D
Auburn University Montgomery M
Augusta State University M
Austin Peay State University M
Avila University M
Azusa Pacific University M,D
Ball State University M
Barry University M,O
Bayamón Central University M
Baylor University M,D
Biola University M,D
Boston College M,D
Boston University M,D
Bowling Green State University M,D
Brandeis University M,D
Brenau University M
Bridgewater State College M
Brigham Young University M,D
Brooklyn College of the City University of New York M,D
Brown University D
Bucknell University M
Caldwell College M,D
California Institute of Integral Studies M,D
California Lutheran University M,D

Institution	Degrees
California Polytechnic State University, San Luis Obispo	M
California State Polytechnic University, Pomona	M
California State University, Bakersfield	M
California State University, Chico	M
California State University, Dominguez Hills	M
California State University, Fresno	M
California State University, Fullerton	M
California State University, Long Beach	M
California State University, Los Angeles	M
California State University, Northridge	M
California State University, Sacramento	M
California State University, San Bernardino	M
California State University, San Marcos	M
California State University, Stanislaus	M,O
Cambridge College	M,O
Cameron University	M
Capella University	M,D,O
Cardinal Stritch University	M
Carlos Albizu University	M,D
Carnegie Mellon University	D
Case Western Reserve University	D
Castleton State College	M
The Catholic University of America	M,D
Central Connecticut State University	M
Central Michigan University	M,D,O
Central Washington University	M
Chestnut Hill College	M,D,O
The Citadel, The Military College of South Carolina	M
City College of the City University of New York	M,D
Claremont Graduate University	M,D,O
Clark University	D
Clemson University	M,D
Cleveland State University	M,D,O
The College at Brockport, State University of New York	M
College of Saint Elizabeth	M,O
College of St. Joseph	M
The College of William and Mary	M,D
Colorado State University	M,D
Columbia University	M,D
Concordia University Chicago	M
Concordia University Wisconsin	M
Cornell University	D
Dartmouth College	D
DePaul University	M,D
Drexel University	M,D
Duke University	D
Duquesne University	D
East Carolina University	M
East Central University	M
Eastern Illinois University	M,O
Eastern Kentucky University	M,O
Eastern Michigan University	M,D
Eastern Washington University	M
East Tennessee State University	M
Edinboro University of Pennsylvania	M
Emory University	D
Emporia State University	M
Fairfield University	M,O
Fairleigh Dickinson University, College at Florham	M,O
Fairleigh Dickinson University, Metropolitan Campus	M,D,O
Fayetteville State University	M
Florida Agricultural and Mechanical University	M
Florida Atlantic University	M,D
Florida Institute of Technology	M,D
Florida International University	M,D
Florida State University	M,D
Fordham University	D
Fort Hays State University	M,O
Framingham State College	M
Francis Marion University	M
Frostburg State University	M
Gallaudet University	M,D,O
Gardner-Webb University	M
Geneva College	M
George Fox University	M,D
Georgetown University	D
The George Washington University	D
Georgia Institute of Technology	M,D
Georgia Southern University	M,D
Georgia State University	M,D
Golden Gate University	M,D,O
Governors State University	M
Graduate School and University Center of the City University of New York	D
Hardin-Simmons University	M
Harvard University	D
Hodges University	M
Hofstra University	M,D,O
Hood College	M,O
Houston Baptist University	M
Howard University	M,D
Humboldt State University	M
Hunter College of the City University of New York	M
Idaho State University	M,D
Illinois Institute of Technology	M,D
Illinois State University	M,D,O
Immaculata University	M,D,O
Indiana State University	M,D
Indiana University Bloomington	M,D
Indiana University of Pennsylvania	M,D
Indiana University–Purdue University Indianapolis	M,D
Indiana University South Bend	M
Inter American University of Puerto Rico, Metropolitan Campus	M,D
Inter American University of Puerto Rico, San Germán Campus	M,D
Iona College	M
Iowa State University of Science and Technology	D
Jackson State University	D
Jacksonville State University	M
James Madison University	M,D,O
John F. Kennedy University	M,D,O
The Johns Hopkins University	D
Kansas State University	M,D
Kean University	M
Kent State University	M,D
Lamar University	M
La Salle University	D
Lehigh University	M,D
Lesley University	M,D,O
Lewis & Clark College	M,O
Lipscomb University	M,O
Long Island University, Brooklyn Campus	M,D
Long Island University, C.W. Post Campus	M,D
Louisiana State University and Agricultural and Mechanical College	M,D
Louisiana Tech University	M,D
Loyola University Chicago	M,D
Loyola University Maryland	M,D,O
Lynn University	M,O
Madonna University	M
Marist College	M,O
Marquette University	M,D
Marshall University	M,D
Marywood University	M
McNeese State University	M
Medaille College	M
Mercy College	M
Metropolitan State University	M
Miami University	D
Michigan State University	M,D
Middle Tennessee State University	M
Midwestern State University	M
Millersville University of Pennsylvania	M
Minnesota State University Mankato	M,D
Mississippi State University	M,D
Missouri State University	M
Monmouth University	M,O
Montana State University	M
Montana State University–Billings	M

M—master's degree; P—first professional degree; D—doctorate; O—other advanced degree

Montclair State University	M,O
Morehead State University	M
Morgan State University	M,D
Murray State University	M
National-Louis University	M,O
National University	M
New Jersey City University	M,O
New Mexico Highlands University	M
New Mexico State University	M,D
The New School: A University	M,D
New York University	M,D,O
Norfolk State University	M,D
North Carolina Central University	M
North Carolina State University	D
Northcentral University	M,D,O
North Dakota State University	M,D
Northeastern State University	M
Northeastern University	M,D,O
Northern Arizona University	M
Northern Illinois University	M,D
Northern Michigan University	M
Northwestern State University of Louisiana	M
Northwestern University	D
Northwest Missouri State University	M
Notre Dame de Namur University	M,O
Nova Southeastern University	M,D,O
The Ohio State University	M,D
Ohio University	D
Oklahoma State University	M,D
Old Dominion University	M,D
Our Lady of the Lake University of San Antonio	M,D
Pace University	M
Pacifica Graduate Institute	M,D
Pacific University	M,D
Penn State Harrisburg	M,D
Penn State University Park	M,D
Pepperdine University	M
Pittsburg State University	M
Polytechnic Institute of NYU	M
Pontifical Catholic University of Puerto Rico	M,D
Portland State University	M,D,O
Princeton University	D
Purdue University	D
Queens College of the City University of New York	M
Radford University	M,D,O
Regis University	M,O
Rhode Island College	M
Rice University	M,D
Rochester Institute of Technology	M
Roosevelt University	D
Rowan University	M
Rutgers, The State University of New Jersey, Camden	M
Rutgers, The State University of New Jersey, Newark	D
Rutgers, The State University of New Jersey, New Brunswick	M,D
St. Cloud State University	M
St. John's University (NY)	M,D
Saint Joseph's University	M,O
Saint Louis University	M,D
St. Mary's University (United States)	M
Saint Xavier University	M,O
Salem State College	M
Sam Houston State University	M,D
San Diego State University	M,D
San Francisco State University	M
San Jose State University	M
Seattle University	M
Seton Hall University	M,D,O
Shippensburg University of Pennsylvania	M
Southeastern Louisiana University	M
Southern Connecticut State University	M
Southern Illinois University Carbondale	M,D
Southern Illinois University Edwardsville	M,O
Southern Methodist University	D
Southern Nazarene University	M
Southern New Hampshire University	M,O
Southern Oregon University	M
Southern University and Agricultural and Mechanical College	M
Spalding University	M,D
Stanford University	D
State University of New York at Binghamton	M,D
State University of New York at New Paltz	M
State University of New York at Plattsburgh	M,O
Stephen F. Austin State University	M
Stony Brook University, State University of New York	D
Suffolk University	D
Sul Ross State University	M
Temple University	D
Tennessee State University	M,D
Texas A&M International University	M
Texas A&M University	M,D
Texas A&M University–Commerce	M,D
Texas A&M University–Corpus Christi	M
Texas A&M University–Kingsville	M
Texas A&M University–Texarkana	M
Texas Christian University	M,D
Texas Southern University	M
Texas State University–San Marcos	M
Texas Tech University	M,D
Texas Woman's University	M,D,O
Trevecca Nazarene University	M,D
Tufts University	M,D
Tulane University	M,D
Union College (KY)	M
Union Institute & University	M
University at Albany, State University of New York	M,D,O
University at Buffalo, the State University of New York	M,D
The University of Akron	M,D
The University of Alabama	D
The University of Alabama at Birmingham	M,D
The University of Alabama in Huntsville	M
University of Alaska Anchorage	M,D
University of Alaska Fairbanks	D
The University of Arizona	M,D
University of Arkansas	M,D
University of Arkansas at Little Rock	M
University of Baltimore	M
University of California, Berkeley	D
University of California, Davis	D
University of California, Irvine	D
University of California, Los Angeles	M,D
University of California, Riverside	M,D
University of California, San Diego	D
University of California, Santa Barbara	M,D
University of California, Santa Cruz	D
University of Central Arkansas	M,D
University of Central Florida	M,D
University of Central Missouri	M
University of Central Oklahoma	M
University of Chicago	D
University of Cincinnati	D
University of Colorado at Boulder	M,D
University of Colorado at Colorado Springs	M,D
University of Colorado Denver	D
University of Connecticut	M,D,O
University of Dallas	M
University of Dayton	M
University of Delaware	D
University of Denver	M,D
University of Detroit Mercy	M,D,O
University of Florida	M,D
University of Georgia	M,D
University of Hartford	M,D
University of Hawaii at Manoa	M,D,O
University of Houston	M,D
University of Houston–Clear Lake	M
University of Houston–Victoria	M
University of Idaho	M

University of Illinois at Chicago D
University of Illinois at Urbana–Champaign M,D
University of Indianapolis M,D
The University of Iowa M,D,O
The University of Kansas M,D
University of Kentucky M,D
University of La Verne M,D
University of Louisiana at Lafayette M
University of Louisiana at Monroe M,O
University of Louisville M,D
University of Maine M,D
University of Mary Hardin-Baylor M
University of Maryland, Baltimore County M,D
University of Maryland, College Park M,D
University of Massachusetts Amherst M,D
University of Massachusetts Dartmouth M,O
University of Massachusetts Lowell M
University of Memphis M,D
University of Miami M,D
University of Michigan D,O
University of Minnesota, Twin Cities Campus D
University of Mississippi M,D
University of Missouri–Columbia M,D
University of Missouri–Kansas City M,D
University of Missouri–St. Louis M,D,O
The University of Montana M,D,O
University of Nebraska at Omaha M,D,O
University of Nebraska–Lincoln M,D
University of Nevada, Las Vegas D
University of Nevada, Reno M,D
University of New Hampshire D
University of New Mexico M,D
University of New Orleans M,D
The University of North Carolina at Chapel Hill D
The University of North Carolina at Charlotte M,D
The University of North Carolina at Greensboro M,D
The University of North Carolina Wilmington M
University of North Dakota M,D
University of Northern Colorado M,D
University of Northern Iowa M
University of North Florida M
University of North Texas M,D
University of Notre Dame D
University of Oklahoma M,D
University of Oregon M,D
University of Pennsylvania D
University of Phoenix M
University of Phoenix–Denver Campus M
University of Phoenix–Hawaii Campus M
University of Phoenix–Las Vegas Campus M
University of Phoenix–Louisiana Campus M
University of Phoenix–New Mexico Campus M
University of Phoenix–Oregon Campus M
University of Phoenix–Philadelphia Campus M
University of Phoenix–Phoenix Campus M,O
University of Phoenix–Sacramento Valley Campus M
University of Phoenix–Southern Arizona Campus M,O
University of Phoenix–Southern California Campus M,O
University of Phoenix–Southern Colorado Campus M
University of Pittsburgh M,D
University of Puerto Rico, Río Piedras M,D
University of Rhode Island D
University of Rochester M,D
University of Saint Francis (IN) M
University of Saint Mary M
University of St. Thomas (MN) M,D,O
University of South Alabama M
University of South Carolina M,D
The University of South Dakota M,D
University of Southern California M,D
University of Southern Mississippi M,D
University of South Florida M,D
The University of Tennessee M,D
The University of Tennessee at Chattanooga M
The University of Texas at Arlington M,D
The University of Texas at Austin D
The University of Texas at Brownsville M
The University of Texas at Dallas M,D
The University of Texas at El Paso M,D
The University of Texas at San Antonio M
The University of Texas at Tyler M
The University of Texas of the Permian Basin M
The University of Texas–Pan American M
University of the Pacific M
The University of Toledo M,D
University of Tulsa M,D
University of Utah D
University of Vermont D
University of Virginia M,D
University of Washington D
University of West Florida M
University of West Georgia M,D
University of Wisconsin–Eau Claire M,O
University of Wisconsin–La Crosse M,O
University of Wisconsin–Madison D
University of Wisconsin–Milwaukee M,D
University of Wisconsin–Oshkosh M
University of Wisconsin–Stout M
University of Wisconsin–Whitewater M,O
University of Wyoming M,D
Utah State University M,D
Valdosta State University M,O
Valparaiso University M,O
Vanderbilt University M,D
Villanova University M
Virginia Commonwealth University D
Virginia Polytechnic Institute and State University M,D
Virginia State University M,D
Wake Forest University M
Walden University M,D,O
Washburn University M
Washington State University M,D
Washington University in St. Louis D
Wayne State University M,D
West Chester University of Pennsylvania M,O
Western Carolina University M
Western Illinois University M,O
Western Kentucky University M,O
Western Michigan University M,D
Western New England College D
Western Washington University M
Westfield State College M
West Texas A&M University M
West Virginia University M,D
Wheaton College M,D
Wichita State University M,D
Widener University
William Carey University M
Winthrop University M,O
Wright State University M,D
Xavier University M,D
Yale University D
Yeshiva University M,D
Youngstown State University M

■ PUBLIC ADMINISTRATION

Adelphi University O
Albany State University M
American International College M
American University M,D,O

M—master's degree; P—first professional degree; D—doctorate; O—other advanced degree

Angelo State University M
Anna Maria College M
Appalachian State University M
Argosy University, Orange County M,D,O
Argosy University, Tampa M,D
Arkansas State University M,O
Auburn University M,D
Auburn University Montgomery M,D
Ball State University M
Barry University M
Baylor University M,D
Belhaven College (MS) M
Bellevue University M,D
Bernard M. Baruch College of the City University of New York M
Boise State University M
Boston University M,O
Bowie State University M
Bowling Green State University M
Bridgewater State College M
Brigham Young University M
California Baptist University M
California Lutheran University M
California State Polytechnic University, Pomona M
California State University, Bakersfield M
California State University, Chico M
California State University, Dominguez Hills M
California State University, East Bay M
California State University, Fresno M
California State University, Fullerton M
California State University, Long Beach M
California State University, Los Angeles M
California State University, Northridge M
California State University, Sacramento M
California State University, San Bernardino M
California State University, Stanislaus M
Capella University M,D
Carnegie Mellon University M
Central Michigan University M,O
Cheyney University of Pennsylvania M
City College of the City University of New York M,D
Clark Atlanta University M
Clark University M,O
Clemson University M,D
Cleveland State University M,O
The College at Brockport, State University of New York M,O
College of Charleston M
Columbia University M
Columbus State University M
Concordia University Wisconsin M
Cumberland University M
DePaul University M,O
Drake University M
Duquesne University M,O
East Carolina University M
Eastern Kentucky University M
Eastern Michigan University M,O
Eastern Washington University M
The Evergreen State College M
Fairleigh Dickinson University, College at Florham M
Fairleigh Dickinson University, Metropolitan Campus M,O
Florida Agricultural and Mechanical University M
Florida Atlantic University M,D
Florida Gulf Coast University M
Florida Institute of Technology M
Florida International University M,D
Florida State University M,D,O
Framingham State College M
Gannon University M,O
The George Washington University M,D
Georgia College & State University M
Georgia Southern University M
Georgia State University M,D,O
Governors State University M
Grambling State University M
Grand Valley State University M
Hamline University M,D
Harvard University M
Hodges University M
Hood College M
Howard University M
Idaho State University M
Illinois Institute of Technology M
Indiana State University M
Indiana University Bloomington M,D,O
Indiana University Northwest M,O
Indiana University–Purdue University Indianapolis M
Indiana University South Bend M,O
Iowa State University of Science and Technology M
Jackson State University M,D
James Madison University M
John Jay College of Criminal Justice of the City University of New York M
Kansas State University M
Kean University M
Kennesaw State University M
Kent State University M
Kutztown University of Pennsylvania M
Lamar University M
Lewis University M
Lincoln University (MO) M
Lindenwood University M
Long Island University, Brooklyn Campus M
Long Island University, C.W. Post Campus M,O
Louisiana State University and Agricultural and Mechanical College M,D
Marist College M
Marquette University M
Marywood University M
Metropolitan College of New York M
Metropolitan State University M,O
Midwestern State University M
Minnesota State University Mankato M
Minnesota State University Moorhead M
Mississippi State University M,D
Missouri State University M
Montana State University M
Montana State University–Billings M
Monterey Institute of International Studies M
Morehead State University M
National University M
New York University M,D,O
North Carolina Central University M
North Carolina State University M,D
Northeastern University M,O
Northern Arizona University M,D,O
Northern Illinois University M
Northern Kentucky University M,O
Northern Michigan University M
North Georgia College & State University M
Norwich University M
Notre Dame de Namur University M
Nova Southeastern University M
Oakland University M
Ohio University M
Old Dominion University M,D
Pace University M
Park University M
Penn State Harrisburg M,D
Pepperdine University M
Pontifical Catholic University of Puerto Rico M
Portland State University M,D
Regent University M
Regis College (MA) M,O
Rhode Island College M
Roger Williams University M
Roosevelt University M
Rutgers, The State University of New Jersey, Camden M
Rutgers, The State University of New Jersey, Newark M,D

Institution	Degree
Saginaw Valley State University	M
St. Edward's University	M,O
Saint Louis University	M,D,O
St. Mary's University (United States)	M
St. Thomas University	M,O
Salisbury University	M
Sam Houston State University	M
San Diego State University	M
San Francisco State University	M
San Jose State University	M
Savannah State University	M
Seattle University	M
Seton Hall University	M,O
Shenandoah University	M,D,O
Shippensburg University of Pennsylvania	M
Sonoma State University	M
Southeast Missouri State University	M
Southern Illinois University Carbondale	M
Southern Illinois University Edwardsville	M
Southern University and Agricultural and Mechanical College	M
Southern Utah University	M
State University of New York at Binghamton	M
Stephen F. Austin State University	M
Strayer University	M
Suffolk University	M,O
Sul Ross State University	M
Syracuse University	M,D,O
Tennessee State University	M,D
Texas A&M International University	M
Texas A&M University	M,O
Texas A&M University–Corpus Christi	M
Texas Southern University	M
Texas State University–San Marcos	M
Texas Tech University	M,D
Troy University	M
Tufts University	O
University at Albany, State University of New York	M,D,O
The University of Akron	M
The University of Alabama	M,D
The University of Alabama at Birmingham	M
University of Alaska Anchorage	M
University of Alaska Southeast	M
The University of Arizona	M,D
University of Arkansas	M
University of Arkansas at Little Rock	M
University of Baltimore	M,D
University of Central Florida	M,O
University of Colorado at Colorado Springs	M
University of Colorado Denver	M
University of Connecticut	M,O
University of Dayton	M
University of Delaware	M
University of Evansville	M
The University of Findlay	M
University of Georgia	M,D
University of Guam	M
University of Hawaii at Manoa	M,O
University of Idaho	M
University of Illinois at Chicago	M,D
University of Illinois at Springfield	M,D
The University of Kansas	M,D
University of Kentucky	M,D
University of La Verne	M,D,O
University of Louisville	M
University of Maine	M,D
University of Maryland, College Park	M
University of Massachusetts Amherst	M
University of Memphis	M
University of Michigan–Dearborn	M,O
University of Michigan–Flint	M
University of Missouri–Kansas City	M,D
University of Missouri–St. Louis	M,D,O
The University of Montana	M
University of Nebraska at Omaha	M,D,O
University of Nevada, Las Vegas	M,D,O
University of Nevada, Reno	M
University of New Hampshire	M,O
University of New Haven	M
University of New Mexico	M
University of New Orleans	M
The University of North Carolina at Chapel Hill	M
The University of North Carolina at Charlotte	M
The University of North Carolina at Pembroke	M
The University of North Carolina Wilmington	M
University of North Dakota	M
University of North Florida	M
University of North Texas	M,D
University of Oklahoma	M
University of Pennsylvania	M
University of Phoenix	M
University of Phoenix–Central Florida Campus	M
University of Phoenix–Denver Campus	M
University of Phoenix–Hawaii Campus	M
University of Phoenix–Las Vegas Campus	M
University of Phoenix–Louisiana Campus	M
University of Phoenix–North Florida Campus	M
University of Phoenix–Oregon Campus	M
University of Phoenix–Philadelphia Campus	M
University of Phoenix–Sacramento Valley Campus	M
University of Phoenix–San Diego Campus	M
University of Phoenix–Southern California Campus	M
University of Phoenix–Southern Colorado Campus	M
University of Phoenix–South Florida Campus	M
University of Phoenix–West Florida Campus	M
University of Pittsburgh	M,D,O
University of Puerto Rico, Río Piedras	M
University of Rhode Island	M,O
University of San Francisco	M
University of South Alabama	M
University of South Carolina	M
The University of South Dakota	M,D
University of Southern California	M
University of Southern Indiana	M
University of South Florida	M
The University of Tennessee	M
The University of Tennessee at Chattanooga	M,O
The University of Texas at Arlington	M
The University of Texas at Brownsville	M
The University of Texas at El Paso	M
The University of Texas at San Antonio	M
The University of Texas at Tyler	M
The University of Texas–Pan American	M
University of the District of Columbia	M
The University of Toledo	M,O
University of Utah	M
University of Vermont	M
University of Washington	M,D
University of West Florida	M
University of West Georgia	M,O
University of Wisconsin–Milwaukee	M
University of Wisconsin–Oshkosh	M
University of Wyoming	M
Upper Iowa University	M
Villanova University	M
Virginia Commonwealth University	M,O

M—master's degree; P—first professional degree; D—doctorate; O—other advanced degree

Virginia Polytechnic Institute and State University M,D,O
Walden University M,D,O
Wayland Baptist University M
Wayne State University M
Webster University M,D
West Chester University of Pennsylvania M,O
Western Illinois University M,O
Western International University M
Western Michigan University M,D,O
West Virginia University M
Wichita State University M
Widener University M
Wilmington University M
Wright State University M

■ PUBLIC AFFAIRS

American University M
Arizona State University M,D
Cornell University M
DePaul University M,O
George Mason University M,D
The George Washington University M
Indiana University Bloomington M,D,O
Indiana University Northwest M,O
Indiana University of Pennsylvania M
Indiana University–Purdue University Fort Wayne M,O
Indiana University–Purdue University Indianapolis M
Indiana University South Bend M,O
Jackson State University M
Murray State University M
New Mexico Highlands University M
Northeastern University M,D,O
Notre Dame de Namur University M
The Ohio State University M,D
Park University M
Princeton University M,D,O
Texas A&M University M,O
The University of Alabama in Huntsville M
University of Arkansas at Little Rock M,O
University of Central Florida D
University of Colorado at Colorado Springs M
University of Colorado Denver D
University of Florida M,D,O
University of Idaho M,D
University of Louisville D
University of Massachusetts Boston M
University of Minnesota, Twin Cities Campus M
University of Missouri–Columbia M
University of Missouri–Kansas City M,D
University of Nevada, Las Vegas M,D,O
The University of North Carolina at Greensboro M,O
The University of Texas at Arlington D
The University of Texas at Austin M,D
The University of Texas at Dallas M,D
University of Washington M,D
University of Wisconsin–Madison M
Virginia Commonwealth University M,D,O
Virginia Polytechnic Institute and State University M,D
West Chester University of Pennsylvania M,O
Western Carolina University M
Western Michigan University M,D,O

■ PUBLIC HEALTH—GENERAL

Adelphi University O
Arizona State University M,D,O
Armstrong Atlantic State University M
Austin Peay State University M
Barry University M
Bellevue University M,D
Benedictine University M
Boise State University M
Boston University P,M,D,O
Bowling Green State University M
Brooklyn College of the City University of New York M
Brown University M
California State University, Fresno M
California State University, Fullerton M
California State University, Northridge M
California State University, San Bernardino M
Case Western Reserve University M
Cleveland State University M
Columbia University M,D
Dartmouth College M
Davenport University M
Dominican University of California M
Drexel University M,D,O
East Carolina University M
East Stroudsburg University of Pennsylvania M
East Tennessee State University M,O
Emory University M,D,O
Florida Agricultural and Mechanical University M
Florida International University M,D
Florida State University M
Fort Valley State University M
Georgetown University M,D
The George Washington University M,D,O
Georgia Southern University M,D
Georgia State University M,D,O
Graduate School and University Center of the City University of New York D
Harvard University M,D
Howard University M
Hunter College of the City University of New York M
Idaho State University M,O
Indiana University Bloomington M,D
Indiana University–Purdue University Indianapolis M
The Johns Hopkins University M,D
Kansas State University M
Kent State University M
Michigan State University M
Missouri State University M
Morgan State University M,D
New Mexico State University M
Northern Arizona University M
Northern Illinois University M
Northwestern University M
Nova Southeastern University M
The Ohio State University M,D
Old Dominion University M
Oregon State University M,D
Portland State University M,O
Purdue University M,D
Rutgers, The State University of New Jersey, New Brunswick M,D
St. Catherine University M
Saint Louis University M,D
Saint Xavier University M,O
San Diego State University M,D
San Francisco State University M
San Jose State University M,O
Sarah Lawrence College M
Southern Connecticut State University M
Stony Brook University, State University of New York M
Temple University M,D
Texas A&M University M,D
Touro College M,D
Trinity (Washington) University M
Tufts University M
Tulane University M,D,O
University at Albany, State University of New York M,D
University at Buffalo, the State University of New York M,D
The University of Akron M,D
The University of Alabama at Birmingham M,D
University of Alaska Anchorage M
The University of Arizona M,D
University of California, Berkeley M,D
University of California, Los Angeles M,D
University of California, San Diego D

University of Colorado Denver M,D
University of Connecticut M
University of Florida M
University of Hawaii at Manoa M;D,O
University of Illinois at Chicago M,D
University of Illinois at Springfield M
University of Illinois at Urbana–Champaign M,D
The University of Iowa M,D,O
The University of Kansas M
University of Kentucky M
University of Louisville M,D
University of Maryland, College Park M,D
University of Massachusetts Amherst M,D
University of Massachusetts Lowell M,O
University of Memphis M
University of Miami M
University of Michigan M,D
University of Minnesota, Twin Cities Campus M,D,O
University of Missouri–Columbia M
The University of Montana M,O
University of Nebraska at Omaha M
University of Nevada, Reno M,D
University of New England M,O
University of New Hampshire M,O
University of New Mexico M
The University of North Carolina at Chapel Hill M,D
The University of North Carolina at Charlotte M
University of Northern Colorado M
University of North Florida M,O
University of Pittsburgh M,D,O
University of Rochester M
University of South Carolina M
University of Southern California M
University of Southern Mississippi M
University of South Florida M,D
The University of Tennessee M
The University of Texas at El Paso M
The University of Toledo M,O
University of Utah M,D
University of Virginia M,D
University of West Florida M
University of Wisconsin–La Crosse M
University of Wisconsin–Milwaukee M,D,O
Vanderbilt University M
Walden University M,D
Washington University in St. Louis M,D
Wayne State University M,O
West Chester University of Pennsylvania M,O
Western Kentucky University M
Westminster College (UT) M
West Virginia University M
Wichita State University M
Wright State University M
Yale University M,D

■ PUBLIC HISTORY

Appalachian State University M
Arizona State University M,D
California State University, Sacramento M
Eastern Illinois University M
Florida State University M,D
Georgia College & State University M
Indiana University–Purdue University Indianapolis M
Loyola University Chicago M,D
Middle Tennessee State University M,D
New York University M,D,O
North Carolina State University M
Northeastern University M,D
Northern Kentucky University M
Rutgers, The State University of New Jersey, Camden M
Shippensburg University of Pennsylvania M,O
Simmons College
Sonoma State University M
University at Albany, State University of New York M,D,O
University of Arkansas at Little Rock M
University of Central Florida M
University of Houston M,D
University of Illinois at Springfield M
University of Massachusetts Amherst M,D
University of Massachusetts Boston M
University of South Carolina M,O
The University of Texas at Austin M,D
University of West Florida M
Washington State University M,D

■ PUBLIC POLICY

Albany State University M
American University M
Arizona State University P,M
Baylor University M,D
Boise State University M
Brandeis University M
Brigham Young University M
Brooklyn College of the City University of New York M,D
Brown University M
California Lutheran University M
California State University, Long Beach M
California State University, Sacramento M
Carnegie Mellon University M,D
Claremont Graduate University M,D,O
Clemson University M,D
The College of William and Mary M
Columbia University M
Cornell University M,D
DePaul University M,O
Duke University M,D,O
Duquesne University M,O
Eastern Michigan University M,O
Florida State University M,D,O
George Mason University M,D
Georgetown University M,D
The George Washington University M,D
Georgia Institute of Technology M,D
Georgia State University M,D,O
Graduate School and University Center of the City University of New York M,D
Harvard University M,D
Indiana University Bloomington M,D,O
Indiana University–Purdue University Indianapolis M
Jackson State University M,D
John Jay College of Criminal Justice of the City University of New York M,D
The Johns Hopkins University M
Kent State University M,D
Lincoln University (MO) M
Loyola University Chicago M,D
Mills College M
Mississippi State University M,D
Monmouth University M
The New School: A University D
Northeastern University M,D
Northwestern University D
Pepperdine University M
Princeton University M,D
Regent University M
Regis College (MA) M,O
Rochester Institute of Technology M
Rutgers, The State University of New Jersey, Camden M
Rutgers, The State University of New Jersey, Newark M,D
Rutgers, The State University of New Jersey, New Brunswick M,D
Saint Louis University M,D,O
San Francisco State University M
Seton Hall University M,O
Southern New Hampshire University M,D
Southern University and Agricultural and Mechanical College D

M—master's degree; P—first professional degree; D—doctorate; O—other advanced degree

State University of New York at Binghamton M,D
State University of New York Empire State College M
Stony Brook University, State University of New York M,D
Suffolk University M
Texas A&M University M,O
Tufts University M
University at Albany, State University of New York M,D,O
The University of Arizona M,D
University of Arkansas D
University of California, Berkeley M,D
University of California, Los Angeles M
University of Chicago M,D
University of Colorado at Boulder M,D
University of Delaware M,D
University of Denver M
University of Georgia M,D
University of Hawaii at Manoa O
University of Louisville M
University of Maryland, Baltimore County M,D
University of Maryland, College Park M,D
University of Massachusetts Amherst M
University of Massachusetts Boston D
University of Massachusetts Dartmouth M,O
University of Memphis M
University of Michigan M,D
University of Michigan–Dearborn M
University of Minnesota, Twin Cities Campus M
University of Missouri–St. Louis M,D,O
University of Nebraska–Lincoln M,D,O
University of Nevada, Las Vegas M
The University of North Carolina at Chapel Hill D
The University of North Carolina at Charlotte D
University of Northern Iowa M
University of Oregon M
University of Pennsylvania M,D
University of Pittsburgh M,D,O
University of Rhode Island M,O
University of Southern California M
University of Southern Maine M,D,O
The University of Texas at Austin M,D
The University of Texas at Brownsville M
The University of Texas at Dallas M,D
The University of Texas at El Paso M
University of the Pacific P,M,D
University of Utah M
University of Virginia M
University of Washington M,D
University of Washington, Bothell M
Vanderbilt University M,D
Virginia Commonwealth University D
Virginia Polytechnic Institute and State University M,D,O
Walden University M,D,O
Washington State University M,D
Washington University in St. Louis M
West Virginia University M,D
William Paterson University of New Jersey M

■ PUBLISHING

Carnegie Mellon University M
DePaul University M
Drexel University M
Emerson College M
The George Washington University M
New York University M
Northwestern University M
Pace University M
Rosemont College M
University of Baltimore M
University of Houston–Victoria M

■ QUALITY MANAGEMENT

California State University, Dominguez Hills M
Calumet College of Saint Joseph M
Case Western Reserve University M,D
Dowling College M,O
Eastern Michigan University M,O
Ferris State University M
Florida Institute of Technology M
Hofstra University M
Madonna University M
Marian University (WI) M
Northwest Missouri State University M,O
Penn State University Park M
Regis College (MA) M
Rutgers, The State University of New Jersey, New Brunswick M,D
Saint Joseph's College of Maine M
San Jose State University M
Southern Polytechnic State University M,O
Stevens Institute of Technology M,O
Universidad del Turabo M
The University of Alabama M
University of California, Berkeley O
Upper Iowa University M
Webster University M,D

■ QUANTITATIVE ANALYSIS

Bernard M. Baruch College of the City University of New York M
Drexel University M,D,O
Georgia State University M,D
Lehigh University M
New York University M,D,O
Oklahoma State University M,D
Providence College M
St. John's University (NY) M,O
Syracuse University D
Texas Tech University M,D
University of California, Santa Barbara M,D
University of Cincinnati M,D
University of Connecticut M,O
University of Florida M
University of Illinois at Chicago M,D
University of Missouri–St. Louis M,O
University of North Texas M,D
University of Oregon M
University of Pittsburgh D
University of Puerto Rico, Río Piedras M,D
University of Southern California M,D
The University of Texas at Arlington M,D
Virginia Commonwealth University M
Walden University M,D

■ RADIATION BIOLOGY

Auburn University M,D
Austin Peay State University M
Colorado State University M,D
Georgetown University M
The University of Iowa M,D

■ RANGE SCIENCE

Colorado State University M,D
Kansas State University M,D
Montana State University M,D
New Mexico State University M,D
North Dakota State University M,D
Oregon State University M,D
Sul Ross State University M
Texas A&M University–Kingsville M
Texas Tech University M,D
The University of Arizona M,D
University of California, Berkeley M
University of Idaho M
University of Wyoming M,D
Utah State University M,D

■ READING EDUCATION

Adelphi University M
Alfred University M
Alverno College M
American International College M,D,O
Andrews University M
Angelo State University M
Appalachian State University M
Arcadia University M,D,O
Arkansas State University M,O
Ashland University M
Auburn University M,D,O
Auburn University Montgomery M,O
Aurora University M,D

Institution	Degrees
Austin Peay State University	M,O
Avila University	M,O
Baldwin-Wallace College	M
Barry University	M,D,O
Bellarmine University	M
Benedictine University	M
Bethel University	M,D,O
Bloomsburg University of Pennsylvania	M
Boise State University	M
Boston College	M,O
Boston University	M,D,O
Bowie State University	M
Bowling Green State University	M,O
Bridgewater State College	M,O
Brigham Young University	M
Bucknell University	M
Buffalo State College, State University of New York	M
Butler University	M
California Baptist University	M
California Lutheran University	M
California State University, Bakersfield	M,O
California State University, Chico	M
California State University, Fresno	M
California State University, Fullerton	M
California State University, Los Angeles	M
California State University, Northridge	M
California State University, Sacramento	M
California State University, San Bernardino	M
California State University, Stanislaus	M,O
California University of Pennsylvania	M
Cambridge College	M,D,O
Canisius College	M
Capella University	M,D,O
Cardinal Stritch University	M
Castleton State College	M,O
Central Connecticut State University	M,O
Central Michigan University	M,O
Central Washington University	M
Chapman University	M
Chicago State University	M
The Citadel, The Military College of South Carolina	M
City College of the City University of New York	M
City University of Seattle	M,O
Clarion University of Pennsylvania	M
Clemson University	M
The College at Brockport, State University of New York	M
College of Mount St. Joseph	M
The College of New Jersey	M,O
The College of New Rochelle	M
College of St. Joseph	M
The College of Saint Rose	M,O
The College of William and Mary	M
Concordia University Chicago	M
Concordia University, Nebraska	M
Concordia University Wisconsin	M
Coppin State University	M
Dallas Baptist University	M
Delaware State University	M
DePaul University	M,D
Dominican University	M
Dowling College	M,D,O
Drury University	M
Duquesne University	M
East Carolina University	M
Eastern Connecticut State University	M
Eastern Michigan University	M
Eastern Nazarene College	M,O
Eastern Washington University	M
East Stroudsburg University of Pennsylvania	M
East Tennessee State University	M
Edinboro University of Pennsylvania	M,O
Emporia State University	M
Endicott College	M
Fairleigh Dickinson University, College at Florham	M,O
Fairleigh Dickinson University, Metropolitan Campus	M,O
Fayetteville State University	M
Ferris State University	M
Florida Atlantic University	M
Florida Gulf Coast University	M
Florida International University	M,D
Florida State University	M,D,O
Fordham University	M,D,O
Framingham State College	M
Fresno Pacific University	M
Frostburg State University	M
Furman University	M
Gannon University	M,O
George Fox University	M,D,O
George Mason University	M,O
Georgetown College	M
Georgia Southern University	M
Georgia Southwestern State University	M,O
Georgia State University	M,D,O
Gonzaga University	M
Governors State University	M
Grambling State University	M,D
Grand Valley State University	M
Gwynedd-Mercy College	M
Harding University	M,O
Hardin-Simmons University	M
Harvard University	M
Henderson State University	M
Heritage University	M
Hofstra University	M,D,O
Holy Family University	M
Hood College	M
Houston Baptist University	M
Howard University	M,O
Hunter College of the City University of New York	M,O
Idaho State University	M,O
Illinois State University	M
Indiana University Bloomington	M,D,O
Indiana University of Pennsylvania	M
Indiana University–Purdue University Indianapolis	M,O
Iona College	M
Jacksonville State University	M
Jacksonville University	M
James Madison University	M
The Johns Hopkins University	M,D,O
Johnson State College	M
Kean University	M
Kent State University	M
King's College	M
Kutztown University of Pennsylvania	M
Lehman College of the City University of New York	M
Lesley University	M,D,O
Lewis University	M
Liberty University	M,D,O
Lincoln University (PA)	M
Long Island University, Brentwood Campus	M
Long Island University, Brooklyn Campus	M
Long Island University, C.W. Post Campus	M
Longwood University	M
Loyola Marymount University	M
Loyola University Chicago	M
Loyola University Maryland	M,O
Lynchburg College	M
Madonna University	M
Malone University	M
Manhattanville College	M
Marshall University	M,O
Marygrove College	M
Maryville University of Saint Louis	M,D
Marywood University	M
McDaniel College	M
Medaille College	M
Mercer University	M,D,O
Mercy College	M
Miami University	M
Michigan State University	M
Middle Tennessee State University	M,D
Midwestern State University	M
Millersville University of Pennsylvania	M

M—master's degree; P—first professional degree; D—doctorate; O—other advanced degree

Minnesota State University Moorhead M
Missouri State University M
Monmouth University M,O
Montana State University–Billings M
Montclair State University M,O
Morehead State University M,O
Mount Saint Mary College M
Murray State University M,O
National-Louis University M,D,O
Nazareth College of Rochester M
New Jersey City University M
New York University M
Niagara University M
North Carolina Agricultural and Technical State University M
Northeastern Illinois University M
Northeastern State University M
Northern Illinois University M,D
Northern Michigan University M,O
Northwestern State University of Louisiana M,O
Northwest Missouri State University M
Northwest Nazarene University M
Notre Dame de Namur University M,O
Nova Southeastern University M,O
Oakland University M,D,O
Ohio University M,D
Old Dominion University M,D
Olivet Nazarene University M
Oregon State University M
Our Lady of the Lake University of San Antonio M
Penn State Harrisburg M,D
Penn State University Park M,D
Pittsburg State University M
Plymouth State University M
Portland State University M,D
Providence College M
Purdue University M,D,O
Queens College of the City University of New York M
Queens University of Charlotte M
Radford University M
Regis College (MA) M
Regis University M,O
Rhode Island College M
Rider University M,O
Rivier College M,D,O
Roberts Wesleyan College M,O
Rockford College M
Roger Williams University M
Roosevelt University M
Rowan University M
Rutgers, The State University of New Jersey, New Brunswick M,D
Sacred Heart University M,O
Saginaw Valley State University M
St. Bonaventure University M
Saint Francis University M
St. John Fisher College M
St. John's University (NY) M,D
St. Joseph's College, Long Island Campus M
Saint Joseph's University M,D
Saint Leo University M
Saint Martin's University M
Saint Mary's College of California M
St. Mary's University (United States) M
Saint Mary's University of Minnesota M,O
Saint Michael's College M,O
Saint Peter's College M
St. Thomas Aquinas College M,O
St. Thomas University M,D,O
Saint Xavier University M,O
Salem State College M,O
Salisbury University M
Sam Houston State University M,D
San Diego State University M
San Francisco State University M,O
Seattle Pacific University M
Seattle University M,O
Shippensburg University of Pennsylvania M
Siena Heights University M
Slippery Rock University of Pennsylvania M
Southeastern Oklahoma State University M
Southern Connecticut State University M,O
Southern Illinois University Edwardsville M,O
Southern Oregon University M
State University of New York at Binghamton M
State University of New York at Fredonia M
State University of New York at New Paltz M
State University of New York at Oswego M
State University of New York at Plattsburgh M
State University of New York College at Cortland M
State University of New York College at Geneseo M
State University of New York College at Oneonta M
State University of New York College at Potsdam M
Stetson University M
Sul Ross State University M
Syracuse University M,D
Temple University M,D
Tennessee Technological University M,O
Texas A&M International University M,D
Texas A&M University M,D
Texas A&M University–Commerce M,D
Texas A&M University–Corpus Christi M,D
Texas A&M University–Kingsville M
Texas State University–San Marcos M
Texas Tech University M,D
Texas Woman's University M,D
Towson University M,O
Trevecca Nazarene University M
Trinity (Washington) University M
Union College (KY) M
University at Albany, State University of New York M,D,O
University at Buffalo, the State University of New York M,D,O
University of Alaska Fairbanks M,D,O
The University of Arizona M,D,O
University of Arkansas at Little Rock M,O
University of Bridgeport M,O
University of California, Berkeley M,D
University of California, Riverside M,D
University of California, Santa Cruz M,D
University of Central Arkansas M
University of Central Florida M,O
University of Central Missouri M,O
University of Central Oklahoma M
University of Cincinnati M,D
University of Connecticut M,D,O
University of Dayton M
University of Florida M,D,O
University of Georgia M,D,O
University of Guam M
University of Houston M,D
University of Houston–Clear Lake M
University of Illinois at Chicago M,D
University of La Verne M,O
University of Louisiana at Monroe M,D
University of Louisville M
University of Maine M,D,O
University of Mary M
University of Mary Hardin-Baylor M,D
University of Maryland, College Park M,D,O
University of Massachusetts Amherst M,D,O
University of Massachusetts Lowell M,D,O
University of Memphis M,D
University of Miami M,D,O
University of Michigan M,D
University of Michigan–Flint M
University of Minnesota, Twin Cities Campus M,D,O
University of Missouri–Columbia M,D,O
University of Missouri–Kansas City M,D,O

University of Missouri–St. Louis M,O
University of Nebraska at Kearney M
University of Nebraska at Omaha M
University of Nevada, Reno M,D
University of New England M
University of New Hampshire M
The University of North Carolina at Chapel Hill M,D
The University of North Carolina at Charlotte M
The University of North Carolina at Greensboro M,D,O
The University of North Carolina at Pembroke M
The University of North Carolina Wilmington M
University of North Dakota M
University of Northern Colorado M
University of Northern Iowa M
University of North Texas M,D
University of Oklahoma M,D,O
University of Pennsylvania M,D
University of Pittsburgh M,D
University of Rhode Island M
University of Rio Grande M
University of St. Francis (IL) M
University of St. Thomas (MN) M,D,O
University of San Diego M
University of San Francisco M,D
The University of Scranton M
University of Sioux Falls M,O
University of South Alabama M,O
University of South Carolina M,D
University of Southern Maine M,O
University of Southern Mississippi M,D,O
University of South Florida M,D,O
The University of Tennessee M,D,O
The University of Texas at Brownsville M
The University of Texas at El Paso M,D
The University of Texas at San Antonio M
The University of Texas at Tyler M
The University of Texas of the Permian Basin M
The University of Texas–Pan American M
University of the Incarnate Word M,D
University of Vermont M
University of Virginia M,D,O
University of Washington M,D
University of West Florida M
University of West Georgia M
University of Wisconsin–Eau Claire M
University of Wisconsin–La Crosse M
University of Wisconsin–Milwaukee M
University of Wisconsin–Oshkosh M
University of Wisconsin–River Falls M
University of Wisconsin–Stevens Point M
University of Wisconsin–Superior M
University of Wisconsin–Whitewater M
Ursuline College M
Valdosta State University M,O
Vanderbilt University M
Virginia Commonwealth University M
Wagner College M
Walden University M,D,O
Walla Walla University M
Washburn University M
Washington State University M,D
Wayne State University M,D,O
West Chester University of Pennsylvania M,O
Western Connecticut State University M
Western Illinois University M
Western Kentucky University M
Western New Mexico University M
Westfield State College M
West Texas A&M University M
West Virginia University M
Wheelock College M
Widener University M,D
William Paterson University of New Jersey M
Wilmington University M
Winthrop University M
Worcester State College M,O
Xavier University M
Youngstown State University M

■ REAL ESTATE

American University M
California State University, Sacramento M
Clemson University M
Cleveland State University M,D,O
Columbia University M
Cornell University M
DePaul University M
Drexel University M
Florida International University M
Georgetown University M,D
The George Washington University M
Georgia State University M,D,O
Hofstra University M
The Johns Hopkins University M
Marylhurst University M
Massachusetts Institute of Technology M
New York University M,O
Nova Southeastern University M
Roosevelt University M,O
Texas A&M University M
University of California, Berkeley D
University of Central Florida M
University of Denver M
University of Florida M,D,O
University of Hawaii at Manoa M
University of Illinois at Chicago M
University of Maryland, College Park M
University of Memphis M,D
University of Michigan M,O
University of North Texas M,D
University of Pennsylvania M,D
University of St. Thomas (MN) M
University of Southern California M
The University of Texas at Arlington M,D
University of Wisconsin–Madison M,D
Virginia Commonwealth University M,O
Washington State University D
Woodbury University M

■ RECREATION AND PARK MANAGEMENT

Arizona State University M,D
Bowling Green State University M
Brigham Young University M
California State University, Chico M
California State University, Long Beach M
California State University, Northridge M
California State University, Sacramento M
Central Michigan University M,O
Clemson University M,D
The College at Brockport, State University of New York M
Colorado State University M,D
Delta State University M
East Carolina University M
Eastern Kentucky University M
Florida Agricultural and Mechanical University M
Florida International University M
Florida State University M,D,O
Frostburg State University M
Georgia College & State University M
Georgia Southern University M
Hardin-Simmons University M
Indiana University Bloomington M,D,O
Kent State University M
Lehman College of the City University of New York M
Michigan State University M,D
Middle Tennessee State University M

M—master's degree; P—first professional degree; D—doctorate; O—other advanced degree

Naropa University M
North Carolina Central University M
North Carolina State University M,D
Northwest Missouri State University M
Ohio University M
Old Dominion University M
Penn State University Park M,D
San Francisco State University M
San Jose State University M
South Dakota State University M
Southern Connecticut State University M
Southern Illinois University Carbondale M
Southern University and Agricultural and Mechanical College M
Southwestern Oklahoma State University M
Springfield College M
State University of New York College at Cortland M
State University of New York College of Environmental Science and Forestry M,D
Temple University M
Texas A&M University M,D
Texas State University–San Marcos M
Universidad Metropolitana M
University of Arkansas M,D
University of Florida M,D
University of Idaho M
The University of Iowa M
University of Minnesota, Twin Cities Campus M,D
University of Mississippi M,D
University of Missouri–Columbia M
The University of Montana M,D
University of Nebraska at Omaha M
University of New Hampshire M
The University of North Carolina at Chapel Hill M
The University of North Carolina at Greensboro M
University of North Texas M,O
University of Rhode Island M,D
University of South Alabama M
University of Southern Mississippi M,D
The University of Tennessee M,D
University of Utah M,D
University of Wisconsin–La Crosse M
University of Wisconsin–Milwaukee M,O
Utah State University M,D
Virginia Commonwealth University M
Virginia Polytechnic Institute and State University M,D
Wayne State University M
Western Illinois University M
Western Kentucky University M
West Virginia University M
Winona State University M,O
Wright State University M

■ REHABILITATION COUNSELING

Arkansas State University M,O
Assumption College M,O
Auburn University M,D
Barry University M,O
Bayamón Central University M
Bowling Green State University M
California State University, Fresno M
California State University, Los Angeles M,D
California State University, San Bernardino M
Central Connecticut State University M,O
Coppin State University M
Drake University M
East Carolina University M
East Central University M
Edinboro University of Pennsylvania M,O
Emporia State University M
Florida Atlantic University M,D,O
Florida International University M
Florida State University M,D,O
Fort Valley State University M
The George Washington University M
Georgia State University M
Hofstra University M,O
Hunter College of the City University of New York M
Illinois Institute of Technology M,D
Indiana University–Purdue University Indianapolis M,D
Jackson State University M,O
Kent State University M,O
La Salle University D
Maryville University of Saint Louis M
Michigan State University M,D,O
Minnesota State University Mankato M
Montana State University–Billings M
North Carolina Agricultural and Technical State University M,D
Northeastern University M
Ohio University M,D
Pontifical Catholic University of Puerto Rico M
St. Cloud State University M
St. John's University (NY) M,D,O
Salve Regina University M,O
San Diego State University M
San Francisco State University M
South Carolina State University M
Southern Illinois University Carbondale M,D
Southern University and Agricultural and Mechanical College M
Springfield College M
Syracuse University M
Troy University M,O
University at Albany, State University of New York M
University at Buffalo, the State University of New York M,D,O
The University of Arizona M,D
University of Arkansas M,D
University of Arkansas at Little Rock M,O
University of Florida M
The University of Iowa M,D
University of Kentucky M,D
University of Louisiana at Lafayette M
University of Maryland, College Park M,D,O
University of Maryland Eastern Shore M
University of Massachusetts Boston M,O
University of Memphis M,D
University of Nevada, Las Vegas M,O
The University of North Carolina at Chapel Hill M,D
University of Northern Colorado M,D
University of North Florida M,O
University of North Texas M
University of Pittsburgh M
University of Puerto Rico, Río Piedras M
The University of Scranton M
University of South Alabama M,D
University of South Carolina M,O
University of South Florida M
The University of Tennessee M,D
The University of Texas–Pan American M
University of Wisconsin–Madison M,D
University of Wisconsin–Stout M
Utah State University M
Virginia Commonwealth University M,O
Wayne State University M,D,O
Western Michigan University M
Western Oregon University M
Western Washington University M
West Virginia University M
Wright State University M

■ REHABILITATION SCIENCES

Boston University D
California University of Pennsylvania M

Canisius College M
Central Michigan University M,D
Clarion University of Pennsylvania M
Concordia University Wisconsin M
Drake University M,D,O
East Carolina University M
East Stroudsburg University of Pennsylvania M
Indiana University–Purdue University Indianapolis M,D
Northwestern University D
University at Buffalo, the State University of New York M,D,O
The University of Alabama at Birmingham O
University of Cincinnati D
University of Florida D
University of Illinois at Urbana–Champaign M,D
The University of Iowa D
The University of Kansas M,D
University of Kentucky D
University of Maryland Eastern Shore M
University of Northern Iowa M,D
University of North Texas M
University of Pittsburgh M,D,O
University of South Carolina M,O
University of Washington M,D
University of Wisconsin–La Crosse M
University of Wisconsin–Madison M
Virginia Commonwealth University D
Wayne State University M,O

■ RELIABILITY ENGINEERING

Arizona State University M
The University of Arizona M
University of Maryland, College Park M,D,O

■ RELIGION

Arizona State University M,D
Azusa Pacific University M
Baylor University M,D
Bellarmine University M
Biola University P,M,D
Bob Jones University P,M,D,O
Boston University M,D
Brown University D
California Institute of Integral Studies M,D
California State University, Long Beach M
Cardinal Stritch University M
The Catholic University of America P,M,D,O
Chestnut Hill College M,O
Christian Brothers University M
Claremont Graduate University M,D
Columbia University M,D
Concordia University Chicago M
Cornell University D
Drew University M,D
Duke University M,D
Eastern Mennonite University P,M,O
Edgewood College M
Emory University D,O
Florida International University M
Florida State University M,D
Fordham University M,D,O
George Fox University P,M,D,O
George Mason University M
Georgetown University M,D
The George Washington University M
Georgia State University M
Gonzaga University M
Graceland University (IA) M
Hardin-Simmons University M
Harvard University D
Holy Names University M,O
Hope International University M
Indiana University Bloomington M,D
John Carroll University M
La Salle University M
La Sierra University P,M
Lee University M
Liberty University P,M,D
Lipscomb University P,M
Loyola University Chicago P,M,O
Miami University M
Missouri State University M
Mount St. Mary's College M
Naropa University M
New York University M,O
Northwest Nazarene University P,M
Oklahoma City University M
Olivet Nazarene University M
Pepperdine University P,M
Point Loma Nazarene University M
Princeton University D
Providence College M
Rice University D
Sacred Heart University M
Santa Clara University M
Seton Hall University M
Southern Methodist University M,D
Southern Nazarene University M
Stanford University M,D
Syracuse University M,D
Temple University M,D
Trevecca Nazarene University M
Union University M,D
University of California, Berkeley D
University of California, Santa Barbara M,D
University of Chicago P,M,D
University of Colorado at Boulder M
University of Denver M,D
University of Detroit Mercy M
University of Florida M,D
University of Georgia M
University of Hawaii at Manoa M
The University of Iowa M,D
The University of Kansas M
University of Michigan M,D
University of Minnesota, Twin Cities Campus M,D
University of Missouri–Columbia M
University of Mobile M
The University of North Carolina at Chapel Hill M,D
The University of North Carolina at Charlotte M
University of North Texas M,D
University of Notre Dame M
University of Pennsylvania D
University of Pittsburgh M,D
University of St. Thomas (MN) M
University of South Carolina M
University of South Florida M
The University of Tennessee M,D
University of the Incarnate Word M
University of Virginia M,D
University of Washington M,D
Vanderbilt University M,D
Vanguard University of Southern California M
Wake Forest University M
Wayland Baptist University M
Western Michigan University M
Wheaton College M
Yale University D

■ RELIGIOUS EDUCATION

Andrews University M,D,O
Azusa Pacific University M
Biola University P,M,D
Boston College P,M,D,O
Brandeis University M
Brigham Young University M
Campbell University P,M,D
The Catholic University of America P,M,D,O
Concordia University Chicago M
Concordia University, Nebraska M
Concordia University, St. Paul M,O
Dallas Baptist University M
Fordham University M,D,O
Gardner-Webb University P,D
Georgian Court University M,O
Gratz College M,D,O
Inter American University of Puerto Rico, Metropolitan Campus D
La Sierra University P,M
Loyola Marymount University M
Loyola University Chicago M
Oral Roberts University P,M,D
Pfeiffer University M

M—master's degree; P—first professional degree; D—doctorate; O—other advanced degree

Pontifical Catholic University of Puerto Rico M
Regent University M,D,O
Towson University M
Trinity International University P,M,D,O
University of St. Thomas (MN) M
University of San Francisco M,D
Wheaton College M
Yeshiva University M,D,O

■ REPRODUCTIVE BIOLOGY

Cornell University M,D
Northwestern University D
University of Colorado Denver D
University of Hawaii at Manoa M,D
University of Wyoming M,D
West Virginia University M,D

■ RHETORIC

Abilene Christian University M
Ball State University M
Bob Jones University P,M,D,O
Bowling Green State University M,D
California State University, Dominguez Hills M,O
California State University, Northridge M
California State University, Stanislaus M,O
Carnegie Mellon University M,D
The Catholic University of America M,D
Clemson University D
Duquesne University M,D
Eastern Washington University M
Florida State University M,D
Georgia State University M,D
Hofstra University M
Idaho State University M
Indiana University Bloomington M,D
Indiana University of Pennsylvania M,D
Iowa State University of Science and Technology M,D
Kansas State University M
Kent State University M,D
Miami University M,D
Michigan State University M,D
Michigan Technological University M,D
New Mexico Highlands University M
New Mexico State University M,D
North Carolina State University D
Rensselaer Polytechnic Institute M,D
San Diego State University M
Southern Illinois University Carbondale M,D
Syracuse University M,D
Texas State University–San Marcos M
Texas Tech University M,D
Texas Woman's University M,D
The University of Alabama M,D
The University of Arizona D
University of Arkansas at Little Rock M
University of California, Berkeley D
The University of Iowa M,D
University of Louisiana at Lafayette M,D
University of Louisville M,D
University of Nebraska–Lincoln M,D
The University of North Carolina at Greensboro M,D
The University of Texas at El Paso M,D
University of Utah M,D
University of Wisconsin–Madison M,D
University of Wisconsin–Milwaukee M,D,O
Virginia Commonwealth University M
Wright State University M

■ ROMANCE LANGUAGES

Appalachian State University M
Boston University M,D
Clark Atlanta University M,D
Columbia University M,D
Cornell University M,D
Hunter College of the City University of New York M
The Johns Hopkins University D
Michigan State University M,D
New York University M,D
Northern Illinois University M
Queens College of the City University of New York M
San Diego State University M
Stony Brook University, State University of New York M
Texas Tech University M,D
University at Buffalo, the State University of New York M,D
The University of Alabama M,D
University of California, Berkeley D
University of Chicago M,D
University of Cincinnati M,D
University of Georgia M,D
University of Miami D
University of Michigan D
University of Missouri–Columbia M,D
University of Missouri–Kansas City M
University of New Orleans M
The University of North Carolina at Chapel Hill M,D
University of Notre Dame M
University of Oregon M,D
University of Pennsylvania M,D
The University of Texas at Austin M,D
University of Virginia M,D
University of Washington M,D
Washington University in St. Louis M,D

■ RURAL PLANNING AND STUDIES

California State University, Chico M
Cornell University M
Iowa State University of Science and Technology M,D
University of Alaska Fairbanks M
The University of Montana M
University of West Georgia M
University of Wyoming M
Virginia Polytechnic Institute and State University M,D

■ RURAL SOCIOLOGY

Auburn University M
Cornell University M,D
Iowa State University of Science and Technology M,D
The Ohio State University M,D
Penn State University Park M,D
South Dakota State University M,D
University of Missouri–Columbia M,D
The University of Montana M
University of Wisconsin–Madison M,D

■ RUSSIAN

American University O
Boston College M
Brown University M,D
Columbia University M,D
Harvard University D
Hofstra University M
Kent State University M,D
New York University M
Penn State University Park M,D
Princeton University D
Stanford University M,D
University at Albany, State University of New York M,O
The University of Arizona M
University of California, Berkeley D
University of Michigan M,D
The University of North Carolina at Chapel Hill M,D
University of Oregon M
The University of Tennessee D
University of Washington M,D
Wayne State University M,D
Yale University D

■ SAFETY ENGINEERING

Indiana University Bloomington M,D
Murray State University M
National University M
New Jersey Institute of Technology M
University of Minnesota, Duluth M
University of Southern California M,D,O
West Virginia University M

■ SCANDINAVIAN LANGUAGES

Cornell University M,D

Harvard University	D
University of California, Berkeley	D
University of California, Los Angeles	M
University of Massachusetts Amherst	M,D
University of Minnesota, Twin Cities Campus	M,D
University of Washington	M,D
University of Wisconsin–Madison	M,D

■ SCHOOL NURSING

Cambridge College	M,D,O
Eastern University	M,O
Kean University	M
Kutztown University of Pennsylvania	M,O
Monmouth University	M,O
Saint Joseph's University	M,O
Seton Hall University	M
University of Illinois at Chicago	M
West Chester University of Pennsylvania	M,O
Wright State University	M

■ SCHOOL PSYCHOLOGY

Abilene Christian University	M
Adelphi University	M
Alabama Agricultural and Mechanical University	M,O
Alfred University	M,D,O
Alliant International University–San Diego	M,D,O
Andrews University	M,O
Appalachian State University	M
Arcadia University	M
Argosy University, Sarasota	M,D,O
Arkansas State University	M,O
Assumption College	M,O
Auburn University	M,D,O
Azusa Pacific University	M
Ball State University	M,D,O
Barry University	M,O
Bowling Green State University	M,O
Brigham Young University	M,D,O
Brooklyn College of the City University of New York	M,O
Bucknell University	M
California Baptist University	M
California State University, Los Angeles	M,D
California State University, Northridge	M
California State University, Sacramento	M
California University of Pennsylvania	M
Canisius College	M
Capella University	M,D,O
Central Connecticut State University	M,O
Central Michigan University	D,O
Central Washington University	M
Chapman University	M,D,O
The Citadel, The Military College of South Carolina	M,O
City University of Seattle	M,O
Cleveland State University	M,D,O
The College of New Rochelle	M
College of St. Joseph	M
The College of Saint Rose	M,O
The College of William and Mary	M,O
Duquesne University	M,D,O
East Carolina University	
Eastern Illinois University	M,O
Eastern Kentucky University	M,O
Eastern University	M,O
Eastern Washington University	M
Edinboro University of Pennsylvania	M,O
Emporia State University	M,O
Fairfield University	M,O
Fairleigh Dickinson University, Metropolitan Campus	M,D
Florida Agricultural and Mechanical University	M
Florida International University	M,O
Florida State University	M,O
Fordham University	M,D,O
Fort Hays State University	O
Francis Marion University	M
Fresno Pacific University	M
Gallaudet University	M,O
Gardner-Webb University	M
George Fox University	M,O
George Mason University	M
Georgia Southern University	M,O
Georgia State University	M,D,O
Grand Valley State University	M
Hofstra University	M,D,O
Howard University	M,D,O
Humboldt State University	M
Idaho State University	M,D,O
Illinois State University	D,O
Immaculata University	M,D,O
Indiana State University	M,D,O
Indiana University Bloomington	M,D,O
Indiana University of Pennsylvania	D,O
Inter American University of Puerto Rico, Metropolitan Campus	M,D
Inter American University of Puerto Rico, San Germán Campus	M,D
Iona College	M
James Madison University	M,D,O
The Johns Hopkins University	M,O
Kean University	D,O
Kent State University	M,D,O
La Sierra University	M,O
Lehigh University	M,D,O
Lesley University	M
Lewis & Clark College	M,O
Lindenwood University	M,D,O
Long Island University, Brooklyn Campus	M
Louisiana State University and Agricultural and Mechanical College	M,D
Louisiana State University in Shreveport	O
Loyola Marymount University	M
Loyola University Chicago	M,D,O
Marist College	M,O
Marshall University	O
Marywood University	M,O
McNeese State University	M
Mercy College	M
Miami University	M,O
Michigan State University	M,D,O
Middle Tennessee State University	M,O
Millersville University of Pennsylvania	M
Minnesota State University Mankato	M,D
Minnesota State University Moorhead	M,O
Minot State University	O
Mississippi State University	M,D,O
Montana State University	M,D,O
Montclair State University	M,O
National-Louis University	M,D,O
National University	M
New Jersey City University	M,O
New Mexico Highlands University	M
New Mexico State University	M,D,O
Niagara University	M,O
Nicholls State University	M,O
North Carolina State University	D
Northeastern University	M,D,O
Northern Arizona University	M,D
Northwest Nazarene University	M
Nova Southeastern University	O
Our Lady of the Lake University of San Antonio	M,D
Penn State University Park	M,D
Pittsburg State University	O
Purdue University Calumet	M
Queens College of the City University of New York	M,O
Radford University	M,D,O
Rider University	O
Roberts Wesleyan College	M
Rochester Institute of Technology	M,O
Rowan University	M,O
Rutgers, The State University of New Jersey, New Brunswick	M,D
St. John's University (NY)	M,D
San Diego State University	M
Seattle University	M,O
Seton Hall University	O
Southeast Missouri State University	M,O

M—master's degree; P—first professional degree; D—doctorate; O—other advanced degree

Southern Connecticut State University M,O
Southern Illinois University Edwardsville O
Southwestern Oklahoma State University M
State University of New York at Oswego M,O
State University of New York at Plattsburgh M,O
Stephen F. Austin State University M
Syracuse University M,D,O
Tarleton State University M,O
Temple University M,D
Tennessee State University M,D
Texas A&M University M,D
Texas State University–San Marcos M
Texas Woman's University M,D,O
Towson University O
Trinity University M
Troy University M
Tufts University M,O
Union College (KY) M
Universidad del Turabo M
University at Albany, State University of New York M,D,O
University at Buffalo, the State University of New York M,D,O
The University of Akron M
The University of Arizona M,D,O
University of California, Berkeley
University of California, Riverside M,D
University of California, Santa Barbara M,D
University of Central Arkansas M,D
University of Central Florida O
University of Cincinnati D,O
University of Connecticut M,D,O
University of Dayton M,O
University of Delaware M,D,O
University of Denver M,D,O
University of Detroit Mercy O
University of Florida M,D,O
University of Hartford M
University of Houston–Clear Lake M
University of Houston–Victoria M
University of Idaho O
The University of Iowa M,D,O
The University of Kansas D,O
University of Kentucky M,D,O
University of Louisiana at Monroe M,O
University of Mary M
University of Mary Hardin-Baylor M
University of Maryland, College Park M,D,O
University of Massachusetts Amherst D
University of Massachusetts Boston M,O
University of Memphis M,D
University of Minnesota, Twin Cities Campus M,D,O
University of Missouri–Columbia M,D,O
University of Missouri–St. Louis D,O
The University of Montana M,D,O
University of Nebraska at Kearney M,O
University of Nebraska at Omaha M,D,O
University of Nebraska–Lincoln M,D,O
The University of North Carolina at Chapel Hill M,D
The University of North Carolina at Greensboro M,D,O
University of Northern Colorado D,O
University of Northern Iowa M,O
University of North Texas M
University of Oklahoma M,D
University of Phoenix–Denver Campus M
University of Phoenix–Las Vegas Campus M
University of Phoenix–Southern Colorado Campus M,O
University of Phoenix–Utah Campus M
University of Rhode Island M,D
University of South Alabama M,D
University of South Carolina D
University of Southern Maine M,D
University of Southern Mississippi M,D
University of South Florida M,D,O
The University of Tennessee M,D,O
The University of Tennessee at Chattanooga O
The University of Texas at Austin M,D
The University of Texas at San Antonio M
The University of Texas at Tyler M
The University of Texas–Pan American M
University of the Pacific M,D,O
The University of Toledo M,D,O
University of Utah M,D
University of Virginia M,D,O
University of Washington M,D
University of Wisconsin–Eau Claire M,O
University of Wisconsin–La Crosse M,O
University of Wisconsin–Milwaukee D,O
University of Wisconsin–River Falls M,O
University of Wisconsin–Stout M,O
University of Wisconsin–Whitewater M,O
Utah State University M,D
Valdosta State University M,O
Valparaiso University
Walden University M,D,O
Washington State University M,D,O
Wayne State University M,D,O
Western Carolina University M
Western Illinois University M,O
Western Kentucky University M,O
Western New Mexico University M
Wichita State University M,D,O
Worcester State College M,O
Yeshiva University D
Youngstown State University M

■ SCIENCE EDUCATION

Alabama State University M,O
Albany State University M
Alverno College M
Andrews University M,D,O
Antioch University New England M
Arcadia University M,D,O
Arkansas State University M,O
Armstrong Atlantic State University M
Auburn University M,D,O
Ball State University M,D
Belmont University M
Bemidji State University M
Benedictine University M
Bennington College M
Bethel University (TN) M
Bloomsburg University of Pennsylvania M
Boise State University M,D
Boston College M,D
Boston University M,D,O
Bowling Green State University M
Bridgewater State College M
Brigham Young University M,D
Brooklyn College of the City University of New York M,O
Brown University M
Buffalo State College, State University of New York M
California State University, Chico M
California State University, Fullerton M
California State University, Northridge M
California State University, San Bernardino M
Cambridge College M,D,O
Central Michigan University M
Chatham University M
The Citadel, The Military College of South Carolina M
City College of the City University of New York M
Clarion University of Pennsylvania M
Clemson University M
Cleveland State University M
The College at Brockport, State University of New York M
College of Charleston M

The College of William and Mary M
Columbia University M,D,O
Columbus State University M,O
Converse College M
Cornell University M,D
Delaware State University M,D
Delta State University M
Drake University M
Duquesne University M
East Carolina University M
Eastern Connecticut State University M
Eastern Kentucky University M
Eastern Michigan University M
East Stroudsburg University of Pennsylvania M
Fairleigh Dickinson University, Metropolitan Campus M
Fitchburg State College M
Florida Agricultural and Mechanical University M
Florida Institute of Technology M,D,O
Florida International University M,D
Florida State University M,D,O
Fresno Pacific University M
Gannon University M
George Mason University M,O
Georgia Southern University M
Georgia State University M,D,O
Grambling State University M,D,O
Harding University M,O
Hardin-Simmons University M,D
Harvard University M
Heritage University M
Hofstra University M
Hood College M
Hunter College of the City University of New York M,O
Illinois Institute of Technology M,D
Indiana State University M,D
Indiana University Bloomington M,D,O
Inter American University of Puerto Rico, Metropolitan Campus M
Inter American University of Puerto Rico, San Germán Campus M
Iona College M
Ithaca College M
Jackson State University M,D
John Carroll University M
The Johns Hopkins University M,O
Johnson State College M
Kean University M
Kutztown University of Pennsylvania M,O
Lawrence Technological University M
Lehman College of the City University of New York M
Lesley University M,D,O
Lewis University M
Long Island University, C.W. Post Campus M
Louisiana Tech University M,D
Loyola University Chicago M
Lynchburg College M
Manhattanville College M
McNeese State University M
Michigan State University M
Michigan Technological University M
Middle Tennessee State University M
Mills College M,D
Minnesota State University Mankato M
Minot State University M
Mississippi College M,D,O
Missouri State University M
Montclair State University M,D,O
Morgan State University M,D
National-Louis University M,O
New Mexico Institute of Mining and Technology M
New York University M
North Carolina Agricultural and Technical State University M
North Carolina State University M,D
North Dakota State University M,D,O
Northeastern State University M
Northern Arizona University M
Northern Michigan University M
North Georgia College & State University M,O
Northwestern State University of Louisiana M
Northwest Missouri State University M
Nova Southeastern University M,O
Ohio University M
Old Dominion University M
Oregon State University M,D
Our Lady of the Lake University of San Antonio M
Penn State Great Valley M
Penn State University Park M,D
Plymouth State University M
Portland State University M,D
Purdue University M,D,O
Purdue University Calumet M
Queens College of the City University of New York M,O
Quinnipiac University M
Regis University M,O
Rensselaer Polytechnic Institute M
Rider University O
Rutgers, The State University of New Jersey, New Brunswick M,D
Saginaw Valley State University M
St. John Fisher College M
Salem State College M
San Diego State University M,D
Shippensburg University of Pennsylvania M
Slippery Rock University of Pennsylvania M
South Carolina State University M
Southeast Missouri State University M
Southern Connecticut State University M,O
Southern Illinois University Edwardsville M
Southern University and Agricultural and Mechanical College D
Southwestern Oklahoma State University M
Stanford University M,D
State University of New York at Binghamton M
State University of New York at Fredonia M
State University of New York at New Paltz M
State University of New York at Plattsburgh M
State University of New York College at Cortland M
State University of New York College at Potsdam M
Stony Brook University, State University of New York M,D,O
Syracuse University D
Temple University M,D
Texas A&M University M,D
Texas Christian University M,D
Texas State University–San Marcos M
Texas Woman's University M,D
Towson University M
University at Albany, State University of New York M,D
University at Buffalo, the State University of New York M,D,O
The University of Alabama in Huntsville M,D
University of California, Berkeley M,D
University of California, Los Angeles M,D
University of California, San Diego D
University of California, Santa Cruz M,D
University of Central Florida M,D,O
University of Chicago D
University of Cincinnati M,D,O
University of Connecticut M,D
University of Florida M,D,O
University of Georgia M,D,O
University of Houston M,D
University of Idaho M,D

M—master's degree; P—first professional degree; D—doctorate; O—other advanced degree

University of Illinois at Urbana–Champaign M,D
University of Indianapolis M
The University of Iowa M,D
University of Maine M,O
University of Maryland, Baltimore County M,O
University of Massachusetts Lowell M,D,O
University of Miami D
University of Michigan M,D
University of Michigan–Dearborn M
University of Minnesota, Twin Cities Campus M
University of Missouri–Columbia M,D,O
University of Nebraska at Kearney M
University of New Hampshire M,D
The University of North Carolina at Chapel Hill M
The University of North Carolina at Greensboro M,D,O
The University of North Carolina at Pembroke M
University of Northern Colorado M,D
University of Northern Iowa M
University of Oklahoma M,D,O
University of Pittsburgh M,D
University of Puerto Rico, Río Piedras M,D
University of St. Francis (IL) M
University of San Diego M
University of South Alabama M,O
University of South Carolina M,D
University of Southern Mississippi M,D
University of South Florida M,D,O
The University of Tampa M
The University of Tennessee M,D,O
The University of Texas at Austin M,D
The University of Texas at Dallas M
University of the Incarnate Word M
The University of Toledo M
University of Tulsa M
University of Utah M,D
University of Vermont M,D
University of Virginia M,D,O
University of Washington M,D
University of Washington, Tacoma M
The University of West Alabama M
University of West Florida M
University of West Georgia M,O
University of Wisconsin–Madison M,D
University of Wisconsin–River Falls M
University of Wisconsin–Stevens Point M
University of Wyoming M
Ursuline College M
Vanderbilt University M,D
Walden University M,D,O
Wayne State College M
Wayne State University M,D,O
West Chester University of Pennsylvania M,O
Western Carolina University M
Western Kentucky University M
Western Michigan University M,D
Western Oregon University M
Western Washington University M
Widener University M,D
Wilkes University M,D
Wright State University M
Youngstown State University M

■ SECONDARY EDUCATION

Adelphi University M
Alabama Agricultural and Mechanical University M,O
Alabama State University M,O
Alcorn State University M,O
American International College M,D,O
American University M,O
Andrews University M,D,O
Arcadia University M,D,O
Argosy University, Orange County M,D
Argosy University, Sarasota M,D,O
Argosy University, Tampa M,D,O
Argosy University, Twin Cities M,D,O
Arizona State University M,D,O
Arkansas State University M,D,O
Arkansas Tech University M,O
Armstrong Atlantic State University M
Auburn University M,D,O
Auburn University Montgomery M,O
Augusta State University M,O
Austin Peay State University M,O
Ball State University M
Belhaven College (MS) M
Bellarmine University M
Belmont University M
Benedictine University M
Bennington College M
Bethel University M,D,O
Bob Jones University P,M,D,O
Boston College M
Bowie State University M
Brandeis University M
Brenau University M,O
Bridgewater State College M
Brooklyn College of the City University of New York M,O
Brown University M
Butler University M
California State University, Bakersfield M
California State University, Fullerton M
California State University, Long Beach M
California State University, Los Angeles M
California State University, Northridge M
California State University, San Bernardino M
California State University, Stanislaus M,O
California University of Pennsylvania M
Campbell University M
Canisius College M
Carlow University M
Carson-Newman College M
The Catholic University of America M,D,O
Central Connecticut State University M
Central Michigan University M,O
Chapman University M
Charleston Southern University M
Chatham University M
Chestnut Hill College M
Chicago State University M
The Citadel, The Military College of South Carolina M
City College of the City University of New York M,O
Clemson University M
College of Mount St. Joseph M
The College of New Jersey M
College of St. Joseph M
The College of Saint Rose M,O
College of Staten Island of the City University of New York M
The College of William and Mary M
Columbus State University M,O
Concordia University (OR) M
Concordia University Chicago M
Concordia University, Nebraska M
Converse College M
Creighton University M
Dallas Baptist University M
Delta State University M,O
DePaul University M,D
Dowling College M,D,O
Drake University M
Drury University M
Duquesne University M
D'Youville College M,O
Eastern Connecticut State University M
Eastern Kentucky University M
Eastern Michigan University M
Eastern Nazarene College M,O
Eastern Oregon University M
East Stroudsburg University of Pennsylvania M
East Tennessee State University M
Emmanuel College M,O
Emory University M,D,O
Emporia State University M

Fairfield University M,O
Fayetteville State University M
Fitchburg State College M
Florida Agricultural and Mechanical University M
Fordham University M,D,O
Francis Marion University M
Fresno Pacific University M
Friends University M
Frostburg State University M
Gallaudet University M,D,O
George Fox University M,D,O
George Mason University M,O
The George Washington University M
Georgia College & State University M,O
Georgia Southern University M
Georgia Southwestern State University M,O
Georgia State University M,D,O
Grand Canyon University M,D
Grand Valley State University M,O
Hampton University M
Harding University M,O
Hawai'i Pacific University M
Hofstra University M,O
Holy Family University M
Hood College M,O
Howard University M,O
Hunter College of the City University of New York M
Idaho State University M,O
Immaculata University M,D,O
Indiana University Bloomington M,D,O
Indiana University Northwest M
Indiana University–Purdue University Fort Wayne M,O
Indiana University South Bend M
Indiana University Southeast M
Ithaca College M
Jackson State University M,D,O
Jacksonville State University M
James Madison University M
John Carroll University M
The Johns Hopkins University M,O
Johnson & Wales University D
Johnson State College M,O
Jones International University M
Kennesaw State University M
Kent State University M
Kutztown University of Pennsylvania M,O
Lee University M,O
Lehigh University M,D,O
Le Moyne College M,O
Lewis & Clark College M
Lewis University M
Liberty University M,D,O
Lincoln University (MO) M,O
Long Island University, C.W. Post Campus M
Longwood University M
Louisiana State University and Agricultural and Mechanical College M,D,O
Louisiana Tech University M,D
Loyola Marymount University M
Loyola University Chicago M
Maharishi University of Management M
Manhattanville College M
Mansfield University of Pennsylvania M
Marshall University M
Marygrove College M
Marymount University M
Maryville University of Saint Louis M,D
Marywood University M
McDaniel College M
McNeese State University M
Mercer University M,D,O
Mercy College M
Miami University M
Middle Tennessee State University M,O
Mills College M,D
Minnesota State University Mankato M,O
Mississippi College M,D,O
Mississippi State University M,D,O
Missouri State University M,O
Montana State University–Billings M
Morehead State University M,O
Morgan State University M
Mount Saint Mary College M
Mount St. Mary's College M
Murray State University M,O
National-Louis University M
New Jersey City University M
Niagara University M,O
Norfolk State University M
North Carolina State University M
Northern Arizona University M
Northern Illinois University M,D
Northern Michigan University M
North Georgia College & State University M,O
Northwestern State University of Louisiana M,O
Northwestern University M
Northwest Missouri State University M,O
Nova Southeastern University M,O
Oakland University M
Ohio University M,D
Old Dominion University M
Olivet Nazarene University M
Our Lady of the Lake University of San Antonio M
Pacific University M
Park University M
Piedmont College M,O
Pittsburg State University M
Plymouth State University M
Portland State University M,D
Prescott College M,D
Providence College M
Queens College of the City University of New York M,O
Quinnipiac University M
Regis University M,O
Rhode Island College M
Roberts Wesleyan College M,O
Rochester Institute of Technology M
Rockford College M
Rollins College M
Roosevelt University M
Rowan University M
Sacred Heart University M,O
Saginaw Valley State University M
St. John's University (NY) M
Saint Joseph's University M,D
Saint Mary's University of Minnesota M,O
St. Thomas Aquinas College M,O
Saint Xavier University M,O
Salem State College M
Samford University M,D,O
San Diego State University M
San Francisco State University M
San Jose State University M,O
Seattle Pacific University M,O
Shenandoah University M,D,O
Siena Heights University M
Simmons College M,O
Slippery Rock University of Pennsylvania M
South Carolina State University M
Southeast Missouri State University M
Southern Illinois University Edwardsville M
Southern New Hampshire University M,O
Southern Oregon University M
Southern University and Agricultural and Mechanical College M
Southwestern Oklahoma State University M
Spalding University M
Springfield College M
Spring Hill College M
State University of New York at Binghamton M
State University of New York at Fredonia M
State University of New York at New Paltz M
State University of New York at Oswego M

M—master's degree; P—first professional degree; D—doctorate; O—other advanced degree

State University of New York at Plattsburgh M
State University of New York College at Cortland M
State University of New York College at Geneseo M
State University of New York College at Oneonta M
State University of New York College at Potsdam M
Stephen F. Austin State University M,D
Suffolk University M,O
Sul Ross State University M
Tarleton State University M,O
Tennessee Technological University M,O
Texas A&M University–Commerce M,D
Texas A&M University–Corpus Christi M
Texas A&M University–Kingsville M
Texas Christian University M
Texas Southern University M,D
Texas State University–San Marcos M
Texas Tech University M,D
Towson University M
Trevecca Nazarene University M
Trinity (Washington) University M
Troy University M,O
Tufts University M,D
Union College (KY) M
The University of Akron M,D
The University of Alabama M,D,O
The University of Alabama at Birmingham M
University of Alaska Fairbanks M,D,O
University of Alaska Southeast M
The University of Arizona M,D
University of Arkansas M,O
University of Arkansas at Little Rock M
University of Bridgeport M,O
University of California, Irvine M,D
University of Central Missouri M,O
University of Central Oklahoma M
University of Cincinnati M
University of Connecticut M,D,O
University of Dayton M
University of Great Falls M
University of Guam M
University of Houston M,D
University of Illinois at Chicago M,D
University of Indianapolis M
The University of Iowa M,D
University of Louisiana at Monroe M
University of Louisville M
University of Maine M,O
University of Maryland, Baltimore County M
University of Maryland, College Park M,D,O
University of Massachusetts Amherst M,D,O
University of Massachusetts Boston M,D,O
University of Massachusetts Dartmouth M,O
University of Memphis M,D
University of Missouri–St. Louis M,O
University of Montevallo M
University of Nebraska at Omaha M
University of Nevada, Reno M
University of New Hampshire M
University of New Mexico M,O
University of North Alabama M
The University of North Carolina at Chapel Hill M
The University of North Carolina at Charlotte M
University of North Dakota D
University of North Florida M
University of North Texas M,O
University of Oklahoma M,D,O
University of Pennsylvania M
University of Phoenix M
University of Phoenix–Central Florida Campus M
University of Phoenix–Denver Campus M
University of Phoenix–Hawaii Campus M
University of Phoenix–New Mexico Campus M
University of Phoenix–North Florida Campus M
University of Phoenix–Oregon Campus M
University of Phoenix–Phoenix Campus M
University of Phoenix–Sacramento Valley Campus M,O
University of Phoenix–San Diego Campus M
University of Phoenix–Southern Arizona Campus M,O
University of Phoenix–Southern California Campus M
University of Phoenix–Southern Colorado Campus M,O
University of Phoenix–South Florida Campus M
University of Phoenix–Utah Campus M
University of Phoenix–West Florida Campus M
University of Pittsburgh M,D
University of Puerto Rico, Río Piedras M,D
University of Puget Sound M
University of Rhode Island M
University of St. Francis (IL) M
University of St. Thomas (MN) M,O
The University of Scranton M
University of South Alabama M,O
University of South Carolina M,D
The University of South Dakota M
University of Southern Indiana M
University of Southern Mississippi M,D,O
University of South Florida M,D,O
The University of Tennessee M,D,O
The University of Tennessee at Chattanooga M,O
The University of Tennessee at Martin M
The University of Texas–Pan American M
University of the Incarnate Word M
The University of Toledo M,D,O
University of Utah M,D
University of Washington, Tacoma M
The University of West Alabama M
University of West Florida M
University of West Georgia M,O
University of Wisconsin–Eau Claire M
University of Wisconsin–La Crosse M
University of Wisconsin–Milwaukee M
University of Wisconsin–Platteville M
University of Wisconsin–Whitewater M
Utah State University M
Valdosta State University M,O
Vanderbilt University M
Villanova University M
Virginia Commonwealth University M,O
Wagner College M
Wake Forest University M
Washington State University M,D
Washington University in St. Louis M
Wayne State University M,D,O
West Chester University of Pennsylvania M,O
Western Kentucky University M,O
Western New Mexico University M
Western Oregon University M
Western Washington University M
Westfield State College M
West Virginia University M,D
Wheaton College M
Whitworth University M
Wilkes University M,D
William Carey University M,O
William Woods University M,O
Wilmington University M
Winthrop University M
Worcester State College M
Wright State University M

Xavier University	M
Youngstown State University	M

■ SLAVIC LANGUAGES

Boston College	M
Brown University	M,D
Columbia University	M,D
Cornell University	M,D
Duke University	M
Florida State University	M
Harvard University	D
Indiana University Bloomington	M,D
New York University	M
Northwestern University	D
The Ohio State University	M,D
Princeton University	D
Stanford University	M,D
University of California, Berkeley	D
University of California, Los Angeles	M,D
University of Chicago	M,D
University of Illinois at Urbana–Champaign	M,D
The University of Kansas	M,D
University of Michigan	M,D
The University of North Carolina at Chapel Hill	M,D
University of Pittsburgh	M,D
University of Southern California	M,D
The University of Texas at Austin	M,D
University of Virginia	M,D
University of Washington	M,D
University of Wisconsin–Madison	M,D
University of Wisconsin–Milwaukee	M,O
Yale University	D

■ SOCIAL PSYCHOLOGY

Alvernia University	M
American University	M
Andrews University	M
Appalachian State University	M
Arcadia University	M
Argosy University, Sarasota	M,D,O
Arizona State University	D
Auburn University	M,D,O
Ball State University	M
Bowling Green State University	M,D
Brandeis University	M,D
Brigham Young University	M,D
Brooklyn College of the City University of New York	M,D
Brown University	D
California Institute of Integral Studies	M,D
California State University, Fullerton	M
Canisius College	M
Carnegie Mellon University	D
Central Connecticut State University	M
Claremont Graduate University	M,D,O
Clark University	D
The College of New Rochelle	M
College of St. Joseph	M
Columbia University	M,D
Cornell University	M,D
Creighton University	M
DePaul University	M,D
Eastern Michigan University	M,O
Eastern University	M,O
Florida Agricultural and Mechanical University	M
Florida State University	D
Francis Marion University	M
The George Washington University	M,D
Graduate School and University Center of the City University of New York	D
Harvard University	D
Henderson State University	M
Hofstra University	M,D,O
Howard University	M,D
Hunter College of the City University of New York	M
Indiana University Bloomington	M,D
Indiana Wesleyan University	M
Iowa State University of Science and Technology	D
Lamar University	M
Lesley University	M,D,O
Lewis & Clark College	M
Loyola University Chicago	M,D
Lynchburg College	M
Marymount University	
Miami University	D
Minnesota State University Mankato	M,D,O
Missouri State University	M
Montclair State University	M,D,O
Naropa University	M
National-Louis University	M,O
New York University	M,D,O
Norfolk State University	M
North Carolina Central University	M
North Carolina State University	M
North Dakota State University	M,D
Northern Arizona University	M
Northern Kentucky University	M,O
North Georgia College & State University	M
Northwestern University	D
Northwest Nazarene University	M
The Ohio State University	M,D
Penn State Harrisburg	M,D
Penn State University Park	M,D
Pittsburg State University	M
Regent University	M,D,O
Regis University	M,O
Rutgers, The State University of New Jersey, Newark	D
Rutgers, The State University of New Jersey, New Brunswick	D
St. Cloud State University	M
Saint Joseph College	M
Saint Martin's University	M
St. Mary's University (United States)	M
Shippensburg University of Pennsylvania	M,O
Southeastern Oklahoma State University	M
Springfield College	M
Stony Brook University, State University of New York	D
Syracuse University	M,D
Temple University	D
Texas A&M University	M,D
University at Albany, State University of New York	M,D,O
University at Buffalo, the State University of New York	M,D
The University of Akron	M
University of Alaska Anchorage	M,D
University of Alaska Fairbanks	M,D
University of Central Arkansas	M
University of Connecticut	M,D,O
University of Dayton	M,O
University of Delaware	D
University of Florida	M,D
University of Hawaii at Manoa	M,D,O
University of Houston	M,D
The University of Iowa	M,D
University of La Verne	D
University of Maine	M,D
University of Mary	M
University of Mary Hardin-Baylor	M
University of Maryland, College Park	M,D
University of Massachusetts Amherst	M,D
University of Massachusetts Lowell	M
University of Michigan	D
University of Minnesota, Twin Cities Campus	D
University of Missouri–Kansas City	M,D
University of Missouri–St. Louis	M,D,O
University of Montevallo	M
University of Nebraska–Lincoln	M,D
University of Nevada, Reno	D
University of New Haven	M,O
The University of North Carolina at Chapel Hill	D
The University of North Carolina at Charlotte	M
The University of North Carolina at Greensboro	M,D
University of Oklahoma	M
University of Oregon	M,D
University of Phoenix	M

M—master's degree; P—first professional degree; D—doctorate; O—other advanced degree

University of Phoenix–Denver Campus	M
University of Phoenix–Hawaii Campus	M
University of Phoenix–Phoenix Campus	M,O
University of Phoenix–Southern Colorado Campus	M
University of Rochester	M,D
The University of Scranton	M
University of South Carolina	M,D
University of Southern California	M,D
The University of Tennessee at Martin	M
The University of Toledo	M,D,O
University of Washington	D
University of Wisconsin–Madison	D
University of Wisconsin–Milwaukee	M,D
University of Wisconsin–Superior	M
University of Wisconsin–Whitewater	M
Walden University	M,D,O
Washington State University	M,D
Washington University in St. Louis	D
Western Carolina University	M
Western Connecticut State University	M
Western Illinois University	M,O
Wichita State University	M,D
Wilmington University	M
Yale University	D

■ SOCIAL SCIENCES

Arizona State University	M,D
Arkansas Tech University	M
Ball State University	M
California Institute of Technology	M,D
California State University, Chico	M
California State University, San Bernardino	M
California University of Pennsylvania	M
Carnegie Mellon University	D
The Citadel, The Military College of South Carolina	M
Columbia University	M
Eastern Michigan University	M,O
Edinboro University of Pennsylvania	M
Florida Agricultural and Mechanical University	M
George Mason University	M,D,O
Hollins University	M,O
Humboldt State University	M
Indiana University Bloomington	P,M,D,O
The Johns Hopkins University	M,D
Lincoln University (MO)	M
Long Island University, Brooklyn Campus	M,O
Long Island University, C.W. Post Campus	M
Massachusetts Institute of Technology	D
Michigan State University	M
Middle Tennessee State University	M
Mississippi College	M,O
Montclair State University	M,O
The New School: A University	M,D
New York University	M,O
North Dakota State University	M,D
Northwestern University	M,O
Nova Southeastern University	M,O
Nyack College	M
Ohio University	M
Queens College of the City University of New York	M
Regis University	M,O
St. Edward's University	M,O
Southern Oregon University	M
Southern University and Agricultural and Mechanical College	M
Stony Brook University, State University of New York	M,O
Syracuse University	M,D
Texas A&M International University	M
Texas A&M University–Commerce	M
Towson University	M
University of California, Irvine	M,D
University of California, Santa Cruz	D
University of Chicago	M,D
University of Colorado Denver	M
University of Florida	M
University of Idaho	M
University of Illinois at Springfield	M
The University of Kansas	M,D
University of Maryland, Baltimore County	D
University of Michigan	D
University of Michigan–Flint	M
University of Northern Iowa	M
The University of Texas at Tyler	M
University of Washington	M,D
University of Wisconsin–Madison	D
Worcester Polytechnic Institute	M,D,O
Yale University	M,D

■ SOCIAL SCIENCES EDUCATION

Alabama State University	M,O
Andrews University	M,D,O
Appalachian State University	M
Arcadia University	M,D,O
Arkansas State University	M,O
Arkansas Tech University	M
Armstrong Atlantic State University	M
Auburn University	M,D,O
Belmont University	M
Bennington College	M
Bethel University (TN)	M
Bob Jones University	P,M,D,O
Boston College	M
Boston University	M,D,O
Bridgewater State College	M
Brooklyn College of the City University of New York	M,O
Brown University	M
Buffalo State College, State University of New York	M
California State University, Chico	M
California State University, Fresno	M
California State University, San Bernardino	M,D
Cambridge College	M,D,O
Campbell University	M
Chaminade University of Honolulu	M
Chatham University	M
The Citadel, The Military College of South Carolina	M
City College of the City University of New York	M,O
Clarion University of Pennsylvania	M
The College at Brockport, State University of New York	M
College of St. Joseph	M
The College of William and Mary	M
Columbus State University	M,O
Converse College	M
Delta State University	M
Drake University	M
Duquesne University	M
East Carolina University	M
Eastern Kentucky University	M
East Stroudsburg University of Pennsylvania	M
Emporia State University	M
Fayetteville State University	M
Fitchburg State College	M,O
Florida Agricultural and Mechanical University	M
Florida International University	M,D
Florida State University	M,D,O
Framingham State College	M
Georgia Southern University	M
Georgia State University	M,D,O
Grambling State University	M
Harding University	M,O
Hofstra University	M
Hunter College of the City University of New York	M
Indiana University Bloomington	M,D,O
Iona College	M
Ithaca College	M
The Johns Hopkins University	M,O
Kutztown University of Pennsylvania	M,O

Lehman College of the City University of New York M
Lewis University M
Louisiana Tech University M,D
Manhattanville College M
Miami University M
Michigan State University M,D
Mills College M,D
Minnesota State University Mankato M
Mississippi College M,D,O
Missouri State University M
Montclair State University M,O
New York University M,D,O
North Carolina Agricultural and Technical State University M
North Carolina State University M
North Dakota State University M,D,O
North Georgia College & State University M,O
Northwestern State University of Louisiana M
Northwest Missouri State University M
Nova Southeastern University M,O
Ohio University M,D
Penn State University Park M,D
Portland State University M
Purdue University M,D,O
Queens College of the City University of New York M,O
Quinnipiac University M
Rhode Island College M
Rider University O
Rivier College M
Rutgers, The State University of New Jersey, New Brunswick M,D
St. John Fisher College M
South Carolina State University M
Southern Illinois University Edwardsville M
Southwestern Oklahoma State University M
Stanford University M,D
State University of New York at Binghamton M
State University of New York at New Paltz M
State University of New York at Plattsburgh M
State University of New York College at Cortland M
State University of New York College at Potsdam M
Stony Brook University, State University of New York M,O
Syracuse University M
Texas A&M University–Commerce M
Texas State University–San Marcos D
Trinity (Washington) University M
University at Buffalo, the State University of New York M,D,O
The University of Alabama in Huntsville M
University of California, Santa Cruz M
University of Central Florida M,D
University of Cincinnati M,D,O
University of Connecticut M,D,O
University of Florida M,D,O
University of Georgia M,D,O
University of Houston M,D
University of Indianapolis M
The University of Iowa M,D
University of Maine M,O
University of Michigan M,D
University of Minnesota, Twin Cities Campus M
University of Missouri–Columbia M,D,O
University of New Orleans M
The University of North Carolina at Chapel Hill M
The University of North Carolina at Greensboro M,D,O
The University of North Carolina at Pembroke M
University of Oklahoma M,D,O
University of Pittsburgh M,D
University of Puerto Rico, Río Piedras M,D
University of St. Francis (IL) M
University of South Carolina M,D
University of Southern Mississippi M,D,O
University of South Florida M,D,O
The University of Tampa M
The University of Tennessee M,D,O
The University of Toledo M
University of Virginia M,D,O
University of Washington M,D
The University of West Alabama M
University of West Georgia M,O
University of Wisconsin–Eau Claire M
University of Wisconsin–River Falls M
Ursuline College M
Virginia Commonwealth University M,O
Wayne State College M
Wayne State University M,D,O
Webster University M,O
West Chester University of Pennsylvania M,O
Western Oregon University M
Widener University M,D
Wilkes University M,D
William Carey University M,O
Worcester State College M

■ SOCIAL WORK

Abilene Christian University M
Adelphi University M,D
Alabama Agricultural and Mechanical University M
Andrews University M
Appalachian State University M
Arizona State University M,D
Arkansas State University M
Augsburg College M
Aurora University M
Barry University M,D
Baylor University M
Boise State University M
Boston College M,D
Boston University M,D
Bridgewater State College M
Brigham Young University M
California State University, Bakersfield M
California State University, Chico M
California State University, Dominguez Hills M
California State University, East Bay M
California State University, Fresno M
California State University, Fullerton M
California State University, Long Beach M
California State University, Los Angeles M
California State University, Northridge M
California State University, Sacramento M
California State University, San Bernardino M
California State University, Stanislaus M
California University of Pennsylvania M
Case Western Reserve University M,D
The Catholic University of America M,D
Chicago State University M
Clark Atlanta University M,D
Cleveland State University M
The College at Brockport, State University of New York M
Colorado State University M
Columbia University M,D
Cornell University M,D
Delaware State University M
Dominican University M
East Carolina University M
Eastern Michigan University M,O
Eastern Washington University M
East Tennessee State University M
Edinboro University of Pennsylvania M

M—master's degree; P—first professional degree; D—doctorate; O—other advanced degree

Fayetteville State University M
Florida Agricultural and Mechanical University M
Florida Atlantic University M
Florida Gulf Coast University M
Florida International University M,D
Florida State University M,D
Fordham University M,D
Gallaudet University M
George Mason University M
Georgia State University M
Governors State University M
Graduate School and University Center of the City University of New York D
Grambling State University M
Grand Valley State University M
Gratz College M,O
Hawai'i Pacific University M
Howard University M,D
Humboldt State University M
Hunter College of the City University of New York M,D
Illinois State University M
Indiana University Northwest M
Indiana University–Purdue University Indianapolis M,D,O
Indiana University South Bend M
Inter American University of Puerto Rico, Metropolitan Campus M
Jackson State University M,D
Kean University M
Kennesaw State University M
Kutztown University of Pennsylvania M
Long Island University, C.W. Post Campus M
Louisiana State University and Agricultural and Mechanical College M,D
Marywood University M,D
Michigan State University M,D
Middle Tennessee State University M
Millersville University of Pennsylvania M
Missouri State University M
Molloy College M
Monmouth University M
Morgan State University M,D
Nazareth College of Rochester M
Newman University M
New Mexico Highlands University M
New Mexico State University M
New York University M,D
Norfolk State University M,D
North Carolina Agricultural and Technical State University M
North Carolina State University M
Northwest Nazarene University M
The Ohio State University M,D
Ohio University M
Our Lady of the Lake University of San Antonio M
Pontifical Catholic University of Puerto Rico M
Portland State University M,D
Radford University M
Rhode Island College M
Roberts Wesleyan College M
Rutgers, The State University of New Jersey, New Brunswick M,D
St. Ambrose University M
St. Catherine University M
St. Cloud State University M
Saint Louis University M
Salem State College M
Salisbury University M
San Diego State University M
San Francisco State University M
San Jose State University M,O
Savannah State University M
Shippensburg University of Pennsylvania M,O
Simmons College M,D
Southern Connecticut State University M
Southern Illinois University Carbondale M
Southern Illinois University Edwardsville M
Southern University at New Orleans M
Spalding University M
Springfield College M
State University of New York at Binghamton M
Stephen F. Austin State University M
Stony Brook University, State University of New York M,D
Syracuse University M
Temple University M
Texas A&M University–Commerce M
Texas State University–San Marcos M
Tulane University M
University at Albany, State University of New York M,D
University at Buffalo, the State University of New York M,D
The University of Akron M
The University of Alabama M,D
University of Alaska Anchorage M,O
University of Arkansas M
University of Arkansas at Little Rock M
University of California, Berkeley M,D
University of California, Los Angeles M,D
University of Central Florida M,O
University of Chicago M,D
University of Cincinnati M
University of Denver M,D,O
University of Georgia M,D,O
University of Guam M
University of Hawaii at Manoa M,D
University of Houston M,D
University of Illinois at Chicago M,D
University of Illinois at Urbana–Champaign M,D
The University of Iowa M,D
University of Kentucky M,D
University of Louisville M,D,O
University of Maine M
University of Maryland, College Park
University of Michigan M,D
University of Minnesota, Duluth M
University of Minnesota, Twin Cities Campus M,D
University of Missouri–Columbia M
University of Missouri–Kansas City M
University of Missouri–St. Louis M,O
The University of Montana M
University of Nebraska at Omaha M
University of Nevada, Las Vegas M,O
University of Nevada, Reno M
University of New England M,O
University of New Hampshire M,O
The University of North Carolina at Chapel Hill M,D
The University of North Carolina at Charlotte M
The University of North Carolina at Greensboro M
The University of North Carolina Wilmington M
University of North Dakota M
University of Northern Iowa M
University of Oklahoma M
University of Pennsylvania M,D
University of Pittsburgh M,D,O
University of Puerto Rico, Río Piedras M,D
University of St. Francis (IL) M
University of St. Thomas (MN) M
University of South Carolina M,D
University of Southern California M,D
University of Southern Indiana M
University of Southern Maine M
University of Southern Mississippi M
University of South Florida M,D
The University of Tennessee M,D
The University of Texas at Arlington M,D
The University of Texas at Austin M,D
The University of Texas at San Antonio M
The University of Texas–Pan American M
The University of Toledo M

University of Utah M,D
University of Vermont M
University of Washington M,D
University of Washington, Tacoma M
University of West Florida M
University of Wisconsin–Madison M,D
University of Wisconsin–Milwaukee M,D,O
University of Wisconsin–Oshkosh M
University of Wyoming M
Valdosta State University M
Virginia Commonwealth University M,D
Walden University M,D
Walla Walla University M
Washburn University M
Washington University in St. Louis M,D
Wayne State University M,D,O
West Chester University of Pennsylvania M
Western Carolina University M
Western Kentucky University M
Western Michigan University M
Western New Mexico University M
West Virginia University M
Wheelock College M
Wichita State University M
Widener University M,D
Winthrop University M
Yeshiva University M,D

■ SOCIOLOGY

American University M,O
Arizona State University M,D
Arkansas State University M,O
Auburn University M
Ball State University M
Baylor University M,D
Boston College M,D
Boston University M,D
Bowling Green State University M,D
Brandeis University M,D
Brigham Young University M
Brooklyn College of the City University of New York M,D
Brown University M,D
California State University, Bakersfield M
California State University, Dominguez Hills M,O
California State University, East Bay M
California State University, Fullerton M
California State University, Los Angeles M
California State University, Northridge M
California State University, Sacramento M
California State University, San Marcos M
Case Western Reserve University M,D
The Catholic University of America M
City College of the City University of New York M
Clark Atlanta University M
Clemson University M
Cleveland State University M
Colorado State University M,D
Columbia University M,D
Cornell University M,D
DePaul University M
Drake University M
Duke University M,D
East Carolina University M
Eastern Michigan University M
East Tennessee State University M
Emory University M,D
Fayetteville State University M
Florida Agricultural and Mechanical University M
Florida Atlantic University M
Florida International University M,D
Florida State University M,D
Fordham University M
The George Washington University M
Georgia Southern University M
Georgia State University M,D
Graduate School and University Center of the City University of New York D
Harvard University D
Hofstra University M
Howard University M,D
Humboldt State University M
Hunter College of the City University of New York M
Idaho State University M
Illinois State University M
Indiana University Bloomington M,D
Indiana University of Pennsylvania M
Indiana University–Purdue University Fort Wayne M
Indiana University–Purdue University Indianapolis M
Iowa State University of Science and Technology M,D
Jackson State University M
The Johns Hopkins University D
Kansas State University M,D
Kean University M
Kent State University M,D
Lehigh University M
Lincoln University (MO) M
Louisiana State University and Agricultural and Mechanical College M,D
Loyola University Chicago M,D
Marshall University M
Michigan State University M,D
Middle Tennessee State University M
Minnesota State University Mankato M
Mississippi State University M,D
Montclair State University M
Morehead State University M
Morgan State University M
New Mexico Highlands University M
New Mexico State University M
The New School: A University M,D
New York University M,D
Norfolk State University M
North Carolina Central University M
North Carolina State University M,D
North Dakota State University M,D
Northeastern University M,D
Northern Arizona University M
Northern Illinois University M
Northwestern University D
The Ohio State University M,D
Ohio University M
Oklahoma State University M,D
Old Dominion University M
Penn State University Park M,D
Portland State University M,D,O
Prairie View A&M University M
Princeton University D,O
Purdue University M,D
Queens College of the City University of New York M
Roosevelt University M
Rutgers, The State University of New Jersey, New Brunswick M,D
St. John's University (NY) M
Sam Houston State University M
San Diego State University M
San Jose State University M
Shippensburg University of Pennsylvania M
Southeastern Louisiana University M
Southern Connecticut State University M
Southern Illinois University Carbondale M,D
Southern Illinois University Edwardsville M
Stanford University D
State University of New York at Binghamton M,D
State University of New York Institute of Technology M
Stony Brook University, State University of New York M,D

M—master's degree; P—first professional degree; D—doctorate; O—other advanced degree

Syracuse University M,D
Temple University M,D
Texas A&M International University M
Texas A&M University M,D
Texas A&M University–Commerce M
Texas A&M University–Kingsville M
Texas Southern University M
Texas State University–San Marcos M
Texas Tech University M
Texas Woman's University M,D
Tulane University M,D
University at Albany, State University of New York M,D,O
University at Buffalo, the State University of New York M,D
The University of Akron M,D
The University of Alabama at Birmingham M,D
The University of Arizona D
University of Arkansas M
University of California, Berkeley M,D
University of California, Davis M,D
University of California, Irvine M,D
University of California, Los Angeles M,D
University of California, Riverside M,D
University of California, San Diego D
University of California, Santa Barbara D
University of California, Santa Cruz D
University of Central Florida M,D,O
University of Central Missouri M
University of Chicago D
University of Cincinnati M,D
University of Colorado at Boulder D
University of Colorado at Colorado Springs M
University of Colorado Denver M
University of Connecticut M,D
University of Delaware M,D
University of Florida M,D
University of Georgia M,D
University of Hawaii at Manoa M,D
University of Houston M
University of Houston–Clear Lake M
University of Illinois at Chicago M,D
University of Illinois at Urbana–Champaign M,D
University of Indianapolis M
The University of Iowa M,D
The University of Kansas M,D
University of Kentucky M,D
University of Louisville M
University of Maryland, Baltimore County M,O
University of Maryland, College Park M,D
University of Massachusetts Amherst M,D
University of Massachusetts Boston M
University of Massachusetts Lowell M,O
University of Memphis M
University of Miami M,D
University of Michigan D,O
University of Minnesota, Duluth M
University of Minnesota, Twin Cities Campus M,D
University of Mississippi M
University of Missouri–Columbia M,D
University of Missouri–Kansas City M,D
University of Missouri–St. Louis M
The University of Montana M
University of Nebraska–Lincoln M,D
University of Nevada, Las Vegas M,D
University of Nevada, Reno M
University of New Hampshire M,D
University of New Mexico M,D
University of New Orleans M
The University of North Carolina at Chapel Hill M,D
The University of North Carolina at Charlotte M
The University of North Carolina at Greensboro M
The University of North Carolina Wilmington M
University of North Dakota M
University of Northern Colorado M
University of Northern Iowa M
University of North Florida M
University of North Texas M,D
University of Notre Dame D
University of Oklahoma M,D
University of Oregon M,D
University of Pennsylvania M,D
University of Pittsburgh M,D
University of Puerto Rico, Río Piedras M
University of South Alabama M
University of South Carolina M,D
University of Southern California D
University of South Florida M,D
The University of Tennessee M,D
The University of Texas at Arlington M
The University of Texas at Austin M,D
The University of Texas at Dallas M
The University of Texas at El Paso M
The University of Texas at San Antonio M
The University of Texas at Tyler M
The University of Texas–Pan American M
The University of Toledo M
University of Utah M,D
University of Virginia M,D
University of Washington M,D
University of West Georgia M
University of Wisconsin–Madison M,D
University of Wisconsin–Milwaukee M
University of Wyoming M
Utah State University M,D
Valdosta State University M
Vanderbilt University M,D
Virginia Commonwealth University M
Virginia Polytechnic Institute and State University M,D
Washington State University M,D
Wayne State University M,D
West Chester University of Pennsylvania M,O
Western Illinois University M
Western Kentucky University M
Western Michigan University M,D
West Virginia University M
Wichita State University M
William Paterson University of New Jersey M
Yale University D

■ SOFTWARE ENGINEERING

Andrews University M
Arizona State University M
Auburn University M,D
Bowling Green State University M
Brandeis University M,O
California State University, East Bay M
California State University, Fullerton M
California State University, Northridge M
California State University, Sacramento M
Carnegie Mellon University M,D
Carroll University M
Cleveland State University M,D
Colorado Technical University Colorado Springs M,D
Colorado Technical University Denver M
Colorado Technical University Sioux Falls M
DePaul University M,D
Drexel University M,D,O
East Tennessee State University M
Embry-Riddle Aeronautical University (FL) M
Fairfield University M
Florida Agricultural and Mechanical University M
Florida Institute of Technology M,D
Florida State University M,D
Gannon University M
George Mason University M,D,O

Grand Valley State University	M
Hawai'i Pacific University	M
Illinois Institute of Technology	M,D
Jacksonville State University	M
Kansas State University	M,D
Loyola University Chicago	M
Loyola University Maryland	M
Marist College	M,O
Mercer University	M
Miami University	M,O
Monmouth University	M,O
National University	M
New Jersey Institute of Technology	M,D
North Dakota State University	M,D,O
Northern Kentucky University	M,O
Oakland University	M
Penn State Great Valley	M
Polytechnic Institute of NYU	O
Portland State University	M,D
Regis University	M,O
Rochester Institute of Technology	M
St. Mary's University (United States)	M
San Francisco State University	M
San Jose State University	M
Santa Clara University	M,D,O
Seattle University	M
Southern Methodist University	M,D
Southern Polytechnic State University	M,O
Stevens Institute of Technology	M,D,O
Stony Brook University, State University of New York	M,D,O
Strayer University	M
Texas State University–San Marcos	M
Texas Tech University	M,D
Towson University	D,O
The University of Alabama in Huntsville	M,D,O
University of Alaska Fairbanks	M
University of Colorado at Colorado Springs	M
University of Connecticut	M,D
University of Detroit Mercy	M
University of Houston–Clear Lake	M
University of Massachusetts Dartmouth	M,O
University of Michigan–Dearborn	M
University of Missouri–Kansas City	M,D
University of New Haven	M
University of St. Thomas (MN)	M,O
The University of Scranton	M
University of South Carolina	M,D
University of Southern California	M,D
The University of Texas at Arlington	M,D
The University of Texas at Dallas	M,D
University of Washington, Tacoma	M
University of West Florida	M
University of West Georgia	M,O
University of Wisconsin–La Crosse	M
Villanova University	M
Walden University	M,O
West Virginia University	M
Widener University	M
Winthrop University	M,O

■ SPANISH

American University	M,O
Arizona State University	M,D
Arkansas Tech University	M
Auburn University	M
Baylor University	M
Bennington College	M
Boston College	M,D
Boston University	M,D
Bowling Green State University	M
Brigham Young University	M
Brooklyn College of the City University of New York	M,D
California State University, Bakersfield	M
California State University, Fresno	M
California State University, Fullerton	M
California State University, Long Beach	M
California State University, Los Angeles	M
California State University, Northridge	M
California State University, Sacramento	M
California State University, San Bernardino	M
California State University, San Marcos	M
The Catholic University of America	M,D
Central Connecticut State University	M,O
Central Michigan University	M
City College of the City University of New York	M
Cleveland State University	M
Columbia University	M,D
Cornell University	D
Duke University	D
Eastern Michigan University	M,O
Emory University	D,O
Florida Atlantic University	M
Florida International University	M,D
Florida State University	M,D
Framingham State College	M
Georgetown University	M,D
Georgia Southern University	M
Georgia State University	M,O
Graduate School and University Center of the City University of New York	D
Harvard University	M,D
Hofstra University	M
Howard University	M
Hunter College of the City University of New York	M
Illinois State University	M
Indiana University Bloomington	M,D
Inter American University of Puerto Rico, Metropolitan Campus	M
Iona College	M
The Johns Hopkins University	D
Kansas State University	M
Kean University	M
Kent State University	M,D
Lehman College of the City University of New York	M
Long Island University, C.W. Post Campus	M
Loyola University Chicago	M
Marquette University	M
Marshall University	M
Miami University	M
Michigan State University	M,D
Millersville University of Pennsylvania	M
Minnesota State University Mankato	M
Mississippi State University	M
Missouri State University	M
Montclair State University	M,O
New Mexico State University	M
New York University	M,D
North Carolina State University	M
Northern Illinois University	M
Nova Southeastern University	M,O
The Ohio State University	M,D
Ohio University	M
Penn State University Park	M,D
Pontifical Catholic University of Puerto Rico	M,O
Portland State University	M
Princeton University	D
Purdue University	M,D
Queens College of the City University of New York	M
Rice University	M
Rider University	O
Roosevelt University	M
Rutgers, The State University of New Jersey, New Brunswick	M,D
St. John's University (NY)	M,O
Saint Louis University	M
Salem State College	M
San Diego State University	M
San Francisco State University	M
San Jose State University	M

M—master's degree; P—first professional degree; D—doctorate; O—other advanced degree

Simmons College M
Stanford University M,D
State University of New York at Binghamton M,O
Syracuse University M
Temple University M,D
Texas A&M International University M,D
Texas A&M University M,D
Texas A&M University–Commerce M,D
Texas A&M University–Kingsville M
Texas State University–San Marcos M
Texas Tech University M,D
Tulane University M,D
University at Albany, State University of New York M,D
University at Buffalo, the State University of New York M,D
The University of Akron M
The University of Alabama M,D
The University of Arizona M,D
University of Arkansas M
University of California, Berkeley D
University of California, Davis M,D
University of California, Irvine M,D
University of California, Los Angeles M
University of California, Riverside M,D
University of California, San Diego M
University of California, Santa Barbara M,D
University of Central Florida M
University of Chicago M,D
University of Cincinnati M,D
University of Colorado at Boulder M,D
University of Colorado Denver M
University of Connecticut M,D
University of Delaware M
University of Florida M,D
University of Georgia M
University of Hawaii at Manoa M
University of Houston M,D
University of Illinois at Chicago M,D
University of Illinois at Urbana–Champaign M,D
The University of Iowa M,D
The University of Kansas M,D
University of Louisville M
University of Maryland, College Park M,D
University of Massachusetts Amherst M,D
University of Memphis M
University of Miami M,D
University of Michigan D
University of Minnesota, Twin Cities Campus M,D
University of Mississippi M
University of Missouri–Columbia M,D
The University of Montana M
University of Nebraska–Lincoln M,D
University of Nevada, Las Vegas M,O
University of Nevada, Reno M
University of New Hampshire M
University of New Mexico M,D
The University of North Carolina at Chapel Hill M,D
The University of North Carolina at Charlotte M
The University of North Carolina at Greensboro M,O
University of Northern Colorado M
University of Northern Iowa M
University of North Texas M
University of Notre Dame M
University of Oklahoma M,D
University of Oregon M
University of Pennsylvania M,D
University of Pittsburgh M,D
University of Rhode Island M
University of South Carolina M,D
University of South Florida M
The University of Tennessee M,D
The University of Texas at Arlington M
The University of Texas at Austin M,D
The University of Texas at Brownsville M
The University of Texas at El Paso M
The University of Texas at San Antonio M,O
The University of Texas of the Permian Basin M
The University of Texas–Pan American M
The University of Toledo M
University of Utah M,D
University of Virginia M,D
University of Washington M
University of Wisconsin–Madison M,D
University of Wisconsin–Milwaukee M,O
University of Wyoming M
Vanderbilt University M,D
Washington State University M
Washington University in St. Louis M,D
Wayne State University M
West Chester University of Pennsylvania M,O
Western Michigan University M,D
West Virginia University M
Wichita State University M
Winthrop University M
Worcester State College M
Yale University D

■ SPECIAL EDUCATION

Abilene Christian University M
Adams State College M
Adelphi University M,O
Alabama Agricultural and Mechanical University M,O
Alabama State University M
Albany State University M
Alcorn State University M,O
American International College M,D,O
American University M
Andrews University M,D,O
Appalachian State University M
Arcadia University M,D,O
Arizona State University M,D,O
Arkansas State University M,D,O
Armstrong Atlantic State University M
Ashland University M
Assumption College M
Auburn University M,D
Auburn University Montgomery M,O
Augusta State University M,O
Austin Peay State University M,O
Azusa Pacific University M
Baldwin-Wallace College M
Ball State University M,D,O
Barry University M,D,O
Bayamón Central University M
Bellarmine University M
Belmont University M
Bemidji State University M
Benedictine University M
Bethel University (TN) M
Bethel University M,D,O
Bloomsburg University of Pennsylvania M
Bob Jones University P,M,D,O
Boise State University M
Boston College M,O
Boston University M,D,O
Bowie State University M
Bowling Green State University M
Brenau University M,O
Bridgewater State College M
Brigham Young University M,D,O
Brooklyn College of the City University of New York M
Buffalo State College, State University of New York M
Butler University M
Caldwell College M
California Baptist University M
California Lutheran University M
California State University, Bakersfield M
California State University, Chico M
California State University, Dominguez Hills M
California State University, East Bay M
California State University, Fresno M
California State University, Fullerton M

California State University, Long Beach M
California State University, Los Angeles M,D
California State University, Northridge M
California State University, Sacramento M
California State University, San Bernardino M
California State University, Stanislaus M,D
California University of Pennsylvania M
Cambridge College M,D,O
Canisius College M
Cardinal Stritch University M
Carlow University M
Castleton State College M,O
The Catholic University of America M,D,O
Centenary College M
Central Connecticut State University M,O
Central Michigan University M
Central Washington University M
Chapman University M
Chatham University M
Cheyney University of Pennsylvania M
Chicago State University M
City College of the City University of New York M
City University of Seattle M,O
Claremont Graduate University M,D,O
Clarion University of Pennsylvania M
Clemson University M
Cleveland State University M
College of Charleston M
The College of New Jersey M,O
The College of New Rochelle M
College of St. Joseph M
The College of Saint Rose M,O
College of Santa Fe M
College of Staten Island of the City University of New York M
The College of William and Mary M
Columbus State University M,O
Concordia University, St. Paul M,O
Concordia University Wisconsin M
Converse College M
Coppin State University M
Creighton University M
Daemen College M
Delaware State University M
Delta State University M
DePaul University M,D
DeSales University M
Dominican College M
Dominican University M
Dominican University of California O
Dowling College M,D,O
Drake University M
Drury University M
Duquesne University M
D'Youville College M,O
East Carolina University M
Eastern Illinois University M
Eastern Kentucky University M
Eastern Michigan University M,O
Eastern Nazarene College M,O
Eastern New Mexico University M
Eastern Washington University M
East Stroudsburg University of Pennsylvania M
East Tennessee State University M,D
Edgewood College M,D,O
Edinboro University of Pennsylvania M,O
Elmhurst College M
Elon University M
Emporia State University M
Endicott College M
Fairfield University M,O
Fairleigh Dickinson University, Metropolitan Campus M
Ferris State University M
Fitchburg State College M
Florida Atlantic University M,D
Florida Gulf Coast University M
Florida International University M,D,O
Florida State University M,D,O
Fontbonne University M
Fordham University M,D,O
Fort Hays State University M
Framingham State College M
Francis Marion University M
Freed-Hardeman University M,O
Fresno Pacific University M
Frostburg State University M
Furman University M
Gallaudet University M,D,O
Geneva College M
George Mason University M,O
Georgetown College M
The George Washington University M,D,O
Georgia College & State University M
Georgia Southern University M
Georgia Southwestern State University M,O
Georgia State University M,D
Gonzaga University M
Governors State University M
Graceland University (IA) M
Grand Canyon University M,D
Grand Valley State University M
Gwynedd-Mercy College M
Hampton University M
Harding University M,O
Henderson State University M
Heritage University M
High Point University M
Hofstra University M,D,O
Holy Family University M
Holy Names University M,O
Hood College M
Howard University M,O
Hunter College of the City University of New York M
Idaho State University M,D,O
Illinois State University M,D
Immaculata University M,D,O
Indiana University Bloomington M,D,O
Indiana University of Pennsylvania M
Indiana University–Purdue University Fort Wayne M
Indiana University–Purdue University Indianapolis M,O
Indiana University South Bend M
Inter American University of Puerto Rico, Metropolitan Campus M
Inter American University of Puerto Rico, San Germán Campus M
Iowa State University of Science and Technology M,D
Jackson State University M,O
Jacksonville State University M
James Madison University M
The Johns Hopkins University M,D,O
Johnson State College M
Kansas State University M,D
Kean University M
Keene State College M,O
Kennesaw State University M
Kent State University M,D,O
Kutztown University of Pennsylvania M,O
Lamar University M,D
Lee University M,O
Lehigh University M,D,O
Lehman College of the City University of New York M
Le Moyne College M,O
Lesley University M,D,O
Lewis & Clark College M
Lewis University M
Liberty University M,D,O
Lincoln University (MO) M,O
Lipscomb University M
Long Island University, Brentwood Campus M
Long Island University, Brooklyn Campus M
Long Island University, C.W. Post Campus M
Longwood University M
Louisiana Tech University M,D

M—master's degree; P—first professional degree; D—doctorate; O—other advanced degree

Loyola Marymount University M
Loyola University Chicago M
Loyola University Maryland M,O
Lynchburg College M
Lynn University M,D
Madonna University M
Malone University M
Manhattan College M
Manhattanville College M
Marshall University M
Marymount University M
Marywood University M
McDaniel College M
McNeese State University M
Medaille College M
Mercy College M,O
Mercyhurst College M,O
Miami University M
Michigan State University M,D,O
MidAmerica Nazarene University M
Middle Tennessee State University M,O
Midwestern State University M
Millersville University of Pennsylvania M
Minnesota State University Mankato M,O
Minnesota State University Moorhead M
Minot State University M
Mississippi College M,D,O
Mississippi State University M,D,O
Missouri State University M,D
Monmouth University M,O
Montana State University–Billings M
Montclair State University M,O
Morehead State University M,O
Morningside College M
Mount Saint Mary College M
Mount St. Mary's College M
Murray State University M
National-Louis University M,O
National University M
New Jersey City University M
New Mexico Highlands University M
New Mexico State University M,D
New York University M
Niagara University M,O
Norfolk State University M
North Carolina Central University M
North Carolina State University M
Northeastern Illinois University M
Northeastern University M,D,O
Northern Arizona University M
Northern Illinois University M,D
Northern Kentucky University M,O
Northern Michigan University M
North Georgia College & State University M,O
Northwestern State University of Louisiana M,O
Northwestern University M,D
Northwest Missouri State University M
Northwest Nazarene University M
Notre Dame de Namur University M,O
Nova Southeastern University M,D,O
Nyack College M
Oakland University M,O
Ohio University M,D
Old Dominion University M,D
Our Lady of the Lake University of San Antonio M
Pacific University M
Park University M
Penn State Great Valley M
Penn State University Park M,D
Pittsburg State University M
Plymouth State University M,D,O
Portland State University M,D
Prairie View A&M University M
Prescott College M,D
Providence College M
Purdue University M,D,O
Purdue University Calumet M
Queens College of the City University of New York M
Radford University M
Regent University M,D,O
Regis College (MA) M
Regis University M,O
Rhode Island College M,O
Rider University M,O
Rivier College M,D,O
Roberts Wesleyan College M,O
Rochester Institute of Technology M
Rockford College M
Roosevelt University M
Rowan University M
Rutgers, The State University of New Jersey, New Brunswick M,D
Saginaw Valley State University M
St. Ambrose University M
St. Cloud State University M
St. John Fisher College M,O
St. John's University (NY) M
Saint Joseph College M
St. Joseph's College, Long Island Campus M
Saint Joseph's University M,D
Saint Louis University M,D
Saint Martin's University M
Saint Mary's College of California M
Saint Mary's University of Minnesota M,O
Saint Michael's College M,O
Saint Peter's College M
St. Thomas Aquinas College M,O
St. Thomas University M,D,O
Saint Xavier University M,O
Salem State College M
Sam Houston State University M,D
San Diego State University M
San Francisco State University M,D,O
San Jose State University M,O
Santa Clara University M,O
Seattle University M,O
Seton Hill University M,O
Shippensburg University of Pennsylvania M
Silver Lake College M
Simmons College M,D,O
Slippery Rock University of Pennsylvania M
Sonoma State University M
South Carolina State University M
Southeastern Louisiana University M
Southeast Missouri State University M
Southern Connecticut State University M,O
Southern Illinois University Carbondale M
Southern Illinois University Edwardsville M,O
Southern New Hampshire University M,O
Southern Oregon University M
Southern University and Agricultural and Mechanical College M,D
Southwestern College (KS) M
Southwestern Oklahoma State University M
Southwest Minnesota State University M
Spalding University M
Spring Arbor University M
Springfield College M
State University of New York at Binghamton M
State University of New York at New Paltz M
State University of New York at Oswego M
State University of New York at Plattsburgh M
State University of New York College at Cortland M
State University of New York College at Potsdam M
Stephen F. Austin State University M
Syracuse University M,D
Tarleton State University M,O
Temple University M,D
Tennessee State University M,D
Tennessee Technological University M,O
Texas A&M International University M
Texas A&M University M,D
Texas A&M University–Commerce M,D

Texas A&M University–Corpus Christi M
Texas A&M University–Kingsville M
Texas A&M University–Texarkana M
Texas Christian University M
Texas State University–San Marcos M
Texas Tech University M,D
Texas Woman's University M,D
Towson University M
Trinity (Washington) University M
Union College (KY) M
Universidad del Turabo M
Universidad Metropolitana M
University at Albany, State University of New York M
University at Buffalo, the State University of New York M,D,O
The University of Akron M
The University of Alabama M,D,O
The University of Alabama at Birmingham M
University of Alaska Anchorage M,O
The University of Arizona M,D,O
University of Arkansas M
University of Arkansas at Little Rock M,O
University of California, Berkeley D
University of California, Los Angeles D
University of California, Riverside M,D
University of California, Santa Barbara M,D
University of Central Arkansas M
University of Central Florida M,D
University of Central Missouri M,O
University of Central Oklahoma M
University of Cincinnati M,D
University of Colorado at Colorado Springs M,D
University of Connecticut M,D,O
University of Dayton M
University of Detroit Mercy M
The University of Findlay M
University of Florida M,D,O
University of Georgia M,D,O
University of Guam M
University of Hawaii at Manoa M,D
University of Houston M,D
University of Houston–Victoria M
University of Idaho M,O
University of Illinois at Chicago M,D
University of Illinois at Urbana–Champaign M,D,O
The University of Iowa M,D
The University of Kansas M,D
University of Kentucky M,D
University of La Verne M
University of Louisville M
University of Maine M,O
University of Mary M
University of Maryland, College Park M,D,O
University of Maryland Eastern Shore M
University of Massachusetts Amherst M,D,O
University of Massachusetts Boston M
University of Memphis M,D
University of Miami M,D,O
University of Michigan–Dearborn M
University of Michigan–Flint M
University of Minnesota, Twin Cities Campus M,D,O
University of Missouri–Columbia M,D
University of Missouri–Kansas City M,D,O
University of Missouri–St. Louis M,O
University of Nebraska at Kearney M
University of Nebraska at Omaha M
University of Nebraska–Lincoln M,D,O
University of Nevada, Las Vegas M,D,O
University of Nevada, Reno M,D
University of New Hampshire M,O
University of New Mexico M,D,O
University of New Orleans M,D,O
University of North Alabama M
The University of North Carolina at Charlotte M,D
The University of North Carolina at Greensboro M,D,O
University of North Dakota M,D
University of Northern Colorado M,D
University of Northern Iowa M,D
University of North Florida M
University of North Texas M,D,O
University of Oklahoma M,D
University of Phoenix M
University of Phoenix–Hawaii Campus M
University of Phoenix–Phoenix Campus M
University of Phoenix–Southern Arizona Campus M,O
University of Phoenix–Utah Campus M
University of Pittsburgh M,D
University of Puerto Rico, Río Piedras M
University of Rio Grande M
University of St. Francis (IL) M
University of Saint Francis (IN) M
University of Saint Mary M
University of St. Thomas (MN) M,O
University of San Diego M
The University of Scranton M
University of South Alabama M,O
University of South Carolina M,D
The University of South Dakota M
University of Southern Maine M
University of Southern Mississippi M,D,O
University of South Florida M,D
The University of Tennessee M,D,O
The University of Tennessee at Chattanooga M,O
The University of Texas at Austin M,D
The University of Texas at Brownsville M
The University of Texas at El Paso M
The University of Texas at San Antonio M
The University of Texas at Tyler M
The University of Texas of the Permian Basin M
The University of Texas–Pan American M
University of the District of Columbia M
University of the Incarnate Word M,D
University of the Pacific M,D
University of the Southwest M
The University of Toledo M,D,O
University of Utah M,D
University of Vermont M
University of Virginia M,D,O
University of Washington M,D
University of Washington, Tacoma M
The University of West Alabama M
University of West Florida M
University of West Georgia M,O
University of Wisconsin–Eau Claire M
University of Wisconsin–La Crosse M
University of Wisconsin–Madison M,D
University of Wisconsin–Milwaukee M,D,O
University of Wisconsin–Oshkosh M
University of Wisconsin–Stevens Point M
University of Wisconsin–Superior M
University of Wisconsin–Whitewater M
University of Wyoming M,D,O
Ursuline College M
Utah State University M,D,O
Valdosta State University M,O
Vanderbilt University M,D
Virginia Commonwealth University M,D
Virginia Polytechnic Institute and State University D,O
Walden University M,D,O
Walla Walla University M
Washburn University M
Washington University in St. Louis M,D
Waynesburg University M,D

M—master's degree; P—first professional degree; D—doctorate; O—other advanced degree

Wayne State College M
Wayne State University M,D,O
Webster University M,O
West Chester University of Pennsylvania M,O
Western Connecticut State University M
Western Illinois University M
Western Kentucky University M
Western New Mexico University M
Western Oregon University M
Westfield State College M
West Texas A&M University M
West Virginia University M,D
Wheelock College M
Whitworth University M
Wichita State University M
Widener University M,D
Wilkes University M,D
William Carey University M,O
William Paterson University of New Jersey M
William Woods University M,O
Wilmington University M
Winona State University M
Winthrop University M
Worcester State College M
Wright State University M
Xavier University M
Youngstown State University M

■ SPEECH AND INTERPERSONAL COMMUNICATION

Arizona State University M,D
Arkansas State University M,O
Ball State University M
Bob Jones University P,M,D,O
Bowling Green State University M,D
Brooklyn College of the City University of New York M,D
California State University, Fullerton M
California State University, Los Angeles M
California State University, Northridge M
Central Michigan University M
Colorado State University M
Drake University M
Eastern Illinois University M
Florida State University M,D
Georgia State University M,D
Hofstra University M
Idaho State University M
Indiana University Bloomington M,D
Kansas State University M
Louisiana Tech University M
Marquette University M
Miami University M
Minnesota State University Mankato M
Montclair State University M
New York University M,D
North Dakota State University M,D
Northeastern Illinois University M
Northeastern University D
Northwestern University M,D
Ohio University D
Portland State University M,O
Rensselaer Polytechnic Institute M,D
San Francisco State University M
San Jose State University M
Seton Hall University M
Southern Illinois University Carbondale M,D
Southern Illinois University Edwardsville M
Texas A&M University–Commerce M
Texas Christian University M
The University of Alabama M
University of Arkansas at Little Rock M
University of California, Santa Barbara D
University of Central Florida M
University of Central Missouri M
University of Denver M,D
University of Georgia M,D
University of Hawaii at Manoa M
University of Houston M
University of Maryland, College Park M,D
University of Nebraska–Lincoln M,D
University of Nevada, Reno M
University of South Carolina M,D
University of Southern California M,D
University of Southern Mississippi M,D
The University of Tennessee M,D
University of Wisconsin–Madison M,D
University of Wisconsin–Stevens Point M
University of Wisconsin–Superior M
Wake Forest University M
Washington University in St. Louis M,D
Wayne State University M,D

■ SPORT PSYCHOLOGY

Argosy University, Orange County M
Barry University M
California State University, Fresno M
California State University, Long Beach M
California University of Pennsylvania M
Capella University M,D,O
Chatham University M,D
Cleveland State University M
Eastern Washington University M
Florida State University M,D,O
John F. Kennedy University M
Purdue University M,D
Southern Connecticut State University M
Springfield College M,D,O
University of Florida M,D
The University of Iowa M,D
University of Rhode Island M,D
The University of Texas at Austin M,D
West Virginia University M,D

■ SPORTS MANAGEMENT

Ashland University M
Barry University M
Belmont University M
Boise State University M
Bowling Green State University M
Brooklyn College of the City University of New York M
California Baptist University M
California State University, Long Beach M
California University of Pennsylvania M
Canisius College M
Cardinal Stritch University M
Central Michigan University M,O
The Citadel, The Military College of South Carolina M
Cleveland State University M
The College at Brockport, State University of New York M
Columbia University M
Concordia University (CA) M
Concordia University, St. Paul M,O
Drexel University M
Duquesne University M
Eastern Kentucky University M
Eastern Michigan University M
Eastern Washington University M
East Stroudsburg University of Pennsylvania M
East Tennessee State University M
Endicott College M
Fairleigh Dickinson University, Metropolitan Campus M
Florida International University M
Florida State University M,D,O
Georgetown University M,D
The George Washington University M,O
Georgia Southern University M
Georgia State University M
Gonzaga University M
Grambling State University M
Henderson State University M
Hofstra University M
Holy Names University M
Howard University M
Indiana State University M
Indiana University Bloomington M,D,O
Indiana University of Pennsylvania M
Ithaca College M
Kent State University M

Lindenwood University M
Lynn University M,D
Manhattanville College M
Marshall University M
Millersville University of Pennsylvania M
Mississippi State University M
Missouri State University M
Montana State University–Billings M
Montclair State University M,O
Morehead State University M
Neumann University M
New Mexico Highlands University M
New York University M,O
North Carolina Central University M
North Carolina State University M,D
North Dakota State University M
Northern Illinois University M
Nova Southeastern University M,O
Ohio University M
Old Dominion University M
St. Cloud State University M
St. Edward's University M,O
St. John's University (NY) M
Saint Leo University M
St. Thomas University M,O
San Diego State University M
Seattle University M
Seton Hall University M
Slippery Rock University of Pennsylvania M
Southeast Missouri State University M
Southern New Hampshire University M,D,O
Springfield College M,D,O
State University of New York College at Cortland M
Temple University M,D
Tiffin University M
Troy University M
The University of Alabama M,D
University of Central Florida M,O
University of Dallas M
University of Florida M,D
The University of Iowa M
University of Louisville M
University of Massachusetts Amherst M,D
University of Miami M
University of Michigan M,D
University of Minnesota, Twin Cities Campus M,D,O
University of Nevada, Las Vegas M,D
University of New Haven M
The University of North Carolina at Chapel Hill M
The University of North Carolina at Charlotte M
University of Northern Colorado M,D
University of Northern Iowa M,D
University of Rhode Island M,D
University of San Francisco M
University of South Carolina M
University of Southern Maine M,O
University of Southern Mississippi M,D
The University of Tennessee M,D
University of the Incarnate Word M,O
University of Wisconsin–La Crosse M
Valparaiso University M
Washington State University M,D,O
Wayne State College M
Wayne State University M
West Chester University of Pennsylvania M,O
Western Carolina University M
Western Illinois University M
Western Michigan University M
Western New England College M
West Virginia University M,D
Wichita State University M
Winona State University M,O
Xavier University M

■ STATISTICS

American University M,O
Arizona State University M,D
Auburn University M,D
Ball State University M
Baylor University M,D
Bernard M. Baruch College of the City University of New York M
Bowling Green State University M,D
Brigham Young University M
California State University, East Bay M
California State University, Sacramento M
Carnegie Mellon University M,D
Case Western Reserve University M,D
Central Connecticut State University M,O
Claremont Graduate University M,D
Clemson University M,D
Colorado State University M,D
Columbia University M,D
Cornell University M,D
Duke University D
Florida Atlantic University M,D
Florida International University M
Florida State University M,D,O
George Mason University M,D,O
Georgetown University M
The George Washington University M,D,O
Georgia Institute of Technology M,D
Georgia State University M,D
Hampton University M
Harvard University M,D
Indiana University Bloomington M,D
Iowa State University of Science and Technology M,D
James Madison University M
The Johns Hopkins University M,D
Kansas State University M,D
Kean University M
Lehigh University M,D
Louisiana State University and Agricultural and Mechanical College M
Louisiana Tech University M
Loyola University Chicago M
McNeese State University M
Miami University M
Michigan State University M,D
Minnesota State University Mankato M
Mississippi State University M,D
Missouri University of Science and Technology M,D
Montana State University M,D
Montclair State University M,D,O
Murray State University M
New Mexico State University M,D
New York University M,D
North Carolina State University M,D
North Dakota State University M,D,O
Northern Arizona University M
Northern Illinois University M
Northwestern University M,D
Oakland University O
The Ohio State University M,D
Oklahoma State University M,D
Oregon State University M,D
Penn State University Park M,D
Portland State University M,D
Purdue University M,D,O
Rice University M,D
Rochester Institute of Technology M,O
Rutgers, The State University of New Jersey, New Brunswick M,D
St. John's University (NY) M
Sam Houston State University M
San Diego State University M
San Jose State University M
South Dakota State University M,D
Southern Illinois University Carbondale M,D
Southern Methodist University M,D
Stanford University M,D
State University of New York at Binghamton M,D
Stephen F. Austin State University M
Stevens Institute of Technology M,O
Stony Brook University, State University of New York M,D
Temple University M,D
Texas A&M University M,D
Texas Tech University M

M—master's degree; P—first professional degree; D—doctorate; O—other advanced degree

Tulane University M,D
University at Albany, State University of New York M,D,O
The University of Akron M
University of Alaska Fairbanks M,D
The University of Arizona M,D
University of Arkansas M
University of California, Berkeley M,D
University of California, Davis M,D
University of California, Los Angeles M,D
University of California, Riverside M,D
University of California, San Diego M,D
University of California, Santa Barbara M,D
University of California, Santa Cruz M,D
University of Central Florida M,O
University of Central Oklahoma M
University of Chicago M,D
University of Cincinnati M,D
University of Connecticut M,D
University of Delaware M
University of Denver M
University of Florida M,D
University of Georgia M,D
University of Houston–Clear Lake M
University of Idaho M
University of Illinois at Chicago M,D
University of Illinois at Urbana–Champaign M,D
The University of Iowa M,D,O
University of Kentucky M,D
University of Maryland, Baltimore County M,D
University of Maryland, College Park M,D
University of Massachusetts Amherst M,D
University of Memphis M,D
University of Michigan M,D
University of Minnesota, Twin Cities Campus M,D
University of Missouri–Columbia M,D
University of Missouri–Kansas City M,D
University of Nebraska–Lincoln M,D
University of New Hampshire M,D,O
University of New Mexico M,D
The University of North Carolina at Chapel Hill M,D
University of North Florida M
University of Pennsylvania M,D
University of Pittsburgh M,D
University of Puerto Rico, Mayagüez Campus M
University of Rhode Island M,D,O
University of Rochester M,D
University of South Carolina M,D,O
The University of South Dakota M,D
University of Southern California M,D
University of Southern Maine M
University of South Florida M,D,O
The University of Tennessee M,D
The University of Texas at Austin M
The University of Texas at Dallas M,D
The University of Texas at El Paso M
The University of Texas at San Antonio M,D
University of the Incarnate Word M
The University of Toledo M,D
University of Utah M,D
University of Vermont M
University of Virginia M,D
University of Washington M,D
University of Wisconsin–Madison M,D
University of Wyoming M,D
Utah State University M,D
Virginia Commonwealth University M,O
Virginia Polytechnic Institute and State University M,D
Washington State University M
Washington University in St. Louis M,D
Wayne State University M,D
Western Michigan University M,D
West Virginia University M,D
Wichita State University M,D
Yale University M,D
Youngstown State University M

■ STRUCTURAL BIOLOGY

Brandeis University M,D
Carnegie Mellon University D
Cornell University M,D
Duke University O
Florida State University D
Harvard University D
Illinois State University M,D
Iowa State University of Science and Technology D
Massachusetts Institute of Technology D
Mayo Graduate School D
Michigan State University D
New York University P,M,D
Northwestern University D
Stanford University D
Stony Brook University, State University of New York D
Syracuse University D
Tulane University M,D
University at Albany, State University of New York M,D
University at Buffalo, the State University of New York M,D
University of California, San Diego D
University of Connecticut M,D
University of Minnesota, Twin Cities Campus D
University of Pittsburgh D
University of Washington D
Yale University D

■ STRUCTURAL ENGINEERING

Auburn University M,D
California State University, Northridge M
The Catholic University of America M,D,O
Cornell University M,D
Drexel University M,D
Illinois Institute of Technology M,D
Iowa State University of Science and Technology M,D
Lehigh University M,D
Louisiana State University and Agricultural and Mechanical College M,D
Marquette University M,D
Massachusetts Institute of Technology M,D,O
Northwestern University M,D
Ohio University M,D
Oregon State University M,D
Penn State University Park M,D
Princeton University M,D
Rensselaer Polytechnic Institute M,D
Stevens Institute of Technology M,D,O
Texas A&M University M,D
Tufts University M,D
University at Buffalo, the State University of New York M,D
The University of Alabama in Huntsville M,D
University of California, Berkeley M,D
University of California, San Diego M,D
University of Central Florida M,D,O
University of Colorado at Boulder M,D
University of Dayton M
University of Delaware M,D
University of Maine M,D
University of Memphis M,D
University of Michigan M,D,O
University of Missouri–Columbia M,D
University of North Dakota M
University of Oklahoma M,D
University of Rhode Island M,D
University of Washington M,D
Washington University in St. Louis M,D
Western Michigan University M
Worcester Polytechnic Institute M,D,O

■ STUDENT AFFAIRS

Alliant International University–San Diego M,D,O
Arkansas State University M,O
Arkansas Tech University M,O
Ashland University M
Azusa Pacific University M

Bloomsburg University of Pennsylvania M
Bob Jones University P,M,D,O
Bowling Green State University M
Buffalo State College, State University of New York M
California State University, Bakersfield M
California State University, Long Beach M,D
Canisius College M
Central Michigan University M,D,O
The Citadel, The Military College of South Carolina M
Claremont Graduate University M,D,O
Cleveland State University M,O
College of Saint Elizabeth M,O
The College of Saint Rose M,O
Colorado State University M,D
Concordia University Wisconsin M
Creighton University M
Eastern Illinois University M
Fresno Pacific University M
Grambling State University M,D
Hampton University M
Illinois State University M
Indiana State University M,D,O
Indiana University–Purdue University Indianapolis M,O
Kansas State University M,D
Kent State University M
Lewis University M
Miami University M
Minnesota State University Mankato M,D,O
Mississippi State University M,D,O
Missouri State University M
New York University M,D
Northeastern University M
Northern Arizona University M
Northern Kentucky University M,O
Northwestern State University of Louisiana M,O
Nova Southeastern University M,O
The Ohio State University M
Ohio University M,D
Oregon State University M
Penn State University Park M,D
Radford University M
Regent University M,D,O
St. Cloud State University M
St. Edward's University M
Saint Louis University M,D,O
San Jose State University M
Seton Hall University M
Shippensburg University of Pennsylvania M,O
Slippery Rock University of Pennsylvania M
Springfield College M,O
Syracuse University M
Tennessee Technological University M,O
University of Bridgeport M
University of Central Arkansas M
University of Central Florida M,D,O
University of Central Missouri M
University of Dayton M,O
University of Florida M,D,O
University of Georgia M,D,O
The University of Iowa M,D
University of Maryland, College Park M,D,O
University of Memphis M,D
University of Miami M,D,O
University of Minnesota, Twin Cities Campus M,D,O
University of Mississippi M,D,O
University of Northern Colorado D
University of Northern Iowa M
University of Rhode Island M
University of St. Thomas (MN) M,D,O
University of South Carolina M
University of Southern California M
University of South Florida M,D,O
The University of Tennessee M
University of Virginia M,D,O
University of West Florida M
University of Wisconsin–La Crosse M
University of Wyoming M,D
Washington State University M,D,O
Western Illinois University M
Western Kentucky University M,O

■ SUPPLY CHAIN MANAGEMENT

American University M
Arizona State University M,D
California State University, East Bay M
Case Western Reserve University M
Clarkson University M
Eastern Michigan University M,O
Elmhurst College M
Howard University M
Lehigh University M,D,O
Michigan State University M,D
North Carolina State University M
Penn State University Park M,D
Rutgers, The State University of New Jersey, Newark D
Strayer University M
Syracuse University M,D
The University of Akron M
The University of Alabama in Huntsville M,O
University of Dallas M
University of Florida M,D
University of La Verne M
University of Massachusetts Dartmouth M,O
University of Memphis M,D
University of Michigan M,D
University of Minnesota, Twin Cities Campus M
University of Missouri–St. Louis M,D,O
The University of North Carolina at Greensboro M,D,O
University of San Diego M,O
University of Southern California M,D,O
The University of Texas at Austin D
The University of Texas at Dallas M
University of Wisconsin–Madison M
University of Wisconsin–Whitewater M
Walden University M,D
Wright State University M

■ SURVEYING SCIENCE AND ENGINEERING

The Ohio State University M,D

■ SURVEY METHODOLOGY

University of Maryland, College Park M,D
University of Michigan M,D,O
University of Nebraska–Lincoln M,D

■ SUSTAINABILITY MANAGEMENT

Alliant International University–San Diego M,D
Antioch University New England M
City University of Seattle M,O
Colorado State University M
Columbia University M
Dominican University of California M
Duquesne University M
Goddard College M
Illinois Institute of Technology M
Lipscomb University M
Maharishi University of Management M,D
Michigan Technological University O
Rochester Institute of Technology D
University of California, Berkeley O
University of Maine M
Walden University M,D

■ SUSTAINABLE DEVELOPMENT

American University M,D,O
Appalachian State University M
Arizona State University M,D
Brandeis University M
California State University, Stanislaus M
City College of the City University of New York M
Clark University M
Columbia University M,D
Dominican University of California M
Florida Atlantic University M,O

M—master's degree; P—first professional degree; D—doctorate; O—other advanced degree

George Mason University M,D,O
Hawai'i Pacific University M
Iowa State University of Science and Technology M,D
Lesley University M
Michigan Technological University O
Northern Arizona University M
Philadelphia University M
Rochester Institute of Technology D
SIT Graduate Institute M
Slippery Rock University of Pennsylvania M
University of Connecticut M
University of Georgia M,D
University of Maryland, College Park M
University of Massachusetts Lowell M,D,O
University of Michigan M,D
University of Southern California M,D,O
University of Washington P,M,D
University of Wisconsin–Madison M
Walden University M,D,O
Wayne State University O
Western Illinois University M,O
West Virginia University D

■ SYSTEMS BIOLOGY

Dartmouth College D
Harvard University D
Massachusetts Institute of Technology D
Michigan State University D
Rutgers, The State University of New Jersey, New Brunswick D
University of California, San Diego D
University of Chicago D
University of Southern California D
Virginia Commonwealth University D

■ SYSTEMS ENGINEERING

Arizona State University M
Auburn University M,D
Boston University M,D
California Institute of Technology M,D
California State University, Fullerton M
California State University, Northridge M
Carnegie Mellon University M
Case Western Reserve University M,D
The Catholic University of America M,D,O
Colorado School of Mines M,D
Colorado Technical University Colorado Springs M
Colorado Technical University Denver M
Cornell University M
Embry-Riddle Aeronautical University (FL) M
Florida Institute of Technology M
George Mason University M,D,O
The George Washington University M,D,O
Georgia Institute of Technology M,D
Indiana University–Purdue University Fort Wayne M
Iowa State University of Science and Technology M
The Johns Hopkins University M,O
Lehigh University M,D
Loyola Marymount University M
Massachusetts Institute of Technology M,D
Mississippi State University M,D
Missouri University of Science and Technology M,D
National University M
North Carolina Agricultural and Technical State University M,D
Northeastern University M
Oakland University M,D
The Ohio State University M,D
Ohio University M
Old Dominion University M,D
Oregon State University M,D
Polytechnic Institute of NYU M
Portland State University M,O
Regis University M,O
Rensselaer Polytechnic Institute M,D
Rochester Institute of Technology M,D
Rutgers, The State University of New Jersey, New Brunswick M,D
San Jose State University M
Southern Methodist University M,D
Southern Polytechnic State University M,O
Stevens Institute of Technology M,D,O
Stony Brook University, State University of New York M,D,O
Texas Tech University M,D
The University of Alabama in Huntsville M,D
The University of Arizona M,D
University of Arkansas at Little Rock O
University of Central Florida M,D,O
University of Florida M,D,O
University of Houston M,D
University of Houston–Clear Lake M
University of Idaho M
University of Illinois at Urbana–Champaign M,D
University of Maryland, Baltimore County M,O
University of Maryland, College Park M,O
University of Michigan M,D
University of Michigan–Dearborn M,D
University of Minnesota, Twin Cities Campus M
The University of North Carolina at Charlotte D
University of Pennsylvania M,D
University of Rhode Island M,D
University of St. Thomas (MN) M,O
University of Southern California M,D,O
The University of Texas at Arlington M
University of Virginia M,D
University of Wisconsin–Madison M,D
Virginia Polytechnic Institute and State University M
Walden University M,O
Western International University M
Worcester Polytechnic Institute M,D,O

■ SYSTEMS SCIENCE

Arizona State University M
Arkansas Tech University M
Claremont Graduate University M,D,O
Eastern Illinois University M,O
Fairleigh Dickinson University, Metropolitan Campus M
Florida Institute of Technology M
Hood College M
Louisiana State University and Agricultural and Mechanical College M,D
Louisiana State University in Shreveport M
Miami University M
Oakland University M
Portland State University M,D,O
Southern Methodist University M,D
State University of New York at Binghamton M,D
Stevens Institute of Technology M,D
Strayer University M
University of Central Florida M
University of Michigan–Dearborn M,D
The University of North Carolina at Charlotte M,D
The University of North Carolina Wilmington M
Washington University in St. Louis M,D
Worcester Polytechnic Institute M,D,O

■ TAXATION

American International College M
American University M,O
Bentley University M
Bernard M. Baruch College of the City University of New York M
Boise State University M
Boston University P,M
Bryant University M
California Polytechnic State University, San Luis Obispo M
California State University, East Bay M

California State University, Fullerton M
California State University, Los Angeles M
California State University, Northridge M
Capital University M
Chapman University P,M
Cleveland State University M
DePaul University M
Fairfield University M,O
Fairleigh Dickinson University, College at Florham M,O
Fairleigh Dickinson University, Metropolitan Campus M
Florida Atlantic University M
Florida Gulf Coast University M
Florida International University M
Florida State University M,D
Fontbonne University M
Fordham University M
Georgetown University P,M,D
Georgia State University M
Golden Gate University P,M,D,O
Grand Valley State University M
Hofstra University M
Illinois Institute of Technology P,M
Long Island University, Brooklyn Campus M
Long Island University, C.W. Post Campus M,O
Loyola Marymount University P,M
Mississippi State University M
New York University P,M,D,O
Northeastern University M,O
Northern Illinois University M
Northern Kentucky University M,O
Northwestern University P,M
Nova Southeastern University M
Pace University M
Philadelphia University M
Robert Morris University M
Rutgers, The State University of New Jersey, Newark M
St. John's University (NY) M,O
St. Mary's University (United States) M
St. Thomas University P,M
San Jose State University M
Seton Hall University M
Southern Methodist University P,M,D
Southern New Hampshire University M,D,O
Strayer University M
Suffolk University M,O
Temple University P,M,D
Texas Tech University M,D
Universidad del Turabo M
University at Albany, State University of New York M
The University of Akron M
The University of Alabama M,D
The University of Alabama in Huntsville M,O
University of Arkansas at Little Rock M,O
University of Baltimore P,M
University of Central Florida M
University of Denver M
University of Florida P,M,D
University of Hartford M,O
University of Hawaii at Manoa M
University of Illinois at Urbana–Champaign M,D
University of Memphis M
University of Miami M
University of Michigan P,M,D
University of Minnesota, Twin Cities Campus M
University of Mississippi M,D
University of Missouri–Kansas City P,M
University of New Haven M
University of New Mexico M
University of New Orleans M
The University of North Carolina at Greensboro M,O
University of North Texas M,D
University of San Diego P,M,O
University of Southern California M
The University of Texas at Arlington M
The University of Texas at Dallas M
The University of Texas at San Antonio M,D
University of the Pacific P,M,D
University of Tulsa M
University of Washington P,M,D
Villanova University M
Virginia Commonwealth University M
Wake Forest University M
Washington State University M
Wayne State University M,D
Widener University M

■ TECHNICAL COMMUNICATION

Boise State University M
Bowling Green State University M,D
Colorado State University M,D
Drexel University M
Eastern Michigan University M,O
Eastern Washington University M
Harvard University M
Lawrence Technological University M
Michigan Technological University M,D
Minnesota State University Mankato M,O
New Jersey Institute of Technology M
North Carolina State University M
Polytechnic Institute of NYU O
Rensselaer Polytechnic Institute M
Rochester Institute of Technology O
Southern Polytechnic State University M,O
Texas State University–San Marcos M
University of California, Berkeley O
University of Colorado Denver M
University of Nebraska at Omaha M,O
University of Washington M,D

■ TECHNICAL WRITING

Carnegie Mellon University M
Colorado State University M,D
Drexel University M
Fitchburg State College M,O
Illinois Institute of Technology M,D
James Madison University M
The Johns Hopkins University M
Massachusetts Institute of Technology M
Metropolitan State University M
Miami University M
Northern Arizona University M
Polytechnic Institute of NYU M
Regis University M,O
Texas Tech University M,D
The University of Alabama in Huntsville M,O
University of Arkansas at Little Rock M
University of California, Santa Cruz O
University of Central Florida M,D,O
The University of North Carolina at Greensboro M,D,O

■ TECHNOLOGY AND PUBLIC POLICY

Carnegie Mellon University M,D
Eastern Michigan University M
The George Washington University M
Massachusetts Institute of Technology M,D
Rensselaer Polytechnic Institute M,D
Rochester Institute of Technology M
St. Cloud State University M
Stony Brook University, State University of New York M,D,O
University of Minnesota, Twin Cities Campus M
The University of Texas at Austin M
Western Illinois University M

■ TELECOMMUNICATIONS

Ball State University M
Boston University M

M—master's degree; P—first professional degree; D—doctorate; O—other advanced degree

California State University, East Bay M
The Catholic University of America M,D
Claremont Graduate University M,D,O
DePaul University M,D
Drexel University M
Florida International University M
George Mason University M,D,O
The George Washington University M,D
Illinois Institute of Technology M,D
Indiana University Bloomington M
Iona College M,O
The Johns Hopkins University M,O
Michigan State University M
National University M
Ohio University M
Pace University M,D,O
Polytechnic Institute of NYU M
Polytechnic Institute of NYU, Westchester Graduate Center M
Rochester Institute of Technology M
Roosevelt University M
Saint Mary's University of Minnesota M
Southern Methodist University M,D
State University of New York Institute of Technology M
Stevens Institute of Technology M,D,O
Syracuse University M
Universidad del Turabo M
University of Arkansas M
University of California, San Diego M,D
University of California, Santa Cruz M,D
University of Colorado at Boulder M
University of Denver M,O
University of Hawaii at Manoa O
University of Houston M
University of Louisiana at Lafayette M
University of Maryland, College Park M
University of Massachusetts Dartmouth M,D,O
University of Missouri–Kansas City M,D
University of Oklahoma M
University of Pennsylvania M
University of Pittsburgh M,D,O
University of Southern California M,D,O
The University of Texas at Dallas M,D
Widener University M

■ TELECOMMUNICATIONS MANAGEMENT

Alaska Pacific University M
Carnegie Mellon University M
George Mason University M,D,O
Hawai'i Pacific University M
Morgan State University M
Murray State University M
Northeastern University M,D
Oklahoma State University M,D
Polytechnic Institute of NYU M
San Diego State University M
Santa Clara University M,D,O
Stevens Institute of Technology M,D,O
Strayer University M
Syracuse University M,O
University of Colorado at Boulder M
University of Denver M,O
University of Pennsylvania M
University of San Francisco M
University of Wisconsin–Stout M
Webster University M,D

■ TERATOLOGY

West Virginia University M,D

■ TEXTILE DESIGN

California State University, Los Angeles M
Cornell University M,D
Drexel University M
Illinois State University M
James Madison University M
Kent State University M
Marywood University M
Missouri State University M
Philadelphia University M
Sul Ross State University M
Syracuse University M
Temple University M
University of California, Davis M
University of Cincinnati M
University of Massachusetts Dartmouth M,O
University of Minnesota, Twin Cities Campus M,D,O
The University of North Carolina at Greensboro M,D

■ TEXTILE SCIENCES AND ENGINEERING

Auburn University D
Clemson University M,D
Cornell University M,D
Georgia Institute of Technology M,D
North Carolina State University M,D
Philadelphia University M,D
University of Massachusetts Dartmouth M
The University of Texas at Austin M

■ THANATOLOGY

Brooklyn College of the City University of New York M
Hood College M,O

■ THEATER

Antioch University McGregor M
Arcadia University M,D,O
Arizona State University M,D
Arkansas State University M,O
Baylor University M
Bob Jones University P,M,D,O
Boston University M,O
Bowling Green State University M,D
Brandeis University M
Brigham Young University M
Brooklyn College of the City University of New York M,D
Brown University M,D
California State University, Fullerton M
California State University, Long Beach M
California State University, Los Angeles M
California State University, Northridge M
California State University, Sacramento M
California State University, San Bernardino M
Carnegie Mellon University M
Case Western Reserve University M
The Catholic University of America M
Central Washington University M
Columbia University M,D
Cornell University D
DePaul University M
Drake University M
Eastern Michigan University M
Emerson College M
Florida Atlantic University M
Florida State University M,D
Fontbonne University M
The George Washington University M
Graduate School and University Center of the City University of New York D
Hollins University M
Humboldt State University M
Hunter College of the City University of New York M
Idaho State University M
Illinois State University M
Indiana University Bloomington M,D
Kansas State University M
Kent State University M
Lamar University M
Lindenwood University M
Long Island University, C.W. Post Campus M
Louisiana State University and Agricultural and Mechanical College M,D
Mary Baldwin College M
Miami University M
Michigan State University M
Minnesota State University Mankato M
Missouri State University M

Montclair State University	M
Naropa University	M
The New School: A University	M
New York University	M,D,O
Northern Illinois University	M
Northwestern University	M,D
The Ohio State University	M,D
Ohio University	M
Oklahoma City University	M
Oklahoma State University	M
Pace University	M
Penn State University Park	M
Pittsburg State University	M
Point Park University	M
Portland State University	M
Purchase College, State University of New York	M
Purdue University	M
Regent University	M,D
Rhode Island College	M
Roosevelt University	M
Rowan University	M
Rutgers, The State University of New Jersey, New Brunswick	M
St. John's University (NY)	M,D,O
San Diego State University	M
San Francisco State University	M
San Jose State University	M
Sarah Lawrence College	M
Southern Illinois University Carbondale	M,D
Southern Methodist University	M
Stanford University	D
State University of New York at Binghamton	M
Stony Brook University, State University of New York	M
Temple University	M
Texas A&M University–Commerce	M
Texas State University–San Marcos	M
Texas Tech University	M,D
Texas Woman's University	M
Towson University	M
Tufts University	M,D
Tulane University	M
University at Albany, State University of New York	M
The University of Akron	M
The University of Alabama	M
The University of Arizona	M
University of Arkansas	M
University of California, Berkeley	D
University of California, Davis	M,D
University of California, Irvine	M,D
University of California, Los Angeles	M,D
University of California, San Diego	M,D
University of California, Santa Barbara	M,D
University of California, Santa Cruz	O
University of Central Florida	M
University of Central Missouri	M
University of Cincinnati	M,D
University of Colorado at Boulder	M,D
University of Connecticut	M
University of Delaware	M
University of Florida	M
University of Georgia	M,D
University of Hawaii at Manoa	M,D
University of Houston	M
University of Idaho	M
University of Illinois at Urbana–Champaign	M,D
The University of Iowa	M
The University of Kansas	M,D
University of Kentucky	M
University of Louisville	M
University of Maryland, College Park	M,D
University of Massachusetts Amherst	M
University of Memphis	M
University of Michigan	M,D
University of Minnesota, Twin Cities Campus	M,D
University of Missouri–Columbia	M,D
University of Missouri–Kansas City	M
The University of Montana	M
University of Nebraska at Omaha	M
University of Nebraska–Lincoln	M
University of Nevada, Las Vegas	M
University of New Mexico	M
University of New Orleans	M
The University of North Carolina at Chapel Hill	M
The University of North Carolina at Charlotte	M
The University of North Carolina at Greensboro	M
University of North Dakota	M
University of Oklahoma	M
University of Oregon	M,D
University of Pittsburgh	M,D
University of Portland	M
University of San Diego	M
University of South Carolina	M,D
The University of South Dakota	M
University of Southern California	M
University of Southern Mississippi	M
The University of Tennessee	M
The University of Texas at Austin	M,D
The University of Texas–Pan American	M
University of Virginia	M
University of Washington	M,D
University of Wisconsin–Madison	M,D
University of Wisconsin–Milwaukee	M
University of Wisconsin–Superior	M
Utah State University	M
Villanova University	M
Virginia Commonwealth University	M
Virginia Polytechnic Institute and State University	M
Wayne State University	M,D
Western Illinois University	M
West Virginia University	M
Yale University	M,D,O

■ THEOLOGY

Abilene Christian University	P,M
Anderson University (IN)	P,M,D
Andrews University	P,M,D,O
Azusa Pacific University	M,D
Barry University	M,D
Baylor University	P,M,D
Biola University	P,M,D
Bob Jones University	P,M,D,O
Boston College	P,M,D,O
Boston University	P,M,D
California Institute of Integral Studies	M,D
Campbell University	P,M,D
The Catholic University of America	P,M,D,O
Chaminade University of Honolulu	M
Claremont Graduate University	M,D
College of Mount St. Joseph	M
College of Saint Elizabeth	M
Concordia University (CA)	M
Concordia University, St. Paul	M,O
Creighton University	M
Drew University	P,M,D,O
Duke University	P,M,D
Duquesne University	M,D
Eastern Mennonite University	P,M,O
Eastern University	P,M,D
Emory University	P,M,D
Fordham University	M,D
Franciscan University of Steubenville	M
Freed-Hardeman University	P,M
Friends University	M
Gardner-Webb University	P,D
George Fox University	P,M,D,O
Georgetown University	D
Georgian Court University	M,O
Hardin-Simmons University	P,M
Harvard University	P,M,D
Houston Baptist University	M
Howard University	P,M,D
Indiana Wesleyan University	P,M

M—master's degree; P—first professional degree; D—doctorate; O—other advanced degree

Inter American University of Puerto Rico, Metropolitan Campus D
Lakeland College M
La Salle University M
Lee University M
Liberty University P,M,D
Lipscomb University P,M
Loyola Marymount University M
Loyola University Chicago P,M,D,O
Loyola University New Orleans M,O
Lubbock Christian University M
Madonna University M
Malone University M
Marquette University M,D
Marylhurst University P,M
Mercer University P,M,D
Mount St. Mary's University P,M
Naropa University P
Oakland City University P,D
Ohio Dominican University M
Oklahoma Christian University P,M
Olivet Nazarene University M
Oral Roberts University P,M,D
Philadelphia Biblical University P,M
Pontifical Catholic University of Puerto Rico P
Providence College M
Regent University P,M,D
St. Bonaventure University M,O
St. Catherine University M
St. John's University (NY) P,M,O
Saint Louis University M,D
St. Mary's University (United States) M
Saint Michael's College M,O
St. Thomas University M,D,O
Samford University P,M,D
Seattle University P,M,O
Seton Hall University P,M
Southern Methodist University P,M,D
Southern Nazarene University M
Spring Arbor University M
Spring Hill College M
Trevecca Nazarene University M
Trinity International University P,M,D,O
University of Chicago P,M,D
University of Dallas M
University of Dayton M,D
University of Denver D
University of Dubuque P,M,D
University of Mobile M
University of Notre Dame P,M,D
University of St. Thomas (MN) P,M
University of St. Thomas (TX) P,M
University of San Francisco M
The University of Scranton M
Ursuline College M
Valparaiso University M,O
Vanderbilt University P,M
Vanguard University of Southern California M
Villanova University M
Walsh University M
Wheaton College M,D
Xavier University M
Xavier University of Louisiana M
Yale University P,M

■ THEORETICAL CHEMISTRY

Carnegie Mellon University M,D
Cornell University D
Georgetown University D
The University of Tennessee M,D
Vanderbilt University M,D
West Virginia University M,D
Yale University D

■ THEORETICAL PHYSICS

Cornell University M,D
Delaware State University D
Harvard University D
Rutgers, The State University of New Jersey, New Brunswick M,D
West Virginia University M,D

■ THERAPIES—DANCE, DRAMA, AND MUSIC

Antioch University New England M
Appalachian State University M
Arizona State University M,D
California Institute of Integral Studies M,D
Columbia College Chicago M,O
Drexel University M,O
East Carolina University M
Florida State University M,D
Georgia College & State University M
Immaculata University M
Lesley University M,D,O
Loyola University New Orleans M
Maryville University of Saint Louis M
Marywood University M,O
Michigan State University M,D
Molloy College M
Montclair State University M,O
Naropa University M
Nazareth College of Rochester M
New York University M
Ohio University M,O
Radford University M
Shenandoah University M,D,O
State University of New York at New Paltz M
Temple University M,D
The University of Kansas M
University of Miami M,D,O
University of the Pacific M
Western Michigan University M

■ TOXICOLOGY

American University M
Brown University M,D
Columbia University M,D
Cornell University M,D
Dartmouth College D
Duke University D,O
Florida Agricultural and Mechanical University M,D
The George Washington University M
Indiana University–Purdue University Indianapolis M,D
Iowa State University of Science and Technology M,D
The Johns Hopkins University M,D
Long Island University, Brooklyn Campus M,D
Louisiana State University and Agricultural and Mechanical College M
Massachusetts Institute of Technology M,D
Michigan State University M,D
New York University M,D
North Carolina State University M,D
Northeastern University M
Northwestern University D
The Ohio State University M,D
Oregon State University M,D
Purdue University M,D
Rutgers, The State University of New Jersey, New Brunswick M,D
St. John's University (NY) M
San Diego State University M,D
Texas A&M University M,D
Texas Southern University M,D
Texas Tech University M,D
University at Albany, State University of New York M,D
University at Buffalo, the State University of New York M,D
The University of Alabama at Birmingham M,D
University of California, Davis M,D
University of California, Irvine M,D
University of California, Los Angeles D
University of California, Riverside M,D
University of California, Santa Cruz M,D
University of Colorado Denver D
University of Connecticut M,D
University of Florida M,D,O
University of Georgia M,D
The University of Iowa M,D
The University of Kansas M,D
University of Kentucky M,D
University of Louisville M,D
University of Maryland Eastern Shore M,D
University of Michigan M,D
University of Minnesota, Duluth M,D

University of Minnesota, Twin Cities Campus M,D
The University of Montana M,D
University of Nebraska–Lincoln M,D
University of New Mexico M,D
The University of North Carolina at Chapel Hill M,D
University of Rhode Island M,D
University of Rochester M,D
University of South Alabama M
University of Southern California M,D
University of Utah D
University of Washington M,D
University of Wisconsin–Madison M,D
Utah State University M,D
Virginia Commonwealth University M,D
Washington State University M,D
Wayne State University M,D
West Virginia University M,D
Wright State University M

■ TRANSCULTURAL NURSING

Augsburg College M

■ TRANSLATIONAL BIOLOGY

The University of Iowa M,D

■ TRANSLATION AND INTERPRETATION

American University M,O
College of Charleston O
Georgia State University O
Kent State University M,D
Marygrove College O
Montclair State University M,O
Monterey Institute of International Studies M
New York University M,D
Rutgers, The State University of New Jersey, New Brunswick M,D
State University of New York at Binghamton M,O
University at Albany, State University of New York M,O
University of Arkansas M
University of Denver M,O
The University of Iowa M
University of Nevada, Las Vegas M,O
University of Puerto Rico, Río Piedras M,O
The University of Texas at San Antonio M,O
University of Wisconsin–Milwaukee M,O

■ TRANSPERSONAL AND HUMANISTIC PSYCHOLOGY

John F. Kennedy University M
Naropa University M
Seattle University M

■ TRANSPORTATION AND HIGHWAY ENGINEERING

Auburn University M,D
Cornell University M,D
Illinois Institute of Technology M,D
Iowa State University of Science and Technology M,D
Louisiana State University and Agricultural and Mechanical College M,D
Marquette University M,D
Massachusetts Institute of Technology M,D,O
Morgan State University M
New Jersey Institute of Technology M,D
Northwestern University M,D
Ohio University M,D
Oregon State University M,D
Penn State University Park M,D
Polytechnic Institute of NYU M,D
Rensselaer Polytechnic Institute M,D
South Carolina State University M
Texas A&M University M,D
Texas Southern University M
The University of Alabama in Huntsville M,D
University of Arkansas M
University of California, Berkeley M,D
University of California, Davis M,D
University of California, Irvine M,D
University of Central Florida M,D,O
University of Dayton M
University of Delaware M,D
University of Memphis M,D
University of Missouri–Columbia M,D
University of Nevada, Las Vegas M,D
University of Rhode Island M
University of Southern California M,D,O
University of Washington M,D
Villanova University M
Western Michigan University M

■ TRANSPORTATION MANAGEMENT

Arizona State University M,O
Florida Institute of Technology M
George Mason University M
Iowa State University of Science and Technology M
Morgan State University M
New Jersey Institute of Technology M,D
North Dakota State University M,D
Polytechnic Institute of NYU M
San Jose State University M
State University of New York Maritime College M
Texas Southern University M

University at Buffalo, the State University of New York M,D,O
University of California, Davis M,D
University of California, Santa Barbara M,D
University of Central Missouri M,O
University of Denver M
The University of Tennessee M,D
University of Washington O
Wilmington University M

■ TRAVEL AND TOURISM

Arizona State University M,D
Boston University M
California State University, Fullerton M
California State University, Northridge M
Clemson University M,D
Eastern Michigan University M,O
East Stroudsburg University of Pennsylvania M
Florida Atlantic University M,O
The George Washington University M,O
Hawai'i Pacific University M
Indiana University Bloomington M,D,O
New York University M,O
North Carolina State University M,D
Old Dominion University M
Purdue University M,D
Rochester Institute of Technology M
Saint Xavier University M,O
Schiller International University (United States) M
Strayer University M
Temple University M
University of Central Florida M
University of Hawaii at Manoa M
University of Massachusetts Amherst M
University of New Orleans M
University of South Carolina M
The University of Tennessee M
Virginia Polytechnic Institute and State University M,D
Western Illinois University M

■ URBAN AND REGIONAL PLANNING

Alabama Agricultural and Mechanical University M
Arizona State University M,D
Auburn University M
Ball State University M
Boston University M
California Polytechnic State University, San Luis Obispo M
California State Polytechnic University, Pomona M
California State University, Chico M
The Catholic University of America M
Clark University M

M—master's degree; P—first professional degree; D—doctorate; O—other advanced degree

Clemson University M
Cleveland State University M,O
Columbia University M,D
Cornell University M,D
Delta State University M
DePaul University M,O
Eastern Kentucky University M
Eastern Michigan University M,O
Eastern University M
Eastern Washington University M
East Tennessee State University M
Florida Atlantic University M,O
Florida State University M,D
Georgia Institute of Technology M,D
Georgia State University M,D,O
Harvard University M,D
Hunter College of the City University of New York M
Iowa State University of Science and Technology M
Jackson State University M
Kansas State University M
Lesley University M
Massachusetts Institute of Technology M,D
Michigan State University M,D
Minnesota State University Mankato M,O
Missouri State University M
Morgan State University M
New York University M,O
The Ohio State University M,D
Portland State University M
Rutgers, The State University of New Jersey, New Brunswick M,D
San Diego State University M
San Jose State University M,O
State University of New York College of Environmental Science and Forestry M,D
Temple University M
Texas A&M University M,D
Texas Southern University M,D
Tufts University M
University at Albany, State University of New York M
University at Buffalo, the State University of New York M
The University of Akron M
The University of Arizona M
University of California, Berkeley M,D
University of California, Davis M
University of California, Irvine M,D
University of California, Los Angeles M,D
University of Central Florida M,O
University of Cincinnati M
University of Colorado Denver M,D
University of Florida M,D
University of Hawaii at Manoa M,D,O
University of Idaho M
University of Illinois at Chicago M,D
University of Illinois at Urbana–Champaign M,D
The University of Iowa M
The University of Kansas M
University of Louisville M
University of Maryland, College Park M,D
University of Massachusetts Amherst M,D
University of Memphis M
University of Michigan M,D,O
University of Minnesota, Twin Cities Campus M
University of Nebraska–Lincoln M,D
University of New Mexico M
University of New Orleans M
The University of North Carolina at Chapel Hill M,D
University of Oklahoma M
University of Oregon M
University of Pennsylvania M,D,O
University of Pittsburgh M,O
University of Puerto Rico, Río Piedras M
University of Southern California D
University of Southern Maine M,O
The University of Texas at Arlington M
The University of Texas at Austin M,D
The University of Texas at San Antonio M,O
The University of Toledo M,O
University of Utah M,D
University of Virginia M,O
University of Washington M,D
University of Wisconsin–Madison M,D
University of Wisconsin–Milwaukee M,O
Utah State University M,D
Vanderbilt University M
Virginia Commonwealth University M,O
Virginia Polytechnic Institute and State University M,D
Wayne State University M
West Chester University of Pennsylvania M,O
West Virginia University M,D

■ URBAN DESIGN

Arizona State University M
Ball State University M
Carnegie Mellon University M,D
The Catholic University of America M
City College of the City University of New York M
Cleveland State University M,O
Cornell University M,D
Georgia Institute of Technology M,D
Harvard University M
Kent State University M,O
New York Institute of Technology M
Prairie View A&M University M
Rice University M,D
State University of New York College of Environmental Science and Forestry M
University at Buffalo, the State University of New York M
University of California, Berkeley M,D
University of California, Los Angeles M,D
University of Colorado Denver M
University of Miami M
University of Michigan M
University of New Mexico O
University of Pennsylvania D
The University of Texas at Austin M,D
University of Washington M,D,O
Washington University in St. Louis M

■ URBAN EDUCATION

Alvernia University M
Brown University M
Cardinal Stritch University M,D
Claremont Graduate University M,D,O
Cleveland State University D
College of Mount Saint Vincent M,O
Columbia College Chicago M
DePaul University M,D
Florida International University M
Graduate School and University Center of the City University of New York D
Harvard University D
Holy Names University M,O
The Johns Hopkins University M,O
Kean University D
Loyola Marymount University M
Marygrove College M
Mercy College M
Morgan State University M,D
New Jersey City University M
Norfolk State University M
Northeastern Illinois University M
Nova Southeastern University M,O
Roberts Wesleyan College M,O
Simmons College M,O
Temple University M,D
Texas A&M University M,D
University of Central Florida M,D,O
University of Illinois at Chicago M,D
University of Massachusetts Boston M,D,O
University of Nebraska at Omaha M,O
University of Southern California D
University of Wisconsin–Milwaukee M,D
Vanderbilt University M
Virginia Commonwealth University D

■ URBAN STUDIES

Boston University M
Brooklyn College of the City University of New York M,D
Cleveland State University M,D,O
Eastern University M
East Tennessee State University M
Fordham University M
Graduate School and University Center of the City University of New York M,D
Hunter College of the City University of New York M
Long Island University, Brooklyn Campus M
Massachusetts Institute of Technology M,D
Minnesota State University Mankato M,O
New Jersey City University M
New Jersey Institute of Technology D
The New School: A University M
Norfolk State University M
Northeastern University M,O
Old Dominion University D
Portland State University M,D
Queens College of the City University of New York M
Rutgers, The State University of New Jersey, Newark M,D
Saint Louis University M,D,O
Savannah State University M
Southern Connecticut State University M
Temple University M
Tufts University M
University at Albany, State University of New York M,D,O
The University of Akron M,D
University of California, Irvine M,D
University of Central Oklahoma M
University of Delaware M,D
University of Louisville D
University of New Orleans M,D
University of Wisconsin–Milwaukee M,D
Virginia Polytechnic Institute and State University M,D
Wright State University M

■ VETERINARY MEDICINE

Auburn University P
Colorado State University P
Cornell University P
Iowa State University of Science and Technology P,M
Kansas State University P
Louisiana State University and Agricultural and Mechanical College P
Michigan State University P
Mississippi State University P
North Carolina State University P,M
The Ohio State University P
Oklahoma State University P
Oregon State University P
Purdue University P
Texas A&M University P,M
Tufts University P
University of California, Davis P
University of Florida P
University of Georgia P
University of Illinois at Urbana–Champaign P
University of Maryland, College Park P
University of Minnesota, Twin Cities Campus P
University of Missouri–Columbia P
University of Pennsylvania P
The University of Tennessee P
University of Wisconsin–Madison P
Virginia Polytechnic Institute and State University P
Washington State University P,M,D

■ VETERINARY SCIENCES

Auburn University M,D
Clemson University M,D
Colorado State University M,D
Drexel University M
Iowa State University of Science and Technology M,D
Kansas State University M
Louisiana State University and Agricultural and Mechanical College M,D
Michigan State University M,D
Mississippi State University M,D
Montana State University M,D
North Carolina State University M,D
North Dakota State University M,D
The Ohio State University M,D
Oklahoma State University M,D
Oregon State University D
Penn State University Park D
Purdue University M,D
South Dakota State University M,D
Texas A&M University M
Tufts University M,D
University of California, Davis M,O
University of Florida M,D,O
University of Georgia M,D
University of Idaho M,D
University of Illinois at Urbana–Champaign M,D
University of Kentucky M,D
University of Maryland, College Park M,D
University of Minnesota, Twin Cities Campus M,D
University of Missouri–Columbia M,D
University of Nebraska–Lincoln M,D
University of Washington M
University of Wisconsin–Madison M,D
Utah State University M,D
Virginia Polytechnic Institute and State University M,D
Washington State University M,D

■ VIROLOGY

Case Western Reserve University D
Mayo Graduate School D
The Ohio State University M,D
Purdue University M,D
Rutgers, The State University of New Jersey, New Brunswick M,D
University of California, San Diego D
The University of Iowa M,D
University of Minnesota, Twin Cities Campus D
University of Pennsylvania D
University of Pittsburgh M,D
Yale University D

■ VISION SCIENCES

Emory University M
Nova Southeastern University P,M
The University of Alabama at Birmingham M,D
The University of Alabama in Huntsville M,D
University of California, Berkeley M,D
University of Chicago D
University of Houston M,D
University of Missouri–St. Louis M,D

■ VITICULTURE AND ENOLOGY

California State University, Fresno M
University of California, Davis M,D

■ VOCATIONAL AND TECHNICAL EDUCATION

Alabama Agricultural and Mechanical University M
Alcorn State University M,O
Appalachian State University M
Ball State University M
Bemidji State University M
Bowling Green State University M
Buffalo State College, State University of New York M
California Baptist University M
California State University, Long Beach M
California State University, Sacramento M
California State University, San Bernardino M
California University of Pennsylvania M
Cambridge College M,D,O

M—master's degree; P—first professional degree; D—doctorate; O—other advanced degree

Central Connecticut State University M,O
Chicago State University M
Clarion University of Pennsylvania M
Colorado State University M,D
East Carolina University M
Eastern Kentucky University M
Eastern Michigan University M
East Tennessee State University M
Fitchburg State College M
Florida Agricultural and Mechanical University M
Georgia Southern University M
Idaho State University M
Indiana State University M
Inter American University of Puerto Rico, Metropolitan Campus M
Iowa State University of Science and Technology M,D
Jackson State University M
James Madison University M
Kent State University M,O
Louisiana State University and Agricultural and Mechanical College M,D
Marshall University M
Middle Tennessee State University M
Millersville University of Pennsylvania M
Mississippi State University M,D,O
Murray State University M
North Carolina Agricultural and Technical State University M,D
North Dakota State University M,D,O
Northern Arizona University M
Nova Southeastern University D
The Ohio State University D
Old Dominion University M,D
Our Lady of the Lake University of San Antonio M
Penn State University Park M,D
Pittsburg State University M,O
Purdue University M,D,O
Rhode Island College M
Saint Martin's University M
South Carolina State University M
Southern Illinois University Carbondale M,D
Southern New Hampshire University M,O
State University of New York at Oswego M
Temple University M,D
Texas State University–San Marcos M
Trevecca Nazarene University M
The University of Akron M
University of Arkansas M,D
University of California, Berkeley O
University of Central Florida M
University of Central Missouri M,O
University of Georgia M,D,O
University of Idaho M,D,O
University of Illinois at Urbana–Champaign M,D,O
University of Kentucky M
University of Maryland Eastern Shore M
University of Minnesota, Twin Cities Campus M,D,O
University of Missouri–Columbia M,D,O
University of Nebraska–Lincoln M,D,O
University of Northern Iowa M,D
University of North Texas M,D
University of Southern Mississippi M
University of South Florida M,D,O
The University of Texas at Tyler M,D
The University of Toledo M,O
University of West Florida M
University of Wisconsin–Platteville M
University of Wisconsin–Stout M,O
Utah State University M
Virginia Polytechnic Institute and State University M,D,O
Virginia State University M,O
Wayne State College M
Wayne State University M,D,O
Western Michigan University M
Westfield State College M,O
Wilmington University M
Wright State University M

■ WATER RESOURCES

Albany State University M
Colorado State University M,D
Duke University M
Eastern Michigan University M,O
Humboldt State University M
Inter American University of Puerto Rico, San Germán Campus M
Missouri University of Science and Technology M,D
Montclair State University M,D,O
Rutgers, The State University of New Jersey, New Brunswick M,D
State University of New York College of Environmental Science and Forestry M,D
University of Alaska Fairbanks M,D
The University of Arizona M,D
University of California, Riverside M,D
University of Florida M,D
University of Idaho M,D
The University of Kansas M
University of Minnesota, Twin Cities Campus M,D
University of Nevada, Las Vegas M
University of New Hampshire M
University of New Mexico M
University of Oklahoma M,D
University of the Pacific P,M,D
University of Wisconsin–Madison M
University of Wyoming M,D
Utah State University M,D

■ WATER RESOURCES ENGINEERING

Cornell University M,D
George Mason University M,D,O
Louisiana State University and Agricultural and Mechanical College M,D
Marquette University M,D
New Mexico Institute of Mining and Technology M
Ohio University M,D
Oregon State University M,D
Penn State University Park M,D
Princeton University M,D
Stevens Institute of Technology M,D,O
Texas A&M University M,D
Tufts University M,D
The University of Alabama in Huntsville M,D
University of California, Berkeley M,D
University of Colorado at Boulder M,D
University of Dayton M
University of Delaware M,D
University of Memphis M,D
University of Missouri–Columbia M,D
The University of Texas at Austin M,D
University of Washington M,D
Utah State University M,D
Villanova University M

■ WESTERN EUROPEAN STUDIES

American University M,D,O
Boston College M,D
Brown University M,D
California State University, Long Beach M
The Catholic University of America M,D
Central Michigan University M,D,O
Claremont Graduate University M,D,O
Columbia University M,O
Cornell University M,D
East Carolina University M
Georgetown University M
The George Washington University M
Indiana University Bloomington M
Mississippi State University M,D
New York University M
San Diego State University M
University of Connecticut M
University of Nevada, Reno D
University of Pittsburgh O
Washington State University M,D

■ WOMEN'S HEALTH NURSING

Case Western Reserve University M,D

Columbia University O
Emory University M
Georgia Southern University M,D,O
Georgia State University M,D,O
Hampton University M
Indiana University–Purdue University Fort Wayne M,O
Indiana University–Purdue University Indianapolis M,D
The Johns Hopkins University M,O
Kent State University M,D
Loyola University Chicago M
Old Dominion University M
Seton Hall University M
Stony Brook University, State University of New York M,O
Texas Woman's University M,D
University at Buffalo, the State University of New York M,D,O
University of Cincinnati M,D
University of Colorado at Colorado Springs M,D
University of Delaware M,O
University of Illinois at Chicago M
University of Minnesota, Twin Cities Campus M
University of Missouri–Kansas City M,D
The University of North Carolina at Chapel Hill M,D,O
University of Pennsylvania M
University of South Carolina M
The University of Texas at El Paso M,O
Vanderbilt University M,D
Virginia Commonwealth University M,D,O
Wilmington University M

■ WOMEN'S STUDIES

Brandeis University M
California Institute of Integral Studies M,D
Claremont Graduate University M,D
Clark Atlanta University M,D
Cornell University M,D
Drew University M
Duke University O
Eastern Michigan University M
Emory University D,O
Florida Atlantic University M,O
George Mason University M
The George Washington University M,D,O
Georgia State University M,O
Graduate School and University Center of the City University of New York M,D
Lesley University M
Minnesota State University Mankato M,O
The Ohio State University M,D
Old Dominion University M,D
Roosevelt University M,O
Rutgers, The State University of New Jersey, New Brunswick M,D
San Diego State University M
San Francisco State University M
Sarah Lawrence College M
Southern Connecticut State University M
Suffolk University M
Texas Woman's University M
Towson University M,O
University at Albany, State University of New York M,D
The University of Alabama M
The University of Arizona M,D
University of California, Los Angeles M,D
University of California, Santa Barbara M,D
University of Cincinnati M,O
University of Florida M,O
University of Georgia O
University of Hawaii at Manoa O
The University of Iowa D
University of Louisville M,O
University of Maryland, Baltimore County O
University of Maryland, College Park M,D
University of Massachusetts Boston M,D,O
University of Michigan D,O
University of Minnesota, Twin Cities Campus D
University of Nevada, Las Vegas O
University of New Mexico O
The University of North Carolina at Greensboro M,D,O
University of Northern Iowa M
University of Pittsburgh O
University of South Carolina O
University of South Florida M
University of Washington D
University of Wisconsin–Madison M,D
Washington State University M,D
West Chester University of Pennsylvania M,O

■ WRITING

Abilene Christian University M
Adelphi University M
American University M
Antioch University Los Angeles M,O
Antioch University McGregor M
Arizona State University M
Ashland University M
Ball State University M,D
Belmont University M
Bennington College M
Boise State University M
Boston University M,D
Bowling Green State University M,D
Brooklyn College of the City University of New York M
Brown University M
California State University, Fresno M
California State University, Long Beach M
California State University, Northridge M
California State University, Sacramento M
California State University, San Bernardino M
California State University, San Marcos M
California State University, Stanislaus M,O
Carlow University M
Carnegie Mellon University M
Central Michigan University M
Chapman University M
Chatham University M
Chicago State University M
City College of the City University of New York M
Claremont Graduate University M,D
Clemson University M
Cleveland State University M
The College at Brockport, State University of New York M
Colorado State University M
Columbia College Chicago M
Columbia University M
Cornell University M,D
Creighton University M
DePaul University M
Eastern Kentucky University M
Eastern Michigan University M,O
Eastern Washington University M
Emerson College M
Fairfield University M
Fairleigh Dickinson University, College at Florham M
Florida Atlantic University M
Florida International University M
Florida State University M,D
George Mason University M
Georgia College & State University M
Georgia State University M,D
Goddard College M
Hofstra University M
Hollins University M
Hunter College of the City University of New York M
Illinois State University M
Indiana State University M
Indiana University Bloomington M,D
Indiana University of Pennsylvania M,D

M—master's degree; P—first professional degree; D—doctorate; O—other advanced degree

Institution	Degrees
The Johns Hopkins University	M
Kennesaw State University	M
Kent State University	M,D
La Sierra University	M
Lesley University	M
Lindenwood University	M,O
Long Island University, Brooklyn Campus	M
Longwood University	M
Louisiana State University and Agricultural and Mechanical College	M,D
Loyola Marymount University	M
Manhattanville College	M
Massachusetts Institute of Technology	M
McNeese State University	M
Miami University	M,D
Michigan State University	M,D
Mills College	M
Minnesota State University Mankato	M,O
Minnesota State University Moorhead	M
Murray State University	M
Naropa University	M
National-Louis University	M
National University	M
New Mexico Highlands University	M
New Mexico State University	M,D
The New School: A University	M
New York University	M,D
North Carolina State University	M
Northeastern Illinois University	M
Northern Arizona University	M
Northern Michigan University	M
Northwestern University	M
Oklahoma City University	M
Oklahoma State University	M,D
Old Dominion University	M
Our Lady of the Lake University of San Antonio	M
Pacific Lutheran University	M
Pacific University	M
Penn State University Park	M,D
Purdue University	M,D
Queens College of the City University of New York	M
Queens University of Charlotte	M
Rhode Island College	M
Rivier College	M
Roosevelt University	M
Rosemont College	M
Rowan University	M
Rutgers, The State University of New Jersey, Camden	M
Rutgers, The State University of New Jersey, Newark	M
Rutgers, The State University of New Jersey, New Brunswick	M
Saint Joseph's University	M
Saint Mary's College of California	M
Saint Xavier University	M,O
Salisbury University	M
San Diego State University	M
San Francisco State University	M
San Jose State University	M,O
Sarah Lawrence College	M
Seattle Pacific University	M
Seton Hall University	M
Seton Hill University	M
Slippery Rock University of Pennsylvania	M
Sonoma State University	M
Southern Illinois University Carbondale	M
Southern Illinois University Edwardsville	M
Southern New Hampshire University	M,O
Spalding University	M
Stony Brook University, State University of New York	M
Syracuse University	M,D
Temple University	M
Texas State University–San Marcos	M
Towson University	M
Union Institute & University	M
The University of Akron	M
The University of Alabama	M,D
University of Alaska Anchorage	M
University of Alaska Fairbanks	M
The University of Arizona	M
University of Arkansas	M
University of Arkansas at Little Rock	M
University of Baltimore	M
University of California, Berkeley	O
University of California, Davis	M,D
University of California, Irvine	M
University of California, Riverside	M
University of California, Santa Cruz	M
University of Central Florida	M
University of Central Oklahoma	M
University of Colorado at Boulder	M,D
University of Florida	M,D
University of Georgia	M,D
University of Houston	M,D
University of Idaho	M
University of Illinois at Chicago	M,D
University of Illinois at Urbana–Champaign	M,D
The University of Iowa	M,D
The University of Kansas	M,D
University of Louisiana at Lafayette	M,D
University of Louisville	M
University of Maryland, College Park	M,D
University of Massachusetts Amherst	M,D
University of Massachusetts Dartmouth	M,O
University of Memphis	M,D,O
University of Miami	M,D
University of Michigan	M
University of Missouri–St. Louis	M,O
The University of Montana	M
University of Nebraska at Kearney	M
University of Nebraska at Omaha	M,O
University of Nebraska–Lincoln	M,D
University of Nevada, Las Vegas	M,D
University of New Hampshire	M,D
University of New Mexico	M,D
The University of North Carolina at Greensboro	M
The University of North Carolina Wilmington	M
University of North Florida	M
University of North Texas	M,D
University of Notre Dame	M
University of Oklahoma	M
University of Oregon	M
University of Pennsylvania	M,D
University of Pittsburgh	M,D
University of San Francisco	M
University of South Carolina	M,D
University of Southern California	M,D
University of Southern Maine	M
The University of Texas at Austin	M,D
The University of Texas at El Paso	M,D
The University of Texas at San Antonio	M,D,O
The University of Toledo	M,O
University of Utah	M,D
University of Virginia	M
University of Washington	M,D
University of West Florida	M
University of Wisconsin–Madison	M,D
University of Wisconsin–Milwaukee	M,D,O
University of Wyoming	M
Utah State University	M
Vanderbilt University	M
Virginia Commonwealth University	M
Washington University in St. Louis	M
Wayne State University	M,D
Western Connecticut State University	M
Western Kentucky University	M
Western Michigan University	M,D
Westminster College (UT)	M
West Virginia University	M
Wichita State University	M
Wilkes University	M
Wright State University	M

■ ZOOLOGY

Institution	Degrees
Auburn University	M,D

Colorado State University	M,D
Cornell University	M,D
Emporia State University	M
Illinois State University	M,D
Indiana University Bloomington	M,D
Miami University	M,D
Michigan State University	M,D
Montana State University	M,D
North Carolina State University	M,D
North Dakota State University	M,D
Oklahoma State University	M,D
Oregon State University	M,D
Southern Illinois University Carbondale	M,D
Texas A&M University	M,D
Texas Tech University	M,D
University of Alaska Fairbanks	M,D
University of California, Davis	M
University of Chicago	D
University of Connecticut	M,D
University of Florida	M,D
University of Hawaii at Manoa	M,D
University of Illinois at Urbana–Champaign	M,D
University of Maine	M,D
The University of Montana	M,D
University of New Hampshire	M,D
University of North Dakota	M,D
University of Oklahoma	M,D
University of Wisconsin–Madison	M,D
University of Wisconsin–Oshkosh	M
University of Wyoming	M,D
Virginia Polytechnic Institute and State University	M,D
Washington State University	M,D
Western Illinois University	M,O

M—master's degree; P—first professional degree; D—doctorate; O—other advanced degree

Profiles of Institutions Offering Graduate and Professional Work

Alabama

■ ALABAMA AGRICULTURAL AND MECHANICAL UNIVERSITY
Huntsville, AL 35811
http://www.aamu.edu/

State-supported, coed, university. CGS member. *Graduate faculty:* 309 full-time (121 women), 69 part-time/adjunct (42 women). *Computer facilities:* 1,000 computers available on campus for general student use. A campuswide network can be accessed from student residence rooms and from off campus. *General application contact:* Dr. Frank Archer, Dean, School of Graduate Studies, 256-372-5266.

School of Graduate Studies
Dr. Michael Orok, Dean, School of Graduate Studies

School of Agricultural and Environmental Sciences
Dr. Robert Taylor, Dean
Programs in:
agribusiness (MS)
agricultural and environmental sciences (MS, MURP, PhD)
animal sciences (MS)
environmental science (MS)
family and consumer sciences (MS)
food science (MS, PhD)
plant and soil science (PhD)
urban and regional planning (MURP)

School of Arts and Sciences
Dr. Matthew Edwards, Dean
Programs in:
arts and sciences (MS, MSW, PhD)
biology (MS)
physics (MS, PhD)
social work (MSW)

School of Business
Dr. Barbara A. P. Jones, Dean
Programs in:
business (MBA)
management and marketing (MBA)

School of Education
Dr. Larry Powers, Dean
Programs in:
communicative disorders (M Ed, MS)
early childhood education (MS Ed, Ed S)
education (M Ed, Ed S)
elementary education (MS Ed, Ed S)
higher administration (MS)
music (MS)
music education (M Ed)
physical education (M Ed, MS)
psychology and counseling (MS, Ed S)
special education (M Ed, MS)

School of Engineering and Technology
Dr. Trent Montgomery, Dean
Programs in:
computer science (MS)
engineering and technology (M Ed, MS)
industrial technology (M Ed, MS)

■ ALABAMA STATE UNIVERSITY
Montgomery, AL 36101-0271
http://www.alasu.edu/

State-supported, coed, comprehensive institution. *Computer facilities:* 380 computers available on campus for general student use. A campuswide network can be accessed from student residence rooms and from off campus. Online class registration, e-mail are available. *General application contact:* Dean of Graduate Studies, 334-229-4274.

School of Graduate Studies
Programs in:
instrumental music (M Ed)
vocal/choral music (M Ed)

College of Arts and Sciences
Programs in:
arts and sciences (M Ed, MS, Ed S)
biological sciences (MS)
mathematics (M Ed, MS, Ed S)

College of Business Administration
Programs in:
accountancy (M Acc)
business administration (M Acc)

College of Education
Programs in:
biology education (M Ed, Ed S)
early childhood education (M Ed, Ed S)
education (M Ed, MS, Ed D, Ed S)
educational administration (M Ed, Ed D, Ed S)
educational leadership, policy and law (Ed D)
elementary education (M Ed, Ed S)
English/language arts (M Ed)
general counseling (MS, Ed S)
guidance and counseling (M Ed, MS, Ed S)
health education (M Ed)
history education (M Ed, Ed S)
library education media (M Ed, Ed S)
mathematics education (M Ed)
physical education (M Ed)
school counseling (M Ed, Ed S)
secondary education (M Ed, Ed S)
social studies (Ed S)
special education (M Ed)

College of Health Sciences
Programs in:
health sciences (DPT)
physical therapy (DPT)

■ AUBURN UNIVERSITY
Auburn University, AL 36849
http://www.auburn.edu/

State-supported, coed, university. CGS member. *Graduate faculty:* 1,224 full-time (392 women), 139 part-time/adjunct (58 women). *Computer facilities:* Computer purchase and lease plans are available. 1,722 computers available on campus for general student use. A campuswide network can be accessed from student residence rooms and from off campus. Online class registration, pay Bursar online, course materials available online are available. *Graduate expenses:* Tuition, state resident: full-time $5880; part-time $243 per credit hour. Tuition, nonresident: full-time $17,640; part-time $729 per credit hour. International tuition: $17,846 full-time. Tuition and fees vary according to program and reciprocity agreements. *General application contact:* Dr. George Flowers, Dean of the Graduate School, 334-844-2125.

College of Veterinary Medicine
Dr. Timothy R. Boosinger, Dean
Program in:
veterinary medicine (DVM, MS, PhD)

Graduate Programs in Veterinary Medicine
Dr. Timothy R. Boosinger, Dean
Program in:
biomedical sciences (MS, PhD)

Graduate School
Dr. George Flowers, Dean
Programs in:
cell and molecular biology (PhD)
integrated textile and apparel sciences (PhD)
rural sociology (MS)
sociology (MA, MS)
sociology, anthropology, criminology, and social work (MA, MS)

College of Agriculture
Dr. Richard Guthrie, Dean
Programs in:
agricultural economics (M Ag, MS)
agriculture (M Ag, M Aq, MS, PhD)
agronomy and soils (M Ag, MS, PhD)
animal sciences (M Ag, MS, PhD)
applied economics (PhD)
entomology (M Ag, MS, PhD)
fisheries and allied aquacultures (M Aq, MS, PhD)
horticulture (M Ag, MS, PhD)
plant pathology (M Ag, MS, PhD)
poultry science (M Ag, MS, PhD)

College of Architecture, Design, and Construction
Prof. Dan D. Bennett, Dean
Programs in:
architecture, design, and construction (MBS, MCP, MDB, MID, MLA)
building science (MBS)
community planning (MCP)
construction management (MBS)
design-build (MDB)
industrial design (MID)
landscape architecture (MLA)

College of Business
Dr. Paul M. Bobrowski, Dean

Programs in:
- accountancy (M Acc)
- business (M Acc, MBA, MMIS, MS, PhD)
- business administration (MBA)
- economics (MS)
- finance (MS)
- human resource management (PhD)
- management (MS, PhD)
- management information systems (MMIS, PhD)

College of Education
Dr. Frances Kochan, Dean
Programs in:
- adult education (M Ed, MS, Ed D)
- business education (M Ed, MS, PhD)
- collaborative teacher special education (M Ed, MS)
- community agency counseling (M Ed, MS, Ed D, PhD, Ed S)
- counseling psychology (PhD)
- counselor education (Ed D, PhD)
- curriculum and instruction (M Ed, MS, Ed D, Ed S)
- curriculum supervision (M Ed, MS, Ed D, Ed S)
- early childhood education (M Ed, MS, PhD, Ed S)
- early childhood special education (M Ed, MS)
- education (M Ed, MS, Ed D, PhD, Ed S)
- educational psychology (PhD)
- elementary education (M Ed, MS, PhD, Ed S)
- exercise science (M Ed, MS, PhD)
- foreign languages (M Ed, MS)
- health promotion (M Ed, MS)
- higher education administration (M Ed, MS, Ed D, Ed S)
- kinesiology (PhD)
- media instructional design (MS)
- media specialist (M Ed)
- music education (M Ed, MS, PhD, Ed S)
- physical education/teacher education (M Ed, MS, Ed D, Ed S)
- postsecondary education (PhD)
- reading education (PhD, Ed S)
- rehabilitation counseling (M Ed, MS, PhD)
- school administration (M Ed, MS, Ed D, Ed S)
- school counseling (M Ed, MS, Ed D, PhD, Ed S)
- school psychometry (M Ed, MS, Ed D, PhD, Ed S)
- secondary education (M Ed, MS, PhD, Ed S)

College of Human Sciences
Dr. June Henton, Dean
Programs in:
- apparel and textiles (MS)
- human development and family studies (MS, PhD)
- human sciences (MS, PhD)
- nutrition and food science (MS, PhD)

College of Liberal Arts
Dr. Anne-Katrin Gramberg, Dean
Programs in:
- applied behavior analysis in developmental disabilities (MS)
- audiology (MCD, MS, Au D)
- clinical psychology (PhD)
- communication (MA)
- English (MA, MTPC, PhD)
- experimental psychology (PhD)
- history (MA, PhD)
- industrial/organizational psychology (PhD)
- liberal arts (MA, MCD, MHS, MPA, MS, MTPC, Au D, PhD)
- mass communications (MA)
- public administration (MPA, PhD)
- Spanish (MA, MHS)
- speech pathology (MCD, MS)

College of Sciences and Mathematics
Dr. Stewart W. Schneller, Dean
Programs in:
- analytical chemistry (MS, PhD)
- applied mathematics (MAM, MS)
- biochemistry (MS, PhD)
- botany (MS, PhD)
- geography (MS)
- geology (MS)
- inorganic chemistry (MS, PhD)
- mathematics (MS, PhD)
- microbiology (MS, PhD)
- organic chemistry (MS, PhD)
- physical chemistry (MS, PhD)
- physics (MS, PhD)
- probability and statistics (M Prob S)
- sciences and mathematics (M Prob S, MAM, MS, PhD)
- statistics (MS)
- zoology (MS, PhD)

Ginn College of Engineering
Dr. Larry Benefield, Dean
Programs in:
- aerospace engineering (MAE, MS, PhD)
- chemical engineering (M Ch E, MS, PhD)
- computer science and software engineering (MS, MSWE, PhD)
- construction engineering and management (MCE, MS, PhD)
- electrical and computer engineering (MEE, MS, PhD)
- engineering (M Ch E, M Mtl E, MAE, MCE, MEE, MISE, MME, MS, MSWE, PhD)
- environmental engineering (MCE, MS, PhD)
- geotechnical/materials engineering (MCE, MS, PhD)
- hydraulics/hydrology (MCE, MS, PhD)
- industrial and systems engineering (MISE, MS, PhD)
- materials engineering (M Mtl E, MS, PhD)
- mechanical engineering (MME, MS, PhD)
- structural engineering (MCE, MS, PhD)
- transportation engineering (MCE, MS, PhD)

School of Forestry and Wildlife Sciences
Dr. Richard W. Brinker, Dean
Programs in:
- forest economics (PhD)
- forestry (MS, PhD)
- natural resource conservation (MNR)
- wildlife sciences (MS, PhD)

Harrison School of Pharmacy
Dr. R. Lee Evans, Dean
Programs in:
- pharmacal sciences (MS, PhD)
- pharmaceutical sciences (PhD)
- pharmacy (Pharm D, MS, PhD)
- pharmacy care systems (MS, PhD)

■ AUBURN UNIVERSITY MONTGOMERY
Montgomery, AL 36124-4023
http://www.aum.edu/

State-supported, coed, comprehensive institution. *Graduate faculty:* 84 full-time (27 women), 12 part-time/adjunct (4 women). *Computer facilities:* 500 computers available on campus for general student use. A campuswide network can be accessed from student residence rooms and from off campus. Online class registration is available. *Graduate expenses:* Tuition, state resident: full-time $5088; part-time $212 per credit. Tuition, nonresident: full-time $15,264; part-time $636 per credit. Required fees: $234. *General application contact:* Ronnie McKinney, Associate Director of Enrollment Services, 334-244-3598.

School of Business
Dr. Jane Goodson, Dean
Program in:
- business (MBA)

School of Education
Dr. Jennifer A. Brown, Dean
Programs in:
- counseling (M Ed, Ed S)
- early childhood education (M Ed, Ed S)
- education (M Ed, Ed S)
- education administration (M Ed, Ed S)
- elementary education (M Ed, Ed S)
- physical education (M Ed)
- reading education (M Ed, Ed S)
- secondary education (M Ed, Ed S)
- special education (M Ed, Ed S)

School of Liberal Arts
Dr. Steven Daniell, Interim Dean
Program in:
- liberal arts (MLA)

School of Sciences
Dr. Bayo Lawal, Dean
Programs in:
- justice and public safety (MSJPS)
- psychology (MSPG)
- public administration and political science (MPA, MPS, PhD)
- sciences (MPA, MPS, MSJPS, MSPG, PhD)

■ JACKSONVILLE STATE UNIVERSITY
Jacksonville, AL 36265-1602
http://www.jsu.edu/

State-supported, coed, comprehensive institution. *Graduate faculty:* 125 full-time (45 women), 5 part-time/adjunct (0 women). *Computer facilities:* 330 computers available on campus for general student use. A campuswide network can be accessed from student residence rooms and from off campus. *Graduate expenses:* Tuition, state resident: full-time $4560; part-time $225 per credit hour. Tuition, nonresident: full-time $9120; part-time $450 per credit hour. *General application contact:* Dr. William D. Carr, Dean of the College of Graduate Studies and Continuing Education, 256-782-5329.

College of Graduate Studies and Continuing Education
Dr. William D. Carr, Dean

College of Arts and Sciences
Dr. Earl Wade, Dean
Programs in:
- arts and sciences (MA, MPA, MS)
- biology (MS)
- computer systems and software design (MS)
- criminal justice (MS)
- emergency management (MS)
- English (MA)
- history (MA)
- liberal studies (MA)
- mathematics (MS)
- music (MA)
- political science (MPA)
- psychology (MS)

College of Commerce and Business Administration
Dr. William Fielding, Dean
Program in:
- commerce and business administration (MBA)

College of Education and Professional Studies
Dr. John Hammett, Dean
Programs in:
- early childhood education (MS Ed)
- education (Ed S)
- education and professional studies (MS, MS Ed, Ed S)
- educational administration (MS Ed, Ed S)
- elementary education (MS Ed)
- guidance and counseling (MS)
- health and physical education (MS Ed)
- instructional media (MS Ed)
- reading specialist (MS Ed)
- secondary education (MS Ed)
- special education (MS Ed)

College of Nursing
Dr. Sarah Latham, Dean
Program in:
- nursing (MSN)

■ SAMFORD UNIVERSITY
Birmingham, AL 35229
http://www.samford.edu/

Independent-religious, coed, university. *Graduate faculty:* 144 full-time (60 women), 38 part-time/adjunct (14 women). *Computer facilities:* 330 computers available on campus for general student use. A campuswide network can be accessed from student residence rooms. Online class registration is available. *Graduate expenses:* Tuition: full-time $24,800; part-time $1007 per credit. Required fees: $110 per semester. *General application contact:* Brian E. Willett, Director of Admissions, 205-726-2902.

Beeson School of Divinity
Dr. Timothy George, Dean
Program in:
- divinity (M Div, MTS, D Min)

Brock School of Business
Dr. Beck Taylor, Dean
Program in:
- business (M Acc, MBA)

Cumberland School of Law
John L. Carroll, Dean
Program in:
- law (JD, MCL)

Howard College of Arts and Sciences
Dr. David W. Chapman, Dean
Program in:
- arts and sciences (MSEM)

Ida V. Moffett School of Nursing
Dr. Nena F. Sanders, Dean
Programs in:
- advance practice (DNP)
- anesthesia (MSN)
- education (MSN)
- family nurse practitioner (MSN)
- management (MSN)
- nurse educator (DNP)
- nurse manager (DNP)

McWhorter School of Pharmacy
Dr. Bobby G. Bryant, Dean
Program in:
- pharmacy (Pharm D)

Orlean Bullard Beeson School of Education and Professional Studies
Dr. Jean Ann Box, Dean
Programs in:
- early childhood education (Ed S)
- early childhood/elementary education (MS Ed)
- educational administration (Ed S)
- educational leadership (Ed D)
- elementary education (Ed S)
- gifted education (MS Ed)
- instructional leadership (MS Ed)
- secondary collaboration (MS Ed)

School of the Arts
Dr. Joseph H. Hopkins, Dean
Programs in:
- church music (MM)
- music (MME)
- piano pedagogy (MM)

■ SPRING HILL COLLEGE
Mobile, AL 36608-1791
http://www.shc.edu/

Independent-religious, coed, comprehensive institution. *Graduate faculty:* 22 full-time (7 women), 11 part-time/adjunct (6 women). *Computer facilities:* 194 computers available on campus for general student use. A campuswide network can be accessed from student residence rooms and from off campus. Online class registration is available. *Graduate expenses:* Tuition: full-time $4860; part-time $270 per credit hour. Tuition and fees vary according to program. *General application contact:* Donna B. Tarasavage, Director of Marketing and Recruiting, Graduate and Continuing Studies, 251-380-3094.

Graduate Programs
Ramona Marsalis Hill, Associate Provost of Graduate and Continuing Studies
Programs in:
- business administration (MBA)
- clinical nurse leader (MSN)
- early childhood education (MAT, MS Ed)
- elementary education (MAT, MS Ed)
- liberal arts (MLA)
- secondary education (MAT, MS Ed)
- theology (MA, MPS, MTS)

■ TROY UNIVERSITY
Troy, AL 36082
http://www.troy.edu/

State-supported, coed, comprehensive institution. *Graduate faculty:* 259 full-time (61 women), 310 part-time/adjunct (112 women). *Computer facilities:* 1,570 computers available on campus for general student use. A campuswide network can be accessed from student residence rooms and from off campus. Online class registration is available. *Graduate expenses:* Tuition, state resident: full-time $4800; part-time $200 per credit hour. Tuition, nonresident: full-time $9600; part-time $400 per credit hour. Required fees: $140 per term. *General application contact:* Brenda K. Campbell, Director of Graduate Admissions, 334-670-3178.

Graduate School
Dr. Dianne Barron, Associate Provost/Dean of Graduate School

College of Arts and Sciences
Dr. William S. Richardson, Dean
Programs in:
- arts and sciences (MPA, MS)
- computer and information science (MS)

criminal justice (MS)
education (MPA)
environmental analysis and management (MS)
health care administration (MPA)
international relations (MS)
justice administration (MPA)
management information systems (MPA)
national security affairs (MPA)
nonprofit management (MPA)
public human resources management (MPA)
public management (MPA)

College of Business
Dr. Don Hines, Dean
Programs in:
business (EMBA, MBA, MS, MSM)
business administration (EMBA, MBA)
human resources management (MS)
management (MS, MSM)

College of Communication and Fine Arts
Program in:
communication and fine arts (MS)

College of Education
Programs in:
adult education (MS)
clinical mental health (MS)
community counseling (MS, Ed S)
counselor education (MS)
early childhood education (MS, MSE, Ed S)
education (M Ed, MS, MSE, Ed S)
educational administration/leadership (MS, Ed S)
guidance services (MS)
K–6 elementary and collaborative education (MS, MSE, Ed S)
postsecondary education (M Ed)
rehabilitation counseling (Ed S)
school counseling (Ed S)
school psychology (MS)
secondary education (MS, Ed S)
student affairs counseling (MS)
teacher education-multiple levels (MS, Ed S)

College of Health and Human Services
Dr. Edith Smith, Interim Dean
Programs in:
health and human services (MS, MSN)
nursing (MSN)
sport and fitness management (MS)

■ THE UNIVERSITY OF ALABAMA
Tuscaloosa, AL 35487
http://www.ua.edu/

State-supported, coed, university. CGS member. *Graduate faculty:* 770 full-time (261 women), 16 part-time/adjunct (10 women). *Computer facilities:* 2,200 computers available on campus for general student use. A campuswide network can be accessed from student residence rooms and from off campus. Online class registration is available. *Graduate expenses:* Tuition, state resident: full-time $6400. Tuition, nonresident: full-time $18,000. *General application contact:* Louise F. Labosier, Admissions Officer, 205-348-5921.

Graduate School
Dr. David A. Francko, Dean

Capstone College of Nursing
Dr. Sara E. Barger, Dean
Program in:
nursing (MSN, DNP)

College of Arts and Sciences
Dr. Robert F. Olin, Dean
Programs in:
acting (MFA)
American studies (MA)
anthropology (MA, PhD)
applied mathematics (PhD)
arranging (MM)
art history (MA)
arts and sciences (MA, MATESOL, MFA, MM, MPA, MS, DMA, PhD)
biological sciences (MS, PhD)
chemistry (MS, PhD)
choral conducting (MM, DMA)
clinical psychology (PhD)
composition (MM, DMA)
composition and rhetoric (PhD)
costume design (MFA)
creative writing (MFA)
criminal justice (MS)
directing (MFA)
experimental psychology (PhD)
French (MA, PhD)
French and Spanish (PhD)
geography (MS)
geological sciences (MS, PhD)
German (MA)
history (MA, PhD)
literature (MA, PhD)
mathematics (MA, PhD)
music education (MA, PhD)
music history (MM)
performance (MM, DMA)
physics (MS, PhD)
political science (MA, PhD)
public administration (MPA)
pure mathematics (PhD)
rhetoric and composition (MA)
Romance languages (MA, PhD)
scene design/technical production (MFA)
Spanish (MA, PhD)
speech language pathology (MS)
stage management (MFA)
studio art (MA, MFA)
teaching English as a second language (MATESOL)
theatre (MFA)
theatre management/administration (MFA)
theory (MM)
wind conducting (MM, DMA)
women's studies (MA)

College of Communication and Information Sciences
Dr. Jennings Bryant, Associate Dean for Graduate Studies
Programs in:
advertising and public relations (MA)
book arts (MFA)
communication and information sciences (MA, MFA, MLIS, PhD)
communication studies (MA)
journalism (MA)
library and information studies (MLIS, PhD)
mass communications (PhD)
telecommunication and film (MA)

College of Education
Dr. James E. McLean, Dean
Programs in:
alternative sport pedagogy (MA)
choral music education (MA)
collaborative teacher program (M Ed, Ed S)
early intervention (M Ed, Ed S)
education (M Ed, MA, Ed D, PhD, Ed S)
educational administration (Ed D, PhD)
educational leadership (MA, Ed S)
educational studies in psychology, research methodology and counseling (MA, Ed D, PhD, Ed S)
elementary education (MA, Ed D, PhD, Ed S)
exercise science (MA, PhD)
gifted education (M Ed, Ed S)
higher education administration (MA, Ed D, PhD)
human performance (MA)
instructional leadership (Ed D, PhD)
instrumental music education (MA)
multiple abilities program (M Ed)
music education (Ed D, PhD, Ed S)
secondary education (MA, Ed D, PhD, Ed S)
special education (Ed D, PhD)
sport management (MA)
sport pedagogy (MA, PhD)

College of Engineering
Dr. Charles Karr, Dean
Programs in:
aerospace engineering (MAE)
chemical and biological engineering (MS Ch E, PhD)
civil engineering (MSCE, PhD)
computer science (MS, PhD)
electrical engineering (MS, PhD)
engineering (MAE, MES, MS, MS Ch E, MS Met E, MSCE, MSIE, PhD)
engineering science and mechanics (MES, PhD)
environmental engineering (MS)
industrial engineering (MSIE)
materials science (PhD)
mechanical engineering (MS, PhD)
metallurgical and materials engineering (MS Met E, PhD)

College of Human Environmental Sciences
Dr. Milla D. Boschung, Dean
Programs in:
clothing, textiles, and interior design (MSHES)

The University of Alabama (continued)
- consumer sciences (MS)
- family financial planning and counseling (MS)
- health education and promotion (PhD)
- health studies (MA)
- human development and family studies (MSHES)
- human environmental sciences (MA, MS, MSHES, PhD)
- human nutrition and hospitality management (MSHES)
- interactive technology (MS)
- quality management (MS)
- restaurant and meeting management (MS)
- rural community health (MS)
- sport management (MS)

Manderson Graduate School of Business
Dr. J. Barry Mason, Dean
Programs in:
- accounting (M Acc, PhD)
- applied statistics (MS, PhD)
- business (EMBA, M Acc, MA, MBA, MS, MTA, PhD)
- economics (MA, PhD)
- finance (MS, PhD)
- general commerce and business (EMBA, MBA)
- information systems, statistics, and management science—applied statistics (MS, PhD)
- information systems, statistics, and management science—operations management (MS, PhD)
- management (MA, MS, PhD)
- marketing (MS, PhD)
- operations management (MS, PhD)
- tax accounting (MTA)

School of Social Work
Dr. James P. Adams, Dean
Program in:
- social work (MSW, PhD)

School of Law
Kenneth C. Randall, Dean
Program in:
- law (JD, LL M, LL M in Tax)

■ THE UNIVERSITY OF ALABAMA AT BIRMINGHAM

Birmingham, AL 35294
http://www.uab.edu/

State-supported, coed, university. CGS member. *Computer facilities:* 550 computers available on campus for general student use. A campuswide network can be accessed from student residence rooms and from off campus. Online class registration, transcript requests are available. *General application contact:* Julie Bryant, Director of Graduate Admissions, 205-934-8227.

Graduate Programs in Joint Health Sciences
Dr. Robert R. Rich, Vice President/Dean, School of Medicine
Programs in:
- basic medical sciences (MSBMS)
- biochemistry and molecular genetics (PhD)
- cell biology (PhD)
- cellular and molecular biology (PhD)
- cellular and molecular physiology (PhD)
- genetics (PhD)
- integrative biomedical sciences (PhD)
- microbiology (PhD)
- neurobiology (PhD)
- neuroscience (PhD)
- pathology (PhD)
- pharmacology (PhD)
- pharmacology and toxicology (PhD)
- physiology and biophysics (PhD)
- toxicology (PhD)

School of Arts and Humanities
Bert Brouwer, Dean
Programs in:
- art history (MA)
- arts and humanities (MA)
- communication management (MA)
- English (MA)

School of Business
Dr. David R. Klock, Dean
Programs in:
- accounting and information systems (M Acct)
- business (M Acct, MBA, PhD)
- management (MBA)

School of Dentistry
Dr. Huw F. Thomas, Dean
Programs in:
- dentistry (DMD, MS, MSBMS, PhD)
- dentistry and oral biology (MS)

School of Education
Dr. Michael J. Froning, Dean
Programs in:
- arts education (MA Ed)
- counseling (MA)
- early childhood education (MA Ed, PhD)
- education (MA, MA Ed, Ed D, PhD, Ed S)
- educational leadership (MA Ed, Ed D, PhD, Ed S)
- elementary education (MA Ed)
- health education (MA Ed)
- health education and health promotion (PhD)
- high school education (MA Ed)
- physical education (MA Ed)
- special education (MA Ed)

School of Engineering
Dr. Linda C. Lucas, Dean
Programs in:
- biomedical engineering (MSBME, PhD)
- civil engineering (MSCE, PhD)
- computer engineering (PhD)
- electrical engineering (MSEE)
- engineering (MS Mt E, MSBME, MSCE, MSEE, MSME, PhD)
- environmental health engineering (PhD)
- materials engineering (MS Mt E, PhD)
- materials science (PhD)
- mechanical engineering (MSME, PhD)

School of Health Professions
Dr. Harold P. Jones, Dean
Programs in:
- administration-health services (PhD)
- clinical nutrition (MS)
- clinical nutrition and dietetics (MS, Certificate)
- dietetic internship (Certificate)
- health administration (MSHA)
- health informatics (MS)
- health professions (MNA, MS, MSHA, DPT, Dr Sc PT, PhD, Certificate)
- low vision rehabilitation (Certificate)
- nurse anesthesia (MNA)
- nutrition sciences (PhD)
- occupational therapy (MS, Certificate)
- physical therapy (DPT, Dr Sc PT)
- physician assistant (MS)

School of Medicine
Dr. Robert R. Rich, Vice President/Dean, School of Medicine
Program in:
- medicine (MD, MSBMS, PhD)

School of Natural Sciences and Mathematics
Dr. Lowell E. Wenger, Dean
Programs in:
- applied mathematics (PhD)
- biology (MS, PhD)
- chemistry (MS, PhD)
- computer and information sciences (MS, PhD)
- mathematics (MS)
- natural sciences and mathematics (MS, PhD)
- physics (MS, PhD)

School of Nursing
Dr. Doreen C. Harper, Dean
Program in:
- nursing (MSN, PhD)

School of Optometry
Dr. John F. Amos, Dean
Programs in:
- optometry (OD, MS, PhD)
- vision science (MS, PhD)

School of Public Health
Dr. Max Michael, Dean
Programs in:
- biostatistics (MS, PhD)
- environmental health (PhD)
- epidemiology (PhD)
- health care organization and policy (MPH, MSPH)
- health education and health promotion (PhD)
- public health (MPH, MS, MSPH, DPH, PhD)

School of Social and Behavioral Sciences
Dr. Jean Ann Linney, Dean
Programs in:
- anthropology (MA)
- criminal justice (MSCJ)
- forensic science (MSFS)

history (MA)
medical sociology (PhD)
psychology (MA, PhD)
public administration (MPA)
social and behavioral sciences (MA, MPA, MSCJ, MSFS, PhD)
sociology (MA)

■ THE UNIVERSITY OF ALABAMA IN HUNTSVILLE

Huntsville, AL 35899
http://www.uah.edu/

State-supported, coed, university. CGS member. *Graduate faculty:* 196 full-time (51 women), 24 part-time/adjunct (5 women). *Computer facilities:* 1,153 computers available on campus for general student use. A campuswide network can be accessed from student residence rooms and from off campus. Online class registration is available. *Graduate expenses:* Tuition, state resident: full-time $5214; part-time $323 per credit hour. Tuition, nonresident: full-time $11,444; part-time $705 per credit hour. Required fees: $540; $120 per semester. Tuition and fees vary according to course load. *General application contact:* Dr. Debra Moriarity, Dean of Graduate Studies, 256-824-6002.

School of Graduate Studies
Dr. Debra Moriarity, Dean of Graduate Studies

College of Business Administration
Dr. James Simpson, Acting Dean
Programs in:
accounting (M Acc, Certificate)
business administration (M Acc, MBA, MSIS, Certificate)
economics and information systems (MSIS, Certificate)
human resource management (Certificate)
management (MBA)

College of Engineering
Dr. Phillip Farrington, Acting Dean
Programs in:
aerospace engineering (MSE)
chemical engineering (MSE)
civil and environmental engineering (PhD)
civil engineering (MSE)
computer engineering (MSE, PhD)
electrical engineering (MSE, PhD)
engineering (MSE, MSOR, MSSE, PhD)
industrial and systems engineering (PhD)
industrial engineering (MSE)
mechanical engineering (MSE, PhD)
operations research (MSOR)
optical science and engineering (PhD)
optics and photonics (MSE)
software engineering (MSSE)

College of Liberal Arts
Glenn Dasher, Acting Dean
Programs in:
English (MA)
history (MA)
liberal arts (MA, Certificate)
psychology (MA)
public affairs (MA)
teaching of English to speakers of other languages (Certificate)
technical communications (Certificate)

College of Nursing
Dr. Fay Raines, Dean, College of Nursing
Programs in:
family nurse practitioner (Certificate)
nursing (MSN, DNP)
nursing education (Certificate)

College of Science
Dr. Jack Fix, Dean
Programs in:
applied mathematics (PhD)
atmospheric and environmental science (MS, PhD)
biological sciences (MS)
chemistry (MS)
computer science (MS, PhD)
mathematics (MA, MS)
optics and photonics technology (MS)
physics (MS, PhD)
science (MA, MS, MSSE, PhD, Certificate)
software engineering (MSSE, Certificate)

Interdisciplinary Studies
Dr. Debra Moriarity, Dean of Graduate Studies
Programs in:
biotechnology science and engineering (PhD)
information assurance and cybersecurity (Certificate)
interdisciplinary studies (MS, PhD, Certificate)
materials science (MS, PhD)
modeling and simulation (MS, PhD, Certificate)
optical science and engineering (PhD)

■ UNIVERSITY OF MOBILE

Mobile, AL 36613
http://www.umobile.edu/

Independent-religious, coed, comprehensive institution. *Graduate faculty:* 16 full-time (6 women), 6 part-time/adjunct (3 women). *Computer facilities:* 110 computers available on campus for general student use. A campuswide network can be accessed from student residence rooms and from off campus. Online class registration is available. *Graduate expenses:* Tuition: full-time $7560; part-time $420 per credit hour. Required fees: $240; $120 per semester. *General application contact:* Dr. Anne B. Lowery, Dean, School of Business, 251-442-2332.

Graduate Programs
Dr. Anne B. Lowery, Dean
Programs in:
biblical/theological studies (MA)
business administration (MBA)
education (MA)
marriage and family counseling (MA)
nursing (MSN)
religious studies (MA)

■ UNIVERSITY OF MONTEVALLO

Montevallo, AL 35115
http://www.montevallo.edu/

State-supported, coed, comprehensive institution. *Computer facilities:* 340 computers available on campus for general student use. A campuswide network can be accessed from student residence rooms and from off campus. Online class registration is available. *Graduate expenses:* Tuition, state resident: full-time $5280; part-time $220 per credit hour. Tuition, nonresident: full-time $10,560; part-time $440 per credit hour. Required fees: $482; $113 per semester. One-time fee: $25 part-time. *General application contact:* Rebecca Hartley, Coordinator for Graduate Studies, 205-665-6350.

College of Arts and Sciences
Dr. Mary Beth Armstrong, Dean
Programs in:
arts and sciences (MA, MS)
English literature (MA)
speech-language pathology (MS)

College of Education
Dr. Jack Riley, Dean
Programs in:
community counseling (M Ed)
education (M Ed, Ed S)
elementary education (M Ed)
instructional leadership (M Ed, Ed S)
marriage and family (M Ed)
school counseling (M Ed)
secondary/high school education (M Ed)

■ UNIVERSITY OF NORTH ALABAMA

Florence, AL 35632-0001
http://www.una.edu/

State-supported, coed, comprehensive institution. *Graduate faculty:* 11 full-time (5 women), 75 part-time/adjunct (27 women). *Computer facilities:* 1,000 computers available on campus for general student use. A campuswide network can be accessed from student residence rooms and from off campus. Online class registration is available. *Graduate expenses:* Tuition, state resident: full-time $4704; part-time $196 per credit hour. Tuition, nonresident: full-time $9408; part-time $392 per credit hour. Required fees: $882. Tuition and fees vary according to course load and program. *General application contact:* Kim Mauldin, Director of Admissions, 256-765-4608.

College of Arts and Sciences
Dr. Vagn Hansen, Dean

University of North Alabama (continued)
Programs in:
arts and sciences (MA, MAEN, MSCJ)
criminal justice (MSCJ)
English (MAEN)
history and political science (MA)

College of Business
Dr. Kerry Gatlin, Dean
Program in:
business (MBA)

College of Education
Dr. Donna Jacobs, Dean
Programs in:
collaborative teacher special education (MA Ed)
counseling (MA Ed)
education (MA, MA Ed, Ed S)
education leadership (Ed S)
elementary education (MA Ed, Ed S)
learning disabilities (MA Ed)
mentally retarded (MA Ed)
mild learning handicapped (MA Ed)
non-school-based counseling (MA)
non-school-based teaching (MA)
secondary education (MA Ed, Ed S)

College of Nursing and Allied Health
Dr. Birdie Bailey, Dean
Program in:
nursing and allied health (MSN)

■ UNIVERSITY OF SOUTH ALABAMA

Mobile, AL 36688-0002

http://www.southalabama.edu/

State-supported, coed, university. CGS member. *Graduate faculty:* 355 full-time (119 women), 5 part-time/adjunct (2 women). *Computer facilities:* 500 computers available on campus for general student use. A campuswide network can be accessed from student residence rooms and from off campus. Online class registration is available. *Graduate expenses:* Tuition, state resident: full-time $4656. Tuition, nonresident: full-time $9312. *General application contact:* Dr. B. Keith Harrison, Dean, Graduate School, 251-460-6310.

College of Medicine
Dr. Ronald Balczon, Director of Graduate Studies
Programs in:
biochemistry and molecular biology (PhD)
cell biology and neuroscience (PhD)
medicine (MD, PhD)
microbiology and immunology (PhD)
pharmacology (PhD)
physiology (PhD)

Graduate School
Dr. B. Keith Harrison, Dean of the Graduate School
Program in:
environmental toxicology (MS)

College of Allied Health Professions
Dr. Julio F. Turrens, Director of Graduate Studies
Programs in:
allied health professions (MHS, MS, Au D, DPT, PhD)
audiology (Au D)
communication sciences and disorders (PhD)
occupational therapy (MS)
physical therapy (DPT)
physician assistant studies (MHS)
speech and hearing sciences (MS)

College of Arts and Sciences
Dr. S. L. Varghese, Director of Graduate Studies
Programs in:
arts and sciences (MA, MPA, MS, PhD, Certificate)
biological sciences (MS)
communication (MA)
English (MA)
gerontology (Certificate)
history (MA)
marine sciences (MS, PhD)
mathematics (MS)
psychology (MS)
public administration (MPA)
sociology (MA)

College of Education
Dr. Abigail Baxter, Director of Graduate Studies
Programs in:
community counseling (MS)
early childhood education (M Ed)
education (M Ed, MS, PhD, Ed S)
educational administration (Ed S)
educational leadership (M Ed)
educational media (M Ed, MS)
elementary education (M Ed)
exercise science (MS)
health education (M Ed)
instructional design and development (MS, PhD)
physical education (M Ed)
reading education (M Ed)
rehabilitation counseling (MS)
school counseling (M Ed)
school psychometry (M Ed)
science education (M Ed)
secondary education (M Ed)
special education (M Ed, Ed S)
therapeutic recreation (MS)

College of Engineering
Dr. Thomas G. Thomas, Director of Graduate Studies
Programs in:
chemical engineering (MS Ch E)
civil engineering (MSCE)
electrical engineering (MSEE)
engineering (MS Ch E, MSCE, MSEE, MSME)
mechanical engineering (MSME)

College of Nursing
Dr. Rosemary Rhodes, Director of Graduate Education
Programs in:
adult health nursing (MSN)
community/mental health nursing (MSN)
maternal/child nursing (MSN)
nursing (DNP)

Mitchell College of Business
Dr. John Gamble, Director of Graduate Studies
Programs in:
accounting (M Acct)
business (M Acct, MBA)
general management (MBA)

School of Computer and Information Sciences
Dr. Roy Daigle, Director of Graduate Studies
Programs in:
computer science (MS)
information systems (MS)

■ THE UNIVERSITY OF WEST ALABAMA

Livingston, AL 35470

http://www.uwa.edu/

State-supported, coed, comprehensive institution. *Computer facilities:* 400 computers available on campus for general student use. A campuswide network can be accessed from student residence rooms. *General application contact:* Dean of Graduate Studies, 205-652-3647 Ext. 421.

School of Graduate Studies

College of Education
Programs in:
continuing education (MSCE)
early childhood education (M Ed)
education (M Ed, MAT, MSCE)
elementary education (M Ed)
guidance and counseling (M Ed, MSCE)
library media (M Ed)
physical education (M Ed, MAT)
school administration (M Ed)
secondary education (MAT)
special education (M Ed)

College of Liberal Arts
Programs in:
history (MAT)
language arts (MAT)
liberal arts (MAT)
social science (MAT)

College of Natural Sciences and Mathematics
Programs in:
biological sciences (MAT)
mathematics (MAT)
natural sciences and mathematics (MAT)

Alaska

■ ALASKA PACIFIC UNIVERSITY

Anchorage, AK 99508-4672

http://www.alaskapacific.edu/

Independent, coed, comprehensive institution. *Computer facilities:* 105 computers available on campus for general student use. A campuswide network can be accessed from student residence rooms. Online class registration is available. *General application contact:* Director of Admissions, 907-564-8248.

Graduate Programs

Programs in:
- business administration (MBA)
- counseling psychology (MSCP)
- environmental science (MSES, MSOEE)
- health services administration (MBA)
- information and communication technology (MBAICT)
- investment (CGS)
- outdoor and environmental education (MSOEE)
- self-designed study (MA)
- teaching (MAT)
- teaching (K-8) (MAT)

■ UNIVERSITY OF ALASKA ANCHORAGE

Anchorage, AK 99508-8060

http://www.uaa.alaska.edu/

State-supported, coed, comprehensive institution. CGS member. *Graduate faculty:* 140 full-time (82 women). *Computer facilities:* Computer purchase and lease plans are available. 500 computers available on campus for general student use. A campuswide network can be accessed from student residence rooms and from off campus. Online class registration is available. *Graduate expenses:* Tuition, state resident: full-time $5418; part-time $301 per credit. Tuition, nonresident: full-time $11,070; part-time $615 per credit. Required fees: $580; $56 per semester. Tuition and fees vary according to course level, course load, program, reciprocity agreements and student level. *General application contact:* Elisa Mattison, Director, Graduate School, 907-786-1096.

College of Arts and Sciences

Programs in:
- anthropology (MA)
- arts and sciences (MA, MFA, MS, PhD)
- biological sciences (MS)
- clinical psychology (MS)
- clinical-community psychology with rural-indigenous emphasis (PhD)
- creative writing and literary arts (MFA)
- English (MA)
- interdisciplinary studies (MA, MS)

College of Business and Public Policy

Programs in:
- business administration (MBA)
- business and public policy (MBA, MPA, MS, Certificate)
- global supply chain management (MS)
- public administration (MPA)
- supply chain management (Certificate)

College of Education

Programs in:
- adult education (M Ed)
- counseling and guidance (M Ed)
- early childhood special education (M Ed)
- education (M Ed, MAT, Certificate)
- educational leadership (M Ed)
- master teacher (M Ed)
- principal licensure (Certificate)
- special education (M Ed, Certificate)
- superintendent (Certificate)
- teaching (MAT)

College of Health and Social Welfare

Program in:
- health and social welfare (MPH, MS, MSW, Certificate)

Division of Health Sciences

Program in:
- public health practice (MPH)

School of Nursing

Programs in:
- family nurse practitioner (Certificate)
- nursing (MS)
- nursing education (Certificate)
- psychiatric nurse practitioner (Certificate)

School of Social Work

Programs in:
- clinical social work practice (Certificate)
- social work (MSW)
- social work management (Certificate)

School of Engineering

Programs in:
- applied environmental science and technology (M AEST, MS)
- arctic engineering (MS)
- civil engineering (MCE, MS)
- engineering (M AEST, MCE, MS, Certificate)
- engineering management (MS)
- port and coastal engineering (Certificate)
- project management (MS)
- science management (MS)

■ UNIVERSITY OF ALASKA FAIRBANKS

Fairbanks, AK 99775-7520

http://www.uaf.edu/

State-supported, coed, university. CGS member. *Graduate faculty:* 311 full-time (98 women), 91 part-time/adjunct (45 women). *Computer facilities:* Computer purchase and lease plans are available. 125 computers available on campus for general student use. A campuswide network can be accessed from student residence rooms and from off campus. Online class registration, university portal; campus wireless access are available. *Graduate expenses:* Tuition, state resident: full-time $5418; part-time $301 per credit. Tuition, nonresident: full-time $11,070; part-time $615 per credit. Required fees: $849; $25 per credit. $78 per semester. Tuition and fees vary according to course load and reciprocity agreements. *General application contact:* Lael Oldmixon, Interim Director of Admissions, 907-474-7500.

College of Engineering and Mines

Dr. Douglas J. Goering, Dean

Programs in:
- arctic engineering (MS, PhD)
- civil engineering (MCE, MS, PhD)
- electrical engineering (MEE, MS, PhD)
- engineering (PhD)
- engineering and mines (MCE, MEE, MS, PhD)
- engineering and science management (MS, PhD)
- engineering management (MS, PhD)
- environmental engineering (MS, PhD)
- environmental quality science (MS)
- geological engineering (MS, PhD)
- mechanical engineering (MS)
- mineral preparation engineering (MS)
- mining engineering (MS, PhD)
- petroleum engineering (MS, PhD)
- science management (MS)

College of Liberal Arts

Ron Davis, Dean

Programs in:
- anthropology (MA, PhD)
- applied linguistics (MA)
- art (MFA)
- ceramics (MFA)
- clinical-community psychology (PhD)
- computer art (MFA)
- conducting (MA)
- creative writing (MFA)
- cross cultural studies (MA)
- drawing (MFA)
- environmental politics and policy (MA)
- justice (MA)
- liberal arts (MA, MFA, PhD)
- literature (MA)
- music education (MA)
- music history (MA)
- music theory/composition (MA)
- Native arts (MFA)
- Northern history (MA)
- painting (MFA)
- performance (MA)
- photography (MFA)
- printmaking (MFA)
- professional communications (MA)
- sculpture (MFA)

College of Natural Sciences and Mathematics

Dr. Joan Braddock, Dean

University of Alaska Fairbanks (continued)
Programs in:
atmospheric science (MS, PhD)
biochemistry and molecular biology (MS, PhD)
biological sciences (MS, PhD)
biology (MAT, MS)
chemistry (MA, MS)
computational physics (MS)
computer science (MS)
environmental chemistry (MS, PhD)
geology (MS, PhD)
geophysics (MS, PhD)
mathematics (MAT, PhD)
natural sciences and mathematics (MA, MAT, MS, MSE, PhD)
physics (MAT, MS, PhD)
software engineering (MSE)
space physics (MS, PhD)
statistics (MS)
wildlife biology (MS)

College of Rural and Community Development
Jennifer Carroll, Acting Vice Chancellor
Programs in:
rural and community development (MA)
rural development (MA)

Graduate School for Interdisciplinary Studies
Lawrence Duffy, Interim Dean
Program in:
interdisciplinary studies (MA, MS, PhD)

School of Education
Dr. Eric C. Madsen, Dean
Programs in:
counseling (M Ed)
curriculum and instruction (M Ed)
education (M Ed, PhD)
elementary education (M Ed)
guidance and counseling (M Ed)
language and literacy (M Ed)
reading (M Ed)
secondary education (M Ed)

School of Fisheries and Ocean Sciences
Dr. Denis Wiesenberg, Dean
Programs in:
fisheries (MS, PhD)
marine biology (MS, PhD)
marine sciences and limnology (MS, PhD)
oceanography (PhD)
seafood science and nutrition (MS, PhD)

School of Management
Dr. Mark Herrmann, Dean
Programs in:
capital markets (MBA)
general management (MBA)
management (MBA, MS)
resource and applied economics (MS)

School of Natural Resources and Agricultural Sciences
Dr. Carol E. Lewis, Dean
Program in:
natural resource management (MS)

■ UNIVERSITY OF ALASKA SOUTHEAST
Juneau, AK 99801
http://www.uas.alaska.edu/

State-supported, coed, comprehensive institution. *Computer facilities:* 75 computers available on campus for general student use. A campuswide network can be accessed from student residence rooms and from off campus. Online class registration is available. *General application contact:* Administrative Assistant, 866-465-6424.

Graduate Programs
Programs in:
business administration (MBA)
early childhood education (M Ed, MAT)
educational technology (M Ed)
elementary education (MAT)
public administration (MPA)
reading (M Ed)
secondary education (MAT)

Arizona

■ ARIZONA STATE UNIVERSITY
Tempe, AZ 85287
http://www.asu.edu/

State-supported, coed, university. CGS member. *Computer facilities:* Computer purchase and lease plans are available. 5,000 computers available on campus for general student use. A campuswide network can be accessed from student residence rooms and from off campus. Online class registration is available. *General application contact:* Graduate Admissions, 480-965-6113.

Graduate College
Program in:
statistics (MS)

College of Design
Programs in:
architecture (M Arch)
arts/media/engineering (MSD)
building design (MS)
design (PhD)
healthcare and healing environments (MSD)
history, theory, and criticism (PhD)
industrial design (MSD)
interaction design (MSD)
interior design (MSD)
landscape architecture (MLA)
new product innovation (MSD)
planning (MUEP)
transportation systems (Certificate)
urban design (MUD)
visual communication design (MSD)

College of Liberal Arts and Sciences
Programs in:
American media and popular culture (MAS)
anthropology (PhD)
applied mathematics for the life and social sciences (PhD)
astrophysics (MS, PhD)
audiology (Au D)
behavioral neuroscience (PhD)
biological design (PhD)
biology (MNS, MS, PhD)
biology and society (PhD)
chemistry and biochemistry (MS, PhD)
Chinese (MA)
clinical psychology (PhD)
cognition, action and perception (PhD)
communication (MA, PhD)
communication disorders (MS)
computational biosciences (PSM, PhD)
creative writing (MFA)
developmental psychology (PhD)
East/Southeast Asian history (MA, PhD)
English (MA, PhD)
environmental social science (PhD)
European history (MA, PhD)
family and human development (MS, PhD)
film analysis (MLS)
French (MA)
gender studies (PhD)
geographic education (MAS)
geographic information systems (MAS)
geography (MA, PhD)
geological sciences (MS, PhD)
German (MA)
human and social dimensions of science and technology (PhD)
humanities (MA, MAS, MFA, MLS, MTESOL, PhD)
infant-family practice (MAS)
Japanese (MA)
justice studies (MS, PhD)
kinesiology (PhD)
Latin American studies (MA, PhD)
liberal arts and sciences (MA, MAS, MFA, MLS, MNS, MS, MTESOL, PSM, Au D, PhD)
marriage and family therapy (MAS)
mathematics (MA, MNS, PhD)
microbiology (MNS, MS, PhD)
molecular and cellular biology (MS, PhD)
museum studies in anthropology (MA)
nanoscience (PSM)
natural sciences (MA, MNS, MS, PSM, Au D, PhD)
neuroscience (PhD)
North American history (MA, PhD)
philosophy (MA, PhD)
physics (MNS, MS, PhD)
plant biology (MNS, MS, PhD)
political science (MA, PhD)
public history (MA)
quantitative psychology (PhD)
religious studies (MA, PhD)
screenwriting (MAS)
social psychology (PhD)
social science and health (PhD)

social sciences (MA, MAS, MS, PhD)
sociology (MA, PhD)
Spanish (MA, PhD)
speech and hearing science (PhD)
teaching English to speakers of other languages (MTESOL)

College of Nursing and Healthcare Innovation
Programs in:
child and adolescent mental health intervention specialist (Graduate Certificate)
community and public health practice (Graduate Certificate)
community health (MS)
evidence-based practice in nursing (Graduate Certificate)
exercise and wellness (MS, PhD)
healthcare innovation (MHI)
nurse education in academic and practice settings (Graduate Certificate)
nurse educator (MS)
nursing (MS)
nursing and healthcare innovation (PhD)
nursing practice (DNP)
nutrition (MS)
physical activity, nutrition and wellness (PhD)

College of Public Programs
Programs in:
community resources and development (PhD)
criminal justice (MA)
criminology and criminal justice (MS, PhD)
nonprofit studies (MNpS)
public affairs (MPA, MPP, PhD)
recreation and tourism studies (MS)
social work (MSW, PhD)

College of Teacher Education and Leadership
Programs in:
educational administration and supervision (M Ed)
elementary education (M Ed, Certificate)
leadership/innovation (administration) (Ed D)
leadership/innovation (teaching) (Ed D)
physical education (MPE)
secondary education (M Ed, Certificate)
special education (M Ed)

College of Technology and Innovation
Programs in:
aeronautical management technology (MS)
applied biological sciences (MS)
applied psychology (MS)
computing studies (MCST)
electronic systems (MS)
mechanical and manufacturing engineering technology (MS)
technology (MS)
technology and innovation (MCST, MS)
technology management (MS)

Herberger College of the Arts
Programs in:
art (MA, MFA, PhD)
arts (MA, MFA, MM, DMA, PhD)
composition (MM)
creative writing (playwriting) (MFA)
dance (MFA)
music (MA, DMA)
music education (MM)
music therapy (MM)
performance (MM)
theatre (MA, MFA, PhD)

Ira A. Fulton School of Engineering
Programs in:
aerospace engineering (MS, MSE, PhD)
bioengineering (MS, PhD)
biomedical informatics (MS, PhD)
chemical engineering (MS, MSE, PhD)
civil and environmental engineering (MS, MSE, PhD)
computer science (MCS, MS, PhD)
construction (MS)
electrical engineering (MS, MSE, PhD)
embedded systems (M Eng)
engineering (M Eng, MCS, MS, MSE, PhD)
enterprise systems innovation and management (MSE)
industrial engineering (MS, MSE, PhD)
materials science and engineering (MS, MSE, PhD)
mechanical engineering (MS, MSE, PhD)
modeling and simulation (M Eng)
quality and reliability engineering (M Eng)
semiconductor processing and packaging (MSE)
software engineering (MSE)
systems engineering (M Eng)

Mary Lou Fulton College of Education
Programs in:
counseling (M Ed, MC)
counseling psychology (PhD)
curriculum and instruction (M Ed, MA, Ed D, PhD)
education (M Ed, MA, MC, Ed D, PhD)
educational administration and supervision (M Ed, Ed D)
educational leadership and policy studies (M Ed, MA, Ed D, PhD)
educational psychology (M Ed, MA, PhD)
educational technology (M Ed, PhD)
higher and post-secondary education (M Ed)
psychology in education (M Ed, MA, MC, PhD)
social and philosophical foundations of education (MA)
special education (M Ed, MA)

New College of Interdisciplinary Arts and Sciences
Programs in:
communication studies (MA)
interdisciplinary studies (MA)
social justice and human rights (MA)

School of Aging and Lifespan Development
Programs in:
aging and lifespan development (MS)
gerontology (Certificate)

School of Sustainability
Program in:
sustainability (MA, MS, PhD)

Walter Cronkite School of Journalism and Mass Communication
Program in:
journalism and mass communication (MMC)

W.P. Carey School of Business
Programs in:
accountancy (M Acc, M Tax, PhD)
agribusiness (MS, PhD)
applied leadership and management (MALM)
business (M Acc, M Tax, MALM, MBA, MHSM, MS, PhD)
business administration (MBA)
commerce (MS)
economics (PhD)
finance (MBA, PhD)
health sector management (MBA, MHSM)
information management (MS)
information systems (PhD)
management (MBA, PhD)
marketing (MBA, PhD)
supply chain management (MBA, PhD)
urban health (MPH)

Sandra Day O'Connor College of Law

Dean Paul Schiff Berman, Dean and Foundation Professor of Law
Programs in:
biotechnology and genomics (LL M)
law (JD)
legal studies (MLS)
tribal policy, law and government (LL M)

■ DEVRY UNIVERSITY

Phoenix, AZ 85021-2995
http://www.devry.edu/

Proprietary, coed, comprehensive institution. *Computer facilities:* Computer purchase and lease plans are available. 436 computers available on campus for general student use. A campuswide network can be accessed from off campus. Online class registration is available. *General application contact:* Student Application Contact, 602-870-9222.

Keller Graduate School of Management

Program in:
management (MAFM, MBA, MHRM, MISM, MNCM, MPA, MPM, Graduate Certificate)

■ GRAND CANYON UNIVERSITY
Phoenix, AZ 85017-1097
http://www.gcu.edu/

Independent-religious, coed, university. CGS member. *Graduate faculty:* 69 full-time (34 women), 432 part-time/adjunct (300 women). *Computer facilities:* 65 computers available on campus for general student use. A campuswide network can be accessed from student residence rooms and from off campus. Online class registration is available. *General application contact:* Becky Schildt, Online Enrollment Manager, 800-557-9551.

College of Business
Kim Donaldson, Dean
Programs in:
- accounting (MBA)
- executive fire service leadership (MS)
- finance (MBA)
- general management (MBA)
- health systems management (MBA)
- leadership (MBA, MS)
- management of information system (MBA)
- marketing (MBA)
- six sigma (MBA)

College of Education
Dr. Cindy K. Knott, Dean
Programs in:
- curriculum and instruction (M Ed)
- education administration (M Ed)
- elementary education (M Ed)
- organizational leadership (Ed D)
- secondary education (M Ed)
- special education (M Ed)
- teaching (MA)

College of Nursing and Health Sciences
Dr. Fran Roberts, Vice President
Programs in:
- addiction counseling (MS)
- nursing (MS)
- professional counseling (MS)

■ NORTHCENTRAL UNIVERSITY
Prescott Valley, AZ 86314
http://www.ncu.edu/

Proprietary, coed, comprehensive institution. *Computer facilities:* A campuswide network can be accessed from off campus. Online class registration is available.

■ NORTHERN ARIZONA UNIVERSITY
Flagstaff, AZ 86011
http://www.nau.edu/

State-supported, coed, university. CGS member. *Computer facilities:* Computer purchase and lease plans are available. 903 computers available on campus for general student use. A campuswide network can be accessed from student residence rooms and from off campus. Online class registration is available. *General application contact:* Director of Graduate Admissions, 928-523-4348.

Graduate College

College of Arts and Letters
Programs in:
- applied linguistics (PhD)
- arts and letters (MA, MAT, MM, PhD, Certificate)
- choral conducting (MM)
- creative writing (MA)
- English (MA)
- general English (MA)
- history (MA, PhD)
- instrumental conducting (MM)
- instrumental performance (MM)
- literacy, technology and professional writing (MA)
- literature (MA)
- music education (MM)
- musicology (MM)
- secondary English education (MA)
- Spanish (MAT)
- sustainable communities (MA)
- teaching English as a second language (MA)
- teaching English as a second language/ applied linguistics (MA, PhD, Certificate)
- teaching English as a second language/ English as a second language (Certificate)
- theory and composition (MM)
- vocal performance (MM)

College of Education
Programs in:
- bilingual education (M Ed)
- career and technical education (M Ed)
- community college/higher education (M Ed)
- community counseling (MA)
- counseling psychology (PhD)
- curriculum and instruction (Ed D)
- early childhood education (M Ed)
- education (M Ed, MA, Ed D, PhD, Certificate)
- educational foundations (M Ed)
- educational leadership (Ed D)
- educational technology (M Ed, Certificate)
- elementary education (M Ed)
- human relations (M Ed)
- learning and instruction (PhD)
- multicultural education (M Ed)
- school counseling (M Ed)
- school leadership (M Ed)
- school psychology (PhD)
- secondary education (M Ed)
- special education (M Ed)
- student affairs (M Ed)

College of Engineering, Forestry and Natural Sciences
Programs in:
- applied physics (MS)
- biological sciences (MS, PhD)
- chemistry (MS)
- civil engineering (MSE)
- computer science (MSE)
- earth science (MAT, MS)
- electrical engineering (MSE)
- engineering (M Eng, MSE)
- engineering, forestry and natural sciences (M Eng, MAT, MF, MS, MSE, MSF, PhD)
- environmental engineering (MSE)
- environmental sciences and policy (MS)
- forestry (MF, MSF, PhD)
- geology (MAT, MS)
- mathematics (MAT, MS)
- mechanical engineering (MSE)
- quaternary sciences (MS)
- science education (MAT)
- statistics (MS)

College of Health and Human Services
Programs in:
- clinical speech pathology (MS)
- family nurse practitioner (MSN)
- health and human services (M Ad, MPH, MS, MSN, DPT)
- health sciences (M Ad, MPH)
- nursing (MSN)
- nursing education (MSN)
- physical therapy (DPT)

College of Social and Behavioral Sciences
Programs in:
- applied communication (MA)
- applied criminology (MS)
- applied geographic information science (MS)
- applied health psychology (MA)
- applied sociology (MA)
- archaeology (MA)
- clinical psychology (MA)
- criminal justice policy and planning (Certificate)
- cultural anthropology (MA)
- general psychology (MA)
- geographic information systems (Certificate)
- linguistic anthropology (MA)
- political science (MA, PhD, Certificate)
- public administration (MPA)
- public management (Certificate)
- rural geography (MA)
- social and behavioral sciences (MA, MPA, MS, PhD, Certificate)
- sociology (MA)
- teaching of psychology (MA)

The W. A. Franke College of Business
Program in:
- business (MBA)

■ PRESCOTT COLLEGE

Prescott, AZ 86301

http://www.prescott.edu/

Independent, coed, comprehensive institution. *Graduate faculty:* 4 full-time (2 women), 206 part-time/adjunct (113 women). *Computer facilities:* 50 computers available on campus for general student use. A campuswide network can be accessed from student residence rooms and from off campus. *Graduate expenses:* Tuition: full-time $13,608; part-time $567 per credit. Required fees: $50 per term. One-time fee: $182. Tuition and fees vary according to degree level. *General application contact:* Lea Detweiler, Admissions Counselor, 928-350-2112.

Graduate Programs

Dr. Paul Burkhardt, Dean, Adult Degree and Graduate Programs
Programs in:
- adventure education (MA)
- adventure-based psychotherapy (MA)
- counseling psychology (MA)
- early childhood special education (MA)
- ecopsychology (MA)
- ecotherapy (MA)
- education (MA)
- elementary education (MA)
- environmental education leadership and administration (MA)
- environmental studies (MA)
- equine-assisted experiential learning (MA)
- equine-assisted mental health (MA)
- expressive arts therapy (MA)
- humanities (MA)
- school guidance counseling (MA)
- secondary education (MA)
- somatic psychology (MA)
- special education: learning disability (MA)
- special education: mental retardation (MA)
- special education: serious emotional disability (MA)
- student-directed independent study (MA)
- sustainability education (PhD)

■ THE UNIVERSITY OF ARIZONA

Tucson, AZ 85721

http://www.arizona.edu/

State-supported, coed, university. CGS member. *Graduate faculty:* 1,626. *Computer facilities:* 3,000 computers available on campus for general student use. A campuswide network can be accessed from student residence rooms and from off campus. Online class registration is available. *Graduate expenses:* Tuition, state resident: full-time $6880; part-time $420 per credit hour. Tuition, nonresident: full-time $21,592; part-time $900 per credit hour. *General application contact:* Graduate College Admissions Information Desk, 520-621-3471.

College of Medicine

Programs in:
- biochemistry (MS, PhD)
- cell biology and anatomy (PhD)
- immunobiology (MS, PhD)
- medicine (MD, MPH, MS, PhD)

College of Optical Sciences

Dr. James Wyant, Dean
Program in:
- optical sciences (MS, PhD)

Graduate College

Dr. Andrew Comrie, Dean
Programs in:
- American Indian studies (MA, PhD)
- applied mathematics (MS, PMS, PhD)
- biomedical engineering (MS, PhD)
- cancer biology (PhD)
- genetics (MS, PhD)
- insect science (MS, PhD)
- mathematical sciences (PMS)
- neuroscience (PhD)
- physiological sciences (MS, PhD)
- second language acquisition and teaching (PhD)
- statistics (MS, PhD)

College of Agriculture and Life Sciences

Dr. Eugene G. Sander, Dean
Programs in:
- agricultural and biosystems engineering (MS, PhD)
- agricultural and resource economics (MS)
- agricultural education (M Ag Ed, MS)
- agriculture and life sciences (M Ag Ed, MHE Ed, MS, PhD)
- animal sciences (MS, PhD)
- arid lands resource sciences (PhD)
- entomology (MS, PhD)
- family and consumer sciences (MS, PhD)
- family and consumer sciences education (MS)
- family studies and human development (PhD)
- microbiology (MS, PhD)
- natural resources (MS, PhD)
- nutritional sciences (MS, PhD)
- pathobiology (MS, PhD)
- plant pathology (PhD)
- plant sciences (MS, PhD)
- rangeland science and management (MS, PhD)
- retailing and consumer sciences (MS, PhD)
- soil, water and environmental science (MS, PhD)
- watershed resources (MS, PhD)
- wildlife, fisheries conservation, and management (MS, PhD)

College of Architecture and Landscape Architecture

Janice A. Cervelli, Dean
Programs in:
- architecture (M Arch)
- architecture and landscape architecture (M Arch, ML Arch, MS)
- landscape architecture (ML Arch)
- planning (MS)

College of Education

Dr. Ronald Marx, Dean
Programs in:
- bilingual education (M Ed)
- bilingual/multicultural education (MA)
- bilingual/multicultural learning disabilities (MA, Ed D, PhD)
- deaf and hard of hearing (MA, Ed D, PhD)
- education (M Ed, MA, MS, Ed D, PhD, Ed S)
- educational leadership (M Ed, Ed D, Ed S)
- educational psychology (MA, PhD, Ed S)
- gifted and talented (MA, Ed D, PhD)
- higher education (MA, PhD)
- language, reading and culture (MA, Ed D, PhD, Ed S)
- learning disabilities (MA, Ed D, PhD)
- rehabilitation (MA, PhD)
- school counseling and guidance (M Ed)
- school psychology (PhD, Ed S)
- severe and profound multiple disabilities (MA, Ed D, PhD)
- special education (MA)
- teaching and teacher education (M Ed, MA, Ed D, PhD)
- visual impairment (MA, Ed D, PhD)

College of Engineering

Dr. Thomas W. Peterson, Dean
Programs in:
- aerospace engineering (MS, PhD)
- chemical engineering (MS, PhD)
- civil engineering (MS, PhD)
- electrical and computer engineering (M Eng, MS, PhD)
- engineering (M Eng, ME, MS, PhD, Certificate)
- engineering mechanics (MS, PhD)
- environmental engineering (MS, PhD)
- geological engineering (MS, PhD)
- hydrology and water resources (MS, PhD)
- industrial engineering (MS)
- materials science and engineering (MS, PhD)
- mechanical engineering (MS, PhD)
- mine health and safety (Certificate)
- mine information and production technology (Certificate)
- mining engineering (M Eng, Certificate)
- reliability and quality engineering (MS)
- rock mechanics (Certificate)
- systems and industrial engineering (MS, PhD)
- systems engineering (MS, PhD)

College of Fine Arts

Dr. Maurice Sevigny, Dean
Programs in:
- art education (MA)
- art history (MA, PhD)

The University of Arizona (continued)
composition (MM, A Mus D)
conducting (MM, A Mus D)
fine arts (MA, MFA, MM, A Mus D, PhD)
history and theory of art (PhD)
media arts (MA)
music education (MM, PhD)
music theory (MM, PhD)
musicology (MM)
performance (MM, A Mus D)
studio art (MFA)
theatre arts (MA, MFA)

College of Humanities
Dr. Mary Wildner-Bassett, Interim Dean
Programs in:
classics (MA)
creative writing (MFA)
East Asian studies (MA, PhD)
English (MA, PhD)
French (MA)
German (MA)
humanities (MA, MFA, PhD)
rhetoric, composition and the teaching of English (PhD)
Russian (MA)
Spanish (MA, PhD)

College of Nursing
Dr. Carolyn Murdaugh, Interim Dean
Programs in:
health care informatics (Certificate)
nurse practitioner (MS, Certificate)
nursing (DNP, PhD)
rural health (Certificate)

College of Pharmacy
Dr. J. Lyle Bootman, Dean
Programs in:
medical pharmacology (MS, PhD)
medicinal and natural products chemistry (MS, PhD)
perfusion science (MS)
pharmaceutical economics (MS, PhD)
pharmaceutics and pharmacokinetics (MS, PhD)
pharmacy (Pharm D, MS, PhD)

College of Science
Dr. Joaquin Ruiz, Dean
Programs in:
applied and industrial physics (PMS)
applied biosciences (PSM)
applied science and business (PMS)
astronomy (MS, PhD)
atmospheric sciences (MS, PhD)
chemistry (MA, MS, PhD)
computer science (MS, PhD)
ecology and evolutionary biology (MS, PhD)
geosciences (MS, PhD)
mathematical sciences (PMS)
mathematics (MA, MS, PhD)
molecular and cellular biology (MS, PhD)
physics (MS, PhD)
planetary sciences (MS, PhD)
science (MA, MS, PMS, PSM, Au D, PhD)
speech, language, and hearing sciences (MS, Au D, PhD)

College of Social and Behavioral Sciences
Dr. Edward Donnerstein, Dean
Programs in:
anthropology (MA, PhD)
communication (MA, PhD)
geography (MA, PhD)
history (MA, PhD)
human language technology (MS)
information resources and library science (MA, PhD)
Latin American studies (MA)
linguistics and anthropology (PhD)
Native American linguistics (MA)
Near Eastern studies (MA, PhD)
philosophy (MA, PhD)
political science (MA, PhD)
psychology (MA, PhD)
social and behavioral sciences (MA, MS, PhD)
sociology (PhD)
theoretical linguistics (PhD)
women's studies (MA, PhD)

Eller College of Management
Dr. Paul R. Portney, Dean
Programs in:
accounting (M Ac)
business administration (MBA)
economics (MA, PhD)
finance (MS, PhD)
management (M Ac, MA, MBA, MPA, MS, PhD)
management information systems (MS)
marketing (MS, PhD)
public administration (MPA)
public administration and policy (PhD)

Mel and Enid Zuckerman College of Public Health
Dr. Iman Hakim, Interim Dean
Programs in:
biostatistics (PhD)
epidemiology (MS, PhD)
public health (MPH, Dr PH, PhD)

James E. Rogers College of Law
Toni M. Massaro, Dean
Programs in:
indigenous peoples law and policy (LL M)
international trade and business law (LL M)
law (JD)

■ UNIVERSITY OF PHOENIX
Phoenix, AZ 85034-7209
http://www.uopxonline.com/

Proprietary, coed, comprehensive institution. *Computer facilities:* Computer purchase and lease plans are available. A campuswide network can be accessed from off campus. Online class registration is available.

The Artemis School

College of Education
Programs in:
administration and supervision (MAEd)
adult education and training (MAEd)
curriculum and instruction (MAEd)
curriculum and instruction-adult education (MAEd)
curriculum and instruction-computer education (MAEd)
curriculum and instruction-English and language arts education (MAEd)
curriculum and instruction-English as a second language (MAEd)
curriculum and instruction-mathematics education (MAEd)
curriculum education (MAEd)
early childhood (MAEd)
elementary teacher education (MAEd)
secondary teacher education (MAEd)
special education (MAEd)

College of Health and Human Services
Programs in:
administration of justice and security (MS)
community counseling (MSC)
education (MHA)
family nurse practitioner (MSN)
gerontology (MHA)
health administration (MHA)
health care education (MSN)
health care management (MBA, MSN)
informatics (MHA)
marriage, family, and child therapy (MSC)
nursing (MSN)
nursing for nurse practitioners (MSN)
psychology (MS)

John Sperling School of Business
Program in:
business (MBA, MIS, MM, MSA)

College of Graduate Business and Management
Programs in:
accountancy (MSA)
accounting (MBA)
business administration (MBA)
global management (MBA)
human resources management (MBA, MM)
management (MM)
marketing (MBA)
public administration (MBA, MM)

College of Information Systems and Technology
Programs in:
e-business (MBA)
management (MIS)
technology management (MBA)

School of Advanced Studies
Programs in:
business administration (DBA)
education (Ed D)
health administration (DHA)
organizational management (DM)

■ UNIVERSITY OF PHOENIX–PHOENIX CAMPUS

Phoenix, AZ 85040-1958

http://www.phoenix.edu/

Proprietary, coed, comprehensive institution. CGS member. *Computer facilities:* Computer purchase and lease plans are available. A campuswide network can be accessed from off campus. *General application contact:* Campus Information Center, 480-804-7600.

The Artemis School

College of Education

Programs in:
- administration and supervision (MA Ed)
- adult education and training (MA Ed)
- curriculum and instruction (MA Ed)
- early childhood education (MA Ed)
- elementary teacher education (MA Ed)
- secondary teacher education (MA Ed)
- special education (MA Ed)

College of Health and Human Services

Programs in:
- community counseling (MSC)
- education (MHA)
- family nurse practitioner (MSN)
- gerontology (MHA)
- health administration (MHA)
- health care education (MSN)
- health care management (MBA)
- informatics (MHA)
- marriage, family, and child therapy (MSC)
- nurse practitioner (Certificate)
- nursing (MSN)
- nursing health care education (Certificate)
- psychology (MS)

The John Sperling School of Business

Program in:
- business (MBA, MIS, MM, MS)

College of Graduate Business and Management

Programs in:
- accountancy (MS)
- accounting (MBA)
- business administration (MBA)
- global management (MBA)
- human resources management (MBA, MM)
- management (MM)
- marketing (MBA)

College of Information Systems and Technology

Programs in:
- management (MIS)
- technology management (MBA)

■ UNIVERSITY OF PHOENIX–SOUTHERN ARIZONA CAMPUS

Tucson, AZ 85711

http://www.phoenix.edu/

Proprietary, coed, comprehensive institution. *Computer facilities:* Computer purchase and lease plans are available. A campuswide network can be accessed from off campus. Online class registration is available. *General application contact:* Campus Information Center, 520-881-6512.

The Artemis School

College of Education

Programs in:
- administration and supervision (MA Ed)
- adult education and training (MA Ed)
- curriculum instruction (MA Ed)
- educational counseling (MA Ed)
- elementary teacher education (MA Ed)
- school counseling (MSC)
- secondary teacher education (MA Ed)
- special education (MA Ed, Certificate)

College of Health and Human Services

Programs in:
- administration of justice and security (MS)
- family nurse practitioner (MSN, Certificate)
- health administration (MHA)
- health care management (MBA)
- marriage, family and child therapy (MSC)
- nursing (MSN)
- psychology (MS)

John Sperling School of Business

Program in:
- business (MBA, MIS, MM, MS)

College of Graduate Business and Management

Programs in:
- accountancy (MS)
- accounting (MBA)
- business administration (MBA)
- global management (MBA)
- human resources management (MBA)
- management (MM)
- marketing (MBA)

College of Information Systems and Technology

Programs in:
- information systems (MIS)
- technology management (MBA)

■ WESTERN INTERNATIONAL UNIVERSITY

Phoenix, AZ 85021-2718

http://www.wintu.edu/

Proprietary, coed, comprehensive institution. *Graduate faculty:* 149 part-time/adjunct (49 women). *Computer facilities:* Computer purchase and lease plans are available. 50 computers available on campus for general student use. A campuswide network can be accessed from off campus. Online class registration is available. *General application contact:* Karen Janitell, Director of Enrollment, 602-943-2311 Ext. 1063.

Graduate Programs in Business

Dr. Deborah DeSimone, Chief Academic Officer

Programs in:
- business (MA, MBA, MPA, MS)
- business administration (MBA)
- finance (MBA)
- information system engineering (MS)
- information technology (MBA)
- innovative leadership (MA)
- international business (MBA)
- management (MBA)
- marketing (MBA)
- organization development (MBA)
- public administration (MPA)

Arkansas

■ ARKANSAS STATE UNIVERSITY

Jonesboro, State University, AR 72467

http://www.astate.edu/

State-supported, coed, university. CGS member. *Graduate faculty:* 225 full-time (87 women), 60 part-time/adjunct (33 women). *Computer facilities:* Computer purchase and lease plans are available. 510 computers available on campus for general student use. A campuswide network can be accessed from student residence rooms and from off campus. Online class registration is available. *Graduate expenses:* Tuition, state resident: full-time $3744; part-time $208 per credit hour. Tuition, nonresident: full-time $9540; part-time $530 per credit hour. International tuition: $7938 full-time. Required fees: $896; $47 per credit hour. $25 per term. One-time fee: $50. Tuition and fees vary according to course load and program. *General application contact:* Dr. Andrew Sustich, Dean of the Graduate School, 870-972-3029.

Graduate School

Dr. Andrew Sustich, Dean of the Graduate School

College of Agriculture and Technology

Dr. Gregory Phillips, Dean

Programs in:
- agricultural education (MSA, SCCT)
- agriculture (MSA)
- molecular biosciences (PhD)
- vocational-technical administration (MS, SCCT)

Arkansas State University (continued)

College of Business
Dr. Len Frey, Dean
Programs in:
- accountancy (M Acc)
- business (EMBA, M Acc, MBA, MS, MSE, SCCT)
- business administration (EMBA, MBA)
- business administration education (SCCT)
- business education (SCCT)
- business technology education (MSE)
- information systems and e-commerce (MS)

College of Communications
Dr. Russell Shain, Dean
Programs in:
- communication studies and theatre arts (MA)
- communication studies and theatre arts education (SCCT)
- communications (MA, MSMC, SCCT)
- journalism (MSMC)
- radio-television (MSMC)

College of Education
Dr. Don Maness, Interim Dean
Programs in:
- college student personnel services (MS)
- community college administration education (SCCT)
- counselor education (Ed S)
- curriculum and instruction (MSE)
- early childhood education (MSE)
- early childhood services (MS)
- education (MRC, MS, MSE, Ed D, Certificate, Ed S, SCCT)
- education theory and practice (MSE)
- educational leadership (MSE, Ed D, Ed S)
- exercise science (MS)
- middle level education (MSE)
- physical education (MS, MSE, SCCT)
- reading (MSE, SCCT)
- rehabilitation counseling (MRC)
- school counseling (MSE)
- special education (MSE)
- student affairs (Certificate)

College of Engineering
Dr. Ricky Clifft, Associate Dean
Program in:
- engineering (MEM)

College of Fine Arts
Dr. Daniel Reeves, Dean
Programs in:
- art (MA)
- communication studies and theatre arts (MA)
- communication studies and theatre arts education (SCCT)
- fine arts (MA, MM, MME, SCCT)
- music education (MME, SCCT)
- performance (MM)

College of Humanities and Social Sciences
Dr. Gloria Gibson, Dean
Programs in:
- criminal justice (MA, Certificate)
- English (MA)
- English education (MSE, SCCT)
- heritage studies (MA, PhD)
- history (MA)
- history education (SCCT)
- humanities and social sciences (MA, MPA, MSE, PhD, Certificate, SCCT)
- political science (MA)
- political science education (SCCT)
- public administration (MPA)
- social science education (MSE)
- sociology (MA)
- sociology education (SCCT)

College of Nursing and Health Professions
Dr. Susan Hanrahan, Dean
Programs in:
- aging studies (Certificate)
- communication disorders (MCD)
- health sciences (MS)
- nurse anesthesia (MSN)
- nursing (MSN)
- nursing and health professions (MCD, MPT, MS, MSN, MSW, DPT, Certificate)
- physical therapy (MPT, DPT)
- social work (MSW)

College of Sciences and Mathematics
Dr. Andrew Sustich, Interim Dean
Programs in:
- biological sciences (MA)
- biology (MS)
- biology education (MSE, SCCT)
- chemistry (MS)
- chemistry education (MSE, SCCT)
- computer science (MS)
- environmental sciences (MS, PhD)
- mathematics (MS)
- mathematics education (MSE)
- sciences and mathematics (MA, MS, MSE, PhD, SCCT)

■ ARKANSAS TECH UNIVERSITY
Russellville, AR 72801
http://www.atu.edu/

State-supported, coed, comprehensive institution. *Graduate faculty:* 62 full-time (30 women), 6 part-time/adjunct (5 women). *Computer facilities:* Computer purchase and lease plans are available. 700 computers available on campus for general student use. A campuswide network can be accessed from student residence rooms and from off campus. Online class registration is available. *Graduate expenses:* Tuition, state resident: full-time $1575; part-time $175 per credit hour. Tuition, nonresident: full-time $3150; part-time $350 per credit hour. Tuition and fees vary according to course load. *General application contact:* Dr. Eldon G. Clary, Dean of Graduate School, 479-968-0398.

Graduate School
Dr. Eldon G. Clary, Dean of Graduate School

School of Community Education
Dr. Mary Ann Rollans, Dean
Program in:
- emergency management and homeland security (MS)

School of Education
Dr. C. Glenn Sheets, Dean
Programs in:
- college student personnel (MSE)
- educational leadership (M Ed, Ed S)
- English education (M Ed)
- gifted education (MSE)
- instructional improvement (M Ed)
- secondary education (M Ed)
- teaching, learning and leadership (M Ed)

School of Liberal and Fine Arts
Dr. Georgena Duncan, Dean
Programs in:
- communication (MLA)
- English (M Ed, MA)
- fine arts (MLA)
- history (MA)
- multi-media journalism (MA)
- social science (MLA)
- social studies (M Ed)
- Spanish (MA, MLA)
- teaching English as a second language (MA, MLA)

School of Physical and Life Sciences
Dr. Richard Cohoon, Dean
Programs in:
- fisheries and wildlife biology (MS)
- nursing (MSN)

School of Systems Science
Dr. William Hoefler, Dean
Programs in:
- engineering (M Engr)
- information technology (MS)
- mathematics (M Ed)

■ HARDING UNIVERSITY
Searcy, AR 72149-0001
http://www.harding.edu/

Independent-religious, coed, comprehensive institution. *Graduate faculty:* 36 full-time (11 women), 106 part-time/adjunct (41 women). *Computer facilities:* 465 computers available on campus for general student use. A campuswide network can be accessed from student residence rooms and from off campus. Online class registration is available. *Graduate expenses:* Tuition: full-time $9360; part-time $520 per credit hour. Required fees: $21 per credit hour. Tuition and fees vary according to course load and program. *General application contact:* Dr. Cheri Yecke, Dean of Graduate Programs, 501-279-4335.

College of Bible and Religion
Dr. Monte Cox, Dean
Programs in:
- Bible and religion (M Min, MS)
- marriage and family therapy (MS)
- mental health counseling (MS)
- ministry (M Min)

College of Business Administration
Glen Metheny, Director of Graduate Studies
Programs in:
accounting (MBA)
health care management (MBA)
information technology (MBA)
international business (MBA)
leadership and organizational management (MBA)

College of Communication
Dr. Rebecca O. Weaver, Chair, Department of Communication Sciences and Disorders/Graduate Program Director
Program in:
speech-language pathology (MS)

College of Education
Pat Bashaw, Chair
Programs in:
advanced studies in teaching and learning (M Ed)
art (MSE)
behavioral science (MSE)
counseling (MS, Ed S)
early childhood special education (M Ed, MSE)
education (MSE)
educational leadership (M Ed, Ed S)
elementary education (M Ed)
English (MSE)
family and consumer science (MSE)
French (MSE)
history/social science (MSE)
kinesiology (MSE)
math (MSE)
physical science (MSE)
reading (M Ed)
secondary education (M Ed)
Spanish (MSE)
special education licensure (M Ed)
teaching (MAT)
teaching English as a second language (M Ed)

College of Pharmacy
Dr. Julie Ann Hixson-Wallace, Dean
Program in:
pharmacy (Pharm D)

College of Sciences
Michael Murphy, Director
Program in:
physician assistant studies (MS)

■ HENDERSON STATE UNIVERSITY

Arkadelphia, AR 71999-0001

http://www.hsu.edu/

State-supported, coed, comprehensive institution. CGS member. *Graduate faculty:* 70 full-time (25 women), 14 part-time/adjunct (4 women). *Computer facilities:* 125 computers available on campus for general student use. A campuswide network can be accessed from student residence rooms and from off campus. Online class registration is available. *Graduate expenses:* Tuition, state resident: full-time $2448; part-time $204 per credit hour. Tuition, nonresident: full-time $4896; part-time $408 per credit hour. Required fees: $754. Tuition and fees vary according to course load. *General application contact:* Dr. Marck L. Beggs, Graduate Dean, 870-230-5126.

Graduate Studies
Dr. Marck L. Beggs, Graduate Dean

Ellis College of Arts and Sciences
Dr. Maralyn Sommer, Dean
Program in:
arts and sciences (MLA)

School of Business Administration
Dr. Margaret Hoskins, Interim Dean
Program in:
business administration (MBA)

School of Education
Dr. Judy Harrison, Dean
Programs in:
community counseling (MS)
early childhood (P-4) (MSE)
education (MAT)
educational leadership (Ed S)
elementary school counseling (MSE)
middle school (MSE)
reading (MSE)
recreation (MS)
school administration (MSE)
secondary school counseling (MSE)
special education (MSE)
sports administration (MS)

■ JOHN BROWN UNIVERSITY

Siloam Springs, AR 72761-2121

http://www.jbu.edu/

Independent-religious, coed, comprehensive institution. *Graduate faculty:* 11 full-time (2 women), 43 part-time/adjunct (10 women). *Computer facilities:* 100 computers available on campus for general student use. A campuswide network can be accessed from student residence rooms and from off campus. Online class registration is available. *Graduate expenses:* Tuition: full-time $7740; part-time $430 per credit hour. *General application contact:* Lori Walker, Director of Recruitment, Graduate and Professional Studies, 479-524-7343.

Graduate Business Division
Dr. Joe Walenciak, Program Director
Programs in:
business administration (MBA)
leadership and ethics (MS)

Graduate Counseling Division
Dr. John V. Carmack, Program Director
Programs in:
community counseling (MS)
marriage and family therapy (MS)
school counseling (MS)

Graduate Studies Division of Christian Ministry
Dr. Dan Lambert, Director
Programs in:
leadership and ethics (MA)
ministry leadership (MA)
pastoral counseling (MA)
youth ministry (MA)

■ UNIVERSITY OF ARKANSAS

Fayetteville, AR 72701-1201

http://www.uark.edu/

State-supported, coed, university. CGS member. *Graduate faculty:* 655 full-time (169 women), 13 part-time/adjunct (2 women). *Computer facilities:* Computer purchase and lease plans are available. 2,457 computers available on campus for general student use. A campuswide network can be accessed from student residence rooms and from off campus. Online class registration is available. *General application contact:* Lynn Mosesso, Director of Graduate and International Recruitment and Admissions, 479-575-6246.

Graduate School
Dr. Patricia R. Koski, Associate Dean
Programs in:
cell and molecular biology (MS, PhD)
classical studies (MA)
comparative literature (PhD)
environmental dynamics (PhD)
microelectronics and photonics (MS, PhD)
public policy (PhD)
space and planetary sciences (MS, PhD)

College of Education and Health Professions
Dr. M. Reed Greenwood, Dean
Programs in:
childhood education (MAT)
communication disorders (MS)
counseling (MS, PhD, Ed S)
curriculum and instruction (M Ed, MAT, MS, Ed D, PhD, Ed S)
education and health professions (M Ed, MAT, MS, MSN, Ed D, PhD, Ed S)
education policy (PhD)
educational leadership (M Ed, Ed D, Ed S)
educational statistics and research methods (MS, PhD)
educational technology (M Ed)
elementary education (M Ed, Ed S)
health science (MS, PhD)
higher education (M Ed, Ed D, Ed S)
kinesiology (MS, PhD)
middle-level education (MAT)
nursing (MSN)
physical education (M Ed, MAT)
recreation (M Ed, Ed D)
rehabilitation (MS, PhD)
secondary education (M Ed, MAT, Ed S)
special education (M Ed, MAT)
vocational education (MAT)
workforce development education (M Ed, Ed D)

College of Engineering
Ashok Saxena, Dean

University of Arkansas (continued)
Programs in:
biological and agricultural engineering (MSE, PhD)
biological engineering (MSBE)
biomedical engineering (MSBME)
chemical engineering (MS Ch E, MSE, PhD)
civil engineering (MS En E, MSCE, MSE, MSTE, PhD)
computer engineering (MS Cmp E, MSE, PhD)
computer science (MS, PhD)
electrical engineering (MSEE, PhD)
engineering (MS, MS Cmp E, MS Ch E, MS En E, MS Tc E, MSBE, MSBME, MSCE, MSE, MSEE, MSIE, MSME, MSOR, MSTE, PhD)
environmental engineering (MS En E, MSE)
industrial engineering (MS, MSE, MSIE, MSOR, PhD)
mechanical engineering (MSE, MSME, PhD)
operations management (MS)
operations research (MSE, MSOR)
telecommunications engineering (MS Tc E)
transportation engineering (MSE, MSTE)

Dale Bumpers College of Agricultural, Food and Life Sciences
Dr. Lalit Verma, Dean
Programs in:
agricultural and extension education (MS)
agricultural economics (MS)
agricultural, food and life sciences (MS, PhD)
agronomy (MS, PhD)
animal science (MS, PhD)
entomology (MS, PhD)
food science (MS, PhD)
horticulture (MS)
human environmental sciences (MS)
plant pathology (MS)
plant science (PhD)
poultry science (MS, PhD)

J. William Fulbright College of Arts and Sciences
Dr. Bill Schwab, Dean
Programs in:
anthropology (MA, PhD)
applied physics (MS)
art (MFA)
arts and sciences (MA, MFA, MM, MPA, MS, MSW, PhD)
biological sciences (MA, MS, PhD)
chemistry (MS, PhD)
communication (MA)
creative writing (MFA)
drama (MA, MFA)
English (MA, PhD)
French (MA)
geography (MA)
geology (MS)
German (MA)
history (MA, PhD)
journalism (MA)
mathematics (MS, PhD)
music (MM)
philosophy (MA, PhD)
physics (MS, PhD)
physics education (MA)
political science (MA, MPA)
psychology (MA, PhD)
public administration (MPA)
secondary mathematics (MA)
social work (MSW)
sociology (MA)
Spanish (MA)
statistics (MS)
translation (MFA)

Sam M. Walton College of Business Administration
Dr. Dan Worrell, Dean
Programs in:
accounting (M Acc)
business administration (M Acc, MA, MBA, MIS, PhD)
economics (MA, PhD)
information systems (MIS)

School of Law
Cynthia Nance, Dean
Programs in:
agricultural law (LL M)
law (JD)

■ UNIVERSITY OF ARKANSAS AT LITTLE ROCK

Little Rock, AR 72204-1099
http://www.ualr.edu/

State-supported, coed, university. CGS member. *Computer facilities:* 500 computers available on campus for general student use. A campuswide network can be accessed from off campus. *General application contact:* Dean of the Graduate School, 501-569-3206.

Graduate School

Clinton School of Public Service
Program in:
public service (MPS, Graduate Certificate)

College of Arts, Humanities, and Social Science
Programs in:
applied psychology (MAP)
art education (MA)
art history (MA)
arts, humanities, and social science (MA, MALS, MAP, Graduate Certificate)
gerontology (Graduate Certificate)
philosophy and liberal studies (MALS)
professional and technical writing (MA)
public history (MA)
second languages (MA)
studio art (MA)

College of Business Administration
Programs in:
accountancy (M Acc, Graduate Certificate)
business administration (MBA)
construction management (Graduate Certificate)
management (Graduate Certificate)
management information system (MIS)
management information systems (Graduate Certificate)
management information systems leadership (Graduate Certificate)
taxation (MS, Graduate Certificate)

College of Education
Programs in:
adult education (M Ed)
college student affairs (MA)
counselor education (M Ed)
early childhood education (M Ed)
education (M Ed, MA, Ed D, Ed S, Graduate Certificate)
educational administration (M Ed, Ed D, Ed S)
educational administration and supervision (Ed D)
higher education administration (Ed D)
higher education: two-year college teaching (MA)
learning systems technology (M Ed)
literacy coach (Graduate Certificate)
middle childhood education (M Ed)
orientation and mobility of the blind (Graduate Certificate)
reading (M Ed, Ed S)
reading education (M Ed, Ed S, Graduate Certificate)
rehabilitation counseling (MA, Graduate Certificate)
rehabilitation of the blind (MA)
school counseling (M Ed)
secondary education (M Ed)
special education (M Ed)
teaching advanced placement (Graduate Certificate)
teaching deaf and hard of hearing (M Ed)
teaching the gifted and talented (M Ed)
teaching the visually impaired (M Ed)

College of Professional Studies
Programs in:
advanced direct practice (MSW)
applied communication studies (MA)
conflict mediation (Graduate Certificate)
criminal justice (MA, MS, PhD)
health sciences (MS)
journalism (MA)
management and community practice (MSW)
marriage and family therapy (Graduate Certificate)
nonprofit management (Graduate Certificate)
professional studies (MA, MPA, MS, MSW, Graduate Certificate)
public administration (MPA)
social work (MSW, Graduate Certificate)

College of Science and Mathematics
Programs in:
applied statistics (Graduate Certificate)
biology (MS)
chemistry (MA, MS)
geospatial technology (Graduate Certificate)
integrated science and mathematics (MS)
mathematical sciences (MS)
science and mathematics (MA, MS, Graduate Certificate)

George W. Donughey College of Engineering and Information Technology
Programs in:
applied science (MS, PhD)
bioinformatics (MS, PhD)
computer and information science (MS)
engineering and information technology (MS, PhD, Graduate Certificate)
information quality (MS)
systems engineering (Graduate Certificate)

William H. Bowen School of Law
Program in:
law (JD)

■ UNIVERSITY OF ARKANSAS AT MONTICELLO

Monticello, AR 71656
http://www.uamont.edu/

State-supported, coed, comprehensive institution. *Computer facilities:* 400 computers available on campus for general student use. A campuswide network can be accessed from student residence rooms and from off campus. Online class registration is available. *General application contact:* Director, Office of Admissions, 870-460-1026.

School of Education
Programs in:
education (M Ed, MAT)
educational leadership (M Ed)

School of Forest Resources
Program in:
forest resources (MS)

■ UNIVERSITY OF CENTRAL ARKANSAS

Conway, AR 72035-0001
http://www.uca.edu/

State-supported, coed, university. CGS member. *Computer facilities:* 608 computers available on campus for general student use. A campuswide network can be accessed from student residence rooms and from off campus. Online class registration is available. *General application contact:* Admissions Assistant, 501-450-5065.

Graduate School

College of Business Administration
Programs in:
accounting (M Acc)
business administration (M Acc, MBA, MS)
community and economic development (MS)

College of Education
Programs in:
collaborative instructional specialist (ages 0–8) (MSE)
collaborative instructional specialist (grades 4–12) (MSE)
college student personnel (MS)
early childhood education (MSE)
education (MAT, MS, MSE, Ed S)
education media and library science (MS)
educational leadership—district level (Ed S)
elementary school counseling (MS)
reading education (MSE)
school counseling (MS)
school leadership (MS)
secondary school counseling (MS)
special education (MSE)
teaching (MAT)
teaching and learning (MSE)
training systems (MS)

College of Fine Arts and Communication
Programs in:
choral conducting (MM)
digital filmmaking (MFA)
fine arts and communication (MFA, MM)
instrumental conducting (MM)
music education (MM)
music theory (MM)
performance (MM)

College of Health and Behavioral Sciences
Programs in:
clinical nurse specialist (MSN)
communication sciences and disorders (PhD)
community service counseling (MS)
counseling psychology (MS)
family and consumer sciences (MS)
health and behavioral sciences (MS, MSN, DPT, PhD)
health education (MS)
health systems (MS)
kinesiology (MS)
nurse practitioner (MSN)
occupational therapy (MS)
physical therapy (DPT, PhD)
school psychology (MS, PhD)
speech-language pathology (MS)

College of Liberal Arts
Programs in:
English (MA)
foreign languages (MA)
geographic information systems (MGIS, Certificate)
history (MA)
liberal arts (MA, MGIS, Certificate)

College of Natural Sciences and Math
Programs in:
applied computing (MS)
applied mathematics (MS)
biological science (MS)
math education (MA)
natural sciences and math (MA, MS)

California

■ ALLIANT INTERNATIONAL UNIVERSITY–SAN DIEGO

San Diego, CA 92131-1799
http://www.alliant.edu/

Independent, coed, graduate-only institution. *Computer facilities:* 55 computers available on campus for general student use. A campuswide network can be accessed from student residence rooms and from off campus. Online class registration is available. *General application contact:* Alliant International University Central Contact Center, 866-U-ALLIANT.

California School of Professional Psychology
Programs in:
clinical psychology (PhD, Psy D)
marital and family therapy (MA, Psy D)
professional psychology (MA, PhD, Psy D)

Graduate School of Education
Programs in:
education (MA, Ed D, Psy D, Certificate, Credential)
educational administration (MA)
educational leadership and management (K-12) (Ed D)
educational psychology (Psy D)
higher education (Ed D, Certificate)
preliminary administrative services (Credential)
preliminary single subject (Credential)
professional clear multiple subject (Credential)
professional clear single subject (Credential)
pupil personnel services (Credential)
school psychology (MA)
student personnel services (Certificate)
teacher education (MA)
teaching English to speakers of other languages (MA, Ed D, Certificate)

Marshall Goldsmith School of Management
Program in:
management (MA, MBA, MIBA, MS, DBA, PhD)

Alliant International University–San Diego (continued)

Business and Management Division
Programs in:
business administration (MBA)
information and technology management (DBA)
international business (MIBA, DBA)
strategic business (DBA)
sustainable management (MBA)

International Studies Division
Program in:
international relations (MA)

Organizational Psychology Division
Programs in:
clinical/industrial organizational psychology (PhD)
consulting psychology (PhD)
industrial/organizational psychology (MA, MS, PhD)
organizational behavior (MA)

■ ANTIOCH UNIVERSITY LOS ANGELES
Culver City, CA 90230
http://www.antiochla.edu/

Independent, coed, upper-level institution. *Computer facilities:* 12 computers available on campus for general student use. A campuswide network can be accessed from off campus. Online class registration is available. *General application contact:* Information Contact, 310-578-1090.

Graduate Programs
Programs in:
clinical psychology (MA)
creative writing (MFA)
education (MA)
human resource development (MA)
leadership (MA)
organizational development (MA)
pedagogy of creative writing (Certificate)
psychology (MA)

■ ANTIOCH UNIVERSITY SANTA BARBARA
Santa Barbara, CA 93101-1581
http://www.antiochsb.edu/

Independent, coed, upper-level institution. *Graduate faculty:* 13 full-time (9 women), 42 part-time/adjunct (21 women). *Computer facilities:* 14 computers available on campus for general student use. A campuswide network can be accessed from off campus. Online class registration is available. *Graduate expenses:* Tuition: full-time $17,025; part-time $570 per unit. Required fees: $26. Tuition and fees vary according to course load, degree level and program. *General application contact:* Steve Weir, Director of Marketing and Enrollment Management, 805-962-8179 Ext. 152.

Program in Clinical Psychology
Dr. Michele Harway, Director
Program in:
clinical psychology (Psy D)

Program in Education/Teacher Credentialing
Michele Britton Bass, Chair
Program in:
education/teacher credentialing (MA)

Program in Organizational Management
Dr. Esther Lopez-Mulnix, Chair
Program in:
organizational management (MA)

Program in Psychology
Dr. Catherine Radecki-Bush, Chair
Program in:
psychology (MA)

■ ARGOSY UNIVERSITY, ORANGE COUNTY
Santa Ana, CA 92704
http://www.argosy.edu/orangecounty/

Proprietary, coed, university. CGS member.

College of Business
Programs in:
accounting (DBA, Adv C)
customized professional concentration (MBA, DBA)
finance (MBA, Certificate)
healthcare administration (MBA)
information systems (DBA, Adv C)
information systems management (MBA)
international business (MBA, DBA, Adv C, Certificate)
management (MBA, MSM, DBA, Adv C)
marketing (MBA, DBA, Adv C, Certificate)
public administration (MBA, Certificate)

College of Education
Programs in:
community college executive leadership (Ed D)
educational leadership (MA Ed, Ed D)
instructional leadership (MA Ed, Ed D)

College of Psychology and Behavioral Sciences
Programs in:
child and adolescent psychology (Psy D)
counseling psychology (Ed D)
forensic psychology (MA)
marriage and family therapy (MA)
organizational leadership (Ed D)
psychology and behavioral sciences (MA, Ed D, Psy D, Postdoctoral Respecialization Certificate)
sport-exercise psychology (MA)

■ AZUSA PACIFIC UNIVERSITY
Azusa, CA 91702-7000
http://www.apu.edu/

Independent-religious, coed, university. CGS member. *Graduate faculty:* 115 full-time (64 women), 9 part-time/adjunct (1 woman). *Computer facilities:* Computer purchase and lease plans are available. 300 computers available on campus for general student use. A campuswide network can be accessed from off campus. Online class registration is available. *Graduate expenses:* Tuition: full-time $9180; part-time $510 per unit. Required fees: $700; $700 per year. Tuition and fees vary according to degree level and program. *General application contact:* Linda Witte, Graduate Admissions Office, 626-969-3434.

College of Liberal Arts and Sciences
Programs in:
fine arts in visual art (MFA)
liberal arts and sciences (MA, MFA)
teaching English to speakers of other languages (MA)

Haggard School of Theology
Programs in:
Christian education (MAR)
Christian non-profit leadership (MA)
divinity (M Div)
ministry (D Min)
ministry management (MAMM)
pastoral studies (MAPS)
religion: Biblical studies (MAR)
religion: theology and ethics (MAR)
theology (M Div, MA, MAMM, MAPS, MAR, MAWL, D Min)
worship leadership (MAWL)

School of Behavioral and Applied Sciences
Programs in:
behavioral and applied sciences (M Ed, MA, MLOS, DPT, Ed D, Psy D)
clinical psychology (MA, Psy D)
college student affairs (M Ed)
entry-level (DPT)
higher education leadership (Ed D)
leadership and organizational studies (MLOS)
organizational leadership (MA)
transitional (DPT)

School of Business and Management
Programs in:
business administration (MBA)
human and organizational development (MA)
international business (MBA)
strategic management (MBA)

School of Education
Programs in:
curriculum and instruction in a multicultural setting (MA)
education (M Ed, MA, Ed D)
educational counseling (MA)
educational leadership (Ed D)
educational psychology (MA)
educational technology (M Ed)
language development (MA)
physical education (M Ed)
pupil personnel services (MA)
school administration (MA)
school librarianship (MA)
special education (MA)
teaching (MA)

School of Music
Programs in:
education (M Mus)
performance (M Mus)

School of Nursing
Programs in:
nursing (MSN)
nursing education (PhD)

■ BIOLA UNIVERSITY
La Mirada, CA 90639-0001
http://www.biola.edu/

Independent-religious, coed, university. *Computer facilities:* 165 computers available on campus for general student use. A campuswide network can be accessed from student residence rooms and from off campus. Online class registration is available. *General application contact:* Director of Graduate Admissions, 562-903-4752.

Crowell School of Business
Program in:
business (MBA)

Rosemead School of Psychology
Program in:
psychology (MA, PhD, Psy D)

School of Arts and Sciences
Program in:
arts and sciences (MA Ed)

School of Intercultural Studies
Programs in:
applied linguistics (MA)
intercultural education (PhD)
intercultural studies (MAICS)
missiology (D Miss)
missions (MA)
teaching English to speakers of other languages (MA, Certificate)

School of Professional Studies
Programs in:
Christian apologetics (MA)
organizational leadership (MA)

Talbot School of Theology
Programs in:
Bible exposition (MA)
biblical and theological studies (MA)
Christian education (MACE)
Christian ministry and leadership (MA)
divinity (M Div)
education (PhD)
ministry (MA Min)
New Testament (MA)
Old Testament (MA)
philosophy of religion and ethics (MA)
spiritual formation (MA)
spiritual formation and soul care (MA)
theology (MA, Th M, D Min)

■ CALIFORNIA BAPTIST UNIVERSITY
Riverside, CA 92504-3206
http://www.calbaptist.edu/

Independent-religious, coed, comprehensive institution. *Graduate faculty:* 47 full-time (23 women), 23 part-time/adjunct (11 women). *Computer facilities:* Computer purchase and lease plans are available. 279 computers available on campus for general student use. A campuswide network can be accessed from student residence rooms and from off campus. Online class registration is available. *Graduate expenses:* Tuition: full-time $8172; part-time $454 per credit hour. Required fees: $510. *General application contact:* Gail Ronveaux, Dean of Graduate Enrollment, 951-343-5045.

Program in Athletic Training
Dr. Nicole MacDonald, Director
Program in:
athletic training (MS)

Program in Business Administration
Dr. Andrew Herrity, Dean, School of Business
Program in:
management (MBA)

Program in Counseling Ministry
Dr. Nathan Lewis, Director
Program in:
counseling ministry (MA)

Program in Counseling Psychology
Dr. Gary Collins, Director and Associate Dean, School of Business
Programs in:
professional counseling (MS)
professional ministry (MS)

Program in Education
Dr. Mary Crist, Dean, School of Education
Programs in:
cross-cultural language and academic development (MA)
educational leadership (MS)
educational leadership and faith-based instruction (MS)
educational technology (MS)
instructional computer applications (MS)
reading (MS)
school counseling (MS)
school psychology (MS)
special education (MS)
special education in mild/moderate disabilities (MS)
special education in moderate/severe disabilities (MS)
teaching (MS)
teaching and learning (MS Ed)

Program in English
Dr. Jennifer Newton, Director
Programs in:
English pedagogy (MA)
literature (MA)
teaching English as a second language (TESOL) (MA)

Program in Forensic Psychology
Dr. Anne-Marie Larsen, Director
Program in:
forensic psychology (MA)

Program in Kinesiology
Dr. Sean Sullivan, Chair, Department of Kinesiology
Programs in:
physical education pedagogy (MS)
sport management (MS)

Program in Music
Dr. Gary Bonner, Dean, School of Music
Programs in:
conducting (MM)
music education (MM)
performance (MM)

Program in Nursing
Dr. Constance Milton, Dean, School of Nursing
Program in:
nursing (MS)

Program in Public Administration
Dr. Patricia Kircher, Director
Program in:
public administration (MPA)

■ CALIFORNIA INSTITUTE OF INTEGRAL STUDIES
San Francisco, CA 94103
http://www.ciis.edu/

Independent, coed, upper-level institution. CGS member. *Graduate faculty:* 57 full-time, 91 part-time/adjunct. *Computer facilities:* A campuswide network can be accessed from off campus. *Graduate expenses:* Tuition: part-time $815 per contact hour. Required fees: $135 per semester. Tuition and fees vary according to degree level. *General application contact:* Cori Watkins, Admissions Inquiries Coordinator, 415-575-6151.

California Institute of Integral Studies (continued)

School of Consciousness and Transformation

Programs in:
- cultural anthropology and social transformation (MA)
- East-West psychology (MA, PhD)
- integrative health studies (MA)
- philosophy and religion (MA, PhD)
- social and cultural anthropology (PhD)
- transformative leadership (MA)
- transformative studies (PhD)

School of Professional Psychology

Programs in:
- clinical psychology (Psy D)
- community mental health (MA)
- drama therapy (MA)
- expressive arts therapy (MA)
- integral counseling psychology (MA)
- integral counseling, psychology-weekend (MA)
- somatic psychology (MA)

■ CALIFORNIA INSTITUTE OF TECHNOLOGY

Pasadena, CA 91125-0001

http://www.caltech.edu/

Independent, coed, university. CGS member. *Computer facilities:* Computer purchase and lease plans are available. 600 computers available on campus for general student use. A campuswide network can be accessed from student residence rooms and from off campus. Online class registration is available. *General application contact:* Graduate Office, 626-395-3812.

Division of Biology

Programs in:
- biochemistry and molecular biophysics (MS, PhD)
- cell biology and biophysics (PhD)
- developmental biology (PhD)
- genetics (PhD)
- immunology (PhD)
- molecular biology (PhD)
- neurobiology (PhD)

Division of Chemistry and Chemical Engineering

Prof. Jacqueline K. Barton, Chair

Programs in:
- biochemistry and molecular biophysics (MS, PhD)
- chemical engineering (MS, PhD)
- chemistry (MS, PhD)

Division of Engineering and Applied Science

Programs in:
- aeronautics (MS, PhD, Engr)
- applied and computational mathematics (MS, PhD)
- applied mechanics (MS, PhD)
- applied physics (MS, PhD)
- bioengineering (MS, PhD)
- civil engineering (MS, PhD, Engr)
- computation and neural systems (MS, PhD)
- computer science (MS, PhD)
- control and dynamical systems (MS, PhD)
- electrical engineering (MS, PhD, Engr)
- environmental science and engineering (MS, PhD)
- materials science (MS, PhD)
- mechanical engineering (MS, PhD, Engr)

Division of Geological and Planetary Sciences

Dr. Kenneth A. Farley, Chairman

Programs in:
- geobiology (PhD)
- geochemistry (MS, PhD)
- geology (MS, PhD)
- geophysics (MS, PhD)
- planetary science (MS, PhD)

Division of Physics, Mathematics and Astronomy

Programs in:
- astronomy (PhD)
- mathematics (PhD)
- physics (PhD)

Division of the Humanities and Social Sciences

Programs in:
- humanities and social sciences (MS, PhD)
- social science (MS, PhD)

■ CALIFORNIA LUTHERAN UNIVERSITY

Thousand Oaks, CA 91360-2787

http://www.callutheran.edu/

Independent-religious, coed, comprehensive institution. CGS member. *Graduate faculty:* 34 full-time (18 women), 80 part-time/adjunct (42 women). *Computer facilities:* 300 computers available on campus for general student use. A campuswide network can be accessed from student residence rooms and from off campus. Online class registration is available. *General application contact:* Information Contact, 805-493-3127.

Graduate Studies

Dr. Leanne Neilson, Provost/Vice President for Academic Affairs

Programs in:
- clinical psychology (MS, Psy D)
- marital and family therapy (MS)
- public policy and administration (MPPA)

School of Business

Dr. Ronald Hagler, Director

Programs in:
- business (IMBA)
- entrepreneurship (MBA, Certificate)
- finance (MBA, Certificate)
- financial planning (MBA, Certificate)
- information systems and technology (MS)
- information technology management (MBA, Certificate)
- international business (MBA, Certificate)
- management and organization behavior (MBA)
- management and organizational behavior (Certificate)
- marketing (MBA, Certificate)

School of Education

Dr. Carol Bartell, Dean

Programs in:
- counseling and guidance (MS)
- curriculum and instruction (MA)
- educational leadership (MA, Ed D)
- educational leadership (k-12) (Ed D)
- higher education leadership (Ed D)
- reading education (MA)
- special education (MS)
- teaching (M Ed)

■ CALIFORNIA POLYTECHNIC STATE UNIVERSITY, SAN LUIS OBISPO

San Luis Obispo, CA 93407

http://www.calpoly.edu/

State-supported, coed, comprehensive institution. CGS member. *Graduate faculty:* 168 full-time (40 women), 30 part-time/adjunct (12 women). *Computer facilities:* A campuswide network can be accessed from student residence rooms and from off campus. Online class registration is available. *Graduate expenses:* Tuition, nonresident: full-time $10,170; part-time $226 per unit. Required fees: $5751; $1265 per quarter. *General application contact:* Dr. James Maraviglia, Assistant Vice President for Admissions, Recruitment and Financial Aid, 805-756-2311.

College of Agriculture, Food and Environmental Sciences

Dr. David J. Wehner, Dean

Programs in:
- agribusiness (MS)
- agriculture (MS)
- agriculture, food and environmental sciences (MS)
- forestry sciences (MS)

College of Architecture and Environmental Design

R. Thomas Jones, Dean

Programs in:
- architecture (MS)
- architecture and environmental design (MCRP, MS)
- city and regional planning (MCRP)

College of Education

Dr. Bonnie Konopak, Dean

Program in:
- education (MA)

College of Engineering
Dr. Mohammad Noori, Dean
Programs in:
aerospace engineering (MS)
civil and environmental engineering (MS)
computer science (MS)
electrical engineering (MS)
engineering (MS)
general engineering (MS)
industrial engineering (MS)
mechanical engineering (MS)

College of Liberal Arts
Dr. Linda Halisky, Dean
Programs in:
English (MA)
history (MA)
liberal arts (MA, MPP, MS)
political science (MPP)
psychology (MS)

College of Science and Mathematics
Dr. Philip S. Bailey, Dean
Programs in:
biological sciences (MS)
kinesiology (MS)
mathematics (MS)
polymers and coating science (MS)
science and mathematics (MS)

Orfalea College of Business
Dr. David P. Christy, Dean
Programs in:
business (MBA)
industrial and technical studies (MS)
taxation (MSA)

■ CALIFORNIA STATE POLYTECHNIC UNIVERSITY, POMONA

Pomona, CA 91768-2557
http://www.csupomona.edu/

State-supported, coed, comprehensive institution. CGS member. *Graduate faculty:* 559 full-time (238 women), 456 part-time/adjunct (171 women). *Computer facilities:* Computer purchase and lease plans are available. 1,850 computers available on campus for general student use. A campuswide network can be accessed from student residence rooms and from off campus. Online class registration is available. *Graduate expenses:* Tuition, nonresident: full-time $7232; part-time $226 per credit. Required fees: $4272. One-time fee: $2694 part-time. Tuition and fees vary according to course load. *General application contact:* Scott J. Duncan, Director, Admissions, 909-869-3258.

Academic Affairs
Dr. Marten L. denBoer, Provost/Vice President for Academic Affairs

College of Agriculture
Dr. Lester C. Young, Interim Dean
Program in:
agriculture (MS)

College of Business Administration
Dr. Lynn H. Turner, Interim Dean
Program in:
business administration (MBA, MSBA, PMBA)

College of Education and Integrative Studies
Dr. Peggy Kelly, Dean
Program in:
education and integrative studies (MA)

College of Engineering
Dr. Edward Hohmann, Dean
Programs in:
civil engineering (MS)
electrical engineering (MSEE)
engineering (MSE)
engineering management (MS)
mechanical engineering (MS)

College of Environmental Design
Dr. Kyle D. Brown, Interim Dean
Programs in:
architecture (M Arch)
environmental design (M Arch, M Land Arch, MS, MURP)
landscape architecture (M Land Arch)
regenerative studies (MS)
urban and regional planning (MURP)

College of Letters, Arts, and Social Sciences
Dr. Carol P. Richardson, Dean
Programs in:
economics (MS)
English (MA)
history (MA)
kinesiology (MS)
letters, arts, and social sciences (MA, MPA, MS)
psychology (MS)
public administration (MPA)

College of Science
Dr. Donald O. Straney, Dean
Programs in:
applied mathematics (MS)
biological sciences (MS)
chemistry (MS)
computer science (MS)
pure mathematics (MS)
science (MS)

■ CALIFORNIA STATE UNIVERSITY, BAKERSFIELD

Bakersfield, CA 93311-1022
http://www.csubak.edu/

State-supported, coed, comprehensive institution. *Computer facilities:* 600 computers available on campus for general student use. A campuswide network can be accessed from student residence rooms and from off campus. Online class registration is available. *General application contact:* Associate Dean, 661-664-2161.

Division of Graduate Studies
Programs in:
administration (MS)
interdisciplinary studies (MA)

School of Business and Public Administration
Programs in:
business administration (MBA)
business and public administration (MBA, MPA, MSA)
health care management (MSA)
public administration (MPA)

School of Education
Programs in:
bilingual/multicultural education (MA Ed)
curriculum and instruction (MA Ed)
early childhood education (MA)
education (MA, MA Ed, MS, Certificate)
educational administration (MA)
educational technology (MA Ed)
reading/literacy (MA Ed, Certificate)
school counseling (MS)
special education (MA)
student affairs (MS)

School of Humanities and Social Sciences
Programs in:
anthropology (MA)
counseling psychology (MS)
English (MA)
history (MA)
humanities and social sciences (MA, MS, MSW)
psychology (MA)
social work (MSW)
sociology (MA)
Spanish (MA)

School of Natural Sciences and Mathematics
Programs in:
biology (MS)
geology (MS)
hydrogeology (MS)
natural sciences and mathematics (MA, MS)
nursing (MS)
petroleum geology (MS)
teaching mathematics (MA)

■ CALIFORNIA STATE UNIVERSITY, CHICO

Chico, CA 95929-0722
http://www.csuchico.edu/

State-supported, coed, comprehensive institution. CGS member. *Computer facilities:* Computer purchase and lease plans are available. 1,167 computers available on campus for general student use. A campuswide network can be accessed from student residence rooms and from off campus. Online class registration, student account information, calendar, transcripts are available. *General application contact:* School of Graduate, International, and Interdisciplinary Studies, 530-898-6880.

California State University, Chico (continued)

Graduate School
Programs in:
- interdisciplinary studies (MA, MS)
- science teaching (MS)
- simulation science (MS)
- teaching international languages (MA)

College of Behavioral and Social Sciences
Programs in:
- applied psychology (MA)
- behavioral and social sciences (MA, MPA, MS, MSW)
- geography (MA)
- health administration (MPA)
- local government management (MPA)
- marriage and family therapy (MS)
- museum studies (MA)
- political science (MA)
- psychological science (MA)
- psychology (MA)
- public administration (MPA)
- rural and town planning (MA)
- social science (MA)
- social science education (MA)
- social work (MSW)

College of Business
Programs in:
- business (MBA)
- business administration (MBA)

College of Communication and Education
Programs in:
- communication and education (MA)
- communication science and disorders (MA)
- communication studies (MA)
- curriculum and instruction (MA)
- education (MA)
- kinesiology (MA)
- linguistically and culturally diverse learners (MA)
- reading/language arts (MA)
- recreation administration (MA)
- special education (MA)

College of Engineering, Computer Science, and Technology
Programs in:
- computer engineering (MS)
- computer science (MS)
- electronics engineering (MS)
- engineering, computer science, and technology (MS)

College of Humanities and Fine Arts
Programs in:
- art history (MA)
- English (MA)
- fine arts (MFA)
- history (MA)
- humanities and fine arts (MA, MFA)
- music (MA)

College of Natural Sciences
Programs in:
- biological sciences (MS)
- botany (MS)
- environmental science (MS)
- geosciences (MS)
- hydrology/hydrogeology (MS)
- math education (MS)
- natural sciences (MS)
- nursing (MS)
- nutrition education (MS)
- nutritional sciences (MS)

■ CALIFORNIA STATE UNIVERSITY, DOMINGUEZ HILLS

Carson, CA 90747-0001

http://www.csudh.edu/

State-supported, coed, comprehensive institution. CGS member. *Graduate faculty:* 112 full-time (70 women), 143 part-time/adjunct (107 women). *Computer facilities:* 256 computers available on campus for general student use. A campuswide network can be accessed from student residence rooms. Online class registration is available. *Graduate expenses:* Tuition, nonresident: part-time $339 per unit. Required fees: $1300 per semester. *General application contact:* Dr. Gayle Ball-Parker, Director of Admissions, 310-243-3645.

College of Arts and Humanities
Dr. George Arasimowicz, Dean
Programs in:
- arts and humanities (MA, MS, Certificate)
- English (MA)
- humanities (MA)
- negotiation, conflict resolution and peacebuilding (MA)
- rhetoric and composition (Certificate)
- teaching English as a second language (Certificate)

College of Business Administration and Public Policy
Dr. James Strong, Dean
Programs in:
- business administration (MBA)
- business administration and public policy (MBA, MPA)
- public administration (MPA)

College of Extended and International Education
Dr. Margaret Gordon, Dean
Programs in:
- extended and international education (MA, MS)
- humanities (MA)
- quality assurance (MS)

College of Natural and Behavioral Sciences
Dr. Laura Robles, Interim Dean
Programs in:
- biology (MS)
- clinical psychology (MA)
- computer science (MSCS)
- natural and behavioral sciences (MA, MS, MSCS, Certificate)
- social research (Certificate)
- sociology (MA)
- teaching of mathematics (MA)

College of Professional Studies
Dr. Mitchell T. Maki, Dean

School of Education
Dr. Sharon Russell, Acting Director
Programs in:
- counseling (MA)
- curriculum and instruction (MA)
- early childhood (MA)
- education (MA, Certificate)
- educational administration (MA)
- individualized education (MA)
- mild/moderate (MA)
- moderate/severe (MA)
- multicultural education (MA)
- special education (MA)
- technology-based education (MA, Certificate)

School of Health and Human Services
Dr. Mitchell T. Maki, Dean
Programs in:
- health and human services (MA, MS, MSN, MSW)
- health sciences (MS)
- marital and family therapy (MS)
- nursing (MSN)
- occupational therapy (MS)
- physical education administration (MA)
- social work (MSW)

■ CALIFORNIA STATE UNIVERSITY, EAST BAY

Hayward, CA 94542-3000

http://www.csueastbay.edu/

State-supported, coed, comprehensive institution. CGS member. *Graduate faculty:* 365. *Computer facilities:* 700 computers available on campus for general student use. A campuswide network can be accessed from student residence rooms and from off campus. Online class registration is available. *General application contact:* Rita Nakasone, Graduate Prospect Specialist, 510-885-3286.

Academic Programs and Graduate Studies
Dr. Carl Bellone, Associate Vice President
Programs in:
- interdisciplinary studies (MA, MS, Certificate)
- multimedia (MA)

College of Business and Economics
Dr. Terri Swartz, Dean
Programs in:
- accounting (MBA)
- business administration (MS)
- business and economics (MA, MBA, MS)
- business economics (MBA)

e-business (MBA)
economics (MA, MBA)
economics for teachers (MBA)
entrepreneurship (MBA)
finance (MBA)
human resources management (MBA)
information technology management (MBA)
international business (MBA)
management sciences (MBA)
marketing management (MBA)
new ventures/small business management (MBA)
operations and materials management (MBA)
strategic management (MBA)
supply chain management (MBA)
taxation (MS)
telecommunications (MS)

College of Education and Allied Studies
Dr. Deidre Badejo, Dean
Programs in:
counseling (MS)
education (MS)
education and allied studies (MS)
educational leadership (MS)
physical education (MS)
special education (MS)
specializing in urban teaching leadership (MS)

College of Letters, Arts, and Social Sciences
Dr. Deidre Badejo, Dean
Programs in:
anthropology (MA)
communication (MA)
English (MA)
geography (MA)
health care administration (MS)
history (MA)
letters, arts, and social sciences (MA, MPA, MS, MSW)
music (MA)
public administration (MPA)
social work (MSW)
sociology (MA)
speech pathology and audiology (MS)

College of Science
Dr. Michael Leung, Dean
Programs in:
actuarial statistics (MS)
biochemistry (MS)
biological sciences (MS)
biostatistics (MS)
chemistry (MS)
computational statistics (MS)
computer science (MS)
engineering management (MS)
geology (MS)
marine sciences (MS)
mathematical statistics (MS)
mathematics (MS)
multimedia (MA)
science (MA, MS)
statistics (MS)
telecommunication (MS)
theoretical and applied statistics (MS)

■ CALIFORNIA STATE UNIVERSITY, FRESNO
Fresno, CA 93740-8027
http://www.csufresno.edu/

State-supported, coed, comprehensive institution. CGS member. *Computer facilities:* 859 computers available on campus for general student use. A campuswide network can be accessed from student residence rooms and from off campus. Online class registration is available. *General application contact:* Administrative Analyst/Specialist, 559-278-2448.

Division of Graduate Studies

College of Agricultural Sciences and Technology
Programs in:
agricultural sciences and technology (MS)
animal science (MS)
family and consumer sciences (MS)
food science and nutritional sciences (MS)
industrial technology (MS)
plant science (MS)
viticulture and enology (MS)

College of Arts and Humanities
Programs in:
art (MA)
arts and humanities (MA, MFA)
communication (MA)
composition theory (MA)
creative writing (MFA)
linguistics (MA)
literature (MA)
mass communication and journalism (MA)
music (MA)
music education (MA)
performance (MA)
Spanish (MA)

College of Engineering and Computer Science
Programs in:
civil engineering (MS)
electrical engineering (MS)
engineering and computer science (MS)
mechanical engineering (MS)

College of Health and Human Services
Programs in:
communicative disorders (MA)
exercise science (MA)
health and human services (MA, MPH, MPT, MS, MSW, DPT)
health policy and management (MPH)
health promotion (MPH)
nursing (MS)
physical therapy (MPT, DPT)
social work education (MSW)
sport psychology (MA)

College of Science and Mathematics
Programs in:
biology (MA)
biotechnology (MBT)
chemistry (MS)
computer science (MS)
geology (MS)
marine sciences (MS)
mathematics (MA)
physics (MS)
psychology (MA, MS)
science and mathematics (MA, MBT, MS)
teaching (MA)

College of Social Sciences
Programs in:
criminology (MS)
history-teaching option (MA)
history-traditional track (MA)
international relations (MA)
public administration (MPA)
social sciences (MA, MPA, MS)

Craig School of Business
Programs in:
accountancy (MS)
business (MBA, MS)
business administration (MBA)

School of Education and Human Development
Programs in:
counseling and student services (MS)
education (MA)
education and human development (MA, MS, Ed D)
educational leadership (Ed D)
marriage and family therapy (MS)
rehabilitation counseling (MS)
special education (MA)

■ CALIFORNIA STATE UNIVERSITY, FULLERTON
Fullerton, CA 92834-9480
http://www.fullerton.edu/

State-supported, coed, comprehensive institution. CGS member. *Computer facilities:* 2,000 computers available on campus for general student use. A campuswide network can be accessed from student residence rooms and from off campus. Online class registration is available. *General application contact:* Admissions/Applications, 657-278-2371.

Graduate Studies
Dr. Dorota Huizinga, Associate Vice President, Graduate Programs and Research

College of Communications
Dr. Rick Pullen, Dean
Programs in:
communications (MA)
communications—advertising (MA)
communications—entertainment and tourism (MA)
communications—journalism (MA)
communications—public relations (MA)
communicative disorders (MA)
speech communication (MA)

College of Education
Dr. Claire Cavallaro, Dean

California State University, Fullerton (continued)

Programs in:
- bilingual/bicultural education (MS)
- education (MS, Ed D)
- educational leadership (MS, Ed D)
- elementary curriculum and instruction (MS)
- instructional design and technology (MS)
- middle school mathematics (MS)
- reading (MS)
- secondary education (MS)
- special education (MS)
- teacher induction (MS)

College of Engineering and Computer Science
Dr. Raman Unnikrishnan, Dean
Programs in:
- civil engineering and engineering mechanics (MS)
- computer science (MS)
- electrical engineering (MS)
- engineering and computer science (MS)
- mechanical engineering (MS)
- software engineering (MS)
- systems engineering (MS)

College of Health and Human Development
Dr. Roberta Rikli, Dean
Programs in:
- counseling (MS)
- health and human development (MPH, MS, MSW)
- kinesiology (MS)
- nursing (MS)
- public health (MPH)
- social work (MSW)

College of Humanities and Social Sciences
Dr. Thomas Klammer, Dean
Programs in:
- American studies (MA)
- analysis of specific language structures (MA)
- anthropological linguistics (MA)
- anthropology (MA)
- applied linguistics (MA)
- clinical/community psychology (MS)
- communication and semantics (MA)
- comparative literature (MA)
- disorders of communication (MA)
- English (MA)
- environmental sciences (MS)
- experimental phonetics (MA)
- French (MA)
- geography (MA)
- German (MA)
- gerontology (MS)
- history (MA)
- humanities and social sciences (MA, MPA, MS)
- political science (MA)
- psychology (MA)
- public administration (MPA)
- sociology (MA)
- Spanish (MA)
- teaching English to speakers of other languages (MS)

College of Natural Science and Mathematics
Dr. Steven Murray, Dean
Programs in:
- applied mathematics (MA)
- biological science (MS)
- chemistry (MS)
- geochemistry (MS)
- geological sciences (MS)
- mathematics (MA)
- mathematics for secondary school teachers (MA)
- natural science and mathematics (MA, MAT, MS)
- physics (MA)
- teaching science (MAT)

College of the Arts
Jerry Samuelson, Dean
Programs in:
- acting (MFA)
- acting and directing (MA)
- art (MA, MFA)
- art history (MA)
- arts (MA, MFA, MM)
- dance (MA)
- design (MA)
- directing (MFA)
- dramatic literature/criticism (MA)
- music education (MA)
- music history and literature (MA)
- oral interpretation (MA)
- performance (MM)
- piano pedagogy (MA)
- playwriting (MA)
- technical theater (MA)
- technical theater and design (MFA)
- television (MA)
- theatre for children (MA)
- theatre history (MA)
- theory-composition (MM)

Mihaylo College of Business and Economics
Dr. Anil Puri, Dean
Programs in:
- accounting (MBA, MS)
- business and economics (MA, MBA, MS)
- business economics (MBA)
- e-commerce (MBA)
- economics (MA)
- entrepreneurship (MBA)
- finance (MBA)
- information systems (MS)
- information systems (decision sciences) (MS)
- information systems (e-commerce) (MS)
- information technology (MS)
- international business (MBA)
- management (MBA)
- management science (MBA)
- marketing (MBA)
- taxation (MS)

■ CALIFORNIA STATE UNIVERSITY, LONG BEACH

Long Beach, CA 90840
http://www.csulb.edu/

State-supported, coed, comprehensive institution. CGS member. *Graduate faculty:* 427 full-time (184 women), 170 part-time/adjunct (78 women). *Computer facilities:* 2,000 computers available on campus for general student use. A campuswide network can be accessed from off campus. *Graduate expenses:* Tuition, nonresident: full-time $11,160; part-time $372 per unit. Required fees: $4100; $1261 per semester. *General application contact:* Rachel Brophy, Student Programs Coordinator, 562-985-4546.

Graduate Studies
Dr. Cecile Lindsay, Director
Program in:
- interdisciplinary studies (MA, MS)

College of Business Administration
Dr. Michael E. Solt, Dean
Programs in:
- accelerated (MBA)
- evening (MBA)
- fully employed (MBA)
- theatre management (MBA)

College of Education
Dr. Marquita Grenot-Scheyer, Dean
Programs in:
- counseling (MS)
- education (MA, Ed D)
- marriage and family therapy (MS)
- school counseling (MS)
- special education (MS)

College of Engineering
Dr. Forouzan Golshani, Dean
Programs in:
- aerospace engineering (MSAE)
- civil engineering (MSCE)
- computer engineering and computer science (MS)
- electrical engineering (MSEE)
- engineering (MS, MSAE, MSCE, MSE, MSEE, MSME, PhD)
- engineering and industrial applied mathematics (PhD)
- interdisciplinary engineering (MSE)
- management engineering (MSE)
- mechanical engineering (MSME)

College of Health and Human Services
Dr. Ronald Vogel, Dean
Programs in:
- adapted physical education (MA)
- adult clinical nurse specialist (MS)
- children, youth and families (MSW)
- coaching and student athlete development (MA)
- communicative disorders (MA)
- concurrent degree in nursing/health care administration (MS)
- criminal justice (MS)
- emergency services administration (MS)

exercise physiology and nutrition (MS)
exercise science (MS)
family and consumer sciences (MA)
food science (MS)
gerontology (MS)
health and human services (MA, MPA, MPH, MPT, MS, MSN, MSW, Certificate)
health care administration (MS, Certificate)
health science (MS)
hospitality foodservice and hotel management (MS)
individualized studies (MA)
kinesiology (MA)
nursing (MSN)
nutritional science (MS)
nutritional sciences/dietetics and food administration (MS)
occupational studies (MA)
older adults and families (MSW)
pedagogical studies (MA)
physical therapy (MPT)
public policy and administration (MPA)
recreation administration (MS)
sport and exercise psychology (MS)
sport management (MA)
sports medicine and injury studies (MS)

College of Liberal Arts
Dr. Gerry Riposa, Dean
Programs in:
Africa and the Middle East (MA)
ancient/Medieval Europe (MA)
anthropology (MA)
applied anthropology (MA)
Asia (MA)
Asian American studies (Certificate)
Asian studies (MA)
communication studies (MA)
creative writing (MFA)
economics (MA)
English (MA)
French (MA)
general linguistics (MA)
geography (MA)
German (MA)
human factors (MS)
language and culture (MA)
Latin America (MA)
liberal arts (MA, MFA, MS, Certificate)
modern Europe (MA)
philosophy (MA)
political science (MA)
psychology (MA)
religious studies (MA)
Spanish (MA)
special concentration (MA)
teaching English as a second language (MA)
United States (MA)
world (MA)

College of Natural Sciences and Mathematics
Dr. Laura Kingsford, Dean
Programs in:
applied physics (MS)
biochemistry (MS)
biology (MS)
chemistry (MS)
general physics (MS)
geology (MS)
geophysics (MS)
mathematics (MS)
microbiology (MS)
natural sciences and mathematics (MS)

College of the Arts
Dr. Donald Para, Dean
Programs in:
acting (MFA)
art education (MA)
art history (MFA)
arts (MA, MFA, MM)
composition (MM)
conducting-choral (MM)
conducting-instrumental (MM)
dance (MA, MFA)
dramatic writing (MFA)
instrument/vocal performance (MM)
jazz studies (MM)
music (MA)
opera performance (MM)
studio art (MA)
technical theatre/design (MFA)
theatre management (MFA)

■ CALIFORNIA STATE UNIVERSITY, LOS ANGELES

Los Angeles, CA 90032-8530
http://www.calstatela.edu/

State-supported, coed, comprehensive institution. CGS member. *Graduate faculty:* 263 full-time (119 women), 101 part-time/adjunct (49 women). *Computer facilities:* 1,500 computers available on campus for general student use. A campuswide network can be accessed from student residence rooms and from off campus. Online class registration is available. *Graduate expenses:* Tuition, nonresident: part-time $226 per credit. Required fees: $4019. *General application contact:* Dr. Jose L. Galvan, Dean of Graduate Studies, 323-343-3820.

Graduate Studies
Dr. Jose L. Galvan, Dean of Graduate Studies

Charter College of Education
Dr. Mary Falvey, Dean
Programs in:
applied and advanced studies in education (MA)
counseling (MS)
education (MA, MS, PhD)
elementary teaching (MA)
reading (MA)
secondary teaching (MA)
special education (MA, PhD)

College of Arts and Letters
Dr. Terry Allison, Dean
Programs in:
art (MA)
arts and letters (MA, MFA, MM)
English (MA)
fine arts (MFA)
French (MA)
music composition (MM)
music education (MA)
musicology (MA)
performance (MM)
philosophy (MA)
Spanish (MA)
speech communication (MA)
television, film and theatre (MFA)
theater arts (MA)

College of Business and Economics
Dr. Philip Romero, Acting Dean
Programs in:
accountancy (MS)
accounting (MBA)
analytical quantitative economics (MA)
business and economics (MA, MBA, MS)
business economics (MA, MBA, MS)
business information systems (MBA)
economics (MA)
finance and banking (MBA, MS)
health care management (MS)
international business (MBA, MS)
management (MBA, MS)
management information systems (MS)
marketing management (MBA, MS)
office management (MBA)

College of Engineering, Computer Science, and Technology
Dr. Keith Moo-Young, Dean
Programs in:
civil engineering (MS)
computer science (MS)
electrical engineering (MS)
engineering, computer science, and technology (MA, MS)
industrial and technical studies (MA)
mechanical engineering (MS)

College of Health and Human Services
Dr. Beatrice Yorker, Dean
Programs in:
child development (MA)
criminal justice (MS)
criminalistics (MS)
health and human services (MA, MS, MSW)
health science (MA)
nursing (MS)
nutritional science (MS)
physical education and kinesiology (MA, MS)
social work (MSW)
speech and hearing (MA)
speech-language pathology (MA)

College of Natural and Social Sciences
Dr. James Henderson, Dean
Programs in:
analytical chemistry (MS)
anthropology (MA)
biochemistry (MS)
biology (MS)
chemistry (MS)

California State University, Los Angeles (continued)

geography (MA)
geological sciences (MS)
history (MA)
inorganic chemistry (MS)
Latin American studies (MA)
mathematics (MS)
Mexican-American studies (MA)
natural and social sciences (MA, MS)
organic chemistry (MS)
physical chemistry (MS)
physics (MS)
political science (MA)
psychology (MA, MS)
public administration (MS)
sociology (MA)

■ CALIFORNIA STATE UNIVERSITY, NORTHRIDGE

Northridge, CA 91330

http://www.csun.edu/

State-supported, coed, comprehensive institution. CGS member. *Graduate faculty:* 726 full-time (312 women), 1,107 part-time/adjunct (507 women). *Computer facilities:* A campuswide network can be accessed from student residence rooms and from off campus. Online class registration is available. *General application contact:* Dr. Mack Johnson, Associate Vice President, 818-677-2138.

Graduate Studies

Dr. Mack Johnson, Associate Vice President
Program in:
interdisciplinary studies (MA, MS)

College of Arts, Media, and Communication
Robert Bucker, Dean
Programs in:
art education (MA)
art history (MA)
arts, media, and communication (MA, MFA, MM)
communication studies (MA)
composition (MM)
conducting (MM)
mass communication (MA)
music education (MA)
performance (MM)
screenwriting (MA)
studio art (MA, MFA)
theatre (MA)
visual communications (MA, MFA)

College of Business and Economics
Dr. William Jennings, Dean
Program in:
business and economics (MBA)

College of Education
Dr. Michael E. Spagna, Dean
Programs in:
counseling (MS)
curriculum and instruction (MA)
early childhood special education (MA)
education (MA, MA Ed, MS, Ed D)
education of the deaf and hard of hearing (MA)
educational administration (MA)
educational leadership (Ed D)
educational psychology (MA Ed)
educational technology (MA)
educational therapy (MA)
English education (MA)
language and literacy (MA)
mathematics education (MA)
mild/moderate disabilities (MA)
moderate/severe disabilities (MA)
multilingual/multicultural education (MA)
secondary science education (MA)
teaching and learning (MA)

College of Engineering and Computer Science
Dr. S. K. Ramesh, Dean
Programs in:
computer science (MS)
electrical engineering (MS)
engineering (MS)
engineering and computer science (MS)
engineering automation (MS)
engineering management (MS)
manufacturing systems engineering (MS)
materials engineering (MS)
mechanical engineering (MS)
software engineering (MS)

College of Health and Human Development
Dr. Sylvia A. Alva, Dean
Programs in:
audiology (MS)
environmental and occupational health (MS)
family and consumer sciences (MS)
health administration (MS)
health and human development (MPH, MPT, MS)
hospitality and tourism (MS)
industrial hygiene (MS)
kinesiology (MS)
physical therapy (MPT)
public health (MPH)
recreational sport management/campus recreation (MS)
speech language pathology (MS)

College of Humanities
Dr. Elizabeth Say, Dean
Programs in:
Chicana and Chicano studies (MA)
creative writing (MA)
humanities (MA)
linguistics (MA)
literature (MA)
rhetoric and composition theory (MA)
Spanish (MA)

College of Science and Mathematics
Dr. Jerry Stinner, Dean
Programs in:
applied mathematics (MS)
biochemistry (MS)
biology (MS)
chemistry (MS)
geology (MS)
mathematics (MS)
mathematics for educational careers (MS)
physics (MS)
science and mathematics (MS)

College of Social and Behavioral Sciences
Dr. Stella Z. Theodoulou, Dean
Programs in:
clinical psychology (MA)
general anthropology (MA)
general-experimental psychology (MA)
geography (MA)
history (MA)
human factors and applied experimental psychology (MA)
political science (MA)
public archaeology (MA)
social and behavioral sciences (MA, MSW)
social work (MSW)
sociology (MA)

The Tseng College of Extended Learning
Joyce Feucht-Haviar, Dean
Programs in:
knowledge management (MKM)
public administration (MPA)
taxation (MS)

■ CALIFORNIA STATE UNIVERSITY, SACRAMENTO

Sacramento, CA 95819-6048

http://www.csus.edu/

State-supported, coed, comprehensive institution. CGS member. *Computer facilities:* Computer purchase and lease plans are available. 700 computers available on campus for general student use. A campuswide network can be accessed from student residence rooms and from off campus. Online class registration, online transcripts are available. *General application contact:* Associate Dean of Graduate Admissions, 916-278-6470.

Graduate Studies

College of Arts and Letters
Programs in:
arts and letters (MA, MM)
communication studies (MA)
creative writing (MA)
foreign languages (MA)
music (MM)
public history (MA)
studio art (MA)
teaching English to speakers of other languages (MA)
theatre and dance (MA)

College of Business Administration
Programs in:
accountancy (MS)
business administration (MBA)

human resources (MBA)
management information science (MS)
urban land development (MBA)

College of Education
Programs in:
bilingual/multicultural education (MA)
career counseling (MS)
curriculum and instruction (MA)
early childhood education (MA)
education (MA, MS)
educational leadership (MA)
generic counseling (MS)
guidance (MA)
reading education (MA)
school counseling (MS)
school psychology (MS)
special education (MA)
vocational rehabilitation (MS)

College of Engineering and Computer Science
Programs in:
civil engineering (MS)
computer systems (MS)
electrical engineering (MS)
engineering and computer science (MS)
mechanical engineering (MS)
software engineering (MS)

College of Health and Human Services
Programs in:
audiology (MS)
criminal justice (MS)
family and children's services (MSW)
health and human services (MS, MSW)
health care (MSW)
mental health (MSW)
nursing (MS)
physical education (MS)
recreation administration (MS)
social justice and corrections (MSW)
speech pathology (MS)

College of Natural Sciences and Mathematics
Programs in:
biological sciences (MA, MS)
chemistry (MS)
immunohematology (MS)
marine science (MS)
mathematics and statistics (MA)
natural sciences and mathematics (MA, MS)

College of Social Sciences and Interdisciplinary Studies
Programs in:
anthropology (MA)
counseling psychology (MA)
French (MA)
German (MA)
government (MA)
international affairs (MA)
public policy and administration (MPPA)
social sciences and interdisciplinary studies (MA, MPPA)
sociology (MA)
Spanish (MA)
theater arts (MA)

■ CALIFORNIA STATE UNIVERSITY, SAN BERNARDINO

San Bernardino, CA 92407-2397
http://www.csusb.edu/

State-supported, coed, comprehensive institution. CGS member. *Graduate faculty:* 238 full-time (101 women), 121 part-time/adjunct (51 women). *Computer facilities:* Computer purchase and lease plans are available. 1,300 computers available on campus for general student use. A campuswide network can be accessed from student residence rooms and from off campus. Online class registration is available. *General application contact:* Olivia Rosas, Director of Admissions, 909-537-5188.

Graduate Studies

Program in:
interdisciplinary studies (MA)

College of Arts and Letters
Dr. Eri F. Yasuhara, Dean
Programs in:
art (MA)
arts and letters (MA, MFA)
communication studies (MA)
creative writing (MFA)
English composition (MA)
integrated marketing communication (MA)
Spanish (MA)
theatre arts (MA)
theatre education (MA)
theatre for youth (MA)

College of Business and Public Administration
Dr. Karen Dill-Bowerman, Dean
Programs in:
business administration (MBA)
business and public administration (MBA, MPA)
for executives (MBA)
public administration (MPA)

College of Education
Dr. Patricia Arlin, Dean
Programs in:
bilingual/cross-cultural education (MA)
correctional and alternative education (MA)
counseling and guidance (MS)
curriculum and instruction (MA)
educational administration (MA)
educational leadership and curriculum (Ed D)
educational psychology and counseling (MA, MS)
elementary education (MA)
English as a second language (MA)
environmental education (MA)
history and English for secondary teachers (MA)
instructional technology (MA)
reading (MA)
rehabilitation counseling (MA)
secondary education (MA)
special education (MA)
special education and rehabilitation counseling (MA)
teaching of science (MA)
vocational and career education (MA)

College of Natural Sciences
Dr. B. Robert Carlson, Dean
Programs in:
biology (MS)
computer science (MS)
health science (MS)
health services administration (MS)
kinesiology (MA Ed)
mathematics (MA)
natural sciences (MA, MA Ed, MAT, MPH, MS)
nursing (MS)
public health (MPH)
teaching mathematics (MAT)

College of Social and Behavioral Sciences
Jamal Nassar, Dean
Programs in:
child development (MA)
clinical psychology (MS)
clinical/counseling psychology (MS)
criminal justice (MA)
environmental sciences (MS)
general/experimental psychology (MA)
industrial/organizational psychology (MS)
national security studies (MA)
organizational psychology (MS)
psychology (MA)
psychology-life span (MA)
social and behavioral sciences (MA, MS, MSW)
social sciences (MA)
social work (MSW)

■ CALIFORNIA STATE UNIVERSITY, SAN MARCOS

San Marcos, CA 92096-0001
http://www.csusm.edu/

State-supported, coed, comprehensive institution. CGS member. *Computer facilities:* 1,100 computers available on campus for general student use. A campuswide network can be accessed from student residence rooms and from off campus. Online class registration is available. *General application contact:* Admissions, 760-750-4848.

College of Arts and Sciences

Programs in:
arts and sciences (MA, MS)
biological sciences (MS)
computer science (MS)
literature and writing studies (MA)
mathematics (MS)
psychology (MA)
sociological practice (MA)
Spanish (MA)

California State University, San Marcos (continued)

College of Business Administration
Programs in:
business management (MBA)
government management (MBA)

College of Education
Program in:
education (MA)

■ CALIFORNIA STATE UNIVERSITY, STANISLAUS
Turlock, CA 95382
http://www.csustan.edu/

State-supported, coed, comprehensive institution. CGS member. *Computer facilities:* 150 computers available on campus for general student use. A campuswide network can be accessed from student residence rooms and from off campus. Online class registration is available. *General application contact:* Graduate School, 209-667-3129.

College of Business Administration
Programs in:
business administration (EMBA, MBA, MSBA)
finance and international finance (MSBA)

College of Education
Programs in:
community college leadership (Ed D)
curriculum and instruction (MA)
education (MA)
educational leadership (Ed D)
educational technology (MA)
middle/junior high studies (Graduate Certificate)
P-12 leadership (Ed D)
physical education (MA)
school administration (MA)
school counseling (MA)
special education (MA)

College of Human and Health Sciences
Programs in:
behavior analysis (MS)
child development (Graduate Certificate)
counseling (MS)
human and health sciences (MA, MS, MSW, Graduate Certificate)
psychology (MA, MS)
social work (MSW)

College of Humanities and Social Sciences
Programs in:
criminal justice (MA)
English (MA)
gerontology (Certificate)
history (MA)
humanities and social sciences (MA, MPA, Certificate)
international relations (MA)
literature (MA)
public administration (MPA)
rhetoric and teaching of writing (MA)
secondary school teachers (MA)
TESOL (MA, Certificate)

College of Natural Sciences
Programs in:
ecology and sustainability (MS)
genetic counseling (MS)
marine sciences (MS)
natural sciences (MS)

College of the Arts
Programs in:
arts (Certificate)
printmaking (Certificate)

Programs in Interdisciplinary Studies
Program in:
interdisciplinary studies (MA, MS)

■ CHAPMAN UNIVERSITY
Orange, CA 92866
http://www.chapman.edu/

Independent-religious, coed, comprehensive institution. *Graduate faculty:* 198 full-time (71 women), 148 part-time/adjunct (54 women). *Computer facilities:* Computer purchase and lease plans are available. 453 computers available on campus for general student use. A campuswide network can be accessed from student residence rooms and from off campus. Online class registration is available. *Graduate expenses:* Tuition: full-time $11,970; part-time $665 per credit. Required fees: $456; $456 per year. Tuition and fees vary according to course load, degree level and program. *General application contact:* Saundra Hoover, Director of Graduate Admissions, 714-997-6786.

Graduate Studies
Dr. Raymond Sfeir, Associate Provost

College of Educational Studies
Dr. Don Cardinal, Dean
Programs in:
administrative services (Tier I) (Credential)
communication sciences and disorders (MS)
curriculum and instruction (MA)
education: cultural and curricular studies (PhD)
education: disability studies (PhD)
education: school psychology (PhD)
educational leadership and administration (MA)
educational psychology (MA, Ed S)
multiple subjects (Credential)
multiple subjects with bilingual emphasis (Credential)
professional clear (Ryan 5th year) (Credential)
pupil personnel services school counseling (Credential)
pupil personnel services school psychology (Credential)
reading Certificate (Credential)
reading education (MA)
school counseling (MA)
school psychology (Ed S)
single subject (Credential)
special education (MA)
special education level I mild/moderate (Credential)
special education level I moderate/severe (Credential)
special education level II mild/moderate (Credential)
special education level II moderate/severe (Credential)
teaching: elementary education (MA)
teaching: secondary education (MA)

Dodge College of Film and Media Arts
Robert Bassett, Dean
Programs in:
film and media arts (MA, MFA)
film and television producing (MFA)
film production (MFA)
film studies (MA)
production design (MFA)
screenwriting (MFA)

The George L. Argyros School of Business and Economics
Dr. Arthur Kraft, Dean
Program in:
business and economics (Exec MBA, MBA)

Schmid College of Science
Dr. Janeen Hill, Interim Dean
Programs in:
food science (MS)
health communication (MS)
marriage and family therapy (MA)
physical therapy (DPT)
science (MA, MS, DPT)

School of Law
Dr. John Eastman, Dean
Programs in:
advocacy and dispute resolution (JD)
entertainment law (JD)
environmental, land use, and real estate (JD)
international law (JD)
law (LL M)
prosecutorial science (LL M)
tax law (JD)
taxation (LL M)

Wilkinson College of Humanities and Social Sciences
Dr. Roberta Lessor, Dean
Programs in:
creative writing (MFA)
English (MA)
humanities and social sciences (MA, MFA)
international studies (MA)

■ CLAREMONT GRADUATE UNIVERSITY
Claremont, CA 91711-6160
http://www.cgu.edu/

Independent, coed, graduate-only institution. CGS member. *Graduate faculty:* 117 full-time (46 women), 14 part-time/adjunct (1 woman). *Computer facilities:* 90 computers available on campus for general student use. A campuswide network can be accessed. Online class registration is available. *Graduate expenses:* Tuition: full-time $33,698; part-time $1465 per unit. Required fees: $310; $155 per semester. Tuition and fees vary according to program. *General application contact:* Julia Evans, Director of Central Recruitment, 909-607-3689.

Graduate Programs
Yi Feng, Provost and Vice President for Academic Affairs
Programs in:
- arts management (MA)
- botany (MS, PhD)
- financial engineering (MSFE)
- public policy and evaluation (MA)

Peter F. Drucker and Masatoshi Ito Graduate School of Management
Ira A. Jackson, Henry Y. Hwang Dean and Professor of Management
Programs in:
- advanced management (MS)
- executive management (EMBA)
- leadership (Certificate)
- management (EMBA, MA, MBA, MS, PhD, Certificate)
- strategy (Certificate)

School of Arts and Humanities
Marc Redfield, Interim Dean
Programs in:
- Africana history (Certificate)
- Africana studies (Certificate)
- American studies (MA, PhD)
- American studies and U.S. history (MA, PhD)
- applied women's studies (MA)
- archival studies (MA)
- arts and humanities (M Phil, MA, MFA, DCM, DMA, PhD, Certificate)
- church music (MA, DCM)
- composition (MA, DMA)
- critical theory (MA, PhD)
- cultural studies (MA, PhD)
- digital media (MA, MFA)
- drawing (MA, MFA)
- early modern studies (MA, PhD)
- English (M Phil, MA, PhD)
- European studies (MA, PhD)
- historical performance practices (MA, DMA)
- installation (MA, MFA)
- literary theory (PhD)
- literature (MA, PhD)
- literature and creative writing (MA)
- literature and film (MA)
- media studies (MA, PhD)
- museum studies (MA)
- musicology (MA, PhD)
- new genre (MA, MFA)
- oral history (MA, PhD)
- painting (MA, MFA)
- performance (MA, MFA, DMA)
- philosophy (MA, PhD)
- photography (MA, MFA)
- sculpture (MA, MFA)

School of Behavioral and Organizational Sciences
Stewart Donaldson, Dean
Programs in:
- advanced study in evaluation (Certificate)
- behavioral and organizational sciences (MA, MS, PhD, Certificate)
- cognitive psychology (MA, PhD)
- developmental psychology (MA, PhD)
- evaluation and applied research methods (MA, PhD)
- health behavior research and evaluation (MA, PhD)
- human resource development and evaluation (MA)
- human resources design (MS)
- industrial/organizational psychology (MA, PhD)
- organizational behavior (MA, PhD)
- organizational psychology (MA, PhD)
- social psychology (MA, PhD)

School of Educational Studies
Margaret Grogan, Dean
Programs in:
- Africana education (Certificate)
- education and policy (MA, PhD)
- higher education/student affairs (MA, PhD)
- human development (MA, PhD)
- public school administration (MA, PhD)
- quantitative evaluation (MA, PhD)
- special education (MA, PhD)
- teacher education (MA)
- teaching and learning (MA, PhD)
- urban leadership (PhD)

School of Information Systems and Technology
Terry Ryan, Dean
Programs in:
- electronic commerce (MS, PhD)
- health information management (MS)
- information systems (Certificate)
- knowledge management (MS, PhD)
- systems development (MS, PhD)
- telecommunications and networking (MS, PhD)

School of Mathematical Sciences
John Angus, Dean
Programs in:
- computational and systems biology (PhD)
- computational mathematics and numerical analysis (MA, MS)
- computational science (PhD)
- engineering and industrial applied mathematics (PhD)
- mathematics (PhD)
- operations research and statistics (MA, MS)
- physical applied mathematics (MA, MS)
- pure mathematics (MA, MS)
- scientific computing (MA, MS)
- systems and control theory (MA, MS)

School of Politics and Economics
Yi Feng, Interim Dean
Programs in:
- American politics (MA, PhD)
- business and financial economics (MA, PhD)
- comparative politics (PhD)
- economic development (Certificate)
- economics (PhD)
- industrial organization (PhD)
- international and development economics (PhD)
- international economics policy and development (MA)
- international money and finance (PhD)
- international political economy (MA)
- international studies (MA)
- neuroeconomics (PhD)
- political economy and public policy (MA)
- political philosophy (PhD)
- political science (PhD)
- politics and economics (MA, PhD, Certificate)
- politics, economics and business (MA)
- public choice and public economics (PhD)
- public policy (MA, PhD)
- world politics (PhD)

School of Religion
Karen Torjesen, Dean
Programs in:
- Hebrew Bible (MA, PhD)
- history of Christianity and religions of North America (MA, PhD)
- New Testament (MA, PhD)
- philosophy of religion and theology (MA, PhD)
- theology, ethics and culture (MA, PhD)
- women's studies in religion (MA, PhD)

■ CONCORDIA UNIVERSITY
Irvine, CA 92612-3299
http://www.cui.edu/

Independent-religious, coed, comprehensive institution. *Computer facilities:* Computer purchase and lease plans are available. 103 computers available on campus for general student use. A campuswide network can be accessed from student residence rooms and from off campus. Online class registration is available. *General application contact:* Information Contact, 800-229-1200.

School of Arts and Sciences
Program in:
- coaching and athletic administration (MA)

Concordia University (continued)

School of Business and Professional Studies

Programs in:
entrepreneurial business administration (MBA)
international studies (MA)

School of Education

Programs in:
curriculum and instruction (MA)
education (M Ed)
educational administration and administrative services credential (MA)

School of Theology

Program in:
theology (MA)

■ DEVRY UNIVERSITY
Pomona, CA 91768-2642
http://www.devry.edu/

Proprietary, coed, comprehensive institution. *Computer facilities:* Computer purchase and lease plans are available. 513 computers available on campus for general student use. A campuswide network can be accessed from off campus. Online class registration is available.

Keller Graduate School of Management

Program in:
management (MAFM, MBA, MHRM, MISM, MNCM, MPA, MPM, Graduate Certificate)

■ DOMINICAN UNIVERSITY OF CALIFORNIA
San Rafael, CA 94901-2298
http://www.dominican.edu/

Independent-religious, coed, comprehensive institution. *Computer facilities:* 260 computers available on campus for general student use. A campuswide network can be accessed from student residence rooms and from off campus. Online class registration, Microsoft Office Applications (Word, Excel, PowerPoint) are available. *Graduate expenses:* Tuition: full-time $14,040; part-time $780 per unit. *General application contact:* Shannon Lovelace, Assistant Director, 415-485-3246.

Graduate Programs

Dr. Kenneth Porada, Provost/Vice President for Academic Affairs

School of Education and Counseling Psychology

Dr. Ed Kujawa, Dean
Programs in:
counseling psychology (MFT, MS)
education (MS)
education and counseling psychology (MFT, MS, Credential)
multiple subject teaching (Credential)
single subject teaching (Credential)
special education (Credential)

School of Arts, Humanities and Social Sciences

Dr. Martha Nelson, Dean
Programs in:
arts, humanities and social sciences (MA)
humanities (MA)

School of Business and Leadership

Dr. Ed Kujawa, Dean
Programs in:
business and leadership (MAM, MBA)
global strategic management (MBA)
management (MAM)
strategic leadership (MBA)
sustainable development (MBA)

School of Health and Natural Sciences

Programs in:
biology (MS)
geriatric and nurse educator (MS)
health and natural sciences (MS)
integrated health practices (clinical nursing specialist) (MS)
occupational therapy (MS)

■ FRESNO PACIFIC UNIVERSITY
Fresno, CA 93702-4709
http://www.fresno.edu/

Independent-religious, coed, comprehensive institution. *Computer facilities:* 90 computers available on campus for general student use. A campuswide network can be accessed from student residence rooms and from off campus. Online class registration is available. *General application contact:* Admissions Coordinator, 559-453-3667.

Graduate Programs

Programs in:
individualized study (MA)
kinesiology (MA)
leadership and organizational studies (MA)
peacemaking and conflict studies (MA)

School of Education

Programs in:
administration (MA Ed)
administrative services (MA Ed)
bilingual/cross-cultural education (MA Ed)
curriculum and teaching (MA Ed)
educational technology (MA Ed)
elementary and middle school mathematics (MA Ed)
foundations, curriculum and teaching (MA Ed)
integrated mathematics/science education (MA Ed)
language development (MA Ed)
language, literacy, and culture (MA Ed)
literacy in multilingual contexts (MA Ed)
mathematics education (MA Ed)
mathematics/science/computer education (MA Ed)
mild/moderate (MA Ed)
moderate/severe (MA Ed)
physical and health impairments (MA Ed)
pupil personnel services (MA Ed)
reading (MA Ed)
reading/English as a second language (MA Ed)
reading/language arts (MA Ed)
school counseling (MA Ed)
school library and information technology (MA Ed)
school psychology (MA Ed)
secondary school mathematics (MA Ed)
special education (MA Ed)
teaching English to speakers of other languages (MA)

■ GOLDEN GATE UNIVERSITY
San Francisco, CA 94105-2968
http://www.ggu.edu/

Independent, coed, university. *Computer facilities:* Computer purchase and lease plans are available. 52 computers available on campus for general student use. A campuswide network can be accessed. Online class registration is available. *General application contact:* Enrollment Services, 415-442-7800.

Ageno School of Business

Terry Connelly, Dean
Programs in:
accounting (MBA)
business administration (EMBA, MBA, DBA)
finance (MBA, MS, Certificate)
financial planning (MS, Certificate)
human resource management (MBA, MS)
human resources management (Certificate)
information technology (MBA)
information technology management (MS, Certificate)
integrated marketing and communications (MS, Certificate)
international business (MBA)
management (MBA)
marketing (MBA, MS, Certificate)
operations management (Certificate)
psychology (MA, Certificate)
public relations (MS, Certificate)

School of Accounting

Program in:
accounting (M Ac, Graduate Certificate)

School of Law

Programs in:
environmental law (LL M)
intellectual property law (LL M)
international legal studies (LL M, SJD)
law (JD)
taxation (LL M)
U.S. legal studies (LL M)

School of Taxation
Mary Canning, Dean
Program in:
taxation (MS, Certificate)

■ HOLY NAMES UNIVERSITY
Oakland, CA 94619-1699
http://www.hnu.edu/

Independent-religious, coed, primarily women, comprehensive institution. *Graduate faculty:* 17 full-time (13 women), 58 part-time/adjunct (37 women). *Computer facilities:* 80 computers available on campus for general student use. A campuswide network can be accessed from student residence rooms and from off campus. *Graduate expenses:* Tuition: full-time $6255; part-time $695 per unit. Required fees: $340. Tuition and fees vary according to course load, program, reciprocity agreements and student's religious affiliation. *General application contact:* Annie Wenzel, Graduate Admissions Office, 510-436-1642.

Graduate Division
Murad Dibbini, Dean of Enrollment Services
Programs in:
administration/management (MS, Certificate)
clinical faculty (MS, Certificate)
community health nursing/case manager (MS)
counseling psychology (MA)
educational therapy (Certificate)
energy and environment management (MBA)
family nurse practitioner (MS, Certificate)
finance (MBA)
forensic psychology (MA, Certificate)
Kodaly specialist certificate (Certificate)
Kodaly summer certificate (Certificate)
level 1 education specialist mild/moderate disabilities (Credential)
level 2 education specialist mild/moderate disabilities (Credential)
management and leadership (MBA)
marketing (MBA)
multiple subject teaching credential (Credential)
music education with Kodaly emphasis (MM)
pastoral counseling (MA, Certificate)
pastoral ministries (MA, Certificate)
piano pedagogy (MM)
piano pedagogy with Suzuki emphasis (MM)
single subject teaching credential (Credential)
sports management (MBA)
teaching English as a second language (TESL) (M Ed)
urban education: educational therapy (M Ed)
urban education: K-12 education (M Ed)
urban education: special education (M Ed)
vocal pedagogy (MM)

Sophia Center in Culture and Spirituality
Dr. James Conlon, Program Director
Program in:
culture and spirituality (MA, Certificate)

■ HOPE INTERNATIONAL UNIVERSITY
Fullerton, CA 92831-3138
http://www.hiu.edu/

Independent-religious, coed, comprehensive institution. *Computer facilities:* 53 computers available on campus for general student use. A campuswide network can be accessed from student residence rooms and from off campus. Online class registration is available. *General application contact:* Director of Graduate and Adult Admissions, 714-879-3901.

School of Graduate and Professional Studies
Programs in:
business administration (MBA)
Christian leadership (MCM)
church music (MA)
church music (Korean track) (MCM)
church planting (MCM)
education (ME)
educational administration (MSM)
intercultural studies (MCM)
international development (MBA, MSM)
management (MBA)
marriage and family therapy (MA, MFT)
nonprofit management (MBA)
worship (MCM)

■ HUMBOLDT STATE UNIVERSITY
Arcata, CA 95521-8299
http://www.humboldt.edu/

State-supported, coed, comprehensive institution. CGS member. *Graduate faculty:* 269 full-time (100 women), 252 part-time/adjunct (154 women). *Computer facilities:* Computer purchase and lease plans are available. 1,191 computers available on campus for general student use. A campuswide network can be accessed from student residence rooms and from off campus. Online class registration is available. *Graduate expenses:* Tuition, nonresident: full-time $6102. Required fees: $5236. *General application contact:* Cynthia Werner, Research and Graduate Studies, 707-826-3949.

Graduate Studies
Dr. Chris Hopper, Interim Dean

College of Arts, Humanities, and Social Sciences
Dr. Ken Ayoob, Interim Dean
Programs in:
arts, humanities, and social sciences (MA, MFA)
English (MA)
environment and community (MA)
sociology (MA)
theatre arts (MA, MFA)

College of Natural Resources and Sciences
Dr. Jim Howard, Dean
Programs in:
biological sciences (MA)
environmental systems (MS)
natural resources (MS)
natural resources and sciences (MA, MS)
psychology (MA)

College of Professional Studies
Dr. Nancy Hurlbut, Interim Dean
Programs in:
athletic training education (MS)
business (MBA)
education (MA)
exercise science/wellness management (MS)
pre-physical therapy (MS)
social work (MSW)
teaching/coaching (MS)

■ JOHN F. KENNEDY UNIVERSITY
Pleasant Hill, CA 94523-4817
http://www.jfku.edu/

Independent, coed, primarily women, upper-level institution. CGS member. *Computer facilities:* 50 computers available on campus for general student use. Online class registration is available. *General application contact:* Vice President, Enrollment Services, 925-969-3509.

Graduate School of Holistic Studies
Programs in:
consciousness studies (MA)
counseling psychology (MA)
dream studies (Certificate)
holistic health education (MA)
holistic studies (MA, MFA, Certificate)
integral psychology (MA, Certificate)
life coaching (Certificate)
somatic psychology (MA)
studio arts (MFA)
transformative arts (MA)
transpersonal psychology (MA)

Graduate School of Professional Psychology
Programs in:
counseling psychology (MA)
organizational psychology (MA, Certificate)
professional psychology (MA, Psy D, Certificate)
psychology (Psy D)
sport psychology (MA)

John F. Kennedy University (continued)

School of Education and Liberal Arts

Programs in:
education (MAT)
education and liberal arts (MA, MAT, Certificate)
museum studies (MA, Certificate)

School of Law

Program in:
law (JD)

School of Management

Programs in:
business administration (MBA)
career coaching (Certificate)
career development (MA, Certificate)
management (MA, MBA, Certificate)
organizational leadership (Certificate)

■ LA SIERRA UNIVERSITY
Riverside, CA 92515
http://www.lasierra.edu/

Independent-religious, coed, comprehensive institution. CGS member. *Computer facilities:* Computer purchase and lease plans are available. 262 computers available on campus for general student use. A campuswide network can be accessed from student residence rooms and from off campus. Online class registration is available. *General application contact:* Director of Admissions, 909-785-2176.

College of Arts and Sciences

Programs in:
arts and sciences (MA)
communication (MA)
English (MA)

School of Business and Management

Programs in:
accounting (MBA)
finance (MBA)
general management (MBA)
human resources management (MBA)
leadership, values, and ethics for business and management (Certificate)
marketing (MBA)

School of Education

Programs in:
administration and leadership (MA, Ed D, Ed S)
counseling (MA)
curriculum and instruction (MA, Ed D, Ed S)
education (MA, MAT, Ed D, Ed S)
educational psychology (Ed S)
school psychology (Ed S)
teaching (MAT)

School of Religion

Programs in:
pastoral ministry (M Div)
religion (MA)
religious education (MA)
religious studies (MA)

■ LOYOLA MARYMOUNT UNIVERSITY
Los Angeles, CA 90045-2659
http://www.lmu.edu/

Independent-religious, coed, comprehensive institution. CGS member. *Graduate faculty:* 297 full-time (116 women), 92 part-time/adjunct (53 women). *Computer facilities:* Computer purchase and lease plans are available. 56 computers available on campus for general student use. A campuswide network can be accessed from student residence rooms and from off campus. Online class registration is available. *Graduate expenses:* Tuition: part-time $872 per credit hour. Tuition and fees vary according to degree level and campus/location. *General application contact:* Chake H. Kouyoumjian, Associate Dean of the Graduate Division, 310-338-2721.

College of Business Administration

Dr. Dennis Draper, Dean
Programs in:
business administration (MBA)
executive business administration (MBA)

College of Fine Arts

Barbara J. Busse, Dean
Programs in:
fine arts (MA)
marital and family therapy (MA)

College of Liberal Arts

Dr. Michael Engh, Dean
Programs in:
English (MA)
liberal arts (MA)
pastoral theology (MA)
philosophy (MA)
theology (MA)

The Bioethics Institute

Dr. James J. Walter, Chair
Program in:
bioethics (MA)

College of Science and Engineering

Dr. Michael Manoogian, Chair
Programs in:
civil engineering (MS, MSE)
computer science (MS)
electrical engineering (MSE)
environmental engineering (MSE)
environmental science (MS)
mechanical engineering (MSE)
science and engineering (MAT, MS, MSE)
systems engineering and leadership (MS)
teaching mathematics (MAT)

Loyola Law School Los Angeles

Victor Gold, Dean
Programs in:
law (JD)
taxation (LL M)

School of Education

Dr. Shane Martin, Dean
Programs in:
bilingual elementary education (MA)
bilingual secondary education (MA)
biliteracy, leadership, and intercultural education (MA)
Catholic inclusive education (MA)
Catholic school administration (MA)
child/adolescent literacy (MA)
counseling (MA)
early childhood education (MA)
education (MA, Ed D)
educational leadership in social justice (Ed D)
elementary education (MA)
general education (MA)
guidance and counseling (MA)
literacy education (MA)
literacy/language arts (MA)
school administration (MA)
school psychology (MA)
secondary education (MA)
special education (MA)
teaching English as a second language (MA)
urban education (MA)

School of Film and Television

Teri Schwartz, Dean
Programs in:
film and television (MFA)
production (film and television) (MFA)
screenwriting (MFA)

■ MILLS COLLEGE
Oakland, CA 94613-1000
http://www.mills.edu/

Independent, Undergraduate: women only; graduate: coed, comprehensive institution. *Graduate faculty:* 96 full-time (59 women), 103 part-time/adjunct (73 women). *Computer facilities:* Computer purchase and lease plans are available. 336 computers available on campus for general student use. A campuswide network can be accessed from student residence rooms and from off campus. Online class registration, online degree audit are available. *Graduate expenses:* Tuition: full-time $25,072; part-time $6272 per course. Required fees: $880. *General application contact:* Marika Benko, Graduate Admission Specialist, 510-430-3309.

Graduate Studies

Carol Langlois, Administrative Dean for Graduate Recruitment and Enrollment
Programs in:
book art and creative writing (MFA)
ceramics (MFA)
composition (MA)
computer science (Certificate)
creative writing, poetry (MFA)
creative writing, prose (MFA)
dance (MA, MFA)
electronic music and recording media (MFA)
English and American literature (MA)
interdisciplinary computer science (MA)

intermedia (MFA)
music performance and literature (MFA)
painting (MFA)
photography (MFA)
pre-medical studies (Certificate)
public policy (MPP)
sculpture (MFA)

Lori I. Lokey Graduate School of Business
Nancy Thornborrow, Dean
Program in:
management (MBA)

School of Education
Joseph Kahne, Chairperson
Programs in:
child life in hospitals (MA)
early childhood education (MA)
education (MA)
educational leadership (MA, Ed D)
infant mental health (MA)

■ MONTEREY INSTITUTE OF INTERNATIONAL STUDIES

Monterey, CA 93940-2691
http://www.miis.edu/

Independent, coed, graduate-only institution. *Computer facilities:* 105 computers available on campus for general student use. A campuswide network can be accessed from off campus. *Graduate expenses:* Tuition: full-time $29,300; part-time $1400 per credit. Required fees: $56. *General application contact:* Admissions Office, 831-647-4123.

Fisher Graduate School of International Business
Dr. Ernest J. Scalberg, Dean
Program in:
international business (MBA)

Graduate School of International Policy Studies
Dr. Edward J. Laurance, Dean
Programs in:
international environmental policy (MA)
international management (MPA)
international policy studies (MA, MPA)
international trade policy (MA)

Graduate School of Language and Educational Linguistics
Dr. Renee Jourdenais, Dean
Programs in:
language and educational linguistics (MATESOL, MATFL)
teaching English to speakers of other languages (MATESOL)
teaching foreign language (MATFL)

Graduate School of Translation and Interpretation
Dr. Chuanyun Bao, Dean
Programs in:
conference interpretation (MA)
translation (MA)
translation and interpretation (MA)
translation and localization management (MA)

James Martin Center for Nonproliferation Studies
Program in:
nonproliferation and terrorism studies (MA)

■ MOUNT ST. MARY'S COLLEGE

Los Angeles, CA 90049-1599
http://www.msmc.la.edu/

Independent-religious, coed, comprehensive institution. *Graduate faculty:* 16 full-time (all women), 23 part-time/adjunct (19 women). *Computer facilities:* 350 computers available on campus for general student use. A campuswide network can be accessed from student residence rooms and from off campus. Online class registration is available. *Graduate expenses:* Tuition: full-time $16,992; part-time $708 per unit. Required fees: $313. One-time fee: $110 full-time. Tuition and fees vary according to course load and program. *General application contact:* Jessica M. Bibeau, Director of Graduate Admission, 213-477-2800 Ext. 2798.

Graduate Division
Programs in:
administrative studies (MS)
business administration (MBA)
counseling psychology (MS)
elementary education (MS)
humanities (MA)
nursing (MS)
physical therapy (DPT)
religious studies (MA)
secondary education (MS)
special education (MS)

■ NATIONAL UNIVERSITY

La Jolla, CA 92037-1011
http://www.nu.edu/

Independent, coed, comprehensive institution. CGS member. *Graduate faculty:* 237 full-time (113 women), 2,626 part-time/adjunct (1,333 women). *Computer facilities:* Computer purchase and lease plans are available. 3,100 computers available on campus for general student use. A campuswide network can be accessed from off campus. Online class registration is available. *Graduate expenses:* Tuition: full-time $8694; part-time $322 per credit hour. Tuition and fees vary according to course load. *General application contact:* Dominick Giovanniello, Associate Regional Dean—San Diego, 800-NAT-UNIV.

Academic Affairs
Dr. Thomas M. Green, Provost

College of Letters and Sciences
Dr. Michael Mcanear, Dean
Programs in:
counseling psychology (MA)
creative writing (MFA)
English (MA)
forensic science (MFS)
history (MA)
human behavior (MA)
letters and sciences (MA, MFA, MFS, MPA)
public administration (MPA)

School of Business and Management
Dr. Thomas M. Green, Interim Dean
Programs in:
accountancy (MS)
alternative dispute resolution (MBA)
business and management (MA, MBA, MS)
corporate and international finance (MS)
e-business (MBA, MS)
financial management (MBA)
human resource management (MBA)
human resources management (MA)
international business (MBA)
knowledge management (MS)
management (MA)
marketing (MBA)
organizational leadership (MBA, MS)
technology management (MBA)

School of Education
Dr. Carl Kalani Beyer, Interim Dean
Programs in:
applied school leadership (MS)
best practices (MA)
cross-cultural teaching (M Ed)
deaf and hard of hearing education (MS)
education (M Ed, MA, MS)
educational administration (MS)
educational counseling (MS)
exceptional student education (MS)
school psychology (MS)
special education (MS)
teacher leadership (MA)
teaching (MA)
teaching/learning in global society (MA)

School of Engineering and Technology
Dr. Howard Evans, Dean
Programs in:
computer science (MS)
database administration (MS)
engineering and technology (MS)
engineering management (MS)
environmental engineering (MS)
homeland security and safety engineering (MS)
information systems (MS)
software engineering (MS)
system engineering (MS)
technology management (MS)
wireless communications (MS)

School of Health and Human Services
Dr. Michael Lacourse, Dean
Programs in:
health and human services (MHA, MHCA, MIH, MS)
integrative health (MIH)

School of Media and Communication
Karla Berry, Dean

National University (continued)
Programs in:
digital cinema (MFA)
educational and instructional technology (MS)
media and communication (MA, MFA, MS)
strategic communication (MA)
video game production and design (MFA)

■ NOTRE DAME DE NAMUR UNIVERSITY

Belmont, CA 94002-1908

http://www.ndnu.edu/

Independent-religious, coed, comprehensive institution. *Graduate faculty:* 28 full-time (13 women), 63 part-time/adjunct (44 women). *Computer facilities:* 80 computers available on campus for general student use. A campuswide network can be accessed from student residence rooms. Online class registration is available. *Graduate expenses:* Tuition: part-time $699 per unit. Required fees: $3 per unit. $35 per semester. *General application contact:* Candace Hallmark, Assistant Director of Graduate Admissions, 650-508-3592.

Division of Academic Affairs
Dr. Richard Giardina, Interim Provost

School of Arts and Humanities
Dr. Arnell R. Etherington, Dean
Programs in:
arts and humanities (MA, MFA, MM, Certificate)
English (MA)
music (MFA, MM)
pedagogy (MM)
performance (MM)
teaching English to speakers of other languages (Certificate)

School of Business and Management
Dr. James Fogal, Dean
Programs in:
business administration (MBA)
business and management (MBA, MPA, MSM)
finance (MBA)
human resource management (MBA)
management (MSM)
managing with information technology (MSM)
marketing (MBA)
operations management (MSM)
project and program management (MSM)
public administration (MPA)
public affairs administration (MPA)

School of Education and Leadership
Dr. Joanne Rossi, Dean
Programs in:
education (MA)
education and leadership (MA, MAT, Certificate)
multiple subject teaching credential (Certificate)
reading (MA, Certificate)
school administration (MA, Certificate)
single subject teaching credential (Certificate)
special education (MA, Certificate)
teaching (MAT)

School of Sciences
Dr. Arnell Etherington, Dean
Programs in:
art therapy psychology (MAAT, MAMFT)
clinical gerontology (Certificate)
clinical psychology (MA)
marital and family therapy (MAMFT)
premedical studies (Certificate)
sciences (MA, MAAT, MACP, MAMFT, Certificate)

■ PACIFICA GRADUATE INSTITUTE

Carpinteria, CA 93013

http://www.pacifica.edu/

Proprietary, coed, graduate-only institution. *Computer facilities:* 5 computers available on campus for general student use. A campuswide network can be accessed from off campus. *General application contact:* Admissions Office, 805-969-3626 Ext. 128.

Graduate Programs
Programs in:
clinical psychology (PhD)
counseling psychology (MA)
depth psychology (MA, PhD)
mythological studies (MA, PhD)

■ PEPPERDINE UNIVERSITY

Malibu, CA 90263

http://www.pepperdine.edu/

Independent-religious, coed, university. CGS member. *Graduate faculty:* 41 full-time (11 women), 43 part-time/adjunct (10 women). *Computer facilities:* Computer purchase and lease plans are available. 292 computers available on campus for general student use. A campuswide network can be accessed from student residence rooms and from off campus. Online class registration is available. *Graduate expenses:* Tuition: full-time $36,442; part-time $1273 per unit. Tuition and fees vary according to degree level and program. *General application contact:* Kristin A. Collins, Director of Admission, 310-506-4392.

Graduate School of Education and Psychology
Dr. Margaret J. Weber, Dean
Programs in:
clinical psychology (MA)
education and psychology (MA, MS, Ed D, Psy D)

Malibu Graduate Business Programs
Dr. Mark Mallinger, Director, Full-Time Programs
Programs in:
business administration (MBA)
international business (MIB)

School of Law
Kenneth W. Starr, Dean
Programs in:
dispute resolution (LL M, MDR)
law (JD, LL M, MDR)

School of Public Policy
Dr. James R. Wilburn, Dean
Programs in:
American politics (MPP)
economics (MPP)
international relations (MPP)
public policy (MPP)
state and local policy (MPP)

Seaver College
Dr. David W. Baird, Dean
Programs in:
American studies (MA)
communication (MA)
history (MA)
ministry (MS)
religion (M Div, MA)

■ POINT LOMA NAZARENE UNIVERSITY

San Diego, CA 92106-2899

http://www.pointloma.edu/

Independent-religious, coed, comprehensive institution. *Computer facilities:* Computer purchase and lease plans are available. 270 computers available on campus for general student use. A campuswide network can be accessed from student residence rooms and from off campus. Online class registration is available. *General application contact:* Associate Director, Graduate Admission, 866-692-4723.

Graduate Studies
Programs in:
biology (MA, MS)
business administration (MBA)
education (MA, Ed S)
nursing (MSN)
religion (M Min, MA)

■ SAINT MARY'S COLLEGE OF CALIFORNIA

Moraga, CA 94575

http://www.stmarys-ca.edu/

Independent-religious, coed, comprehensive institution. CGS member. *Computer facilities:* 325 computers available on campus for general student use. A campuswide network can be accessed from student residence rooms and from off campus. Online class registration, student accounts are available. *General application contact:* Vice Provost for Enrollment, 925-631-4277.

Graduate Business Programs
Programs in:
- business (MBA)
- business administration (MBA)
- executive business administration (MBA)

Kalmanovitz School of Education
Programs in:
- early childhood education and Montessori teacher training (M Ed, MA)
- education (M Ed, MA, MAT, PhD)
- educational leadership (MA, PhD)
- general counseling (MA)
- instruction (M Ed)
- marital and family therapy (MA)
- reading leadership (MA)
- school counseling (MA)
- special education (M Ed, MA)
- teachers for tomorrow (MAT)
- teaching leadership (MA)

School of Liberal Arts
Programs in:
- creative writing (MFA)
- kinesiology (MA)
- leadership (MA)
- liberal arts (MA, MFA)
- liberal studies (MA)

■ SAN DIEGO STATE UNIVERSITY
San Diego, CA 92182
http://www.sdsu.edu/

State-supported, coed, university. CGS member. *Computer facilities:* 400 computers available on campus for general student use. A campuswide network can be accessed from student residence rooms and from off campus. Online class registration is available. *General application contact:* Information Contact, 619-594-5213.

Graduate and Research Affairs
Program in:
- interdisciplinary studies (MA, MS)

College of Arts and Letters
Programs in:
- anthropology (MA)
- applied linguistics and English as a second language (CAL)
- arts and letters (MA, MFA, PhD, CAL)
- Asian studies (MA)
- computational linguistics (MA)
- creative writing (MFA)
- economics (MA)
- English (MA)
- English as a second language/applied linguistics (MA)
- European studies (MA)
- general linguistics (MA)
- geography (MA, PhD)
- history (MA)
- Latin American studies (MA)
- liberal arts and sciences (MA)
- philosophy (MA)
- political science (MA)
- rhetoric and writing (MA)
- sociology (MA)
- Spanish (MA)
- women's studies (MA)

College of Business Administration
Programs in:
- accountancy (MS)
- business administration (MBA, MS)
- entrepreneurship (MS)
- finance (MS)
- human resources management (MS)
- information and decision systems (MS)
- international business (MS)
- management science (MS)
- marketing (MS)
- production and operations management (MS)
- sports business management (MBA)

College of Education
Programs in:
- child development (MS)
- counseling and school psychology (MS)
- education (MA, MS, Ed D, PhD)
- educational leadership (MA)
- educational leadership in post-secondary education (MA)
- educational technology (MA)
- educational technology and teaching and learning (Ed D)
- elementary curriculum and instruction (MA)
- multi-cultural emphasis (PhD)
- policy studies in language and cross cultural education (MA)
- reading education (MA)
- rehabilitation counseling (MS)
- secondary curriculum and instruction (MA)
- special education (MA)

College of Engineering
Programs in:
- aerospace engineering (MS)
- civil engineering (MS)
- electrical engineering (MS)
- engineering (MS, PhD)
- engineering mechanics (MS)
- engineering sciences and applied mechanics (PhD)
- flight dynamics (MS)
- fluid dynamics (MS)
- manufacture and design (MS)
- mechanical engineering (MS)

College of Health and Human Services
Programs in:
- audiology (Au D)
- biometry (MPH)
- communicative disorders (MA)
- environmental health (MPH)
- epidemiology (MPH, PhD)
- gerontology (MS)
- global emergency preparedness and response (MS)
- global health (PhD)
- health and human services (MA, MPH, MS, MSW, Au D, PhD)
- health behavior (PhD)
- health promotion (MPH)
- health services administration (MPH)
- language and communicative disorders (PhD)
- nursing (MS)
- social work (MSW)
- toxicology (MS)

College of Professional Studies and Fine Arts
Programs in:
- advertising and public relations (MA)
- art history (MA)
- city planning (MCP)
- composition (acoustic and electronic) (MM)
- conducting (MM)
- criminal justice administration (MPA)
- criminal justice and criminology (MS)
- critical-cultural studies (MA)
- ethnomusicology (MA)
- exercise physiology (MS)
- interaction studies (MA)
- intercultural and international studies (MA)
- jazz studies (MM)
- musicology (MA)
- new media studies (MA)
- news and information studies (MA)
- nutritional science (MS)
- nutritional sciences (MS)
- performance (MM)
- physical education/kinesiology (MS)
- piano pedagogy (MA)
- professional studies and fine arts (MA, MCP, MFA, MM, MPA, MS)
- public administration (MPA)
- studio arts (MA, MFA)
- telecommunications and media management (MA)
- television, film, and new media production (MA)
- theatre arts (MA, MFA)
- theory (MA)

College of Sciences
Programs in:
- applied mathematics (MS)
- astronomy (MS)
- biology (MA, MS)
- cell and molecular biology (PhD)
- chemistry (MA, MS, PhD)
- clinical psychology (MS, PhD)
- computational science (MS, PhD)
- computer science (MS)
- ecology (MS, PhD)
- geological sciences (MS)
- industrial and organizational psychology (MS)
- mathematics (MA)
- mathematics and science education (PhD)
- microbiology (MS)
- molecular biology (MA, MS)
- physics (MA, MS)
- program evaluation (MS)
- psychology (MA)
- radiological physics (MS)
- regulatory affairs (MS)
- sciences (MA, MS, PhD)
- statistics (MS)

■ SAN FRANCISCO STATE UNIVERSITY

San Francisco, CA 94132-1722

http://www.sfsu.edu/

State-supported, coed, comprehensive institution. CGS member. *Computer facilities:* Computer purchase and lease plans are available. 2,800 computers available on campus for general student use. A campuswide network can be accessed from student residence rooms and from off campus. Online class registration is available. *General application contact:* Director of Graduate Admissions, 415-338-2234.

Division of Graduate Studies

College of Behavioral and Social Sciences

Programs in:
- anthropology (MA)
- behavioral and social sciences (MA, MPA, MS)
- economics (MA)
- geography (MA)
- history (MA)
- human sexuality studies (MA)
- integrated and collaborative services (MPA)
- international relations (MA)
- nonprofit administration (MPA)
- policy analysis (MPA)
- political science (MA)
- psychology (MA, MS)
- public management (MPA)
- urban administration (MPA)

College of Business

Programs in:
- business (MBA, MSBA)
- business administration (MBA)

College of Creative Arts

Programs in:
- art (MFA)
- art history (MA)
- chamber music (MM)
- cinema (MFA)
- cinema studies (MA)
- classical performance (MM)
- composition (MA)
- conducting (MM)
- creative arts (MA, MFA, MM)
- drama (MA)
- industrial arts (MA)
- music education (MA)
- music history (MA)
- radio and television (MA)
- theatre arts (MFA)

College of Education

Programs in:
- adult education (MA Ed, AC)
- communicative disorders (MS)
- early childhood education (MA)
- education (MA, MA Ed, MS, PhD, AC)
- educational administration (MA, AC)
- educational technology (MA)
- elementary education (MA)
- equity and social justice (AC)
- equity and social justice in education (MA Ed)
- language and literacy education (MA)
- mathematics education (MA)
- secondary education (MA Ed)
- special education (MA, PhD, AC)
- special interest (MA Ed)
- training systems development (AC)

College of Ethnic Studies

Programs in:
- Asian American studies (MA)
- ethnic studies (MA)

College of Health and Human Services

Programs in:
- case management (MS)
- counseling (MS)
- family and consumer sciences (MA)
- geriatric care management (MA)
- health and human services (MA, MPH, MS, MSC, MSW, DPT, Dr Sc PT)
- health education (MPH)
- health, wellness and aging (MA)
- kinesiology (MS)
- long-term care administration (MA)
- marriage, family, and child counseling (MSC)
- nursing administration (MS)
- nursing education (MS)
- physical therapy (MS, DPT, Dr Sc PT)
- recreation (MS)
- rehabilitation counseling (MS)
- social work (MSW)

College of Humanities

Programs in:
- Chinese (MA)
- classics (MA)
- communication studies (MA)
- comparative literature (MA)
- composition (MA, Certificate)
- creative writing (MA, MFA)
- French (MA)
- German (MA)
- humanities (MA, MFA, Certificate)
- Italian (MA)
- Japanese (MA)
- linguistics (MA)
- literature (MA)
- museum studies (MA)
- philosophy (MA)
- Spanish (MA)
- teaching composition (Certificate)
- teaching critical thinking (Certificate)
- teaching English to speakers of other languages (MA)
- teaching post-secondary reading (Certificate)
- women studies (MA)

College of Science and Engineering

Programs in:
- applied geosciences (MS)
- biomedical laboratory science (MS)
- cell and molecular biology (MS)
- chemistry (MS)
- computer science (MS)
- computer science: computing and business (MS)
- computer science: computing for life sciences (MS)
- computer science: software and engineering (MS)
- conservation biology (MS)
- ecology and systematic biology (MS)
- embedded electrical and computer systems (MS)
- engineering (MS)
- marine biology (MS)
- marine science (MS)
- mathematics (MA)
- microbiology (MS)
- physics (MS)
- physiology and behavioral biology (MS)
- science and engineering (MA, MS)
- structural/earthquake engineering (MS)

■ SAN JOSE STATE UNIVERSITY

San Jose, CA 95192-0001

http://www.sjsu.edu/

State-supported, coed, comprehensive institution. CGS member. *Computer facilities:* Computer purchase and lease plans are available. A campuswide network can be accessed from student residence rooms and from off campus. Online class registration is available. *General application contact:* Associate Director, Undergraduate and Graduate Admissions, 408-924-2359.

Graduate Studies and Research

Program in:
- interdisciplinary studies (MA, MS)

College of Applied Sciences and Arts

Programs in:
- applied sciences and arts (MA, MLIS, MPH, MS, MSW, PhD, Certificate)
- applied social gerontology (Certificate)
- community health education (MPH)
- gerontology nurse practitioner (MS)
- justice studies (MS)
- kinesiology (MA)
- library and information science (MLIS, PhD)
- mass communications (MS)
- nursing (Certificate)
- nursing administration (MS)
- nursing education (MS)
- nutritional science (MS)
- occupational therapy (MS)
- recreation (MS)
- social work (MSW, Certificate)

College of Education

Programs in:
- child and adolescent development (MA)
- counselor education (MA)
- education (MA, Certificate)
- educational administration (MA)
- elementary education (MA, Certificate)
- higher education administration (MA)
- instructional technology (MA, Certificate)
- school business management (Certificate)

secondary education (Certificate)
special education (MA, Certificate)
speech language pathology (MA)

College of Engineering
Programs in:
aerospace engineering (MS)
chemical engineering (MS)
civil engineering (MS)
computer engineering (MS)
electrical engineering (MS)
engineering (MS)
general engineering (MS)
human factors and ergonomics (MS)
industrial and systems engineering (MS)
materials engineering (MS)
mechanical engineering (MS)
quality assurance (MS)
software engineering (MS)

College of Humanities and the Arts
Programs in:
art education (MA)
art history (MA)
computational linguistics (Certificate)
creative writing (MFA)
digital media (MFA)
digital media in art history and education (MA)
French (MA)
humanities and the arts (MA, MFA, Certificate)
linguistics (MA, Certificate)
literature (MA)
music (MA)
philosophy (MA, Certificate)
photography (MFA)
pictorial arts (MFA)
secondary English education (Certificate)
Spanish (MA)
spatial arts (MFA)
teaching English to speakers of other languages (MA, Certificate)
theatre arts (MA)

College of Science
Programs in:
applied mathematics (MS)
biological sciences (MA, MS)
chemistry (MA, MS)
computational physics (MS)
computer science (MS)
geology (MS)
marine science (MS)
mathematics (MA, MS)
mathematics education (MA)
meteorology (MS)
molecular biology and microbiology (MS)
organismal biology, conservation and ecology (MS)
physics (MS)
physiology (MS)
science (MA, MS)
statistics (MA)

College of Social Sciences
Programs in:
applied anthropology (MA)
applied economics (MA)
clinical psychology (MS)
communication studies (MA)
economics (MA)
environmental studies (MS)
experimental psychology (MA)
geographic information science (Certificate)
geography (MA)
history (MA)
history education (MA)
industrial/organizational psychology (MS)
Mexican-American studies (MA)
psychology (MA)
public administration (MPA)
social sciences (MA, MPA, MS, MUP, Certificate)
sociology (MA)
urban and regional planning (MUP, Certificate)

Lucas Graduate School of Business
Programs in:
accounting (MS)
business (MBA, MS)
business administration (MBA)
taxation (MS)
transportation management (MS)

■ SANTA CLARA UNIVERSITY
Santa Clara, CA 95053
http://www.scu.edu/

Independent-religious, coed, university. CGS member. *Graduate faculty:* 218 full-time (75 women), 131 part-time/adjunct (43 women). *Computer facilities:* Computer purchase and lease plans are available. 800 computers available on campus for general student use. A campuswide network can be accessed from student residence rooms and from off campus. Online class registration is available. *Graduate expenses:* Tuition: full-time $6849; part-time $761 per credit hour. Tuition and fees vary according to course load and program. *General application contact:* Richard Toomey, Associate Vice Provost, Enrollment Management, 408-554-4966.

Leavey School of Business
Dr. Barry Posner, Dean
Programs in:
business (EMBA, MBA, MSIS)
business administration (EMBA, MBA)
information systems (MSIS)

School of Education, Counseling Psychology, and Pastoral Ministries
Dr. Dale Larson, Interim Dean
Programs in:
catechetics (MA)
counseling (MA)
counseling psychology (MA)
education, counseling psychology, and pastoral ministries (MA, Certificate)
educational administration (MA)
interdisciplinary education (MA)
liturgical music (MA)
multiple subject teaching (Certificate)
pastoral liturgy (MA)
single subject teaching (Certificate)
special education (MA, Certificate)
spirituality (MA)
teacher education (Certificate)

School of Engineering
Godfrey Mungal, Dean
Programs in:
analog circuit design (Certificate)
applied mathematics (MSAM)
ASIC design and test (Certificate)
civil engineering (MSCE)
computer science and engineering (MSCSE, PhD, Engineer)
controls (Certificate)
data storage technologies (Certificate)
digital signal processing (Certificate)
dynamics (Certificate)
electrical engineering (MSEE, PhD, Engineer)
engineering (MS, MSAM, MSCE, MSCSE, MSE, MSE Mgt, MSEE, MSME, PhD, Certificate, Engineer)
engineering management (MSE Mgt)
fundamentals of electrical engineering (Certificate)
grid computing (Certificate)
information assurance (Certificate)
materials engineering (Certificate)
mechanical design analysis (Certificate)
mechanical engineering (MSME, PhD, Engineer)
mechatronics systems engineering (Certificate)
networking (Certificate)
software engineering (MS, Certificate)
technology jump-start (Certificate)
telecommunications management (Certificate)
thermofluids (Certificate)

School of Law
Donald Polden, Dean
Programs in:
high technology law (Certificate)
intellectual property law (LL M)
international and comparative law (LL M)
international law (Certificate)
law (JD)
public interest and social justice law (Certificate)
US law for foreign lawyers (LL M)

■ SONOMA STATE UNIVERSITY
Rohnert Park, CA 94928-3609
http://www.sonoma.edu/

State-supported, coed, comprehensive institution. *Graduate faculty:* 60 full-time (32 women), 20 part-time/adjunct (13 women). *Computer facilities:* 400 computers available on campus for general student use. A campuswide network can be accessed from student residence rooms and from off

Sonoma State University (continued)
campus. Online class registration is available. *General application contact:* Elaine Sundberg, Associate Vice Provost, Academic Programs/Graduate Studies, 707-664-2215.

Institute of Interdisciplinary Studies/Special Major
Dr. Ellen Carlton, Coordinator
Program in:
special major (MA, MS)

School of Arts and Humanities
Programs in:
American literature (MA)
arts and humanities (MA)
creative writing (MA)
English literature (MA)
world literature (MA)

School of Business and Economics
Sandra Newton, Coordinator
Programs in:
business administration (MBA)
business and economics (MBA)

School of Education
Dr. Mary Gendernalik-Cooper, Dean
Programs in:
education (MA)
education—curriculum, teaching and learning (MA)
educational leadership (MA)
literacy studies and elementary education (MA)
special education (MA)

School of Science and Technology
Programs in:
environmental biology (MA)
family nurse practitioner (MS)
general biology (MA)
kinesiology (MA)
science and technology (MA, MS)

School of Social Sciences
Programs in:
counseling (MA)
cultural resources management (MA)
history (MA)
marriage, family, and child counseling (MA)
public administration (MPA)
pupil personnel services (MA)
social sciences (MA, MPA)

■ STANFORD UNIVERSITY
Stanford, CA 94305-9991
http://www.stanford.edu/

Independent, coed, university. CGS member. *Computer facilities:* Computer purchase and lease plans are available. 1,000 computers available on campus for general student use. A campuswide network can be accessed from student residence rooms and from off campus. Online class registration is available. *General application contact:* Graduate Admissions, 650-723-4291.

Graduate School of Business
Program in:
business (MBA, PhD)

Law School
Program in:
law (JD, JSM, MLS, JSD)

School of Earth Sciences
Programs in:
earth sciences (MS, PhD, Eng)
earth systems (MS)
geological and environmental sciences (MS, PhD, Eng)
geophysics (MS, PhD)
petroleum engineering (MS, PhD, Eng)

School of Education
Programs in:
administration and policy analysis (Ed D, PhD)
anthropology of education (PhD)
art education (MA, PhD)
child and adolescent development (PhD)
counseling psychology (PhD)
dance education (MA)
economics of education (PhD)
education (MA, Ed D, PhD)
educational linguistics (PhD)
educational psychology (PhD)
English education (MA, PhD)
evaluation (MA)
general curriculum studies (MA, PhD)
higher education (PhD)
history of education (PhD)
interdisciplinary studies (PhD)
international comparative education (MA, PhD)
international education administration and policy analysis (MA)
languages education (MA)
learning, design, and technology (MA, PhD)
mathematics education (MA, PhD)
philosophy of education (PhD)
policy analysis (MA)
prospective principal's program (MA)
science education (MA, PhD)
social studies education (MA, PhD)
sociology of education (PhD)
symbolic systems in education (PhD)
teacher education (MA, PhD)

School of Engineering
Programs in:
aeronautics and astronautics (MS, PhD, Eng)
biomechanical engineering (MS)
chemical engineering (MS, PhD, Eng)
civil and environmental engineering (MS, PhD, Eng)
computer science (MS, PhD)
electrical engineering (MS, PhD, Eng)
engineering (MS, PhD, Eng)
management science and engineering (MS, PhD)
materials science and engineering (MS, PhD, Eng)
mechanical engineering (MS, PhD, Eng)
product design (MS)
scientific computing and computational mathematics (MS, PhD)

School of Humanities and Sciences
Programs in:
anthropological sciences (MA, MS, PhD)
applied physics (MS, PhD)
art history (PhD)
art practice (MFA)
biological sciences (MS, PhD)
biophysics (PhD)
chemistry (PhD)
Chinese (MA, PhD)
classics (MA, PhD)
communication (journalism specialization) (MA)
communication theory and research (PhD)
comparative literature (PhD)
computer-based music theory and acoustics (MA, PhD)
cultural and social anthropology (MA, PhD)
drama (PhD)
economics (PhD)
English (MA, PhD)
financial mathematics (MS)
French (MA, PhD)
German studies (MA, PhD)
history (MA, PhD)
humanities (MA)
humanities and sciences (MA, MFA, MS, DMA, PhD)
international policy studies (MA)
Italian (MA, PhD)
Japanese (MA, PhD)
linguistics (MA, PhD)
mathematics (MS, PhD)
modern thought and literature (PhD)
music composition (MA, DMA)
music history (MA)
music, science, and technology (MA)
musicology (PhD)
philosophy (MA, PhD)
physics (PhD)
political science (MA, PhD)
psychology (PhD)
religious studies (MA, PhD)
Russian (MA)
Slavic languages and literatures (PhD)
sociology (PhD)
Spanish (MA, PhD)
statistics (MS, PhD)

Center for East Asian Studies
Program in:
East Asian studies (MA)

Center for Russian and East European Studies
Program in:
Russian and East European studies (MA)

School of Medicine
Programs in:
bioengineering (MS, PhD)
medicine (MD, MS, PhD)

Graduate Programs in Medicine
Programs in:
biochemistry (PhD)
biomedical informatics (MS, PhD)

cancer biology (PhD)
developmental biology (PhD)
epidemiology (MS, PhD)
genetics (PhD)
health services research (MS)
immunology (PhD)
medicine (MS, PhD)
microbiology and immunology (PhD)
molecular and cellular physiology (PhD)
molecular pharmacology (PhD)
neurosciences (PhD)
structural biology (PhD)

■ UNIVERSITY OF CALIFORNIA, BERKELEY

Berkeley, CA 94720-1500
http://www.berkeley.edu/

State-supported, coed, university. CGS member. *Computer facilities:* A campuswide network can be accessed from student residence rooms and from off campus. Online class registration is available. *General application contact:* Information Contact, 510-642-7405.

Graduate Division

Programs in:
ancient history and Mediterranean archaeology (MA, PhD)
Asian studies (PhD)
bioengineering (PhD)
biophysics (PhD)
Buddhist studies (PhD)
comparative biochemistry (PhD)
demography (MA, PhD)
East Asian studies (MA)
endocrinology (MA, PhD)
energy and resources (MA, MS, PhD)
ethnic studies (PhD)
folklore (MA)
French (PhD)
international and area studies (MA)
Italian (PhD)
Jewish studies (PhD)
Latin American studies (MA)
neuroscience (PhD)
Northeast Asian studies (MA)
performance studies (PhD)
range management (MS)
sociology and demography (PhD)
South Asian studies (MA)
Southeast Asian studies (MA)
Spanish (PhD)
vision science (MS, PhD)

College of Chemistry

Programs in:
chemical engineering (MS, PhD)
chemistry (MS, PhD)

College of Engineering

Programs in:
applied science and technology (PhD)
computer science (MS, PhD)
electrical engineering (MS, PhD)
engineering (M Eng, MS, D Eng, PhD)
engineering and project management (M Eng, MS, D Eng, PhD)
engineering science (M Eng, MS, PhD)
environmental engineering (M Eng, MS, D Eng, PhD)
geoengineering (M Eng, MS, D Eng, PhD)
industrial engineering and operations research (M Eng, MS, D Eng, PhD)
mechanical engineering (M Eng, MS, D Eng, PhD)
nuclear engineering (M Eng, MS, D Eng, PhD)
structural engineering, mechanics and materials (M Eng, MS, D Eng, PhD)
transportation engineering (M Eng, MS, D Eng, PhD)

College of Environmental Design

Programs in:
architecture (M Arch)
building science (MS, PhD)
building structures, construction and materials (MS, PhD)
city and regional planning (MCP, PhD)
design (MA)
design theories, methods, and practices (MS, PhD)
environmental design (M Arch, MA, MCP, MLA, MS, MUD, PhD)
environmental design in developing countries (MS, PhD)
environmental planning (MLA)
history of architecture and urbanism (MS, PhD)
landscape architecture (MLA)
landscape architecture and environmental planning (PhD)
landscape design and site planning (MLA)
social and cultural processes in architecture and urbanism (MS, PhD)
urban and community design (MLA)
urban design (MUD)

College of Letters and Science

Programs in:
African American studies (PhD)
anthropology (PhD)
applied mathematics (PhD)
art practice (MFA)
astrophysics (PhD)
Chinese language (PhD)
classical archaeology (MA, PhD)
classics (MA, PhD)
comparative literature (PhD)
composition (PhD)
Czech (PhD)
economics (PhD)
English (PhD)
ethnomusicology (PhD)
French (PhD)
geography (PhD)
geology (MA, MS, PhD)
geophysics (MA, MS, PhD)
German (PhD)
Greek (MA)
Hindi (MA, PhD)
Hispanic languages and literature (PhD)
history (PhD)
history of art (PhD)
Indonesian (MA, PhD)
integrative biology (PhD)
Italian studies (PhD)
Japanese language (PhD)
Latin (MA)
letters and science (MA, MFA, MS, PhD)
linguistics (PhD)
logic and the methodology of science (PhD)
mathematics (MA, PhD)
medical anthropology (PhD)
molecular and cell biology (PhD)
musicology (PhD)
Near Eastern religions (PhD)
Near Eastern studies (MA, PhD)
philosophy (PhD)
physics (PhD)
Polish (PhD)
political science (PhD)
psychology (PhD)
rhetoric (PhD)
Russian (PhD)
Sanskrit (MA, PhD)
Scandinavian languages and literatures (PhD)
Serbo-Croatian (PhD)
sociology (PhD)
statistics (MA, PhD)
Tamil (MA, PhD)

College of Natural Resources

Programs in:
agricultural and resource economics (PhD)
environmental science, policy, and management (MS, PhD)
forestry (MF)
microbiology (PhD)
molecular and biochemical nutrition (PhD)
molecular toxicology (PhD)
natural resources (MF, MS, PhD)
plant biology (PhD)

Graduate School of Journalism

Program in:
journalism (MJ)

Graduate School of Public Policy

Program in:
public policy (MPP, PhD)

Haas School of Business

Richard K. Lyons, Dean
Programs in:
accounting (PhD)
business (MBA, MFE, PhD)
business administration (MBA, PhD)
business and public policy (PhD)
finance (PhD)
financial engineering (MFE)
marketing (PhD)
organizational behavior and industrial relations (PhD)
real estate (PhD)

School of Education

Programs in:
development in mathematics and science (MA)
developmental teacher educationeducation (MA, Ed D, PhD)

University of California, Berkeley (continued)
- education and single subject credential: English (MA)
- education in mathematics, science, and technology (MA, PhD)
- human development and education (MA, PhD)
- language, literacy, and culture (MA, Ed D, PhD)
- policy and organizational research (MA, PhD)
- principal leadership (MA)
- program evaluation and assessment (Ed D)
- quantitative methods and evaluation (MA, PhD)
- science and mathematics educationsocial and cultural studies in education (MA, PhD)
- special education (PhD)

School of Information Management and Systems
Program in:
- information management and systems (MIMS, PhD)

School of Public Health
Programs in:
- biostatistics (MA, PhD)
- community health education (MPH)
- environmental health sciences (MPH, MS, Dr PH, PhD)
- epidemiology (MPH, MS, PhD)
- health and social behavior (MPH)
- health policy and management (MPH)
- health services and policy analysis (PhD)
- infectious diseases (MPH, PhD)
- infectious diseases and immunity (PhD)
- interdisciplinary (MPH)
- maternal and child health (MPH)
- public health (MA, MPH, MS, Dr PH, PhD)
- public health nutrition (MPH)

School of Social Welfare
Program in:
- social welfare (MSW, PhD)

School of Law
Christopher J. Edley, Dean
Programs in:
- jurisprudence and social policy (PhD)
- law (JD, LL M, JSD)

School of Optometry
Program in:
- optometry (OD, Certificate)

UC Berkeley Extension
Programs in:
- accounting (Certificate)
- alcohol and drug abuse studies (Certificate)
- business administration (Certificate, Diploma)
- business intelligence and SAS analytics software (Certificate)
- clinical research conduct and management (Certificate)
- college admissions and career planning (Certificate)
- construction management (Certificate)
- database management (Certificate)
- designated subjects teaching in adult education (Certificate)
- designated subjects teaching in career and technical education (Certificate)
- editing (Certificate)
- English learner pedagogy (Certificate)
- facilities management (Certificate)
- finance (Certificate, Diploma)
- global business management (Diploma)
- graphic design (Certificate)
- health professions (Certificate)
- human resource management (Certificate)
- HVAC (Certificate)
- information systems and management (Certificate)
- integrated circuit design and techniques (Certificate)
- integrated marketing communications (Certificate)
- interior design and interior architecture (Certificate)
- Java programming (Certificate)
- landscape architecture (Certificate)
- leadership in sustainability and environmental management (Certificate)
- management (Certificate)
- marketing (Certificate, Diploma)
- marketing metrics (Certificate)
- paralegal studies (Certificate)
- personal financial planning (Certificate)
- project human resource management (Certificate)
- project management (Certificate, Diploma)
- project management for biopharmaceuticals (Certificate)
- project quality management (Certificate)
- project risk management (Certificate)
- quality and compliance for biotechnology (Certificate)
- solar energy and green building (Certificate)
- sustainable design (Certificate)
- teaching English as a second language (Certificate)
- technical communication (Certificate)
- UNIX/Linux system administration (Certificate)
- virtual and cloud computing (Certificate)
- visual arts (Certificate)
- wealth management (Certificate)
- writing (Certificate)

■ UNIVERSITY OF CALIFORNIA, DAVIS
Davis, CA 95616
http://www.ucdavis.edu/

State-supported, coed, university. CGS member. *Computer facilities:* 150 computers available on campus for general student use. A campuswide network can be accessed from student residence rooms and from off campus. Online class registration, software packages are available. *General application contact:* Director of Outreach, Recruitment and Retention, 530-752-2119.

College of Engineering
Programs in:
- aeronautical engineering (M Engr, MS, D Engr, PhD, Certificate)
- applied science (MS, PhD)
- biological systems engineering (M Engr, MS, D Engr, PhD)
- biomedical engineering (MS, PhD)
- chemical engineering (MS, PhD)
- civil and environmental engineering (M Engr, MS, D Engr, PhD, Certificate)
- computer science (MS, PhD)
- electrical and computer engineering (MS, PhD)
- engineering (M Engr, MS, D Engr, PhD, Certificate)
- materials science and engineering (MS, PhD)
- mechanical engineering (M Engr, MS, D Engr, PhD, Certificate)
- transportation, technology and policy (MS, PhD)

Graduate School of Management
Nicole W. Biggart, Dean
Programs in:
- business administration (MBA)
- management (MBA)

Graduate Studies
Programs in:
- acting (MFA)
- agricultural and environmental chemistry (MS, PhD)
- agricultural and resource economics (MS, PhD)
- animal behavior (PhD)
- animal biology (MAM, MS, PhD)
- anthropology (MA, PhD)
- applied linguistics (MA, PhD)
- applied mathematics (MS, PhD)
- art (MFA)
- art history (MA)
- atmospheric sciences (MS, PhD)
- avian sciences (MS)
- biochemistry and molecular biology (MS, PhD)
- biophysics (MS, PhD)
- biostatistics (MS, PhD)
- cell and developmental biology (MS, PhD)
- chemistry (MS, PhD)
- child development (MS)
- clinical research (MAS)
- communication (MA)
- community development (MS)
- comparative literature (PhD)
- comparative pathology (MS, PhD)
- composition (MA, PhD)
- conducting (MA, PhD)
- creative writing (MA)
- cultural studies (MA, PhD)
- dramatic art (PhD)
- ecology (MS, PhD)

economics (MA, PhD)
education (MA, Ed D)
English (MA, PhD)
entomology (MS, PhD)
epidemiology (MS, PhD)
exercise science (MS)
food science (MS, PhD)
forensic science (MS)
French (PhD)
genetics (MS, PhD)
geography (MA, PhD)
geology (MS, PhD)
German (MA, PhD)
health informatics (MS)
history (MA, PhD)
horticulture and agronomy (MS)
human development (PhD)
hydrologic sciences (MS, PhD)
immunology (MS, PhD)
instructional studies (PhD)
integrated pest management (MS)
international agricultural development (MS)
linguistics (MA)
mathematics (MA, MAT, PhD)
microbiology (MS, PhD)
molecular, cellular and integrative physiology (MS, PhD)
musicology (MA, PhD)
Native American studies (MA, PhD)
neuroscience (PhD)
nutrition (MS, PhD)
pharmacology/toxicology (MS, PhD)
philosophy (MA, PhD)
physics (MS, PhD)
plant biology (MS, PhD)
plant pathology (MS, PhD)
political science (MA, PhD)
population biology (PhD)
psychological studies (PhD)
psychology (PhD)
sociocultural studies (PhD)
sociology (MA, PhD)
soils and biogeochemistry (MS, PhD)
Spanish (MA, PhD)
statistics (MS, PhD)
textile arts and costume design (MFA)
textiles (MS)
viticulture and enology (MS, PhD)

School of Law

Program in:
law (JD, LL M)

School of Medicine

Dr. Claire Pomeroy, Dean/Vice Chancellor, Human Health Sciences
Program in:
medicine (MD)

School of Veterinary Medicine

Programs in:
preventive veterinary medicine (MPVM)
veterinary medicine (DVM, MPVM, Certificate)

■ UNIVERSITY OF CALIFORNIA, IRVINE

Irvine, CA 92697
http://www.uci.edu/

State-supported, coed, university. CGS member. *Computer facilities:* 1,500 computers available on campus for general student use. A campuswide network can be accessed from student residence rooms and from off campus. Online class registration is available. *General application contact:* Office of Graduate Studies, 949-824-4611.

Office of Graduate Studies

Programs in:
educational administration (Ed D)
educational administration and leadership (Ed D)
elementary and secondary education (MAT)

Claire Trevor School of the Arts

Programs in:
accompanying (MFA)
acting (MFA)
arts (MFA, PhD)
choral conducting (MFA)
composition and technology (MFA)
dance (MFA)
design and stage management (MFA)
directing (MFA)
drama (MFA)
drama and theatre (PhD)
guitar/lute performance (MFA)
instrumental performance (MFA)
jazz instrumental/composition (MFA)
piano performance (MFA)
studio art (MFA)
vocal performance (MFA)

Donald Bren School of Information and Computer Sciences

Programs in:
information and computer science (MS, PhD)
networked systems (MS, PhD)

The Paul Merage School of Business

Programs in:
business administration (MBA)
management (PhD)

School of Biological Sciences

Programs in:
biological science (MS)
biological sciences (MS, PhD)
biotechnology (MS)

School of Engineering

Programs in:
biomedical engineering (MS, PhD)
chemical and biochemical engineering (MS, PhD)
civil and environmental engineering (MS, PhD)
electrical engineering and computer science (MS, PhD)
engineering (MS, PhD)
materials science and engineering (MS, PhD)
mechanical and aerospace engineering (MS, PhD)
networked systems (MS, PhD)

School of Humanities

Programs in:
Chinese (MA, PhD)
classics (MA, PhD)
comparative literature (MA, PhD)
creative writing (MFA)
East Asian languages and literatures (MA, PhD)
English (MA, PhD)
English (summer program) (MA)
English and American literature (PhD)
French (MA, PhD)
German (MA, PhD)
history (MA, PhD)
humanities (MA, MAT, MFA, PhD)
Japanese (MA, PhD)
philosophy (MA, PhD)
Spanish (MA, MAT, PhD)
visual studies (MA, PhD)
writing (MFA)

School of Physical Sciences

Programs in:
chemical and material physics (PhD)
chemical and materials physics (MS, PhD)
chemistry (MS, PhD)
earth system science (MS, PhD)
mathematics (MS, PhD)
physical sciences (MS, PhD)
physics (MS, PhD)

School of Social Ecology

Programs in:
criminology, law and society (MAS, PhD)
planning, policy and design (PhD)
psychology and social behavior (PhD)
social ecology (MA, MAS, MURP, PhD)
urban and regional planning (MURP)

School of Social Sciences

Programs in:
anthropology (MA, PhD)
demographic and social analysis (MA)
economics (MA, PhD)
philosophy (PhD)
political psychology (PhD)
political sciences (PhD)
psychology (PhD)
public choice (MA, PhD)
social networks (PhD)
social networks-social science (MA)
social science (MA, PhD)
social sciences (MA, PhD)
sociology and social relations-social science (MA, PhD)
transportation economics (MA, PhD)
transportation science (MA, PhD)

School of Medicine

Programs in:
biological sciences (MS, PhD)
epidemiology (MS, PhD)
genetic counseling (MS)
medicine (MD, MS, PhD)
pharmacology and toxicology (MS, PhD)

■ UNIVERSITY OF CALIFORNIA, LOS ANGELES

Los Angeles, CA 90095
http://www.ucla.edu/

State-supported, coed, university. CGS member. *Graduate faculty:* 1,835 full-time (475 women). *Computer facilities:* 4,134 computers available on campus for general student use. A campuswide network can be accessed from student residence rooms and from off campus. Online class registration is available. *Graduate expenses:* Tuition, nonresident: full-time $14,694. Required fees: $9669.50. Full-time tuition and fees vary according to course load, degree level, program and student level. *General application contact:* Graduate Admissions Office, 310-825-1711.

David Geffen School of Medicine

Program in:
medicine (MD, MS, PhD)

Graduate Programs in Medicine
Programs in:
anatomy and cell biology (PhD)
biological chemistry (MS, PhD)
biomathematics (MS, PhD)
biomedical physics (MS, PhD)
clinical research (MS)
experimental pathology (MS, PhD)
human genetics (MS, PhD)
medicine (MS, PhD)
microbiology, immunology and molecular genetics (MS, PhD)
molecular and medical pharmacology (PhD)
molecular, cell and developmental biology (PhD)
neuroscience (PhD)
physiology (PhD)

Graduate Division

Dr. Claudia Mitchell-Kernan, Dean

College of Letters and Science
Dr. Judith L. Smith, Vice Provost/Dean
Programs in:
African studies (MA)
Afro-American studies (MA)
American Indian studies (MA)
anthropology (MA, PhD)
applied linguistics (PhD)
applied linguistics and teaching English as a second language (MA)
archaeology (MA, PhD)
art history (MA, PhD)
Asian languages and cultures (MA, PhD)
Asian-American studies (MA)
astronomy (MAT, MS, PhD)
atmospheric sciences (MS, PhD)
biochemistry and molecular biology (MS, PhD)
biological chemistry (PhD)
cellular and molecular pathology (PhD)
chemistry (MS, PhD)
classics (MA, PhD)
comparative literature (MA, PhD)
East Asian studies (MA)
ecology and evolutionary biology (MA, PhD)
economics (MA, PhD)
English (MA, PhD)
French and Francophone studies (MA, PhD)
geochemistry (MS, PhD)
geography (MA, PhD)
geology (MS, PhD)
geophysics and space physics (MS, PhD)
Germanic languages (MA, PhD)
Greek (MA)
Hispanic languages and literature (PhD)
history (MA, PhD)
human genetics (PhD)
Indo-European studies (PhD)
Islamic studies (MA, PhD)
Italian (MA, PhD)
Latin (MA)
Latin American studies (MA)
letters and science (MA, MAT, MS, PhD, Certificate)
linguistics (MA, PhD)
mathematics (MA, MAT, PhD)
microbiology, immunology, and molecular genetics (PhD)
molecular biology (PhD)
molecular toxicology (PhD)
molecular, cellular and integrative physiology (PhD)
musicology (MA, PhD)
Near Eastern languages and cultures (MA, PhD)
neurobiology (PhD)
oral biology (PhD)
philosophy (MA, PhD)
physics (MAT, MS, PhD)
physics education (MAT)
physiological science (MS)
physiology (PhD)
political science (MA, PhD)
Portuguese (MA)
psychology (MA, PhD)
Scandinavian (MA)
Slavic languages and literatures (MA, PhD)
sociology (MA, PhD)
Spanish (MA)
statistics (MS, PhD)
teaching English as a second language (Certificate)
women's studies (MA, PhD)

Graduate School of Education and Information Studies
Programs in:
archival studies (MLIS)
education (M Ed, MA, Ed D, PhD)
education and information studies (M Ed, MA, MLIS, Ed D, PhD, Certificate)
educational leadership (Ed D)
informatics (MLIS)
information studies (PhD)
library and information science (Certificate)
library studies (MLIS)
moving image archive studies (MA)
special education (PhD)

Henry Samueli School of Engineering and Applied Science
Dr. Richard D. Wesel, Associate Dean, Academic and Student Affairs
Programs in:
aerospace engineering (MS, PhD)
biomedical engineering (MS, PhD)
chemical and biomolecular engineering (MS, PhD)
civil and environmental engineering (MS, PhD)
computer science (MS, PhD)
electrical engineering (MS, PhD)
engineering and applied science (MS, PhD)
manufacturing engineering (MS)
materials science and engineering (MS, PhD)
mechanical engineering (MS, PhD)

School of Nursing
Courtney H. Lyder, Dean
Program in:
nursing (MSN, PhD)

School of Public Affairs
Programs in:
public affairs (MA, MPP, MSW, PhD)
public policy (MPP)
social welfare (MSW, PhD)
urban planning (MA, PhD)

School of Public Health
Programs in:
biostatistics (MPH, MS, Dr PH, PhD)
environmental health sciences (MS, PhD)
environmental science and engineering (D Env)
epidemiology (MPH, MS, Dr PH, PhD)
health services (MPH, MS, Dr PH, PhD)
molecular toxicology (PhD)
public health (MPH, MS, D Env, Dr PH, PhD)

School of the Arts and Architecture
Programs in:
architecture and urban design (M Arch, MA, PhD)
art (MA, MFA)
arts and architecture (M Arch, MA, MFA, MM, DMA, PhD)
composition (MA, PhD)
culture and performance (MA, PhD)
dance (MFA)
design/media arts (MFA)
ethnomusicology (MA, PhD)
performance (MM, DMA)

School of Theater, Film and Television
Robert Rosen, Dean
Programs in:
film and television (MA, MFA, PhD)
theater (MA, MFA)
theater and performance studies (PhD)
theater, film and television (MA, MFA, PhD)

UCLA Anderson School of Management
Judy D. Olian, Dean

Program in:
management (MBA, MS, PhD)

School of Dentistry
Programs in:
dentistry (DDS, MS, PhD, Certificate)
oral biology (MS, PhD)

School of Law
Program in:
law (JD, LL M, SJD)

■ UNIVERSITY OF CALIFORNIA, RIVERSIDE
Riverside, CA 92521-0102
http://www.ucr.edu/

State-supported, coed, university. CGS member. *Graduate faculty:* 706 full-time (216 women). *Computer facilities:* Computer purchase and lease plans are available. 793 computers available on campus for general student use. A campuswide network can be accessed from student residence rooms and from off campus. Online class registration, online viewing of financial information are available. *Graduate expenses:* Tuition, nonresident: full-time $4898. Required fees: $10,362. *General application contact:* Graduate Admissions, 951-827-3313.

Graduate Division
Dr. Joseph W. Childers, Dean
Programs in:
anthropology (MA, MS, PhD)
applied statistics (PhD)
archival management (MA)
art history (MA)
biochemistry and molecular biology (MS, PhD)
bioengineering (MS, PhD)
biology (MS, PhD)
biomedical sciences (PhD)
cell, molecular, and developmental biology (MS, PhD)
chemical and environmental engineering (MS, PhD)
chemistry (MS, PhD)
classics (PhD)
comparative literature (MA, PhD)
composition (PhD)
computer science (MS, PhD)
creative writing and writing for the performing arts (MFA)
critical dance studies (PhD)
economics (MA, PhD)
electrical engineering (MS, PhD)
English (MA, PhD)
entomology (MS, PhD)
environmental toxicology (MS, PhD)
ethnic studies (PhD)
ethnomusicology (MA, PhD)
evolution, ecology and organismal biology (MS, PhD)
experimental choreography (MFA)
genomics and bioinformatics (PhD)
geological sciences (MS, PhD)
historic preservation (MA)
history (MA, PhD)
materials science and engineering (MS, PhD)
mathematics (MA, MS, PhD)
mechanical engineering (MS, PhD)
microbiology (MS, PhD)
molecular genetics (PhD)
museum curatorship (MA)
musicology (PhD)
neuroscience (PhD)
philosophy (MA, PhD)
physics (MS, PhD)
plant biology (MS, PhD)
plant genetics (PhD)
plant pathology (MS, PhD)
political science (MA, PhD)
population and evolutionary genetics (PhD)
psychology (MA, PhD)
sociology (MA, PhD)
soil and water sciences (MS, PhD)
Southeast Asian studies (MA)
Spanish (MA, PhD)
statistics (MS)
visual arts (MFA)

A. Gary Anderson Graduate School of Management
Dr. David W. Stewart, Dean
Program in:
management (MBA)

Graduate School of Education
Dr. Steven T. Bossert, Dean
Programs in:
autism (M Ed)
curriculum and instruction (MA)
educational leadership and policy (MA, PhD)
educational psychology (PhD)
general education (M Ed)
higher education administration and policy (PhD)
leadership (M Ed)
reading (M Ed)
school psychology (PhD)
special education (MA, PhD)

■ UNIVERSITY OF CALIFORNIA, SAN DIEGO
La Jolla, CA 92093
http://www.ucsd.edu/

State-supported, coed, university. CGS member. *Computer facilities:* 1,500 computers available on campus for general student use. A campuswide network can be accessed from student residence rooms and from off campus. Online class registration is available. *General application contact:* Graduate Admissions Office, 858-534-1193.

Office of Graduate Studies
Programs in:
acting (MFA)
aerospace engineering (MS, PhD)
anthropology (PhD)
applied mathematics (MA)
applied mechanics (MS, PhD)
applied ocean science (MS, PhD)
applied physics (MS, PhD)
bilingual education (MA)
bioengineering (M Eng, MS, PhD)
bioinformatics (PhD)
biophysics (MS, PhD)
chemical engineering (MS, PhD)
chemistry (MS, PhD)
clinical psychology (PhD)
cognitive science (PhD)
cognitive science/anthropology (PhD)
cognitive science/communication (PhD)
cognitive science/computer science and engineering (PhD)
cognitive science/linguistics (PhD)
cognitive science/neuroscience (PhD)
cognitive science/philosophy (PhD)
cognitive science/psychology (PhD)
cognitive science/sociology (PhD)
communication (MA, PhD)
communication theory and systems (MS, PhD)
comparative literature (MA, PhD)
computer engineering (MS, PhD)
computer science (MS, PhD)
curriculum design (MA)
design (MFA)
directing (MFA)
drama and theatre (PhD)
earth sciences (PhD)
economics (PhD)
economics and international affairs (PhD)
electrical engineering (M Eng)
electronic circuits and systems (MS, PhD)
engineering physics (MS, PhD)
ethnic studies (MA, PhD)
French literature (MA)
German literature (MA)
health law (MAS)
history (MA, PhD)
intelligent systems, robotics and control (MS, PhD)
Judaic studies (MA)
language and communicative disorders (PhD)
Latin American studies (MA)
linguistics (PhD)
literature (PhD)
literatures in English (MA)
marine biodiversity and conservation (MAS)
marine biology (PhD)
materials science and engineering (MS, PhD)
mathematics (MA, PhD)
mathematics and science education (PhD)
mechanical engineering (MS, PhD)
music (MA, DMA, PhD)
oceanography (PhD)
philosophy (PhD)
photonics (MS, PhD)
physics (MS, PhD)
physics/materials physics (MS)
playwriting (MFA)
political science (PhD)
political science and international affairs (PhD)

University of California, San Diego (continued)

psychology (PhD)
public health and epidemiology (PhD)
science studies (PhD)
signal and image processing (MS, PhD)
sociology (PhD)
Spanish literature (MA)
stage management (MFA)
statistics (MS)
structural engineering (MS, PhD)
teacher education (M Ed)
teaching and learning (Ed D)
theatre (PhD)
visual arts (MFA, PhD)

Division of Biological Sciences
Programs in:
biochemistry (PhD)
biology (MS)
cell and developmental biology (PhD)
computational neurobiology (PhD)
ecology, behavior, and evolution (PhD)
genetics and molecular biology (PhD)
immunology, virology, and cancer biology (PhD)
molecular and cellular biology (PhD)
neurobiology (PhD)
plant molecular biology (PhD)
plant systems biology (PhD)
signal transduction (PhD)

Graduate School of International Relations and Pacific Studies
Programs in:
economics and international affairs (PhD)
Pacific international affairs (MPIA)
political science and international affairs (PhD)

Rady School of Management
Program in:
business administration and management (MBA)

School of Medicine
Programs in:
audiology (Au D)
bioinformatics (PhD)
cancer biology/oncology (PhD)
cardiovascular sciences and disease (PhD)
clinical research (MAS)
leadership in healthcare organizations (MAS)
medicine (MD, MAS, Au D, PhD)
microbiology (PhD)
molecular pathology (PhD)
neurological disease (PhD)
neurosciences (PhD)
stem cell and developmental biology (PhD)
structural biology/drug design (PhD)

Graduate Studies in Biomedical Sciences
Programs in:
molecular cell biology (PhD)
pharmacology (PhD)
physiology (PhD)
regulatory biology (PhD)

School of Pharmacy and Pharmaceutical Sciences
Program in:
pharmacy and pharmaceutical sciences (Pharm D)

■ UNIVERSITY OF CALIFORNIA, SANTA BARBARA
Santa Barbara, CA 93106-2014
http://www.ucsb.edu/

State-supported, coed, university. CGS member. *Computer facilities:* 3,000 computers available on campus for general student use. A campuswide network can be accessed from student residence rooms and from off campus. *Graduate expenses:* Tuition, nonresident: full-time $25,149. Required fees: $10,143. Full-time tuition and fees vary according to campus/location, reciprocity agreements and student level. *General application contact:* Graduate Admissions Coordinator, 805-893-2278.

Graduate Division
Dr. Gale M. Morrison, Dean

College of Engineering
Dr. Matthew Tirrell, Dean
Programs in:
chemical engineering (MS, PhD)
computational science and engineering (PhD)
computer science (MS, PhD)
electrical and computer engineering (PhD)
engineering (MS, PhD)
materials science and engineering (MS, PhD)
mechanical engineering (MS, PhD)

College of Letters and Sciences
Dr. David Marshall, Executive Dean
Programs in:
ancient history (MA, PhD)
applied linguistics (PhD)
applied mathematics (MA)
art (MFA)
Asian studies (MA)
Asian Studies (MA)
biochemistry and molecular biology (MS, PhD)
brass (MM)
business economics (MA)
chemistry (MA, MS, PhD)
Chicana and Chicano studies (PhD)
classics (MA)
cognitive science (PhD)
comparative literature (PhD)
composition (MA, PhD)
computational science and engineering (PhD)
conducting (MM, DMA)
East Asian language and cultural studies (PhD)
East Asian literatures (PhD)
economics (PhD)
electronic music and sound design (MA)
English (PhD)
ethnomusicology (MA, PhD)
European archaeology (MA)
European Medieval studies (PhD)
feminist studies (PhD)
film and media studies (PhD)
financial mathematics and statistics (PhD)
French (MA, MABL, PhD)
geography (MA)
geological sciences (MS, PhD)
geophysics (MS)
Germanic languages and literature (MA, PhD)
global and international studies (MA)
global studies (PhD)
Hispanic languages and literature (PhD)
history of art and architecture (PhD)
human development (PhD)
humanities and fine arts (MA, MABL, MFA, MM, MS, DMA, PhD)
keyboard (MM, DMA)
language, interaction and social organization (PhD)
language, interaction, and social organizations (PhD)
Latin American and Iberian studies (MA)
letters and sciences (MA, MFA, MM, MS, DMA, PhD)
literature and theory (PhD)
marine science (MS, PhD)
mathematics (MA, PhD)
mathematics, life, and physical sciences (MA, MS, PhD)
media arts and technology (PhD)
molecular, cellular, and developmental biology (MA, PhD)
multimedia engineering (MS)
musicology (MA, PhD)
North American archeology (MA)
philosophy (PhD)
physics (PhD)
piano accompanying (MM)
political science (MA)
Portuguese (MA)
psychology (MA, PhD)
public history (PhD)
quantitative methods in the social sciences (PhD)
religious studies (MA, PhD)
social sciences (MA, PhD)
sociocultural anthropology (MA)
South American archaeology (MA)
Spanish (MA)
Spanish and Portuguese (MA)
statistics (MA)
statistics and applied probability (PhD)
strings (MM, DMA)
technology and society (PhD)
theater studies (MA, PhD)
theory (MA, PhD)
transportation (PhD)
visual and spatial arts (MA)
voice (MM, DMA)
women's studies (PhD)
woodwinds (MM)

Donald Bren School of Environmental Science and Management
Dr. John Melack, Acting Dean

Program in:
environmental science and management (MESM, PhD)

Gevirtz Graduate School of Education
Dr. Jane Conoley, Chair
Programs in:
counseling, clinical and school psychology (PhD)
education (M Ed, MA, PhD)
educational leadership (Ed D)
school psychology (M Ed)

Summer Sessions
Dr. Loy Lytle, Dean of Summer Sessions
Programs in:
French (MA)
Spanish (MA)

■ UNIVERSITY OF CALIFORNIA, SANTA CRUZ

Santa Cruz, CA 95064
http://www.ucsc.edu/

State-supported, coed, university. CGS member. *Computer facilities:* 320 computers available on campus for general student use. A campuswide network can be accessed from student residence rooms and from off campus. Online class registration is available. *General application contact:* Reporting Analyst for Graduate Admissions, 831-459-5906.

Division of Graduate Studies

Division of Humanities
Programs in:
history (MA, PhD)
history of consciousness (PhD)
humanities (MA, PhD)
linguistics (MA, PhD)
literature (MA, PhD)
philosophy (MA, PhD)

Division of Physical and Biological Sciences
Programs in:
astronomy and astrophysics (PhD)
chemistry and biochemistry (MS, PhD)
earth and planetary sciences (MS, PhD)
ecology and evolutionary biology (MA, PhD)
environmental toxicology (MS, PhD)
mathematics (MA, PhD)
molecular, cellular, and developmental biology (MA, PhD)
ocean sciences (MS, PhD)
physical and biological sciences (MA, MS, PhD, Certificate)
physics (MS, PhD)
science illustration (Certificate)
science writing (Certificate)

Division of Social Sciences
Programs in:
anthropological archaeology (PhD)
applied economics and finance (MS)
cultural anthropology (PhD)
education (MA)
environmental studies (PhD)
international economics (PhD)
language and literacy studies (PhD)
mathematics and science education (PhD)
politics (PhD)
psychology (PhD)
social context and policy studies of education (PhD)
social documentation (MA)
social sciences (MA, MS, PhD)
sociology (PhD)

Division of the Arts
Programs in:
arts (MA, MFA, DMA, PhD, Certificate)
digital arts and new media (MFA)
music (MA, PhD)
music composition (DMA)
theater arts (Certificate)

Jack Baskin School of Engineering
Programs in:
bioinformatics (MS, PhD)
computer engineering (MS, PhD)
computer science (MS, PhD)
electrical engineering (MS, PhD)
engineering (MS, PhD)
network engineering (MS)
statistics and applied mathematics (MS, PhD)

■ UNIVERSITY OF LA VERNE

La Verne, CA 91750-4443
http://www.ulv.edu/

Independent, coed, university. *Graduate faculty:* 73 full-time (32 women), 149 part-time/adjunct (75 women). *Computer facilities:* 250 computers available on campus for general student use. A campuswide network can be accessed from student residence rooms and from off campus. Online class registration, MyULV (online) are available. *Graduate expenses:* Tuition: part-time $575 per credit hour. Required fees: $575 per credit hour. Tuition and fees vary according to degree level, campus/location and program. *General application contact:* Connie Hamlow, Admissions Information Specialist, 909-593-3511 Ext. 4244.

College of Arts and Sciences

Dr. Fred Yaffe, Dean
Programs in:
arts and sciences (MS, Psy D)
clinical-community psychology (Psy D)
counseling (MS)
general counseling (MS)
higher education counseling (MS)
marriage and family therapy (MS)

College of Business and Public Management

Dr. Abe Helou, Dean
Programs in:
accounting (MBA)
business (MBIT)
business administration (MS)
business and public management (MBA, MBA-EP, MBIT, MHA, MPA, MS, DPA, Certificate)
counseling (MS)
executive management (MBA-EP)
finance (MBA, MBA-EP)
financial management (MHA)
gerontology (Certificate)
gerontology administration (MS)
health administration (MHA)
health services management (MBA, MS)
human resources (MHA)
information management (MHA)
information technology (MBA, MBA-EP)
international business (MBA, MBA-EP)
leadership (MBA-EP)
leadership and management (MHA, MS)
managed care (MBA, MHA)
management (MBA, MBA-EP)
marketing (MBA, MBA-EP)
marketing and business development (MHA)
nonprofit management (Certificate)
organizational leadership (Certificate)
public administration (MPA, DPA)

College of Education and Organizational Leadership

Dr. Mark Goor, Dean
Programs in:
advanced teaching skills (M Ed)
child development (MS)
child development/child life (MS)
child life (MS)
education (M Ed)
education (special emphasis) (M Ed)
education and organizational leadership (M Ed, MS, Ed D, Certificate, Credential)
educational management (M Ed, Credential)
multiple subject (Credential)
organizational leadership (Ed D)
preliminary administrative services (Credential)
professional administrative services (Credential)
pupil personnel services (Credential)
reading (M Ed, Certificate, Credential)
reading and language arts specialist (Credential)
school counseling (MS, Credential)
single subject (Credential)
teacher education (Credential)

College of Law

Allen K. Easley, Dean
Program in:
law (JD)

Regional Campus Administration

Dr. Stephen E. Lesniak, Dean
Programs in:
advanced teaching (M Ed)
business (MBA-EP)
business administration (MBA)

University of La Verne (continued)
business organizational management (MS)
cross cultural language and academic development (Credential)
educational management (M Ed)
health administration (MHA)
leadership and management (MS)
multiple subject (Credential)
public administration (MPA)
reading (M Ed)
school counseling (MS)
single subject (Credential)

■ UNIVERSITY OF PHOENIX–SACRAMENTO VALLEY CAMPUS
Sacramento, CA 95833-3632
http://www.phoenix.edu/

Proprietary, coed, comprehensive institution. *Computer facilities:* Computer purchase and lease plans are available. A campuswide network can be accessed from off campus. Online class registration is available. *General application contact:* Campus Information Center, 916-923-2107.

The Artemis School

College of Education
Programs in:
adult education (MA Ed)
curriculum instruction (MA Ed)
elementary teacher education (MA Ed)
secondary teacher education (MA Ed)
teacher education (Certificate)

College of Health and Human Services
Programs in:
administration of justice and security (MS)
community counseling (MSC)
family nurse practitioner (MSN)
health administration (MHA)
health care education (MSN)
health care management (MBA)
marriage, family and child counseling (MSC)
nursing (MSN)
psychology (MS)

John Sperling School of Business
Program in:
business (MBA, MIS, MM)

College of Graduate Business and Management
Programs in:
accounting (MBA)
business administration (MBA)
global management (MBA)
human resources management (MBA, MM)
management (MM)
marketing (MBA)
public administration (MBA, MM)

College of Information Systems and Technology
Programs in:
management (MIS)
technology management (MBA)

■ UNIVERSITY OF PHOENIX–SAN DIEGO CAMPUS
San Diego, CA 92123
http://www.phoenix.edu/

Proprietary, coed, comprehensive institution. *Computer facilities:* Computer purchase and lease plans are available. A campuswide network can be accessed from off campus. Online class registration is available. *General application contact:* Campus Information Center, 888-UOP-INFO.

The Artemis School

College of Education
Programs in:
curriculum and instruction (MA Ed)
elementary teacher education (MA Ed)
secondary teacher education (MA Ed)

College of Health and Human Services
Programs in:
administration of justice and security (MS)
health care education (MSN)
health care management (MBA)
marriage, family and child counseling (MSC)
marriage, family and child therapy (MSC)
nursing (MSN)

John Sperling School of Business
Program in:
business (MBA, MIS, MM)

College of Graduate Business and Management
Programs in:
accounting (MBA)
business administration (MBA)
global management (MBA)
human resources management (MBA, MM)
management (MM)
marketing (MBA)
public administration (MBA)

College of Information Systems and Technology
Programs in:
management (MIS)
technology management (MBA)

■ UNIVERSITY OF PHOENIX–SOUTHERN CALIFORNIA CAMPUS
Costa Mesa, CA 92626
http://www.phoenix.edu/

Proprietary, coed, comprehensive institution. *Computer facilities:* Computer purchase and lease plans are available. A campuswide network can be accessed from off campus. Online class registration is available. *General application contact:* Campus Information Center, 714-378-1878.

The Artemis School

College of Education
Programs in:
adult education and training (MA Ed)
curriculum and instruction (MA Ed)
elementary teacher education (MA Ed)
secondary teacher education (MA Ed)

College of Health and Human Services
Programs in:
administration of justice and security (MS)
family nurse practitioner (MSN, Certificate)
health administration (MHA)
health care education (MSN)
health care management (MBA)
marriage, family and child therapy (MSC)
nursing (MSN)
psychology (MS)

John Sperling School of Business
Program in:
business (MBA, MIS, MM)

College of Graduate Business and Management
Programs in:
accounting (MBA)
business administration (MBA)
global management (MBA)
human resources management (MBA, MM)
management (MM)
marketing (MBA)
public administration (MBA, MM)

College of Information Systems and Technology
Programs in:
information systems (MIS)
technology management (MBA)

■ UNIVERSITY OF REDLANDS
Redlands, CA 92373-0999
http://www.redlands.edu/

Independent, coed, comprehensive institution. *Computer facilities:* 804 computers available on campus for general student use. A campuswide network can be accessed from student residence rooms and from off campus. Online class registration is available. *General application contact:* Information Contact, 909-793-2121 Ext. 3937.

College of Arts and Sciences
Programs in:
arts and sciences (MM, MS)
communicative disorders (MS)
geographic information systems (MS)

School of Music
Program in:
music (MM)

School of Business
Programs in:
business (MBA)
information technology (MS)
management (MA)

School of Education
Program in:
education (MA, Ed D, Certificate)

■ UNIVERSITY OF SAN DIEGO

San Diego, CA 92110-2492

http://www.sandiego.edu/

Independent-religious, coed, university. CGS member. *Graduate faculty:* 141 full-time (73 women), 156 part-time/adjunct (83 women). *Computer facilities:* Computer purchase and lease plans are available. 765 computers available on campus for general student use. A campuswide network can be accessed from student residence rooms and from off campus. Online class registration is available. *Graduate expenses:* Tuition: full-time $19,710; part-time $1129 per unit. Required fees: $154. Full-time tuition and fees vary according to course load and degree level. *General application contact:* Dr. John Mosby, Associate Director of Graduate Admissions, 619-260-4524.

College of Arts and Sciences
Dr. Mary K. Boyd, Dean
Programs in:
arts and sciences (MA, MFA, MS)
dramatic arts (MFA)
history (MA)
international relations (MA)
marine science (MS)

Hahn School of Nursing and Health Science
Dr. Sally Hardin, Dean
Programs in:
accelerated nursing (for RNs) (MSN)
adult clinical nurse specialist (MSN)
adult nurse practitioner (MSN)
clinical nursing (MSN)
entry-level nursing (for non-RNs) (MSN)
executive nurse leader (MSN)
family nurse practitioner (MSN)
nursing (PhD)
nursing practice (DNP)
pediatric nurse practitioner (MSN)

Joan B. Kroc School of Peace Studies
Fr. William Headley, Dean
Program in:
peace and justice studies (MA)

School of Business Administration
Dr. David Pyke, Interim Dean
Programs in:
accountancy (MS)
business administration (MBA)
executive leadership (MSEL)
global leadership (MSGL)
international business administration (IMBA)
real estate (MSRE)
supply chain management (MS, Certificate)
taxation (MS)

School of Law
Kevin Cole, Dean
Programs in:
business and corporate law (LL M)
comparative law (LL M)
general studies (LL M)
international law (LL M)
law (JD)
taxation (LL M, Diploma)

School of Leadership and Education Sciences
Dr. Paula A. Cordeiro, Dean
Programs in:
clinical mental health counseling (MA)
curriculum and teaching (M Ed)
higher education leadership (MA)
leadership and education sciences (M Ed, MA, MAT, PhD, Certificate)
leadership studies (MA, PhD)
literacy, culture and teaching English to speakers of other languages (M Ed)
marital and family therapy (MA)
mathematics, science and technology education (M Ed)
nonprofit leadership and management (MA, Certificate)
school counseling (MA)
special education (M Ed)
teaching (MAT)

■ UNIVERSITY OF SAN FRANCISCO

San Francisco, CA 94117-1080

http://www.usfca.edu/

Independent-religious, coed, university. *Graduate faculty:* 111 full-time (48 women), 271 part-time/adjunct (143 women). *Computer facilities:* Computer purchase and lease plans are available. 350 computers available on campus for general student use. A campuswide network can be accessed from student residence rooms and from off campus. Online class registration is available. *Graduate expenses:* Tuition: full-time $19,350; part-time $1075 per credit hour. Tuition and fees vary according to course load, degree level, campus/location and program. *General application contact:* Information Contact, 415-422-4723.

College of Arts and Sciences
Dr. Jennifer Turpin, Dean
Programs in:
arts and sciences (MA, MFA, MS)
Asia Pacific studies (MA)
biology (MS)
chemistry (MS)
computer science (MS)
economics (MA)
environmental management (MS)
financial analysis (MS)
international and development economics (MA)
international studies (MA)
investor relations (MA)
risk management (MS)
sport management (MA)
theology (MA)
Web science (MS)
writing (MFA)

College of Professional Studies
Dr. John Fitzgibbons, SJ, Dean
Programs in:
health services administration (MPA)
information systems (MS)
nonprofit administration (MNA)
organization development (MS)
project management (MS)
public administration (MPA)

Masagung Graduate School of Management
Dr. Michael Duffy, Dean
Programs in:
business administration (MBA)
business economics (MBA)
e-business (MBA)
entrepreneurship (MBA)
finance (MBA)
international business (MBA)
management (MBA)
marketing (MBA)
telecommunications management and policy (MBA)

School of Education
Dr. Walter Gmelch, Dean
Programs in:
Catholic school leadership (MA, Ed D)
Catholic school teaching (MA)
counseling (MA)
counseling psychology (Ed D)
digital media and learning (MA)
education (MA, Ed D)
international and multicultural education (MA, Ed D)
learning and instruction (MA, Ed D)
multicultural literature for children and young adults (MA)
organization and leadership (MA, Ed D)
teaching (MA)
teaching English as a second language (MA)
teaching reading (MA)

School of Law
Jeffrey Brand, Dean
Programs in:
intellectual property and technology law (LL M)
international transactions and comparative law (LL M)
law (JD, LL M)

School of Nursing
Dr. Judith Karshmer, Dean

University of San Francisco (continued)
Programs in:
clinical nurse leader (MSN)
family nurse practitioner (DNP)
healthcare systems leadership (MSN, DNP)
nursing practice (DNP)

■ UNIVERSITY OF SOUTHERN CALIFORNIA
Los Angeles, CA 90089
http://www.usc.edu/

Independent, coed, university. CGS member. *Graduate faculty:* 2,031 full-time (655 women), 1,101 part-time/adjunct (398 women). *Computer facilities:* Computer purchase and lease plans are available. 2,700 computers available on campus for general student use. A campuswide network can be accessed from student residence rooms and from off campus. Online class registration, online degree progress, financial aid applications, document sharing, calendars, personal Web space, customizable Web portal, course management systems (including data and video) are available. *Graduate expenses:* Tuition: full-time $19,285; part-time $1299 per unit. Required fees: $554; $283 per semester. Tuition and fees vary according to course load and program. *General application contact:* Joseph Sanosa, Associate Director of Graduate Admission, 213-740-1111.

Graduate School
Jean Morrison, Vice Provost for Academic Affairs/Graduate Program Director, Women in Science and Engineering

Annenberg School for Communication and Journalism
Programs in:
broadcast journalism (MA)
communication (MA, PhD)
communication and journalism (MA, MCM, MPD, PhD)
communication management (MCM)
global communicationonline journalism (MA)
print journalism (MA)
public diplomacy (MPD)
specialized journalism (MA)
strategic public relations (MA)

College of Letters, Arts and Sciences
Howard Gillman, Dean
Programs in:
American studies and ethnicity (PhD)
applied mathematics (MS, PhD)
art history (MA, PhD)
biology (MS)
brain and cognitive science (PhD)
chemical physics (PhD)
chemistry (MA, MS, PhD)
classics (MA, PhD)
clinical science (PhD)
comparative literature (MA, PhD)
computational molecular biology (MS)
developmental psychology (PhD)
East Asian languages and cultures (MA, PhD)
East Asian linguistics (PhD)
East Asian studies (MA)
economic development programming (MA)
economics (MA, PhD)
English (MA, PhD)
fiction (MPW)
geographic information science and technology (MS, Graduate Certificate)
geological sciences (MS, PhD)
Hispanic linguistics (MA, PhD)
history (PhD)
history of collecting and display (Graduate Certificate)
human behavior (MHB)
integrative and evolutionary biology (PhD)
Internet (MPW)
letters, arts and sciences (MA, MHB, MPW, MS, PhD, Graduate Certificate)
linguistics (MA, PhD)
literature and creative writing (PhD)
marine environmental biology (MS)
mathematics (PhD)
molecular biology (PhD)
neurobiology (PhD)
neuroscience (MS, PhD)
non-fiction (MPW)
philosophy (MA, PhD)
physics (MA, MS, PhD)
playwriting (MPW)
poetry (MPW)
politics and international relations (PhD)
professional writing (MPW)
psychology (MA)
quantitative methods (PhD)
screenwriting (MPW)
Slavic languages and literatures (MA, PhD)
social psychology (PhD)
sociology (PhD)
statistics (MS)
visual studies (Graduate Certificate)

Davis School of Gerontology
Maria Henke, Assistant Dean
Program in:
gerontology (MA, MS, PhD, Graduate Certificate)

Gould School of Law
Dean Robert Rasmussen, Dean
Programs in:
comparative law for foreign attorneys (MCL)
law (JD)
law for foreign-educated attorneys (LL M)

Marshall School of Business
James Ellis, Dean
Programs in:
accounting (M Acc)
business (M Acc, MBA, MBT, MS, PhD)
business administration (MBA, MM, MS, PhD)
business taxation (MBT)

Roski School of Fine Arts
Ruth Weisberg, Dean
Programs in:
fine arts (MFA, MPAS)
public art studies (MPAS)

Rossier School of Education
Programs in:
education (MAT, ME, MMFT, MS, Ed D, PhD)
educational psychology (Ed D, PhD)
educational psychology/instructional technology (ME)
higher education administration (Ed D)
higher education administration and policy (PhD)
K-12 leadership in urban school settings (Ed D)
K-12 policy and practice (PhD)
marriage, family and child counseling (MMFT)
postsecondary administration and student affairs (ME)
school counseling (ME)
teacher education in multicultural societies (Ed D)
teaching and teaching credential (MAT)
teaching English as a foreign language (ME)
teaching English to speakers of other languages (MS)

School of Architecture
Qingyun Ma, Dean
Program in:
architecture (M Arch, MBS, MHP, ML Arch, MLA, PhD)

School of Cinematic Arts
Elizabeth Daley, Dean
Programs in:
cinema-television (MA)
cinema-television (critical studies) (PhD)
cinematic arts (MA, MFA, PhD, Graduate Certificate)
cinematic arts (media arts and practice) (PhD)
film and video production (MFA)
film, video, and computer animation (MFA)
interactive media (MFA)
motion picture producing (MFA)
writing in screen and television (Graduate Certificate)

School of Dentistry
Harold Slavkin, Dean
Programs in:
biokinesiology (MS, PhD)
craniofacial biology (MS, PhD, Graduate Certificate)
dentistry (DDS, MA, MS, DPT, OTD, PhD, Graduate Certificate)
occupational science (PhD)
occupational therapy (MA, OTD)
physical therapy (DPT)

School of Pharmacy
Pete Vanderveen, Dean

Programs in:
- clinical research design and management (Graduate Certificate)
- food safety (Graduate Certificate)
- molecular pharmacology and toxicology (MS, PhD)
- patient and product safety (Graduate Certificate)
- pharmaceutical economics and policy (MS, PhD)
- pharmaceutical sciences (MS, PhD)
- pharmacy (Pharm D, MS, D Sc, PhD, Graduate Certificate)
- preclinical drug development (Graduate Certificate)
- regulatory science (MS, D Sc)

School of Policy, Planning, and Development
Dr. Jack H. Knott, Head
Programs in:
- health administration (EMHA, MHA)
- international public policy and management (MPPM)
- leadership (EML)
- policy, planning, and development (EMHA, EML, M Pl, MHA, MPA, MPP, MPPM, MRED, MS, DPPD, PhD, Graduate Certificate)
- public administration (MPA)
- public policy (MPP)
- real estate development (MRED)

School of Social Work
Marilyn Flynn, Dean
Programs in:
- community organization, planning and administration (MSW)
- families and children (MSW)
- health (MSW)
- military social work and veterans services (MSW)
- older adults (MSW)
- public child welfare (MSW)
- school settings (MSW)
- social work (MSW, PhD)
- systems of mental illness recovery (MSW)
- work and life (MSW)

School of Theatre
Sergio Ramierez, Director, Academic and Student Services
Programs in:
- acting (MFA)
- applied theatre arts (MA)
- dramatic writing (MFA)

Thornton School of Music
Dr. Robert A. Cutietta, Dean
Programs in:
- choral music (MM)
- composition (MM)
- historical musicology (PhD)
- jazz studies (MM)
- music education (MM)
- performance (MM, DMA)

Viterbi School of Engineering
Dr. Yannis C. Yortsos, Dean
Programs in:
- aerospace and mechanical engineering: computational fluid and solid mechanics (MS)
- aerospace and mechanical engineering: dynamics and control (MS)
- aerospace engineering (MS, PhD, Engr)
- applied mechanics (MS)
- astronautical engineering (Engr, Graduate Certificate)
- biomedical engineering (MS, PhD)
- chemical engineering (MS, PhD, Engr)
- civil engineering (MS, PhD)
- computer engineering (MS, PhD)
- computer networks (MS)
- computer science (MS, PhD)
- computer security (MS)
- computer-aided engineering (ME, Graduate Certificate)
- construction management (MCM)
- digital supply chain management (MS)
- electrical engineering (MS, PhD, Engr)
- engineering (MCM, ME, MS, PhD, Engr, Graduate Certificate)
- engineering management (MS)
- engineering technology commercialization (Graduate Certificate)
- engineering technology communication (Graduate Certificate)
- environmental engineering (MS, PhD)
- environmental quality management (ME)
- game development (MS)
- health systems operations (Graduate Certificate)
- high performance computing and simulations (MS)
- industrial and systems engineering (MS, PhD, Engr)
- intelligent robotics (MS)
- manufacturing engineering (MS)
- materials science and engineering (MS, PhD, Engr)
- mechanical engineering (MS, PhD, Engr)
- medical device and diagnostic engineering (MS)
- multimedia and creative technologies (MS)
- operations research engineering (MS)
- optimization and supply chain management (Graduate Certificate)
- petroleum engineering (MS, PhD, Engr, Graduate Certificate)
- product development engineering (MS)
- safety systems and security (MS)
- software engineering (MS)
- structural design (ME)
- sustainable cities (Graduate Certificate)
- systems architecting and engineering (MS, Graduate Certificate)
- systems safety and security (Graduate Certificate)
- transportation systems (Graduate Certificate)

Keck School of Medicine
Dr. Carmen A. Puliafito, Dean
Programs in:
- genetic, molecular and cellular biology (PhD)
- medicine (MD, MPAP, MPH, MS, PhD)
- systems biology and disease (PhD)

Graduate Programs in Medicine
Dr. Debbie Johnson, Associate Dean for Graduate Affairs
Programs in:
- applied biostatistics/epidemiology (MS)
- biochemistry and molecular biology (MS, PhD)
- biometry/epidemiology (MPH)
- biostatistics (MS, PhD)
- cell and neurobiology (MS, PhD)
- child and family health (MPH)
- epidemiology (PhD)
- experimental and molecular pathology (MS)
- genetic epidemiology and statistical genetics (PhD)
- global health leadership (MPH)
- health behavior research (PhD)
- health communication (MPH)
- health promotion (MPH)
- medicine (MPAP, MPH, MS, PhD)
- molecular epidemiology (MS, PhD)
- molecular microbiology and immunology (MS, PhD)
- pathobiology (PhD)
- physiology and biophysics (MS, PhD)
- primary care physician assistant (MPAP)
- public health (MPH)

■ UNIVERSITY OF THE PACIFIC

Stockton, CA 95211-0197
http://www.pacific.edu/

Independent, coed, university. CGS member. *Graduate faculty:* 276 full-time (112 women), 278 part-time/adjunct (125 women). *Computer facilities:* 350 computers available on campus for general student use. A campuswide network can be accessed from student residence rooms and from off campus. Online class registration is available. *Graduate expenses:* Tuition: full-time $30,380; part-time $950 per unit. Required fees: $300. *General application contact:* Office of Graduate Admissions, 209-946-2344.

Arthur A. Dugoni School of Dentistry
Dr. Arthur A. Dugoni, Dean
Programs in:
- advanced education in general dentistry (Certificate)
- dentistry (DDS, MSD, Certificate)
- international dental studies (DDS)
- oral and maxillofacial surgery (Certificate)

College of the Pacific
Dr. Robert Cox, Dean

University of the Pacific (continued)
Programs in:
biological sciences (MS)
communication (MA)
psychology (MA)
sport sciences (MA)

Conservatory of Music
Dr. Steven Anderson, Dean
Programs in:
music (MA, MM)
music education (MM)
music therapy (MA)

Eberhardt School of Business
Dr. Richard Flaherty, Dean
Program in:
business (MBA)

McGeorge School of Law
Elizabeth Rindskopf Parker, Dean
Programs in:
advocacy (JD)
advocacy practice and teaching (LL M)
criminal justice (JD)
intellectual property (JD)
international legal studies (JD)
international water resources law (LL M, JSD)
law (JD)
public law and policy (JD)
public policy and law (LL M)
tax (JD)
transnational business practice (LL M)

School of Education
Dr. Lynn Beck, Dean
Programs in:
curriculum and instruction (M Ed, MA, Ed D)
education (M Ed)
educational administration (MA, Ed D)
educational psychology (MA, Ed D)
school psychology (Ed S)
special education (MA)

School of International Studies
Dr. Margee Ensign, Dean
Programs in:
intercultural relations (MA)
international studies (MA)

School of Pharmacy and Health Sciences
Dr. Philip Oppenheimer, Dean
Programs in:
pharmaceutical sciences (MS, PhD)
pharmacy (Pharm D)
pharmacy and health sciences (Pharm D, MS, DPT, PhD)
physical therapy (MS, DPT)
speech-language pathology (MS)

■ VANGUARD UNIVERSITY OF SOUTHERN CALIFORNIA
Costa Mesa, CA 92626-9601
http://www.vanguard.edu/

Independent-religious, coed, comprehensive institution. *Graduate faculty:* 15 full-time (7 women), 15 part-time/adjunct (9 women). *Computer facilities:* 150 computers available on campus for general student use. A campuswide network can be accessed from student residence rooms and from off campus. Online class registration is available. *General application contact:* Drake Levasheff, Director of Graduate Admissions, 714-966-5499.

Graduate Program in Business
Dr. David Alford, Dean
Program in:
business (MBA)

Graduate Program in Clinical Psychology
Dr. Jerre White, Director
Program in:
clinical psychology (MS)

Graduate Programs in Education
Dr. Jerry Ternes, Dean
Program in:
education (MA)

Graduate Programs in Religion
Dr. Richard Israel, Associate Dean
Programs in:
leadership studies (MA)
theological studies (MTS)

■ WOODBURY UNIVERSITY
Burbank, CA 91504-1099
http://www.woodbury.edu/

Independent, coed, comprehensive institution. *Computer facilities:* 135 computers available on campus for general student use. A campuswide network can be accessed from off campus. Online class registration is available. *General application contact:* Director of Admissions, 800-784-9663.

School of Architecture
Program in:
real estate development (M Arch)

School of Business and Management
Programs in:
business administration (MBA)
organizational leadership (MA)

Colorado

■ ADAMS STATE COLLEGE
Alamosa, CO 81102
http://www.adams.edu/

State-supported, coed, comprehensive institution. CGS member. *Computer facilities:* 329 computers available on campus for general student use. A campuswide network can be accessed from student residence rooms and from off campus. Online class registration is available. *General application contact:* Information Contact, 719-587-8152.

The Graduate School
Programs in:
art (MA)
counseling (MA)
education (MA)
history (MA)
human performance and physical education (MA)
special education (MA)

■ COLORADO CHRISTIAN UNIVERSITY
Lakewood, CO 80226
http://www.ccu.edu/

Independent-religious, coed, comprehensive institution. *Computer facilities:* 141 computers available on campus for general student use. A campuswide network can be accessed from student residence rooms and from off campus. Online class registration is available. *General application contact:* College of Adult and Graduate Studies, 303-963-3300.

Program in Business Administration
Program in:
business administration (MBA)

Program in Counseling
Program in:
counseling (MA)

Program in Curriculum and Instruction
Program in:
curriculum and instruction (MA)

■ COLORADO SCHOOL OF MINES
Golden, CO 80401-1887
http://www.mines.edu/

State-supported, coed, university. CGS member. *Graduate faculty:* 313 full-time (69 women), 94 part-time/adjunct (21 women). *Computer facilities:* Computer purchase and lease plans are available. 400 computers available on campus for general student use. A campuswide network can be accessed from student residence rooms and from off campus. Online class registration is available. *Graduate expenses:* Tuition, state resident: full-time $9810; part-time $477 per credit hour. Tuition, nonresident: full-time $23,814; part-time $1158 per credit hour. Required fees: $1428.76; $714.38 per semester. *General application contact:* Kay Leaman, Graduate Admissions Coordinator, 303-273-3249.

Graduate School
Dr. Tom M. Boyd, Dean of Graduate Studies

Programs in:
applied chemistry (PhD)
applied physics (MS, PhD)
chemical engineering (MS, PhD)
chemistry (MS, PhD)
engineer of mines (ME)
geochemistry (MS, PhD)
geological engineering (ME, MS, PhD)
geology (MS, PhD)
geophysical engineering (ME, MS, PhD)
geophysics (MS, PhD)
materials science (MS, PhD)
mathematical and computer sciences (MS, PhD)
metallurgical and materials engineering (ME, MS, PhD)
mineral exploration and mining geosciences (PMS)
mining and earth systems engineering (MS)
nuclear engineering (MS, PhD)
petroleum engineering (ME, MS, PhD)
petroleum reservoir systems (PMS)

Division of Economics and Business
Dr. Rod Eggert, Division Head
Programs in:
engineering and technology management (MS)
mineral economics (MS, PhD)

Division of Engineering
Dr. Terence Parker, Division Director
Program in:
engineering systems (ME, MS, PhD)

Division of Environmental Science and Engineering
Dr. Robert Siegrist, Division Director
Program in:
environmental science and engineering (MS, PhD)

Division of Liberal Arts and International Studies
Dr. James Jesudason, Director
Programs in:
international political economy (Graduate Certificate)
liberal arts and international studies (MIPER)
science and technology policy (Graduate Certificate)

■ COLORADO STATE UNIVERSITY
Fort Collins, CO 80523-0015
http://www.colostate.edu/

State-supported, coed, comprehensive institution. CGS member. *Graduate faculty:* 941 full-time (296 women), 43 part-time/adjunct (8 women). *Computer facilities:* Computer purchase and lease plans are available. 2,700 computers available on campus for general student use. A campuswide network can be accessed from student residence rooms and from off campus. Online class registration, personalized portal services including transcripts and financials (billing, financial aid) are available. *Graduate expenses:* Tuition, state resident: full-time $5620; part-time $312.25 per credit. Tuition, nonresident: full-time $17,253; part-time $958.50 per credit. Required fees: $1449.56; $82.35 per credit. *General application contact:* Sandra Dailey, Graduate School Administrative Assistant III, 970-491-6817.

College of Veterinary Medicine and Biomedical Sciences
Dr. Lance Perryman, Dean
Programs in:
biomedical sciences (MS, PhD)
clinical sciences (MS, PhD)
environmental health (MS, PhD)
microbiology (MS, PhD)
pathology (PhD)
radiological health sciences (MS, PhD)
veterinary medicine (DVM)
veterinary medicine and biomedical sciences (DVM, MS, PhD)

Graduate School
Peter K. Dorhout, Vice Provost for Graduate Studies
Programs in:
cell and molecular biology (MS, PhD)
ecology (MS, PhD)
molecular, cellular and integrative neurosciences (PhD)

College of Agricultural Sciences
Dr. Lee Sommers, Interim Dean
Programs in:
agricultural and resource economics (MS, PhD)
agricultural sciences (M Agr, MS, PhD)
animal sciences (MS, PhD)
entomology (MS, PhD)
horticulture (MS, PhD)
plant pathology and weed science (MS, PhD)
soil and crop sciences (MS, PhD)

College of Applied Human Sciences
April C. Mason, Dean
Programs in:
adult education and training (M Ed)
applied human sciences (M Ed, MS, MSW, PhD)
community college leadership (PhD)
construction management (MS)
counseling and career development (M Ed)
design and merchandising (MS)
education and human resource studies (M Ed, PhD)
educational leadership (M Ed, PhD)
food science and human nutrition (MS, PhD)
health and exercise science (MS)
human bioenergetics (PhD)
human development and family studies (MS, PhD)
interdisciplinary studies (PhD)
occupational therapy (MS)
organizational performance and change (M Ed, PhD)
social work (MSW)
student affairs in higher education (MS)

College of Business
Dr. John Hoxmeier, Associate Dean
Programs in:
accounting (M Acc)
business (M Acc, MBA, MMP, MS, MSBA)
business administration (MBA)
computer information systems (MSBA)
financial risk management (MSBA)
global social and sustainable enterprise (MSBA)
management practice (MMP)

College of Engineering
Dr. Sandra L. Woods, Dean
Programs in:
atmospheric science (MS, PhD)
chemical engineering (MS, PhD)
civil engineering (ME, MS, PhD)
electrical engineering (MEE, MS, PhD)
engineering (ME, MEE, MS, PhD)
mechanical engineering (ME, MS, PhD)

College of Liberal Arts
Dr. Ann Gill, Dean
Programs in:
anthropology (MA)
art (MFA)
communication studies (MA)
creative writing (MFA)
economics (MA, PhD)
English (MA)
foreign languages and literatures (MA)
history (MA)
liberal arts (MA, MFA, MM, MS, PhD)
music (MM)
philosophy (MA)
political science (MA, PhD)
public communication and technology (MS, PhD)
sociology (MA, PhD)
technical communication (MS)

College of Natural Sciences
Dr. Jan Nerger, Interim Dean
Programs in:
biochemistry (MS, PhD)
botany (MS, PhD)
chemistry (MS, PhD)
computer science (MCS, MS, PhD)
mathematics (MAT, MS, PhD)
natural sciences (MAT, MCS, MS, PhD)
physics (MS, PhD)
psychology (MS, PhD)
statistics (MS, PhD)
zoology (MS, PhD)

School of Biomedical Engineering
Dr. Susan James, Director
Program in:
biomedical engineering (ME, MS, PhD)

Warner College of Natural Resources
Dr. Joseph T. O'Leary, Dean
Programs in:
earth sciences (PhD)
fish, wildlife and conservation biology (MFWCB)
fishery and wildlife biology (MFWB, MS, PhD)
forest sciences (MS, PhD)
geosciences (MS)
human dimensions of natural resources (MS, PhD)

Colorado State University (continued)
natural resources (MFWB, MFWCB, MNRS, MS, PhD)
natural resources stewardship (MNRS)
rangeland ecosystem science (MS, PhD)
watershed science (MS)

■ COLORADO TECHNICAL UNIVERSITY COLORADO SPRINGS

Colorado Springs, CO 80907-3896
http://www.coloradotech.edu/

Proprietary, coed, university. *Computer facilities:* 400 computers available on campus for general student use. A campuswide network can be accessed. *General application contact:* Graduate Admissions, 719-590-6720.

Graduate Studies

Programs in:
accounting (MBA, MSA)
business administration (MBA)
computer engineering (MSCE)
computer science (DCS)
computer systems security (MSCS)
criminal justice (MSM)
database systems (MSCS)
electrical engineering (MSEE)
finance (MBA)
human resources management (MBA)
information systems security (MSM)
logistics/supply chain management (MBA)
management (DM)
marketing (MBA)
mediation and dispute resolution (MBA)
operations management (MBA)
project management (MBA)
software engineering (MSCS)
systems engineering (MS)
technology management (MBA)

■ COLORADO TECHNICAL UNIVERSITY DENVER

Greenwood Village, CO 80111
http://www.coloradotech.edu/

Proprietary, coed, comprehensive institution. *Computer facilities:* 230 computers available on campus for general student use. A campuswide network can be accessed. *General application contact:* Director of Admissions, 303-694-6600.

Program in Computer Engineering

Program in:
computer engineering (MS)

Program in Computer Science

Programs in:
computer systems security (MSCS)
database systems (MSCS)
software engineering (MSCS)

Program in Electrical Engineering

Program in:
electrical engineering (MS)

Program in Information Science

Program in:
information systems security (MSM)

Program in Systems Engineering

Program in:
systems engineering (MS)

Programs in Business Administration and Management

Programs in:
accounting (MBA)
business administration (MBA)
business administration and management (EMBA)
finance (MBA)
human resource management (MBA)
marketing (MBA)
mediation and dispute resolution (MBA)
operations management (MBA)
project management (MBA)
technology management (MBA)

■ JONES INTERNATIONAL UNIVERSITY

Centennial, CO 80112
http://www.jonesinternational.edu/

Proprietary, coed, university. *Computer facilities:* Online class registration is available. *General application contact:* Associate Director of Admissions, 800-811-JONES Ext. 5663.

Graduate School of Education

Programs in:
adult education (M Ed)
corporate training and knowledge management (M Ed)
curriculum and instruction (M Ed)
e-learning technology and design (M Ed)
educational leadership and administration (M Ed)
educational leadership and administration: principal and administrator licensure (M Ed)
elementary curriculum instruction and assessment (M Ed)
higher education leadership and administration (M Ed)
K-12 instructional technology (M Ed)
K-12 instructional technology: teacher licensure (M Ed)
secondary curriculum instruction and assessment (M Ed)
technology and design (M Ed)

School of Business

Programs in:
accounting (MBA)
business communication (MABC)
entrepreneurship (MABC, MBA)
finance (MBA)
global enterprise management (MBA)
health care management (MBA)
information security management (MBA)
information technology management (MBA)
leadership and influence (MABC)
leading the customer-driven organization (MABC)
negotiation and conflict management (MBA)
project management (MABC, MBA)

■ NAROPA UNIVERSITY

Boulder, CO 80302-6697
http://www.naropa.edu/

Independent, coed, comprehensive institution. *Graduate faculty:* 52 full-time (29 women), 158 part-time/adjunct (106 women). *Computer facilities:* 75 computers available on campus for general student use. A campuswide network can be accessed from student residence rooms and from off campus. Online class registration is available. *Graduate expenses:* Tuition: full-time $14,767; part-time $726 per credit hour. Required fees: $45 per term. *General application contact:* Office of Admissions, 303-546-3572.

Graduate Programs

Susan Boyle, Dean of Admissions
Programs in:
art therapy (MA)
body psychotherapy (MA)
contemplative education (MA)
contemplative psychotherapy (MA)
counseling psychology (MA)
creative writing (MFA)
dance/movement therapy (MA)
divinity (M Div)
ecopsychology (MA)
environmental leadership (MA)
Indo-Tibetan Buddhism (MA)
Indo-Tibetan Buddhism with language (MA)
religious studies (MA)
religious studies with language (MA)
theater: contemporary performance (MFA)
theater: Lecoq-based actor-created theater (MFA)
transpersonal psychology (MA)
wilderness therapy (MA)
writing and poetics (MFA)

■ REGIS UNIVERSITY

Denver, CO 80221-1099
http://www.regis.edu/

Independent-religious, coed, comprehensive institution. *Computer facilities:* 300 computers available on campus for general student use. A campuswide network can be accessed from student residence rooms and from off campus. Online class registration is available. *General application contact:* Information Contact, 303-458-4300.

College for Professional Studies

Programs in:
- accounting (MS)
- adult learning, training, and development (M Ed)
- business administration (MBA)
- community counseling (MAC)
- computer information technology (MSOL)
- counseling children and adolescents (Post-Graduate Certificate)
- criminology (MA)
- curriculum, instruction, and assessment (M Ed)
- early childhood (M Ed)
- educational technology (Certificate)
- elementary (M Ed)
- emerging markets (MBA)
- ESL (M Ed)
- executive internal management (Certificate)
- executive leadership (Certificate)
- finance (MBA)
- finance and accounting (MBA)
- fine arts (M Ed)
- fine arts administration (Certificate)
- human resource management (MSOL)
- instructional technology (M Ed)
- international business (MBA)
- language and communication (MA)
- leadership (Certificate)
- marketing (MBA)
- marriage and family therapy (Post-Graduate Certificate)
- mediation (Certificate)
- nonprofit management (MNM)
- operations management (MBA)
- organization leadership (MS)
- organizational leadership (MSOL)
- professional leadership (M Ed)
- program management (Certificate)
- project leadership and management (MSOL, Certificate)
- project management (Certificate)
- psychology (MA)
- reading (M Ed)
- resource development (Certificate)
- secondary (M Ed)
- self-designed (M Ed)
- self-designed major (MA)
- social justice, peace, and reconciliation (Certificate)
- social science (MA)
- space studies (M Ed)
- special education (M Ed)
- strategic business (Certificate)
- strategic human resource (Certificate)
- teacher licensure (M Ed)
- technical communication (Certificate)
- technical management (Certificate)

School of Computer and Information Sciences

Programs in:
- database administration with IBM DB2 (Certificate)
- database administration with Oracle (Certificate)
- database development (Certificate)
- database technologies (MA)
- enterprise Java software development (Certificate)
- executive information technologies (Certificate)
- information assurance (MA, Certificate)
- information technology management (MA)
- software and information systems (M Sc)
- software engineering (MA, Certificate)
- storage area networks (Certificate)
- systems engineering (MA, Certificate)

Regis College

Program in:
- education (MA)

Rueckert-Hartman School for Health Professions

Programs in:
- clinical leadership for physician assistants (MS)
- family nurse practitioner (MSN)
- health informatics (Postbaccalaureate Certificate)
- health services administration (MS)
- healthcare education (Certificate)
- leadership in healthcare systems (MSN)
- neonatal nurse practitioner (MSN)
- nursing (MSN)
- pharmacy (Pharm D)
- physical therapy (DPT, TDPT)

■ UNIVERSITY OF COLORADO AT BOULDER

Boulder, CO 80309

http://www.colorado.edu/

State-supported, coed, university. CGS member. *Graduate faculty:* 1,038 full-time (313 women). *Computer facilities:* Computer purchase and lease plans are available. 1,855 computers available on campus for general student use. A campuswide network can be accessed from student residence rooms and from off campus. Online class registration, standard and academic software, student government voting are available. *General application contact:* Philip Distefano, Chancellor, 303-492-8908.

ATLAS Institute (Alliance for Technology, Learning, and Society)

Program in:
- technology, media, and society (PhD)

Graduate School

College of Arts and Sciences

Todd T. Gleeson, Dean

Programs in:
- animal behavior (MA)
- anthropology (MA, PhD)
- applied mathematics (MS, PhD)
- art history (MA)
- arts and sciences (MA, MFA, MS, Au D, PhD)
- astrophysics (MS, PhD)
- atmospheric and oceanic sciences (MS, PhD)
- audiology (Au D, PhD)
- biochemistry (PhD)
- biology (MA, PhD)
- cellular structure and function (MA, PhD)
- ceramics (MFA)
- chemical physics (PhD)
- chemistry (MS)
- Chinese (MA, PhD)
- classics (MA, PhD)
- clinical research and practice in audiology (PhD)
- communication (MA, PhD)
- comparative literature and humanities (MA, PhD)
- dance (MFA)
- developmental biology (MA, PhD)
- drawing (MFA)
- economics (MA, PhD)
- environmental biology (MA, PhD)
- environmental studies (MS, PhD)
- evolutionary biology (MA, PhD)
- French (MA, PhD)
- geography (MA, PhD)
- geology (MS, PhD)
- geophysics (PhD)
- German (MA)
- Hispanic linguistics (MA)
- history (MA, PhD)
- integrative physiology (MS, PhD)
- international affairs (MA)
- Japanese (MA, PhD)
- linguistics (MA, PhD)
- liquid crystal science and technology (PhD)
- literature (MA, PhD)
- mathematical physics (PhD)
- mathematics (MA, MS, PhD)
- medical physics (PhD)
- medieval/early modern Hispanic literatures (PhD)
- molecular biology (MA, PhD)
- museum and field studies (MS)
- neurobiology (MA)
- optical sciences and engineering (PhD)
- painting (MFA)
- philosophy (MA, PhD)
- photography and media arts (MFA)
- physics (MS, PhD)
- planetary science (MS, PhD)
- political science (MA, PhD)
- population biology (MA)
- population genetics (PhD)
- printmaking (MFA)
- psychology and neuroscience (MA, PhD)
- public policy (MA)
- religious studies (MA)
- sculpture (MFA)
- sociology (PhD)
- Spanish literature (MA, PhD)
- speech, language and hearing science (MA)
- speech-language pathology (MA, PhD)
- speech-language-hearing sciences (PhD)
- theatre (MA, PhD)

College of Engineering and Applied Science

Robert Davis, Dean

University of Colorado at Boulder (continued)
Programs in:
- aerospace engineering sciences (ME, MS, PhD)
- building systems (MS, PhD)
- chemical and biological engineering (ME, MS, PhD)
- computer science (ME, MS, PhD)
- construction engineering and management (MS, PhD)
- electrical and computer engineering (ME, MS)
- electrical engineering (PhD)
- engineering and applied science (ME, MS, PhD)
- environmental engineering (MS, PhD)
- geoenvironmental engineering (MS, PhD)
- geotechnical engineering (MS, PhD)
- mechanical engineering (ME, MS, PhD)
- operations and logistics (ME)
- quality and process (ME)
- research and development (ME)
- structural engineering (MS, PhD)
- telecommunications (ME, MS)
- water resources engineering (MS, PhD)

College of Music
Programs in:
- church music (M Mus)
- composition (M Mus, D Mus A)
- conducting (M Mus, D Mus A)
- music education (M Mus Ed, PhD)
- music literature (M Mus)
- musicology (PhD)
- pedagogy (M Mus, D Mus A)
- performance (M Mus, D Mus A)

School of Education
Lorrie Shepard, Dean
Programs in:
- education (MA, PhD)
- educational and psychological studies (MA, PhD)
- instruction and curriculum (MA, PhD)
- research and evaluation methodologies (PhD)
- social multicultural and bilingual foundations (MA, PhD)

School of Journalism and Mass Communication
Programs in:
- communication (PhD)
- mass communication research (MA)
- media studies (PhD)
- newsgathering (MA)

Leeds School of Business
Dennis Ahlburg, Dean
Programs in:
- accounting (MS, PhD)
- business (MBA, MS, PhD)
- business administration (MBA, MS, PhD)
- finance (PhD)
- information systems (PhD)
- marketing (PhD)
- operations (PhD)
- strategic, organizational, and entrepreneurial studies (PhD)

School of Law
Program in:
- law (JD)

■ UNIVERSITY OF COLORADO AT COLORADO SPRINGS
Colorado Springs, CO 80933-7150
http://www.uccs.edu/

State-supported, coed, comprehensive institution. *Graduate faculty:* 278 full-time (137 women), 90 part-time/adjunct (48 women). *Computer facilities:* 250 computers available on campus for general student use. A campuswide network can be accessed from student residence rooms and from off campus. *General application contact:* Michael Sanderson, Graduate Recruitment Coordinator, 719-255-3072.

Graduate School
Dr. Janenne Nelson, Dean

Beth-El College of Nursing and Health Sciences
Dr. Nancy Smith, Dean
Programs in:
- adult health nurse practitioner and clinical specialist (MSN)
- family practitioner (MSN)
- gerontology (MSN)
- neonatal nurse practitioner and clinical specialist (MSN)
- nursing administration (MSN)
- nursing practice (DNP)
- women nurse practitioner (MSN)

College of Education
Dr. LaVonne Neal, Dean
Programs in:
- counseling and human services (MA)
- curriculum and instruction (MA)
- educational administration (MA)
- educational leadership (MA, PhD)
- special education (MA)

College of Engineering and Applied Science
Dr. Ramaswami Dandapani, Dean
Programs in:
- computer science (MS)
- electrical engineering (MS, PhD)
- engineering (PhD)
- engineering and applied science (ME, MS, PhD)
- engineering management (ME)
- information operations (ME)
- manufacturing (ME)
- mechanical engineering (MS)
- software engineering (ME)
- space operations (ME)
- space systems (MS)

College of Letters, Arts and Sciences
Dr. Tom Christensen, Dean
Programs in:
- applied mathematics (MS)
- biology (M Sc)
- chemistry (M Sc)
- communications (MA)
- geography and environmental studies (MA)
- history (MA)
- letters, arts and sciences (M Sc, MA, MS, PhD)
- mathematics (M Sc)
- physics (M Sc)
- psychology (MA, PhD)
- sociology (MA)

Graduate School of Business Administration
Dr. Venkateshwar Reddy, Dean
Programs in:
- accounting (MBA)
- finance (MBA)
- general health care administration (MBA)
- information systems (MBA)
- international business management (MBA)
- marketing (MBA)
- service management/technology management (MBA)

Graduate School of Public Affairs
Dr. Terry Schwartz, Dean
Programs in:
- criminal justice (MCJ)
- public administration (MPA)

■ UNIVERSITY OF COLORADO DENVER
Denver, CO 80217-3364
http://www.cudenver.edu/

State-supported, coed, university. CGS member. *Graduate faculty:* 2,474 full-time (1,199 women), 788 part-time/adjunct (430 women). *Computer facilities:* 750 computers available on campus for general student use. A campuswide network can be accessed from student residence rooms and from off campus. Online class registration is available. *General application contact:* Graduate School Admissions, 303-556-2400.

Business School
Dr. Sueann Ambron, Dean
Programs in:
- accounting (MS)
- business (MBA, MS, MSIB, PhD)
- business administration (MBA)
- computer science and information systems (PhD)
- finance (MS)
- health administration (MS)
- information systems (MS)
- international business (MSIB)
- management and organization (MS)
- marketing (MS)

College of Architecture and Planning
Mark Gelernter, Dean

Programs in:
- architecture (M Arch)
- architecture and planning (M Arch, MLA, MUD, MURP, PhD)
- design and planning (PhD)
- landscape architecture (MLA)
- urban and regional planning (MURP)
- urban design (MUD)

College of Arts and Media
Dr. David Dynak, Dean
Programs in:
- arts and media (MS)
- recording arts (MS)

College of Engineering and Applied Science
Dr. Paul Rakowski, Assistant Dean of Student Services
Programs in:
- civil engineering (MS, PhD)
- computer science and engineering (MS)
- computer science and information systems (PhD)
- electrical engineering (M Eng, MS)
- engineering and applied science (M Eng, MS, PhD)
- geographic information systems (M Eng)
- mechanical engineering (M Eng, MS)

College of Liberal Arts and Sciences
Dr. Daniel Howard, Dean
Programs in:
- anthropology (MA)
- applied linguistics (MA)
- applied mathematics (MS, PhD)
- applied science (MIS)
- biology (MS)
- chemistry (MS)
- clinical health psychology (PhD)
- communication (MA)
- computer science (MIS)
- economics (MA)
- English studies (MA)
- environmental sciences (MS)
- health and behavioral sciences (PhD)
- history (MA)
- humanities (MH)
- liberal arts and sciences (MA, MH, MIS, MS, MSS, PhD, Certificate)
- literature (MA)
- mathematics (MIS)
- political science (MA)
- psychology (PhD)
- social science (MSS)
- sociology (MA)
- Spanish (MA)
- teaching English to speakers of other languages (Certificate)
- teaching of writing (MA)
- technical communication (MS)

College of Nursing
Dr. Patricia Moritz, Dean
Programs in:
- nursing (MS, DNP, PhD, Post Master's Certificate)
- nursing practice (DNP)

Colorado School of Public Health
Programs in:
- analytic health sciences (PhD)
- analytical health sciences (PhD)
- bioinformatics (PhD)
- biostatistics (MS)
- epidemiology (PhD)
- health services research (PhD)
- public health (MPH, MS, PhD)

Graduate School of Public Affairs
Paul Teske, Dean
Programs in:
- criminal justice (MCJ)
- public administration (MPA)
- public affairs (MCJ, MPA, PhD)

Program in Genetic Counseling
Program in:
- genetic counseling (MS)

School of Dental Medicine
Dr. Denise K. Kassebaum, Dean
Program in:
- dental medicine (DDS)

School of Education and Human Development
Lynn K. Rhodes, Dean
Programs in:
- administrative leadership and professional studies (MA, Ed S)
- counseling psychology and counselor education (MA)
- curriculum and instruction (MA)
- early childhood education (MA)
- education and human development (MA, PhD, Ed S)
- educational leadership and innovation (PhD)
- information and learning technologies (MA)

School of Medicine
Dr. Richard Krugman, Dean
Programs in:
- child health associate/physician assistant (MPAS)
- medicine (MD, MPAS, MS, DPT, PhD)
- physical therapy (DPT)

Programs in Biomedical Sciences
Dr. Steven Anderson, Director
Programs in:
- biochemistry and molecular genetics (PhD)
- biomedical sciences (MS, PhD)
- biomolecular structure (PhD)
- biophysics and genetics (MS, PhD)
- cancer biology (PhD)
- cell and developmental biology (PhD)
- cell biology, stem cells and development (PhD)
- clinical science (MS, PhD)
- immunology (PhD)
- microbiology (PhD)
- microbiology and immunology (PhD)
- molecular biology (PhD)
- neuroscience (PhD)
- pathology (PhD)
- pharmacology (PhD)
- physiology (PhD)
- reproductive sciences (PhD)

School of Pharmacy
Ralpha Altiere, Dean
Programs in:
- pharmaceutical sciences (PhD)
- pharmacy (Pharm D, PhD)
- toxicology (PhD)

■ UNIVERSITY OF DENVER
Denver, CO 80208
http://www.du.edu/

Independent, coed, university. CGS member. *Graduate faculty:* 453 full-time (182 women), 497 part-time/adjunct (240 women). *Computer facilities:* Computer purchase and lease plans are available. 200 computers available on campus for general student use. A campuswide network can be accessed from student residence rooms and from off campus. Online class registration is available. *General application contact:* Information Contact, 303-871-2706.

College of Education
Dr. Cheryl Lovell, Associate Dean
Programs in:
- counseling psychology (MA, PhD)
- curriculum and instruction (MA, PhD, Certificate)
- educational administration and policy studies (Certificate)
- educational psychology (MA, PhD, Ed S)
- higher education and adult studies (MA, PhD)
- library and information science (MLIS)
- library and information sciences (Certificate)
- school administration (PhD)

College of Law
Jose Roberto Juarez, Dean
Programs in:
- American and comparative law (LL M)
- international natural resources law (LL M, MRLS)
- law (JD, LL M, MRLS, MSLA, MT, Certificate)
- legal administration (MSLA, Certificate)
- taxation (LL M, MT)

Daniels College of Business
Dr. Chris Riordan, Dean
Programs in:
- business (IMBA, M Acc, MBA, MS)
- business administration (MBA)
- business intelligence (MS)
- data mining (MS)
- finance (IMBA, MBA, MS)
- general business administration (IMBA, MBA, MS)
- information technology and electronic commerce (IMBA, MBA)
- international business/management (IMBA, MBA)
- management (MS)
- marketing (IMBA, MBA, MS)

University of Denver (continued)

School of Accountancy
Dr. Ronald Kucic, Director
Programs in:
accountancy (M Acc)
accounting (MBA)

School of Real Estate and Construction Management
Dr. Mark Levine, Director
Programs in:
construction management (IMBA, MS)
real estate (IMBA, MBA, MS)

Division of Arts, Humanities and Social Sciences
Dr. Anne McCall, Dean
Programs in:
anthropology (MA)
arts, humanities and social sciences (MA, MFA, MM, MPP, MS, PhD, Certificate)
economics (MA)
English (MA, PhD)
psychology (MA, PhD)
public policy (MPP)
religious studies (MA)

Lamont School of Music
Joseph Docksey, Director
Programs in:
composition (MA)
conducting (MA)
jazz and commercial music (Certificate)
music (MM)
music education (MA)
music history and literature (MA)
Orff-Schulwerk (MA)
performance (MA)
piano pedagogy (MA)
Suzuki pedagogy (MA)
Suzuki teaching (Certificate)
theory (MA)

School of Art and Art History
Dr. Annette Stott, Director
Programs in:
art history (MA)
art history/museum studies (MA)
electronic media arts and design (MFA)

School of Communication
Programs in:
advertising management (MS)
communication (MA, MS, PhD)
digital media studies (MA)
human communication studies (MA, PhD)
international and intercultural communication (MA)
mass communications (MA)
public relations (MS)
video production (MA)

Faculty of Natural Sciences and Mathematics
Dr. Alayne Parson, Dean
Programs in:
applied mathematics (MA, MS)
biological sciences (MS, PhD)
chemistry (MA, MS, PhD)
computer science (MS)
geography (MA, MS, PhD)
mathematics (PhD)
natural sciences and mathematics (MA, MS, PhD)
physics and astronomy (MS, PhD)

Graduate School of Professional Psychology
Dr. Peter Buirski, Dean
Programs in:
clinical psychology (Psy D)
psychology (MA)

Graduate School of Social Work
Dr. James Herbert Williams, Dean
Program in:
social work (MSW, PhD, Certificate)

Graduate Studies
Dr. James Moran, Vice Provost
Program in:
religious and theological studies (PhD)

Conflict Resolution Institute
Dr. Karen Feste, Director
Program in:
conflict resolution (MA)

Intermodal Transportation Institute
Cathryne C. Johnson, Executive Director
Program in:
intermodal transportation (MS)

Josef Korbel School of International Studies
Brad Miller, Director of Graduate Admissions
Program in:
international studies (MA, PhD)

School of Engineering and Computer Science
Dr. Rahmat Shoureshi, Dean
Programs in:
bioengineering (MS)
computer engineering (MS)
computer science (MS, PhD)
computer science and engineering (MS)
electrical engineering (MS)
engineering (MS, PhD)
engineering and computer science (MS, PhD)
materials science (PhD)
mechanical engineering (MS)
mechatronics (MS)

University College
Dr. James Davis, Dean
Programs in:
applied communication (MAS, MPS, Certificate)
computer information systems (MAS, Certificate)
environmental policy and management (MAS, Certificate)
geographic information systems (MAS, Certificate)
human resource administration (MPS, Certificate)
knowledge and information technologies (MAS)
liberal studies (MLS, Certificate)
modern languages (MLS, Certificate)
organizational leadership (MPS, Certificate)
security management (Certificate)
technology management (MAS, Certificate)
telecommunications (MAS, Certificate)

■ UNIVERSITY OF NORTHERN COLORADO
Greeley, CO 80639
http://www.unco.edu/

State-supported, coed, university. CGS member. *Graduate faculty:* 293 full-time (130 women). *Computer facilities:* Computer purchase and lease plans are available. 1,169 computers available on campus for general student use. A campuswide network can be accessed from student residence rooms and from off campus. Online class registration is available. *Graduate expenses:* Tuition, state resident: full-time $4370; part-time $242.75 per credit hour. Tuition, nonresident: full-time $12,366; part-time $687 per credit hour. Required fees: $664.20; $36.90 per credit hour. *General application contact:* Linda Sisson, Graduate Student Admission Coordinator, 970-351-1807.

Graduate School
Dr. Robbyn Wacker, Assistant Vice President, Research and Extended Studies/Dean of Graduate School

College of Education and Behavioral Sciences
Dr. Eugene P. Sheehan, Dean
Programs in:
applied psychology and counselor education (MA, PhD, Psy D, Ed S)
applied statistics and research methods (MS, PhD)
clinical counseling (MA)
counseling psychology (Psy D)
counselor education and supervision (PhD)
early childhood education (MA)
education and behavioral sciences (MA, MAT, MS, Ed D, PhD, Psy D, Ed S)
educational leadership (MA, Ed D, Ed S)
educational media (MA)
educational psychology (MA, PhD)
educational research, leadership and technology (MA, MS, Ed D, PhD, Ed S)
educational studies (MAT, Ed D)
educational technology (MA, PhD)
higher education and student affairs leadership (PhD)
interdisciplinary studies (MA)
psychological sciences (MA, PhD)
reading (MA)
school counseling (MA)
school library education (MA)

school psychology (PhD, Ed S)
special education (MA, Ed D)
teacher education (MA, MAT, Ed D)

College of Humanities and Social Sciences
Dr. David Caldwell, Dean
Programs in:
clinical sociology (MA)
communication (MA)
communication studies (MA)
English (MA)
history (MA)
humanities and social sciences (MA)
modern languages and cultural studies (MA)
social sciences (MA)
Spanish/teaching (MA)

College of Natural and Health Sciences
Dr. Denise A. Battles, Dean
Programs in:
audiology (Au D)
biological education (PhD)
biological sciences (MS)
chemistry education (PhD)
chemistry, earth sciences and physics (MA, MS, PhD)
chemistry: education (MS)
chemistry: research (MS)
clinical nurse specialist in chronic illness (MS)
earth sciences (MA)
exercise science (MS, PhD)
family nurse practitioner (MS)
gerontology (MA)
human rehabilitation (PhD)
human sciences (MA, MPH, Au D, PhD)
mathematical teaching (MA)
mathematics (MA, PhD)
mathematics education (PhD)
mathematics: liberal arts (MA)
natural and health sciences (MA, MPH, MS, Au D, PhD)
nursing education (MS, PhD)
public health education (MPH)
rehabilitation counseling (MA)
speech language pathology (MA)
sport administration (MS, PhD)
sport pedagogy (MS, PhD)

College of Performing and Visual Arts
Dr. Andrew J. Svedlow, Dean
Programs in:
collaborative keyboard (MM)
conducting (MM)
instrumental performance (MM)
jazz studies (MM)
music conducting (DA)
music education (MM, DA)
music history and literature (MM, DA)
music performance (DA)
music theory and composition (MM, DA)
performing and visual arts (MA, MM, DA)
visual arts (MA)
vocal performance (MM)

■ UNIVERSITY OF PHOENIX–DENVER CAMPUS

Lone Tree, CO 80124-5453
http://www.phoenix.edu/

Proprietary, coed, comprehensive institution. *Computer facilities:* A campuswide network can be accessed from off campus. *General application contact:* Campus Information Center, 303-694-9093.

The Artemis School

College of Education
Programs in:
administration and supervision (MAEd)
curriculum instruction (MAEd)
elementary teacher education (MAEd)
school counseling (MSC)
secondary teacher education (MAEd)

College of Health and Human Services
Programs in:
administration of justice and security (MS)
community counseling (MSC)
health administration (MHA)
health care management (MBA)
marriage, family and child therapy (MSC)
nursing (MSN)
psychology (MS)

John Sperling School of Business

Program in:
business (MBA, MIS, MM, MSA)

College of Graduate Business and Management
Programs in:
accountancy (MSA)
accounting (MBA)
business administration (MBA)
e-business (MBA)
global management (MBA)
human resources management (MBA, MM)
management (MM)
marketing (MBA)
public administration (MBA, MM)

College of Information Systems and Technology
Programs in:
e-business (MBA)
management (MIS)
technology management (MBA)

■ UNIVERSITY OF PHOENIX–SOUTHERN COLORADO CAMPUS

Colorado Springs, CO 80919-2335
http://www.phoenix.edu/

Proprietary, coed, comprehensive institution. *Computer facilities:* Computer purchase and lease plans are available. A campuswide network can be accessed from off campus. Online class registration is available. *General application contact:* Campus Information Center, 719-599-5282.

The Artemis School

College of Education
Programs in:
administration and supervision (MA Ed)
curriculum and instruction (MA Ed)
elementary teacher education (MA Ed)
principal licensure certification (Certificate)
school counseling (MSC)
secondary teacher education (MA Ed)

College of Health and Human Services
Programs in:
administration of justice and security (MS)
community counseling (MSC)
education (MHA)
gerontology (MHA)
health administration (MHA)
health care management (MBA)
marriage, family and child therapy (MSC)
nursing (MSN)
psychology (MS)

John Sperling School of Business

Program in:
business (MBA, MM)

College of Graduate Business and Management
Programs in:
accounting (MBA)
business administration (MBA)
global management (MBA)
human resources management (MBA, MM)
management (MM)
marketing (MBA)
public administration (MM)

College of Information Systems and Technology
Program in:
technology management (MBA)

Connecticut

■ CENTRAL CONNECTICUT STATE UNIVERSITY

New Britain, CT 06050-4010
http://www.ccsu.edu/

State-supported, coed, comprehensive institution. CGS member. *Graduate faculty:* 343 full-time (140 women), 410 part-time/adjunct (182 women). *Computer facilities:* 1,000 computers available on campus for general student use. A campuswide network can be accessed from student residence rooms and from off campus. Online class registration is available. *Graduate expenses:* Full-time $4377; part-time $420 per credit.

Central Connecticut State University (continued)
Tuition, state resident: full-time $6566; part-time $420 per credit. Tuition, nonresident: full-time $12,195; part-time $420 per credit. Required fees: $3462. One-time fee: $62 part-time. *General application contact:* Patricia Gardner, Graduate Admissions, 860-832-2350.

School of Graduate Studies
Patricia Gardner, Graduate Admissions

School of Arts and Sciences
Dr. Susan Pease, Dean
Programs in:
anesthesia (MS)
art education (MS, Certificate)
arts and sciences (MA, MS, Certificate)
biological sciences (MA, MS)
biology (Certificate)
community psychology (MA)
computer information technology (MS)
criminal justice (MS)
data mining (MS, Certificate)
English (MA, Certificate)
French (MA)
general health (MS)
general psychology (MA)
geography (MS)
graphic information design (MA)
health psychology (MA)
history (MA, Certificate)
international studies (MS)
Italian (Certificate)
mathematics (MA, MS, Certificate)
modern language (MA, Certificate)
music education (MS, Certificate)
natural sciences (MS)
organizational communication (MS)
physics and earth science (MS, Certificate)
public history (MA)
public relations/promotions (Certificate)
social studies (Certificate)
Spanish (MA, MS, Certificate)
Spanish language and Hispanic culture (MA)
teaching English to speakers of other languages (MS, Certificate)

School of Business
Dr. Siamack Shojai, Dean
Programs in:
business (MS, Certificate)
business education (MS, Certificate)

School of Education and Professional Studies
Dr. Mitchell Sakofs, Dean
Programs in:
early childhood education (MS)
education and professional studies (MS, Ed D, Certificate, Sixth Year Certificate)
educational foundations policy/secondary education (MS)
educational leadership (MS, Ed D, Sixth Year Certificate)
educational technology and media (MS)
elementary education (MS, Certificate)
marriage and family therapy (MS)
physical education (MS, Certificate)
professional counseling (MS, Certificate)
reading and language arts (MS, Sixth Year Certificate)
school counseling (MS)
special education (Certificate)
special education for special educators (MS)
special education for teachers certified in areas other than education (MS)
student development in higher education (MS)

School of Technology
Dr. Zdzislaw Kremens, Dean
Programs in:
biomolecular sciences (MA)
engineering (MS)
technology (MA, MS, Certificate)
technology education (MS, Certificate)
technology management (MS)

■ EASTERN CONNECTICUT STATE UNIVERSITY
Willimantic, CT 06226-2295
http://www.easternct.edu/

State-supported, coed, comprehensive institution. *Graduate faculty:* 11 full-time (6 women), 16 part-time/adjunct (10 women). *Computer facilities:* Computer purchase and lease plans are available. 637 computers available on campus for general student use. A campuswide network can be accessed from student residence rooms and from off campus. Online class registration is available. *Graduate expenses:* Tuition, state resident: full-time $4000; part-time $400 per credit. Tuition, nonresident: full-time $12,000. Required fees: $50 per term. *General application contact:* Graduate Division, School of Education and Professional Studies, 860-465-5292.

School of Education and Professional Studies/Graduate Division
Dr. Patricia A. Kleine, Dean
Programs in:
early childhood education (MS)
education and professional studies (MS)
educational technology (MS)
elementary education (MS)
organizational management (MS)
reading and language arts (MS)
science education (MS)
secondary education (MS)

■ FAIRFIELD UNIVERSITY
Fairfield, CT 06824-5195
http://www.fairfield.edu/

Independent-religious, coed, comprehensive institution. *Graduate faculty:* 141 full-time (75 women), 65 part-time/adjunct (24 women). *Computer facilities:* Computer purchase and lease plans are available. 220 computers available on campus for general student use. A campuswide network can be accessed from student residence rooms and from off campus. Online class registration is available. *Graduate expenses:* Tuition: full-time $9450; part-time $525 per credit hour. Required fees: $25 per semester. Tuition and fees vary according to course load and program. *General application contact:* Marianne Gumpper, Director of Graduate and Continuing Studies Admissions, 203-254-4184.

Charles F. Dolan School of Business
Dr. Norman A. Solomon, Dean
Programs in:
accounting (MBA, MS, CAS)
finance (MBA, MS, CAS)
general management (MBA)
human resource management (MBA, CAS)
information systems and operations (MBA)
information systems and operations management (CAS)
international business (MBA, CAS)
marketing (MBA, CAS)
taxation (MBA, MS)

College of Arts and Sciences
Dr. Robbin Crabtree, Dean
Programs in:
American studies (MA)
communication (MA)
creative writing (MFA)
mathematics (MS)

Graduate School of Education and Allied Professions
Dr. Susan D. Franzosa, Dean
Programs in:
applied psychology (MA)
bilingual education (CAS)
community counseling (MA, CAS)
education and allied professions (MA, CAS)
elementary education (MA)
marriage and family therapy (MA)
media/educational technology (MA)
school counseling (MA, CAS)
school media specialist (MA)
school psychology (MA, CAS)
secondary education (MA)
special education (MA, CAS)
teaching and foundations (MA, CAS)
TESOL, foreign language and bilingual/multicultural education (MA, CAS)

School of Engineering
Dr. Evangelos Hadjimichael, Dean
Programs in:
electrical and computer engineering (MS)
management of technology (MS)
mechanical engineering (MS)
software engineering (MS)

School of Nursing
Dr. Jeanne M. Novotny, Dean
Programs in:
clinical nurse leader (MSN)

family nurse practitioner (MSN, PMC)
healthcare management (MSN)
nurse anesthesia (MSN)
psychiatric nurse practitioner (MSN, PMC)

■ QUINNIPIAC UNIVERSITY
Hamden, CT 06518-1940
http://www.quinnipiac.edu/

Independent, coed, comprehensive institution. *Graduate faculty:* 101 full-time (42 women), 92 part-time/adjunct (41 women). *Computer facilities:* Computer purchase and lease plans are available. 600 computers available on campus for general student use. A campuswide network can be accessed from student residence rooms and from off campus. Online class registration, e-commerce 'Q' card for local merchants, food service, dorm card access are available. *Graduate expenses:* Tuition: full-time $14,600; part-time $730 per credit. Required fees: $630; $30 per credit. *General application contact:* Information Contact, 800-462-1944.

Division of Education
Dr. Cynthia Dubea, Dean
Programs in:
biology (MAT)
education (MAT)
elementary education (MAT)
English (MAT)
history/social studies (MAT)
mathematics (MAT)
Spanish (MAT)

School of Business
Dr. Kim McKeage, Director of Master of Business Administration
Programs in:
accounting (MBA)
business (MBA, MS)
chartered financial analyst (MBA)
finance (MBA)
health care management (MBA)
healthcare management (MBA)
information systems management (MS)
international business (MBA)
management (MBA)
marketing (MBA)

School of Communications
Programs in:
communications (MS)
interactive communications (MS)
journalism (MS)
public relations (MS)

School of Health Sciences
Dr. Edward O'Connor, Dean
Programs in:
adult nurse practitioner (MSN, Post Master's Certificate)
biomedical sciences (MHS)
cardiovascular perfusion (MHS)
family nurse practitioner (MSN, Post Master's Certificate)
health sciences (MHS, MHS, MOT, MPT, MS, MSN, DPT, Post Master's Certificate)
laboratory management (MHS)
microbiology (MHS)
molecular and cell biology (MS)
occupational therapy (MOT)
pathologists' assistant (MHS)
physical therapy (MPT, DPT)
physician assistant (MHS)
radiologist assistant (MHS)

School of Law
Brad Saxton, Dean
Programs in:
health law (LL M)
law (JD)

■ SACRED HEART UNIVERSITY
Fairfield, CT 06825-1000
http://www.sacredheart.edu/

Independent-religious, coed, comprehensive institution. *Computer facilities:* 330 computers available on campus for general student use. A campuswide network can be accessed from student residence rooms and from off campus. Online class registration is available. *General application contact:* Dean of Graduate Admissions, 203-365-7619.

Graduate Programs

College of Arts and Sciences
Programs in:
arts and sciences (MA, MS, CPS)
chemistry (MS)
computer science (MS)
criminal justice (MA)
database (CPS)
information technology (MS, CPS)
information technology and network security (CPS)
interactive multimedia (CPS)
religious studies (MA)
Web development (CPS)

College of Education and Health Professions
Programs in:
administration (CAS)
clinical nurse leader (MSN)
clinical practice in health care (DNP)
education and health professions (MAT, MS, MSN, MSOT, DNP, DPT, CAS)
educational technology (MAT)
elementary education (MAT)
exercise science and nutrition (MS)
family nurse practitioner (MSN)
geriatric health and wellness (MS)
leadership in health care (DNP)
occupational therapy (MSOT)
patient care services administration (MSN)
physical therapy (DPT)
reading (CAS)
secondary education (MAT)
teaching (CAS)

John F. Welch College of Business
Program in:
business (MBA)

■ SAINT JOSEPH COLLEGE
West Hartford, CT 06117-2700
http://www.sjc.edu/

Independent-religious, Undergraduate: women only; graduate: coed, comprehensive institution. *Computer facilities:* A campuswide network can be accessed from student residence rooms and from off campus. Online class registration is available. *Graduate expenses:* Tuition: part-time $560 per credit. Required fees: $30 per credit. *General application contact:* Graduate Admissions Office, 860-231-5261.

Department of Biology
Program in:
biology (MS)

Department of Business Administration
Program in:
management (MS)

Department of Chemistry
Programs in:
biochemistry (MS)
chemistry (MS)

Department of Counselor Education
Programs in:
community counseling (MA)
school counseling (MA)

Department of Education
Programs in:
education (MA)
special education (MA)

Department of Marriage and Family Therapy
Program in:
marriage and family therapy (MA)

Department of Nursing
Programs in:
family nurse practitioner (MS)
nursing (Post Master's Certificate)

Department of Nutrition
Program in:
nutrition (MS)

Institute in Gerontology
Program in:
human development/gerontology (MA, Certificate)

■ SOUTHERN CONNECTICUT STATE UNIVERSITY
New Haven, CT 06515-1355
http://www.southernct.edu/

State-supported, coed, comprehensive institution. CGS member. *Computer facilities:*

Southern Connecticut State University (continued)
800 computers available on campus for general student use. A campuswide network can be accessed from student residence rooms and from off campus. Online class registration is available. *General application contact:* Assistant Dean, 203-392-5240.

School of Graduate Studies

School of Arts and Sciences
Programs in:
- art education (MS)
- arts and sciences (MA, MS, Diploma)
- biology (MS)
- biology for nurse anesthetists (MS)
- chemistry (MS)
- English (MA, MS)
- environmental education (MS)
- history (MA, MS)
- mathematics (MS)
- multicultural-bilingual education/ teaching English to speakers of other languages (MS)
- political science (MS)
- psychology (MA)
- science education (MS, Diploma)
- sociology (MS)
- urban studies (MS)
- women's studies (MA)

School of Business
Programs in:
- business (MBA)
- business administration (MBA)

School of Communication, Information and Library Science
Programs in:
- communication, information and library science (MLS, MS, Diploma)
- computer science (MS)
- library science (MLS)
- library/information studies (Diploma)

School of Education
Programs in:
- classroom teacher specialist (Diploma)
- community counseling (MS)
- counseling (Diploma)
- education (MS, MS Ed, Ed D, Diploma)
- educational foundations (Diploma)
- educational leadership (Ed D, Diploma)
- elementary education (MS)
- foundational studies (Diploma)
- human performance (MS)
- physical education (MS)
- reading (MS, Diploma)
- research, statistics, and measurement (MS)
- school counseling (MS)
- school health education (MS)
- school psychology (MS, Diploma)
- special education (MS Ed, Diploma)
- sport psychology (MS)

School of Health and Human Services
Programs in:
- audiology (MS)
- health and human services (MFT, MPH, MS, MSN, MSW)
- marriage and family therapy (MFT)
- nursing administration (MSN)
- nursing education (MSN)
- public health (MPH)
- recreation and leisure studies (MS)
- social work (MSW)
- speech pathology (MS)

■ UNIVERSITY OF BRIDGEPORT
Bridgeport, CT 06604
http://www.bridgeport.edu/

Independent, coed, comprehensive institution. CGS member. *Graduate faculty:* 117 full-time (41 women), 435 part-time/adjunct (188 women). *Computer facilities:* Computer purchase and lease plans are available. 500 computers available on campus for general student use. A campuswide network can be accessed from student residence rooms and from off campus. Online class registration is available. *Graduate expenses:* Tuition: full-time $19,820; part-time $595 per credit hour. Required fees: $75 per semester. *General application contact:* Barbara L. Maryak, Associate Vice President for Admissions, 203-576-4552.

Acupuncture Institute
Dr. Jennifer Brett, Director
Program in:
- acupuncture (MS)

College of Chiropractic
Dr. Francis A. Zolli, Dean
Program in:
- chiropractic (DC)

College of Naturopathic Medicine
Dr. Guru Sandesh Singh Khalsa, Dean
Program in:
- naturopathic medicine (ND)

Fones School of Dental Hygiene
Dr. Margaret H. Zayan, Dean
Program in:
- dental hygiene (MS)

International College
Dr. Thomas J. Ward, Dean
Program in:
- global development and peace (MA)

Nutrition Institute
Dr. David M. Brady, Director
Program in:
- human nutrition (MS)

School of Business
Paul Lerman, Dean
Programs in:
- business (MBA)
- business administration (MBA)

School of Education and Human Resources
Dr. Paul C. Paese, Dean
Program in:
- education and human resources (MS, Ed D, Diploma)

Division of Education
Dr. Paul C. Paese, Dean
Programs in:
- computer specialist (Diploma)
- early childhood education (MS, Diploma)
- education (MS, Ed D, Diploma)
- educational management (Ed D, Diploma)
- elementary education (MS, Diploma)
- intermediate administrator or supervisor (Diploma)
- international education (Diploma)
- leadership (Ed D)
- reading specialist (MS, Diploma)
- secondary education (MS, Diploma)

Division of Human Resources
Dr. Tracy Ryan, Director, Division of Counseling and Human Resources
Programs in:
- college student personnel (MS)
- community counseling (MS)
- human resource development (MS)
- human service (MS)

School of Engineering
Dr. Tarek M. Sobh, Vice President for Graduate Studies and Research/Dean, School of Engineering
Programs in:
- computer engineering (MS)
- computer science (MS)
- computer science and engineering (PhD)
- electrical engineering (MS)
- engineering (MS, PhD)
- mechanical engineering (MS)
- technology management (MS)

■ UNIVERSITY OF CONNECTICUT
Storrs, CT 06269
http://www.uconn.edu/

State-supported, coed, university. CGS member. *Graduate faculty:* 1,330 full-time (438 women). *Computer facilities:* Computer purchase and lease plans are available. 1,318 computers available on campus for general student use. A campuswide network can be accessed from student residence rooms and from off campus. Online class registration is available. *Graduate expenses:* Tuition, state resident: full-time $4455; part-time $495 per credit. Tuition, nonresident: full-time $11,565; part-time $1285 per credit. Required fees: $842 per semester. *General application contact:* Anne K. Lanzit, Associate Director of Graduate Admissions, 860-486-3617.

Graduate School
Suman Singha, Dean and Vice President, Research and Graduate Education

Center for Continuing Studies
Susan W. Nesbitt, Director

Programs in:
- continuing studies (MPS)
- homeland security leadership (MPS)
- humanitarian services administration (MPS)
- labor relations (MPS)
- occupational safety and health management (MPS)
- personnel (MPS)

College of Agriculture and Natural Resources
Kirklyn M. Kerr, Dean
Programs in:
- agricultural and resource economics (MS, PhD)
- agriculture and natural resources (MS, PhD)
- allied health sciences (MS)
- animal science (MS, PhD)
- natural resources management and engineering (MS, PhD)
- nutritional sciences (MS, PhD)
- pathobiology (MS, PhD)
- plant and soil sciences (MS, PhD)

College of Liberal Arts and Sciences
Ross D. MacKinnon, Dean
Programs in:
- actuarial science (MS, PhD)
- African studies (MA)
- anthropology (MA, PhD)
- applied financial mathematics (MS)
- applied genomics (MS, PSM)
- audiology (Au D, PhD)
- behavioral neuroscience (PhD)
- biobehavioral science (PhD)
- biochemistry (MS, PhD)
- biophysics and structural biology (MS, PhD)
- biopsychology (PhD)
- biotechnology (MS)
- botany (MS, PhD)
- cell and developmental biology (MS, PhD)
- chemistry (MS, PhD)
- clinical psychology (MA, PhD)
- cognition and instruction (PhD)
- communication processes (MA)
- communication processes and marketing communication (PhD)
- comparative literature and cultural studies (MA, PhD)
- comparative physiology (MS, PhD)
- culture, health and human development (Graduate Certificate)
- developmental psychology (MA, PhD)
- ecological psychology (PhD)
- ecology (MS, PhD)
- economics (MA, PhD)
- endocrinology (MS, PhD)
- English (MA, PhD)
- entomology (MS, PhD)
- European studies (MA)
- experimental psychology (PhD)
- French (MA, PhD)
- general psychology (MA, PhD)
- genetics (MS, PhD)
- genetics, genomics, and bioinformatics (MS, PhD)
- geographic information systems (Certificate)
- geography (MS, PhD)
- geological sciences (MS, PhD)
- German (MA, PhD)
- health psychology (Graduate Certificate)
- history (MA, PhD)
- human development and family studies (MA, PhD)
- industrial/organizational psychology (PhD)
- international studies (MA, Graduate Certificate)
- Italian (MA, PhD)
- Italian history and culture (MA)
- Judaic studies (MA)
- language and cognition (PhD)
- Latin American studies (MA)
- liberal arts and sciences (MA, MPA, MS, PSM, Au D, PhD, Certificate, Graduate Certificate)
- linguistics (MA, PhD)
- marine sciences (MS, PhD)
- mathematics (MS, PhD)
- medieval studies (MA, PhD)
- microbial systems analysis (MS, PSM)
- microbiology (MS, PhD)
- neurobiology (MS, PhD)
- neuroscience (PhD)
- nonprofit management (Graduate Certificate)
- occupational health psychology (Graduate Certificate)
- philosophy (MA, PhD)
- physics (MS, PhD)
- plant cell and molecular biology (MS, PhD)
- political science (MA, PhD)
- public administration (MPA, Graduate Certificate)
- public financial management (Graduate Certificate)
- quantitative research methods (Graduate Certificate)
- social psychology (MA, PhD)
- sociology (MA, PhD)
- Spanish (MA, PhD)
- speech-language pathology (MA, PhD)
- statistics (MS, PhD)
- survey research (MA, Graduate Certificate)
- zoology (MS, PhD)

Neag School of Education
Richard L. Schwab, Dean
Programs in:
- adult learning (MA, PhD)
- agriculture (MA)
- agriculture education (PhD, Post-Master's Certificate)
- bilingual and bicultural education (MA, PhD, Post-Master's Certificate)
- cognition and instruction (MA, PhD, Post-Master's Certificate)
- counseling psychology (MA, PhD, Post-Master's Certificate)
- education (MA, DPT, Ed D, PhD, Post-Master's Certificate)
- education policy analysis (PhD)
- educational administration (Ed D, PhD, Post-Master's Certificate)
- elementary education (MA, PhD, Post-Master's Certificate)
- English education (MA, PhD, Post-Master's Certificate)
- exercise science (MA, PhD)
- gifted and talented education (MA, PhD, Post-Master's Certificate)
- higher education and student affairs (MA)
- history and social sciences education (MA, PhD, Post-Master's Certificate)
- learning technology (MA, PhD, Post-Master's Certificate)
- mathematics education (MA, PhD, Post-Master's Certificate)
- measurement, evaluation, and assessment (MA, PhD, Post-Master's Certificate)
- physical therapy (DPT)
- reading education (MA, PhD, Post-Master's Certificate)
- school counseling (MA, Post-Master's Certificate)
- school psychology (MA, PhD, Post-Master's Certificate)
- science education (MA, PhD)
- secondary education (MA, PhD, Post-Master's Certificate)
- special education (MA, PhD, Post-Master's Certificate)
- sport management and sociology (MA, PhD)
- world languages education (MA, PhD, Post-Master's Certificate)

School of Business
P. Christopher Earley, Dean
Programs in:
- accounting (MS, PhD)
- business administration (Exec MBA, MBA, PhD)
- finance (PhD)
- health care management and insurance studies (MBA)
- management (PhD)
- management consulting (MBA)
- marketing (PhD)
- marketing intelligence (MBA)

School of Engineering
Mun Y. Choi, Dean
Programs in:
- biomedical engineering (MS, PhD)
- chemical engineering (MS, PhD)
- civil engineering (MS, PhD)
- computer science (MS, PhD)
- electrical engineering (MS, PhD)
- engineering (M Eng, MS, PhD)
- environmental engineering (MS, PhD)
- materials science and engineering (MS, PhD)
- mechanical engineering (MS, PhD)
- metallurgy and materials engineering (MS, PhD)

School of Fine Arts
David G. Woods, Dean
Programs in:
- acting (MFA)
- art history (MA)

University of Connecticut (continued)
conducting (M Mus, DMA)
costume design (MFA)
fine arts (M Mus, MA, MFA, DMA, PhD, Performer's Certificate)
historical musicology (MA)
lighting design (MFA)
music (Performer's Certificate)
music education (M Mus, PhD)
music theory (MA)
music theory and history (PhD)
performance (M Mus, DMA)
puppetry (MA, MFA)
scenic design (MFA)
studio art (MFA)

School of Nursing
Anne R. Bavier, Dean
Program in:
nursing (MS, PhD, Post-Master's Certificate)

School of Pharmacy
Robert L. McCarthy, Dean
Programs in:
medicinal chemistry (MS, PhD)
pharmaceutics (MS, PhD)
pharmacology (MS, PhD)
pharmacology and toxicology (MS, PhD)
pharmacy (Pharm D, MS, PhD)
toxicology (MS, PhD)

School of Social Work
David E. Cournoyer, Interim Dean
Program in:
social work (MSW, PhD)

University of Connecticut Health Center
Lawrence Klobutcher, Associate Dean
Programs in:
biomedical science (PhD)
clinical and translational research (MS)
dental science (M Dent Sc)
health (M Dent Sc, MPH, MS, PhD)
public health (MPH)

School of Law
Jeremy Paul, Dean
Program in:
law (JD)

■ UNIVERSITY OF HARTFORD
West Hartford, CT 06117-1599
http://www.hartford.edu/

Independent, coed, comprehensive institution. CGS member. *Computer facilities:* 400 computers available on campus for general student use. A campuswide network can be accessed from student residence rooms and from off campus. Online class registration, student Web pages are available. *General application contact:* Assistant Director of Graduate Admissions, 860-768-4373.

Barney School of Business
Programs in:
business (MBA, MSAT, Certificate)
business administration (MBA)
professional accounting (Certificate)
taxation (MSAT)

College of Arts and Sciences
Programs in:
arts and sciences (MA, MS, Psy D)
biology (MS)
clinical practices (MA, Psy D)
communication (MA)
general experimental psychology (MA)
neuroscience (MS)
organizational behavior (MS)
psychology (MA)
school psychology (MS)

College of Education, Nursing, and Health Professions
Programs in:
administration and supervision (CAGS)
community/public health nursing (MSN)
counseling (M Ed, MS, Sixth Year Certificate)
early childhood education (M Ed)
education, nursing, and health professions (M Ed, MS, MSN, MSPT, DPT, Ed D, CAGS, Sixth Year Certificate)
educational leadership (Ed D, CAGS)
educational technology (M Ed)
elementary education (M Ed)
nursing education (MSN)
nursing management (MSN)
physical therapy (MSPT, DPT)

College of Engineering, Technology and Architecture
Programs in:
architecture (M Arch)
engineering (M Eng)
engineering, technology and architecture (M Arch, M Eng)

Hartford Art School
Program in:
art (MFA)

The Hartt School
Programs in:
choral conducting (MM Ed)
composition (MM, DMA, Artist Diploma, Diploma)
conducting (MM, DMA, Artist Diploma, Diploma)
early childhood education (MM Ed)
instrumental conducting (MM Ed)
Kodály (MM Ed)
music (CAGS)
music education (DMA, PhD)
music history (MM)
music theory (MM)
pedagogy (MM Ed)
performance (MM, MM Ed, DMA, Artist Diploma, Diploma)
research (MM Ed)
technology (MM Ed)

■ UNIVERSITY OF NEW HAVEN
West Haven, CT 06516-1916
http://www.newhaven.edu/

Independent, coed, comprehensive institution. CGS member. *Graduate faculty:* 103 full-time (21 women), 120 part-time/adjunct (24 women). *Computer facilities:* Computer purchase and lease plans are available. 300 computers available on campus for general student use. A campuswide network can be accessed from student residence rooms and from off campus. Online class registration, computer repair services are available. *Graduate expenses:* Tuition: full-time $15,075; part-time $670 per credit. Required fees: $240; $45 per trimester. Tuition and fees vary according to course load and program. *General application contact:* Eloise Gormley, Director of Graduate Admissions, 203-932-7449.

Graduate School
Dr. Ira Kleinfeld, Associate Provost and Dean of Graduate Studies

College of Arts and Sciences
Dr. Ronald Nowaczyk, Dean
Programs in:
arts and sciences (MA, MS, Certificate)
cellular and molecular biology (MS)
community psychology (MA, Certificate)
education (MS)
environmental sciences (MS)
human nutrition (MS)
industrial and organizational psychology (MA, Certificate)

College of Business
Dr. Richard Highfield, Dean
Programs in:
accounting (MBA)
business (EMBA, MBA, MPA, MS)
business administration (EMBA, MBA)
business policy and strategy (MBA)
corporate taxation (MS)
finance (MBA)
finance and financial services (MS)
financial accounting (MS)
health care administration (MS)
health care management (MBA, MPA)
human resources management (MBA)
industrial relations (MS)
international business (MBA)
managerial accounting (MS)
marketing (MBA)
personnel and labor relations (MPA)
public relations (MBA)
public taxation (MS)
sports management (MBA)
taxation (MS)
technology management (MBA)

Henry C. Lee College of Criminal Justice and Forensic Sciences
Dr. Richard Ward, Dean
Programs in:
advanced investigation (MS)
correctional counseling (MS)

criminal justice and forensic sciences (MS)
criminal justice management (MS)
criminalistics (MS)
fire science (MS)
forensic science (MS)
industrial hygiene (MS)
national security and public safety (MS)
occupational safety and health management (MS)
security management (MS)

Tagliatela College of Engineering
Dr. Barry Farbrother, Dean
Programs in:
applications software (MS)
civil engineering design (Certificate)
electrical engineering (MSEE)
engineering (EMS, MS, MSEE, MSIE, MSME, Certificate)
engineering management (EMS)
environmental engineering (MS)
industrial engineering (MSIE)
logistics (Certificate)
management information systems (MS)
mechanical engineering (MSME)
systems software (MS)

■ WESTERN CONNECTICUT STATE UNIVERSITY
Danbury, CT 06810-6885
http://www.wcsu.edu/

State-supported, coed, comprehensive institution. CGS member. *Graduate faculty:* 53 full-time (21 women), 43 part-time/adjunct (21 women). *Computer facilities:* 928 computers available on campus for general student use. A campuswide network can be accessed from student residence rooms and from off campus. Online class registration is available. *Graduate expenses:* Tuition, state resident: full-time $4377; part-time $363 per credit. Tuition, nonresident: full-time $12,195; part-time $363 per credit. Required fees: $3574; $60 per credit. Part-time tuition and fees vary according to degree level and program. *General application contact:* Chris Shankle, Associate Director of Graduate Studies, 203-837-9005.

Division of Graduate Studies
Dr. Ellen D. Durnin, Dean, Division of Graduate Studies

Ancell School of Business
Dr. Allen Morton, Dean
Programs in:
accounting (MBA)
business (MBA, MHA, MS)
business administration (MBA)
health administration (MHA)
justice administration (MS)

School of Arts and Sciences
Dr. Linda Vaden-Goad, Dean
Programs in:
arts and sciences (MA, MFA)
biological and environmental sciences (MA)
earth and planetary sciences (MA)
English (MA)
history (MA)
literature option (MA)
mathematics (MA)
professional writing (MFA)
TESOL option (MA)
theoretical mathematics (MA)
writing option (MA)

School of Professional Studies
Dr. Lynne Clark, Dean
Programs in:
adult nurse practitioner (MSN)
clinical nurse specialist (MSN)
community counseling (MS)
curriculum (MS)
English education (MS)
instructional leadership (Ed D)
instructional technology (MS)
mathematics education (MS)
reading (MS)
school counseling (MS)
special education (MS)

School of Visual and Performing Arts
Dr. Carol A. Hawkes, Dean
Programs in:
illustration (MFA)
music education (MS)
painting (MFA)
visual and performing arts (MFA, MS)

■ YALE UNIVERSITY
New Haven, CT 06520
http://www.yale.edu/

Independent, coed, university. CGS member. *Computer facilities:* Computer purchase and lease plans are available. 350 computers available on campus for general student use. A campuswide network can be accessed from student residence rooms and from off campus. Online class registration is available. *General application contact:* Admissions Information, 203-432-2772.

Divinity School
Dr. Harold W. Attridge, Dean
Program in:
divinity (M Div, MAR, STM)

Graduate School of Arts and Sciences
Programs in:
African studies (MA)
African-American studies (PhD)
American studies (PhD)
anthropology (M Phil, MA, PhD)
applied mathematics (M Phil, MS, PhD)
Arabic and Islamic studies (MA, PhD)
archaeological studies (MA)
archaeology of the ancient Near East (MA, PhD)
arts and sciences (M Phil, MA, MS, PhD, M E Sc/MA)
Assyriology (MA, PhD)
astronomy (PhD)
behavioral neuroscience (PhD)
biochemistry, molecular biology and chemical biology (PhD)
biogeochemistry (PhD)
biophysical chemistry (PhD)
cell biology (PhD)
cellular and developmental biology (PhD)
cellular and molecular physiology (PhD)
classics (M Phil, MA, PhD)
climate dynamics (PhD)
clinical psychology (PhD)
cognitive psychology (PhD)
comparative and historical sociology (PhD)
comparative literature (PhD)
computer science (MS, PhD)
cultural sociology and social theory (PhD)
developmental psychology (PhD)
East Asian languages and literatures (PhD)
East Asian languages and literatures and film studies (PhD)
East Asian studies (MA)
ecology and evolutionary biology (PhD)
economics (PhD)
Egyptology (MA, PhD)
English language and literature (MA, PhD)
environmental sciences (PhD)
experimental pathology (MS, PhD)
film studies (PhD)
forestry (PhD)
French (M Phil, MA, PhD)
genetics (PhD)
geochemistry (PhD)
geophysics (PhD)
German (PhD)
Graeco-Arabic studies (MA, PhD)
history (M Phil, MA, PhD)
history of art (PhD)
history of science and medicine (MS, PhD)
immunobiology (PhD)
inorganic chemistry (PhD)
international and development economics (MA)
international relations (MA, M E Sc/MA)
Italian language and literature (PhD)
Latin American literature (PhD)
linguistics (PhD)
Luso-Brazilian and Spanish/Spanish American literatures (PhD)
mathematics (M Phil, MS, PhD)
medieval Slavic literature and philology (PhD)
medieval studies (M Phil, PhD)
meteorology (PhD)
molecular biophysics and biochemistry (PhD)
music history (MA)
music theory (MA)
neurobiology (PhD)
neuroscience (PhD)
Northwest Semitic, Bible, comparative Semitics (MA, PhD)
oceanography (PhD)
organic chemistry (PhD)

Yale University (continued)
paleontology (PhD)
paleooceanography (PhD)
petrology (PhD)
philosophy (PhD)
physical and theoretical chemistry (PhD)
physics (PhD)
plant sciences (PhD)
Polish literature (PhD)
political science (PhD)
religious studies (PhD)
Renaissance studies (PhD)
Russian and East European studies (MA)
Russian literature (PhD)
Slavic languages and literatures and film studies (PhD)
social stratification and the life course (PhD)
social/personality psychology (PhD)
solar and terrestrial physics (PhD)
Spanish peninsular literature (PhD)
statistics (MA, PhD)
tectonics (PhD)

School of Engineering and Applied Science
Programs in:
applied physics (MS, PhD)
biomedical engineering (MS, PhD)
chemical engineering (MS, PhD)
electrical engineering (MS, PhD)
engineering and applied science (MS, PhD)
environmental engineering (MS, PhD)
mechanical engineering (MS, PhD)

School of Architecture
Program in:
architecture (M Arch, M Env Des, MEM)

School of Art
Robert Storr, Dean
Programs in:
graphic design (MFA)
painting/printmaking (MFA)
photography (MFA)
sculpture (MFA)

School of Drama
Program in:
drama (MFA, DFA, Certificate)

School of Forestry and Environmental Studies
Program in:
forestry and environmental studies (MEM, MES, MF, MFS, PhD)

School of Medicine
Programs in:
biological and biomedical sciences (PhD)
computational biology and bioinformatics (PhD)
immunology (PhD)
medicine (MD, MM Sc, MPH, MS, PhD, MM Sc/MPH)
microbiology (PhD)
molecular biophysics and biochemistry (PhD)
molecular cell biology, genetics, and development (PhD)
neurobiology (PhD)
neuroscience (PhD)
pharmacological sciences and molecular medicine (PhD)
pharmacology (PhD)
physician associate (MM Sc, MM Sc/MPH)
physiology and integrative medical biology (PhD)

School of Public Health
Programs in:
biostatistics (MPH, MS, PhD)
chronic disease epidemiology (MPH, PhD)
environmental health sciences (MPH, PhD)
epidemiology of microbial diseases (MPH, PhD)
global health (MPH)
health management (MPH)
health policy and administration (MPH, PhD)
parasitology (PhD)
social and behavioral sciences (MPH)

School of Music
Robert Blocker, Dean
Program in:
music (MM, MMA, DMA, AD, Certificate)

School of Nursing
Dr. Margaret Grey, Dean
Program in:
nursing (MSN, PhD, Post Master's Certificate)

Yale Law School
Harold Hongju Koh, Dean
Program in:
law (JD, LL M, MSL, JSD)

Yale School of Management
Programs in:
accounting (PhD)
business administration (MBA, PhD)
financial economics (PhD)
management (MBA, PhD)
marketing (PhD)

Delaware

■ DELAWARE STATE UNIVERSITY
Dover, DE 19901-2277
http://www.desu.edu/

State-supported, coed, university. CGS member. *Computer facilities:* Computer purchase and lease plans are available. 641 computers available on campus for general student use. A campuswide network can be accessed from student residence rooms and from off campus. Online class registration is available. *General application contact:* Senior Administrator for Research, 302-857-6800.

Graduate Programs
Programs in:
applied chemistry (MS, PhD)
applied mathematics (MS)
applied mathematics and theoretical physics (PhD)
applied optics (MS)
biological sciences (MA, MS)
biology education (MS)
chemistry (MS, PhD)
French (MA)
historic preservation (MA)
mathematics (MS)
mathematics education (MS)
molecular and cellular neuroscience (MS)
natural resources (MS)
neuroscience (PhD)
nursing (MS)
optics (PhD)
physics (MS)
physics teaching (MS)
plant science (MS)
social work (MSW)
Spanish (MA)
sport administration (MS)

College of Business Administration
Program in:
business administration (MBA)

College of Education
Programs in:
adult literacy and basic education (MA)
art education (MA)
curriculum and instruction (MA)
education (MA, Ed D)
educational leadership (MA, Ed D)
science education (MA)
special education (MA)
teaching (MA)

■ UNIVERSITY OF DELAWARE
Newark, DE 19716
http://www.udel.edu/

State-related, coed, university. CGS member. *Computer facilities:* 908 computers available on campus for general student use. A campuswide network can be accessed from student residence rooms and from off campus. Online class registration, e-mail, personal Web page are available. *General application contact:* Assistant Provost for Graduate Studies, 302-831-8916.

Alfred Lerner College of Business and Economics
Programs in:
accounting (MS)
business administration (MBA)
business and economics (MA, MBA, MS, PhD)
economics (MA, MS, PhD)

economics for entrepreneurship and educators (MA)
finance (MS)
hospitality information management (MS)
information systems and technology management (MS)

College of Agriculture and Natural Resources
Programs in:
agricultural economics (MS)
agriculture and natural resources (MA, MS, PhD)
agriculture and technical education (MA)
animal sciences (MS, PhD)
bioresources engineering (MS)
entomology and applied ecology (MS, PhD)
food sciences (MS)
operations research (MS, PhD)
plant and soil sciences (MS, PhD)
public horticulture (MS)
statistics (MS)

College of Arts and Sciences
Programs in:
acting (MFA)
applied mathematics (MS, PhD)
art (MA, MFA)
art history (MA, PhD)
arts and sciences (MA, MALS, MFA, MM, MS, DPT, PhD)
behavioral neuroscience (PhD)
biochemistry (MA, MS, PhD)
biomechanics and movement science (MS, PhD)
biotechnology (MS)
cancer biology (MS, PhD)
cell and extracellular matrix biology (MS, PhD)
cell and systems physiology (MS, PhD)
chemistry (MA, MS, PhD)
climatology (PhD)
clinical psychology (PhD)
cognitive psychology (PhD)
communication (MA)
composition (MM)
computer and information sciences (MS, PhD)
criminology (MA, PhD)
developmental biology (MS, PhD)
early American culture (MA)
ecology and evolution (MS, PhD)
English and American literature (MA, PhD)
foreign languages and literatures (MA)
foreign languages pedagogy (MA)
geography (MA, MS)
history (MA, PhD)
history of technology and industrialization (MA, PhD)
liberal studies (MALS)
linguistics (MA, PhD)
mathematics (MS, PhD)
microbiology (MS, PhD)
molecular biology and genetics (MS, PhD)
music education (MM)
performance (MM)
physical therapy (DPT)
physics and astronomy (MS, PhD)
political science and international relations (MA, PhD)
practicing art conservation (MS)
social psychology (PhD)
sociology (MA, PhD)
stage management (MFA)
technical production (MFA)

College of Engineering
Programs in:
chemical engineering (M Ch E, PhD)
electrical and computer engineering (MSECE, PhD)
engineering (M Ch E, MAS, MCE, MEM, MMSE, MSECE, MSME, PhD)
environmental engineering (MAS, MCE, PhD)
geotechnical engineering (MAS, MCE, PhD)
materials science and engineering (MMSE, PhD)
mechanical engineering (MEM, MSME, PhD)
ocean engineering (MAS, MCE, PhD)
structural engineering (MAS, MCE, PhD)
transportation engineering (MAS, MCE, PhD)
water resource engineering (MAS, MCE, PhD)

College of Health Sciences
Programs in:
adult nurse practitioner (MSN, PMC)
cardiopulmonary clinical nurse specialist (MSN, PMC)
cardiopulmonary clinical nurse specialist/adult nurse practitioner (MSN, PMC)
exercise science (MS)
family nurse practitioner (MSN, PMC)
gerontology clinical nurse specialist (MSN, PMC)
gerontology clinical nurse specialist geriatric nurse practitioner (PMC)
gerontology clinical nurse specialist/ geriatric nurse practitioner (MSN)
health promotion (MS)
health sciences (MS, MSN, PMC)
health services administration (MSN, PMC)
human nutrition (MS)
nursing of children clinical nurse specialist (MSN, PMC)
nursing of children clinical nurse specialist/pediatric nurse practitioner (MSN, PMC)
oncology/immune deficiency clinical nurse specialist (MSN, PMC)
oncology/immune deficiency clinical nurse specialist/adult nurse practitioner (MSN, PMC)
perinatal/women's health clinical nurse specialist (MSN, PMC)
perinatal/women's health clinical nurse specialist/women's health nurse practitioner (MSN, PMC)
psychiatric nursing clinical nurse specialist (MSN, PMC)

College of Human Services, Education and Public Policy
Programs in:
counseling in higher education (M Ed, MA)
human development and family studies (MS, PhD)
human services, education and public policy (M Ed, MA, MEEP, MI, MPA, MS, Ed D, PhD, Ed S)

Center for Energy and Environmental Policy
Programs in:
community development and nonprofit leadership (MA)
energy and environmental policy (MA)
environmental and energy policy (MEEP, PhD)
governance, planning and management (PhD)
historic preservation (MA)
social and urban policy (PhD)
technology, environment and society (PhD)
urban affairs and public policy (MA, PhD)

School of Education
Programs in:
education (PhD)
educational leadership (Ed D)
higher education (M Ed)
instruction (MI)
reading (M Ed)
school leadership (M Ed)
school psychology (MA, Ed S)
teaching English as a second language (TESL) (MA)

School of Urban Affairs and Public Policy
Programs in:
public administration (MPA)
urban affairs and public policy (MPA)

College of Marine and Earth Studies
Programs in:
geology (MS, PhD)
marine policy (MS)
marine studies (MMP, MS, PhD)
oceanography (MS, PhD)

■ WESLEY COLLEGE
Dover, DE 19901-3875
http://www.wesley.edu/

Independent-religious, coed, comprehensive institution. *Computer facilities:* Computer purchase and lease plans are available. 225 computers available on campus for general student use. A campuswide network can be accessed from student residence rooms and from off campus. Online class registration is available. *General application contact:* Director of Graduate Admissions, 302-736-2343.

Wesley College (continued)

Business Program

Programs in:
- environmental management (MBA)
- executive leadership (MBA)
- management (MBA)

Education Program

Program in:
- education (M Ed, MA Ed, MAT)

Environmental Studies Program

Program in:
- environmental studies (MS)

Nursing Program

Program in:
- nursing (MSN)

■ WILMINGTON UNIVERSITY

New Castle, DE 19720-6491
http://www.wilmu.edu/

Independent, coed, comprehensive institution. *Computer facilities:* 600 computers available on campus for general student use. A campuswide network can be accessed. Online class registration is available. *General application contact:* Director of Admissions, 302-356-4636 Ext. 256.

College of Social and Behavioral Sciences

Programs in:
- administration of human services (MS)
- administration of justice (MS)
- community counseling (MS)

College of Business

Programs in:
- business administration (MBA)
- finance (MBA)
- health care administration (MBA, MS)
- homeland security (MBA, MS)
- human resource management (MS)
- management (MS)
- management information systems (MBA)
- organizational leadership (MS)
- public administration (MS)
- transportation and logistics (MBA, MS)

College of Education

Programs in:
- applied education technology (M Ed)
- career and technical education (M Ed)
- elementary and secondary school counseling (M Ed)
- elementary special education (M Ed)
- elementary studies (M Ed)
- instruction: gifted and talented (M Ed)
- instruction: teaching and learning (M Ed)
- literacy (M Ed)
- reading (M Ed)
- school leadership (M Ed)
- secondary teaching (MAT)

College of Technology

Programs in:
- corporate training (MS)
- information assurance (MS)
- information systems technologies (MS)
- Internet web design (MS)
- management information systems (MS)

College of Health Professions

Programs in:
- adult nurse practitioner (MSN)
- family nurse practitioner (MSN)
- gerontology (MSN)
- leadership (MSN)
- nursing (MSN)
- women's nurse practitioner (MSN)

Program in Innovation and Leadership

Programs in:
- education innovation (Ed D)
- organizational leadership (Ed D)

District of Columbia

■ AMERICAN UNIVERSITY

Washington, DC 20016-8001
http://www.american.edu/

Independent-religious, coed, university. CGS member. *Graduate faculty:* 591 full-time (274 women), 500 part-time/adjunct (224 women). *Computer facilities:* 700 computers available on campus for general student use. A campuswide network can be accessed from student residence rooms and from off campus. Online class registration, printers, scanners, online course support are available. *Graduate expenses:* Tuition: full-time $21,204; part-time $1178 per credit hour. Required fees: $380. Part-time tuition and fees vary according to course load and program. *General application contact:* 202-885-1000.

College of Arts and Sciences

Dr. Peter Starr, Dean

Programs in:
- anthropology (PhD)
- applied microeconomics (Certificate)
- applied science (MS)
- applied statistics (Certificate)
- art history (MA)
- arts and sciences (M Ed, MA, MAT, MFA, MS, PhD, Certificate)
- arts management (MA, Certificate)
- behavior, cognition, and neuroscience (PhD)
- biology (MA, MS)
- chemistry (MS)
- clinical psychology (PhD)
- computer science (MS, Certificate)
- creative writing (MFA)
- economics (MA, PhD)
- environmental science (MS)
- ethics, peace, and global affairs (MA)
- experimental/biological psychology (MA)
- French (Certificate)
- general psychology (MA)
- history (MA, PhD)
- interdisciplinary studies (MA)
- international economic relations (Certificate)
- literature (MA)
- marine science (MS)
- mathematics (MA)
- painting, sculpture and printmaking (MFA)
- personality/social psychology (MA)
- philosophy (MA)
- psychology (MA, PhD)
- public anthropology (MA, Certificate)
- Russian (Certificate)
- social research (Certificate)
- sociology (MA)
- Spanish: Latin American studies (MA, Certificate)
- statistics (MS, Certificate)
- teaching English to speakers of other languages (MA, Certificate)
- toxicology (MS)
- translation (Certificate)

School of Education, Teaching, and Health

Dr. Sarah Irvine-Belson, Dean

Programs in:
- curriculum and instruction (M Ed, Certificate)
- early childhood education (MAT, Certificate)
- elementary education (MAT)
- English for speakers of other languages (MAT, Certificate)
- health promotion management (MS)
- international training and development (MAT)
- international training and education (MA)
- nutrition education (Certificate)
- secondary teaching (MAT, Certificate)
- special education (MA)
- special education: learning disabilities (MA)

Kogod School of Business

Dr. Richard Durand, Dean

Programs in:
- accounting (MS, Certificate)
- business (MBA, MS, Certificate)
- consulting (MBA)
- corporate finance: commercial banking (MBA)
- corporate finance: corporate financial management (MBA)
- corporate finance: investment banking (MBA)
- entrepreneurship (MBA)
- finance (MS, Certificate)
- global emerging markets (MBA)
- information systems (MS, Certificate)
- international business (Certificate)

international trade and global supply chain management (MBA)
leadership (MBA)
marketing management (MBA)
marketing research (MBA)
real estate (MS)
taxation (MS, Certificate)

School of Communication

Dean Larry Kirkman, Dean
Programs in:
broadcast journalism (MA)
communication (MA, MFA)
film and electronic media (MFA)
film and video (MA)
interactive journalism (MA)
international media (MA)
news media studies (MA)
print journalism (MA)
producing film and video (MA)
producing for film and video (MA)
public communication (MA)

School of International Service

Dr. Louis W. Goodman, Dean
Programs in:
comparative and regional studies (Certificate)
cross-cultural communication (Certificate)
development management (MS)
ethics, peace, and global affairs (MA)
European studies (Certificate)
global environmental policy (MA, Certificate)
international affairs (MA)
international communication (MA, Certificate)
international development (MA, Certificate)
international development management (Certificate)
international economic policy (Certificate)
international economic relations (Certificate)
international media (MA)
international peace and conflict resolution (MA, Certificate)
international relations (PhD)
international service (MIS)
peace building (Certificate)
the Americas (Certificate)
United States foreign policy (Certificate)

School of Public Affairs

Dr. William Leo Grande, Dean
Programs in:
advanced organization development (Certificate)
fundamentals of organization development (Certificate)
justice, law and society (MS, PhD)
key executive leadership (MPA)
leadership for organizational change (Certificate)
non-profit management (Certificate)
organization development (MSOD)
organizational change (Certificate)
political science (MA, PhD)
public administration (MPA, PhD)
public affairs (MA, MPA, MPP, MS, MSOD, PhD, Certificate)
public financial management (Certificate)
public management (Certificate)
public policy (MPP)
public policy analysis (Certificate)
women, policy and political leadership (Certificate)

Washington College of Law

Dr. Claudio Grossman, Dean
Programs in:
human rights and the law (Certificate)
international legal studies (LL M, Certificate)
judicial sciences (SJD)
law (JD, LL M, SJD, Certificate)
law and government (LL M)

■ THE CATHOLIC UNIVERSITY OF AMERICA

Washington, DC 20064
http://www.cua.edu/

Independent-religious, coed, university. CGS member. *Graduate faculty:* 352 full-time (128 women), 342 part-time/adjunct (155 women). *Computer facilities:* Computer purchase and lease plans are available. 450 computers available on campus for general student use. A campuswide network can be accessed from student residence rooms and from off campus. Online class registration, internet 2, video streaming, online voting, pedagogical software are available. *Graduate expenses:* Tuition: full-time $30,520; part-time $1195 per credit hour. Required fees: $50; $25 per semester. One-time fee: $425. *General application contact:* Christine Mica, Dean, University Admissions, 202-319-5305.

The Benjamin T. Rome School of Music

Murry Sidlin, Dean
Programs in:
chamber music (MM)
composition (MM, DMA)
music (Certificate)
musicology (MA, PhD)
orchestral conducting (MM)
orchestral instruments (DMA)
piano pedagogy (MM, DMA)
piano performance (MM)
sacred music (MMSM, DMA)
vocal pedagogy (MM)
vocal performance (MM)

Columbus School of Law

Program in:
law (JD)

Metropolitan College

Dr. Sara Thompson, Dean
Programs in:
human resource management (MA)
management (MS)

National Catholic School of Social Service

Dr. James R. Zabora, Dean
Programs in:
clinical (MSW)
combined (clinical and macro) (MSW)
contract research and theory in clinical social work (PhD)
macro (MSW)
research and theory in macro social work (PhD)

School of Architecture and Planning

Randall Ott, Dean
Programs in:
cultural studies/sacred space (M Arch)
design technologies (M Arch)
digital media (M Arch)
urban design (M Arch)

School of Arts and Sciences

Dr. Lawrence R. Poos, Dean
Programs in:
acting, directing, and playwriting (MFA)
American government (MA, PhD)
ancient Near East (Biblical Hebrew/Aramaic) (PhD)
Ancient Near East (Biblical Hebrew/Aramaic) (MA)
anthropology (MA)
applied experimental psychology (PhD)
Arabic (PhD)
arts and sciences (MA, MFA, MS, PhD, Certificate)
Catholic educational leadership (PhD)
cell and microbial biology (MS, PhD)
chemistry (MS)
Christian Near East (Biblical Hebrew/Aramaic) (MA)
clinical laboratory science (MS, PhD)
clinical psychology (PhD)
comparative literature (MA)
Congressional and presidential studies (MA)
Coptic (MA, PhD)
early Christian studies (MA, PhD)
education (Certificate)
educational psychology (PhD)
English language and literature (MA, PhD)
general psychology (MA)
Greek and Latin (MA, PhD)
human factors (MA)
international affairs (MA)
international political economics (MA)
Irish studies (MA)
Latin (MA)
learning and instruction (MA)
medieval and Byzantine studies (MA, PhD, Certificate)
Medieval Europe (MA, PhD)
modern Europe (PhD)
physics (MS, PhD)
political theory (MA, PhD)
religion and society in the late Medieval and early modern world (MA)
rhetoric (MA, PhD)
secondary education (MA)

The Catholic University of America (continued)

sociology (MA)
Spanish (MA, PhD)
special education (MA)
Syriac (MA)
theatre education (MA)
theatre history and criticism (MA)
United States (MA)
world politics (MA, PhD)

School of Canon Law
Sr. Rose McDermott, Interim Dean
Program in:
canon law (JCD, JCL)

School of Engineering
Dr. Charles C. Nguyen, Dean
Programs in:
active control and smart materials/systems (MME, MSE, PhD)
antennas and electromagnetic propagation (MEE, MSCS, D Engr)
bioimaging (MEE, MSCS, PhD)
bioinformatics and intelligent information systems (MEE, D Engr, PhD)
bioinstrumentation (MBE, MSE, D Engr)
biomechanics (MBE, D Engr, PhD)
biosignal processing and medical imaging (MBE, MSE, PhD)
combustion (MME, MSE, D Engr)
computational fluid dynamics (MME, MSE, D Engr)
controls (MME, MSE, D Engr, PhD)
distributed and real-time systems (MEE, MSCS, D Engr, PhD)
dynamics (MME, MSE, PhD)
electronic packaging (MME, MSE, PhD)
engineering (MBE, MCE, MEE, MME, MSCS, MSE, D Engr, PhD, Certificate)
engineering management (MSE, Certificate)
environmental engineering (MCE, MSE, D Engr, PhD, Certificate)
environmental engineering and management (MCE, MSE, PhD, Certificate)
environmental engineering and management (D Engr)
fluid and solid mechanics (MCE, MSE, PhD, Certificate)
geotechnical engineering (MCE, MSE, PhD, Certificate)
high speed communications and networking (MSCS, D Engr, PhD)
home care technologies (MBE, MSE, D Engr)
human thermal comfort (MME, MSE, D Engr, PhD)
HVAC and refrigeration (MME, MSE, D Engr, PhD)
information security (MEE, MSCS, PhD)
management of construction (MCE, MSE, D Engr, PhD)
MEMS (MSE, D Engr, PhD)
micro-optics (MEE, MSCS, D Engr, PhD)
nano-mechanics (MME, D Engr, PhD)
rehabilitation engineering (MBE, MSE, D Engr)
signal and image processing (MEE, MSCS, D Engr)
structural engineering (MSE, D Engr, PhD)
systems engineering (MSE, D Engr, PhD, Certificate)
telemedicine (MBE, MSE, D Engr)
thermal/fluid sciences (MME, MSE, D Engr, PhD)
vibrations (MSE, D Engr, PhD)

School of Library and Information Science
Dr. Kimberly B. Kelley, Dean
Program in:
library and information science (MSLS)

School of Nursing
Dr. Nalini N. Jairath, Dean
Programs in:
adult health specialist with functional role as nurse educator (MSN)
adult nurse practitioner (MSN)
community/public health nurse specialist educator (MSN)
family nurse practitioner (MSN)
geriatric nurse practitioner (MSN)
immigrant, refugee, and global health clinical nurse specialist (MSN)
nursing (DNP, PhD, Certificate)
pediatric nurse practitioner (MSN)
promoting healthy families in vulnerable communities (MSN)
psychiatric-mental health nursing (MSN)

School of Philosophy
Rev. Kurt J. Pritzl, OP, Dean
Program in:
philosophy (MA, PhD, Ph L)

School of Theology and Religious Studies
Msgr. Kevin W. Irwin, Dean
Programs in:
Biblical studies (STB, MA, PhD, STL)
Catholic educational leadership (MA)
church history (PhD)
Hispanic pastoral leadership (Certificate)
Hispanic/Latino ministry (M Div)
historical theology (STB, STD)
history of religions (Hinduism/Islam) (MA, PhD)
liturgical studies/sacramental theology (MA, PhD, STD, STL)
moral theology/ethics (STB, MA, PhD, STD, STL)
pastoral studies (M Div, Certificate)
religion and culture (PhD)
religious education/catechetics (MA, MRE, PhD)
spirituality (STB, PhD, STD, STL)
systematic and historical theology (MA, PhD, STD, STL)

■ GALLAUDET UNIVERSITY
Washington, DC 20002-3625
http://www.gallaudet.edu/

Independent, coed, university. CGS member. *Computer facilities:* 240 computers available on campus for general student use. A campuswide network can be accessed from student residence rooms and from off campus. Online class registration is available. *General application contact:* Coordinator of Prospective Graduate Student Services, 202-651-5647.

The Graduate School
Programs in:
administration (MS)
administration and supervision (PhD)
change leadership on deaf education (Ed S)
early childhood education (MA, Ed S)
education of deaf and hard of hearing students and multihandicapped deaf and hard of hearing students (MA, Ed S)
elementary education (MA, Ed S)
hearing, speech, and language sciences (MA, MS, Au D)
individualized program of study (PhD)
international development (MA, Certificate)
interpretation (MA)
leadership (Certificate)
leisure services administration (MS)
linguistics (MA, PhD)
management (Certificate)
mental health counseling (MA)
parent/infant specialty (MA, Ed S)
school counseling (MA)
secondary education (MA, Ed S)
special education administration (PhD)

College of Arts and Sciences
Programs in:
arts and sciences (MA, MSW, PhD, Psy S)
clinical psychology (PhD)
developmental psychology (MA)
school psychology (MA, Psy S)
social work (MSW)

■ GEORGETOWN UNIVERSITY
Washington, DC 20057
http://www.georgetown.edu/

Independent-religious, coed, university. CGS member. *Computer facilities:* 400 computers available on campus for general student use. A campuswide network can be accessed from student residence rooms and from off campus. Online class registration, online grade reports are available. *General application contact:* Dean of the Graduate School, 202-687-5974.

Graduate School of Arts and Sciences
Programs in:
- American government (MA, PhD)
- analytical chemistry (PhD)
- Arab studies (MA, Certificate)
- Arabic area studies (PhD)
- arts and sciences (IEMBA, MA, MALS, MAT, MBA, MPM, MPP, MPS, MS, DLS, PhD, Certificate)
- bilingual education (Certificate)
- biochemistry (PhD)
- bioethics (MA)
- biology (MS, PhD)
- British and American literature (MA)
- communication, culture, and technology (MA)
- comparative government (PhD)
- computational chemistry (PhD)
- computer science (MS)
- conflict resolution (MA)
- democracy and governance (MA)
- econometrics (PhD)
- economic development (PhD)
- economic theory (PhD)
- German (MA, MS, PhD)
- global history (MA)
- global, international and comparative history (MA)
- history (MA, PhD)
- industrial organization (PhD)
- inorganic chemistry (PhD)
- international law and government (MA)
- international macro and finance (PhD)
- international relations (PhD)
- international trade (PhD)
- Islamic studies (MA, PhD)
- labor economics (PhD)
- language and communication (MA)
- linguistics (MA, MS, PhD)
- macroeconomics (PhD)
- materials chemistry (PhD)
- mathematics and statistics (MS)
- organic chemistry (PhD)
- philosophy (PhD)
- physical chemistry (PhD)
- political theory (PhD)
- psychology (PhD)
- public economics and political economics (PhD)
- Russian and East European studies (MA)
- Spanish (MS, PhD)
- teaching English as a second language (MAT, Certificate)
- teaching English as a second language and bilingual education (MAT)
- theology (PhD)
- theoretical chemistry (PhD)

BMW Center for German and European Studies
Program in:
- German and European studies (MA)

Center for Latin American Studies
Program in:
- Latin American studies (MA)

Edmund A. Walsh School of Foreign Service
Programs in:
- foreign service (MS)
- security studies (MA)

The Georgetown Public Policy Institute
Program in:
- public policy (MPM, MPP)

McDonough School of Business
Program in:
- business administration (IEMBA, MBA)

Programs in Biomedical Sciences
Programs in:
- biochemistry and molecular biology (MS, PhD)
- biohazardous threat agents and emerging infectious diseases (MS)
- biomedical sciences (MS, PhD)
- biostatistics (MS)
- cell biology (PhD)
- general microbiology and immunology (MS)
- global infectious diseases (PhD)
- health physics (MS)
- microbiology and immunology research (PhD)
- neuroscience (PhD)
- pathology (MS, PhD)
- pharmacology (MS, PhD)
- physiology and biophysics (MS, PhD)
- radiobiology (MS)
- science policy and advocacy (MS)

School of Continuing Studies
Programs in:
- American studies (MALS)
- Catholic studies (MALS)
- classical civilizations (MALS)
- ethics and the professions (MALS)
- human resources management (MPS)
- humanities (MALS)
- individualized study (MALS)
- international affairs (MALS)
- Islam and Muslim-Christian relations (MALS)
- journalism (MPS)
- liberal studies (DLS)
- literature and society (MALS)
- medieval and early modern European studies (MALS)
- public relations (MPS)
- real estate (MPS)
- religious studies (MALS)
- social and public policy (MALS)
- sports industry management (MPS)
- the theory and practice of American democracy (MALS)
- visual culture (MALS)

School of Nursing & Health Studies
Programs in:
- acute care nurse practitioner (MS)
- clinical nurse specialist (MS)
- family nurse practitioner (MS)
- nurse anesthesia (MS)
- nurse-midwifery (MS)
- nursing education (MS)

Law Center
Programs in:
- general (LL M)
- global health law (LL M)
- international and comparative law (LL M)
- international business and economic law (LL M)
- international legal studies (LL M)
- law (JD, SJD)
- securities and financial regulation (LL M)
- taxation (LL M)

National Institutes of Health Sponsored Programs
Program in:
- biomedical sciences (MS, PhD)

School of Medicine
Program in:
- medicine (MD)

■ THE GEORGE WASHINGTON UNIVERSITY
Washington, DC 20052
http://www.gwu.edu/

Independent, coed, university. CGS member. *Graduate faculty:* 1,705 full-time (707 women), 3,213 part-time/adjunct (1,190 women). *Computer facilities:* 550 computers available on campus for general student use. A campuswide network can be accessed from student residence rooms and from off campus. *General application contact:* Kristin Williams, Assistant Vice President for Graduate and Special Enrollment Management, 202-994-0467.

College of Professional Studies
Kathleen M. Burke, Dean
Programs in:
- healthcare corporate compliance (Graduate Certificate)
- law firm management (MPS, Graduate Certificate)
- molecular biotechnology (MPS)
- paralegal studies (MPS, Graduate Certificate)
- publishing (MPS)

Graduate School of Political Management
Dr. Christopher Arterton, Dean
Programs in:
- legislative affairs (MA)
- PAC management (Graduate Certificate)
- political management (MA)

Columbian College of Arts and Sciences
Peg Barratt, Dean
Programs in:
- American studies (PhD)
- analytical chemistry (MS, PhD)
- anthropology (MA)
- applied mathematics (MA, MS, PhD)
- applied social psychology (PhD)
- art history (MA)
- art therapy (MA)

The George Washington University (continued)

arts and sciences (MA, MFA, MFS, MPA, MPP, MS, PhD, Psy D, Certificate, Graduate Certificate)
biological sciences (MS, PhD)
biostatistics (MS, PhD)
ceramics (MFA)
classical acting (MFA)
clinical psychology (PhD)
cognitive neuroscience (PhD)
crime scene investigation (MFS)
criminology (MA)
design (MFA)
drawing/painting (MFA)
economics (MA, PhD)
English (MA, PhD)
epidemiology (MS, PhD)
folklife (MA)
forensic chemistry (MFS)
forensic molecular biology (MFS)
forensic toxicology (MFS)
geography (MA)
high-technology crime investigation (MFS)
Hinduism and Islam (MA)
historic preservation (MA)
history (MA, PhD)
hominid paleobiology (MS, PhD)
human resources management (MA)
industrial/organizational psychology (PhD)
inorganic chemistry (MS, PhD)
interior design (MFA)
international development (MA)
material culture (MA)
materials science (MS, PhD)
museum studies (MA, Certificate)
museum training (MA)
new media (MFA)
organic chemistry (MS, PhD)
organizational management (MA)
photography (MFA)
physical chemistry (MS, PhD)
physics (MA, PhD)
political science (MA, PhD)
professional psychology (Psy D)
pure mathematics (MA, MS, PhD)
sculpture (MFA)
security management (MFS)
sociology (MA)
speech-language pathology (MA)
statistics (MS, PhD)
survey design and data analysis (Graduate Certificate)
women's studies (MA, Certificate)

Institute for Biomedical Sciences
Dr. Linda L. Werling, Director
Programs in:
biochemistry and molecular genetics (PhD)
microbiology and immunology (PhD)
molecular and cellular oncology (PhD)
molecular medicine (PhD)
neurosciences (PhD)
pharmacology and physiology (PhD)

School of Media and Public Affairs
Lee W. Huebner, Director
Program in:
media and public affairs (MA)

Trachtenberg School of Public Policy and Public Administration
Dr. Joseph J. Cordes, Director
Programs in:
budget and public finance (MPA)
environmental and resource policy (MA)
federal policy, politics, and management (MPA)
international development management (MPA)
managing public organizations (MPA)
managing state and local governments (MPA)
nonprofit management (MPA)
philosophy and social policy (MA)
policy analysis and evaluation (MPA)
public administration (MPA)
public policy (MA, MPP)
public policy and administration (PhD)
public-private policy and management (MPA)
women's studies (MA)

Elliott School of International Affairs
Michael Brown, Dean
Programs in:
Asian studies (MA)
European and Eurasian studies (MA)
global communication (MA)
international affairs (MA, MIPP, MIS)
international development studies (MA)
international policy and practice (MIPP)
international science and technology policy (MA)
international studies (MIS)
international trade and investment policy (MA)
Latin American and hemispheric studies (MA)
Middle East studies (MA)
security policy studies (MA)

Graduate School of Education and Human Development
Dr. Mary Hatwood Futrell, Dean
Programs in:
community counseling (MA Ed)
counseling (PhD, Ed S)
counseling: school, community and rehabilitation (MA Ed)
curriculum and instruction (MA Ed, Ed D, Ed S)
early childhood special education (MA Ed)
education and human development (M Ed, MA Ed, MAT, Ed D, PhD, Certificate, Ed S, Graduate Certificate)
education policy (Ed D)
education policy studies (MA Ed)
educational administration (Ed D)
educational administration and policy studies (Ed D)
educational leadership and administration (MA Ed, Certificate, Ed S)
educational technology leadership (MA Ed)
elementary education (M Ed)
higher education administration (MA Ed, Ed D, Ed S)
human and organizational learning (MA Ed, Ed D, Graduate Certificate)
human resource development (MA Ed)
international education (MA Ed)
leadership development (Graduate Certificate)
museum education (MAT)
rehabilitation counseling (MA Ed)
school counseling (MA Ed)
secondary education (M Ed)
special education (Ed D, Ed S)
special education for children with emotional and behavioral disabilities (MA Ed)
transition special education (MA Ed, Certificate)

Law School
Frederick M. Lawrence, Dean
Program in:
law (JD, LL M, SJD)

School of Business
Dr. Susan M. Phillips, Dean
Programs in:
accountancy (M Accy, MBA, PhD)
business (M Accy, MBA, MS, MSF, MSIST, MTA, PMBA, PhD, Professional Certificate)
event and meeting management (MTA)
event management (Professional Certificate)
finance (MSF, PhD)
finance and investments (MBA)
hospitality management (MTA, Professional Certificate)
information and decision systems (PhD)
information systems (MSIST)
information systems development (MSIST)
information systems management (MBA)
information systems project management (MSIST)
international business (MBA, PhD)
management (MBA, PhD)
management information systems (MSIST)
management of science, technology, and innovation (MBA, PhD)
marketing (MBA, PhD)
project management (MS)
real estate and urban development (MBA)
sports business management (Professional Certificate)
sports management (MTA)
strategic management and public policy (MBA, PhD)
sustainable destination management (MTA)
tourism administration (MTA)
tourism and hospitality management (MBA)
tourism destination management (Professional Certificate)

School of Engineering and Applied Science
David S. Dolling, Dean

Programs in:
- civil and environmental engineering (MS, D Sc, App Sc, Engr)
- computer science (MS, D Sc)
- electrical and computer engineering (MS, D Sc)
- engineering and applied science (MS, D Sc, App Sc, Engr, Graduate Certificate)
- engineering management and systems engineering (MS, D Sc, App Sc, Engr, Graduate Certificate)
- mechanical and aerospace engineering (MS, D Sc, App Sc, Engr, Graduate Certificate)
- telecommunication and computers (MS)

School of Medicine and Health Sciences

Dr. Jean Johnson, Senior Associate Dean

Programs in:
- adult nurse practitioner (MSN, Post Master's Certificate)
- biochemistry and molecular biology (MS)
- biochemistry and molecular genetics (PhD)
- clinical practice management (MSHS)
- clinical research administration (MSHS)
- clinical research administration for nurses (MSN)
- emergency services management (MSHS)
- end-of-life care (MSHS, MSN)
- family nurse practitioner (MSN, Post Master's Certificate)
- genomics and bioinformatics (MS)
- immunohematology (MSHS)
- medicine (MD)
- medicine and health sciences (MD, MS, MSHS, MSN, DNP, DPT, PhD, Post Master's Certificate)
- nursing (DNP)
- nursing leadership and management (MSN)
- physical therapy (DPT)
- physician assistant (MSHS)

School of Public Health and Health Services

Dr. Josef J. Reum, Associate Dean

Programs in:
- biostatistics (MPH)
- community-oriented primary care (MPH)
- environmental and occupational health (Dr PH)
- environmental health science and policy (MPH)
- epidemiology (MPH)
- exercise science (MS)
- global health (Dr PH)
- health behavior (Dr PH)
- health management and leadership (MHSA)
- health policy (MPH, MS)
- health promotion (MPH)
- health services administration (Specialist)
- maternal and child health (MPH)
- microbiology and emerging infectious diseases (MSPH)
- public health (MPH)
- public health and health services (MHSA, MPH, MS, MSPH, Dr PH, Specialist)
- public health communication and marketing (MPH)
- public health management (MPH)

■ HOWARD UNIVERSITY

Washington, DC 20059-0002

http://www.howard.edu/

Independent, coed, university. CGS member. *Computer facilities:* 6,343 computers available on campus for general student use. A campuswide network can be accessed from student residence rooms and from off campus. Online class registration, student residential network are available. *General application contact:* Associate Dean for Student Relations, 202-806-4676.

College of Dentistry

Programs in:
- advanced education program general dentistry (Certificate)
- dentistry (DDS)
- general dentistry (Certificate)
- oral and maxillofacial surgery (Certificate)
- orthodontics (Certificate)
- pediatric dentistry (Certificate)

College of Engineering, Architecture, and Computer Sciences

Program in:
- engineering, architecture, and computer sciences (M Eng, MCS, MS, PhD)

School of Engineering and Computer Science

Programs in:
- chemical engineering (MS)
- civil engineering (M Eng)
- electrical engineering (M Eng, PhD)
- engineering and computer science (M Eng, MCS, MS, PhD)
- mechanical engineering (M Eng, PhD)
- systems and computer science (MCS)

College of Medicine

Programs in:
- biochemistry and molecular biology (PhD)
- biotechnology (MS)
- medicine (MD, MPH, MS, PhD)
- microbiology (PhD)
- pharmacology (MS, PhD)
- public health (MPH)

College of Pharmacy, Nursing and Allied Health Sciences

Program in:
- pharmacy, nursing and allied health sciences (Pharm D, MSN, Certificate)

Division of Nursing

Programs in:
- nurse practitioner (Certificate)
- primary family health nursing (MSN)

School of Pharmacy

Program in:
- pharmacy (Pharm D)

Graduate School

Programs in:
- African diaspora (MA, PhD)
- African history (MA, PhD)
- African studies (MA, PhD)
- analytical chemistry (MS, PhD)
- anatomy (MS, PhD)
- applied mathematics (MS, PhD)
- atmospheric (MS, PhD)
- atmospheric sciences (MS, PhD)
- biochemistry (MS, PhD)
- biology (MS, PhD)
- biophysics (PhD)
- clinical psychology (PhD)
- developmental psychology (PhD)
- economics (MA, PhD)
- English (MA, PhD)
- environmental (MS, PhD)
- exercise physiology (MS)
- experimental psychology (PhD)
- French (MA)
- health education (MS)
- inorganic chemistry (MS, PhD)
- Latin America and the Caribbean (MA, PhD)
- mathematics (MS, PhD)
- neuropsychology (PhD)
- nutrition (MS, PhD)
- organic chemistry (MS, PhD)
- personality psychology (PhD)
- philosophy (MA)
- physical chemistry (MS, PhD)
- physics (MS, PhD)
- physiology (PhD)
- political science (MA, MAPA, PhD)
- psychology (MS)
- public administration (MAPA)
- public history (MA)
- social psychology (PhD)
- sociology (MA, PhD)
- Spanish (MA)
- sports studies (MS)
- United States history (MA, PhD)
- urban recreation (MS)

Division of Fine Arts

Programs in:
- 3D reality (sculpture and ceramics) (MFA)
- applied music (MM)
- art history (MA)
- design (MFA)
- electronic studio (MFA)
- fine arts (MFA)
- history of art and visual culture (MA)
- instrument (MM Ed)
- jazz studies (MM)
- organ (MM Ed)
- painting (MFA)
- photography (MFA)
- piano (MM Ed)
- voice (MM Ed)

Howard University (continued)

School of Business
Programs in:
accounting (MBA)
business (MBA)
entrepreneurship (MBA)
finance (MBA)
general management (MBA)
human resources management (MBA)
information systems (MBA)
international business (MBA)
marketing (MBA)
supply chain management (MBA)

School of Communications
Programs in:
communication sciences (PhD)
communications (MA, MFA, MS, PhD)
film (MFA)
intercultural communication (MA, PhD)
organizational communication (MA, PhD)
speech pathology (MS)

Division of Mass Communication and Media Studies
Programs in:
mass communication (MA, PhD)
media studies (MA, PhD)

School of Divinity
Program in:
theology (M Div, MARS, D Min)

School of Education
Dr. Leslie T. Fenwick, Head
Programs in:
counseling and guidance (M Ed, MA, CAGS)
counseling psychology (M Ed, MA, PhD, CAGS)
early childhood education (M Ed, MA, MAT, CAGS)
education (M Ed, MA, MAT, MS, Ed D, PhD, CAGS)
educational administration (M Ed, MA, CAGS)
educational administration and policy (M Ed, MA, Ed D, CAGS)
educational psychology (M Ed, MA, Ed D, PhD, CAGS)
elementary education (M Ed)
human development (MS)
reading (M Ed, MA, MAT, CAGS)
school psychology (M Ed, MA, Ed D, PhD, CAGS)
secondary education (M Ed, MA, MAT, CAGS)
special education (M Ed, MA, CAGS)

School of Law
Program in:
law (JD, LL M)

School of Social Work
Program in:
social work (MSW, PhD)

■ STRAYER UNIVERSITY
Washington, DC 20005-2603
http://www.strayer.edu/

Proprietary, coed, comprehensive institution. *Computer facilities:* 1,500 computers available on campus for general student use. A campuswide network can be accessed. Online class registration is available. *General application contact:* Campus Manager, 202-408-2400.

Graduate Studies
Programs in:
accounting (MS)
acquisition (MBA)
business administration (MBA)
communications technology (MS)
educational management (M Ed)
finance (MBA)
health services administration (MHSA)
hospitality and tourism management (MBA)
human resource management (MBA)
information systems (MS)
management (MBA)
management information systems (MS)
marketing (MBA)
professional accounting (MS)
public administration (MPA)
supply chain management (MBA)
technology in education (M Ed)

■ TRINITY (WASHINGTON) UNIVERSITY
Washington, DC 20017-1094
http://www.trinitydc.edu/

Independent-religious, Undergraduate: women only; graduate: coed, comprehensive institution. *Computer facilities:* A campuswide network can be accessed from student residence rooms and from off campus. Online class registration is available. *General application contact:* Director of Admissions for School of Education and School of Professional Studies, 202-884-9400.

School of Education
Programs in:
counseling (MA)
early childhood education (MAT)
educating for change (M Ed)
educational administration (MSA)
elementary education (MAT)
school counseling (MA)
secondary education (MAT)
special education (MAT)
teaching English as a second language (MAT)
teaching English to speakers of other languages (M Ed)
the teaching of reading (M Ed)

School of Professional Studies
Programs in:
business administration (MBA)
communication (MA)
international security studies (MA)
organizational management (MSA)

■ UNIVERSITY OF THE DISTRICT OF COLUMBIA
Washington, DC 20008-1175
http://www.udc.edu/

District-supported, coed, comprehensive institution. CGS member. *Computer facilities:* 1,500 computers available on campus for general student use. A campuswide network can be accessed. Online class registration is available. *General application contact:* Processor, Graduate Applications, 202-274-5008.

College of Arts and Sciences
Programs in:
arts and sciences (MA, MS, MST)
clinical psychology (MS)
counseling (MS)
early childhood education (MA)
English composition and rhetoric (MA)
mathematics (MST)
special education (MA)
speech and language pathology (MS)

David A. Clarke School of Law
Program in:
law (JD)

School of Business and Public Administration
Programs in:
business administration (MBA)
business and public administration (MBA, MPA)
public administration (MPA)

Florida

■ AMERICAN INTERCONTINENTAL UNIVERSITY SOUTH FLORIDA
Weston, FL 33326
http://www.aiuniv.edu/

Proprietary, coed, comprehensive institution. *Computer facilities:* 40 computers available on campus for general student use. A campuswide network can be accessed. Online class registration is available. *General application contact:* Vice President, Academic Affairs, 954-446-6119.

Program in Information Technology
Programs in:
Internet security (MIT)
wireless computer forensics (MIT)

Program in Instructional Technology
Program in:
instructional technology (M Ed)

Program in International Business
Programs in:
accounting and finance (MBA)
human resource management (MBA)
management (MBA)
marketing (MBA)

■ ARGOSY UNIVERSITY, SARASOTA
Sarasota, FL 34235
http://www.argosy.edu/sarasota/

Proprietary, coed, university. CGS member.

College of Business
Programs in:
accounting (DBA, Adv C)
customized professional concentration (MBA, DBA)
finance (MBA, Certificate)
healthcare administration (MBA)
information systems (DBA, Adv C, Certificate)
information systems management (MBA)
international business (MBA, DBA, Adv C, Certificate)
management (MBA, MSM, DBA, Adv C)
marketing (MBA, DBA, Adv C, Certificate)

College of Education
Programs in:
community college executive leadership (Ed D)
educational leadership (MA Ed, Ed D, Ed S)
instructional leadership (MA Ed, Ed D, Ed S)

College of Health Sciences
Program in:
healthcare administration (Certificate)

College of Psychology and Behavioral Sciences
Programs in:
community counseling (MA)
counseling psychology (Ed D)
counselor education and supervision (Ed D)
forensic psychology (MA)
marriage and family therapy (MA)
mental health counseling (MA)
organizational leadership (Ed D)
pastoral community counseling (Ed D)
school counseling (MA, Ed S)
school psychology (MA)

■ ARGOSY UNIVERSITY, TAMPA
Tampa, FL 33614
http://www.argosy.edu/tampa/

Proprietary, coed, university. CGS member.

College of Business
Programs in:
accounting (DBA)
customized professional concentration (MBA, DBA)
finance (MBA)
healthcare administration (MBA)
information systems (DBA)
information systems management (MBA)
international business (MBA, DBA)
management (MBA, MSM, DBA)
marketing (MBA, DBA)
public administration (MBA)

College of Education
Programs in:
community college executive leadership (Ed D)
educational leadership (MA Ed, Ed D, Ed S)
instructional leadership (MA Ed, Ed D, Ed S)

College of Health Sciences
Program in:
healthcare administration (Certificate)

College of Psychology and Behavioral Sciences
Programs in:
clinical psychology (MA, Psy D)
counselor education and supervision (Ed D)
marriage and family therapy (MA)
mental health counseling (MA)
organizational leadership (Ed D)
school counseling (MA)

■ BARRY UNIVERSITY
Miami Shores, FL 33161-6695
http://www.barry.edu/

Independent-religious, coed, university. *Computer facilities:* 368 computers available on campus for general student use. A campuswide network can be accessed from student residence rooms and from off campus. Online class registration, Blackboard are available. *General application contact:* Director of Graduate Admissions, 305-899-3113.

Andreas School of Business
Programs in:
accounting (MSA)
business (MBA, MSA, MSM, Certificate)
business administration (MBA)
finance (Certificate)
health services administration (Certificate)
international business (Certificate)
management (MSM)
management information systems (Certificate)
marketing (Certificate)

College of Health Sciences
Programs in:
anesthesiology (MS)
biology (MS)
biomedical sciences (MS)
health care leadership (Certificate)
health care planning and informatics (Certificate)
health sciences (MS, Certificate)
health services administration (MS)
histotechnology (Certificate)
long term care management (Certificate)
medical group practice management (Certificate)
occupational therapy (MS)
quality improvement and outcomes management (Certificate)

School of Adult and Continuing Education
Programs in:
administrative studies (MA)
adult and continuing education (MA, MPA, MS)
information technology (MS)
public administration (MPA)

School of Arts and Sciences
Programs in:
arts and sciences (MA, MFA, MS, D Min, Certificate, SSP)
broadcasting (Certificate)
clinical psychology (MS)
communication (MA)
liberal studies (MA)
ministry (D Min)
organizational communication (MS)
pastoral ministry for Hispanics (MA)
pastoral theology (MA)
photography (MA, MFA)
practical theology (MA)
school psychology (MS, SSP)

School of Education
Programs in:
accomplished teacher (Ed S)
advanced teaching and learning with technology (Certificate)
counseling (MS, PhD, Ed S)
culture, language and literacy (TESOL) (PhD)
curriculum evaluation and research (PhD)
distance education (Certificate)
early childhood (Ed S)
early childhood education (PhD)
education (MS, Ed D, PhD, Certificate, Ed S)
education for teachers of students with hearing impairments (MS)
educational computing and technology (MS, Ed S)
educational leadership (MS, Ed D, Certificate, Ed S)

Barry University (continued)
educational technology (PhD)
elementary (Ed S)
elementary education (MS, PhD)
elementary education/ESOL (MS)
ESOL (Ed S)
exceptional student education (MS, Ed S)
gifted (Ed S)
higher education administration (MS)
higher education technology integration (Certificate)
human resource development (PhD)
human resource development and administration (MS)
human resources: not for profit and religious organizations (Certificate)
K-12 technology integration (Certificate)
leadership (PhD)
marital, couple and family counseling/therapy (MS, Ed S)
mental health counseling (MS, Ed S)
Montessori (Ed S)
Montessori education (MS, Ed S)
PKP/elementary (Ed S)
pre-k/primary (MS)
pre-k/primary/ESOL (MS)
reading (Ed S)
reading, language and cognition (PhD)
rehabilitation counseling (MS, Ed S)
school counseling (MS, Ed S)
technology and TESOL (MS, Ed S)
TESOL (MS)
TESOL international (MS)

School of Graduate Medical Sciences
Programs in:
anatomy (MS)
medical sciences (DPM, MCMS, MPH, MS)
physician assistant (MCMS)
podiatric medicine and surgery (DPM)
public health (MPH)

School of Human Performance and Leisure Sciences
Programs in:
athletic training (MS)
biomechanics (MS)
exercise science (MS)
general movement science (MS)
human performance and leisure sciences (MS)
sport and exercise psychology (MS)
sport management (MS)

School of Law
Program in:
law (JD)

School of Nursing
Programs in:
acute care nurse practitioner (MSN)
family nurse practitioner (MSN)
nurse practitioner (Certificate)
nursing (MSN, PhD, Certificate)
nursing administration (MSN, PhD, Certificate)
nursing education (MSN, Certificate)

School of Social Work
Program in:
social work (MSW, PhD)

■ DEVRY UNIVERSITY
Miramar, FL 33027-4150
http://www.devry.edu/

Proprietary, coed, comprehensive institution. *Computer facilities:* Computer purchase and lease plans are available. 124 computers available on campus for general student use.

Keller Graduate School of Management
Program in:
management (MAFM, MBA, MHRM, MISM, MNCM, MPA, MPM, Graduate Certificate)

■ DEVRY UNIVERSITY
Orlando, FL 32839
http://www.devry.edu/

Proprietary, coed, comprehensive institution. *Computer facilities:* Computer purchase and lease plans are available. 310 computers available on campus for general student use. A campuswide network can be accessed from off campus. Online class registration is available.

Keller Graduate School of Management
Program in:
management (MAFM, MBA, MHRM, MISM, MNCM, MPA, MPM, Graduate Certificate)

■ EMBRY-RIDDLE AERONAUTICAL UNIVERSITY
Daytona Beach, FL 32114-3900
http://www.embryriddle.edu/

Independent, coed, comprehensive institution. *Graduate faculty:* 51 full-time (6 women), 10 part-time/adjunct (3 women). *Computer facilities:* 1,013 computers available on campus for general student use. A campuswide network can be accessed from student residence rooms and from off campus. Online class registration is available. *Graduate expenses:* Tuition: full-time $13,200; part-time $1100 per credit hour. *General application contact:* Keath Deaton, Associate Director, International and Graduate Admissions, 800-388-3728.

Daytona Beach Campus Graduate Program
Dr. Richard H. Heist, Executive Vice President and Chief Academic Officer
Programs in:
aeronautics (MBAA, MSA, MSAE, MSE, MSEP, MSHFS, MSME)
aerospace engineering (MSAE)
applied aviation sciences (MSA)
business administration in aviation (MBAA)
engineering physics (space science) (MSEP)
human factors engineering (MSHFS)
mechanical engineering (MSME)
software engineering (MSE)
systems engineering (MSHFS)

■ EMBRY-RIDDLE AERONAUTICAL UNIVERSITY WORLDWIDE
Daytona Beach, FL 32114-3900
http://www.embryriddle.edu/

Independent, coed, comprehensive institution. *Graduate faculty:* 68 full-time (9 women), 316 part-time/adjunct (52 women). *Graduate expenses:* Tuition: full-time $8304; part-time $346 per credit hour. *General application contact:* Bill Hampton, Executive Director of Enrollment Management, 386-226-6910.

Worldwide Headquarters
Dr. Martin A. Smith, Executive Vice President
Programs in:
aeronautics (MAS)
management (MSM, MSM/MBAA)
project management (MSPM)
space education (MSSE)
technical management (MSTM)

■ EVEREST UNIVERSITY
Clearwater, FL 33759
http://www.everest.edu/

Proprietary, coed, comprehensive institution. *Computer facilities:* A campuswide network can be accessed. *General application contact:* Information Contact, 727-725-2688.

Graduate School of Business
Program in:
business (MBA)

■ FLORIDA AGRICULTURAL AND MECHANICAL UNIVERSITY
Tallahassee, FL 32307-3200
http://www.famu.edu/

State-supported, coed, university. CGS member. *Computer facilities:* A campuswide network can be accessed from student residence rooms and from off campus. *General application contact:* Dean of Graduate Studies, Research, and Continuing Education, 850-599-3315.

College of Law
Program in:
law (JD)

Division of Graduate Studies, Research, and Continuing Education

College of Arts and Sciences
Programs in:
African American history (MASS)
arts and sciences (MASS, MS, MSW, PhD)
biology (MS)
chemistry (MS)
community psychology (MS)
criminal justice (MASS)
economics (MASS)
history (MASS)
history and political sciences (MASS, MSW)
physics (MS, PhD)
political science (MASS)
public administration (MASS)
public management (MASS)
school psychology (MS)
social work (MSW)
sociology (MASS)
software engineering (MS)

College of Education
Programs in:
administration and supervision (M Ed, MS Ed, PhD)
adult education (M Ed, MS Ed)
biology (M Ed)
business education (MBE)
chemistry (MS Ed)
early childhood and elementary education (M Ed, MS Ed)
education (M Ed, MBE, MS Ed, PhD)
educational leadership (PhD)
English (MS Ed)
guidance and counseling (M Ed, MS Ed)
health, physical education, and recreation (M Ed, MS Ed)
history (MS Ed)
industrial education (M Ed, MS Ed)
math (MS Ed)
physics (MS Ed)

College of Engineering Science, Technology, and Agriculture
Programs in:
agribusiness (MS)
animal science (MS)
engineering science, technology, and agriculture (MS)
engineering technology (MS)
entomology (MS)
food science (MS)
international programs (MS)
plant science (MS)

College of Pharmacy and Pharmaceutical Sciences
Programs in:
environmental toxicology (PhD)
medicinal chemistry (MS, PhD)
pharmaceutics (MS, PhD)
pharmacology/toxicology (MS, PhD)
pharmacy administration (MS)
pharmacy and pharmaceutical sciences (Pharm D, MPH, MS, Ex Doc, PhD)
public health (MPH)

FAMU-FSU College of Engineering
Programs in:
biomedical engineering (MS, PhD)
chemical engineering (MS, PhD)
civil engineering (MS, PhD)
electrical engineering (MS, PhD)
engineering (MS, PhD)
environmental engineering (MS, PhD)
industrial engineering (MS, PhD)
mechanical engineering (MS, PhD)

School of Allied Health Sciences
Programs in:
health administration (MS)
physical therapy (MPT)

School of Architecture
Programs in:
architectural studies (MS Arch)
architecture (professional) (M Arch)
landscape architecture (MLA)

School of Business and Industry
Programs in:
accounting (MBA)
finance (MBA)
management information systems (MBA)
marketing (MBA)

School of Journalism and Graphic Communication
Program in:
journalism (MS)

School of Nursing
Program in:
nursing (MS)

Environmental Sciences Institute

Dr. Henry Neal Williams, Director
Program in:
environmental sciences (MS, PhD)

■ FLORIDA ATLANTIC UNIVERSITY

Boca Raton, FL 33431-0991

http://www.fau.edu/

State-supported, coed, university. CGS member. *Graduate faculty:* 1,063 full-time (478 women), 510 part-time/adjunct (265 women). *Computer facilities:* 1,000 computers available on campus for general student use. A campuswide network can be accessed from student residence rooms and from off campus. Online class registration is available. *Graduate expenses:* Tuition, state resident: full-time $4867; part-time $270.40 per credit hour. Tuition, nonresident: full-time $16,486; part-time $915.87 per credit hour. *General application contact:* Joanna Arlington, Manager, Graduate Admissions, 561-297-2428.

Barry Kaye College of Business

Dr. Dennis Coates, Dean
Programs in:
business (Exec MBA, M Ac, M Tax, MBA, MHA, MS, PhD, Certificate)
economics (MS)
finance (MS, PhD)
global entrepreneurship (MBA)
international business (MBA, MS)
management (PhD)
management information systems (MS)
music business administration (MS)

School of Accounting
Dr. Somnath Bhattacharya, Director
Programs in:
accounting (M Ac, M Tax, PhD)
taxation (M Tax)

Charles E. Schmidt College of Science

Dr. Gary W. Perry, Dean
Programs in:
applied mathematics and statistics (MS)
biological sciences (MS, MST)
chemistry (MS, MST, PhD)
environmental sciences (MS)
geography (MA)
geology (MS)
mathematical sciences (MS, MST, PhD)
physics (MS, PhD)
psychology (MA, PhD)
science (MA, MS, MST, PhD)

Center for Complex Systems and Brain Sciences
Dr. Janet Blanks, Director
Program in:
complex systems and brain sciences (PhD)

Christine E. Lynn College of Nursing

Dr. Anne J. Boykin, Dean
Program in:
nursing (MS, DNP, PhD, Post Master's Certificate)

College of Architecture, Urban and Public Affairs

Dr. Rosalyn Carter, Dean
Program in:
architecture, urban and public affairs (MNM, MPA, MS, MSW, MURP, PhD, Certificate)

School of Criminology and Criminal Justice
Dr. Gordon Bazemore, Chair
Program in:
criminology and criminal justice (MS)

School of Public Administration
Dr. Hugh T. Miller, Director
Programs in:
nonprofit management (MNM)
public administration (MNM, MPA, PhD)

School of Social Work
Dr. Michele Hawkins, Director
Program in:
social work (MSW)

School of Urban and Regional Planning
Dr. Jaap Vos, Chair

Florida Atlantic University (continued)
Programs in:
economic development and tourism (Certificate)
environmental planning (Certificate)
sustainable community planning (Certificate)
urban and regional planning (MURP)
visual planning technology (Certificate)

College of Biomedical Science
Dr. Michael L. Friedland, Dean
Programs in:
biomedical science (MS)
integrative biology (PhD)

College of Education
Dr. Valerie J. Bristor, Dean
Programs in:
adult and community education (M Ed, PhD, Ed S)
counselor education (M Ed, PhD, Ed S)
curriculum and instruction (M Ed, Ed D, Ed S)
early childhood education (M Ed)
education (M Ed, MS, Ed D, PhD, Ed S)
educational leadership (M Ed, PhD, Ed S)
elementary education (M Ed)
environmental education (M Ed)
exceptional student education (M Ed, Ed D)
exercise science and health promotion (MS)
higher education (M Ed, PhD)
K-12 school leadership (M Ed, PhD, Ed S)
marriage and family therapy (Ed S)
mental health counseling (M Ed, Ed S)
multicultural education (M Ed)
reading education (M Ed)
rehabilitation counseling (M Ed)
school counseling (M Ed, Ed S)
social foundations of education (M Ed)
speech-language pathology (MS)
teaching English to speakers of other languages (TESOL) (M Ed)

College of Engineering and Computer Science
Dr. Karl K. Stevens, Dean
Programs in:
civil engineering (MS)
computer engineering (MS, PhD)
computer science (MS, PhD)
electrical engineering (MS, PhD)
engineering and computer science (MS, PhD)
mechanical engineering (MS, PhD)
ocean engineering (MS, PhD)

Dorothy F. Schmidt College of Arts and Letters
Dr. Manjunath Pendakur, Dean
Programs in:
acting (MFA)
anthropology (MA)
art education (MAT)
arts and letters (MA, MAT, MFA, PhD, Certificate)
British and American literature (MA)
ceramics (MFA)
commercial music (MA)
comparative literature (MA)
comparative studies (PhD)
computer art (MFA)
creative nonfiction (MFA)
creative writing (MA)
design and technology (MFA)
environmental studies (Certificate)
fiction (MFA)
French (MA)
graphic design (MFA)
history (MA)
liberal studies (MA)
linguistics (MA)
multicultural literatures and literacies (MA)
music history/literature (MA)
painting (MFA)
performance (MA)
poetry (MFA)
political science (MA, MAT)
science fiction and fantasy (MA)
sociology (MA)
Spanish (MA)
teaching English (MAT)

School of Communication and Multimedia Studies
Dr. Susan S. Reilly, Director
Programs in:
communication studies (MA)
film and video (Certificate)
film studies (MA)
multimedia journalism studies (MA)

Women's Studies Center
Dr. Josephine Beoku-Betts, Director
Program in:
women's studies (MA, Certificate)

■ FLORIDA GULF COAST UNIVERSITY
Fort Myers, FL 33965-6565
http://www.fgcu.edu/

State-supported, coed, comprehensive institution. CGS member. *Graduate faculty:* 324 full-time (154 women), 249 part-time/adjunct (113 women). *Computer facilities:* Computer purchase and lease plans are available. 323 computers available on campus for general student use. A campuswide network can be accessed from student residence rooms and from off campus. Online class registration, online admissions and advising are available. *General application contact:* Michael Savarese, Director of Graduate Studies, 239-590-7988.

College of Arts and Sciences
Dr. Donna Price Henry, Dean
Programs in:
arts and sciences (MA, MS)
English (MA)
environmental science (MS)
history (MA)

College of Education
Dr. Marci Greene, Dean
Programs in:
behavior disorders (MA)
counseling (MA)
early childhood education (M Ed)
education (M Ed, MA)
educational leadership (M Ed, MA)
educational technology (M Ed, MA)
elementary curriculum (M Ed)
elementary education (MA)
English education (M Ed)
mental retardation (MA)
reading education (M Ed)
specific learning disabilities (MA)
varying exceptionalities (MA)

College of Health Professions
Dr. Denise Heinemann, Dean
Programs in:
health professions (MS, MSN, DPT)
health sciences (MS)
occupational therapy (MS)
physical therapy (MS, DPT)

School of Nursing
Dr. Marianne Rodgers, Director
Program in:
nursing (MSN)

College of Professional Studies
Dr. Kenneth Millar, Dean
Programs in:
criminal forensic studies (MS)
criminal justice (MPA)
criminal justice studies (MS)
environmental policy (MPA)
general public administration (MPA)
management (MPA)
professional studies (MPA, MS, MSW)
social work (MSW)

Lutgert College of Business
Dr. Richard Pegnetter, Dean
Programs in:
accounting and taxation (MS)
business (MBA, MS)
business administration (MBA)
computer and information systems (MS)

■ FLORIDA INSTITUTE OF TECHNOLOGY
Melbourne, FL 32901-6975
http://www.fit.edu/

Independent, coed, university. *Graduate faculty:* 161 full-time (26 women), 150 part-time/adjunct (27 women). *Computer facilities:* 400 computers available on campus for general student use. A campuswide network can be accessed from student residence rooms and from off campus. Online class registration is available. *Graduate expenses:* Tuition: part-time $980 per credit hour. *General application contact:* Thomas M. Shea, Director of Graduate Admissions, 321-674-7577.

Graduate Programs

College of Aeronautics
Dr. Winston E. Scott, Dean

Programs in:
airport development and management (MSA)
applied aviation safety (MSA)
aviation human factors (MS)

College of Business
Dr. Robert E. Niebuhr, Dean
Programs in:
accounting and finance (MBA)
business (EMBA, MBA)
healthcare management (MBA)
management (MBA)
marketing (MBA)

College of Engineering
Dr. Thomas Waite, Dean
Programs in:
aerospace engineering (MS, PhD)
biological oceanography (MS)
chemical engineering (MS, PhD)
chemical oceanography (MS)
civil engineering (MS, PhD)
coastal zone management (MS)
computer engineering (MS, PhD)
computer science (MS, PhD)
earth remote sensing (MS)
electrical engineering (MS, PhD)
engineering (MS, PhD)
engineering management (MS)
environmental resource management (MS)
environmental science (MS, PhD)
geological oceanography (MS)
mechanical engineering (MS, PhD)
meteorology (MS)
ocean engineering (MS, PhD)
oceanography (MS, PhD)
physical oceanography (MS)
software engineering (MS)
systems engineering (MS)

College of Psychology and Liberal Arts
Dr. Mary Beth Kenkel, Dean
Programs in:
applied behavior analysis (MS)
clinical psychology (Psy D)
communication (MS)
humanities and communication (MS)
industrial/organizational psychology (MS, PhD)
psychology (MS, PhD, Psy D)

College of Science
Dr. Gordon L. Nelson, Dean
Programs in:
applied mathematics (MS, PhD)
biological sciences (PhD)
biotechnology (MS)
cell and molecular biology (MS, PhD)
chemistry (MS, PhD)
computer education (MS)
ecology (MS)
elementary science education (M Ed)
environmental education (MS)
informal science education (M Ed)
marine biology (MS)
mathematics education (MS, Ed D, PhD, Ed S)
operations research (MS, PhD)
physics (MS, PhD)
science (M Ed, MAT, MS, Ed D, PhD, Ed S)
science education (MS, Ed D, PhD, Ed S)
space sciences (MS, PhD)
teaching (MAT)

University College
Dr. Clifford Bragdon, Dean
Programs in:
acquisition and contract management (MS, PMBA)
aerospace engineering (MS)
business administration (PMBA)
computer information systems (MS)
computer science (MS)
e-business (PMBA)
electrical engineering (MS)
engineering management (MS)
human resource management (PMBA)
human resources management (MS)
information systems (PMBA)
information technology (MS)
logistics management (MS)
management (MS)
materiel acquisition management (MS)
mechanical engineering (MS)
operations research (MS)
project management (MS)
public administration (MPA)
quality management (MS)
software engineering (MS)
space systems (MS)
space systems management (MS)
systems management (MS)

■ FLORIDA INTERNATIONAL UNIVERSITY

Miami, FL 33199
http://www.fiu.edu/

State-supported, coed, university. CGS member. *Graduate faculty:* 843 full-time (315 women), 16 part-time/adjunct (4 women). *Computer facilities:* A campuswide network can be accessed from student residence rooms and from off campus. Online class registration, online financial aid and cashier's information are available. *Graduate expenses:* Tuition, state resident: full-time $7167; part-time $298.64 per credit hour. Tuition, nonresident: full-time $19,265; part-time $802.71 per credit hour. Required fees: $319 per semester. *General application contact:* Nanett Rojas, Assistant Director of Graduate Admissions, 305-348-7442.

Alvah H. Chapman, Jr. Graduate School of Business

Anna M. Pietraszek, Associate Director, Chapman Graduate School Admissions
Programs in:
business (EMBA, IMBA, M Acc, MBA, MIB, MIS, MSF, MSHRM, MSRE, MST, PhD)
business administration (EMBA, IMBA, MBA, PhD)
decision sciences and information systems (MIS)
finance (MSF)
human resources management (MSHRM)
international business (MIB)
real estate (MSRE)

School of Accounting
Dr. Sharon Lassar, Director
Programs in:
accounting (M Acc)
taxation (MST)

College of Architecture and the Arts

Dr. Brian Schriner, Acting Dean
Program in:
architecture and the arts (M Arch, MFA, MID, MLA, MM, MS)

School of Architecture
Prof. Brian Schriner, Interim Dean
Programs in:
architecture (M Arch, MID, MLA)
interior design (MID)
landscape architecture (MLA)

School of Art and Art History
Prof. Brian Schriner, Interim Dean
Program in:
visual arts (MFA)

School of Music
Kathleen Wilson, Director
Programs in:
music (MM)
music education (MS)

College of Arts and Sciences

Dr. Kenneth Furton, Dean
Programs in:
African-new world studies (MA)
arts and sciences (MA, MFA, MPA, MS, PhD)
Asian studies (MA)
biology (MS, PhD)
chemistry (MS, PhD)
comparative sociology (MA, PhD)
creative writing (MFA)
criminal justice (MS)
earth sciences (MS, PhD)
economics (MA, PhD)
English (MA, MFA)
environmental studies (MS)
forensic science (MS)
history (MA, PhD)
international relations (MA, PhD)
Latin American and Caribbean studies (MA)
liberal studies (MA)
linguistics (MA)
mathematical sciences (MS)
physics (MS, PhD)
political science (MS, PhD)
psychology (MS, PhD)
public administration (MPA, PhD)
religious studies (MA)
Spanish (MA, PhD)
statistics (MS)

Florida International University (continued)

College of Education

Programs in:
- adult education (MS)
- adult education in human resource development (Ed D)
- advanced athletic injury training/sports medicine (MS)
- advanced teacher preparation (MS)
- art education (MAT, MS, Ed D)
- conflict resolution and consensus building (Certificate)
- counselor education (MS)
- curriculum and instruction (Ed S)
- curriculum development (MS)
- curriculum studies (PhD)
- early childhood education (MS, Ed D)
- education (MA, MAT, MS, Ed D, PhD, Certificate, Ed S)
- educational administration and supervision (Ed D)
- educational leadership (MS, Certificate, Ed S)
- elementary education (MS, Ed D)
- English education (MAT, MS, Ed D)
- exceptional student education (MS, Ed D)
- exercise and sports science (MS)
- foreign language education (Certificate)
- foreign language education—teaching English to speakers of other languages (TESOL) (Certificate)
- foreign language education- teaching English to speakers of other languages (TESOL) (MS)
- French education—initial teacher preparation (MAT)
- higher education (Ed D)
- higher education administration (MS)
- human resource development (MS)
- international and intercultural development education (Ed D)
- international and intercultural developmental education (MS)
- language, literacy and culture (PhD)
- learning technologies (MS, Ed D, PhD)
- leisure services (MS)
- mathematics education (MAT, MS, Ed D, PhD)
- mental health counseling (MS)
- modern language education/bilingual education (MS, Ed D)
- parks and recreation management (MS)
- physical education (MS)
- reading education (MS, Ed D)
- rehabilitation counseling (MS)
- school counseling (MS)
- school psychology (Ed S)
- science education (MAT, MS, Ed D, PhD)
- social studies education (MAT, MS, Ed D)
- Spanish education—initial teacher preparation (MAT)
- special education (MS)
- sports management (MS)
- strength and conditioning (MS)
- teaching English (MS)
- therapeutic recreation (MS)
- urban education (MS)

College of Engineering and Computing

Dr. Amir Mirmiran, Dean

Programs in:
- biomedical engineering (MS, PhD)
- civil engineering (MS, PhD)
- computer engineering (MS)
- construction management (MS)
- electrical engineering (MS, PhD)
- engineering and computing (MS, PhD)
- environmental engineering (MS)
- materials science and engineering (MS, PhD)
- mechanical engineering (MS, PhD)
- telecommunications and networking (MS)

School of Computing and Information Sciences

Dr. Yi Deng, Director

Program in:
- computing and information sciences (MS, PhD)

College of Law

Dr. Leonard Strickman, Dean

Program in:
- law (JD)

College of Nursing and Health Sciences

Dr. Divina Grossman, Dean

Programs in:
- nursing (MSN, PhD)
- nursing and health sciences (MS, MSN, DPT, PhD)
- occupational therapy (MS)
- physical therapy (DPT)
- speech-language pathology (MS)

School of Hospitality and Tourism Management

Dr. Joseph West, Dean

Programs in:
- hospitality and tourism management (MS)
- hospitality management (MS)

School of Journalism and Mass Communication

Dr. Lillian Kopenhaver, Dean

Program in:
- mass communication (MS)

Stempel College of Public Health and Social Work

Dr. Fernando Trevino, Interim Dean

Programs in:
- biostatistics (MPH)
- community nutrition (MPH, PhD)
- dietetics and nutrition (MS, PhD)
- environmental and occupational health (MPH, PhD)
- epidemiology (MPH, PhD)
- general public health (MPH)
- health policy and management (MPH)
- health promotion and disease prevention (PhD)
- health promotion and diseases prevention (MPH)
- public health and social work (MHSA, MPH, MS, MSW, PhD)

School of Social Work

Dr. Paul Stuart, Director

Program in:
- social work (MSW, PhD)

■ FLORIDA STATE UNIVERSITY

Tallahassee, FL 32306

http://www.fsu.edu/

State-supported, coed, university. CGS member. *Graduate faculty:* 1,179 full-time (415 women), 176 part-time/adjunct (86 women). *Computer facilities:* 3,821 computers available on campus for general student use. A campuswide network can be accessed from student residence rooms and from off campus. Online class registration, course home pages, course search, online fee payment are available. *Graduate expenses:* Tuition, state resident: full-time $5537.52. Tuition, nonresident: full-time $14,432. One-time fee: $20 full-time. *General application contact:* Melanie Booker, Associate Director for Graduate Admissions, 850-644-3420.

College of Law

Donald J. Weidner, Dean

Program in:
- law (JD, LL M)

College of Medicine

Dr. J. Ocie Harris, Dean

Programs in:
- biomedical sciences (PhD)
- medicine (MD)

The Graduate School

Dr. Nancy Marcus, Dean, The Graduate School

Programs in:
- computational materials science and mechanics (MS)
- functional materials (MS)
- nanoscale materials, composite materials, and interfaces (MS)
- polymers and bio-inspired materials (MS)

College of Arts and Sciences

Dr. Joseph Travis, Dean

Programs in:
- American and Florida studies (MA, Certificate)
- analytical chemistry (MS, PhD)
- anthropology (MA, MS, PhD)
- applied behavior analysis (MS)
- applied computational mathematics (MS, PhD)
- applied statistics (MS)
- arts and sciences (MA, MFA, MS, PhD, Certificate)
- biochemistry (MS, PhD)
- biochemistry, molecular and cell biology (PhD)
- biomedical mathematics (MS, PhD)
- biostatistics (MS, PhD)

cell and molecular biology and genetics (MS, PhD)
classical archaeology (MA)
classical civilization (MA)
classics (MA, PhD)
clinical psychology (PhD)
cognitive psychology (PhD)
computational structural biology (PhD)
computer science (MS, PhD)
creative writing (MFA)
developmental psychology (PhD)
ecology and evolutionary biology (MS, PhD)
English (PhD)
financial mathematics (MS, PhD)
French (MA, PhD)
geological sciences (MS, PhD)
geophysical fluid dynamics (PhD)
German (MA)
Greek (MA)
Greek and Latin (MA)
historical administration (MA)
history (MA, PhD)
history and philosophy of science (MA)
humanities (PhD)
information security (MS)
inorganic chemistry (MS, PhD)
interdisciplinary humanities (PhD)
Italian (MA)
Italian studies (MA)
Latin (MA)
literature (MA)
mathematical statistics (MS, PhD)
meteorology (MS, PhD)
molecular biophysics (PhD)
neuroscience (PhD)
oceanography (MS, PhD)
organic chemistry (MS, PhD)
philosophy (MA, PhD)
physical chemistry (MS, PhD)
physics (MS, PhD)
pure mathematics (MS, PhD)
religion (MA, PhD)
rhetoric and composition (MA)
Slavic languages and literatures (MA)
Slavic languages/Russian (MA)
social psychology (PhD)
software engineering (MS)
Spanish (MA, PhD)

College of Business
Dr. Caryn Beck-Dudley, Dean
Programs in:
accounting (M Acc)
business administration (MBA, PhD)
insurance (MSM)
management information systems (MS)

College of Communication
Dr. Gary Heald, Interim Dean
Programs in:
communication (Adv M, MA, MS, PhD)
communication sciences and disorders (Adv M, MS, PhD)
corporate and public communication (MA, MS)
integrated marketing communication (MA, MS)
mass communication (PhD)
media and communication studies (MA, MS)
speech communication (PhD)

College of Criminology and Criminal Justice
Dr. Thomas Blomberg, Dean
Program in:
criminology and criminal justice (MA, MSC, PhD)

College of Education
Dr. Marcy P. Driscoll, Dean
Programs in:
counseling/school psychology (PhD)
early childhood education (MS, Ed D, PhD, Ed S)
education (MS, Ed D, PhD, Ed S)
educational administration/leadership (MS, Ed D, PhD, Ed S)
educational leadership/administration (MS, Ed D, PhD, Ed S)
educational policy and planning analysis (PhD, Ed S)
educational psychology (MS, PhD, Ed S)
elementary education (MS, Ed D, PhD, Ed S)
emotional disturbance/learning disabilities (MS)
English education (MS, PhD, Ed S)
higher education (MS, Ed D, PhD, Ed S)
history and philosophy of education (MS, PhD, Ed S)
instructional systems (MS, PhD, Ed S)
international and intercultural education (PhD)
learning and cognition (MS, PhD, Ed S)
mathematics education (MS, PhD, Ed S)
measurement and statistics (MS, PhD, Ed S)
mental health counseling (PhD)
mental retardation (MS)
open and distance learning (MS)
performance improvement and human resources (MS)
physical education (MS, Ed D, PhD, Ed S)
program evaluation (MS, PhD, Ed S)
psychological services (MS, PhD, Ed S)
reading education/language arts (MS, Ed D, PhD, Ed S)
recreation management (MS)
rehabilitation counseling (MS, PhD, Ed S)
school psychology (MS, Ed S)
science education (MS, PhD, Ed S)
social science education (MS, PhD, Ed S)
social, history and philosophy of education (MS, PhD, Ed S)
sociocultural and international developmental education (MS, PhD, Ed S)
special education (MS, PhD, Ed S)
sport management (MS, Ed D, PhD)
sports psychology (MS, PhD)
visual disabilities (MS)

College of Human Sciences
Dr. Billie J. Collier, Dean
Programs in:
exercise science (MS, PhD)
family and child sciences (MS)
family relations (PhD)
human sciences (MS, PhD)
marriage and family therapy (PhD)
nutrition and food sciences (MS, PhD)

College of Information
Dr. Lawrence Dennis, Dean
Program in:
library and information studies (MS, PhD, Specialist)

College of Motion Picture, Television, and Recording Arts
Frank Patterson, Dean
Programs in:
production (MFA)
screen and play writing (MFA)

College of Music
Don Gibson, Dean
Programs in:
accompanying (MM)
arts administration (MA)
choral conducting (MM)
composition (MM, DM)
ethnomusicology (MM)
general music (MA)
instrumental accompanying (MM)
instrumental conducting (MM)
jazz studies (MM)
music education (MM Ed, PhD)
music theory (MM, PhD)
music therapy (MM)
musicology (MM, PhD)
opera (MM)
performance (MM, DM)
piano pedagogy (MM)
piano technology (MA)
vocal accompanying (MM)

College of Nursing
Dr. Lisa Ann Plowfield, Dean
Programs in:
family nurse practitioner (MSN, Certificate)
nurse educator (MSN, Certificate)

College of Social Sciences
Dr. David W. Rasmussen, Dean
Programs in:
Asian studies (MA)
demography and population health (MS, Certificate)
economics (MS, PhD)
geographic information science (MS)
geography (MA, MS, PhD)
international affairs (MA, MS)
political science (MA, MS, PhD)
public administration and policy (MPA, PhD, Certificate)
public health (MPH)
Russian and East European studies (MA)
social sciences (MA, MPA, MPH, MS, MSP, PhD, Certificate)
sociology (MA, MS, PhD)
urban and regional planning (MSP, PhD)

College of Social Work
Dr. Nicholas Mazza, Dean

Florida State University (continued)
Programs in:
clinical social work (MSW)
social policy and administration (MSW)
social work (PhD)

College of Visual Arts, Theatre and Dance
Dr. Sally E. McRorie, Dean
Programs in:
American dance studies (MA)
art education (MA, MS, Ed D, PhD, Ed S)
art history (MA, PhD)
dance (MFA)
interior design (MA, MFA, MS)
museum studies (Certificate)
studio and related studies (MA)
studio art (MFA)
visual arts, theatre and dance (MA, MFA, MS, Ed D, PhD, Certificate, Ed S)

FAMU-FSU College of Engineering
Programs in:
biomedical engineering (MS, PhD)
chemical engineering (MS, PhD)
civil and environmental engineering (MS, PhD)
electrical engineering (MS, PhD)
engineering (MS, PhD)
industrial engineering (MS, PhD)
mechanical engineering (MS, PhD)

School of Theatre
Cameron Jackson, Director
Programs in:
acting (MFA)
directing (MFA)
lighting, costume, and scenic design (MFA)
technical production (MFA)
theater management (MFA)
theatre (MA, MS, PhD)

■ HODGES UNIVERSITY
Naples, FL 34119
http://www.hodges.edu/

Independent, coed, comprehensive institution. *Graduate faculty:* 13 full-time (4 women), 3 part-time/adjunct (2 women). *Computer facilities:* 500 computers available on campus for general student use. A campuswide network can be accessed. *Graduate expenses:* Tuition: part-time $600 per credit hour. *General application contact:* Rita Lampus, Vice President of Student Enrollment Management, 239-513-1122.

Graduate Programs
Terry McMahan, President
Programs in:
business administration (MBA)
computer information technology (MS)
criminal justice (MCJ)
education (MPS)
information systems management (MIS)
interdisciplinary (MPS)
law (MPS)
management (MSM)
professional studies (MPS)
psychology (MPS)
public administration (MPA)

■ JACKSONVILLE UNIVERSITY
Jacksonville, FL 32211-3394
http://www.ju.edu/

Independent, coed, comprehensive institution. *Computer facilities:* 450 computers available on campus for general student use. A campuswide network can be accessed from student residence rooms and from off campus. Online class registration is available. *General application contact:* Executive Director, Transfer and Graduate Enrollment, 904-256-7144.

College of Arts and Sciences
Program in:
arts and sciences (MAT, MSN, Certificate)

School of Education
Programs in:
computer sciences (MAT)
early childhood education (Certificate)
elementary education (MAT)
integrated learning with educational technology (MAT)
mathematics education (MAT)
music education (MAT)
reading education (MAT)
second career as a teacher (Certificate)
second careers as a teacher (Certificate)

School of Nursing
Program in:
nursing (MSN)

School of Orthodontics
Program in:
orthodontics (Certificate)

Davis College of Business
Programs in:
business (Exec MBA, MBA)
business administration (Exec MBA, MBA)

■ LYNN UNIVERSITY
Boca Raton, FL 33431-5598
http://www.lynn.edu/

Independent, coed, comprehensive institution. *Computer facilities:* Computer purchase and lease plans are available. 150 computers available on campus for general student use. A campuswide network can be accessed from student residence rooms and from off campus. Online class registration is available. *General application contact:* Assistant Director of Graduate Admissions, 561-237-7916 Ext. 7845.

College of Arts and Sciences
Programs in:
applied psychology (MS)
criminal justice administration (MS)
emergency planning and administration (MS, Certificate)

College of Business and Management
Programs in:
aviation management (MBA)
financial valuation and investment management (MBA)
global leadership (PhD)
hospitality management (MBA)
international business (MBA)
marketing (MBA)
mass communication and media management (MBA)
sports and athletics administration (MBA)

Conservatory of Music
Programs in:
music performance (MM)
professional performance (Certificate)

Donald and Helen Ross College of Education
Programs in:
exceptional student education (M Ed)
global leadership (PhD)

Eugene M. and Christine E. Lynn College of International Communication
Program in:
mass communication (MS)

■ NOVA SOUTHEASTERN UNIVERSITY
Fort Lauderdale, FL 33314-7796
http://www.nova.edu/

Independent, coed, university. CGS member. *Computer facilities:* 2,708 computers available on campus for general student use. A campuswide network can be accessed from student residence rooms and from off campus. Online class registration is available. *General application contact:* Information Contact, 800-541-6682.

Center for Psychological Studies
Karen Grosby, Dean
Programs in:
clinical pharmacology (MS)
clinical psychology (PhD, Psy D, SPS)
mental health counseling (MS)
psychological studies (MS, PhD, Psy D, Psy S, SPS)
school guidance and counseling (MS)
school psychology (Psy S)

Criminal Justice Institute
Dr. Tammy Kushner, Director
Program in:
criminal justice (MHS, MS)

Fischler School of Education and Human Services
Dr. H. Wells Singleton, Provost/Dean

Programs in:
adult education (Ed D)
athletic administration (MS)
brain research (MS, Ed S)
charter school education/leadership (MS)
child and youth studies (Ed D)
child protection (MHS)
cognitive and behavioral disabilities (MS)
computer science education (Ed S)
computer science education (K-12) (MS)
computing and information technology (Ed D)
curriculum and teaching (Ed S)
curriculum, instruction and technology (MS)
curriculum, instruction, management and administration (Ed S)
early childhood education (MS)
early literacy and reading (Ed S)
early literacy education (MS)
education (MS)
education and human services (MA, MHS, MS, Ed D, SLPD, Ed S)
education technology (MS)
educational leaders (Ed D)
educational leadership (Ed D)
educational leadership (administration K–12) (MS, Ed S)
educational media (Ed S)
educational media (K-12) (MS)
elementary education (MS, Ed S)
English education (MS, Ed S)
environmental education (MS)
exceptional student education (MS)
gifted education (MS, Ed S)
health care education (Ed D)
health professions education (MS)
higher education (Ed D)
higher education leadership (Ed D)
human services administration (Ed D)
instructional leadership (Ed D)
instructional technology and distance education (MS, Ed D)
interdisciplinary arts education (MS)
leadership (MS)
management and administration of educational programs (MS)
mathematics (MS)
mathematics education (Ed S)
multicultural early intervention (MS)
organizational leadership (Ed D)
pre-kindergarten/primary (MS)
preschool education (MS)
reading (MS)
reading and TESOL (MS)
reading education (Ed S)
science (MS)
science education (Ed S)
secondary education (MS)
social studies (MS, Ed S)
Spanish language (MS)
special education (Ed D)
special education and reading (MS)
speech language pathology (Ed D)
speech-language pathology (MS, SLPD)
substance abuse counseling and education (MS)
teaching and learning (MA, MS)
teaching English to speakers of other languages (MS, Ed S)
technology management and administration (Ed S)
urban studies education (MS)
vocational, occupational and technical education (Ed D)

Graduate School of Computer and Information Sciences

Dr. Amon Seagull, Interim Dean
Programs in:
computer information systems (MS, PhD)
computer science (MS, PhD)
computing technology in education (PhD)
information security (MS)
information systems (MS, PhD)
management information systems (MS)

Graduate School of Humanities and Social Sciences

Dr. Honggang Yang, Dean
Programs in:
college student affairs (MS)
college student personnel administration (Certificate)
conflict analysis and resolution (MS, PhD)
conflict analysis and resolution studies (Certificate)
cross-disciplinary studies (MA)
family studies (Certificate)
family systems healthcare (Certificate)
family therapy (MS, DMFT, PhD, Certificate)
health care conflict resolution (Certificate)
humanities and social sciences (MA, MS, DMFT, PhD, Certificate)
marriage and family therapy (DMFT)
peace studies (Certificate)
qualitative research (Certificate)

Health Professions Division

Dr. Frederick Lippman, Chancellor
Program in:
health professions (DMD, DO, OD, Pharm D, MBS, MH Sc, MMS, MOT, MPH, MS, MSN, Au D, DHSc, DPT, OTD, PhD, TDPT)

College of Allied Health and Nursing

Dr. Richard Davis, Dean
Programs in:
allied health and nursing (MH Sc, MMS, MOT, MSN, Au D, DHSc, DPT, OTD, PhD, TDPT)
audiology (Au D)
health science (MH Sc, DHSc)
medical science/physician assistant (MMS)
nursing (MSN, PhD)
occupational therapy (MOT, OTD, PhD)
physical therapy (DPT, PhD, TDPT)

College of Dental Medicine

Dr. Robert A. Uchin, Dean
Programs in:
dental medicine (DMD)
dentistry (MS)

College of Medical Sciences

Dr. Harold E. Laubach, Dean
Program in:
biomedical sciences (MBS)

College of Optometry

Dr. David Loshin, Dean
Programs in:
clinical vision research (MS)
optometry (OD)

College of Osteopathic Medicine

Dr. Anthony J. Silavgni, Dean
Programs in:
osteopathic medicine (DO)
public health (MPH)

College of Pharmacy

Dr. Andres Malave, Dean
Program in:
pharmacy (Pharm D)

H. Wayne Huizenga School of Business and Entrepreneurship

Dr. Randolph A. Pohlman, Dean
Programs in:
accounting (DBA)
business administration (MBA)
business and entrepreneurship (M Acc, M Tax, MBA, MIBA, MPA, MS, MSHRM, DBA)
entrepreneurship (MBA)
finance (DBA)
human resource management (DBA)
human resources management (MSHRM)
international business (DBA)
international business administration (MIBA)
leadership (MS)
management (DBA)
operations management (DBA)
public administration (MPA)
real estate development (MS)
taxation (M Tax)

Oceanographic Center

Dr. Richard Dodge, Dean
Programs in:
coastal zone management (MS)
marine biology (MS, PhD)
marine biology and oceanography (PhD)
marine environmental science (MS)
oceanography (PhD)
physical oceanography (MS)

Shepard Broad Law Center

Joseph D. Harbaugh, Dean
Programs in:
education law (MS, Certificate)
employment law (MS)
health law (MS)
law (JD)

■ PALM BEACH ATLANTIC UNIVERSITY
West Palm Beach, FL 33416-4708
http://www.pba.edu/

Independent-religious, coed, comprehensive institution. *Graduate faculty:* 35 full-time (20 women), 13 part-time/adjunct (5 women). *Computer facilities:* 460 computers available on campus for general student use. A campuswide network can be accessed from student residence rooms and from off campus. Online class registration is available. *Graduate expenses:* Tuition: full-time $8010; part-time $445 per credit hour. Required fees: $99 per semester. Tuition and fees vary according to course load, degree level and campus/location. *General application contact:* Joe Sharp, Dean of Admissions, 888-468-6722.

Gregory School of Pharmacy
Dr. Daniel Brown, Dean
Program in:
pharmacy (Pharm D)

MacArthur School of Leadership
Dr. Jim Laub, Dean
Program in:
organizational leadership (MS)

Rinker School of Business
Dr. Edgar Langlois, Dean
Program in:
business (MBA)

School of Education and Behavioral Studies
Dr. Phillip Henry, Program Director
Program in:
counseling psychology (MSCP)

■ ROLLINS COLLEGE
Winter Park, FL 32789-4499
http://www.rollins.edu/

Independent, coed, comprehensive institution. *Graduate faculty:* 26 full-time (6 women). *Computer facilities:* 240 computers available on campus for general student use. A campuswide network can be accessed from student residence rooms and from off campus. Online class registration is available. *General application contact:* Information Contact, 407-646-2000.

Crummer Graduate School of Business
Dr. Craig M. McAllaster, Dean
Program in:
business (MBA)

Hamilton Holt School
Dr. James C. Eck, Acting Dean
Programs in:
elementary education (M Ed, MAT)
human resources (MA)
liberal studies (MLS)
mental health counseling (MA)
secondary education (MAT)

■ SAINT LEO UNIVERSITY
Saint Leo, FL 33574-6665
http://www.saintleo.edu/

Independent-religious, coed, comprehensive institution. *Computer facilities:* Computer purchase and lease plans are available. 1,243 computers available on campus for general student use. A campuswide network can be accessed from student residence rooms and from off campus. Online class registration is available. *General application contact:* Director, Graduate/Weekend and Evening Admission, 800-707-8846.

Graduate Business Studies
Programs in:
accounting (MBA)
business (MBA)
criminal justice (MBA)
health services management (MBA)
human resource administration (MBA)
information security management (MBA)
sport business (MBA)

Graduate Pastoral Studies
Program in:
pastoral studies (MA)

Graduate Studies in Criminal Justice
Programs in:
criminal justice (MS)
critical incident management (MS)

Graduate Studies in Education
Programs in:
education (MAT)
educational leadership (M Ed)
exceptional student education (M Ed)
instructional design (MS)
instructional leadership (M Ed)
reading (M Ed)

■ ST. THOMAS UNIVERSITY
Miami Gardens, FL 33054-6459
http://www.stu.edu/

Independent-religious, coed, comprehensive institution. *Computer facilities:* 60 computers available on campus for general student use. A campuswide network can be accessed. *General application contact:* Assistant Director of Admissions, 305-628-6546.

Biscayne College
Programs in:
guidance and counseling (MS, Post-Master's Certificate)
marriage and family therapy (MS, Post-Master's Certificate)
mental health counseling (MS)

School of Business
Programs in:
accounting (MBA)
business (M Acc, MBA, MIB, MS, MSM, Certificate)
business administration (M Acc, MBA, Certificate)
general management (MSM, Certificate)
health management (MBA, MSM, Certificate)
human resource management (MBA, MSM, Certificate)
international business (MBA, MIB, MSM, Certificate)
justice administration (MSM, Certificate)
management accounting (MSM, Certificate)
public management (MSM, Certificate)
sports administration (MS)

School of Law
Programs in:
international human rights (LL M)
international taxation (LL M)
law (JD)

School of Leadership Studies
Programs in:
art management (MA)
electronic media (MA)
executive management (MPS)
Hispanic media (MA, Certificate)
leadership studies (MA, MPS, MS, Ed D, Certificate)

Institute for Education
Programs in:
earth/space science (Certificate)
educational administration (MS, Certificate)
educational leadership (Ed D)
elementary education (MS)
ESOL (Certificate)
gifted education (Certificate)
instructional technology (MS, Certificate)
professional/studies (Certificate)
reading (MS, Certificate)
special education (MS)

School of Theology and Ministry
Program in:
theology and ministry (MA, PhD, Certificate)

Institute for Pastoral Ministries
Programs in:
pastoral ministries (MA, Certificate)
practical theology (PhD)

■ SCHILLER INTERNATIONAL UNIVERSITY
Largo, FL 33770
http://www.schiller.edu/

Independent, coed, comprehensive institution. *Computer facilities:* 42 computers available on campus for general student use. A campuswide network can be accessed. *General application contact:* Associate Director of Admissions, 727-736-5082.

MBA Programs, Florida
Programs in:
financial planning (MBA)
information technology (MBA)
international business (MBA)
international hotel and tourism management (MBA)

■ STETSON UNIVERSITY
DeLand, FL 32723
http://www.stetson.edu/

Independent, coed, comprehensive institution. *Graduate faculty:* 80 full-time (34 women), 65 part-time/adjunct (24 women). *Computer facilities:* 458 computers available on campus for general student use. A campuswide network can be accessed from student residence rooms and from off campus. Online class registration is available. *General application contact:* Office of Graduate Studies, 386-822-7075.

College of Arts and Sciences
Dr. Grady Ballenger, Dean
Programs in:
arts and sciences (M Ed, MA, MS)
education (M Ed, MS)
educational leadership (M Ed)
marriage and family therapy (MS)
mental health counseling (MS)
reading education (M Ed)
school guidance and family consultation (MS)

Division of Humanities
Dr. Grady Ballenger, Dean
Programs in:
English (MA)
humanities (MA)

College of Law
Dr. Darby Dickerson, Dean
Program in:
law (JD, LL M)

School of Business Administration
Dr. James Scheiner, Dean
Programs in:
accounting (M Acc)
business administration (M Acc, MBA)

■ UNIVERSITY OF CENTRAL FLORIDA
Orlando, FL 32816
http://www.ucf.edu/

State-supported, coed, university. CGS member. *Graduate faculty:* 1,137 full-time (423 women), 528 part-time/adjunct (285 women). *Computer facilities:* Computer purchase and lease plans are available. 3,276 computers available on campus for general student use. A campuswide network can be accessed from student residence rooms and from off campus. Online class registration is available. *Graduate expenses:* Tuition, state resident: part-time $384 per credit. Tuition, nonresident: part-time $1076 per credit. Required fees: $9 per credit. *General application contact:* Dr. Patricia Bishop, Vice Provost and Dean of Graduate Studies, 407-823-2766.

College of Arts and Humanities
Dr. Jose Fernandez, Dean
Programs in:
acting (MA)
arts and humanities (MA, MFA, MS, PhD, Certificate)
creative writing (MFA)
English (MA, MFA)
history (MA)
literature (MA)
music (MA)
professional writing (Certificate)
public history (MA)
rhetoric and composition (MA)
Spanish (MA)
studio art and the computer (MFA)
teaching English to speakers of other languages (MA, Certificate)
technical communication (MA)
texts and technology (PhD)
theatre for young audiences (MFA)

Division of Film and Digital Media
Dr. Jose Maunez-Cuadra, Interim Chair
Programs in:
entrepreneurial digital cinema (MFA)
interactive entertainment (MS)
visual language and interactive media (MA, MFA)

College of Business Administration
Dr. Thomas L. Keon, Dean
Programs in:
business administration (MBA, MS, MSA, MSBM, MSM, MST, PhD, Graduate Certificate)
economics (MS, PhD)
entrepreneurship (Graduate Certificate)
finance (PhD)
human resources and change management (MSM)
management information systems (MS)
marketing (PhD)
sport business management (MSBM)
technology ventures (Graduate Certificate)

Dr. P. Phillips School of Real Estate
Program in:
real estate (MS)

Kenneth G. Dixon School of Accounting
Dr. Robin W. Roberts, Director
Programs in:
accounting (MSA, MST)
taxation (MST)

College of Education
Dr. Sandra L. Robinson, Dean
Programs in:
applied learning and instruction (MA)
art education (M Ed, MA)
autism spectrum disorders (Certificate)
biology (MA)
career and technical education (MA)
career counseling (Certificate)
chemistry (MA)
communication sciences and disorders (PhD)
community college education (Certificate)
counselor education (M Ed, MA, PhD, Ed S)
curriculum and instruction (M Ed, MA, Ed D, Ed S)
e-learning (MA)
e-learning professional development (Certificate)
early childhood development and education (MS)
early childhood education (MS)
education (M Ed, MA, MS, Ed D, PhD, Certificate, Ed S)
educational leadership (M Ed, MA, Ed D, Ed S)
educational media (M Ed)
educational technology (MA)
elementary education (M Ed, MA, PhD)
English language arts education (M Ed, MA)
exceptional education (M Ed, MA)
gifted education (Certificate)
global and comparative education (Certificate)
health/wellness and applied exercise physiology (MA)
higher education (PhD)
higher education/community college education (MA)
higher education/student personnel (MA)
hospitality education (PhD)
initial teacher professional preparation (Certificate)
instructional design for simulations (Certificate)
instructional systems (MA)
instructional technology (PhD)
instructional technology/media (M Ed, MA, Certificate)
instructional technology/media and e-learning (MA)
instructional/educational technology (Certificate)
K-8 mathematics and science education (M Ed, Certificate)
marriage and family therapy (MA, Certificate)
mathematics education (M Ed, MA, PhD)
mental health counseling (MA)
middle school mathematics (MA)
middle school science (MA)
physics (MA)
play therapy (Certificate)
pre-kindergarten handicapped endorsement (Certificate)
reading education (M Ed, Certificate)
school counseling (M Ed, MA, Ed S)
school psychology (Ed S)

University of Central Florida (continued)
- science education (M Ed, MA, PhD)
- severe and profound disabilities (Certificate)
- social science education (M Ed, MA)
- special education (Certificate)
- sport and fitness (MA)
- sport leadership and coaching (MA)
- sports leadership (Certificate)
- teacher leadership (M Ed)
- teaching excellence (Certificate)
- urban education (Certificate)

College of Engineering and Computer Science
Dr. Marwan Simaan, Interim Dean
Programs in:
- aerospace engineering (MSAE)
- applied operations research (Certificate)
- civil engineering (MS, MSCE, PhD, Certificate)
- computer-integrated manufacturing (MS)
- construction engineering (Certificate)
- design for usability (Certificate)
- digital forensics (MS)
- engineering and computer science (MS, MS Cp E, MS Env E, MSAE, MSCE, MSEE, MSIE, MSME, MSMSE, PMS, PhD, Certificate)
- engineering management (MS)
- environmental engineering (MS, MS Env E, PhD)
- human engineering/ergonomics (MS)
- industrial engineering (MSIE, PhD)
- industrial ergonomics and safety (Certificate)
- interactive simulation and training systems (MS)
- manufacturing engineering (MS)
- materials science and engineering (MSMSE, PhD)
- mechanical engineering (MSME, PhD, Certificate)
- modeling and simulation (PMS)
- operations research (MS)
- project engineering (Certificate)
- quality assurance (Certificate)
- quality engineering (MS)
- simulation modeling and analysis (MS)
- structural engineering (Certificate)
- surface water modeling (Certificate)
- systems engineering (MS, Certificate)
- systems simulation for engineers (Certificate)
- technology (MS)
- training simulation (Certificate)
- transportation engineering (Certificate)

School of Electrical Engineering and Computer Science
Dr. Issa Batarseh, Director
Programs in:
- communications systems (Certificate)
- computer engineering (MS Cp E, PhD)
- computer science (MS, PhD)
- digital forensics (MS)
- electrical engineering (MSEE, PhD, Certificate)
- electronic circuits (Certificate)

College of Graduate Studies
Dr. Patricia Bishop, Vice Provost and Dean
Programs in:
- interdisciplinary studies (MA, MS)
- modeling and simulation (MS, PhD)

College of Health and Public Affairs
Dr. Michael Frumkin, Dean
Programs in:
- child language disorders (Certificate)
- communication sciences and disorders (MA)
- corrections leadership (Certificate)
- crime analysis (Certificate)
- criminal justice (MS)
- emergency management and homeland security (Certificate)
- health and public affairs (MA, MNM, MPA, MS, MSW, DPT, PhD, Certificate)
- health services administration (MS, Certificate)
- juvenile justice leadership (Certificate)
- medical speech-language pathology (Certificate)
- multicultural/multilingual speech-language pathology (Certificate)
- non-profit management (MNM, Certificate)
- physical therapy (DPT)
- police leadership (Certificate)
- public administration (MPA, Certificate)
- public affairs (PhD)
- urban and regional planning (Certificate)

School of Social Work
Dr. John Ronnau, Director
Programs in:
- addictions (Certificate)
- aging studies (Certificate)
- children's services (Certificate)
- school social work (Certificate)
- social work (MSW)
- social work administration (Certificate)

College of Medicine
Dr. Deborah C. German, Dean
Program in:
- medicine (MS, PhD)

Burnett School of Biomedical Sciences
Dr. Pappachan E. Kolattukudy, Director
Programs in:
- biomedical sciences (MS, PhD)
- biotechnology (MS)
- molecular biology and microbiology (MS)

College of Nursing
Dr. Jean D. Leuner, Dean
Programs in:
- adult nurse practitioner (MSN, Post-Master's Certificate)
- clinical nurse leader (MSN, Post-Master's Certificate)
- clinical nurse specialist (MSN, Post-Master's Certificate)
- family nurse practitioner (MSN, Post-Master's Certificate)
- leadership and management (MSN)
- nurse educator (MSN)
- nursing (PhD)
- nursing education (Post-Master's Certificate)
- nursing practice (DNP)
- pediatric nurse practitioner (MSN, Post-Master's Certificate)

College of Optics and Photonics
Dr. Bahaa E. Saleh, Dean and Director
Program in:
- optics (MS, PhD)

College of Sciences
Dr. Peter Panousis, Dean
Programs in:
- actuarial science (MS)
- anthropology (MA)
- applied experimental and human factors psychology (MA, PhD)
- applied mathematics (Certificate)
- applied sociology (MA)
- biology (MS)
- chemistry (MS, PhD)
- clinical psychology (MA, MS, PhD)
- computer forensics (Certificate)
- conservation biology (PhD, Certificate)
- data mining (MS)
- domestic violence (MA)
- environmental politics (MA)
- forensic analysis (MS)
- forensic biochemistry (MS)
- industrial chemistry (MS)
- industrial mathematics (MS)
- industrial/organizational psychology (MS, PhD)
- international studies (MA)
- mathematical science (MS)
- mathematics (PhD)
- Maya studies (Certificate)
- physics (MS, PhD)
- political analysis and policy (MA)
- SAS data mining (Certificate)
- sciences (MA, MS, PhD, Certificate)
- sociology (PhD)
- statistical computing (MS)

Nicholson School of Communication
Dr. Robert Chandler, Director
Programs in:
- business communication (MA)
- interpersonal communication (MA)
- mass communication (MA)

Rosen College of Hospitality Management
Dr. Abraham C. Pizam, Dean
Program in:
- hospitality and tourism management (MS)

■ UNIVERSITY OF FLORIDA
Gainesville, FL 32611
http://www.ufl.edu/

State-supported, coed, university. CGS member. *Computer facilities:* 2,200 computers available on campus for general student use. A campuswide network can be accessed from student residence rooms and from off campus. Online class registration is available. *General application contact:* Graduate Admissions, 352-392-3261.

College of Dentistry

Programs in:
- dentistry (DMD, MS, PhD, Certificate)
- endodontics (MS, Certificate)
- foreign trained dentistry (Certificate)
- oral biology (PhD)
- orthodontics (MS, Certificate)
- periodontology (MS, Certificate)
- prosthodontics (MS, Certificate)

College of Medicine

Programs in:
- biochemistry and molecular biology (MS, PhD)
- biomedical sciences (PhD)
- clinical investigation (MS)
- epidemiology (MS)
- genetics (PhD)
- imaging science and technology (MS, PhD)
- immunology and microbiology (PhD)
- immunology and molecular pathology (PhD)
- medicine (MD, MPAS, MPH, MS, PhD)
- molecular cell biology (PhD)
- molecular genetics and microbiology (MS, PhD)
- neuroscience (MS, PhD)
- pharmacology and therapeutics (PhD)
- physician assistant (MPAS)
- physiology and functional genomics (PhD)
- physiology and pharmacology (PhD)
- public health (MPH)

College of Pharmacy

Programs in:
- clinical pharmaceutical sciences (PhD)
- forensic DNA and serology (MS, Certificate)
- forensic drug chemistry (MS, Certificate)
- forensic toxicology (MS, Certificate)
- medicinal chemistry (Pharm D, MSP, PhD)
- pharmaceutical sciences (MSP, PhD)
- pharmaceutics (PhD)
- pharmacodynamics (MSP, PhD)
- pharmacology (PhD)
- pharmacy (Pharm D, MS, MSP, PhD, Certificate)
- pharmacy health care administration (MSP, PhD)
- pharmacy practice (PhD)

College of Veterinary Medicine

Programs in:
- forensic toxicology (Certificate)
- veterinary medical sciences (MS, PhD)
- veterinary medicine (DVM, MS, PhD, Certificate)

Graduate School

College of Agricultural and Life Sciences

Programs in:
- agricultural and life sciences (MAB, MFAS, MFRC, MFYCS, MS, DPM, PhD)
- agricultural education and communication (MS, PhD)
- agronomy (MS, PhD)
- anatomy and development (MS, PhD)
- animal sciences (MS, PhD)
- biochemistry and molecular biology (MS, PhD)
- breeding and genetics (MS, PhD)
- ecology (MS, PhD)
- entomology and nematology (MS, PhD)
- family, youth, and community sciences (MFYCS, MS)
- fisheries and aquatic sciences (MFAS, MS, PhD)
- food and resource economics (MAB, MS, PhD)
- food science (MS, PhD)
- forest resources and conservation (MFRC, MS, PhD)
- microbiology and cell science (MS, PhD)
- nutritional sciences (MS, PhD)
- plant biotechnology (MS, PhD)
- plant breeding and genetics (MS, PhD)
- plant medicine (DPM)
- plant molecular and cellular biology (MS, PhD)
- plant pathology (MS, PhD)
- plant production and nutrient management (MS, PhD)
- postharvest biology (MS, PhD)
- soil and water science (MS, PhD)
- stress physiology (MS, PhD)
- sustainable/organic practice (MS, PhD)
- taxonomy (MS, PhD)
- tissue culture (MS, PhD)
- weed science (MS, PhD)
- wildlife ecology and conservation (MS, PhD)

College of Design, Construction and Planning

Programs in:
- architecture (M Arch, MSAS, PhD)
- building construction (MBC, MICM, MSBC, PhD)
- design, construction and planning (M Arch, MAURP, MBC, MICM, MID, MLA, MSAS, MSBC, PhD)
- interior design (MID, PhD)
- landscape architecture (MLA, PhD)
- urban and regional planning (MAURP, PhD)

College of Education

Programs in:
- bilingual/ESOL education (M Ed, MAE, Ed D, PhD, Ed S)
- curriculum and instruction (M Ed, MAE, Ed D, PhD, Ed S)
- early childhood education (Ed D, PhD, Ed S)
- education (M Ed, MAE, Ed D, PhD, Ed S)
- educational leadership (M Ed, MAE, Ed D, PhD, Ed S)
- educational psychology (M Ed, MAE, Ed D, PhD, Ed S)
- elementary education (M Ed, MAE)
- English education (M Ed, MAE)
- higher education administration (Ed D, PhD, Ed S)
- marriage and family counseling (M Ed, MAE, Ed D, PhD, Ed S)
- mathematics education (M Ed, MAE)
- mental health counseling (M Ed, MAE, Ed D, PhD, Ed S)
- reading education (M Ed, MAE)
- research and evaluation methodology (M Ed, MAE, Ed D, PhD, Ed S)
- school counseling and guidance (M Ed, MAE, Ed D, PhD, Ed S)
- school psychology (M Ed, MAE, Ed D, PhD, Ed S)
- science education (M Ed, MAE)
- social foundations (M Ed, MAE, Ed D, PhD)
- social studies education (M Ed, MAE)
- special education (M Ed, MAE, Ed D, PhD, Ed S)
- student personnel in higher education (M Ed, MAE)

College of Engineering

Programs in:
- aerospace engineering (ME, MS, PhD, Engr)
- agricultural and biological engineering (ME, MS, PhD, Engr)
- biomedical engineering (ME, MS, PhD, Certificate)
- chemical engineering (ME, MS, PhD)
- civil engineering (MCE, MS, PhD, Engr)
- coastal and oceanographic engineering (ME, MS, PhD, Engr)
- computer engineering (ME, MS, PhD)
- computer science (MS)
- digital arts and sciences (MS)
- electrical and computer engineering (ME, MS, PhD, Engr)
- engineering (MCE, ME, MS, PhD, Certificate, Engr)
- environmental engineering sciences (ME, MS, PhD, Engr)
- industrial and systems engineering (ME, MS, PhD, Engr)
- materials science and engineering (ME, MS, PhD, Engr)
- mechanical engineering (ME, MS, PhD, Engr)
- nuclear engineering sciences (ME, MS, PhD, Engr)

College of Fine Arts

Programs in:
- art (MFA)
- art education (MA)
- art history (MA, PhD)
- choral conducting (MM, PhD)
- composition/theory (MM, PhD)
- digital arts and sciences (MA)

University of Florida (continued)
ethnomusicology (PhD)
fine arts (MA, MFA, MM, PhD)
instrumental conducting (MM, PhD)
museology (museum studies) (MA)
music (MM, PhD)
music education (MM, PhD)
music history and literature (MM)
musicology (PhD)
performance (MM)
sacred music (MM)
theatre (MFA)

College of Health and Human Performance
Programs in:
athletic training/sport medicine (MS, PhD)
biomechanics (MS, PhD)
clinical exercise physiology (MS)
exercise physiology (MS, PhD)
health and human performance (PhD)
health behavior (PhD)
health communication (Graduate Certificate)
health education and behavior (MS)
human performance (MS)
motor learning/control (MS, PhD)
recreational studies (MS)
sport and exercise psychology (MS)

College of Journalism and Communications
Programs in:
advertising (M Adv)
journalism (MAMC)
mass communication (MAMC, PhD)
public relations (MAMC)
telecommunication (MAMC)

College of Liberal Arts and Sciences
Programs in:
African studies (Certificate)
anthropology (MA, PhD)
astronomy (MS, PhD)
behavior analysis (PhD)
behavioral neuroscience (MS, PhD)
botany (M Ag, MS, MST, PhD)
chemistry (MS, MST, PhD)
classical studies (MA, PhD)
cognitive and sensory processes (PhD)
communication sciences and disorders (MA, Au D, PhD)
counseling psychology (PhD)
creative writing (MFA)
criminology and law (MA, PhD)
developmental psychology (PhD)
English (MA, PhD)
French (MA, PhD)
gender and development (Graduate Certificate)
geography (MA, MS, PhD)
geology (MS, MST, PhD)
German (MA, PhD)
history (MA, PhD)
international development policy and administration (MA, Certificate)
international relations (MA, MAT)
Latin (MA, MAT, ML)
Latin American studies (MA, Certificate)
liberal arts and sciences (M Ag, M Stat, MA, MAT, MFA, ML, MS, MS Stat, MST, MWS, Au D, PhD, Certificate, Graduate Certificate)
linguistics (MA, PhD)
mathematics (MA, MAT, MS, MST, PhD)
philosophy (MA, PhD)
physics (MS, MST, PhD)
political campaigning (MA, Certificate)
political science (MA, MAT, PhD)
public affairs (MA, Certificate)
religion (MA, PhD)
social psychology (MS, PhD)
sociology (MA, PhD)
Spanish (MA, PhD)
statistics (M Stat, MS Stat, PhD)
teaching English as a second language (Certificate)
women's studies (MA, MWS, Graduate Certificate)
zoology (MS, MST, PhD)

College of Nursing
Programs in:
nursing (MSN)
nursing sciences (PhD)

College of Public Health and Health Professions
Programs in:
audiology (Au D)
biostatistics (MPH)
clinical and health psychology (PhD)
environmental health (MPH)
epidemiology (MPH)
health administration (MHA)
health services research (PhD)
occupational therapy (MHS, MOT)
physical therapy (DPT)
public health and health professions (MHA, MHS, MOT, MPH, Au D, DPT, PhD)
public health management and policy (MPH)
public health practice (MPH)
rehabilitation counseling (MHS)
rehabilitation science (PhD)
social and behavioral sciences (MPH)

School of Natural Resources and Environment
Program in:
interdisciplinary ecology (MS, PhD)

Warrington College of Business Administration
Programs in:
accounting (MBA)
arts administration (MBA)
business administration (M Acc, MA, MAIB, MBA, MS, PhD, Certificate)
business strategy and public policy (MBA)
competitive strategy (MBA)
decision and information sciences (MBA, MS, PhD)
economics (MA, PhD)
electronic commerce (MBA)
finance (MBA, PhD)
financial services (Certificate)
general business (MBA)
global management (MBA)
Graham-Buffett security analysis (MBA)
health administration (MBA)
human resources management (MBA)
insurance (PhD)
international business (MAIB)
international studies (MBA)
Latin American business (MBA)
management (MBA, MS, PhD)
marketing (MBA)
real estate and urban analysis (PhD)
sports administration (MBA)
supply chain management (MS)

Interdisciplinary Concentration in Animal Molecular and Cellular Biology
Program in:
animal molecular and cellular biology (MS, PhD)

Levin College of Law
Robert Jerry, Dean
Programs in:
comparative law (LL M)
environmental law (LL M)
international taxation (LL M)
law (JD)
taxation (LL M, SJD)

■ UNIVERSITY OF MIAMI
Coral Gables, FL 33124
http://www.miami.edu/

Independent, coed, university. CGS member. *Graduate faculty:* 917 full-time (256 women), 13 part-time/adjunct (5 women). *Computer facilities:* Computer purchase and lease plans are available. 1,800 computers available on campus for general student use. A campuswide network can be accessed from student residence rooms and from off campus. Online class registration, online student account information are available. *Graduate expenses:* Tuition: full-time $25,632; part-time $1424 per credit. Required fees: $274; $102 per semester. Tuition and fees vary according to course load, campus/location and program. *General application contact:* Office of Graduate Studies, 305-284-4154.

Graduate School
Dr. Terri A. Scandura, Dean
Programs in:
advanced professional studies (MS Ed, Ed S)
bilingual and bicultural counseling (Certificate)
biochemistry and molecular biology (PhD)
cancer biology (PhD)
comparative law (LL M)
counseling (MS Ed, Certificate)
counseling and research (MS Ed)
counseling psychology (PhD)
early childhood special education (Ed S)
education (MS Ed, PhD, Certificate, Ed S)

elementary education-initial certification/TESOL (MS Ed)
epidemiology (PhD)
estate planning (LL M)
exceptional student education, pre–K disabilities and ESOL (MS Ed, Ed S)
exceptional student education, pre-k disabilities and ESOL (MS Ed, Ed S)
exceptional student education, reading and ESOL (MS Ed, Ed S)
exercise physiology (MS Ed, PhD)
higher education administration (MS Ed, Ed D, Certificate)
higher education administration/ enrollment management (Certificate)
higher education leadership (Ed D)
inter-American law (LL M)
international administration (MAIA)
international law (LL M)
language and literacy learning in multilingual settings (PhD)
law (JD)
marriage and family therapy (MS Ed)
mathematics and science education (PhD)
medicine (MD, MPH, MSPH, DPT, PhD)
mental health counseling (MS Ed)
microbiology and immunology (PhD)
molecular and cellular pharmacology (PhD)
molecular cell and developmental biology (PhD)
neuroscience (PhD)
ocean and coastal law (LL M)
physical therapy (DPT, PhD)
physiology and biophysics (PhD)
public health (MPH, MSPH)
reading (MS Ed, Ed S)
real property development (LL M)
research, measurement, and evaluation (MS Ed, PhD)
special education (PhD)
sport administration (MS Ed)
sports medicine (MS Ed)
taxation (LL M)
teaching and learning (PhD, Certificate)

College of Arts and Sciences
Dr. Michael R. Halleran, Dean
Programs in:
adult clinical (PhD)
art history (MA)
arts and sciences (MA, MAIA, MALS, MFA, MPA, MS, PhD)
behavioral neuroscience (PhD)
biology (MS, PhD)
ceramics/glass (MFA)
chemistry (MS)
child clinical (PhD)
computer science (MS, PhD)
creative writing (MFA)
developmental psychology (PhD)
English (MA, PhD)
genetics and evolution (MS, PhD)
geography (MA)
graphic design/multimedia (MFA)
health clinical (PhD)
history (MA, PhD)
inorganic chemistry (PhD)
international studies (MA, PhD)
Latin American studies (MA)
liberal studies (MALS)
mathematics (MA, MS, PhD)
organic chemistry (PhD)
painting (MFA)
philosophy (MA, PhD)
photography/digital imaging (MFA)
physical chemistry (PhD)
physics (MS, PhD)
political science (MPA)
printmaking (MFA)
psychology (MS)
romance studies (PhD)
sculpture (MFA)
sociology (MA, PhD)

College of Engineering
Dr. James M. Tien, Dean
Programs in:
architectural engineering (MSAE)
biomedical engineering (MSBE, PhD)
civil engineering (MSCE, PhD)
electrical and computer engineering (MSECE, PhD)
engineering (MS, MSAE, MSBE, MSCE, MSECE, MSEVH, MSIE, MSME, MSOES, PhD)
environmental health and safety (MS)
ergonomics (PhD)
industrial engineering (MSIE, PhD)
management of technology (MS)
mechanical and aerospace engineering (MSME, PhD)
occupational ergonomics and safety (MS, MSOES)

Frost School of Music
Shelton Berg, Dean
Programs in:
accompanying and chamber music (MM, DMA)
choral conducting (MM, DMA)
composition (MM, DMA)
electronic music (MM)
instrumental conducting (MM, DMA)
instrumental performance (MM, DMA, AD)
jazz composition (DMA)
jazz pedagogy (MM)
jazz performance (MM, DMA)
keyboard performance and pedagogy (MM, DMA)
media writing and production (MM)
multiple woodwinds (MM, DMA)
music (MM, MS, DMA, PhD, AD, Spec M)
music business and entertainment industries (MM)
music education (MM, PhD, Spec M)
music engineering (MS)
music theory (MM)
music therapy (MM)
musicology (MM)
piano performance (MM, DMA, AD)
studio jazz writing (MM)
vocal pedagogy (DMA)
vocal performance (MM, DMA, AD)

Rosenstiel School of Marine and Atmospheric Science
Dr. Roni Avissar, Dean
Programs in:
applied marine physics (MS, PhD)
marine affairs and policy (MA, MS)
marine and atmospheric chemistry (MS, PhD)
marine and atmospheric science (MA, MS, PhD)
marine biology and fisheries (MA, MS, PhD)
marine geology and geophysics (MS, PhD)
meteorology (MS, PhD)
physical oceanography (MS, PhD)

School of Architecture
Teofilo Victoria, Director of Graduate Studies
Programs in:
architecture (M Arch)
suburb and town design (M Arch)

School of Business Administration
Dr. Anuj Mehrotra, Vice Dean
Programs in:
accounting (MBA)
business administration (MA, MBA, MP Acc, MS, MS Tax, MSPM, PhD)
computer information systems (MBA)
economic development (MA, PhD)
environmental economics (PhD)
executive and professional (MBA)
finance (MBA)
human resource economics (MA, PhD)
international business (MBA)
international economics (MA, PhD)
macroeconomics (PhD)
management (MBA)
management science (MBA)
marketing (MBA)
professional accounting (MP Acc)
professional management (MSPM)
taxation (MS Tax)

School of Communication
Dr. Sam L. Grogg, Dean
Programs in:
communication (PhD)
communication studies (MA)
film studies (MA, PhD)
motion pictures (MFA)
print journalism (MA)
public relations (MA)
Spanish language journalism (MA)
television broadcast journalism (MA)

School of Nursing and Health Studies
Dr. Nilda Peragallo, Dean
Programs in:
acute care (MSN)
nursing (PhD)
primary care (MSN)

■ UNIVERSITY OF NORTH FLORIDA

Jacksonville, FL 32224-2645
http://www.unf.edu/

State-supported, coed, comprehensive institution. *Graduate faculty:* 405 full-time (162 women). *Computer facilities:* Computer purchase and lease plans are available. 750 computers available on campus for general

University of North Florida (continued)
student use. A campuswide network can be accessed from student residence rooms and from off campus. Online class registration, applications software are available. *Graduate expenses:* Tuition, state resident: full-time $5782.08; part-time $240.92 per credit hour. Tuition, nonresident: full-time $19,974; part-time $832.26 per credit hour. Required fees: $952.80; $39.70 per credit hour. *General application contact:* Kiersten Jarvis, Graduate Coordinator, The Graduate School, 904-620-1360.

Brooks College of Health
Dr. Pamela Chally, Dean
Programs in:
community health (MPH)
geriatric management (MSH)
health (MHA, MPH, MPT, MS, MSH, MSN, Certificate)
health administration (MHA)
health behavior research and evaluation (Certificate)
nutrition (MSH)
physical therapy (MPT)
rehabilitation counseling (MS)

School of Nursing
Dr. Lillia Loriz, Chair
Programs in:
advanced practice nursing (MSN)
primary care nurse practitioner (Certificate)

Coggin College of Business
Dr. John P. McAllister, Dean
Programs in:
accounting (M Acct)
business (M Acct, MBA)
business administration (MBA)

College of Arts and Sciences
Dr. Barbara Hetrick, Dean
Programs in:
applied ethics (Graduate Certificate)
applied sociology (MS)
arts and sciences (MA, MAC, MPA, MS, MSCJ, Graduate Certificate)
biology (MA, MS)
counseling psychology (MAC)
criminal justice (MSCJ)
English (MA)
European history (MA)
general psychology (MA)
mathematical sciences (MS)
practical philosophy and applied ethics (MA)
public administration (MPA)
statistics (MS)
US history (MA)

College of Computing, Engineering, and Construction
Dr. Neal Coulter, Dean
Program in:
computer and information sciences (MS)

College of Education and Human Services
Dr. Larry Daniel, Dean
Programs in:
counselor education (M Ed)
deaf education (M Ed)
disability services (M Ed)
education and human services (M Ed, Ed D)
educational leadership (M Ed, Ed D)
exceptional student education (M Ed)
instructional leadership (M Ed)
mental health counseling (M Ed)
school counseling (M Ed)

Division of Curriculum and Instruction
Dr. Ronghua Ouyang, Chair
Programs in:
elementary education (M Ed)
secondary education (M Ed)

■ UNIVERSITY OF PHOENIX–CENTRAL FLORIDA CAMPUS

Maitland, FL 32751-7057
http://www.phoenix.edu/

Proprietary, coed, comprehensive institution. *Computer facilities:* Computer purchase and lease plans are available. A campuswide network can be accessed from off campus. Online class registration is available. *General application contact:* Campus Information Center, 407-667-0555.

The Artemis School

College of Education
Programs in:
administration and supervision (MA Ed)
curriculum and instruction (MA Ed)
curriculum and instruction-computer education (MA Ed)
curriculum and instruction-mathematics education (MA Ed)
early childhood education (MA Ed)
elementary teacher education (MA Ed)
secondary teacher education (MA Ed)

College of Health and Human Services
Programs in:
health administration (MHA)
health and human services (MSN)
health care management (MBA)
nursing (MSN)
nursing/health care education (MSN)

John Sperling School of Business
Program in:
business (MBA, MIS, MM)

College of Graduate Business and Management
Programs in:
accounting (MBA)
business administration (MBA)
business and management (MM)
global management (MBA)
human resources management (MBA, MM)
management (MM)
marketing (MBA)
public administration (MBA, MM)

College of Information Systems and Technology
Programs in:
management (MIS)
technology management (MBA)

■ UNIVERSITY OF PHOENIX–NORTH FLORIDA CAMPUS

Jacksonville, FL 32216-0959
http://www.phoenix.edu/

Proprietary, coed, comprehensive institution. *Computer facilities:* A campuswide network can be accessed from off campus. Online class registration is available. *General application contact:* Campus Information Center, 904-636-6645.

The Artemis School

College of Education
Programs in:
administration and supervision (MA Ed)
curriculum and instruction (MA Ed)
early childhood education (MA Ed)
elementary teacher education (MA Ed)
secondary teacher education (MA Ed)

College of Health and Human Services
Programs in:
health administration (MHA)
health care education (MSN)
health care management (MBA)
nursing (MSN)

John Sperling School of Business
Program in:
business (MBA, MIS, MM)

College of Graduate Business and Management
Programs in:
accounting (MBA)
business administration (MBA)
global management (MBA)
human resources management (MBA, MM)
management (MM)
marketing (MBA)
public administration (MBA, MM)

College of Information Systems and Technology
Programs in:
information systems (MIS)
management (MIS)

■ UNIVERSITY OF PHOENIX–SOUTH FLORIDA CAMPUS

Fort Lauderdale, FL 33309
http://www.phoenix.edu/

Proprietary, coed, comprehensive institution. *Computer facilities:* Computer purchase and lease plans are available. A campuswide network can be accessed from off campus.

Online class registration is available. *General application contact:* Campus Information Center, 954-832-5503.

The Artemis School

College of Education
Programs in:
administration and supervision (MA Ed)
curriculum and instruction (MA Ed)
early childhood education (MA Ed)
elementary teacher education (MA Ed)
secondary teacher education (MA Ed)

College of Health and Human Services
Programs in:
health administration (MHA)
health care education (MSN)
health care management (MBA)
nursing (MSN)

John Sperling School of Business
Program in:
business (MBA, MIS, MM)

College of Graduate Business and Management
Programs in:
accounting (MBA)
business administration (MBA)
global management (MBA)
human resource management (MBA)
human resources management (MM)
management (MM)
marketing (MBA)
public administration (MBA, MM)

College of Information Systems and Technology
Programs in:
management (MIS)
technology management (MBA)

■ UNIVERSITY OF PHOENIX–WEST FLORIDA CAMPUS
Temple Terrace, FL 33637
http://www.phoenix.edu/

Proprietary, coed, comprehensive institution. *Computer facilities:* Computer purchase and lease plans are available. A campuswide network can be accessed from off campus. Online class registration is available. *General application contact:* Campus Information Center, 813-626-7911.

The Artemis School

College of Education
Programs in:
administration and supervision (MA Ed)
curriculum and instruction (MA Ed)
curriculum and technology (MA Ed)
early childhood education (MA Ed)
elementary teacher education (MA Ed)
secondary teacher education (MA Ed)

College of Health and Human Services
Programs in:
health administration (MHA)
health care education (MSN)
health care management (MBA)
nursing (MSN)

The John Sperling School of Business
Program in:
business (MBA, MIS, MM)

College of Graduate Business and Management
Programs in:
accounting (MBA)
business administration (MBA)
global management (MBA)
human resources management (MBA, MM)
management (MM)
marketing (MBA)
public administration (MBA, MM)

College of Information Systems and Technology
Programs in:
information systems (MIS)
technology management (MBA)

■ UNIVERSITY OF SOUTH FLORIDA
Tampa, FL 33620-9951
http://www.usf.edu/

State-supported, coed, university. CGS member. *Graduate faculty:* 1,094 full-time (426 women), 135 part-time/adjunct (75 women). *Computer facilities:* Computer purchase and lease plans are available. 825 computers available on campus for general student use. A campuswide network can be accessed from student residence rooms and from off campus. Online class registration is available. *Graduate expenses:* Tuition, state resident: full-time $2624.40; part-time $291.60 per credit hour. Tuition, nonresident: full-time $7822; part-time $869.13 per credit hour. *General application contact:* Dr. Karen Liller, Interim Dean, Graduate School/Associate Vice President for Research and Innovation, 813-974-2846.

Center for Entrepreneurship
Dr. Michael W. Fountain, Director
Program in:
entrepreneurship (MS, Graduate Certificate)

College of Medicine
Stephen K. Klasko, Dean
Programs in:
aging and neuroscience (MSMS)
allergy, immunology and infectious disease (PhD)
anatomy (PhD)
biochemistry and molecular biology (MS, PhD)
clinical and translational research (MSMS, PhD)
health sciences (MSMS)
medical microbiology and immunology (PhD)
medical science (MSMS)
medicine (MD, MS, MSMS, DPT, PhD)
molecular medicine (PhD)
molecular pharmacology and physiology (PhD)
neuroscience (PhD)
pathology (PhD)
pharmacology and therapeutics (PhD)
physiology and biophysics (PhD)
women's health (MSMS)

School of Physical Therapy
David Newman, Coordinator
Program in:
physical therapy (MS, DPT)

Graduate School
Dr. Karen D. Liller, Interim Dean
Programs in:
applied behavior analysis (MA)
cancer biology (PhD)

College of Arts and Sciences
Dr. Eric Eisenberg, Interim Dean
Programs in:
Africana studies (MLA)
aging studies (PhD)
American studies (MA)
analytical chemistry (MS, PhD)
applied anthropology (MA, PhD)
applied physics (PhD)
arts and sciences (MA, MFA, MLA, MPA, MS, MSW, MURP, Au D, PhD, Graduate Certificate)
biochemistry (MS, PhD)
cell biology and molecular biology (MS)
classics: latin/greek (MA)
clinical psychology (MA, PhD)
coastal marine biology (MS)
coastal marine biology and ecology (PhD)
cognitive and neural sciences (MA, PhD)
communication (MA, PhD)
communication sciences and disorders (MA, MS, Au D, PhD)
computational chemistry (MS, PhD)
conservation biology (MS, PhD)
criminal justice administration (MA)
criminology (MA, PhD)
Cuban studies (Graduate Certificate)
English (MA, MFA, PhD)
environmental chemistry (MS, PhD)
environmental science and policy (MS)
French (MA)
geography (MA, MURP, PhD)
geology (MS, PhD)
gerontology (MA)
history (MA, PhD)
industrial-organizational psychology (MA, PhD)
inorganic chemistry (MS, PhD)
Latin American and Caribbean studies (Graduate Certificate)

University of South Florida (continued)
Latin American Caribbean and Latino Studies (MA)
Latin American, Caribbean and Latino studies (MA)
liberal arts (MLA)
library and information science (MA)
linguistics (MA)
linguistics: ESL (MA)
mass communications (MA)
mathematics (MA, PhD, Graduate Certificate)
molecular and cell biology (PhD)
organic chemistry (MS)
philosophy (MA, PhD)
physical chemistry (MS, PhD)
physics (MS)
political science (MA)
polymer chemistry (MS, PhD)
public administration (MPA)
rehabilitation and mental health counseling (MA)
religious studies (MA)
social work (MSW, PhD)
sociology (MA, PhD)
Spanish (MA)
statistics (MA, Graduate Certificate)
women's studies (MA)

College of Business Administration
Dr. Robert Forsythe, Dean
Programs in:
accounting (M Acc)
business administration (M Acc, MA, MBA, MS, MSM, PhD)
economics (MA, PhD)
finance (MS)
management information systems (MS)

College of Education
Programs in:
adult education (MA, Ed D, PhD, Ed S)
behavior disorders (MA)
career and technical education (MA)
career and workforce education (PhD)
college student affairs (M Ed)
counselor education (MA, PhD, Ed S)
early childhood education (M Ed, MA, PhD)
education (M Ed, MA, MAT, Ed D, PhD, Ed S)
educational leadership (M Ed, Ed D, Ed S)
elementary education (MA, MAT)
English education (M Ed, MA, MAT, PhD)
exceptional student education (MA, MAT)
exercise science (MA)
foreign language education/ESOL (M Ed, MA, MAT)
gifted education (MA)
higher education/community college teaching (MA, Ed D, PhD)
instructional technology (M Ed, PhD, Ed S)
interdisciplinary (PhD, Ed S)
mathematics education (M Ed, MA, MAT, PhD, Ed S)
measurement and evaluation (M Ed, PhD, Ed S)
mental retardation (MA)
physical education teacher preparation (MA)
reading/language arts (MA, PhD, Ed S)
school psychology (PhD, Ed S)
science education (M Ed, MA, MAT, PhD)
second language acquisition/instructional technology (PhD)
secondary education (M Ed, PhD)
secondary education/TESOL (M Ed)
social science education (M Ed, MA, MAT)
special education (PhD)
specific learning disabilities (MA)
teaching and learning in the content area (PhD)
vocational education (Ed S)

College of Engineering
Dr. John Wieneck, Dean
Programs in:
biomedical engineering (MSBE, MSES, PhD)
chemical engineering (MCHE, ME, MSCH, MSES, PhD)
civil and environmental engineering (MEVE, MSES, MSEV)
civil engineering (MCE, MSCE, PhD)
computer science (MSCP, MSCS)
computer science and engineering (ME, MSES, PhD)
electrical engineering (ME, MSEE, MSES, PhD)
engineering (ME)
engineering management (MSEM)
engineering science (PhD)
industrial engineering (MIE, MSIE, PhD)
materials science and engineering (MSE)
mechanical engineering (ME, MME, MSES, MSME, PhD)

College of Marine Science
Dr. William T. Hogarth, Dean
Program in:
marine science (MS, PhD)

College of Nursing
Dr. Patricia A. Burns, Dean
Program in:
nursing (MS, DNP, PhD)

College of Public Health
Dr. Donna J. Petersen, Dean
Programs in:
community and family health (MPH, MSPH, DPH, PhD)
environmental and occupational health (MPH, MSPH, PhD)
epidemiology and biostatistics (MPH, MSPH, PhD)
global health (MPH, MSPH, DPH, PhD)
health policy and management (MHA, MPH, MSPH, PhD)
public health (MHA, MPH, MSPH, DPH, PhD)
public health practice (MPH)

College of The Arts
Ron Jones, Dean
Programs in:
architecture and community design (M Arch)
art history (MA)
chamber music (MM)
composition (MM)
conducting (MM)
electro-acoustic music (MM)
jazz studies (MM)
music (MA)
performance (MM)
piano pedagogy (MM)
studio art (MFA)
theory (MM)
visual and performing arts (M Arch, MA, MFA, MM, PhD)

■ THE UNIVERSITY OF TAMPA

Tampa, FL 33606-1490
http://www.ut.edu/

Independent, coed, comprehensive institution. CGS member. *Graduate faculty:* 57 full-time (27 women), 28 part-time/adjunct (15 women). *Computer facilities:* Computer purchase and lease plans are available. 528 computers available on campus for general student use. A campuswide network can be accessed from student residence rooms and from off campus. Online class registration is available. *Graduate expenses:* Tuition: full-time $7552; part-time $472 per credit hour. Required fees: $70; $70 per year. *General application contact:* Karen Full, Director of Admissions, Graduate and Continuing Studies, 813-257-3642.

John H. Sykes College of Business
Dr. Don Morrill, Associate Dean, Graduate and Continuing Studies
Programs in:
accounting (MBA, MS)
economics (MBA)
entrepreneurship and innovation (MBA)
finance (MBA, MS)
information systems management (MBA)
international business (MBA)
management (MBA)
marketing (MBA, MS)
nonprofit management (MBA)

Nursing Program
Dr. Maria Warda, Director
Programs in:
adult nurse practitioner (MSN)
family nurse practitioner (MSN)

Program in Teaching
Dr. Martha Harrison, Associate Professor of Education
Programs in:
curriculum and instruction (M Ed)
math education (MAT)
science education (MAT)
social science education (MAT)

■ UNIVERSITY OF WEST FLORIDA

Pensacola, FL 32514-5750
http://www.uwf.edu/

State-supported, coed, comprehensive institution. CGS member. *Graduate faculty:* 126 full-time (44 women), 31 part-time/adjunct (14 women). *Computer facilities:* Computer purchase and lease plans are available. 1,100 computers available on campus for general student use. A campuswide network can be accessed from student residence rooms and from off campus. Online class registration is available. *Graduate expenses:* Tuition, state resident: full-time $6095; part-time $253.97 per credit hour. Tuition, nonresident: full-time $21,919; part-time $913.31 per credit hour. *General application contact:* Terry McCray, Assistant Director of Graduate Admissions, 850-473-7718.

College of Arts and Sciences: Arts
Dr. Jane Halonen, Dean
Programs in:
arts and sciences: arts (MA)
communication arts (MA)
counseling (MA)
counseling-licensed mental health counselor (MA)
creative writing (MA)
general (MA)
historic preservation (MA)
history (MA)
industrial-organizational (MA)
interdisciplinary humanities (MA)
literature (MA)
political science (MA)
public history (MA)

Division of Anthropology and Archaeology
Dr. John Bratten, Interim Chair
Programs in:
anthropology (MA)
historical archaeology (MA)

College of Arts and Sciences: Sciences
Dr. Jane Halonen, Dean
Programs in:
arts and sciences: sciences (MA, MPH, MS, MST)
computer science (MS)
environmental science (MS)
mathematical sciences (MS)
software engineering (MS)

School of Allied Health and Life Sciences
Dr. George L. Stewart, Chairperson
Programs in:
allied health and life sciences (MA, MPH, MS, MST)
biological chemistry (MS)
biology (MS)
biology education (MST)
biotechnology (MS)
coastal zone studies (MS)
environmental biology (MS)
public health (MPH)

College of Business
Dr. F. Edward Ranelli, Dean
Programs in:
accounting (M Acc, MA)
business (M Acc, MA, MBA)
business administration (MBA)

College of Professional Studies
Dr. Donald Chu, Dean
Programs in:
acquisition and contract administration (MSA)
biomedical/pharmaceutical (MSA)
career and technical studies (M Ed)
clinical teaching (MA)
college student personnel administration (M Ed)
criminal justice administration (MSA)
curriculum and instruction (Ed D, Ed S)
curriculum and instruction: special education (M Ed)
education (M Ed, MA)
education leadership (MSA)
educational leadership (M Ed, Ed S)
elementary education (M Ed)
guidance and counseling (M Ed)
habilitative science (MA)
healthcare administration (MSA)
instructional technology (M Ed)
middle and secondary level education and ESOL (M Ed)
nursing administration (MSA)
primary education (M Ed)
public administration (MSA)
reading education (M Ed)
special education (M Ed)

Division of Health, Leisure, and Exercise Science
Dr. John Todorovich, Chairperson
Programs in:
exercise science (MS)
health education (MS)
health, leisure, and exercise science (MS)
physical education (MS)

School of Justice Studies and Social Work
Program in:
social work (MSW)

Georgia

■ ALBANY STATE UNIVERSITY

Albany, GA 31705-2717
http://www.asurams.edu/

State-supported, coed, primarily women, comprehensive institution. CGS member. *Graduate faculty:* 79 full-time (29 women), 15 part-time/adjunct (12 women). *Computer facilities:* 1,000 computers available on campus for general student use. A campuswide network can be accessed from student residence rooms and from off campus. Online class registration is available. *Graduate expenses:* Tuition, state resident: full-time $4296; part-time $154 per semester hour. Tuition, nonresident: full-time $15,338; part-time $614 per semester hour. Required fees: $306 per semester. Tuition and fees vary according to course load. *General application contact:* Diane P. Frink, Graduate Admissions Counselor, 229-430-5118.

College of Arts and Humanities
Dr. Leroy Bynum, Dean
Programs in:
arts and humanities (MPA, MS)
community and economic development (MPA)
criminal justice (MPA)
fiscal management (MPA)
general management (MPA)
health administration and policy (MPA)
human resources management (MPA)
public policy (MPA)
water resource management and policy (MPA)

College of Business
Dr. Michael Rogers, Interim Dean
Program in:
business (MBA)

College of Education
Dr. Wilburn Campbell, Dean
Programs in:
biology (M Ed)
chemistry (M Ed)
early childhood education (M Ed)
education (M Ed, Certificate, Ed S)
educational leadership (M Ed, Certificate, Ed S)
English education (M Ed)
health and physical education (M Ed)
middle grades education (M Ed)
music education (M Ed)
school counseling (M Ed)
special education (M Ed)

College of Sciences and Health Professions
Dr. Joyce Johnson, Dean
Programs in:
criminal justice (MS)
criminal justice and forensic science (MS)
mathematics education (M Ed)
nursing (MSN)
science education (M Ed)

■ AMERICAN INTERCONTINENTAL UNIVERSITY BUCKHEAD CAMPUS

Atlanta, GA 30326-1016
http://www.aiuniv.edu/

Proprietary, coed, comprehensive institution. CGS member. *Computer facilities:* 313

American InterContinental University Buckhead Campus (continued)
computers available on campus for general student use. A campuswide network can be accessed. Online class registration is available. *General application contact:* Vice President Admissions and Marketing, 404-965-5719.

Program in Business Administration

Programs in:
accounting and finance (MBA)
management (MBA)
marketing (MBA)

■ AMERICAN INTERCONTINENTAL UNIVERSITY DUNWOODY CAMPUS
Atlanta, GA 30328
http://www.aiuniv.edu/

Proprietary, coed, comprehensive institution. CGS member. *Computer facilities:* A campuswide network can be accessed. Online class registration is available. *General application contact:* Information Contact, 888-754-4422 Ext. 8072.

Program in Global Technology Management

Program in:
global technology management (MBA)

Program in Information Technology

Program in:
information technology (MIT)

■ ARMSTRONG ATLANTIC STATE UNIVERSITY
Savannah, GA 31419-1997
http://www.armstrong.edu/

State-supported, coed, primarily women, comprehensive institution. *Computer facilities:* 230 computers available on campus for general student use. A campuswide network can be accessed from student residence rooms and from off campus. Online class registration is available. *General application contact:* Assistant Vice President for Academic Affairs, Graduate Studies and Sponsored Programs, 912-921-5711.

School of Graduate Studies

Programs in:
adult education (M Ed)
computer science (MS)
criminal justice (MS)
curriculum and instruction (M Ed)
early childhood education (M Ed)
education (M Ed)
elementary education (M Ed)
health services administration (MHSA)
history (MA)
liberal and professional studies (MALPS)
middle grades education (M Ed)
nursing (MSN)
physical therapy (DPT)
public health (MPH)
secondary education (M Ed)
special education (M Ed)
sports health sciences (MSSM)

■ AUGUSTA STATE UNIVERSITY
Augusta, GA 30904-2200
http://www.aug.edu/

State-supported, coed, comprehensive institution. *Graduate faculty:* 50 full-time (24 women), 34 part-time/adjunct (25 women). *Computer facilities:* 325 computers available on campus for general student use. A campuswide network can be accessed from off campus. Online class registration is available. *Graduate expenses:* Tuition, state resident: full-time $2520; part-time $140 per credit hour. Tuition, nonresident: full-time $10,080; part-time $560 per credit hour. Required fees: $546; $273 per semester. *General application contact:* Katherine Sweeney, Director of Admissions/Registrar, 706-737-1405.

Graduate Studies

Dr. Samuel Sullivan, Vice President for Academic Affairs

College of Arts and Sciences
Dr. Robert R. Parham, Dean
Programs in:
arts and sciences (MPA, MS)
political science (MPA)
psychology (MS)

College of Education
Dr. Richard Harrison, Dean
Programs in:
counseling/guidance (M Ed)
curriculum/instruction (M Ed)
education (M Ed, MAT, Ed S)
educational leadership (M Ed, Ed S)
health and physical education (M Ed)
special education (M Ed, Ed S)
teaching/learning (MAT, Ed S)

Hull College of Business
Dr. Marc D. Miller, Dean
Program in:
business (MBA)

■ BRENAU UNIVERSITY
Gainesville, GA 30501
http://www.brenau.edu/

Independent, women only, comprehensive institution. *Graduate faculty:* 54 full-time (35 women), 69 part-time/adjunct (34 women). *Computer facilities:* 200 computers available on campus for general student use. A campuswide network can be accessed from student residence rooms. Online class registration is available. *General application contact:* Michelle Leavell, Graduate Admissions Specialist, 770-538-4390.

Graduate Programs

Dr. James Southerland, Vice President for Academic Services/Dean of Faculty

School of Business and Mass Communication
Dr. William S. Lightfoot, Dean
Programs in:
accounting (MBA)
advanced management studies (MBA)
business administration (MBA)
healthcare management (MBA)
organizational leadership (MS)
project management (MBA)

School of Education
Dr. Lora Bailey, Dean
Programs in:
early childhood (Ed S)
early childhood education (M Ed, MAT)
middle grades (Ed S)
middle grades education (M Ed, MAT)
secondary education (MAT)
special education (M Ed, MAT)

School of Fine Arts and Humanities
Dr. Andrea Birch, Dean
Program in:
interior design (MID)

School of Health and Science
Dr. Gale Starich, Dean
Programs in:
family nurse practitioner (MSN)
nurse educator (MSN)
nursing management (MSN)
occupational therapy (MS)
psychology (MS)

■ CLARK ATLANTA UNIVERSITY
Atlanta, GA 30314
http://www.cau.edu/

Independent-religious, coed, university. CGS member. *Graduate faculty:* 97 full-time (28 women), 29 part-time/adjunct (13 women). *Computer facilities:* 650 computers available on campus for general student use. A campuswide network can be accessed from student residence rooms. Online class registration is available. *Graduate expenses:* Tuition: full-time $12,240; part-time $680 per credit hour. Required fees: $710; $355 per semester. *General application contact:* Michelle Clark-Davis, Graduate Program Admissions, 404-880-8709.

School of Arts and Sciences

Dr. Shirley Williams-Kirksey, Dean
Programs in:
African-American studies (MA, DAH)
Africana women's studies (MA, DAH)
arts and sciences (MA, MPA, MS, DAH, PhD)
biology (MS, PhD)
chemistry (MS, PhD)
computer and information science (MS)
criminal justice (MA)
English (MA, DAH)

history (MA, DAH)
mathematical sciences (MS)
physics (MS)
political science (MA, PhD)
public administration (MPA)
Romance languages (MA, DAH)
sociology (MA)

School of Business Administration
Dr. Edward Davis, Interim Dean
Programs in:
accounting (MA)
business administration (MA, MBA)
economics (MA)

School of Education
Dr. Trevor Turner, Interim Dean
Programs in:
counseling and psychological studies (MA)
curriculum (MA, MAT)
education (MA, MAT, Ed D, Ed S)
educational leadership (MA, Ed D, Ed S)

School of Social Work
Dr. Vimala Pillari, Interim Dean
Program in:
social work (MSW, PhD)

■ COLUMBUS STATE UNIVERSITY
Columbus, GA 31907-5645
http://www.colstate.edu/

State-supported, coed, comprehensive institution. *Graduate faculty:* 59 full-time (28 women), 36 part-time/adjunct (15 women). *Computer facilities:* 311 computers available on campus for general student use. A campuswide network can be accessed from student residence rooms and from off campus. Online class registration is available. *Graduate expenses:* Full-time $3410; part-time $143 per credit hour. Tuition, state resident: full-time $3411; part-time $143 per credit hour. Tuition, nonresident: full-time $13,634; part-time $569 per credit hour. Required fees: $1348. *General application contact:* Katie Thornton, Graduate Admissions Specialist, 706-568-2035.

Graduate Studies
Dr. Inessa Levi, Vice President for Academic Affairs

College of Arts and Letters
Dr. James Patrick McHenry, Acting Dean
Programs in:
art education (M Ed)
arts and letters (M Ed, MM, MPA)
justice administration (MPA)
music education (MM)

College of Education
Dr. David Rock, Dean
Programs in:
accomplished teaching (M Ed)
community counseling (MS)
curriculum and leadership (Ed D)
early childhood education (M Ed, Ed S)
education (M Ed, MS, Ed D, Ed S)
educational leadership (M Ed, Ed S)
instructional technology (MS)
middle grades education (M Ed, Ed S)
physical education (M Ed)
school counseling (M Ed)
secondary education (M Ed, Ed S)
special education (M Ed)

College of Science
Dr. Glenn Stokes, Dean
Programs in:
applied computer science (MS)
environmental science (MS)
health services administration (MPA)
science (MPA, MS)

D. Abbott Turner College of Business
Dr. Linda U. Hadley, Dean
Program in:
business administration (MBA)

■ DEVRY UNIVERSITY
Decatur, GA 30030-2556
http://www.devry.edu/

Proprietary, coed, comprehensive institution. *Computer facilities:* Computer purchase and lease plans are available. A campuswide network can be accessed from off campus. Online class registration is available.

Keller Graduate School of Management
Program in:
management (MAFM, MBA, MHRM, MISM, MNCM, MPA, MPM, Graduate Certificate)

■ EMORY UNIVERSITY
Atlanta, GA 30322-1100
http://www.emory.edu/

Independent-religious, coed, university. CGS member. *Graduate faculty:* 3,129 full-time (1,172 women), 547 part-time/adjunct (286 women). *Computer facilities:* Computer purchase and lease plans are available. 600 computers available on campus for general student use. A campuswide network can be accessed from student residence rooms and from off campus. Online class registration is available. *Graduate expenses:* Tuition: full-time $32,800; part-time $1025 per credit hour. Tuition and fees vary according to course load and program. *General application contact:* Kharen Fulton, Director of Admissions, 404-727-0184.

Candler School of Theology
Missy Page, Registrar
Programs in:
formation and witness (M Div)
leadership in church and community (M Div)
religion and race (M Div)
religion, health and science (M Div)
scripture and interpretation (M Div)
society and personality (M Div)
theology (MTS, Th M, Th D)
theology and ethics (M Div)
theology and the arts (M Div)
traditions of the church (M Div)
women and religion (M Div)

Goizueta Business School
Program in:
business (EMBA, MBA, WEMBA, PhD)

Graduate School of Arts and Sciences
Programs in:
anthropology (PhD)
art history (PhD)
arts and sciences (M Ed, MA, MAT, MM, MPH, MS, MSM, MSPH, PhD, Certificate, DAST)
biophysics (PhD)
biostatistics (MPH, MSPH, PhD)
chemistry (PhD)
choral conducting (MM, MSM)
clinical psychology (PhD)
clinical research (MS)
cognition and development (PhD)
comparative literature (PhD, Certificate)
computer science (MS)
condensed matter physics (PhD)
economics (PhD)
English (PhD)
film studies (Certificate)
French (PhD, Certificate)
French and educational studies (PhD)
history (PhD)
Jewish studies (MA)
mathematics (PhD)
Middle Eastern studies (PhD)
neuroscience and animal behavior (PhD)
non-linear physics (PhD)
nursing (PhD)
organ performance (MM, MSM)
philosophy (PhD)
political science (PhD)
psychoanalytic studies (PhD)
public health informatics (MSPH)
radiological physics (PhD)
religion (PhD)
sociology (MA, PhD)
soft condensed matter physics (PhD)
solid-state physics (PhD)
Spanish (PhD, Certificate)
statistical physics (PhD)
women studies (Certificate)
women's studies (PhD)

Division of Biological and Biomedical Sciences
Dr. Keith Wilkinson, Director
Programs in:
biochemistry, cell and developmental biology (PhD)
biological and biomedical sciences (PhD)
genetics and molecular biology (PhD)
immunology and molecular pathogenesis (PhD)
microbiology and molecular genetics (PhD)

Emory University (continued)
molecular and systems pharmacology (PhD)
neuroscience (PhD)
nutrition and health sciences (PhD)
population biology, ecology and evolution (PhD)

Division of Educational Studies
Programs in:
educational studies (MA, PhD, DAST)
middle grades teaching (M Ed, MAT)
secondary teaching (M Ed, MAT)

Division of Religion
Program in:
religion (PhD)

Graduate Institute of Liberal Arts
Program in:
liberal arts (PhD)

Nell Hodgson Woodruff School of Nursing
Programs in:
adult and elder health advanced practice nursing (MSN)
emergency nurse practitioner (MSN)
family nurse practitioner (MSN)
family nurse-midwife (MSN)
leadership in healthcare (MSN)
nurse midwifery (MSN)
nursing administration (MSN)
pediatric advanced nursing practice (MSN)
public health nursing (MSN)
women's health nurse practitioner (MSN)

Rollins School of Public Health
Programs in:
applied epidemiology (MPH)
behavioral sciences and health education (MPH)
biostatistics and bioinformatics (MPH, MSPH)
environmental and occupational health (MPH, MSPH)
epidemiology (MPH, MSPH, PhD)
global demography (MSPH)
global environmental health (MPH)
health policy (MPH)
health policy research (MSPH)
health services management (MPH)
healthcare outcomes (MPH)
prevention science (MPH)
public health (MPH, MSPH, PhD, MM Sc/MPH)
public health informatics (MSPH)
public nutrition (MSPH)

School of Law
David F. Partlett, Dean
Program in:
law (JD, LL M, Certificate)

School of Medicine
Programs in:
anesthesiology (MM Sc)
anesthesiology/patient monitoring systems (MM Sc)
biomedical engineering (PhD)
medicine (MD, MM Sc, DPT, PhD)
ophthalmic technology (MM Sc)
physical therapy (DPT)
physician assistant (MM Sc)

■ FORT VALLEY STATE UNIVERSITY
Fort Valley, GA 31030-4313
http://www.fvsu.edu/

State-supported, coed, comprehensive institution. *Computer facilities:* 633 computers available on campus for general student use. A campuswide network can be accessed from off campus. Online grade reports available. *General application contact:* Director of Admissions, 478-825-6672.

College of Graduate Studies and Extended Education
Programs in:
animal science (MS)
environmental health (MPH)
guidance and counseling (Ed S)
mental health counseling (MS)
rehabilitation counseling (MS)

■ GEORGIA COLLEGE & STATE UNIVERSITY
Milledgeville, GA 31061
http://www.gcsu.edu/

State-supported, coed, comprehensive institution. *Graduate faculty:* 321 full-time (164 women). *Computer facilities:* Computer purchase and lease plans are available. 180 computers available on campus for general student use. A campuswide network can be accessed from student residence rooms and from off campus. Online class registration is available. *Graduate expenses:* Full-time $3942; part-time $219 per semester hour. Tuition, state resident: full-time $3942; part-time $876 per semester hour. Tuition, nonresident: full-time $15,768; part-time $876 per semester hour. Required fees: $930; $465 per semester. One-time fee: $100. Tuition and fees vary according to campus/location. *General application contact:* Maryllis Wolfgang, Director, Graduate Admissions, 478-445-6289.

Graduate School
Maryllis Wolfgang, Director of Graduate Programs

College of Arts and Sciences
Kenneth Proctor, Dean
Programs in:
biology (MS)
creative writing (MFA)
criminal justice (MS)
English (MA)
history (advanced studies option) (MA)
history (predoctoral option) (MA)
liberal arts and sciences (MA, MFA, MM Ed, MPA, MS, MSA)
logistics (MSA)
logistics management (MSA)
music and theatre (MM Ed)
public administration (MPA)
public history (MA)

College of Health Sciences
Dr. Sandra Gangstead, Dean
Programs in:
adult health (MSN)
family nurse practitioner (MSN)
health promotion (M Ed)
health sciences (M Ed, MMT, MSN)
music therapy (MMT)
nursing administration (MSN)
outdoor education (M Ed)

The John H. Lounsbury College of Education
Dr. Linda Irwin-Devitis, Dean
Programs in:
curriculum and instruction (Ed S)
early childhood education (M Ed, Ed S)
education (M Ed, MAT, Ed S)
educational leadership (M Ed, Ed S)
instructional technology (M Ed)
middle grades education (M Ed, Ed S)
secondary education (M Ed, MAT)
special education (M Ed, MAT)
special education and educational leadership (M Ed, MAT, Ed S)

The J. Whitney Bunting School of Business
Dr. Dale Young, Interim Dean
Programs in:
accountancy (MACCT)
business (MBA)
information systems (MIS)

■ GEORGIA INSTITUTE OF TECHNOLOGY
Atlanta, GA 30332-0001
http://www.gatech.edu/

State-supported, coed, primarily men, university. CGS member. *Computer facilities:* Computer purchase and lease plans are available. 2,018 computers available on campus for general student use. A campuswide network can be accessed from student residence rooms and from off campus. Online class registration is available. *General application contact:* Manager, Graduate Academic and Enrollment Services, 404-894-4612.

Graduate Studies and Research
Programs in:
algorithms, combinatorics, and optimization (PhD)
statistics (MS Stat)

College of Architecture
Programs in:
architecture (M Arch, MCRP, MS, PhD)
building construction (PhD)
city and regional planning (PhD)
economic development (MCRP)

environmental planning and management (MCRP)
geographic information systems (MCRP)
integrated facility management (MS)
integrated project delivery systems (MS)
land and community development (MCRP)
land use planning (MCRP)
residential construction development (MS)
transportation (MCRP)
urban design (MCRP)

College of Computing
Programs in:
algorithms, combinatorics, and optimization (PhD)
computational science and engineering (MS, PhD)
computer science (MS, MSCS, PhD)
human computer interaction (MSHCI)
human-centered computing (PhD)
information security (MS)

College of Engineering
Programs in:
aerospace engineering (MS, MSAE, PhD)
algorithms, combinatorics, and optimization (PhD)
bioengineering (MS Bio E, PhD)
bioinformatics (PhD)
biomedical engineering (MS Bio E, PhD)
chemical engineering (MS Ch E, PhD)
civil engineering (MS, MSCE, PhD)
electrical and computer engineering (MS, MSEE, PhD)
engineering (MS, MS Bio E, MS Ch E, MS Env E, MS Poly, MS Stat, MSAE, MSCE, MSEE, MSESM, MSHS, MSIE, MSME, MSNE, MSOR, PhD)
engineering science and mechanics (MS, MSESM, PhD)
environmental engineering (MS, MS Env E, PhD)
health systems (MSHS)
industrial and systems engineering (MS, MS Stat, MSIE, PhD)
industrial engineering (MS, MSIE)
materials science and engineering (MS, PhD)
mechanical engineering (MS, MS Bio E, MSME, PhD)
medical physics (MS)
nuclear and radiological engineering (MSNE, PhD)
nuclear and radiological engineering and medical physics (MS, MSNE, PhD)
operations research (MSOR, PhD)
paper science and engineering (MS, PhD)
polymer, textile and fiber engineering (MS, PhD)
polymers (MS Poly)
statistics (MS Stat)

College of Management
Programs in:
accounting (MBA, PhD)
e-commerce (Certificate)
engineering entrepreneurship (MBA)
entrepreneurship (Certificate)
finance (MBA, PhD)
information technology management (MBA, PhD)
international business (MBA, Certificate)
management (EMBA, MBA, MS, PhD, Certificate)
management of technology (Certificate)
marketing (MBA, PhD)
operations management (MBA, PhD)
organizational behavior (MBA, PhD)
quantitative and computational finance (MS)
strategic management (MBA, PhD)

College of Sciences
Programs in:
algorithms, combinatorics, and optimization (PhD)
applied biology (MS, PhD)
applied mathematics (MS)
atmospheric chemistry, aerosols and clouds (MS, PhD)
bioinformatics (MS, PhD)
biology (MS)
chemistry and biochemistry (MS, MS Chem, PhD)
dynamics of weather and climate (MS, PhD)
geochemistry (MS, PhD)
geophysics (MS, PhD)
human computer interaction (MSHCI)
mathematics (PhD)
oceanography (MS, PhD)
paleoclimate (MS, PhD)
physics (MS, PhD)
planetary science (MS, PhD)
prosthetics and orthotics (MS)
psychology (MS, MS Psy, PhD)
quantitative and computational finance (MS)
remote sensing (MS, PhD)
sciences (MS, MS Chem, MS Phys, MS Psy, MS Stat, MSA Phy, MSHCI, PhD)
statistics (MS Stat)

Ivan Allen College of Policy and International Affairs
Programs in:
digital media (MS, PhD)
economics (MS)
history and sociology of technology and science (MS, PhD)
human computer interaction (MSHCI)
international affairs (MS Int A, PhD)
policy and international affairs (MS, MS Int A, MS Pub P, MSHCI, MSIDT, PhD)
public policy (MS Pub P, PhD)

■ GEORGIA SOUTHERN UNIVERSITY
Statesboro, GA 30460
http://www.georgiasouthern.edu/

State-supported, coed, university. CGS member. *Graduate faculty:* 482 full-time (215 women), 19 part-time/adjunct (9 women). *Computer facilities:* 2,385 computers available on campus for general student use. A campuswide network can be accessed from student residence rooms and from off campus. Online class registration is available. *Graduate expenses:* Tuition, state resident: full-time $3840; part-time $160 per semester hour. Tuition, nonresident: full-time $15,336; part-time $639 per semester hour. Required fees: $1152. *General application contact:* Office of Graduate Admissions, 912-478-5384.

Jack N. Averitt College of Graduate Studies
Dr. Dick Diebolt, Associate Dean of Graduate Studies and Research

Allen E. Paulson College of Science and Technology
Dr. Bret Danilowicz, Dean
Programs in:
biology (MS)
mathematics (MS)
mechanical and electrical engineering technology (M Tech)
science and technology (M Tech, MS)

College of Business Administration
Dr. Ron Shiffler, Dean
Programs in:
accounting (M Acc)
applied economics (MS)
business administration (M Acc, MBA, MS)

College of Education
Dr. Lucindia Chance, Dean
Programs in:
accomplished teaching (M Ed)
art education (MAT)
business education (MAT)
counselor education (M Ed, Ed S)
curriculum studies (Ed D)
early childhood education (MAT)
education (M Ed, MAT, Ed D, Ed S)
educational administration (Ed D)
educational leadership (M Ed, Ed S)
English education (M Ed, MAT)
French education (M Ed)
health and physical education (M Ed)
higher education (M Ed)
instructional technology (M Ed)
mathematics education (M Ed, MAT)
middle grades education (M Ed, MAT)
reading education (M Ed)
school psychology (M Ed, Ed S)
science education (M Ed, MAT)
secondary and p-12 education (M Ed)
social science education (M Ed, MAT)
Spanish education (MAT)
special education (M Ed, MAT)
teaching and learning (Ed S)
technology education (M Ed)

College of Health and Human Sciences
Dr. Frederick Whitt, Dean
Programs in:
clinical nurse specialist (MSN, Certificate)

Georgia Southern University (continued)
health and human sciences (MS, MSN, DNP, Certificate)
health and kinesiology (MS)
nurse practitioner (MSN, Certificate)
nursing science (DNP)
recreation administration (MS)
rural community health nurse practitioner (MSN)
rural community health nurse specialist (Certificate)
rural family nurse practitioner (MSN, Certificate)
sport management (MS)
women's health nurse practitioner (MSN, Certificate)

College of Liberal Arts and Social Sciences
Dr. Sue M. Moore, Dean
Programs in:
English (MA)
fine arts (MFA)
history (MA)
liberal arts and social sciences (MA, MFA, MM, MPA, MS, Psy D)
music (MM)
psychology (MS, Psy D)
public administration (MPA)
sociology and anthropology (MA)
Spanish (MA)

Jiann-Ping Hsu College of Public Health
Dr. Charlie Hardy, Dean
Programs in:
biostatistics (MPH, Dr PH)
community health behavior and education (Dr PH)
community health education (MPH)
environmental health sciences (MPH)
epidemiology (MPH)
health services administration (MHSA)
health services policy management (MPH)
public health (MHSA, MPH, Dr PH)
public health leadership (Dr PH)

■ GEORGIA SOUTHWESTERN STATE UNIVERSITY
Americus, GA 31709-4693
http://www.gsw.edu/

State-supported, coed, comprehensive institution. *Computer facilities:* 550 computers available on campus for general student use. A campuswide network can be accessed from student residence rooms and from off campus. Online class registration is available.

Graduate Studies

School of Business Administration
Program in:
business administration (MBA)

School of Computer and Information Sciences
Programs in:
computer information systems (MS)
computer science (MS)

School of Education
Programs in:
early childhood education (M Ed, Ed S)
health and physical education (M Ed)
middle grades education (M Ed, Ed S)
reading (M Ed)
secondary education (M Ed)
special education (M Ed)

■ GEORGIA STATE UNIVERSITY
Atlanta, GA 30303-3083
http://www.gsu.edu/

State-supported, coed, university. CGS member. *Graduate faculty:* 707 full-time (299 women). *Computer facilities:* 1,000 computers available on campus for general student use. A campuswide network can be accessed from student residence rooms and from off campus. Online class registration is available. *Graduate expenses:* Tuition, state resident: full-time $5722; part-time $239 per credit hour. Tuition, nonresident: full-time $22,878; part-time $954 per credit hour. Required fees: $600 per semester. *General application contact:* Daniel Niccum, Associate Director, 404-413-2049.

Andrew Young School of Policy Studies
Dr. W. Bartley Hildreth, Dean
Programs in:
disaster management (Certificate)
economics (MA, PhD)
non-profit management (Certificate)
planning and economic development (Certificate)
policy studies (MA, MPA, MPP, MS, PhD, Certificate)
public administration (MPA)
public policy (MPP, PhD)

College of Arts and Sciences
Dr. Lauren B. Adamson, Dean
Programs in:
anthropology (MA)
applied and environmental microbiology (MS, PhD)
applied linguistics (MA, PhD)
arts and sciences (M Mu, MA, MA Ed, MFA, MHP, MS, PhD, Certificate, Graduate Certificate)
astronomy (PhD)
cellular and molecular biology and physiology (MS, PhD)
chemistry (MS, PhD)
computer science (MS, PhD)
creative writing (MA, MFA, PhD)
English (MA, PhD)
fiction (MFA)
fiction/poetry (MA, MFA)
film/video/digital imaging (MA)
French (MA, Certificate)
geographic information systems (Certificate)
geography (MA)
geology (MA)
German (MA, Certificate)
heritage preservation (MHP, Certificate)
history (MA, PhD)
human communication and social influence (MA)
hydrogeology (Certificate)
Latin American studies (Certificate)
literary studies (MA, PhD)
mass communication (MA)
mathematics (MA, MS)
mathematics and statistics (PhD)
molecular genetics and biochemistry (MS, PhD)
moving image studies (PhD)
neurobiology and behavior (MS, PhD)
philosophy (MA)
physics (MS, PhD)
poetry (MFA)
political science (MA, PhD)
psychology (MA, PhD)
public communication (PhD)
religious studies (MA)
rhetoric and composition (MA, PhD)
sociology (MA, PhD)
Spanish (MA, Certificate)
translation and interpretation (Certificate)

Ernest G. Welch School of Art and Design
Programs in:
art and design (MA, MA Ed, MFA)
art education (MA Ed)
art history (MA)
studio art (MFA)

Gerontology Institute
Dr. Frank J. Whittington, Director
Program in:
gerontology (MA)

School of Music
W. Dwight Coleman, Director
Program in:
music (M Mu)

Women's Studies Institute
Dr. Susan Talburt, Director
Program in:
women's studies (MA, Graduate Certificate)

College of Education
Dr. Randy W. Kamphaus, Dean
Programs in:
art education (Ed S)
behavior and learning disabilities (M Ed)
communication disorders (M Ed)
counseling psychology (PhD)
counselor education and practice (PhD)
early childhood education (M Ed, MAT, PhD, Ed S)
education (M Ed, MAT, MLM, MS, PhD, Ed S)
education of students with exceptionalities (PhD)

educational leadership (M Ed, PhD, Ed S)
educational psychology (MS, PhD)
educational research (MS, PhD)
English education (M Ed, Ed S)
exercise science (MS)
health and physical education (M Ed)
instructional technology (MS, PhD, Ed S)
kinesiology (PhD)
library media technology (MLM, PhD, Ed S)
library science/media (MLM, MS, PhD, Ed S)
mathematics education (M Ed, PhD, Ed S)
middle childhood education (M Ed, Ed S)
multiple and severe disabilities (M Ed, MAT)
music education (PhD)
professional counseling (MS, PhD, Ed S)
reading instruction (M Ed, PhD, Ed S)
reading, language and literacy (M Ed)
reading, language, and literacy (PhD, Ed S)
rehabilitation counseling (MS)
research, measurements and statistics (PhD)
school counseling (M Ed, Ed S)
school psychology (M Ed, PhD, Ed S)
science education (M Ed, PhD, Ed S)
secondary education (M Ed, PhD, Ed S)
social foundations of education (MS, PhD)
social studies education (M Ed, PhD, Ed S)
sports administration (MS)
sports medicine (MS)
teaching English as a second language (M Ed)

College of Health and Human Sciences
Programs in:
criminal justice (MS)
health and human sciences (MPH, MS, MSW, DPT, PhD, Certificate)

Byrdine F. Lewis School of Nursing
Dr. Barbara C. Woodring, Director
Programs in:
adult health (MS)
adult health nursing (Certificate)
child health (MS)
family nurse practitioner (MS, Certificate)
health promotion, protection and restoration (PhD)
perinatal/women's health (MS)
psychiatric mental health nursing (Certificate)
psychiatric/mental health (MS)
women's health nursing (Certificate)

Institute of Public Health
Dr. Michael P. Eriksen, Director
Program in:
public health (MPH, Certificate)

School of Health Professions
Dr. Lynda Goodfellow, Director
Programs in:
health professions (MS, DPT)
nutrition (MS)
physical therapy (DPT)
respiratory therapy (MS)

School of Social Work
Dr. Nancy Kropf, Director
Program in:
community partnerships (MSW)

College of Law
Program in:
law (JD)

J. Mack Robinson College of Business
Programs in:
accounting/information systems (MBA)
actuarial science (MAS, MBA)
business (EMBA, MAS, MBA, MHA, MIB, MPA, MS, MSHA, MSIS, MSRE, MTX, PMBA, PhD, Certificate)
business analysis (MBA, MS)
computer information systems (MBA, MSIS, PhD)
decision sciences (PhD)
economics (MBA, MS)
enterprise risk management (MBA)
entrepreneurship (MBA)
finance (MBA, MS, PhD)
general business (MBA)
general business administration (EMBA, PMBA)
human resources management (MBA, MS)
information systems consulting (MBA)
information systems risk management (MBA)
international business and information technology (MBA)
international entrepreneurship (MBA)
management (MBA, PhD)
marketing (MBA, MS, PhD)
operations management (MBA, MS)
organization change (MS)
personal financial planning (MBA, MS, Certificate)
personnel employee relations (PhD)
real estate (MBA, MSRE, PhD, Certificate)
risk management and insurance (MBA, MS, PhD, Certificate)
strategic management (PhD)

Institute of Health Administration
Dr. Andrew T. Sumner, Director
Program in:
health administration (MBA, MHA, MSHA)

Institute of International Business
Dr. Tamer Cavusgil, Director
Program in:
international business (MBA, MIB)

School of Accountancy
Dr. Galen R. Sevcik, Interim Director
Programs in:
accountancy (MBA, MPA, MTX, PhD, Certificate)
taxation (MTX)

■ KENNESAW STATE UNIVERSITY
Kennesaw, GA 30144-5591
http://www.kennesaw.edu/

State-supported, coed, comprehensive institution. CGS member. *Graduate faculty:* 221 full-time (88 women), 34 part-time/adjunct (12 women). *Computer facilities:* Computer purchase and lease plans are available. 1,087 computers available on campus for general student use. A campuswide network can be accessed from student residence rooms and from off campus. Online class registration is available. *Graduate expenses:* Tuition, state resident: full-time $3668; part-time $153 per semester hour. Tuition, nonresident: full-time $14,670; part-time $612 per semester hour. Required fees: $474 per semester. *General application contact:* Vilma Marquez, Admissions Counselor, 770-420-4377.

College of Health and Human Services
Dr. Richard Sowell, Dean
Programs in:
advanced care management and leadership (MSN)
applied exercise and health science (MS)
health and human services (MS, MSN, MSW)
primary care nurse practitioner (MSN)
social work (MSW)

College of Humanities and Social Sciences
Dr. Richard Vengroff, Dean
Programs in:
conflict management (MSCM)
humanities and social sciences (MAPW, MPA, MSCM)
professional writing (MAPW)
public administration (MPA)

College of Science and Mathematics
Dr. Laurence I. Peterson, Dean
Programs in:
applied computer science (MSaCS)
applied statistics (MSAS)
information systems (MSIS)
science and mathematics (MSAS, MSIS, MSaCS)

Leland and Clarice C. Bagwell College of Education
Dr. Arlinda Eaton, Dean
Programs in:
adolescent education (M Ed)
education (M Ed, MAT, Ed D, Ed S)
educational leadership (M Ed)
educational leadership technology (M Ed)
elementary and early childhood education (M Ed)
leadership for learning (Ed D, Ed S)
secondary English or mathematics (MAT)

Kennesaw State University (continued)
special education (M Ed)
teaching English to speakers of other languages (M Ed, MAT)

Michael J. Coles College of Business
Dr. Timothy Mescon, Dean
Programs in:
accounting (M Acc)
business (M Acc, MBA)
business administration (MBA)

■ MERCER UNIVERSITY
Macon, GA 31207-0003
http://www.mercer.edu/

Independent-religious, coed, university. *Graduate faculty:* 126 full-time (57 women), 27 part-time/adjunct (10 women). *Computer facilities:* 500 computers available on campus for general student use. A campuswide network can be accessed from student residence rooms and from off campus. Online class registration is available. *General application contact:* 478-301-2700.

Graduate Studies, Cecil B. Day Campus
Richard V. Swindle, Senior Vice President

College of Pharmacy and Health Sciences
Dr. Hewitt W. Matthews, Dean
Programs in:
medical sciences (MS)
pharmacy (Pharm D, PhD)

Eugene W. Stetson School of Business and Economics (Atlanta)
Jim W. Westbrook, Coordinator for Academic Affairs
Program in:
business administration (MBA, XMBA)

Georgia Baptist College of Nursing
Dr. Susan S. Gunby, Dean/Professor
Programs in:
nurse education (Certificate)
nursing (MSN, PhD)

James and Carolyn McAfee School of Theology
Dr. R. Alan Culpepper, Dean
Program in:
theology (M Div, MACM, D Min)

Tift College of Education (Atlanta)
Dr. Carl R. Martray, Dean
Programs in:
curriculum and instruction (PhD)
early childhood education (M Ed, MAT)
educational leadership (PhD, Ed S)
middle grades education (M Ed, MAT)
reading education (M Ed)
secondary education (M Ed, MAT)
teacher leadership (Ed S)

Graduate Studies, Macon Campus

Eugene W. Stetson School of Business and Economics (Macon)
Dr. William S. Mounts, Dean
Program in:
business and economics (MBA)

School of Engineering
Dr. Michael S. Leonard, Interim Dean
Programs in:
biomedical engineering (MSE)
computer engineering (MSE)
electrical engineering (MSE)
engineering management (MSE)
environmental engineering (MSE)
environmental systems (MS)
mechanical engineering (MSE)
software engineering (MSE)
software systems (MS)
technical communications management (MS)
technical management (MS)

School of Music
John E. Simon, Director of Graduate Studies
Programs in:
choral conducting (MM)
church music (MM)
performance (MM)

Tift College of Education (Macon)
Dr. Carl R. Martray, Dean
Programs in:
collaborative education (M Ed)
curriculum and instruction (PhD)
educational leadership (PhD, Ed S)

School of Medicine
Program in:
medicine (MD, MFT, MPH, MSA)

Walter F. George School of Law
Daisy H. Floyd, Dean
Program in:
law (JD)

■ NORTH GEORGIA COLLEGE & STATE UNIVERSITY
Dahlonega, GA 30597
http://www.ngcsu.edu/

State-supported, coed, comprehensive institution. *Computer facilities:* 470 computers available on campus for general student use. A campuswide network can be accessed from student residence rooms and from off campus. Online class registration is available. *General application contact:* Director of Graduate Studies and External Programs, 706-864-1528.

Graduate Studies
Programs in:
community counseling (MS)
early childhood education (M Ed)
educational leadership (Ed S)
family nurse practitioner (MSN)
middle grades education (M Ed)
nursing education (MSN)
physical therapy (DPT)
public administration (MPA)
secondary education (M Ed)
special education (M Ed)

■ PIEDMONT COLLEGE
Demorest, GA 30535-0010
http://www.piedmont.edu/

Independent-religious, coed, comprehensive institution. CGS member. *Computer facilities:* 150 computers available on campus for general student use. A campuswide network can be accessed from student residence rooms and from off campus. *General application contact:* Director of Graduate Studies, 706-778-8500 Ext. 1181.

School of Business
Program in:
business (MBA)

School of Education
Programs in:
early childhood education (MA, MAT)
instruction (Ed S)
secondary education (MA, MAT)

■ SAVANNAH STATE UNIVERSITY
Savannah, GA 31404
http://www.savannahstate.edu/

State-supported, coed, comprehensive institution. *Computer facilities:* 440 computers available on campus for general student use. A campuswide network can be accessed. *General application contact:* Director of Admissions, 912-356-2345.

Program in Business Administration
Program in:
business administration (MBA)

Program in Marine Science
Program in:
marine science (MS)

Program in Public Administration
Program in:
public administration (MPA)

Program in Social Work
Program in:
social work (MSW)

Program in Urban Studies
Program in:
urban studies (MS)

■ SOUTHERN POLYTECHNIC STATE UNIVERSITY
Marietta, GA 30060-2896
http://www.spsu.edu/

State-supported, coed, comprehensive institution. *Graduate faculty:* 62 full-time (21 women), 17 part-time/adjunct (7 women). *Computer facilities:* 1,300 computers available on campus for general student use. A campuswide network can be accessed from student residence rooms and from off campus. Online class registration is available. *Graduate expenses:* Tuition, state resident: full-time $2752; part-time $172 per semester hour. Tuition, nonresident: full-time $10,992; part-time $687 per semester hour. Required fees: $365 per semester. *General application contact:* Nikki Palamiotis, Director of Graduate Studies, 678-915-4276.

Division of Engineering
Dr. Tom Currin, Associate Dean
Program in:
- systems engineering (MS, Graduate Certificate)

School of Architecture, Civil Engineering Technology and Construction
Dr. Wilson Barnes, Dean
Programs in:
- architecture, civil engineering technology and construction (MS)
- construction management (MS)

School of Arts and Sciences
Dr. Alan Gabrielli, Dean
Programs in:
- arts and sciences (MS, Graduate Certificate)
- communications management (Graduate Certificate)
- content development (Graduate Certificate)
- information design and communication (MS)
- instructional design (Graduate Certificate)
- technical and professional communication (Graduate Certificate)
- visual communication and graphics (Graduate Certificate)

School of Computing and Software Engineering
Dr. Han Reichgelt, Dean
Programs in:
- business continuity (Graduate Certificate)
- computer science (MS, Graduate Certificate, Graduate Transition Certificate)
- computing and software engineering (MS, MS SwE, MSIT, Graduate Certificate, Graduate Transition Certificate)
- information security and assurance (Graduate Certificate)
- information technology (MSIT, Graduate Certificate, Graduate Transition Certificate)
- software engineering (MSSWE, Graduate Certificate)

School of Engineering Technology and Management
Dr. Jeff Ray, Dean
Programs in:
- accounting (MSA)
- business administration (MBA, Graduate Certificate)
- engineering technology and management (MBA, MS, MSA, Graduate Certificate)
- engineering technology/electrical (MS)
- quality assurance (MS, Graduate Certificate)

■ UNIVERSITY OF GEORGIA
Athens, GA 30602
http://www.uga.edu/

State-supported, coed, university. CGS member. *Graduate faculty:* 1,177 full-time (349 women), 54 part-time/adjunct (13 women). *Computer facilities:* 3,100 computers available on campus for general student use. A campuswide network can be accessed from student residence rooms and from off campus. Online class registration is available. *General application contact:* Krista Haynes, Director of Graduate Admissions, 706-425-1789.

College of Pharmacy
Dr. Svein Oie, Dean
Programs in:
- clinical trials design and management (Certificate)
- pharmaceutical and biomedical regulatory affairs (Certificate)
- pharmacy (MS, PhD)
- pharmacy and biomedical regulatory affairs (Certificate)

College of Public Health
Dr. Phillip L. Williams, Dean
Programs in:
- environmental health science (MS, PhD)
- health promotion and behavior (MA, MPH, PhD)
- public health (MA, MPH, MS, PhD, Certificate)

Institute of Gerontology
Dr. Leonard W. Poon, Director
Program in:
- gerontology (Certificate)

College of Veterinary Medicine
Dr. Sheila W. Allen, Dean
Programs in:
- food animal medicine (MFAM)
- infectious diseases (MS, PhD)
- pathology (MS, PhD)
- pharmacology (MS, PhD)
- physiology (MS, PhD)
- physiology and pharmacology (MS, PhD)
- population health (MAM, MFAM)
- toxicology (MS, PhD)
- veterinary anatomy (MS)
- veterinary anatomy and radiology (MS)
- veterinary medicine (DVM, MAM, MFAM, MS, PhD)

Graduate School
Program in:
- law (LL M)

Biomedical and Health Sciences Institute
Dr. Harry A. Dailey, Director
Program in:
- neuroscience (PhD)

College of Agricultural and Environmental Sciences
Dr. J. Scott Angle, Dean
Programs in:
- agricultural and environmental sciences (MA Ext, MADS, MAE, MAL, MCCS, MFT, MPPPM, MS, PhD)
- agricultural economics (MAE, MS, PhD)
- agricultural engineering (MS)
- agricultural leadership, education, and communication (MA Ext, MAL)
- animal and dairy science (PhD)
- animal and dairy sciences (MADS)
- animal nutrition (PhD)
- animal science (MS)
- biological and agricultural engineering (PhD)
- biological engineering (MS)
- crop and soil science (MS, PhD)
- crop and soil sciences (MCCS)
- dairy science (MS)
- entomology (MS, PhD)
- environmental economics (MS)
- food science (MS, PhD)
- food technology (MFT)
- horticulture (MS, PhD)
- plant pathology (MS, PhD)
- plant protection and pest management (MPPPM)
- poultry science (MS, PhD)

College of Arts and Sciences
Dr. Garnett Stokes, Dean
Programs in:
- analytical chemistry (MS, PhD)
- anthropology (MA, PhD)
- applied mathematical science (MAMS)
- archaeological resource management (MS)
- art (MFA, PhD)
- art history (MA)
- artificial intelligence (MS)
- arts and sciences (MA, MAMS, MAT, MFA, MM, MS, DMA, PhD, Certificate)
- biochemistry and molecular biology (MS, PhD)
- cellular biology (MS, PhD)
- classical languages (MA)
- comparative literature (MA, PhD)
- computer science (MS, PhD)
- creative writing (MFA, PhD)
- English (MA, MAT, PhD)
- French (MA)
- genetics (MS, PhD)
- geography (MA, MS, PhD)
- geology (MS, PhD)
- German (MA)
- Greek (MA)
- history (MA, PhD)
- inorganic chemistry (MS, PhD)
- Latin (MA)
- linguistics (MA, PhD)

University of Georgia (continued)
marine sciences (MS, PhD)
mathematics (MA, PhD)
microbiology (MS, PhD)
music (MA, MM, DMA, PhD)
organic chemistry (MS, PhD)
philosophy (MA, PhD)
physical chemistry (MS, PhD)
physics (MS, PhD)
plant biology (MS, PhD)
psychology (MS, PhD)
religion (MA)
Romance languages (MA, PhD)
sociology (MA, PhD)
Spanish (MA)
speech communication (MA, PhD)
statistics (MS, PhD)
theatre (MFA, PhD)
women's studies (Certificate)

College of Education
Dr. Arthur M. Horne, Interim Dean
Programs in:
adult education (M Ed, Ed D, PhD, Ed S)
art education (MA Ed, Ed D, PhD, Ed S)
college student affairs administration (M Ed, PhD)
communication science and disorders (M Ed, MA, PhD, Ed S)
counseling and student personnel (PhD)
counseling psychology (PhD)
early childhood education (M Ed, MAT, PhD, Ed S)
education (M Ed, MA, MA Ed, MAT, MM Ed, MS, Ed D, PhD, Ed S)
education of the gifted (Ed D)
educational administration and policy (M Ed, PhD, Ed S)
educational leadership (Ed D)
educational psychology (M Ed, MA, Ed D, PhD, Ed S)
elementary education (PhD)
English education (M Ed, Ed S)
higher education (PhD)
human resource and organizational design (M Ed)
human resources and organization design (M Ed)
instructional technology (M Ed, PhD, Ed S)
kinesiology (MS, PhD)
language and literacy education (PhD)
mathematics education (M Ed, Ed D, PhD, Ed S)
middle school education (M Ed, PhD, Ed S)
music education (MM Ed, Ed D, Ed S)
occupational studies (MAT, Ed D, PhD, Ed S)
professional counseling (M Ed)
professional school counseling (Ed S)
reading education (M Ed, Ed D, Ed S)
recreation and leisure studies (M Ed, MA, PhD)
science education (M Ed, Ed D, PhD, Ed S)
social foundations of education (PhD)
social studies education (M Ed, Ed D, PhD, Ed S)
special education (M Ed, Ed D, PhD, Ed S)
teaching additional languages (M Ed, Ed S)

College of Environment and Design
Dean Daniels J. Nadenicek, Acting Dean
Programs in:
environmental planning and design (MEPD)
historic preservation (MHP)
landscape architecture (MLA)

College of Family and Consumer Sciences
Dr. Laura Dunn Jolly, Dean
Programs in:
child and family development (MS, PhD)
early childhood education (MAT)
family and consumer sciences (MAT, MFCS, MS, PhD)
foods and nutrition (MFCS, MS, PhD)
historic costume and textiles (MS)
housing and consumer economics (MS, PhD)
merchandising/international trade (MS)
textile analysis (PhD)
textile chemical processes (PhD)
textile products and standards (PhD)
textile science (MS)

School of Ecology
Dr. John L. Gittleman, Dean
Programs in:
conservation ecology and sustainable development (MS)
ecology (MS, PhD)

School of Forestry and Natural Resources
Dr. Michael C. Clutter, Dean
Program in:
forestry and natural resources (MFR, MS, PhD)

School of Social Work
Dr. Maurice C. Daniels, Dean
Programs in:
non-profit organizations (MA, Certificate)
social work (MA, MSW, PhD, Certificate)

Terry College of Business
Dr. Robert T. Sumichrast, Dean
Programs in:
accounting (M Acc)
business (M Acc, MA, MBA, MIT, MMR, PhD)
business administration (MA, MBA, PhD)
economics (MA, PhD)
Internet technology (MIT)
marketing research (MMR)

Grady School of Journalism and Mass Communication
Dr. E. Culpepper Clark, Dean
Programs in:
journalism and mass communication (MA)
mass communication (PhD)

School of Law
Dean Rebecca H. White, Dean
Program in:
law (JD)

School of Public and International Affairs
Dr. Thomas P. Lauth, Dean
Programs in:
political science (MA, PhD)
public administration (MPA, PhD)
public and international affairs (MA, MPA, PhD)

■ UNIVERSITY OF WEST GEORGIA
Carrollton, GA 30118
http://www.westga.edu/

State-supported, coed, comprehensive institution. CGS member. *Graduate faculty:* 241 full-time (137 women), 16 part-time/adjunct (8 women). *Computer facilities:* 1,000 computers available on campus for general student use. A campuswide network can be accessed from student residence rooms and from off campus. Online class registration is available. *Graduate expenses:* Tuition, state resident: full-time $2844; part-time $158 per semester hour. Tuition, nonresident: full-time $11,340; part-time $630 per semester hour. Required fees: $1120; $41.56 per semester hour. $186 per semester. Tuition and fees vary according to course load. *General application contact:* Dr. Charles W. Clark, Dean, 678-839-6508.

Graduate School
Dr. Charles W. Clark, Interim Dean

College of Arts and Sciences
Dr. Donadrian Rice, Interim Dean
Programs in:
applied computer science (MS)
arts and sciences (M Mus, MA, MPA, MS, MSN, Psy D, Certificate)
biology (MS)
criminology (MA)
English (MA)
geographic information systems (Certificate)
geosciences (Certificate)
history (MA, Certificate)
human centered computing (Certificate)
individual, organizational, and community transformation: consciousness and society (Psy D)
museum studies (Certificate)
music education (M Mus)
nursing (MSN)
performance (M Mus)
psychology (MA, Psy D)
public administration (MPA)
public management (Certificate)

rural and small town planning (MS)
sociology (MA)
software development (Certificate)
system and network administration (Certificate)
teaching and applied mathematics (MS)
Web technologies (Certificate)

College of Education
Dr. Kim Metcalf, Dean
Programs in:
administration and supervision (M Ed, Ed S)
art education (M Ed)
art teacher education (Ed S)
biology/secondary education (Ed S)
business education (M Ed, Ed S)
early childhood education (M Ed, Ed S)
economics/secondary teacher education (Ed S)
education (M Ed, Ed D, Ed S)
education-French (M Ed)
education-Spanish (M Ed)
English teacher education (Ed S)
French language teacher education (Ed S)
guidance and counseling (M Ed, Ed S)
history teacher education (Ed S)
mathematics teacher education (Ed S)
media (M Ed, Ed S)
middle grades education (M Ed, Ed S)
physical education (M Ed)
reading education (M Ed)
school improvement (Ed D)
science teacher education (Ed S)
secondary education (M Ed, Ed S)
social science teacher education (Ed S)
Spanish language teacher education (Ed S)
special education-general (M Ed, Ed S)
speech-language pathology (M Ed)

Richards College of Business
Dr. Faye S. McIntyre, Dean
Programs in:
accounting and finance (MP Acc)
business (MBA, MP Acc)
business administration (MBA)

■ VALDOSTA STATE UNIVERSITY
Valdosta, GA 31698
http://www.valdosta.edu/

State-supported, coed, university. CGS member. *Graduate faculty:* 211 full-time (92 women). *Computer facilities:* Computer purchase and lease plans are available. 1,550 computers available on campus for general student use. A campuswide network can be accessed from student residence rooms. Online class registration, online classes are available. *General application contact:* Dr. Karla Hull.

Graduate School
Programs in:
business administration (MBA)
clinical/counseling psychology (MS)
criminal justice (MS)
early childhood education (M Ed, Ed S)
educational leadership (M Ed, Ed D, Ed S)
English (MA)
history (MA)
industrial/organizational psychology (MS)
library and information science (MLIS)
marriage and family therapy (MS)
middle grades education (M Ed, Ed S)
reading education (M Ed)
school counseling (M Ed, Ed S)
school psychology (Ed S)
secondary education (M Ed, Ed S)
sociology (MS)
special education (M Ed, Ed S)

Division of Social Work
Dr. Martha Giddings, Director
Program in:
social work (MSW)

Guam

■ UNIVERSITY OF GUAM
Mangilao, GU 96923
http://www.uog.edu/

Territory-supported, coed, comprehensive institution. *Computer facilities:* 150 computers available on campus for general student use. *General application contact:* Program Coordinator, Graduate Studies Office, 671-735-2173.

Office of Graduate Studies

College of Liberal Arts and Social Sciences
Programs in:
ceramics (MA)
English (MA)
graphics (MA)
liberal arts and social sciences (MA)
Micronesian studies (MA)
painting (MA)

College of Natural and Applied Sciences
Programs in:
environmental science (MS)
natural and applied sciences (MS, MSW)
social work (MSW)
tropical marine biology (MS)

School of Business and Public Administration
Programs in:
business administration (PMBA)
business and public administration (MPA, PMBA)
public administration (MPA)

School of Education
Programs in:
administration and supervision (M Ed)
counseling (MA)
education (M Ed, MA)
language and literacy (M Ed)
secondary education (M Ed)
special education (M Ed)
teaching English to speakers of other languages (M Ed)

Hawaii

■ CHAMINADE UNIVERSITY OF HONOLULU
Honolulu, HI 96816-1578
http://www.chaminade.edu/

Independent-religious, coed, comprehensive institution. *Computer facilities:* 90 computers available on campus for general student use. A campuswide network can be accessed from student residence rooms and from off campus. Online class registration is available. *General application contact:* Assistant to the Provost, 808-739-4674.

Graduate Services
Programs in:
business administration (MBA)
counseling psychology (MSCP)
criminal justice administration (MSCJA)
forensic science (MSFS)
homeland security (Certificate)
pastoral leadership (MAPL)
pastoral theology (MPT)
social science via peace education (M Ed)

■ HAWAI'I PACIFIC UNIVERSITY
Honolulu, HI 96813
http://www.hpu.edu/

Independent, coed, comprehensive institution. *Graduate faculty:* 83 full-time (32 women), 34 part-time/adjunct (7 women). *Computer facilities:* 590 computers available on campus for general student use. A campuswide network can be accessed from student residence rooms and from off campus. Online class registration is available. *Graduate expenses:* Tuition: full-time $10,800; part-time $600 per credit. *General application contact:* Danny Lam, Assistant Director of Graduate Admissions, 808-544-1135.

College of Business Administration
Dr. Aytun Ozturk, Dean
Programs in:
accounting/CPA (MBA)
e-business (MBA)

Hawai'i Pacific University (continued)
economics (MBA)
finance (MBA)
human resource management (MA)
information systems (MBA)
international business (MBA)
management (MBA)
marketing (MBA)
organizational change (MBA)
travel industry management (MBA)

College of Communication
Dr. Steven Combs, Dean
Program in:
communication (MA)

College of International Studies
Dr. Carlos Juarez, Dean
Program in:
teaching English as a second language (MA)

College of Liberal Arts
Dr. William Potter, Associate Vice President and Dean
Programs in:
diplomacy and military studies (MA)
secondary education (M Ed)
social work (MSW)

College of Natural Sciences
Dr. Andrew Brittain, Vice President, Research/Dean
Program in:
marine science (MS)

College of Professional Studies
Dr. Gordon Jones, Dean
Programs in:
global leadership and sustainable development (MA)
human resource management (MA)
information systems (MSIS)
knowledge management (MSIS)
organizational change (MA)
software engineering (MSIS)
telecommunications security (MSIS)

School of Nursing
Dr. Patricia Lange-Otsuka, Associate Dean of Nursing for Administration
Programs in:
community clinical nurse specialist (MSN)
community clinical nurse specialist educator option (MSN)
family nurse practitioner (MSN)

■ UNIVERSITY OF HAWAII AT MANOA
Honolulu, HI 96822
http://www.uhm.hawaii.edu/

State-supported, coed, university. CGS member. *Computer facilities:* Computer purchase and lease plans are available. 81 computers available on campus for general student use. A campuswide network can be accessed from student residence rooms and from off campus. Online class registration is available. *General application contact:* Director of Graduate Admissions, 808-956-8544.

Graduate Division
Programs in:
communication and information sciences (PhD)
ecology, evolution and conservation biology (MS, PhD)
marine biology (MS, PhD)

College of Arts and Humanities
Programs in:
American studies (MA, PhD)
art (MA)
art history (MA)
arts and humanities (M Mus, MA, MFA, PhD, Graduate Certificate)
dance (MA, MFA)
historic preservation (Graduate Certificate)
history (MA, PhD)
museum studies (Graduate Certificate)
music (M Mus, MA, PhD)
philosophy (MA, PhD)
religion (MA)
speech (MA)
theatre (MA, MFA, PhD)
visual arts (MFA)

College of Education
Programs in:
counseling and guidance (M Ed)
curriculum and instruction (PhD)
curriculum studies (M Ed)
disability and diversity studies (Graduate Certificate)
early childhood education (M Ed)
education (M Ed, M Ed T, MS, PhD, Graduate Certificate)
educational administration (M Ed)
educational foundations (M Ed)
educational policy studies (PhD)
educational psychology (M Ed, PhD)
educational technology (M Ed)
exceptionalities (PhD)
kinesiology (MS, PhD)
special education (M Ed)
teaching (M Ed T)

College of Engineering
Programs in:
civil and environmental engineering (MS, PhD)
electrical engineering (MS, PhD)
engineering (MS, PhD)
mechanical engineering (MS, PhD)

College of Language, Linguistics and Literature
Programs in:
Chinese (MA, PhD)
English (MA, PhD)
English as a second language (MA, Graduate Certificate)
French (MA)
Japanese (MA, PhD)
Korean (MA, PhD)
language, linguistics and literature (MA, PhD, Graduate Certificate)
linguistics (MA, PhD)
second language acquisition (PhD)
Spanish (MA)

College of Natural Sciences
Programs in:
advanced library and information science (Graduate Certificate)
astronomy (MS, PhD)
botany (MS, PhD)
chemistry (MS, PhD)
computer science (MS, PhD)
library and information science (MLI Sc, Graduate Certificate)
mathematics (MA, PhD)
microbiology (MS, PhD)
natural sciences (MA, MLI Sc, MS, PhD, Graduate Certificate)
physics (MS, PhD)
zoology (MS, PhD)

College of Social Sciences
Programs in:
advanced women's studies (Graduate Certificate)
anthropology (MA, PhD)
clinical psychology (PhD)
communication (MA)
community and cultural psychology (PhD)
community and culture (MA)
community planning and social policy (MURP)
conflict resolution (Graduate Certificate)
disaster preparedness and emergency management (Graduate Certificate)
economics (MA, PhD)
environmental planning and management (MURP)
geography (MA, PhD)
land use and infrastructure planning (MURP)
ocean policy (Graduate Certificate)
political science (MA, PhD)
psychology (MA, PhD, Graduate Certificate)
public administration (MPA, Graduate Certificate)
public policy (Graduate Certificate)
social sciences (MA, MPA, MURP, PhD, Graduate Certificate)
sociology (MA, PhD)
telecommunication and information resource management (Graduate Certificate)
urban and regional planning (PhD, Graduate Certificate)
urban and regional planning in Asia and Pacific (MURP)

College of Tropical Agriculture and Human Resources
Programs in:
animal sciences (MS)
bioengineering (MS)
entomology (MS, PhD)
food science (MS)
molecular bioscience and bioengineering (MS)
molecular biosciences and bioengineering (PhD)
natural resources and environmental management (MS, PhD)
nutrition (PhD)

nutritional sciences (MS, PhD)
tropical agriculture and human resources (MS, PhD)
tropical plant and soil sciences (MS, PhD)
tropical plant pathology (MS, PhD)

School of Hawaiian Knowledge
Programs in:
Hawaiian (MA)
Hawaiian studies (MA)

School of Nursing and Dental Hygiene
Mary Boland, Dean
Programs in:
clinical nurse specialist (MS)
nurse practitioner (MS)
nursing (PhD, Graduate Certificate)
nursing administration (MS)

School of Ocean and Earth Science and Technology
Programs in:
high-pressure geophysics and geochemistry (MS, PhD)
hydrogeology and engineering geology (MS, PhD)
marine geology and geophysics (MS, PhD)
meteorology (MS, PhD)
ocean and earth science and technology (MS, PhD)
ocean and resources engineering (MS, PhD)
oceanography (MS, PhD)
planetary geosciences and remote sensing (MS, PhD)
seismology and solid-earth geophysics (MS, PhD)
volcanology, petrology, and geochemistry (MS, PhD)

School of Pacific and Asian Studies
Programs in:
Asian studies (MA, Graduate Certificate)
Chinese studies (Graduate Certificate)
Japanese studies (Graduate Certificate)
Korean studies (Graduate Certificate)
Pacific and Asian studies (MA, Graduate Certificate)
Pacific Island studies (MA, Graduate Certificate)
Philippine studies (Graduate Certificate)
Southeast Asian studies (Graduate Certificate)

School of Social Work
Jon Matsuoka, Dean
Programs in:
social welfare (PhD)
social work (MSW)

School of Travel Industry Management
Program in:
travel industry management (MS)

Shidler College of Business
Programs in:
accounting (M Acc)
accounting law (M Acc)
Asian business studies (MBA)
Asian finance (PhD)
business (EMBA, M Acc, MBA, MHRM, MS, PhD)
Chinese business studies (MBA)
decision sciences (MBA)
entrepreneurship (MBA)
executive business administration (EMBA)
finance (MBA)
finance and banking (MBA)
financial engineering (MS)
global information technology management (PhD)
human resources management (MBA)
information management (MBA)
information systems (M Acc)
information technology (MBA)
international accounting (PhD)
international business (MBA)
international marketing (PhD)
international organization and strategy (PhD)
Japanese business studies (MBA)
marketing (MBA)
organizational behavior (MBA)
organizational management (MBA)
real estate (MBA)
student-designed track (MBA)
taxation (M Acc)
Vietnam focused business administration (EMBA)

John A. Burns School of Medicine
Programs in:
cell and molecular biology (MS, PhD)
communication sciences and disorders (MS)
developmental and reproductive biology (MS, PhD)
epidemiology (PhD)
global health and population studies (Graduate Certificate)
medicine (MD, MPH, MS, Dr PH, PhD, Graduate Certificate)
public health (MPH, MS, Dr PH)

Graduate Programs in Biomedical Sciences
Programs in:
biomedical sciences (MS, PhD)
tropical medicine (MS, PhD)

School of Architecture
Program in:
architecture (D Arch)

William S. Richardson School of Law
Program in:
law (JD, LL M, Graduate Certificate)

■ UNIVERSITY OF PHOENIX–HAWAII CAMPUS
Honolulu, HI 96813-4317
http://www.phoenix.edu/

Proprietary, coed, comprehensive institution. *Computer facilities:* A campuswide network can be accessed from off campus. *General application contact:* Campus Information Center, 808-536-2686.

The Artemis School

College of Education
Programs in:
administration and supervision (MA Ed)
curriculum and instruction (MA Ed)
elementary education (MA Ed)
secondary education (MA Ed)
special education (MA Ed)
teacher education for elementary licensure (MA Ed)

College of Health and Human Services
Programs in:
administration of justice and security (MS)
community counseling (MSC)
education (MHA)
family nurse practitioner (MSN)
gerontology (MHA)
health administration (MHA)
health care management (MBA)
marriage, family and child therapy (MSC)
nursing (MSN)
nursing/health care education (MSN)
psychology (MS)

John Sperling School of Business
Program in:
business (MBA, MIS, MM)

College of Graduate Business and Management
Programs in:
accounting (MBA)
business administration (MBA)
global management (MBA)
human resources management (MBA, MM)
management (MM)
marketing (MBA)
public administration (MBA, MM)

College of Information Systems and Technology
Programs in:
information systems (MIS)
technology management (MBA)

Idaho

■ BOISE STATE UNIVERSITY
Boise, ID 83725-0399
http://www.boisestate.edu/

State-supported, coed, university. CGS member. *Graduate faculty:* 658. *Computer facilities:* 900 computers available on campus for general student use. A campuswide network can be accessed from student residence rooms and from off

Boise State University (continued)
campus. Online class registration is available. *Graduate expenses:* Tuition, state resident: full-time $3763; part-time $204 per credit. Tuition, nonresident: full-time $11,467; part-time $204 per credit. Required fees: $1741; $81 per credit. *General application contact:* Dr. John R. Pelton, Dean, 208-426-3647.

Graduate College

Dr. John R. Pelton, Dean

College of Arts and Sciences
Programs in:
art education (MA)
arts and sciences (MA, MFA, MM, MS, PhD)
biology (MA, MS)
creative writing (MFA)
earth science (MS)
English (MA, MFA)
geology (MS, PhD)
geophysics (MS, PhD)
interdisciplinary studies (MA, MS)
music (MM)
music education (MM)
pedagogy (MM)
performance (MM)
raptor biology (MS)
technical communication (MA)
visual arts (MFA)

College of Business and Economics
Programs in:
accountancy (MSA)
business administration (MBA)
business and economics (MBA, MSA)
information technology management (MBA)
taxation (MSA)

College of Education
Programs in:
athletic administration (MPE)
counseling (MA)
counselor education (MA)
curriculum and instruction (Ed D)
curriculum instruction (MA)
early childhood education (M Ed, MA)
education (M Ed, MA, MET, MPE, MS, MS Ed, Ed D)
educational leadership (M Ed)
educational technology (MET, MS, MS Ed)
exercise and sports studies (MS)
physical education (MPE)
reading (MA)
special education (M Ed, MA)

College of Engineering
Programs in:
civil engineering (M Engr, MS)
computer engineering (M Engr, MS)
computer science (MS)
electrical and computer engineering (PhD)
electrical engineering (M Engr, MS)
engineering (M Engr, MS, PhD)
instructional and performance technology (MS)
materials science and engineering (M Engr, MS)
mechanical engineering (M Engr, MS)

College of Health Science
Program in:
health science (MHS)

College of Social Sciences and Public Affairs
Programs in:
communication (MA)
criminal justice administration (MA)
environmental and natural resources policy and administration (MPA)
general public administration (MPA)
history (MA)
social sciences and public affairs (MA, MPA, MSW)
social work (MSW)
state and local government policy and administration (MPA)

■ IDAHO STATE UNIVERSITY
Pocatello, ID 83209
http://www.isu.edu/

State-supported, coed, university. CGS member. *Graduate faculty:* 273 full-time (83 women), 7 part-time/adjunct (3 women). *Computer facilities:* 519 computers available on campus for general student use. A campuswide network can be accessed from student residence rooms and from off campus. Online class registration is available. *Graduate expenses:* Tuition, state resident: full-time $3114; part-time $276 per credit hour. Tuition, nonresident: full-time $12,318; part-time $404 per credit hour. Required fees: $2360. Tuition and fees vary according to course load and reciprocity agreements. *General application contact:* Dr. Thomas Jackson, Dean, 208-282-2390.

Office of Graduate Studies

Dr. Thomas Jackson, Dean
Programs in:
general interdisciplinary (M Ed, MA, MNS)
waste management and environmental science (MS)

College of Arts and Sciences
Dr. Scott Hughes, Interim Dean
Programs in:
anthropology (MA, MS)
applied physics (PhD)
art (MFA)
arts and sciences (MA, MFA, MNS, MPA, MS, DA, PhD, Post-Master's Certificate, Postbaccalaureate Certificate)
biology (MNS, MS, DA, PhD)
chemistry (MNS, MS)
clinical laboratory science (MS)
clinical psychology (PhD)
communication and rhetorical studies (MA)
English (MA, DA, PhD, Post-Master's Certificate)
geographic information science (MS)
geology (MNS, MS)
geophysics/hydrology (MS)
geotechnology (Postbaccalaureate Certificate)
health physics (MS)
historical resources management (MA)
mathematics (MS, DA)
mathematics for secondary teachers (MA)
microbiology (MS)
physics (MNS)
political science (MA, DA)
psychology (MS)
public administration (MPA)
sociology (MA)
theatre (MA)

College of Business
Dr. Ken Smith, Dean
Programs in:
business administration (MBA, Postbaccalaureate Certificate)
computer information systems (MS, Postbaccalaureate Certificate)

College of Education
Dr. Deborah Hedeen, Dean
Programs in:
child and family studies (M Ed)
curriculum leadership (M Ed)
education (M Ed)
educational administration (M Ed, 6th Year Certificate, Ed S)
educational foundations (5th Year Certificate)
educational leadership (Ed D)
elementary education (M Ed)
human exceptionality (M Ed)
instructional design (PhD)
instructional technology (M Ed)
physical education (MPE)
school psychology (Ed S)
special education (Ed S)

College of Engineering
Dr. Richard Jacobsen, Dean
Programs in:
civil engineering (MS)
engineering (MS, PhD, Postbaccalaureate Certificate)
engineering and applied science (PhD)
environmental engineering (MS)
measurement and control engineering (MS)
mechanical engineering (MS)
nuclear science and engineering (MS, PhD, Postbaccalaureate Certificate)

College of Pharmacy
Dr. Joseph Steiner, Dean
Programs in:
biopharmaceutical analysis (PhD)
biopharmaceutics (PhD)
pharmaceutical chemistry (MS)
pharmaceutical science (PhD)
pharmaceutics (MS)
pharmacognosy (MS)
pharmacokinetics (PhD)
pharmacology (MS, PhD)
pharmacy (Pharm D)
pharmacy administration (MS, PhD)

College of Technology
Dr. Marilyn Davis, Dean

Programs in:
- human resource training and development (MTD)
- technology (MTD)

Kasiska College of Health Professions
Dr. Linda Hatzenbuehler, Dean
Programs in:
- advanced general dentistry (Post-Doctoral Certificate)
- audiology (MS, Au D)
- counseling (M Coun, Ed S)
- counselor education and counseling (PhD)
- deaf education (MS)
- dental hygiene (MS)
- dietetics (Certificate)
- family medicine (Post-Master's Certificate)
- health education (MHE)
- health professions (M Coun, MHE, MOT, MPAS, MPH, MS, Au D, DPT, PhD, Certificate, Ed S, Post-Doctoral Certificate, Post-Master's Certificate, Postbaccalaureate Certificate)
- Nursing (MS, Post-Master's Certificate)
- occupational therapy (MOT)
- physical therapy (DPT)
- physician assistant studies (MPAS)
- public health (MPH)
- speech language pathology (MS)

■ NORTHWEST NAZARENE UNIVERSITY
Nampa, ID 83686-5897
http://www.nnu.edu/

Independent-religious, coed, comprehensive institution. *Graduate faculty:* 48 full-time (19 women), 72 part-time/adjunct (25 women). *Computer facilities:* Computer purchase and lease plans are available. 400 computers available on campus for general student use. A campuswide network can be accessed from student residence rooms and from off campus. Online class registration, various software packages are available. *General application contact:* Dr. Mark Maddix, Director, Graduate Studies, 208-467-8817.

Graduate Studies
Dr. Mark Maddix, Director, Graduate Studies
Programs in:
- business administration (MBA)
- Christian education (MA)
- community counseling (MS)
- curriculum and instruction (M Ed)
- educational leadership (M Ed)
- exceptional child (M Ed)
- marriage and family counseling (MS)
- missional leadership (MA)
- pastoral ministry (MA)
- reading education (M Ed)
- religion (M Div)
- school counseling (M Ed, MS)
- social work (MSW)
- spiritual formation (MA)

■ UNIVERSITY OF IDAHO
Moscow, ID 83844-2282
http://www.uidaho.edu/

State-supported, coed, university. CGS member. *Graduate faculty:* 430 full-time (110 women), 119 part-time/adjunct (20 women). *Computer facilities:* 670 computers available on campus for general student use. A campuswide network can be accessed from student residence rooms and from off campus. Online class registration, student evaluations of teaching are available. *General application contact:* Dr. Margrit von Braun, Dean of the College of Graduate Studies, 208-885-6243.

College of Graduate Studies
Dr. Margrit von Braun, Dean of the College of Graduate Studies
Programs in:
- bioinformatics and computational biology (MS, PhD)
- bioregional planning (MS)
- environmental science (MS, PhD)
- interdisciplinary studies (MA, MS)
- neuroscience (MS, PhD)
- water resources (MS, PhD)

College of Agricultural and Life Sciences
Dr. John Hammel, Dean
Programs in:
- agricultural and life sciences (M Engr, MS, PhD)
- agricultural economics (MS)
- agricultural education (MS)
- animal physiology (PhD)
- animal science (MS, PhD)
- applied economics (MS)
- biochemistry (MS)
- entomology (MS, PhD)
- family and consumer sciences (MS)
- food science (MS, PhD)
- microbiology, molecular biology and biochemistry (PhD)
- plant science (MS, PhD)
- soil and land resources (MS, PhD)
- soil science (MS, PhD)
- veterinary science (MS)

College of Art and Architecture
Dr. Mark Elison Hoversten, Dean
Programs in:
- architecture and interior design (M Arch, MA, MS)
- art (MAT, MFA)
- art and architecture (M Arch, MA, MAT, MFA, MS)
- landscape architecture (MS)

College of Business and Economics
Dr. John Morris, Dean
Programs in:
- accounting (M Acct, MS)
- business and economics (EMBA, M Acct, MBA, MS)

College of Education
Dr. Paul Rowland, Dean
Programs in:
- adult and organizational learning (M Ed, MS, Ed S)
- counseling and human services (M Ed, MS, Ed D, PhD, Ed S)
- curriculum and instruction (Ed D, PhD)
- education (M Ed, MAT, MS, Ed D, PhD, Ed S, Ed Sp PTE)
- educational leadership (M Ed, MS, Ed S)
- physical education (M Ed, MS)
- professional-technical and technology education (M Ed, MS, Ed D, PhD, Ed Sp PTE)
- recreation (MS)
- school psychology (Ed S)
- special education (M Ed, MS, Ed S)

College of Engineering
Dr. Donald Blackletter, Dean
Programs in:
- agricultural engineering (M Engr, MS)
- biological and agricultural engineering (M Engr, MS, PhD)
- chemical engineering (M Engr, MA, MS, PhD)
- Civil Engineering (MS, PhD)
- computer engineering (M Engr, MS)
- computer science (MS, PhD)
- electrical engineering (M Engr, MS, PhD)
- engineering (MS, PhD)
- engineering management (M Engr, MS)
- environmental engineering (M Engr, MS)
- geological engineering (MS)
- materials science and engineering (MS, PhD)
- mechanical engineering (M Engr, MS, PhD)
- metallurgical engineering (MS)
- nuclear engineering (M Engr, PhD)
- systems engineering (M Engr)

College of Letters, Arts and Social Sciences
Dr. Katherine Aiken, Dean
Programs in:
- anthropology (MA)
- creative writing (MFA)
- English (MA, MAT, MFA)
- history (MA, MAT, PhD)
- letters, arts and social sciences (M Mus, MA, MAT, MFA, MPA, MS, PhD)
- music (M Mus, MA)
- political science (MA, PhD)
- psychology (MS)
- public administration (MPA)
- teaching English as a second language (MA)
- theatre arts (MFA)

College of Natural Resources
Dr. William James McLaughlin, Acting Dean
Programs in:
- conservation social sciences (MS)
- fishery resources (MS)
- forest products (MS)
- forest resources (MS)
- natural resources (MNR, MS, PhD)
- rangeland ecology and management (MS)
- wildlife resources (MS)

University of Idaho (continued)

College of Science
Dr. Scott Wood, Dean
Programs in:
- biological sciences (M Nat Sci)
- biology (MS, PhD)
- chemistry (MAT, MS, PhD)
- Geography (MS, PhD)
- geology (MS, PhD)
- hydrology (MS)
- mathematics (MAT, MS, PhD)
- physics (MS, PhD)
- physics education (MAT)
- science (M Nat Sci, MAT, MS, PhD)
- statistics (MS)

College of Law
Donald L. Burnett, Dean
Program in:
- law (JD)

Illinois

■ AURORA UNIVERSITY
Aurora, IL 60506-4892
http://www.aurora.edu/

Independent, coed, comprehensive institution. *Graduate faculty:* 39 full-time (19 women), 168 part-time/adjunct (89 women). *Computer facilities:* 90 computers available on campus for general student use. A campuswide network can be accessed from student residence rooms and from off campus. Learning Management System available. *Graduate expenses:* Tuition: full-time $19,512; part-time $542 per semester hour. Tuition and fees vary according to degree level, campus/location and program. *General application contact:* Dr. Donna DeSpain, Dean of Adult and Graduate Studies, 800-742-5281.

College of Arts and Sciences
Dr. Lora Delacey, Dean
Program in:
- mathematics (MS)

College of Education
Dr. Donald C. Wold, Dean
Programs in:
- curriculum and instruction (Ed D)
- education (MAT)
- education and administration (Ed D)
- educational leadership (MEL)
- reading instruction (MA)

College of Professional Studies
Dr. Michael Carroll, Dean

Dunham School of Business
Dr. Shawn Green, Director
Program in:
- business (MBA)

School of Social Work
Dr. Fred Mckenzie, Dean
Program in:
- social work (MSW)

George Williams College of Aurora University
Dr. Rita Yerkes, Dean

School of Experiential Leadership
Programs in:
- administration of leisure services (MS)
- outdoor pursuits recreation administration (MS)

■ BENEDICTINE UNIVERSITY
Lisle, IL 60532-0900
http://www.ben.edu/

Independent-religious, coed, comprehensive institution. *Computer facilities:* 200 computers available on campus for general student use. A campuswide network can be accessed from student residence rooms and from off campus. Online class registration is available. *General application contact:* Director, Admissions, 630-829-6200.

Graduate Programs
Programs in:
- accountancy (MSA)
- accounting (MBA)
- administration of health care institutions (MPH)
- clinical exercise physiology (MS)
- clinical psychology (MS)
- curriculum and instruction and collaborative teaching (M Ed)
- dietetics (MPH)
- disaster management (MPH)
- elementary education (MA Ed)
- entrepreneurship and managing innovation (MBA)
- financial management (MBA)
- health administration (MBA)
- health education (MPH)
- health information systems (MPH)
- higher education and organizational change (Ed D)
- human resource management (MBA)
- information systems security (MBA)
- international business (MBA)
- leadership and administration (M Ed)
- management and organizational behavior (MS)
- management consulting (MBA)
- management information systems (MBA)
- marketing management (MBA)
- nutrition and wellness (MS)
- operations management and logistics (MBA)
- organizational development (PhD)
- organizational leadership (MBA)
- reading and literacy (M Ed)
- science content and process (MSSCP)
- secondary education (MA Ed)
- special education (MA Ed)

■ BRADLEY UNIVERSITY
Peoria, IL 61625-0002
http://www.bradley.edu/

Independent, coed, comprehensive institution. CGS member. *Computer facilities:* Computer purchase and lease plans are available. 2,000 computers available on campus for general student use. A campuswide network can be accessed from student residence rooms and from off campus. Online class registration is available. *General application contact:* Director, Graduate Admissions, 309-677-2375.

Graduate School

College of Education and Health Sciences
Programs in:
- curriculum and instruction (MA, Certificate)
- education and health sciences (MA, MSN, DPT, Certificate)
- human development counseling (MA)
- leadership in educational administration (MA)
- leadership in human service administration (MA)
- nurse administered anesthesia (MSN)
- nursing administration (MSN)
- physical therapy (DPT)

College of Engineering and Technology
Programs in:
- civil engineering and construction (MSCE)
- electrical engineering (MSEE)
- engineering and technology (MSCE, MSEE, MSIE, MSME, MSMFE)
- industrial engineering (MSIE)
- manufacturing engineering (MSIE)
- mechanical engineering (MSME)

College of Liberal Arts and Sciences
Programs in:
- biology (MS)
- chemistry (MS)
- computer information systems (MS)
- computer science (MS)
- English (MA)
- liberal arts and sciences (MA, MLS, MS)
- liberal studies (MLS)

Foster College of Business Administration
Programs in:
- accounting (MSA)
- business administration (MBA, MSA)

Slane College of Communications and Fine Arts
Programs in:
- ceramics (MA, MFA)
- communications and fine arts (MA, MFA)
- drawing/illustration (MA, MFA)
- interdisciplinary art (MA, MFA)
- painting (MA, MFA)
- photography (MA, MFA)
- printmaking (MA, MFA)
- sculpture (MA, MFA)
- visual communication and design (MA, MFA)

■ CHICAGO STATE UNIVERSITY

Chicago, IL 60628

http://www.csu.edu/

State-supported, coed, comprehensive institution. *Computer facilities:* Computer purchase and lease plans are available. 75 computers available on campus for general student use. A campuswide network can be accessed from student residence rooms and from off campus. Online class registration is available. *General application contact:* Admissions and Records Officer II, 773-995-2404.

School of Graduate and Professional Studies

College of Arts and Sciences

Programs in:
- arts and sciences (MA, MFA, MS, MSW)
- biological sciences (MS)
- computer science (MS)
- counseling (MA)
- creative writing (MFA)
- criminal justice (MS)
- English (MA)
- geography and economic development (MA)
- history, philosophy, and political science (MA)
- mathematics (MS)
- social work (MSW)

College of Education

Programs in:
- bilingual education (M Ed)
- curriculum and instruction (MS Ed)
- early childhood education (MAT, MS Ed)
- education (M Ed, MA, MAT, MS Ed, Ed D)
- educational leadership (MA, Ed D)
- elementary education (MAT)
- general administration (MA)
- higher education administration (MA)
- instructional foundations (MS Ed)
- library information and media studies (MS Ed)
- middle school education (MAT)
- physical education (MS Ed)
- reading (MS Ed)
- secondary education (MAT)
- special education (M Ed)
- teaching of reading (MS Ed)
- technology and education (MS Ed)

■ COLUMBIA COLLEGE CHICAGO

Chicago, IL 60605-1996

http://www.colum.edu/

Independent, coed, comprehensive institution. *Graduate faculty:* 128. *Computer facilities:* 730 computers available on campus for general student use. A campuswide network can be accessed. *Graduate expenses:* Tuition: full-time $15,992; part-time $633 per credit hour. *General application contact:* Royal Dawson, Director of Institutional Research, 312-369-7478.

Graduate School

Dr. Keith Cleveland, Office of Provost/Senior Vice President

Programs in:
- architectural studies (MFA)
- arts, entertainment and media management (MA)
- creative writing (MFA)
- dance/movement therapy (MA, Certificate)
- elementary education (MAT)
- English (MAT)
- film and video (MFA)
- interdisciplinary arts (MA, MAT)
- interdisciplinary book and paper arts (MFA)
- interior design (MFA)
- multicultural education (MA)
- photography (MA, MFA)
- poetry (MFA)
- public affairs journalism (MA)
- teaching of writing (MA)
- urban teaching (MA)

■ CONCORDIA UNIVERSITY CHICAGO

River Forest, IL 60305-1499

http://www.cuchicago.edu/

Independent-religious, coed, comprehensive institution. CGS member. *Computer facilities:* 85 computers available on campus for general student use. A campuswide network can be accessed from student residence rooms and from off campus. Online class registration is available. *General application contact:* Director of Graduate Admissions, 708-209-3454.

College of Education

Programs in:
- Christian education (MA)
- curriculum and instruction (MA)
- early childhood education (MAT)
- elementary education (MAT)
- reading education (MA)
- school leadership (MA, Ed D, CAS)
- secondary education (MAT)

College of Graduate and Innovative Programs

Programs in:
- business administration (MBA)
- church music (MCM)
- community counseling (MA)
- educational technology (MA)
- gerontology (MA)
- human services (MA)
- liberal studies (MA)
- music (MA)
- psychology (MA)
- religion (MA)
- school counseling (MA, CAS)

■ DEPAUL UNIVERSITY

Chicago, IL 60604-2287

http://www.depaul.edu/

Independent-religious, coed, university. CGS member. *Graduate faculty:* 899 full-time (406 women), 943 part-time/adjunct (430 women). *Computer facilities:* 1,500 computers available on campus for general student use. A campuswide network can be accessed from student residence rooms and from off campus. Online class registration is available. *General application contact:* Information Contact, 312-362-6709.

Charles H. Kellstadt Graduate School of Business

Robert T. Ryan, Assistant Dean and Director

Programs in:
- applied economics (MBA)
- behavioral finance (MBA)
- brand management (MBA)
- business (M Acc, MA, MBA, MS, MSA, MSEPA, MSF, MSHR, MSMA, MSRE, MST)
- computational finance (MS)
- customer relationship management (MBA)
- economics (MA)
- economics and policy analysis (MA)
- entrepreneurship (MBA)
- finance (MBA, MSF)
- financial analysis (MBA)
- financial management and control (MBA)
- health sector management (MBA)
- human resource management (MBA, MSHR)
- integrated marketing communication (MBA)
- international business (MBA)
- international marketing and finance (MBA)
- leadership/change management (MBA)
- management planning and strategy (MBA)
- managerial finance (MBA)
- marketing analysis (MSMA)
- marketing and management (MBA)
- marketing strategy and analysis (MBA)
- marketing strategy and planning (MBA)
- new product management (MBA)
- operations management (MBA)
- real estate (MS)
- real estate finance and investment (MBA)
- sales leadership (MBA)
- strategy, execution and valuation (MBA)

School of Accountancy and Management Information Systems

Programs in:
- accountancy (M Acc, MSA)
- business information technology (MS)
- e-business (MBA, MS)
- financial management and control (MBA)
- management accounting (MBA)

DePaul University (continued)
management information systems (MBA)
taxation (MST)

College of Communication
Dr. Jacqueline Taylor, Dean
Programs in:
journalism (MA)
media, culture and society (MA)
organizational and multicultural communication (MA)
public relations and advertising (MA)

College of Computing and Digital Media
Dr. David Miller, Dean
Programs in:
business information technology (MS)
computational finance (MS)
computer game development (MS)
computer graphics and motion technology (MS)
computer science (MS, PhD)
computer, information and network security (MS)
digital cinema (MFA, MS)
e-commerce technology (MS)
human-computer interaction (MS)
information systems (MS)
information technology (MA)
information technology project management (MS)
software engineering (MS)
telecommunications systems (MS)

College of Law
Glen Weissenberger, Dean
Programs in:
health law (LL M)
intellectual property law (LL M)
international law (LL M)
law (JD)
tax law (LL M)

College of Liberal Arts and Sciences
Charles Suchar, Dean
Programs in:
advanced practice nursing (MS)
applied mathematics (MS)
applied physics (MS)
applied statistics (MS, Certificate)
biochemistry (MS)
biological sciences (MA, MS)
chemistry (MS)
clinical psychology (MA, PhD)
English (MA)
experimental psychology (MA, PhD)
general psychology (MS)
history (MA)
industrial/organizational psychology (MA, PhD)
interdisciplinary studies (MA, MS)
liberal arts and sciences (MA, MS, PhD, Certificate)
masters entry into nursing practice (MS)
mathematics education (MA)
nurse anesthesia (MS)
philosophy (MA, PhD)
polymer chemistry and coatings technology (MS)
sociology (MA)
writing and publishing (MA)

School for New Learning
Dr. Russ Rogers, Program Director
Programs in:
applied technology (MS)
educating adults (MA)
integrated professional studies (MA)

School of Education
Dr. Marie Donovan, Dean
Programs in:
bilingual and bicultural education (M Ed, MA)
curriculum studies (M Ed, MA, Ed D)
education (Ed D)
educational leadership (M Ed, MA, Ed D)
human development and learning (MA)
human services and counseling (M Ed, MA)
reading and learning disabilities (M Ed, MA)
social culture studies in education and development (M Ed, MA)
teaching and learning (early childhood, elementary and secondary) (M Ed)
teaching and learning (early childhood, elementary, and secondary) (MA)

School of Music
Dr. Donald E. Casey, Dean
Programs in:
applied music (performance) (MM, Certificate)
jazz studies (MM)
music composition (MM)
music education (MM)

School of Public Service
Dr. J. Patrick Murphy, Director
Programs in:
financial administration management (Certificate)
health administration (Certificate)
health law and policy (MS)
international public services (MS)
leadership and policy studies (MS)
metropolitan planning (Certificate)
public administration (MPA)
public service management (MS)
public services (Certificate)

The Theatre School
John Culbert, Dean
Programs in:
acting (MFA)
arts leadership (MFA)
directing (MFA)

■ DOMINICAN UNIVERSITY
River Forest, IL 60305-1099
http://www.dom.edu/

Independent-religious, coed, comprehensive institution. *Graduate faculty:* 53 full-time (28 women), 169 part-time/adjunct (101 women). *Computer facilities:* Computer purchase and lease plans are available. 625 computers available on campus for general student use. A campuswide network can be accessed from student residence rooms and from off campus. Online class registration, online student account information, online financial aid information are available. *Graduate expenses:* Tuition: full-time $12,060; part-time $670 per credit hour. *General application contact:* Mary Ann Rowan, Vice President of Enrollment Management, 708-524-6544.

Edward A. and Lois L. Brennan School of Business
Dr. Arvid Johnson, Dean
Programs in:
accounting (MSA)
business administration (MBA)
computer information systems (MSCIS)
management information systems (MSMIS)
organization management (MSOM)

Graduate School of Library and Information Science
Dr. Susan Roman, Dean
Programs in:
library and information science (MLIS, PhD)
special studies (CSS)

Graduate School of Social Work
Dr. Mark Rodgers, Dean
Program in:
social work (MSW)

School of Education
Dr. Colleen Reardon, Dean
Programs in:
curriculum and instruction (MA Ed)
early childhood education (MS)
education (MAT)
educational administration (MA)
elementary (online) (MS)
English as a second language (online) (MS)
reading (online) (MS)
special education (MS)

School of Leadership and Continuing Studies
Dr. Bryan J. Watkins, Executive Director
Programs in:
leadership (MA)
organizational leadership (MSOL)

■ EASTERN ILLINOIS UNIVERSITY
Charleston, IL 61920-3099
http://www.eiu.edu/

State-supported, coed, comprehensive institution. CGS member. *Computer facilities:* Computer purchase and lease plans are available. 976 computers available on campus for general student use. A campuswide network can be accessed from student residence rooms and from off campus. Online class registration is available. *General application contact:* Director of Graduate Admissions, 217-581-7489.

Graduate School

College of Arts and Humanities
Programs in:
art (MA)
art education (MA)
arts and humanities (MA)
communication studies (MA)
English (MA)
historical administration (MA)
history (MA)
music (MA)

College of Education and Professional Studies
Programs in:
clinical counseling (MS)
college student affairs (MS)
education and professional studies (MS, MS Ed, Ed S)
educational administration (MS Ed, Ed S)
elementary education (MS Ed)
physical education (MS)
school counseling (MS)
special education (MS Ed)

College of Sciences
Programs in:
biological sciences (MS)
chemistry (MS)
clinical psychology (MA)
communication disorders and sciences (MS)
economics (MA)
mathematics (MA)
mathematics and computer science (MA)
mathematics education (MA)
natural sciences (MS)
political science (MA)
psychology (MA, SSP)
school psychology (SSP)

Lumpkin College of Business and Applied Sciences
Programs in:
accountancy (Certificate)
business and applied sciences (MA, MBA, MS, Certificate)
computer technology (Certificate)
dietetics (MS)
family and consumer sciences (MS)
general management (MBA)
gerontology (MA)
quality systems (Certificate)
technology (MS)
technology security (Certificate)
work performance improvement (Certificate)

■ ELMHURST COLLEGE

Elmhurst, IL 60126-3296
http://www.elmhurst.edu/

Independent-religious, coed, comprehensive institution. *Graduate faculty:* 17 full-time (11 women), 21 part-time/adjunct (5 women). *Computer facilities:* 620 computers available on campus for general student use. A campuswide network can be accessed from student residence rooms and from off campus. Online class registration is available. *Graduate expenses:* Tuition: part-time $675 per semester hour. Tuition and fees vary according to program. *General application contact:* Elizabeth D. Kuebler, Director of Adult and Graduate Admission, 630-617-3069.

Graduate Programs
Dr. John E. Bohnert, Dean of Graduate Studies
Programs in:
business administration (MBA)
computer network systems (MS)
early childhood special education (M Ed)
English studies (MA)
industrial/organizational psychology (MA)
nursing (MSN)
professional accountancy (MPA)
supply chain management (MS)
teacher leadership (M Ed)

■ GOVERNORS STATE UNIVERSITY

University Park, IL 60466-0975
http://www.govst.edu/

State-supported, coed, upper-level institution. CGS member. *Computer facilities:* 165 computers available on campus for general student use. A campuswide network can be accessed from off campus. *General application contact:* Associate Director of Admission, 708-534-4492.

College of Arts and Sciences
Programs in:
analytical chemistry (MS)
art (MA)
arts and sciences (MA, MS)
communication studies (MA)
computer science (MS)
English (MA)
environmental biology (MS)
instructional and training technology (MA)
media communication (MA)
political and justice studies (MA)

College of Business and Public Administration
Programs in:
accounting (MS)
business administration (MBA)
business and public administration (MBA, MPA, MS)
management information systems (MS)
public administration (MPA)

College of Education
Programs in:
counseling (MA)
early childhood education (MA)
education (MA)
educational administration and supervision (MA)
multi-categorical special education (MA)
psychology (MA)
reading (MA)

College of Health Professions
Programs in:
addictions studies (MHS)
communication disorders (MHS)
health administration (MHA)
health professions (MHA, MHS, MOT, MPT, MSN, MSW, DPT)
nursing (MSN)
occupational therapy (MOT)
physical therapy (MPT, DPT)
social work (MSW)

■ ILLINOIS INSTITUTE OF TECHNOLOGY

Chicago, IL 60616-3793
http://www.iit.edu/

Independent, coed, university. CGS member. *Graduate faculty:* 364 full-time (71 women), 263 part-time/adjunct (57 women). *Computer facilities:* 500 computers available on campus for general student use. A campuswide network can be accessed from student residence rooms. Online class registration is available. *General application contact:* Morgan Frederick, Office of Graduate Admissions, 866-472-3448.

Chicago-Kent College of Law
Programs in:
family law (LL M)
financial services (LL M)
international intellectual property (LL M)
international law (LL M)
law (JD)
taxation (LL M)

Graduate College
Dr. Ali Cinar, Dean/Vice Provost

Armour College of Engineering
Dr. Natacha DePaola, Dean
Programs in:
architectural engineering (M Arch E)
biological engineering (MBE)
biomedical engineering (PhD)
biomedical imaging and signals (MBMI)
chemical engineering (M Ch E, MS, PhD)
civil engineering (MS, PhD)
computer engineering (MS, PhD)
construction engineering and management (MCEM)
electrical and computer engineering (MECE)
electrical engineering (MS, PhD)
electricity markets (MEM)
engineering (M Arch E, M Ch E, M Env E, M Geoenv E, M Trans E, MBE, MBMI, MCEM, MECE, MEM, MFPE, MGE, MGE, MMAE, MME, MMME, MNE, MPE, MPW, MS, MSE, MTSE, MVM, PhD)
environmental engineering (M Env E, MS, PhD)
food process engineering (MFPE)
food processing engineering (MS)
gas engineering (MGE)

Illinois Institute of Technology (continued)
geoenvironmental engineering (M Geoenv E)
geotechnical engineering (MGE)
manufacturing engineering (MME, MS)
materials science and engineering (MMME, MS, PhD)
mechanical and aerospace engineering (MMAE, MS, PhD)
network engineering (MNE)
power engineering (MPE)
public works (MPW)
structural engineering (MSE)
telecommunications and software engineering (MTSE)
transportation engineering (M Trans E)
VLSI and microelectronics (MVM)

Center for Professional Development
C. Robert Carlson, Director
Programs in:
industrial technology and management (MITO)
information technology and management (MITM)

College of Architecture
Donna V. Robertson, John and Jeanne Rowe Chair
Programs in:
architecture (M Ar, PhD)
integrated building delivery (M IBD)
landscape architecture (MLA)

College of Science and Letters
Dr. R. Russell Betts, Dean
Programs in:
analytical chemistry (M Ch)
applied mathematics (MS, PhD)
biology (MBS, MS, PhD)
chemistry (M Ch, M Chem, MS, PhD)
collegiate mathematics education (PhD)
computer science (MCS, MS, PhD)
food safety and technology (MFST, MS)
health physics (MHP)
information architecture (MS)
materials and chemical synthesis (M Ch)
mathematical finance (MMF)
mathematics education (MME, MS, PhD)
molecular biochemistry and biophysics (MS, PhD)
nonprofit management (MPA)
physics (MHP, MS, PhD)
public administration (MPA)
public safety and crisis management (MPA)
science and letters (M Ch, M Chem, MBS, MCS, MFST, MHP, MME, MMF, MPA, MS, MSE, MST, MTSE, PhD)
science education (MS, MSE, PhD)
teaching (MST)
technical communication (PhD)
technical communication and information design (MS)
telecommunications and software engineering (MTSE)

Institute of Design
Rachel Williams Smothers, Director of Admissions and Retention
Program in:
design (M Des, MSDM, PhD)

Institute of Psychology
Dr. M. Ellen Mitchell, Dean
Programs in:
clinical psychology (PhD)
industrial/organizational psychology (PhD)
personnel/human resource development (MS)
psychology (MS)
rehabilitation counseling (MS)
rehabilitation counselor education (PhD)

Stuart School of Business
Dr. Harvey Kahalas, Dean
Programs in:
business (MBA, MMF, MS, PhD)
environmental management and sustainability (MS)
finance (MS)
financial management (MBA)
innovation and emerging enterprises (MBA)
management science (PhD)
marketing (MBA)
marketing communication (MS)
mathematical finance (MMF)
sustainable enterprise (MBA)

■ ILLINOIS STATE UNIVERSITY
Normal, IL 61790-2200
http://www.ilstu.edu/

State-supported, coed, university. CGS member. *Computer facilities:* Computer purchase and lease plans are available. 2,275 computers available on campus for general student use. A campuswide network can be accessed from student residence rooms and from off campus. Online class registration is available. *General application contact:* Associate Vice President of Research, Graduate Studies and International Education, 309-438-2583.

Graduate School

College of Applied Science and Technology
Programs in:
agribusiness (MS)
applied science and technology (MA, MS)
criminal justice sciences (MA, MS)
family and consumer sciences (MA, MS)
health education (MS)
information technology (MS)
physical education (MS)
technology (MS)

College of Arts and Sciences
Programs in:
animal behavior (MS)
arts and sciences (MA, MS, MSW, PhD, SSP)
bacteriology (MS)
biochemistry (MS)
biological sciences (MS)
biology (PhD)
biophysics (MS)
biotechnology (MS)
botany (MS, PhD)
cell biology (MS)
chemistry (MS)
communication (MA, MS)
communication sciences and disorders (MA, MS)
conservation biology (MS)
developmental biology (MS)
ecology (MS, PhD)
economics (MA, MS)
English (MA, MS, PhD)
English studies (PhD)
entomology (MS)
evolutionary biology (MS)
French (MA)
French and German (MA)
French and Spanish (MA)
genetics (MS, PhD)
German (MA)
German and Spanish (MA)
historical archaeology (MA, MS)
history (MA, MS)
hydrogeology (MS)
immunology (MS)
mathematics (MA, MS, PhD)
mathematics education (PhD)
microbiology (MS, PhD)
molecular biology (MS)
molecular genetics (MS)
neurobiology (MS)
neuroscience (MS)
parasitology (MS)
physiology (MS, PhD)
plant biology (MS)
plant molecular biology (MS)
plant sciences (MS)
politics and government (MA, MS)
psychology (MA, MS)
school psychology (PhD, SSP)
social work (MSW)
sociology (MA, MS)
Spanish (MA)
structural biology (MS)
writing (MA, MS)
zoology (MS, PhD)

College of Business
Programs in:
accounting (MPA, MS)
business (MBA, MPA, MS)
business administration (MBA)

College of Education
Programs in:
college student personnel administration (MS)
curriculum and instruction (MS, MS Ed, Ed D)
education (MS, MS Ed, Ed D, PhD)
educational administration (MS, MS Ed, Ed D, PhD)
educational policies (Ed D)
postsecondary education (Ed D)
reading (MS Ed)
special education (MS, MS Ed, Ed D)
supervision (Ed D)

College of Fine Arts
Programs in:
art history (MA, MS)
arts technology (MS)
ceramics (MFA, MS)
drawing (MFA, MS)
fibers (MFA, MS)
fine arts (MA, MFA, MM, MM Ed, MS)
glass (MFA, MS)
graphic design (MFA, MS)
metals (MFA, MS)
music (MM, MM Ed)
painting (MFA, MS)
photography (MFA, MS)
printmaking (MFA, MS)
sculpture (MFA, MS)
theatre (MA, MFA, MS)

Mennonite College of Nursing
Programs in:
family nurse practitioner (PMC)
nursing (MSN, PhD)

■ LEWIS UNIVERSITY
Romeoville, IL 60446
http://www.lewisu.edu/

Independent-religious, coed, comprehensive institution. CGS member. *Graduate faculty:* 70 full-time (37 women), 124 part-time/adjunct (59 women). *Computer facilities:* Computer purchase and lease plans are available. 310 computers available on campus for general student use. A campuswide network can be accessed from student residence rooms and from off campus. Online class registration, online help, online billing, online financial aid, online application, online housing application are available. *General application contact:* Julie Nickel, Assistant Director, Graduate and Adult Admission, 800-897-9000.

College of Arts and Sciences
Dr. Bonnie Bondavalli, Dean
Programs in:
arts and sciences (MA, MS)
aviation and transportation (MS)
child and adolescent counseling (MA)
criminal/social justice (MS)
higher education/student services (MA)
mental health counseling (MA)
organizational management (MA)
public administration (MA)
public safety administration (MS)
school counseling and guidance (MA)
training and development (MA)

College of Business
Dr. Rami Khasawneh, Dean
Programs in:
accounting (MBA)
business (MBA, MS)
business administration (MBA)
custom elective option (MBA)
e-business (MBA)
finance (MBA, MS)
healthcare management (MBA)
human resources management (MBA)
information security (MS)
international business (MBA)
management (MS)
management information systems (MBA)
marketing (MBA)
project management (MBA)
technology and operations management (MBA)

College of Education
Dr. Jeanette Mines, Dean
Programs in:
advanced study in education (CAS)
biology (MA)
chemistry (MA)
curriculum and teacher leadership (MA Ed)
educational leadership (M Ed, MA)
educational leadership for teaching and learning (Ed D)
elementary education (MA)
English (MA)
English as a second language (M Ed)
general administrative (CAS)
history (MA)
instructional technology (M Ed)
math (MA)
physics (MA)
psychology and social science (MA)
reading and literacy (M Ed, MA)
secondary education (MA)
special education (MA)
superintendent endorsement (CAS)

College of Nursing and Health Professions
Dr. Peggy Rice, Dean
Programs in:
adult nurse practitioner (MSN)
nursing administration (MSN)
nursing and health professions (MSN)
nursing education (MSN)

■ LOYOLA UNIVERSITY CHICAGO
Chicago, IL 60660
http://www.luc.edu/

Independent-religious, coed, university. CGS member. *Graduate faculty:* 975 full-time (384 women), 698 part-time/adjunct (230 women). *Computer facilities:* Computer purchase and lease plans are available. 800 computers available on campus for general student use. A campuswide network can be accessed from student residence rooms and from off campus. Online class registration is available. *Graduate expenses:* Tuition: full-time $13,500; part-time $750 per credit hour. Required fees: $60 per semester. Full-time tuition and fees vary according to program. *General application contact:* Janice K. Atkinson, Director, Graduate and Professional Enrollment Management, 312-915-8902.

Graduate School
Dr. Samuel Attoh, Dean
Programs in:
applied social psychology (MA, PhD)
applied sociology (MA)
applied statistics (MS)
biochemistry (MS, PhD)
biology (MA, MS)
cell and molecular physiology (MS, PhD)
cell biology, neurobiology and anatomy (MS, PhD)
chemistry (MS, PhD)
clinical psychology (MA, PhD)
computer science (MS)
criminal justice (MA)
developmental psychology (MA, PhD)
English (MA, PhD)
health care ethics (MA)
history (MA, PhD)
human perception (MS)
immunology (PhD)
information technology (MS)
mathematics and statistics (MS)
microbiology (MS)
molecular biology (PhD)
neuroscience (MS, PhD)
pharmacology and experimental therapeutics (MS, PhD)
philosophy (MA, PhD)
political science (MA, PhD)
public history (MA)
public policy (MPP)
social philosophy (MA)
sociology (MA, PhD)
software technology (MS)
Spanish (MA)
theology (MA, PhD)

Marcella Niehoff School of Nursing
Dr. Mary K. Walker, Dean
Programs in:
acute care (Certificate)
acute care clinical nurse specialist (MSN)
acute care nurse practitioner (MSN)
adult clinical nurse specialist (MSN, Certificate)
adult nurse practitioner (MSN)
cardiac health (Certificate)
cardiovascular health (Certificate)
cardiovascular health and disease management clinical nurse specialist (MSN, Certificate)
critical care/trauma (MSN)
emergency nurse practitioner (Certificate)
family nurse practitioner (MSN)
family practice nurse practitioner (Certificate)
informatics (Certificate)
manager care (Certificate)
nursing (MSN, DNP, PhD, Certificate)
nursing oncology (Certificate)
nursing practice (DNP)
oncology clinical nurse specialist (MSN)
oncology nursing (Certificate)
outcomes performance management (Certificate)
population-based infection control and environmental safety (MSN, Certificate)
women's health nurse practitioner (MSN)

Loyola University Chicago (continued)

Graduate School of Business

Programs in:
- accountancy (MS, MSA)
- business administration (MBA)
- finance (MS)
- healthcare management (MBA)
- human resources and employee relations (MS, MSHR)
- information systems and operations management (MS)
- information systems management (MS)
- integrated marketing communications (MS)
- marketing (MS, MSIMC)
- strategic financial services (MBA)

Institute of Human Resources and Employee Relations

Program in:
- human resources and employee relations (MSHR)

Institute of Pastoral Studies

Dr. Robert A. Ludwig, Director

Programs in:
- divinity (M Div)
- pastoral care and counseling (MA)
- pastoral counseling (MA, Certificate)
- pastoral studies (MA)
- religious education (MA, Certificate)
- social justice (MA, Certificate)
- spiritual direction (Certificate)
- spirituality (MA)

School of Education

Dr. David Prasse, Dean

Programs in:
- administration and supervision (M Ed, Ed D, Certificate)
- community counseling (M Ed, MA)
- counseling psychology (PhD)
- cultural and educational policy studies (M Ed, MA, Ed D, PhD)
- curriculum and instruction (M Ed, Ed D)
- education (M Ed, MA, Ed D, PhD, Certificate, Ed S)
- educational psychology (M Ed)
- elementary education (M Ed)
- higher education (M Ed, PhD)
- instructional leadership (M Ed)
- reading specialist (M Ed)
- research methods (M Ed, MA, PhD)
- school counseling (M Ed, Certificate)
- school psychology (M Ed, PhD, Ed S)
- school technology (M Ed)
- science education (M Ed)
- secondary education (M Ed)
- special education (M Ed)

School of Law

David N. Yellen, Dean

Programs in:
- business law (LL M, MJ)
- child and family law (LL M, MJ)
- health law (LL M, MJ, D Law, SJD)
- law (JD)

School of Social Work

Program in:
- social work (MSW, PhD, PGC)

Stritch School of Medicine

Program in:
- medicine (MD)

■ NATIONAL-LOUIS UNIVERSITY

Chicago, IL 60603

http://www.nl.edu/

Independent, coed, university. *Graduate faculty:* 254 full-time (173 women), 856 part-time/adjunct (574 women). *Computer facilities:* A campuswide network can be accessed from off campus. Online class registration is available. *General application contact:* Dr. Larry Poselli, Vice President of Enrollment Management, 312-261-3550.

College of Arts and Sciences

Programs in:
- addictions counseling (Certificate)
- addictions treatment (Certificate)
- arts and sciences (M Ed, MA, MS, Ed D, Certificate)
- career counseling and development studies (Certificate)
- community counseling (MS)
- community wellness and prevention (Certificate)
- counseling (Certificate)
- cultural psychology (MA)
- eating disorders counseling (Certificate)
- employee assistance programs (MS, Certificate)
- gerontology administration (Certificate)
- gerontology counseling (MS, Certificate)
- health psychology (MA)
- human development (MA)
- human services administration (MS, Certificate)
- long-term care administration (Certificate)
- organizational psychology (MA)
- psychology (Certificate)
- school counseling (MS)
- written communication (MS)

Division of Language and Academic Development

Judith Kent, Associate Professor

Programs in:
- adult education (Ed D)
- adult literacy and developmental studies (M Ed, Certificate)
- adult, continuing, and literacy education (M Ed, Certificate)

College of Management and Business

Chrisopher Multhauf, Executive Dean

Programs in:
- business administration (MBA)
- human resource management and development (MS)
- management (MS)
- management and business (MBA, MS)

National College of Education

Dr. Alison Hilsobeck, Dean

Programs in:
- administration and supervision (M Ed, CAS, Ed S)
- adult education (Ed D)
- curriculum and instruction (M Ed, MS Ed, CAS)
- curriculum and social inquiry (Ed D)
- early childhood administration (M Ed, CAS)
- early childhood curriculum and instruction specialist (M Ed, MS Ed, CAS)
- early childhood education (M Ed, MAT, CAS)
- education (M Ed, MAT, MS Ed, Ed D, CAS, Ed S)
- educational leadership (Ed D)
- educational leadership/superintendent endorsement (Ed D)
- educational psychology (CAS, Ed S)
- educational psychology/human learning and development (M Ed, MS Ed)
- educational psychology/school psychology (Ed D)
- elementary education (MAT)
- general special education (M Ed, MAT, CAS)
- human learning and development (Ed D)
- interdisciplinary studies in curriculum and instruction (M Ed)
- language and literacy (M Ed, MS Ed, CAS)
- learning disabilities (M Ed, CAS)
- learning disabilities/behavior disorders (M Ed, MAT, CAS)
- mathematics education (M Ed, MS Ed, CAS)
- reading and language (M Ed, MS Ed, Ed D, CAS)
- reading recovery (CAS)
- reading specialist (M Ed, MS Ed, CAS)
- school psychology (M Ed, Ed S)
- science education (M Ed, MS Ed, CAS)
- secondary education (MAT)
- technology in education (M Ed, MS Ed, CAS)

■ NORTH CENTRAL COLLEGE

Naperville, IL 60566-7063

http://www.noctrl.edu/

Independent-religious, coed, comprehensive institution. *Computer facilities:* 325 computers available on campus for general student use. A campuswide network can be accessed from student residence rooms and from off campus. Online class registration, software packages are available. *General application contact:* Graduate Admissions Counselor, 630-637-5812.

Graduate Programs

Programs in:
- business administration (MBA)
- computer science (MS)
- curriculum and instruction (MA Ed)

leadership and administration (MA Ed)
leadership studies (MLD)
liberal studies (MALS)
management information systems (MS)
reading (MA)
special education (MA)
teaching (MAT)
teaching children with learning disabilities (MA)

■ NORTHEASTERN ILLINOIS UNIVERSITY

Chicago, IL 60625-4699
http://www.neiu.edu/

State-supported, coed, comprehensive institution. CGS member. *Computer facilities:* 360 computers available on campus for general student use. A campuswide network can be accessed from off campus. Online class registration, productivity software are available. *General application contact:* Assistant to the Dean—Admission, 773-442-6008.

Graduate College

College of Arts and Sciences
Programs in:
arts and sciences (MA, MS)
biology (MS)
chemistry (MS)
communication, media and theatre (MA)
composition/writing (MA)
computer science (MS)
earth science (MS)
English (MA)
geography and environmental studies (MA)
gerontology (MA)
history (MA)
linguistics (MA)
literature (MA)
mathematics (MA, MS)
mathematics for elementary school teachers (MA)
music (MA)
political science (MA)

College of Business and Management
Programs in:
accounting (MBA)
finance (MBA)
management (MBA)
marketing (MBA)

College of Education
Programs in:
bilingual/bicultural education (MAT, MSI)
early childhood special education (MA)
educating children with behavior disorders (MA)
educating individuals with mental retardation (MA)
education (MA, MAT, MSI)
educational administration and supervision (MA)
educational leadership (MA)
gifted education (MA)
guidance and counseling (MA)
human resource development (MA)
inner city studies (MA)
instruction (MSI)
language arts (MAT, MSI)

■ NORTHERN ILLINOIS UNIVERSITY

De Kalb, IL 60115-2854
http://www.niu.edu/

State-supported, coed, university. CGS member. *Computer facilities:* 1,500 computers available on campus for general student use. A campuswide network can be accessed from student residence rooms and from off campus. Online class registration is available. *General application contact:* Associate Dean, Graduate School, 815-753-0395.

College of Law

Malcolm Morris, Interim Dean
Program in:
law (JD)

Graduate School

Dr. Bradley G. Bond, Dean of the Graduate School and Vice President for Research
Programs in:
accountancy (MAS, MST)
adult and higher education (MS Ed, Ed D)
allied health and communicative disorders (MA, MPT, Au D)
anthropology (MA)
applied family and child studies (MS)
art (MA, MFA, MS)
biological sciences (MS, PhD)
business (MAS, MBA, MS, MST)
business administration (MBA)
chemistry (MS, PhD)
communication studies (MA)
communicative disorders (MA, Au D)
computer science (MS)
counseling (MS Ed, Ed D)
curriculum and instruction (MS Ed, Ed D)
early childhood education (MS Ed)
economics (MA, PhD)
education (MS, MS Ed, Ed D, Ed S)
educational administration (MS Ed, Ed D, Ed S)
educational psychology (MS Ed, Ed D)
educational research and evaluation (MS)
electrical engineering (MS)
elementary education (MS Ed)
engineering and engineering technology (MS)
English (MA, PhD)
foundations of education (MS Ed)
French (MA)
geography (MS)
geology (MS, PhD)
health and human sciences (MA, MPH, MPT, MS, Au D)
history (MA, PhD)
industrial engineering (MS)
industrial management (MS)
instructional technology (MS Ed, Ed D)
liberal arts and sciences (MA, MPA, MS, PhD)
literacy education (MS Ed)
management information systems (MS)
mathematical sciences (PhD)
mathematics (MS)
mechanical engineering (MS)
music (MM, Performer's Certificate)
nursing (MS)
nutrition and dietetics (MS)
philosophy (MA)
physical education (MS Ed)
physical therapy (MPT)
physics (MS, PhD)
political science (MA, PhD)
psychology (MA, PhD)
public administration (MPA)
public health (MPH)
school business management (MS Ed)
sociology (MA)
Spanish (MA)
special education (MS Ed)
sport management (MS)
statistics (MS)
theatre and dance (MFA)
visual and performing arts (MA, MFA, MM, MS, Performer's Certificate)

College of Business
Dr. Denise Schoenbachler, Dean
Programs in:
accountancy (MAS, MST)
business (MAS, MBA, MS, MST)
business administration (MBA)
management information systems (MS)

College of Education
Dr. Lemuel W. Watson, Dean
Programs in:
adult and higher education (MS Ed, Ed D)
counseling (MS Ed, Ed D)
curriculum and instruction (MS Ed, Ed D)
early childhood education (MS Ed)
education (MS, MS Ed, Ed D, Ed S)
educational administration (MS Ed, Ed D, Ed S)
educational psychology (MS Ed, Ed D)
educational research and evaluation (MS)
elementary education (MS Ed)
foundations of education (MS Ed)
instructional technology (MS Ed, Ed D)
literacy education (MS Ed)
physical education (MS Ed)
school business management (MS Ed)
special education (MS Ed)
sport management (MS)

College of Engineering and Engineering Technology
Dr. Promod Vohra, Acting Dean
Programs in:
electrical engineering (MS)
engineering and engineering technology (MS)

Northern Illinois University (continued)
industrial engineering (MS)
industrial management (MS)
mechanical engineering (MS)

College of Health and Human Sciences
Dr. Shirley Richmond, Dean
Programs in:
allied health and communicative disorders (MA, MPT, Au D)
applied family and child studies (MS)
communicative disorders (MA, Au D)
health and human sciences (MA, MPH, MPT, MS, Au D)
nursing (MS)
nutrition and dietetics (MS)
physical therapy (MPT)
public health (MPH)

College of Liberal Arts and Sciences
Dr. Christopher McCord, Acting Dean
Programs in:
anthropology (MA)
biological sciences (MS, PhD)
chemistry (MS, PhD)
communication studies (MA)
computer science (MS)
economics (MA, PhD)
English (MA, PhD)
French (MA)
geography (MS)
geology (MS, PhD)
history (MA, PhD)
liberal arts and sciences (MA, MPA, MS, PhD)
mathematical sciences (PhD)
mathematics (MS)
philosophy (MA)
physics (MS, PhD)
political science (MA, PhD)
psychology (MA, PhD)
public administration (MPA)
sociology (MA)
Spanish (MA)
statistics (MS)

College of Visual and Performing Arts
Dr. Rich Holly, Dean
Programs in:
art (MA, MFA, MS)
music (MM, Performer's Certificate)
theatre and dance (MFA)
visual and performing arts (MA, MFA, MM, MS, Performer's Certificate)

■ NORTH PARK UNIVERSITY
Chicago, IL 60625-4895
http://www.northpark.edu/

Independent-religious, coed, comprehensive institution. *Computer facilities:* A campuswide network can be accessed from student residence rooms and from off campus. *General application contact:* Vice President for Admissions and Financial Aid, 773-244-5500.

School of Business and Nonprofit Management
Program in:
business and nonprofit management (MBA, MHEA, MHRM, MM, MNA)

School of Education
Program in:
education (MA)

School of Nursing
Programs in:
advanced practice nursing (MS)
leadership and management (MS)

■ NORTHWESTERN UNIVERSITY
Evanston, IL 60208
http://www.northwestern.edu/

Independent, coed, university. CGS member. *Computer facilities:* 678 computers available on campus for general student use. A campuswide network can be accessed from student residence rooms and from off campus. Online class registration is available. *General application contact:* Student Services.

The Graduate School
Programs in:
African studies (Certificate)
biochemistry, molecular biology, and cell biology (PhD)
biotechnology (PhD)
cell and molecular biology (PhD)
clinical investigation (MSCI, Certificate)
clinical psychology (PhD)
counseling psychology (MA)
developmental biology and genetics (PhD)
genetic counseling (MS)
hormone action and signal transduction (PhD)
law and social science (Certificate)
liberal studies (MA)
literature (MA)
management and organizations and sociology (PhD)
marital and family therapy (MS)
mathematical methods in social science (MS)
neuroscience (PhD)
public health (MPH)
structural biology, biochemistry, and biophysics (PhD)

Center for International and Comparative Studies
Program in:
international and comparative studies (Certificate)

Institute for Neuroscience
Program in:
neuroscience (PhD)

Judd A. and Marjorie Weinberg College of Arts and Sciences
Programs in:
anthropology (PhD)
art history (PhD)
arts and sciences (MA, MFA, MS, PhD, Certificate)
astrophysics (PhD)
brain, behavior and cognition (PhD)
chemistry (PhD)
clinical psychology (PhD)
cognitive psychology (PhD)
comparative literary studies (PhD)
economics (MA, PhD)
eighteenth-century studies (Certificate)
English (MA, PhD)
French (PhD)
French and comparative literature (PhD)
geological sciences (MS, PhD)
German literature and critical thought (PhD)
history (PhD)
Italian studies (Certificate)
linguistics (MA, PhD)
mathematics (PhD)
neurobiology and physiology (MS)
personality (PhD)
philosophy (PhD)
physics (MS, PhD)
political science (MA, PhD)
Slavic languages and literature (PhD)
social psychology (PhD)
sociology (PhD)
statistics (MS, PhD)
visual arts (MFA)

Kellogg School of Management
Programs in:
accounting (PhD)
business administration (MBA)
finance (PhD)
management (MBA, PhD)
management and organizations (PhD)
managerial economics and strategy (PhD)
marketing (PhD)

School of Communication
Programs in:
audiology and hearing sciences (MA, PhD)
clinical audiology (Au D)
communication (MA, MFA, MSC, Au D, PhD)
communication studies (MA, PhD)
communication systems strategy and management (MSC)
directing (MFA)
learning disabilities (MA, PhD)
managerial communication (MSC)
performance studies (MA, PhD)
radio/television/film (MA, MFA, PhD)
speech and language pathology (MA, PhD)
speech and language pathology and learning disabilities (MA)
stage design (MFA)
theatre (MA)
theatre and drama (PhD)

School of Education and Social Policy
Mark P. Hoffman, Graduate Student Administrative Liaison

Programs in:
advanced teaching (MS)
education and social policy (MS)
elementary education and policy (MS)
higher education administration (MS)
human development and social policy (PhD)
learning and organizational change (MS)
learning sciences (MA, PhD)
secondary teaching (MS)

Henry and Leigh Bienen School of Music
Programs in:
collaborative arts (DM)
conducting (MM, DM)
jazz (MM)
music (MM, DM, PhD, CP)
music composition (DM)
music education (MM, PhD)
music technology (MM)
music technology/new media (DM)
music theory (MM, PhD)
musicology (MM, PhD)
performance (MM)
piano performance (MM, DM, CP)
piano performance and collaborative arts (MM)
piano performance and pedagogy (MM)
string performance and pedagogy (MM)
strings (MM, DM)
strings, winds and percussion (CP)
voice (MM, DM, CP)
winds and percussion (MM, DM)

Law School
David Van Zandt, Dean
Programs in:
executive (LL M)
international human rights (LL M)
law (JD, LL M)
tax (LL M in Tax)
two-year accelerated (JD)

McCormick School of Engineering and Applied Science
Programs in:
applied mathematics (MS, PhD)
biomedical engineering (MS, PhD)
chemical engineering (MS, PhD)
computational biology and bioinformatics (MS)
computer science (MS, PhD)
electrical and computer engineering (MS, PhD)
electronic materials (MS, PhD, Certificate)
engineering and applied science (MEM, MIT, MME, MMM, MPD, MS, PhD, Certificate)
engineering management (MEM)
environmental engineering and science (MS, PhD)
fluid mechanics (MS, PhD)
geotechnical engineering (MS, PhD)
industrial engineering and management science (MS, PhD)
information technology (MIT)
manufacturing engineering (MME)
materials science and engineering (MS, PhD)
mechanical engineering (MS, PhD)
mechanics of materials and solids (MS, PhD)
operations research (MS, PhD)
project management (MS)
solid mechanics (MS, PhD)
structural engineering and materials (MS, PhD)
theoretical and applied mechanics (MS, PhD)
transportation systems analysis and planning (MS, PhD)

Segal Design Institute
Program in:
engineering design and innovation (MS)

Medill School of Journalism
Programs in:
advertising/sales promotion (MSIMC)
broadcast journalism (MSJ)
direct database and e-commerce marketing (MSIMC)
general studies (MSIMC)
integrated marketing communications (MSIMC)
magazine publishing (MSJ)
new media (MSJ)
public relations (MSIMC)
reporting and writing (MSJ)

Northwestern University Feinberg School of Medicine
Programs in:
cancer biology (PhD)
cell biology (PhD)
clinical investigation (MSCI)
developmental biology (PhD)
evolutionary biology (PhD)
immunology and microbial pathogenesis (PhD)
medicine (MD, MS, MSCI, DPT, PhD)
molecular biology and genetics (PhD)
movement and rehabilitation science (PhD)
neurobiology (PhD)
pharmacology and toxicology (PhD)
physical therapy (DPT)
structural biology and biochemistry (PhD)

■ OLIVET NAZARENE UNIVERSITY
Bourbonnais, IL 60914-2271
http://www.olivet.edu/

Independent-religious, coed, comprehensive institution. *Computer facilities:* Computer purchase and lease plans are available. A campuswide network can be accessed from student residence rooms and from off campus. Online class registration is available. *General application contact:* Dean, 800-648-1463.

Graduate School
Programs in:
business administration (MBA)
practical ministries (MPM)

Division of Education
Programs in:
curriculum and instruction (MAE)
elementary education (MAT)
library information specialist (MAE)
reading specialist (MAE)
school leadership (MAE)
secondary education (MAT)

Division of Religion
Programs in:
biblical literature (MA)
religion (MA)
theology (MA)

Program in Organizational Leadership
Program in:
organizational leadership (MOL)

■ ROCKFORD COLLEGE
Rockford, IL 61108-2393
http://www.rockford.edu/

Independent, coed, comprehensive institution. *Graduate faculty:* 16 full-time (5 women), 61 part-time/adjunct (39 women). *Computer facilities:* 75 computers available on campus for general student use. A campuswide network can be accessed from student residence rooms and from off campus. *Graduate expenses:* Tuition: full-time $11,250; part-time $625 per credit hour. Required fees: $30 per semester. Tuition and fees vary according to course load and program. *General application contact:* Michele Mehren, Office Manager for Graduate Studies, 815-226-4041.

Graduate Studies
Dr. Michelle M. McReynolds, MAT Director
Programs in:
business administration (MBA)
education (MAT)
elementary education (MAT)
instructional strategies (MAT)
reading (MAT)
secondary education (MAT)
special education (MAT)

■ ROOSEVELT UNIVERSITY
Chicago, IL 60605-1394
http://www.roosevelt.edu/

Independent, coed, comprehensive institution. CGS member. *Graduate faculty:* 210 full-time (86 women), 543 part-time/adjunct (247 women). *Computer facilities:* 300 computers available on campus for general student use. A campuswide network can be accessed from student residence rooms and from off campus. Online class registration is available. *Graduate expenses:* Tuition: full-time $14,730; part-time $709 per credit. Required fees: $175 per semester. Tuition and fees vary according to course load and program. *General application contact:* Joanne Canyon-Heller, Coordinator of Graduate Admission, 877-APPLY RU.

Roosevelt University (continued)

Graduate Division
Dr. Janett Trubatch, Dean of Graduate Studies

Chicago College of Performing Arts
Rudy Marcozzi, Interim Dean
Programs in:
- directing and dramaturgy (MFA)
- music (MM)
- musical theatre (MFA)
- performing arts (MA, MFA, MM, Diploma)
- piano pedagogy (Diploma)
- theatre (MA, MFA)
- theatre-directing (MA)
- theatre-performance (MFA)

College of Arts and Sciences
Lynn Weiner, Dean
Programs in:
- anthropology (MA)
- applied economics (MA)
- arts and sciences (MA, MFA, MPA, MS, MSC, MSIMC, MSJ, MST, Psy D, Certificate)
- biotechnology and chemical science (MS)
- clinical professional psychology (MA, Psy D)
- computer science (MSC)
- creative writing (MFA)
- economics (MA)
- English (MA)
- history (MA)
- industrial/organizational psychology (MA)
- integrated marketing communications (MSIMC)
- journalism (MSJ)
- mathematical sciences (MS)
- mathematics (MS)
- political science (MA)
- psychology (Psy D)
- public administration (MPA)
- sociology (MA)
- Spanish (MA)
- telecommunications (MST)
- women's and gender studies (MA, Certificate)

College of Education
George Olson, Interim Dean
Programs in:
- counseling and human services (MA)
- early childhood education (MA)
- education (MA, Ed D)
- educational leadership (MA, Ed D)
- elementary education (MA)
- reading teacher education (MA)
- secondary education (MA)
- special education (MA)
- teacher leadership (MA)

College of Professional Studies
John Cicero, Dean
Programs in:
- hospitality management (MS)
- training and development (MA)

Walter E. Heller College of Business Administration
Joe Chan, Interim Dean
Programs in:
- accounting (MSA)
- business administration (MBA, MS, MSA, MSHRM, MSIB, MSIS, Certificate)
- commercial real estate development (Certificate)
- human resource management (MSHRM)
- information systems (MSIS)
- international business (MSIB)
- real estate (MBA, MS)

■ SAINT XAVIER UNIVERSITY
Chicago, IL 60655-3105
http://www.sxu.edu/

Independent-religious, coed, comprehensive institution. *Computer facilities:* 306 computers available on campus for general student use. A campuswide network can be accessed from student residence rooms and from off campus. Online class registration is available. *General application contact:* Vice President of Enrollment Services, 773-298-3050.

Graduate Studies

Graham School of Management
Programs in:
- e-commerce (MBA)
- employee health benefits (Certificate)
- finance (MBA, MS)
- financial analysis and investments (MBA)
- financial planning (MBA, Certificate)
- financial trading and practice (MBA, Certificate)
- generalist/administration (MBA)
- health administration (MBA, MS)
- managed care (Certificate)
- management (MBA, MS)
- marketing (MBA)
- public and non-profit management (MBA)
- public health (MPH)
- service management (MBA)
- training and performance management (MBA)

School of Arts and Sciences
Programs in:
- adult counseling (Certificate)
- applied computer science in Internet information systems (MS)
- arts and sciences (MA, MS, CAS, Certificate)
- child/adolescent counseling (Certificate)
- core counseling (Certificate)
- counseling psychology (MA)
- English (CAS)
- literary studies (MA)
- mathematics and computer science (MA)
- speech-language pathology (MS)
- teaching of writing (MA)
- writing pedagogy (CAS)

School of Education
Programs in:
- counseling (MA)
- counselor education (MA)
- curriculum and instruction (MA)
- early childhood education (MA)
- education (CAS)
- educational administration (MA)
- elementary education (MA)
- field-based education (MA)
- general educational studies (MA)
- individualized program (MA)
- learning disabilities (MA)
- reading (MA)
- secondary education (MA)

School of Nursing
Programs in:
- adult health clinical nurse specialist (MS)
- family nurse practitioner (MS, PMC)
- leadership in community health nursing (MS)
- psychiatric-mental health clinical nurse specialist (MS)
- psychiatric-mental health clinical specialist (PMC)

■ SOUTHERN ILLINOIS UNIVERSITY CARBONDALE
Carbondale, IL 62901-4701
http://www.siuc.edu

State-supported, coed, university. CGS member. *Computer facilities:* Computer purchase and lease plans are available. 1,776 computers available on campus for general student use. A campuswide network can be accessed from student residence rooms and from off campus. Online class registration is available. *General application contact:* Associate Dean of the Graduate School, 618-536-7791.

Graduate School
Programs in:
- molecular, cellular and systemic physiology (MS)
- pharmacology (MS, PhD)
- physiology (MS, PhD)

College of Agriculture
Programs in:
- agribusiness economics (MS)
- agriculture (MS)
- animal science (MS)
- food and nutrition (MS)
- forestry (MS)
- horticultural science (MS)
- plant and soil science (MS)

College of Applied Science
Programs in:
- applied science (M Arch, MSPA)
- architecture (M Arch)
- physician assistant studies (MSPA)

College of Business and Administration
Programs in:
- accountancy (M Acc, PhD)

business administration (MBA, PhD)
business and administration (M Acc, MBA, PhD)

College of Education
Programs in:
behavior analysis and therapy (MS)
behavioral analysis and therapy (MS)
communication disorders and sciences (MS)
community health education (MPH)
counselor education (MS Ed, PhD)
curriculum and instruction (MS Ed, PhD)
education (MPH, MS, MS Ed, MSW, PhD, Rh D)
educational administration (MS Ed, PhD)
educational psychology (MS Ed, PhD)
health education (MS Ed, PhD)
higher education (MS Ed)
human learning and development (MS Ed)
measurement and statistics (PhD)
physical education (MS Ed)
recreation (MS Ed)
rehabilitation (Rh D)
rehabilitation administration and services (MS)
rehabilitation counseling (MS)
social work (MSW)
special education (MS Ed)
workforce education and development (MS Ed, PhD)

College of Engineering
Programs in:
biomedical engineering (ME, MS)
civil engineering (MS)
electrical and computer engineering (MS, PhD)
electrical systems (PhD)
engineering (ME, MS, PhD)
fossil energy (PhD)
manufacturing systems (MS)
mechanical engineering and energy processes (MS)
mechanics (PhD)
mining engineering (MS)

College of Liberal Arts
Programs in:
administration of justice (MA)
anthropology (MA, PhD)
applied linguistics (MA)
ceramics (MFA)
clinical psychology (MA, MS, PhD)
composition (MA, PhD)
composition and theory (MM)
counseling psychology (MA, MS, PhD)
creative writing (MFA)
drawing (MFA)
economics (MA, MS, PhD)
experimental psychology (MA, MS, PhD)
fiber/weaving (MFA)
foreign languages and literatures (MA)
geography (MS, PhD)
glass (MFA)
history (MA, PhD)
history and literature (MM)
jewelry (MFA)
liberal arts (MA, MFA, MM, MPA, MS, PhD)
metalsmithing/blacksmithing (MFA)
music education (MM)
opera/music theater (MM)
painting (MFA)
performance (MM)
philosophy (MA, PhD)
piano pedagogy (MM)
political science (MA, PhD)
printmaking (MFA)
public administration (MPA)
sculpture (MFA)
sociology (MA, PhD)
speech communication (MA, MS, PhD)
speech/theater (PhD)
teaching English to speakers of other languages (MA)
theater (MFA)

College of Mass Communication and Media Arts
Programs in:
journalism (PhD)
mass communication and media arts (MA, MFA, PhD)
media theory and research (MA)
professional media and media management studies (MA)

College of Science
Programs in:
biological sciences (MS)
chemistry and biochemistry (MS, PhD)
computer science (MS, PhD)
environmental resources and policy (PhD)
geology (MS, PhD)
mathematics (MA, MS, PhD)
molecular biology, microbiology, and biochemistry (MS, PhD)
physics (MS, PhD)
plant biology (MS, PhD)
science (MA, MS, PhD)
statistics (MS)
zoology (MS, PhD)

School of Law
Programs in:
general law (LL M, MLS)
health law and policy (LL M, MLS)
law (JD)
legal studies (MLS)

■ SOUTHERN ILLINOIS UNIVERSITY EDWARDSVILLE

Edwardsville, IL 62026-0001
http://www.siue.edu/

State-supported, coed, comprehensive institution. CGS member. *Graduate faculty:* 462 full-time (178 women). *Computer facilities:* 600 computers available on campus for general student use. A campuswide network can be accessed from student residence rooms and from off campus. Online class registration, online job finder are available. *Graduate expenses:* Tuition, state resident: full-time $5838. Tuition, nonresident: full-time $14,596. Required fees: $1525. *General application contact:* Michelle Robinson, Coordinator of Graduate Recruitment, 618-650-2811.

Graduate Studies and Research
Dr. Stephen L. Hansen, Associate Provost for Research and Dean of Graduate School

College of Arts and Sciences
Dr. John Danley, Acting Dean
Programs in:
American and English literature (MA, Postbaccalaureate Certificate)
art therapy counseling (MA)
arts and sciences (MA, MFA, MM, MPA, MS, MSW, Postbaccalaureate Certificate)
biology (MA, MS)
biotechnology management (MS)
chemistry (MS)
corporate and organizational communication (Postbaccalaureate Certificate)
creative writing (MA)
environmental science management (MS)
environmental sciences (MS)
geography (MS)
history (MA)
mass communications (MS, Postbaccalaureate Certificate)
mathematics (MS)
media literacy (Postbaccalaureate Certificate)
museum studies (Postbaccalaureate Certificate)
music education (MM)
music performance (MM)
physics (MS)
piano pedagogy (Postbaccalaureate Certificate)
public administration and policy analysis (MPA)
school social work (MSW)
sociology and criminal justice studies (MA)
speech communication (MA, Postbaccalaureate Certificate)
studio art (MFA)
teaching English as a second language (MA, Postbaccalaureate Certificate)
teaching of writing (MA, Postbaccalaureate Certificate)
vocal pedagogy (Postbaccalaureate Certificate)

School of Business
Dr. Gary Giamartino, Dean
Programs in:
accounting (MSA)
business (MA, MBA, MMR, MS, MSA)
computer management and information systems (MS)
economics and finance (MA, MS)
general business (MBA)
management information systems (MBA)
marketing research (MMR)
project management (MBA)

Southern Illinois University Edwardsville (continued)

School of Education
Dr. Bette Bergeron, Interim Dean
Programs in:
art (MS Ed)
biology (MS Ed)
chemistry (MS Ed)
clinical child and school psychology (MS)
clinical-adult psychology (MA)
curriculum and instruction (MS Ed)
earth and space sciences (MS Ed)
education (MA, MAT, MS, MS Ed, Ed S, Post-Master's Certificate, Postbaccalaureate Certificate, SD)
educational administration (MS Ed, Ed S)
English/language arts (MS Ed)
exercise physiology (Postbaccalaureate Certificate)
foreign languages (MS Ed)
history (MS Ed)
industrial-organizational psychology (MA)
instructional technology (MS Ed)
kinesiology (MS Ed)
learning, culture, and society (MS Ed)
literacy education (MS Ed)
literacy specialist (Post-Master's Certificate)
mathematics (MS Ed)
pedagogy administration (Postbaccalaureate Certificate)
physics (MS Ed)
school psychology (SD)
secondary education (MS Ed)
special education (MS Ed)
speech language pathology (MS)
sport and exercise behavior (Postbaccalaureate Certificate)
teaching (MAT)
web-based learning (Postbaccalaureate Certificate)

School of Engineering
Dr. Hasan Sevim, Dean
Programs in:
civil engineering (MS)
computer science (MS)
electrical engineering (MS)
engineering (MS)
industrial engineering (MS)
mechanical engineering (MS)

School of Nursing
Dr. Marcia Maurer, Dean
Programs in:
family nurse practitioner (MS, Post-Master's Certificate)
health care and nursing administration (MS, Post-Master's Certificate)
nurse anesthesia (MS, Post-Master's Certificate)
nurse educator (MS, Post-Master's Certificate)
nursing (MS, Post-Master's Certificate)

School of Dental Medicine
Dr. Ann Boyle, Dean
Program in:
dental medicine (DMD)

School of Pharmacy
Dr. Philip J. Medon, Head
Program in:
pharmacy (Pharm D)

■ TRINITY INTERNATIONAL UNIVERSITY
Deerfield, IL 60015-1284
http://www.tiu.edu/

Independent-religious, coed, university. *Computer facilities:* 130 computers available on campus for general student use. A campuswide network can be accessed from student residence rooms and from off campus. Online class registration is available. *General application contact:* Director of Admissions, 800-345-8337.

Trinity Evangelical Divinity School
Programs in:
Biblical and Near Eastern archaeology and languages (MA)
Christian studies (MA, Certificate)
Christian thought (MA)
church history (MA, Th M)
congregational ministry: pastor-teacher (M Div)
congregational ministry: team ministry (M Div)
counseling ministries (MA)
counseling psychology (MA)
cross-cultural ministry (M Div)
educational studies (PhD)
evangelism (MA)
history of Christianity in America (MA)
intercultural studies (MA, PhD)
leadership and ministry management (D Min)
military chaplaincy (D Min)
ministry (MA)
mission and evangelism (Th M)
missions and evangelism (D Min)
New Testament (MA, Th M)
Old Testament (Th M)
Old Testament and Semitic languages (MA)
pastoral care (M Div)
pastoral care and counseling (D Min)
pastoral counseling and psychology (Th M)
pastoral theology (Th M)
philosophy of religion (MA)
preaching (D Min)
religion (MA)
research ministry (M Div)
systematic theology (Th M)
theological studies (PhD)
urban ministry (MA)

Trinity Graduate School
Programs in:
bioethics (MA)
communication and culture (MA)
counseling psychology (MA)
instructional leadership (M Ed)
teaching (MA)

Trinity Law School
Program in:
law (JD)

■ UNIVERSITY OF CHICAGO
Chicago, IL 60637-1513
http://www.uchicago.edu/

Independent, coed, university. CGS member. *Graduate faculty:* 2,160 full-time (683 women), 760 part-time/adjunct (280 women). *Computer facilities:* 1,000 computers available on campus for general student use. A campuswide network can be accessed from student residence rooms and from off campus. Online class registration is available. *General application contact:* Martha Jackson, Manager, Office of Graduate Affairs, 773-702-7813.

Divinity School
Program in:
divinity (M Div, AM, AMRS, PhD)

Division of Social Sciences
Programs in:
anthropology (PhD)
comparative human development (PhD)
conceptual and historical studies of science (PhD)
economics (PhD)
history (PhD)
international relations (AM)
Latin American and Caribbean studies (AM)
Middle Eastern studies (AM)
political science (PhD)
psychology (PhD)
social sciences (AM, PhD)
social thought (PhD)
sociology (PhD)

Division of the Biological Sciences
Dr. James Madara, Dean
Programs in:
biochemistry and molecular biology (PhD)
biological sciences (MD, MS, PhD)
cancer biology (PhD)
cell and molecular biology (PhD)
cell physiology (PhD)
cellular and molecular physiology (PhD)
cellular differentiation (PhD)
computational neuroscience (PhD)
developmental biology (PhD)
developmental endocrinology (PhD)
developmental genetics (PhD)
developmental neurobiology (PhD)
ecology and evolution (PhD)
evolutionary biology (PhD)
functional and evolutionary biology (PhD)
gene expression (PhD)
genetics, genomics and systems biology (PhD)
health studies (MS, PhD)
human genetics (PhD)

immunology (PhD)
integrative neuroscience (PhD)
interdisciplinary scientist training (PhD)
medical physics (PhD)
microbiology (PhD)
molecular metabolism and nutrition (PhD)
neurobiology (PhD)
ophthalmology and visual science (PhD)
organismal biology and anatomy (PhD)
pathology (PhD)
pharmacological and physiological sciences (PhD)

Pritzker School of Medicine
Program in:
medicine (MD)

Division of the Humanities
Programs in:
ancient philosophy (AM, PhD)
anthropology and linguistics (PhD)
art history (AM, PhD)
cinema and media studies (AM, PhD)
classical archaeology (AM, PhD)
classical languages and literatures (AM, PhD)
comparative literature (AM, PhD)
East Asian languages and civilizations (AM, PhD)
English language and literature (AM, PhD)
French (AM, PhD)
Germanic languages and literatures (AM, PhD)
humanities (AM, MA, MFA, PhD)
Italian (AM, PhD)
linguistics (AM, PhD)
music (AM, PhD)
Near Eastern languages and civilizations (AM, PhD)
philosophy (AM, PhD)
Slavic languages and literatures (AM, PhD)
South Asian languages and civilizations (AM, PhD)
Spanish (AM, PhD)
visual arts (MFA)

Division of the Physical Sciences
Programs in:
applied mathematics (SM, PhD)
astronomy and astrophysics (MS, PhD)
atmospheric sciences (SM, PhD)
biophysical science (PhD)
chemistry (PhD)
computer science (SM, PhD)
earth sciences (SM, PhD)
financial mathematics (MS)
mathematics (SM, PhD)
paleobiology (PhD)
physical sciences (MS, SM, PhD)
physics (PhD)
planetary and space sciences (SM, PhD)
statistics (SM, PhD)

Full-time MBA Program
Stacey Kole, Deputy Dean of full-time MBA Program
Programs in:
business (IMBA, MBA, PhD)
business administration (MBA)
executive business administration (MBA)
international business administration (IMBA)

Irving B. Harris Graduate School of Public Policy Studies
Programs in:
environmental science and policy (MS)
public policy studies (AM, MPP, PhD)

The Law School
Saul Levmore, Dean
Program in:
law (JD, LL M, MCL, DCL, JSD)

School of Social Service Administration
Programs in:
social service administration (PhD)
social work (AM)

■ UNIVERSITY OF ILLINOIS AT CHICAGO
Chicago, IL 60607-7128
http://www.uic.edu/

State-supported, coed, university. CGS member. *Computer facilities:* 800 computers available on campus for general student use. A campuswide network can be accessed from student residence rooms and from off campus. Online class registration is available. *General application contact:* Graduate College Receptionist, 312-413-2550.

College of Dentistry
Programs in:
dentistry (DDS, MS, PhD)
oral sciences (MS, PhD)

College of Medicine
Programs in:
biochemistry and molecular genetics (PhD)
cellular and systems neuroscience and cell biology (PhD)
medical education (MHPE)
medicine (MD, MHPE, MS, PhD)
microbiology and immunology (PhD)
neuroscience (PhD)
pharmacology (PhD)
physiology and biophysics (MS, PhD)
surgery (MS)

College of Pharmacy
Programs in:
biopharmaceutical sciences (PhD)
forensic science (MS)
medicinal chemistry (MS, PhD)
pharmacognosy (MS, PhD)
pharmacy (Pharm D, MS, PhD)
pharmacy administration (MS, PhD)

Center for Pharmaceutical Biotechnology
Program in:
pharmaceutical biotechnology (PhD)

Graduate College
Program in:
neuroscience (PhD)

College of Applied Health Sciences
Programs in:
applied health sciences (MS, DPT, OTD, PhD)
biomedical visualization (MS)
disability and human development (MS)
disability studies (PhD)
health informatics (MS)
kinesiology (MS, PhD)
nutrition (MS, PhD)
occupational therapy (MS, OTD)
physical therapy (MS, DPT)

College of Architecture and Art
Programs in:
architecture (M Arch, MS Arch)
architecture and art (M Arch, MA, MFA, MS Arch, PhD)
architecture in health design (MS Arch)
art history (MA, PhD)
electronic visualization (MFA)
film animation (MFA)
graphic design (MFA)
industrial design (MFA)
photography (MFA)
studio arts (MFA)

College of Education
Programs in:
curriculum studies (PhD)
education (M Ed, Ed D, PhD)
educational psychology (PhD)
educational studies (M Ed)
elementary education (M Ed)
literacy, language and culture (M Ed, PhD)
policy studies (M Ed)
policy studies in urban education (PhD)
secondary education (M Ed)
special education (M Ed, PhD)
urban education leadership (Ed D)

College of Engineering
Programs in:
bioengineering (MS, PhD)
chemical engineering (MS, PhD)
civil engineering (MS, PhD)
computer science (MS, PhD)
electrical and computer engineering (MS, PhD)
energy engineering (MEE)
engineering (M Eng, MEE, MS, PhD)
industrial engineering (MS)
industrial engineering and operations research (PhD)
materials engineering (MS, PhD)
mechanical engineering (MS, PhD)

College of Liberal Arts and Sciences
Programs in:
anthropology (MA, PhD)
applied mathematics (MS, PhD)
biological sciences (MS, PhD)
chemistry (MS, PhD)
communication (MA, PhD)
computational finance (MS, PhD)
computer science (MS, PhD)
criminal justice (MA, PhD)

University of Illinois at Chicago (continued)

earth and environmental sciences (MS, PhD)
economics (MA, PhD)
elementary (MST)
English (MA, PhD)
environmental and urban geography (MA)
environmental studies (MA)
French (MA)
Germanic studies (MA, PhD)
Hispanic linguistics (MA, PhD)
Hispanic literary and cultural studies (MA, PhD)
Hispanic studies (MA, PhD)
history (MA, MAT, PhD)
liberal arts and sciences (MA, MAT, MS, MST, DA, PhD)
linguistics (MA)
mathematics (DA)
mathematics and information sciences for industry (MS)
philosophy (MA, PhD)
physics (MS, PhD)
political science (MA, PhD)
probability and statistics (PhD)
psychology (PhD)
pure mathematics (MS, PhD)
secondary (MST)
sociology (MA, PhD)
statistics (MS)
teaching English to speakers of other languages/applied linguistics (MA)
teaching of mathematics (MST)
urban geography (MA)

College of Nursing
Programs in:
acute care clinical nurse specialist (MS)
acute care nurse practitioner (MS)
administrative studies in nursing (MS)
adult nurse practitioner (MS)
adult/geriatric nurse practitioner (MS)
advanced community health nurse specialist (MS)
family nurse practitioner (MS)
geriatric clinical nurse specialist (MS)
geriatric nurse practitioner (MS)
mental health clinical nurse specialist (MS)
mental health nurse practitioner (MS)
nurse midwifery (MS)
nursing (MS, DNP, PhD)
nursing practice (DNP)
nursing science (PhD)
occupational health/advanced community health nurse specialist (MS)
occupational health/family nurse practitioner (MS)
pediatric clinical nurse specialist (MS)
pediatric nurse practitioner (MS)
perinatal clinical nurse specialist (MS)
school/advanced community health nurse specialist (MS)
school/family nurse practitioner (MS)
women's health nurse practitioner (MS)

College of Urban Planning and Public Affairs
Programs in:
public administration (MPA, PhD)
urban planning and policy (MUPP, PhD)
urban planning and public affairs (MPA, MUPP, PhD)

Jane Addams College of Social Work
Program in:
social work (MSW, PhD)

Liautaud Graduate School of Business
Programs in:
accounting (MS)
business (MA, MBA, MS, PhD)
business administration (MBA, PhD)
business statistics (PhD)
management information systems (MS, PhD)
real estate (MA)

School of Public Health
Programs in:
biostatistics (MS, PhD)
cancer epidemiology (MS, PhD)
clinical translational science (MS)
community health sciences (MPH, MS, Dr PH, PhD)
environmental and occupational health sciences (MPH, MS, Dr PH, PhD)
epidemiology (MPH, MS, Dr PH, PhD)
health policy (PhD)
health policy and administration (Dr PH)
health services research (PhD)
healthcare (MHA)
public health (MHA, MPH, MS, Dr PH, PhD)
public health policy management (MPH)
quantitative methods (MPH)

■ UNIVERSITY OF ILLINOIS AT SPRINGFIELD

Springfield, IL 62703-5407
http://www.uis.edu/

State-supported, coed, comprehensive institution. CGS member. *Graduate faculty:* 180 full-time (70 women), 68 part-time/adjunct (26 women). *Computer facilities:* 475 computers available on campus for general student use. A campuswide network can be accessed from student residence rooms and from off campus. Online class registration is available. *Graduate expenses:* Tuition, state resident: full-time $6144; part-time $256 per credit hour. Tuition, nonresident: full-time $13,980; part-time $582.50 per credit hour. Required fees: $1800. *General application contact:* Dr. Lynn Pardie, Office of Graduate Studies, 800-252-8533.

Graduate Programs

Dr. Lynn Pardie, Office of Graduate Studies

College of Business and Management
Dr. Ronald McNeil, Dean
Programs in:
accountancy (MA)
business administration (MBA)
business and management (MA, MBA, MS)
management information systems (MS)

College of Education and Human Services
Dr. Larry Stonecipher, Dean
Programs in:
alcoholism and substance abuse (MA)
child and family services (MA)
education and human services (MA)
educational leadership (MA)
gerontology (MA)
human development counseling (MA)
social services administration (MA)
teacher leadership (MA)

College of Liberal Arts and Sciences
Dr. Margot Duley, Dean
Programs in:
biology (MS)
communication (MA)
computer science (MS)
English (MA)
history (MA)
interdisciplinary studies (MA)
liberal arts and sciences (MA, MS)

College of Public Affairs and Administration
Dr. Pinky Sue Wassenberg, Dean
Programs in:
environmental science (MS)
environmental studies (MA)
legal studies (MA)
political studies (MA)
public administration (MPA, DPA)
public affairs and administration (MA, MPA, MPH, MS, DPA)
public affairs reporting (MA)
public health (MPH)

■ UNIVERSITY OF ILLINOIS AT URBANA–CHAMPAIGN

Champaign, IL 61820
http://www.uiuc.edu/

State-supported, coed, university. CGS member. *Graduate faculty:* 2,083 full-time (626 women), 154 part-time/adjunct (54 women). *Computer facilities:* Computer purchase and lease plans are available. 3,400 computers available on campus for general student use. A campuswide network can be accessed from student residence rooms and from off campus. Online class registration is available. *General application contact:* William Welburn, Associate Dean, 217-333-6715.

College of Law

Bruce Smith, Dean
Program in:
law (JD, LL M, MCL, JSD)

College of Veterinary Medicine

Herbert Whiteley, Dean

Programs in:
- pathobiology (MS, PhD)
- veterinary biosciences (MS, PhD)
- veterinary clinical medicine (MS, PhD)
- veterinary medical science (DVM)
- veterinary medicine (DVM, MS, PhD)

Graduate College
Debasish Dutta, Dean

College of Agricultural, Consumer and Environmental Sciences
Robert A. Easter, Dean
Programs in:
- agricultural and consumer economics (MS, PhD)
- agricultural education (MS)
- agricultural engineering (MS, PhD)
- agricultural, consumer and environmental sciences (MS, PhD)
- animal sciences (MS, PhD)
- bioinformatics: animal sciences (MS)
- bioinformatics: crop sciences (MS)
- crop sciences (MS, PhD)
- food science and human nutrition (MS, PhD)
- human and community development (MS, PhD)
- natural resources and environmental science (MS, PhD)
- nutritional sciences (MS, PhD)

College of Applied Health Sciences
Tanya Gallagher, Dean
Programs in:
- applied health sciences (MA, MPH, MS, MSPH, Au D, PhD)
- audiology (Au D)
- community health (MS, MSPH, PhD)
- kinesiology (MS, PhD)
- public health (MPH)
- recreation, sport and tourism (MS, PhD)
- rehabilitation (MS)
- speech and hearing science (MA, PhD)

College of Business
Lawrence M. Debrock, Interim Dean
Programs in:
- accountancy (MAS, MS, PhD)
- business (MAS, MBA, MS, PhD)
- business administration (MS, PhD)
- finance (MS, PhD)
- taxation (MS)
- technology management (MS)

College of Education
Mary A. Kalantzis, Dean
Programs in:
- curriculum and instruction (Ed M, MA, MS, Ed D, PhD, CAS)
- early childhood education (Ed M)
- education (Ed M, MA, MS, Ed D, PhD, CAS)
- education, organization and leadership (Ed M, MS, Ed D, PhD, CAS)
- educational policy studies (Ed M, MA, PhD)
- educational psychology (Ed M, MA, MS, PhD, CAS)
- elementary education (Ed M)
- human resource education (Ed M, MS, Ed D, PhD, CAS)
- secondary education (Ed M)
- special education (Ed M, MS, Ed D, PhD, CAS)

College of Engineering
Dr. Ilesanmi Adesida, Dean
Programs in:
- aerospace engineering (MS, PhD)
- bioengineering (MS, PhD)
- bioinformatics (MS)
- civil engineering (MS)
- computer science (MCS, MS, PhD)
- electrical and computer engineering (MS, PhD)
- engineering (MCS, MS, PhD)
- environmental engineering in civil engineering (MS, PhD)
- environmental science in civil engineering (MS, PhD)
- industrial engineering (MS, PhD)
- materials science and engineering (MS, PhD)
- mechanical engineering (MS, PhD)
- nuclear engineering (MS, PhD)
- physics (MS, PhD)
- systems and entrepreneurial engineering (MS, PhD)
- teaching of physics (MS)
- theoretical and applied mechanics (MS, PhD)

College of Fine and Applied Arts
Robert F. Graves, Dean
Programs in:
- architectural studies (MS)
- architecture (M Arch, PhD)
- art and design (Ed M, MA, MFA, PhD)
- art education (Ed M, MA, PhD)
- art history (MA, PhD)
- crafts (MFA)
- dance (MFA)
- fine and applied arts (Ed M, M Arch, M Mus, MA, MFA, MLA, MME, MS, MUP, DMA, Ed D, PhD, AD, CAS)
- graphic design (MFA)
- industrial design (MFA)
- landscape architecture (MLA, PhD)
- metals (MFA)
- music (M Mus, DMA, AD)
- music education (MME, MS, Ed D, PhD, CAS)
- musicology (PhD)
- painting (MFA)
- photography (MFA)
- regional planning (PhD)
- sculpture (MFA)
- theatre (MA, MFA, PhD)
- urban planning (MUP)

College of Liberal Arts and Sciences
Ruth Watkins, Dean
Programs in:
- African studies (MA)
- animal biology (ecology, ethology and evolution) (MS, PhD)
- anthropology (MA, PhD)
- applied mathematics (MS)
- applied mathematics: actuarial science (MS)
- applied statistics (MS)
- Asian studies (MA)
- astrochemistry (PhD)
- astronomy (PhD)
- atmospheric sciences (MS, PhD)
- biochemistry (MS, PhD)
- bioinformatics: chemical and biomolecular engineering (MS)
- biophysics and computational biology (MS, PhD)
- cell and developmental biology (PhD)
- chemical engineering (MS, PhD)
- chemical physics (PhD)
- chemical sciences (MA, MS, PhD)
- chemistry (MA, MS, PhD)
- classical philology (PhD)
- classics (MA)
- communication (MA)
- comparative literature (MA, PhD)
- creative writing (MFA)
- earth, society and environment (MA, MS, PhD)
- East Asian languages and cultures (PhD)
- ecology, evolution and conservation biology (MS, PhD)
- economics (MS, PhD)
- English (MA, PhD)
- entomology (MS, PhD)
- French (MA, PhD)
- geography (MA, MS, PhD)
- geology (MS, PhD)
- German (MA, PhD)
- history (MA, PhD)
- integrative biology (MS, MST, PhD)
- Italian (MA, PhD)
- Latin American studies (MA)
- liberal arts and sciences (MA, MFA, MS, MST, PhD)
- linguistics (MA, PhD)
- literatures, cultures and linguistics (MA, MS, PhD)
- mathematics (MA, MS, PhD)
- microbiology (MS, PhD)
- molecular and cellular biology (MS, PhD)
- molecular and integrative physiology (MS, PhD)
- neuroscience (PhD)
- philosophy (MA, PhD)
- physiological and molecular plant biology (PhD)
- plant biology (MS, PhD)
- policy economics (MS)
- political science (MA, PhD)
- Portuguese (MA, PhD)
- psychology (MA, MS, PhD)
- Russian, East European and Eurasian studies (MA)
- Slavic languages and literatures (MA, PhD)
- sociology (MA, PhD)
- Spanish (MA, PhD)
- statistics (PhD)
- teaching of chemistry (MS)
- teaching of earth sciences (MS)
- teaching of English as a second language (MA)
- teaching of Latin (MA)
- teaching of mathematics (MS)

College of Media
Ronald E. Yates, Dean

University of Illinois at Urbana–Champaign (continued)
Programs in:
advertising (MS)
communications and media (PhD)
journalism (MS)
media (MS, PhD)

Graduate School of Library and Information Science
John Unsworth, Dean
Programs in:
bioinformatics: library and information science (MS)
library and information science (MS, PhD, CAS)
library and information science: digital libraries (CAS)

School of Labor and Employment Relations
Dr. Joel Cutcher Gershenfeld, Dean
Program in:
human resources and industrial relations (MHRIR, PhD)

School of Social Work
Wynne S. Korr, Dean
Programs in:
advocacy, leadership, and social change (MSW)
children, youth and family services (MSW)
social work (PhD)

Institute of Aviation
Alex Kirlik, Acting Head
Program in:
human factors (MS)

■ UNIVERSITY OF ST. FRANCIS
Joliet, IL 60435-6169
http://www.stfrancis.edu/

Independent-religious, coed, comprehensive institution. *Graduate faculty:* 37 full-time (25 women), 90 part-time/adjunct (46 women). *Computer facilities:* 365 computers available on campus for general student use. A campuswide network can be accessed from student residence rooms and from off campus. Online class registration, billing/payment are available. *Graduate expenses:* Tuition: part-time $560 per credit hour. Part-time tuition and fees vary according to program. *General application contact:* Sandra Sloka, Director of Admissions for Graduate and Degree Completion Programs, 800-735-7500.

College of Arts and Sciences
Dr. Robert Kase, Dean
Program in:
social work (MSW)

College of Business and Health Administration
Dr. Michael LaRocco, Dean
Program in:
business (MBA, MSM)

School of Business
Program in:
business (MBA, MSM)

School of Professional Studies
Dr. Michael LaRocco, Dean
Programs in:
health administration (MS)
training and development (MS)

College of Education
Dr. John Gambro, Dean
Programs in:
educational leadership (MS)
elementary education certification (M Ed)
reading (MS)
secondary education certification (M Ed)
special education (M Ed)
teaching and learning (MS)

College of Nursing and Allied Health
Dr. Maria Connolly, Dean
Programs in:
nursing (MSN)
nursing practice (DNP)
physician assistant studies (MS)

■ WESTERN ILLINOIS UNIVERSITY
Macomb, IL 61455-1390
http://www.wiu.edu/

State-supported, coed, comprehensive institution. CGS member. *Computer facilities:* 1,000 computers available on campus for general student use. A campuswide network can be accessed from student residence rooms and from off campus. Online class registration is available. *Graduate expenses:* Tuition, state resident: full-time $5696; part-time $237.34 per credit hour. Tuition, nonresident: full-time $11,392; part-time $474.68 per credit hour. Required fees: $1453; $60.55 per credit hour. *General application contact:* Evelyn A. Hoing, Assistant Director of Graduate Studies, 309-298-1806.

School of Graduate Studies
Dr. Judith Dallinger, Director of Graduate Studies/Associate Provost

College of Arts and Sciences
Dr. Susan Martinelli-Fernandez, Interim Dean
Programs in:
applied math (Certificate)
arts and sciences (MA, MLAS, MS, Certificate, SSP)
biological sciences (MS)
chemistry (MS)
clinical/community mental health (MS)
community development (Certificate)
English (MA, Certificate)
environmental geographic information systems (Certificate)
general psychology (MS)
geography (MA)
history (MA)
liberal arts and sciences (MLAS)
mathematics (MS)
physics (MS)
political science (MA)
psychology (MS, SSP)
public and non-profit management (Certificate)
school psychology (SSP)
sociology (MA)
zoo and aquarium studies (Certificate)

College of Business and Technology
Dr. Tom Erekson, Dean
Programs in:
accountancy (M Acct)
business administration (MBA)
business and technology (M Acct, MA, MBA, MS, Certificate)
computer science (MS)
economics (MA, Certificate)
manufacturing engineering systems (MS)

College of Education and Human Services
Dr. Bernard N. DiGrino, Interim Dean
Programs in:
college student personnel (MS)
counseling (MS Ed)
distance learning (Certificate)
education and human services (MA, MS, MS Ed, Ed D, Certificate, Ed S)
educational and interdisciplinary studies (MS Ed)
educational leadership (MS Ed, Ed D, Ed S)
elementary education (MS Ed)
graphic applications (Certificate)
health education (MS)
health services administration (Certificate)
instructional design and technology (MS)
kinesiology (MS)
law enforcement and justice administration (MA)
multimedia (Certificate)
police executive administration (Certificate)
reading (MS Ed)
recreation, park, and tourism administration (MS)
special education (MS Ed)
sport management (MS)
technology integration in education (Certificate)
training development (Certificate)

College of Fine Arts and Communication
Dr. Paul K. Kreider, Dean
Programs in:
acting (MFA)
communication (MA)
communication sciences and disorders (MS)
costume design (MFA)
directing (MFA)
fine arts and communication (MA, MFA, MM, MS)

lighting design/theatre technology (MFA)
museum studies (MA)
music (MM)
scenic design (MFA)

■ WHEATON COLLEGE
Wheaton, IL 60187-5593
http://www.wheaton.edu/

Independent-religious, coed, comprehensive institution. CGS member. *Computer facilities:* Computer purchase and lease plans are available. 125 computers available on campus for general student use. A campuswide network can be accessed from student residence rooms and from off campus. Online class registration, financial information, degree requirements evaluation are available. *General application contact:* Director of Graduate Admissions, 630-752-5195.

Graduate School
Programs in:
biblical and theological studies (MA, PhD)
biblical archaeology (MA)
biblical exegesis (MA)
biblical studies (MA)
Christian formation and ministry (MA)
clinical psychology (MA, Psy D)
counseling ministries (MA)
elementary level (MAT)
evangelism (MA)
general history of Christianity (MA)
historical and systematic theology (MA)
intercultural studies (MA)
intercultural studies/teaching English as a second language (MA)
missions (MA)
religion in American life (MA)
secondary level (MAT)
teaching English as a second language (Certificate)

Indiana

■ ANDERSON UNIVERSITY
Anderson, IN 46012-3495
http://www.anderson.edu/

Independent-religious, coed, comprehensive institution. *Computer facilities:* 250 computers available on campus for general student use. A campuswide network can be accessed from student residence rooms and from off campus. Online class registration, microcomputer software are available. *General application contact:* Director of Seminary Advancement, 765-641-4526.

Falls School of Business
Programs in:
accountancy (MA)
business administration (MBA, DBA)

School of Education
Program in:
education (M Ed)

School of Theology
Programs in:
missions (MA)
theology (M Div, MTS, D Min)

■ BALL STATE UNIVERSITY
Muncie, IN 47306-1099
http://www.bsu.edu/

State-supported, coed, university. CGS member. *Graduate faculty:* 712. *Computer facilities:* 1,500 computers available on campus for general student use. A campuswide network can be accessed from student residence rooms and from off campus. *General application contact:* Dr. Robert J. Morris, Associate Provost for Research and Dean of the Graduate School, 765-285-1300.

Graduate School
Dr. Robert J. Morris, Associate Provost for Research and Dean of the Graduate School

College of Applied Science and Technology
Dr. Mitchell Whaley, Dean
Programs in:
applied gerontology (MA)
applied science and technology (MA, MAE, MS, PhD, Graduate Certificate)
family and consumer sciences (MA, MS)
human bioenergetics (PhD)
industry and technology (MA, MAE)
nursing (MS)
physical education (MA, MAE, MS, PhD)
wellness management (MA, MS)

College of Architecture and Planning
Dr. Guillermo Vasquez de Velasco, Dean
Programs in:
architecture (M Arch)
architecture and planning (M Arch, MLA, MS, MUD, MURP)
historic preservation (M Arch, MS)
landscape architecture (MLA)
urban design (MUD)
urban planning (MURP)

College of Communication, Information, and Media
Roger Lavery, Dean
Programs in:
communication, information, and media (MA, MS)
digital storytelling (MA)
information and communication sciences (MS)
journalism (MA)
public relations (MA)
speech, public address, forensics, and rhetoric (MA)

College of Fine Arts
Dr. Robert Kvam, Dean
Programs in:
art (MA)
art education (MA, MAE)
fine arts (MA, MAE, MM, DA, Graduate Certificate)
music education (MA, MM, DA)

College of Sciences and Humanities
Dr. Michael Maggioto, Dean
Programs in:
actuarial science (MA)
anthropology (MA)
applied linguistics (PhD)
biology (MA, MAE, MS)
biology education (Ed D)
chemistry (MA, MS)
clinical psychology (MA)
cognitive and social processes (MA)
computer science (MA, MS)
earth sciences (MA)
English (MA, PhD)
geology (MA, MS)
health education (MA, MAE)
history (MA)
linguistics (MA, PhD)
linguistics and teaching English to speakers of other languages (MA)
mathematical statistics (MA)
mathematics (MA, MAE, MS)
mathematics education (MAE)
natural resources (MA, MS)
physics (MA, MS)
physiology (MA, MS)
political science (MA)
public administration (MPA)
sciences and humanities (MA, MAE, MPA, MS, Au D, Ed D, PhD, Graduate Certificate)
social sciences (MA)
sociology (MA)
speech pathology and audiology (MA, Au D)
teaching English to speakers of other languages (MA)

Miller College of Business
Programs in:
accounting (MS)
business (MAE, MBA, MS)
business administration (MBA)
business education (MAE)

Teachers College
Dr. John E. Jacobson, Dean
Programs in:
adult and community education (MA)
adult education (MA, Ed D)
adult, community, and higher education (Ed D)
counseling psychology (MA, PhD)
curriculum (MAE, Ed S)
curriculum and instruction (MAE, Ed S)
education (MA, MAE, Ed D, PhD, Ed S, Graduate Certificate)
educational administration (MAE, Ed D)
educational psychology (MA, PhD, Ed S)
educational studies (MAE, PhD)
elementary education (MAE, Ed D, PhD)
executive development (MA)

Ball State University (continued)
school psychology (MA, PhD, Ed S)
school superintendency (Ed S)
secondary education (MA)
social psychology (MA)
special education (MA, MAE, Ed D, Ed S)
student affairs administration in higher education (MA)

■ BUTLER UNIVERSITY
Indianapolis, IN 46208-3485
http://www.butler.edu/

Independent, coed, comprehensive institution. *Graduate faculty:* 66 full-time (26 women), 36 part-time/adjunct (20 women). *Computer facilities:* 450 computers available on campus for general student use. A campuswide network can be accessed from student residence rooms and from off campus. Online class registration is available. *General application contact:* Pamela Bender, Student Services Specialist, 317-940-8100.

College of Business Administration
Dr. Chuck Williams, Dean
Program in:
business administration (MBA, MP Acc)

College of Education
Dr. Ena Shelley, Dean
Programs in:
administration (MS)
elementary education (MS)
reading (MS)
school counseling (MS)
secondary education (MS)
special education (MS)

College of Liberal Arts and Sciences
Dr. Judi Morrel, Interim Dean
Programs in:
English (MA)
history (MA)
liberal arts and sciences (MA)

College of Pharmacy
Dr. Mary Andritz, Dean
Programs in:
pharmaceutical science (Pharm D, MS)
physician assistance studies (MS)

Jordan College of Fine Arts
Dr. Peter Alexander, Dean
Programs in:
composition (MM)
conducting (MM)
fine arts (MM)
music (MM)
music education (MM)
music history (MM)
organ (MM)
performance (MM)

■ CALUMET COLLEGE OF SAINT JOSEPH
Whiting, IN 46394-2195
http://www.ccsj.edu/

Independent-religious, coed, comprehensive institution. *Computer facilities:* 104 computers available on campus for general student use. A campuswide network can be accessed from off campus. Online class registration is available.

Program in Leadership in Teaching
Program in:
leadership in teaching (MS Ed)

Program in Public Safety Administration
Program in:
public safety administration (MS)

Program in Quality Assurance
Program in:
quality assurance (MS)

■ INDIANA STATE UNIVERSITY
Terre Haute, IN 47809-1401
http://www.indstate.edu/

State-supported, coed, university. CGS member. *Computer facilities:* Computer purchase and lease plans are available. 600 computers available on campus for general student use. A campuswide network can be accessed from student residence rooms and from off campus. Online class registration is available. *General application contact:* Assistant to the Dean, 800-444-GRAD.

School of Graduate Studies
Program in:
technology management (PhD)

College of Arts and Sciences
Programs in:
arts and sciences (MA, MFA, MM, MPA, MS, PhD, Psy D, CAS)
ceramics (MA, MFA)
clinical psychology (Psy D)
communication studies (MA, MS)
criminology and criminal justice (MA, MS)
dietetics (MS)
drawing (MA, MFA)
ecology (PhD)
English teaching (MA)
family and consumer sciences education (MS)
general psychology (MA, MS)
geography (MA)
geology (MS)
graphic design (MA, MFA)
history (MA)
inter-area option (MS)
life sciences (MS)
linguistics/teaching English as a second language (MA)
literature (MA)
math teaching (MA, MS)
mathematics and computer science (MA)
mathematics and computer sciences (MS)
microbiology (PhD)
music performance (MM)
painting (MA, MFA)
photography (MA, MFA)
physical geography (PhD)
physiology (PhD)
political science (MA, MS)
printmaking (MA, MFA)
public administration (MPA)
radio, television and film (MA, MS)
science education (MS)
sculpture (MA, MFA)
TESL/TEFL (CAS)

College of Business
Program in:
business (MBA)

College of Education
Programs in:
counseling psychology (MS, PhD)
counselor education (PhD)
curriculum and instruction (M Ed, PhD)
early childhood education (M Ed)
education (M Ed, MS, PhD, Ed S)
educational administration (PhD)
educational technology (MS)
elementary education (M Ed)
leadership in higher education (PhD)
mental health counseling (MS)
school administration (Ed S)
school administration and supervision (M Ed)
school counseling (M Ed)
school psychology (PhD, Ed S)
student affairs in higher education (MS)

College of Nursing, Health and Human Services
Programs in:
adult fitness (MA, MS)
athletic training (MS)
coaching (MA, MS)
community health promotion (MA, MS)
exercise science (MA, MS)
health and safety education (MA, MS)
nursing (MS)
nursing, health and human services (MA, MS)
occupational safety management (MA, MS)
recreation and sport management (MA, MS)

College of Technology
Programs in:
career and technical education (MS)
electronics and computer technology (MS)
human resource development (MS)
industrial technology (MS)
technology (MS)
technology education (MS)

■ INDIANA UNIVERSITY BLOOMINGTON

Bloomington, IN 47405-7000

http://www.iub.edu/

State-supported, coed, university. CGS member. *Graduate faculty:* 1,080 full-time (328 women), 4 part-time/adjunct (2 women). *Computer facilities:* A campuswide network can be accessed from student residence rooms and from off campus. Online class registration, various software packages are available. *Graduate expenses:* Part-time $291.97 per credit hour. Tuition, state resident: part-time $291.97 per credit hour. Tuition, nonresident: part-time $850.33 per credit hour. Required fees: $110 per semester. Tuition and fees vary according to course load and program. *General application contact:* Information Contact, 812-855-0661.

Jacobs School of Music

Gwyn Richards, Dean
Programs in:
- church music (DM)
- music (MA, MM, MM/MLS, MME, MS, DM, DME, PhD, AD, Performance Diploma, Spec)
- music literature and performance (DM)
- performance (MM)
- performance and church music (MM)

Kelley School of Business

Daniel Smith, Dean
Programs in:
- business (MBA, MPA, MS, DBA, PhD)
- business economics and public policy (PhD)

Maurer School of Law

Lauren K. Robel, Dean
Programs in:
- comparative law (MCL)
- juridical science (SJD)
- law (JD, LL M)
- law and social sciences (PhD)
- legal studies (Certificate)

School of Education

Dr. Gerardo Gonzalez, Dean
Programs in:
- art education (MS, Ed D, PhD)
- counseling (MS, PhD, Ed S)
- counseling psychology (PhD)
- counselor education (MS, Ed S)
- curriculum studies (Ed D, PhD)
- education (MS, Ed D, PhD, Ed S)
- education policy studies (PhD)
- educational leadership (MS, Ed D, PhD, Ed S)
- educational psychology (MS, PhD)
- elementary education (MS, Ed D, PhD, Ed S)
- higher education (MS, Ed D, PhD)
- history and philosophy of education (MS)
- history of education (PhD)
- inquiry methodology (PhD)
- instructional systems technology (MS, PhD, Ed S)
- international and comparative education (MS, PhD)
- learning and developmental sciences (MS, PhD)
- literacy, culture, and language education (MS, Ed D, PhD, Ed S)
- mathematics education (MS, Ed D, PhD)
- philosophy of education (PhD)
- school psychology (PhD, Ed S)
- science education (MS, Ed D, PhD)
- secondary education (MS, Ed D, PhD)
- social studies education (MS, PhD)
- special education (MS, Ed D, PhD, Ed S)
- student affairs administration (MS)

School of Health, Physical Education and Recreation

Dr. Robert Goodman, Dean
Programs in:
- adapted physical education (MS)
- applied sport science (MS)
- athletic administration/sport management (MS)
- athletic training (MS)
- biomechanics (MS)
- ergonomics (MS)
- exercise physiology (MS)
- fitness management (MS)
- health behavior (PhD)
- health promotion (MS)
- health, physical education and recreation (MPH, MS, PhD, Re Dir)
- human development/family studies (MS)
- human performance (PhD)
- leisure behavior (PhD)
- motor learning/control (MS)
- nutrition science (MS)
- outdoor recreation (MS)
- public health (MPH)
- recreation (Re Dir)
- recreation administration (MS)
- recreational sports administration (MS)
- safety management (MS)
- school and college health programs (MS)
- therapeutic recreation (MS)
- tourism management (MS)

School of Informatics

Dr. David Leake, Associate Dean for Graduate Studies
Programs in:
- bioinformatics (MS)
- chemical informatics (MS)
- computer science (MS, PhD)
- health informatics (MS)
- human computer interaction (MS)
- informatics (PhD)
- laboratory informatics (MS)
- media arts and science (MS)
- music informatics (MS)
- security informatics (MS)

School of Journalism

Bradley Hamm, Dean
Programs in:
- journalism (MA, MAT)
- mass communication (PhD)

School of Library and Information Science

Dr. Blaise Cronin, Dean
Program in:
- library and information science (MIS, MLS, PhD, Sp LIS)

School of Optometry

Dr. P. Sarita Soni, Interim Dean
Program in:
- optometry (OD, MS, PhD)

School of Public and Environmental Affairs

Charles Kurt Zorn, Interim Dean
Programs in:
- environmental science (MSES, PhD)
- nonprofit management (Certificate)
- public affairs (MPA, PhD)
- public and environmental affairs (MA, MPA, MSES, PhD, Certificate)
- public management (Certificate)
- public policy (PhD)

University Graduate School

Dr. James Wimbush, Dean

College of Arts and Sciences

Dr. Bennett Bertenthal, Dean
Programs in:
- acting (MFA)
- African American and African diaspora studies (MA)
- African languages and linguistics (PhD)
- African studies (MA)
- analytical chemistry (PhD)
- anthropology (MA, PhD)
- applied mathematics–numerical analysis (MA, PhD)
- arts and sciences (MA, MAT, MFA, MS, Au D, PhD, Certificate)
- astronomy (MA, PhD)
- astrophysics (PhD)
- audiology (Au D)
- auditory sciences (PhD)
- biochemistry (PhD)
- biogeochemistry (MS, PhD)
- biological chemistry (PhD)
- biology and behavior (PhD)
- biology teaching (MAT)
- biotechnology (MA)
- Central Eurasian studies (MA, PhD)
- chemistry (MAT)
- Chinese (MA, PhD)
- classical studies (MA, MAT, PhD)
- clinical science (PhD)
- cognitive psychology (PhD)
- cognitive science (PhD)
- comparative literature (MA, MAT, PhD)
- composition, literacy, and culture (PhD)
- computational linguistics (MA, PhD)
- creative writing (MA, MFA)
- criminal justice (MA, PhD)
- criminology (MA, PhD)
- cross-cultural perspectives of crime and justice (MA, PhD)
- design and technology (MFA)
- developmental psychology (PhD)
- directing (MFA)
- East Asian languages and cultures (PhD)

Indiana University Bloomington (continued)

East Asian studies (MA)
economic geology (MS, PhD)
economics (MA, PhD)
evolution, ecology, and behavior (MA, PhD)
film and media studies (PhD)
fine arts (MA, MFA, PhD)
folklore (MA, PhD)
French (MA, PhD)
gender studies (PhD)
genetics (PhD)
geobiology (MS, PhD)
geography (MA, MAT, MS, PhD)
geophysics, structural geology and tectonics (MS, PhD)
German philology and linguistics (PhD)
German studies (MA, PhD)
Hispanic linguistics (MA, PhD)
Hispanic literature (MA)
history (MA, MAT, PhD)
history and philosophy of science (MA, PhD)
history of art (MA, PhD)
hydrogeology (MS, PhD)
inorganic chemistry (PhD)
Italian (MA, PhD)
Japanese (MA, PhD)
language (MA)
language pedagogy (MA)
language sciences (PhD)
Latin American and Caribbean studies (MA)
law and society (MA, PhD)
linguistics (MA, PhD)
literature (MA, PhD)
Luso-Brazilian literature (MA)
Luso-Brazilian studies (PhD)
mass communications (PhD)
mathematics education (MAT)
medieval German studies (PhD)
microbiology (MA, PhD)
mineralogy (MS, PhD)
molecular, cellular, and developmental biology (PhD)
Near Eastern languages and cultures (MA, PhD)
neuroscience (PhD)
performance and ethnography (PhD)
philosophy (MA, PhD)
physical chemistry (PhD)
physics (MAT, MS, PhD)
plant sciences (MA, PhD)
playwriting (MFA)
political science (MA, PhD)
probability-statistics (MA, PhD)
psychological and brain sciences (MA)
psychology and the law (MA)
pure mathematics (MA)
religious studies (MA, PhD)
rhetoric and public culture (PhD)
Russian and East European studies (MA, Certificate)
second language studies (MA, PhD)
Slavic languages and literatures (MA, MAT, PhD)
social psychology (PhD)
sociology (MA, PhD)
Spanish literatures (PhD)
speech and hearing sciences (MA, PhD)
speech and voice sciences (PhD)
speech-language pathology (MA)
stratigraphy and sedimentology (MS, PhD)
teaching German (MAT)
teaching Spanish (MAT)
telecommunications (MA, MS, PhD)
TESOL and applied linguistics (MA)
theatre and drama (MAT)
theatre history (MA, PhD)
theory (MA, PhD)
West European studies (MA)
writing (MA)
zoology (MA, PhD)

■ INDIANA UNIVERSITY NORTHWEST

Gary, IN 46408-1197
http://www.iun.edu/

State-supported, coed, comprehensive institution. *Computer facilities:* A campuswide network can be accessed from off campus. Online class registration is available. *General application contact:* Admissions Counselor, 219-980-6760.

Division of Social Work

Program in:
social work (MSW)

School of Business and Economics

Programs in:
accountancy (M Acc)
accounting (Certificate)
business administration (MBA)

School of Education

Programs in:
elementary education (MS Ed)
secondary education (MS Ed)

School of Public and Environmental Affairs

Programs in:
criminal justice (MPA)
environmental affairs (Graduate Certificate)
health services administration (MPA)
human services administration (MPA)
nonprofit management (Graduate Certificate)
public management (MPA, Graduate Certificate)

■ INDIANA UNIVERSITY–PURDUE UNIVERSITY FORT WAYNE

Fort Wayne, IN 46805-1499
http://www.ipfw.edu/

State-supported, coed, comprehensive institution. CGS member. *Graduate faculty:* 196 full-time (73 women), 11 part-time/adjunct (2 women). *Computer facilities:* Computer purchase and lease plans are available. 472 computers available on campus for general student use. A campuswide network can be accessed from student residence rooms and from off campus. Online class registration, student academic records are available. *Graduate expenses:* Tuition, state resident: full-time $4376; part-time $243 per credit. Tuition, nonresident: full-time $10,337; part-time $574 per credit. Required fees: $503; $27.95 per credit. Tuition and fees vary according to course load. *General application contact:* Susan Humphreys, Graduate Applications Coordinator, 260-481-6145.

College of Arts and Sciences

Dr. Carl Drummond, Dean
Programs in:
applied mathematics (MS)
applied statistics (Certificate)
arts and sciences (MA, MAT, MLS, MS, Certificate)
biology (MS)
English (MA, MAT)
liberal studies (MLS)
mathematics (MS)
operations research (MS)
professional communication (MA, MS)
sociological practice (MA)
speech and language pathology (MA)
TENL (teaching English as a new language) (Certificate)

College of Engineering, Technology, and Computer Science

Dr. Gerard Voland, Dean
Programs in:
applied computer science (MS)
computer engineering (MS)
electrical engineering (MS)
engineering, technology, and computer science (MS)
industrial technology/manufacturing (MS)
information technology/advanced computer applications (MS)
mechanical engineering (MS)
organizational leadership and supervision (MS)
systems engineering (MS)

College of Health and Human Services

Dr. Linda M. Finke, Dean
Programs in:
adult nursing practice (MS)
health and human services (MS, Certificate)
nursing administration (MS, Certificate)
nursing education (MS)
women's health nursing practice (MS)

Division of Public and Environmental Affairs

Dr. Jane Grant, Interim Assistant Dean and Graduate Program Director
Programs in:
public affairs (MPA)
public management (MPM, Certificate)

School of Business and Management Sciences
Dr. Otto Chang, Dean
Program in:
business administration (MBA)

School of Education
Dr. Barry Kanpol, Dean
Programs in:
counselor education (MS Ed)
education (MS Ed, Certificate)
educational administration (MS Ed)
elementary education (MS Ed, Certificate)
secondary education (MS Ed, Certificate)
special education (MS Ed)

■ INDIANA UNIVERSITY–PURDUE UNIVERSITY INDIANAPOLIS

Indianapolis, IN 46202-2896
http://www.iupui.edu/

State-supported, coed, university. *Computer facilities:* A campuswide network can be accessed from student residence rooms and from off campus. Online class registration is available. *General application contact:* Director, Graduate Studies and Associate Dean, 317-274-1577.

Department of Economics
Program in:
economics (MA)

Department of English
Programs in:
English (MA)
teaching English (MA)

Department of History
Programs in:
history (MA)
public history (MA)

Herron School of Art and Design
Programs in:
art education (MAE)
furniture design (MFA)
printmaking (MFA)
sculpture (MFA)
visual communication (MFA)

Indiana University School of Medicine
Programs in:
anatomy and cell biology (MS, PhD)
behavioral health science (MPH)
biochemistry and molecular biology (PhD)
epidemiology (MPH)
genetic counseling (MS)
health policy and management (MPH)
medical and molecular genetics (MS, PhD)
medicine (MD, MPH, MS, DPT, PhD)
microbiology and immunology (MS, PhD)
pathology and laboratory medicine (MS, PhD)
pharmacology (MS, PhD)
toxicology (MS, PhD)

School of Health and Rehabilitation Sciences
Programs in:
health sciences education (MS)
nutrition and dietetics (MS)
occupational therapy (MS)
physical therapy (DPT)

Kelley School of Business
Programs in:
accounting (MSA)
business (MBA)

School of Continuing Studies
Program in:
adult education (MS)

School of Dentistry
Program in:
dentistry (DDS, MS, MSD, PhD, Certificate)

School of Education
Programs in:
computer education (Certificate)
curriculum and instruction (MS)
early childhood (MS)
educational leadership (MS, Certificate)
English as a second language (Certificate)
higher education and student affairs (MS)
kindergarten (Certificate)
language education (MS)
reading (Certificate)
school counseling (MS)
special education (MS, Certificate)

School of Engineering and Technology
Programs in:
biomedical engineering (MS, MS Bm E, PhD)
computer-aided mechanical engineering (Certificate)
electrical and computer engineering (MS, MSECE, PhD)
engineering (interdisciplinary) (MSE)
engineering and technology (MS, MS Bm E, MSE, MSECE, MSME, PhD, Certificate)
mechanical engineering (MSME, PhD)

School of Informatics
Programs in:
informatics (PhD)
media arts and science (MS)

School of Law
Program in:
law (JD, LL M, SJD)

School of Liberal Arts
Programs in:
American philosophy (Certificate)
bioethics (Certificate)
family/gender studies (MA)
geographic information systems (MS, Certificate)
liberal arts (MA, MS, XMA, PhD, Certificate)
medical sociology (MA)
museum studies (MS, Certificate)
philanthropic studies (MA, XMA, PhD)
philosophy (MA)
political science (MA, Certificate)
work/occupations (MA)

Center on Philanthropy
Program in:
philanthropic studies (MA, PhD)

School of Library and Information Science
Program in:
library and information science (MLS)

School of Music
Program in:
music technology (MS)

School of Nursing
Programs in:
acute care nurse practitioner (MSN)
adult health clinical nurse specialist (MSN)
adult health nursing (MSN)
adult nurse practitioner (MSN)
adult psychiatric/mental health nursing (MSN)
child psychiatric/mental health nursing (MSN)
community health nursing (MSN)
family nurse practitioner (MSN)
neonatal nurse practitioner (MSN)
nursing science (PhD)
pediatric clinical nurse specialist (MSN)
women's health nurse practitioner (MSN)

School of Physical Education and Tourism Management
Program in:
physical education (MS)

School of Public and Environmental Affairs
Programs in:
health administration (MHA)
public affairs (MPA)

School of Science
Programs in:
applied mathematics (MS, PhD)
applied statistics (MS)
biology (MS, PhD)
chemistry (MS, PhD)
clinical rehabilitation psychology (MS)
computer science (MS, PhD)
geology (MS)
industrial/organizational psychology (MS)
math education (MS)
mathematics (MS, PhD)
physics (MS, PhD)
psychobiology of addictions (MS, PhD)
science (MS, PhD)

Indiana University–Purdue University Indianapolis (continued)

School of Social Work
Program in:
social work (MSW, PhD, Certificate)

■ INDIANA UNIVERSITY SOUTH BEND

South Bend, IN 46634-7111
http://www.iusb.edu/

State-supported, coed, comprehensive institution. *Computer facilities:* A campuswide network can be accessed. Online class registration is available. *General application contact:* Admissions Counselor, 574-520-4839.

College of Liberal Arts and Sciences
Programs in:
applied mathematics and computer science (MS)
applied psychology (MA)
English (MA)
liberal studies (MLS)

School of Business and Economics
Programs in:
accounting (MSA)
business administration (MBA)
management of information technologies (MS)

School of Education
Programs in:
counseling and human services (MS Ed)
elementary education (MS Ed)
secondary education (MS Ed)
special education (MS Ed)

School of Public and Environmental Affairs
Programs in:
health systems administration and policy (MPA)
health systems management (Certificate)
nonprofit management (Certificate)
public and community services administration and policy (MPA)
public management (Certificate)
urban affairs (Certificate)

School of Social Work
Program in:
social work (MSW)

School of the Arts
Programs in:
music (MM)
studio teaching (MM)

■ INDIANA UNIVERSITY SOUTHEAST

New Albany, IN 47150-6405
http://www.ius.edu/

State-supported, coed, comprehensive institution. *Computer facilities:* A campuswide network can be accessed from off campus. Online class registration is available. *General application contact:* Admissions Counselor, 812-941-2212.

Program in Liberal Studies
Program in:
liberal studies (MLS)

School of Business
Programs in:
business administration (MBA)
strategic finance (MS)

School of Education
Programs in:
counselor education (MS Ed)
elementary education (MS Ed)
secondary education (MS Ed)

■ INDIANA WESLEYAN UNIVERSITY

Marion, IN 46953-4974
http://www.indwes.edu/

Independent-religious, coed, comprehensive institution. *Graduate faculty:* 66 full-time (28 women), 308 part-time/adjunct (131 women). *Computer facilities:* 675 computers available on campus for general student use. A campuswide network can be accessed from student residence rooms. *Graduate expenses:* Tuition: full-time $7020; part-time $390 per credit hour. One-time fee: $290 full-time; $85 part-time. Full-time tuition and fees vary according to course load. *General application contact:* Dr. Jim Freemyer, Director of Graduate Education, 765-677-2278.

College of Adult and Professional Studies
Bradford Sample, Dean
Programs in:
accounting (MBA)
applied management (MBA)
business administration (MBA)
curriculum and instruction (M Ed)
health care (MBA)
human resources (MBA)
management (MS)

College of Graduate Studies
Dr. Jim Fuller, Dean
Programs in:
addictions counseling (MS)
community counseling (MS)
divinity (M Div)
marriage and family counseling (MS)
organizational leadership (Ed D)
school counseling (MS)

School of Nursing
Dr. Barbara Ihrke, Executive Director of Nursing Programs
Programs in:
community health nursing (MS)
nursing (Post Master's Certificate)
nursing administration (MS)
nursing education (MS)
primary care nursing (MS)

Wesley Seminary
Programs in:
divinity (M Div)
ministerial leadership (MA)
ministry (MA)
youth ministries (MA)

■ OAKLAND CITY UNIVERSITY

Oakland City, IN 47660-1099
http://www.oak.edu/

Independent-religious, coed, comprehensive institution. *Computer facilities:* 92 computers available on campus for general student use. A campuswide network can be accessed from student residence rooms and from off campus. *General application contact:* Counselor for Graduate Admissions, 812-749-1404.

Chapman Seminary
Program in:
religious studies (M Div, D Min)

School of Adult and Extended Learning
Program in:
management (MS Mgt)

School of Education and Technology
Programs in:
educational leadership (Ed D)
teaching (MA)

■ PURDUE UNIVERSITY

West Lafayette, IN 47907
http://www.purdue.edu/

State-supported, coed, university. CGS member. *Graduate faculty:* 1,779 full-time (447 women), 334 part-time/adjunct (76 women). *Computer facilities:* Computer purchase and lease plans are available. 5,783 computers available on campus for general student use. A campuswide network can be accessed from student residence rooms and from off campus. Online class registration is available. *General application contact:* Marcia Fritzlen, Graduate School Admissions, 765-494-2600.

College of Engineering
Dr. Audeen Fentiman, Associate Dean
Programs in:
agricultural and biological engineering (MS, MSABE, MSE, PhD)
biomedical engineering (MSBME, PhD)
engineering (MS, MSAAE, MSABE, MSBME, MSCE, MSChE, MSE, MSECE, MSIE, MSME, MSMSE, MSNE, PhD, Certificate)
engineering professional education (MS, MSE)

School of Aeronautics and Astronautics Engineering
Prof. Anastansios Lyrintzis, Graduate Chair

Program in:
aeronautics and astronautics engineering (MS, MSAAE, MSE, PhD)

School of Chemical Engineering
Dr. James D. Lister, Director, Graduate Studies
Program in:
chemical engineering (MSChE, PhD)

School of Civil Engineering
Dr. Timothy M. Whalen, Director of Academic Programs
Program in:
civil engineering (MS, MSCE, MSE, PhD)

School of Electrical and Computer Engineering
Stan Zak, Graduate Coordinator
Program in:
electrical and computer engineering (MS, MSE, MSECE, PhD)

School of Engineering Education
David Radcliffe, Graduate Chair
Program in:
engineering education (PhD)

School of Industrial Engineering
Dr. C. Richard Liu, Graduate Committee Chair
Program in:
industrial engineering (MS, MSIE, PhD)

School of Materials Engineering
Dr. Carol Handwerker, Graduate Coordinator
Program in:
materials engineering (MSMSE, PhD)

School of Mechanical Engineering
Anil K. Bajaj, Associate Head
Program in:
mechanical engineering (MS, MSE, MSME, PhD, Certificate)

School of Nuclear Engineering
Program in:
nuclear engineering (MS, MSNE, PhD)

College of Pharmacy and Pharmacal Sciences

Program in:
pharmacy and pharmacal sciences (Pharm D, MS, PhD, Certificate)

Graduate Programs in Pharmacy and Pharmacal Sciences
Programs in:
analytical medicinal chemistry (PhD)
clinical pharmacy (MS, PhD)
computational and biophysical medicinal chemistry (PhD)
industrial and physical pharmacy (MS, PhD, Certificate)
medicinal and bioorganic chemistry (PhD)
medicinal biochemistry and molecular biology (PhD)
medicinal chemistry and molecular pharmacology (MS, PhD)
molecular pharmacology and toxicology (PhD)
natural products and pharmacognosy (PhD)
nuclear pharmacy (MS)
pharmaceutics (PhD)
pharmacy administration (MS, PhD)
pharmacy practice (MS, PhD)
radiopharmaceutical chemistry and nuclear pharmacy (PhD)
regulatory quality compliance (MS, Certificate)

Graduate School

Program in:
life sciences (PhD)

Center for Education and Research in Information Assurance and Security (CERIAS)
Program in:
information security (MS)

College of Agriculture
Dr. Victor L. Lechtenberg, Dean
Programs in:
agricultural economics (MS, PhD)
agriculture (EMBA, M Agr, MA, MS, MSF, PhD)
agronomy (MS, PhD)
animal sciences (MS, PhD)
aquaculture, fisheries, aquatic science (MSF)
aquaculture, fisheries, aquatic sciences (MS, PhD)
biochemistry (MS, PhD)
botany and plant pathology (MS, PhD)
entomology (MS, PhD)
food and agricultural business (EMBA)
food science (MS, PhD)
forest biology (MS, MSF, PhD)
horticulture (M Agr, MS, PhD)
natural resources and environmental policy (MS, MSF)
natural resources environmental policy (PhD)
quantitative resource analysis (MS, MSF, PhD)
wildlife science (MS, MSF, PhD)
wood science and technology (MS, MSF, PhD)
youth development and agricultural education (MA, PhD)

College of Consumer and Family Sciences
Programs in:
consumer and family sciences (MS, PhD)
consumer behavior (MS, PhD)
developmental studies (MS, PhD)
family and consumer economics (MS, PhD)
family studies (MS, PhD)
hospitality and tourism management (MS, PhD)
marriage and family therapy (MS, PhD)
nutrition (MS, PhD)
retail management (MS, PhD)
textile science (MS, PhD)

College of Liberal Arts
Programs in:
American studies (MA, PhD)
anthropology (MS, PhD)
art and design (MA)
audiology (MS, Au D, PhD)
communication (MA, MS, PhD)
comparative literature (MA, PhD)
creative writing (MFA)
exercise, human physiology of movement and sport (PhD)
French (MA, MAT, PhD)
German (MA, MAT, PhD)
health and fitness (MS)
health promotion (MS)
health promotion and disease prevention (PhD)
history (MA, PhD)
liberal arts (MA, MAT, MFA, MS, Au D, PhD)
linguistics (MS, PhD)
literature (MA, PhD)
movement and sport science (MS)
pedagogy and administration (MS)
pedagogy of physical activity and health (PhD)
philosophy (MA, PhD)
political science (MA, PhD)
psychological sciences (PhD)
psychology of sport and exercise, and motor behavior (PhD)
sociology (MS, PhD)
Spanish (MA, MAT, PhD)
speech and hearing science (MS, PhD)
speech-language pathology (MS, PhD)
theatre (MA, MFA)

College of Science
Programs in:
analytical chemistry (MS, PhD)
biochemistry (MS, PhD)
biophysics (PhD)
cell and developmental biology (PhD)
chemical education (MS, PhD)
computer sciences (MS, PhD)
earth and atmospheric sciences (MS, PhD)
ecology, evolutionary and population biology (MS, PhD)
genetics (MS, PhD)
inorganic chemistry (MS, PhD)
mathematics (MS, PhD)
microbiology (MS, PhD)
molecular biology (PhD)
neurobiology (MS, PhD)
organic chemistry (MS, PhD)
physical chemistry (MS, PhD)
physics (MS, PhD)
plant physiology (PhD)
science (MS, PhD, Certificate)
statistics (MS, PhD, Certificate)

College of Technology
Programs in:
industrial technology (MS)
technology (MS)

Krannert School of Management
Programs in:
business administration (MBA)
economics (PhD)

Purdue University (continued)
finance (MSF)
general business (MBA)
human resource management (MSHRM)
industrial administration (MSIA)
international management (MBA)
management (EMBA, MBA, MS, MSF, MSHRM, MSIA, PhD)
organizational behavior and human resource management (PhD)

School of Education
Programs in:
administration (MS Ed, PhD, Ed S)
agricultural and extension education (PhD, Ed S)
agriculture and extension education (MS, MS Ed)
art education (PhD)
consumer and family sciences and extension education (MS Ed, PhD, Ed S)
counseling and development (MS Ed, PhD)
curriculum studies (MS Ed, PhD, Ed S)
education (MS, MS Ed, PhD, Ed S)
education of the gifted (MS Ed)
educational psychology (MS Ed, PhD)
educational technology (MS Ed, PhD, Ed S)
elementary education (MS Ed)
foreign language education (MS Ed, PhD, Ed S)
foundations of education (MS Ed, PhD)
higher education administration (MS Ed, PhD)
industrial technology (PhD, Ed S)
language arts (MS Ed, PhD, Ed S)
literacy (MS Ed, PhD, Ed S)
mathematics/science education (MS, MS Ed, PhD, Ed S)
social studies (MS Ed, PhD)
social studies education (Ed S)
special education (MS Ed, PhD)
vocational/industrial education (MS Ed, PhD, Ed S)
vocational/technical education (MS Ed, PhD, Ed S)

School of Health Sciences
Program in:
health sciences (MS, PhD)

School of Veterinary Medicine
Programs in:
anatomy (MS, PhD)
basic medical sciences (MS, PhD)
comparative epidemiology and public health (MS)
comparative epidemiology and public heath (PhD)
comparative microbiology and immunology (MS, PhD)
comparative pathobiology (MS, PhD)
interdisciplinary studies (PhD)
lab animal medicine (MS)
pharmacology (MS, PhD)
physiology (MS, PhD)
veterinary anatomic pathology (MS)
veterinary clinical pathology (MS)
veterinary clinical sciences (MS, PhD)
veterinary medicine (DVM, MS, PhD)

■ PURDUE UNIVERSITY CALUMET
Hammond, IN 46323-2094
http://www.calumet.purdue.edu/

State-supported, coed, comprehensive institution. *Computer facilities:* 1,500 computers available on campus for general student use. A campuswide network can be accessed from student residence rooms and from off campus. Online class registration, Student Web Page Publishing are available. *General application contact:* Assistant to the Graduate School, 219-989-2257.

Graduate School

School of Education
Programs in:
counseling (MS Ed)
educational administration (MS Ed)
human services (MS Ed)
instructional technology (MS Ed)
mental health counseling (MS Ed)
school counseling (MS Ed)
special education (MS Ed)

School of Engineering, Mathematics, and Science
Programs in:
biology (MS)
biology teaching (MS)
biotechnology (MS)
computer engineering (MSE)
electrical engineering (MSE)
engineering (MS)
engineering, mathematics, and science (MAT, MS, MSE)
mathematics (MAT, MS)
mechanical engineering (MSE)

School of Liberal Arts and Social Sciences
Programs in:
communication (MA)
English (MA)
history (MA)
liberal arts and social sciences (MA, MS)
marriage and family therapy (MS)

School of Management
Programs in:
accountancy (M Acc)
business administration (MBA)
business administration for executives (EMBA)

School of Nursing
Program in:
nursing (MS)

■ UNIVERSITY OF EVANSVILLE
Evansville, IN 47722
http://www.evansville.edu/

Independent-religious, coed, comprehensive institution. *Graduate faculty:* 17 full-time (6 women), 14 part-time/adjunct (5 women). *Computer facilities:* 385 computers available on campus for general student use. A campuswide network can be accessed from student residence rooms and from off campus. Online class registration is available. *Graduate expenses:* Tuition: full-time $7212. Tuition and fees vary according to course load, degree level and program. *General application contact:* Carla Doty, Director of Continuing Education, 812-488-2981.

Center for Adult Education
Carla S. Doty, Director of Continuing Education
Program in:
public service administration (MS)

College of Education and Health Sciences
Dr. Lynn Penland, Dean
Programs in:
education and health sciences (MS, DPT)
health services administration (MS)
physical therapy (DPT)

College of Engineering and Computer Science
Dr. Philip Gerhart, Dean
Programs in:
electrical engineering and computer science (MS)
engineering and computer science (MS)

Schroeder Family School of Business Administration
Dr. Robert Clark, Dean
Program in:
executive business administration (MBA)

■ UNIVERSITY OF INDIANAPOLIS
Indianapolis, IN 46227-3697
http://www.uindy.edu/

Independent-religious, coed, comprehensive institution. *Graduate faculty:* 94 full-time (52 women), 53 part-time/adjunct (28 women). *Computer facilities:* 218 computers available on campus for general student use. A campuswide network can be accessed from student residence rooms and from off campus. *General application contact:* Dr. E. John McIlvried, Associate Provost for Graduate Programs and International Programs, 317-788-3274.

Graduate Programs
Dr. E. John McIlvried, Associate Provost for Graduate Programs and International Programs

Center for Aging and Community
Dr. Ellen Miller, Executive Director
Program in:
gerontology (MS, Certificate)

College of Arts and Sciences
Dr. Daniel Briere, Dean

Programs in:
- applied sociology (MA)
- art (MA)
- arts and sciences (MA, MS)
- English (MA)
- history (MA)
- human biology (MS)
- international relations (MA)

Krannert School of Physical Therapy
Dr. Mary Huer, Dean of Health Sciences
Program in:
- physical therapy (MHS, DHS, DPT, TDPT)

School of Business
Dr. Mitch B. Shapiro, Dean
Program in:
- business (EMBA, MBA, Graduate Certificate)

School of Education
Dr. Kathy Moran, Dean
Programs in:
- art education (MAT)
- biology (MAT)
- chemistry (MAT)
- curriculum and instruction (MA)
- earth sciences (MAT)
- education (MA, MAT)
- educational leadership (MA)
- elementary education (MA)
- English (MAT)
- French (MAT)
- math (MAT)
- physical education (MAT)
- physics (MAT)
- secondary education (MA)
- social studies (MAT)
- Spanish (MAT)

School of Nursing
Dr. Mary McHugh, Dean
Programs in:
- family practice (post-RN) (MSN)
- gerontological nurse practitioner (MSN)
- nurse-midwifery (MSN)
- nursing (MSN)
- nursing administration (MSN)
- nursing education (MSN)

School of Occupational Therapy
Dr. Mary Huer, Dean of Health Sciences
Program in:
- occupational therapy (MHS, MOT, DHS)

School of Psychological Sciences
Dr. E. John McIlvried, Dean
Programs in:
- clinical psychology (Psy D)
- clinical psychology/mental health counseling (MA)

■ UNIVERSITY OF NOTRE DAME

Notre Dame, IN 46556
http://www.nd.edu/

Independent-religious, coed, university. CGS member. *Computer facilities:* 261 computers available on campus for general student use. A campuswide network can be accessed from student residence rooms and from off campus. Online class registration is available. *General application contact:* Dr. Barbara Turpin, Director of Graduate Admissions, 574-631-7706.

Graduate School
Dr. Gregory Sterling, Dean of the Graduate School

College of Arts and Letters
Dr. John T. McGreevy, Dean
Programs in:
- art history (MA)
- arts and letters (M Div, M Ed, MA, MFA, MMS, MSM, MTS, PhD)
- cognitive psychology (PhD)
- counseling psychology (PhD)
- creative writing (MFA)
- design (MFA)
- developmental psychology (PhD)
- early Christian studies (MA)
- economics and econometrics (MA, PhD)
- educational initiatives (M Ed, MA)
- English (MA, PhD)
- French and Francophone studies (MA)
- history (MA, PhD)
- history and philosophy of science (MA, PhD)
- humanities (M Div, MA, MFA, MMS, MSM, MTS, PhD)
- Iberian and Latin American studies (MA)
- international peace studies (MA, PhD)
- Italian studies (MA)
- literature (PhD)
- medieval studies (MMS, PhD)
- philosophy (PhD)
- political science (PhD)
- quantitative psychology (PhD)
- Romance literatures (MA)
- social science (M Ed, MA, PhD)
- sociology (PhD)
- studio art (MFA)
- theology (M Div, MA, MSM, MTS, PhD)

College of Engineering
Dr. Peter Kilpatrick, Dean
Programs in:
- aerospace and mechanical engineering (M Eng, PhD)
- aerospace engineering (MS Aero E)
- bioengineering (MS Bio E)
- chemical and biomolecular engineering (MS Ch E, PhD)
- civil engineering (MSCE)
- civil engineering and geological sciences (PhD)
- computer science and engineering (MSCSE, PhD)
- electrical engineering (MSEE, PhD)
- engineering (M Eng, MEME, MS, MS Aero E, MS Bio E, MS Ch E, MS Env E, MSCE, MSCSE, MSEE, MSME, PhD)
- environmental engineering (MS Env E)
- geological sciences (MS)
- mechanical engineering (MEME, MSME)

College of Science
Dr. Gregory Crawford, Dean
Programs in:
- algebra (PhD)
- algebraic geometry (PhD)
- applied mathematics (MSAM)
- aquatic ecology, evolution and environmental biology (MS, PhD)
- biochemistry (MS, PhD)
- cellular and molecular biology (MS, PhD)
- complex analysis (PhD)
- differential geometry (PhD)
- genetics (MS, PhD)
- inorganic chemistry (MS, PhD)
- logic (PhD)
- organic chemistry (MS, PhD)
- partial differential equations (PhD)
- physical chemistry (MS, PhD)
- physics (MS, PhD)
- physiology (MS, PhD)
- science (MS, MSAM, PhD)
- topology (PhD)
- vector biology and parasitology (MS, PhD)

School of Architecture
Prof. Philip Bess, Director of Graduate Studies
Programs in:
- architectural design and urbanism (M ADU)
- architecture (M Arch)

Law School
Patricia A. O'Hara, Dean
Programs in:
- human rights (LL M, JSD)
- international and comparative law (LL M)
- law (JD)

Mendoza College of Business
Programs in:
- accountancy (MS)
- administration (MNA)
- business (MBA, MNA, MS)
- business administration (MBA)
- executive business administration (MBA)

■ UNIVERSITY OF SAINT FRANCIS

Fort Wayne, IN 46808-3994
http://www.sf.edu/

Independent-religious, coed, comprehensive institution. *Computer facilities:* Computer purchase and lease plans are available. 297 computers available on campus for general student use. A campuswide network can be accessed from student residence rooms. Online class registration is available. *General application contact:* Admissions Counselor, 260-434-3279.

Graduate School
Programs in:
- business administration (MBA)
- fine art (MA)
- general psychology (MS)
- mental health counseling (MS)

University of Saint Francis (continued)
nursing (MSN)
pastoral counseling (MS)
physician assistant studies (MS)
school counseling (MS Ed)
special education (MS Ed)

■ UNIVERSITY OF SOUTHERN INDIANA
Evansville, IN 47712-3590
http://www.usi.edu/

State-supported, coed, comprehensive institution. CGS member. *Graduate faculty:* 64 full-time (27 women), 10 part-time/adjunct (8 women). *Computer facilities:* 306 computers available on campus for general student use. A campuswide network can be accessed from student residence rooms and from off campus. Online class registration is available. *Graduate expenses:* Tuition, state resident: full-time $4374; part-time $243 per credit hour. Tuition, nonresident: full-time $8622; part-time $479 per credit hour. Required fees: $220; $22.75 per term. Tuition and fees vary according to course load and reciprocity agreements. *General application contact:* Dr. Peggy F. Harrel, Director, Graduate Studies, 812-465-7015.

Graduate Studies
Dr. Peggy F. Harrel, Director

College of Business
Dr. Mohammed F. Khayum, Dean
Programs in:
accountancy (MSA)
business (MBA, MSA)
business administration (MBA)

College of Education and Human Services
Dr. Julie Edmister, Dean
Programs in:
education and human services (MS, MSW)
elementary education (MS)
secondary education (MS)
social work (MSW)

College of Liberal Arts
Dr. David L. Glassman, Dean
Programs in:
liberal arts (MA, MPA)
liberal studies (MA)
public administration (MPA)

College of Nursing and Health Professions
Dr. Nadine Coudret, Dean
Programs in:
health administration (MHA)
nursing (MSN, DNP)
nursing and health professions (MHA, MSN, MSOT, DNP)
occupational therapy (MSOT)

College of Science and Engineering
Dr. Scott A. Gordon, Dean
Programs in:
industrial management (MS)
science and engineering (MS)

■ VALPARAISO UNIVERSITY
Valparaiso, IN 46383
http://www.valpo.edu/

Independent-religious, coed, comprehensive institution. *Graduate faculty:* 30 full-time (10 women), 130 part-time/adjunct (60 women). *Computer facilities:* 901 computers available on campus for general student use. A campuswide network can be accessed from student residence rooms and from off campus. Online class registration, Web academic information, degree audit are available. *General application contact:* Dr. David L. Rowland, Dean, Graduate Studies and Continuing Education, 219-464-5313.

Graduate Division
Dr. David L. Rowland, Dean, Graduate Studies and Continuing Education
Programs in:
business management (for counseling students) (Certificate)
Chinese studies (MA)
clinical mental health counseling (MA)
community counseling (MA)
English (MALS, Post-Master's Certificate)
English studies and communication (MA)
ethics and values (MALS, Post-Master's Certificate)
gerontology (MALS, Post-Master's Certificate)
history (MALS, Post-Master's Certificate)
human behavior and society (MALS, Post-Master's Certificate)
information technology (MS)
initial licensure (M Ed)
international commerce and policy (MS)
international economics and finance (MS)
liberal studies (MALS, Post-Master's Certificate)
school psychologysports administration (MS)
teaching and learning (M Ed)
teaching of English to speakers of other languages (TESOL) (Certificate)
theology (MALS, Post-Master's Certificate)
theology and ministry (MALS, Post-Master's Certificate)

College of Business Administration
Bruce MacLean, Director of Graduate Programs in Management
Programs in:
business administration (MBA)
engineering management (MEM)
management (Certificate)

College of Nursing
Dr. Janet Brown, Dean
Programs in:
management (Certificate)
nursing (MSN, Post-Master's Certificate)
nursing education (MSN)

School of Law
Program in:
law (JD, LL M)

Iowa

■ DRAKE UNIVERSITY
Des Moines, IA 50311-4516
http://www.drake.edu/

Independent, coed, university. *Graduate faculty:* 32 full-time (14 women), 58 part-time/adjunct (25 women). *Computer facilities:* 1,000 computers available on campus for general student use. A campuswide network can be accessed from student residence rooms and from off campus. Online class registration is available. *General application contact:* Ann J. Martin, Graduate Coordinator, 515-271-2034.

College of Business and Public Administration
Dr. Charles Edwards, Dean
Program in:
business and public administration (M Acc, MBA, MFM, MPA)

College of Pharmacy and Health Sciences
Dr. Raylene Rospond, Dean
Programs in:
pharmaceutical sciences (Pharm D)
pharmacy and health sciences (Pharm D)
pharmacy practice (Pharm D)

Law School
David Walker, Dean
Program in:
law (JD)

School of Education
Dr. Janet McMahill, Dean
Programs in:
adult learning and organizational development (MS)
adult learning and performance development (MS)
art (MAT)
biology (MAT)
business (MAT)
chemistry (MAT)
community agency counseling (MS)
education (MAT, MS, MSE, MST, Ed D, Ed S)
education leadership (MSE, Ed D, Ed S)
effective teaching, learning and leadership (MSE)
elementary education (MST)
English (MAT)
general science (MAT)
guidance counseling (MS)
history-American (MAT)
history-world (MAT)
journalism (MAT)
mathematics (MAT)

mental health counseling (MS)
physical science (MAT)
physics (MAT)
rehabilitation administration (MS)
rehabilitation counseling (MS)
rehabilitation placement (MS)
secondary education (MAT)
sociology (MAT)
special education (MSE)
speech (MAT)
speech communication (MAT)
teacher education (MST)
theatre (MAT)

School of Journalism and Mass Communication
Dr. Charles Edwards, Dean
Programs in:
communication leadership (MCL)
journalism and mass communication (MCL)

■ GRACELAND UNIVERSITY
Lamoni, IA 50140
http://www.graceland.edu/

Independent-religious, coed, comprehensive institution. *Graduate faculty:* 15 full-time (13 women), 56 part-time/adjunct (43 women). *Computer facilities:* 106 computers available on campus for general student use. A campuswide network can be accessed from student residence rooms and from off campus. Online class registration is available. *Graduate expenses:* Tuition: part-time $360 per semester hour. Required fees: $65 per course. One-time fee: $230 part-time. Tuition and fees vary according to program. *General application contact:* Cathy Porter, Program Consultant, 816-833-0524 Ext. 4816.

Community of Christ Seminary
Dr. Don H. Compier, Dean
Programs in:
Christian ministry (MACM)
religion (MAR)

Gleazer School of Education
Dr. Nancy Halferty, Dean
Programs in:
collaborative learning and teaching (M Ed)
differentiated instruction (M Ed)
instructional leadership (M Ed)
mild/moderate special education (M Ed)
quality schools (M Ed)
technology integration (M Ed)

School of Nursing
Dr. Claudia D. Horton, Dean
Programs in:
family nurse practitioner (MSN, PMC)
health care administration (MSN, PMC)
nurse educator (MSN, PMC)

■ IOWA STATE UNIVERSITY OF SCIENCE AND TECHNOLOGY
Ames, IA 50011
http://www.iastate.edu/

State-supported, coed, university. CGS member. *Graduate faculty:* 1,388 full-time (380 women), 182 part-time/adjunct (76 women). *Computer facilities:* Computer purchase and lease plans are available. 2,400 computers available on campus for general student use. A campuswide network can be accessed from student residence rooms and from off campus. Online class registration, network services are available. *Graduate expenses:* Tuition, state resident: full-time $6446; part-time $359 per credit. Tuition, nonresident: full-time $17,330; part-time $963 per credit. Required fees: $790; $249.25 per semester. Tuition and fees vary according to course load and program. *General application contact:* Information Contact, 515-294-5836.

College of Veterinary Medicine
Dr. John Thomson, Dean
Programs in:
biomedical sciences (MS, PhD)
veterinary clinical sciences (MS)
veterinary diagnostic and production animal medicine (MS)
veterinary medicine (DVM, MS, PhD)
veterinary microbiology (MS, PhD)
veterinary microbiology and preventive medicine (MS, PhD)
veterinary pathology (MS, PhD)
veterinary preventative medicine (MS)

Graduate College
Dr. David K. Holger, Associate Provost for Academic Progress and Dean of the Graduate College
Programs in:
bioinformatics and computational biology (PhD)
biorenewable resources and technology (MS, PhD)
ecology and evolutionary biology (MS, PhD)
environmental sciences (MS, PhD)
genetics (MS, PhD)
human-computer interaction (MS, PhD)
immunobiology (MS, PhD)
information assurance (MS)
interdisciplinary graduate studies (MA, MS)
interdisciplinary studies (MA, MBA, MS, PhD)
microbiology (MS, PhD)
molecular, cellular, and developmental biology (MS, PhD)
neuroscience (MS, PhD)
nutritional sciences (MS, PhD)
plant biology (MS, PhD)
sustainable agriculture (MS, PhD)
toxicology (MS, PhD)
transportation (MS)

College of Agriculture
Dr. Wendy Wintersteen, Dean
Programs in:
agricultural education and studies (MS, PhD)
agricultural meteorology (MS, PhD)
agriculture (M Ag, MS, PhD)
agronomy (MS)
animal breeding and genetics (MS, PhD)
animal physiology (MS)
animal psychology (PhD)
animal science (MS, PhD)
biochemistry (MS, PhD)
biophysics (MS, PhD)
crop production and physiology (MS, PhD)
entomology (MS, PhD)
forestry (MS, PhD)
genetics (MS, PhD)
horticulture (MS, PhD)
industrial agriculture and technology (MS, PhD)
meat science (MS, PhD)
molecular, cellular, and developmental biology (MS, PhD)
plant breeding (MS, PhD)
plant pathology (MS, PhD)
soil science (MS, PhD)
toxicology (MS, PhD)
wildlife ecology (MS)

College of Business
Dr. Labh S. Hira, Dean
Programs in:
accounting (M Acc)
business (M Acc, MBA, MS)
business administration (MBA, MS)
information systems (MS)

College of Design
Mark Engelbrecht, Dean
Programs in:
architectural studies (MSAS)
architecture (M Arch)
art and design (MA)
community and regional planning (MCRP)
design (M Arch, MA, MCRP, MFA, MLA, MS, MSAS)
graphic design (MFA)
integrated visual arts (MFA)
interior design (MFA)
landscape architecture (MLA)
transportation (MS)

College of Engineering
Dr. Jonathan Wickert, Dean
Programs in:
aerospace engineering (M Eng, MS, PhD)
agricultural and biosystems engineering (M Eng, MS, PhD)
chemical and biological engineering (M Eng, MS, PhD)
civil engineering (MS, PhD)
computer engineering (M Eng, MS, PhD)
electrical engineering (M Eng, MS, PhD)
engineering (M Eng, MS, PhD)
engineering mechanics (M Eng, MS, PhD)

Iowa State University of Science and Technology (continued)

industrial engineering (M Eng, MS, PhD)
materials science and engineering (MS, PhD)
mechanical engineering (MS, PhD)
mechanical engineering (coursework only) (M Eng)
operations research (MS)
systems engineering (M Eng)

College of Human Sciences
Dr. Pamela White, Dean
Programs in:
counselor education (M Ed, MS)
curriculum and instructional technology (M Ed, MS, PhD)
educational administration (M Ed, MS)
educational leadership (PhD)
elementary education (M Ed, MS)
family and consumer sciences (MFCS)
family and consumer sciences education and studies (M Ed, MS, PhD)
food science and technology (MS, PhD)
foodservice and lodging management (MFCS, MS, PhD)
higher education (M Ed, MS)
historical, philosophical, and comparative studies in education (M Ed, MS)
human development and family studies (MFCS, MS, PhD)
human sciences (M Ed, MFCS, MS, PhD)
kinesiology (MS, PhD)
nutrition (MS, PhD)
organizational learning and human resource development (M Ed, MS)
research and evaluation (MS)
special education (M Ed, MS)
textiles and clothing (MFCS, MS, PhD)

College of Liberal Arts and Sciences
Dr. Michael Whiteford, Dean
Programs in:
agricultural economics (MS, PhD)
agricultural history and rural studies (PhD)
anthropology (MA)
applied mathematics (MS, PhD)
applied physics (MS, PhD)
astrophysics (MS, PhD)
chemistry (MS, PhD)
cognitive psychology (PhD)
computer science (MS, PhD)
condensed matter physics (MS, PhD)
counseling psychology (PhD)
earth science (MS, PhD)
ecology, evolution, and organismal biology (MS, PhD)
economics (MS, PhD)
English (MA)
environmental science (MS, PhD)
genetics, developmental and cell biology (MS, PhD)
geology (MS, PhD)
high energy physics (MS, PhD)
history (MA)
history of technology and science (MA, PhD)
journalism and mass communication (MS)
liberal arts and sciences (MA, MPA, MS, MSM, PhD)
mathematics (MS, PhD)
meteorology (MS, PhD)
nuclear physics (MS, PhD)
physics (MS, PhD)
political science (MA)
public administration (MPA)
rhetoric and professional communication (PhD)
rural sociology (MS, PhD)
school mathematics (MSM)
social psychology (PhD)
sociology (MS, PhD)
statistics (MS, PhD)

■ MAHARISHI UNIVERSITY OF MANAGEMENT
Fairfield, IA 52557
http://www.mum.edu/

Independent, coed, university. *Computer facilities:* 20 computers available on campus for general student use. A campuswide network can be accessed from student residence rooms and from off campus. *General application contact:* Director of Admissions, 641-472-1110.

Graduate Studies
Programs in:
accounting (MBA)
business administration (PhD)
computer science (MS)
Maharishi Vedic science (MA, PhD)
sustainability (MBA)
teaching elementary education (MA)
teaching secondary education (MA)

■ MORNINGSIDE COLLEGE
Sioux City, IA 51106
http://www.morningside.edu/

Independent-religious, coed, comprehensive institution. *Computer facilities:* 800 computers available on campus for general student use. A campuswide network can be accessed from student residence rooms and from off campus. Online class registration, academic and financial records are available. *General application contact:* Director, 712-274-5269.

Graduate Division
Programs in:
professional educator (MAT)
special education: instructional strategist I: mild/moderate elementary (K-6) (MAT)
special education: instructional strategist II-mild/moderate secondary (7-12) (MAT)
special education: K-12 instructional strategist II-behavior disorders/ learning disabilities (MAT)
special education: K-12 instructional strategist II-mental disabilities (MAT)

■ ST. AMBROSE UNIVERSITY
Davenport, IA 52803-2898
http://www.sau.edu/

Independent-religious, coed, comprehensive institution. *Graduate faculty:* 63 full-time (26 women), 44 part-time/adjunct (20 women). *Computer facilities:* 276 computers available on campus for general student use. A campuswide network can be accessed from student residence rooms and from off campus. Online class registration, online course syllabi, online class listings, and online payments are available. *Graduate expenses:* Tuition: part-time $672 per contact hour. Tuition and fees vary according to degree level, program and reciprocity agreements. *General application contact:* Elizabeth Loveless, Director of Graduate Student Recruitment, 563-333-6271.

College of Arts and Sciences
Dr. Aron R. Aji, Dean
Programs in:
arts and sciences (MCJ, MOL, MPS, MSW)
criminal justice (MCJ)
juvenile justice education (MCJ)
pastoral studies (MPS)
social work (MSW)

College of Business
Dr. John P. Byrne, Dean
Programs in:
accounting (MAC)
business (MAC, MBA, MOL, MSITM, DBA)
business administration (DBA)
health care (MBA)
human resources (MBA)
information technology management (MSITM)
organizational leadership (MOL)

College of Education and Health Sciences
Dr. Robert Ristow, Dean
Programs in:
education and health sciences (M Ed, MEA, MOT, MSN, DPT)
educational administration (MEA)
nursing (MSN)
occupational therapy (MOT)
physical therapy (DPT)
special education (M Ed)
teaching (M Ed)

■ UNIVERSITY OF DUBUQUE

Dubuque, IA 52001-5099

http://www.dbq.edu/

Independent-religious, coed, comprehensive institution. *Computer facilities:* 220 computers available on campus for general student use. A campuswide network can be accessed from student residence rooms and from off campus. Intranet available. *General application contact:* Graduate Program Coordinator, 563-589-3300.

Program in Business Administration
Program in:
business administration (MBA)

Program in Communication
Programs in:
information technologies communication (MAC)
leadership and management (MAC)
strategic and corporate communication (MAC)

Theological Seminary
Program in:
theology (M Div, MAR, D Min)

■ THE UNIVERSITY OF IOWA

Iowa City, IA 52242-1316

http://www.uiowa.edu/

State-supported, coed, university. CGS member. *Graduate faculty:* 1,585 full-time (468 women), 87 part-time/adjunct (23 women). *Computer facilities:* Computer purchase and lease plans are available. 1,200 computers available on campus for general student use. A campuswide network can be accessed from student residence rooms and from off campus. Online class registration, online degree process, financial aid summary, bills are available. *General application contact:* Emil Rinderspacher, Senior Associate Director of Admissions, 319-335-1525.

College of Dentistry
Programs in:
dental public health (MS)
dentistry (DDS, MS, PhD, Certificate)
endodontics (MS, Certificate)
operative dentistry (MS, Certificate)
oral and maxillofacial pathology (Certificate)
oral and maxillofacial radiology (Certificate)
oral and maxillofacial surgery (MS, Certificate)
oral pathology, radiology and medicine (MS, Certificate)
oral science (MS, PhD)
orthodontics (MS, Certificate)
pediatric dentistry (Certificate)
periodontics (MS, Certificate)
preventive and community dentistry (MS)
prosthodontics (MS, Certificate)
stomatology (MS)

College of Law
Carolyn Jones, Dean
Program in:
law (JD, LL M)

College of Pharmacy
Program in:
pharmacy (MS, PhD)

Graduate College
Programs in:
applied mathematical and computational sciences (PhD)
bioinformatics and computational biology (Certificate)
genetics (PhD)
health informatics (MS, PhD, Certificate)
human toxicology (MS, PhD)
immunology (PhD)
information science (MS, PhD, Certificate)
molecular and cellular biology (PhD)
neuroscience (PhD)
second language acquisition (PhD)
translational biomedicine (MS, PhD)
urban and regional planning (MA, MS)

College of Education
Programs in:
administration and research (PhD)
art education (PhD)
community/rehabilitation counseling (MA)
counseling psychology (PhD)
counselor education and supervision (PhD)
curriculum and supervision (MA, PhD)
curriculum supervision (MA)
developmental reading (MA)
early childhood education and care (MA)
education (MA, MAT, PhD, Ed S)
educational administration (MA, PhD, Ed S)
educational measurement and statistics (MA, PhD)
educational psychology (MA, PhD)
elementary education (MA, PhD)
English education (MA, MAT)
foreign language education (MA, MAT)
foreign language/ESL education (PhD)
higher education (MA, PhD, Ed S)
language, literature and culture (PhD)
math education (PhD)
mathematics education (MA)
rehabilitation counselor education (PhD)
school counseling (MA)
school psychology (PhD, Ed S)
secondary education (MA, MAT, PhD)
social foundations (MA, PhD)
social studies (MA, PhD)
special education (MA, PhD)
student development (MA, PhD)

College of Engineering
Programs in:
biomedical engineering (MS, PhD)
chemical and biochemical engineering (MS, PhD)
civil and environmental engineering (MS, PhD)
electrical and computer engineering (MS, PhD)
engineering (MS, PhD)
engineering design and manufacturing (MS, PhD)
ergonomics (MS, PhD)
information and engineering management (MS, PhD)
mechanical engineering (MS, PhD)
operations research (MS, PhD)
quality engineering (MS, PhD)

College of Liberal Arts and Sciences
Programs in:
African American world studies (MA)
American studies (MA, PhD)
anthropology (MA, PhD)
art (MA, MFA)
art history (MA, PhD)
Asian languages and literature (MA)
astronomy (MS)
biology (MS, PhD)
cell and developmental biology (MS, PhD)
chemistry (MS, PhD)
classics (MA, PhD)
communication research (MA, PhD)
comparative literature (MA, PhD)
comparative literature translation (MFA)
computer science (MCS, MS, PhD)
dance (MFA)
English (PhD)
evolution (MS, PhD)
exercise science (MS)
film and video production (MA, MFA)
film studies (MA, PhD)
French (MA, PhD)
genetics (MS, PhD)
geography (MA, PhD)
geoscience (MS, PhD)
German (MA, PhD)
history (MA, PhD)
integrative physiology (PhD)
leisure and recreational sport management (MA)
liberal arts and sciences (MA, MCS, MFA, MS, MSW, Au D, DMA, PhD)
linguistics (MA, PhD)
linguistics with TESL (MA)
literary criticism (PhD)
literary history (PhD)
literary studies (MA)
mass communication (PhD)
mathematics (MS, PhD)
media communication (MA)
music (MA, MFA, DMA, PhD)
neural and behavioral sciences (PhD)
neurobiology (MS, PhD)
nonfiction writing (MFA)
philosophy (MA, PhD)
physics (MS, PhD)
plant biology (MS, PhD)
political science (MA, PhD)

The University of Iowa (continued)
professional journalism (MA)
professional speech pathology and audiology (MA, Au D)
psychology (MA, PhD)
psychology of sport and physical activity (MA, PhD)
religious studies (MA, PhD)
rhetorical studies (MA, PhD)
rhetorical theory and stylistics (PhD)
science education (MS, PhD)
social work (MSW, PhD)
sociology (MA, PhD)
Spanish (MA, PhD)
speech and hearing science (PhD)
sports studies (MA, PhD)
statistics and actuarial science (MS, PhD)
theatre arts (MFA)
therapeutic recreation (MA)
women's studies (PhD)
writer's workshop (MFA)

College of Nursing
Program in:
nursing (MSN, DNP, PhD)

College of Public Health
Programs in:
biostatistics (MS, PhD)
clinical investigation (MS)
community and behavioral health (MS, PhD)
epidemiology (MS, PhD)
health management and policy (MHA, PhD)
occupational and environmental health (MS, PhD, Certificate)
public health (MHA, MPH, MS, PhD, Certificate)

School of Library and Information Science
Program in:
library and information science (MA)

Henry B. Tippie College of Business
Programs in:
accountancy (M Ac)
accounting (PhD)
business (M Ac, MBA, PhD)
business administration (PhD)
economics (PhD)

Henry B. Tippie School of Management
Programs in:
accounting (MBA)
corporate finance (MBA)
entrepreneurship (MBA)
finance (MBA)
individually designed concentration (MBA)
investment management (MBA)
management information systems (MBA)
marketing (MBA)
nonprofit management (MBA)
operations management (MBA)
strategic management and consulting (MBA)

Roy J. and Lucille A. Carver College of Medicine
Dr. Paul B. Rothman, Dean
Programs in:
anatomy and biology (PhD)
biochemistry (PhD)
biology (PhD)
chemistry (PhD)
free radical and radiation biology (PhD)
genetics (PhD)
human toxicology (PhD)
immunology (PhD)
medicine (MD, MA, MPAS, MS, DPT, PhD)
microbiology (PhD)
molecular and cellular biology (PhD)
molecular physiology and biophysics (PhD)
neuroscience (PhD)
pharmacology (PhD)
speech and hearing (PhD)

Graduate Programs in Medicine
Dr. Paul B. Rothman, Dean
Programs in:
anatomy and cell biology (PhD)
biochemistry (MS, PhD)
free radical and radiation biology (MS, PhD)
general microbiology and microbial physiology (MS, PhD)
immunology (MS, PhD)
medicine (MA, MPAS, MS, DPT, PhD)
microbial genetics (MS, PhD)
molecular physiology and biophysics (PhD)
pathogenic bacteriology (MS, PhD)
pathology (MS)
pharmacology (MS, PhD)
physical therapy (DPT)
physician assistant (MPAS)
rehabilitation science (PhD)
virology (MS, PhD)

■ UNIVERSITY OF NORTHERN IOWA
Cedar Falls, IA 50614
http://www.uni.edu/

State-supported, coed, comprehensive institution. CGS member. *Computer facilities:* Computer purchase and lease plans are available. 1,900 computers available on campus for general student use. A campuswide network can be accessed from student residence rooms and from off campus. Online class registration, course registration, student account, degree audit, program of study are available. *Graduate expenses:* Tuition, state resident: full-time $6446. Tuition, nonresident: full-time $14,874. Required fees: $852. *General application contact:* Laurie S. Russell, Record Analyst, 319-273-2623.

Graduate College
Dr. Sue Joseph, Interim Dean
Programs in:
philanthropy and nonprofit development (MA)
public policy (MPP)
women's and gender studies (MA)

College of Business Administration
Dr. Farzad Moussavi, Dean
Programs in:
accounting (M Acc)
business administration (M Acc, MBA)

College of Education
Dr. William Callahan, Dean
Programs in:
communication and training technology (MA)
community health education (Ed D)
counseling (MA, MAE, Ed D)
curriculum and instruction (MAE, Ed D)
early childhood education (MAE)
education (MA, MAE, Ed D, Ed S)
educational administration (Ed D)
educational leadership (MAE, Ed D)
educational media (MA)
educational psychology (MAE)
educational technology (MA)
elementary education (MAE)
elementary principal (MAE)
elementary reading and language arts (MAE)
health education (MA, Ed D)
leisure services (MA, Ed D)
middle school/junior high education (MAE)
physical education (MA)
postsecondary education (MAE)
professional development for teachers (MAE)
program administration (MA)
reading (MAE)
reading education (MAE)
rehabilitation studies (Ed D)
school counseling (MAE)
school library media studies (MA)
school psychology (Ed S)
scientific basis of physical education (MA)
secondary principal (MAE)
secondary reading (MAE)
special education (MAE, Ed D)
student affairs (MAE)
teaching/coaching (MA)
youth/human services administration (MA)

College of Humanities and Fine Arts
Dr. Reinhold Bubser, Dean
Programs in:
art (MA)
art education (MA)
audiology (MA)
communication studies (MA)
composition (MM)
conducting (MM)
English (MA)
French (MA)
German (MA)
humanities and fine arts (MA, MM)
jazz pedagogy (MM)

music (MA, MM)
music education (MA, MM)
music history (MM)
performance (MM)
piano performance and pedagogy (MM)
Spanish (MA)
speech pathology (MA)
teaching English to speakers of other languages (MA)
teaching English to speakers of other languages/French (MA)
teaching English to speakers of other languages/German (MA)
teaching English to speakers of other languages/Spanish (MA)
two languages (MA)

College of Natural Sciences
Dr. Joel Haack, Dean
Programs in:
biology (MA, MS, PSM)
chemistry (MA, MS, PSM)
computer science (MA, MS)
environmental health (MS)
environmental science (MS)
environmental technology (MS)
industrial technology (MA, PSM, DIT)
mathematics (MA)
mathematics for middle grades (MA)
natural sciences (MA, MS, PSM, DIT)
physics (MA, PSM)
science education (MA)

College of Social and Behavioral Sciences
Dr. John Johnson, Interim Dean
Programs in:
criminology (MA)
geography (MA)
history (MA)
political science (MA)
psychology (MA)
social and behavioral sciences (MA, MSW)
social science (MA)
social work (MSW)
sociology (MA)

■ UPPER IOWA UNIVERSITY
Fayette, IA 52142-1857
http://www.uiu.edu/

Independent, coed, comprehensive institution. *Computer facilities:* 75 computers available on campus for general student use. A campuswide network can be accessed. *General application contact:* Online Program Office Manager, 515-369-7777.

Online Master's Programs
Programs in:
accounting (MBA)
corporate financial management (MBA)
global business (MBA)
health and human services (MPA)
homeland security (MPA)
human resources management (MBA)
justice administration (MPA)
organizational development (MBA)
public personnel management (MPA)
quality management (MBA)

Kansas

■ BENEDICTINE COLLEGE
Atchison, KS 66002-1499
http://www.benedictine.edu/

Independent-religious, coed, comprehensive institution. *Graduate faculty:* 5 full-time (1 woman), 13 part-time/adjunct (6 women). *Computer facilities:* 80 computers available on campus for general student use. A campuswide network can be accessed from student residence rooms and from off campus. Online class registration is available. *Graduate expenses:* Tuition: full-time $21,000; part-time $530 per credit hour. *General application contact:* Donna Bonnel, Administrative of Graduation Programs, 913-367-5340 Ext. 2524.

Executive Master of Business Administration Program
Dr. Antonio J. Soave, Executive Director, School of Business
Program in:
business administration (EMBA)

Master of Arts Program in School Leadership
Dr. Cheryl Reding, Director
Program in:
school leadership (MA)

Traditional Business Administration Program
Dr. Antonio J. Soave, Director
Program in:
business administration (MBA)

■ EMPORIA STATE UNIVERSITY
Emporia, KS 66801-5087
http://www.emporia.edu/

State-supported, coed, comprehensive institution. CGS member. *Graduate faculty:* 260 full-time (120 women), 33 part-time/adjunct (20 women). *Computer facilities:* 410 computers available on campus for general student use. A campuswide network can be accessed from student residence rooms and from off campus. Online class registration, various software packages are available. *Graduate expenses:* Tuition, state resident: full-time $3976; part-time $166 per credit hour. Tuition, nonresident: full-time $12,028; part-time $501 per credit hour. Required fees: $51 per credit hour. Tuition and fees vary according to campus/location. *General application contact:* Mary Sewell, Admissions Coordinator, 800-950-GRAD.

School of Graduate Studies
Dr. Gerrit Bleeker, Dean

College of Liberal Arts and Sciences
Dr. Steven Brown, Dean
Programs in:
American history (MA, MAT)
anthropology (MAT)
botany (MS)
earth science (MS)
economics (MAT)
English (MA)
environmental biology (MS)
general biology (MS)
geography (MAT)
geospatial analysis (Postbaccalaureate Certificate)
history (MA)
liberal arts and sciences (MA, MAT, MM, MS, Postbaccalaureate Certificate)
mathematics (MS)
microbial and cellular biology (MS)
music education (MM)
performance (MM)
physical science (MS)
political science (MAT)
social sciences (MAT)
social studies education (MAT)
sociology (MAT)
teaching English to speakers of other languages (MA)
world history (MA, MAT)
zoology (MS)

School of Business
Dr. Joseph Wen, Dean
Programs in:
business (MBA, MSBE)
business administration (MBA)
business education (MSBE)

School of Library and Information Management
Dr. Gwen Alexander, Interim Dean
Programs in:
archives studies (Certificate)
legal information management (Certificate)
library and information management (MLS, PhD, Certificate)

The Teachers College
Dr. J. Phillip Bennett, Dean
Programs in:
art therapy (MS)
behavior disorders (MS)
clinical psychology (MS)
curriculum and instruction (MS)
curriculum leadership (MS)
early childhood curriculum (MS)
early childhood education (MS)
early childhood special education (MS)
education (MS, Ed S)
educational administration (MS)
effective practitioner (MS)
elementary administration (MS)
elementary subject matter (MS)
elementary/secondary administration (MS)
English as a second language (MS)

Emporia State University (continued)
general psychology (MS)
gifted, talented, and creative (MS)
industrial/organizational psychology (MS)
instructional design and technology (MS)
interrelated special education (MS)
learning disabilities (MS)
master teacher (MS)
mental health counseling (MS)
mental retardation (MS)
national board certification (MS)
physical education (MS)
psychology (MS)
reading (MS)
rehabilitation counseling (MS)
school counseling (MS)
school psychology (MS, Ed S)
secondary administration (MS)
secondary subject matter (MS)
special education (MS)

■ FORT HAYS STATE UNIVERSITY

Hays, KS 67601-4099
http://www.fhsu.edu/

State-supported, coed, comprehensive institution. CGS member. *Graduate faculty:* 127 full-time (31 women). *Computer facilities:* Computer purchase and lease plans are available. 813 computers available on campus for general student use. A campuswide network can be accessed from student residence rooms and from off campus. *Graduate expenses:* Tuition, state resident: full-time $3131; part-time $174 per credit hour. Tuition, nonresident: full-time $8317; part-time $462 per credit hour. Full-time tuition and fees vary according to course level, course load and degree level. *General application contact:* Dr. Timothy R. Crowley, Dean, 785-628-4236.

Graduate School

College of Arts and Sciences
Programs in:
arts and sciences (MA, MFA, MLS, MS, Ed S)
communication (MS)
English (MA)
geography (MS)
geology (MS)
geosciences (MS)
history (MA)
liberal studies (MLS)
psychology (MS)
school psychology (Ed S)
studio art (MFA)

College of Business and Leadership
Programs in:
business and leadership (MBA)
management (MBA)

College of Education and Technology
Programs in:
counseling (MS)
education (MSE)
education and technology (MS, MSE, Ed S)
educational administration (MS, Ed S)
instructional technology (MS)
special education (MS)

College of Health and Life Sciences
Programs in:
biology (MS)
health and human performance (MS)
health and life sciences (MS, MSN)
nursing (MSN)
speech-language pathology (MS)

■ FRIENDS UNIVERSITY

Wichita, KS 67213
http://www.friends.edu/

Independent, coed, comprehensive institution. *Graduate faculty:* 19 full-time (7 women). *Computer facilities:* 190 computers available on campus for general student use. A campuswide network can be accessed from student residence rooms and from off campus. *General application contact:* Craig Davis, Director of Graduate Admissions, 800-794-6945 Ext. 5573.

Graduate School

Division of Business, Technology, and Leadership
Programs in:
business administration (MBA)
business law (MBL)
business, technology, and leadership (MBA, MBL, MHCL, MMIS, MSM, MSOD, MSOM)
health care leadership (MHCL)
management (MSM)
management information systems (MMIS)
operations management (MSOM)
organization development (MSOD)

Division of Science, Arts, and Education
Programs in:
Christian ministry (MACM)
elementary education (MAT)
family therapy (MSFT)
science, arts, and education (MACM, MAT, MSFT)
secondary education (MAT)

■ KANSAS STATE UNIVERSITY

Manhattan, KS 66506
http://www.ksu.edu/

State-supported, coed, university. CGS member. *Graduate faculty:* 913 full-time (246 women), 138 part-time/adjunct (28 women). *Computer facilities:* 326 computers available on campus for general student use. A campuswide network can be accessed from student residence rooms and from off campus. Online class registration is available. *Graduate expenses:* Tuition, state resident: full-time $6466; part-time $269.40 per credit hour. Tuition, nonresident: full-time $14,874; part-time $619.75 per credit hour. Required fees: $673; $23.40 per credit hour. Tuition and fees vary according to campus/location. *General application contact:* Dr. Carol W. Shanklin, Dean, 785-532-6191.

College of Veterinary Medicine
Ralph Richardson, Dean
Programs in:
anatomy and physiology (MS, PhD)
biomedical science (MS)
clinical sciences (MS)
diagnostic medicine/pathobiology (MS, PhD)
physiology (PhD)
veterinary medicine (DVM, MS, PhD)

Graduate School

Dr. Carol W. Shanklin, Dean

College of Agriculture
Fred Cholick, Dean
Programs in:
agricultural economics (MAB, MS, PhD)
agriculture (MAB, MS, PhD)
animal breeding and genetics (MS, PhD)
crop science (MS, PhD)
entomology (MS, PhD)
food science (MS, PhD)
genetics (MS, PhD)
grain science and industry (MS, PhD)
horticulture (MS, PhD)
meat science (MS, PhD)
monogastric nutrition (MS, PhD)
physiology (MS, PhD)
plant pathology (MS, PhD)
range management (MS, PhD)
ruminant nutrition (MS, PhD)
soil science (MS, PhD)
weed science (MS, PhD)

College of Architecture, Planning and Design
Dennis Law, Dean
Programs in:
architecture (M Arch)
architecture, planning and design (M Arch, MLA, MRCP)
landscape architecture and regional and community planning (MLA)
regional and community planning (MRCP)

College of Arts and Sciences
Stephen White, Dean
Programs in:
analytical chemistry (MS)
art (MFA)
arts and sciences (MA, MFA, MM, MPA, MS, PhD)
biochemistry (MS, PhD)
biological chemistry (MS)
biology (MS, PhD)
chemistry (PhD)
economics (MA, PhD)
English (MA)
French (MA)
geography (MA, PhD)
geology (MS)
German (MA)

history (MA)
inorganic chemistry (MS)
international service (MA)
kinesiology (MS)
mass communications (MS)
materials chemistry (MS)
mathematics (MS, PhD)
microbiology (PhD)
music education (MM)
music education/band conducting (MM)
music history and literature (MM)
organic chemistry (MS)
performance (MM)
performance with pedagogy emphasis (MM)
physical chemistry (MS)
political science (MA)
psychology (MS, PhD)
public administration (MPA)
rhetoric/communication (MA)
security studies (MA, PhD)
sociology (MA, PhD)
Spanish (MA)
statistics (MS, PhD)
theatre (MA)
theory and composition (MM)

College of Business Administration
Yar M. Ebadi, Dean
Programs in:
accounting (M Acc)
business administration (M Acc, MBA)

College of Education
Michael Holen, Dean
Programs in:
academic advising (MS)
adult and continuing education (MS, Ed D)
college student development (MS)
counselor education and supervision (PhD)
curriculum and instruction (MS, Ed D, PhD)
education (MS, Ed D, PhD)
educational administration (MS, Ed D)
school counseling (MS)
special education (MS)

College of Engineering
John English, Dean
Programs in:
architectural engineering (MS)
bioengineering (MS, PhD)
biological and agricultural engineering (MS)
chemical engineering (MS)
civil engineering (MS)
communications systems (MS, PhD)
computer engineering (MS, PhD)
computer science (MS, PhD)
control systems (MS, PhD)
electromagnetics (MS, PhD)
engineering (PhD)
engineering management (MEM)
industrial engineering (MS, PhD)
instrumentation (MS, PhD)
mechanical engineering (MS)
nuclear engineering (MS)
operations research (MS)
power systems (MS, PhD)
signal processing (MS, PhD)
software engineering (MSE)
solid-state electronics (MS, PhD)

College of Human Ecology
Virginia Moxley, Dean
Programs in:
apparel and textiles (MS, PhD)
dietetics and administration (MS)
family life education and consultation (PhD)
family studies and human services (MS)
food science (MS, PhD)
food service and hospitality management (MS)
food service, hospitality management, and administrative dietetics (PhD)
human ecology (MS, PhD)
human nutrition (MS, PhD)
institutional management (PhD)
lifespan and human development (PhD)
marriage and family therapy (PhD)
public health (MS)

■ MIDAMERICA NAZARENE UNIVERSITY
Olathe, KS 66062-1899
http://www.mnu.edu/

Independent-religious, coed, comprehensive institution. *Graduate faculty:* 18 full-time (6 women), 39 part-time/adjunct (19 women). *Computer facilities:* 85 computers available on campus for general student use. A campuswide network can be accessed from student residence rooms and from off campus. *General application contact:* Kevin Mokhtarian, Admissions Coordinator, 913-971-3436.

Graduate Studies in Counseling
Dr. Todd Frye, Director
Programs in:
counseling (MAC)
play therapy (PMC)

Graduate Studies in Education
Dr. Martin Dunlap, Director
Programs in:
ESOL (M Ed)
professional teaching (M Ed)
special education (MA)
technology enhanced teaching (M Ed)

Graduate Studies in Management
Dr. Willadee Wehmeyer, Director
Programs in:
management (MBA)
organizational administration (MA)

■ NEWMAN UNIVERSITY
Wichita, KS 67213-2097
http://www.newmanu.edu/

Independent-religious, coed, comprehensive institution. *Graduate faculty:* 19 full-time (5 women), 36 part-time/adjunct (27 women). *Computer facilities:* 130 computers available on campus for general student use. A campuswide network can be accessed from student residence rooms. Online class registration is available. *General application contact:* Linda Kay Sabala, Director of Graduate Admissions, 316-942-4291 Ext. 2230.

School of Business
Dr. Joe Goetz, Dean of the College of Professional Studies and Director of the School of Business
Programs in:
international business (MBA)
leadership (MBA)
management (MBA)
technology (MBA)

School of Education
Dr. Guy Glidden, Director
Programs in:
building leadership (MS Ed)
curriculum and instruction (MS Ed)

School of Nursing and Allied Health
Dr. Sharon Niemann, Director
Program in:
nurse anesthesia (MS)

School of Social Work
Dr. Kevin Brown, Director
Program in:
social work (MSW)

■ PITTSBURG STATE UNIVERSITY
Pittsburg, KS 66762
http://www.pittstate.edu/

State-supported, coed, comprehensive institution. CGS member. *Computer facilities:* 425 computers available on campus for general student use. A campuswide network can be accessed from student residence rooms and from off campus. Online class registration is available. *General application contact:* Assistant Director, 620-235-4223.

Graduate School

College of Arts and Sciences
Programs in:
applied communication (MA)
applied physics (MS)
art education (MA)
arts and sciences (MA, MM, MS, MSN)
biology (MS)
chemistry (MS)
communication education (MA)
English (MA)
history (MA)
instrumental music education (MM)
mathematics (MS)
music history/music literature (MM)
nursing (MSN)
performance (MM)
physics (MS)
professional physics (MS)
studio art (MA)
theatre (MA)
theory and composition (MM)
vocal music education (MM)

Pittsburg State University (continued)

College of Education
Programs in:
behavioral disorders (MS)
classroom reading teacher (MS)
community college and higher education (Ed S)
community counseling (MS)
counselor education (MS)
early childhood education (MS)
education (MAT, MS, Ed S)
educational leadership (MS)
educational technology (MS)
elementary education (MS)
general school administration (Ed S)
learning disabilities (MS)
mentally retarded (MS)
physical education (MS)
psychology (MS)
reading (MS)
reading specialist (MS)
school counseling (MS)
school psychology (Ed S)
secondary education (MS)
special education (MS)
teaching (MAT)

College of Technology
Programs in:
engineering technology (MET)
human resource development (MS)
industrial education (Ed S)
technical teacher education (MS)
technology (MS)
technology education (MS)

Kelce College of Business
Programs in:
accounting (MBA)
business (MBA)
general administration (MBA)

■ SOUTHWESTERN COLLEGE

Winfield, KS 67156-2499

http://www.sckans.edu/

Independent-religious, coed, comprehensive institution. *Graduate faculty:* 7 full-time (2 women), 35 part-time/adjunct (18 women). *Computer facilities:* 30 computers available on campus for general student use. A campuswide network can be accessed from student residence rooms and from off campus. Online class registration is available. *Graduate expenses:* Tuition: full-time $6970; part-time $387 per credit. Tuition and fees vary according to class time, course load, campus/location and program. *General application contact:* Office of Graduate Admissions, 620-229-6000.

Fifth-Year Graduate Programs
Dr. James Sheppard, Vice President for Academic Affairs
Programs in:
leadership (MS)
management (MBA)
specialized ministries (MA)

Master of Education Programs
Dr. David Hofmeister, Director of Teacher Education
Programs in:
curriculum and instruction (M Ed)
special education (M Ed)
teaching (MA)

Professional Studies Programs
Gail Cullen, Director of Academic Affairs
Programs in:
business administration (MBA)
leadership (MS)
management (MS)
security administration (MS)
specialized ministries (MA)

■ THE UNIVERSITY OF KANSAS

Lawrence, KS 66045

http://www.ku.edu

State-supported, coed, university. CGS member. *Graduate faculty:* 1,800. *Computer facilities:* 1,500 computers available on campus for general student use. A campuswide network can be accessed from student residence rooms and from off campus. Online class registration is available. *Graduate expenses:* Tuition, state resident: full-time $6122; part-time $255.10 per credit hour. Tuition, nonresident: full-time $14,629; part-time $609.55 per credit hour. Required fees: $847; $70.56 per credit hour. Tuition and fees vary according to course load and program. *General application contact:* Graduate Studies, 785-864-8040.

Graduate Studies
Dr. Sara Rosen, Associate Vice Provost and Dean of Graduate Studies

College of Liberal Arts and Sciences
Dr. Greg B. Simpson, Interim Dean
Programs in:
African and African-American studies (MA)
African Studies (Graduate Certificate)
American studies (MA, PhD)
anthropology (MA, PhD)
applied behavioral science (MA)
arts (MA)
audiology (PhD)
behavioral psychology (PhD)
biochemistry and biophysics (MA, PhD)
biological sciences (MA, PhD)
botany (MA, PhD)
Brazilian studies (Graduate Certificate)
Central American and Mexican studies (Graduate Certificate)
chemistry (MS, PhD)
child language (MA, PhD)
classics (MA)
clinical child psychology (MA, PhD)
cognitive (PhD)
collection conservation (Graduate Certificate)
communication studies (MA, PhD)
computational physics and astronomy (MS)
creative writing (MFA)
developmental (PhD)
East Asian languages and cultures (MA)
ecology and evolutionary biology (MA, PhD)
economics (MA, PhD)
English (MA, PhD)
entomology (MA, PhD)
film and media studies (PhD)
French (MA, PhD)
geography (MA, PhD)
geology (MS, PhD)
German (MA, PhD)
gerontology (MA, PhD, Graduate Certificate)
global and international studies (MA)
global indigenous nations studies (MA)
history (MA, PhD)
history of art (MA, PhD)
Latin American studies (MA)
liberal arts and sciences (MA, MFA, MPA, MS, PhD, Graduate Certificate)
linguistics (MA, PhD)
mathematics (MA, PhD)
microbiology (MA, PhD)
molecular, cellular, and developmental biology (MA, PhD)
museum studies (MA)
philosophy (MA, PhD)
physics (MS, PhD)
political science (MA, PhD)
psychology (MA, PhD)
public administration (MPA, PhD)
quantitative (PhD)
religious studies (MA)
Russian, East European and Eurasian studies (MA)
Slavic languages and literatures (MA, PhD)
sociology (MA, PhD)
Spanish (MA, PhD)
speech-language pathology (MA, PhD)
theatre (MA)
theatre design (MFA)
visual art education (MA)
visual arts education (MA)

School of Architecture, Design, and Planning
John C. Gaunt, Dean
Programs in:
architecture (PhD)
architecture, design, and planning (M Arch, MA, MFA, MUP, PhD, AC)
design (MA, MFA)
design management (MA)
facility management (AC)
interaction design (MA)
management option (M Arch)
professional track (M Arch)
urban planning (MUP)

School of Business
William L. Fuerst, Dean
Programs in:
accounting (M Acc)
animal health (MBA)
business (PhD)

finance (MBA)
human resources management (MBA)
information systems (MBA)
international business (MBA)
management (MBA)
marketing (MBA)
strategic management (MBA)
supply chain management (MS)

School of Education
Dr. Rick Ginsberg, Dean
Programs in:
counseling psychology (MS, PhD)
curriculum and instruction (MA, MS Ed, Ed D, PhD)
education (MA, MS, MS Ed, Ed D, PhD, Ed S)
educational administration (MS Ed, Ed D, PhD)
educational policy and leadership (Ed D, PhD)
educational psychology and research (MS Ed, PhD)
foundations (PhD)
foundations of education (MS Ed)
health and physical education (MS Ed, Ed D, PhD)
higher education (MS Ed, Ed D)
higher education administration (MS Ed)
historical, philosophical, and social foundations of education (MS Ed)
policy studies (PhD)
school psychology (PhD, Ed S)
special education (MS Ed, Ed D, PhD)

School of Engineering
Dr. Stuart R. Bell, Dean
Programs in:
aerospace engineering (ME, MS, DE, PhD)
architectural engineering (MS)
bioengineering (PhD)
chemical engineering (MS)
chemical/petroleum engineering (PhD)
civil engineering (MCE, MS, DE, PhD)
computer engineering (MS)
computer science (MS, PhD)
construction management (MCM)
electrical engineering (MS, DE, PhD)
engineering (MCE, MCM, ME, MS, DE, PhD)
engineering management (MS)
environmental engineering (MS, PhD)
environmental science (MS, PhD)
information technology (MS)
mechanical engineering (MS, DE, PhD)
petroleum engineering (MS)
water resources science (MS)

School of Journalism and Mass Communications
Ann Brill, Dean
Program in:
journalism (MS)

School of Music
Dr. Alicia Ann Clair, Interim Dean
Programs in:
music (MM, MME, DMA, PhD)
music education (MME, PhD)
music therapy (MME)

School of Pharmacy
Kenneth L. Audus, Dean
Programs in:
hospital pharmacy (MS)
medicinal chemistry (MS, PhD)
neurosciences (MS, PhD)
pharmaceutical chemistry (MS, PhD)
pharmacology and toxicology (MS, PhD)
pharmacy (MS, PhD)

School of Social Welfare
Mary Ellen Kondrat, Dean
Programs in:
social welfare (MSW)
social work (PhD)

School of Law
Gail B. Agrawal, Dean
Program in:
law (JD)

University of Kansas Medical Center
Dr. Allen Rawitch, Vice Chancellor for Academic Affairs and Dean of Graduate Studies
Program in:
medicine (MD, MA, MHSA, MOT, MPH, MS, Au D, DNP, DPT, OTD, PhD, Certificate, PMC)

School of Allied Health
Dr. Karen L. Miller, Dean
Programs in:
allied health (MA, MOT, MS, Au D, DPT, OTD, PhD, Certificate)
audiology (MA, Au D, PhD)
dietetic internship (Certificate)
dietetics and nutrition (MS)
molecular biotechnology (MS)
nurse anesthesia (MS)
occupational therapy (MOT, MS, OTD)
physical therapy and rehabilitation science (DPT, PhD)
speech-language pathology (MA, PhD)
therapeutic science (PhD)

School of Medicine
Programs in:
anatomy and cell biology (MA, PhD)
biochemistry and molecular biology (MS, PhD)
biomedical sciences (MA, MPH, MS, PhD)
health policy and management (MHSA)
medicine (MD, MA, MHSA, MPH, MS, PhD)
microbiology, molecular genetics and immunology (PhD)
molecular and integrative physiology (MS, PhD)
neuroscience (MS, PhD)
pathology and laboratory medicine (MA, PhD)
pharmacology (MS, PhD)
preventive medicine (MPH, MS)
toxicology (MS, PhD)

School of Nursing
Dr. Karen L. Miller, Dean
Programs in:
family nurse practitioner (PMC)
health care informatics (PMC)
health professions educator (PMC)
nurse midwife (PMC)
nursing (MS, DNP, PhD)
organizational leadership (PMC)
psychiatric/mental health nurse practitioner (PMC)
public health nursing (PMC)

■ UNIVERSITY OF SAINT MARY

Leavenworth, KS 66048-5082

http://www.stmary.edu/

Independent-religious, coed, comprehensive institution. *Computer facilities:* 380 computers available on campus for general student use. A campuswide network can be accessed from student residence rooms. Online class registration is available. *General application contact:* Graduate Dean, 913-345-8288.

Graduate Programs
Programs in:
business administration (MBA)
curriculum and instruction (MAT)
education (MA, MAT)
management (MS)
psychology (MA)
special education (MA)
teaching (MA)

■ WASHBURN UNIVERSITY

Topeka, KS 66621

http://www.washburn.edu/

City-supported, coed, comprehensive institution. CGS member. *Computer facilities:* 1,200 computers available on campus for general student use. A campuswide network can be accessed from student residence rooms and from off campus. Online class registration is available. *General application contact:* Dean, 785-670-1561.

College of Arts and Sciences
Programs in:
arts and sciences (M Ed, MA, MLS)
clinical psychology (MA)
curriculum and instruction (M Ed)
educational leadership (M Ed)
liberal studies (MLS)
reading (M Ed)
special education (M Ed)

School of Applied Studies
Programs in:
applied studies (MCJ, MSW)
clinical social work (MSW)
criminal justice (MCJ)

School of Business
Dr. David L. Sollars, Dean
Program in:
business (MBA)

School of Law
Thomas J. Romig, Dean

Washburn University (continued)
Program in:
law (JD)

■ WICHITA STATE UNIVERSITY
Wichita, KS 67260
http://www.wichita.edu/

State-supported, coed, university. CGS member. *Computer facilities:* 1,500 computers available on campus for general student use. A campuswide network can be accessed from student residence rooms and from off campus. Online class registration is available. *General application contact:* Dean of the Graduate School, 316-978-3095.

Graduate School

College of Education
Programs in:
communications sciences (MA, PhD)
counseling (M Ed)
curriculum and instruction (M Ed)
education (M Ed, MA, Ed D, PhD, Ed S)
education administration (M Ed, Ed D)
educational psychology (M Ed)
physical education (M Ed)
school psychology (Ed S)
special education (M Ed)
sports administration (M Ed)

College of Engineering
Programs in:
aerospace engineering (MS, PhD)
electrical engineering (MS, PhD)
engineering (MEM, MS, PhD)
industrial and manufacturing engineering (MEM, MS, PhD)
mechanical engineering (MS, PhD)

College of Fine Arts
Programs in:
art education (MA)
fine arts (MA, MFA, MM, MME)
music (MM)
music education (MME)
studio arts (MFA)

College of Health Professions
Programs in:
clinical nurse specialist (MSN)
health professions (MPH, MPT, MSN)
nurse midwifery (MSN)
nurse practitioner (MSN)
nursing and health care systems administration (MSN)
physical therapy (MPT)
public health (MPH)

Fairmount College of Liberal Arts and Sciences
Programs in:
anthropology (MA)
applied mathematics (PhD)
biological sciences (MS)
chemistry (MS, PhD)
communication (MA)
community/clinical psychology (PhD)
computer science (MS)
creative writing (MA, MFA)
criminal justice (MA)
English (MA, MFA)
environmental science (MS)
geology (MS)
gerontology (MA)
history (MA)
human factors (PhD)
liberal arts and sciences (MA, MFA, MPA, MS, MSW, PhD)
mathematics (MS)
physics (MS)
political science (MA)
psychology (MA)
public administration (MPA)
social work (MSW)
sociology (MA)
Spanish (MA)
statistics (MS)

W. Frank Barton School of Business
Programs in:
accountancy (MPA)
business (EMBA, MBA, MS)
business economics (MA)
economic analysis (MA)
economics (MA)
professional accountancy (MPA)

Kentucky

■ BELLARMINE UNIVERSITY
Louisville, KY 40205-0671
http://www.bellarmine.edu/

Independent-religious, coed, comprehensive institution. *Graduate faculty:* 54 full-time (29 women), 50 part-time/adjunct (32 women). *Computer facilities:* 350 computers available on campus for general student use. A campuswide network can be accessed from student residence rooms and from off campus. Online class registration is available. *General application contact:* Dr. Sara Yount, Dean of Graduate Admission, 502-452-8401.

Annsley Frazier Thornton School of Education
Dr. Cindy Gnadinger, Dean
Programs in:
early elementary education (MA, MAT)
instructional leadership and school administration/school principal (MA)
learning and behavior disorders (MA)
middle school education (MA, MAT)
reading and writing endorsement (MA)
secondary school education (MAT)
Waldorf inspired curriculum (MA)

Bellarmine College of Arts and Sciences
Dr. Gregory Hillis, Program Director
Program in:
spirituality (MA)

Center for Interdisciplinary Technology and Entrepreneurship
Dr. Michael D. Mattei, Dean of Continuing and Professional Studies
Program in:
technology and entrepreneurship (MAIT)

Donna and Allan Lansing School of Nursing and Health Sciences
Dr. Susan H. Davis, Dean
Programs in:
family nurse practitioner (MSN)
nursing administration (MSN)
nursing education (MSN)
nursing practice (DNP)
physical therapy (DPT)

School of Communication
Dr. Ruth Wagoner, Director of Graduate Studies
Program in:
communication (MA, MS)

W. Fielding Rubel School of Business
Dr. Daniel L. Bauer, Dean
Program in:
business (EMBA, MBA)

■ EASTERN KENTUCKY UNIVERSITY
Richmond, KY 40475-3102
http://www.eku.edu/

State-supported, coed, comprehensive institution. CGS member. *Computer facilities:* 1,200 computers available on campus for general student use. A campuswide network can be accessed from student residence rooms and from off campus. Online class registration is available. *General application contact:* Dean, 859-622-1742.

The Graduate School

College of Arts and Sciences
Programs in:
arts and sciences (MA, MFA, MM, MPA, MS, PhD, Psy S)
biological sciences (MS)
chemistry (MS)
choral conducting (MM)
clinical psychology (MS)
community development (MPA)
community health administration (MPA)
creative writing (MFA)
ecology (MS)
English (MA)
general public administration (MPA)
geology (MS, PhD)
history (MA)
industrial/organizational psychology (MS)
mathematical sciences (MS)
performance (MM)
political science (MA)
school psychology (Psy S)
theory/composition (MM)

College of Business and Technology
Programs in:
business administration (MBA)
business and technology (MBA, MS)
industrial education (MS)
industrial technology (MS)
occupational training and development (MS)
technical administration (MS)
technology education (MS)

College of Education
Programs in:
communication disorders (MA Ed)
education (MA, MA Ed, MAT)
elementary education (MA Ed)
human services (MA)
instructional leadership (MA Ed)
library science (MA Ed)
mental health counseling (MA)
music education (MA Ed)
school counseling (MA Ed)
secondary and higher education (MA Ed)
secondary education (MA Ed)
teaching (MAT)

College of Health Sciences
Programs in:
community health (MPH)
community nutrition (MS)
environmental health science (MPH)
exercise and sport science (MS)
exercise and wellness (MS)
health sciences (MPH, MS, MSN)
occupational therapy (MS)
recreation and park administration (MS)
rural community health care (MSN)
rural health family nurse practitioner (MSN)
sports administration (MS)

College of Justice and Safety
Programs in:
correctional and juvenile justice studies (MS)
criminal justice (MS)
criminal justice education (MS)
justice and safety (MS)
loss prevention and safety (MS)
police studies (MS)

■ GEORGETOWN COLLEGE
Georgetown, KY 40324-1696
http://www.georgetowncollege.edu/

Independent-religious, coed, comprehensive institution. *Graduate faculty:* 15 full-time (9 women), 14 part-time/adjunct (8 women). *Computer facilities:* Computer purchase and lease plans are available. 175 computers available on campus for general student use. A campuswide network can be accessed from student residence rooms and from off campus. Online class registration is available. *Graduate expenses:* Tuition: part-time $270 per credit hour. Required fees: $270 per credit hour. *General application contact:* Dr. Eve Proffitt, Associate Dean of Graduate Education, 502-863-8176.

Department of Education
Programs in:
reading and writing (MA Ed)
special education (MA Ed)
teaching (MA Ed)

■ MOREHEAD STATE UNIVERSITY
Morehead, KY 40351
http://www.moreheadstate.edu/

State-supported, coed, comprehensive institution. *Graduate faculty:* 151 full-time (57 women), 15 part-time/adjunct (5 women). *Computer facilities:* Computer purchase and lease plans are available. 2,045 computers available on campus for general student use. A campuswide network can be accessed from student residence rooms and from off campus. Online class registration is available. *Graduate expenses:* Tuition, state resident: full-time $6084; part-time $338 per credit hour. Tuition, nonresident: full-time $15,804; part-time $878 per credit hour. *General application contact:* Michelle Barber, Graduate Admissions Counselor, 606-783-2039.

Graduate Programs
Susan Maxey, Associate Vice President for Graduate and Undergraduate Programs

Caudill College of Humanities
Dr. Scott McBride, Interim Dean
Programs in:
art education (MA)
communication (MA)
criminology (MA)
English (MA)
general sociology (MA)
gerontology (MA)
humanities (MA, MM)
music education (MM)
music performance (MM)
studio art (MA)

College of Business
Dr. Robert L. Albert, Dean
Programs in:
business (MBA, MSIS)
information systems (MSIS)

College of Education
Dr. Cathy Gunn, Dean
Programs in:
adult and higher education (MA, Ed S)
counseling (MA Ed, Ed S)
curriculum and instruction (Ed S)
education (MA, MA Ed, MAT, Ed S)
elementary education (MA Ed)
exercise physiology (MA)
health and physical education (MA)
instructional leadership (Ed S)
school administration (MA)
secondary education (MA Ed)
special education (MA Ed)
sports management (MA)
teaching (MAT)

College of Science and Technology
Dr. Gerald DeMoss, Dean
Programs in:
biology (MS)
clinical psychology (MS)
counseling psychology (MS)
experimental/general psychology (MS)
industrial technology (MS)
regional analysis and public policy (MS)
science and technology (MS)

Institute for Regional Analysis and Public Policy
Dr. David Rudy, Dean
Program in:
public administration (MPA)

■ MURRAY STATE UNIVERSITY
Murray, KY 42071
http://www.murraystate.edu/

State-supported, coed, comprehensive institution. CGS member. *Computer facilities:* Computer purchase and lease plans are available. 1,800 computers available on campus for general student use. A campuswide network can be accessed from student residence rooms and from off campus. Billing accounts available. *General application contact:* University Coordinator of Graduate Studies, 270-809-3027.

College of Business and Public Affairs
Programs in:
business administration (MBA)
business and public affairs (MA, MBA, MPAC, MS)
economics (MS)
mass communications (MA, MS)
organizational communication (MA, MS)
professional accountancy (MPAC)
telecommunications systems management (MS)

College of Education
Programs in:
advanced learning behavior disorders (MA Ed)
community and agency counseling (Ed S)
early childhood education (MA Ed)
education (MA Ed, MS, Ed D, PhD, Ed S)
elementary education (MA Ed, Ed S)
elementary education/reading and writing (MA Ed, Ed S)
health, physical education, and recreation (MA)
human development and leadership (MS)
industrial and technical education (MS)
learning disabilities (MA Ed)
middle school education (MA Ed, Ed S)
moderate/severe disorders (MA Ed)
reading and writing (MA Ed)
school administration (MA Ed, Ed S)
school guidance and counseling (MA Ed, Ed S)
secondary education (MA Ed, Ed S)
special education (MA Ed)

Murray State University (continued)

College of Health Sciences and Human Services

Programs in:
- clinical nurse specialist (MSN)
- environmental science (MS)
- exercise and leisure studies (MS)
- family nurse practitioner (MSN)
- health sciences and human services (MS, MSN)
- industrial hygiene (MS)
- nurse anesthesia (MSN)
- safety management (MS)
- speech-language pathology (MS)

College of Humanities and Fine Arts

Programs in:
- clinical psychology (MA, MS)
- creative writing (MFA)
- English (MA)
- history (MA)
- humanities and fine arts (MA, MFA, MME, MPA, MS)
- music education (MME)
- psychology (MA, MS)
- public administration (MPA)
- public affairs (MPA)
- teaching English to speakers of other languages (MA)

College of Science, Engineering and Technology

Programs in:
- biological sciences (MAT, MS, PhD)
- chemistry (MS)
- geosciences (MS)
- management of technology (MS)
- mathematics (MA, MAT, MS)
- science, engineering and technology (MA, MAT, MS, PhD)
- water science (MS)

School of Agriculture

Programs in:
- agriculture (MS)
- agriculture education (MS)

■ NORTHERN KENTUCKY UNIVERSITY

Highland Heights, KY 41099

http://www.nku.edu/

State-supported, coed, comprehensive institution. CGS member. *Graduate faculty:* 150 full-time (72 women), 67 part-time/adjunct (35 women). *Computer facilities:* 500 computers available on campus for general student use. A campuswide network can be accessed from student residence rooms and from off campus. Online class registration, course specific software, office software are available. *Graduate expenses:* Tuition, state resident: full-time $6642. Tuition, nonresident: full-time $11,682. *General application contact:* Dr. Peg Griffin, Director of Graduate Programs, 859-572-5224.

Office of Graduate Programs

Dr. Salina Shrofel, Graduate Dean/Associate Provost for Research

College of Arts and Sciences

Dr. Kevin Corcoran, Dean

Programs in:
- arts and sciences (MA, MPA, MS, Certificate)
- civic engagement (Certificate)
- English (MA)
- industrial psychology (Certificate)
- industrial-organizational psychology (MS)
- integrative studies (MA)
- non-profit management (Certificate)
- occupational health psychology (Certificate)
- organizational psychology (Certificate)
- public administration (MPA)
- public history (MA)

College of Business

Dr. John Beehler, Dean

Programs in:
- accountancy (M Acc)
- advanced taxation (Certificate)
- business (M Acc, MBA, MS, Certificate)
- business administration (MBA)
- entrepreneurship (Certificate)
- executive leadership and organizational change (MS)
- finance (Certificate)
- international business (Certificate)
- marketing (Certificate)
- project management (Certificate)

College of Education and Human Services

Dr. Elaine McNally Jarchow, Dean

Programs in:
- college student development administration (Certificate)
- community counseling (MS, Certificate)
- education (MA)
- educational leadership (Ed D)
- instructional leadership (MA)
- school counseling (MA, Certificate)
- school superintendent (Certificate)
- special education (Certificate)
- teacher as a leader (MA)
- teaching (MA, Certificate)
- temporary school counseling provision (Certificate)

College of Informatics

Dr. Douglas Perry, Dean

Programs in:
- business informatics (MS, Certificate)
- communication (MA)
- computer science (MSCS)
- corporate information security (Certificate)
- enterprise resource planning (Certificate)
- health informatics (MS, Certificate)
- informatics (MA, MS, MSCS, Certificate)
- secure software engineering (Certificate)

School of Nursing and Health Professions

Dr. Denise C. Robinson, Program Director

Programs in:
- nurse practitioner advancement (Certificate)
- nursing (MSN, Post-Master's Certificate)

Salmon P. Chase College of Law

Dennis R. Honabach, Dean

Program in:
- law (JD)

■ SPALDING UNIVERSITY

Louisville, KY 40203-2188

http://www.spalding.edu/

Independent-religious, coed, comprehensive institution. CGS member. *Graduate faculty:* 28 full-time (20 women), 27 part-time/adjunct (20 women). *Computer facilities:* 80 computers available on campus for general student use. A campuswide network can be accessed. Online class registration is available. *Graduate expenses:* Tuition: full-time $11,340; part-time $630 per credit hour. Tuition and fees vary according to program. *General application contact:* Admissions Office, 502-585-7111.

Graduate Studies

Dr. Randy Strickland, Senior Vice President for Academic Affairs

College of Business and Communication

Dr. Diane Tobin, Dean

Program in:
- business communication (MS)

College of Education

Dr. Beverly Keepers, Dean

Programs in:
- education (MA, MAT, Ed D)
- elementary school education (MAT)
- general education (MA)
- high school education (MAT)
- leadership education (Ed D)
- middle school education (MAT)
- school administration (MA)
- special education (learning and behavioral disorders) (MAT)

College of Health and Natural Sciences

Dr. John James, Interim Dean

Programs in:
- adult nurse practitioner (MSN)
- family nurse practitioner (MSN)
- health and natural sciences (MS, MSN)
- leadership in nursing and healthcare (MSN)
- occupational therapy (advanced-level) (MS)
- occupational therapy (entry-level) (MS)
- pediatric nurse practitioner (MSN)

College of Social Sciences and Humanities

Dr. John James, Dean

Programs in:
- applied behavior analysis (MA)

clinical psychology (MA, Psy D)
social sciences and humanities (MA, MFA, MSW, Psy D)
social work (MSW)
writing (MFA)

■ SULLIVAN UNIVERSITY

Louisville, KY 40205
http://www.sullivan.edu/

Proprietary, coed, comprehensive institution. *Graduate faculty:* 13 full-time (7 women), 11 part-time/adjunct (4 women). *Computer facilities:* 225 computers available on campus for general student use. A campuswide network can be accessed from student residence rooms and from off campus. *General application contact:* Beverly Horsley, Admissions Officer, 502-456-6505.

School of Business

Dr. Eric S. Harter, Dean of Graduate School
Programs in:
business administration (MBA)
collaborative leadership (MSCL)
conflict management (MSCM)
dispute resolution (MSDR)
executive business administration (EMBA)
human resource leadership (MSHRL)
information technology (MSMIT)
management and information technology (MBIT)
pharmacy (Pharm D)

■ THOMAS MORE COLLEGE

Crestview Hills, KY 41017-3495
http://www.thomasmore.edu/

Independent-religious, coed, comprehensive institution. *Graduate faculty:* 14 full-time (3 women), 8 part-time/adjunct (4 women). *Computer facilities:* 100 computers available on campus for general student use. A campuswide network can be accessed from student residence rooms and from off campus. Online class registration is available. *Graduate expenses:* Tuition: full-time $10,555; part-time $499 per credit hour. Tuition and fees vary according to program. *General application contact:* Nathan Hartman, Director of Lifelong Learning, 859-344-3602.

Program in Business Administration

Nathan Hartman, Director of Lifelong Learning
Program in:
business administration (MBA)

Program in Teaching

Joyce Hamberg, Director
Program in:
teaching (MAT)

■ UNION COLLEGE

Barbourville, KY 40906-1499
http://www.unionky.edu/

Independent-religious, coed, comprehensive institution. *Computer facilities:* 230 computers available on campus for general student use. A campuswide network can be accessed from student residence rooms and from off campus. Online class registration is available. *General application contact:* Dean of Graduate Academic Affairs, 606-546-1210.

Graduate Programs

Programs in:
clinical psychology (MA)
counseling psychology (MA)
elementary education (MA)
health (MA Ed)
health and physical education (MA)
middle grades (MA)
music education (MA)
principalship (MA)
reading specialist (MA)
school psychology (MA)
secondary education (MA)
special education (MA)

■ UNIVERSITY OF KENTUCKY

Lexington, KY 40506-0032
http://www.uky.edu/

State-supported, coed, university. CGS member. *Graduate faculty:* 2,027 full-time (603 women), 166 part-time/adjunct (34 women). *Computer facilities:* 1,400 computers available on campus for general student use. A campuswide network can be accessed from student residence rooms and from off campus. Online class registration, various software packages are available. *General application contact:* Dr. Brian Jackson, Senior Associate Dean, 859-257-8176.

College of Dentistry

Program in:
dentistry (DMD)

College of Law

Program in:
law (JD)

College of Medicine

Program in:
medicine (MD)

College of Pharmacy

Dr. Patrick McNamara, Interim Dean
Program in:
pharmacy (Pharm D)

Graduate School

Dr. Jeannine Blackwell, Dean
Programs in:
biomedical engineering (MSBE, PBME, PhD)
dentistry (MS)
health administration (MHA)
nutritional sciences (MSNS, PhD)
pharmaceutical sciences (MS, PhD)
public administration (MPA, MPP, PhD)

College of Agriculture
Dr. Michael Reed, Dean
Programs in:
agricultural economics (MS, PhD)
agriculture (MS, MSFAM, MSFOR, PhD)
animal sciences (MS, PhD)
biosystems and agricultural engineering (MS, PhD)
career, technology and leadership education (MS)
crop science (MS, PhD)
entomology (MS, PhD)
family studies, human development, and resource management (MSFAM, PhD)
forestry (MSFOR)
hospitality and dietetic administration (MS)
plant and soil science (MS)
plant pathology (MS, PhD)
plant physiology (PhD)
soil science (PhD)
veterinary science (MS, PhD)

College of Arts and Sciences
Dr. Steven Hoch, Dean
Programs in:
anthropology (MA, PhD)
applied mathematics (MS)
arts and sciences (MA, MS, PhD)
biology (MS, PhD)
chemistry (MS, PhD)
classics (MA)
clinical psychology (MA)
English (MA, PhD)
experimental psychology (MA)
French (MA)
geography (MA, PhD)
geology (MS, PhD)
German (MA)
Hispanic studies (MA, PhD)
history (MA, PhD)
mathematics (MA, MS, PhD)
philosophy (MA, PhD)
physics (MS, PhD)
political science (MA, PhD)
sociology (MA, PhD)
statistics (MS, PhD)
teaching world languages (MA)

College of Communications and Information Studies
Dr. Derek R. Lane, Dean
Programs in:
communication (MA, PhD)
communications and information studies (MA, MSLS, PhD)
library science (MA, MSLS)

College of Design
Dr. Allison Carll-White, Dean
Programs in:
architecture (M Arch)
design (M Arch, MAIDM, MHP, MSIDM)
historic preservation (MHP)
interior design, merchandising, and textiles (MAIDM, MSIDM)

University of Kentucky (continued)

College of Education
Dr. Roy Remer, Dean
Programs in:
administration and supervision (Ed S)
counseling psychology (MS Ed, PhD, Ed S)
curriculum and instruction (MA Ed, Ed D)
early childhood special education (MS Ed)
education (M Ed, MA Ed, MRC, MS, MS Ed, Ed D, PhD, Ed S)
educational and counseling psychology (MS Ed)
educational policy studies and evaluation (Ed D)
educational psychology (Ed D, PhD, Ed S)
exercise science (PhD)
higher education (MS Ed, PhD)
instruction and administration (Ed D)
instruction system design (MS Ed)
kinesiology (MS, Ed D)
middle school education (MS Ed)
rehabilitation counseling (MRC)
school administration (M Ed)
school psychometrist and school psychology (MA Ed)
special education (MS Ed)
special education leadership personnel preparation (Ed D)

College of Engineering
Dr. G. T. Lineberry, Dean
Programs in:
chemical engineering (MS, PhD)
civil engineering (MCE, MSCE, PhD)
computer science (MS, PhD)
electrical engineering (MSEE, PhD)
engineering (M Eng, MCE, MME, MS, MS Ch E, MS Min, MSCE, MSEE, MSEM, MSMAE, MSME, MSMSE, PhD)
manufacturing systems engineering (MSMSE)
materials science and engineering (MSMAE, PhD)
mechanical engineering (MSME, PhD)
mining engineering (MME, MS Min, PhD)

College of Fine Arts
Dr. Robert Shay, Dean
Programs in:
art education (MA)
art history (MA)
art studio (MFA)
fine arts (MA, MFA, MM, DMA, PhD)
music (PhD)
music composition (MM)
music education (MM)
music performance (MM)
music theory (MA)
musical arts (DMA)
musicology (MA)
theatre (MA)

College of Health Sciences
Dr. Patrick Kitzman, Dean
Programs in:
clinical sciences (MS, DS)
communication disorders (MSCD)
health physics (MSHP)
health sciences (MS, MSCD, MSHP, MSPAS, MSPT, MSRMP, DS, PhD)
physical therapy (MSPT)
physician assistant studies (MSPAS)
radiological medical physics (MSRMP)
rehabilitation sciences (PhD)

College of Public Health
Dr. Bill Pfeifle, Dean
Programs in:
gerontology (PhD)
public health (MPH, PhD)

College of Social Work
Dr. Janet Ford, Dean
Program in:
social work (MSW, PhD)

Gatton College of Business and Economics
Dr. Devanathan Sudharshan, Dean
Programs in:
accounting (MSACC)
business administration (MBA, PhD)
business and economics (MBA, MS, MSACC, PhD)
economics (MS, PhD)

Graduate School Programs from the College of Medicine
Dr. Jeffrey Davidson, Dean of College of Medicine
Programs in:
anatomy (PhD)
biochemistry (PhD)
medical science (MS)
medicine (MS, PhD)
microbiology (PhD)
pharmacology (PhD)
physiology (MS, PhD)
toxicology (MS, PhD)

Graduate School Programs in the College of Nursing
Dr. Terry Lennie, Dean
Program in:
nursing (MSN, PhD)

Patterson School of Diplomacy and International Commerce
Dr. Evan Hillebrand, Director of Graduate Studies
Program in:
diplomacy and international commerce (MA)

■ UNIVERSITY OF LOUISVILLE

Louisville, KY 40292-0001

http://www.louisville.edu/

State-supported, coed, university. CGS member. *Graduate faculty:* 1,552 full-time (554 women), 572 part-time/adjunct (286 women). *Computer facilities:* Computer purchase and lease plans are available. 425 computers available on campus for general student use. A campuswide network can be accessed from student residence rooms and from off campus. Online class registration is available. *General application contact:* Libby Leggett, Information Contact, 502-852-3108.

Graduate School

Dr. William M. Pierce, Interim Dean

College of Arts and Sciences
Dr. J. Blaine Hudson, Dean
Programs in:
administration of planning organizations (MUP)
African and Diaspora studies (MA)
African-American studies (MA)
analytical chemistry (MS, PhD)
applied and industrial mathematics (PhD)
art history (MA, PhD)
arts and sciences (MA, MFA, MPA, MS, MUP, PhD, Certificate)
biochemistry (MS, PhD)
biology (MS, PhD)
chemical physics (PhD)
clinical psychology (MA, PhD)
communication (MA)
creative art (MA)
creative writing (MA)
curatorial studies (MA)
English (MA)
English rhetoric and composition (PhD)
environmental biology (PhD)
experimental psychology (PhD)
French (MA)
history (MA)
housing and community development (MUP)
human resources management (MPA)
humanities (MA, PhD)
inorganic chemistry (MS, PhD)
justice administration (MS)
land use and environmental planning (MUP)
literature (MA)
mathematics (MA)
non-profit management (MPA)
organic chemistry (MS, PhD)
performance (MFA)
philosophy (MA)
physical chemistry (MS, PhD)
physics (MS, PhD)
political science (MA)
psychology (MA)
public administration (MPA)
public policy and administration (MPA)
rhetoric and composition (MA, PhD)
sociology (MA)
Spanish (MA)
spatial analysis (MUP)
urban and public affairs (PhD)
urban planning (MUP)
urban planning and development (PhD)
urban policy and administration (PhD)
women's and gender studies (MA, Certificate)

College of Business
Dr. Charles Moyer, Dean
Programs in:
accountancy (MAC)
business (MAC, MBA, PhD)
business administration (MBA)
entrepreneurship (PhD)

College of Education and Human Development
Dr. Blake Haselton, Interim Dean
Programs in:
art education (MAT)
counseling and personnel services (M Ed, PhD)
curriculum and instruction (PhD)
early elementary education (M Ed, MAT)
education and human development (M Ed, MA, MAT, MS, Ed D, PhD, Ed S)
educational and counseling psychology (M Ed, PhD)
educational leadership and organizational development (Ed D, PhD)
exercise physiology (MS)
health education (M Ed)
higher education (MA)
human resource education (MS)
instructional technology (M Ed)
interdisciplinary early childhood education (M Ed, MAT)
middle school education (M Ed, MAT)
music education (MAT)
p-12 educational administration (M Ed, Ed S)
physical education (MAT)
reading education (M Ed)
secondary education (M Ed, MAT)
special education (M Ed, MAT)
sport administration (MS)

Interdisciplinary Studies
Program in:
interdisciplinary studies (MA, MS)

J.B. Speed School of Engineering
Dr. Mickey R. Wilhelm, Dean
Programs in:
chemical engineering (M Eng, MS, PhD)
civil and environmental engineering (M Eng, MS, PhD)
computer engineering and computer science (M Eng, MS)
computer science (MS)
computer science and engineering (PhD)
electrical and computer engineering (M Eng, MS, PhD)
engineering (M Eng, MS, PhD)
engineering management (M Eng)
industrial engineering (M Eng, MS, PhD)
mechanical engineering (M Eng, MS)

Raymond A. Kent School of Social Work
Dr. Terry Singer, Dean
Programs in:
marriage and family therapy (PMC)
social work (MSSW, PhD)

School of Music
Dr. Christopher Doane, Dean
Programs in:
music education (MME)
music history (MM, PhD)
music history and literature (MM)
music literature (PhD)
music performance (MM)
music theory and composition (MM)
musicology (PhD)
performance (MM)
theory and composition (MM)

School of Nursing
Dr. Marcia J. Hern, Dean
Programs in:
adult nurse practitioner (MSN)
family nurse practitioner (MSN)
health professions education (MSN)
neonatal nurse practitioner (MSN)
nursing research (PhD)
psychiatric mental health nurse practitioner (MSN)

School of Public Health and Information Sciences
Dr. Richard D. Clover, Dean
Programs in:
biostatistics (PhD)
biostatistics-decision science (MS)
clinical research, epidemiology and statistics (MS, Certificate)
epidemiology (MS)
public health (MPH)
public health and information sciences (MPH, MS, PhD, Certificate)
public health sciences (PhD)

Louis D. Brandeis School of Law
James Ming Chen, Dean
Program in:
law (JD)

School of Dentistry
Dr. John J. Sauk, Dean
Programs in:
dentistry (DMD, MS)
oral biology (MS)

School of Medicine
Dr. Edward C. Halperin, Dean
Programs in:
anatomical sciences and neurobiology (MS, PhD)
audiology (Au D)
biochemistry and molecular biology (MS, PhD)
communicative disorders (MS)
medicine (MD, MS, Au D, PhD)
microbiology and immunology (MS, PhD)
pharmacology and toxicology (MS, PhD)
physiology and biophysics (MS, PhD)

■ WESTERN KENTUCKY UNIVERSITY

Bowling Green, KY 42101
http://www.wku.edu/

State-supported, coed, comprehensive institution. CGS member. *Computer facilities:* Computer purchase and lease plans are available. 1,300 computers available on campus for general student use. A campuswide network can be accessed from student residence rooms and from off campus. Online class registration is available. *General application contact:* Interim Dean, Graduate Studies, 270-745-3696.

Graduate Studies

College of Education and Behavioral Sciences
Programs in:
business and marketing education (MA Ed, MAE)
counseling (MA Ed)
counselor education (Ed S)
education and behavioral science (MA Ed)
education and behavioral sciences (MA, MAE, MS, Ed S)
educational administration (MAE)
elementary education (MA Ed, MAE, Ed S)
exceptional child education (MAE)
interdisciplinary early child education (MAE)
library media education (MS)
literacy (MAE)
middle grades education (MAE)
middle years education (MA Ed)
psychology (MA)
school administration (Ed S)
school psychology (Ed S)
secondary education (MA Ed, MAE, Ed S)
student affairs (MA Ed)

College of Health and Human Services
Programs in:
communication disorders (MS)
health and human services (MHA, MPH, MS, MSN, MSW)
healthcare administration (MHA)
nursing (MSN)
physical education (MS)
public health (MPH)
recreation (MS)
social work (MSW)

Gordon Ford College of Business
Programs in:
business (MBA)
business administration (MBA)

Ogden College of Science and Engineering
Programs in:
agriculture (MA Ed, MS)
biology (MA Ed, MS)
chemistry (MA Ed, MS)
computer science (MS)
geography and geology (MAE, MS)
mathematics (MA Ed, MS)
science and engineering (MA Ed, MAE, MS)

Potter College of Arts and Letters
Programs in:
art education (MA Ed)
arts and letter (MA, MA Ed, MPA)
communication (MA)
education (MA)
English (MA Ed)
folk studies (MA)

Western Kentucky University (continued)
history (MA, MA Ed)
literature (MA)
music (MA Ed)
political science (MPA)
sociology (MA)
teaching English as a second language (MA)
writing (MA)

Louisiana

■ GRAMBLING STATE UNIVERSITY
Grambling, LA 71245
http://www.gram.edu/

State-supported, coed, university. CGS member. *Graduate faculty:* 52 full-time (28 women), 15 part-time/adjunct (7 women). *Computer facilities:* 600 computers available on campus for general student use. A campuswide network can be accessed from student residence rooms and from off campus. Online class registration is available. *Graduate expenses:* Tuition, state resident: full-time $3637; part-time $134 per credit hour. Tuition, nonresident: full-time $7651; part-time $134 per credit hour. Required fees: $1225; $430 per semester. *General application contact:* Katina Crowe, Special Assistant to Associate Vice President/Dean, 318-274-2158.

School of Graduate Studies and Research
Dr. Janet Guyden, Associate Vice President/Dean, School of Graduate Studies and Research

College of Arts and Sciences
Dr. Connie Walton, Dean
Programs in:
arts and sciences (MAT, MPA)
health service administration (MPA)
human resource management (MPA)
public management (MPA)
social sciences (MAT)
state and local government (MPA)

College of Education
Dr. Sean Warner, Dean
Programs in:
curriculum and instruction (Ed D)
developmental education (MS, Ed D)
education (MS, Ed D)
educational leadership (MS, Ed D)
sports administration (MS)

College of Professional Studies
Dr. Rama Tunuguntla, Interim Dean
Programs in:
criminal justice (MS)
family nurse practitioner (MSN, PMC)
mass communication (MA)
nurse educator (MSN)
social work (MSW)

■ LOUISIANA STATE UNIVERSITY AND AGRICULTURAL AND MECHANICAL COLLEGE
Baton Rouge, LA 70803
http://www.lsu.edu/

State-supported, coed, university. CGS member. *Graduate faculty:* 1,282 full-time (330 women), 14 part-time/adjunct (2 women). *Computer facilities:* 7,000 computers available on campus for general student use. A campuswide network can be accessed from student residence rooms and from off campus. Online class registration, free software for download, personal Web sites, storage, discounts on hardware, virtual computer lab are available. *General application contact:* Dr. Renee Renegar, Office of Graduate Admissions, 225-578-1641.

Graduate School
Dr. David Constant, Interim Dean

College of Agriculture
Dr. Kenneth Koonce, Dean
Programs in:
agricultural economics and agribusiness (MS, PhD)
agriculture (M App St, MS, MSBAE, PhD)
agriculture and extension education and youth development (MS, PhD)
agronomy (MS, PhD)
animal sciences (MS, PhD)
applied statistics (M App St)
biological and agricultural engineering (MSBAE)
career and technical education (MS, PhD)
comprehensive vocational education (MS, PhD)
engineering science (MS, PhD)
entomology (MS, PhD)
extension and international education (MS, PhD)
fisheries (MS)
food science (MS, PhD)
forestry (MS, PhD)
horticulture (MS, PhD)
human ecology (MS, PhD)
human resource and leadership development (MS, PhD)
industrial education (MS)
plant health (MS, PhD)
plant, environmental and soil science (MS, PhD)
vocational agriculture education (MS, PhD)
vocational business education (MS)
vocational home economics education (MS)
wildlife (MS)
wildlife and fisheries science (PhD)

College of Art and Design
David Cronrath, Dean
Programs in:
architecture (M Arch)
art and design (M Arch, MA, MFA, MLA)
art history (MA)
ceramics (MFA)
graphic design (MFA)
landscape architecture (MLA)
painting and drawing (MFA)
photography (MFA)
printmaking (MFA)
sculpture (MFA)
studio art (MFA)

College of Arts and Sciences
Dr. Guillermo Ferreya, Dean
Programs in:
anthropology (MA)
arts and sciences (MA, MALA, MFA, MS, PhD)
biological psychology (MA, PhD)
clinical psychology (MA, PhD)
cognitive psychology (MA, PhD)
communication sciences and disorders (MA, PhD)
communication studies (MA, PhD)
comparative literature (MA, PhD)
creative writing (MFA)
developmental psychology (MA, PhD)
English (MA, PhD)
French literature and linguistics (MA, PhD)
geography (MA, MS, PhD)
Hispanic studies (MA)
history (MA, PhD)
industrial/organizational psychology (MA, PhD)
liberal arts (MALA)
linguistics (MA, PhD)
mathematics (MS, PhD)
philosophy (MA)
political science (MA, PhD)
school psychology (MA, PhD)
sociology (MA, PhD)

College of Basic Sciences
Dr. Kevin Carman, Dean
Programs in:
astronomy (PhD)
astrophysics (PhD)
basic sciences (MNS, MS, MSSS, PhD)
biochemistry (MS, PhD)
biological science (MS, PhD)
chemistry (MS, PhD)
computer science (MSSS, PhD)
geology and geophysics (MS, PhD)
medical physics (MS)
natural sciences (MNS)
physics (MS, PhD)
systems science (MSSS)

College of Education
Dr. Jayne Fleener, Dean
Programs in:
counseling (M Ed, MA, Ed S)
education (M Ed, MA, MS, PhD, Ed S)
educational administration (M Ed, MA, PhD, Ed S)
educational technology (MA)
elementary education (M Ed)
higher education (PhD)
kinesiology (MS, PhD)
research methodology (PhD)
secondary education (M Ed)

College of Engineering
Dr. Richard Koubek, Dean
Programs in:
chemical engineering (MS Ch E, PhD)
electrical and computer engineering (MSEE, PhD)
engineering (MS Ch E, MS Pet E, MSCE, MSEE, MSES, MSIE, MSME, PhD)
engineering science (MSES, PhD)
environmental engineering (MSCE, PhD)
geotechnical engineering (MSCE, PhD)
industrial engineering (MSIE)
mechanical engineering (MSME, PhD)
petroleum engineering (MS Pet E, PhD)
structural engineering and mechanics (MSCE, PhD)
transportation engineering (MSCE, PhD)
water resources (MSCE, PhD)

College of Music and Dramatic Arts
Dr. Lawrence Kaptain, Interim Dean
Programs in:
acting (MFA)
directing (MFA)
music (MM, DMA, PhD)
music and dramatic arts (MFA, MM, DMA, PhD)
music education (PhD)
theatre (PhD)
theatre design/technology (MFA)

E. J. Ourso College of Business
Dr. Eli Jones, Interim Dean
Programs in:
accounting (MS, PhD)
business (EMBA, MBA, MPA, MS, PMBA, PhD)
business administration (PhD)
economics (MS, PhD)
finance (MS)
information systems and decision sciences (MS, PhD)
public administration (MPA)

Manship School of Mass Communication
Dr. John Maxwell Hamilton, Dean
Program in:
mass communication (MMC, PhD)

School of Library and Information Science
Dr. Beth M. Paskoff, Dean
Program in:
library and information science (MLIS, CAS)

School of Social Work
Dr. Christian Molidor, Dean
Program in:
social work (MSW, PhD)

School of the Coast and Environment
Dr. Ed Laws, Dean
Programs in:
environmental planning and management (MS)
environmental toxicology (MS)
oceanography and coastal sciences (MS, PhD)
the coast and environment (MS, PhD)

Paul M. Hebert Law Center
Jack M. Weiss, Chancellor
Program in:
law (LL M, MCL)

School of Veterinary Medicine
Dr. Peter Haynes, Dean
Programs in:
comparative biomedical sciences (MS, PhD)
pathobiological sciences (MS, PhD)
veterinary clinical sciences (MS, PhD)
veterinary medicine (DVM, MS, PhD)

■ LOUISIANA STATE UNIVERSITY IN SHREVEPORT
Shreveport, LA 71115-2399
http://www.lsus.edu/

State-supported, coed, comprehensive institution. *Computer facilities:* A campuswide network can be accessed. Online class registration is available. *Graduate expenses:* Tuition, state resident: full-time $2385; part-time $132 per credit hour. Tuition, nonresident: full-time $6697; part-time $372 per credit hour. Required fees: $42 per credit hour. Tuition and fees vary according to course load. *General application contact:* Yvonne Yarbrough, Secretary, Graduate Studies, 318-797-5247.

College of Business Administration
Program in:
business administration (MBA)

College of Education and Human Development
Programs in:
counseling psychology (MS)
education (M Ed)
education and human development (M Ed, MS, SSP)
education curriculum and instruction (M Ed)
educational leadership (M Ed)
school psychology (SSP)

College of Liberal Arts
Programs in:
health administration (MHA)
human services administration (MS)
liberal arts (MA, MHA, MS)

College of Sciences
Programs in:
computer systems technology (MS)
sciences (MS)

■ LOUISIANA TECH UNIVERSITY
Ruston, LA 71272
http://www.latech.edu/

State-supported, coed, university. *Computer facilities:* 1,800 computers available on campus for general student use. A campuswide network can be accessed from student residence rooms and from off campus. *General application contact:* Dean of the Graduate School, 318-257-2924.

Graduate School

College of Applied and Natural Sciences
Programs in:
applied and natural sciences (MS)
biological sciences (MS)
dietetics (MS)
human ecology (MS)

College of Business
Programs in:
business (MBA, MPA, DBA)
business administration (MBA, DBA)
business economics (MBA, DBA)
finance (MBA, DBA)
marketing (MBA, DBA)
professional accountancy (MBA, MPA, DBA)

College of Education
Programs in:
counseling (MA)
counseling psychology (PhD)
curriculum and instruction (MS, Ed D)
education (M Ed, MA, MS, Ed D, PhD)
educational leadership (Ed D)
health and exercise sciences (MS)
industrial/organizational psychology (MA)
secondary education (M Ed)
special education (MA)

College of Engineering and Science
Programs in:
applied computational analysis and modeling (PhD)
biomedical engineering (MS, PhD)
chemical engineering (MS, PhD)
chemistry (MS)
civil engineering (MS, PhD)
computer science (MS)
electrical engineering (MS, PhD)
engineering (PhD)
engineering and science (MS, PhD)
industrial engineering (MS)
mathematics and statistics (MS)
mechanical engineering (MS, PhD)
physics (MS)

College of Liberal Arts
Programs in:
art and graphic design (MFA)
English (MA)
history (MA)
interior design (MFA)
liberal arts (MA, MFA)
photography (MFA)
speech (MA)
speech pathology and audiology (MA)
studio art (MFA)

■ LOYOLA UNIVERSITY NEW ORLEANS
New Orleans, LA 70118-6195
http://www.loyno.edu/

Independent-religious, coed, comprehensive institution. *Computer facilities:* Computer

Loyola University New Orleans (continued)
purchase and lease plans are available. 525 computers available on campus for general student use. A campuswide network can be accessed from student residence rooms and from off campus. Online class registration is available. *Graduate expenses:* Tuition: full-time $13,146; part-time $626 per credit hour. Required fees: $876; $229 per semester. *General application contact:* Salvadore A. Liberto, Vice President for Enrollment Management and Associate Provost, 504-865-3240.

College of Law
Brian Bromberger, Dean
Program in:
law (JD, LL M)

College of Music and Fine Arts
Dr. Donald R. Boomgaarden, Dean
Programs in:
music therapy (MMT)
performance (MM)

College of Social Sciences
Dr. Luis F. Miron, Dean
Programs in:
counseling (MS)
criminal justice (MCJ)
social sciences (MCJ, MPS, MRE, MS, MSN, Certificate)

Loyola Institute for Ministry
Dr. Tom Ryan, Director
Programs in:
pastoral studies (MPS)
religious education (MRE)
theology and ministry (Certificate)

School of Nursing
Dr. Ann H. Cary, Director
Programs in:
adult nurse practitioner (MSN)
family nurse practitioner (MSN)
health care systems management (MSN)
nursing (MSN, DNP)

Joseph A. Butt, S.J., College of Business
Dr. William B. Locander, Dean
Programs in:
business (MBA)
business administration (MBA)

■ MCNEESE STATE UNIVERSITY
Lake Charles, LA 70609
http://www.mcneese.edu/

State-supported, coed, comprehensive institution. *Graduate faculty:* 115 full-time (38 women), 6 part-time/adjunct (4 women). *Computer facilities:* 700 computers available on campus for general student use. A campuswide network can be accessed from student residence rooms and from off campus. Online class registration is available. *Graduate expenses:* Tuition, state resident: full-time $2386. Required fees: $885. Tuition and fees vary according to course load. *General application contact:* Dr. George F. Mead, Interim Dean of Dore' School of Graduate Studies, 337-475-5396.

Doré School of Graduate Studies
Dr. George F. Mead, Interim Dean

Burton College of Education
Dr. Wayne R. Fetter, Dean
Programs in:
addiction treatment (MA)
applied behavior analysis (MA)
counseling psychology (MA)
curriculum and instruction (M Ed)
early childhood education (M Ed)
education (M Ed, MA, MAT, MS, Ed S)
educational leadership (M Ed, Ed S)
educational technology (Ed S)
educational technology leadership (M Ed)
elementary education (M Ed)
elementary education grades 1-5 (MAT)
exercise physiology (MS)
general/experimental psychology (MA)
health promotion (MS)
instructional technology (MS)
nutrition and wellness (MS)
school counseling (M Ed)
secondary education (M Ed)
secondary education grades 6-12 (MAT)
special education—mild/moderate grades 1-12 (MAT)
special education mild/moderate grades 1-12 (M Ed)
teaching (MAT)

College of Business
Dr. Mitchell Adrian, Dean
Programs in:
accounting (MBA)
business (MBA)

College of Engineering and Engineering Technology
Dr. Nikos Kiritsis, Dean
Programs in:
chemical engineering (M Eng)
civil engineering (M Eng)
electrical engineering (M Eng)
engineering management (M Eng)
mechanical engineering (M Eng)

College of Liberal Arts
Dr. Ray Miles, Dean
Programs in:
creative writing (MFA)
English (MA)
Kodaly studies (MM Ed)
liberal arts (MA, MFA, MM Ed)
music education (MM Ed)
vocal (MM Ed)

College of Nursing
Dr. Peggy L. Wolfe, Dean
Programs in:
clinical nurse specialist (MSN)
nurse educator (MSN)
nurse practitioner (MSN)
nursing leadership and administration (MSN)

College of Science
Dr. George F. Mead, Dean
Programs in:
agricultural sciences (MS)
chemistry (MS)
chemistry education (MS)
environmental and chemical science (MS)
environmental and chemical sciences (MS)
environmental science education (MS)
environmental sciences (MS)
mathematical science (MS)
science (MS)

■ NICHOLLS STATE UNIVERSITY
Thibodaux, LA 70310
http://www.nicholls.edu

State-supported, coed, comprehensive institution. *Computer facilities:* 1,500 computers available on campus for general student use. A campuswide network can be accessed from student residence rooms and from off campus. Online class registration, course management system—Blackboard are available. *General application contact:* Director, University Graduate Studies, 985-448-4191.

Graduate Studies

College of Arts and Sciences
Programs in:
arts and sciences (MS)
community/technical college mathematics (MS)
marine and environmental biology (MS)

College of Business Administration
Program in:
business administration (MBA)

College of Education
Programs in:
administration and supervision (M Ed)
counselor education (M Ed)
curriculum and instruction (M Ed)
education (M Ed, MA, SSP)
psychological counseling (MA)
school psychology (SSP)

■ NORTHWESTERN STATE UNIVERSITY OF LOUISIANA
Natchitoches, LA 71497
http://www.nsula.edu/

State-supported, coed, comprehensive institution. CGS member. *Computer facilities:* A campuswide network can be accessed from student residence rooms and from off campus. Online class registration is available. *General application contact:* Dr. Steven G. Horton, Associate Provost/Dean, Graduate Studies, Research, and Information Systems, 318-357-5851.

Graduate Studies and Research
Dr. Steven G. Horton, Associate Provost/Dean, Graduate Studies, Research, and Information Systems

Programs in:
clinical psychology (MS)
English (MA)
health and human performance (MS)
heritage resources (MA)

College of Education
Dr. Vickie Gentry, Chair
Programs in:
adult and continuing education (M Ed)
business and distributive education (M Ed)
counseling (M Ed, Ed S)
counseling and guidance (M Ed, Ed S)
curriculum and instruction (M Ed)
early childhood education (M Ed)
early childhood education and teaching (M Ed)
education (M Ed, MA, MAT, Ed S)
education leadership (M Ed)
educational leadership (Ed S)
educational technology (M Ed, Ed S)
educational technology leadership (M Ed)
elementary education (MAT)
elementary teaching (M Ed, Ed S)
English education (M Ed)
home economics education (M Ed)
mathematics education (M Ed)
middle school education (MAT)
reading (M Ed, Ed S)
school counseling (MA)
science education (M Ed)
secondary education (MAT)
secondary teaching (M Ed, Ed S)
social sciences education (M Ed)
special education (MA)
student personnel services (MA)
teacher education and professional development, specific levels and methods (M Ed)

College of Nursing
Dr. Norann Planchock, Director
Program in:
nursing (MSN)

School of Creative and Performing Arts
William E. Brent, Chairman
Programs in:
art (MA)
fine and graphic arts (MA)
music (MM)

■ SOUTHEASTERN LOUISIANA UNIVERSITY
Hammond, LA 70402
http://www.selu.edu/

State-supported, coed, comprehensive institution. CGS member. *Graduate faculty:* 142 full-time (60 women). *Computer facilities:* 1,603 computers available on campus for general student use. A campuswide network can be accessed from student residence rooms and from off campus. Online class registration, campus Webmail, student newspaper, transcripts, bookstore are available. *Graduate expenses:* Tuition, state resident: full-time $2376. Tuition, nonresident: full-time $6876. Required fees: $1105. *General application contact:* Sandra Meyers, Graduate Admissions Analyst, 985-549-2066.

College of Arts, Humanities and Social Sciences
Dr. Bryan DePoy, Interim Dean
Programs in:
applied sociology (MS)
arts, humanities and social sciences (M Mus, MA, MS)
English (MA)
history (MA)
music (M Mus)
organizational communication (MA)
psychology (MA)

College of Business
Dr. Randy Settoon, Dean
Program in:
business administration (MBA)

College of Education and Human Development
Dr. Diane Allen, Dean
Programs in:
counselor education (M Ed)
curriculum and instruction (M Ed)
education and human development (M Ed, MAT, Ed D)
educational leadership (M Ed, Ed D)
educational technology leadership (M Ed)
elementary education (MAT)
special education (M Ed)

College of Nursing and Health Sciences
Dr. Donnie Booth, Dean
Programs in:
communication sciences and disorders (MS)
health and kinesiology (MA)
nursing and health sciences (MA, MS, MSN)

School of Nursing
Dr. Barbara Moffett, Director
Program in:
nursing (MSN)

College of Science and Technology
Dr. Daniel McCarthy, Dean
Programs in:
biology (MS)
integrated science and technology (MS)
science and technology (MS)

■ SOUTHERN UNIVERSITY AND AGRICULTURAL AND MECHANICAL COLLEGE
Baton Rouge, LA 70813
http://www.subr.edu/

State-supported, coed, university. CGS member. *Computer facilities:* 1,500 computers available on campus for general student use. A campuswide network can be accessed from student residence rooms and from off campus. Online class registration is available. *General application contact:* Director of Graduate Admissions and Recruitment, 225-771-5390.

College of Business
Program in:
business (MBA)

Graduate School
Programs in:
science/mathematics education (PhD)
special education (M Ed, PhD)

College of Agricultural, Family and Consumer Sciences
Program in:
urban forestry (MS)

College of Arts and Humanities
Programs in:
arts and humanities (MA)
mass communications (MA)
social sciences (MA)

College of Education
Programs in:
administration and supervision (M Ed)
counselor education (MA)
education (M Ed, MA, MS, PhD)
educational leadership (M Ed)
elementary education (M Ed)
media (M Ed)
mental health counseling (MA)
secondary education (M Ed)
therapeutic recreation (MS)

College of Engineering
Program in:
engineering (ME)

College of Sciences
Programs in:
analytical chemistry (MS)
biochemistry (MS)
biology (MS)
environmental sciences (MS)
information systems (MS)
inorganic chemistry (MS)
mathematics (MS)
micro/minicomputer architecture (MS)
operating systems (MS)
organic chemistry (MS)
physical chemistry (MS)
physics (MS)
rehabilitation counseling (MS)
sciences (MA, MS)

Nelson Mandela School of Public Policy and Urban Affairs
Programs in:
criminal justice (MS)
public administration (MPA)
public policy (PhD)
public policy and urban affairs (MA, MPA, MS, PhD)
social sciences (MA)

School of Nursing
Programs in:
educator/administrator (PhD)
family health nursing (MSN)

Southern University and Agricultural and Mechanical College (continued)
family nurse practitioner (Post Master's Certificate)
geriatric nurse practitioner/gerontology (PhD)

Southern University Law Center
Program in:
law (JD)

■ SOUTHERN UNIVERSITY AT NEW ORLEANS
New Orleans, LA 70126-1009
http://www.suno.edu/

State-supported, coed, primarily women, comprehensive institution. *Computer facilities:* 100 computers available on campus for general student use. A campuswide network can be accessed. Online class registration is available. *General application contact:* Director of Student Affairs, 504-286-5376.

School of Social Work
Program in:
social work (MSW)

■ TULANE UNIVERSITY
New Orleans, LA 70118-5669
http://www.tulane.edu/

Independent, coed, university. CGS member. *Computer facilities:* 556 computers available on campus for general student use. A campuswide network can be accessed from student residence rooms and from off campus. Online class registration is available. *General application contact:* Dean, 504-865-5100.

A. B. Freeman School of Business
Program in:
business (EMBA, M Acct, M Fin, MBA, PMBA, PhD)

Program in Liberal Arts
Program in:
liberal arts (MLA)

School of Architecture
Program in:
architecture (M Arch, MPS)

School of Law
Programs in:
admiralty (LL M)
American business law (LL M)
energy and environment (LL M)
international and comparative law (LL M)
law (JD, LL M, SJD)

School of Liberal Arts
Programs in:
anthropology (MA, PhD)
art (MFA)
art history (MA)
classical studies (MA)
design and technical production (MFA)
economics (MA, PhD)
English (MA, PhD)
French (MA, PhD)
history (MA, PhD)
liberal arts (MA, MFA, MS, PhD)
music (MA, MFA)
philosophy (MA, PhD)
political science (MA, PhD)
Portuguese (MA)
sociology (MA, PhD)
Spanish (MA)
Spanish and Portuguese (PhD)

The Payson Center for International Development and Technology Transfer
Program in:
international development (MS, PhD)

Roger Thayer Stone Center for Latin American Studies
Program in:
Latin American studies (MA, PhD)

School of Medicine
Program in:
medicine (MD, MBS, MS, PhD)

Graduate Programs in Biomedical Sciences
Programs in:
biochemistry (MS, PhD)
biomedical sciences (MBS, MS, PhD)
human genetics (MBS, PhD)
microbiology and immunology (MS, PhD)
molecular and cellular biology (PhD)
neuroscience (MS, PhD)
pharmacology (MS, PhD)
physiology (MS, PhD)
structural and cellular biology (MS, PhD)

School of Public Health and Tropical Medicine
Programs in:
biostatistics (MS, MSPH, PhD, Sc D)
clinical tropical medicine and travelers health (Diploma)
environmental health sciences (MPH, MSPH, Dr PH, PhD)
epidemiology (MPH, MS, Dr PH, PhD)
health education and communication (MPH)
health systems management (MHA, MMM, MPH, PhD, Sc D)
international health and development (MPH, Dr PH, PhD)
maternal and child health (MPH, Dr PH)
nutrition (MPH)
parasitology (MSPH, PhD)
public health and tropical medicine (MHA, MMM, MPH, MPHTM, MS, MSPH, Dr PH, PhD, Sc D, Diploma)
vector borne infectious diseases (MS, PhD)

School of Science and Engineering
Programs in:
applied mathematics (MS)
biomedical engineering (MS, PhD)
cell and molecular biology (MS, PhD)
chemical and biomolecular engineering (PhD)
chemistry (MS, PhD)
earth and environmental sciences (MS, PhD)
ecology and evolutionary biology (MS, PhD)
interdisciplinary studies (PhD)
mathematics (MS, PhD)
neuroscience (MS, PhD)
physics (PhD)
psychology (MS, PhD)
science and engineering (M Eng, MS, PhD)
statistics (MS)

School of Social Work
Program in:
social work (MSW)

■ UNIVERSITY OF LOUISIANA AT LAFAYETTE
Lafayette, LA 70504
http://www.louisiana.edu/

State-supported, coed, university. CGS member. *Computer facilities:* 600 computers available on campus for general student use. A campuswide network can be accessed from off campus. Online class registration is available. *General application contact:* Dean, 337-482-6965.

BI Moody III College of Business Administration MBA Program
Program in:
business administration (MBA)

College of Education
Program in:
education (M Ed, Ed D)

Graduate Studies and Research in Education
Programs in:
administration and supervision (M Ed)
curriculum and instruction (M Ed)
education of the gifted (M Ed)
educational leadership (M Ed, Ed D)

College of Engineering
Programs in:
chemical engineering (MSE)
civil engineering (MSE)
computer engineering (MS, PhD)
engineering (MS, MSE, MSET, MSTC, PhD)
engineering and technology management (MSET)
mechanical engineering (MSE)
petroleum engineering (MSE)
telecommunications (MSTC)

Center for Advanced Computer Studies
Programs in:
computer engineering (MS, PhD)
computer science (MS, PhD)

College of Liberal Arts
Programs in:
British and American literature (MA)
communicative disorders (MS, PhD)
creative writing (PhD)
Francophone studies (PhD)
French (MA)
history (MA)
liberal arts (MA, MS, PhD)
literature (PhD)
mass communications (MS)
psychology (MS)
rehabilitation counseling (MS)
rhetoric (PhD)

College of Nursing
Program in:
nursing (MSN)

College of Sciences
Programs in:
biology (MS)
computer science (MS, PhD)
environmental and evolutionary biology (PhD)
geology (MS)
mathematics (MS, PhD)
physics (MS)
sciences (MS, PhD)

Institute of Cognitive Science
Program in:
cognitive science (PhD)

College of the Arts
Program in:
arts (M Arch, MM)

School of Architecture
Program in:
architecture (M Arch)

School of Music
Programs in:
conducting (MM)
pedagogy (MM)
vocal and instrumental performance (MM)

Department of Counselor Education
Program in:
counselor education (MS)

■ UNIVERSITY OF LOUISIANA AT MONROE

Monroe, LA 71209-0001
http://www.ulm.edu/

State-supported, coed, university. *Graduate faculty:* 108 full-time (49 women), 29 part-time/adjunct (10 women). *Computer facilities:* A campuswide network can be accessed from student residence rooms and from off campus. Online class registration is available. *General application contact:* Dr. Lisa Colvin, Interim Graduate Studies and Research Director, 318-342-1036.

Graduate School
Dr. Lisa Colvin, Interim Graduate Studies and Research Director
Programs in:
pharmaceutical sciences (MS)
pharmacy (Pharm D, MS, PhD)

College of Arts and Sciences
Dr. Jeffrey D. Cass, Dean
Programs in:
arts and sciences (MA, MM, MS, CGS)
biology (MS)
communication (MA)
criminal justice (MA)
English (MA)
gerontology (MA, CGS)
history (MA)
music (MM)
visual and performing arts (MM)

College of Business Administration
Dr. Ronald Berry, Dean
Program in:
business administration (MBA)

College of Education and Human Development
Dr. Sandra M. Lemoine, Dean
Programs in:
administration and supervision (M Ed)
applied exercise physiology (MS)
clinical exercise physiology (MS)
counseling (M Ed)
curriculum and instruction (M Ed, Ed D)
education (M Ed, MA, MAT, MS, Ed D, PhD, SSP)
educational leadership (M Ed, Ed D)
elementary education (M Ed, MAT)
elementary education (1-5) (M Ed)
general psychology (MS)
grades 1-5 (M Ed)
marriage and family therapy (MA, PhD)
multiple levels grades K-12 (MAT)
reading education (K-12) (M Ed)
school psychology (MS, SSP)
secondary education 6-12 (M Ed, MAT)
SPED-academically gifted education (K-12) (M Ed)
SPED-early intervention education (birth-3) (M Ed)
SPED-educational diagnostics education (PreK-12) (M Ed)
substance abuse counseling (MA)

College of Health Sciences
Dr. Denny Ryman, Dean
Programs in:
health sciences (MS)
speech-language pathology (MS)

■ UNIVERSITY OF NEW ORLEANS

New Orleans, LA 70148
http://www.uno.edu/

State-supported, coed, university. CGS member. *Graduate faculty:* 591. *Computer facilities:* 1,129 computers available on campus for general student use. A campuswide network can be accessed from student residence rooms and from off campus. Online class registration, classes in Blackboard are available. *General application contact:* Amanda M. Athey, Assistant Dean, 504-280-1155.

Graduate School
Dr. Scott L. Whittenburg, Dean

College of Business Administration
Dr. James W. Logan, Dean
Programs in:
accounting (MS)
business administration (MBA, MS, PhD)
economics and finance (MS)
financial economics (PhD)
health care management (MS)
hospitality and tourism management (MS)
taxation (MS)

College of Education and Human Development
Dr. James Meza, Dean
Programs in:
counselor education (M Ed, PhD, GCE)
curriculum and instruction (M Ed, PhD, GCE)
education and human development (M Ed, PhD, GCE)
educational leadership (M Ed, PhD, GCE)
special education (M Ed, PhD, GCE)

College of Engineering
Dr. Russell Trahan, Dean
Programs in:
engineering (MS, PhD, Certificate)
engineering and applied sciences (PhD)
engineering management (MS, Certificate)
mechanical engineering (MS)

College of Liberal Arts
Dr. Susan Krantz, Dean
Programs in:
arts administration (MA)
English (MA, MAET)
English teaching (MAET)
film production (MFA)
fine arts (MFA)
foreign languages (MA)
geography (MA)
history (MA)
history teaching (MAHT)
liberal arts (MA, MAET, MAHT, MFA, MM, MPA, MS, MURP, PhD)
music (MM)
political science (MA, PhD)
public administration (MPA)
sociology (MA)
theatre directing (MFA)
theatre performance (MFA)
urban and regional planning (MURP)
urban planning and regional studies (MS, MURP, PhD)
urban studies (MS, PhD)

College of Sciences
Dr. Steven G. Johnson, Dean

University of New Orleans (continued)
Programs in:
biological sciences (MS, PhD)
chemistry (MS, PhD)
computer science (MS)
earth and environmental sciences (MS)
mathematics (MS)
physics (MS, PhD)
psychology (MS, PhD)
sciences (MS, PhD)

■ UNIVERSITY OF PHOENIX–LOUISIANA CAMPUS

Metairie, LA 70001-2082
http://www.phoenix.edu/

Proprietary, coed, comprehensive institution. *Computer facilities:* A campuswide network can be accessed from off campus. *General application contact:* Campus Information Center, 504-461-8852.

The Artemis School

College of Education
Programs in:
curriculum and instruction (MA Ed)
early childhood education (MA Ed)

College of Health and Human Services
Programs in:
administration of justice and security (MS)
health administration (MHA)
health care management (MBA)
nursing (MSN)
psychology (MS)

John Sperling School of Business

Program in:
business (MBA, MIS, MM)

College of Graduate Business and Management
Programs in:
accounting (MBA)
business administration (MBA)
global management (MBA)
human resources management (MBA, MM)
management (MM)
marketing (MBA)
public administration (MBA)

College of Information Systems and Technology
Programs in:
information systems/management (MIS)
technology management (MBA)

■ XAVIER UNIVERSITY OF LOUISIANA

New Orleans, LA 70125-1098
http://www.xula.edu/

Independent-religious, coed, comprehensive institution. CGS member. *Computer facilities:* 250 computers available on campus for general student use. A campuswide network can be accessed from student residence rooms and from off campus. *General application contact:* Director of Graduate Admissions, 504-520-7487.

College of Pharmacy

Program in:
pharmacy (Pharm D)

Graduate School

Programs in:
curriculum and instruction (MA)
education administration and supervision (MA)
guidance and counseling (MA)

Institute for Black Catholic Studies
Program in:
pastoral theology (Th M)

Maine

■ HUSSON UNIVERSITY

Bangor, ME 04401-2999
http://www.husson.edu/

Independent, coed, comprehensive institution. *Computer facilities:* 57 computers available on campus for general student use. A campuswide network can be accessed from student residence rooms and from off campus. Online class registration is available. *General application contact:* Dean of Graduate Studies, 207-941-7062.

School of Graduate and Professional Studies

Programs in:
advanced practice psychiatric nursing (MSN, PMC)
counseling psychology (MS)
criminal justice administration (MS)
family and community nurse practitioner (MSN, PMC)
health care management (MSB)
nonprofit management (MSB)
occupational therapy (MSOT)
physical therapy (DPT)
school counseling (MS)

■ SAINT JOSEPH'S COLLEGE OF MAINE

Standish, ME 04084-5263
http://www.sjcme.edu/

Independent-religious, coed, comprehensive institution. *Computer facilities:* Computer purchase and lease plans are available. 102 computers available on campus for general student use. A campuswide network can be accessed from student residence rooms. *General application contact:* Admissions Department/Graduate and Professional Studies, 800-752-4723.

Department of Nursing

Programs in:
nursing (MS)
nursing administration and leadership (Certificate)
nursing and health care education (Certificate)

Program in Business Administration

Program in:
quality leadership (MBA)

Program in Health Services Administration

Program in:
health services administration (MHSA)

Program in Teacher Education

Program in:
teacher education (MS)

■ UNIVERSITY OF MAINE

Orono, ME 04469
http://www.umaine.edu/

State-supported, coed, university. CGS member. *Computer facilities:* Computer purchase and lease plans are available. 500 computers available on campus for general student use. A campuswide network can be accessed from student residence rooms and from off campus. Online class registration, online housing and financial aid information are available. *General application contact:* Associate Dean of the Graduate School, 207-581-3219.

Graduate School

Programs in:
biomedical sciences (PhD)
information systems (MS)
interdisciplinary studies (PhD)
liberal studies (MA)
teaching (MST)

Climate Change Institute
Program in:
climate change (MS)

College of Business, Public Policy and Health
Programs in:
accounting (MS)
business administration (MBA)
business and sustainability (MBA)
business, public policy and health (MA, MBA, MPA, MS, MSW, PhD, CAS)
economics (MA)
financial economics (MA)
nursing (MS, CAS)
public administration (MPA, PhD)
social work (MSW)

College of Education and Human Development
Programs in:
counselor education (M Ed, MA, MS, Ed D, CAS)
curriculum, assessment, and instruction (M Ed)

educational leadership (M Ed, Ed D, CAS)
elementary and secondary education (M Ed)
elementary education (M Ed, MAT, MS, CAS)
higher education (M Ed, MA, MS, Ed D, CAS)
human development (MS)
human development and family relations (MS)
instructional technology (M Ed)
kinesiology and physical education (M Ed, MS)
literacy education (M Ed, MA, MS, Ed D, CAS)
science education (M Ed, MS, CAS)
secondary education (M Ed, MA, MAT, MS, CAS)
social studies education (M Ed, MA, MS, CAS)
special education (M Ed, CAS)

College of Engineering
Programs in:
biological engineering (MS)
chemical engineering (MS, PhD)
civil engineering (MS, PhD)
computer engineering (MS)
electrical engineering (MS, PhD)
engineering (MS, PhD)
mechanical engineering (MS, PhD)
spatial information science and engineering (MS, PhD)

College of Liberal Arts and Sciences
Programs in:
chemistry (MS, PhD)
clinical psychology (PhD)
communication (MA)
communication sciences and disorders (MA)
computer science (MS, PhD)
developmental psychology (MA)
engineering physics (M Eng)
English (MA)
experimental psychology (MA, PhD)
French (MA, MAT)
history (MA, PhD)
liberal arts and sciences (M Eng, MA, MAT, MM, MS, PhD)
mathematics (MA)
music (MM)
physics (MS, PhD)
social psychology (MA)

College of Natural Sciences, Forestry, and Agriculture
Programs in:
animal sciences (MPS, MS)
biochemistry (MPS, MS)
biochemistry and molecular biology (PhD)
biological sciences (PhD)
botany and plant pathology (MS)
earth sciences (MS, PhD)
ecology and environmental science (MS, PhD)
ecology and environmental sciences (MS, PhD)
entomology (MS)
food and nutritional sciences (PhD)
food science and human nutrition (MS)
forest resources (PhD)
forestry (MF, MS)
horticulture (MS)
marine biology (MS, PhD)
marine policy (MS)
microbiology (MPS, MS, PhD)
natural sciences, forestry, and agriculture (MF, MPS, MS, MWC, PhD)
oceanography (MS, PhD)
plant science (PhD)
plant, soil, and environmental sciences (MS)
resource economics and policy (MS)
resource utilization (MS)
wildlife conservation (MWC)
wildlife ecology (MS, PhD)
zoology (MS, PhD)

■ UNIVERSITY OF NEW ENGLAND

Biddeford, ME 04005-9526
http://www.une.edu/

Independent, coed, comprehensive institution. *Computer facilities:* Computer purchase and lease plans are available. 150 computers available on campus for general student use. A campuswide network can be accessed from student residence rooms and from off campus. Online class registration is available. *General application contact:* Assistant Director of Graduate Admissions, 207-221-4225.

College of Arts and Sciences
Programs in:
applied biosciences (MS)
arts and sciences (MS, MS Ed, CAGS)
educational leadership (CAGS)
general studies (MS Ed)
literacy (MS Ed)
marine science (MS)
teaching methodologies (MS Ed)

College of Health Professions
Programs in:
health professions (MS, MSW, DPT, Certificate)
nurse anesthesia (MS)
occupational therapy (MS)
physical therapy (DPT)
physician assistant (MS)
post professional occupational therapy (MS)
post professional physical therapy (DPT)

School of Social Work
Programs in:
addictions counseling (Certificate)
gerontology (Certificate)
social work (MSW)

College of Osteopathic Medicine
Programs in:
osteopathic medicine (DO, MPH, Certificate)
public health (MPH, Certificate)

■ UNIVERSITY OF SOUTHERN MAINE

Portland, ME 04104-9300
http://www.usm.maine.edu/

State-supported, coed, comprehensive institution. CGS member. *Computer facilities:* 485 computers available on campus for general student use. A campuswide network can be accessed from student residence rooms and from off campus. Online class registration is available. *General application contact:* Office of Graduate Studies Assistant Director, 207-780-4812.

College of Arts and Sciences
Programs in:
American and New England studies (MA)
arts and sciences (MA, MFA, MM, MS, MSW)
biology (MS)
creative writing (MFA)
music (MM)
social work (MSW)
statistics (MS)

College of Education and Human Development
Betty Lou Whitford, Dean
Programs in:
adult education (MS)
adult learning (CAS)
applied behavior analysis (Certificate)
applied literacy (MS Ed)
assistant principal (Certificate)
athletic administration (Certificate)
counseling (MS, CAS)
early language and literacy (Certificate)
education and human development (MS, MS Ed, Psy D, CAS, Certificate)
educational leadership (MS Ed, CAS)
English as a second language (MS Ed, CAS)
literacy education (MS Ed, CAS, Certificate)
mental health rehabilitation technician/community (Certificate)
middle-level education (Certificate)
professional educator (MS Ed)
school psychology (MS, Psy D)
self-design in special education (MS)
teaching all students (MS)
teaching and learning (MS Ed)

College of Nursing and Health Professions
Programs in:
adult health nursing (PMC)
clinical nurse leader (MS)
clinical nurse specialist psychiatric-mental health nursing (MS)
family nursing (PMC)
medical/surgical nursing (MS)
nurse practitioner adult health nursing (MS)
nurse practitioner family nursing (MS)
nurse practitioner psychiatric/mental health nursing (MS)
psychiatric-mental health nursing (PMC)

University of Southern Maine (continued)

Edmund S. Muskie School of Public Service
Programs in:
child and family policy (Certificate)
community planning and development (MCPD, Certificate)
health policy and management (MS, Certificate)
non-profit management (Certificate)
public policy (PhD)
public policy and management (MPPM)
public service (MCPD, MPPM, MS, PhD, Certificate)

Lewiston-Auburn College
Program in:
leadership studies (MLS)

Program in Occupational Therapy
Program in:
occupational therapy (MOT)

School of Applied Science, Engineering, and Technology
Programs in:
applied medical sciences (MS)
applied science, engineering, and technology (MS)
computer science (MS)
manufacturing systems (MS)

School of Business
Programs in:
accounting (MSA)
business administration (MBA)

University of Maine School of Law
Peter R. Pitegoff, Dean
Program in:
law (JD)

Maryland

BOWIE STATE UNIVERSITY

Bowie, MD 20715-9465
http://www.bowiestate.edu/

State-supported, coed, comprehensive institution. CGS member. *Computer facilities:* 3,144 computers available on campus for general student use. A campuswide network can be accessed from student residence rooms and from off campus. Online class registration is available. *General application contact:* Dean, 301-860-3406.

Graduate Programs
Programs in:
administration of nursing services (MS)
applied and computational mathematics (MS)
business administration (MBA)
computer science (MS, App Sc D)
counseling psychology (MA)
educational leadership (Ed D)
elementary and secondary school administration (M Ed)
elementary education (M Ed)
English (MA)
family nurse practitioner (MS)
guidance and counseling (M Ed)
human resource development (MA)
information systems analyst (Certificate)
management information systems (MS)
mental halth counseling (MA)
nursing education (MS)
organizational communication (MA, Certificate)
public administration (MPA)
reading education (M Ed)
school administration and supervision (M Ed)
secondary education (M Ed)
special education (M Ed)
teaching (MAT)

COLLEGE OF NOTRE DAME OF MARYLAND

Baltimore, MD 21210-2476
http://www.ndm.edu/

Independent-religious, Undergraduate: women only; graduate: coed, comprehensive institution. *Computer facilities:* 60 computers available on campus for general student use. A campuswide network can be accessed from student residence rooms and from off campus. Online class registration, online classroom assignments and information are available. *General application contact:* Graduate Admissions Coordinator, 410-532-5317.

Graduate Studies
Programs in:
contemporary communication (MA)
instructional leadership for changing populations (PhD)
leadership in teaching (MA)
liberal studies (MA)
management (MA)
nonprofit management (MA)
teaching (MA)
teaching English to speakers of other languages (MA)

COPPIN STATE UNIVERSITY

Baltimore, MD 21216-3698
http://www.coppin.edu/

State-supported, coed, comprehensive institution. CGS member. *Computer facilities:* A campuswide network can be accessed from off campus. *General application contact:* Dean, Graduate Studies and Research Evaluation, 410-951-3090.

Division of Graduate Studies

Division of Arts and Sciences
Programs in:
alcohol and substance abuse counseling (MS)
arts and sciences (M Ed, MA, MS)
criminal justice (MS)
human services administration (MS)
rehabilitation counseling (M Ed)

Division of Education
Programs in:
adult and general education (MS)
curriculum and instruction (M Ed, MAT, MS)
reading education (MS)
special education (M Ed)
teacher education (MAT)
teaching (MAT)

Helene Fuld School of Nursing
Programs in:
family nurse practitioner (PMC)
nursing (MSN)

FROSTBURG STATE UNIVERSITY

Frostburg, MD 21532-1099
http://www.frostburg.edu/

State-supported, coed, comprehensive institution. *Graduate faculty:* 64 full-time (25 women), 20 part-time/adjunct (8 women). *Computer facilities:* 577 computers available on campus for general student use. A campuswide network can be accessed from student residence rooms and from off campus. Online class registration is available. *Graduate expenses:* Tuition, state resident: full-time $5706; part-time $317 per credit hour. Tuition, nonresident: full-time $6552; part-time $364 per credit hour. Required fees: $77 per credit hour. $11 per semester. One-time fee: $30 part-time. *General application contact:* Vickie Mazer, Director, Graduate Services, 301-687-7053.

Graduate School
Vickie Mazer, Director, Graduate Services

College of Business
Dr. Ahmad Tootoonchi, Interim Dean
Programs in:
business (MBA)
business administration (MBA)

College of Education
Dr. Kenneth Witmer, Dean
Programs in:
curriculum and instruction (M Ed)
education (M Ed, MAT, MS)
educational administration and supervision (M Ed)
educational technology (M Ed)
elementary (M Ed)
elementary education (M Ed)
elementary teaching (MAT)
interdisciplinary education (M Ed)
parks and recreational management (MS)

reading (M Ed)
school counseling (M Ed)
secondary (M Ed)
secondary education (M Ed)
secondary teaching (MAT)
special education (M Ed)

College of Liberal Arts and Sciences
Dr. Joseph Hoffman, Dean
Programs in:
applied computer science (MS)
applied ecology and conservation biology (MS)
counseling psychology (MS)
fisheries and wildlife management (MS)
liberal arts and sciences (MS)

■ HOOD COLLEGE
Frederick, MD 21701-8575
http://www.hood.edu/

Independent, coed, comprehensive institution. CGS member. *Graduate faculty:* 31 full-time (15 women), 78 part-time/adjunct (39 women). *Computer facilities:* Computer purchase and lease plans are available. 283 computers available on campus for general student use. A campuswide network can be accessed from student residence rooms and from off campus. Online class registration is available. *Graduate expenses:* Tuition: full-time $6480. Required fees: $100; $50 per semester. *General application contact:* Dr. Allen Flora, Dean of Graduate School, 301-696-3811.

Graduate School
Dr. Allen P. Flora, Dean of the Graduate School
Programs in:
accounting (MBA)
administration and management (MBA)
biomedical science (MS)
ceramic arts (Certificate)
ceramics (MFA)
computer and information sciences (MS)
computer science (MS)
curriculum and instruction (MS)
educational leadership (MS)
environmental biology (MS)
finance (MBA)
human resource management (MBA)
human sciences (MA)
humanities (MA)
information systems (MBA)
management of information technology (MS)
marketing (MBA)
mathematics education (MS)
public management (MBA)
reading specialization (MS)
regulatory compliance (Certificate)
secondary mathematics education (Certificate)
thanatology (MA, Certificate)

■ THE JOHNS HOPKINS UNIVERSITY
Baltimore, MD 21218-2699
http://www.jhu.edu/

Independent, coed, university. CGS member. *Graduate faculty:* 3,597 full-time (1,388 women), 442 part-time/adjunct (142 women). *Computer facilities:* Computer purchase and lease plans are available. 140 computers available on campus for general student use. A campuswide network can be accessed from student residence rooms and from off campus. Online class registration is available. *Graduate expenses:* Tuition: full-time $37,700; part-time $2035 per course. *General application contact:* Graduate Admissions Office, 410-516-8174.

Bloomberg School of Public Health
Dr. Michael J. Klag, Dean
Programs in:
biochemistry and molecular biology (MHS, Sc M, PhD)
bioethics and policy (PhD)
bioinformatics (MHS)
biostatistics (MHS, Sc M, PhD)
cancer epidemiology (MHS, Sc M, PhD, Sc D)
cardiovascular disease epidemiology (MHS, Sc M, PhD, Sc D)
child and adolescent health and development (Dr PH, PhD)
children's mental health services (PhD)
clinical epidemiology (MHS, Sc M, PhD, Sc D)
clinical investigation (MHS, Sc M, PhD)
clinical trials (PhD, Sc D)
demography (MHS)
drug dependence epidemiology (PhD)
economic evaluation and policy (PhD)
environmental health engineering (PhD)
environmental health sciences (MHS, Dr PH)
epidemiology (Dr PH)
epidemiology (general) (MHS, Sc M, PhD, Sc D)
epidemiology of aging (MHS, Sc M, PhD, Sc D)
genetic counseling (Sc M)
global disease epidemiology and control (MHS, PhD)
health and public policy (PhD)
health care management and leadership (Dr PH)
health education and health communication (MHS)
health finance and management (MHA, MHS)
health policy (MHS)
health services research and policy (PhD)
health systems (MHS, PhD)
human genetics/genetic epidemiology (MHS, Sc M, PhD, Sc D)
human nutrition (MHS, PhD)
infectious disease epidemiology (MHS, Sc M, PhD, Sc D)
international health (Dr PH)
mental health (MHS, Dr PH)
molecular microbiology and immunology (MHS, Sc M, PhD)
occupational and environmental health (PhD)
occupational and environmental hygiene (MHS, MHS)
occupational/environmental epidemiology (MHS, Sc M, PhD, Sc D)
physiology (PhD)
population and health (Dr PH, PhD)
population, family and reproductive health (MHS)
psychiatric epidemiology (PhD)
public health (MHA, MHS, MPH, Sc M, Dr PH, PhD, Sc D)
reproductive, perinatal women's health (Dr PH, PhD)
social and behavioral interventions (MHS, PhD)
social and behavioral sciences (PhD, Sc D)
toxicology (PhD)

Carey Business School
Dr. Yash Gupta, Dean
Programs in:
business administration (MBA)
business of health (MBA, Certificate)
business of medicine (Certificate)
business of nursing (Certificate)
competitive intelligence (Certificate)
finance (MS, Certificate)
financial management (Certificate)
information and telecommunication systems (Certificate)
information security management (Certificate)
information technology (MS, Certificate)
information technology and telecommunication systems for business (MS)
investments (Certificate)
leadership and management in the life sciences (MBA, Certificate)
leadership development (Certificate)
management (MS, Certificate)
marketing (MS)
medical services management (MBA)
organization development and strategic human resources (MS)
real estate (MS)
senior living and health care real estate (Certificate)
skilled facilitator (Certificate)

Engineering for Professionals
Dr. Allan Bjerkaas, Associate Dean
Programs in:
applied and computational mathematics (MS, Post-Master's Certificate)
applied biomedical engineering (MS, Post-Master's Certificate)
applied physics (MS, Post-Master's Certificate)

The Johns Hopkins University (continued)
bioinformatics (MS, Post-Master's Certificate)
chemical and biomolecular engineering (M Ch E)
civil engineering (MCE)
computer science (MS, Post-Master's Certificate)
electrical and computer engineering (MS, Post-Master's Certificate)
engineering (M Ch E, M Mat SE, MCE, MEE, MME, MS, MSE, Graduate Certificate, Post-Master's Certificate)
environmental engineering (MS, Graduate Certificate, Post-Master's Certificate)
environmental engineering and science (MEE, MS, Graduate Certificate, Post-Master's Certificate)
environmental planning and management (MS, Post-Master's Certificate)
information assurance (MS)
information systems and technology (MS, Post-Master's Certificate)
materials science and engineering (M Mat SE, MSE)
mechanical engineering (MME)
systems engineering (MS, Graduate Certificate, Post-Master's Certificate)
technical management (MS, Graduate Certificate, Post-Master's Certificate)
telecommunications and networking (MS)

G. W. C. Whiting School of Engineering

Dr. Nicholas P. Jones, Interim Dean
Programs in:
bioengineering innovation and design (MSE)
biomaterials (MSEM)
biomedical engineering (MSE, PhD)
chemical and biomolecular engineering (MSE, PhD)
civil engineering (MCE, MSE, PhD)
communications science (MSEM)
computational medicine (PhD)
computer science (MSE, PhD)
discrete mathematics (MA, MSE, PhD)
electrical and computer engineering (MSE, PhD)
engineering (M Ch E, M Mat SE, MA, MCE, MEE, MME, MS, MSE, MSEM, MSSI, PhD, Certificate, Post-Master's Certificate)
financial mathematics (MSE)
fluid mechanics (MSEM)
geography and environmental engineering (MA, MS, MSE, PhD)
materials science and engineering (MSEM)
mechanical engineering (MSEM)
mechanics and materials (MSEM)
nano-biotechnology (MSEM)
nanomaterials and nanotechnology (MSEM)
operations research/optimization/decision science (MA, MSE, PhD)
probability and statistics (MSEM)
smart product and device design (MSEM)
statistics/probability/stochastic processes (MA, MSE, PhD)
systems analysis, management and environmental policy (MSEM)

Information Security Institute
Dr. Gerald M. Masson, Director
Program in:
information security (MSSI)

National Institutes of Health Sponsored Programs

Dr. Allen Shearn, Chair
Programs in:
biology (PhD)
cell, molecular, and developmental biology and biophysics (PhD)

Paul H. Nitze School of Advanced International Studies

Sidney Jackson, Director of Admissions
Programs in:
international development (MA, Certificate)
international public policy (MIPP)
international relations (PhD)
international studies (Certificate)
Japan studies (MA)
Korea Studies (MA)
South Asia studies (MA)
Southeast Asia studies (MA)

Peabody Conservatory

Jeffrey Sharkey, Director
Program in:
music (MA, MM, DMA, AD, GPD)

School of Education

Dr. Ralph Fessler, Dean
Programs in:
adult learning (Certificate)
advanced methods for differentiated instruction and inclusive education (Certificate)
assistive technology (Certificate)
clinical community counseling (Certificate)
counseling (MS, CAGS)
counseling at-risk youth (Certificate)
data-based decision making and organizational improvement (Certificate)
early intervention/preschool special education specialist (Certificate)
earth/space science (Certificate)
education (MAT, MS, Ed D, CAGS, Certificate)
education of students with autism and other pervasive developmental disorders (Certificate)
education of students with severe disabilities (Certificate)
educational leadership for independent schools (Certificate)
educational studies (MS)
effective teaching of reading (Certificate)
elementary education (MAT)
English as a second language instruction (Certificate)
English for speakers of other languages (MAT)
gifted education (Certificate)
K-8 mathematics lead-teacher (Certificate)
K-8 science lead-teacher (Certificate)
leadership for school, family, and community collaboration (Certificate)
leadership in technology integration (Certificate)
mind, brain, and teaching (Certificate)
organizational counseling (Certificate)
out-of-school time leadership (Certificate)
play therapy (Certificate)
reading (MS)
school administration and supervision (MS, Certificate)
secondary education (MAT)
special education (MS, Ed D, CAGS)
teacher development and leadership (MS, Ed D, Certificate)
teacher leadership (Certificate)
technology for educators (MS)
urban education (Certificate)

Division of Public Safety Leadership
Dr. Sheldon Greenberg, Associate Dean
Programs in:
intelligence analysis (MS)
management (MS)

School of Medicine

Dr. Edward D. Miller, Dean of Medical Faculty and Chief Executive Officer
Program in:
medicine (MD, MA, MS, PhD)

Division of Health Sciences Informatics
Dr. Harold P. Lehmann, Director, Training Program
Program in:
health sciences informatics (MS)

Graduate Programs in Medicine
Dr. Peter Maloney, Associate Dean for Graduate Programs
Programs in:
biochemistry, cellular and molecular biology (PhD)
biological chemistry (PhD)
cellular and molecular medicine (PhD)
cellular and molecular physiology (PhD)
functional anatomy and evolution (PhD)
human genetics (PhD)
immunology (PhD)
medical and biological illustration (MA)
medicine (MA, MS, PhD)
molecular biophysics (MS, PhD)
neuroscience (PhD)
pathobiology (PhD)
pharmacology and molecular sciences (PhD)
physiology (PhD)

School of Nursing

Dr. Martha N. Hill, Dean

Programs in:
- adult acute/critical care (MSN, Certificate)
- adult and pediatric primary care (MSN)
- adult or pediatric primary care (Certificate)
- business of nursing (Certificate)
- clinical nurse specialist (MSN)
- clinical nurse specialist and health systems management (MSN)
- emergency preparedness/disaster response (Certificate)
- family primary care (MSN, Certificate)
- health systems management (MSN)
- nursing (MSN, DNP, PhD, Certificate)
- public health nursing (MSN)
- women's health (Certificate)

Zanvyl Krieger School of Arts and Sciences

Dr. Adam Falk, Dean
Programs in:
- anthropology (PhD)
- applied economics (MA)
- arts and sciences (MA, MFA, MS, PhD, Certificate)
- astronomy (PhD)
- bioinformatics (MS)
- biology (PhD)
- bioscience regulatory affairs (MS)
- biotechnology (MS)
- chemistry (PhD)
- chemistry-biology (PhD)
- classics (PhD)
- cognitive science (PhD)
- communication in contemporary society (MA)
- earth and planetary sciences (MA, PhD)
- economics (PhD)
- English and American literature (PhD)
- environmental sciences and policy (MS)
- fiction writing (MFA)
- French (PhD)
- German (PhD)
- government (MA, Certificate)
- history (PhD)
- history of art (MA, PhD)
- history of science and technology (MA, PhD)
- Italian (PhD)
- liberal arts (MA, Certificate)
- mathematics (PhD)
- molecular biophysics (PhD)
- museum studies (MA)
- national securities study (Certificate)
- Near Eastern studies (PhD)
- philosophy (MA, PhD)
- physics (PhD)
- poetry (MFA)
- political science (MA, PhD)
- psychological and brain sciences (PhD)
- romance languages (PhD)
- science writing (MA)
- sociology (PhD)
- Spanish (PhD)
- writing (MA, MFA)

Humanities Center
Prof. Ruth Leys, Chair
Program in:
- humanities (PhD)

Institute for Public Policy
Dr. Sandra J. Newman, Director
Program in:
- public policy (MA)

■ LOYOLA UNIVERSITY MARYLAND

Baltimore, MD 21210-2699

http://www.loyola.edu/

Independent-religious, coed, comprehensive institution. CGS member. *Graduate faculty:* 262 full-time (134 women), 144 part-time/adjunct (71 women). *Computer facilities:* Computer purchase and lease plans are available. A campuswide network can be accessed from student residence rooms and from off campus. Online class registration is available. *General application contact:* Maureen Faux, Interim Director, Graduate Admissions, 410-617-5020.

Graduate Programs

Rev. Brian Linnane, President

College of Arts and Sciences
Dr. James Buckley, Dean
Programs in:
- administration and supervision (M Ed, MA, CAS)
- arts and sciences (M Ed, MA, MMS, MS, PhD, Psy D, CAS)
- clinical psychology (MS, Psy D, CAS)
- computer science (MS)
- counseling psychology (MS, CAS)
- curriculum and instruction (M Ed, MA, CAS)
- educational technology (M Ed)
- liberal studies (MMS)
- Montessori education (M Ed, CAS)
- pastoral counseling (MS, PhD, CAS)
- reading (M Ed, CAS)
- school counseling (M Ed, CAS)
- software engineering (MS)
- special education (M Ed, CAS)
- speech-language pathology and audiology (MS, CAS)
- spiritual and pastoral care (MA)

Sellinger School of Business and Management
Dr. Karyl Leggio, Dean
Programs in:
- accounting (MBA)
- business and management (MBA, MSF)
- executive business administration (MBA)
- finance (MBA)
- general business (MBA)
- international business (MBA)
- management (MBA)
- management information systems (MBA)
- marketing (MBA)

■ MCDANIEL COLLEGE

Westminster, MD 21157-4390

http://www.mcdaniel.edu/

Independent, coed, comprehensive institution. *Computer facilities:* 340 computers available on campus for general student use. A campuswide network can be accessed from student residence rooms and from off campus. Online class registration is available. *General application contact:* Dean of Graduate and Professional Studies, 410-857-2500.

Graduate and Professional Studies

Programs in:
- curriculum and instruction (MS)
- education of the deaf (MS)
- educational administration (MS)
- elementary education (MS)
- guidance and counseling (MS)
- human resources development (MS)
- human services management in special education (MS)
- liberal studies (MLA)
- media/library science (MS)
- physical education (MS)
- reading education (MS)
- secondary education (MS)
- special education (MS)

■ MORGAN STATE UNIVERSITY

Baltimore, MD 21251

http://www.morgan.edu/

State-supported, coed, university. CGS member. *Graduate faculty:* 222. *Computer facilities:* 285 computers available on campus for general student use. A campuswide network can be accessed from student residence rooms and from off campus. Online class registration, engineering lab supercomputer are available. *General application contact:* Dr. Dean Campbell, Graduate Recruitment Specialist, 443-885-3185.

School of Graduate Studies

Dr. Mark Garrison, Interim Dean

Clarence M. Mitchell, Jr. School of Engineering
Dr. Eugene DeLoatch, Dean
Programs in:
- civil engineering (M Eng, D Eng)
- electrical engineering (M Eng, D Eng)
- industrial engineering (M Eng, D Eng)
- transportation (MS)

College of Liberal Arts
Dr. Burney J. Hollis, Dean
Programs in:
- African-American studies (MA)
- economics (MA)
- English (MA, PhD)
- history (MA, PhD)
- international studies (MA)
- liberal arts (MA, MS, PhD)
- music (MA)
- psychometrics (MS, PhD)
- sociology (MA, MS)
- telecommunications management (MS)

Earl G. Graves School of Business and Management
Dr. Otis A. Thomas, Dean

Morgan State University (continued)
Programs in:
business administration (MBA, PhD)
business and management (MBA, PhD)

Institute of Architecture and Planning
Mahendra Parekh, Interim Director
Programs in:
architecture (M Arch)
city and regional planning (MCRP)
landscape architecture (MLA, MSLA)

School of Community Health and Policy
Dr. Allan Noonan, Dean
Programs in:
nursing (MS, PhD)
public health (MPH, Dr PH)

School of Computer, Mathematical, and Natural Sciences
Dr. Joseph Whittaker, Dean
Programs in:
bioenvironmental science (PhD)
bioinformatics (MS)
biology (MS)
chemistry (MS)
computer, mathematical, and natural sciences (MA, MS, PhD)
mathematics (MA)

School of Education and Urban Studies
Dr. Patricia L. Welch, Dean
Programs in:
education and urban studies (MAT, MS, MSW, Ed D, PhD)
educational administration and supervision (MS)
elementary and middle school education (MS)
elementary education (MAT)
high school education (MAT)
higher education administration (PhD)
higher education-community college leadership (Ed D)
mathematics education (MS, Ed D)
middle school education (MAT)
science education (MS, Ed D)
social work (MSW, PhD)
urban educational leadership (Ed D)

■ MOUNT ST. MARY'S UNIVERSITY

Emmitsburg, MD 21727-7799

http://www.msmary.edu/

Independent-religious, coed, comprehensive institution. *Graduate faculty:* 25 full-time (6 women), 18 part-time/adjunct (9 women). *Computer facilities:* 150 computers available on campus for general student use. A campuswide network can be accessed from student residence rooms and from off campus. Online class registration, tuition payment, course management system are available. *Graduate expenses:* Tuition: full-time $7938; part-time $441 per credit hour. Tuition and fees vary according to program. *General application contact:* David Rehm, Vice President for Academic Affairs, 301-447-5218.

Graduate Seminary
Rev. Steven P. Rohlfs, Vice President/ Rector
Program in:
theology (M Div, MA)

Program in Business Administration
Dr. Carolyn Jacobson, Director, MBA Program
Program in:
business administration (MBA)

Program in Education
Laura Frazier, Director
Program in:
education (M Ed, MAT)

■ ST. JOHN'S COLLEGE

Annapolis, MD 21404

http://www.stjohnscollege.edu/

Independent, coed, comprehensive institution. *Computer facilities:* 16 computers available on campus for general student use. A campuswide network can be accessed from student residence rooms and from off campus. *General application contact:* Office of Graduate Admissions, 410-263-2371.

Graduate Institute in Liberal Education
Program in:
liberal arts (MALA)

■ SALISBURY UNIVERSITY

Salisbury, MD 21801-6837

http://www.salisbury.edu/

State-supported, coed, comprehensive institution. *Graduate faculty:* 88 full-time (43 women), 21 part-time/adjunct (15 women). *Computer facilities:* Computer purchase and lease plans are available. 423 computers available on campus for general student use. A campuswide network can be accessed from student residence rooms and from off campus. Online class registration, accounts for all students are available. *Graduate expenses:* Part-time $270 per credit hour. Tuition, state resident: part-time $270 per credit hour. Tuition, nonresident: part-time $566 per credit hour. Required fees: $52 per credit hour. *General application contact:* Melissa Boog, Associate Director of Admissions, 410-543-6161.

Graduate Division
Melissa Boog, Associate Director of Admissions
Programs in:
accounting track (MBA)
applied health physiology (MS)
composition, language and rhetoric (MA)
educational leadership (M Ed)
general track (MBA)
geographic information systems and public administration (MS)
history (MA)
literature (MA)
mathematics education (MSME)
nursing (MS)
reading specialist (M Ed)
social work (MSW)
teaching (MA)
teaching English to speakers of other languages (MA)

■ TOWSON UNIVERSITY

Towson, MD 21252-0001

http://www.towson.edu/

State-supported, coed, university. CGS member. *Computer facilities:* 1,200 computers available on campus for general student use. A campuswide network can be accessed from student residence rooms and from off campus. Online class registration is available. *General application contact:* Information Contact, 410-704-2501.

College of Graduate Studies and Research
Programs in:
accounting and business advisory services (MS)
applied and industrial mathematics (MS)
applied gerontology (MS, Certificate)
applied information technology (D Sc)
art education (M Ed)
audiology (Au D)
biology (MS)
clinical psychology (MA)
clinician-administrator transition (Certificate)
communications management (MS)
computer science (MS)
counseling psychology (CAS)
database management (Certificate)
early childhood education (M Ed, CAS)
elementary education (M Ed)
environmental science (MS, Certificate)
family-professional collaboration (Certificate)
forensic science (MS)
geography and environmental planning (MA)
health science (MS)
human resource development (MS)
humanities (MA)
information security and assurance (Certificate)
information systems management (Certificate)
instructional design and training (MS)
instructional technology (Ed D)
integrated homeland security management (MS)
interactive media design (Certificate)
Internet application development (Certificate)
kinesiology (MS)
management and leadership development (Certificate)
mathematics education (MS)

music education (MS, Certificate)
music performance and composition (MM)
networking technologies (Certificate)
nursing (MS)
nursing education (Certificate)
occupational science (Sc D)
occupational therapy (MS)
organizational change (CAS)
physician assistant studies (MS)
professional studies (MA)
professional writing (MS)
reading (M Ed)
reading education (CAS)
school psychology (CAS)
science education (MS)
secondary education (M Ed)
security assessment and management (Certificate)
social science (MS)
software engineering (Certificate)
special education leadership (M Ed)
speech-language pathology (MS)
strategic public relations and integrated communications (Certificate)
studio arts (MFA)
teaching (MAT)
theatre (MFA)
women's studies (MS, Certificate)

Arts Integration Institute
Program in:
arts integration (Certificate)

Baltimore Hebrew Institute
Programs in:
Jewish communal service (MAJCS)
Jewish education (MAJE)
Jewish studies (MAJS)

Joint University of Baltimore/ Towson University (UB/Towson) MBA Program
Program in:
business administration (MBA)

■ UNIVERSITY OF BALTIMORE

Baltimore, MD 21201-5779
http://www.ubalt.edu/

State-supported, coed, comprehensive institution. *Graduate faculty:* 166 full-time (68 women), 186 part-time/adjunct (61 women). *Computer facilities:* Computer purchase and lease plans are available. 135 computers available on campus for general student use. A campuswide network can be accessed from off campus. Online class registration is available. *Graduate expenses:* Tuition, state resident: part-time $568 per credit. Tuition, nonresident: part-time $824 per credit. Required fees: $250 per semester. *General application contact:* Kevin Nies, Assistant Director, Office of Graduate Admission, 410-837-6780.

Graduate School
Miriam King, Senior Vice President for Enrollment Management

Merrick School of Business
Dr. Darlene Smith, Dean
Programs in:
accounting and business advisory services (MS)
accounting fundamentals (Graduate Certificate)
business (MBA, MS, Graduate Certificate)
business/finance (MS)
business/marketing and venturing (MS)
forensic accounting (Graduate Certificate)
taxation (MS)

The Yale Gordon College of Liberal Arts
Dr. Larry Thomas, Dean
Programs in:
applied psychology (MS)
communications design (DCD)
creative writing and publishing arts (MFA)
criminal justice (MS)
health systems management (MS)
human services administration (MS)
human-computer interaction (MS)
integrated design (MFA)
interaction design and information technology (MS)
legal and ethical studies (MA)
liberal arts (MA, MFA, MPA, MS, DCD, DPA)
negotiations and conflict management (MS)
public administration (MPA, DPA)
publications design (MA)

Joint University of Baltimore/ Towson University (UB/Towson) MBA Program
Ron Desi, Director
Program in:
business administration (MBA)

School of Law
Phillip J. Closius, Dean
Programs in:
law (JD)
law of the United States (LL M)
taxation (LL M)

■ UNIVERSITY OF MARYLAND, BALTIMORE COUNTY

Baltimore, MD 21250
http://www.umbc.edu/

State-supported, coed, university. CGS member. *Graduate faculty:* 432 full-time, 168 part-time/adjunct. *Computer facilities:* 875 computers available on campus for general student use. A campuswide network can be accessed from student residence rooms and from off campus. Online class registration, student account information are available. *General application contact:* Kathryn Nee, Coordinator of Domestic Admissions, 410-455-2944.

Graduate School
Dr. Janet c. Rutledge, Interim Vice Provost for Graduate Education
Programs in:
aging policy for the elderly (PhD)
epidemiology of aging (PhD)
marine-estuarine-environmental sciences (MS, PhD)
social, cultural, and behavioral sciences (PhD)

College of Arts, Humanities and Social Sciences
Dr. John Jeffries, Dean
Programs in:
administration, planning, and policy (MS)
American contemporary music (Postbaccalaureate Certificate)
applied behavioral analysis (MA)
applied developmental psychology (PhD)
applied sociology (MA, Postbaccalaureate Certificate)
arts, humanities and social science (MA, MAT, MFA, MPP, MPS, MS, PhD, Certificate, Postbaccalaureate Certificate)
computer/web-based instruction (Postbaccalaureate Certificate)
distance education (Postbaccalaureate Certificate)
early childhood education (MAT)
economic policy analysis (MA)
education (MA, MAT, Postbaccalaureate Certificate)
elementary education (MAT)
elementary/middle science education (Postbaccalaureate Certificate)
emergency health services (MS)
emergency management (Postbaccalaureate Certificate)
gender and women's studies (Postbaccalaureate Certificate)
geographic information systems (MPS, Certificate)
geography and environmental systems (MPS, MS, PhD, Certificate)
historical studies (MA)
human services psychology (MA, PhD)
human services psychology/clinical (PhD)
imaging and digital arts (MFA)
industrial organizational psychology (MPS)
intercultural communication (MA)
language, literacy, and culture (PhD)
math education (Postbaccalaureate Certificate)
nonprofit sector (Postbaccalaureate Certificate)
preventive medicine and epidemiology (MS)
psychology (MPS)
public policy (MPP, PhD)
secondary education (MAT)
STEM education (Postbaccalaureate Certificate)
teaching (MAT)
teaching English as a second language (MA)

University of Maryland, Baltimore County (continued)

College of Engineering and Information Technology
Dr. Warren DeVries, Dean
Programs in:
- biochemical regulatory engineering (Postbaccalaureate Certificate)
- chemical and biochemical engineering (MS, PhD)
- civil and environmental engineering (MS, PhD)
- civil engineering (MS, PhD)
- computer engineering (MS, PhD)
- computer science (MS, PhD)
- electrical engineering (MS, PhD)
- engineering and information technology (MS, PhD, Postbaccalaureate Certificate)
- engineering management (MS, Postbaccalaureate Certificate)
- human-centered computing (MS, PhD)
- information systems (MS, PhD)
- mechanical engineering (MS, PhD, Postbaccalaureate Certificate)
- mechatronics (Postbaccalaureate Certificate)
- systems engineering (MS, Postbaccalaureate Certificate)

College of Natural and Mathematical Sciences
Dr. Philip J. Rous, Dean
Programs in:
- applied mathematics (MS, PhD)
- applied molecular biology (MS)
- applied physics (MS, PhD)
- astrophysics (PhD)
- atmospheric physics (MS, PhD)
- biochemistry (MS, PhD)
- biological sciences (MS, PhD)
- biostatistics (PhD)
- chemistry (MS, PhD)
- environmental statistics (MS)
- molecular and cell biology (PhD)
- natural and mathematical sciences (MS, PhD)
- neurosciences and cognitive sciences (PhD)
- optics (MS, PhD)
- quantum optics (PhD)
- solid state physics (MS, PhD)
- statistics (MS, PhD)

Continuing and Professional Studies
Program in:
- biotechnology management (Graduate Certificate)

■ UNIVERSITY OF MARYLAND, COLLEGE PARK

College Park, MD 20742
http://www.maryland.edu/

State-supported, coed, university. CGS member. *Graduate faculty:* 2,967 full-time (1,055 women), 900 part-time/adjunct (397 women). *Computer facilities:* Computer purchase and lease plans are available. 11,097 computers available on campus for general student use. A campuswide network can be accessed from student residence rooms and from off campus. Online class registration, student account information, financial aid summary are available. *Graduate expenses:* Tuition, state resident: full-time $9129; part-time $471 per credit hour. Tuition, nonresident: full-time $18,381; part-time $1016 per credit hour. Required fees: $1137; $374 per year. Tuition and fees vary according to course level, course load and program. *General application contact:* Dr. Charles Caramello, Dean of Graduate School, 301-405-0376.

Academic Affairs

Dr. Charles Caramello, Dean of the Graduate School

A. James Clark School of Engineering
Dr. Darryll Pines, Dean
Programs in:
- aerospace engineering (M Eng)
- bioengineering (MS, PhD)
- chemical engineering (M Eng, MS, PhD)
- civil and environmental engineering (M Eng, MS, PhD)
- civil engineering (M Eng)
- electrical and computer engineering (M Eng, MS, PhD)
- electrical engineering (M Eng, MS, PhD)
- electronic packaging and reliability (MS, PhD)
- engineering (Certificate)
- engineering and public policy (MS)
- fire protection engineering (M Eng)
- manufacturing and design (MS, PhD)
- materials science and engineering (M Eng, MS, PhD)
- mechanical engineering (M Eng)
- mechanics and materials (MS, PhD)
- nuclear engineering (ME, MS, PhD)
- reliability engineering (M Eng, MS, PhD)
- systems engineering (M Eng)
- telecommunications (MS)
- thermal and fluid sciences (MS, PhD)

College of Agriculture and Natural Resources
Dr. Cheng-i Wei, Dean
Programs in:
- agriculture and natural resources (DVM, MS, PhD)
- agriculture economics (MS, PhD)
- agronomy (MS, PhD)
- animal sciences (MS, PhD)
- environmental science and technology (MS, PhD)
- food science (MS, PhD)
- horticulture (PhD)
- natural resource sciences (MS, PhD)
- nutrition (MS, PhD)
- resource economics (MS, PhD)
- veterinary medical sciences (MS, PhD)
- veterinary medicine (DVM, MS, PhD)

College of Arts and Humanities
Dr. James F. Harris, Dean
Programs in:
- American studies (MA, PhD)
- Arabic (Graduate Certificate)
- art (MFA)
- art history (MA, PhD)
- arts and humanities (M Ed, MA, MFA, MM, MPS, DMA, Ed D, PhD, Graduate Certificate)
- classics (MA)
- communication (MA, PhD)
- comparative literature (MA, PhD)
- creative writing (MA, MFA, PhD)
- dance (MFA)
- English language and literature (MA, PhD)
- ethnomusicology (MA)
- French (MA)
- French language and literature (MA)
- German (MA)
- Germanic language and literature (MA, PhD)
- history (MA, PhD)
- Japanese (MA)
- Jewish studies (MA)
- languages, literature, and cultures (MA, PhD)
- linguistics (MA, PhD)
- modern French studies (PhD)
- music (M Ed, MA, MM, DMA, Ed D, PhD)
- Persian (MPS, Graduate Certificate)
- philosophy (MA, PhD)
- Russian (MA)
- second language instruction (PhD)
- second language learning (PhD)
- second language measurement and assessment (PhD)
- second language use (PhD)
- Spanish (MA)
- Spanish and Portuguese (MA, PhD)
- theatre (MA, MFA, PhD)
- women's studies (MA, PhD)

College of Behavioral and Social Sciences
Dr. Edward Montgomery, Dean
Programs in:
- American politics (PhD)
- applied anthropology (MAA)
- audiology (MA, PhD)
- behavioral and social sciences (MA, MAA, MS, Au D, PhD)
- clinical psychology (PhD)
- comparative politics (PhD)
- criminology and criminal justice (MA, PhD)
- developmental psychology (PhD)
- economics (MA, PhD)
- experimental psychology (PhD)
- geography (MA, PhD)
- hearing and speech sciences (Au D)
- industrial psychology (MA, MS, PhD)
- international relations (PhD)
- language pathology (MA, PhD)
- neuroscience (PhD)
- neurosciences and cognitive sciences (PhD)
- political economy (PhD)
- political theory (PhD)
- social psychology (PhD)

sociology (MA, PhD)
speech (MA, PhD)
survey methodology (MS, PhD)

College of Chemical and Life Sciences
Dr. Norma M. Allewell, Dean
Programs in:
analytical chemistry (MS, PhD)
behavior, ecology, and systematics (PhD)
behavior, ecology, evolution, and systematics (MS, PhD)
biochemistry (MS, PhD)
biology (MS, PhD)
cell biology and molecular genetics (MS, PhD)
chemical and life sciences (MLS, MS, PhD)
chemistry (MS, PhD)
entomology (MS, PhD)
inorganic chemistry (MS, PhD)
life sciences (MLS)
marine-estuarine-environmental sciences (MS, PhD)
molecular and cellular biology (PhD)
organic chemistry (MS, PhD)
physical chemistry (MS, PhD)
plant biology (MS, PhD)
sustainable development and conservation biology (MS)

College of Computer, Mathematical and Physical Sciences
Dr. Stephen Halperin, Dean
Programs in:
applied mathematics (MS, PhD)
astronomy (MS, PhD)
atmospheric and oceanic science (MS, PhD)
chemical physics (MS, PhD)
computer science (MS, PhD)
computer, mathematical and physical sciences (MA, MS, PhD)
geology (MS, PhD)
mathematical statistics (MA, PhD)
mathematics (MA, PhD)
physics (MS, PhD)

College of Education
Donna L. Wiseman, Dean
Programs in:
college student personnel (M Ed, MA)
college student personnel administration (PhD)
community counseling (CAGS)
community/career counseling (M Ed, MA)
counseling and personnel services (M Ed, MA, PhD)
counseling psychology (PhD)
counselor education (PhD)
curriculum and educational communications (M Ed, MA, Ed D, PhD)
early childhood/elementary education (M Ed, MA, Ed D, PhD)
education (M Ed, MA, Ed D, PhD, AGSC, CAGS)
education leadership, higher education and international education (MA, Ed D, PhD)
education policy studies (M Ed, MA, PhD)
human development (M Ed, MA, Ed D, PhD)
measurement (MA, PhD)
program evaluation (MA, PhD)
reading (M Ed, MA, PhD, CAGS)
rehabilitation counseling (M Ed, MA, AGSC)
school counseling (M Ed, MA)
school psychology (M Ed, MA, PhD)
secondary education (M Ed, MA, Ed D, PhD, CAGS)
social foundations of education (M Ed, MA, Ed D, PhD, CAGS)
special education (M Ed, MA, PhD, CAGS)
statistics (MA, PhD)
teaching English to speakers of other languages (M Ed)

College of Information Studies
Dr. Jennifer Preece, Dean
Program in:
information studies (MIM, MLS, PhD)

Phillip Merrill College of Journalism
Lee Thornton, Acting Dean
Programs in:
broadcast journalism (MA)
journalism (MA)
journalism and media studies (PhD)
online news (MA)
public affairs reporting (MA)

Robert H. Smith School of Business
Dr. Anand Anandalingam, Dean
Programs in:
business (EMBA, MBA, MS, PhD)
business administration (EMBA, MBA)
business and management (MS, PhD)

School of Architecture, Planning and Preservation
Garth Rockcastle, Dean
Programs in:
architecture (M Arch)
architecture, planning and preservation (M Arch, MCP, MHP, MRED, PhD, Certificate)
historic preservation (MHP, Certificate)
real estate development (MRED)
urban and regional planning/design (PhD)
urban studies and planning (MCP)

School of Public Health
Dr. Robert Gold, Dean
Programs in:
biostatistics (MPH)
community health education (MPH)
environmental health sciences (MPH)
epidemiology (MPH, PhD)
family studies (PhD)
health services administration (MHA, PhD)
kinesiology (MA, PhD)
marriage and family therapy (MS)
maternal and child health (PhD)
public health (MA, MHA, MPH, MS, PhD)
public/community health (PhD)

School of Public Policy
Dr. Donald Kettl, Dean
Programs in:
policy studies (PhD)
public management (MPM)
public policy (MPM, MPP, PhD)

■ UNIVERSITY OF MARYLAND EASTERN SHORE

Princess Anne, MD 21853-1299
http://www.umes.edu/

State-supported, coed, university. CGS member. *Computer facilities:* 200 computers available on campus for general student use. A campuswide network can be accessed. Online class registration is available. *General application contact:* Associate Vice President for Academic Affairs, 410-651-6507.

Graduate Programs
Programs in:
applied computer science (MS)
career and technology education (M Ed)
criminology and criminal justice (MS)
education leadership (Ed D)
food and agricultural sciences (MS)
food science and technology (PhD)
guidance and counseling (M Ed)
marine-estuarine-environmental sciences (MS, PhD)
organizational leadership (PhD)
physical therapy (DPT)
rehabilitation counseling (MS)
special education (M Ed)
teaching (MAT)
toxicology (MS, PhD)

■ UNIVERSITY OF MARYLAND UNIVERSITY COLLEGE

Adelphi, MD 20783
http://www.umuc.edu/

State-supported, coed, comprehensive institution. CGS member. *Graduate faculty:* 175 full-time (64 women), 451 part-time/adjunct (158 women). *Computer facilities:* 375 computers available on campus for general student use. A campuswide network can be accessed from off campus. Online class registration is available. *Graduate expenses:* Tuition, state resident: full-time $7416; part-time $412 per credit hour. Tuition, nonresident: full-time $11,862; part-time $659 per credit hour. Required fees: $180; $10 per credit hour. *General application contact:* Coordinator, Graduate Admissions, 301-985-7155.

Graduate School of Management and Technology
Dr. Michael S. Frank, Vice President and Dean of Graduate Studies
Programs in:
accounting and financial management (MS, Certificate)

University of Maryland University College (continued)
- accounting and information technology (MS, Certificate)
- biotechnology studies (MS, Certificate)
- business administration (Exec MBA, MBA, Certificate)
- distance education (MDE, Certificate)
- education (M Ed)
- environmental management (MS, Certificate)
- financial management and information systems (MS, Certificate)
- health administration informatics (MS, Certificate)
- health care administration (MS, Certificate)
- information technology (Exec MS, MS, Certificate)
- international management (MIM, Certificate)
- management (MS, Certificate)
- management and technology (Exec MBA, Exec MS, M Ed, MBA, MDE, MIM, MS, DM, Certificate)
- technology management (Exec MS, MS, Certificate)

Center for Human Resource Development
Program in:
- human resource development (MA)

School of Business Administration
Programs in:
- accounting (MBA)
- accounting and taxation (MSAT)
- business administration (MBA, MPA, MS, MSAT)
- corporate/public communication (MBA)
- finance (MBA)
- general business (MBA)
- hospitality, hotel and service management (MBA)
- international business (MBA)
- international business practice (MBA)
- management (MBA)
- management information systems (MBA)
- marketing (MBA)
- nonprofit management (MS)
- organization development (MS)
- public administration (MPA)

School of Health Sciences
Programs in:
- health sciences (MSN, MSOT, DPT)
- nursing administration (MSN)
- nursing education (MSN)
- occupational therapy (MSOT)
- physical therapy (DPT)

Massachusetts

■ AMERICAN INTERNATIONAL COLLEGE
Springfield, MA 01109-3189
http://www.aic.edu/

Independent, coed, comprehensive institution. *Computer facilities:* Computer purchase and lease plans are available. 175 computers available on campus for general student use. A campuswide network can be accessed from student residence rooms and from off campus. Online class registration is available. *General application contact:* Director of Graduate Admissions, 413-205-3700.

School of Arts, Education and Sciences
Programs in:
- arts, education and sciences (M Ed, MA, MS, Ed D, CAGS)
- clinical psychology (MA)
- early childhood education (M Ed, CAGS)
- education (Ed D)
- educational psychology (MA, Ed D)
- elementary education (M Ed, CAGS)
- forensic psychology (MS)
- middle/secondary education (M Ed, CAGS)
- moderate disabilities (M Ed, CAGS)
- reading (M Ed, CAGS)
- school adjustment counseling (MA, CAGS)
- school administration (M Ed, CAGS)
- school guidance counseling (MA, CAGS)
- teaching (MA)

■ ANNA MARIA COLLEGE
Paxton, MA 01612
http://www.annamaria.edu/

Independent-religious, coed, comprehensive institution. *Graduate faculty:* 18 full-time (8 women), 42 part-time/adjunct (16 women). *Computer facilities:* 63 computers available on campus for general student use. A campuswide network can be accessed from student residence rooms. Student account information available. *Graduate expenses:* Tuition: part-time $1400 per course. *General application contact:* Dennis Braun, Director, Graduate Studies and Continuing Education, 508-849-3293.

Graduate Division
Dr. Jack P. Calareso, President
Programs in:
- art and visual art (MA)
- business administration (MBA, AC)
- counseling psychology (MA)
- criminal justice (MS)
- early childhood education (M Ed)
- education (CAGS)
- elementary education (M Ed)
- emergency management (MS, Graduate Certificate)
- English language arts (M Ed)
- fire science (MA)
- justice administration (MS)
- occupational and environmental health and safety (MS)
- pastoral ministry (MA)
- public administration (MPA)
- security management (MA)
- teacher of visual art (M Ed)
- visual arts (M Ed)

■ ASSUMPTION COLLEGE
Worcester, MA 01609-1296
http://www.assumption.edu/

Independent-religious, coed, comprehensive institution. CGS member. *Graduate faculty:* 18 full-time (5 women), 44 part-time/adjunct (18 women). *Computer facilities:* Computer purchase and lease plans are available. 300 computers available on campus for general student use. A campuswide network can be accessed from student residence rooms and from off campus. Online class registration is available. *Graduate expenses:* Tuition: part-time $468 per credit hour. Required fees: $20 per semester. One-time fee: $100. *General application contact:* Adrian O. Dumas, Director of Graduate Enrollment Management and Services, 508-767-7365.

Graduate School
Dr. Mary Lou Anderson, Dean
Programs in:
- accounting (MBA)
- business administration (CAGS)
- child and family interventions (MA)
- cognitive and behavioral therapies (MA)
- finance/economics (MBA)
- general business (MBA)
- general psychology (MA)
- human resources (MBA)
- international business (MBA)
- management (MBA)
- marketing (MBA)
- nonprofit leadership (MBA)
- rehabilitation counseling (MA, CAGS)
- school counseling (MA, CAGS)
- special education (MA)

■ BENTLEY UNIVERSITY
Waltham, MA 02452-4705
http://www.bentley.edu

Independent, coed, comprehensive institution. *Graduate faculty:* 285 full-time (110 women), 199 part-time/adjunct (78 women). *Computer facilities:* Computer purchase and lease plans are available. 4,789 computers available on campus for general student use. A campuswide network can be accessed from student residence rooms and from off campus. Online class registration, grade checking, online admission, Blackboard, resume review, student employment, interlibrary loan, free software downloads for popular Microsoft titles and many academic applications are available. *Graduate expenses:* Tuition: full-time $25,200; part-time $3150 per course. Required fees: $404; $105 per year. Tuition and fees vary according to course load. *General application contact:* Sharon Hill, Assistant Dean/Director of Graduate Admissions, 781-891-2108.

McCallum Graduate School of Business

Dr. Michael J. Page, Vice President for Academic Affairs/Dean of Business
Programs in:
accountancy (PhD)
accounting (GBC)
accounting information systems (GBC)
business (GSS)
business administration (MBA)
business ethics (GBC)
data analysis (GBC)
finance (MSF)
financial planning (GBC)
fraud and forensic accounting (GBC)
human factors in information design (MSHFID)
information technology (MSIT)
marketing analytics (MSMA)
taxation (MST)

■ BOSTON COLLEGE

Chestnut Hill, MA 02467-3800
http://www.bc.edu/

Independent-religious, coed, university. CGS member. *Graduate faculty:* 679. *Computer facilities:* Computer purchase and lease plans are available. 1,000 computers available on campus for general student use. A campuswide network can be accessed from student residence rooms and from off campus. Online class registration is available. *Graduate expenses:* Tuition: part-time $1148 per credit. *General application contact:* Robert V. Howe, Associate Dean, 617-552-3265.

The Carroll School of Management

Dr. Jeffrey L. Ringuest, Associate Dean for Graduate Programs
Programs in:
accounting (MSA)
business administration (MBA)
finance (MSF, PhD)
management (MBA, MSA, MSF, PhD)
organization studies (PhD)

Graduate School of Arts and Sciences

Dr. David Quigley, Dean
Programs in:
arts and sciences (M Div, MA, MS, MST, MTS, Th M, PhD, STD, STL)
biochemistry (PhD)
biology (PhD)
classics (MA)
economics (PhD)
English (MA, PhD)
European national studies (MA)
French (MA, PhD)
geology and geophysics (MS)
Greek (MA)
history (MA, PhD)
inorganic chemistry (PhD)
Italian (MA)
Latin (MA)
linguistics (MA)
mathematics (MA)
medieval language (PhD)
medieval studies (MA)
organic chemistry (PhD)
philosophy (MA, PhD)
physical chemistry (PhD)
physics (MS, PhD)
political science (MA, PhD)
psychology (MA, PhD)
Russian and Slavic languages and literature (MA)
science education (MST)
Slavic studies (MA)
sociology (MA, PhD)
Spanish (MA, PhD)
theology (PhD)

School of Theology and Ministry

Programs in:
church leadership (MA)
divinity (M Div)
pastoral ministry (MA)
religious education (MA, PhD)
sacred theology (STD, STL)
social justice/social ministry (MA)
spiritual direction (MA)
theological studies (MTS)
theology (Th M, PhD)
youth ministry (MA)

Graduate School of Social Work

Dr. Alberto Godenzi, Dean
Program in:
social work (MSW, PhD)

Law School

John H. Garvey, Dean
Program in:
law (JD)

Lynch Graduate School of Education

Programs in:
biology (MST)
chemistry (MST)
counseling psychology (MA, PhD)
curriculum and instruction (M Ed, PhD, CAES)
developmental and educational psychology (MA, PhD)
early childhood education/teacher option (M Ed)
early childhood/specialist option (MA)
education (M Ed, MA, MAT, MST, Ed D, PhD, CAES)
educational administration (M Ed, CAES)
educational research, measurement, and evaluation (M Ed, PhD)
elementary education (M Ed)
English (MAT)
French (MAT)
geology (MST)
higher education (MA, PhD)
history (MAT)
Latin and classical humanities (MAT)
mathematics (MST)
physics (MST)
professional school administrator (Ed D)
reading specialist (M Ed, CAES)
religious education (M Ed, CAES)
secondary education (M Ed, MAT, MST)
secondary teaching (M Ed)
Spanish (MAT)
special needs: moderate disabilities (M Ed, CAES)
special needs: severe disabilities (M Ed)

William F. Connell School of Nursing

Dr. Susan Gennaro, Dean
Programs in:
adult health nursing (MS)
community health nursing (MS)
family health (MS)
forensic nursing (MS)
gerontology (MS)
maternal/child health nursing (MS)
nurse anesthesia (MS)
nursing (PhD)
palliative care (MS)
psychiatric-mental health nursing (MS)

■ BOSTON UNIVERSITY

Boston, MA 02215
http://www.bu.edu/

Independent, coed, university. CGS member. *Computer facilities:* Computer purchase and lease plans are available. 750 computers available on campus for general student use. A campuswide network can be accessed from student residence rooms and from off campus. Online class registration, research and educational networks are available. *Graduate expenses:* Tuition: full-time $36,540; part-time $1142 per credit. Required fees: $224 per semester. Tuition and fees vary according to course level, course load and program.

College of Communication

Thomas Fiedler, Dean
Programs in:
advertising (MS)
broadcast journalism (MS)
business and economics journalism (MS)
communication (MFA, MS)
communication research (MS)
communication studies (MS)
film production (MFA)
film studies (MFA)
media ventures (MS)
photojournalism (MS)
print journalism (MS)
public relations (MS)
science journalism (MS)
screenwriting (MFA)
television production (MS)

College of Engineering

Dr. Kenneth R. Lutchen, Dean
Programs in:
biomedical engineering (M Eng, MS, PhD)
computer engineering (MS, PhD)
electrical engineering (MS, PhD)
engineering (M Eng, MS, PhD)

Boston University (continued)
general engineering (MS)
materials science and engineering (MS, PhD)
mechanical engineering (MS, PhD)
photonics (MS)
systems engineering (M Eng, MS, PhD)

College of Fine Arts

Walt Meissner, Interim Dean
Programs in:
art education (MA)
collaborative piano (MM, DMA)
composition (MM, DMA)
conducting (MM, Artist Diploma, Performance Diploma)
costume design (MFA)
costume production (MFA)
directing (MFA)
fine arts (MFA, MM, DMA, Artist Diploma, Certificate, Performance Diploma)
graphic design (MFA)
historical performance (MM, DMA, Artist Diploma, Performance Diploma)
lighting design (MFA)
music education (MM, DMA)
music theory (MM)
musicology (MM)
opera performance (Certificate)
painting (MFA)
performance (MM, DMA, Artist Diploma, Performance Diploma)
scene design (MFA)
sculpture (MFA)
studio teaching (MA)
technical production (MFA, Certificate)
theatre crafts (Certificate)
theatre education (MFA)

College of Health and Rehabilitation Sciences—Sargent College

Dr. Gloria S. Waters, Dean
Programs in:
applied anatomy and physiology (MS, PhD)
audiology (PhD)
health and rehabilitation sciences (MS, MSOT, D Sc, DPT, OTD, PhD, CAGS)
nutrition (MS)
occupational therapy (MS, MSOT, OTD)
physical therapy (DPT)
rehabilitation sciences (D Sc)
speech-language pathology (MS, PhD, CAGS)

Goldman School of Dental Medicine

Dr. Jeffrey W. Hutter, Interim Dean
Programs in:
advanced general dentistry (CAGS)
dental medicine (DMD, MS, MSD, D Sc, D Sc D, PhD, CAGS)
dental public health (MS, MSD, D Sc D, CAGS)
dentistry (DMD)
endodontics (MSD, D Sc D, CAGS)
implantology (CAGS)
operative dentistry (MSD, D Sc D, CAGS)
oral and maxillofacial surgery (MSD, D Sc D, CAGS)
oral biology (MSD, D Sc, D Sc D, PhD)
orthodontics (MSD, D Sc D, CAGS)
pediatric dentistry (MSD, D Sc D, CAGS)
periodontology (MSD, D Sc D, CAGS)
prosthodontics (MSD, D Sc D, CAGS)

Graduate School of Arts and Sciences

J. Scott Whittaker, Associate Dean
Programs in:
African American studies (MA)
African studies (Certificate)
American and New England studies (PhD)
anthropology (PhD)
applied anthropology (MA)
applied linguistics (MA, PhD)
archaeological heritage management (MA)
archaeology (MA, PhD)
art history (MA, PhD)
arts and sciences (MA, MAEP, MAPE, MFA, MS, PhD, Certificate)
astronomy (MA, PhD)
bioinformatics (MS, PhD)
biology (MA, PhD)
biostatistics (MA, PhD)
cellular biophysics (PhD)
chemistry (MA, PhD)
classical studies (MA, PhD)
cognitive and neural systems (MA, PhD)
composition (MA)
computer science (MA, PhD)
creative writing (MA)
earth sciences (MA, PhD)
economic policy (MAEP)
economics (MA, PhD)
energy and environmental analysis (MA)
English (MA, PhD)
environmental remote sensing and GIs (MA)
French language and literature (MA, PhD)
geoarchaeology (MA)
geography (MA)
geography and environment (PhD)
Hispanic language and literatures (MA, PhD)
history (MA, PhD)
international relations (MA)
international relations and environmental policy (MA)
international relations and environmental policy management (MA)
international relations and international communication (MA)
mathematical finance (MA)
mathematics (MA, PhD)
molecular biology, cell biology, and biochemistry (MA, PhD)
museum studies (Certificate)
music education (MA)
music history/theory (PhD)
musicology (MA, PhD)
neuroscience (MA, PhD)
philosophy (MA, PhD)
physics (MA, PhD)
political economy (MAPE)
political science (MA, PhD)
preservation studies (MA)
psychology (MA, PhD)
religious and theological studies (MA, PhD)
sociology (MA, PhD)
sociology and social work (PhD)

Editorial Institute

Archie Burnett, Co-Director
Program in:
editorial studies (MA, PhD)

Metropolitan College

Dr. Jay Halfond, Dean
Programs in:
actuarial science (MS)
advertising (MS)
arts administration (MS, Graduate Certificate)
banking and financial management (MSM)
business continuity in emergency management (MSM)
city planning (MCP)
computer information systems (MS)
computer science (MS)
criminal justice (MCJ)
economics development and tourism management (MSAS)
electronic commerce, systems, and technology (MSAS)
financial economics (MSAS)
fundraising management (Graduate Certificate)
gastronomy (MLA)
health communication (MS)
human resource management (MSM)
innovation and technology (MSAS)
insurance management (MSM)
interdisciplinary studies (MLA)
international market management (MSM)
multinational commerce (MSAS)
project management (MSM)
telecommunications (MS)
urban affairs (MUA)

School of Education

Programs in:
administration, training, and policy studies (Ed D)
bilingual education (Ed M, CAGS)
counseling (Ed M, CAGS)
counseling psychology (Ed D)
curriculum and teaching (Ed M, MAT, Ed D, CAGS)
developmental studies (Ed M, Ed D, CAGS)
early childhood education (Ed M, Ed D, CAGS)
education (Ed M, MAT, Ed D, CAGS)
education of the deaf (Ed M, CAGS)

educational administration (Ed M)
educational media and technology (Ed M, Ed D, CAGS)
elementary education (Ed M)
English and language arts education (Ed M, CAGS)
health education (Ed M, CAGS)
human resource education (Ed M, CAGS)
international educational development (Ed M)
Latin and classical studies (MAT)
literacy and language (Ed D)
mathematics education (Ed M, MAT, Ed D, CAGS)
modern foreign language education (Ed M, MAT)
physical education and coaching (Ed M, Ed D, CAGS)
policy, planning, and administration (Ed M, CAGS)
reading education (Ed M, Ed D, CAGS)
science education (Ed M, MAT, Ed D, CAGS)
social studies education (Ed M, MAT, Ed D, CAGS)
special education (Ed M, Ed D, CAGS)
teaching of English to speakers of other languages (Ed M, CAGS)

School of Law
Maureen A. O'Rourke, Dean
Programs in:
American law (LL M)
banking (LL M)
intellectual property law (LL M)
law (JD)
taxation (LL M)

School of Management
Louis Lataif, Dean
Programs in:
accounting (DBA)
advanced accounting (Certificate)
business administration (Exec MBA, MBA, DBA, Certificate)
entrepreneurship (MBA)
finance (MBA)
health sector management (MBA)
information systems (DBA)
international management (MBA)
investment management (MSIM)
management (Exec MBA, MA, MBA, MS, MSIM, DBA, PhD, Certificate)
management policy (DBA)
marketing (MBA, DBA)
mathematical finance (MA, MS, PhD)
operations management (DBA)
organizational behavior (DBA)
public and nonprofit management (MBA)
strategy and business analysis (MBA)

School of Medicine
Dr. Karen H. Antman, Dean
Programs in:
immunology (PhD)
medicine (MD, MA, MS, PhD)

Division of Graduate Medical Sciences
Dr. Carl Franzblau, Associate Dean
Programs in:
biochemistry (MA, PhD)
cell and molecular biology (PhD)
medical sciences (MA, MS, PhD)
microbiology (MA, PhD)
molecular medicine (PhD)
pharmacology and experimental therapeutics (MA, PhD)

School of Public Health
Dr. Robert F. Meenan, Dean
Programs in:
biostatistics (MA, MPH, PhD)
environmental health (MPH, PhD)
epidemiology (M Sc, MPH, PhD)
health behavior, health promotion, and disease prevention (MPH)
health law, bioethics and human rights (MPH)
health policy and management (MPH)
health services research (M Sc, PhD)
international health (MPH, Dr PH, Certificate)
maternal and child health (MPH, Dr PH)
public health (M Sc, MA, MPH, Dr PH, PhD, Certificate)
social behavioral sciences (Dr PH)

School of Social Work
Gail Steketee, Interim Dean
Programs in:
clinical practice with groups (MSW)
clinical practice with individuals and families (MSW)
macro social work practice (MSW)
social work and sociology (PhD)

School of Theology
Dr. Ray Hart, Interim Dean
Program in:
theology (M Div, MSM, MTS, STM, D Min, Th D)

■ BRANDEIS UNIVERSITY
Waltham, MA 02454-9110
http://www.brandeis.edu/

Independent, coed, university. *Graduate faculty:* 360 full-time (138 women), 176 part-time/adjunct (86 women). *Computer facilities:* Computer purchase and lease plans are available. 104 computers available on campus for general student use. A campuswide network can be accessed from student residence rooms and from off campus. Online class registration, educational software are available. *Graduate expenses:* Tuition: full-time $36,122; part-time $4515 per course. Required fees: $294; $294 per year. Full-time tuition and fees vary according to course load, program and student level. *General application contact:* 781-736-3410.

Graduate School of Arts and Sciences
Dr. Gregory L. Freeze, Dean
Programs in:
acting (MFA)
ancient Greek and Roman studies (MA, Graduate Certificate)
anthropology (MA, PhD)
anthropology and women's and gender studies (MA)
anthropology and women's and gender studies (MA)
arts and sciences (MA, MAT, MFA, MS, PhD, Certificate, Graduate Certificate, Postbaccalaureate Certificate)
biochemistry (MS, PhD)
biophysics and structural biology (MS, PhD)
brain, body and behavior (PhD)
coexistence and conflict (MA)
cognitive neuroscience (PhD)
composition and theory (MA, MFA, PhD)
computational linguistics (MA)
cultural production (MA)
design (MFA)
English and American literature (MA, PhD)
English and women's studies (MA)
English and women's and gender studies (MA)
general psychology (MA)
genetic counseling (MS)
genetics (PhD)
global studies (MA)
history (MA, PhD)
inorganic chemistry (MS, PhD)
Jewish day school (MAT)
Jewish professional leadershipmathematics (MA, PhD, Postbaccalaureate Certificate)
microbiology (PhD)
molecular and cell biology (MS, PhD)
molecular biology (PhD)
music and women's studies (MA)
music and women's and gender studies (MA)
musicology (MA, MFA, PhD)
Near Eastern and Judaic studies (MA, PhD)
Near Eastern and Judaic studies and sociology (PhD)
Near Eastern and Judaic studies and women's studies (MA)
Near Eastern and Judaic studies and women's and gender studies (MA)
neurobiology (PhD)
neuroscience (MS, PhD)
organic chemistry (MS, PhD)
philosophy (MA)
physical chemistry (MS, PhD)
physics (MS, PhD)
politics (MA, PhD)
premedical studies (Certificate)
public education elementary (MAT)
public policy and gender studies (MA)
secondary education (English, history, biology, Bible) (MAT)
social policy and sociology (PhD)
social/developmental psychology (PhD)
sociology (MA, PhD)

Brandeis University (continued)
- sociology and women's and gender studies (MA)
- sociology and women's and gender studies (MA)
- studio art (Certificate)
- sustainable international development and women's/gender studies (MA)
- teaching of Hebrew (MAT)
- women's and gender studies (MA)

Michtom School of Computer Science
Dr. Richard Alterman, Graduate Chair
Programs in:
- computer science (MA, PhD)
- computer science and IT entrepreneurship (MA)

The Heller School for Social Policy and Management
Stuart Altman, Dean
Programs in:
- aging (MPP)
- aging services management (MBA)
- assets and inequalities (PhD)
- behavioral health (MPP)
- child, youth, and family management (MBA)
- children, youth and families (MPP, PhD)
- general social policy (MPP)
- health (MPP)
- health and behavioral health (PhD)
- health care management (MBA)
- international development (MA)
- international health policy and management (MS)
- poverty alleviation and development (MPP)
- social impact management (MBA)
- social policy and management (MBA)
- sustainable development (MA, MBA)

International Business School
Programs in:
- finance (MSF)
- international business (MBAi)
- international economics and finance (MA, PhD)
- international finance/international economics (MBAi)

Rabb School of Continuing Studies, Division of Graduate Professional Studies
Sybil P. Smith, Executive Director
Programs in:
- bioinformatics (MS, Graduate Certificate)
- information assurance (MS, Graduate Certificate)
- information technology management (MS, Graduate Certificate)
- management of projects and programs (MS, Graduate Certificate)
- software engineering (MSE, Graduate Certificate)
- virtual team management and communication (MS, Graduate Certificate)

■ BRIDGEWATER STATE COLLEGE
Bridgewater, MA 02325-0001
http://www.bridgew.edu/

State-supported, coed, comprehensive institution. CGS member. *Computer facilities:* 900 computers available on campus for general student use. A campuswide network can be accessed from student residence rooms and from off campus. Online class registration, student account information, application software are available. *General application contact:* Assistant Dean School of Graduate Studies-Enrollment Management, 508-531-2919.

School of Graduate Studies

School of Arts and Sciences
Programs in:
- art (MAT)
- arts and sciences (MA, MAT, MPA, MS, MSW)
- biological sciences (MAT)
- computer science (MS)
- criminal justice (MS)
- English (MA, MAT)
- history (MAT)
- mathematics (MAT)
- physical sciences (MAT)
- physics (MAT)
- psychology (MA)
- public administration (MPA)
- social work (MSW)

School of Business
Programs in:
- accounting and finance (MSM)
- business (MSM)
- management (MSM)

School of Education and Allied Science
Programs in:
- counseling (M Ed, CAGS)
- early childhood education (M Ed)
- education and allied science (M Ed, MAT, MS, CAGS)
- educational leadership (M Ed, CAGS)
- elementary education (M Ed)
- health promotion (M Ed)
- instructional technology (M Ed)
- physical education (MS)
- reading (M Ed, CAGS)
- secondary education (MAT)
- special education (M Ed)

■ CAMBRIDGE COLLEGE
Cambridge, MA 02138-5304
http://www.cambridgecollege.edu/

Independent, coed, comprehensive institution. *Graduate faculty:* 18 full-time (8 women), 814 part-time/adjunct (478 women). *Computer facilities:* A campuswide network can be accessed. Online class registration is available. *Graduate expenses:* Tuition: full-time $6960; part-time $435 per credit. One-time fee: $140 full-time. Tuition and fees vary according to degree level, campus/location and program. *General application contact:* Farah Favanbakhsh, Assistant Vice President of Undergraduate Admissions, 617-868-1000 Ext. 1124.

School of Education
Dr. Jo-Ann Testaverde, Acting Dean
Programs in:
- art education (M Ed)
- autism spectrum disorders (M Ed)
- behavioral management (M Ed)
- early childhood teacher (M Ed)
- education specialist: curriculum and instruction (CAGS)
- educational leadership (Ed D)
- elementary teacher (M Ed)
- English as a second language (M Ed)
- general science (M Ed)
- health/family and consumer sciences (M Ed)
- history (M Ed)
- humane education (M Ed)
- individualized (M Ed)
- information technology literacy (M Ed)
- instructional technology (M Ed)
- interdisciplinary studies (M Ed)
- library teacher (M Ed)
- literacy education (M Ed)
- mathematics (M Ed)
- mathematics education (M Ed)
- middle school mathematics and science (M Ed)
- school administration (M Ed, CAGS)
- school guidance counselor (M Ed)
- school nurse education (M Ed)
- science (M Ed)
- science education (M Ed)
- special education administrator (CAGS)
- special education/moderate disabilities (M Ed)
- teaching skills and methodologies (M Ed)
- workforce education (M Ed)

School of Management
Dr. Mary Ann Joseph, Acting Dean
Programs in:
- business negotiation and conflict resolution (M Mgt)
- general business (M Mgt)
- health care informatics (M Mgt)
- healthcare management (M Mgt)
- leadership in human organizational dynamics (M Mgt)
- non-profit and public organization management (M Mgt)
- small business development (M Mgt)
- technology management (M Mgt)

School of Psychology and Counseling
Dr. Niti Seth, Dean
Programs in:
- addiction counseling (M Ed)
- counseling psychology (M Ed)
- counseling psychology: forensic counseling (M Ed)
- marriage and family therapy (M Ed)
- mental health and addiction counseling (M Ed)
- mental health counseling (M Ed)

mental health counseling for school guidance counselors (Certificate)
mental health, addiction and school adjustment counseling (M Ed)
psychological studies (M Ed)
school adjustment counseling (M Ed)
school guidance counseling (M Ed)

■ CLARK UNIVERSITY

Worcester, MA 01610-1477

http://www.clarku.edu/

Independent, coed, university. CGS member. *Graduate faculty:* 189 full-time (80 women), 68 part-time/adjunct (27 women). *Computer facilities:* 96 computers available on campus for general student use. A campuswide network can be accessed from student residence rooms and from off campus. Online class registration, online course support are available. *Graduate expenses:* Tuition: full-time $34,900; part-time $1091 per credit hour. Required fees: $30. *General application contact:* Denise Robertson, Graduate School Coordinator, 508-793-7676.

Graduate School
Dr. Nancy Budwig, Director
Programs in:
American history (PhD)
biology (MA, PhD)
chemistry (MA, PhD)
clinical psychology (PhD)
community development and planning (MA)
developmental psychology (PhD)
economics (PhD)
education (MA Ed)
English (MA)
environmental science and policy (MA)
geographic information science (MA)
geographic information science for development and environment (MA)
geography (PhD)
history (MA, CAGS)
holocaust history (PhD)
international development and social change (MA)
physics (MA, PhD)
social-personality psychology (PhD)

College of Professional and Continuing Education
Dr. Thomas Massey, Director
Programs in:
information technology (MIT)
liberal studies (MALA)
professional and continuing education (MALA, MIT, MPA, MSPC, CAGS, Certificate)
professional communication (MSPC)
public administration (MPA, Certificate)

Graduate School of Management
Dr. Edward Ottensmeyer, Dean
Programs in:
accounting (MBA)
finance (MBA)
global business (MBA)
health care management (MBA)
management (MBA, MSF)
management of information technology (MBA)
marketing (MBA)

■ EASTERN NAZARENE COLLEGE

Quincy, MA 02170-2999

http://www.enc.edu/

Independent-religious, coed, comprehensive institution. *Computer facilities:* 98 computers available on campus for general student use. A campuswide network can be accessed from student residence rooms and from off campus. Online class registration is available. *General application contact:* Graduate Studies Recruiter, 617-774-6703.

Adult and Graduate Studies
Program in:
marriage and family therapy (MS)

Division of Education
Programs in:
early childhood education (M Ed, Certificate)
elementary education (M Ed, Certificate)
English as a second language (M Ed, Certificate)
instructional enrichment and development (M Ed, Certificate)
middle school education (M Ed, Certificate)
moderate special needs education (M Ed, Certificate)
principal (Certificate)
program development and supervision (M Ed, Certificate)
secondary education (M Ed, Certificate)
special education administrator (Certificate)
supervisor (Certificate)
teacher of reading (M Ed, Certificate)

■ EMERSON COLLEGE

Boston, MA 02116-4624

http://www.emerson.edu/

Independent, coed, comprehensive institution. CGS member. *Graduate faculty:* 162 full-time (70 women), 242 part-time/adjunct (118 women). *Computer facilities:* Computer purchase and lease plans are available. 480 computers available on campus for general student use. A campuswide network can be accessed from student residence rooms and from off campus. Online class registration is available. *Graduate expenses:* Tuition: full-time $17,720; part-time $886 per credit. Required fees: $60 per year. One-time fee: $170. *General application contact:* Office of Graduate Admission, 617-824-8610.

Graduate Studies
Dr. Donna Schroth, Director

School of Communication
Dr. Janis Andersen, Dean
Programs in:
communication (MA, MS)
communication disorders (MS)
communication management (MA)
global marketing communication and advertising (MA)
health communication (MA)
integrated marketing communication (MA)
journalism (MA)

School of the Arts
Grafton Nunes, Dean
Programs in:
arts (MA, MFA)
creative writing (MFA)
media art (MFA)
publishing and writing (MA)
theatre education (MA)
visual and media arts (MFA)

■ EMMANUEL COLLEGE

Boston, MA 02115

http://www.emmanuel.edu/

Independent-religious, coed, comprehensive institution. *Graduate faculty:* 31 part-time/adjunct (4 women). *Computer facilities:* Computer purchase and lease plans are available. 145 computers available on campus for general student use. A campuswide network can be accessed from student residence rooms and from off campus. Online class registration, software applications are available. *Graduate expenses:* Tuition: part-time $1950 per course. *General application contact:* Enrollment Counselor, 617-735-9700.

Graduate Programs
Dr. Judith Marley, Dean, Graduate and Professional Programs
Programs in:
educational leadership (CAGS)
elementary education (MAT)
human resource management (MS, Certificate)
management (MSM)
management and leadership (Certificate)
research administration (Certificate)
school administration (M Ed)
secondary education (MAT)

■ ENDICOTT COLLEGE

Beverly, MA 01915-2096

http://www.endicott.edu/

Independent, coed, comprehensive institution. *Graduate faculty:* 19 full-time (6 women), 46 part-time/adjunct (22 women). *Computer facilities:* Computer purchase and lease plans are available. 167 computers available on campus for general student use. A campuswide network can be accessed from student residence rooms and from off campus. Online class registration is available. *Graduate expenses:* Tuition: part-time $311 per credit hour. Tuition and fees vary according to program. *General application contact:* Dr. Mary Huegel, Dean of Graduate and Professional Studies, 978-232-2084.

Endicott College (continued)

Apicius International School of Hospitality

Program in:
organizational management (M Ed)

Van Loan School of Graduate and Professional Studies

Dr. Mary Huegel, Dean of Graduate and Professional Studies

Programs in:
arts and learning (M Ed)
business administration (MBA)
computer systems technology (MSIT)
initial and professional licensure (M Ed)
integrative learning (M Ed)
Montessori early childhood education (M Ed)
organizational management (M Ed)
sport management (M Ed)

■ FITCHBURG STATE COLLEGE

Fitchburg, MA 01420-2697

http://www.fsc.edu/

State-supported, coed, comprehensive institution. *Computer facilities:* Computer purchase and lease plans are available. 150 computers available on campus for general student use. A campuswide network can be accessed from student residence rooms and from off campus. Online class registration is available. *Graduate expenses:* Tuition, state resident: full-time $3600; part-time $150 per credit. Tuition, nonresident: full-time $3600; part-time $150 per credit. Required fees: $109 per credit. *General application contact:* Director of Admissions, 978-665-3144.

Division of Graduate and Continuing Education

Catherine Canney, Dean, Graduate and Continuing Education

Programs in:
accounting (MBA)
applied communications (MS, Certificate)
arts education (M Ed)
biology and teaching biology (MA, MAT)
computer science (MS)
criminal justice (MS)
curriculum and teaching (M Ed)
early childhood education (M Ed)
educational technology (Certificate)
elementary education (M Ed)
elementary school guidance counseling (MS)
English and teaching English (secondary level) (MA, MAT, Certificate)
fine arts director (Certificate)
forensic nursing (MS, Certificate)
guided studies (M Ed)
higher education administration (CAGS)
history and teaching history (secondary level) (MA, MAT, Certificate)
human resource management (MBA)
interdisciplinary studies (CAGS)
library media (MS)
management (MBA)
marriage and family therapy (Certificate)
mental health counseling (MS)
middle school education (M Ed)
non-licensure (M Ed, CAGS)
occupational education (M Ed)
professional mentoring for teachers (Certificate)
reading specialist (M Ed)
school principal (M Ed, CAGS)
science education (M Ed)
secondary education (M Ed)
secondary school guidance counseling (MS)
supervisor director (M Ed, CAGS)
teaching students with moderate disabilities (M Ed)
teaching students with severe disabilities (M Ed)
technical and professional writing (MS)
technology education (M Ed)
technology leader (M Ed, CAGS)

■ FRAMINGHAM STATE COLLEGE

Framingham, MA 01701-9101

http://www.framingham.edu/

State-supported, coed, comprehensive institution. *Computer facilities:* Computer purchase and lease plans are available. 232 computers available on campus for general student use. A campuswide network can be accessed from student residence rooms and from off campus. Online class registration is available. *General application contact:* Dean of Graduate and Continuing Education, 508-626-4550.

Division of Graduate and Continuing Education

Programs in:
art (M Ed)
business administration (MBA)
counseling psychology (MA)
curriculum and instructional technology (M Ed)
dietetics (MS)
early childhood education (M Ed)
educational leadership (MA)
elementary education (M Ed)
English (M Ed)
food science and nutrition science (MS)
health care administration (MA)
history (M Ed)
human nutrition: education and media technologies (MS)
human resource management (MA)
literacy and language (M Ed)
mathematics (M Ed)
nursing education (MSN)
nursing leadership (MSN)
public administration (MA)
Spanish (M Ed)
special education (M Ed)
teaching of English as a second language (M Ed)

■ HARVARD UNIVERSITY

Cambridge, MA 02138

http://www.harvard.edu/

Independent, coed, university. CGS member. *Graduate faculty:* 2,517. *Computer facilities:* Computer purchase and lease plans are available. 605 computers available on campus for general student use. A campuswide network can be accessed from student residence rooms and from off campus. Online class registration is available. *Graduate expenses:* Tuition: full-time $32,556. Required fees: $1426. Full-time tuition and fees vary according to program and student level. *General application contact:* Admissions Office, 617-495-1814.

Cyprus International Institute for the Environment and Public Health in Association with Harvard School of Public Health

Program in:
environmental health (MS)

Extension School

Programs in:
applied sciences (CAS)
biotechnology (ALM)
educational technologies (ALM)
educational technology (CET)
English for graduate and professional studies (DGP)
environmental management (ALM, CEM)
information technology (ALM)
journalism (ALM)
liberal arts (ALM)
management (ALM, CM)
mathematics for teaching (ALM)
museum studies (ALM)
premedical studies (Diploma)
publication and communication (CPC)

Graduate School of Arts and Sciences

Programs in:
African and African American studies (PhD)
African history (PhD)
Akkadian and Sumerian (AM, PhD)
American history (PhD)
ancient art (PhD)
ancient Near Eastern art (PhD)
ancient, medieval, early modern, and modern Europe (PhD)
anthropology and Middle Eastern studies (PhD)
Arabic (AM, PhD)
archaeology (PhD)
architecture (PhD)
Armenian (AM, PhD)
arts and sciences (AM, ME, MFS, SM, PhD)
astronomy (PhD)
astrophysics (PhD)
baroque art (PhD)
biblical history (AM, PhD)
biochemical chemistry (PhD)

biological anthropology (PhD)
biological sciences in dental medicine (PhD)
biology (PhD)
biophysics (PhD)
biostatistics (PhD)
business economics (PhD)
Byzantine art (PhD)
Byzantine Greek (PhD)
chemical biology (PhD)
chemical physics (PhD)
Chinese (PhD)
Chinese studies (AM)
classical archaeology (PhD)
classical art (PhD)
classical philology (PhD)
classical philosophy (PhD)
comparative literature (PhD)
composition (AM, PhD)
critical theory (PhD)
descriptive linguistics (PhD)
diplomatic history (PhD)
earth and planetary sciences (AM, PhD)
East Asian history (PhD)
economic and social history (PhD)
economics (PhD)
economics and Middle Eastern studies (PhD)
eighteenth-century literature (PhD)
experimental physics (PhD)
fine arts and Middle Eastern studies (PhD)
forest science (MFS)
French (AM, PhD)
German (PhD)
health policy (PhD)
Hebrew (AM, PhD)
historical linguistics (PhD)
history and Middle Eastern studies (PhD)
history of American civilization (PhD)
history of science (AM, PhD)
Indian art (PhD)
Indian philosophy (AM, PhD)
Indo-Muslim culture (AM, PhD)
information, technology and management (PhD)
Inner Asian and Altaic studies (PhD)
inorganic chemistry (PhD)
intellectual history (PhD)
Iranian (AM, PhD)
Irish (PhD)
Islamic art (PhD)
Italian (AM, PhD)
Japanese (PhD)
Japanese and Chinese art (PhD)
Japanese studies (AM)
Jewish history and literature (AM, PhD)
Korean (PhD)
Korean studies (AM)
landscape architecture (PhD)
Latin American history (PhD)
legal anthropology (AM)
literature: nineteenth-century to the present (PhD)
mathematics (PhD)
medical anthropology (AM)
medical engineering/medical physics (PhD)
medieval art (PhD)
medieval Latin (PhD)
medieval literature and language (PhD)
modern art (PhD)
modern British and American literature (PhD)
molecular and cellular biology (PhD)
Mongolian (PhD)
Mongolian studies (AM)
musicology (AM)
musicology and ethnomusicology (PhD)
Near Eastern history (PhD)
neurobiology (PhD)
oceanic history (PhD)
oral literature (PhD)
organic chemistry (PhD)
organizational behavior (PhD)
Pali (AM, PhD)
Persian (AM, PhD)
philosophy (PhD)
physical chemistry (PhD)
Polish (PhD)
political economy and government (PhD)
political science (PhD)
Portuguese (AM, PhD)
psychology (PhD)
public policy (PhD)
regional studies–Middle East (AM)
regional studies-Russia, Eastern Europe, and Central Asia (AM)
Renaissance and modern architecture (PhD)
Renaissance art (PhD)
Renaissance literature (PhD)
Russian (PhD)
Sanskrit (AM, PhD)
Scandinavian (PhD)
Semitic philology (AM, PhD)
Serbo-Croatian (PhD)
Slavic philology (PhD)
social anthropology (AM, PhD)
social change and development (AM)
social policy (PhD)
social psychology (PhD)
sociology (PhD)
Spanish (AM, PhD)
statistics (AM, PhD)
study of religion (PhD)
Syro-Palestinian archaeology (AM, PhD)
systems biology (PhD)
theoretical linguistics (PhD)
theoretical physics (PhD)
theory (AM, PhD)
Tibetan (AM, PhD)
Turkish (AM, PhD)
Ukrainian (PhD)
urban planning (PhD)
Urdu (AM, PhD)
Vietnamese (PhD)
Vietnamese studies (AM)
Welsh (PhD)

Division of Medical Sciences
Programs in:
biological chemistry and molecular pharmacology (PhD)
cell biology (PhD)
genetics (PhD)
microbiology and molecular genetics (PhD)
pathology (PhD)

School of Engineering and Applied Sciences
Cherry Murray, Dean
Programs in:
applied mathematics (ME, SM, PhD)
applied physics (ME, SM, PhD)
computer science (ME, SM, PhD)
engineering science (ME)
engineering sciences (SM, PhD)

Graduate School of Design
Programs in:
architecture (M Arch)
design (M Arch, M Des S, MAUD, MLA, MLAUD, MUP, Dr DES)
design studies (M Des S)
landscape architecture (MLA)
urban planning (MUP)
urban planning and design (MAUD, MLAUD)

Graduate School of Education
Dr. Kathleen McCartney, Dean
Programs in:
arts in education (Ed M)
culture, communities and education (Ed D)
education (Ed M, Ed D)
education policy and management (Ed M)
education policy, leadership and instructional practice (Ed D)
higher education (Ed M, Ed D)
human development and education (Ed D)
human development and psychology (Ed M)
international education policy (Ed M)
language and literacy (Ed M)
learning and teaching (Ed M)
mid-career mathematics and science (teaching certificate) (Ed M)
mind brain and education (Ed M)
quantitative policy analysis in education (Ed D)
risk and prevention (Ed M)
school leadership (Ed M)
special studies (Ed M)
teaching and curriculum (teaching certificate) (Ed M)
technology innovation and education (Ed M)
urban superintendency (Ed D)

Harvard Business School
Programs in:
accounting and management (DBA)
business (MBA, DBA, PhD)
business administration (MBA)
business economics (PhD)
health policy management (PhD)
management (DBA)
marketing (DBA)
organizational behavior (PhD)
science, technology and management (PhD)
strategy (DBA)
technology and operations management (DBA)

Harvard Divinity School
William A. Graham, Dean

Harvard University (continued)
Program in:
divinity (M Div, MTS, Th M, PhD, Th D)

Harvard Medical School
Dr. Jeffrey S. Flier, Dean of the Faculty of Medicine
Program in:
medicine (MD, M Eng, SM, PhD, Sc D)

Division of Health Sciences and Technology
Programs in:
biomedical engineering (M Eng)
biomedical enterprise (SM)
biomedical informatics (SM)
health sciences and technology (MD, M Eng, SM, PhD, Sc D)
medical engineering (PhD)
medical engineering/medical physics (Sc D)
medical physics (PhD)
medical sciences (MD)
speech and hearing bioscience and technology (PhD, Sc D)

John F. Kennedy School of Government
Dr. David Ellwood, Dean
Programs in:
government (MPA, MPAID, MPP, MPPUP, PhD)
political economy and government (PhD)
public administration (MPA)
public administration/international development (MPAID)
public policy (MPP, PhD)
public policy and urban planning (MPPUP)

Law School
Programs in:
international and comparative law (JD)
law (JD, LL M, SJD)
law and business (JD)
law and government (JD)
law and social change (JD)
law, science and technology (JD)

School of Dental Medicine
Programs in:
advanced general dentistry (Certificate)
dental medicine (DMD, M Med Sc, D Med Sc, Certificate)
dental public health (Certificate)
endodontics (Certificate)
general practice residency (Certificate)
oral biology (M Med Sc, D Med Sc)
oral implantology (Certificate)
oral medicine (Certificate)
oral pathology (Certificate)
oral surgery (Certificate)
orthodontics (Certificate)
pediatric dentistry (Certificate)
periodontics (Certificate)
prosthodontics (Certificate)

School of Public Health
Dr. Julio Frenk, Dean of the Faculty
Programs in:
biological sciences in public health (PhD)
biostatistics (SM, PhD)
cancer epidemiology (SM, DPH)
cardiovascular epidemiology (SM, DPH, SD)
clinical effectiveness (MPH)
clinical epidemiology (SM, DPH, SD)
environmental health (MOH, SM, DPH, PhD, SD)
environmental/occupational epidemiology (SM, SD)
epidemiologic methods (DPH, SD)
epidemiology (SM, DPH, SD)
epidemiology of aging (SM, DPH, SD)
family and community health (MPH)
genetics and complex diseases (PhD)
global health (MPH)
global health and population (SM, DPH, SD)
health care management and policy (MPH)
health policy (PhD)
health policy and management (SM, SD)
immunology and infectious diseases (PhD, SD)
infectious diseases (SM, DPH, SD)
molecular/genetic epidemiology (DPH, SD)
neuroepidemiology (DPH, SD)
nutrition (DPH, PhD, SD)
nutritional epidemiology (DPH, SD)
occupational and environmental health (MPH)
occupational health (MOH, SM, DPH, SD)
oral and dental health epidemiology (SM, SD)
pharmacoepidemiology (SM, DPH, SD)
physiology (PhD, SD)
psychiatric epidemiology (SM, DPH)
public health (MOH, MPH, SM, DPH, PhD, SD)
public health nutrition (DPH, SD)
quantitative methods (MPH)
reproductive epidemiology (SM, SD)
society, human development and health (SM, DPH, SD)

■ LESLEY UNIVERSITY
Cambridge, MA 02138-2790
http://www.lesley.edu/

Independent, coed, comprehensive institution. CGS member. *Graduate faculty:* 84 full-time (62 women), 427 part-time/adjunct (294 women). *Computer facilities:* 175 computers available on campus for general student use. A campuswide network can be accessed from student residence rooms and from off campus. Online class registration is available. *Graduate expenses:* Tuition: full-time $13,770; part-time $765 per credit hour. Required fees: $150. Tuition and fees vary according to course load, degree level, campus/location and program. *General application contact:* Graduate Studies, 800-LESLEYU.

Graduate School of Arts and Social Sciences
Programs in:
clinical mental health counseling (MA)
counseling psychology (MA, CAGS)
creative arts in learning (CAGS)
creative writing (MFA)
ecological teaching and learning (MS)
environmental education (MS)
expressive therapies (MA, PhD, CAGS)
independent studies (CAGS)
independent study (MA)
individualized studies (MA)
integrative holistic health (MA)
intercultural relations (MA, CAGS)
interdisciplinary studies (MA)
professional counseling (MA)
school counseling (MA)
urban environmental leadership (MA)
visual arts (MFA)
women's studies (MA)

Division of Expressive Therapies
Programs in:
art (MA)
dance (MA)
expressive therapies (MA, PhD, CAGS)
music (MA)

School of Education
Programs in:
curriculum and instruction (M Ed, CAGS)
early childhood education (M Ed)
educational studies (PhD)
elementary education (M Ed)
individually designed (M Ed)
middle school education (M Ed)
moderate special needs (M Ed)
reading (M Ed, CAGS)
science in education (M Ed)
severe special needs (M Ed)
special needs (CAGS)
technology in education (M Ed, CAGS)

■ MASSACHUSETTS INSTITUTE OF TECHNOLOGY
Cambridge, MA 02139-4307
http://www.mit.edu/

Independent, coed, university. CGS member. *Graduate faculty:* 998 full-time (195 women), 11 part-time/adjunct (3 women). *Computer facilities:* Computer purchase and lease plans are available. 1,100 computers available on campus for general student use. A campuswide network can be accessed from student residence rooms and from off campus. Online class registration is available. *Graduate expenses:* Tuition: full-time $36,140; part-time $565 per unit. Required fees: $250. *General application contact:* Stuart Schmill, Dean of Admissions, 617-253-2917.

MIT Sloan School of Management
David C. Schmittlein, Dean

Program in:
- management (M Fin, MBA, MS, SM, PhD)

Operations Research Center

Program in:
- operations research (SM, PhD)

School of Architecture and Planning

Prof. Adèle Naudé Santos, Dean
Programs in:
- architecture (M Arch, PhD)
- architecture and planning (M Arch, MCP, SM, SM Arch S, SM Vis S, SMBT, SMRED, PhD)
- architecture studies (SM Arch S)
- building technology (SMBT)
- city planning (MCP)
- media arts and sciences (SM, PhD)
- media technology (SM)
- urban and regional planning (PhD)
- urban and regional studies (PhD)
- urban studies and planning (SM)
- visual studies (SM Vis S)

Center for Real Estate

Program in:
- real estate (MSRED)

School of Engineering

Prof. Subra Suresh, Dean
Programs in:
- aeronautics and astronautics (SM, PhD, Sc D, EAA)
- aerospace computational engineering (PhD, Sc D)
- air transportation systems (PhD, Sc D)
- air-breathing propulsion (PhD, Sc D)
- aircraft systems engineering (PhD, Sc D)
- applied biosciences (PhD, Sc D)
- archaeological materials (PhD, Sc D)
- autonomous systems (Sc D)
- bio- and polymeric materials (PhD, Sc D)
- bioengineering (PhD, Sc D)
- biological oceanography (PhD, Sc D)
- biomedical engineering (M Eng)
- chemical engineering (SM, PhD, Sc D)
- chemical engineering practice (SM, PhD)
- chemical oceanography (PhD, Sc D)
- civil and environmental engineering (M Eng, SM, PhD, Sc D, CE)
- civil and environmental systems (PhD, Sc D)
- civil engineering (PhD, Sc D)
- coastal engineering (PhD, Sc D)
- communications and networks (PhD, Sc D)
- computation for design and optimization (SM)
- computational and systems biology (PhD)
- computer science (PhD, Sc D, ECS)
- construction engineering and management (PhD, Sc D)
- controls (Sc D)
- electrical engineering (PhD, Sc D, EE)
- electrical engineering and computer science (M Eng, SM, PhD, Sc D)
- electronic, photonic and magnetic materials (PhD, Sc D)
- emerging, fundamental and computational studies in materials science (Sc D)
- emerging, fundamental, and computational studies in materials science (PhD)
- engineering (M Eng, SM, PhD, Sc D, CE, EAA, ECS, EE, Mat E, Mech E, Met E, NE, Naval E)
- environmental biology (PhD, Sc D)
- environmental chemistry (PhD, Sc D)
- environmental engineering (PhD, Sc D)
- environmental fluid mechanics (PhD, Sc D)
- genetic toxicology (PhD, Sc D)
- geotechnical and geoenvironmental engineering (PhD, Sc D)
- humans in aerospace (PhD, Sc D)
- hydrology (PhD, Sc D)
- information technology (PhD, Sc D)
- manufacturing (M Eng)
- materials and structures (Sc D)
- materials engineering (Mat E)
- materials science and engineering (M Eng, SM, PhD, Sc D)
- mechanical engineering (SM, PhD, Sc D, Mech E)
- metallurgical engineering (Met E)
- molecular and systems bacterial pathogenesis (PhD, Sc D)
- molecular and systems toxicology and pharmacology (PhD, Sc D)
- molecular systems toxicology (PhD, Sc D)
- naval architecture and marine engineering (SM, PhD, Sc D)
- naval engineering (Naval E)
- nuclear science and engineering (SM, PhD, Sc D, NE)
- ocean engineering (SM, PhD, Sc D)
- oceanographic engineering (SM, PhD, Sc D)
- space propulsion (PhD, Sc D)
- space systems (PhD, Sc D)
- structural and environmental materials (PhD, Sc D)
- structures and materials (PhD, Sc D)
- toxicology (SM, PhD, Sc D)
- transportation (PhD, Sc D)

Engineering Systems Division

Prof. Yossi Sheffi, Director
Programs in:
- engineering and management (SM)
- engineering systems (SM, PhD)
- logistics (M Eng)
- technology and policy (SM)
- technology, management and policy (PhD)

School of Humanities, Arts, and Social Sciences

Prof. Deborah Fitzgerald, Dean
Programs in:
- comparative media studies (SM)
- economics (SM, PhD)
- history, anthropology, and science, technology and society (PhD)
- humanities, arts, and social sciences (SM, PhD)
- linguistics (PhD)
- philosophy (PhD)
- political science (SM, PhD)
- science writing (SM)

School of Science

Prof. Marc A. Kastner, Dean
Programs in:
- atmospheric chemistry (PhD, Sc D)
- atmospheric science (SM, PhD, Sc D)
- biochemistry (PhD)
- biological chemistry (PhD, Sc D)
- biological oceanography (PhD)
- biology (PhD)
- biophysical chemistry and molecular structure (PhD)
- cell biology (PhD)
- climate physics and chemistry (PhD, Sc D)
- cognitive science (PhD)
- computational and systems biology (PhD)
- developmental biology (PhD)
- earth and planetary sciences (SM)
- genetics (PhD)
- geochemistry (PhD, Sc D)
- geology (PhD, Sc D)
- geophysics (PhD, Sc D)
- geosystems (SM)
- immunology (PhD)
- inorganic chemistry (PhD, Sc D)
- marine geology and geophysics (SM)
- mathematics (PhD)
- microbiology (PhD)
- molecular biology (PhD)
- neurobiology (PhD)
- neuroscience (PhD)
- oceanography (SM)
- organic chemistry (PhD, Sc D)
- physical chemistry (PhD, Sc D)
- physical oceanography (PhD, Sc D)
- physics (SM, PhD)
- planetary sciences (PhD, Sc D)
- science (SM, PhD, Sc D)

Whitaker College of Health Sciences and Technology

Dr. Ram Sasisekharan, Director
Programs in:
- biomedical engineering (M Eng)
- biomedical enterprise (SM)
- biomedical informatics (SM)
- health sciences and technology (MD, M Eng, SM, PhD, Sc D)
- medical engineering (PhD)
- medical engineering and medical physics (Sc D)
- medical physics (PhD)
- medical sciences (MD)
- speech and hearing bioscience and technology (PhD, Sc D)

■ NORTHEASTERN UNIVERSITY
Boston, MA 02115-5096
http://www.northeastern.edu/

Independent, coed, university. CGS member. *Computer facilities:* 1,993 computers available on campus for general student use. A campuswide network can be accessed from student residence rooms and from off campus. Online class registration is available. *General application contact:* Information Contact, 617-373-2000.

Bouvé College of Health Sciences Graduate School
Programs in:
applied behavior analysis (MS)
applied educational psychology (MS)
audiology (Au D)
biotechnology (PSM)
clinical exercise physiology (MS)
college student development and counseling (MS)
counseling psychology (MS, PhD, CAGS)
health sciences (Pharm D, MS, MS Ed, PSM, Au D, DPT, PhD, CAGS, CAS)
pharmaceutical sciences (PhD)
pharmacology (MS)
pharmacy (Pharm D)
physician assistant (MS)
school counseling (MS)
school psychology (MS, PhD, CAGS)
special needs and intensive special needs (MS Ed)
speech-language pathology (MS)
toxicology (MS)

School of Nursing
Programs in:
critical care-acute care nurse practitioner (MS, CAS)
critical care-neonatal nurse practitioner (MS, CAS)
nurse anesthesia (MS, CAGS)
nursing (MS, PhD, CAGS, CAS)
nursing administration (MS)
primary care nursing (MS, CAS)
psychiatric-mental health nursing (MS, CAS)

College of Arts and Sciences
Programs in:
analytical chemistry (PhD)
applied mathematics (MS)
arts and sciences (M Arch, MA, MAW, MPA, MS, MSOR, PMS, PSM, PhD, Certificate)
bioinformatics (PMS)
biology (MS, PhD)
biotechnology (MS)
chemistry (MS, PhD)
cinema studies (Certificate)
development administration (MPA)
economics (MA, PhD)
English (MA, PhD)
experimental psychology (MA, PhD)
health administration and policy (MPA)
history (MA)
inorganic chemistry (PhD)
law, policy, and society (MS, PhD)
marine biology (MS)
mathematics (MS, PhD)
operations research (MSOR)
organic chemistry (PhD)
physical chemistry (PhD)
physics (MS, PhD)
political science (MA)
public administration (MPA, Certificate)
public and international affairs (PhD)
public history (MA)
sociology (MA, PhD)
state and local government (MPA)
studio art (MFA)
urban studies (Certificate)
women's studies (Certificate)
world history (PhD)

School of Journalism
Program in:
journalism (MA)

College of Computer and Information Science
Programs in:
computer and information science (PhD)
computer science (MS)
health informatics (MS)
information assurance (MS)
telecommunication systems management (MS)

College of Criminal Justice
Program in:
criminal justice (MS, PhD)

College of Engineering
Programs in:
chemical engineering (MS, PhD)
civil and environmental engineering (MS, PhD)
computer engineering (PhD)
computer systems engineering (MS)
electrical engineering (MS, PhD)
energy systems (MS)
engineering (MS, PSM, PhD, Certificate)
engineering management (MS)
industrial engineering (MS, PhD)
information systems (MS, Certificate)
mechanical engineering (MS, PhD)
operations research (MS)
telecommunication systems management (MS)

Graduate School of Business Administration
Programs in:
business administration (EMBA, MBA, MSF, MST, CAGS)
finance (MSF)

Graduate School of Professional Accounting
Programs in:
professional accounting (MST, CAGS)
taxation (MST, CAGS)

School of Architecture
Program in:
architecture (M Arch)

School of Law
Program in:
law (JD)

School of Technological Entrepreneurship
Program in:
technological entrepreneurship (MS)

■ REGIS COLLEGE
Weston, MA 02493
http://www.regiscollege.edu/

Independent-religious, coed, comprehensive institution. *Computer facilities:* 201 computers available on campus for general student use. A campuswide network can be accessed from student residence rooms and from off campus. Online class registration is available. *Graduate expenses:* Tuition: part-time $676 per credit. *General application contact:* Christine Petherick, Administrative Coordinator, Planning and Enrollment, 866-438-7330.

Department of Education
Dr. Leona McCaughey-Oreszak, Program Director
Programs in:
elementary teacher (MAT)
reading (MAT)
special education (MAT)

Department of Health Product Regulation
Charles Burr, Director
Program in:
health product regulation (MS)

Department of Management and Leadership
Dr. Phillip Jutras, Director
Program in:
leadership and organizational change (MS)

Department of Organizational and Professional Communication
Dr. Joan Murray, Director
Program in:
organizational and professional communication (MS)

Program in Public Administration
Claudia Pouravelis, Director of Graduate Admission
Programs in:
nonprofit administration (Graduate Certificate)
public administration (MPA)
public policymaking (Graduate Certificate)

School of Nursing and Health Professions
Dr. Antoinette Hays, Dean

Programs in:
nurse educator (Certificate)
nurse practitioner (Certificate)
nursing (MS)

■ SALEM STATE COLLEGE
Salem, MA 01970-5353
http://www.salemstate.edu/

State-supported, coed, comprehensive institution. CGS member. *Graduate faculty:* 338 full-time (173 women), 433 part-time/adjunct (242 women). *Computer facilities:* Computer purchase and lease plans are available. 426 computers available on campus for general student use. A campuswide network can be accessed from student residence rooms and from off campus. Online class registration is available. *General application contact:* Dr. Marc Glasser, Dean of the Graduate School, 978-542-6323.

School of Graduate Studies
Dr. Marc Glasser, Dean of the School of Graduate Studies
Programs in:
advanced practice in rehabilitation (MSN)
art (MAT)
bilingual education (M Ed)
biology (MAT)
business administration (MBA)
chemistry (MAT)
counseling and psychological services (MS)
criminal justice (MS)
direct entry nursing (MSN)
early childhood education (M Ed)
educational leadership (CAGS)
elementary education (M Ed)
English (MA, MAT)
English as a second language (MAT)
field-based education (M Ed)
general science (MAT)
geo-information science (MS)
higher education in student affairs (M Ed)
history (MA, MAT)
humanities (M Ed)
innovative practices (CAGS)
library media studies (M Ed)
mathematics (MAT, MS)
middle school (MAT)
nursing (MSN)
occupational therapy (MS)
physical education 5-12 (M Ed)
physical education K-9 (M Ed)
reading (M Ed, CAGS)
reading, literacy and language (CAGS)
school business officer (M Ed)
school counseling (M Ed)
secondary education (M Ed)
social work (MSW)
Spanish (MAT)
special education (M Ed, MAT)
teaching English as a second language (MAT)
technology in education (M Ed)

■ SIMMONS COLLEGE
Boston, MA 02115
http://www.simmons.edu/

Independent, Undergraduate: women only; graduate: coed, university. CGS member. *Computer facilities:* Computer purchase and lease plans are available. 350 computers available on campus for general student use. A campuswide network can be accessed from student residence rooms and from off campus. Online class registration is available. *General application contact:* Donna M. Dolan, Registrar, 617-521-2111.

College of Arts and Sciences Graduate Studies
Dr. Diane Raymond, Dean
Programs in:
applied behavior analysis (PhD)
arts and sciences (MA, MAT, MFA, MS, MS Ed, PhD, CAGS, Ed S)
assistive technology (MS Ed, Ed S)
behavioral education (MS Ed, Ed S)
children's literature (MA)
communications management (MS)
educational leadership (MS Ed, CAGS)
elementary education (MAT, CAGS)
English (MA)
gender/cultural studies (MA)
general education (CAGS)
general purposes (MS)
health professions education (PhD)
language and literacy (MS Ed, Ed S)
middle school education (MAT, CAGS)
moderate disabilities (Ed S)
moderate special needs (MS Ed)
professional license (CAGS)
professional license: elementary (MS Ed)
professional license: middle/high (MS Ed)
secondary education (MAT, CAGS)
severe disabilities (Ed S)
severe special needs (MS Ed)
Spanish (MA)
special education (MS Ed, PhD, Ed S)
special education administration (MS Ed, PhD, Ed S)
teacher preparation (MAT, MS, MS Ed, CAGS)
teaching English as a second language (MAT, CAGS)
urban education (MS Ed, CAGS)
writing for children (MFA)

Graduate School of Library and Information Science
Dr. Michele V. Cloonan, Dean
Programs in:
history and archives managementlibrary and information science (PhD)
school library teacher (MS, Certificate)

School of Health Sciences
Dr. Gerald P. Koocher, Dean
Programs in:
didactic program in dietetics (Certificate)
health care administration (MHA, CAGS)
health professions education (PhD, CAGS)
health sciences (MHA, MS, DPT, PhD, CAGS, Certificate)
nursing practice (PhD)
nutrition (dietetic internship) (Certificate)
nutrition and health promotion (MS)
physical therapy (DPT)
primary health care nursing (MS, CAGS)
sports nutrition (Certificate)

School of Management
Dr. Deborah Merrill-Sands, Dean
Programs in:
entrepreneurship (Certificate)
management (MBA)

School of Social Work
Dr. Stefan Krug, Dean
Program in:
clinical social work (MSW, PhD)

■ SPRINGFIELD COLLEGE
Springfield, MA 01109-3797
http://www.spfldcol.edu/

Independent, coed, comprehensive institution. *Graduate faculty:* 171 full-time (75 women), 151 part-time/adjunct (75 women). *Computer facilities:* Computer purchase and lease plans are available. 95 computers available on campus for general student use. A campuswide network can be accessed from student residence rooms and from off campus. *Graduate expenses:* Tuition: full-time $9132; part-time $761 per semester hour. Required fees: $150. Tuition and fees vary according to course load. *General application contact:* Donald James Shaw, Director of Graduate Admissions, 413-748-3479.

Graduate Programs
Dr. Mary Ann Coughlin, Assistant Vice President for Academic Affairs
Programs in:
adapted physical education (M Ed, MPE, MS)
advanced level coaching (M Ed, MPE, MS)
alcohol rehabilitation/substance abuse counseling (M Ed, MS)
art therapy (M Ed, MS, CAGS)
athletic administration (M Ed, MPE, MS)
athletic counseling (M Ed, MS, CAGS)
athletic training (MS)
counseling and secondary education (M Ed, MS)
deaf counseling (M Ed, MS)
developmental disabilities (M Ed, MS)
early childhood education (M Ed, MS)
education (M Ed, MS)
educational administration (M Ed, MS)
educational studies (M Ed, MS)

Springfield College (continued)
- elementary education (M Ed, MS)
- exercise physiology (MS)
- exercise science and sport studies (PhD)
- general counseling and casework (M Ed, MS)
- general physical education (PhD, CAGS)
- health care management (M Ed, MS)
- health education licensure (MPE, MS)
- health education licensure program (M Ed)
- health promotion and disease prevention (MS)
- human services (MS)
- industrial/organizational psychology (M Ed, MS, CAGS)
- marriage and family therapy (M Ed, MS, CAGS)
- mental health counseling (M Ed, MS, CAGS)
- occupational therapy (M Ed, MS, CAGS)
- physical education licensure (MPE, MS)
- physical education licensure program (M Ed)
- physical therapy (DPT)
- physician assistant (MS)
- psychiatric rehabilitation/mental health counseling (M Ed, MS)
- recreational management (M Ed, MS)
- school guidance and counseling (M Ed, MS, CAGS)
- secondary education (M Ed, MS)
- special education (M Ed, MS)
- special services (M Ed, MS)
- sport management (M Ed, MS)
- sport psychology (MS)
- student personnel in higher education (M Ed, MS, CAGS)
- teaching and administration (MS)
- therapeutic recreational management (M Ed, MS)

School of Social Work
Dr. Francine Vecchiolla, Dean
Programs in:
- advanced generalist (weekday and weekend) (MSW)
- advanced standing (MSW)

■ SUFFOLK UNIVERSITY
Boston, MA 02108-2770
http://www.suffolk.edu/

Independent, coed, comprehensive institution. *Graduate faculty:* 243 full-time (94 women), 115 part-time/adjunct (43 women). *Computer facilities:* Computer purchase and lease plans are available. 539 computers available on campus for general student use. A campuswide network can be accessed from student residence rooms and from off campus. Online class registration is available. *Graduate expenses:* Tuition: full-time $31,550; part-time $1052 per credit. Required fees: $10 per year. Tuition and fees vary according to program. *General application contact:* Judith Reynolds, Director of Graduate Admissions, 617-573-8302.

College of Arts and Sciences
Dr. Kenneth S. Greenberg, Dean
Programs in:
- administration of higher education (M Ed, CAGS)
- arts and sciences (M Ed, MA, MAC, MS, MSCJS, MSCS, MSE, MSEP, MSIE, MSPS, PhD, CAGS, Graduate Certificate)
- clinical psychology (PhD)
- communication studies (MAC)
- crime and justice studies (MSCJS)
- economic policy (MSEP)
- economics (MSE, PhD)
- ethics and public policy (MS)
- foundations of education (M Ed)
- global human resources (Graduate Certificate)
- human resource, learning and performance (MS, CAGS, Graduate Certificate)
- human resources (MS, Graduate Certificate)
- integrated marketing communication (MAC)
- international economics (MSIE)
- international relations (MSPS)
- leadership (CAGS)
- mental health counseling (MS, CAGS)
- middle school teaching (M Ed)
- organizational communication (MAC)
- organizational development (CAGS, Graduate Certificate)
- organizational learning and development (MS, Graduate Certificate)
- political science (MSPS)
- professional politics (MSPS, CAGS)
- public relations and advertising (MAC)
- school counseling (M Ed, CAGS)
- school teaching (M Ed, CAGS)
- secondary school teaching (M Ed)
- software engineering and databases (MSCS)
- women's health (MA)

Law School
Programs in:
- business law and financial services (JD)
- civil litigation (JD)
- global law and technology (LL M)
- health care and biotechnology law (JD)
- intellectual property law (JD)
- international law (JD)
- U.S. law for international business lawyers (LL M)

New England School of Art and Design
William Davis, Director
Programs in:
- graphic design (MA)
- interior design (MA)

Sawyer Business School
Dr. William J. O'Neill, Dean
Programs in:
- accounting (MBA, MSA, GDPA)
- business (EMBA, GMBA, MBA, MBAH, MHA, MPA, MSA, MSF, MSFSB, MST, APC, CASPA, CPASF, GDPA)
- business administration (APC)
- corporate financial executive track (MBA)
- entrepreneurship (MBA)
- executive business administration (EMBA)
- finance (MSF, MSFSB, CPASF)
- global business administration (GMBA)
- health administration (MBA)
- international business (MBA)
- marketing (MBA)
- nonprofit management (MPA)
- organizational behavior (MBA)
- public administration (CASPA)
- state and local government (MPA)
- strategic management (MBA)
- taxation (MBA, MST)

■ TUFTS UNIVERSITY
Medford, MA 02155
http://www.tufts.edu/

Independent, coed, university. CGS member. *Graduate faculty:* 768 full-time (300 women), 459 part-time/adjunct (217 women). *Computer facilities:* Computer purchase and lease plans are available. 300 computers available on campus for general student use. A campuswide network can be accessed from student residence rooms and from off campus. Online class registration is available. *Graduate expenses:* Tuition: full-time $36,632. Required fees: $660. Tuition and fees vary according to course level, course load, degree level, program and student level. *General application contact:* Information Contact, 617-628-5000.

Cummings School of Veterinary Medicine
Programs in:
- animals and public policy (MS)
- comparative biomedical sciences (PhD)
- veterinary medicine (DVM, MS, PhD)

Fletcher School of Law and Diplomacy
Program in:
- law and diplomacy (LL M, MA, MAHA, MALD, MIB, PhD)

The Gerald J. and Dorothy R. Friedman School of Nutrition Science and Policy
Programs in:
- humanitarian assistance (MAHA)
- nutrition (MS, PhD)

Graduate School of Arts and Sciences
Lynne Pepall, Dean
Programs in:
- analytical chemistry (MS, PhD)
- art history (MA)

arts and sciences (MA, MAT, MFA, MPP, MS, OTD, PhD, CAGS, Certificate)
bioengineering (Certificate)
biology (MS, PhD)
bioorganic chemistry (MS, PhD)
biotechnology (Certificate)
biotechnology engineering (Certificate)
child development (MA, PhD, CAGS)
classical archaeology (MA)
classics (MA)
community development (MA)
community environmental studies (Certificate)
computer science (Certificate)
computer science minor (Certificate)
dance (MA, PhD)
drama (MA)
dramatic literature and criticism (PhD)
early childhood education (MAT)
economics (MS)
education (MA, MAT, MS, PhD)
English (MA, PhD)
environmental chemistry (MS, PhD)
environmental management (Certificate)
environmental policy (MA)
epidemiology (Certificate)
ethnomusicology (MA)
French (MA)
German (MA)
health and human welfare (MA)
history (MA, PhD)
housing policy (MA)
human-computer interaction (Certificate)
inorganic chemistry (MS, PhD)
international environment/development policy (MA)
management of community organizations (Certificate)
manufacturing engineering (Certificate)
mathematics (MA, MS, PhD)
microwave and wireless engineering (Certificate)
middle and secondary education (MA, MAT)
museum studies (Certificate)
music history and literature (MA)
music theory and composition (MA)
occupational therapy (Certificate)
organic chemistry (MS, PhD)
philosophy (MA)
physical chemistry (MS, PhD)
physics (MS, PhD)
program evaluation (Certificate)
psychology (MS, PhD)
public policy (MPP)
school psychology (MA, CAGS)
secondary education (MA)
studio art (MFA)
theater history (PhD)

Sackler School of Graduate Biomedical Sciences
Programs in:
biochemistry (PhD)
biomedical sciences (MS, PhD)
cell, molecular and developmental biology (PhD)
cellular and molecular physiology (PhD)
genetics (PhD)
immunology (PhD)
integrated studies (PhD)
molecular microbiology (PhD)
neuroscience (PhD)
pharmacology and experimental therapeutics (PhD)

Division of Clinical Care Research
Program in:
clinical care research (MS, PhD)

School of Dental Medicine
Programs in:
dental medicine (DMD, MS, Certificate)
dentistry (Certificate)

School of Engineering
Linda Abriola, Dean
Programs in:
biomedical engineering (ME, MS, PhD)
chemical and biological engineering (ME, MS, PhD)
civil engineering (ME, MS, PhD)
computer science (MS, PhD)
electrical engineering (MS, PhD)
engineering (ME, MS, MSEM, PhD)
environmental engineering (ME, MS, PhD)
human factors (MS)
mechanical engineering (ME, MS, PhD)

The Gordon Institute
Robert Hannemann, Director
Program in:
engineering management (MSEM)

School of Medicine
Dr. Michael Rosenblatt, Dean
Programs in:
biomedical sciences (MS)
health communication (MS)
medicine (MD, MPH, MS)
pain research, education and policy (MS)
public health (MPH)

■ UNIVERSITY OF MASSACHUSETTS AMHERST

Amherst, MA 01003
http://www.umass.edu/

State-supported, coed, university. CGS member. *Graduate faculty:* 1,247 full-time (410 women). *Computer facilities:* 450 computers available on campus for general student use. A campuswide network can be accessed from student residence rooms and from off campus. Online class registration, online housing assignments, bill payment, Learning Management System, file storage, web hosting, blogs are available. *Graduate expenses:* Tuition, state resident: full-time $2640. Tuition, nonresident: full-time $9936. One-time fee: $332 full-time. Tuition and fees vary according to course load. *General application contact:* Jean M. Ames, Supervisor of Admissions, 413-545-0722.

Graduate School
Dr. John R. Mullin, Dean
Programs in:
biological chemistry and molecular biophysics (PhD)
biomedicine (PhD)
cellular and developmental biology (PhD)
civil engineering and business administrationenvironmental engineering and business administrationinterdisciplinary studies (MS, PhD)
marine science and technology (MS)
mechanical engineering and business administrationneuroscience and behavior (MS, PhD)
organismic and evolutionary biology (MS, PhD)
plant biology (MS, PhD)

College of Engineering
Dr. Michael Malone, Dean
Programs in:
chemical engineering (MS, PhD)
civil engineering (MS, PhD)
electrical and computer engineering (MS, PhD)
engineering (MS, PhD)
environmental engineering (MS)
industrial engineering and operations research (MS, PhD)
mechanical engineering (MS, PhD)

College of Humanities and Fine Arts
Dr. Joel W. Martin, Dean
Programs in:
Afro-American studies (MA, PhD)
ancient history (MA)
architecture (M Arch, MS)
architecture and design (M Arch)
art (MA, MFA)
art history (MA)
Asian languages and literatures (MA)
British Empire history (MA)
Chinese (MA)
comparative literature (MA, PhD)
creative writing (MFA)
English and American literature (MA, PhD)
European (medieval and modern) history (MA, PhD)
French (MA, MAT)
French and Francophone studies (MA, MAT)
German and Scandinavian studies (MA, PhD)
Hispanic literatures, cultures and linguistics (MA, MAT, PhD)
historic preservation (MS)
humanities and fine arts (M Arch, MA, MAT, MFA, MM, MS, PhD)
interior design (MS)
Islamic history (MA)
Italian studies (MAT)
Japanese (MA)
Latin American history (MA, PhD)
Latin and classical humanities (MAT)
linguistics (MA, PhD)
modern global history (MA)
music (MM, PhD)
philosophy (MA, PhD)

University of Massachusetts Amherst (continued)

public history (MA)
science and technology history (MA)
teaching Spanish (MAT)
theater (MFA)
U.S. history (MA, PhD)

College of Natural Resources and the Environment
Dr. Steven D. Goodwin, Dean
Programs in:
entomology (MS, PhD)
food science (MS, PhD)
forest resources (MS, PhD)
landscape architecture (MLA)
mammalian and avian biology (MS, PhD)
microbiology (MS, PhD)
natural resources and the environment (MLA, MRP, MS, PhD)
plant and soil sciences (MS, PhD)
regional planning (MRP, PhD)
resource economics (MS, PhD)
soil science (MS)
wildlife and fisheries conservation (MS, PhD)

College of Natural Sciences and Mathematics
Dr. James F. Kurose, Dean
Programs in:
applied mathematics (MS)
astronomy (MS, PhD)
biochemistry (MS)
chemistry (MS, PhD)
computer science (MS, PhD)
geography (MS)
geosciences (MS, PhD)
mathematics and statistics (MS, PhD)
natural sciences and mathematics (MS, PhD)
physics (MS, PhD)
polymer science and engineering (MS, PhD)

College of Social and Behavioral Sciences
Dr. Janet Rifkin, Dean
Programs in:
anthropology (MA, PhD)
clinical psychology (MS, PhD)
cognitive psychology (MS, PhD)
communication (MA, PhD)
developmental science (MS, PhD)
economics (MA, PhD)
labor studies (MS)
political science (MA, PhD)
psychology of peace and violence (MS, PhD)
public policy and administration (MPPA)
social and behavioral sciences (MA, MPPA, MS, PhD)
social psychology (MS, PhD)
sociology (MA, PhD)
union leadership and administration (MS)

Isenberg School of Management
Dr. D. Anthony Butterfield, Dean
Programs in:
accounting (MS)
business administration (MBA)
hospitality and tourism management (MS)
management (MBA, MS, PMBA, PhD)
sport management (MS, PhD)

School of Education
Dr. Christine B. McCormick, Dean
Programs in:
bilingual, English as a second language, and multicultural education (M Ed, CAGS)
child and family studies (Ed D, CAGS)
child study and early education (M Ed)
education (M Ed, Ed D, PhD, CAGS)
educational administration (M Ed, CAGS)
educational policy and leadership (Ed D)
elementary teacher education (M Ed, CAGS)
higher education (M Ed, CAGS)
international education (M Ed)
language, literacy and culture (Ed D)
learning, media and technology (CAGS)
mathematics, science, and learning technologies (Ed D)
policy studies in education (CAGS)
reading and writing (M Ed)
research and evaluation methods (Ed D)
school counselor education (M Ed, CAGS)
school psychology (CAGS)
secondary teacher education (M Ed, CAGS)
social justice education (M Ed, Ed D, CAGS)
special education (M Ed, Ed D, CAGS)
teacher education and school improvement (Ed D)

School of Nursing
Dr. M. Christine King, Graduate Program Director
Program in:
nursing (MS, DNP, PhD)

School of Public Health and Health Sciences
Dr. C. Marjorie Aelion, Dean
Programs in:
communication disorders (MA, Au D, PhD)
kinesiology (MS, PhD)
nutrition (MPH, MS)
public health (PhD)
public health and health sciences (MA, MPH, MS, Au D, PhD)

■ UNIVERSITY OF MASSACHUSETTS BOSTON

Boston, MA 02125-3393
http://www.umb.edu/

State-supported, coed, university. CGS member. *Computer facilities:* 350 computers available on campus for general student use. A campuswide network can be accessed from off campus. Online class registration is available. *General application contact:* Graduate Admissions Coordinator, 617-287-6400.

Office of Graduate Studies

College of Liberal Arts
Programs in:
American studies (MA)
applied sociology (MA)
archival methods (MA)
bilingual education (MA)
clinical psychology (PhD)
English (MA)
English as a second language (MA)
foreign language pedagogy (MA)
historical archaeology (MA)
history (MA)
liberal arts (MA, PhD)

College of Management
Programs in:
business administration (MBA)
management (MBA)

College of Nursing and Health Sciences
Program in:
nursing (MS, PhD)

College of Public and Community Service
Programs in:
dispute resolution (MA, Certificate)
human services (MS)
public and community service (MA, MS, Certificate)

College of Science and Mathematics
Programs in:
applied physics (MS)
biology (MS)
biotechnology and biomedical science (MS)
chemistry (MS)
computer science (MS, PhD)
environmental biology (PhD)
environmental sciences (MS)
environmental, earth and ocean sciences (PhD)
molecular, cellular and organismal biology (PhD)
science and mathematics (MS, PhD)

Division of Continuing Education
Programs in:
continuing education (Certificate)
women in politics and government (Certificate)

Graduate College of Education
Programs in:
critical and creative thinking (MA, Certificate)
education (M Ed, Ed D)
educational administration (M Ed, CAGS)
elementary and secondary education/certification (M Ed)
family therapy (M Ed, CAGS)
forensic counseling (M Ed, CAGS)
higher education administration (Ed D)
instructional design (M Ed)
mental health counseling (M Ed, CAGS)
rehabilitation counseling (M Ed, CAGS)
school guidance counseling (M Ed, CAGS)

school psychology (M Ed, CAGS)
special education (M Ed)
teacher certification (M Ed)
urban school leadership (Ed D)

John W. McCormack Graduate School of Policy Studies
Programs in:
gerontology (MA, MS, PhD, Certificate)
gerontology research (MA)
management in aging services (MA)
public affairs (MS)
public policy (PhD)
women in politics and government (Certificate)

■ UNIVERSITY OF MASSACHUSETTS DARTMOUTH

North Dartmouth, MA 02747-2300

http://www.umassd.edu/

State-supported, coed, university. *Graduate faculty:* 279 full-time (104 women), 156 part-time/adjunct (80 women). *Computer facilities:* 368 computers available on campus for general student use. A campuswide network can be accessed from student residence rooms and from off campus. Online class registration is available. *Graduate expenses:* Tuition, state resident: full-time $2071; part-time $86.29 per credit. Tuition, nonresident: full-time $8099; part-time $337.46 per credit. Required fees: $7946. Tuition and fees vary according to class time, course load and reciprocity agreements. *General application contact:* Elan Turcotte-Shamski, Graduate Admissions Officer, 508-999-8604.

Graduate School

Scott Webster, Director for Graduate Studies and Admissions
Program in:
biomedical engineering and biotechnology (PhD)

Charlton College of Business
Dr. Dan Braha, Assistant Dean
Programs in:
accounting (Postbaccalaureate Certificate)
business (MBA, PMC, Postbaccalaureate Certificate)
business administration (MBA)
e-commerce (PMC)
finance (PMC)
general management (PMC)
leadership (PMC)
management (Postbaccalaureate Certificate)
marketing (PMC)
supply chain management (PMC)

College of Arts and Sciences
Dr. William Hogan, Dean
Programs in:
arts and sciences (MA, MS, PhD, PMC, Postbaccalaureate Certificate)
behavior analyst (PMC)
biology (MS)
chemistry (MS, PhD)
clinical psychology (MA)
general psychology (MA)
Luso-Afro-Brazilian studies (PhD)
marine biology (MS)
Portuguese (MA)
professional writing (MA, Postbaccalaureate Certificate)

College of Engineering
Dr. Robert Peck, Dean
Programs in:
acoustics (Postbaccalaureate Certificate)
civil and environmental engineering (MS)
communications (Postbaccalaureate Certificate)
computer engineering (MS, PhD)
computer networks and distributed systems (Postbaccalaureate Certificate)
computer science (MS)
computer systems (Postbaccalaureate Certificate)
computer systems engineering (Postbaccalaureate Certificate)
digital signal processing (Postbaccalaureate Certificate)
electrical engineering (MS, PhD)
electrical engineering systems (Postbaccalaureate Certificate)
engineering (MS, PhD, Postbaccalaureate Certificate)
mechanical engineering (MS)
physics (MS)
software development and design (Postbaccalaureate Certificate)
textile chemistry (MS)
textile technology (MS)

College of Nursing
Dr. Gail Russell, Director
Programs in:
adult health/adult nurse practitioner (MS)
adult health/advanced practice (MS)
adult nurse practitioner (PMC)
community nursing/advanced practice (MS)
individualized nursing (PMC)
nursing (PhD)

College of Visual and Performing Arts
Adrian Tio, Dean
Programs in:
art education (MAE)
ceramics (MFA, Postbaccalaureate Certificate)
digital media (MFA)
drawing (MFA)
fibers (MFA)
fibers/textiles (Postbaccalaureate Certificate)
graphic design (MFA)
illustration (MFA)
jewelry/metals (MFA, Postbaccalaureate Certificate)
painting (MFA)
photography (MFA)
printmaking (MFA)
sculpture (MFA)
typography (MFA)
visual and performing arts (MAE, MFA, Postbaccalaureate Certificate)
wood/furniture design (MFA, Postbaccalaureate Certificate)

School of Education, Public Policy, and Civic Engagement
Dr. Ismael Ramirez-Soto, Interim Dean
Programs in:
education, public policy, and civic engagement (MAT, MPP, Postbaccalaureate Certificate)
elementary education (MAT, Postbaccalaureate Certificate)
environmental policy (Postbaccalaureate Certificate)
middle school education (MAT)
principal initial licensure (Postbaccalaureate Certificate)
public policy (MPP)
secondary school education (MAT)

School of Marine Science and Technology
Dr. Avijit Gangopadhyay, Associate Dean
Program in:
marine science and technology (MS, PhD)

■ UNIVERSITY OF MASSACHUSETTS LOWELL

Lowell, MA 01854-2881

http://www.uml.edu/

State-supported, coed, university. *Computer facilities:* Computer purchase and lease plans are available. 4,000 computers available on campus for general student use. A campuswide network can be accessed from student residence rooms and from off campus. Online class registration is available. *General application contact:* Graduate Admissions Office, 978-934-2390.

College of Arts and Sciences

Programs in:
analytical chemistry (PhD)
applied mathematics (MS)
applied mechanics (PhD)
applied physics (MS, PhD)
arts and sciences (MA, MM, MS, PhD, Sc D, Graduate Certificate)
atmospheric science (MS, PhD)
biochemistry (PhD)
biological sciences (MS)
biotechnology (MS)
chemistry (MS, PhD)
community social psychology (MA)
computational mathematics (PhD)
computer science (MS, PhD, Sc D)
criminal justice and criminology (MA)
environmental studies (PhD)

University of Massachusetts Lowell (continued)

- green chemistry (PhD)
- inorganic chemistry (PhD)
- mathematics (MS)
- music education (MM)
- organic chemistry (PhD)
- physics (MS, PhD)
- polymer science (MS)
- radiological science and protection (MS)
- regional economic and social development (MA, Graduate Certificate)
- sound recording technology (MM)

College of Management

Programs in:
- business administration (MBA)
- foundations of business (Graduate Certificate)
- new venture creation (Graduate Certificate)

Graduate School of Education

Programs in:
- administration, planning, and policy (CAGS)
- curriculum and instruction (M Ed, CAGS)
- educational administration (M Ed)
- language arts and literacy (Ed D)
- leadership in schooling (Ed D)
- math and science education (Ed D)
- reading and language (M Ed, CAGS)

James B. Francis College of Engineering

Programs in:
- chemical engineering (MS Eng, D Eng, PhD)
- civil and environmental engineering (MS Eng, Certificate)
- computer engineering (MS Eng)
- elastomers (Graduate Certificate)
- electrical engineering (MS Eng, D Eng)
- energy engineering (MS Eng, D Eng, PhD)
- engineering (MS Eng, MSES, D Eng, PhD, Certificate, Graduate Certificate)
- environmental engineering (MSES, D Eng)
- environmental studies (MSES, PhD, Certificate)
- mechanical engineering (MS Eng, D Eng, PhD)
- medical plastics design and manufacturing (Graduate Certificate)
- plastics design (Graduate Certificate)
- plastics engineering (MS Eng, D Eng, PhD)
- plastics engineering fundamentals (Graduate Certificate)
- plastics materials (Graduate Certificate)
- plastics processing (Graduate Certificate)
- polymer science/plastics engineering (PhD)
- sustainable infrastructure for developing nations (Certificate)

School of Health and Environment

Programs in:
- adult psychiatric and mental health nursing (MS, Graduate Certificate)
- cleaner production and pollution prevention (MS, Sc D)
- clinical laboratory sciences (MS)
- clinical pathology (Graduate Certificate)
- environmental risk assessment (Certificate)
- epidemiology (MS, Sc D)
- ergonomics and safety (MS, Sc D)
- family health nursing (MS)
- gerontological nursing (MS, Graduate Certificate)
- geropsychiatric nursing (Graduate Certificate)
- health and environment (MS, DPT, PhD, Sc D, Certificate, Graduate Certificate)
- health management and policy (MS, Graduate Certificate)
- identification and control of ergonomic hazards (Certificate)
- job stress and healthy job redesign (Certificate)
- nursing (PhD)
- nursing education (Graduate Certificate)
- nutritional sciences (Graduate Certificate)
- occupational and environmental hygiene (MS, Sc D)
- palliative and end-of-life nursing care (Graduate Certificate)
- physical therapy (DPT)
- public health laboratory sciences (Graduate Certificate)
- radiological health physics and general work environment protection (Certificate)
- work environment policy (MS, Sc D)

■ WESTERN NEW ENGLAND COLLEGE

Springfield, MA 01119

http://www.wnec.edu/

Independent, coed, comprehensive institution. *Graduate faculty:* 61 full-time (16 women), 80 part-time/adjunct (23 women). *Computer facilities:* Computer purchase and lease plans are available. 460 computers available on campus for general student use. A campuswide network can be accessed from student residence rooms and from off campus. Online class registration is available. *General application contact:* Assistant Vice President, Graduate Studies and Continuing Education, 413-782-1517.

School of Arts and Sciences

Dr. Saeed Ghahramani, Dean

Programs in:
- arts and sciences (M Ed, MAET, MAMT, PhD)
- behavior analysis (PhD)
- elementary education (M Ed)
- English for teachers (MAET)
- mathematics for teachers (MAMT)

School of Business

Dr. Julie Siciliano, Dean

Programs in:
- accounting (MSA)
- business (MBA, MSA)
- general business (MBA)
- sport management (MBA)

School of Engineering

Dr. S. Hossein Cheraghi, Dean

Programs in:
- electrical engineering (MSE)
- engineering (MSE, MSEM)
- mechanical engineering (MSE)
- production management (MSEM)

School of Law

Programs in:
- estate planning/elder law (LL M)
- law (JD)

■ WESTFIELD STATE COLLEGE

Westfield, MA 01086

http://www.wsc.ma.edu/

State-supported, coed, comprehensive institution. *Graduate faculty:* 21 full-time (9 women), 29 part-time/adjunct (10 women). *Computer facilities:* Computer purchase and lease plans are available. 275 computers available on campus for general student use. A campuswide network can be accessed from student residence rooms and from off campus. Online class registration, online transcripts and billing information are available. *General application contact:* Michelle Janke, Admissions Coordinator, 413-572-8022.

Division of Graduate and Continuing Education

Dr. Kimberly Tobin, Dean of Graduate and Continuing Education

Programs in:
- applied behavior analysis (MA)
- criminal justice (MS)
- early childhood education (M Ed)
- elementary education (M Ed)
- English (MA)
- history (M Ed)
- mental health counseling (MA)
- occupational education (M Ed, CAGS)
- physical education (M Ed)
- reading (M Ed)
- school administration (M Ed, CAGS)
- school guidance (MA)
- secondary education (M Ed)
- special education (M Ed)
- technology for educators (M Ed)

■ WHEELOCK COLLEGE

Boston, MA 02215-4176

http://www.wheelock.edu/

Independent, coed, primarily women, comprehensive institution. *Computer facilities:* 120 computers available on campus for general student use. A campuswide network can be accessed from student residence rooms and from off campus. Online class registration is available. *General application contact:* Associate Director of Graduate Admissions, 617-879-2206.

Graduate Programs

Program in:
education (MS, MSW)

Division of Arts and Sciences
Program in:
human development (MS)

Division of Child and Family Studies
Programs in:
family studies (MS)
family support and parent education (MS)
family, culture, and society (MS)

Division of Education
Programs in:
early childhood education (MS)
education leadership (MS)
elementary education (MS)
language, literacy, and reading (MS)
teaching students with moderate disabilities (MS)

Division of Social Work
Program in:
social work (MSW)

■ WORCESTER POLYTECHNIC INSTITUTE

Worcester, MA 01609-2280
http://www.wpi.edu/

Independent, coed, university. CGS member. *Graduate faculty:* 134 full-time (27 women), 50 part-time/adjunct (8 women). *Computer facilities:* Computer purchase and lease plans are available. 500 computers available on campus for general student use. A campuswide network can be accessed from student residence rooms and from off campus. Online class registration, online course content are available. *General application contact:* Lynne Dougherty, Administrative Assistant, 508-831-5301.

Graduate Studies and Research

Programs in:
advanced computer science (Advanced Certificate)
advanced computer systems (Advanced Certificate)
applied mathematics (MS)
applied statistics (MS)
artificial intelligence (Graduate Certificate)
artificial intelligence data and knowledge (Advanced Certificate)
biochemistry (MS, PhD)
biology and biotechnology (MS)
biomedical engineering (M Eng, MS, PhD, Graduate Certificate)
bioscience administration (MS)
biotechnology (PhD)
building regulatory integration in construction management (Advanced Certificate)
chemical engineering (MS, PhD)
chemistry (MS, PhD)
civil engineering (MS, PhD)
clinical engineering (M Eng)
compilers and languages (Advanced Certificate)
computational fields (Advanced Certificate, Graduate Certificate)
computational mechanics (Advanced Certificate)
computer and communication networks (Advanced Certificate, Graduate Certificate)
computer and communications networks (MS, Graduate Certificate)
computer based support systems for construction management (Advanced Certificate)
computer science (PhD)
computer systems database design graphics (Graduate Certificate)
construction project management (MS, Graduate Certificate)
customized management (Graduate Certificate)
data and knowledge based systems (Advanced Certificate)
electrical engineering (MS, PhD)
environmental engineering (MS, Graduate Certificate)
financial mathematics (MS)
fire protection engineering (MS, PhD)
geotechnical engineering (Graduate Certificate)
image processing (Graduate Certificate)
image science (Advanced Certificate)
impact engineering (MS)
industrial mathematics (MS, Graduate Certificate)
industrial statistics (Graduate Certificate)
information security (Graduate Certificate)
information security management (Graduate Certificate)
information technology (MS)
interdisciplinary social science (PhD)
management of technology (Graduate Certificate)
manufacturing engineering (MS, PhD, Graduate Certificate)
manufacturing engineering management (MS)
marketing and technological innovation (MS)
master builder (Graduate Certificate)
master builder environmental engineering (M Eng)
materials process engineering (MS)
materials science and engineering (MS, PhD, Advanced Certificate)
materials/transportation (Graduate Certificate)
mathematical sciences (PhD)
mathematics (MME)
mechanical engineering (MS, PhD, Advanced Certificate)
operations design and leadership (MS)
physics (MS, PhD)
power systems management (MS)
robotics (MS)
social science (PhD)
software engineering (Graduate Certificate)
structural engineering (Graduate Certificate)
system dynamics (MS, Graduate Certificate)
systems engineering (MS)
systems modeling (MS)
technology (MBA)
technology marketing (Graduate Certificate)
visualization programming languages (Graduate Certificate)
waste minimization and management (Advanced Certificate)

■ WORCESTER STATE COLLEGE

Worcester, MA 01602-2597
http://www.worcester.edu/

State-supported, coed, comprehensive institution. *Graduate faculty:* 30 full-time (20 women), 19 part-time/adjunct (10 women). *Computer facilities:* Computer purchase and lease plans are available. 500 computers available on campus for general student use. A campuswide network can be accessed from student residence rooms and from off campus. Online class registration is available. *Graduate expenses:* Tuition, state resident: full-time $2700; part-time $150 per credit. Tuition, nonresident: full-time $2700; part-time $150 per credit. Required fees: $1530; $85 per credit. *General application contact:* Nicole Brown, Assistant Dean of Graduate and Continuing Education, 508-929-8787.

Graduate Studies

Dr. William H. White, Associate Vice President for Continuing Education and Outreach/Dean of the Graduate School
Programs in:
accounting (MS)
biotechnology (MS)
community health nursing (MS)
early childhood education (M Ed)
elementary education (M Ed)
English (M Ed)
health care administration (MS)
health education (M Ed)
history (M Ed)
leadership and administration (M Ed, CAGS)
middle school education (M Ed)
moderate special needs (M Ed)
non-profit management (MS)
occupational therapy (MOT)
organizational leadership (MS)
reading (M Ed, CAGS)
school psychology (M Ed, CAGS)
secondary education (M Ed)
Spanish (M Ed)
speech-language pathology (MS)

Michigan

■ ANDREWS UNIVERSITY

Berrien Springs, MI 49104

http://www.andrews.edu/

Independent-religious, coed, university. CGS member. *Graduate faculty:* 162 full-time (49 women), 20 part-time/adjunct (13 women). *Computer facilities:* Computer purchase and lease plans are available. 130 computers available on campus for general student use. A campuswide network can be accessed from student residence rooms and from off campus. Online class registration, degree audit are available. *Graduate expenses:* Tuition: full-time $18,360; part-time $765 per credit hour. Required fees: $476; $765 per credit hour. $238 per semester. Tuition and fees vary according to degree level. *General application contact:* Carolyn Hurst, Supervisor of Graduate Admission, 800-253-2874.

School of Graduate Studies

Dr. Emilio Garcia-Marenko, Interim Dean

College of Arts and Sciences

Dr. Keith Mattingly, Dean

Programs in:

- arts and sciences (M Mus, MA, MAT, MS, MSA, MSMT, MSW, Dr Sc PT, TDPT)
- biology (MAT, MS)
- clinical and laboratory sciences (MSMT)
- communication (MA)
- community services management (MSA)
- English (MA, MAT)
- history (MA, MAT)
- international development (MSA)
- international language studies (MAT)
- mathematics and physical science (MS)
- music (M Mus, MA)
- nursing (MS)
- nutrition (MS)
- physical therapy (DPT, Dr Sc PT, TDPT)
- social work (MSW)

College of Technology

Dr. Verlyn Benson, Head

Programs in:

- software engineering (MS)
- technology (MS)

Division of Architecture

Carey Carscallen, Director

Program in:

- architecture (M Arch)

School of Business

Dr. Allen Stembridge, Dean

Programs in:

- accounting, economics and finance (MBA, MSA)
- business (MBA, MSA)
- management and marketing (MBA, MSA)

School of Education

Dr. James R. Jeffery, Dean

Programs in:

- community counseling (MA)
- counseling psychology (PhD)
- curriculum and instruction (MA, Ed D, PhD, Ed S)
- education (MA, MAT, MS, Ed D, PhD, Ed S)
- educational administration and leadership (MA, Ed D, PhD, Ed S)
- educational and developmental psychology (MA, Ed D, PhD)
- educational psychology (Ed D, PhD)
- elementary education (MAT)
- leadership (MA, Ed D, PhD)
- reading (MA)
- school counseling (MA)
- school psychology (Ed S)
- secondary education (MAT)
- special education (MS)
- special education/learning disabilities (MS)
- teacher education (MAT)

Seventh-day Adventist Theological Seminary

Dr. Denis Fortin, Dean

Programs in:

- ministry (M Div, D Min)
- pastoral ministry (MA)
- religious education (MA, Ed D, PhD, Ed S)
- theology (M Th, Th D)
- youth ministry (MA)

■ AQUINAS COLLEGE

Grand Rapids, MI 49506-1799

http://www.aquinas.edu/

Independent-religious, coed, comprehensive institution. *Graduate faculty:* 38 full-time (24 women), 24 part-time/adjunct (13 women). *Computer facilities:* Computer purchase and lease plans are available. 153 computers available on campus for general student use. A campuswide network can be accessed from student residence rooms and from off campus. *Graduate expenses:* Tuition: full-time $9000; part-time $500 per credit hour. *General application contact:* Lynn Atkins-Rykert, Executive Assistant, School of Management, 616-632-2924.

School of Education

Nanette Clatterbuck, Dean

Program in:

- education (MAT, ME, MS)

School of Management

Cynthia VanGelderen, Dean

Program in:

- management (M Mgt)

■ CENTRAL MICHIGAN UNIVERSITY

Mount Pleasant, MI 48859

http://www.cmich.edu/

State-supported, coed, university. CGS member. *Graduate faculty:* 349 full-time (134 women), 52 part-time/adjunct (26 women). *Computer facilities:* Computer purchase and lease plans are available. 3,000 computers available on campus for general student use. A campuswide network can be accessed from student residence rooms and from off campus. Online class registration, Blackboard are available. *Graduate expenses:* Tuition, state resident: full-time $3717; part-time $413 per credit. Tuition, nonresident: full-time $6894; part-time $766 per credit. *General application contact:* Judith L. Prince, Director of Graduate Student Services, 989-774-1059.

Central Michigan University Off-Campus Programs

Dr. Merodie Hancock, Vice President and Executive Director

Programs in:

- acquisitions administration (MSA, Certificate)
- adult education (MA)
- community college (MA)
- education (MA)
- educational administration (Ed S)
- educational administration and community leadership (Ed D)
- general administration (MSA, Certificate)
- guidance and development (MA)
- health administration (DHA)
- health services administration (MSA, Certificate)
- human resources administration (MSA, Certificate)
- humanities (MA)
- information resource management (MSA, Certificate)
- instructional (MA)
- international administration (MSA, Certificate)
- leadership (MSA, Certificate)
- professional counseling (MA)
- public administration (MSA, Certificate)
- public management (MPA)
- SAP (MBA)
- school counseling (MA)
- school principalship (MA)
- sport administration (MA)
- state and local government (MPA)
- value-driven organization (MBA)
- vehicle design and manufacturing administration (MSA, Certificate)

College of Graduate Studies

Dr. Roger Coles, Interim Dean, College of Graduate Studies

Programs in:

- acquisitions administration (MSA, Graduate Certificate)
- general administration (MSA, Graduate Certificate)
- health services administration (MSA, Graduate Certificate)
- human resource administration (Graduate Certificate)
- human resources administration (MSA)
- information resource management (MSA, Graduate Certificate)

international administration (MSA, Graduate Certificate)
leadership (MSA)
organizational communication (MSA, Graduate Certificate)
public administration (MSA, Graduate Certificate)
recreation and park administration (MSA)
sport administration (MSA)

College of Business Administration
Dr. Michael Fields, Dean
Programs in:
accounting (MBA)
business computing (Graduate Certificate)
business economics (MBA)
business information systems (MS, Graduate Certificate)
economics (MA)
finance (MBA)
finance and law (MBA)
human resource management (MBA)
information systems (MS)
international business (MBA)
management (MBA)
management information systems (MBA)
management information systems/SAP (MBA)
marketing (MBA)
marketing and hospitality services administration (MBA)

College of Communication and Fine Arts
Dr. Salma Ghanem, Dean
Programs in:
communication and fine arts (MA, MM)
conducting (MM)
electronic media management (MA)
electronic media studies (MA)
film theory and criticism (MA)
interpersonal and public communication (MA)
media production (MA)
music composition (MM)
music education (MM)
music performance (MM)
piano pedagogy (MM)

College of Education and Human Services
Dr. Kathy Koch, Interim Dean
Programs in:
apparel product development and merchandising technology (MS)
autism (Graduate Certificate)
counseling (MA)
education and human services (MA, MS, Ed D, Ed S, Graduate Certificate)
educational leadership (MA, Ed D)
educational technology (MA)
elementary education (MA)
general educational administration (Ed S)
human development and family studies (MA)
middle level education (MA)
nutrition and dietetics (MS)
reading and literacy K-12 (MA)
recreation and park administration (MA)
school principalship (MA)
secondary education (MA)
special education (MA)
therapeutic recreation (MA)

College of Humanities and Social and Behavioral Sciences
Dr. Gary Shapiro, Dean
Programs in:
applied experimental psychology (PhD)
clinical psychology (MA, PhD)
English composition and communication (MA)
English language and literature (MA)
European history (Graduate Certificate)
experimental psychology (MS, PhD)
history (MA, PhD)
humanities (MA)
humanities and social and behavioral sciences (MA, MPA, MS, PhD, Graduate Certificate, S Psy S)
industrial and organizational psychology (MA, PhD)
modern history (Graduate Certificate)
neuroscience (MS, PhD)
political science (MA)
professional development in public administration (Graduate Certificate)
psychological services (S Psy S)
public administration (MPA, Graduate Certificate)
public management (MPA)
school psychology (PhD, S Psy S)
Spanish (MA)
state and local government (MPA)
teaching English to speakers of other languages (TESOL) (MA)
United States history (Graduate Certificate)

College of Science and Technology
Dr. Ian R. Davison, Dean
Programs in:
biology (MS)
chemistry (MS)
computer science (MS)
conservation biology (MS)
industrial management and technology (MA)
mathematics (MA, PhD)
physics (MS)
science and technology (MA, MS, PhD, Graduate Certificate)
science of advanced materials (PhD)
teaching chemistry (MA)

The Herbert H. and Grace A. Dow College of Health Professions
Dr. Chris Ingersoll, Dean
Programs in:
audiology (Au D)
health professions (MA, MS, Au D, DHA, DPT)
health sciences (DHA)
physical education (MA)
physical therapy (DPT)
physician assistant (MS)
speech-language pathology (MA)
sport education (MA)

■ CORNERSTONE UNIVERSITY

Grand Rapids, MI 49525-5897
http://www.cornerstone.edu/

Independent-religious, coed, comprehensive institution. *Computer facilities:* Computer purchase and lease plans are available. 531 computers available on campus for general student use. A campuswide network can be accessed from student residence rooms and from off campus. Online class registration is available. *General application contact:* Graduate Admissions Director, 616-222-1559.

Graduate Programs
Programs in:
business administration (MBA)
education (MA Ed)
management (MSM)
teaching English to speakers of other languages (MA, Graduate Certificate)

■ DAVENPORT UNIVERSITY

Grand Rapids, MI 49503
http://www.davenport.edu/

Independent, coed, comprehensive institution. *Computer facilities:* Computer purchase and lease plans are available. 3,647 computers available on campus for general student use. A campuswide network can be accessed from student residence rooms. Online class registration is available. *General application contact:* Program Coordinator, 616-233-2597.

Sneden Graduate School
Programs in:
accounting (MBA)
business administration (EMBA)
finance (MBA)
health care management (MBA)
human resources (MBA)
information assurance (MS)
public health (MPH)
strategic management (MBA)

■ EASTERN MICHIGAN UNIVERSITY

Ypsilanti, MI 48197
http://www.emich.edu/

State-supported, coed, comprehensive institution. CGS member. *Graduate faculty:* 705 full-time (329 women). *Computer facilities:* 1,500 computers available on campus for general student use. A campuswide network can be accessed from student residence rooms and from off campus. Online class registration is available. *Graduate expenses:* Tuition, state resident: full-time $9636; part-time $401.50 per credit hour. Tuition, nonresident: full-time $18,996; part-time $791.50 per credit hour. Required fees: $36.60 per credit hour. $43 per term. One-time fee: $88. Tuition and fees vary according to course level, course load, degree

Eastern Michigan University (continued)
level, program and reciprocity agreements.
General application contact: Graduate Admissions, 734-487-2400.

Graduate School

Dr. Deborah deLaski-Smith, Interim Dean

Academic Affairs Division

Programs in:
- individualized studies (MA, MS)
- integrated marketing communications (MS)

College of Arts and Sciences

Dr. Thomas Venner, Dean
Programs in:
- African-American studies (Graduate Certificate)
- applied economics (MA)
- applied statistics (MA)
- art (MA)
- art education (MA)
- artificial intelligence (Graduate Certificate)
- arts administration (MA)
- arts and sciences (MA, MFA, MLS, MM, MPA, MS, PhD, Graduate Certificate)
- bioinformatics (MS, Graduate Certificate)
- cell and molecular biology (MS)
- chemistry (MS)
- children's literature (MA)
- clinical behavioral psychology (MS)
- clinical psychology (MS, PhD)
- communication (MA)
- community college biology teaching (MS)
- computer science (MA, MS)
- creative writing (MA)
- criminology and criminal justice (MA)
- drama/theatre for the young (MA, MFA)
- earth science education (MS)
- ecology and organismal biology (MS)
- economics (MA)
- English linguistics (MA)
- English studies for teachers (MA)
- foreign languages (MA, Graduate Certificate)
- French (MA)
- general biology (MS)
- general science (MS)
- geographic information systems (MS, Graduate Certificate)
- geography (MA, MS)
- geography and geology (MA, MS, Graduate Certificate)
- German (MA)
- German for business (Graduate Certificate)
- GIS educator (Graduate Certificate)
- GIS professional (Graduate Certificate)
- GIS-planning (MS)
- health economics (MA)
- heritage interpretation and tourism (MS)
- Hispanic language and cultures (Graduate Certificate)
- historic preservation (MS, Graduate Certificate)
- history (MA, Graduate Certificate)
- international economics and development (MA)
- interpretation/performance studies (MA)
- Japanese business practices (Graduate Certificate)
- language and international trade (MA)
- language technology (Graduate Certificate)
- literature (MA, Graduate Certificate)
- local government management (Graduate Certificate)
- management of public healthcare services (Graduate Certificate)
- mathematics (MA)
- mathematics education (MA)
- music composition (MM)
- music education (MM)
- music pedagogy (MM)
- music performance (MM)
- physics (MS)
- physics education (MS)
- political science (MPA, Graduate Certificate)
- psychology (MS)
- public administration (MPA, Graduate Certificate)
- public budget management (Graduate Certificate)
- public land planning (Graduate Certificate)
- public management (Graduate Certificate)
- public personnel management (Graduate Certificate)
- public policy analysis (Graduate Certificate)
- schools, society and violence (MA)
- social science (MA, MLS, Graduate Certificate)
- social science and American culture (MLS)
- sociology (MA)
- sociology—family specialty (MA)
- Spanish (MA)
- state and local history (Graduate Certificate)
- studio art (MA, MFA)
- teaching English to speakers of other languages (MA, Graduate Certificate)
- teaching of writing (MA, Graduate Certificate)
- technical communications (MA, Graduate Certificate)
- theatre arts (MA)
- theatre arts-arts administration (MA)
- trade and development (MA)
- urban and regional planning (MS)
- water resources (MS, Graduate Certificate)
- women's and gender studies (MLS)
- written communication (MA, Graduate Certificate)
- written communications (MA)

College of Business

Dr. David Mielke, Dean
Programs in:
- accounting (MS)
- accounting information systems (MS)
- business (MBA, MS, MSHROD, MSIS, Graduate Certificate)
- business administration (MBA)
- e-business (MBA)
- enterprise business intelligence (MBA)
- entrepreneurship (MBA, Graduate Certificate)
- finance (MBA)
- human resources (MBA)
- human resources management and organizational development (MSHROD)
- information systems (MBA, MSIS)
- internal auditing (MBA)
- international business (MBA)
- nonprofit management (MBA)
- supply chain management (MBA)

College of Education

Dr. Vernon C. Polite, Dean
Programs in:
- autism spectrum disorders (MA)
- cognitive impairment (MA)
- college counseling (MA)
- college student personnel (MA)
- community college leadership (Graduate Certificate)
- community counseling (MA)
- counseling (MA, Graduate Certificate, Post Master's Certificate)
- culture and diversity (MA)
- curriculum and instruction (MA)
- early childhood education (MA)
- education (MA, Ed D, PhD, Graduate Certificate, Post Master's Certificate, SPA)
- educational assessment (Graduate Certificate)
- educational leadership (MA, Ed D, SPA)
- educational media and technology (MA, Graduate Certificate)
- educational psychology (MA)
- educational psychology and assessment (MA, Graduate Certificate)
- educational studies (PhD)
- elementary education (MA)
- emotional impairment (MA)
- hearing impairment (MA)
- helping interventions in a multicultural society (Graduate Certificate)
- higher education general administration (MA)
- higher education student affairs (MA)
- K-12 administration (MA)
- K-12 education (MA)
- leadership (MA, Ed D, Graduate Certificate, SPA)
- learning disabilities (MA)
- mentally impaired (MA)
- middle school education (MA)
- physical/other health impairment (MA)
- reading (MA)
- school counseling (MA)
- school counselor (MA)
- school counselor licensure (Post Master's Certificate)
- secondary school education (MA)

social foundations (MA)
special education (MA, SPA)
special education-administration and supervision (SPA)
special education-curriculum development (SPA)
speech and language pathology (MA)
visual impairment (MA)

College of Health and Human Services
Dr. Deborah deLaski-Smith, Interim Dean
Programs in:
adapted physical education (MS)
clinical research administration (MS, Graduate Certificate)
community building (Graduate Certificate)
exercise physiology (MS)
family and children's services (MSW)
gerontology (Graduate Certificate)
gerontology-dementia (Graduate Certificate)
health administration (MHA, MS, Graduate Certificate)
health and human services (MHA, MOT, MPA, MS, MSN, MSW, Graduate Certificate)
health education (MS)
health promotion and human performance (MS, Graduate Certificate)
health sciences (MHA, MOT, MS, Graduate Certificate)
human nutrition (MS)
human nutrition-coordinated program in dietetics (MS)
mental health and chemical dependency (MSW)
nonprofit management (Graduate Certificate)
nursing (MSN)
occupational therapy (MOT, MS)
orthotics (Graduate Certificate)
orthotics/prosthetics (MS)
physical education pedagogy (MS)
prosthetics (Graduate Certificate)
quality improvement in health care systems (Graduate Certificate)
services to the aging (MSW)
sports management (MS)
sports medicine-biomechanics (MS)
sports medicine-corporate adult fitness (MS)
sports medicine-exercise physiology (MS)
teaching in health care systems (MSN, Graduate Certificate)

College of Technology
Dr. Morell Boone, Dean
Programs in:
apparel, textile merchandising (MS)
CAD/CAM (MS)
career, technical and workforce education (MS)
computer aided technology (MS)
construction management (MS)
engineering management (MS)
engineering technology (MS, Graduate Certificate)
hotel and restaurant management (MS, Graduate Certificate)
information assurance (MLS, Graduate Certificate)
interdisciplinary technology (MLS)
interior design (MS)
legal administration (Graduate Certificate)
polymer technology (MS)
quality (MS, Graduate Certificate)
quality management (MS)
technology (MLS, MS, PhD, Graduate Certificate)
technology studies (MLS, MS)

■ FERRIS STATE UNIVERSITY
Big Rapids, MI 49307
http://www.ferris.edu/

State-supported, coed, comprehensive institution. CGS member. *Computer facilities:* 2,373 computers available on campus for general student use. A campuswide network can be accessed from student residence rooms and from off campus. Online class registration is available. *General application contact:* Dean Enrollment Services/Director Admissions and Records, 231-591-2100.

College of Allied Health Sciences
Program in:
allied health sciences (MS)

School of Nursing
Programs in:
nursing (MS)
nursing administration (MS)
nursing education (MS)
nursing informatics (MS)

College of Business
Programs in:
application development (MSISM)
database administration (MSISM)
e-business (MSISM)
information systems (MBA)
networking (MSISM)
quality management (MBA)
security (MSISM)

College of Education and Human Services
Program in:
education and human services (M Ed, MS, MSCTE)

School of Criminal Justice
Program in:
criminal justice administration (MS)

School of Education
Programs in:
administration (MSCTE)
curriculum and instruction (M Ed)
education technology (MSCTE)
instructor (MSCTE)
post-secondary administration (MSCTE)
training and development (MSCTE)

College of Pharmacy
Program in:
pharmacy (Pharm D)

Kendall College of Art and Design
Program in:
art and design (MFA)

Michigan College of Optometry
Program in:
optometry (OD)

■ GRAND VALLEY STATE UNIVERSITY
Allendale, MI 49401-9403
http://www.gvsu.edu/

State-supported, coed, comprehensive institution. CGS member. *Graduate faculty:* 181 full-time (81 women), 63 part-time/adjunct (31 women). *Computer facilities:* 2,600 computers available on campus for general student use. A campuswide network can be accessed from student residence rooms and from off campus. Online class registration, transcript, degree audit, credit card payments are available. *General application contact:* Tracey James-Heer, Associate Director for Graduate Recruitment, 616-331-2025.

College of Community and Public Service
George Grant, Dean
Program in:
community and public service (MHA, MPA, MS, MSW)

School of Criminal Justice
Dr. William Crawley, Director
Program in:
criminal justice (MS)

School of Public and Nonprofit Administration
Dr. Mark Hoffman, Director
Programs in:
health administration (MHA)
public and nonprofit administration (MHA, MPA)

School of Social Work
Program in:
social work (MSW)

College of Education
Dr. Elaine C. Collins, Dean
Programs in:
adult and higher education (M Ed)
college student affairs leadership (M Ed)
early childhood developmental delay (M Ed)
early childhood education (M Ed)
education (M Ed, Ed S)
educational differentiation (M Ed)
educational leadership (M Ed)
educational technology integration (M Ed)
elementary education (M Ed)

Grand Valley State University (continued)
emotional impairment (M Ed)
learning disabilities (M Ed)
middle level education (M Ed)
reading and language arts (M Ed)
school counseling (M Ed)
school library media services (M Ed)
secondary level education (M Ed)
special education administration (M Ed)
teaching English to speakers of other languages (M Ed)

College of Health Professions
Dr. Roy Olson, Dean
Programs in:
health professions (MPAS, MS, DPT)
occupational therapy (MS)
physical therapy (DPT)
physician assistant studies (MPAS)

College of Liberal Arts and Sciences
Dr. Frederick Antczak, Dean
Programs in:
biology (MS)
biomedical sciences (MHS)
biostatistics (MS)
cell and molecular biology (MS)
English (MA)
liberal arts and sciences (MA, MHS, MS)

School of Communications
Dr. Alex Nesterenko, Director
Program in:
communications (MS)

Kirkhof College of Nursing
Dr. Cynthia McCurren, Dean
Programs in:
advanced practice (MSN)
case management (MSN)
nursing administration (MSN)
nursing education (MSN)
nursing practice (DNP)

Padnos College of Engineering and Computing
Dr. Paul Plotkowski, Dean
Programs in:
engineering and computing (MS, MSE)
medical and bioinformatics (MS)

School of Computing and Information Systems
Paul Leidig, Director
Program in:
computer information systems (MS)

School of Engineering
Dr. Charles Standridge, Acting Director
Programs in:
electrical and computer engineering (MSE)
manufacturing operations (MSE)
mechanical engineering (MSE)
product design and manufacturing engineering (MSE)

Seidman College of Business
Dr. H. James Williams, Dean
Programs in:
accounting (MSA)
business (MBA, MSA, MST)
business administration (MBA)
taxation (MST)

■ LAWRENCE TECHNOLOGICAL UNIVERSITY

Southfield, MI 48075-1058

http://www.ltu.edu/

Independent, coed, university. *Graduate faculty:* 57 full-time (18 women), 91 part-time/adjunct (21 women). *Computer facilities:* Computer purchase and lease plans are available. 60 computers available on campus for general student use. A campuswide network can be accessed from student residence rooms and from off campus. Online class registration, degree audit, Blackboard, SCT Banner (student information) are available. *Graduate expenses:* Tuition: part-time $763 per credit hour. Required fees: $115 per semester. Tuition and fees vary according to course level, degree level, campus/location and program. *General application contact:* Director of Admissions, 248-204-3160.

College of Architecture and Design
Glen LeRoy, Dean
Programs in:
architecture (M Arch)
interior design (MID)

College of Arts and Sciences
Dr. Hsiao-Ping Moore, Dean
Programs in:
computer science (MS)
educational technology (MET)
science education (MSE)
technical communication (MS)

College of Engineering
Dr. Devdas Shetty, Dean
Programs in:
automotive engineering (MAE)
civil engineering (MCE)
construction engineering management (MS)
electrical and computer engineering (MS)
engineering management (ME)
manufacturing systems (MEMS, DE)
mechanical engineering (MS)
mechatronic systems engineering (MS)

College of Management
Dr. Lou DeGennaro, Dean
Programs in:
business administration (MBA, DBA)
information systems (MS)
information technology (DM)
operations management (MS)

■ MADONNA UNIVERSITY

Livonia, MI 48150-1173

http://www.madonna.edu/

Independent-religious, coed, comprehensive institution. *Computer facilities:* 179 computers available on campus for general student use. A campuswide network can be accessed from student residence rooms and from off campus. Online class registration is available. *General application contact:* Coordinator of Graduate Admissions and Records, 734-432-5667.

Department of English
Program in:
teaching English to speakers of other languages (MATESOL)

Department of Psychology
Program in:
clinical psychology (MSCP)

Program in Health Services
Program in:
health services (MSHS)

Program in Hospice
Program in:
hospice (MSH)

Program in Liberal Studies
Program in:
liberal studies (MALS)

Program in Nursing
Programs in:
adult health: chronic health conditions (MSN)
adult nurse practitioner (MSN)
nursing administration (MSN)

Program in Religious Studies
Program in:
pastoral ministry (MA)

Programs in Education
Programs in:
Catholic school leadership (MSA)
educational leadership (MSA)
learning disabilities (MAT)
literacy education (MAT)
teaching and learning (MAT)

School of Business
Programs in:
business administration (MBA)
international business (MSBA)
leadership studies (MSBA)
leadership studies in criminal justice (MSBA)
quality and operations management (MSBA)

■ MARYGROVE COLLEGE

Detroit, MI 48221-2599

http://www.marygrove.edu/

Independent-religious, coed, primarily women, comprehensive institution. *Computer facilities:* Computer purchase and lease plans are available. 115 computers available on campus for general student use. A campuswide network can be accessed from student residence rooms. *General application contact:* Director, Graduate Admissions, 313-927-1390.

Graduate Division
Programs in:
- art of teaching (MAT)
- educational leadership (MA)
- English (MA)
- Griot (M Ed)
- human resource management (MA)
- modern language translation (Certificate)
- reading and literacy (M Ed)
- Sage (M Ed)
- social justice (MA)

■ MICHIGAN STATE UNIVERSITY
East Lansing, MI 48824
http://www.msu.edu/

State-supported, coed, university. CGS member. *Graduate faculty:* 1,992 full-time (638 women), 18 part-time/adjunct (6 women). *Computer facilities:* Computer purchase and lease plans are available. 2,100 computers available on campus for general student use. A campuswide network can be accessed from student residence rooms and from off campus. Online class registration is available. *Graduate expenses:* Tuition, state resident: part-time $434 per credit hour. Tuition, nonresident: part-time $892.75 per credit hour. Required fees: $312 per term. *General application contact:* Dr. Karen Klomparens, Dean of the Graduate School and Associate Provost for Graduate Education, 517-355-0301.

College of Human Medicine
Dr. Marsha D. Rappley, Dean
Programs in:
- biochemistry and molecular biology (MS, PhD)
- epidemiology (MS, PhD)
- human medicine (MD, MPH, MS, PhD)
- human medicine/medical scientist training program (MD)
- microbiology (MS)
- microbiology and molecular genetics (PhD)
- pharmacology and toxicology (MS, PhD)
- physiology (MS, PhD)
- public health (MPH)

College of Osteopathic Medicine
Dr. William D. Strampel, Dean
Programs in:
- biochemistry and molecular biology (MS, PhD)
- integrative pharmacology (MS)
- microbiology (MS)
- microbiology and molecular genetics (PhD)
- osteopathic medicine (DO, MS, PhD)
- pharmacology and toxicology (MS, PhD)
- pharmacology and toxicology-environmental toxicology (PhD)
- physiology (MS, PhD)

College of Veterinary Medicine
Dr. Christopher M. Brown, Dean
Programs in:
- animal science–environmental toxicology (PhD)
- biochemistry and molecular biology–environmental toxicology (PhD)
- chemistry–environmental toxicology (PhD)
- comparative medicine and integrative biology (MS, PhD)
- comparative medicine and integrative biology–environmental toxicology (PhD)
- crop and soil sciences–environmental toxicology (PhD)
- environmental engineering–environmental toxicology (PhD)
- environmental geosciences–environmental toxicology (PhD)
- fisheries and wildlife–environmental toxicology (PhD)
- food safety (MS)
- food safety and toxicology (MS)
- food science–environmental toxicology (PhD)
- forestry–environmental toxicology (PhD)
- genetics–environmental toxicology (PhD)
- human nutrition–environmental toxicology (PhD)
- industrial microbiology (MS, PhD)
- integrative toxicology (PhD)
- large animal clinical sciences (MS, PhD)
- microbiology (MS, PhD)
- microbiology and molecular genetics (MS, PhD)
- microbiology–environmental toxicology (PhD)
- pathobiology and diagnostic investigation (MS, PhD)
- pathology (MS, PhD)
- pathology–environmental toxicology (PhD)
- pharmacology and toxicology (MS, PhD)
- pharmacology and toxicology–environmental toxicology (PhD)
- physiology (MS, PhD)
- small animal clinical sciences (MS)
- veterinary medicine (DVM)
- veterinary medicine/medical scientist training program (DVM)
- zoology–environmental toxicology (PhD)

The Graduate School
Dr. Karen Klomparens, Dean of the Graduate School and Associate Provost for Graduate Education

College of Agriculture and Natural Resources
Dr. Jeffrey D. Armstrong, Dean
Programs in:
- agricultural economics (MS, PhD)
- agricultural, food, and resource economics (MS, PhD)
- agriculture and natural resources (MA, MIPS, MS, MURP, PhD)
- animal science (MS, PhD)
- animal science-environmental toxicology (PhD)
- biosystems engineering (MS, PhD)
- community, agriculture, recreation, and resource studies (MS, PhD)
- construction management (MS, PhD)
- crop and soil sciences (MS, PhD)
- crop and soil sciences-environmental toxicology (PhD)
- entomology (MS, PhD)
- environmental design (MA)
- fisheries and wildlife (MS, PhD)
- fisheries and wildlife—environmental toxicology (PhD)
- food science (MS, PhD)
- food science—environmental toxicology (PhD)
- forestry (MS, PhD)
- forestry-environmental toxicology (PhD)
- horticulture (MS, PhD)
- human nutrition (MS, PhD)
- human nutrition-environmental toxicology (PhD)
- integrated pest management (MS)
- interior design and facilities management (MA)
- international planning studies (MIPS)
- packaging (MS, PhD)
- plant breeding and genetics (MS, PhD)
- plant breeding and genetics-crop and soil sciences (MS)
- plant breeding, genetics and biotechnology-crop and soil sciences (PhD)
- plant breeding, genetics and biotechnology-forestry (MS, PhD)
- plant breeding, genetics and biotechnology-horticulture (MS, PhD)
- plant pathology (MS, PhD)
- urban and regional planning (MURP)

College of Arts and Letters
Dr. Karin A. Wurst, Dean
Programs in:
- African American and African studies (MA, PhD)
- American studies (MA, PhD)
- applied Spanish linguistics (MA)
- arts and letters (MA, MFA, PhD)
- critical studies in literacy and pedagogy (MA)
- digital rhetoric and professional writing (MA)
- English (PhD)
- French (MA)
- French language and literature (PhD)
- German studies (MA, PhD)
- Hispanic cultural studies (PhD)
- Hispanic literatures (MA)
- history (MA, PhD)
- history-secondary school teaching (MA)
- linguistics (MA, PhD)
- literature in English (MA)

Michigan State University (continued)
philosophy (MA, PhD)
rhetoric and writing (PhD)
second language studies (PhD)
studio art (MFA)
teaching English to speakers of other languages (MA)
theatre (MA, MFA)

College of Communication Arts and Sciences
Dr. Bradley S. Greenberg, Interim Dean
Programs in:
advertising (MA)
communication (MA, PhD)
communication arts and sciences (MA, MS, PhD)
communication arts and sciences–media and information studies (PhD)
communicative sciences and disorders (MA, PhD)
digital media arts and technology (MA)
health communication (MA)
information and telecommunication management (MA)
information, policy and society (MA)
journalism (MA)
public relations (MA)
retailing (MS, PhD)
serious game design (MA)

College of Education
Dr. Carole Ames, Dean
Programs in:
counseling (MA)
curriculum, instruction and teacher education (PhD, Ed S)
education (MA, MS, PhD, Ed S)
education for professional teachers (MA)
educational policy (PhD)
educational psychology and educational technology (PhD)
educational technology (MA)
higher, adult and lifelong education (MA, PhD)
K–12 educational administration (MA, PhD, Ed S)
kinesiology (MS, PhD)
literacy instruction (MA)
measurement and quantitative methods (PhD)
rehabilitation counseling (MA)
rehabilitation counselor education (PhD)
school psychology (MA, PhD, Ed S)
special education (MA, PhD)
student affairs administration (MA)
teaching and curriculum (MA)

College of Engineering
Dr. Satish Udpa, Dean
Programs in:
chemical engineering (MS, PhD)
civil engineering (MS, PhD)
computer science (MS, PhD)
electrical engineering (MS, PhD)
engineering (MS, PhD)
engineering mechanics (MS, PhD)
environmental engineering (MS, PhD)
environmental engineering-environmental toxicology (PhD)
materials science and engineering (MS, PhD)
mechanical engineering (MS, PhD)

College of Music
Prof. James B. Forger, Dean
Programs in:
collaborative piano (M Mus)
jazz studies (M Mus)
music (PhD)
music composition (M Mus, DMA)
music conducting (M Mus, DMA)
music education (M Mus)
music performance (M Mus, DMA)
music theory (M Mus)
music therapy (M Mus)
musicology (MA)
piano pedagogy (M Mus)

College of Natural Science
Dr. R. James Kirkpatrick, Dean
Programs in:
applied mathematics (MS, PhD)
applied statistics (MS)
astrophysics and astronomy (MS, PhD)
biochemistry and molecular biology (MS, PhD)
biochemistry and molecular biology/environmental toxicology (PhD)
biological, physical and general science for teachers (MAT, MS)
biomedical laboratory operations (MS)
cell and molecular biology (MS, PhD)
cell and molecular biology/environmental toxicology (PhD)
chemical physics (PhD)
chemistry (MS, PhD)
chemistry-environmental toxicology (PhD)
clinical laboratory sciences (MS)
computational chemistry (MS)
ecology, evolutionary biology and behavior (PhD)
environmental geosciences (MS, PhD)
environmental geosciences-environmental toxicology (PhD)
genetics (MS, PhD)
genetics–environmental toxicology (PhD)
geological sciences (MS, PhD)
industrial mathematics (MS)
mathematics (MAT, MS, PhD)
mathematics education (MS, PhD)
natural science (MAT, MS, PhD)
neuroscience (MS, PhD)
physics (MS, PhD)
physiology (MS, PhD)
plant biology (MS, PhD)
plant breeding, genetics and biotechnology—plant biology (MS, PhD)
quantitative biology (PhD)
statistics (MS, PhD)
zoo and aquarium management (MS)
zoology (MS, PhD)
zoology-environmental toxicology (PhD)

College of Nursing
Dr. Mary Mundt, Dean
Program in:
nursing (MSN, PhD)

College of Social Science
Dr. Marietta L. Baba, Dean
Programs in:
anthropology (MA, PhD)
Chicano/Latino studies (PhD)
child development (MA)
clinical social work (MSW)
community services (MS)
criminal justice (MS, PhD)
economics (MA, PhD)
family and child ecology (PhD)
family studies (MA)
forensic science (MS)
geographic information science (MS)
geography (MS, PhD)
human resources and labor relations (MLRHR)
industrial relations and human resources (PhD)
law enforcement intelligence and analysis (MS)
marriage and family therapy (MA)
organizational and community practice (MSW)
political science (MA, PhD)
professional applications in anthropology (MA)
psychology (MA, PhD)
public policy (MPP)
social science (MA, MIPS, MLRHR, MPP, MS, MSW, MURP, PhD)
social work (PhD)
sociology (MA, PhD)
youth development (MA)

Eli Broad Graduate School of Management
Dr. Elvin C. Lashbrooke, Acting Dean
Programs in:
accounting (MS)
business administration (MBA, PhD)
business research (MBA)
corporate business administration (MBA)
finance (MS)
foodservice business management (MS)
hospitality business management (MS)
integrative management (MBA)
management (MBA, MS, PhD)
marketing (MBA, PhD)
supply chain management (MS)

■ MICHIGAN TECHNOLOGICAL UNIVERSITY

Houghton, MI 49931-1295
http://www.mtu.edu/

State-supported, coed, university. CGS member. *Computer facilities:* 1,555 computers available on campus for general student use. A campuswide network can be accessed from student residence rooms and from off campus. Online class registration is available. *General application contact:* Senior Staff Assistant, 906-487-2327.

Graduate School

College of Engineering
Programs in:
biomedical engineering (PhD)

chemical engineering (MS, PhD)
civil engineering (ME, MS, PhD)
computational science and engineering (PhD)
electrical engineering (MS, PhD)
engineering (ME, MS, PhD)
engineering mechanics (MS)
environmental engineering (ME, MS, PhD)
environmental engineering science (MS)
geological engineering (MS, PhD)
geology (MS, PhD)
geophysics (MS)
materials science and engineering (MS, PhD)
mechanical engineering (MS, PhD)
mechanical engineering-engineering mechanics (PhD)
mining engineering (MS, PhD)

College of Sciences and Arts
Programs in:
applied science education (MS)
atmospheric sciences (PhD)
biological sciences (MS, PhD)
chemistry (MS, PhD)
computational science and engineering (PhD)
computer science (MS, PhD)
engineering physics (PhD)
environmental policy (MS)
industrial archaeology (MS)
industrial heritage and archeology (PhD)
mathematical sciences (MS, PhD)
physics (MS, PhD)
rhetoric and technical communication (MS, PhD)
sciences and arts (MS, PhD)

School of Business and Economics
Programs in:
applied natural resource economics (MS)
business administration (MBA)
business and economics (MBA, MS)

School of Forest Resources and Environmental Science
Programs in:
applied ecology (MS)
forest ecology and management (MS)
forest molecular genetics and biotechnology (MS, PhD)
forest resources and environmental science (MF, MS, PhD)
forest science (PhD)
forestry (MF, MS)

Sustainable Futures Institute
Program in:
sustainability (Certificate)

■ NORTHERN MICHIGAN UNIVERSITY
Marquette, MI 49855-5301
http://www.nmu.edu/

State-supported, coed, comprehensive institution. CGS member. *Computer facilities:* 9,900 computers available on campus for general student use. A campuswide network can be accessed from student residence rooms and from off campus. Online class registration is available. *General application contact:* Dean of Graduate Studies and Research, 906-227-2300.

College of Graduate Studies

College of Arts and Sciences
Programs in:
arts and sciences (MA, MFA, MPA, MS)
biology (MS)
creative writing (MFA)
literature (MA)
pedagogy (MA)
psychology (MS)
public administration (MPA)
writing (MA)

College of Professional Studies
Programs in:
administration and supervision (MA Ed, Ed S)
criminal justice (MS)
elementary education (MA Ed)
exercise science (MS)
learning disabilities (MA Ed)
literacy leadership (Ed S)
nursing (MSN)
reading (MA Ed)
reading education (MA Ed, Ed S)
reading specialist (MA Ed)
school guidance counseling (MA Ed)
science education (MS)
secondary education (MA Ed)

■ OAKLAND UNIVERSITY
Rochester, MI 48309-4401
http://www.oakland.edu/

State-supported, coed, university. CGS member. *Graduate faculty:* 225 full-time (88 women), 86 part-time/adjunct (47 women). *Computer facilities:* A campuswide network can be accessed from student residence rooms and from off campus. Online class registration is available. *General application contact:* Katherine Z. Rowley, Associate Director of Graduate Study and Lifelong Learning, 248-370-3167.

Graduate Study and Lifelong Learning
Claire K. Rammel, Executive Director

College of Arts and Sciences
Ronald A. Sudol, Dean
Programs in:
applied mathematical sciences (PhD)
applied statistics (MS)
arts and sciences (MA, MM, MPA, MS, PhD, Certificate)
biological sciences (MA, MS)
biological sciences: health and environmental chemistry (PhD)
biomedical sciences: biological communications (PhD)
chemistry (MS)
English (MA)
history (MA)
industrial applied mathematics (MS)
liberal studies (MA)
linguistics (MA)
mathematics (MA)
medical physics (PhD)
music (MM)
music education (PhD)
physics (MS)
public administration (MPA)
statistical methods (Certificate)
teaching English as a second language (Certificate)

School of Business Administration
Dr. Jonathan Silberman, Dean
Programs in:
accounting (M Acc, Certificate)
business administration (M Acc, MBA, MS, Certificate)
economics (Certificate)
entrepreneurship (Certificate)
finance (Certificate)
general management (Certificate)
human resource management (Certificate)
information technology management (MS)
international business (Certificate)
management information systems (Certificate)
marketing (Certificate)
production and operations management (Certificate)

School of Education and Human Services
Dr. Mary L. Otto, Dean
Programs in:
advanced microcomputer applications (Certificate)
counseling (MA, PhD, Certificate)
early childhood education (M Ed, PhD, Certificate)
early mathematics education (Certificate)
education and human services (M Ed, MA, MAT, MTD, PhD, Certificate, Ed S)
education studies (M Ed)
educational leadership (M Ed, PhD)
higher education (Certificate)
higher education administration (Certificate)
human resource development (MTD)
microcomputer applications (Certificate)
reading (Certificate)
reading and language arts (MAT)
reading education (PhD)
reading, language arts and literature (Certificate)
school administration (Ed S)
secondary education (MAT)
special education (M Ed, Certificate)

School of Engineering and Computer Science
Dr. Pieter A. Frick, Dean
Programs in:
computer science (MS)
electrical and computer engineering (MS)
embedded systems (MS)
engineering and computer science (MS, PhD)

Oakland University (continued)
engineering management (MS)
information systems engineering (MS)
mechanical engineering (MS, PhD)
software engineering (MS)
systems engineering (MS, PhD)

School of Health Sciences
Dr. Kenneth R. Hightower, Dean
Programs in:
complimentary medicine and wellness (Certificate)
exercise science (MS, Certificate)
health sciences (MS, MSPT, DPT, Dr Sc PT, Certificate)
neurological rehabilitation (Certificate)
orthopedic manual physical therapy (Certificate)
orthopedic physical therapy (Certificate)
pediatric rehabilitation (Certificate)
physical therapy (MSPT, DPT, Dr Sc PT)
safety management (MS)
teaching and learning for rehabilitation professionals (Certificate)

School of Nursing
Dr. Linda Thompson, Dean
Programs in:
adult gerontological nurse practitioner (MSN, Certificate)
adult health (MSN)
family nurse practitioner (MSN, Certificate)
nurse anesthetist (MSN, Certificate)
nursing (MSN, DNP, Certificate)
nursing education (MSN, Certificate)
nursing practice (DNP)

■ SAGINAW VALLEY STATE UNIVERSITY

University Center, MI 48710
http://www.svsu.edu/

State-supported, coed, comprehensive institution. *Graduate faculty:* 154 full-time (92 women), 74 part-time/adjunct (47 women). *Computer facilities:* 1,033 computers available on campus for general student use. A campuswide network can be accessed from student residence rooms and from off campus. Online class registration is available. *Graduate expenses:* Tuition, state resident: full-time $8620; part-time $359.15 per credit hour. Tuition, nonresident: full-time $16,526; part-time $688.60 per credit hour. Required fees: $350.40; $14.60 per credit hour. Tuition and fees vary according to campus/location. *General application contact:* P. Laine Blasch, Graduate Recruitment Coordinator, 989-964-2182.

College of Arts and Behavioral Sciences
Dr. Mary Hedberg, Dean
Programs in:
administrative science (MA)
arts and behavioral sciences (MA)
communication and digital media design (MA)

College of Business and Management
Dr. Marwan A. Wafa, Dean
Programs in:
business administration (MBA)
business and management (MBA)

College of Education
Dr. Steve P. Barbus, Dean
Programs in:
adapted physical activity (MAT)
chief business officers (M Ed)
e-learning (MA)
early childhood education (MAT)
education (M Ed, MA, MAT, Ed S)
education leadership (Ed S)
educational administration and supervision (M Ed)
elementary (MAT)
elementary classroom teaching (MAT)
instructional technology (MAT)
learning and behavioral disorders (MAT)
middle school (MAT)
middle school classroom teaching (MAT)
principalship (M Ed)
reading education (MAT)
secondary classroom teaching (MAT)
secondary school (MAT)
special education (MAT)
superintendency (M Ed)

Crystal M. Lange College of Nursing and Health Sciences
Dr. Janalou Blecke, Dean
Programs in:
clinical nurse specialist (MSN)
health leadership (MS)
health system nurse specialist (MSN)
nurse practitioner (MSN)
nursing (MSN)
nursing and health sciences (MS, MSN, MSOT)
occupational therapy (MSOT)

■ SIENA HEIGHTS UNIVERSITY

Adrian, MI 49221-1796
http://www.sienaheights.edu/

Independent-religious, coed, comprehensive institution. *Computer facilities:* 75 computers available on campus for general student use. A campuswide network can be accessed from student residence rooms and from off campus. Online class registration is available. *General application contact:* Dean, Graduate College, 517-264-7663.

Graduate College
Programs in:
early childhood education (MA)
educational leadership (MA)
elementary education (MA)
elementary education/reading (MA)
mathematics education (MA)
middle school education (MA)
Montessori education (MA)
secondary education (MA)
secondary education/reading (MA)

■ SPRING ARBOR UNIVERSITY

Spring Arbor, MI 49283-9799
http://www.arbor.edu/

Independent-religious, coed, comprehensive institution. *Graduate faculty:* 28 full-time (10 women), 119 part-time/adjunct (53 women). *Computer facilities:* 230 computers available on campus for general student use. A campuswide network can be accessed from student residence rooms and from off campus. Online class registration is available. *Graduate expenses:* Tuition: full-time $5280; part-time $440 per credit hour. Required fees: $240; $150. Tuition and fees vary according to program. *General application contact:* John Ball, Coordinator of Admissions, 517-750-1459.

School of Arts and Sciences
Dr. Wally Metts, Chair of the Department of Communication
Programs in:
communication (MA)
spiritual formation and leadership (MA)

School of Business and Management
Dr. James Coe, Dean, School of Business Management
Program in:
business and management (MBA)

School of Education
Dr. Linda Sherrill, Dean of Education
Programs in:
education (MAE)
special education (MSE)

School of Graduate and Professional Studies
Dr. Robert Hamill, Dean of Graduate and Professional Studies
Programs in:
counseling (MAC)
family studies (MAFS)
nursing (MSN)
organizational management (MAOM)

■ UNIVERSITY OF DETROIT MERCY

Detroit, MI 48221
http://www.udmercy.edu/

Independent-religious, coed, university. *General application contact:* Vice President, Enrollment Management, 313-993-1245.

College of Business Administration
Programs in:
business administration (EMBA, MBA, MS, MSCIS, Certificate)
business turnaround management (MS, Certificate)
computer information systems (MSCIS)
information assurance (MS)

College of Engineering and Science

Programs in:
- chemistry (MS)
- civil and environmental engineering (ME, DE)
- computer engineering (ME, DE)
- computer science (MSCS)
- computer science education (MATM)
- computer systems applications (MSCS)
- engineering and science (M Eng Mgt, MATM, ME, MS, MSCS, DE)
- engineering management (M Eng Mgt)
- mathematics education (MATM)
- mechanical engineering (ME, DE)
- mechatronics systems (ME, DE)
- signals and systems (ME, DE)
- software engineering (MSCS)

College of Health Professions

Programs in:
- family nurse practitioner (MSN, Certificate)
- health professions (MHSA, MS, MSN, Certificate)
- health services administration (MHSA)
- health systems management (MSN)
- nurse anesthesiology (MS)
- physician assistant (MS)

College of Liberal Arts and Education

Programs in:
- addiction counseling (MA)
- addiction studies (Certificate)
- clinical psychology (MA, PhD)
- community counseling (MA)
- counseling (MA)
- criminal justice (MA)
- curriculum and instruction (MA)
- educational administration (MA)
- emotionally impaired (MA)
- industrial/organizational psychology (MA)
- intelligence analysis (MS)
- learning disabilities (MA)
- liberal arts and education (MA, MALS, MS, PhD, Certificate, Spec)
- liberal studies (MALS)
- religious studies (MA)
- school counseling (MA)
- school psychology (Spec)
- security administration (MS)
- special education (MA)

School of Architecture

Program in:
- architecture (M Arch)

School of Dentistry

Programs in:
- dentistry (DDS, MS, Certificate)
- endodontics (MS, Certificate)
- orthodontics (MS, Certificate)
- periodontics (MS, Certificate)

School of Law

Program in:
- law (JD)

■ UNIVERSITY OF MICHIGAN

Ann Arbor, MI 48109
http://www.umich.edu/

State-supported, coed, university. CGS member. *Graduate faculty:* 5,290 full-time (1,851 women), 1,230 part-time/adjunct (606 women). *Computer facilities:* Computer purchase and lease plans are available. 2,254 computers available on campus for general student use. A campuswide network can be accessed from student residence rooms and from off campus. Online class registration, personal webpages are available. *Graduate expenses:* Tuition, state resident: full-time $16,162. Tuition, nonresident: full-time $32,876. Tuition and fees vary according to course level, course load, degree level, program and student level. *General application contact:* Admissions Office, 734-764-8129.

College of Pharmacy

Programs in:
- medicinal chemistry (PhD)
- pharmaceutical sciences (PhD)
- pharmacy (Pharm D, PhD)
- social and administrative sciences (PhD)

Horace H. Rackham School of Graduate Studies

Dr. Janet A. Weiss, Dean of the Graduate School and Vice President for Academic Affairs

Programs in:
- bioinformatics (MS, PhD)
- biological chemistry (PhD)
- biomedical sciences (MS, PhD)
- biophysics (PhD)
- cell and developmental biology (PhD)
- cellular and molecular biology (PhD)
- education and psychology (PhD)
- English and education (PhD)
- human genetics (MS, PhD)
- immunology (PhD)
- microbiology and immunology (PhD)
- modern Middle Eastern and North African studies (AM)
- molecular and cellular pathology (PhD)
- molecular and integrative physiology (PhD)
- neuroscience (PhD)
- pharmacology (PhD)
- survey methodology (MS, PhD, Certificate)

College of Engineering

Prof. David C. Munson, Chair

Programs in:
- aerospace engineering (M Eng, MS, MSE, PhD)
- atmospheric (MS)
- atmospheric and space sciences (PhD)
- automotive engineering (M Eng)
- biomedical engineering (MS, MSE, PhD)
- chemical engineering (MSE, PhD, Ch E)
- civil engineering (MSE, PhD, CE)
- computer science and engineering (MS, MSE, PhD)
- concurrent marine design (M Eng)
- construction engineering and management (M Eng, MSE)
- electrical engineering (MS, MSE, PhD)
- electrical engineering systems (MS, MSE, PhD)
- energy systems engineering (MESE)
- engineering (M Eng, MESE, MS, MSE, D Eng, PhD, CE, Certificate, Ch E, Mar Eng, Nav Arch, Nuc E)
- environmental engineering (MSE, PhD)
- financial engineering (MS)
- geoscience and remote sensing (PhD)
- global automotive and manufacturing engineering (M Eng)
- industrial and operations engineering (MS, MSE, PhD)
- integrated microsystems (M Eng)
- macromolecular science and engineering (MS, MSE, PhD)
- manufacturing (M Eng, D Eng)
- materials science and engineering (MS, PhD)
- mechanical engineering (MSE, PhD)
- naval architecture and marine engineering (MS, MSE, PhD, Mar Eng, Nav Arch)
- nuclear engineering (Nuc E)
- nuclear engineering and radiological sciences (MSE, PhD)
- nuclear science (MS, PhD)
- pharmaceutical engineering (M Eng)
- space and planetary sciences (PhD)
- space engineering (M Eng)
- space sciences (MS)
- structural engineering (M Eng)

College of Literature, Science, and the Arts

Dr. Terrence J. McDonald, Dean

Programs in:
- American culture (AM, PhD)
- analytical chemistry (PhD)
- ancient Israel/Hebrew Bible (AM, PhD)
- anthropology (PhD)
- anthropology and history (PhD)
- applied and interdisciplinary mathematics (AM, MS, PhD)
- applied economics (AM)
- applied physics (PhD)
- applied statistics (AM)
- Arabic (AM, PhD)
- Armenian (AM, PhD)
- Asian languages and cultures (MA, PhD)
- Asian studies: China (AM, Graduate Certificate)
- astronomy and astrophysics (PhD)
- biopsychology (PhD)
- chemical biology (PhD)
- Christianity in late antiquity (PhD)
- classical art and archaeology (PhD)
- classical studies (PhD)
- clinical psychology (PhD)
- cognition and perception (PhD)
- communication studies (PhD)
- comparative literature (PhD)
- creative writing (MFA)

University of Michigan (continued)
developmental psychology (PhD)
early Christian studies (AM, PhD)
ecology and evolutionary biology (MS, PhD)
ecology and evolutionary biology-Frontiers (MS)
economics (AM, PhD)
Egyptology (AM, PhD)
English and education (PhD)
English and women's studies (PhD)
English language and literature (PhD)
French (PhD)
general linguistics (PhD)
geology (MS, PhD)
German (AM, PhD)
Greek (AM)
Greek and Roman history (PhD, Certificate)
Hebrew (AM)
Hebrew literature (PhD)
history (PhD)
history and women's studies (PhD)
history of art (PhD)
inorganic chemistry (PhD)
Islamic studies (AM, PhD)
Japanese studies (AM)
Latin (AM)
lesbian, gay, bisexual, transgender, queer (LGBTQ)
studies (Certificate)
linguistics and Germanic languages and literatures (PhD)
literature, science, and the arts (AM, MA, MAT, MFA, MS, PhD, Certificate, Graduate Certificate)
material chemistry (PhD)
mathematics (AM, MS, PhD)
medieval and early modern studies (Certificate)
Mesopotamian and ancient Near Eastern studies (AM, PhD)
molecular, cellular, and developmental biology (MS, PhD)
oceanography: marine geology and geochemistry (MS, PhD)
organic chemistry (PhD)
Persian (AM, PhD)
personality and social contexts (PhD)
philosophy (AM, PhD)
physical chemistry (PhD)
physics (MS, PhD)
political science (AM, PhD)
psychology and women's studies (PhD)
public policy and economics (PhD)
public policy and sociology (PhD)
Rabbinic literature (PhD)
Romance linguistics (PhD)
Russian (AM)
Russian and East European studies (AM, Certificate)
screen arts and cultures (PhD, Certificate)
Slavic languages and literatures (PhD)
social psychology (PhD)
social work and economics (PhD)
social work and political science (PhD)
social work and sociology (PhD)
sociology (PhD)
sociology and women's studies (PhD)
South Asian studies (MA, Certificate)
Southeast Asian studies (MA, Graduate Certificate)
Spanish (PhD)
statistics (AM, PhD)
teaching Latin (MAT)
teaching of Arabic as a foreign language (AM)
Turkish (AM, PhD)
women's studies (Certificate)
women's studies and sociology (PhD)

Gerald R. Ford School of Public Policy
Program in:
public policy (MPA, MPP, PhD)

School of Art and Design
Bryan Rogers, Dean
Program in:
art and design (MFA)

School of Education
Deborah Loewenberg Ball, Dean
Programs in:
academic affairs and student development (PhD)
cross specialization (PhD)
curriculum development (MA)
development (AM)
early childhood education (MA, PhD)
education (AM, MA, MS, PhD)
educational administration and policy (MA, PhD)
educational foundations and policy (MA, PhD)
English education (MA)
English language learning in school settings (MA)
higher education (AM)
individually designed concentration (PhD)
learning technologies (MA, PhD)
literacy, language, and culture (MA, PhD)
mathematics education (MA, PhD)
medical and professional education (AM)
organizational behavior and management (PhD)
postsecondary science education (MS)
public policy (PhD)
research methods (MA)
research, evaluation, and assessment (PhD)
science education (MA, PhD)
social studies education (MA)
teaching and teacher education (PhD)

School of Information
Programs in:
archives and records management (MS)
human-computer interaction (MS)
information (MS, PhD)
information economics, management and policy (MS)
library and information services (MS)

School of Kinesiology
Dr. Gregory D. Cartee, Interim Dean
Programs in:
kinesiology (MS, PhD)
sport management (AM)

The School of Music, Theatre, and Dance
Christopher Kendall, Dean
Programs in:
composition (MA, MM, A Mus D)
composition and theory (PhD)
conducting (MM, A Mus D)
design (MFA)
media arts (MA)
modern dance performance and choreography (MFA)
music education (MM, PhD, Spec M)
music, theatre, and dance (MA, MFA, MM, A Mus D, PhD, Spec M)
musicology (MA, PhD)
performance (MM, A Mus D, Spec M)
theatre (PhD)
theory (MA, PhD)

School of Nursing
Programs in:
adult acute care nurse practitioner (MS)
adult nurse practitioner (Post Master's Certificate)
adult primary care/adult nurse practitioner (MS)
community care (Post Master's Certificate)
community care/home care (MS)
community health nursing (MS, Post Master's Certificate)
family nurse practitioner (MS, Post Master's Certificate)
gerontology nurse practitioner (MS)
gerontology nursing (MS)
gerontology-clinical nurse specialist (MS)
infant, child, adolescent health nurse practitioner (MS)
medical-surgical clinical nurse specialist (MS)
nurse midwifery (MS, Post Master's Certificate)
nursing (MS, PhD, Post Master's Certificate)
nursing business and health systems (MS)
occupational health nursing (MS)
parent-child nursing (MS, Post Master's Certificate)
psychiatric mental health nurse practitioner (MS)
psychiatric mental health nursing (MS)
psychiatric mental health nursing-clinical nurse specialist (MS)

Jean and Samuel Frankel Center for Judaic Studies
Prof. Deborah Dash Moore, Director
Program in:
Judaic studies (MA, Graduate Certificate)

Law School
Evan H. Caminker, Dean
Programs in:
comparative law (MCL)
international tax (LL M)
law (JD, LL M, SJD)

Medical School
Program in:
medicine (MD, MS, PhD)

Ross School of Business at the University of Michigan
Dr. Robert J. Dolan, Dean
Programs in:
business (M Acc, MBA)
business administration (PhD)
supply chain management (MSCM)

School of Dentistry
Programs in:
biomaterials (MS)
dental hygiene (MS)
dentistry (DDS, MS, PhD, Certificate)
endodontics (MS)
oral health sciences (PhD)
orthodontics (MS)
pediatric dentistry (MS)
periodontics (MS)
prosthodontics (MS)
restorative dentistry (MS)

School of Natural Resources and Environment
Dr. Rosina Bierbaum, Dean
Programs in:
aquatic sciences: research and management (MS)
behavior, education and communication (MS)
conservation biology (MS)
environmental informatics (MS)
environmental justice (MS)
environmental policy and planning (MS)
industrial ecology (Certificate)
landscape architecture (MLA, PhD)
natural resources and environment (MS, PhD)
spatial analysis (Certificate)
sustainable systems (MS)
terrestrial ecosystems (MS)

School of Public Health
Kenneth E. Warner, Dean
Programs in:
biostatistics (MPH, MS, PhD)
clinical research design and statistical analysis (MS)
dental public health (MPH)
environmental health sciences (MS, PhD)
environmental quality and health (MPH)
epidemiological science (PhD)
epidemiology (MPH)
health behavior and health education (MPH, PhD)
health management and policy (MHSA, MPH, MS)
health services organization and policy (PhD)
hospital and molecular epidemiology (MPH)
human nutrition (MPH)
industrial hygiene (MPH, MS)
international health (MPH)
nutritional sciences (MS)
occupational and environmental epidemiology (MPH)
public health (MHSA, MPH, MS, PhD)
toxicology (MPH, MS, PhD)

School of Social Work
Programs in:
social work (MSW, PhD)
social work and social science (PhD)

Taubman College of Architecture and Urban Planning
Monica Ponce de Leon, Dean
Programs in:
architecture (M Arch, M Sc, PhD)
architecture and urban planning (M Arch, M Sc, MUD, MUP, PhD, Certificate)
real estate development (Certificate)
urban and regional planning (MUP, PhD, Certificate)
urban design (MUD)
urban planning (MUP)

■ UNIVERSITY OF MICHIGAN–DEARBORN
Dearborn, MI 48128-1491
http://www.umd.umich.edu/

State-supported, coed, comprehensive institution. *Graduate faculty:* 294 full-time (104 women), 191 part-time/adjunct (75 women). *Computer facilities:* Computer purchase and lease plans are available. 350 computers available on campus for general student use. A campuswide network can be accessed from off campus. Online class registration, Tuition and application payments accepted online are available. *General application contact:* Kimberly Lewandowski, Graduate Programs Coordinator, 313-593-1494.

College of Arts, Sciences, and Letters
Dr. Kathryn Anderson-Levitt, Dean
Programs in:
applied and computational mathematics (MS)
arts, sciences, and letters (MA, MPA, MPP, MS, Certificate)
assessment and evaluation (Certificate)
clinical health psychology (MS)
environmental science (MS)
health psychology (MS)
liberal studies (MA)
nonprofit leadership (Certificate)
public administration (MPA)
public policy (MPP)

College of Business
Dr. Kim Schatzel, Dean
Programs in:
accounting (MS)
finance (MS)
management (MBA)

College of Engineering and Computer Science
Dr. Subrata Sengupta, Dean
Programs in:
automotive systems engineering (MSE, PhD)
computer and information science (MS)
computer engineering (MSE)
electrical engineering (MSE)
engineering and computer science (MS, MSE, D Eng, PhD)
engineering management (MS)
industrial and systems engineering (MSE)
information systems and technology (MS)
information systems engineering (PhD)
manufacturing systems engineering (MSE, D Eng)
mechanical engineering (MSE)
software engineering (MS)

School of Education
Dr. Paul Zionts, Dean
Programs in:
education (M Ed, MA, MAT, MPA, MS, Certificate)
emotional impairments endorsement (M Ed)
inclusion specialist (M Ed)
learning disabilities endorsement (M Ed)
science education (MS)
teaching (MAT)

■ UNIVERSITY OF MICHIGAN–FLINT
Flint, MI 48502-1950
http://www.umflint.edu/

State-supported, coed, comprehensive institution. CGS member. *Graduate faculty:* 81 full-time (44 women), 42 part-time/adjunct (21 women). *Computer facilities:* Computer purchase and lease plans are available. 251 computers available on campus for general student use. A campuswide network can be accessed from student residence rooms and from off campus. Online class registration is available. *Graduate expenses:* Tuition, state resident: full-time $9973; part-time $415.50 per credit. Tuition, nonresident: full-time $14,960; part-time $623.30 per credit. Required fees: $368; $141 per term. Tuition and fees vary according to course level, course load, degree level and student level. *General application contact:* Bradley T. Maki, Director of Graduate Admissions, 810-762-3171.

College of Arts and Sciences
Dr. D. J. Trela, Dean
Programs in:
arts and sciences (MA, MS)
biology (MS)
computer science and information systems (MS)
English (MA)
social sciences (MA)

Graduate Programs
Dr. Vahid Lotfi, Associate Provost and Dean of Graduate Programs

University of Michigan–Flint (continued)
Programs in:
American culture (MLS)
public administration (MPA)

School of Education and Human Services

Dr. Susanne Chandler, Dean
Programs in:
early childhood education (MA)
education (MA)
education and human services (MA)
elementary education with teaching certification (MA)
literacy (K-12) (MA)
special education (MA)
technology in education (MA)

School of Health Professions and Studies

Dr. Betty Velthouse, Interim Dean
Programs in:
anesthesia (MSA)
health education (MS)
health professions and studies (MS, MSA, DNP, DPT)
nursing (DNP)
online transitional (DPT)
traditional entry-level (DPT)

School of Management

Dr. Jack A. Helmuth, Dean
Program in:
management (MBA)

■ UNIVERSITY OF PHOENIX–WEST MICHIGAN CAMPUS

Walker, MI 49544
http://www.phoenix.edu/

Proprietary, coed, comprehensive institution. *Computer facilities:* Computer purchase and lease plans are available. A campuswide network can be accessed from off campus. Online class registration is available. *General application contact:* Campus Information Center, 888-345-9699.

The Artemis School

College of Education

Programs in:
administration and supervision (MA Ed)
curriculum and instruction (MA Ed)

College of Health and Human Services

Programs in:
health care management (MBA)
nursing (MSN)

The John Sperling School of Business

Program in:
business (MBA)

College of Graduate Business and Management

Programs in:
accounting (MBA)
business administration (MBA)
global management (MBA)
human resource management (MBA)

College of Information Systems and Technology

Programs in:
e-business (MBA)
technology management (MBA)

■ WAYNE STATE UNIVERSITY

Detroit, MI 48202
http://www.wayne.edu/

State-supported, coed, university. CGS member. *Computer facilities:* 1,800 computers available on campus for general student use. A campuswide network can be accessed from student residence rooms and from off campus. Online class registration is available. *General application contact:* Director, 313-577-9753.

College of Education

Program in:
education (M Ed, MA, MAT, Ed D, PhD, Certificate, Ed S)

Division of Administrative and Organizational Studies

Programs in:
administration and supervision-secondary (Ed S)
college and university teaching (Certificate)
curriculum and instruction (PhD)
educational leadership (M Ed, Ed S)
educational leadership and policy studies (Ed D, PhD)
elementary education curriculum and instruction (MA, Ed S)
general administration and supervision (Ed D, PhD, Ed S)
higher education (Ed D, PhD)
instructional technology (M Ed, Ed D, PhD, Ed S)
secondary curriculum and instruction (M Ed, Ed S)

Division of Kinesiology, Health and Sports Studies

Programs in:
health education (M Ed)
kinesiology (M Ed)
physical education (M Ed)
recreation and park services (MA)
sports administration (MA)

Division of Teacher Education

Programs in:
adult and continuing education (M Ed)
art education (M Ed)
bilingual/bicultural education (M Ed, MAT)
business education (M Ed, MAT)
career and technical education (M Ed, Ed D, PhD, Ed S)
curriculum and instruction (Ed D, PhD, Ed S)
distributive education (M Ed, MAT)
early childhood education (M Ed)
elementary education (M Ed, MAT, Ed D, PhD, Ed S)
elementary education curriculum and instruction (M Ed)
English education (M Ed)
English education-secondary (M Ed, Ed S)
foreign language education (M Ed)
general education (Ed D, Ed S)
health occupations education (M Ed)
industrial education (M Ed)
mathematics education (M Ed, Ed S)
pre-school and parent education (M Ed)
reading (M Ed, Ed D, Ed S)
reading, languages and literature (Ed D)
school music-vocal (M Ed)
science education (M Ed, MAT, Ed S)
secondary education (MAT)
secondary school reading (M Ed)
social studies education (M Ed, Ed S)
special education (M Ed, Ed D, PhD, Ed S)
teacher education (MAT, Ed D, PhD)

Division of Theoretical and Behavioral Foundations

Programs in:
counseling (M Ed, MA, Ed D, PhD, Ed S)
education evaluation and research (M Ed, Ed D, PhD)
educational psychology (M Ed, Ed D, PhD, Ed S)
educational sociology (M Ed, Ed D, PhD, Ed S)
history and philosophy of education (M Ed, Ed D, PhD)
rehabilitation counseling and community inclusion (MA, Ed S)
school and community psychology (MA, Ed S)
school clinical psychology (Ed S)

College of Engineering

Programs in:
biomedical engineering (MS, PhD)
chemical engineering (MS, PhD)
civil engineering (MS, PhD)
computer engineering (MS, PhD)
electrical engineering (MS, PhD)
electronics and computer control systems (MS)
engineering (MS, PhD, Certificate)
engineering management (MS)
environmental auditing (Certificate)
hazardous materials management on public lands (Certificate)
hazardous waste (MS, Certificate)
hazardous waste control (Certificate)
hazardous waste management (MS)
industrial engineering (MS, PhD)
manufacturing engineering (MS)
materials science and engineering (MS, PhD, Certificate)

mechanical engineering (MS, PhD)
metallurgical engineering (MS, PhD)
polymer engineering (Certificate)
sustainable engineering (Certificate)

Division of Engineering Technology
Program in:
engineering technology (MS)

College of Fine, Performing and Communication Arts
Programs in:
art (MA, MFA)
art history (MA)
choral conducting (MM)
communication studies (MA, PhD)
composition (MM)
design and merchandising (MA)
dispute resolution (MADR, Certificate)
fine, performing and communication arts (MA, MADR, MFA, MM, PhD, Certificate)
music (MA, MM)
music education (MM)
orchestral studies (Certificate)
performance (MM)
public relations and organizational communication (MA)
radio-TV-film (MA, PhD)
speech communication (MA, PhD)
theatre (MA, MFA, PhD)
theory (MM)

College of Liberal Arts and Sciences
Programs in:
anthropology (MA, PhD)
applied mathematics (MA, PhD)
audiology (MA, MS, Au D, PhD)
behavioral and cognitive neuroscience (PhD)
biological sciences (MA, MS, PhD)
chemistry (MA, MS, PhD)
classics (MA)
classics, Greek, and Latin (MA)
clinical psychology (PhD)
cognitive and social psychology (PhD)
communication disorders and science (MA, PhD)
comparative literature (MA)
computer science (MA, MS, PhD)
criminal justice (MPA)
economic development (Certificate)
economics (MA, PhD)
English (MA, PhD)
French (MA)
geography (MA)
geology (MA, MS)
German (MA)
German and Slavic studies (MA, PhD)
history (MA, PhD)
human development (MA)
industrial relations (MAIR)
industrial/organizational psychology (PhD)
Italian (MA)
language learning (MA)
Latin (MA)
liberal arts and sciences (MA, MAIR, MPA, MS, MUP, Au D, PhD, Certificate)
linguistics (MA)
mathematical statistics (MA, PhD)
mathematics (MA, MS, PhD)
modern languages (PhD)
molecular biotechnology (MS)
Near Eastern and Asian studies (MA)
Near Eastern studies (MA)
nutrition and food science (MA, MS, PhD)
philosophy (MA, PhD)
physics (MA, MS, PhD)
political science (MA, MPA, PhD)
psychology (MA, MS, PhD)
public administration (MPA)
Russian (MA)
scientific computing (Certificate)
sociology (MA, PhD)
Spanish (MA)
speech-language pathology (MA, PhD)
urban planning (MUP)

College of Nursing
Programs in:
adult acute care nursing (MSN)
adult primary care nursing (MSN)
advanced practice nursing with women, neonates and children (MSN)
community health nursing (MSN)
neonatal nurse practitioner (Certificate)
nursing (MSN, PhD, Certificate)
nursing education (Certificate)
psychiatric mental health nurse practitioner (MSN, Certificate)
transcultural nursing (MSN, Certificate)

Eugene Applebaum College of Pharmacy and Health Sciences
Programs in:
clinical laboratory science (MS)
clinical laboratory sciences (MS, Certificate)
experimental technology in pharmaceutical sciences (Certificate)
health systems pharmacy management (MS)
hospital pharmacy (MS)
medical technology (Certificate)
medicinal chemistry (MS, PhD)
nurse anesthesia (MS)
nursing anesthesia (MS, Certificate)
occupational and environmental health sciences (MPH, MS, Certificate, Post-Master's Certificate)
occupational therapy (MOT, MS)
pediatric nurse anesthesia (Certificate)
pharmaceutical administration (MS, PhD)
pharmaceutical sciences (MS, PhD)
pharmaceutics (MS, PhD)
pharmacology (MS, PhD)
pharmacy (Pharm D)
pharmacy and health sciences (Pharm D, MOT, MPH, MPT, MS, PhD, Certificate, Post-Master's Certificate)
physical therapy (MPT)
physician assistant studies (MS)

Graduate School
Programs in:
alcohol and drug abuse studies (Certificate)
archival administration (Certificate)
developmental disabilities (Certificate)
gerontology (Certificate)
infant mental health (Certificate)
library and information science (MLIS, Spec)
library science (MS, Spec)
molecular and cellular toxicology (MS, PhD)
molecular biology and genetics (MS, PhD)

Law School
Program in:
law (JD, LL M, PhD)

School of Business Administration
Programs in:
accounting (MS)
business administration (MBA, PhD)
interdisciplinary studies (PhD)
taxation (MS)

School of Medicine
Program in:
medicine (MD, MPH, MS, PhD, Certificate)

Graduate Programs in Medicine
Programs in:
anatomy (MS, PhD)
basic medical science (MS)
biochemistry and molecular biology (MS, PhD)
cancer biology (MS, PhD)
cellular and clinical neurobiology (PhD)
community health (MS)
community health services (Certificate)
immunology and microbiology (MS, PhD)
medical physics (PhD)
medical research (MS)
medicine (MPH, MS, PhD, Certificate)
pathology (MS, PhD)
pharmacology (MS, PhD)
physiology (MS, PhD)
psychiatry and behavioral neurosciences (MS)
public health (MPH)
public health practice (Certificate)
radiological physics (MS)
rehabilitation science administration (Certificate)
rehabilitation sciences (MS)

School of Social Work
Programs in:
interdisciplinary studies (PhD)
social work (MSW)
social work practice with families and couples (Certificate)

■ WESTERN MICHIGAN UNIVERSITY

Kalamazoo, MI 49008-5202

http://www.wmich.edu/

State-supported, coed, university. CGS member. *Computer facilities:* Computer purchase and lease plans are available. 2,000 computers available on campus for general student use. A campuswide network can be accessed from student residence rooms and from off campus. Online class registration is available. *General application contact:* Admissions and Orientation, 616-387-2000.

Graduate College

College of Arts and Sciences
Programs in:
anthropology (MA)
applied and computational mathematics (MS)
applied economics (MA, PhD)
applied statistics (MS)
arts and sciences (MA, MDA, MFA, MPA, MS, PhD, Graduate Certificate)
behavior analysis (MA, PhD)
biological sciences (MS, PhD)
chemistry (MA, PhD)
clinical psychology (MA, PhD)
communication (MA)
comparative religion (MA)
creative writing (MFA)
development administration (MDA)
earth science (MA, MS)
electron microscopy (MS)
English (MA, PhD)
English education (MA, PhD)
experimental psychology (MA)
geography (MA)
geosciences (MA, MS, PhD)
health care administration (Graduate Certificate)
history (MA, PhD)
industrial/organizational psychology (MA)
mathematics (MA, PhD)
mathematics education (MA, PhD)
medieval studies (MA)
molecular biotechnology (MS)
nonprofit leadership and administration (Graduate Certificate)
philosophy (MA)
physics (MA, PhD)
political science (MA, PhD)
professional writing (MA)
public administration (PhD)
public affairs and administration (MPA)
science education (MA, PhD)
sociology (MA, PhD)
Spanish (MA, PhD)
statistics (MS, PhD)

College of Education
Programs in:
career and technical education (MA)
counseling psychology (MA, PhD)
counselor education (MA, PhD)
education (MA, Ed D, PhD, Ed S, Graduate Certificate)
educational leadership (MA, Ed D, PhD, Ed S)
educational technology (MA)
evaluation, measurement and research (MA, PhD, Graduate Certificate)
exercise and sports medicine (MS)
family and consumer sciences (MA)
human resources development (MA)
marriage and family therapy (MA)
physical education (MA)
socio-cultural foundations and educational thought (MA)

College of Engineering and Applied Sciences
Programs in:
civil engineering (MS)
computer engineering (MSE, PhD)
computer science (MS, PhD)
electrical and computer engineering (PhD)
electrical engineering (MSE)
engineering and applied sciences (MS, MSE, PhD)
engineering management (MS)
industrial engineering (MSE)
manufacturing engineering (MS)
mechanical engineering (MSE, PhD)
paper and imaging science and engineering (MS, PhD)

College of Fine Arts
Programs in:
art education (MA)
composition (MM)
conducting (MM)
fine arts (MA, MFA, MM)
music education (MM)
music therapy (MM)
performance (MM)
studio design (MFA)

College of Health and Human Services
Programs in:
audiology (Au D)
blind rehabilitation (MA)
health and human services (MA, MS, MSW, Au D)
occupational therapy (MS)
physician assistant (MS)
social work (MSW)
speech-language pathology (MA)

Haworth College of Business
Programs in:
accountancy (MSA)
business (MBA, MSA)
finance (MBA)

Minnesota

■ ARGOSY UNIVERSITY, TWIN CITIES

Eagan, MN 55121

http://www.argosy.edu/twincities

Proprietary, coed, university.

College of Business
Programs in:
accounting (DBA)
customized professional concentration (MBA, DBA)
finance (MBA)
healthcare administration (MBA)
information systems (DBA)
information systems management (MBA)
international business (MBA, DBA)
management (MBA, MSM, DBA)
marketing (MBA, DBA)

College of Education
Programs in:
educational leadership (MA Ed, Ed D, Ed S)
instructional leadership (MA Ed, Ed D, Ed S)

College of Health Sciences
Program in:
health services management (MS)

College of Psychology and Behavioral Sciences
Programs in:
clinical psychology (MA, Psy D)
forensic counseling (Post-Graduate Certificate)
forensic psychology (MA)
marriage and family therapy (MA, DMFT)
organizational leadership (Ed D)

■ AUGSBURG COLLEGE

Minneapolis, MN 55454-1351

http://www.augsburg.edu/

Independent-religious, coed, comprehensive institution. *Graduate faculty:* 30 full-time (19 women), 18 part-time/adjunct (8 women). *Computer facilities:* 260 computers available on campus for general student use. A campuswide network can be accessed from student residence rooms and from off campus. Online class registration is available. *General application contact:* Nathan Gorr, Director, Weekend College and Graduate Admissions, 612-330-1101 Ext. 1390.

Program in Business Administration
Steven Zitnick, Director
Program in:
business administration (MBA)

Program in Education
Vicki Olson, Professor
Program in:
education (MAE)

Program in Leadership
Dr. Norma Noonan, Director
Program in:
leadership (MA)

Program in Physicians Assistant Studies
Dawn B. Ludwig, Director

Program in:
physicians assistant studies (MS)

Program in Social Work
Dr. Lois A. Bosch, Director
Program in:
social work (MSW)

Program in Transcultural Community Health Nursing
Dr. Cheryl J. Leuning, Director
Program in:
transcultural community health nursing (MA)

■ BEMIDJI STATE UNIVERSITY
Bemidji, MN 56601-2699
http://www.bemidjistate.edu/

State-supported, coed, comprehensive institution. *Computer facilities:* Computer purchase and lease plans are available. 1,200 computers available on campus for general student use. A campuswide network can be accessed from student residence rooms and from off campus. Online class registration is available. *General application contact:* Interim Dean, School of Graduate/Professional Studies, 218-755-3732.

School of Graduate Studies

College of Arts and Letters
Programs in:
arts and letters (MA, MS)
English (MA, MS)

College of Professional Studies
Programs in:
education (M Ed, MS)
professional studies (M Ed, M Sp Ed, MS)
special education (M Sp Ed, MS)
sport studies (MS)
technical education (MS)
technology/career technical education (MS)

College of Social and Natural Sciences
Programs in:
biology (MS)
environmental studies (MS)
mathematics (MS)
psychology (MS)
science (MS)
social and natural sciences (MS)

■ BETHEL UNIVERSITY
St. Paul, MN 55112-6999
http://www.bethel.edu/

Independent-religious, coed, comprehensive institution. *Computer facilities:* Computer purchase and lease plans are available. 400 computers available on campus for general student use. A campuswide network can be accessed from student residence rooms and from off campus. Online class registration is available. *General application contact:* Director of Admissions, 651-635-8000 Ext. 8017.

Graduate School
Programs in:
business administration (MBA)
child and adolescent mental health (Certificate)
Christian health ministry (MA)
communication (MA)
counseling psychology (MA)
education K-12 (MA)
educational administration (Ed D)
gerontology (MA)
healthcare leadership (MA)
literacy (Certificate)
literacy education (MA)
nursing education (MA, Certificate)
organizational leadership (MA)
post-secondary teaching (Certificate)
secondary education (MA)
special education (M Ed)

■ CAPELLA UNIVERSITY
Minneapolis, MN 55402
http://www.capella.edu/

Proprietary, coed, upper-level institution. CGS member. *Computer facilities:* Online class registration is available. *General application contact:* Enrollment Services Office, 888-CAPELLA.

Harold Abel School of Psychology
Dr. Deborah Bushway, Dean
Programs in:
child and adolescent development (MS)
clinical psychology (MS, Psy D)
counseling psychology (MS)
educational psychology (MS, PhD)
evaluation, research, and measurement (MS)
general psychology (MS, PhD)
industrial/organizational psychology (MS, PhD)
leadership coaching psychology (MS)
organizational leader development (MS)
school psychology (MS)
sport psychology (MS)

School of Business and Technology
Programs in:
accounting (MBA)
business (Certificate)
finance (MBA)
general business (MBA)
health care management (MBA)
information technology (MS, Certificate)
information technology management (MBA)
marketing (MBA)
organization and management (MBA, MS, PhD)
project management (MBA)

School of Public Service Leadership
Programs in:
criminal justice (MS, PhD)
emergency management (MS, PhD)
general human services (MS, PhD)
general public administration (MPA, DPA)
gerontology (MS)
health care administration (MS, PhD)
health management and policy (MSPH)
management of nonprofit agencies (MS, PhD)
nurse educator (MS)
public safety leadership (MS, PhD)
social and community services (MS, PhD)
social behavioral sciences (MSPH)

■ THE COLLEGE OF ST. SCHOLASTICA
Duluth, MN 55811-4199
http://www.css.edu/

Independent-religious, coed, comprehensive institution. *Computer facilities:* 222 computers available on campus for general student use. A campuswide network can be accessed from student residence rooms and from off campus. Online class registration, student account information and transcripts online are available. *General application contact:* Graduate Recruitment Counselor, 218-723-6285.

Graduate Studies
Programs in:
computer information systems (MA, Certificate)
educational media and technology (M Ed)
exercise physiology (MA)
health information management (MA, Certificate)
management (MA, Certificate)
nursing (MA, PMC)
occupational therapy (MA)
physical therapy (DPT)
teaching (M Ed, Certificate)

■ CONCORDIA UNIVERSITY, ST. PAUL
St. Paul, MN 55104-5494
http://www.csp.edu/

Independent-religious, coed, comprehensive institution. CGS member. *Graduate faculty:* 29 full-time (19 women), 76 part-time/adjunct (43 women). *Computer facilities:* A campuswide network can be accessed from student residence rooms and from off campus. Online class registration is available. *General application contact:* Kimberly Craig, Director of Graduate and Cohort Admission, 651-603-6223.

College of Business and Organizational Leadership
Dr. Bruce Corrie, Dean

Concordia University, St. Paul (continued)
Programs in:
business and organizational leadership (MBA)
criminal justice leadership (MA)
human resources management (MA)
organizational management (MA)

College of Education
Prof. Lonn Maly, Dean
Programs in:
curriculum and instruction (MA Ed)
differentiated instruction (MA Ed)
early childhood education (MA Ed)
educational leadership (MA Ed)
family life education (MA)
special education (Certificate)
sports management (MA)

College of Vocation and Ministry
Dr. David Lumpp, Dean
Programs in:
Christian education (Certificate)
Christian outreach (MA)

■ HAMLINE UNIVERSITY
St. Paul, MN 55104-1284
http://www.hamline.edu/

Independent-religious, coed, comprehensive institution. *Graduate faculty:* 92 full-time (51 women), 259 part-time/adjunct (167 women). *Computer facilities:* 150 computers available on campus for general student use. A campuswide network can be accessed from student residence rooms and from off campus. Online class registration is available. *Graduate expenses:* Tuition: full-time $6400; part-time $400 per credit. Required fees: $6 per credit. One-time fee: $205. Tuition and fees vary according to degree level and program. *General application contact:* Rae A. Lenway, Director, Graduate Recruitment and Admission, 651-523-2900.

Graduate School of Liberal Studies
Mary Francois Rockcastle, Dean
Program in:
liberal studies (MALS, MFA, CALS)

School of Business
Julian Schuster, Dean
Programs in:
business (MBA)
nonprofit management (MANM)
public administration (MPA, DPA)

School of Education
Barbara Swanson, Interim Dean
Program in:
education (MA Ed, MAESL, MAT, Ed D)

School of Law
Donald M. Lewis, Dean
Program in:
law (JD, LL M)

■ MAYO GRADUATE SCHOOL
Rochester, MN 55905
http://www.mayo.edu/mgs/index.html

Independent, coed, graduate-only institution. *Computer facilities:* A campuswide network can be accessed from off campus. *General application contact:* Admissions Coordinator, 507-538-1160.

Graduate Programs in Biomedical Sciences
Programs in:
biochemistry and structural biology (PhD)
biomedical engineering (PhD)
biomedical sciences (PhD)
cell biology and genetics (PhD)
immunology (PhD)
molecular biology (PhD)
molecular neuroscience (PhD)
molecular pharmacology and experimental therapeutics (PhD)
tumor biology (PhD)
virology and gene therapy (PhD)

■ METROPOLITAN STATE UNIVERSITY
St. Paul, MN 55106-5000
http://www.metrostate.edu/

State-supported, coed, comprehensive institution. *Computer facilities:* 550 computers available on campus for general student use. A campuswide network can be accessed from off campus. Online class registration is available. *General application contact:* Office of Graduate Admissions, 651-793-1212.

College of Arts and Sciences
Programs in:
computer science (MS)
liberal studies (MA)
technical communication (MS)

College of Management
Programs in:
business administration (MBA)
information management (MMIS)
MIS generalist (Graduate Certificate)
MIS systems analysis (Graduate Certificate)
nonprofit management (MPNA)
project management (Graduate Certificate)
public administration (MPNA)
systems management (MMIS)

College of Nursing and Health Sciences
Program in:
nursing (MSN, DNP)

College of Professional Studies
Program in:
psychology (MA)

■ MINNESOTA STATE UNIVERSITY MANKATO
Mankato, MN 56001
http://www.mnsu.edu/

State-supported, coed, university. CGS member. *Computer facilities:* Computer purchase and lease plans are available. 900 computers available on campus for general student use. A campuswide network can be accessed from student residence rooms and from off campus. Online class registration is available. *General application contact:* Information Contact, 507-389-2321.

College of Graduate Studies
Dean Anne Blackhurst, Dean
Program in:
cross-disciplinary studies (MS)

College of Allied Health and Nursing
Dr. Kaye Herth, Dean
Programs in:
allied health and nursing (MA, MS, MSN, MT, DNP, SP)
communication disorders (MS)
community health (MS)
family nursing (MSN)
health science (MS, MT)
human performance (MA, MS, MT, SP)
managed care (MSN)
nursing (DNP)
rehabilitation counseling (MS)
school health (MS)

College of Arts and Humanities
Dr. Terrance Flaherty, Interim Dean
Programs in:
art education (MS)
arts and humanities (MA, MAT, MFA, MM, MS, MT, Certificate)
creative writing (MFA)
design/technology (MFA)
English (MA, MS)
English literature (MA)
forensics (MFA)
French (MAT, MS)
music (MM, MT)
performance (MFA)
Spanish (MAT, MS)
speech communication (MA, MS, MT)
studio art (MA)
teaching art (MAT, MT)
teaching English (MS, MT)
teaching English as a second language (MA, Certificate)
technical communication (Certificate)
theatre arts (MA, MFA)

College of Business
Dr. Kevin Elliott, Graduate Coordinator
Programs in:
accounting and business law (MBA)
finance (MBA)
management (MBA)
marketing and international business (MBA)

College of Education
Dr. Michael Miller, Dean

Programs in:
- college student affairs (MS)
- computer services administration (MS)
- counselor education and supervision (Ed D)
- curriculum and instruction (SP)
- early education for exceptional children (MS)
- education (MAT, MS, Ed D, Certificate, SP)
- educational administration (Certificate)
- educational leadership (MS, Ed D)
- educational technology (MS)
- elementary and early childhood education (MS)
- elementary school administration (MS, SP)
- emotional/behavioral disorders (MS, Certificate)
- experiential education (MS, Certificate, SP)
- general school administration (MS)
- higher education administration (MS)
- learning disabilities (MS, Certificate)
- library media education (MS, Certificate, SP)
- marriage and family counseling (Certificate)
- professional community counseling (MS)
- professional school counseling (MS)
- secondary administration (MS, SP)
- talent development and gifted education (MS, Certificate, SP)
- teaching and learning (MAT, MS, Certificate)
- vocational-technical administration (MS)

College of Science, Engineering and Technology
Dean John Knox, Dean
Programs in:
- biology (MS)
- biology education (MS)
- computer science (MS, Graduate Certificate)
- database technologies (Certificate)
- electrical and computer engineering and technology (MSE)
- environmental sciences (MS)
- manufacturing engineering technology (MS)
- mathematics (MA, MS)
- mathematics education (MAT, MS)
- physics (MS)
- physics and astronomy (MT)
- science, engineering and technology (MA, MAT, MS, MSE, MT, Certificate, Graduate Certificate)
- statistics (MS)

College of Social and Behavioral Sciences
Dr. John Alessio, Dean
Programs in:
- anthropology (MS)
- clinical psychology (MA)
- ethnic studies (MS)
- geography (MS)
- geography education (MT)
- gerontology (MS, Certificate)
- history (MA, MS)
- industrial/organizational psychology (MA)
- local government (Certificate)
- psychology (MT)
- public administration (MAPA)
- school psychology (Psy D)
- social and behavioral sciences (MA, MAPA, MS, MT, Psy D, Certificate)
- social studies (MS)
- sociology (MA)
- sociology: corrections (MS)
- sociology: human services planning and administration (MS)
- teaching history (MS, MT)
- urban and regional studies (MA)
- urban planning (Certificate)
- women's studies (MS, Certificate)

■ MINNESOTA STATE UNIVERSITY MOORHEAD
Moorhead, MN 56563-0002
http://www.mnstate.edu/

State-supported, coed, comprehensive institution. *Computer facilities:* Computer purchase and lease plans are available. 450 computers available on campus for general student use. A campuswide network can be accessed from student residence rooms and from off campus. Online class registration is available. *General application contact:* Graduate Studies Office, 218-477-2344.

Graduate Studies

College of Arts and Humanities
Programs in:
- arts and humanities (MFA, MLA)
- creative writing (MFA)
- liberal studies (MLA)

College of Education and Human Services
Programs in:
- counseling and student affairs (MS)
- curriculum and instruction (MS)
- educational leadership (MS, Ed S)
- nursing (MS)
- reading (MS)
- special education (MS)
- speech-language pathology (MS)

College of Social and Natural Sciences
Programs in:
- public, human services, and health administration (MS)
- school psychology (MS, Psy S)
- social and natural sciences (MS, Psy S)

■ ST. CATHERINE UNIVERSITY
St. Paul, MN 55105-1789
http://www.stkate.edu/

Independent-religious, Undergraduate: women only; graduate: coed, comprehensive institution. CGS member. *Graduate faculty:* 93 full-time (74 women). *Computer facilities:* Computer purchase and lease plans are available. 350 computers available on campus for general student use. A campuswide network can be accessed from student residence rooms and from off campus. Transcript available. *Graduate expenses:* Tuition: part-time $687 per credit. Required fees: $20 per term. Tuition and fees vary according to course load and program. *General application contact:* Sylvia Alexander-Sedey, Senior Admissions Counselor, 651-690-6933.

Graduate Programs
Susan Cochrane, Dean of Professional Studies
Programs in:
- education–curriculum and instruction (MA)
- holistic health studies (MA)
- library and information science (MLIS)
- nursing (MA, DNP)
- occupational therapy (MA)
- organizational leadership (MA)
- physical therapy (DPT)
- social work (MSW)
- theology (MA)

■ ST. CLOUD STATE UNIVERSITY
St. Cloud, MN 56301-4498
http://www.stcloudstate.edu/

State-supported, coed, comprehensive institution. CGS member. *Graduate faculty:* 540 full-time (194 women), 34 part-time/adjunct (16 women). *Computer facilities:* Computer purchase and lease plans are available. 1,489 computers available on campus for general student use. A campuswide network can be accessed from student residence rooms and from off campus. Online class registration is available. *Graduate expenses:* Tuition, state resident: full-time $4404.20; part-time $275.20 per credit. Tuition, nonresident: full-time $6885; part-time $430.35 per credit. Required fees: $29.58 per credit. Tuition and fees vary according to course level, degree level, campus/location and reciprocity agreements. *General application contact:* Annette Day, Director of Graduate Admissions, 320-308-2113.

School of Graduate Studies
Dr. Dennis Nunes, Dean

College of Education
Dr. Glen Palm, Interim Dean
Programs in:
- applied behavior analysis (MS)
- child and family studies (MS)
- college counseling and student development (MS)
- community counseling (MS)
- curriculum and instruction (MS)
- educable mentally handicapped (MS)
- education (MS, Ed D, Spt)
- educational administration and leadership (MS)

St. Cloud State University (continued)
- educational leadership and community psychology (Spt)
- emotionally disturbed (MS)
- exercise science (MS)
- gifted and talented (MS)
- higher education administration (MS, Ed D)
- information media (MS)
- learning disabled (MS)
- marriage and family therapy (MS)
- physical education (MS)
- rehabilitation counseling (MS)
- school counseling (MS)
- social responsibility (MS)
- special education (MS)
- sports management (MS)
- trainable mentally retarded (MS)

College of Fine Arts and Humanities
Todd DeVriese, Dean
Programs in:
- communication sciences and disorders (MS)
- conducting and literature (MM)
- English (MA, MS)
- fine arts and humanities (MA, MM, MS)
- mass communication (MS)
- music education (MM)
- piano pedagogy (MM)
- teaching English as a second language (MA)

College of Science and Engineering
Dr. David DeGroote, Chairperson
Programs in:
- applied statistics (MS)
- biological sciences (MA, MS)
- computer science (MS)
- electrical engineering (MS)
- engineering management (MEM)
- environmental and technological studies (MS)
- mathematics (MS)
- mechanical engineering (MS)
- regulatory affairs and services (MS)
- science and engineering (MA, MEM, MS)

College of Social Sciences
Dr. Sharon Cogdill, Interim Dean
Programs in:
- applied economics (MS)
- criminal justice administration (MS)
- criminal justice counseling (MS)
- cultural resource management archeology (MS)
- geography (MS)
- gerontology (MS)
- history (MA, MS)
- industrial-organizational psychology (MS)
- public and nonprofit institutions (MS)
- public safety executive leadership (MS)
- social sciences (MA, MS, MSW)
- social work (MSW)

G.R. Herberger College of Business
Michele Mumm, Graduate Director
Programs in:
- information assurance (MS)
- management and finance (MBA)
- marketing and general business (MBA)

■ SAINT MARY'S UNIVERSITY OF MINNESOTA
Winona, MN 55987-1399
http://www.smumn.edu/

Independent-religious, coed, comprehensive institution. *Graduate faculty:* 9 full-time (2 women), 386 part-time/adjunct (196 women). *Computer facilities:* 200 computers available on campus for general student use. A campuswide network can be accessed from student residence rooms and from off campus. Online class registration is available. *General application contact:* Becky Copper, Director of Admissions for Graduate and Professional Programs, 612-728-5207.

Schools of Graduate and Professional Programs
James M. Bedtke, Vice President, Schools of Graduate and Professional Programs

Graduate School of Business and Technology
Programs in:
- arts and cultural management (MA)
- business administration (MBA)
- business and technology (MA, MBA, MS, Certificate)
- geographic information science (MS, Certificate)
- human development (MA)
- human resource management (MA)
- information technology management (MS)
- international business (MA)
- management (MA)
- organizational leadership (MA)
- philanthropy and development (MA)
- project management (MS, Certificate)
- public safety administration (MA)

Graduate School of Education
Programs in:
- behavioral disorders (Certificate)
- Catholic school leadership (MA)
- curriculum, assessment and instruction (Ed S)
- education (MA)
- education-Wisconsin (MA)
- educational administration (Ed S)
- educational leadership (MA)
- gifted and talented instruction (Certificate)
- instruction (MA, Certificate)
- K-12 reading teacher (Certificate)
- learning disabilities (Certificate)
- literacy education (MA)
- special education (MA)
- teaching and learning (M Ed)

Graduate School of Health and Human Services
Programs in:
- Canon law (Certificate)
- counseling and psychological services (MA, Psy D)
- health and human services (MA, MS, Psy D, Certificate)
- health and human services administration (MA)
- marriage and family therapy (MA, Certificate)
- nurse anesthesia (MS)
- pastoral administration (MA)
- pastoral ministries (MA)

■ SOUTHWEST MINNESOTA STATE UNIVERSITY
Marshall, MN 56258
http://www.smsu.edu/

State-supported, coed, comprehensive institution. *Graduate faculty:* 6 full-time (3 women), 16 part-time/adjunct (9 women). *Computer facilities:* 420 computers available on campus for general student use. A campuswide network can be accessed from student residence rooms and from off campus. Online class registration is available. *Graduate expenses:* Tuition, state resident: full-time $5462; part-time $288 per credit. Tuition, nonresident: full-time $5462; part-time $288 per credit. Required fees: $36 per credit. Tuition and fees vary according to campus/location and program. *General application contact:* LeAnn Thooft, Interim Admissions Director, 507-537-6286.

Department of Business and Public Affairs
Dr. William Thomas, Professor
Programs in:
- business administration (MBA)
- management (MS)

Department of Education
Dr. Donna Burgraff, Dean of Business, Education and Professional Studies
Programs in:
- education (MS)
- special education (MS)

■ UNIVERSITY OF MINNESOTA, DULUTH
Duluth, MN 55812-2496
http://www.d.umn.edu/

State-supported, coed, comprehensive institution. *Computer facilities:* Computer purchase and lease plans are available. 465 computers available on campus for general student use. A campuswide network can be accessed from student residence rooms and from off campus. Online class registration is available. *General application contact:* Executive Administrative Specialist, 218-726-7523.

Graduate School
Program in:
- toxicology (MS, PhD)

College of Education and Human Service Professions
Programs in:
- communication sciences and disorders (MA)
- education (Ed D)
- education and human service professions (MA, MSW, Ed D)
- social work (MSW)

College of Liberal Arts
Programs in:
- criminology (MA)
- English (MA)
- liberal arts (MA, MLS)
- liberal studies (MLS)

College of Science and Engineering
Programs in:
- applied and computational mathematics (MS)
- chemistry and biochemistry (MS)
- computer science (MS)
- electrical and computer engineering (MSECE)
- engineering management (MSEM)
- environmental health and safety (MEHS)
- geological sciences (MS, PhD)
- integrated biosciences (MS, PhD)
- physics (MS)
- science and engineering (MEHS, MS, MSECE, MSEM, PhD)

Labovitz School of Business and Economics
Programs in:
- business administration (MBA)
- business and economics (MBA)

School of Fine Arts
Programs in:
- fine arts (MFA, MM)
- graphic design (MFA)
- music education (MM)
- performance (MM)

Medical School
Programs in:
- biochemistry, molecular biology and biophysics (MS, PhD)
- medicine (MD, MS, PhD)
- microbiology, immunology and molecular pathobiology (MS, PhD)
- pharmacology (MS, PhD)
- physiology (MS, PhD)

■ UNIVERSITY OF MINNESOTA, TWIN CITIES CAMPUS

Minneapolis, MN 55455-0213
http://www.umn.edu/tc/

State-supported, coed, university. CGS member. *Computer facilities:* Computer purchase and lease plans are available. A campuswide network can be accessed from student residence rooms and from off campus. Online class registration, e-mail are available. *General application contact:* Information Contact, 612-625-3014.

Carlson School of Management
Dr. Alison Davis-Blake, Dean
Programs in:
- accountancy (M Acc)
- accounting (MBA, PhD)
- business administration (MBA, PhD)
- business taxation (MBT)
- entrepreneurship (MBA)
- finance (MBA, PhD)
- healthcare management (MBA)
- human resources and industrial relations (MA, PhD)
- information and decision sciences (MBA, PhD)
- international business (MBA)
- management (EMBA, M Acc, MA, MBA, MBT, MS, MSMOT, PhD)
- marketing and logistics management (MBA, PhD)
- operations and management science (MBA, PhD)
- strategic management and organization (MBA, PhD)
- supply chain management (MBA)

College of Pharmacy
Programs in:
- experimental and clinical pharmacology (MS, PhD)
- medicinal chemistry (MS, PhD)
- pharmaceutics (PhD)
- pharmacy (Pharm D, MS, PhD)
- social and administrative pharmacy (MS, PhD)
- social, administrative and clinical pharmacy (MS, PhD)

College of Veterinary Medicine
Dr. Trevor Ames, Dean
Programs in:
- comparative and molecular bioscience (MS, PhD)
- veterinary medicine (MS, PhD)

Graduate School
Programs in:
- biophysical sciences and medical physics (MS, PhD)
- genetic counseling (MS)
- health informatics (MHI, MS, PhD)
- history of science, technology and medicine (MA, PhD)
- integrative biology and physiology (PhD)
- microbial engineering (MS)
- microbiology, immunology and cancer biology (PhD)
- molecular, cellular, developmental biology and genetics (PhD)
- neuroscience (MS, PhD)
- scientific computation (MS, PhD)
- stem cell biology (MS, PhD)

College of Biological Sciences
Programs in:
- biochemistry, molecular biology and biophysics (PhD)
- biological science (MBS)
- biological sciences (MBS, MS, PhD)
- ecology, evolution, and behavior (MS, PhD)
- plant biological sciences (MS, PhD)

College of Design
Programs in:
- apparel (MA, MS, PhD)
- architecture (M Arch)
- design (M Arch, MA, MFA, MLA, MS, PhD, Postbaccalaureate Certificate)
- design communication (MA, MS, PhD)
- housing studies (MA, MS, PhD, Postbaccalaureate Certificate)
- interactive design (MFA)
- interior design (MA, MS, PhD)
- landscape architecture (MLA, MS)
- sustainable design (MS)

College of Education and Human Development
Dr. Jean K. Quam, Dean
Programs in:
- adapted physical education (MA, PhD)
- adult education (M Ed, MA, Ed D, PhD, Certificate)
- agricultural, food and environmental education (M Ed, MA, Ed D, PhD)
- art education (M Ed, MA, PhD)
- biomechanics (MA)
- biomechanics and neural control (PhD)
- business and industry education (M Ed, MA, Ed D, PhD)
- business education (M Ed)
- child psychology (MA, PhD)
- children's literature (M Ed, MA, PhD)
- Chinese (M Ed)
- coaching (Certificate)
- comparative and international development education (MA, PhD)
- counseling and student personnel psychology (MA, PhD, Ed S)
- curriculum and instruction (MA, PhD)
- developmental adapted physical education (M Ed)
- disability policy and services (Certificate)
- early childhood education (M Ed, MA, PhD)
- earth science (M Ed)
- education and human development (M Ed, MA, MSW, Ed D, PhD, Certificate, Ed S)
- educational administration (MA, Ed D, PhD)
- educational psychology (PhD)
- elementary education (M Ed, MA, PhD)
- elementary special education (M Ed)
- English (M Ed)
- English as a second language (M Ed)
- English education (MA, PhD)
- environmental education (M Ed)
- evaluation studies (MA, PhD)
- exercise physiology (MA, PhD)
- family education (M Ed, MA, Ed D, PhD)
- French (M Ed)
- German (M Ed)
- Hebrew (M Ed)
- higher education (MA, PhD)
- human factors/ergonomics (MA, PhD)
- human resource development (M Ed, MA, Ed D, PhD, Certificate)
- instructional systems and technology (M Ed, MA, PhD)

University of Minnesota, Twin Cities Campus (continued)

international/comparative sport (MA, PhD)
Japanese (M Ed)
kinesiology (M Ed, MA, PhD, Certificate)
language arts (MA, PhD)
language immersion education (Certificate)
leisure services/management (MA, PhD)
life sciences (M Ed)
literacy education (MA)
marketing education (M Ed)
marriage and family therapy (MA, PhD)
mathematics (M Ed)
mathematics education (MA, PhD)
middle school science (M Ed)
motor development (MA, PhD)
motor learning/control (MA, PhD)
outdoor education/recreation (MA, PhD)
physical education (M Ed)
postsecondary administration (Ed D)
program evaluation (Certificate)
psychological foundations of education (MA, PhD, Ed S)
reading education (MA, PhD)
recreation, park, and leisure studies (M Ed, MA, PhD)
school psychology (MA, PhD, Ed S)
school-to-work (Certificate)
science (M Ed)
science education (MA, PhD)
second languages and cultures (M Ed)
second languages and cultures education (MA, PhD)
social studies (M Ed)
social studies education (MA, PhD)
social work (MSW, PhD)
Spanish (M Ed)
special education (M Ed, MA, PhD, Ed S)
sport and exercise science (M Ed)
sport management (M Ed, MA, PhD)
sport psychology (MA, PhD)
sport sociology (MA, PhD)
staff development (Certificate)
talent development and gifted education (Certificate)
teacher leadership (M Ed)
teaching (M Ed)
technical education (Certificate)
technology education (M Ed, MA)
technology enhanced learning (Certificate)
therapeutic recreation (MA, PhD)
work and human resource education (M Ed, MA, Ed D, PhD)
writing education (M Ed, MA, PhD)
youth development leadership (M Ed)

College of Food, Agricultural and Natural Resource Sciences
Programs in:
animal science (MS, PhD)
applied economics (MS, PhD)
applied plant sciences (MS, PhD)
bioproducts and biosystems science engineering and management (MS, PhD)
conservation biology (MS, PhD)
entomology (MS, PhD)
food science (MS, PhD)
food, agricultural and natural resource sciences (MS, PhD)
natural resources science and management (MS, PhD)
nutrition (MS, PhD)
plant pathology (MS, PhD)
soil science (MS, PhD)
water resources science (MS, PhD)

College of Liberal Arts
Programs in:
American studies (PhD)
ancient and medieval art and archaeology (MA, PhD)
anthropology (MA, PhD)
art (MFA)
art history (MA, PhD)
Asian literatures, cultures, and media (PhD)
audiology (Au D)
biological psychopathology (PhD)
classics (MA, PhD)
clinical psychology (PhD)
cognitive and biological psychology (PhD)
communication studies (MA, PhD)
comparative literature (PhD)
comparative studies in discourse and society (PhD)
counseling psychology (PhD)
design technology (MFA)
economics (PhD)
English (MA, MFA, PhD)
English as a second language (MA)
feminist studies (PhD)
French (MA, PhD)
geographic information science (MGIS)
geography (MA, MGIS, PhD)
Germanic studies: German and Scandinavian studies track (PhD)
Germanic studies: German track (MA, PhD)
Germanic studies: Germanic medieval studies track (MA, PhD)
Germanic studies: Scandinavian studies track (MA)
Germanic studies: teaching track (MA)
Greek (MA, PhD)
health journalism (professional program) (MA)
Hispanic and Luso-Brazilian literatures and linguistics (PhD)
Hispanic linguistics (MA)
Hispanic literature (MA)
history (MA, PhD)
industrial/organizational psychology (PhD)
Latin (MA, PhD)
liberal arts (MA, MFA, MGIS, MM, MS, Au D, DMA, PhD)
linguistics (MA, PhD)
Lusophone literature (MA)
mass communication (MA, PhD)
music (MA, MM, DMA, PhD)
personality, individual differences, and behavior genetics (PhD)
philosophy (MA, PhD)
political science (PhD)
quantitative/psychometric methods (PhD)
religions in antiquity (MA)
school psychology (PhD)
social psychology (PhD)
sociology (MA, PhD)
speech-language pathology (MA)
speech-language-hearing sciences (PhD)
statistics (MS, PhD)
strategic communication (professional program) (MA)
theatre arts and dance (MA, PhD)

Hubert H. Humphrey Institute of Public Affairs
Programs in:
advanced policy analysis methods (MPP)
economic and community development (MPP)
environmental planning (MURP)
foreign policy (MPP)
housing and community development (MURP)
land use and urban design (MURP)
public affairs (MPA, MPP, MS, MURP)
public and nonprofit leadership and management (MPP)
regional, economic and workforce development (MURP)
science technology and environmental policy (MPP)
science, technology, and environmental policy (MS)
social policy (MPP)
transportation planning (MURP)
women and public policy (MPP)

School of Nursing
Programs in:
adolescent nursing (MS)
adult health clinical nurse specialist (MS)
advanced clinical specialist in gerontology (MS)
children with special health care needs (MS)
family nurse practitioner (MS)
gerontological nurse practitioner (MS)
nurse anesthetist (MS)
nurse midwifery (MS)
nursing (MN, MS, DNP, PhD)
nursing and health care systems administration (MS)
pediatric clinical nurse specialist (MS)
pediatric nurse practitioner (MS)
psychiatric mental health clinical nurse specialist (MS)
public health nursing (MS)
women's health nurse practitioner (MS)

Institute of Technology
Programs in:
aerospace engineering (M Aero E)
aerospace engineering and mechanics (MS, PhD)
biomedical engineering (MS, PhD)

chemical engineering (M Ch E, MS Ch E, PhD)
chemistry (MS, PhD)
civil engineering (MCE, MS, PhD)
computer and information sciences (MCIS, MS, PhD)
computer engineering (M Comp E, MS)
electrical engineering (MEE, MSEE, PhD)
geological engineering (M Geo E, MS, PhD)
geology (MS, PhD)
geophysics (MS, PhD)
history of science and technology (MA, PhD)
industrial engineering (MSIE, PhD)
materials science and engineering (M Mat SE, MS Mat SE, PhD)
mechanical engineering (MSME, PhD)
technology (M Aero E, M Ch E, M Comp E, M Geo E, M Mat SE, MA, MCE, MCIS, MCS, MEE, MS, MS Ch E, MS Mat SE, MSEE, MSIE, MSISE, MSME, MSMOT, MSST, PhD)

School of Mathematics
Program in:
mathematics (MS, PhD)

School of Physics and Astronomy
Programs in:
astronomy (MS, PhD)
astrophysics (MS, PhD)
physics (MS, PhD)

Technological Leadership Institute
Dr. Massoud Amin, Director
Programs in:
infrastructure systems engineering (MSISE)
management of technology (MSMOT)
security technologies (MS, MSST)

Law School
David Wippman, Dean
Program in:
law (JD, LL M)

Medical School
Programs in:
medicine (MD, MA, MS, DPT, PhD)
pharmacology (MS, PhD)
physical therapy (DPT)

Graduate Programs in Medicine
Program in:
medicine (MA)

School of Dentistry
Programs in:
dentistry (DDS, MS, PhD, Certificate)
endodontics (MS, Certificate)
oral biology (MS, PhD)
oral health services for older adults (geriatrics) (MS, Certificate)
orthodontics (MS)
pediatric dentistry (MS)
periodontology (MS)
prosthodontics (MS)
temporomandibular joint disorders (MS)

School of Public Health
Programs in:
biostatistics (MPH, MS, PhD)
clinical research (MS)
community health education (MPH)
core concepts (Certificate)
environmental and occupational epidemiology (MPH, MS, PhD)
environmental chemistry (MS, PhD)
environmental health policy (MPH, MS, PhD)
environmental infectious diseases (MPH, MS, PhD)
environmental toxicology (MPH, MS, PhD)
epidemiology (MPH, PhD)
exposure sciences (MS)
food safety and biosecurity (Certificate)
general environmental health (MPH, MS)
global environmental health (MPH, MS, PhD)
health services research, policy, and administration (MS, PhD)
healthcare administration (MHA)
industrial hygiene (MPH, MS, PhD)
maternal and child health (MPH)
occupational health and safety (Certificate)
occupational health nursing (MPH, MS, PhD)
occupational medicine (MPH)
preparedness, response and recovery (Certificate)
public health (MHA, MPH, MS, PhD, Certificate)
public health administration and policy (MPH)
public health nutrition (MPH)
public health practice (MPH)

■ UNIVERSITY OF ST. THOMAS
St. Paul, MN 55105-1096
http://www.stthomas.edu/

Independent-religious, coed, university. *Computer facilities:* 1,549 computers available on campus for general student use. A campuswide network can be accessed from student residence rooms and from off campus. Online class registration is available. *General application contact:* Dr. Angeline Barretta-Herman, Associate Vice President for Academic Affairs, 651-962-6033.

Graduate Studies
Dr. Susan J. Huber, Executive Vice President for Academic Affairs

College of Arts and Sciences
Programs in:
art history (MA)
arts and sciences (MA)
Catholic studies (MA)
English (MA)
music education (MA)

Graduate School of Professional Psychology
Dr. Burton Nolan, Associate Dean
Programs in:
counseling psychology (MA, Psy D)
marriage and family psychology (Certificate)

Opus College of Business
Dr. Christopher Puto, Dean
Programs in:
accountancy (MS)
advanced studies in business analysis (Certificate)
business (MBA, MBC, MS, MSDD, MSS, Certificate)
business administration (MBA)
business communication (MBC)
computer security (Certificate)
health care business administration (MBA)
information systems (Certificate)
real estate (MS)
software design and development (Certificate)
software engineering (MS)
software management (MS)
software systems (MSS)

Saint Paul Seminary School of Divinity
Programs in:
divinity (M Div, MA, MARE)
religious education (MARE)
theology (MA)

School of Education
Dr. Bruce H. Kramer, Interim Dean
Programs in:
athletics and activities administration (MA)
autism spectrum disorders (Certificate)
community education administration (MA)
critical pedagogy (Ed D)
curriculum and instruction (MA, Ed S)
director of special education (Ed S)
e-learning (Certificate)
education (MA, MAT, Ed D, Certificate, Ed S)
educational leadership (Ed S)
educational leadership and administration (MA)
elementary (MAT)
gifted, creative, and talented education (MA, Certificate)
human resource management (Certificate)
human resources and change leadership (MA)
international leadership (Certificate)
leadership (Ed D)
leadership in student affairs (MA, Certificate)
learning technologies (Certificate)
learning technology (MA, Certificate)
multicultural education (Certificate)
organization development (Certificate)
Orton-Gillingham reading (Certificate)
police leadership (MA)
public policy and leadership (MA, Certificate)
reading (MA, Certificate)
special education (MA)

University of St. Thomas (continued)

School of Engineering
Programs in:
- engineering and technology management (Certificate)
- manufacturing systems (MS)
- manufacturing systems engineering (MMSE)
- systems engineering (MS)
- technology management (MS)

School of Law
Thomas M. Mengler, Dean
Program in:
- law (JD)

School of Social Work
Dr. Barbara W. Shank, Dean and Professor
Program in:
- social work (MSW)

■ WALDEN UNIVERSITY
Minneapolis, MN 55401
http://www.waldenu.edu/

Proprietary, coed, upper-level institution. CGS member. *Graduate faculty:* 72 full-time, 1,422 part-time/adjunct. *Graduate expenses:* Tuition: full-time $12,877; part-time $520 per credit. Required fees: $1230. Tuition and fees vary according to course load, degree level and program. *General application contact:* Jennifer Hall, Director of Enrollment, 866-4-WALDEN.

Graduate Programs
Jonathan A. Kaplan, President

NTU School of Engineering and Applied Science
Colin Wightman, Interim Associate Dean
Programs in:
- competitive product management (Certificate)
- engineering management (Certificate)
- software engineering (MS)
- software project management (Certificate)
- software testing (Certificate)
- systems engineering (MS, Certificate)
- technical project management (Certificate)

Richard W. Riley College of Education and Leadership
Victoria Reid, Vice President
Programs in:
- administrator leadership for teaching and learning (Ed D, Ed S)
- early childhood education (birth-grade 3) (MAT)
- education (MS, PhD)
- educational technology (Ed S)
- higher education and adult learning (Ed D)
- special education: emotional/behavioral disorders (K-12) (MAT)
- special education: learning disabilities (K-12) (MAT)
- teacher leadership (Ed D, Ed S)

School of Counseling and Social Service
Dr. Savitri Dixon-Saxon, Associate Dean
Programs in:
- human services (PhD)
- mental health counseling (MS)

School of Health Sciences
Dr. Joanne Flowers, Associate Dean
Programs in:
- clinical research administration (MS)
- health services (PhD)
- healthcare administration (MHA)
- public health (MPH, PhD)

School of Management
Dr. Wanda Gravett, Associate Dean
Programs in:
- applied management and decision sciences (PhD)
- business information management (MISM)
- enterprise information security (MISM)
- entrepreneurship (MBA, DBA)
- finance (MBA, DBA)
- global supply chain management (DBA)
- human resource management (MBA)
- information systems management (DBA)
- international business (DBA)
- IT strategy and governance (MISM)
- leadership (MBA, DBA)
- management (MS)
- managing global software and service supply chains (MISM)
- marketing (MBA, DBA)
- project management (MBA)
- risk management (MBA)
- self-designed (MBA, DBA)
- social impact management (DBA)
- sustainable futures (MBA)
- technology (MBA)
- technology entrepreneurship (DBA)

School of Nursing
Dr. Sara Torres, Associate Dean
Programs in:
- nursing (Post-Master's Certificate)
- nursing education (MS)
- nursing informatics (MS)
- nursing leadership and management (MS)

School of Psychology
Dr. Nina Nabors, Associate Dean
Programs in:
- clinical assessment (Post-Doctoral Certificate)
- clinical child psychology (Post-Doctoral Certificate)
- clinical psychology (Post-Doctoral Certificate)
- counseling psychology (Post-Doctoral Certificate)
- forensic psychology (MS)
- general psychology (Post-Doctoral Certificate)
- health psychology (Post-Doctoral Certificate)
- organizational psychology (Post-Doctoral Certificate)
- organizational psychology and development (Certificate)
- psychology (MS, PhD)
- school psychology (Post-Doctoral Certificate)
- teaching online (Post-Master's Certificate)

School of Public Policy and Administration
Dr. Mark Gordon, Interim Associate Dean
Programs in:
- general public policy and administration (MPA)
- government management (Certificate)
- health policy (MPA)
- homeland security policy (MPA)
- interdisciplinary policy studies (MPA)
- law and public policy (MPA)
- local government management for sustainable communities (MPA)
- nonprofit management (Certificate)
- nonprofit management and leadership (MPA, MS)
- policy analysis (MPA)
- public management and leadership (MPA)
- public policy and administration (PhD)
- terrorism, mediation, and peace (MPA)

■ WINONA STATE UNIVERSITY
Winona, MN 55987-5838
http://www.winona.edu/

State-supported, coed, comprehensive institution. *Graduate faculty:* 57 full-time (38 women). *Computer facilities:* Computer purchase and lease plans are available. 1,400 computers available on campus for general student use. A campuswide network can be accessed from student residence rooms and from off campus. Online class registration is available. *Graduate expenses:* Tuition, state resident: full-time $5280. Tuition, nonresident: full-time $7940. Required fees: $540. *General application contact:* Dr. Nancy Jannik, Director of Graduate Studies, 507-457-5010.

College of Education
Sally Standiford, Dean
Programs in:
- community counseling (MS)
- education (MS, Ed S)
- educational leadership (Ed S)
- general school leadership (MS)
- K-12 principalship (MS)
- outdoor education/adventure based leadership (MS)
- professional development (MS)
- school counseling (MS)
- special education (MS)
- sports management (MS)
- teacher leadership (MS)

College of Liberal Arts
Dr. Troy Paino, Dean

Programs in:
English (MA, MS)
liberal arts (MA, MS)

College of Nursing and Health Sciences
Dr. William J. McBreen, Dean
Programs in:
adult nurse practitioner (MS, Post Master's Certificate)
clinical nurse specialist (MS, Post Master's Certificate)
family nurse practitioner (MS, Post Master's Certificate)
nurse administrator (MS)
nurse educator (MS, Post Master's Certificate)
nursing (DNP)

Mississippi

■ ALCORN STATE UNIVERSITY
Alcorn State, MS 39096-7500
http://www.alcorn.edu/

State-supported, coed, comprehensive institution. CGS member. *Computer facilities:* 500 computers available on campus for general student use. A campuswide network can be accessed from student residence rooms and from off campus. Online class registration is available. *General application contact:* Administrative Assistant to the Dean, School of Graduate Studies, 601-877-6122.

School of Graduate Studies
Program in:
workforce education leadership (MS)

School of Agriculture and Applied Science
Programs in:
agricultural economics (MS Ag)
agronomy (MS Ag)
animal science (MS Ag)

School of Arts and Sciences
Programs in:
arts and sciences (MS)
biology (MS)
computer and information sciences (MS)

School of Business
Program in:
business (MBA)

School of Nursing
Program in:
rural nursing (MSN)

School of Psychology and Education
Programs in:
agricultural education (MS Ed)
elementary education (MS Ed, Ed S)
guidance and counseling (MS Ed)
industrial education (MS Ed)
secondary education (MS Ed)
special education (MS Ed)

■ BELHAVEN COLLEGE
Jackson, MS 39202-1789
http://www.belhaven.edu/

Independent-religious, coed, comprehensive institution. *Graduate faculty:* 18 full-time (7 women), 18 part-time/adjunct (8 women). *Computer facilities:* 36 computers available on campus for general student use. A campuswide network can be accessed from student residence rooms and from off campus. Online class registration is available. *General application contact:* Dr. Audrey Kelleher, Vice President for Adult and Graduate Marketing and Development, 407-804-1424.

School of Business
Dr. Ralph Mason, Dean, School of Business
Programs in:
business administration (MBA)
business management (MSM)
public administration (MPA)

School of Education
Dr. Sandra L. Rasberry, Dean
Programs in:
elementary education (M Ed, MAT)
secondary education (M Ed, MAT)

■ DELTA STATE UNIVERSITY
Cleveland, MS 38733-0001
http://www.deltastate.edu/

State-supported, coed, comprehensive institution. *Graduate faculty:* 74 full-time (37 women), 20 part-time/adjunct (9 women). *Computer facilities:* Computer purchase and lease plans are available. 350 computers available on campus for general student use. A campuswide network can be accessed from student residence rooms and from off campus. Online class registration is available. *Graduate expenses:* Tuition, state resident: full-time $4450; part-time $247 per credit hour. Tuition, nonresident: full-time $11,182; part-time $621 per credit hour. *General application contact:* Dr. Albert Nylander, Dean of Graduate Studies, 662-846-4875.

Graduate Programs
Dr. Ann Lotven, Provost and Vice President for Academic Affairs

College of Arts and Sciences
Programs in:
arts and sciences (M Ed, MSCD, MSCJ, MSNS)
biological science (MSNS)
community development (MS)
criminal justice (MS)
English education (M Ed)
history education (M Ed)
mathematics education (M Ed)
physical science (MSNS)
social science secondary education (M Ed)

College of Business
Programs in:
accountancy (MPAC)
business (MBA, MCA, MPA)
commercial aviation (MCA)
management (MBA)
marketing (MBA)

College of Education
Programs in:
administration and supervision (M Ed)
administrative and supervision (Ed S)
counseling (M Ed)
counselor education (Ed D)
education (M Ed, MAT, Ed D, Ed S)
educational administration and supervision (Ed S)
educational leadership (M Ed, Ed D)
elementary education (M Ed, MAT, Ed D, Ed S)
higher education (Ed D)
physical education and recreation (M Ed)
secondary education (Ed S)
special education (M Ed)
teaching (Ed D)

School of Nursing
Programs in:
family nurse practitioner (MSN)
nurse administrator (MSN)
nurse educator (MSN)

■ JACKSON STATE UNIVERSITY
Jackson, MS 39217
http://www.jsums.edu/

State-supported, coed, university. CGS member. *Computer facilities:* 300 computers available on campus for general student use. A campuswide network can be accessed from off campus. Online class registration is available. *General application contact:* Dean of the Graduate School, 601-979-2455.

Graduate School

College of Public Service
Programs in:
communicative disorders (MS)
public service (MS)

School of Business
Programs in:
accounting (MPA)
business (MBA, MPA, PhD)
business administration (MBA)

School of Education
Programs in:
community and agency counseling (MS)
early childhood education (MS Ed, Ed D)
education (MS, MS Ed, Ed D, PhD, Ed S)
education administration (Ed S)
educational administration (MS Ed, PhD)
elementary education (MS Ed, Ed S)

Jackson State University (continued)
guidance and counseling (MS, MS Ed, Ed S)
health, physical education and recreation (MS Ed)
rehabilitative counseling (MS Ed)
rehabilitative counseling service (MS Ed)
secondary education (MS Ed, Ed S)
special education (MS Ed, Ed S)

School of Liberal Arts
Programs in:
clinical psychology (PhD)
criminology and justice service (MA)
English (MA)
history (MA)
liberal arts (MA, MAT, MM Ed, MPPA, MS, PhD)
mass communications (MS)
music education (MM Ed)
political science (MA)
public policy and administration (MPPA, PhD)
sociology (MA)
teaching English (MAT)
urban and regional planning (MS)

School of Science and Technology
Programs in:
biology education (MST)
chemistry (MS, PhD)
computer science (MS)
environmental science (MS, PhD)
hazardous materials management (MS)
industrial arts education (MS Ed)
mathematics (MS)
mathematics education (MST)
science and technology (MS, MS Ed, MST, PhD)
science education (MST)

School of Social Work
Program in:
social work (MSW, PhD)

■ MISSISSIPPI COLLEGE
Clinton, MS 39058
http://www.mc.edu/

Independent-religious, coed, comprehensive institution. *Graduate faculty:* 103 full-time (40 women), 85 part-time/adjunct (32 women). *Computer facilities:* 340 computers available on campus for general student use. A campuswide network can be accessed from student residence rooms and from off campus. Online class registration is available. *Graduate expenses:* Tuition: full-time $7830; part-time $435 per hour. Required fees: $98 per semester. Tuition and fees vary according to course load, campus/location, program and student level. *General application contact:* Dr. Debbie C. Norris, Graduate Dean, 601-925-3260.

Graduate School
Dr. Debbie C. Norris, Graduate Dean
Programs in:
health services administration (MHSA)
liberal studies (MLS)

College of Arts and Sciences
Dr. Ron Howard, Dean
Programs in:
administration of justice (MSS)
applied communication (MSC)
applied music performance (MM)
art (M Ed, MA, MFA)
arts and sciences (M Ed, MA, MCS, MFA, MM, MS, MSC, MSS, Certificate)
biological science (M Ed)
biology (MCS)
biology-biological sciences (MS)
biology-medical sciences (MS)
chemistry and biochemistry (MCS, MS)
Christian studies and the arts (M Ed, MA, MFA, MM, MSC)
computer science (M Ed, MS)
conducting (MM)
English (M Ed, MA)
history (M Ed, MA, MSS)
humanities and social sciences (M Ed, MA, MS, MSS, Certificate)
mathematics (M Ed, MCS, MS)
music education (MM)
music performance: organ (MM)
paralegal studies (Certificate)
political science (MSS)
public relations and corporate communication (MSC)
science and mathematics (M Ed, MCS, MS)
social sciences (M Ed, MSS)
teaching English to speakers of other languages (MA, MS)
vocal pedagogy (MM)

School of Business
Dr. Marcelo Eduardo, Dean
Programs in:
accounting (Certificate)
business administration (MBA)
business education (M Ed)
finance (MBA, Certificate)

School of Education
Dr. Don Locke, Dean
Programs in:
art (M Ed)
athletic administration (MS)
biological science (M Ed)
business education (M Ed)
computer science (M Ed)
counseling (Ed S)
dyslexia therapy (M Ed)
education (M Ed, MS, Ed D, Ed S)
educational leadership (M Ed, Ed D, Ed S)
elementary education (M Ed, Ed S)
English (M Ed)
higher education administration (MS)
marriage and family counseling (MS)
mathematics (M Ed)
mental health counseling (MS)
school counseling (M Ed)
secondary education (M Ed)
social studies (history) (M Ed)
teaching arts (M Ed)

School of Law
Programs in:
civil law studies (Certificate)
law (JD)

■ MISSISSIPPI STATE UNIVERSITY
Mississippi State, MS 39762
http://www.msstate.edu/

State-supported, coed, university. CGS member. *Graduate faculty:* 558 full-time (137 women), 51 part-time/adjunct (24 women). *Computer facilities:* 1,000 computers available on campus for general student use. A campuswide network can be accessed from student residence rooms and from off campus. Online class registration, campuswide wireless Internet access are available. *Graduate expenses:* Tuition, state resident: full-time $5151; part-time $286.25 per hour. Tuition, nonresident: full-time $12,503; part-time $408.50 per hour. International tuition: $12,833 full-time. Tuition and fees vary according to course load. *General application contact:* Karin Lee, Manager, Graduate Programs, 662-325-8095.

Bagley College of Engineering
Dr. Sarah A. Rajala, Dean
Programs in:
aerospace engineering (MS)
civil engineering (MS)
computer engineering (MS, PhD)
computer science (MS, PhD)
electrical engineering (MS, PhD)
engineering (PhD)
industrial engineering (MS)
mechanical engineering (MS)

David C. Swalm School of Chemical Engineering
Dr. Mark White, Director
Programs in:
chemical engineering (MS)
engineering (PhD)

College of Agriculture and Life Sciences
Dr. Melissa Mixon, Interim Dean and Vice President
Programs in:
agribusiness management (MABM)
agricultural life sciences (MS, PhD)
agricultural science (PhD)
agriculture (MS)
agriculture and life sciences (MABM, MLA, MS, PhD, Ed S)
agriculture life sciences (MS)
agriculture sciences (PhD)
biological engineering (MS)
biomedical engineering (MS, PhD)
engineering (PhD)
food science, nutrition and health promotion (MS, PhD)
landscape architecture (MLA)
life sciences (PhD)
molecular biology (PhD)

School of Human Sciences
Dr. Gary Jackson, Director
Programs in:
agricultural sciences (PhD)
agriculture and extension education (MS)
education (Ed S)

College of Architecture, Art and Design
James L. West, Dean
Program in:
architecture, art and design (MS)

School of Architecture
Dr. Larry Barrow, Director
Program in:
architecture (MS)

College of Arts and Sciences
Dr. Gary Myers, Dean/Professor
Programs in:
applied anthropology (MA)
arts and sciences (MA, MPPA, MS, PhD)
biological sciences (MS, PhD)
chemistry (MS, PhD)
cognitive science (PhD)
engineering (PhD)
English (MA)
foreign language (MA)
geosciences (MS)
history (MA)
mathematical sciences (PhD)
mathematics (MS)
physics (MS)
political science (MA)
psychology (MS)
public policy and administration (MPPA, PhD)
sociology (MS, PhD)
statistics (MS)

College of Business
Dr. Lynne Richardson, Dean
Programs in:
applied economics (PhD)
business administration (MBA, PhD)
business and industry (MA, MBA, MPA, MSBA, MSIS, MTX, PhD)
economics (MA)
finance (MSBA)
information systems (MSIS)
marketing (PhD)
project management (MBA)

School of Accountancy
Dr. Louis Dawkins, Director
Programs in:
accounting (MPA)
taxation (MTX)

College of Education
Dr. Richard Blackbourn, Dean
Programs in:
college/postsecondary student counseling and personnel services (PhD)
community college education (MAT)
community college leadership (PhD)
counselor education (MS)
counselor education/student counseling and guidance services (PhD)
curriculum and instruction (PhD)
education (MAT, MS, MSIT, Ed D, PhD, Ed S)
educational psychology (MS, PhD)
elementary education (MS, PhD)
elementary, middle school, and secondary education administration (PhD)
instructional systems and workforce development (PhD)
instructional technology (MSIT)
physical education (MS)
school administration (MS)
secondary education (MS, PhD)
secondary teacher alternate route (MAT)
special education (MS)
technology (MS)
workforce educational leadership (MS)

College of Forest Resources
Dr. George M. Hopper, Dean
Programs in:
forest resources (MS, PhD)
forestry (MS)
wildlife and fisheries science (MS)

College of Veterinary Medicine
Programs in:
environmental toxicology (PhD)
veterinary medical science (MS, PhD)
veterinary medicine (DVM, MS, PhD)

■ MISSISSIPPI UNIVERSITY FOR WOMEN
Columbus, MS 39701-9998
http://www.muw.edu/

State-supported, coed, primarily women, comprehensive institution. *Computer facilities:* 300 computers available on campus for general student use. A campuswide network can be accessed from student residence rooms and from off campus. Online class registration, various software packages are available. *General application contact:* Director, Graduate School, 601-329-7150.

Graduate School

College of Education and Human Sciences
Programs in:
differentiated instruction (M Ed)
gifted studies (M Ed)
teaching (MAT)

College of Nursing and Speech-Language Pathology
Programs in:
nursing (MSN, PMC)
speech/language pathology (MS)

Division of Health and Kinesiology
Program in:
health education (MS)

■ MISSISSIPPI VALLEY STATE UNIVERSITY
Itta Bena, MS 38941-1400
http://www.mvsu.edu/

State-supported, coed, comprehensive institution. *Computer facilities:* 275 computers available on campus for general student use. A campuswide network can be accessed from student residence rooms and from off campus. Online class registration is available. *General application contact:* Office of Admissions, 601-254-3344.

Department of Criminal Justice and Social Work
Program in:
criminal justice (MS)

Department of Education
Programs in:
education (MAT)
elementary education (MA)

Department of Natural Science and Environmental Health
Programs in:
bioinformatics (MS)
environmental health (MS)

■ UNIVERSITY OF MISSISSIPPI
Oxford, University, MS 38677
http://www.olemiss.edu/

State-supported, coed, university. CGS member. *Computer facilities:* 1,200 computers available on campus for general student use. A campuswide network can be accessed from student residence rooms and from off campus. Online class registration, application for admission, registration for orientation are available. *General application contact:* Dr. Christy M. Wyandt, Associate Dean of Graduate School, 662-915-7474.

Graduate School
Dr. Maurice Eftink, Dean

College of Liberal Arts
Dr. Glenn Hopkins, Dean
Programs in:
anthropology (MA)
art education (MA)
art history (MA)
biology (MS, PhD)
chemistry and biochemistry (MS, DA, PhD)
classics (MA)
clinical psychology (PhD)
economics (MA, PhD)
English (MA, MFA, PhD)
experimental psychology (PhD)
fine arts (MFA)
French (MA)
German (MA)
history (MA, PhD)
journalism (MA)
liberal arts (MA, MFA, MM, MS, MSS, DA, PhD)
mathematics (MA, MS, PhD)
music (MM, DA)
philosophy (MA)
physics (MA, MS, PhD)
political science (MA, PhD)
psychology (MA)
sociology (MA, MSS)
Southern studies (MA)
Spanish (MA)

School of Accountancy
Dr. Mark Wilder, Interim Dean

University of Mississippi (continued)
Programs in:
accountancy (M Acc, PhD)
taxation accounting (M Tax)

School of Applied Sciences
Dr. Linda Chitwood, Dean
Programs in:
applied sciences (MA, MS, PhD)
communicative disorders (MS)
exercise science (MS)
exercise science and leisure management (PhD)
family and consumer sciences (MS)
legal studies (MS)
park and recreation management (MA)
wellness (MS)

School of Business Administration
Dr. Brian Reithel, Dean
Programs in:
business administration (MBA, PhD)
systems management (MS)

School of Education
Dr. Tom Burnham, Dean
Programs in:
counselor education (M Ed, PhD, Specialist)
curriculum and instruction (M Ed, Ed D, Ed S)
education (PhD)
educational leadership (PhD)
educational leadership and counselor education (M Ed, MA, Ed D, Ed S)
higher education/student personnel (MA)

School of Engineering
Programs in:
computational engineering science (MS, PhD)
engineering science (MS, PhD)

School of Pharmacy
Dr. Barbara G. Wells, Dean
Programs in:
medicinal chemistry (PhD)
pharmaceutical sciences (MS)
pharmaceutics (PhD)
pharmacognosy (PhD)
pharmacology (PhD)
pharmacy (Pharm D, MS, PhD)
pharmacy administration (PhD)

School of Law
Dr. Samuel Davis, Dean
Program in:
law (JD)

■ UNIVERSITY OF SOUTHERN MISSISSIPPI
Hattiesburg, MS 39406-0001
http://www.usm.edu/

State-supported, coed, university. CGS member. *Graduate faculty:* 572 full-time (221 women), 12 part-time/adjunct (4 women). *Computer facilities:* Computer purchase and lease plans are available. 600 computers available on campus for general student use. A campuswide network can be accessed from student residence rooms and from off campus. Online class registration is available. *General application contact:* Dr. Susan Siltanen, University Director, 601-266-4369.

Graduate School
Dr. Susan Siltanen, University Director

College of Arts and Letters
Dr. Denise Von Hermann, Dean
Programs in:
anthropology (MA)
art education (MAE)
arts and letters (MA, MAE, MATL, MFA, MM, MME, MS, DMA, PhD)
conducting (MM)
English (MA, PhD)
French (MATL)
history (MA, MS, PhD)
history and literature (MM)
international development (PhD)
mass communication (MA, MS, PhD)
music education (MME, PhD)
performance (MM)
performance and pedagogy (DMA)
philosophy (MA)
political science (MA, MS)
public relations (MS)
Spanish (MATL)
speech communication (MA, MS, PhD)
teaching English to speakers of other languages (TESOL) (MATL)
theatre (MFA)
theory and composition (MM)
woodwind performance (MM)

College of Business
Dr. Harold Doty, Dean
Programs in:
accountancy (MPA)
business (MBA, MPA)
business administration (MBA)

College of Education and Psychology
Dr. Wanda Maulding, Interim Chair
Programs in:
adult education (M Ed, Ed D, PhD, Ed S)
alternative secondary teacher education (MAT)
business technology education (MS)
child and family studies (MS)
clinical psychology (MA, PhD)
counseling psychology (PhD)
early childhood education (M Ed, Ed S)
early intervention (MS)
education and psychology (M Ed, MA, MAT, MLIS, MS, Ed D, PhD, Ed S, SLS)
education of the gifted (M Ed, Ed D, PhD, Ed S)
educational administration (M Ed, Ed D, PhD, Ed S)
elementary education (M Ed, Ed D, PhD, Ed S)
experimental psychology (MA, PhD)
higher education (PhD)
instructional technology (MS)
library and information science (MLIS, SLS)
marriage and family therapy (MS)
psychology (MS)
reading (M Ed, MS, Ed S)
school psychology (MA, PhD)
secondary education (M Ed, MS, Ed D, PhD, Ed S)
special education (M Ed, Ed D, PhD, Ed S)
technical occupational education (MS)

College of Health
Dr. Michael Forster, Dean
Programs in:
adult health nursing (MSN)
community health nursing (MSN)
epidemiology and biostatistics (MPH)
ethics (PhD)
family nurse practitioner (MSN)
health (MA, MPH, MS, MSN, MSW, Au D, Ed D, PhD)
health education (MPH)
health policy/administration (MPH)
human performance (MS, Ed D, PhD)
interscholastic athletic administration (MS)
leadership (PhD)
medical technology (MS)
nursing service administration (MSN)
nutrition and food systems (MS, PhD)
occupational/environmental health (MPH)
policy analysis (PhD)
psychiatric nursing (MSN)
public health nutrition (MPH)
recreation and leisure management (MS)
social work (MSW)
speech and hearing sciences (MA, MS, Au D)
sport administration (MS)
sport and coaching education (MS)
sport management (MS)
sports and high performance materials (MS)

College of Science and Technology
Dr. Rex Gandy, Dean
Programs in:
administration of justice (PhD)
analytical chemistry (MS, PhD)
architecture and construction visualization (MS)
biochemistry (MS, PhD)
coastal sciences (MS, PhD)
computational science (MS, PhD)
computational science: mathematics (PhD)
computer science (MS, PhD)
construction management and technology (MS)
corrections (MA, MS)
economic development (MS)
engineering technology (MS)
environmental biology (MS, PhD)
geography (MS, PhD)
geology (MS)
human capital development (PhD)
hydrographic science (MS)
inorganic chemistry (MS, PhD)
juvenile justice (MA, MS)
law enforcement (MA, MS)
logistics management and technology (MS)

marine biology (MS, PhD)
marine science (MS, PhD)
mathematics (MS)
microbiology (MS, PhD)
molecular biology (MS, PhD)
organic chemistry (MS, PhD)
physical chemistry (MS, PhD)
physics (MS)
polymer science (MS)
polymer science and engineering (PhD)
science and mathematics education (MS, PhD)
science and technology (MA, MS, PhD)
workforce training and development (MS)

■ WILLIAM CAREY UNIVERSITY

Hattiesburg, MS 39401-5499

http://www.wmcarey.edu/

Independent-religious, coed, comprehensive institution. *Computer facilities:* 50 computers available on campus for general student use. A campuswide network can be accessed from student residence rooms and from off campus. *General application contact:* Clerical Assistant, Graduate Admissions, 601-318-6774.

School of Business
Program in:
business (MBA)

School of Education
Programs in:
art education (M Ed)
art of teaching (M Ed)
elementary education (M Ed, Ed S)
English education (M Ed)
gifted education (M Ed)
history and social science (M Ed)
mild/moderate disabilities (M Ed)
secondary education (M Ed)

School of Nursing
Program in:
nursing (MSN)

School of Psychology and Counseling
Program in:
counseling psychology (MS)

Missouri

■ AVILA UNIVERSITY

Kansas City, MO 64145-1698

http://www.avila.edu/

Independent-religious, coed, comprehensive institution. *Graduate faculty:* 25 full-time (14 women), 57 part-time/adjunct (29 women). *Computer facilities:* 180 computers available on campus for general student use. A campuswide network can be accessed from student residence rooms and from off campus. Online class registration is available. *Graduate expenses:* Tuition: full-time $7776; part-time $432 per credit hour. Required fees: $414; $24 per credit hour. Tuition and fees vary according to program. *General application contact:* Office of Admissions, 816-501-2400.

Department of Psychology
Dr. Regina Staves, Director of Graduate Psychology
Programs in:
counseling psychology (MS)
general psychology (MS)

Program in Organizational Development
Dr. Lacey Smith, Assistant Dean
Programs in:
organizational development (MS)
project management (Graduate Certificate)

School of Business
Dr. Richard Woodall, Dean, School of Business
Programs in:
accounting (MBA)
finance (MBA)
general management (MBA)
health care administration (MBA)
international business (MBA)
management information systems (MBA)
marketing (MBA)

School of Education
Deana Angotti, Director of Graduate Education
Programs in:
education (MA)
English for speakers of other languages (Advanced Certificate)
special reading (Advanced Certificate)

■ COLUMBIA COLLEGE

Columbia, MO 65216-0002

http://www.ccis.edu/

Independent-religious, coed, comprehensive institution. *Graduate faculty:* 14 full-time (6 women), 40 part-time/adjunct (9 women). *Computer facilities:* 83 computers available on campus for general student use. A campuswide network can be accessed from student residence rooms and from off campus. Online class registration is available. *Graduate expenses:* Tuition: full-time $3420; part-time $285 per semester hour. Full-time tuition and fees vary according to campus/location. *General application contact:* White Samantha, Director of Admissions, 573-875-7352.

Master of Arts in Teaching Program
Dr. Kristina Miller, MAT Graduate Program Coordinator
Program in:
teaching (MAT)

Master of Business Administration Program
Dr. Diane Suhler, MBA Graduate Program Coordinator
Program in:
business administration (MBA)

Master of Science in Criminal Justice Program
Dr. Joseph Carrier, MSCJ Graduate Program Coordinator
Program in:
criminal justice (MSCJ)

■ DRURY UNIVERSITY

Springfield, MO 65802

http://www.drury.edu/

Independent, coed, comprehensive institution. *Computer facilities:* 323 computers available on campus for general student use. A campuswide network can be accessed from student residence rooms and from off campus. Online class registration, digital imaging lab, online bill payment/student information are available. *General application contact:* Graduate Programs Office Coordinator, 417-873-6948.

Breech School of Business Administration
Program in:
business administration (MBA)

Graduate Programs in Education
Programs in:
elementary education (M Ed)
gifted education (M Ed)
human services (M Ed)
instructional mathematics K-8 (M Ed)
instructional technology (M Ed)
middle school teaching (M Ed)
secondary education (M Ed)
special education (M Ed)
special reading (M Ed)

Hammons School of Architecture
Program in:
architecture (M Arch)

Program in Communication
Program in:
communication (MA)

Program in Criminology/Criminal Justice
Programs in:
criminal justice (MS)
criminology (MA)

Program in Studio Art and Theory
Program in:
studio art and theory (MA)

■ FONTBONNE UNIVERSITY

St. Louis, MO 63105-3098

http://www.fontbonne.edu/

Independent-religious, coed, primarily women, comprehensive institution. *Graduate*

Fontbonne University (continued)
faculty: 46 full-time (30 women), 139 part-time/adjunct (66 women). *Computer facilities:* Computer purchase and lease plans are available. 285 computers available on campus for general student use. A campuswide network can be accessed from student residence rooms and from off campus. Online class registration is available. *Graduate expenses:* Tuition: part-time $540 per credit hour. Required fees: $270 per year. *General application contact:* Peggy Musen, Vice President of Enrollment Management, 314-889-1400.

Graduate Programs
Dr. Nancy Blattner, Vice President and Dean for Academic and Student Affairs
Programs in:
art (MA)
computer education (MS)
early intervention in deaf education (MA)
education (MA)
family and consumer sciences (MA)
fine arts (MFA)
speech-language pathology (MS)
theater education (MA)

College of Global Business and Professional Studies
Dean Linda Maurer, Dean of the College of Global Business and Professional Studies
Programs in:
accounting (MS)
business administration (MBA)
options in business administration (MBA)
options in management (MM)
taxation (MST)

■ LINCOLN UNIVERSITY
Jefferson City, MO 65102
http://www.lincolnu.edu/

State-supported, coed, comprehensive institution. *Graduate faculty:* 27 full-time (9 women), 9 part-time/adjunct (3 women). *Computer facilities:* Computer purchase and lease plans are available. 250 computers available on campus for general student use. A campuswide network can be accessed from student residence rooms. Online class registration is available. *Graduate expenses:* Tuition, state resident: full-time $4185; part-time $232.50 per credit hour. Tuition, nonresident: full-time $7767; part-time $431.50 per credit hour. Required fees: $270; $15 per credit hour. One-time fee: $20. Tuition and fees vary according to course load. *General application contact:* Dr. Linda S. Bickel, Dean of the School of Graduate Studies and Continuing Education, 573-681-5247.

School of Graduate Studies and Continuing Education
Dr. Linda S. Bickel, Dean of the School of Graduate Studies and Continuing Education

College of Business and Professional Studies
Dr. Linda S. Bickel, Dean
Programs in:
business administration (MBA)
business and professional studies (MBA)

College of Liberal Arts, Education and Journalism
Dr. Ann Harris, Dean
Programs in:
educational leadership (Ed S)
guidance and counseling (M Ed)
history (MA)
liberal arts, education and journalism (M Ed, MA, Ed S)
school administration and supervision (M Ed)
school teaching (M Ed)
social science (MA)
sociology (MA)
sociology/criminal justice (MA)

■ LINDENWOOD UNIVERSITY
St. Charles, MO 63301-1695
http://www.lindenwood.edu/

Independent-religious, coed, comprehensive institution. *Graduate faculty:* 91 full-time (39 women), 317 part-time/adjunct (139 women). *Computer facilities:* Computer purchase and lease plans are available. 160 computers available on campus for general student use. A campuswide network can be accessed from student residence rooms and from off campus. Online class registration, WebCT are available. *Graduate expenses:* Tuition: full-time $12,700; part-time $360 per credit hour. *General application contact:* Brett Barger, Dean of Evening Admissions and Extension Campuses, 636-949-4934.

Graduate Programs
Dr. Jann Weitzel, Vice President of Academic Affairs and Provost

College of Individualized Education
Dan Kemper, Dean of Lindenwood College for Individual Education
Programs in:
administration (MSA)
business administration (MBA)
communication (MS)
communications (MA)
criminal justice and administration (MS)
gerontology (MA)
health management (MS)
human resource management (MS)
information technology (MBA, Certificate)
management (MSA)
managing information technology (MS)
marketing (MSA)
writing (MFA)

School of Business and Entrepreneurship
Ed Morris, Dean of Management
Programs in:
accounting (MBA, MS)
business administration (MBA)
entrepreneurial studies (MBA, MS)
finance (MBA, MS)
human resource management (MBA)
human resources (MS)
international business (MBA, MS)
management (MBA, MS)
management information systems (MBA, MS)
marketing (MBA, MS)
public management (MBA, MS)
sport management (MA)

School of Education
Dr. Cynthia Bice, Dean of Education
Programs in:
education (MA)
educational administration (MA, Ed D, Ed S)
instructional leadership (Ed D, Ed S)
library media (MA)
professional and school counseling (MA)
professional counseling (MA)
school counseling (MA)
teaching (MA)

School of Fine and Performing Arts
Donnell Walsh, Dean of Fine Arts
Programs in:
arts management (MA)
communication arts (MA)
studio art (MA, MFA)
theatre (MA, MFA)

School of Humanities
Dr. Ana Schnellmann, Dean of Humanities
Program in:
American studies (MA)

■ MARYVILLE UNIVERSITY OF SAINT LOUIS
St. Louis, MO 63141-7299
http://www.maryville.edu/

Independent, coed, comprehensive institution. *Graduate faculty:* 45 full-time (30 women), 38 part-time/adjunct (23 women). *Computer facilities:* Computer purchase and lease plans are available. 489 computers available on campus for general student use. A campuswide network can be accessed from student residence rooms and from off campus. Online class registration, specialized software, university catalog are available. *Graduate expenses:* Tuition: full-time $19,650; part-time $605 per credit hour. Required fees: $100 per semester. Part-time tuition and fees vary according to degree level and program. *General application contact:* Denise Evans, Assistant Vice President, Adult and Continuing Education, 314-529-9676.

College of Arts and Sciences
Dr. Dan Sparling, Dean
Programs in:
actuarial science (MS)
arts and sciences (MS)

The John E. Simon School of Business
Dr. Pamela Horwitz, Dean
Programs in:
accounting (MBA, PGC)
business studies (PGC)
e-marketing (MBA, PGC)
management (MBA, PGC)
marketing (MBA, PGC)

School of Education
Dr. Sam Hausfather, Dean
Programs in:
art education (MA Ed)
early childhood education (MA Ed)
educational leadership (Ed D)
educational leadership: principal certification (MA Ed)
elementary education (MA Ed)
elementary education/English (MA Ed)
elementary education/psychology (MA Ed)
environmental education (MA Ed)
gifted education (MA Ed)
literacy specialist (MA Ed)
middle grades education (MA Ed)
secondary teaching and inquiry (MA Ed)
teacher as leader (MA Ed)

School of Health Professions
Dr. Charles Gulas, Dean
Programs in:
adult nurse practitioner (MSN)
family nurse practitioner (MSN)
health professions (MARC, MMT, MOT, MSN, DPT)
marriage and family therapy (MARC)
music therapy (MARC)
nursing education (MSN)
occupational therapy (MOT)
physical therapy (DPT)
substance abuse (MARC)

■ MISSOURI BAPTIST UNIVERSITY
St. Louis, MO 63141-8660
http://www.mobap.edu/

Independent-religious, coed, comprehensive institution. *Computer facilities:* 122 computers available on campus for general student use. A campuswide network can be accessed from student residence rooms and from off campus.

■ MISSOURI STATE UNIVERSITY
Springfield, MO 65804-0094
http://www.missouristate.edu/

State-supported, coed, comprehensive institution. CGS member. *Graduate faculty:* 426 full-time (132 women), 137 part-time/adjunct (43 women). *Computer facilities:* Computer purchase and lease plans are available. 1,800 computers available on campus for general student use. A campuswide network can be accessed from student residence rooms and from off campus. Online class registration is available. *Graduate expenses:* Tuition, state resident: full-time $3852; part-time $214 per credit hour. Tuition, nonresident: full-time $7524; part-time $418 per credit hour. Required fees: $230 per semester. Tuition and fees vary according to course level and course load. *General application contact:* Eric Eckert, Coordinator of Admissions and Recruitment, 417-836-5331.

Graduate College
Dr. Frank A. Einhellig, Associate Provost and Dean of the Graduate College
Programs in:
applied communication (MS)
criminal justice (MS)
environmental management (MS)
project management (MS)
sports management (MS)

College of Arts and Letters
Dr. Carey Adams, Dean
Programs in:
arts and letters (MA, MM, MS Ed)
communication and mass media (MA)
English and writing (MA)
music (MM)
secondary education (MS Ed)
theatre (MA)

College of Business Administration
Dr. Danny Arnold, Dean
Programs in:
accountancy (M Acc)
business administration (M Acc, MBA, MHA, MS, MS Ed)
computer information systems (MS)
health administration (MHA)
secondary education (MS Ed)
technology and construction management (MS)

College of Education
Dr. Dennis Kear, Dean
Programs in:
counseling (MS)
early childhood and family development (MS)
education (MAT, MS, MS Ed, Ed S)
educational administration (MS Ed, Ed S)
elementary education (MS Ed)
elementary principal (Ed S)
instructional media technology (MS Ed)
reading (MS Ed)
reading education (MS Ed)
secondary education (MS Ed)
secondary principal (Ed S)
special education (MS Ed)
student affairs (MS)
superintendent (Ed S)
teaching (MAT)

College of Health and Human Services
Dr. Helen Reid, Dean
Programs in:
audiology (Au D)
cell and molecular biology (MS)
communication sciences and disorders (MS)
family nurse practitioner (MSN)
health and human services (MPH, MS, MS Ed, MSN, MSW, Au D, DPT)
health promotion and wellness management (MS)
nurse anesthesia (MS)
nurse educator (MSN)
nursing (MSN)
physical therapy (DPT)
physician assistant studies (MS)
psychology (MS)
public health (MPH)
secondary education (MS Ed)
social work (MSW)

College of Humanities and Public Affairs
Dr. Victor Matthews, Dean
Programs in:
criminology (MS)
defense and strategic studies (MS)
history (MA)
humanities and public affairs (MA, MIAA, MPA, MS, MS Ed)
international affairs and administration (MIAA)
public administration (MPA)
religious studies (MA)
secondary education (MS Ed)

College of Natural and Applied Sciences
Dr. Tamera Jahnke, Dean
Programs in:
biology (MS)
chemistry (MS)
computer science (MNAS)
geospatial sciences (MS)
materials science (MS)
mathematics (MS)
natural and applied science (MNAS)
natural and applied sciences (MNAS, MS, MS Ed)
physics, astronomy, and materials science (MNAS)
plant science (MS)
secondary education (MS Ed)

■ MISSOURI UNIVERSITY OF SCIENCE AND TECHNOLOGY
Rolla, MO 65409
http://www.mst.edu/

State-supported, coed, primarily men, university. CGS member. *Computer facilities:* Computer purchase and lease plans are available. 980 computers available on campus for general student use. A campuswide network can be accessed from student residence rooms and from off campus. Online class registration is available. *General application contact:* Admissions Coordinator, 573-341-6013.

Missouri University of Science and Technology (continued)

Graduate School

Programs in:
- aerospace engineering (MS, PhD)
- applied and environmental biology (MS)
- applied mathematics (MS)
- business and information technology (MBA)
- ceramic engineering (MS, DE, PhD)
- chemical engineering (MS, DE, PhD)
- chemistry (MS, MST, PhD)
- civil engineering (MS, DE, PhD)
- computer science (MS, PhD)
- construction engineering (MS, DE, PhD)
- engineering management (MS, DE, PhD)
- environmental engineering (MS)
- fluid mechanics (MS, DE, PhD)
- geological engineering (MS, DE, PhD)
- geology and geophysics (MS, PhD)
- geotechnical engineering (MS, DE, PhD)
- hydrology and hydraulic engineering (MS, DE, PhD)
- information science and technology (MS)
- manufacturing engineering (M Eng, MS)
- mathematics (MST, PhD)
- mechanical engineering (MS, DE, PhD)
- metallurgical engineering (MS, PhD)
- mining engineering (MS, DE, PhD)
- nuclear engineering (MS, DE, PhD)
- petroleum engineering (MS, DE, PhD)
- physics (MS, MST, PhD)
- systems engineering (MS, PhD)

School of Engineering

Programs in:
- computer engineering (MS, DE, PhD)
- electrical engineering (MS, DE, PhD)
- engineering (M Eng, MS, DE, PhD)

■ NORTHWEST MISSOURI STATE UNIVERSITY

Maryville, MO 64468-6001

http://www.nwmissouri.edu/

State-supported, coed, comprehensive institution. *Computer facilities:* Computer purchase and lease plans are available. 6,450 computers available on campus for general student use. A campuswide network can be accessed from student residence rooms and from off campus. Online class registration, online courses with library and databases are available. *General application contact:* Dean of Graduate School, 660-562-1145.

Graduate School

College of Arts and Sciences

Programs in:
- arts and sciences (MA, MS, MS Ed, Certificate)
- biology (MS)
- English (MA)
- English with speech emphasis (MA)
- geographic information sciences (MS, Certificate)
- history (MA)
- teaching English (option 1) (MS Ed)
- teaching English with speech emphasis (MS Ed)
- teaching history (MS Ed)
- teaching mathematics (MS Ed)
- teaching music (MS Ed)
- teaching: science (MS Ed)

College of Education and Human Services

Programs in:
- applied health science (MS)
- education and human services (MS, MS Ed, Certificate, Ed S)
- educational leadership (MS Ed, Ed S)
- educational leadership: elementary (MS Ed)
- educational leadership: secondary (MS Ed)
- elementary principalship (Ed S)
- English language learners (Certificate)
- guidance and counseling (MS Ed)
- health and physical education (MS Ed)
- higher education leadership (MS)
- reading (MS Ed)
- recreation (MS)
- secondary individualized prescribed programs (MS Ed)
- secondary principalship (Ed S)
- special education (MS Ed)
- superintendency (Ed S)
- teaching secondary (MS Ed)
- teaching: early childhood (MS Ed)
- teaching: elementary self contained (MS Ed)
- teaching: English language learners (MS Ed)
- teaching: middle school (MS Ed)

Melvin and Valorie Booth College of Business and Professional Studies

Programs in:
- accounting (MBA)
- agricultural economics (MBA)
- agriculture (MS)
- applied computer science (MS)
- business administration (MBA)
- business and professional studies (MBA, MS, MS Ed, Certificate)
- health management (MBA)
- information technology management (MBA)
- instructional technology (Certificate)
- quality (MBA, MS)
- quality management (Certificate)
- teaching agriculture (MS Ed)
- teaching instructional technology (MS Ed)

■ PARK UNIVERSITY

Parkville, MO 64152-3795

http://www.park.edu/

Independent, coed, comprehensive institution. CGS member. *Computer facilities:* 143 computers available on campus for general student use. A campuswide network can be accessed from student residence rooms. Online class registration is available. *General application contact:* Recruiter, 816-842-6182 Ext. 5530.

College of Graduate and Professional Studies

Programs in:
- adult education (M Ed)
- at-risk students (M Ed)
- disaster and emergency management (MPA)
- educational administration (M Ed)
- entrepreneurship (MBA)
- general business (MBA)
- general education (M Ed)
- government/business relations (MPA)
- healthcare/services management (MBA, MPA)
- international business (MBA)
- K-12 certification (MAT)
- management information systems (MBA)
- management of information systems (MPA)
- middle school certification (MAT)
- multi-cultural education (M Ed)
- nonprofit management (MPA)
- public management (MPA)
- school law (M Ed)
- secondary school certification (MAT)
- special education (M Ed)

■ ROCKHURST UNIVERSITY

Kansas City, MO 64110-2561

http://www.rockhurst.edu/

Independent-religious, coed, comprehensive institution. CGS member. *Graduate faculty:* 59 full-time (31 women), 23 part-time/adjunct (9 women). *Computer facilities:* Computer purchase and lease plans are available. 227 computers available on campus for general student use. A campuswide network can be accessed from student residence rooms and from off campus. Online class registration, wireless network are available. *General application contact:* Cheryl Hooper, Director of Graduate Recruitment, 816-501-4097.

Helzberg School of Management

Dr. James Daley, Dean

Program in:
- management (MBA)

School of Graduate and Professional Studies

Dr. Donna Calvert, Dean

Programs in:
- arts and sciences (M Ed, MOT, MS, DPT)
- communication sciences and disorders (MS)
- education (M Ed)
- occupational therapy (MOT)
- physical therapy (DPT)

■ SAINT LOUIS UNIVERSITY

St. Louis, MO 63103-2097

http://www.slu.edu/

Independent-religious, coed, university. CGS member. *Computer facilities:* 300 computers available on campus for general student use. A campuswide network can be accessed from student residence rooms and from off campus. Online class registration is available. *General application contact:* Associate Dean of Graduate School Admissions, 314-977-3827.

Graduate School

Programs in:
- anatomy (MS-R, PhD)
- biochemistry and molecular biology (PhD)
- biomedical sciences (MS-R, PhD)
- molecular microbiology and immunology (PhD)
- pathology (PhD)
- pharmacological and physiological science (PhD)

Center for Advanced Dental Education

Programs in:
- endodontics (MSD)
- orthodontics (MSD)
- periodontics (MSD)

Center for Health Care Ethics

Programs in:
- clinical health care ethics (Certificate)
- health care ethics (PhD)

College of Arts and Sciences

Programs in:
- American studies (MA, MA-R, PhD)
- arts and sciences (M Pr Met, MA, MA-R, MS, MS-R, PhD)
- biology (MS, MS-R, PhD)
- chemistry (MS, MS-R, PhD)
- clinical psychology (MS-R, PhD)
- communication (MA, MA-R)
- communication sciences and disorders (MA, MA-R)
- English (MA, MA-R, PhD)
- experimental psychology (MS-R, PhD)
- French (MA)
- geophysics (PhD)
- geoscience (MS)
- historical theology (MA, PhD)
- history (MA, MA-R, PhD)
- industrial-organizational psychology (PhD)
- mathematics (MA, MA-R, PhD)
- meteorology (M Pr Met, MS-R, PhD)
- philosophy (MA, MA-R, PhD)
- political science (MA)
- psychology (PhD)
- Spanish (MA)
- theology (MA)

College of Education and Public Service

Programs in:
- Catholic school leadership (MA)
- counseling and family therapy (PhD)
- curriculum and instruction (MA, Ed D, PhD)
- education and public service (MA, MA-R, MAPA, MAT, MAUA, MSW, MUPRED, Ed D, PhD, Certificate, Ed S)
- educational administration (MA, Ed D, PhD, Ed S)
- educational foundations (MA, Ed D, PhD)
- geographic information systems (Certificate)
- higher education (MA, Ed D, PhD)
- human development counseling (MA)
- marriage and family therapy (Certificate)
- organizational development (Certificate)
- public administration (MAPA)
- public policy analysis (PhD)
- school counseling (MA, MA-R)
- social work (MSW)
- special education (MA)
- student personnel administration (MA)
- teaching (MAT)
- urban affairs (MAUA)
- urban planning and real estate development (MUPRED)

Doisy College of Health Sciences

Programs in:
- athletic training (MAT)
- health sciences (MAT, MMS, MOT, MS, MSN, MSN-R, DNP, DPT, PhD, Certificate)
- medical dietetics (MS)
- nursing (MSN, MSN-R, DNP, PhD, Certificate)
- nutrition and physical performance (MS)
- occupational science and occupational therapy (MOT)
- physical therapy (DPT)
- physician assistant education (MMS)

John Cook School of Business

Programs in:
- accounting (M Acct, MBA)
- business (EMIB, M Acct, MBA, MSF, PhD)
- business administration (MBA)
- executive international business (EMIB)
- finance (MBA, MSF)
- international business (MBA)

Parks College of Engineering, Aviation, and Technology

Programs in:
- biomedical engineering (MS, MS-R, PhD)
- engineering, aviation, and technology (MS, MS-R, PhD)

School of Medicine

Program in:
- medicine (MD)

School of Public Health

Programs in:
- biosecurity (Certificate)
- community health (MPH, MS, MSPH)
- health administration (MHA)
- health management and policy (MHA, MPH, PhD)
- health policy (MPH)
- public health (PhD)
- public health studies (PhD)

School of Law

Program in:
- law (JD, LL M)

■ SOUTHEAST MISSOURI STATE UNIVERSITY

Cape Girardeau, MO 63701-4799

http://www.semo.edu/

State-supported, coed, comprehensive institution. CGS member. *Graduate faculty:* 212 full-time (86 women). *Computer facilities:* 1,311 computers available on campus for general student use. A campuswide network can be accessed from student residence rooms. Online class registration is available. *Graduate expenses:* Part-time $213.30 per credit hour. Tuition, state resident: part-time $213.30 per credit hour. Tuition, nonresident: part-time $393.30 per credit hour. Required fees: $23.70 per credit hour. *General application contact:* Dr. Fred Janzow, Dean of the School of Graduate Studies, 573-651-2192.

School of Graduate Studies

Dr. Fred Janzow, Vice Provost and Dean of the School of Graduate Studies

Programs in:
- applied chemistry (MNS)
- biology (MNS)
- communication disorders (MA)
- community wellness and leisure (MPA)
- counseling (MA, Ed S)
- counseling education (Ed S)
- criminal justice and sociology (MS)
- educational administration (MA, Ed S)
- educational studies (MA)
- elementary education (MA)
- English (MA)
- exceptional child education (MA)
- higher education (MA)
- history (MA)
- human environmental studies (MA)
- mathematics (MNS)
- mental health counseling (MA)
- middle level education (MA)
- music education (MME)
- nursing (MSN)
- nutrition and exercise science (MS)
- public administration (MPA)
- school counseling (MA)
- teaching English to speakers of other languages (MA)
- technology management (MS)

Godwin Center for Science and Mathematics Education

Dr. Rachel Morgan Theall, Director of Graduate Program in Science Education

Program in:
- science education (MNS)

Southeast Missouri State University (continued)

Harrison College of Business
Dr. Kenneth A. Heischmidt, Director, Graduate Programs in Business
Programs in:
- accounting (MBA)
- entrepreneurship (MBA)
- environmental management (MBA)
- financial management (MBA)
- general management (MBA)
- health administration (MBA)
- industrial management (MBA)
- international business (MBA)
- sport management (MBA)

■ SOUTHWEST BAPTIST UNIVERSITY
Bolivar, MO 65613-2597
http://www.sbuniv.edu/

Independent-religious, coed, comprehensive institution. *Graduate faculty:* 15 full-time (7 women), 49 part-time/adjunct (30 women). *Computer facilities:* 261 computers available on campus for general student use. A campuswide network can be accessed from student residence rooms and from off campus. Online class registration is available. *General application contact:* Dr. Gordon Dutile, Provost, 417-328-1601.

Program in Business
Shelly Francka, Director of Graduate Studies in Business
Programs in:
- business administration (MBA)
- health administration (MBA)

Program in Education
Dr. Mick Arnold, Director, Graduate Studies in Education
Programs in:
- education (MS)
- educational administration (MS, Ed S)

Program in Physical Therapy
Dr. Steve Lesh, Director
Program in:
- physical therapy (DPT)

■ TRUMAN STATE UNIVERSITY
Kirksville, MO 63501-4221
http://www.truman.edu/

State-supported, coed, comprehensive institution. CGS member. *Computer facilities:* Computer purchase and lease plans are available. 965 computers available on campus for general student use. A campuswide network can be accessed from student residence rooms and from off campus. Online class registration is available. *General application contact:* Graduate Office Secretary, 660-785-4109.

Graduate School

College of Arts and Sciences
Programs in:
- arts and sciences (MA, MS)
- biology (MS)
- English (MA)
- music (MA)

School of Business
Programs in:
- accounting (M Ac)
- business (M Ac)

School of Health Sciences and Education
Programs in:
- communication disorders (MA)
- education (MAE)
- health sciences and education (MA, MAE)

■ UNIVERSITY OF CENTRAL MISSOURI
Warrensburg, MO 64093
http://www.ucmo.edu/

State-supported, coed, comprehensive institution. CGS member. *Computer facilities:* 10,000 computers available on campus for general student use. A campuswide network can be accessed from student residence rooms and from off campus. Online class registration is available. *General application contact:* Interim Assistant for Research/Dean of the Graduate School, 660-543-4950.

The Graduate School

College of Arts, Humanities and Social Sciences
Programs in:
- arts, humanities and social sciences (MA, MS)
- communication (MA)
- English (MA)
- history (MA)
- music (MA)
- speech communication (MA)
- teaching English as a second language (MA)
- theatre (MA)

College of Education
Programs in:
- college student personnel administration (MS)
- counseling (MS)
- counselor education (MS, Ed S)
- curriculum and instruction (Ed S)
- education (MS, MSE, Ed D, Ed S)
- educational leadership (Ed D)
- educational technology (MSE)
- elementary education (MSE)
- human service/guidance counseling (Ed S)
- human services/ technology and occupational education (Ed S)
- human services/learning resources (Ed S)
- K–12 education (MSE)
- library science and information services (MS, Ed S)
- literacy education (MSE)
- school administration (MSE, Ed S)
- secondary education (MSE)
- secondary education/business and office education (MSE)
- special education (MSE, Ed S)
- special education/human services (Ed S)
- technology and occupational education (MS)

College of Health and Human Services
Programs in:
- criminal justice (MS)
- fire science (MS)
- health and human services (MA, MS, Ed S)
- human services/public services (Ed S)
- industrial hygiene (MS)
- industrial safety management (MS)
- loss control (MS)
- occupational safety management (MS)
- physical education/exercise and sports science (MS)
- psychology (MS)
- public safety (MS)
- rural family nursing (MS)
- security (MS)
- social gerontology (MS)
- sociology (MA)
- speech pathology and audiology (MS)
- transportation safety (MS)

College of Science and Technology
Programs in:
- applied mathematics (MS)
- aviation safety (MS)
- biology (MS)
- industrial management (MS)
- mathematics (MS)
- science and technology (MS)

Harmon College of Business Administration
Programs in:
- accountancy (MA)
- business administration (MA, MBA, MS)
- information technology (MS)

■ UNIVERSITY OF MISSOURI–COLUMBIA
Columbia, MO 65211
http://www.missouri.edu/

State-supported, coed, university. CGS member. *Graduate faculty:* 1,678 full-time (520 women), 70 part-time/adjunct (32 women). *Computer facilities:* 1,080 computers available on campus for general student use. A campuswide network can be accessed from student residence rooms and from off campus. Online class registration, telephone registration are available. *General application contact:* Terrence Grus, Director of Graduate Admissions and Academic Records, 573-882-6312.

College of Veterinary Medicine
Dr. Neil Olson, Dean

Programs in:
- laboratory animal medicine (MS)
- pathobiology (MS, PhD)
- veterinary biomedical sciences (MS)
- veterinary clinical sciences (MS)
- veterinary medicine (DVM)
- veterinary medicine and surgery (MS)
- veterinary pathobiology (MS, PhD)

Graduate School

Dr. Pamela Benoit, Vice-Provost for Advanced Studies and Dean of the Graduate School

Programs in:
- dispute resolution (LL M)
- genetics (PhD)
- health administration (MHA)
- health informatics (MHA)
- health services management (MHA)
- neuroscience (MS, PhD)
- public health (MPH)

College of Agriculture, Food and Natural Resources

Dr. Thomas L. Payne, Dean

Programs in:
- agricultural economics (MS, PhD)
- agricultural education (MS, PhD)
- agriculture, food and natural resources (MS, PhD)
- animal sciences (MS, PhD)
- biochemistry (MS, PhD)
- entomology (MS, PhD)
- food science (MS, PhD)
- foods and food systems management (MS)
- horticulture (MS, PhD)
- human nutrition (MS)
- plant microbiology and pathology (MS, PhD)
- plant sciences (MS, PhD)
- rural sociology (MS, PhD)

College of Arts and Sciences

Dr. Michael J. O'Brien, Dean

Programs in:
- analytical chemistry (MS, PhD)
- anthropology (MA, PhD)
- applied mathematics (MS)
- art (MFA)
- art history and archaeology (MA, PhD)
- arts and sciences (MA, MFA, MM, MS, MST, PhD)
- classical studies (MA, PhD)
- communication (MA, PhD)
- economics (MA, PhD)
- English (MA, PhD)
- evolutionary biology and ecology (MA, PhD)
- French (MA, PhD)
- genetic, cellular and developmental biology (MA, PhD)
- geography (MA)
- geological sciences (MS, PhD)
- German (MA)
- history (MA, PhD)
- inorganic chemistry (MS, PhD)
- literature (MA)
- mathematics (MA, MST, PhD)
- music (MA, MM)
- neurobiology and behavior (MA, PhD)
- organic chemistry (MS, PhD)
- philosophy (MA, PhD)
- physical chemistry (MS, PhD)
- physics and astronomy (MS, PhD)
- political science (MA, PhD)
- psychological sciences (MA, MS, PhD)
- religious studies (MA)
- sociology (MA, PhD)
- Spanish (MA, PhD)
- statistics (MA, PhD)
- teaching (MA)
- theatre (MA, PhD)

College of Education

Dr. Rose Porter, Interim Dean

Programs in:
- administration and supervision of special education (PhD)
- agricultural education (M Ed, PhD, Ed S)
- art education (M Ed, PhD, Ed S)
- behavior disorders (M Ed, PhD)
- business and office education (M Ed, PhD, Ed S)
- counseling psychology (M Ed, MA, PhD, Ed S)
- curriculum development of exceptional students (M Ed, PhD)
- early childhood education (M Ed, PhD, Ed S)
- early childhood special education (M Ed, PhD)
- education (M Ed, MA, Ed D, PhD, Ed S)
- education administration (M Ed, MA, Ed D, PhD, Ed S)
- educational psychology (M Ed, MA, PhD, Ed S)
- educational technology (M Ed, Ed S)
- elementary education (M Ed, PhD, Ed S)
- English education (M Ed, PhD, Ed S)
- foreign language education (M Ed, PhD, Ed S)
- general special education (M Ed, MA, PhD)
- health education and promotion (M Ed, PhD)
- higher and adult education (M Ed, MA, Ed D, PhD, Ed S)
- information science and learning technology (PhD)
- learning and instruction (M Ed)
- learning disabilities (M Ed, PhD)
- library science (MA)
- marketing education (M Ed, PhD, Ed S)
- mathematics education (M Ed, PhD, Ed S)
- mental retardation (M Ed, PhD)
- music education (M Ed, PhD, Ed S)
- reading education (M Ed, PhD, Ed S)
- school psychology (M Ed, MA, PhD, Ed S)
- science education (M Ed, PhD, Ed S)
- social studies education (M Ed, PhD, Ed S)
- vocational education (M Ed, PhD, Ed S)

College of Engineering

Dr. James E. Thompson, Dean

Programs in:
- agricultural engineering (MS)
- biological engineering (MS, PhD)
- chemical engineering (MS, PhD)
- civil engineering (MS, PhD)
- computer science (MS, PhD)
- electrical and computer engineering (MS, PhD)
- engineering (ME, MS, PhD)
- environmental engineering (MS, PhD)
- geotechnical engineering (MS, PhD)
- industrial and manufacturing systems engineering (MS, PhD)
- mechanical and aerospace engineering (MS, PhD)
- structural engineering (MS, PhD)
- transportation and highway engineering (MS)
- water resources (MS, PhD)

College of Human Environmental Science

Dr. Stephen R. Jorgensen, Dean

Programs in:
- design with digital media (MA, MS)
- environmental design (MS)
- exercise physiology (MA, PhD)
- human development and family studies (MA, MS, PhD)
- human environmental science (MA, MS, PhD)
- nutritional sciences (MS, PhD)
- personal financial planning (MS)
- textile and apparel management (MA, MS)

Harry S Truman School of Public Affairs

Dr. Bart Wechsler, Director

Program in:
- public affairs (MPA)

Informatics Institute

Dr. Chi-Ren Shyu, Director

Program in:
- informatics (PhD)

Nuclear Science and Engineering Institute

Dr. Wynn Volkert, Department Chair

Program in:
- nuclear power engineering (MS, PhD)

Robert J. Trulaske, Sr. College of Business

Dr. Bruce Walker, Dean

Programs in:
- accountancy (M Acc, PhD)
- business (M Acc, MBA, PhD)
- business administration (MBA, PhD)

School of Journalism

Dr. Esther Thorson, Associate Dean

Program in:
- journalism (MA, PhD)

School of Natural Resources

Dr. Mark Ryan, Director

Programs in:
- atmospheric science (MS, PhD)
- fisheries and wildlife (MS, PhD)
- forestry (MS, PhD)
- natural resources (MNR, MS, PhD)
- parks, recreation and tourism (MS)
- soil science (MS, PhD)

University of Missouri–Columbia (continued)

School of Social Work
Dr. Marjorie Sable, Director
Program in:
social work (MSW)

Sinclair School of Nursing
Dr. Roxanne W. McDaniel, Department Chair
Program in:
nursing (MS, PhD)

School of Health Professions
Dr. Richard E. Oliver, Dean
Programs in:
communication science and disorders (MHS)
diagnostic medical ultrasound (MHS)
health professions (MHS, MOT, MPT)
occupational therapy (MOT)
physical therapy (MPT)

School of Law
Dr. R. Lawrence Dessem, Dean
Program in:
law (JD, LL M)

School of Medicine
Dr. Robert Churchill, Interim Dean
Programs in:
medicine (MD, MS, PhD)
public health (MS)

Graduate Programs in Medicine
Dr. Roberta Churchill, Interim Dean
Programs in:
medicine (MS, PhD)
molecular microbiology and immunology (MS, PhD)
pathology and anatomical sciences (MS)
pharmacology (MS, PhD)
physiology (MS, PhD)

■ UNIVERSITY OF MISSOURI–KANSAS CITY
Kansas City, MO 64110-2499
http://www.umkc.edu/

State-supported, coed, university. CGS member. *Graduate faculty:* 698 full-time (297 women), 467 part-time/adjunct (234 women). *Computer facilities:* Computer purchase and lease plans are available. 728 computers available on campus for general student use. A campuswide network can be accessed from student residence rooms and from off campus. Online class registration is available. *Graduate expenses:* Tuition, state resident: full-time $5376; part-time $298.70 per credit hour. Tuition, nonresident: full-time $13,882; part-time $771.20 per credit hour. Required fees: $640.28; $34.65 per contact hour. $30 per semester. Tuition and fees vary according to course load and program. *General application contact:* Jennifer DeHaemeas, Director of Admissions, 816-235-1111.

College of Arts and Sciences
Dr. Karen Vorst, Dean
Programs in:
acting (MFA)
analytical chemistry (MS, PhD)
art history (MA, PhD)
arts and sciences (MA, MFA, MS, MSW, PhD)
criminal justice and criminology (MS)
design technology (MFA)
economics (MA, PhD)
English (MA, PhD)
environmental and urban geosciences (MS)
geosciences (PhD)
history (MA, PhD)
inorganic chemistry (MS, PhD)
mathematics and statistics (MA, MS, PhD)
organic chemistry (MS, PhD)
physical chemistry (MS, PhD)
physics (MS, PhD)
political science (MA, PhD)
polymer chemistry (MS, PhD)
psychology (MA, PhD)
Romance languages and literatures (MA)
sociology (MA, PhD)
studio art (MA)
theatre (MA)

School of Social Work
Dr. Michael Smith, Program Director
Program in:
social work (MSW)

Conservatory of Music
Peter Witte, Dean
Programs in:
composition (MM, DMA)
conducting (MM, DMA)
music (MA)
music education (MME, PhD)
music history and literature (MM)
music theory (MM)
performance (MM, DMA)

Henry W. Bloch School of Business and Public Administration
Dr. Teng-Kee Tan, Dean
Programs in:
accounting (MS)
business administration (MBA)
entrepreneurship and innovation (PhD)
public affairs (MPA, PhD)

School of Biological Sciences
Dr. Lawrence A. Dreyfus, Dean
Programs in:
biology (MA)
cell biology and biophysics (PhD)
cellular and molecular biology (MS)
molecular biology and biochemistry (PhD)

School of Computing and Engineering
Dr. Kevin Z. Truman, Dean
Programs in:
civil engineering (MS)
computer and electrical engineering (PhD)
computer science (MS)
computer science and informatics (PhD)
computing (PhD)
electrical engineering (MS)
engineering (PhD)
mechanical engineering (MS)
telecommunications (PhD)

School of Dentistry
Dr. Marsha Pyle, Dean
Programs in:
advanced education in dentistry (Graduate Dental Certificate)
dental hygiene education (MS)
dental specialties (Graduate Dental Certificate)
dentistry (DDS)
diagnostic sciences (Graduate Dental Certificate)
oral and maxillofacial surgery (Graduate Dental Certificate)
oral biology (MS, PhD)
orthodontics and dentofacial orthopedics (Graduate Dental Certificate)
pediatric dentistry (Graduate Dental Certificate)
periodontics (Graduate Dental Certificate)
prosthodontics (Graduate Dental Certificate)

School of Education
Dr. Linda Edwards, Dean
Programs in:
administration (Ed D)
counseling and guidance (MA, Ed S)
counseling psychology (PhD)
curriculum and instruction (MA, Ed S)
education (PhD)
educational administration (Ed S)
reading education (MA, Ed S)
special education (MA)

School of Graduate Studies
Dr. Ronald MacQuarrie, Dean
Program in:
interdisciplinary studies (PhD)

School of Law
Ellen Y. Suni, Dean
Program in:
law (JD, LL M)

School of Medicine
Dr. Betty Drees, Dean
Program in:
medicine (MD)

School of Nursing
Dr. Lora Lacey-Haun, Dean
Programs in:
adult clinical nurse specialist (MSN)
family nurse practitioner (MSN)
neonatal nurse practitioner (MSN)
nurse educator (MSN)
nurse executive (MSN)
nursing (PhD)
pediatric nurse practitioner (MSN)

School of Pharmacy
Dr. Robert W. Piepho, Dean

Programs in:
- pharmaceutical sciences (MS, PhD)
- pharmacy (Pharm D)

■ UNIVERSITY OF MISSOURI–ST. LOUIS
St. Louis, MO 63121
http://www.umsl.edu/

State-supported, coed, university. CGS member. *Graduate faculty:* 423 full-time (163 women). *Computer facilities:* Computer purchase and lease plans are available. 1,280 computers available on campus for general student use. A campuswide network can be accessed from student residence rooms and from off campus. Online class registration is available. *Graduate expenses:* Tuition, state resident: full-time $5377; part-time $298.70 per credit hour. Tuition, nonresident: full-time $13,381; part-time $472.50 per credit hour. Required fees: $4078; $52 per credit hour. *General application contact:* Graduate Admissions, 314-516-5458.

College of Arts and Sciences
Dr. Tereas Thiel, Interim Dean
Programs in:
- advanced social perspective (MA)
- American literature (MA)
- American politics (MA)
- applied mathematics (MA, PhD)
- applied physics (MS)
- arts and sciences (MA, MFA, MS, MSW, PhD, Certificate, Graduate Certificate)
- astrophysics (MS)
- behavioral neuroscience (PhD)
- biology (MS, PhD)
- biotechnology (Certificate)
- chemistry (MS, PhD)
- clinical psychology respecialization (Certificate)
- community conflict intervention (MA)
- community psychology (PhD)
- comparative politics (MA)
- computer science (MS, PhD)
- creative writing (MFA)
- criminology and criminal justice (MA, PhD)
- English (MA)
- English literature (MA)
- general economics (MA)
- general psychology (MA)
- gerontology (MS, Certificate)
- industrial/organizational psychology (PhD)
- international politics (MA)
- linguistics (MA)
- long term care administration (Certificate)
- managerial economics (Certificate)
- mathematics (PhD)
- museum studies (MA, Certificate)
- philosophy (MA)
- physics (PhD)
- political process and behavior (MA)
- political science (PhD)
- program design and evaluation research (MA)
- public administration and public policy (MA)
- social policy planning and administration (MA)
- teaching of writing (Graduate Certificate)
- tropical biology and conservation (Certificate)
- urban and regional politics (MA)

School of Social Work
Dr. Margaret Sherraden, Graduate Program Director
Program in:
- social work (MS, MSW, Certificate)

College of Business Administration
Karl Kottemann, Assistant Director
Programs in:
- accounting (MBA)
- business administration (M Acc, MBA, MSIS, PhD, Certificate)
- finance (MBA)
- human resource management (Certificate)
- information systems (MSIS, PhD)
- logistics and supply chain management (MBA, PhD, Certificate)
- management (MBA)
- marketing (MBA)
- marketing management (Certificate)
- operations (MBA)
- quantitative management science (MBA)

College of Education
Dr. Kathleen Haywood, Director of Graduate Studies
Programs in:
- adult and higher education (Ed D)
- counseling (PhD)
- counselor education (Ed D)
- education (M Ed, Ed D, PhD, Certificate, Ed S)
- educational administration (Ed D)
- educational leadership and policy studies (PhD)
- educational psychology (PhD)

Division of Counseling
Dr. Mark Pope, Chair
Programs in:
- community counseling (M Ed)
- elementary school counseling (M Ed)
- secondary school counseling (M Ed)

Division of Educational Leadership and Policy Studies
Dr. E. Paulette Savage, Chair
Programs in:
- adult and higher education (M Ed)
- educational administration (M Ed, Ed S)
- institutional research (Certificate)

Division of Educational Psychology, Research, and Evaluation
Dr. Matthew Keefer, Chairperson
Programs in:
- education (Ed D)
- educational psychology (PhD)
- program evaluation and assessment (Certificate)
- school psychology (Ed S)

Division of Teaching and Learning
Dr. Joseph Polman, Chair
Programs in:
- elementary education (M Ed)
- secondary education (M Ed)
- secondary school teaching (Certificate)
- special education (M Ed)
- teaching English to speakers of other languages (Certificate)

College of Fine Arts and Communication
Dr. John Hylton, Dean
Programs in:
- communication (MA)
- fine arts and communication (MA, MME)
- music education (MME)

College of Nursing
Dean Juliann Sebastian, Dean
Programs in:
- family nurse practitioner (MSN)
- nurse practitioner (Post Master's Certificate)
- nursing (DNP, PhD)

College of Optometry
Dr. Larry J. Davis, Dean
Programs in:
- optometry (OD, MS, PhD)
- vision science (MS, PhD)

Graduate School
Dr. Judith Walker de Felix, Dean
Programs in:
- health policy (MPPA)
- local government management (MPPA)
- managing human resources and organization (MPPA)
- nonprofit organization management (MPPA)
- nonprofit organization management and leadership (Certificate)
- policy research and analysis (MPPA)

■ WASHINGTON UNIVERSITY IN ST. LOUIS
St. Louis, MO 63130-4899
http://www.wustl.edu/

Independent, coed, university. CGS member. *Computer facilities:* Computer purchase and lease plans are available. 2,500 computers available on campus for general student use. A campuswide network can be accessed from student residence rooms and from off campus. Online class registration is available. *General application contact:* Information Contact, 314-935-6880.

Washington University in St. Louis (continued)

George Warren Brown School of Social Work

Programs in:
- public health (MPH)
- social work (MSW, PhD)

Graduate School of Arts and Sciences

Programs in:
- American history (MA, PhD)
- anthropology (PhD)
- art history (MA, PhD)
- arts and sciences (MA, MA Ed, MAT, MFAW, MM, PhD)
- Asian history (MA, PhD)
- British history (MA, PhD)
- chemistry (PhD)
- Chinese (MA)
- Chinese and comparative literature (PhD)
- classical archaeology (MA, PhD)
- classics (MA)
- clinical psychology (PhD)
- comparative literature (MA, PhD)
- earth and planetary sciences (MA)
- East Asian studies (MA)
- economics (PhD)
- educational research (PhD)
- elementary education (MA Ed)
- English and American literature (MA, PhD)
- European history (MA, PhD)
- French (MA, PhD)
- general experimental psychology (PhD)
- Germanic languages and literature (MA, PhD)
- Japanese (MA)
- Japanese and comparative literature (PhD)
- Latin American history (MA, PhD)
- mathematics (MA, PhD)
- Middle Eastern history (MA, PhD)
- movement science (PhD)
- music (MM, PhD)
- philosophy (MA, PhD)
- philosophy/neuroscience/psychology (PhD)
- physics (PhD)
- planetary sciences (PhD)
- political economy and public policy (MA)
- political science (PhD)
- secondary education (MA Ed, MAT)
- social psychology (PhD)
- social work (PhD)
- Spanish (MA, PhD)
- statistics (MA)
- writing (MFAW)

Division of Biology and Biomedical Sciences

Programs in:
- biochemistry (PhD)
- chemical biology (PhD)
- computational biology (PhD)
- developmental biology (PhD)
- ecology (PhD)
- environmental biology (PhD)
- evolution, ecology and population biology (PhD)
- evolutionary biology (PhD)
- genetics (PhD)
- immunology (PhD)
- molecular biophysics (PhD)
- molecular cell biology (PhD)
- molecular genetics (PhD)
- molecular microbiology and microbial pathogenesis (PhD)
- neurosciences (PhD)
- plant biology (PhD)

Henry Edwin Sever Graduate School of Engineering and Applied Science

Programs in:
- biomedical engineering (MS, D Sc, PhD)
- chemical engineering (MS, D Sc)
- computer engineering (MS, PhD)
- computer science (MS, PhD)
- electrical engineering (MS, D Sc, PhD)
- engineering and applied science (MCE, MCM, MEM, MIM, MS, MSCE, MSE, MSEE, MSEE, MTM, D Sc, PhD)
- environmental engineering (MS, D Sc)
- mechanical, aerospace and structural engineering (MS, D Sc, PhD)
- systems science and mathematics (MS, D Sc, PhD)

Olin Business School

Programs in:
- accounting (MS)
- business (EMBA, M Acc, MBA, MS, PhD)
- business administration (EMBA, MBA)
- finance (MS)

Sam Fox School of Design and Visual Arts

Programs in:
- architecture (M Arch, MLA)
- design and visual arts (M Arch, MFA, MLA, MUD)
- urban design (MUD)

Graduate School of Art

Dean Franklin Spector, Dean

Program in:
- art (MFA)

School of Law

Program in:
- law (JD, LL M, MJS, JSD)

School of Medicine

Dr. Larry Shapiro, Dean

Programs in:
- audiology (Au D)
- clinical (MS)
- clinical investigation (MS)
- computational (MS)
- deaf education (MS)
- genetic epidemiology (Certificate)
- medicine (MD, MS, MSOT, Au D, DPT, OTD, PhD, Certificate, PPDPT)
- movement science (PhD)
- occupational therapy (MSOT, OTD)
- physical therapy (DPT, PhD, PPDPT)
- speech and hearing sciences (PhD)

■ WEBSTER UNIVERSITY

St. Louis, MO 63119-3194

http://www.webster.edu/

Independent, coed, comprehensive institution. *Graduate faculty:* 82 full-time, 1,513 part-time/adjunct. *Computer facilities:* 450 computers available on campus for general student use. A campuswide network can be accessed from student residence rooms. Online class registration is available. *Graduate expenses:* Tuition: part-time $550 per credit hour. Tuition and fees vary according to degree level, campus/location and program. *General application contact:* Matt Nolan, Director of Graduate and Evening Student Admissions, 314-968-7089.

College of Arts and Sciences

Dr. David Carl Wilson, Dean

Programs in:
- arts and sciences (MA, MS, MSN)
- counseling (MA)
- environmental management (MS)
- gerontology (MA)
- international nongovernmental organizations (MA)
- international relations (MA)
- legal analysis (MA)
- legal studies (MA)
- nurse anesthesia (MS)
- nursing (MSN)
- patent agency (MA)
- professional science management and leadership (MA)

Leigh Gerdine College of Fine Arts

Peter Sargent, Dean

Programs in:
- art (MA)
- arts management and leadership (MFA)
- church music (MM)
- composition (MM)
- conducting (MM)
- fine arts (MA, MFA, MM)
- jazz studies (MM)
- music (MA)
- music education (MM)
- performance (MM)
- piano (MM)

School of Business and Technology

Dr. Benjamin Ola Akande, Dean

Programs in:
- business (MA)
- business and organizational security management (MA, MBA)
- business and technology (MA, MBA, MHA, MPA, MS, DM, Certificate)
- computer resources and information management (MA, MBA)
- computer science/distributed systems (MS, Certificate)

environmental management (MBA, MS)
finance (MA, MBA)
health care management (MA)
health services management (MA, MBA)
human resources development (MA, MBA)
human resources management (MA, MBA)
international business (MA, MBA)
management (DM)
management and leadership (MA, MBA)
marketing (MA, MBA)
procurement and acquisitions management (MA, MBA)
public administration (MA)
quality management (MA)
space systems operations management (MS)
telecommunications management (MA, MBA)

School of Communications
Debra Carpenter, Dean
Programs in:
advertising and marketing communications (MA)
communications (MA)
communications management (MA)
media communications (MA)
media literacy (MA)
public relations (MA)

School of Education
Dr. Brenda Fyfe, Dean
Programs in:
administrative leadership (Ed S)
communications (MAT)
early childhood education (MAT)
education (MAT, Ed S)
education leadership (Ed S)
educational technology (MAT)
mathematics (MAT)
multidisciplinary studies (MAT)
school systems, superintendency and leadership (Ed S)
social science (MAT)
special education (MAT)

■ WILLIAM WOODS UNIVERSITY

Fulton, MO 65251-1098
http://www.williamwoods.edu/

Independent-religious, coed, comprehensive institution. *Computer facilities:* 105 computers available on campus for general student use. A campuswide network can be accessed from student residence rooms. Online class registration is available. *General application contact:* Administrative Assistant, 800-995-3199.

Graduate and Adult Studies
Programs in:
administration (Ed S)
agriculture (MBA)
athletic/activities administration (M Ed)
curriculum and instruction (M Ed)
curriculum leadership (Ed S)
elementary administration (M Ed)
health management (MBA)
human resources (MBA)
principalship (Ed S)
secondary administration (M Ed)
special education director (M Ed)

Montana

■ MONTANA STATE UNIVERSITY

Bozeman, MT 59717
http://www.montana.edu/

State-supported, coed, university. CGS member. *Graduate faculty:* 553 full-time (195 women), 265 part-time/adjunct (150 women). *Computer facilities:* 850 computers available on campus for general student use. A campuswide network can be accessed from student residence rooms and from off campus. Online class registration is available. *Graduate expenses:* Tuition, state resident: full-time $4103; part-time $227.95 per credit. Tuition, nonresident: full-time $12,438; part-time $691 per credit. Required fees: $1118.60; $98.85 per credit. Tuition and fees vary according to course load and program. *General application contact:* Dr. Carl A. Fox, Vice Provost for Graduate Education, 406-994-4145.

College of Graduate Studies
Dr. Carl A. Fox, Vice Provost for Graduate Education

College of Agriculture
Dr. Jeffrey S. Jacobsen, Dean
Programs in:
agricultural education (MS)
agriculture (MS, PhD)
animal and range sciences (MS, PhD)
ecology and environmental sciences (PhD)
land rehabilitation (interdisciplinary) (MS)
land resources and environmental sciences (MS)
plant pathology (MS)
plant sciences (MS, PhD)
veterinary molecular biology (MS, PhD)

College of Arts and Architecture
Susan Agre-Kippenhan, Dean
Programs in:
architecture (M Arch)
art (MFA)
arts and architecturé (M Arch, MFA)
science and natural history filmmaking (MFA)

College of Business
Dr. Dan Moshavi, Dean
Program in:
professional accountancy (MP Ac)

College of Education, Health, and Human Development
Larry Baker, Dean
Programs in:
adult and higher education (Ed D)
curriculum and instruction (Ed D, Ed S)
education (M Ed)
education, health, and human development (M Ed, MS, Ed D, Ed S)
educational leadership (Ed D, Ed S)
health and human development (MS)

College of Engineering
Dr. Robert Marley, Dean
Programs in:
chemical engineering (MS)
CHMYical engineering (MS)
civil engineering (MS)
computer science (MS, PhD)
construction engineering management (MCEM)
electrical engineering (MS)
engineering (PhD)
environmental engineering (MS)
industrial and management engineering (MS)
mechanical engineering (MS)

College of Letters and Science
Dr. Paula Lutz, Interim Dean
Programs in:
biochemistry (MS, PhD)
biological sciences (MS, PhD)
chemistry (MS, PhD)
earth sciences (MS, PhD)
ecological and environmental statistics (MS)
ecology and environmental sciences (PhD)
English (MA)
fish and wildlife biology (PhD)
fish and wildlife management (MS)
history (MA, PhD)
letters and science (MA, MPA, MS, PhD)
mathematics (MS, PhD)
microbiology (MS, PhD)
Native American studies (MA)
neuroscience (MS, PhD)
physics (MS, PhD)
psychology (MS)
public administration (MPA)
statistics (MS, PhD)

College of Nursing
Dr. Elizabeth Kinion, Dean
Programs in:
clinical nurse specialist (CNS) (MN, Post-Master's Certificate)
family nurse practitioner (MN, Post-Master's Certificate)
nursing education (Certificate)

■ MONTANA STATE UNIVERSITY–BILLINGS

Billings, MT 59101-0298
http://www.msubillings.edu/

State-supported, coed, comprehensive institution. *Computer facilities:* Computer purchase and lease plans are available. 1,000 computers available on campus for general student use. A campuswide network can be accessed from student residence rooms and from off campus. Online class

Montana State University–Billings (continued)
registration, online degree programs are available. *General application contact:* Graduate Studies Counselor, 406-657-2053.

College of Allied Health Professions

Programs in:
- allied health professions (MHA, MS, MSRC)
- athletic training (MS)
- health administration (MHA)
- rehabilitation and human services (MSRC)
- sport management (MS)

College of Arts and Sciences

Programs in:
- arts and sciences (MPA, MS)
- psychology (MS)
- public administration (MPA)
- public relations (MS)

College of Education

Programs in:
- advanced studies (MS Sp Ed)
- early childhood education (M Ed)
- education (M Ed, MS Sp Ed, Certificate)
- educational technology (M Ed)
- general curriculum (M Ed)
- interdisciplinary studies (M Ed)
- reading (M Ed)
- school counseling (M Ed)
- secondary education (M Ed)
- special education (MS Sp Ed)
- special education generalist (MS Sp Ed)
- teaching (Certificate)

■ UNIVERSITY OF GREAT FALLS

Great Falls, MT 59405
http://www.ugf.edu/

Independent-religious, coed, comprehensive institution. *Computer facilities:* 110 computers available on campus for general student use. A campuswide network can be accessed from student residence rooms and from off campus. Online class registration is available. *General application contact:* Coordinator of Graduate Studies, 406-791-5332.

Graduate Studies

Dr. Katrina Stark, Associate Dean for Graduate Studies
Programs in:
- counseling psychology (MSC)
- criminal justice (MSM)
- education (M Ed)
- human development (MSM)
- management (MSM)
- secondary teaching (MAT)

■ THE UNIVERSITY OF MONTANA

Missoula, MT 59812-0002
http://www.umt.edu/

State-supported, coed, university. CGS member. *Computer facilities:* 545 computers available on campus for general student use. A campuswide network can be accessed from student residence rooms and from off campus. Online class registration is available. *General application contact:* Dean of the Graduate School, 406-243-2572.

Graduate School

Programs in:
- individual interdisciplinary programs (IIP) (PhD)
- interdisciplinary studies (MIS)

College of Arts and Sciences

Programs in:
- anthropology (MA)
- applied geoscience (PhD)
- arts and sciences (MA, MFA, MPA, MS, PhD, Ed S)
- biochemistry (MS)
- biochemistry and microbiology (MS, PhD)
- chemistry (MS, PhD)
- clinical psychology (PhD)
- communication studies (MA)
- computer science (MS)
- creative writing (MFA)
- criminology (MA)
- cultural heritage (MA)
- cultural heritage studies (PhD)
- ecology of infectious disease (PhD)
- economics (MA)
- environmental studies (MS)
- experimental psychology (PhD)
- fiction (MFA)
- forensic anthropology (MA)
- French (MA)
- geography (MA)
- geology (MS, PhD)
- German (MA)
- historical anthropology (PhD)
- history (MA, PhD)
- integrative microbiology and biochemistry (PhD)
- linguistics (MA)
- literature (MA)
- mathematics (MA, PhD)
- mathematics education (MA)
- microbial ecology (MS, PhD)
- microbiology (MS)
- non-fiction (MFA)
- organismal biology and ecology (MS, PhD)
- philosophy (MA)
- poetry (MFA)
- political science (MA, MPA)
- public administration (MPA)
- rural and environmental change (MA)
- school psychology (MA, PhD, Ed S)
- sociology (MA)
- Spanish (MA)
- teaching (MA)

College of Forestry and Conservation

Programs in:
- ecosystem management (MEM, MS)
- fish and wildlife biology (PhD)
- forestry (MS, PhD)
- recreation management (MS)
- resource conservation (MS)
- wildlife biology (MS)

College of Health Professions and Biomedical Sciences

Programs in:
- biomedical and pharmaceutical sciences (MS, PhD)
- biomedical sciences (PhD)
- health professions and biomedical sciences (Pharm D, MPH, MS, MSW, DPT, PhD, CPH)
- neuroscience (MS, PhD)
- pharmaceutical sciences (MS)
- pharmacy (Pharm D)
- physical therapy (DPT)
- public health (MPH, CPH)
- social work (MSW)
- toxicology (MS, PhD)

School of Business Administration

Programs in:
- accounting (M Acct)
- business administration (M Acct, MBA)

School of Education

Programs in:
- counselor education (MA, Ed D, Ed S)
- counselor education and supervision (Ed D)
- curriculum and instruction (M Ed, Ed D)
- education (M Ed, MA, MS, Ed D, Ed S)
- educational leadership (M Ed, Ed D, Ed S)
- exercise science (MS)
- health and human performance (MS)
- health promotion (MS)
- mental health counseling (MA)
- school counseling (MA)

School of Fine Arts

Programs in:
- fine arts (MA, MFA)
- music (MM)

School of Journalism

Program in:
- journalism (MA)

School of Law

Program in:
- law (JD)

Nebraska

■ BELLEVUE UNIVERSITY

Bellevue, NE 68005-3098
http://www.bellevue.edu/

Independent, coed, comprehensive institution. *Computer facilities:* 1,000 computers available on campus for general student use. A campuswide network can be accessed from off campus. Online class registration is available. *General application contact:* Director of Graduate Enrollment, 402-682-4045.

Graduate School
Programs in:
acquisition and contract management (MS)
business administration (MBA)
clinical counseling (MS)
computer information systems (MS)
healthcare administration (MA, MHA, MS)
human capital management (MS, PhD)
human services (MA, MS)
instructional design and development (MS)
leadership (MA)
management (MA)
management information systems (MS)
organizational performance (MS)
public administration (MPA)
public health (MPH)
security management (MS)

■ CONCORDIA UNIVERSITY, NEBRASKA
Seward, NE 68434-1599
http://www.cune.edu/

Independent-religious, coed, comprehensive institution. *Computer facilities:* 186 computers available on campus for general student use. A campuswide network can be accessed from student residence rooms and from off campus. Online class registration, academic plans, human resource data are available. *General application contact:* Dean of Graduate Studies, 402-643-7464.

Graduate Programs in Education
Programs in:
early childhood education (M Ed)
education (M Ed, MPE, MS)
elementary and secondary education (M Ed)
elementary education (M Ed)
family life ministry (MS)
parish education (MPE)
reading education (M Ed)
secondary education (M Ed)

■ CREIGHTON UNIVERSITY
Omaha, NE 68178-0001
http://www.creighton.edu/

Independent-religious, coed, university. CGS member. *Graduate faculty:* 287. *Computer facilities:* Computer purchase and lease plans are available. A campuswide network can be accessed from student residence rooms and from off campus. Online class registration, financial aid information are available. *Graduate expenses:* Tuition: full-time $11,250; part-time $625 per credit hour. Required fees: $121 per semester. *General application contact:* Jami E. Monico, Senior Program Coordinator, 402-280-2870.

Graduate School
Dr. Gail M. Jensen, Dean

College of Arts and Sciences
Dr. Robert J. Lueger, Dean
Programs in:
arts and sciences (M Ed, MA, MLS, MS)
atmospheric sciences (MS)
Christian spirituality (MA)
college student affairs (MS)
community counseling (MS)
counselor education (MS)
creative writing (MA)
educational leadership (MS)
elementary school guidance (MS)
elementary teaching (M Ed)
international relations (MA)
liberal studies (MLS)
literature (MA)
ministry (MA)
physics (MS)
secondary school administration (MS)
secondary school guidance (MS)
secondary teaching (M Ed)
special populations in education (MS)
teaching (M Ed)
theology (MA)

Eugene C. Eppley College of Business Administration
Dr. Robert Moorman, Director
Programs in:
business administration (MBA)
information technology management (MS)
securities and portfolio management (MSAPM)

School of Dentistry
Program in:
dentistry (DDS)

School of Law
Eric A. Chiappinelli, Dean and Professor of Law
Programs in:
law (JD, MS, Certificate)
negotiation and dispute resolution (MS, Certificate)

School of Medicine
Programs in:
biomedical sciences (MS, PhD)
clinical anatomy (MS)
medical microbiology and immunology (MS, PhD)
medicine (MD, MS, PhD)
pharmaceutical sciences (MS)
pharmacology (MS, PhD)

School of Nursing
Dr. Eleanor V. Howell, Dean
Program in:
nursing (MS, DNP)

School of Pharmacy and Health Professions
Dr. J. Chris Bradberry, Dean
Programs in:
occupational therapy (OTD)
pharmaceutical sciences (MS)
pharmacy (Pharm D)
pharmacy and health professions (Pharm D, MS, DPT, OTD)
physical therapy (DPT)

■ DOANE COLLEGE
Crete, NE 68333-2430
http://www.doane.edu/

Independent-religious, coed, comprehensive institution. *Computer facilities:* Computer purchase and lease plans are available. 246 computers available on campus for general student use. A campuswide network can be accessed from student residence rooms and from off campus. Online class registration is available. *General application contact:* Assistant Dean, 402-464-1223.

Program in Counseling
Program in:
counseling (MAC)

Program in Education
Programs in:
curriculum and instruction (M Ed)
educational leadership (M Ed)

Program in Management
Program in:
management (MA)

■ UNIVERSITY OF NEBRASKA AT KEARNEY
Kearney, NE 68849-0001
http://www.unk.edu/

State-supported, coed, comprehensive institution. CGS member. *Computer facilities:* 277 computers available on campus for general student use. A campuswide network can be accessed from student residence rooms and from off campus. Online class registration, online degree audit, online personal information update, online bill viewing and payment, online financial aid awards and acceptance are available. *General application contact:* Graduate Dean, 308-856-8843.

College of Graduate Study

College of Business and Technology
Programs in:
business administration (MBA)
business and technology (MBA)

College of Education
Programs in:
adapted physical education (MA Ed)
counseling (MS Ed, Ed S)
curriculum and instruction (MS Ed)
education (MA Ed, MS Ed, Ed S)
educational administration (MA Ed, Ed S)
exercise science (MA Ed)
instructional technology (MS Ed)
master teacher (MA Ed)

University of Nebraska at Kearney (continued)
- reading education (MA Ed)
- school psychology (Ed S)
- special education (MA Ed)
- speech pathology (MS Ed)
- supervisor (MA Ed)

College of Fine Arts and Humanities
Programs in:
- art education (MA Ed)
- creative writing (MA)
- fine arts and humanities (MA, MA Ed)
- French (MA Ed)
- German (MA Ed)
- literature (MA)
- music education (MA Ed)
- Spanish (MA Ed)

College of Natural and Social Sciences
Programs in:
- biology (MS)
- history (MA)
- natural and social sciences (MA, MS, MS Ed)
- science education (MS Ed)

■ UNIVERSITY OF NEBRASKA AT OMAHA
Omaha, NE 68182
http://www.unomaha.edu/

State-supported, coed, university. CGS member. *Computer facilities:* Computer purchase and lease plans are available. 2,000 computers available on campus for general student use. A campuswide network can be accessed from student residence rooms and from off campus. Online class registration is available. *General application contact:* Director, Graduate Studies, 402-554-2341.

Graduate Studies and Research
Programs in:
- public health (MPH)
- writing (MFA)

College of Arts and Sciences
Programs in:
- advanced writing (Certificate)
- arts and sciences (MA, MAT, MS, PhD, Certificate, Ed S)
- biology (MS)
- developmental psychology (PhD)
- English (MA)
- geographic information science (Certificate)
- geography (MA)
- history (MA)
- industrial/organizational psychology (MS, PhD)
- language teaching (MA)
- mathematics (MA, MAT, MS)
- political science (MS)
- psychobiology (PhD)
- psychology (MA)
- school psychology (MS, Ed S)
- teaching English to speakers of other languages (Certificate)
- technical communication (Certificate)

College of Business Administration
Programs in:
- accounting (M Acc)
- business administration (EMBA, M Acc, MA, MBA, MS)
- economics (MA, MS)

College of Communication, Fine Arts and Media
Programs in:
- communication (MA)
- communication, fine arts and media (MA, MM)
- music (MM)
- theatre (MA)

College of Education
Programs in:
- community counseling (MA, MS)
- counseling gerontology (MA, MS)
- education (MA, MS, Ed D, Certificate, Ed S)
- educational administration and supervision (MS, Ed D, Ed S)
- elementary education (MA, MS)
- health, physical education, and recreation (MA, MS)
- instruction in urban schools (Certificate)
- instructional technology (Certificate)
- reading education (MS)
- school counseling (MA, MS)
- secondary education (MA, MS)
- special education (MS)
- speech-language pathology (MA, MS)
- student affairs practice in higher education (MA, MS)

College of Information Science and Technology
Programs in:
- computer science (MA, MS)
- information science and technology (MA, MS, PhD, Certificate)
- information technology (PhD)
- management information systems (MS)

College of Public Affairs and Community Service
Programs in:
- criminal justice (MA, MS, PhD)
- gerontology (Certificate)
- public administration (MPA, PhD)
- public affairs and community service (MA, MPA, MS, MSW, PhD, Certificate)
- public management (Certificate)
- social gerontology (MA)
- social work (MSW)
- urban studies (MS)

■ UNIVERSITY OF NEBRASKA–LINCOLN
Lincoln, NE 68588
http://www.unl.edu/

State-supported, coed, university. CGS member. *Graduate faculty:* 1,070 full-time (306 women), 11 part-time/adjunct (3 women). *Computer facilities:* 600 computers available on campus for general student use. A campuswide network can be accessed from student residence rooms and from off campus. Online class registration is available. *Graduate expenses:* Tuition, state resident: full-time $4275; part-time $237.50 per credit hour. Tuition, nonresident: full-time $11,525; part-time $640.25 per credit hour. Required fees: $1068; $10.35 per credit hour. $440.70 per semester. Tuition and fees vary according to course load and program. *General application contact:* Dr. Ellen Weissinger, Dean of Graduate Studies, 402-472-2875.

College of Law
Steven Willborn, Dean
Programs in:
- law (JD)
- legal studies (MLS)
- space and telecommunications law (LL M)

Graduate College
Dr. Prem Paul, Vice Chancellor for Research and Dean of Graduate Studies
Programs in:
- environmental health, occupational health and toxicology (MS, PhD)
- survey research and methodology (MS, PhD)

College of Agricultural Sciences and Natural Resources
Dr. Steven S. Waller, Dean
Programs in:
- agribusiness (MBA)
- agricultural economics (MS, PhD)
- agricultural sciences and natural resources (M Ag, MA, MBA, MS, PhD)
- agronomy (MS, PhD)
- animal science (MS, PhD)
- biochemistry (MS, PhD)
- community development (M Ag)
- distance education specialization (MS)
- entomology (MS, PhD)
- food science and technology (MS, PhD)
- geography (PhD)
- horticulture (MS, PhD)
- leadership development (MS)
- leadership education (MS)
- mechanized systems management (MS)
- natural resources (MS, PhD)
- nutrition (MS, PhD)
- nutrition outreach education specialization (MS)
- statistics (MS, PhD)
- teaching and extension education specialization (MS)
- veterinary science (MS)

College of Architecture
Wayne Drummond, Dean
Programs in:
- architecture (M Arch, MCRP, MS, PhD)
- community and regional planning (MCRP)
- interior design (MS)

College of Arts and Sciences
Dr. Richard Hoffmann, Dean
Programs in:
- analytical chemistry (PhD)

anthropology (MA)
arts and sciences (M Sc T, MA, MAT, MS, PhD, Graduate Certificate)
astronomy (MS, PhD)
biochemistry (PhD)
bioinformatics (MS, PhD)
biological sciences (MA, MS, PhD)
biopsychology (PhD)
chemistry (MS)
classics and religious studies (MA)
clinical psychology (PhD)
cognitive psychology (PhD)
composition and rhetoric (MA, PhD)
computer engineering (MS, PhD)
computer science (MS, PhD)
creative writing (MA, PhD)
developmental psychology (PhD)
French (MA, PhD)
geography (MA, PhD)
geosciences (MS, PhD)
German (MA, PhD)
history (MA, PhD)
information technology (PhD)
inorganic chemistry (PhD)
instructional communication (MA, PhD)
interpersonal communication (MA, PhD)
literature studies (MA, PhD)
marketing, communication studies, and advertising (MA, PhD)
materials chemistry (PhD)
mathematics (MA, MAT, MS, PhD)
mathematics and computer science (PhD)
organic chemistry (PhD)
organizational communication (MA, PhD)
philosophy (MA, PhD)
physical chemistry (PhD)
physics (MS, PhD)
political science (MA, PhD)
professional archaeology (MA)
psychology (MA)
public policy analysis (Graduate Certificate)
rhetoric and culture (MA, PhD)
social/personality psychology (PhD)
sociology (MA, PhD)
Spanish (MA, PhD)

College of Business Administration
Cynthia H. Milligan, Dean
Programs in:
accountancy (MPA, PhD)
actuarial science (MS)
business (MA, MBA, PhD)
business administration (MA, MBA, MPA, MS, PhD)
economics (MA, PhD)
finance (MA, PhD)
management (MA, PhD)
marketing (MA, PhD)

College of Education and Human Sciences
Dr. Marjorie J. Kostelnik, Dean
Programs in:
administration, curriculum and instruction (Ed D, PhD)
adult and continuing education (MA)
audiology and hearing science (Au D)
audiology research (PhD)
child development/early childhood education (MS, PhD)
child, youth and family studies (MS)
clinical audiology (Au D)
cognition, learning and development (MA)
community nutrition and health promotion (MS)
counseling psychology (MA)
education and human sciences (M Ed, MA, MS, MST, Au D, Ed D, PhD, Certificate, Ed S)
educational administration (M Ed, MA, Ed D, Certificate)
educational psychology (MA, Ed S)
educational studies (Ed D, PhD)
family and consumer sciences education (MS, PhD)
family financial planning (MS)
family science (MS, PhD)
gerontology (PhD)
human sciences (PhD)
marriage and family therapy (MS)
medical family therapy (PhD)
merchandising (MS)
nutrition (MS, PhD)
nutrition and exercise (MS)
nutrition and health sciences (MS, PhD)
psychological studies in education (PhD)
quantitative, qualitative, and psychometric methods (MA)
school psychology (MA, Ed S)
special education (M Ed, MA, Ed S)
speech-language pathology and audiology (MS, Au D)
teaching, learning and teacher education (M Ed, MA, MST, Ed D, PhD)
textile history/quilt studies (MA)
textile science (MS)
textile-apparel (MA)
textiles, clothing and design (MA, MS)
vocational and adult education (M Ed, MA)
youth development (MS)

College of Engineering
Dr. David H. Allen, Dean
Programs in:
agricultural and biological systems engineering (MS, PhD)
architectural engineering (M Eng, MAE, MS, PhD)
chemical and biomolecular engineering (MS, PhD)
chemical and materials engineering (PhD)
civil engineering (MS, PhD)
electrical engineering (MS, PhD)
engineering (M Eng, MAE, MEE, MS, PhD)
engineering management (M Eng)
engineering mechanics (MS, PhD)
environmental engineering (MS, PhD)
industrial and management systems engineering (MS, PhD)
manufacturing systems engineering (MS)
mechanical engineering (MS, PhD)
mechanized systems management (MS)

College of Fine and Performing Arts
Dr. Giacomo Oliva, Dean
Programs in:
acting (MFA)
art and art history (MA, MFA)
art history (MA)
composition (MM, DMA)
conducting (MM, DMA)
costume (MFA)
directing (MFA)
fine and performing arts (MA, MFA, MM, DMA, PhD)
music education (MM, PhD)
music history (MM)
music theory (MM)
performance (MM, DMA)
piano pedagogy (MM)
stage design (MFA)
studio art (MFA)
woodwind specialties (MM)

College of Journalism and Mass Communications
Dr. Will Norton, Dean
Programs in:
marketing, communication and advertising (MA)
professional journalism (MA)

■ WAYNE STATE COLLEGE

Wayne, NE 68787
http://www.wsc.edu/

State-supported, coed, comprehensive institution. CGS member. *Computer facilities:* Computer purchase and lease plans are available. 365 computers available on campus for general student use. A campuswide network can be accessed from student residence rooms and from off campus. Online class registration is available. *General application contact:* Director of Graduate Studies, 402-375-7121.

Department of Health, Human Performance and Sport
Programs in:
exercise science (MSE)
organizational management (MS)

School of Business and Technology
Program in:
business and technology (MBA)

School of Education and Counseling
Programs in:
alternative education (MSE)
business and information technology education (MSE)
communication arts education (MSE)
counseling (MSE)
counselor education (MSE)
curriculum and instruction (MSE)
early childhood education (MSE)
education and counseling (MSE, Ed S)
educational administration (MSE, Ed S)
elementary administration (MSE)
elementary and secondary administration (MSE)

Wayne State College (continued)
elementary education (MSE)
English as a second language (MSE)
English education (MSE)
family and consumer sciences education (MSE)
guidance and counseling (MSE)
industrial technology and vocational education (MSE)
learning communities (MSE)
mathematics education (MSE)
music education (MSE)
school counseling (MSE)
science education (MSE)
secondary administration (MSE)
social science education (MSE)
special education (MSE)

Nevada

■ UNIVERSITY OF NEVADA, LAS VEGAS

Las Vegas, NV 89154-9900
http://www.unlv.edu/

State-supported, coed, university. CGS member. *Graduate faculty:* 706 full-time (242 women), 143 part-time/adjunct (65 women). *Computer facilities:* 2,100 computers available on campus for general student use. A campuswide network can be accessed from student residence rooms and from off campus. Online class registration is available. *Graduate expenses:* Tuition, state resident: part-time $198 per credit. Tuition, nonresident: part-time $415.75 per credit. Required fees: $4 per credit. $252 per semester. Tuition and fees vary according to course load. *General application contact:* Frederick Krauss, Director of Graduate Outreach, 702-895-5773.

Graduate College

Dr. Ronald Smith, Vice President for Research and Dean of the Graduate College

College of Business
Dr. Paul Jarley, Dean
Programs in:
accounting (MS)
business (EMBA, MA, MBA, MS)
business administration (EMBA, MBA)
economics (MA)
management information systems (MS)

College of Education
Dr. William Speer, Interim Dean
Programs in:
addiction studies (Advanced Certificate)
community mental health (MS)
curriculum and instruction (M Ed, Ed D, PhD)
early childhood education (M Ed)
education (M Ed, MS, Ed D, Exec Ed D, PhD, Advanced Certificate, Ed S)
educational leadership (M Ed, MS, Ed D, Exec Ed D, PhD)
educational psychology (MS, PhD)
learning and technology (PhD)
physical education (M Ed, MS)
rehabilitation counseling (Advanced Certificate)
school counseling (M Ed)
school psychology (Ed S)
special education (MS, Ed D, PhD, Ed S)
sports education leadership (PhD)
teacher education (PhD)

College of Fine Arts
Dr. Jeffrey Koep, Dean
Programs in:
architecture (M Arch)
art (MFA)
fine arts (M Arch, MA, MFA, MM, DMA)
music (MM)
musical arts (DMA)
screenwriting (MFA)
theatre arts (MA, MFA)

College of Liberal Arts
Dr. Chris Hudgins, Dean
Programs in:
anthropology (MA, PhD)
creative writing (MFA)
English (MA, PhD)
ethics and policy studies (MA)
Hispanic studies (MA)
history (MA, PhD)
liberal arts (MA, MFA, PhD, Certificate)
political science (PhD)
psychology (PhD)
sociology (MA, PhD)
Spanish translation (Certificate)
women's studies (Certificate)

College of Science
Dr. Wanda Taylor, Interim Dean
Programs in:
astronomy (MS)
biochemistry (MS)
chemistry (MS, PhD)
geoscience (MS, PhD)
life sciences (MS, PhD)
mathematical sciences (MS, PhD)
physics (PhD)
radiochemistry (PhD)
science (MA, MS, PhD)
water resources management (MS)

Greenspun College of Urban Affairs
Dr. E. Lee Bernick, Dean
Programs in:
communication studies (MA)
criminal justice (MA)
crisis and emergency management (MS)
environmental studies (MS, PhD)
forensic social work (Advanced Certificate)
journalism and media studies (MA)
marriage and family therapy (MS, Advanced Certificate)
non-profit management (Certificate)
public administration (MPA)
public affairs (PhD)
public management (Certificate)
social work (MSW)
urban affairs (MA, MPA, MS, MSW, PhD, Advanced Certificate, Certificate)

Howard R. Hughes College of Engineering
Dr. Eric Sandgren, Dean
Programs in:
aerospace engineering (MS)
biomedical engineering (MS)
civil and environmental engineering (MS, PhD)
computer science (MS, PhD)
construction management (MS)
electrical and computer engineering (MSE, PhD)
engineering (MS, MSE, PhD)
informatics (MS, PhD)
materials and nuclear engineering (MS)
mechanical engineering (MS)
transportation (MS)

School of Allied Health Sciences
Dr. Carolyn Yucha, Interim Dean
Programs in:
exercise physiology (MS)
health physics (MS)
health sciences (MS, DPT)
kinesiology (MS)
physical therapy (DPT)

School of Community Health Sciences
Dr. Mary Guinan, Dean
Programs in:
community health sciences (M Ed, MHA, MPH)
health care administration (MHA)
health care promotion (M Ed)
public health (MPH)

School of Nursing
Dr. Carolyn Yucha, Interim Dean
Programs in:
family nurse practitioner (Advanced Certificate)
nursing (MS, PhD)
nursing education (Advanced Certificate)

William F. Harrah College of Hotel Administration
Dr. Stuart Mann, Dean
Programs in:
food and beverage management (Certificate)
hospitality administration (MHA, PhD)
hotel administration (MS)
sport and leisure services management (MS)

William S. Boyd School of Law

John V. White, Dean
Program in:
law (JD)

■ UNIVERSITY OF NEVADA, RENO

Reno, NV 89557

http://www.unr.edu/

State-supported, coed, university. CGS member. *Graduate faculty:* 1,035 full-time (321 women). *Computer facilities:* Computer purchase and lease plans are available. 500 computers available on campus for general student use. A campuswide network can be accessed from student residence rooms and from off campus. Online class registration is available. *Graduate expenses:* Tuition, state resident: full-time $1710; part-time $1140 per semester. Tuition, nonresident: full-time $7115. Required fees: $158 per semester. *General application contact:* Lisa Oliveto, Recruitment Coordinator, 775-327-2361.

Graduate School

Dr. Marsha Read, Interim Dean
Programs in:
atmospheric sciences (MS, PhD)
Basque studies (PhD)
biomedical engineering (MS, PhD)
cell and molecular biology (MS, PhD)
cellular and molecular pharmacology and physiology (PhD)
chemical physics (PhD)
ecology, evolution, and conservation biology (PhD)
environmental sciences and health (MS, PhD)
hydrogeology (MS, PhD)
hydrology (MS, PhD)
social psychology (PhD)

College of Agriculture, Biotechnology and Natural Resources
Dr. David Thawley, Dean
Programs in:
agriculture, biotechnology and natural resources (MS, PhD)
animal science (MS)
biochemistry (MS, PhD)
biotechnology (MS)
natural resources and environmental sciences (MS)
nutrition (MS)
resource economics (MS, PhD)

College of Business Administration
Dr. Greg Mosier, Dean
Programs in:
accounting and information systems (M Acc)
business administration (M Acc, MA, MBA, MS)
economics (MA, MS)
finance (MS)
information systems (MS)

College of Education
Dr. William E. Sparkman, Dean
Programs in:
counseling and educational psychology (M Ed, MA, MS, Ed D, PhD, Ed S)
curriculum and instruction (PhD)
curriculum, teaching and learning (Ed D, PhD)
education (M Ed, MA, MS, Ed D, PhD, Ed S)
educational leadership (M Ed, MA, MS, Ed D, PhD, Ed S)
educational specialties (M Ed, MA, MS, Ed D, PhD)
elementary education (M Ed, MA, MS)
human development and family studies (MS)
literacy studies (M Ed, MA, Ed D, PhD)
secondary education (M Ed, MA, MS)
special education (M Ed, MA, MS, Ed D, PhD)
special education and disability studies (PhD)
teaching English to speakers of other languages (MA)

College of Engineering
Dr. Emmanuel Maragakis, Dean
Programs in:
chemical engineering (MS, PhD)
civil and environmental engineering (MS, PhD)
computer engineering (MS)
computer science (MS)
computer science and engineering (MS, PhD)
electrical engineering (MS, PhD)
engineering (MS, PhD)
materials science and engineering (MS, PhD)
mechanical engineering (MS, PhD)

College of Liberal Arts
Dr. Heather Hardy, Dean
Programs in:
anthropology (MA, PhD)
behavior analysis (MA, PhD)
clinical psychology (MA, PhD)
cognitive brain science (MA, PhD)
criminal justice (MA)
English (MA, MATE, PhD)
fine arts (MFA)
French (MA)
German (MA)
history (MA, PhD)
judicial studies (MJS, PhD)
justice management (MJM)
liberal arts (MA, MATE, MFA, MJM, MJS, MM, MPA, PhD)
music (MA, MM)
philosophy (MA)
political science (MA, PhD)
public administration (MPA)
public administration and policy (MPA)
social research and justice studies (MA, MJM, MJS, PhD)
sociology (MA)
Spanish (MA)
speech communications (MA)

College of Science
Dr. Jeff Thompson, Acting Dean
Programs in:
biology (MS)
chemistry (MS, PhD)
earth sciences and engineering (MS, PhD)
geochemistry (MS, PhD)
geography (MS, PhD)
geological engineering (MS, PhD)
geology (MS, PhD)
geophysics (MS, PhD)
land use planning (MS)
mathematics (MS)
mining engineering (MS)
physics (MS, PhD)
science (MATM, MS, PhD)
teaching mathematics (MATM)

Division of Health Sciences
Dr. John McDonald, Vice President
Programs in:
health and human sciences (MPH, MS, MSN, MSW, PhD)
nursing (MSN)
public health (MPH, PhD)
social work (MSW)
speech pathology (PhD)
speech pathology and audiology (MS)

Donald W. Reynolds School of Journalism
Dr. Donica Mensing, Graduate Program Director
Program in:
journalism (MA)

School of Medicine

Dr. Ole Thienhaus, Dean
Program in:
medicine (MD)

■ UNIVERSITY OF PHOENIX–LAS VEGAS CAMPUS

Las Vegas, NV 89128

http://www.phoenix.edu/

Proprietary, coed, comprehensive institution. *Computer facilities:* A campuswide network can be accessed from off campus. *General application contact:* Campus Information Center, 702-638-7249.

The Artemis School

College of Education
Programs in:
administration and supervision (MA Ed)
curriculum and instruction (MA Ed)
school counseling (MSC)
teacher education-elementary licensure (MA Ed)

College of Health and Human Services
Programs in:
administration of justice and security (MS)
health administration (MHA)
health care management (MBA)
marriage, family, and child therapy (MSC)
mental health counseling (MSC)
nursing (MSN)
nursing/health care education (MSN)
psychology (MS)

University of Phoenix–Las Vegas Campus (continued)

John Sperling School of Business
Program in:
business (MBA, MIS, MM)

College of Graduate Business and Management
Programs in:
accounting (MBA)
business administration (MBA)
global management (MBA)
human resources management (MBA, MM)
management (MM)
marketing (MBA)
public administration (MM)

College of Information Systems and Technology
Programs in:
information systems (MIS)
technology management (MBA)

New Hampshire

■ ANTIOCH UNIVERSITY NEW ENGLAND

Keene, NH 03431-3552
http://www.antiochne.edu/

Independent, coed, graduate-only institution. *Computer facilities:* 25 computers available on campus for general student use. A campuswide network can be accessed from off campus. Online class registration is available. *General application contact:* Co-Director of Admissions, 800-490-3310.

Graduate School
Programs in:
administration and supervision (M Ed)
autism spectrum disorders (Certificate)
clinical mental health counseling (MA)
clinical psychology (Psy D)
conservation biology (MS)
dance/movement therapy and counseling (M Ed, MA)
early childhood education (M Ed)
elementary education (M Ed)
environmental advocacy and organizing (MS)
environmental education (MS)
environmental studies (MS, PhD)
experienced educators (M Ed)
individualized study (MS)
integrated learning (M Ed)
marriage and family therapy (MA, PhD)
organizational and environmental sustainability (MBA)
organizational development (Certificate)
organizational leadership and management (MS)
resource management and conservation (MS)
science teacher certification (MS)
Waldorf teacher training (M Ed)

■ DARTMOUTH COLLEGE

Hanover, NH 03755
http://www.dartmouth.edu/

Independent, coed, university. CGS member. *Graduate faculty:* 339 full-time (88 women), 83 part-time/adjunct (29 women). *Computer facilities:* Computer purchase and lease plans are available. 200 computers available on campus for general student use. A campuswide network can be accessed from student residence rooms and from off campus. Online class registration is available. *Graduate expenses:* Tuition: full-time $36,690. Required fees: $50. *General application contact:* Gary Hutchins, Assistant Dean, School of Arts and Sciences, 603-646-2107.

Arts and Sciences Graduate Programs
Dr. Brian Pogue, Dean of Graduate Studies
Programs in:
arts and sciences (AM, MALS, MS, PhD)
biomedical physiology (PhD)
cancer biology and molecular therapeutics (PhD)
cardiovascular diseases (PhD)
chemistry (PhD)
cognitive neuroscience (PhD)
comparative literature (AM)
computer science (MS, PhD)
earth sciences (MS, PhD)
ecology and evolutionary biology (PhD)
electro-acoustic music (AM)
liberal studies (MALS)
mathematics (PhD)
molecular pharmacology, toxicology and experimental therapeutics (PhD)
neuroscience (PhD)
pharmacology and toxicology (PhD)
physics and astronomy (MS, PhD)
physiology (PhD)
psychology (PhD)

The Dartmouth Institute
Programs in:
evaluative clinical sciences (MS, PhD)
public health (MPH)

Dartmouth Medical School
Dr. William Green, Dean
Program in:
medicine (MD)

Graduate Program in Molecular and Cellular Biology
Programs in:
biochemistry (PhD)
biological sciences (PhD)
genetics (PhD)
immunology (PhD)
microbiology and immunology (PhD)
molecular and cellular biology (PhD)
molecular pathogenesis (PhD)

Program in Experimental and Molecular Medicine
Dr. Murray Korc, Director
Programs in:
biomedical physiology (PhD)
cancer biology and molecular therapeutics (PhD)
cardiovascular diseases (PhD)
molecular pharmacology, toxicology and experimental therapeutics (PhD)
neuroscience (PhD)

Thayer School of Engineering
Dr. Joseph J. Helbie, Dean
Programs in:
biotechnology and biochemical engineering (MS, PhD)
computer engineering (MS, PhD)
electrical engineering (MS, PhD)
engineering (MEM, MS, PhD)
engineering management (MEM)
engineering physics (MS, PhD)
manufacturing systems (MS, PhD)
materials sciences and engineering (MS, PhD)
mechanical engineering (MS, PhD)

Tuck School of Business at Dartmouth
Program in:
business (MBA)

■ KEENE STATE COLLEGE

Keene, NH 03435
http://www.keene.edu/

State-supported, coed, comprehensive institution. *Graduate faculty:* 16 full-time (11 women), 5 part-time/adjunct (4 women). *Computer facilities:* Computer purchase and lease plans are available. 500 computers available on campus for general student use. A campuswide network can be accessed from student residence rooms and from off campus. Online class registration, personal Web pages are available. *Graduate expenses:* Tuition, state resident: full-time $6600; part-time $386 per credit. Tuition, nonresident: full-time $14,450; part-time $416 per credit. Required fees: $2178; $86 per credit. *General application contact:* Peggy Richmond, Director of Admissions, 603-358-2276.

School of Professional and Graduate Studies
Dr. Melinda Treadwell, Dean
Programs in:
curriculum and instruction (M Ed)
educational leadership (M Ed)
special education (M Ed)
teacher certification (Postbaccalaureate Certificate)

■ PLYMOUTH STATE UNIVERSITY

Plymouth, NH 03264-1595
http://www.plymouth.edu/

State-supported, coed, comprehensive institution. *Computer facilities:* Computer purchase and lease plans are available. 500 computers available on campus for general student use. A campuswide network can be accessed from student residence rooms and from off campus. Online class registration, degree audit, academic history, account status are available. *General application contact:* Director of Recruitment and Outreach, 603-535-2737.

College of Graduate Studies
Program in:
- business (MBA)

Graduate Studies in Education
Programs in:
- applied meteorology (MS)
- athletic training (M Ed, MS)
- counselor education (M Ed)
- education (M Ed, MAT, MS, Ed D, CAGS)
- educational leadership (M Ed)
- elementary education (M Ed)
- English education (M Ed)
- environmental science and policy (MS)
- health education (M Ed)
- k-12 education (M Ed)
- learning, leadership and community (Ed D)
- mathematics education (M Ed)
- reading and writing specialist (M Ed)
- science (MS)
- science education (MS)
- secondary education (M Ed)
- special education administration (M Ed)
- special education k-12 (M Ed)
- teaching (MAT)

■ RIVIER COLLEGE
Nashua, NH 03060
http://www.rivier.edu/

Independent-religious, coed, comprehensive institution. *Graduate faculty:* 36 full-time (18 women), 64 part-time/adjunct (34 women). *Computer facilities:* 93 computers available on campus for general student use. A campuswide network can be accessed from student residence rooms and from off campus. *Graduate expenses:* Tuition: full-time $5208; part-time $434 per credit. *General application contact:* Mathew Kittredge, Director of Graduate Admissions, 603-897-8129.

School of Graduate Studies
Sr. Therese LaRochelle, Vice President of Academic Affairs
Programs in:
- business administration (MBA)
- computer information systems (MS)
- computer science (MS)
- curriculum and instruction (M Ed)
- early childhood education (M Ed)
- educational administration (M Ed)
- educational studies (M Ed)
- elementary education (M Ed)
- elementary education and general special education (M Ed)
- emotional and behavioral disorders (M Ed)
- English (MA, MAT)
- general social education (M Ed)
- leadership and learning (Ed D, CAGS)
- learning disabilities (M Ed)
- learning disabilities and reading (M Ed)
- mathematics (MAT)
- mental health counseling (MA)
- organizational leadership (EMBA)
- reading (M Ed)
- school counseling (M Ed)
- social studies education (MAT)
- Spanish (MAT)
- writing and literature (MA)

Division of Nursing
Dr. Paula Williams, Head
Programs in:
- family nurse practitioner (MS)
- nursing education (MS)

■ SOUTHERN NEW HAMPSHIRE UNIVERSITY
Manchester, NH 03106-1045
http://www.snhu.edu/

Independent, coed, comprehensive institution. *Computer facilities:* Computer purchase and lease plans are available. 557 computers available on campus for general student use. A campuswide network can be accessed from student residence rooms and from off campus. Online class registration is available. *General application contact:* Director of Graduate Enrollment Services, 603-644-3102 Ext. 3338.

School of Business
Programs in:
- accounting (MS)
- business administration (MBA, Certificate)
- finance (MS)
- hospitality and tourism leadership (Certificate)
- information technology (MS, Certificate)
- information technology/international business (Certificate)
- integrated marketing communications (Certificate)
- international business (MS, DBA)
- marketing (MS)
- operations and project management (MS)
- organizational leadership (MS)
- project management (Certificate)
- sport management (MS)

School of Community Economic Development
Program in:
- community economic development (MA, MBA, MS, PhD)

School of Education
Programs in:
- business education (MS)
- child development (M Ed)
- computer technology education (Certificate)
- curriculum and instruction (M Ed)
- education (M Ed, CAS)
- elementary education (M Ed)
- general special education (Certificate)
- school business administrator (Certificate)
- secondary education (M Ed)
- training and development (Certificate)

School of Liberal Arts
Programs in:
- clinical services for adults psychiatric disabilities (Certificate)
- clinical services for children and adolescents with psychiatric disabilities (Certificate)
- clinical services for persons with co-occurring substance abuse and psychiatric disabilities (Certificate)
- community mental health (MS)
- fiction writing (MFA)
- non-fiction writing (MFA)
- teaching English as a foreign language (MS)

■ UNIVERSITY OF NEW HAMPSHIRE
Durham, NH 03824
http://www.unh.edu/

State-supported, coed, university. CGS member. *Graduate faculty:* 607 full-time (199 women). *Computer facilities:* Computer purchase and lease plans are available. 345 computers available on campus for general student use. A campuswide network can be accessed from student residence rooms and from off campus. Online class registration is available. *Graduate expenses:* Tuition, state resident: full-time $9720; part-time $540 per credit hour. Tuition, nonresident: full-time $23,200; part-time $954 per credit hour. Required fees: $1446; $361.50 per term. *General application contact:* Dovev Levine, Graduate Admissions Office, 603-862-3000.

Center for Graduate and Professional Studies
Kate Ferreira, Director
Programs in:
- business administration (MBA)
- counseling (M Ed)
- education (M Ed, MAT)
- educational administration and supervision (M Ed, CAGS)
- industrial statistics (Certificate)
- public administration (MPA)
- public health (MPH, Certificate)
- social work (MSW)

Graduate School
Dr. Harry J. Richards, Dean
Programs in:
- college teaching (MST)
- earth and environmental science (PhD)
- environmental education (MA)

University of New Hampshire (continued)
interdisciplinary studies (Postbaccalaureate Certificate)
natural resources and earth system science (PhD)
natural resources and environmental studies (PhD)

College of Engineering and Physical Sciences
Dr. Joe Klewicki, Dean
Programs in:
applied mathematics (MS)
chemical engineering (MS, PhD)
chemistry (MS, MST, PhD)
chemistry education (PhD)
civil engineering (MS, PhD)
computer science (MS, PhD)
earth sciences (MS)
electrical engineering (MS, PhD)
engineering and physical sciences (MS, MST, PhD, Postbaccalaureate Certificate)
hydrology (MS)
industrial statistics (Postbaccalaureate Certificate)
materials science (MS, PhD)
mathematics (MS, MST, PhD)
mathematics education (PhD)
mechanical engineering (MS, PhD)
ocean engineering (MS, PhD)
ocean mapping (MS, Postbaccalaureate Certificate)
physics (MS, PhD)
statistics (MS)
systems design (PhD)

College of Liberal Arts
Dr. Marilyn Hoskin, Dean
Programs in:
counseling (M Ed, MA)
early childhood education (M Ed)
education (PhD)
educational administration (M Ed, CAGS)
elementary education (M Ed, MAT)
English (MFA, PhD)
English education (MST)
history (MA, PhD)
justice studies (MA)
language and linguistics (MA)
liberal arts (M Ed, MA, MALS, MAT, MFA, MPA, MST, PhD, CAGS, Postbaccalaureate Certificate)
liberal studies (MALS)
literature (MA)
museum studies (MA)
music education (MA)
music history (MA)
painting (MFA)
political science (MA)
psychology (PhD)
public administration (MPA)
reading (M Ed)
secondary education (M Ed, MAT)
sociology (MA, PhD)
Spanish (MA)
special education (M Ed, Postbaccalaureate Certificate)
special needs (M Ed)
teacher leadership (M Ed, Postbaccalaureate Certificate)
writing (MA)

College of Life Sciences and Agriculture
Tom Brady, Dean
Programs in:
animal and nutritional sciences (PhD)
animal science (MS)
biochemistry (MS, PhD)
environmental conservation (MS)
forestry (MS)
genetics (MS, PhD)
life sciences and agriculture (MS, PhD)
microbiology (MS, PhD)
nutritional sciences (MS)
plant biology (MS, PhD)
resource administration (MS)
resource economics (MS)
soil science (MS)
water resources management (MS)
wildlife (MS)
zoology (MS, PhD)

School of Health and Human Services
Dr. Barbara Arrington, Dean
Programs in:
communication sciences and disorders (Postbaccalaureate Certificate)
early childhood intervention (MS)
family studies (MS)
health and human services (MPH, MS, MSW, Postbaccalaureate Certificate)
kinesiology (MS)
language and literature disabilities (MS)
marriage and family therapy (MS)
nursing (MS, Postbaccalaureate Certificate)
occupational therapy (MS, Postbaccalaureate Certificate)
public health (MPH, Postbaccalaureate Certificate)
recreation administration (MS)
social work (MSW, Postbaccalaureate Certificate)
therapeutic recreation (MS)

Whittemore School of Business and Economics
Dr. Daniel Innis, Dean
Programs in:
accounting (MS)
business administration (MBA)
business and economics (MA, MBA, MS, PhD, Postbaccalaureate Certificate)
economics (MA, PhD)
executive business administration (MBA)
health management (MBA)
management of technology (MS, Postbaccalaureate Certificate)

New Jersey

■ CALDWELL COLLEGE
Caldwell, NJ 07006-6195
http://www.caldwell.edu/

Independent-religious, coed, comprehensive institution. CGS member. *Computer facilities:* 197 computers available on campus for general student use. A campuswide network can be accessed from student residence rooms and from off campus. Online class registration is available. *General application contact:* Graduate Admissions Counselor, 973-618-3408.

Graduate Studies
Programs in:
accounting (MBA)
applied behavior analysis (MA, PhD)
art therapy (MA)
business administration (MBA)
counseling psychology (MA)
curriculum and instruction (MA)
educational administration (MA)
pastoral ministry (MA)
school counseling (MA)
special education (MA)

■ CENTENARY COLLEGE
Hackettstown, NJ 07840-2100
http://www.centenarycollege.edu/

Independent-religious, coed, comprehensive institution. *Computer facilities:* Computer purchase and lease plans are available. 100 computers available on campus for general student use. A campuswide network can be accessed from student residence rooms and from off campus. Online class registration is available. *General application contact:* Dean, 908-852-1400 Ext. 2322.

Program in Business Administration
Program in:
business administration (MBA)

Program in Counseling Psychology
Programs in:
counseling (MA)
counseling psychology (MA)

Program in Education
Programs in:
instructional leadership (MA)
special education (MA)

Program in Professional Accounting
Program in:
professional accounting (MS)

■ THE COLLEGE OF NEW JERSEY

Ewing, NJ 08628

http://www.tcnj.edu/

State-supported, coed, comprehensive institution. CGS member. *Computer facilities:* Computer purchase and lease plans are available. 782 computers available on campus for general student use. A campuswide network can be accessed from student residence rooms and from off campus. Online class registration is available. *Graduate expenses:* Part-time $557 per credit. Tuition, state resident: part-time $557 per credit. Tuition, nonresident: part-time $845 per credit. Required fees: $135 per credit. *General application contact:* Susan L. Hydro, Assistant Dean, Office of Graduate Studies, 609-771-2300.

Graduate Division

Program in:
- overseas education (M Ed, Certificate)

School of Culture and Society

Dr. Benjamin Rifkin, Dean
Programs in:
- culture and society (MA)
- English (MA)

School of Education

Dr. William Behre, Dean, School of Education
Programs in:
- community counseling: human services (MA)
- community counseling: substance abuse and addiction (MA, Certificate)
- developmental reading (M Ed)
- education (M Ed, MA, MAT, MS, Certificate, Ed S)
- educational leadership (M Ed, Certificate)
- educational technology (MS)
- elementary education (M Ed, MAT)
- elementary teaching (MAT)
- English as a second language (M Ed)
- marriage and family therapy (Ed S)
- reading certification (Certificate)
- school counseling (MA)
- school personnel licensure: preschool-grade 3 (M Ed, MAT)
- secondary education (MAT)
- special education (M Ed, MAT)
- special education with learning disabilities (Certificate)
- teaching English as a second language (M Ed, Certificate)

School of Nursing, Health and Exercise Science

Dr. Susan Bakewell-Sachs, Dean
Programs in:
- health (MAT)
- health education (M Ed, MAT)
- nursing (MSN, Certificate)
- nursing, health and exercise science (M Ed, MAT, MSN, Certificate)
- physical education (M Ed, MAT)

■ COLLEGE OF SAINT ELIZABETH

Morristown, NJ 07960-6989

http://www.cse.edu/

Independent-religious, Undergraduate: women only; graduate: coed, comprehensive institution. CGS member. *Graduate faculty:* 27 full-time (14 women), 57 part-time/adjunct (33 women). *Computer facilities:* 127 computers available on campus for general student use. A campuswide network can be accessed from student residence rooms and from off campus. *Graduate expenses:* Tuition: part-time $759 per credit. Required fees: $380 per semester. *General application contact:* Donna Tatarka, Dean of Admission, 973-290-4705.

Department of Business Administration and Economics

Dr. Kathleen Reddick, Director of the Graduate Program in Management
Program in:
- management (MS)

Department of Education

Dr. Alan H. Markowitz, Director of Graduate Education Programs
Programs in:
- accelerated certification for teachers (Certificate)
- assistive technology (Certificate)
- education: human services leadership (MA)
- educational leadership (MA, Ed D)
- educational technology (MA)

Department of Foods and Nutrition

Dr. Jean C. Burge, Director of the Graduate Program in Nutrition
Programs in:
- dietetic internship (Certificate)
- nutrition (MS)

Department of Health Professions and Related Sciences

Linda Hunter, Director of the Graduate Program in Health Care Management
Program in:
- health care management (MS)

Department of Nursing

Dr. Sharon Hellwig, Director of Graduate Program in Nursing
Program in:
- nursing (MSN)

Department of Psychology

Dr. Valerie Scott, Director of the Graduate Program in Counseling Psychology
Programs in:
- counseling psychology (MA)
- forensic psychology (MA)
- student affairs in higher education (Certificate)

Department of Theology

Sr. Kathleen Flanagan, Director of the Graduate Program in Theology
Program in:
- theology (MA)

■ DREW UNIVERSITY

Madison, NJ 07940-1493

http://www.drew.edu/

Independent-religious, coed, university. CGS member. *Computer facilities:* Computer purchase and lease plans are available. 200 computers available on campus for general student use. A campuswide network can be accessed from student residence rooms and from off campus. Online class registration is available. *General application contact:* Director of Graduate Admissions, 973-408-3110.

Caspersen School of Graduate Studies

Programs in:
- anthropology of religion (MA, PhD)
- Christian social ethics (MA, PhD)
- English literature (MA, PhD)
- historical studies (MA, PhD)
- holocaust and genocide studies (Certificate)
- interdisciplinary studies (M Litt, D Litt)
- liturgical studies (MA, PhD)
- medical humanities (MMH, DMH, CMH)
- Methodist studies (PhD)
- modern history and literature (MA, PhD)
- philosophy of religion (MA, PhD)
- psychology and religion (MA, PhD)
- religion in ancient Israel (MA, PhD)
- sociology of religion (MA, PhD)
- systematic theology (MA, PhD)
- the New Testament and early Christianity (MA, PhD)
- theological ethics (MA, PhD)
- Wesleyan and Methodist studies (MA, PhD)
- women's studies (MA)

The Theological School

Program in:
- theology (M Div, MTS, STM, D Min, Certificate)

■ FAIRLEIGH DICKINSON UNIVERSITY, COLLEGE AT FLORHAM

Madison, NJ 07940-1099

http://www.fdu.edu/

Independent, coed, comprehensive institution. *Computer facilities:* Computer purchase and lease plans are available. 140 computers available on campus for general student use. A campuswide network can be accessed from student residence rooms and from off campus. Online class registration is available. *General application contact:* Susan Brooman, University Director, Graduate Admissions, 973-443-8905.

Fairleigh Dickinson University, College at Florham (continued)

Anthony J. Petrocelli College of Continuing Studies
Kenneth Vehrkens, Dean
Program in:
continuing studies (MAS, MPA, MS)

International School of Hospitality and Tourism Management
Program in:
hospitality management studies (MS)

Public Administration Institute
Dr. William Roberts, Head
Program in:
public administration (MPA)

School of Administrative Science
Program in:
administrative science (MAS)

Maxwell Becton College of Arts and Sciences
Dr. Geoffrey Weinman, Dean
Programs in:
arts and sciences (MA, MFA, MS, Certificate)
biology (MS)
chemistry (MS)
corporate and organizational communication (MA)
counseling (MA)
creative writing (MFA)
industrial/organizational psychology (MA)
organizational behavior (MA, Certificate)
organizational leadership (Certificate)

Silberman College of Business
Dr. William Moore, Dean
Programs in:
accounting (MS)
business (EMBA, MBA, MS, Certificate)
business administration (MBA)
entrepreneurial studies (MBA, Certificate)
evolving technology (Certificate)
finance (MBA, Certificate)
health care and life sciences (EMBA)
international business (MBA, Certificate)
international taxation (Certificate)
management (EMBA, MBA, Certificate)
marketing (MBA, Certificate)
pharmaceutical studies (MBA, Certificate)
taxation (MS, Certificate)

Center for Human Resource Management Studies
Dr. Gerard Farias, Head
Programs in:
human resource management (MBA)
human resource management studies (MBA)

University College: Arts, Sciences, and Professional Studies
Patti Mills, Dean
Program in:
arts, sciences, and professional studies (MA, MAT, Certificate)

Peter Sammartino School of Education
Programs in:
education for certified teachers (MA, Certificate)
educational leadership (MA)
instructional technology (Certificate)
literacy/reading (Certificate)
teaching (MAT)

■ FAIRLEIGH DICKINSON UNIVERSITY, METROPOLITAN CAMPUS

Teaneck, NJ 07666-1914
http://www.fdu.edu/

Independent, coed, comprehensive institution. *Computer facilities:* Computer purchase and lease plans are available. 160 computers available on campus for general student use. A campuswide network can be accessed from student residence rooms and from off campus. Online class registration is available. *General application contact:* Susan Brooman, University Director of Graduate Admissions, 201-692-2554.

Anthony J. Petrocelli College of Continuing Studies
Kenneth T. Vehrkens, Dean
Programs in:
continuing studies (MAS, MPA, MS, MSA, MSHS, Certificate)
sports administration (MSA)

International School of Hospitality and Tourism Management
Dr. Richard Wisch, Director
Program in:
hospitality management (MS)

Public Administration Institute
Dr. William Roberts, Director
Programs in:
public administration (MPA, Certificate)
public non-profit management (Certificate)

School of Administrative Science
Ronald Calissi, Director/Executive Associate Dean
Programs in:
administrative science (MAS, MSHS, Certificate)
homeland security (MSHS)

Silberman College of Business
Dr. William Moore, Dean
Programs in:
accounting (MS, Certificate)
business (EMBA, MBA, MS, Certificate)
business administration (MBA)
chemical studies (Certificate)
entrepreneurial studies (MBA, Certificate)
executive management (EMBA)
finance (MBA, Certificate)
healthcare and life sciences (EMBA)
international business (MBA)
management (MBA, Certificate)
management information systems (Certificate)
marketing (MBA, Certificate)
pharmaceutical studies (MBA, Certificate)
taxation (MS)

Center for Human Resources Management Studies
Programs in:
human resource management (MBA, Certificate)
human resources management studies (MBA, Certificate)

University College: Arts, Sciences, and Professional Studies
Patti Mills, Dean
Programs in:
arts, sciences, and professional studies (MA, MAT, MS, MSEE, MSN, DNP, PhD, Psy D, Certificate)
English and literature (MA)
systems science (MS)

Henry P. Becton School of Nursing and Allied Health
Programs in:
medical technology (MS)
nursing (MSN, Certificate)
nursing practice (DNP)

Peter Sammartino School of Education
Dr. Vicki Cohen, Director
Programs in:
dyslexia specialist (Certificate)
education for certified teachers (MA)
educational leadership (MA)
instructional technology (Certificate)
learning disabilities (MA)
literacy/reading (Certificate)
multilingual education (MA)
teacher of the handicapped (Certificate)
teaching (MAT)

School of Art and Media Studies
Programs in:
art and media studies (MA)
media and communications (MA)

School of Computer Sciences and Engineering
Dr. Alfredo Tan, Director
Programs in:
computer engineering (MS)
computer science (MS)
e-commerce (MS)
electrical engineering (MSEE)
management information systems (MS)
mathematical foundation (MS)

School of History, Political and International Studies
Programs in:
history (MA)
international studies (MA)
political science (MA)

School of Natural Sciences
Dr. Irwin Isquith, Director

Programs in:
biology (MS)
chemistry (MS)
science (MA)

School of Psychology
Programs in:
clinical psychology (MA, PhD)
clinical psychopharmacology (MA)
forensic psychology (MA)
general-theoretical psychology (MA, Certificate)
school psychology (MA, Psy D)

■ GEORGIAN COURT UNIVERSITY
Lakewood, NJ 08701-2697
http://www.georgian.edu/

Independent-religious, Undergraduate: women only; graduate: coed, comprehensive institution. *Graduate faculty:* 55 full-time (31 women), 64 part-time/adjunct (37 women). *Computer facilities:* 192 computers available on campus for general student use. A campuswide network can be accessed. Online class registration is available. *Graduate expenses:* Tuition: full-time $12,276; part-time $682 per credit. Required fees: $400 per year. Tuition and fees vary according to campus/location. *General application contact:* Eugene Soltys, Director of Graduate Admissions, 732-987-2770.

School of Arts and Humanities
Dr. Linda James, Dean
Programs in:
Catholic school leadership (Certificate)
parish business management (Certificate)
pastoral administration (Certificate)
pastoral ministry (Certificate)
religious education (Certificate)
theology (MA, Certificate)

School of Business
Binetta Dolan, Dean
Programs in:
accounting (Certificate)
business administration (MBA)

School of Education
Dr. Jacqueline Kress, Dean
Programs in:
administration and leadership (MA)
education (MA)

School of Sciences and Mathematics
Dr. Linda James, Dean
Programs in:
biology (MS)
counseling psychology (MA)
holistic health (Certificate)
holistic health studies (MA)
mathematics (MA)
professional counselor (Certificate)
school psychology (Certificate)

■ KEAN UNIVERSITY
Union, NJ 07083
http://www.kean.edu/

State-supported, coed, comprehensive institution. CGS member. *Graduate faculty:* 218 full-time (115 women). *Computer facilities:* 1,700 computers available on campus for general student use. A campuswide network can be accessed from student residence rooms and from off campus. Online class registration is available. *Graduate expenses:* Tuition, state resident: full-time $10,128; part-time $422 per credit. Tuition, nonresident: full-time $13,728; part-time $572 per credit. Required fees: $2570; $107 per credit. Part-time tuition and fees vary according to course load, degree level and program. *General application contact:* Steven Koch, Pre-Admissions Coordinator, 908-737-4723.

College of Business and Public Administration
Dr. Alfred Ntoko, Dean
Programs in:
accounting (MS)
business and public administration (MA, MPA, MS)
criminal justice (MA)
environmental management (MPA)
health services administration (MPA)
non-profit management (MPA)
public administration (MPA)

College of Education
Dr. Susan Polirstok, Dean
Programs in:
administration in early childhood and family studies (MA)
adult literacy (MA)
advanced curriculum and teaching (MA)
alcohol and drug abuse counseling (MA)
basic skills (MA)
bilingual/bicultural education (MA)
business and industry counseling (MA)
classroom instruction (MA)
community/agency counseling (MA)
earth science (MA)
education (MA, MS)
education for family living (MA)
exercise science (MS)
high incidence disabilities (MA)
low incidence disabilities (MA)
mathematics/science/computer education (MA)
reading specialization (MA)
school counseling (MA)
speech language pathology (MA)
teaching (MA)
teaching English as a second language (MA)
world languages (Spanish) (MA)

College of Humanities and Social Sciences
Dr. Kenneth Dollarhide, Dean
Programs in:
advanced standing (MSW)
communication studies (MA)
educational psychology (MA)
human behavior and organizational psychology (MA)
humanities and social sciences (MA, MSW, Diploma)
marriage and family therapy (Diploma)
political science (MA)
psychological services (MA)
school psychology (Diploma)
social work (MSW)
sociology and social justice (MA)

College of Natural, Applied and Health Sciences
Dr. Jeffrey H. Toney, Dean
Programs in:
clinical management (MSN)
community health (MSN)
computer applications (MA)
computing, statistics and mathematics (MS)
natural, applied and health sciences (MA, MS, MSN)
occupational therapy (MS)
school nursing (MSN)
supervision of math education (MA)
teaching of math (MA)

Nathan Weiss Graduate College
Dr. Kristie Reilly, Vice President of Research and Graduate Studies and Dean
Programs in:
biotechnology (MS)
executive management (MBA)
global management (MBA)
Holocaust and genocide studies (MA)
school and clinical psychology (Psy D)
school business administration (MA)
supervisors and principals (MA)
urban leadership (Ed D)

School of Visual and Performing Arts
Dr. Holly Logue, Dean
Programs in:
certification (MA)
graphic communication technology management (MS)
liberal studies (MA)
studio/research (MA)
supervision (MA)
visual and performing arts (MA, MS)

■ MONMOUTH UNIVERSITY
West Long Branch, NJ 07764-1898
http://www.monmouth.edu/

Independent, coed, comprehensive institution. *Graduate faculty:* 134 full-time (66 women), 69 part-time/adjunct (45 women). *Computer facilities:* 695 computers available on campus for general student use. A campuswide network can be accessed from student residence rooms and from off campus. Online class registration is available. *Graduate expenses:* Tuition: full-time $13,914; part-time $773 per credit. Required

Monmouth University (continued)
fees: $628; $157 per semester. *General application contact:* Kevin Roane, Director, Office of Graduate Admission, 732-571-3452.

Graduate School
Dr. Datta V. Naik, Dean
Programs in:
community and international development (MSW)
computer science (MS)
corporate and public communication (MA)
criminal justice administration (MA, Certificate)
English (MA)
history (MA)
human resources communication (Certificate)
liberal arts (MA)
media studies (Certificate)
practice with families and children (MSW)
professional counseling (PMC)
psychological counseling (MA)
public policy (MA)
public relations (Certificate)
software development (Certificate)
software engineering (MS, Certificate)

Leon Hess Business School
Donald Smith, Program Director
Programs in:
accounting (MBA)
business administration (MBA)
health care management (MBA, Certificate)

The Marjorie K. Unterberg School of Nursing and Health Studies
Dr. Janet Mahoney, Director
Programs in:
advanced practice nursing (Post-Master's Certificate)
nursing (MSN)
school nursing (Certificate)
substance awareness coordinator (Certificate)

School of Education
Dr. Terri Rothman, Program Director
Programs in:
education (M Ed)
educational counseling (MS Ed)
elementary education (MAT)
learning disabilities-teacher consultant (Certificate)
principal studies (MS Ed)
reading specialist (MS Ed, Certificate)
special education (MS Ed)
supervisor (Certificate)
teacher of the handicapped (Certificate)

■ MONTCLAIR STATE UNIVERSITY
Montclair, NJ 07043-1624
http://www.montclair.edu/

State-supported, coed, comprehensive institution. CGS member. *Graduate faculty:* 524 full-time (248 women), 873 part-time/adjunct (485 women). *Computer facilities:* Computer purchase and lease plans are available. 218 computers available on campus for general student use. A campuswide network can be accessed from student residence rooms and from off campus. Online class registration is available. *General application contact:* Ben Enoma, Director of the Office of Graduate Admissions and Support Services, 973-655-5147.

The Office of Graduate Admissions and Support Services
Dr. Joan Ficke, Vice Provost for Academic Affairs

College of Education and Human Services
Dr. Ada Beth Cutler, Dean
Programs in:
administration and supervision (MA)
advanced counseling (Certificate)
American Dietetic Association (Certificate)
counseling and guidance (MA)
counselor education (PhD)
critical thinking (M Ed)
early childhood education and teaching students with disabilities (MAT)
early childhood special education (M Ed, Certificate)
early childhood/elementary education (M Ed)
education (M Ed)
education and human services (M Ed, MA, MAT, MS, Ed D, PhD, Certificate)
educational technology (M Ed)
elementary education with disabilities (MAT)
elementary school teacher (Certificate)
food safety instructor (Certificate)
health and physical education (Certificate)
health education (MA)
learning disabilities (Certificate)
learning disabled teacher consultant (Certificate)
mathematics education (Ed D)
nutrition and exercise science (MS, Certificate)
nutrition and food science (MS)
philosophy for children (M Ed, Ed D, Certificate)
physical education (MA, Certificate)
principal (Certificate)
reading (MA, Certificate)
reading specialist (Certificate)
school administrator (Certificate)
school business administrator (Certificate)
school counselor (Certificate)
school library media specialist (Certificate)
substance awareness coordinator (Certificate)
teaching (MAT, Certificate)

College of Humanities and Social Sciences
Dr. Morrissey, Dean
Programs in:
applied linguistics (MA)
applied sociology (MA)
audiology (Sc D)
child advocacy (MA, Certificate)
conflict management in the workplace (Certificate)
dispute resolution (MA)
educational psychology (MA)
English (MA, Certificate)
French (MA, Certificate)
governance, compliance and regulation (MA)
humanities and social sciences (MA, Sc D, Certificate)
intellectual property (MA)
Italian (Certificate)
law and governance (MA)
legal management, information and technology (MA)
paralegal studies (Certificate)
psychology (MA, Certificate)
public child welfare (MA)
school psychologist (Certificate)
social sciences (MA)
social studies (Certificate)
Spanish (MA, Certificate)
speech/language pathology (MA)
teacher of English as a second language (Certificate)
translating and interpreting Spanish (Certificate)

College of Science and Mathematics
Dr. Robert Prezant, Dean
Programs in:
applied mathematics (MS)
applied statistics (MS)
biology (MS)
chemical business (MS)
chemistry (MS)
CISCO (Certificate)
earth science (Certificate)
environmental management (MA, D Env M, PhD)
environmental studies (MS)
geographic information science (Certificate)
geoscience (MS, Certificate)
informatics (MS)
math pedagogy (Ed D)
mathematics (MS)
molecular biology (Certificate)
object oriented computing (Certificate)
physical science (Certificate)
science and mathematics (MA, MS, D Env M, Ed D, PhD, Certificate)
teaching middle grades math (MS, Certificate)

School of Business
Dr. William Turner, Dean
Programs in:
accounting (MBA, Certificate)
business (MBA, Certificate)
business economics (MBA)
finance (MBA, Certificate)
international business (MBA, Certificate)
management (MBA, Certificate)
management information systems (MBA, Certificate)
marketing (Certificate)

School of the Arts
Dr. Geoffrey Newman, Dean
Programs in:
- art education (MA, Certificate)
- art history (MA)
- arts (MA, MFA, AD, Certificate)
- music (AD)
- music education (MA)
- music therapy (MA)
- organizational communication (MA)
- performance (MA, Certificate)
- public relations (MA)
- speech communication (MA)
- studio arts (MA, MFA)
- theatre (MA)
- theory/composition (MA)

■ NEW JERSEY CITY UNIVERSITY
Jersey City, NJ 07305-1597
http://www.njcu.edu/

State-supported, coed, comprehensive institution. *Computer facilities:* 1,400 computers available on campus for general student use. A campuswide network can be accessed from student residence rooms and from off campus. Online class registration is available. *General application contact:* Dean of Graduate Studies, 201-200-3409.

Graduate Studies and Continuing Education

College of Arts and Sciences
Programs in:
- art (MFA)
- art education (MA)
- arts and sciences (MA, MFA, MM, PD)
- counseling (MA)
- educational psychology (MA, PD)
- mathematics education (MA)
- music education (MA)
- performance (MM)
- school psychology (PD)
- studio art (MFA)

College of Education
Programs in:
- basics and urban studies (MA)
- bilingual/bicultural education and English as a second language (MA)
- early childhood education (MA)
- education (MA, MAT)
- educational administration and supervision (MA)
- educational technology (MA)
- elementary education (MAT)
- elementary school reading (MA)
- reading specialist (MA)
- secondary education (MAT)
- secondary school reading (MA)
- special education (MA)

College of Professional Studies
Programs in:
- accounting (MS)
- community health education (MS)
- criminal justice (MS)
- finance (MS)
- health administration (MS)
- law enforcement (MS)
- school health education (MS)

■ NEW JERSEY INSTITUTE OF TECHNOLOGY
Newark, NJ 07102
http://www.njit.edu/

State-supported, coed, university. CGS member. *Graduate faculty:* 396 full-time (67 women), 263 part-time/adjunct (48 women). *Computer facilities:* Computer purchase and lease plans are available. 1,938 computers available on campus for general student use. A campuswide network can be accessed from student residence rooms and from off campus. Online class registration is available. *Graduate expenses:* Tuition, state resident: full-time $13,780; part-time $750 per credit. Tuition, nonresident: full-time $19,580; part-time $1033 per credit. Required fees: $1956; $197 per credit. *General application contact:* Kathryn Kelly, Director of Admissions, 973-596-3300.

Office of Graduate Studies
Dr. Ronald Kane, Dean of Graduate Studies

College of Computing Science
Dr. Narain Gehani, Chairperson
Programs in:
- bioinformatics (MS)
- business and information systems (MS)
- computer science (MS, PhD)
- computing and business (MS)
- computing science (MS, PhD)
- emergency management and business continuity (MS)
- information systems (MS, PhD)
- software engineering (MS)

College of Science and Liberal Arts
Dr. Fadi P. Deek, Dean
Programs in:
- applied mathematics (MS)
- applied physics (MS, PhD)
- applied statistics (MS)
- biology (MS, PhD)
- biostatistics (MS)
- chemistry (MS, PhD)
- computational biology (MS)
- computing biology (MS)
- environmental policy studies (MS)
- environmental science (MS, PhD)
- history (MA, MAT)
- material science and engineering (MS)
- materials science and engineering (PhD)
- mathematics science (PhD)
- professional and technical communication (MS)
- science and liberal arts (MA, MAT, MS, PhD)

Newark College of Engineering
Dr. Sunil Saigal, Dean
Programs in:
- biomedical engineering (MS, PhD)
- chemical engineering (MS, PhD)
- civil engineering (MS, PhD)
- computer engineering (MS, PhD)
- electrical engineering (MS, PhD)
- engineering (MS, PhD, Engineer)
- engineering management (MS)
- engineering science (MS)
- environmental engineering (MS, PhD)
- industrial engineering (MS, PhD)
- Internet engineering (MS)
- manufacturing engineering (MS)
- mechanical engineering (MS, PhD, Engineer)
- occupational safety and health engineering (MS)
- pharmaceutical engineering (MS)
- power and energy systems (MS)
- transportation (MS, PhD)

School of Architecture
Urs P. Gauchat, Dean
Programs in:
- architecture (M Arch, MIP, MS, PhD)
- infrastructure planning (MIP)
- urban systems (PhD)

School of Management
Dr. Robert English, Interim Dean
Programs in:
- management of business administration (MBA)
- management of technology (MS)

■ PRINCETON UNIVERSITY
Princeton, NJ 08544-1019
http://www.princeton.edu/

Independent, coed, university. CGS member. *Computer facilities:* Computer purchase and lease plans are available. 500 computers available on campus for general student use. A campuswide network can be accessed from student residence rooms and from off campus. Online class registration, academic applications and courseware, printing, network file space, Web site hosting, media lab, broadcast center are available. *General application contact:* Graduate Admissions Office, 609-258-3034.

Graduate School
Programs in:
- anthropology (PhD)
- applied and computational mathematics (PhD)
- applied physics (M Eng, MSE, PhD)
- astronomy (PhD)
- atmospheric and oceanic sciences (PhD)
- chemical engineering (M Eng, MSE, PhD)
- chemistry (PhD)
- civil and environmental engineering (MSE)
- classical and hellenic studies (PhD)
- classical art and archaeology (PhD)
- classical philosophy (PhD)
- comparative literature (PhD)
- composition (PhD)
- computational methods (M Eng, MSE)
- computer science (MSE, PhD)
- demography (PhD, Certificate)

Princeton University (continued)
dynamics and control systems (M Eng, MSE, PhD)
East Asian art and archaeology (PhD)
East Asian studies (PhD)
ecology and evolutionary biology (PhD)
economics (PhD)
economics and demography (PhD)
electrical engineering (M Eng, PhD)
energy and environmental policy (M Eng, MSE, PhD)
energy conversion, propulsion, and combustion (M Eng, MSE, PhD)
English (PhD)
environmental engineering and water resources (M Eng, PhD)
financial engineering (M Eng, MSE)
flight science and technology (M Eng, MSE, PhD)
fluid mechanics (M Eng, MSE, PhD)
French language and literature (PhD)
geosciences (PhD)
German (PhD)
history (PhD)
history (the ancient world) (PhD)
history of science (PhD)
industrial chemistry (MS)
literature and philology (PhD)
mathematics (PhD)
mechanics, materials, and structures (PhD)
molecular biology (PhD)
musicology (PhD)
Near Eastern studies (MA, PhD)
neuroscience (PhD)
ocean sciences and marine biology (PhD)
operations research and financial engineering (PhD)
philosophy (PhD)
philosophy of science (PhD)
physics (PhD)
plasma physics (PhD)
political philosophy (PhD)
politics (PhD)
psychology (PhD)
public affairs and demography (PhD)
religion (PhD)
Russian and Slavic linguistics (PhD)
Russian literature (PhD)
sociology (PhD)
sociology and demography (PhD)
Spanish and Portuguese languages and cultures (PhD)
structural engineering (M Eng)

Bendheim Center for Finance
Program in:
finance (M Fin)

School of Architecture
Program in:
architecture (M Arch, PhD)

Woodrow Wilson School of Public and International Affairs
Programs in:
public affairs (MPA, PhD)
public policy (MPP)

Princeton Institute for the Science and Technology of Materials (PRISM)
Program in:
materials (PhD)

Princeton Neuroscience Institute
Program in:
neuroscience (PhD)

■ RAMAPO COLLEGE OF NEW JERSEY
Mahwah, NJ 07430-1680
http://www.ramapo.edu/

State-supported, coed, comprehensive institution. *Graduate faculty:* 9 full-time (6 women), 25 part-time/adjunct (14 women). *Computer facilities:* 1,058 computers available on campus for general student use. A campuswide network can be accessed from student residence rooms and from off campus. Online class registration is available. *Graduate expenses:* Tuition, state resident: part-time $472.20 per credit. Tuition, nonresident: part-time $606.85 per credit. Required fees: $43.80 per credit. Part-time tuition and fees vary according to reciprocity agreements. *General application contact:* Dr. Beth E. Barnett, Vice President of Academic Affairs and Provost, Office Of The Provost, 201-684-7529.

Master of Science in Educational Technology Program
Dr. Angela Cristini, Dean of the Masters in Educational Technology Program/ Executive Director of Special Programs, Office Of The Provost
Program in:
educational technology (MS)

Master of Science in Nursing Program
Dr. Kathleen M. Burke, Assistant Dean
Program in:
nursing education (MSN)

Program in Liberal Studies
Dr. Anthony T. Padovano, Director
Program in:
liberal studies (MALS)

■ THE RICHARD STOCKTON COLLEGE OF NEW JERSEY
Pomona, NJ 08240-0195
http://www.stockton.edu/

State-supported, coed, comprehensive institution. CGS member. *Graduate faculty:* 46 full-time (27 women), 16 part-time/adjunct (12 women). *Computer facilities:* 865 computers available on campus for general student use. A campuswide network can be accessed from student residence rooms and from off campus. Online class registration is available. *Graduate expenses:* Tuition, state resident: full-time $8526; part-time $474 per credit. Tuition, nonresident: full-time $13,125; part-time $729 per course. Required fees: $2030; $113 per credit. *General application contact:* Ann Mari Tarsitano, Director of Graduate Recruitment and Marketing, 609-652-4298.

School of Graduate and Continuing Education
Dr. Deborah M. Figart, Dean of Graduate Studies
Programs in:
business administration (MBA)
criminal justice (MA)
education (MA)
Holocaust and genocide studies (MA)
instructional technology (MA)
nursing (MSN)
occupational therapy (MSOT)
paralegal (Certificate)
physical therapy (DPT)

■ RIDER UNIVERSITY
Lawrenceville, NJ 08648-3001
http://www.rider.edu/

Independent, coed, comprehensive institution. *Computer facilities:* Computer purchase and lease plans are available. 300 computers available on campus for general student use. A campuswide network can be accessed from student residence rooms and from off campus. Online class registration is available. *General application contact:* Director of Graduate Admissions, 609-896-5036.

College of Business Administration
Programs in:
accountancy (M Acc)
business administration (M Acc, MBA)

Department of Graduate Education, Leadership and Counseling
Programs in:
alternative route in special education (Certificate)
business education (Certificate)
counseling services (MA, Certificate, Ed S)
curriculum, instruction and supervision (MA, Certificate)
director of school counseling (Certificate)
educational administration (MA, Certificate)
elementary education (Certificate)
English as a second language (Certificate)
English education (Certificate)
mathematics education (Certificate)
organizational leadership (MA)
preschool to grade 3 (Certificate)
principal (Certificate)
reading specialist (Certificate)
reading/language arts (MA, Certificate)
school administrator (Certificate)
school counseling services (Certificate)

school psychology (Certificate, Ed S)
science education (Certificate)
social studies education (Certificate)
special education (MA, Certificate)
supervisor (Certificate)
teacher certification (Certificate)
teacher of students with disabilities (Certificate)
teacher of the handicapped (Certificate)
teaching (MA)
world languages (Certificate)

■ ROWAN UNIVERSITY

Glassboro, NJ 08028-1701
http://www.rowan.edu/

State-supported, coed, comprehensive institution. CGS member. *Graduate faculty:* 116 full-time (50 women), 56 part-time/adjunct (24 women). *Computer facilities:* 1,200 computers available on campus for general student use. A campuswide network can be accessed from student residence rooms and from off campus. Online class registration, online library are available. *Graduate expenses:* Tuition, state resident: full-time $10,624; part-time $590 per credit. Tuition, nonresident: full-time $10,624; part-time $590 per credit. Required fees: $2258; $124.90 per credit. *General application contact:* Dr. Mira Lalovic-Hand, Dean, College of Professional and Continuing Education, 856-256-5120.

Graduate School

Dr. Mira Lalovic-Hand, Assistant Provost/Director of the Graduate School

College of Communication
Dr. Mira Lalovic-Hand, Interim Associate Provost/Director of Graduate School
Programs in:
communication (MA)
public relations (MA)
writing (MA)

College of Education
Dr. Mira Lalovic-Hand, Interim Associate Provost/Director of Graduate School
Programs in:
business administration (MA)
collaborative teaching (MST)
counseling in educational settings (MA)
education (M Ed, MA, MST, MST, Ed D, Ed S)
educational leadership (MA, Ed D)
elementary education (MST)
elementary school teaching (MA)
higher education administration (MA)
learning disabilities (MA)
music education (MA)
principal preparation (MA)
reading education (MA)
school administration (MA)
school and public librarianship (MA)
school business administration (MA)
school psychology (MA, Ed S)
secondary education (MST)
special education (MA)
standards-based practice (M Ed)
subject matter teaching (MA)
supervision and curriculum development (MA)
teacher leadership (M Ed)

College of Engineering
Dr. Dianne Dorland, Dean
Programs in:
engineering (MEM, MS)
engineering management (MEM)

College of Fine and Performing Arts
Dr. Mira Lalovic-Hand, Interim Associate Provost/Director of Graduate School
Programs in:
fine and performing arts (MA, MM, MST)
performance (MM)
theatre (MA)
theatre education (MST)

College of Liberal Arts and Sciences
Dr. Mira Lalovic-Hand, Interim Associate Provost/Director of Graduate School
Programs in:
criminal justice (MA)
liberal arts and sciences (MA)
mathematics (MA)
mental health counseling (MA)
mental health counseling and applied psychology (MA)

William G. Rohrer College of Business
Dr. Mira Lalovic-Hand, Interim Associate Provost/Director of Graduate School
Program in:
business (MBA)

■ RUTGERS, THE STATE UNIVERSITY OF NEW JERSEY, CAMDEN

Camden, NJ 08102-1401
http://www.rutgers.edu/

State-supported, coed, university. *Computer facilities:* 184 computers available on campus for general student use. A campuswide network can be accessed from student residence rooms and from off campus. Online grade reports available. *General application contact:* Information Contact, 856-225-6149.

Graduate School of Arts and Sciences

Programs in:
American and public history (MA)
biology (MS)
chemistry (MS)
childhood studies (MA, PhD)
computer science (MS)
creative writing (MFA)
criminal justice (MA)
education policy and leadership (MPA)
English (MA)
international public service and development (MPA)
liberal studies (MALS)
mathematics (MS)
physical therapy (DPT)
psychology (MA)
public management (MPA)

School of Business

Program in:
business (MBA)

School of Law

Program in:
law (JD)

■ RUTGERS, THE STATE UNIVERSITY OF NEW JERSEY, NEWARK

Newark, NJ 07102
http://www.rutgers.edu/

State-supported, coed, university. CGS member. *Computer facilities:* 708 computers available on campus for general student use. A campuswide network can be accessed from student residence rooms and from off campus. Online grade reports available. *General application contact:* Information Contact, 973-353-5205.

Graduate School

Programs in:
accounting (PhD)
accounting information systems (PhD)
American political system (MA)
American studies (MA, PhD)
analytical chemistry (MS, PhD)
applied physics (MS, PhD)
biochemistry (MS, PhD)
biology (MS, PhD)
cognitive neuroscience (PhD)
cognitive science (PhD)
computational biology (MS)
computer information systems (PhD)
creative writing (MFA)
economics (MA)
English (MA)
environmental geology (MS)
environmental science (MS, PhD)
finance (PhD)
health care administration (MPA)
history (MA, MAT)
human resources administration (MPA)
information technology (PhD)
inorganic chemistry (MS, PhD)
integrative neuroscience (PhD)
international business (PhD)
international relations (MA)
jazz history and research (MA)
liberal studies (MALS)
management science (PhD)
marketing (PhD)
mathematical sciences (PhD)
nursing (MS)
organic chemistry (MS, PhD)
organization management (PhD)
perception (PhD)
physical chemistry (MS, PhD)
psychobiology (PhD)

Rutgers, The State University of New Jersey, Newark (continued)
- public administration (PhD)
- public management (MPA)
- public policy analysis (MPA)
- social cognition (PhD)
- urban systems (PhD)
- urban systems and issues (MPA)

Division of Global Affairs
Program in:
- global affairs (MS, PhD)

School of Criminal Justice
Program in:
- criminal justice (MA, PhD)

Rutgers Business School–Newark and New Brunswick
Programs in:
- accounting (PhD)
- accounting information systems (PhD)
- business (M Accy, MBA, MQF, PhD, Certificate)
- business environment (MBA)
- customized concentration (MBA)
- finance (PhD)
- finance and economics (MBA, MQF)
- global business (MBA)
- government financial management (Certificate)
- governmental accounting (M Accy)
- individualized study (PhD)
- information technology (PhD)
- international business (PhD)
- management and business strategy (MBA)
- management science (PhD)
- management science and information systems (MBA)
- marketing (MBA)
- organizational management (PhD)
- professional accounting (MBA)
- supply chain management (PhD)
- taxation (M Accy)

School of Law
Program in:
- law (JD)

■ RUTGERS, THE STATE UNIVERSITY OF NEW JERSEY, NEW BRUNSWICK

Piscataway, NJ 08854-8097
http://www.rutgers.edu/

State-supported, coed, university. CGS member. *Computer facilities:* 1,450 computers available on campus for general student use. A campuswide network can be accessed from student residence rooms and from off campus. Online grade reports available. *General application contact:* Information Contact, 732-932-7711.

Edward J. Bloustein School of Planning and Public Policy
Programs in:
- planning and public policy (MCRP, MCRS, MPAP, MPH, MPP, Dr PH, PhD)
- public health (MPH, Dr PH, PhD)
- public policy (MPAP, MPP)
- urban planning and policy development (MCRP, MCRS, PhD)

Ernest Mario School of Pharmacy
Programs in:
- medicinal chemistry (MS, PhD)
- pharamceutical science (PhD)
- pharmaceutical science (MS)
- pharmacy (Pharm D)

Graduate School
Programs in:
- African-American history (PhD)
- air pollution and resources (MS, PhD)
- American politics (PhD)
- anthropology (MA, PhD)
- applied mathematics (MS, PhD)
- applied microbiology (MS, PhD)
- applied statistics (MS)
- aquatic biology (MS, PhD)
- aquatic chemistry (MS, PhD)
- art history (MA, PhD)
- astronomy (MS, PhD)
- atmospheric science (MS, PhD)
- behavioral neuroscience (PhD)
- bilingualism and second language acquisition (MA, PhD)
- biochemistry (PhD)
- biological chemistry (MS, PhD)
- biomedical engineering (MS, PhD)
- biophysics (PhD)
- biostatistics (MS)
- cell and developmental biology (MS, PhD)
- cellular and molecular pharmacology (PhD)
- chemical and biochemical engineering (MS, PhD)
- chemistry and physics of aerosol and hydrosol systems (MS, PhD)
- civil and environmental engineering (MS, PhD)
- classics (MA, MAT, PhD)
- clinical microbiology (MS, PhD)
- clinical psychology (PhD)
- cognitive psychology (PhD)
- communications and solid-state electronics (MS, PhD)
- comparative literature (MA, PhD)
- comparative politics (PhD)
- computational biology and molecular biophysics (PhD)
- computational molecular biology (PhD)
- computer engineering (MS, PhD)
- computer science (MS, PhD)
- condensed matter physics (MS, PhD)
- control systems (MS, PhD)
- curatorial studies (Certificate)
- data mining (MS)
- design and control (MS, PhD)
- digital signal processing (MS, PhD)
- early American history (PhD)
- early modern European history (PhD)
- east Asian history (PhD)
- ecology and evolution (MS, PhD)
- economics (MA, PhD)
- elementary particle physics (MS, PhD)
- endocrinology and animal biosciences (MS, PhD)
- entomology (MS, PhD)
- environmental chemistry (MS, PhD)
- environmental microbiology (MS, PhD)
- environmental toxicology (MS, PhD)
- exposure assessment (PhD)
- fate and effects of pollutants (MS, PhD)
- fluid mechanics (MS, PhD)
- food and business economics (MS)
- food science (M Phil, MS, PhD)
- French (MA, PhD)
- French studies (MAT)
- geography (MA, MS, PhD)
- geological sciences (MS, PhD)
- German (MAT, PhD)
- German literature (MA, PhD)
- global and comparative history (PhD)
- historic preservation (Certificate)
- history (PhD)
- history of diplomacy and foreign relations (PhD)
- history of technology, environment and health (PhD)
- history of the Atlantic cultures and African diaspora (PhD)
- horticulture and plant technology (MS, PhD)
- immunology (MS, PhD)
- industrial and systems engineering (MS, PhD)
- industrial-occupational toxicology (MS, PhD)
- information technology (MS)
- inorganic chemistry (MS, PhD)
- interdisciplinary classical studies and ancient history (MA, PhD)
- interdisciplinary health psychology (PhD)
- intermediate energy nuclear physics (MS)
- international relations (PhD)
- Italian (MA, PhD)
- Italian literature and literary criticism (MA)
- language, literature and culture (MAT)
- Latin American history (PhD)
- linguistics (PhD)
- literatures in English (PhD)
- manufacturing systems engineering (MS)
- materials science and engineering (MS, PhD)
- mathematics (MS, PhD)
- mechanics (MS, PhD)
- medieval history (PhD)
- microbial biochemistry (MS, PhD)
- microbiology and molecular genetics (MS, PhD)
- modern European history (PhD)
- molecular and cellular biology (MS, PhD)
- molecular genetics (MS, PhD)
- neuroscience (PhD)

nineteenth and twentieth century American history (PhD)
nuclear physics (MS, PhD)
nutritional sciences (MS, PhD)
nutritional toxicology (MS, PhD)
oceanography (MS, PhD)
operations research (PhD)
organic chemistry (MS, PhD)
organismal and population biology (MS, PhD)
pharmaceutical toxicology (MS, PhD)
philosophy (PhD)
physical chemistry (MS, PhD)
physics (MST)
plant pathology (MS, PhD)
political theory (PhD)
pollution prevention and control (MS, PhD)
public law (PhD)
quality and productivity management (MS)
quality and reliability engineering (MS)
social psychology (PhD)
sociology (MA, PhD)
solid mechanics (MS, PhD)
Spanish (MA, MAT, PhD)
Spanish literature (MA, PhD)
statistics (MS, PhD)
surface science (PhD)
theoretical physics (MS, PhD)
thermal sciences (MS, PhD)
translation (MA)
virology (MS, PhD)
water and wastewater treatment (MS, PhD)
water resources (MS, PhD)
women and politics (PhD)
women's and gender history (PhD)
women's and gender studies (MA, PhD)

Graduate School of Applied and Professional Psychology
Programs in:
applied and professional psychology (Psy M, Psy D)
clinical psychology (Psy M, Psy D)
organizational psychology (Psy M, Psy D)
school psychology (Psy M, Psy D)

Graduate School of Education
Programs in:
counseling psychology (Ed M)
early childhood/elementary education (Ed M, Ed D)
education (Ed M, Ed D, PhD)
educational administration and supervision (Ed M, Ed D)
educational policy (PhD)
educational psychology (PhD)
educational statistics, measurement and evaluation (Ed M)
English as a second language education (Ed M)
English education (Ed M)
language education (Ed M, Ed D)
learning, cognition and development (Ed M)
literacy education (Ed M, Ed D)
mathematics education (Ed M, Ed D, PhD)
reading education (Ed M)
science education (Ed M, Ed D)
social and philosophical foundations of education (Ed M, Ed D)
social studies education (Ed M, Ed D)
special education (Ed M, Ed D)

Mason Gross School of the Arts
Programs in:
acting (MFA)
arts (MFA, MM, DMA, AD)
collaborative piano (MM, DMA)
conducting: choral (MM, DMA)
conducting: instrumental (MM, DMA)
conducting: orchestral (MM, DMA)
design (MFA)
directing (MFA)
drawing (MFA)
jazz studies (MM)
music (DMA, AD)
music education (MM, DMA)
music performance (MM)
painting (MFA)
playwriting (MFA)
sculpture (MFA)
stage management (MFA)

School of Communication, Information and Library Studies
Programs in:
communication and information studies (MCIS)
communication, information and library studies (MCIS, MLS, PhD)
communication, library and information science and media studies (PhD)
library and information science (MLS)

School of Management and Labor Relations
Programs in:
human resource management (MHRM)
industrial relations and human resources (PhD)
labor and employment relations (MLER)

School of Social Work
Program in:
social work (MSW, PhD)

■ SAINT PETER'S COLLEGE
Jersey City, NJ 07306-5997
http://www.spc.edu/

Independent-religious, coed, comprehensive institution. *Computer facilities:* 150 computers available on campus for general student use. A campuswide network can be accessed from student residence rooms and from off campus. *General application contact:* Graduate Admissions Coordinator, 201-761-6470.

Graduate Programs in Education
Programs in:
administration and supervision (MA)
elementary teacher (Certificate)
reading specialist (MA)
special education (MA)
supervisor of instruction (Certificate)
teaching (MA, Certificate)

MBA Programs
Programs in:
finance (MBA)
health care administration (MBA)
international business (MBA)
management (MBA)
management information systems (MBA)
marketing (MBA)

Nursing Program
Programs in:
adult nurse practitioner (MSN)
case management (MSN)
RN to MSN bridge (MSN)

Program in Accountancy
Program in:
accountancy (MS)

■ SETON HALL UNIVERSITY
South Orange, NJ 07079-2697
http://www.shu.edu/

Independent-religious, coed, university. CGS member. *Computer facilities:* Computer purchase and lease plans are available. 300 computers available on campus for general student use. A campuswide network can be accessed from student residence rooms and from off campus. Online class registration is available. *General application contact:* Sarah Caron, Director, Graduate Admissions, 973-275-2892.

College of Arts and Sciences
Dr. Joseph R. Marbach, Dean
Programs in:
analytical chemistry (MS, PhD)
arts and sciences (MA, MHA, MPA, MS, PhD, Graduate Certificate)
Asian languages (MA)
Asian studies (MA)
biochemistry (MS, PhD)
biology (MS)
biology/business administration (MS)
chemistry (MS)
corporate and professional communication (MA)
English (MA)
experimental psychology (MS)
healthcare administration (MHA, Graduate Certificate)
history (MA)
Holocaust studies (MA)
inorganic chemistry (MS, PhD)
intercultural communication (MA)
Jewish-Christian Studies (MA)
microbiology (MS)

Seton Hall University (continued)
molecular bioscience (PhD)
molecular bioscience/neuroscience (PhD)
museum professions (MA)
nonprofit organization management (MPA)
organic chemistry (MS, PhD)
organizational communication (MA)
physical chemistry (MS, PhD)
public administration (MPA, Graduate Certificate)
public relations (MA)
strategic communication and leadership (MA)
strategic communication planning (MA)
teaching Chinese language and culture (MA)

College of Education and Human Services
Dr. Joseph V. De Pierro, Dean
Programs in:
bilingual education (Ed S)
Catholic school teaching EPICS (MA)
college student personnel administration (MA)
counseling psychology (MA, PhD)
education and human services (MA, MS, Ed D, Exec Ed D, PhD, Ed S)
education media specialist (MA)
education research, assessment and program evaluation (PhD)
higher education administration (Ed D, PhD)
human resource training and development (MA)
instructional design (MA)
K–12 administration and supervision (Ed D, Exec Ed D, Ed S)
K–12 leadership, management and policy (Ed D, Exec Ed D, Ed S)
marriage and family therapy (MS, PhD, Ed S)
professional development (MA)
psychological studies (MA)
school psychology (Ed S)

College of Nursing
Programs in:
acute care nurse practitioner (MSN)
adult nurse practitioner (MSN)
advanced practice in acute care nursing (MSN)
advanced practice in primary health care (MSN)
gerontological nurse practitioner (MSN)
health systems administration (MSN)
nursing (MA, MSN, PhD)
nursing case management (MSN)
nursing education (MA)
pediatric nurse practitioner (MSN)
school nurse (MSN)
women's health nurse practitioner (MSN)

Immaculate Conception Seminary School of Theology
Programs in:
pastoral ministry (M Div, MA)
theology (MA)

School of Health and Medical Sciences
Programs in:
athletic training (MS)
health and medical sciences (MS, DPT, PhD)
health sciences (MS, PhD)
occupational therapy (MS)
physician assistant (MS)
professional physical therapy (DPT)
speech-language pathology (MS)

School of Law
Program in:
law (JD, LL M, MSJ)

Stillman School of Business
Dr. Karen E. Boroff, Dean
Programs in:
accounting (MBA, MS)
business (MBA, MS, Certificate)
finance (MBA)
financial markets, institutions and instruments (MBA)
healthcare management (MBA)
information systems (MBA)
international business (MS, Certificate)
management (MBA)
marketing (MBA)
pharmaceutical management (MBA)
professional accounting (MS)
sport management (MBA)
taxation (MS)

Whitehead School of Diplomacy and International Relations
Ursula Sanjamino, Assistant Dean of Graduate Studies
Program in:
diplomacy and international relations (MA)

■ STEVENS INSTITUTE OF TECHNOLOGY
Hoboken, NJ 07030
http://www.stevens.edu/

Independent, coed, university. CGS member. *Computer facilities:* 175 computers available on campus for general student use. A campuswide network can be accessed from student residence rooms and from off campus. Online class registration, online account information, debit dining program, laundry status are available. *General application contact:* Graduate Admissions, 800-496-4935.

Graduate School

Charles V. Schaefer Jr. School of Engineering
Programs in:
advanced manufacturing (Certificate)
air pollution technology (Certificate)
analytical chemistry (PhD, Certificate)
applied mathematics (MS)
applied optics (Certificate)
applied statistics (Certificate)
armament engineering (M Eng)
bioinformatics (PhD, Certificate)
biomedical chemistry (Certificate)
biomedical engineering (M Eng, Certificate)
chemical biology (MS, PhD, Certificate)
chemical engineering (M Eng, PhD, Engr)
chemical physiology (Certificate)
chemistry (MS, PhD)
civil engineering (M Eng, PhD, Certificate, Engr)
computational fluid mechanics and heat transfer (Certificate)
computer and electrical engineering (M Eng)
computer architecture and digital system design (M Eng)
computer engineering (M Eng, PhD, Certificate)
computer graphics (Certificate)
computer science (MS, PhD)
computer systems (M Eng, Certificate)
construction accounting/estimating (Certificate)
construction engineering (Certificate)
construction law/disputes (Certificate)
construction management (MS, Certificate)
construction/quality management (Certificate)
data communications and networks (M Eng)
database management systems (Certificate)
design and production management (Certificate)
digital signal processing (Certificate)
digital systems design (M Eng)
distributed systems (Certificate)
electrical engineering (M Eng, PhD, Certificate)
elements of computer science (Certificate)
engineered software systems (M Eng)
engineering (M Eng, MS, PhD, Certificate, Engr)
engineering physics (M Eng)
enterprise computing (Certificate)
enterprise security and information assurance (Certificate)
environmental compatibility in engineering (Certificate)
environmental engineering (M Eng, PhD, Certificate)
environmental processes (M Eng, Certificate)
geotechnical engineering (Certificate)
geotechnical/geoenvironmental engineering (M Eng, Engr)
groundwater and soil pollution control (M Eng, Certificate)
health informatics (Certificate)
hydrologic modeling (M Eng)
image processing and multimedia (M Eng)
information system security (M Eng)
information systems (M Eng)

inland and coastal environmental hydrodynamics (M Eng, Certificate)
integrated product development (M Eng)
manufacturing technologies (M Eng)
maritime systems (MS)
materials science (M Eng, PhD)
mathematics (MS, PhD)
mechanical engineering (M Eng, PhD)
microdevices and microsystems (Certificate)
microelectronics and photonics (Certificate)
microelectronics and photonics science and technology (M Eng)
multimedia experience and management (Certificate)
networks and systems administration (Certificate)
ocean engineering (M Eng, PhD)
organic chemistry (PhD)
pharmaceutical manufacturing (M Eng, MS, Certificate)
physical chemistry (PhD)
physics (MS, PhD)
plasma and surface physics (Certificate)
polymer chemistry (PhD, Certificate)
power generation (Certificate)
product architecture and engineering (M Eng)
real-time and embedded systems (Certificate)
robotics and control (Certificate)
security and privacy (Certificate)
service oriented computing (Certificate)
signal processing for communications (M Eng)
software design (Certificate)
stochastic systems (MS, Certificate)
stormwater management (M Eng)
structural analysis and design (Certificate)
structural engineering (M Eng, Engr)
systems reliability and design (M Eng)
telecommunications systems engineering (M Eng)
theoretical computer science (Certificate)
vibration and noise control (Certificate)
water quality control (Certificate)
water resources engineering (M Eng)
wireless communications (M Eng, Certificate)

School of Systems and Enterprises
Programs in:
agile systems and enterprises (Certificate)
engineering management (M Eng, PhD)
enterprise systems (MS, PhD)
financial engineering (MS)
software engineering (MS)
space systems engineering (M Eng, Certificate)
systems and enterprises (M Eng, MS, PhD, Certificate)
systems and supportability engineering (Certificate)
systems design and operational effectiveness (M Eng)
systems engineering (M Eng, PhD)
systems engineering management (Certificate)

Wesley J. Howe School of Technology Management
Programs in:
business (MS)
computer science (MS)
e-commerce (MS)
engineering management (MBA)
enterprise systems (MS)
entrepreneurial information technology (MS)
financial engineering (MBA)
general management (MS)
global innovation management (MS)
human resource management (MS)
information architecture (MS)
information management (MBA, MS, PhD, Certificate)
information security (MS)
information technology in financial services (MBA)
information technology in financial services industry (MS)
information technology in the pharmaceutical industry (MBA, MS)
information technology outsourcing (MBA)
information technology outsourcing management (MS)
management of wireless networks (MS)
online security, technology and business (MS)
pharmaceutical management (MBA)
professional communications (Certificate)
project management (MBA, MS, Certificate)
software engineering (MS)
technical management (MS)
technology commercialization (MS)
technology management (EMBA, EMTM, MBA, MS, PhD, Certificate)
technology management for experienced professionals (EMTM, MS, Certificate)
telecommunications (MS)
telecommunications management (MBA, PhD, Certificate)

■ WILLIAM PATERSON UNIVERSITY OF NEW JERSEY

Wayne, NJ 07470-8420
http://www.wpunj.edu/

State-supported, coed, comprehensive institution. CGS member. *Computer facilities:* Computer purchase and lease plans are available. 700 computers available on campus for general student use. A campuswide network can be accessed from student residence rooms and from off campus. Online class registration is available. *General application contact:* Director, 973-720-3579.

Christos M. Cotsakos College of Business
Program in:
business (MBA)

College of Education
Programs in:
counseling services (M Ed)
education (M Ed, MAT)
educational leadership (M Ed)
elementary education (M Ed, MAT)
reading (M Ed)
special education (M Ed)

College of Science and Health
Programs in:
biotechnology (MS)
general biology (MA)
limnology and terrestrial ecology (MA)
molecular biology (MA)
nursing (MSN)
physiology (MA)
science and health (MA, MS, MSN)
speech pathology (MS)

College of the Arts and Communication
Programs in:
art (MFA)
arts and communication (MA, MFA, MM)
communication and media studies (MA)
music (MM)
visual arts (MA)

College of the Humanities and Social Sciences
Programs in:
clinical and counseling psychology (MA)
English (MA)
history (MA)
humanities and social sciences (MA)
public policy and international affairs (MA)
sociology (MA)

New Mexico

■ COLLEGE OF SANTA FE

Santa Fe, NM 87505-7634
http://www.csf.edu

Independent, coed, comprehensive institution. *Computer facilities:* 84 computers available on campus for general student use. A campuswide network can be accessed from student residence rooms and from off campus. Online class registration is available. *General application contact:* Interim Dean of Enrollment, 505-473-6188.

Department of Business Administration
Programs in:
finance (MBA)
human resources (MBA)

College of Santa Fe (continued)

Department of Education
Programs in:
at-risk youth (MA)
curriculum and instruction (MA)
multicultural special education (MA)

■ EASTERN NEW MEXICO UNIVERSITY

Portales, NM 88130

http://www.enmu.edu/

State-supported, coed, comprehensive institution. CGS member. *Graduate faculty:* 73 full-time (27 women), 2 part-time/adjunct (1 woman). *Computer facilities:* 476 computers available on campus for general student use. A campuswide network can be accessed from student residence rooms and from off campus. Online class registration is available. *Graduate expenses:* Tuition, state resident: full-time $2748; part-time $114.50 per hour. Tuition, nonresident: full-time $8292; part-time $345.50 per hour. Required fees: $978; $40.75 per unit. *General application contact:* Dr. Linda Weems, Dean, Graduate School, 575-562-2147.

Graduate School
Dr. Linda Weems, Dean, Graduate School

College of Business
Dr. Sue Stockly, Graduate Coordinator
Program in:
business (MBA)

College of Education and Technology
Dr. Jerry Harmon, Dean
Programs in:
counseling (MA)
education (M Ed)
education and technology (M Ed, M Sp Ed, MA, MS)
physical education (MS)
school counseling (M Ed)
special education (M Ed, M Sp Ed)

College of Liberal Arts and Sciences
Dr. Mary Ayala, Dean
Programs in:
anthropology (MA)
biology (MS)
chemistry (MS)
communicative arts and sciences (MA)
English (MA)
liberal arts and sciences (MA, MS)
mathematical sciences (MA)
speech pathology and audiology (MS)

■ NEW MEXICO HIGHLANDS UNIVERSITY

Las Vegas, NM 87701

http://www.nmhu.edu/

State-supported, coed, comprehensive institution. CGS member. *Graduate faculty:* 152 full-time (72 women). *Computer facilities:* 500 computers available on campus for general student use. A campuswide network can be accessed from student residence rooms and from off campus. Online class registration is available. *Graduate expenses:* Tuition, state resident: full-time $2880; part-time $120 per credit hour. Tuition, nonresident: full-time $4234; part-time $176 per credit hour. International tuition: $5645 full-time. One-time fee: $20. *General application contact:* Diane Trujillo, Administrative Assistant, Graduate Studies, 505-454-3266.

Graduate Studies
Dr. Gilbert Rivera, Vice President for Academic Affairs

College of Arts and Sciences
Dr. Roy Lujan, Dean
Programs in:
anthropology (MA)
applied sociology (MA)
arts and sciences (MA, MS)
chemistry (MS)
English (MA)
life science (MS)
media arts and computer science (MS)
psychology (MS)

School of Business
Dr. Charles Swim, Dean
Program in:
business administration (MBA)

School of Education
Dr. Michael Anderson, Interim Dean
Programs in:
curriculum and instruction (MA)
education (MA)
educational leadership (MA)
exercise and sport sciences (MA)
guidance and counseling (MA)
human performance and sport (MA)
special education (MA)
sports administration (MA)
teacher education (MA)

School of Social Work
Dr. Alfredo Garcia, Dean
Programs in:
bilingual/bicultural social work practice (MSW)
clinical practice (MSW)
government non-profit management (MSW)

■ NEW MEXICO INSTITUTE OF MINING AND TECHNOLOGY

Socorro, NM 87801

http://www.nmt.edu/

State-supported, coed, university. *Computer facilities:* 225 computers available on campus for general student use. A campuswide network can be accessed from student residence rooms and from off campus. Online class registration is available. *General application contact:* Dean of Graduate Studies, 505-835-5513.

Graduate Studies
Programs in:
advanced mechanics (MS)
applied math (PhD)
astrophysics (MS, PhD)
atmospheric physics (MS, PhD)
biochemistry (MS)
biology (MS)
chemistry (MS)
computer science (MS, PhD)
electrical engineering (MS)
engineering management (MEM)
environmental chemistry (PhD)
environmental engineering (MS)
explosives engineering (MS)
explosives technology and atmospheric chemistry (PhD)
geochemistry (MS, PhD)
geology (MS, PhD)
geology and geochemistry (MS, PhD)
geophysics (MS, PhD)
hydrology (MS, PhD)
instrumentation (MS)
materials engineering (MS, PhD)
mathematical physics (PhD)
mathematics (MS)
mining and mineral engineering (MS)
operations research (MS)
petroleum engineering (MS, PhD)
science teaching (MST)

■ NEW MEXICO STATE UNIVERSITY

Las Cruces, NM 88003-8001

http://www.nmsu.edu/

State-supported, coed, university. CGS member. *Graduate faculty:* 413 full-time (164 women), 64 part-time/adjunct (31 women). *Computer facilities:* Computer purchase and lease plans are available. 751 computers available on campus for general student use. A campuswide network can be accessed from student residence rooms and from off campus. Online class registration, online financial aid are available. *Graduate expenses:* Tuition, state resident: full-time $3890; part-time $212.85 per credit. Tuition, nonresident: full-time $13,916; part-time $630.55 per credit. Required fees: $1218; $609 per semester. *General application contact:* Elena Luna, Coordinator, 575-646-3498.

Graduate School
Dr. Linda Lacey, Dean
Programs in:
interdisciplinary studies (MA, MS, PhD)
molecular biology (MS, PhD)

College of Agriculture, Consumer and Environmental Sciences
Dr. Lowell Catlett, Interim Dean
Programs in:
agribusiness (M Ag, MBA)
agricultural and extension education (MA)
agricultural biology (MS)
agricultural economics (MS)

agriculture, consumer and environmental sciences (M Ag, MA, MBA, MS, DED, PhD)
animal science (M Ag, MS, PhD)
economics (MA)
family and consumer sciences (MS)
horticulture (MS)
plant and environmental sciences (MS, PhD)
range science (M Ag, MS, PhD)
wildlife science (MS)

College of Arts and Sciences
Dr. Pamela Jansma, Interim Dean
Programs in:
anthropology (MA)
art history (MA)
arts and sciences (MA, MAG, MCJ, MFA, MM, MPA, MS, PhD)
astronomy (MS, PhD)
biology (MS, PhD)
ceramics (MA, MFA)
chemistry and biochemistry (MS, PhD)
communication studies (MA)
computer science (MS, PhD)
conducting (MM)
creative writing (MFA)
criminal justice (MCJ)
design (MA, MFA)
drawing (MFA)
English (MA)
geography (MAG)
geological sciences (MS)
government (MA, MPA)
history (MA)
mathematical sciences (MS, PhD)
metals (MA, MFA)
music education (MM)
painting (MFA)
performance (MM)
photography (MFA)
physics (MS, PhD)
printmaking (MA, MFA)
psychology (MA, PhD)
public history (MA)
rhetoric and professional communication (PhD)
sculpture (MA, MFA)
sociology (MA)
Spanish (MA)

College of Business
Dr. Garrey Carruthers, Dean
Programs in:
accounting and information systems (M Acct)
business (M Acct, MA, MBA, MS, DED, PhD)
business administration (MBA, PhD)
economic development (DED)
economics (MA)
experimental statistics (MS)

College of Education
Dr. Michael Morehead, Dean
Programs in:
communication disorders (MA)
counseling and guidance (MA)
counseling psychology (PhD)
curriculum and instruction (MAT, Ed D, PhD, Ed S)
education (MA, MAT, Ed D, PhD, Ed S)
educational administration (MA, PhD)
educational management and development (Ed D)
general education (MA)
school psychology (Ed S)
special education (MA, Ed D, PhD)

College of Engineering
Dr. Steven Castillo, Dean
Programs in:
chemical engineering (MS Ch E, PhD)
civil engineering (MSCE, PhD)
electrical and computer engineering (MSEE, PhD)
engineering (MS Ch E, MS Env E, MSCE, MSEE, MSIE, MSME, PhD)
environmental engineering (MS Env E)
industrial engineering (MSIE, PhD)
mechanical engineering (MSME, PhD)

College of Health and Social Services
Dr. Robert Rhodes, Interim Dean
Programs in:
community health education (MPH)
community/public health (MSN)
health and social services (MPH, MSN, MSW)
medical-surgical (adult health) (MSN)
nursing administration (MSN)
psychiatric/mental health (MSN)
social work (MSW)

■ ST. JOHN'S COLLEGE
Santa Fe, NM 87505-4599
http://www.stjohnscollege.edu/

Independent, coed, comprehensive institution. *Computer facilities:* Computer purchase and lease plans are available. 25 computers available on campus for general student use. A campuswide network can be accessed from student residence rooms and from off campus. *General application contact:* Associate Director of Graduate Admissions, 505-984-6083.

Graduate Institute in Liberal Education
Programs in:
Eastern classics (MA)
liberal arts (MA)
liberal education (MA)

■ UNIVERSITY OF NEW MEXICO
Albuquerque, NM 87131-2039
http://www.unm.edu/

State-supported, coed, university. CGS member. *Computer facilities:* 470 computers available on campus for general student use. A campuswide network can be accessed from student residence rooms and from off campus. Online class registration is available. *General application contact:* Enrollment Management Specialist, 505-277-2711.

Graduate School
Programs in:
computational science and engineering (Graduate Certificate)
nanoscience and microsystems (MS, PhD)
water resources (MWR)

College of Arts and Sciences
Programs in:
American studies (MA, PhD)
anthropology (MA, MS, PhD)
arts and sciences (MA, MFA, MS, PhD, Graduate Certificate)
biology (MS, PhD)
biomedical physics (MS, PhD)
chemistry (MS, PhD)
clinical psychology (MS, PhD)
communication (MA, PhD)
comparative literature and cultural studies (MA)
creative writing (MFA)
earth and planetary sciences (MS, PhD)
economics (MA, PhD)
English (MA, MFA, PhD)
French (MA)
French studies (PhD)
geography (MS)
German studies (MA)
history (MA, PhD)
Latin American studies (MA, PhD)
linguistics (MA, PhD)
mathematics (MS, PhD)
optical science and engineering (MS, PhD)
philosophy (MA, PhD)
physics (MS, PhD)
political science (MA, PhD)
Portuguese (MA)
psychology (PhD)
sociology (MA, PhD)
Spanish (MA)
Spanish and Portuguese (PhD)
speech and hearing sciences (MS)
statistics (MS, PhD)
women studies (Graduate Certificate)

College of Education
Programs in:
art education (MA)
counselor education (MA, PhD)
education (MA, MS, Ed D, PhD, EDSPC, Graduate Certificate)
educational leadership (MA, Ed D, EDSPC)
educational linguistics (Ed D, PhD)
educational psychology (MA, PhD)
elementary education (MA, EDSPC)
family studies (MA, PhD)
health education (MS)
intensive social, language and behavioral needs (Graduate Certificate)
language, literacy and sociocultural studies (MA, Ed D, PhD)
multicultural teacher and childhood education (Ed D, PhD, EDSPC)
nutrition (MS)
organizational learning and instructional technologies (MA, PhD, EDSPC)

University of New Mexico (continued)
physical education (MS, Ed D, PhD, EDSPC)
physical education, sports and exercise science (PhD)
secondary education (MA, EDSPC)
special education (MA, Ed D, PhD, EDSPC)

College of Fine Arts
Programs in:
art history (MA, PhD)
dramatic writing (MFA)
fine arts (M Mu, MA, MFA, PhD)
music (M Mu)
studio arts (MFA)
theater and dance (MA)

College of Nursing
Program in:
nursing (MSN, PhD)

College of Pharmacy
Programs in:
pharmaceutical sciences (MS, PhD)
pharmacy (Pharm D, MS, PhD)

School of Architecture and Planning
Programs in:
architecture (M Arch)
architecture and planning (M Arch, MCRP, MLA, Graduate Certificate)
community and regional planning (MCRP)
historic preservation and regionalism (Graduate Certificate)
landscape architecture (MLA)
town design (Graduate Certificate)

School of Engineering
Programs in:
chemical engineering (MS, PhD)
civil engineering (MS)
computer engineering (MS, PhD)
computer science (MS, PhD)
construction management (MCM)
electrical engineering (MS, PhD)
engineering (PhD)
manufacturing engineering (MEME)
mechanical engineering (MS)
nuclear engineering (MS, PhD)

School of Public Administration
Program in:
public administration (MPA)

Robert O. Anderson Graduate School of Management
Douglas M. Brown, Dean
Programs in:
accounting (MBA)
advanced accounting (M Acct)
finance (MBA)
human resources management (MBA)
international management (MBA)
international management in Latin America (MBA)
management (EMBA, M Acct, MBA)
management information systems (MBA)
management of technology (MBA)
marketing management (MBA)
operations management (MBA)
policy and planning (MBA)
professional accounting (M Acct)
tax accounting (M Acct)

School of Law
Leo Romero, Dean
Program in:
law (JD)

School of Medicine
Programs in:
biochemistry and molecular biology (MS, PhD)
cell biology and physiology (MS, PhD)
clinical laboratory science (MS)
dental hygiene (MS)
medicine (MD, MOT, MPH, MPT, MS, PhD)
molecular genetics and microbiology (MS, PhD)
neuroscience (MS, PhD)
occupational therapy (MOT)
pathology (MS, PhD)
physical therapy (MPT)
public health (MPH)
toxicology (MS, PhD)

■ UNIVERSITY OF PHOENIX–NEW MEXICO CAMPUS
Albuquerque, NM 87109-4645
http://www.phoenix.edu/

Proprietary, coed, comprehensive institution. *Computer facilities:* A campuswide network can be accessed from off campus. *General application contact:* Campus Information Center, 505-821-4800.

The Artemis School

College of Education
Programs in:
administration and supervision (MAEd)
curriculum and instruction (MAEd)
elementary teacher education (MAEd)
school counseling (MSC)
secondary teacher education (MAEd)

College of Health and Human Services
Programs in:
administration of justice and security (MS)
health administration (MHA)
health care education (MSN)
health care management (MBA)
marriage and family therapy (MSC)
nursing (MSN)
psychology (MS)

John Sperling School of Business
Program in:
business (MBA, MIS, MM, MS)

College of Graduate Business and Management
Programs in:
accounting (MBA)
business administration (MBA)
global management (MBA)
human resource management (MBA)
human resources management (MM)
management (MM)
marketing (MBA)

College of Information Systems and Technology
Programs in:
e-business (MBA)
information systems (MS)
technology management (MBA)

■ UNIVERSITY OF THE SOUTHWEST
Hobbs, NM 88240-9129
http://www.usw.edu/

Independent, coed, comprehensive institution. *Graduate faculty:* 6 full-time (5 women), 3 part-time/adjunct (1 woman). *Computer facilities:* 35 computers available on campus for general student use. A campuswide network can be accessed from student residence rooms. Online class registration is available. *Graduate expenses:* Tuition: full-time $5400; part-time $425 per credit hour. *General application contact:* Dr. Steve Hill, Dean/Recruiting, 505-392-6561 Ext. 1010.

Graduate Programs
Dr. Dennis G. Atherton, Provost
Programs in:
business administration (MBA)
curriculum and instruction (MSE)
early childhood education (MSE)
educational administration (MSE)
educational counseling (MSE)
educational diagnostician (MSE)
school business administration (MSE)
special education (MSE)

■ WESTERN NEW MEXICO UNIVERSITY
Silver City, NM 88062-0680
http://www.wnmu.edu/

State-supported, coed, comprehensive institution. *Computer facilities:* 85 computers available on campus for general student use. A campuswide network can be accessed from student residence rooms. Online class registration, online classes in Spanish are available. *General application contact:* Director of Admissions, 505-538-6106.

Graduate Division
Programs in:
business administration (MBA)
interdisciplinary studies (MA)
occupational therapy (MOT)
social work (MSW)

School of Education
Programs in:
bilingual education (MAT)

counseling (MA)
educational leadership (MA)
elementary education (MAT)
reading (MAT)
school psychology (MA)
secondary education (MAT)
special education (MAT)
TESOL (teaching English to speakers of other languages) (MAT)

New York

■ ADELPHI UNIVERSITY

Garden City, NY 11530-0701
http://www.adelphi.edu/

Independent, coed, university. *Graduate faculty:* 295 full-time (155 women), 639 part-time/adjunct (450 women). *Computer facilities:* 772 computers available on campus for general student use. A campuswide network can be accessed from student residence rooms and from off campus. Online class registration, payment, drop/add classes, check application status are available. *Graduate expenses:* Tuition: full-time $25,700; part-time $775 per credit hour. Required fees: $500. Tuition and fees vary according to course load, degree level, campus/location, program and student level. *General application contact:* Christine Murphy, Director of Admissions, 516-877-3050.

Derner Institute of Advanced Psychological Studies

Dr. Jeau Lau Chin, Dean
Programs in:
clinical psychology (PhD)
general psychology (MA)
mental health counseling (MA)
school psychology (MA)

Graduate School of Arts and Sciences

Dr. Steven Rubin, Dean
Programs in:
art and art history (MA)
arts and sciences (MA, MFA, MS)
biology (MS)
creative writing (MFA)
environmental studies (MS)
physics (MS)

School of Business

Dr. Rakesh Gupta, Associate Dean
Programs in:
accounting (MBA)
business (MBA, Certificate)
finance (MBA)
human resources management (Certificate)
management information systems (MBA)
management/human resource management (MBA)
marketing/e-commerce (MBA)

School of Education

Dr. Ronald Feingold, Dean
Programs in:
adolescent education (MA)
aging (Certificate)
art education (MA)
audiology (MS, DA)
birth through grade 2 (Certificate)
birth-grade 12 (MS)
birth-grade 6 (MS)
childhood special education (Certificate)
childhood special education studies (MS)
community health education (MA, Certificate)
early childhood education (Certificate)
education (MA, MS, DA, Certificate)
educational leadership and technology (MA, Certificate)
elementary teachers pre K-6 (MA)
grades 1-6 (MA, MS)
grades 5-12 (MS)
in-service (MA, MS)
inclusive setting, grades 1-6 preservice or in-service track (MS)
physical/educational human performance science (MA)
pre-certification (MA)
preservice (MS)
school health education (MA)
special education (MS, Certificate)
speech-language pathology (MS, DA)
teaching English to speakers of other languages (MA, Certificate)

School of Nursing

Dr. Patrick Coonan, Dean
Program in:
nursing (MS, PhD, Certificate)

School of Social Work

Dr. Andrew Safyer, Dean
Programs in:
social welfare (DSW)
social work (MSW, PhD)

University College

Program in:
emergency management (Certificate)

■ ALFRED UNIVERSITY

Alfred, NY 14802-1205
http://www.alfred.edu/

Independent, coed, university. CGS member. *Computer facilities:* Computer purchase and lease plans are available. 450 computers available on campus for general student use. A campuswide network can be accessed from student residence rooms and from off campus. Online class registration is available. *General application contact:* Coordinator of Graduate Admissions, 607-871-2141.

Graduate School

Programs in:
school counseling (MS Ed, CAS)
school psychology (MA, Psy D, CAS)

College of Business

Program in:
business administration (MBA)

Division of Education

Programs in:
literacy teacher (MS Ed)
numeracy (MS)

New York State College of Ceramics

Programs in:
biomedical materials engineering science (MS)
ceramic art (MFA)
ceramic engineering (MS)
ceramics (MFA, MS, PhD)
electrical engineering (MS)
electronic integrated arts (MFA)
glass art (MFA)
glass science (MS, PhD)
materials science and engineering (MS, PhD)
mechanical engineering (MS)
sculpture (MFA)

■ BERNARD M. BARUCH COLLEGE OF THE CITY UNIVERSITY OF NEW YORK

New York, NY 10010-5585
http://www.baruch.cuny.edu/

State and locally supported, coed, comprehensive institution. *Computer facilities:* 1,300 computers available on campus for general student use. A campuswide network can be accessed. Online class registration is available. *General application contact:* Office of Graduate Admissions, 646-312-1300.

School of Public Affairs

David Birdsell, Dean
Programs in:
educational leadership (MS Ed)
higher education administration (MS Ed)
nonprofit administration (MPA)
public affairs (MPA, MS Ed, AC)
public management (MPA)

Weissman School of Arts and Sciences

Programs in:
arts and sciences (MA, MS)
corporate communication (MA)
financial engineering (MS)
industrial organizational psychology (MS)

Zicklin School of Business

Programs in:
accounting (MBA, MS, PhD)
business (MBA, MS, PhD, Certificate)
business administration (MBA)
computer information systems (MBA, MS, PhD)
decision sciences (MBA, MS)
economics (MBA)
entrepreneurship (MBA)
finance (MBA, MS, PhD)
general business (MBA)
general management and policy (MBA)
health care administration (MBA)

Bernard M. Baruch College of the City University of New York (continued)
- human resources management (MBA)
- industrial and labor relations (MS)
- industrial and organizational psychology (MBA, MS, PhD, Certificate)
- international executive education (MBA)
- management planning systems (PhD)
- management science (MBA)
- marketing (MBA, MS, PhD)
- organization and policy studies (PhD)
- organizational behavior (MBA)
- statistics (MBA, MS)
- taxation (MBA, MS)

■ BROOKLYN COLLEGE OF THE CITY UNIVERSITY OF NEW YORK

Brooklyn, NY 11210-2889

http://www.brooklyn.cuny.edu/

State and locally supported, coed, comprehensive institution. *Computer facilities:* 800 computers available on campus for general student use. A campuswide network can be accessed from off campus. Online class registration is available. *Graduate expenses:* Tuition, state resident: full-time $7360; part-time $310 per credit hour. Tuition, nonresident: full-time $13,800; part-time $575 per credit hour. *General application contact:* Office of Admissions, 718-951-5001.

Division of Graduate Studies

Dr. Louise Hainline, Dean

Programs in:
- accounting (MS)
- acting (MFA)
- applied physics (MA)
- art history (MA, PhD)
- audiology (Au D)
- biology (MA, PhD)
- chemistry (MA, PhD)
- community health (MA, MPH, MS)
- community health education (MA)
- computer science (MA, PhD)
- computer science and health science (MS)
- creative writing (MFA)
- criticism and history (MA)
- design and technical production (MFA)
- digital art (MFA)
- directing (MFA)
- dramaturgy (MFA)
- drawing and painting (MFA)
- economics (MA)
- English (MA, PhD)
- exercise science and rehabilitation (MS)
- experimental psychology (MA)
- fiction (MFA)
- French (MA)
- geology (MA, PhD)
- grief counseling (CAS)
- health care management (MPH)
- health care policy and administration (MPH)
- history (MA, PhD)
- industrial and organizational psychology (MA)
- information systems (MS)
- international affairs (MA)
- Judaic studies (MA)
- liberal studies (MA)
- mathematics (MA, PhD)
- mental health counseling (MA)
- modern languages and literature (PhD)
- nutrition (MS)
- parallel and distributed computing (Advanced Certificate)
- performance and interactive media arts (MFA, CAS)
- performing arts management (MFA)
- photography (MFA)
- physical education (MS)
- physics (MA, PhD)
- playwriting (MFA)
- poetry (MFA)
- political science (MA, PhD)
- political science, urban policy and administration (MA)
- printmaking (MFA)
- psychology (PhD)
- public health (MPH)
- sculpture (MFA)
- sociology (MA, PhD)
- Spanish (MA)
- speech (MA)
- speech and hearing sciences (PhD)
- speech pathology (MS)
- television and radio (MS)
- television production (MFA)
- thanatology (MA)
- theater (PhD)

Conservatory of Music

Dr. Bruce MacIntyre, Chairperson

Programs in:
- composition (MM)
- music (DMA, PhD)
- music education (MA)
- musicology (MA)
- performance (MM)
- performance practice (MA)

School of Education

Dr. Deborah Shanley, Dean

Programs in:
- adolescence science education (MAT)
- art teacher (MA)
- bilingual education (MS Ed)
- biology (MA)
- biology teacher (MA)
- birth-grade 2 (MS Ed)
- chemistry (MA)
- chemistry teacher (MA)
- earth science (MA)
- education (MA, MAT, MS Ed, CAS)
- educational leadership (MS Ed)
- English teacher (MA)
- French teacher (MA)
- general science (MA)
- guidance and counseling (CAS)
- health and nutrition sciences: health teacher (MS Ed)
- liberal arts (MS Ed)
- mathematics (MS Ed)
- mathematics teacher (MA)
- middle childhood education (math) (MS Ed)
- music education (CAS)
- music teacher (MA)
- physical education teacher (MS Ed)
- physics (MA)
- physics teacher (MA)
- school psychologist (MS Ed, CAS)
- school psychologist-bilingual (CAS)
- science/environmental education (MS Ed)
- social studies teacher (MA)
- Spanish teacher (MA)
- teacher of students with disabilities (MS Ed)

■ BUFFALO STATE COLLEGE, STATE UNIVERSITY OF NEW YORK

Buffalo, NY 14222-1095

http://www.buffalostate.edu/

State-supported, coed, comprehensive institution. CGS member. *Graduate faculty:* 274 full-time (92 women), 57 part-time/adjunct (20 women). *Computer facilities:* 1,700 computers available on campus for general student use. A campuswide network can be accessed from student residence rooms and from off campus. Online class registration is available. *Graduate expenses:* Full-time $3940; part-time $328 per credit. Tuition, state resident: full-time $3940; part-time $328 per credit. Tuition, nonresident: full-time $6625; part-time $552 per credit. International tuition: $6625 full-time. Required fees: $575; $23.95 per credit. *General application contact:* The Graduate School, 716-878-5601.

The Graduate School

Dr. Kevin Railey, Associate Provost/Dean

Program in:
- multidisciplinary studies (MA, MS)

Faculty of Applied Science and Education

Programs in:
- adult education (MS, Certificate)
- applied science and education (MPS, MS, MS Ed, CAS, Certificate)
- business and marketing education (MS Ed)
- career and technical education (MS Ed)
- childhood education (grades 1-6) (MS Ed)
- creative studies (MS)
- criminal justice (MS)
- early childhood and childhood curriculum and instruction (MS Ed)
- early childhood education (birth-grade 2) (MS Ed)
- educational computing (MS Ed)
- educational leadership and facilitation (CAS)
- elementary education (MS Ed)
- human resources development (Certificate)

industrial technology (MS)
literacy specialist (MPS, MS Ed)
literacy specialist (birth-grade 6) (MS Ed)
literacy specialist (grades 5-12) (MPS)
special education (MS Ed)
special education: adolescents (MS Ed)
special education: childhood (MS Ed)
special education: early childhood (MS Ed)
speech language pathology (MS Ed)
student personnel administration (MS)
teaching bilingual exceptional individuals (MS Ed)
technology education (MS Ed)

Faculty of Arts and Humanities
Programs in:
art conservation (CAS)
art education (MS Ed)
arts and humanities (MA, MS Ed, CAS)
conservation of historic works and art works (MA)
English (MA)
secondary education (MS Ed)

Faculty of Natural and Social Sciences
Programs in:
applied economics (MA)
biology (MA)
chemistry (MA)
history (MA)
mathematics education (MS Ed)
natural and social sciences (MA, MS Ed)
secondary education (MS Ed)
secondary education physics (MS Ed)

■ CANISIUS COLLEGE
Buffalo, NY 14208-1098
http://www.canisius.edu/

Independent-religious, coed, comprehensive institution. *Graduate faculty:* 99 full-time (40 women), 128 part-time/adjunct (65 women). *Computer facilities:* Computer purchase and lease plans are available. 500 computers available on campus for general student use. A campuswide network can be accessed from student residence rooms and from off campus. Online class registration, online accounts are available. *Graduate expenses:* Tuition: full-time $33,750; part-time $680 per credit hour. Required fees: $18.50 per credit hour. *General application contact:* Graduate Education Office, 716-888-2545.

Graduate Division
Dr. Scott A. Chadwick, Vice President for Academic Affairs

College of Arts and Sciences
Dr. Paula McNutt, Dean
Programs in:
arts and sciences (MS)
communication and leadership (MS)

Richard J. Wehle School of Business
Dr. Antone Alber, Dean
Programs in:
accounting (MBA)
business (MBA, MBAPA, MS)
business administration (MBA)
international business (MS)
professional accounting (MBAPA)

School of Education and Human Services
Dr. Margaret C. McCarthy, Dean
Programs in:
adolescence education (grades 7-12) (MS)
childhood education (grades 1-6) (MS)
college student personnel administration (MS)
community mental health counseling (MS)
deaf education (MS)
differentiated instruction (MS Ed)
education and human services (MS, MS Ed)
educational administration and supervision (MS)
general counseling (MS)
general education (MS Ed)
health and human performance (MS)
initial teacher certification (elementary education) (MS)
initial teacher certification (secondary education) (MS)
literacy (MS Ed)
physical education (MS)
physical education (Pre-K to Grade 12) (MS)
school counseling (MS)
special education (MS)
sport administration (MS)

■ CITY COLLEGE OF THE CITY UNIVERSITY OF NEW YORK
New York, NY 10031-9198
http://www.ccny.cuny.edu/

State and locally supported, coed, comprehensive institution. *Graduate faculty:* 519 full-time (199 women), 610 part-time/adjunct (291 women). *Computer facilities:* 4,000 computers available on campus for general student use. A campuswide network can be accessed from off campus. Online class registration is available. *Graduate expenses:* Tuition, state resident: full-time $6400; part-time $270 per credit. Tuition, nonresident: full-time $12,000; part-time $500 per credit. Required fees: $260.70; $80.35 per semester. One-time fee: $125. Tuition and fees vary according to course level, course load, degree level, program and student level. *General application contact:* Chad K. Austein, Assistant Director of Graduate Admissions, 212-650-6977.

Graduate School
Program in:
sustainability in the urban environment (MS)

College of Liberal Arts and Science
Programs in:
advertising design (MFA)
art history (MA)
art history and museum studies (MA)
biochemistry (MA, PhD)
biology (MA, PhD)
ceramic design (MFA)
chemistry (MA, PhD)
clinical psychology (PhD)
creative writing (MA, MFA)
earth and environmental science (PhD)
earth systems science (MA)
economics (MA)
English and American literature (MA)
experimental cognition (PhD)
fine arts (MFA)
general psychology (MA)
history (MA)
humanities and arts (MA, MFA)
international relations (MA)
language and literacy (MA)
liberal arts and science (MA, MFA, MPA, PhD)
mathematics (MA)
media arts production (MFA)
mental health counseling (MA)
museum studies (MA)
music (MA)
painting (MFA)
physics (MA, PhD)
printmaking (MFA)
psychology (MA, PhD)
public service management (MPA)
science (MA, PhD)
sculpture (MFA)
sociology (MA)
Spanish (MA)
wood and metal design (MFA)

Grove School of Engineering
Programs in:
biomedical engineering (ME, PhD)
chemical engineering (ME, MS, PhD)
civil engineering (ME, MS, PhD)
computer sciences (MS, PhD)
electrical engineering (ME, MS, PhD)
engineering (ME, MS, PhD)
mechanical engineering (ME, MS, PhD)

School of Architecture and Environmental Studies
Programs in:
architecture (M Arch, PD)
landscape architecture (PD)
urban design (MUP)

School of Education
Programs in:
administration and supervision (MS, AC)
adolescent mathematics education (MA, AC)
bilingual education (MS)
childhood education (MS)
education (MA, MS, AC)
English education (MA)
middle school mathematics education (MS)
science education (MA)
social studies education (AC)
teaching students with disabilities (MA)

■ CLARKSON UNIVERSITY

Potsdam, NY 13699

http://www.clarkson.edu/

Independent, coed, university. *Graduate faculty:* 139 full-time (29 women), 9 part-time/adjunct (3 women). *Computer facilities:* Computer purchase and lease plans are available. 400 computers available on campus for general student use. A campuswide network can be accessed from student residence rooms and from off campus. Online class registration is available. *Graduate expenses:* Tuition: part-time $1011 per credit hour.

Graduate School

Coulter School of Engineering
Dr. Goodarz Ahmadi, Dean
Programs in:
chemical engineering (ME, MS, PhD)
civil and environmental engineering (PhD)
civil engineering (ME, MS)
computer engineering (ME, MS)
electrical and computer engineering (PhD)
electrical engineering (ME, MS)
engineering (ME, MS, PhD)
environmental science and engineering (MS, PhD)
interdisciplinary engineering science (MS, PhD)
mechanical engineering (ME, MS, PhD)

Division of Health Sciences
Dr. Scott D. Minor, Associate Dean
Programs in:
health sciences (DPT)
physical therapy (DPT)

School of Arts and Sciences
Dr. Peter Turner, Dean
Programs in:
analytical chemistry (MS, PhD)
arts and sciences (MS, PhD)
computer science (MS)
information technology (MS)
inorganic chemistry (MS, PhD)
mathematics (MS, PhD)
organic chemistry (MS, PhD)
physical chemistry (MS, PhD)
physics (MS, PhD)

School of Business
Dr. Timothy Sugrue, Dean
Programs in:
business (MBA, MS)
engineering and global operations management (MS)
environmental management (MBA)
general business administration (MBA)
global supply chain management (MBA)
innovation and new venture management (MBA)

■ THE COLLEGE AT BROCKPORT, STATE UNIVERSITY OF NEW YORK

Brockport, NY 14420-2997

http://www.brockport.edu/

State-supported, coed, comprehensive institution. CGS member. *Computer facilities:* 700 computers available on campus for general student use. A campuswide network can be accessed from student residence rooms and from off campus. Online class registration is available. *General application contact:* Danielle A. Welch, Graduate Admissions Counselor, 585-395-5465.

Office of the Vice Provost

Programs in:
accounting (MS)
forensic accounting (MS)
liberal studies (MA)

School of Arts, Humanities and Social Sciences

Programs in:
arts, humanities and social sciences (MA, MFA)
communication (MA)
dance (MA, MFA)
English (MA)
history (MA)
visual studies (MFA)

School of Education and Human Services

Programs in:
adolescence biology education (MS Ed)
adolescence chemistry education (MS Ed)
adolescence earth science education (MS Ed)
adolescence education (MS Ed)
adolescence English education (MS Ed)
adolescence mathematics education (MS Ed)
adolescence physics education (MS Ed)
adolescence social studies education (MS Ed)
alternate adolescence English inclusive education (MS Ed)
alternate adolescence inclusive education (MS Ed)
alternate adolescence mathematics inclusive education (MS Ed)
alternate adolescence science inclusive education (MS Ed)
alternate adolescence social studies inclusive education (MS Ed)
arts administration (AGC)
bilingual education (MS Ed, AGC)
childhood curriculum specialist (MS Ed)
childhood literacy (MS Ed)
college counseling (MS Ed)
education and human services (MPA, MS, MS Ed, MSW, AGC, CAS)
educational administration (CAS)
mental health counseling (MS)
nonprofit management (AGC)
public administration (MPA)
school business administration (CAS)
school counseling (MS Ed, CAS)
social work (MSW)

School of Health and Human Performance

Programs in:
health and human performance (MS, MS Ed)
health education (MS Ed)
physical education (MS Ed)
recreation and leisure (MS)

School of Science and Mathematics

Programs in:
biological sciences (MS)
computational science (MS)
environmental science and biology (MS)
mathematics (MA)
psychology (MA)
science and mathematics (MA, MS)

■ COLLEGE OF MOUNT SAINT VINCENT

Riverdale, NY 10471-1093

http://www.mountsaintvincent.edu/

Independent, coed, comprehensive institution. *Computer facilities:* 200 computers available on campus for general student use. A campuswide network can be accessed from student residence rooms and from off campus. Online class registration is available. *General application contact:* Dean, School of Professional and Continuing Studies, 718-405-3373.

School of Professional and Continuing Studies

Programs in:
adult nurse practitioner (MSN, PMC)
family nurse practitioner (MSN, PMC)
instructional technology and global perspectives (Certificate)
middle level education (Certificate)
multicultural studies (Certificate)
nurse educator (PMC)
nursing administration (MSN)
nursing for the adult and aged (MSN)
urban and multicultural education (MS Ed)

■ THE COLLEGE OF NEW ROCHELLE

New Rochelle, NY 10805-2308

http://www.cnr.edu/

Independent, coed, primarily women, comprehensive institution. CGS member. *Computer facilities:* Computer purchase and lease plans are available. 120 computers available on campus for general student use. A campuswide network can be accessed from student residence rooms and from off campus. Online class registration is available. *General application contact:* Dean of the Graduate School, 914-654-5320.

Graduate School

Programs in:
- acute care nurse practitioner (MS, Certificate)
- clinical specialist in holistic nursing (MS, Certificate)
- family nurse practitioner (MS, Certificate)
- nursing and health care management (MS)
- nursing education (Certificate)

Division of Art and Communication Studies

Programs in:
- art education (MA)
- art therapy (MS)
- art therapy/counseling (MS)
- communication studies (MS, Certificate)
- studio art (MS)

Division of Education

Programs in:
- bilingual education (Certificate)
- creative teaching and learning (MS Ed, Certificate)
- dual certification: school building leader/school district leader (MS)
- elementary education/early childhood education (MS Ed)
- literacy education (MS Ed)
- school administration and supervision (MS, Advanced Certificate, Advanced Diploma)
- school building leader (MS, Advanced Certificate)
- school district leader (MS, Advanced Diploma)
- special education (MS Ed)
- teaching English as a second language (MS Ed)
- teaching English as a second language and multilingual/multicultural education (MS Ed, Certificate)

Division of Human Services

Programs in:
- career development (MS)
- community-school psychology (MS)
- gerontology (MS, Certificate)
- guidance and counseling (MS)
- mental health counseling (Certificate)

■ THE COLLEGE OF SAINT ROSE

Albany, NY 12203-1419

http://www.strose.edu/

Independent, coed, comprehensive institution. CGS member. *Computer facilities:* 575 computers available on campus for general student use. A campuswide network can be accessed from student residence rooms and from off campus. Online class registration is available. *General application contact:* Assistant Vice President for Graduate Admission, 518-454-5136.

Graduate Studies

School of Arts and Humanities

Programs in:
- art education (MS Ed, Certificate)
- arts and humanities (MA, MS Ed, Certificate)
- English (MA)
- history/political science (MA)
- music (MA)
- music education (MS Ed, Certificate)
- public communications (MA)

School of Business

Programs in:
- accounting (MS)
- business (MBA, MS, Certificate)
- business administration (MBA)
- not-for-profit management (Certificate)

School of Education

Programs in:
- applied technology education (MS Ed)
- bilingual pupil personnel services (Certificate)
- business and marketing (MS Ed)
- childhood education (MS Ed)
- college student personnel (MS Ed)
- college student services administration (MS Ed)
- communication disorders (MS Ed)
- community counseling (MS Ed)
- counseling (MS Ed)
- curriculum and instruction (MS Ed)
- early childhood education (MS Ed)
- education (MS, MS Ed, Certificate)
- educational administration and supervision (MS Ed, Certificate)
- educational leadership and administration (MS Ed)
- educational leadership and administrationûschool building leader (Certificate)
- educational leadership and administrationûschool district leader (Certificate)
- educational psychology (MS Ed)
- elementary education (K-6) (MS Ed)
- literacy: birth-grade 6 (MS Ed)
- literacy: grades 5-12 (MS Ed)
- reading (Certificate)
- school administrator and supervisor (Certificate)
- school counseling (MS Ed)
- school psychology (MS, Certificate)
- secondary education (MS Ed, Certificate)
- special education (MS Ed)
- teacher education (MS Ed, Certificate)

School of Mathematics and Sciences

Programs in:
- computer information systems (MS)
- mathematics and sciences (MS)

■ COLLEGE OF STATEN ISLAND OF THE CITY UNIVERSITY OF NEW YORK

Staten Island, NY 10314-6600

http://www.csi.cuny.edu/

State and locally supported, coed, comprehensive institution. CGS member. *Graduate faculty:* 50 full-time (23 women), 19 part-time/adjunct (11 women). *Computer facilities:* 1,254 computers available on campus for general student use. A campuswide network can be accessed from off campus. Online class registration is available. *Graduate expenses:* Tuition, state resident: full-time $6400; part-time $270 per credit. Tuition, nonresident: full-time $12,000; part-time $500 per credit. Required fees: $378; $113 per semester. *General application contact:* Sasha Spence, Assistant Director of Graduate Recruitment and Admissions, 718-982-2699.

Graduate Programs

Dr. William J. Fritz, Provost and Senior Vice President for Academic Affairs

Programs in:
- adolescence education (MS Ed)
- adult health nursing (MS, 6th Year Certificate)
- biology (MS)
- business management (MS)
- childhood education (MS Ed)
- cinema and media studies (MA)
- computer science (MS)
- cultural competence (6th Year Certificate)
- English (MA)
- gerontological nursing (MS, 6th Year Certificate)
- history (MA)
- leadership in education (6th Year Certificate)
- liberal studies (MA)
- mental health counseling (MA)
- nursing education (6th Year Certificate)
- special education (MS Ed)

Center for Developmental Neuroscience and Developmental Disabilities

Dr. Probal Banerjee, Coordinator

Program in:
- neuroscience, mental retardation and developmental disabilities (MS)

Center for Environmental Science

Dr. Alfred Levine, Director

Program in:
- environmental science (MS)

■ COLUMBIA UNIVERSITY

New York, NY 10027

http://www.columbia.edu/

Independent, coed, university. CGS member. *Graduate faculty:* 3,608 full-time (1,394 women), 1,053 part-time/adjunct (412 women). *Computer facilities:* Computer purchase and lease plans are available. 400

Columbia University (continued)
computers available on campus for general student use. A campuswide network can be accessed from student residence rooms and from off campus. Online class registration is available. *Graduate expenses:* Tuition: full-time $34,364; part-time $1362 per credit. Required fees: $1769; $73 per credit. $760 per term. One-time fee: $95. Part-time tuition and fees vary according to course load, degree level, program and student level. *General application contact:* Information Contact, 212-854-1754.

College of Dental Medicine
Programs in:
- advanced education in general dentistry (Certificate)
- biomedical informatics (MA, PhD)
- dental and oral surgery (DDS)
- dental medicine (DDS, MA, MS, PhD, Certificate)
- endodontics (Certificate)
- orthodontics (MS, Certificate)
- periodontics (MS, Certificate)
- prosthodontics (MS, Certificate)
- science education (MA)

College of Physicians and Surgeons
Programs in:
- anatomy (M Phil, MA, PhD)
- anatomy and cell biology (PhD)
- biochemistry and molecular biophysics (M Phil, PhD)
- biomedical informatics (M Phil, MA, PhD)
- biomedical sciences (M Phil, MA, PhD)
- biophysics (PhD)
- cellular, molecular and biophysical studies (M Phil, MA, PhD)
- genetics (M Phil, MA, PhD)
- medicine (MD, M Phil, MA, MS, DN Sc, DPT, Ed D, PhD, Adv C)
- movement science (Ed D)
- neurobiology and behavior (PhD)
- occupational therapy (professional) (MS)
- occupational therapy administration or education (post-professional) (MS)
- pathobiology (M Phil, MA, PhD)
- pharmacology (M Phil, MA, PhD)
- pharmacology-toxicology (M Phil, MA, PhD)
- physical therapy (DPT)
- physiology and cellular biophysics (M Phil, MA, PhD)

Institute of Human Nutrition
Program in:
- nutrition (MS, PhD)

Columbia University Mailman School of Public Health
Dr. Linda P. Fried, Dean/Professor
Programs in:
- biostatistics (MPH, MS, Dr PH, PhD)
- environmental health sciences (MPH, Dr PH, PhD)
- epidemiology (MPH, MS, Dr PH, PhD)
- health policy and management (Exec MPH, MPH)
- population and family health (MPH)
- public health (Exec MPH, MPH, MS, Dr PH, PhD)
- sociomedical sciences (MPH, Dr PH, PhD)

Fu Foundation School of Engineering and Applied Science
Dr. Feniosky Pena-Mora, Dean
Programs in:
- applied physics (Eng Sc D)
- applied physics and applied mathematics (MS, PhD, Engr)
- biomedical engineering (MS, Eng Sc D, PhD)
- chemical engineering (MS, Eng Sc D, PhD)
- civil engineering (MS, Eng Sc D, PhD, Engr)
- computer engineering (MS)
- computer science (MS, Eng Sc D, PhD, Engr)
- construction engineering and management (MS)
- earth and environmental engineering (MS, Eng Sc D, PhD)
- electrical engineering (MS, Eng Sc D, PhD, Engr)
- engineering and applied science (MS, Eng Sc D, PhD, Engr)
- engineering management systems (MS)
- engineering mechanics (MS, Eng Sc D, PhD, Engr)
- financial engineering (MS)
- industrial engineering (Engr)
- industrial engineering and operations research (MS, Eng Sc D, PhD)
- materials science and engineering (MS, Eng Sc D, PhD)
- mechanical engineering (MS, Eng Sc D, PhD, Engr)
- medical physics (MS)
- metallurgical engineering (Engr)
- mining engineering (Engr)
- solid state science and engineering (MS, Eng Sc D, PhD)

Graduate School of Architecture, Planning, and Preservation
Programs in:
- advanced architectural design (MS)
- architecture (M Arch, PhD)
- architecture, planning, and preservation (M Arch, MS, PhD, Certificate)
- historic preservation (MS, Certificate)
- real estate development (MS)
- urban planning (MS, PhD)

Graduate School of Arts and Sciences
Programs in:
- African-American studies (MA)
- American studies (MA)
- arts and sciences (M Phil, MA, DMA, PhD, Certificate)
- climate and society (MA)
- conservation biology (MA)
- East Asian regional studies (MA)
- East Asian studies (MA)
- French cultural studies (MA)
- human rights studies (MA)
- Islamic culture studies (MA)
- Jewish studies (MA)
- medieval studies (MA)
- modern European studies (MA)
- quantitative methods in the social sciences (MA)
- Russian, Eurasian and East European regional studies (MA)
- South Asian studies (MA)
- sustainable development (PhD)
- theatre (M Phil, MA, PhD)
- Yiddish studies (MA)

Division of Humanities
Programs in:
- archaeology (M Phil, MA, PhD)
- art history and archaeology (M Phil, MA, PhD)
- classics (M Phil, MA, PhD)
- comparative literature (M Phil, MA, PhD)
- East Asian languages and cultures (M Phil, MA, PhD)
- English literature (M Phil, MA, PhD)
- French and Romance philology (M Phil, PhD)
- Germanic languages (M Phil, MA, PhD)
- Hebrew language and literature (M Phil, MA, PhD)
- humanities (M Phil, MA, DMA, PhD)
- Italian (M Phil, MA, PhD)
- Jewish studies (M Phil, MA, PhD)
- literature-writing (M Phil, MA, PhD)
- Middle Eastern languages and cultures (M Phil, MA, PhD)
- modern art (MA)
- music (M Phil, MA, DMA, PhD)
- Oriental studies (M Phil, MA, PhD)
- philosophy (M Phil, MA, PhD)
- religion (M Phil, MA, PhD)
- Romance languages (MA)
- Russian literature (M Phil, MA, PhD)
- Slavic languages (M Phil, MA, PhD)
- South Asian languages and cultures (M Phil, MA, PhD)
- Spanish and Portuguese (M Phil, MA, PhD)

Division of Natural Sciences
Programs in:
- astronomy (M Phil, MA, PhD)
- atmospheric and planetary science (M Phil, PhD)
- biological sciences (M Phil, MA, PhD)
- chemical physics (M Phil, PhD)
- conservation biology (Certificate)
- ecology and evolutionary biology (PhD)
- environmental policy (Certificate)
- experimental psychology (M Phil, MA, PhD)
- geochemistry (M Phil, MA, PhD)
- geodetic sciences (M Phil, MA, PhD)
- geophysics (M Phil, MA, PhD)
- inorganic chemistry (M Phil, MA, PhD)
- mathematics (M Phil, MA, PhD)
- natural sciences (M Phil, MA, PhD, Certificate)

oceanography (M Phil, MA, PhD)
organic chemistry (M Phil, MA, PhD)
philosophical foundations of physics (MA)
physics (M Phil, PhD)
psychobiology (M Phil, MA, PhD)
social psychology (M Phil, MA, PhD)
statistics (M Phil, MA, PhD)

Division of Social Sciences
Programs in:
American history (M Phil, MA, PhD)
anthropology (M Phil, MA, PhD)
economics (M Phil, MA, PhD)
history (M Phil, MA, PhD)
political science (M Phil, MA, PhD)
social sciences (M Phil, MA, PhD)
sociology (M Phil, MA, PhD)

Graduate School of Business
Programs in:
accounting (MBA)
business (PhD)
business administration (EMBA, MBA)
decision, risk, and operations (MBA)
entrepreneurship (MBA)
finance and economics (MBA)
global business administration (EMBA)
human resource management (MBA)
international business (MBA)
management/leadership (MBA)
marketing (MBA)
media (MBA)
real estate (MBA)
social enterprise (MBA)

Graduate School of Journalism
Program in:
journalism (MA, MS, PhD)

School of Continuing Education
Programs in:
actuarial science (MS)
bioethics (MS)
construction administration (MS)
fundraising management (MS)
information and archive management (MS)
landscape design (MS)
negotiation and conflict resolution (MS)
sports management (MS)
strategic communications (MS)
sustainability management (MS)
technology management (Exec MS)

School of International and Public Affairs
Programs in:
development practice (MPA)
environmental science and policy (MPA)
international affairs (MIA)
international and public affairs (MA, MIA, MPA, Certificate)
public policy and administration (MPA)

The East Central Europe Center
Program in:
East Central European studies (Certificate)

The Harriman Institute
Program in:
Russian, Eurasian, and Eastern European studies (Certificate)

Institute for the Study of Europe
Program in:
European studies (Certificate)

Institute of African Studies
Program in:
African studies (Certificate)

Institute of Latin American Studies
Programs in:
Latin American and Caribbean studies (MA)
Latin American studies (Certificate)

Middle East Institute
Program in:
Middle East studies (Certificate)

Southern Asian Institute
Program in:
Southern Asian studies (Certificate)

Weatherhead East Asian Institute
Program in:
Asian studies (Certificate)

School of Law
Program in:
law (JD, LL M, JSD)

School of Nursing
Programs in:
acute care nurse practitioner (MS, Adv C)
adult nurse practitioner (MS, Adv C)
family nurse practitioner (MS, Adv C)
geriatric nurse practitioner (MS, Adv C)
neonatal nurse practitioner (MS, Adv C)
nurse anesthesia (MS, Adv C)
nurse midwifery (MS)
nursing (MS, DN Sc, DNP, Adv C)
nursing practice (DNP)
nursing science (DN Sc)
oncology nursing (MS, Adv C)
pediatric nurse practitioner (MS, Adv C)
psychiatric mental health nursing (MS, Adv C)
women's health nurse practitioner (Adv C)

School of Social Work
Program in:
social work (MSSW, PhD)

School of the Arts
Programs in:
arts (MA, MFA)
directing (MFA)
fiction (MFA)
film studies (MA)
new genres (MFA)
nonfiction (MFA)
painting (MFA)
photography (MFA)
poetry (MFA)
printmaking (MFA)
producing (MFA)
screen writing (MFA)
sculpture (MFA)

Theatre Arts Division
Programs in:
acting (MFA)
directing (MFA)
dramaturgy (MFA)
playwriting (MFA)
stage management (MFA)
theater management (MFA)

■ CORNELL UNIVERSITY
Ithaca, NY 14853-0001
http://www.cornell.edu/

Independent, coed, university. CGS member. *Graduate faculty:* 1,553 full-time (410 women), 80 part-time/adjunct (18 women). *Computer facilities:* Computer purchase and lease plans are available. 2,650 computers available on campus for general student use. A campuswide network can be accessed from student residence rooms and from off campus. Online class registration is available. *Graduate expenses:* Tuition: full-time $29,500. Required fees: $70. Full-time tuition and fees vary according to degree level, program and student level. *General application contact:* Graduate School Application Requests, Caldwell Hall, 607-255-5820.

College of Veterinary Medicine
Dr. Michael Kotlikoff, Dean
Program in:
veterinary medicine (DVM)

Cornell Law School
Program in:
law (JD, LL M, JSD)

Graduate School
Dr. Alison G. Power, Dean
Programs in:
acarology (MS, PhD)
advanced composites and structures (M Eng)
advanced materials processing (M Eng, MS, PhD)
aerospace engineering (M Eng, MS, PhD)
African history (MA, PhD)
African studies (MPS)
African-American literature (PhD)
African-American studies (MPS)
agricultural economics (MPS, MS, PhD)
agricultural education (MAT)
agriculture and life sciences (M Eng, MAT, MFS, MLA, MPS, MS, PhD)
agronomy (MS, PhD)
algorithms (M Eng, PhD)
American art (PhD)
American history (MA, PhD)
American literature after 1865 (PhD)
American literature to 1865 (PhD)
American politics (PhD)
American studies (PhD)
analytical chemistry (PhD)
ancient art and archaeology (PhD)
ancient history (MA, PhD)
ancient Near Eastern studies (MA, PhD)
ancient philosophy (PhD)
animal breeding (MS, PhD)
animal cytology (MS, PhD)

Cornell University (continued)
animal genetics (MS, PhD)
animal nutrition (MPS, MS, PhD)
animal science (MPS, MS, PhD)
apiculture (MS, PhD)
apparel design (MA, MPS)
applied economics (PhD)
applied entomology (MS, PhD)
applied linguistics (MA, PhD)
applied logic and automated reasoning (M Eng, PhD)
applied mathematics (PhD)
applied mathematics and computational methods (M Eng, MS, PhD)
applied physics (PhD)
applied probability and statistics (PhD)
applied research in human-environment relations (MS)
applied statistics (MPS)
aquatic entomology (MS, PhD)
aquatic science (MPS, MS, PhD)
Arabic and Islamic studies (MA, PhD)
archaeological anthropology (PhD)
artificial intelligence (M Eng, PhD)
arts and sciences (MA, MFA, MPA, MPS, MS, DMA, PhD)
Asian art (PhD)
Asian religions (PhD)
astronomy (PhD)
astrophysics (PhD)
atmospheric science (MS, PhD)
baroque art (PhD)
basic analytical economics (PhD)
behavioral biology (PhD)
behavioral physiology (MS, PhD)
biblical studies (MA, PhD)
bio-organic chemistry (PhD)
biochemical engineering (M Eng, MS, PhD)
biochemistry (PhD)
biological anthropology (PhD)
biological control (MS, PhD)
biological engineering (M Eng, MPS, MS, PhD)
biology (7-12) (MAT)
biomechanical engineering (M Eng, MS, PhD)
biomedical engineering (M Eng, MS, PhD)
biometry (MS, PhD)
biophysical chemistry (PhD)
biophysics (PhD)
biopsychology (PhD)
cardiovascular and respiratory physiology (MS, PhD)
cell biology (PhD)
cellular and molecular medicine (MS, PhD)
cellular and molecular toxicology (MS, PhD)
cellular immunology (MS, PhD)
chemical biology (PhD)
chemical physics (PhD)
chemical reaction engineering (M Eng, MS, PhD)
chemistry (7-12) (MAT)
Chinese linguistics (MA, PhD)
Chinese philology (MA, PhD)
classical and statistical thermodynamics (M Eng, MS, PhD)
classical archaeology (PhD)
classical Chinese literature (MA, PhD)
classical Japanese literature (MA, PhD)
classical myth (PhD)
classical rhetoric (PhD)
cognition (PhD)
collective bargaining, labor law and labor history (MILR, MPS, MS, PhD)
colonial and postcolonial literature (PhD)
combustion (M Eng, MS, PhD)
communication (MPS, MS, PhD)
communication research methods (MS, PhD)
community and regional society (MS)
community and regional sociology (MPS, PhD)
community development process (MPS)
community nutrition (MPS, MS, PhD)
comparative and functional anatomy (MS, PhD)
comparative biomedical sciences (MS, PhD)
comparative literature (PhD)
comparative politics (PhD)
composition (DMA)
computational behavioral biology (PhD)
computational biology (PhD)
computational cell biology (PhD)
computational ecology (PhD)
computational macromolecular biology (PhD)
computational organismal biology (PhD)
computer engineering (M Eng, PhD)
computer graphics (M Eng, PhD)
computer science (M Eng, PhD)
computer vision (M Eng, PhD)
concurrency and distributed computing (M Eng, PhD)
consumer policy (PhD)
controlled environment agriculture (MPS, PhD)
controlled environment horticulture (MS)
creative writing (MFA)
cultural studies (PhD)
curriculum and instruction (MPS, MS, PhD)
cytology (MS, PhD)
dairy science (MPS, MS, PhD)
decision theory (MS, PhD)
development policy (MPS)
developmental and reproductive biology (MS, PhD)
developmental biology (MS, PhD)
developmental psychology (PhD)
drama and the theatre (PhD)
dramatic literature (PhD)
dynamics and space mechanics (MS, PhD)
early modern European history (MA, PhD)
earth science (7-12) (MAT)
East Asian linguistics (MA, PhD)
East Asian studies (MA)
ecological and environmental plant pathology (MPS, MS, PhD)
ecology (MS, PhD)
econometrics and economic statistics (PhD)
economic and social statistics (MILR, MS, PhD)
economic development (MPS)
economic development and planning (PhD)
economic geology (M Eng, MS, PhD)
economic theory (PhD)
economy and society (MA, PhD)
ecotoxicology and environmental chemistry (MS, PhD)
electrical engineering (M Eng, PhD)
electrical systems (M Eng, PhD)
electrophysics (M Eng, PhD)
endocrinology (MS, PhD)
energy (M Eng, MPS, MS, PhD)
energy and power systems (M Eng, MS, PhD)
engineering (M Eng, MPS, MS, PhD)
engineering geology (M Eng, MS, PhD)
engineering management (M Eng, MS, PhD)
engineering physics (M Eng)
engineering statistics (MS, PhD)
English history (MA, PhD)
English linguistics (MA, PhD)
English poetry (PhD)
English Renaissance to 1660 (PhD)
environmental and comparative physiology (MS, PhD)
environmental archaeology (MA)
environmental engineering (M Eng, MPS, MS, PhD)
environmental fluid mechanics and hydrology (M Eng, MS, PhD)
environmental geophysics (M Eng, MS, PhD)
environmental information science (MS, PhD)
environmental management (MPS)
environmental systems engineering (M Eng, MS, PhD)
epidemiological plant pathology (MPS, MS, PhD)
evaluation (PhD)
evolutionary biology (PhD)
experimental design (MS, PhD)
experimental physics (MS, PhD)
extension, and adult education (MPS, MS, PhD)
facilities planning and management (MS)
family and social welfare policy (PhD)
fiber science (MS, PhD)
field crop science (MS, PhD)
fishery science (MPS, MS, PhD)
fluid dynamics, rheology and biorheology (M Eng, MS, PhD)
fluid mechanics (M Eng, MS, PhD)
food chemistry (MPS, MS, PhD)
food engineering (MPS, MS, PhD)
food microbiology (MPS, MS, PhD)
food processing engineering (M Eng, MPS, MS, PhD)
food processing waste technology (MPS, MS, PhD)
food science (MFS, MPS, MS, PhD)

forest science (MPS, MS, PhD)
French history (MA, PhD)
French linguistics (PhD)
French literature (PhD)
gastrointestinal and metabolic physiology (MS, PhD)
gender and life course (MA, PhD)
general geology (M Eng, MS, PhD)
general linguistics (MA, PhD)
general space sciences (PhD)
genetics (PhD)
geobiology (M Eng, MS, PhD)
geochemistry and isotope geology (M Eng, MS, PhD)
geohydrology (M Eng, MS, PhD)
geomorphology (M Eng, MS, PhD)
geophysics (M Eng, MS, PhD)
geotechnical engineering (M Eng, MS, PhD)
geotectonics (M Eng, MS, PhD)
German area studies (MA, PhD)
German history (MA, PhD)
German intellectual history (MA, PhD)
Germanic linguistics (MA, PhD)
Germanic literature (MA, PhD)
Greek and Latin language and linguistics (PhD)
Greek language and literature (PhD)
greenhouse crops (MPS, MS, PhD)
health administration (MHA)
health management and policy (PhD)
heat and mass transfer (M Eng, MS, PhD)
heat transfer (M Eng, MS, PhD)
Hebrew and Judaic studies (MA, PhD)
Hispanic literature (PhD)
histology (MS, PhD)
historical archaeology (MA)
history and philosophy of science and technology (MA, PhD)
history of science (MA, PhD)
horticultural business management (MPS, MS, PhD)
horticultural physiology (MPS, MS, PhD)
hospitality management (MMH)
hotel administration (MS, PhD)
housing and design (MS)
human computer interaction (PhD)
human development and family studies (PhD)
human ecology (MA, MHA, MPS, MS, PhD)
human experimental psychology (PhD)
human factors and ergonomics (MS)
human nutrition (MPS, MS, PhD)
human resource studies (MILR, MPS, MS, PhD)
human-environment relations (MS)
immunochemistry (MS, PhD)
immunogenetics (MS, PhD)
immunopathology (MS, PhD)
Indo-European linguistics (MA, PhD)
industrial and labor relations problems (MILR, MPS, MS, PhD)
industrial organization and control (PhD)
infection and immunity (MS, PhD)
infectious diseases (MS, PhD)
information organization and retrieval (M Eng, PhD)
information systems (PhD)
infrared astronomy (PhD)
inorganic chemistry (PhD)
insect behavior (MS, PhD)
insect biochemistry (MS, PhD)
insect ecology (MS, PhD)
insect genetics (MS, PhD)
insect morphology (MS, PhD)
insect pathology (MS, PhD)
insect physiology (MS, PhD)
insect systematics (MS, PhD)
insect toxicology and insecticide chemistry (MS, PhD)
integrated pest management (MS, PhD)
interior design (MA, MPS)
international agriculture (M Eng, MPS, MS, PhD)
international agriculture and development (MPS)
international and comparative labor (MILR, MPS, MS, PhD)
international communication (MS, PhD)
international economics (PhD)
international food science (MPS, MS, PhD)
international nutrition (MPS, MS, PhD)
international planning (MPS)
international population (MPS)
international relations (PhD)
Italian linguistics (PhD)
Italian literature (PhD)
Japanese linguistics (MA, PhD)
kinetics and catalysis (M Eng, MS, PhD)
Korean literature (MA, PhD)
labor economics (MILR, MPS, MS, PhD)
landscape architecture (MLA)
landscape horticulture (MPS, MS, PhD)
Latin American archaeology (MA)
Latin American history (MA, PhD)
Latin language and literature (PhD)
lesbian, bisexual, and gay literature studies (PhD)
literary criticism and theory (PhD)
local government organizations and operations (MPS)
local roads (M Eng, MPS, MS, PhD)
machine systems (M Eng, MPS, MS, PhD)
manufacturing systems engineering (PhD)
marine geology (MS, PhD)
materials and manufacturing engineering (M Eng, MS, PhD)
materials chemistry (PhD)
materials engineering (M Eng, PhD)
materials science (M Eng, PhD)
mathematical programming (PhD)
mathematical statistics (MS, PhD)
mathematics (PhD)
mathematics (7-12) (MAT)
mechanical systems and design (M Eng, MS, PhD)
mechanics of materials (MS, PhD)
medical and veterinary entomology (MS, PhD)
medieval and Renaissance Latin literature (PhD)
medieval archaeology (MA, PhD)
medieval art (PhD)
medieval Chinese history (MA, PhD)
medieval history (MA, PhD)
medieval literature (PhD)
medieval music (PhD)
medieval philology and linguistics (PhD)
medieval philosophy (PhD)
Mediterranean and Near Eastern archaeology (MA)
membrane and epithelial physiology (MS, PhD)
methodology (MA, PhD)
methods of social research (MPS, MS, PhD)
microbiology (PhD)
mineralogy (M Eng, MS, PhD)
modern art (PhD)
modern Chinese history (MA, PhD)
modern Chinese literature (MA, PhD)
modern European history (MA, PhD)
modern Japanese history (MA, PhD)
modern Japanese literature (MA, PhD)
molecular and cell biology (PhD)
molecular and cellular physiology (MS, PhD)
molecular biology (PhD)
molecular plant pathology (MPS, MS, PhD)
monetary and macroeconomics (PhD)
multiphase flows (M Eng, MS, PhD)
musicology (PhD)
mycology (MPS, MS, PhD)
neural and sensory physiology (MS, PhD)
neurobiology (PhD)
nineteenth century (PhD)
nuclear engineering (M Eng, MS, PhD)
nuclear science (MS, PhD)
nursery crops (MPS, MS, PhD)
nutrition of horticultural crops (MPS, MS, PhD)
nutritional and food toxicology (MS, PhD)
nutritional biochemistry (MPS, MS, PhD)
Old and Middle English (PhD)
old Norse (MA, PhD)
operating systems (M Eng, PhD)
operations research and industrial engineering (M Eng)
organic chemistry (PhD)
organizational behavior (MILR, MPS, MS, PhD)
organizations (MA, PhD)
organometallic chemistry (PhD)
paleobotany (MS, PhD)
paleontology (M Eng, MS, PhD)
parallel computing (M Eng, PhD)
performance practice (DMA)
personality and social psychology (PhD)
petroleum geology (M Eng, MS, PhD)
petrology (M Eng, MS, PhD)
pharmacology (MS, PhD)
philosophy (PhD)
phonetics (MA, PhD)
phonological theory (MA, PhD)

Cornell University (continued)

physical chemistry (PhD)
physics (MS, PhD)
physics (7-12) (MAT)
physiological genomics (MS, PhD)
physiology of reproduction (MPS, MS, PhD)
planetary geology (M Eng, MS, PhD)
planetary studies (PhD)
plant breeding (MPS, MS, PhD)
plant cell biology (MS, PhD)
plant disease epidemiology (MPS, MS, PhD)
plant ecology (MS, PhD)
plant genetics (MPS, MS, PhD)
plant molecular biology (MS, PhD)
plant morphology, anatomy and biomechanics (MS, PhD)
plant pathology (MPS, MS, PhD)
plant physiology (MS, PhD)
plant propagation (MPS, MS, PhD)
plant protection (MPS)
policy analysis (MA, PhD)
political methodology (PhD)
political sociology/social movements (MA, PhD)
political thought (PhD)
polymer chemistry (PhD)
polymer science (MS, PhD)
polymers (M Eng, MS, PhD)
pomology (MPS, MS, PhD)
population and development (MPS, MS, PhD)
population medicine and epidemiology (MS, PhD)
Precambrian geology (M Eng, MS, PhD)
premodern Islamic history (MA, PhD)
premodern Japanese history (MA, PhD)
probability (MS, PhD)
program development and planning (MPS)
programming environments (M Eng, PhD)
programming languages and methodology (M Eng, PhD)
prose fiction (PhD)
public affairs (MPA)
public finance (PhD)
public garden management (MPS, MS, PhD)
public policy (MPA, PhD)
Quaternary geology (M Eng, MS, PhD)
racial and ethnic relations (MA, PhD)
radio astronomy (PhD)
radiophysics (PhD)
remote sensing (M Eng, MS, PhD)
Renaissance art (PhD)
Renaissance history (MA, PhD)
reproductive physiology (MS, PhD)
resource economics (MPS, MS, PhD)
resource policy and management (MPS, MS, PhD)
Restoration and eighteenth century (PhD)
restoration ecology (MPS, MS, PhD)
risk assessment, management and public policy (MS, PhD)
robotics (M Eng, PhD)
rock mechanics (M Eng, MS, PhD)
Romance linguistics (MA, PhD)
rural and environmental sociology (MPS, MS, PhD)
Russian history (MA, PhD)
sampling (MS, PhD)
science and environmental communication (MS, PhD)
science and technology policy (MPS)
scientific computing (M Eng, PhD)
second language acquisition (MA, PhD)
sedimentology (M Eng, MS, PhD)
seismology (M Eng, MS, PhD)
semantics (MA, PhD)
sensory evaluation (MPS, MS, PhD)
Slavic linguistics (MA, PhD)
social aspects of information (PhD)
social networks (MA, PhD)
social psychology (MA, PhD)
social psychology of communication (MS, PhD)
social stratification (MA, PhD)
social studies of science and technology (MA, PhD)
sociocultural anthropology (PhD)
sociolinguistics (MA, PhD)
soil and water engineering (M Eng, MPS, MS, PhD)
soil science (MS, PhD)
solid mechanics (MS, PhD)
South Asian linguistics (MA, PhD)
South Asian studies (MA)
Southeast Asian art (PhD)
Southeast Asian history (MA, PhD)
Southeast Asian linguistics (MA, PhD)
Southeast Asian studies (MA)
Spanish linguistics (PhD)
state, economy, and society (MPS, MS, PhD)
statistical computing (MS, PhD)
stochastic processes (MS, PhD)
Stone Age archaeology (MA)
stratigraphy (M Eng, MS, PhD)
structural and functional biology (MS, PhD)
structural engineering (M Eng, MS, PhD)
structural geology (M Eng, MS, PhD)
structural mechanics (M Eng, MS)
structures and environment (M Eng, MPS, MS, PhD)
surface science (M Eng, MS, PhD)
syntactic theory (MA, PhD)
systematic botany (MS, PhD)
systems engineering (M Eng)
taxonomy of ornamental plants (MPS, MS, PhD)
textile science (MS, PhD)
theatre history (PhD)
theatre theory and aesthetics (PhD)
theoretical astrophysics (PhD)
theoretical chemistry (PhD)
theoretical physics (MS, PhD)
theory and criticism (PhD)
theory of computation (M Eng, PhD)
theory of music (MA)
transportation engineering (MS, PhD)
transportation systems engineering (M Eng)
turfgrass science (MPS, MS, PhD)
twentieth century (PhD)
urban horticulture (MPS, MS, PhD)
uses and effects of communication (MS, PhD)
vegetable crops (MPS, MS, PhD)
water resource systems (M Eng, MS, PhD)
weed science (MPS, MS, PhD)
wildlife science (MPS, MS, PhD)
women's literature (PhD)

Field of Environmental Management

Program in:
environmental management (MPS)

Graduate Field in the Law School

Program in:
law (JSD)

Graduate Field of Management

Programs in:
accounting (PhD)
behavioral decision theory (PhD)
finance (PhD)
marketing (PhD)
organizational behavior (PhD)
production and operations management (PhD)

Graduate Fields of Architecture, Art and Planning

Programs in:
architectural design (M Arch)
architectural science (MS)
architecture, art and planning (M Arch, MA, MFA, MPSRE, MRP, MS, PhD)
building technology and environmental science (MS)
city and regional planning (MRP, PhD)
computer graphics (MS)
creative visual arts (MFA)
environmental planning and design (MRP, PhD)
environmental studies (MA, MS, PhD)
historic preservation planning (MA)
history of architecture (MA, PhD)
history of urban development (MA, PhD)
international development planning (MRP, PhD)
international spatial problems (MA, MS, PhD)
location theory (MA, MS, PhD)
multiregional economic analysis (MA, MS, PhD)
peace science (MA, MS, PhD)
planning methods (MA, MS, PhD)
planning theory and systems analysis (MRP, PhD)
real estate (MPSRE)
regional economics and development planning (MRP, PhD)
regional science (MRP, PhD)
social and health systems planning (MRP, PhD)
theory and criticism of architecture (M Arch)
urban and regional economics (MA, MS, PhD)
urban and regional theory (MRP, PhD)
urban design (M Arch)
urban planning history (MRP, PhD)

Johnson Graduate School of Management
Dr. L. Joseph Thomas, Dean
Program in:
management (MBA)

■ DAEMEN COLLEGE
Amherst, NY 14226-3592
http://www.daemen.edu/

Independent, coed, comprehensive institution. *Graduate faculty:* 28 full-time (16 women), 61 part-time/adjunct (48 women). *Computer facilities:* 99 computers available on campus for general student use. A campuswide network can be accessed from student residence rooms and from off campus. Online class registration is available. *Graduate expenses:* Tuition: part-time $740 per credit hour. Tuition and fees vary according to course load and program. *General application contact:* Karl Shallowhorn, Associate Director of Graduate Admissions, 716-839-8225.

Department of Accounting and Business Administration
Dr. Linda J. Kuechler, Chair
Program in:
global business (MS)

Department of Nursing
Dr. Mary Lou Rusin, Chair
Programs in:
adult nurse practitioner (MS, Certificate)
nursing education (MS, Post Master's Certificate)
nursing executive leadership (MS, Post Master's Certificate)
palliative care nursing (MS, Certificate)

Department of Physical Therapy
Dr. Sharon L. Held, Chair
Programs in:
orthopedic manual physical therapy (Advanced Certificate)
physical therapy (DPT, TDPT)

Education Department
Dr. Mary H. Fox, Chair
Programs in:
adolescence education (MS)
childhood education (MS)
childhood special education (MS)

Physician Assistant Department
Gregg L. Shutts, Director
Program in:
physician assistant (MS)

Program in Executive Leadership and Change
Dr. John S. Frederick, Executive Director
Program in:
executive leadership and change (MS)

■ DOMINICAN COLLEGE
Orangeburg, NY 10962-1210
http://www.dc.edu/

Independent, coed, comprehensive institution. *Computer facilities:* 150 computers available on campus for general student use. A campuswide network can be accessed from student residence rooms and from off campus. Web portal, Black Board available. *General application contact:* Director of Admissions, 845-848-7896 Ext. 15.

Division of Allied Health
Programs in:
allied health (MS, DPT)
occupational therapy (MS)
physical therapy (MS, DPT)

Division of Nursing
Programs in:
family nurse practitioner (MSN)
nursing (MSN)

Division of Teacher Education
Programs in:
childhood education (MS Ed)
teacher education (MS Ed)
teacher of students with disabilities (MS Ed)
teacher of visually impaired (MS Ed)

MBA Program
Program in:
business administration (MBA)

■ DOWLING COLLEGE
Oakdale, NY 11769-1999
http://www.dowling.edu/

Independent, coed, comprehensive institution. *Computer facilities:* 227 computers available on campus for general student use. A campuswide network can be accessed from student residence rooms and from off campus. Online class registration is available. *General application contact:* Director of Admissions Operations, 631-244-3227.

Graduate Programs in Education
Programs in:
educational administration (Ed D, PD)
human development and learning (MS Ed)
literacy (MS Ed)
literacy/special education (MS Ed)
secondary education (MS Ed)
special education (MS Ed)

Programs in Arts and Sciences
Programs in:
integrated math and science (MS)
liberal studies (MA)

School of Business
Programs in:
aviation management (MBA, Certificate)
banking and finance (MBA, Certificate)
general management (MBA)
public management (MBA, Certificate)
total quality management (MBA, Certificate)

■ D'YOUVILLE COLLEGE
Buffalo, NY 14201-1084
http://www.dyc.edu/

Independent, coed, comprehensive institution. *Graduate faculty:* 79 full-time (47 women), 91 part-time/adjunct (56 women). *Computer facilities:* 72 computers available on campus for general student use. A campuswide network can be accessed from student residence rooms and from off campus. Online class registration is available. *Graduate expenses:* Tuition: full-time $12,150; part-time $675 per credit hour. Required fees: $2 per credit hour. $37 per semester. One-time fee: $115. Tuition and fees vary according to degree level and program. *General application contact:* Linda Fisher, Graduate Admissions Director, 716-829-8400.

Department of Business
Dr. Susan Kowalewski, Chair
Programs in:
business administration (MBA)
international business (MS)

Department of Dietetics
Dr. Charlotte Baumgart, Chair
Program in:
dietetics (MS)

Department of Education
Dr. Kushnood Haq, Chair
Programs in:
elementary education (MS Ed, Teaching Certificate)
secondary education (MS Ed, Teaching Certificate)
special education (MS Ed)

Department of Health Services Administration
Dr. Walter Iwanenko, Chair
Programs in:
clinical research associate (Certificate)
health services administration (MS, Certificate)
long term care administration (Certificate)

Department of Holistic Health Studies
Dr. Peter Hagman, Director, Chiropractic Program
Program in:
chiropractic (DC)

Department of Nursing
Dr. Kathleen Mariano, Chair
Programs in:
community health nursing/education (MSN)
community health nursing/high risk parents and children (MSN)
community health nursing/management (MSN)
family nurse practitioner (MS, Post-Master's Certificate)

D'Youville College (continued)
- nursing and health-related professions (Certificate)
- nursing with clinical focus choice (MSN)

Department of Physical Therapy
Dr. Lynn Rivers, Chair
Programs in:
- advanced orthopedic physical therapy (Certificate)
- manual physical therapy (Certificate)
- physical therapy (MPT, MS, DPT)

Doctoral Programs
Dr. Mark Garrison, Director of Doctoral Programs
Programs in:
- educational leadership (Ed D)
- health education (Ed D)
- health policy (Ed D)

Occupational Therapy Department
Dr. Amy Nwora, Chair
Program in:
- occupational therapy (MS)

Physician Assistant Department
Dr. Maureen F. Finney, Chair
Program in:
- physician assistant (MS)

■ FORDHAM UNIVERSITY
New York, NY 10458
http://www.fordham.edu/

Independent-religious, coed, university. CGS member. *Graduate faculty:* 502 full-time, 416 part-time/adjunct. *Computer facilities:* Computer purchase and lease plans are available. 1,400 computers available on campus for general student use. A campuswide network can be accessed from student residence rooms and from off campus. Online class registration is available. *General application contact:* Charlene Dundie, Director of Graduate Admissions, 718-817-4420.

Graduate School of Arts and Sciences
Dr. Nancy A. Busch, Dean
Programs in:
- applied developmental psychology (PhD)
- arts and sciences (MA, MS, PhD, Certificate)
- biological sciences (MS, PhD)
- classical Greek and Latin literature (MA)
- classics (PhD)
- clinical psychology (PhD)
- computer science (MS)
- economics (MA, PhD)
- elections and campaign management (MA)
- English language and literature (MA, PhD)
- history (MA, PhD)
- humanities and sciences (MA)
- international political economy and development (MA, Certificate)
- Latin American and Latino studies (MA, Certificate)
- philosophical resources (MA)
- philosophy (MA, PhD)
- psychometrics (PhD)
- public communications (MA)
- sociology (MA)
- theology (MA, PhD)
- urban studies (MA)

Center for Ethics Education Program
Dr. Celia Fisher, Director
Programs in:
- ethics and society (MA)
- health care ethics (Certificate)

Center for Medieval Studies
Dr. Maryanne Kowaleski, Director
Program in:
- medieval studies (MA, Certificate)

Graduate School of Business Administration
Programs in:
- accounting (MBA)
- business administration (EMBA, MBA, MS, MTA)
- communications and media management (MBA)
- executive business administration (EMBA)
- finance (MBA, MS)
- information systems (MBA, MS)
- management systems (MBA)
- marketing (MBA)
- media management (MS)
- taxation (MS)
- taxation and accounting (MTA)

Graduate School of Education
Program in:
- education (MAT, MS, MSE, MST, Ed D, PhD, Adv C)

Division of Curriculum and Teaching
Programs in:
- adult education (MS, MSE)
- bilingual teacher education (MSE)
- curriculum and teaching (MSE)
- early childhood education (MSE)
- elementary education (MST)
- language, literacy, and learning (PhD)
- reading education (MSE, Adv C)
- secondary education (MAT, MSE)
- special education (MSE, Adv C)
- teaching English as a second language (MSE)

Division of Educational Leadership, Administration and Policy
Programs in:
- administration and supervision (MSE, Adv C)
- administration and supervision for church leaders (PhD)
- educational administration and supervision (Ed D, PhD)
- human resource program administration (MS)

Division of Psychological and Educational Services
Programs in:
- counseling and personnel services (MSE, Adv C)
- counseling psychology (PhD)
- educational psychology (MSE, PhD)
- school psychology (PhD)
- urban and urban bilingual school psychology (Adv C)

Graduate School of Religion and Religious Education
Programs in:
- pastoral counseling and spiritual care (MA)
- pastoral ministry/spirituality/pastoral counseling (D Min)
- religion and religious education (MA)
- religious education (MS, PhD, PD)
- spiritual direction (Certificate)

Graduate School of Social Service
Program in:
- social work (PhD)

School of Law
Programs in:
- banking, corporate and finance law (LL M)
- intellectual property and information law (LL M)
- international business and trade law (LL M)
- law (JD)

■ GRADUATE SCHOOL AND UNIVERSITY CENTER OF THE CITY UNIVERSITY OF NEW YORK
New York, NY 10016-4039
http://www.gc.cuny.edu/

State and locally supported, coed, graduate-only institution. CGS member. *General application contact:* Director of Admissions, 212-817-7470.

Graduate Studies
Dr. Linda Edwards, Acting Provost and Senior Vice President for Academic Affairs
Programs in:
- accounting (PhD)
- anthropological linguistics (PhD)
- archaeology (PhD)
- architecture (PhD)
- audiology (Au D)
- basic applied neurocognition (PhD)
- behavioral science (PhD)
- biochemistry (PhD)
- biology (PhD)
- biomedical engineering (PhD)
- biopsychology (PhD)
- chemical engineering (PhD)
- chemistry (PhD)
- civil engineering (PhD)

classics (MA, PhD)
clinical psychology (PhD)
comparative literature (MA, PhD)
computer science (PhD)
criminal justice (PhD)
cultural anthropology (PhD)
developmental psychology (PhD)
earth and environmental sciences (PhD)
economics (PhD)
educational psychology (PhD)
electrical engineering (PhD)
English (PhD)
environmental psychology (PhD)
experimental psychology (PhD)
finance (PhD)
French (PhD)
Germanic languages and literatures (MA, PhD)
graphic arts (PhD)
Hispanic and Luso-Brazilian literatures and languages (PhD)
history (PhD)
industrial psychology (PhD)
learning processes (PhD)
liberal studies (MA)
linguistics (MA, PhD)
management planning systems (PhD)
mathematics (PhD)
mechanical engineering (PhD)
music (DMA, PhD)
neuropsychology (PhD)
nursing science (DNS)
painting (PhD)
philosophy (MA, PhD)
photography (PhD)
physical anthropology (PhD)
physical therapy (DPT)
physics (PhD)
political science (MA, PhD)
psychology (PhD)
public health (DPH)
sculpture (PhD)
social personality (PhD)
social welfare (DSW, PhD)
sociology (PhD)
speech and hearing sciences (PhD)
theatre (PhD)
urban education (PhD)

Interdisciplinary Studies
Programs in:
language in social context (PhD)
medieval studies (PhD)
public policy (MA, PhD)
urban studies (MA, PhD)
women's studies (MA, PhD)

■ HOFSTRA UNIVERSITY
Hempstead, NY 11549
http://www.hofstra.edu/

Independent, coed, university. CGS member. *Graduate faculty:* 271 full-time (116 women), 193 part-time/adjunct (83 women). *Computer facilities:* Computer purchase and lease plans are available. 1,628 computers available on campus for general student use. A campuswide network can be accessed from student residence rooms and from off campus. Online class registration, Gmail/ Google Apps for students; Emergency Notification System; Online course management system; Online card services balance update; Online portfolio are available. *Graduate expenses:* Tuition: full-time $15,300; part-time $850 per credit. Required fees: $970; $165 per term. Tuition and fees vary according to program. *General application contact:* Carol Drummer, Dean of Graduate Admissions, 516-463-4876.

College of Liberal Arts and Sciences
Dr. Bernard J. Firestone, Dean
Programs in:
applied linguistics (MA)
applied mathematics (MS)
applied organizational psychology (PhD)
applied social research and policy analysis (MA)
audiology (Au D)
biology (MA, MS)
clinical psychology (MA, PhD)
comparative arts and culture (MA)
computer science (MA, MS)
English and creative writing (MA)
English literature (MA)
industrial/organizational psychology (MA)
liberal arts and sciences (MA, MS, Au D, PhD, Psy D, CAS)
mathematics (MA)
school-community psychology (MS, Psy D, CAS)
Spanish (MA)
speech-language pathology (MA)

New College
Dr. Barry Nass, Vice Dean
Program in:
interdisciplinary studies (MA)

Frank G. Zarb School of Business
Salvatore F. Sodano, Dean
Programs in:
accounting (MS)
business (EMBA, MBA, MS)
business administration (MBA)
finance (MS)
human resource management (MS)
information technology (MS)
marketing (MS)
marketing research (MS)
quantitative finance (MS)
real estate (MBA)
taxation (MS)

School of Communication
Dr. Cliff Jernigan, Acting Dean
Programs in:
communication (MA, MFA)
documentary studies and production (MFA)
journalism (MA)
speech communication and rhetorical studies (MA)

School of Education, Health, and Human Services
Dr. David Foulk, Dean
Programs in:
bilingual education (MA)
bilingual extension education (CAS)
business education (MS Ed)
community health (MS)
counseling (MA, MS Ed, Advanced Certificate, PD)
creative arts therapy (MA)
early childhood and childhood education (MS Ed)
early childhood education (MA, MS Ed)
early childhood special education (MS Ed, Advanced Certificate)
education, health, and human services (MA, MHA, MS, MS Ed, Ed D, PhD, Advanced Certificate, CAS, PD)
educational and policy leadership (MS Ed, Ed D, CAS)
educational leadership (CAS)
educational technology (CAS)
elementary education (MA, MS Ed)
elementary education—math, science, and technology (MA)
English education (MA, MS Ed)
fine arts education (MA, MS Ed)
foreign language education (MA, MS Ed)
foundations of education (MA, CAS)
gerontology (MS, Advanced Certificate)
gifted education (Advanced Certificate)
health administration (MHA)
health education (MS)
inclusive early childhood special education (MS Ed)
inclusive elementary special education (MS Ed)
inclusive secondary special education (MS Ed)
learning and teaching (Ed D)
literacy studies (MA, MS Ed, Ed D, PhD, CAS, PD)
literacy studies and special education (MS Ed)
marriage and family therapy (MA)
mathematics education (MA, MS Ed)
mental health counseling (MA)
middle level education (Advanced Certificate)
middle school extension (grades 5-6) (Advanced Certificate)
middle school extension (grades 7-9) (Advanced Certificate)
music education (MA, MS Ed)
physical education (MA, MS)
rehabilitation administration (PD)
rehabilitation counseling (MS Ed, PD)
rehabilitation counseling in mental health (MS Ed)
school counselor (MS Ed)
school counselor-bilingual extension (Advanced Certificate)
science education (MA, MS Ed)
secondary education (Advanced Certificate)
social studies education (MA, MS Ed)
special education (MA, MS Ed, Advanced Certificate, PD)
special education assessment and diagnosis (Advanced Certificate)

Hofstra University (continued)

- teaching students with severe or multiple disabilities (Advanced Certificate)
- TESL/bilingual education (MA, MS Ed, CAS)
- TESOL (MS Ed, CAS)
- wind conducting (MA)

School of Law

Nora V. Demleitner, Dean
Programs in:

- American legal studies (LL M)
- family law (LL M)
- law (JD)

■ HUNTER COLLEGE OF THE CITY UNIVERSITY OF NEW YORK

New York, NY 10021-5085
http://www.hunter.cuny.edu/

State and locally supported, coed, comprehensive institution. *Graduate faculty:* 315 full-time (166 women), 290 part-time/adjunct (169 women). *Computer facilities:* 750 computers available on campus for general student use. A campuswide network can be accessed. *Graduate expenses:* Tuition, state resident: full-time $6400; part-time $270 per credit. Tuition, nonresident: full-time $15,000; part-time $500 per credit. Required fees: $399 per semester. *General application contact:* William Zlata, Director for Graduate Admissions, 212-772-4482.

Graduate School

William Zlata, Director of Admissions

School of Arts and Sciences
Dr. Shirley Clay Scott, Dean
Programs in:

- accounting (MS)
- analytical geography (MA)
- anthropology (MA)
- applied and evaluative psychology (MA)
- applied mathematics (MA)
- applied social research (MS)
- art history (MA)
- arts and sciences (MA, MFA, MS, MUP, PhD, Certificate)
- biochemistry (MA, PhD)
- biological sciences (MA, PhD)
- biopsychology and comparative psychology (MA)
- British and American literature (MA)
- chemistry (PhD)
- creative writing (MFA)
- earth system science (MA)
- economics (MA)
- English education (MA)
- environmental and social issues (MA)
- fiction (MFA)
- fine arts (MFA)
- French (MA)
- French education (MA)
- geographic information science (Certificate)
- geographic information systems (MA)
- history (MA)
- integrated media arts (MA, MFA)
- Italian (MA)
- Italian education (MA)
- mathematics for secondary education (MA)
- music (MA)
- music education (MA)
- nonfiction (MFA)
- physics (MA, PhD)
- poetry (MFA)
- pure mathematics (MA)
- social, cognitive, and developmental psychology (MA)
- Spanish (MA)
- Spanish education (MA)
- studio art (MFA)
- teaching earth science (MA)
- teaching Latin (MA)
- theatre (MA)
- urban affairs (MS)
- urban planning (MUP)
- urban studies/affairs (MS)

School of Education
Dr. David Steiner, Dean
Programs in:

- bilingual education (MS)
- biology education (MA)
- blind or visually impaired (MS Ed)
- chemistry education (MA)
- corrective reading (K–12) (MS Ed)
- deaf or hard of hearing (MS Ed)
- early childhood education (MS)
- earth science (MA)
- education (MA, MS, MS Ed, AC)
- educational supervision and administration (AC)
- elementary education (MS)
- English education (MA)
- French education (MA)
- Italian education (MA)
- literacy education (MS)
- mathematics education (MA)
- music education (MA)
- physics education (MA)
- rehabilitation counseling (MS Ed)
- school counseling (MS Ed)
- school counseling with bilingual extension (MS Ed)
- school counselor (MS Ed)
- severe/multiple disabilities (MS Ed)
- social studies education (MA)
- Spanish education (MA)
- special education (MS Ed)
- teaching English as a second language (MA)

School of Social Work
Dr. Jacqueline B. Mondros, Dean/Professor
Program in:

- social work (MSW, DSW)

Schools of the Health Professions
Lauren N. Sherwen, Dean
Programs in:

- adult nurse practitioner (MS)
- audiology (MS)
- community health education (MPH)
- community health nursing (MS)
- environmental and occupational health education (MS)
- epidemiology and biostatistics (MPH)
- gerontological nurse practitioner (MS)
- health policy management (MPH)
- health professions (MPH, MS, DPT, AC)
- health sciences (MPH, MS, DPT)
- nursing (MS, AC)
- nutrition and public health (MPH)
- psychiatric nursing (MS, AC)
- speech language pathology (MS)
- teacher of speech and hearing handicapped (MS)

■ IONA COLLEGE

New Rochelle, NY 10801-1890
http://www.iona.edu/

Independent-religious, coed, comprehensive institution. *Graduate faculty:* 117 full-time (42 women), 64 part-time/adjunct (28 women). *Computer facilities:* Computer purchase and lease plans are available. 625 computers available on campus for general student use. A campuswide network can be accessed from student residence rooms and from off campus. Online class registration is available. *Graduate expenses:* Tuition: part-time $755 per credit. Required fees: $175 per term. *General application contact:* Kevin Cavanagh, Assistant Vice President for College Admissions, 914-633-2120.

Hagan School of Business

Dr. Vincent Calluzo, Dean
Programs in:

- business (MBA, PMC)
- financial management (MBA, PMC)
- human resource management (MBA, PMC)
- information systems (MBA, PMC)
- international business (PMC)
- management (MBA, PMC)
- marketing (MBA)

School of Arts and Science

Dr. Brian J. Nickerson, Dean
Programs in:

- arts and science (MA, MS, MS Ed, MST, Certificate)
- biology education (MS Ed, MST)
- computer science (MS)
- criminal justice (MS)
- educational leadership (MS Ed)
- educational technology (MS, Certificate)
- English (MA)
- English education (MS Ed, MST)
- experimental psychology (MA)
- family counseling (MS, Certificate)
- health service administration (MS, Certificate)
- history (MA)
- industrial-organizational psychology (MA)
- Italian (MA)
- journalism (MS)
- literacy education (MS Ed)

mathematics education (MS Ed, MST)
mental health counseling (MA)
pastoral counseling (MS)
psychology (MA)
public relations (MA)
school psychology (MA)
social studies education (MS Ed, MST)
Spanish (MA)
Spanish education (MS Ed, MST)
teaching in childhood education (MST)
telecommunications (MS, Certificate)

■ ITHACA COLLEGE

Ithaca, NY 14850-7020

http://www.ithaca.edu/

Independent, coed, comprehensive institution. CGS member. *Graduate faculty:* 149 full-time (64 women), 10 part-time/adjunct (8 women). *Computer facilities:* Computer purchase and lease plans are available. 640 computers available on campus for general student use. A campuswide network can be accessed from student residence rooms and from off campus. Online class registration is available. *Graduate expenses:* Tuition: full-time $18,090; part-time $603 per hour. *General application contact:* Rob Gearhart, Interim Dean, Graduate and Professional Studies, 607-274-3527.

Division of Graduate and Professional Studies

Rob Gearhart, Interim Dean, Graduate and Professional Studies

Roy H. Park School of Communications

Dr. Diane Gayeski, Interim Dean, Roy H. Park School of Communications
Program in:
communications (MS)

School of Business

Dr. Mark Cordano, Interim Dean, School of Business
Programs in:
accountancy (MBA)
business (MBA)
business administration (MBA)

School of Health Sciences and Human Performance

Dr. Steven Siconolfi, Dean, School of Health Sciences and Human Performance
Programs in:
exercise and sport sciences (MS)
health education (MS)
health sciences and human performance (MS, DPT)
occupational therapy (MS)
physical education (MS)
physical therapy (MS, DPT)
speech pathology (MS)
sport management (MS)
teacher of students with speech and language disabilities (MS)

School of Humanities and Sciences

Dr. Leslie Lewis, Dean, School of Humanities and Sciences
Programs in:
biology 7-12 (MAT)
chemistry 7-12 (MAT)
childhood education (MS)
English 7-12 (MAT)
French 7-12 (MAT)
humanities and sciences (MAT, MS)
math 7-12 (MAT)
physics 7-12 (MAT)
social studies 7-12 (MAT)
Spanish (MAT)

School of Music

Dr. Gregory Woodward, Dean
Programs in:
composition (MM)
conducting (MM)
music (MM, MS)
music education (MM, MS)
performance (MM)
Suzuki pedagogy (MM)

■ JOHN JAY COLLEGE OF CRIMINAL JUSTICE OF THE CITY UNIVERSITY OF NEW YORK

New York, NY 10019-1093

http://www.jjay.cuny.edu/

State and locally supported, coed, comprehensive institution. *Computer facilities:* 1,750 computers available on campus for general student use. A campuswide network can be accessed from off campus. Online class registration is available. *General application contact:* Director of Graduate Admissions, 212-237-8864.

Graduate Studies

Programs in:
criminal justice (MA, PhD)
criminology and deviance (PhD)
forensic computing (MS)
forensic psychology (PhD)
forensic science (PhD)
law and philosophy (PhD)
organizational behavior (PhD)
protection management (MS)
public administration (MPA)
public policy (PhD)

■ LEHMAN COLLEGE OF THE CITY UNIVERSITY OF NEW YORK

Bronx, NY 10468-1589

http://www.lehman.cuny.edu/

State and locally supported, coed, comprehensive institution. *Computer facilities:* 800 computers available on campus for general student use. A campuswide network can be accessed from student residence rooms. Online class registration is available. *General application contact:* Director of Graduate Admissions, 718-960-8856.

Division of Arts and Humanities

Programs in:
art (MA, MFA)
arts and humanities (MA, MAT, MFA)
English (MA)
history (MA)
music (MAT)
Spanish (MA)
speech-language pathology and audiology (MA)

Division of Education

Programs in:
bilingual special education (MS Ed)
business education (MS Ed)
early childhood education (MS Ed)
early special education (MS Ed)
education (MA, MS Ed)
elementary education (MS Ed)
emotional handicaps (MS Ed)
English education (MS Ed)
guidance and counseling (MS Ed)
learning disabilities (MS Ed)
mathematics 7–12 (MS Ed)
mental retardation (MS Ed)
music education (MS Ed)
reading teacher (MS Ed)
science education (MS Ed)
social studies 7–12 (MA)
teachers of special education (MS Ed)
teaching English to speakers of other languages (MS Ed)

Division of Natural and Social Sciences

Programs in:
accounting (MS)
adult health nursing (MS)
biology (MA)
clinical nutrition (MS)
community nutrition (MS)
computer science (MS)
dietetic internship (MS)
health education and promotion (MA)
health N–12 teacher (MS Ed)
mathematics (MA)
natural and social sciences (MA, MS, MS Ed, PhD)
nursing of older adults (MS)
nutrition (MS)
parent-child nursing (MS)
pediatric nurse practitioner (MS)
plant sciences (PhD)
recreation (MA, MS Ed)
recreation education (MA, MS Ed)

■ LE MOYNE COLLEGE

Syracuse, NY 13214

http://www.lemoyne.edu/

Independent-religious, coed, comprehensive institution. *Graduate faculty:* 40 full-time (18 women), 60 part-time/adjunct (30 women). *Computer facilities:* Computer purchase and lease plans are available. 325 computers available on campus for general student use. A campuswide network can be accessed from student residence rooms and from off campus. Online class registration, ECHO (campus-wide portal) are available. *Graduate*

Le Moyne College (continued)

expenses: Tuition: full-time $10,800; part-time $600 per credit hour. Required fees: $25 per semester. *General application contact:* Kristen P. Trapasso, Director of Graduate Admission, 315-445-4265.

Department of Education
Dr. William D. Silky, Visiting Chair, Education Department and Director of Graduate Education
Programs in:
adolescent education (MS Ed, MST)
adolescent education/special education (MS Ed, MST)
childhood education (MS Ed)
childhood education/special education (MS Ed)
elementary education (MS Ed)
general professional education (MS Ed)
inclusive childhood education (MST)
middle child specialist/special education (MS Ed)
middle childhood specialist (MS Ed)
school building leadership (MS Ed, CAS)
school district business leader (MS Ed, CAS)
school district leadership (MS Ed, CAS)
secondary education (MS Ed)
special education (MS Ed)

Department of Nursing
Barbara M. Carranti, Clinical Assistant Professor and Interim Chair of Department of Nursing
Programs in:
nursing administration (MS)
nursing education (CAS)

Department of Physician Assistant Studies
Mary E. Springston, Clinical Assistant Professor and Director of Department of Physician Assistant Studies
Program in:
physician assistant studies (MS)

Division of Management
Dr. George Kulick, Director of MBA Program
Program in:
management (MBA)

■ LONG ISLAND UNIVERSITY, BRENTWOOD CAMPUS

Brentwood, NY 11717
http://www.liu.edu/

Independent, coed, upper-level institution. *Computer facilities:* Computer purchase and lease plans are available. *General application contact:* Director of Admissions, 631-273-5112 Ext. 26.

School of Education
Programs in:
childhood education (MS)
early childhood education (MS)
literacy (MS)
mental health counseling (MS)
school counseling (MS)
special education (MS)

School of Public Service
Program in:
criminal justice (MS)

■ LONG ISLAND UNIVERSITY, BROOKLYN CAMPUS

Brooklyn, NY 11201-8423
http://www.liu.edu/

Independent, coed, university. *Computer facilities:* A campuswide network can be accessed from student residence rooms and from off campus. Online class registration is available. *General application contact:* Director of Graduate Admissions, 718-488-1011.

Arnold and Marie Schwartz College of Pharmacy and Health Sciences
Programs in:
cosmetic science (MS)
drug regulatory affairs (MS)
industrial pharmacy (MS)
pharmaceutical sciences (MS, PhD)
pharmaceutics (PhD)
pharmacology/toxicology (MS)
pharmacy administration (MS)
pharmacy and health sciences (MS, PhD)
social and administrative sciences (MS)

Richard L. Conolly College of Liberal Arts and Sciences
Programs in:
biology (MS)
chemistry (MS)
clinical psychology (PhD)
economics (MA)
English literature (MA)
history (MS)
liberal arts and sciences (MA, MS, PhD, Certificate)
media arts (MA)
political science (MA)
professional and creative writing (MA)
psychology (MA, PhD)
speech-language pathology (MS)
teaching of writing (MA)
United Nations studies (Certificate)
urban studies (MA)

School of Business, Public Administration and Information Sciences
Programs in:
accounting (MS)
business administration (MBA)
business, public administration and information sciences (MBA, MPA, MS)
computer science (MS)
human resources management (MS)
public administration (MPA)
taxation (MS)

School of Education
Programs in:
bilingual education (MS Ed)
computers in education (MS)
counseling and development (MS, MS Ed, Certificate)
education (MS, MS Ed, Certificate)
elementary education (MS Ed)
leadership and policy (MS)
mathematics education (MS Ed)
reading (MS Ed)
school psychology (MS Ed)
secondary education (MS Ed)
special education (MS Ed)
teaching English to speakers of other languages (MS Ed)

School of Health Professions
Programs in:
adapted physical education (MS)
athletic training and sports sciences (MS)
community mental health (MS)
exercise physiology (MS)
family health (MS)
health management (MS)
health professions (MS, DPT, TDPT)
health sciences (MS)
physical therapy (DPT, TDPT)

School of Nursing
Programs in:
adult nurse practitioner (MS, Certificate)
nurse executive (MS)
nursing (MS, Certificate)

■ LONG ISLAND UNIVERSITY, C.W. POST CAMPUS

Brookville, NY 11548-1300
http://www.liu.edu/

Independent, coed, comprehensive institution. *Computer facilities:* 357 computers available on campus for general student use. A campuswide network can be accessed from student residence rooms and from off campus. Online class registration is available. *General application contact:* Director of Graduate and International Admissions, 516-299-2900 Ext. 3952.

College of Information and Computer Science
Dr. Mary Westermann-Cicio, Acting Dean
Programs in:
information and computer science (MS, PhD, Certificate)
information systems (MS)
information technology education (MS)
management engineering (MS)

Palmer School of Library and Information Science
Programs in:
- archives and records management (Certificate)
- information studies (PhD)
- library and information science (MS)
- library media specialist (MS)
- public library management (Certificate)

College of Liberal Arts and Sciences
Dr. Katherine Hill-Miller, Dean
Programs in:
- applied mathematics (MS)
- biology (MS)
- biology education (MS)
- clinical psychology (Psy D)
- earth science (MS)
- earth science education (MS)
- English (MA)
- English for adolescence education (MS)
- environmental studies (MS)
- history (MA)
- interdisciplinary studies (MA, MS)
- liberal arts and sciences (MA, MS, Psy D)
- mathematics education (MS)
- mathematics for secondary school teachers (MS)
- political science/international studies (MA)
- psychology (MA)
- Spanish (MA)
- Spanish education (MS)

College of Management
Francis Bonsignore, Dean
Programs in:
- criminal justice (MS)
- fraud examination (MS)
- gerontology (Certificate)
- health care administration (MPA)
- health care administration/gerontology (MPA)
- management (MBA, MPA, MS, MSW, Certificate)
- nonprofit management (MPA, Certificate)
- public administration (MPA)
- security administration (MS)
- social work (MSW)

School of Business
Programs in:
- accounting and taxation (Certificate)
- business administration (Certificate)
- finance (MBA, Certificate)
- general business administration (MBA)
- international business (MBA, Certificate)
- management (MBA, Certificate)
- management information systems (MBA, Certificate)
- marketing (MBA, Certificate)

School of Professional Accountancy
Dr. Charles Barragato, Director
Programs in:
- accounting (MS)
- taxation (MS)

School of Education
Dr. Robert Manheimer, Dean
Programs in:
- adolescence education (MS)
- adolescence education: biology (MS)
- adolescence education: earth science (MS)
- adolescence education: English (MS)
- adolescence education: mathematics (MS)
- adolescence education: social studies (MS)
- adolescence education: Spanish (MS)
- art education (MS)
- bilingual education (MS)
- childhood education (MS)
- childhood education/literacy (MS)
- childhood education/special education (MS)
- computers in education (MS)
- early childhood education (MS)
- education (MA, MS, MS Ed, Ed D, AC)
- educational leadership (Ed D)
- literacy (MS Ed)
- mental health counseling (MS)
- middle childhood education (MS)
- music education (MS)
- school administration and supervision (MS Ed)
- school building leader (AC)
- school counseling (MS)
- school district business leader (AC)
- school district leader (AC)
- special education (MS Ed)
- speech language pathology (MA)
- teaching and learning (Ed D)
- teaching English to speakers of other languages (MS)

School of Health Professions and Nursing
Dr. Theodora T. Grauer, Dean
Programs in:
- cardiovascular perfusion (MS)
- clinical laboratory management (MS)
- clinical nurse specialist (MS)
- dietetic internship (Certificate)
- family nurse practitioner (MS, Certificate)
- health professions and nursing (MS, Certificate)
- medical biology (MS)
- nutrition (MS)

School of Visual and Performing Arts
Rhoda Grauer, Acting Dean
Programs in:
- art (MA)
- art education (MS)
- clinical art therapy (MA)
- fine art and design (MFA)
- interactive multimedia (MA)
- music (MA)
- music education (MS)
- theatre (MA)
- visual and performing arts (MA, MFA, MS)

■ MANHATTAN COLLEGE
Riverdale, NY 10471
http://www.manhattan.edu/

Independent-religious, coed, comprehensive institution. *Computer facilities:* 375 computers available on campus for general student use. A campuswide network can be accessed from student residence rooms and from off campus. Online class registration is available. *General application contact:* Provost, 718-862-7303.

Graduate Division

School of Education
Programs in:
- 5 year dual childhood/special education (MS Ed)
- counseling (MA, Diploma)
- dual childhood/special education (MS Ed)
- mental health counseling (MA)
- school building leadership (MS Ed, Diploma)
- school counseling (MA)
- special education (MS Ed)

School of Engineering
Programs in:
- chemical engineering (MS)
- civil engineering (MS)
- computer engineering (MS)
- electrical engineering (MS)
- environmental engineering (ME, MS)
- mechanical engineering (MS)

■ MANHATTANVILLE COLLEGE
Purchase, NY 10577-2132
http://www.manhattanville.edu/

Independent, coed, comprehensive institution. *Computer facilities:* Computer purchase and lease plans are available. 240 computers available on campus for general student use. A campuswide network can be accessed from student residence rooms and from off campus. Online class registration is available. *Graduate expenses:* Tuition: full-time $13,680; part-time $760 per credit. Required fees: $45 per semester. *General application contact:* Graduate Admissions, 914-323-5464.

Graduate Programs
Dr. Edgar Schick, Interim Provost
Programs in:
- finance (MS)
- integrated marketing communications (MS)
- international management (MS)
- leadership and strategic management (MS)
- liberal studies (MA)
- organizational management and human resource development (MS)
- sport business management (MS)
- writing (MA)

School of Education
Dr. Shelley Wepner, Dean

Manhattanville College (continued)

Programs in:
- biology (MAT)
- biology and special education (MPS)
- chemistry (MAT)
- chemistry and special education (MPS)
- child and early childhood education (MAT, MPS)
- childhood and early childhood education (MAT)
- childhood and special education (MPS)
- childhood education (MAT)
- early childhood education (birth-grade 2) (MAT)
- education (M Ed, MAT, MPS)
- educational leadership (MPS)
- English (MAT)
- English and special education (MPS)
- English as a second language (MAT)
- literacy (MPS)
- literacy (birth-grade 6) (MPS)
- literacy (birth-grade 6)
- and special education (grades 1-6) (MPS)
- literacy and special education (MPS)
- math (MAT)
- math and special education (MPS)
- music education (MAT)
- physical education and sport pedagogy (MAT)
- second language (MAT)
- social studies (MAT)
- social studies and special education (MPS)
- special education (MPS)
- special education (birth-grade 2) (MPS)
- special education (birth-grade 6) (MPS)
- special education childhood (MPS)
- teaching English as a second language (MPS)
- visual arts education (MAT)

■ MARIST COLLEGE

Poughkeepsie, NY 12601-1387

http://www.marist.edu/

Independent, coed, comprehensive institution. *Computer facilities:* Computer purchase and lease plans are available. 761 computers available on campus for general student use. A campuswide network can be accessed from student residence rooms and from off campus. Online class registration, admissions application, billing, transcript, degree audit, online financial aid summary are available. *General application contact:* Director of Admissions, 845-575-3800.

Graduate Programs

School of Communication and the Arts

Program in:
- organizational communication and leadership (MA)

School of Computer Science and Mathematics

Programs in:
- information systems (MS, Adv C)
- software development (MS)
- technology management (MS)

School of Management

Programs in:
- business administration (MBA, Adv C)
- executive leadership (Adv C)
- public administration (MPA)
- technology management (MS)

School of Social and Behavioral Sciences

Programs in:
- counseling psychology (MA)
- education (M Ed)
- education psychology (MA)
- school psychology (MA, Adv C)

■ MEDAILLE COLLEGE

Buffalo, NY 14214-2695

http://www.medaille.edu/

Independent, coed, comprehensive institution. *Graduate faculty:* 41 full-time (25 women), 101 part-time/adjunct (58 women). *Computer facilities:* 120 computers available on campus for general student use. A campuswide network can be accessed from student residence rooms and from off campus. Online class registration is available. *Graduate expenses:* Tuition: full-time $15,480; part-time $645 per credit hour. *General application contact:* Jacqueline Matheny, Executive Director of Marketing and Enrollment, 716-932-2541.

Program in Business Administration—Amherst

Jennifer Bavifard, Associate Dean for Special Programs

Programs in:
- business administration (MBA)
- organizational leadership (MA)

Program in Business Administration—Rochester

Jennifer Bavifard, Branch Campus Director

Programs in:
- business administration (MBA)
- organizational leadership (MA)

Program in Education

Dr. Robert DiSibio, Director of Graduate Programs

Programs in:
- curriculum and instruction (MS Ed)
- education preparation (MS Ed)
- literacy (MS Ed)
- special education (MS)

Programs in Psychology

Dr. Judith Horowitz, Dean of Adult and Graduate Studies

Programs in:
- mental health counseling (MA)
- psychology (MA)

■ MERCY COLLEGE

Dobbs Ferry, NY 10522-1189

http://www.mercy.edu/

Independent, coed, comprehensive institution. CGS member. *Graduate faculty:* 82 full-time (45 women), 211 part-time/adjunct (113 women). *Computer facilities:* 680 computers available on campus for general student use. A campuswide network can be accessed from student residence rooms and from off campus. Online class registration is available. *Graduate expenses:* Tuition: full-time $12,330; part-time $685 per credit. Required fees: $240; $120 per semester. Tuition and fees vary according to program. *General application contact:* Allison Rickards, Senior Associate Director of Recruitment, 877-MERCY-GO.

School of Business

Dr. Geofrey Mills, Dean

Programs in:
- business administration (MBA)
- human resource management (MS)
- organizational leadership (MS)
- public accounting (MS)

School of Education

Dr. Andrew Peiser, Interim Dean

Programs in:
- adolescence education, grades 7-12 (MS)
- applied behavior analysis (Post Master's Certificate)
- bilingual education (MS)
- childhood education, grade 1-6 (MS)
- early childhood education, birth-grade 2 (MS)
- early childhood education/students with disabilities (MS)
- individualized certification plan for teachers (ICPT) (MS)
- middle childhood education, grades 5-9 (MS)
- school building leadership (MS, Advanced Certificate)
- teaching English to speakers of other languages (TESOL) (MS)
- teaching literacy (MS)
- urban education (MS)

School of Health and Natural Sciences

Dr. Pat Chute, Dean

Programs in:
- communication disorders (MS)
- nursing (MS)
- nursing administration (MS)
- nursing education (MS, Certificate)
- occupational therapy (MS)
- physical therapy (MS, DPT)
- physician assistant (MS)
- physician assistant studies (MS)

School of Liberal Arts

Sean Dugan, Interim Dean for the School of Liberal Arts

Programs in:
- English literature (MA)
- information assurance and security (MS)
- Internet business systems (MS)

School of Social and Behavioral Sciences

Hind Rassam Culhane, Interim Dean

Programs in:
- alcohol and substance abuse counseling (Certificate)
- counseling (MS, Certificate)
- health services management (MPA, MS)
- marriage and family therapy (MS)
- mental health counseling (MS)
- psychology (MS)
- retirement counseling (Certificate)
- school counseling (Certificate)
- school counseling and bilingual extension (Certificate)
- school psychology (MS)

■ METROPOLITAN COLLEGE OF NEW YORK

New York, NY 10013

http://www.metropolitan.edu/

Independent, coed, primarily women, comprehensive institution. *Computer facilities:* 150 computers available on campus for general student use. A campuswide network can be accessed from off campus. *General application contact:* Graduate Admissions Coordinator, 212-343-1234 Ext. 2709.

Program in Childhood Education

Program in:
- childhood education (MS)

Program in General Management

Program in:
- general management (MBA)

Program in Media Management

Program in:
- media management (MBA)

Program in Public Administration

Program in:
- public administration (MPA)

■ MOLLOY COLLEGE

Rockville Centre, NY 11571-5002

http://www.molloy.edu/

Independent, coed, comprehensive institution. *Graduate faculty:* 18 full-time (all women), 4 part-time/adjunct (3 women). *Computer facilities:* 391 computers available on campus for general student use. A campuswide network can be accessed from off campus. Online class registration is available. *Graduate expenses:* Tuition: full-time $12,870; part-time $715 per credit. Required fees: $620; $620 per contact hour. One-time fee: $60 full-time. *General application contact:* Dr. Mary O'Shaughnessy, Interim Associate Dean/Director, Graduate Program, 516-678-5000 Ext. 6838.

Department of Nursing

Programs in:
- adult nurse practitioner (Advanced Certificate)
- clinical nurse specialist: adult health (Advanced Certificate)
- family nurse practitioner (Advanced Certificate)
- nurse practitioner psychiatry (Advanced Certificate)
- nursing (MS)
- nursing administration (Advanced Certificate)
- nursing administration with informatics (Advanced Certificate)
- nursing education (Advanced Certificate)
- nursing informatics (Advanced Certificate)
- pediatric nurse practitioner (Advanced Certificate)

Graduate Business Programs

Programs in:
- accounting (MBA)
- accounting and management (MBA)
- management (MBA)
- personal financial planning and accounting (MBA)
- personal financial planning and management (MBA)

Graduate Social Work Program

Program in:
- social work (MSW)

Music Therapy Graduate Program

Program in:
- music therapy (MS)

Program in Criminal Justice

Program in:
- criminal justice (MS)

■ MOUNT SAINT MARY COLLEGE

Newburgh, NY 12550-3494

http://www.msmc.edu/

Independent, coed, comprehensive institution. *Graduate faculty:* 24 full-time (15 women), 22 part-time/adjunct (15 women). *Computer facilities:* Computer purchase and lease plans are available. 570 computers available on campus for general student use. A campuswide network can be accessed from student residence rooms and from off campus. Online class registration, intranet are available. *Graduate expenses:* Tuition: full-time $13,356; part-time $742 per credit. Required fees: $50 per semester. *General application contact:* Graduate Coordinator, 845-561-0800.

Division of Business

Dr. Moira Tolan, Coordinator

Programs in:
- business (MBA)
- financial planning (MBA)

Division of Education

Dr. Theresa Lewis, Coordinator

Programs in:
- adolescence and special education (MS Ed)
- adolescence education (MS Ed)
- childhood and special education (MS Ed)
- childhood education (MS Ed)
- literacy and special education (MS Ed)
- literacy/childhood (MS Ed)
- middle school (5-6) (MS Ed)
- middle school (7-9) (MS Ed)
- special education (1-6) (MS Ed)
- special education (7-12) (MS Ed)

Division of Nursing

Dr. Karen Baldwin, Coordinator

Programs in:
- adult nurse practitioner (MS)
- clinical nurse specialist-adult health (MS)

■ NAZARETH COLLEGE OF ROCHESTER

Rochester, NY 14618-3790

http://www.naz.edu/

Independent, coed, comprehensive institution. *Computer facilities:* 240 computers available on campus for general student use. A campuswide network can be accessed from student residence rooms and from off campus. Online class registration is available. *General application contact:* Director, Graduate Admissions, 585-389-2050.

Graduate Studies

Programs in:
- art education (MS Ed)
- art therapy (MS)
- business education (MS Ed)
- communication sciences and disorders (MS)
- educational technology/computer education (MS Ed)
- gerontological nurse practitioner (MS)
- human resource management (MS)
- inclusive education-adolescence level (MS Ed)
- inclusive education-childhood level (MS Ed)
- inclusive education-early childhood level (MS Ed)
- liberal studies (MA)
- literacy education (MS Ed)
- management (MS)
- music education (MS Ed)
- music therapy (MS)
- physical therapy (MS, DPT)
- social work (MSW)
- teaching English to speakers of other languages (MS Ed)

■ THE NEW SCHOOL: A UNIVERSITY

New York, NY 10011

http://www.newschool.edu/

Independent, coed, university. *Graduate faculty:* 177 full-time (72 women), 304 part-time/adjunct (121 women). *Graduate*

The New School: A University (continued)
expenses: Tuition: full-time $27,144; part-time $1508 per credit. Required fees: $355 per semester. *General application contact:* Christy Kalan, Assistant Vice President for Enrollment Operations, 212-229-5155 Ext. 3580.

Mannes College The New School for Music
Joel Lester, Dean
Program in:
music performance (MM, PD)

Milano The New School for Management and Urban Policy
Dr. Lisa Servon, Dean
Programs in:
health services management and policy (MS)
human resources management (MS, Adv C)
management and urban policy (MS, PhD, Adv C)
medical group practice management (Adv C)
nonprofit management (MS)
organizational change management (MS)
public and urban policy (PhD)
urban policy analysis and management (MS)

The New School for Drama
Robert LuPone, Director
Programs in:
acting (MFA)
directing (MFA)
playwriting (MFA)

The New School for General Studies
Dr. Linda Dunne, Dean
Programs in:
communication theory (MA)
creative writing (MFA)
general studies (MA, MFA, MS)
global management, trade, and finance (MA, MS)
international development (MA, MS)
international media and communication (MA, MS)
international politics and diplomacy (MA, MS)
media studies (MA)
service, civic, and non-profit management (MS)
teaching English to speakers of other languages (MA)

The New School for Social Research
Dr. Michael Schober, Dean
Programs in:
anthropology (MA, DS Sc, PhD)
clinical psychology (PhD)
economics (MA, DS Sc, PhD)
general psychology (MA, PhD)
global finance (MS)
historical studies (MA, PhD)
liberal studies (MA)
philosophy (MA, DS Sc, PhD)
political science (MA, DS Sc, PhD)
social research (MA, MS, DS Sc, PhD)
sociology (MA, DS Sc, PhD)

Parsons The New School for Design
Programs in:
architecture (M Arch)
design (M Arch, MA, MFA)
design and technology (MFA)
fine arts (MFA)
history of decorative arts (MA)
interior design (MFA)
lighting design (MFA)
photography (MFA)

■ NEW YORK INSTITUTE OF TECHNOLOGY
Old Westbury, NY 11568-8000
http://www.nyit.edu/

Independent, coed, university. CGS member. *Computer facilities:* 815 computers available on campus for general student use. A campuswide network can be accessed from student residence rooms and from off campus. E-mail available. *Graduate expenses:* Tuition: part-time $783 per credit. *General application contact:* Dr. Jacquelyn Nealon, Vice President for Enrollment Services, 516-686-7925.

Graduate Division
Dr. Richard Pizer, Provost and Vice President for Academic Affairs

School of Architecture and Design
Judith DiMaio, Dean
Program in:
urban and regional design (M Arch)

School of Arts and Sciences
Dr. Roger Yu, Dean
Programs in:
arts and sciences (MA)
communication arts (MA)

School of Education
Dr. Michael Uttendorfer, Dean
Programs in:
distance learning (Advanced Certificate)
district leadership and technology (Professional Diploma)
education (MS, Advanced Certificate, Professional Diploma)
elementary education (MS)
instructional technology (MS)
mental health counseling and school counseling (MS)
multimedia (Advanced Certificate)
school counseling (MS)
school leadership and technology (Professional Diploma)

School of Engineering and Computing Sciences
Dr. Nada Anid, Dean
Programs in:
computer science (MS)
electrical engineering and computer engineering (MS)
energy management (MS)
energy technology (Advanced Certificate)
engineering and computing sciences (MS, Advanced Certificate)
environmental management (Advanced Certificate)
environmental technology (MS)
facilities management (Advanced Certificate)

School of Health Professions, Behavioral, and Life Sciences
Dr. Chukuka Enwemeka, Dean
Programs in:
clinical nutrition (MS)
health professions, behavioral, and life sciences (MPS, MS, DPT)
human relations (MPS)
occupational therapy (MS)
physical therapy (MS, DPT)
physician assistant (MS)

School of Management
Dr. Jess Boronico, Dean
Programs in:
accounting (Advanced Certificate)
business administration (MBA)
finance (Advanced Certificate)
human resources administration (Advanced Certificate)
human resources management and labor relations (MS)
international business (Advanced Certificate)
labor relations (Advanced Certificate)
management (MBA, MS, Advanced Certificate)
management of information systems (Advanced Certificate)
marketing (Advanced Certificate)

New York College of Osteopathic Medicine
Dr. Thomas Scandalis, Dean
Program in:
osteopathic medicine (DO)

■ NEW YORK UNIVERSITY
New York, NY 10012-1019
http://www.nyu.edu/

Independent, coed, university. CGS member. *Graduate faculty:* 3,695 full-time (1,442 women), 3,540 part-time/adjunct (1,615 women). *Computer facilities:* 4,500 computers available on campus for general student use. A campuswide network can be accessed from student residence rooms and from off campus. Online class registration is available. *Graduate expenses:* Tuition: full-time $28,944; part-time $1206 per credit. Required fees: $2094. Part-time tuition and fees vary according to course load and program. *General application contact:* New York University Information, 212-998-1212.

College of Dentistry
Programs in:
- clinical research (MS)
- dentistry (DDS, MS, PhD, Advanced Certificate)
- endodontics (Advanced Certificate)
- oral and maxillofacial surgery (Advanced Certificate)
- orthodontics (Advanced Certificate)
- pediatric dentistry (Advanced Certificate)
- periodontics (Advanced Certificate)
- prosthodontics (Advanced Certificate)
- prosthodontics (implantology) (Advanced Certificate)

College of Nursing
Dr. Terry Fulmer, Dean
Programs in:
- advanced practice nursing: adult acute care (MS, Advanced Certificate)
- advanced practice nursing: adult primary care (MS, Advanced Certificate)
- advanced practice nursing: adult primary care/geriatrics (MS)
- advanced practice nursing: children with special needs (Advanced Certificate)
- advanced practice nursing: geriatrics (MS, Advanced Certificate)
- advanced practice nursing: holistic nursing (MS, Advanced Certificate)
- advanced practice nursing: home health nursing (Advanced Certificate)
- advanced practice nursing: mental health (MS)
- advanced practice nursing: mental health nursing (Advanced Certificate)
- advanced practice nursing: pediatrics (MS, Advanced Certificate)
- advanced practice nursing: pediatrics/children with special needs (MS)
- midwifery (MS, Advanced Certificate)
- nursing (MS, PhD, Advanced Certificate)
- nursing administration (MS, Advanced Certificate)
- nursing education (MS, Advanced Certificate)
- nursing informatics (MS, Advanced Certificate)
- palliative care (MS, Advanced Certificate)
- research and theory development in nursing science (PhD)

Gallatin School of Individualized Study
Dr. Susanne L. Wofford, Dean
Program in:
- individualized study (MA)

Graduate School of Arts and Science
Catharine R. Stimpson, Dean
Programs in:
- African diaspora (PhD)
- African history (PhD)
- Africana studies (MA)
- American studies (MA, PhD)
- anthropology (MA, PhD)
- anthropology and French studies (PhD)
- applied economic analysis (Advanced Certificate)
- archival management and historical editing (Advanced Certificate)
- arts and science (MA, MFA, MS, PhD, Advanced Certificate)
- Atlantic history (PhD)
- bioethics (MA)
- biology (PhD)
- biomaterials science (MS)
- biomedical journalism (MS)
- cancer and molecular biology (PhD)
- chemistry (MS, PhD)
- classics (MA, PhD)
- cognition and perception (PhD)
- community psychology (PhD)
- comparative literature (MA, PhD)
- composition and theory (MA, PhD)
- computational biology (PhD)
- computers in biological research (MS)
- creative writing (MA, MFA)
- cultural reporting and criticism (MA)
- culture and mediadevelopmental genetics (PhD)
- early music performance (Advanced Certificate)
- East Asian studies (MA, PhD)
- economics (MA, PhD)
- English and American literature (MA, PhD)
- environmental health sciences (MS, PhD)
- ethnomusicology (MA, PhD)
- French studies and sociology (PhD)
- French studies/history (PhD)
- French studies/journalism (MA)
- general biology (MS)
- general psychology (MA)
- German studies and critical thought (MA, PhD)
- Hebrew and Judaic studies (MA, PhD)
- Hebrew and Judaic studies/history (PhD)
- Hebrew and Judaic studies/museum studies (MA)
- history (MA, PhD)
- humanities and social thought (MA)
- immunology and microbiology (PhD)
- industrial/organizational psychology (MA)
- Irish and Irish American studies (MA)
- Italian (MA, PhD)
- Italian studies (MA)
- journalism (MA)
- Latin American and Caribbean studies/journalism (MA)
- linguistics (MA, PhD)
- Middle Eastern history (MA)
- Middle Eastern studies/history (PhD)
- molecular genetics (PhD)
- museum studies (MA, Advanced Certificate)
- Near Eastern studies/journalism (MA)
- neurobiology (PhD)
- oral biology (MS)
- philosophy (MA, PhD)
- physics (MS, PhD)
- plant biology (PhD)
- poetics and theory (Advanced Certificate)
- political campaign management (MA)
- politics (MA, PhD)
- Portuguese (MA, PhD)
- psychotherapy and psychoanalysis (Advanced Certificate)
- public history (Advanced Certificate)
- recombinant DNA technology (MS)
- religion (Advanced Certificate)
- religious studies (MA)
- Russian literature (MA)
- science and environmental reporting (Advanced Certificate)
- Slavic literature (MA)
- social theory (Advanced Certificate)
- social/personality psychology (PhD)
- sociology (MA, PhD)
- Spanish (PhD)
- Spanish and Latin American literatures and cultures (MA)
- Spanish language and translation (MA)
- trauma and violence transdisciplinary studies (MA, Advanced Certificate)
- world history (MA)

Center for European Studies
Katherine Fleming, Director
Program in:
- European studies (MA)

Center for French Civilization and Culture
Judith Miller, Chair
Programs in:
- French (PhD)
- French civilization (PhD)
- French civilization and culture (MA, PhD, Advanced Certificate)
- French language and civilization (MA)
- French literature (MA)
- French studies (MA, PhD, Advanced Certificate)
- French studies and anthropology (PhD)
- French studies and history (PhD)
- French studies and journalism (MA)
- French studies and sociology (PhD)
- Romance languages and literatures (MA)

Center for Latin American and Caribbean Studies
Tom Abercrombie, Director
Program in:
- Latin American and Caribbean studies (MA)

Center for Neural Science
J. Anthony Movshon, Chair
Program in:
- neural science (PhD)

Courant Institute of Mathematical Sciences
Fedor Bogomolov, Director of Graduate Studies
Programs in:
- atmosphere ocean science and mathematics (PhD)
- computer science (MS, PhD)
- information systems (MS)
- mathematics (MS, PhD)

New York University (continued)
- mathematics and statistics/operations research (MS)
- mathematics in finance (MS)
- scientific computing (MS)

Hagop Kevorkian Center for Near Eastern Studies
Timothy Mitchell, Chair
Programs in:
- Middle Eastern and Islamic studies (MA, PhD)
- Middle Eastern and Islamic studies/ history (PhD)
- Near Eastern studies (MA, PhD)
- Near Eastern studies (museum studies) (MA)
- Near Eastern studies/journalism (MA)

Institute for Law and Society
Lewis Kornhauser, Director
Program in:
- law and society (MA, PhD)

Institute of Fine Arts
Mariet Westermann, Chair
Programs in:
- architectural studies (PhD)
- art history and archaeology (MA, PhD)
- classical art and archaeology (PhD)
- conservation trainingcuratorial studies (PhD)
- East and South Asian art (PhD)
- Near Eastern art and archaeology (PhD)

Leonard N. Stern School of Business
Programs in:
- accounting (MBA, PhD)
- economics (MBA, PhD)
- entertainment, media and technology (MBA)
- finance (MBA, PhD)
- general marketing (MBA)
- information systems (MBA, PhD)
- information, operations and management sciences (MBA, PhD)
- management and organizations (MBA, PhD, APC)
- management organizations (MBA)
- marketing (MBA, PhD)
- operations management (MBA, PhD)
- organization theory (PhD)
- organizational behavior (PhD)
- product management (MBA)
- statistics (MBA, PhD)
- strategy (PhD)

NYU in Madrid
Programs in:
- creative writing in Spanish (MFA)
- Spanish (PhD)
- Spanish and Latin American literatures and cultures (MA)
- Spanish language and translation (MA)

NYU in Paris
Program in:
- teaching French as a foreign language (MA)

Robert F. Wagner Graduate School of Public Service
Prof. Ellen Schall, Dean
Programs in:
- health finance (MPA)
- health policy analysis (MPA)
- health policy and management (Advanced Certificate)
- health services management (MPA)
- housing (Advanced Certificate)
- international health (MPA)
- international public service organizations management (MS)
- management (MS)
- public administration (PhD)
- public and nonprofit management and policy (MPA, Advanced Certificate)
- public economics (Advanced Certificate)
- public service (MPA, MS, MUP, PhD, Advanced Certificate)
- quantitative analysis and computer applications for policy and planning (Advanced Certificate)
- urban planning (MUP)

School of Continuing and Professional Studies
Robert Lapiner, Dean

Center for Advanced Digital Applications
Michael Hosenfeld, Director
Program in:
- digital imaging and design (MS)

Center for Global Affairs
Dr. Vera Jelinek, Assistant Dean and Director
Program in:
- global affairs (MS)

Division for Media Industry Studies and Design
Bonnie Blake, Dean
Programs in:
- graphic communications management and technology (MA)
- publishing (MS)

Division of Programs in Business
Dr. Anthony Davidson, Assistant Dean
Programs in:
- benefits and compensation (Advanced Certificate)
- brand management (MS)
- corporate and organizational communications (MS)
- database technologies (MS)
- digital marketing (MS)
- enterprise and risk management (Advanced Certificate)
- enterprise risk management (MS)
- human resource development (MS)
- human resource management (MS, Advanced Certificate)
- information technologies (Advanced Certificate)
- interactive marketing (MS)
- leadership and human capital management (MS, Advanced Certificate)
- management and systems (MS, Advanced Certificate)
- marketing analytics (MS)
- organizational and executive coaching (Advanced Certificate)
- organizational effectiveness (MS)
- public relations and corporate communications (MS)
- public relations management (MS)
- strategy and leadership (MS, Advanced Certificate)
- systems management (MS)

The George Heyman Jr. Center for Philanthropy and Fundraising
Lewis Brindle, Director
Program in:
- fundraising (MS)

The Preston Robert Tisch Center for Hospitality, Tourism, and Sports Management
Dr. Lalia Rach, Associate Dean
Programs in:
- customer relationship management (MS)
- hospitality industry studies (MS, Advanced Certificate)
- sports business (MS, Advanced Certificate)
- tourism and travel management (MS, Advanced Certificate)
- tourism development (MS)
- tourism planning and analysis (MS)

Schack Institute of Real Estate
D. Kenneth Patton, Divisional Dean
Programs in:
- construction management (MS, Advanced Certificate)
- construction management for the development process (MS)
- development (MS)
- finance and investment (MS)
- project management (MS)
- real estate (MS, Advanced Certificate)
- strategic real estate management (MS)

School of Law
Richard L. Revesz, Dean
Programs in:
- law (JD, LL M, JSD)
- law and business (Advanced Certificate)
- taxation (Advanced Certificate)

School of Medicine
Programs in:
- biomedical sciences (PhD)
- clinical investigation (MS)
- medicine (MD, MS, PhD)

Sackler Institute of Graduate Biomedical Sciences
Programs in:
- cellular and molecular biology (PhD)
- computational biology (PhD)
- developmental genetics (PhD)
- immunology (PhD)
- medical and molecular parasitology (PhD)
- microbiology (PhD)
- molecular oncology (PhD)

molecular oncology and immunology (PhD)
molecular pharmacology (PhD)
neuroscience and physiology (PhD)
pathobiology (PhD)
pharmacology (PhD)
structural biology (PhD)

Silver School of Social Work
Dr. Suzanne England, Dean
Program in:
social work (MSW, PhD)

Steinhardt School of Culture, Education, and Human Development
Dr. Mary Brabeck, Dean
Programs in:
advanced occupational therapy (MA)
art education (MA)
art therapy (MA)
bilingual education (MA, PhD, Advanced Certificate)
biology grades 7-12 (MA)
business education (MA, Advanced Certificate)
business education in higher education (MA)
chemistry grades 7-12 (MA)
childhood education (MA, PhD, Advanced Certificate)
childhood special education (MA)
clinical nutrition (MS)
communication sciences and disorders (MA, PhD)
community health (MPH)
community public health (MPH, PhD)
counseling and guidance (MA, Advanced Certificate)
counseling for mental health and wellness (MA)
counseling psychology (PhD)
counselor education (MA, PhD, Advanced Certificate)
culture, education, and human development (MA, MFA, MM, MPH, MS, DPS, DPT, Ed D, PhD, Advanced Certificate)
dance education (MA)
drama therapy (MA)
dual certification: educational theatre and social studies (MA)
dual degree: educational theatre and social studies (MA)
early childhood and childhood education (MA, PhD, Advanced Certificate)
early childhood education (MA, PhD, Advanced Certificate)
early childhood special education (MA)
education and Jewish studies (MA, PhD)
education and jewish studies (MA)
education and Jewish studies (PhD)
education and social policy (MA)
educational and developmental psychology (MA, PhD)
educational communication and technology (MA, PhD, Advanced Certificate)
educational leadership (MA, Ed D, PhD, Advanced Certificate)
educational psychology (MA)
educational theatre (MA, Ed D, PhD, Advanced Certificate)
educational theatre for colleges and communities (MA, PhD)
educational theatre with English 7-12 (MA)
English education (MA, PhD, Advanced Certificate)
environmental conservation education (MA)
food studies (MA)
food studies and food management (MA, PhD)
foods and nutrition (MS)
for-profit sector (MA)
foreign language education (MA, Advanced Certificate)
foreign language education/TESOL (MA)
higher and postsecondary education (Ed D, PhD)
higher education (MA, Ed D, PhD)
higher education administration (Ed D)
higher education/student personnel administration (MA)
history of education (MA, PhD)
instrumental performance (MM)
international community health (MPH)
international education (MA, PhD, Advanced Certificate)
literacy education (MA)
mathematics education (MA)
media, culture, and communication (MA, PhD)
multilingual/multicultural studies (MA, PhD, Advanced Certificate)
music business (MA)
music education (MA, Ed D, PhD, Advanced Certificate)
music performance and composition (MM, PhD)
music technology (MM)
music theory and composition (MM)
music therapy (MA)
not-for-profit sector (MA)
nutrition and dietetics (MS, PhD)
occupational therapy (MA, MS, DPS)
orthopedic physical therapy (Advanced Certificate)
performing arts administration (MA)
physical therapists pathokinesiology (MA)
physical therapy (DPT)
physics grades 7-12 (MA)
piano performance (MM)
politics and advocacy (MA)
practicing physical therapist (DPT)
psychological development (PhD)
psychology and social intervention (PhD)
public health (PhD)
public health nutrition (MPH)
research in occupational therapy (PhD)
research in physical therapy (PhD)
school building leader (MA)
school district leader (Advanced Certificate)
science education (MA)
social studies education (MA)
sociology of education (MA, PhD)
special education (MA)
studio art (MA, MFA)
teaching and learning (Ed D, PhD)
teaching educational theatre, all grades (MA)
teaching English to speakers of other languages (MA, PhD, Advanced Certificate)
visual arts administration (MA)
visual culture (MA, PhD)
visual culture and education (PhD)
visual culture: costume studies (MA)
visual culture: theory (MA, PhD)
vocal performance (MM)
workplace learning (Advanced Certificate)

Tisch School of the Arts
Dr. Mary Schmidt Campbell, Dean
Programs in:
acting (MFA)
arts (MA, MFA, MPS, PhD)
arts politics (MA)
cinema studies (MA, PhD)
dance (MFA)
design for stage and film (MFA)
dramatic writing (MFA)
interactive telecommunications (MPS)
moving image archiving and preservation (MA)
musical theatre writing (MFA)
performance studies (MA, PhD)

Kanbar Institute of Film and Television
John Tintori, Chair
Program in:
film and television (MFA)

Tisch School of the Arts Asia
Dean Pari Sara Shirazi, Vice Dean/ President
Programs in:
animation and digital arts (MFA)
dramatic writing (MFA)
film production (MFA)

■ NIAGARA UNIVERSITY
Niagara Falls, Niagara University, NY 14109
http://www.niagara.edu/

Independent-religious, coed, comprehensive institution. *Graduate faculty:* 36 full-time (16 women), 44 part-time/adjunct (20 women). *Computer facilities:* 175 computers available on campus for general student use. A campuswide network can be accessed from student residence rooms. Online class registration is available. *Graduate expenses:* Tuition: full-time $12,330; part-time $685 per contact hour. Required fees: $25 per semester. Tuition and fees vary according to program. *General application contact:* Carlos Tejada, Associate Dean for Graduate Recruitment, 716-286-8769.

Niagara University (continued)

Graduate Division of Arts and Sciences
Dr. Nancy McGlen, Dean
Programs in:
arts and sciences (MA, MS)
criminal justice administration (MS)
interdisciplinary studies (MA)

Graduate Division of Business Administration
Dr. Peggy Choong, Director
Programs in:
business (MBA)
commerce (MBA)

Graduate Division of Education
Dr. Debra A. Colley, Dean
Programs in:
administration/supervision (Certificate)
early childhood and childhood education (MS Ed)
educational administration/supervision (MS Ed)
educational leadership (MS Ed, Certificate)
educational leadership school district building (MS Ed)
foundations of teaching (MA, MS Ed)
literacy instruction (MS Ed)
mental health counseling (MS, Certificate)
middle and adolescence education (MS Ed)
school business administration (Certificate)
school business leadership (MS Ed)
school counseling (MS Ed, Certificate)
school district administration (Certificate)
school psychology (MS, Certificate)
special education (grades 1-12) (MS Ed)
teacher education (Certificate)

■ NYACK COLLEGE
Nyack, NY 10960-3698
http://www.nyack.edu

Independent-religious, coed, comprehensive institution. *Computer facilities:* 180 computers available on campus for general student use. A campuswide network can be accessed. Online class registration is available. *General application contact:* Director of Admissions, 800-33-NYACK.

Alliance Graduate School of Counseling
Program in:
counseling (MA)

School of Adult and Distance Education
Program in:
organizational leadership (MS)

School of Business
Programs in:
accounting (MBA)
business administration (MBA)

School of Education
Programs in:
childhood education (MS)
childhood special education (MS)
inclusive education (MS)

■ PACE UNIVERSITY
New York, NY 10038
http://www.pace.edu/

Independent, coed, university. CGS member. *Computer facilities:* Computer purchase and lease plans are available. 250 computers available on campus for general student use. A campuswide network can be accessed from student residence rooms and from off campus. Online class registration is available. *General application contact:* Donna Hoyt, Dean of Admissions, 212-346-1531.

Dyson College of Arts and Sciences
Dr. Nira Hermann, Dean
Programs in:
acting (MFA)
arts and sciences (MA, MFA, MPA, MS, MS Ed, Psy D)
counseling-substance abuse (MS)
directing (MFA)
environmental science (MS)
forensic science (MS)
government management (MPA)
health care administration (MPA)
loss and grief (MS)
mental health (MS)
nonprofit management (MPA)
physician assistant (MS)
playwriting (MFA)
psychology (MA, MS, MS Ed, Psy D)
publishing (MS)
school psychology (MS Ed)
school-clinical child psychology (MS Ed, Psy D)
school-clinical psychology (Psy D)
substance abuse (MS)

Lienhard School of Nursing
Dr. Harriet Feldman, Dean
Programs in:
family nurse practitioner (MS)
nursing (Advanced Certificate)
nursing education (MA)
nursing practice (DNP)

Lubin School of Business
Joseph R. Baczko, Dean
Programs in:
banking and finance (MBA)
business (MBA, MS, DPS, APC)
corporate economic planning (MBA)
corporate financial management (MBA)
financial economics (MBA)
financial management (MBA)
information systems (MBA)
international business (MBA)
international economics (MBA)
investment management (MBA, MS)
management (MBA)
management science (MBA)
managerial accounting (MBA)
marketing management (MBA)
marketing research (MBA)
operations management (MBA)
professional studies (DPS)
public accounting (MBA, MS)
taxation (MBA, MS)

School of Education
Dr. Harriet Feldman, Interim Dean
Programs in:
administration and supervision (MS Ed)
curriculum and instruction (MS)
education (MST)
school business management (Certificate)

School of Law
Programs in:
comparative legal studies (LL M)
environmental law (LL M, SJD)
law (JD)
real estate law (LL M)

Seidenberg School of Computer Science and Information Systems
Dr. Constance Knapp, Interim Dean
Programs in:
computer communications and networks (Certificate)
computer science (MS)
computing studies (DPS)
information systems (MS)
object-oriented programming (Certificate)
telecommunications (MS, Certificate)

■ POLYTECHNIC INSTITUTE OF NYU
Brooklyn, NY 11201-2990
http://www.poly.edu/

Independent, coed, university. CGS member. *Computer facilities:* Computer purchase and lease plans are available. 1,334 computers available on campus for general student use. A campuswide network can be accessed from student residence rooms and from off campus. Online class registration is available. *General application contact:* Associate Provost for Graduate School, 718-260-3482.

Department of Chemical and Biological Sciences
Programs in:
bioinformatics (MS)
biomedical engineering (MS, PhD)
biotechnology (MS)
biotechnology and entrepreneurship (MS)
chemistry (MS)
materials chemistry (PhD)
polymer science and engineering (MS)

Department of Civil Engineering
Programs in:
civil engineering (MS, PhD)
construction management (MS)

environmental engineering (MS)
environmental science (MS)
transportation management (MS)
transportation planning and engineering (MS, PhD)

Department of Computer and Information Science
Programs in:
computer science (MS, PhD)
cyber security (Graduate Certificate)
software engineering (Graduate Certificate)

Department of Electrical and Computer Engineering
Programs in:
computer engineering (MS, Certificate)
electrical engineering (MS, PhD)
electrophysics (MS)
image processing (Certificate)
systems engineering (MS)
telecommunication networks (MS)
wireless communications (Certificate)

Department of Finance and Risk Engineering
Programs in:
financial engineering (MS, Advanced Certificate)
financial technology management (Advanced Certificate)
risk management (Advanced Certificate)

Department of Humanities and Social Sciences
Programs in:
environment-behavior studies (MS)
history of science (MS)
integrated digital media (MS, Graduate Certificate)
technical communication (Graduate Certificate)
technical writing and specialized journalism (MS)

Department of Management
Programs in:
management (MBA, MS, PhD)
management of technology (MS)
organizational behavior (MS)
technology management (MBA, PhD)
telecommunications and information management (MS)

Department of Mathematics
Program in:
mathematics (MS, PhD)

Department of Mechanical and Aerospace Engineering
Programs in:
industrial engineering (MS)
manufacturing engineering (MS)
materials science (MS)
mechanical engineering (MS, PhD)

Department of Physics
Program in:
physics (MS, PhD)

Othmer-Jacobs Department of Chemical and Biological Engineering
Program in:
chemical engineering (MS, PhD)

■ POLYTECHNIC INSTITUTE OF NYU, WESTCHESTER GRADUATE CENTER
Hawthorne, NY 10532-1507
http://www.poly.edu/west/

Independent, coed, graduate-only institution. *Computer facilities:* 30 computers available on campus for general student use. A campuswide network can be accessed from off campus. *General application contact:* Graduate Admissions, 718-260-3482.

Graduate Programs
Programs in:
chemical engineering (MS)
chemistry (MS)
computer engineering (MS)
computer science (MS, PhD)
electrical engineering (MS, PhD)
information systems engineering (MS)
materials chemistry (PhD)
telecommunication networks (MS)

Department of Management
Programs in:
capital markets (MS)
computational finance (MS)
financial engineering (MS, AC)
financial technology (MS)
financial technology management (AC)
information management (AC)
management (MS)
management of technology (MS)

■ PURCHASE COLLEGE, STATE UNIVERSITY OF NEW YORK
Purchase, NY 10577-1400
http://www.purchase.edu/

State-supported, coed, comprehensive institution. *Graduate faculty:* 97. *Computer facilities:* 600 computers available on campus for general student use. A campuswide network can be accessed from student residence rooms and from off campus. Online class registration is available. *Graduate expenses:* Tuition, state resident: full-time $6900; part-time $288 per credit. Tuition, nonresident: full-time $10,920; part-time $455 per credit. Required fees: $1461; $0.85 per credit. One-time fee: $75 full-time. *General application contact:* Sabrina Johnston, Admissions Counselor, 914-251-6479.

Conservatory of Dance
Stacey-Jo Marine, Interim Associate Dean
Program in:
dance (MFA)

Conservatory of Music
Robert Thompson, Interim Dean
Programs in:
composition (MM)
instrumental performance (MM)
jazz studies (MM)
studio composition (MM)
voice and opera studies (MM)

Conservatory of Theatre Arts and Film
Gregory Taylor, Interim Dean
Programs in:
theatre design (MFA)
theatre technology (MFA)

Division of Humanities
Louise Yelin, Dean, Division of Humanities
Program in:
art history (MA)

School of Art and Design
Denise Mullen, Dean
Program in:
art and design (MFA)

■ QUEENS COLLEGE OF THE CITY UNIVERSITY OF NEW YORK
Flushing, NY 11367-1597
http://www.qc.cuny.edu/

State and locally supported, coed, comprehensive institution. CGS member. *Graduate faculty:* 628 full-time (267 women), 693 part-time/adjunct (344 women). *Computer facilities:* Computer purchase and lease plans are available. 2,300 computers available on campus for general student use. A campuswide network can be accessed from off campus. Online class registration is available. *General application contact:* Mario Caruso, Director of Graduate Admissions, 718-997-5200.

Division of Graduate Studies
Dr. Richard Bodnar, Acting Dean of Research and Graduate Services

Arts and Humanities Division
Dr. Tamara Evans, Dean
Programs in:
applied linguistics (MA)
art history (MA)
arts and humanities (MA, MFA, MS Ed)
creative writing (MA)
English language and literature (MA)
fine arts (MFA)
French (MA)
Italian (MA)
music (MA)
Spanish (MA)
speech pathology (MA)
teaching English to speakers of other languages (MS Ed)

Division of Education
Dr. Penny Hammrich, Dean
Programs in:
art (MS Ed)

Queens College of the City University of New York (continued)

bilingual education (MS Ed)
biology (MS Ed, AC)
chemistry (MS Ed, AC)
childhood education (MA)
counselor education (MS Ed)
early childhood education (MA)
earth sciences (MS Ed, AC)
education (MA, MS Ed, AC)
educational leadership (AC)
elementary education (MS Ed, AC)
English (MS Ed, AC)
French (MS Ed, AC)
Italian (MS Ed, AC)
literacy (MS Ed)
mathematics (MS Ed, AC)
music (MS Ed, AC)
physics (MS Ed, AC)
school psychology (MS Ed, AC)
social studies (MS Ed, AC)
Spanish (MS Ed, AC)
special education (MS Ed)

Mathematics and Natural Sciences Division
Dr. Thomas Strekas, Dean
Programs in:
biochemistry (MA)
biology (MA)
chemistry (MA)
clinical behavioral applications in mental health settings (MA)
computer science (MA)
earth and environmental sciences (MA)
home economics (MS Ed)
mathematics (MA)
mathematics and natural sciences (MA, MS Ed, PhD)
physical education and exercise sciences (MS Ed)
physics (MA, PhD)
psychology (MA)

Social Science Division
Dr. Elizabeth Hendrey, Dean
Programs in:
accounting (MS)
history (MA)
liberal studies (MALS)
library and information studies (MLS, AC)
social science (MA, MALS, MASS, MLS, MS, AC)
social sciences (MASS)
sociology (MA)
urban studies (MA)

■ RENSSELAER POLYTECHNIC INSTITUTE

Troy, NY 12180-3590
http://www.rpi.edu/

Independent, coed, university. CGS member. *Graduate faculty:* 401 full-time (87 women), 95 part-time/adjunct (19 women). *Computer facilities:* Computer purchase and lease plans are available. 1,081 computers available on campus for general student use. A campuswide network can be accessed from student residence rooms and from off campus. Online class registration, billing are available. *General application contact:* James G. Nondorf, Vice President for Enrollment, 518-276-6216.

Graduate School

Dr. Stanley M. Dunn, Vice Provost and Dean of Graduate Education

Lally School of Management and Technology
Dr. David A. Gautschi, Dean
Programs in:
business (MBA)
financial engineering and risk analytics (MS)
management (MS, PhD)
technology commercialization and entrepreneurship (MS)

School of Architecture
Programs in:
architectural acoustics (MS)
architectural sciences (PhD)
architectural sciences (built ecologies) (MS)
architecture (M Arch, MS, PhD)
lighting (MS)

School of Engineering
Programs in:
aerospace engineering (M Eng, MS, PhD)
biomedical engineering (MS, PhD)
ceramics and glass science (M Eng, MS, PhD)
chemical and biological engineering (M Eng, MS, PhD)
civil engineering (M Eng, MS, D Eng, PhD)
composites (M Eng, MS, PhD)
computer and systems engineering (M Eng, MS, D Eng, PhD)
decision sciences and engineering systems (PhD)
electric power engineering (M Eng, MS, D Eng, PhD)
electrical engineering (M Eng, MS, D Eng, PhD)
electronic materials (M Eng, MS, PhD)
engineering (M Eng, MS, D Eng, PhD)
engineering physics (MS, PhD)
environmental engineering (M Eng, MS, D Eng, PhD)
geotechnical engineering (M Eng, MS, D Eng, PhD)
industrial and management engineering (M Eng, MS)
mechanical engineering (M Eng, MS, PhD)
mechanics of composite materials and structures (M Eng, MS, D Eng, PhD)
metallurgy (M Eng, MS, PhD)
nuclear engineering (M Eng, MS, PhD)
nuclear engineering and science (PhD)
polymers (M Eng, MS, PhD)
structural engineering (M Eng, MS, D Eng, PhD)
transportation engineering (M Eng, MS, D Eng, PhD)

School of Humanities and Social Sciences
Programs in:
cognitive science (PhD)
communication and rhetoric (MS, PhD)
ecological economics (PhD)
ecological economics, values, and policy (MS)
economics (MS)
electronic arts (MFA, PhD)
human-computer interaction (MS)
humanities and social sciences (MFA, MS, PhD)
science and technology studies (MS, PhD)
technical communication (MS)

School of Science
Programs in:
analytical chemistry (MS, PhD)
applied mathematics (MS)
applied science (MS)
biochemistry (MS, PhD)
biophysics (MS, PhD)
cell biology (MS, PhD)
computer science (MS, PhD)
developmental biology (MS, PhD)
geochemistry (PhD)
geology (MS, PhD)
geophysics (PhD)
hydrogeology (MS, PhD)
information technology (MS)
inorganic chemistry (MS, PhD)
mathematics (MS, PhD)
microbiology (MS, PhD)
molecular biology (MS, PhD)
multidisciplinary science (MS, PhD)
natural sciences (MS)
organic chemistry (MS, PhD)
petrology (PhD)
physical chemistry (MS, PhD)
physics (MS, PhD)
polymer chemistry (MS, PhD)
science (MS, PhD)

■ ROBERTS WESLEYAN COLLEGE

Rochester, NY 14624-1997
http://www.roberts.edu/

Independent-religious, coed, comprehensive institution. *Computer facilities:* 250 computers available on campus for general student use. A campuswide network can be accessed from student residence rooms and from off campus. Online class registration is available. *General application contact:* Office of Admissions, 800-777-4RWC.

Division of Adult Professional Studies

Program in:
health administration (MS)

Division of Business

Programs in:
nonprofit leadership (Certificate)
strategic leadership (MS)
strategic marketing (MS)

Division of Nursing
Programs in:
nursing administration (MSN)
nursing education (MSN)

Division of Social Sciences
Programs in:
counseling in ministry (MA)
school counseling (MS)
school psychology (MS)

Division of Social Work
Programs in:
child and family practice (MSW)
congregational and community practice (MSW)
mental health practice (MSW)

Division of Teacher Education
Programs in:
adolescence education (M Ed)
childhood and special education (M Ed)
literacy education (M Ed)
urban education (M Ed)

■ ROCHESTER INSTITUTE OF TECHNOLOGY
Rochester, NY 14623-5603
http://www.rit.edu/

Independent, coed, comprehensive institution. CGS member. *Computer facilities:* Computer purchase and lease plans are available. 2,500 computers available on campus for general student use. A campuswide network can be accessed from student residence rooms and from off campus. Online class registration, student account information are available. *Graduate expenses:* Tuition: full-time $30,174; part-time $848 per credit hour. Required fees: $207. Tuition and fees vary according to course load. *General application contact:* Diane Ellison, Assistant Vice President, Graduate Enrollment Services, 585-475-2229.

Graduate Enrollment Services
Diane Ellison, Assistant Vice President, Graduate Enrollment Services

B. Thomas Golisano College of Computing and Information Sciences
Dr. Jorge Diaz-Herrera, Dean
Programs in:
computer science (MS)
computing and information sciences (MS, PhD, AC)
database administration (AC)
game design and development (MS)
human computer interaction (MS)
information assurance (AC)
information technology (MS, AC)
interactive multimedia development (AC)
network planning and design (AC)
networking and systems administration (MS, AC)
security and information assurance (MS)
software development and management (MS)
software engineering (MS)

College of Applied Science and Technology
Dr. H. Fred Walker, Dean
Programs in:
applied science and technology (MS, AC)
elements of health care leadership (AC)
environmental management (MS)
facility management (MS)
health information resources (AC)
health systems administration (MS, AC)
health systems administration executive leader (MS)
health systems-finance (AC)
hospitality-tourism management (MS)
human resources development (MS)
manufacturing and mechanical systems integration (MS)
multidisciplinary studies (MS, AC)
packaging science (MS)
professional studies (MS)
service leadership and innovation (MS)
technical information design (AC)
telecommunications engineering technology (MS)

College of Imaging Arts and Sciences
Frank Cost, Interim Dean
Programs in:
ceramics (MFA)
computer graphics design (MFA)
fine arts (MFA, MST)
fine arts studio (MST)
glass (MFA)
graphic design (MFA)
imaging arts (MFA)
imaging arts and sciences (MFA, MS, MST)
industrial design (MFA)
medical illustration (MFA)
metal crafts and jewelry (MFA)
painting (MFA)
print media (MS)
printmaking (MFA)
visual art (MST)
woodworking and furniture design (MFA)

College of Liberal Arts
Dr. Robert Ulin, Dean
Programs in:
communication and media technologies (MS)
criminal justice (MS)
liberal arts (MS, AC)
psychology (MS)
school psychology (MS, AC)
science, technology and public policy (MS)

College of Science
Dr. Sophia Maggelakis, Interim Dean
Programs in:
astrophysical sciences and technology (MS, PhD)
bioinformatics (MS)
chemistry (MS)
clinical chemistry (MS)
color science (MS, PhD)
environmental science (MS)
imaging science (MS, PhD)
industrial and applied mathematics (MS)
materials science and engineering (MS)
science (MS, PhD)

E. Philip Saunders College of Business
Dr. Ashok Rao, Dean
Programs in:
accounting (MBA)
business (Exec MBA, MBA, MS)
business administration (MBA)
executive business administration (Exec MBA)
finance (MS)
innovation management (MS)
management (MS)

Golisano Institute for Sustainability
Dr. Nabil Nasr, Assistant Provost and Director
Program in:
sustainability (PhD)

Kate Gleason College of Engineering
Dr. Harvey Palmer, Dean
Programs in:
applied statistics (MS)
computer engineering (MS)
electrical engineering (MSEE)
engineering (ME, MS, MSEE, PhD, AC)
engineering management (ME)
industrial engineering (ME, MS)
manufacturing engineering (ME, MS)
manufacturing leadership (MS)
mechanical engineering (ME, MS)
microelectronic engineering (MS)
microelectronic manufacturing engineering (ME)
microsystems engineering (PhD)
product development (MS)
statistical quality (AC)
systems engineering (ME)

National Technical Institute for the Deaf
Dr. Alan Hurwitz, Vice President and Dean
Programs in:
deaf studies (MS)
secondary education (MS)

■ ST. BONAVENTURE UNIVERSITY
St. Bonaventure, NY 14778-2284
http://www.sbu.edu/

Independent-religious, coed, comprehensive institution. CGS member. *Computer facilities:* 200 computers available on campus for general student use. A campuswide network can be accessed from student residence rooms and from off campus. Online class registration is available. *General application contact:* Information Contact, 716-375-2021.

St. Bonaventure University (continued)
School of Graduate Studies

School of Arts and Sciences
Programs in:
arts and sciences (MA)
English (MA)

School of Business
Programs in:
accounting and finance (MBA)
general business (MBA)
international business (MBA)
management and marketing (MBA)
professional leadership (MS)

School of Education
Programs in:
community mental health counselor (Adv C)
counseling education-school (MS Ed)
education (MS, MS Ed, Adv C)
educational leadership (MS Ed)
literacy (MS Ed)
school building leader (Adv C)
school counselor (Adv C)
school district leader (Adv C)
supervisor of curriculum and instruction (Adv C)

School of Franciscan Studies
Program in:
Franciscan studies (MA, Adv C)

■ ST. JOHN FISHER COLLEGE
Rochester, NY 14618-3597
http://www.sjfc.edu/

Independent-religious, coed, comprehensive institution. *Graduate faculty:* 75 full-time (38 women), 34 part-time/adjunct (19 women). *Computer facilities:* 525 computers available on campus for general student use. A campuswide network can be accessed from student residence rooms and from off campus. Online class registration is available. *Graduate expenses:* Tuition: part-time $655 per credit hour. Required fees: $25 per semester. *General application contact:* Holly Smith, Assistant Director of Graduate Admissions, 585-385-8161.

Ralph C. Wilson Jr. School of Education
Dr. Julius G. Adams, Acting Dean of the School of Education
Programs in:
adolescence English (MS Ed)
adolescence French (MS Ed)
adolescence social studies (MS Ed)
adolescence Spanish (MS Ed)
childhood education/special education (MS Ed)
education (MS, MS Ed, Ed D, Certificate)
educational leadership (MS Ed)
executive leadership (Ed D)
literacy birth to grade 6 (MS)
literacy grades 5 to 12 (MS)
organizational learning and human resource development (MS)
special education (MS, Certificate)

Ronald L. Bittner School of Business
Dr. Selim Ilter, Dean
Programs in:
business (MBA)
business administration and management (MBA)

School of Arts and Sciences
Dr. David Pate, Dean of the School of Arts and Sciences
Programs in:
arts and sciences (MS)
international studies (MS)
mathematics/science/technology education (MS)

Wegmans School of Nursing
Dr. Diane Cooney-Miner, Dean of the Wegmans School of Nursing
Programs in:
advanced practice nursing (MS)
clinical nurse specialist (Certificate)
family nurse practitioner (Certificate)
mental health counseling (MS)
nurse educator (Certificate)
nursing (MS, DNP, Certificate)
nursing practice (DNP)

Wegmans School of Pharmacy
Dr. Scott A. Swigart, Dean
Program in:
pharmacy (Pharm D)

■ ST. JOHN'S UNIVERSITY
Queens, NY 11439
http://www.stjohns.edu/

Independent-religious, coed, university. CGS member. *Graduate faculty:* 696 full-time (291 women), 824 part-time/adjunct (334 women). *Computer facilities:* Computer purchase and lease plans are available. 13,107 computers available on campus for general student use. A campuswide network can be accessed from student residence rooms and from off campus. Online class registration, various software packages are available. *Graduate expenses:* Tuition: full-time $20,760; part-time $865 per credit. Required fees: $300; $150 per semester. Tuition and fees vary according to program. *General application contact:* Kathleen Davis, Director of Graduate Admissions, 718-990-2790.

College of Pharmacy and Allied Health Professions
Dr. Robert Mangione, Dean
Programs in:
pharmaceutical sciences (MS, PhD)
pharmacy (Pharm D, MS, PhD)
pharmacy administration (MS)
pharmacy and allied health professions (Pharm D, MS, PhD)
toxicology (MS)

College of Professional Studies
Dr. Kathleen Voute MacDonald, Dean
Programs in:
criminal justice and legal studies (MPS)
sport management (MPS)

Institute for Biotechnology
Dr. Diana Bartelt, Director
Program in:
biological/pharmaceutical biotechnology (MS)

The Peter J. Tobin College of Business
Dr. Steven Papamarcos, Dean
Programs in:
accounting (MBA, MS, Adv C)
business (MBA, MS, Adv C)
computer information systems and decision sciences (MBA, Adv C)
finance (MBA, MS, Adv C)
international business (MBA, Adv C)
management (MBA, Adv C)
marketing (MBA, Adv C)
taxation (MBA, MS, Adv C)

School of Risk Management and Actuarial Science
Dr. James Barrese, Chair
Program in:
risk management and actuarial science (MBA, MS)

St. John's College of Liberal Arts and Sciences
Dr. Jeffrey Fagen, Dean
Programs in:
algebra (MA)
analysis (MA)
applied mathematics (MA)
biological sciences (MS, PhD)
chemistry (MS)
clinical psychology (PhD)
clinical psychology-child (PhD)
clinical psychology-general (PhD)
computer science (MA)
criminology and justice (MA)
English (MA, DA)
general experimental psychology (MA)
geometry-topology (MA)
government and politics (MA, Adv C)
government information specialisthistory (MA)
international law and diplomacy (Adv C)
languages and literatures (Adv C)
liberal arts and sciences (M Div, MA, MLS, MS, Au D, DA, PhD, Psy D, Adv C, Advanced Diploma, Certificate)
liberal studies (MA)
library and information science (MLS, Adv C)
logic and foundations (MA)
modern world history (DA)
pastoral ministry (Certificate)
philosophy (MA)
priestly studies (M Div)
probability and statistics (MA)
school psychology (MS, Psy D)
sociology (MA)
Spanish (MA)

speech, communication sciences and theatre (MA, Au D, Advanced Diploma)
theology (MA, Certificate)

Institute of Asian Studies
Dr. Bernadette Li, Chair
Programs in:
Asian and African cultural studies (Adv C)
Asian studies (Adv C)
Chinese studies (MA, Adv C)
East Asian culture studies (Adv C)
East Asian studies (MA)

The School of Education
Dr. Jerrold Ross, Dean
Programs in:
administration and supervision (Ed D, PD)
adolescent education (MS Ed)
bilingual school counseling (MS Ed, PD)
bilingual/multicultural education/ teaching English to speakers of other languages (MS Ed)
childhood education (MS Ed)
early childhood education (MS Ed)
education (MS Ed, Ed D, PhD, PD)
educational administration and supervision (Ed D, PD)
instructional leadership (Ed D, PD)
literacy (MS Ed, PhD)
mental health counseling (MS Ed)
school building leadership (MS Ed, PD)
school counseling (MS Ed, PD)
school district leadership (PD)
teaching children with disabilities in childhood education (MS Ed)
teaching literacy 5-12 (MS Ed)
teaching literacy B-12 (MS Ed)
teaching literacy B-6 (MS Ed)

School of Law
Michael A. Simons, Dean
Programs in:
bankruptcy (LL M)
law (JD, LL M)
U.S. legal studies (LL M)

■ ST. JOSEPH'S COLLEGE, LONG ISLAND CAMPUS

Patchogue, NY 11772-2399
http://www.sjcny.edu/

Independent, coed, comprehensive institution. *Computer facilities:* 245 computers available on campus for general student use. A campuswide network can be accessed from off campus. Online class registration is available. *General application contact:* Coordinator of Graduate Admissions, 631-447-3383.

Executive MBA Program
Program in:
business administration (EMBA)

Program in Accounting
Program in:
accounting (MBA)

Program in Infant/Toddler Early Childhood Special Education
Program in:
infant/toddler early childhood special education (MA)

Program in Literacy and Cognition
Program in:
literacy and cognition (MA)

Program in Management
Programs in:
health care (AC)
health care management (MS)
human resource management (AC)
human resources management (MS)
organizational management (MS)

Program in Nursing
Program in:
nursing (MS)

■ ST. THOMAS AQUINAS COLLEGE

Sparkill, NY 10976
http://www.stac.edu/

Independent, coed, comprehensive institution. *Computer facilities:* Computer purchase and lease plans are available. 200 computers available on campus for general student use. A campuswide network can be accessed from student residence rooms and from off campus. Online class registration is available. *General application contact:* Director of Admissions, 845-398-4102.

Division of Business Administration
Programs in:
business administration (MBA)
finance (MBA)
management (MBA)
marketing (MBA)

Division of Teacher Education
Programs in:
adolescence education (MST)
childhood and special education (MST)
childhood education (MST)
educational leadership (MS Ed)
reading (MS Ed, PMC)
special education (MS Ed, PMC)
teaching (MS Ed)

■ SARAH LAWRENCE COLLEGE

Bronxville, NY 10708-5999
http://www.sarahlawrence.edu/

Independent, coed, comprehensive institution. CGS member. *Graduate faculty:* 134 part-time/adjunct (78 women). *Computer facilities:* Computer purchase and lease plans are available. 110 computers available on campus for general student use. A campuswide network can be accessed from student residence rooms and from off campus. *Graduate expenses:* Tuition: full-time $26,544; part-time $1106 per credit. Required fees: $450. Tuition and fees vary according to program. *General application contact:* Susan Guma, Dean of Graduate Studies, 914-395-2373.

Graduate Studies
Susan Guma, Dean of Graduate Studies
Programs in:
art of teaching (MS Ed)
child development (MA)
creative non-fiction (MFA)
dance (MFA)
fiction (MFA)
health advocacy (MA)
human genetics (MS)
individualized study (MA)
poetry (MFA)
theater (MFA)
women's history (MA)

■ STATE UNIVERSITY OF NEW YORK AT BINGHAMTON

Binghamton, NY 13902-6000
http://www.binghamton.edu/

State-supported, coed, university. CGS member. *Graduate faculty:* 461 full-time (162 women), 211 part-time/adjunct (92 women). *Computer facilities:* 992 computers available on campus for general student use. A campuswide network can be accessed from student residence rooms and from off campus. Online class registration, course management system, personal Web space are available. *Graduate expenses:* Tuition, state resident: full-time $6900; part-time $288 per credit. Tuition, nonresident: full-time $10,920; part-time $455 per credit. Required fees: $1130. Part-time tuition and fees vary according to course load, program and student level. *General application contact:* Dr. Nancy E. Stamp, Vice Provost and Dean of the Graduate School, 607-777-2070.

Graduate School
Dr. Nancy E. Stamp, Vice Provost and Dean of the Graduate School

College of Community and Public Affairs
Dr. Patricia Ingraham, Dean
Programs in:
community and public affairs (MPA, MSW)
public administration (MPA)
social work (MSW)

Decker School of Nursing
Dr. Joyce Ferrario, Dean
Program in:
nursing (MS, PhD, Certificate)

School of Arts and Sciences
Dr. Jean-Pierre Mileur, Dean

State University of New York at Binghamton (continued)
Programs in:
analytical chemistry (PhD)
anthropology (MA, PhD)
applied physics (MS)
art history (MA, PhD)
arts and sciences (MA, MM, MS, PhD, Certificate)
behavioral neuroscience (MA, PhD)
biological sciences (MA, PhD)
chemistry (MA, MS)
clinical psychology (MA, PhD)
cognitive and behavioral science (MA, PhD)
comparative literature (MA, PhD)
computer science (MA, PhD)
economics (MA, PhD)
economics and finance (MA, PhD)
English (MA, PhD)
French (MA)
geography (MA)
geological sciences (MA, PhD)
history (MA, PhD)
inorganic chemistry (PhD)
Italian (MA)
music (MA, MM)
organic chemistry (PhD)
philosophy (MA, PhD)
philosophy, interpretation and culture (MA, PhD)
physical chemistry (PhD)
physics (MA, MS)
political science (MA, PhD)
probability and statistics (MA, PhD)
public policy (MA, PhD)
social, political, ethical and legal philosophy (MA, PhD)
sociology (MA, PhD)
Spanish (MA, Certificate)
theater (MA)
translation (Certificate)
translation research and instruction (Certificate)

School of Education
Dr. Susan Strahle, Interim Dean
Programs in:
biology education (MAT, MS Ed, MST)
childhood education (MS Ed)
earth science education (MAT, MS Ed, MST)
education (MAT, MS Ed, MST, Ed D)
educational theory and practice (Ed D)
English education (MAT, MS Ed, MST)
French education (MAT, MST)
literacy education (MS Ed)
mathematical sciences education (MAT, MS Ed, MST)
physics (MAT, MS Ed, MST)
social studies (MAT, MS Ed, MST)
Spanish education (MAT, MST)
special education (MS Ed)

School of Management
Dr. Upinder S. Dhillon, Dean
Programs in:
accounting (MS, PhD)
business administration (MBA, PhD)
health care professional executive (MBA)
management (MBA, MS, PhD)

Thomas J. Watson School of Engineering and Applied Science
Dr. Seshu Desu, Dean
Programs in:
computer science (M Eng, MS, PhD)
electrical and computer engineering (M Eng, MS, PhD)
engineering and applied science (M Eng, MS, MSAT, PhD)
materials science and engineering (MS, PhD)
mechanical engineering (M Eng, MS, PhD)
systems science and industrial engineering (M Eng, MS, MSAT, PhD)

■ STATE UNIVERSITY OF NEW YORK AT FREDONIA
Fredonia, NY 14063-1136
http://www.fredonia.edu/

State-supported, coed, comprehensive institution. CGS member. *Graduate faculty:* 50 full-time (26 women), 24 part-time/adjunct (12 women). *Computer facilities:* Computer purchase and lease plans are available. 500 computers available on campus for general student use. A campuswide network can be accessed from student residence rooms and from off campus. Online class registration is available. *Graduate expenses:* Tuition, state resident: full-time $8370; part-time $349 per credit hour. Tuition, nonresident: full-time $13,250; part-time $552 per credit hour. Required fees: $1289; $53.55 per credit hour. *General application contact:* Dr. Kevin P. Kearns, Associate Vice President of Graduate Studies and Research, 716-673-3808.

Graduate Studies
Programs in:
accounting (MS)
biology (MS, MS Ed)
chemistry (MS)
curriculum and instruction science education (MS Ed)
English (MA, MS Ed)
interdisciplinary studies (MA, MS)
mathematical sciences (MS Ed)
speech pathology and audiology (MS, MS Ed)

College of Education
Programs in:
educational administration (CAS)
elementary education (MS Ed)
literacy (MS Ed)
secondary education (MS Ed)
teaching English to speakers of other languages (MS Ed)

School of Music
Programs in:
music (MM)
music education (MM)

■ STATE UNIVERSITY OF NEW YORK AT NEW PALTZ
New Paltz, NY 12561
http://www.newpaltz.edu/

State-supported, coed, comprehensive institution. *Graduate faculty:* 144 full-time (81 women), 49 part-time/adjunct (31 women). *Computer facilities:* 600 computers available on campus for general student use. A campuswide network can be accessed from student residence rooms and from off campus. Online class registration is available. *General application contact:* Caroline Murphy, Graduate Admissions Advisor, 845-257-3285.

Graduate School
Dr. Laurel M. Garrick Duhaney, Associate Provost for Academic Affairs/ Dean of the Graduate School

School of Business
Dr. Hadi Salavitabar, Dean
Programs in:
business administration (MBA)
public accountancy (MBA)

School of Education
Dr. Robert Michael, Dean
Programs in:
adolescence (7-12) (MS Ed)
adolescence education: biology (MS Ed)
adolescence education: English (MS Ed)
adolescence education: social studies (MS Ed)
adolescence special education and literacy education (MS Ed)
alternative certificate: school district leader (transition D) (CAS)
childhood (1-6) (MS Ed)
childhood education (MS Ed)
childhood education (1-6) (MST)
childhood special education and literacy education (MS Ed)
early childhood (B-2) (MS Ed)
education (MAT, MPS, MS Ed, MST, CAS)
English as a second language (MS Ed)
humanistic/multicultural education (MPS)
literacy education (5-12) (MS Ed)
literacy education (B-6) (MS Ed)
literacy education and adolescence special education (MS Ed)
literacy education and childhood education and childhood special education (MS Ed)
school business leadership (CAS)
school leadership (MS Ed, CAS)
second language education (MS Ed)
special education (MS Ed)

School of Fine and Performing Arts
Dr. Mary Haefeli, Dean
Programs in:
ceramics (MFA)
fine and performing arts (MA, MFA, MS, MS Ed)
interdisciplinary (MA)

metal (MFA)
music therapy (MS)
painting/drawing (MFA)
printmaking (MFA)
sculpture (MFA)
visual arts education (MS Ed)

School of Liberal Arts and Sciences
Dr. James Schiffer, Dean
Programs in:
communication disorders (MS)
English (MA)
liberal arts and sciences (MA, MS)
mental health counseling (MS)
psychology (MA)
school counseling (MS)

School of Science and Engineering
Dr. Daniel Jelski, Dean
Programs in:
biology (MA)
computer science (MS)
electrical engineering (MS)
science and engineering (MA, MS)

■ STATE UNIVERSITY OF NEW YORK AT OSWEGO

Oswego, NY 13126
http://www.oswego.edu/

State-supported, coed, comprehensive institution. CGS member. *Computer facilities:* 750 computers available on campus for general student use. A campuswide network can be accessed from student residence rooms and from off campus. Online class registration is available. *General application contact:* Dean of Graduate Studies, 315-312-3152.

Graduate Studies

College of Arts and Sciences
Programs in:
art (MA)
arts and sciences (MA, MS)
chemistry (MS)
English (MA)
history (MA)
human computer interaction (MA)

School of Business
Programs in:
business (MBA)
business administration (MBA)

School of Education
Programs in:
agriculture (MS Ed)
art education (MAT)
business and marketing (MS Ed)
counseling services (MS, CAS)
education (MAT, MS, MS Ed, CAS)
educational administration and supervision (CAS)
elementary education (MS Ed)
family and consumer sciences (MS Ed)
health careers (MS Ed)
human services/counseling (MS)
literacy education (MS Ed)
school building leadership (CAS)
school psychology (MS, CAS)
secondary education (MS Ed)
special education (MS Ed)
technical education (MS Ed)
technology (MS Ed)
trade education (MS Ed)

■ STATE UNIVERSITY OF NEW YORK AT PLATTSBURGH

Plattsburgh, NY 12901-2681
http://www.plattsburgh.edu/

State-supported, coed, comprehensive institution. *Graduate faculty:* 72 full-time (38 women), 56 part-time/adjunct (30 women). *Computer facilities:* Computer purchase and lease plans are available. 343 computers available on campus for general student use. A campuswide network can be accessed from student residence rooms and from off campus. Online class registration, online library databases are available. *Graduate expenses:* Tuition, state resident: full-time $7880; part-time $328 per credit hour. Required fees: $1060. *General application contact:* Marguerite Adelman, Assistant Director of Graduate Admissions, 518-564-4723.

Division of Education, Health, and Human Services

Dr. David Hill, Dean
Programs in:
adolescence education (MST)
biology 7-12 (MST)
birth to grade 2 (MS Ed)
birth-grade 6 (MS Ed)
chemistry 7-12 (MST)
childhood education (grades 1-6) (MST)
college/agency counseling (MS)
earth science 7-12 (MST)
education, health, and human services (MA, MS, MS Ed, MST, CAS)
educational leadership (CAS)
English 7-12 (MST)
French 7-12 (MST)
grades 1 to 6 (MS Ed)
grades 5-12 (MS Ed)
grades 7 to 12 (MS Ed)
mathematics 7-12 (MST)
physics 7-12 (MST)
school counselor (MS Ed, CAS)
social studies 7-12 (MST)
Spanish 7-12 (MST)
speech-language pathology (MA)
teacher education: curriculum and instruction (MS Ed)

Faculty of Arts and Science

Dr. Kathleen Lavoie, Dean
Programs in:
arts and science (MA, MS, CAS)
natural science (MS)
school psychology (MA, CAS)

School of Business and Economics

Dr. Raymond Guydosh, Interim Dean
Programs in:
business and economics (MA)
liberal studies (MA)

■ STATE UNIVERSITY OF NEW YORK COLLEGE AT CORTLAND

Cortland, NY 13045
http://www.cortland.edu/

State-supported, coed, comprehensive institution. *Computer facilities:* 832 computers available on campus for general student use. A campuswide network can be accessed from student residence rooms and from off campus. *General application contact:* Assistant Director of Graduate Studies, 607-753-4800.

Graduate Studies

School of Arts and Sciences
Programs in:
American civilization and culture (CAS)
arts and sciences (MA, MAT, MS Ed, CAS)
biology (MAT, MS Ed)
chemistry (MAT, MS Ed)
earth science (MAT, MS Ed)
English (MA, MAT, MS Ed)
French (MS Ed)
history (MA, MS Ed)
mathematics (MAT, MS Ed)
physics (MAT, MS Ed)
second language education (MS Ed)
social studies (MS Ed)
Spanish (MS Ed)

School of Education
Programs in:
childhood/early child education (MS Ed, MST)
educational leadership (CAS)
literacy (MS Ed)
teaching students with disabilities (MS Ed)

School of Professional Studies
Programs in:
exercise science and sport studies (MS)
health education (MS Ed, MST)
international sport management (MS)
physical education (MS Ed)
professional studies (MS, MS Ed, MST)
recreation and leisure studies (MS, MS Ed)
sport management (MS)

■ STATE UNIVERSITY OF NEW YORK COLLEGE AT GENESEO

Geneseo, NY 14454-1401
http://www.geneseo.edu/

State-supported, coed, comprehensive institution. *Graduate faculty:* 38 full-time (18 women), 12 part-time/adjunct (7 women). *Computer facilities:* Computer purchase and lease plans are available. 900 computers available on campus for general student use.

State University of New York College at Geneseo (continued)
A campuswide network can be accessed from student residence rooms and from off campus. Online class registration is available. *Graduate expenses:* Tuition, state resident: full-time $7635; part-time $349 per credit hour. Tuition, nonresident: full-time $12,085; part-time $552 per credit hour. One-time fee: $28.28 part-time. *General application contact:* Dr. Terence Bazzett, Associate Dean of the College, 585-245-5541.

Graduate Studies
Dr. Mary Radosh, Dean of the College
Program in:
communicative disorders and sciences (MA)

School of Business
Dr. Michael Schinski, Interim Dean
Program in:
accounting (MS)

School of Education
Dr. Osman Alawiye, Chairperson
Programs in:
childhood multicultural education (1-6) (MS Ed)
early childhood education (MS Ed)
elementary education (MS Ed)
reading (MS Ed)
secondary education (MS Ed)

■ STATE UNIVERSITY OF NEW YORK COLLEGE AT ONEONTA

Oneonta, NY 13820-4015
http://www.oneonta.edu/

State-supported, coed, comprehensive institution. *Computer facilities:* Computer purchase and lease plans are available. 700 computers available on campus for general student use. A campuswide network can be accessed from student residence rooms and from off campus. Online class registration is available. *Graduate expenses:* Tuition, state resident: full-time $6900. Tuition, nonresident: full-time $10,920. Part-time tuition and fees vary according to program. *General application contact:* Dean, 607-436-2523.

Graduate Education
Programs in:
biology (MA)
earth sciences (MA)
history museum studies (MA)
nutrition and dietetics (MS)

Division of Education
Dr. Joanne Curran, Associate Dean
Programs in:
adolescence education (MS Ed)
childhood education (MS Ed)
educational psychology and counseling (MS Ed, CAS)
elementary education and reading (MS Ed)
family and consumer science education (MS Ed)
literacy education (MS Ed)
school counselor K-12 (MS Ed, CAS)
secondary education (MS Ed)

■ STATE UNIVERSITY OF NEW YORK COLLEGE AT POTSDAM

Potsdam, NY 13676
http://www.potsdam.edu/

State-supported, coed, comprehensive institution. *Graduate faculty:* 59 full-time (29 women), 16 part-time/adjunct (13 women). *Computer facilities:* Computer purchase and lease plans are available. 470 computers available on campus for general student use. A campuswide network can be accessed from student residence rooms and from off campus. Online class registration, online access to financial aid status, unofficial transcripts, billing, meal plan and housing sign ups are available. *Graduate expenses:* Tuition, state resident: full-time $7390; part-time $328 per credit hour. Tuition, nonresident: full-time $12,085; part-time $552 per credit hour. Required fees: $952; $43.70 per credit hour. *General application contact:* Peter Cutler, Graduate Admissions Counselor, 315-267-3154.

Crane School of Music
Dr. Alan Solomon, Dean
Programs in:
composition (MM)
history and literature (MM)
music education (MM)
music theory (MM)
performance (MM)

School of Arts and Sciences
Dr. Galen K. Pletcher, Dean
Programs in:
arts and sciences (MA)
English and communication (MA)
mathematics (MA)

School of Education and Professional Studies
Dr. William Amoriell, Dean
Programs in:
birth-grade 2 (MS Ed)
childhood education (grades 1-6) (MST)
childhood instruction (MST)
curriculum and instruction (MS Ed)
education and professional studies (MS Ed, MST)
educational technology specialist (MS Ed)
English (MST)
grades 1-6 (MS Ed)
grades 5-9 (MS Ed)
grades 7-12 (MS Ed)
human performance technology (MS Ed)
information technology (MS Ed)
literacy educator (MS Ed)
literacy specialist (MS Ed)
mathematics (with grades 5-6 extension) (MST)
organizational leadership (MS Ed)
science (MST)
social studies (MS Ed)
Social Studies (with grades 5-6 extension) (MST)
technology educator (MS Ed)

■ STATE UNIVERSITY OF NEW YORK COLLEGE OF ENVIRONMENTAL SCIENCE AND FORESTRY

Syracuse, NY 13210-2779
http://www.esf.edu/

State-supported, coed, university. CGS member. *Computer facilities:* Computer purchase and lease plans are available. 150 computers available on campus for general student use. A campuswide network can be accessed from student residence rooms and from off campus. Online class registration is available. *General application contact:* Dean, Instruction and Graduate Studies, 315-470-6599.

Department of Chemistry
Programs in:
biochemistry (MPS, MS, PhD)
environmental and forest chemistry (MPS, MS, PhD)
organic chemistry (MPS)
organic chemistry of natural products (MS, PhD)
polymer chemistry (MPS, MS, PhD)

Department of Construction Management and Wood Products Engineering
Program in:
environmental and resources engineering (MPS, MS, PhD)

Department of Environmental and Forest Biology
Programs in:
applied ecology (MPS)
chemical ecology (MPS, MS, PhD)
conservation biology (MPS, MS, PhD)
ecology (MPS, MS, PhD)
entomology (MPS, MS, PhD)
environmental interpretation (MPS, MS, PhD)
environmental physiology (MPS, MS, PhD)
fish and wildlife biology (MPS, MS, PhD)
forest pathology and mycology (MPS, MS, PhD)
plant biotechnology (MPS)
plant science and biotechnology (MPS, MS, PhD)

Department of Environmental Resources and Forest Engineering
Program in:
- environmental and resources engineering (MPS, MS, PhD)

Department of Environmental Studies
Program in:
- environmental studies (MPS, MS)

Department of Forest and Natural Resources Management
Programs in:
- environmental and natural resource policy (MS, PhD)
- environmental and natural resources policy (MPS)
- forest management and operations (MF)
- forestry ecosystems science and applications (MPS, MS, PhD)
- natural resources management (MPS, MS, PhD)
- quantitative methods and management in forest science (MPS, MS, PhD)
- recreation and resource management (MPS, MS, PhD)
- watershed management and forest hydrology (MPS, MS, PhD)

Department of Landscape Architecture
Programs in:
- community design and planning (MLA, MS)
- cultural landscape studies and conservation (MLA, MS)
- landscape and urban ecology (MLA, MS)

Department of Paper and Bioprocess Engineering
Program in:
- environmental and resources engineering (MPS, MS, PhD)

Program in Environmental Science
Programs in:
- environmental and community land planning (MPS, MS, PhD)
- environmental and natural resources policy (PhD)
- environmental communication and participatory processes (MPS, MS, PhD)
- environmental policy and democratic processes (MPS, MS, PhD)
- environmental systems and risk management (MPS, MS, PhD)
- water and wetland resource studies (MPS, MS, PhD)

■ STATE UNIVERSITY OF NEW YORK EMPIRE STATE COLLEGE
Saratoga Springs, NY 12866-4391
http://www.esc.edu/

State-supported, coed, comprehensive institution. *Computer facilities:* 100 computers available on campus for general student use. A campuswide network can be accessed from off campus. Online class registration is available. *General application contact:* Assistant Director, 518-587-2100 Ext. 2393.

Graduate Studies
Programs in:
- business administration (MBA)
- business and policy studies (MA)
- labor and policy studies (MA)
- liberal studies (MA)
- social policy (MA)
- teaching (MA)

■ STATE UNIVERSITY OF NEW YORK INSTITUTE OF TECHNOLOGY
Utica, NY 13504-3050
http://www.sunyit.edu/

State-supported, coed, comprehensive institution. *Computer facilities:* 244 computers available on campus for general student use. A campuswide network can be accessed from student residence rooms and from off campus. Online class registration, various other software applications are available. *General application contact:* Director of Admissions, 315-792-7500.

School of Arts and Sciences
Programs in:
- applied sociology (MS)
- information design and technology (MS)

School of Business
Programs in:
- accountancy (MS)
- business administration in technology management (MBA)
- health services administration (MS)
- technology management (MBA)

School of Information Systems and Engineering Technology
Programs in:
- advanced technology (MS)
- computer and information science (MS)
- telecommunications (MS)

School of Nursing and Health Systems
Programs in:
- adult nurse practitioner (MS, CAS)
- family nurse practitioner (MS, CAS)
- gerontological nurse practitioner (MS, CAS)
- nursing administration (MS, CAS)
- nursing education (MS, CAS)

■ STATE UNIVERSITY OF NEW YORK MARITIME COLLEGE
Throggs Neck, NY 10465-4198
http://www.sunymaritime.edu/

State-supported, coed, primarily men, comprehensive institution. *Computer facilities:* 110 computers available on campus for general student use. A campuswide network can be accessed from student residence rooms and from off campus. Online class registration is available. *General application contact:* Director, 718-409-7285.

Program in International Transportation Management
Program in:
- international transportation management (MS)

■ STONY BROOK UNIVERSITY, STATE UNIVERSITY OF NEW YORK
Stony Brook, NY 11794
http://www.sunysb.edu/

State-supported, coed, university. CGS member. *Graduate faculty:* 1,298 full-time (417 women), 480 part-time/adjunct (193 women). *Computer facilities:* Computer purchase and lease plans are available. 2,600 computers available on campus for general student use. A campuswide network can be accessed from student residence rooms and from off campus. Online class registration is available. *General application contact:* Dr. Kent Marks, Assistant Dean, Admissions and Records, 631-632-4723.

Graduate School
Dr. Lawrence B. Martin, Dean

College of Arts and Sciences
Dr. Nancy Squires, Interim Dean
Programs in:
- Africana studies (MA)
- anthropology (MA, PhD)
- applied ecology (MA)
- art history and criticism (MA, PhD)
- arts and sciences (MA, MAPP, MAT, MFA, MM, MS, DMA, PhD, Certificate)
- astronomy (PhD)
- biochemistry and molecular biology (PhD)
- biochemistry and structural biology (PhD)
- biological sciences (MA)
- biopsychology (PhD)
- cellular and developmental biology (PhD)

Stony Brook University, State University of New York (continued)

chemistry (MS, PhD)
clinical psychology (PhD)
cognitive/experimental psychology (PhD)
comparative literature (MA, PhD)
composition studies (Certificate)
cultural studies (PhD)
dramaturgy (MFA)
earth science (MAT)
ecology and evolution (PhD)
economics (MA, PhD)
English (MA, PhD)
English education (MAT)
ethnomusicology (MA, PhD)
French (MA)
genetics (PhD)
geosciences (MS, PhD)
Hispanic languages and literature (MA, PhD)
history (MA, PhD)
immunology and pathology (PhD)
Italian (MA)
linguistics (MA, PhD)
mathematics (MA, MAT, PhD)
modern research instrumentation (MS)
molecular and cellular biology (MA, PhD)
music history/theory (MA, PhD)
music performance (MM, DMA)
neuroscience (PhD)
philosophy (MA, PhD)
physics (MA, MAT, MS, PhD)
physics education (MAT)
political science (MA, PhD)
public policy (MAPP)
Romance languages (MA)
social and health psychology (PhD)
sociology (MA, PhD)
studio art (MFA)
teaching English to speakers of other languages (MA)
theatre arts (MA, MFA)

College of Business
Joseph McDonnell, Interim Dean
Programs in:
business (MBA, MS, Certificate)
finance (MBA, Certificate)
health care management (MBA, Certificate)
human resource management (Certificate)
human resources (MBA)
information systems management (MBA, Certificate)
management (MBA)
marketing (MBA)
technology management (MS)

College of Engineering and Applied Sciences
Dr. Yacov Shamash, Dean
Programs in:
applied mathematics and statistics (MS, PhD)
biomedical engineering (MS, PhD, Certificate)
computer science (MS, PhD)
educational technology (MS)
electrical and computer engineering (MS, PhD)
energy and environmental systems (MS, Advanced Certificate)
engineering and applied sciences (MS, PhD, Advanced Certificate, Certificate)
global operations management (MS)
information systems (Certificate)
information systems engineering (MS)
materials science and engineering (MS, PhD)
mechanical engineering (MS, PhD)
medical physics (MS, PhD)
software engineering (Certificate)
technology, policy, and innovation (PhD)

School of Marine and Atmospheric Sciences
Dr. David O. Conover, Dean and Director
Programs in:
atmospheric sciences (MS, PhD)
marine and atmospheric sciences (MS, PhD)
marine sciences (MS, PhD)

School of Professional Development
Dr. Paul J. Edelson, Dean
Programs in:
biology-grade 7-12 (MAT)
chemistry-grade 7-12 (MAT)
coaching (Graduate Certificate)
computer integrated engineering (Graduate Certificate)
earth science-grade 7-12 (MAT)
educational computing (Graduate Certificate)
educational leadership (Advanced Certificate)
English-grade 7-12 (MAT)
environmental management (Graduate Certificate)
environmental/occupational health and safety (Graduate Certificate)
French-grade 7-12 (MAT)
German-grade 7-12 (MAT)
human resource management (Graduate Certificate)
information systems management (Graduate Certificate)
Italian-grade 7-12 (MAT)
liberal studies (MA)
liberal studies online (MA)
mathematics-grade 7-12 (MAT)
operation research (Graduate Certificate)
physics-grade 7-12 (MAT)
school administration and supervision (Graduate Certificate)
school building leadership (Graduate Certificate)
school district administration (Graduate Certificate)
school district business leadership (Advanced Certificate)
school district leadership (Graduate Certificate)
social science and the professions (MPS)
social studies-grade 7-12 (MAT)
Spanish-grade 7-12 (MAT)
waste management (Graduate Certificate)

Stony Brook Southampton
Dr. Robert Reeves, Director
Programs in:
fiction (MFA)
poetry (MFA)
scientific writing (MFA)
scriptwriting (MFA)

Stony Brook University Medical Center
Steven L. Strongwater, Chief Executive Officer
Program in:
medicine (DDS, MD, MPH, MS, MSW, DNP, DPT, PhD, Advanced Certificate, Certificate)

Health Sciences Center
Dr. Craig A. Lehmann, Interim Executive Dean
Programs in:
adult health nurse practitioner (Certificate)
adult health/primary care nursing (MS)
child health nurse practitioner (Certificate)
child health nursing (MS)
dental medicine (DDS, MS, PhD, Certificate)
endodontics (Certificate)
family nurse practitioner (MS, Certificate)
health care management (Advanced Certificate)
health care policy and management (MS)
health sciences (DDS, MD, MS, MSW, DNP, DPT, PhD, Advanced Certificate, Certificate)
mental health/psychiatric nursing (MS, Certificate)
neonatal nurse practitioner (Certificate)
neonatal nursing (MS)
nurse midwifery (MS, Certificate)
nursing (MS, DNP, Certificate)
nursing practice (DNP)
occupational therapy (MS)
oral biology and pathology (MS, PhD)
orthodontics (Certificate)
perinatal women's health nursing (MS, Certificate)
periodontics (Certificate)
physical therapy (DPT)
physician assistant (MS)
social welfare (PhD)
social work (MSW)

School of Medicine
Dr. Richard N. Fine, Dean
Programs in:
anatomical sciences (PhD)
community health (MPH)
evaluation sciences (MPH)
family violence (MPH)

health economics (MPH)
medical scientistmedicine (MD, MPH, PhD)
molecular and cellular pharmacology (PhD)
molecular microbiology (PhD)
physiology and biophysics (PhD)
population health (MPH)
population health and clinical outcomes research (PhD)
substance abuse (MPH)

■ SYRACUSE UNIVERSITY

Syracuse, NY 13244
http://www.syracuse.edu/

Independent, coed, university. CGS member. *Graduate faculty:* 959 full-time (343 women), 550 part-time/adjunct (270 women). *Computer facilities:* Computer purchase and lease plans are available. 2,955 computers available on campus for general student use. A campuswide network can be accessed from student residence rooms and from off campus. Online class registration, online services, networked client and server computing are available. *Graduate expenses:* Tuition: full-time $19,242; part-time $1069 per credit hour. Required fees: $1218. *General application contact:* Diana Hahn, Associate Director, Graduate Recruitment and Retention, 315-443-4492.

College of Law

Hannah Arterian, Dean
Programs in:
law (JD)

Graduate School

College of Arts and Sciences
Programs in:
applied statistics (MS)
art history (MA)
arts and sciences (MA, MFA, MS, Au D, PhD)
audiology (Au D, PhD)
biology (MS, PhD)
chemistry (MS, PhD)
clinical psychology (PhD)
college science teaching (PhD)
composition and cultural rhetoric (PhD)
creative writing (MFA)
earth sciences (MA, MS, PhD)
English (MA, PhD)
experimental psychology (PhD)
forensic science (MS)
French and Francophone studies (MA)
linguistic studies (MA)
mathematics (MS, PhD)
Pan-African studies (MA)
philosophy (MA, PhD)
physics (MS, PhD)
religion (MA, PhD)
school psychology (PhD)
social psychology (PhD)
Spanish language, literature and culture (MA)
speech language pathology (MS, PhD)
structural biology, biochemistry and biophysics (PhD)

College of Human Ecology
Programs in:
child and family studies (MA, MS, PhD)
human ecology (MA, MS, MSW, PhD)
marriage and family therapy (MA)
nutrition science (MA, MS)
social work (MSW)

College of Visual and Performing Arts
Programs in:
art photography (MFA)
art video (MFA)
ceramics (MFA)
communication and rhetorical studies (MA)
computer art (MFA)
conducting (M Mu)
fiber arts/material studies (MFA)
film (MFA)
illustration (MFA)
jewelry and metalsmithing (MFA)
museum studies (MA)
music composition (M Mus)
organ (M Mus)
painting (MFA)
percussion (M Mus)
piano (M Mus)
printmaking (MFA)
sculpture (MFA)
strings (M Mus)
visual and performing arts (M Mu, M Mus, MA, MFA, MS)
voice (M Mus)
wind instruments (M Mus)

L. C. Smith College of Engineering and Computer Science
Programs in:
bioengineering (ME, MS, PhD)
chemical engineering (MS, PhD)
civil engineering (MS, PhD)
computer and information science and engineering (PhD)
computer engineering (MS, CE)
computer science (MS)
electrical and computer engineering (PhD)
electrical engineering (MS, EE)
engineering and computer science (ME, MS, PhD, CE, EE)
engineering management (MS)
environmental engineering (MS, PhD)
mechanical and aerospace engineering (MS, PhD)
microwave engineering (CAS)

Maxwell School of Citizenship and Public Affairs
Programs in:
anthropology (MA, PhD)
citizenship and public affairs (EMPA, MA, MPA, MS Sc, PhD, CAS)
conflict resolution (CAS)
economics (MA, PhD)
geography (MA, PhD)
health services management and policy (CAS)
history (MA, PhD)
political science (MA, PhD)
public administration (EMPA, MPA, PhD, CAS)
social sciences (MS Sc, PhD)
sociology (MA, PhD)

School of Architecture
Program in:
architecture (M Arch I, M Arch II)

School of Education
Programs in:
art education (CAS)
art education/professional certification (MS)
art education: preparation (MS)
childhood education: (1-6)
preparation (MS)
community counseling (MS)
counselor education (PhD)
cultural foundations of education (MS, PhD)
disability studies (CAS)
early childhood special education (MS)
education (M Mus, MS, Ed D, PhD, CAS)
educational leadership (MS, Ed D, CAS)
educational technology (CAS)
English education (MS, PhD)
English education: preparation 7-12 (MS)
exercise science (MS)
higher education (MS, PhD)
inclusive special education (grades 1-6) (MS)
inclusive special education (grades 7-12) (MS)
inclusive special education: severe/multiple disabilities (MS)
instructional design, development, and evaluation (MS, PhD, CAS)
lifelong learning and continuing education (CAS)
literacy education: birth-grade 6 (MS)
mathematics education (PhD)
mathematics education: preparation 7-12 (MS)
music education/professional certification (M Mus, MS)
music education: teacher preparation (MS)
professional practice in educational technology (CAS)
reading education (PhD)
rehabilitation and community counseling (MS)
rehabilitation counseling (MS)
school counseling (MS, CAS)
science education (PhD)
social studies education: preparation 7-12 (MS)
special education (PhD)
student affairs counseling (MS)
teaching and curriculum (MS, PhD, CAS)
teaching English language learners (MS)

School of Information Studies
Programs in:
digital libraries (CAS)
information management (MS, DPS)

Syracuse University (continued)
information science and technology (PhD)
information security management (CAS)
information studies (MS, DPS, PhD, CAS)
information systems and telecommunications management (CAS)
library and information science (MS)
library and information science: school media (MS)
school media (CAS)
telecommunications and network management (MS)

S. I. Newhouse School of Public Communications
Programs in:
advertising (MA)
arts journalism (MA)
broadcast journalism (MS)
communications management (MS)
documentary film and history (MA)
magazine, newspaper and online journalism (MA)
mass communications (PhD)
media management (MS)
media studies (MA)
photography (MS)
public communications (MA, MS, PhD)
public relations (MS)
television, radio, and film (MA)

Martin J. Whitman School of Management
Programs in:
accounting (MBA, PhD)
entrepreneurship (MBA)
finance (MBA, PhD)
management (MBA, MS Acct, MSF, PhD)
management information systems (PhD)
managerial statistics (PhD)
marketing (MBA, PhD)
operations management (PhD)
organizational behavior (PhD)
strategy and human resources (PhD)
supply chain management (MBA, PhD)

■ TOURO COLLEGE
New York, NY 10010
http://www.touro.edu/

Independent, coed, comprehensive institution. *Computer facilities:* A campuswide network can be accessed from off campus. Online class registration is available.

School of Health Sciences
Programs in:
acupuncture (MS)
occupational therapy (MS)
oriental medicine (MSOM)
physical therapy (DPT)
public health (MPH)
speech-language pathology (MS)

Graduate School of Jewish Studies
Program in:
Jewish studies (MA)

Jacob D. Fuchsberg Law Center
Programs in:
law (JD)
U.S. law for foreign lawyers (LL M)

■ UNIVERSITY AT ALBANY, STATE UNIVERSITY OF NEW YORK
Albany, NY 12222-0001
http://www.albany.edu/

State-supported, coed, university. CGS member. *Graduate faculty:* 652 full-time (238 women), 621 part-time/adjunct (284 women). *Computer facilities:* 500 computers available on campus for general student use. A campuswide network can be accessed from student residence rooms and from off campus. Online class registration is available. *Graduate expenses:* Tuition, state resident: full-time $7880; part-time $328 per credit. Tuition, nonresident: full-time $13,250; part-time $552 per credit. Required fees: $1173. *General application contact:* Michael DeRensis, Director, Graduate Admissions, 518-442-3980.

College of Arts and Sciences
Programs in:
African studies (MA)
Afro-American studies (MA)
anthropology (MA, PhD)
art (MA, MFA)
arts and sciences (MA, MFA, MRP, MS, DA, PhD, Certificate)
atmospheric science (MS, PhD)
autism (Certificate)
biodiversity, conservation, and policy (MS)
biopsychology (PhD)
chemistry (MS, PhD)
clinical psychology (PhD)
communication (MA)
demography (Certificate)
ecology, evolution, and behavior (MS, PhD)
economics (MA, PhD)
English (MA, PhD)
forensic molecular biology (MS)
French (MA, PhD)
general/experimental psychology (PhD)
geographic information systems and spatial analysis (Certificate)
geography (MA, Certificate)
geology (MS, PhD)
history (MA, PhD)
industrial/organizational psychology (PhD)
Italian (MA)
Latin American, Caribbean, and US Latino studies (MA, Certificate)
liberal studies (MA)
mathematics (PhD)
molecular, cellular, developmental, and neural biology (MS, PhD)
philosophy (MA, PhD)
physics (MS, PhD)
psychology (MA)
public history (Certificate)
regional planning (MRP)
regulatory economics (Certificate)
Russian (MA, Certificate)
Russian translation (Certificate)
secondary teaching (MA)
social/personality psychology (PhD)
sociology (MA, PhD)
sociology and communication (PhD)
Spanish (MA, PhD)
statistics (MA)
theatre (MA)
urban policy (Certificate)
women's studies (MA, DA)

College of Computing and Information
Programs in:
computer science (MS, PhD)
information science (MS, PhD, CAS)
information studies (MS, CAS)

College of Nanoscale Science and Engineering
Program in:
nanoscale science and engineering (MS, PhD)

Nelson A. Rockefeller College of Public Affairs and Policy
Programs in:
administrative behavior (PhD)
comparative and development administration (MPA, PhD)
human resources (MPA)
legislative administration (MPA)
nonprofit leadership and management (Certificate)
planning and policy analysis (CAS)
policy analysis (MPA)
political science (MA, PhD)
program analysis and evaluation (PhD)
public affairs and policy (MA)
public finance (MPA, PhD)
public management (MPA, PhD)
women and public policy (Certificate)

School of Business
Programs in:
accounting (MS)
business (MBA, MS)
finance (MBA)
human resource systems (MBA)
information technology management (MBA)
marketing (MBA)
taxation (MS)

School of Criminal Justice
Program in:
criminal justice (MA, PhD)

School of Education
Programs in:
counseling psychology (MS, PhD, CAS)

curriculum and instruction (MS, Ed D, CAS)
curriculum planning and development (MA)
education (MA, MS, Ed D, PhD, Psy D, CAS)
educational administration and policy studies (MS, PhD, CAS)
educational communications (MS, CAS)
educational psychology (Ed D)
educational psychology and statistics (MS)
measurements and evaluation (Ed D)
reading (MS, Ed D, CAS)
rehabilitation counseling (MS)
school counselor (CAS)
school psychology (Psy D, CAS)
special education (MS)
statistics and research design (Ed D)

School of Public Health
Programs in:
biochemistry, molecular biology, and genetics (MS, PhD)
cell and molecular structure (MS, PhD)
environmental and analytical chemistry (MS, PhD)
environmental and occupational health (MS, PhD)
epidemiology and biostatistics (MS, PhD)
health policy, management, and behavior (MS)
immunobiology and immunochemistry (MS, PhD)
molecular pathogenesis (MS, PhD)
neuroscience (MS, PhD)
public health (MPH, MS, Dr PH, PhD, Certificate)
toxicology (MS, PhD)

School of Social Welfare
Program in:
social welfare (MSW, PhD)

■ UNIVERSITY AT BUFFALO, THE STATE UNIVERSITY OF NEW YORK
Buffalo, NY 14260
http://www.buffalo.edu/

State-supported, coed, university. CGS member. *Graduate faculty:* 1,277 full-time (418 women), 1,122 part-time/adjunct (417 women). *Computer facilities:* Computer purchase and lease plans are available. 2,000 computers available on campus for general student use. A campuswide network can be accessed from student residence rooms and from off campus. Online class registration is available. *General application contact:* Christopher S. Connor, Director of Graduate Enrollment Management Services, 716-645-3482.

Graduate School
Dr. Myron A. Thompson, Associate Provost and Executive Director of the Graduate School

College of Arts and Sciences
Dr. Bruce D. McCombe, Dean
Programs in:
American studies (MA, PhD)
anthropology (MA, PhD)
art (MFA)
art history (MA, Certificate)
arts and sciences (MA, MFA, MM, MS, Au D, PhD, Certificate)
audiology (Au D)
behavioral neuroscience (PhD)
biological sciences (MA, MS, PhD)
chemistry (MA, PhD)
classics (MA, PhD)
clinical psychology (PhD)
cognitive psychology (PhD)
communication (MA, PhD)
communicative disorders and sciences (MA, PhD)
comparative literature (MA, PhD)
critical museum studies (Certificate)
economics (MA, MS, PhD)
English (MA, PhD)
evolution, ecology and behavior (MS, PhD, Certificate)
financial economics (Certificate)
fine arts (MFA)
French (MA, PhD)
general psychology (MA)
geographic information science (Certificate)
geography (MA, MS, PhD)
geology (MA, MS, PhD)
health services (Certificate)
historical musicology and music theory (PhD)
history (MA, PhD)
humanities (film studies concentration) (MA)
information and Internet economics (Certificate)
international economics (Certificate)
law and regulation (Certificate)
linguistics (MA, PhD)
mathematics (MA, PhD)
media arts production (MFA)
medicinal chemistry (MS, PhD)
music composition (MA, PhD)
music history (MA)
music performance (MM)
music theory (MA)
new media design (Certificate)
philosophy (MA, PhD)
physics (MS, PhD)
political science (MA, PhD)
social-personality psychology (PhD)
sociology (MA, PhD)
Spanish (MA, PhD)
transportation and business geographics (Certificate)
urban and regional economics (Certificate)

Graduate Programs in Cancer Research and Biomedical Sciences at Roswell Park Cancer Institute
Dr. Arthur M. Michalek, Dean
Programs in:
cancer pathology and prevention (PhD)
cellular and molecular biology (PhD)
immunology (PhD)
interdisciplinary biomedical and natural sciences (MS)
molecular and cellular biophysics (PhD)
molecular and cellular biophysics and biochemistry (PhD)
molecular pharmacology and cancer therapeutics (PhD)
natural and biomedical sciences (MS)

Graduate School of Education
Dr. Mary H. Gresham, Dean
Programs in:
adolescence education (Certificate)
biology (Ed M)
chemistry (Ed M)
childhood education (Ed M)
counseling/school psychology (PhD)
counselor education (PhD)
early childhood and childhood education with bilingual extension (Ed M)
early childhood education (Ed M)
earth science (Ed M)
education (Ed M, MA, MLS, MS, Ed D, PhD, Certificate)
educational administration (Ed M, Ed D, PhD)
educational psychology (MA, PhD)
elementary education (Ed D, PhD)
English (Ed M)
English education (PhD)
English for speakers of other languages (Ed M)
foreign and second language education (PhD)
French (Ed M)
general education (Ed M)
German (Ed M)
gifted education (Certificate)
higher education (PhD)
higher education administration (Ed M)
Italian (Ed M)
Japanese (Ed M)
Latin (Ed M)
library and information studies (MLS, Certificate)
literary specialist (Ed M)
mathematics (Ed M)
mathematics education (PhD)
mental health counseling (MS)
mentoring teachers (Certificate)
music education (Ed M, Certificate)
physics (Ed M)
reading education (PhD)
rehabilitation counseling (MS)
Russian (Ed M)
school administrator and supervisor (Certificate)
school business and human resource administration (Certificate)
school counseling (Ed M, Certificate)
school psychology (MA)
science education (PhD)
social foundations (PhD)
social studies (Ed M)
Spanish (Ed M)
special education (PhD)
specialist in education administration (Certificate)

University at Buffalo, the State University of New York (continued)
teaching and leading for diversity (Certificate)
teaching English to speakers of other languages (Ed M)

Law School
Dr. Makau Mutua, Dean
Programs in:
criminal law (LL M)
general law for international students (LL M)
law (JD)

School of Architecture and Planning
Brian Carter, Dean
Programs in:
architecture (M Arch)
architecture and planning (M Arch, MUP)
planning (MUP)

School of Dental Medicine
Dr. Richard N. Buchanan, Dean
Programs in:
advanced education in general dentistry (Certificate)
biomaterials (MS)
combined prosthodontics (Certificate)
dental medicine (DDS, MS, PhD, Certificate)
endodontics (Certificate)
general practice residency (Certificate)
oral and maxillofacial pathology (Certificate)
oral and maxillofacial surgery (Certificate)
oral biology (PhD)
oral diagnostic sciences (MS)
oral sciences (MS)
orthodontics (MS, Certificate)
pediatric dentistry (Certificate)
periodontics (Certificate)
temporomandibular disorders and oralfacial pain (Certificate)

School of Engineering and Applied Sciences
Dr. Harvey G. Stenger, Dean
Programs in:
aerospace engineering (MS, PhD)
chemical and biological engineering (M Eng, MS, PhD)
civil engineering (M Eng, MS, PhD)
computer science and engineering (MS, PhD)
electrical engineering (M Eng, MS, PhD)
engineering and applied sciences (M Eng, MS, PhD)
engineering science (MS)
industrial and systems engineering (M Eng, MS, PhD)
mechanical engineering (MS, PhD)

School of Management
Arjang Assad, Dean
Programs in:
accounting (MS)
business administration (MBA)
finance (MS)
information assurance (Certificate)
management (PhD)
management information systems (MS)
supply chains and operations management (MS)

School of Medicine and Biomedical Sciences
Dr. Michael E. Cain, Dean of Medicine
Programs in:
anatomical sciences (MA, PhD)
biochemical pharmacology (MS)
biochemistry (MA, PhD)
biomedical sciences (PhD)
biophysics (MS, PhD)
biotechnology (MS)
medicine (MD)
medicine and biomedical sciences (MD, MA, MS, PhD)
microbiology and immunology (MA, PhD)
neuroscience (MS, PhD)
pathology (MA, PhD)
pharmacology (MA, PhD)
physiology (MA, PhD)
structural biology (MS, PhD)

School of Nursing
Dr. Jean K. Brown, Interim Dean
Programs in:
acute care nurse practitioner (MS, Certificate)
adult health nursing (MS, Certificate)
child health nursing (MS)
family nurse practitioner (Certificate)
family nursing (MS)
geriatric nurse practitioner (MS, Certificate)
maternal and women's health nurse practitioner (Certificate)
maternal and women's health nursing (MS)
nurse anesthetist (MS)
nursing (PhD)
nursing education (Certificate)
pediatric nurse practitioner (Certificate)
psychiatric/mental health nurse practitioner (Certificate)
psychiatric/mental health nursing (MS)

School of Pharmacy and Pharmaceutical Sciences
Dr. Wayne K. Anderson, Dean
Programs in:
pharmaceutical sciences (MS, PhD)
pharmacy (Pharm D)
pharmacy and pharmaceutical sciences (Pharm D, MS, PhD)

School of Public Health and Health Professions
Dr. Lynn Kozlowski, Dean
Programs in:
assistive and rehabilitation technology (Certificate)
biostatistics (MA, PhD)
community health (PhD)
epidemiology (MS, PhD)
exercise science (MS, PhD)
nutrition (MS)
occupational therapy (MS)
physical therapy (DPT)
public health (MPH)
public health and health professions (MA, MPH, MS, DPT, PhD, Certificate)

School of Social Work
Dr. Nancy J. Smyth, Dean
Program in:
social work (MSW, PhD)

■ UNIVERSITY OF ROCHESTER

Rochester, NY 14627-0250
http://www.rochester.edu/

Independent, coed, university. CGS member. *Computer facilities:* Computer purchase and lease plans are available. 450 computers available on campus for general student use. A campuswide network can be accessed from student residence rooms and from off campus. Online class registration is available. *General application contact:* Dean of Graduate Studies, 585-275-3540.

The College, Arts and Sciences
Programs in:
arts and sciences (MA, MS, PhD)
biology (MS, PhD)
brain and cognitive sciences (MS, PhD)
chemistry (MS, PhD)
clinical psychology (PhD)
computer science (MS, PhD)
developmental psychology (PhD)
economics (MA, PhD)
English (MA, PhD)
geological sciences (MS, PhD)
history (MA, PhD)
mathematics (MA, MS, PhD)
philosophy (MA, PhD)
physics (MA, MS, PhD)
physics and astronomy (PhD)
political science (MA, PhD)
psychology (MA)
social-personality psychology (PhD)
visual and cultural studies (MA, PhD)

The College, School of Engineering and Applied Sciences
Programs in:
biomedical engineering (MS, PhD)
chemical engineering (MS, PhD)
electrical and computer engineering (MS, PhD)
engineering and applied sciences (MS, PhD)
materials science (MS, PhD)
mechanical engineering (MS, PhD)

Institute of Optics
Program in:
optics (MS, PhD)

Eastman School of Music
Programs in:
composition (MA, MM, DMA, PhD)
conducting (MM, DMA)
education (MA, PhD)

jazz studies/contemporary media (MM)
music education (MM, DMA)
musicology (MA, PhD)
pedagogy of music theory (MA)
performance and literature (MM, DMA)
piano accompanying and chamber music (MM, DMA)
theory (MA, PhD)

Margaret Warner Graduate School of Education and Human Development
Program in:
education and human development (MAT, MS, Ed D, PhD)

School of Medicine and Dentistry
Programs in:
medicine (MD)
medicine and dentistry (MD, MA, MPH, MS, PhD, Certificate)

Graduate Programs in Medicine and Dentistry
Programs in:
biochemistry (MS, PhD)
biomedical genetics (MS, PhD)
biophysics (MS, PhD)
epidemiology (MS, PhD)
health services research and policy (PhD)
marriage and family therapy (MS)
medical statistics (MS)
medicine and dentistry (MA, MPH, MS, PhD)
microbiology (MS, PhD)
neurobiology and anatomy (MS, PhD)
neuroscience (MS, PhD)
oral biology (MS)
pathology (MS, PhD)
pharmacology (MS, PhD)
physiology (MS, PhD)
public health (MPH)
statistics (MA, PhD)
toxicology (MS, PhD)

School of Nursing
Dr. Kathy P. Parker, Dean
Programs in:
acute care nurse practitioner (MS)
adult nurse practitioner (MS)
adult psychiatric mental health nurse practitioner (MS)
care of children and families/pediatric nurse practitioner (MS)
care of children and families/pediatric nurse practitioner with pediatric behavioral health (MS)
care of children and families/pediatric nurse practitioner/neonatal nurse practitioner (MS)
child and adolescent psychiatric mental health nurse practitioner (MS)
clinical nurse leader (MS)
disaster response and emergency preparedness (MS)
family nurse practitioner (MS)
health practice research (PhD)
health promotion, education and technology (MS)
nursing (Certificate)

William E. Simon Graduate School of Business Administration
Program in:
business administration (MBA, MS, PhD)

■ UTICA COLLEGE
Utica, NY 13502-4892
http://www.utica.edu/

Independent, coed, comprehensive institution. *Graduate faculty:* 65 full-time (28 women). *Computer facilities:* 179 computers available on campus for general student use. A campuswide network can be accessed from student residence rooms. Online class registration is available. *Graduate expenses:* Tuition: full-time $22,611; part-time $840 per credit hour. Required fees: $50 per semester. Tuition and fees vary according to class time, course load, degree level and program. *General application contact:* John D. Rowe, Director of Graduate Admissions, 315-792-3824.

Department of Physical Therapy
Dr. Shauna Malta, Director of Physical Therapy
Program in:
physical therapy (DPT, TDPT)

Liberal Studies Program
Dr. Lawrence Aaronson, Coordinator, Liberal Studies
Program in:
liberal studies (MS)

Program in Accountancy
Dr. Hartwell Herring, MBA Director
Program in:
accountancy (MBA)

Program in Economic Crime and Fraud Management
Dr. R. Bruce McBride, Director of Economic Crime Graduate Programs
Program in:
economic crime and fraud management (MBA)

Program in Economic Crime Management
Dr. R. Bruce McBride, Director of Economic Crime Graduate Programs
Program in:
economic crime management (MS)

Program in Health Care Administration
Dr. Dana Hart, Head
Program in:
health care administration (MS)

Program in Occupational Therapy
Sally Townsend, Director, Occupational Therapy Program
Program in:
occupational therapy (MS)

Teacher Education Programs
Dr. Lois Fisch, Director, Institute for Excellence in Education
Program in:
teacher education (MS, MS Ed, CAS)

■ WAGNER COLLEGE
Staten Island, NY 10301-4495
http://www.wagner.edu/

Independent, coed, comprehensive institution. *Computer facilities:* 225 computers available on campus for general student use. A campuswide network can be accessed from student residence rooms and from off campus. Online class registration is available. *General application contact:* Assistant Coordinator of Graduate Studies, 718-390-3464.

Division of Graduate Studies
Programs in:
accelerated business administration (MBA)
accounting (MS)
adolescent education (MS Ed)
advanced physician assistant studies (MS)
childhood education (MS Ed)
early childhood education (birth-grade 2) (MS Ed)
educational leadership (Certificate)
family nurse practitioner (Certificate)
finance (MBA)
health care administration (MBA)
international business (MBA)
literacy (B-6) (MS Ed)
management (Exec MBA, MBA)
marketing (MBA)
microbiology (MS)
middle level education (5-9) (MS Ed)
nursing (MS)
school building leader (Certificate)
school district leader (Certificate)

■ YESHIVA UNIVERSITY
New York, NY 10033-3201
http://www.yu.edu/

Independent, coed, university. CGS member. *General application contact:* Associate Director of Admissions, 212-960-5277.

Azrieli Graduate School of Jewish Education and Administration
Program in:
Jewish education and administration (MS, Ed D, Specialist)

Benjamin N. Cardozo School of Law
David G. Martinidez, Dean of Admissions
Programs in:
comparative legal thought (LL M)
general studies (LL M)
intellectual property law (LL M)
law (JD)

Yeshiva University (continued)

Bernard Revel Graduate School of Jewish Studies
Program in:
Jewish studies (MA, PhD)

Ferkauf Graduate School of Psychology
Programs in:
clinical psychology (Psy D)
health psychology (PhD)
mental health counseling psychology (MA)
psychology (MA, PhD, Psy D)
school/clinical-child psychology (Psy D)

Sy Syms School of Business
Program in:
accounting (MS)

Wurzweiler School of Social Work
Dr. Sheldon R. Gelman, Dean
Program in:
social work (MSW, PhD)

North Carolina

■ APPALACHIAN STATE UNIVERSITY
Boone, NC 28608
http://www.appstate.edu/

State-supported, coed, comprehensive institution. CGS member. *Graduate faculty:* 471 full-time (180 women), 90 part-time/adjunct (51 women). *Computer facilities:* 2,500 computers available on campus for general student use. A campuswide network can be accessed from student residence rooms and from off campus. Online class registration is available. *Graduate expenses:* Tuition, state resident: full-time $2600; part-time $700 per course. Tuition, nonresident: full-time $5000; part-time $3300 per course. Required fees: $2150; $330 per course. Tuition and fees vary according to campus/location. *General application contact:* Sandy Krause, Director of Admissions and Recruiting, 828-262-2130.

Cratis D. Williams Graduate School
Dr. Edelma D. Huntley, Dean of Research and Graduate Studies
Programs in:
accounting (MS)
business administration (MBA)
cell and molecular (MS)
child development (MA)
clinical health psychology (MA)
community counseling (MA)
computer science (MS)
criminal justice (MS)
curriculum specialist (MA)
educational administration (Ed S)
educational leadership (Ed D)
educational media (MA)
elementary education (MA)
engineering physics (MS)
English (MA)
English education (MA)
exercise science (MS)
family and consumer science (MA)
family and consumer science education (MA)
general (MS)
general experimental psychology (MA)
geography (MA)
gerontology (MA)
higher education (MA, Ed S)
history (MA)
history education (MA)
industrial and organizational psychology (MA)
industrial technology (MA)
library science (MLS)
marriage and family therapy (MA)
mathematics (MA)
mathematics education (MA)
middle grades education (MA)
political science (MA)
public administration (MPA)
public history (MA)
reading education (MA)
romance languages (MA)
school administration (MSA)
school counseling (MA)
social work (MSW)
special education (MA)
speech-language pathology (MA)
student development (MA)
technology education (MA)

Center for Appalachian Studies
Dr. Pat Beaver, Director
Programs in:
culture (MA)
music (MA)
sustainable development (MA)

School of Music
Dr. William Harbinson, Dean
Programs in:
music education (MM)
music performance (MM)
music therapy (MMT)

■ CAMPBELL UNIVERSITY
Buies Creek, NC 27506
http://www.campbell.edu/

Independent-religious, coed, university. *Computer facilities:* 256 computers available on campus for general student use. A campuswide network can be accessed from student residence rooms and from off campus. Online class registration is available. *General application contact:* Director of Graduate Admissions for Business and Education, 910-893-1200 Ext. 1318.

Graduate and Professional Programs

Divinity School
Programs in:
Christian education (MA)
divinity (M Div)
ministry (D Min)

Lundy-Fetterman School of Business
Program in:
business (MBA, MTIM)

Norman Adrian Wiggins School of Law
Program in:
law (JD)

School of Education
Programs in:
administration (MSA)
community counseling (MA)
elementary education (M Ed)
English education (M Ed)
interdisciplinary studies (M Ed)
mathematics education (M Ed)
middle grades education (M Ed)
physical education (M Ed)
school counseling (M Ed)
secondary education (M Ed)
social science education (M Ed)

School of Pharmacy
Programs in:
clinical research (MS)
pharmaceutical science (MS)
pharmacy (Pharm D)

■ DUKE UNIVERSITY
Durham, NC 27708-0586
http://www.duke.edu/

Independent-religious, coed, university. CGS member. *Computer facilities:* Computer purchase and lease plans are available. 450 computers available on campus for general student use. A campuswide network can be accessed from student residence rooms and from off campus. Online class registration is available. *General application contact:* Associate Dean for Academic Services, 919-684-3913.

Divinity School
Dr. L. Gregory Jones, Dean
Program in:
theology (M Div, MTS, Th M, Th D)

Duke Global Health Institute
Program in:
global health (MS)

The Fuqua School of Business
Programs in:
business (EMBA, GEMBA, MBA, MMS, WEMBA, PhD, Certificate)
cross continent executive business administration (EMBA)
executive business administration (EMBA)

global executive business administration (GEMBA)
health sector management (Certificate)
weekend executive business administration (WEMBA)

Graduate School

Programs in:
art, art history and visual studies (PhD)
biological and biologically inspired materials (PhD, Certificate)
biological chemistry (PhD, Certificate)
biological psychology (PhD)
biology (PhD)
business administration (PhD)
cell biology (PhD)
cellular and molecular biology (PhD)
chemistry (PhD)
classical studies (PhD)
clinical psychology (PhD)
cognitive neuroscience (PhD, Certificate)
cognitive psychology (PhD)
computational biology and bioinformatics (PhD)
computer science (MS, PhD)
crystallography of macromolecules (PhD)
developmental biology (PhD, Certificate)
developmental psychology (PhD)
East Asian studies (AM, Certificate)
ecology (PhD, Certificate)
economics (AM, PhD)
English (PhD)
enzyme mechanisms (PhD)
experimental psychology (PhD)
French (PhD)
genetics and genomics (PhD)
German studies (PhD)
gross anatomy and physical anthropology (PhD)
health psychology (PhD)
history (AM, PhD)
human social development (PhD)
humanities (AM)
immunology (PhD)
integrated toxicology and environmental health (PhD, Certificate)
Latin American studies (PhD)
liberal studies (AM)
lipid biochemistry (PhD)
literature (PhD)
mathematics (PhD)
medical physics (MS, PhD)
medieval and Renaissance studies (Certificate)
membrane structure and function (PhD)
molecular cancer biology (PhD)
molecular genetics (PhD)
molecular genetics and microbiology (PhD)
music composition (AM, PhD)
musicology (AM, PhD)
natural resource economics/policy (AM, PhD)
natural resource science/ecology (AM, PhD)
natural resource systems science (AM, PhD)
neuroanatomy (PhD)
neurobiology (PhD)
neurochemistry (PhD)
nucleic acid structure and function (PhD)
pathology (PhD)
performance practice (AM, PhD)
pharmacology (PhD)
philosophy (AM, PhD)
physical anthropology (PhD)
physics (PhD)
political science (AM, PhD)
protein structure and function (PhD)
religion (MA, PhD)
Slavic languages and literatures (AM)
social/cultural anthropology (PhD)
sociology (AM, PhD)
Spanish (PhD)
structural biology and biophysics (Certificate)
teaching (MAT)
women's studies (Certificate)

Center for Latin American and Caribbean Studies

Program in:
Latin American and Caribbean studies (Certificate)

Division of Earth and Ocean Sciences

Program in:
earth and ocean sciences (MS, PhD)

Duke Sanford Institute of Public Policy

Programs in:
international development policy (AM, Certificate)
public policy (AM, MPP, PhD, Certificate)

Institute of Statistics and Decision Sciences

Program in:
statistics and decision sciences (PhD)

Pratt School of Engineering

Programs in:
biomedical engineering (MS, PhD)
civil and environmental engineering (MS, PhD),
electrical and computer engineering (MS, PhD)
engineering (MEM, MS, PhD)
engineering management (MEM)
environmental engineering (MS, PhD)
materials science (MS, PhD)
mechanical engineering (MS, PhD)

Nicholas School of the Environment

Programs in:
coastal environmental management (MEM)
DEL-environmental leadership (MEM)
energy and environment (MEM)
environmental economics and policy (MEM)
environmental health and security (MEM)
forest resource management (MF)
global environmental change (MEM)
resource ecology (MEM)
water and air resources (MEM)

School of Law

Program in:
law (JD, LL M, MLS, SJD)

School of Medicine

Dr. Edward G. Buckley, Vice Dean, Medical Education
Programs in:
clinical leadership program (MHS)
clinical research (MHS)
medicine (MD, MHS, DPT)
pathologists' assistant (MHS)
physician assistant (MHS)

Physical Therapy Division

Dr. Pam Duncan, Interim Chief and Professor
Program in:
physical therapy (DPT)

School of Nursing

Programs in:
adult acute care (Certificate)
adult cardiovascular (Certificate)
adult oncology/HIV (Certificate)
adult primary care (Certificate)
clinical nurse specialist (MSN)
clinical research management (MSN, Certificate)
family (Certificate)
gerontology (Certificate)
health and nursing ministries (MSN, Certificate)
health systems leadership and outcomes (Certificate)
leadership in community based long term care (MSN, Certificate)
neonatal (Certificate)
neonatal/pediatric in rural health (MSN, Certificate)
nurse anesthetist (MSN, Certificate)
nurse practitioner (MSN)
nursing (MSN, PhD, Certificate)
nursing and healthcare leadership (MSN)
nursing education (MSN)
nursing informatics (MSN, Certificate)
pediatric (Certificate)
pediatric acute care (Certificate)

■ EAST CAROLINA UNIVERSITY

Greenville, NC 27858-4353
http://www.ecu.edu/

State-supported, coed, university. CGS member. *Computer facilities:* Computer purchase and lease plans are available. 2,083 computers available on campus for general student use. A campuswide network can be accessed from student residence rooms and from off campus. Online class registration is available. *General application contact:* Dean of Graduate School, 252-328-6012.

East Carolina University (continued)

Brody School of Medicine

Programs in:
- anatomy and cell biology (PhD)
- biochemistry and molecular biology (PhD)
- medicine (MD, MPH, PhD)
- microbiology and immunology (PhD)
- Pathology (PhD)
- pharmacology (PhD)
- physiology (PhD)
- public health (MPH)

Graduate School

Program in:
- coastal resources management (PhD)

College of Business

Programs in:
- accounting (MS)
- business (MBA, MS, MSA)
- management (MBA)

College of Education

Programs in:
- adult education (MA Ed)
- behavior/emotional disabilities (MA Ed)
- counselor education (MS, Ed S)
- education (MA, MA Ed, MLS, MS, MSA, Ed D, CAS, Ed S)
- educational administration and supervision (Ed S)
- educational leadership (Ed D)
- elementary education (MA Ed)
- English education (MA Ed)
- higher education administration (Ed D)
- information technologies (MS)
- instruction technology specialist (MA Ed)
- learning disabilities (MA Ed)
- library science (MLS, CAS)
- low incidence disabilities (MA Ed)
- mathematics (MA Ed)
- mental retardation (MA Ed)
- middle grade education (MA Ed)
- reading education (MA Ed)
- school administration (MSA)
- science education (MA, MA Ed)
- social studies education (MA Ed)
- supervision (MA Ed)
- vocation education (MA Ed)

College of Fine Arts and Communication

Programs in:
- art and design (MA, MA Ed, MFA)
- fine arts and communication (MA, MA Ed, MFA, MM)
- health communication (MA)
- music education (MM)
- music therapy (MM)
- performance (MM)
- theory and composition (MM)

College of Health and Human Performance

Programs in:
- bioenergetics (PhD)
- environmental health (MS)
- exercise and sport science (MA, MA Ed)
- health and human performance (MA, MA Ed, MS, PhD)
- health education (MA, MA Ed)
- recreation and leisure services administration (MS)
- therapeutic recreation administration (MS)

College of Human Ecology

Programs in:
- child development and family relations (MS)
- criminal justice (MS)
- human ecology (MS, MSW)
- marriage and family therapy (MS)
- nutrition (MS)
- social work (MSW)

College of Nursing

Program in:
- nursing (MSN, PhD)

College of Technology and Computer Science

Programs in:
- computer network professional (Certificate)
- computer science (MS)
- industrial technology (MS)
- information assurance (Certificate)
- occupational safety (MS)
- technology and computer science (MS, PhD, Certificate)
- technology management (PhD)
- Website developer (Certificate)

School of Allied Health Sciences

Programs in:
- allied health sciences (MPT, MS, MSOT, DPT, PhD)
- communication sciences and disorders (PhD)
- occupational therapy (MSOT)
- physical therapy (MPT, DPT)
- physician assistant studies (MS)
- rehabilitation counseling (MS)
- speech, language and auditory pathology (MS)
- substance abuse and clinical counseling (MS)
- vocational evaluation (MS)

Thomas Harriot College of Arts and Sciences

Programs in:
- American history (MA)
- anthropology (MA)
- applied and biomedical physics (MS)
- applied mathematics (MA)
- applied resource economics (MS)
- arts and sciences (MA, MA Ed, MPA, MS, PhD)
- biology (MS)
- chemistry (MS)
- clinical psychology (MA)
- English (MA)
- European history (MA)
- general psychology (MA)
- geography (MA)
- geology (MS)
- health psychology (PhD)
- international studies (MA)
- maritime history (MA)
- mathematics (MA)
- medical physics (MS)
- molecular biology/biotechnology (MS)
- physics (PhD)
- public administration (MPA)
- sociology (MA)

■ ELON UNIVERSITY

Elon, NC 27244-2010

http://www.elon.edu/

Independent-religious, coed, comprehensive institution. CGS member. *Graduate faculty:* 71 full-time (33 women), 34 part-time/adjunct (16 women). *Computer facilities:* 850 computers available on campus for general student use. A campuswide network can be accessed from student residence rooms and from off campus. Online class registration is available. *General application contact:* Art Fadde, Director of Graduate Admissions, 800-334-8448 Ext. 3.

Program in Business Administration

Dr. William Burpit, Director

Program in:
- business administration (MBA)

Program in Education

Dr. Judith B. Howard, Director

Programs in:
- elementary education (M Ed)
- gifted education (M Ed)
- special education (M Ed)

Program in Interactive Media

Dr. David Alan Copeland, Director

Program in:
- interactive media (MA)

Program in Law

George Johnson, Dean

Program in:
- law (JD)

Program in Physical Therapy

Dr. Elizabeth A. Rogers, Chair

Program in:
- physical therapy (DPT)

■ FAYETTEVILLE STATE UNIVERSITY

Fayetteville, NC 28301-4298

http://www.uncfsu.edu/

State-supported, coed, comprehensive institution. CGS member. *Computer facilities:* Computer purchase and lease plans are available. 600 computers available on campus for general student use. A campuswide network can be accessed from student residence rooms and from off campus. Online class registration is available. *General application contact:* Associate Vice-Chancellor for Enrollment Management, 910-672-1784.

Graduate School
Programs in:
- biology (MA Ed, MS)
- business administration (MBA)
- criminal justice (MA)
- educational leadership (Ed D)
- elementary education (MA Ed)
- English (MA)
- history (MA, MA Ed)
- mathematics (MA Ed, MS)
- middle grades (MA Ed)
- political science (MA, MA Ed)
- psychology (MA)
- reading (MA Ed)
- school administration (MSA)
- social work (MSW)
- sociology (MA)
- special education (MA Ed)

■ GARDNER-WEBB UNIVERSITY
Boiling Springs, NC 28017
http://www.gardner-webb.edu/

Independent-religious, coed, comprehensive institution. *Graduate faculty:* 50 full-time (18 women), 18 part-time/adjunct (5 women). *Computer facilities:* 150 computers available on campus for general student use. A campuswide network can be accessed from student residence rooms and from off campus. Online class registration is available. *Graduate expenses:* Tuition: part-time $290 per credit hour. *General application contact:* Dr. Jackson Rainer, Dean, Graduate School, 704-406-4724.

Graduate School
Dr. Gayle B. Price, Dean
Programs in:
- English (MA)
- English education (MA)
- sport science and pedagogy (MA)

School of Education
Dr. Donna Simmons, Chair
Programs in:
- curriculum and instruction (Ed D)
- educational leadership (Ed D)
- elementary education (MA)
- middle grades education (MA)
- school administration (MA)

School of Nursing
Dr. Gayle B. Price, Dean
Program in:
- nursing (MSN, PMC)

School of Psychology
Dr. David Carscaddon, Chair
Programs in:
- mental health counseling (MA)
- school counseling (MA)

Graduate School of Business
Dr. Anthony Negbenebor, Director
Program in:
- business (IMBA, M Acc, MBA)

M. Christopher White School of Divinity
Programs in:
- Christian education (M Div)
- ministry (D Min)
- missiology (M Div)
- pastoral care and counseling (M Div)
- pastoral ministry (M Div)

■ HIGH POINT UNIVERSITY
High Point, NC 27262-3598
http://www.highpoint.edu/

Independent-religious, coed, comprehensive institution. CGS member. *Computer facilities:* Computer purchase and lease plans are available. 950 computers available on campus for general student use. A campuswide network can be accessed from student residence rooms and from off campus. Online class registration is available. *General application contact:* Dean of Norcross Graduate School, 336-841-9198.

Norcross Graduate School
Programs in:
- business administration (MBA)
- educational leadership (M Ed)
- elementary education (M Ed)
- history (MA)
- nonprofit management (MA)
- special education (M Ed)
- sport studies (MS)

■ NORTH CAROLINA AGRICULTURAL AND TECHNICAL STATE UNIVERSITY
Greensboro, NC 27411
http://www.ncat.edu/

State-supported, coed, university. CGS member. *Computer facilities:* 250 computers available on campus for general student use. A campuswide network can be accessed from off campus. Online class registration is available. *General application contact:* Interim Dean of the Graduate School, 336-334-7920.

Graduate School

College of Arts and Sciences
Programs in:
- art education (MS)
- arts and sciences (MA, MAT, MS, MSW)
- biology (MS)
- biology education (MAT)
- chemistry (MS)
- English (MA)
- English and Afro-American literature (MA)
- English education (MS)
- history education (MAT, MS)
- mathematics education (MS)
- social studies education (MS)
- sociology and social work (MSW)

College of Engineering
Programs in:
- chemical engineering (MS Ch E)
- civil engineering (MSCE)
- computer science (MSCS)
- electrical engineering (MSEE, PhD)
- engineering (MS Ch E, MSCE, MSCS, MSE, MSEE, MSIE, MSME, PhD)
- industrial engineering (MSIE, PhD)
- mechanical engineering (MSME, PhD)

School of Agriculture and Environmental Sciences
Programs in:
- agricultural economics (MS)
- agricultural education (MS)
- agriculture and environmental sciences (MS)
- animal health science (MS)
- food and nutrition (MS)
- plant, soil and environmental science (MS)

School of Education
Programs in:
- adult education (MS)
- counselor education (MS)
- education (MA Ed, MAT, MS)
- elementary education (MA Ed)
- human resources-agency counseling (MS)
- human resources-rehabilitation counseling (MS)
- instructional technology (MS)
- leadership studies (PhD)
- physical education (MAT, MS)
- reading (MA Ed)
- school administration (MS)
- teaching (MAT)

School of Technology
Programs in:
- construction management (MSIT)
- electronics and computer technology (MSIT)
- industrial arts education (MS)
- industrial technology (MS, MSIT)
- occupational safety and health (MSIT)
- safety and driver education (MS)
- technology (MS, MSIT, PhD)
- technology education (MS)
- technology management (PhD)
- vocational-industrial education (MS)
- workforce development director (MS)

■ NORTH CAROLINA CENTRAL UNIVERSITY
Durham, NC 27707-3129
http://www.nccu.edu/

State-supported, coed, comprehensive institution. CGS member. *Computer facilities:* Computer purchase and lease plans are available. 175 computers available on campus for general student use. A campuswide network can be accessed from student residence rooms and from off campus. Online class registration is available. *General application contact:* Vice Chancellor for Academic Affairs and Provost, 919-560-6230.

North Carolina Central University (continued)

Division of Academic Affairs

College of Behavioral and Social Sciences
Programs in:
athletic administration (MS)
behavioral and social sciences (MA, MPA, MS)
criminal justice (MS)
family and consumer sciences (MS)
physical education (MS)
psychology (MA)
public administration (MPA)
recreation administration (MS)
sociology (MA)
therapeutic recreation (MS)

College of Liberal Arts
Programs in:
English (MA)
history (MA)
jazz studies (MM)
liberal arts (MA, MM)

College of Science and Technology
Programs in:
applied mathematics (MS)
biology (MS)
chemistry (MS)
earth sciences (MS)
mathematics education (MS)
physics (MS)
pure mathematics (MS)
science and technology (MS)

School of Business
Program in:
business (MBA)

School of Education
Programs in:
career counseling (MA)
communication disorders (M Ed)
community agency counseling (MA)
curriculum and instruction (MA)
education (M Ed, MA, MAT, MSA)
educational technology (MA)
instructional technology (M Ed)
school administration (MSA)
school counseling (MA)
special education (M Ed, MAT)

School of Law
Program in:
law (JD)

School of Library and Information Sciences
Program in:
library and information sciences (MIS, MLS)

■ NORTH CAROLINA STATE UNIVERSITY

Raleigh, NC 27695
http://www.ncsu.edu/

State-supported, coed, university. CGS member. *Computer facilities:* Computer purchase and lease plans are available. 3,000 computers available on campus for general student use. A campuswide network can be accessed from student residence rooms and from off campus. Online class registration, course materials, online homework submission, online testing/quizzes, financial aid/cashier's office account balances, wiki space, blogging service, Web space, online storage space, on-site OS and virus removal, online/hybrid courses are available. *General application contact:* Office of Graduate Admissions, 919-515-2871.

College of Veterinary Medicine

Programs in:
cell biology (MS, PhD)
infectious disease (MS, PhD)
pathology (MS, PhD)
pharmacology (MS, PhD)
population medicine (MS, PhD)
specialized veterinary medicine (MSpVM)
veterinary medicine (DVM, MS, MSpVM, MVPH, PhD)
veterinary public health (MVPH)

Graduate School

College of Agriculture and Life Sciences
Programs in:
agricultural and extension education (Ed D)
agricultural and resource economics (MS)
agricultural education (MAE, MS, Certificate)
agriculture and life sciences (M Tox, MAE, MB, MBAE, MFG, MFM, MFS, MG, MMB, MN, MP, MS, MZS, Ed D, PhD, Certificate)
animal and poultry science (PhD)
animal science (MS)
biochemistry (PhD)
bioinformatics (MB, PhD)
biological and agricultural engineering (MBAE, MS, PhD, Certificate)
crop science (MS, PhD)
entomology (MS, PhD)
environmental and molecular toxicology (M Tox, MS, PhD)
extension education (MS)
financial mathematics (MFM)
food science (MFS, MS, PhD)
functional genomics (MFG, MS, PhD)
genetics (MG, MS, PhD)
genomic sciences (MS, PhD)
horticultural science (MS, PhD, Certificate)
immunology (MS, PhD)
microbial biotechnology (MMB)
microbiology (MMB, MS, PhD)
nutrition (MN, MS, PhD)
physiology (MP, MS, PhD)
plant biology (MS, PhD)
plant pathology (MS, PhD)
poultry science (MS)
soil science (MS, PhD)
zoology (MS, MZS, PhD)

College of Design
Programs in:
architecture (M Arch)
art and design (MAD)
design (M Arch, MAD, MGD, MID, MLA, PhD)
graphic design (MGD)
industrial design (MID)
landscape architecture (MLA)

College of Education
Programs in:
adult and community college education (M Ed, MS, Ed D)
agency counseling (M Ed, MS)
business and marketing education (M Ed, MS)
counselor education (M Ed, MS, PhD)
curriculum and instruction (M Ed, MS, MS Ed, PhD)
education (M Ed, MS, MS Ed, MSA, Ed D, PhD, Certificate)
educational administration and supervision (Ed D)
educational research and policy analysis (PhD)
elementary education (M Ed)
higher education administration (M Ed, MS, Ed D)
human resource development (MS)
instructional technology (M Ed, MS)
mathematics education (M Ed, MS, PhD)
middle grades education (M Ed, MS)
school administration (MSA)
science education (M Ed, MS, PhD)
secondary English education (M Ed, MS Ed)
social studies education (M Ed)
special education (M Ed, MS)
technology education (M Ed, MS, Ed D)
training and development (M Ed, Ed D, Certificate)

College of Engineering
Programs in:
aerospace engineering (MS, PhD)
biomedical engineering (MS, PhD)
chemical engineering (M Ch E, MS, PhD)
civil engineering (MCE, MS, PhD)
computer engineering (MS, PhD)
computer networking (MS)
computer science (MC Sc, MS, PhD)
electrical engineering (MS, PhD)
engineering (M Ch E, M Eng, MC Sc, MCE, MIE, MIMS, MMSE, MNE, MOR, MS, PhD)
industrial engineering (MIE, MS, PhD)
integrated manufacturing systems engineering (MIMS)
materials science and engineering (MMSE, MS, PhD)
mechanical engineering (MS, PhD)
nuclear engineering (MNE, MS, PhD)
operations research (MOR, MS, PhD)

College of Humanities and Social Sciences
Programs in:
anthropology (MA)
bioarchaeology (MA)
communication (MS)

communication, rhetoric, and digital media (PhD)
creative writing (MFA)
cultural anthropology (MA)
developmental psychology (PhD)
English (MA, MFA, MS)
environmental anthropology (MA)
ergonomics and experimental psychology (PhD)
French language and literature (MA)
history (MA)
humanities and social sciences (M Soc, MA, MFA, MIS, MPA, MS, MSW, PhD, Certificate)
industrial/organizational psychology (PhD)
international studies (MIS)
liberal studies (MA)
nonprofit management (Certificate)
psychology in the public interest (PhD)
public administration (MPA, PhD)
public history (MA)
school psychology (PhD)
social work (MSW)
sociology (M Soc, MS, PhD)
Spanish language and literature (MA)
technical communication (MS)

College of Management
Programs in:
accounting (MAC)
analytics (MS)
biosciences management (MBA)
economics (M Econ, MA, PhD)
entrepreneurship and technology commercialization (MBA)
financial management (MBA)
innovation management (MBA)
management (M Econ, MA, MAC, MBA, MS, PhD)
marketing management (MBA)
services management and consulting (MBA)
supply chain management (MBA)

College of Natural Resources
Programs in:
fisheries and wildlife sciences (MFWS, MS, PhD)
forestry and environmental resources (MF, MS, PhD)
natural resource management (MPRTM, MS)
natural resources (MF, MFWS, MNR, MPRTM, MS, MWPS, PhD)
park and recreation management (MPRTM, MS)
parks, recreation and tourism management (PhD)
recreational sport management (MPRTM, MS)
spatial information science (MPRTM, MS)
tourism policy and development (MPRTM, MS)
wood and paper science (MS, MWPS, PhD)

College of Physical and Mathematical Sciences
Programs in:
applied mathematics (MS, PhD)
biomathematics (M Biomath, MS, PhD)
chemistry (MS, PhD)
marine, earth, and atmospheric sciences (MS, PhD)
mathematics (MS, PhD)
meteorology (MS, PhD)
oceanography (MS, PhD)
physical and mathematical sciences (M Biomath, M Stat, MS, PhD)
physics (MS, PhD)
statistics (M Stat, MS, PhD)

College of Textiles
Programs in:
fiber and polymer science (PhD)
textile and apparel technology and management (MS, MT)
textile chemistry (MS)
textile engineering (MS)
textile technology management (PhD)
textiles (MS, MT, PhD)

■ PFEIFFER UNIVERSITY
Misenheimer, NC 28109-0960
http://www.pfeiffer.edu/

Independent-religious, coed, comprehensive institution. *Computer facilities:* 114 computers available on campus for general student use. A campuswide network can be accessed from student residence rooms. Online class registration is available. *General application contact:* Assistant Dean, 704-521-9116 Ext. 253.

Program in Business Administration
Programs in:
business administration (MBA)
organizational management (MS)

Program in Health Administration
Program in:
health administration (MHA)

Program in Organizational Change and Leadership
Program in:
organizational change and leadership (MS)

School of Education
Programs in:
elementary education (MS)
teaching (MAT)

School of Religion and Christian Education
Program in:
religion and Christian education (MACE)

■ QUEENS UNIVERSITY OF CHARLOTTE
Charlotte, NC 28274-0002
http://www.queens.edu/

Independent-religious, coed, comprehensive institution. *Graduate faculty:* 31 full-time (11 women), 11 part-time/adjunct (8 women). *Computer facilities:* Computer purchase and lease plans are available. 125 computers available on campus for general student use. A campuswide network can be accessed from student residence rooms and from off campus. *General application contact:* Robert Mobley, Director of Graduate Admissions, McColl School of Business, 704-337-2224.

College of Arts and Sciences
Dr. Betty J. Powell, Dean
Program in:
creative writing (MFA)

McColl School of Business
Terry Broderick, Dean
Program in:
business administration (EMBA, MBA)

Presbyterian School of Nursing
Dr. William K. Cody, Dean
Program in:
nursing management (MSN)

School of Communication
Van King, Dean
Program in:
organizational and strategic communication (MA)

Wayland H. Cato, Jr. School of Education
Dr. Darrel L. Miller, Dean
Programs in:
education in literacy (M Ed)
elementary education (MAT)
school administration (MSA)

■ THE UNIVERSITY OF NORTH CAROLINA AT CHAPEL HILL
Chapel Hill, NC 27599
http://www.unc.edu/

State-supported, coed, university. CGS member. *Computer facilities:* Computer purchase and lease plans are available. 600 computers available on campus for general student use. A campuswide network can be accessed from student residence rooms and from off campus. Online class registration is available. *General application contact:* Director of Admissions and Enrollment Services, 919-966-2611.

Eshelman School of Pharmacy
Dr. Robert A. Blouin, Dean
Program in:
pharmacy (MS, PhD)

The University of North Carolina at Chapel Hill (continued)

Graduate School
Programs in:
materials science (MS, PhD)
public policy (PhD)
Russian and east European studies (MA)

College of Arts and Sciences
Programs in:
acting (MFA)
anthropology (MA, PhD)
art history (MA, PhD)
arts and sciences (MA, MCRP, MFA, MPA, MRP, MS, MSRA, PhD, Certificate)
athletic training (MA)
biological psychology (PhD)
botany (MA, MS, PhD)
cell biology, development, and physiology (MA, MS, PhD)
cell motility and cytoskeleton (PhD)
chemistry (MA, MS, PhD)
city and regional planning (MCRP)
classical archaeology (MA, PhD)
classics (MA, PhD)
clinical psychology (PhD)
cognitive psychology (PhD)
communication studies (MA, PhD)
comparative literature (MA, PhD)
computer science (MS, PhD)
costume production (MFA)
developmental psychology (PhD)
ecology (MA, MS, PhD)
ecology and behavior (MA, MS, PhD)
economics (MS, PhD)
English (MA, PhD)
exercise physiology (MA)
folklore (MA)
French (MA, PhD)
genetics and molecular biology (MA, MS, PhD)
geography (MA, PhD)
geological sciences (MS, PhD)
history (MA, PhD)
Italian (MA, PhD)
Latin American studies (Certificate)
linguistics (MA, PhD)
literature and linguistics (MA, PhD)
marine sciences (MS, PhD)
mathematics (MA, MS, PhD)
morphology, systematics, and evolution (MA, MS, PhD)
music (MA, PhD)
operations research (MS, PhD)
philosophy (MA, PhD)
physics (MS, PhD)
planning (PhD)
Polish literature (PhD)
political science (MA, PhD)
Portuguese (MA, PhD)
public administration (MPA)
public policy analysis (PhD)
quantitative psychology (PhD)
recreation and leisure studies (MSRA)
religious studies (MA, PhD)
Romance languages (MA, PhD)
Romance philology (MA, PhD)
Russian literature (MA, PhD)
Serbo-Croatian literature (PhD)
Slavic linguistics (MA, PhD)
social psychology (PhD)
sociology (MA, PhD)
Spanish (MA, PhD)
sport administration (MA)
statistics (MS, PhD)
studio art (MFA)
technical production (MFA)
trans-Atlantic studies (MA)

School of Education
Dr. Jill Fitzgerald, Interim Dean
Programs in:
culture, curriculum and change (MA, PhD)
early childhood, intervention and literacy (MA, PhD)
education (M Ed, MA, MAT, MSA, Ed D, PhD)
education for experienced teachers (K-12) (M Ed)
education for experienced teachers, early childhood intervention and family support (M Ed)
educational leadership (Ed D)
educational psychology, measurement and evaluation (MA, PhD)
English (Grades 9-12) (MAT)
French (Grades K-12) (MAT)
German (Grades K-12) (MAT)
Japanese (Grades K-12) (MAT)
Latin (Grades 9-12) (MAT)
mathematics (Grades 9-12) (MAT)
music (Grades K-12) (MAT)
school administration (MSA)
school counseling (M Ed)
school psychology (M Ed, MA, PhD)
science (Grades 9-12) (MAT)
social studies (Grades 9-12) (MAT)
Spanish (Grades K-12) (MAT)

School of Information and Library Science
Program in:
information and library science (MSIS, MSLS, PhD, CAS)

School of Journalism and Mass Communication
Dr. Jean Folkerts, Dean
Program in:
mass communication (MA, PhD)

School of Public Health
Programs in:
air, radiation and industrial hygiene (MPH, MS, MSEE, MSPH, PhD)
aquatic and atmospheric sciences (MPH, MS, MSPH, PhD)
biostatistics (MPH, MS, Dr PH, PhD)
environmental engineering (MPH, MS, MSEE, MSPH, PhD)
environmental health sciences (MPH, MS, MSPH, PhD)
environmental management and policy (MPH, MS, MSPH, PhD)
epidemiology (MPH, PhD)
health behavior and health education (MPH, PhD)
health care and prevention (MPH)
health policy and administration (MHA, MPH, MSPH, Dr PH, PhD)
leadership (MPH)
maternal and child health (MPH, MSPH, Dr PH, PhD)
nutrition (MPH, Dr PH, PhD)
nutritional biochemistry (MS)
occupational health nursing (MPH)
professional practice program (MPH)
public health (MHA, MPH, MS, MSEE, MSPH, Dr PH, PhD)
public health nursing (MS)

School of Social Work
Program in:
social work (MSW, PhD)

Kenan-Flagler Business School
Programs in:
accounting (PhD)
business (MAC, MBA, PhD)
business administration (MBA, PhD)
finance (PhD)
marketing (PhD)
operations management (PhD)
organizational behavior (PhD)
strategy (PhD)

National Institutes of Health Sponsored Programs
Program in:
cell motility and cytoskeleton (PhD)

School of Dentistry
Programs in:
dental hygiene (MS)
dentistry (DDS, MS, PhD)
endodontics (MS)
epidemiology (PhD)
operative dentistry (MS)
oral and maxillofacial pathology (MS)
oral and maxillofacial radiology (MS)
oral biology (PhD)
orthodontics (MS)
pediatric dentistry (MS)
periodontology (MS)
prosthodontics (MS)

School of Law
Program in:
law (JD)

School of Medicine
Programs in:
allied health sciences (MPT, MS, Au D, DPT, PhD)
audiology (Au D)
biochemistry and biophysics (MS, PhD)
biomedical engineering (MS, PhD)
cell and developmental biology (PhD)
cell and molecular physiology (PhD)
experimental pathology (PhD)
genetics and molecular biology (MS, PhD)
human movement science (MS, PhD)
immunology (MS, PhD)
medicine (MD, MPT, MS, Au D, DPT, PhD)
microbiology (MS, PhD)
microbiology and immunology (MS, PhD)

neurobiology (PhD)
occupational science (MS, PhD)
pathology and laboratory medicine (PhD)
pharmacology (PhD)
physical therapy (MPT, MS, DPT)
physical therapy—off campus (DPT)
physical therapy—on campus (DPT)
rehabilitation counseling and psychology (MS)
speech and hearing sciences (MS, Au D, PhD)
toxicology (MS, PhD)

School of Nursing
Program in:
nursing (MSN, PhD, PMC)

■ THE UNIVERSITY OF NORTH CAROLINA AT CHARLOTTE
Charlotte, NC 28223-0001
http://www.uncc.edu/

State-supported, coed, university. CGS member. *Graduate faculty:* 796 full-time (310 women), 81 part-time/adjunct (37 women). *Computer facilities:* 1,400 computers available on campus for general student use. A campuswide network can be accessed from student residence rooms and from off campus. Online class registration is available. *Graduate expenses:* Tuition, state resident: full-time $2919; part-time $122 per credit hour. Tuition, nonresident: full-time $13,126; part-time $547 per credit hour. Required fees: $1779; $91 per credit hour. Tuition and fees vary according to program. *General application contact:* Dr. Thomas L. Reynolds, Dean and Associate Provost, 704-687-3372.

Graduate School
Dr. Thomas L. Reynolds, Dean and Associate Provost

Belk College of Business
Dr. Stephen Ott, Interim Dean
Programs in:
accounting (M Acc)
business (M Acc, MBA, MS, PhD)
business administration (MBA, PhD)
economics (MS)
mathematical finance (MS)
sports marketing management (MBA)

College of Arts and Architecture
Kenneth A. Lambla, Dean
Program in:
arts and architecture (M Arch)

College of Arts and Sciences
Dr. Nancy A. Gutierrez, Dean
Programs in:
applied mathematics (MS, PhD)
applied physics (MS)
arts and sciences (MA, MPA, MS, PhD)
biology (MA, MS, PhD)
chemistry (MS)
communication studies (MA)
community/clinical psychology (MA)
criminal justice (MS)
earth sciences (MS)
English (MA)
English education (MA)
geography (MA)
geography and urban and regional analysis (PhD)
gerontology (MA)
health psychology (PhD)
history (MA)
industrial/organizational psychology (MA)
Latin American studies (MA)
liberal studies (MA)
mathematics (MS)
mathematics education (MA)
optical science and engineering (MS, PhD)
organizational science (PhD)
public administration (MPA)
public policy (PhD)
religious studies (MA)
sociology (MA)
Spanish (MA)

College of Computing and Informatics
Dr. Mirsad Hadzikadic, Dean
Programs in:
computer science (MS)
computing and informatics (MS, PMS, PhD, Certificate)
health information technology (PMS, Certificate)
information technology (MS, PhD)

College of Education
Dr. Mary Lynne Calhoun, Dean
Programs in:
art education (K-12) (MAT)
counseling (MA, PhD)
curriculum and supervision (M Ed)
dance education (K-12) (MAT)
education (M Ed, MA, MAT, MSA, Ed D, PhD, CAS)
educational administration (CAS)
educational leadership (Ed D)
elementary education (M Ed)
elementary education (K-6) (MAT)
English as a second language (K-12) (MAT)
foreign language education (K-12) (MAT)
general teacher education (MAT)
instructional systems technology (M Ed)
middle grades and secondary education (M Ed)
middle grades education (6-9) (MAT)
music education (K-12) (MAT)
reading, language and literacy (M Ed)
school administration (MSA)
secondary education (9-12) (MAT)
special education (M Ed, PhD)
special education (K-12) (MAT)
teaching English as a second language (M Ed)
theatre education (K-12) (MAT)
urban education (PhD)
urban literacy (PhD)
urban math (PhD)

College of Health and Human Services
Dr. Karen Schmaling, Dean
Programs in:
clinical exercise physiology (MS)
health and human services (MHA, MS, MSN, MSPH, MSW, PhD)
health care administration (MHA)
health services research (PhD)
nursing advanced clinical (MSN)
nursing anesthesia (MSN)
nursing systems population (MSN)
public health (MSPH)
social work (MSW)

The William States Lee College of Engineering
Dr. Robert E. Johnson, Dean
Programs in:
civil engineering (MSCE)
electrical engineering (MSEE, PhD)
engineering (MS, MSCE, MSE, MSEE, MSME, PhD)
engineering management (MS)
infrastructure and environmental systems (PhD)
infrastructure and environmental systems design (PhD)
infrastructure and environmental systems management (PhD)
infrastructure and environmental systems science (PhD)
mechanical engineering (MSME, PhD)

■ THE UNIVERSITY OF NORTH CAROLINA AT GREENSBORO
Greensboro, NC 27412-5001
http://www.uncg.edu/

State-supported, coed, university. CGS member. *Computer facilities:* Computer purchase and lease plans are available. 500 computers available on campus for general student use. A campuswide network can be accessed from student residence rooms and from off campus. Online class registration is available. *General application contact:* Director of Graduate Admissions, 336-334-4884.

Graduate School
Programs in:
conflict resolution (MA, Certificate)
genetic counseling (MS)
gerontology (MS, Certificate)
liberal studies (MALS)

Bryan School of Business and Economics
Programs in:
accounting (MS)
accounting systems (MS)
applied economics (MA)
business administration (MBA, PMC, Postbaccalaureate Certificate)
business and economics (MA, MBA, MS, PhD, Certificate, PMC, Postbaccalaureate Certificate)

The University of North Carolina at Greensboro (continued)
- economics (PhD)
- financial accounting and reporting (MS)
- financial analysis (PMC)
- financial economics (MA)
- information systems (PhD)
- information technology (Certificate)
- information technology and management (MS)
- supply chain management (Certificate)
- tax concentration (MS)

College of Arts and Sciences
Programs in:
- acting (MFA)
- advanced Spanish language and Hispanic cultural studies (Certificate)
- American literature (PhD)
- applied geography (MA)
- arts and sciences (M Ed, MA, MFA, MPA, MS, PhD, Certificate)
- biochemistry (MS)
- biology (MS)
- chemistry (MS)
- clinical psychology (MA, PhD)
- cognitive psychology (MA, PhD)
- communication studies (MA)
- computer science (MS)
- creative writing (MFA)
- criminology (MA)
- design (MFA)
- developmental psychology (MA, PhD)
- directing (MFA)
- English (M Ed, MA, PhD, Certificate)
- English literature (PhD)
- film and video production (MFA)
- French (MA)
- geographic information science (Certificate)
- geography (PhD)
- historic preservation (Certificate)
- history (MA)
- Latin (M Ed)
- mathematics (MA, PhD)
- museum studies (Certificate)
- nonprofit management (Certificate)
- public affairs (MPA)
- rhetoric and composition (PhD)
- social psychology (MA, PhD)
- sociology (MA)
- Spanish (MA, Certificate)
- studio arts (MFA)
- theater education (M Ed)
- theater for youth (MFA)
- U.S. history (PhD)
- urban and economic development (Certificate)
- women's and gender studies (MA, Certificate)

School of Education
Programs in:
- advanced school counseling (PMC)
- college teaching and adult learning (Certificate)
- counseling and counselor education (PhD)
- counseling and educational development (MS)
- couple and family counseling (PMC)
- cross-categorical special education (M Ed)
- curriculum and instruction (M Ed)
- curriculum and teaching (PhD)
- education (M Ed, MLIS, MS, MSA, Ed D, PhD, Certificate, Ed S, PMC)
- educational leadership (Ed D, Ed S)
- educational research, measurement and evaluation (PhD)
- English as a second language (Certificate)
- higher education (M Ed, PhD)
- interdisciplinary studies in special education (M Ed)
- leadership early care and education (Certificate)
- library and information studies (MLIS)
- school administration (MSA)
- school counseling (PMC)
- special education (M Ed, PhD)
- supervision (M Ed)
- teacher education and development (PhD)

School of Health and Human Performance
Programs in:
- community health education (MPH, Dr PH)
- dance (MA, MFA)
- exercise and sports science (M Ed, MS, Ed D, PhD)
- health and human performance (M Ed, MA, MFA, MPH, MS, Dr PH, Ed D, PhD)
- parks and recreation management (MS)
- speech language pathology (PhD)
- speech pathology and audiology (MA)

School of Human Environmental Sciences
Programs in:
- consumer, apparel, and retail studies (MS, PhD)
- historic preservation (Certificate)
- human development and family studies (M Ed, MS, PhD)
- human environmental sciences (M Ed, MS, MSW, PhD, Certificate)
- interior architecture (MS)
- museum studies (Certificate)
- nutrition (MS, PhD)
- social work (MSW)

School of Music
Programs in:
- composition (MM)
- education (MM)
- music education (PhD)
- performance (MM, DMA)

School of Nursing
Programs in:
- adult clinical nurse specialist (MSN, PMC)
- adult/gerontological nurse practitioner (MSN, PMC)
- nurse anesthesia (MSN, PMC)
- nursing (PhD)
- nursing administration (MSN)
- nursing education (MSN)

■ THE UNIVERSITY OF NORTH CAROLINA AT PEMBROKE

Pembroke, NC 28372-1510
http://www.uncp.edu/

State-supported, coed, comprehensive institution. CGS member. *Computer facilities:* 650 computers available on campus for general student use. A campuswide network can be accessed from student residence rooms and from off campus. Online class registration is available. *General application contact:* Dean of Graduate Studies, 910-521-6271.

Graduate Studies
Programs in:
- art education (MA, MAT)
- English education (MA, MAT)
- mathematics education (MA, MAT)
- music education (MA, MAT)
- physical education (MA, MAT)
- public administration (MPA)
- science education (MA)
- service agency counseling (MA)
- social studies education (MA, MAT)

School of Business
Programs in:
- business (MBA)
- business administration (MBA)

School of Education
Programs in:
- elementary education (MA Ed)
- middle grades education (MA Ed, MAT)
- reading education (MA Ed)
- school administration (MSA)
- school counseling (MA Ed)

■ THE UNIVERSITY OF NORTH CAROLINA WILMINGTON

Wilmington, NC 28403-3297
http://www.uncw.edu/

State-supported, coed, comprehensive institution. CGS member. *Graduate faculty:* 285 full-time (107 women), 29 part-time/adjunct (12 women). *Computer facilities:* Computer purchase and lease plans are available. 1,170 computers available on campus for general student use. A campuswide network can be accessed from student residence rooms and from off campus. Online class registration is available. *Graduate expenses:* Tuition, state resident: full-time $4838. Tuition, nonresident: full-time $14,898. Tuition and fees vary according to course load, campus/location and program. *General application contact:* Dr. Robert D. Roer, Dean, Graduate School and Research, 910-962-4117.

Center for Marine Science
Dr. Daniel Baden, Director
Program in:
- marine science (MS)

College of Arts and Sciences
Dr. David Cordle, Dean
Programs in:
- applied gerontology (MS)
- arts and sciences (MA, MALS, MFA, MPA, MS, MSW, PhD, Graduate Certificate)
- biology (MS)
- chemistry and biochemistry (MS)
- coastal management (MA)
- computer science and information systems (MS)
- creative writing (MFA)
- criminology (MA)
- English (MA)
- environmental education and interpretation (MA)
- environmental management (MA)
- geology (MS)
- Hispanic studies (Graduate Certificate)
- history (MA)
- individualized study (MA)
- liberal studies (MALS)
- marine biology (MS, PhD)
- marine science (MS)
- mathematical sciences (MS)
- psychology (MA)
- public and international affairs (MPA)
- public sociology (MA)
- social work (MSW)

School of Business
Dr. Lawrence Clark, Dean
Programs in:
- accountancy (MSA)
- business (MBA, MSA)
- business administration (MBA)

School of Education
Dr. Karen Wetherill, Interim Dean
Programs in:
- curriculum, instruction and supervision (M Ed)
- education (M Ed, MAT, MS, MSA, Ed D)
- educational leadership (M Ed, MSA, Ed D)
- elementary education (M Ed)
- instructional technology (MS)
- language and literacy education (M Ed)
- middle grades education (M Ed)

School of Nursing
Dr. Julie S. Taylor, Graduate Program Coordinator
Programs in:
- family nurse practitioner (MSN)
- nurse educator (MSN)

■ WAKE FOREST UNIVERSITY
Winston-Salem, NC 27109
http://www.wfu.edu/

Independent, coed, university. CGS member. *Graduate faculty:* 1,900. *Computer facilities:* 150 computers available on campus for general student use. A campuswide network can be accessed from student residence rooms and from off campus. Online class registration, financial information online, drop-add, transcript requests are available.

Babcock Graduate School of Management
Steve Reinemund, Dean
Programs in:
- accountancy (MSA)
- assurance services (MSA)
- business administration (MA, MBA)
- entrepreneurship (MBA)
- finance (MBA)
- health care (MBA)
- management (MA, MBA, MSA)
- marketing (MBA)
- operations management (MBA)
- tax consulting (MSA)
- transaction services (MSA)

Graduate School of Arts and Sciences
Dr. Lorna G. Moore, Dean
Programs in:
- accountancy (MSA)
- analytical chemistry (MS, PhD)
- arts and sciences (MA, MA Ed, MALS, MS, MSA, PhD)
- biology (MS, PhD)
- computer science (MS)
- counseling (MA)
- English (MA)
- health and exercise science (MS)
- inorganic chemistry (MS, PhD)
- liberal studies (MALS)
- mathematics (MA)
- organic chemistry (MS, PhD)
- physical chemistry (MS, PhD)
- physics (MS, PhD)
- psychology (MA)
- religion (MA)
- secondary education (MA Ed)
- speech communication (MA)

School of Law
Program in:
- law (JD, LL M, SJD)

School of Medicine
Program in:
- medicine (MD, MS, PhD)

Graduate Programs in Medicine
Programs in:
- biochemistry (PhD)
- cancer biology (PhD)
- comparative medicine (MS)
- health sciences research (MS)
- medicine (MS, PhD)
- microbiology and immunology (PhD)
- molecular and cellular pathobiology (MS, PhD)
- molecular genetics and genomics (PhD)
- molecular medicine (MS, PhD)
- neurobiology and anatomy (PhD)
- neuroscience (PhD)
- pharmacology (PhD)
- physiology (PhD)

Virginia Tech-Wake Forest University School of Biomedical Engineering and Sciences
Program in:
- biomedical engineering (MS, PhD)

■ WESTERN CAROLINA UNIVERSITY
Cullowhee, NC 28723
http://www.wcu.edu/

State-supported, coed, comprehensive institution. CGS member. *Computer facilities:* Computer purchase and lease plans are available. 181 computers available on campus for general student use. A campuswide network can be accessed from student residence rooms and from off campus. Online class registration, student Web pages, online music services are available. *General application contact:* Admissions Specialist, 828-227-7398.

Graduate School

College of Arts and Sciences
Programs in:
- applied mathematics (MS)
- arts and sciences (MA, MPA, MS)
- biology (MS)
- chemistry (MS)
- English (MA)
- history (MA)
- political science and public affairs (MPA)
- science and entrepreneurship (MS)
- teaching English as a second language or foreign language (MA)

College of Business
Programs in:
- accountancy (M Ac)
- business administration (MBA)
- entrepreneurship (ME)
- project management (MPM)
- sport management (MS)

College of Education and Allied Professions
Programs in:
- biology, two-year college teaching (MA Ed)
- community college administration (MA Ed)
- community college and higher education (MA Ed)
- community college teaching (MA Ed)
- community counseling (M Ed, MS)
- comprehensive education (MA Ed)
- counseling (M Ed, MA Ed, MS)
- education and allied professions (M Ed, MA, MA Ed, MAT, MS, MSA, Ed D, Ed S)
- educational leadership (MA Ed, MSA, Ed D, Ed S)
- educational supervision (MA Ed)
- English, two-year college teaching (MA Ed)
- general psychology (MA)
- human resources (MS)

Western Carolina University (continued)
mathematics, two-year college teaching (MA Ed)
physical education, two-year college teaching (MA Ed)
school counseling (MA Ed)
school psychology (MA)
teaching (MAT)
teaching degrees (MA Ed, MAT)

College of Fine and Performing Arts
Programs in:
art and design (MFA)
fine and performing arts (MFA, MM)
music (MM)

College of Health and Human Sciences
Programs in:
communication sciences and disorders (MS)
health and human sciences (MHS, MPT, MS, MSN, MSW)
health sciences (MHS)
nursing (MSN)
physical therapy (MPT)
social work (MSW)

Kimmel School of Construction Management and Technology
Programs in:
construction management (MCM)
construction management and technology (MCM, MS)
engineering and technology (MS)

North Dakota

■ MINOT STATE UNIVERSITY
Minot, ND 58707-0002
http://www.minotstateu.edu/

State-supported, coed, comprehensive institution. *Computer facilities:* Computer purchase and lease plans are available. 460 computers available on campus for general student use. A campuswide network can be accessed from student residence rooms and from off campus. Online class registration is available. *Graduate expenses:* Full-time $5527; part-time $230.30 per credit hour. Tuition, state resident: full-time $8291; part-time $345.45 per credit hour. Tuition, nonresident: full-time $14,758; part-time $614.90 per credit hour. Required fees: $865; $36.03 per credit hour. Tuition and fees vary according to course load and reciprocity agreements. *General application contact:* Administrative Assistant, 701-858-3250 Ext. 3150.

Graduate School
Dr. Linda Cresap, Dean
Programs in:
audiology (MS)
criminal justice (MS)
education of the deaf (MS)
elementary education (M Ed)
information systems (MSIS)
learning disabilities (MS)
management (MS)
mathematics (MAT)
school psychology (Ed Sp)
science (MAT)
special education strategist (MS)
speech-language pathology (MS)

Division of Music
Sandra Starr, Chairperson
Program in:
music education (MME)

■ NORTH DAKOTA STATE UNIVERSITY
Fargo, ND 58105
http://www.ndsu.edu/

State-supported, coed, university. CGS member. *Graduate faculty:* 510 full-time (140 women), 21 part-time/adjunct (6 women). *Computer facilities:* Computer purchase and lease plans are available. 500 computers available on campus for general student use. A campuswide network can be accessed from student residence rooms. Online class registration is available. *General application contact:* Dr. David A. Wittrock, Dean, 701-231-7033.

College of Graduate and Interdisciplinary Studies
Dr. David A. Wittrock, Dean
Programs in:
cellular and molecular biology (PhD)
environmental and conservation sciences (MS, PhD)
food safety (MS, PhD)
genomics and bioinformatics (MS, PhD)
materials and nanotechnology (PhD)
natural resources management (MS, PhD)
transportation and logistics (PhD)

College of Agriculture, Food Systems, and Natural Resources
Dr. Kenneth F. Grafton, Dean
Programs in:
agribusiness and applied economics (MS)
agriculture, food systems, and natural resources (MS, PhD)
animal science (MS, PhD)
cereal science (MS, PhD)
crop and weed sciences (MS)
entomology (MS, PhD)
environment and conservation science (MS, PhD)
environmental and conservation science (PhD)
environmental conservation science (MS)
food safety (MS)
horticulture (MS)
international agribusiness (MS)
microbiology (MS)
molecular pathogenesis (PhD)
natural resource management (MS, PhD)
plant pathology (MS, PhD)
plant sciences (PhD)
range sciences (MS, PhD)
soil sciences (MS, PhD)

College of Arts, Humanities and Social Sciences
Dr. Thomas J. Riley, Dean
Programs in:
arts, humanities and social sciences (M Ed, MA, MM, MS, DMA, PhD)
communication (PhD)
criminal justice (MS, PhD)
emergency management (MS, PhD)
English (MA, MS)
history (MA, MS, PhD)
mass communication (MA, MS)
music (M Ed, MM, DMA)
social science (MA, MS)
sociology (MS)
speech communication (MA, MS)

College of Business
Dr. Ron Johnson, Dean
Program in:
business (MBA)

College of Engineering and Architecture
Dr. Gary R. Smith, Dean
Programs in:
agricultural and biosystems engineering (MS, PhD)
civil engineering (MS, PhD)
construction management (MS)
electrical and computer engineering (MS, PhD)
engineering (PhD)
engineering and architecture (MS, PhD)
environmental engineering (MS, PhD)
industrial and manufacturing engineering (PhD)
industrial engineering and management (MS)
manufacturing engineering (MS)
mechanical engineering and applied mechanics (MS, PhD)
natural resource management (MS)
natural resources management (PhD)
transportation and logistics (PhD)

College of Human Development and Education
Dr. Virginia Clark Johnson, Dean
Programs in:
agricultural education (M Ed, MS)
agricultural extension education (MS)
child development and family science (MS)
counseling (M Ed, MS, PhD)
couple and family therapy (MS)
curriculum and instruction (M Ed, MS)
dietetics (MS)
education (PhD)
educational leadership (M Ed, MS, Ed S)
entry level athletic training (MS)
exercise science (MS)

family and consumer sciences education (M Ed, MS)
family financial planning (MS)
gerontology (MS, PhD)
history education (M Ed, MS)
human development (PhD)
human development and education (M Ed, MS, Ed D, PhD, Ed S)
institutional analysis (Ed D)
mathematics education (M Ed, MS)
music education (M Ed, MS)
nutrition science (MS)
occupational and adult education (Ed D)
pedagogy (M Ed, MS)
physical education and athletic administration (M Ed, MS)
public health (MS)
science education (M Ed, MS)
sport pedagogy (MS)
sports recreation management (MS)

College of Pharmacy, Nursing and Allied Sciences
Dr. Charles D. Peterson, Dean
Programs in:
nursing (MS, DNP)
pharmaceutical sciences (MS, PhD)
pharmacy, nursing and allied sciences (MS, DNP, PhD)

College of Science and Mathematics
Dr. Kevin McCaul, Dean
Programs in:
applied mathematics (MS, PhD)
applied statistics (MS, Certificate)
biochemistry (MS, PhD)
biology (MS)
botany (MS, PhD)
cellular and molecular biology (PhD)
chemistry (MS, PhD)
clinical psychology (MS)
coatings and polymeric materials (MS, PhD)
cognitive and visual neuroscience (PhD)
computer science (MS, PhD)
environmental and conservation sciences (MS, PhD)
genomics (PhD)
health and social psychology (PhD)
mathematics (MS, PhD)
natural resources management (MS, PhD)
operations research (MS)
physics (MS, PhD)
psychology (MS)
science and mathematics (MS, PhD, Certificate)
software engineering (MS, PhD, Certificate)
statistics (PhD)
zoology (MS, PhD)

■ UNIVERSITY OF MARY

Bismarck, ND 58504-9652

http://www.umary.edu/

Independent-religious, coed, comprehensive institution. *Graduate faculty:* 41 full-time (21 women), 34 part-time/adjunct (13 women). *Computer facilities:* 235 computers available on campus for general student use. A campuswide network can be accessed from student residence rooms and from off campus. Online class registration is available. *Graduate expenses:* Tuition: full-time $6700; part-time $430 per credit hour. Required fees: $430 per credit hour. One-time fee: $40 full-time. Tuition and fees vary according to course load and program. *General application contact:* Dr. Kathy Perrin, Director of Graduate Studies, 701-355-8119.

Department of Occupational Therapy
Dr. Janeene Sibla, Program Director
Programs in:
entry level (MSOT)
post professional (MSOT)

Department of Physical Therapy
Dr. Joellen Marie Roller, Program Director
Program in:
physical therapy (DPT)

Division of Nursing
Glenda Reemts, Director
Programs in:
family nurse practitioner (MSN)
nurse administrator (MSN)
nursing educator (MSN)

Division of Social and Behavioral Sciences
James Renner, Program Director for Counseling Graduate Studies
Programs in:
addiction counseling (MSC)
community counseling (MSC)
school counseling (MSC)

Gary Tharaldson School of Business
Dr. Shanda Traiser, Director of the School of Accelerated and Distance Education
Programs in:
health care (MBA)
human resource management (MBA)
management (MBA)
project management (MPM)
strategic leadership (MSSL)

Program in Education
Dr. Rebecca Yunker Salveson, Director
Programs in:
college teaching (M Ed)
curriculum, instruction and assessment (M Ed)
early childhood education (M Ed)
early childhood special education (M Ed)
elementary education administration (M Ed)
emotional disorders (M Ed)
learning disabilities (M Ed)
reading (M Ed)
secondary education administration (M Ed)
special education (M Ed)
special education strategist (M Ed)

■ UNIVERSITY OF NORTH DAKOTA

Grand Forks, ND 58202

http://www.und.nodak.edu/

State-supported, coed, university. CGS member. *Computer facilities:* Computer purchase and lease plans are available. 1,100 computers available on campus for general student use. A campuswide network can be accessed from student residence rooms and from off campus. Online class registration is available. *General application contact:* Director of Admissions and Assistance, 701-777-2945.

Graduate School
Program in:
earth system science and policy (MEM, MS, PhD)

College of Arts and Sciences
Programs in:
arts and sciences (M Ed, M Mus, MA, MFA, MS, DA, DMEd, PhD)
botany (MS, PhD)
chemistry (MS, PhD)
clinical psychology (PhD)
communication (MA, PhD)
communication sciences and disorders (PhD)
counseling psychology (PhD)
criminal justice (PhD)
ecology (MS, PhD)
English (MA, PhD)
entomology (MS, PhD)
environmental biology (MS, PhD)
experimental psychology (PhD)
fisheries/wildlife (MS, PhD)
forensic psychology (MA, MS)
genetics (MS, PhD)
geography (MA, MS)
history (MA, DA, PhD)
linguistics (MA)
mathematics (M Ed, MS)
music (M Mus)
music education (M Mus, DMEd)
physics (MS, PhD)
psychology (MA)
sociology (MA)
speech-language pathology (MS)
theatre arts (MA)
visual arts (MFA)
zoology (MS, PhD)

College of Business and Public Administration
Programs in:
accountancy (M Acc)
applied economics (MSAE)
business administration (MBA)
business and public administration (M Acc, MBA, MPA, MSAE)
public administration (MPA)

College of Education and Human Development
Programs in:
counseling (MA)
early childhood education (MS)

University of North Dakota (continued)
education and human development (M Ed, MA, MS, MSW, Ed D, PhD, Specialist)
education/general studies (MS)
educational leadership (M Ed, MS, Ed D, PhD, Specialist)
elementary education (M Ed, MS)
instructional design and technology (M Ed, MS)
kinesiology (MS)
measurement and statistics (Ed D, PhD)
reading education (M Ed, MS)
secondary education (Ed D, PhD)
social work (MSW)
special education (Ed D, PhD)

College of Nursing
Program in:
nursing (MS, PhD)

John D. Odegard School of Aerospace Sciences
Programs in:
aerospace sciences (MS, PhD)
atmospheric sciences (MS, PhD)
aviation (MS)
computer science (MS)
space studies (MS)

School of Engineering and Mines
Programs in:
chemical engineering (M Engr, MS)
civil engineering (M Engr)
electrical engineering (M Engr, MS)
engineering (PhD)
engineering and mines (M Engr, MA, MS, PhD)
environmental engineering (M Engr, MS)
geological engineering (M Engr, MS)
geology (MA, MS, PhD)
mechanical engineering (M Engr, MS)
sanitary engineering (M Engr)

School of Law
Program in:
law (JD)

School of Medicine and Health Sciences
Programs in:
anatomy (MS, PhD)
biochemistry (MS, PhD)
clinical laboratory science (MS)
medicine (MD, MOT, MPAS, MPT, MS, DPT, PhD)
medicine and health sciences (MD, MOT, MPAS, MPT, MS, DPT, PhD)
microbiology and immunology (MS, PhD)
occupational therapy (MOT)
pharmacology (MS, PhD)
physical therapy (MPT, DPT)
physician assistant (MPAS)
physiology (MS, PhD)

Ohio

■ ANTIOCH UNIVERSITY MCGREGOR
Yellow Springs, OH 45387-1609
http://www.mcgregor.edu/

Independent, coed, upper-level institution. *Graduate faculty:* 14 full-time (7 women), 59 part-time/adjunct (34 women). *Computer facilities:* 32 computers available on campus for general student use. A campuswide network can be accessed. Online class registration is available. *Graduate expenses:* Tuition: full-time $20,016; part-time $417 per credit hour. Required fees: $150 per quarter. *General application contact:* Seth Gordon, Assistant Director of Admissions, 937-769-1800 Ext. 1825.

Graduate Programs
Darlene Robertson, Dean of Students
Programs in:
community college management (MA)
conflict analysis and management (MA)
liberal and professional studies (MA)
management (MA)

School of Education
Dr. Zak Shariff, Director
Program in:
education (M Ed)

■ ASHLAND UNIVERSITY
Ashland, OH 44805-3702
http://www.exploreashland.com/

Independent-religious, coed, comprehensive institution. CGS member. *Graduate faculty:* 72 full-time (34 women), 181 part-time/adjunct (90 women). *Computer facilities:* Computer purchase and lease plans are available. 760 computers available on campus for general student use. A campuswide network can be accessed from student residence rooms and from off campus. Online class registration is available. *Graduate expenses:* Tuition: part-time $419 per credit hour. Tuition and fees vary according to degree level and program. *General application contact:* Dr. W. Gregory Gerrick, Dean, Graduate School, 419-289-5750.

College of Arts and Sciences
Dr. Dawn Weber, Dean
Programs in:
American history and government (MAHG)
arts and sciences (MAHG, MFA)
creative writing (MFA)

Dauch College of Business and Economics
Dr. Beverly Heimann, Chair
Program in:
business and economics (MBA)

Dwight Schar College of Education
Dr. James P. Van Keuren, Dean
Programs in:
adapted physical education (M Ed)
administration (M Ed)
applied exercise science (M Ed)
business manager (M Ed)
classroom instruction (M Ed)
curriculum specialist (M Ed)
education (M Ed, Ed D)
educational leadership studies (Ed D)
intervention specialist-mild/moderate (M Ed)
intervention specialist-moderate/intensive (M Ed)
literacy (M Ed)
principalship (M Ed)
pupil services (M Ed)
school treasurer (M Ed)
sport education (M Ed)
sport management (M Ed)
superintendency (M Ed)
talent development (M Ed)

■ BALDWIN-WALLACE COLLEGE
Berea, OH 44017-2088
http://www.bw.edu/

Independent-religious, coed, comprehensive institution. *Graduate faculty:* 30 full-time (10 women), 25 part-time/adjunct (5 women). *Computer facilities:* 465 computers available on campus for general student use. A campuswide network can be accessed from student residence rooms. Online class registration is available. *Graduate expenses:* Tuition: full-time $12,330; part-time $690 per credit hour. *General application contact:* Winifred W. Gerhardt, Director of Admission for the Evening and Weekend College, 440-826-2222.

Graduate Programs
Mary Lou Higgerson, Vice President for Academic Affairs and Dean of the College

Division of Business
Wayne Cunningham, Chairperson, Business Administration
Programs in:
accounting (MBA)
business administration-systems management (MBA)
entrepreneurship (MBA)
executive management (MBA)
health care management (MBA)
human resources (MBA)
international management (MBA)

Division of Education
Karen Kaye, Chair
Programs in:
educational technology (MA Ed)
leadership in higher education (MA Ed)
mild/moderate educational needs (MA Ed)

reading (MA Ed)
school leadership (MA Ed)
teaching and learning (M Ed, MA Ed)

■ BOWLING GREEN STATE UNIVERSITY

Bowling Green, OH 43403
http://www.bgsu.edu/

State-supported, coed, university. CGS member. *Computer facilities:* Computer purchase and lease plans are available. 1,563 computers available on campus for general student use. A campuswide network can be accessed from student residence rooms. Online class registration is available. *General application contact:* Assistant Dean for Graduate Admissions and Studies, 419-372-7713.

Graduate College

College of Arts and Sciences
Programs in:
2-D studio art (MA, MFA)
3-D studio art (MA, MFA)
American culture studies (MA, PhD)
applied philosophy (PhD)
applied statistics (MS)
art education (MA)
art history (MA)
arts and sciences (MA, MAT, MFA, MPA, MS, PhD)
biological sciences (MAT, MS, PhD)
chemistry (MAT, MS)
clinical psychology (MA, PhD)
communication studies (MA, PhD)
computer art (MA)
computer science (MS)
creative writing (MFA)
demography and population studies (MA)
design (MFA)
developmental psychology (MA, PhD)
digital arts (MFA)
English (MA, PhD)
experimental psychology (MA, PhD)
fiction (MFA)
French (MA, MAT)
French education (MAT)
geology (MS)
geophysics (MS)
German (MA, MAT)
graphics (MFA)
history (MA, MAT, PhD)
industrial/organizational psychology (MA, PhD)
institutional theory and history (PhD)
literature (MA)
mathematics (MA, MAT, PhD)
philosophy (MA)
photochemical sciences (PhD)
physics (MAT, MS)
poetry (MFA)
popular culture (MA)
public administration (MPA)
public history (MA)
quantitative psychology (MA, PhD)
rhetoric and writing (PhD)
scientific and technical communication (MA)
social psychology (MA)
sociology (PhD)
Spanish (MA, MAT)
Spanish education (MAT)
statistics (PhD)
theatre and film (MA, PhD)

College of Business Administration
Programs in:
accountancy (M Acc)
applied statistics (MS)
business (MBA)
business administration (M Acc, MA, MBA, MOD, MS)
economics (MA)
organization development (MOD)

College of Education and Human Development
Programs in:
assistive technology (M Ed)
business education (M Ed)
classroom technology (M Ed)
college student personnel (MA)
counseling (M Ed, MA)
cross-cultural and international education (MA)
curriculum (M Ed)
curriculum and teaching (M Ed)
developmental kinesiology (M Ed)
early childhood intervention (M Ed)
education and human development (M Ed, MA, MFCS, MRC, Ed D, PhD, Ed S, Sp Ed)
education and intervention services (M Ed, MA, MRC, Ed S, Sp Ed)
educational administration and supervision (M Ed, Ed S)
food and nutrition (MFCS)
gifted education (M Ed)
hearing impaired intervention (M Ed)
higher education administration (PhD)
human development and family studies (MFCS)
leadership and policy studies (M Ed, MA, Ed D, PhD, Ed S)
leadership studies (Ed D)
master teaching (M Ed)
mental health counseling (MA)
mild/moderate intervention (M Ed)
moderate/intensive intervention (M Ed)
reading (M Ed, Ed S)
recreation and leisure (M Ed)
rehabilitation counseling (MRC)
school counseling (M Ed)
school psychology (M Ed, Sp Ed)
special education (M Ed)
sport administration (M Ed)

College of Health and Human Services
Programs in:
communication disorders (PhD)
criminal justice (MSCJ)
health and human services (MPH, MS, MSCJ, PhD)
public health (MPH)
speech-language pathology (MS)

College of Musical Arts
Programs in:
composition (MM)
contemporary music (DMA)
ethnomusicology (MM)
music education (MM)
music history (MM)
music theory (MM)
performance (MM)

College of Technology
Programs in:
career and technology education (M Ed)
construction management (MIT)
manufacturing technology (MIT)
technology (M Ed, MIT)

Interdisciplinary Studies
Program in:
interdisciplinary studies (M Ed, MA, MS, PhD)

■ CAPITAL UNIVERSITY

Columbus, OH 43209-2394
http://www.capital.edu/

Independent-religious, coed, comprehensive institution. *Computer facilities:* 454 computers available on campus for general student use. A campuswide network can be accessed from student residence rooms and from off campus. Online class registration is available. *General application contact:* Professor and Director of the MSN Program, 614-236-6393.

Conservatory of Music

Program in:
music education (MM)

Law School

Programs in:
business (LL M)
business and taxation (LL M)
law (JD, LL M, MT)
taxation (LL M, MT)

School of Management

Program in:
management (MBA)

School of Nursing

Programs in:
administration (MSN)
legal studies (MSN)
theological studies (MSN)

■ CASE WESTERN RESERVE UNIVERSITY

Cleveland, OH 44106
http://www.case.edu/

Independent, coed, university. CGS member. *Graduate faculty:* 2,646 full-time (905 women). *Computer facilities:* Computer purchase and lease plans are available. 415 computers available on campus for general student use. A campuswide network can be accessed from student residence rooms and from off campus. Online class registration, software library, online reference databases,

Case Western Reserve University (continued)
electronic books and journals are available. *Graduate expenses:* Tuition: full-time $31,000; part-time $1292 per credit hour. Required fees: $22. *General application contact:* Susan M. Benedict, Admissions Coordinator, 216-368-4400.

Frances Payne Bolton School of Nursing

Programs in:
- acute care cardiovascular nursing (MSN)
- acute care nurse practitioner (MSN, DNP)
- acute care/flight nurse (MSN)
- adult nurse practitioner (MSN, DNP)
- community health nursing (MSN)
- family nurse practitioner (MSN, DNP)
- gerontological nurse practitioner (MSN, DNP)
- graduate entry/pre-licensure option (DNP)
- medical-surgical nursing (MSN, DNP)
- midwifery/family nursing (DNP)
- neonatal nurse practitioner (MSN, DNP)
- nurse anesthesia (MSN)
- nurse midwifery (MSN)
- nurse practitioner (MSN)
- nursing (MSN, DNP, PhD)
- nursing informatics (MSN)
- pediatric nurse practitioner (MSN, DNP)
- post-licensure option (DNP)
- psychiatric-mental health nurse practitioner (MSN, DNP)
- women's health nurse practitioner (MSN, DNP)

Mandel School of Applied Social Sciences

Programs in:
- social administration (MSSA)
- social welfare (PhD)

School of Dental Medicine

Programs in:
- advanced general dentistry (Certificate)
- dental medicine (DMD, MSD, Certificate)
- dentistry (DMD, MSD, Certificate)
- endodontics (MSD, Certificate)
- oral surgery (Certificate)
- orthodontics (MSD, Certificate)
- pedodontics (MSD, Certificate)
- periodontics (MSD, Certificate)

School of Graduate Studies

Dr. Charles E. Rozek, Dean
Programs in:
- acting (MFA)
- anthropology (MA, PhD)
- applied mathematics (MS, PhD)
- art education (MA)
- art history (MA, PhD)
- art history and museum studies (MA, PhD)
- astronomy (MS, PhD)
- biology (MS, PhD)
- chemistry (MS, PhD)
- clinical psychology (PhD)
- cognitive linguistics (MA)
- contemporary dance (MFA)
- dance (MA)
- early music (MA, D Mus A)
- English (MA, PhD)
- experimental psychology (PhD)
- French (MA)
- geological sciences (MS, PhD)
- history (MA, PhD)
- mathematics (MS, PhD)
- music education (MA, PhD)
- music history (MA)
- musicology (PhD)
- physics (MS, PhD)
- political science (MA, PhD)
- sociology (MA, PhD)
- speech-language pathology (MA, PhD)
- statistics (MS, PhD)
- theater (MFA)
- world literature (MA)

The Case School of Engineering

Norman C. Tien, Dean
Programs in:
- aerospace engineering (MS, PhD)
- biomedical engineering (MS, PhD)
- ceramics and materials science (MS)
- chemical engineering (MS, PhD)
- civil engineering (MS, PhD)
- computer engineering (MS, PhD)
- computing and information science (MS, PhD)
- electrical engineering (MS, PhD)
- engineering (ME, MEM, MS, PhD)
- engineering mechanics (MS)
- fluid and thermal engineering sciences (MS, PhD)
- integration of management and engineering (MEM)
- macromolecular science (MS, PhD)
- materials science and engineering (MS, PhD)
- mechanical engineering (MS, PhD)
- systems and control engineering (MS, PhD)

Cleveland Clinic Lerner Research Institute–Molecular Medicine PhD Program

Dr. Martha Cathcart, Director
Program in:
- molecular medicine (PhD)

School of Law

Robert H. Rawson, Interim Dean
Programs in:
- law (JD)
- U.S. legal studies (LL M)

School of Medicine

Programs in:
- clinical research (MS)
- medicine (MD, MA, MPH, MS, PhD)

Graduate Programs in Medicine

Programs in:
- anesthesiology (MS)
- applied anatomy (MS)
- biochemical research (MS)
- biochemistry (MS, PhD)
- bioethics (MA)
- biological anthropology (MS)
- biomedical sciences (PhD)
- biostatistics (MS, PhD)
- cancer biology (PhD)
- cell and molecular physiology (MS)
- cell biology (MS, PhD)
- cell physiology (PhD)
- cellular biology (MS, PhD)
- dietetics (MS)
- epidemiology (MS, PhD)
- genetic and molecular epidemiology (MS, PhD)
- genetic counseling (MS)
- health services research (MS, PhD)
- human, molecular, and developmental genetics and genomics (PhD)
- immunology (MS, PhD)
- medicine (MA, MPH, MS, PhD)
- microbiology (PhD)
- molecular biology (PhD)
- molecular medicine (PhD)
- molecular virology (PhD)
- molecular/cellular biophysics (PhD)
- neurobiology (PhD)
- neuroscience (PhD)
- nutrition (MS, PhD)
- pathology (MS, PhD)
- pharmacology (PhD)
- physiology and biophysics (PhD)
- public health (MPH)
- public health nutrition (MS)
- RNA biology (PhD)
- systems physiology (PhD)

Weatherhead School of Management

N. Mohan Reddy, Head
Programs in:
- accountancy (M Acc, PhD)
- banking and finance (MBA)
- business administration (EMBA, MBA)
- economics (MBA)
- information systems (MBA)
- labor and human resource policy (MBA)
- management (MS, MSM, EDM)
- management for liberal arts graduates (MSM)
- management policy (MBA)
- marketing (MBA)
- operations research (MSM, PhD)
- organizational behavior and analysis (MBA, MPOD, MS)
- positive organization development and change (MS)
- supply chain (MSM)

Mandel Center for Nonprofit Organizations

Wendy Jelinek, Director
Program in:
- nonprofit organizations (MNO, CNM)

■ CLEVELAND STATE UNIVERSITY

Cleveland, OH 44115
http://www.csuohio.edu/

State-supported, coed, university. CGS member. *Graduate faculty:* 383 full-time (145 women), 151 part-time/adjunct (55 women). *Computer facilities:* Computer purchase and lease plans are available. 600 computers available on campus for general student use. A campuswide network can be accessed. Online class registration is available. *General application contact:* Deborah L. Brown, Interim Assistant Director, Graduate Admissions, 216-523-7572.

Cleveland-Marshall College of Law

Geoffrey S. Mearns, Dean
Programs in:
- business law (JD)
- civil litigation and dispute resolution (JD)
- criminal law (JD)
- employment labor law (JD)
- law (JD, LL M)

College of Graduate Studies

Dr. Vera Vogelsang-Coombs, Dean, College of Graduate Studies

College of Education and Human Services
Dr. James A. McLoughlin, Dean
Programs in:
- accelerated degree in adult learning and development (M Ed)
- adult learning and development (M Ed)
- art education (M Ed)
- chemical dependency counseling (Certificate)
- clinical nursing leader (MSN)
- community agency counseling (M Ed)
- community health education (M Ed)
- counseling (PhD)
- counseling and pupil personnel administration (Ed S)
- counseling psychology (PhD)
- early childhood education (M Ed)
- early childhood mental health counseling (Certificate)
- education and human services (M Ed, MPH, MSN, PhD, Certificate, Ed S)
- educational administration and supervision (M Ed)
- executive track (MSN)
- exercise science (M Ed)
- foreign language education (M Ed)
- forensic nursing (MSN)
- human performance (M Ed)
- leadership and lifelong learning (PhD)
- learning and development (PhD)
- mathematics and science education (M Ed)
- middle childhood education (M Ed)
- nursing education (MSN)
- physical education pedagogy (M Ed)
- policy studies (PhD)
- population health nursing (MSN)
- public health (MPH)
- school administration (PhD, Ed S)
- school counseling (M Ed)
- school health education (M Ed)
- special education (M Ed)
- sport and exercise psychology (M Ed)
- sports management (M Ed)
- teaching English to speakers of other languages (M Ed)

College of Liberal Arts and Social Sciences
Dr. Gregory M. Sadlek, Dean
Programs in:
- applied communication theory and methodology (MA)
- art education (M Ed)
- art history (MA)
- bioethics (MA, Certificate)
- composition (MM)
- creative writing (MFA)
- culture, communication and health care (Certificate)
- economics (MA)
- English (MA)
- French (M Ed)
- history (MA)
- liberal arts and social sciences (M Ed, MA, MFA, MM, MSW, Certificate)
- museum studies (MA)
- music education (MM)
- performance (MM)
- philosophy (MA)
- social work (MSW)
- sociology (MA)
- Spanish (M Ed, MA)

College of Science
Dr. Bette R. Bonder, Dean
Programs in:
- adult development and aging (PhD)
- analytical chemistry (MS)
- applied optics (MS)
- biology (MS)
- clinical chemistry (MS)
- clinical psychology (MA)
- clinical/bioanalytical chemistry (PhD)
- condensed matter physics (MS)
- consumer/industrial research (MA)
- diversity management (MA)
- environmental chemistry (MS)
- environmental science (MS)
- experimental research psychology (MA)
- health sciences (MS)
- inorganic chemistry (MS)
- mathematics (MA, MS)
- medical physics (MS)
- museum studies for natural historians (MS)
- occupational therapy (MOT)
- online health sciences (MS)
- optics and materials (MS)
- optics and medical imaging (MS)
- organic chemistry (MS)
- physical chemistry (MS)
- physical therapy (DPT)
- physician's assistant (MS)
- regulatory biology (PhD)
- school psychology (Psy S)
- science (MA, MOT, MS, DPT, PhD, Psy S)
- speech pathology and audiology (MA)

Fenn College of Engineering
Dr. Paul P. Lin, Associate Dean
Programs in:
- accelerated program civil engineering (MS)
- accelerated program environmental engineering (MS)
- applied biomedical engineering (D Eng)
- chemical engineering (MS, D Eng)
- civil engineering (MS, D Eng)
- electrical engineering (MS, D Eng)
- engineering (MS, D Eng)
- engineering mechanics (MS)
- environmental engineering (MS)
- industrial engineering (MS, D Eng)
- mechanical engineering (MS, D Eng)
- software engineering (MS)

Maxine Goodman Levin College of Urban Affairs
Dr. Edward W. Hill, Dean
Programs in:
- environmental studies (MAES)
- geographic information systems (Certificate)
- local and urban management (Certificate)
- non-profit management (Certificate)
- nonprofit administration and leadership (MNAL)
- nonprofit management (Certificate)
- public administration (MPA)
- urban affairs (MAES, MNAL, MPA, MS, MUPDD, PhD, Certificate)
- urban economic development (Certificate)
- urban planning, design, and development (MUPDD)
- urban real estate development (Certificate)
- urban real estate development and finance (Certificate)
- urban studies (MS)
- urban studies and public affairs (PhD)

Nance College of Business Administration
Dr. Robert F. Scherer, Dean
Programs in:
- business administration (AMBA, EMBA, M Acc, MBA, MCIS, MLRHR, DBA, Graduate Certificate)
- computer and information science (MCIS)
- executive business administration (EMBA)
- finance (DBA)
- financial accounting/audit (M Acc)
- global business (Graduate Certificate)
- health care administration (MBA)
- information systems (DBA)
- labor relations and human resources (MLRHR)
- marketing (MBA, DBA)
- marketing analytics (Graduate Certificate)
- off-campus programs (MBA)
- operations management (DBA)
- taxation (M Acc)

■ COLLEGE OF MOUNT ST. JOSEPH

Cincinnati, OH 45233-1670
http://www.msj.edu/

Independent-religious, coed, comprehensive institution. CGS member. *Graduate faculty:* 40 full-time (23 women), 17 part-time/

College of Mount St. Joseph (continued)
adjunct (15 women). *Computer facilities:* Computer purchase and lease plans are available. 270 computers available on campus for general student use. A campuswide network can be accessed from student residence rooms and from off campus. Online class registration, computer-aided instruction are available. *Graduate expenses:* Tuition: full-time $11,400; part-time $475 per credit hour. Required fees: $100 per semester. Tuition and fees vary according to program. *General application contact:* Marilyn Hoskins, Assistant Director of Admissions for Graduate Recruitment, 513-244-4723.

Graduate Education Program
Dr. Mifrando Obach, Chair
Programs in:
- adolescent young adult education (MA)
- art (MA)
- inclusive early childhood education (MA)
- instructional leadership (MA)
- middle childhood education (MA)
- multicultural special education (MA)
- music (MA)
- reading (MA)

Graduate Program in Religious Studies
Dr. John Trokan, Chair
Program in:
- spiritual and pastoral care (MA)

Master of Nursing Program
Dr. Darla Vale, Chair, Health Sciences Department
Program in:
- nursing (MN)

Master of Science in Organizational Leadership Program
Joseph Ahern, Interim Chair
Program in:
- organizational leadership (MS)

Physical Therapy Program
Dr. Darla Vale, Chair, Health Sciences Department
Program in:
- physical therapy (MPT, DPT)

■ DEVRY UNIVERSITY
Columbus, OH 43209-2705
http://www.devry.edu/

Proprietary, coed, comprehensive institution. *Computer facilities:* 408 computers available on campus for general student use. A campuswide network can be accessed from off campus. Online class registration is available.

Keller Graduate School of Management
Program in:
- management (MAFM, MBA, MHRM, MISM, MNCM, MPA, MPM, Graduate Certificate)

■ FRANCISCAN UNIVERSITY OF STEUBENVILLE
Steubenville, OH 43952-1763
http://www.franciscan.edu/

Independent-religious, coed, comprehensive institution. *Computer facilities:* Computer purchase and lease plans are available. 126 computers available on campus for general student use. A campuswide network can be accessed from student residence rooms and from off campus. Online class registration is available. *General application contact:* Director of Graduate Enrollment, 800-783-6220.

Graduate Programs
Programs in:
- administration (MS Ed)
- business (MBA)
- counseling (MA)
- nursing (MSN)
- philosophy (MA)
- teaching (MS Ed)
- theology and Christian ministry (MA)

■ HEIDELBERG UNIVERSITY
Tiffin, OH 44883-2462
http://www.heidelberg.edu/

Independent-religious, coed, comprehensive institution. *Computer facilities:* 125 computers available on campus for general student use. A campuswide network can be accessed from student residence rooms and from off campus. Online class registration is available. *General application contact:* Graduate Studies Office, 419-448-2288.

Program in Business
Program in:
- business (MBA)

Program in Counseling
Program in:
- counseling (MA)

Program in Education
Program in:
- education (MA)

■ JOHN CARROLL UNIVERSITY
University Heights, OH 44118-4581
http://www.jcu.edu/

Independent-religious, coed, comprehensive institution. CGS member. *Computer facilities:* 210 computers available on campus for general student use. A campuswide network can be accessed from student residence rooms and from off campus. Online class registration is available. *General application contact:* Records Management Assistant, 216-397-1925.

Graduate School
Programs in:
- administration (M Ed, MA)
- biology (MA, MS)
- clinical counseling (Certificate)
- communications management (MA)
- community counseling (MA)
- educational and school psychology (M Ed, MA)
- English (MA)
- history (MA)
- humanities (MA)
- integrated science (MA)
- mathematics (MA, MS)
- nonprofit administration (MA)
- professional teacher education (M Ed, MA)
- religious studies (MA)
- school based adolescent-young adult education (M Ed)
- school based early childhood education (M Ed)
- school based middle childhood education (M Ed)
- school based multi-age education (M Ed)
- school counseling (M Ed, MA)

John M. and Mary Jo Boler School of Business
Programs in:
- accountancy (MS)
- business (MBA)

■ KENT STATE UNIVERSITY
Kent, OH 44242-0001
http://www.kent.edu/

State-supported, coed, university. CGS member. *Computer facilities:* Computer purchase and lease plans are available. 1,700 computers available on campus for general student use. A campuswide network can be accessed from student residence rooms and from off campus. Online class registration is available. *General application contact:* Division of Research and Graduate Studies, 330-672-2661.

College of Architecture and Environmental Design
Programs in:
- architecture (M Arch)
- preservation architecture (Certificate)
- urban design (M Arch, MUD, Certificate)

College of Arts and Sciences
Programs in:
- analytical chemistry (MS, PhD)
- anthropology (MA)
- applied geology (PhD)
- applied mathematics (MA, MS, PhD)
- arts and sciences (MA, MFA, MLS, MPA, MS, PhD)
- biochemistry (MS, PhD)
- chemical physics (MS, PhD)
- chemistry (MA, MS, PhD)
- clinical psychology (MA, PhD)

comparative literature (MA)
computer science (MA, MS, PhD)
creative writing (MFA)
ecology (MS, PhD)
English (PhD)
English for teachers (MA)
experimental psychology (MA, PhD)
French literature (MA)
French, Spanish, German and Latin pedagogy (MA)
geography (MA, PhD)
geology (MS)
German literature (MA)
history (MA, PhD)
inorganic chemistry (MS, PhD)
justice studies (MA)
liberal studies (MLS)
literature and writing (MA)
organic chemistry (MS, PhD)
philosophy (MA)
physical chemistry (MS, PhD)
physics (MA, MS, PhD)
physiology (MS, PhD)
political science (MA)
public administration (MPA)
public policy (PhD)
pure mathematics (MA, MS, PhD)
rhetoric and composition (PhD)
sociology (MA, PhD)
Spanish literature (MA)
teaching English as a second language (MA)
translation (MA)
translation studies (PhD)

College of Communication and Information

Programs in:
communication and information (MA, MFA, MLIS, MS, PhD)
information architecture and knowledge management (MS)

School of Communication Studies
Program in:
communication studies (MA, PhD)

School of Journalism and Mass Communication
Program in:
journalism and mass communication (MA)

School of Library and Information Science
Program in:
library and information science (MLIS)

School of Visual Communication Design
Program in:
visual communication design (MA, MFA)

College of Nursing

Programs in:
adult nurse practitioner (MSN)
family nurse practitioner (MSN)
geriatric nurse practitioner (MSN)
nursing (PhD)
nursing and health care management (MSN)
nursing of adults (clinical nurse specialist) (MSN)
pediatric nurse practitioner (MSN)
psychiatric/mental health nursing (MSN)
women's health nursing (MSN)

College of Technology

Program in:
technology (MT)

College of the Arts

Program in:
arts (MA, MFA, MM, PhD)

Hugh A. Glauser School of Music
Programs in:
composition (MA)
conducting (MM)
ethnomusicology (MA)
music education (MM, PhD)
musicology (MA)
musicology-ethnomusicology (PhD)
performance (MM)
theory (MA)
theory and composition (PhD)

School of Art
Programs in:
art education (MA)
art history (MA)
crafts (MA, MFA)
fine art (MA, MFA)

School of Theatre and Dance
Programs in:
acting (MFA)
design and technology (MFA)
theatre (MA, MFA)

Graduate School of Education, Health, and Human Services

Dr. Daniel Mahony, Dean
Programs in:
career technical teacher education (M Ed, MA, Ed S)
community counseling (M Ed, MA)
counseling (Ed S)
counseling and human development services (PhD)
cultural foundations (M Ed, MA, PhD)
curriculum and instruction (M Ed, MA, PhD, Ed S)
early childhood education (M Ed, MA, MAT)
education, health, and human services (M Ed, MA, MAT, MPH, MS, Au D, PhD, Ed S)
educational administration (PhD, Ed S)
educational psychology (M Ed, MA, PhD)
evaluation and measurement (M Ed, MA, PhD)
health education and promotion (M Ed, MA, PhD)
higher education administration and student personnel (M Ed, MA)
instructional technology (M Ed, MA)
intervention specialist (M Ed, MA)
junior high/middle school (M Ed, MA)
K-12 leadership (M Ed, MA, PhD, Ed S)
math specialization (M Ed, MA)
public health (MPH)
reading (M Ed, MA)
rehabilitation counseling (M Ed, MA, Ed S)
school counseling (M Ed, MA)
school psychology (M Ed, PhD, Ed S)
secondary education (MAT)
special education (PhD, Ed S)

School of Exercise, Leisure and Sport
Wayne Munson, Director
Programs in:
exercise, leisure and sport (MA, PhD)
exercise, leisure, and sport (MA)
physical education (PhD)

School of Family and Consumer Studies
Dr. Rhonda Richardson, Director
Programs in:
family and consumer studies (MA, MS)
family studies (MA)
nutrition (MS)

School of Speech Pathology and Audiology
Dr. Lynne B. Rowan, Director
Programs in:
audiology (Au D, PhD)
speech pathology and audiology (MA, Au D, PhD)

Graduate School of Management

Dr. Frederick W. Schroath, Associate Dean
Programs in:
accounting (MS, PhD)
business administration (MBA)
economics (MA)
finance (PhD)
financial engineering (MSFE)
management (MA, MBA, MS, MSFE, PhD)
management systems (PhD)
marketing (PhD)

School of Biomedical Sciences

Programs in:
biological anthropology (PhD)
biomedical sciences (MS, PhD)
cellular and molecular biology (MS, PhD)
neuroscience (MS, PhD)
pharmacology (MS, PhD)
physiology (MS, PhD)

■ MALONE UNIVERSITY

Canton, OH 44709-3897
http://www.malone.edu/

Independent-religious, coed, comprehensive institution. *Graduate faculty:* 37 full-time (20 women), 36 part-time/adjunct (18 women). *Computer facilities:* Computer purchase and lease plans are available. 200 computers available on campus for general student use. A campuswide network can be accessed

Malone University (continued)
from student residence rooms and from off campus. Online class registration, online advising, online financial aid information, and online credit card payments are available. *Graduate expenses:* Tuition: part-time $435 per semester hour. Tuition and fees vary according to program. *General application contact:* David L. Kleffman, Assistant Director of Enrollment, 330-471-8447.

Graduate Program in Business

Dr. Julia A. Frankland, Director
Program in:
business (MBA)

Graduate Program in Christian Ministries

Dr. D. Nathan Phinney, Interim Director
Programs in:
Christian leadership in sports ministry (MA)
Christian ministries (MA)
leadership in the Christian church (MA)

Graduate Program in Counselor and Guidance Education

Dr. Brock M. Reiman, Associate Dean of Graduate Studies/Director of the Graduate Program in Counselor and Guidance Education
Programs in:
clinical counseling (MA)
school counseling (MA)

Graduate Program in Education

Dr. Alice E. Christie, Director
Programs in:
curriculum and instruction (MA)
curriculum, instruction, and professional development (MA)
instructional technology (MA)
intervention specialist (MA)
reading (MA)

Graduate Program in Nursing

Dr. Loretta M. Reinhart, Interim Director
Programs in:
clinical nurse specialist (MSN)
family nurse practitioner (MSN)

■ MIAMI UNIVERSITY

Oxford, OH 45056
http://www.muohio.edu/

State-related, coed, university. CGS member. *Computer facilities:* Computer purchase and lease plans are available. 1,200 computers available on campus for general student use. A campuswide network can be accessed from student residence rooms and from off campus. Online class registration is available. *General application contact:* Associate Provost for Research and Dean of the Graduate School, 513-529-3734.

Graduate School

College of Arts and Sciences

Programs in:
analytical chemistry (MS, PhD)
arts and sciences (MA, MAT, MGS, MS, MS Stat, MTSC, PhD)
biochemistry (MS, PhD)
biological sciences (MAT)
botany (MA, MAT, MS, PhD)
chemical education (MS, PhD)
chemistry (MS, PhD)
clinical psychology (PhD)
comparative religion (MA)
composition and rhetoric (MA, PhD)
creative writing (MA)
criticism (PhD)
English and American literature and language (PhD)
English education (MAT)
experimental psychology (PhD)
French (MA)
geography (MA)
geology (MA, MS, PhD)
gerontology (MGS)
history (MA, PhD)
inorganic chemistry (MS, PhD)
library theory (PhD)
literature (MA, MAT, PhD)
mass communication (MA)
mathematics (MA, MAT, MS)
mathematics/operations research (MS)
microbiology (MS, PhD)
organic chemistry (MS, PhD)
philosophy (MA)
physical chemistry (MS, PhD)
physics (MAT, MS)
political science (MA, MAT, PhD)
social gerontology (PhD)
social psychology (PhD)
Spanish (MA)
speech communication (MA)
speech pathology and audiology (MA, MS)
statistics (MS Stat)
technical and scientific communication (MTSC)
zoology (MA, MS, PhD)

Farmer School of Business

Programs in:
accountancy (M Acc)
business administration (MBA)
economics (MA)
finance (MBA)
general management (MBA)
management information systems (MBA)
marketing (MBA)
quality and process improvement (MBA)

Institute of Environmental Sciences

Program in:
environmental sciences (M En S)

School of Education and Allied Professions

Programs in:
adolescent education (MAT)
child and family studies (MS)
college student personnel services (MS)
curriculum and teacher leadership (M Ed)
education and allied professions (M Ed, MAT, MS, Ed D, PhD, Ed S)
educational administration (Ed D, PhD)
educational leadership (M Ed, MS)
educational psychology (M Ed)
elementary education (M Ed, MAT)
elementary mathematics education (M Ed)
exercise and health studies (MS)
reading education (M Ed)
school psychology (MS, Ed S)
secondary education (M Ed, MAT)
special education (M Ed)
sport studies (MS)

School of Engineering and Applied Science

Programs in:
computer science (MCS)
computer science and systems analysis (MCS)
paper science and engineering (MS)
software development (Certificate)

School of Fine Arts

Programs in:
architecture (M Arch)
art education (MA)
fine arts (M Arch, MA, MFA, MM)
music education (MM)
music performance (MM)
studio art (MFA)
theatre (MA)

■ MUSKINGUM UNIVERSITY

New Concord, OH 43762
http://www.muskingum.edu/

Independent-religious, coed, comprehensive institution. *Computer facilities:* A campuswide network can be accessed from student residence rooms and from off campus. *General application contact:* Director of Graduate Studies, 614-826-8037.

Graduate Programs in Education

Program in:
education (MAE, MAT)

■ OHIO DOMINICAN UNIVERSITY

Columbus, OH 43219-2099
http://www.ohiodominican.edu/

Independent-religious, coed, comprehensive institution. *Computer facilities:* 198 computers available on campus for general student use. A campuswide network can be accessed from student residence rooms and from off campus. Online class registration is available. *General application contact:* Graduate Admissions Recruiter, 614-251-4725.

Graduate Programs

Programs in:
liberal studies (MA)
TESOL (MA)

Division of Business
Program in:
business (MBA)

Division of Education
Program in:
education (M Ed)

Division of Theology, Arts and Ideas
Program in:
theology (MA)

■ THE OHIO STATE UNIVERSITY

Columbus, OH 43210
http://www.osu.edu/

State-supported, coed, university. CGS member. *Computer facilities:* 800 computers available on campus for general student use. A campuswide network can be accessed from student residence rooms and from off campus. Online class registration is available. *General application contact:* Information Contact, 614-292-9444.

College of Dentistry
Programs in:
dentistry (DDS, MS, PhD)
oral biology (PhD)

College of Medicine
Program in:
medicine (MD, MOT, MPT, MS, PhD)

School of Allied Medical Professions
Programs in:
allied medicine (MS)
circulation technology (MS)
occupational therapy (MOT)
physical therapy (MPT)

School of Biomedical Science
Programs in:
anatomy (MS, PhD)
biomedical science (MD, MS, PhD)
experimental pathobiology (MS)
immunology (PhD)
medical genetics (PhD)
medical science (PhD)
medicine (MD)
molecular virology (PhD)
molecular virology, immunology and medical genetics (MS, PhD)
neuroscience (PhD)
pathology assistant (MS)
pharmacology (PhD)

College of Optometry
Programs in:
optometry (OD, MS, PhD)
vision science (MS, PhD)

College of Pharmacy
Dr. Robert W. Brueggemeier, Dean
Programs in:
medicinal chemistry and pharmacognosy (MS, PhD)
pharmaceutical administration (MS, PhD)
pharmaceutics (MS, PhD)
pharmacology (PhD)
pharmacy (Pharm D, MS, PhD)
pharmacy practice and administration (MS, PhD)

College of Public Health
Program in:
public health (MHA, MHROD, MPH, MS, PhD)

College of Veterinary Medicine
Programs in:
anatomy and cellular biology (MS, PhD)
pathobiology (MS, PhD)
pharmacology (MS, PhD)
toxicology (MS, PhD)
veterinary clinical sciences (MS, PhD)
veterinary medicine (DVM, MS, PhD)
veterinary physiology (MS, PhD)
veterinary preventive medicine (MS, PhD)

Graduate School
Program in:
biochemistry (PhD)

College of Biological Sciences
Programs in:
biological sciences (MS, PhD)
biophysics (MS, PhD)
cell and developmental biology (MS, PhD)
entomology (MS, PhD)
environmental science (MS, PhD)
evolution, ecology, and organismal biology (MS, PhD)
genetics (MS, PhD)
microbiology (MS, PhD)
molecular biology (MS, PhD)
molecular, cellular and developmental biology (MS, PhD)
plant biology (MS, PhD)

College of Education and Human Ecology
Programs in:
education and human ecology (M Ed, MA, MS, PhD)
educational policy and leadership (M Ed, MA, PhD)
family and consumer sciences education (M Ed, MS)
family resource management (MS, PhD)
food service management (MS, PhD)
foods (MS, PhD)
higher education and student affairs (MA)
hospitality management (MS, PhD)
human development and family science (M Ed, MS, PhD)
nutrition (MS, PhD)
physical activity and educational services (M Ed, MA, PhD)
teaching and learning (M Ed, MA, PhD)
textiles and clothing (MS, PhD)

College of Engineering
Programs in:
aeronautical and astronautical engineering (MS, PhD)
architecture (M Arch, M Land Arch, MAS, MCRP, PhD)
biomedical engineering (MS, PhD)
chemical engineering (MS, PhD)
city and regional planning (MCRP, PhD)
civil engineering (MS, PhD)
computer and information science (MS, PhD)
computer science and engineering (MS)
electrical engineering (MS, PhD)
engineering (M Arch, M Land Arch, MAS, MCRP, MS, MWE, PhD)
engineering mechanics (MS, PhD)
engineering physics (MS, PhD)
geodetic science and surveying (MS, PhD)
industrial and systems engineering (MS, PhD)
landscape architecture (M Land Arch)
materials science and engineering (MS, PhD)
mechanical engineering (MS, PhD)
nuclear engineering (MS, PhD)
welding engineering (MS, MWE, PhD)

College of Food, Agricultural, and Environmental Sciences
Programs in:
agricultural economics and rural sociology (MS, PhD)
animal sciences (MS, PhD)
environment and natural resources (MS, PhD)
food science and nutrition (MS, PhD)
food, agricultural, and biological engineering (MS, PhD)
food, agricultural, and environmental sciences (M Ed, MS, PhD)
horticulture and crop science (MS, PhD)
human and community resource development (M Ed, MS, PhD)
human dimensions in natural resources (MS, PhD)
natural resources (MS, PhD)
plant pathology (MS, PhD)
rural sociology (MS, PhD)
soil science (MS, PhD)
vocational education (PhD)

College of Humanities
Programs in:
African-American and African studies (MA)
ancient Greek (MA)
Chinese (MA, PhD)
classics (MA, PhD)
comparative studies (MA, PhD)
English (MA, MFA, PhD)
French (MA, PhD)
Germanic languages and literatures (MA, PhD)
Greek studies (MA, PhD)
history (MA, PhD)
humanities (MA, MFA, PhD)
Italian (MA)
Japanese (MA, PhD)
Latin studies (MA, PhD)
linguistics (MA, PhD)
modern Greek (MA, PhD)

The Ohio State University (continued)
- Near Eastern languages and cultures (MA, PhD)
- philosophy (MA, PhD)
- Slavic and East European studies (MA)
- Slavic languages and literatures (MA, PhD)
- Spanish and Portuguese (MA, PhD)
- women's studies (MA, PhD)

College of Mathematical and Physical Sciences
Programs in:
- astronomy (MS, PhD)
- biostatistics (PhD)
- chemical physics (MS, PhD)
- chemistry (MS, PhD)
- earth sciences (MS, PhD)
- geodetic science (MS)
- geological sciences (MS, PhD)
- mathematical and physical sciences (M Appl Stat, MA, MS, PhD)
- mathematics (MA, MS, PhD)
- physics (MS, PhD)
- statistics (M Appl Stat, MS, PhD)

College of Nursing
Program in:
- nursing (MS, PhD)

College of Social and Behavioral Sciences
Programs in:
- anthropology (MA, PhD)
- atmospheric sciences (MS, PhD)
- audiology (Au D)
- behavioral neuroscience (PhD)
- clinical psychology (PhD)
- cognitive psychology (PhD)
- communication (MA, PhD)
- developmental psychology (PhD)
- economics (MA, PhD)
- geography (MA, PhD)
- hearing science (PhD)
- journalism and communication (MA)
- mental retardation and developmental disabilities (PhD)
- political science (MA, PhD)
- psychology (MA)
- quantitative psychology (PhD)
- social and behavioral science (MA, MS, Au D, PhD)
- social and behavioral sciences (MA, MS, Au D, PhD)
- social psychology (PhD)
- sociology (MA, PhD)
- speech hearing science (MA)
- speech-language pathology (MA, PhD)
- speech-language science (PhD)

College of Social Work
Program in:
- social work (MSW, PhD)

College of the Arts
Programs in:
- art (MFA)
- art education (MA, PhD)
- arts (M Mus, MA, MFA, DMA, PhD, CAL)
- arts policy and administration (MA)
- choreography (MFA)
- dance (MA, MFA, PhD)
- dance and technology (MFA)
- dance studies (PhD)
- history of art (MA, PhD)
- industrial, interior, and visual communication design (MA, MFA)
- Labanotation (MFA)
- lighting (MFA)
- music (M Mus, MA, DMA, PhD)
- performance (MFA)
- photography and cinema (MA)
- theatre (MA, MFA, PhD)

Max M. Fisher College of Business
Programs in:
- accounting (M Acc, MA, MS)
- accounting and MIS (PhD)
- business (M Acc, MA, MBA, MBLE, MLHR, PhD)
- business administration (MA, MBA, PhD)
- business logistics engineering (MBLE)
- finance (MA, PhD)
- labor and human resources (MLHR, PhD)

John Glenn School of Public Affairs
Program in:
- public affairs (MA, MPA, PhD)

Moritz College of Law
Program in:
- law (JD, LL M, MSL)

■ OHIO UNIVERSITY
Athens, OH 45701-2979
http://www.ohio.edu/

State-supported, coed, university. CGS member. *Computer facilities:* Computer purchase and lease plans are available. 1,500 computers available on campus for general student use. A campuswide network can be accessed from student residence rooms and from off campus. Online class registration is available. *General application contact:* Graduate College, 740-593-2800.

College of Osteopathic Medicine
Dr. John A. Brose, Dean
Program in:
- osteopathic medicine (DO)

Graduate College

Center for International Studies
Programs in:
- African studies (MA)
- communications and development studies (MA)
- development studies (MA)
- international studies (MA)
- Latin American studies (MA)
- Southeast Asian studies (MA)

College of Arts and Sciences
Programs in:
- applied economics (MA)
- applied linguistics/TESOL (MA)
- arts and sciences (MA, MFE, MPA, MS, MSS, MSW, PhD)
- astronomy (MS, PhD)
- biological sciences (MS, PhD)
- cell biology and physiology (MS, PhD)
- chemistry and biochemistry (MS, PhD)
- clinical psychology (PhD)
- ecology and evolutionary biology (MS, PhD)
- English language and literature (MA, PhD)
- environmental and plant biology (MS, PhD)
- environmental geochemistry (MS)
- environmental geology (MS)
- environmental studies (MS)
- environmental/hydrology (MS)
- exercise physiology and muscle biology (MS, PhD)
- experimental psychology (PhD)
- financial economics (MFE)
- French (MA)
- geography (MA)
- geology (MS)
- geology education (MS)
- geomorphology/surficial processes (MS)
- geophysics (MS)
- history (MA, PhD)
- hydrogeology (MS)
- mathematics (MS, PhD)
- microbiology (MS, PhD)
- molecular and cellular biology (MS, PhD)
- neuroscience (MS, PhD)
- organizational psychology (PhD)
- philosophy (MA)
- physics (MS, PhD)
- political science (MA)
- public administration (MPA)
- sedimentology (MS)
- social sciences (MSS)
- social work (MSW)
- sociology (MA)
- Spanish (MA)
- structure/tectonics (MS)

College of Business
Programs in:
- business (EMBA, MBA)
- business administration (EMBA, MBA)

College of Education
Programs in:
- adolescent to young adult education (M Ed)
- college student personnel (M Ed)
- community/agency counseling (M Ed)
- computer education and technology (M Ed)
- counselor education (PhD)
- cultural studies in education (PhD)
- curriculum and instruction (M Ed, PhD)
- early childhood/special education (M Ed)
- education (M Ed, Ed D, PhD)
- educational administration (M Ed, Ed D)
- educational research and evaluation (M Ed, PhD)
- higher education (M Ed, PhD)

instructional technology (PhD)
mathematics education (PhD)
middle child education (M Ed)
reading and language arts (PhD)
reading education (M Ed)
rehabilitation counseling (M Ed)
school counseling (M Ed)
social studies education (PhD)
special education (M Ed, PhD)

College of Fine Arts
Programs in:
accompanying (MM)
art history (MA)
ceramics (MFA)
composition (MM)
conducting (MM)
film (MFA)
film studies (MA)
fine arts (MA, MFA, MM, PhD, Certificate)
graphic design (MFA)
history/literature (MM)
interdisciplinary arts (PhD)
music education (MM)
music therapy (MM)
painting (MFA)
performance (MM, Certificate)
performance/pedagogy (MM)
photography (MFA)
printmaking (MFA)
sculpture (MFA)
theater (MA, MFA)
theory (MM)

College of Health and Human Services
Programs in:
athletic training education (MS)
audiology (Au D)
child development and family life (MS)
coaching education (MS)
early childhood education (MS)
family studies (MS)
food and nutrition (MS)
health and human services (MA, MHA, MPH, MS, MSA, Au D, DPT, PhD)
health sciences (MHA, MPH)
hearing science (PhD)
physical therapy (DPT)
physiology of exercise (MS)
recreation studies (MS)
speech language pathology (MA)
speech-language science (PhD)
sports administration and facility management (MSA)

Russ College of Engineering and Technology
Programs in:
biomedical engineering (MS)
chemical engineering (MS, PhD)
civil (PhD)
computer science (MS)
construction (MS)
electrical engineering (MS, PhD)
engineering and technology (MS, PhD)
environmental (MS)
geotechnical and environmental engineering (MS)
industrial (PhD)
industrial and manufacturing systems engineering (MS)
integrated engineering (PhD)
manufacturing engineering (MS)
mechanical (PhD)
mechanical engineering (MS, PhD)
structures (MS)
transportation (MS)
water resources and structures (MS)

Scripps College of Communication
Programs in:
communication (MA, MCTP, MS, PhD)
communication studies (PhD)
information and telecommunication systems (MCTP)
journalism (MS, PhD)
mass communication (PhD)
media arts and studies (MA)
visual communication (MA)

■ OTTERBEIN COLLEGE
Westerville, OH 43081
http://www.otterbein.edu/

Independent-religious, coed, comprehensive institution. *Computer facilities:* 146 computers available on campus for general student use. A campuswide network can be accessed from student residence rooms and from off campus. Online class registration is available. *General application contact:* Administrative Assistant, Office of Graduate Programs, 614-823-3210.

Department of Business, Accounting and Economics
Program in:
business, accounting and economics (MBA)

Department of Education
Program in:
education (MAE, MAT)

Department of Nursing
Programs in:
adult nurse practitioner (MSN, Certificate)
clinical nurse leader (MSN)
family nurse practitioner (MSN, Certificate)
nurse service administration (MSN)

■ TIFFIN UNIVERSITY
Tiffin, OH 44883-2161
http://www.tiffin.edu/

Independent, coed, comprehensive institution. *Computer facilities:* Computer purchase and lease plans are available. 60 computers available on campus for general student use. A campuswide network can be accessed from student residence rooms and from off campus. Online class registration is available. *General application contact:* Director of Graduate Admissions, 800-968-6446 Ext. 3445.

Program in Business Administration
Programs in:
general management (MBA)
leadership (MBA)
safety and security management (MBA)
sports management (MBA)

Program in Criminal Justice
Programs in:
crime analysis (MSCJ)
criminal behavior (MSCJ)
forensic psychology (MSCJ)
homeland security administration (MSCJ)
justice administration (MSCJ)

Program in Humanities
Program in:
humanities (MH)

■ UNION INSTITUTE & UNIVERSITY
Cincinnati, OH 45206-1925
http://www.tui.edu/

Independent, coed, university. *Computer facilities:* Computer purchase and lease plans are available. A campuswide network can be accessed from off campus. Online class registration is available. *General application contact:* Admissions Office, 513-861-6400.

Doctor of Education Program
Programs in:
educational leadership (Ed D)
higher education (Ed D)

Online MA Programs
Programs in:
health and wellness (MA)
history and culture (MA)
leadership (MA)
literature and writing (MA)
psychology (MA)

Online Master of Education Program
Program in:
education (M Ed)

PhD Program in Interdisciplinary Studies
Program in:
interdisciplinary studies (PhD)

Program in Clinical Psychology
Program in:
clinical psychology (Psy D)

Program in Education (Florida Campus)
Program in:
education (M Ed, Ed S)

Program in Education (Vermont Campus)
Program in:
education (M Ed)

Union Institute & University (continued)

Program in Psychology and Counseling
Program in:
psychology and counseling (MA)

■ THE UNIVERSITY OF AKRON
Akron, OH 44325
http://www.uakron.edu/

State-supported, coed, university. CGS member. *Graduate faculty:* 486 full-time (166 women), 445 part-time/adjunct (225 women). *Computer facilities:* Computer purchase and lease plans are available. 3,100 computers available on campus for general student use. A campuswide network can be accessed from student residence rooms and from off campus. Online class registration, library laptops for student checkout are available. *Graduate expenses:* Tuition, state resident: full-time $6164; part-time $342 per credit hour. Tuition, nonresident: full-time $10,574; part-time $588 per credit hour. Required fees: $806. *General application contact:* Dr. Mark Tausig, Associate Dean, 330-972-6266.

Graduate School
Dr. George R. Newkome, Vice President for Research and Dean of the Graduate School

Buchtel College of Arts and Sciences
Dr. Chand Midha, Interim Dean
Programs in:
applied cognitive aging (MA, PhD)
applied mathematics (MS)
applied politics (MA)
arts and sciences (MA, MFA, MPA, MS, PhD)
biology (MS)
chemistry (MS, PhD)
composition (MA)
computer science (MS)
counseling psychology (MA, PhD)
creative writing (MFA)
earth science (MS)
economics (MA)
environmental geology (MS)
geographic information science (MS)
geology (MS)
geophysics (MS)
history (MA, PhD)
industrial/gerontological psychology (PhD)
industrial/organizational psychology (MA, PhD)
integrated bioscience (PhD)
literature (MA)
mathematics (MS)
physics (MS)
political science (MA)
psychology (MA)
public administration (MPA)
sociology (MA, PhD)
Spanish (MA)
statistics (MS)
urban planning (MA)
urban studies (MA, PhD)
urban studies and public affairs (PhD)

College of Business Administration
Dr. Raj Aggrawal, Dean
Programs in:
accountancy (MS)
accounting-information systems (MS)
business administration (MBA, MS, MSM, MT)
electronic business (MBA)
entrepreneurship (MBA)
finance (MBA)
international business (MBA)
international business for international executive (MBA)
management (MBA)
management of technology (MBA)
management-health services administration (MSM)
management-human resources (MSM)
management-information systems (MSM)
management-supply chain management (MSM)
strategic marketing (MBA)
taxation (MT)

College of Education
Dr. Cynthia Capers, Interim Dean
Programs in:
classroom guidance for teachers (MA, MS)
community counseling (MA, MS)
counseling psychology (PhD)
counselor education and supervision (PhD)
education (MA, MS, Ed D, PhD)
educational leadership (Ed D)
elementary education (MA, MS, PhD)
elementary education—literacy (MA)
elementary education with licensure (MS)
exercise physiology/adult fitness (MA, MS)
higher education administration (MA, MS)
marriage and family therapy (MA, MS)
physical education K–12 (MA, MS)
principalship (MA, MS)
school counseling (MA, MS)
school psychology (MS)
secondary education (MA, MS, PhD)
secondary education with licensure (MS)
special education (MA, MS)
sports science/coaching (MA, MS)
technical education (MS)

College of Engineering
Dr. George Haritos, Dean
Programs in:
biomedical engineering (MS, PhD)
chemical and biomolecular engineering (MS, PhD)
civil engineering (MS, PhD)
electrical and computer engineering (MS, PhD)
engineering (MS, PhD)
engineering (biomedical engineering specialization) (MS)
engineering (management specialization) (MS)
engineering (polymer specialization) (MS)
engineering applied mathematics (PhD)
interdisciplinary engineering (PhD)
mechanical engineering (MS, PhD)

College of Fine and Applied Arts
Dr. James Lynn, Interim Dean
Programs in:
arts administration (MA)
audiology (Au D)
child and family development (MA)
child development (MA)
child life (MA)
clothing, textiles and interiors (MA)
communication (MA)
composition (MM)
family development (MA)
fine and applied arts (MA, MM, MS, Au D)
music education (MM)
music history and literature (MM)
music technology (MM)
nutrition and dietetics (MS)
performance (MM)
social work (MS)
speech-language pathology (MA)
theatre arts (MA)
theory (MM)

College of Nursing
Dr. Margaret Wineman, Dean
Programs in:
nursing (MSN, PhD)
public health (MPH)

College of Polymer Science and Polymer Engineering
Dr. Stephen Cheng, Dean
Programs in:
polymer engineering (MS, PhD)
polymer science (MS, PhD)

School of Law
Martin H. Belsky, Dean
Program in:
law (JD)

■ UNIVERSITY OF CINCINNATI
Cincinnati, OH 45221
http://www.uc.edu/

State-supported, coed, university. CGS member. *Computer facilities:* A campuswide network can be accessed from student residence rooms and from off campus. Online class registration is available. *General application contact:* Associate Senior Vice President and University Dean, 513-556-2872.

College of Law
Louis D. Bilionois, Dean
Program in:
law (JD)

College of Pharmacy
Program in:
pharmacy (Pharm D, MS, PhD)

Division of Pharmaceutical Sciences
Program in:
pharmaceutical sciences (MS, PhD)

Division of Pharmacy Practice
Program in:
pharmacy practice (Pharm D)

Graduate School
Program in:
neuroscience (PhD)

College-Conservatory of Music
Programs in:
arts administration (MA)
choral conducting (MM, DMA)
composition (MM, DMA)
directing (MFA)
keyboard studies (MM, DMA, AD)
music (MA, MFA, MM, DMA, PhD, AD)
music education (MM)
music history (MM)
music theory (MM, PhD)
musicology (PhD)
orchestral conducting (MM, DMA)
performance (MM, DMA, AD)
theater design and production (MFA)
voice and opera (MM, DMA)
wind conducting (MM, DMA)

College of Allied Health Sciences
Programs in:
allied health sciences (MA, MS, Au D, DPT, PhD)
blood transfusion medicine (MS)
cellular therapies (MS)
communication sciences and disorders (MA, Au D, PhD)
medical genetics (MS)
nutritional science (MS)
rehabilitation science (DPT)

College of Business
Programs in:
accounting (MS, PhD)
business (MBA, MS, PhD)
business administration (MBA)
finance (PhD)
information systems (MS, PhD)
management (PhD)
marketing (MS, PhD)
quantitative analysis (MS)
quantitative analysis and operations management (PhD)

College of Design, Architecture, Art, and Planning
Programs in:
architecture (M Arch)
art education (MA)
art history (MA)
community planning (MCP)
design, architecture, art, and planning (M Arch, M Des, MA, MCP, MFA, PhD)
fashion design (M Des)
fine arts (MFA)
graphic design (M Des)
industrial design (M Des)
interaction design (M Des)
planning (MCP)
product development (M Des)
regional development planning (PhD)

College of Education, Criminal Justice, and Human Services
Programs in:
community health (MS)
counseling (Ed D)
counselor education (CAGS)
criminal justice (MS, PhD)
curriculum and instruction (M Ed, Ed D)
deaf studies (Certificate)
early childhood education (M Ed)
education, criminal justice, and human services (M Ed, MA, MS, Ed D, PhD, CAGS, Certificate, Ed S)
educational leadership (M Ed, Ed S)
educational studies (M Ed, Ed D, PhD, Ed S)
health education (MS, PhD)
health promotion and education (M Ed)
human services (M Ed, MA, MS, Ed D, PhD, CAGS, Ed S)
mental health (MA)
middle childhood education (M Ed)
postsecondary literacy instruction (Certificate)
reading/literacy (M Ed, Ed D)
school counseling (M Ed)
school psychology (PhD, Ed S)
secondary education (M Ed)
special education (M Ed, Ed D)
teaching English as a second language (M Ed, Ed D, Certificate)
teaching science (MS)
urban educational leadership (Ed D)

College of Engineering
Programs in:
aerospace engineering and engineering mechanics (MS, PhD)
bioinformatics (PhD)
biomechanics (PhD)
ceramic science and engineering (MS, PhD)
chemical engineering (MS, PhD)
civil engineering (MS, PhD)
computer engineering (MS)
computer science (MS)
computer science and engineering (PhD)
electrical engineering (MS, PhD)
engineering (MS, PhD)
environmental engineering (MS, PhD)
environmental sciences (MS, PhD)
health physics (MS)
industrial engineering (MS, PhD)
materials science and engineering (MS, PhD)
materials science and metallurgical engineering (MS, PhD)
mechanical engineering (MS, PhD)
medical imaging (PhD)
metallurgical engineering (MS, PhD)
nuclear engineering (MS, PhD)
polymer science and engineering (MS, PhD)
tissue engineering (PhD)

College of Medicine
Programs in:
biomedical sciences (MS, PhD)
cell and cancer biology (PhD)
cell biophysics (PhD)
environmental and industrial hygiene (MS, PhD)
environmental and occupational medicine (MS)
environmental genetics and molecular toxicology (MS, PhD)
epidemiology and biostatistics (MS, PhD)
immunobiology (MS, PhD)
medical physics (MS)
medicine (MD, MS, PhD)
molecular and developmental biology (PhD)
molecular genetics, biochemistry and microbiology (MS, PhD)
occupational safety and ergonomics (MS, PhD)
pathology (PhD)
pharmacology (PhD)
physiology (PhD)

College of Nursing
Dr. Andrea R. Lindell, Dean
Programs in:
clinical nurse specialist (MSN)
nurse anesthesia (MSN)
nurse midwifery (MSN)
nurse practitioner (MSN)
nursing (PhD)

McMicken College of Arts and Sciences
Programs in:
analytical chemistry (MS, PhD)
anthropology (MA)
applied economics (MA)
applied mathematics (MS, PhD)
arts and sciences (MA, MALER, MAT, MS, PhD, Certificate)
biochemistry (MS, PhD)
biological sciences (MS, PhD)
classics (MA, PhD)
clinical psychology (PhD)
communication (MA)
English (MA, MAT, PhD)
experimental psychology (PhD)
French (MA, PhD)
geography (MA, PhD)
geology (MS, PhD)
German studies (MA, PhD)
history (MA, PhD)
inorganic chemistry (MS, PhD)
interdisciplinary studies (PhD)
labor and employment relations (MALER)
mathematics education (MAT)
organic chemistry (MS, PhD)
organizational leadership (MALER)
philosophy (MA, PhD)
physical chemistry (MS, PhD)
physics (MS, PhD)
political science (MA, PhD)

University of Cincinnati (continued)
polymer chemistry (MS, PhD)
pure mathematics (MS, PhD)
Romance languages and literatures (PhD)
sensors (PhD)
sociology (MA, PhD)
Spanish (MA, PhD)
statistics (MS, PhD)
women's, gender, and sexuality studies (MA, Certificate)

School of Social Work
Program in:
social work (MSW)

■ UNIVERSITY OF DAYTON
Dayton, OH 45469-1300
http://www.udayton.edu/

Independent-religious, coed, university. CGS member. *Graduate faculty:* 161 full-time (44 women), 9 part-time/adjunct (3 women). *Computer facilities:* Computer purchase and lease plans are available. 250 computers available on campus for general student use. A campuswide network can be accessed from student residence rooms and from off campus. Online class registration, applications, admission/enrollment status, virtual orientation, online digital resources, online courses, assistive technology, learning management system, multimedia labs, payment, cyber cafes, centrally-licensed, downloadable software and training are available. *Graduate expenses:* Tuition: full-time $6950; part-time $1737.50 per semester. Required fees: $25 per semester. Tuition and fees vary according to course level, course load, degree level and program. *General application contact:* Angela Jones-Glukhov, Associate Director of Graduate Admissions, 937-229-4305.

Graduate School
Dr. F. Thomas Eggemeier, Dean of the Graduate School

College of Arts and Sciences
Dr. Paul Benson, Dean
Programs in:
applied mathematics (MAS)
arts and sciences (MA, MAS, MCS, MFM, MME, MPA, MS, PhD)
biology (MS, PhD)
chemistry (MS)
clinical psychology (MA)
communication (MA)
computer science (MCS)
English (MA)
financial mathematics (MFM)
general psychology (MA)
mathematics (MME)
pastoral ministry (MA)
public administration (MPA)
theological studies (MA)
theology (PhD)

School of Business Administration
Janice M. Glynn, Director, MBA Program
Programs in:
accounting (MBA)
business intelligence (MBA)
entrepreneurship (MBA)
finance (MBA)
international business (MBA)
marketing (MBA)
MIS (MBA)
operations management (MBA)
technology-enhanced business/e-commerce (MBA)

School of Education and Allied Professions
Dr. Thomas J. Lasley, Dean
Programs in:
adolescent/young adult (MS Ed)
art education (MS Ed)
college student personnel (MS Ed)
community counseling (MS Ed)
early childhood education (MS Ed)
education administration (Ed S)
education and allied professions (MS Ed, DPT, PhD, Ed S)
educational leadership (MS Ed, PhD, Ed S)
exercise science (MS Ed)
higher education administration (MS Ed)
human services (MS Ed)
inclusive early childhood (MS Ed)
interdisciplinary education (MS Ed)
intervention specialist education, mild/moderate (MS Ed)
literacy (MS Ed)
middle childhood (MS Ed)
multi-age education (MS Ed)
music education (MS Ed)
physical therapy (DPT)
school counseling (MS Ed)
school psychology (MS Ed, Ed S)
teacher as child/youth development specialist (MS Ed)
teacher as leader (MS Ed)
technology in education (MS Ed)

School of Engineering
Dr. Malcolm W. Daniels, Interim Dean
Programs in:
aerospace engineering (MSAE, DE, PhD)
chemical engineering (MS Ch E)
electrical and computer engineering (MSEE, DE, PhD)
electro-optics (MSEO, PhD)
engineering (MS, MS Ch E, MS Mat E, MSAE, MSCE, MSE, MSEE, MSEM, MSEM, MSEO, MSME, MSMS, DE, PhD)
engineering management (MSEM)
engineering mechanics (MSEM)
environmental engineering (MSCE)
geotechnical engineering (MSCE)
materials engineering (MS Mat E, DE, PhD)
mechanical engineering (MSME, DE, PhD)
renewable and clean energy (MS)
structural engineering (MSCE)
transport engineering (MSCE)
water resources engineering (MSCE)

School of Law
Lisa A. Kloppenberg, Dean
Program in:
law (JD, LL M, MSL)

■ THE UNIVERSITY OF FINDLAY
Findlay, OH 45840-3653
http://www.findlay.edu/

Independent-religious, coed, comprehensive institution. CGS member. *Graduate faculty:* 106 full-time, 4 part-time/adjunct. *Computer facilities:* Computer purchase and lease plans are available. 200 computers available on campus for general student use. A campuswide network can be accessed from student residence rooms and from off campus. Online class registration is available. *General application contact:* Heather Riffle, Assistant to the Dean, Graduate and Professional Studies, 419-434-4640.

Graduate and Professional Studies
Dr. Thomas Dillion, Dean, Graduate and Professional Studies
Programs in:
administration (MA Ed)
early childhood (MA Ed)
elementary education (MA Ed)
human resource development (MA Ed)
leadership (MA Ed)
special education (MA Ed)
technology (MA Ed)
web instruction (MA Ed)

College of Business
Dr. Paul Sears, Dean
Programs in:
financial management (MBA)
human resource management (MBA)
international management (MBA)
management (MBA)
marketing (MBA)
public management (MBA)

College of Health Professions
Dr. Andrea Koepke, Dean
Programs in:
athletic training (MAT)
health professions (MAT, MOT, MPT)
occupational therapy (MOT)
physical therapy (MPT)

College of Liberal Arts
Dr. Gary Johnson, Dean
Programs in:
bilingual and multicultural education (MA)
liberal arts (MA, MALS)
liberal studies (MALS)
teaching English to speakers of other languages (MA)

College of Pharmacy
Program in:
pharmacy (Pharm D)

College of Sciences
Dr. Terry Schwaner, Dean

Programs in:
environmental, safety and health management (MSEM)
sciences (MSEM)

■ UNIVERSITY OF RIO GRANDE

Rio Grande, OH 45674
http://www.rio.edu/

Independent, coed, comprehensive institution. *Graduate faculty:* 4 full-time (1 woman), 17 part-time/adjunct (8 women). *Computer facilities:* 300 computers available on campus for general student use. A campuswide network can be accessed from student residence rooms and from off campus. Online class registration is available. *Graduate expenses:* Tuition: full-time $8096; part-time $508 per credit hour. *General application contact:* Dreama Hudson, Graduate Secretary, 740-245-7167.

Graduate School

Dr. Greg Miller, Coordinator
Program in:
classroom teaching (M Ed)

■ THE UNIVERSITY OF TOLEDO

Toledo, OH 43606-3390
http://www.utoledo.edu/

State-supported, coed, university. CGS member. *Computer facilities:* Computer purchase and lease plans are available. 5,000 computers available on campus for general student use. A campuswide network can be accessed from student residence rooms and from off campus. Online class registration, online transcripts, student account are available. *General application contact:* Recruitment Coordinator, 419-530-8582.

College of Graduate Studies

College of Arts and Sciences
Programs in:
analytical chemistry (MS, PhD)
applied mathematics (MS, PhD)
arts and sciences (MA, MLS, MMP, MPA, MS, PhD, Certificate)
behavioral (PhD)
biological chemistry (MS, PhD)
biology (MS, PhD)
biology (ecology track) (MS, PhD)
clinical psychology (PhD)
communication studies (Certificate)
economics (MA)
English as a second language (MA)
experimental psychology (MA)
French (MA)
geographic information systems and applied geographics (Certificate)
geography (MA)
geology (MS)
German (MA)
health care policy (MPA)
healthcare policy (Certificate)
history (MA, PhD)
inorganic chemistry (MS, PhD)
liberal studies (MLS)
literature (MA)
mathematics (MA, PhD)
municipal administration (MPA, Certificate)
organic chemistry (MS, PhD)
performance (MMP)
philosophy (MA)
physical chemistry (MS, PhD)
physics (MS, PhD)
planning (MA)
political science (MA)
public administration (MPA, Certificate)
sociology (MA)
Spanish (MA)
statistics (MS, PhD)
teaching of writing (Certificate)

College of Business Administration
Programs in:
accounting (MBA, MSA)
business administration (EMBA, MBA, MSA, DME)
business administration-general (MBA)
finance and business economics (MBA)
human resource management (MBA)
information systems (MBA)
international business (MBA)
management (MBA)
manufacturing management (MBA, DME)
marketing (MBA)
operations management (MBA)

College of Education
Programs in:
art education (ME)
career and technical education (Ed S)
career and technical training (ME)
curriculum and instruction (ME, DE, PhD, Ed S)
early childhood education (ME, Ed S)
education (MAE, ME, MES, MME, DE, PhD, Ed S)
education and biology (MES)
education and chemistry (MES)
education and economics (MAE)
education and English (MAE)
education and French (MAE)
education and geology (MES)
education and German (MAE)
education and history (MAE)
education and mathematics (MAE, MES)
education and physics (MES)
education and political science (MAE)
education and sociology (MAE)
education and Spanish (MAE)
educational administration and supervision (ME, DE, Ed S)
educational media (DE, PhD, Ed S)
educational psychology (ME, DE, PhD)
educational research and measurement (ME, PhD)
educational sociology (DE, PhD)
educational technology (ME)
educational theory and social foundations (ME)
elementary education (DE, PhD, Ed S)
English as a second language (MAE)
foundations of education (DE, PhD)
gifted and talented (PhD, Ed S)
health education (ME)
higher education (ME, PhD)
history of education (DE, PhD)
middle childhood education (ME)
music education (MME)
philosophy of education (DE, PhD)
physical education (ME)
secondary education (ME, DE, PhD, Ed S)
special education (ME, DE, PhD, Ed S)

College of Engineering
Dr. Nagi Naganathan, Professor and Dean
Programs in:
bioengineering (MS, PhD)
biomedical engineering (PhD)
chemical engineering (MS, PhD)
civil engineering (MS, PhD)
computer science (MS, PhD)
electrical engineering (MS, PhD)
engineering (MS, PhD)
general engineering (MS)
industrial engineering (MS, PhD)
mechanical engineering (MS, PhD)

College of Health Science and Human Service
Programs in:
community counseling (MA)
counselor education (MA, PhD, Ed S)
counselor education and school psychology (MA, PhD, Ed S)
counselor education and supervision (PhD)
criminal justice (MA, Certificate)
exercise science (MSX, PhD)
guidance/counselor education (PhD)
health and rehabilitative services (MA)
health education (PhD)
health science and human service (MA, MS, MSBS, MSW, MSX, DPT, OTD, PhD, Certificate, Ed S)
human donation science (MS, Certificate)
juvenile justice (Certificate)
kinesiology (MSX, PhD)
occupational therapy (OTD)
physical therapy (DPT)
physician assistant studies (MSBS)
recreation and leisure (MA)
school counseling (MA)
school psychology (MA, Ed S)
severe behavioral spectrum (Certificate)
social work (MSW)
speech-language pathology (MA)

College of Medicine
Programs in:
anatomic pathology (Certificate)
biochemistry and molecular biology (MSBS)
bioinformatics and proteomics/genomics (MSBS, Certificate)

The University of Toledo (continued)
biostatistics and epidemiology (Certificate)
cancer biology (MSBS, PhD)
cardiovascular and metabolic diseases (MSBS, PhD)
contemporary gerontological practice (Certificate)
diagnostic radiology (MSBS)
emergency response (Certificate)
gerontology (Certificate)
global health (Certificate)
infection, immunity and transplantation (MSBS)
infection, immunology and transplantation (PhD)
medical physics (MSBS)
medical physics-clinical radiation oncology (MSBS)
medical sciences (MSBS)
medicine (MPH, MS, MSBS, MSOH, PhD, Certificate, PhD/MSBS)
neurosciences and neurological disorders (MS, PhD)
occupational health (MSOH, Certificate)
oral biology (MSBS)
orthopedic science (MSBS)
pathology (Certificate)
public health (MPH, Certificate)
radiation oncology (MSBS)
surgery (MSBS)
urology (MSBS)

College of Nursing
Programs in:
adult health practitioner/clinical nurse specialist (MSN)
adult nurse practitioner (Certificate)
entry-level nursing initiative (GEMINI) (MSN)
family nurse practitioner (MSN, Certificate)
nursing education (Certificate)
pediatric nurse practitioner (Certificate)
pediatric nurse practitioner/clinical nurse specialist (MSN)
RN to MSN (MSN)

College of Pharmacy
Programs in:
administrative pharmacy (MSPS)
industrial pharmacy (MSPS)
medicinal and biological chemistry (MS, PhD)
pharmacology toxicology (MSPS)
pharmacy (MS, MSPS, PhD)

College of Law
Douglas E. Ray, Dean
Program in:
law (JD)

■ URSULINE COLLEGE
Pepper Pike, OH 44124-4398
http://www.ursuline.edu/

Independent-religious, Undergraduate: women only; graduate: coed, comprehensive institution. *Graduate faculty:* 12 full-time (11 women), 27 part-time/adjunct (19 women). *Computer facilities:* 72 computers available on campus for general student use. A campuswide network can be accessed from student residence rooms. *Graduate expenses:* Tuition: full-time $13,590; part-time $775 per credit hour. Required fees: $220; $70 per semester. *General application contact:* Brandi Rizzo, Graduate Recruiter, 440-646-8146.

School of Graduate Studies
Dr. Alison Benders, Dean of Graduate Studies
Programs in:
art education (MA)
art therapy counseling (MA)
care management (MSN)
early childhood education (MA)
education (MA)
educational administration (MA)
historic preservation (MA)
language arts education (MA)
liberal studies (MALS)
life science education (MA)
management (MM, MMT)
math education (MA)
middle school education (MA)
ministry (MA)
nurse practitioner (MSN)
nursing education (MSN)
palliative care (MSN)
social studies education (MA)
special education (MA)

■ WALSH UNIVERSITY
North Canton, OH 44720-3396
http://www.walsh.edu/

Independent-religious, coed, comprehensive institution. CGS member. *Graduate faculty:* 22 full-time (13 women), 31 part-time/adjunct (16 women). *Computer facilities:* 357 computers available on campus for general student use. A campuswide network can be accessed from student residence rooms and from off campus. Online class registration is available. *Graduate expenses:* Tuition: full-time $9450; part-time $525 per credit. Part-time tuition and fees vary according to course load and program. *General application contact:* Brett Freshour, Vice President of Enrollment Management, 330-490-7286.

Graduate Studies
Dr. Laurence Bove, Provost
Programs in:
business administration (MBA)
education (MA)
mental health counseling (MA)
physical therapy (DPT)
school counseling (MA)
theology (MA)

■ WRIGHT STATE UNIVERSITY
Dayton, OH 45435
http://www.wright.edu/

State-supported, coed, university. CGS member. *Computer facilities:* Computer purchase and lease plans are available. 450 computers available on campus for general student use. A campuswide network can be accessed from student residence rooms and from off campus. Online class registration is available. *General application contact:* Associate Director of Graduate Admissions and Records, 937-775-2957.

School of Graduate Studies
Program in:
interdisciplinary studies (MA, MS)

College of Education and Human Services
Programs in:
adolescent young adult (M Ed, MA)
advanced curriculum and instruction (Ed S)
advanced educational leadership (Ed S)
career, technology and vocational education (M Ed, MA)
chemical dependency (MRC)
classroom teacher education (M Ed, MA)
computer/technology education (M Ed, MA)
counseling (M Ed, MA, MS)
curriculum and instruction: teacher leader (MA)
early childhood education (M Ed, MA)
education and human services (M Ed, MA, MRC, MS, MST, Ed S)
educational administrative specialist: teacher leader (M Ed)
educational administrative specialist: vocational education administration (M Ed, MA)
educational leadership (M Ed, MA)
gifted educational needs (M Ed, MA)
health, physical education, and recreation (M Ed, MA)
higher education-adult education (Ed S)
intervention specialist (M Ed, MA)
library/media (M Ed, MA)
middle childhood education (M Ed, MA)
mild to moderate educational needs (M Ed, MA)
moderate to intensive educational needs (M Ed, MA)
multi-age (M Ed, MA)
pupil personnel services (M Ed, MA)
rehabilitation counseling (MRC)
severe disabilities (MRC)
student affairs in higher education-administration (M Ed, MA)
superintendent (Ed S)
vocational education (M Ed, MA)
workforce education (M Ed, MA)

College of Engineering and Computer Science
Programs in:
biomedical and human factors engineering (MSE)
biomedical engineering (MSE)
computer engineering (MSCE)
computer science (MS)
computer science and engineering (MS, MSCE, PhD)
electrical engineering (MSE)
engineering (PhD)

engineering and computer science (MS, MSCE, MSE, PhD)
human factors engineering (MSE)
materials science and engineering (MSE)
mechanical and materials engineering (MSE)
mechanical engineering (MSE)

College of Liberal Arts
Programs in:
composition and rhetoric (MA)
criminal justice and social problems (MA)
English (MA)
history (MA)
humanities (M Hum)
international and comparative politics (MA)
liberal arts (M Hum, M Mus, MA, MPA)
literature (MA)
music education (M Mus)
performance (M Mus)
public administration (MPA)
teaching English to speakers of other languages (MA)

College of Nursing and Health
Programs in:
acute care nurse practitioner (MS)
administration of nursing and health care systems (MS)
adult health (MS)
child and adolescent health (MS)
community health (MS)
family nurse practitioner (MS)
nurse practitioner (MS)
nursing and health (MS)
school nurse (MS)

College of Science and Mathematics
Programs in:
anatomy (MS)
applied mathematics (MS)
applied statistics (MS)
biochemistry and molecular biology (MS)
biological sciences (MS)
biomedical sciences (PhD)
chemistry (MS)
earth science education (MST)
environmental sciences (PhD)
geological sciences (MS)
geophysics (MS)
human factors and industrial/organizational psychology (MS, PhD)
mathematics (MS)
medical physics (MS)
microbiology and immunology (MS)
physics (MS)
physics education (MST)
physiology and biophysics (MS)
science and mathematics (MS, MST, PhD)

Raj Soin College of Business
Programs in:
accountancy (M Acc, MBA)
accounting (MBA)
business (M Acc, MBA, MIS, MS)
business administration (MBA)
business economics (MBA)
finance (MBA)
flexible business (MBA)
health care management (MBA)
information systems (MIS)
international business (MBA)
logistics and supply chain management (MS)
management information technology (MBA)
management, innovation and change (MBA)
marketing (MBA)
project management (MBA)
social and applied economics (MS)
supply chain management (MBA)

School of Medicine
Programs in:
aerospace medicine (MS)
health promotion and education (MPH)
medicine (MD, MPH, MS, PhD)
pharmacology and toxicology (MS)
public health management (MPH)
public health nursing (MPH)

School of Professional Psychology
Program in:
clinical psychology (Psy D)

■ XAVIER UNIVERSITY
Cincinnati, OH 45207
http://www.xu.edu/

Independent-religious, coed, comprehensive institution. *Graduate faculty:* 161 full-time (72 women), 136 part-time/adjunct (70 women). *Computer facilities:* Computer purchase and lease plans are available. 250 computers available on campus for general student use. A campuswide network can be accessed from student residence rooms and from off campus. Online class registration is available. *General application contact:* Roger Bosse, Interim Director of Graduate Studies, 513-745-3357.

College of Arts and Sciences
Dr. Janice B. Walker, Dean
Programs in:
arts and sciences (MA)
English (MA)
theology (MA)

College of Social Sciences, Health and Education
Dr. Mark Meyers, Dean
Programs in:
clinical nurse leader (MSN)
clinical psychology (Psy D)
criminal justice (MS)
forensic nursing (MSN)
health services administration (MHSA)
healthcare law (MSN)
nursing administration (MSN)
occupational therapy (MOT)
psychology (MA)
school nursing (MSN)
social sciences, health and education (M Ed, MA, MHSA, MOT, MS, MSN, Psy D)
sport administration (M Ed)

School of Education
Dr. Jennifer Fager, Associate Dean
Programs in:
community counseling (MA)
education (M Ed, MA)
educational administration (M Ed)
elementary education (M Ed)
human resource development (M Ed)
Montessori (M Ed)
multicultural literature for children (M Ed)
reading (M Ed)
school counseling (MA)
secondary education (M Ed)
special education (M Ed)

Williams College of Business
Dr. Ali Malekzadeh, Dean
Programs in:
business (Exec MBA, MBA)
business administration (Exec MBA, MBA)
e-commerce (MBA)
finance (MBA)
international business (MBA)
management information systems (MBA)
marketing (MBA)

■ YOUNGSTOWN STATE UNIVERSITY
Youngstown, OH 44555-0001
http://www.ysu.edu/

State-supported, coed, comprehensive institution. CGS member. *Computer facilities:* 100 computers available on campus for general student use. A campuswide network can be accessed from student residence rooms and from off campus. Online class registration is available. *General application contact:* Dean of Graduate Studies and Research, 330-941-3091.

Graduate School

Beeghly College of Education
Programs in:
adolescent/young adult education (MS Ed)
community counseling (MS Ed)
content area concentration (MS Ed)
early childhood education (MS Ed)
education (MS Ed, Ed D)
educational administration (MS Ed)
educational leadership (Ed D)
educational technology (MS Ed)
gifted and talented education (MS Ed)
literacy (MS Ed)
middle childhood education (MS Ed)
school counseling (MS Ed)
special education (MS Ed)

Youngstown State University (continued)

Bitonte College of Health and Human Services
Programs in:
criminal justice (MS)
health and human services (MHHS, MPH, MS, MSN, DPT)
nursing (MSN)
physical therapy (DPT)
public health (MPH)

College of Fine and Performing Arts
Programs in:
fine and performing arts (MM)
jazz studies (MM)
music education (MM)
music history and literature (MM)
music theory and composition (MM)
performance (MM)

College of Liberal Arts and Social Sciences
Programs in:
applied behavior analysis (MS)
economics (MA)
English (MA)
environmental studies (MS)
financial economics (MA)
history (MA)
industrial/institutional management (Certificate)
liberal arts and social sciences (MA, MS, Certificate)
risk management (Certificate)

College of Science, Technology, Engineering and Mathematics
Programs in:
analytical chemistry (MS)
applied mathematics (MS)
biochemistry (MS)
chemistry education (MS)
civil and environmental engineering (MSE)
computer engineering (MSE)
computer science (MS)
computing and information systems (MCIS)
electrical engineering (MSE)
environmental biology (MS)
industrial and systems engineering (MSE)
inorganic chemistry (MS)
mechanical engineering (MSE)
molecular biology, microbiology, and genetic (MS)
organic chemistry (MS)
physical chemistry (MS)
physiology and anatomy (MS)
science, technology, engineering and mathematics (MCIS, MSE)
secondary mathematics (MS)
statistics (MS)

Williamson College of Business Administration
Programs in:
accounting (MBA)
business administration (MBA, Certificate)
enterprise resource planning (Certificate)
marketing (MBA)

Oklahoma

■ CAMERON UNIVERSITY
Lawton, OK 73505-6377
http://www.cameron.edu/

State-supported, coed, comprehensive institution. *Computer facilities:* 540 computers available on campus for general student use. A campuswide network can be accessed from student residence rooms and from off campus. Online courses, student information system available. *General application contact:* Graduate Admissions/ Enrollment Coordinator, 580-581-2987.

Office of Graduate Studies
Programs in:
behavioral sciences (MS)
business administration (MBA)
education (M Ed)
educational leadership (MS)
entrepreneurial studies (MS)
teaching (MAT)

■ EAST CENTRAL UNIVERSITY
Ada, OK 74820-6899
http://www.ecok.edu/

State-supported, coed, comprehensive institution. CGS member. *Graduate faculty:* 48. *Computer facilities:* 500 computers available on campus for general student use. A campuswide network can be accessed. *Graduate expenses:* Tuition, state resident: full-time $1175; part-time $130.50 per credit hour. Tuition, nonresident: full-time $3335; part-time $370.50 per credit hour. Required fees: $38 per credit hour. *General application contact:* Dr. G. Richard Wetherill, Interim Dean, 580-559-5709 Ext. 709.

School of Graduate Studies
Programs in:
administration (MSHR)
counseling (MSHR)
criminal justice (MSHR)
education (M Ed)
psychology (MSPS)
rehabilitation counseling (MSHR)

■ NORTHEASTERN STATE UNIVERSITY
Tahlequah, OK 74464-2399
http://www.nsuok.edu/

State-supported, coed, comprehensive institution. *Graduate faculty:* 121 full-time (35 women), 10 part-time/adjunct (5 women). *Computer facilities:* Computer purchase and lease plans are available. 897 computers available on campus for general student use. A campuswide network can be accessed from student residence rooms and from off campus. *General application contact:* Donna Trout, Graduate Program Coordinator, 918-449-6000 Ext. 6123.

College of Optometry
Program in:
optometry (OD)

Graduate College
Dr. Thomas L. Jackson, Dean

College of Business and Technology
Dr. John Schleede, Dean
Programs in:
accounting and financial analysis (MS)
business administration (MBA)
business and technology (MBA, MS)
industrial management (MS)

College of Education
Dr. Kay Grant, Head
Programs in:
collegiate scholarship and services (MS)
counseling psychology (MS)
early childhood education (M Ed)
education (M Ed, MS, MS Ed)
health and kinesiology (MS Ed)
higher education administration and services (MS)
library media and information technology (MS Ed)
mathematics education (M Ed)
reading (M Ed)
school administration (M Ed)
school counseling (M Ed)
teaching (M Ed)

College of Liberal Arts
Dr. Paul Westbrook, Interim Dean
Programs in:
American studies (MA)
communication (MA)
criminal justice (MS)
English (MA)
liberal arts (MA, MS)

College of Science and Health Professions
Dr. Doug Penisten, Interim Dean
Programs in:
science and health professions (M Ed, MS)
science education (M Ed)
speech-language pathology (MS)

■ OKLAHOMA CHRISTIAN UNIVERSITY
Oklahoma City, OK 73136-1100
http://www.oc.edu/

Independent-religious, coed, comprehensive institution. *Graduate faculty:* 11 full-time (0 women). *Computer facilities:* 101 computers available on campus for general student use. A campuswide network can be accessed from student residence rooms and from off campus. Online class registration is available. *General application contact:* Dustin Crawford, Graduate School of Theology Admissions Counselor, 405-425-5485.

Graduate School of Theology
Dr. John Harrison, Chair

Programs in:
family life ministry (MA)
ministry (M Div, MA)
youth ministry (MA)

■ OKLAHOMA CITY UNIVERSITY

Oklahoma City, OK 73106-1402

http://www.okcu.edu/

Independent-religious, coed, comprehensive institution. *Computer facilities:* Computer purchase and lease plans are available. 402 computers available on campus for general student use. A campuswide network can be accessed from student residence rooms and from off campus. Online class registration is available. *General application contact:* Director, Graduate Admissions, 800-633-7242.

Kramer School of Nursing
Program in:
nursing (MSN)

Margaret E. Petree College of Performing Arts
Programs in:
costume design (MA)
performing arts (MA, MFA, MM)
technical theater (MA)
theater (MA)
theater for young audiences (MA)

Ann Lacy School of American Dance and Arts Management
Program in:
dance (MFA)

Wanda L. Bass School of Music
Programs in:
composition (MM)
conducting (MM)
musical theatre (MM)
opera performance (MM)
performance (MM)

Meinders School of Business
Programs in:
accounting (MSA)
business (MBA, MSA)
finance (MBA)
health administration (MBA)
information technology (MBA)
integrated marketing communications (MBA)
international business (MBA)
marketing (MBA)

Petree College of Arts and Sciences
Programs in:
art (MLA)
arts and sciences (M Ed, MA, MCJ, MLA, MS)
general studies (MLA)
leadership/management (MLA)
literature (MLA)
mass communications (MLA)
philosophy (MLA)
writing (MLA)

Division of Computer Science
Program in:
computer science (MS)

Division of Education and Kinesiology Exercise Studies
Programs in:
applied behavioral studies (M Ed)
early childhood education (M Ed)
education and kinesiology exercise studies (M Ed, MA)
elementary education (M Ed)
teaching English to speakers of other languages (MA)

Division of Sociology and Justice Studies
Program in:
criminal justice (MCJ)

School of Law
Program in:
law (JD)

Wimberly School of Religion and Graduate Theological Center
Program in:
religion and theology (M Rel, MAR)

■ OKLAHOMA STATE UNIVERSITY

Stillwater, OK 74078

http://www.okstate.edu/

State-supported, coed, university. CGS member. *Graduate faculty:* 1,030 full-time (320 women), 212 part-time/adjunct (103 women). *Computer facilities:* Computer purchase and lease plans are available. A campuswide network can be accessed from student residence rooms and from off campus. Online class registration is available. *Graduate expenses:* Tuition, state resident: part-time $154.85 per credit hour. Tuition, nonresident: part-time $602 per credit hour. Required fees: $73.85 per credit hour. One-time fee: $50 part-time. Tuition and fees vary according to course load and campus/location. *General application contact:* Dr. Gordon Emslie, Dean, 405-744-6368.

Center for Veterinary Health Sciences
Programs in:
veterinary biomedical sciences (MS, PhD)
veterinary health sciences (DVM, MS, PhD)
veterinary medicine (DVM)

College of Agricultural Science and Natural Resources
Dr. Robert E. Whitson, Dean
Programs in:
agricultural economics (M Ag, MS, PhD)
agricultural education, communications and leadership (M Ag, MS, PhD)
agricultural science and natural resources (M Ag, MS, PhD)
animal breeding and reproduction (PhD)
animal nutrition (PhD)
animal sciences (M Ag, MS)
biochemistry and molecular biology (MS, PhD)
biomechanical engineering (MS, PhD)
bioprocessing and biotechnology (MS, PhD)
crop science (PhD)
entomology (MS, PhD)
environmental and natural resources (MS, PhD)
environmental science (PhD)
food processing (MS, PhD)
food science (MS, PhD)
horticulture (M Ag, MS)
international agriculture (M Ag)
natural resource ecology and management (M Ag, MS, PhD)
plant and soil sciences (M Ag, MS)
plant pathology (PhD)
plant science (PhD)
soil science (PhD)

College of Arts and Sciences
Dr. Peter M. A. Sherwood, Dean
Programs in:
applied history (MA)
applied mathematics (MS)
arts and sciences (MA, MFA, MM, MS, PhD)
botany (MS)
chemistry (MS, PhD)
clinical psychology (PhD)
communications sciences and disorders (MS)
computer science (MS, PhD)
creative writing (MA)
English (MFA)
environmental science (PhD)
fire and emergency management administration (MS, PhD)
general psychology (MS)
geography (MS, PhD)
history (PhD)
lifespan development psychology (PhD)
literature (PhD)
mathematics (pure and applied) (PhD)
mathematics (pure) (MS)
mathematics education (MS, PhD)
microbiology and molecular genetics (MS, PhD)
pedagogy and performance (MM)
philosophy (MA)
photonics (MS, PhD)
physics (MS, PhD)
plant science (PhD)
political science (MA)
sociology (MS, PhD)
statistics (MS, PhD)
theatre (MA)
zoology (MS, PhD)

School of Geology
Dr. Jay Gregg, Head
Program in:
geology (MS, PhD)

School of Journalism and Broadcasting
Dr. Derina Holtzhausen, Director

Oklahoma State University (continued)
Program in:
mass communication (MS)

College of Education
Dr. Pamela Fry, Dean
Program in:
education (MS, Ed D, PhD, Ed S)

School of Applied Health and Educational Psychology
Dr. John Romans, Head
Program in:
applied behavioral studies (Ed D)

School of Educational Studies
Dr. Bert Jacobson, Head
Program in:
higher education (Ed D)

School of Teaching and Curriculum Leadership
Dr. Christine Ormsbee, Head
Program in:
teaching and curriculum leadership (MS, PhD)

College of Engineering, Architecture and Technology
Dr. Karl N. Reid, Dean
Program in:
engineering, architecture and technology (MS, PhD)

School of Chemical Engineering
Dr. Khaled A. M. Gasem, Head
Program in:
chemical engineering (MS, PhD)

School of Civil and Environmental Engineering
Dr. John Veenstra, Head
Programs in:
civil engineering (MS)
environmental engineering (PhD)

School of Electrical and Computer Engineering
Dr. Keith Teague, Head
Program in:
electrical and computer engineering (MS, PhD)

School of Industrial Engineering and Management
Dr. William J. Kolarik, Head
Program in:
industrial engineering and management (PhD)

School of Mechanical and Aerospace Engineering
Dr. Lawrence L. Hoberock, Head
Program in:
mechanical engineering (MS, PhD)

College of Human Environmental Sciences
Dr. Stephan Wilson, Dean
Programs in:
design, housing and merchandising (MS, PhD)
human development and family science (MS, PhD)
human environmental sciences (MS)
nutritional sciences (MS, PhD)

School of Hotel and Restaurant Administration
Dr. Richard Ghiselli, Head
Program in:
hotel and restaurant administration (MS, PhD)

Graduate College
Dr. Gordon Emslie, Dean
Programs in:
environmental science (MS)
natural and applied science (MS)
photonics (PhD)
plant science (PhD)

William S. Spears School of Business
Dr. Sara M. Freedman, Dean
Programs in:
business (MBA, MS, PhD)
business administration (MBA, PhD)
economics and legal studies in business (MS, PhD)
finance (PhD)
management (MS, PhD)
management information systems (MS)
management science and information systems (PhD)
marketing (MBA, PhD)
quantitative financial economics (MS)
telecommunications management (MS)

School of Accounting
Dr. Don Hansen, Head
Program in:
accounting (MS, PhD)

■ ORAL ROBERTS UNIVERSITY
Tulsa, OK 74171-0001
http://www.oru.edu/

Independent-religious, coed, comprehensive institution. *Computer facilities:* 382 computers available on campus for general student use. A campuswide network can be accessed from student residence rooms and from off campus. Online class registration is available. *General application contact:* Graduate Admissions Coordinator, 918-495-6989.

School of Business
Programs in:
accounting (MBA)
entrepreneurship (MBA)
finance (MBA)
international business (MBA)
management (MBA)
marketing (MBA)
non-profit management (M Man, MBA)
organizational dynamics (M Man)
sales marketing (M Man)

School of Education
Programs in:
Christian school administration (K-12) (MA Ed, Ed D)
Christian school curriculum development (MA Ed)
college and higher education administration (MA Ed, Ed D)
public school administration (K-12) (MA Ed, Ed D)
public school teaching (MA Ed)
teaching English as a second language (MA Ed)

School of Theology and Missions
Programs in:
biblical literature (MA)
Christian counseling (MA)
Christian education (MA)
divinity (M Div)
missions (MA)
practical theology (MA)
theological/historical studies (MA)
theology (D Min)

■ SOUTHEASTERN OKLAHOMA STATE UNIVERSITY
Durant, OK 74701-0609
http://www.sosu.edu/

State-supported, coed, comprehensive institution. *Graduate faculty:* 97 full-time (33 women), 8 part-time/adjunct (3 women). *Computer facilities:* 518 computers available on campus for general student use. A campuswide network can be accessed from student residence rooms. Online class registration, campus Blackboard classes are available. *General application contact:* Carrie Williamson, Graduate Secretary, 580-745-2200.

Department of Aviation Science
Dr. David Conway, Director
Program in:
aerospace administration and logistics (MS)

School of Arts and Sciences
Dr. Teresa Golden, Graduate Coordinator
Program in:
technology (MT)

School of Behavioral Sciences
Dr. Daniel Weigel, Program Coordinator
Program in:
community counseling (MBS)

School of Business
Dr. Buddy Gaster, Dean
Program in:
business (MBA, MS)

School of Education
Dr. Muhammad Betz, Chair
Programs in:
elementary education (M Ed)
math specialist (M Ed)

reading specialist (M Ed)
school administration (M Ed)
school counseling (M Ed)

■ SOUTHERN NAZARENE UNIVERSITY
Bethany, OK 73008
http://www.snu.edu/

Independent-religious, coed, comprehensive institution. *Computer facilities:* Computer purchase and lease plans are available. 120 computers available on campus for general student use. A campuswide network can be accessed from student residence rooms and from off campus. *General application contact:* Dean of Graduate College, 405-491-6316.

Graduate College
Program in:
theology (MA)

School of Business
Program in:
business (MBA, MS Mgt)

School of Education
Programs in:
curriculum and instruction (MA)
educational leadership (MA)

School of Nursing
Programs in:
nursing education (MS)
nursing leadership (MS)

School of Psychology
Programs in:
counseling psychology (MSCP)
marriage and family therapy (MA)

■ SOUTHWESTERN OKLAHOMA STATE UNIVERSITY
Weatherford, OK 73096-3098
http://www.swosu.edu/

State-supported, coed, comprehensive institution. *Computer facilities:* 270 computers available on campus for general student use. A campuswide network can be accessed from student residence rooms and from off campus. *General application contact:* Information Contact, 580-774-3790.

College of Arts and Sciences
Programs in:
art education (M Ed)
arts and sciences (M Ed, MM)
English (M Ed)
mathematics (M Ed)
music education (MM)
natural sciences (M Ed)
performance (MM)
social sciences (M Ed)

College of Pharmacy
Program in:
pharmacy (Pharm D)

College of Professional and Graduate Studies

School of Behavioral Sciences and Education
Programs in:
community counseling (M Ed)
early childhood education (M Ed)
educational administration (M Ed)
elementary education (M Ed)
health sciences and microbiology (M Ed)
kinesiology (M Ed)
parks and recreation management (M Ed)
school counseling (M Ed)
school psychology (MS)
school psychometry (M Ed)
secondary education (M Ed)
special education (M Ed)

School of Business and Technology
Program in:
business and technology (MBA)

■ UNIVERSITY OF CENTRAL OKLAHOMA
Edmond, OK 73034-5209
http://www.uco.edu/

State-supported, coed, comprehensive institution. CGS member. *Computer facilities:* 400 computers available on campus for general student use. A campuswide network can be accessed from student residence rooms and from off campus. Online class registration is available. *General application contact:* Interim Dean, Graduate College, 405-974-3341.

College of Graduate Studies and Research

College of Arts, Media, and Design
Programs in:
arts, media, and design (MFA, MM)
design and interior design (MFA)
music education (MM)
performance (MM)

College of Business Administration
Program in:
business administration (MBA)

College of Education
Programs in:
adult education (M Ed)
community services (M Ed)
counseling psychology (MS)
early childhood education (M Ed)
education (M Ed, MA, MS)
educational administration (M Ed)
elementary education (M Ed)
family and child studies (MS)
family and consumer science education (MS)
general education (M Ed)
general psychology (MA)
gerontology (M Ed)
guidance and counseling (M Ed)
instructional media (M Ed)
interior design (MS)
nutrition-food management (MS)
professional health occupations (M Ed)
reading (M Ed)
secondary education (M Ed)
special education (M Ed)
speech-language pathology (M Ed)

College of Liberal Arts
Programs in:
composition skills (MA)
contemporary literature (MA)
creative writing (MA)
criminal justice management and administration (MA)
history (MA)
international affairs (MA)
liberal arts (MA)
museum studies (MA)
political science (MA)
social studies teaching (MA)
Southwestern studies (MA)
teaching English as a second language (MA)
traditional studies (MA)
urban affairs (MA)

College of Mathematics and Science
Programs in:
applied mathematical sciences (MS)
biology (MS)
chemistry (MS)
mathematics and science (MS)
physics and engineering (MS)

■ UNIVERSITY OF OKLAHOMA
Norman, OK 73019-0390
http://www.ou.edu/

State-supported, coed, university. CGS member. *Graduate faculty:* 1,101 full-time (334 women), 173 part-time/adjunct (70 women). *Computer facilities:* Computer purchase and lease plans are available. 3,600 computers available on campus for general student use. A campuswide network can be accessed from student residence rooms and from off campus. Online class registration is available. *Graduate expenses:* Tuition, state resident: full-time $3744; part-time $156 per credit hour. Tuition, nonresident: full-time $13,577; part-time $565.70 per credit hour. Required fees: $2415.40; $90.10 per credit hour. *General application contact:* Patricia Lynch, Director of Admissions, 405-325-2251.

College of Law
Dr. Andrew M. Coats, Dean
Program in:
law (JD)

Graduate College
Lee Williams, Dean/Vice President of Research
Program in:
interdisciplinary studies (MA, MS, PhD)

College of Architecture
Charles W. Graham, Dean

University of Oklahoma (continued)
Programs in:
architecture (M Arch, MLA, MRCP, MS, MSAUS, MSCA)
construction science (MS)
landscape architecture (MLA)
regional and city planning (MRCP)

College of Arts and Sciences
Paul B. Bell, Dean and Vice Provost
Programs in:
anthropology (MA, PhD)
arts and sciences (M Nat Sci, MA, MHR, MLIS, MPA, MS, MSKM, MSW, PhD, Certificate)
astrophysics (MS, PhD)
botany (MS, PhD)
cellular and behavioral neurobiology (PhD)
chemistry and biochemistry (MS, PhD)
communication (MA, PhD)
ecology and evolutionary biology (PhD)
economics (MA, PhD)
English (MA, PhD)
French (MA, PhD)
German (MA)
health and exercise science (MS, PhD)
history (MA, PhD)
history of science (MA, PhD)
human relations (MHR)
knowledge management (MSKM)
library and information studies (MLIS)
mathematics (MA, MS, PhD)
microbiology (MS, PhD)
Native American studies (MA)
organizational dynamics (MS)
philosophy (MA, PhD)
physics (MS, PhD)
political science (MA, MPA, PhD)
psychology (MS, PhD)
public administration (MPA)
school library media specialist (Certificate)
social work (MSW)
sociology (MA, PhD)
Spanish (MA, PhD)
zoology (M Nat Sci, MS, PhD)

College of Atmospheric and Geographic Sciences
Dr. John T. Snow, Dean
Programs in:
atmospheric and geographic sciences (M Pr Met, MA, MS Metr, PhD)
geography (MA, PhD)
meteorology (M Pr Met, MS Metr, PhD)

College of Earth and Energy
Doug Elmore, Associate Provost/Director
Programs in:
earth and energy (MS, PhD)
geological engineering (MS, PhD)
geology (MS, PhD)
geophysics (MS)
natural gas engineering (MS)
petroleum engineering (MS, PhD)

College of Education
Dr. Joan Karen Smith, Dean
Programs in:
adult and higher education (M Ed, PhD)
community counseling (M Ed)
counseling psychology (PhD)
education (Certificate)
educational administration, curriculum and supervision (M Ed, Ed D, PhD)
educational studies (M Ed, PhD)
historical, philosophical, and social foundations of education (M Ed, PhD)
instructional leadership and academic curriculum (M Ed, PhD)
instructional psychology (M Ed, PhD)
school counseling (M Ed)
special education (M Ed, PhD)

College of Engineering
Dr. Thomas Landers, Dean
Programs in:
aerospace engineering (MS, PhD)
air (M Env Sc)
bioengineering (MS, PhD)
chemical engineering (MS, PhD)
civil engineering (MS, PhD)
computer science (MS, PhD)
electrical and computer engineering (MS, PhD)
engineering (M Env Sc, MS, D Engr, PhD)
engineering physics (MS, PhD)
environmental engineering (MS)
environmental science (M Env Sc, PhD)
geotechnical engineering (MS)
groundwater management (M Env Sc)
hazardous solid waste (M Env Sc)
industrial engineering (MS, PhD)
mechanical engineering (MS, PhD)
occupational safety and health (M Env Sc)
process design (M Env Sc)
structures (MS)
telecommunication systems engineering (MS)
water quality resources (M Env Sc)

College of Fine Arts
Dr. Rich Taylor, Dean
Programs in:
acting (MFA)
art (MA, MFA)
art history (MA, MFA)
ceramics (MFA)
choral conducting (M Mus)
conducting (M Mus Ed, DMA)
dance (MFA)
design (MFA)
directing (MFA)
drama (MA)
film and video (MFA)
fine arts (M Mus, M Mus Ed, MA, MFA, DMA, PhD)
general (M Mus Ed)
instrumental (M Mus Ed)
instrumental conducting (M Mus)
music composition (M Mus, DMA)
music education (M Mus Ed, PhD)
music theory (M Mus)
musicology (M Mus)
organ (M Mus, DMA)
painting (MFA)
photography (MFA)
piano (M Mus, DMA)
printmaking (MFA)
visual communications (MFA)
voice (M Mus, DMA)
wind/percussion/string (M Mus, DMA)

College of Liberal Studies
Dr. James Pappas, Dean and Vice President for University Outreach
Programs in:
administrative leadership (MLS)
integrated studies (MLS)
interprofessional human and health services (MLS)
museum studies (MLS)

Gaylord College of Journalism and Mass Communication
Joe Foote, Dean
Programs in:
advertising and public relations (MA)
information gathering and distribution (MA)
journalism and mass communication (MA)
mass communication management and policy (MA)
professional writing (MPW)
telecommunication and new technology (MA)

Michael F. Price College of Business
Dr. Kenneth Evans, Dean
Programs in:
accounting (M Acc)
business administration (MBA, PhD)
management (MS)
management information systems (MS)

School of International and Area Studies
Dr. Millie C. Audas, Director
Program in:
international studies (MA)

■ UNIVERSITY OF TULSA
Tulsa, OK 74104-3189
http://www.utulsa.edu/

Independent-religious, coed, university. CGS member. *Graduate faculty:* 184 full-time (49 women), 21 part-time/adjunct (8 women). *Computer facilities:* Computer purchase and lease plans are available. 900 computers available on campus for general student use. A campuswide network can be accessed from student residence rooms and from off campus. Online class registration is available. *Graduate expenses:* Tuition: full-time $15,408; part-time $899 per credit hour. Required fees: $3.33 per credit hour. One-time fee: $200 full-time. Tuition and fees vary according to course load and program. *General application contact:* Dr. Janet A. Haggerty, Associate Vice President of Research and Dean of the Graduate School, 918-631-2336.

College of Law
Janet Levit, Dean

Programs in:
- American Indian and indigenous law (LL M)
- American law for foreign lawyers (LL M)
- comparative and international law (Certificate)
- entrepreneurial law (Certificate)
- health law (Certificate)
- law (JD)
- lawyering skills (Certificate)
- Native American law (Certificate)
- public policy and regulation (Certificate)
- resources, energy, and environmental law (Certificate)

Graduate School
Dr. Janet A. Haggerty, Associate Vice President of Research and Dean of the Graduate School

College of Arts and Sciences
Dr. Dale Thomas Benediktson, Dean
Programs in:
- anthropology (MA)
- art (MA, MFA, MTA)
- arts and sciences (MA, MFA, MS, MSMSE, MTA, PhD)
- clinical psychology (MA, PhD)
- education (MA)
- English language and literature (MA, MTA, PhD)
- history (MA, MTA)
- industrial/organizational psychology (MA, PhD)
- mathematics and science education (MSMSE)
- speech-language pathology (MS)
- teaching arts (MTA)

College of Engineering and Natural Sciences
Dr. Steve J. Bellovich, Dean
Programs in:
- biochemistry (MS)
- biological sciences (MS, MTA, PhD)
- chemical engineering (ME, MSE, PhD)
- chemistry (MS, PhD)
- computer science (MS, PhD)
- electrical engineering (ME, MSE)
- engineering and natural sciences (ME, MS, MSE, MTA, PhD)
- engineering physics (MS)
- geosciences (MS, PhD)
- mathematical sciences (MS, MTA)
- mechanical engineering (ME, MSE, PhD)
- petroleum engineering (ME, MSE, PhD)
- physics (MS)

Collins College of Business
Dr. W. Gale Sullenburger, Dean
Programs in:
- accounting (MBA)
- business (M Tax, MBA, MS)
- business administration (MBA)
- corporate finance (MS)
- energy management (MBA)
- finance (MS)
- finance/applied mathematicsinternational business (MBA)
- investments and portfolio management (MS)
- management information systems (MBA)
- risk management (MS)
- taxation (MBA)

Oregon

■ CONCORDIA UNIVERSITY
Portland, OR 97211-6099
http://www.cu-portland.edu/

Independent-religious, coed, comprehensive institution. *Computer facilities:* 100 computers available on campus for general student use. A campuswide network can be accessed from student residence rooms and from off campus. Online class registration is available. *General application contact:* Graduate Admissions Counselor, 503-280-8501.

College of Education
Programs in:
- curriculum and instruction (elementary) (M Ed)
- educational administration (M Ed)
- elementary education (MAT)
- secondary education (MAT)

School of Management
Program in:
- management (MBA)

■ EASTERN OREGON UNIVERSITY
La Grande, OR 97850-2899
http://www.eou.edu/

State-supported, coed, comprehensive institution. *Computer facilities:* Computer purchase and lease plans are available. 75 computers available on campus for general student use. A campuswide network can be accessed from student residence rooms and from off campus. Online class registration is available. *General application contact:* Coordinator of Graduate Studies, 541-962-3399.

School of Education and Business
Programs in:
- education (MS)
- education and business (MS, MTE)
- elementary education (MTE)
- secondary education (MTE)

■ GEORGE FOX UNIVERSITY
Newberg, OR 97132-2697
http://www.georgefox.edu/

Independent-religious, coed, university. *Graduate faculty:* 88 full-time (37 women), 92 part-time/adjunct (52 women). *Computer facilities:* Computer purchase and lease plans are available. 140 computers available on campus for general student use. A campuswide network can be accessed from student residence rooms and from off campus. Online class registration is available. *General application contact:* Bonnie Nakashimada, Director for Graduate and SPS Admissions and Regional Sites, 503-554-6149.

George Fox Evangelical Seminary
Dr. Chuck Conniry, Vice President and Dean, George Fox Evangelical Seminary
Programs in:
- divinity (M Div)
- ministry (D Min)
- ministry leadership (MA)
- spiritual formation (MA)
- spiritual formation and discipleship (Certificate)
- theological studies (MA)

Graduate Department of Clinical Psychology
Dr. Wayne Adams, Professor and Chairperson, Graduate Department of Clinical Psychology
Program in:
- clinical psychology (MA, Psy D)

School of Education
Dr. Linda Samek, Dean, School of Education
Programs in:
- continuing administrator license (Certificate)
- counseling (MA, Certificate, Ed S)
- curriculum and instruction (M Ed)
- educational foundations and leadership (M Ed, Ed D)
- higher education (M Ed)
- initial administrator license (Certificate)
- library media (Certificate)
- literacy (M Ed)
- marriage and family therapy (MA, Certificate)
- mental health trauma (Certificate)
- reading (M Ed)
- school counseling (MA, Certificate)
- school psychology (Certificate, Ed S)
- secondary education (M Ed)
- teaching (MAT)
- teaching plus ESOL (MAT)
- teaching plus ESOL/bilingual (MAT)
- teaching plus reading (MAT)

School of Management
Dr. Ken Armstrong, Professor of Management and Dean, School of Management

George Fox University (continued)
Programs in:
executive management (D Mgt)
management (MBA)
management education (D Mgt)

■ LEWIS & CLARK COLLEGE
Portland, OR 97219-7899
http://www.lclark.edu/

Independent, coed, comprehensive institution. CGS member. *Graduate faculty:* 36 full-time (25 women), 75 part-time/adjunct (48 women). *Computer facilities:* Computer purchase and lease plans are available. 158 computers available on campus for general student use. A campuswide network can be accessed from student residence rooms and from off campus. Online class registration is available. *Graduate expenses:* Tuition: full-time $5087; part-time $677 per credit hour. Tuition and fees vary according to course level and campus/location. *General application contact:* Becky Haas, Director of Admissions, 503-768-6200.

Graduate School of Education and Counseling
Dr. Scott Fletcher, Dean
Programs in:
addictions treatment (MA, MS)
community counseling (MA, MS)
early childhood/elementary education (MAT)
education (M Ed, MAT, Ed D)
education and counseling (M Ed, MA, MAT, MS, Ed D, Ed S)
educational leadership (M Ed, Ed D)
marriage, couple and family therapy (MA, MS)
middle level/high school education (MAT)
psychological and cultural studies (MA, MS)
school counseling (M Ed)
school psychology (Ed S)
special education (M Ed)

Lewis & Clark Law School
Programs in:
environmental and natural resources law (LL M)
law (JD)

■ MARYLHURST UNIVERSITY
Marylhurst, OR 97036-0261
http://www.marylhurst.edu/

Independent-religious, coed, primarily women, comprehensive institution. *Graduate faculty:* 12 full-time (8 women), 73 part-time/adjunct (41 women). *Computer facilities:* 40 computers available on campus for general student use. A campuswide network can be accessed. Online class registration is available. *Graduate expenses:* Tuition: full-time $11,988; part-time $444 per quarter hour. Required fees: $297; $11 per quarter hour. *General application contact:* Office of Admissions, 503-636-8141 Ext. 6268.

Department of Art Therapy Counseling
Christine Turner, Chair
Programs in:
art therapy (PGC)
art therapy counseling (MA)
counseling (PGC)

Department of Business Administration
Bob Hanks, Director of Business and Real Estate Programs
Programs in:
finance (MBA)
general management (MBA)
health care management (MBA)
marketing (MBA)
nonprofit management (MBA)
organizational behavior (MBA)
real estate (MBA)
sustainable business (MBA)

Department of Education
Dr. Thomas Ruhl, Chair
Program in:
education (M Ed, MA)

Department of Interdisciplinary Studies
Dr. Debrah B. Bokowski, Chair
Program in:
interdisciplinary studies (MA)

Department of Religious Studies–Applied Theology Program
Dr. Jerry Roussell, Chair
Program in:
applied theology (MA)

Department of Religious Studies–Divinity Program
Dr. Jerry Roussell, Chair
Program in:
divinity (M Div)

■ OREGON STATE UNIVERSITY
Corvallis, OR 97331
http://www.oregonstate.edu/

State-supported, coed, university. CGS member. *Graduate faculty:* 1,148 full-time (431 women), 237 part-time/adjunct (131 women). *Computer facilities:* Computer purchase and lease plans are available. 1,300 computers available on campus for general student use. A campuswide network can be accessed from student residence rooms and from off campus. Online class registration is available. *Graduate expenses:* Tuition, state resident: full-time $9396; part-time $348 per credit. Tuition, nonresident: full-time $15,228; part-time $564 per credit. *General application contact:* Dr. Sally K. Francis, Dean of the Graduate School, 541-737-4881.

College of Pharmacy
Dr. Wayne A. Kradjan, Dean
Program in:
pharmacy (Pharm D, MS, PhD)

College of Veterinary Medicine
Dr. Cyril Clarke, Dean
Programs in:
comparative veterinary medicine (PhD)
veterinary medicine (DVM, MS, PhD)

Graduate School
Dr. Sally K. Francis, Dean
Programs in:
environmental sciences (MA, MS, PhD)
interdisciplinary studies (MAIS)
molecular and cellular biology (MS, PhD)
plant physiology (MS, PhD)
water resources engineering (MS, PhD)

College of Agricultural Sciences
Dr. Thayne R. Dutson, Dean
Programs in:
agricultural and resource economics (M Agr, MAIS, MS, PhD)
agricultural education (M Agr, MAIS, MAT, MS)
agricultural sciences (M Ag, M Agr, MA, MAIS, MAT, MS, PhD)
animal science (M Agr, MAIS, MS, PhD)
crop science (M Agr, MAIS, MS, PhD)
economics (MS, PhD)
fisheries science (M Agr, MAIS, MS, PhD)
food science and technology (M Agr, MAIS, MS, PhD)
genetics (MA, MAIS, MS, PhD)
horticulture (M Ag, MAIS, MS, PhD)
poultry science (M Agr, MAIS, MS, PhD)
rangeland ecology and management (M Agr, MAIS, MS, PhD)
soil science (M Agr, MAIS, MS, PhD)
toxicology (MS, PhD)
wildlife science (MAIS, MS, PhD)

College of Business
Dr. Ilene K. Kleinsorge, Dean
Program in:
business (MAIS, MBA, Certificate)

College of Education
Dr. Sam Stern, Dean
Programs in:
adult education and higher education leadership (Ed M, MAIS)
college student service administration (Ed M, MS)
counseling (MS, PhD)
education (Ed M, MAIS, MAT, MS, Ed D, PhD)
elementary education (MAT)
family and consumer sciences education (MAT, MS)
general education (Ed M, MAIS, MS, Ed D, PhD)
language arts education (MAT)
music education (MAT)

College of Engineering
Dr. Ronald L. Adams, Dean

Programs in:
biological and ecological engineering (M Eng, MS, PhD)
chemical engineering (M Eng, MS, PhD)
chemical, biological and environmental engineering (M Eng, MS, PhD)
civil engineering (MS, PhD)
coastal and ocean engineering (M Oc E, PhD)
coastal engineering (MS)
computer science (M Eng, MAIS, MS, PhD)
construction engineering management (MBE, PhD)
electrical and computer engineering (M Eng, MS, PhD)
engineering (M Eng, M Engr, M Oc E, MA, MAIS, MBE, MHP, MS, PhD)
geotechnical engineering (MS, PhD)
human systems engineering (MS, PhD)
industrial engineering (MS, PhD)
information systems engineering (MS, PhD)
manufacturing engineering (M Engr)
manufacturing systems engineering (MS, PhD)
materials science (MAIS, MS, PhD)
mechanical engineering (MS, PhD)
nano/micro fabrication (MS, PhD)
nuclear engineering (M Eng, MS, PhD)
radiation health physics (MA, MHP, MS, PhD)
structural engineering (MS, PhD)
transportation engineering (MS, PhD)
water engineering (MS, PhD)

College of Forestry
Hal J. Salwasser, Dean
Programs in:
forest ecosystems and society (MAIS, MF, MS, PhD)
forest engineering (MF, MS)
forest hydrology (MF, MS, PhD)
forest operations (MF)
forest products (MAIS, MF, MS, PhD)
forest soil science (MF, MS, PhD)
forestry (MAIS, MF, MS, PhD)
timber harvesting (PhD)
wood science and technology (MF, MS, PhD)

College of Health and Human Sciences
Dr. Tammy Bray, Dean
Programs in:
design and human environment (MA, MAIS, MS, PhD)
environmental health and occupational safety management (MAIS, MS)
exercise and sport science (MS, PhD)
gerontology (MAIS)
health and human sciences (MA, MAIS, MAT, MPH, MS, PhD)
health management and policy (MS, PhD)
health promotion and health behavior (MAIS, MAT, MS, PhD)
human development and family studies (MS, PhD)
movement studies in disabilities (MAIS, MS)
nutrition and exercise sciences (MAIS)
nutrition and food management (MS)
physical education teacher education (MAT, MS)
public health (MPH, PhD)

College of Liberal Arts
Dr. Kay F. Schaffer, Dean
Programs in:
anthropology (MAIS)
applied anthropology (MA)
applied ethics (MA)
contemporary Hispanic studies (MA)
economics (MA, MS, PhD)
English (MA, MAIS, MFA)
foreign language education (MAT)
history of science (MA, PhD)
interdisciplinary studies (MAIS)
interdisciplinary study (MAIS)
liberal arts (MA, MAIS, MAT, MFA, MS, PhD)
music education (MAT)

College of Oceanic and Atmospheric Sciences
Dr. Mark R. Abbott, Dean
Programs in:
atmospheric sciences (MA, MS, PhD)
geophysics (MA, MS, PhD)
marine resource management (MA, MS)
oceanic and atmospheric sciences (MA, MS, PhD)
oceanography (MA, MS, PhD)

College of Science
Dr. Sherman H. Bloomer, Dean
Programs in:
analytical chemistry (MS, PhD)
applied physics (MS)
biochemistry and biophysics (MA, MAIS, MS, PhD)
biology education (MS)
chemistry (MA, MAIS)
chemistry education (MS)
ecology (MA, MAIS, MS, PhD)
general science (MA, MS, PhD)
genetics (MA, MAIS, MS, PhD)
geography (MA, MAIS, MS, PhD)
geology (MA, MAIS, MS, PhD)
inorganic chemistry (MS, PhD)
integrated science education (MS)
mathematics (MA, MAIS, MS, PhD)
mathematics education (MA, MS, PhD)
microbiology (MA, MAIS, MS, PhD)
molecular and cellular biology (MA, MAIS, MS, PhD)
mycology (MA, MAIS, MS, PhD)
nuclear and radiation chemistry (MS, PhD)
operations research (MA, MS)
organic chemistry (MS, PhD)
physical chemistry (MS, PhD)
physics (MA, MS, PhD)
physics education (MS)
plant pathology (MA, MAIS, MS, PhD)
plant physiology (MA, MAIS, MS, PhD)
science (MA, MAIS, MAT, MS, PhD)
science education (MA, MS, PhD)
statistics (MA, MS, PhD)
structural botany (MA, MAIS, MS, PhD)
systematics (MA, MAIS, MS, PhD)
zoology (MA, MAIS, MS, PhD)

■ PACIFIC UNIVERSITY
Forest Grove, OR 97116-1797
http://www.pacificu.edu/

Independent, coed, comprehensive institution. *Graduate faculty:* 104 full-time (58 women), 105 part-time/adjunct (61 women). *Computer facilities:* Computer purchase and lease plans are available. 315 computers available on campus for general student use. A campuswide network can be accessed from student residence rooms and from off campus. Web space, printing, student and academic information, WebCT, computer peripherals available. *General application contact:* Jon-Erik Larsen, Director of Graduate and Professional Admissions, 503-352-7221.

College of Education
Programs in:
early childhood education (MAT)
education (MAE)
elementary education (MAT)
high school education (MAT)
middle school education (MAT)
special education (MAT)
visual function in learning (M Ed)

College of Optometry
Program in:
optometry (OD, MS)

Healthcare Administration Program
Program in:
healthcare administration (MHA)

Program in Writing
Program in:
writing (MFA)

School of Occupational Therapy
Program in:
occupational therapy (MOT)

School of Physical Therapy
Programs in:
entry level (DPT)
post-professional (DPT)

School of Physician Assistant Studies
Randy Randolph, Director
Program in:
physician assistant studies (MHS, MS)

School of Professional Psychology
Programs in:
clinical psychology (MS, Psy D)
counseling psychology (MA)

■ PORTLAND STATE UNIVERSITY
Portland, OR 97207-0751
http://www.pdx.edu/

State-supported, coed, university. CGS member. *Graduate faculty:* 724 full-time (317 women), 583 part-time/adjunct (298 women). *Computer facilities:* 875 computers available on campus for general student use. A campuswide network can be accessed from student residence rooms and from off campus. Online class registration is available. *General application contact:* Information Contact, 503-725-3511.

Graduate Studies
Dr. William H. Feyerherm, Vice Provost for Sponsored Research/Dean of Graduate Studies
Programs in:
computational intelligence (Certificate)
computer modeling and simulation (Certificate)
systems science (MS)
systems science/anthropology (PhD)
systems science/business administration (PhD)
systems science/civil engineering (PhD)
systems science/economics (PhD)
systems science/engineering management (PhD)
systems science/general (PhD)
systems science/mathematical sciences (PhD)
systems science/mechanical engineering (PhD)
systems science/psychology (PhD)
systems science/sociology (PhD)

College of Liberal Arts and Sciences
Dr. Marvin Kaiser, Dean
Programs in:
anthropology (MA)
applied economics (MA, MS)
biology (MA, MS, PhD)
chemistry (MA, MS, PhD)
conflict resolution (MA, MS)
economics (PhD)
English (MA)
environmental management (MEM)
environmental sciences and resources (PhD)
environmental sciences/biology (PhD)
environmental sciences/chemistry (PhD)
environmental sciences/civil engineering (PhD)
environmental sciences/geography (PhD)
environmental sciences/geology (PhD)
environmental sciences/physics (PhD)
environmental studies (MS)
foreign literature and language (MA)
French (MA)
general arts and letters education (MAT, MST)
general economics (MA, MS)
general science education (MAT, MST)
general social science education (MAT, MST)
general speech communication (MA, MS, Certificate)
geography (MA, MAT, MS, MST, PhD)
geology (MA, MS)
German (MA)
history (MA)
Japanese (MA)
liberal arts and sciences (MA, MAT, MEM, MS, MST, MST, PhD, Certificate)
mathematical sciences (PhD)
mathematics education (PhD)
physics (MA, MS, PhD)
psychology (MA, MS, PhD)
science/environmental science (MST)
science/geology (MAT, MST)
sociology (MA, MS, PhD)
Spanish (MA)
speech-language pathology (MA, MS)
statistics (MS)
teaching English to speakers of other languages (MA)

College of Urban and Public Affairs
Dr. Lawrence Wallack, Dean
Programs in:
aging (Certificate)
criminology and criminal justice (MS, PhD)
government (MA, MAT, MPA, MS, MST, PhD)
health administration (MPA, MPH)
health education (MA, MS)
health education and health promotion (MPH)
health studies (MPA, MPH)
political science (MA, MAT, MS, MST, PhD)
public administration (MPA)
public administration and policy (PhD)
urban and public affairs (MA, MAT, MPA, MPH, MS, MST, MURP, MUS, PhD, Certificate)
urban and regional planning (MURP)
urban studies (MUS, PhD)
urban studies and planning (MURP, MUS, PhD)

Graduate School of Social Work
Dr. Kristine E. Nelson, Dean
Programs in:
social work (MSW)
social work and social research (PhD)

Maseeh College of Engineering and Computer Science
Richard I. Knight, Interim Dean
Programs in:
civil and environmental engineering (M Eng, MS, PhD)
civil and environmental engineering management (M Eng)
computer science (MS, PhD)
electrical and computer engineering (M Eng, MS, PhD)
engineering and computer science (M Eng, ME, MS, MSE, PhD, Certificate)
engineering and technology management (M Eng)
engineering management (MS)
environmental sciences and resources (PhD)
manufacturing engineering (ME)
manufacturing management (M Eng)
mechanical engineering (M Eng, MS, PhD)
software engineering (MSE)
systems engineering (M Eng)
systems engineering fundamentals (Certificate)
systems science (PhD)
systems science/engineering management (PhD)

School of Business Administration
Dr. Scott Dawson, Dean
Programs in:
business administration (MBA, MIM, MSFA, PhD)
financial analysis (MSFA)
human resource management (MBA)
international management (MIM)

School of Education
Dr. Randy Hitz, Dean
Programs in:
counselor education (MA, MS)
early childhood education (MA, MS)
education (M Ed, MA, MAT, MS, MST, Ed D)
educational leadership (MA, MS, Ed D)
educational leadership: curriculum and instruction (Ed D)
educational media/school librarianship (MA, MS)
elementary education (M Ed, MAT, MST)
postsecondary, adult and continuing education (Ed D)
reading (MA, MS)
secondary education (M Ed, MAT, MST)
special and counselor education (Ed D)
special education (MA, MS)

School of Fine and Performing Arts
Barbara Sestak, Dean
Programs in:
conducting (MMC)
drawing (MFA)
fine and performing arts (MA, MAT, MFA, MMC, MMP, MS, MST)
mixed media (MFA)
music education (MAT, MST)
painting (MFA)
performance (MMP)
printmaking (MFA)
sculpture (MFA)
theater arts (MA, MS)

■ SOUTHERN OREGON UNIVERSITY
Ashland, OR 97520
http://www.sou.edu/

State-supported, coed, comprehensive institution. *Computer facilities:* 750 computers available on campus for general student use. A campuswide network can be accessed from student residence rooms and from off campus. Online class registration is available. *General application contact:* Director of Admissions, 541-552-6411.

Graduate Studies

School of Arts and Letters
Program in:
music (MA, MS)

School of Business
Program in:
business (MA Ed, MIM, MS Ed)

School of Sciences
Programs in:
environmental education (MA, MS)
mathematics/computer science (MA, MS)
science (MA, MS)

School of Social Sciences
Programs in:
applied psychology (MAP)
elementary education (MA Ed, MS Ed)
human service-organizational training and development (MA, MS)
secondary education (MA Ed, MS Ed)
social science (MA, MS)
social science, health and physical education (MA, MA Ed, MAP, MAT, MS, MS Ed)
teaching (MAT)

■ UNIVERSITY OF OREGON
Eugene, OR 97403
http://www.uoregon.edu/

State-supported, coed, university. CGS member. *Computer facilities:* Computer purchase and lease plans are available. 1,700 computers available on campus for general student use. A campuswide network can be accessed from student residence rooms and from off campus. Online class registration is available. *General application contact:* Information Contact, 541-346-5129.

Graduate School

Program in:
applied information management (MS)

Charles H. Lundquist College of Business
Programs in:
accounting (M Actg, PhD)
business (M Actg, MA, MBA, MS, PhD)
decision sciences (MA, MS)
finance (PhD)
management (PhD)
management: general business (MBA)
marketing (PhD)

College of Arts and Sciences
Programs in:
anthropology (MA, MS, PhD)
arts and sciences (MA, MFA, MS, PhD)
Asian studies (MA)
biochemistry (MA, MS, PhD)
chemistry (MA, MS, PhD)
Chinese (MA, PhD)
classical civilization (MA)
classics (MA)
clinical psychology (PhD)
cognitive psychology (MA, MS, PhD)
comparative literature (MA, PhD)
computer and information science (MA, MS, PhD)
creative writing (MFA)
developmental psychology (MA, MS, PhD)
ecology and evolution (MA, MS, PhD)
economics (MA, MS, PhD)
English (MA, PhD)
environmental science, studies, and policy (PhD)
environmental studies (MA, MS)
French (MA)
geography (MA, MS, PhD)
geological sciences (MA, MS, PhD)
Germanic languages and literatures (MA, PhD)
Greek (MA)
history (MA, PhD)
human physiology (MS, PhD)
independent study: folklore (MA, MS)
international studies (MA)
Italian (MA)
Japanese (MA, PhD)
Latin (MA)
linguistics (MA, PhD)
marine biology (MA, MS, PhD)
mathematics (MA, MS, PhD)
molecular, cellular and genetic biology (PhD)
neuroscience and development (PhD)
philosophy (MA, PhD)
physics (MA, MS, PhD)
physiological psychology (MA, MS, PhD)
political science (MA, MS, PhD)
psychology (MA, MS, PhD)
Romance languages (MA, PhD)
Russian and East European Studies (MA)
social/personality psychology (MA, MS, PhD)
sociology (MA, MS, PhD)
Spanish (MA)
theater arts (MA, MFA, MS, PhD)

College of Education
Program in:
education (M Ed, MA, MS, D Ed, PhD)

School of Architecture and Allied Arts
Programs in:
architecture (M Arch)
architecture and allied arts (M Arch, MA, MCRP, MFA, MI Arch, MLA, MPA, MS, PhD)
art (MFA)
art history (MA, PhD)
arts management (MA, MS)
community and regional planning (MCRP)
historic preservation (MS)
interior architecture (MI Arch)
landscape architecture (MLA)
media management (MA, MS)
public policy and management (MA, MPA, MS)

School of Journalism and Communication
Program in:
journalism and communication (MA, MS, PhD)

School of Music
Programs in:
composition (M Mus, DMA, PhD)
conducting (M Mus)
dance (MA, MS)
jazz studies (M Mus)
music (M Mus, MA, MS, DMA, PhD)
music education (M Mus, DMA, PhD)
music history (PhD)
music theory (PhD)
performance (M Mus, DMA)
piano pedagogy (M Mus)

School of Law

Program in:
law (JD, MA, MS)

■ UNIVERSITY OF PHOENIX–OREGON CAMPUS
Tigard, OR 97223
http://www.phoenix.edu/

Proprietary, coed, comprehensive institution. *Computer facilities:* Computer purchase and lease plans are available. A campuswide network can be accessed from off campus. Online class registration is available. *General application contact:* Campus Information Center, 503-403-2900.

The Artemis School

College of Education
Programs in:
curriculum and instruction (MA Ed)
early childhood education (MA Ed)
elementary education (MA Ed)
secondary education (MA Ed)

College of Health and Human Services
Programs in:
administration of justice and security (MS)
health administration (MHA)
health care management (MBA)
nursing (MSN)
psychology (MS)

The John Sperling School of Business

Program in:
business (MBA, MIS, MM)

College of Graduate Business and Management
Programs in:
accounting (MBA)
business administration (MBA)
global management (MBA)
human resource management (MM)
human resources management (MBA)
management (MM)
marketing (MBA)
public administration (MM)

University of Phoenix–Oregon Campus (continued)

College of Information Systems and Technology
Programs in:
- information systems (MIS)
- technology management (MBA)

■ UNIVERSITY OF PORTLAND
Portland, OR 97203-5798
http://www.up.edu/

Independent-religious, coed, comprehensive institution. *Graduate faculty:* 84 full-time (26 women), 11 part-time/adjunct (5 women). *Computer facilities:* 575 computers available on campus for general student use. A campuswide network can be accessed from student residence rooms and from off campus. Online class registration is available. *Graduate expenses:* Tuition: full-time $7380; part-time $8.20 per credit hour. *General application contact:* Dr. Thomas G. Greene, Assistant to the Provost and Dean of the Graduate School, 503-943-7107.

Graduate School
Dr. Thomas G. Greene, Assistant to the Provost and Dean of the Graduate School

College of Arts and Sciences
Rev. Stephen Rowan, Dean
Programs in:
- arts and sciences (MA, MFA, MS)
- communication (MA)
- directing (MFA)
- drama (MFA)
- management communication (MS)
- music (MA)
- pastoral ministry (MA)

Dr. Robert B. Pamplin, Jr. School of Business
Dr. Howard Feldman, Associate Dean
Program in:
- business (MBA)

School of Education
Dr. Maria Ciriello, OP, Dean
Program in:
- education (M Ed, MA, MAT)

School of Engineering
Dr. Zia Yamayee, Dean
Program in:
- engineering (ME)

School of Nursing
Programs in:
- clinical nurse leader (MS)
- nursing (DNP)

■ WESTERN OREGON UNIVERSITY
Monmouth, OR 97361-1394
http://www.wou.edu/

State-supported, coed, comprehensive institution. *Computer facilities:* 411 computers available on campus for general student use. A campuswide network can be accessed from student residence rooms and from off campus. Online class registration is available. *General application contact:* Associate Provost for Retention and Enrollment Management, 503-838-8919.

Graduate Programs

College of Education
Programs in:
- bilingual education (MS Ed)
- deaf education (MS Ed)
- early childhood special education (MS Ed)
- education (MAT, MS, MS Ed)
- health (MS Ed)
- humanities (MAT, MS Ed)
- information technology (MS Ed)
- initial licensure (MAT)
- mathematics (MAT, MS Ed)
- rehabilitation counseling (MS)
- science (MAT, MS Ed)
- secondary education (MAT, MS Ed)
- social science (MAT, MS Ed)
- special education (MS Ed)

College of Liberal Arts and Sciences
Programs in:
- contemporary music (MM)
- criminal justice (MA, MS)
- liberal arts and sciences (MA, MM, MS)

■ WILLAMETTE UNIVERSITY
Salem, OR 97301-3931
http://www.willamette.edu/

Independent-religious, coed, comprehensive institution. *Graduate faculty:* 47 full-time (14 women), 52 part-time/adjunct (20 women). *Computer facilities:* 400 computers available on campus for general student use. A campuswide network can be accessed from student residence rooms and from off campus. Online class registration is available. *General application contact:* Office of Graduate Admissions, 503-370-6300.

College of Law
Symeon C. Symeonides, Dean
Program in:
- law (JD, LL M)

George H. Atkinson Graduate School of Management
Debra J. Ringold, Dean
Programs in:
- early career MBA (full-time) (MBA)
- MBA for career change (full-time) (MBA)
- MBA for professionals (part-time) (MBA)

School of Education
Program in:
- teaching (MAT)

Pennsylvania

■ ALVERNIA UNIVERSITY
Reading, PA 19607-1799
http://www.alvernia.edu/

Independent-religious, coed, comprehensive institution. *Computer facilities:* 180 computers available on campus for general student use. A campuswide network can be accessed from student residence rooms. Online class registration is available. *General application contact:* Coordinator of Graduate Admissions and Student Services, 610-796-8296.

Graduate Studies
Programs in:
- business (MBA)
- community counseling (MA)
- leadership (PhD)
- liberal studies (MALS)
- occupational therapy (MSOT)
- urban education (M Ed)

■ ARCADIA UNIVERSITY
Glenside, PA 19038-3295
http://www.arcadia.edu/

Independent-religious, coed, comprehensive institution. CGS member. *Graduate faculty:* 71 full-time, 135 part-time/adjunct. *Computer facilities:* 120 computers available on campus for general student use. A campuswide network can be accessed from student residence rooms and from off campus. Online class registration is available. *General application contact:* Information Contact, 215-572-2910.

Graduate Studies
John Hoffman, Dean of Graduate Studies
Programs in:
- allied health (MSHE, MSPH)
- art education (M Ed, MA Ed)
- biology education (MA Ed)
- business administration (MBA)
- chemistry education (MA Ed)
- child development (CAS)
- community counseling (MACP)
- computer education (M Ed, CAS)
- computer education 7–12 (MA Ed)
- early childhood education (M Ed, CAS)
- educational leadership (M Ed, CAS)
- educational psychology (CAS)
- elementary education (M Ed, CAS)
- English (MAE)
- English education (MA Ed)
- environmental education (MA Ed, CAS)
- fine arts, theater, and music (MAH)
- forensic science (MSFS)
- genetic counseling (MSGC)
- history education (MA Ed)
- history, philosophy, and religion (MAH)
- international peace and conflict management (MAIPCR)

international relations and diplomacy (MA)
language arts (M Ed, CAS)
literature and language (MAH)
mathematics education (M Ed, MA Ed, CAS)
medical science and community health (MM Sc, MSHE, MSPH)
music education (MA Ed)
physical therapy (DPT)
psychology (MA Ed)
pupil personnel services (CAS)
reading (M Ed, CAS)
school counseling (MACP)
school library science (M Ed)
science education (M Ed, CAS)
secondary education (M Ed, CAS)
special education (M Ed, Ed D, CAS)
theater arts (MA Ed)
written communication (MA Ed)

■ BLOOMSBURG UNIVERSITY OF PENNSYLVANIA
Bloomsburg, PA 17815-1301
http://www.bloomu.edu/

State-supported, coed, comprehensive institution. CGS member. *Computer facilities:* Computer purchase and lease plans are available. 1,440 computers available on campus for general student use. A campuswide network can be accessed from student residence rooms and from off campus. Online class registration is available. *General application contact:* Administrative Assistant, 570-389-4015.

School of Graduate Studies

College of Business
Programs in:
business (M Ed, MBA)
business administration (MBA)
business education (M Ed)

College of Liberal Arts
Programs in:
clinical athletic training (MS)
exercise science (MS)
liberal arts (MS)

College of Professional Studies
Programs in:
adult and family nurse practitioner (MSN)
adult health and illness (MSN)
audiology (Au D)
community health (MSN)
curriculum and instruction (M Ed)
early childhood education (MS)
education (M Ed, MS)
education of the deaf/hard of hearing (MS)
elementary education (M Ed)
exceptionality programs (MS)
guidance counseling and student affairs (M Ed)
health sciences (MS, MSN, Au D)
nursing (MSN)
nursing administration (MSN)
reading (M Ed)
special education (MS)
speech pathology (MS)

College of Science and Technology
Programs in:
biology (MS)
biology education (M Ed)
instructional technology (MS)
radiologist assistant (MS)
science and technology (M Ed, MS)

■ BUCKNELL UNIVERSITY
Lewisburg, PA 17837
http://www.bucknell.edu/

Independent, coed, comprehensive institution. CGS member. *Computer facilities:* 970 computers available on campus for general student use. A campuswide network can be accessed from student residence rooms and from off campus. Online class registration is available. *General application contact:* Director of Graduate Studies, 570-577-1304.

Graduate Studies

College of Arts and Sciences
Programs in:
animal behavior (MA, MS)
arts and sciences (MA, MS, MS Ed)
biology (MA, MS)
chemistry (MA, MS)
classroom teaching (MS Ed)
educational research (MS Ed)
elementary and secondary counseling (MA, MS Ed)
elementary and secondary principalship (MA, MS Ed)
English (MA)
mathematics (MA, MS)
psychology (MA, MS)
reading (MA, MS Ed)
school psychology (MS Ed)
supervision of curriculum and instruction (MA, MS Ed)

College of Engineering
Programs in:
chemical engineering (MS, MS Ch E)
civil and environmental engineering (MS, MSCE, MSEV)
electrical engineering (MS, MSEE)
engineering (MS, MS Ch E, MSCE, MSEE, MSEV, MSME)
mechanical engineering (MS, MSME)

■ CABRINI COLLEGE
Radnor, PA 19087-3698
http://www.cabrini.edu/

Independent-religious, coed, comprehensive institution. CGS member. *Graduate faculty:* 6 full-time (3 women), 106 part-time/adjunct (61 women). *Computer facilities:* 460 computers available on campus for general student use. A campuswide network can be accessed from student residence rooms. Online class registration, account balances and other services are available. *Graduate expenses:* Tuition: part-time $540 per credit hour. Required fees: $45 per semester. Tuition and fees vary according to campus/location. *General application contact:* Bruce D. Bryde, Director of Enrollment and Recruiting, 610-902-8291.

Graduate and Professional Studies

Dr. Dennis R. Dougherty, Interim Dean for Graduate and Professional Studies
Programs in:
biotechnology (Certificate)
education (M Ed)
instructional systems technology (MS)
organization leadership (MS)

■ CALIFORNIA UNIVERSITY OF PENNSYLVANIA
California, PA 15419-1394
http://www.cup.edu/

State-supported, coed, comprehensive institution. CGS member. *Computer facilities:* 1,220 computers available on campus for general student use. A campuswide network can be accessed from student residence rooms. Online class registration is available. *General application contact:* Director of Graduate Admissions and Recruitment, 724-938-4029.

School of Graduate Studies and Research

Program in:
legal studies (MS)

College of Liberal Arts
Programs in:
liberal arts (MA)
social science—criminal justice (MA)

School of Education
Programs in:
athletic training (MS)
communication disorders (MS)
education (M Ed, MAT, MS, MSW)
exercise science and health promotion (MS)
fitness and wellness (MS)
guidance and counseling (M Ed, MS)
mentally and/or physically handicapped education (M Ed)
performance enhancement and injury prevention (MS)
reading specialist (M Ed)
rehabilitation sciences (MS)
school administration (M Ed)
school psychology (MS)
secondary education (MAT)
social work (MSW)
sport management (MS)
sport psychology (MS)
technology education (M Ed)

School of Science and Technology
Programs in:
business administration (MSBA)
multimedia technology (MS)
science and technology (MS, MSBA)

■ CARLOW UNIVERSITY
Pittsburgh, PA 15213-3165
http://www.carlow.edu/

Independent-religious, coed, primarily women, comprehensive institution. CGS member. *Graduate faculty:* 25 full-time (20 women), 56 part-time/adjunct (37 women). *Computer facilities:* 151 computers available on campus for general student use. A campuswide network can be accessed from student residence rooms and from off campus. Online class registration is available. *Graduate expenses:* Tuition: part-time $700 per credit. *General application contact:* Jo Danhires, Administrative Assistant, Admissions, 412-578-6059.

Humanities Division
Dr. Ellie Wymard, Director of MFA Program
Program in:
creative writing (MFA)

School for Social Change
Dr. Robert A. Reed, Chair, Department of Psychology and Counseling
Programs in:
professional counseling (MS)
professional counseling: school counseling (MS)
professional leadership: management for nonprofit organizations (MS)
professional leadership: organizational influence and policy (MS)
professional leadership: training and development (MS)

School of Education
Dr. Roberta Schomburg, Associate Dean and Director
Programs in:
art education (M Ed)
early childhood education (M Ed)
early childhood supervision (M Ed)
education (M Ed)
educational leadership (M Ed)
educational praxis (MA)
elementary education (M Ed)
instructional technology specialist (M Ed)
secondary education (M Ed)
special education (M Ed)

School of Management
Dr. Enrique Mu, Director, MBA Program
Program in:
business administration (MBA)

School of Nursing
Dr. Clare M. Hopkins, Associate Dean and Director
Programs in:
family nurse practitioner (MSN)
home health advanced practice nursing (MSN)
nursing (DNP)
nursing case management/leadership (MSN)
nursing leadership (MSN)

■ CARNEGIE MELLON UNIVERSITY
Pittsburgh, PA 15213-3891
http://www.cmu.edu/

Independent, coed, university. CGS member. *Computer facilities:* 444 computers available on campus for general student use. A campuswide network can be accessed from student residence rooms and from off campus. Online class registration is available. *General application contact:* Information Contact, 412-268-2000.

Carnegie Institute of Technology
Programs in:
advanced infrastructure systems (MS, PhD)
bioengineering (MS, PhD)
biomedical engineering (MS)
chemical engineering (M Ch E, MS, PhD)
civil and environmental engineering (MS, PhD)
civil and environmental engineering/engineering and public policy (PhD)
civil engineering (MS, PhD)
colloids, polymers and surfaces (MS)
computational science and engineering (MS, PhD)
electrical and computer engineering (MS, PhD)
engineering and public policy (PhD)
environmental engineering (MS, PhD)
environmental management and science (MS, PhD)
materials science and engineering (MS, PhD)
mechanical engineering (MS, PhD)
product development (MPD)
technology (M Ch E, MPD, MS, PhD)

Information Networking Institute
Dr. Dena Haritos Tsamitis, Director
Programs in:
information networking (MS)
information security technology and management (MS)
information technology—information security (MS)
information technology—mobility (MS)
information technology—software management (MS)

Center for the Neural Basis of Cognition
Program in:
neural basis of cognition (PhD)

College of Fine Arts
Program in:
fine arts (M Des, M Sc, MAM, MET, MFA, MM, MPD, MS, MSA, PhD)

School of Architecture
Programs in:
architectural engineering construction management (M Sc)
architecture (MSA)
architecture, engineering, and construction management (PhD)
building performance and diagnostics (M Sc, PhD)
computational design (M Sc, PhD)
sustainable design (M Sc)
urban design (M Sc)

School of Art
Program in:
art (MFA)

School of Design
Programs in:
communication planning and information design (M Des)
design (PhD)
design theory (PhD)
interaction design (M Des, PhD)
new product development (PhD)
product development (MPD)
typography and information design (PhD)

School of Drama
Programs in:
design (MFA)
directing (MFA)
dramatic writing (MFA)
production technology and management (MFA)

School of Music
Programs in:
composition (MM)
conducting (MM)
instrumental performance (MM)
music and technology (MS)
music education (MM)
vocal performance (MM)

College of Humanities and Social Sciences
Programs in:
African and African-American diaspora (PhD)
behavioral decision research (PhD)
behavioral decision research and psychology (PhD)
cognitive neuroscience (PhD)
cognitive psychology (PhD)
communication planning and design (M Des)
culture and power (PhD)
developmental psychology (PhD)
editing and publishing (MAPW)
gender and the family (PhD)
history (MA, MS)
history and policy (MA)
humanities and social sciences (M Des, MA, MAPW, MS, PhD)
labor and politics (PhD)
literary and cultural studies (MA, PhD)
logic and computation (MS)
logic, computation and methodology (PhD)
machine learning and statistics (PhD)
mathematical finance (PhD)
philosophy (MA)
policy and non-profit communication (MAPW)

professional writing (MAPW)
public and media relations / corporate communications (MAPW)
rhetoric (MA, PhD)
science or healthcare communication (MAPW)
science, technology, medicine and environment (PhD)
second language acquisition (PhD)
social and decision science (PhD)
social/personality/health psychology (PhD)
statistics (MS, PhD)
statistics and public policy (PhD)
strategy, entrepeneurship, and technological change (PhD)
technical writing (MAPW)
writing for new media (MAPW)
writing for print media (MAPW)

Center for Innovation in Learning
Program in:
instructional science (PhD)

H. John Heinz III College
Programs in:
arts management (MAM)
entertainment industry management (MEIM)
public policy and management (MAM, MEIM, MIS, MISM, MMM, MPM, MS, MSED, MSHCPM, MSISPM, MSIT, PhD)

School of Information Systems and Management
Programs in:
information security policy and management (MSISPM)
information systems and management (MISM, MSISPM, MSIT)
information systems management (MISM)
information technology (MSIT)

School of Public Policy and Management
Programs in:
biotechnology and management (MS)
health care policy and management (MSHCPM)
medical management (MMM)
public management (MPM)
public policy and management (MMM, MPM, MS, MSHCPM, PhD)

Joint CMU-Pitt PhD Program in Computational Biology
Program in:
computational biology (PhD)

Mellon College of Science
Programs in:
algorithms, combinatorics, and optimization (PhD)
applied mathematics (PhD)
applied physics (PhD)
biochemistry (PhD)
biophysics (PhD)
biotechnology and management (MS)
cell biology (PhD)
chemistry (PhD)
colloids, polymers and surfaces (MS)
computational biology (MS)
computational finance (MS)
developmental biology (PhD)
genetics (PhD)
mathematical finance (PhD)
mathematical sciences (MS, DA, PhD)
molecular biology (PhD)
molecular biophysics and structural biology (PhD)
neuroscience (PhD)
physics (MS, PhD)
pure and applied logic (PhD)
science (MS, DA, PhD)

School of Computer Science
Programs in:
algorithms, combinatorics, and optimization (PhD)
computer science (MS, PhD)
entertainment technology (MET)
human-computer interaction (MHCI, PhD)
machine learning (PhD)
pure and applied logic (PhD)
software engineering (MSE, PhD)

Language Technologies Institute
Program in:
language technologies (MLT, PhD)

Robotics Institute
Program in:
robotics (MS, PhD)

Tepper School of Business
Programs in:
accounting (PhD)
algorithms, combinatorics, and optimization (MS, PhD)
business management and software engineering (MBMSE)
civil engineering and industrial management (MS)
computational finance (MSCF)
economics (PhD)
electronic commerce (MS)
environmental engineering and management (MEEM)
finance (PhD)
financial economics (PhD)
industrial administration (MBA)
information systems (PhD)
management of manufacturing and automation (PhD)
marketing (PhD)
mathematical finance (PhD)
operations research (PhD)
organizational behavior and theory (PhD)
political economy (PhD)
production and operations management (PhD)
public policy and management (MS, MSED)
software engineering and business management (MS)

■ CHATHAM UNIVERSITY
Pittsburgh, PA 15232-2826
http://www.chatham.edu/

Independent, Undergraduate: women only; graduate: coed, university. CGS member. *Graduate faculty:* 88 full-time, 79 part-time/adjunct. *Computer facilities:* 250 computers available on campus for general student use. A campuswide network can be accessed from student residence rooms and from off campus. Online class registration is available. *Graduate expenses:* Tuition: part-time $686 per credit. Tuition and fees vary according to program. *General application contact:* Michael May, Director of Graduate Admissions, 412-365-1141.

Program in Accounting
Program in:
accounting (M Acc)

Program in Biology
Dr. Lisa Lambert, Director
Programs in:
environmental biology-non-thesis track (MS)
environmental biology-thesis track (MS)
human biology-non-thesis track (MS)
human biology-thesis track (MS)

Program in Business Administration
Programs in:
business administration (MBA)
healthcare professionals (MBA)

Program in Counseling Psychology
Dr. Mary Beth Mannarino, Director
Programs in:
child, adolescent and family (MSCP)
counseling psychology (Psy D)
health and holistic (MSCP)
infant mental health (MSCP)
organization and supervision (MSCP)
sport and exercise (MSCP)

Program in Education
Dr. Tracey Johnson, Director
Programs in:
early childhood education (MAT)
elementary education (MAT)
English—secondary (MAT)
environmental education (K-12) (MAT)
secondary art (MAT)
secondary biology education (MAT)
secondary chemistry education (MAT)
secondary English education (MAT)
secondary math education (MAT)
secondary physics education (MAT)
secondary social studies education (MAT)
special education (MAT)

Program in Film and Digital Technology
Dr. Prajna Parasher, Director
Program in:
emerging media (MFA)

Chatham University (continued)

Program in Health Science
Dr. Janet Littrell, Dean, College of Continuing Education and Professional Studies
Program in:
health science (MHS)

Program in Interior Architecture
Prof. Lori Anthony, Director
Program in:
interior architecture (MIA, MSIA)

Program in Landscape Architecture
Prof. Lisa Kunst Vavaro, Director
Programs in:
landscape architecture (ML Arch)
landscape studies (MA)

Program in Nursing
Dr. Carol Patton, Director
Programs in:
education/leadership (MSN)
nursing (DNP)

Program in Occupational Therapy
Dr. Joyce Salls, Director
Program in:
occupational therapy (MOT, OTD)

Program in Physical Therapy
Dr. Patricia Downey, Director
Program in:
physical therapy (DPT, TDPT)

Program in Physician Assistant Studies
Luis Ramos, Director
Program in:
physician assistant studies (MPAS)

Program in Wellness
Dr. Janet Littrell, Dean, College of Continuing Education and Professional Studies
Program in:
wellness (MA)

Program in Writing
Dr. Sheryl St. Germain, Director
Programs in:
children's writing (MFA)
fiction (MFA)
non-fiction (MFA)
poetry (MFA)
professional writing (MPW)
screenwriting (MFA)

■ CHESTNUT HILL COLLEGE
Philadelphia, PA 19118-2693
http://www.chc.edu/

Independent-religious, coed, comprehensive institution. CGS member. *Graduate faculty:* 28 full-time (17 women), 84 part-time/adjunct (53 women). *Computer facilities:* 60 computers available on campus for general student use. A campuswide network can be accessed from student residence rooms. Online class registration is available. *Graduate expenses:* Tuition: part-time $510 per credit hour. *General application contact:* Jayne Mashett, Director of Graduate Admissions, 215-248-7020.

School of Graduate Studies
Dr. Steven Guerriero, Dean of the School of Graduate Studies
Programs in:
administration of human services (MS)
adult and aging services (CAS)
clinical and counseling psychology (MA, MS, CAS)
clinical psychology (Psy D)
early childhood education (M Ed)
educational leadership (M Ed)
elementary education (M Ed)
holistic spirituality (MA)
holistic spirituality and healthcare (MA)
holistic spirituality and spiritual direction (MA)
holistic spirituality/health care (CAS)
instructional technology (MS, CAS)
leadership development (CAS)
secondary education (M Ed)
spiritual direction (CAS)
spirituality (CAS)
supervision of spiritual directors (CAS)

■ CHEYNEY UNIVERSITY OF PENNSYLVANIA
Cheyney, PA 19319-0200
http://www.cheyney.edu/

State-supported, coed, comprehensive institution. *Graduate faculty:* 6 full-time (1 woman), 3 part-time/adjunct (2 women). *Computer facilities:* Computer purchase and lease plans are available. 250 computers available on campus for general student use. A campuswide network can be accessed from student residence rooms and from off campus. Online class registration, online tutorials, various software packages, online payment/online Praxis study guide are available. *General application contact:* Dr. Ivan Banks, Provost, 610-399-2271.

School of Education and Professional Studies
Dr. Ivan Banks, Provost
Programs in:
adult and continuing education (MS)
early childhood education (Certificate)
education and professional studies (M Ed, MAT, MPA, MS, Certificate)
educational administration and supervision (M Ed, Certificate)
educational administration of adult and continuing education (M Ed, MS)
elementary and secondary principalship (Certificate)
elementary education (M Ed, MAT)
public administration (MPA)
special education (M Ed, MS)

■ CLARION UNIVERSITY OF PENNSYLVANIA
Clarion, PA 16214
http://www.clarion.edu/

State-supported, coed, comprehensive institution. CGS member. *Computer facilities:* 400 computers available on campus for general student use. A campuswide network can be accessed from student residence rooms and from off campus. Online class registration is available. *General application contact:* Assistant Vice President for Academic Affairs, 814-393-2337.

Office of Research and Graduate Studies

College of Arts and Sciences
Programs in:
arts and sciences (MA, MS)
biology (MS)
English (MA)
mass media arts, journalism, and communication studies (MS)

College of Business Administration
Program in:
business administration (MBA)

College of Education and Human Services
Programs in:
curriculum and instruction (M Ed)
early childhood (M Ed)
education (M Ed)
education and human services (M Ed, MS, MSLS, CAS)
English (M Ed)
history (M Ed)
library science (MSLS, CAS)
literacy (M Ed)
reading (M Ed)
rehabilitative sciences (MS)
science (M Ed)
science education (M Ed)
special education (MS)
speech language pathology (MS)
technology (M Ed)

School of Nursing
Program in:
nursing (MSN)

■ DESALES UNIVERSITY
Center Valley, PA 18034-9568
http://www.desales.edu

Independent-religious, coed, comprehensive institution. *Graduate faculty:* 41. *Computer facilities:* 200 computers available on campus for general student use. A campuswide network can be accessed from student residence rooms and from off campus. Online class registration is available. *Graduate expenses:* Tuition: full-time $16,720. Required fees: $800. Tuition and fees vary according to program. *General application contact:* Caryn Stopper, Director of Graduate Admissions, 610-282-1100 Ext. 1768.

Graduate Division
Caryn Stopper, Director of Graduate Admissions
Programs in:
accounting (MBA)
adult advanced practice nurse specialist (MSN)
business administration (MBA)
certified nurse midwives (MSN)
certified nurse practitioners (MSN)
computer information systems (MBA)
criminal justice (MACJ)
elementary education (M Ed)
family nurse practitioner (MSN)
finance (MBA)
health care systems management (MBA)
information systems (MSIS)
interdisciplinary (M Ed)
management (MBA)
marketing (MBA)
mathematics (M Ed)
nurse educator (MSN)
physician assistant studies (MSPAS)
project management (MBA)
self-design (MBA)
special education (M Ed)
technology in education (K-12) (M Ed)
TESOL/ESL (M Ed)

■ DREXEL UNIVERSITY
Philadelphia, PA 19104-2875
http://www.drexel.edu/

Independent, coed, university. CGS member. *Computer facilities:* 6,500 computers available on campus for general student use. A campuswide network can be accessed from student residence rooms and from off campus. Online class registration is available. *General application contact:* Director of Graduate Admissions, 215-895-6700.

College of Arts and Sciences
Programs in:
arts and sciences (MA, MS, PhD)
biological sciences (MS, PhD)
chemistry (MS, PhD)
clinical psychology (PhD)
communication (MS)
environmental policy (MS)
environmental science (MS, PhD)
forensic psychology (PhD)
health psychology (PhD)
human nutrition (MS)
law-psychology (PhD)
mathematics (MS, PhD)
neuropsychology (PhD)
physics (MS, PhD)
psychology (MS)
public communication (MS)
publication management (MS)
science communication (MS)
science, technology and society (MS)
technical communication (MS)

College of Engineering
Programs in:
architectural / building systems engineering (MS, PhD)
biochemical engineering (MS)
chemical engineering (MS, PhD)
civil engineering (MS, PhD)
computer engineering (MS)
computer science (MS, PhD)
electrical and computer engineering (PhD)
electrical engineering (MSEE)
engineering (MS, MSEE, MSSE, PhD, Certificate)
engineering management (MS, Certificate)
environmental engineering (MS, PhD)
geotechnical, geoenvironmental and geosynthetics (MS, PhD)
geotechnical, geoenvironmental and geosynthetics engineering (MS, PhD)
hydraulics, hydrology and water resources engineering (MS, PhD)
materials engineering (MS, PhD)
mechanical engineering (MS, PhD)
software engineering (MSSE)
structures (MS)
telecommunications engineering (MSEE)

College of Media Arts and Design
Programs in:
arts administration (MS)
design (MS)
digital media (MS)
fashion design (MS)
interior design (MS)
media arts (MS)
performing arts (MS)
television management (MS)

College of Medicine
Program in:
medicine (MD, MLAS, MMS, MS, PhD, Certificate)

Biomedical Graduate Programs
Programs in:
biochemistry (MS, PhD)
biomedical sciences (MLAS, MMS, MS, PhD, Certificate)
laboratory animal science (MLAS)
medical science (MMS, Certificate)
microbiology and immunology (MS, PhD)
molecular and cell biology and genetics (MS, PhD)
molecular pathobiology (MS, PhD)
neuroscience (MS, PhD)
pharmacology and physiology (MS, PhD)

College of Nursing and Health Professions
Programs in:
art therapy (MA, PMC)
couples and family therapy (PhD)
dance/movement therapy (MA, PMC)
emergency and public safety services (MS)
family therapy (MFT)
hand and upper quarter rehabilitation (MHS, Certificate, PPDPT)
movement science (PhD)
music therapy (MA, PMC)
nurse anesthesia (MSN)
nursing (MSN)
nursing and health professions (MA, MFT, MHS, MS, MSN, DPT, PhD, Certificate, PMC, PPDPT)
orthopedics (MHS, PhD, PPDPT)
pediatrics (MHS, PhD, PPDPT)
physical therapy (DPT)
physician assistant studies (MHS)

The iSchool at Drexel, College of Information Science and Technology
Dr. David E. Fenske, Dean and Isaac L. Auerbach Professor of Information Science
Programs in:
archival studies (MS)
competitive intelligence and knowledge management (MS)
digital libraries (MS)
healthcare informatics (Certificate)
information science and technology (PMC)
information studies (PhD)
information studies and technology (Advanced Certificate)
information systems (MSIS)
library and information science (MS)
library and information services (MS)
school library media (MS)
software engineering (MSSE)
youth services (MS)

LeBow College of Business
Programs in:
accounting (MS)
business administration (MBA, PhD, APC)
business and administration (MBA, MS, PhD, APC)
finance (MS)

School of Biomedical Engineering, Science and Health Systems
Programs in:
biomedical engineering (MS, PhD)
biomedical science (MS, PhD)
biostatistics (MS)
clinical/rehabilitation engineering (MS)

School of Education
Programs in:
educational administration (MS)
educational administration and collaborative learning (MS)
educational leadership and learning technology (PhD)
global and international education (MS)
graduate intern teaching (Certificate)
higher education (MS)
instructional technology (Spt)
post-bachelor's teaching (Certificate)
school principal (Certificate)
school superintendent (Certificate)
science of instruction (MS)
teaching English as a second language (Certificate)
teaching, learning and curriculum (MS)

Drexel University (continued)

School of Journalism

Program in:
- journalism (MA)

School of Public Health

Programs in:
- biostatistics (MS)
- epidemiology (PhD)
- epidemiology and biostatistics (Certificate)
- public health (MPH, MS, PhD, Certificate)

School of Technology and Professional Studies

Programs in:
- construction management (MS)
- engineering technology (MS)
- food science (MS)
- hospitality management (MS)
- professional studies: creativity studies (MS)
- professional studies: e-learning leadership (MS)
- professional studies: homeland security management (MS)
- project management (MS)
- property management (MS)
- sport management (MS)

■ DUQUESNE UNIVERSITY

Pittsburgh, PA 15282-0001

http://www.duq.edu/

Independent-religious, coed, university. CGS member. *Computer facilities:* Computer purchase and lease plans are available. 1,000 computers available on campus for general student use. A campuswide network can be accessed from student residence rooms and from off campus. Online class registration is available. *Graduate expenses:* Tuition: part-time $819 per credit. Required fees: $78 per credit. Tuition and fees vary according to course load. *General application contact:* Dr. Ralph L. Pearson, Provost and Academic Vice President, 412-396-6054.

Bayer School of Natural and Environmental Sciences

Dr. David W. Seybert, Dean

Programs in:
- biological sciences (MS, PhD)
- biotechnology (MS)
- chemistry (MS, PhD)
- environmental management (MEM, Certificate)
- environmental science (Certificate)
- environmental science and management (MS)
- forensic science and law (MS)
- natural and environmental sciences (MEM, MS, PhD, Certificate)

Graduate School of Liberal Arts

Dr. Evan Stoddard, Acting Dean

Programs in:
- archival, museum, and editing studies (MA)
- clinical psychology (PhD)
- communication (MA)
- computational mathematics (MA, MS)
- English (MA, PhD)
- health care ethics (MA, DHCE, PhD, Certificate)
- history (MA)
- liberal arts (MA, MS, DHCE, PhD, Certificate)
- multimedia technology (MS, Certificate)
- pastoral ministry (MA)
- philosophy (MA, PhD)
- religious education (MA)
- rhetoric (PhD)
- systematic theology (PhD)
- theology (MA)

Graduate Center for Social and Public Policy

Dr. Joseph Yenerall, Director

Programs in:
- conflict resolution and peace studies (Certificate)
- social and public policy (MA, Certificate)

John F. Donahue Graduate School of Business

Alan R. Miciak, Dean

Programs in:
- accountancy (MS)
- business administration (MBA)
- information systems management (MSISM)
- sustainability (MBA)

John G. Rangos, Sr. School of Health Sciences

Dr. Gregory H. Frazer, Dean

Programs in:
- health management systems (MHMS)
- health sciences (PhD)
- occupational therapy (MS)
- physical therapy (DPT)
- physician assistant (MPA)
- speech–language pathology (MS)

Mary Pappert School of Music

Dr. Edward W. Kocher, Dean

Programs in:
- music composition (MM)
- music education (MM)
- music performance (MM, AD)
- music technology (MM)
- music theory (MM)
- sacred music (MM)

Mylan School of Pharmacy

Dr. J. Douglas Bricker, Dean

Program in:
- pharmacy (Pharm D, MS, PhD)

Graduate School of Pharmaceutical Sciences

Dr. James K. Drennen, Associate Dean for Research and Graduate Programs

Programs in:
- medicinal chemistry (MS, PhD)
- pharmaceutical administration (MS)
- pharmaceutics (MS, PhD)
- pharmacology (MS, PhD)
- pharmacy administration (MS)

School of Education

Dr. Olga Welch, Dean

Programs in:
- child psychology (MS Ed)
- community counseling (MS Ed)
- counselor education (MS Ed, Ed D)
- counselor education and supervision (Ed D)
- early childhood education (MS Ed)
- education (MS Ed, Ed D, PhD, CAGS, Post-Master's Certificate)
- educational leaders (Ed D)
- educational studies (MS Ed)
- elementary education (MS Ed)
- elementary education/early childhood (MS Ed)
- English as a second language (MS Ed)
- instructional technology (MS Ed, Ed D)
- marriage and family therapy (MS Ed)
- reading and language arts (MS Ed)
- school administration (MS Ed)
- school administration and supervision (MS Ed, Post-Master's Certificate)
- school counseling (MS Ed)
- school psychology (MS Ed, PhD, CAGS)
- school supervision (MS Ed)
- secondary education (MS Ed)
- special education (MS Ed)

School of Law

Ken Gormley, Interim Dean

Program in:
- law (JD, LL M)

School of Leadership and Professional Advancement

Dr. Dorothy Bassett, Dean

Programs in:
- community leadership (MS)
- leadership and business ethics (MS)
- leadership and information technology (MS)
- leadership and liberal studies (MA)
- sports leadership (MS)

School of Nursing

Dr. Eileen Zungolo, Dean/Professor

Programs in:
- acute care nursing (Post-Master's Certificate)
- family nurse practitioner (MSN, Post-Master's Certificate)
- forensic nursing (MSN, Post-Master's Certificate)
- nursing (MSN, DNP, PhD, Post-Master's Certificate)
- nursing education (MSN)
- nursing practice (DNP)
- transcultural/international nursing (Post-Master's Certificate)

■ EASTERN UNIVERSITY

St. Davids, PA 19087-3696

http://www.eastern.edu/

Independent-religious, coed, comprehensive institution. *Computer facilities:* 60 computers available on campus for general student use. A campuswide network can be accessed from student residence rooms and from off campus. *General application contact:* Graduate Admissions Office, 800-732-7669.

Department of Counseling Psychology
Programs in:
community/clinical counseling (MA)
school counseling (MA, Certificate)
school psychology (MS, Certificate)

Graduate Education Programs
Programs in:
multicultural education (M Ed)
school health services (M Ed)
school nurse (Certificate)

Office of Interdisciplinary Programs
Program in:
organizational leadership (PhD)

Palmer Theological Seminary
Programs in:
marriage and family (D Min)
renewal of the church for mission (D Min)
theology (M Div, MTS, D Min)

School for Social Change
Program in:
urban studies (MA)

School of Leadership and Development
Programs in:
economic development (MBA)
international development (MA)
nonprofit management (MS)
organizational leadership (MA)

School of Management Studies
Programs in:
health administration (MBA)
management (MBA)

■ EAST STROUDSBURG UNIVERSITY OF PENNSYLVANIA

East Stroudsburg, PA 18301-2999

http://www.esu.edu/

State-supported, coed, comprehensive institution. CGS member. *Graduate faculty:* 85 full-time (39 women), 20 part-time/adjunct (7 women). *Computer facilities:* 500 computers available on campus for general student use. A campuswide network can be accessed from student residence rooms and from off campus. Online class registration, online classes are available. *Graduate expenses:* Tuition, state resident: full-time $6430; part-time $357 per credit. Tuition, nonresident: full-time $10,288; part-time $572 per credit. *General application contact:* Kevin Quintero, Associate Provost for Enrollment Management, 570-422-3890.

Graduate School
Dr. Marilyn Wells, Graduate Dean

College of Arts and Sciences
Dr. Marilyn Wells, Provost
Programs in:
arts and sciences (M Ed, MA, MS)
biology (M Ed, MS)
computer science (MS)
history (M Ed, MA)
political science (M Ed, MA)

College of Business and Management
Dr. Alla Wilson, Dean
Programs in:
business and management (MS)
management and leadership (MS)
sports management (MS)

College of Education
Dr. Pamela Kramer, Dean
Programs in:
education (M Ed)
elementary education (M Ed)
instructional technology (M Ed)
professional and secondary education (M Ed)
reading (M Ed)
special education (M Ed)

College of Health Sciences
Dr. Mark Kilker, Dean
Programs in:
cardiac rehabilitation and exercise science (MS)
community health education (MPH)
health and physical education (M Ed)
health education (MS)
health sciences (M Ed, MPH, MS)
speech pathology and audiology (MS)

■ EDINBORO UNIVERSITY OF PENNSYLVANIA

Edinboro, PA 16444

http://www.edinboro.edu/

State-supported, coed, comprehensive institution. *Graduate faculty:* 71 full-time (35 women). *Computer facilities:* Computer purchase and lease plans are available. 997 computers available on campus for general student use. A campuswide network can be accessed from student residence rooms and from off campus. Online class registration, software are available. *Graduate expenses:* Tuition, state resident: full-time $6430; part-time $357 per credit. Tuition, nonresident: full-time $8038; part-time $572 per credit. International tuition: $15,171.58 full-time. Required fees: $2113; $60 per credit. Tuition and fees vary according to course load. *General application contact:* Dr. R. Scott Baldwin, Dean of Graduate Studies and Research, 814-732-2856.

Graduate Studies and Research
Dr. R. Scott Baldwin, Dean

School of Education
Dr. Kenneth Adams, Dean
Programs in:
behavior management (Certificate)
character education (Certificate)
counseling (MA)
education (M Ed, MA, Certificate)
educational leadership (M Ed)
educational psychology (M Ed)
elementary education (M Ed)
letter of eligibility (Certificate)
reading (M Ed, Certificate)
special education (M Ed)

School of Liberal Arts
Dr. Terry L. Smith, Dean
Programs in:
art (MA)
clinical psychology (MA)
communications and media studies (MA)
fine arts (MFA)
liberal arts (MA, MFA, MSW)
social sciences (MA)
social work (MSW)
speech language pathology (MA)

School of Science, Management and Technology
Dr. Eric Randall, Dean
Programs in:
biology (MS)
family nurse practitioner (MSN)
science, management and technology (MS, MSN)

■ GANNON UNIVERSITY

Erie, PA 16541-0001

http://www.gannon.edu/

Independent-religious, coed, comprehensive institution. CGS member. *Graduate faculty:* 86 full-time (35 women), 64 part-time/adjunct (21 women). *Computer facilities:* 350 computers available on campus for general student use. A campuswide network can be accessed from student residence rooms and from off campus. Online class registration is available. *Graduate expenses:* Tuition: full-time $13,050; part-time $725 per credit. Required fees: $502; $16 per credit. Tuition and fees vary according to course load, degree level, campus/location and program. *General application contact:* Kara Morgan, Assistant Director of Graduate Admissions, 814-871-5831.

School of Graduate Studies
Michael J. O'Neill, Dean

College of Engineering and Business
Dr. Melanie Hatch, Dean
Programs in:
accounting (Certificate)
business (MBA, MPA, Certificate)
business administration (MBA)
computer and information science (MSCIS)
electrical engineering (MSEE)
embedded software engineering (MSES)

Gannon University (continued)
- engineering and business (M Ed, MBA, MPA, MS, MSCIS, MSEE, MSEM, MSES, MSME, Certificate)
- engineering and computer science (M Ed, MS, MSCIS, MSEE, MSEM, MSES, MSME, Certificate)
- engineering management (MSEM)
- environmental and occupational science and health (Certificate)
- environmental science and engineering (MS)
- finance (Certificate)
- human resources management (Certificate)
- investments (Certificate)
- marketing (Certificate)
- mechanical engineering (MSME)
- natural and environmental sciences (M Ed)
- public administration (MPA, Certificate)
- risk management (Certificate)

College of Humanities, Education, and Social Sciences
Dr. Timothy Downs, Dean
Programs in:
- advanced counselor studies (Certificate)
- community counseling (MS, Certificate)
- counseling psychology (PhD)
- curriculum and instruction (M Ed)
- early intervention (MS)
- education (M Ed, MS, PhD, Certificate)
- educational computing technology (M Ed)
- educational leadership (M Ed)
- English (MA)
- English as a second language (Certificate)
- gerontology (Certificate)
- humanities (MA, MS, PhD, Certificate)
- humanities, education, and social sciences (M Ed, MA, MS, PhD, Certificate)
- instructional technology specialist (Certificate)
- organizational learning and leadership (PhD)
- pastoral studies (MA, Certificate)
- principal certification (Certificate)
- reading (M Ed, Certificate)
- school counselor preparation (Certificate)
- superintendent letter of eligibility certification (Certificate)

Morosky College of Health Professions and Sciences
Dr. Carolynn Masters, Dean
Programs in:
- anesthesia (MSN)
- business administration (MSN)
- family nurse practitioner (Certificate)
- health professions (MPAS, MS, MSN, DPT, Certificate)
- health professions and sciences (MPAS, MS, MSN, DPT, Certificate)
- medical-surgical nursing (MSN)
- nurse anesthesia (Certificate)
- nursing rural practitioner (MSN)
- occupational therapy (MS)
- physical therapy (DPT)
- physician assistant (MPAS)

■ GENEVA COLLEGE
Beaver Falls, PA 15010-3599
http://www.geneva.edu/

Independent-religious, coed, comprehensive institution. *Computer facilities:* 150 computers available on campus for general student use. A campuswide network can be accessed from student residence rooms and from off campus. Online class registration is available. *General application contact:* Information Contact, 724-846-5100.

Program in Business Administration
Program in:
- business administration (MBA)

Program in Counseling
Programs in:
- marriage and family (MA)
- mental health (MA)
- school counseling (MA)

Program in Higher Education
Programs in:
- campus ministry (MA)
- college teaching (MA)
- educational leadership (MA)
- student affairs administration (MA)

Program in Organizational Leadership
Program in:
- organizational leadership (MS)

Program in Special Education
Program in:
- special education (M Ed)

■ GRATZ COLLEGE
Melrose Park, PA 19027
http://www.gratzcollege.edu/

Independent-religious, coed, comprehensive institution. *Computer facilities:* 2 computers available on campus for general student use. A campuswide network can be accessed from off campus. *General application contact:* Director of Admissions, 215-635-7300 Ext. 140.

Graduate Programs
Programs in:
- classical studies (MA)
- education (MA)
- Holocaust studies (Certificate)
- Jewish communal service (MA, Certificate)
- Jewish education (MA, Ed D, Certificate)
- Jewish music (MA, Certificate)
- Jewish studies (MA, Certificate)
- modern studies (MA)

■ GWYNEDD-MERCY COLLEGE
Gwynedd Valley, PA 19437-0901
http://www.gmc.edu/

Independent-religious, coed, comprehensive institution. *Graduate faculty:* 9 full-time (7 women), 17 part-time/adjunct (11 women). *Computer facilities:* Computer purchase and lease plans are available. 218 computers available on campus for general student use. A campuswide network can be accessed from student residence rooms and from off campus. Online class registration is available. *Graduate expenses:* Tuition: part-time $555 per credit hour. *General application contact:* Information Contact, 800-342-5462.

Center for Lifelong Learning
Joseph Coleman, Executive Director
Program in:
- lifelong learning (MSM)

School of Education
Dr. Lorraine Cavaliere, Dean
Programs in:
- educational administration (MS)
- master teacher (MS)
- reading (MS)
- school counseling (MS)
- special education (MS)

School of Nursing
Dr. Andrea D. Hollingsworth, Dean
Programs in:
- clinical nurse specialist (MSN)
- nurse practitioner (MSN)

■ HOLY FAMILY UNIVERSITY
Philadelphia, PA 19114-2094
http://www.holyfamily.edu/

Independent-religious, coed, primarily women, comprehensive institution. *Graduate faculty:* 18 full-time (11 women), 51 part-time/adjunct (25 women). *Computer facilities:* 450 computers available on campus for general student use. A campuswide network can be accessed from student residence rooms. Online class registration is available. *Graduate expenses:* Tuition: part-time $555 per credit. Required fees: $85 per semester. One-time fee: $25 part-time. *General application contact:* Gidget Marie Montelibano, Graduate Admissions Counselor, 267-341-3358.

Division of Extended Learning
Honour Moore, Associate Vice President, Division of Extended Learning
Programs in:
- business administration (MBA)
- finance (MBA)
- health care administration (MBA)

Graduate School
Margaret Wendling Bacheler, Director of Graduate Admissions

School of Arts and Sciences
Dr. Regina Hobaugh, Dean of the School of Arts and Sciences
Programs in:
- counseling psychology (MS)
- criminal justice (MA)

School of Business
Dr. Jan Duggar, Dean of the School of Business
Programs in:
- human resources management (MS)
- information systems management (MS)

School of Education
Dr. Leonard Soroka, Dean of the School of Education
Programs in:
- education (M Ed)
- education leadership (M Ed)
- elementary education (M Ed)
- reading specialist (M Ed)
- secondary education (M Ed)
- special education (M Ed)

School of Nursing
Dr. Christine Rosner, Dean of the School of Nursing
Programs in:
- community health nursing (MSN)
- nursing administration (MSN)
- nursing education (MSN)

■ IMMACULATA UNIVERSITY
Immaculata, PA 19345
http://www.immaculata.edu/

Independent-religious, coed, primarily women, comprehensive institution. CGS member. *Computer facilities:* 254 computers available on campus for general student use. A campuswide network can be accessed from student residence rooms. *General application contact:* Director of Graduate Admission, 610-647-4400 Ext. 3215.

College of Graduate Studies
Programs in:
- applied communication (MA)
- clinical psychology (Psy D)
- counseling psychology (MA, Certificate)
- cultural and linguistic diversity (MA)
- educational leadership and administration (MA, Ed D)
- elementary education (Certificate)
- music therapy (MA)
- nursing (MSN)
- nutrition education (MA)
- nutrition education/approved pre-professional practice program (MA)
- organization studies (MA)
- school principal (Certificate)
- school superintendent (Certificate)
- secondary education (Certificate)
- special education (Certificate)

■ INDIANA UNIVERSITY OF PENNSYLVANIA
Indiana, PA 15705-1087
http://www.iup.edu/

State-supported, coed, university. CGS member. *Graduate faculty:* 284 full-time (122 women), 10 part-time/adjunct (5 women). *Computer facilities:* Computer purchase and lease plans are available. 3,500 computers available on campus for general student use. A campuswide network can be accessed from student residence rooms and from off campus. Online class registration is available. *Graduate expenses:* Tuition, state resident: full-time $6430; part-time $357 per credit. Tuition, nonresident: full-time $10,288; part-time $572 per credit. Required fees: $1547.50; $107 per credit. $283 per year. *General application contact:* Donna Griffith, Assistant Dean, 724-357-2222.

School of Graduate Studies and Research
Dr. Timothy Mack, Dean

College of Education and Educational Technology
Dr. Mary Ann Rafoth, Dean
Programs in:
- administration and leadership studies (D Ed)
- adult education and communication technology (MA)
- adult education and communications technology (MA)
- communications media and instructional technology (PhD)
- communications technology (MA)
- community counseling (MA)
- counselor education (M Ed)
- curriculum and instruction (M Ed, D Ed)
- education (M Ed, Certificate)
- education and educational technology (M Ed, MA, MS, D Ed, PhD, Certificate)
- education of exceptional persons (M Ed)
- educational psychology (M Ed, Certificate)
- elementary education (M Ed)
- literacy (M Ed)
- principal (Certificate)
- reading (M Ed)
- school psychology (D Ed, Certificate)
- speech-language pathology (MS)
- student affairs in higher education (MA)

College of Fine Arts
Michael Hood, Dean
Programs in:
- art (MA, MFA)
- fine arts (MA, MFA)
- music (MA)
- music education (MA)
- music history and literature (MA)
- music theory and composition (MA)
- performance (MA)

College of Health and Human Services
Dr. Carleen Zoni, Dean
Programs in:
- aquatics administration and facilities management (MS)
- criminology (MA, PhD)
- exercise science (MS)
- food and nutrition (MS)
- health and human services (MA, MS, PhD, Certificate)
- industrial and labor relations (MA)
- nursing (MS)
- safety sciences (MS, Certificate)
- sport management (MS)
- sport science (MS)

College of Humanities and Social Sciences
Dr. Yaw Asamoah, Dean
Programs in:
- administration and leadership studies (PhD)
- composition and teaching English to speakers of other languages (MA, MAT, PhD)
- generalist (MA)
- geography (MA, MS)
- history (MA)
- humanities and social sciences (MA, MAT, MS, PhD)
- literature (MA)
- literature and criticism (MA, PhD)
- public affairs (MA)
- rhetoric and linguistics (PhD)
- sociology (MA)
- teaching English (MAT)
- teaching English to speakers of other languages (MA)

College of Natural Sciences and Mathematics
Dr. Gerald Buriok, Interim Dean
Programs in:
- applied mathematics (MS)
- biology (MS)
- chemistry (MA, MS)
- clinical psychology (Psy D)
- elementary and middle school mathematics education (M Ed)
- mathematics education (M Ed)
- natural sciences and mathematics (M Ed, MA, MS, Psy D)
- physics (MA, MS)
- psychology (MA)
- science for disaster response (MS)

Eberly College of Business and Information Technology
Dr. Robert Camp, Dean
Programs in:
- business (M Ed, MBA)
- business administration (MBA)
- business/workforce development (M Ed)

■ KING'S COLLEGE
Wilkes-Barre, PA 18711-0801
http://www.kings.edu/

Independent-religious, coed, comprehensive institution. *Graduate faculty:* 14 full-time (8 women), 16 part-time/adjunct (10 women). *Computer facilities:* Computer purchase and lease plans are available. 470 computers available on campus for general student use.

King's College (continued)
A campuswide network can be accessed from student residence rooms and from off campus. Online class registration is available. *General application contact:* Dr. Elizabeth S. Lott, Director of Graduate Programs, 570-208-5991.

Program in Physician Assistant Studies
Dr. Elizabeth S. Lott, Director of Graduate Programs
Program in:
physician assistant studies (MSPAS)

Program in Reading
Dr. Elizabeth S. Lott, Director of Graduate Programs
Program in:
reading (M Ed)

William G. McGowan School of Business
Dr. John J. Ryan, Director
Program in:
health care administration (MS)

■ KUTZTOWN UNIVERSITY OF PENNSYLVANIA
Kutztown, PA 19530-0730
http://www.kutztown.edu/

State-supported, coed, comprehensive institution. CGS member. *Graduate faculty:* 86 full-time (42 women), 7 part-time/adjunct (4 women). *Computer facilities:* Computer purchase and lease plans are available. 950 computers available on campus for general student use. A campuswide network can be accessed from student residence rooms. Online class registration is available. *Graduate expenses:* Tuition, state resident: full-time $6430; part-time $357 per credit. Tuition, nonresident: full-time $10,288; part-time $572 per credit. Required fees: $1360; $72 per credit. $67 per semester. *General application contact:* Dr. Linda Matthews, Interim Dean of Graduate Studies, 610-683-4201.

College of Graduate Studies and Extended Learning
Dr. Linda Matthews, Interim Dean of Graduate Studies
Programs in:
agency counseling (MA)
counselor education (M Ed)
marital and family therapy (MA)
student affairs in higher education (M Ed)

College of Business
Dr. William Dempsey, Dean
Programs in:
business (MBA)
business administration (MBA)

College of Education
Dr. Darrell Garber, Dean
Programs in:
biology (M Ed)
curriculum and instruction (M Ed)
early childhood education (Certificate)
education (M Ed, MLS, Certificate)
elementary education (M Ed, Certificate)
English (M Ed)
instructional technology (M Ed, Certificate)
library science (MLS, Certificate)
mathematics (M Ed)
reading (M Ed)
secondary education (Certificate)
social studies (M Ed)
special education (Certificate)

College of Liberal Arts and Sciences
Dr. Anne E. Zayaitz, Acting Dean
Programs in:
computer science (MS)
electronic media (MS)
English (MA)
liberal arts and sciences (MA, MPA, MS, MSN, MSW, Certificate)
public administration (MPA)
school nursing (MSN, Certificate)
social work (MSW)

College of Visual and Performing Arts
Dr. William Mowder, Dean
Programs in:
art education (M Ed, Certificate)
music education (Certificate)
visual and performing arts (M Ed, Certificate)

■ LA ROCHE COLLEGE
Pittsburgh, PA 15237-5898
http://www.laroche.edu/

Independent-religious, coed, comprehensive institution. *Graduate faculty:* 6 full-time (4 women), 6 part-time/adjunct (2 women). *Computer facilities:* Computer purchase and lease plans are available. 186 computers available on campus for general student use. A campuswide network can be accessed. Online class registration is available. *Graduate expenses:* Tuition: full-time $9450; part-time $525 per credit. *General application contact:* Hope Schiffgens, Director of Graduate Studies and Adult Education, 412-536-1266.

School of Graduate Studies and Adult Education
Dr. Jean Forti, Interim Dean
Programs in:
human resources management (MS, Certificate)
nurse anesthesia (MS)
nursing education (MSN)
nursing management (MSN)

■ LA SALLE UNIVERSITY
Philadelphia, PA 19141-1199
http://www.lasalle.edu/

Independent-religious, coed, comprehensive institution. *Computer facilities:* Computer purchase and lease plans are available. 1,100 computers available on campus for general student use. A campuswide network can be accessed from student residence rooms and from off campus. Online class registration, Blackboard Course Management System are available. *General application contact:* Director of Marketing/Graduate Enrollment, 215-951-1946.

Program in Instructional Technology Management
Program in:
instructional technology management (MS)

School of Arts and Sciences
Programs in:
arts and sciences (MA, MS, Psy D)
bilingual/bicultural studies (Spanish) (MA)
Central and Eastern European studies (MA)
clinical psychology (Psy D)
clinical-counseling psychology (MA)
computer information science (MS)
education (MA)
family psychology (Psy D)
history (MA)
information technology leadership (MS)
pastoral studies (MA)
professional communication (MA)
rehabilitation psychology (Psy D)
religion (MA)
theological studies (MA)

School of Business
Program in:
business (MBA, MS, Certificate)

School of Nursing and Health Sciences
Programs in:
nursing (MSN, Certificate)
nursing and health sciences (MS, MSN, Certificate)
speech-language-hearing science (MS)

■ LEHIGH UNIVERSITY
Bethlehem, PA 18015-3094
http://www.lehigh.edu/

Independent, coed, university. CGS member. *Graduate faculty:* 331 full-time (78 women), 65 part-time/adjunct (23 women). *Computer facilities:* Computer purchase and lease plans are available. 588 computers available on campus for general student use. A campuswide network can be accessed from student residence rooms and from off campus. Online class registration is available. *General application contact:* Information Contact, 610-758-3000.

College of Arts and Sciences
Dr. Michael Stavola, Associate Dean of Graduate Studies
Programs in:
American studies (MA)

applied mathematics (MS, PhD)
arts and sciences (MA, MS, PhD)
biochemistry (PhD)
chemistry (MS, PhD)
earth and environmental sciences (MS, PhD)
English (MA, PhD)
environmental policy design (MA)
history (MA, PhD)
human cognition and development (MS, PhD)
integrative biology and neuroscience (PhD)
mathematics (MS, PhD)
molecular biology (MS, PhD)
photonics (MS)
physics (MS, PhD)
politics and policy (MA)
polymer science (MS, PhD)
polymer science and engineering (MS, PhD)
sociology (MA)
statistics (MS)

College of Business and Economics
Martin K. Saffer, Graduate Business Programs
Programs in:
accounting (MS)
accounting and information analysis (MS)
analytical finance (MS)
business administration (MBA)
economics (MS, PhD)
entrepreneurship (Certificate)
finance (MS)
health and bio-pharmaceutical economics (MS)
project management (Certificate)
supply chain management (Certificate)

College of Education
Dr. Gary M. Sasso, Dean
Programs in:
counseling and human services (M Ed)
counseling psychology (PhD)
education (M Ed, MS, Ed D, PhD, Certificate, Ed S)
educational leadership (M Ed, Ed D, Certificate)
elementary and secondary school counseling (M Ed)
elementary education (M Ed)
globalization and educational change (M Ed)
instructional technology (MS)
international counseling (M Ed, Certificate)
learning sciences and technology (PhD)
school psychology (M Ed, PhD, Ed S)
secondary education (M Ed)
secondary school counseling (M Ed)
special education (M Ed, PhD)
technology use in schools (Certificate)
TESOL (Certificate)

P.C. Rossin College of Engineering and Applied Science
Dr. John P. Coulter, Associate Dean of Graduate Studies and Research
Programs in:
analytical finance (MS)
applied mathematics (MS, PhD)
biological chemical engineering (M Eng)
chemical engineering (M Eng, PhD)
civil engineering (M Eng, MS, PhD)
computational engineering and mechanics (MS, PhD)
computer engineering (M Eng, MS, PhD)
computer science (M Eng, MS, PhD)
electrical engineering (M Eng, MS, PhD)
engineering and applied science (M Eng, MS, PhD)
environmental engineering (MS, PhD)
industrial engineering (M Eng, MS, PhD)
information and systems engineering (M Eng, MS)
management science (MS)
manufacturing systems engineering (MS)
materials science and engineering (M Eng, MS, PhD)
mechanical engineering (M Eng, MS, PhD)
photonics (MS)
polymer science/engineering (M Eng, MS, PhD)
quality engineering (MS)
structural engineering (M Eng, MS, PhD)
wireless network engineering (MS)

Center for Polymer Science and Engineering
Dr. Raymond A. Pearson, Director
Program in:
polymer science and engineering (M Eng, MS, PhD)

■ LINCOLN UNIVERSITY
Lincoln University, PA 19352
http://www.lincoln.edu/

State-related, coed, comprehensive institution. *Computer facilities:* 167 computers available on campus for general student use. A campuswide network can be accessed from student residence rooms and from off campus. *General application contact:* Acting Director, Graduate Program in Human Services, 610-932-8300 Ext. 3360.

Graduate Center
Programs in:
administration (MSA)
early childhood education (M Ed)
elementary education (M Ed)
human services (M Hum Svcs)
reading (MSR)

■ LOCK HAVEN UNIVERSITY OF PENNSYLVANIA
Lock Haven, PA 17745-2390
http://www.lhup.edu/

State-supported, coed, comprehensive institution. *Graduate faculty:* 12 full-time (5 women), 6 part-time/adjunct (1 woman). *Computer facilities:* 290 computers available on campus for general student use. A campuswide network can be accessed from student residence rooms and from off campus. Online class registration is available. *Graduate expenses:* Tuition, state resident: full-time $6430; part-time $357 per credit hour. Tuition, nonresident: full-time $10,288; part-time $572 per credit hour. Required fees: $1988; $144 per credit hour. One-time fee: $25. Tuition and fees vary according to course load. *General application contact:* Jerry Falco, Assistant Director of Admissions, 570-484-3869.

Department of Education
Dr. Edward Jensen, Coordinator
Programs in:
alternative education (M Ed)
teaching and learning (M Ed)

Department of Health Science
Program in:
physician assistant in rural primary care (MHS)

Department of Liberal Arts
Dr. Ellen P. O'Hara-Mays, Graduate Coordinator
Program in:
liberal arts (MLA)

■ MANSFIELD UNIVERSITY OF PENNSYLVANIA
Mansfield, PA 16933
http://www.mansfield.edu/

State-supported, coed, comprehensive institution. *Graduate faculty:* 23 full-time (16 women), 14 part-time/adjunct (12 women). *Computer facilities:* 661 computers available on campus for general student use. A campuswide network can be accessed from student residence rooms and from off campus. Online class registration is available. *General application contact:* Christina Hale, Assistant Director of Enrollment Services/Graduate Admissions, 570-662-4806.

Graduate Studies
Dr. Deborah Erickson, Associate Provost
Programs in:
art education (M Ed)
band conducting (MA)
choral conducting (MA)
elementary education (M Ed)
library science (M Ed)
nursing (MSN)
performance (MA)
secondary education (MS)

■ MARYWOOD UNIVERSITY
Scranton, PA 18509-1598
http://www.marywood.edu/

Independent-religious, coed, comprehensive institution. CGS member. *Computer facilities:* 367 computers available on campus for

Marywood University (continued)
general student use. A campuswide network can be accessed from student residence rooms. Online class registration is available. *General application contact:* Director of University Admissions, 866-279-9663 Ext. 6002.

Academic Affairs

College of Education and Human Development
Programs in:
- addiction (MA)
- child/clinical school psychology (MA)
- clinical psychology (Psy D)
- clinical services (MA)
- counseling (Certificate)
- early childhood intervention (MS)
- education (M Ed)
- education and human development (M Ed, MA, MAT, MS, PhD, Psy D, Certificate, Ed S)
- educational administration (PhD)
- elementary education (MAT)
- elementary school counseling (MS)
- general (MA)
- general theoretical psychology (MA)
- health promotion (PhD)
- higher education administration (MS, PhD)
- human development (PhD)
- instructional leadership (M Ed, PhD)
- mental health counseling (MA)
- pastoral (MA)
- psychology (MA)
- reading education (MS)
- school leadership (MS)
- school psychology (Ed S)
- secondary education (MAT)
- secondary school counseling (MS)
- social work (PhD)
- special education (MS)
- special education administration and supervision (MS)
- speech-language pathology (MS)

College of Health and Human Services
Programs in:
- clinical physician assistant (MS)
- criminal justice (MPA)
- dietetic internships (Certificate)
- gerontology (MS, Certificate)
- health and human services (MHSA, MPA, MS, MSW, Certificate)
- health services administration (MHSA)
- long-term care management (MHSA)
- managed care (MHSA)
- nursing administration (MS)
- nutrition (MS)
- physician assistant studies (MS)
- public administration (MPA)
- social work (MSW)
- sports nutrition and exercise science (MS)

College of Liberal Arts and Sciences
Programs in:
- biotechnology (MS)
- criminal justice (MS)
- liberal arts and sciences (MS)

Insalaco College of Creative Arts and Management
Programs in:
- advertising design (MA, MFA)
- art education (MA)
- art therapy (MA, Certificate)
- ceramics (MA)
- clay (MA, MFA)
- communication arts (MA, Certificate)
- corporate communication (MS, Certificate)
- creative arts and management (MA, MBA, MFA, MMT, MS, Certificate)
- e-business (MS, Certificate)
- fibers (MFA)
- finance and investments (MBA)
- general management (MBA)
- graphic design (MA, MFA)
- health communication (MS, Certificate)
- illustration (MA, MFA)
- information sciences (MS)
- instructional technology (MS, Certificate)
- interdisciplinary (MA)
- interior architecture (MA)
- library science/information science (MS)
- library science/information specialist (Certificate)
- management information systems (MBA)
- media management (MA)
- metals (MFA)
- music education (MA)
- music therapy (MMT, Certificate)
- painting (MA, MFA)
- photography (MA, MFA)
- printmaking (MA, MFA)
- production (MA)
- sculpture (MA)
- studio art (MA)
- visual arts (MFA)
- vocal pedagogy (Certificate)
- weaving (MA)

School of Architecture
Program in:
- architecture (M Arch)

■ MERCYHURST COLLEGE
Erie, PA 16546
http://www.mercyhurst.edu/

Independent-religious, coed, comprehensive institution. *Computer facilities:* 350 computers available on campus for general student use. A campuswide network can be accessed from student residence rooms and from off campus. Online class registration is available. *General application contact:* Academic Coordinator, 814-824-2985.

Graduate Program
Programs in:
- administration of justice (MS)
- applied intelligence (MS, Certificate)
- bilingual/bicultural special education (MS)
- educational leadership (Certificate)
- forensic and biological anthropology (MS)
- organizational leadership (MS, Certificate)
- special education (MS)

■ MILLERSVILLE UNIVERSITY OF PENNSYLVANIA
Millersville, PA 17551-0302
http://www.millersville.edu/

State-supported, coed, comprehensive institution. CGS member. *Graduate faculty:* 204 full-time (105 women), 93 part-time/adjunct (55 women). *Computer facilities:* 705 computers available on campus for general student use. A campuswide network can be accessed from student residence rooms and from off campus. Online class registration is available. *Graduate expenses:* Tuition, state resident: full-time $6430; part-time $357 per credit. Tuition, nonresident: full-time $10,288; part-time $572 per credit. Required fees: $1937; $73.50 per credit. One-time fee: $88 part-time. Tuition and fees vary according to course load. *General application contact:* Dr. Victor S. DeSantis, Dean of Graduate and Professional Studies, 717-872-3099.

Graduate School
Dr. Victor S. DeSantis, Dean of Graduate and Professional Studies

School of Education
Dr. Jane S. Bray, Dean
Programs in:
- athletic coaching (M Ed)
- athletic management (M Ed)
- clinical psychology (MS)
- early childhood education (M Ed)
- education (M Ed, MS)
- elementary education (M Ed)
- gifted education (M Ed)
- language and literacy education (M Ed)
- language and literacy education-ESL option (M Ed)
- leadership for teaching and learning (M Ed)
- psychology (MS)
- school counseling (M Ed)
- school psychology (MS)
- special education (M Ed)
- sport management (M Ed)
- technology education (M Ed)

School of Humanities and Social Sciences
Dr. John N. Short, Dean
Programs in:
- art education (M Ed)
- emergency management (MS)
- English (MA)
- English education (M Ed)
- French (M Ed, MA)
- German (M Ed, MA)
- history (MA)

humanities and social sciences (M Ed, MA, MS, MSW)
social work (MSW)
Spanish (M Ed, MA)

School of Science and Mathematics
Dr. Edward C. Shane, Dean
Programs in:
biology (MS)
mathematics (M Ed)
nursing (MSN)
science and mathematics (M Ed, MS, MSN)

■ MISERICORDIA UNIVERSITY
Dallas, PA 18612-1098
http://www.misericordia.edu/

Independent-religious, coed, primarily women, comprehensive institution. *Graduate faculty:* 24 full-time (16 women), 29 part-time/adjunct (15 women). *Computer facilities:* Computer purchase and lease plans are available. 100 computers available on campus for general student use. A campuswide network can be accessed from student residence rooms and from off campus. Online class registration, Student Leadership Transcript are available. *Graduate expenses:* Tuition: part-time $525 per credit. *General application contact:* Larree Brown, Coordinator of Part-Time Undergraduate and Graduate Programs, 570-674-6451.

College of Health Sciences
Dr. Jean A. Dyer, Dean of Health Sciences
Programs in:
health sciences (MSN, MSOT, MSPT, MSSLP, DPT, OTD)
nursing (MSN)
occupational therapy (MSOT, OTD)
physical therapy (MSPT, DPT)
speech-language pathology (MSSLP)

College of Professional Studies and Social Sciences
Tom O'Neill, Dean of Adult and Continuing Education
Programs in:
business administration (MBA)
education/curriculum (MS)
organizational management (MS)

■ NEUMANN UNIVERSITY
Aston, PA 19014-1298
http://www.neumann.edu/

Independent-religious, coed, comprehensive institution. *Graduate faculty:* 22 full-time (17 women), 58 part-time/adjunct (35 women). *Computer facilities:* Computer purchase and lease plans are available. 400 computers available on campus for general student use. A campuswide network can be accessed from student residence rooms and from off campus. Online class registration is available. *General application contact:* Kittie D. Pain, Associate Director of Admissions, Graduate and Adult Programs, 610-558-5613.

Program in Education
Dr. Andrew DeSanto, Coordinator, Division of Education and Human Services
Program in:
education (MS)

Program in Nursing and Health Sciences
Dr. Kathleen Hoover, Dean, Division of Nursing and Health Services
Program in:
nursing and health sciences (MS)

Program in Pastoral Counseling
Dr. Leonard DiPaul, Executive Director
Programs in:
pastoral counseling (MS, CAS)
spiritual direction (CSD)

Program in Physical Therapy
Dr. Robert Post, Director
Program in:
physical therapy (DPT)

Program in Sports Management
Dr. Sandra L. Slabik, Coordinator
Program in:
sports management (MS)

Program in Strategic Leadership
Dr. Fredenick Loomis, Coordinator, Division of Continuing Adult and Professional Studies
Program in:
strategic leadership (MS)

Programs in Education
Jannay Morrow, Dean of Studies
Program in:
education (Ed D)

■ PENN STATE GREAT VALLEY
Malvern, PA 19355-1488
http://www.gv.psu.edu/

State-related, coed, graduate-only institution. *Computer facilities:* 331 computers available on campus for general student use. A campuswide network can be accessed from off campus. Online class registration is available. *General application contact:* Assistant Director of Admissions, 610-648-3315.

Graduate Studies
Dr. Craig Edelbrock, Chancellor

Education Division
Dr. Roy Clariana, Division Head
Programs in:
curriculum and instruction (M Ed)
instructional leadership (M Ed)
science education (M Ed)
special education (M Ed, MS)
technology integration for educators (M Ed)
training design for corporations (M Ed)

Engineering Division
Dr. James A. Nemes, Division Head
Programs in:
engineering management (MEM)
information science (MS)
software engineering (MSE)

Management Division
Dr. Daniel Indro, Division Head
Programs in:
biotechnology and health industry management (MBA)
business administration (MBA)
finance (M Fin)
leadership development (MLD)
management of information technology (MBA)
new ventures and entrepreneurial studies (MBA)

■ PENN STATE HARRISBURG
Middletown, PA 17057-4898
http://www.hbg.psu.edu/

State-related, coed, comprehensive institution. *Computer facilities:* Computer purchase and lease plans are available. 500 computers available on campus for general student use. A campuswide network can be accessed from student residence rooms and from off campus. Online class registration is available. *General application contact:* Director of Admissions, 717-948-6250.

Graduate School
Dr. Madlyn L. Hanes, Chancellor

School of Behavioral Sciences and Education
Dr. William D. Milheim, Director
Programs in:
applied behavior analysis (MA)
applied clinical psychology (MA)
applied psychological research (MA)
community psychology and social change (MA)
health education (M Ed)
literacy education (M Ed)
teaching and curriculum (M Ed)
training and development (M Ed)

School of Business Administration
Dr. Stephen P. Schappe, Acting Director
Programs in:
business administration (MBA, MS)
information systems (MS)

School of Humanities
Dr. Kathryn Robinson, Director
Programs in:
American studies (MA, PhD)
humanities (MA)

School of Public Affairs
Dr. Steven A. Peterson, Director

Penn State Harrisburg (continued)
Programs in:
criminal justice (MA)
health administration (MHA)
public administration (MPA, PhD)

School of Science, Engineering and Technology
Dr. Omid Ansary, Director
Programs in:
computer science (MS)
electrical engineering (M Eng)
engineering management (MPS)
engineering science (M Eng)
environmental engineering (M Eng)
environmental pollution control (MEPC, MS)

■ PENN STATE UNIVERSITY PARK

State College, University Park, PA 16802-1503

http://www.psu.edu/

State-related, coed, university. CGS member. *Computer facilities:* Computer purchase and lease plans are available. 4,800 computers available on campus for general student use. A campuswide network can be accessed from student residence rooms and from off campus. Online class registration is available. *General application contact:* Director, Graduate Enrollment Services, 814-865-1834.

Graduate School
Dr. Eva J. Pell, Vice President, Research and Dean of the Graduate School
Programs in:
acoustics (M Eng, MS, PhD)
bioengineering (MS, PhD)
biogeochemistry (dual) (PhD)
business administration (MBA)
cell and developmental biology (PhD)
demography (dual) (MA)
ecology (MS, PhD)
environmental pollution control (MEPC, MS)
genetics (MS, PhD)
human dimensions of natural resources and the environment (dual) (MA, MS, PhD)
immunology and infectious diseases (MS)
integrative biosciences (MS, PhD)
materials science and engineering (PhD)
operations research (dual) (M Eng, MA, MS, PhD)
physiology (MS, PhD)
plant physiology (MS, PhD)
quality and manufacturing management (MMM)

College of Agricultural Sciences
Dr. Bruce A. McPheron, Dean
Programs in:
agricultural and biological engineering (MS, PhD)
agricultural and extension education (M Ed, MS, PhD)
agricultural sciences (M Agr, M Ed, MFR, MS, PhD)
agricultural, environmental and regional economics (M Agr, MS, PhD)
agronomy (M Agr, MS, PhD)
animal science (M Agr, MS, PhD)
entomology (MS, PhD)
food science (MS, PhD)
forest resources (MFR, MS, PhD)
horticulture (M Agr, MS, PhD)
pathobiology (PhD)
plant pathology (MS, PhD)
rural sociology (M Agr, MS, PhD)
soil science (M Agr, PhD)
wildlife and fisheries sciences (MFR, MS, PhD)
youth and family education (M Ed)

College of Arts and Architecture
Dr. Barbara O. Korner, Dean
Programs in:
architecture (M Arch)
art (MFA)
art education (M Ed, MS, PhD)
art history (MA, PhD)
arts and architecture (M Arch, M Ed, M Mus, MA, MFA, MLA, MME, MS, PhD)
composition/theory (M Mus)
conducting (M Mus)
landscape architecture (MLA, MS)
music education (MME, PhD)
music theory (MA)
music theory and history (MA)
musicology (MA)
performance (M Mus)
piano performance (PhD)
piano, pedagogy and performance (M Mus)
theatre (MFA)
voice performance and pedagogy (M Mus)

College of Communications
Dr. Douglas A. Anderson, Dean
Programs in:
communications (MA, PhD)
mass communications (PhD)
media studies (MA)
telecommunications studies (MA)

College of Earth and Mineral Sciences
Dr. William E. Easterling, Dean
Programs in:
earth and mineral sciences (MS, PhD)
energy and geo-environmental engineering (MS, PhD)
geography (MS, PhD)
geosciences (MS, PhD)
materials science and engineering (MS, PhD)
meteorology (MS, PhD)

College of Education
Dr. David H. Monk, Dean
Programs in:
adult education (M Ed, D Ed, PhD)
college student affairs (M Ed)
counseling psychology (PhD)
counselor education (M Ed, MS)
counselor education, counseling psychology and rehabilitation services (D Ed)
curriculum and supervision (M Ed, MS, D Ed, PhD)
early childhood education (M Ed, MS, D Ed, PhD)
education (M Ed, MA, MS, D Ed, PhD)
educational leadership (M Ed, MS, D Ed, PhD)
educational psychology (MS, PhD)
educational theory and policy (MA, PhD)
elementary education (M Ed, MS, D Ed, PhD)
higher education (M Ed, D Ed, PhD)
instructional systems (M Ed, MS, D Ed, PhD)
language and literacy education (M Ed, MS, D Ed, PhD)
mathematics education (M Ed, MS, D Ed, PhD)
school psychology (M Ed, MS, PhD)
science education (M Ed, MS, D Ed, PhD)
social studies education (M Ed, MS, PhD)
special education (M Ed, MS, PhD)
workforce education and development (M Ed, MS, D Ed, PhD)
world language education (M Ed, MS, D Ed, PhD)

College of Engineering
Dr. David N. Wormley, Dean
Programs in:
aerospace engineering (M Eng, MS, PhD)
architectural engineering (M Eng, MS, PhD)
chemical engineering (MS, PhD)
civil engineering (M Eng, MS, PhD)
computer science and engineering (M Eng, MS, PhD)
electrical engineering (MS, PhD)
engineering (M Eng, MMM, MS, PhD)
engineering mechanics (M Eng, MS, PhD)
engineering science (M Eng, MS, PhD)
engineering science and mechanics (M Eng, MS, PhD)
environmental engineering (M Eng, MS, PhD)
industrial engineering (M Eng, MS, PhD)
manufacturing engineering (M Eng)
mechanical engineering (M Eng, MS, PhD)
nuclear engineering (M Eng, MS, PhD)
structural engineering (M Eng, MS, PhD)
transportation and highway engineering (M Eng, MS, PhD)
water resources engineering (M Eng, MS, PhD)

College of Health and Human Development
Dr. Ann C. Crouter, Dean

Programs in:
- biobehavioral health (MS, PhD)
- communication sciences and disorders (MS, PhD)
- health and human development (M Ed, MHA, MS, PhD)
- health policy and administration (MHA, MS, PhD)
- hospitality management (MS, PhD)
- hotel, restaurant, and institutional management (MHRIM, MS, PhD)
- human development and family studies (MS, PhD)
- human nutrition (M Ed)
- kinesiology (MS, PhD)
- leisure studies (MS, PhD)
- nursing (MS, PhD)
- nutrition (MS, PhD)
- recreation, park and tourism management (M Ed)

College of Information Sciences and Technology
Dr. Henry Foley, Dean
Program in:
- information sciences and technology. (MS, PhD)

College of the Liberal Arts
Dr. Susan Welch, Dean
Programs in:
- anthropology (MA, PhD)
- applied linguistics (PhD)
- classical American philosophy (MA, PhD)
- clinical psychology (MS, PhD)
- cognitive psychology (MS, PhD)
- communication arts and sciences (MA, PhD)
- comparative literature (MA, PhD)
- contemporary European philosophy (MA, PhD)
- crime, law, and justice (MA, PhD)
- developmental psychology (MS, PhD)
- economics (MA, PhD)
- English (MA, MFA, PhD)
- French (MA, PhD)
- German (MA, PhD)
- history (MA, PhD)
- history of philosophy (MA, PhD)
- human resources and employment relations (MPS, MS, Postbaccalaureate Certificate)
- industrial/organizational psychology (MS, PhD)
- liberal arts (MA, MFA, MPS, MS, PhD, Postbaccalaureate Certificate)
- political science (MA, PhD)
- psychobiology (MS, PhD)
- Russian and comparative literature (MA)
- social psychology (MS, PhD)
- sociology (MA, PhD)
- Spanish (MA, PhD)
- teaching English as a second language (MA)

Eberly College of Science
Dr. Daniel J. Larson, Dean
Programs in:
- applied statistics (MAS)
- astronomy and astrophysics (MS, PhD)
- biochemistry, microbiology, and molecular biology (MS, PhD)
- biology (MS, PhD)
- biotechnology (MS)
- cell and developmental biology (MS, PhD)
- chemistry (MS, PhD)
- mathematics (M Ed, MA, D Ed, PhD)
- molecular evolutionary biology (MS, PhD)
- physics (M Ed, MS, D Ed, PhD)
- science (M Ed, MA, MAS, MS, D Ed, PhD)
- statistics (MA, MAS, MS, PhD)

The Mary Jean and Frank P. Smeal College of Business Administration
Dr. James B. Thomas, Dean
Programs in:
- business (MBA)
- business administration (MBA)
- supply chain management (MPS)

■ PHILADELPHIA BIBLICAL UNIVERSITY
Langhorne, PA 19047-2990
http://www.pbu.edu/

Independent-religious, coed, comprehensive institution. *Graduate faculty:* 16 full-time (5 women), 18 part-time/adjunct (9 women). *Computer facilities:* Computer purchase and lease plans are available. 90 computers available on campus for general student use. A campuswide network can be accessed from student residence rooms and from off campus. Online class registration is available. *Graduate expenses:* Tuition: full-time $9450; part-time $525 per credit. Required fees: $10; $10 per year. Tuition and fees vary according to program. *General application contact:* Binu Abraham, Assistant Director, Graduate Admissions, 800-572-2472.

School of Biblical Studies
Dr. O. Herbert Hirt, Dean
Program in:
- biblical studies (M Div, MSB)

School of Business and Leadership
Ron Ferner, Dean
Program in:
- organizational leadership (MSOL)

School of Church and Community Ministries
Donald Cheyney, Dean
Program in:
- Christian counseling (MSCC)

School of Education
Dr. Martha MacCullough, Dean
Programs in:
- educational leadership and administration (MS El)
- teacher education (MS Ed)

■ PHILADELPHIA UNIVERSITY
Philadelphia, PA 19144-5497
http://www.philau.edu/

Independent, coed, comprehensive institution. *Computer facilities:* 400 computers available on campus for general student use. A campuswide network can be accessed from student residence rooms and from off campus. Online class registration is available. *General application contact:* Director of Graduate Admissions, 215-951-2943.

School of Architecture
Programs in:
- architecture (MS)
- construction management (MS)
- sustainable design (MS)

School of Business Administration
Programs in:
- business (MBA, MS, PhD)
- business administration (MBA)
- finance (MBA)
- health care management (MBA)
- international business (MBA)
- marketing (MBA)
- taxation (MS)

School of Design and Media
Programs in:
- design and media (MS)
- digital design (MS)

School of Engineering and Textiles
Programs in:
- engineering and textiles (MS, PhD)
- fashion apparel studies (MS)
- textile design (MS)
- textile engineering (MS, PhD)

School of Science and Health
Programs in:
- disaster medicine and management (MS)
- midwifery (MS)
- nurse midwifery (Postbaccalaureate Certificate)
- occupational therapy (MS)
- physician assistant studies (MS)
- science and health (MS, Postbaccalaureate Certificate)

■ POINT PARK UNIVERSITY
Pittsburgh, PA 15222-1984
http://www.pointpark.edu/

Independent, coed, comprehensive institution. *Graduate faculty:* 34 full-time, 49 part-time/adjunct. *Computer facilities:* 247 computers available on campus for general student use. A campuswide network can be accessed from student residence rooms. Online class registration is available. *Graduate expenses:* Tuition: full-time $11,880; part-time $660 per credit. Required fees:

Point Park University (continued)
$486; $27 per credit. *General application contact:* Kathy Ballas, Associate Director, Graduate and Adult Enrollment, 412-392-3812.

Conservatory of Performing Arts
Ronald Allan-Lindblom, Dean/Artistic Producing Director
Program in:
theatre arts-acting (MFA)

Program in Environmental Studies
Program in:
environmental studies (MS)

School of Arts and Sciences
Dr. Karen McIntyre, Dean
Programs in:
arts and sciences (MA, MS)
criminal justice administration (MS)
curriculum and instruction (MA)
educational administration (MA)
engineering management (MS)
journalism and mass communication (MA)

School of Business
Dr. Soren Hogsgaard, Dean
Programs in:
business (MBA)
organizational leadership (MA)

■ ROBERT MORRIS UNIVERSITY
Moon Township, PA 15108-1189
http://www.rmu.edu/

Independent, coed, university. *Computer facilities:* Computer purchase and lease plans are available. 300 computers available on campus for general student use. A campuswide network can be accessed from student residence rooms and from off campus. Online class registration, online payment are available. *Graduate expenses:* Tuition: part-time $730 per credit hour. Required fees: $15 per credit hour. Part-time tuition and fees vary according to degree level, campus/location and program. *General application contact:* Edward J. Lamm, Assistant Dean, Graduate Admissions, 412-397-5200.

Graduate Studies
Dr. David L. Jamison, Provost/Senior Vice President for Academic Affairs

School of Business
Dr. Derya A. Jacobs, Dean
Programs in:
business administration and management (MBA)
human resource management (MS)
nonprofit management (MS)
taxation (MS)

School of Communications and Information Systems
Dr. Barbara J. Levine, Acting Dean
Programs in:
communication and information systems (MS)
competitive intelligence systems (MS)
information security and assurance (MS)
information systems and communications (D Sc)
information systems management (MS)
information technology project management (MS)
Internet information systems (MS)
organizational studies (MS)

School of Education and Social Sciences
Dr. John E. Graham, Dean
Programs in:
business education (MS)
education (Postbaccalaureate Certificate)
instructional leadership (MS)
instructional management and leadership (PhD)

School of Engineering, Mathematics and Science
Dr. Joe Iannelli, Department Head, Engineering
Program in:
engineering management (MS)

School of Nursing and Health Sciences
Dr. Lynda J. Davidson, Dean
Program in:
nursing (MS, DNP)

■ ROSEMONT COLLEGE
Rosemont, PA 19010-1699
http://www.rosemont.edu/

Independent-religious, coed, comprehensive institution. *Computer facilities:* 100 computers available on campus for general student use. A campuswide network can be accessed from student residence rooms and from off campus. Online class registration is available. *General application contact:* Director, Enrollment and Student Services, 610-527-0200 Ext. 2187.

Schools of Graduate and Professional Studies
Dr. Judith Renyi, Dean of Graduate Studies
Programs in:
business administration (MBA)
creative writing (MFA)
elementary certification (MA)
English and publishing (MA)
English literature (MA)
human services (MA)
management (MSM)
school counseling (MA)

■ SAINT FRANCIS UNIVERSITY
Loretto, PA 15940-0600
http://www.francis.edu/

Independent-religious, coed, comprehensive institution. *Computer facilities:* Computer purchase and lease plans are available. 60 computers available on campus for general student use. A campuswide network can be accessed from student residence rooms and from off campus. Online class registration is available. *General application contact:* Associate Vice President for Academic Affairs, 814-472-3085.

Department of Occupational Therapy
Dr. Donald Walkovich, Chair
Program in:
occupational therapy (MOT)

Department of Physical Therapy
Dr. Kay Malek, Interim Department Chair/Assistant Professor
Program in:
physical therapy (DPT)

Department of Physician Assistant Sciences
Donna L. Yeisley, Director
Programs in:
health science (MHS)
medical science (MMS)
physician assistant sciences (MPAS)

Graduate Education Program
Dr. Janette D. Kelly, Director, Graduate Education
Programs in:
education (M Ed)
leadership (M Ed)
reading (M Ed)

Graduate School of Business and Human Resource Management
Programs in:
business administration (MBA)
business and human resource management (MBA, MHRM)
human resource management (MHRM)

■ SAINT JOSEPH'S UNIVERSITY
Philadelphia, PA 19131-1395
http://www.sju.edu/

Independent-religious, coed, comprehensive institution. *Graduate faculty:* 140 full-time (49 women), 130 part-time/adjunct (45 women). *Computer facilities:* Computer purchase and lease plans are available. 670 computers available on campus for general student use. A campuswide network can be accessed from student residence rooms and from off campus. Online class registration is available. *Graduate expenses:* Tuition: part-time $745 per credit. Tuition and fees vary according to course load, degree level and program. *General application contact:* Coralee Dixon, Assistant Director, Graduate Admissions, 610-660-1101.

College of Arts and Sciences
Dr. Sabrina DeTurk, Associate Dean/Executive Director of Graduate Programs

Programs in:
- administration/police executive (MS)
- adult learning and training (MS, Certificate)
- arts and sciences (MA, MS, Ed D, Certificate, Post-Master's Certificate)
- behavior analysis (MS, Post-Master's Certificate)
- biology (MA, MS)
- computer science (MS)
- criminal justice (MS, Post-Master's Certificate)
- criminology (MS)
- educational leadership (Ed D)
- elementary education (MS)
- environmental protection and safety management (MS, Post-Master's Certificate)
- federal law (MS)
- gerontological counseling (MS)
- gerontological services (Post-Master's Certificate)
- health administration (MS, Post-Master's Certificate)
- health education (MS, Post-Master's Certificate)
- health informatics (Post-Master's Certificate)
- healthcare ethics (Certificate)
- homeland security (MS, Certificate)
- human services administration (MS)
- instructional technology (MS)
- intelligence and crime (MS)
- mathematics and computer science (Post-Master's Certificate)
- nurse anesthesia (MS)
- organization dynamics and leadership (MS, Certificate)
- organizational psychology and development (MS, Certificate)
- probation, parole, and corrections (MS)
- professional education (MS)
- psychology (MS)
- public safety (Post-Master's Certificate)
- public safety management (MS, Certificate)
- reading specialist (MS)
- school nurse certification (MS)
- secondary education (MS)
- special education (MS)
- training and organizational development (MS)
- writing studies (MA)

Erivan K. Haub School of Business
Dr. Joseph A. DiAngelo, Dean
Programs in:
- accounting (MBA)
- business (MBA, MS, Post Master's Certificate)
- business intelligence (MS)
- executive business administration (MBA)
- executive pharmaceutical marketing (Post Master's Certificate)
- finance (MBA)
- financial services (MS)
- food marketing (MBA, MS)
- general business (MBA)
- health and medical services administration (MBA)
- human resource management (MBA, MS)
- international business (MBA)
- international marketing (MS)
- management (MBA)
- marketing (MBA)
- pharmaceutical marketing (MBA)

■ SETON HILL UNIVERSITY
Greensburg, PA 15601
http://www.setonhill.edu/

Independent-religious, coed, comprehensive institution. *Graduate faculty:* 23 full-time (12 women), 23 part-time/adjunct (12 women). *Computer facilities:* Computer purchase and lease plans are available. 300 computers available on campus for general student use. A campuswide network can be accessed from student residence rooms and from off campus. Online class registration is available. *Graduate expenses:* Tuition: full-time $12,510; part-time $695 per credit hour. Required fees: $200; $100 per semester. Tuition and fees vary according to course load and program. *General application contact:* Tracey Bartos, Director of Graduate and Adult Studies, 724-838-4283.

Program in Art Therapy
Program in:
- art therapy (MA, Certificate)

Program in Business Administration
Program in:
- business administration (MBA)

Program in Elementary Education
Program in:
- elementary education (MA, Teaching Certificate)

Program in Genocide and Holocaust Studies
Program in:
- genocide and Holocaust studies (Certificate)

Program in Inclusive Education
Program in:
- inclusive education (MA)

Program in Marriage and Family Therapy
Program in:
- marriage and family therapy (MA)

Program in Physician Assistant
Program in:
- physician assistant (MS)

Program in Special Education
Program in:
- special education (MA, Teaching Certificate)

Program in Writing Popular Fiction
Program in:
- writing popular fiction (MA)

■ SHIPPENSBURG UNIVERSITY OF PENNSYLVANIA
Shippensburg, PA 17257-2299
http://www.ship.edu/

State-supported, coed, comprehensive institution. CGS member. *Graduate faculty:* 155 full-time (60 women), 24 part-time/adjunct (15 women). *Computer facilities:* 1,100 computers available on campus for general student use. A campuswide network can be accessed from student residence rooms and from off campus. Online class registration, personal Web pages are available. *Graduate expenses:* Tuition, state resident: full-time $6430; part-time $357 per credit. Tuition, nonresident: full-time $10,288; part-time $572 per credit. Required fees: $1127; $38 per credit. One-time fee: $44 part-time. *General application contact:* Renee Payne, Associate Dean of Graduate Admissions, 717-477-1231.

School of Graduate Studies
Dr. Tracy Schoolcraft, Dean of Graduate Studies/Associate Provost

College of Arts and Sciences
Dr. James Mike, Dean
Programs in:
- applied history (MA, Certificate)
- arts and sciences (MA, MPA, MS, Certificate)
- biology (MS)
- communication studies (MS)
- computer science (MS)
- geoenvironmental studies (MS)
- organizational development and leadership (MS)
- psychology (MS)
- public administration (MPA)

College of Education and Human Services
Dr. James R. Johnson, Dean
Programs in:
- Adlerian studies (Certificate)
- administration of justice (MS)
- advanced study in counseling (Certificate)
- aging (Certificate)
- alcohol and drug counseling (Certificate)
- counseling (M Ed, MS)
- couple and family counseling (Certificate)
- curriculum and instruction (M Ed)
- education and human services (M Ed, MS, MSW, Certificate)
- reading (M Ed)
- school administration principal K-12 (M Ed)
- social work (MSW)
- special education (M Ed)

Shippensburg University of Pennsylvania (continued)

John L. Grove College of Business
Dr. Patricia Wolf, Director/Assistant Dean
Programs in:
advanced studies in business (Certificate)
business administration (MBA)

■ SLIPPERY ROCK UNIVERSITY OF PENNSYLVANIA

Slippery Rock, PA 16057-1383

http://www.sru.edu/

State-supported, coed, comprehensive institution. *Graduate faculty:* 67 full-time (37 women), 9 part-time/adjunct (7 women). *Computer facilities:* Computer purchase and lease plans are available. 1,323 computers available on campus for general student use. A campuswide network can be accessed from student residence rooms and from off campus. Online class registration is available. *Graduate expenses:* Tuition, state resident: full-time $6430; part-time $357 per credit. Tuition, nonresident: full-time $10,288; part-time $572 per credit. Required fees: $2062; $158 per credit. *General application contact:* Angela Piverotto, Director of Graduate Admissions, 724-738-2051.

Graduate Studies (Recruitment)

Angela Piverotto, Director of Graduate Studies

College of Education
Dr. Jay Hertzog, Dean
Programs in:
community counseling (MA)
education (M Ed, MA, MS)
elementary guidance and counseling (M Ed)
master teacher (M Ed)
physical education (M Ed)
reading (M Ed)
secondary education in math/science (M Ed)
secondary guidance and counseling (M Ed)
sport management (MS)
student personnel (MA)
supervision (M Ed)

College of Health, Environment, and Science
Dr. Susan Hannam, Dean
Programs in:
environmental education (M Ed)
health, environment, and science (M Ed, MS, DPT)
physical therapy (DPT)
resource management (MS)
sustainable systems (MS)

College of Humanities, Fine and Performing Arts
Dr. Diana Dreyer, Interim Dean
Programs in:
history (MA)
humanities, fine and performing arts (MA)
literature and composition (MA)
professional writing (MA)

■ TEMPLE UNIVERSITY

Philadelphia, PA 19122-6096

http://www.temple.edu/

State-related, coed, university. CGS member. *Computer facilities:* Computer purchase and lease plans are available. 3,587 computers available on campus for general student use. A campuswide network can be accessed from student residence rooms and from off campus. Online class registration, student accounts, Web hosting are available. *General application contact:* Coordinator of Outreach, 215-204-6575.

Ambler College

Program in:
community and regional planning (MS)

Graduate School

College of Education
Programs in:
adult and organizational development (Ed M)
applied behavioral analysis (MS Ed)
career and technical education (MS Ed)
counseling psychology (Ed M, PhD)
early childhood education and elementary education (MS Ed)
education (Ed M, MS Ed, Ed D, PhD)
educational administration (Ed M, Ed D)
educational psychology (Ed M, PhD)
English education (MS Ed)
language arts education (Ed D)
math/science education (Ed D)
mathematics education (MS Ed)
school psychology (Ed M, PhD)
science education (MS Ed)
second and foreign language education (MS Ed)
special education (MS Ed)
teaching English as a second language (MS Ed)
urban education (Ed M, Ed D)

College of Engineering
Programs in:
civil engineering (MSE)
electrical engineering (MSE)
engineering (MS, MSE, PhD)
mechanical engineering (MSE)

College of Liberal Arts
Programs in:
African American studies (MA, PhD)
anthropology (PhD)
clinical psychology (PhD)
cognitive psychology (PhD)
creative writing (MA)
criminal justice (MA, PhD)
developmental psychology (PhD)
English (MA, PhD)
geography (MA)
history (MA, PhD)
liberal arts (MA, MLA, PhD)
philosophy (MA, PhD)
political science (MA, PhD)
religion (MA, PhD)
social psychology (PhD)
sociology (MA, PhD)
Spanish (MA, PhD)
urban studies (MA)

College of Science and Technology
Programs in:
applied mathematics (MA)
biology (MS, PhD)
chemistry (MA, PhD)
computer and information sciences (MS, PhD)
geology (MS)
mathematics (PhD)
physics (MA, PhD)
pure mathematics (MA)
science and technology (MA, MS, PhD)

Esther Boyer College of Music and Dance
Programs in:
choral activities (MM)
composition (MM, DMA)
dance (Ed M, MFA, PhD)
instrumental studies (MM, DMA)
keyboard instruction (MM, DMA)
music and dance (Ed M, MFA, MM, MMT, DMA, PhD)
music education (MM, PhD)
music history (MM)
music theory (MM)
music therapy (MMT, PhD)
voice and opera (MM, DMA)

Fox School of Business
Dr. M. Moshe Porat, Dean
Programs in:
accounting (MBA, PhD)
accounting and financial management (MS)
actuarial science (MS)
business (EMBA, IMBA, MBA, MHM, MS, PhD)
business management (MBA)
entrepreneurship (PhD)
finance (MS, PhD)
financial engineering (MS)
financial management (MBA)
healthcare and life sciences innovation (MBA)
healthcare financial management (MS)
healthcare management (MHM)
human resource administration (PhD)
human resource management (MBA, MS)
international business (IMBA, PhD)
IT management (MBA)
management information systems (MS, PhD)
marketing (MS, PhD)
marketing management (MBA)
pharmaceutical management (MBA)
risk management and insurance (PhD)
statistics (MS, PhD)

strategic management (EMBA, MBA, PhD)
tourism and sport (PhD)

School of Communications and Theater
Programs in:
acting (MFA)
broadcasting, telecommunications and mass media (MA)
communication management (MS)
communications and theater (MA, MFA, MJ, MS, PhD)
design (MFA)
directing (MFA)
film and media arts (MFA)
journalism (MJ)
mass media and communication (PhD)

School of Social Administration
Programs in:
social administration (MSW)
social work (MSW)

School of Tourism and Hospitality Management
Programs in:
sport and recreation administration (Ed M)
tourism and hospitality management (Ed M, MTHM)

Tyler School of Art
Programs in:
art (Ed M, MA, MFA, PhD)
art and art education (Ed M)
art history (MA, PhD)
ceramics/glass (MFA)
fibers and fabric design (MFA)
graphic and interactive design (MFA)
metals/jewelry/CAD-CAM (MFA)
painting (MFA)
photography (MFA)
printmaking (MFA)
sculpture (MFA)

Health Sciences Center
Program in:
health sciences (DMD, DPM, MD, Pharm D, Ed M, MA, MOT, MPH, MS, MSN, DPT, PhD, Certificate)

College of Health Professions
Programs in:
communication sciences (PhD)
community health education (MPH)
environmental health (MS)
epidemiology (MS)
health professions (Ed M, MA, MOT, MPH, MS, MSN, DPT, PhD)
health studies (PhD)
kinesiology (Ed M, PhD)
linguistics (MA)
nursing (MSN)
occupational therapy (MOT, MS)
physical therapy (DPT, PhD)
public health (Ed M, MPH, MS, PhD)
school health education (Ed M)
speech-language-hearing (MA)
therapeutic recreation (Ed M)

School of Dentistry
Programs in:
advanced education in general dentistry (Certificate)
dentistry (DMD, MS, Certificate)
endodontology (Certificate)
oral biology (MS)
orthodontics (Certificate)
periodontology (Certificate)

School of Medicine
Programs in:
anatomy and cell biology (MS, PhD)
biochemistry (MS, PhD)
medicine (MD, MS, PhD)
microbiology and immunology (MS, PhD)
molecular biology and genetics (PhD)
neuroscience (MS, PhD)
pathology and laboratory medicine (PhD)
pharmacology (PhD)
physiology (PhD)

School of Pharmacy
Programs in:
medicinal chemistry (MS, PhD)
pharmaceutics (MS, PhD)
pharmacodynamics (MS, PhD)
pharmacy (Pharm D, MS, PhD)
quality assurance/regulatory affairs (MS)

School of Podiatric Medicine
Program in:
podiatric medicine (DPM)

James E. Beasley School of Law
Programs in:
law (JD)
legal education (SJD)
taxation (LL M)
transnational law (LL M)
trial advocacy (LL M)

■ UNIVERSITY OF PENNSYLVANIA
Philadelphia, PA 19104
http://www.upenn.edu/

Independent, coed, university. CGS member. *Graduate faculty:* 2,524 full-time (730 women), 1,639 part-time/adjunct (589 women). *Computer facilities:* Computer purchase and lease plans are available. 1,295 computers available on campus for general student use. A campuswide network can be accessed from student residence rooms and from off campus. Online class registration, billing information, financial aid application, status, academic records, student services are available. *Graduate expenses:* Tuition: full-time $24,720; part-time $4583 per course. Required fees: $2074; $338 per course. Tuition and fees vary according to course load, degree level, campus/location and program. *General application contact:* Karen Lawrence, Assistant Vice Provost for Graduate Education, 215-898-1842.

Annenberg School for Communication
Dr. Michael X. Delli Carpini, Dean
Program in:
communication (PhD)

Graduate School of Education
Dr. Andrew Porter, Graduate Dean
Programs in:
applied psychology and human development (M Phil, MS Ed, PhD)
counseling and psychological services (PhD)
counseling psychology (M Phil)
education (M Phil, MS Ed, Ed D, PhD)
education, culture and society (MS Ed, PhD)
educational leadership (MS Ed, Ed D, PhD)
educational linguistics (PhD)
elementary and secondary education (MS Ed)
foundations and practices in education (MS Ed, Ed D, PhD)
human development (MS Ed, PhD)
intercultural communication (MS Ed, Ed D, PhD)
learning science and technologies (MS Ed)
policy, management and evaluation (M Phil, MS Ed, Ed D, PhD)
reading, writing, and literacy (MS Ed, Ed D, PhD)
teaching English to speakers of other languages (MS Ed)
teaching English to speakers of other languages and intercultural communication (MS Ed, PhD)

Law School
Michael A. Fitts, Dean
Program in:
law (JD, LL CM, LL M, SJD)

School of Arts and Sciences
Dr. Ralph M. Rosen, Associate Dean for Graduate Studies
Programs in:
ancient history (AM, PhD)
anthropology (AM, MS, PhD)
applied mathematics and computational science (PhD)
art and archaeology of the Mediterranean world (AM, PhD)
arts and sciences (AM, MA, MBA, MES, MGA, MLA, MS, PhD)
biology (PhD)
chemistry (MS, PhD)
classical studies (AM, PhD)
comparative literature (AM, PhD)
criminology (MA, MS, PhD)
demography (AM, PhD)
earth and environmental science (MS, PhD)
East Asian languages and civilization (AM, PhD)
economics (AM, PhD)
English (AM, PhD)
French (AM, PhD)
Germanic languages (AM, PhD)

University of Pennsylvania (continued)
history (AM, PhD)
history and sociology of science (AM, PhD)
history of art (AM, PhD)
international studies (AM)
Italian (AM, PhD)
linguistics (AM, PhD)
literary theory (AM, PhD)
mathematics (AM, PhD)
medical physics (MS)
music (AM, PhD)
near eastern languages and civilization (AM, PhD)
organizational dynamics (MS)
philosophy (AM, PhD)
physics (PhD)
political science (AM, PhD)
psychology (PhD)
religious studies (PhD)
sociology (AM, PhD)
South Asian regional studies (AM, PhD)
Spanish (AM, PhD)

College of Liberal and Professional Studies
Dr. Kristine Billmyer, Associate Dean/ Director
Programs in:
environmental studies (MES)
individualized study (MLA)

Fels Institute of Government
David B. Thornburgh, Director
Program in:
government (MGA)

Joseph H. Lauder Institute of Management and International Studies
Mauro Guillen, Director
Programs in:
international studies (MA)
management and international studies (MBA)

School of Dental Medicine
Dr. Denis Kinane, Dean
Program in:
dental medicine (DMD)

School of Design
Patricia Woldar, Associate Dean
Programs in:
architecture (M Arch, PhD)
city and regional planning (MCP, PhD, Certificate)
conservation and heritage management (Certificate)
design (M Arch, MCP, MFA, MLA, MS, PhD, Certificate)
fine arts (MFA)
historic conservation (Certificate)
historic preservation (MS)
landscape architecture and regional planning (MLA)
landscape studies (Certificate)
real estate design and development (PhD, Certificate)
urban design (PhD, Certificate)

School of Engineering and Applied Science
Eduardo D. Glandt, Dean
Programs in:
applied mechanics (MSE, PhD)
bioengineering (MSE, PhD)
biotechnology (MS)
chemical engineering (MSE, PhD)
computer and information science (MCIT, MSE, PhD)
computer graphics and game technology (MSE)
electrical and systems engineering (MSE, PhD)
engineering and applied science (EMBA, MCIT, MS, MSE, PhD, AC)
materials science and engineering (MSE, PhD)
mechanical engineering (MSE, PhD)
technology management (EMBA)
telecommunications and networking (MSE)

School of Medicine
Dr. Arthur M. Rubenstein, Dean
Program in:
medicine (MD, MS, MSCE, PhD)

Biomedical Graduate Studies
Dr. Susan R. Ross, Director
Programs in:
biochemistry and molecular biophysics (PhD)
biomedical studies (MS, PhD)
biostatistics (MS, PhD)
cancer biology (PhD)
cell biology and physiology (PhD)
developmental biology (PhD)
developmental stem cell regenerative biology (PhD)
gene therapy and vaccines (PhD)
genetics and gene regulation (PhD)
genomics and computational biology (PhD)
immunology (PhD)
microbiology, virology, and parasitology (PhD)
neuroscience (PhD)
pharmacology (PhD)

Center for Clinical Epidemiology and Biostatistics
Dr. Harold I. Feldman, Director
Programs in:
clinical epidemiology (MSCE)
epidemiology (PhD)

School of Nursing
Programs in:
acute care nurse practitioner (MSN)
administration/consulting (MSN)
adult and special populations (MSN)
adult health nurse practitioner (MSN)
adult oncology nurse practitioner (MSN)
child and family (MSN)
family health nurse practitioner (MSN, Certificate)
geropsychiatrics (MSN)
health leadership (MSN)
neonatal nurse practitioner (MSN)
nurse anesthetist (MSN)
nurse midwifery (MSN)
nursing (MSN, PhD, Certificate)
nursing and health care administration (MSN, PhD)
pediatric acute/chronic care nurse practitioner (MSN)
pediatric critical care nurse practitioner (MSN)
pediatric nurse practitioner (MSN)
pediatric oncology nurse practitioner (MSN)
perinatal advanced practice nurse specialist (MSN)
primary care (MSN)
women's healthcare nurse practitioner (MSN)

School of Social Policy and Practice
Programs in:
social policy and practice (MSW, PhD)
social welfare (PhD)
social work (MSW)

School of Veterinary Medicine
Program in:
veterinary medicine (VMD)

Wharton School
Programs in:
accounting (PhD)
applied economics (PhD)
business (MBA, PhD)
business administration (MBA)
business and public policy (MBA, PhD)
ethics and legal studies (PhD)
finance (MBA, PhD)
health care management (MBA, PhD)
health care management and economics (PhD)
insurance and risk management (MBA, PhD)
legal studies and business ethics (MBA, PhD)
management (MBA, PhD)
marketing (PhD)
operations and information management (PhD)
real estate (MBA, PhD)
statistics (MBA, PhD)

The Wharton MBA Program for Executives
Program in:
executive business administration (MBA)

■ UNIVERSITY OF PHOENIX–PHILADELPHIA CAMPUS
Wayne, PA 19087-2121
http://www.phoenix.edu/

Proprietary, coed, comprehensive institution. *Computer facilities:* Computer purchase and lease plans are available. A campuswide network can be accessed from off campus. Online class registration is available. *General application contact:* Campus Information Center, 610-989-0880.

The Artemis School

College of Health and Human Services
Programs in:
administration of justice and security (MS)
health administration (MHA)
health care education (MSN)
health care management (MBA)
nursing (MSN)
psychology (MS)

The John Sperling School of Business

Program in:
business (MBA, MIS, MM)

College of Graduate Business and Management
Programs in:
accounting (MBA)
business administration (MBA)
global management (MBA)
human resources management (MBA, MM)
management (MM)
marketing (MBA)
public administration (MM)

College of Information Systems and Technology
Programs in:
information systems (MIS)
technology management (MBA)

■ UNIVERSITY OF PITTSBURGH

Pittsburgh, PA 15260
http://www.pitt.edu/

State-related, coed, university. CGS member. *Graduate faculty:* 3,898 full-time (1,462 women), 771 part-time/adjunct (379 women). *Computer facilities:* Computer purchase and lease plans are available. 1,150 computers available on campus for general student use. A campuswide network can be accessed from student residence rooms and from off campus. Online class listings, online tuition payment available. *Graduate expenses:* Tuition, state resident: full-time $15,772; part-time $640 per credit. Tuition, nonresident: full-time $27,996; part-time $1147 per credit. Required fees: $690; $175 per term. *General application contact:* Information Contact, 412-624-4141.

Graduate School of Public and International Affairs

Dr. John T.S. Keeler, Dean and Professor
Programs in:
development planning (MPPM)
development policy (PhD)
foreign and security policy (PhD)
international development (MPPM)
international political economy (MPPM, PhD)
international security studies (MPPM)
management of non profit organizations (MPPM)
metropolitan management and regional development (MPPM)
policy analysis and evaluation (MPPM)
public administration (PhD)
public and international affairs (MID, MPA, MPIA, MPPM, PhD, MPA/MID)
public policy (PhD)

Division of International Development
Dr. Louis Picard, Director, International Development Divisions
Programs in:
development planning and environmental sustainability (MID)
human security (MID)
nongovernmental organizations and civil society (MID)

Division of Public and Urban Affairs
Dr. David Y. Miller, Director, Public and Urban Affairs Division
Programs in:
policy research and analysis (MPA)
public and nonprofit management (MPA, MPA/MID)
urban and regional affairs (MPA)

International Affairs Division
Dr. Martin Staniland, Director, International Affairs and International Development Divisions
Programs in:
global political economy (MPIA)
human security (MPIA)
security and intelligence studies (MPIA)

Graduate School of Public Health

Dr. Donald S. Burke, Dean
Programs in:
behavioral and community health sciences (MPH, Dr PH)
bioscience of infectious diseases (MPH)
biostatistics (MPH, MS, Dr PH, PhD)
community and behavioral intervention of infectious diseases (MPH)
environmental and occupational health (MPH, MS, PhD)
epidemiology (MPH, MS, Dr PH, PhD)
genetic counseling (MS)
health policy and management (MHA, MPH)
human genetics (MS, PhD)
infectious diseases and microbiology (MS, Dr PH, PhD)
lesbian, gay, bisexual and transgender health and wellness (Certificate)
LGBT health and wellness (Certificate)
minority health and health disparities (Certificate)
occupational medicine (MPH)
program evaluation (Certificate)
public health (MHA, MPH, MS, Dr PH, PhD, Certificate)
public health and aging (Certificate)
public health awareness and disaster response (Certificate)
public health genetics (MPH, Certificate)
public health preparedness (Certificate)
risk assessment (Certificate)

Joint CMU-Pitt PhD Program in Computational Biology

Dr. Ivet Bahar, Director
Program in:
computational biology (PhD)

Katz Graduate School of Business

Dr. John T. Delaney, Dean
Programs in:
accounting (MAC, PhD)
business (EMBA, MAC, MBA, MS, MSIS, PhD)
business administration (MBA)
finance (MBA, PhD)
information science (PhD)
information systems (MBA, MSIS)
international business (MBA)
international business administration (MBA)
management of information systems (MS)
marketing (MBA, PhD)
operations/decision sciences/artificial intelligence (PhD)
organizational behavior and human resource management (MBA, PhD)
strategic planning (PhD)
strategy, environment and organizations (MBA)

School of Arts and Sciences

Dr. Nicole Constable, Associate Dean, Graduate Studies and Research
Programs in:
anthropology (MA, PhD)
applied linguistics (PhD)
applied mathematics (MA, MS)
applied statistics (MA, MS)
arts and sciences (MA, MFA, MS, PM Sc, PMS, PhD, Certificate, Doctoral Certificate, Master's Certificate)
chemistry (MS, PhD)
classics (MA, PhD)
communication (MA, PhD)
composition and theory (MA, PhD)
computer science (MS, PhD)
cultural and critical studies (PhD)
East Asian studies (MA)
ecology and evolution (PhD)
economics (PhD)
English (MA)
ethnomusicology (MA, PhD)
financial mathematics (PMS)
French (MA, PhD)
geographical information systems (PM Sc)
geology and planetary science (MS, PhD)
German studies (MA, PhD)
Hispanic languages and literatures (MA, PhD)
Hispanic linguistics (MA, PhD)
historical musicology (MA, PhD)

University of Pittsburgh (continued)
history (MA, PhD)
history and philosophy of science (MA, PhD)
history of art and architecture (MA, PhD)
intelligent systems (MS, PhD)
Italian (MA)
linguistics (MA)
mathematics (MA, MS, PhD)
molecular, cellular, and developmental biology (PhD)
performance pedagogy (MFA)
philosophy (MA, PhD)
physics (MS, PhD)
political science (MA, PhD)
psychology (MS, PhD)
religion (PhD)
religious studies (MA)
Slavic languages and literatures (MA, PhD)
sociolinguistics (PhD)
sociology (MA, PhD)
statistics (MA, MS, PhD)
TESOL—teaching English to speakers of other languages (Certificate)
theatre and performance studies (MA, PhD)
women's studies (Doctoral Certificate, Master's Certificate)
writing (MFA)

Center for Bioethics and Health Law
Dr. Lisa S. Parker, Director of Graduate Education
Program in:
bioethics (MA)

Center for Neuroscience
Dr. Alan Sved, Co-Director, Graduate Program
Programs in:
neurobiology (PhD)
neuroscience (PhD)

School of Dental Medicine
Dr. Thomas W. Braun, Dean
Programs in:
craniofacial and maxillofacial surgery (Certificate)
dental anesthesia (Certificate)
dental medicine (DMD, MDS, Certificate)
endodontics (MDS, Certificate)
general dentistry (Certificate)
general practice residency (Certificate)
oral and maxillofacial pathology (Certificate)
oral and maxillofacial surgery (Certificate)
orthodontics and dentofacial orthopedics (MDS, Certificate)
pediatric dentistry (MDS, Certificate)
periodontics (MDS, Certificate)
prosthodontics (MDS, Certificate)

School of Education
Dr. Alan Lesgold, Dean
Programs in:
applied developmental psychology (M Ed, MS, PhD)
cognitive studies (PhD)
developmental movement (MS)
early childhood education (M Ed)
early education of disabled students (M Ed)
education (M Ed, MA, MAT, MS, Ed D, PhD)
education of students with mental and physical disabilities (M Ed)
elementary education (M Ed, MAT)
English/communications education (M Ed, MAT)
exercise physiology (MS, PhD)
foreign languages education (M Ed, MAT)
general special education (M Ed)
higher education (M Ed, Ed D)
higher education management (M Ed, Ed D)
mathematics education (M Ed, MAT, Ed D)
reading education (M Ed, Ed D)
research methodology (M Ed, MA, PhD)
school leadership (M Ed, Ed D)
science education (M Ed, MAT, MS, Ed D)
secondary education (M Ed, MAT, MS, Ed D, PhD)
social and comparative analysis in education (M Ed, MA, Ed D, PhD)
social studies education (M Ed, MAT)
special education (M Ed, Ed D, PhD)
vision studies (M Ed)

School of Engineering
Dr. Gerald D. Holder, Dean
Programs in:
bioengineering (MSBENG, PhD)
chemical engineering (MS Ch E, PhD)
civil and environmental engineering (MSCEE, PhD)
electrical engineering (MSEE, PhD)
engineering (MS Ch E, MSBENG, MSCEE, MSEE, MSIE, MSME, MSPE, PhD)
industrial engineering (MSIE, PhD)
mechanical engineering and materials science (MSME, PhD)
petroleum engineering (MSPE)

School of Health and Rehabilitation Sciences
Dr. Clifford E. Brubaker, Dean
Programs in:
assistive rehabilitation technology (Certificate)
communication science and disorders (MA, MS, Au D, CScD, PhD)
dietetics (MS)
disability studies (Certificate)
health and rehabilitation sciences (MA, MOT, MS, Au D, CScD, DPT, PhD, Certificate)
occupational therapy (MOT)
physical therapy (DPT)
rehabilitation science (PhD)

School of Information Sciences
Dr. Ronald L. Larsen, Dean and Professor
Programs in:
information science (MSIS, PhD, Certificate)
information sciences (MLIS, MSIS, MST, PhD, Certificate)
library and information science (MLIS, PhD, Certificate)
telecommunications and networking (MST, PhD, Certificate)

School of Law
Mary Crossley, Dean
Programs in:
business law (MSL)
civil litigation (Certificate)
constitutional law (MSL)
criminal law and justice (MSL)
disabilities law (MSL)
dispute resolution (MSL)
education law (MSL)
elder and estate planning law (MSL)
employment and labor law (MSL)
environment and real estate law (MSL)
environmental law, science and policy (Certificate)
family law (MSL)
general law and jurisprudence (MSL)
health law (Certificate)
intellectual property and technology (MSL)
intellectual property and technology law (Certificate)
international and comparative law (LL M, MSL)
international law (Certificate)
law (JD, LL M, MSL, Certificate)
personal injury and civil litigation (MSL)
regulatory law (MSL)
self-designed (MSL)
sports and entertainment law (MSL)

School of Medicine
Dr. Arthur S. Levine, Dean and Senior Vice Chancellor, Health Sciences
Programs in:
biochemistry and molecular genetics (MS, PhD)
biomedical informatics (MS, PhD, Certificate)
cell biology and molecular physiology (MS, PhD)
cellular and molecular pathology (MS, PhD)
clinical and translational science (PhD)
clinical research (MS, Certificate)
immunology (MS, PhD)
integrative molecular biology (PhD)
interdisciplinary biomedical sciences (PhD)
medical education (MS, Certificate)
medicine (MD, MS, PhD, Certificate)
molecular biophysics and structural biology (PhD)
molecular pharmacology (PhD)
molecular virology and microbiology (MS, PhD)
neurobiology (PhD)

School of Nursing
Programs in:
- acute care nurse practitioner (MSN)
- adult nurse practitioner (MSN)
- anesthesia nursing (MSN)
- family nurse practitioner (MSN)
- medical/surgical clinical nurse specialist (MSN)
- nursing (MSN, DNP, PhD)
- nursing administration (MSN)
- nursing education (MSN)
- nursing informatics (MSN)
- nursing practice (DNP)
- nursing research (MSN)
- pediatric nurse practitioner (MSN)
- psychiatric and mental health clinical nurse specialist (MSN)
- psychiatric primary care nurse practitioner (MSN)

School of Pharmacy
Dr. Patricia Dowley Kroboth, Dean
Programs in:
- pharmaceutical sciences (MS, PhD)
- pharmacy (Pharm D, MS, PhD)

School of Social Work
Dr. Larry E. Davis, Dean
Programs in:
- gerontology (Certificate)
- social work (MSW, PhD)

University Center for International Studies
Lawrence F. Feick, Director, University Center for International Studies
Programs in:
- African studies (Certificate)
- Asian studies (Certificate)
- European Union studies (Certificate)
- global studies (Certificate)
- Latin American studies (Certificate)
- Russian and East European studies (Certificate)
- West European studies (Certificate)

■ THE UNIVERSITY OF SCRANTON
Scranton, PA 18510
http://www.scranton.edu/

Independent-religious, coed, comprehensive institution. CGS member. *Graduate faculty:* 135 full-time (57 women), 68 part-time/adjunct (29 women). *Computer facilities:* Computer purchase and lease plans are available. 927 computers available on campus for general student use. A campuswide network can be accessed from student residence rooms and from off campus. Online class registration is available. *General application contact:* Joseph M. Roback, Director of Admissions, 570-941-4385.

College of Graduate and Continuing Education
Dr. W. Jeffrey Welsh, Dean
Programs in:
- accounting (MBA)
- adult health nursing (MSN)
- biochemistry (MA, MS)
- chemistry (MA, MS)
- clinical chemistry (MA, MS)
- community counseling (MS)
- curriculum and instruction (MA, MS)
- early childhood education (MA, MS)
- educational administration (MS)
- elementary education (MS)
- English as a second language (MS)
- family nurse practitioner (MSN, PMC)
- finance (MBA)
- general business administration (MBA)
- health administration (MHA)
- history (MA)
- human resources (MS)
- human resources administration (MS)
- human resources development (MS)
- international business (MBA)
- management information systems (MBA)
- marketing (MBA)
- nurse anesthesia (MSN, PMC)
- occupational therapy (MS)
- operations management (MBA)
- organizational leadership (MS)
- physical therapy (MPT, DPT)
- professional counseling (CAGS)
- reading education (MS)
- rehabilitation counseling (MS)
- school counseling (MS)
- secondary education (MS)
- software engineering (MS)
- special education (MS)
- theology (MA)

■ VILLANOVA UNIVERSITY
Villanova, PA 19085-1699
http://www.villanova.edu/

Independent-religious, coed, comprehensive institution. CGS member. *Graduate faculty:* 274. *Computer facilities:* Computer purchase and lease plans are available. 6,609 computers available on campus for general student use. A campuswide network can be accessed from student residence rooms and from off campus. Online class registration, learning management system, Web-based laundry reservation, electronic portfolios, data vaulting, calendar system, basketball ticket lottery, printing are available. *General application contact:* Dr. Gerald Long, Dean, Graduate School of Liberal Arts and Sciences, 610-519-7093.

College of Engineering
Dr. Gary A. Gabriele, Dean
Programs in:
- chemical engineering (MSChE)
- civil engineering (MSCE)
- communication systems engineering (Certificate)
- computer architectures (Certificate)
- computer engineering (MSCPE, Certificate)
- electric power systems (Certificate)
- electrical engineering (MSEE, Certificate)
- electro mechanical systems (Certificate)
- electro-mechanical systems (Certificate)
- engineering (MSCPE, MSChE, MSEE, MSME, MSTE, MSWREE, PhD, Certificate)
- high frequency systems (Certificate)
- intelligent systems (Certificate)
- machinery dynamics (Certificate)
- mechanical engineering (MSME)
- thermofluid systems (Certificate)
- transportation engineering (MSTE)
- water resources and environmental engineering (MSWREE)
- wireless and digital communications (Certificate)

College of Nursing
Dr. Marguerite K. Schlag, Assistant Dean and Director, Graduate Program
Programs in:
- adult nurse practitioner (MSN, Post Master's Certificate)
- geriatric nurse practitioner (MSN, Post Master's Certificate)
- health care administration (MSN)
- nurse anesthetist (MSN, Post Master's Certificate)
- nursing (PhD)
- nursing education (MSN, Post Master's Certificate)
- pediatric nurse practitioner (MSN, Post Master's Certificate)

Graduate School of Liberal Arts and Sciences
Dr. Gerald Long, Dean
Programs in:
- applied statistics (MS)
- biology (MA, MS)
- chemistry (MS)
- communication (MA)
- community counseling (MS)
- computer science (MS)
- counseling and human relations (MS)
- criminology, law and society (MA)
- educational leadership (MA)
- elementary school counseling (MS)
- elementary teacher education (MA)
- English (MA)
- higher education (MA)
- Hispanic studies (MA)
- history (MA)
- human resource development (MS)
- humanities and Augustinian tradition (MA)
- liberal arts and sciences (MA, MPA, MS, PhD)
- liberal studies (MA)
- mathematical sciences (MA)
- philosophy (PhD)
- political science (MA, MPA)
- psychology (MS)
- public administration (MPA)
- secondary school counseling (MS)
- secondary teacher education (MA)
- software engineering (MS)
- theatre (MA)
- theology (MA)

Villanova University (continued)

School of Law
Mark A. Sargent, Dean
Programs in:
- law (JD, LL M)
- tax (LL M)

Villanova School of Business
Simone L. Pollard, Assistant Dean of Graduate Business Programs
Programs in:
- accountancy (MAC)
- business (EMBA, MAC, MBA, MSF)
- corporate management (general) (MBA)
- executive business administration (EMBA)
- finance (MBA)
- international business (MBA)
- management information systems (MBA)
- marketing (MBA)

■ WAYNESBURG UNIVERSITY

Waynesburg, PA 15370-1222
http://www.waynesburg.edu/

Independent-religious, coed, comprehensive institution. *Computer facilities:* 150 computers available on campus for general student use. A campuswide network can be accessed from student residence rooms and from off campus. Online class registration is available. *General application contact:* Director, 412-854-3600.

Graduate and Professional Studies
Programs in:
- business (MBA)
- counseling psychology (MA)
- education (MAT)
- nursing (MSN)
- nursing practice (DNP)
- special education (M Ed)
- technology (M Ed)

■ WEST CHESTER UNIVERSITY OF PENNSYLVANIA

West Chester, PA 19383
http://www.wcupa.edu/

State-supported, coed, comprehensive institution. CGS member. *Computer facilities:* Computer purchase and lease plans are available. 1,200 computers available on campus for general student use. A campuswide network can be accessed from student residence rooms and from off campus. Online class registration is available. *Graduate expenses:* Tuition, state resident: full-time $6430; part-time $357 per credit. Tuition, nonresident: full-time $10,288; part-time $572 per credit. Required fees: $652.50; $50 per credit. $67 per semester. *General application contact:* Office of Graduate Studies, 610-436-2943.

Office of Graduate Studies
Dr. Janet Hickman, Interim Dean

College of Arts and Sciences
Dr. Lori Vermeulen, Dean
Programs in:
- applied statistics (MS, Certificate)
- arts and sciences (M Ed, MA, MS, MSA, Certificate, Teaching Certificate)
- biology (MS, Teaching Certificate)
- biology—thesis (MS)
- business ethics (Certificate)
- clinical chemistry (MS)
- clinical mental health (Certificate)
- clinical psychology (MA)
- communication studies (MA)
- computer science (MS, Certificate)
- computer security (Certificate)
- earth-space science (Teaching Certificate)
- English (MA, Teaching Certificate)
- English—non-thesis option (MA)
- French (M Ed, MA, Teaching Certificate)
- general psychology (MA)
- general science (Teaching Certificate)
- German (Teaching Certificate)
- gerontology (Certificate)
- healthcare ethics (Certificate)
- history (M Ed, MA)
- holocaust and genocide studies (MA, Certificate)
- industrial psychology (MA)
- information systems (Certificate)
- Latin (Teaching Certificate)
- leadership for women (MSA, Certificate)
- long term health care (MSA)
- mathematics (MA, Teaching Certificate)
- philosophy (MA)
- physical science: earth science (MA)
- social studies/history (Teaching Certificate)
- Spanish (M Ed, MA, Teaching Certificate)
- TESL (MA, Certificate)
- Web technology (Certificate)

College of Business and Public Affairs
Dr. Christopher Fiorentino, Dean
Programs in:
- administration (Certificate)
- business (Certificate)
- business administration: economics-finance (MBA)
- business administration: tech-electronic (MBA)
- business and public affairs (MA, MBA, MS, MSA, MSW, Certificate)
- criminal justice (MS)
- executive (MBA)
- general business (MBA)
- geographic technology (Certificate)
- geography (MA)
- human resource management (MSA, Certificate)
- individualized (MSA)
- management (MBA)
- non profit administration (Certificate)
- nonprofit administration (MSA)
- public administration (MSA)
- regional planning (MSA)
- social work (MSW)
- training and development (MSA)

College of Education
Dr. Joseph Malak, Dean
Programs in:
- autism (Certificate)
- counseling (Teaching Certificate)
- counseling and educational psychology (M Ed, MS, Certificate, Teaching Certificate)
- early childhood and special education (M Ed, Certificate, Teaching Certificate)
- early childhood education (M Ed, Teaching Certificate)
- educational research (MS)
- elementary education (M Ed, Teaching Certificate)
- elementary school counseling (M Ed)
- entrepreneurial education (Certificate)
- higher education counseling (MS)
- literacy (M Ed, Certificate, Teaching Certificate)
- professional and secondary education (M Ed, MS, Certificate, Teaching Certificate)
- professional counselor license preparation (Certificate)
- reading (M Ed, Teaching Certificate)
- secondary education (M Ed)
- secondary school counseling (M Ed)
- special education (M Ed, Teaching Certificate)
- teaching and learning with technology (Certificate)

College of Health Sciences
Dr. Donald E. Barr, Dean
Programs in:
- adapted physical education (Certificate)
- communicative disorders (MA)
- emergency preparedness (Certificate)
- exercise physiology (MS)
- health and physical education (Teaching Certificate)
- health care administration (Certificate)
- health sciences (M Ed, MA, MPH, MS, MSA, MSN, Certificate, Teaching Certificate)
- integrative health (Certificate)
- nursing (MSN)
- nursing education (MSN, Certificate)
- parish nursing (Certificate)
- physical education (MS)
- public health (MPH)
- school health (M Ed)
- school nursing (Teaching Certificate)
- speech correction (Teaching Certificate)
- sport and athletic administration (MSA)

College of Visual and Performing Arts
Dr. Timothy Blair, Dean
Programs in:
- 21st Century music education (Certificate)
- accompanying (MM)
- Kodaly methodology (Certificate)

music education (MM, Teaching Certificate)
music education-technology (MM)
music history (MA)
music technology (Certificate)
music: theory and composition (MM)
Orff-Schulwerk (Certificate)
performance (MM)
piano pedagogy (MM, Certificate)
visual and performing arts (MA, MM, Certificate, Teaching Certificate)

■ WIDENER UNIVERSITY
Chester, PA 19013-5792
http://www.widener.edu/

Independent, coed, comprehensive institution. CGS member. *Graduate faculty:* 194 full-time (97 women), 152 part-time/adjunct (61 women). *Computer facilities:* 345 computers available on campus for general student use. A campuswide network can be accessed from student residence rooms and from off campus. Online class registration is available. *General application contact:* Dr. Roberta Nolan, Assistant to Associate Provost for Graduate Studies, 610-499-4125.

College of Arts and Sciences
Dr. Matthew Poslusny, Dean
Programs in:
arts and sciences (MA, MPA)
criminal justice (MA)
liberal studies (MA)
public administration (MPA)

Graduate Programs in Engineering
Nora J. Kogut, Assistant Dean
Programs in:
chemical engineering (M Eng)
civil engineering (M Eng)
computer and software engineering (M Eng)
engineering management (M Eng)
management and technology (MSMT)
mechanical engineering (M Eng)
telecommunications engineering (M Eng)

School of Business Administration
Dr. Savas Ozatalay, Dean
Programs in:
accounting information systems (MS)
business administration (MBA, MHA, MHR, MS)
health and medical services administration (MBA, MHA)
human resource management (MHR, MS)
taxation (MS)

School of Human Service Professions
Dr. Stephen C. Wilhite, Dean
Program in:
human service professions (M Ed, MS, MSW, DPT, Ed D, PhD, Psy D)

Center for Education
Dr. Michael W. LeDoux, Associate Dean
Programs in:
adult education (M Ed)
counseling in higher education (M Ed)
counselor education (M Ed)
early childhood education (M Ed)
educational foundations (M Ed)
educational leadership (M Ed)
educational psychology (M Ed)
elementary education (M Ed)
English and language arts (M Ed)
health education (M Ed)
higher education leadership (Ed D)
home and school visitor (M Ed)
human sexuality (M Ed)
mathematics education (M Ed)
middle school education (M Ed)
principalship (M Ed)
reading and language arts (Ed D)
reading education (M Ed)
school administration (Ed D)
science education (M Ed)
social studies education (M Ed)
special education (M Ed)
technology education (M Ed)

Center for Social Work Education
Dr. Paula T. Silver, Associate Dean and Director
Program in:
social work education (MSW, PhD)

Institute for Graduate Clinical Psychology
Dr. Virginia Brabender, Associate Dean/Director
Program in:
clinical psychology (Psy D)

Institute for Physical Therapy Education
Dr. Robin L. Dole, Associate Dean and Director
Program in:
physical therapy education (MS, DPT)

School of Law at Harrisburg
Linda L. Ammons, Dean
Program in:
law (JD)

School of Law at Wilmington
Linda L. Ammons, Dean
Programs in:
corporate law and finance (LL M)
health law (LL M, MJ, D Law)
juridical science (SJD)
law (JD)

School of Nursing
Dr. Mary B. Walker, Assistant Dean for Graduate Studies
Program in:
nursing (MSN, DN Sc, PhD, PMC)

■ WILKES UNIVERSITY
Wilkes-Barre, PA 18766-0002
http://www.wilkes.edu/

Independent, coed, comprehensive institution. CGS member. *Computer facilities:* Computer purchase and lease plans are available. 570 computers available on campus for general student use. A campuswide network can be accessed from student residence rooms and from off campus. Online class registration is available. *General application contact:* Kathleen Houlihan, Director of Graduate Studies, 570-408-3235.

College of Graduate and Professional Studies
Dr. Michael Speziale, Dean

College of Arts, Humanities and Social Sciences
Dr. Darin Fields, Dean
Programs in:
arts, humanities and social sciences (MA, MFA)
creative writing (MA, MFA)

College of Science and Engineering
Dr. Dale Bruns, Dean
Programs in:
electrical engineering (MSEE)
engineering operations and strategy (MS)
mathematics (MS, MS Ed)
science and engineering (MS, MS Ed, MSEE)

Jay S. Sidhu School of Business and Leadership
Dr. Paul Browne, Dean
Programs in:
accounting (MBA)
entrepreneurship (MBA)
finance (MBA)
human resource management (MBA)
international business (MBA)
management (MBA)
marketing (MBA)

Nesbitt College of Pharmacy and Nursing
Dr. Bernard Graham, Dean
Programs in:
nursing (MSN)
pharmacy (Pharm D)
pharmacy and nursing (Pharm D, MSN)

School of Education
Dr. Michael Speziale, Dean
Programs in:
classroom technology (MS Ed)
educational computing (MS Ed)
educational development and strategies (MS Ed)
educational leadership (MS Ed)
educational technology (Ed D)
elementary education (MS Ed)
higher education administration (Ed D)
instructional technology (MS Ed)
K-12 administration (Ed D)
online teaching (MS Ed)
school business leadership (MS Ed)
secondary education (MS Ed)
special education (MS Ed)

Puerto Rico

■ BAYAMÓN CENTRAL UNIVERSITY

Bayamón, PR 00960-1725

http://www.ucb.edu.pr/

Independent-religious, coed, comprehensive institution. *Computer facilities:* A campuswide network can be accessed. *General application contact:* Director of Admissions, 787-786-3030 Ext. 2100.

Graduate Programs

Programs in:
- accounting (MBA)
- administration and supervision (MA Ed)
- commercial education (MA Ed)
- education of the autistic (MA Ed)
- elementary education (K–3) (MA Ed)
- elementary education (K–6) (MA Ed)
- finance (MBA)
- general business (MBA)
- guidance and counseling (MA Ed)
- management (MBA)
- management of security and protection (MBA)
- marketing (MBA)
- organizational psychology (MA)
- pre-elementary teacher (MA Ed)
- psychology (MA)
- rehabilitation counseling (MA Ed)
- special education (MA Ed)

■ CARLOS ALBIZU UNIVERSITY

San Juan, PR 00901

http://www.albizu.edu/

Independent, coed, primarily women, university. *Graduate faculty:* 22 full-time (11 women), 52 part-time/adjunct (38 women). *Computer facilities:* 55 computers available on campus for general student use. A campuswide network can be accessed. *Graduate expenses:* Tuition: full-time $6912; part-time $288 per credit. Required fees: $512 per semester. Tuition and fees vary according to degree level. *General application contact:* Carlos Rodriguez, Director of Students Affairs, 787-725-6500 Ext. 21.

Graduate Programs

Dr. Jose J. Cabiya, Chancellor

Programs in:
- clinical psychology (MS, PhD, Psy D)
- general psychology (PhD)
- industrial/organizational psychology (MS, PhD)
- speech and language pathology (MS)

■ INTER AMERICAN UNIVERSITY OF PUERTO RICO, METROPOLITAN CAMPUS

San Juan, PR 00919-1293

http://metro.inter.edu/

Independent, coed, comprehensive institution. CGS member. *Computer facilities:* 400 computers available on campus for general student use. A campuswide network can be accessed from student residence rooms and from off campus. Online class registration is available. *General application contact:* Information Contact, 787-765-1270.

Graduate Programs

Programs in:
- accounting (MBA)
- administration of clinical laboratories (MS)
- advanced clinical services (MSW)
- advanced social work administration (MSW)
- American history (PhD)
- Christian education (PhD)
- clinical services (MSW)
- commerical education (MA)
- counseling psychology (MA, PhD)
- criminal justice (MA)
- curriculum and instruction (Ed D)
- educational administration (Ed D)
- educational computing (MA)
- elementary education (MA)
- English (MA)
- environmental evaluation and protection (MS)
- finance (MBA)
- general business (MBA)
- guidance and counseling (MA, Ed D)
- higher education administration (MA)
- history (MA, PhD)
- human resources (MBA)
- industrial management (MBA)
- industrial/organizational psychology (MA, PhD)
- international business (MIB)
- labor relations (MA)
- management information systems (MBA)
- marketing (MBA)
- molecular microbiology (MS)
- music education (MM)
- occupational education (MA)
- open information systems (MS)
- pastoral theology (PhD)
- school psychology (MA, PhD)
- social work administration (MSW)
- Spanish (MA)
- special education (MA)
- special education administration (Ed D)
- teaching English as a second language (MA)
- teaching of math (MA)
- teaching of physical education (MA)
- teaching of science (MA)
- theological studies (PhD)
- training and sport performance (MA)
- women's wtudies (MA)

■ INTER AMERICAN UNIVERSITY OF PUERTO RICO, SAN GERMÁN CAMPUS

San Germán, PR 00683-5008

http://www.sg.inter.edu/

Independent, coed, university. *Computer facilities:* 1,800 computers available on campus for general student use. A campuswide network can be accessed from student residence rooms. Online class registration is available. *General application contact:* Director of Graduate Studies Center, 787-264-1912 Ext. 7357.

Graduate Studies Center

Programs in:
- accounting (MBA)
- administration and supervision (MA, Ed D)
- applied mathematics (MA)
- business education (MA)
- ceramics (MFA)
- counseling psychology (MA, PhD)
- curriculum and instruction (Ed D)
- drawing (MFA)
- elementary education (MA)
- engraving (MFA)
- environmental biology (MS)
- environmental chemistry (MS)
- finance (MBA)
- financial accounting (M Acc)
- guidance and counseling (MA, Ed D)
- human resources (PhD)
- human resources management (MBA)
- industrial management (MBA)
- international business (PhD)
- interregional and international business (PhD)
- library and information sciences (MLS)
- management information systems (MBA)
- managerial accounting (M Acc)
- marketing management (MBA)
- music education (MA)
- painting (MFA)
- photography (MFA)
- physical education and scientific analysis of human body movement (MA)
- school psychology (MA, PhD)
- science education (MA)
- sculpture (MFA)
- special education (MA)
- teaching English as a second language (MA)
- water analysis (MS)

■ PONTIFICAL CATHOLIC UNIVERSITY OF PUERTO RICO

Ponce, PR 00717-0777

http://www.pucpr.edu/

Independent-religious, coed, university. *Computer facilities:* 419 computers available on campus for general student use. A campuswide network can be accessed from off campus. *General application contact:* Director of Admissions, 787-841-2000 Ext. 1000.

College of Arts and Humanities

Programs in:
- arts and humanities (MA, Professional Certificate)
- grammar and writing (Professional Certificate)
- Hispanic studies (MA)
- history (MA)
- theology and philosophy (M Div)

College of Business Administration

Programs in:
- accounting (MBA)
- business administration (MBA, PhD)
- finance (MBA)
- general business (MBA)
- human resources (MBA)
- international business (MBA)
- management (MBA)
- management information systems (MBA)
- marketing (MBA)
- office administration (MBA, MS)

College of Education

Programs in:
- business teacher education (M Ed, PhD)
- counselor education (M Ed)
- curriculum and instruction (M Ed, PhD)
- education (M Ed, MA Ed, MRE, PhD)
- education-general (M Ed, MA Ed)
- educational leadership and administration (PhD)
- educational psychology (M Ed)
- English as a second language (M Ed)

College of Sciences

Programs in:
- chemistry (MS)
- environmental sciences (MS)
- medical technology (Certificate)
- medical-surgical nursing (MS)
- mental health and psychiatric nursing (MS)
- sciences (MS, Certificate)

Institute of Graduate Studies in Behavioral Science and Community Affairs

Programs in:
- clinical psychology (MA, MS, PhD, Psy D)
- clinical social work (MSW)
- criminology (MA)
- industrial psychology (MS, PhD)
- psychology (PhD)
- public administration (MA)
- vocational rehabilitation counseling (MSS)

School of Law

Program in:
- law (JD)

■ UNIVERSIDAD DEL TURABO
Gurabo, PR 00778-3030
http://www.suagm.edu/ut/

Independent, coed, university. CGS member. *Computer facilities:* A campuswide network can be accessed from off campus. *General application contact:* Director of Admissions and Financial Aid, 787-743-7979 Ext. 4352.

Graduate Programs

Programs in:
- administration of school libraries (M Ed)
- athletic training (MPE)
- bilingual education (M Ed)
- coaching (MPE)
- curriculum and instruction and appropriate environment (D Ed)
- curriculum and teaching (M Ed)
- education administration and supervision (M Ed)
- educational administration (M Ed)
- educational leadership (D Ed)
- environmental biology (DS)
- environmental chemistry (DS)
- environmental sciences (MS, DS)
- guidance counseling (M Ed)
- library service and information technology (M Ed)
- pollution management (DS)
- special education (M Ed)
- teaching at primary level (M Ed)
- teaching English as a second language (M Ed)
- teaching of fine arts (M Ed)
- wellness (MPE)

School in Business Administration

Programs in:
- accounting (MBA)
- business administration (MBA, DBA)
- human resources (MBA)
- logistics and materials management (MBA)
- management (MBA)
- management of information systems (MBA, DBA)
- marketing (MBA)
- materials management (MBA)
- office systems management (MBA)
- project management (MBA)
- quality management (MBA)

School of Engineering

Programs in:
- engineering (MS Eng)
- telecommunication and network administration (MS Eng)

School of Health Sciences

Programs in:
- clinical nurse leader (MSN)
- family nurse practitioner (MSN, Advanced Certificate)
- family nurse practitioner—adult nursing (MSN)
- health sciences (MS, MSN, ND, Advanced Certificate)
- naturopathiy (ND)
- speech and language pathology (MS)

School of Social Sciences and Humanities

Programs in:
- arts administration (MA)
- counseling psychology (MA, DS)
- criminal justice studies (MA)
- forensic science (MA)
- human services administration (MA)
- social sciences and humanities (MA, MSS)

■ UNIVERSIDAD METROPOLITANA
San Juan, PR 00928-1150
http://www.suagm.edu/umet/

Independent, coed, comprehensive institution. *Computer facilities:* 50 computers available on campus for general student use. A campuswide network can be accessed from off campus. Online class registration is available. *General application contact:* Director of Admissions and Financial Aid, 787-766-1717 Ext. 6587.

Graduate Programs in Education

Programs in:
- administration and supervision (M Ed)
- curriculum and teaching (M Ed)
- educational administration and supervision (M Ed)
- environmental education (M Ed)
- fitness management (M Ed)
- managing leisure services (M Ed)
- pre-school centers administration (M Ed)
- pre-school education (M Ed)
- special education (M Ed)
- teaching of physical education (M Ed)

School of Business Administration

Programs in:
- accounting (MBA)
- finance (MBA)
- human resources management (MBA)
- international business (MBA)
- management (MBA)
- management information systems (MBA)
- marketing (MBA)
- public accounting (Certificate)

School of Environmental Affairs

Programs in:
- conservation and management of natural resources (MSEM)
- environmental education (MA)
- environmental planning (MSEM)
- environmental risk and assessment management (MSEM)

School of Social Sciences, Humanities and Communications

Programs in:
- communications (MA)
- interdisciplinary Puerto Rican studies (MA)

■ UNIVERSITY OF PUERTO RICO, MAYAGÜEZ CAMPUS

Mayagüez, PR 00681-9000

http://www.uprm.edu

Commonwealth-supported, coed, university. CGS member. *Computer facilities:* 1,066 computers available on campus for general student use. A campuswide network can be accessed from off campus. Online class registration is available. *General application contact:* Student Affairs Official, 787-265-3809.

Graduate Studies

College of Agricultural Sciences
Programs in:
agricultural economics (MS)
agricultural education (MS)
agricultural extension (MS)
agricultural sciences (MS)
agronomy (MS)
cattle industry (MS)
crop protection (MS)
food science and technology (MS)
horticulture (MS)
soils (MS)

College of Arts and Sciences
Programs in:
applied mathematics (MS)
arts and sciences (MA, MS, PhD)
biology (MS)
chemistry (MS, PhD)
computational sciences (MS)
English education (MA)
geology (MS)
Hispanic studies (MA)
marine sciences (MS, PhD)
physics (MS)
pure mathematics (MS)
statistics (MS)

College of Business Administration
Programs in:
business administration (MBA)
finance (MBA)
human resources (MBA)
industrial management (MBA)

College of Engineering
Programs in:
chemical engineering (ME, MS, PhD)
civil engineering (ME, MS, PhD)
computer engineering (ME, MS)
computing information science and engineering (PhD)
electrical engineering (ME, MS)
engineering (ME, MS, PhD)
industrial engineering (MS)
management systems (MS)
mechanical engineering (ME, MS)

■ UNIVERSITY OF PUERTO RICO, RÍO PIEDRAS

San Juan, PR 00931-3300

http://www.uprrp.edu/

Commonwealth-supported, coed, university. CGS member. *Computer facilities:* 170 computers available on campus for general student use. A campuswide network can be accessed from student residence rooms. Online class registration is available. *General application contact:* Admission Office Director, 787-764-0000 Ext. 5653.

College of Business Administration
Programs in:
accounting (MBA)
finance (MBA, PhD)
general business (MBA)
human resources management (MBA)
international trade and business (MBA, PhD)
marketing (MBA)
operations management (MBA)
quantitative methods (MBA)

College of Education
Programs in:
biology education (M Ed)
chemistry education (M Ed)
child education (M Ed)
curriculum and teaching (Ed D)
education (M Ed, MS, Ed D)
educational research and evaluation (M Ed)
exercise sciences (MS)
family ecology and nutrition (M Ed)
guidance and counseling (M Ed, Ed D)
history education (M Ed)
mathematics education (M Ed)
physics education (M Ed)
school administration and supervision (M Ed, Ed D)
Spanish education (M Ed)
special education (M Ed)
teaching English as a second language (M Ed)

College of Humanities
Programs in:
Caribbean history (PhD)
Caribbean linguistics (PhD)
Caribbean literature (PhD)
comparative literature (MA)
English (MA)
Hispanic studies (MA)
history (MA)
humanities (MA, PhD, Certificate)
Latin American literature (PhD)
linguistics (MA)
philosophy (MA)
Puerto Rican history (PhD)
Puerto Rican literature (PhD)
Spanish linguistics (PhD)
Spanish literature (PhD)
translation (MA, Certificate)

College of Natural Sciences
Programs in:
chemical physics (PhD)
chemistry (MS, PhD)
ecology/systematics (MS, PhD)
environmental sciences (MS)
evolution/genetics (MS, PhD)
mathematics (MS, PhD)
molecular/cellular biology (MS, PhD)
natural sciences (MS, PhD)
neuroscience (MS, PhD)
physics (MS)

College of Social Sciences
Programs in:
clinical psychology (MA)
economics (MA)
industrial organizational psychology (MA)
investigative academic psychology (MA)
psychology (PhD)
social sciences (MA, MPA, MRC, MSW, PhD)
social-community psychology (MA)
sociology (MA)

Graduate School of Rehabilitation Counseling
Program in:
rehabilitation counseling (MRC)

Graduate School of Social Work
Program in:
social work (MSW, PhD)

School of Public Administration
Program in:
public administration (MPA)

Graduate School of Information Sciences and Technologies
Programs in:
administration of academic libraries (PMC)
administration of public libraries (PMC)
administration of special libraries (PMC)
consultant in information services (PMC)
documents and files administration (Post-Graduate Certificate)
electronic information resources analyst (Post-Graduate Certificate)
librarianship (Post-Graduate Certificate)
librarianship and information services (MLS)
master librarian (Post-Graduate Certificate)
specialist in legal information (PMC)

Graduate School of Planning
Program in:
planning (MP)

School of Architecture
Program in:
architecture (M Arch)

School of Communication
Programs in:
communication (MA)
communication theory and research (MA)
journalism (MA)

School of Law
Program in:
law (JD, LL M)

Rhode Island

■ BROWN UNIVERSITY

Providence, RI 02912

http://www.brown.edu/

Independent, coed, university. CGS member. *Computer facilities:* Computer purchase and lease plans are available. 500 computers available on campus for general student use. A campuswide network can be accessed from student residence rooms and from off campus. Online class registration is available. *General application contact:* Admission Office, 401-863-2600.

Graduate School

Programs in:
- acting and directing (MFA)
- American civilization (MA, PhD)
- ancient Judaism (PhD)
- anthropology (AM, PhD)
- behavioral neuroscience (PhD)
- biochemistry (PhD)
- chemistry (AM, Sc M, PhD)
- classics (MA, PhD)
- cognitive processes (PhD)
- cognitive science (Sc M, PhD)
- comparative literature (PhD)
- computer science (Sc M, PhD)
- early Christianity (PhD)
- economics (PhD)
- Egyptology (AM, PhD)
- electronic music and multimedia (PhD)
- elementary education 1-6 (MAT)
- ethnomusicology (PhD)
- French studies (PhD)
- geological sciences (MA, Sc M, PhD)
- German (PhD)
- Hispanic studies (MA, PhD)
- history (MA, PhD)
- history of art and architecture (MA, PhD)
- Italian studies (PhD)
- linguistics (AM, PhD)
- literatures and cultures in English (MA, PhD)
- mathematics (M Sc, MA, PhD)
- museum studies (AM)
- neuroscience (PhD)
- nonfiction writing (MFA)
- philosophy (MA, PhD)
- physics (Sc M, PhD)
- political science (PhD)
- public humanities (MA)
- religion and critical thought (PhD)
- religion in the ancient Mediterranean (PhD)
- religion, culture, and comparison (PhD)
- Russian language and literature (AM)
- secondary biology (MAT)
- secondary English (MAT)
- secondary history/social studies (MAT)
- sensation and perception (PhD)
- Slavic languages (AM)
- Slavic studies (PhD)
- social/developmental (PhD)
- sociology (MA, PhD)
- teaching (MAT)
- theatre and performance studies (PhD)
- theatre arts (AM)
- urban education policy (AM)

A. Alfred Taubman Center for Public Policy and American Institutions

Program in:
- public policy and American institutions (MPA, MPP)

Center for Environmental Studies

Dr. Phil Brown, Interim Director

Program in:
- environmental studies (AM)

Center for Portuguese and Brazilian Studies

Programs in:
- Brazilian studies (AM)
- Portuguese and Brazilian studies (AM, PhD)
- Portuguese Bilingual Education and Cross-Cultural Studies (AM)

Division of Applied Mathematics

Program in:
- applied mathematics (Sc M, PhD)

Division of Biology and Medicine

Programs in:
- artificial organs, biomaterials, and cell technology (MA, Sc M, PhD)
- biochemistry (M Med Sc, Sc M, PhD)
- biology (MA, PhD)
- biology and medicine (M Med Sc, MA, MPH, MS, Sc M, PhD)
- biomedical engineering (MS, PhD)
- biostatistics (MS, PhD)
- cancer biology (PhD)
- cell biology (M Med Sc, Sc M, PhD)
- developmental biology (M Med Sc, Sc M, PhD)
- ecology and evolutionary biology (PhD)
- epidemiology (MS, PhD)
- health services research (MS, PhD)
- immunology (M Med Sc, Sc M, PhD)
- immunology and infection (PhD)
- medical science (PhD)
- molecular microbiology (M Med Sc, Sc M, PhD)
- molecular pharmacology and physiology (MA, Sc M, PhD)
- neuroscience (PhD)
- pathobiology (Sc M)
- public health (MPH)
- statistical science (MS, PhD)
- toxicology and environmental pathology (PhD)

Division of Engineering

Programs in:
- biomedical engineering (Sc M, PhD)
- electrical sciences and computer engineering (Sc M, PhD)
- fluid, thermal and chemical processes (Sc M, PhD)
- materials science and engineering (Sc M, PhD)
- mechanics of solids (Sc M, PhD)

Joukowsky Institute for Archaeology and the Ancient World

Program in:
- archaeology and the ancient world (PhD)

National Institutes of Health Sponsored Programs

Program in:
- neuroscience (PhD)

Program in Medicine

Program in:
- medicine (MD)

■ BRYANT UNIVERSITY

Smithfield, RI 02917-1284

http://www.bryant.edu/

Independent, coed, comprehensive institution. *Graduate faculty:* 38 full-time (9 women), 2 part-time/adjunct (0 women). *Computer facilities:* Computer purchase and lease plans are available. 467 computers available on campus for general student use. A campuswide network can be accessed from student residence rooms and from off campus. Online class registration, e-mail, online library, wireless network, student Web hosts are available. *Graduate expenses:* Tuition: part-time $26,928 per degree program. One-time fee: $750 part-time. *General application contact:* Kristopher T. Sullivan, Assistant Dean of the Graduate School, 401-232-6230.

Graduate School of Business

Dr. Jack W. Trifts, Dean of the College of Business

Programs in:
- business administration (MBA)
- general business (MBA)
- professional accountancy (MPAC)
- taxation (MST)

■ JOHNSON & WALES UNIVERSITY

Providence, RI 02903-3703

http://www.jwu.edu/

Independent, coed, comprehensive institution. *Computer facilities:* 400 computers available on campus for general student use. A campuswide network can be accessed from student residence rooms and from off campus. Online class registration is available. *General application contact:* Director of Graduate Admissions, 401-598-1015.

The Alan Shawn Feinstein Graduate School

Programs in:
- accounting (MBA)
- business education and secondary special education (MAT)
- elementary education and elementary special education (MAT)

Johnson & Wales University (continued)
elementary education and elementary/ secondary special education (MAT)
elementary education and secondary special education (MAT)
event leadership (MBA)
financial management (MBA)
food service education and secondary special education (MAT)
higher education (Ed D)
international trade (MBA)
K-12 (Ed D)
marketing (MBA)
organizational leadership (MBA)
teaching and learning (M Ed)

■ PROVIDENCE COLLEGE
Providence, RI 02918
http://www.providence.edu/

Independent-religious, coed, comprehensive institution. *Graduate faculty:* 42 full-time (13 women), 53 part-time/adjunct (27 women). *Computer facilities:* Computer purchase and lease plans are available. 278 computers available on campus for general student use. A campuswide network can be accessed from student residence rooms and from off campus. Online class registration is available. *Graduate expenses:* Tuition: part-time $333 per credit hour. One-time fee: $170 part-time. Tuition and fees vary according to program. *General application contact:* Dr. Thomas F. Flaherty, Dean, Graduate Studies, 401-865-2247.

Graduate Studies
Dr. Thomas F. Flaherty, Dean, Graduate Studies
Programs in:
administration (M Ed)
American history (MA)
biblical studies (MABS)
counseling (M Ed)
early Christian studies (MA Th)
elementary administration (M Ed)
elementary special education (M Ed)
European history (MA)
literacy (M Ed)
mathematics (MAT)
secondary administration (M Ed)
special education (M Ed)
St. Thomas Aquinas studies (MA Th, MTS)

School of Business
Dr. MaryJane Lenon, Director, MBA Program
Programs in:
accountancy (MBA)
economics (MBA)
entrepreneurship (MBA)
finance (MBA)
international business (MBA)
management (MBA)
marketing (MBA)
not-for-profit (MBA)
quantitative (MBA)

■ RHODE ISLAND COLLEGE
Providence, RI 02908-1991
http://www.ric.edu/

State-supported, coed, comprehensive institution. *Graduate faculty:* 128 full-time (62 women), 50 part-time/adjunct (35 women). *Computer facilities:* Computer purchase and lease plans are available. 675 computers available on campus for general student use. A campuswide network can be accessed from student residence rooms and from off campus. Online class registration is available. *Graduate expenses:* Tuition, state resident: full-time $6816; part-time $284 per credit hour. Tuition, nonresident: full-time $13,920; part-time $580 per credit hour. Required fees: $454; $16 per credit. $68 per term. *General application contact:* Graduate Studies, 401-456-8700.

School of Graduate Studies

Faculty of Arts and Sciences
Dr. Earl Simson, Interim Dean
Programs in:
art education (MA, MAT)
arts and sciences (MA, MAT, MFA, MM Ed, MPA)
biology (MA)
creative writing (MA)
English (MA)
history (MA)
mathematics (MA)
media studies (MA)
music education (MAT, MM Ed)
psychology (MA)
public administration (MPA)
theatre (MFA)

Feinstein School of Education and Human Development
Dr. Roger Eldridge, Interim Dean
Programs in:
counseling (MA)
early childhood education (M Ed)
education (PhD)
education and human development (M Ed, MA, MAT, PhD, CAGS, CGS)
educational leadership (M Ed)
elementary education (M Ed, MAT)
English (MAT)
French (MAT)
health education (M Ed)
history (MAT)
math (MAT)
physical education (CGS)
reading (M Ed)
school administration (M Ed)
school counseling (CAGS)
secondary education (MAT)
Spanish (MAT)
special education (M Ed, CAGS)
teaching English as a second language (M Ed)
technology education (M Ed)

School of Management
David Blanchette, Interim Dean
Programs in:
accounting (MP Ac)
financial planning (CGS)
management (MP Ac, CGS)

School of Nursing
Dr. Jane Williams, Dean
Program in:
nursing (MSN)

School of Social Work
Sue Pearlmutter, Interim Dean
Program in:
social work (MSW)

■ ROGER WILLIAMS UNIVERSITY
Bristol, RI 02809
http://www.rwu.edu/

Independent, coed, comprehensive institution. *Graduate faculty:* 34 full-time (15 women), 30 part-time/adjunct (8 women). *Computer facilities:* 410 computers available on campus for general student use. A campuswide network can be accessed from student residence rooms and from off campus. Online class registration is available. *Graduate expenses:* Tuition: full-time $33,450; part-time $1251 per credit hour. Required fees: $570. Tuition and fees vary according to class time, program and reciprocity agreements. *General application contact:* Lori Vales, Graduate Admission Coordinator, 401-254-6200.

Feinstein College of Arts and Sciences
Dean Robert Cole, Dean
Programs in:
arts and sciences (MA, MPA)
forensic psychology (MA)
public administration (MPA)

School of Architecture, Art and Historic Preservation
Dean Stephen White, Dean
Program in:
architecture (M Arch)

School of Education
Dr. Mieko Kamii, Dean of the School of Education
Programs in:
education (MA, MAT)
elementary education (MAT)
literacy (MA)

School of Engineering, Computing and Construction Management
Program in:
construction management (MSCM)

School of Justice Studies
Dr. Stephanie Manzi, Dean
Program in:
criminal justice (MS)

School of Law
Program in:
law (JD)

■ SALVE REGINA UNIVERSITY

Newport, RI 02840-4192

http://www.salve.edu/

Independent-religious, coed, comprehensive institution. *Graduate faculty:* 19 full-time (9 women), 47 part-time/adjunct (19 women). *Computer facilities:* Computer purchase and lease plans are available. 163 computers available on campus for general student use. A campuswide network can be accessed from student residence rooms and from off campus. Online class registration is available. *Graduate expenses:* Tuition: part-time $395 per credit. Required fees: $40 per term. Tuition and fees vary according to degree level. *General application contact:* Kelly Alverson, Graduate Admissions Counselor, 401-341-2153.

Graduate Studies

Dr. Thomas M. Sabbagh, Dean of Graduate Studies and Continuing Education

Programs in:
- business administration (MBA)
- business studies (Certificate)
- expressive and creative arts (CAGS)
- healthcare administration and management (MS, Certificate)
- holistic counseling (MA)
- holistic leadership (MA, CAGS)
- homeland security (Certificate)
- human resources management (Certificate)
- humanities (MA, PhD, CAGS)
- international relations (MA, Certificate)
- justice and homeland security (MS)
- law enforcement leadership (MS)
- management (Certificate)
- mental health (CAGS)
- mental health counseling (CAGS)
- organizational development (Certificate)
- rehabilitation counseling (MA)

■ UNIVERSITY OF RHODE ISLAND

Kingston, RI 02881

http://www.uri.edu

State-supported, coed, university. CGS member. *Computer facilities:* Computer purchase and lease plans are available. 552 computers available on campus for general student use. A campuswide network can be accessed from student residence rooms and from off campus. Online class registration is available. *Graduate expenses:* Tuition, state resident: full-time $8024; part-time $446 per credit. Tuition, nonresident: full-time $21,046; part-time $1169 per credit. Required fees: $1056; $26 per credit. $30 per semester. One-time fee: $95 part-time. *General application contact:* Harold D. Bibb, Associate Dean of the Graduate School, 401-874-2262.

Graduate School

Harold Bibb, Associate Dean of the Graduate School

College of Arts and Sciences

Winifed Brownell, Dean

Programs in:
- applied mathematical sciences (MS, PhD)
- applied mathematics (PhD)
- arts and sciences (MA, MLIS, MM, MPA, MS, PhD, Certificate, Graduate Certificate)
- behavioral science (PhD)
- chemistry (MS, PhD)
- clinical psychology (MA, PhD)
- communication studies (MA)
- computer science (MS, PhD)
- digital forensics (Graduate Certificate)
- English (MA, PhD)
- history (MA)
- library and information studies (MLIS)
- mathematics (MS, PhD)
- music (MM)
- physics (MS, PhD)
- political science (MA)
- public policy and administration (MA, MPA, Certificate)
- school psychology (MS, PhD)
- Spanish (MA)
- statistics (MS)

College of Business Administration

Mark Higgins, Dean

Programs in:
- accounting (MS)
- business administration (PhD)
- finance (MBA)
- finance and insurance (PhD)
- international business (MBA)
- international sports management (MBA)
- management (MBA)
- management science (MBA)
- management science and information systems (PhD)
- marketing (MBA, PhD)

College of Engineering

Dr. Raymond Wright, Interim Dean

Programs in:
- biomedical engineering (MS, PhD)
- chemical engineering (MS, PhD)
- computer engineering (MS, PhD)
- design/systems (MS, PhD)
- electrical engineering (MS, PhD)
- engineering (MS, MSCE, PhD)
- environmental engineering (MSCE)
- fluid mechanics (MS, PhD)
- geotechnical engineering (MSCE, PhD)
- industrial and manufacturing engineering (PhD)
- manufacturing systems engineering (MS)
- ocean engineering (MS, PhD)
- solid mechanics (MS, PhD)
- structural engineering (MS, PhD)
- thermal sciences (MS, PhD)
- transportation engineering (MSCE)

College of Human Science and Services

Dr. W. Lynn McKinney, Dean

Programs in:
- adapted physical education (MS)
- adult education (MA)
- audiology (Au D)
- college student personnel (MS)
- cultural studies of sport and physical culture (MS)
- education (PhD)
- elementary education (MA)
- exercise science (MS)
- human development and family studies (MS)
- human science and services (MA, MM, MS, Au D, DPT, PhD)
- marriage and family therapy (MS)
- music education (MM)
- physical education pedagogy (MS)
- physical therapy (DPT)
- psychosocial/behavioral aspects of physical activity (MS)
- reading education (MA)
- secondary education (MA)
- speech-language pathology (MS)
- textiles, fashion merchandising and design (MS)

College of Nursing

Dr. Dayle Joseph, Dean

Programs in:
- administration (MS)
- clinical nurse leader (MS)
- clinical specialist in gerontology (MS)
- clinical specialist in psychiatric/mental health (MS)
- family nurse practitioner (MS)
- gerontological nurse practitioner (MS)
- nursing (PhD)
- nursing education (MS)

College of Pharmacy

Dr. Ronald Jordan, Interim Dean

Programs in:
- biomedical and pharmaceutical sciences (MS, PhD)
- medicinal chemistry and pharmacognosy (MS, PhD)
- pharmaceutical sciences (MS, PhD)
- pharmaceutics and pharmacokinetics (MS, PhD)
- pharmacology and toxicology (MS, PhD)
- pharmacy (Pharm D, MS, PhD)
- pharmacy practice (MS, PhD)

College of the Environment and Life Sciences

Dr. Jeffrey Seemann, Dean

Programs in:
- animal health and disease (MS)
- animal science (MS)
- aquaculture (MS)
- aquatic pathology (MS)
- biochemistry (MS, PhD)
- biological sciences (MS, PhD)
- biotechnology (MS)
- clinical laboratory science (MS)
- clinical laboratory sciences (MS)
- cytopathology (MS)
- entomology (MS, PhD)
- environment and life sciences (MA, MESM, MMA, MS, PhD)

University of Rhode Island (continued)
environmental and natural resource economics (MS, PhD)
environmental science and management (MESM)
environmental sciences (MS, PhD)
fisheries (MS)
food science (MS, PhD)
marine affairs (MA, MMA, PhD)
microbiology (MS, PhD)
molecular genetics (MS, PhD)
nutrition (MS, PhD)
plant sciences (MS, PhD)

Graduate School of Oceanography
Dr. David Farmer, Dean
Program in:
oceanography (MO, MS, PhD)

Labor Research Center
Dr. Richard Scholl, Director
Program in:
labor relations and human resources (MS)

South Carolina

■ BOB JONES UNIVERSITY
Greenville, SC 29614
http://www.bju.edu/

Independent-religious, coed, university. *Computer facilities:* Computer purchase and lease plans are available. 450 computers available on campus for general student use. A campuswide network can be accessed from student residence rooms and from off campus. Online class registration is available.

■ CHARLESTON SOUTHERN UNIVERSITY
Charleston, SC 29423-8087
http://www.charlestonsouthern.edu/

Independent-religious, coed, comprehensive institution. *Graduate faculty:* 19 full-time (5 women), 6 part-time/adjunct (2 women). *Computer facilities:* 250 computers available on campus for general student use. A campuswide network can be accessed from student residence rooms and from off campus. Online class registration, online course work are available. *Graduate expenses:* Tuition: full-time $8832; part-time $368 per credit hour. Required fees: $30. One-time fee: $30. Tuition and fees vary according to course load and program. *General application contact:* Alison Harrison, Graduate Enrollment Counselor, 843-863-7534.

Department of Criminal Justice
Dr. Jacqueline Fish, Chair
Program in:
criminal justice (MSCJ)

Program in Business
Dr. Scott Pearson, Director of the MBA Program
Programs in:
accounting (MBA)
finance (MBA)
health care administration (MBA)
information systems (MBA)
organizational development (MBA)

School of Education
Dr. Norma Harper, Dean
Programs in:
administration and supervision (M Ed)
elementary education (M Ed)
secondary education (M Ed)

■ THE CITADEL, THE MILITARY COLLEGE OF SOUTH CAROLINA
Charleston, SC 29409
http://www.citadel.edu

State-supported, coed, comprehensive institution. *Graduate faculty:* 70 full-time (24 women), 19 part-time/adjunct (7 women). *Computer facilities:* 350 computers available on campus for general student use. A campuswide network can be accessed from student residence rooms and from off campus. Online class registration is available. *Graduate expenses:* Tuition, state resident: full-time $5850; part-time $325 per credit hour. Tuition, nonresident: full-time $9612; part-time $534 per credit hour. Required fees: $15 per semester.

Citadel Graduate College
Brig. Gen. Samuel M. Hines, Provost/ Dean of the College
Programs in:
biology (MA)
computer and information science (MS)
English (MA)
health, exercise, and sport science (MS)
history (MA)
mathematics education (MAE)
physical education (MAT)
psychology (MA)
social science (MA)

School of Business Administration
Dr. Ronald F. Green, Dean
Programs in:
business administration (MBA)
sport management (MBA)

School of Education
Dr. Tony Johnson, Dean
Programs in:
biology (MAT)
education (M Ed, MA, MAT, Ed S)
elementary/secondary school administration and supervision (M Ed)
elementary/secondary school counseling (M Ed)
English language arts (MAT)
literacy education (M Ed)
mathematics (MAT)
school psychology (MA, Ed S)
school superintendency (Ed S)
social studies (MAT)
student affairs and college counseling (M Ed)

■ CLEMSON UNIVERSITY
Clemson, SC 29634
http://www.clemson.edu/

State-supported, coed, university. CGS member. *Graduate faculty:* 802 full-time (214 women), 235 part-time/adjunct (83 women). *Computer facilities:* Computer purchase and lease plans are available. 1,250 computers available on campus for general student use. A campuswide network can be accessed from student residence rooms and from off campus. Online class registration is available. *General application contact:* Information Contact, 864-656-3195.

Graduate School
Dr. J. Bruce Rafert, Dean

College of Agriculture, Forestry and Life Sciences
Dr. Alan Sams, Dean
Programs in:
agricultural education (M Ag Ed)
agriculture, forestry and life sciences (M Ag Ed, MFR, MS, PhD)
animal and veterinary sciences (MS, PhD)
applied economics and statistics (MS)
biochemistry and molecular biology (MS, PhD)
biological sciences (MS, PhD)
biosystems engineering (MS, PhD)
entomology (PhD)
environmental toxicology (MS, PhD)
food technology (PhD)
food, nutrition, and culinary science (MS)
forest resources (MFR, MS, PhD)
genetics (MS, PhD)
microbiology (MS, PhD)
packaging science (MS)
plant and environmental sciences (MS, PhD)
wildlife and fisheries biology (MS, PhD)

College of Architecture, Arts, and Humanities
Dr. Clifton Egan, Interim Dean
Programs in:
architecture (M Arch, MS)
architecture, arts, and humanities (M Arch, MA, MCRP, MCSM, MFA, MLA, MRED, MS, PhD)
city and regional planning (MCRP)
construction science and management (MCSM)
developmental planning (MCRP)
digital production arts (MFA)
English (MA)

environmental design and planning (PhD)
historic preservation (MS)
history (MA)
landscape architecture (MLA)
professional communication (MA)
real estate development (MRED)
rhetorics, communication and information design (PhD)
visual arts (MFA)

College of Business and Behavioral Science
Dr. Claude C. Lilly, Dean
Programs in:
accountancy and legal studies (MP Acc)
applied economics (PhD)
applied psychology (MS)
applied sociology (MS)
business administration (MBA)
business and behavioral science (MA, MBA, MP Acc, MPA, MRED, MS, PhD)
economics (MA)
graphic communications (MS)
human factors psychology (PhD)
industrial/organizational psychology (PhD)
management (MS, PhD)
marketing (MS)
policy studies (PhD)
public administration (MPA)

College of Engineering and Science
Dr. Esin Gulari, Dean
Programs in:
applied and pure mathematics (MS, PhD)
automotive engineering (MS, PhD)
bioengineering (MS, PhD)
chemical engineering (MS, PhD)
chemistry (MS, PhD)
civil engineering (MS, PhD)
computational mathematics (MS, PhD)
computer engineering (MS, PhD)
computer science (MS, PhD)
electrical engineering (M Engr, MS, PhD)
engineering and science (M Engr, MS, PhD)
environmental engineering and science (M Engr, MS, PhD)
environmental health physics (MS)
hydrogeology (MS)
industrial engineering (MS, PhD)
materials science and engineering (MS, PhD)
mechanical engineering (MS, PhD)
operations research (MS, PhD)
physics (MS, PhD)
polymer and fiber science (MS, PhD)
statistics (MS, PhD)

College of Health, Education, and Human Development
Dr. Larry Allen, Dean
Programs in:
administration and supervision (M Ed, Ed S)
community counseling (M Ed)
counselor education (M Ed)
curriculum and instruction (PhD)
educational leadership (M Ed, PhD)
elementary education (M Ed)
English (M Ed)
health, education, and human development (M Ed, MAT, MHRD, MPRTM, MS, PhD, Ed S)
human resource development (MHRD)
mathematics (M Ed)
middle grades education (MAT)
natural sciences (M Ed)
nursing (MS)
parks, recreation, and tourism management (MPRTM, MS, PhD)
reading (M Ed)
school counseling (M Ed)
secondary education (M Ed)
special education (M Ed)
student affairs (M Ed)
youth development (MS)

Institute on Family and Neighborhood Life
Dr. Gary B. Melton, Director
Program in:
family and neighborhood life (PhD)

■ COLLEGE OF CHARLESTON
Charleston, SC 29424-0001
http://www.cofc.edu/

State-supported, coed, comprehensive institution. CGS member. *Graduate faculty:* 210 full-time (93 women), 38 part-time/adjunct (20 women). *Computer facilities:* Computer purchase and lease plans are available. 578 computers available on campus for general student use. A campuswide network can be accessed from student residence rooms and from off campus. Online class registration is available. *Graduate expenses:* Tuition, state resident: part-time $368 per credit hour. Tuition, nonresident: part-time $893 per credit hour. Required fees: $30 per course. One-time fee: $45 part-time. *General application contact:* Susan Hallatt, Director of Admissions, 843-953-5614.

Graduate School
Dr. Amy Thompson McCandless, Dean of the Graduate School

School of Business and Economics
Dr. Alan Shao, Dean
Programs in:
accountancy (MS)
business and economics (MS)

School of Education, Health, and Human Performance
Dr. Frances Welch, Dean
Programs in:
early childhood education (MAT)
education, health, and human performance (M Ed, MAT, Certificate)
elementary education (MAT)
English to speakers of other languages (Certificate)
languages (M Ed)
performing arts education (MAT)
science and mathematics for teachers (M Ed)
special education (MAT)

School of Humanities and Social Sciences
Dr. Cynthia Lowenthal, Dean
Programs in:
communication (MA)
English (MA)
history (MA)
humanities and social sciences (MA, MPA, Certificate)
organizational and corporate communication (Certificate)
public administration (MPA)

School of Languages, Cultures, and World Affairs
Dr. David Cohen, Dean
Programs in:
bilingual legal interpreting (MA, Certificate)
healthcare and medical interpreting (Certificate)
languages, cultures, and world affairs (MA, Certificate)

School of Sciences and Mathematics
Dr. George Pothering, Dean
Programs in:
computer and information sciences (MS)
environmental studies (MS)
marine biology (MS)
mathematics (MS)
sciences and mathematics (MS, Certificate)

School of the Arts
Dr. Valerie B. Morris, Dean
Programs in:
arts (MPA, MS, Certificate)
arts management (MPA, Certificate)
historic preservation (MS)

■ COLUMBIA COLLEGE
Columbia, SC 29203-5998
http://www.columbiacollegesc.edu/

Independent-religious, Undergraduate: women only; graduate: coed, comprehensive institution. *Graduate faculty:* 5 full-time (3 women), 28 part-time/adjunct (17 women). *Computer facilities:* Computer purchase and lease plans are available. 150 computers available on campus for general student use. A campuswide network can be accessed from student residence rooms. Online class registration is available. *Graduate expenses:* Tuition: full-time $3015; part-time $335 per semester hour. *General application contact:* Carolyn Emeneker, Director of Graduate School and Evening College Admissions, 803-786-3766.

Graduate Programs
Dr. Laurie B. Hopkins, Provost and Vice President for Academic Affairs

Columbia College (continued)

Programs in:
- divergent learning (M Ed)
- human behavior and conflict management (MA)
- interpersonal relations/conflict management (Certificate)
- organizational behavior/conflict management (Certificate)

■ CONVERSE COLLEGE
Spartanburg, SC 29302-0006
http://www.converse.edu/

Independent, Undergraduate: women only; graduate: coed, comprehensive institution. *Computer facilities:* 72 computers available on campus for general student use. A campuswide network can be accessed from student residence rooms and from off campus. Online class registration is available. *General application contact:* Dr., 864-596-9082.

Carroll McDaniel Petrie School of Music

Programs in:
- instrumental performance (M Mus)
- music education (M Mus)
- piano pedagogy (M Mus)
- vocal performance (M Mus)

School of Education and Graduate Studies

Programs in:
- administration and supervision (Ed S)
- art education (M Ed)
- biology (MAT)
- chemistry (MAT)
- curriculum and instruction (Ed S)
- early childhood education (MAT)
- education (Ed S)
- elementary education (M Ed, MAT)
- English (M Ed, MAT, MLA)
- gifted education (M Ed)
- history (MLA)
- leadership (M Ed)
- learning disabilities (MAT)
- liberal arts (MLA)
- marriage and family therapy (Ed S)
- mathematics (M Ed, MAT)
- mental disabilities (MAT)
- natural sciences (M Ed)
- political science (MLA)
- secondary education (M Ed, MAT)
- social sciences (M Ed, MAT)
- special education (M Ed, MAT)

■ FRANCIS MARION UNIVERSITY
Florence, SC 29501-0547
http://www.fmarion.edu/

State-supported, coed, comprehensive institution. *Graduate faculty:* 114 full-time (35 women), 10 part-time/adjunct (5 women). *Computer facilities:* 551 computers available on campus for general student use. A campuswide network can be accessed from student residence rooms and from off campus. Online class registration, Blackboard are available. *Graduate expenses:* Tuition, state resident: full-time $7547; part-time $377.35 per credit hour. Tuition, nonresident: full-time $15,094; part-time $754.70 per credit hour. Required fees: $22 per credit hour. $30 per semester. *General application contact:* Rannie Gamble, Administrative Manager, 843-661-1286.

Graduate Programs

Programs in:
- applied clinical psychology (MS)
- applied community psychology (MS)
- school psychology (MS)

School of Business

Dr. M. Barry O'Brien, Dean

Programs in:
- business (MBA)
- health management (MBA)

School of Education

Dr. James R. Faulkenberry, Dean

Programs in:
- early childhood education (M Ed)
- elementary education (M Ed)
- learning disabilities (M Ed, MAT)
- remedial education (M Ed)
- secondary education (M Ed)

■ FURMAN UNIVERSITY
Greenville, SC 29613
http://www.furman.edu/

Independent, coed, comprehensive institution. *Graduate faculty:* 23 full-time (11 women), 10 part-time/adjunct (6 women). *Computer facilities:* Computer purchase and lease plans are available. 425 computers available on campus for general student use. A campuswide network can be accessed from student residence rooms and from off campus. Online class registration is available. *General application contact:* Dr. Troy M. Terry, Director of Graduate Studies, 864-294-2213.

Graduate Division

Dr. Troy M. Terry, Director of Graduate Studies

Programs in:
- chemistry (MS)
- curriculum and instruction (MA)
- early childhood education (MA)
- English as a second language (MA)
- literacy (MA)
- school leadership (MA)
- special education (MA)

■ SOUTH CAROLINA STATE UNIVERSITY
Orangeburg, SC 29117-0001
http://www.scsu.edu/

State-supported, coed, comprehensive institution. CGS member. *Graduate faculty:* 51 full-time (28 women), 22 part-time/adjunct (10 women). *Computer facilities:* 300 computers available on campus for general student use. A campuswide network can be accessed. Online class registration is available. *Graduate expenses:* Tuition, state resident: full-time $7806; part-time $434 per credit hour. Tuition, nonresident: full-time $15,298; part-time $850 per credit hour. *General application contact:* Dr. Thomas Thompson, Dean of the School of Graduate Studies, 803-516-4734.

School of Graduate Studies

Dr. Thomas Thompson, Dean of the School of Graduate Studies

Programs in:
- agribusiness (MS)
- agribusiness and entrepreneurship (MBA)
- early childhood and special education (M Ed)
- early childhood education (MAT)
- educational leadership (Ed D, Ed S)
- elementary counselor education (M Ed)
- elementary education (M Ed, MAT)
- engineering (MAT)
- general science (MAT)
- individual and family development (MS)
- mathematics (MAT)
- nutritional sciences (MS)
- rehabilitation counseling (MA)
- secondary counselor education (M Ed)
- secondary education (M Ed)
- special education (M Ed)
- speech/language pathology (MA)
- transportation (MS)

■ SOUTHERN WESLEYAN UNIVERSITY
Central, SC 29630-1020
http://www.swu.edu/

Independent-religious, coed, comprehensive institution. *Computer facilities:* Computer purchase and lease plans are available. 85 computers available on campus for general student use. A campuswide network can be accessed from student residence rooms and from off campus. Online class registration is available. *General application contact:* Regional Enrollment Manager, 800-808-1653.

Program in Business Administration

Program in:
- business administration (MBA)

Program in Christian Ministries

Program in:
- Christian ministries (M Min)

Program in Education

Program in:
- education (M Ed)

Program in Management

Program in:
- management (MSM)

■ UNIVERSITY OF SOUTH CAROLINA

Columbia, SC 29208

http://www.sc.edu/

State-supported, coed, university. CGS member. *Computer facilities:* Computer purchase and lease plans are available. 2,800 computers available on campus for general student use. A campuswide network can be accessed from student residence rooms and from off campus. Online class registration is available. *General application contact:* Director of Graduate Admissions, 803-777-4243.

The Graduate School

Program in:
gerontology (Certificate)

Arnold School of Public Health

Programs in:
biostatistics (MPH, MSPH, Dr PH, PhD)
communication sciences and disorders (MCD, MSP, PhD)
environmental health science (MS)
environmental quality (MPH, MS, MSPH, PhD)
epidemiology (MPH, MSPH, Dr PH, PhD)
exercise science (MS, DPT, PhD)
general public health (MPH)
hazardous materials management (MPH, MSPH, PhD)
health education (MAT)
health promotion, education, and behavior (MPH, MS, MSPH, Dr PH, PhD)
health services policy and management (MHA, MPH, Dr PH, PhD)
industrial hygiene (MPH, MSPH, PhD)
physical activity and public health (MPH)
public health (MAT, MCD, MHA, MPH, MS, MSP, MSPH, DPT, Dr PH, PhD, Certificate)
school health education (Certificate)

College of Arts and Sciences

Programs in:
anthropology (MA, PhD)
applied statistics (CAS)
archives (MA)
art education (IMA, MA, MAT)
art history (MA)
art studio (MA)
arts and sciences (IMA, M Math, MA, MAT, MFA, MIS, MMA, MPA, MS, PSM, PhD, CAS, Certificate)
biology (MS, PhD)
biology education (IMA, MAT)
chemistry and biochemistry (IMA, MAT, MS, PhD)
clinical/community psychology (MA, PhD)
comparative literature (MA, PhD)
creative writing (MFA)
criminology and criminal justice (MA, PhD)
ecology, evolution and organismal biology (MS, PhD)
English (MA, PhD)
English education (MAT)
experimental psychology (MA, PhD)
foreign languages (MAT)
French (MA)
general psychology (MA)
geography (MA, MS, PhD)
geography education (IMA)
geological sciences (MS, PhD)
German (MA)
historic preservation (MA)
history (MA, PhD)
industrial statistics (MIS)
international studies (MA, PhD)
linguistics (MA, PhD)
marine science (MS, PhD)
mathematics (MA, MS, PhD)
mathematics education (M Math, MAT)
media arts (MMA)
molecular, cellular, and developmental biology (MS, PhD)
museum (MA)
museum management (Certificate)
philosophy (MA, PhD)
physics and astronomy (IMA, MAT, MS, PSM, PhD)
political science (MA, MPA, PhD)
public administration (MPA)
public history (MA, Certificate)
religious studies (MA)
school psychology (PhD)
sociology (MA, PhD)
Spanish (MA)
statistics (MS, PhD)
studio art (MFA)
teaching English to speakers of other languages (Certificate)
theater (MA, MAT, MFA)
women's studies (Certificate)

College of Education

Programs in:
art education (IMA, MAT)
business education (IMA, MAT)
counseling education (PhD, Ed S)
curriculum and instruction (Ed D)
early childhood education (M Ed, Ed D, PhD)
education (IMA, M Ed, MAT, MS, MT, Ed D, PhD, Certificate, Ed S)
educational administration (M Ed, PhD, Ed S)
educational psychology, research (M Ed, PhD)
educational technology (M Ed)
elementary education (MAT, Ed D, PhD)
English (MAT)
foreign language (MAT)
foundations in education (PhD)
health education (MAT)
higher education and student affairs (M Ed)
higher education leadership (Certificate)
language and literacy (M Ed, PhD)
mathematics (MAT)
physical education (IMA, MAT, MS, PhD)
science (IMA, MAT)
secondary (Ed D)
secondary education (IMA, MAT, MT, Ed D, PhD)
social studies (MAT)
special education (M Ed, MAT, PhD)
teaching (M Ed, Ed S)
theatre and speech (MAT)

College of Engineering and Computing

Programs in:
chemical engineering (ME, MS, PhD)
civil engineering (ME, MS, PhD)
computer science and engineering (ME, MS, PhD)
electrical engineering (ME, MS, PhD)
engineering and computing (ME, MS, PhD)
mechanical engineering (ME, MS, PhD)
nuclear engineering (ME, MS, PhD)
software engineering (MS)

College of Hospitality, Retail, and Sport Management

Programs in:
hospitality, retail, and sport management (MIHTM, MR, MS)
hotel, restaurant and tourism management (MIHTM)
live sport and entertainment events (MS)
public assembly facilities management (MS)
retailing (MR)

College of Mass Communications and Information Studies

Programs in:
journalism and mass communications (MA, MMC, PhD)
library and information science (MLIS, PhD, Certificate, Specialist)
mass communications and information studies (MA, MLIS, MMC, PhD, Certificate, Specialist)

College of Nursing

Programs in:
acute care clinical specialist (MSN)
acute care nurse practitioner (MSN, Certificate)
adult nurse practitioner (MSN)
advanced practice clinical nursing (MSN, Certificate)
advanced practice nursing in primary care (MSN, Certificate)
advanced practice nursing in psychiatric mental health (MSN, Certificate)
clinical nursing (MSN)
community mental health and psychiatric health nursing (MSN)
community/public health clinical nurse specialist (MSN)
family nurse practitioner (MSN)
health nursing (MSN)
nursing administration (MSN)
nursing practice (DNP)
nursing science (PhD)
pediatric nurse practitioner (MSN)
psychiatric/mental health nurse practitioner (MSN)

University of South Carolina (continued)
psychiatric/mental health specialist (MSN)
women's health nurse practitioner (MSN)

College of Social Work
Program in:
social work (MSW, PhD)

Moore School of Business
Programs in:
accountancy (M Acc)
business administration (MBA, PhD)
business measurement and assurance (M Acc)
economics (MA, PhD)
human resources (MHR)
international business administration (IMBA)

School of Music
Programs in:
composition (MM, DMA)
conducting (MM, DMA)
jazz studies (MM)
music education (MM Ed, PhD)
music history (MM)
music performance (Certificate)
music theory (MM)
opera theater (MM)
performance (MM, DMA)
piano pedagogy (MM, DMA)

School of the Environment
Programs in:
earth and environmental resources management (MEERM)
environment (MEERM)

School of Law
Program in:
law (JD)

School of Medicine
Programs in:
biomedical science (MBS, PhD)
genetic counseling (MS)
medicine (MD, MBS, MNA, MRC, MS, PhD, Certificate)
nurse anesthesia (MNA)
psychiatric rehabilitation (Certificate)
rehabilitation counseling (MRC, Certificate)

South Carolina College of Pharmacy
Programs in:
pharmaceutical sciences (MS, PhD)
pharmacy (Pharm D, MS, PhD)

■ WINTHROP UNIVERSITY
Rock Hill, SC 29733
http://www.winthrop.edu/

State-supported, coed, comprehensive institution. CGS member. *Computer facilities:* Computer purchase and lease plans are available. 250 computers available on campus for general student use. A campuswide network can be accessed from student residence rooms and from off campus. Online class registration is available. *General application contact:* Information Contact, 800-411-7041.

College of Arts and Sciences
Programs in:
arts and sciences (MA, MLA, MS, SSP)
biology (MS)
English (MA)
history (MA)
human nutrition (MS)
liberal arts (MLA)
psychology (MS, SSP)
social work (MA)
Spanish (MA)

College of Business Administration
Programs in:
business administration (MBA, MS, Certificate)
software development (MS)
software project management (Certificate)

College of Education
Programs in:
agency counseling (M Ed)
education (M Ed, MAT, MS)
educational leadership (M Ed)
middle level education (M Ed)
physical education (MS)
reading education (M Ed)
school counseling (M Ed)
secondary education (M Ed, MAT)
special education (M Ed)

College of Visual and Performing Arts
Programs in:
art (MFA)
art administration (MA)
art education (MA)
conducting (MM)
music education (MME)
performance (MM)
visual and performing arts (MA, MFA, MM, MME)

South Dakota

■ COLORADO TECHNICAL UNIVERSITY SIOUX FALLS
Sioux Falls, SD 57108
http://www.ctu-siouxfalls.com/

Proprietary, coed, comprehensive institution. *Computer facilities:* 25 computers available on campus for general student use. A campuswide network can be accessed. *General application contact:* Admissions Manager, 605-361-0200 Ext. 103.

Program in Computing
Programs in:
computer systems security (MSCS)
software engineering (MSCS)

Program in Criminal Justice
Program in:
criminal justice (MSM)

Programs in Business Administration and Management
Programs in:
business administration (MBA)
business management (MSM)
health science management (MSM)
human resources management (MSM)
information technology (MSM)
organizational leadership (MSM)
project management (MBA)
technology management (MBA)

■ MOUNT MARTY COLLEGE
Yankton, SD 57078-3724
http://www.mtmc.edu/

Independent-religious, coed, comprehensive institution. *Computer facilities:* Computer purchase and lease plans are available. 25 computers available on campus for general student use. A campuswide network can be accessed from student residence rooms and from off campus. Online class registration is available. *General application contact:* Vice President of Enrollment, 800-658-4552.

Graduate Studies Division
Programs in:
business administration (MBA)
nurse anesthesia (MS)
pastoral ministries (MPM)

■ SOUTH DAKOTA STATE UNIVERSITY
Brookings, SD 57007
http://www.sdstate.edu/

State-supported, coed, university. CGS member. *Computer facilities:* Computer purchase and lease plans are available. 692 computers available on campus for general student use. A campuswide network can be accessed from student residence rooms and from off campus. Online class registration is available. *General application contact:* Linda Winkler, Registration Officer, 605-688-4182.

Graduate School
Dr. Kevin Kephart, Dean

College of Agriculture and Biological Sciences
Dr. Donald Marshall, Acting Dean
Programs in:
agriculture and biological sciences (MS, PhD)
agriculture and biosystems engineering (MS, PhD)
agronomy (PhD)
animal science (MS, PhD)
animal sciences (MS, PhD)
biological sciences (MS, PhD)

economics (MS)
plant science (MS)
rural sociology (MS)
sociology (PhD)
wildlife and fisheries sciences (MS, PhD)

College of Arts and Science
Dr. Jerry Jorgensen, Dean
Programs in:
arts and science (MA, MS, PhD)
chemistry (MS, PhD)
communication studies and journalism (MS)
English (MA)
geography (MS)

College of Engineering
Dr. Lewis Brown, Dean
Programs in:
biological sciences (MS, PhD)
computational science and statistics (PhD)
electrical engineering (PhD)
engineering (MS)
geospatial science and engineering (PhD)
industrial management (MS)
mathematics (MS)

College of Education and Human Sciences
Dr. Jane Hegland, Acting Dean
Programs in:
apparel merchandising and interior design (MFCS)
counseling and human resource development (MS)
curriculum and instruction (M Ed)
dietetics (MS)
education and human sciences (M Ed, MFCS, MS, PhD)
educational administration (M Ed)
health, physical education and recreation (MS)
human development, consumer and family sciences (MFCS)
nutrition, food science and hospitality (MFCS)
nutritional sciences (MS, PhD)

College of Nursing
Dr. Sandra J. Bunkers, Department Head, Graduate Nursing
Program in:
nursing (MS, PhD)

College of Pharmacy
Dr. Dennis Hedge, Dean
Programs in:
biological science (MS)
pharmaceutical sciences (PhD)
pharmacy (Pharm D, MS, PhD)

■ UNIVERSITY OF SIOUX FALLS

Sioux Falls, SD 57105-1699
http://www.usiouxfalls.edu/

Independent-religious, coed, comprehensive institution. *Graduate faculty:* 19 full-time (11 women), 17 part-time/adjunct (9 women). *Computer facilities:* 150 computers available on campus for general student use. A campuswide network can be accessed from student residence rooms and from off campus. Online class registration is available. *General application contact:* Student Contact, 605-331-5000.

Fredrikson School of Education
Dawn Olson, Director of Graduate Programs in Education
Programs in:
leadership (M Ed)
reading (M Ed)
superintendent (Ed S)
teaching (M Ed)
technology (M Ed)

John T. Vucurevich School of Business
Rebecca T. Murdock, Director
Program in:
business (MBA)

■ THE UNIVERSITY OF SOUTH DAKOTA

Vermillion, SD 57069-2390
http://www.usd.edu/

State-supported, coed, university. CGS member. *Computer facilities:* 917 computers available on campus for general student use. A campuswide network can be accessed from student residence rooms and from off campus. Online class registration is available. *General application contact:* Registration Officer, 605-677-6287.

Graduate School
Programs in:
administrative studies (MS)
interdisciplinary studies (MA)

College of Arts and Sciences
Programs in:
American political institutions (PhD)
arts and sciences (MA, MNS, MPA, MS, Au D, PhD)
audiology (Au D)
biology (MA, MNS, MS, PhD)
chemistry (MNS, MS, PhD)
clinical psychology (MA, PhD)
communication studies (MA)
communications disorders (MA)
computational sciences and statistics (PhD)
computer science (MS)
English (MA, PhD)
history (MA)
human factors (MA, PhD)
mathematics (MA, MNS, MS)
physics (MS, PhD)
political science (MA)
public administration (MPA, PhD)
public policy (PhD)
speech-language pathology (MA)

College of Fine Arts
Programs in:
art (MFA)
fine arts (MA, MFA, MM)
music (MM)
theatre (MA, MFA)

School of Business
Programs in:
business (MBA, MP Acc)
business administration (MBA)
professional accountancy (MP Acc)

School of Education
Programs in:
counseling and psychology in education (MA, PhD, Ed S)
curriculum and instruction (Ed D, Ed S)
education (MA, MS, Ed D, PhD, Ed S)
educational administration (MA, Ed D, Ed S)
elementary education (MA)
health, physical education and recreation (MA)
secondary education (MA)
special education (MA)
technology for education and training (MS, Ed S)

School of Law
Program in:
law (JD)

School of Medicine and Health Sciences
Programs in:
cardiovascular research (MS, PhD)
cellular and molecular biology (MS, PhD)
medicine (MD)
medicine and health science (MD, MS, DPT, PhD)
molecular microbiology and immunology (MS, PhD)
neuroscience (MS, PhD)
occupational therapy (MS)
physical therapy (DPT)
physician assistant studies (MS)
physiology and pharmacology (MS, PhD)

Tennessee

■ AUSTIN PEAY STATE UNIVERSITY

Clarksville, TN 37044
http://www.apsu.edu/

State-supported, coed, comprehensive institution. CGS member. *Graduate faculty:* 97 full-time (46 women), 14 part-time/adjunct (10 women). *Computer facilities:* Computer purchase and lease plans are available. 760 computers available on campus for general student use. A campuswide network can be accessed from student residence rooms and from off campus. Online class registration is available. *Graduate expenses:* Tuition, state resident: full-time $5772; part-time $305 per credit hour. Tuition, nonresident: full-time $16,664; part-time $778 per credit hour. Required fees: $1224. *General application contact:* Dr. Charles Pinder, Dean, College of Graduate Studies, 931-221-7414.

Austin Peay State University (continued)

College of Graduate Studies

Dr. Charles Pinder, Dean, College of Graduate Studies

College of Arts and Letters

Dixie Webb, Interim Dean

Programs in:
- arts and letters (M Mu, MA)
- communication arts (MA)
- English (MA)
- military history (MA)
- music education (M Mu)
- music performance (M Mu)

College of Professional Programs and Social Sciences

Dr. David Denton, Dean

Programs in:
- administration and supervision (Ed S)
- advanced practice (MSN)
- counseling (MS)
- counseling and guidance (Ed S)
- curriculum and instruction (MA Ed)
- educational leadership studies (MA Ed)
- elementary education (Ed S)
- family nurse practitioner (MSN)
- K-6 education (MAT)
- management (MS)
- nursing administration (MSN)
- nursing education (MSN)
- nursing informatics (MSN)
- psychology (MA)
- public and community health (MS)
- reading (MA Ed)
- secondary education (MAT, Ed S)
- social sciences (MA, MA Ed, MAT, MS, MSN, Ed S)
- special education (MAT)

College of Science and Mathematics

Dr. Jaime Taylor, Interim Dean

Programs in:
- clinical laboratory science (MS)
- radiologic science (MS)
- science and mathematics (MS)

■ BELMONT UNIVERSITY

Nashville, TN 37212-3757

http://www.belmont.edu/

Independent-religious, coed, comprehensive institution. *Graduate faculty:* 113 full-time (58 women), 43 part-time/adjunct (24 women). *Computer facilities:* Computer purchase and lease plans are available. 400 computers available on campus for general student use. A campuswide network can be accessed from student residence rooms and from off campus. Online class registration, individual student information via BANNER Web are available. *Graduate expenses:* Tuition: full-time $14,270; part-time $810 per credit hour. Required fees: $530; $280 per year. Tuition and fees vary according to degree level and program. *General application contact:* Dr. Kathryn Baugher, Dean of Enrollment Services, 615-460-6785.

College of Arts and Sciences

Dr. Bryce Sullivan, Dean

Programs in:
- arts and sciences (M Ed, MA, MAT, MSA)
- literature (MA)
- writing (MA)

School of Education

Dr. Trevor F. Hutchins, Associate Dean

Programs in:
- education (M Ed)
- elementary education (MAT)
- English (MAT)
- history (MAT)
- mathematics (MAT)
- middle grade education (MAT)
- science (MAT)
- secondary education (MAT)
- special education (MAT)
- sports administration (MSA)

College of Health Sciences

Dr. Jack Williams, Dean

Program in:
- health sciences (Pharm D, MSN, MSOT, DPT, OTD)

School of Nursing

Dr. Leslie J. Higgins, Director, Graduate Program

Program in:
- nursing (MSN)

School of Occupational Therapy

Dr. Ruth Ford, Associate Dean

Program in:
- occupational therapy (MSOT, OTD)

School of Pharmacy

Dr. Phil Johnston, Dean

Program in:
- pharmacy (Pharm D)

School of Physical Therapy

Dr. John S. Halle, Associate Dean

Program in:
- physical therapy (DPT)

College of Visual and Performing Arts

Dr. Cynthia R. Curtis, Dean

Program in:
- visual and performing arts (MM)

School of Music

Dr. Robert Gregg, Director

Programs in:
- church music (MM)
- composition (MM)
- music education (MM)
- pedagogy (MM)
- performance (MM)

Jack C. Massey Graduate School of Business

Dr. Patrick Raines, Dean

Program in:
- business (M Acc, MBA)

■ BETHEL UNIVERSITY

McKenzie, TN 38201

http://www.bethel-college.edu/

Independent-religious, coed, comprehensive institution. *Computer facilities:* Computer purchase and lease plans are available. 8 computers available on campus for general student use. A campuswide network can be accessed from student residence rooms. Online class registration is available. *General application contact:* Chair, Division of Education and Health Sciences, 731-352-4025.

Program in Education

Programs in:
- administration and supervision (MA Ed)
- biology education K8-12 (MAT)
- elementary education (MAT)
- English education K8-12 (MAT)
- history education K8-12 (MAT)
- physical education K8-12 (MAT)
- special education K8-12 (MAT)

■ CARSON-NEWMAN COLLEGE

Jefferson City, TN 37760

http://www.cn.edu/

Independent-religious, coed, comprehensive institution. *Graduate faculty:* 14 full-time (8 women), 5 part-time/adjunct (2 women). *Computer facilities:* 200 computers available on campus for general student use. A campuswide network can be accessed from student residence rooms and from off campus. *Graduate expenses:* Tuition: full-time $5310. Required fees: $200. *General application contact:* Graduate Admissions and Services Adviser, 865-473-3468.

Division of Nursing

Programs in:
- family nurse practitioner (MSN)
- nurse educator (MSN)

Graduate Program in Education

Programs in:
- curriculum and instruction (M Ed)
- educational leadership (M Ed)
- elementary education (MAT)
- school counseling (MS)
- secondary education (MAT)
- teaching English as a second language (MATESL)

■ CHRISTIAN BROTHERS UNIVERSITY

Memphis, TN 38104-5581

http://www.cbu.edu/

Independent-religious, coed, comprehensive institution. *Graduate faculty:* 9 full-time (6 women), 18 part-time/adjunct (7 women). *Computer facilities:* 310 computers available on campus for general student use. A campuswide network can be accessed from student residence rooms and from off campus. Online class registration, online class listings, course assignments are available. *General application contact:* Dr. Patrick B. Wilson, Dean, Graduate and Professional Studies Programs, 901-321-3296.

Graduate and Professional Studies
Dr. Patrick B. Wilson, Dean

School of Arts
Dr. Marius Carriere, Dean
Programs in:
- Catholic studies (MACS)
- curriculum and instruction (M Ed)
- educational leadership (MSEL)
- teacher-leadership (M Ed)
- teaching (MAT)

School of Business
Dr. Scott Lawyer, Dean
Programs in:
- business (MBA)
- executive leadership (MAEL)
- financial planning (Certificate)
- project management (Certificate)

School of Engineering
Dr. Eric B. Welch, Dean
Program in:
- engineering (MEM, MSEM)

■ CUMBERLAND UNIVERSITY
Lebanon, TN 37087-3408
http://www.cumberland.edu/

Independent, coed, comprehensive institution. *Computer facilities:* 150 computers available on campus for general student use. A campuswide network can be accessed from student residence rooms and from off campus. *General application contact:* Vice President for Enrollment Management, 615-444-2562 Ext. 1225.

Program in Business Administration
Program in:
- business administration (MBA)

Program in Education
Program in:
- education (MAE)

Program in Organizational Leadership and Human Relations Management
Program in:
- organizational leadership and human relations management (MS)

Program in Public Service Administration
Program in:
- public service administration (MS)

■ EAST TENNESSEE STATE UNIVERSITY
Johnson City, TN 37614
http://www.etsu.edu/

State-supported, coed, university. CGS member. *Computer facilities:* Computer purchase and lease plans are available. 1,400 computers available on campus for general student use. A campuswide network can be accessed from student residence rooms. Online class registration is available. *General application contact:* Assistant Dean, 423-439-4221.

James H. Quillen College of Medicine
Programs in:
- anatomy (MS, PhD)
- biochemistry (MS, PhD)
- biophysics (MS, PhD)
- medicine (MD, MS, PhD)
- microbiology (MS, PhD)
- pharmacology (MS, PhD)
- physiology (MS, PhD)

School of Graduate Studies

College of Arts and Sciences
Programs in:
- applied sociology (MA)
- art education (MA)
- art history (MA)
- arts and sciences (MA, MFA, MS, MSW)
- biology (MS)
- chemistry (MS)
- clinical psychology (MA)
- communication (MA)
- criminal justice and criminology (MA)
- English (MA)
- general psychology (MA)
- general sociology (MA)
- history (MA)
- mathematics (MS)
- microbiology (MS)
- social work (MSW)
- studio art (MA, MFA)

College of Business and Technology
Programs in:
- accountancy (M Acc)
- business administration (MBA, Certificate)
- business and technology (M Acc, MBA, MCM, MPM, MS, Certificate)
- city management (MCM)
- clinical nutrition (MS)
- community development (MPM)
- computer science (MS)
- digital media (MS)
- engineering technology (MS)
- general administration (MPM)
- health care management (Certificate)
- industrial arts/technology education (MS)
- information systems science (MS)
- municipal service management (MPM)
- software engineering (MS)
- urban and regional economic development (MPM)
- urban and regional planning (MPM)

College of Education
Programs in:
- 7-12 (MAT)
- administrative endorsement (M Ed, Ed D, Ed S)
- advanced practitioner (M Ed)
- classroom leadership (Ed D)
- classroom technology (M Ed)
- community agency counseling (M Ed, MA)
- comprehensive concentration (M Ed)
- counseling (M Ed, MA)
- early childhood education (M Ed, MA)
- early childhood general (M Ed)
- early childhood special education (M Ed)
- early childhood teaching (M Ed)
- education (M Ed, MA, MAT, Ed D, Ed S)
- educational communication (M Ed)
- educational leadership (M Ed, Ed D, Ed S)
- educational media/educational technology (M Ed)
- elementary and secondary (school counseling) (M Ed, MA)
- elementary education (M Ed, MAT)
- exercise physiology (MA)
- fitness leadership (MA)
- K-12 (MAT)
- marriage and family therapy (M Ed, MA)
- modified concentration (M Ed)
- physical education (M Ed, MA)
- post secondary and private sector leadership (Ed D)
- reading and storytelling (M Ed, MA)
- reading education (M Ed, MA)
- school leadership (Ed D)
- school library media (M Ed)
- school system leadership (Ed S)
- secondary education (M Ed, MAT)
- sports management (MA)
- sports sciences (MA)
- teacher leadership (Ed S)

College of Nursing
Programs in:
- advanced nursing practice (Post Master's Certificate)
- health care management (Certificate)
- nursing (MSN, DSN)

College of Public and Allied Health
Programs in:
- audiology (MS, Au D)
- communicative disorders (MS)
- community health (MPH)
- environmental health (MSEH)
- epidemiology (Certificate)
- gerontology (Certificate)
- health care management (Certificate)
- physical therapy (DPT)
- public and allied health (MPH, MS, MSEH, Au D, DPT, Certificate)
- public health (MPH)
- public health administration (MPH)
- special education audiology pre-K-12 (MS)
- special education speech pathology pre-K-12 (MS)
- speech pathology (MS)

Division of Cross-Disciplinary Studies
Program in:
- liberal studies (MALS)

■ FREED-HARDEMAN UNIVERSITY
Henderson, TN 38340-2399
http://www.fhu.edu/

Independent-religious, coed, comprehensive institution. *Graduate faculty:* 32 full-time (7 women), 10 part-time/adjunct (2 women). *Computer facilities:* Computer purchase and lease plans are available. 250 computers available on campus for general student use. A campuswide network can be accessed from student residence rooms and from off campus. Online class registration is available. *Graduate expenses:* Tuition: full-time $4284; part-time $357 per credit hour. Required fees: $16 per credit hour. *General application contact:* Dr. Samuel T. Jones, Vice President for Academics, 731-989-6004.

Program in Business Administration
Dr. Tom Deberry, Director of Graduate Studies, School of Business
Programs in:
accounting (MBA)
corporate responsibility (MBA)
leadership (MBA)

Program in Counseling
Dr. Mike Cravens, Graduate Director
Program in:
counseling (MS)

Program in Education
Dr. Elizabeth Saunders, Graduate Director
Programs in:
curriculum and instruction (M Ed)
school counseling (M Ed)
school leadership (Ed S)

School of Biblical Studies
Dr. Mark Blackwelder, Director of Graduate Studies
Programs in:
biblical studies (M Div, M Min, MA)
divinity (M Div)
ministry (M Min)
New Testament (MA)

■ LEE UNIVERSITY
Cleveland, TN 37320-3450
http://www.leeuniversity.edu/

Independent-religious, coed, comprehensive institution. *Graduate faculty:* 60 full-time (19 women), 16 part-time/adjunct (7 women). *Computer facilities:* 450 computers available on campus for general student use. A campuswide network can be accessed from off campus. Online class registration is available. *Graduate expenses:* Tuition: full-time $10,824; part-time $451 per credit. Required fees: $270; $200 per semester. Tuition and fees vary according to course load and program. *General application contact:* Vicki Glasscock, Graduate Admissions Director, 423-614-8059.

College of Arts and Sciences
Dr. Doyle Goff, Director
Programs in:
mental health counseling (MS)
school counseling (MS)

Program in Education
Dr. Gary Riggins, Director
Programs in:
classroom teaching (M Ed)
education specialist (Ed S)
educational leadership (M Ed)
elementary/secondary education (MAT)
special education (elementary) (M Ed)
special education (secondary) (M Ed, MAT)
special education (severe disabilities) (M Ed)

Program in Music
Dr. Jim W. Burns, Director
Programs in:
church music (MCM)
music education (MME)
performance (MMMP)

Program in Religion
Dr. Michael Fuller, Director
Programs in:
biblical studies (MA)
theological studies (MA)
youth and family ministry (MA)

■ LINCOLN MEMORIAL UNIVERSITY
Harrogate, TN 37752-1901
http://www.lmunet.edu/

Independent, coed, comprehensive institution. *Computer facilities:* A campuswide network can be accessed from student residence rooms. Online class registration is available. *Graduate expenses:* Tuition: full-time $5580; part-time $310 per credit hour. Tuition and fees vary according to degree level and program.

Carter and Moyers School of Education
Dr. Fred Bedelle, Dean, School of Education
Programs in:
administration and supervision (M Ed, Ed S)
counseling and guidance (M Ed)
curriculum and instruction (M Ed, Ed S)
English (M Ed)

Caylor School of Nursing
Dr. Mary Anne Modrcin, Dean
Programs in:
family nurse practitioner (MSN)
nurse anesthesia (MSN)

DeBusk College of Osteopathic Medicine
Dr. Ray Stowers, Vice President and Dean
Program in:
osteopathic medicine (DO)

School of Business
Dr. Jack McCann, Dean
Program in:
business (MBA)

■ LIPSCOMB UNIVERSITY
Nashville, TN 37204-3951
http://www.lipscomb.edu/

Independent-religious, coed, comprehensive institution. CGS member. *Computer facilities:* 203 computers available on campus for general student use. A campuswide network can be accessed from student residence rooms. Online class registration is available. *General application contact:* Associate Provost for Graduate Studies, 615-966-5711.

Hazelip School of Theology
Programs in:
biblical studies (MA)
Christian studies (MA)
divinity (M Div)
ministry (MA)
New Testament (MA)
Old Testament (MA)
theological studies (MTS)
theology (MA)

Institute for Conflict Management
Program in:
conflict management (MA, Certificate)

MBA Program
Programs in:
accounting (MBA)
business administration (general) (MBA)
conflict management (MBA)
financial services (MBA)
healthcare management (MBA)
leadership (MBA)
nonprofit management (MBA)
sustainable practice (MBA)

Program in Accountancy
Program in:
accountancy (M Acc)

Program in Counseling
Programs in:
counseling psychology (Certificate)
professional counseling (MS)
psychology (MS)

Program in Education
Programs in:
English language learners (MAT)
instructional leadership (M Ed)
learning and teaching (MALT)
school administration and supervision (M Ed)
special education instruction, K-12 (MASE)

Program in Pharmacy
Program in:
pharmacy (Pharm D)

■ MIDDLE TENNESSEE STATE UNIVERSITY

Murfreesboro, TN 37132

http://www.mtsu.edu/

State-supported, coed, university. CGS member. *Graduate faculty:* 416 full-time (175 women), 10 part-time/adjunct (3 women). *Computer facilities:* 2,400 computers available on campus for general student use. A campuswide network can be accessed from student residence rooms and from off campus. Online class registration is available. *General application contact:* Dr. Michael Allen, Dean and Vice Provost for Research, 615-898-2840.

College of Graduate Studies

Dr. Michael Allen, Dean and Vice Provost for Research
Programs in:
gerontology (Graduate Certificate)
health care management (Graduate Certificate)

College of Basic and Applied Sciences
Dr. Thomas Cheatham, Dean
Programs in:
aerospace education (M Ed)
aviation administration (MS)
basic and applied sciences (M Ed, MS, MSN, MST, DA, Graduate Certificate)
biology (MS)
biostatistics (MS)
biotechnology (MS)
chemistry (MS, DA)
computer science (MS)
engineering technology and industrial studies (MS)
family nurse practitioner (MSN, Graduate Certificate)
health care informatics (MS)
mathematics (MS, MST)
nursing (MSN, Graduate Certificate)

College of Continuing Education and Distance Learning
Dr. David Gotcher, Program Director
Program in:
social sciences (MPS)

College of Education and Behavioral Science
Dr. Terry Whiteside, Interim Dean
Programs in:
administration and supervision (M Ed, Ed S)
child development and family studies (MS)
clinical psychology (MA)
criminal justice administration (MCJ)
curriculum and instruction (M Ed, Ed S)
dyslexic studies (Graduate Certificate)
early childhood education (M Ed)
education and behavioral science (M Ed, MA, MCJ, MS, PhD, Ed S, Graduate Certificate)
elementary education (M Ed, Ed S)
English as a second language (M Ed, Ed S)
exercise science (MS)
health, physical education and recreation (MS)
human performance (PhD)
industrial/organizational psychology (MA)
literacy studies (PhD)
mental health counseling (M Ed)
middle school education (M Ed)
nutrition and food science (MS)
professional counseling (M Ed, Ed S)
psychology (MA)
reading (M Ed)
school counseling (M Ed)
school psychology (Ed S)
secondary education (M Ed)
special education (M Ed)
teaching and learning (M Ed)
technology and curriculum design (Ed S)

College of Liberal Arts
Dr. John McDaniel, Dean
Programs in:
English (MA, PhD)
English as a second language (M Ed)
foreign language (MAT)
geosciences (Graduate Certificate)
history (MA, PhD)
liberal arts (M Ed, MA, MAT, MSW, PhD, Graduate Certificate)
music (MA)
public history (MA, PhD)
social work (MSW)
sociology (MA)

College of Mass Communication
Dr. John Omachionu, Interim Dean
Programs in:
mass communication (MFA, MS)
recording arts and technologies (MFA)

Jennings A. Jones College of Business
Dr. E. James Burton, Dean
Programs in:
accounting (MS)
business (MA, MBA, MBE, MS, PhD)
business education (MBE)
computer information systems (MS)
economics (MA, PhD)
information systems (MS)
management and marketing (MBA)

■ TENNESSEE STATE UNIVERSITY

Nashville, TN 37209-1561

http://www.tnstate.edu/

State-supported, coed, comprehensive institution. CGS member. *Graduate faculty:* 151 full-time (63 women), 20 part-time/adjunct (11 women). *Computer facilities:* 1,025 computers available on campus for general student use. A campuswide network can be accessed from student residence rooms and from off campus. Online class registration is available. *General application contact:* Deborah Chisom, Director of Graduate School Admissions, 615-963-5962.

The School of Graduate Studies and Research

Dr. Helen Barrett, Dean

College of Arts and Sciences
Dr. Gloria Johnson, Interim Dean
Programs in:
arts and sciences (MA, MCJ, MS, PhD)
biological sciences (MS, PhD)
chemistry (MS)
criminal justice (MCJ)
English (MA)
mathematical sciences (MS)
music education (MS)

College of Business
Dr. Tilden J. Curry, Dean
Program in:
business (MBA)

College of Education
Dr. Peter Millett, Dean
Programs in:
administration and supervision (M Ed, Ed D, Ed S)
counseling and guidance (MS)
counseling psychology (PhD)
curriculum and instruction (M Ed, Ed D)
education (M Ed, MA Ed, MS, Ed D, PhD, Ed S)
elementary education (M Ed, MA Ed, Ed D)
human performance and sports science (MA Ed)
psychology (MS, PhD)
school psychology (MS, PhD)
special education (M Ed, MA Ed, Ed D)

College of Engineering, Technology, and Computer Science
Dr. Lonnie Sharpe, Dean
Programs in:
computer and information systems engineering (MS, PhD)
engineering (ME)

College of Health Sciences
Dr. Kathleen McEnerney, Dean
Programs in:
health sciences (MPT, MS, DPT)
physical therapy (MPT, DPT)
speech and hearing science (MS)

Institute of Government
Dr. Ann-Marie Rizzo, Director
Program in:
public administration (MPA, PhD)

School of Agriculture and Consumer Sciences
Dr. Chandra Reddy, Dean
Program in:
agricultural sciences (MS)

School of Nursing
Dr. Bernadeen Fleming, Interim Dean
Programs in:
family nurse practitioner (MSN)
holistic nursing (MSN)
nursing administration (MSN)
nursing education (MSN)
nursing informatics (MSN)

■ TENNESSEE TECHNOLOGICAL UNIVERSITY

Cookeville, TN 38505

http://www.tntech.edu/

State-supported, coed, university. CGS member. *Computer facilities:* 800 computers available on campus for general student use. A campuswide network can be accessed from student residence rooms and from off campus. Online class registration is available. *General application contact:* Associate Vice President for Research and Graduate Studies, 931-372-3233.

Graduate School

College of Arts and Sciences
Programs in:
arts and sciences (MA, MS, PhD)
chemistry (MS)
computer science (MS)
English (MA)
environmental biology (MS)
environmental sciences (PhD)
fish, game, and wildlife management (MS)
mathematics (MS)

College of Business
Program in:
business (MBA)

College of Education
Programs in:
curriculum (MA, Ed S)
early childhood education (MA, Ed S)
education (MA, PhD, Ed S)
educational psychology (MA, Ed S)
educational psychology and student personnel (MA, Ed S)
elementary education (MA, Ed S)
exceptional learning (PhD)
exercise science, physical education and wellness (MA)
instructional leadership (MA, Ed S)
library science (MA, Ed S)
reading (MA, Ed S)
secondary education (MA, Ed S)
special education (MA, Ed S)

College of Engineering
Programs in:
chemical engineering (MS, PhD)
civil engineering (MS, PhD)
electrical engineering (MS, PhD)
engineering (MS, PhD)
mechanical engineering (MS, PhD)

School of Nursing

Program in:
nursing (MSN)

■ TREVECCA NAZARENE UNIVERSITY

Nashville, TN 37210-2877

http://www.trevecca.edu/

Independent-religious, coed, comprehensive institution. *Graduate faculty:* 43 full-time (19 women), 42 part-time/adjunct (20 women). *Computer facilities:* 200 computers available on campus for general student use. A campuswide network can be accessed from student residence rooms and from off campus. *General application contact:* Glenda Bolling, Director of Non-Traditional and Graduate Admissions, 615-248-1320.

Graduate Division

Dr. Stephen M. Pusey, Provost and Chief Academic Officer
Programs in:
biblical studies (MA)
business (MBA, MSM)
business administration (MBA)
clinical counseling (Ed D)
counseling (MA)
counseling psychology (MA)
management (MSM)
marriage and family therapy (MMFT)
physician assistant (MS)
preaching and practical theology (MA)
systematic theology/historical theology (MA)

School of Education
Dr. Esther Swink, Dean/Director of Graduate Education Programs
Programs in:
educational leadership (M Ed)
English language learners (PreK-12) (M Ed)
instructional effectiveness (M Ed)
instructional technology (M Ed)
leadership and professional practice (Ed D)
library and information science (MLI Sc)
reading PreK-12 (M Ed)
teaching (MAT)
teaching 7-12 (MAT)
teaching K-6 (MAT)

■ TUSCULUM COLLEGE

Greeneville, TN 37743-9997

http://www.tusculum.edu/

Independent-religious, coed, comprehensive institution. *Computer facilities:* 200 computers available on campus for general student use. A campuswide network can be accessed from student residence rooms and from off campus. Online class registration is available. *General application contact:* Director of Admissions, 423-636-7300 Ext. 5901.

Graduate School

Programs in:
adult education (MA Ed)
K–12 (MA Ed)
organizational management (MAOM)

■ UNION UNIVERSITY

Jackson, TN 38305-3697

http://www.uu.edu/

Independent-religious, coed, comprehensive institution. *Computer facilities:* 236 computers available on campus for general student use. A campuswide network can be accessed from student residence rooms and from off campus. Online class registration is available. *General application contact:* Director of Enrollment Services, 731-661-5008.

Institute for International and Intercultural Studies

Program in:
international and intercultural studies (MAIS)

McAfee School of Business Administration

Program in:
business administration (MBA)

School of Christian Studies

Programs in:
Christian studies (MCS)
expository preaching (D Min)

School of Education

Programs in:
education (M Ed, MA Ed)
education administration generalist (Ed S)
educational leadership (Ed D)
educational supervision (Ed S)
higher education (Ed D)

School of Nursing

Programs in:
executive leadership (DNP)
nurse anesthesia (DNP)
nurse anesthetist (PMC)
nurse practitioner (DNP)
nursing education (MSN, PMC)

■ UNIVERSITY OF MEMPHIS

Memphis, TN 38152

http://www.memphis.edu/

State-supported, coed, university. CGS member. *Graduate faculty:* 574 full-time (205 women), 70 part-time/adjunct (38 women). *Computer facilities:* 2,000 computers available on campus for general student use. A campuswide network can be accessed from off campus. Online class registration is available. *Graduate expenses:* Tuition, state resident: full-time $6242; part-time $330 per credit hour. Tuition, nonresident: full-time $17,828; part-time $815 per credit hour. Required fees: $1156; $70 per credit hour. *General application contact:* Information Contact, 901-678-2531.

Cecil C. Humphreys School of Law

Dr. Kevin H. Smith, Dean
Program in:
law (JD)

Graduate School

Dr. Karen D. Weddle-West, Vice Provost for Graduate Studies

College of Arts and Sciences
Dr. Henry A. Kurtz, Dean

Programs in:
- anthropology (MA)
- applied computer science (MS)
- applied mathematics (MS)
- applied statistics (PhD)
- arts and sciences (MA, MCRP, MFA, MHA, MPA, MPH, MS, PhD, Graduate Certificate)
- bioinformatics (MS)
- biology (MS, PhD)
- chemistry (MS, PhD)
- city and regional planning (MCRP)
- clinical psychology (PhD)
- computer science (MS, PhD)
- computer sciences (MS)
- creative writing (MFA)
- criminology and criminal justice (MA)
- earth sciences (MA, MS, PhD, Graduate Certificate)
- English (MA, Graduate Certificate)
- experimental psychology (PhD)
- French (MA)
- general psychology (MS)
- health administration (MHA)
- history (MA, PhD)
- interdisciplinary studies (MA, MS, Graduate Certificate)
- mathematics (MS, PhD)
- nonprofit administration (MPA)
- philosophy (MA, PhD)
- physics (MS)
- political science (MA)
- public health (MPH)
- public management and policy (MPA)
- school psychology (MA, PhD)
- sociology (MA)
- Spanish (MA)
- statistics (MS, PhD)
- urban management and planning (MPA)
- writing and language studies (PhD)

College of Communication and Fine Arts
Dr. Richard R. Ranta, Dean
Programs in:
- applied music (M Mu, DMA)
- architecture (M Arch)
- art (Graduate Certificate)
- art history (MA)
- ceramics (MFA)
- communication (MA)
- communication and fine arts (M Arch, M Mu, MA, MFA, DMA, PhD, Graduate Certificate)
- communication arts (PhD)
- composition (M Mu, DMA)
- conducting (M Mu, DMA)
- film and video production (MA)
- general journalism (MA)
- graphic design (MFA)
- historical musicology (PhD)
- interior design (MFA)
- jazz and studio performance (M Mu)
- journalism administration (MA)
- music education (M Mu, DMA)
- musicology (M Mu)
- painting (MFA)
- printmaking/photography (MFA)
- sculpture (MFA)
- theatre (MFA)

College of Education
Dr. Donald J. Wagner, Dean
Programs in:
- adult education (Ed D)
- clinical nutrition (MS)
- community education (Ed D)
- counseling (MS, Ed D)
- counseling psychology (PhD)
- early childhood education (MAT, MS, Ed D)
- education (M Ed, MAT, MS, Ed D, PhD, Ed S, Graduate Certificate)
- educational leadership (Ed D)
- educational psychology and research (MS, PhD)
- elementary education (MAT)
- exercise and sport science (MS)
- health promotion (MS)
- higher education (Ed D)
- instruction and curriculum (MS, Ed D)
- instruction design and technology (MS, Ed D)
- leadership (MS)
- middle grades education (MAT)
- physical education teacher education (MS)
- policy studies (Ed D)
- reading (MS, Ed D)
- school administration and supervision (MS)
- secondary education (MAT)
- special education (MAT, MS, Ed D)
- sport and leisure commerce (MS)
- student personnel (MS)

Fogelman College of Business and Economics
Rajiv Grover, Dean
Programs in:
- accounting (MBA, MS, PhD)
- accounting systems (MS)
- business and economics (IMBA, MA, MBA, MS, PhD)
- economics (MA, PhD)
- executive business administration (MBA)
- finance (PhD)
- finance, insurance, and real estate (MBA, MS)
- international business administration (IMBA)
- management (MBA, MS, PhD)
- management information systems (MBA, MS, PhD)
- management science (MBA)
- marketing (MBA, MS)
- marketing and supply chain management (PhD)
- real estate development (MS)
- taxation (MS)

Herff College of Engineering
Dr. Richard C. Warder, Dean
Programs in:
- automatic control systems (MS)
- biomedical engineering (MS, PhD)
- biomedical systems (MS)
- civil engineering (PhD)
- communications and propagation systems (MS)
- computer engineering technology (MS)
- design and mechanical engineering (MS)
- electrical engineering (PhD)
- electronics engineering technology (MS)
- energy systems (MS)
- engineering (MS, PhD)
- engineering computer systems (MS)
- environmental engineering (MS)
- foundation engineering (MS)
- industrial engineering (MS)
- manufacturing engineering technology (MS)
- mechanical engineering (PhD)
- mechanical systems (MS)
- power systems (MS)
- structural engineering (MS)
- transportation engineering (MS)
- water resources engineering (MS)

School of Audiology and Speech-Language Pathology
Dr. Maurice Mendel, Dean
Program in:
- audiology and speech-language pathology (MA, Au D, PhD)

University College
Dr. Dan Lattimore, Dean
Programs in:
- liberal studies (MALS)
- merchandising and consumer science (MS)
- strategic leadership (MPS)

Loewenberg School of Nursing
Dr. Marjorie Luttrell, Dean
Program in:
- nursing (MSN, Graduate Certificate)

■ THE UNIVERSITY OF TENNESSEE
Knoxville, TN 37996
http://www.tennessee.edu/

State-supported, coed, university. CGS member. *Graduate faculty:* 1,172 full-time (390 women), 16 part-time/adjunct (6 women). *Computer facilities:* Computer purchase and lease plans are available. 600 computers available on campus for general student use. A campuswide network can be accessed from student residence rooms and from off campus. Online class registration, Blackboard Course Management System are available. *Graduate expenses:* Part-time $348 per credit hour. Tuition, state resident: full-time $6262. Tuition, nonresident: full-time $18,920; part-time $1052 per credit hour. Required fees: $812; $36 per credit hour. Tuition and fees vary according to program. *General application contact:* Michael Ickowitz, Associate Director of Graduate and International Admissions, 865-974-3251.

College of Law
Dr. Karen R. Britton, Director of Admissions, Financial Aid and Career Services
Programs in:
- business transactions (JD)
- law (JD)

The University of Tennessee (continued)

Graduate School

Programs in:
- aviation systems (MS)
- comparative and experimental medicine (MS, PhD)

College of Agricultural Sciences and Natural Resources

Programs in:
- agricultural education (MS)
- agricultural extension education (MS)
- agricultural sciences and natural resources (MS, PhD)
- animal anatomy (PhD)
- biosystems engineering (MS, PhD)
- biosystems engineering technology (MS)
- breeding (MS, PhD)
- entomology (MS, PhD)
- floriculture (MS)
- food science and technology (MS, PhD)
- forestry (MS)
- integrated pest management and bioactive natural products (PhD)
- landscape design (MS)
- management (MS, PhD)
- nutrition (MS, PhD)
- physiology (MS, PhD)
- plant pathology (MS, PhD)
- public horticulture (MS)
- turfgrass (MS)
- wildlife and fisheries science (MS)
- woody ornamentals (MS)

College of Architecture and Design

Programs in:
- architecture (professional) (M Arch)
- architecture (research) (M Arch)
- architecture and design (M Arch, MA, MLA, MS)
- landscape architecture (MLA)
- landscape architecture (research) (MA, MS)

College of Arts and Sciences

Programs in:
- accompanying (MM)
- American history (PhD)
- analytical chemistry (MS, PhD)
- applied linguistics (PhD)
- applied mathematics (MS)
- archaeology (MA, PhD)
- arts and sciences (M Math, MA, MFA, MM, MPA, MS, PhD)
- audiology (MA)
- behavior (MS, PhD)
- biochemistry, cellular and molecular biology (MS, PhD)
- biological anthropology (MA, PhD)
- ceramics (MFA)
- chemical physics (PhD)
- choral conducting (MM)
- clinical psychology (PhD)
- composition (MM)
- computer science (MS, PhD)
- costume design (MFA)
- criminology (MA, PhD)
- cultural anthropology (MA, PhD)
- drawing (MFA)
- ecology (MS, PhD)
- energy, environment, and resource policy (MA, PhD)
- English (MA, PhD)
- environmental chemistry (MS, PhD)
- European history (PhD)
- evolutionary biology (MS, PhD)
- experimental psychology (MA, PhD)
- French (MA, PhD)
- genome science and technology (MS, PhD)
- geography (MS, PhD)
- geology (MS, PhD)
- German (MA, PhD)
- graphic design (MFA)
- hearing science (PhD)
- history (MA)
- inorganic chemistry (MS, PhD)
- instrumental conducting (MM)
- inter-area studies (MFA)
- Italian (PhD)
- jazz (MM)
- lighting design (MFA)
- mathematical ecology (PhD)
- mathematics (M Math, MS, PhD)
- media arts (MFA)
- medical ethics (MA, PhD)
- microbiology (MS, PhD)
- modern foreign languages (PhD)
- music education (MM)
- music theory (MM)
- musicology (MM)
- organic chemistry (MS, PhD)
- painting (MFA)
- performance (MFA, MM)
- philosophy (MA, PhD)
- physical chemistry (MS, PhD)
- physics (MS, PhD)
- piano pedagogy and literature (MM)
- plant physiology and genetics (MS, PhD)
- political economy (MA, PhD)
- political science (MA, MPA, PhD)
- polymer chemistry (MS, PhD)
- Portuguese (PhD)
- printmaking (MFA)
- psychology (MA)
- public administration (MPA)
- religious studies (MA)
- Russian (PhD)
- scene design (MFA)
- sculpture (MFA)
- Spanish (MA)
- speech and hearing science (PhD)
- speech and language pathology (PhD)
- speech and language science (PhD)
- speech pathology (MA)
- theatre technology (MFA)
- theoretical chemistry (PhD)
- watercolor (MFA)
- zoo-archaeology (MA, PhD)

College of Business Administration

Programs in:
- accounting (M Acc, PhD)
- business administration (M Acc, MA, MBA, MS, PhD)
- economics (MA, PhD)
- finance (MBA, PhD)
- industrial and organizational psychology (PhD)
- industrial statistics (MS)
- logistics and transportation (MBA, PhD)
- management (PhD)
- management science (MS, PhD)
- marketing (MBA, PhD)
- operations management (MBA)
- professional business administration (MBA)
- statistics (MS, PhD)
- systems (M Acc)
- taxation (M Acc)
- teacher licensure (MS)
- training and development (MS)

College of Communication and Information

Programs in:
- advertising (MS, PhD)
- broadcasting (MS, PhD)
- communications (MS, PhD)
- information sciences (MS, PhD)
- journalism (MS, PhD)
- public relations (MS, PhD)
- speech communication (MS, PhD)

College of Education, Health and Human Sciences

Programs in:
- adult education (MS)
- applied educational psychology (MS)
- art education (MS)
- biomechanics/sports medicine (MS, PhD)
- child and family studies (MS, PhD)
- collaborative learning (Ed D)
- college student personnel (MS)
- community health (PhD)
- community health education (MPH)
- consumer services management (MS)
- counseling education (PhD)
- cultural studies in education (PhD)
- curriculum (MS, Ed S)
- curriculum, educational research and evaluation (Ed D, PhD)
- early childhood education (MS, PhD)
- early childhood special education (MS)
- education of deaf and hard of hearing (MS)
- education, health and human sciences (MPH, MS, Ed D, PhD, Ed S)
- educational administration and policy studies (Ed D, PhD)
- educational administration and supervision (MS, Ed S)
- educational psychology (Ed D, PhD)
- elementary education (MS, Ed S)
- elementary teaching (MS)
- English education (MS, Ed S)
- exercise physiology (MS, PhD)
- exercise science (MS, PhD)
- foreign language/ESL education (MS, Ed S)
- gerontology (MPH)
- health planning/administration (MPH)
- health promotion and health education (MS)
- hospitality management (MS)
- hotel, restaurant, and tourism management (MS)

instructional technology (MS, Ed D, PhD, Ed S)
literacy, language and ESL education (PhD)
literacy, language education, and ESL education (Ed D)
mathematics education (MS, Ed S)
mental health counseling (MS)
modified and comprehensive special education (MS)
nutrition (MS)
nutrition science (PhD)
reading education (MS, Ed S)
recreation and leisure studies (MS)
rehabilitation counseling (MS)
retail and consumer sciences (MS)
retailing and consumer sciences (PhD)
safety (MS)
school counseling (MS, Ed S)
school psychology (PhD, Ed S)
science education (MS, Ed S)
secondary teaching (MS)
social foundations (MS)
social science education (MS, Ed S)
socio-cultural foundations of sports and education (PhD)
special education (Ed S)
sport management (MS)
sport studies (MS, PhD)
teacher education (Ed D, PhD)
textile science (MS, PhD)
therapeutic recreation (MS)
tourism (MS)

College of Engineering
Dr. Way Kuo, Dean
Programs in:
aerospace engineering (MS, PhD)
applied artificial intelligence (MS)
biomedical engineering (MS, PhD)
chemical engineering (MS, PhD)
civil engineering (MS, PhD)
composite materials (MS, PhD)
computational mechanics (MS, PhD)
computer engineering (MS, PhD)
computer science (MS, PhD)
electrical engineering (MS, PhD)
engineering (MS, PhD)
engineering management (MS)
engineering science (MS, PhD)
environmental engineering (MS)
fluid mechanics (MS, PhD)
human factors engineering (MS)
industrial engineering (MS, PhD)
information engineering (MS)
manufacturing systems engineering (MS)
materials science and engineering (MS, PhD)
mechanical engineering (MS, PhD)
optical engineering (MS, PhD)
polymer engineering (MS, PhD)
radiological engineering (MS, PhD)
solid mechanics (MS, PhD)

College of Nursing
Program in:
nursing (MSN, PhD)

College of Social Work
Programs in:
clinical social work practice (MSSW)
social welfare management and community practice (MSSW)
social work (PhD)

College of Veterinary Medicine
Program in:
veterinary medicine (DVM)

■ THE UNIVERSITY OF TENNESSEE AT CHATTANOOGA

Chattanooga, TN 37403-2598
http://www.utc.edu/

State-supported, coed, comprehensive institution. CGS member. *Graduate faculty:* 150 full-time (60 women), 19 part-time/adjunct (9 women). *Computer facilities:* 300 computers available on campus for general student use. A campuswide network can be accessed from student residence rooms and from off campus. Online class registration is available. *Graduate expenses:* Tuition, state resident: full-time $6150; part-time $281 per credit hour. Tuition, nonresident: full-time $16,710; part-time $867 per credit hour. Required fees: $1100; $128 per credit hour. $550 per semester. *General application contact:* Dr. Stephanie Bellar, Interim Dean of Graduate Studies, 423-425-4666.

Graduate School
Dr. Stephanie Bellar, Dean of Graduate Studies

College of Arts and Sciences
Dr. Herb Burhenn, Dean
Programs in:
arts and sciences (MA, MM, MPA, MS, MSCJ, Postbaccalaureate Certificate)
criminal justice (MSCJ)
English (MA)
environmental sciences (MS)
industrial/organizational psychology (MS)
music (MM)
public administration (MPA, Postbaccalaureate Certificate)
research psychology (MS)

College of Business
Dr. Richard P. Casavant, Dean
Programs in:
accountancy (M Acc)
business (M Acc, MBA)
business administration (MBA)

College of Engineering and Computer Science
Dr. William Sutton, Dean
Programs in:
chemical engineering (MS)
civil engineering (MS)
computational engineering (MS, PhD)
computer science (MS, Graduate Certificate)
electrical engineering (MS)
engineering and computer science (MS, PhD, Graduate Certificate)
engineering management (MS, Graduate Certificate)
industrial engineering (MS)
mechanical engineering (MS)

College of Health, Education and Professional Studies
Dr. Mary Tanner, Dean
Programs in:
administration (MSN)
adult health (MSN)
certified nurse anesthetist (Post-Master's Certificate)
counseling (M Ed)
education (M Ed, MSN, Post-Master's Certificate)
educational leadership (Ed D)
educational specialist (Ed S)
educational technology (Ed S)
elementary education (M Ed)
family nurse practitioner (MSN, Post-Master's Certificate)
health and human performance (MS)
health, education and professional studies (M Ed, MS, MSN, DPT, Ed D, Ed S, Post-Master's Certificate)
learning and leadership (Ed D)
nurse anesthesia (MSN)
physical therapy (DPT)
school leadership (M Ed, Post-Master's Certificate)
school psychology (Ed S)
secondary education (M Ed)
special education (M Ed)

■ THE UNIVERSITY OF TENNESSEE AT MARTIN

Martin, TN 38238-1000
http://www.utm.edu/

State-supported, coed, comprehensive institution. *Graduate faculty:* 146. *Computer facilities:* 725 computers available on campus for general student use. A campuswide network can be accessed from student residence rooms and from off campus. Online class registration, online fee payments, degree progress, financial aid data, housing applications, transcripts are available. *Graduate expenses:* Tuition, state resident: full-time $6084; part-time $340 per semester hour. Tuition, nonresident: full-time $16,726; part-time $932 per semester hour. *General application contact:* Linda S. Arant, Student Services Specialist, 731-881-7012.

Graduate Programs
Dr. Victoria S. Seng, Assistant Vice Chancellor and Dean of Graduate Studies

College of Agriculture and Applied Sciences
Dr. James Byford, Dean
Programs in:
agricultural and natural resources management (MSANR)
agriculture and applied sciences (MSANR, MSFCS)

The University of Tennessee at Martin (continued)

dietetics (MSFCS)
general family and consumer sciences (MSFCS)

College of Business and Public Affairs
Dr. Ernest Moser, Dean
Programs in:
business (MBA)
business and public affairs (MBA)

College of Education and Behavioral Sciences
Dr. Mary Lee Hall, Dean
Programs in:
advanced elementary (MS Ed)
advanced secondary (MS Ed)
community counseling (MS Ed)
education and behavioral sciences (MS Ed)
educational administration and supervision (MS Ed)
initial licensure comprehensive (MS Ed)
initial licensure elementary (MS Ed)
initial licensure secondary (MS Ed)
school counseling (MS Ed)

■ VANDERBILT UNIVERSITY

Nashville, TN 37240-1001
http://www.vanderbilt.edu/

Independent, coed, university. CGS member. *Computer facilities:* 400 computers available on campus for general student use. A campuswide network can be accessed from student residence rooms and from off campus. Productivity and educational software available. *General application contact:* Walter B. Bieschke, Program Coordinator for Graduate Admissions, 615-343-6321.

Divinity School

Program in:
divinity (M Div, MTS)

Graduate School

Dr. Dennis G. Hall, Associate Provost for Research and Dean of the Graduate School
Programs in:
analytical chemistry (MAT, MS, PhD)
anthropology (MA, PhD)
astronomy (MS)
biochemistry (MS, PhD)
biological sciences (MS, PhD)
biomedical informatics (MS, PhD)
cancer biology (MS, PhD)
cell and developmental biology (MS, PhD)
classics (MA)
community research and action (MS, PhD)
creative writing (MFA)
earth and environmental sciences (MS)
economic development (MA)
economics (MA, MAT, PhD)
English (MA, MAT, PhD)
French (MA, MAT, PhD)
German (MA, MAT, PhD)
history (MA, MAT, PhD)
human genetics (PhD)
inorganic chemistry (MAT, MS, PhD)
Latin (MAT)
Latin American studies (MA)
leadership and policy studies (PhD)
learning, teaching and diversity (MS, PhD)
liberal arts and science (MLAS)
mathematics (MA, MAT, MS, PhD)
microbiology and immunology (MS, PhD)
molecular physiology and biophysics (MS, PhD)
neuroscience (PhD)
nursing science (PhD)
organic chemistry (MAT, MS, PhD)
pathology (PhD)
pharmacology (PhD)
philosophy (MA, PhD)
physical chemistry (MAT, MS, PhD)
physics (MA, MAT, MS, PhD)
political science (MA, MAT, PhD)
Portuguese (MA)
psychological sciences (MA, PhD)
religion (MA, PhD)
sociology (MA, PhD)
Spanish (MA, MAT, PhD)
Spanish and Portuguese (PhD)
theoretical chemistry (MAT, MS, PhD)

Center for Medicine, Health, and Society
Dr. Arlene Tuchman, Director
Program in:
medicine, health, and society (MA)

Owen Graduate School of Management

Programs in:
business administration (MBA)
executive business administration (MBA)
finance (PhD)
management (MBA, MSF, PhD)
marketing (PhD)
operations management (PhD)
organization studies (PhD)

Peabody College

Dr. Camilla P. Benbow, Dean
Programs in:
child studies (M Ed)
community development and action (M Ed)
education (M Ed, MPP, Ed D)
education policy (MPP)
educational leadership and policy (Ed D)
elementary education (M Ed)
English language learners (M Ed)
higher education (M Ed)
higher education, leadership and policy (Ed D)
human development counseling (M Ed)
human resource development (M Ed)
international education policy and management (M Ed)
learning and instruction (M Ed)
learning, diversity, and urban studies (M Ed)
organizational leadership (M Ed)
reading education (M Ed)
secondary education (M Ed)
special education (M Ed)

School of Engineering

Dr. Kenneth F. Galloway, Dean
Programs in:
biomedical engineering (M Eng, MS, PhD)
chemical and biomolecular engineering (M Eng, MS, PhD)
civil engineering (M Eng, MS, PhD)
computer science (M Eng, MS, PhD)
electrical engineering (M Eng, MS, PhD)
engineering (M Eng, MS, PhD)
environmental engineering (M Eng, MS, PhD)
environmental management (MS, PhD)
materials science (M Eng, MS, PhD)
mechanical engineering (M Eng, MS, PhD)

School of Medicine

Programs in:
audiology (Au D, PhD)
biomedical and biological sciences (PhD)
chemical and physical biology (PhD)
clinical investigation (MS)
education of the deaf (MED)
hearing and speech sciences (MS)
medical physics (MS)
medicine (MED, MPH, MS, Au D, PhD)
public health (MPH)
speech-language-pathology (MS)

School of Nursing

Dr. Colleen Conway-Welch, Dean
Programs in:
adult acute care nurse practitioner (MSN)
adult health nurse practitioner/forensic (MSN)
adult nurse practitioner/cardiovascular disease management and prevention (MSN)
adult nurse practitioner/palliative care (MSN)
clinical management (clinical nurse leader/specialist) (MSN)
family nurse practitioner (MSN)
gerontology nurse practitioner (MSN)
health systems management (MSN)
neonatal nurse practitioner (MSN)
nurse midwifery (MSN)
nursing informatics (MSN)
nursing practice (DNP)
nursing science (PhD)
nutrition (MS)
pediatric acute care nurse practitioner (MSN)
pediatric primary care nurse practitioner (MSN)
psychiatric-mental health nurse practitioner (MSN)
women's health nurse practitioner (MSN)

Vanderbilt University Law School
G. Todd Morton, Assistant Dean for Admissions
Programs in:
law (JD, LL M)
law and economics (PhD)

Texas

■ ABILENE CHRISTIAN UNIVERSITY

Abilene, TX 79699-9100

http://www.acu.edu/

Independent-religious, coed, comprehensive institution. CGS member. *Graduate faculty:* 13 full-time (2 women), 69 part-time/adjunct (23 women). *Computer facilities:* Computer purchase and lease plans are available. 724 computers available on campus for general student use. A campuswide network can be accessed from student residence rooms and from off campus. Online class registration is available. *Graduate expenses:* Tuition: full-time $10,728; part-time $596 per hour. Required fees: $1090; $53.50 per hour. $10 per term. Tuition and fees vary according to campus/location. *General application contact:* William Horn, Graduate Admissions Counselor, 325-674-2656.

Graduate School
Dr. Carol G. Williams, Graduate Dean
Program in:
liberal arts (MLA)

College of Arts and Sciences
Dr. Greg Straughn, Interim Dean
Programs in:
arts and sciences (MA, MS, Certificate)
clinical psychology (MS)
communication (MA)
composition/rhetoric (MA)
conflict resolution (Certificate)
conflict resolution and reconciliation (MA)
counseling psychology (MS)
gerontology (MS, Certificate)
literature (MA)
organizational and human resource development (MS)
psychology (MS)
school psychology (MS)
writing (MA)

College of Biblical Studies
Dr. Jack Reese, Dean
Programs in:
biblical studies (M Div, MA, MACM, MMFT, D Min)
Christian ministry (MACM)
divinity (M Div)
history and theology (MA)
marriage and family therapy (MMFT)
ministry (D Min)
missions (MA)
New Testament (MA)
Old Testament (MA)

College of Business Administration
Bill Fowler, Department Chair
Program in:
business administration (M Acc)

College of Education and Human Services
Dr. Malesa Breeding, Dean
Programs in:
communication sciences and disorders (MS)
curriculum and instruction (M Ed)
education and human services (M Ed, MS, MSSW)
higher education (M Ed)
leadership of learning (M Ed)
social work (MSSW)
special education (M Ed)

School of Nursing
Dr. Amy Toone, Dean
Programs in:
education and administration (MSN)
family nurse practitioner (MSN)

■ AMBERTON UNIVERSITY

Garland, TX 75041-5595

http://www.amberton.edu/

Independent-religious, coed, upper-level institution. *Computer facilities:* 30 computers available on campus for general student use. *General application contact:* Adviser, 972-279-6511 Ext. 180.

Graduate School
Programs in:
counseling (MA)
general business (MBA)
human relations and business (MA, MS)
management (MBA)
professional development (MA)

■ ANGELO STATE UNIVERSITY

San Angelo, TX 76909

http://www.angelo.edu/

State-supported, coed, comprehensive institution. CGS member. *Graduate faculty:* 70 full-time (27 women), 2 part-time/adjunct (0 women). *Computer facilities:* Computer purchase and lease plans are available. 715 computers available on campus for general student use. A campuswide network can be accessed from student residence rooms and from off campus. Online class registration, Online courses. Other online services: pay tuition, purchase books, purchase parking permits, university calendar, library card catalog and library resources. Discounted hardware and software programs for personally owned computers. are available. *General application contact:* Theresa Fortin, Graduate Admissions Assistant, 325-942-2169.

College of Graduate Studies
Dr. Brian J. May, Dean of the College of Graduate Studies
Program in:
interdisciplinary studies (MA, MS)

College of Business and Professional Studies
Dr. Corbett Gaulden, Dean
Programs in:
accounting (MBA)
business (MBA, MPAC)
business administration (MBA)
professional accountancy (MPAC)

College of Education
Dr. John J. Miazga, Dean of the College of Education
Programs in:
curriculum and instruction (MA)
education (M Ed, MA, MS)
educational diagnostics (M Ed)
guidance and counseling (M Ed)
kinesiology (MS)
reading specialist (M Ed)
school administration (M Ed)
student development and leadership in higher education (M Ed)

College of Liberal and Fine Arts
Dr. Kevin Lambert, Dean
Programs in:
communication systems management (MA)
English (MA)
history (MA)
liberal and fine arts (MA, MPA, MS)
psychology (MS)
public administration (MPA)

College of Nursing and Allied Health
Dr. Leslie M. Mayrand, Dean
Programs in:
adult nurse practitioner (MSN)
nurse educator (MSN)
nursing and allied health (MSN, DPT)
physical therapy (DPT)

College of Sciences
Dr. Grady Blount, Dean
Programs in:
animal science (MS)
biology (MS)
sciences (MS)

■ BAYLOR UNIVERSITY

Waco, TX 76798

http://www.baylor.edu/

Independent-religious, coed, university. CGS member. *Graduate faculty:* 350. *Computer facilities:* 1,668 computers available on campus for general student use. A campuswide network can be accessed from student residence rooms and from off campus. Online class registration is available. *General application contact:* Suzanne Keener, Administrative Assistant, 254-710-3588.

George W. Truett Seminary
Dr. David E. Garland, Dean

Baylor University (continued)
Program in:
theology (M Div, MTS, D Min)

Graduate School
Dr. Larry Lyon, Dean
Programs in:
clinical orthopedics (D Sc)
emergency medicine (D Sc PA)
health care administration (MHA)
health sciences (MHA, MPT, MS, D Sc, D Sc PA, DPT)
nutrition (MS)
physical therapy (MPT, DPT)

College of Arts and Sciences
Programs in:
air science and environment (IMES)
American studies (MA)
applied sociology (PhD)
arts and sciences (IMES, MA, MES, MFA, MIJ, MPPA, MS, MSCP, MSCSD, MSW, PhD, Psy D)
biology (MA, MS, PhD)
chemistry (MS, PhD)
church-state studies (MA, PhD)
clinical psychology (MSCP, Psy D)
communication sciences and disorders (MA, MSCSD)
communication studies (MA)
directing (MFA)
earth science (MA)
English (MA, PhD)
environmental biology (MS)
environmental studies (MES, MS)
geology (MS, PhD)
history (MA)
international journalism (MIJ)
international studies (MA)
journalism (MA)
limnology (MS)
mathematics (MS, PhD)
museum studies (MA)
neuroscience (MA, PhD)
philosophy (MA, PhD)
physics (MA, MS, PhD)
political science (MA, PhD)
public policy and administration (MPPA)
religion (MA, PhD)
sociology (MA)
Spanish (MA)
statistics (MA, PhD)

Hankamer School of Business
Dr. Gary Carini, Director of Graduate Programs
Programs in:
accounting and business law (M Acc, MT)
business (M Acc, MA, MBA, MBAIM, MIM, MS, MS Eco, MSIS, MT)
business administration (MBA)
economics (MS Eco)
information systems (MSIS)
information systems management (MBA)
international economics (MA, MS)
international management (MBA, MBAIM, MIM)

Institute of Biomedical Studies
Dr. Chris Kearney, Graduate Program Director
Program in:
biomedical studies (MS, PhD)

Louise Herrington School of Nursing
Dr. Mary Brucker, Graduate Program Director
Programs in:
family nurse practitioner (MSN)
neonatal nurse practitioner (MSN)
nursing administration and management (MSN)

School of Education
Programs in:
curriculum and instruction (MA, MS Ed, Ed D, Ed S)
education (MA, MS Ed, Ed D, PhD, Ed S)
educational administration (MS Ed, Ed S)
educational psychology (MA, MS Ed, PhD, Ed S)
exercise, nutrition and preventive health (PhD)
health, human performance and recreation (MS Ed)

School of Engineering and Computer Science
Dr. Greg Speegle, Graduate Program Director
Programs in:
biomedical engineering (MSBE)
computer science (MS)
electrical and computer engineering (MSECE)
engineering (ME, MSBE, MSECE, MSME)
mechanical engineering (MSME)

School of Music
Dr. David Music, Graduate Program Director
Programs in:
church music (MM)
collaborative piano (MM)
composition (MM)
conducting (MM)
music history and literature (MM)
music theory (MM)
performance (MM)
piano pedagogy and performance (MM)

School of Law
Dr. Bradley J. B. Toben, Dean
Program in:
law (JD)

School of Social Work
Dr. Dennis Myers, Associate Dean for Graduate Studies
Program in:
social work (MSW)

■ DALLAS BAPTIST UNIVERSITY

Dallas, TX 75211-9299
http://www.dbu.edu/

Independent-religious, coed, comprehensive institution. *Graduate faculty:* 68 full-time (30 women), 113 part-time/adjunct (47 women). *Computer facilities:* 190 computers available on campus for general student use. A campuswide network can be accessed from student residence rooms and from off campus. Online class registration is available. *Graduate expenses:* Tuition: part-time $558 per credit hour. *General application contact:* Kit P. Montgomery, Director of Graduate Programs, 214-333-5242.

College of Adult Education
Dr. Donovan Fredrickson, Dean
Programs in:
accounting (MA)
adult education (MA, MLA)
arts (MLA)
Christian ministry (MLA)
church leadership (MA)
counseling (MA)
criminal justice (MA)
English (MLA)
English as a second language (MA, MLA)
finance (MA)
fine arts (MLA)
higher education (MA)
history (MLA)
leadership studies (MA)
management (MA)
management information systems (MA)
marketing (MA)
missions (MA, MLA)
political science (MLA)

College of Business
Dr. Charlene Conner, Dean
Programs in:
accounting (MBA)
business (MA, MBA)
business communication (MA, MBA)
conflict resolution management (MA, MBA)
e-business (MBA)
entrepreneurship (MBA)
finance (MBA)
general management (MA)
health care management (MA, MBA)
human resource management (MA)
international business (MBA)
leading the non-profit organization (MBA)
management (MBA)
management information systems (MBA)
marketing (MBA)
performance management (MA)
project management (MBA)
technology and engineering management (MBA)

College of Humanities and Social Sciences
Dr. Michael Williams, Dean
Programs in:
counseling (MA)
humanities and social sciences (MA)

Dorothy M. Bush College of Education
Dr. Charles Carona, Dean

Programs in:
curriculum and instruction (M Ed)
education (M Ed, MAT)
educational leadership (M Ed)
elementary (MAT)
English as a second language (M Ed, MAT)
hi-level (MAT)
kinesiology (M Ed)
master reading teacher (M Ed)
reading specialist (M Ed)
school counseling (M Ed)
secondary (MAT)

Gary Cook School of Leadership
Dr. Rick Gregory, Dean
Programs in:
adult ministry (MA)
business communication (MA)
business ministry (MA)
childhood ministry (MA)
Christian education and business administration (MA, MBA)
Christian education/missions (MA)
Christian education: childhood ministry (MA)
Christian education: student ministry (MA)
collegiate ministry (MA)
communication ministry (MA)
counseling ministry (MA)
education in higher education (M Ed)
education ministry (MA)
ESL (MA)
general ministry (MA)
general studies (MA)
global studies (MA)
international business (MA)
leadership (M Ed, MA, MBA)
missions (MA)
missions ministry (MA)
student ministry (MA)
worship leadership (MA)
worship ministry (MA)
worship/missions (MA)

■ DEVRY UNIVERSITY
Irving, TX 75063-2439
http://www.devry.edu/

Proprietary, coed, comprehensive institution. *Computer facilities:* Computer purchase and lease plans are available. 442 computers available on campus for general student use. A campuswide network can be accessed from off campus. Online class registration is available.

Keller Graduate School of Management
Program in:
management (MAFM, MBA, MHRM, MISM, MNCM, MPM, Graduate Certificate)

■ HARDIN-SIMMONS UNIVERSITY
Abilene, TX 79698-0001
http://www.hsutx.edu/

Independent-religious, coed, comprehensive institution. *Graduate faculty:* 80 full-time (30 women), 19 part-time/adjunct (5 women). *Computer facilities:* 217 computers available on campus for general student use. A campuswide network can be accessed from student residence rooms and from off campus. *Graduate expenses:* Tuition: full-time $10,620; part-time $590 per credit hour. Required fees: $590; $110 per semester. Tuition and fees vary according to course load and degree level. *General application contact:* Dr. Gary Stanlake, Dean of Graduate Studies, 325-670-1298.

The Acton MBA in Entrepreneurship
Program in:
entrepreneurship (MBA)

Graduate School
Dr. Gary Stanlake, Dean of Graduate Studies

Cynthia Ann Parker College of Liberal Arts
Dr. Alan R. Stafford, Dean
Programs in:
English (MA)
family psychology (MA)
history (MA)
liberal arts (MA)

Holland School of Sciences and Mathematics
Dr. Christopher McNair, Dean
Programs in:
environmental management (MS)
physical therapy (DPT)
sciences and mathematics (MS, DPT)

Irvin School of Education
Dr. Pam Williford, Dean
Programs in:
counseling and human development (M Ed)
education (M Ed)
gifted education (M Ed)
kinesiology, sport, and recreation (M Ed)
reading specialist education (M Ed)

Kelley College of Business
Dr. Nancy Kucinski, Director
Program in:
business (MBA)

Logsdon School of Theology
Dr. Thomas V. Brisco, Dean
Programs in:
family ministry (MA)
religion (MA)
theology (M Div)

Patty Hanks Shelton School of Nursing
Dr. Amy Toone, Director
Programs in:
advanced healthcare delivery (MSN)
family nurse practitioner (MSN)

School of Music
Dr. Leigh Anne Hunsaker, Director
Programs in:
church music (MM)
music education (MM)
music performance (MM)
theory-composition (MM)

■ HOUSTON BAPTIST UNIVERSITY
Houston, TX 77074-3298
http://www.hbu.edu/

Independent-religious, coed, comprehensive institution. *Computer facilities:* 95 computers available on campus for general student use. A campuswide network can be accessed from student residence rooms. Online class registration is available. *General application contact:* Coordinator of Graduate Admissions, 281-649-3295.

College of Arts and Humanities
Programs in:
arts and humanities (MATS, MLA)
liberal arts (MLA)
theological studies (MATS)

College of Business and Economics
Programs in:
accounting (MACCT)
business administration (MBA, MSM)
business and economics (MACCT, MBA, MSHA, MSHRM, MSM)
health administration (MSHA)
human resources management (MSHRM)

College of Education and Behavioral Sciences
Programs in:
bilingual education (M Ed)
Christian counseling (MACC)
counselor education (M Ed)
curriculum and instruction (M Ed)
education and behavioral sciences (M Ed, MACC, MAP)
educational administration (M Ed)
educational diagnostician (M Ed)
psychology (MAP)
reading education (M Ed)

■ LAMAR UNIVERSITY
Beaumont, TX 77710
http://www.lamar.edu/

State-supported, coed, university. CGS member. *Graduate faculty:* 185 full-time (61 women), 20 part-time/adjunct (4 women). *Computer facilities:* 120 computers available on campus for general student use. A campuswide network can be accessed from student residence rooms and from off campus. *Graduate expenses:* Tuition, state resident: full-time $5000; part-time $195 per credit. Tuition, nonresident: full-time $12,376; part-time $476 per credit. Required

Lamar University (continued)
fees: $1570. *General application contact:* Sandy Drane, Coordinator of Graduate Admissions, 409-880-8356.

College of Graduate Studies

College of Arts and Sciences
Dr. Brenda S. Nichols, Dean
Programs in:
- applied criminology (MS)
- arts and sciences (MA, MPA, MS, MSN)
- biology (MS)
- chemistry (MS)
- community/clinical psychology (MS)
- computer science (MS)
- English (MA)
- history (MA)
- industrial/organizational psychology (MS)
- mathematics (MS)
- nursing administration (MSN)
- nursing education (MSN)
- public administration (MPA)

College of Business
Dr. Enrique R. Venta, Dean
Programs in:
- accounting (MBA)
- experiential business and entrepreneurship (MBA)
- financial management (MBA)
- healthcare administration (MBA)
- information systems (MBA)
- management (MBA)

College of Education and Human Development
Dr. H. Lowery-Moore, Dean
Programs in:
- counseling and development (M Ed, Certificate)
- education administration (M Ed)
- education and human development (M Ed, MS, DE, Ed D, Certificate)
- educational leadership (DE)
- family and consumer science (MS)
- kinesiology (MS)
- principal (Certificate)
- professional pedagogy (Ed D)
- school superintendent (Certificate)
- supervision (M Ed)
- technology application (Certificate)
- vocational home economics (Certificate)

College of Engineering
Dr. Jack Hopper, Chair
Programs in:
- chemical engineering (ME, MES, DE, PhD)
- civil engineering (ME, MES, DE)
- electrical engineering (ME, MES, DE)
- engineering (ME, MEM, MES, MS, DE, PhD)
- engineering management (MEM)
- environmental engineering (MS)
- environmental studies (MS)
- industrial engineering (ME, MES, DE)
- mechanical engineering (ME, MES, DE)

College of Fine Arts and Communication
Dr. Russ A. Schultz, Dean
Programs in:
- art history (MA)
- audiology (MS, Au D)
- deaf studies and deaf education (MS, Ed D)
- fine arts and communication (MA, MM, MM Ed, MS, Au D, Ed D)
- music education (MM Ed)
- music performance (MM)
- photography (MA)
- speech language pathology (MS)
- studio art (MA)
- theatre (MS)
- visual design (MA)

■ LETOURNEAU UNIVERSITY
Longview, TX 75607-7001
http://www.letu.edu/

Independent-religious, coed, comprehensive institution. *Computer facilities:* Computer purchase and lease plans are available. 191 computers available on campus for general student use. A campuswide network can be accessed from student residence rooms and from off campus. Online class registration is available. *Graduate expenses:* Tuition: full-time $11,603; part-time $595 per credit hour. Required fees: $975; $50 per credit hour. One-time fee: $75 full-time. *General application contact:* Assistant Vice President for Enrollment Management and Market Research, 903-233-4000.

School of Graduate and Professional Studies
Programs in:
- business administration (MBA)
- curriculum and instruction (M Ed)
- educational administration (M Ed)
- teaching and learning (M Ed)

■ LUBBOCK CHRISTIAN UNIVERSITY
Lubbock, TX 79407-2099
http://www.lcu.edu/

Independent-religious, coed, comprehensive institution. *Computer facilities:* 159 computers available on campus for general student use. A campuswide network can be accessed from student residence rooms and from off campus. Online class registration is available. *General application contact:* Administrative Assistant, 806-720-7662.

Graduate Biblical Studies
Programs in:
- Bible and ministry (MS)
- biblical interpretation (MA)

■ MIDWESTERN STATE UNIVERSITY
Wichita Falls, TX 76308
http://www.mwsu.edu/

State-supported, coed, comprehensive institution. *Computer facilities:* 402 computers available on campus for general student use. A campuswide network can be accessed from student residence rooms and from off campus. Online class registration is available. *General application contact:* Director of Admissions, 800-842-1922.

Graduate Studies

College of Business Administration
Programs in:
- business administration (MBA)
- health services administration (MBA)

College of Education
Programs in:
- curriculum and instruction (ME)
- education (M Ed, MA, ME)
- educational leadership and technology (ME)
- general counseling (MA)
- human resource development (MA)
- reading education (M Ed)
- school counseling (M Ed)
- special education (M Ed)
- training and development (MA)

College of Health Sciences and Human Services
Programs in:
- family nurse practitioner (MSN)
- health sciences and human services (MHA, MPA, MSK, MSN, MSR)
- health services administration (MHA, MSN)
- kinesiology (MSK)
- nurse educator (MSN)
- public administration (MPA)
- public administration (administrative justice) (MPA)
- public administration (health services administration)
- with certificate (MPA)
- public administration (health services) (MPA)
- radiologic administration (MSR)
- radiologic education (MSR)
- radiologic sciences (MSR)
- radiologist assistant (MSR)

College of Humanities and Social Sciences
Programs in:
- English (MA)
- history (MA)
- humanities and social sciences (MA)
- political science (MA)
- psychology (MA)

College of Science and Mathematics
Programs in:
- biology (MS)
- computer science (MS)
- science and mathematics (MS)

■ OUR LADY OF THE LAKE UNIVERSITY OF SAN ANTONIO

San Antonio, TX 78207-4689
http://www.ollusa.edu/

Independent-religious, coed, comprehensive institution. *Computer facilities:* 230 computers available on campus for general student use. A campuswide network can be accessed from student residence rooms and from off campus. Online class registration is available. *Graduate expenses:* Tuition: full-time $11,970; part-time $665 per credit hour. Required fees: $500; $250 per term. *General application contact:* Information Contact, 210-434-6711 Ext. 2314.

College of Arts and Sciences

Dr. Mary Francine Danis, Dean
Programs in:
- English (MA)
- English and communication arts (MA)
- English and literature (MA)
- English education (MA)
- writing (MA)

School of Business and Leadership

Dr. Robert Bisking, Dean
Programs in:
- accounting/finance (MBA)
- healthcare management (MBA)
- information systems and security (MS)
- leadership studies (PhD)
- management (MBA)
- nonprofit management (MS)
- organizational leadership (MS)

School of Professional Studies

Dr. Teresita Aguilar, Dean
Programs in:
- bilingual (M Ed)
- communication and learning disorders (MA)
- counseling psychology (MS, Psy D)
- curriculum and instruction (M Ed)
- early childhood education (M Ed)
- early elementary education (M Ed)
- English as a second language (M Ed)
- generic special education (M Ed)
- human sciences (MA)
- integrated math teaching (M Ed)
- integrated science teaching (M Ed)
- intermediate education (M Ed)
- learning resources specialist (M Ed)
- marriage and family therapy (MS)
- master technology teacher (M Ed)
- principal (M Ed)
- psychology (MS, Psy D)
- reading specialist (M Ed)
- school counseling (M Ed)
- school psychology (MS)
- secondary education (M Ed)

Worden School of Social Service

Dr. Walter Calvo, Director
Program in:
- social service (MSW)

■ PRAIRIE VIEW A&M UNIVERSITY

Prairie View, TX 77446-0519
http://www.pvamu.edu/

State-supported, coed, comprehensive institution. *Computer facilities:* 3,000 computers available on campus for general student use. A campuswide network can be accessed from student residence rooms and from off campus. Online class registration is available. *General application contact:* Office of Graduate Admissions, 936-857-3311.

College of Agriculture and Human Sciences

Programs in:
- agricultural economics (MS)
- animal sciences (MS)
- interdisciplinary human sciences (MS)
- soil science (MS)

College of Arts and Sciences

Programs in:
- arts and sciences (MA, MS)
- biology (MS)
- chemistry (MS)
- English (MA)
- mathematics (MS)

Division of Social Work, Behavioral and Political Science
Program in:
- sociology (MA)

College of Business

Programs in:
- accounting (MS)
- general business administration (MBA)

College of Education

Programs in:
- counseling (MA, MS Ed)
- curriculum and instruction (M Ed, MS Ed)
- education (M Ed, MA, MS, MS Ed, PhD)
- educational administration (M Ed, MS Ed)
- educational leadership (PhD)
- health education (M Ed, MS)
- physical education (M Ed, MS)
- special education (M Ed, MS Ed)

College of Engineering

Programs in:
- computer information systems (MSCIS)
- computer science (MSCS)
- electrical engineering (MSEE, PhDEE)
- engineering (MS Engr)

College of Juvenile Justice and Psychology

Programs in:
- clinical adolescent psychology (PhD)
- juvenile forensic psychology (MSJFP)
- juvenile justice (MSJJ, PhD)

College of Nursing

Programs in:
- family nurse practitioner (MSN)
- nursing administration (MSN)
- nursing education (MSN)

School of Architecture

Programs in:
- architecture (M Arch)
- community development (MCD)

■ RICE UNIVERSITY

Houston, TX 77251-1892
http://www.rice.edu/

Independent, coed, university. CGS member. *Computer facilities:* 523 computers available on campus for general student use. A campuswide network can be accessed from student residence rooms and from off campus. Online class registration is available. *General application contact:* Office of Graduate Studies, 713-348-4002.

Graduate Programs

Program in:
- education (MAT)

George R. Brown School of Engineering
Programs in:
- bioengineering (MS, PhD)
- biostatistics (PhD)
- chemical and biomolecular engineering (MS, PhD)
- chemical engineering (M Ch E)
- circuits, controls, and communication systems (MS, PhD)
- civil engineering (MCE, MS, PhD)
- computational and applied mathematics (MA, MCAM, PhD)
- computational finance (PhD)
- computational science and engineering (MCSE, PhD)
- computer science (MCS, MS, PhD)
- computer science and engineering (MS, PhD)
- computer science in bioinformatics (MCS)
- electrical engineering (MEE)
- engineering (M Ch E, M Stat, MA, MBE, MCAM, MCE, MCS, MCSE, MEE, MEE, MES, MME, MMS, MS, PhD)
- environmental engineering (MEE, MES, MS, PhD)
- environmental science (MEE, MES, MS, PhD)
- lasers, microwaves, and solid-state electronics (MS, PhD)
- materials science (MMS, MS, PhD)
- mechanical engineering (MME, MS, PhD)
- statistics (M Stat, MA, PhD)

Jesse H. Jones Graduate School of Management
Program in:
- business administration (EMBA, MBA, PMBA)

Rice University (continued)

School of Architecture
Programs in:
architecture (M Arch, D Arch)
urban design (M Arch UD)

School of Humanities
Programs in:
English (MA, PhD)
French studies (MA, PhD)
history (MA, PhD)
humanities (MA, PhD)
linguistics (MA, PhD)
philosophy (MA, PhD)
religious studies (PhD)
Spanish (MA)

School of Social Sciences
Programs in:
anthropology (MA, PhD)
cognitive sciences (MA, PhD)
economics (MA, PhD)
industrial-organizational/social psychology (MA, PhD)
political science (MA, PhD)
psychology (MA, PhD)
social sciences (MA, PhD)

Shepherd School of Music
Programs in:
composition (MM, DMA)
conducting (MM)
history (MM)
performance (MM, DMA)
theory (MM)

Wiess School of Natural Sciences
Programs in:
biochemistry and cell biology (MA, PhD)
chemistry (MA)
earth science (MA, PhD)
ecology and evolutionary biology (MA, MS, PhD)
inorganic chemistry (PhD)
mathematics (MA, PhD)
natural sciences (MA, MS, MST, PhD)
organic chemistry (PhD)
physical chemistry (PhD)
physics (MA)
physics and astronomy (MS, MST, PhD)

Wiess School–Professional Science Master's Programs
Programs in:
environmental analysis and decision making (MS)
geophysics (MS)
nanoscale physics (MS)
professional science (MS)

Rice Quantum Institute
Program in:
quantum physics (MS, PhD)

■ ST. EDWARD'S UNIVERSITY
Austin, TX 78704
http://www.gotostedwards.com/

Independent-religious, coed, comprehensive institution. *Graduate faculty:* 51 full-time (15 women), 73 part-time/adjunct (29 women). *Computer facilities:* 649 computers available on campus for general student use. A campuswide network can be accessed from student residence rooms and from off campus. Online class registration is available. *Graduate expenses:* Tuition: full-time $13,752; part-time $764 per credit hour. Required fees: $50 per semester. Full-time tuition and fees vary according to course load and program. *General application contact:* Bridget S. Davidson, Director, Center for Academic Progress, 512-428-1061.

New College
Dr. H. Ramsey Fowler, Dean
Programs in:
college student development (MA)
counseling (MA)
global issues (MLA)
humanities (MLA)
liberal arts (Certificate)
social sciences (MLA)

School of Education
Dr. Karen Jenlink, Dean
Programs in:
curriculum leadership (Certificate)
education (MA, Certificate)
instructional technology (Certificate)
mentoring and supervision (Certificate)
sports management (Certificate)
teaching (MA)

School of Management and Business
Marsha Kelliher, Dean
Programs in:
accounting (M Ac)
administration (Certificate)
business management (MBA)
computer information systems (MS)
conflict resolution (Certificate)
corporate finance (MBA, Certificate)
digital media management (MBA)
entrepreneurship (MBA, Certificate)
family mediation (Certificate)
global business (MBA, Certificate)
human resource management (MBA, Certificate)
human services (MA)
management and business (M Ac, MA, MBA, MS, Certificate)
management information systems (MBA, Certificate)
marketing (MBA, Certificate)
mediation (Certificate)
operations management (MBA, Certificate)
organization development and training (Certificate)
organizational leadership and ethics (MS)
project management (MS)

■ ST. MARY'S UNIVERSITY
San Antonio, TX 78228-8507
http://www.stmarytx.edu/

Independent-religious, coed, comprehensive institution. *Graduate faculty:* 47 full-time (18 women), 55 part-time/adjunct (18 women). *Computer facilities:* Computer purchase and lease plans are available. 100 computers available on campus for general student use. A campuswide network can be accessed from student residence rooms and from off campus. Online class registration is available. *Graduate expenses:* Tuition: full-time $12,006; part-time $667 per credit hour. Required fees: $440; $220 per semester. *General application contact:* Dr. Henry Flores, Dean of the Graduate School, 210-436-3101.

Graduate School
Dr. Henry Flores, Dean of the Graduate School
Programs in:
Catholic principalship (Certificate)
Catholic school administrators (Certificate)
Catholic school leadership (MA, Certificate)
Catholic school teachers (Certificate)
clinical psychology (MA, MS)
communication studies (MA)
community counseling (MA)
computer information systems (MS)
computer science (MS)
counseling (Sp C)
counseling education and supervision (PhD)
educational leadership (MA, Certificate)
electrical engineering (MS)
electrical/computer engineering (MS)
engineering administration (MS)
engineering computer applications (MS)
engineering management (MS)
engineering systems management (MS)
English literature and language (MA)
industrial engineering (MS)
industrial/organizational psychology (MA, MS)
inter-American administration (MPA)
international relations (MA)
marriage and family relations (Certificate)
marriage and family therapy (MA, PhD)
mental health (MA)
mental health and substance abuse counseling (Certificate)
operations research (MS)
pastoral ministry (MA)
political communications and applied science (MA)
political science (MA)
principalship (mid-management) (Certificate)
public administration (MPA)
public management (MPA)
reading (MA)
software engineering (MS)
substance abuse (MA)
theology (MA)

Bill Greehey School of Business
Dr. Orion J. Welch, Interim Dean
Programs in:
accounting (M Acc)
business administration (MBA)
finance (MBA)

international business (MBA)
management (MBA)
taxation (M Acc)

School of Law
Dr. Charles Cantu, Interim Dean
Program in:
law (JD)

■ SAM HOUSTON STATE UNIVERSITY
Huntsville, TX 77341
http://www.shsu.edu/

State-supported, coed, university. CGS member. *Graduate faculty:* 222 full-time (84 women), 41 part-time/adjunct (20 women). *Computer facilities:* 600 computers available on campus for general student use. A campuswide network can be accessed from student residence rooms and from off campus. Online class registration is available. *Graduate expenses:* Tuition, state resident: full-time $3564; part-time $198 per credit hour. Tuition, nonresident: full-time $8622; part-time $479 per credit hour. Required fees: $1290. Tuition and fees vary according to course load and campus/location. *General application contact:* Dr. Mitchell Muehsam, Dean of Graduate Studies and Associate Vice President for Academic Affairs, 936-294-1971.

College of Arts and Sciences
Dr. Jaimie Hebert, Dean
Programs in:
agriculture (MS)
arts and sciences (MA, MFA, MM, MS)
biology (MA, MS)
chemistry (MS)
computing and information science (MS)
dance (MFA)
industrial technology (MA)
mathematics (MA, MS)
statistics (MS)

School of Music
Dr. James Bankhead, Chair
Programs in:
music (MM)
music education (MM)

College of Business Administration
Dr. Leroy Ashorn, Acting Dean
Programs in:
accounting (MS)
business administration (MBA)
finance (MS)
general business and finance (MS)

College of Criminal Justice
Dr. Vincent Webb, Dean
Programs in:
criminal justice (MS, PhD)
criminal justice and criminology (MA)
criminal justice management (MS)
forensic science (MS)
security studies (MS)
victim services management (MS)

College of Education and Applied Science
Dr. Genevieve Brown, Dean
Programs in:
administration (M Ed, MA)
counseling (M Ed, MA)
counselor education (MA, PhD)
curriculum and instruction (M Ed, MA)
education and applied science (M Ed, MA, MLS, Ed D, PhD)
educational leadership (Ed D)
health and kinesiology (M Ed, MA)
instructional leadership (M Ed, MA)
instructional technology (M Ed)
library science (MLS)
reading (M Ed, MA, Ed D)
special education (M Ed, MA)

College of Humanities and Social Sciences
Dr. John deCastro, Dean
Programs in:
clinical psychology (PhD)
dietetics (MS)
English (MA)
family and consumer sciences (MS)
history (MA)
humanities and social sciences (MA, MPA, MS, PhD)
political science (MA)
psychology (MA)
public administration (MPA)
sociology (MA)

■ SOUTHERN METHODIST UNIVERSITY
Dallas, TX 75275
http://www.smu.edu/

Independent-religious, coed, university. CGS member. *Graduate faculty:* 656 full-time (232 women), 378 part-time/adjunct (147 women). *Computer facilities:* 758 computers available on campus for general student use. A campuswide network can be accessed from student residence rooms and from off campus. Online class registration, online billing/payment processing are available. *General application contact:* Dr. James E. Quick, Associate Vice President for Research and Dean of Graduate Studies, 214-768-4345.

Annette Caldwell Simmons School of Education and Human Development
Dr. David J. Chard, Leon Simmons Endowed Dean
Programs in:
bilingual/ESL education (MBE)
counseling (MS)
dispute resolution (MA, Certificate)
dispute resolution and counseling (MA, Certificate)
education (M Ed, PhD)
educational preparation (Certificate)
gifted and talented focus (MBE)
learning therapist (Certificate)
liberal studies (MLS)
teaching and learning (MBE, PhD, Certificate)

Bobby B. Lyle School of Engineering
Dr. Geoffrey Orsak, Dean
Programs in:
applied science (MS, PhD)
civil engineering (MS, PhD)
computer engineering (MS Cp E, PhD)
computer science (MS, PhD)
electrical engineering (MSEE, PhD)
electronic and optical packaging (MS)
engineering (MS, MS Cp E, MSEE, MSEM, MSIEM, MSME, DE, PhD)
engineering management (MSEM, DE)
environmental engineering (MS)
environmental science (MS)
facilities management (MS)
information engineering and management (MSIEM)
manufacturing systems management (MS)
mechanical engineering (MSME, PhD)
operations research (MS, PhD)
security engineering (MS)
software engineering (MS)
systems engineering (MS, PhD)
telecommunications (MS)

Cox School of Business
Dr. Albert W. Niemi, Dean
Programs in:
accounting (MBA, MSA)
business (Exec MBA)
business administration (MBA)
entrepreneurship (MS)
finance (MBA)
information technology and operations management (MBA)
management (MSM)
marketing (MBA)
strategy and entrepreneurship (MBA)

Dedman College
Programs in:
anthropology (PhD)
applied economics (MA)
applied geophysics (MS)
biological sciences (MA, MS, PhD)
chemistry (MS, PhD)
clinical psychology (PhD)
computational and applied mathematics (MS, PhD)
economics (MA, PhD)
English (MA, PhD)
geology (MS, PhD)
geophysics (MS, PhD)
history (MA, PhD)
medical anthropology (MA)
medieval studies (MA)
physics (MS, PhD)
religious studies (MA, PhD)
statistical science (MS, PhD)

Dedman School of Law
John B. Attanasio, Dean
Programs in:
foreign law school graduates (LL M)

Southern Methodist University (continued)
law (JD, SJD)
law-general (LL M)
taxation (LL M)

Meadows School of the Arts
Jose Antonio Bowen, Dean
Programs in:
acting (MFA)
art history (MA)
arts (MA, MFA, MM, MSM, Certificate)
conducting (MM)
dance (MFA)
design (MFA)
music composition (MM)
music education (MM)
music history (MM)
music theory (MM)
performance (MM, Certificate)
piano performance and pedagogy (MM)
sacred music (MSM)
studio art (MFA)

Division of Arts Administration
Dr. P. Gregory Warden, Interim Chair

Division of Communication Arts
Rick Worland, Chair
Program in:
communication arts (MA)

Perkins School of Theology
Dr. William B. Lawrence, Dean
Program in:
theology (M Div, CMM, MSM, MTS, D Min)

■ STEPHEN F. AUSTIN STATE UNIVERSITY

Nacogdoches, TX 75962
http://www.sfasu.edu/

State-supported, coed, comprehensive institution. *Computer facilities:* 1,000 computers available on campus for general student use. A campuswide network can be accessed from student residence rooms and from off campus. Online class registration is available. *General application contact:* Associate Vice President for Graduate Studies and Research, 936-468-2807.

Graduate School

College of Applied Arts and Science
Programs in:
applied arts and science (MA, MIS, MSW)
communication (MA)
interdisciplinary studies (MIS)
mass communication (MA)
social work (MSW)

College of Business
Programs in:
business (MBA, MPAC, MS)
computer science (MS)
management and marketing (MBA)
professional accountancy (MPAC)

College of Education
Programs in:
athletic training (MS)
counseling (MA)
early childhood education (M Ed)
education (M Ed, MA, MS, Ed D)
educational leadership (Ed D)
elementary education (M Ed)
human sciences (MS)
kinesiology (M Ed)
school psychology (MA)
secondary education (M Ed)
special education (M Ed)
speech pathology (MS)

College of Fine Arts
Programs in:
art (MA)
design (MFA)
drawing (MFA)
fine arts (MA, MFA, MM)
music (MA, MM)
painting (MFA)
sculpture (MFA)

College of Forestry and Agriculture
Programs in:
agriculture (MS)
forestry (MF, MS, PhD)
forestry and agriculture (MF, MS, PhD)

College of Liberal Arts
Programs in:
English (MA)
history (MA)
liberal arts (MA, MPA)
psychology (MA)
public administration (MPA)

College of Sciences and Mathematics
Programs in:
biology (MS)
biotechnology (MS)
chemistry (MS)
environmental science (MS)
geology (MS, MSNS)
mathematics (MS)
mathematics education (MS)
physics (MS)
sciences and mathematics (MS, MSNS)
statistics (MS)

■ SUL ROSS STATE UNIVERSITY

Alpine, TX 79832
http://www.sulross.edu/

State-supported, coed, comprehensive institution. *Computer facilities:* 200 computers available on campus for general student use. A campuswide network can be accessed from student residence rooms and from off campus. *General application contact:* Dean of Admissions and Records, 915-837-8050.

Division of Agricultural and Natural Resource Science
Programs in:
agricultural and natural resource science (M Ag, MS)
animal science (M Ag, MS)
range and wildlife management (M Ag, MS)

Rio Grande College of Sul Ross State University
Programs in:
business administration (MBA)
teacher education (M Ed)

School of Arts and Sciences
Programs in:
art education (M Ed)
art history (M Ed)
arts and sciences (M Ed, MA, MS)
biology (MS)
Earth and physical sciences (MS)
English (MA)
history (MA)
political science (MA)
psychology (MA)
public administration (MA)
studio art (M Ed)

School of Professional Studies
Programs in:
bilingual education (M Ed)
business administration (MBA)
counseling (M Ed)
criminal justice (MS)
educational diagnostics (M Ed)
elementary education (M Ed)
physical education (M Ed)
professional studies (M Ed, MBA, MS)
reading specialist (M Ed)
school administration (M Ed)
secondary education (M Ed)
supervision (M Ed)

■ TARLETON STATE UNIVERSITY

Stephenville, TX 76402
http://www.tarleton.edu/

State-supported, coed, comprehensive institution. *Graduate faculty:* 140 full-time (49 women), 42 part-time/adjunct (21 women). *Computer facilities:* 1,000 computers available on campus for general student use. A campuswide network can be accessed from student residence rooms and from off campus. Online class registration is available. *Graduate expenses:* Tuition, state resident: full-time $2853; part-time $158.50 per credit hour. Tuition, nonresident: full-time $7551; part-time $419.50 per credit hour. Required fees: $1040; $42 per credit hour. $124 per semester. Tuition and fees vary according to course load and campus/location. *General application contact:* Dr. Linda M. Jones, Dean, 254-968-9104.

College of Graduate Studies
Dr. Linda M. Jones, Dean
Program in:
liberal studies (MS)

College of Agriculture and Human Sciences
Dr. Don Cawthon, Dean
Programs in:
agriculture (MS)
agriculture and human sciences (MS)
agriculture education (MS)

College of Business Administration
Programs in:
business administration (MBA, MS)
human resource management (MS)
information systems (MS)
management and leadership (MS)

College of Education
Dr. Jill Burk, Dean
Programs in:
counseling and psychology (M Ed)
curriculum and instruction (M Ed)
education (M Ed, Ed D, Certificate)
educational administration (M Ed)
educational leadership (Ed D, Certificate)
physical education (M Ed)
secondary education (Certificate)
special education (Certificate)

College of Liberal and Fine Arts
Dr. Dean A. Minix, Dean
Programs in:
criminal justice (MCJ)
English (MA)
history (MA)
liberal and fine arts (MA, MCJ, MM)
music education (MM)
political science (MA)

College of Science and Technology
Dr. James Pierce, Dean
Programs in:
biology (MS)
environmental science (MS)
mathematics (MS)
science and technology (MS)

■ TEXAS A&M INTERNATIONAL UNIVERSITY

Laredo, TX 78041-1900
http://www.tamiu.edu/

State-supported, coed, comprehensive institution. CGS member. *Graduate faculty:* 79 full-time (21 women), 13 part-time/adjunct (3 women). *Computer facilities:* 410 computers available on campus for general student use. A campuswide network can be accessed from student residence rooms and from off campus. Online class registration is available. *General application contact:* Dr. Jeff Brown, Dean, Office of Graduate Studies, 956-326-2596.

Office of Graduate Studies and Research
Dr. Jeff Brown, Dean
Programs in:
educational administration (MS Ed)
generic special education (MS Ed)
school counseling (MS)

College of Arts and Sciences
Dr. Thomas R. Mitchell, Interim Dean
Programs in:
arts and sciences (MA, MACP, MPA, MS, PhD)
biology (MS)
counseling psychology (MACP)
criminal justice (MS)
English (MA)
Hispanic studies (PhD)
history (MA)
mathematical and physical science (MA)
political science (MA)
psychology (MS)
public administration (MPA)
sociology (MA)
Spanish (MA)

College of Business Administration
Dr. Antonio Rodriguez, Associate Dean
Programs in:
accounting (MP Acc)
business administration (MBA, MP Acc, MSIS)
information systems (MSIS)
international banking (MBA)
international trade (MBA)

College of Education
Dr. Humberto Gonzalez, Dean
Programs in:
bilingual education (PhD)
curriculum and instruction (MS, PhD)
early childhood education (PhD)
education (MS, MS Ed, PhD)
reading (MS)

College of Nursing and Health Sciences
Natalie Burkhalter, Interim Dean
Program in:
nursing and health sciences (MSN)

■ TEXAS A&M UNIVERSITY

College Station, TX 77843
http://www.tamu.edu/

State-supported, coed, university. CGS member. *Graduate faculty:* 1,633. *Computer facilities:* 1,483 computers available on campus for general student use. A campuswide network can be accessed from student residence rooms and from off campus. Online class registration is available. *Graduate expenses:* Tuition, state resident: full-time $3838.50. Tuition, nonresident: full-time $8897. Required fees: $2359.60. *General application contact:* Graduate Admissions, 979-458-0427.

College of Agriculture and Life Sciences
Dr. Mark Hussey, Interim Vice Chancellor
Programs in:
agricultural economics (MAB, MS, PhD)
agricultural education (M Ed, MS, Ed D, PhD)
agriculture (M Agr)
agriculture and life sciences (M Agr, M Ed, M Eng, MAB, MS, DE, Ed D, PhD)
agronomy (M Agr, MS, PhD)
animal breeding (MS, PhD)
animal science (M Agr, MS, PhD)
biochemistry (MS, PhD)
biological and agricultural engineering (M Agr, M Eng, MS, DE, PhD)
biophysics (MS)
dairy science (M Agr, MS)
entomology (M Agr, MS, PhD)
forestry (MS, PhD)
genetics (PhD)
horticulture (PhD)
horticulture and floriculture (M Agr, MS)
molecular and environmental plant sciences (MS, PhD)
natural resources development (M Agr)
nutrition and food science (M Agr, MS, PhD)
physiology of reproduction (MS, PhD)
plant pathology (MS, PhD)
plant protection (M Agr)
poultry science (M Agr, MS, PhD)
recreation resources development (M Agr)
recreation, park, and tourism sciences (MS, PhD)
soil science (MS, PhD)
wildlife and fisheries sciences (M Agr, MS, PhD)

College of Architecture
Jorge Vanegas, Interim Dean
Programs in:
architecture (M Arch, MS Arch, PhD)
construction management (MS)
land development (MSLD)
landscape architecture (MLA)
urban and regional science (PhD)
urban planning (MUP)
visualization science (MS)

College of Education and Human Development
Doug Palmer, Dean
Programs in:
counseling psychology (PhD)
curriculum and instruction (M Ed, MS, PhD)
education and human development (M Ed, MS, Ed D, PhD)
educational administration and human resource development (M Ed, MS, Ed D, PhD)
educational psychology (PhD)
educational technology (M Ed)
gifted and talented education (M Ed, MS)
health education (M Ed, MS, Ed D, PhD)
Hispanic bilingual education (M Ed, PhD)
human learning and development (MS)
intelligence, creativity, and giftedness (PhD)
kinesiology (M Ed, MS, Ed D, PhD)

Texas A&M University (continued)
- learning, development, and instruction (PhD)
- mathematics education (M Ed, MS, PhD)
- multicultural/urban/ESL/international education (M Ed, MS, PhD)
- reading/language arts (M Ed, MS, PhD)
- research, measurement and statistics (MS)
- research, measurement, and statistics (PhD)
- school counseling (M Ed)
- school psychology (PhD)
- science education (M Ed, MS, PhD)
- social studies education (M Ed, MS, PhD)
- special education (M Ed, PhD)

College of Engineering
Dr. G. Kemble Bennett, Dean
Programs in:
- aerospace engineering (M Eng, MS, PhD)
- biomedical engineering (M Eng, MS, D Eng, PhD)
- chemical engineering (M Eng, MS, PhD)
- computer engineering (M En, M Eng, MS, PhD)
- computer science (MCS, MS, PhD)
- construction engineering and management (M Eng, MS, D Eng, PhD)
- electrical engineering (MS, PhD)
- engineering (M En, M Eng, MCS, MID, MS, D Eng, PhD)
- engineering technology and industrial distribution (MID)
- environmental engineering (M Eng, MS, D Eng, PhD)
- geotechnical engineering (M Eng, MS, D Eng, PhD)
- health physics (MS)
- industrial and systems engineering (M Eng, MS)
- industrial engineering (D Eng, PhD)
- materials engineering (M Eng, MS, D Eng, PhD)
- mechanical engineering (M Eng, MS, D Eng, PhD)
- nuclear engineering (M Eng, MS, PhD)
- ocean engineering (M Eng, MS, D Eng, PhD)
- petroleum engineering (M Eng, MS, PhD)
- structural engineering (M Eng, MS, D Eng, PhD)
- transportation engineering (M Eng, MS, D Eng, PhD)
- water resources engineering (M Eng, MS, D Eng, PhD)

College of Geosciences
Dr. Bjorn Kjerfve, Dean
Programs in:
- atmospheric sciences (MS, PhD)
- geography (MS, PhD)
- geology (MS, PhD)
- geophysics (MS, PhD)
- geosciences (MS, PhD)
- oceanography (MS, PhD)

College of Liberal Arts
Dr. Charles A. Johnson, Dean
Programs in:
- anthropology (MA, PhD)
- behavioral and cellular neuroscience (MS, PhD)
- clinical psychology (MS, PhD)
- cognitive psychology (MS, PhD)
- communication (MA, PhD)
- developmental psychology (MS, PhD)
- economics (MS, PhD)
- English (MA, PhD)
- Hispanic studies (MA, PhD)
- history (MA, PhD)
- industrial/organizational psychology (MS, PhD)
- liberal arts (MA, MS, PhD)
- philosophy (MA, PhD)
- political science (MA, PhD)
- social psychology (MS, PhD)
- sociology (MS, PhD)

College of Science
H. Joseph Newton, Dean
Programs in:
- applied physics (PhD)
- biology (MS, PhD)
- botany (MS, PhD)
- chemistry (MS, PhD)
- mathematics (MS, PhD)
- microbiology (MS, PhD)
- molecular and cell biology (PhD)
- neuroscience (MS, PhD)
- physics (MS, PhD)
- science (MS, PhD)
- statistics (MS, PhD)
- zoology (MS, PhD)

College of Veterinary Medicine
Dr. H. Richard Adams, Dean
Programs in:
- epidemiology (MS)
- food safety/toxicology (MS)
- genetics (MS, PhD)
- physiology and pharmacology (MS, PhD)
- toxicology (MS, PhD)
- veterinary anatomy (MS, PhD)
- veterinary medicine (DVM, MS, PhD)
- veterinary medicine and surgery (MS)
- veterinary microbiology (MS, PhD)
- veterinary parasitology (MS)
- veterinary pathology (MS, PhD)
- veterinary public health (MS)

George Bush School of Government and Public Service
A. Benton Cocanougher, Dean
Programs in:
- advanced international affairs (Certificate)
- homeland security (Certificate)
- international affairs (MPIA)
- nonprofit management (Certificate)
- public service and administration (MPSA)

Mays Business School
Programs in:
- accounting (MS, PhD)
- business (EMBA, MBA, MLERE, MS, PhD)
- business administration (EMBA, MBA)
- finance (MS, PhD)
- human resource management (MS)
- management (PhD)
- management information systems (MS, PhD)
- management science (PhD)
- marketing (MS, PhD)
- production and operations management (PhD)
- real estate (MLERE)

■ TEXAS A&M UNIVERSITY–COMMERCE
Commerce, TX 75429-3011
http://www.tamu-commerce.edu/

State-supported, coed, university. CGS member. *Computer facilities:* Computer purchase and lease plans are available. 405 computers available on campus for general student use. A campuswide network can be accessed from student residence rooms and from off campus. Online class registration is available. *General application contact:* Graduate Admissions Adviser, 843-886-5167.

Graduate School

College of Arts and Sciences
Programs in:
- agricultural education (M Ed, MS)
- agricultural sciences (M Ed, MS)
- art (MA, MS)
- art history (MA)
- arts and sciences (M Ed, MA, MFA, MM, MS, PhD)
- biological and earth sciences (M Ed, MS)
- chemistry (M Ed, MS)
- college teaching of English (PhD)
- computer science (MS)
- English (MA, MS)
- fine arts (MFA)
- history (MA, MS)
- mathematics (MA, MS)
- music (MA, MS)
- music composition (MA, MM)
- music education (MA, MM, MS)
- music literature (MA)
- music performance (MA, MM)
- music theory (MA, MM)
- physics (M Ed, MS)
- social sciences (M Ed, MS)
- sociology (MA, MS)
- Spanish (MA)
- studio art (MA)
- theatre (MA, MS)

College of Business and Technology
Programs in:
- business administration (MBA)
- business and technology (MA, MBA, MS)
- economics (MA, MS)
- industrial technology (MS)
- technology management (MS)

College of Education and Human Services
Programs in:
bilingual/ESL education (M Ed, MS)
cognition and instruction (PhD)
counseling (M Ed, MS, PhD)
early childhood education (M Ed, MS)
education and human services (M Ed, MA, MS, MSW, Ed D, PhD)
educational administration (M Ed, Ed D)
educational technology (M Ed, MS)
elementary education (M Ed, MS)
exercise physiology (MS)
health and human performance (M Ed)
health promotion (MS)
health, kinesiology and sports studies (Ed D)
higher education (MS, Ed D)
learning technology and information systems (M Ed, MS)
motor performance (MS)
psychology (MA, MS)
reading (M Ed, MS)
secondary education (M Ed, MS)
social work (MSW)
special education (M Ed, MA, MS)
sport studies (MS)
supervision, curriculum and instruction: elementary education (Ed D)
supervision, curriculum, and instruction (Ed D)
training and development (MS)

■ TEXAS A&M UNIVERSITY–CORPUS CHRISTI

Corpus Christi, TX 78412-5503
http://www.tamucc.edu/

State-supported, coed, comprehensive institution. CGS member. *Computer facilities:* 500 computers available on campus for general student use. A campuswide network can be accessed from student residence rooms and from off campus. Online class registration is available. *General application contact:* Graduate Admissions Coordinator, 361-825-2177.

Graduate Studies and Research

College of Business
Programs in:
accounting (M Acc)
health care administration (MBA)
international business (MBA)

College of Education
Programs in:
counseling (MS, PhD)
counselor education (PhD)
curriculum and instruction (MS, Ed D)
early childhood education (MS)
educational administration (MS)
educational leadership (Ed D)
educational technology (MS)
elementary education (MS)
kinesiology (MS)
reading (MS)
secondary education (MS)
special education (MS)

College of Liberal Arts
Programs in:
English (MA)
history (MA)
psychology (MA)
public administration (MPA)
studio arts (MA, MFA)

College of Nursing and Health Sciences
Programs in:
clinical nurse specialist (MSN)
family nurse practitioner (MSN)
health care administration (MSN)
leadership in nursing systems (MSN)

College of Science and Technology
Programs in:
applied and computational mathematics (MS)
biology (MS)
coastal and marine system science (PhD)
computer science (MS)
curriculum content (MS)
environmental science (MS)
mariculture (MS)
science and technology (MS, PhD)

■ TEXAS A&M UNIVERSITY–KINGSVILLE

Kingsville, TX 78363
http://www.tamuk.edu/

State-supported, coed, university. *General application contact:* Dean, College of Graduate Studies, 361-593-2808.

College of Graduate Studies

College of Agriculture and Home Economics
Programs in:
agribusiness (MS)
agricultural education (MS)
agriculture and home economics (MS, PhD)
animal sciences (MS)
human sciences (MS)
plant and soil sciences (MS, PhD)
range and wildlife management (MS)
wildlife science (PhD)

College of Arts and Sciences
Programs in:
applied geology (MS)
art (MA, MS)
arts and sciences (MA, MM, MS)
biology (MS)
chemistry (MS)
communication (MS)
English (MA, MS)
gerontology (MS)
history and political science (MA, MS)
mathematics (MS)
music education (MM)
psychology (MA, MS)
sociology (MA, MS)
Spanish (MA)

College of Business Administration
Program in:
business administration (MBA, MS)

College of Education
Programs in:
adult education (M Ed)
bilingual education (MA, MS, Ed D)
early childhood education (M Ed)
education (M Ed, MA, MS, Ed D, PhD)
elementary education (MA, MS)
English as a second language (M Ed)
guidance and counseling (MA, MS)
health and kinesiology (MA, MS)
higher education administration leadership (PhD)
reading (MS)
school administration (MA, MS, Ed D)
secondary education (MA, MS)
special education (M Ed)
supervision (MA, MS)

College of Engineering
Programs in:
chemical engineering (ME, MS)
civil engineering (ME, MS)
computer science (MS)
electrical engineering (ME, MS)
engineering (ME, MS, PhD)
environmental engineering (ME, MS, PhD)
industrial engineering (ME, MS)
mechanical engineering (ME, MS)
natural gas engineering (ME, MS)

■ TEXAS A&M UNIVERSITY–TEXARKANA

Texarkana, TX 75505-5518
http://www.tamut.edu/

State-supported, coed, upper-level institution. *Computer facilities:* 133 computers available on campus for general student use. A campuswide network can be accessed from off campus. Online class registration is available. *General application contact:* Director of Admissions and Registrar, 903-223-3068.

Graduate Studies and Research

College of Education and Liberal Arts
Programs in:
adult education (MS)
curriculum and instruction (M Ed)
education (MS)
educational administration (M Ed)
English (MA)
instructional technology (MS)
interdisciplinary studies (MA, MS)
special education (MS)

College of Business
Programs in:
accounting (MSA)
business administration (MBA, MS)

College of Health and Behavioral Sciences
Program in:
counseling psychology (MS)

■ TEXAS CHRISTIAN UNIVERSITY

Fort Worth, TX 76129-0002

http://www.tcu.edu/

Independent-religious, coed, university. CGS member. *Graduate faculty:* 506 full-time (209 women), 305 part-time/adjunct (150 women). *Computer facilities:* A campuswide network can be accessed from student residence rooms and from off campus. Online class registration is available. *Graduate expenses:* Tuition: full-time $17,640. *General application contact:* Admissions, TCU Graduate Studies Office, 817-257-7515.

AddRan College of Liberal Arts

Dr. Andrew Schoolmaster, Dean
Programs in:
- English (MA, PhD)
- history (MA, PhD)
- liberal arts (MA, PhD)

College of Communication

Dr. David Whillock, Dean
Programs in:
- communication (MS)
- communication in human relations (MS)

Schieffer School of Journalism
Dr. John Tisdale, Director
Programs in:
- advertising/public relations (MS)
- news-editorial (MS)

College of Education

Dr. Mary M. Patton, Dean
Programs in:
- counseling (M Ed)
- curriculum studies (M Ed)
- education (M Ed, PhD, Certificate)
- educational administration (M Ed)
- educational studies: science education (PhD)
- elementary education (M Ed, Certificate)
- middle school education (M Ed)
- school counseling (Certificate)
- science education (M Ed)
- secondary education (M Ed)
- special education (M Ed)

College of Fine Arts

Dr. Scott Sullivan, Dean
Programs in:
- art history (MA)
- fine arts (M Mus, MA, MFA, MM Ed, Artist Diploma)
- studio art (MFA)

School of Music
Dr. Richard Gipson, Director
Programs in:
- conducting (M Mus)
- music education (MM Ed)
- musicology (M Mus)
- organ performance (M Mus)
- piano (Artist Diploma)
- piano pedagogy (M Mus)
- piano performance (M Mus)
- string performance (M Mus)
- theory/composition (M Mus)
- vocal performance (M Mus)
- voice pedagogy (M Mus)
- wind and percussion performance (M Mus)

College of Science and Engineering

Dr. Demetrius Kouris, Dean
Programs in:
- biology (MA, MS)
- chemistry (MA, MS, PhD)
- earth sciences (MS)
- ecology (MS)
- geology (MS)
- mathematics (MAT)
- physics (MA, MS, PhD)
- psychology (MA, MS, PhD)
- science and engineering (MA, MAT, MS, PhD)

Graduate Studies

Dr. Bonnie Melhart, Associate Provost for Academic Affairs
Program in:
- liberal arts (MLA)

Harris College of Nursing and Health Sciences

Dr. Paulette Burns, Dean
Programs in:
- adult nursing (MSN)
- kinesiology (MS)
- nursing (DNP)
- nursing and health sciences (MS, MSN, MSNA, DNP)
- speech-language pathology (MS)

School of Nurse Anesthesia
Dr. Kay K. Sanders, Director
Program in:
- nurse anesthesia (MSNA)

The Neeley School of Business at TCU

Dr. Homer Erekson, Dean
Programs in:
- accounting (M Ac)
- business administration (MBA)
- international management (MIM)

■ TEXAS SOUTHERN UNIVERSITY

Houston, TX 77004-4584

http://www.tsu.edu/

State-supported, coed, university. CGS member. *Graduate faculty:* 179 full-time (77 women), 37 part-time/adjunct (13 women). *Computer facilities:* 500 computers available on campus for general student use. A campuswide network can be accessed from student residence rooms and from off campus. Online class registration, Blackboard Learning and Community Portal System (E-education) are available. *Graduate expenses:* Tuition, state resident: full-time $1912; part-time $96 per credit hour. Tuition, nonresident: full-time $6302; part-time $343 per credit hour. Required fees: $3542. *General application contact:* Dr. Gregory Maddox, Interim Dean of the Graduate School, 713-313-7011 Ext. 4410.

College of Education

Programs in:
- bilingual education (M Ed)
- counseling (M Ed)
- counselor education (Ed D)
- curriculum and instruction (Ed D)
- education (M Ed, MS, Ed D)
- educational administration (M Ed, Ed D)
- health education (MS)
- human performance (MS)
- secondary education (M Ed)

College of Liberal Arts and Behavioral Sciences

Dr. Merline Pitre, Dean
Programs in:
- English (MA)
- fine arts (MA)
- history (MA)
- human services and consumer sciences (MS)
- liberal arts and behavioral sciences (MA, MS)
- music (MA)
- psychology (MA)
- sociology (MA)

College of Pharmacy and Health Sciences

Dr. Barbara Hayes, Dean
Program in:
- pharmacy and health sciences (Pharm D, MS, PhD)

Jesse H. Jones School of Business

Dr. Joseph Boyd, Dean
Programs in:
- business (MBA, MS)
- business administration (MBA)
- management information systems (MS)

School of Public Affairs

Dr. Theophilus Herrington, Dean
Programs in:
- administration of justice (MS, PhD)
- public administration (MPA)
- public affairs (MPA, MS, PhD)
- urban planning and environmental policy (MS, PhD)

School of Science and Technology

Dr. John Sapp, Interim Dean
Programs in:
- biology (MS)
- chemistry (MS)
- computer science (MS)
- environmental toxicology (MS, PhD)
- industrial technology (MS)
- mathematics (MS)
- science and technology (MS, PhD)
- transportation, planning and management (MS)

Tavis Smiley School of Communication

Dr. James Ward, Dean

Program in:
communication (MA)

Thurgood Marshall School of Law
Dr. McKen V. Carrington, Dean
Program in:
law (JD)

■ TEXAS STATE UNIVERSITY–SAN MARCOS
San Marcos, TX 78666
http://www.txstate.edu/

State-supported, coed, university. CGS member. *Graduate faculty:* 377 full-time (163 women), 81 part-time/adjunct (42 women). *Computer facilities:* Computer purchase and lease plans are available. 1,453 computers available on campus for general student use. A campuswide network can be accessed from student residence rooms and from off campus. Online class registration is available. *Graduate expenses:* Full-time $5280; part-time $220 per credit hour. Tuition, state resident: full-time $5280; part-time $220 per credit hour. Tuition, nonresident: full-time $12,024; part-time $501 per credit hour. Required fees: $1576; $42 per credit hour. $302 per semester. Tuition and fees vary according to course load. *General application contact:* Dr. J. Michael Willoughby, Dean of Graduate School, 512-245-2581.

Graduate School
Dr. J. Michael Willoughby, Dean
Programs in:
applied sociology (MAIS)
biology (MSIS)
criminal justice (MSIS)
educational administration and psychological services (MAIS)
elementary mathematics, science, and technology (MSIS)
health, physical education, and recreation (MAIS)
interdisciplinary studies in political science (MAIS)
international studies (MA)
modern languages (MAIS)
occupational education (MAIS, MSIS)
psychology (MAIS)

College of Applied Arts
Dr. Jaime Chahin, Dean
Programs in:
agriculture (M Ed)
applied arts (M Ed, MS, MSCJ, MSW, PhD)
criminal justice (MSCJ, PhD)
family and child studies (MS)
human nutrition (MS)
management of technical education (M Ed)
social work (MSW)

College of Education
Dr. Rosalinda Barrera, Dean
Programs in:
athletic training (MS)
counseling and guidance (M Ed)
developmental and adult education (MA, PhD)
early childhood education (M Ed, MA)
education (M Ed, MA, MSRLS, PhD)
educational administration (M Ed, MA)
elementary education (M Ed, MA)
elementary education-bilingual/bicultural (M Ed, MA)
health education (M Ed)
physical education (M Ed)
professional counseling (MA)
reading education (M Ed)
recreation and leisure services (MSRLS)
school psychology (MA)
secondary education (M Ed, MA)
special education (M Ed)

College of Fine Arts and Communication
Dr. T. Richard Cheatham, Dean
Programs in:
communication design (MFA)
communication studies (MA)
fine arts and communication (MA, MFA, MM)
journalism and mass communication (MA)
music education (MM)
music performance (MM)
theatre arts (MA)

College of Health Professions
Dr. Ruth Welborn, Dean
Programs in:
communication disorders (MA, MSCD)
health administration (MHA, MS)
health professions (MA, MHA, MS, MSCD, DPT)
health services research (MS)
healthcare human resources (MS)
physical therapy (DPT)

College of Liberal Arts
Dr. Ann Marrie Ellis, Dean
Programs in:
anthropology (MA)
applied geography (MAG)
creative writing (MFA)
environmental geography (PhD)
environmental geography, geography education, and geography information science (PhD)
geographic information science (MAG)
geography (MAG, MS)
geography education (PhD)
health psychology (MA)
history (M Ed, MA)
information science (PhD)
land/area studies (MAG)
legal studies (MA)
liberal arts (M Ed, MA, MAG, MFA, MPA, MS, PhD)
literature (MA)
political science (MA, MPA)
public administration (MPA)
resource and environmental studies (MAG)
rhetoric and composition (MA)
sociology (MA, MS)
Spanish (MA)
technical communication (MA)

College of Science
Dr. Hector E. Flores, Dean
Programs in:
aquatic resources (MS, PhD)
biochemistry (MS)
biology (M Ed, MA, MS)
chemistry (MA, MS)
computer science (MA, MS)
industrial mathematics (MS)
industrial technology (MST)
mathematics (M Ed, MS, PhD)
mathematics education (PhD)
middle school mathematics teaching (M Ed)
physics (MS)
population and conservation biology (MS)
science (M Ed, MA, MS, MST, PhD)
software engineering (MS)
wildlife ecology (MS)

Emmett and Miriam McCoy College of Business Administration
Dr. Denise Smart, Dean
Programs in:
accounting (M Acy)
accounting and information technology (MS)
business administration (M Acy, MBA, MS)

■ TEXAS TECH UNIVERSITY
Lubbock, TX 79409
http://www.ttu.edu/

State-supported, coed, university. CGS member. *Graduate faculty:* 725 full-time (217 women), 42 part-time/adjunct (10 women). *Computer facilities:* Computer purchase and lease plans are available. 3,000 computers available on campus for general student use. A campuswide network can be accessed from student residence rooms and from off campus. Online class registration, online degree plans, accounts, transcripts, schedules are available. *Graduate expenses:* Part-time $194 per credit hour. Tuition, state resident: full-time $4648; part-time $194 per credit hour. Tuition, nonresident: full-time $11,392; part-time $475 per credit hour. Required fees: $2206; $69 per credit hour. $389 per semester. *General application contact:* Dr. Duane Crawford, Assistant Dean of Graduate Admissions and Recruitment, 806-742-2781.

Center for Biotechnology and Genomics
Dr. David B. Knaff, Advisor
Programs in:
biotechnology (MS)
science and agricultural biotechnology (MS)

Graduate School
Dr. Fred Hartmeister, Dean

Texas Tech University (continued)
Programs in:
heritage management (MS)
interdisciplinary studies (MA, MS)
museum science (MA)

College of Agricultural Sciences and Natural Resources
Dr. John M. Burns, Dean
Programs in:
agribusiness (MAB)
agricultural and applied economics (MS, PhD)
agricultural communication (MS)
agricultural education (MS, Ed D)
agricultural sciences and natural resources (M Agr, MAB, MLA, MS, Ed D, PhD)
animal science (MS, PhD)
crop science (MS)
entomology (MS)
fisheries science (MS, PhD)
food science (MS)
horticulture (MS)
landscape architecture (MLA)
plant and soil science (PhD)
range science (MS, PhD)
soil science (MS)
wildlife science (MS, PhD)

College of Architecture
David Andrew Vernooy, Dean
Programs in:
architecture (M Arch, MS, PhD)
land-use planning, management, and design (PhD)

College of Arts and Sciences
Dr. Jane L. Winer, Dean
Programs in:
anthropology (MA)
applied linguistics (MA)
applied physics (MS)
arts and sciences (MA, MPA, MS, PhD)
atmospheric sciences (MS)
biological informatics (MS)
biology (MS, PhD)
chemistry (MS, PhD)
classics (MA)
clinical psychology (PhD)
communication studies (MA)
counseling psychology (MA, PhD)
economics (MA, PhD)
English (MA, PhD)
environmental toxicology (MS, PhD)
exercise and sport sciences (MS)
experimental psychology (MA, PhD)
geoscience (MS, PhD)
German (MA)
history (MA, PhD)
mathematics (MA, MS, PhD)
microbiology (MS)
philosophy (MA)
physics (MS, PhD)
political science (MA, PhD)
psychology (MA, PhD)
public administration (MPA)
Romance language (MA)
Romance languages-French (MA)
Romance languages-Spanish (MA, PhD)
sociology (MA)
sports health (MS)
statistics (MS)
technical communication (MA)
technical communication and rhetoric (PhD)
zoology (MS, PhD)

College of Education
Dr. Charles Ruch, Interim Dean
Programs in:
bilingual education (M Ed)
counselor education (M Ed, PhD)
curriculum and instruction (M Ed, PhD)
education (M Ed, Ed D, PhD)
educational leadership (M Ed, Ed D)
educational psychology (M Ed, PhD)
elementary education (M Ed)
higher education (M Ed, Ed D, PhD)
instructional technology (M Ed, Ed D)
language and literacy education (M Ed)
secondary education (M Ed)
special education (M Ed, Ed D)

College of Engineering
Dr. Jon C. Strauss, Interim Dean
Programs in:
chemical engineering (MS Ch E, PhD)
civil engineering (MSCE, PhD)
computer science (MS, PhD)
electrical engineering (MSEE, PhD)
engineering (M Engr, MENVEGR, MS, MS Ch E, MSCE, MSEE, MSETM, MSIE, MSME, MSMSE, MSPE, MSSEM, PhD)
environmental engineering (MENVEGR)
environmental technology and management (MSETM)
industrial engineering (MSIE, PhD)
manufacturing systems and engineering (MSMSE)
mechanical engineering (MSME, PhD)
petroleum engineering (MSPE, PhD)
software engineering (MS)
systems and engineering management (MSSEM, PhD)
wind science and engineering (PhD)

College of Human Sciences
Dr. Linda C. Hoover, Dean
Programs in:
family and consumer sciences education (MS, PhD)
gerontology (MS)
hospitality administration (PhD)
human development and family studies (MS, PhD)
human sciences (MS, PhD)
interior and environmental design (MS, PhD)
marriage and family therapy (MS, PhD)
nutritional sciences (MS, PhD)
personal financial planning (MS, PhD)
restaurant, hotel and institutional management (MS)
restaurant, hotel, and institutional management (MS, PhD)

College of Mass Communications
Dr. Jerry C. Hudson, Dean
Program in:
mass communications (MA, PhD)

College of Visual and Performing Arts
Dr. Carol Edwards, Dean
Programs in:
art (MFA)
art education (MAE)
arts (PhD)
composition (MM, DMA)
conducting (DMA)
fine arts (PhD)
fine arts-art (PhD)
fine arts-music (PhD)
music (MM Ed, PhD)
music theory (MM)
musicology (MM)
pedagogy (MM)
performance (MM, DMA)
piano pedagogy (DMA)
theatre arts (MA, MFA, PhD)
visual and performing arts (MA, MAE, MFA, MM, MM Ed, DMA, PhD)

Jerry S. Rawls College of Business Administration
Dr. Allen T. McInnes, Dean
Programs in:
accounting (PhD)
agricultural business (MBA)
audit/financial reporting (MSA)
business administration (IMBA, MBA, MS, MSA, PhD, Certificate)
business statistics (MS, PhD)
entrepreneurship (MBA)
finance (MS, PhD)
general business (MBA)
health organization management (MBA)
international business (MBA)
management (PhD)
management and leadership skills (MBA)
management information systems (MBA, MS, PhD)
marketing (MBA, PhD)
production and operations management (MS, PhD)
statistics (MBA)
taxation (MSA)

School of Law
Walter Burl Huffman, Dean
Program in:
law (JD)

■ TEXAS WESLEYAN UNIVERSITY
Fort Worth, TX 76105-1536
http://www.txwes.edu/

Independent-religious, coed, comprehensive institution. *Graduate faculty:* 37 full-time (11 women), 40 part-time/adjunct (13 women). *Computer facilities:* 77 computers available on campus for general student use. A campuswide network can be accessed from student residence rooms. Online class registration is available. *General application contact:* Holly Kiser, Director of Admissions, 817-531-4458.

Graduate Programs
Dr. Allen Henderson, Provost

Programs in:
- business administration (MBA)
- education (M Ed)
- health services administration (MS)
- management (MiM)
- mental health/school counseling (MSP)
- nurse anesthesia (MHS, MSNA, DNAP)
- professional counseling (MA)

School of Law
Frederic White, Dean
Program in:
- law (JD)

■ TEXAS WOMAN'S UNIVERSITY
Denton, TX 76201
http://www.twu.edu/

State-supported, coed, primarily women, university. CGS member. *Graduate faculty:* 308 full-time (224 women), 196 part-time/adjunct (141 women). *Computer facilities:* 800 computers available on campus for general student use. A campuswide network can be accessed from student residence rooms and from off campus. Online class registration is available. *Graduate expenses:* Tuition, state resident: full-time $3564; part-time $198 per semester hour. Tuition, nonresident: full-time $8622; part-time $479 per semester hour. Required fees: $1158; $64 per semester hour. Tuition and fees vary according to course load. *General application contact:* Samuel Wheeler, Assistant Director of Admissions, 940-898-3188.

Graduate School
Dr. Jennifer L. Martin, Vice Provost and Dean of the Graduate School

College of Arts and Sciences
Dr. Ann Staton, Dean
Programs in:
- art (MA, MFA)
- arts (MA, MFA, PhD)
- arts and sciences (MA, MBA, MFA, MHSM, MS, PhD, SSP)
- biology (MS)
- biology teaching (MS)
- business administration (MBA)
- chemistry (MS)
- chemistry teaching (MS)
- counseling psychology (MA, PhD)
- dance (MA, MFA, PhD)
- drama (MA)
- English (MA)
- government (MA)
- health systems management (MHSM)
- history (MA)
- mathematics (MA, MS)
- mathematics teaching (MS)
- molecular biology (PhD)
- music (MA)
- rhetoric (PhD)
- school psychology (PhD, SSP)
- science teaching (MS)
- sociology (MA, PhD)
- women's studies (MA)

College of Health Sciences
Dr. Jimmy Ishee, Dean
Programs in:
- education of the deaf (MS)
- exercise and sports nutrition (MS)
- food science (MS)
- food systems administration (MS)
- health care administration (MHA)
- health sciences (MA, MHA, MOT, MS, DPT, Ed D, PhD)
- health studies (MS, Ed D, PhD)
- kinesiology (MS, PhD)
- nutrition (MS, PhD)
- occupational therapy (MA, MOT, PhD)
- physical therapy (MS, DPT, PhD)
- speech-language pathology (MS)

College of Nursing
Dr. Patricia Holden-Huchton, Interim Dean
Programs in:
- acute care nurse practitioner (MS)
- adult health clinical nurse specialist (MS)
- adult health nurse practitioner (MS)
- child health clinical nurse specialist (MS)
- community health (MS)
- family nurse practitioner (MS)
- health systems management (MS)
- nursing education (MS)
- nursing practice (DNP)
- nursing science (PhD)
- pediatric nurse practitioner (MS)
- women's health clinical nurse specialist (MS)
- women's health nurse practitioner (MS)

College of Professional Education
Dr. Nan L. Restine, Dean
Programs in:
- administration (M Ed, MA)
- child development (MS, PhD)
- counseling and development (MS)
- early childhood education (M Ed, MA, MS, Ed D)
- elementary education (MA)
- family studies (MS, PhD)
- family therapy (MS, PhD)
- library science (MA, MLS, PhD)
- professional education (M Ed, MA, MAT, MLS, MS, Ed D, PhD)
- reading education (M Ed, MA, MS, Ed D, PhD)
- special education (M Ed, MA, PhD)
- teaching (MAT)
- teaching, learning, and curriculum (M Ed)

■ TRINITY UNIVERSITY
San Antonio, TX 78212-7200
http://www.trinity.edu/

Independent-religious, coed, comprehensive institution. *Graduate faculty:* 21 full-time (10 women), 8 part-time/adjunct. *Computer facilities:* Computer purchase and lease plans are available. 450 computers available on campus for general student use. A campuswide network can be accessed from student residence rooms and from off campus. Online class registration is available. *General application contact:* Office of the Registrar, 210-999-7201.

Department of Business Administration
Dr. Petrea K. Sandlin, Director of the Accounting Program
Program in:
- accounting (MS)

Department of Education
Dr. Paul Kelleher, Chair
Programs in:
- school administration (M Ed)
- school psychology (MA)
- teacher education (MAT)

Department of Health Care Administration
Dr. Mary E. Stefl, Chair
Program in:
- health care administration (MS)

■ UNIVERSITY OF DALLAS
Irving, TX 75062-4736
http://www.udallas.edu/

Independent-religious, coed, university. *Graduate faculty:* 125 full-time, 101 part-time/adjunct. *Computer facilities:* Computer purchase and lease plans are available. 125 computers available on campus for general student use. A campuswide network can be accessed from student residence rooms and from off campus. Online class registration is available. *Graduate expenses:* Tuition: full-time $11,880; part-time $660 per credit hour. Required fees: $270; $15 per credit hour. *General application contact:* Dr. David Sweet, Dean, 972-721-5288.

Braniff Graduate School of Liberal Arts
Programs in:
- American studies (MAS)
- art (MA, MFA)
- English literature (MA, MEL)
- humanities (M Hum, MA)
- liberal arts (M Hum, M Pol, M Psych, M Th, MA, MAS, MCSL, MEL, MFA, MPM, MRE, MTS, PhD)
- philosophy (MA)
- politics (M Pol, MA)
- psychology (M Psych, MA)
- theology (M Th, MA)

Institute of Philosophic Studies
Programs in:
- literature (PhD)
- philosophy (PhD)
- politics (PhD)

Graduate School of Management
Programs in:
- accounting (MBA, MS)
- business management (MBA, MM)
- corporate finance (MBA, MM)
- engineering management (MBA, MM)
- entrepreneurship (MBA, MM)
- financial services (MBA, MM)
- global business (MBA, MM)

University of Dallas (continued)
- health services management (MBA, MM)
- human resource management (MBA, MM, MS)
- information assurance (MBA, MM, MS)
- information technology (MBA, MM, MS)
- information technology service management (MBA, MS)
- marketing management (MBA, MM)
- not-for-profit management (MBA)
- organization development (MBA)
- project management (MBA, MM)
- service management (MBA, MM)
- sports and entertainment management (MBA, MM)
- strategic leadership (MBA, MM)
- supply chain management (MBA)
- supply chain management and market logistics (MM)
- technologies management (MM)

School of Ministry
Program in:
- ministry (MCSL, MPM, MRE, MTS)

■ UNIVERSITY OF HOUSTON

Houston, TX 77204
http://www.uh.edu/

State-supported, coed, university. CGS member. *Graduate faculty:* 653 full-time (167 women), 416 part-time/adjunct (168 women). *Computer facilities:* Computer purchase and lease plans are available. 625 computers available on campus for general student use. A campuswide network can be accessed from student residence rooms and from off campus. Online class registration is available. *Graduate expenses:* Tuition, state resident: full-time $5164; part-time $287 per credit. Tuition, nonresident: full-time $10,222; part-time $568 per credit. *General application contact:* Jeff Fuller, Executive Associate Director of Admission, 832-842-9047.

Bauer College of Business
Dr. Arthur Warga, Dean
Programs in:
- accountancy (M Acy)
- accounting (PhD)
- business (M Acy, MBA, MS, PhD)
- decision and information sciences (MBA, PhD)
- finance (MS)
- management (PhD)
- marketing and entrepreneurship (PhD)

College of Architecture
Joseph Mashburn, Dean
Program in:
- architecture (M Arch, MS)

College of Education
Robert K. Wimpelberg, Dean
Programs in:
- allied health (M Ed, Ed D)
- art education (M Ed)
- bilingual education (M Ed)
- counseling psychology (M Ed, PhD)
- curriculum and instruction (Ed D)
- early childhood education (M Ed)
- education (M Ed, MS, Ed D, PhD)
- education of the gifted (M Ed)
- educational administration (M Ed, Ed D)
- educational psychology (M Ed)
- educational psychology and individual differences (PhD)
- elementary education (M Ed)
- exercise science (MS)
- health education (M Ed)
- higher education (M Ed)
- historical, social, and cultural foundations of education (M Ed, Ed D)
- human nutrition (MS)
- human space exploration sciences (MS)
- kinesiology (PhD)
- mathematics education (M Ed)
- physical education (M Ed, Ed D)
- reading and language arts education (M Ed)
- science education (M Ed)
- second language education (M Ed)
- secondary education (M Ed)
- social studies education (M Ed)
- special education (M Ed, Ed D)
- teaching (M Ed)

College of Liberal Arts and Social Sciences
Dr. Joseph Pratt, Interim Dean
Programs in:
- anthropology (MA)
- applied English linguistics (MA)
- clinical psychology (PhD)
- economics (MA, PhD)
- English and American literature (MA, PhD)
- French (MA)
- history (MA, PhD)
- industrial/organizational psychology (PhD)
- interior design (MA)
- liberal arts and social sciences (MA, MFA, MM, DMA, PhD)
- literature and creative writing (MA, MFA, PhD)
- painting (MA)
- philosophy (MA)
- photography (MA)
- political science (MA, PhD)
- psychology (MA)
- public history (MA)
- sculpture (MA)
- social psychology (PhD)
- sociology (MA)
- Spanish (MA, PhD)
- speech language pathology (MA)

Moores School of Music
David Ashley White, Chairperson
Programs in:
- accompanying (MM)
- applied music (MM)
- composition (MM, DMA)
- conducting (DMA)
- music education (MM, DMA)
- music literature (MM)
- music performance and pedagogy (MM)
- music theory (MM)
- performance (DMA)

School of Communication
Beth Olson, Chairperson
Programs in:
- mass communication studies (MA)
- public relations studies (MA)
- speech communication (MA)

School of Theatre
Steven Wallace, Chairperson
Program in:
- theatre (MA, MFA)

College of Natural Sciences and Mathematics
Dr. John L. Bear, Dean
Programs in:
- biochemistry (MA, MS, PhD)
- biology (MA, MS, PhD)
- chemistry (MA, MS, PhD)
- computer science (MA, MS, PhD)
- geology (MA, MS, PhD)
- geophysics (MA, MS, PhD)
- mathematics (MA, MS, PhD)
- natural sciences and mathematics (MA, MS, PhD)
- physics (MA, MS, PhD)

College of Optometry
Earl Smith, Dean
Programs in:
- optometry (OD, MS Phys Op, PhD)
- physiological optics/vision science (MS Phys Op, PhD)

College of Pharmacy
Dr. Mustafa F. Lokhandwala, Dean
Programs in:
- hospital pharmacy (MSPHR)
- medical chemistry and pharmacology (MS)
- pharmaceutics (MS, PhD)
- pharmacology (MS, PhD)
- pharmacy (Pharm D)
- pharmacy administration (MSPHR)

College of Technology
William Fitzgibbon, Interim Dean
Programs in:
- engineering technology (M Tech)
- human development and consumer science (MS)
- information and logistics technology (MS)
- technology (M Tech, MS)

Conrad N. Hilton College of Hotel and Restaurant Management
John Bowen, Dean
Program in:
- hotel and restaurant management (MHM, MS)

Cullen College of Engineering
Dr. Joseph Tedesco, Dean

Programs in:
- aerospace engineering (MS, PhD)
- biomedical engineering (MS)
- chemical engineering (M Ch E, MS Ch E, PhD)
- civil and environmental engineering (MCE, MS Env E, MSCE, PhD)
- computer and systems engineering (MS, PhD)
- electrical and computer engineering (MEE, MSEE, PhD)
- engineering (M Ch E, MCE, MEE, MIE, MME, MS, MS Ch E, MS Env E, MSCE, MSEE, MSIE, MSME, PhD)
- environmental engineering (MS, PhD)
- industrial engineering (MIE, MSIE, PhD)
- materials engineering (MS, PhD)
- mechanical engineering (MME, MSME)
- petroleum engineering (MS)

Graduate School of Social Work
Dr. Ira C. Colby, Dean
Program in:
- social work (MSW, PhD)

Law Center
Raymond Nimmer, Interim Dean
Program in:
- law (JD, LL M)

■ UNIVERSITY OF HOUSTON–CLEAR LAKE
Houston, TX 77058-1098
http://www.uhcl.edu/

State-supported, coed, upper-level institution. CGS member. *Computer facilities:* 715 computers available on campus for general student use. A campuswide network can be accessed from off campus. Online class registration is available. *General application contact:* Assistant Director of Admissions, Recruitment and Communications, 281-283-2540.

School of Business
Programs in:
- accounting (MS)
- business (MA, MBA, MHA, MS)
- business administration (MBA)
- environmental management (MS)
- finance (MS)
- healthcare administration (MHA)
- human resource management (MA)
- management information systems (MS)
- professional accounting (MS)

School of Education
Programs in:
- counseling (MS)
- curriculum and instruction (MS)
- early childhood education (MS)
- education (MS, Ed D)
- educational leadership (Ed D)
- educational management (MS)
- instructional technology (MS)
- multicultural studies (MS)
- reading (MS)
- school library and information science (MS)

School of Human Sciences and Humanities
Programs in:
- behavioral sciences (MA)
- clinical psychology (MA)
- criminology (MA)
- cross cultural studies (MA)
- family therapy (MA)
- fitness and human performance (MA)
- history (MA)
- human sciences and humanities (MA)
- humanities (MA)
- literature (MA)
- school psychology (MA)

School of Science and Computer Engineering
Programs in:
- biological sciences (MS)
- biotechnology (MS)
- chemistry (MS)
- computer engineering (MS)
- computer information systems (MS)
- computer science (MS)
- environmental science (MS)
- mathematical sciences (MS)
- physics (MS)
- science and computer engineering (MS)
- software engineering (MS)
- statistics (MS)
- system engineering (MS)

■ UNIVERSITY OF HOUSTON–VICTORIA
Victoria, TX 77901-4450
http://www.uhv.edu/

State-supported, coed, upper-level institution. *Graduate faculty:* 81 full-time (33 women). *Computer facilities:* 150 computers available on campus for general student use. A campuswide network can be accessed from off campus. Online class registration is available. *General application contact:* Admissions and Records, 361-570-4114.

School of Arts and Sciences
Programs in:
- arts and sciences (MA, MAIS, MS)
- computer science (MS)
- counseling psychology (MA)
- interdisciplinary studies (MAIS)
- publishing (MS)
- school psychology (MA)

School of Business Administration
Programs in:
- accounting (MBA)
- economic development and entrepreneurship (MS)
- finance (GMBA, MBA)
- general business (MBA)
- international business (MBA)
- management (GMBA, MBA)
- marketing (MBA)

School of Education and Human Development
Programs in:
- administration and supervision (M Ed)
- counseling (M Ed)
- curriculum and instruction (M Ed)
- special education (M Ed)

School of Nursing
Program in:
- nursing (MSN)

■ UNIVERSITY OF MARY HARDIN-BAYLOR
Belton, TX 76513
http://www.umhb.edu/

Independent-religious, coed, comprehensive institution. *Graduate faculty:* 30 full-time (18 women), 10 part-time/adjunct (2 women). *Computer facilities:* Computer purchase and lease plans are available. 275 computers available on campus for general student use. A campuswide network can be accessed from student residence rooms and from off campus. Online class registration is available. *Graduate expenses:* Tuition: full-time $11,340; part-time $630 per credit hour. Required fees: $1350; $75 per credit hour. $50 per semester. Tuition and fees vary according to degree level. *General application contact:* Sherry Rosenblad, Director of Graduate Admissions, 254-295-4020.

Graduate Studies in Business Administration
Dr. Chrisann Merriman, Graduate Program Director, MBA Program
Programs in:
- accounting (MBA)
- management (MBA)

Graduate Studies in Counseling and Psychology
Dr. Raylene B. Statz, Graduate Program Director
Programs in:
- community counseling (MA)
- marriage and family Christian counseling (MA)
- psychology and counseling (MA)
- school counseling and psychology (MA)

Graduate Studies in Education
Dr. Austin Vasek, Graduate Program Director
Programs in:
- educational administration (M Ed, Ed D)
- educational psychology (M Ed)
- exercise and sport science (M Ed)
- general studies (M Ed)
- reading education (M Ed)

Graduate Studies in Information Systems
Dr. Patrick Jaska, Graduate Program Director
Program in:
- information systems (MS)

University of Mary Hardin-Baylor (continued)

Graduate Studies in Nursing
Dr. Margaret Prydun, Program Director
Program in:
nursing (MSN)

■ UNIVERSITY OF NORTH TEXAS

Denton, TX 76203
http://www.unt.edu/

State-supported, coed, university. CGS member. *Graduate faculty:* 886 full-time, 264 part-time/adjunct. *Computer facilities:* 725 computers available on campus for general student use. A campuswide network can be accessed from student residence rooms and from off campus. Online class registration is available. *General application contact:* Dr. Donna Hughes, Director of Admissions, 940-565-2383.

College of Information
Programs in:
applied technology, training and development (M Ed, MS, Ed D, PhD)
computer education and cognitive systems (MS)
educational computing (PhD)
information (M Ed, MS, Ed D, PhD)
information science (MS, PhD)
library science (MS)

Robert B. Toulouse School of Graduate Studies
Dr. Michael Monticino, Dean

College of Arts and Sciences
Dr. Warren Burggren, Dean
Programs in:
arts and sciences (MA, MFA, MJ, MS, Au D, PhD, Graduate Certificate)
audiology (Au D)
biochemistry (MS, PhD)
biology (MA, MS, PhD)
chemistry (MS, PhD)
clinical psychology (PhD)
communication studies (MA, MS)
counseling psychology (MA, MS, PhD)
creative writing (MA)
economic research (MS)
economics (MA, MS)
English (MA, PhD)
environmental science (MS, PhD)
experimental psychology (MA, MS, PhD)
French (MA)
geography (MS)
health psychology and behavioral medicine (PhD)
history (MA, MS, PhD)
journalism (MA, MJ)
labor and industrial relations (MS)
mathematics (MA, MS, PhD)
molecular biology (MA, MS, PhD)
narrative journalism (Graduate Certificate)
philosophy (MA, PhD)
physics (MA, MS, PhD)
political science (MA, MS, PhD)
radio, television and film (MA, MFA, MS)
Spanish (MA)
speech-language pathology (MA, MS)

College of Business Administration
Dr. O. Finley Graves, Dean
Programs in:
accounting (MS, PhD)
business administration (MBA, MS, PhD)
business computer information systems (PhD)
decision technologies (MS)
finance (PhD)
finance, insurance, real estate, and law (MS)
information technology (MS)
managementmanagement science (PhD)
marketing and logistics (PhD)
real estate (MS)
taxation (MS)

College of Education
Dr. Jean Keller, Dean
Programs in:
adolescent (Certificate)
adult (Certificate)
alternative initial certification (Certificate)
autism intervention (M Ed)
behavioral specialist (Certificate)
child/play therapy (Certificate)
college/university (Certificate)
community (Certificate)
community college (MS)
counseling (M Ed, MS, PhD, Certificate)
couple and family (Certificate)
curriculum and instruction (M Ed, Ed D, PhD)
development and family studies (MS, Certificate)
early childhood education (MS, Ed D)
EC-12 certification (M Ed)
education (M Ed, MS, Ed D, PhD, Certificate)
educational administration (M Ed, Ed D, PhD)
educational psychology (MS)
educational research (PhD)
elementary school (M Ed, MS)
emotional disorders/behavioral disorders (M Ed)
group (Certificate)
higher education (M Ed, MS, Ed D, PhD, Certificate)
higher education (Certificate)
inclusion specialist (Certificate)
kinesiology (MS)
mild/moderate disability (Certificate)
re-integration-traumatic brain injury (Certificate)
reading education (M Ed, MS, Ed D, PhD)
recreation and leisure studies (MS, Certificate)
recreation management (Certificate)
school psychology (MS)
secondary education (M Ed, Certificate)
secondary school (M Ed)
special education (M Ed, MS, PhD, Certificate)
transition (M Ed)
transition emotional disorders/behavioral disorders (Certificate)
traumatic brain injury (M Ed)
university (M Ed)

College of Engineering
Dr. Reza Mirshams, Associate Dean
Programs in:
computer science (MS)
computer science and engineering (PhD)
electrical engineering (MS)
engineering (MS, PhD)
engineering technology (MS)
materials science and engineering (MS, PhD)

College of Music
Dr. James C. Scott, Dean
Programs in:
composition (MM, DMA)
jazz studies (MM)
music (MA)
music education (MM, MME, PhD)
music theory (MM, PhD)
musicology (MM, PhD)
performance (MM, DMA)

College of Public Affairs and Community Service
Dr. Tom Evenson, Dean
Programs in:
aging (Certificate)
applied anthropology (MA, MS)
applied economics (MS)
applied gerontology (PhD)
behavior analysis (MS)
criminal justice (MS)
general studies in aging (MA, MS)
global and comparative (PhD)
health and illness (PhD)
long term care, senior housing, and aging services (MA, MS)
public administration (MPA)
public administration and management (PhD)
public affairs and community service (MA, MPA, MS, PhD, Certificate)
rehabilitation counseling (MS)
social stratification and inequality (PhD)
sociology (MA, MS)

College of Visual Arts and Design
Dr. Robert Milnes, Dean
Programs in:
art education (MA, PhD)
art history (MA)
art museum education (Certificate)
arts leadership (Certificate)
design (MFA)
metalsmithing and jewelry (MFA)
visual arts and design (MA, MFA, MS, PhD, Certificate)

Interdisciplinary Studies
Donna Hughes, Head
Program in:
interdisciplinary studies (MA, MS)

School of Merchandising and Hospitality Management
Dr. Judith C. Forney, Dean
Programs in:
hospitality management (MS)
merchandising (MS)

■ UNIVERSITY OF ST. THOMAS
Houston, TX 77006-4696
http://www.stthom.edu/

Independent-religious, coed, comprehensive institution. CGS member. *Graduate faculty:* 83 full-time (32 women), 30 part-time/adjunct (14 women). *Computer facilities:* A campuswide network can be accessed from student residence rooms and from off campus. Online class registration is available. *Graduate expenses:* Tuition: full-time $13,554; part-time $753 per credit. Required fees: $224; $224 per year. *General application contact:* Dr. Dominic Aquila, Dean, Arts and Sciences, 713-942-5049.

Cameron School of Business
Dr. Bahman Mirshab, Dean
Program in:
business (MBA, MSA)

Center for Thomistic Studies
Dr. Mary Catherine Sommers, Director
Program in:
philosophy (MA, PhD)

Program in Liberal Arts
Dr. Ravi Srinivas, Dean
Program in:
liberal arts (MLA)

School of Education
Dr. Robert M. LeBlanc, Dean
Program in:
education (M Ed)

School of Theology
Dr. Sandra C. Magie, Dean
Program in:
theology (M Div, MAPS, MAT)

■ THE UNIVERSITY OF TEXAS AT ARLINGTON
Arlington, TX 76019
http://www.uta.edu/

State-supported, coed, university. CGS member. *Graduate faculty:* 527 full-time (156 women), 128 part-time/adjunct (57 women). *Computer facilities:* 1,000 computers available on campus for general student use. A campuswide network can be accessed from student residence rooms and from off campus. Online class registration is available. *Graduate expenses:* Tuition, state resident: full-time $6500. Tuition, nonresident: full-time $11,558. *General application contact:* Dr. Phil Cohen, Dean of Graduate Studies, 817-272-3186.

Graduate School
Dr. Phil Cohen, Dean of Graduate Studies

College of Business
Dr. Daniel Himarios, Dean
Programs in:
accounting (MP Acc, MS, PhD)
business (MA, MBA, MP Acc, MS, MSHRM, PhD)
business statistics (PhD)
economics (MA)
finance (MBA, PhD)
health care administration (MS)
human resources (MSHRM)
information systems (MBA, MS, PhD)
management (MBA, PhD)
management sciences (MBA)
marketing (MBA, PhD)
marketing research (MS)
operations management (PhD)
quantitative finance (MS)
real estate (MBA, MS)
taxation (MS)

College of Education
Dr. Jeanne M. Gerlach, Dean
Programs in:
curriculum and instruction (M Ed)
educational leadership and policy studies (M Ed)
K-16 educational, leadership and policy studies (PhD)
physiology of exercise (MS)
teaching (M Ed T)

College of Engineering
Dr. Bill D. Carroll, Dean
Programs in:
aerospace engineering (M Engr, MS, PhD)
bioengineering (MS, PhD)
civil engineering (M Engr, MS, PhD)
computer science and engineering (M Engr, M Sw En, MS, PhD)
electrical engineering (M Engr, MS, PhD)
engineering (M Engr, M Sw En, MS, PhD)
engineering management (MS)
industrial engineering (MS, PhD)
logistics (MS)
materials science and engineering (M Engr, MS, PhD)
mechanical engineering (M Engr, MS, PhD)
systems engineering (MS)

College of Liberal Arts
Dr. Beth S. Wright, Dean
Programs in:
anthropology (MA)
art and art history (MFA)
communication (MA)
criminology and criminal justice (MA)
education (MM)
English (MA)
French (MA)
history (MA)
humanities (MA)
liberal arts (MA, MFA, MM, PhD)
linguistics (MA, PhD)
literature (PhD)
performance (MM)
political science (MA)
sociology (MA)
Spanish (MA)
teaching English to speakers of other languages (MA)
transatlantic history (PhD)

College of Science
Dr. Paul B. Paulus, Interim Dean
Programs in:
biology (MS)
chemistry (MS, PhD)
environmental and earth sciences (MS, PhD)
environmental science (MS, PhD)
experimental psychology (PhD)
geology (MS, PhD)
health psychology (PhD)
industrial organizational psychology (MS)
mathematics (MA, MS, PhD)
physics (MS)
physics and applied physics (PhD)
psychology (MS)
quantitative biology (PhD)
science (MA, MS, PhD)

School of Architecture
Donald Gatzke, Dean
Programs in:
architecture (M Arch, MLA)
landscape architecture (MLA)

School of Nursing
Dr. Elizabeth C. Poster, Dean
Programs in:
administration/supervision of nursing (MSN)
nurse practitioner (MSN)
nursing science (PhD)
teaching of nursing (MSN)

School of Social Work
Dr. Phillip Popple, Interim Dean
Program in:
social work (MSSW, PhD)

School of Urban and Public Affairs
Dr. Barbara Becker, Dean
Programs in:
city and regional planning (MCRP)
interdisciplinary science (MA)
public administration (MPA)
urban and public affairs (MA, MCRP, MPA, PhD)

■ THE UNIVERSITY OF TEXAS AT AUSTIN
Austin, TX 78712-1111
http://www.utexas.edu/

State-supported, coed, university. CGS member. *Computer facilities:* Computer purchase and lease plans are available. 500 computers available on campus for general student use. A campuswide network can be accessed from student residence rooms and from off campus. Online class registration is

The University of Texas at Austin (continued)
available. *General application contact:* Director, Graduate and International Admissions Center, 512-475-7398.

Graduate School
Programs in:
computational and applied mathematics (MA, PhD)
technology commercialization (MS)
writing (MFA)

Cockrell School of Engineering
Programs in:
aerospace engineering (MSE, PhD)
architectural engineering (MSE)
biomedical engineering (MS, PhD)
chemical engineering (MSE, PhD)
civil engineering (MS, PhD)
electrical and computer engineering (MSE, PhD)
energy and earth resources (MA)
engineering (MA, MS, MSE, PhD)
engineering mechanics (MS, PhD)
environmental and water resources engineering (MS, PhD)
materials science and engineering (MS, PhD)
mechanical engineering (MS, PhD)
operations research and industrial engineering (MS, PhD)
petroleum engineering (MS, PhD)

College of Communication
Programs in:
advertising (MA, PhD)
audiology (Au D, PhD)
communication (MA, MFA, Au D, PhD)
communication studies (MA, PhD)
film and video production (MFA)
journalism (MA, PhD)
radio-television-film (MA, PhD)
screenwriting (MFA)
speech language pathology (MA, PhD)

College of Education
Programs in:
academic educational psychology (M Ed, MA)
behavioral health (PhD)
counseling psychology (PhD)
counselor education (M Ed)
curriculum and instruction (M Ed, MA, Ed D, PhD)
education (M Ed, MA, Ed D, PhD)
educational administration (M Ed, Ed D, PhD)
exercise and sport psychology (M Ed, MA)
foreign language education (MA, PhD)
health education (M Ed, MA, Ed D, PhD)
human development and culture (PhD)
kinesiology (M Ed, MA)
learning, cognition and instruction (PhD)
quantitative methods (PhD)
school psychology (PhD)
science and mathematics education (M Ed, MA, PhD)
special education (M Ed, MA, Ed D, PhD)

College of Fine Arts
Programs in:
acting (MFA)
art education (MA)
art history (MA, PhD)
dance (MFA)
design (MFA)
directing (MFA)
drama and theatre for youth (MFA)
fine arts (M Music, MA, MFA, DMA, PhD)
music (M Music, DMA, PhD)
performance as public practice (MA, MFA, PhD)
playwriting (MFA)
studio art (MFA)
theatre technology (MFA)
theatrical design (MFA)

College of Liberal Arts
Programs in:
African Diaspora studies (MA, PhD)
American studies (MA, PhD)
Arabic (MA, PhD)
archaeology (MA, PhD)
Asian cultures and languages (MA, PhD)
Asian studies (MA)
classics (MA, PhD)
comparative literature (MA, PhD)
creative writing (MA)
economics (MA, MS Econ, PhD)
English (MA, PhD)
folklore and public culture (MA, PhD)
French (MA, PhD)
French linguistics (MA, PhD)
geography and the environment (MA, PhD)
Germanic studies (MA, PhD)
government (PhD)
Hebrew (MA)
Hispanic linguistics (MA, PhD)
Hispanic literature (MA, PhD)
history (MA, PhD)
Italian studies (MA, PhD)
Latin American studies (MA, PhD)
liberal arts (MA, MS Econ, PhD)
linguistic anthropology (MA, PhD)
linguistics (MA, PhD)
Luso-Brazilian literature (MA, PhD)
Mexican American studies (MA)
Middle Eastern studies (MA, PhD)
philosophy (PhD)
physical anthropology (MA, PhD)
psychology (PhD)
Romance linguistics (MA, PhD)
Russian, East European, and Eurasian studies (MA)
Slavic languages (MA, PhD)
social anthropology (MA, PhD)
sociology (MA, PhD)

College of Natural Sciences
Programs in:
analytical chemistry (MA, PhD)
astronomy (MA, PhD)
biochemistry (MA, PhD)
biological sciences (MA, PhD)
computer sciences (MA, MSCS, PhD)
ecology, evolution and behavior (MA, PhD)
human development and family sciences (MA, PhD)
inorganic chemistry (MA, PhD)
marine science (MS, PhD)
mathematics (MA, PhD)
microbiology (PhD)
natural sciences (MA, MS, MS Stat, MSCS, PhD)
nutrition (MA)
nutritional sciences (MA, PhD)
organic chemistry (MA, PhD)
physical chemistry (MA, PhD)
physics (MA, MS, PhD)
plant biology (MA, PhD)
statistics (MS Stat)
textile and apparel technology (MS)

College of Pharmacy
Program in:
pharmacy (Pharm D, MS, PhD)

Institute for Cellular and Molecular Biology
Program in:
cellular and molecular biology (PhD)

The Institute for Neuroscience
Program in:
neuroscience (PhD)

Jackson School of Geosciences
Program in:
geosciences (MA, MS, PhD)

Lyndon B. Johnson School of Public Affairs
Programs in:
global policy studies (MGPS)
public affairs (MP Aff)
public policy (PhD)

McCombs School of Business
Programs in:
accounting (MPA, PhD)
business (MBA, MPA, PhD)
business administration (MBA)
finance (PhD)
information systems (PhD)
management (PhD)
marketing (PhD)
risk analysis and decision making (PhD)
supply chain and operations management (PhD)

School of Architecture
Programs in:
architecture (M Arch)
community and regional planning (MSCRP, PhD)
historic preservation (MS)
history of architecture (MA, PhD)
landscape architecture (MLA)
urban design (MSUD)

School of Information
Program in:
information (MS, PhD)

School of Nursing
Program in:
nursing (MSN, PhD)

School of Social Work
Program in:
social work (MSSW, PhD)

School of Law
Lawrence Sager, Dean
Program in:
law (JD, LL M)

■ THE UNIVERSITY OF TEXAS AT BROWNSVILLE
Brownsville, TX 78520-4991
http://www.utb.edu/

State-supported, coed, comprehensive institution. CGS member. *Computer facilities:* Computer purchase and lease plans are available. 332 computers available on campus for general student use. A campuswide network can be accessed from student residence rooms and from off campus. Online class registration is available. *General application contact:* Dean, Graduate Studies, 956-882-8812.

Graduate Studies

College of Liberal Arts
Programs in:
behavioral sciences (MAIS)
English (MA)
government (MAIS)
history (MAIS)
interdisciplinary studies (MAIS)
liberal arts (MA, MAIS, MPPM)
public policy and management (MPPM)
Spanish (MA)

College of Science, Mathematics and Technology
Programs in:
biological sciences (MS, MSIS)
mathematics (MS)
physics (MS)

School of Business
Program in:
business (MBA)

School of Education
Programs in:
bilingual education (M Ed)
counseling and guidance (M Ed)
curriculum and instruction (M Ed)
early childhood education (M Ed)
educational administration (M Ed)
educational technology (M Ed)
English as a second language (M Ed)
reading specialist (M Ed)
special education/educational diagnostician (M Ed)

School of Health Sciences
Program in:
health sciences (MSN)

■ THE UNIVERSITY OF TEXAS AT DALLAS
Richardson, TX 75083-0688
http://www.utdallas.edu/

State-supported, coed, university. CGS member. *Graduate faculty:* 393 full-time (81 women), 60 part-time/adjunct (20 women). *Computer facilities:* Computer purchase and lease plans are available. 630 computers available on campus for general student use. A campuswide network can be accessed from student residence rooms and from off campus. Online class registration is available. *Graduate expenses:* Tuition, state resident: full-time $8320. Tuition, nonresident: full-time $15,054. Part-time tuition and fees vary according to course load. *General application contact:* Dr. Austin Cunningham, Dean for Graduate Studies, 972-883-2234.

Erik Jonsson School of Engineering and Computer Science
Dr. Mark Spong, Dean
Programs in:
computer engineering (MS, PhD)
computer science (MS, PhD)
electrical engineering (MSEE, PhD)
engineering and computer science (MS, MSEE, MSME, MSTE, PhD)
materials science and engineering (MS, PhD)
materials science engineering (PhD)
mechanical engineering (MSME)
microelectronics (MSEE, PhD)
software engineering (MS, PhD)
telecommunications (MSEE, MSTE, PhD)

School of Arts and Humanities
Dr. Dennis M. Kratz, Dean
Programs in:
arts and technology (MFA)
emerging media and communications (MA)
humanities (MA, MAT, PhD)

School of Behavioral and Brain Sciences
Dr. Bert Moore, Dean
Programs in:
applied cognition and neuroscience (MS)
audiology (Au D)
behavioral and brain sciences (MS, Au D, PhD)
cognition and neuroscience (PhD)
communication disorders (MS)
communication sciences (PhD)
early childhood disorders (MS)
psychological sciences (MS, PhD)

School of Economic, Political and Policy Sciences
Dr. Brian Berry, Dean
Programs in:
applied sociology (MS)
criminology (MS, PhD)
economic, political and policy sciences (MA, MPA, MPP, MS, PhD)
economics (MS, PhD)
geospatial sciences (MS, PhD)
international political economy (MS)
legislative studies (MA)
political science (PhD)
public affairs (MPA, PhD)
public policy (MPP)
public policy and political economy (PhD)

School of Interdisciplinary Studies
Dr. George Fair, Dean
Program in:
interdisciplinary studies (MA)

School of Management
Dr. Hasan Pirkul, Dean
Programs in:
accounting (PhD)
audit and professional (MS)
cohort (MBA)
electronic commerce (MS)
executive business administration (EMBA)
finance (MS, PhD)
financial analysis (MS)
global leadership (EMBA)
global online (MBA)
health care systems (MS)
healthcare management (EMBA, MS)
information management (MS)
information security and assurance (MS)
information systems (PhD)
innovation and entrepreneurship (MS)
internal audit (MS)
international management (MA, PhD)
international services (MS)
management (EMBA, MA, MBA, MS, PhD)
managerial (MS)
marketing (PhD)
organizations and strategy (MS)
professional business administration (MBA)
project management (EMBA)
supply chain management (MS)
taxation (MS)

School of Natural Sciences and Mathematics
Dr. Myron B. Salamon, Dean
Programs in:
applied mathematics (MS, PhD)
applied physics (MS)
bioinformatics and computational biology (MS)
biotechnology (MS)
chemistry (MS, PhD)
engineering mathematics (MS)
geochemistry (MS, PhD)
geophysics (MS)
geospatial information sciences (MS, PhD)
hydrogeology (MS, PhD)
mathematical science (MS)
mathematics education (MAT)
molecular and cell biology (MS, PhD)
natural sciences and mathematics (MAT, MS, PhD)
physics (MS, PhD)
science education (MAT)
sedimentary, stratigraphy, paleontology (PhD)
statistics (MS, PhD)
stratigraphy, paleontology (MS)
structural geology and tectonics (MS, PhD)

■ THE UNIVERSITY OF TEXAS AT EL PASO

El Paso, TX 79968-0001

http://www.utep.edu/

State-supported, coed, university. CGS member. *Computer facilities:* A campuswide network can be accessed from student residence rooms and from off campus. *General application contact:* Dean of the Graduate School, 915-747-5491 Ext. 7886.

Graduate School

Programs in:
- environmental science and engineering (PhD)
- materials science and engineering (PhD)

College of Business Administration

Programs in:
- accounting (M Acc)
- business administration (M Acc, MBA, MS)
- economics (MS)

College of Education

Programs in:
- education (M Ed, MA, Ed D, PhD)
- educational administration (M Ed)
- educational diagnostics (M Ed)
- educational leadership and administration (Ed D)
- guidance and counseling (M Ed)
- instruction (M Ed)
- reading education (M Ed)
- special education (M Ed)
- teaching, learning, and culture (PhD)

College of Engineering

Programs in:
- civil engineering (MS, PhD)
- computer engineering (MS)
- computer science (MS, PhD)
- electrical and computer engineering (PhD)
- electrical engineering (MS)
- engineering (MEENE, MIT, MS, MSENE, PhD)
- environmental engineering (MEENE, MSENE)
- industrial engineering (MS)
- information technology (MIT)
- manufacturing engineering (MS)
- mechanical engineering (MS)
- metallurgical and materials engineering (MS)

College of Health Sciences

Programs in:
- health education (MS)
- health sciences (MOT, MPH, MPT, MS, PhD)
- interdisciplinary health sciences (PhD)
- kinesiology (MS)
- occupational therapy (MOT)
- physical therapy (MPT)
- public health (MPH)
- speech-language pathology (MS)

College of Liberal Arts

Programs in:
- art education (MA)
- border history (MA)
- clinical psychology (MA)
- communication (MA)
- creative writing in English (MFA)
- creative writing in Spanish (MFA)
- English and American literature (MA)
- experimental psychology (MA)
- history (MA, PhD)
- liberal arts (MA, MAIS, MAT, MFA, MM, PhD)
- linguistics (MA)
- music education (MM)
- music performance (MM)
- political science (MA)
- psychology (PhD)
- rhetoric and composition (PhD)
- rhetoric and writing studies (MA)
- sociology (MA)
- studio art (MA)
- teaching English (MAT)

College of Science

Programs in:
- applied mathematics (MS)
- bioinformatics (MS)
- biological sciences (MS, PhD)
- chemistry (MS, PhD)
- geological sciences (MS, PhD)
- geophysics (MS, PhD)
- interdisciplinary studies (MSIS)
- mathematics (MAT, MS)
- physics (MS)
- science (MAT, MS, MSIS, PhD)
- statistics (MS)

Institute for Policy and Economic Development

Programs in:
- intelligence and national security studies (MS)
- leadership studies (MLS)
- public administration (MPA)

School of Nursing

Programs in:
- evidence-based practice (Certificate)
- family nurse practitioner (MSN, Certificate)
- health care leadership and management (Certificate)
- nurse clinician educator (MSN)
- nurse educator (Certificate)
- nursing systems management (MSN)
- women's health care nurse practitioner (MSN)

■ THE UNIVERSITY OF TEXAS AT SAN ANTONIO

San Antonio, TX 78249-0617

http://www.utsa.edu/

State-supported, coed, university. CGS member. *Computer facilities:* 800 computers available on campus for general student use. A campuswide network can be accessed from student residence rooms. Online class registration is available. *General application contact:* Dean of the Graduate School, 210-458-4330.

College of Business

Programs in:
- accountancy (M Accy)
- applied statistics (PhD)
- business (Exec MBA, M Accy, MA, MBA, MS, MSIT, MSMOT, PhD)
- business administration-accounting (PhD)
- business administration-finance (PhD)
- business administration-information technology (PhD)
- business administration-marketing (PhD)
- business administration-organizational management (PhD)
- business economics (MBA)
- business finance (MBA)
- economics (MA)
- executive business administration (Exec MBA)
- finance (MS)
- information systems (MBA)
- information technology (MSIT)
- international business (MBA)
- management accounting (MBA)
- management science (MBA)
- management technology (MSMOT)
- marketing management (MBA)
- statistics (MS)
- taxation (MBA)

College of Education and Human Development

Programs in:
- bicultural-bilingual studies (MA)
- counseling (MA)
- counselor education and supervision (PhD)
- culture, literacy, and language (PhD)
- curriculum and instruction (MA)
- early childhood education (MA)
- education and human development (M Ed, MA, MA Ed, MS, Ed D, PhD, Graduate Certificate)
- educational leadership (M Ed, Ed D)
- health and kinesiology (MS)
- instructional technology (MA)
- kinesiology and health promotion (MA Ed)
- reading (MA)
- school psychology (MA)
- special education (MA)
- teaching English as a second language (MA)

College of Engineering

Programs in:
- biomedical engineering (MS, PhD)
- civil engineering (MSCE)
- computer engineering (MS)
- electrical engineering (MSEE, PhD)
- engineering (MS, MSCE, MSEE, MSME, PhD)
- environmental science and engineering (PhD)
- mechanical engineering (MSME)

College of Liberal and Fine Arts

Programs in:
- anthropology (MA, PhD)

art history (MA)
communication (MA)
creative writing (Graduate Certificate)
English (MA, PhD)
history (MA)
keyboard pedagogy (Graduate Certificate)
keyboard performance (Graduate Certificate)
liberal and fine arts (MA, MFA, MM, MS, PhD, Graduate Certificate)
music (MM)
political science (MA)
psychology (MS)
sociology (MS)
Spanish (MA)
Spanish translation studies (Graduate Certificate)
studio art (MFA)

College of Public Policy

Programs in:
applied demography (PhD)
justice policy (MS)
public administration (MPA)
public policy (MPA, MS, MSW, PhD)
social work (MSW)

College of Sciences

Programs in:
applied/industrial mathematics (MS)
biology (MS, PhD)
biotechnology (MS)
chemistry (MS, PhD)
computer science (MS, PhD)
environmental sciences (MS)
geology (MS)
mathematics (MS)
physics (MS, PhD)
sciences (MS, PhD)

■ THE UNIVERSITY OF TEXAS AT TYLER

Tyler, TX 75799-0001
http://www.uttyler.edu/

State-supported, coed, comprehensive institution. CGS member. *Graduate faculty:* 173 full-time (64 women). *Computer facilities:* 139 computers available on campus for general student use. A campuswide network can be accessed from student residence rooms and from off campus. Online class registration is available. *General application contact:* Dr. Alecia Wolf, Graduate Services Coordinator, 903-566-7457.

College of Arts and Sciences

Programs in:
art and art history (MA, MAIS, MFA)
arts and sciences (MA, MAIS, MAT, MFA, MPA, MS, MSIS)
biology (MS)
communication (MA)
criminal justice (MS)
English (MA)
history (MA)
interdisciplinary studies (MAIS, MSIS)
mathematics (MS, MSIS)
political science (MA)
public administration (MPA)
sociology (MS)

College of Business and Technology

Program in:
business and technology (MBA, MS, PhD)

School of Business Administration
Dr. Mary Fischer, Interim Dean and Professor of Accounting
Programs in:
business administration (MBA)
general management (MBA)
health care (MBA)

School of Human Resource Development and Technology
Dr. W. Clayton Allen, Chair
Programs in:
human resource development (MS, PhD)
industrial management (MS)
industrial safety (MS)

College of Education and Psychology

Programs in:
clinical psychology (MS)
counseling psychology (MA)
education and psychology (M Ed, MA, MS, MSIS)
educational leadership (M Ed)
interdisciplinary studies (MSIS)
school counseling (MA)

School of Education
Dr. Michael Odell, Interim Director
Programs in:
early childhood education (M Ed, MA)
reading (M Ed, MA)
special education (M Ed, MA)

College of Engineering and Computer Science

Dr. Jim Nelson, Dean
Programs in:
civil engineering (MS)
computer science (MS)
electrical engineering (MS)
engineering and computer science (MS, MSIS)
interdisciplinary studies (MSIS)
mechanical engineering (MS)

College of Nursing and Health Sciences

Programs in:
health and kinesiology (M Ed, MA)
kinesiology (MS)
nurse practitioner (MSN)
nursing (PhD)
nursing administration (MSN)
nursing and health sciences (M Ed, MA, MS, MSN, PhD)
nursing education (MSN)

■ THE UNIVERSITY OF TEXAS OF THE PERMIAN BASIN

Odessa, TX 79762-0001
http://www.utpb.edu/

State-supported, coed, comprehensive institution. *Computer facilities:* 170 computers available on campus for general student use. A campuswide network can be accessed from student residence rooms and from off campus. Online class registration is available. *General application contact:* Director of Graduate Studies, 915-552-2530.

Office of Graduate Studies

College of Arts and Sciences
Programs in:
applied research psychology (MA)
arts and sciences (MA, MS)
biology (MS)
clinical psychology (MA)
computer science (MS)
criminal justice administration (MS)
English (MA)
geology (MS)
history (MA)
kinesiology (MS)
political science (MPA)
Spanish (MA)

School of Business
Programs in:
accountancy (MPA)
business (MBA, MPA)
management (MBA)

School of Education
Programs in:
bilingual/English as a second language education (MA)
counseling (MA)
early childhood education (MA)
education (MA)
educational leadership (MA)
professional education (MA)
reading (MA)
special education (MA)

■ THE UNIVERSITY OF TEXAS–PAN AMERICAN

Edinburg, TX 78541-2999
http://www.utpa.edu/

State-supported, coed, comprehensive institution. CGS member. *Computer facilities:* A campuswide network can be accessed from off campus. Online class registration is available. *Graduate expenses:* Tuition, state resident; full-time $3379; part-time $188 per credit hour. Tuition, nonresident: full-time $8437; part-time $469 per credit hour. Required fees: $785; $116.05 per credit hour. $137.20 per semester. *General application contact:* Graduate Student Recruiter, 956-381-3661.

The University of Texas–Pan American (continued)

College of Arts and Humanities
Programs in:
art (MFA)
arts and humanities (M Mus, MA, MAIS, MFA, MSIS)
communication (MA)
English (MA, MAIS)
English as a second language (MA)
ethnomusicology (M Mus)
history (MA, MAIS)
interdisciplinary studies (MAIS)
music education (M Mus)
performance (M Mus)
Spanish (MA)
theatre (MA)

College of Business Administration
Programs in:
accounting (M Acc, MS)
business administration (M Acc, MBA, MS, PhD)
computer information systems (PhD)
economics (PhD)
finance (PhD)
management (PhD)
marketing (PhD)

College of Education
Programs in:
bilingual education (M Ed)
counseling (M Ed)
early childhood education (M Ed)
education (M Ed, MA, MS, Ed D)
educational diagnostician (M Ed)
educational leadership (M Ed, Ed D)
elementary education (M Ed)
gifted education (M Ed)
kinesiology (MS)
reading (M Ed)
school psychology (MA)
secondary education (M Ed)
special education (M Ed)

College of Health Sciences and Human Services
Programs in:
adult health nursing (MSN)
communication sciences and disorders (MS)
family nurse practitioner (MSN)
health sciences and human services (MS, MSN, MSSW)
occupational therapy (MS)
pediatric nurse practitioner (MSN)
rehabilitation counseling (MS)
social work (MSSW)

College of Science and Engineering
Programs in:
biology (MS)
chemistry (MS)
computer science (MS)
electrical engineering (MS)
manufacturing engineering (MS)
mathematical science (MS)
mathematics teaching (MS)
mechanical engineering (MS)
science and engineering (MS)

College of Social and Behavioral Sciences
Programs in:
criminal justice (MS)
psychology (MA)
public administration (MPA)
social and behavioral sciences (MA, MPA, MS)
sociology (MS)

■ UNIVERSITY OF THE INCARNATE WORD

San Antonio, TX 78209-6397
http://www.uiw.edu/

Independent-religious, coed, comprehensive institution. *Graduate faculty:* 76 full-time (40 women), 49 part-time/adjunct (26 women). *Computer facilities:* Computer purchase and lease plans are available. 175 computers available on campus for general student use. A campuswide network can be accessed from student residence rooms. Online class registration is available. *Graduate expenses:* Tuition: full-time $11,520; part-time $640 per credit hour. Required fees: $1494; $83 per credit hour. One-time fee: $50. Tuition and fees vary according to degree level and program. *General application contact:* Janet Kaufman, Graduate Admissions Counselor, 210-829-6005.

Feik School of Pharmacy
Dr. Arcelia Johnson-Fannin, Founding Dean
Program in:
pharmacy (Pharm D)

School of Graduate Studies and Research
Dr. Kevin Vichcales, Dean

College of Humanities, Arts, and Social Sciences
Dr. Bob Connelly, Dean
Programs in:
humanities, arts, and social sciences (MA)
multidisciplinary studies (MA)
religious studies (MA)

Dreeben School of Education
Dr. Denise Staudt, Dean
Programs in:
adult education (M Ed, MA)
all-level teaching (MAT)
cross-cultural education (M Ed, MA)
early childhood literacy (M Ed, MA)
education (M Ed, MA, MAT, PhD)
elementary teaching (MAT)
general education (M Ed, MA)
Higher Education (PhD)
instructional technology (M Ed, MA)
international education and entrepreneurship (PhD)
kinesiology (M Ed, MA)
literacy (M Ed, MA)
mathematics education (PhD)
organizational leadership (PhD)
organizational learning and learning (M Ed, MA)
reading (M Ed, MA)
secondary teaching (MAT)
special education (M Ed, MA)
teacher leadership (M Ed, MA)

H-E-B School of Business and Administration
Dr. Shawn Daly, Dean
Programs in:
accounting (MS)
adult education (MAA)
applied administration (MAA)
business and administration (MAA, MBA, MS, Certificate)
communication arts (MAA)
general business (MBA)
healthcare administration (MAA)
instructional technology (MAA)
international business (MBA, Certificate)
international business strategy (MBA)
nutrition (MAA)
organizational development (MAA, Certificate)
project management (Certificate)
sports management (MAA, MBA)

School of Interactive Media and Design
Dr. Cheryl Anderson, Dean
Programs in:
communication arts (MA)
instructional technology (MA)
interactive media and design (MA)

School of Mathematics, Science, and Engineering
Dr. Glen Edward James, Dean
Programs in:
administration (MS)
biology (MA, MS)
mathematics teaching (MA)
mathematics, science, and engineering (MA, MS)
medical nutrition therapy (MS)
multidisciplinary sciences (MA)
nutrition education and health promotion (MS)
nutrition services administration (MS)
research statistics (MS)

School of Nursing and Health Professions
Dr. Kathleen Light, Dean
Programs in:
kinesiology (MS)
nursing (MSN)
nursing and health professions (MS, MSN, Certificate)
sport management (MS, Certificate)
sport pedagogy (Certificate)

School of Optometry
Dr. Hani Ghazi-Birry, Founding Dean
Program in:
optometry (OD)

■ WAYLAND BAPTIST UNIVERSITY
Plainview, TX 79072-6998
http://www.wbu.edu/

Independent-religious, coed, comprehensive institution. *Graduate faculty:* 40 full-time (13 women), 5 part-time/adjunct (0 women). *Computer facilities:* Computer purchase and lease plans are available. 241 computers available on campus for general student use. A campuswide network can be accessed from student residence rooms and from off campus. Online class registration is available. *Graduate expenses:* Tuition: part-time $310 per credit hour. Required fees: $9 per credit hour. $60 per semester. *General application contact:* Dr. Bobby Hall, Vice President of Academic Services, 806-291-3410.

Graduate Programs
Dr. Bobby Hall, Vice President of Academic Services
Programs in:
- Christian ministry (MCM)
- counseling (MA)
- education (M Ed)
- general business (MBA)
- government administration (MPA)
- health care administration (MBA)
- homeland security (MPA)
- human resource management (MBA)
- international management (MBA)
- justice administration (MPA)
- management (MA, MBA)
- management information systems (MBA)
- multidisciplinary science (MS)
- religion (MA)

■ WEST TEXAS A&M UNIVERSITY
Canyon, TX 79016-0001
http://www.wtamu.edu/

State-supported, coed, comprehensive institution. *Computer facilities:* 1,200 computers available on campus for general student use. A campuswide network can be accessed from student residence rooms and from off campus. Online class registration is available. *General application contact:* Dean of the Graduate School, 806-651-2730.

College of Agriculture, Nursing, and Natural Sciences
Programs in:
- agricultural business and economics (MS)
- agriculture (PhD)
- agriculture, nursing, and natural sciences (MS, MSN, PhD)
- animal science (MS)
- biology (MS)
- chemistry (MS)
- engineering technology (MS)
- environmental science (MS)
- mathematics (MS)
- nursing (MSN)
- plant science (MS)

College of Business
Programs in:
- accounting (MP Acc)
- accounting/business administration (MPA)
- business (MBA, MP Acc, MPA, MS)
- business administration (MBA)
- finance and economics (MS)
- professional accounting (MPA)

College of Education and Social Sciences
Programs in:
- administration (M Ed)
- counseling education (M Ed)
- criminal justice (MA)
- curriculum and instruction (M Ed)
- education and social sciences (M Ed, MA, MS)
- educational diagnostician (M Ed)
- educational technology (M Ed)
- history (MA)
- political science (MA)
- professional counseling (MA)
- psychology (MA)
- reading (M Ed)
- special education (M Ed)
- sports and exercise science (MS)

College of Fine Arts and Humanities
Programs in:
- art (MA)
- communication (MA)
- communication disorders (MS)
- English (MA)
- fine arts and humanities (MA, MFA, MM, MS)
- music (MA)
- performance (MM)
- studio art (MFA)

Program in Interdisciplinary Studies
Program in:
- interdisciplinary studies (MA, MS)

Utah

■ BRIGHAM YOUNG UNIVERSITY
Provo, UT 84602-1001
http://www.byu.edu/

Independent-religious, coed, university. CGS member. *Graduate faculty:* 1,048 full-time (177 women), 2 part-time/adjunct (1 woman). *Computer facilities:* Computer purchase and lease plans are available. 2,000 computers available on campus for general student use. A campuswide network can be accessed from student residence rooms and from off campus. Online class registration is available. *Graduate expenses:* Tuition: full-time $5160; part-time $287 per credit hour. Tuition and fees vary according to program and student's religious affiliation. *General application contact:* Graduate Studies, 801-422-4091.

Graduate Studies
Bonnie Brinton, Dean

College of Family, Home, and Social Sciences
Dr. David B. Magleby, Dean
Programs in:
- anthropology (MA)
- clinical psychology (PhD)
- family, home, and social sciences (MA, MPP, MS, MSW, PhD)
- general psychology (MS)
- geography (MS)
- marriage and family therapy (MS, PhD)
- marriage, family and human development (MS, PhD)
- psychology (PhD)
- public policy (MPP)
- social work (MSW)
- sociology (MS)

College of Fine Arts and Communications
Dr. Stephen M. Jones, Dean
Programs in:
- art education (MA)
- art history (MA)
- composition (MM)
- conducting (MM)
- fine arts and communications (MA, MFA, MM)
- mass communications (MA)
- music education (MA, MM)
- musicology (MA)
- performance (MM)
- studio art (MFA)
- theatre and media arts (MA)

College of Health and Human Performance
Sara Lee Gibb, Dean
Programs in:
- athletic training (MS)
- exercise physiology (MS, PhD)
- health and human performance (MPH, MS, PhD)
- health promotion (MS, PhD)
- health science (MPH)
- physical medicine and rehabilitation (PhD)
- youth and family recreation (MS)

College of Humanities
Dr. John R. Rosenberg, Dean
Programs in:
- comparative literature (MA)
- comparative studies (MA)
- English (MA)
- French studies (MA)
- general linguistics (MA)
- German studies (MA)
- humanities (MA, Certificate)
- language acquisition and teaching (MA)

Brigham Young University (continued)
Portuguese linguistics (MA)
Portuguese literature (MA)
Spanish linguistics (MA)
Spanish teaching (MA)
Spanish/Latin American Literature (MA)
Spanish/Peninsular literature (MA)
teaching English as a second language (MA, Certificate)

College of Life Sciences
Dr. Rodney J. Brown, Dean
Programs in:
biological science education (MS)
biology (MS, PhD)
environmental science (MS)
food science (MS)
genetics and biotechnology (MS)
life sciences (MS, PhD)
microbiology (MS, PhD)
molecular biology (MS, PhD)
neuroscience (MS, PhD)
nutrition (MS)
physiology and developmental biology (MS, PhD)
wildlife and wildlands conservation (MS, PhD)

College of Nursing
Dr. Beth Vaughan Cole, Dean
Program in:
family nurse practitioner (MS)

College of Physical and Mathematical Sciences
Dr. Scott D. Sommerfeldt, Chair
Programs in:
applied statistics (MS)
biochemistry (MS, PhD)
chemistry (MS, PhD)
computer science (MS, PhD)
geological sciences (MS)
mathematics (MS, PhD)
mathematics education (MA)
physical and mathematical sciences (MA, MS, PhD)
physics (MS, PhD)
physics and astronomy (PhD)

College of Religious Education
Dr. Terry B. Ball, Dean
Program in:
religious education (MA)

David O. McKay School of Education
Dr. K. Richard Young, Dean
Programs in:
counseling psychology (PhD)
education (M Ed, MA, MS, PhD, Ed S)
educational leadership and foundations (M Ed, PhD)
instructional psychology and technology (MS, PhD)
literacy education (MA)
school psychology (Ed S)
special education (MS)
speech-language pathology (MS)
teacher education (MA)

Ira A. Fulton College of Engineering and Technology
Dr. Alan R. Parkinson, Dean
Programs in:
chemical engineering (MS, PhD)
civil engineering (MS, PhD)
construction management (MS)
electrical and computer engineering (MS, PhD)
engineering and technology (MS, PhD)
information technology (MS)
manufacturing systems (MS)
mechanical engineering (MS, PhD)
technology and engineering education (MS)

J. Reuben Clark Law School
James D. Gordon, Dean
Program in:
law (JD, LL M)

Marriott School of Management
Dr. Gary C. Cornia, Dean
Programs in:
accountancy (M Acc)
business administration (MBA)
information systems (MISM)
management (EMPA, M Acc, MBA, MISM, MPA)
public administration (EMPA, MPA)

■ SOUTHERN UTAH UNIVERSITY
Cedar City, UT 84720-2498
http://www.suu.edu/

State-supported, coed, comprehensive institution. *Computer facilities:* 300 computers available on campus for general student use. A campuswide network can be accessed from student residence rooms and from off campus. *General application contact:* Provost, 435-586-7704.

College of Education
Programs in:
education (M Ed, MS)
sports conditioning (MS)

College of Humanities and Social Sciences
Programs in:
communication (MA)
humanities and social sciences (MA, MS)
public administration (MS)

College of Performing and Visual Arts
Programs in:
arts administration (MFA)
performing and visual arts (MFA)

College of Science
Programs in:
forensic science (MS)
science (MS)

School of Business
Programs in:
accounting (M Acc)
business (M Acc, MBA)
business administration (MBA)

■ UNIVERSITY OF PHOENIX–UTAH CAMPUS
Salt Lake City, UT 84123-4617
http://www.phoenix.edu/

Proprietary, coed, comprehensive institution. *Computer facilities:* Computer purchase and lease plans are available. A campuswide network can be accessed from off campus. Online class registration is available. *General application contact:* Campus Information Center, 801-263-1444.

The Artemis School

College of Education
Programs in:
administration and supervision (MA Ed)
curriculum and instruction (MA Ed)
elementary teacher education (MA Ed)
school counseling (MSC)
secondary teacher education (MA Ed)
special education (MA Ed)

College of Health and Human Services
Programs in:
health care management (MBA)
healthcare education (MSN)
mental health counseling (MSC)
nursing (MSN)

John Sperling School of Business
Program in:
business (MBA, MIS, MM)

College of Graduate Business and Management
Programs in:
accounting (MBA)
business administration (MBA)
global management (MBA)
human resource management (MBA, MM)
management (MM)
marketing (MBA)
technology management (MBA)

College of Information Systems and Technology
Program in:
information systems and technology (MIS)

■ UNIVERSITY OF UTAH
Salt Lake City, UT 84112-1107
http://www.utah.edu/

State-supported, coed, university. CGS member. *Computer facilities:* 8,000 computers available on campus for general student use. A campuswide network can be accessed from student residence rooms and from off campus. Online class registration, online classes are available. *Graduate expenses:* Tuition, state resident: full-time $3656; part-time $149.44 per credit hour. Tuition, nonresident: full-time $12,908; part-time $525.98 per credit hour. Required fees: $672; $700 per year. Tuition and fees vary according to course load, degree level, program, reciprocity agreements and student level. *General application contact:* Office of Admissions, 801-581-7283.

The Graduate School
Dr. David S. Chapman, Dean
Programs in:
biological chemistry (PhD)
biostatistics (MST)
biotechnology (PSM)
business (MST)
computational science (PSM)
econometrics (MST)
economics (MST)
educational psychology (MST)
environmental science (PSM)
mathematics (MST)
molecular biology (PhD)
science instrumentation (PSM)
sociology (MST)
statistics (M Stat)

College of Architecture and Planning
Prof. Brenda Scheer, Director
Programs in:
architectural studies (MS)
architecture (M Arch)
architecture and planning (M Arch, MCMP, MS, PhD)
city and metropolitan planning (MCMP)
metropolitan planning, policy and design (PhD)

College of Education
Michael Hardman, Dean
Programs in:
counseling psychology (PhD)
early childhood hearing impairments (M Ed, MS)
early childhood special education (M Ed, PhD)
early childhood vision impairments (M Ed, MS)
education (M Ed, M Phil, M Stat, MA, MAT, MS, Ed D, PhD)
education, culture, and society (M Ed, MA, MS, PhD)
educational leadership and policy (M Ed, M Phil, Ed D, PhD)
educational psychology (MA)
elementary education (MAT)
hearing impairments (M Ed, MS)
mild/moderate disabilities (MS, PhD)
professional counseling (MS)
professional practice (M Ed)
professional psychology (M Ed)
research in special education (MS)
school counseling (M Ed, MS)
school psychology (MS, PhD)
secondary education (MAT)
severe disabilities (MS)
statistics (M Stat)
teaching and learning (M Ed, M Phil, MA, MS, PhD)
vision impairments (M Ed)

College of Engineering
Dr. Richard B. Brown, Dean
Programs in:
bioengineering (ME, MS, PhD)
chemical engineering (ME, MS, PhD)
civil engineering (MS, PhD)
computational engineering and science (MS)
computational science (MS)
computer science (M Phil, MS, PhD)
computing (MS, PhD)
electrical engineering (M Phil, ME, MS, PhD, EE)
engineering (M Phil, ME, MS, PhD, EE)
environmental engineering (ME, MS, PhD)
materials science and engineering (MS, PhD)
mechanical engineering (M Phil, ME, MS, PhD)
nuclear engineering (ME, MS, PhD)

College of Fine Arts
Dr. Raymond Tymas Jones, Dean and Associate Vice-President for the Arts
Programs in:
art history (MA)
ballet (MFA)
ceramics (MFA)
community-based art education (MFA)
drawing (MFA)
film studies (MFA)
fine arts (M Mus, MA, MFA, DMA, PhD)
graphic design (MFA)
modern dance (MA, MFA)
music (M Mus, MA, DMA, PhD)
painting (MFA)
photography/digital imaging (MFA)
printmaking (MFA)
sculpture/intermedia (MFA)

College of Health
Dr. James E. Graves, Dean
Programs in:
audiology (Au D, PhD)
exercise and sport science (MS, PhD)
health (M Phil, MA, MOT, MS, Au D, DPT, Ed D, PhD, PPDPT)
health promotion and education (M Phil, MS, Ed D, PhD)
nutrition (MS)
occupational therapy (MOT)
parks, recreation, and tourism (M Phil, MS, Ed D, PhD)
physical therapy (DPT, PPDPT)
speech-language pathology (MA, MS, PhD)

College of Humanities
Dr. Robert D. Newman, Dean and Associate Vice President of Interdisciplinary Studies
Programs in:
American studies (MA, PhD)
anthropology (MA)
applied linguistics (MA, PhD)
Arabic (MA, PhD)
Arabic and linguistics (MA, PhD)
Asian studies (MA)
British American literature (MA, PhD)
communication (M Phil, MA, MS, PhD)
comparative literary and cultural studies (MA, PhD)
creative writing (MA, MFA, PhD)
French (MA, MALP)
German (MA, MALP, PhD)
Hebrew (MA)
history (MA, PhD)
humanities (M Phil, MA, MALP, MAT, MFA, MS, PhD)
language pedagogy (MALP)
linguistics (MA, PhD)
literature (PhD)
Persian (MA, PhD)
philosophy (MA, MS, PhD)
political science (MA, PhD)
rhetoric and composition (PhD)
rhetoric/composition (MA, PhD)
Spanish (MA, MALP, PhD)
Turkish (MA)
world languages with secondary teaching licensure (MA)

College of Mines and Earth Sciences
Dr. Francis H. Brown, Dean
Programs in:
atmospheric sciences (MS, PhD)
environmental engineering (ME, MS, PhD)
geological engineering (ME, MS, PhD)
geology (MS, PhD)
geophysics (MS, PhD)
metallurgical engineering (ME, MS, PhD)
mines and earth sciences (ME, MS, PhD)
mining engineering (ME, MS, PhD)

College of Nursing
Dr. Maureen Keefe, Dean
Programs in:
gerontology (MS, Certificate)
nursing (MS, DNP, PhD, Certificate)

College of Pharmacy
Dr. John W. Mauger, Dean
Programs in:
medicinal chemistry (MS, PhD)
pharmaceutics and pharmaceutical chemistry (MS, PhD)
pharmacology and toxicology (PhD)
pharmacotherapy (MS)
pharmacy (Pharm D, MS, PhD)

College of Science
Pierre V. Sokolsky, Dean
Programs in:
biology (MS, PhD)
chemical physics (PhD)
chemistry (M Phil, MA, MS, PhD)
mathematics (M Phil, M Stat, MA, MS, PhD)
medical physics (PhD)
physics (MA, MS, PhD)
science (M Phil, M Stat, MA, MS, PhD)
science teacher education (MS)

College of Social and Behavioral Science
J. Steven Ott, Dean
Programs in:
anthropology (M Phil, MA, MS, PhD)
clinical psychology (PhD)
econometrics (M Stat)
economics (M Phil, MA, MS)
geography (MA, MS, PhD)

University of Utah (continued)
human development and social policy (MS)
international affairs and global enterprises (MS)
political science (MA, MS, PhD)
psychology (PhD)
public administration (Exec MPA, MPA)
public policy (MPP)
social and behavioral science (Exec MPA, M Phil, M Stat, MA, MPA, MPP, MS, PhD, Certificate)
sociology (M Stat, MA, MS, PhD)

College of Social Work
Dr. Jannah H. Mather, Dean
Program in:
social work (MSW, PhD)

David Eccles School of Business
Dr. Jack Brittain, Dean
Programs in:
accounting (M Acc, PhD)
business (EMBA, M Acc, M Stat, MBA, MS, PhD)
business administration (EMBA, M Stat, MBA, PhD)
finance (MS, PhD)

School of Medicine

Programs in:
biochemistry (MS, PhD)
biostatistics (M Stat)
experimental pathology (PhD)
human genetics (MS, PhD)
laboratory medicine and biomedical science (MS)
medical informatics (MS, PhD, Certificate)
medicine (MD, M Phil, M Stat, MPAS, MPH, MS, MSPH, PhD, Certificate)
neurobiology and anatomy (PhD)
neuroscience (PhD)
oncological sciences (M Phil, MS, PhD)
physician assistant (MPAS)
physiology (PhD)
public health (MPH, MSPH, PhD)

S.J. Quinney College of Law

Program in:
law (JD, LL M)

■ UTAH STATE UNIVERSITY

Logan, UT 84322
http://www.usu.edu/

State-supported, coed, university. CGS member. *Computer facilities:* 925 computers available on campus for general student use. A campuswide network can be accessed from student residence rooms and from off campus. Online class registration is available. *General application contact:* Admissions Officer, School of Graduate Studies, 435-797-1190.

School of Graduate Studies

College of Agriculture
Programs in:
agricultural systems technology (MS)
agriculture (MDA, MFMS, MS, PhD)
animal science (MS, PhD)
biometeorology (MS, PhD)
bioveterinary science (MS, PhD)
dairy science (MS)
dietetic administration (MDA)
ecology (MS, PhD)
family and consumer sciences education (MS)
food microbiology and safety (MFMS)
nutrition and food sciences (MS, PhD)
nutrition science (MS, PhD)
plant science (MS, PhD)
soil science (MS, PhD)
toxicology (MS, PhD)

College of Business
Programs in:
accountancy (M Acc)
applied economics (MS)
business (M Acc, MA, MBA, MS, Ed D, PhD)
business administration (MBA)
business education (MS)
business information systems (MS)
business information systems and education (Ed D)
economics (MA, MS, PhD)
education (PhD)
human resource management (MS)

College of Education and Human Services
Programs in:
audiology (Au D, Ed S)
business information systems (Ed D, PhD)
clinical/counseling/school psychology (PhD)
communication disorders and deaf education (M Ed)
communicative disorders and deaf education (MA, MS)
curriculum and instruction (Ed D, PhD)
disability disciplines (PhD)
education and human services (M Ed, MA, MFHD, MRC, MS, Au D, Ed D, PhD, Ed S)
elementary education (M Ed, MA, MS)
family and human development (MFHD)
family, consumer, and human development (MS, PhD)
health, physical education and recreation (M Ed, MS)
instructional technology (M Ed, MS, PhD, Ed S)
rehabilitation counselor education (MRC)
research and evaluation (PhD)
research and evaluation methodology (PhD)
school counseling (MS)
school psychology (MS)
secondary education (M Ed, MA, MS)
special education (M Ed, MS, Ed S)

College of Engineering
Programs in:
aerospace engineering (MS, PhD)
biological and agricultural engineering (MS, PhD)
civil and environmental engineering (ME, MS, PhD, CE)
electrical engineering (ME, MS, PhD)
engineering (ME, MS, PhD, CE)
industrial technology (MS)
irrigation engineering (MS, PhD)
mechanical engineering (ME, MS, PhD)

College of Humanities, Arts and Social Sciences
Programs in:
advanced technical practice (MFA)
American studies (MA, MS)
art (MA, MFA)
bioregional planning (MS)
design (MFA)
English (MA, MS)
folklore (MA, MS)
history (MA, MS)
humanities, arts and social sciences (MA, MFA, MLA, MS, MSLT, MSS, PhD)
interior design (MS)
journalism and communication (MA, MS)
landscape architecture (MLA)
political science (MA, MS)
second language teaching (MSLT)
sociology (MA, MS, MSS, PhD)
theatre arts (MA, MFA)
western American literature and culture (MA, MS)

College of Natural Resources
Programs in:
bioregional planning (MS)
ecology (MS, PhD)
fisheries biology (MS, PhD)
forestry (MS, PhD)
geography (MA, MS)
human dimensions of ecosystem science and management (MS, PhD)
natural resources (MA, MNR, MS, PhD)
range science (MS, PhD)
recreation resource management (MS, PhD)
watershed science (MS, PhD)
wildlife biology (MS, PhD)

College of Science
Programs in:
biochemistry (MS, PhD)
biology (MS, PhD)
chemistry (MS, PhD)
computer science (MCS, MS, PhD)
ecology (MS, PhD)
geology (MS)
industrial mathematics (MS)
mathematical sciences (PhD)
mathematics (M Math, MS)
physics (MS, PhD)
science (M Math, MCS, MS, PhD)
statistics (MS)

■ WEBER STATE UNIVERSITY

Ogden, UT 84408-1001
http://www.weber.edu/

State-supported, coed, comprehensive institution. *Computer facilities:* 558 computers available on campus for general student use. A campuswide network can be accessed from student residence rooms and from off campus. Online class registration is available. *General application contact:* Director of Admissions, 801-626-6046.

College of Arts and Humanities

Programs in:
arts and humanities (MENG)
English (MENG)

College of Health Professions

Programs in:
health administration (MHA)
health professions (MHA)

College of Social and Behavioral Sciences

Programs in:
criminal justice (MCJ)
social and behavioral sciences (MCJ)

Jerry and Vickie Moyes College of Education

Programs in:
athletic training (MSAT)
curriculum and instruction (M Ed)
education (M Ed, MSAT)

John B. Goddard School of Business and Economics

Programs in:
accountancy (M Acc)
business administration (MBA)
business and economics (M Acc, MBA)

■ WESTMINSTER COLLEGE

Salt Lake City, UT 84105-3697
http://www.westminstercollege.edu/

Independent, coed, comprehensive institution. *Graduate faculty:* 51 full-time (33 women), 14 part-time/adjunct (5 women). *Computer facilities:* 403 computers available on campus for general student use. A campuswide network can be accessed from student residence rooms and from off campus. Online class registration is available. *Graduate expenses:* Tuition: part-time $840 per credit hour. Tuition and fees vary according to course load and program. *General application contact:* Joel Bauman, Vice President of Enrollment Services, 801-832-2200.

The Bill and Vieve Gore School of Business

John Groesbeck, Dean
Programs in:
business administration (MBA, Certificate)
technology management (MBATM)

Program in Counseling Psychology

Janine Wanlass, Director
Program in:
counseling psychology (MSPC)

Program in Professional Communication

Dr. Helen Hodgson, Director
Program in:
professional communication (MPC)

School of Education

Robert Shaw, Interim Dean
Program in:
education (M Ed, MAT)

School of Nursing and Health Sciences

Dr. Sheryl Steadman, Dean
Programs in:
family nurse practitioner (MSN)
nurse anesthesia (MSNA)
nurse education (MSNED)
nursing (MSN)
nursing education (MSN)
public health (MPH)

Vermont

■ BENNINGTON COLLEGE

Bennington, VT 05201
http://www.bennington.edu/

Independent, coed, comprehensive institution. *Graduate faculty:* 40 full-time (16 women), 33 part-time/adjunct (16 women). *Computer facilities:* 100 computers available on campus for general student use. A campuswide network can be accessed from student residence rooms and from off campus. *Graduate expenses:* Tuition: full-time $20,640; part-time $2890 per course. One-time fee: $75. Tuition and fees vary according to program. *General application contact:* Ken Himmelman, Dean of Admissions and Financial Aid, 802-440-4312.

Graduate Programs

Duncan Dobbelmann, Associate Dean for Academic Services
Programs in:
allied and health sciences (Certificate)
art education (MAT)
creative writing (MFA)
dance (MFA)
early childhood (MAT)
education (MATSL)
elementary education (MAT)
English education (MAT)
foreign language education (MAT, MATSL)
French (MATSL)
mathematics education (MAT)
music (MFA)
music education (MAT)
science education (MAT)
secondary education (MAT)
social science education (MAT)
Spanish (MATSL)

■ CASTLETON STATE COLLEGE

Castleton, VT 05735
http://www.castleton.edu/

State-supported, coed, comprehensive institution. *Computer facilities:* Computer purchase and lease plans are available. 225 computers available on campus for general student use. A campuswide network can be accessed from student residence rooms. *General application contact:* Director of Admissions, 802-468-1213.

Division of Graduate Studies

Programs in:
curriculum and instruction (MA Ed)
educational leadership (MA Ed, CAGS)
forensic psychology (MA)
language arts and reading (MA Ed, CAGS)
special education (MA Ed, CAGS)

■ COLLEGE OF ST. JOSEPH

Rutland, VT 05701-3899
http://www.csj.edu/

Independent-religious, coed, comprehensive institution. *Computer facilities:* 30 computers available on campus for general student use. A campuswide network can be accessed. *General application contact:* Director of Admissions, 802-773-5900 Ext. 3262.

Graduate Programs

Division of Business

Program in:
business administration (MBA)

Division of Education

Programs in:
elementary education (M Ed)
English (M Ed)
general education (M Ed)
reading (M Ed)
secondary education (M Ed)
social studies (M Ed)
special education (M Ed)

Division of Psychology and Human Services

Programs in:
alcohol and substance abuse counseling (MS)
clinical mental health counseling (MS)
clinical psychology (MS)
community counseling (MS)
school guidance counseling (MS)

■ GODDARD COLLEGE

Plainfield, VT 05667-9432

http://www.goddard.edu/

Independent, coed, comprehensive institution. *Graduate faculty:* 5 full-time (2 women), 84 part-time/adjunct (60 women). *Computer facilities:* 55 computers available on campus for general student use. A campuswide network can be accessed from student residence rooms and from off campus. Library services available. *Graduate expenses:* Tuition: full-time $14,446. Full-time tuition and fees vary according to campus/location and program. Part-time tuition and fees vary according to course load and program. *General application contact:* Josh Castle, Associate Dean for Enrollment, 800-906-8312.

Graduate Programs

Robert Kenny, Vice President

Programs in:
- community education (MA)
- consciousness studies (MA)
- creative writing (MFA)
- environmental studies (MA)
- health arts and sciences (MA)
- interdisciplinary arts (MFA)
- organizational development (MA)
- psychology and counseling (MA)
- sexual orientation (MA)
- socially responsible business and sustainable communities (MA)
- teacher licensure (MA)
- transformative language arts (MA)

■ JOHNSON STATE COLLEGE

Johnson, VT 05656-9405

http://www.johnsonstatecollege.edu/

State-supported, coed, comprehensive institution. *Graduate faculty:* 11 full-time (6 women), 15 part-time/adjunct (12 women). *Computer facilities:* 131 computers available on campus for general student use. A campuswide network can be accessed from student residence rooms and from off campus. Online class registration is available. *Graduate expenses:* Tuition, state resident: part-time $390 per credit. Tuition, nonresident: part-time $842 per credit. *General application contact:* Catherine H. Higley, Program Coordinator, 800-635-2356 Ext. 1244.

Graduate Program in Education

Programs in:
- applied behavior analysis (MA Ed)
- children's mental health (MA Ed)
- curriculum and instruction (MA Ed)
- gifted and talented (MA Ed)
- literacy (MA Ed)
- science education (MA Ed)
- secondary education (MA Ed, CAGS)
- special education (MA Ed)

Program in Counseling

Program in:
- counseling (MA)

Program in Studio Arts

Programs in:
- drawing (MFA)
- mixed media (MFA)
- painting (MFA)
- sculpture (MFA)

■ NORWICH UNIVERSITY

Northfield, VT 05663

http://www.norwich.edu/

Independent, coed, primarily men, comprehensive institution. *Graduate faculty:* 2 full-time (0 women), 173 part-time/adjunct (34 women). *Computer facilities:* 200 computers available on campus for general student use. A campuswide network can be accessed from student residence rooms and from off campus. *Graduate expenses:* Tuition: full-time $16,000. Full-time tuition and fees vary according to degree level and program. *General application contact:* Sally Burkart, Administrative Assistant, 802-485-2567.

School of Graduate Studies

Dr. William Clemments, Dean

Programs in:
- business administration (MBA)
- civil engineering (MCE)
- corrections administration (MJA)
- information assurance (MS)
- international commerce (MA)
- international conflict management (MA)
- international terrorism (MA)
- justice administration (MJA)
- law administration (MJA)
- military history (MA)
- nursing administration (MSN)
- organizational leadership (MSOL)
- public administration (MPA)

■ SAINT MICHAEL'S COLLEGE

Colchester, VT 05439

http://www.smcvt.edu/

Independent-religious, coed, comprehensive institution. *Computer facilities:* Computer purchase and lease plans are available. 375 computers available on campus for general student use. A campuswide network can be accessed from student residence rooms and from off campus. Online class registration is available. *General application contact:* Director of Admissions and Marketing, Graduate Programs, 802-654-2251.

Graduate Programs

Programs in:
- administration (M Ed, CAGS)
- administration and management (MSA, CAMS)
- arts in education (CAGS)
- clinical psychology (MA)
- curriculum and instruction (M Ed, CAGS)
- information technology (CAGS)
- reading (M Ed)
- special education (M Ed, CAGS)
- teaching English as a second language (MATESL, Certificate)
- technology (M Ed)
- theology (MA, CAS, Certificate)

■ SIT GRADUATE INSTITUTE

Brattleboro, VT 05302-0676

http://www.sit.edu/

Independent, coed, graduate-only institution. *Graduate faculty:* 27 full-time (12 women), 19 part-time/adjunct (8 women). *Computer facilities:* 55 computers available on campus for general student use. A campuswide network can be accessed from student residence rooms and from off campus. *General application contact:* Information Contact, 800-336-1616.

Graduate Programs

Adam Weinberg, President/CEO of World Learning and SIT

Programs in:
- conflict transformation (MA)
- English for speakers of other languages (MAT)
- French (MAT)
- global management (MGM)
- intercultural service, leadership, and management (MA)
- international education (MA)
- management (MS)
- social justice in intercultural relations (MA)
- Spanish (MAT)
- sustainable development (MA)

■ UNIVERSITY OF VERMONT

Burlington, VT 05405

http://www.uvm.edu/

State-supported, coed, university. CGS member. *Graduate faculty:* 702 full-time, 604 part-time/adjunct. *Computer facilities:* Computer purchase and lease plans are available. 475 computers available on campus for general student use. A campuswide network can be accessed from student residence rooms and from off campus. Online class registration, Web pages, online course support are available. *Graduate expenses:* Tuition, state resident: part-time $488 per credit. Tuition, nonresident: part-time $1232 per credit. *General application contact:* Dr. Patricia Stokowski, Interim Dean, 802-656-3160.

College of Medicine

Dr. Frederick Moria, Dean

Programs in:
biochemistry (MS, PhD)
clinical and translational science (MS, PhD)
medicine (MD, MS, PhD)
microbiology and molecular genetics (MS, PhD)
molecular physiology and biophysics (MS, PhD)
neuroscience (PhD)
pathology (MS)
pharmacology (MS, PhD)

Graduate College
Dr. Patricia Stokowski, Interim Dean
Program in:
cell and molecular biology (MS, PhD)

College of Agriculture and Life Sciences
Dr. Thomas C. Vogelmann, Dean
Programs in:
agriculture and life sciences (MPA, MS, MSD, PhD)
animal sciences (MS, PhD)
animal, nutrition and food sciences (PhD)
community development and applied economics (MS)
dietetics (MSD)
field naturalist (MS)
microbiology and molecular genetics (MS, PhD)
nutritional sciences (MS)
plant and soil science (MS, PhD)
plant biology (MS, PhD)
public administration (MPA)

College of Arts and Sciences
Dr. Eleanor Miller, Dean
Programs in:
arts and sciences (MA, MAT, MS, MST, PhD)
biology (MS, PhD)
biology education (MST)
chemistry (MS, PhD)
clinical psychology (PhD)
communication sciences (MS)
English (MA)
French (MA)
geology (MS)
German (MA)
Greek (MA)
Greek and Latin (MAT)
historic preservation (MS)
history (MA)
Latin (MA)
physics (MS)
psychology (PhD)

College of Education and Social Services
Dr. Fayneese Miller, Dean
Programs in:
counseling (MS)
curriculum and instruction (M Ed, MAT)
education and social services (M Ed, MAT, MS, MSW, Ed D)
educational leadership (M Ed)
educational leadership and policy studies (Ed D)
educational studies (M Ed)
higher education and student affairs administration (M Ed)
interdisciplinary studies (M Ed)
reading and language arts (M Ed)
social work (MSW)
special education (M Ed)

College of Engineering and Mathematics
Dr. Domenico Grasso, Dean
Programs in:
biomedical engineering (MS)
biostatistics (MS)
civil and environmental engineering (MS, PhD)
computer science (MS, PhD)
electrical engineering (MS, PhD)
engineering and mathematics (MS, MST, PhD)
materials science (MS, PhD)
mathematics (MS, MST, PhD)
mathematics education (MST)
mechanical engineering (MS, PhD)
statistics (MS)

College of Nursing and Health Sciences
Dr. Betty Rambur, Dean
Programs in:
nursing (MS)
nursing and health sciences (MS, DPT)
physical therapy (DPT)

The Rubenstein School of Environment and Natural Resources
Mary Watzin, Director/Coordinator
Programs in:
environment and natural resources (MS, PhD)
natural resources (MS, PhD)

School of Business Administration
Dr. R. DeWitt, Dean
Programs in:
accounting (M Acc)
business administration (M Acc, MBA)

Virginia

■ THE COLLEGE OF WILLIAM AND MARY
Williamsburg, VA 23187-8795
http://www.wm.edu/

State-supported, coed, university. CGS member. *Graduate faculty:* 628 full-time (232 women), 173 part-time/adjunct (72 women). *Computer facilities:* Computer purchase and lease plans are available. 350 computers available on campus for general student use. A campuswide network can be accessed from student residence rooms and from off campus. Online class registration is available. *Graduate expenses:* Tuition, state resident: full-time $6400; part-time $300 per credit hour. Tuition, nonresident: full-time $19,720; part-time $800 per credit hour. Required fees: $3860. *General application contact:* Dr. Laurie Sanderson, Dean of Graduate Studies and Research, 757-221-2468.

Faculty of Arts and Sciences
Dr. Laurie Sanderson, Dean of Graduate Studies and Research
Programs in:
American studies (MA, PhD)
anthropology (MA, PhD)
applied science (MS, PhD)
arts and sciences (MA, MPP, MS, PhD, Psy D)
biology (MS)
chemistry (MA, MS)
clinical psychology (Psy D)
computational operations research (MS)
computer science (MS, PhD)
general experimental psychology (MA)
history (MA, PhD)
physics (MS, PhD)
public policy (MPP)

Mason School of Business
Dr. Lawrence Pulley, Dean
Programs in:
accounting (M Acc)
business administration (EMBA, MBA)

School of Education
Dr. Virginia McLaughlin, Dean
Programs in:
community and addictions counseling (M Ed)
community counseling (M Ed)
counselor education (PhD)
curriculum and educational technology (Ed D, PhD)
curriculum leadership (Ed D, PhD)
education (M Ed, MA Ed, Ed D, PhD, Ed S)
educational leadership (M Ed)
educational policy, planning, and leadership (Ed D, PhD)
elementary education (MA Ed)
family counseling (M Ed)
gifted education (MA Ed)
gifted education administration (M Ed)
reading education (MA Ed)
school counseling (M Ed)
school psychology (M Ed, Ed S)
secondary education (MA Ed)
special education (MA Ed)

Virginia Institute of Marine Science
Dr. John T. Wells, Dean/Director
Program in:
marine science (MS, PhD)

William and Mary Law School
Davison M. Douglas, Dean and Hanson Professor of Law
Program in:
law (JD, LL M)

■ DEVRY UNIVERSITY
Arlington, VA 22202
http://www.devry.edu/

Proprietary, coed, comprehensive institution. *Computer facilities:* Computer purchase and lease plans are available. 380 computers available on campus for general student use. A campuswide network can be accessed from off campus. Online class registration is available.

Keller Graduate School of Management
Program in:
management (MAFM, MBA, MHRM, MISM, MNCM, MPA, MPM, Graduate Certificate)

■ EASTERN MENNONITE UNIVERSITY
Harrisonburg, VA 22802-2462
http://www.emu.edu/

Independent-religious, coed, comprehensive institution. *Graduate faculty:* 22 full-time (7 women), 22 part-time/adjunct (6 women). *Computer facilities:* 152 computers available on campus for general student use. A campuswide network can be accessed from student residence rooms and from off campus. Online class registration is available. *Graduate expenses:* Tuition: part-time $455 per credit hour. Tuition and fees vary according to program. *General application contact:* Don A. Yoder, Director of Seminary and Graduate Admissions, 540-432-4257.

Eastern Mennonite Seminary
Dr. Ervin R. Stutzman, Seminary Dean
Programs in:
church leadership (MA)
divinity (M Div)
ministry studies (Certificate)
online theological studies (Certificate)
religion (MA)
theological studies (Certificate)

Program in Business Administration
Dr. Ronald L. Stoltzfus, Co-Director, MBA Program
Program in:
business administration (MBA)

Program in Conflict Transformation
Dr. David Brubaker, Academic Director
Program in:
conflict transformation (MA, Graduate Certificate)

Program in Counseling
Dr. P. David Glanzer, Professor of Counselor Education
Program in:
counseling (MA)

Program in Education
Dr. Donovan D. Steiner, Director
Program in:
education (MA)

■ GEORGE MASON UNIVERSITY
Fairfax, VA 22030
http://www.gmu.edu/

State-supported, coed, university. CGS member. *Graduate faculty:* 1,249 full-time (511 women), 972 part-time/adjunct (461 women). *Computer facilities:* Computer purchase and lease plans are available. 1,545 computers available on campus for general student use. A campuswide network can be accessed from student residence rooms and from off campus. Online class registration is available. *Graduate expenses:* Tuition, state resident: full-time $6894; part-time $287.25 per credit. Tuition, nonresident: full-time $20,286; part-time $853.75 per credit. Required fees: $1986; $82.75. *General application contact:* Dan Robb, Director of Graduate Admissions, 703-993-9700.

College of Education and Human Development
Jeffrey Gorrell, Dean
Programs in:
counseling and development (M Ed)
early childhood education (M Ed)
education (PhD)
education and human development (M Ed, MA, MS, PhD, Graduate Certificate)
education leadership (M Ed)
educational psychology (MS)
English as a second language (M Ed)
exercise, science and health (MS)
gifted child education (M Ed)
history (M Ed)
instructional technology (M Ed)
library media (M Ed)
literacy and reading (M Ed)
mathematics (M Ed)
new professional studies (MA)
physical education (M Ed)
science (M Ed)
secondary education (M Ed)
special education (M Ed, Graduate Certificate)
teacher leadership (M Ed)

School of Recreation, Health and Tourism
David Wiggins, Director
Program in:
exercise, fitness, and health promotion (MS)

College of Health and Human Services
Dr. Shirley S. Travis, Dean
Programs in:
epidemiology (Certificate)
global health (MS)
health administration and policy (MS)
health and human services (MPH, MS, MSN, MSW, PhD, Certificate)
health science (MS)
nutrition (Certificate)
public health (MPH)
social work (MSW)

School of Nursing
Dr. Shirley S. Travis, Dean
Programs in:
epidemiology and biostatistics (MS)
nurse educator (MSN)
nurse practitioner (MSN)
nursing (MSN, PhD)
nursing administration (MSN)
nursing education (Certificate)

College of Humanities and Social Sciences
Jack Censer, Dean
Programs in:
anthropology (MA, MAIS)
applied developmental psychology (MA, PhD)
art history (MA)
biodefense (MS, PhD)
biopsychology (MA, PhD)
clinical psychology (MA, PhD)
communications (MA, PhD)
community college teaching (MAIS)
creative writing (MFA)
cultural studies (PhD)
economic systems design (Graduate Certificate)
economics (MA, PhD)
English (MA)
English literature (MA)
folklore (MAIS)
foreign languages (MA)
global interaction (MAIS)
higher education (MAIS)
history (MA, PhD)
human factors engineering psychology (MA, PhD)
humanities and social sciences (MA, MAIS, MFA, MPA, MS, DA Ed, PhD, Certificate, Graduate Certificate)
individualized studies (MAIS)
industrial/organizational psychology (MA, PhD)
justice, law, and crime policy (MA, PhD)
linguistics (MA)
philosophy (MA)
political science (MA, PhD)
professional writing and editing (MA, Certificate)
psychology (MA, PhD)
public administration (MPA)
religion, cultures, and values (MAIS)
school psychology (MA)
sociology (MA, PhD)
teaching English as a second language (Certificate)
teaching writing and literature (MA)
video-based production (MAIS)
women and gender studies (MAIS)
women's studies (MAIS)
zoo and aquarium leadership (MAIS)

Higher Education Program
John O'Connor, Director

Programs in:
college teaching (Certificate)
community college education (DA Ed)

College of Science
Programs in:
applied and engineering physics (MS)
biodefense (MS, PhD)
bioinformatics and computational biology (MS, PhD, Certificate)
biology (MS, PhD)
chemistry (MS)
chemistry and biochemistry (MS)
climate dynamics (PhD)
computational and data sciences (MS, PhD, Certificate)
computational social science (PhD)
computational techniques and applications (Certificate)
earth systems and geoinformation sciences (MS, PhD, Certificate)
environmental science and policy (MS, PhD)
geographic and cartographic sciences (MS)
geography (MS)
mathematical sciences (MS, PhD)
mathematics (MS, PhD)
nanotechnology and nanoscience (Certificate)
neuroscience (PhD)
physical sciences (PhD)
physics and astronomy (MS)
remote sensing and earth image processing (Certificate)

College of Visual and Performing Arts
William Reeder, Dean
Programs in:
art and visual technology (MA, MFA)
art education (MAT)
artist certificate (Certificate)
arts management (MA)
composition (MA, MM)
conducting (MA, MM)
dance (MFA)
music (MM)
music education (MA, MM, Certificate)
pedagogy and performance (MA)
performance (MA, MM)
visual and performing arts (MA, MAT, MFA, MM, Certificate)

Institute for Conflict Analysis and Resolution
Dr. Sara Cobb, Director
Program in:
conflict analysis and resolution (MS, PhD)

School of Law
Dean Daniel D. Polsby, Dean
Programs in:
intellectual property (LL M)
law (JD)
law and economics (LL M)

School of Management
Richard Klimoski, Dean
Programs in:
accounting (MS)
business administration (EMBA, MBA)
management (EMBA, MBA, MS)
technology management (MS)

School of Public Policy
Dr. Kingsley Haynes, Dean
Programs in:
international commerce and policy (MA)
organization development and knowledge management (MS)
peace operations (MNPS)
public policy (MA, MNPS, MPP, MS, PhD)
transportation policy, operations and logistics (MA)

Volgenau School of Information Technology and Engineering
Lloyd Griffiths, Dean
Programs in:
advanced networking protocols for telecommunications (Certificate)
applied information technology (MS)
architecture-based systems integration (Certificate)
biometrics (Certificate)
biostatistics (Certificate)
civil and infrastructure engineering (MS, PhD)
civil infrastructure and security engineering (Certificate)
command, control, communication, computing and intelligence (Certificate)
communications and networking (Certificate)
computational modeling (Certificate)
computer engineering (MS)
computer forensics (MS)
computer games technology (Certificate)
computer networking (Certificate)
computer science (MS, PhD)
data mining (Certificate)
database management (Certificate)
discovery, design, and innovation (Certificate)
electrical and computer engineering (PhD)
electrical engineering (MS)
electronic commerce (Certificate)
epidemiology and biostatistics (MS)
federal statistics (Certificate)
foundations of information systems (Certificate)
information engineering (Certificate)
information security and assurance (MS)
information systems (MS, Certificate)
information technology (PhD, Engr)
information technology and engineering (MS, PhD, Certificate, Engr)
intelligence agents (Certificate)
leading technical enterprises (Certificate)
military operations research (Certificate)
network technology and applications (Certificate)
networks, system integration and testing (Certificate)
operations research (MS)
signal processing (Certificate)
software architecture (Certificate)
software engineering (MS, Certificate)
statistical science (MS, PhD)
sustainability and the environment (Certificate)
systems engineering (MS)
systems engineering and operations research (PhD)
systems engineering software intensive systems (Certificate)
telecom systems modeling (Certificate)
telecommunications (MS)
telecommunications forensics and security (Certificate)
VLSI design/manufacturing (Certificate)
water resources engineering (Certificate)
Web-based software engineering (Certificate)
wireless communication (Certificate)

■ HAMPTON UNIVERSITY

Hampton, VA 23668
http://www.hamptonu.edu/

Independent, coed, university. CGS member. *Computer facilities:* 1,300 computers available on campus for general student use. A campuswide network can be accessed from student residence rooms and from off campus. Online class registration is available. *General application contact:* Vice President for Research and Dean of Graduate College, 757-727-5310.

Graduate College
Programs in:
advanced adult nursing (MS)
atmospheric physics (MS, PhD)
biology (MS)
business (MBA)
chemistry (MS)
college student development (MA)
communicative sciences and disorders (MA)
community agency counseling (MA)
community health nursing (MS)
community mental health/psychiatric nursing (MS)
computational mathematics (MS)
computer science (MS)
counseling (MA)
early childhood education (MT)
elementary education (MA)
environmental science (MS)
family nursing (MS)
gerontological nursing for the nurse practitioner (MS)
medical physics (MS, PhD)
medical science (MS)
middle school education (MT)
music education (MT)
nonlinear science (MS)
nuclear physics (MS, PhD)
optical physics (MS, PhD)
pastoral counseling (MA)
pediatric nursing (MS)
physical therapy (DPT)
school counseling (MA)

Hampton University (continued)
secondary education (MT)
special education (MA, MT)
statistics and probability (MS)
teaching (MT)
women's health nursing (MS)

■ HOLLINS UNIVERSITY
Roanoke, VA 24020-1603
http://www.hollins.edu/

Independent, Undergraduate: women only; graduate: coed, comprehensive institution. *Graduate faculty:* 20 full-time (7 women), 30 part-time/adjunct (18 women). *Computer facilities:* Computer purchase and lease plans are available. 100 computers available on campus for general student use. A campuswide network can be accessed from student residence rooms and from off campus. Online class registration, applications software are available. *Graduate expenses:* Tuition: full-time $26,720; part-time $590 per credit hour. Required fees: $280. *General application contact:* Cathy S. Koon, Manager of Graduate Services, 540-362-6326.

Graduate Programs
Dr. Jeanine S. Stewart, Vice President for Academic Affairs
Programs in:
children's literature (MA, MFA)
creative writing (MFA)
dance (MFA)
humanities (MALS)
interdisciplinary studies (MALS)
justice and legal studies (MALS)
liberal studies (CAS)
playwriting (MFA)
screenwriting and film studies (MA, MFA)
social science (MALS)
teaching (MAT)
visual and performing arts (MALS)

■ JAMES MADISON UNIVERSITY
Harrisonburg, VA 22807
http://www.jmu.edu/

State-supported, coed, comprehensive institution. CGS member. *Graduate faculty:* 243 full-time (116 women), 72 part-time/adjunct (42 women). *Computer facilities:* Computer purchase and lease plans are available. 600 computers available on campus for general student use. A campuswide network can be accessed from student residence rooms and from off campus. Online class registration is available. *Graduate expenses:* Tuition, state resident: full-time $7008; part-time $292 per credit hour. Tuition, nonresident: full-time $20,352; part-time $848 per credit hour. *General application contact:* Dr. Reid Linn, Dean, The Graduate School, 540-568-6131.

The Graduate School
Dr. Reid Linn, Dean

College of Arts and Letters
Dr. David K. Jeffrey, Dean
Programs in:
arts and letters (MA, MPA, MS)
English (MA)
history (MA)
political science (MA, MPA)
public administration (MPA)
writing, rhetoric, and technical communication (MA, MS)

College of Business
Dr. Robert D. Reid, Dean
Programs in:
accounting (MS)
business (MBA, MS)
business administration (MBA)

College of Education
Dr. Phillip M. Wishon, Dean
Programs in:
adult education/human resource development (MS Ed)
early childhood education (M Ed)
education (M Ed, MAT, MS Ed)
educational leadership (M Ed)
elementary education (M Ed)
exceptional education (M Ed)
middle education (MAT)
reading education (M Ed)
secondary education (MAT)

College of Integrated Science and Technology
Dr. Sharon E. Lovell, Interim Dean
Programs in:
assessment and measurement (PhD)
audiology (Au D, PhD)
clinical audiology (PhD)
college student personnel administration (M Ed)
combined-integrated clinical and school psychology (PhD, Psy D)
community counseling psychology (M Ed, MA, Ed S)
computer science (MS)
health education (MS, MS Ed)
integrated science and technology (M Ed, MA, MOT, MPAS, MS, MS Ed, MSN, Au D, PhD, Psy D, Ed S)
kinesiology (MS)
nursing (MSN)
occupational therapy (MOT)
physician assistant studies (MPAS)
psychological sciences (MA)
school counseling (Ed S)
school psychology (M Ed, MA, Ed S)
speech-language pathology (MS, PhD)

College of Science and Mathematics
Dr. David F. Brakke, Dean
Programs in:
biology (MS)
mathematics and statistics (M Ed)
science and mathematics (M Ed, MS)

College of Visual and Performing Arts
Dr. George Sparks, Dean
Programs in:
art education (MA)
art history (MA)
ceramics (MFA)
conducting (MM)
drawing/painting (MFA)
metal/jewelry (MFA)
music education (MM)
musical arts (DMA)
performance (MM)
photography (MFA)
printmaking (MFA)
sculpture (MFA)
studio art (MA)
theory-composition (MM)
visual and performing arts (MA, MFA, MM, DMA)
weaving/fibers (MFA)

■ LIBERTY UNIVERSITY
Lynchburg, VA 24502
http://www.liberty.edu/

Independent-religious, coed, comprehensive institution. *Computer facilities:* 600 computers available on campus for general student use. A campuswide network can be accessed from student residence rooms and from off campus. Online class registration is available. *Graduate expenses:* Tuition: part-time $1779 per semester. Required fees: $150 per semester. *General application contact:* Kyle A. Falce, Director of Graduate Admissions, 800-424-9596.

College of Arts and Sciences
Programs in:
counseling (MA)
nursing (MSN)
pastoral care and counseling (PhD)
professional counseling (PhD)

Liberty Theological Seminary and Graduate School
Programs in:
religious studies (M Div, MA, MAR, MRE, D Min)
theology (Th M)

School of Business
Program in:
business (MBA, MS)

School of Communications
Program in:
communications (MA)

School of Education
Programs in:
administration and supervision (M Ed)
curriculum and instruction (M Ed)
early childhood education (M Ed)
education specialist (Ed S)
educational leadership (Ed D)
elementary education (M Ed)
gifted education (M Ed)
reading specialist (M Ed)
school counseling (M Ed)
secondary education (M Ed)
special education (M Ed)

School of Law
Program in:
law (JD)

■ LONGWOOD UNIVERSITY
Farmville, VA 23909
http://www.longwood.edu/

State-supported, coed, comprehensive institution. CGS member. *Computer facilities:* Computer purchase and lease plans are available. 270 computers available on campus for general student use. A campuswide network can be accessed from student residence rooms and from off campus. Online class registration is available. *General application contact:* Assistant Dean of Graduate Studies, 434-395-2707.

Office of Graduate Studies
Programs in:
6-12 initial teaching/licensure (MA)
creative writing (MA)
criminal justice (MS)
English education and writing (MA)
literature (MA)

College of Business and Economics
Program in:
retail management (MBA)

College of Education and Human Services
Programs in:
communication sciences and disorders (MS)
community and college counseling (MS)
curriculum and instruction specialist-elementary (MS)
curriculum and instruction specialist-secondary (MS)
educational leadership (MS)
guidance and counseling (MS)
literacy and culture (MS)
school library media (MS)

■ LYNCHBURG COLLEGE
Lynchburg, VA 24501-3199
http://www.lynchburg.edu/

Independent-religious, coed, comprehensive institution. *Graduate faculty:* 35 full-time (17 women), 9 part-time/adjunct (4 women). *Computer facilities:* 300 computers available on campus for general student use. A campuswide network can be accessed from student residence rooms. Online class registration is available. *Graduate expenses:* Tuition: full-time $6750; part-time $375 per credit. *General application contact:* Dr. Edward Polloway, Vice President for Community Advancement and Dean of Graduate Studies, 434-544-8655.

Graduate Studies
Dr. Edward Polloway, Vice President for Graduate and Community Advancement

School of Business and Economics
Dr. Joe Turek, Dean, School of Business and Economics
Program in:
business (MBA)

School of Communications and the Arts
Dr. Edward Polloway, Vice President for Graduate and Community Advancement
Program in:
music (MA)

School of Education and Human Development
Dr. Jan Stenette, Dean
Programs in:
community counseling (M Ed)
counselor education (M Ed)
curriculum and instruction (M Ed)
educational leadership (M Ed)
English education (M Ed)
reading (M Ed)
school counseling (M Ed)
science education (M Ed)
special education (M Ed)

School of Health Sciences and Human Performance
Programs in:
clinical nurse leader (MSN)
nursing education (MSN)
physical therapy (DPT)

School of Humanities and Social Sciences
Dr. Edward Polloway, Vice President for Graduate and Community Advancement
Programs in:
English (MA)
history (MA)

■ MARY BALDWIN COLLEGE
Staunton, VA 24401-3610
http://www.mbc.edu/

Independent, Undergraduate: women only; graduate: coed, comprehensive institution. *Computer facilities:* 244 computers available on campus for general student use. A campuswide network can be accessed from student residence rooms and from off campus. Online class registration is available. *General application contact:* Executive Director of Admissions and Financial Aid, 540-887-7260.

Graduate Studies
Programs in:
acting (M Litt)
directing (M Litt)
elementary education (MAT)
middle grades education (MAT)
Shakespeare and Renaissance literature in performance (M Litt, MFA)
teaching (M Litt, MAT)

■ MARYMOUNT UNIVERSITY
Arlington, VA 22207-4299
http://www.marymount.edu/

Independent-religious, coed, comprehensive institution. CGS member. *Graduate faculty:* 70 full-time (48 women), 55 part-time/adjunct (31 women). *Computer facilities:* 260 computers available on campus for general student use. A campuswide network can be accessed from student residence rooms. Online class registration, online drive space are available. *Graduate expenses:* Tuition: full-time $12,420; part-time $690 per credit hour. Required fees: $126; $7 per credit hour. Tuition and fees vary according to degree level. *General application contact:* Francesca Reed, Director, Graduate Admissions, 703-284-5901.

Academic Outreach Program
Dr. Donald Shandler, Assistant Vice President for Graduate and Adult Education
Programs in:
health care management (MS)
management studies (Certificate)
organization development (Certificate)

School of Arts and Sciences
Dr. Teresa Reed, Dean
Programs in:
arts and sciences (MA)
humanities (MA)
interior design (MA)
literature and languages (MA)

School of Business Administration
James Ryerson, Dean
Programs in:
business administration (MA, MBA, MS, Certificate)
computer security and information assurance (Certificate)
forensic computing (Certificate)
health care informatics (Certificate)
health care management (MS)
human resource management (MA, Certificate)
information technology (MS, Certificate)
information technology project management: technology leadership (Certificate)
instructional design (Certificate)
leadership (Certificate)
legal administration (MA)
management (MS)
organization development (Certificate)
paralegal studies (Certificate)
project management (Certificate)

School of Education and Human Services
Dr. Wayne Lesko, Dean
Programs in:
Catholic school leadership (M Ed, Certificate)
community counseling (MA, Certificate)
community counseling and forensic psychologyeducation and human services (M Ed, MA, Certificate)
elementary education (M Ed)
English as a second language (M Ed)
forensic psychology (MA)

Marymount University (continued)
learning disabilities (M Ed)
pastoral and spiritual care (MA)
pastoral counseling (MA, Certificate)
professional studies (M Ed)
school counseling (MA)
secondary education (M Ed)

School of Health Professions
Dr. Tess Cappello, Dean
Programs in:
family nurse practitioner (MSN, Certificate)
health professions (MS, MSN, DPT, Certificate)
health promotion management (MS)
nursing education (MSN, Certificate)
physical therapy (DPT)
RN to MSN (MSN)

■ NORFOLK STATE UNIVERSITY
Norfolk, VA 23504
http://www.nsu.edu/

State-supported, coed, comprehensive institution. CGS member. *Computer facilities:* Computer purchase and lease plans are available. A campuswide network can be accessed. Online class registration is available. *General application contact:* Director, Office of Graduate Studies, 757-823-8015.

School of Graduate Studies

School of Education
Programs in:
early childhood education (MAT)
education (MA, MAT)
pre-elementary education (MA)
principal preparation (MA)
secondary education (MAT)
severe disabilities (MA)
teaching (MA)
urban education/administration (MA)

School of Liberal Arts
Programs in:
applied sociology (MS)
community/clinical psychology (MA)
criminal justice (MA)
liberal arts (MA, MFA, MM, MS, Psy D)
media and communication (MA)
music (MM)
music education (MM)
performance (MM)
psychology (Psy D)
theory and composition (MM)
urban affairs (MA)
visual studies (MA, MFA)

School of Science and Technology
Programs in:
computer science (MS)
electronics engineering (MS)
materials science (MS)
optical engineering (MS)
science and technology (MS)

School of Social Work
Program in:
social work (MSW, PhD)

■ OLD DOMINION UNIVERSITY
Norfolk, VA 23529
http://www.odu.edu/

State-supported, coed, university. CGS member. *Graduate faculty:* 589 full-time (208 women), 128 part-time/adjunct (69 women). *Computer facilities:* Computer purchase and lease plans are available. 2,035 computers available on campus for general student use. A campuswide network can be accessed from student residence rooms and from off campus. Online class registration, online courses are available. *Graduate expenses:* Tuition, state resident: full-time $7704; part-time $321 per credit. Tuition, nonresident: full-time $19,104; part-time $796 per credit. Required fees: $99 per semester. One-time fee: $40. *General application contact:* Lakeisha Phelps, Director of Admissions, 757-683-3648.

College of Arts and Letters
Dr. Chandra deSilva, Dean
Programs in:
applied linguistics (MA)
applied sociology (MA)
arts and letters (MA, MFA, MME, PhD)
conflict and cooperation (PhD)
creative writing (MFA)
criminology and criminal justice (PhD)
English (MA, PhD)
history (MA)
humanities (MA)
music education (MME)
U.S. foreign policy (MA)

College of Business and Public Administration
Dr. Nancy Bagranoff, Dean
Programs in:
accounting (MS)
business and economic forecasting (MBA)
business and public administration (MA, MBA, MPA, MS, PhD)
economics (MA)
finance (PhD)
financial analysis and valuation (MBA)
information technology (PhD)
information technology and enterprise integration (MBA)
international business (MBA)
maritime and port management (MBA)
marketing (PhD)
public administration (MPA)
public administration and urban policy (PhD)
strategic management (PhD)

College of Health Sciences
Dr. Andrew Balas, Dean
Programs in:
community health professions (MS)
environmental health (MS)
health care administration (MS)
health sciences (MPH, MS, MSN, DNP, DPT, PhD)
health services research (PhD)
long-term care administration (MS)
nursing practice (DNP)
public health (MPH)
wellness and promotion (MS)

School of Dental Hygiene
Prof. Michele L. Darby, Graduate Program Director
Program in:
dental hygiene (MS)

School of Nursing
Dr. Laurel Garzon, Graduate Program Director
Programs in:
family nurse practitioner (MSN)
nurse anesthesia (MSN)
nurse educator (MSN)
nurse midwifery (MSN)
women's health nurse practitioner (MSN)

School of Physical Therapy
Dr. Martha Walker, Graduate Program Director
Program in:
physical therapy (DPT)

College of Sciences
Dr. Chris Platsoucas, Dean
Programs in:
analytical chemistry (MS)
applied experimental psychology (PhD)
biochemistry (MS)
biology (MS)
biomedical sciences (PhD)
chemistry (PhD)
clinical psychology (Psy D)
computational and applied mathematics (MS, PhD)
computer science (MS, PhD)
ecological sciences (PhD)
environmental chemistry (MS)
human factors psychology (PhD)
industrial/organizational psychology (PhD)
ocean and earth sciences (MS)
oceanography (PhD)
organic chemistry (MS)
physical chemistry (MS)
physics (MS, PhD)
psychology (MS, PhD)
sciences (MS, PhD, Psy D)

Darden College of Education
Dr. William H. Graves, Dean
Programs in:
athletic training (MS Ed)
biology (MS Ed)
business and industry training (MS)
career and technical education (MS, PhD)
chemistry (MS Ed)
community college leadership (PhD)
community college teaching (MS)
counseling (MS Ed, PhD, Ed S)
curriculum and instruction (MS Ed)
early childhood education (MS Ed, PhD)
education (MS, MS Ed, PhD, Ed S)

educational leadership (MS Ed, PhD, Ed S)
educational media (MS Ed)
educational training (MS Ed)
elementary education (MS Ed)
English (MS Ed)
exercise and wellness (MS Ed)
higher education (MS Ed, PhD, Ed S)
human movement science (PhD)
human resources training (PhD)
instructional design and technology (PhD)
instructional technology (MS Ed)
library science (MS Ed)
literacy leadership (PhD)
middle school education (MS Ed)
physical education (MS Ed)
principal preparation (MS Ed)
reading education (MS Ed)
recreation and tourism studies (MS Ed)
secondary education (MS Ed)
special education (MS Ed, PhD)
speech-language pathology (MS Ed)
sport management (MS Ed)
technology education (PhD)

Frank Batten College of Engineering and Technology

Dr. Oktay Baysal, Dean
Programs in:
aerospace engineering (ME, MS, D Eng, PhD)
civil and environmental engineering (D Eng)
civil engineering (ME, MS, PhD)
computer engineering (ME, MS)
design and manufacturing (ME)
electrical and computer engineering (PhD)
electrical engineering (ME, MS)
engineering and technology (ME, MEM, MS, D Eng, PhD)
engineering management (MEM, MS, PhD)
engineering management and systems engineering (D Eng)
environmental engineering (ME, MS, PhD)
mechanical engineering (ME, MS, D Eng, PhD)
modeling and simulation (ME, MS, D Eng, PhD)
motorsports (ME)
systems engineering (ME)

■ RADFORD UNIVERSITY
Radford, VA 24142
http://www.radford.edu/

State-supported, coed, comprehensive institution. CGS member. *Graduate faculty:* 222 full-time (109 women), 44 part-time/adjunct (34 women). *Computer facilities:* 756 computers available on campus for general student use. A campuswide network can be accessed from student residence rooms and from off campus. Online class registration, online financial aid status and student accounts payable are available. *Graduate expenses:* Tuition, state resident: full-time $4845; part-time $202 per credit. Tuition, nonresident: full-time $11,483; part-time $478 per credit. Required fees: $2349; $98 per credit. *General application contact:* Graduate Admissions, 540-831-5431.

College of Graduate and Professional Studies

Dr. Dennis Grady, Dean

College of Business and Economics

Dr. Faye W. Gilbert, Dean
Programs in:
business administration (MBA)
business and economics (MBA)

College of Education and Human Development

Dr. Patricia Shoemaker, Dean
Programs in:
community counseling (MS)
content area studies (MS)
curriculum and instruction (MS)
deaf and hard of hearing (MS)
early childhood education (MS)
early childhood special education (MS)
education (MS)
education and human development (MS)
educational leadership (MS)
educational technology (MS)
high incidence disabilities (MS)
library media (MS)
literacy education (MS)
school counseling (MS)
severe disabilities (MS)
special education (MS)
student administration counseling (MS)
student affairs counseling (MS)

College of Humanities and Behavioral Sciences

Dr. Brian Conniff, Dean
Programs in:
clinical psychology (MA, MS)
corporate and professional communication (MS)
counseling psychology (Psy D)
criminal justice (MA, MS)
English (MA, MS)
experimental psychology (MA)
general psychology (MS)
humanities and behavioral sciences (MA, MS, Psy D, Ed S)
industrial/organizational psychology (MA, MS)
school psychology (Ed S)

College of Visual and Performing Arts

Dr. Joseph P. Scartelli, Dean
Programs in:
art (MFA)
music (MA)
music education (MS)
music therapy (MS)
visual and performing arts (MA, MFA, MS)

Waldron College of Health and Human Services

Dr. Raymond Linville, Dean
Programs in:
adult clinical nurse specialist (MSN)
family nurse practitioner (MSN)
health and human services (MA, MS, MSN, MSW)
social work (MSW)
speech-language pathology (MS)

■ REGENT UNIVERSITY
Virginia Beach, VA 23464-9800
http://www.regent.edu/

Independent, coed, comprehensive institution. CGS member. *Graduate faculty:* 179 full-time (59 women), 397 part-time/adjunct (192 women). *Computer facilities:* 200 computers available on campus for general student use. A campuswide network can be accessed from student residence rooms and from off campus. Online class registration is available. *Graduate expenses:* Tuition: full-time $15,141; part-time $721 per credit hour. Required fees: $200; $100 per semester. Tuition and fees vary according to course level, course load, degree level and program. *General application contact:* Matthew Chadwick, Director of Admissions, 800-373-5504.

Graduate School

Dr. Carlos Campo, Vice President for Academic Affairs

Robertson School of Government

Dr. Charles W. Dunn, Dean
Programs in:
health care policy and administration (MA)
international politics (MA)
law and public policy (MA)
Mid-East Politics (MA)
political leadership and management (MA)
political management (MA)
public administration (MA)
public policy (MA)
terrorism and homeland defense (MA)
world economies and political development (MA)

School of Communication and the Arts

Michael Patrick, Dean
Programs in:
acting (MFA)
acting and directing (MFA)
cinema arts/television arts (MA)
communication (MA, PhD)
digital media (MA)
directing for cinema/TV (MA)
journalism (MA)
producing for cinema/TV (MA)
script and screenwriting (MFA)
theatre (MA)

School of Divinity

Dr. Michael Palmer, Dean
Programs in:
Biblical studies (MA)
leadership and renewal (D Min)

Regent University (continued)
missiology (M Div, MA)
practical theology (M Div, MA)
renewal studies (PhD)

School of Education
Dr. Alan A. Arroyo, Dean
Programs in:
career switcher (M Ed)
Christian school program (M Ed)
cross-categorical special education (M Ed)
education (M Ed, Ed D)
education licensure (M Ed)
educational leadership (M Ed)
elementary education (M Ed)
individualized degree plan (M Ed)
leadership in character education (M Ed)
master teacher (M Ed)
mathematics education (M Ed)
special education leadership (Ed S)
student affairs (M Ed)
TESOL (M Ed)

School of Global Leadership and Entrepreneurship
Dr. Bruce Winston, Dean
Programs in:
business administration (MBA)
management (MA)
organizational leadership (MA, PhD, Certificate)
strategic foresight (MA)
strategic leadership (DSL)

School of Law
Jeffrey Brauch, Dean
Programs in:
American legal studies (LL M)
law (JD)

School of Psychology and Counseling
Dr. Rosemarie Hughes, Dean
Programs in:
clinical psychology (MA, Psy D)
counseling (MA)
counseling studies (CAGS)
counselor education and supervision (PhD)

■ SHENANDOAH UNIVERSITY
Winchester, VA 22601-5195
http://www.su.edu/

Independent-religious, coed, comprehensive institution. *Graduate faculty:* 115 full-time (65 women), 56 part-time/adjunct (34 women). *Computer facilities:* Computer purchase and lease plans are available. 175 computers available on campus for general student use. A campuswide network can be accessed from student residence rooms and from off campus. Online class registration, online student account information are available. *Graduate expenses:* Tuition: full-time $16,900; part-time $670 per credit. *General application contact:* David Anthony, Dean of Admissions, 540-665-4581.

Byrd School of Business
Dr. Randy Boxx, Dean
Programs in:
business administration (MBA)
health care management (Certificate)
information systems and computer technology (Certificate)

School of Education and Human Development
Dr. Steven E. Humphries, Dean
Programs in:
advanced professional teaching English to speakers of other languages (Certificate)
education (MSE)
elementary education (Certificate)
ESL (Certificate)
middle school education (Certificate)
organizational leadership (D Ed)
professional studies (Certificate)
professional studies for VA licensure (Certificate)
professional teaching English to speakers of other languages (Certificate)
public management (Certificate)
secondary education (Certificate)

School of Health Professions
Program in:
health professions (MS, MSN, DPT, Certificate)

Division of Athletic Training
Dr. Rose A. Schmieg, Director
Program in:
athletic training (MS)

Division of Nursing
Dr. Kathryn Ganske, Director
Programs in:
family nurse practitioner (Certificate)
health systems management (Certificate)
nurse-midwifery (Certificate)
nursing (MSN)
psychiatric mental health nurse practitioner (Certificate)

Division of Occupational Therapy
Dr. Deborah A. Marr, Director
Program in:
occupational therapy (MS)

Division of Physical Therapy
Dr. Karen Abraham-Justice, Director
Program in:
physical therapy and non-traditional physical therapy (DPT)

Division of Physician Assistant Studies
Anthony A. Miller, Director
Program in:
physician assistant studies (MS)

School of Pharmacy
Dr. Alan McKay, Dean
Program in:
pharmacy and non-traditional pharmacy (Pharm D)

Shenandoah Conservatory
Dr. Laurence A. Kaptain, Dean
Programs in:
arts administration (MS)
church music (MM, Certificate)
composition (MM)
conducting (MM)
dance accompanying (MM)
music (MS)
music education (MME, DMA)
music therapy (MMT, Certificate)
pedagogy (MM, DMA)
performance (MM, DMA, Artist Diploma)
piano accompanying (MM)

■ UNIVERSITY OF MARY WASHINGTON
Fredericksburg, VA 22401-5358
http://www.umw.edu/

State-supported, coed, comprehensive institution. *Computer facilities:* Computer purchase and lease plans are available. 306 computers available on campus for general student use. A campuswide network can be accessed from student residence rooms and from off campus. Online class registration is available. *General application contact:* Associate Dean of Admissions, 540-286-8017.

College of Graduate and Professional Studies
Programs in:
business administration (MBA)
education (M Ed)
management information systems (MSMIS)

■ UNIVERSITY OF RICHMOND
Richmond, University of Richmond, VA 23173
http://www.richmond.edu/

Independent, coed, comprehensive institution. *Computer facilities:* Computer purchase and lease plans are available. 700 computers available on campus for general student use. A campuswide network can be accessed from student residence rooms and from off campus. Online class registration is available. *General application contact:* Director of the Graduate School, 804-289-8417.

Robins School of Business
Program in:
business (MBA)

School of Law
Program in:
law (JD)

■ UNIVERSITY OF VIRGINIA
Charlottesville, VA 22903
http://www.virginia.edu/

State-supported, coed, university. CGS member. *Graduate faculty:* 2,171 full-time (688 women), 197 part-time/adjunct (94 women). *Computer facilities:* Computer purchase and lease plans are available. A campuswide network can be accessed from student residence rooms and from off campus. Online class registration, online course management tool are available. *Graduate expenses:* Tuition, state resident: full-time $10,452. Tuition, nonresident: full-time $20,010. Required fees: $2176. Part-time tuition and fees vary according to course load and program. *General application contact:* Dean, 434-924-0311.

College and Graduate School of Arts and Sciences
Meredith Jung-En Woo, Dean
Programs in:
anthropology (MA, PhD)
art and architectural history (MA, PhD)
arts and sciences (MA, MFA, MS, PhD)
astronomy (MS, PhD)
biology (MA, MS, PhD)
chemistry (MA, MS, PhD)
classical art and archaeology (MA, PhD)
classics (MA, PhD)
creative writing (MFA)
drama (MFA)
East Asian studies (MA)
economics (MA, PhD)
English (MA, PhD)
environmental sciences (MA, MS, PhD)
foreign affairs (MA, PhD)
French (MA, PhD)
German (MA, PhD)
government (MA, PhD)
history (MA, PhD)
history of art and architecture (MA, PhD)
immunology (PhD)
Italian (MA)
linguistics (MA)
math education (MA)
mathematics (MA, PhD)
music (MA, PhD)
philosophy (MA, PhD)
physics (MA, MS, PhD)
physics education (MA)
psychology (MA, PhD)
religious studies (MA, PhD)
Slavic languages and literatures (MA, PhD)
sociology (MA, PhD)
Spanish (MA, PhD)
statistics (MS, PhD)

Center for Biomedical Ethics
Margaret Mohrmann, Director
Program in:
bioethics (MA)

Curry School of Education
Robert C. Pianta, Dean
Programs in:
administration and supervision (M Ed, Ed D, PhD, Ed S)
applied developmental science (M Ed, PhD)
clinical and school psychology (PhD)
communication disorders (M Ed)
counselor education (M Ed, Ed D, PhD, Ed S)
curriculum and instruction (M Ed, Ed D, PhD, Ed S)
early childhood-developmental risk (MT)
education (M Ed, MT, Ed D, PhD, Ed S)
education evaluation (PhD)
educational evaluation (M Ed)
educational policy studies (M Ed, Ed D)
educational psychology (M Ed, Ed D, PhD, Ed S)
educational research (Ed D, PhD)
elementary (M Ed, MT, Ed D, PhD)
English (M Ed, Ed D)
English education (MT, PhD)
foreign language (M Ed)
foreign language education (MT)
gifted education (M Ed)
health and physical education (M Ed, Ed D)
higher education (M Ed, Ed D, PhD, Ed S)
instructional technology (M Ed, PhD, Ed S)
kinesiology (M Ed, MT, Ed D, PhD)
math education (PhD)
mathematics (M Ed, Ed D)
reading (M Ed, Ed D, Ed S)
reading education (PhD)
research statistics and evaluation (Ed D, PhD)
school psychology (Ed D, PhD)
science (Ed D)
science education (PhD)
social foundations (PhD)
social studies (M Ed)
social studies education (MT, PhD)
special education (M Ed, Ed D, PhD, Ed S)
student affairs practice (M Ed)
world languages education (MT)

Darden Graduate School of Business Administration
Robert F. Bruner, Dean
Program in:
business administration (MBA, PhD)

Frank Batten Sr. School of Leadership and Public Policy
Harry Harding, Dean
Programs in:
leadership and public policy (MPP)
public policy (MPP)

McIntire School of Commerce
Programs in:
accounting (MS)
commerce (MSC)
financial services (MSC)
management of information technology (MS)
marketing and management (MSC)

School of Architecture
Karen Van Lengen, Dean
Programs in:
architectural history (M Arch H, PhD)
architecture (M Arch)
landscape architecture (M Land Arch)
urban and environmental planning (MUEP, JD/MUEP)

School of Engineering and Applied Science
James H. Aylor, Dean
Programs in:
biomedical engineering (ME, MS, PhD)
chemical engineering (ME, MS, PhD)
civil engineering (ME, MS, PhD)
computer engineering (ME, MS, PhD)
computer science (MCS, MS, PhD)
electrical engineering (ME, MS, PhD)
engineering and applied science (MCS, ME, MEP, MMSE, MS, PhD)
engineering physics (MEP, MS, PhD)
materials science (MMSE, MS, PhD)
mechanical and aerospace engineering (ME, MS, PhD)
systems and information engineering (ME, MS, PhD)

School of Law
Paul G. Mahoney, Dean
Program in:
law (JD, LL M, SJD, JD/MUEP)

School of Medicine
Steven T. DeKosky, Vice President and Dean
Programs in:
biochemistry (PhD)
biological and physical sciences (MS)
biophysics (PhD)
cell biology (PhD)
clinical investigation and patient-oriented research (MS)
clinical research (MS)
experimental pathology (PhD)
informatics in medicine (MS)
medicine (MD, MPH, MS, PhD)
microbiology (PhD)
neuroscience (PhD)
pharmacology (PhD)
physiology (PhD)
public health (MPH)
surgery (MS)

School of Nursing
Dorrie K. Fontaine, Dean
Programs in:
acute and specialty care (MSN)
acute care nurse practitioner (MSN)
clinical nurse leadership (MSN)
community-public health leadership (MSN)
nursing (DNP, PhD)
psychiatric mental health counseling (MSN)

■ VIRGINIA COMMONWEALTH UNIVERSITY
Richmond, VA 23284-9005
http://www.vcu.edu/

State-supported, coed, university. CGS member. *Computer facilities:* Computer purchase and lease plans are available. 1,600 computers available on campus for general student use. A campuswide network can be accessed from student residence rooms and from off campus. Online class

Virginia Commonwealth University (continued)
registration is available. *General application contact:* Recruitment Coordinator, Graduate School, 804-828-6916.

Graduate School

Program in:
interdisciplinary studies (MIS)

College of Humanities and Sciences

Programs in:
account management (MS)
account planning (MS)
analytical chemistry (MS, PhD)
applied mathematics (MS)
applied social research (CASR)
art direction (MS)
biology (MS)
chemical physics (PhD)
clinical psychology (PhD)
copywriting (MS)
counseling psychology (PhD)
creative brand management (MS)
creative media planning (MS)
creative writing (MFA)
criminal justice (MS, CCJA)
English (MA)
fiction (MFA)
fictional poetry (MFA)
forensic science (MS)
gender violence intervention (Certificate)
general psychology (PhD)
geographic information systems (Certificate)
government and public affairs (MA, MPA, MS, MURP, PhD, CASR, CCJA, CPM, CURP, Certificate, Graduate Certificate)
historic preservation planning (Certificate)
history (MA)
homeland security and emergency preparedness (MA, Graduate Certificate)
humanities and sciences (MA, MFA, MPA, MS, MURP, PhD, CASR, CCJA, CPM, CURP, Certificate, Graduate Certificate)
inorganic chemistry (MS, PhD)
literature (MA)
mass communications (MS, PhD)
mathematics (MS)
media, art, and text (PhD)
medical physics (MS, PhD)
nanosciences (PhD)
nonprofit management (Graduate Certificate)
operations research (MS)
organic chemistry (MS, PhD)
physical chemistry (MS, PhD)
physics and applied physics (MS)
planning information systems (Certificate)
poetry (MFA)
political science and public administration (MPA)
public management (CPM)
public policy and administration (PhD)
scholastic journalism (MS)
sociology (MS, CASR, Certificate)
statistical sciences and operations research (MS, Certificate)
strategic public relations (MS)
urban and regional planning (MURP)
urban revitalization (CURP)
writing and rhetoric (MA)

School of Allied Health Professions

Programs in:
advanced physical therapy (MS)
aging studies (CAS)
allied health professions (MHA, MS, MSHA, MSNA, MSOT, PhD, CAS, CPC)
clinical laboratory sciences (MS)
entry-level physical therapy (MS)
gerontology (MS, PhD)
health administration (MHA, MSHA, PhD)
health related sciences (PhD)
health services organization and research (PhD)
nurse anesthesia (MSNA)
occupational therapy (MS, MSOT)
patient counseling (MS, CPC)
physical therapy (PhD)
physiology (PhD)
radiation sciences (PhD)
rehabilitation counseling (MS, CPC)
rehabilitation leadership (PhD)

School of Business

Programs in:
accounting (M Acc, MBA, PhD)
business (M Acc, M Tax, MA, MBA, MS, PhD, Certificate, Postbaccalaureate Certificate)
business administration (MBA, Postbaccalaureate Certificate)
decision sciences (MBA)
economics (MA, MBA, MS)
finance, insurance, and real estate (MS)
information systems (MS, PhD)
management (Certificate)
marketing and business law (Certificate)
real estate and urban land development (Certificate)
taxation (M Tax)

School of Education

Programs in:
adult literacy (M Ed)
adults with disabilities (M Ed)
athletic training (MSAT)
counselor education (M Ed)
curriculum and instruction (M Ed)
early childhood (M Ed)
early education (MT)
education (M Ed, MS, MSAT, MT, PhD, Certificate)
educational leadership (PhD)
educational psychology (PhD)
emotionally disturbed (M Ed, MT)
health and movement sciences (MS)
human resource development (M Ed)
instructional leadership (PhD)
learning disabilities (M Ed)
mentally retarded (M Ed, MT)
middle education (MT)
reading (M Ed)
recreation, parks and sports leadership (MS)
rehabilitation and movement science (PhD)
research and evaluation (PhD)
secondary education (MT, Certificate)
severely/profoundly handicapped (M Ed)
special education (MT)
special education and disability leadership (PhD)
urban services leadership (PhD)

School of Engineering

Programs in:
biomedical engineering (MS, PhD)
chemical and life science engineering (MS, PhD)
computer science (MS, PhD, Certificate)
electrical engineering (MS, PhD)
engineering (PhD)
mechanical engineering (MS, PhD)
nuclear engineering (MS)

School of Life Sciences

Programs in:
bioinformatics (MS)
environmental communication (MIS)
environmental health (MIS)
environmental policy (MIS)
environmental sciences (MIS)
integrative life sciences (PhD)
life sciences (MIS, MS, PhD)

School of Nursing

Programs in:
adult health nursing (MS)
child health nursing (MS)
family health nursing (MS)
health system (PhD)
immunocompetence (PhD)
nurse practitioner (MS, Certificate)
nursing administration (MS)
psychiatric-mental health nursing (MS)
risk and resilience (PhD)
women's health nursing (MS)

School of Social Work

Program in:
social work (MSW, PhD)

School of the Arts

Programs in:
acting (MFA)
architectural history (MA)
art education (MAE)
art history (MA, PhD)
ceramics (MFA)
costume design (MFA)
design/visual communications (MFA)
directing (MFA)
education (MM)
fibers (MFA)
furniture design (MFA)
glassworking (MFA)
graphic design (MFA)
historical studies (MA)
interior environment (MFA)
jewelry/metalworking (MFA)
kinetic imaging (MFA)
museum studies (MA)
music (MM)

painting (MFA)
pedagogy (MFA)
photography and film (MFA)
printmaking (MFA)
scene design/technical theater (MFA)
sculpture (MFA)
theatre (MFA)

Medical College of Virginia-Professional Programs

Program in:
medicine (DDS, MD, Pharm D, MPH, MS, PhD)

School of Dentistry
Program in:
dentistry (DDS, MS)

School of Medicine
Programs in:
anatomy (MS, PhD)
anatomy and neurobiology (MS, PhD)
anatomy and physical therapy (PhD)
biochemistry (MS, PhD)
biostatistics (MS, PhD)
epidemiology and community health (PhD)
genetic counseling (MS)
human genetics (PhD)
medicine (MD, MPH, MS, PhD)
microbiology and immunology (MS, PhD)
molecular biology and genetics (MS, PhD)
neuroscience (MS, PhD)
pathology (MS, PhD)
pharmacology (PhD)
pharmacology and toxicology (MS)
physiology (MS, PhD)

School of Pharmacy
Programs in:
pharmaceutics (Pharm D, MS, PhD)
pharmacy (Pharm D, MS, PhD)

Program in Pre-Medical Basic Health Sciences

Programs in:
anatomy (CBHS)
biochemistry (CBHS)
human genetics (CBHS)
microbiology (CBHS)
pharmacology (CBHS)
physiology (CBHS)

■ VIRGINIA POLYTECHNIC INSTITUTE AND STATE UNIVERSITY

Blacksburg, VA 24061
http://www.vt.edu/

State-supported, coed, university. CGS member. *Computer facilities:* 8,000 computers available on campus for general student use. A campuswide network can be accessed from student residence rooms and from off campus. Online class registration is available. *General application contact:* Graduate School Receptionist, 540-231-9563.

Graduate School

College of Agriculture and Life Sciences
Programs in:
agribusiness (MS)
agricultural economics (MS, PhD)
agricultural extension education (MS, PhD)
agriculture and life sciences (MS, PhD)
animal science (MS, PhD)
applied economics (MS)
crop and soil environmental sciences (MS, PhD)
developmental and international economics (PhD)
econometrics (PhD)
entomology (MS, PhD)
food science and technology (MS, PhD)
horticulture (MS, PhD)
human nutrition, foods and exercise (MS, PhD)
life sciences (MS, PhD)
macro and micro economics (PhD)
markets and industrial organizations (PhD)
plant pathology (MS, PhD)
plant physiology and weed science (MS, PhD)
plant protection (MS)
poultry science (MS, PhD)
public and regional/urban economics (PhD)
resource and environmental economics (PhD)

College of Architecture and Urban Studies
Programs in:
architecture (M Arch, MS)
architecture and urban studies (M Arch, MLA, MPA, MPIA, MS, MURP, PhD, CAGS)
architecture design research (PhD)
building construction (MS)
environmental design and planning (PhD)
environmental planning and policy (MURP)
government and international affairs (MPIA)
housing, community and economic development (MURP)
international development planning (MURP)
land use and physical planning (MURP)
landscape architecture (MLA)
planning, governance and globalization (PhD)
public administration and policy (MPA, PhD, CAGS)
urban and regional planning (MURP)

College of Engineering
Programs in:
aerospace engineering (M Eng, MS, PhD)
biological systems engineering (M Eng, MS, PhD)
chemical engineering (M Eng, MS, PhD)
civil engineering (M Eng, MS, PhD)
computer engineering (M Eng, MS, PhD)
computer science (MS, PhD)
electrical engineering (M Eng, MS, PhD)
engineering (M Eng, MEA, MIS, MS, PhD)
engineering administration (MEA)
engineering education (PhD)
engineering mechanics (MS, PhD)
environmental engineering (M Eng, MS)
environmental sciences and engineering (MS)
industrial engineering (M Eng, MS, PhD)
information systems (MIS)
materials science and engineering (M Eng, MS, PhD)
mechanical engineering (M Eng, MS, PhD)
mining and minerals engineering (M Eng, MS, PhD)
ocean engineering (MS)
operations research (M Eng, MS, PhD)
systems engineering (M Eng, MS)

College of Liberal Arts and Human Sciences
Programs in:
administration and supervision of special education (Ed D, PhD, Ed S)
adult development and aging (MS, PhD)
adult learning and human resource development (MS, PhD)
apparel business and economics (MS, PhD)
apparel product design and analysis (MS, PhD)
apparel quality analysis (MS, PhD)
career and technical education (MS Ed, Ed D, PhD, Ed S)
child development (MS, PhD)
communication (MA)
consumer studies (MS, PhD)
counselor education (MA Ed, Ed D, PhD, Ed S)
creative writing (MFA)
curriculum and instruction (MA Ed, Ed D, PhD, Ed S)
directing and public dialogue (MFA)
education (MA Ed, MS Ed, Ed D, PhD, Ed S)
educational leadership (MA Ed, Ed D, PhD)
educational psychology (PhD)
educational research and evaluation (PhD)
English (MA)
family financial management (MS, PhD)
family studies (MS, PhD)
foreign languages and literatures (MA)
health and physical education (MS Ed)
health promotion (MS)
higher education (MA Ed, PhD)
history (MA)
household equipment (MS, PhD)
housing (MS, PhD)
instructional design and technology (MA, Ed D, PhD, Ed S)

Virginia Polytechnic Institute and State University (continued)
interior design (MS, PhD)
liberal arts and human sciences (MA, MA Ed, MFA, MS, MS Ed, Ed D, PhD, Ed S)
marriage and family therapy (MS, PhD)
mathematics education (MA Ed, PhD)
philosophy (MA)
political science (MA)
resource management (MS, PhD)
rhetoric and writing (PhD)
science and technology studies (MS, PhD)
secondary English education (MA Ed)
social, political, ethical and cultural thought (PhD, Graduate Certificate)
sociology (MS, PhD)
stage management (MFA)
theatre design and technology (MFA)

College of Natural Resources
Programs in:
fisheries and wildlife sciences (MS, PhD)
forest biology (MF, MS, PhD)
forest biometry (MF, MS, PhD)
forest management/economics (MF, MS, PhD)
forest products marketing (MF, MS, PhD)
geography (MS, PhD)
industrial forestry operations (MF, MS, PhD)
natural resources (MF, MNR, MS, PhD)
outdoor recreation (MF, MS, PhD)
wood science and engineering (MF, MS, PhD)

College of Science
Programs in:
applied mathematics (MS, PhD)
applied physics (MS, PhD)
bio-behavioral sciences (PhD)
botany (MS, PhD)
chemistry (MS, PhD)
clinical psychology (PhD)
developmental psychology (PhD)
ecology and evolutionary biology (MS, PhD)
economics (MA, PhD)
genetics and developmental biology (MS, PhD)
geological sciences (MS, PhD)
geophysics (MS, PhD)
industrial/organizational psychology (PhD)
mathematical physics (MS, PhD)
microbiology (MS, PhD)
physics (MS, PhD)
psychology (MS)
pure mathematics (MS, PhD)
science (MA, MS, PhD)
statistics (MS, PhD)
zoology (MS, PhD)

Intercollege
Programs in:
biomedical engineering and sciences (MS, PhD)
genetics, bioinformatics and computational biology (PhD)
information technology (MIT)
interdisciplinary studies (MIT, MS, PhD)
macromolecular science and engineering (MS, PhD)

Pamplin College of Business
Programs in:
accounting and information systems (MACIS, PhD)
business (MACIS, MBA, MS, PhD)
business administration (MBA)
business information technology (MS, PhD)
finance (PhD)
hospitality and tourism management (MS, PhD)
management (PhD)
marketing (PhD)

Virginia-Maryland Regional College of Veterinary Medicine
Programs in:
biomedical and veterinary sciences (MS, PhD)
veterinary medicine (DVM, MS, PhD)

■ VIRGINIA STATE UNIVERSITY
Petersburg, VA 23806-0001
http://www.vsu.edu/

State-supported, coed, comprehensive institution. *Computer facilities:* 750 computers available on campus for general student use. A campuswide network can be accessed from student residence rooms and from off campus. Online class registration is available. *General application contact:* Dean, Graduate Studies, Research, and Outreach, 804-524-5985.

School of Graduate Studies, Research, and Outreach
Program in:
interdisciplinary studies (MIS)

School of Agriculture
Programs in:
agriculture (MS)
plant science (MS)

School of Engineering, Science and Technology
Programs in:
behavioral and community health sciences (PhD)
biology (MS)
clinical health psychology (PhD)
clinical psychology (MS)
computer science (MS)
engineering, science and technology (M Ed, MS)
general psychology (MS)
mathematics (MS)
mathematics education (M Ed)
physics (MS)

School of Liberal Arts and Education
Programs in:
career and technical studies (M Ed, MS, CAGS)
economics (MA)
education (M Ed, MS)
educational administration and supervision (M Ed, MS)
English (MA)
history (MA)
liberal arts and education (M Ed, MA, MS, CAGS)

Washington

■ ANTIOCH UNIVERSITY SEATTLE
Seattle, WA 98121-1814
http://www.antiochsea.edu/

Independent, coed, university. *General application contact:* Dean of Student and Enrollment Services, 206-441-5352 Ext. 5200.

Graduate Programs
Programs in:
education (MA)
psychology (MA, Psy D)

Center for Creative Change
Programs in:
environment and community (MA)
management (MS)
organizational psychology (MA)
strategic communications (MA)
whole system design (MA)

■ CENTRAL WASHINGTON UNIVERSITY
Ellensburg, WA 98926
http://www.cwu.edu/

State-supported, coed, comprehensive institution. CGS member. *Computer facilities:* Computer purchase and lease plans are available. 720 computers available on campus for general student use. A campuswide network can be accessed from student residence rooms and from off campus. Online class registration is available. *General application contact:* Admissions Program Coordinator, 509-963-3103.

Graduate Studies, Research and Continuing Education
Program in:
individual studies (M Ed, MA, MS)

College of Arts and Humanities
Programs in:
art (MA, MFA)
arts and humanities (MA, MFA, MM)
English (MA)
history (MA)

music (MM)
teaching English as a second language (MA)
theatre production (MA)

College of Business
Programs in:
accounting (MPA)
business (MPA)

College of Education and Professional Studies
Programs in:
education and professional studies (M Ed, MS)
engineering technology (MS)
family and consumer sciences education (MS)
family studies (MS)
health, physical education and nutrition (MS)
master teacher (M Ed)
nutrition (MS)
reading education (M Ed)
special education (M Ed)

College of the Sciences
Programs in:
biological sciences (MS)
chemistry (MS)
experimental psychology (MS)
geological sciences (MS)
mathematics (MAT)
mental health counseling (MS)
resource management (MS)
school counseling (M Ed)
school psychology (M Ed)
sciences (M Ed, MAT, MS)

■ CITY UNIVERSITY OF SEATTLE
Bellevue, WA 98005
http://www.cityu.edu/

Independent, coed, comprehensive institution. *Graduate faculty:* 31 full-time (16 women), 1,142 part-time/adjunct (633 women). *Computer facilities:* 145 computers available on campus for general student use. A campuswide network can be accessed from off campus. Online class registration is available. *Graduate expenses:* Tuition: part-time $586 per credit. One-time fee: $50. Tuition and fees vary according to program. *General application contact:* Information Contact, 800-426-5596.

Graduate Division
Dr. Steven Olswang, Interim Provost

Division of Arts and Sciences
Judy Hinrichs, Interim Dean
Program in:
counseling psychology (MA)

Gordon Albright School of Education
Judy Hinrichs, Dean
Programs in:
curriculum and instruction (M Ed)
educational leadership (M Ed)
educational leadership: administrator certification (Certificate)
executive leadership: superintendent certification (Certificate)
guidance and counseling (M Ed)
leadership (M Ed)
leadership and school counseling (M Ed)
professional certification for teachers (Certificate)
reading and literacy (M Ed)
reading and literacy in education (M Ed)
teacher certification (elementary K-8) (MIT)
teacher certification (special education K-12) (MIT)
technology, curriculum, and instruction (M Ed)

School of Management
Dr. Kurt Kirstein, Dean
Programs in:
accounting (Certificate)
change leadership (MBA, Certificate)
financial management (MBA, Certificate)
general management (MBA)
general management-Europe (MBA)
global leadership (Certificate)
global marketing (MBA)
individualized study (MBA)
information security (MS)
information systems (MBA)
leadership (MA)
marketing (MBA, Certificate)
project management (MBA, MS, Certificate)
sustainable business (Certificate)
technology management (MBA, MS, Certificate)

■ EASTERN WASHINGTON UNIVERSITY
Cheney, WA 99004-2431
http://www.ewu.edu/

State-supported, coed, comprehensive institution. CGS member. *Computer facilities:* Computer purchase and lease plans are available. 812 computers available on campus for general student use. A campuswide network can be accessed from student residence rooms and from off campus. Online class registration is available. *General application contact:* Associate Dean for Graduate Studies, 509-359-6297.

Graduate Studies
Program in:
interdisciplinary studies (MA, MS)

College of Arts and Letters
Programs in:
arts and letters (M Ed, MA, MFA)
composition (MA)
creative writing (MFA)
French education (M Ed)
instrumental/vocal performance (MA)
literature (MA)
music education (MA)
music history and literature (MA)
rhetoric, composition, and technical communication (MA)
teaching English as a second language (MA)

College of Business and Public Administration
Programs in:
business administration (MBA)
business and public administration (MBA, MPA, MURP)
public administration (MPA)
urban and regional planning (MURP)

College of Education and Human Development
Programs in:
adult education (M Ed)
applied psychology (MS)
curriculum development (M Ed)
early childhood education (M Ed)
education and human development (M Ed, MS)
educational leadership (M Ed)
elementary teaching (M Ed)
exercise science (MS)
foundations of education (M Ed)
instructional media and technology (M Ed)
literacy (M Ed)
mental health counseling (MS)
school counseling (MS)
school psychology (MS)
special education (M Ed)
sport and exercise psychology (MS)
sports administration/pedagogy (MS)

College of Science, Health and Engineering
Programs in:
biology (MS)
communication disorders (MS)
computer and technology-supported education (M Ed)
computer science (MS)
dental hygiene (MS)
mathematics (MS)
occupational therapy (MOT)
physical therapy (DPT)
science, health and engineering (M Ed, MA, MOT, MS, DPT)
teaching mathematics (MA)

College of Social and Behavioral Sciences
Programs in:
clinical psychology (MS)
communication studies (MSC)
experimental psychology (MS)
history (MA)
psychology (MS)
school psychology (MS)
social and behavioral sciences (MA, MS, MSC)

Intercollegiate College of Nursing
Program in:
nursing (MN)

School of Social Work and Human Services
Program in:
social work and human services (MSW)

■ THE EVERGREEN STATE COLLEGE
Olympia, WA 98505
http://www.evergreen.edu/

State-supported, coed, comprehensive institution. *Graduate faculty:* 17 full-time (8 women), 12 part-time/adjunct (5 women). *Computer facilities:* 375 computers available on campus for general student use. A campuswide network can be accessed from student residence rooms and from off campus. Online class registration, online payment and student accounts history are available. *Graduate expenses:* Tuition, state resident: full-time $6567; part-time $219 per credit. Tuition, nonresident: full-time $20,004; part-time $667 per credit. Required fees: $7.85 per credit. $50 per quarter. Tuition and fees vary according to course load.

Graduate Programs
Dr. Don Bantz, Vice President and Provost
Programs in:
English as a second language (M Ed)
environmental studies (MES)
mathematics (M Ed)
public administration (MPA)
teaching (MIT)

■ GONZAGA UNIVERSITY
Spokane, WA 99258
http://www.gonzaga.edu/

Independent-religious, coed, comprehensive institution. *Computer facilities:* Computer purchase and lease plans are available. 625 computers available on campus for general student use. A campuswide network can be accessed from student residence rooms and from off campus. Online class registration is available. *General application contact:* Dean of Admissions, 509-323-6592.

College of Arts and Sciences
Programs in:
arts and sciences (MA)
pastoral ministry (MA)
philosophy (MA)
religious studies (MA)
spirituality (MA)

Program in Teaching English as a Second Language
Program in:
teaching English as a second language (MATESL)

School of Business Administration
Program in:
business administration (M Acc, MBA)

School of Education
Programs in:
administration and curriculum (MAA)
anesthesiology education (M Anesth Ed)
counseling psychology (MAC, MAP)
education (M Anesth Ed, M Ed, MA Ed Ad, MAA, MAC, MAP, MASPAA, MAT, MES, MIT)
educational administration (MA Ed Ad)
initial teaching (MIT)
literacy (M Ed)
special education (MES)
sports and athletic administration (MASPAA)
teaching at-risk students (MAT)

School of Law
Program in:
law (JD)

School of Professional Studies
Programs in:
communication and leadership studies (MA)
leadership studies (PhD)
nursing (MSN)
organizational leadership (MOL)

■ HERITAGE UNIVERSITY
Toppenish, WA 98948-9599
http://www.heritage.edu/

Independent, coed, comprehensive institution. *Computer facilities:* 158 computers available on campus for general student use. A campuswide network can be accessed from off campus. *General application contact:* Coordinator of Administrative Services, 509-865-8635.

Graduate Programs in Education
Programs in:
bilingual education/ESL (M Ed)
biology (M Ed)
counseling (M Ed)
educational administration (M Ed)
English and literature (M Ed)
professional studies (M Ed)
reading/literacy (M Ed)
special education (M Ed)
teaching (MIT)

■ PACIFIC LUTHERAN UNIVERSITY
Tacoma, WA 98447
http://www.plu.edu/

Independent-religious, coed, comprehensive institution. *Computer facilities:* 435 computers available on campus for general student use. A campuswide network can be accessed from student residence rooms and from off campus. Online class registration is available. *General application contact:* Senior Office Assistant, 253-535-7151.

Division of Graduate Studies

Division of Humanities
Program in:
creative writing (MFA)

Division of Social Sciences
Programs in:
marriage and family therapy (MA)
social sciences (MA)

School of Business
Program in:
business administration (MBA)

School of Education
Programs in:
education (MAE)
educational leadership (MAE)
initial teaching certification (MAE)

School of Nursing
Programs in:
client systems management (MSN)
entry level nursing (MSN)
family nurse practitioner (MSN)
health care systems management (MSN)
nursing (MSN)

■ SAINT MARTIN'S UNIVERSITY
Lacey, WA 98503-1297
http://www.stmartin.edu/

Independent-religious, coed, comprehensive institution. *Computer facilities:* 80 computers available on campus for general student use. A campuswide network can be accessed from student residence rooms. Online class registration is available. *General application contact:* Information Contact, 360-438-4311.

Graduate Programs
Programs in:
administration (M Ed)
civil engineering (MCE)
counseling psychology (MAC)
engineering management (M Eng Mgt)
English as a second language (M Ed)
guidance and counseling (M Ed)
reading (M Ed)
special education (M Ed)
teaching (MIT)
technology in education (M Ed)

Division of Economics and Business Administration
Program in:
economics and business administration (MBA)

■ SEATTLE PACIFIC UNIVERSITY
Seattle, WA 98119-1997
http://www.spu.edu/

Independent-religious, coed, comprehensive institution. *Graduate faculty:* 31 full-time (11 women). *Computer facilities:* 150 computers available on campus for general student use. A campuswide network can be accessed from student residence rooms and from off campus. Online class registration is available. *Graduate expenses:* Tuition: part-time $659 per credit hour. One-time fee: $50 part-time. Tuition and fees vary according to program. *General application contact:* John Glancy, Director, Graduate Admissions/ Marketing, 206-281-2325.

Educational Leadership Program

Dr. Richard Smith, Chair
Programs in:
educational leadership (M Ed, Ed D)
principal (Certificate)
superintendent (Certificate)

Industrial Organizational Psychology Program

Dr. Robert B. McKenna, Chair
Program in:
industrial organizational psychology (MA, PhD)

Literacy Program

Dr. William Nagy, Co-Chair
Program in:
literacy (M Ed)

MA in Teaching English to Speakers of Other Languages Program

Dr. Kathryn Bartholomew, Chair
Programs in:
K-12 certification (MA)
teaching English to speakers of other languages (MA)

Master of Business Administration (MBA) Program

Gary Karns, Graduate Director
Program in:
business administration (MBA)

Master's in Information Systems Management (MS-ISM) Program

Gary Karns, Graduate Director
Program in:
information systems management (MS)

Master of Arts in Teaching Program

Dr. Richard Schuerman, Chair
Programs in:
alternate routes to certification (Certificate)
teaching (MAT)

Masters of Fine Arts in Creative Writing Program

Dr. Gregory Wolfe, Director
Program in:
creative writing (MFA)

Medical Family Therapy Certificate Program

Dr. Claudia Grauf-Grounds, Chair
Program in:
medical family therapy (Certificate)

M Ed in Curriculum and Instruction Program

Dr. Andrew Lumpe, Chair
Program in:
reading/language arts education (M Ed)

MS in Marriage and Family Therapy Program

Dr. Claudia Grauf-Grounds, Chair
Program in:
marriage and family therapy (MS)

MS in Nursing Program

Dr. Susan Casey, Director
Programs in:
administration (MSN)
adult/gerontology nurse practitioner (MSN)
clinical nurse specialist (MSN)
family nurse practitioner (MSN)
informatics (MSN)
nurse educator (MSN)

PhD in Clinical Psychology Program

Dr. Jay Skidmore, Chair
Program in:
clinical psychology (PhD)

Post-Master's Nurse Practitioner Certificate Program

Susan Casey, Associate Dean
Programs in:
adult/gerontological nurse practitioner (Certificate)
family nurse practitioner (Certificate)

School Counseling Program

Dr. Cher Edwards, Chair
Program in:
school counseling (M Ed, PhD, Certificate)

■ SEATTLE UNIVERSITY

Seattle, WA 98122-1090
http://www.seattleu.edu/

Independent-religious, coed, comprehensive institution. *Computer facilities:* 401 computers available on campus for general student use. A campuswide network can be accessed from student residence rooms and from off campus. Online class registration is available. *General application contact:* Associate Dean of Graduate Admissions, 206-296-5900.

Albers School of Business and Economics

Programs in:
business administration (MBA, MIB, Certificate)
business and economics (EMBA, MBA, MIB, MPAC, MSF, Certificate)
finance (MSF, Certificate)
professional accounting (MPAC)

Center for Leadership Formation
Program in:
leadership formation (EMBA, Certificate)

College of Arts and Sciences

Programs in:
arts and sciences (MA Psych, MACJ, MNPL, MPA, MSAL)
criminal justice (MACJ)
existential and phenomenological therapeutic psychology (MA Psych)

The Center for Nonprofit and Social Enterprise Management
Program in:
nonprofit and social enterprise management (MNPL)

Center for the Study of Sport and Exercise
Program in:
sport and exercise (MSAL)

Institute of Public Service
Program in:
public service (MPA)

College of Education

Programs in:
adult education and training (M Ed, MA, Certificate)
counseling and school psychology (MA, Certificate, Ed S)
curriculum and instruction (M Ed, MA, Certificate)
education (M Ed, MA, MIT, Ed D, Certificate, Ed S, Post-Master's Certificate)
educational administration (M Ed, MA, Certificate, Ed S)
educational leadership (Ed D)
literacy (M Ed, Post-Master's Certificate)
special education (M Ed, MA, Certificate)
student development administration (M Ed, MA)
teacher education (MIT)
teaching English to speakers of other languages (M Ed, MA, Certificate)

College of Nursing

Programs in:
advanced practice nursing immersion (MSN)
leadership in community nursing (MSN)
nursing (MSN)
primary care nurse practitioner (MSN)

College of Science and Engineering

Programs in:
science and engineering (MSE)
software engineering (MSE)

School of Law

Kellye Y. Testy, Dean
Program in:
law (JD, JD/MATL)

School of Theology and Ministry

Programs in:
divinity (M Div)
pastoral counseling (MA)
pastoral studies (MAPS)
theology and ministry (M Div, MA, MAPS, MATS, Certificate)
transforming spirituality (MATS, Certificate)

■ UNIVERSITY OF PUGET SOUND

Tacoma, WA 98416

http://www.ups.edu/

Independent, coed, comprehensive institution. *Graduate faculty:* 24 full-time (16 women), 9 part-time/adjunct (7 women). *Computer facilities:* 320 computers available on campus for general student use. A campuswide network can be accessed from student residence rooms and from off campus. Online class registration, financial aid, admission, student employment are available. *Graduate expenses:* Tuition: full-time $29,820; part-time $4260 per unit. Tuition and fees vary according to program. *General application contact:* Dr. George H. Mills, Vice President for Enrollment, 253-879-3211.

Graduate Studies

Dr. Sarah Y. Moore, Associate Dean

School of Education

Dr. John Woodward, Dean

Programs in:
- education (M Ed, MAT)
- elementary education (MAT)
- mental health counseling (M Ed)
- pastoral counseling (M Ed)
- school counseling (M Ed)
- secondary education (MAT)

School of Occupational Therapy and Physical Therapy

Programs in:
- occupational therapy (MOT, MSOT)
- occupational therapy and physical therapy (MOT, MSOT, DPT)
- physical therapy (DPT)

■ UNIVERSITY OF WASHINGTON

Seattle, WA 98195

http://www.washington.edu/

State-supported, coed, university. CGS member. *Computer facilities:* 2,000 computers available on campus for general student use. A campuswide network can be accessed from student residence rooms and from off campus. Online class registration is available. *General application contact:* Information Contact, 206-543-2100.

Graduate School

Programs in:
- biology for teachers (MS)
- education (M Ed, Professional Certificate)
- global trade, transportation and logistics studies (Certificate)
- museology (MA)
- Near and Middle Eastern studies (PhD)
- quantitative ecology and resource management (MS, PhD)

College of Architecture and Urban Planning

Programs in:
- architecture (M Arch, MS)
- architecture and urban planning (M Arch, MLA, MS, MSCM, MSCPI, MUP, PhD, Certificate)
- built environment (PhD)
- construction management (MSCM)
- design computing (Certificate)
- design firm leadership and management (Certificate)
- historic preservation (Certificate)
- landscape architecture (MLA)
- lighting (Certificate)
- strategic planning for critical infrastructures (MSCPI)
- urban design (Certificate)
- urban design and planning (PhD)
- urban planning (MUP)

College of Arts and Sciences

Programs in:
- acting (MFA)
- animal behavior (PhD)
- anthropology (MA, PhD)
- applied mathematics (MS, PhD)
- art (MFA)
- art history (MA, PhD)
- arts and sciences (MA, MAIS, MAT, MC, MFA, MM, MS, Au D, DMA, PhD)
- astronomy (MS, PhD)
- atmospheric sciences (MS, PhD)
- audiology (Au D)
- biology (PhD)
- Buddhist studies (MA, PhD)
- Central Asian studies (MAIS)
- chemistry (MS, PhD)
- child psychology (PhD)
- China studies (MAIS)
- Chinese language and literature (MA, PhD)
- choral conducting (MM, DMA)
- classics (MA, PhD)
- classics and philosophy (PhD)
- clinical psychology (PhD)
- cognition and perception (PhD)
- communication (MA, MC, PhD)
- comparative literature (MA, PhD)
- comparative religion (MAIS)
- computational linguistics (MA)
- costume design (MFA)
- creative writing (MFA)
- dance (MFA)
- design (MFA)
- developmental psychology (PhD)
- directing (MFA)
- dramatic theory (PhD)
- East European studies (MAIS)
- economics (PhD)
- English as a second language (MAT)
- English literature and language (MA, MAT, PhD)
- ethnomusicology (MA)
- French (MA, PhD)
- French and Italian studies (MA, PhD)
- geography (MA, PhD)
- geology (MS, PhD)
- geophysics (MS, PhD)
- Germanics (MA, PhD)
- Hispanic literary and cultural studies (MA)
- history (MA, PhD)
- industrial design (MFA)
- international studies (MAIS)
- Italian (MA)
- Japan studies (MAIS)
- Japanese language and literature (MA, PhD)
- Korea studies (MAIS)
- Korean language and literature (MA, PhD)
- lighting design (MFA)
- linguistics (MA, PhD)
- mathematics (MA, MS, PhD)
- Middle Eastern studies (MAIS)
- music (MA, MM, DMA, PhD)
- music education (MA, PhD)
- music history (MA, PhD)
- Near Eastern languages and civilization (MA)
- numerical analysis (MS)
- optimization (MS)
- painting and drawing (MFA)
- philosophy (MA, PhD)
- photography (MFA)
- physics (MS, PhD)
- political science (MA, PhD)
- quantitative psychology (PhD)
- Romance linguistics (MA, PhD)
- Russian literature (MA, PhD)
- Russian studies (MAIS)
- Russian, East European and Central Asian studies (MAIS)
- Scandinavian studies (MA, PhD)
- scenic design (MFA)
- Slavic linguistics (MA, PhD)
- social psychology and personality (PhD)
- sociology (MA, PhD)
- South Asian language and literature (MA, PhD)
- South Asian studies (MAIS)
- Spanish and Portuguese (MA)
- speech and hearing sciences (PhD)
- speech-language pathology (MS)
- statistics (MS, PhD)
- theatre and performance history (PhD)
- visual communication design (MFA)
- women studies (PhD)

College of Education

Programs in:
- curriculum and instruction (M Ed, Ed D, PhD)
- early childhood special education (M Ed)
- educational leadership and policy studies (M Ed, Ed D, PhD)
- educational psychology (M Ed, PhD)
- emotional and behavioral disabilities (M Ed)
- human development and cognition (M Ed)
- instructional leadership (M Ed)
- intercollegiate athletic leadership (M Ed)
- learning disabilities (M Ed)
- learning sciences (M Ed, PhD)
- low-incidence disabilities (M Ed)

measurement, statistics and research design (M Ed)
school psychology (M Ed)
severe disabilities (M Ed)
special education (M Ed, Ed D, PhD)
teacher education (MIT)

College of Engineering
Dr. Matthew O'Donnell, Dean
Programs in:
aeronautics and astronautics (MSAA)
bioengineering (MME, MS, PhD)
chemical engineering (MS Ch E, MSE, PhD)
composite materials and structures (MAE)
computer science (MS, PhD)
construction engineering (MSCE)
electrical engineering (MSEE, PhD)
engineering (MAE, MME, MS, MS Ch E, MSAA, MSCE, MSE, MSEE, MSHCDE, MSIE, MSMSE, MSTC, PhD)
environmental engineering (MS, MSCE, MSE, PhD)
hydrology, water resources, and environmental fluid mechanics (MS, MSCE, MSE, PhD)
industrial and systems engineering (MSIE, PhD)
interdisciplinary Japanese (MSTC)
materials science and engineering (MS, MSE, MSMSE, PhD)
materials science and engineering nanotechnology (PhD)
mechanical engineering (MS, MSE, PhD)
structural and geotechnical engineering and mechanics (MS, MSCE, MSE, PhD)
transportation and construction engineering (MS, MSE, PhD)
transportation engineering (MSCE)
user-centered design (MSHCDE, PhD)

College of Forest Resources
Programs in:
bioresource science and engineering (MS, PhD)
environmental horticulture (MEH)
environmental horticulture and urban forestry (MS, PhD)
forest ecology (MS, PhD)
forest management (MFR)
forest soils (MS, PhD)
forest systems and bioenergy (MS, PhD)
restoration ecology (MS, PhD)
social sciences (MS, PhD)
sustainable resource management (MS, PhD)
wildlife science (MS, PhD)

College of Ocean and Fishery Sciences
Programs in:
aquatic and fishery sciences (MS, PhD)
biological oceanography (MS, PhD)
chemical oceanography (MS, PhD)
marine affairs (MMA, Graduate Certificate)
marine geology and geophysics (MS, PhD)
ocean and fishery sciences (MMA, MS, PhD, Graduate Certificate)
physical oceanography (MS, PhD)

Daniel J. Evans School of Public Affairs
Programs in:
public administration (MPA)
public policy and management (PhD)

The Information School
Dr. Harry Bruce, Dean
Programs in:
information management (MSIM)
information science (PhD)
library and information science (MLIS)

Michael G. Foster School of Business
James Jiambalvo, Dean
Programs in:
auditing and assurance (MP Acc)
business (PhD)
business administration (evening) (MBA)
business administration (full-time) (MBA)
executive business administration (MBA)
global business administration (MBA)
global executive business administration (MBA)
taxation (MP Acc)
technology management (MBA)

School of Dentistry
Programs in:
dental surgery (DDS)
dentistry (DDS, MS, MSD, PhD, Certificate)
endodontics (MSD, Certificate)
oral biology (MS, MSD, PhD)
oral medicine (MSD)
orthodontics (MSD, Certificate)
pediatric dentistry (MSD, Certificate)
periodontics (MSD, PhD, Certificate)
prosthodontics (MSD, Certificate)

School of Law
Programs in:
Asian law (LL M, PhD)
intellectual property law and policy (LL M)
law (JD)
law of sustainable international development (LL M)
taxation (LL M)

School of Medicine
Programs in:
biochemistry (PhD)
bioethics (MA)
biological structure (PhD)
biomedical and health informatics (MS, PhD)
comparative medicine (MS)
experimental and molecular pathology (PhD)
genome sciences (PhD)
immunology (MS, PhD)
laboratory medicine (MS)
medicine (MD, MA, MOT, MS, DPT, PhD)
microbiology (PhD)
molecular and cellular biology (PhD)
neurobiology and behavior (PhD)
occupational therapy (MOT)
pharmacology (PhD)
physical therapy (DPT)
physiology and biophysics (PhD)
rehabilitation science (PhD)

School of Nursing
Program in:
nursing (MN, MS, DNP, PhD, Graduate Certificate)

School of Public Health
Dr. Patricia Wahl, Dean
Programs in:
bioinformatics (PhD)
biostatistics (MPH, MS, PhD)
cancer prevention and control (PhD)
clinical research (MS)
community oriented public health practice (MPH)
economics or finance (PhD)
environmental and occupational health (MPH)
environmental and occupational hygiene (PhD)
environmental health (MS)
epidemiology (MPH, MS, PhD)
evaluation sciences (PhD)
executive program (MHA)
genetic epidemiology (MS)
global health (MPH)
global health—peace corps international (MPH)
health behavior and health promotion (PhD)
health care and population health research (MPH)
health policy analysis and process (PhD)
health policy and analysis and process (MPH)
health services (MS, PhD)
health services administration (EMHA, MHA)
in residence program (MHA)
maternal/child health (MPH)
nutritional sciences (MPH, MS, PhD)
occupational and environmental exposure sciences (MS)
occupational and environmental medicine (MPH)
occupational health (PhD)
pathobiology (PhD)
population health and social determinants (PhD)
public health (EMHA, MHA, MPH, MS, PhD)
public health genetics (MPH, MS, PhD)
social and behavioral sciences (MPH)
sociology and demography (PhD)
statistical genetics (PhD)
toxicology (MS, PhD)

School of Social Work
Program in:
social work (MSW, PhD)

School of Social Work, Tacoma Campus
Program in:
social work (MSW)

University of Washington (continued)

School of Pharmacy
Programs in:
medicinal chemistry (PhD)
pharmaceutics (MS, PhD)
pharmacy (Pharm D, MS, PhD)

■ UNIVERSITY OF WASHINGTON, BOTHELL

Bothell, WA 98011-8246

http://www.uwb.edu

State-supported, coed, comprehensive institution. *Computer facilities:* 315 computers available on campus for general student use. A campuswide network can be accessed from off campus. Online class registration, online course management system are available. *General application contact:* Jill Orcutt, Director of Admissions.

Program in Business Administration
Prof. Steven Holland, Director of Business Program
Program in:
business administration (MA)

Program in Education
Prof. Linda Watts, Interim Director
Program in:
education (MA)

Program in Nursing
Prof. Mary Baroni, Nursing Program Director
Program in:
nursing (MA)

Program in Policy Studies
Prof. Bruce Burgett, Interim Director, Interdisciplinary Studies Program
Program in:
policy studies (MA)

■ UNIVERSITY OF WASHINGTON, TACOMA

Tacoma, WA 98402-3100

http://www.tacoma.washington.edu/

State-supported, coed, comprehensive institution. *Graduate faculty:* 98 full-time (54 women), 6 part-time/adjunct (1 woman). *Computer facilities:* 138 computers available on campus for general student use. A campuswide network can be accessed from student residence rooms and from off campus. Online class registration, (online courseware-Blackboard) are available. *Graduate expenses:* Tuition, state resident: full-time $10,476; part-time $498 per credit. Tuition, nonresident: full-time $22,947; part-time $1092 per credit. Tuition and fees vary according to course load, degree level and program. *General application contact:* Joan Abe, Director of Admissions, 206-543-5929.

Graduate Programs
Dr. Patricia Spakes, Chancellor
Programs in:
accounting (MBA)
certified financial analyst (MBA)
computing and software systems (MS)
educational administrator (M Ed)
interdisciplinary studies (MA)
K-8 teacher education (M Ed)
nursing (MN)
professional certification (M Ed)
secondary science education (M Ed)
social work (MSW)
special education (M Ed)

■ WALLA WALLA UNIVERSITY

College Place, WA 99324-1198

http://www.wallawalla.edu/

Independent-religious, coed, comprehensive institution. *Graduate faculty:* 29 full-time (16 women), 22 part-time/adjunct (15 women). *Computer facilities:* Computer purchase and lease plans are available. 118 computers available on campus for general student use. A campuswide network can be accessed from student residence rooms and from off campus. Online class registration, online forum, online classifieds, online student directory are available. *Graduate expenses:* Tuition: full-time $25,584; part-time $492 per credit. Tuition and fees vary according to course load. *General application contact:* Dr. Joe G. Galusha, Dean of Graduate Studies, 509-527-2421.

Graduate School
Dr. Joe G. Galusha, Dean of Graduate Studies
Program in:
biology (MS)

School of Education and Psychology
Dr. Julian Melgosa, Dean
Programs in:
counseling psychology (MA)
curriculum and instruction (M Ed, MA, MAT)
educational leadership (M Ed, MA, MAT)
literacy instruction (M Ed, MA, MAT)
students at risk (M Ed, MA, MAT)
teaching (MAT)

School of Social Work
Dr. Pamela Cress, Dean, Wilma Hepker School of Sociology and Social Work
Program in:
social work (MSW)

■ WASHINGTON STATE UNIVERSITY

Pullman, WA 99164

http://www.wsu.edu/

State-supported, coed, university. CGS member. *Computer facilities:* 2,500 computers available on campus for general student use. A campuswide network can be accessed from student residence rooms and from off campus. Online class registration is available. *General application contact:* Graduate School Admissions, 800-GRADWSU.

College of Veterinary Medicine
Dr. Bryan K. Slinker, Dean
Programs in:
neuroscience (MS, PhD)
veterinary and comparative anatomy, pharmacology, and physiology (MS, PhD)
veterinary clinical sciences (MS)
veterinary medicine (DVM, MS, PhD)
veterinary microbiology and pathology (MS, PhD)
veterinary science (MS, PhD)

Graduate School
Program in:
interdisciplinary studies (PhD)

College of Agricultural, Human, and Natural Resource Sciences
Programs in:
agribusiness (MA, Certificate)
agricultural economics (MA, PhD)
agricultural, human, and natural resource sciences (MA, MS, MSLA, PhD, Certificate)
agriculture (MS)
animal sciences (MS, PhD)
apparel, merchandising, design and textiles (MA)
applied economics (MA)
applied statistics (MS)
crop sciences (MS, PhD)
economics (MA, PhD, Certificate)
entomology (MS, PhD)
food science (MS, PhD)
horticulture (MS, PhD)
human development (MA)
interdisciplinary (PhD)
interior design (MA)
international business economics (Certificate)
landscape architecture (MSLA)
molecular plant sciences (MS, PhD)
plant pathology (MS, PhD)
soil sciences (MS, PhD)
theoretical statistics (MS)

College of Business
Programs in:
accounting and business law (M Acc)
accounting and information systems (M Acc)
accounting and taxation (M Acc)
business (M Acc, MBA, PhD)
business administration (MBA, PhD)
finance, insurance and real estate (PhD)

College of Education
Programs in:
counseling psychology (Ed M, MA, PhD, Certificate)
curriculum and instruction (Ed D, PhD)
diverse languages (M Ed, MA)
education (Ed M, M Ed, MA, MIT, MS, Ed D, PhD, Certificate)
educational leadership (M Ed, MA, Ed D, PhD)

educational psychology (Ed M, MA, PhD)
elementary education (M Ed, MA, MIT)
exercise science (MS)
higher education (Ed M, MA, Ed D, PhD)
higher education with sport management (Ed M)
literacy education (M Ed, MA, PhD)
math education (PhD)
school psychologist (Certificate)
secondary education (M Ed, MA)

College of Engineering and Architecture
Programs in:
architecture (M Arch)
architecture design theory (MS)
biological and agricultural engineering (MS, PhD)
chemical engineering (MS, PhD)
chemical engineering and bioengineering (MS, PhD)
civil engineering (MS, PhD)
computer engineering (MS, PhD)
computer science (MS, PhD)
electrical engineering (MS, PhD)
electrical engineering and computer science (MS, PhD)
engineering and architecture (M Arch, MS, PhD)
environmental engineering (MS)
material science engineering (MS)
mechanical and materials engineering (MS, PhD)
mechanical engineering (MS, PhD)

College of Liberal Arts
Programs in:
archaeology (MA, PhD)
ceramics (MFA)
clinical psychology (PhD)
composition (MA)
crime and deviance (MA, PhD)
criminal justice (MA, PhD)
cultural anthropology (MA, PhD)
digital media (MFA)
drawing (MFA)
early and modern European history (MA, PhD)
English (MA, PhD)
environmental history (MA, PhD)
environments, community and demographics (MA, PhD)
ethnic studies (MA, PhD)
evolutionary anthropology (MA, PhD)
experimental psychology (PhD)
feminist studies (MA, PhD)
foreign languages with emphasis in Spanish (MA)
health communications (MA, PhD)
history (MA, PhD)
institutions and social organizations (MA, PhD)
intercultural and international communications (MA, PhD)
jazz (MA)
Latin American history (MA, PhD)
liberal arts (MA, MFA, MS, PhD)
literature (MA, PhD)
media and society (MA, PhD)
media process and effects (MA, PhD)
modern East Asia history (MA, PhD)
music (MA)
music education (MA)
organizational communications (MA, PhD)
painting (MFA)
performance (MA)
philosophy (MA)
photography (MFA)
political science (MA, PhD)
political sociology (MA, PhD)
print making (MFA)
psychology (MS)
public history (MA, PhD)
sculpture (MFA)
social inequality (MA, PhD)
social psychology and life course (MA, PhD)
teaching of English (MA)
US history (MA, PhD)
women's history (MA, PhD)
world history (MA, PhD)

College of Pharmacy
Programs in:
health policy and administration (MHPA)
human nutrition (MS)
nutrition (PhD)
pharmaceutical science (Pharm D)
pharmacology and toxicology (MS, PhD)
pharmacy (Pharm D, MHPA, MS, PhD)

College of Sciences
Programs in:
applied mathematics (MS, PhD)
biochemistry and biophysics (MS, PhD)
biological sciences (MS, PhD)
biology (MS)
botany (MS, PhD)
chemistry (MS, PhD)
earth and environmental sciences (MS, PhD)
environmental and natural resource sciences (PhD)
environmental science (MS, PhD)
genetics and cell biology (MS, PhD)
geology (MS, PhD)
materials science (PhD)
mathematics teaching (MS, PhD)
microbiology (MS, PhD)
molecular biosciences (MS, PhD)
natural resource sciences (MS)
physics (MS, PhD)
sciences (MS, PhD)
zoology (MS, PhD)

■ WESTERN WASHINGTON UNIVERSITY

Bellingham, WA 98225-5996

http://www.wwu.edu/

State-supported, coed, comprehensive institution. CGS member. *Computer facilities:* 2,408 computers available on campus for general student use. A campuswide network can be accessed from student residence rooms and from off campus. Online class registration is available. *General application contact:* Graduate Office Admissions, 360-650-3170.

Graduate School

College of Business and Economics
Program in:
business and economics (MBA, MP Acc)

College of Fine and Performing Arts
Programs in:
fine and performing arts (M Mus, MA)
music (M Mus)

College of Humanities and Social Sciences
Programs in:
anthropology (MA)
communication sciences and disorders (MA)
English (MA)
exercise science (MS)
experimental psychology (MS)
history (MA)
humanities and social sciences (M Ed, MA, MS)
mental health counseling (MS)
political science (MA)
school counseling (M Ed)
sport psychology (MS)

College of Sciences and Technology
Programs in:
biology (MS)
chemistry (MS)
computer science (MS)
geology (MS)
mathematics (MS)
natural science/science education (M Ed)
sciences and technology (M Ed, MS)

Huxley College of the Environment
Programs in:
environment (M Ed, MS)
environmental education (M Ed)
environmental science (MS)
geography (MS)
marine and estuarine science (MS)

Woodring College of Education
Programs in:
continuing and college education (M Ed)
education (M Ed, MA, MIT)
educational administration (M Ed)
elementary education (M Ed)
rehabilitation counseling (MA)
secondary education (MIT)
special education (M Ed)
student affairs administration (M Ed)

■ WHITWORTH UNIVERSITY

Spokane, WA 99251-0001

http://www.whitworth.edu/

Independent-religious, coed, comprehensive institution. *Computer facilities:* 300 computers available on campus for general student use. A campuswide network can be accessed from student residence rooms and from off campus. Online class registration is available. *General application contact:* Office of Admissions, 509-777-1000.

Whitworth University (continued)

School of Education
Program in:
education (M Ed, MAT, MIT)

Graduate Studies in Education
Programs in:
administration (M Ed)
counseling (M Ed)
elementary education (M Ed)
gifted and talented (MAT)
school counselors (M Ed)
secondary education (M Ed)
social agency/church setting (M Ed)
special education (MAT)
teaching (MIT)

School of Global Commerce and Management
Mary Alberts, Director, Graduate Studies in Business
Programs in:
business administration (MBA)
global commerce and management (MBA, MIM)
international management (MIM)

West Virginia

■ MARSHALL UNIVERSITY
Huntington, WV 25755
http://www.marshall.edu/

State-supported, coed, university. CGS member. *Graduate faculty:* 369 full-time (145 women), 147 part-time/adjunct (101 women). *Computer facilities:* 1,461 computers available on campus for general student use. A campuswide network can be accessed from student residence rooms and from off campus. Online class registration is available. *General application contact:* Graduate Admissions, 304-746-1900.

Academic Affairs Division
Dr. Gayle Ormiston, Provost and Senior Vice President for Academic Affairs

College of Education and Human Services
Dr. Rosalyn Anstine Templeton, Executive Dean
Programs in:
adult and technical education (MS)
counseling (MA, Ed S)
early childhood education (MA)
education (MAT)
education and human services (MA, MAT, MS, Ed D, Ed S)
education and professional development (MA, Ed D, Ed S)
elementary education (MA)
exercise science (MS)
exercise science, sport and recreation (MS)
family and consumer sciences (MA)
human development and allied technology (MA, MS)
leadership studies (MA, Ed D, Ed S)
reading education (MA, Ed S)
school psychology (Ed S)
secondary education (MA)
special education (MA)
sport administration (MS)

College of Fine Arts
Dr. Donald Van Horn, Dean
Programs in:
art (MA)
fine arts (MA)
music (MA)

College of Health Professions
Dr. Shortie McKinney, Dean
Programs in:
communication disorders (MA)
dietetics (MS)
health professions (MA, MS, MSN)
nursing (MSN)

College of Information Technology and Engineering
Dr. Betsy Dulin, Dean
Programs in:
applied science and technology (MS)
engineering (MSE)
environmental science (MS)
information systems (MS)
information technology and engineering (MS, MSE)
safety (MS)
technology management (MS)

College of Liberal Arts
Dr. David J. Pittenger, Dean
Programs in:
clinical psychology (MA)
communication studies (MA)
criminal justice (MS)
English (MA)
general psychology (MA)
geography (MA, MS)
history (MA)
humanities (MA)
industrial and organizational psychology (MA)
Latin (MA)
liberal arts (MA, MS, Psy D)
political science (MA)
psychology (Psy D)
sociology (MA)
Spanish (MA)

College of Science
Dr. Wayne Elmore, Interim Dean
Programs in:
biological science (MA, MS)
chemistry (MS)
mathematics (MA, MS)
physical science (MS)
science (MA, MS)

Lewis College of Business
Dr. Chong Kim, Dean
Programs in:
business (IMBA, MBA, MS, DMPNA, Graduate Certificate)
business administration (IMBA, MBA)
business management foundations (Graduate Certificate)
health care administration (MS, DMPNA)
human resource management (MS)
management (IMBA, MBA, MS, DMPNA, Graduate Certificate)

School of Journalism and Mass Communications
Dr. Corley F. Dennison, Dean
Program in:
journalism and mass communications (MAJ)

Joan C. Edwards School of Medicine
Programs in:
biomedical sciences (MS, PhD)
medicine (MD, MS, PhD)

■ MOUNTAIN STATE UNIVERSITY
Beckley, WV 25802-9003
http://www.mountainstate.edu/

Independent, coed, comprehensive institution. *Graduate faculty:* 23 full-time (12 women), 56 part-time/adjunct (25 women). *Computer facilities:* Computer purchase and lease plans are available. 185 computers available on campus for general student use. A campuswide network can be accessed from student residence rooms and from off campus. Online class registration is available. *Graduate expenses:* Tuition: full-time $4020; part-time $335 per contact hour. *General application contact:* Dinah Rock, Coordinator of Graduate Academic Services, 304-929-1588.

Graduate Studies
Dr. Brian Holloway, Dean, School of Graduate Studies
Programs in:
administration/education (MSN)
criminal justice administration (MCJA)
family nurse practitioner (MSN)
health science (MHS)
interdisciplinary studies (MA, MS)
nurse anesthesia (MSN)
physician assistant (MSPA)
registered nurse anesthetist (Certificate)
strategic leadership (MSSL)

■ WEST VIRGINIA UNIVERSITY
Morgantown, WV 26506
http://www.wvu.edu/

State-supported, coed, university. CGS member. *Computer facilities:* Computer purchase and lease plans are available. 2,500 computers available on campus for general student use. A campuswide network can be accessed from student residence rooms and from off campus. Online class registration is available. *General application contact:* Information Contact, 800-344-WVU1.

College of Business and Economics

Programs in:

- business administration (MBA)
- business and economics (MA, MBA, MPA, MSIR, PhD)
- industrial relations (MSIR)

Division of Accounting

Program in:

- accounting (MPA)

Division of Economics and Finance

Programs in:

- business analysis (MA)
- developmental financial economics (PhD)
- environmental and resource economics (PhD)
- international economics (PhD)
- mathematical economics (MA)
- monetary economics (PhD)
- public finance (PhD)
- public policy (MA)
- regional and urban economics (PhD)
- statistics and economics (MA)

College of Creative Arts

Programs in:

- acting (MFA)
- art education (MA)
- art history (MA)
- ceramics (MFA)
- creative arts (MA, MFA, MM, DMA, PhD)
- graphic design (MFA)
- music composition (MM, DMA)
- music education (MM, PhD)
- music history (MM)
- music performance (MM, DMA)
- music theory (MM)
- painting (MFA)
- printmaking (MFA)
- sculpture (MFA)
- studio art (MA)
- theatre design/technology (MFA)

College of Engineering and Mineral Resources

Programs in:

- aerospace engineering (MSAE, PhD)
- chemical engineering (MS Ch E, PhD)
- civil engineering (MSCE, MSE, PhD)
- computer engineering (PhD)
- computer science (MSCS, PhD)
- electrical engineering (MSEE, PhD)
- engineering (MSE)
- engineering and mineral resources (MS, MS Ch E, MS Min E, MSAE, MSCE, MSCS, MSE, MSEE, MSIE, MSME, MSPNGE, MSSE, PhD)
- industrial engineering (MSE, MSIE, PhD)
- industrial hygiene (MS)
- mechanical engineering (MSME, PhD)
- mining engineering (MS Min E, PhD)
- occupational safety and health (PhD)
- petroleum and natural gas engineering (MSPNGE, PhD)
- safety management (MS)
- software engineering (MSSE)

College of Human Resources and Education

Programs in:

- audiology (Au D)
- autism spectrum disorder (5-adult) (MA)
- autism spectrum disorder (K-6) (MA)
- child development and family studies (MA)
- counseling (MA)
- counseling psychology (PhD)
- curriculum and instruction (Ed D)
- early intervention/early childhood special education (MA)
- educational leadership (Ed D)
- educational psychology (MA)
- elementary education (MA)
- gifted education (1-12) (MA)
- higher education administration (MA)
- higher education curriculum and teaching (MA)
- human resources and education (MA, MS, Au D, Ed D, PhD)
- instructional design and technology (MA, Ed D)
- low vision (PreK-adult) (MA)
- multicategorical special education (5-adult) (MA)
- multicategorical special education (K-6) (MA)
- public school administration (MA)
- reading (MA)
- rehabilitation counseling (MS)
- secondary education (MA)
- severe/multiple disabilities (K-adult) (MA)
- special education (MA, Ed D)
- speech-language pathology (MS)
- vision impairments (PreK-adult) (MA)

College of Law

Program in:

- law (JD)

Davis College of Agriculture, Forestry and Consumer Sciences

Programs in:

- agricultural and extension education (MS, PhD)
- agricultural and resource economics (MS)
- agricultural sciences (PhD)
- agriculture, forestry and consumer sciences (M Agr, MS, MSF, PhD)
- agronomy (MS)
- animal and food sciences (PhD)
- animal and nutritional sciences (MS)
- animal breeding (MS, PhD)
- biochemical and molecular genetics (MS, PhD)
- breeding (MS)
- cytogenetics (MS, PhD)
- descriptive embryology (MS, PhD)
- developmental genetics (MS)
- entomology (MS)
- environmental microbiology (MS)
- experimental morphogenesis/teratology (MS)
- food sciences (MS)
- forest resource science (PhD)
- forestry (MSF)
- horticulture (MS)
- human and community development (PhD)
- human genetics (MS, PhD)
- immunogenetics (MS, PhD)
- life cycles of animals and plants (MS, PhD)
- molecular aspects of development (MS, PhD)
- mutagenesis (MS, PhD)
- natural resource economics (PhD)
- nutrition (MS)
- oncology (MS, PhD)
- physiology (MS)
- plant and soil sciences (PhD)
- plant genetics (MS, PhD)
- plant pathology (MS)
- population and quantitative genetics (MS, PhD)
- production management (MS)
- recreation, parks and tourism resources (MS)
- regeneration (MS, PhD)
- reproduction (MS)
- reproductive physiology (MS, PhD)
- resource management (PhD)
- resource management and sustainable development (PhD)
- teaching vocational-agriculture (MS)
- teratology (PhD)
- toxicology (MS, PhD)
- wildlife and fisheries resources (MS)

Eberly College of Arts and Sciences

Programs in:

- African history (MA, PhD)
- African-American history (MA, PhD)
- American history (MA, PhD)
- American public policy and politics (MA)
- analytical chemistry (MS, PhD)
- Appalachian/regional history (MA, PhD)
- applied mathematics (MS, PhD)
- applied physics (MS, PhD)
- arts and sciences (MA, MALS, MFA, MLS, MPA, MS, MSW, PhD)
- astrophysics (MS, PhD)
- behavior analysis (PhD)
- cell and molecular biology (MS, PhD)
- chemical physics (MS, PhD)
- clinical psychology (MA, PhD)
- communication in instruction (MA)
- communication studies (PhD)
- communication theory and research (MA)
- condensed matter physics (MS, PhD)
- corporate and organizational communication (MA)
- creative writing (MFA)
- development psychology (PhD)
- discrete mathematics (PhD)
- East Asian history (MA, PhD)
- elementary particle physics (MS, PhD)
- energy and environmental resources (MA)
- English (MA, PhD)
- environmental and evolutionary biology (MS, PhD)

West Virginia University (continued)

European history (MA, PhD)
forensic biology (MS, PhD)
French (MA)
genomic biology (MS, PhD)
geographic information systems (PhD)
geography (MA, PhD)
geography-regional development (PhD)
geology (MS, PhD)
geomorphology (MS, PhD)
geophysics (MS, PhD)
GIS/cartographic analysis (MA)
history of science and technology (MA, PhD)
hydrogeology (MS, PhD)
inorganic chemistry (MS, PhD)
interdisciplinary mathematics (MS)
international and comparative public policy and politics (MA)
Latin American history (MA)
liberal studies (MALS)
linguistics (MA)
literary/cultural studies (MA, PhD)
materials physics (MS, PhD)
mathematics for secondary education (MS)
neurobiology (MS, PhD)
organic chemistry (MS, PhD)
paleontology (MS, PhD)
petroleum geology (PhD)
petrology (MS, PhD)
physical chemistry (MS, PhD)
plasma physics (MS, PhD)
political science (PhD)
psychology (MS)
public policy analysis (PhD)
pure mathematics (MS)
regional development (MA)
solid state physics (MS, PhD)
Spanish (MA)
statistical physics (MS, PhD)
statistics (MS)
stratigraphy (MS, PhD)
structure (MS, PhD)
teaching English to speakers of other languages (MA)
theoretical chemistry (MS, PhD)
theoretical physics (MS, PhD)
writing (MA)

School of Applied Social Sciences
Programs in:
aging and health care (MSW)
applied social research (MA)
applied social sciences (MA, MLS, MPA, MSW)
children and families (MSW)
community mental health (MSW)
community organization and social administration (MSW)
direct (clinical)
social work practice (MSW)
legal studies (MLS)
public administration (MPA)

Perley Isaac Reed School of Journalism
Programs in:
integrated marketing communications (MS)
journalism (MSJ)

School of Dentistry
Programs in:
dentistry (DDS, MS)
endodontics (MS)
orthodontics (MS)
prosthodontics (MS)

Division of Dental Hygiene
Program in:
dental hygiene (MS)

School of Medicine
Programs in:
community health/preventative medicine (MPH)
medicine (MD, MOT, MPH, MS, DPT, PhD)
occupational therapy (MOT)
physical therapy (DPT)
public health (MPH)
public health sciences (PhD)

Graduate Programs at the Health Sciences Center
Programs in:
biochemistry and molecular biology (MS, PhD)
cancer cell biology (PhD)
cellular and integrative physiology (MS, PhD)
exercise physiology (MS, PhD)
health sciences (MS, PhD)
immunology and microbial pathogenesis (MS, PhD)
neuroscience (PhD)
pharmaceutical and pharmacological sciences (MS, PhD)

School of Nursing
Programs in:
nurse practitioner (Certificate)
nursing (MSN, DNP, PhD)

School of Pharmacy
Programs in:
administrative pharmacy (PhD)
behavioral pharmacy (MS, PhD)
biopharmaceutics/pharmacokinetics (MS, PhD)
clinical pharmacy (Pharm D)
industrial pharmacy (MS)
medicinal chemistry (MS, PhD)
pharmaceutical chemistry (MS, PhD)
pharmaceutics (MS, PhD)
pharmacology and toxicology (MS)
pharmacy (MS)
pharmacy administration (MS)

School of Physical Education
Programs in:
athletic coaching education (MS)
athletic training (MS)
physical education/teacher education (MS, PhD)
sport and exercise psychology (PhD)
sport management (MS)

■ WHEELING JESUIT UNIVERSITY
Wheeling, WV 26003-6295
http://www.wju.edu/

Independent-religious, coed, comprehensive institution. CGS member. *Computer facilities:* 243 computers available on campus for general student use. A campuswide network can be accessed from student residence rooms and from off campus. Online class registration is available. *General application contact:* Director of Business Development, 304-243-2250.

Center for Professional and Graduate Studies
Program in:
organizational leadership (MSOL)

Department of Business
Programs in:
accounting (MS)
business administration (MBA)

Department of Nursing
Program in:
nursing (MSN)

Department of Physical Therapy
Program in:
physical therapy (DPT)

Wisconsin

■ ALVERNO COLLEGE
Milwaukee, WI 53234-3922
http://www.alverno.edu/

Independent-religious, Undergraduate: women only; graduate: coed, comprehensive institution. *Computer facilities:* 400 computers available on campus for general student use. A campuswide network can be accessed from student residence rooms and from off campus. E-mail available. *General application contact:* Director, Graduate and Adult Admissions, 414-382-6133.

School of Business
Program in:
business (MBA)

School of Education
Programs in:
adaptive education (MA)
administrative leadership (MA)
adult education and organizational development (MA)
adult educational and instructional design (MA)
adult educational and instructional technology (MA)
instructional leadership (MA)

instructional technology for K-12 settings (MA)
professional development (MA)
reading education (MA)
reading education with adaptive education (MA)
science education (MA)
teaching in alternative schools (MA)

School of Nursing
Program in:
nursing (MSN)

■ CARDINAL STRITCH UNIVERSITY
Milwaukee, WI 53217-3985
http://www.stritch.edu/

Independent-religious, coed, comprehensive institution. *Computer facilities:* 290 computers available on campus for general student use. A campuswide network can be accessed from student residence rooms and from off campus. *General application contact:* Information Contact, 800-347-8822 Ext. 4042.

College of Arts and Sciences
Programs in:
arts and sciences (MA, MM, MS)
clinical psychology (MA)
history (MA)
lay ministries (MA)
ministry (MA)
piano (MM)
religious studies (MA)
sport management (MS)
visual studies (MA)

College of Business and Management
Program in:
business and management (MBA, MSM)

College of Education
Programs in:
education (MA, MAT, ME, MS, Ed D, PhD)
educational leadership (MS)
instructional technology (ME, MS)
leadership for the advancement of learning and service (Ed D, PhD)
literacy/English as a second language (MA)
reading/language arts (MA)
reading/learning disability (MA)
special education (MA)
teaching (MAT)
urban education (MA)

College of Nursing
Program in:
nursing (MSN)

■ CARROLL UNIVERSITY
Waukesha, WI 53186-5593
http://www.cc.edu/

Independent-religious, coed, comprehensive institution. *Graduate faculty:* 24 full-time (11 women), 26 part-time/adjunct (21 women). *Computer facilities:* Computer purchase and lease plans are available. 250 computers available on campus for general student use. A campuswide network can be accessed from student residence rooms and from off campus. Online class registration is available. *Graduate expenses:* Tuition: full-time $21,560; part-time $345 per credit. Required fees: $400. *General application contact:* Tami Bartunek, Graduate Admission Counselor, 262-524-7643.

Graduate Program in Education
Dr. Bruce Strom, Chair
Programs in:
education (M Ed)
learning and teaching (M Ed)

Program in Physical Therapy
Dr. Jane F. Hopp, Dean, Natural and Health Sciences
Program in:
physical therapy (MPT, DPT)

Program in Software Engineering
Dr. Chenglie Hu, Associate Professor of Computer Science and Program Director
Program in:
software engineering (MSE)

■ CONCORDIA UNIVERSITY WISCONSIN
Mequon, WI 53097-2402
http://www.cuw.edu/

Independent-religious, coed, comprehensive institution. *Computer facilities:* 100 computers available on campus for general student use. A campuswide network can be accessed from student residence rooms and from off campus. *General application contact:* Graduate Admissions, 262-243-4551.

Graduate Programs
Programs in:
art education (MS Ed)
curriculum and instruction (MS Ed)
early childhood (MS Ed)
educational administration (MS Ed)
environmental education (MS Ed)
family studies (MS Ed)
professional counseling (MPC)
reading (MS Ed)
school counseling (MS Ed)
special education (MS Ed)

School of Arts and Sciences
Programs in:
arts and sciences (MCM)
church music (MCM)

School of Business and Legal Studies
Programs in:
business and legal studies (MBA, MSSPA)
finance (MBA)
health care administration (MBA)
human resource management (MBA)
international business (MBA)
international business-bilingual English/Chinese (MBA)
management (MBA)
management information systems (MBA)
managerial communications (MBA)
marketing (MBA)
public administration (MBA)
risk management (MBA)
student personnel administration (MSSPA)

School of Health and Human Services
Programs in:
family nurse practitioner (MSN)
geriatric nurse practitioner (MSN)
health and human services (MOT, MSN, MSPT, MSRS, DPT)
nurse educator (MSN)
occupational therapy (MOT)
physical therapy (MSPT, DPT)
rehabilitation science (MSRS)

■ EDGEWOOD COLLEGE
Madison, WI 53711-1997
http://www.edgewood.edu/

Independent-religious, coed, primarily women, comprehensive institution. *Graduate faculty:* 189. *Computer facilities:* Computer purchase and lease plans are available. 146 computers available on campus for general student use. A campuswide network can be accessed from student residence rooms and from off campus. Online class registration is available. *Graduate expenses:* Tuition: part-time $655 per credit. *General application contact:* Paula O'Malley, Director for Admissions and Recruitment, 608-663-2217.

Program in Business
Dr. Charles Taylor, Dean
Programs in:
accountancy (MS)
business (MBA)

Program in Education
Dr. Joseph Schmiedicke, Dean
Programs in:
director of instruction (Certificate)
director of special education and pupil services (Certificate)
education (MA Ed)
educational administration (MA)
educational leadership (Ed D)
program coordinator (Certificate)
school business administration (Certificate)
school principalship K-12 (Certificate)

Program in Marriage and Family Therapy
Dr. Peter Fabian, Director
Program in:
marriage and family therapy (MS)

Program in Nursing
Dr. Margaret Noreuil, Dean

Edgewood College (continued)
Program in:
nursing (MS)

Program in Religious Studies
Dr. John Leonard, Chairperson
Program in:
religious studies (MA)

■ LAKELAND COLLEGE
Sheboygan, WI 53082-0359
http://www.lakeland.edu/

Independent-religious, coed, comprehensive institution. *Computer facilities:* Computer purchase and lease plans are available. 157 computers available on campus for general student use. A campuswide network can be accessed from student residence rooms and from off campus. *General application contact:* Graduate Program Coordinator, 920-565-1256.

Graduate Studies Division
Programs in:
accounting (MBA)
counseling (MA)
education (M Ed)
finance (MBA)
healthcare management (MBA)
project management (MBA)
theology (MAT)

■ MARIAN UNIVERSITY
Fond du Lac, WI 54935-4699
http://www.mariancollege.edu/

Independent-religious, coed, comprehensive institution. CGS member. *Graduate faculty:* 22 full-time (13 women), 67 part-time/adjunct (43 women). *Computer facilities:* Computer purchase and lease plans are available. 315 computers available on campus for general student use. A campuswide network can be accessed from student residence rooms and from off campus. Online class registration is available. *Graduate expenses:* Tuition: part-time $380 per credit hour. Tuition and fees vary according to program. *General application contact:* Dr. Deborah Golias, Interim Vice President for Academic Affairs, 920-923-7604.

Business Division
Donna Innes, Assistant Provost and Dean of PACE
Program in:
organizational leadership and quality (MS)

School of Education
Donna Innes, Dean, School of Education
Programs in:
educational leadership (MA, PhD)
teacher development (MA)

School of Nursing
Dr. James C. McCann, Dean, School of Nursing
Programs in:
adult nurse practitioner (MSN)
nurse educator (MSN)

■ MARQUETTE UNIVERSITY
Milwaukee, WI 53201-1881
http://www.marquette.edu/

Independent-religious, coed, university. CGS member. *Graduate faculty:* 652 full-time (252 women), 444 part-time/adjunct (183 women). *Computer facilities:* 1,200 computers available on campus for general student use. A campuswide network can be accessed from student residence rooms and from off campus. Online class registration, AV Software are available. *Graduate expenses:* Tuition: full-time $15,120; part-time $840 per credit hour. *General application contact:* Erin Fox, Assistant Director for Recruitment, 414-288-5319.

Graduate School
Dr. William Wiener, Vice Provost for Research/Dean
Programs in:
interdisciplinary studies (PhD)
public service (MAPS)
transfusion medicine (MS)

College of Arts and Sciences
Dr. Jeanne Hossenlopp, Dean
Programs in:
American literature (PhD)
analytical chemistry (MS, PhD)
ancient philosophy (MA, PhD)
arts and sciences (MA, MAT, MS, PhD)
bioanalytical chemistry (MS, PhD)
bioinformatics (MS)
biophysical chemistry (MS, PhD)
British and American literature (MA)
British empiricism and analytic philosophy (MA, PhD)
British literature (PhD)
cell biology (MS, PhD)
chemical physics (MS, PhD)
Christian philosophy (MA, PhD)
clinical psychology (MS)
computational sciences (PhD)
computers (MS)
computing (MS)
developmental biology (MS, PhD)
early modern European philosophy (MA, PhD)
ecology (MS, PhD)
endocrinology (MS, PhD)
ethics (MA, PhD)
European history (MA, PhD)
evolutionary biology (MS, PhD)
genetics (MS, PhD)
German philosophy (MA, PhD)
historical theology (MA, PhD)
inorganic chemistry (MS, PhD)
international affairs (MA)
mathematics education (MS)
medieval history (MA)
medieval philosophy (MA, PhD)
microbiology (MS, PhD)
molecular biology (MS, PhD)
muscle and exercise physiology (MS, PhD)
neurobiology (MS, PhD)
organic chemistry (MS, PhD)
phenomenology and existentialism (MA, PhD)
philosophy of religion (MA, PhD)
physical chemistry (MS, PhD)
political science (MA)
psychology (PhD)
religious studies (PhD)
Renaissance and Reformation (MA)
reproductive physiology (MS, PhD)
social and applied philosophy (MA)
Spanish (MA, MAT)
systematic theology (MA, PhD)
theology (MA)
theology and society (PhD)
United States history (MA, PhD)

College of Communication
Dr. Ana Garner, Dean
Programs in:
advertising and public relations (MA)
broadcasting and electronic communications (MA)
communications studies (MA)
journalism (MA)
mass communications (MA)
religious communications (MA)
science, health and environmental communications (MA)

College of Education
Dr. Bill Henk, Dean
Program in:
education (MA, Ed D, PhD, Spec)

College of Engineering
Dr. Stan V. Jaskolski, Dean
Programs in:
bioinstrumentation/computers (MS, PhD)
biomechanics/biomaterials (MS, PhD)
computing (MS)
construction and public works management (MS, PhD)
electrical engineering (MS, PhD)
engineering (MS, PhD)
engineering management (MS)
environmental/water resources engineering (MS, PhD)
functional imaging (PhD)
healthcare technologies management (MS)
mechanical engineering (MS, PhD)
structural/geotechnical engineering (MS, PhD)
systems physiology (MS, PhD)
transportation planning and engineering (MS, PhD)

College of Health Sciences
Dr. Jack C. Brooks, Dean
Programs in:
health sciences (MS, DPT)
physical therapy (DPT)
physician assistant studies (MS)
speech-language pathology (MS)

College of Nursing
Dr. Lea Acord, Dean

Programs in:
- adult nurse practitioner (Certificate)
- advanced practice nursing (MSN)
- gerontological nurse practitioner (Certificate)
- neonatal nurse practitioner (Certificate)
- nurse-midwifery (Certificate)
- nursing (PhD)
- pediatric nurse practitioner (Certificate)

Graduate School of Management
Dr. David Shrock, Dean
Programs in:
- accounting (MSA)
- business administration (MBA)
- business economics (MSAE)
- entrepreneurship (Graduate Certificate)
- financial economics (MSAE)
- human resources (MSHR)
- international economics (MSAE)
- management (MBA, MSA, MSAE, MSHR, Graduate Certificate)

Law School
Program in:
- law (JD)

School of Dentistry
Programs in:
- advanced training in general dentistry (MS)
- dental biomaterials (MS)
- dentistry (DDS, MS)
- endodontics (MS)
- orthodontics (MS)
- prosthodontics (MS)

■ MOUNT MARY COLLEGE
Milwaukee, WI 53222-4597
http://www.mtmary.edu/

Independent-religious, Undergraduate: women only; graduate: coed, comprehensive institution. CGS member. *Graduate faculty:* 15 full-time (13 women), 47 part-time/adjunct (35 women). *Computer facilities:* 80 computers available on campus for general student use. A campuswide network can be accessed from student residence rooms and from off campus. Online class registration is available. *Graduate expenses:* Tuition: part-time $545 per credit. *General application contact:* Dr. Douglas J. Mickelson, Associate Dean for Graduate and Continuing Education, 414-256-1252.

Graduate Programs
Dr. Douglas J. Mickelson, Associate Dean for Graduate and Continuing Education
Programs in:
- administrative dietetics (MS)
- art therapy (MS)
- business administration (MBA)
- clinical dietetics (MS)
- community counseling (MS)
- education (MA)
- English (MA)
- nutrition education (MS)
- occupational therapy (MS)
- professional development (MA)

■ SILVER LAKE COLLEGE
Manitowoc, WI 54220-9319
http://www.sl.edu/

Independent-religious, coed, primarily women, comprehensive institution. *Graduate faculty:* 7 full-time (all women), 63 part-time/adjunct (36 women). *Computer facilities:* 50 computers available on campus for general student use. A campuswide network can be accessed from off campus. Online class registration is available. *Graduate expenses:* Tuition: part-time $395 per credit. *General application contact:* Jamie Grant, Associate Director of Admissions, 800-236-4752 Ext. 186.

Division of Graduate Studies
Programs in:
- administrative leadership (MA Ed)
- management and organizational behavior (MS)
- music education-Kodaly emphasis (MM)
- special education (MASE)
- teacher leadership (MA Ed)

■ UNIVERSITY OF WISCONSIN–EAU CLAIRE
Eau Claire, WI 54702-4004
http://www.uwec.edu/

State-supported, coed, comprehensive institution. CGS member. *Graduate faculty:* 334 full-time (126 women), 11 part-time/adjunct (5 women). *Computer facilities:* 1,150 computers available on campus for general student use. A campuswide network can be accessed from student residence rooms and from off campus. Online class registration is available. *Graduate expenses:* Tuition, state resident: full-time $6426; part-time $400.60 per credit. Tuition, nonresident: full-time $17,560; part-time $975.32 per credit. One-time fee: $56 full-time. *General application contact:* Kristina Anderson, Director of Admissions, 715-836-5415.

College of Arts and Sciences
Dr. Donald Christian, Dean
Programs in:
- arts and sciences (MA, MSE, Ed S)
- English (MA)
- history (MA)
- school psychology (MSE, Ed S)

College of Business
Dr. V. Thomas Dock, Dean
Programs in:
- business (MBA)
- business administration (MBA)

College of Education and Human Sciences
Dr. Gail Scukanec, Dean
Programs in:
- communication sciences and disorders (MS)
- education and human sciences (MAT, MEPD, MS, MSE, MST)
- education and professional development (MEPD)
- elementary education (MST)
- English (MST)
- history/social science (MAT, MST)
- mathematics (MAT, MST)
- reading (MST)
- special education (MSE)

College of Nursing and Health Sciences
Dr. Mary Zwygart-Stauffacher, Associate Dean
Programs in:
- nursing (MSN)
- nursing and health sciences (MSN)

■ UNIVERSITY OF WISCONSIN–LA CROSSE
La Crosse, WI 54601-3742
http://www.uwlax.edu/

State-supported, coed, comprehensive institution. CGS member. *Graduate faculty:* 169 full-time (76 women), 18 part-time/adjunct (13 women). *Computer facilities:* 600 computers available on campus for general student use. A campuswide network can be accessed from student residence rooms and from off campus. Online class registration is available. *Graduate expenses:* Tuition, state resident: full-time $6485; part-time $360 per credit hour. Tuition, nonresident: full-time $16,830; part-time $935 per credit hour. Required fees: $846. Tuition and fees vary according to program and reciprocity agreements. *General application contact:* Kathryn Kiefer, Associate Director of Admissions, 608-785-8939.

Office of University Graduate Studies
Dr. Vijendra Agarwal, Director

College of Business Administration
Dr. Bruce May, Associate Dean
Program in:
- business administration (MBA)

College of Liberal Studies
Dr. Ruthann Benson, Dean
Programs in:
- college student development and administration (MS Ed)
- elementary education (MEPD)
- emotional disturbance (MS Ed)
- K–12 (MEPD)
- learning disabilities (MS Ed)
- liberal studies (MEPD, MS Ed, Ed S)
- professional development (MEPD)
- reading (MS Ed)
- school psychology (MS Ed, Ed S)
- secondary education (MEPD)
- special education (MS Ed)
- student affairs administration (MS Ed)

College of Science and Health
Dr. Bruce Riley, Interim Dean

University of Wisconsin–La Crosse (continued)
Programs in:
- aquatic sciences (MS)
- athletic training (MS)
- biology (MS)
- cellular and molecular biology (MS)
- clinical exercise physiology (MS)
- clinical microbiology (MS)
- community health education (MPH, MS)
- human performance (MS)
- microbiology (MS)
- nurse anesthesia (MS)
- occupational therapy (MS)
- physical education teaching (MS)
- physical therapy (MSPT, DPT)
- physician assistant studies (MS)
- physiology (MS)
- recreation (MS)
- school health education (MS)
- science and health (MPH, MS, MSE, MSPT, DPT)
- software engineering (MSE)
- special/adapted physical education (MS)
- sport administration (MS)

■ UNIVERSITY OF WISCONSIN–MADISON
Madison, WI 53706-1380
http://www.wisc.edu/

State-supported, coed, university. CGS member. *Graduate faculty:* 3,239 full-time (946 women), 818 part-time/adjunct (425 women). *Computer facilities:* A campuswide network can be accessed from student residence rooms and from off campus. Online class registration is available. *General application contact:* Information Contact, 608-262-2433.

Development Studies Program
Program in:
- development studies (PhD)

Graduate School
Dr. Martin Cadwallader, Dean
Programs in:
- biophysics (PhD)
- cellular and molecular biology (PhD)
- engine systems (ME)
- neuroscience (PhD)
- professional practice (ME)

College of Agricultural and Life Sciences
Programs in:
- agricultural and applied economics (MA, MS, PhD)
- agricultural and life sciences (MA, MPS, MS, PhD)
- agroecology (MS)
- agronomy (MS, PhD)
- animal sciences (MS, PhD)
- bacteriology (MS)
- biochemistry (PhD)
- biological systems engineering (MS, PhD)
- dairy science (MS, PhD)
- entomology (MS, PhD)
- food science (MS, PhD)
- forest and wildlife ecology (MS, PhD)
- genetic counseling (MS)
- genetics (PhD)
- horticulture (MS, PhD)
- landscape architecture (MA, MS)
- life sciences communication (MPS, MS)
- mass communication (PhD)
- nutritional sciences (MS, PhD)
- plant breeding and plant genetics (MS, PhD)
- plant pathology (MS, PhD)
- soil science (MS, PhD)

College of Engineering
Programs in:
- biomedical engineering (MS, PhD)
- chemical engineering (MS, PhD)
- civil and environmental engineering (MS, PhD)
- electrical engineering (MS, PhD)
- energy systems (ME)
- engine systems (ME)
- engineering (ME, MS, PhD, PDD)
- engineering mechanics (MS, PhD)
- environmental chemistry and technology (MS, PhD)
- geological engineering (MS, PhD)
- industrial and systems engineering (MS, PhD)
- limnology and marine science (MS, PhD)
- manufacturing systems engineering (MS)
- materials engineering (MS, PhD)
- materials science (MS, PhD)
- mechanical engineering (MS, PhD)
- nuclear engineering and engineering physics (MS, PhD)
- polymers (ME)

College of Letters and Science
Programs in:
- African history (MA, PhD)
- African languages and literature (MA, PhD)
- Afro-American studies (MA)
- applied English linguistics (MA)
- archaeology (PhD)
- area studies (MA)
- art history (MA, PhD)
- astronomy (PhD)
- atmospheric and oceanic sciences (MS, PhD)
- biological anthropology (PhD)
- biology of brain and behavior (PhD)
- biometry (MS)
- botany (MS, PhD)
- cartography and geographic information systems (MS)
- Central Asian history (MA, PhD)
- chemistry (MS, PhD)
- Chinese literature (MA, PhD)
- Chinese thought (MA, PhD)
- choral (MM, DMA)
- civilizations and cultures (PhD)
- classics (MA, PhD)
- clinical psychology (PhD)
- cognitive neurosciences (PhD)
- communication science (MA, PhD)
- comparative literature (MA, PhD)
- comparative world history (MA, PhD)
- composition (MM, DMA)
- composition and rhetoric (PhD)
- computer sciences (MS, PhD)
- creative writing (MFA)
- cultural anthropology (PhD)
- curriculum and instruction (MS, PhD)
- developmental psychology (PhD)
- East Asian history (MA, PhD)
- economics (PhD)
- English language and linguistics (PhD)
- ethnomusicology (MA, PhD)
- European history (MA, PhD)
- family and consumer journalism (PhD)
- film (MA, PhD)
- folklore (PhD)
- French (MA, PhD)
- French studies (MFS, Certificate)
- gender and women's history (MA, PhD)
- geographic information systems (Certificate)
- geography (MS, PhD)
- geology (MS, PhD)
- geophysics (MS, PhD)
- German (MA, PhD)
- Greek (MA)
- Hebrew and Semitic studies (MA, PhD)
- historical musicology (PhD)
- history of medicine (MA)
- history of science (MA, PhD)
- instrumental (MM, DMA)
- international public affairs (MPIA)
- Italian (MA, PhD)
- Japanese linguistics (MA, PhD)
- Japanese literature (MA, PhD)
- journalism and mass communication (MA)
- languages and cultures of Asia (MA)
- languages and literatures (PhD)
- Latin (MA)
- Latin American and Caribbean history (MA, PhD)
- Latin American, Caribbean and Iberian studies (MA)
- letters and science (MA, MFA, MFS, MM, MPA, MPIA, MS, MSW, DMA, PhD, Certificate)
- library and information studies (MA, PhD)
- linguistics (MA, PhD)
- literary studies (MA, PhD)
- literature (MA, PhD)
- mass communication (PhD)
- mathematics (PhD)
- media and cultural studies (MA, PhD)
- Middle Eastern history (MA, PhD)
- music (MA, MM, DMA, PhD)
- music education (MM)
- music history (MA)
- music performance (MM, DMA)
- music theory (MA, PhD)
- normal aspects of speech, language and hearing (MS, PhD)
- orchestral (MM, DMA)
- perception (PhD)
- philology (PhD)
- philosophy (MA, PhD)

physics (MA, MS, PhD)
political science (PhD)
Portuguese (MA, PhD)
psychology (PhD)
public affairs (MPA, MPIA)
religions of Asia (PhD)
rhetoric (MA, PhD)
rural sociology (MS)
Slavic languages and literature (MA, PhD)
social and personality psychology (PhD)
social welfare (PhD)
social work (MSW)
sociology (MS, PhD)
South Asian history (MA, PhD)
Southeast Asian history (MA, PhD)
Southeast Asian studies (MA)
Spanish (MA, PhD)
speech-language pathology (MS, PhD)
statistics (MS, PhD)
theatre and drama (MA, MFA, PhD)
United States history (MA, PhD)
urban and regional planning (MS, PhD)
zoology (MA, MS, PhD)

Gaylord Nelson Institute for Environmental Studies
William Bland, Chair
Programs in:
conservation biology and sustainable development (MS)
environment and resources (MS, PhD)
environmental monitoring (MS, PhD)
environmental studies (MS, PhD)
water resources management (MS)

School of Education
Programs in:
administration (Certificate)
art (MA, MFA)
art education (MA)
counseling (MS)
counseling psychology (MS, PhD)
curriculum and instruction (MS, PhD)
education (MA, MFA, MS, PhD, Certificate)
education and mathematics (MA)
educational policy (MS, PhD)
educational policy studies (MA, PhD)
educational psychology (MS, PhD)
French education (MA)
German education (MA)
kinesiology (MS, PhD)
music education (MS)
occupational therapy (MS, PhD)
rehabilitation psychology (MA, MS, PhD)
science education (MS)
Spanish education (MA)
special education (MA, MS, PhD)
therapeutic science (MS)

School of Human Ecology
Programs in:
consumer behavior and family economics (MS, PhD)
design studies (MFA, MS, PhD)
human development and family studies (MS, PhD)

Wisconsin School of Business
Dr. Michael M. Knetter, Dean
Programs in:
accountancy (M Acc)
accounting and information systems (PhD)
actuarial science (MS)
actuarial science, risk management and insurance (PhD)
applied corporate finance (MBA)
applied security analysis (MBA)
arts administration (MBA)
brand and product management (MBA)
business (M Acc, MBA, MS, PhD)
business administration (MBA)
entrepreneurial management (MBA)
finance, investment, and banking (PhD)
information systems (PhD)
management and human resources (PhD)
marketing (PhD)
marketing research (MBA)
operations and information management (PhD)
operations and technology management (MBA)
quantitative finance (MS)
real estate (MBA)
real estate and urban land economics (PhD)
risk management and insurance (MBA)
strategic human resource management (MBA)
strategic management in the life and engineering sciences (MBA)
supply chain management (MBA)

Law School
Program in:
law (JD, LL M, SJD)

School of Medicine and Public Health
Dr. Robert N. Golden, Dean
Programs in:
biomolecular chemistry (MS, PhD)
cancer biology (PhD)
clinical research (PhD)
endocrinology-reproductive physiology (MS, PhD)
epidemiology (MS)
genetics and medical genetics (MS, PhD)
health physics (MS)
health services research (MS, PhD)
medical physics (MS, PhD)
medicine (MD, MPH, MS, PhD)
medicine and public health (MD, MPH, MS, PhD)
microbiology (PhD)
molecular and cellular pharmacology (PhD)
pathology and laboratory medicine (PhD)
physiology (PhD)
population health sciences (MPH, MS, PhD)
social and behavioral health sciences (MS, PhD)

Molecular and Environmental Toxicology Center
Dr. Christopher Bradfield, Director
Program in:
molecular and environmental toxicology (MS, PhD)

School of Nursing
Dr. Katharyn A. May, Dean
Program in:
nursing (PhD)

School of Pharmacy
Programs in:
pharmaceutical sciences (PhD)
pharmacy (Pharm D, MS, PhD)
social and administrative sciences in pharmacy (MS, PhD)

School of Veterinary Medicine
Dr. Daryl D. Buss, Dean
Programs in:
comparative biomedical sciences (MS, PhD)
veterinary medicine (DVM, MS, PhD)

■ UNIVERSITY OF WISCONSIN–MILWAUKEE
Milwaukee, WI 53201-0413
http://www.uwm.edu/

State-supported, coed, university. CGS member. *Graduate faculty:* 848 full-time (340 women). *Computer facilities:* 1,000 computers available on campus for general student use. A campuswide network can be accessed from student residence rooms and from off campus. Online class registration is available. *Graduate expenses:* Tuition, state resident: full-time $7320; part-time $165 per credit. Tuition, nonresident: full-time $17,840; part-time $714 per credit. Tuition and fees vary according to campus/location, program and reciprocity agreements. *General application contact:* General Information Contact, 414-229-4982.

Graduate School
Colin Scanes, Dean of Graduate School/ Vice Chancellor for Research and Economic Development
Program in:
multidisciplinary studies (PhD)

College of Engineering and Applied Science
Dr. Michael R. Lovell, Dean
Programs in:
civil engineering (MS)
computer science (MS, PhD)
electrical and computer engineering (MS)
engineering (PhD)
engineering and applied science (MS, PhD, Certificate)
engineering management (MS)
engineering mechanics (MS)
industrial and management engineering (MS)
manufacturing engineering (MS)
materials engineering (MS)
mechanical engineering (MS)
medical informatics (PhD)

University of Wisconsin–Milwaukee (continued)

College of Health Sciences
Johannes Britz, Acting Dean
Programs in:
clinical laboratory science (MS)
communication sciences and disorders (MS)
ergonomics (Certificate)
health sciences (MS, DPT, PhD, Certificate)
healthcare informatics (MS, Certificate)
kinesiology/human movement sciences (MS)
occupational therapy (MS)
physical therapy (DPT)
therapeutic recreation (Certificate)

College of Letters and Sciences
G. Richard Meadows, Dean
Programs in:
Africology (PhD)
anthropology (PhD)
art history (MA)
art museum studies (Certificate)
biogeochemistry (PhD)
biological sciences (MS, PhD)
chemistry (MS, PhD)
classics and Hebrew studies (MAFLL)
clinical psychology (MS, PhD)
communication (MA, PhD)
comparative literature (MAFLL)
creative writing (PhD)
economics (MA, PhD)
English (MA)
French and Italian (MAFLL)
geography (MA, MS, PhD)
geological sciences (MS, PhD)
German (MAFLL)
global history (PhD)
history (MA)
human resources and labor relations (MHRLR)
international human resources and labor relations (Certificate)
letters and sciences (MA, MAFLL, MHRLR, MLS, MPA, MS, PhD, Certificate)
liberal studies (MLS)
linguistics (PhD)
mathematics (MS, PhD)
media studies (MA)
mediation and negotiation (Certificate)
modern studies (PhD)
museum studies (Certificate)
philosophy (MA)
physics (MS, PhD)
political science (MA, PhD)
professional writing (PhD)
professional writing and communication (Certificate)
psychology (MS, PhD)
public administration (MPA)
rhetoric and composition (PhD)
rhetorical leadership (Certificate)
Slavic studies (MAFLL)
sociology (MA)
Spanish (MA)
translation (Certificate)
urban history (PhD)
urban studies (MS, PhD)

College of Nursing
Karen Morin, Representative
Programs in:
family nursing practitioner (Post Master's Certificate)
health professional education (Certificate)
nursing (MS, PhD)
public health (Certificate)

Peck School of the Arts
Wade Hobgood, Dean
Programs in:
art (MA, MFA)
art education (MA, MFA, MS)
arts (MA, MFA, MM, MS, Certificate)
chamber music performance (Certificate)
dance (MFA)
film (MFA)
music composition (MM)
music education (MM)
music history and literature (MM)
opera and vocal arts (Certificate)
string pedagogy (MM)
theatre (MFA)

School of Architecture and Urban Planning
Robert Greenstreet, Dean
Programs in:
architecture (PhD)
architecture and urban planning (M Arch, MUP, PhD, Certificate)
geographic information systems (Certificate)
preservation studies (Certificate)
urban planning (MUP)

School of Education
Alfonzo Thurman, Dean
Programs in:
administrative leadership (Certificate)
administrative leadership and supervision in education (MS)
adult and continuing education (PhD)
assistive technology and accessible design (Certificate)
counseling (school, community) (MS)
counseling psychology (PhD)
cultural foundations of education (MS)
curriculum and instruction (PhD)
curriculum planning and instruction improvement (MS)
early childhood education (MS)
education (MS, PhD, Certificate, Ed S)
educational administration (PhD)
educational and media technology (PhD)
educational psychology (PhD)
elementary education (MS)
exceptional education (MS)
junior high/middle school education (MS)
learning and development (MS)
multicultural studies (PhD)
reading education (MS)
research methodology (MS, PhD)
school psychology (PhD)
secondary education (MS)
social foundations of education (PhD)
teaching in an urban setting (MS)

School of Information Studies
Johannes Britz, Dean
Programs in:
advanced studies in library and information science (CAS)
archives and records administration (CAS)
information studies (MLIS, PhD)

School of Social Welfare
Stan Stojkovic, Dean
Programs in:
administration (MS)
applied gerontology (Certificate)
corrections (MS)
law enforcement (MS)
marriage and family therapy (Certificate)
non-profit management (Certificate)
social welfare (MS, MSW, PhD, Certificate)
social work (MSW, PhD)

Sheldon B. Lubar School of Business
V. Kanti Prasad, Dean
Programs in:
business (MBA, PhD, Certificate)
executive business administration (Exec MBA)
management science (MS, PhD)
nonprofit management and leadership (Certificate)

■ UNIVERSITY OF WISCONSIN–OSHKOSH
Oshkosh, WI 54901
http://www.uwosh.edu/

State-supported, coed, comprehensive institution. *Computer facilities:* 475 computers available on campus for general student use. A campuswide network can be accessed from student residence rooms and from off campus. Online class registration is available. *General application contact:* Director of Graduate Services, 920-424-0007.

The Office of Graduate Studies
Program in:
social work (MSW)

College of Business
Programs in:
business (GMBA, MBA)
business administration (MBA)
global business administration (GMBA)

College of Education and Human Services
Programs in:
counseling (MSE)
cross-categorical (MSE)
curriculum and instruction (MSE)
early childhood: exceptional education needs (MSE)
education and human services (MS, MSE)
educational leadership (MS)
non-licensure (MSE)
reading education (MSE)

College of Letters and Science
Programs in:
biology (MS)

English (MA)
experimental psychology (MS)
general agency (MPA)
health care (MPA)
industrial/organizational psychology (MS)
letters and science (MA, MPA, MS, MSW)
mathematics education (MS)

College of Nursing
Programs in:
adult health and illness (MSN)
family nurse practitioner (MSN)

■ UNIVERSITY OF WISCONSIN–PLATTEVILLE
Platteville, WI 53818-3099
http://www.uwplatt.edu/

State-supported, coed, comprehensive institution. *Graduate faculty:* 5 full-time (2 women), 90 part-time/adjunct (16 women). *Computer facilities:* 1,200 computers available on campus for general student use. A campuswide network can be accessed from student residence rooms and from off campus. Online class registration is available. *General application contact:* Lisa Popp, School of Graduate Studies, 608-342-1322.

School of Graduate Studies
Dr. David P. Van Buren, Dean

College of Engineering, Mathematics and Science
Dr. Rich Shultz, Dean
Programs in:
computer science (MS)
engineering, mathematics and science (MS)

College of Liberal Arts and Education
Dr. Mittie Nimocks, Dean
Programs in:
adult education (MSE)
counselor education (MSE)
elementary education (MSE)
liberal arts and education (MSE)
middle school education (MSE)
secondary education (MSE)
vocational and technical education (MSE)

Distance Learning Center
Dawn Drake, Executive Director
Programs in:
criminal justice (MS)
engineering (MS)
project management (MS)

■ UNIVERSITY OF WISCONSIN–RIVER FALLS
River Falls, WI 54022-5001
http://www.uwrf.edu/

State-supported, coed, comprehensive institution. CGS member. *Computer facilities:* Computer purchase and lease plans are available. 387 computers available on campus for general student use. A campuswide network can be accessed from student residence rooms and from off campus. Online class registration is available. *General application contact:* Program Assistant II, 715-425-3843.

Outreach and Graduate Studies

College of Agriculture, Food, and Environmental Sciences
Programs in:
agricultural education (MS)
agriculture, food, and environmental sciences (MS)

College of Arts and Science
Programs in:
arts and science (MA, MSE)
fine arts (MSE)
mathematics education (MSE)
science education (MSE)
social science education (MSE)
teaching English to speakers of other languages (MA)

College of Business and Economics
Program in:
business and economics (MBA, MM)

College of Education and Professional Studies
Programs in:
communicative disorders (MS)
counseling (MSE)
education and professional studies (MS, MSE, Ed S)
elementary education (MSE)
professional development shared inquiry communities (MSE)
reading (MSE)
school psychology (MSE, Ed S)
secondary education-communicative disorders (MSE)

■ UNIVERSITY OF WISCONSIN–STEVENS POINT
Stevens Point, WI 54481-3897
http://www.uwsp.edu/

State-supported, coed, comprehensive institution. *Graduate faculty:* 259 full-time (93 women), 4 part-time/adjunct (1 woman). *Computer facilities:* 634 computers available on campus for general student use. A campuswide network can be accessed from student residence rooms and from off campus. Online class registration is available. *General application contact:* Catherine Glennon, Director of Admissions, 715-346-2441.

College of Fine Arts and Communication
Jeff Morin, Dean
Programs in:
fine arts and communication (MA, MM Ed)
interpersonal communication (MA)
mass communication (MA)
music (MM Ed)
organizational communication (MA)
public relations (MA)

College of Letters and Science
Dr. Charles Clark, Interim Dean
Programs in:
biology (MST)
business and economics (MBA)
English (MST)
history (MST)
letters and science (MBA, MST)

College of Natural Resources
Dr. Christine Thomas, Dean
Program in:
natural resources (MS)

College of Professional Studies

School of Communicative Disorders
Dr. Gary Cumley, Head
Program in:
communicative disorders (MS, Au D)

School of Education
Programs in:
education—general/reading (MSE)
education—general/special (MSE)
educational administration (MSE)
elementary education (MSE)
guidance and counseling (MSE)

School of Health Promotion and Human Development
Dr. Marty Loy, Head
Programs in:
human and community resources (MS)
nutritional sciences (MS)

■ UNIVERSITY OF WISCONSIN–STOUT
Menomonie, WI 54751
http://www.uwstout.edu/

State-supported, coed, comprehensive institution. *Graduate faculty:* 146 full-time (60 women), 36 part-time/adjunct (25 women). *Computer facilities:* Computer purchase and lease plans are available. 590 computers available on campus for general student use. A campuswide network can be accessed from student residence rooms and from off campus. Online class registration, all undergraduates receive a laptop computer are available. *Graduate expenses:* Tuition, state resident: full-time $6227; part-time $345.93 per credit. Tuition, nonresident: full-time $9998; part-time $555.42 per credit. International tuition: $10,512 full-time. Tuition and fees vary according to course load, program and reciprocity agreements. *General application contact:* Anne E. Johnson, Graduate Student Evaluator (Admissions and Assistantship Coordinator), 715-232-1322.

Graduate School
Dr. Claudia Johnston, Director, Office of Graduate Studies

College of Human Development
Dr. John Wesolek, Dean

University of Wisconsin–Stout (continued)
Programs in:
applied psychology (MS)
family studies and human development (MS)
food and nutritional sciences (MS)
human development (MS)
marriage and family therapy (MS)
mental health counseling (MS)
vocational rehabilitation (MS)

College of Technology, Engineering, and Management
Dr. Carol Mooney, Interim Dean
Programs in:
information and communication technologies (MS)
manufacturing engineering (MS)
risk control (MS)
technology management (MS)
technology, engineering, and management (MS)
training and development (MS)

School of Education
Dr. Mary Hopkins-Best, Interim Dean
Programs in:
career and technical education (MS, Ed S)
education (MS, MS Ed, Ed S)
industrial/technology education (MS)
school counseling (MS)
school psychology (MS Ed, Ed S)

■ UNIVERSITY OF WISCONSIN–SUPERIOR
Superior, WI 54880-4500
http://www.uwsuper.edu/

State-supported, coed, comprehensive institution. *Computer facilities:* Computer purchase and lease plans are available. 200 computers available on campus for general student use. A campuswide network can be accessed from student residence rooms and from off campus. Online class registration is available. *General application contact:* Program Assistant/Status Examiner, 715-394-8295.

Graduate Division
Programs in:
art education (MA)
art history (MA)
art therapy (MA)
arts administration (MA)
community counseling (MSE)
educational administration (MSE, Ed S)
educational psychology (MSE)
elementary school counseling (MSE)
emotional/behavior disabilities (MSE)
human relations (MSE)
instruction (MSE)
learning disabilities (MSE)
mass communication (MA)
secondary school counseling (MSE)
special education (MSE)
speech communication (MA)
studio arts (MA)
teaching reading (MSE)
theater (MA)

■ UNIVERSITY OF WISCONSIN–WHITEWATER
Whitewater, WI 53190-1790
http://www.uww.edu/

State-supported, coed, comprehensive institution. *Computer facilities:* Computer purchase and lease plans are available. 1,300 computers available on campus for general student use. A campuswide network can be accessed from student residence rooms and from off campus. Online class registration is available. *General application contact:* School of Graduate Studies, 262-472-1006.

School of Graduate Studies

College of Arts and Communications
Programs in:
arts and communications (MS)
corporate communication (MS)
mass communication (MS)

College of Business and Economics
Programs in:
accounting (MPA)
business and economics (MBA, MPA, MS, MS Ed)
finance (MBA)
general business education (MS)
human resource management (MBA)
information technology management (MBA)
international business (MBA)
management (MBA)
marketing (MBA)
operations and supply chain management (MBA)
post-secondary business education (MS)
school business management (MS Ed)
secondary business education (MS)
technology and training (MBA)

College of Education
Programs in:
communicative disorders (MS)
community counseling (MS Ed)
curriculum and instruction (MS)
education (MS, MS Ed)
higher education (MS Ed)
reading (MS Ed)
safety (MS)
school counseling (MS Ed)
special education (MS Ed)

College of Letters and Sciences
Programs in:
letters and sciences (MS Ed, Ed S)
school psychology (Ed S)

■ VITERBO UNIVERSITY
La Crosse, WI 54601-4797
http://www.viterbo.edu/

Independent-religious, coed, primarily women, comprehensive institution. *Computer facilities:* 314 computers available on campus for general student use. A campuswide network can be accessed from student residence rooms and from off campus. Online class registration, Blackboard courses are available. *General application contact:* Information Contact, 608-796-3000.

Graduate Program in Business
Program in:
business (MBA)

Graduate Program in Education
Program in:
education (MA)

Graduate Program in Nursing
Dr. Bonnie Nesbitt, Director
Program in:
nursing (MSN)

Wyoming

■ UNIVERSITY OF WYOMING
Laramie, WY 82070
http://www.uwyo.edu/

State-supported, coed, university. CGS member. *Graduate faculty:* 684 full-time (223 women), 29 part-time/adjunct (19 women). *Computer facilities:* Computer purchase and lease plans are available. 1,269 computers available on campus for general student use. A campuswide network can be accessed from student residence rooms and from off campus. Online class registration is available. *General application contact:* Michell Anderson, Graduate Admissions Coordinator, 307-766-3802.

College of Agriculture
Dr. Frank D. Galey, Dean
Programs in:
agricultural and applied economics (MS)
agriculture (MS, PhD)
agroecology (MS)
agronomy (MS, PhD)
animal sciences (MS, PhD)
early childhood development (MS)
entomology (MS, PhD)
entomology/water resources (MS, PhD)
family and consumer sciences (MS)
food science and human nutrition (MS)
molecular biology (MS, PhD)
pathobiology (MS)
rangeland ecology and watershed management (MS, PhD)
rangeland ecology and watershed management/water resources (MS, PhD)
reproductive biology (MS, PhD)
soil science (MS)
soil science/water resources (PhD)

College of Arts and Sciences
B. Oliver Walter, Dean
Programs in:
American studies (MA)

anthropology (MA, PhD)
arts and sciences (MA, MAT, MFA, MM, MME, MP, MPA, MS, MST, PhD)
botany (MS, PhD)
botany/water resources (MS)
chemistry (MS, PhD)
communication (MA)
community and regional planning and natural resources (MP)
creative writing (MFA)
English (MA)
French (MA)
geography (MA, MP, MST)
geography/water resources (MA)
geology (MS, PhD)
geophysics (MS, PhD)
German (MA)
history (MA, MAT)
international peace corps (MA)
international studies (MA)
mathematics (MA, MAT, MS, MST, PhD)
mathematics/computer science (PhD)
music education (MME)
performance (MM)
philosophy (MA)
political science (MA)
psychology (MA, MS, PhD)
public administration (MPA)
rural planning and natural resources (MP)
sociology (MA)
Spanish (MA)
statistics (MS, PhD)
zoology and physiology (MS, PhD)

College of Business
Dr. Brent A. Hathaway, Dean
Programs in:
accounting (MS)
business (MBA, MS, PhD)
business administration (MBA)
economics (MS, PhD)
economics and finance (MS, PhD)
finance (MS)

College of Education
Dr. Kay Persichitte, Dean
Programs in:
adult and postsecondary education (MA, Ed D, PhD, Ed S)
community mental health (MS)
counselor education and supervision (PhD)
curriculum and instruction (MA, Ed D, PhD)
distance education (Ed D, PhD)
education (MA, MS, MST, Ed D, PhD, Certificate, Ed S)
educational leadership (MA, Ed D, Certificate)
instructional technology (MS, Ed D, PhD)
school counseling (MS)
special education (MA, PhD, Ed S)
student affairs (MS)

Science and Mathematics Teaching Center
Dr. Robert L. Mayes, Director
Program in:
science and mathematics teaching (MS, MST)

College of Engineering and Applied Sciences
Dr. Robert Ettema, Dean
Programs in:
atmospheric science (MS, PhD)
chemical engineering (MS, PhD)
civil engineering (MS, PhD)
computer science (MS, PhD)
electrical engineering (MS, PhD)
engineering and applied sciences (MS, PhD)
environmental engineering (MS)
mechanical engineering (MS, PhD)
petroleum engineering (MS, PhD)

College of Health Sciences
Dr. Beverky O. Sullivan, Interim Dean
Program in:
health sciences (Pharm D, MS, MSW)

Division of Communication Disorders
Dr. Teresa Ukrainetz, Director
Program in:
speech-language pathology (MS)

Division of Kinesiology and Health
Dr. Mark Byra, Director
Program in:
kinesiology and health (MS)

Division of Social Work
Dr. Mona C.S. Schultz, Director
Program in:
social work (MSW)

Fay W. Whitney School of Nursing
Dr. Mary E. Burman, Dean and Professor
Program in:
nursing (MS)

School of Pharmacy
John H. Vandel, Dean
Program in:
pharmacy (Pharm D)

College of Law
Denise Burke, Assistant Dean
Program in:
law (JD)

Graduate Program in Molecular and Cellular Life Sciences
Dr. David S. Fay, Director
Program in:
molecular and cellular life sciences (PhD)

Program in Ecology
Steve Jackson, Director
Program in:
ecology (MS, PhD)

Index

Alphabetical Listing of Schools

NOTES

NOTES

NOTES

NOTES

Peterson's
Book Satisfaction Survey

Give Us Your Feedback

Thank you for choosing Peterson's as your source for personalized solutions for your education and career achievement. Please take a few minutes to answer the following questions. Your answers will go a long way in helping us to produce the most user-friendly and comprehensive resources to meet your individual needs.

When completed, please tear out this page and mail it to us at:

Publishing Department
Peterson's, a Nelnet company
2000 Lenox Drive
Lawrenceville, NJ 08648

You can also complete this survey online at **www.petersons.com/booksurvey.**

1. What is the ISBN of the book you have purchased? (The ISBN can be found on the book's back cover in the lower right-hand corner.) ____________________

2. Where did you purchase this book?

❑ Retailer, such as Barnes & Noble
❑ Online reseller, such as Amazon.com
❑ Petersons.com
❑ Other (please specify) ____________________

3. If you purchased this book on Petersons.com, please rate the following aspects of your online purchasing experience on a scale of 4 to 1 (4 = Excellent and 1 = Poor).

	4	3	2	1
Comprehensiveness of Peterson's Online Bookstore page	❑	❑	❑	❑
Overall online customer experience	❑	❑	❑	❑

4. Which category best describes you?

❑ High school student
❑ Parent of high school student
❑ College student
❑ Graduate/professional student
❑ Returning adult student
❑ Teacher
❑ Counselor
❑ Working professional/military
❑ Other (please specify) ____________________

5. Rate your overall satisfaction with this book.

Extremely Satisfied	Satisfied	Not Satisfied
❑	❑	❑

6. **Rate each of the following aspects of this book on a scale of 4 to 1 (4 = Excellent and 1 = Poor).**

	4	3	2	1
Comprehensiveness of the information	❑	❑	❑	❑
Accuracy of the information	❑	❑	❑	❑
Usability	❑	❑	❑	❑
Cover design	❑	❑	❑	❑
Book layout	❑	❑	❑	❑
Special features *(e.g., CD, flashcards, charts, etc.)*	❑	❑	❑	❑
Value for the money	❑	❑	❑	❑

7. **This book was recommended by:**
   - ❑ Guidance counselor
   - ❑ Parent/guardian
   - ❑ Family member/relative
   - ❑ Friend
   - ❑ Teacher
   - ❑ Not recommended by anyone—I found the book on my own
   - ❑ Other (please specify) ______________________________

8. **Would you recommend this book to others?**

Yes	Not Sure	No
❑	❑	❑

9. **Please provide any additional comments.**

____

____

____

____

____

Remember, you can tear out this page and mail it to us at:

Publishing Department
Peterson's, a Nelnet company
2000 Lenox Drive
Lawrenceville, NJ 08648

or you can complete the survey online at **www.petersons.com/booksurvey.**

Your feedback is important to us at Peterson's, and we thank you for your time!

If you would like us to keep in touch with you about new products and services, please include your e-mail address here: ____